Fourth Edition — 1990

Baseball Card Price Guide

Jeff Kurowski, Editor

Special Consultants:

Dan Albaugh	Mary Huston
Bill Bossert	Rob Lifson
Bill Goodwin	John Spalding

Copyright 1990 by Krause Publications, Inc.
Library of Congress Catalog Number: 87-080033
ISBN: 0-87341-131-5

Krause Publications, Inc.
700 E. State St.
Iola, WI 54990

ACKNOWLEDGEMENTS

Dozens of individuals have made countless valuable contributions which have been incorporated into the *Sports Collectors Digest Baseball Card Price Guide* and the *Standard Catalog of Baseball Cards*. While all cannot be acknowledged, special appreciation is extended to the following principal contributors who have exhibited a special dedication by creating, revising or verifying listings and technical data, reviewing market valuations or loaning cards for photography.

Extra special thanks goes out to the following individuals for their efforts in completing this project.

John Brigandi
 (*Brigand Coin Co.*)
Steve Ellingboe
David Festberg
 (*Baseball and Hobby Shop*)
Richard Galasso

Walter, David, Joel Hall
 (*Hall's Nostalgia*)
David Kohler
Howie Levy
 (*Blue Chip Sportcard*)
Bil Mendel
Marty Perry

Stan Pietruska
 (*Pro Sports Investments*)
Kevin Savage
 (*The Sports Gallery*)
Pete Waldman
Kit Young

Johnny Adams, Jr.
Ken Agona
 (*Sports Cards Plus*)
Gary Agostino
Lisa Albano
Mark Anker
Steve Applebaum
John Beisiegel
Karen Bell
Cathy Black
Mike Bodner
Brian Boston
Mike Boyd
Lou Brown
Dan Bruner
 (*The Card King*)
Greg Bussineau
 (*Superior Sports Cards*)
Billy Caldwell
 (*Packman*)
Len Caprisecca
Tony Carrafiell
 (*Delco Sports Cards*)
Lee Champion
Dwight Chapin
Chriss Christiansen
Shane Cohen
 (*Grand Slam Sports Collectibles*)
Charles Conlon
Eric Cooper
 (*All Star Cards*)
Bryan Couling
Clyde Cripe
Jim Cumpton
Robert Curtiss
Tom Daniels
 (*T&J Sports Cards*)
Tom Day
 (*Major League Marketing*)
Dick DeCourcy
 (*Georgia Music & Sports*)
Mike Del Gado
 (*All American Sportscards*)
Larry Dluhy
 (*Texas Trading Cards*)
John Dorsey
Curtis Earl
Joe Esposito
 (*B&E Collectibles*)
Doak Ewing

Shirley Eross
 (*Hobbyrama Sports By Eross*)
Jay Finglass
Nick Flaviano
Jeff Fritsch
Larry Fritsch
Tom Galic
Tony Galovich
 (*American Card Exchange*)
Frank Giffune
Richard Gilkeson
Dick Goddard
Jack Goodman
Audre Gold
 (*Au Sports Memorabilia*)
Mike Gordon
Howard Gordon
Bob Gray
Paul Green
Wayne Grove
 (*First Base*)
Gerry Guenther
Don Guilbert
Tom Guilfoile
Gary Hamilton
Tom Harbin
Rick Hawksley
Herbert Hecht
Bill Henderson
Gregg Hitesman
Jim Horne
Ron Hosmer
Marvin Huck
Robert Jacobsen
Donn Jennings
Scott Jensen
LouAnne Johnson
 (*Baseball Card News*)
Jim Johnston
Stewart Jones
Larry Jordon
Judy Kay
 (*Kay's Baseball Cards*)
Allan Kaye
Michael Keedy
Mark Kemmerle
Rick Keplinger
John King
John Kittleson
 (*Sports Collectibles*)
Bob Koehler

Steve Lacasse
Lee Lasseigne
William Lawrence
Morley Leeking
Don Lepore
Rod Lethbridge
Paul Lewicki
Neil Lewis
 (*Leaf, Inc.*)
Ken & Norman Liss
 (*Topps, Inc.*)
Jeff Litteral
Mark MacRae
Paul Marchant
Bill Mastro
Jay McCracken
 (*Upper Deck*)
Tony McLaughlin
Don McPherson
John Mehlin
Blake Meyer
 (*Lone Star Sportcard Co.*)
Dick Millerd
Minnesota Sports Collectibles
Keith Mitchell
J.A. Monaco
Joe Morano
Brian Morris
Mike Mowery
Peter Muldavin
Mark Murphy
 (*The Baseball Card "Kid"*)
Vincent Murray
 (*Fleer Corp.*)
David Musser
 (*D.M.B.'s Baseball Cards*)
Steve Myland
Frank Nagy
Chuck Nobriga
Mark Nochta
Wayne Nochta
Keith Olbermann
Joe Pasternack
 (*Card Collectors Co.*)
Tom Pfirrman
 (*Baseball Card Corner*)
Dan Piepenbrok
 (*Uneeda Hobbie*)
Paul Pollard
Ed Ransom

Fred Rapoport
 (*Yesterday's Heroes*)
Tom Reid
Bob Richardson
Gavin Riley
Ron Ritzler
Mike Rodell
Mike Rogers
Chris Ronan
Rocky Rosato
Alan Rosen
John Rumierz
Bob Rund
Jon Sands
 (*Howard's Coin Shop*)
Stephen Schauer
Dave Schwartz
 (*Dave's Sportscards*)
Robert Scott
Corey Shanus
Dan Shedrick
 (*Major League Marketing*)
Max Silberman
Barry Sloate
Joe Smith
Mark Soltan
Kevin Spears
Gene Speranza
David Spivack
Don Steinbach
 (*Sports Collectors Store*)
Dan Stickney
Larry Stone
Doug Stultz
Joe Szeremet
Erik Teller
K.J. Terplak
Dick Tinsley
Scott Torrey
Rich Unruh
Jack Urban
Joe Valle
 (*Cardboard Dreams*)
Eric Waller
Gary Walter
Ken Weimer
Dale Weselowski
 (*Ab D. Cards of Winnipeg*)
E.C. Wharton-Tigar
Charles Williamson
Ted Zanidakis

INTRODUCTORY NOTE

The fourth edition of the *Sports Collectors Digest Baseball Card Price Guide* is the end result of many years of accumulating and confirming baseball card checklists. This volume includes numerous baseball card sets that have never been checklisted in any price guide. Because of production deadlines only the major sets (Donruss, Fleer, Score, Sportflics, Topps and Upper Deck) of 1990 have been checklisted and priced.

A new feature has been added the *Sports Collectors Digest Baseball Card Price Guide.* A special section has been devoted to checklists and values of minor league baseball cards. Also included is a special alphabetical rookie card section (1948-1990). Additionally, all rookie cards found in the major regular issue sets will be noted in italic type.

ROOKIE/FIRST CARD DESIGNATIONS

A player's name in italic type indicates a rookie card. An (FC) designation indicates a player's first card for that particular company. FCs will be found in 1981-90 Donruss, Fleer, Score and Topps sets. They will also be located in the Donruss Rookies, Fleer Update, Topps Traded and Score Traded sets.

BASEBALL CARD HISTORY

In 1887 - over 100 years ago - the first nationally distributed baseball cards were issued by Goodwin & Co. of New York City. The 1½" x 2½" cards featured posed studio photographs glued to stiff cardboard. They were inserted into cigarette packages with such exotic brand names as Old Judge, Gypsy Queen and Dog's Head. Poses were formal, with artificial backgrounds and bare-handed players fielding balls suspended on strings to simulate action.

Then, as now, baseball cards were intended to stimulate product sales. What could be more American than using the diamond heroes of the national pastime to gain an edge on the competition? It is a tradition that has continued virtually unbroken for a century.

Following Goodwin's lead a year later, competitors began issuing baseball cards with their cigarettes, using full-color lithography to bring to life painted portraits of the era's top players.

After a few short years of intense competition, the cigarette industry's leading firms formed a monopoly and cornered the market. By the mid-1890's, there was little competition, and no reason to issue baseball cards. The first great period of baseball card issues came to an end.

The importing of Turkish tobaccos in the years just prior to 1910 created a revolution in American smoking habits. With dozens of new firms entering the market, the idea of using baseball cards to boost sales was revived.

In the years from 1909-1912, dozens of different sets of cards were produced to be given away in cigarette packages. There was a greater than ever variety in sizes, shapes and designs, from the extremely popular 1½" x 2⅝" color lithographed set of 500+ players which collectors call T206, to the large (5" x 8") Turkey Red brand cards. There were double folders, featuring two players on the same card, and triple folders; which had two player portraits and an action scene. Gold ink and embossed designs were also tried to make each competing company's cards attractive and popular.

It was this era that saw the issue of the "King of Baseball Cards", the T206 Honus Wagner card, worth $95,000.00.

The zeal with which America's youngsters pursued their fathers, uncles, and neighbors for cigarette cards in the years just prior to World War I convinced the nation's confectioners that baseball cards could also be used to boost candy sales.

While baseball cards had been produced by candy companies on a limited basis as far back as the 1880s, by the early 1920s the concept was being widely used in the industry. The highly competitive caramel business was a major force in this new marketing strategy, offering a baseball card in each package of candy. Not to be outdone, Cracker Jack began including baseball cards in each box. The 1914-1915 Cracker Jack cards are important because they were the most popular of the candy cards to include players form a short-lived third major league, the Federal League.

Generally, candy cards of the era were not as colorful or well-printed as the earlier tobacco cards, due to a shortage of paper and ink-making ingredients caused by World War I.

The association of bubble gum and baseball cards is a phenomenon of only the past half-century. In the early 1930s techniques were developed using rubber tree products to give the elasticity necessary for blowing bubbles.

During this era the standard method of selling a slab of bubble gum and a baseball card in a colorfully wax-wrapped 1¢ package was developed. Bubble gum - and baseball cards - production in this era was centered in Massachusetts, where National Chicle Company (Cambridge) and Goudey Gum Company (Boston) were headquartered.

Most bubble gum cards produced in the early 1930s featured a roughly square (about 2½") format, with players depicted in colorful paintings. For the first time, considerable attention was paid to the backs of the cards, where biographical details, career highlights and past season statistics were presented.

In 1939, a new company entered the baseball card market - Gum, Inc., of Philadelphia. Its "Play Ball" gum was the major supplier of baseball cards until 1941, when World War II caused a shortage of the materials necessary both for the production of bubble gum and the printing of baseball cards.

Three years after the end of World War II baseball cards returned on a national scale, with two companies competing for the bubble gum market. In Philadelphia, the former Gum, Inc., reappeared on the market as Bowman Gum, Inc.

Bowman's first baseball card set appeared in 1948, very similar in format to the cards which had existed prior to the war, black and white player photos on nearly square (2" x 2½") cardboard. The 1948 Bowman effort was modest, with only 48 cards. The following year, color was added to the photos. For 1950, Bowman replaced the re-rouched photos with original color painting of players, many of which were repeated a year later in the 1951 issue. Also new for 1951 was a larger card size, 2" x 3⅛".

Bowman had little national competition in this era. 1948-1949, Leaf Gum in Chicago produced a 98-card set that is the only bubble gum issue of the era to include a Joe DiMaggio card.

While Bowman dominated the post-war era through 1951, in that year Topps began production of its first baseball cards, issuing three different small sets of cards and serving warning that it was going to become a major force in the baseball card field.

In 1952, Brooklyn-based Topps entered the baseball card market in a big way. Not only was its 407-card set the largest single-year issue ever produced, but its 2⅝" x 3¾" format was the largest-size baseball card ever offered for over-the-counter sale. Other innovations in Topps' premiere issue for 1952 included the first-ever use of team logos in card design, and on the back of the card, the first use of line statistics to document the player's previous year and career performance. By contrast, Bowman's set for 1952 remained in the smaller format, had 72 fewer cards and showed little change in design from 1951.

CLASSIC REPRINTS

THE MONSTER-T206 Classic Tobacco card set, nicknamed "the monster" is recognized as the most popular card set ever issued. Vintage 1909-1911 the 524 card set includes such famous cards as the rare Honus Wagner, Magie error, Plank, 4 different Ty Cobbs and almost 100 other Hall of Famers. Set only **$39.95**

Free with every order 1933 Super Goudey reprint set which includes 4 different Babe Ruth cards. Just mention **Krause** when you order. Free 80 page catalog with every order.

OTHER REPRINTS

1st Baseball Card Circa 1850 .... $1.50
N172 Old Judge Series one 50 cards 5.00
1880 Allen and Ginter large card set 6 cards 3.95
1886-87 Landmark Reprint A & G, Goodwin 24 cards 5.95
1898-1946 Negro League 115 cards 9.95
1911 T201 Mecca Double Folder 50 cards 100 players 14.95
1907 A.C. Dietsch Postcard Tigers 15 cards 6.00
1915 Cracker Jack 176 cards 24.00
1933 Goudey Set 240 cards with four different Babe Ruths 32.95
1933 Goudey Sport Kings 96 cards 10.00
1934 Goudey 96 cards 10.00
1934 36 Diamond Stars 108 cards 10.00
1935 Goudey 36 cards 5.00
1935 National Chicle Football 36 cards 5.00
1933 Goudey Large Card Premium 4 cards 3.95
1936 Goudey 25 cards 5.00
1938 Goudey 48 cards 7.00
1939 Play Ball 162 cards 22.00
1940 Play Ball 240 cards 25.00
1941 Play Ball 72 cards 8.95
1941 Goudey Reprint 33 cards 8.00
1948 Sport Thrill set 20 cards 7.00
1948 Bowman Reprint 48 cards 6.95
1949 Bowman 240 cards 24.95
1949 Bowman Pacific Coast League 36 cards 6.95
1951 Bowman Reprint 324 cards 39.95
1952 Bowman Reprint on 4 uncut sheets 252 cards plus 36 extra cards on the sheets 120.00
1952 Red Man 33 cards 19.95
1954 Dan Dee Potato Set 29 cards 9.95
1954 WIlson Weiner 20 cards 8.00
1959 Home Run Derby 19 cards 5.95
1953 Johnston Cookie Braves 25 cards 8.00
1954 Johnston Cookie Braves 35 cards 9.00
1955 Johnston Cookie Braves 35 cards 9.00
1989 Lou Gehrig Postcard set 8 cards 8.00

Visit our well stocked store, open 7 days a week 12-7 p.m.
We are nestled next to the Museum of Natural History.

Watch our weekly TV show "The Baseball Card Show" every Monday nite 7:30 p.m.
Manhattan cable TV Channel J.

Please add $3.00 for shipping and handling on your order.
NY State residents add sale tax.

CALL TOLL FREE FOR ORDERS 1-800-822-0028

Make all checks payable to : CARD COLLECTOR'S COMPANY

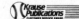

RICHARD GELMAN
C/O CARD COLLECTOR'S COMPANY
105 West 77 Street, New York City, NY 10024 • 212-873-6999

Just as clearly as Topps won the 1952 baseball card battle, Bowman came back in 1953 with what is often considered the finest baseball card set ever produced. For the first time ever, actual color photographs were reproduced on baseball cards in Bowman's 160-card set. To allow the full impact of the new technology, there were no other design elements on the front of the card and Bowman adopted a larger format, 2½" x 3¾".

And so the competition went for five years, each company trying to gain an edge by signing players to exclusive contracts and creating new and exciting card designs each year. Gradually, Topps became the dominant force in the baseball card market. In late 1955, Bowman admitted defeat and the company was sold to Topps.

Baseball cards entered a new era in 1957. After years of intense competition, Topps enjoyed a virtual monopoly that was rarely seriously challenged in the next 25 years. One such challenge in the opening years of the 1960s came from Post cereal, which from 1961-1963 issued 200-card sets on the backs of its cereal boxes.

In 1957, Topps' baseball cards were issued in a new size - 2½" x 3½" - that would become the industry-wide standard that prevails to this day. It was also that year that Topps first used full-color photographs for its cards, rather than paintings or re-touched black and white photos. Another innovation in the 1957 set was the introduction of complete major and/or minor league statistics on the card backs. This feature quickly became a favorite with youngsters and provided fuel for endless schoolyard debates about whether one player was better than another.

In the ensuing five years, major league baseball underwent monumental changes. In 1958, the Giants and Dodgers left New York for California. In 1961-1962 expansion came to the major leagues, with new teams springing up from coast to coast and border to border.

The Topps baseball cards of the era preserve those days when modern baseball was in its formative stages.

In 1963, for the first time in seven years, it looked as if there might once again be two baseball card issues to choose from. After three years of issuing "old-timers" cards sets, Fleer issued a 66-card set of current players. Topps took Fleer to court, where the validity of Topps' exclusive contracts with baseball players to appear on bubble gum cards was upheld. It was the last major challenge to Topps for nearly 20 years.

The 1960's offered baseball card collecting at its traditional finest. Youngsters would wait and worry through the long winter, watching candy store shelves for the first appearance of the brightly colored 5¢ card packs in the spring. A cry of "They're in!" could empty a playground in seconds as youngsters rushed to the corner store to see what design innovations Topps had come up with for the new year. Then, periodically through the summer, new series would be released, offering a new challenge to complete. As the season wore down, fewer and fewer stores carried the final few series, and it became a real struggle to complete the "high numbers" from a given year's set. But is was all part of the fun of buying baseball cards in the 1960s.

The early 1970s brought some important changes to the baseball card scene. The decade's first two Topps issues were stunning in that the traditional white border was dropped in favor of gray in 1970, and black in 1971. In 1972, Topps' card design was absolutely psychedelic, with brightly colored frames around the player photos, and comic book typography popping out all over. The design for the 1973 cards was more traditional, but the photos were not. Instead of close-up portraits or posed "action" shots, many cards in the 1973 Topps set featured actual game action photos. Unfortunately, too many of those photos made it hard to tell which player was which, and the set was roundly panned by collectors.

But most significantly, 1973 marked the last year in which baseball cards were issued by series through the course of the summer. On the positive side, this eliminated the traditionally scarce "high numbers" produced toward the end of the season. On the negative side, it meant players who had been traded in the pre-season could no longer be shown in their "correct" uniforms, and outstanding new players had to wait a full year before their rookie cards would debut.

This marketing change made a significant impact on the hobby and helped spur a tremendous growth period in the late 1970s. By offering all of its cards at once, Topps made it easy for baseball card dealers to offer complete sets early in the year. Previously, collectors had to either assemble their sets by buying packs of cards, or wait until all series had been issued to buy a set from a dealer. It was in this era that many of today's top baseball card dealers got their start or made the switch to baseball cards as a full-time business.

During this era, the first significant national competition to Topps' baseball card monopoly in many years was introduced. Hostess, a bakery products company, began distributing baseball cards printed on the bottoms of packages of its snack cakes, while the Kellogg's company distributed simulated 3-D cards in boxes of its cereals. The eagerness with which collectors gobbled up these issues showed that the hobby was ready for a period of unprecedented growth.

The baseball card hobby literally boomed in 1981. A Federal court broke Topps' monopoly on the issue of baseball cards with bubble gum and Fleer of Philadelphia and Donruss of Memphis, entered the field as the first meaningful competition in nearly 20 years.

That same year also marked a beginning of the resurgence in the number of regional baseball card issues. Over the next few years, dozens of such sets came onto the market, helping to boost sales of everything from snack cakes to soda pop and police public relations. By 1984, more than half of the teams in the major leagues were issueing some type of baseball cards on a regional basis. The hobby had not enjoyed such diversity of issue since the mid-1950s.

While yet another court decision cost Fleer and Donruss the right to sell their baseball cards with bubble gum, both companies remained in the market and gained strength.

Topps' major contribution in this era was the introduction of annual "Traded" sets which offered cards of the year's new rookies as well as cards of traded players in their "correct" uniforms.

The mid-1980s showed continued strong growth in the number of active baseball card collectors, as well as the number of new baseball card issues. Topps, still the industry's leader, expanded the number and variety of its baseball issues with many different test issues and on-going specialty sets, including oversize cards, 3-D plastic cards, metal "cards" and much more.

After three years of over-production of its baseball card sets, Donruss, in 1984, significantly limited the number of cards printed, creating a situation in which demand exceeded supply, causing the value of Donruss cards to rise above Topps for the first time.

In 1984, Fleer followed Topps' lead and produced a season's-end "Update" set. Because the quantitiy of sets printed was extremely limited, and because it contains many of today's hottest young players, the 1984 Fleer Update set has become the most valuable baseball card issue produced in recent times.

In 1986, a fourth company joined the baseball "card wars." Called "Sprotflics," the cards were produced by a subsidiary of the Wrigley Gum company, and featured three different photos on each card in a simulated 3-D effect. For 1987, a fourth national baseball card set called Score entered the scene. A fifth national baseball card set (Upper Deck) was created for 1989.

Baseball card collecting entered its second century in 1987 and the hobby has never been stronger. It is the fastest growing hobby in the country. With more collectors and more new cards than ever before, 1990 looks like another growth year for baseball cards.

HOW TO USE THIS CATALOG

This catalog has been uniquely designed to serve the needs of both beginning and advanced collectors. It provides a comprehensive guide to more than 100 years of baseball card issues, arranged so that even the most novice collector can consult it with confidence and erase.

The following explanations summarize the general practices used in preparing this catalog's listings. However, because of specialized requirements which may vary from card set to card set, these must not be considered ironclad. Where these standards have been set aside, appropriate notations are incorporated.

ARRANGEMENT

Because the most important feature in identifying, and pricing, a baseball card is its set of origin, this catalog has been alphabetically arranged according to the name by which the set is mostly popularly known to collectors.

Those sets that were issued for more than one year are then listed chronologically, from earliest to most recent.

Within each set, the cards are lsited by their designated card number, or in the absence of card numbers, alphabetically according to the last name of the player pictured.

IDENTIFICATION

While most modern baseball cards are well identified on front, back or both, as to date and issue, such has not always been the case. In general, the back of the card is more usefull in identifying the set of origin than the front. The issuer or sponsor's name will usually appera on the back since, after all, baseball cards were first issued as a promotional item to stimulate sales of other products. As often as not, that issuer's name is the name by which the set is known to collectors and under which it will be found listed in this catalog.

Virtually every set listed in this catalog is accompanied by a photograph of a representative card. If all else fails, a comparison of an unknown card with the photos in this book will usually produce a match.

As a special feature, each set listed in this catalog has been cross-indexed by its date of issue. This will allow identification in some difficult cases since a baseball card's general age, if not specific year of issue, can usually be fixed by studying the biographical or statistical information on the back of the card. The last year mentioned in either the biography or stats is usually the year which preceded the year of issue.

PHOTOGRAPHS

A photograph of the front and back of at least one representative card from virtually every set listed in this catalog has been incorporated into the listings to aid in identification.

Photographs have been printed in reduced size. The actual size of cards in each set is given in the introductory text preceding its listing.

DATING

The dating of baseball cards by year of issue on the front of back of the card itself is a relatively new phenomenon. In most cases, to accurately determine a date of issue for an unidentified card, it must be studied for clues. As mentioned, the biography, career summary or statistics on the back of the card are the best way to pinpoint a year of issue. In most cases, the year of issue will be the year after the last season mentioned on the card.

Luckily for today's collector, earlier generations have done much of the research in deter- mining year of issue for those cards which bear no clues. the painstaking task of matching players' listed and/or pictured team against their career records often allowed an issue date to be determined.

In come cases, particular card sets were issued over a period of more than one calendar year, but since they are collected together as a single set, their specific year of issue is not important. Such sets will be listed with their complete known range of issue years, as 1909-1911 T206, or 1948-1949 Leaf, etc.

NUMBERING

While many baseball card issues as far back as the 1880s have contained card numbers assigned by the issuer, to facilitate the collecting of a complete set, the practice has by no means been universal. Even today, not every set bears card numbers.

Logically, those baseball cards which were numbered by their manufacturer are presented in that numerical order within the listings of this catalog. The many unnumbered issues, however, have been assigned Sports Collectors Digest Baseball Card Price Guide numbers to facilitate their universal identification within the hobby, especially when buying and selling by mail. In all cases, numbers which have been assigned, or which otherwise do not appear on the card through error or by design, are shown in this catalog within parenthesis. In virtually all cases, unless a more natural system suggested itself by the unique nature of a particular set, the assignment of Sports Collectors Digest Baseball Card Price Guide numbers by the cataloging staff has been done by alphabetical arrangement of the player's last names or the card's principal title.

Significant collectible variations of any particular card are noted within the listings by the application of a suffix letter within parentheses. In instances of variations, the suffix "a" is assigned to the variation which was created first.

NAMES

The identification of a player by full name on the front of his baseball card has been a common practice only since the 1920s. Prior to that, the player's last name and team were the more usual information found on the card front.

As a standard practice, the listings in the Sports Collectors Digest Baseball Card Price Guide present the player's name exactly as it appears on the front of the card, if his full name is given there. If the player's full name only appears on the back, rather than the front, of the card, the listing corresponds to that designation.

In cases where only the player's last name is given on the card, the cataloging staff has included the first name by which he was most often known for ease of identification.

Cards which contain misspelled first or last name, or even wrong initials, will have included in their listings the incorrect information, with a correction accompanying in parentheses. This extends, also, to cases where the name on the card does not correspond to the player actually picured.

GRADING

It is necessary that some sort of card grading standard be used so that buyer and seller (especially when dealing by mail) may reach an informed agreement on the value of a card. Each card set's listings are priced in the three grades of preservation in which those cards are most commonly encountered in the day to day buying and selling of the hobby marketplace.

Older cards are listed in grades of Near Mint (NR MT), Excellent (EX) and Very Good (VG), reflecting the basic fact that few cards were able to survive for 25, 50 or even 100 years in a close semblance to the condition of their issue. The pricing of cards in these three conditions will allow readers to accurately price cards which fall in intermediate grades, such as EX-MT, or VG-EX.

More recent issues, which have been preserved in top condition in considerable number, are listed in the grades of Mint (MT), Near Mint and Excellent, reflective of the fact that there exists in the current market little or no demand for cards of the recent past in grades below Excellent.

In general, although grades below Very Good are not priced in this catalog, close approximations of low-grade card values may figured on the following formula; Good condition cards are valued at about 50% of VG price, with Fair cads priced about 50% of Good. Cards in Poor condition have no market value except in the cases of the rarest and most expensive cards. In such cases, value has to be negotiated individually.

For the benefit of the reader, we present herewith the grading guide which was originally formulated by *Baseball Cards* magazine and *Sports Collectors Digest* in 1981, and has been continually refined since that time. These grading definitions have been used in the pricing of cards in this catalog, but they are by no means a universally accepted grading standard. The potential buyer of a basebll card should keep that in mind when encountering cards of nominally the same grade, but at a price which differs widely from that quoted in this book. Ultimately, the collector himself, must formulate his own personal grading standards in deciding whether cards available for purchase meet the needs of his own collection.

No collector or dealer is required to adhere to the grading standards presented herewith - or to any other published grading standards - but all are invited to do so. The editors of the *Sports Collectors Digest Baseball Card Price Guide* are eager to work toward the development of a standardized system of card grading that will be consistent with the realities of the hobby marketplace. Contact the editors.

Mint (MT): A perfect card. Well-centered, with parallel borders which appear equal to the naked eye. Four sharp, square corners. No creases, edge dents, surface scratches, paper flaws, loss of luster, yellowing or fading, regardless of age. No imperfectly printed card - out of register, badly cut or ink flawed - or card stained by contact with gum, wax or other substances can be considered truly Mint, even if new out of the pack.

Near Mint (NR MT): A nearly perfect card. At first glance, a Near Mint card appears perfect; upon closer examination, however, a minor flaw will be discovered. On well-centered cards, three of the four corners must be perfectly sharp; only one corner showing a minor imperfection upon close inspection. A slightly off-cente card with one or more borders being noticeable unequal - but still present - would also fit this grade.

Excellent (EX): Corners are still fairly sharp with only moderate wear. Card borders may be off center. No creases. May have very minor gum, wax or product stains, front or back. Surfaces may show slight loss of luster from rubbing across other cards.

Very Good (VG): Shows obvious handling. Corners rounded and/or perhaps showing minor creases. Other minor creases may be visible. Surfaces may exhibit loss of luster, but all printing is intact. May show major gum, wax or other packaging stains. No major creases, tape marks or extraneous markings or writing. Exhibits honest wear.

Good (G): A well-worn card, but exhibits no intentional damage or abuse. May have major or multiple creases. Corners rounded well beyond the border.

Fair: Shows excessive wear, along with damage or abuse. Will show all of the wear characteristics of a Good card, along with such damage as thumb tack holes in or near margins, evidence of having been taped or pasted, perhaps small tears around the edges, or creases so heavy as to break the cardboard. Backs may show minor added pen or pencil writing, or be missing small bits of paper. Still, a basically complete card.

Poor: A card that has been tortured to death. Corners or other areas may be torn off. Card may have been trimmed, show holes from paper punch or have been used for BB gun practice. Front may have extraneous pen or pencil writing, or other defacement. Major portions of front or back design may be missing. Not a pretty sight.

In addition to these seven widely-used grading terms, collectors will often encounter intermediate grades, such as VG-EX (Very Good to Excellent), EX-MT (Excellent to Mint), or NR MT-MT (Near Mint to Mint). Persons who describe a card with such grades are usually trying to convey that the card has all the characteristics of the lower grade, with enough of the higher grade to merit mention. Such cards are usually priced at a point midway between the two grades.

VALUATIONS

Values quoted in this book represent the current retail market and are compiled from recommendations provided and verified through the author's day to day involvement in the publication of the hobby's leading advertising periodicals, as well as the input of specialized consultants.

It should be stressed, however, that this book is intended to serve only as an aid in evaluating cards; actual market conditions are constantly changing. This is especially true of the cards of current players, whose on-field performance during the course of a season can greatly affect the value of their cards - upwards or downwards.

Publication of this catalog is not intended as a solicitation to buy or sell the listed cards by the editors, publishers or contributors.

Again, the values listed here are retail prices; what a collector can expect to pay when buying a card from a dealer. The wholesale price; that which a collector can expect to receive from a dealer when selling cards will be significantly lower. Most dealers operate on a 100% mark-up, generally paying about 50% of a card's retail value. On some high-demand cards, dealers will pay up to 75% or even 100% or more of retail value, anticipating continued price increases. Conversely, for many low-demand cards, such as common players' cards of recent years, dealers may pay 25% or even less of retail.

It should also be noted that with several hundred thousand valuations quoted in this book, there are bound to be a few compilations or typographical errors which will creep into the final product; a fact readers should remember if they encounter a listing at a fraction of, or several times, the card's actual current retail price. The editors welcome the correction of any such errors discovered. Write: *Sports Collectors Digest Baseball Card Price Guide,* 700 E. State St., Iola, WI 54990.

SETS

Collectors may note that the complete set prices for newer issues quoted in htese listings are usually significantly lower than the total of the value of the individula cards which comprise the set.

This reflects two factors in the baseball card market. First, a seller is often willing to take a lower composite price for a complete set as a "volume discount," and to avoid inventorying a large number of common player or other

lower-demand cards.

Second, to a degree, the value of common cards can be said to be inflated as a result of having built-in overhead charge to justify the dealer's time in sorting cards, carrying them in stock and filling orders. This accounts for the fact that even brand new baseball cards, which cost the dealer around 1¢ each when bought in bulk, carry individual price tags of 3¢ or higher.

ERRORS/VARIATIONS

It is often hard for the beginning collector to understand that an error on a baseball card, in and of itself, does not usually add premium value to that card. It is usually only when the correcting of an error in a subsequent printing

Minor errors such as wrong stats or personal data creates a variation that premium value attaches to an error. misspellings, inconsistencies, etc. - usually affecting the back of the card - are very common, especially in recent years. Unless a corrected variation was also printed, these

errors are not noted in the listings of this book because they are not generally perceived by collectors to have premium value.

On the other hand, major effort has been expended to include the most complete listings ever for collectible variation cards. Many scarce and valuable variations - dozens of them never before cataloged - are included in these listings because they are widely collected and often have significant premium value.

COUNTERFEITS/REPRINTS

As the value of baseball cards has risen in the past 10-20 years, certain cards and sets have become too expensive for the average collector to obtain. This, along with changes in the technology of color printing, have given rise to increasing numbers of counterfeit and reprint cards.

While both terms describe essentially the same thing - a modern copy which attempts to duplicate as closely as possible an original baseball card - there are differences which are important to the collector.

Generally, a counterfeit is made with the intention of deceiving somebody into believing it is genuine, and thus paying large amounts of money for it. The counterfeiter takes every pain to try to make his fakes look as authentic as possible. In recent years, the 1963 Pete Rose, 1984 Donruss Don Mattingly and more than 30 superstar cards of the late 1960s-early 1980s have been counterfeited - all were quickly detected because of the differences in

quality of cardboard on which they were printed.

A reprint, on the other hand, while it may have been made to look as close as possible to an original card, is made with the intention of allowing collectors to buy them as substitutes for cards they may never be otherwise able to afford. The big difference is that a reprint is generally marked as such, usually on the back of the card. In other cases, like the Topps 1952 reprint set, the replicas are printed in a size markedly different from the originals.

Collectors should be aware, however, that unscrupulous persons will sometimes cut off or otherwise obliterate the distinguishing word - "Reprint," "Copy", - or modern copyright date on the back of a reprint card in an attempt to pass it as genuine.

A collector's best defense against reprints and counterfeits is to acquire a knowledge of the "look" and "feel" of genuine baseball cards of various eras and issues.

UNLISTED CARDS

Readers who have cards or sets which are not covered in this edition are invited to correspond with the editor for purposes of adding to the compilation work now in progress.

Address: *Sports Collectors Digest Baseball Card Price Guide,* 700 E. State St., Iola, WI 54990.

Contributions will be acknowledged in future editions.

COLLECTOR ISSUES

There exists within the hobby a great body of cards which do not fall under the scope of this catalog by virtue of their nature of having been issued solely for the collector market. Known as "collector issues," these cards and sets are distinguished from "legitimate" issues in not having been created as a sales promotional item for another product or

service — bubble gum, soda, snack cakes, dog food, cigarettes, gasoline, etc.

By their nature, and principally because the person issuing them is always free to print and distribute more of the same if they should ever attain any real value, collector issues are generally regarded by collectors as having little or no premium value.

NEW ISSUES

Because new baseball cards are being issued all the time, the cataloging of them remains an on-going challenge. The editor will attempt to keep abreast of new issues so that they may be added to future editions of this book.

Readers are invited to submit news of new issues, especially limited-edition or regionally issued cards to the editors. Address: *Sports Collectors Digest Baseball Card Price Guide,* 700 E. State St., Iola, WI 54990.

14

Table of Contents

BILL HENDERSON'S CARDS
"King of the Commons"
2320 RUGER AVE. - KP
JANESVILLE, WISCONSIN 53545
1-608-755-0922

"ALWAYS BUYING"
Call or Write
for Quote

"ALWAYS BUYING"
Call or Write
for Quote

	HI # OR SCARCE SERIES	COMMONS EACH	EX/MT TO MINT CONDITION (scarce series)	GROUP LOTS FOR SALE — 50 Diff.	100 Diff.	300 Asst.	500 Asst.	VG+ -EX 50	100	200 Different
1948 BOWMAN	(37-48) 25.00	15.00								
1949 BOWMAN	(145-240) 80.00	15.00		675.				400.		
1950-51 BOWMAN	50 (1-72) 51 (253-324) 50.00	15.00	51 (2-36) 20.00	675.				400.		
1952 TOPPS	(311-407) P.O.R.	30.00	(2-80) 60.00	1350.				800.		
1952 BOWMAN	(217-252) 30.00	15.00	(2-36) 20.00	695.				400.		
1953 TOPPS	(220-280) 80.00	20.00	(2-165) 30.00	900.				600.		
1953 BOWMAN	(129-160) 40.00	30.00	(113-128) 50.00	1350.				800.		
1954 TOPPS		12.00	(51-75) 25.00	546.				480.		
1954 BOWMAN		7.00	(129-224) 8.00	315.	600.			210.		
1955 TOPPS	(161-210) 18.00	7.00	(151-160) 12.00	315.				210.		
1955 BOWMAN	(225-320) 15.-20. Umps	6.00	(2-96) 8.00	270.	500.			180.	350.	
1956 TOPPS		7.00	(181-260) 12.00	315.				210.	400.	
1957 TOPPS	(265-352) 17.50	5.00	(353-407) 5.00	220.	420.			155.	300.	
1958 TOPPS		3.50	(1-110) 5.00	155.	300.	850.		105.	200.	
1959 TOPPS	(507-572) 12.50	3.50	(1-110) 4.00	135.	260.	750.		90.	175.	385.
1960 TOPPS	(523-572) 12.50	1.75	(441-506) 3.50	85.	165.	450.	790.	52.	100.	190.
1961 TOPPS	(523-589) 25.00	1.50	(371-522) 2.00	65.	125.	360.	700.	45.	80.	155.
1962 TOPPS	(523-590) 12.50	1.50	(371-522) 2.00	65.	125.	360.		45.	80.	155.
1963 TOPPS	(447-576) 8.00	1.00	(197-446) 2.00	45.	90.			32.	60.	
1964 TOPPS	(523-587) 7.50	1.00	(371-522) 2.00	45.	90.			32.	60.	115.
1965 TOPPS	(447-522) 3.00 (523-598) 5.00	1.00	(371-446) 1.50	45.	90.			32.	60.	115.
1966 TOPPS	(523-598) 15.00	1.00	(447-522) 4.00	45.	90.			32.	60.	115.
1967 TOPPS	(534-609) 10.00	1.00	(458-533) 4.00	45.	90.			32.	60.	115.
1968 TOPPS		.75	(458-533) 1.00	35.	65.			23.	45.	85.
1969 TOPPS	(589-664) 1.00	.60	(219-327) 1.00	28.	55.	155.		18.	35.	65.
1970 TOPPS	(634-720) 2.50	.45	(547-633) 1.25	22.	42.	120.	190.	14.	26.	50.
1971 TOPPS	(644-752) 2.50	.45	(524-643) 1.50	22.	42.	120.		14.	26.	50.
1972 TOPPS	(657-787) 3.00	.45	(526-656) 1.50	22.	42.	*120.		14.	26.	50.
1973 TOPPS	(528-660) 2.00	.35	(397-528) .60	16.	32.	*90.		12.	22.	40.
1974 TOPPS		.35		16.	32.	*90.			22.	40.
1975 TOPPS	(8-132 .50)	.35		16.	32.	*90.			22.	40.
1976-77		.20			18.	*50.	* 85.		10.	18.
1978-1980		.15			13.	*38.	* 65.		8.	15.
1981 thru 1990 Topps, Fleer or Donruss Specify Year		.10			8.	*22.	*35.		5.	10.
& Company except below					Per Yr.	Per Yr.	Per Yr.			
1984-86 DONRUSS		.15			7.	13.	*38.	* 60.		

SPECIAL IN VG + -EX CONDITION-POSTPAID

250	58-62	300.
500	58-62	550.
250	60-69	170.
500	60-69	320.
1000	60-69	600.
250	70-79	50.
500	70-79	90.
1000	70-79	160.
250	80-84	15.
500	80-84	28.
1000	80-84	55.

*These lots are all different.
Special 1 Different from each year 1949-80 $130.00 postpaid.
Special 100 Different from each year 1956-80 $2600.00 postpaid.
Special 10 Different from each year 1956-80 $280.00 postpaid.

All lot groups are my choice only.

All assorted lots will contain as many different as possible.
Please list alternates whenever possible.
Send your want list and I will fill them at the above price for commons. High numbers, specials, scarce series, and stars extra.
You can use your Master Card or VISA to charge your purchases
Minimum order $7.50 - Postage and handling .50 per 100 cards (minimum $1.75)

Also interested in purchasing your collection.
Groups include various years of my choice.

SETS AVAILABLE
Topps 1988, 1989, 1990

$19.95 ea. $2.50 UPS
6 for $19.75 ea. $9.00 UPS
18 for $19.25 ea. $20.00 UPS
54 for $18.75 ea. $60.00 UPS

Mix or Match

Gregg Olson

1983 Affiliated Food Rangers

This 28-card set, featuring the Texas Rangers, was issued as a promotion by the Affiliated Food Stores chain of Arlington, Texas, late during the 1983 baseball season. Complete sets were given out free to youngsters 13 and under at the 9/3/83 Rangers game. The cards measure 2-3/8" by 3-1/2" and feature a full-color photo on the front. Also on the front, located inside a blue box, is the player's name, uniform number, and the words "1983 Rangers." The card backs contain a small player photo plus biographical and statistical information, along with the Affiliated logo and a brief promotional message. A total of 10,000 sets were reportedly printed. Cards are numbered by the players' uniform numbers in the checklist that follows.

		MT	NR MT	EX
Complete Set:		7.00	5.25	2.75
Common Player:		.10	.08	.04
1	Bill Stein	.10	.08	.04
2	Mike Richardt	.10	.08	.04
3	Wayne Tolleson	.10	.08	.04
5	Billy Sample	.10	.08	.04
6	Bobby Jones	.10	.08	.04
7	Bucky Dent	.30	.25	.12
8	Bobby Johnson	.10	.08	.04
9	Pete O'Brien	1.00	.70	.40
10	Jim Sundberg	.15	.11	.06
11	Doug Rader	.10	.08	.04
12	Dave Hostetler	.10	.08	.04
14	Larry Biittner	.10	.08	.04
15	Larry Parrish	.35	.25	.14
17	Mickey Rivers	.20	.15	.08
21	Odell Jones	.10	.08	.04
24	Dave Schmidt	.15	.11	.06
25	Buddy Bell	.50	.40	.20
26	George Wright	.10	.08	.04
28	Frank Tanana	.20	.15	.08
29	John Butcher	.10	.08	.04
32	Jon Matlack	.15	.11	.06
40	Rick Honeycutt	.15	.11	.06
41	Dave Tobik	.10	.08	.04
44	Danny Darwin	.15	.11	.06
46	Jim Anderson	.10	.08	.04
48	Mike Smithson	.10	.08	.04
49	Charlie Hough	.35	.25	.14
----	Coaching Staff (Rich Donnelly, Glenn Ezell, Merv Rettenmund, Dick Such, Wayne Terwilliger)	.10	.08	.04

NOTE: A card number in parentheses ( ) indicates the set is unnumbered.

1989 Ames 20/20 Club

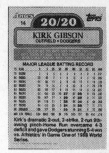

This 33-card set was produced by Topps for the Ames toy store chain. As its name implies, the special boxed set highlights members of the 20/20 club, players who have recorded 20 home runs and 20 stolen bases in the same season. The glossy cards feature action or posed photos on the front with the player's name at the top and "Ames 20/20 Club" along the bottom. The Topps logo appears in the upper right corner.

		MT	NR MT	EX
Complete Set:		5.00	3.75	2.00
Common Player:		.09	.07	.04
1	Jesse Barfield	.09	.07	.04
2	Kevin Bass	.09	.07	.04
3	Don Baylor	.09	.07	.04
4	George Bell	.12	.09	.05
5	Barry Bonds	.12	.09	.05
6	Phil Bradley	.09	.07	.04
7	Ellis Burks	.40	.30	.15
8	Jose Canseco	.70	.50	.30
9	Joe Carter	.15	.11	.06
10	Kal Daniels	.09	.07	.04
11	Eric Davis	.40	.30	.15
12	Mike Davis	.09	.07	.04
13	Andre Dawson	.12	.09	.05
14	Kirk Gibson	.09	.07	.04
15	Pedro Guerrero	.12	.09	.05
16	Rickey Henderson	.50	.40	.20
17	Bo Jackson	1.00	.70	.40
18	Howard Johnson	.20	.15	.08
19	Jeffrey Leonard	.09	.07	.04
20	Kevin McReynolds	.12	.09	.05
21	Dale Murphy	.09	.07	.04
22	Dwayne Murphy	.09	.07	.04
23	Dave Parker	.12	.09	.05
24	Kirby Puckett	.50	.40	.20
25	Juan Samuel	.09	.07	.04
26	Ryne Sandberg	.20	.15	.08
27	Mike Schmidt	.80	.60	.30
28	Darryl Strawberry	.25	.20	.10
29	Alan Trammell	.09	.07	.04
30	Andy Van Slyke	.09	.07	.04
31	Devon White	.09	.07	.04
32	Dave Winfield	.12	.09	.05
33	Robin Yount	.30	.25	.12

1986 Ault Foods Blue Jays

The Ault Foods Blue Jays set is comprised of 24 full-color stickers. Designed to be placed in a special album, the stickers measure 2" by 3" in size. The attractive album measures 9" by 12" and is printed on glossy stock. While the stickers carry no information except for the player's last name and uniform number, the 20-page album contains extensive personal and statistical information about each of the 24 players.

	MT	NR MT	EX
Complete Set:	33.00	25.00	14.00

BELL

		NR MT	EX	VG
Common Player:		.60	.45	.25
Album:		5.00	3.75	2.00
1	Tony Fernandez	2.75	2.00	1.00
5	Rance Mulliniks	.60	.45	.25
7	Damaso Garcia	.60	.45	.25
11	George Bell	4.00	3.00	1.50
12	Ernie Whitt	.90	.70	.35
13	Buck Martinez	.60	.45	.25
15	Lloyd Moseby	1.25	.90	.50
16	Garth Iorg	.60	.45	.25
17	Kelly Gruber	.90	.70	.35
18	Jim Clancy	.90	.70	.35
22	Jimmy Key	2.00	1.50	.80
23	Cecil Fielder	.90	.70	.35
25	Steve Davis	.60	.45	.25
26	Willie Upshaw	.90	.70	.35
29	Jesse Barfield	2.50	2.00	1.00
31	Jim Acker	.60	.45	.25
33	Doyle Alexander	.90	.70	.35
36	Bill Caudill	.60	.45	.25
37	Dave Stieb	2.00	1.50	.80
39	Don Gordon	.60	.45	.25
44	Cliff Johnson	.60	.45	.25
46	Gary Lavelle	.60	.45	.25
50	Tom Henke	1.25	.90	.50
53	Dennis Lamp	.60	.45	.25

1948 Babe Ruth Story

The Philadelphia Gum Co., in 1948, created a card set about the movie "The Babe Ruth Story", which starred William Bendix and Claire Trevor. The set, whose American Card Catalog designation is R421, contains 28 black and white, numbered cards which measure 2" by 2-1/2". The Babe Ruth Story set was originally intended to consist of sixteen cards. Twelve additional cards (#'s 17-28) were added when Ruth died before the release of the film. The card backs include a offer for an autographed photo of William Bendix, starring as the Babe, for five Swell Bubble Gum wrappers and five cents.

	NR MT	EX	VG
Complete Set:	900.00	350.00	220.00
Common Player: 1-16	12.00	6.00	3.50
Common Player: 17-28	35.00	17.50	10.50

		NR MT	EX	VG
1	"The Babe Ruth Story" In The Making	30.00	15.00	9.00
2	Bat Boy Becomes the Babe... William Bendix	12.00	6.00	3.50
3	Claire Hodgson...Claire Trevor	12.00	6.00	3.50
4	Babe Ruth and Claire Hodgson	12.00	6.00	3.50
5	Brother Matthias...Charles Bickford	12.00	6.00	3.50
6	Phil Conrad...Sam Levene	12.00	6.00	3.50
7	Night Club Singer...Gertrude Niesen	12.00	6.00	3.50
8	Baseball's Famous Deal...Jack Dunn (William Frawley)	12.00	6.00	3.50
9	Mr. & Mrs. Babe Ruth	12.00	6.00	3.50
10	Babe Ruth, Claire Ruth, and Brother Matthias	12.00	6.00	3.50
11	Babe Ruth and Miller Huggins (Fred Lightner)	12.00	6.00	3.50
12	Babe Ruth At Bed Of Ill Boy Johnny Sylvester (Gregory Marshall)	12.00	6.00	3.50
13	Sylvester Family Listening To Game	12.00	6.00	3.50
14	"When A Feller Needs a Friend" (With Dog At Police Station)	12.00	6.00	3.50
15	Dramatic Home Run	12.00	6.00	3.50
16	The Homer That Set the Record (#60)	12.00	6.00	3.50
17	"The Slap That Started Baseball's Famous Career"	35.00	17.50	10.50
18	The Babe Plays Santa Claus	35.00	17.50	10.50
19	Meeting Of Owner And Manager	35.00	17.50	10.50
20	"Broken Window Paid Off"	35.00	17.50	10.50
21	Babe In A Crowd Of Autograph Collectors	35.00	17.50	10.50
22	Charley Grimm And William Bendix	35.00	17.50	10.50
23	Ted Lyons And William Bendix	35.00	17.50	10.50
24	Lefty Gomez, William Bendix, And Bucky Harris	40.00	20.00	12.00
25	Babe Ruth and William Bendix	65.00	33.00	20.00
26	Babe Ruth And William Bendix	65.00	33.00	20.00
27	Babe Ruth And Claire Trevor	65.00	33.00	20.00
28	William Bendix, Babe Ruth, And Claire Trevor	70.00	35.00	21.00

1988 Baseball Immortals

One of the most popular of the "collectors' issues", this set is produced with the permission of Major League Baseball by Renata Galasso Inc. and TCMA. The set features players in the Baseball Hall of Fame and was first issued in 1980. Each year since 1980 the set has been updated to include new inductees. The cards measure 2-1/2" by 3-1/2" and have colorful borders. The card fronts include the player's name, position and year of induction. The backs feature a short biography and a trivia question. The photos used are color; most players who were active before 1950 have colored black and white photos. The designation "first printing" appears on all cards issued 1981 and after.

		MT	NR MT	EX
Complete Set:		12.00	9.00	4.75
Common Player:		.03	.02	.01
1	Babe Ruth	.15	.11	.06

PAYING TOP DOLLAR

- Over 10,000 + store and mail order customers need your cards.
- We have a six figure bank balance to support our buying commitment.
- All transactions and payments are mailed within 24 hours.

WE WANT TO BUY!

We will pay cash for the following:
Large and Small collections - Star cards - Baseball sets - Unopened Boxes & Cases - Football, Basketball, - Hockey sets - Hartland Statues - All Sports Memorabilia - Tobacco Cards etc.

- *Please feel FREE TO CALL AND discuss any transactions!*

FREE
1990 illustrated catalog is available. Included in it is a variety of material 1910-1980's, including stars, complete sets, unopened material, rookie cards, Hartlands, bulk lots, etc. Please send two 25 cents stamps.

14038 Beach Blvd. A-1
Westminster, CA 92683
(714) 895-4401
FAX (714) 891-8078
Call David Kohler or Joe Kohler

#	Name	MT	NR MT	EX
2	Ty Cobb	.10	.08	.04
3	Walter Johnson	.07	.05	.03
4	Christy Mathewson	.07	.05	.03
5	Honus Wagner	.07	.05	.03
6	Morgan Bulkeley	.03	.02	.01
7	Ban Johnson	.03	.02	.01
8	Larry Lajoie	.05	.04	.02
9	Connie Mack	.05	.04	.02
10	John McGraw	.05	.04	.02
11	Tris Speaker	.05	.04	.02
12	George Wright	.03	.02	.01
13	Cy Young	.07	.05	.03
14	Grover Alexander	.05	.04	.02
15	Alexander Cartwright	.03	.02	.01
16	Henry Chadwick	.03	.02	.01
17	Cap Anson	.05	.04	.02
18	Eddie Collins	.05	.04	.02
19	Charles Comiskey	.03	.02	.01
20	Candy Cummings	.03	.02	.01
21	Buck Ewing	.03	.02	.01
22	Lou Gehrig	.10	.08	.04
23	Willie Keeler	.03	.02	.01
24	Hoss Radbourne	.03	.02	.01
25	George Sisler	.05	.04	.02
26	Albert Spalding	.03	.02	.01
27	Rogers Hornsby	.07	.05	.03
28	Judge Landis	.03	.02	.01
29	Roger Bresnahan	.03	.02	.01
30	Dan Brouthers	.03	.02	.01
31	Fred Clarke	.03	.02	.01
32	James Collins	.03	.02	.01
33	Ed Delahanty	.03	.02	.01
34	Hugh Duffy	.03	.02	.01
35	Hughie Jennings	.03	.02	.01
36	Mike "King" Kelly	.03	.02	.01
37	James O'Rourke	.03	.02	.01
38	Wilbert Robinson	.03	.02	.01
39	Jesse Burkett	.03	.02	.01
40	Frank Chance	.03	.02	.01
41	Jack Chesbro	.03	.02	.01
42	John Evers	.03	.02	.01
43	Clark Griffith	.03	.02	.01
44	Thomas McCarthy	.03	.02	.01
45	Joe McGinnity	.03	.02	.01
46	Eddie Plank	.03	.02	.01
47	Joe Tinker	.03	.02	.01
48	Rube Waddell	.03	.02	.01
49	Ed Walsh	.03	.02	.01
50	Mickey Cochrane	.05	.04	.02
51	Frankie Frisch	.03	.02	.01
52	Lefty Grove	.05	.04	.02
53	Carl Hubbell	.05	.04	.02
54	Herb Pennock	.03	.02	.01
55	Pie Traynor	.03	.02	.01
56	Three Finger Brown	.03	.02	.01
57	Charlie Gehringer	.05	.04	.02
58	Kid Nichols	.03	.02	.01
59	Jimmie Foxx	.07	.05	.03
60	Mel Ott	.05	.04	.02
61	Harry Heilmann	.03	.02	.01
62	Paul Waner	.03	.02	.01
63	Ed Barrow	.03	.02	.01
64	Chief Bender	.03	.02	.01
65	Tom Connolly	.03	.02	.01
66	Dizzy Dean	.07	.05	.03
67	Bill Klem	.03	.02	.01
68	Al Simmons	.03	.02	.01
69	Bobby Wallace	.03	.02	.01
70	Harry Wright	.03	.02	.01
71	Bill Dickey	.05	.04	.02
72	Rabbit Maranville	.03	.02	.01
73	Bill Terry	.05	.04	.02
74	Home Run Baker	.03	.02	.01
75	Joe DiMaggio	.10	.08	.04
76	Gabby Hartnett	.03	.02	.01
77	Ted Lyons	.03	.02	.01
78	Ray Schalk	.03	.02	.01
79	Dazzy Vance	.03	.02	.01
80	Joe Cronin	.05	.04	.02
81	Hank Greenberg	.05	.04	.02
82	Sam Crawford	.03	.02	.01
83	Joe McCarthy	.03	.02	.01
84	Zack Wheat	.03	.02	.01
85	Max Carey	.03	.02	.01
86	Billy Hamilton	.03	.02	.01
87	Bob Feller	.07	.05	.03
88	Bill McKechnie	.03	.02	.01
89	Jackie Robinson	.10	.08	.04
90	Edd Roush	.03	.02	.01
91	John Clarkson	.03	.02	.01
92	Elmer Flick	.03	.02	.01
93	Sam Rice	.03	.02	.01
94	Eppa Rixey	.03	.02	.01
95	Luke Appling	.03	.02	.01
96	Red Faber	.03	.02	.01
97	Burleigh Grimes	.03	.02	.01
98	Miller Huggins	.03	.02	.01
99	Tim Keefe	.03	.02	.01
100	Heinie Manush	.03	.02	.01
101	John Ward	.03	.02	.01
102	Pud Galvin	.03	.02	.01
103	Casey Stengel	.07	.05	.03
104	Ted Williams	.10	.08	.04
105	Branch Rickey	.03	.02	.01
106	Red Ruffing	.03	.02	.01
107	Lloyd Waner	.03	.02	.01
108	Kiki Cuyler	.03	.02	.01
109	Goose Goslin	.03	.02	.01
110	Joe (Ducky) Medwick	.03	.02	.01
111	Roy Campanella	.07	.05	.03
112	Stan Coveleski	.03	.02	.01
113	Waite Hoyt	.03	.02	.01
114	Stan Musial	.10	.08	.04
115	Lou Boudreau	.03	.02	.01
116	Earle Combs	.03	.02	.01
117	Ford Frick	.03	.02	.01
118	Jesse Haines	.03	.02	.01
119	Dave Bancroft	.03	.02	.01
120	Jake Beckley	.03	.02	.01
121	Chick Hafey	.03	.02	.01
122	Harry Hooper	.03	.02	.01
123	Joe Kelley	.03	.02	.01
124	Rube Marquard	.03	.02	.01
125	Satchel Paige	.05	.04	.02
126	George Weiss	.03	.02	.01
127	Yogi Berra	.07	.05	.03
128	Josh Gibson	.03	.02	.01
129	Lefty Gomez	.05	.04	.02
130	Will Harridge	.03	.02	.01
131	Sandy Koufax	.07	.05	.03
132	Buck Leonard	.03	.02	.01
133	Early Wynn	.03	.02	.01
134	Ross Youngs	.03	.02	.01
135	Roberto Clemente	.10	.08	.04
136	Billy Evans	.03	.02	.01
137	Monte Irvin	.03	.02	.01
138	George Kelly	.03	.02	.01
139	Warren Spahn	.07	.05	.03
140	Mickey Welch	.03	.02	.01
141	Cool Papa Bell	.03	.02	.01
142	Jim Bottomley	.03	.02	.01
143	Jocko Conlan	.03	.02	.01
144	Whitey Ford	.03	.02	.01
145	Mickey Mantle	.15	.11	.08
146	Sam Thompson	.03	.02	.01
147	Earl Averill	.03	.02	.01
148	Bucky Harris	.03	.02	.01
149	Billy Herman	.03	.02	.01
150	Judy Johnson	.03	.02	.01
151	Ralph Kiner	.05	.04	.02
152	Oscar Charleston	.03	.02	.01
153	Roger Connor	.03	.02	.01
154	Cal Hubbard	.03	.02	.01
155	Bob Lemon	.03	.02	.01
156	Fred Lindstrom	.03	.02	.01
157	Robin Roberts	.03	.02	.01
158	Ernie Banks	.05	.04	.02
159	Martin Dihigo	.03	.02	.01
160	John Henry Lloyd	.03	.02	.01
161	Al Lopez	.03	.02	.01
162	Amos Rusie	.03	.02	.01
163	Joe Sewell	.03	.02	.01
164	Addie Joss	.03	.02	.01
165	Larry MacPhail	.03	.02	.01
166	Eddie Mathews	.03	.02	.01
167	Warren Giles	.03	.02	.01
168	Willie Mays	.12	.09	.05
169	Hack Wilson	.03	.02	.01
170	Duke Snider	.07	.05	.03
171	Al Kaline	.05	.04	.02
172	Chuck Klein	.03	.02	.01
173	Tom Yawkey	.03	.02	.01
174	Bob Gibson	.05	.04	.02
175	Rube Foster	.03	.02	.01
176	Johnny Mize	.03	.02	.01
177	Hank Aaron	.12	.09	.05
178	Frank Robinson	.05	.04	.02
179	Happy Chandler	.03	.02	.01
180	Travis Jackson	.03	.02	.01
181	Brooks Robinson	.05	.04	.02
182	Juan Marichal	.03	.02	.01
183	George Kell	.03	.02	.01

ℱans

The home of the 1939 Lou Gehrig
All-Star Pin loaned for exhibit to the
National Baseball Hall of Fame and
Museum, Cooperstown, NY

Our reputation for integrity, customer satisfaction, real-price appraisals and exhibition quality memorabilia speaks for itself.....

ℱans is always buying and selling Baseball's historic rarities.

We are actively buying and selling quality memorabilia relating to the History
of Baseball, especially its famous players, personalities, teams, historic
events, autographed bats, photos, single-signed and team balls with
deceased Hall of Famers. Call, write, send xerox, description or FAX with
asking price for a prompt and entirely confidential response.

Nobody pays more or faster for baseball's historic rarities

Stephan A. Tuchman and Richard E. Russek

FAMOUS AMERICAN NAME SALES, INC.

EXHIBITION QUALITY SPORTS COLLECTIBLES AND MEMORABILIA

184 Hempstead Avenue, West Hempstead, New York 11552 • 516 486-1400 • 800 552-9836 • FAX 516 486-1716

		MT	NR MT	EX
184	Walter Alston	.03	.02	.01
185	Harmon Killebrew	.05	.04	.02
186	Luis Aparicio	.03	.02	.01
187	Don Drysdale	.05	.04	.02
188	Pee Wee Reese	.05	.04	.02
189	Rick Ferrell	.03	.02	.01
190	Willie McCovey	.05	.04	.02
191	Ernie Lombardi	.03	.02	.01
192	Bobby Doerr	.03	.02	.01
193	Arky Vaughan	.03	.02	.01
194	Enos Slaughter	.03	.02	.01
195	Lou Brock	.05	.04	.02
196	Hoyt Wilhelm	.03	.02	.01
197	Billy Williams	.03	.02	.01
198	"Catfish" Hunter	.03	.02	.01
199	Ray Dandridge	.03	.02	.01

1987 Baseball Super Stars Discs

Produced by Mike Schecter and Associates, the "Baseball Super Stars" disc set was released as part of a promotion for various brands of iced tea mixes in many parts of the country. Among the brands participating in the promotion were Acme, Alpha Beta, Bustelo, Key, King Kullen, Lady Lee, Our Own and Weis. The discs were issued in three-part folding panels with each disc measuring 2-1/2" in diameter. The disc fronts feature a full-color photo inside a bright yellow border. Two player discs were included in each panel along with a coupon disc offering either an uncut press sheet of the set or a facsimile autographed ball.

		MT	NR MT	EX
Complete Panel Set:		6.00	4.50	2.50
Complete Singles Set:		2.00	1.50	.80
Common Panel:		.25	.20	.10
Common Single Player:		.05	.04	.02
Panel		.90	.70	.35
1	Darryl Strawberry	.20	.15	.08
2	Roger Clemens	.20	.15	.08
Panel		.35	.25	.14
3	Ron Darling	.08	.06	.03
4	Keith Hernandez	.10	.08	.04
Panel		1.25	.90	.50
5	Tony Pena	.05	.04	.02
6	Don Mattingly	.70	.50	.30
Panel		.90	.70	.35
7	Eric Davis	.25	.20	.10
8	Gary Carter	.12	.09	.05
Panel		.80	.60	.30
9	Dave Winfield	.12	.09	.05
10	Wally Joyner	.20	.15	.08
Panel		.50	.40	.20
11	Mike Schmidt	.15	.11	.06
12	Robby Thompson	.05	.04	.02
Panel		.90	.70	.35
13	Wade Boggs	.35	.25	.14
14	Cal Ripken Jr.	.12	.09	.05
Panel		.90	.70	.35
15	Dale Murphy	.20	.15	.08
16	Tony Gwynn	.15	.11	.06
Panel		1.25	.90	.50
17	Jose Canseco	.40	.30	.15

		MT	NR MT	EX
18	Rickey Henderson	.20	.15	.08
Panel		.25	.20	.10
19	Lance Parrish	.08	.06	.03
20	Dave Righetti	.08	.06	.03

1988 Baseball Super Stars Discs

The "Second Annual Collector's Edition" of Baseball Super Stars Discs is very similar to the 1987 issue. A set of 20 discs (2-1/2" diameter) featuring full-color baseball player photos was inserted in specially marked cannisters of iced tea and fruit drinks. Each tripled-fold insert consists of 2 player discs and one redemption card. Player discs are bright blue, yellow, red and green with a diamond design framing the player closeup. The player name appears upper left, the set logo appears upper right. Personalized disc series were issued for Tetley, Weis, Key Food and A&P supermarkets (untitled series were also sold at Lucky, Skaggs, Alpha Beta, Acme King Kullen, Laneco and Krasdale stores). The series name (i.e. Weis Winners) is printed below the player photo.

		MT	NR MT	EX
Complete Panel Set:		6.00	4.50	2.50
Complete Singles Set:		2.00	1.50	.80
Common Panel:		.60	.45	.25
Common Single Player:		.05	.04	.02
Panel		1.00	.70	.40
1	Wade Boggs	.35	.25	.14
2	Ellis Burks	.20	.15	.08
Panel		1.25	.90	.50
3	Don Mattingly	.70	.50	.30
4	Mark McGwire	.25	.20	.10
Panel		.70	.50	.30
5	Matt Nokes	.10	.08	.04
6	Kirby Puckett	.20	.15	.08
Panel		.80	.60	.30
7	Billy Ripken	.08	.06	.03
8	Kevin Seitzer	.15	.11	.06
Panel		.90	.70	.35
9	Roger Clemens	.20	.15	.08
10	Will Clark	.40	.30	.15
Panel		.80	.60	.30
11	Vince Coleman	.10	.08	.04
12	Eric Davis	.25	.20	.10
Panel		.70	.50	.30
13	Dave Magadan	.05	.04	.02
14	Dale Murphy	.20	.15	.08
Panel		.80	.60	.30
15	Benito Santiago	.10	.08	.04
16	Mike Schmidt	.30	.25	.12
Panel		.60	.45	.25
17	Darryl Strawberry	.20	.15	.08
18	Steve Bedrosian	.05	.04	.02
Panel		.80	.60	.30
19	Dwight Gooden	.20	.15	.08
20	Fernando Valenzuela	.05	.04	.03

A player's name In *italic* type Indicates a rookie card. An (FC) Indicates a player's first card for that particular card company.

1934 Batter-Up

National Chicle's 192-card "Batter-Up" set was issued from 1934 through 1936. The blank-backed cards are die-cut, enabling collectors of the era to fold the top of the card over so that it could stand upright on its own support. The cards can be found in black and white or a variety of color tints. Card numbers 1-80 measure 2-3/8" by 3-1/4" in size, while the high-numbered cards (#'s 81-192) measure 1/4" smaller in width. The high-numbered cards are significantly more difficult to find than the lower numbers. The set's ACC designation is R318.

	NR MT	EX	VG
Complete Set:	13500.00	6750.00	4050.
Common Player: 1-80	40.00	20.00	12.00
Common Player: 81-192	75.00	37.00	22.00

		NR MT	EX	VG
1	Wally Berger	75.00	30.00	12.00
2	Ed Brandt	40.00	20.00	12.00
3	Al Lopez	75.00	30.00	12.00
4	Dick Bartell	40.00	20.00	12.00
5	Carl Hubbell	90.00	45.00	27.00
6	Bill Terry	90.00	45.00	27.00
7	Pepper Martin	40.00	20.00	12.00
8	Jim Bottomley	75.00	37.00	22.00
9	Tommy Bridges	40.00	20.00	12.00
10	Rick Ferrell	75.00	37.00	22.00
11	Ray Benge	40.00	20.00	12.00
12	Wes Ferrell	40.00	20.00	12.00
13	Bill Cissell	40.00	20.00	12.00
14	Pie Traynor	75.00	37.00	22.00
15	Roy Mahaffey	40.00	20.00	12.00
16	Chick Hafey	75.00	37.00	22.00
17	Lloyd Waner	75.00	37.00	22.00
18	Jack Burns	40.00	20.00	12.00
19	Buddy Myer	40.00	20.00	12.00
20	Bob Johnson	40.00	20.00	12.00
21	Arky Vaughn (Vaughan)	75.00	37.00	22.00
22	Red Rolfe	40.00	20.00	12.00
23	Lefty Gomez	100.00	45.00	27.00
24	Earl Averill	50.00	25.00	15.00
25	Mickey Cochrane	75.00	37.00	22.00
26	Van Mungo	40.00	20.00	12.00
27	Mel Ott	125.00	56.00	35.00
28	Jimmie Foxx	150.00	60.00	38.00
29	Jimmy Dykes	40.00	20.00	12.00
30	Bill Dickey	125.00	56.00	35.00
31	Lefty Grove	100.00	45.00	27.00
32	Joe Cronin	75.00	37.00	22.00
33	Frankie Frisch	100.00	45.00	27.00
34	Al Simmons	75.00	37.00	22.00
35	Rogers Hornsby	150.00	60.00	38.00
36	Ted Lyons	75.00	37.00	22.00
37	Rabbit Maranville	75.00	37.00	22.00
38	Jimmie Wilson	40.00	20.00	12.00
39	Willie Kamm	40.00	20.00	12.00
40	Bill Hallahan	40.00	20.00	12.00
41	Gus Suhr	40.00	20.00	12.00
42	Charlie Gehringer	100.00	45.00	27.00
43	Joe Heving	40.00	20.00	12.00
44	Adam Comorosky	40.00	20.00	12.00
45	Tony Lazzeri	75.00	37.00	22.00
46	Sam Leslie	40.00	20.00	12.00
47	Bob Smith	40.00	20.00	12.00
48	Willis Hudlin	40.00	20.00	12.00
49	Carl Reynolds	40.00	20.00	12.00
50	Fred Schulte	40.00	20.00	12.00

		NR MT	EX	VG
51	Cookie Lavagetto	40.00	20.00	12.00
52	Hal Schumacher	40.00	20.00	12.00
53	Doc Cramer	40.00	20.00	12.00
54	Si Johnson	40.00	20.00	12.00
55	Ollie Bejma	40.00	20.00	12.00
56	Sammy Byrd	40.00	20.00	12.00
57	Hank Greenberg	100.00	45.00	27.00
58	Bill Knickerbocker	40.00	20.00	12.00
59	Billy Urbanski	40.00	20.00	12.00
60	Ed Morgan	40.00	20.00	12.00
61	Eric McNair	40.00	20.00	12.00
62	Ben Chapman	40.00	20.00	12.00
63	Roy Johnson	40.00	20.00	12.00
64	"Dizzy" Dean	300.00	120.00	75.00
65	Zeke Bonura	40.00	20.00	12.00
66	Firpo Marberry	40.00	20.00	12.00
67	Gus Mancuso	40.00	20.00	12.00
68	Joe Vosmik	40.00	20.00	12.00
69	Earl Grace	40.00	20.00	12.00
70	Tony Piet	40.00	20.00	12.00
71	Rollie Hemsley	40.00	20.00	12.00
72	Fred Fitzsimmons	40.00	20.00	12.00
73	Hack Wilson	75.00	37.00	22.00
74	Chick Fullis	40.00	20.00	12.00
75	Fred Frankhouse	40.00	20.00	12.00
76	Ethan Allen	40.00	20.00	12.00
77	Heinie Manush	50.00	25.00	15.00
78	Rip Collins	40.00	20.00	12.00
79	Tony Cuccinello	40.00	20.00	12.00
80	Joe Kuhel	40.00	20.00	12.00
81	Thomas Bridges	75.00	37.00	22.00
82	Clinton Brown	75.00	37.00	22.00
83	Albert Blanche	75.00	37.00	22.00
84	"Boze" Berger	75.00	37.00	22.00
85	Goose Goslin	200.00	80.00	50.00
86	Vernon Gomez	275.00	110.00	69.00
87	Joe Glen (Glenn)	75.00	37.00	22.00
88	"Cy" Blanton	75.00	37.00	22.00
89	Tom Carey	75.00	37.00	22.00
90	Ralph Birkhofer	75.00	37.00	22.00
91	Frank Gabler	75.00	37.00	22.00
92	Dick Coffman	75.00	37.00	22.00
93	Ollie Bejma	75.00	37.00	22.00
94	Leroy Earl Parmalee	75.00	37.00	22.00
95	Carl Reynolds	75.00	37.00	22.00
96	Ben Cantwell	75.00	37.00	22.00
97	Curtis Davis	75.00	37.00	22.00
98	Wallace Moses, Billy Webb	75.00	37.00	22.00
99	Ray Benge	75.00	37.00	22.00
100	"Pie" Traynor	200.00	80.00	50.00
101	Phil. Cavarretta	75.00	37.00	22.00
102	"Pep" Young	75.00	37.00	22.00
103	Willis Hudlin	75.00	37.00	22.00
104	Mickey Haslin	75.00	37.00	22.00
105	Oswald Bluege	75.00	37.00	22.00
106	Paul Andrews	75.00	37.00	22.00
107	Edward A. Brandt	75.00	37.00	22.00
108	Dan Taylor	75.00	37.00	22.00
109	Thornton T. Lee	75.00	37.00	22.00
110	Hal Schumacher	75.00	37.00	22.00
111	Minter Hayes, Ted Lyons	150.00	60.00	38.00
112	Odell Hale	75.00	37.00	22.00
113	Earl Averill	150.00	60.00	38.00
114	Italo Chelini	75.00	37.00	22.00
115	Ivy Andrews, Jim Bottomley	150.00	60.00	38.00
116	Bill Walker	75.00	37.00	22.00
117	Bill Dickey	275.00	110.00	69.00
118	Gerald Walker	75.00	37.00	22.00
119	Ted Lyons	150.00	60.00	38.00
120	Elden Auker (Eldon)	75.00	37.00	22.00
121	Wild Bill Hallahan	75.00	37.00	22.00
122	Freddy Lindstrom	175.00	70.00	44.00
123	Oral C. Hildebrand	75.00	37.00	22.00
124	Luke Appling	175.00	70.00	44.00
125	"Pepper" Martin	80.00	40.00	24.00
126	Rick Ferrell	175.00	70.00	44.00
127	Ival Goodman	75.00	37.00	22.00
128	Joe Kuhel	75.00	37.00	22.00
129	Ernest Lombardi	175.00	70.00	44.00
130	Charles Gehringer	250.00	100.00	63.00
131	Van L. Mungo	80.00	40.00	24.00
132	Larry French	75.00	37.00	22.00
133	"Buddy" Myer	75.00	37.00	22.00
134	Mel Harder	75.00	37.00	22.00
135	Augie Galan	75.00	37.00	22.00
136	"Gabby" Hartnett	175.00	70.00	44.00
137	Stan Hack	75.00	37.00	22.00
138	Billy Herman	175.00	70.00	44.00
139	Bill Jurges	75.00	37.00	22.00
140	Bill Lee	75.00	37.00	22.00
141	"Zeke" Bonura	75.00	37.00	22.00

		NR MT	EX	VG
142	Tony Piet	75.00	37.00	22.00
143	Paul Dean	125.00	56.00	35.00
144	Jimmy Foxx	350.00	140.00	88.00
145	Joe Medwick	175.00	70.00	44.00
146	Rip Collins	75.00	37.00	22.00
147	Melo Almada	75.00	37.00	22.00
148	Allan Cooke	75.00	37.00	22.00
149	Moe Berg	75.00	37.00	22.00
150	Adolph Camilli	75.00	37.00	22.00
151	Oscar Melillo	75.00	37.00	22.00
152	Bruce Campbell	75.00	37.00	22.00
153	Lefty Grove	300.00	120.00	75.00
154	John Murphy	75.00	37.00	22.00
155	Luke Sewell	75.00	37.00	22.00
156	Leo Durocher	175.00	70.00	44.00
157	Lloyd Waner	175.00	70.00	44.00
158	Guy Bush	75.00	37.00	22.00
159	Jimmy Dykes	75.00	37.00	22.00
160	Steve O'Neill	75.00	37.00	22.00
161	Gen. Crowder	75.00	37.00	22.00
162	Joe Cascarella	75.00	37.00	22.00
163	"Bud" Hafey	75.00	37.00	22.00
164	"Gilly" Campbell	75.00	37.00	22.00
165	Ray Hayworth	75.00	37.00	22.00
166	Frank Demaree	75.00	37.00	22.00
167	John Babich	75.00	37.00	22.00
168	Marvin Owen	75.00	37.00	22.00
169	Ralph Kress	75.00	37.00	22.00
170	"Mule" Haas	75.00	37.00	22.00
171	Frank Higgins	75.00	37.00	22.00
172	Walter Berger	75.00	37.00	22.00
173	Frank Frisch	200.00	80.00	50.00
174	Wess Ferrell (Wes)	75.00	37.00	22.00
175	Pete Fox	75.00	37.00	22.00
176	John Vergez	75.00	37.00	22.00
177	William Rogell	75.00	37.00	22.00
178	"Don" Brennan	75.00	37.00	22.00
179	James Bottomley	125.00	62.00	37.00
180	Travis Jackson	175.00	70.00	44.00
181	Robert Rolfe	80.00	40.00	24.00
182	Frank Crosetti	125.00	56.00	35.00
183	Joe Cronin	175.00	70.00	44.00
184	"Schoolboy" Rowe	80.00	40.00	24.00
185	"Chuck" Klein	175.00	70.00	44.00
186	Lon Warneke	75.00	37.00	22.00
187	Gus Suhr	75.00	37.00	22.00
188	Ben Chapman	80.00	40.00	24.00
189	Clint. Brown	75.00	37.00	22.00
190	Paul Derringer	75.00	37.00	22.00
191	John Burns	75.00	37.00	22.00
192	John Broaca	175.00	60.00	25.00

		NR MT	EX	VG
Common Player:		50.00	25.00	15.00
(1a)	Hank Aaron (name in white)	300.00	137.00	82.00
(1b)	Hank Aaron (name in yellow)	300.00	137.00	82.00
(2)	Richie Ashburn	225.00	110.00	70.00
(3)	Ernie Banks	325.00	150.00	90.00
(4)	Ken Boyer	175.00	87.00	52.00
(5)	Orlando Cepeda	70.00	35.00	21.00
(6)	Bob Cerv	125.00	62.00	37.00
(7)	Rocco Colavito	175.00	87.00	52.00
(8)	Del Crandall	50.00	25.00	15.00
(9)	Jim Davenport	50.00	25.00	15.00
(10)	Don Drysdale	225.00	112.00	67.00
(11)	Nellie Fox	175.00	87.00	52.00
(12)	Jackie Jensen	150.00	75.00	45.00
(13)	Harvey Kuenn	150.00	75.00	45.00
(14)	Mickey Mantle	950.00	475.00	300.00
(15)	Willie Mays	300.00	150.00	90.00
(16)	Bill Mazeroski	60.00	30.00	18.00
(17)	Roy McMillan	50.00	25.00	15.00
(18)	Billy Pierce	125.00	62.00	37.00
(19)	Roy Sievers	125.00	62.00	37.00
(20)	Duke Snider	400.00	200.00	125.00
(21)	Gus Triandos	125.00	62.00	37.00
(22)	Bob Turley	60.00	30.00	18.00
(23)	Vic Wertz	125.00	62.00	37.00

1960 Bazooka

Three-card panels were found on the bottoms of Bazooka bubble gum boxes in 1960. The blank-backed set is comprised of 36 cards with the card number located at the bottom of each full-color card. The individual cards measure 1-13/16" by 2-3/4"; the panels measure 2-3/4" by 5-1/2" in size. Prices, in the checklist that follows, are given for complete panels and individual cards.

		NR MT	EX	VG
Complete Panel Set:		1200.00	600.00	350.00
Complete Singles Set:		700.00	350.00	210.00
Common Panel:		45.00	22.00	13.50
Common Single Player:		6.00	3.00	1.75
Panel		70.00	35.00	21.00
1	Ernie Banks	40.00	20.00	12.00
2	Bud Daley	6.00	3.00	1.75
3	Wally Moon	6.00	3.00	1.75
Panel		100.00	50.00	30.00
4	Hank Aaron	60.00	30.00	18.00
5	Milt Pappas	8.00	4.00	2.50
6	Dick Stuart	8.00	4.00	2.50
Panel		125.00	62.00	37.00
7	Bob Clemente	50.00	30.00	15.00
8	Yogi Berra	40.00	20.00	12.00
9	Ken Boyer	10.00	5.00	3.00
Panel		40.00	20.00	12.00
10	Orlando Cepeda	15.00	7.50	4.50
11	Gus Triandos	8.00	4.00	2.50
12	Frank Malzone	8.00	4.00	2.50
Panel		70.00	35.00	21.00
13	Willie Mays	50.00	30.00	15.00
14	Camilo Pascual	6.00	3.00	1.75
15	Bob Cerv	6.00	3.00	1.75
Panel		70.00	35.00	21.00
16	Vic Power	6.00	3.00	1.75
17	Larry Sherry	6.00	3.00	1.75
18	Al Kaline	40.00	20.00	12.00

1959 Bazooka

The 1959 Bazooka set, consisting of 23 full-color, unnumbered cards, was issued on boxes of Bazooka one-cent bubble gum. The individually wrapped pieces of Bazooka gum were produced by Topps Chewing Gum. The blank-backed cards measure 2-13/16" by 4-15/16" Nine cards were first issued, with 14 being added to the set later. The nine more plentiful cards are #'s 1, 5, 8, 9, 14, 15, 16, 17 and 22. Complete boxes would command a 75" premium over the prices in the checklist that follows.

	NR MT	EX	VG
Complete Set:	4000.00	2000.00	1200.

Panel		NR MT	EX	VG
Panel		100.00	50.00	30.00
19	Warren Spahn	35.00	17.50	10.50
20	Harmon Killebrew	30.00	15.00	9.00
21	Jackie Jensen	12.00	6.00	3.50
Panel		115.00	57.00	34.00
22	Luis Aparicio	25.00	12.50	7.50
23	Gil Hodges	30.00	15.00	9.00
24	Richie Ashburn	30.00	15.00	9.00
Panel		90.00	45.00	27.00
25	Nellie Fox	30.00	15.00	9.00
26	Robin Roberts	30.00	15.00	9.00
27	Joe Cunningham	6.00	3.00	1.75
Panel		100.00	50.00	30.00
28	Early Wynn	25.00	12.50	7.50
29	Frank Robinson	40.00	20.00	12.00
30	Rocky Colavito	15.00	7.50	4.50
Panel		200.00	100.00	60.00
31	Mickey Mantle	175.00	75.00	45.00
32	Glen Hobbie	6.00	3.00	1.75
33	Roy McMillan	6.00	3.00	1.75
Panel		45.00	22.00	13.50
34	Harvey Kuenn	10.00	5.00	3.00
35	Johnny Antonelli	6.00	3.00	1.75
36	Del Crandall	8.00	4.00	2.50

		NR MT	EX	VG
Panel		75.00	37.00	22.00
22	Jim Perry	6.00	3.00	1.75
23	Willie Mays	50.00	25.00	15.00
24	Bill Mazeroski	10.00	5.00	3.00
Panel		50.00	25.00	15.00
25	Gus Triandos	6.00	3.00	1.75
26	Don Drysdale	25.00	12.50	7.50
27	Frank Herrera	8.00	4.00	2.50
Panel		50.00	25.00	15.00
28	Earl Battey	6.00	3.00	1.75
29	Warren Spahn	30.00	15.00	9.00
30	Gene Woodling	8.00	4.00	2.50
Panel		60.00	30.00	18.00
31	Frank Robinson	30.00	15.00	9.00
32	Pete Runnels	8.00	4.00	2.50
33	Woodie Held	6.00	3.00	1.75
Panel		45.00	22.00	13.50
34	Norm Larker	6.00	3.00	1.75
35	Luis Aparicio	20.00	10.00	6.00
36	Bill Tuttle	6.00	3.00	1.75

1961 Bazooka

TED KLUSZEWSKI
LOS ANGELES ANGELS   1st base
NO. 18 OF 36 CARDS

Similar in design to the 1960 Bazooka set, the 1961 edition consists of 36 cards issued in panels of three on the bottom of Bazooka bubble gum boxes. The full-color cards, which measure 1-13/16" by 2-3/4" individually and 2-3/4" by 5-1/2" as panels, are numbered 1 through 36. The backs are blank.

		NR MT	EX	VG
Complete Panel Set:		1000.00	500.00	300.00
Complete Singles Set:		600.00	300.00	180.00
Common Panel:		40.00	20.00	12.00
Common Single Player:		6.00	3.00	1.75
Panel		200.00	100.00	60.00
1	Art Mahaffey	8.00	4.00	2.50
2	Mickey Mantle	150.00	75.00	45.00
3	Ron Santo	10.00	5.00	3.00
Panel		80.00	40.00	24.00
4	Bud Daley	6.00	3.00	1.75
5	Roger Maris	50.00	25.00	15.00
6	Eddie Yost	6.00	3.00	1.75
Panel		45.00	22.00	13.50
7	Minnie Minoso	10.00	5.00	3.00
8	Dick Groat	10.00	5.00	3.00
9	Frank Malzone	8.00	4.00	2.50
Panel		50.00	25.00	15.00
10	Dick Donovan	6.00	3.00	1.75
11	Ed Mathews	25.00	12.50	7.50
12	Jim Lemon	6.00	3.00	1.75
Panel		40.00	20.00	12.00
13	Chuck Estrada	6.00	3.00	1.75
14	Ken Boyer	10.00	5.00	3.00
15	Harvey Kuenn	10.00	5.00	3.00
Panel		40.00	20.00	12.00
16	Ernie Broglio	6.00	3.00	1.75
17	Rocky Colavito	12.00	6.00	3.50
18	Ted Kluszewski	12.00	6.00	3.50
Panel		115.00	57.00	34.00
19	Ernie Banks	50.00	25.00	15.00
20	Al Kaline	40.00	20.00	12.00
21	Ed Bailey	6.00	3.00	1.75

1962 Bazooka

KEN BOYER
ST. LOUIS CARDINALS   3rd base

In 1962, Bazooka increased the size of its set to 45 full-color cards. The set is unnumbered and was issued in panels of three on the bottoms of bubble gum boxes. The individual cards measure 1-13/16" by 2-3/4" in size, whereas the panels are 2-3/4" by 5-1/2". In the checklist that follows the cards have been numbered by panel using the name of the player who appears on the left side of the panel. Panel #'s 1-3, 31-33 and 43-45 were supposedly issued in shorter supply and command a higher price.

		NR MT	EX	VG
Complete Panel Set:		2200.00	950.00	575.00
Complete Singles Set:		1000.00	500.00	300.00
Common Panel:		30.00	15.00	9.00
Common Single Player:		6.00	3.00	1.75
Panel		400.00	200.00	125.00
(1)	Bob Allison	75.00	38.00	23.00
(2)	Ed Mathews	150.00	70.00	45.00
(3)	Vada Pinson	75.00	38.00	23.00
Panel		50.00	25.00	15.00
(4)	Earl Battey	6.00	3.00	1.75
(5)	Warren Spahn	25.00	12.50	7.50
(6)	Lee Thomas	6.00	3.00	1.75
Panel		40.00	20.00	12.00
(7)	Orlando Cepeda	15.00	7.50	4.50
(8)	Woodie Held	6.00	3.00	1.75
(9)	Bob Aspromonte	6.00	3.00	1.75
Panel		100.00	50.00	30.00
(10)	Dick Howser	8.00	4.00	2.50
(11)	Bob Clemente	40.00	20.00	12.00
(12)	Al Kaline	30.00	15.00	9.00
Panel		80.00	40.00	24.00
(13)	Joey Jay	6.00	3.00	1.75
(14)	Roger Maris	40.00	20.00	12.00
(15)	Frank Howard	12.00	6.00	3.50
Panel		70.00	35.00	21.00
(16)	Sandy Koufax	40.00	20.00	12.00
(17)	Jim Gentile	6.00	3.00	1.75
(18)	Johnny Callison	8.00	4.00	2.50
Panel		30.00	15.00	9.00
(19)	Jim Landis	6.00	3.00	1.75
(20)	Ken Boyer	10.00	5.00	3.00

		NR MT	EX	VG
(21)	Chuck Schilling	6.00	3.00	1.75
Panel		225.00	112.00	67.00
(22)	Art Mahaffey	8.00	4.00	2.50
(23)	Mickey Mantle	150.00	75.00	45.00
(24)	Dick Stuart	8.00	4.00	2.50
Panel		80.00	40.00	24.00
(25)	Ken McBride	6.00	3.00	1.75
(26)	Frank Robinson	30.00	15.00	9.00
(27)	Gil Hodges	25.00	12.50	7.50
Panel		100.00	50.00	30.00
(28)	Milt Pappas	8.00	4.00	2.50
(29)	Hank Aaron	50.00	25.00	15.00
(30)	Luis Aparicio	20.00	10.00	6.00
Panel		400.00	200.00	125.00
(31)	Johnny Romano	75.00	38.00	23.00
(32)	Ernie Banks	200.00	100.00	60.00
(33)	Norm Siebern	75.00	38.00	23.00
Panel		40.00	20.00	12.00
(34)	Ron Santo	10.00	5.00	3.00
(35)	Norm Cash	8.00	4.00	2.50
(36)	Jim Piersall	8.00	4.00	2.50
Panel		70.00	35.00	21.00
(37)	Don Schwall	6.00	3.00	1.75
(38)	Willie Mays	40.00	20.00	12.00
(39)	Norm Larker	6.00	3.00	1.75
Panel		70.00	35.00	21.00
(40)	Bill White	8.00	4.00	2.50
(41)	Whitey Ford	30.00	15.00	9.00
(42)	Rocky Colavito	12.00	6.00	3.50
Panel		400.00	200.00	125.00
(43)	Don Zimmer	75.00	38.00	23.00
(44)	Harmon Killebrew	150.00	70.00	45.00
(45)	Gene Woodling	75.00	38.00	23.00

		NR MT	EX	VG
Panel		70.00	35.00	21.00
13	Camilo Pascual (hands at waist)	5.00	2.50	1.50
14	Bob Clemente (portrait)	40.00	20.00	12.00
15	Johnny Callison (wearing pinstripe uniform)	8.00	4.00	2.50
Panel		120.00	60.00	36.00
16	Carl Yastrzemski (kneeling)	60.00	30.00	18.00
17	Don Drysdale	25.00	12.50	7.50
18	Johnny Romano (portrait)	5.00	2.50	1.50
Panel		30.00	15.00	9.00
19	Al Jackson	8.00	4.00	2.50
20	Ralph Terry	8.00	4.00	2.50
21	Bill Monbouquette	5.00	2.50	1.50
Panel		95.00	47.00	28.00
22	Orlando Cepeda	15.00	7.50	4.50
23	Stan Musial	50.00	25.00	15.00
24	Floyd Robinson (no pinstripes on uniform)	5.00	2.50	1.50
Panel		30.00	15.00	9.00
25	Chuck Hinton (batting)	5.00	2.50	1.50
26	Bob Purkey	5.00	2.50	1.50
27	Ken Hubbs	12.00	6.00	3.50
Panel		60.00	30.00	18.00
28	Bill White	8.00	4.00	2.50
29	Ray Herbert	5.00	2.50	1.50
30	Brooks Robinson (glove in front)	30.00	15.00	9.00
Panel		60.00	30.00	18.00
31	Frank Robinson (batting, uniform number doesn't show)	40.00	20.00	12.00
32	Lee Thomas	5.00	2.50	1.50
33	Rocky Colavito (Detroit)	10.00	5.00	3.00
Panel		60.00	30.00	18.00
34	Al Kaline (kneeling)	30.00	15.00	9.00
35	Art Mahaffey	5.00	2.50	1.50
36	Tommy Davis (batting follow-thru)	8.00	4.00	2.50

1963 Bazooka

The 1963 Bazooka issue reverted back to a 12-panel, 36-card set, but saw a change in the size of the cards. Individual cards measure 1-9/16" by 2-1/2", while panels are 2-1/2" by 4-11/16" in size. The card design was altered also, with the player's name, team and position situated in a white oval space at the bottom of the card. The full-color, blank-backed set is numbered 1-36. Five Bazooka All-Time Greats cards were inserted in each box of bubble gum.

		NR MT	EX	VG
Complete Panel Set:		1000.00	500.00	300.00
Complete Singles Set:		600.00	300.00	180.00
Common Panel:		30.00	15.00	9.00
Common Single Player:		5.00	2.50	1.50
Panel		250.00	125.00	75.00
1	Mickey Mantle (batting righty)	150.00	75.00	45.00
2	Bob Rodgers	5.00	2.50	1.50
3	Ernie Banks	30.00	15.00	9.00
Panel		50.00	25.00	15.00
4	Norm Siebern	5.00	2.50	1.50
5	Warren Spahn (portrait)	30.00	15.00	9.00
6	Bill Mazeroski	10.00	5.00	3.00
Panel		115.00	57.00	34.00
7	Harmon Killebrew (batting)	30.00	15.00	9.00
8	Dick Farrell (portrait)	5.00	2.50	1.50
9	Hank Aaron (glove in front)	50.00	25.00	15.00
Panel		70.00	35.00	21.00
10	Dick Donovan	5.00	2.50	1.50
11	Jim Gentile (batting)	5.00	2.50	1.50
12	Willie Mays (bat in front)	40.00	20.00	12.00

1963 Bazooka All-Time Greats

Consisting of 41 cards, the Bazooka All-Time Greats set was issued as inserts (5 per box) in boxes of Bazooka bubble gum. A black and white head-shot of the player is placed inside a gold plaque within a white border. The card backs have black print on white and white and yellow and contain a brief biography of the player. The numbered cards measure 1-9/16" by 2-1/2" in size. The cards can be found with silver fronts instead of gold. The silver are worth double the values listed in the following checklist.

		NR MT	EX	VG
Complete Set:		175.00	87.00	52.00
Common Player:		2.50	1.25	.70
1	Joe Tinker	3.50	1.75	1.00
2	Harry Heilmann	2.50	1.25	.70
3	Jack Chesbro	3.00	1.50	.90
4	Christy Mathewson	5.00	2.50	1.50
5	Herb Pennock	3.00	1.50	.90
6	Cy Young	5.00	2.50	1.50
7	Big Ed Walsh	2.50	1.25	.70
8	Nap Lajoie	3.50	1.75	1.00
9	Eddie Plank	2.50	1.25	.70
10	Honus Wagner	8.00	4.00	2.50
11	Chief Bender	2.50	1.25	.70
12	Walter Johnson	8.00	4.00	2.50
13	Three-Fingered Brown	2.50	1.25	.70
14	Rabbit Maranville	2.50	1.25	.70

		NR MT	EX	VG
15	Lou Gehrig	20.00	10.00	6.00
16	Ban Johnson	2.50	1.25	.70
17	Babe Ruth	35.00	17.50	10.50
18	Connie Mack	5.00	2.50	1.50
19	Hank Greenberg	3.50	1.75	1.00
20	John McGraw	3.50	1.75	1.00
21	Johnny Evers	2.50	1.25	.70
22	Al Simmons	2.50	1.25	.70
23	Jimmy Collins	2.50	1.25	.70
24	Tris Speaker	3.50	1.75	1.00
25	Frank Chance	2.50	1.25	.70
26	Fred Clarke	2.50	1.25	.70
27	Wilbert Robinson	2.50	1.25	.70
28	Dazzy Vance	2.50	1.25	.70
29	Pete Alexander	3.50	1.75	1.00
30	Judge Landis	2.50	1.25	.70
31	Wee Willie Keeler	2.50	1.25	.70
32	Rogers Hornsby	3.50	1.75	1.00
33	Hugh Duffy	2.50	1.25	.70
34	Mickey Cochrane	3.50	1.75	1.00
35	Ty Cobb	20.00	10.00	6.00
36	Mel Ott	3.50	1.75	1.00
37	Clark Griffith	2.50	1.25	.70
38	Ted Lyons	2.50	1.25	.70
39	Cap Anson	3.50	1.75	1.00
40	Bill Dickey	3.50	1.75	1.00
41	Eddie Collins	3.50	1.75	1.00

		NR MT	EX	VG
Panel		75.00	37.00	22.00
16	Carl Yastrzemski (batting)	50.00	25.00	15.00
17	Billy Williams (kneeling)	20.00	10.00	6.00
18	Johnny Romano (batting)	5.00	2.50	1.50
Panel		55.00	27.00	16.50
19	Jim Maloney	5.00	2.50	1.50
20	Norm Cash	8.00	4.00	2.50
21	Willie McCovey	30.00	15.00	9.00
Panel		25.00	12.50	7.50
22	Jim Fregosi (batting)	6.00	3.00	1.75
23	George Altman	5.00	2.50	1.50
24	Floyd Robinson (wearing pinstripe uniform)	5.00	2.50	1.50
Panel		25.00	12.50	7.50
25	Chuck Hinton (portrait)	5.00	2.50	1.50
26	Ron Hunt (batting)	8.00	4.00	2.50
27	Gary Peters (pitching)	5.00	2.50	1.50
Panel		60.00	30.00	18.00
28	Dick Ellsworth	5.00	2.50	1.50
29	Elston Howard (holding bat)	12.00	6.00	3.50
30	Brooks Robinson (kneeling with glove)	30.00	15.00	9.00
Panel		110.00	55.00	33.00
31	Frank Robinson (uniform number shows)	40.00	20.00	12.00
32	Sandy Koufax (glove in front)	40.00	20.00	12.00
33	Rocky Colavito (Kansas City)	10.00	5.00	3.00
Panel		65.00	32.00	19.50
34	Al Kaline (holding two bats)	30.00	15.00	9.00
35	Ken Boyer (head to waist shot)	10.00	5.00	3.00
36	Tommy Davis (batting)	8.00	4.00	2.50

1964 Bazooka

The 1964 Bazooka set is identical in design and size to the previous year's effort. However, different photographs were used from year to year by Topps, issuer of Bazooka bubble gum. The 1964 set consists of 36 full-color, blank-backed cards numbered 1 through 36. Individual cards measure 1-9/16" by 2-1/2"; three-card panels measure 2-1/2" by 4-11/16". Sheets of ten full-color baseball stamps were inserted in each box of bubble gum.

		NR MT	EX	VG
Complete Panel Set:		1000.00	500.00	300.00
Complete Singles Set:		600.00	300.00	180.00
Common Panel:		25.00	12.50	7.50
Common Single Player:		5.00	2.50	1.50
Panel		220.00	110.00	66.00
1	Mickey Mantle (portrait)	175.00	87.00	52.00
2	Dick Groat	8.00	4.00	2.50
3	Steve Barber	5.00	2.50	1.50
Panel		40.00	20.00	12.00
4	Ken McBride	5.00	2.50	1.50
5	Warren Spahn (head to waist shot)	30.00	15.00	9.00
6	Bob Friend	6.00	3.00	1.75
Panel		115.00	57.00	34.00
7	Harmon Killebrew (portrait)	30.00	15.00	9.00
8	Dick Farrell (hands above head)	5.00	2.50	1.50
9	Hank Aaron (glove to left)	60.00	30.00	18.00
Panel		70.00	35.00	21.00
10	Rich Rollins	5.00	2.50	1.50
11	Jim Gentile (portrait)	5.00	2.50	1.50
12	Willie Mays (looking to left)	50.00	25.00	15.00
Panel		70.00	35.00	21.00
13	Camilo Pascual (pitching follow-thru)	5.00	2.50	1.50
14	Bob Clemente (throwing)	50.00	25.00	15.00
15	Johnny Callison (batting, screen showing)	8.00	4.00	2.50

1964 Bazooka Stamps

Occasionally mislabeled "Topps Stamps," the 1964 Bazooka Stamps set was produced by Topps, but was found only in boxes of 1¢ Bazooka bubble gum. Issued in sheets of ten, 100 color stamps make up the set. Each stamp measures 1" by 1-1/2" in size. While the stamps are not individually numbered, the sheets are numbered one through ten. The stamps are commonly found as complete sheets of ten and are priced in that fashion in the checklist that follows.

		NR MT	EX	VG
Complete Sheet Set:		350.00	175.00	105.00
Common Sheet:		12.00	6.00	3.50
1	Max Alvis, Ed Charles, Dick Ellsworth, Jimmie Hall, Frank Malzone, Milt Pappas, Vada Pinson, Tony Taylor, Pete Ward, Bill White	12.00	6.00	3.50
2	Bob Aspromonte, Larry Jackson, Willie Mays, Al McBean, Bill Monbouquette, Bobby Richardson, Floyd Robinson, Frank Robinson, Norm Siebern, Don Zimmer	40.00	20.00	12.00
3	Ernie Banks, Bob Clemente, Curt Flood, Jesse Gonder, Woody Held, Don Lock, Dave Nicholson, Joe Pepitone, Brooks Robinson, Carl Yastrzemski	60.00	30.00	18.00
4	Hank Aguirre, Jim Grant, Harmon Killebrew, Jim Maloney, Juan Marichal, Bill Mazeroski, Juan Pizarro, Boog Powell, Ed Roebuck, Ron Santo	30.00	15.00	9.00
5	Jim Bouton, Norm Cash, Orlando Cepeda, Tommy Harper, Chuck Hinton, Albie Pearson, Ron Perranoski, Dick Radatz, Johnny Romano, Carl Willey	18.00	9.00	5.50

		NR MT	EX	VG
6	Steve Barber, Jim Fregosi, Tony Gonzalez, Mickey Mantle, Jim O'Toole, Gary Peters, Rich Rollins, Warren Spahn, Dick Stuart, Joe Torre	125.00	62.00	37.00
7	Felipe Alou, George Altman, Ken Boyer, Rocky Colavito, Jim Davenport, Tommy Davis, Bill Freehan, Bob Friend, Ken Johnson, Billy Moran	18.00	9.00	5.50
8	Earl Battey, Ernie Broglio, Johnny Callison, Donn Clendenon, Don Drysdale, Jim Gentile, Elston Howard, Claude Osteen, Billy Williams, Hal Woodeshick	25.00	12.50	7.50
9	Hank Aaron, Jack Baldschun, Wayne Causey, Moe Drabowsky, Dick Groat, Frank Howard, Al Jackson, Jerry Lumpe, Ken McBride, Rusty Staub	40.00	20.00	12.00
10	Ray Culp, Vic Davalillo, Dick Farrell, Ron Hunt, Al Kaline, Sandy Koufax, Ed Mathews, Willie McCovey, Camilo Pascual, Lee Thomas	50.00	25.00	15.00

1965 Bazooka

The 1965 Bazooka set is identical to the 1963 and 1964 sets. Different players were added each year and different photographs were used for those players being included again. Individual cards cut from the boxes measure 1-9/16" by 2-1/2". Complete three-card panels measure 2-1/2" by 4-11/16". Thirty-six full-color, blank-backed, numbered cards comprise the set. Prices are given for individual cards and complete panels in the checklist that follows.

		NR MT	EX	VG
Complete Panel Set:		1100.00	550.00	325.00
Complete Singles Set:		600.00	300.00	180.00
Common Panel:		25.00	12.50	7.50
Common Single Player:		5.00	2.50	1.50
Panel		225.00	115.00	70.00
1	Mickey Mantle (batting lefty)	175.00	87.00	52.00
2	Larry Jackson	5.00	2.50	1.50
3	Chuck Hinton	5.00	2.50	1.50
Panel		30.00	15.00	9.00
4	Tony Oliva	10.00	5.00	3.00
5	Dean Chance	5.00	2.50	1.50
6	Jim O'Toole	5.00	2.50	1.50
Panel		95.00	47.00	28.00
7	Harmon Killebrew (bat on shoulder)	25.00	12.50	7.50
8	Pete Ward	5.00	2.50	1.50
9	Hank Aaron (batting)	40.00	20.00	12.00
Panel		70.00	35.00	21.00
10	Dick Radatz	5.00	2.50	1.50
11	Boog Powell	10.00	5.00	3.00
12	Willie Mays (looking down)	35.00	17.50	10.50
Panel		65.00	32.00	19.50
13	Bob Veale	5.00	2.50	1.50
14	Bob Clemente (batting)	35.00	17.50	10.50
15	Johnny Callison (batting, no screen in background)	8.00	4.00	2.50
Panel		45.00	22.00	13.50
16	Joe Torre	8.00	4.00	2.50
17	Billy Williams (batting)	20.00	10.00	6.00
18	Bob Chance	5.00	2.50	1.50
Panel		30.00	15.00	9.00

		NR MT	EX	VG
19	Bob Aspromonte	5.00	2.50	1.50
20	Joe Christopher	5.00	2.50	1.50
21	Jim Bunning	12.00	6.00	3.50
Panel		70.00	35.00	21.00
22	Jim Fregosi (portrait)	8.00	4.00	2.50
23	Bob Gibson	25.00	12.50	7.50
24	Juan Marichal	20.00	10.00	6.00
Panel		25.00	12.50	7.50
25	Dave Wickersham	5.00	2.50	1.50
26	Ron Hunt (throwing)	8.00	4.00	2.50
27	Gary Peters (portrait)	5.00	2.50	1.50
Panel		70.00	35.00	21.00
28	Ron Santo	10.00	5.00	3.00
29	Elston Howard (with glove)	12.00	6.00	3.50
30	Brooks Robinson (portrait)	30.00	15.00	9.00
Panel		95.00	47.00	28.00
31	Frank Robinson (portrait)	35.00	17.50	10.50
32	Sandy Koufax (hands over head)	35.00	17.50	10.50
33	Rocky Colavito (Cleveland)	10.00	5.00	3.00
Panel		60.00	30.00	18.00
34	Al Kaline (portrait)	25.00	12.50	7.50
35	Ken Boyer (portrait)	10.00	5.00	3.00
36	Tommy Davis (fielding)	8.00	4.00	2.50

1966 Bazooka

The 1966 Bazooka set was increased to 48 cards. Issued in panels of three on the bottoms of boxes of bubble gum, the full-color cards are blank-backed and numbered. Individual cards measure 1-9/16" by 2-1/2", whereas panels measure 2-1/2" by 4-11/16".

		NR MT	EX	VG
Complete Panel Set:		1400.00	700.00	425.00
Complete Singles Set:		775.00	387.00	232.00
Common Panel:		25.00	12.50	7.50
Common Single Player:		5.00	2.50	1.50
Panel		65.00	32.00	19.50
1	Sandy Koufax	35.00	17.50	10.50
2	Willie Horton	6.00	3.00	1.75
3	Frank Howard	8.00	4.00	2.50
Panel		40.00	20.00	12.00
4	Richie Allen	10.00	5.00	3.00
5	Mel Stottlemyre	8.00	4.00	2.50
6	Tony Conigliaro	10.00	5.00	3.00
Panel		250.00	125.00	70.00
7	Mickey Mantle	175.00	87.00	52.00
8	Leon Wagner	5.00	2.50	1.50
9	Ed Kranepool	6.00	3.00	1.75
Panel		70.00	35.00	21.00
10	Juan Marichal	20.00	10.00	6.00
11	Harmon Killebrew	25.00	12.50	7.50
12	Johnny Callison	6.00	3.00	1.75
Panel		55.00	27.00	16.50
13	Roy McMillan	5.00	2.50	1.50
14	Willie McCovey	25.00	12.50	7.50
15	Rocky Colavito	10.00	5.00	3.00
Panel		65.00	32.00	19.50
16	Willie Mays	35.00	17.50	10.50
17	Sam McDowell	8.00	4.00	2.50
18	Vern Law	6.00	3.00	1.75
Panel		50.00	25.00	15.00
19	Jim Fregosi	6.00	3.00	1.75
20	Ron Fairly	6.00	3.00	1.75
21	Bob Gibson	25.00	12.50	7.50
Panel		70.00	35.00	21.00

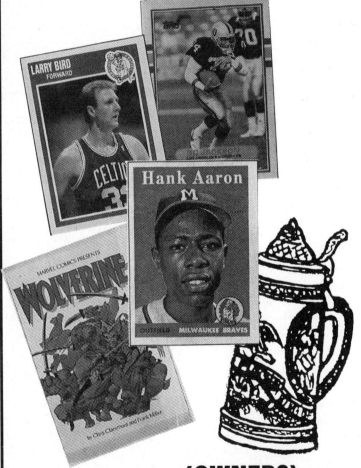

		NR MT	EX	VG
22	Carl Yastrzemski	40.00	20.00	12.00
23	Bill White	8.00	4.00	2.50
24	Bob Aspromonte	5.00	2.50	1.50
Panel		55.00	27.00	16.50
25	Dean Chance (California)	5.00	2.50	1.50
26	Bob Clemente	35.00	17.50	10.50
27	Tony Cloninger	5.00	2.50	1.50
Panel		70.00	35.00	21.00
28	Curt Blefary	5.00	2.50	1.50
29	Milt Pappas	5.00	2.50	1.50
30	Hank Aaron	40.00	20.00	12.00
Panel		60.00	30.00	18.00
31	Jim Bunning	12.00	6.00	3.50
32	Frank Robinson (portrait)	30.00	15.00	9.00
33	Bill Skowron	8.00	4.00	2.50
Panel		60.00	30.00	18.00
34	Brooks Robinson	30.00	15.00	9.00
35	Jim Wynn	6.00	3.00	1.75
36	Joe Torre	8.00	4.00	2.50
Panel		145.00	72.00	43.00
37	Jim Grant	5.00	2.50	1.50
38	Pete Rose	80.00	40.00	24.00
39	Ron Santo	10.00	5.00	3.00
Panel		60.00	30.00	18.00
40	Tom Tresh	8.00	4.00	2.50
41	Tony Oliva	10.00	5.00	3.00
42	Don Drysdale	25.00	12.50	7.50
Panel		25.00	12.50	7.50
43	Pete Richert	5.00	2.50	1.50
44	Bert Campaneris	8.00	4.00	2.50
45	Jim Maloney	5.00	2.50	1.50
Panel		70.00	35.00	21.00
46	Al Kaline	25.00	12.50	7.50
47	Eddie Fisher	5.00	2.50	1.50
48	Billy Williams	20.00	10.00	6.00

		NR MT	EX	VG
Panel		50.00	25.00	15.00
13	Denny McLain	12.00	6.00	3.50
14	Willie McCovey	25.00	12.50	7.50
15	Rocky Colavito	10.00	5.00	3.00
Panel		65.00	32.00	19.50
16	Willie Mays	35.00	17.50	10.50
17	Sam McDowell	6.00	3.00	1.75
18	Jim Kaat	12.00	6.00	3.50
Panel		50.00	25.00	15.00
19	Jim Fregosi	6.00	3.00	1.75
20	Ron Fairly	6.00	3.00	1.75
21	Bob Gibson	25.00	12.50	7.50
Panel		70.00	35.00	21.00
22	Carl Yastrzemski	40.00	20.00	12.00
23	Bill White	6.00	3.00	1.75
24	Bob Aspromonte	5.00	2.50	1.50
Panel		60.00	30.00	18.00
25	Dean Chance (Minnesota)	5.00	2.50	1.50
26	Bob Clemente	35.00	17.50	10.50
27	Tony Cloninger	5.00	2.50	1.50
Panel		70.00	35.00	21.00
28	Curt Blefary	5.00	2.50	1.50
29	Phil Regan	5.00	2.50	1.50
30	Hank Aaron	40.00	20.00	12.00
Panel		60.00	30.00	18.00
31	Jim Bunning	12.00	6.00	3.50
32	Frank Robinson (batting)	25.00	12.50	7.50
33	Ken Boyer	10.00	5.00	3.00
Panel		60.00	30.00	18.00
34	Brooks Robinson	30.00	15.00	9.00
35	Jim Wynn	6.00	3.00	1.75
36	Joe Torre	8.00	4.00	2.50
Panel		140.00	70.00	42.00
37	Tommy Davis	6.00	3.00	1.75
38	Pete Rose	90.00	45.00	27.00
39	Ron Santo	10.00	5.00	3.00
Panel		60.00	30.00	18.00
40	Tom Tresh	8.00	4.00	2.50
41	Tony Oliva	10.00	5.00	3.00
42	Don Drysdale	25.00	12.50	7.50
Panel		25.00	12.50	7.50
43	Pete Richert	5.00	2.50	1.50
44	Bert Campaneris	6.00	3.00	1.75
45	Jim Maloney	5.00	2.50	1.50
Panel		70.00	35.00	21.00
46	Al Kaline	25.00	12.50	7.50
47	Matty Alou	6.00	3.00	1.75
48	Billy Williams	20.00	10.00	6.00

1967 Bazooka

The 1967 Bazooka set is identical in design to the Bazooka sets of 1964-1966. Issued in panels of three on the bottoms of bubble gum boxes, the set is made up of 48 full-color, blank-backed, numbered cards. Individual cards measure 1-9/16" by 2-1/2"; complete panels measure 2-1/2" by 4-11/16" in size.

		NR MT	EX	VG
Complete Panel Set:		1400.00	700.00	425.00
Complete Singles Set:		775.00	387.00	232.00
Common Panel:		25.00	12.50	7.50
Common Single Player:		5.00	2.50	1.50
Panel		25.00	12.50	7.50
1	Rick Reichardt	5.00	2.50	1.50
2	Tommy Agee	5.00	2.50	1.50
3	Frank Howard	8.00	4.00	2.50
Panel		35.00	17.50	10.50
4	Richie Allen	10.00	5.00	3.00
5	Mel Stottlemyre	8.00	4.00	2.50
6	Tony Conigliaro	10.00	5.00	3.00
Panel		225.00	110.00	70.00
7	Mickey Mantle	175.00	87.00	52.00
8	Leon Wagner	5.00	2.50	1.50
9	Gary Peters	5.00	2.50	1.50
Panel		70.00	35.00	21.00
10	Juan Marichal	20.00	10.00	6.00
11	Harmon Killebrew	25.00	12.50	7.50
12	Johnny Callison	6.00	3.00	1.75

1968 Bazooka

The design of the 1968 Bazooka set is radically different from previous years. The player cards are situated on the sides of the boxes with the box back containing "Tipps From The Topps." Four unnumbered player cards, measuring 1-1/4" by 3-1/8", are featured on each box. The box back includes a small player photo plus illustrated tips on various aspects of the game of baseball. The boxes are numbered 1-15 on the top panels. There are 56 different player cards

in the set, with four of the cards (Agee, Drysdale, Rose, Santo) being used twice to round out the set of fifteen boxes.

		NR MT	EX	VG
Complete Box Set:		2100.00	1050.00	630.00
Complete Singles Set:		1300.00	650.00	390.00
Common Box:		110.00	55.00	33.00
Common Single Player:		5.00	2.50	1.50
Box		175.00	87.00	52.00
(1)	Clete Boyer	9.00	4.50	2.75
1	Maury Wills (Bunting)	20.00	10.00	6.00
(2)	Paul Casanova	7.00	3.50	2.00
(3)	Al Kaline	25.00	12.50	7.50
(4)	Tom Seaver	60.00	30.00	18.00
Box		150.00	75.00	45.00
2	Carl Yastrzemski (Batting)	50.00	25.00	15.00
(5)	Matty Alou	9.00	4.50	2.75
(6)	Bill Freehan	9.00	4.50	2.75
(7)	Jim Hunter	20.00	10.00	6.00
(8)	Jim Lefebvre	7.00	3.50	2.00
Box		110.00	55.00	33.00
3	Bert Campaneris (Stealing bases)	20.00	10.00	6.00
(9)	Bobby Knoop	7.00	3.50	2.00
(10)	Tim McCarver	12.00	6.00	3.50
(11)	Frank Robinson	20.00	10.00	6.00
(12)	Bob Veale	7.00	3.50	2.00
Box		90.00	45.00	27.00
4	Maury Wills (Sliding)	20.00	10.00	6.00
(13)	Joe Azcue	7.00	3.50	2.00
(14)	Tony Conigliaro	12.00	6.00	3.50
(15)	Ken Holtzman	9.00	4.50	2.75
(16)	Bill White	9.00	4.50	2.75
Box		150.00	75.00	45.00
5	Julian Javier (The Double Play)	20.00	10.00	6.00
(17)	Hank Aaron	40.00	20.00	12.00
(18)	Juan Marichal	20.00	10.00	6.00
(19)	Joe Pepitone	12.00	6.00	3.50
(20)	Rico Petrocelli	9.00	4.50	2.75
Box		175.00	87.00	52.00
6	Orlando Cepeda (Playing 1st Base)	25.00	12.50	7.50
(21)	Tommie Agee	5.00	2.50	1.50
(22)	Don Drysdale	10.00	5.00	3.00
(23)	Pete Rose	60.00	30.00	18.00
(24)	Ron Santo	5.00	2.50	1.50
Box		110.00	55.00	33.00
7	Bill Mazeroski (Playing 2nd Base)	20.00	10.00	6.00
(25)	Jim Bunning	12.00	6.00	3.50
(26)	Frank Howard	12.00	6.00	3.50
(27)	John Roseboro	9.00	4.50	2.75
(28)	George Scott	9.00	4.50	2.75
Box		150.00	75.00	45.00
8	Brooks Robinson (Playing 3rd Base)	50.00	25.00	15.00
(29)	Tony Gonzalez	7.00	3.50	2.00
(30)	Willie Horton	9.00	4.50	2.75
(31)	Harmon Killebrew	25.00	12.50	7.50
(32)	Jim McGlothlin	7.00	3.50	2.00
Box		110.00	55.00	33.00
9	Jim Fregosi (Playing Shortstop)	20.00	10.00	6.00
(33)	Max Alvis	7.00	3.50	2.00
(34)	Bob Gibson	20.00	10.00	6.00
(35)	Tony Oliva	12.00	6.00	3.50
(36)	Vada Pinson	12.00	6.00	3.50
Box		110.00	55.00	33.00
10	Joe Torre (Catching)	25.00	12.50	7.50
(37)	Dean Chance	7.00	3.50	2.00
(38)	Tommy Davis	9.00	4.50	2.75
(39)	Ferguson Jenkins	15.00	7.50	4.50
(40)	Rick Monday	9.00	4.50	2.75
Box		275.00	137.00	82.00
11	Jim Lonborg (Pitching)	25.00	12.50	7.50
(41)	Curt Flood	9.00	4.50	2.75
(42)	Joel Horlen	7.00	3.50	2.00
(43)	Mickey Mantle	125.00	62.00	37.00
(44)	Jim Wynn	7.00	3.50	2.00
Box		150.00	75.00	45.00
12	Mike McCormick (Fielding the Pitcher's Position)	20.00	10.00	6.00
(45)	Bob Clemente	35.00	17.50	10.50
(46)	Al Downing	9.00	4.50	2.75
(47)	Don Mincher	7.00	3.50	2.00
(48)	Tony Perez	15.00	7.50	4.50
Box		175.00	87.00	52.00
13	Frank Crosetti (Coaching)	35.00	17.50	10.50
(49)	Rod Carew	35.00	17.50	10.50
(50)	Willie McCovey	25.00	12.50	7.50

		NR MT	EX	VG
(51)	Ron Swoboda	7.00	3.50	2.00
(52)	Earl Wilson	7.00	3.50	2.00
Box		150.00	75.00	45.00
14	Willie Mays (Playing the Outfield)	50.00	25.00	15.00
(53)	Richie Allen	12.00	6.00	3.50
(54)	Gary Peters	7.00	3.50	2.00
(55)	Rusty Staub	10.00	5.00	3.00
(56)	Billy Williams	20.00	10.00	6.00
Box		175.00	87.00	52.00
15	Lou Brock (Base Running)	40.00	20.00	12.00
(57)	Tommie Agee	5.00	2.50	1.50
(58)	Don Drysdale	10.00	5.00	3.00
(59)	Pete Rose	60.00	30.00	18.00
(60)	Ron Santo	5.00	2.50	1.50

1969 Bazooka

Issued over a two-year span, the 1969-70 Bazooka set utilized the box bottom and sides. The box bottom, entitled "Baseball Extra," features an historic event in baseball. The bottom panels are numbered 1 through 12. Two "All-Time Great" cards were located on each side of the box. These cards are not numbered and have no distinct borders. Individual cards measure 1-1/4" by 3-1/8"; the "Baseball Extra" panels measure 3" by 6-1/4". The prices in the checklist that follows are for complete boxes only. Cards/panels cut from the boxes have a greatly reduced value - 25 per cent of the complete box prices for all cut pieces.

		NR MT	EX	VG
Complete Box Set:		200.00	100.00	60.00
Common Box:		10.00	5.00	3.00
1	No-Hit Duel By Toney And Vaughn (Mordecai Brown, Ty Cobb, Willie Keeler, Eddie Plank)	15.00	7.50	4.50
2	Alexander Conquers Yanks (Rogers Hornsby, Ban Johnson, Walter Johnson, Al Simmons)	10.00	5.00	3.00
3	Yanks Lazzeri Sets A.L. Hit Record (Hugh Duffy, Lou Gehrig, Tris Speaker, Joe Tinker)	15.00	7.50	4.50
4	Home Run Almost Hit Out Of Stadium (Grover Alexander, Chief Bender, Christy Mathewson, Cy Young)	10.00	5.00	3.00
5	Four Consecutive Homers By Gehrig (Frank Chance, Mickey Cochrane, John McGraw, Babe Ruth)	25.00	12.50	7.50
6	No-Hit Game By Walter Johnson (Johnny Evers, Walter Johnson, John McGraw, Cy Young)	10.00	5.00	3.00
7	Twelve RBI's By Bottomley (Ty Cobb, Eddie Collins, Johnny Evers, Lou Gehrig)	15.00	7.50	4.50
8	Ty Ties Record (Mickey Cochrane, Eddie Collins, Met Ott, Honus Wagner)	10.00	5.00	3.00
9	Babe Ruth Hits Three Homers In Game (Cap Anson, Jack Chesbro, Al Simmons, Tris Speaker)	25.00	12.50	7.50

		NR MT	EX	VG
10	Calls Shot In Series Game (Nap Lajoie, Connie Mack, Rabbit Maranville, Ed Walsh)			
		25.00	12.50	7.50
11	Ruth's 60th Homer Sets New Record (Frank Chance, Nap Lajoie, Mel Ott, Joe Tinker)			
		25.00	12.50	7.50
12	Double Shutout By Ed Reulbach (Rogers Hornsby, Rabbit Maranville, Christy Mathewson, Honus Wagner)			
		10.00	5.00	3.00

		NR MT	EX	VG
(26)	Luis Aparicio	6.00	3.00	1.75
(27)	Bobby Murcer	3.00	1.50	.90
(28)	Rico Petrocelli	2.00	1.00	.60
(29)	Sam McDowell	2.00	1.00	.60
(30)	Clarence Gaston	1.25	.60	.40
(31)	Brooks Robinson	6.50	3.25	2.00
(32)	Hank Aaron	15.00	7.50	4.50
(33)	Larry Dierker	1.25	.60	.40
(34)	Rusty Staub	2.00	1.00	.60
(35)	Bob Gibson	7.00	3.50	2.00
(36)	Amos Otis	1.25	.60	.40

1971 Bazooka Unnumbered Set

This Bazooka set was issued in 1971, consisting of 36 full-color, blank-backed, unnumbered cards. Issued in panels of three on the bottoms of Bazooka bubble gum boxes, individual cards measure 2" by 2-5/8" whereas complete panels measure 2-5/8" by 5-5/16". In the checklist that follows, the cards have been numbered by panel using the name of the player who appears on the left portion of the panel.

	NR MT	EX	VG
Complete Panel Set:	325.00	162.00	97.00
Complete Singles Set:	190.00	95.00	57.00
Common Panel:	10.00	5.00	3.00
Common Single Player:	1.25	.60	.40
Panel	30.00	15.00	9.00
Panel	40.00	20.00	12.00
Panel	25.00	12.50	7.50
Panel	25.00	12.50	7.50
Panel	15.00	7.50	4.50
Panel	30.00	15.00	9.00
Panel	15.00	7.50	4.50
Panel	30.00	15.00	9.00
Panel	15.00	7.50	4.50
Panel	10.00	5.00	3.00
Panel	30.00	15.00	9.00
Panel	15.00	7.50	4.50
(1) Tommie Agee	1.25	.60	.40
(2) Harmon Killebrew	7.00	3.50	2.00
(3) Reggie Jackson	15.00	7.50	4.50
(4) Bert Campaneris	1.25	.60	.40
(5) Pete Rose	25.00	12.50	7.50
(6) Orlando Cepeda	3.00	1.50	.90
(7) Rico Carty	2.00	1.00	.60
(8) Johnny Bench	15.00	7.50	4.50
(9) Tommy Harper	1.25	.60	.40
(10) Bill Freehan	2.00	1.00	.60
(11) Roberto Clemente	15.00	7.50	4.50
(12) Claude Osteen	1.25	.60	.40
(13) Jim Fregosi	2.00	1.00	.60
(14) Billy Williams	6.00	3.00	1.75
(15) Dave McNally	1.25	.60	.40
(16) Randy Hundley	1.25	.60	.40
(17) Willie Mays	15.00	7.50	4.50
(18) Jim Hunter	6.00	3.00	1.75
(19) Juan Marichal	6.00	3.00	1.75
(20) Frank Howard	3.00	1.50	.90
(21) Bill Melton	1.25	.60	.40
(22) Willie McCovey	7.00	3.50	2.00
(23) Carl Yastrzemski	12.00	6.00	3.50
(24) Clyde Wright	1.25	.60	.40
(25) Jim Merritt	1.25	.60	.40

1971 Bazooka Numbered Set

The 1971 Bazooka numbered set is a proof set produced by the company after the unnumbered set was released. The set is comprised of 48 cards as opposed to the 36 cards which make up the unnumbered set. Issued in panels of three, the nine cards not found in the unnumbered set are #'s 1-3, 13-15 and 43-45. All other cards are identical to those found in the unnumbered set. The cards, which measure 2" by 2-5/8", contain full-color photos and are blank-backed.

	NR MT	EX	VG
Complete Panel Set:	700.00	350.00	210.00
Complete Singles Set:	400.00	200.00	125.00
Common Panel:	10.00	5.00	3.00
Common Single Player:	2.00	1.00	.60
Panel	55.00	27.00	16.50
1 Tim McCarver	8.00	4.00	2.50
2 Frank Robinson	25.00	12.50	7.50
3 Bill Mazeroski	8.00	4.00	2.50
Panel	45.00	22.00	13.50
4 Willie McCovey	12.00	6.00	3.50
5 Carl Yastrzemski	20.00	10.00	6.00
6 Clyde Wright	2.00	1.00	.60
Panel	20.00	10.00	6.00
7 Jim Merritt	2.00	1.00	.60
8 Luis Aparicio	9.00	4.50	2.75
9 Bobby Murcer	5.00	2.50	1.50
Panel	10.00	5.00	3.00
10 Rico Petrocelli	3.00	1.50	.90
11 Sam McDowell	3.00	1.50	.90
12 Clarence Gaston	2.00	1.00	.60
Panel	55.00	27.00	16.50
13 Ferguson Jenkins	10.00	5.00	3.00
14 Al Kaline	25.00	12.50	7.50
15 Ken Harrelson	7.00	3.50	2.00
Panel	45.00	22.00	13.50
16 Tommie Agee	2.00	1.00	.60
17 Harmon Killebrew	12.00	6.00	3.50
18 Reggie Jackson	20.00	10.00	6.00
Panel	20.00	10.00	6.00
19 Juan Marichal	9.00	4.50	2.75
20 Frank Howard	5.00	2.50	1.50
21 Bill Melton	2.00	1.00	.60
Panel	55.00	27.00	16.50
22 Brooks Robinson	15.00	7.50	4.50
23 Hank Aaron	30.00	15.00	9.00
24 Larry Dierker	2.00	1.00	.60
Panel	20.00	10.00	6.00
25 Jim Fregosi	3.00	1.50	.90
26 Billy Williams	10.00	5.00	3.00
27 Dave McNally	2.00	1.00	.60

		NR MT	EX	VG
Panel		30.00	15.00	9.00
28	Rico Carty	3.00	1.50	.90
29	Johnny Bench	18.00	9.00	5.50
30	Tommy Harper	2.00	1.00	.60
Panel		60.00	30.00	18.00
31	Bert Campaneris	2.00	1.00	.60
32	Pete Rose	35.00	17.50	10.50
33	Orlando Cepeda	6.00	3.00	1.75
Panel		45.00	22.00	13.50
34	Maury Wills	6.00	3.00	1.75
35	Tom Seaver	20.00	10.00	6.00
36	Tony Oliva	6.00	3.00	1.75
Panel		30.00	15.00	9.00
37	Bill Freehan	3.00	1.50	.90
38	Roberto Clemente	25.00	12.50	7.50
39	Claude Osteen	2.00	1.00	.60
Panel		20.00	10.00	6.00
40	Rusty Staub	3.00	1.50	.90
41	Bob Gibson	10.00	5.00	3.00
42	Amos Otis	2.00	1.00	.60
Panel		25.00	12.50	7.50
43	Jim Wynn	4.00	2.00	1.25
44	Rich Allen	10.00	5.00	3.00
45	Tony Conigliaro	5.00	2.50	1.50
Panel		40.00	20.00	12.00
46	Randy Hundley	2.00	1.00	.60
47	Willie Mays	30.00	15.00	9.00
48	Jim Hunter	9.00	4.50	2.75

		MT	NR MT	EX
20	Benny Santiago	.20	.15	.08
21	Darryl Strawberry	.60	.45	.25
22	Todd Worrell	.20	.15	.08

1989 Bazooka

This 22-card set marks the second consecutive year Bazooka has issued following a 17-year absence. Full color action and posed player shots are bordered by a white frame. Other features of this standard-size includes a "Shining Stars" logo across the top, a yellow stripe enclosing the player's name at the bottom, and the Topps/Bazooka logo in the bottom right corner. Flip sides are printed in red and blue, and contain a large but faint Bazooka logo, the Topps baseball logo, card number, team name, player's name and position, followed by batting or pitching records, personal information and brief highlights. Topps produced this 22-card set in 1989 to be included (one card per box) in specially-marked boxes of its Bazooka brand bubblegum. The player photos have the words "Shining Star" along the top, while the player's name appears along the bottom of the card, along with the Topps Bazooka logo in the lower right corner. The cards are numbered alphabetically.

		MT	NR MT	EX
Complete Set:		7.00	5.25	2.75
Common Player:		.15	.11	.06
1	Tim Belcher	.20	.15	.08
2	Damon Berryhill	.15	.11	.06
3	Wade Boggs	.80	.60	.30
4	Jay Buhner	.15	.11	.06
5	Jose Canseco	.80	.60	.30
6	Vince Coleman	.15	.11	.06
7	Cecil Espy	.15	.11	.06
8	Dave Gallagher	.15	.11	.06
9	Ron Gant	.15	.11	.06
10	Kirk Gibson	.15	.11	.06
11	Paul Gibson	.15	.11	.06
12	Mark Grace	.60	.45	.25
13	Tony Gwynn	.35	.25	.14
14	Rickey Henderson	.40	.30	.15
15	Orel Hershiser	.25	.20	.10
16	Gregg Jefferies	.50	.40	.20
17	Rickey Jordan	.25	.20	.10
18	Chris Sabo	.15	.11	.06
19	Gary Sheffield	.50	.40	.20
20	Darryl Strawberry	.50	.40	.20
21	Frank Viola	.20	.15	.08
22	Walt Weiss	.15	.11	.06

1988 Bazooka

This 22-card set from Topps marks the first Bazooka issue since 1971. Full-color player photos are bordered in white, with the player name printed on a red, white and blue bubble gum box in the lower right corner. Flip sides are also red, white and blue, printed vertically. A large, but faint, Bazooka logo backs the Topps baseball logo, team name, card number, player's name and position, followed by batting records, personal information and brief career highlights. Cards were sold inside specially marked 59¢ and 79¢ Bazooka gum and candy boxes, one card per box.

		MT	NR MT	EX
Complete Set:		10.00	7.50	4.00
Common Player:		.20	.15	.08
1	George Bell	.25	.20	.10
2	Wade Boggs	.90	.70	.35
3	Jose Canseco	1.25	.90	.50
4	Roger Clemens	.60	.45	.25
5	Vince Coleman	.20	.15	.08
6	Eric Davis	.60	.45	.25
7	Tony Fernandez	.20	.15	.08
8	Dwight Gooden	.60	.45	.25
9	Tony Gwynn	.40	.30	.15
10	Wally Joyner	.40	.30	.15
11	Don Mattingly	2.00	1.50	.80
12	Willie McGee	.20	.15	.08
13	Mark McGwire	.90	.70	.35
14	Kirby Puckett	.50	.40	.20
15	Tim Raines	.30	.25	.12
16	Dave Righetti	.20	.15	.08
17	Cal Ripken	.35	.25	.14
18	Juan Samuel	.20	.15	.08
19	Ryne Sandberg	.30	.25	.12

1958 Bell Brand Dodgers

Celebrating the Dodgers first year of play in Los Angeles, Bell Brand inserted ten different unnumbered cards in their bags of potato chips and corn chips. The cards, which measure 3" by 4", have a sepia-colored photo inside a 1/4" green woodgrain border. The card backs feature statistical and biographical information and include the Bell Brand

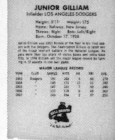

logo. Roy Campanella is included in the set despite a career-ending car wreck that prevented him from ever playing in Los Angeles.

		NR MT	EX	VG
Complete Set:		1000.00	500.00	300.00
Common Player:		25.00	12.50	7.50
1	Roy Campanella	125.00	56.00	35.00
2	Gino Cimoli	100.00	50.00	30.00
3	Don Drysdale	90.00	45.00	27.00
4	Junior Gilliam	30.00	15.00	9.00
5	Gil Hodges	90.00	45.00	27.00
6	Sandy Koufax	125.00	56.00	35.00
7	Johnny Podres	100.00	50.00	30.00
8	Pee Wee Reese	75.00	37.00	22.00
9	Duke Snider	200.00	100.00	60.00
10	Don Zimmer	25.00	12.50	7.50

1960 Bell Brand Dodgers

CLEM LABINE
Right-Hand Pitcher   L.A. Dodgers

Bell Brand returned with a baseball card set in 1960 that was entirely different in style to their previous effort. The cards, which measure 2-1/2" by 3-1/2", feature beautiful, full-color photos. The backs carry a short player biography, the 1960 Dodgers home schedule, and the Bell Brand logo. Twenty different numbered cards were inserted in various size bags of potato chips and corn chips. Although sealed in cellophane, the cards were still subject to grease stains. Cards #'s 6, 12 and 18 are the scarcest in the set.

		NR MT	EX	VG
Complete Set:		625.00	300.00	200.00
Common Player:		12.00	6.00	3.50
1	Norm Larker	12.00	6.00	3.50
2	Duke Snider	50.00	25.00	15.00
3	Danny McDevitt	12.00	6.00	3.50
4	Jim Gilliam	18.00	9.00	5.50
5	Rip Repulski	12.00	6.00	3.50
6	Clem Labine	80.00	40.00	24.00
7	John Roseboro	12.00	6.00	3.50
8	Carl Furillo	18.00	9.00	5.50
9	Sandy Koufax	90.00	45.00	27.00
10	Joe Pignatano	12.00	6.00	3.50

		NR MT	EX	VG
11	Chuck Essegian	12.00	6.00	3.50
12	John Klippstein	70.00	35.00	21.00
13	Ed Roebuck	12.00	6.00	3.50
14	Don Demeter	12.00	6.00	3.50
15	Roger Craig	18.00	9.00	5.50
16	Stan Williams	12.00	6.00	3.50
17	Don Zimmer	18.00	9.00	5.50
18	Walter Alston	100.00	50.00	30.00
19	Johnny Podres	18.00	9.00	5.50
20	Maury Wills	30.00	15.00	9.00

1961 Bell Brand Dodgers

NORM LARKER
INFIELDER   L.A. DODGERS

The 1961 Bell Brand set is identical in format to the previous year, although printed on thinner stock. Cards can be distinguished from the 1960 set by the 1961 schedule on the backs. The cards, which measure 2-7/16" by 3-1/2", are numbered by the player's uniform number. Twenty different cards were inserted into various size potato chip and corn chip packages, each card being sealed in a cellophane wrapper.

		NR MT	EX	VG
Complete Set:		375.00	185.00	110.00
Common Player:		10.00	5.00	3.00
3	Willie Davis	15.00	7.50	4.50
4	Duke Snider	50.00	30.00	15.00
5	Norm Larker	10.00	5.00	3.00
8	John Roseboro	10.00	5.00	3.00
9	Wally Moon	10.00	5.00	3.00
11	Bob Lillis	10.00	5.00	3.00
12	Tom Davis	12.00	6.00	3.50
14	Gil Hodges	25.00	12.50	7.50
16	Don Demeter	10.00	5.00	3.00
19	Jim Gilliam	15.00	7.50	4.50
22	John Podres	15.00	7.50	4.50
24	Walter Alston	25.00	12.50	7.50
30	Maury Wills	25.00	12.50	7.50
32	Sandy Koufax	55.00	28.00	16.50
34	Norm Sherry	10.00	5.00	3.00
37	Ed Roebuck	10.00	5.00	3.00
38	Roger Craig	12.00	6.00	3.50
40	Stan Williams	10.00	5.00	3.00
43	Charlie Neal	10.00	5.00	3.00
51	Larry Sherry	10.00	5.00	3.00

1962 Bell Brand Dodgers

The 1962 Bell Brand set is identical in style to the previous two years and cards can be distinguished by the 1962 Dodgers schedule on the back. The set consists of 20 cards, each measuring 2-7/16" by 3-1/2" and numbered by the player's uniform number. Printed on glossy stock, the 1962 set was less susceptible to grease stains.

		NR MT	EX	VG
Complete Set:		375.00	185.00	110.00
Common Player:		10.00	5.00	3.00
3	Willie Davis	15.00	7.50	4.50

WALLY MOON
OUTFIELDER · L.A. DODGERS

#	Player	NR MT	EX	VG
4	Duke Snider	50.00	30.00	15.00
6	Ron Fairly	10.00	5.00	3.00
8	John Roseboro	10.00	5.00	3.00
9	Wally Moon	10.00	5.00	3.00
12	Tom Davis	12.00	6.00	3.50
16	Ron Perranoski	12.00	6.00	3.50
19	Jim Gilliam	15.00	7.50	4.50
20	Daryl Spencer	10.00	5.00	3.00
22	John Podres	15.00	7.50	4.50
24	Walter Alston	25.00	12.50	7.50
25	Frank Howard	15.00	7.50	4.50
30	Maury Wills	25.00	12.50	7.50
32	Sandy Koufax	55.00	28.00	16.50
34	Norm Sherry	10.00	5.00	3.00
37	Ed Roebuck	10.00	5.00	3.00
40	Stan Williams	10.00	5.00	3.00
51	Larry Sherry	10.00	5.00	3.00
53	Don Drysdale	35.00	17.50	10.50
56	Lee Walls	10.00	5.00	3.00

1951 Berk Ross

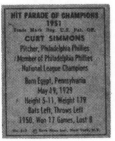

Entitled "Hit Parade of Champions," the 1951 Berk Ross set features 72 stars of various sports. The cards, which measure 2-1/16" by 2-1/2" and have tinted color photographs, were issued in boxes containing two-card panels. The issue is divided into four subsets with the first ten players of each series being baseball players. Only the baseball players are listed in the checklist that follows. Complete panels are valued 50 per cent higher than the sum of the individual cards.

		NR MT	EX	VG
Complete Set:		550.00	275.00	162.00
Common Player:		6.00	3.00	1.75
1-1	Al Rosen	10.00	5.00	3.00
1-2	Bob Lemon	10.00	5.00	3.00
1-3	Phil Rizzuto	15.00	7.50	4.50
1-4	Hank Bauer	10.00	5.00	3.00
1-5	Billy Johnson	8.00	4.00	2.50
1-6	Jerry Coleman	8.00	4.00	2.50
1-7	Johnny Mize	15.00	7.50	4.50
1-8	Dom DiMaggio	8.50	4.25	2.50
1-9	Richie Ashburn	8.50	4.25	2.50
1-10	Del Ennis	7.00	3.50	2.00
2-1	Stan Musial	55.00	28.00	16.50

		NR MT	EX	VG
2-2	Warren Spahn	18.00	9.00	5.50
2-3	Tommy Henrich	10.00	5.00	3.00
2-4	Larry "Yogi" Berra	30.00	15.00	9.00
2-5	Joe DiMaggio	90.00	45.00	27.00
2-6	Bobby Brown	10.00	5.00	3.00
2-7	Granville Hamner	6.00	3.00	1.75
2-8	Willie Jones	6.00	3.00	1.75
2-9	Stanley Lopata	6.00	3.00	1.75
2-10	Mike Goliat	6.00	3.00	1.75
3-1	Ralph Kiner	15.00	7.50	4.50
3-2	Billy Goodman	6.00	3.00	1.75
3-3	Allie Reynolds	10.00	5.00	3.00
3-4	Vic Raschi	10.00	5.00	3.00
3-5	Joe Page	8.00	4.00	2.50
3-6	Eddie Lopat	10.00	5.00	3.00
3-7	Andy Seminick	6.00	3.00	1.75
3-8	Dick Sisler	6.00	3.00	1.75
3-9	Eddie Waitkus	6.00	3.00	1.75
3-10	Ken Heintzelman	6.00	3.00	1.75
4-1	Gene Woodling	10.00	5.00	3.00
4-2	Cliff Mapes	8.00	4.00	2.50
4-3	Fred Sanford	8.00	4.00	2.50
4-4	Tommy Bryne	8.00	4.00	2.50
4-5	Eddie (Whitey) Ford	20.00	10.00	6.00
4-6	Jim Konstanty	7.00	3.50	2.00
4-7	Russ Meyer	6.00	3.00	1.75
4-8	Robin Roberts	15.00	7.50	4.50
4-9	Curt Simmons	7.00	3.50	2.00
4-10	Sam Jethroe	8.50	4.25	2.50

1952 Berk Ross

Although the card size is different (2" by 3"), the style of the fronts and backs of the 1952 Berk Ross set is similar to the previous year's effort. Seventy-two unnumbered cards make up the set. Rizzuto is included twice in the set and the Blackwell and Fox cards have transposed backs. The cards were issued individually rather than as two-card panels like in 1951.

		NR MT	EX	VG
Complete Set:		4000.00	2000.00	1175.
Common Player:		9.00	4.50	2.75
(1)	Richie Ashburn	30.00	15.00	9.00
(2)	Hank Bauer	15.00	7.50	4.50
(3)	Larry "Yogi" Berra	75.00	37.00	22.00
(4)	Ewell Blackwell (photo actually Nelson Fox)	12.00	6.00	3.50
(5)	Bobby Brown	15.00	7.50	4.50
(6)	Jim Busby	9.00	4.50	2.75
(7)	Roy Campanella	125.00	56.00	35.00
(8)	Chico Carrasquel	9.00	4.50	2.75
(9)	Jerry Coleman	12.00	6.00	3.50
(10)	Joe Collins	12.00	6.00	3.50
(11)	Alvin Dark	12.00	6.00	3.50
(12)	Dom DiMaggio	15.00	7.50	4.50
(13)	Joe DiMaggio	600.00	300.00	175.00
(14)	Larry Doby	12.00	6.00	3.50
(15)	Bobby Doerr	25.00	12.50	7.50
(16)	Bob Elliot (Elliott)	9.00	4.50	2.75
(17)	Del Ennis	10.00	5.00	3.00
(18)	Ferris Fain	9.00	4.50	2.75
(19)	Bob Feller	65.00	33.00	20.00
(20)	Nelson Fox (photo actually Ewell Blackwell)	15.00	7.50	4.50
(21)	Ned Garver	9.00	4.50	2.75

		NR MT	EX	VG
(22)	Clint Hartung	9.00	4.50	2.75
(23)	Jim Hearn	9.00	4.50	2.75
(24)	Gil Hodges	50.00	30.00	15.00
(25)	Monte Irvin	30.00	15.00	9.00
(26)	Larry Jansen	9.00	4.50	2.75
(27)	George Kell	25.00	12.50	7.50
(28)	Sheldon Jones	9.00	4.50	2.75
(29)	Monte Kennedy	9.00	4.50	2.75
(30)	Ralph Kiner	40.00	20.00	12.00
(31)	Dave Koslo	9.00	4.50	2.75
(32)	Bob Kuzava	12.00	6.00	3.50
(33)	Bob Lemon	30.00	15.00	9.00
(34)	Whitey Lockman	9.00	4.50	2.75
(35)	Eddie Lopat	15.00	7.50	4.50
(36)	Sal Maglie	12.00	6.00	3.50
(37)	Mickey Mantle	1000.00	500.00	300.00
(38)	Billy Martin	50.00	30.00	15.00
(39)	Willie Mays	350.00	175.00	100.00
(40)	Gil McDougal (McDougald)	15.00	7.50	4.50
(41)	Orestes Minoso	12.00	6.00	3.50
(42)	Johnny Mize	35.00	17.50	10.50
(43)	Tom Morgan	12.00	6.00	3.50
(44)	Don Mueller	9.00	4.50	2.75
(45)	Stan Musial	200.00	80.00	50.00
(46)	Don Newcombe	15.00	7.50	4.50
(47)	Ray Noble	9.00	4.50	2.75
(48)	Joe Ostrowski	12.00	6.00	3.50
(49)	Mel Parnell	9.00	4.50	2.75
(50)	Vic Raschi	15.00	7.50	4.50
(51)	Pee Wee Reese	65.00	33.00	20.00
(52)	Allie Reynolds	15.00	7.50	4.50
(53)	Bill Rigney	10.00	5.00	3.00
(54)	Phil Rizzuto (bunting)	55.00	28.00	16.50
(55)	Phil Rizzuto (swinging)	55.00	28.00	16.50
(56)	Robin Roberts	25.00	12.50	7.50
(57)	Eddie Robinson	9.00	4.50	2.75
(58)	Jackie Robinson	200.00	100.00	60.00
(59)	Elwin "Preacher" Roe	12.00	6.00	3.50
(60)	Johnny Sain	12.00	6.00	3.50
(61)	Albert "Red" Schoendienst	12.00	6.00	3.50
(62)	Duke Snider	125.00	56.00	35.00
(63)	George Spencer	9.00	4.50	2.75
(64)	Eddie Stanky	12.00	6.00	3.50
(65)	Henry Thompson	9.00	4.50	2.75
(66)	Bobby Thomson	15.00	7.50	4.50
(67)	Vic Wertz	10.00	5.00	3.00
(68)	Waldon Westlake	9.00	4.50	2.75
(69)	Wes Westrum	10.00	5.00	3.00
(70)	Ted Williams	300.00	120.00	75.00
(71)	Gene Woodling	15.00	7.50	4.50
(72)	Gus Zernial	9.00	4.50	2.75

		MT	NR MT	EX
1	Mike Schmidt	.50	.40	.20
2	Eddie Murray	.35	.25	.14
3	Dale Murphy	.40	.30	.15
4	Dave Winfield	.30	.25	.12
5	Jim Rice	.30	.25	.12
6	Cecil Cooper	.12	.09	.05
7	Dwight Evans	.15	.11	.06
8	Rickey Henderson	.40	.30	.15
9	Robin Yount	.35	.25	.14
10	Andre Dawson	.25	.20	.10
11	Gary Carter	.35	.25	.14
12	Keith Hernandez	.30	.25	.12
13	George Brett	.40	.30	.15
14	Bill Buckner	.09	.07	.04
15	Tony Armas	.09	.07	.04
16	Harold Baines	.15	.11	.06
17	Don Baylor	.12	.09	.05
18	Steve Garvey	.35	.25	.14
19	Lance Parrish	.20	.15	.08
20	Dave Parker	.15	.11	.06
21	Buddy Bell	.09	.07	.04
22	Cal Ripken	.40	.30	.15
23	Bob Horner	.12	.09	.05
24	Tim Raines	.30	.25	.12
25	Jack Clark	.15	.11	.06
26	Leon Durham	.09	.07	.04
27	Pedro Guerrero	.15	.11	.06
28	Kent Hrbek	.15	.11	.06
29	Kirk Gibson	.20	.15	.08
30	Ryne Sandberg	.30	.25	.12
31	Wade Boggs	1.00	.70	.40
32	Don Mattingly	1.75	1.25	.70
33	Darryl Strawberry	.60	.45	.25

1987 Bohemian Hearth Bread Padres

Bohemian Hearth Bread Company of San Diego issued a 22-card set highlighting the San Diego Padres. Produced in conjunction with Mike Schechter Associates, the cards are the standard 2-1/2" by 3-1/2" size. The card fronts contain a full-color photo encompassed by a yellow border. The Bohemian Hearth Bread logo is located in the upper left corner of the card. The card backs are printed in light brown ink on a cream color card stock and carry player personal and statistical information.

1987 Boardwalk And Baseball

The 33-card "Top Run Makers" set was produced by Topps for distribution by the recreation amusement park "Boardwalk and Baseball," located near Orlando, Fla. The cards, which measure 2-1/2" by 3-1/2", feature fronts which contain full-color player photos and the park's logo (B/B). The card backs are printed in black and pink on white stock and offer personal data and career statistics. The set was issued in a specially designed box.

		MT	NR MT	EX
Complete Set:		5.00	3.75	2.00
Common Player:		.09	.07	.04

		MT	NR MT	EX
Complete Set:		50.00	37.50	20.00
Common Player:		.50	.40	.20
1	Garry Templeton	1.75	1.25	.70
4	Jose Cora	.60	.45	.25
5	Randy Ready	.50	.40	.20
6	Steve Garvey	5.00	3.75	2.00
7	Kevin Mitchell	6.00	4.50	2.50
8	John Kruk	3.75	2.75	1.50
9	Benito Santiago	8.00	6.00	3.25
10	Larry Bowa	1.00	.70	.40
11	Tim Flannery	.50	.40	.20
14	Carmelo Martinez	1.00	.70	.40
16	Marvell Wynne	.50	.40	.20
19	Tony Gwynn	12.00	9.00	4.75
21	James Steels	.50	.40	.20
22	Stan Jefferson	1.50	1.25	.60

		MT	NR MT	EX
30	Eric Show	1.00	.70	.40
31	Ed Whitson	.50	.40	.20
34	Storm Davis	1.00	.70	.40
37	Craig Lefferts	.50	.40	.20
40	Andy Hawkins	1.00	.70	.40
41	Lance McCullers	1.25	.90	.50
43	Dave Dravecky	1.25	.90	.50
54	Rich Gossage	2.50	2.00	1.00

		NR MT	EX	VG
38	Al "Red" Schoendienst	80.00	40.00	24.00
39	Augie Galan	20.00	10.00	6.00
40	Marty Marion	40.00	20.00	12.50
41	Rex Barney	25.00	12.50	7.50
42	Ray Poat	20.00	10.00	6.00
43	Bruce Edwards	20.00	10.00	6.00
44	Johnny Wyrostek	20.00	10.00	6.00
45	Hank Sauer	20.00	10.00	6.00
46	Herman Wehmeier	20.00	10.00	6.00
47	Bobby Thomson	50.00	30.00	15.00
48	George "Dave" Koslo	40.00	7.50	4.50

1948 Bowman

Bowman Gum Co.'s premiere set was produced in 1948, making it one of the first major issues of the post-war period. Forty-eight black and white cards comprise the set, with each card measuring 2-1/16" by 2-1/2" in size. The card backs, printed in black ink on grey stock, include the card number and the player's name, team, position, and a short biography. Twelve cards (#'s 7, 8, 13, 16, 20, 22, 24, 26, 29, 30 and 34) were printed in short supply when they were removed from the 36-card printing sheet to make room for the set's high numbers (#'s 37-48). These 24 cards command a higher price than the remaining cards in the set.

		NR MT	EX	VG
Complete Set:		2300.00	1150.00	575.00
Common Player: 1-36		12.00	6.00	3.50
Common Player: 37-48		20.00	10.00	6.00

		NR MT	EX	VG
1	Bob Elliott	70.00	7.00	4.25
2	Ewell (The Whip) Blackwell	20.00	10.00	6.00
3	Ralph Kiner	70.00	35.00	21.00
4	Johnny Mize	60.00	30.00	18.00
5	Bob Feller	110.00	50.00	28.00
6	*Larry (Yogi) Berra*	375.00	175.00	100.00
7	Pete (Pistol Pete) Reiser	40.00	20.00	12.00
8	Phil (Scooter) Rizzuto	175.00	70.00	44.00
9	Walker Cooper	12.00	6.00	3.50
10	Buddy Rosar	12.00	6.00	3.50
11	Johnny Lindell	18.00	9.00	5.50
12	Johnny Sain	25.00	12.50	7.50
13	Willard Marshall	30.00	15.00	9.00
14	Allie Reynolds	30.00	15.00	9.00
15	Eddie Joost	12.00	6.00	3.50
16	Jack Lohrke	30.00	15.00	9.00
17	Enos (Country) Slaughter	80.00	40.00	24.00
18	Warren Spahn	175.00	70.00	44.00
19	Tommy (The Clutch) Henrich	25.00	12.50	7.50
20	Buddy Kerr	30.00	15.00	9.00
21	Ferris Fain	15.00	7.50	4.50
22	Floyd (Bill) Bevins (Bevens)	40.00	20.00	12.00
23	Larry Jansen	12.00	6.00	3.50
24	Emil (Dutch) Leonard	30.00	15.00	9.00
25	Barney McCoskey (McCosky)	12.00	6.00	3.50
26	Frank Shea	40.00	20.00	12.00
27	Sid Gordon	12.00	6.00	3.50
28	Emil (The Antelope) Verban	30.00	15.00	9.00
29	Joe Page	40.00	20.00	12.00
30	"Whitey" Lockman	30.00	15.00	9.00
31	Bill McCahan	12.00	6.00	3.50
32	Bill Rigney	15.00	7.50	4.50
33	Bill (The Bull) Johnson	18.00	9.00	5.50
34	Sheldon (Available) Jones	30.00	15.00	9.00
35	George (Snuffy) Stirnweiss	18.00	9.00	5.50
36	Stan Musial	475.00	225.00	125.00
37	Clint Hartung	20.00	10.00	6.00

1949 Bowman

In 1949, Bowman increased the size of its issue to 240 numbered cards. The cards, which measure 2-1/16" by 2-1/2", are black and white photos overprinted with various pastel colors. Beginning with card #109 in the set, Bowman inserted the player's names on the card fronts. Twelve cards (#'s 4, 78, 83, 85, 88, 98, 109, 124, 127, 132 and 143) which were produced in the first four series of printings, were reprinted in the seventh series with either a card front or back modification. These variations are noted in the checklist that follows. Card #'s 1-3 and 5-73 can be found with either white or grey backs. The complete set of value in the following checklist does not include the higher priced variation cards.

		NR MT	EX	VG
Complete Set:		12000.00	6000.00	3000.00
Common Player: 1-36		10.00	5.00	3.00
Common Player: 37-73		12.00	6.00	3.50
Common Player: 74-144		10.00	5.00	3.00
Common Player: 145-240		60.00	30.00	18.00

		NR MT	EX	VG
1	Vernon Bickford	75.00	7.50	3.00
2	Carroll "Whitey" Lockman	15.00	5.00	3.00
3	Bob Porterfield	15.00	7.50	4.50
4a	Jerry Priddy (no name on front)	12.00	6.00	3.50
4b	Jerry Priddy (name on front)	40.00	20.00	12.00
5	Hank Sauer	10.00	5.00	3.00
6	Phil Cavarretta	12.00	6.00	3.50
7	Joe Dobson	10.00	5.00	3.00
8	Murry Dickson	10.00	5.00	3.00
9	Ferris Fain	12.00	6.00	3.50
10	Ted Gray	10.00	5.00	3.00
11	Lou Boudreau	45.00	23.00	13.50
12	Cass Michaels	10.00	5.00	3.00
13	Bob Chesnes	10.00	5.00	3.00
14	*Curt Simmons*	20.00	10.00	6.00
15	Ned Garver	10.00	5.00	3.00
16	Al Kozar	10.00	5.00	3.00
17	Earl Torgeson	10.00	5.00	3.00
18	Bobby Thomson	20.00	10.00	6.00
19	*Bobby Brown*	30.00	15.00	9.00
20	Gene Hermanski	12.00	6.00	3.50
21	Frank Baumholtz	10.00	5.00	3.00
22	Harry "P-Nuts" Lowrey	10.00	5.00	3.00
23	Bobby Doerr	60.00	30.00	18.00
24	Stan Musial	425.00	175.00	100.00
25	Carl Scheib	10.00	5.00	3.00
26	George Kell	45.00	23.00	13.50
27	Bob Feller	90.00	45.00	27.00
28	Don Kolloway	10.00	5.00	3.00
29	Ralph Kiner	60.00	30.00	18.00
30	Andy Seminick	10.00	5.00	3.00

	NR MT	EX	VG
31 Dick Kokos	10.00	5.00	3.00
32 Eddie Yost	10.00	5.00	3.00
33 Warren Spahn	110.00	50.00	28.00
34 Dave Koslo	10.00	5.00	3.00
35 Vic Raschi	20.00	10.00	6.00
36 Harold "Peewee" Reese	150.00	60.00	38.00
37 John Wyrostek	12.00	6.00	3.50
38 Emil "The Antelope" Verban	12.00	6.00	3.50
39 Bill Goodman	12.00	6.00	3.50
40 George "Red" Munger	12.00	6.00	3.50
41 Lou Brissie	12.00	6.00	3.50
42 Walter "Hoot" Evers	12.00	6.00	3.50
43 Dale Mitchell	12.00	6.00	3.50
44 Dave Philley	12.00	6.00	3.50
45 Wally Westlake	12.00	6.00	3.50
46 *Robin Roberts*	125.00	56.00	35.00
47 Johnny Sain	18.00	9.00	5.50
48 Willard Marshall	12.00	6.00	3.50
49 Frank Shea	18.00	9.00	5.50
50 Jackie Robinson	525.00	210.00	131.00
51 Herman Wehmeier	12.00	6.00	3.50
52 Johnny Schmitz	12.00	6.00	3.50
53 Jack Kramer	12.00	6.00	3.50
54 Marty "Slats" Marion	16.00	8.00	4.75
55 Eddie Joost	12.00	6.00	3.50
56 Pat Mullin	12.00	6.00	3.50
57 Gene Bearden	12.00	6.00	3.50
58 Bob Elliott	12.00	6.00	3.50
59 Jack "Lucky" Lohrke	12.00	6.00	3.50
60 Larry "Yogi" Berra	250.00	100.00	63.00
61 Rex Barney	14.00	7.00	4.25
62 Grady Hatton	12.00	6.00	3.50
63 Andy Pafko	14.00	7.00	4.25
64 Dom "The Little Professor" DiMaggio	20.00	10.00	6.00
65 Enos "Country" Slaughter	50.00	25.00	15.00
66 Elmer Valo	12.00	6.00	3.50
67 Alvin Dark	16.00	8.00	4.75
68 Sheldon "Available" Jones	12.00	6.00	3.50
69 Tommy "The Clutch" Henrich	25.00	12.50	7.50
70 Carl Furillo	30.00	15.00	9.00
71 Vern "Junior" Stephens	12.00	6.00	3.50
72 Tommy Holmes	14.00	7.00	4.25
73 Billy Cox	14.00	7.00	4.25
74 Tom McBride	10.00	5.00	3.00
75 Eddie Mayo	10.00	5.00	3.00
76 Bill Nicholson	10.00	5.00	3.00
77 Ernie (Jumbo and Tiny) Bonham	10.00	5.00	3.00
78a Sam Zoldak (no name on front)	12.00	6.00	3.50
78b Sam Zoldak (name on front)	40.00	20.00	12.00
79 Ron Northey	10.00	5.00	3.00
80 Bill McCahan	10.00	5.00	3.00
81 Virgil "Red" Stallcup	10.00	5.00	3.00
82 Joe Page	16.00	8.00	4.75
83a Bob Scheffing (no name on front)	12.00	6.00	3.50
83b Bob Scheffing (name on front)	40.00	20.00	12.00
84 *Roy Campanella*	500.00	200.00	125.00
85a Johnny "Big John" Mize (no name on front)	50.00	25.00	15.00
85b Johnny "Big John" Mize (name on front)	110.00	50.00	28.00
86 Johnny Pesky	12.00	6.00	3.50
87 Randy Gumpert	10.00	5.00	3.00
88a Bill Salkeld (no name on front)	12.00	6.00	3.50
88b Bill Salkeld (name on front)	40.00	20.00	12.00
89 Mizell "Whitey" Platt	10.00	5.00	3.00
90 Gil Coan	10.00	5.00	3.00
91 Dick Wakefield	10.00	5.00	3.00
92 Willie "Puddin-Head" Jones	10.00	5.00	3.00
93 Ed Stevens	10.00	5.00	3.00
94 James "Mickey" Vernon	12.00	6.00	3.50
95 Howie Pollett	10.00	5.00	3.00
96 Taft Wright	10.00	5.00	3.00
97 Danny Litwhiler	10.00	5.00	3.00
98a Phil Rizzuto (no name on front)	80.00	40.00	24.00
98b Phil Rizzuto (name on front)	150.00	60.00	38.00
99 Frank Gustine	10.00	5.00	3.00
100 Gil Hodges	150.00	60.00	38.00
101 Sid Gordon	10.00	5.00	3.00
102 Stan Spence	10.00	5.00	3.00
103 Joe Tipton	10.00	5.00	3.00
104 Ed Stanky	12.00	6.00	3.50
105 Bill Kennedy	10.00	5.00	3.00
106 Jake Early	10.00	5.00	3.00
107 Eddie Lake	10.00	5.00	3.00
108 Ken Heintzelman	10.00	5.00	3.00
109a Ed Fitzgerald (Fitz Gerald) (script name on back)	12.00	6.00	3.50
109b Ed Fitzgerald (Fitz Gerald) (printed name on back)	40.00	20.00	12.00
110 Early Wynn	80.00	40.00	24.00
111 Al "Red" Schoendienst	60.00	30.00	18.00
112 Sam Chapman	10.00	5.00	3.00
113 Ray Lamanno	10.00	5.00	3.00
114 Allie Reynolds	30.00	15.00	9.00
115 Emil "Dutch" Leonard	10.00	5.00	3.00
116 Joe Hatten	12.00	6.00	3.50
117 Walker Cooper	10.00	5.00	3.00
118 Sam Mele	10.00	5.00	3.00
119 Floyd Baker	10.00	5.00	3.00
120 Cliff Fannin	10.00	5.00	3.00
121 Mark Christman	10.00	5.00	3.00
122 George Vico	10.00	5.00	3.00
123 Johnny Blatnick	10.00	5.00	3.00
124a Danny Murtaugh (script name on back)	12.00	6.00	3.50
124b Danny Murtaugh (printed name on back)	40.00	20.00	12.00
125 Ken Keltner	12.00	6.00	3.50
126a Al Brazle (script name on back)	12.00	6.00	3.50
126b Al Brazle (printed name on back)	40.00	20.00	12.00
127a Henry "Heeney" Majeski (script name on back)	12.00	6.00	3.50
127b Henry "Heeney" Majeski (printed name on back)	40.00	20.00	12.00
128 Johnny Vander Meer	16.00	8.00	4.75
129 Bill "The Bull" Johnson	16.00	8.00	4.75
130 Harry "The Hat" Walker	12.00	6.00	3.50
131 Paul Lehner	10.00	5.00	3.00
132a Al Evans (script name on back)	12.00	6.00	3.50
132b Al Evans (printed name on back)	40.00	20.00	12.00
133 Aaron Robinson	10.00	5.00	3.00
134 Hank Borowy	10.00	5.00	3.00
135 Stan Rojek	10.00	5.00	3.00
136 Henry "Hank" Edwards	10.00	5.00	3.00
137 Ted Wilks	10.00	5.00	3.00
138 Warren "Buddy" Rosar	10.00	5.00	3.00
139 Hank "Bow-Wow" Arft	10.00	5.00	3.00
140 Rae Scarborough (Ray)	10.00	5.00	3.00
141 Ulysses "Tony" Lupien	10.00	5.00	3.00
142 Eddie Waitkus	10.00	5.00	3.00
143a Bob Dillinger (script name on back)	12.00	6.00	3.50
143b Bob Dillinger (printed name on back)	40.00	20.00	12.00
144 Milton "Mickey" Haefner	10.00	5.00	3.00
145 Sylvester "Blix" Donnelly	50.00	25.00	15.00
146 Myron "Mike" McCormick	55.00	27.00	16.50
147 Elmer "Bert" Singleton	50.00	25.00	15.00
148 Bob Swift	50.00	25.00	15.00
149 Roy Partee	55.00	27.00	16.50
150 Alfred "Allie" Clark	50.00	25.00	15.00
151 Maurice "Mickey" Harris	50.00	25.00	15.00
152 Clarence Maddern	50.00	25.00	15.00
153 Phil Masi	50.00	25.00	15.00
154 Clint Hartung	50.00	25.00	15.00
155 Fermin "Mickey" Guerra	50.00	25.00	15.00
156 Al "Zeke" Zarilla	50.00	25.00	15.00
157 Walt Masterson	50.00	25.00	15.00
158 Harry "The Cat" Brecheen	50.00	25.00	15.00
159 Glen Moulder	50.00	25.00	15.00
160 Jim Blackburn	50.00	25.00	15.00
161 John "Jocko" Thompson	50.00	25.00	15.00
162 Elwin "Preacher" Roe	125.00	56.00	35.00
163 Clyde McCullough	50.00	25.00	15.00
164 Vic Wertz	55.00	27.00	16.50
165 George "Snuffy" Stirnweiss	60.00	30.00	18.00
166 Mike Tresh	50.00	25.00	15.00
167 Boris "Babe" Martin	50.00	25.00	15.00
168 Doyle Lade	50.00	25.00	15.00
169 Jeff Heath	50.00	25.00	15.00
170 Bill Rigney	55.00	27.00	16.50
171 Dick Fowler	50.00	25.00	15.00
172 Eddie Pellagrini	50.00	25.00	15.00
173 Eddie Stewart	50.00	25.00	15.00
174 Terry Moore	55.00	27.00	16.50
175 Luke Appling	100.00	45.00	27.00
176 Ken Raffensberger	50.00	25.00	15.00
177 Stan Lopata	50.00	25.00	15.00
178 Tommy Brown	55.00	27.00	16.50
179 Hugh Casey	55.00	27.00	16.50
180 Connie Berry	50.00	25.00	15.00
181 Gus Niarhos	60.00	30.00	18.00
182 Hal Peck	50.00	25.00	15.00
183 Lou Stringer	50.00	25.00	15.00
184 Bob Chipman	50.00	25.00	15.00
185 Pete Reiser	55.00	27.00	16.50
186 John "Buddy" Kerr	50.00	25.00	15.00
187 Phil Marchildon	50.00	25.00	15.00
188 Karl Drews	50.00	25.00	15.00

		NR MT	EX	VG
189	Earl Wooten	50.00	25.00	15.00
190	Jim Hearn	50.00	25.00	15.00
191	Joe Haynes	50.00	25.00	15.00
192	Harry Gumbert	50.00	25.00	15.00
193	Ken Trinkle	50.00	25.00	15.00
194	Ralph Branca	100.00	45.00	27.00
195	Eddie Bockman	50.00	25.00	15.00
196	Fred Hutchinson	55.00	27.00	16.50
197	Johnny Lindell	60.00	30.00	18.00
198	Steve Gromek	50.00	25.00	15.00
199	Cecil "Tex" Hughson	50.00	25.00	15.00
200	Jess Dobernic	50.00	25.00	15.00
201	Sibby Sisti	50.00	25.00	15.00
202	Larry Jansen	50.00	25.00	15.00
203	Barney McCosky	50.00	25.00	15.00
204	Bob Savage	50.00	25.00	15.00
205	Dick Sisler	50.00	25.00	15.00
206	Bruce Edwards	55.00	27.00	16.50
207	Johnny "Hippity" Hopp	50.00	25.00	15.00
208	Paul "Dizzy" Trout	55.00	27.00	16.50
209	Charlie "King Kong" Keller	90.00	45.00	27.00
210	Joe "Flash" Gordon	55.00	27.00	16.50
211	Dave "Boo" Ferris	50.00	25.00	15.00
212	Ralph Hamner	50.00	25.00	15.00
213	Charles "Red" Barrett	50.00	25.00	15.00
214	*Richie Ashburn*	425.00	175.00	100.00
215	Kirby Higbe	50.00	25.00	15.00
216	Lynwood "Schoolboy" Rowe	50.00	25.00	15.00
217	Marino Pieretti	50.00	25.00	15.00
218	Dick Kryhoski	60.00	30.00	18.00
219	Virgil "Fire" Trucks	55.00	27.00	16.50
220	Johnny McCarthy	50.00	25.00	15.00
221	Bob Muncrief	50.00	25.00	15.00
222	Alex Kellner	50.00	25.00	15.00
223	Bob Hoffman (Hofman)	50.00	25.00	15.00
224	*Leroy "Satchel" Paige*	1100.00	440.00	275.00
225	*Gerry Coleman*	90.00	45.00	27.00
226	Edwin "Duke" Snider	900.00	360.00	225.00
227	Fritz Ostermueller	50.00	25.00	15.00
228	Jackie Mayo	50.00	25.00	15.00
229	Ed Lopat	110.00	50.00	28.00
230	Augie Galan	50.00	25.00	15.00
231	Earl Johnson	50.00	25.00	15.00
232	George McQuinn	60.00	30.00	18.00
233	*Larry Doby*	125.00	56.00	35.00
234	Truett "Rip" Sewell	55.00	27.00	16.50
235	Jim Russell	50.00	25.00	15.00
236	Fred Sanford	60.00	30.00	18.00
237	Monte Kennedy	50.00	25.00	15.00
238	Bob Lemon	200.00	80.00	50.00
239	Frank McCormick	60.00	25.00	15.00
240	Norman "Babe" Young (photo actually Bobby Young)	100.00	45.00	27.00

		NR MT	EX	VG
Complete Set:		5600.00	2800.00	1675.
Common Player:		150.00	75.00	45.00
1	Lee Anthony	150.00	75.00	45.00
2	George Metkovich	150.00	75.00	45.00
3	Ralph Hodgin	150.00	75.00	45.00
4	George Woods	150.00	75.00	45.00
5	Xavier Rescigno	150.00	75.00	45.00
6	Mickey Grasso	150.00	75.00	45.00
7	Johnny Rucker	150.00	75.00	45.00
8	Jack Brewer	150.00	75.00	45.00
9	Dom D'Allessandro	150.00	75.00	45.00
10	Charlie Gassaway	150.00	75.00	45.00
11	Tony Freitas	150.00	75.00	45.00
12	Gordon Maltzberger	150.00	75.00	45.00
13	John Jensen	150.00	75.00	45.00
14	Joyner White	150.00	75.00	45.00
15	Harvey Storey	150.00	75.00	45.00
16	Dick Lajeski	150.00	75.00	45.00
17	Albie Glossop	150.00	75.00	45.00
18	Bill Raimondi	150.00	75.00	45.00
19	Ken Holcombe	150.00	75.00	45.00
20	Don Ross	150.00	75.00	45.00
21	Pete Coscarart	150.00	75.00	45.00
22	Tony York	150.00	75.00	45.00
23	Jake Mooty	150.00	75.00	45.00
24	Charles Adams	150.00	75.00	45.00
25	Les Scarsella	150.00	75.00	45.00
26	Joe Marty	150.00	75.00	45.00
27	Frank Kelleher	150.00	75.00	45.00
28	Lee Handley	150.00	75.00	45.00
29	Herman Besse	150.00	75.00	45.00
30	John Lazor	150.00	75.00	45.00
31	Eddie Malone	150.00	75.00	45.00
32	Maurice Van Robays	150.00	75.00	45.00
33	Jim Tabor	150.00	75.00	45.00
34	Gene Handley	150.00	75.00	45.00
35	Tom Seats	150.00	75.00	45.00
36	Ora Burnett	150.00	75.00	45.00

1950 Bowman

The quality of the 1950 Bowman issue showed a marked improvement over the company's previous efforts. The cards are beautiful color art reproductions of actual photographs and measure 2-1/16" by 2-1/2" in size. The card backs include the same type of information as found in the previous year's issue but are designed in a horizontal format. Cards found in the first two series of the set (#'s 1-72) are the scarcest in the issue. The backs of the final 72 cards in the set (#'s 181-252) can be found with or without the copyright line at the bottom of the card, the "without" version being the less common.

1949 Bowman
Pacific Coast League

One of the scarcest issues of the post-war period, the 1949 Bowman PCL set was issued only on the West Coast. Like the 1949 Bowman regular issue, the cards contain black and white photos overprinted with various pastel colors. Thirty-six cards, which measure 2-1/16" by 2-1/2", make up the set. It is believed that the cards may have been issued only in sheets and not sold in gum packs.

		NR MT	EX	VG
Complete Set:		7000.00	3500.00	1750.
Common Player: 1-72		25.00	12.50	7.50
Common Player: 73-252		10.00	5.00	3.00
1	Mel Parnell	225.00	25.00	8.00
2	Vern Stephens	40.00	20.00	12.50
3	Dom DiMaggio	30.00	15.00	9.00
4	Gus Zernial	25.00	12.50	7.50
5	Bob Kuzava	25.00	12.50	7.50
6	Bob Feller	125.00	56.00	35.00
7	Jim Hegan	25.00	12.50	7.50

		NR MT	EX	VG			NR MT	EX	VG
8	George Kell	50.00	25.00	15.00	99	Billy Goodman	10.00	5.00	3.00
9	Vic Wertz	25.00	12.50	7.50	100	Vic Raschi	20.00	10.00	6.00
10	Tommy Henrich	40.00	20.00	12.00	101	Bobby Brown	20.00	10.00	6.00
11	Phil Rizzuto	100.00	45.00	27.00	102	Billy Johnson	15.00	7.50	4.50
12	Joe Page	30.00	15.00	9.00	103	Eddie Joost	10.00	5.00	3.00
13	Ferris Fain	25.00	12.50	7.50	104	Sam Chapman	10.00	5.00	3.00
14	Alex Kellner	25.00	12.50	7.50	105	Bob Dillinger	10.00	5.00	3.00
15	Al Kozar	25.00	12.50	7.50	106	Cliff Fannin	10.00	5.00	3.00
16	*Roy Sievers*	30.00	15.00	9.00	107	Sam Dente	10.00	5.00	3.00
17	Sid Hudson	25.00	12.50	7.50	108	Rae Scarborough (Ray)	10.00	5.00	3.00
18	Eddie Robinson	25.00	12.50	7.50	109	Sid Gordon	10.00	5.00	3.00
19	Warren Spahn	110.00	50.00	28.00	110	Tommy Holmes	12.00	6.00	3.50
20	Bob Elliott	25.00	12.50	7.50	111	Walker Cooper	10.00	5.00	3.00
21	Harold Reese	150.00	60.00	38.00	112	Gil Hodges	80.00	40.00	24.00
22	Jackie Robinson	500.00	200.00	125.00	113	Gene Hermanski	12.00	6.00	3.50
23	*Don Newcombe*	80.00	40.00	24.00	114	Wayne Terwilliger	10.00	5.00	3.00
24	Johnny Schmitz	25.00	12.50	7.50	115	Roy Smalley	10.00	5.00	3.00
25	Hank Sauer	25.00	12.50	7.50	116	Virgil "Red" Stallcup	10.00	5.00	3.00
26	Grady Hatton	25.00	12.50	7.50	117	Bill Rigney	12.00	6.00	3.50
27	Herman Wehmeier	25.00	12.50	7.50	118	Clint Hartung	10.00	5.00	3.00
28	Bobby Thomson	40.00	20.00	12.00	119	Dick Sisler	10.00	5.00	3.00
29	Ed Stanky	25.00	12.50	7.50	120	John Thompson	10.00	5.00	3.00
30	Eddie Waitkus	25.00	12.50	7.50	121	Andy Seminick	10.00	5.00	3.00
31	Del Ennis	25.00	12.50	7.50	122	Johnny Hopp	10.00	5.00	3.00
32	Robin Roberts	80.00	40.00	25.00	123	Dino Restelli	10.00	5.00	3.00
33	Ralph Kiner	80.00	40.00	25.00	124	Clyde McCullough	10.00	5.00	3.00
34	Murry Dickson	25.00	12.50	7.50	125	Del Rice	10.00	5.00	3.00
35	Enos Slaughter	50.00	25.00	15.00	126	Al Brazle	10.00	5.00	3.00
36	Eddie Kazak	25.00	12.50	7.50	127	Dave Philley	10.00	5.00	3.00
37	Luke Appling	50.00	25.00	15.00	128	Phil Masi	10.00	5.00	3.00
38	Bill Wight	25.00	12.50	7.50	129	Joe "Flash" Gordon	12.00	6.00	3.50
39	Larry Doby	40.00	20.00	12.00	130	Dale Mitchell	10.00	5.00	3.00
40	Bob Lemon	50.00	25.00	15.00	131	Steve Gromek	10.00	5.00	3.00
41	Walter "Hoot" Evers	25.00	12.50	7.50	132	James Vernon	12.00	6.00	3.50
42	Art Houtteman	25.00	12.50	7.50	133	Don Kolloway	10.00	5.00	3.00
43	Bobby Doerr	50.00	25.00	15.00	134	Paul "Dizzy" Trout	12.00	6.00	3.50
44	Joe Dobson	25.00	12.50	7.50	135	Pat Mullin	10.00	5.00	3.00
45	Al "Zeke" Zarilla	25.00	12.50	7.50	136	Warren Rosar	10.00	5.00	3.00
46	Larry "Yogi" Berra	300.00	120.00	75.00	137	Johnny Pesky	12.00	6.00	3.50
47	Jerry Coleman	35.00	17.50	10.50	138	Allie Reynolds	25.00	12.50	7.50
48	Leland "Lou" Brissie	25.00	12.50	7.50	139	Johnny Mize	60.00	30.00	18.00
49	Elmer Valo	25.00	12.50	7.50	140	Pete Suder	10.00	5.00	3.00
50	Dick Kokos	25.00	12.50	7.50	141	Joe Coleman	10.00	5.00	3.00
51	Ned Garver	25.00	12.50	7.50	142	*Sherman Lollar*	12.00	6.00	3.50
52	Sam Mele	25.00	12.50	7.50	143	Eddie Stewart	10.00	5.00	3.00
53	Clyde Vollmer	25.00	12.50	7.50	144	Al Evans	10.00	5.00	3.00
54	Gil Coan	25.00	12.50	7.50	145	Jack Graham	10.00	5.00	3.00
55	John "Buddy" Kerr	25.00	12.50	7.50	146	Floyd Baker	10.00	5.00	3.00
56	*Del Crandell (Crandall)*	30.00	15.00	9.00	147	*Mike Garcia*	12.00	6.00	3.50
57	Vernon Bickford	25.00	12.50	7.50	148	Early Wynn	60.00	30.00	18.00
58	Carl Furillo	40.00	20.00	12.00	149	Bob Swift	10.00	5.00	3.00
59	Ralph Branca	40.00	20.00	12.00	150	George Vico	10.00	5.00	3.00
60	Andy Pafko	22.00	11.00	6.50	151	Fred Hutchinson	12.00	6.00	3.50
61	Bob Rush	25.00	12.50	7.50	152	Ellis Kinder	10.00	5.00	3.00
62	Ted Kluszewski	30.00	15.00	9.00	153	Walt Masterson	10.00	5.00	3.00
63	Ewell Blackwell	22.00	11.00	6.50	154	Gus Niarhos	10.00	5.00	3.00
64	Alvin Dark	30.00	15.00	9.00	155	Frank "Spec" Shea	15.00	7.50	4.50
65	Dave Koslo	25.00	12.50	7.50	156	Fred Sanford	15.00	7.50	4.50
66	Larry Jansen	25.00	12.50	7.50	157	Mike Guerra	10.00	5.00	3.00
67	Willie Jones	25.00	12.50	7.50	158	Paul Lehner	10.00	5.00	3.00
68	Curt Simmons	25.00	12.50	7.50	159	Joe Tipton	10.00	5.00	3.00
69	Wally Westlake	25.00	12.50	7.50	160	Mickey Harris	10.00	5.00	3.00
70	Bob Chesnes	25.00	12.50	7.50	161	Sherry Robertson	10.00	5.00	3.00
71	Al Schoendienst	60.00	30.00	18.00	162	Eddie Yost	10.00	5.00	3.00
72	Howie Pollet	25.00	12.50	7.50	163	Earl Torgeson	10.00	5.00	3.00
73	Willard Marshall	10.00	5.00	3.00	164	Sibby Sisti	10.00	5.00	3.00
74	*Johnny Antonelli*	15.00	7.50	4.50	165	Bruce Edwards	12.00	6.00	3.50
75	Roy Campanella	250.00	100.00	63.00	166	Joe Hatten	12.00	6.00	3.50
76	Rex Barney	12.00	6.00	3.50	167	Elwin Roe	25.00	12.50	7.50
77	Edwin "Duke" Snider	225.00	100.00	60.00	168	Bob Scheffing	10.00	5.00	3.00
78	Mickey Owen	10.00	5.00	3.00	169	Hank Edwards	10.00	5.00	3.00
79	Johnny Vander Meer	12.00	6.00	3.50	170	Emil Leonard	10.00	5.00	3.00
80	Howard Fox	10.00	5.00	3.00	171	Harry Gumbert	10.00	5.00	3.00
81	Ron Northey	10.00	5.00	3.00	172	Harry Lowrey	10.00	5.00	3.00
82	Carroll Lockman	10.00	5.00	3.00	173	Lloyd Merriman	10.00	5.00	3.00
83	Sheldon Jones	10.00	5.00	3.00	174	Henry Thompson	10.00	5.00	3.00
84	Richie Ashburn	45.00	23.00	13.50	175	Monte Kennedy	10.00	5.00	3.00
85	Ken Heintzelman	10.00	5.00	3.00	176	Sylvester Donnelly	10.00	5.00	3.00
86	Stan Rojek	10.00	5.00	3.00	177	Hank Borowy	10.00	5.00	3.00
87	Bill Werle	10.00	5.00	3.00	178	Eddy Fitzgerald (Fitz Gerald)	10.00	5.00	3.00
88	Marty Marion	12.00	6.00	3.50	179	Charles Diering	10.00	5.00	3.00
89	George Munger	10.00	5.00	3.00	180	Harry Walker	12.00	6.00	3.50
90	Harry Brecheen	12.00	6.00	3.50	181	Marino Pieretti	10.00	5.00	3.00
91	Cass Michaels	10.00	5.00	3.00	182	Sam Zoldak	10.00	5.00	3.00
92	Hank Majeski	10.00	5.00	3.00	183	Mickey Haefner	10.00	5.00	3.00
93	Gene Bearden	10.00	5.00	3.00	184	Randy Gumpert	10.00	5.00	3.00
94	Lou Boudreau	40.00	20.00	12.00	185	Howie Judson	10.00	5.00	3.00
95	Aaron Robinson	10.00	5.00	3.00	186	Ken Keltner	12.00	6.00	3.50
96	Virgil "Fire" Trucks	12.00	6.00	3.50	187	Lou Stringer	10.00	5.00	3.00
97	Maurice McDermott	10.00	5.00	3.00	188	Earl Johnson	10.00	5.00	3.00
98	Ted Williams	500.00	200.00	125.00	189	Owen Friend	10.00	5.00	3.00

		NR MT	EX	VG
190	Ken Wood	10.00	5.00	3.00
191	Dick Starr	10.00	5.00	3.00
192	Bob Chipman	10.00	5.00	3.00
193	Harold "Pete" Reiser	12.00	6.00	3.50
194	Billy Cox	15.00	7.50	4.50
195	Phil Cavaretta (Cavarretta)	12.00	6.00	3.50
196	Doyle Lade	10.00	5.00	3.00
197	Johnny Wyrostek	10.00	5.00	3.00
198	Danny Litwhiler	10.00	5.00	3.00
199	Jack Kramer	10.00	5.00	3.00
200	Kirby Higbe	10.00	5.00	3.00
201	Pete Castiglione	10.00	5.00	3.00
202	Cliff Chambers	10.00	5.00	3.00
203	Danny Murtaugh	12.00	6.00	3.50
204	Granville Hamner	10.00	5.00	3.00
205	Mike Goliat	10.00	5.00	3.00
206	Stan Lopata	10.00	5.00	3.00
207	Max Lanier	10.00	5.00	3.00
208	Jim Hearn	10.00	5.00	3.00
209	Johnny Lindell	10.00	5.00	3.00
210	Ted Gray	10.00	5.00	3.00
211	Charlie Keller	10.00	5.00	3.00
212	Gerry Priddy	10.00	5.00	3.00
213	Carl Scheib	10.00	5.00	3.00
214	Dick Fowler	10.00	5.00	3.00
215	Ed Lopat	20.00	10.00	6.00
216	Bob Porterfield	15.00	7.50	4.50
217	Casey Stengel	100.00	50.00	30.00
218	Cliff Mapes	15.00	7.50	4.50
219	*Hank Bauer*	40.00	20.00	12.00
220	Leo Durocher	40.00	20.00	12.00
221	Don Mueller	10.00	5.00	3.00
222	Bobby Morgan	12.00	6.00	3.50
223	Jimmy Russell	12.00	6.00	3.50
224	Jack Banta	12.00	6.00	3.50
225	Eddie Sawyer	10.00	5.00	3.00
226	Jim Konstanty	12.00	6.00	3.50
227	Bob Miller	10.00	5.00	3.00
228	Bill Nicholson	10.00	5.00	3.00
229	Frank Frisch	40.00	20.00	12.00
230	Bill Serena	10.00	5.00	3.00
231	Preston Ward	10.00	5.00	3.00
232	*Al "Flip" Rosen*	40.00	20.00	12.00
233	Allie Clark	10.00	5.00	3.00
234	*Bobby Shantz*	20.00	10.00	6.00
235	Harold Gilbert	10.00	5.00	3.00
236	Bob Cain	10.00	5.00	3.00
237	Bill Salkeld	10.00	5.00	3.00
238	Vernal Jones	10.00	5.00	3.00
239	Bill Howerton	10.00	5.00	3.00
240	Eddie Lake	10.00	5.00	3.00
241	Neil Berry	10.00	5.00	3.00
242	Dick Kryhoski	10.00	5.00	3.00
243	Johnny Groth	10.00	5.00	3.00
244	Dale Coogan	10.00	5.00	3.00
245	Al Papai	10.00	5.00	3.00
246	*Walt Dropo*	12.00	6.00	3.50
247	Irv Noren	10.00	5.00	3.00
248	*Sam Jethroe*	12.00	6.00	3.50
249	George Stirnweiss	10.00	5.00	3.00
250	Ray Coleman	10.00	5.00	3.00
251	John Lester Moss	15.00	5.00	3.00
252	Billy DeMars	70.00	7.50	3.00

1951 Bowman

In 1951, Bowman increased the numbers of cards in its set for the third consecutive year when it issued 324 cards. The cards are, like 1950, color art reproductions of actual photographs but now measured 2-1/16" by 3-1/8" in size. The player's name is situated in a small, black box on the card front. Several of the card fronts are enlargements of the 1950 version. The high-numbered series of the set (#'s 253-324), which includes the rookie cards of Mantle and Mays, are the scarcest of the issue.

		NR MT	EX	VG
Complete Set:		16000.00	8000.00	4000.
Common Player: 1-36		12.00	6.00	3.50
Common Player: 37-252		10.00	5.00	3.00
Common Player: 253-324		40.00	20.00	12.00
1	*Ed "Whitey" Ford*	1250.00	150.00	70.00
2	Larry "Yogi" Berra	400.00	160.00	100.00
3	Robin Roberts	50.00	25.00	15.00
4	Del Ennis	12.00	6.00	3.50
5	Dale Mitchell	12.00	6.00	3.50
6	Don Newcombe	30.00	15.00	9.00
7	Gil Hodges	65.00	33.00	20.00
8	Paul Lehner	12.00	6.00	3.50
9	Sam Chapman	12.00	6.00	3.50
10	Al "Red" Schoendienst	60.00	30.00	18.00
11	George "Red" Munger	12.00	6.00	3.50
12	Hank Majeski	12.00	6.00	3.50
13	Ed Stanky	15.00	7.50	4.50
14	Alvin Dark	18.00	9.00	5.50
15	Johnny Pesky	15.00	7.50	4.50
16	Maurice McDermott	12.00	6.00	3.50
17	Pete Castiglione	12.00	6.00	3.50
18	Gil Coan	12.00	6.00	3.50
19	Sid Gordon	12.00	6.00	3.50
20	Del Crandall	15.00	7.50	4.50
21	George "Snuffy" Stirnweiss	12.00	6.00	3.50
22	Hank Sauer	12.00	6.00	3.50
23	Walter "Hoot" Evers	12.00	6.00	3.50
24	Ewell Blackwell	15.00	7.50	4.50
25	Vic Raschi	20.00	10.00	6.00
26	Phil Rizzuto	75.00	38.00	23.00
27	Jim Konstanty	12.00	6.00	3.50
28	Eddie Waitkus	12.00	6.00	3.50
29	Allie Clark	12.00	6.00	3.50
30	Bob Feller	100.00	50.00	30.00
31	Roy Campanella	225.00	100.00	60.00
32	Duke Snider	200.00	80.00	50.00
33	Bob Hooper	12.00	6.00	3.50
34	Marty Marion	15.00	7.50	4.50
35	Al Zarilla	12.00	6.00	3.50
36	Joe Dobson	12.00	6.00	3.50
37	Whitey Lockman	10.00	5.00	3.00
38	Al Evans	10.00	5.00	3.00
39	Ray Scarborough	10.00	5.00	3.00
40	*Dave "Gus" Bell*	12.00	6.00	3.50
41	Eddie Yost	12.00	6.00	3.50
42	Vern Bickford	10.00	5.00	3.00
43	Billy DeMars	10.00	5.00	3.00
44	Roy Smalley	10.00	5.00	3.00
45	Art Houtteman	10.00	5.00	3.00
46	George Kell	50.00	25.00	15.00
47	Grady Hatton	10.00	5.00	3.00
48	Ken Raffensberger	10.00	5.00	3.00
49	Jerry Coleman	15.00	7.50	4.50
50	Johnny Mize	50.00	25.00	15.00
51	Andy Seminick	10.00	5.00	3.00
52	Dick Sisler	10.00	5.00	3.00
53	Bob Lemon	40.00	20.00	12.00
54	Ray Boone	12.00	6.00	3.50
55	Gene Hermanski	12.00	6.00	3.50
56	Ralph Branca	30.00	15.00	9.00
57	Alex Kellner	10.00	5.00	3.00
58	Enos Slaughter	50.00	25.00	15.00
59	Randy Gumpert	10.00	5.00	3.00
60	Alfonso Carrasquel	10.00	5.00	3.00
61	Jim Hearn	10.00	5.00	3.00
62	Lou Boudreau	50.00	25.00	15.00
63	Bob Dillinger	10.00	5.00	3.00
64	Bill Werle	10.00	5.00	3.00
65	Mickey Vernon	12.00	6.00	3.50
66	Bob Elliott	10.00	5.00	3.00
67	Roy Sievers	12.00	6.00	3.50
68	Dick Kokos	10.00	5.00	3.00
69	Johnny Schmitz	10.00	5.00	3.00
70	Ron Northey	10.00	5.00	3.00
71	Jerry Priddy	10.00	5.00	3.00
72	Lloyd Merriman	10.00	5.00	3.00
73	Tommy Byrne	15.00	7.50	4.50
74	Billy Johnson	15.00	7.50	4.50
75	Russ Meyer	10.00	5.00	3.00
76	Stan Lopata	10.00	5.00	3.00

#	Player	NR MT	EX	VG
77	Mike Goliat	10.00	5.00	3.00
78	Early Wynn	50.00	25.00	15.00
79	Jim Hegan	10.00	5.00	3.00
80	Harold "Peewee" Reese	125.00	56.00	35.00
81	Carl Furillo	25.00	12.50	7.50
82	Joe Tipton	10.00	5.00	3.00
83	Carl Scheib	10.00	5.00	3.00
84	Barney McCosky	10.00	5.00	3.00
85	Eddie Kazak	10.00	5.00	3.00
86	Harry Brecheen	12.00	6.00	3.50
87	Floyd Baker	10.00	5.00	3.00
88	Eddie Robinson	10.00	5.00	3.00
89	Henry Thompson	10.00	5.00	3.00
90	Dave Koslo	10.00	5.00	3.00
91	Clyde Vollmer	10.00	5.00	3.00
92	Vern "Junior" Stephens	12.00	6.00	3.50
93	Danny O'Connell	10.00	5.00	3.00
94	Clyde McCullough	10.00	5.00	3.00
95	Sherry Robertson	10.00	5.00	3.00
96	Sandalio Consuegra	10.00	5.00	3.00
97	Bob Kuzava	10.00	5.00	3.00
98	Willard Marshall	10.00	5.00	3.00
99	Earl Torgeson	10.00	5.00	3.00
100	Sherman Lollar	12.00	6.00	3.50
101	Owen Friend	10.00	5.00	3.00
102	Emil "Dutch" Leonard	10.00	5.00	3.00
103	Andy Pafko	12.00	6.00	3.50
104	Virgil "Fire" Trucks	12.00	6.00	3.50
105	Don Kolloway	10.00	5.00	3.00
106	Pat Mullin	10.00	5.00	3.00
107	Johnny Wyrostek	10.00	5.00	3.00
108	Virgil Stallcup	10.00	5.00	3.00
109	Allie Reynolds	25.00	12.50	7.50
110	Bobby Brown	25.00	12.50	7.50
111	Curt Simmons	12.00	6.00	3.50
112	Willie Jones	10.00	5.00	3.00
113	Bill "Swish" Nicholson	10.00	5.00	3.00
114	Sam Zoldak	10.00	5.00	3.00
115	Steve Gromek	10.00	5.00	3.00
116	Bruce Edwards	12.00	6.00	3.50
117	Eddie Miksis	12.00	6.00	3.50
118	Preacher Roe	25.00	12.50	7.50
119	Eddie Joost	10.00	5.00	3.00
120	Joe Coleman	10.00	5.00	3.00
121	Gerry Staley	10.00	5.00	3.00
122	Joe Garagiola	110.00	50.00	28.00
123	Howie Judson	10.00	5.00	3.00
124	Gus Niarhos	10.00	5.00	3.00
125	Bill Rigney	12.00	6.00	3.50
126	Bobby Thomson	25.00	12.50	7.50
127	Sal Maglie	30.00	15.00	9.00
128	Ellis Kinder	10.00	5.00	3.00
129	Matt Batts	10.00	5.00	3.00
130	Tom Saffell	10.00	5.00	3.00
131	Cliff Chambers	10.00	5.00	3.00
132	Cass Michaels	10.00	5.00	3.00
133	Sam Dente	10.00	5.00	3.00
134	Warren Spahn	90.00	45.00	27.00
135	Walker Cooper	10.00	5.00	3.00
136	Ray Coleman	10.00	5.00	3.00
137	Dick Starr	10.00	5.00	3.00
138	Phil Cavarretta	12.00	6.00	3.50
139	Doyle Lade	10.00	5.00	3.00
140	Eddie Lake	10.00	5.00	3.00
141	Fred Hutchinson	12.00	6.00	3.50
142	Aaron Robinson	10.00	5.00	3.00
143	Ted Kluszewski	25.00	12.50	7.50
144	Herman Wehmeier	10.00	5.00	3.00
145	Fred Sanford	15.00	7.50	4.50
146	Johnny Hopp	15.00	7.50	4.50
147	Ken Heintzelman	10.00	5.00	3.00
148	Granny Hamner	10.00	5.00	3.00
149	Emory "Bubba" Church	10.00	5.00	3.00
150	Mike Garcia	12.00	6.00	3.50
151	Larry Doby	15.00	7.50	4.50
152	Cal Abrams	12.00	6.00	3.50
153	Rex Barney	12.00	6.00	3.50
154	Pete Suder	10.00	5.00	3.00
155	Lou Brissie	10.00	5.00	3.00
156	Del Rice	10.00	5.00	3.00
157	Al Brazle	10.00	5.00	3.00
158	Chuck Diering	10.00	5.00	3.00
159	Eddie Stewart	10.00	5.00	3.00
160	Phil Masi	10.00	5.00	3.00
161	Wes Westrum	12.00	6.00	3.50
162	Larry Jansen	10.00	5.00	3.00
163	Monte Kennedy	10.00	5.00	3.00
164	Bill Wight	10.00	5.00	3.00
165	Ted Williams	450.00	180.00	113.00
166	Stan Rojek	10.00	5.00	3.00
167	Murry Dickson	10.00	5.00	3.00
168	Sam Mele	10.00	5.00	3.00
169	Sid Hudson	10.00	5.00	3.00
170	Sibby Sisti	10.00	5.00	3.00
171	Buddy Kerr	10.00	5.00	3.00
172	Ned Garver	10.00	5.00	3.00
173	Hank Arft	10.00	5.00	3.00
174	Mickey Owen	10.00	5.00	3.00
175	Wayne Terwilliger	10.00	5.00	3.00
176	Vic Wertz	12.00	6.00	3.50
177	Charlie Keller	12.00	6.00	3.50
178	Ted Gray	10.00	5.00	3.00
179	Danny Litwhiler	10.00	5.00	3.00
180	Howie Fox	10.00	5.00	3.00
181	Casey Stengel	70.00	35.00	21.00
182	Tom Ferrick	15.00	7.50	4.50
183	Hank Bauer	25.00	12.50	7.50
184	Eddie Sawyer	10.00	5.00	3.00
185	Jimmy Bloodworth	10.00	5.00	3.00
186	Richie Ashburn	45.00	23.00	13.50
187	Al "Flip" Rosen	20.00	10.00	6.00
188	*Roberto Avila*	12.00	6.00	3.50
189	Erv Palica	12.00	6.00	3.50
190	Joe Hatten	12.00	6.00	3.50
191	Billy Hitchcock	10.00	5.00	3.00
192	Hank Wyse	10.00	5.00	3.00
193	Ted Wilks	10.00	5.00	3.00
194	Harry "Peanuts" Lowrey	10.00	5.00	3.00
195	Paul Richards	15.00	7.50	4.50
196	Bill Pierce	15.00	7.50	4.50
197	Bob Cain	10.00	5.00	3.00
198	*Monte Irvin*	60.00	30.00	18.00
199	Sheldon Jones	10.00	5.00	3.00
200	Jack Kramer	10.00	5.00	3.00
201	Steve O'Neill	10.00	5.00	3.00
202	Mike Guerra	10.00	5.00	3.00
203	*Vernon Law*	15.00	7.50	4.50
204	Vic Lombardi	10.00	5.00	3.00
205	Mickey Grasso	10.00	5.00	3.00
206	Conrado Marrero	10.00	5.00	3.00
207	Billy Southworth	10.00	5.00	3.00
208	Blix Donnelly	10.00	5.00	3.00
209	Ken Wood	10.00	5.00	3.00
210	Les Moss	10.00	5.00	3.00
211	Hal Jeffcoat	10.00	5.00	3.00
212	Bob Rush	10.00	5.00	3.00
213	Neil Berry	10.00	5.00	3.00
214	Bob Swift	10.00	5.00	3.00
215	Kent Peterson	10.00	5.00	3.00
216	Connie Ryan	10.00	5.00	3.00
217	Joe Page	15.00	7.50	4.50
218	Ed Lopat	25.00	12.50	7.50
219	Gene Woodling	25.00	12.50	7.50
220	Bob Miller	10.00	5.00	3.00
221	Dick Whitman	10.00	5.00	3.00
222	Thurman Tucker	10.00	5.00	3.00
223	Johnny Vander Meer	20.00	10.00	6.00
224	Billy Cox	15.00	7.50	4.50
225	Dan Bankhead	15.00	7.50	4.50
226	Jimmy Dykes	15.00	7.50	4.50
227	Bobby Schantz (Shantz)	15.00	7.50	4.50
228	Cloyd Boyer	10.00	5.00	3.00
229	Bill Howerton	10.00	5.00	3.00
230	Max Lanier	10.00	5.00	3.00
231	Luis Aloma	10.00	5.00	3.00
232	Nelson Fox	50.00	25.00	15.00
233	Leo Durocher	35.00	17.50	10.50
234	Clint Hartung	10.00	5.00	3.00
235	Jack "Lucky" Lohrke	10.00	5.00	3.00
236	Warren "Buddy" Rosar	10.00	5.00	3.00
237	Billy Goodman	10.00	5.00	3.00
238	Pete Reiser	15.00	7.50	4.50
239	Bill MacDonald	10.00	5.00	3.00
240	Joe Haynes	10.00	5.00	3.00
241	Irv Noren	10.00	5.00	3.00
242	Sam Jethroe	15.00	7.50	4.50
243	John Antonelli	15.00	7.50	4.50
244	Cliff Fannin	10.00	5.00	3.00
245	John Berardino	15.00	7.50	4.50
246	Bill Serena	10.00	5.00	3.00
247	Bob Ramazotti	10.00	5.00	3.00
248	*Johnny Klippstein*	15.00	7.50	4.50
249	Johnny Groth	10.00	5.00	3.00
250	Hank Borowy	10.00	5.00	3.00
251	Willard Ramsdell	10.00	5.00	3.00
252	Homer "Dixie" Howell	10.00	5.00	3.00
253	*Mickey Mantle*	4800.00	1680.00	720.00
254	*Jackie Jensen*	80.00	40.00	24.00
255	Milo Candini	40.00	20.00	12.00
256	Ken Silvestri	40.00	20.00	12.00
257	Birdie Tebbetts	40.00	20.00	12.00
258	*Luke Easter*	45.00	22.00	13.50

		NR MT	EX	VG
259	Charlie Dressen	45.00	22.00	13.50
260	Carl Erskine	70.00	35.00	21.00
261	Wally Moses	40.00	20.00	12.00
262	Gus Zernial	40.00	20.00	12.00
263	Howie Pollett (Pollet)	40.00	20.00	12.00
264	Don Richmond	40.00	20.00	12.00
265	Steve Bilko	40.00	20.00	12.00
266	Harry Dorish	40.00	20.00	12.00
267	Ken Holcombe	40.00	20.00	12.00
268	Don Mueller	40.00	20.00	12.00
269	Ray Noble	40.00	20.00	12.00
270	Willard Nixon	40.00	20.00	12.00
271	Tommy Wright	40.00	20.00	12.00
272	Billy Meyer	40.00	20.00	12.00
273	Danny Murtaugh	45.00	22.00	13.50
274	George Metkovich	40.00	20.00	12.00
275	Bucky Harris	60.00	30.00	18.00
276	Frank Quinn	40.00	20.00	12.00
277	Roy Hartsfield	40.00	20.00	12.00
278	Norman Roy	40.00	20.00	12.00
279	Jim Delsing	40.00	20.00	12.00
280	Frank Overmire	40.00	20.00	12.00
281	Al Widmar	40.00	20.00	12.00
282	Frank Frisch	60.00	30.00	18.00
283	Walt Dubiel	40.00	20.00	12.00
284	Gene Bearden	40.00	20.00	12.00
285	Johnny Lipon	40.00	20.00	12.00
286	Bob Usher	40.00	20.00	12.00
287	Jim Blackburn	40.00	20.00	12.00
288	Bobby Adams	40.00	20.00	12.00
289	Cliff Mapes	45.00	22.00	13.50
290	Bill Dickey	175.00	70.00	44.00
291	Tommy Henrich	60.00	30.00	18.00
292	Eddie Pellagrini	40.00	20.00	12.00
293	Ken Johnson	40.00	20.00	12.00
294	Jocko Thompson	40.00	20.00	12.00
295	Al Lopez	65.00	33.00	20.00
296	Bob Kennedy	40.00	20.00	12.00
297	Dave Philley	40.00	20.00	12.00
298	Joe Astroth	40.00	20.00	12.00
299	Clyde King	45.00	22.00	13.50
300	Hal Rice	40.00	20.00	12.00
301	Tommy Glaviano	40.00	20.00	12.00
302	Jim Busby	40.00	20.00	12.00
303	Marv Rotblatt	40.00	20.00	12.00
304	Allen Gettel	40.00	20.00	12.00
305	*Willie Mays*	1550.00	575.00	350.00
306	*Jim Piersall*	60.00	30.00	18.00
307	Walt Masterson	40.00	20.00	12.00
308	Ted Beard	40.00	20.00	12.00
309	Mel Queen	40.00	20.00	12.00
310	Erv Dusak	40.00	20.00	12.00
311	Mickey Harris	40.00	20.00	12.00
312	Gene Mauch	50.00	30.00	15.00
313	Ray Mueller	40.00	20.00	12.00
314	Johnny Sain	50.00	25.00	15.00
315	Zack Taylor	40.00	20.00	12.00
316	Duane Pillette	40.00	20.00	12.00
317	*Forrest Burgess*	50.00	25.00	15.00
318	Warren Hacker	40.00	20.00	12.00
319	Red Rolfe	40.00	20.00	12.00
320	Hal White	40.00	20.00	12.00
321	Earl Johnson	40.00	20.00	12.00
322	Luke Sewell	40.00	20.00	12.00
323	*Joe Adcock*	60.00	28.00	16.50
324	Johnny Pramesa	90.00	20.00	12.00

1952 Bowman

MARTY MARION

Coach, Shortstop—St. Louis Browns
Born: Rugsburg, S.C., Dec. 1, 1917
Height: 6-2   Weight: 167
Bats: Right   Throws: Right

"Mr. Shortstop" spent 11 seasons with the St. Louis Cardinals. In 1951 he was manager. Though his team was riddled with sickness and injuries, he brought it into a third-place finish. This year he joins the Browns as coach. Expects to continue playing at short.

No. 85 in the 1952 SERIES

BASEBALL

PICTURE CARDS

©1952 Bowman Gum Division, Haelan Laboratories, Inc., Phila. 44, Pa.—Ptd. in U.S.A.

Bowman reverted back to a 252-card set in 1952,

but retained the card size (2-1/16" by 3-1/8") employed the preceding year. The cards, which are color art reproductions of actual photographs, feature a facsimile autograph on the fronts. Artwork for 15 cards that were never issued was uncovered several years ago and a set featuring those cards was subsequently made available to the collecting public.

		NR MT	EX	VG
Complete Set:		7500.00	3750.00	1875.
Common Player: 1-36		12.00	6.00	3.50
Common Player: 37-216		10.00	5.00	3.00
Common Player: 217-252		20.00	10.00	6.00
1	Larry "Yogi" Berra	600.00	85.00	38.00
2	Bobby Thomson	30.00	10.00	6.00
3	Fred Hutchinson	14.00	7.00	4.25
4	Robin Roberts	45.00	23.00	13.50
5	*Orestes Minoso*	40.00	20.00	12.00
6	Virgil "Red" Stallcup	12.00	6.00	3.50
7	Mike Garcia	14.00	7.00	4.25
8	Harold "Pee Wee" Reese	150.00	60.00	38.00
9	Vern Stephens	12.00	6.00	3.50
10	Bob Hooper	12.00	6.00	3.50
11	Ralph Kiner	45.00	23.00	13.50
12	Max Surkont	12.00	6.00	3.50
13	Cliff Mapes	12.00	6.00	3.50
14	Cliff Chambers	12.00	6.00	3.50
15	Sam Mele	12.00	6.00	3.50
16	Omar Lown	12.00	6.00	3.50
17	Ed Lopat	25.00	12.50	7.50
18	Don Mueller	12.00	6.00	3.50
19	Bob Cain	12.00	6.00	3.50
20	Willie Jones	12.00	6.00	3.50
21	Nelson Fox	30.00	15.00	9.00
22	Willard Ramsdell	12.00	6.00	3.50
23	Bob Lemon	45.00	23.00	13.50
24	Carl Furillo	20.00	10.00	6.00
25	Maurice McDermott	12.00	6.00	3.50
26	Eddie Joost	12.00	6.00	3.50
27	Joe Garagiola	60.00	30.00	18.00
28	Roy Hartsfield	12.00	6.00	3.50
29	Ned Garver	12.00	6.00	3.50
30	Al "Red" Schoendienst	50.00	30.00	15.00
31	Eddie Yost	12.00	6.00	3.50
32	Eddie Miksis	12.00	6.00	3.50
33	*Gil McDougald*	40.00	20.00	12.00
34	Al Dark	16.00	8.00	4.75
35	Gran Hamner	12.00	6.00	3.50
36	Cass Michaels	12.00	6.00	3.50
37	Vic Raschi	18.00	9.00	5.50
38	Whitey Lockman	10.00	5.00	3.00
39	Vic Wertz	12.00	6.00	3.50
40	Emory Church	10.00	5.00	3.00
41	Chico Carrasquel	10.00	5.00	3.00
42	Johnny Wyrostek	10.00	5.00	3.00
43	Bob Feller	75.00	38.00	23.00
44	Roy Campanella	175.00	70.00	44.00
45	Johnny Pesky	12.00	6.00	3.50
46	Carl Scheib	10.00	5.00	3.00
47	Pete Castiglione	10.00	5.00	3.00
48	Vern Bickford	10.00	5.00	3.00
49	Jim Hearn	10.00	5.00	3.00
50	Gerry Staley	10.00	5.00	3.00
51	Gil Coan	10.00	5.00	3.00
52	Phil Rizzuto	55.00	27.00	16.50
53	Richie Ashburn	40.00	20.00	12.00
54	Billy Pierce	12.00	6.00	3.50
55	Ken Raffensberger	10.00	5.00	3.00
56	Clyde King	12.00	6.00	3.50
57	Clyde Vollmer	10.00	5.00	3.00
58	Hank Majeski	10.00	5.00	3.00
59	Murray Dickson (Murry)	10.00	5.00	3.00
60	Sid Gordon	10.00	5.00	3.00
61	Tommy Byrne	10.00	5.00	3.00
62	Joe Presko	10.00	5.00	3.00
63	Irv Noren	10.00	5.00	3.00
64	Roy Smalley	10.00	5.00	3.00
65	Hank Bauer	20.00	10.00	6.00
66	Sal Maglie	20.00	10.00	6.00
67	Johnny Groth	10.00	5.00	3.00
68	Jim Busby	10.00	5.00	3.00
69	Joe Adcock	12.00	6.00	3.50
70	Carl Erskine	18.00	9.00	5.50
71	Vernon Law	12.00	6.00	3.50
72	Earl Torgeson	10.00	5.00	3.00
73	Jerry Coleman	18.00	9.00	5.50
74	Wes Westrum	12.00	6.00	3.50
75	George Kell	40.00	20.00	12.00
76	Del Ennis	12.00	6.00	3.50

		NR MT	EX	VG			NR MT	EX	VG
77	Eddie Robinson	10.00	5.00	3.00	168	Preacher Roe	20.00	10.00	6.00
78	Lloyd Merriman	10.00	5.00	3.00	169	Walt Dropo	10.00	5.00	3.00
79	Lou Brissie	10.00	5.00	3.00	170	Joe Astroth	10.00	5.00	3.00
80	Gil Hodges	45.00	22.00	13.50	171	Mel Queen	10.00	5.00	3.00
81	Billy Goodman	10.00	5.00	3.00	172	Ebba St. Claire	10.00	5.00	3.00
82	Gus Zernial	10.00	5.00	3.00	173	Gene Bearden	10.00	5.00	3.00
83	Howie Pollet	10.00	5.00	3.00	174	Mickey Grasso	10.00	5.00	3.00
84	Sam Jethroe	10.00	5.00	3.00	175	Ransom Jackson	10.00	5.00	3.00
85	Marty Marion	12.00	6.00	3.50	176	Harry Brecheen	12.00	6.00	3.50
86	Cal Abrams	12.00	6.00	3.50	177	Gene Woodling	18.00	9.00	5.50
87	Mickey Vernon	12.00	6.00	3.50	178	Dave Williams	10.00	5.00	3.00
88	Bruce Edwards	10.00	5.00	3.00	179	Pete Suder	10.00	5.00	3.00
89	Billy Hitchcock	10.00	5.00	3.00	180	Eddie Fitzgerald (Fitz Gerald)	10.00	5.00	3.00
90	Larry Jansen	10.00	5.00	3.00	181	Joe Collins	15.00	7.50	4.50
91	Don Kolloway	10.00	5.00	3.00	182	Dave Koslo	10.00	5.00	3.00
92	Eddie Waitkus	10.00	5.00	3.00	183	Pat Mullin	10.00	5.00	3.00
93	Paul Richards	12.00	6.00	3.50	184	Curt Simmons	12.00	6.00	3.50
94	Luke Sewell	10.00	5.00	3.00	185	Eddie Stewart	10.00	5.00	3.00
95	Luke Easter	12.00	6.00	3.50	186	Frank Smith	10.00	5.00	3.00
96	Ralph Branca	18.00	9.00	5.50	187	Jim Hegan	10.00	5.00	3.00
97	Willard Marshall	10.00	5.00	3.00	188	Charlie Dressen	15.00	7.50	4.50
98	Jimmy Dykes	12.00	6.00	3.50	189	Jim Piersall	18.00	9.00	5.50
99	Clyde McCullough	10.00	5.00	3.00	190	Dick Fowler	10.00	5.00	3.00
100	Sibby Sisti	10.00	5.00	3.00	191	*Bob Friend*	15.00	7.50	4.50
101	Mickey Mantle	1400.00	560.00	280.00	192	John Cusick	10.00	5.00	3.00
102	Peanuts Lowrey	10.00	5.00	3.00	193	Bobby Young	10.00	5.00	3.00
103	Joe Haynes	10.00	5.00	3.00	194	Bob Porterfield	10.00	5.00	3.00
104	Hal Jeffcoat	10.00	5.00	3.00	195	Frank Baumholtz	10.00	5.00	3.00
105	Bobby Brown	18.00	9.00	5.50	196	Stan Musial	375.00	150.00	94.00
106	Randy Gumpert	10.00	5.00	3.00	197	Charlie Silvera	15.00	7.50	4.50
107	Del Rice	10.00	5.00	3.00	198	Chuck Diering	10.00	5.00	3.00
108	George Metkovich	10.00	5.00	3.00	199	Ted Gray	10.00	5.00	3.00
109	Tom Morgan	15.00	7.50	4.50	200	Ken Silvestri	10.00	5.00	3.00
110	Max Lanier	10.00	5.00	3.00	201	Ray Coleman	10.00	5.00	3.00
111	Walter "Hoot" Evers	10.00	5.00	3.00	202	Harry Perkowski	10.00	5.00	3.00
112	Forrest "Smokey" Burgess	12.00	6.00	3.50	203	Steve Gromek	10.00	5.00	3.00
113	Al Zarilla	10.00	5.00	3.00	204	Andy Pafko	12.00	6.00	3.50
114	Frank Hiller	10.00	5.00	3.00	205	Walt Masterson	10.00	5.00	3.00
115	Larry Doby	15.00	7.50	4.50	206	Elmer Valo	10.00	5.00	3.00
116	Duke Snider	140.00	58.00	37.00	207	George Strickland	10.00	5.00	3.00
117	Bill Wight	10.00	5.00	3.00	208	Walker Cooper	10.00	5.00	3.00
118	Ray Murray	10.00	5.00	3.00	209	Dick Littlefield	10.00	5.00	3.00
119	Bill Howerton	10.00	5.00	3.00	210	Archie Wilson	10.00	5.00	3.00
120	Chet Nichols	10.00	5.00	3.00	211	Paul Minner	10.00	5.00	3.00
121	Al Corwin	10.00	5.00	3.00	212	Solly Hemus	10.00	5.00	3.00
122	Billy Johnson	10.00	5.00	3.00	213	Monte Kennedy	10.00	5.00	3.00
123	Sid Hudson	10.00	5.00	3.00	214	Ray Boone	12.00	6.00	3.50
124	George Tebbetts	10.00	5.00	3.00	215	Sheldon Jones	10.00	5.00	3.00
125	Howie Fox	10.00	5.00	3.00	216	Matt Batts	10.00	5.00	3.00
126	Phil Cavarretta	12.00	6.00	3.50	217	Casey Stengel	125.00	56.00	35.00
127	Dick Sisler	10.00	5.00	3.00	218	Willie Mays	775.00	300.00	180.00
128	Don Newcombe	20.00	10.00	6.00	219	Neil Berry	25.00	12.50	7.50
129	Gus Niarhos	10.00	5.00	3.00	220	Russ Meyer	25.00	12.50	7.50
130	Allie Clark	10.00	5.00	3.00	221	Lou Kretlow	25.00	12.50	7.50
131	Bob Swift	10.00	5.00	3.00	222	Homer "Dixie" Howell	25.00	12.50	7.50
132	Dave Cole	10.00	5.00	3.00	223	Harry Simpson	25.00	12.50	7.50
133	Dick Kryhoski	10.00	5.00	3.00	224	Johnny Schmitz	27.00	13.50	8.00
134	Al Brazle	10.00	5.00	3.00	225	Del Wilber	25.00	12.50	7.50
135	Mickey Harris	10.00	5.00	3.00	226	Alex Kellner	25.00	12.50	7.50
136	Gene Hermanski	10.00	5.00	3.00	227	Clyde Sukeforth	25.00	12.50	7.50
137	Stan Rojek	10.00	5.00	3.00	228	Bob Chipman	25.00	12.50	7.50
138	Ted Wilks	10.00	5.00	3.00	229	Hank Arft	25.00	12.50	7.50
139	Jerry Priddy	10.00	5.00	3.00	230	Frank Shea	25.00	12.50	7.50
140	Ray Scarborough	10.00	5.00	3.00	231	Dee Fondy	25.00	12.50	7.50
141	Hank Edwards	10.00	5.00	3.00	232	Enos Slaughter	60.00	30.00	18.00
142	Early Wynn	45.00	23.00	13.50	233	Bob Kuzava	32.00	16.00	9.50
143	Sandalio Consuegra	10.00	5.00	3.00	234	Fred Fitzsimmons	25.00	12.50	7.50
144	Joe Hatten	10.00	5.00	3.00	235	Steve Souchock	25.00	12.50	7.50
145	Johnny Mize	50.00	30.00	15.00	236	Tommy Brown	25.00	12.50	7.50
146	Leo Durocher	35.00	17.50	10.50	237	Sherman Lollar	27.00	13.50	8.00
147	Marlin Stuart	10.00	5.00	3.00	238	*Roy McMillan*	27.00	13.50	8.00
148	Ken Heintzelman	10.00	5.00	3.00	239	Dale Mitchell	25.00	12.50	7.50
149	Howie Judson	10.00	5.00	3.00	240	*Billy Loes*	32.00	16.00	9.50
150	Herman Wehmeier	10.00	5.00	3.00	241	Mel Parnell	27.00	13.50	8.00
151	Al "Flip" Rosen	18.00	9.00	5.50	242	Everett Kell	25.00	12.50	7.50
152	Billy Cox	12.00	6.00	3.50	243	George "Red" Munger	25.00	12.50	7.50
153	Fred Hatfield	10.00	5.00	3.00	244	*Lew Burdette*	50.00	30.00	15.00
154	Ferris Fain	12.00	6.00	3.50	245	George Schmees	25.00	12.50	7.50
155	Billy Meyer	10.00	5.00	3.00	246	Jerry Snyder	25.00	12.50	7.50
156	Warren Spahn	80.00	40.00	24.00	247	John Pramesa	25.00	12.50	7.50
157	Jim Delsing	10.00	5.00	3.00	248	Bill Werle	25.00	12.50	7.50
158	Bucky Harris	30.00	15.00	9.00	249	Henry Thompson	25.00	12.50	7.50
159	Dutch Leonard	10.00	5.00	3.00	250	Ivan Delock	25.00	12.50	7.50
160	Eddie Stanky	12.00	6.00	3.50	251	Jack Lohrke	32.00	12.50	7.50
161	Jackie Jensen	25.00	12.50	7.50	252	Frank Crosetti	125.00	30.00	15.00
162	Monte Irvin	35.00	17.50	10.50					
163	Johnny Lipon	10.00	5.00	3.00					
164	Connie Ryan	10.00	5.00	3.00					
165	Saul Rogovin	10.00	5.00	3.00					
166	Bobby Adams	10.00	5.00	3.00					
167	Bob Avila	10.00	5.00	3.00					

NOTE: A card number in parentheses ( ) indicates the set is unnumbered.

1953 Bowman Color

The first set of current major league players featuring actual color photographs, the 160-card 1953 Bowman Color set remains one of the most popular issues of the post-war era. The set is greatly appreciated for its uncluttered look; card fronts that contain no names, teams or facsimile autographs. Bowman increased the size of their cards to a 2-1/2" by 3-3/4" size in order to better compete with Topps Chewing Gum. Bowman copied an idea from the 1952 Topps set and developed card backs that gave player career and previous year statistics. The high-numbered cards (#'s 113-160) are the scarcest of the set, with #'s 113-128 being exceptionally difficult to find.

		NR MT	EX	VG
Complete Set:		10000.00	5000.00	2500.
Common Player: 1-112		25.00	12.50	7.50
Common Player: 113-128		35.00	17.50	10.50
Common Player: 129-160		30.00	15.00	9.00
1	Davey Williams	110.00	15.00	9.00
2	Vic Wertz	35.00	15.00	9.00
3	Sam Jethroe	25.00	12.50	7.50
4	Art Houtteman	25.00	12.50	7.50
5	Sid Gordon	25.00	12.50	7.50
6	Joe Ginsberg	25.00	12.50	7.50
7	Harry Chiti	25.00	12.50	7.50
8	Al Rosen	35.00	17.50	10.50
9	Phil Rizzuto	80.00	40.00	24.00
10	Richie Ashburn	40.00	20.00	12.00
11	Bobby Shantz	30.00	15.00	9.00
12	Carl Erskine	35.00	17.50	10.50
13	Gus Zernial	25.00	12.50	7.50
14	Billy Loes	30.00	15.00	9.00
15	Jim Busby	25.00	12.50	7.50
16	Bob Friend	30.00	15.00	9.00
17	Gerry Staley	25.00	12.50	7.50
18	Nelson Fox	50.00	30.00	15.00
19	Al Dark	30.00	15.00	9.00
20	Don Lenhardt	25.00	12.50	7.50
21	Joe Garagiola	50.00	25.00	15.00
22	Bob Porterfield	25.00	12.50	7.50
23	Herman Wehmeier	25.00	12.50	7.50
24	Jackie Jensen	30.00	15.00	9.00
25	Walter "Hoot" Evers	25.00	12.50	7.50
26	Roy McMillan	25.00	12.50	7.50
27	Vic Raschi	35.00	17.50	10.50
28	Forrest "Smoky" Burgess	30.00	15.00	9.00
29	Roberto Avila	25.00	12.50	7.50
30	Phil Cavarretta	25.00	12.50	7.50
31	Jimmy Dykes	25.00	12.50	7.50
32	Stan Musial	400.00	160.00	100.00
33	Harold "Peewee" Reese	225.00	90.00	56.00
34	Gil Coan	25.00	12.50	7.50
35	Maury McDermott	25.00	12.50	7.50
36	Orestes Minoso	30.00	15.00	9.00
37	Jim Wilson	25.00	12.50	7.50
38	Harry Byrd	25.00	12.50	7.50
39	Paul Richards	25.00	12.50	7.50
40	Larry Doby	35.00	17.50	10.50
41	Sammy White	25.00	12.50	7.50
42	Tommy Brown	25.00	12.50	7.50
43	Mike Garcia	25.00	12.50	7.50
44	Hank Bauer, Yogi Berra, Mickey Mantle	350.00	140.00	88.00
45	Walt Dropo	25.00	12.50	7.50
46	Roy Campanella	200.00	80.00	50.00
47	Ned Garver	25.00	12.50	7.50
48	Hank Sauer	25.00	12.50	7.50
49	Eddie Stanky	25.00	12.50	7.50
50	Lou Kretlow	25.00	12.50	7.50
51	Monte Irvin	45.00	23.00	13.50
52	Marty Marion	30.00	15.00	9.00
53	Del Rice	25.00	12.50	7.50
54	Chico Carrasquel	25.00	12.50	7.50
55	Leo Durocher	45.00	23.00	13.50
56	Bob Cain	25.00	12.50	7.50
57	Lou Boudreau	45.00	23.00	13.50
58	Willard Marshall	25.00	12.50	7.50
59	Mickey Mantle	1200.00	500.00	300.00
60	Granny Hamner	25.00	12.50	7.50
61	George Kell	45.00	23.00	13.50
62	Ted Kluszewski	35.00	17.50	10.50
63	Gil McDougald	35.00	17.50	10.50
64	Curt Simmons	25.00	12.50	7.50
65	Robin Roberts	50.00	25.00	15.00
66	Mel Parnell	25.00	12.50	7.50
67	Mel Clark	25.00	12.50	7.50
68	Allie Reynolds	35.00	17.50	10.50
69	Charlie Grimm	25.00	12.50	7.50
70	Clint Courtney	25.00	12.50	7.50
71	Paul Minner	25.00	12.50	7.50
72	Ted Gray	25.00	12.50	7.50
73	Billy Pierce	25.00	12.50	7.50
74	Don Mueller	25.00	12.50	7.50
75	Saul Rogovin	25.00	12.50	7.50
76	Jim Hearn	25.00	12.50	7.50
77	Mickey Grasso	25.00	12.50	7.50
78	Carl Furillo	35.00	17.50	10.50
79	Ray Boone	25.00	12.50	7.50
80	Ralph Kiner	60.00	30.00	18.00
81	Enos Slaughter	60.00	30.00	18.00
82	Joe Astroth	25.00	12.50	7.50
83	Jack Daniels	25.00	12.50	7.50
84	Hank Bauer	35.00	17.50	10.50
85	Solly Hemus	25.00	12.50	7.50
86	Harry Simpson	25.00	12.50	7.50
87	Harry Perkowski	25.00	12.50	7.50
88	Joe Dobson	25.00	12.50	7.50
89	Sandalio Consuegra	25.00	12.50	7.50
90	Joe Nuxhall	30.00	15.00	9.00
91	Steve Souchock	25.00	12.50	7.50
92	Gil Hodges	100.00	45.00	27.00
93	Billy Martin, Phil Rizzuto	175.00	70.00	44.00
94	Bob Addis	25.00	12.50	7.50
95	Wally Moses	25.00	12.50	7.50
96	Sal Maglie	30.00	15.00	9.00
97	Eddie Mathews	90.00	45.00	27.00
98	Hector Rodriquez	25.00	12.50	7.50
99	Warren Spahn	90.00	45.00	27.00
100	Bill Wight	25.00	12.50	7.50
101	Al "Red" Schoendienst	70.00	35.00	21.00
102	Jim Hegan	25.00	12.50	7.50
103	Del Ennis	25.00	12.50	7.50
104	Luke Easter	25.00	12.50	7.50
105	Eddie Joost	25.00	12.50	7.50
106	Ken Raffensberger	25.00	12.50	7.50
107	Alex Kellner	25.00	12.50	7.50
108	Bobby Adams	25.00	12.50	7.50
109	Ken Wood	25.00	12.50	7.50
110	Bob Rush	25.00	12.50	7.50
111	Jim Dyck	25.00	12.50	7.50
112	Toby Atwell	25.00	12.50	7.50
113	Karl Drews	35.00	17.50	10.50
114	Bob Feller	250.00	100.00	63.00
115	Cloyd Boyer	35.00	17.50	10.50
116	Eddie Yost	35.00	17.50	10.50
117	Duke Snider	475.00	190.00	119.00
118	Billy Martin	200.00	80.00	50.00
119	Dale Mitchell	35.00	17.50	10.50
120	Marlin Stuart	35.00	17.50	10.50
121	Yogi Berra	475.00	190.00	119.00
122	Bill Serena	35.00	17.50	10.50
123	Johnny Lipon	35.00	17.50	10.50
124	Charlie Dressen	45.00	23.00	13.50
125	Fred Hatfield	35.00	17.50	10.50
126	Al Corwin	35.00	17.50	10.50
127	Dick Kryhoski	35.00	17.50	10.50
128	Whitey Lockman	35.00	17.50	10.50
129	Russ Meyer	35.00	17.50	10.50
130	Cass Michaels	30.00	15.00	9.00
131	Connie Ryan	30.00	15.00	9.00
132	Fred Hutchinson	35.00	17.50	10.50
133	Willie Jones	30.00	15.00	9.00
134	Johnny Pesky	35.00	17.50	10.50
135	Bobby Morgan	35.00	17.50	10.50
136	Jim Brideweser	40.00	20.00	12.00
137	Sam Dente	30.00	15.00	9.00

		NR MT	EX	VG
138	Bubba Church	30.00	15.00	9.00
139	Pete Runnels	35.00	17.50	10.50
140	Alpha Brazle	30.00	15.00	9.00
141	Frank "Spec" Shea	30.00	15.00	9.00
142	Larry Miggins	30.00	15.00	9.00
143	Al Lopez	60.00	30.00	18.00
144	Warren Hacker	30.00	15.00	9.00
145	George Shuba	35.00	17.50	10.50
146	Early Wynn	100.00	45.00	27.00
147	Clem Koshorek	30.00	15.00	9.00
148	Billy Goodman	30.00	15.00	9.00
149	Al Corwin	30.00	15.00	9.00
150	Carl Scheib	30.00	15.00	9.00
151	Joe Adcock	40.00	20.00	12.00
152	Clyde Vollmer	30.00	15.00	9.00
153	Ed "Whitey" Ford	350.00	140.00	88.00
154	Omar "Turk" Lown	30.00	15.00	9.00
155	Allie Clark	30.00	15.00	9.00
156	Max Surkont	30.00	15.00	9.00
157	Sherman Lollar	35.00	17.50	10.50
158	Howard Fox	30.00	15.00	9.00
159	Mickey Vernon (Photo actually Floyd Baker)	40.00	17.50	10.50
160	Cal Abrams	100.00	17.50	9.00

		NR MT	EX	VG
31	Gene Woodling	40.00	20.00	12.00
32	Rocky Bridges	22.00	11.00	6.50
33	Bob Kuzava	32.00	16.00	9.50
34	Ebba St. Clair (St. Claire)	22.00	11.00	6.50
35	Johnny Wyrostek	22.00	11.00	6.50
36	Jim Piersall	40.00	20.00	12.00
37	Hal Jeffcoat	22.00	11.00	6.50
38	Dave Cole	22.00	11.00	6.50
39	Casey Stengel	275.00	110.00	69.00
40	Larry Jansen	22.00	11.00	6.50
41	Bob Ramazotti	22.00	11.00	6.50
42	Howie Judson	22.00	11.00	6.50
43	Hal Bevan	22.00	11.00	6.50
44	Jim Delsing	22.00	11.00	6.50
45	Irv Noren	32.00	16.00	9.50
46	Bucky Harris	55.00	28.00	16.50
47	Jack Lohrke	22.00	11.00	6.50
48	Steve Ridzik	22.00	11.00	6.50
49	Floyd Baker	22.00	11.00	6.50
50	Emil "Dutch" Leonard	22.00	11.00	6.50
51	Lou Burdette	40.00	20.00	12.00
52	Ralph Branca	40.00	20.00	12.00
53	Morris Martin	22.00	11.00	6.50
54	Bill Miller	32.00	16.00	9.50
55	Don Johnson	22.00	11.00	6.50
56	Roy Smalley	22.00	11.00	6.50
57	Andy Pafko	27.00	13.50	8.00
58	Jim Konstanty	27.00	13.50	8.00
59	Duane Pillette	22.00	11.00	6.50
60	Billy Cox	27.00	13.50	8.00
61	Tom Gorman	32.00	16.00	9.50
62	Keith Thomas	22.00	11.00	6.50
63	Steve Gromek	27.00	11.00	6.50
64	Andy Hansen	45.00	13.50	6.50

1953 Bowman Black & White

The 1953 Bowman Black and White set is similar in all respects to the 1953 Bowman Color set, except that it lacks color. Purportedly, high costs in producing the color series forced Bowman to issue the set in black and white. Sixty-four cards, which measure 2-1/2" by 3-3/4", comprise the set.

		NR MT	EX	VG
Complete Set:		2200.00	880.00	440.00
Common Player:		22.00	11.00	6.50
1	Gus Bell	80.00	40.00	24.00
2	Willard Nixon	32.00	11.00	6.50
3	Bill Rigney	27.00	13.50	8.00
4	Pat Mullin	22.00	11.00	6.50
5	Dee Fondy	22.00	11.00	6.50
6	Ray Murray	22.00	11.00	6.50
7	Andy Seminick	22.00	11.00	6.50
8	Pete Suder	22.00	11.00	6.50
9	Walt Masterson	22.00	11.00	6.50
10	Dick Sisler	22.00	11.00	6.50
11	Dick Gernert	22.00	11.00	6.50
12	Randy Jackson	22.00	11.00	6.50
13	Joe Tipton	22.00	11.00	6.50
14	Bill Nicholson	22.00	11.00	6.50
15	Johnny Mize	110.00	50.00	28.00
16	Stu Miller	22.00	11.00	6.50
17	Virgil Trucks	27.00	13.50	8.00
18	Billy Hoeft	22.00	11.00	6.50
19	Paul LaPalme	22.00	11.00	6.50
20	Eddie Robinson	22.00	11.00	6.50
21	Clarence "Bud" Podbielan	22.00	11.00	6.50
22	Matt Batts	22.00	11.00	6.50
23	Wilmer Mizell	22.00	11.00	6.50
24	Del Wilber	22.00	11.00	6.50
25	John Sain	50.00	25.00	15.00
26	Preacher Roe	50.00	25.00	15.00
27	Bob Lemon	90.00	45.00	27.00
28	Hoyt Wilhelm	90.00	45.00	27.00
29	Sid Hudson	22.00	11.00	6.50
30	Walker Cooper	22.00	11.00	6.50

1954 Bowman

Bowman's 1954 set consists of 224 full-color cards that measure 2-1/2" by 3-3/4". It is believed that contractual problems caused the pulling of card #66 (Ted Williams) from the set, creating one of the most sought-after scarcities of the post-war era. The Williams card was replaced by Jim Piersall (who is also #210) in subsequent print runs. The set contains over 40 variations, most involving statistical errors on the card backs that were corrected. Neither variation carries a premium value as both varieties appear to have been printed in equal amounts. The complete set price that follows does not include all variations or #66 Williams.

		NR MT	EX	VG
Complete Set:		3500.00	1400.00	700.00
Common Player: 1-224		5.00	2.50	1.50
1	Phil Rizzuto	150.00	60.00	38.00
2	Jack Jensen	10.00	5.00	3.00
3	Marion Fricano	5.00	2.50	1.50
4	Bob Hooper	5.00	2.50	1.50
5	William Hunter	5.00	2.50	1.50
6	Nelson Fox	15.00	7.50	4.50
7	Walter Dropo	5.00	2.50	1.50
8	James F. Busby	5.00	2.50	1.50
9	Dave Williams	5.00	2.50	1.50
10	Carl Daniel Erskine	8.00	4.00	2.50
11	Sid Gordon	5.00	2.50	1.50
12a	Roy McMillan (551/1290 At Bat)	6.00	3.00	1.75

		NR MT	EX	VG
12b	Roy McMillan (557/1296 At Bat)	6.00	3.00	1.75
13	Paul Minner	5.00	2.50	1.50
14	Gerald Staley	5.00	2.50	1.50
15	Richie Ashburn	20.00	10.00	6.00
16	Jim Wilson	5.00	2.50	1.50
17	Tom Gorman	8.00	4.00	2.50
18	Walter "Hoot" Evers	5.00	2.50	1.50
19	Bobby Shantz	7.00	3.50	2.00
20	Artie Houtteman	5.00	2.50	1.50
21	Victor Wertz	6.00	3.00	1.75
22a	Sam Mele (213/1661 Putouts)	6.00	3.00	1.75
22b	Sam Mele (217/1665 Putouts)	6.00	3.00	1.75
23	*Harvey Kuenn*	20.00	10.00	6.00
24	Bob Porterfield	5.00	2.50	1.50
25a	Wes Westrum (1.000/.987 Field Avg.)			
		6.00	3.00	1.75
25b	Wes Westrum (.982/.986 Field Avg.)			
		6.00	3.00	1.75
26a	Billy Cox (1.000/.960 Field Avg.)	7.00	3.50	2.00
26b	Billy Cox (.972/.960 Field Avg.)	7.00	3.50	2.00
27	Richard Roy Cole	5.00	2.50	1.50
28a	Jim Greengrass (Birthplace Addison, N.J.)			
		6.00	3.00	1.75
28b	Jim Greengrass (Birthplace Addison, N.Y.)			
		6.00	3.00	1.75
29	Johnny Klippstein	5.00	2.50	1.50
30	Delbert Rice Jr.	5.00	2.50	1.50
31	"Smoky" Burgess	6.00	3.00	1.75
32	Del Crandall	6.00	3.00	1.75
33a	Victor Raschi (no traded line)	10.00	5.00	3.00
33b	Victor Raschi (with traded line)	15.00	7.50	4.50
34	Sammy White	5.00	2.50	1.50
35a	Eddie Joost (quiz answer is 8)	6.00	3.00	1.75
35b	Eddie Joost (quiz answer is 33)	6.00	3.00	1.75
36	George Strickland	5.00	2.50	1.50
37	Dick Kokos	5.00	2.50	1.50
38a	Orestes Minoso (.895/.961 Field Avg.)			
		8.00	4.00	2.50
38b	Orestes Minoso (.963/.963 Field Avg.)			
		8.00	4.00	2.50
39	Ned Garver	5.00	2.50	1.50
40	Gil Coan	5.00	2.50	1.50
41a	Alvin Dark (.986/.960 Field Avg.)	8.00	4.00	2.50
41b	Alvin Dark (.968/.960 Field Avg.)	8.00	4.00	2.50
42	Billy Loes	7.00	3.50	2.00
43a	Robert B. Friend (20 shutouts in quiz question)	7.00	3.50	2.00
43b	Robert B. Friend (16 shutouts in quiz question)	7.00	3.50	2.00
44	Harry Perkowski	5.00	2.50	1.50
45	Ralph Kiner	40.00	20.00	12.00
46	Eldon Repulski	5.00	2.50	1.50
47a	Granville Hamner (.970/.953 Field Avg.)			
		6.00	3.00	1.75
47b	Granville Hamner (.953/.951 Field Avg.)			
		6.00	3.00	1.75
48	Jack Dittmer	5.00	2.50	1.50
49	Harry Byrd	8.00	4.00	2.50
50	George Kell	25.00	12.50	7.50
51	Alex Kellner	5.00	2.50	1.50
52	Myron N. Ginsberg	5.00	2.50	1.50
53a	Don Lenhardt (.969/.984 Field Avg.)			
		6.00	3.00	1.75
53b	Don Lenhardt (.966/.983 Field Avg.)			
		6.00	3.00	1.75
54	Alfonso Carrasquel	5.00	2.50	1.50
55	Jim Delsing	5.00	2.50	1.50
56	Maurice M. McDermott	5.00	2.50	1.50
57	Hoyt Wilhelm	25.00	12.50	7.50
58	"Pee Wee" Reese	50.00	30.00	15.00
59	Robert D. Schultz	5.00	2.50	1.50
60	Fred Baczewski	5.00	2.50	1.50
61a	Eddie Miksis (.954/.962 Field Avg.)			
		6.00	3.00	1.75
61b	Eddie Miksis (.954/.961 Field Avg.)			
		6.00	3.00	1.75
62	Enos Slaughter	25.00	12.50	7.50
63	Earl Torgeson	5.00	2.50	1.50
64	Ed Mathews	40.00	20.00	12.00
65	Mickey Mantle	625.00	250.00	160.00
66a	Ted Williams	2200.00	900.00	550.00
66b	Jimmy Piersall	80.00	40.00	24.00
67a	Carl Scheib (.306 Pct. with two lines under bio)	6.00	3.00	1.75
67b	Carl Scheib (.306 Pct. with one line under bio)	6.00	3.00	1.75
67c	Carl Scheib (.300 Pct.)	6.00	3.00	1.75
68	Bob Avila	6.00	3.00	1.75
69	Clinton Courtney	5.00	2.50	1.50
70	Willard Marshall	5.00	2.50	1.50
71	Ted Gray	5.00	2.50	1.50

		NR MT	EX	VG
72	Ed Yost	5.00	2.50	1.50
73	Don Mueller	5.00	2.50	1.50
74	James Gilliam	10.00	5.00	3.00
75	Max Surkont	5.00	2.50	1.50
76	Joe Nuxhall	6.00	3.00	1.75
77	Bob Rush	5.00	2.50	1.50
78	Sal A. Yvars	5.00	2.50	1.50
79	Curt Simmons	6.00	3.00	1.75
80a	John Logan (106 Runs)	6.00	3.00	1.75
80b	John Logan (100 Runs)	6.00	3.00	1.75
81a	Jerry Coleman (1.000/.975 Field Avg.)			
		8.00	4.00	2.50
81b	Jerry Coleman (.952/.975 Field Avg.)			
		8.00	4.00	2.50
82a	Bill Goodman (.965/.986 Field Avg.)			
		6.00	3.00	1.75
82b	Bill Goodman (.972/.985 Field Avg.)			
		6.00	3.00	1.75
83	Ray Murray	5.00	2.50	1.50
84	Larry Doby	8.00	4.00	2.50
85a	Jim Dyck (.926/.956 Field Avg.)	6.00	3.00	1.75
85b	Jim Dyck (.947/.960 Field Avg.)	6.00	3.00	1.75
86	Harry Dorish	5.00	2.50	1.50
87	Don Lund	5.00	2.50	1.50
88	Tommy Umphlett	5.00	2.50	1.50
89	Willie May (Mays)	300.00	120.00	75.00
90	Roy Campanella	100.00	45.00	27.00
91	Cal Abrams	5.00	2.50	1.50
92	Kenneth David Raffensberger	5.00	2.50	1.50
93a	Bill Serena (.983/.966 Field Avg.)	6.00	3.00	1.75
93b	Bill Serena (.977/.966 Field Avg.)	6.00	3.00	1.75
94a	Solly Hemus (476/1343 Assists)	6.00	3.00	1.75
94b	Solly Hemus (477/1343 Assists)	6.00	3.00	1.75
95	Robin Roberts	25.00	12.50	7.50
96	Joe Adcock	7.00	3.50	2.00
97	Gil McDougald	12.00	6.00	3.50
98	Ellis Kinder	5.00	2.50	1.50
99a	Peter Suder (.985/.974 Field Avg.)			
		6.00	3.00	1.75
99b	Peter Suder (.978/.974 Field Avg.)			
		6.00	3.00	1.75
100	Mike Garcia	6.00	3.00	1.75
101	*Don James Larsen*	25.00	12.50	7.50
102	Bill Pierce	6.00	3.00	1.75
103a	Stephen Souchock (144/1192 Putouts)			
		6.00	3.00	1.75
103b	Stephen Souchock (147/1195 Putouts)			
		6.00	3.00	1.75
104	Frank Spec Shea	5.00	2.50	1.50
105a	Sal Maglie (quiz answer is 8)	7.00	3.50	2.00
105b	Sal Maglie (quiz answer is 1904)	7.00	3.50	2.00
106	"Clem" Labine	7.00	3.50	2.00
107	Paul E. LaPalme	5.00	2.50	1.50
108	Bobby Adams	5.00	2.50	1.50
109	Roy Smalley	5.00	2.50	1.50
110	Al Schoendienst	30.00	15.00	9.00
111	Murry Monroe Dickson	5.00	2.50	1.50
112	Andy Pafko	6.00	3.00	1.75
113	Allie Reynolds	12.00	6.00	3.50
114	Willard Nixon	5.00	2.50	1.50
115	Don Bollweg	5.00	2.50	1.50
116	Luscious Luke Easter	5.00	2.50	1.50
117	Dick Kryhoski	5.00	2.50	1.50
118	Robert R. Boyd	5.00	2.50	1.50
119	Fred Hatfield	5.00	2.50	1.50
120	Mel Hoderlein	5.00	2.50	1.50
121	Ray Katt	5.00	2.50	1.50
122	Carl Furillo	10.00	5.00	3.00
123	Toby Atwell	5.00	2.50	1.50
124a	Gus Bell (15/27 Errors)	6.00	3.00	1.75
124b	Gus Bell (11/26 Errors)	6.00	3.00	1.75
125	Warren Hacker	5.00	2.50	1.50
126	Cliff Chambers	5.00	2.50	1.50
127	Del Ennis	6.00	3.00	1.75
128	Ebba St Claire	5.00	2.50	1.50
129	Hank Bauer	12.00	6.00	3.50
130	Milt Bolling	5.00	2.50	1.50
131	Joe Astroth	5.00	2.50	1.50
132	Bob Feller	70.00	35.00	21.00
133	Duane Pillette	5.00	2.50	1.50
134	Luis Aloma	5.00	2.50	1.50
135	Johnny Pesky	6.00	3.00	1.75
136	Clyde Vollmer	5.00	2.50	1.50
137	Elmer N. Corwin Jr.	5.00	2.50	1.50
138a	Gil Hodges (.993/.991 Field Avg.)			
		40.00	20.00	12.00
138b	Gil Hodges (.992/.991 Field Avg.)			
		40.00	20.00	12.00
139a	Preston Ward (.961/.992 Field Avg.)			
		6.00	3.00	1.75
139b	Preston Ward (.990/.992 Field Avg.)			
		6.00	3.00	1.75

		NR MT	EX	VG
140a	Saul Rogovin (7-12 Won/Lost with 2 Strikeouts)	6.00	3.00	1.75
140b	Saul Rogovin (7-12 Won/Lost with 62 Strikeouts)	6.00	3.00	1.75
140c	Saul Rogovin (8-12 Won/Lost)	6.00	3.00	1.75
141	Joe Garagiola	35.00	17.50	10.50
142	Al Brazle	5.00	2.50	1.50
143	Puddin Head Jones	5.00	2.50	1.50
144	Ernie Johnson	5.00	2.50	1.50
145a	Billy Martin (.985/.983 Field Avg.)	40.00	20.00	12.00
145b	Billy Martin (.983/.982 Field Avg.)	40.00	20.00	12.00
146	Dick Gernert	5.00	2.50	1.50
147	Joe DeMaestri	5.00	2.50	1.50
148	Dale Mitchell	5.00	2.50	1.50
149	Bob Young	5.00	2.50	1.50
150	Cass Michaels	5.00	2.50	1.50
151	Patrick J. Mullin	5.00	2.50	1.50
152	Mickey Vernon	6.00	3.00	1.75
153a	Whitey Lockman (100/331 Assists)	6.00	3.00	1.75
153b	Whitey Lockman (102/333 Assists)	6.00	3.00	1.75
154	Don Newcombe	10.00	5.00	3.00
155	*Frank J. Thomas*	6.00	3.00	1.75
156a	Everett Lamar Bridges (320/467 Assists)	6.00	3.00	1.75
156b	Everett Lamar Bridges (328/475 Assists)	6.00	3.00	1.75
157	Omar Lown	5.00	2.50	1.50
158	Stu Miller	5.00	2.50	1.50
159	John Lindell	5.00	2.50	1.50
160	Danny O'Connell	5.00	2.50	1.50
161	Yogi Berra	110.00	50.00	28.00
162	Ted Lepcio	5.00	2.50	1.50
163a	Dave Philley (152 Games with no traded line)	7.00	3.50	2.00
163b	Dave Philley (152 Games with traded line)	15.00	7.50	4.50
163c	Dave Philley (157 Games with traded line)	7.00	3.50	2.00
164	Early "Gus" Wynn	25.00	12.50	7.50
165	Johnny Groth	5.00	2.50	1.50
166	Sandalio Consuegra	5.00	2.50	1.50
167	Bill Hoeft	5.00	2.50	1.50
168	Edward Fitzgerald (Fitz Gerald)	5.00	2.50	1.50
169	Larry Jansen	5.00	2.50	1.50
170	Edwin D. Snider	90.00	45.00	27.00
171	Carlos Bernier	5.00	2.50	1.50
172	Andy Seminick	5.00	2.50	1.50
173	Dee V. Fondy Jr.	5.00	2.50	1.50
174a	Peter Paul Castiglione (.966/.959 Field Avg.)	6.00	3.00	1.75
174b	Peter Paul Castiglione (.970/.959 Field Avg.)	6.00	3.00	1.75
175	Melvin E. Clark	5.00	2.50	1.50
176	Vernon Bickford	5.00	2.50	1.50
177	Edward Ford	50.00	30.00	15.00
178	Del Wilber	5.00	2.50	1.50
179a	Morris Martin (44 ERA)	6.00	3.00	1.75
179b	Morris Martin (4.44 ERA)	6.00	3.00	1.75
180	Joe Tipton	5.00	2.50	1.50
181	Lester Moss	5.00	2.50	1.50
182	Sherman Lollar	6.00	3.00	1.75
183	Matt Batts	5.00	2.50	1.50
184	Mickey Grasso	5.00	2.50	1.50
185a	*Daryl Spencer* (.941/.944 Field Avg.)	6.00	3.00	1.75
185b	*Daryl Spencer* (.933/.936 Field Avg.)	6.00	3.00	1.75
186	Russell Meyer	7.00	3.50	2.00
187	Verne Law (Vern)	6.00	3.00	1.75
188	Frank Smith	5.00	2.50	1.50
189	Ransom Jackson	5.00	2.50	1.50
190	Joe Presko	5.00	2.50	1.50
191	Karl A. Drews	5.00	2.50	1.50
192	Selva L. Burdette	7.00	3.50	2.00
193	Eddie Robinson	8.00	4.00	2.50
194	Sid Hudson	5.00	2.50	1.50
195	Bob Cain	5.00	2.50	1.50
196	Bob Lemon	25.00	12.50	7.50
197	Lou Kretlow	5.00	2.50	1.50
198	Virgil Trucks	6.00	3.00	1.75
199	Steve Gromek	5.00	2.50	1.50
200	C. Marrero	5.00	2.50	1.50
201	Bob Thomson	7.00	3.50	2.00
202	George Shuba	7.00	3.50	2.00
203	Vic Janowicz	5.00	2.50	1.50
204	Jack Collum	5.00	2.50	1.50
205	Hal Jeffcoat	5.00	2.50	1.50

		NR MT	EX	VG
206	Steve Bilko	5.00	2.50	1.50
207	Stan Lopata	5.00	2.50	1.50
208	Johnny Antonelli	6.00	3.00	1.75
209	Gene Woodling (photo reversed)	10.00	5.00	3.00
210	Jimmy Piersall	10.00	5.00	3.00
211	Alfred James Robertson Jr.	5.00	2.50	1.50
212a	Owen L. Friend (.964/.957 Field Avg.)	6.00	3.00	1.75
212b	Owen L. Friend (.967/.958 Field Avg.)	6.00	3.00	1.75
213	Dick Littlefield	5.00	2.50	1.50
214	Ferris Fain	6.00	3.00	1.75
215	Johnny Bucha	5.00	2.50	1.50
216a	Jerry Snyder (.988/.988 Field Avg.)	6.00	3.00	1.75
216b	Jerry Snyder (.968/.968 Field Avg.)	6.00	3.00	1.75
217a	Henry Thompson (.956/.951 Field Avg.)	6.00	3.00	1.75
217b	Henry Thompson (.958/.952 Field Avg.)	6.00	3.00	1.75
218	Preacher Roe	10.00	5.00	3.00
219	Hal Rice	5.00	2.50	1.50
220	Hobie Landrith	5.00	2.50	1.50
221	Frank Baumholtz	5.00	2.50	1.50
222	Memo Luna	5.00	2.50	1.50
223	Steve Ridzik	7.00	2.50	1.50
224	William Bruton	20.00	3.50	1.75

1955 Bowman

Bowman produced its final baseball card set in 1955, a popular issue which has player photographs placed inside a television set design. The set consists of 320 cards that measure 2-1/2" by 3-3/4" in size. The high-numbered cards (#'s 225-320) are scarcest in the set and include 31 umpire cards.

		NR MT	EX	VG
	Complete Set:	4200.00	1680.00	840.00
	Common Player: 1-224	5.00	2.50	1.50
	Common Player: 225-320	12.00	6.00	3.50
1	Hoyt Wilhelm	80.00	20.00	6.00
2	Al Dark	12.00	4.00	2.50
3	Joe Coleman	5.00	2.50	1.50
4	Eddie Waitkus	5.00	2.50	1.50
5	Jim Robertson	5.00	2.50	1.50
6	Pete Suder	5.00	2.50	1.50
7	Gene Baker	5.00	2.50	1.50
8	Warren Hacker	5.00	2.50	1.50
9	Gil McDougald	10.00	5.00	3.00
10	Phil Rizzuto	40.00	20.00	12.00
11	Billy Bruton	5.00	2.50	1.50
12	Andy Pafko	6.00	3.00	1.75
13	Clyde Vollmer	5.00	2.50	1.50
14	Gus Keriazakos	5.00	2.50	1.50
15	*Frank Sullivan*	6.00	3.00	1.75
16	Jim Piersall	7.00	3.50	2.00
17	Del Ennis	6.00	3.00	1.75

#	Player	NR MT	EX	VG
18	Stan Lopata	5.00	2.50	1.50
19	Bobby Avila	5.00	2.50	1.50
20	Al Smith	5.00	2.50	1.50
21	Don Hoak	7.00	3.50	2.00
22	Roy Campanella	80.00	40.00	24.00
23	Al Kaline	80.00	40.00	24.00
24	Al Aber	5.00	2.50	1.50
25	Orestes "Minnie" Minoso	10.00	5.00	3.00
26	Virgil Trucks	6.00	3.00	1.75
27	Preston Ward	5.00	2.50	1.50
28	Dick Cole	5.00	2.50	1.50
29	Al "Red" Schoendienst	30.00	15.00	10.50
30	Bill Sarni	5.00	2.50	1.50
31	Johnny Temple	5.00	2.50	1.50
32	Wally Post	5.00	2.50	1.50
33	Nelson Fox	12.00	6.00	3.50
34	Clint Courtney	5.00	2.50	1.50
35	Bill Tuttle	5.00	2.50	1.50
36	Wayne Belardi	5.00	2.50	1.50
37	Harold "Pee Wee" Reese	60.00	30.00	18.00
38	Early Wynn	20.00	10.00	6.00
39	Bob Darnell	6.00	3.00	1.75
40	Vic Wertz	6.00	3.00	1.75
41	Mel Clark	5.00	2.50	1.50
42	Bob Greenwood	5.00	2.50	1.50
43	Bob Buhl	6.00	3.00	1.75
44	Danny O'Connell	5.00	2.50	1.50
45	Tom Umphlett	5.00	2.50	1.50
46	Mickey Vernon	6.00	3.00	1.75
47	Sammy White	5.00	2.50	1.50
48a	Milt Bolling (Frank Bolling back)	6.00	3.00	1.75
48b	Milt Bolling (Milt Bolling back)	15.00	7.50	4.50
49	Jim Greengrass	5.00	2.50	1.50
50	Hobie Landrith	5.00	2.50	1.50
51	Elvin Tappe	5.00	2.50	1.50
52	Hal Rice	5.00	2.50	1.50
53	Alex Kellner	5.00	2.50	1.50
54	Don Bollweg	5.00	2.50	1.50
55	Cal Abrams	5.00	2.50	1.50
56	Billy Cox	5.00	2.50	1.50
57	Bob Friend	6.00	3.00	1.75
58	Frank Thomas	5.00	2.50	1.50
59	Ed "Whitey" Ford	50.00	30.00	15.00
60	Enos Slaughter	20.00	10.00	6.00
61	Paul LaPalme	5.00	2.50	1.50
62	Royce Lint	5.00	2.50	1.50
63	Irv Noren	8.00	4.00	2.50
64	Curt Simmons	6.00	3.00	1.75
65	Don Zimmer	15.00	7.50	4.50
66	George Shuba	6.00	3.00	1.75
67	Don Larsen	15.00	7.50	4.50
68	Elston Howard	20.00	10.00	6.00
69	Bill Hunter	8.00	4.00	2.50
70	Lou Burdette	7.00	3.50	2.00
71	Dave Jolly	5.00	2.50	1.50
72	Chet Nichols	5.00	2.50	1.50
73	Eddie Yost	5.00	2.50	1.50
74	Jerry Snyder	5.00	2.50	1.50
75	Brooks Lawrence	5.00	2.50	1.50
76	Tom Poholsky	5.00	2.50	1.50
77	Jim McDonald	5.00	2.50	1.50
78	Gil Coan	5.00	2.50	1.50
79	Willie Miranda	5.00	2.50	1.50
80	Lou Limmer	5.00	2.50	1.50
81	Bob Morgan	5.00	2.50	1.50
82	Lee Walls	5.00	2.50	1.50
83	Max Surkont	5.00	2.50	1.50
84	George Freese	5.00	2.50	1.50
85	Cass Michaels	5.00	2.50	1.50
86	Ted Gray	5.00	2.50	1.50
87	Randy Jackson	5.00	2.50	1.50
88	Steve Bilko	5.00	2.50	1.50
89	Lou Boudreau	20.00	10.00	6.00
90	Art Ditmar	5.00	2.50	1.50
91	Dick Marlowe	5.00	2.50	1.50
92	George Zuverink	5.00	2.50	1.50
93	Andy Seminick	5.00	2.50	1.50
94	Hank Thompson	5.00	2.50	1.50
95	Sal Maglie	10.00	5.00	3.00
96	Ray Narleski	5.00	2.50	1.50
97	John Podres	12.00	6.00	3.50
98	James "Junior" Gilliam	15.00	7.50	4.50
99	Jerry Coleman	8.00	4.00	2.50
100	Tom Morgan	8.00	4.00	2.50
101a	Don Johnson (Ernie Johnson (Braves) on front)	6.00	3.00	1.75
101b	Don Johnson (Don Johnson (Orioles) on front)	15.00	7.50	4.50
102	Bobby Thomson	8.00	4.00	2.50
103	Eddie Mathews	30.00	15.00	9.00
104	Bob Porterfield	5.00	2.50	1.50
105	Johnny Schmitz	5.00	2.50	1.50
106	Del Rice	5.00	2.50	1.50
107	Solly Hemus	5.00	2.50	1.50
108	Lou Kretlow	5.00	2.50	1.50
109	Vern Stephens	5.00	2.50	1.50
110	Bob Miller	5.00	2.50	1.50
111	Steve Ridzik	5.00	2.50	1.50
112	Gran Hamner	5.00	2.50	1.50
113	Bob Hall	5.00	2.50	1.50
114	Vic Janowicz	5.00	2.50	1.50
115	Roger Bowman	5.00	2.50	1.50
116	Sandalio Consuegra	5.00	2.50	1.50
117	Johnny Groth	5.00	2.50	1.50
118	Bobby Adams	5.00	2.50	1.50
119	Joe Astroth	5.00	2.50	1.50
120	Ed Burtschy	5.00	2.50	1.50
121	Rufus Crawford	5.00	2.50	1.50
122	Al Corwin	5.00	2.50	1.50
123	Marv Grissom	5.00	2.50	1.50
124	Johnny Antonelli	6.00	3.00	1.75
125	Paul Giel	5.00	2.50	1.50
126	Billy Goodman	5.00	2.50	1.50
127	Hank Majeski	5.00	2.50	1.50
128	Mike Garcia	6.00	3.00	1.75
129	Hal Naragon	5.00	2.50	1.50
130	Richie Ashburn	15.00	7.50	4.50
131	Willard Marshall	5.00	2.50	1.50
132a	Harvey Kueen (incorrect spelling on back)	7.00	3.50	2.00
132b	Harvey Kuenn (correct spelling on back)	20.00	10.00	6.00
133	Charles King	5.00	2.50	1.50
134	Bob Feller	55.00	28.00	16.50
135	Lloyd Merriman	5.00	2.50	1.50
136	Rocky Bridges	5.00	2.50	1.50
137	Bob Talbot	5.00	2.50	1.50
138	Davey Williams	5.00	2.50	1.50
139	Billy & Bobby Shantz	7.00	3.50	2.00
140	Bobby Shantz	6.00	3.00	1.75
141	Wes Westrum	6.00	3.00	1.75
142	Rudy Regalado	5.00	2.50	1.50
143	Don Newcombe	8.00	4.00	2.50
144	Art Houtteman	5.00	2.50	1.50
145	Bob Nieman	5.00	2.50	1.50
146	Don Liddle	5.00	2.50	1.50
147	Sam Mele	5.00	2.50	1.50
148	Bob Chakales	5.00	2.50	1.50
149	Cloyd Boyer	5.00	2.50	1.50
150	Bill Klaus	5.00	2.50	1.50
151	Jim Brideweser	5.00	2.50	1.50
152	Johnny Klippstein	5.00	2.50	1.50
153	Eddie Robinson	8.00	4.00	2.50
154	Frank Lary	7.00	3.50	2.00
155	Gerry Staley	5.00	2.50	1.50
156	Jim Hughes	6.00	3.00	1.75
157a	Ernie Johnson (Don Johnson (Orioles) picture on front)	6.00	3.00	1.75
157b	Ernie Johnson (Ernie Johnson (Braves) picture on front)	15.00	7.50	4.50
158	Gil Hodges	40.00	20.00	12.00
159	Harry Byrd	5.00	2.50	1.50
160	Bill Skowron	15.00	7.50	4.50
161	Matt Batts	5.00	2.50	1.50
162	Charlie Maxwell	5.00	2.50	1.50
163	Sid Gordon	5.00	2.50	1.50
164	Toby Atwell	5.00	2.50	1.50
165	Maurice McDermott	5.00	2.50	1.50
166	Jim Busby	5.00	2.50	1.50
167	Bob Grim	8.00	4.00	2.50
168	Larry "Yogi" Berra	75.00	38.00	23.00
169	Carl Furillo	12.00	6.00	3.50
170	Carl Erskine	8.00	4.00	2.50
171	Robin Roberts	20.00	10.00	6.00
172	Willie Jones	5.00	2.50	1.50
173	Al "Chico" Carrasquel	5.00	2.50	1.50
174	Sherman Lollar	6.00	3.00	1.75
175	Wilmer Shantz	5.00	2.50	1.50
176	Joe DeMaestri	5.00	2.50	1.50
177	Willard Nixon	5.00	2.50	1.50
178	Tom Brewer	5.00	2.50	1.50
179	Hank Aaron	170.00	65.00	40.00
180	Johnny Logan	5.00	2.50	1.50
181	Eddie Miksis	5.00	2.50	1.50
182	Bob Rush	5.00	2.50	1.50
183	Ray Katt	5.00	2.50	1.50
184	Willie Mays	170.00	65.00	40.00
185	Vic Raschi	6.00	3.00	1.75
186	Alex Grammas	5.00	2.50	1.50
187	Fred Hatfield	5.00	2.50	1.50
188	Ned Garver	5.00	2.50	1.50
189	Jack Collum	5.00	2.50	1.50

		NR MT	EX	VG
190	Fred Baczewski	5.00	2.50	1.50
191	Bob Lemon	20.00	10.00	6.00
192	George Strickland	5.00	2.50	1.50
193	Howie Judson	5.00	2.50	1.50
194	Joe Nuxhall	6.00	3.00	1.75
195a	Erv Palica (no traded line on back)			
		7.00	3.50	2.00
195b	Erv Palica (traded line on back)	20.00	10.00	6.00
196	Russ Meyer	6.00	3.00	1.75
197	Ralph Kiner	30.00	15.00	9.00
198	Dave Pope	5.00	2.50	1.50
199	Vernon Law	6.00	3.00	1.75
200	Dick Littlefield	5.00	2.50	1.50
201	Allie Reynolds	12.00	6.00	3.50
202	Mickey Mantle	300.00	120.00	75.00
203	Steve Gromek	5.00	2.50	1.50
204a	*Frank Bolling* (Milt Bolling back)	6.00	3.00	1.75
204b	*Frank Bolling* (Frank Bolling back)			
		20.00	10.00	6.00
205	Eldon "Rip" Repulski	5.00	2.50	1.50
206	Ralph Beard	5.00	2.50	1.50
207	Frank Shea	5.00	2.50	1.50
208	Eddy Fitzgerald (Fitz Gerald)	5.00	2.50	1.50
209	Forrest "Smoky" Burgess	6.00	3.00	1.75
210	Earl Torgeson	5.00	2.50	1.50
211	John "Sonny" Dixon	5.00	2.50	1.50
212	Jack Dittmer	5.00	2.50	1.50
213	George Kell	25.00	12.50	7.50
214	Billy Pierce	6.00	3.00	1.75
215	Bob Kuzava	5.00	2.50	1.50
216	Preacher Roe	6.00	3.00	1.75
217	Del Crandall	6.00	3.00	1.75
218	Joe Adcock	6.00	3.00	1.75
219	Whitey Lockman	5.00	2.50	1.50
220	Jim Hearn	5.00	2.50	1.50
221	Hector "Skinny" Brown	5.00	2.50	1.50
222	Russ Kemmerer	5.00	2.50	1.50
223	Hal Jeffcoat	5.00	2.50	1.50
224	Dee Fondy	5.00	2.50	1.50
225	Paul Richards	11.00	5.50	3.25
226	W.F. McKinley (umpire)	15.00	7.50	4.50
227	Frank Baumholtz	10.00	5.00	3.00
228	John M. Phillips	10.00	5.00	3.00
229	Jim Brosnan	11.00	5.50	3.25
230	Al Brazle	10.00	5.00	3.00
231	Jim Konstanty	15.00	7.50	4.50
232	Birdie Tebbetts	10.00	5.00	3.00
233	Bill Serena	10.00	5.00	3.00
234	Dick Bartell	10.00	5.00	3.00
235	J.A. Paparella (umpire)	15.00	7.50	4.50
236	Murray Dickson (Murry)	10.00	5.00	3.00
237	Johnny Wyrostek	10.00	5.00	3.00
238	Eddie Stanky	11.00	5.50	3.25
239	Edwin A. Rommel (umpire)	15.00	7.50	4.50
240	Billy Loes	11.00	5.50	3.25
241	John Pesky	11.00	5.50	3.25
242	Ernie Banks	325.00	130.00	81.00
243	Gus Bell	11.00	5.50	3.25
244	Duane Pillette	10.00	5.00	3.00
245	Bill Miller	10.00	5.00	3.00
246	Hank Bauer	25.00	12.50	7.50
247	Dutch Leonard	10.00	5.00	3.00
248	Harry Dorish	10.00	5.00	3.00
249	Billy Gardner	10.00	5.00	3.00
250	Larry Napp (umpire)	15.00	7.50	4.50
251	Stan Jok	10.00	5.00	3.00
252	Roy Smalley	10.00	5.00	3.00
253	Jim Wilson	10.00	5.00	3.00
254	Bennett Flowers	10.00	5.00	3.00
255	Pete Runnels	11.00	5.50	3.25
256	Owen Friend	10.00	5.00	3.00
257	Tom Alston	10.00	5.00	3.00
258	John W. Stevens (umpire)	15.00	7.50	4.50
259	*Don Mossi*	12.00	6.00	3.50
260	Edwin H. Hurley (umpire)	15.00	7.50	4.50
261	Walt Moryn	11.00	5.50	3.25
262	Jim Lemon	11.00	5.50	3.25
263	Eddie Joost	10.00	5.00	3.00
264	Bill Henry	10.00	5.00	3.00
265	Albert J. Barlick (umpire)	50.00	30.00	15.00
266	Mike Fornieles	10.00	5.00	3.00
267	George (Jim) Honochick (umpire)			
		40.00	20.00	12.00
268	Roy Lee Hawes	10.00	5.00	3.00
269	Joe Amalfitano	10.00	5.00	3.00
270	Chico Fernandez	11.00	5.50	3.25
271	Bob Hooper	10.00	5.00	3.00
272	John Flaherty (umpire)	15.00	7.50	4.50
273	Emory "Bubba" Church	10.00	5.00	3.00
274	Jim Delsing	10.00	5.00	3.00
275	William T. Grieve (umpire)	15.00	7.50	4.50

		NR MT	EX	VG
276	Ivan Delock	10.00	5.00	3.00
277	Ed Runge (umpire)	15.00	7.50	4.50
278	*Charles Neal*	15.00	7.50	4.50
279	Hank Soar (umpire)	15.00	7.50	4.50
280	Clyde McCullough	10.00	5.00	3.00
281	Charles Berry (umpire)	15.00	7.50	4.50
282	Phil Cavarretta	11.00	5.50	3.25
283	Nestor Chylak (umpire)	15.00	7.50	4.50
284	William A. Jackowski (umpire)	15.00	7.50	4.50
285	Walt Dropo	11.00	5.50	3.25
286	Frank E. Secory (umpire)	15.00	7.50	4.50
287	Ron Mrozinski	10.00	5.00	3.00
288	Dick Smith	10.00	5.00	3.00
289	Arthur J. Gore (umpire)	15.00	7.50	4.50
290	Hershell Freeman	10.00	5.00	3.00
291	Frank Dascoli (umpire)	15.00	7.50	4.50
292	Marv Blaylock	10.00	5.00	3.00
293	Thomas D. Gorman (umpire)	15.00	7.50	4.50
294	Wally Moses	10.00	5.00	3.00
295	E. Lee Ballanfant (umpire)	15.00	7.50	4.50
296	*Bill Virdon*	25.00	12.50	7.50
297	L.R. "Dusty" Boggess (umpire)	15.00	7.50	4.50
298	Charlie Grimm	12.00	6.00	3.50
299	Lonnie Warneke (umpire)	15.00	7.50	4.50
300	Tommy Byrne	14.00	7.00	4.25
301	William R. Engeln (umpire)	15.00	7.50	4.50
302	*Frank Malzone*	15.00	7.50	4.50
303	J.B. "Jocko" Conlan (umpire)	75.00	37.00	22.00
304	Harry Chiti	10.00	5.00	3.00
305	Frank Umont (umpire)	15.00	7.50	4.50
306	Bob Cerv	15.00	7.50	4.50
307	R.A. "Babe" Pinelli (umpire)	15.00	7.50	4.50
308	Al Lopez	35.00	17.50	10.50
309	Hal H. Dixon (umpire)	15.00	7.50	4.50
310	Ken Lehman	11.00	5.50	3.25
311	Lawrence J. Goetz (umpire)	15.00	7.50	4.50
312	Bill Wight	10.00	5.00	3.00
313	A.J. Donatelli (umpire)	15.00	7.50	4.50
314	Dale Mitchell	10.00	5.00	3.00
315	Cal Hubbard (umpire)	50.00	25.00	15.00
316	Marion Fricano	10.00	5.00	3.00
317	Wm. R. Summers (umpire)	15.00	7.50	4.50
318	Sid Hudson	10.00	5.00	3.00
319	Albert B. Schroll	12.00	5.00	3.00
320	George D. Susce, Jr.	50.00	6.00	3.50

1989 Bowman

Topps, which purchased the Bowman Co. back in 1955, revived the Bowman name in 1989, issuing a 484-card set modeled after the 1953 Bowman cards. The cards are 2-1/2" by 3-3/4", slightly larger than a current standard-sized card. The fronts contain a full-color player photo, with facsimile autograph on the bottom and the Bowman logo in an upper corner. The unique card backs include a breakdown of the player's stats against each team in his league. A series of "Hot Rookie Stars" highlight the set. The cards were distributed in both wax packs and rack packs. Each pack included a special reproduction of a classic Bowman card with a sweepstakes on the back. The special cards said "reprint" on the front.

	MT	NR MT	EX
Complete Set:	22.00	16.50	9.00
Common Player:	.03	.02	.01

Here's your repli-card . . .

of the world's most valuable baseball card. A high-grade example of the famous 1909 T-206 Honus Wagner card sold for $115,000 in October, 1989 — the highest price ever paid for a baseball card.

Fewer than 50 genuine T-206 Honus Wagner cards are known in all conditions. The most sought-after card in the baseball card hobby, the Wagner brings high prices even in lesser grades. An example grading only Good was sold in December, 1989, for $31,000. New price records continue to be set just about every time a T-206 Wagner is sold.

Return this postcard for a

FREE ISSUE!

Your choice of Baseball Card Price Guide Monthly or Baseball Card News!

CHECK ONE: Please send an issue of

☐ **Baseball Card Price Guide Monthly**

☐ **Baseball Card News**
. . .to the following address:

Name _____

Address _____

City _____

State _____ Zip _____

Complete information above and drop in mail.

Known to collectors . . .

as T-206 is the 524-card issue produced by the American Tobacco Company between 1909-1911. The T-206 designation is taken from the first major card catalog ever produced, Jefferson Burdick's pioneering 1939 *American Card Catalog*. The cards were printed with advertisements for one of 16 different brands of cigarettes on the backs, and were inserted into boxes of 10 cigarettes.

The Honus Wagner card was withdrawn from the issue early in 1909. Press reports of the day said it was because Wagner did not want to encourage smoking among children. It is at least as likely that Wagner, the premier star of his day, objected to not being paid a fee for the use of his picture.

#	Name	MT	NR MT	EX		#	Name	MT	NR MT	EX
1	Oswald Peraza	.05	.04	.02		90	Oddibe McDowell	.05	.04	.02
2	Brian Holton	.05	.04	.02		91	Joe Carter	.15	.11	.06
3	Jose Bautista	.05	.04	.02		92	Frank Tanana	.03	.02	.01
4	Pete Harnisch	.10	.08	.04		93	Jack Morris	.03	.02	.01
5	Dave Schmidt	.03	.02	.01		94	Doyle Alexander	.03	.02	.01
6	Gregg Olson	.50	.40	.20		95	Steve Searcy	.08	.06	.03
7	Jeff Ballard	.10	.08	.04		96	Randy Bockus	.05	.04	.02
8	Bob Melvin	.03	.02	.01		97	Jeff Robinson	.05	.04	.02
9	Cal Ripken	.20	.15	.08		98	Mike Henneman	.05	.04	.02
10	Randy Milligan	.08	.06	.03		99	Paul Gibson	.03	.02	.01
11	Juan Bell	.15	.11	.06		100	Frank Williams	.03	.02	.01
12	Billy Ripken	.05	.04	.02		101	Matt Nokes	.05	.04	.02
13	Jim Trabor	.03	.02	.01		102	Rico Brogna	.15	.11	.06
14	Pete Stanicek	.03	.02	.01		103	Lou Whitaker	.08	.06	.03
15	Steve Finley	.20	.15	.08		104	Al Pedrique	.03	.02	.01
16	Larry Sheets	.03	.02	.01		105	Alan Trammell	.05	.04	.02
17	Phil Bradley	.05	.04	.02		106	Chris Brown	.03	.02	.01
18	Brady Anderson	.10	.08	.04		107	Pat Sheridan	.03	.02	.01
19	Lee Smith	.03	.02	.01		108	Gary Pettis	.03	.02	.01
20	Tom Fischer	.15	.11	.06		109	Keith Moreland	.03	.02	.01
21	Mike Boddicker	.03	.02	.01		110	Mel Stottlemyre Jr.	.15	.11	.06
22	Rob Murphy	.03	.02	.01		111	Bret Saberhagen	.10	.08	.04
23	Wes Gardner	.03	.02	.01		112	Floyd Bannister	.03	.02	.01
24	John Dopson	.10	.08	.04		113	Jeff Montgomery	.05	.04	.02
25	Bob Stanley	.03	.02	.01		114	Steve Farr	.05	.04	.02
26	Roger Clemens	.20	.15	.08		115	Tom Gordon	.80	.60	.30
27	Rich Gedman	.03	.02	.01		116	Charlie Leibrandt	.03	.02	.01
28	Marty Barrett	.03	.02	.01		117	Mark Gubicza	.08	.06	.03
29	Luis Rivera	.03	.02	.01		118	Mike MacFarlane	.03	.02	.01
30	Jody Reed	.05	.04	.02		119	Bob Boone	.05	.04	.02
31	Nick Esasky	.05	.04	.02		120	Kurt Stillwell	.05	.04	.02
32	Wade Boggs	.40	.30	.15		121	George Brett	.15	.11	.06
33	Jim Rice	.10	.08	.04		122	Frank White	.05	.04	.02
34	Mike Greenwell	.40	.30	.15		123	Kevin Seitzer	.08	.06	.03
35	Dwight Evans	.15	.11	.06		124	Willie Wilson	.03	.02	.01
36	Ellis Burks	.25	.20	.10		125	Pat Tabler	.03	.02	.01
37	Chuck Finley	.05	.04	.02		126	Bo Jackson	.90	.70	.35
38	Kirk McCaskill	.05	.04	.02		127	Hugh Walker	.20	.15	.08
39	Jim Abbott	3.75	2.75	1.50		128	Danny Tartabull	.05	.04	.02
40	Bryan Harvey	.05	.04	.02		129	Teddy Higuera	.08	.06	.03
41	Bert Blyleven	.08	.06	.03		130	Don August	.03	.02	.01
42	Mike Witt	.03	.02	.01		131	Juan Nieves	.03	.02	.01
43	Bob McClure	.03	.02	.01		132	Mike Birkbeck	.03	.02	.01
44	Bill Schroeder	.03	.02	.01		133	Dan Plesac	.05	.04	.02
45	Lance Parrish	.05	.04	.02		134	Chris Bosio	.05	.04	.02
46	Dick Schofield	.03	.02	.01		135	Bill Wegman	.03	.02	.01
47	Wally Joyner	.10	.08	.04		136	Chuck Crim	.03	.02	.01
48	Jack Howell	.03	.02	.01		137	B.J. Surhoff	.05	.04	.02
49	Johnny Ray	.03	.02	.01		138	Joey Meyer	.03	.02	.01
50	Chili Davis	.05	.04	.02		139	Dale Sveum	.03	.02	.01
51	Tony Armas	.03	.02	.01		140	Paul Molitor	.08	.06	.03
52	Claudell Washington	.03	.02	.01		141	Jim Gantner	.03	.02	.01
53	Brian Downing	.03	.02	.01		142	Gary Sheffield	1.00	.70	.40
54	Devon White	.10	.08	.04		143	Greg Brock	.03	.02	.01
55	Bobby Thigpen	.08	.06	.03		144	Robin Yount	.25	.20	.10
56	Bill Long	.03	.02	.01		145	Glenn Braggs	.03	.02	.01
57	Jerry Reuss	.03	.02	.01		146	Rob Deer	.03	.02	.01
58	Shawn Hillegas	.03	.02	.01		147	Fred Toliver	.03	.02	.01
59	Melido Perez	.05	.04	.02		148	Jeff Reardon	.03	.02	.01
60	Jeff Bittiger	.05	.04	.02		149	Allan Anderson	.05	.04	.02
61	Jack McDowell	.03	.02	.01		150	Frank Viola	.15	.11	.06
62	Carlton Fisk	.10	.08	.04		151	Shane Rawley	.03	.02	.01
63	Steve Lyons	.03	.02	.01		152	Juan Berenguer	.03	.02	.01
64	Ozzie Guillen	.05	.04	.02		153	Johnny Ard	.20	.15	.08
65	Robin Ventura	.70	.50	.30		154	Tim Laudner	.03	.02	.01
66	Fred Manrique	.03	.02	.01		155	Brian Harper	.03	.02	.01
67	Dan Pasqua	.03	.02	.01		156	Al Newman	.03	.02	.01
68	Ivan Calderon	.03	.02	.01		157	Kent Hrbek	.08	.06	.03
69	Ron Kittle	.03	.02	.01		158	Gary Gaetti	.08	.06	.03
70	Daryl Boston	.03	.02	.01		159	Wally Backman	.03	.02	.01
71	Dave Gallagher	.05	.04	.02		160	Gene Larkin	.03	.02	.01
72	Harold Baines	.08	.06	.03		161	Greg Gagne	.03	.02	.01
73	Charles Nagy	.20	.15	.08		162	Kirby Puckett	.35	.25	.14
74	John Farrell	.03	.02	.01		163	Danny Gladden	.03	.02	.01
75	Kevin Wickander	.25	.20	.10		164	Randy Bush	.03	.02	.01
76	Greg Swindell	.15	.11	.06		165	Dave LaPoint	.03	.02	.01
77	Mike Walker	.15	.11	.06		166	Andy Hawkins	.03	.02	.01
78	Doug Jones	.05	.04	.02		167	Dave Righetti	.05	.04	.02
79	Rich Yett	.03	.02	.01		168	Lance McCullers	.03	.02	.01
80	Tom Candiotti	.03	.02	.01		169	Jimmy Jones	.03	.02	.01
81	Jesse Orosco	.03	.02	.01		170	Al Leiter	.03	.02	.01
82	Bud Black	.03	.02	.01		171	John Candelaria	.03	.02	.01
83	Andy Allanson	.03	.02	.01		172	Don Slaught	.03	.02	.01
84	Pete O'Brien	.05	.04	.02		173	Jamie Quirk	.03	.02	.01
85	Jerry Browne	.05	.04	.02		174	Rafael Santana	.03	.02	.01
86	Brook Jacoby	.03	.02	.01		175	Mike Pagliarulo	.03	.02	.01
87	Mark Lewis	.50	.40	.20		176	Don Mattingly	1.00	.70	.40
88	Luis Aguayo	.03	.02	.01		177	Ken Phelps	.03	.02	.01
89	Cory Snyder	.05	.04	.02		178	Steve Sax	.08	.06	.03
						179	Dave Winfield	.20	.15	.08
						180	Stan Jefferson	.03	.02	.01

#	Player	MT	NR MT	EX
181	Rickey Henderson	.40	.30	.15
182	Bob Brower	.03	.02	.01
183	Roberto Kelly	.10	.08	.04
184	Curt Young	.03	.02	.01
185	Gene Nelson	.03	.02	.01
186	Bob Welch	.03	.02	.01
187	Rick Honeycutt	.03	.02	.01
188	Dave Stewart	.08	.06	.03
189	Mike Moore	.08	.06	.03
190	Dennis Eckersly	.08	.06	.03
191	Eric Plunk	.03	.02	.01
192	Storm Davis	.03	.02	.01
193	Terry Steinbach	.10	.08	.04
194	Ron Hassey	.03	.02	.01
195	Stan Royer	.15	.11	.06
196	Walt Weiss	.15	.11	.06
197	Mark McGwire	.40	.30	.15
198	Carney Lansford	.08	.06	.03
199	Glenn Hubbard	.03	.02	.01
200	Dave Henderson	.05	.04	.02
201	Jose Canseco	.90	.70	.35
202	Dave Parker	.05	.04	.02
203	Scott Bankhead	.05	.04	.02
204	Tom Niedenfuer	.03	.02	.01
205	Mark Langston	.15	.11	.06
206	Eric Hanson	.15	.11	.06
207	Mike Jackson	.03	.02	.01
208	Dave Valle	.03	.02	.01
209	Scott Bradley	.03	.02	.01
210	Harold Reynolds	.08	.06	.03
211	Tino Martinez	.50	.40	.20
212	Rich Renteria	.03	.02	.01
213	Rey Quinones	.03	.02	.01
214	Jim Presley	.03	.02	.01
215	Alvin Davis	.10	.08	.04
216	Edgar Martinez	.03	.02	.01
217	Darnell Coles	.03	.02	.01
218	Jeffrey Leonard	.08	.06	.04
219	Jay Buhner	.03	.02	.01
220	Ken Griffey Jr.	4.00	3.00	1.50
221	Drew Hall	.03	.02	.01
222	Bobby Witt	.03	.02	.01
223	Jamie Moyer	.03	.02	.01
224	Charlie Hough	.03	.02	.01
225	Nolan Ryan	.70	.50	.30
226	Jeff Russell	.05	.04	.02
227	Jim Sundberg	.03	.02	.01
228	Julio Franco	.15	.11	.06
229	Buddy Bell	.03	.02	.01
230	Scott Fletcher	.03	.02	.01
231	Jeff Kunkel	.03	.02	.01
232	Steve Buechele	.03	.02	.01
233	Monty Fariss	.25	.20	.10
234	Rick Leach	.03	.02	.01
235	Ruben Sierra	.40	.30	.15
236	Cecil Espy	.05	.04	.02
237	Rafael Palmeiro	.10	.08	.04
238	Pete Incaviglia	.03	.02	.01
239	Dave Steib	.05	.04	.02
240	Jeff Musselman	.03	.02	.01
241	Mike Flanagan	.03	.02	.01
242	Todd Stottlemyre	.05	.04	.02
243	Jimmy Key	.05	.04	.02
244	Tony Castillo	.10	.08	.04
245	Alex Sanchez	.05	.04	.02
246	Tom Henke	.03	.02	.01
247	John Cerutti	.03	.02	.01
248	Ernie Whitt	.03	.02	.01
249	Bob Brenly	.03	.02	.01
250	Rance Mulliniks	.03	.02	.01
251	Kelly Gruber	.10	.08	.04
252	Ed Sprague	.20	.15	.08
253	Fred McGriff	.40	.30	.15
254	Tony Fernandez	.08	.06	.03
255	Tom Lawless	.03	.02	.01
256	George Bell	.10	.08	.04
257	Jesse Barfield	.05	.04	.02
258	Sandy Alomar	.20	.15	.08
259	Ken Griffey	.30	.25	.12
260	Cal Ripken Sr.	.15	.11	.06
261	Mel Stottlemyre	.15	.11	.06
262	Zane Smith	.03	.02	.01
263	Charlie Puleo	.03	.02	.01
264	Derek Lilliquist	.15	.11	.06
265	Paul Assenmacher	.03	.02	.01
266	John Smoltz	.60	.45	.25
267	Tom Glavine	.10	.08	.04
268	Steve Avery	.50	.40	.20
269	Pete Smith	.05	.04	.02
270	Jody Davis	.03	.02	.01
271	Bruce Benedict	.03	.02	.01
272	Andres Thomas	.03	.02	.01
273	Gerald Perry	.05	.04	.02
274	Ron Gant	.05	.04	.02
275	Darrell Evans	.03	.02	.01
276	Dale Murphy	.08	.06	.03
277	Dion James	.03	.02	.01
278	Lonnie Smith	.08	.06	.03
279	Geronimo Berroa	.05	.04	.02
280	Steve Wilson	.20	.15	.08
281	Rick Suctcliffe	.05	.04	.02
282	Kevin Coffman	.03	.02	.01
283	Mitch Williams	.10	.08	.04
284	Greg Maddux	.05	.04	.02
285	Paul Kilgus	.03	.02	.01
286	Mike Harkey	.10	.08	.04
287	Lloyd McClendon	.05	.04	.02
288	Damon Berryhill	.05	.04	.02
289	Ty Griffin	.60	.45	.25
290	Ryne Sandberg	.15	.11	.06
291	Mark Grace	.60	.45	.25
292	Curt Wilkerson	.03	.02	.01
293	Vance Law	.03	.02	.01
294	Shawon Dunston	.08	.06	.04
295	Jerome Walton	4.00	3.00	1.50
296	Mitch Webster	.03	.02	.01
297	Dwight Smith	1.50	1.25	.60
298	Andre Dawson	.15	.11	.06
299	Jeff Sellers	.03	.02	.01
300	Jose Rijo	.05	.04	.02
301	John Franco	.05	.04	.02
302	Rick Mahler	.03	.02	.01
303	Ron Robinson	.03	.02	.01
304	Danny Jackson	.03	.02	.01
305	Rob Dibble	.08	.06	.04
306	Tom Browning	.03	.02	.01
307	Bo Diaz	.03	.02	.01
308	Manny Trillo	.03	.02	.01
309	Chris Sabo	.15	.11	.06
310	Ron Oester	.03	.02	.01
311	Barry Larkin	.15	.11	.06
312	Todd Benzinger	.05	.04	.02
313	Paul O'Neil	.05	.04	.02
314	Kal Daniels	.05	.04	.02
315	Joel Youngblood	.03	.02	.01
316	Eric Davis	.25	.20	.10
317	Dave Smith	.05	.04	.03
318	Mark Portugal	.03	.02	.01
319	Brian Meyer	.03	.02	.01
320	Jim Deshaies	.05	.04	.02
321	Juan Agosto	.03	.02	.01
322	Mike Scott	.10	.08	.04
323	Rick Rhoden	.03	.02	.01
324	Jim Clancy	.03	.02	.01
325	Larry Anderson	.03	.02	.01
326	Alex Trevino	.03	.02	.01
327	Alan Ashby	.03	.02	.01
328	Craig Reynolds	.03	.02	.01
329	Bill Doran	.03	.02	.01
330	Rafael Ramirez	.03	.02	.01
331	Glenn Davis	.10	.08	.04
332	Willie Ansley	.35	.25	.14
333	Gerald Young	.03	.02	.01
334	Cameron Drew	.10	.08	.04
335	Jay Howell	.05	.04	.03
336	Tim Belcher	.05	.04	.03
337	Fernando Valenzuela	.05	.04	.03
338	Ricky Horton	.03	.02	.01
339	Tim Leary	.03	.02	.01
340	Bill Bene	.15	.11	
341	Orel Hershiser	.20		
342	Mike Scioscia			.02
343	Rick Dempsey		.02	.01
344	Willie Randolph		.02	.01
345	Alfredo Griffin	.03	.02	.01
346	Eddie Murray	.08	.06	.03
347	Mickey Hatcher	.03	.02	.01
348	Mike Sharperson	.03	.02	.01
349	John Shelby	.03	.02	.01
350	Mike Marshall	.03	.02	.01
351	Kirk Gibson	.05	.04	.02
352	Mike Davis	.03	.02	.01
353	Bryn Smith	.03	.02	.01
354	Pascual Perez	.03	.02	.01
355	Kevin Gross	.03	.02	.01
356	Andy McGaffigan	.03	.02	.01
357	Brian Holman	.05	.04	.02
358	Dave Wainhouse	.20	.15	.08
359	Denny Martinez	.03	.02	.01
360	Tim Burke	.03	.02	.01
361	Nelson Santovenia	.08	.06	.04
362	Tim Wallach	.05	.04	.02

		MT	NR MT	EX
363	Spike Owen	.03	.02	.01
364	Rex Hudler	.03	.02	.01
365	Andres Galarraga	.08	.06	.03
366	Otis Nixon	.03	.02	.01
367	Hubie Brooks	.03	.02	.01
368	Mike Aldrete	.03	.02	.01
369	Rock Raines	.08	.06	.03
370	Dave Martinez	.03	.02	.01
371	Bob Ojeda	.03	.02	.01
372	Ron Darling	.05	.04	.02
373	Wally Whitehurst	.20	.15	.08
374	Randy Myers	.05	.04	.02
375	David Cone	.05	.04	.02
376	Doc Gooden	.25	.20	.10
377	Sid Fernandez	.05	.04	.02
378	Dave Proctor	.20	.15	.08
379	Gary Carter	.03	.02	.01
380	Keith Miller	.05	.04	.02
381	Gregg Jefferies	1.50	1.25	.70
382	Tim Teufel	.03	.02	.01
383	Kevin Elster	.03	.02	.01
384	Dave Magadan	.03	.02	.01
385	Keith Hernandez	.05	.04	.02
386	Mookie Wilson	.05	.04	.02
387	Darryl Strawberry	.40	.30	.15
388	Kevin McReynolds	.10	.08	.04
389	Mark Carreon	.05	.04	.02
390	Jeff Parrett	.05	.04	.02
391	Mike Maddux	.03	.02	.01
392	Don Carman	.03	.02	.01
393	Bruce Ruffin	.03	.02	.01
394	Ken Howell	.03	.02	.01
395	Steve Bedrosian	.05	.04	.02
396	Floyd Youmans	.03	.02	.01
397	Larry McWilliams	.03	.02	.01
398	Pat Combs	.40	.30	.15
399	Stev Lake	.03	.02	.01
400	Dickie Thon	.03	.02	.01
401	Ricky Jordan	.35	.25	.14
402	Mike Schmidt	.60	.45	.25
403	Tom Herr	.03	.02	.01
404	Chris James	.03	.02	.01
405	Juan Samuel	.08	.06	.03
406	Von Hayes	.08	.06	.03
407	Ron Jones	.15	.11	.06
408	Curt Ford	.03	.02	.01
409	Bob Walk	.03	.02	.01
410	Jeff Robinson	.03	.02	.01
411	Jim Gott	.03	.02	.01
412	Scott Medvin	.03	.02	.01
413	John Smiley	.03	.02	.01
414	Bob Kipper	.03	.02	.01
415	Brian Fisher	.03	.02	.01
416	Doug Drabek	.03	.02	.01
417	Mike Lavalliere	.03	.02	.01
418	Ken Oberkfell	.03	.02	.01
419	Sid Bream	.03	.02	.01
420	Austin Manahan	.20	.15	.08
421	Jose Lind	.03	.02	.01
422	Bobby Bonilla	.10	.08	.04
423	Glenn Wilson	.03	.02	.01
424	Andy Van Slyke	.10	.08	.04
425	Gary Redus	.03	.02	.01
426	Barry Bonds	.10	.08	.04
427	Don Heinkel	.03	.02	.01
428	Ken Dayley	.03	.02	.01
429	Todd Worrell	.05	.04	.02
430	Brad DuVall	.20	.15	.08
431	Jose Deleon	.03	.02	.01
432	Joe Magrane	.10	.08	.04
433	John Ericks	.20	.15	.08
434	Frank DiPino	.03	.02	.01
435	Tony Pena	.05	.04	.02
436	Ozzie Smith	.08	.06	.03
437	Terry Pendleton	.03	.02	.01
438	Jose Oquendo	.03	.02	.01
439	Tim Jones	.05	.04	.02
440	Pedro Guerrero	.10	.08	.04
441	Milt Thompson	.03	.02	.01
442	Willie McGee	.05	.04	.02
443	Vince Coleman	.05	.04	.02
444	Tom Brunansky	.05	.04	.02
445	Walt Terrell	.03	.02	.01
446	Eric Show	.03	.02	.01
447	Mark Davis	.10	.08	.04
448	Andy Benes	1.00	.70	.40
449	Eddie Whitson	.03	.02	.01
450	Dennis Rasmussen	.03	.02	.01
451	Bruce Hurst	.03	.02	.01
452	Pat Clements	.03	.02	.01
453	Benito Santiago	.10	.08	.04

		MT	NR MT	EX
454	Sandy Alomar Jr.	.60	.45	.25
455	Garry Templeton	.03	.02	.01
456	Jack Clark	.05	.04	.02
457	Tim Flannery	.03	.02	.01
458	Roberto Alomar	.10	.08	.04
459	Camelo Martinez	.03	.02	.01
460	John Kruk	.03	.02	.01
461	Tony Gwynn	.20	.15	.08
462	Jerald Clark	.05	.04	.02
463	Don Robinson	.03	.02	.01
464	Craig Lefferts	.03	.02	.01
465	Kelly Downs	.03	.02	.01
466	Rick Rueschel	.05	.04	.02
467	Scott Garrelts	.03	.02	.01
468	Wil Tejada	.03	.02	.01
469	Kirt Manwaring	.10	.08	.04
470	Terry Kennedy	.03	.02	.01
471	Jose Uribe	.03	.02	.01
472	Royce Clayton	.20	.15	.08
473	Robby Thompson	.05	.04	.02
474	Kevin Mitchell	.80	.60	.30
475	Ernie Riles	.03	.02	.01
476	Will Clark	1.00	.70	.40
477	Donnell Nixon	.03	.02	.01
478	Candy Maldonado	.03	.02	.01
479	Tracy Jones	.03	.02	.01
480	Brett Butler	.05	.04	.02
481	Checklist	.05	.04	.02
482	Checklist	.05	.04	.02
483	Checklist	.05	.04	.02
484	Checklist	.05	.04	.02

1954 Briggs Meats

The Briggs Meat set was issued over a two-year span (1953-54) and features 26 players from the Washington Senators and 12 from the New York City area baseball teams. The set was issued in two-card panels in hot dog packages sold in the Washington, D.C. vicinity. The color cards, which are blank-backed and measure 2-1/4" by 3-1/2", are printed on waxed cardboard. The style of the Senators cards in the set differs from that of the New York players. Poses for the New York players can also be found on cards in the 1954 Dan-Dee Potato Chips and 1953-1955 Stahl-Meyer Franks sets.

		NR MT	EX	VG
	Complete Set	7800.00	3900.00	2340.
	Common Player	100.00	50.00	30.00
(1)	Hank Bauer	150.00	75.00	45.00
(2)	James Busby	100.00	50.00	30.00
(3)	Tommy Byrne	100.00	50.00	30.00
(4)	John Dixon	100.00	50.00	30.00
(5)	Carl Erskine	150.00	75.00	45.00
(6)	Edward Fitzgerald (Fitz Gerald)	100.00	50.00	30.00
(7)	Newton Grasso	100.00	50.00	30.00
(8)	Melvin Hoderlein	100.00	50.00	30.00
(9)	Gil Hodges	250.00	125.00	75.00
(10)	Monte Irvin	175.00	87.00	52.00
(11)	Whitey Lockman	100.00	50.00	30.00
(12)	Mickey Mantle	2200.00	1100.00	660.00
(13)	Conrado Marrero	100.00	50.00	30.00
(14)	Walter Masterson	100.00	50.00	30.00
(15)	Carmen Mauro	100.00	50.00	30.00
(16)	Willie Mays	1000.00	500.00	300.00

		NR MT	EX	VG
(17)	Mickey McDermott	100.00	50.00	30.00
(18)	Gil McDougald	150.00	75.00	45.00
(19)	Julio Moreno	100.00	50.00	30.00
(20)	Don Mueller	100.00	50.00	30.00
(21)	Don Newcombe	150.00	75.00	45.00
(22)	Robert Oldis	100.00	50.00	30.00
(23)	Erwin Porterfield	100.00	50.00	30.00
(24)	Phil Rizzuto	250.00	125.00	75.00
(25)	James Runnels	100.00	50.00	30.00
(26)	John Schmitz	100.00	50.00	30.00
(27)	Angel Scull	100.00	50.00	30.00
(28)	Frank Shea	100.00	50.00	30.00
(29)	Albert Sima	100.00	50.00	30.00
(30)	Duke Snider	500.00	250.00	150.00
(31)	Charles Stobbs	100.00	50.00	30.00
(32)	Willard Terwilliger	100.00	50.00	30.00
(33)	Joe Tipton	100.00	50.00	30.00
(34)	Thomas Umphlett	100.00	50.00	30.00
(35)	Gene Verble	100.00	50.00	30.00
(36)	James Vernon	125.00	62.00	37.00
(37)	Clyde Volmer (Vollmer)	100.00	50.00	30.00
(38)	Edward Yost	100.00	50.00	30.00

1947 Bond Bread
Jackie Robinson

"HOMOGENIZED BOND MAKES A HIT WITH ME EVERY TIME"

Jackie Robinson

FOLKS, WHY NOT EAT THE BREAD THAT JACKIE EATS? HOMOGENIZED BOND!

The major league's first black player, Jackie Robinson, was featured in a 13-card set issued by Bond Bread in 1947. The cards, which measure 2-1/4" by 3-1/2", are black and white photos of Robinson in various action and portrait poses. The unnumbered cards bear three different backs which contain advertising for Bond Bread. Four of the 13 cards make use of a horizontal format. Card #6 in the checklist below is believed to have been issued in greater quantities and perhaps was a promotional card. The back of this card is the only one in the set containing a short biography of Jackie. The ACC designation for the set is D302.

		NR MT	EX	VG
Complete Set:		3800.00	1900.00	1125.
Common Player:		200.00	100.00	60.00
(1)	Batting (awaiting pitch)	300.00	150.00	90.00
(2)	Batting Follow-Thru (white shirtsleeves)			
		300.00	150.00	90.00
(3)	Batting Follow-Thru (no shirtsleeves)			
		300.00	150.00	90.00
(4)	Leaping (scoreboard in background)			
		300.00	150.00	90.00
(5)	Leaping (no scoreboard)	300.00	150.00	90.00
(6)	Portrait (facsimile autograph)	200.00	100.00	60.00
(7)	Portrait (holding glove in air)	300.00	150.00	90.00
(8)	Running (down the baseline)	300.00	150.00	90.00
(9)	Running (about to catch ball)	300.00	150.00	90.00
(10)	Sliding (umpire in picture)	300.00	150.00	90.00
(11)	Stretching For Throw (ball in glove)			
		300.00	150.00	90.00
(12)	Stretching For Throw (no ball visible)			
		300.00	150.00	90.00
(13)	Throwing (ball in hand)	300.00	150.00	90.00

1977 Burger King Yankees

The first Topps-produced set for Burger King restaurants was issued in the New York area in 1977 and featured the A.L. champion New York Yankees. Twenty-two players plus an unnumbered checklist were issued at the beginning of the promotion with card #23 (Lou Piniella) being added to the set at a later date. The Piniella card was issued in limited quantities. The cards, numbered 1 through 23, are 2-1/2" by 3-1/2" in size and have fronts identical to the regular 1977 Topps set except for the following numbers: 2, 6, 7, 13, 14, 15, 17, 20 and 21. These cards feature different poses or major picture-cropping variations. It should be noted that very minor cropping variations between the regular Topps sets and the Burger King issues exist throughout the years the sets were produced.

		NR MT	EX	VG
Complete Set:		45.00	23.00	13.50
Common Player:		.30	.15	.09
1	Yankees Team (Billy Martin)	.90	.45	.25
2	Thurman Munson	4.00	2.00	1.25
3	Fran Healy	.30	.15	.09
4	Jim Hunter	1.50	.70	.45
5	Ed Figueroa	.30	.15	.09
6	Don Gullett	.70	.35	.20
7	Mike Torrez	.70	.35	.20
8	Ken Holtzman	.50	.25	.15
9	Dick Tidrow	.30	.15	.09
10	Sparky Lyle	.50	.25	.15
11	Ron Guidry	1.25	.60	.40
12	Chris Chambliss	.50	.25	.15
13	Willie Randolph	.80	.40	.25
14	Bucky Dent	.80	.40	.25
15	Graig Nettles	1.25	.60	.40
16	Fred Stanley	.30	.15	.09
17	Reggie Jackson	6.00	3.00	1.75
18	Mickey Rivers	.50	.25	.15
19	Roy White	.50	.25	.15
20	Jim Wynn	.70	.35	.20
21	Paul Blair	.70	.35	.20
22	Carlos May	.30	.15	.09
23	Lou Piniella	25.00	12.50	7.50
----	Checklist	.04	.02	.01

A player's name in *italic* type indicates a rookie card. An (FC) indicates a player's first card for that particular card company.

Definitions for grading conditions are located in the Introduction section at the front of this book.

1978 Burger King Astros

JESUS ALOU

Burger King restaurants in the Houston area distributed a Topps-produced 23-card set showcasing the Astros in 1978. The cards are standard size (2-1/2" by 3-1/2") and are numbered 1 through 22. The checklist card is unnumbered. The card fronts are identical to the regular 1978 Topps set with the exception of card numbers 21 and 22, which have different poses. Although not noted in the following checklist, it should be remembered that very minor picture-cropping variations between the regular Topps issues and the 1977-1980 Burger King sets do exist.

		NR MT	EX	VG
	Complete Set:	12.00	6.00	3.50
	Common Player:	.30	.15	.09
1	Bill Virdon	.50	.25	.15
2	Joe Ferguson	.30	.15	.09
3	Ed Herrmann	.30	.15	.09
4	J.R. Richard	.60	.30	.20
5	Joe Niekro	.60	.30	.20
6	Floyd Bannister	.70	.35	.20
7	Joaquin Andujar	.60	.30	.20
8	Ken Forsch	.40	.20	.12
9	Mark Lemongello	.30	.15	.09
10	Joe Sambito	.40	.20	.12
11	Gene Pentz	.30	.15	.09
12	Bob Watson	.40	.20	.12
13	Julio Gonzalez	.30	.15	.09
14	Enos Cabell	.40	.20	.12
15	Roger Metzger	.30	.15	.09
16	Art Howe	.30	.15	.09
17	Jose Cruz	.80	.40	.25
18	Cesar Cedeno	.80	.40	.25
19	Terry Puhl	.40	.20	.12
20	Wilbur Howard	.30	.15	.09
21	Dave Bergman	.60	.30	.20
22	Jesus Alou	.60	.30	.20
----	Checklist	.04	.02	.01

1978 Burger King Rangers

FERGIE JENKINS

Issued by Burger King restaurants in the Dallas-Fort Worth area, this 23-card Topps-produced set features the Texas Rangers. The cards are standard size

(2-1/2" by 3-1/2") and are identical in style to the regular 1978 Topps set with the following exceptions: #'s 5, 8, 10, 12, 17, 21 and 22. An unnumbered checklist card was included with the set.

		NR MT	EX	VG
	Complete Set:	12.00	6.00	3.50
	Common Player:	.30	.15	.09
1	Billy Hunter	.30	.15	.09
2	Jim Sundberg	.50	.25	.15
3	John Ellis	.30	.15	.09
4	Doyle Alexander	.50	.25	.15
5	Jon Matlack	.60	.30	.20
6	Dock Ellis	.30	.15	.09
7	George Medich	.30	.15	.09
8	Fergie Jenkins	1.25	.60	.40
9	Len Barker	.30	.15	.09
10	Reggie Cleveland	.60	.30	.20
11	Mike Hargrove	.40	.20	.12
12	Bump Wills	.60	.30	.20
13	Toby Harrah	.50	.25	.15
14	Bert Campaneris	.50	.25	.15
15	Sandy Alomar	.30	.15	.09
16	Kurt Bevacqua	.30	.15	.09
17	Al Oliver	1.00	.50	.30
18	Juan Beniquez	.30	.15	.09
19	Claudell Washington	.50	.25	.15
20	Richie Zisk	.40	.20	.12
21	John Lowenstein	.60	.30	.20
22	Bobby Thompson	.60	.30	.20
----	Checklist	.04	.02	.01

1978 Burger King Yankees

RICH GOSSAGE

Produced by Topps for Burger King outlets in the New York area for the second year in a row, the 1978 Yankees set contains 22 cards plus an unnumbered checklist. The cards are numbered 1 through 22 and are the standard size of 2-1/2" by 3-1/2". The cards feature the same pictures found in the regular 1978 Topps set except for numbers 10, 11 and 16. Only those variations containing different poses or major picture-cropping differences are noted. Numerous minor picture-cropping variations, that are very insignificant in nature, exist between the regular Topps sets and the Burger King issues of 1977-1980.

		NR MT	EX	VG
	Complete Set:	12.00	6.00	3.50
	Common Player:	.30	.15	.09
1	Billy Martin	.80	.40	.25
2	Thurman Munson	2.50	1.25	.70
3	Cliff Johnson	.30	.15	.09
4	Ron Guidry	1.25	.60	.40
5	Ed Figueroa	.30	.15	.09
6	Dick Tidrow	.30	.15	.09
7	Jim Hunter	1.00	.50	.30
8	Don Gullett	.30	.15	.09
9	Sparky Lyle	.50	.25	.15
10	Rich Gossage	1.25	.60	.40
11	Rawly Eastwick	.70	.35	.20
12	Chris Chambliss	.50	.25	.15
13	Willie Randolph	.50	.25	.15
14	Graig Nettles	.80	.40	.25
15	Bucky Dent	.50	.25	.15

		NR MT	EX	VG
16	Jim Spencer	.70	.35	.20
17	Fred Stanley	.30	.15	.09
18	Lou Piniella	.80	.40	.25
19	Roy White	.50	.25	.15
20	Mickey Rivers	.50	.25	.15
21	Reggie Jackson	2.00	1.00	.60
22	Paul Blair	.30	.15	.09
----	Checklist	.04	.02	.01

1979 Burger King Phillies

Twenty-two Philadelphia Phillies players are featured in the 1979 Burger King issue given out in the Philadelphia area. The Topps-produced set, whose cards measure 2-1/2" by 3-1/2", also includes an unnumbered checklist. The cards are identical to the regular 1979 Topps set except in seven instances. Card numbers 1, 11, 12, 13, 14, 17 and 22 have different poses. Very minor picture-cropping variations between the regular Topps issues and the Burger King sets can be found throughout the four years the cards were produced, but only those variations featuring major changes are noted in the following checklist.

		NR MT	EX	VG
Complete Set:		7.00	3.50	2.00
Common Player:		.20	.10	.06
1	Danny Ozark	.60	.30	.20
2	Bob Boone	.30	.15	.09
3	Tim McCarver	.30	.15	.09
4	Steve Carlton	1.50	.70	.45
5	Larry Christenson	.20	.10	.06
6	Dick Ruthven	.20	.10	.06
7	Ron Reed	.20	.10	.06
8	Randy Lerch	.20	.10	.06
9	Warren Brusstar	.20	.10	.06
10	Tug McGraw	.40	.20	.12
11	Nino Espinosa	.60	.30	.20
12	Doug Bird	.60	.30	.20
13	Pete Rose	3.00	1.50	.90
14	Manny Trillo	.60	.30	.20
15	Larry Bowa	.50	.25	.15
16	Mike Schmidt	2.75	1.50	.80
17	Pete Mackanin	.60	.30	.20
18	Jose Cardenal	.20	.10	.06
19	Greg Luzinski	.40	.20	.12
20	Garry Maddox	.30	.15	.09
21	Bake McBride	.20	.10	.06
22	Greg Gross	.60	.30	.20
----	Checklist	.04	.02	.01

1979 Burger King Yankees

The New York Yankees were featured in a Topps-produced Burger King set for the third consecutive year in 1979. Once again, 22 numbered player cards and an unnumbered checklist made up the set. The cards, which measure 2-1/2" by 3-1/2", are identical to the 1979 Topps regular set except for card numbers 4, 8, 9 and 22 which included new poses. Only different poses or major picture-cropping

variations between the regular Topps set and the Burger King issue are recognized in the checklist that follows. Numerous minor picture cropping variations between the regular Topps issue and the Burger King sets of 1977-1980 exist.

		NR MT	EX	VG
Complete Set:		10.00	5.00	3.00
Common Player:		.30	.15	.09
1	Yankees Team (Bob Lemon)	.50	.25	.15
2	Thurman Munson	2.00	1.00	.60
3	Cliff Johnson	.30	.15	.09
4	Ron Guidry	2.00	1.00	.60
5	Jay Johnstone	.40	.20	.12
6	Jim Hunter	.90	.45	.25
7	Jim Beattie	.30	.15	.09
8	Luis Tiant	.80	.40	.25
9	Tommy John	1.00	.50	.30
10	Rich Gossage	.90	.45	.25
11	Ed Figueroa	.30	.15	.09
12	Chris Chambliss	.50	.25	.15
13	Willie Randolph	.50	.25	.15
14	Bucky Dent	.50	.25	.15
15	Graig Nettles	.70	.35	.20
16	Fred Stanley	.30	.15	.09
17	Jim Spencer	.30	.15	.09
18	Lou Piniella	.70	.35	.20
19	Roy White	.50	.25	.15
20	Mickey Rivers	.50	.25	.15
21	Reggie Jackson	2.00	1.00	.60
22	Juan Beniquez	.60	.30	.15
----	Checklist	.04	.02	.01

1980 Burger King Phillies

Philadelphia-area Burger King outlets issued a 23-card set featuring the Phillies for the second in a row in 1980. The Topps-produced set, whose cards measure 2-1/2" by 3-1/2", contains 22 player cards and an unnumbered checklist. The card fronts are identical in design to the regular 1980 Topps sets with the following exceptions - card numbers 1, 3, 8, 14 and 22 feature new poses. Collectors should note that very minor picture-cropping variations between the regular Topps issues and the Burger King sets exist in all years. Those minor differences are not noted in the checklist that follows. The 1980 Burger King sets were the first to include the Burger King logo on the card backs.

		NR MT	EX	VG
Complete Set:		6.00	3.00	1.75
Common Player:		.15	.08	.05
1	Dallas Green	.50	.25	.15
2	Bob Boone	.25	.13	.08
3	Keith Moreland	.60	.30	.20
4	Pete Rose	2.75	1.50	.80
5	Manny Trillo	.20	.10	.06
6	Mike Schmidt	2.50	1.25	.70
7	Larry Bowa	.40	.20	.12
8	John Vukovich	.50	.25	.15
9	Bake McBride	.15	.08	.05
10	Garry Maddox	.20	.10	.06
11	Greg Luzinski	.30	.15	.09
12	Greg Gross	.15	.08	.05
13	Del Unser	.15	.08	.05
14	Lonnie Smith	.50	.25	.15
15	Steve Carlton	1.25	.60	.40
16	Larry Christenson	.15	.08	.05
17	Nino Espinosa	.15	.08	.05
18	Randy Lerch	.15	.08	.05
19	Dick Ruthven	.15	.08	.05
20	Tug McGraw	.30	.15	.09
21	Ron Reed	.15	.08	.05
22	Kevin Saucier	.50	.25	.15
----	Checklist	.04	.02	.01

1980 Burger King Pitch, Hit & Run

In 1980, Burger King issued, in conjunction with its "Pitch, Hit & Run" promotion, a Topps-produced 34-card set featuring pitchers (card #'s 1-11), hitters (#'s 12-22), and base stealers (#'s 23-33). The card fronts, which carry the Burger King logo, are identical in nature to the regular 1980 Topps set except for numbers 1, 4, 5, 7, 9, 10, 16, 17, 18, 22, 23, 27, 28, 29 and 30, which feature different poses. The cards, which are numbered 1 through 33, measure 2-1/2" by 3-1/2" in size. An unnumbered checklist was included with the set.

		NR MT	EX	VG
Complete Set:		18.00	9.00	5.50
Common Player:		.20	.10	.06
1	Vida Blue	.50	.25	.15
2	Steve Carlton	1.00	.50	.30
3	Rollie Fingers	.30	.15	.09
4	Ron Guidry	.70	.35	.20
5	Jerry Koosman	.40	.20	.12
6	Phil Niekro	.40	.20	.12
7	Jim Palmer	.80	.40	.25
8	J.R. Richard	.20	.10	.06
9	Nolan Ryan	1.25	.60	.40
10	Tom Seaver	1.25	.60	.40
11	Bruce Sutter	.25	.13	.08
12	Don Baylor	.25	.13	.08
13	George Brett	1.25	.60	.40
14	Rod Carew	.90	.45	.25
15	George Foster	.25	.13	.08

		NR MT	EX	VG
16	Keith Hernandez	.90	.45	.25
17	Reggie Jackson	2.25	1.25	.70
18	Fred Lynn	.70	.35	.20
19	Dave Parker	.40	.20	.12
20	Jim Rice	.80	.40	.25
21	Pete Rose	2.50	1.25	.70
22	Dave Winfield	1.25	.60	.40
23	Bobby Bonds	.40	.20	.12
24	Enos Cabell	.20	.10	.06
25	Cesar Cedeno	.20	.10	.06
26	Julio Cruz	.20	.10	.06
27	Ron LeFlore	.40	.20	.12
28	Dave Lopes	.40	.20	.12
29	Omar Moreno	.40	.20	.12
30	Joe Morgan	1.00	.50	.30
31	Bill North	.20	.10	.06
32	Frank Taveras	.20	.10	.06
33	Willie Wilson	.25	.13	.08
----	Checklist	.04	.02	.01

1982 Burger King Braves

A set consisting of 27 "Collector Lids" featuring the Atlanta Braves was issued by Burger King restaurants in 1982. The lids, which measure 3-5/8" in diameter, were placed on a special Coca-Cola cup which listed the scores of the Braves' season-opening 13-game win streak. A black and white photo plus the player's name, position, height, weight, and 1981 statistics are found on the lid front. The unnumbered, blank-backed lids also contain logos for Burger King, Coca-Cola, and the Major League Baseball Players Association.

		MT	NR MT	EX
Complete Set:		40.00	30.00	16.00
Common Player:		1.00	.70	.40
(1)	Steve Bedrosian	2.50	2.00	1.00
(2)	Bruce Benedict	1.00	.70	.40
(3)	Tommy Boggs	1.00	.70	.40
(4)	Brett Butler	2.50	2.00	1.00
(5)	Rick Camp	1.00	.70	.40
(6)	Chris Chambliss	1.25	.90	.50
(7)	Ken Dayley	1.00	.70	.40
(8)	Gene Garber	1.00	.70	.40
(9)	Preston Hanna	1.00	.70	.40
(10)	Terry Harper	1.00	.70	.40
(11)	Bob Horner	3.00	2.25	1.25
(12)	Al Hrabosky	1.25	.90	.50
(13)	Glenn Hubbard	1.00	.70	.40
(14)	Randy Johnson	1.00	.70	.40
(15)	Rufino Linares	1.00	.70	.40
(16)	Rick Mahler	1.50	1.25	.60
(17)	Larry McWilliams	1.00	.70	.40
(18)	Dale Murphy	12.00	9.00	4.75
(19)	Phil Niekro	5.00	3.75	2.00
(20)	Biff Pocoroba	1.00	.70	.40
(21)	Rafael Ramirez	1.00	.70	.40
(22)	Jerry Royster	1.00	.70	.40
(23)	Ken Smith	1.00	.70	.40
(24)	Bob Walk	1.00	.70	.40
(25)	Claudell Washington	1.25	.90	.50
(26)	Bob Watson	1.00	.70	.40
(27)	Larry Whisenton	1.00	.70	.40

1982 Burger King Indians

The 1982 Burger King Indians set was sponsored by WUAB-TV and Burger Kings in the Cleveland vicinity. The cards' green borders encompass a large yellow area which contains a black and white photo plus a baseball tip. Manager Dave Garcia and his four coaches provide the baseball hints. The cards, which measure 3" x 5", are unnumbered and blank-backed.

		MT	NR MT	EX
Complete Set:		18.00	13.50	6.50
Common Player:		1.00	.70	.40
(1)	Dave Garcia (Be In The Game)	1.00	.70	.40
(2)	Dave Garcia (Sportsmanship)	1.00	.70	.40
(3)	Johnny Goryl (Rounding The Bases)	1.00	.70	.40
(4)	Johnny Goryl (3rd Base Running)	1.00	.70	.40
(5)	Tom McCraw (Follow Thru)	1.00	.70	.40
(6)	Tom McCraw (Selecting A Bat)	1.00	.70	.40
(7)	Tom McCraw (Watch The Ball)	1.00	.70	.40
(8)	Mel Queen (Master One Pitch)	1.00	.70	.40
(9)	Mel Queen (Warm Up)	1.00	.70	.40
(10)	Dennis Sommers (Get Down On A Ground Ball)	1.00	.70	.40
(11)	Dennis Sommers (Protect Your Fingers)	1.00	.70	.40
(12)	Dennis Sommers (Tagging First Base)	1.00	.70	.40

1986 Burger King

Burger King restaurants in the Pennsylvania and New Jersey areas issued a 20-card set entitled "All-Pro Series". The cards were issued with the purchase of a Whopper sandwich and came in folded panels of two cards each, along with a coupon card. The card fronts feature a color photo and contain the player's name, team and position plus the Burger King logo. Due to a licensing problem, the team insignias on the players' caps were airbrushed away. The card backs feature black print on white stock and contain brief biographical and statistical information.

		MT	NR MT	EX
Complete Panel Set		10.00	7.50	4.00
Complete Singles Set		6.00	4.50	2.50
Common Panel		.75	.60	.30
Common Single Player		.10	.08	.04
Panel		.70	.50	.30
1	Tony Pena	.10	.08	.04
2	Dave Winfield	.20	.15	.08
Panel		2.00	1.50	.80
3	Fernando Valenzuela	.20	.15	.08
4	Pete Rose	.50	.40	.20
Panel		1.50	1.25	.60
5	Mike Schmidt	.70	.50	.30
6	Steve Carlton	.30	.25	.12
Panel		.70	.50	.30
7	Glenn Wilson	.10	.08	.04
8	Jim Rice	.20	.15	.08
Panel		2.50	2.00	1.00
9	Wade Boggs	.80	.60	.30
10	Juan Samuel	.10	.08	.04
Panel		1.50	1.25	.60
11	Dale Murphy	.40	.30	.15
12	Reggie Jackson	.30	.25	.12
Panel		1.25	.90	.50
13	Kirk Gibson	.20	.15	.08
14	Eddie Murray	.30	.25	.12
Panel		1.00	.70	.40
15	Cal Ripken, Jr.	.30	.25	.12
16	Willie McGee	.10	.08	.04
Panel		1.75	1.25	.70
17	Dwight Gooden	.50	.40	.20
18	Steve Garvey	.25	.20	.10
Panel		3.00	2.25	1.25
19	Don Mattingly	1.50	1.25	.60
20	George Brett	.40	.30	.15

1987 Burger King

The 1987 Burger King "All-Pro 2nd Edition Series" set was part of a giveaway promotion at participating Burger King restaurants. The set is comprised of 20 players on ten different panels. The cards measure 2-1/2" by 3-1/2" each with a three-card panel (includes a coupon card) measuring 7-5/8" by 3-1/2". The card fronts feature a full-color photo and the Burger King logo surrounded by a blue stars-and-stripes border. The backs contain black print on white stock and carry a brief player biography and 1986 career statistics. The set was produced by Mike Schecter Associates and, as with many MSA issues, all team insignias were airbrushed away.

		MT	NR MT	EX
Complete Panel Set:		7.00	5.25	2.75
Complete Singles Set:		4.00	3.00	1.50
Common Panel:		.25	.20	.10
Common Single Player:		.05	.04	.02
Panel		1.25	.90	.50
1	Wade Boggs	.40	.30	.15
2	Gary Carter	.15	.11	.06
Panel		1.00	.70	.40
3	Will Clark	.50	.40	.20
4	Roger Clemens	.20	.15	.08

Panel		MT	NR MT	EX
		.50	.40	.20
5	Steve Garvey	.15	.11	.06
6	Ron Darling	.08	.06	.03
Panel		.25	.20	.10
7	Pedro Guerrero	.08	.06	.03
8	Von Hayes	.05	.04	.02
Panel		.60	.45	.25
9	Rickey Henderson	.25	.20	.10
10	Keith Hernandez	.12	.09	.05
Panel		.60	.45	.25
11	Wally Joyner	.20	.15	.08
12	Mike Krukow	.05	.04	.02
Panel		1.75	1.25	.70
13	Don Mattingly	6.00	4.50	2.50
14	Ozzie Smith	.08	.06	.03
Panel		.50	.40	.20
15	Tony Pena	.05	.04	.02
16	Jim Rice	.15	.11	.06
Panel		.80	.60	.30
17	Ryne Sandberg	.25	.20	.10
18	Mike Schmidt	.40	.30	.15
Panel		.80	.60	.30
19	Darryl Strawberry	.12	.09	.05
20	Fernando Valenzuela	.20	.15	.08

1985 Cain's
Potato Chips Tigers

This 20-card set commemorating the 1984 World champion Tigers was issued by Cain's Potato Chips in the Michigan area in 1985. The yellow-bordered, unnumbered cards measure 2-3/4" in diameter and feature full-color oval photos inside a diamond. The word "Cain's" appears in the upper left corner, while the player's name appears in the lower left with his position directly below the photo. The words "1984 World Champions" are printed in the upper right corner. The backs include 1984 statistics. The cards were inserted in bags of potato chips.

		MT	NR MT	EX
Complete Set:		40.00	30.00	16.00
Common Player:		1.00	.70	.40
(1)	Doug Bair	1.00	.70	.40
(2)	Juan Berenguer	1.00	.70	.40
(3)	Dave Bergman	1.00	.70	.40
(4)	Tom Brookens	1.00	.70	.40
(5)	Marty Castillo	1.00	.70	.40
(6)	Darrell Evans	2.75	2.00	1.00
(7)	Barbaro Garbey	1.00	.70	.40
(8)	Kirk Gibson	3.50	2.75	1.50

		MT	NR MT	EX
(9)	John Grubb	1.00	.70	.40
(10)	Willie Hernandez	1.50	1.25	.60
(11)	Larry Herndon	1.50	1.25	.60
(12)	Chet Lemon	1.50	1.25	.60
(13)	Aurelio Lopez	1.00	.70	.40
(14)	Jack Morris	3.50	2.75	1.50
(15)	Lance Parrish	3.50	2.75	1.50
(16)	Dan Petry	1.50	1.25	.60
(17)	Bill Scherrer	1.00	.70	.40
(18)	Alan Trammell	4.00	3.00	1.50
(19)	Lou Whitaker	3.50	2.75	1.50
(20)	Milt Wilcox	1.00	.70	.40

1986 Cain's
Potato Chips Tigers

For the second year in a row, player discs of the Detroit Tigers were found in boxes of Cain's Potato Chips sold in the Detroit area. Twenty discs make up the set which is branded as a "1986 Annual Collectors' Edition." The discs, which measure 2-3/4" in diameter, have fronts which contain a color photo plus the player's name, team and position. The Cain's logo and the Major League Baseball Players Association's logo also appear. The backs, which display black print on white stock, contain player information plus the card number.

		MT	NR MT	EX
Complete Set:		40.00	30.00	16.00
Common Player:		1.00	.70	.40
1	Tom Brookens	1.00	.70	.40
2	Willie Hernandez	1.50	1.25	.60
3	Dave Bergman	1.00	.70	.40
4	Lou Whitaker	3.50	2.75	1.50
5	Dave LaPoint	1.00	.70	.40
6	Lance Parrish	3.50	2.75	1.50
7	Randy O'Neal	1.00	.70	.40
8	Nelson Simmons	1.00	.70	.40
9	Larry Herndon	1.00	.70	.40
10	Doug Flynn	1.00	.70	.40
11	Jack Morris	3.50	2.75	1.50
12	Dan Petry	1.00	.70	.40
13	Walt Terrell	1.00	.70	.40
14	Chet Lemon	1.50	1.25	.60
15	Frank Tanana	1.50	1.25	.60
16	Kirk Gibson	4.00	3.00	1.50
17	Darrell Evans	2.75	2.00	1.00
18	Dave Collins	1.00	.70	.40
19	John Grubb	1.00	.70	.40
20	Alan Trammell	4.00	3.00	1.50

1987 Cain's
Potato Chips Tigers

Player discs of the Detroit Tigers were inserted in boxes of Cain's Potato Chips for the third consecutive year. The 1987 edition is made up of 20 round cards, each measuring 2-3/4" in diameter. The discs, which were packaged in a cellophane wrapper, feature a full-color photo surrounded by an orange border. The backs are printed in red on white stock. The set was produced by Mike Schecter and Associates.

		MT	NR MT	EX
	Complete Set:	20.00	15.00	8.00
	Common Player:	.60	.45	.25
1	Tom Brookens	.60	.45	.25
2	Darnell Coles	.75	.60	.30
3	Mike Heath	.60	.45	.25
4	Dave Bergman	.60	.45	.25
5	Dwight Lowry	.60	.45	.25
6	Darrell Evans	1.25	.90	.50
7	Alan Trammell	2.75	2.00	1.00
8	Lou Whitaker	2.00	1.50	.80
9	Kirk Gibson	2.75	2.00	1.00
10	Chet Lemon	.75	.60	.30
11	Larry Herndon	.60	.45	.25
12	John Grubb	.60	.45	.25
13	Willie Hernandez	.75	.60	.30
14	Jack Morris	2.00	1.50	.80
15	Dan Petry	.60	.45	.25
16	Walt Terrell	.60	.45	.25
17	Mark Thurmond	.60	.45	.25
18	Pat Sheridan	.60	.45	.25
19	Eric King	.75	.60	.30
20	Frank Tanana	.75	.60	.30

1984 Cereal Series

The Topps-produced 1984 Cereal Series set is identical to the Ralston Purina set from the same year in nearly all aspects. On the card fronts the words "Ralston Purina Company" were replaced by "Cereal Series" and Topps logos were substituted for Ralston checkerboard logos. The set is comprised of 33 cards, each measuring 2-1/2" by 3-1/2." The cards were inserted in unmarked boxes of Chex brand cereals.

		MT	NR MT	EX
	Complete Set	10.00	7.50	4.00
	Common Player	.20	.15	.08
1	Eddie Murray	.70	.50	.30
2	Ozzie Smith	.30	.25	.12

		MT	NR MT	EX
3	Ted Simmons	.20	.15	.08
4	Pete Rose	1.00	.70	.40
5	Greg Luzinski	.20	.15	.08
6	Andre Dawson	.30	.25	.12
7	Dave Winfield	.50	.40	.20
8	Tom Seaver	.50	.40	.20
9	Jim Rice	.50	.40	.20
10	Fernando Valenzuela	.40	.30	.15
11	Wade Boggs	2.00	1.50	.80
12	Dale Murphy	.90	.70	.35
13	George Brett	.90	.70	.35
14	Nolan Ryan	.50	.40	.20
15	Rickey Henderson	.80	.60	.30
16	Steve Carlton	.50	.40	.20
17	Rod Carew	.60	.45	.25
18	Steve Garvey	.50	.40	.20
19	Reggie Jackson	.60	.45	.25
20	Dave Concepcion	.20	.15	.08
21	Robin Yount	.60	.45	.25
22	Mike Schmidt	1.00	.70	.40
23	Jim Palmer	.40	.30	.15
24	Bruce Sutter	.20	.15	.08
25	Dan Quisenberry	.20	.15	.08
26	Bill Madlock	.20	.15	.08
27	Cecil Cooper	.20	.15	.08
28	Gary Carter	.50	.40	.20
29	Fred Lynn	.30	.25	.12
30	Pedro Guerrero	.30	.25	.12
31	Ron Guidry	.30	.25	.12
32	Keith Hernandez	.40	.30	.15
33	Carlton Fisk	.30	.25	.12

1987 Champion Phillies

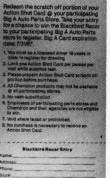

This four card set is interesting in that the players are not identified on the card fronts or backs. The full-color cards, which measure 2-3/4" by 4-5/16", were produced by the Champion Spark Plug Co. as part of a contest held at participating Big A, Car Quest and Pep Boys auto parts stores. Entrants were advised to return the scratch-off coupon portion of the card for a chance to win a Blackbird Racer. Each card contains a scratch-off portion which may have contained an instant prize. Each card can be found with either a Big A, Car Quest or Pep Boys logo in the lower left corner on the card front. The contest was also sponsored in part by the Philadelphia Phillies and radio station WIP.

		MT	NR MT	EX
	Complete Set:	15.00	11.00	6.00
	Common Player:	1.00	.70	.40
(1)	Von Hayes (glove on knee)	2.00	1.50	.80
(2)	Steve Jeltz (#30 on uniform)	1.00	.70	.40
(3)	Juan Samuel (laying on base)	3.00	2.25	1.25
(4)	Mike Schmidt (making throw)	10.00	7.50	4.00

1988 Chef Boyardee

This uncut sheet of 24 cards highlights 12 American and 12 National League players. Full-color player closeup photos are printed beneath a red, white and blue "1988 1st Annual Collector's Edition" header. The player name, team and position appear beneath his photo. Card backs are printed in blue ink on a red background and include biographical information, stats and career highlights including acquisition date and draft date/choice number. The set was produced by American Home Food Products for exclusive distribution via a mail-in offer involving proofs of purchase from the company's Chef Boyardee products.

		MT	NR MT	EX
	Complete Uncut Sheet:	25.00	18.50	10.00
	Complete Singles Set:	15.00	11.00	6.00
	Common Single Player:	.50	.40	.20
1	Mark McGwire	3.00	2.25	1.25
2	Eric Davis	2.00	1.50	.80
3	Jack Morris	.50	.40	.20
4	George Bell	.75	.60	.30
5	Ozzie Smith	.50	.40	.20
6	Tony Gwynn	1.50	1.25	.60
7	Cal Ripken, Jr.	1.25	.90	.50
8	Todd Worrell	.50	.40	.20
9	Larry Parrish	.50	.40	.20
10	Gary Carter	1.00	.70	.40
11	Ryne Sandberg	.75	.60	.30
12	Keith Hernandez	.75	.60	.30
13	Kirby Puckett	1.25	.90	.50
14	Mike Schmidt	1.75	1.25	.70
15	Frank Viola	.50	.40	.20
16	Don Mattingly	4.00	3.00	1.50
17	Dale Murphy	1.50	1.25	.60
18a	Andre Dawson (1987 team is Expos)	.75	.60	.30
18b	Andre Dawson (1987 team is Cubs)	.75	.60	.30
19	Mike Scott	.50	.40	.20
20	Rickey Henderson	1.25	.90	.50
21	Jim Rice	.75	.60	.30
22	Wade Boggs	2.50	2.00	1.00
23	Roger Clemens	1.75	1.25	.70
24	Fernando Valenzuela	.75	.60	.30

1985 Circle K

Produced by Topps for Circle K stores, this 33-card set is entitled "Baseball All Time Home Run Kings". The cards, which measure 2-1/2" by 3-1/2", are numbered on the back according to the player's

position on the all-time career home run list. Joe DiMaggio, who ranked 31st, was not included in the set. The set is skip-numbered from 30 to 32. The glossy card fronts contain the player's name in the lower left corner and feature a color photo, although black and white photos were utilized for a few of the homer kings who played before 1960. The card backs have blue and red print on white stock and contain the player's career batting statistics. The set was issued with a specially designed box.

		MT	NR MT	EX
	Complete Set:	12.00	9.00	4.75
	Common Player:	.15	.11	.06
1	Hank Aaron	.60	.45	.25
2	Babe Ruth	1.25	.90	.50
3	Willie Mays	.60	.45	.25
4	Frank Robinson	.25	.20	.10
5	Harmon Killebrew	.25	.20	.10
6	Mickey Mantle	2.50	2.00	1.00
7	Jimmie Foxx	.25	.20	.10
8	Willie McCovey	.25	.20	.10
9	Ted Williams	.70	.50	.30
10	Ernie Banks	.25	.20	.10
11	Eddie Mathews	.25	.20	.10
12	Mel Ott	.20	.15	.08
13	Reggie Jackson	.40	.30	.15
14	Lou Gehrig	.70	.50	.30
15	Stan Musial	.60	.45	.25
16	Willie Stargell	.20	.15	.08
17	Carl Yastrzemski	.50	.40	.20
18	Billy Williams	.20	.15	.08
19	Mike Schmidt	.40	.30	.15
20	Duke Snider	.40	.30	.15
21	Al Kaline	.25	.20	.10
22	Johnny Bench	.35	.25	.14
23	Frank Howard	.15	.11	.06
24	Orlando Cepeda	.15	.11	.06
25	Norm Cash	.15	.11	.06
26	Dave Kingman	.15	.11	.06
27	Rocky Colavito	.15	.11	.06
28	Tony Perez	.15	.11	.06
29	Gil Hodges	.20	.15	.08
30	Ralph Kiner	.20	.15	.08
32	Johnny Mize	.20	.15	.08
33	Yogi Berra	.35	.25	.14
34	Lee May	.15	.11	.06

1987 Classic Baseball

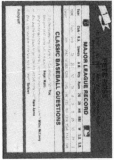

Pete Rose

The "Classic Major League Baseball Board Game" set consists of 100 full-color cards which were used to play the game. Game participants were required to answer trivia questions found on the backs of the cards. The attractive cards measure 2 1/2" by 3 1/2" and are printed on glossy card stock. The card backs carry the player's career statistics besides the Classic Baseball Questions. The game was produced by Game Time, Ltd. of Marietta, Ga., and sold for $19.95 in most retail outlets.

	MT	NR MT	EX
Complete Set:	45.00	34.00	13.50
Common Player:	.10	.08	.04

		MT	NR MT	EX
1	Pete Rose	1.75	1.25	.70
2	Len Dykstra	.30	.25	.12
3	Darryl Strawberry	.80	.60	.30
4	Keith Hernandez	.40	.30	.15
5	Gary Carter	.50	.40	.20
6	Wally Joyner	2.00	1.50	.80
7	Andres Thomas	.15	.11	.06
8	Pat Dodson	.15	.11	.06
9	Kirk Gibson	.30	.25	.12
10	Don Mattingly	3.50	2.75	1.50
11	Dave Winfield	.40	.30	.15
12	Rickey Henderson	.60	.45	.25
13	Dan Pasqua	.15	.11	.06
14	Don Baylor	.15	.11	.06
15	Bo Jackson	25.00	18.00	10.00
16	Pete Incaviglia	.60	.45	.25
17	Kevin Bass	.10	.08	.04
18	Barry Larkin	.40	.30	.15
19	Dave Magadan	.40	.30	.15
20	Steve Sax	.20	.15	.08
21	Eric Davis	1.75	1.25	.70
22	Mike Pagliarulo	.15	.11	.06
23	Fred Lynn	.20	.15	.08
24	Reggie Jackson	.50	.40	.20
25	Larry Parrish	.10	.08	.04
26	Tony Gwynn	.60	.45	.25
27	Steve Garvey	.40	.30	.15
28	Glenn Davis	.20	.15	.08
29	Tim Raines	.40	.30	.15
30	Vince Coleman	.20	.15	.08
31	Willie McGee	.15	.11	.06
32	Ozzie Smith	.80	.60	.30
33	Dave Parker	.20	.15	.08
34	Tony Pena	.10	.08	.04
35	Ryne Sandberg	.80	.60	.30
36	Brett Butler	.10	.08	.04
37	Dale Murphy	.70	.50	.30
38	Bob Horner	.15	.11	.06
39	Pedro Guerrero	.25	.20	.10
40	Brook Jacoby	.15	.11	.06
41	Carlton Fisk	.20	.15	.08
42	Harold Baines	.15	.11	.06
43	Rob Deer	.10	.08	.04
44	Robin Yount	.80	.60	.30
45	Paul Molitor	.20	.15	.08
46	Jose Canseco	2.00	1.50	.80
47	George Brett	.70	.50	.30
48	Jim Presley	.15	.11	.06
49	Rich Gedman	.10	.08	.04
50	Lance Parrish	.20	.15	.08
51	Eddie Murray	.50	.40	.20
52	Cal Ripken, Jr.	.60	.45	.25
53	Kent Hrbek	.25	.20	.10
54	Gary Gaetti	.20	.15	.08
55	Kirby Puckett	.90	.70	.35
56	George Bell	.40	.30	.15
57	Tony Fernandez	.20	.15	.08
58	Jesse Barfield	.15	.11	.06
59	Jim Rice	.40	.30	.15
60	Wade Boggs	2.00	1.50	.80
61	Marty Barrett	.10	.08	.04
62	Mike Schmidt	1.25	.90	.50
63	Von Hayes	.15	.11	.06
64	Jeff Leonard	.10	.08	.04
65	Chris Brown	.15	.11	.06
66	Dave Smith	.10	.08	.04
67	Mike Krukow	.10	.08	.04
68	Ron Guidry	.20	.15	.08
69	Rob Woodward	.15	.11	.06
70	Rob Murphy	.15	.11	.06
71	Andres Galarraga	.25	.20	.10
72	Dwight Gooden	1.25	.90	.50
73	Bob Ojeda	.10	.08	.04
74	Sid Fernandez	.15	.11	.06
75	Jesse Orosco	.10	.08	.04
76	Roger McDowell	.15	.11	.06
77	John Tutor (Tudor)	.15	.11	.06
78	Tom Browning	.15	.11	.06
79	Rick Aguilera	.10	.08	.04
80	Lance McCullers	.15	.11	.06
81	Mike Scott	.20	.15	.08
82	Nolan Ryan	1.00	.70	.40
83	Bruce Hurst	.15	.11	.06
84	Roger Clemens	1.25	.90	.50
85	Oil Can Boyd	.10	.08	.04
86	Dave Righetti	.20	.15	.08
87	Dennis Rasmussen	.10	.08	.04
88	Bret Saberhagan (Saberhagen)	.35	.25	.14
89	Mark Langston	.35	.25	.14
90	Jack Morris	.15	.11	.06
91	Fernando Valenzuela	.25	.20	.10

		MT	NR MT	EX
92	Orel Hershiser	.35	.25	.14
93	Rick Honeycutt	.10	.08	.04
94	Jeff Reardon	.15	.11	.06
95	John Habyan	.10	.08	.04
96	Goose Gossage	.15	.11	.06
97	Todd Worrell	.20	.15	.08
98	Floyd Youmans	.10	.08	.04
99	Don Aase	.10	.08	.04
100	John Franco	.15	.11	.06

1987 Classic Baseball Travel Edition

B.J. Surhoff

Game Time, Ltd. of Marietta, Ga., issued as an update to their Classic Baseball Board Game a 50-card set entitled "Travel Edition." The cards measure 2-1/2" by 3-1/2" and feature the same outstanding quality characteristic of the first release. Numbered from 101 to 150, the "Travel Edition" is an extension of the original set. Besides updating player trades and showcasing rookies, the set offers several highlights from the 1987 season, including Andre Dawson's beaning. All new trivia questions are contained on the card backs.

		MT	NR MT	EX
Complete Set:		15.00	11.00	6.00
Common Player:		.08	.06	.03
101	Mike Schmidt	1.25	.90	.50
102	Eric Davis	1.00	.70	.40
103	Pete Rose	.70	.50	.30
104	Don Mattingly	2.75	2.00	1.00
105	Wade Boggs	1.50	1.25	.60
106	Dale Murphy	.70	.50	.30
107	Glenn Davis	.20	.15	.08
108	Wally Joyner	1.00	.70	.40
109	Bo Jackson	2.00	1.50	.80
110	Cory Snyder	.60	.45	.25
111	Jim Lindeman	.15	.11	.06
112	Kirby Puckett	.90	.70	.35
113	Barry Bonds	.50	.40	.20
114	Roger Clemens	.70	.50	.30
115	Oddibe McDowell	.08	.06	.03
116	Bret Saberhagen	.30	.25	.12
117	Joe Magrane	.30	.25	.12
118	Scott Fletcher	.08	.06	.03
119	Mark McLemore	.08	.06	.03
120	Who Me? (Joe Niekro)	.25	.20	.10
121	Mark McGwire	2.00	1.50	.80
122	Darryl Strawberry	.80	.60	.30
123	Mike Scott	.20	.15	.08
124	Andre Dawson	.50	.40	.20
125	Jose Canseco	2.00	1.50	.80
126	Kevin McReynolds	.25	.20	.10
127	Joe Carter	.20	.15	.08
128	Casey Candaele	.08	.06	.03
129	Matt Nokes	1.00	.70	.40
130	Kal Daniels	.60	.45	.25
131	Pete Incaviglia	.60	.45	.25
132	Benito Santiago	.60	.45	.25
133	Barry Larkin	.60	.45	.25
134	Gary Pettis	.08	.06	.03
135	B.J. Surhoff	.60	.45	.25
136	Juan Nieves	.15	.11	.06
137	Jim Deshaies	.15	.11	.06

		MT	NR MT	EX
138	Pete O'Brien	.15	.11	.06
139	Kevin Seitzer	1.25	.90	.50
140	Devon White	.70	.50	.30
141	Rob Deer	.08	.06	.03
142	Kurt Stillwell	.25	.20	.10
143	Edwin Correa	.08	.06	.03
144	Dion James	.08	.06	.03
145	Danny Tartabull	.40	.30	.15
146	Jerry Browne	.08	.06	.03
147	Ted Higuera	.15	.11	.06
148	Jack Clark	.20	.15	.08
149	Ruben Sierra	.90	.70	.35
150	McGwire/Davis (Eric Davis, Mark McGwire)	1.25	.90	.50

		MT	NR MT	EX
175	Jeff Leonard	.08	.06	.03
176	Cal Ripken, Jr.	.25	.20	.10
177	Pete Incaviglia	.08	.06	.03
178	Devon White	.25	.20	.10
179	Nolan Ryan	3.00	2.25	1.25
180	Ruben Sierra	.70	.50	.25
181	Todd Worrell	.08	.06	.03
182	Glenn Davis	.25	.20	.10
183	Frank Viola	.25	.20	.10
184	Cory Snyder	.40	.30	.15
185	Tracy Jones	.08	.06	.03
186	Terry Steinbach	.70	.50	.25
187	Julio Franco	.15	.11	.06
188	Larry Sheets	.08	.06	.03
189	John Marzano	.08	.06	.03
190	Kevin Elster	.08	.06	.03
191	Vincente Palacios	.08	.06	.03
192	Kent Hrbek	.25	.20	.10
193	Eric Bell	.25	.20	.10
194	Kelly Downs	.08	.06	.03
195	Jose Lind	.10	.08	.04
196	Dave Stewart	.15	.11	.06
197	Jose canseco, Mark McGwire,	2.00	1.50	.80
198	Phil Niekro	.25	.20	.10
199	Phil Niekro	.25	.20	.10
200	Phil Niekro	.25	.20	.10

1988 Classic Baseball
Travel Edition - Red

This 50-card set, numbered 151-200, was produced for use with the travel edition of Game Time's Classic Baseball Board Game. Special cards in the set include a McGwire/Mattingly, an instruction card with McGwire/Canseco, and three different cards featuring Phil Niekro (in different uniforms). A follow-up to the first edition in 1987, the 1988 Red Series was designed for use with the 1988 Blue Series (#'s 201-250). Red Series card fronts have red borders, a yellow Classic logo in the upper left corner and a black and beige player name banner beneath the photo. The card backs are printed in red and pink on white and include the player name, personal info, major league records, a baseball question and space for the player autograph. Classic card series were sold via hobby dealers and retail toy stores nationwide. Game Time Ltd., the set's producer, was purchased by Scoreboard of Cherry Hill, N.J. in 1988.

		MT	NR MT	EX
Complete Set:		12.00	9.00	4.75
Common Player:		.08	.06	.03
151	Don Mattingly, Mark McGwire,	2.00	1.50	.80
152	Don Mattingly	2.00	1.50	.80
153	Mark McGwire	.50	.40	.20
154	Eric Davis	.50	.40	.20
155	Wade Boggs	1.25	.90	.50
156	Dale Murphy	.50	.40	.20
157	Andre Dawson	.25	.20	.10
158	Roger Clemens	.50	.40	.20
159	Kevin Seitzer	.25	.20	.10
160	Benito Santiago	.25	.20	.10
161	Kal Daniels	.25	.20	.10
162	John Kruk	.25	.20	.10
163	Bill Ripken	.08	.06	.03
164	Kirby Puckett	.50	.40	.20
165	Jose Canseco	1.50	1.25	.60
166	Matt Nokes	.25	.20	.10
167	Mike Schmidt	1.00	.70	.40
168	Tim Raines	.25	.20	.10
169	Ryne Sandberg	.25	.20	.10
170	Dave Winfield	.25	.20	.10
171	Dwight Gooden	.70	.50	.30
172	Bret Saberhagen	.20	.15	.08
173	Willie McGee	.08	.06	.03
174	Jack Morris	.08	.06	.03

1988 Classic Baseball
Travel Edition - Blue

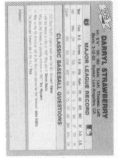

This 50-card set, numbered 201-250, was produced for use with the travel edition of Game Time's Classic Baseball Board Game. Two cards in the set feature two players: Davis/Murphy and McGwire/Mattingly. A follow-up to the first edition in 1987, the 1988 Blue was designed for use with the 1988 Red Series (151-200). Blue Series card fronts have blue borders, a yellow classic logo in the upper left corner and a black and beige player name banner beneath the photo. The card backs are printed in blue on white and include the player name, personal info, major league records, a baseball question and space for the player autograph. Classic card series are sold via hobby dealers and retail toy stores nationwide. Game Time Ltd., the set's producer, was purchased by Scoreboard of Cherry Hill, N.J. in 1988.

		MT	NR MT	EX
Complete Set:		12.00	9.00	4.75
Common Player:		.15	.11	.06
201	Davis/Murphy (Eric Davis, Dale Murphy)	.40	.30	.15
202	B.J. Surhoff	.15	.11	.06
203	John Kruk	.20	.15	.08
204	Sam Horn	.15	.11	.06
205	Jack Clark	.25	.20	.10
206	Wally Joyner	.70	.50	.30
207	Matt Nokes	.50	.40	.20
208	Bo Jackson	2.00	1.50	.80
209	Darryl Strawberry	.80	.60	.30
210	Ozzie Smith	.25	.20	.10
211	Don Mattingly	2.00	1.50	.80
212	Mark McGwire	1.25	.90	.50
213	Eric Davis	1.00	.70	.40
214	Wade Boggs	1.50	1.25	.60

		MT	NR MT	EX
215	Dale Murphy	.70	.50	.30
216	Andre Dawson	.30	.25	.12
217	Roger Clemens	.70	.50	.30
218	Kevin Seitzer	.60	.45	.25
219	Benito Santiago	.30	.25	.12
220	Tony Gwynn	.50	.40	.20
221	Mike Scott	.20	.15	.08
222	Steve Bedrosian	.15	.11	.06
223	Vince Coleman	.25	.20	.10
224	Rick Sutcliffe	.15	.11	.06
225	Will Clark	2.00	1.50	.80
226	Pete Rose	.80	.60	.30
227	Mike Greenwell	1.00	.70	.40
228	Ken Caminiti	.15	.11	.06
229	Ellis Burks	.80	.60	.30
230	Dave Magadan	.15	.11	.06
231	Alan Trammell	.30	.25	.12
232	Paul Molitor	.25	.20	.10
233	Gary Gaetti	.25	.20	.10
234	Rickey Henderon	.60	.45	.25
235	Danny Tartabull	.40	.30	.15
236	Bobby Bonilla	.25	.20	.10
237	Mike Dunne	.20	.15	.08
238	Al Leiter	.70	.50	.30
239	John Farrell	.30	.25	.12
240	Joe Magrane	.15	.11	.06
241	Mike Henneman	.15	.11	.06
242	George Bell	.40	.30	.15
243	Gregg Jefferies	1.50	1.25	.60
244	Jay Buhner	.40	.30	.15
245	Todd Benzinger	.30	.25	.12
246	Matt Williams	.30	.25	.12
247	McGwire/Mattingly (Don Mattingly, Mark McGwire) (no card number on back)	1.50	1.25	.60
248	George Brett	.70	.50	.30
249	Jimmy Key	.20	.15	.08
250	Mark Langston	.20	.15	.08

1989 Classic Baseball

This 100-card set was released by The Score Board accompany two trivia board games. Cards numbered 1-100 correlate with the 1989 Classic Baseball Game, while cards numbered 101-150 belong to the 1989 Classic Travel Series No. 1. The card fronts display full-color photos with the Classic Baseball logo in the upper left corner. The Player's name appears beneath the photo. The flip side includes the card number in the upper left, personal information, and the player's major league record in a boxed area. Another boxed area below the record presents five trivia questions. The lower border of the flip side provides an autograph space. The Classic card series was sold by retail stores and hobby dealers nationwide.

		MT	NR MT	EX
Complete Set:		30.00	22.50	12.00
Common Player:		.08	.06	.03
1	Orel Hershiser	.30	.25	.12
2	Wade Boggs	1.00	.70	.30
3	Jose Canseco	1.75	1.25	.70
4	Mark McGwire	1.00	.70	.30
5	Don Mattingly	1.25	.90	.50
6	Gregg Jefferies	1.00	.70	.40
7	Dwight Gooden	.60	.45	.25

		MT	NR MT	EX
8	Darryl Strawberry	.40	.30	.15
9	Eric Davis	.50	.40	.20
10	Joey Meyer	.08	.06	.03
11	Joe Carter	.15	.11	.06
12	Paul Molitor	.15	.11	.06
13	Mark Grace	2.00	1.50	.80
14	Kurt Stillwell	.08	.06	.03
15	Kirby Puckett	1.00	.70	.30
16	Keith Miller	.08	.06	.03
17	Glenn Davis	.15	.11	.06
18	Will Clark	2.00	1.50	.80
19	Cory Snyder	.15	.11	.06
20	Jose Lind	.08	.06	.03
21	Andres Thomas	.08	.06	.03
22	Dave Smith	.08	.06	.03
23	Mike Scott	.15	.11	.06
24	Kevin McReynolds	.20	.15	.08
25	B.J. Surhoff	.20	.15	.08
26	Mackey Sasser	.08	.06	.03
27	Chad Kreuter	.30	.25	.12
28	Hal Morris	.30	.25	.12
29	Wally Joyner	.40	.30	.15
30	Tony Gwynn	.40	.30	.15
31	Kevin Mitchell	1.75	1.25	.70
32	Dave Winfield	.25	.20	.10
33	Billy Bean	.08	.06	.03
34	Steve Bedrosian	.08	.06	.03
35	Ron Gant	.08	.06	.03
36	Len Dykstra	.08	.06	.03
37	Andre Dawson	.20	.15	.08
38	Brett Butler	.20	.15	.08
39	Rob Deer	.08	.06	.03
40	Tommy John	.08	.06	.03
41	Gary Gaetti	.20	.15	.08
42	Tim Raines	.20	.15	.08
43	George Bell	.20	.15	.08
44	Dwight Evans	.20	.15	.08
45	Denny Martinez	.08	.06	.03
46	Andres Galarraga	.20	.15	.08
47	George Brett	.40	.30	.15
48	Mike Schmidt	1.00	.70	.30
49	Dave Steib	.20	.15	.08
50	Rickey Henderson	.50	.40	.20
51	Craig Biggio	1.00	.70	.30
52	Mark Lemke	.25	.20	.10
53	Chris Sabo	.60	.45	.25
54	Jeff Treadway	.15	.11	.06
55	Kent Hrbek	.15	.11	.06
56	Cal Ripken Jr.	.25	.20	.10
57	Tim Belcher	.15	.11	.06
58	Ozzie Smith	.40	.30	.15
59	Keith Hernandez	.20	.15	.08
60	Pedro Guerrero	.20	.15	.08
61	Greg Swindell	.25	.20	.10
62	Bret Saberhagen	.40	.30	.15
63	John Tudor	.08	.06	.03
64	Gary Carter	.15	.11	.06
65	Kevin Seitzer	.20	.15	.08
66	Jesse Barfield	.20	.15	.08
67	Luis Medina	.35	.25	.14
68	Walt Weiss	.35	.25	.14
69	Terry Steinbach	.60	.45	.25
70	Barry Larkin	.30	.25	.12
71	Pete Rose	1.00	.70	.30
72	Luis Salazar	.08	.06	.03
73	Benito Santiago	.40	.30	.15
74	Kal Daniels	.20	.15	.08
75	Kevin Elster	.08	.06	.03
76	Rob Dibble	.15	.11	.06
77	Bobby Witt	.08	.06	.03
78	Steve Searcy	.25	.20	.10
79	Sandy Alomar	2.00	1.50	.80
80	Chili Davis	.20	.15	.08
81	Alvin Davis	.20	.15	.08
82	Charlie Leibrandt	.08	.06	.03
83	Robin Yount	1.00	.70	.30
84	Mark Carreon	.25	.20	.10
85	Pascual Perez	.08	.06	.03
86	Dennis Rasmussen	.08	.06	.03
87	Ernie Riles	.08	.06	.03
88	Melido Perez	.20	.15	.08
89	Doug Jones	.08	.06	.03
90	Dennis Eckersley	.15	.11	.06
91	Bob Welch	.15	.11	.06
92	Bob Milacki	.35	.25	.14
93	Jeff Robinson	.15	.11	.06
94	Mike Henneman	.15	.11	.06
95	Randy Johnson	.40	.30	.15
96	Ron Jones	.40	.30	.15
97	Jack Armstrong	.08	.06	.03
98	Willie McGee	.08	.06	.03

		MT	NR MT	EX
99	Ryne Sandberg	.40	.30	.15
100	Cone/Jackson	.70	.50	.25
101	Gary Sheffield	1.00	.70	.30
102	Wade Boggs	1.00	.70	.30
103	Jose Canseco	1.25	.90	.50
104	Mark McGwire	1.25	.90	.50
105	Orel Hershiser	.30	.25	.12
106	Don Mattingly	1.25	.90	.50
107	Dwight Gooden	.70	.50	.30
108	Darryl Strawberry	.40	.30	.15
109	Eric Davis	.40	.30	.15
110	Bam Bam Meulens	1.00	.70	.30
111	Andy Van Slyke	.20	.15	.08
112	Al Leiter	.08	.06	.03
113	Matt Nokes	.35	.25	.14
114	Mike Krukow	.08	.06	.03
115	Tony Fernandez	.25	.20	.10
116	Fred McGriff	.70	.50	.25
117	Barry Bonds	.25	.20	.10
118	Gerald Perry	.08	.06	.03
119	Roger Clemens	.40	.30	.15
120	Kirk Gibson	.12	.09	.05
121	Greg Maddux	.30	.25	.12
122	Bo Jackson	1.25	.90	.50
123	Danny Jackson	.08	.06	.03
124	Dale Murphy	.20	.15	.08
125	David Cone	.35	.25	.14
126	Tom Browning	.15	.11	.06
127	Roberto Alomar	.50	.40	.20
128	Alan Trammell	.15	.11	.06
129	Rickey Jordan	.40	.30	.15
130	Ramon Martinez	.50	.40	.20
131	Ken Griffey Jr.	2.00	1.50	.80
132	Gregg Olson	.80	.60	.30
133	Carlos Quintana	.35	.25	.14
134	Dave West	.60	.45	.25
135	Cameron Drew	.30	.25	.12
136	Ted Higuera	.25	.20	.20
137	Sil Campusano	.20	.15	.08
138	Mark Gubicza	.20	.15	.08
139	Mike Boddicker	.08	.06	.03
140	Paul Gibson	.08	.06	.03
141	Jose Rijo	.15	.11	.06
142	John Costello	.08	.06	.03
143	Cecil Espy	.08	.06	.03
144	Frank Viola	.25	.20	.10
145	Erik Hanson	.25	.20	.10
146	Juan Samuel	.08	.06	.03
147	Harold Reynolds	.15	.11	.06
148	Joe Magrane	.15	.11	.06
149	Mike Greenwell	.70	.50	.30
150	Strawberry/Clark	1.50	1.25	.60

		MT	NR MT	EX
155	Mark Grace	.30	.25	.12
156	Jerome Walton	2.25	1.75	.90
157	Bo Jackson	1.00	.70	.40
158	Jack Clark	.05	.04	.02
159	Tom Glavine	.10	.08	.04
160	Eddie Murray	.10	.08	.04
161	John Dopson	.05	.04	.02
162	Ruben Sierra	.35	.25	.14
163	Rafael Palmeiro	.20	.15	.08
164	Nolan Ryan	1.00	.70	.30
165	Barry Larkin	.20	.15	.08
166	Tommy Herr	.05	.04	.02
167	Roberto Kelly	.25	.20	.10
168	Glenn Davis	.10	.08	.04
169	Glenn Braggs	.05	.04	.02
170	Juan Bell	.30	.25	.12
171	Todd Burns	.05	.04	.02
172	Derek Lilliquist	.10	.08	.04
173	Orel Hershiser	.20	.15	.08
174	John Smoltz	.60	.45	.25
175	Guillen/Burks	.30	.25	.12
176	Kirby Puckett	.50	.40	.20
177	Robin Ventura	.80	.60	.30
178	Allan Anderson	.05	.04	.02
179	Steve Sax	.05	.04	.02
180	Will Clark	.80	.60	.30
181	Mike Devereaux	.05	.04	.02
182	Tom Gordon	1.00	.70	.40
183	Rob Murphy	.05	.04	.02
184	Pete O'Brien	.05	.04	.02
185	Cris Carpenter	.10	.08	.04
186	Tom Brunansky	.05	.04	.02
187	Bob Boone	.05	.04	.02
188	Lou Whitaker	.05	.04	.02
189	Dwight Gooden	.30	.25	.12
190	Mark McGwire	.40	.30	.15
191	John Smiley	.05	.04	.02
192	Tommy Gregg	.05	.04	.02
193	Ken Griffey Jr.	2.50	2.00	1.00
194	Bruce Hurst	.05	.04	.02
195	Greg Swindell	.20	.15	.08
196	Nelson Liriano	.05	.04	.02
197	Randy Myers	.05	.04	.02
198	Kevin Mitchell	.70	.50	.30
199	Dante Bichette	.10	.08	.04
200	Deion Sanders	1.00	.70	.40

1989 Classic Update

Jim Abbott

Numbered from 151-200, this 50-card set features rookies and traded players with their new teams. The cards are purple and gray and were sold as part of a board game with baseball trivia questions.

		MT	NR MT	EX
Complete Set:		15.00	11.00	6.00
Common Player:		.05	.04	.02
151	Jim Abbott	1.50	1.25	.60
152	Ellis Burks	.30	.25	.12
153	Mike Schmidt	1.00	.70	.30
154	Gregg Jefferies	.50	.40	.20

1990 Classic Baseball

Jim Abbott

Classic Baseball returned in 1990 with another 150-card set. The cards were again sold as part of a baseball trivia game, and each game included a box designed to store all the cards in the set.

		MT	NR MT	EX
Complete Set:		20.00	15.00	8.00
Common Player:		.05	.04	.02
1	Nolan Ryan	.70	.50	.30
2	Bo Jackson	.40	.30	.15
3	Gregg Olson	.30	.25	.12
4	Tom Gordon	.50	.40	.20
5	Robin Ventura	.80	.60	.30
6	Will Clark	.50	.40	.20
7	Ruben Sierra	.20	.15	.08
8	Mark Grace	.30	.25	.12
9	Luis de los Santos	.05	.04	.02
10	Bernie Williams	1.25	.90	.50

		MT	NR MT	EX
11	Eric Davis	.10	.08	.04
12	Carney Lansford	.05	.04	.02
13	John Smoltz	.10	.08	.04
14	Gary Sheffield	.60	.45	.25
15	Kent Merker	.40	.30	.15
16	Don Mattingly	.50	.40	.20
17	Tony Gwynn	.15	.11	.06
18	Ozzie Smith	.05	.04	.02
19	Frd McGriff	.25	.20	.10
20	Ken Griffey Jr.	1.25	.90	.50
21	Deion Sanders	1.00	.70	.40
22	Jose Canseco	.30	.25	.12
23	Mitch Williams	.20	.15	.08
24	Cal Ripken Jr.	.10	.08	.04
25	Bob Geren	.20	.15	.08
26	Wade Boggs	.15	.11	.06
27	Ryne Sandberg	.15	.11	.06
28	Kirby Puckett	.30	.25	.12
29	Mike Scott	.05	.04	.02
30	Dwight Smith	.80	.60	.30
31	Craig Worthington	.10	.08	.04
32	Ricky Jordan	.15	.11	.06
33	Darryl Strawberry	.10	.08	.04
34	Jerome Walton	1.25	.90	.50
35	John Olerud	3.00	2.25	1.25
36	Tom Glavine	.05	.04	.02
37	Rickey Henderson	.30	.25	.12
38	Rolando Roomes	.10	.08	.04
39	Mickey Tettleton	.10	.08	.04
40	Jim Abbott	.90	.70	.35
41	Dave Righetti	.05	.04	.02
42	Mike LaValliere	.05	.04	.02
43	Rob Dibble	.05	.04	.02
44	Pete Harnisch	.10	.08	.04
45	Jose Offerman	2.00	1.50	.80
46	Walt Weiss	.05	.04	.02
47	Mike Greenwell	.25	.20	.10
48	Barry Larkin	.10	.08	.04
49	Dave Gallagher	.05	.04	.02
50	Junior Felix	.60	.45	.25
51	Roger Clemens	.10	.08	.04
52	Lonnie Smith	.05	.04	.02
53	Jerry Browne	.05	.04	.02
54	Greg Briley	.25	.20	.10
55	Delino Desheilds	1.25	.90	.50
56	Carmelo Martinez	.05	.04	.02
57	Craig Biggio	.20	.15	.08
58	Dwight Gooden	.15	.11	.06
59	Bo,Ruben,Mark	.40	.30	.15
60	Greg Vaughn	1.50	1.25	.60
61	Roberto Alomar	.10	.08	.04
62	Steve Bedrosian	.05	.04	.02
63	Devon White	.05	.04	.02
64	Kevin Mitchell	.40	.30	.15
65	Marquis Grissom	1.25	.90	.50
66	Brian Holman	.05	.04	.02
67	Julio Franco	.10	.08	.04
68	Dave West	.10	.08	.04
69	Harold Baines	.10	.08	.04
70	Eric Anthony	2.00	1.50	.80
71	Glenn Davis	.05	.04	.02
72	Mark Langston	.15	.11	.06
73	Matt Williams	.25	.20	.10
74	Rafael Palmeiro	.05	.04	.02
75	Pete Rose Jr.	1.50	1.25	.60
76	Ramon Martinez	.20	.15	.08
77	Dwight Evans	.10	.08	.04
78	Mackey Sasser	.05	.04	.02
79	Mike Schooler	.05	.04	.02
80	Dennis Cook	.10	.08	.04
81	Orel Hershiser	.20	.15	.08
82	Barry Bonds	.10	.08	.04
83	Geronimo Berroa	.10	.08	.04
84	George Bell	.10	.08	.04
85	Andre Dawson	.10	.08	.04
86	John Franco	.05	.04	.02
87	Clark/Gwynn	.25	.20	.10
88	Glenallen Hill	.35	.25	.14
89	Jeff Ballard	.10	.08	.04
90	Todd Zeile	1.75	1.25	.70
91	Frank Viola	.15	.11	.06
92	Ozzie Guillen	.05	.04	.02
93	Jeff Leonard	.05	.04	.02
94	Dave Smith	.05	.04	.02
95	Dave Parker	.10	.08	.04
96	Jose Gonzales	1.00	.70	.40
97	Dave Steib	.05	.04	.02
98	Charlie Hayes	.15	.11	.06
99	Jesse Barfield	.05	.04	.02
100	Joey Belle	.80	.60	.30
101	Jeff Reardon	.05	.04	.02

		MT	NR MT	EX
102	Bruce Hurst	.05	.04	.02
103	Luis Medina	.05	.04	.02
104	Mike Moore	.10	.08	.04
105	Vince Coleman	.10	.08	.04
106	Alan Trammell	.10	.08	.04
107	Randy Myers	.05	.04	.02
108	Frank Tanana	.05	.04	.02
109	Craig Lefferts	.05	.04	.02
110	John Wetteland	.30	.25	.12
111	Chris Gwynn	.10	.08	.04
112	Mark Carreon	.10	.08	.04
113	Von Hayes	.05	.04	.02
114	Doug Jones	.05	.04	.02
115	Andres Galarraga	.10	.08	.04
116	Carlton Fisk	.10	.08	.04
117	Paul O'Neil	.05	.04	.02
118	Tim Raines	.10	.08	.04
119	Tom Brunansky	.05	.04	.02
120	Andy Benes	.70	.50	.30
121	Mark Portugal	.05	.04	.02
122	Willie Randolph	.05	.04	.02
123	Jeff Blauser	.05	.04	.02
124	Don August	.05	.04	.02
125	Chuck Cary	.05	.04	.02
126	John Smiley	.05	.04	.02
127	Terry Mullholland	.05	.04	.02
128	Harold Reynolds	.05	.04	.02
129	Hubie Brooks	.05	.04	.02
130	Ben McDonald	2.50	2.00	1.00
131	Kevin Ritz	.20	.15	.08
132	Luis Quinones	.05	.04	.02
133	Bam Bam Meulens	.20	.15	.08
134	Bill Spiers	.20	.15	.08
135	Andy Hawkins	.05	.04	.02
136	Alvin Davis	.10	.08	.04
137	Lee Smith	.05	.04	.02
138	Joe Carter	.10	.08	.04
139	Bret Saberhagen	.10	.08	.04
140	Sammy Sosa	.70	.50	.30
141	Matt Nokes	.05	.04	.02
142	Bert Blyleven	.10	.08	.04
143	Bobby Bonilla	.10	.08	.04
144	Howard Johnson	.10	.08	.04
145	Joe Magrane	.05	.04	.02
146	Pedro Guerrero	.10	.08	.04
147	Robin Yount	.25	.20	.10
148	Dan Gladden	.05	.04	.02
149	Steve Sax	.10	.08	.04
150	Clark/Mitchell	.50	.40	.20

1989 Cleveland Indians Team Set

(28) Cory Snyder, OF

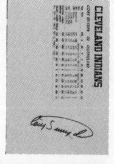

The Cleveland Indians released this oversized (2-3/4" by 4-1/2") 28-card set in 1989. The cards feature a full-color player photo on the front with the "Tribe" logo in the upper left corner. Card backs include major and minor league stat and a facsimile autograph.

	MT	NR MT	EX
Complete Set:	6.00	4.50	2.50
Common Player:	.20	.15	.08
(1) Doc Edwards	.20	.15	.08

		MT	NR MT	EX
(2)	Joel Skinner	.20	.15	.08
(3)	Andy Allanson	.20	.15	.08
(4)	Tom Candiotti	.20	.15	.08
(5)	Doug Jones	.20	.15	.08
(6)	Keith Atherton	.20	.15	.08
(7)	Rich Yett	.20	.15	.08
(8)	John Farrell	.20	.15	.08
(9)	Rod Nichols	.20	.15	.08
(10)	Joe Skalski	.30	.25	.12
(11)	Pete O'Brien	.30	.25	.12
(12)	Jerry Browne	.30	.25	.12
(13)	Brook Jacoby	.30	.25	.12
(14)	Felix Fermin	.20	.15	.08
(15)	Bud Black	.20	.15	.08
(16)	Brad Havens	.20	.15	.08
(17)	Greg Swindell	.40	.30	.15
(18)	Scott Bailes	.20	.15	.08
(19)	Jesse Orosco	.20	.15	.08
(20)	Oddibe McDowell	.30	.25	.12
(21)	Joe Carter	.50	.40	.20
(22)	Cory Snyder	.40	.30	.15
(23)	Louie Medina	.25	.20	.10
(24)	Dave Clark	.25	.20	.10
(25)	Brad Komminsk	.20	.15	.08
(26)	Luis Aguayo	.20	.15	.08
(27)	Pat Keedy	.25	.20	.10
(28)	Tribe Coaches	.20	.15	.08

1981 Coca-Cola

In 1981, Topps produced for Coca-Cola 12-card sets for 11 various American and National League teams. The sets include 11 player cards and one unnumbered header card. The card fronts, which measure 2-1/2" by 3-1/2", are identical in style to the 1981 Topps regular issue save for the Coca-Cola logo. The backs differ only from the '81 Topps regular set in that they are numbered 1-11 and carry the Coca-Cola trademark and copyright line. The backs of the header cards contain an offer for 132-card uncut sheets of 1981 Topps baseball cards.

		MT	NR MT	EX
Complete Set:		18.00	13.50	7.25
Common Player:		.06	.05	.02
1	Tom Burgmeier	.06	.05	.02
2	Dennis Eckersley	.15	.11	.06
3	Dwight Evans	.60	.45	.25
4	Bob Stanley	.10	.08	.04
5	Glenn Hoffman	.06	.05	.02
6	Carney Lansford	.20	.15	.08
7	Frank Tanana	.10	.08	.04
8	Tony Perez	.20	.15	.08
9	Jim Rice	.80	.60	.30
10	Dave Stapleton	.06	.05	.02
11	Carl Yastrzemski	1.50	1.25	.60
----	Header Card	.03	.02	.01
1	Tim Blackwell	.06	.05	.02
2	Bill Buckner	.15	.11	.06
3	Ivan DeJesus	.06	.05	.02
4	Leon Durham	.15	.11	.06
5	Steve Henderson	.06	.05	.02
6	Mike Krukow	.10	.08	.04
7	Ken Reitz	.06	.05	.02

		MT	NR MT	EX
8	Rick Reuschel	.15	.11	.06
9	Scot Thompson	.06	.05	.02
10	Dick Tidrow	.06	.05	.02
11	Mike Tyson	.06	.05	.02
----	Header Card	.03	.02	.01
1	Britt Burns	.10	.08	.04
2	Todd Cruz	.06	.05	.02
3	Rich Dotson	.20	.15	.08
4	Jim Essian	.06	.05	.02
5	Ed Farmer	.06	.05	.02
6	Lamar Johnson	.06	.05	.02
7	Ron LeFlore	.10	.08	.04
8	Chet Lemon	.10	.08	.04
9	Bob Molinaro	.06	.05	.02
10	Jim Morrison	.06	.05	.02
11	Wayne Nordhagen	.06	.05	.02
----	Header Card	.03	.02	.01
1	Johnny Bench	.80	.60	.30
2	Dave Collins	.10	.08	.04
3	Dave Concepcion	.15	.11	.06
4	Dan Driessen	.10	.08	.04
5	George Foster	.25	.20	.10
6	Ken Griffey	.15	.11	.06
7	Tom Hume	.06	.05	.02
8	Ray Knight	.10	.08	.04
9	Ron Oester	.06	.05	.02
10	Tom Seaver	.70	.50	.30
11	Mario Soto	.10	.08	.04
----	Header Card	.03	.02	.01
1	Champ Summers	.06	.05	.02
2	Al Cowens	.06	.05	.02
3	Rich Hebner	.06	.05	.02
4	Steve Kemp	.10	.08	.04
5	Aurelio Lopez	.06	.05	.02
6	Jack Morris	.35	.25	.14
7	Lance Parrish	.35	.25	.14
8	Johnny Wockenfuss	.06	.05	.02
9	Alan Trammell	.50	.40	.20
10	Lou Whitaker	.35	.25	.14
11	Kirk Gibson	.80	.60	.30
----	Header Card	.03	.02	.01
1	Alan Ashby	.06	.05	.02
2	Cesar Cedeno	.15	.11	.06
3	Jose Cruz	.15	.11	.06
4	Art Howe	.06	.05	.02
5	Rafael Landestoy	.06	.05	.02
6	Joe Niekro	.15	.11	.06
7	Terry Puhl	.06	.05	.02
8	J.R. Richard	.15	.11	.06
9	Nolan Ryan	.60	.45	.25
10	Joe Sambito	.06	.05	.02
11	Don Sutton	.35	.25	.14
----	Header Card	.03	.02	.01
1	Willie Aikens	.06	.05	.02
2	George Brett	1.50	1.25	.60
3	Larry Gura	.06	.05	.02
4	Dennis Leonard	.06	.05	.02
5	Hal McRae	.15	.11	.06
6	Amos Otis	.10	.08	.04
7	Dan Quisenberry	.15	.11	.06
8	U.L. Washington	.06	.05	.02
9	John Wathan	.10	.08	.04
10	Frank White	.10	.08	.04
11	Willie Wilson	.15	.11	.06
----	Header Card	.03	.02	.01
1	Neil Allen	.06	.05	.02
2	Doug Flynn	.06	.05	.02
3	Dave Kingman	.15	.11	.06
4	Randy Jones	.06	.05	.02
5	Pat Zachry	.06	.05	.02
6	Lee Mazzilli	.10	.08	.04
7	Rusty Staub	.15	.11	.06
8	Craig Swan	.06	.05	.02
9	Frank Taveras	.06	.05	.02
10	Alex Trevino	.06	.05	.02
11	Joel Youngblood	.06	.05	.02
----	Header Card	.03	.02	.01
1	Bob Boone	.10	.08	.04
2	Larry Bowa	.15	.11	.06
3	Steve Carlton	.60	.45	.25
4	Greg Luzinski	.15	.11	.06
5	Garry Maddox	.10	.08	.04
6	Bake McBride	.06	.05	.02
7	Tug McGraw	.15	.11	.06
8	Pete Rose	2.00	1.50	.80
9	Mike Schmidt	1.75	1.25	.70
10	Lonnie Smith	.06	.05	.02
11	Manny Trillo	.06	.05	.02
----	Header Card	.03	.02	.01
1	Jim Bibby	.06	.05	.02
2	John Candelaria	.10	.08	.04

		MT	NR MT	EX
3	Mike Easler	.10	.08	.04
4	Tim Foli	.06	.05	.02
5	Phil Garner	.06	.05	.02
6	Bill Madlock	.15	.11	.06
7	Omar Moreno	.06	.05	.02
8	Ed Ott	.06	.05	.02
9	Dave Parker	.35	.25	.14
10	Willie Stargell	.50	.40	.20
11	Kent Tekulve	.10	.08	.04
----	Header Card	.03	.02	.01
1	Bob Forsch	.10	.08	.04
2	George Hendrick	.10	.08	.04
3	Keith Hernandez	.50	.40	.20
4	Tom Herr	.15	.11	.06
5	Sixto Lezcano	.06	.05	.02
6	Ken Oberkfell	.06	.05	.02
7	Darrell Porter	.10	.08	.04
8	Tony Scott	.06	.05	.02
9	Lary Sorensen	.06	.05	.02
10	Bruce Sutter	.15	.11	.06
11	Garry Templeton	.10	.08	.04
----	Header Card	.03	.02	.01

1982 Coca-Cola/Brigham's Red Sox

Coca-Cola, in conjunction with Brigham's Ice Cream stores, issued a 23-card set in the Boston area featuring Red Sox players. The Topps-produced cards, which measure 2-1/2" by 3-1/2", are identical in style to the regular 1982 Topps set but contain the Coca-Cola and Brigham's logos in the corners. The cards were distributed in three-card cello packs, including an unnumbered header card.

		MT	NR MT	EX
Complete Set:		5.00	3.75	2.00
Common Player:		.08	.06	.03
1	Gary Allenson	.08	.06	.03
2	Tom Burgmeier	.08	.06	.03
3	Mark Clear	.15	.11	.06
4	Steve Crawford	.08	.06	.03
5	Dennis Eckersley	.30	.25	.12
6	Dwight Evans	.80	.60	.30
7	Rich Gedman	.30	.25	.12
8	Garry Hancock	.08	.06	.03
9	Glen Hoffman (Glenn)	.08	.06	.03
10	Carney Lansford	.20	.15	.08
11	Rick Miller	.08	.06	.03
12	Reid Nichols	.08	.06	.03
13	Bob Ojeda	.20	.15	.08
14	Tony Perez	.30	.25	.12
15	Chuck Rainey	.08	.06	.03
16	Jerry Remy	.08	.06	.03
17	Jim Rice	.80	.60	.30
18	Bob Stanley	.15	.11	.06
19	Dave Stapleton	.08	.06	.03
20	Mike Torrez	.08	.06	.03
21	John Tudor	.30	.25	.12
22	Carl Yastrzemski	1.25	.90	.50
----	Header Card	.05	.04	.02

NOTE: A card number in parentheses ( ) indicates the set is unnumbered.

1982 Coca-Cola Reds

Produced by Topps for Coca-Cola, the set consists of 23 cards featuring the Cincinnati Reds and was distributed in the Cincinnati area. The cards, which are 2-1/2" by 3-1/2" in size, are identical in design to the regular 1982 Topps set but have a Coca-Cola logo on the front and red backs. An unnumbered header card is included in the set.

		MT	NR MT	EX
Complete Set:		5.00	3.75	2.00
Common Player:		.08	.06	.03
1	Johnny Bench	1.00	.70	.40
2	Bruce Berenyi	.08	.06	.03
3	Larry Biittner	.08	.06	.03
4	Cesar Cedeno	.15	.11	.06
5	Dave Concepcion	.25	.20	.10
6	Dan Driessen	.15	.11	.06
7	Greg Harris	.08	.06	.03
8	Paul Householder	.08	.06	.03
9	Tom Hume	.08	.06	.03
10	Clint Hurdle	.08	.06	.03
11	Jim Kern	.08	.06	.03
12	Wayne Krenchicki	.08	.06	.03
13	Rafael Landestoy	.08	.06	.03
14	Charlie Leibrandt	.15	.11	.06
15	Mike O'Berry	.08	.06	.03
16	Ron Oester	.08	.06	.03
17	Frank Pastore	.08	.06	.03
18	Joe Price	.08	.06	.03
19	Tom Seaver	1.00	.70	.40
20	Mario Soto	.15	.11	.06
21	Alex Trevino	.08	.06	.03
22	Mike Vail	.08	.06	.03
----	Header Card	.04	.03	.02

1985 Coca-Cola White Sox

Featuring past and present White Sox players, the cards in this set were given out on Tuesday night home games. The cards, which measure 2-5/8" by 4-1/8", contain a color photo of a current Sox member. A red box at the bottom of the card carries the team logo, the player's name, uniform number and position, plus a small oval portrait of a past Sox player. The card backs contain the Coca-Cola logo and the lifetime hitting or pitching statistics for the current and past player. The set is numbered in the checklist that follows by the player's uniform number with the last three cards being unnumbered.

		MT	NR MT	EX
Complete Set:		14.00	10.50	5.50
Common Player:		.25	.20	.10
0	Oscar Gamble (Zeke Bonura)	.25	.20	.10
1	Scott Fletcher (Luke Appling)	.40	.30	.15
3	Harold Baines (Bill Melton)	.80	.60	.30
5	Luis Salazar (Chico Carrasquel)	.25	.20	.10
7	Marc Hill (Sherm Lollar)	.25	.20	.10
8	Daryl Boston (Jim Landis)	.25	.20	.10
10	Tony LaRussa (Al Lopez)	.40	.30	.15
12	Julio Cruz (Nellie Fox)	.40	.30	.15
13	Ozzie Guillen (Luis Aparicio)	.80	.60	.30
17	Jerry Hairston (Smoky Burgess)	.25	.20	.10
20	Joe DeSa (Carlos May)	.25	.20	.10
22	Joel Skinner (J.C. Martin)	.25	.20	.10
23	Rudy Law (Bill Skowron)	.25	.20	.10
24	Floyd Bannister (Red Faber)	.35	.25	.14
29	Greg Walker (Dick Allen)	.70	.50	.30
30	Gene Nelson (Early Wynn)	.35	.25	.14
32	Tim Hulett (Pete Ward)	.25	.20	.10
34	Richard Dotson (Ed Walsh)	.35	.25	.14
37	Dan Spillner (Thornton Lee)	.25	.20	.10
40	Britt Burns (Gary Peters)	.25	.20	.10
41	Tom Seaver (Ted Lyons)	.80	.60	.30
42	Ron Kittle (Minnie Minoso)	.40	.30	.15
43	Bob James (Hoyt Wilhelm)	.40	.30	.15
44	Tom Paciorek (Eddie Collins)	.35	.25	.14
46	Tim Lollar (Billy Pierce)	.25	.20	.10
50	Juan Agosto (Wilbur Wood)	.25	.20	.10
72	Carlton Fisk (Ray Schalk)	.70	.50	.30
----	Comiskey Park	.50	.40	.20
----	Ribbie and Roobarb (mascots)	.25	.20	.10
----	Nancy Faust (organist)	.25	.20	.10

1986 Coca-Cola White Sox

For the second year in a row, Coca-Cola, in conjunction with the Chicago White Sox, issued a 30-card set. As in 1985, cards were given out at the park on Tuesday night games. Full sets were again available through a fan club offer found in the White Sox program. The cards, which measure 2-5/8" by 4-1/8", feature 25 players plus other White Sox personnel. The cards fronts feature a color photo (an action shot in most instances) and a white bar at the bottom. A black and white bat with "SOX" shown on the barrel is located within the white bar, along with the player's name, position and uniform number. The white and grey backs with black print include the Coca-Cola trademark. Lifetime statistics are shown on all player cards, but there is no personal information such as height, weight or age. The non-player cards are blank-backed save for the name and logo at the top. The cards in the checklist that follows are numbered by the players' uniform numbers, with the last five cards of the set being unnumbered.

		MT	NR MT	EX
Complete Set:		12.00	9.00	4.75
Common Player:		.25	.20	.10
1	Wayne Tolleson	.25	.20	.10
3	Harold Baines	.60	.45	.25
7	Marc Hill	.25	.20	.10
8	Daryl Boston	.25	.20	.10
12	Julio Cruz	.25	.20	.10
13	Ozzie Guillen	.45	.35	.20
17	Jerry Hairston	.25	.20	.10
19	Floyd Bannister	.35	.25	.14
20	Reid Nichols	.25	.20	.10
22	Joel Skinner	.25	.20	.10
24	Dave Schmidt	.25	.20	.10
26	Bobby Bonilla	.70	.50	.30
29	Greg Walker	.40	.30	.15
30	Gene Nelson	.25	.20	.10
32	Tim Hulett	.25	.20	.10
33	Neil Allen	.25	.20	.10
34	Richard Dotson	.35	.25	.14
40	Joe Cowley	.25	.20	.10
41	Tom Seaver	.70	.50	.30
42	Ron Kittle	.35	.25	.14
43	Bob James	.25	.20	.10
44	John Cangelosi	.35	.25	.14
50	Juan Agosto	.25	.20	.10
52	Joel Davis	.25	.20	.10
72	Carlton Fisk	.50	.40	.20
----	Ribbie & Roobarb (mascots)	.25	.20	.10
----	Nancy Faust (organist)	.25	.20	.10
----	Ken "Hawk" Harrelson	.30	.25	.12
----	Tony LaRussa	.30	.25	.12
----	Minnie Minoso	.30	.25	.12

1987 Coca-Cola Tigers

Coca-Cola and S. Abraham & Sons, Inc. issued a set of 18 baseball cards featuring members of the Detroit Tigers. The set is comprised of six four-part folding panels. Each panel includes three player cards (each 2-1/2" by 3-1/2") and one team logo card. A bright yellow border surrounds the full-color photo. The backs are designed on a vertical format and contain personal data and career statistics. The set was produced by Mike Schecter and Associates.

		MT	NR MT	EX
Complete Set:		6.00	4.50	2.50
Complete Singles Set:		2.00	1.50	.80
Common Panel:		.60	.45	.25
Common Single Player:		.05	.04	.02
Panel		1.25	.90	.50
1	Kirk Gibson	.50	.40	.20
2	Larry Herndon	.08	.06	.03
3	Walt Terrell	.10	.08	.04
Panel		1.25	.90	.50
4	Alan Trammell	.50	.40	.20
5	Frank Tanana	.10	.08	.04
6	Pat Sheridan	.05	.04	.02
Panel		.90	.70	.35
7	Jack Morris	.30	.25	.12
8	Mike Heath	.05	.04	.02
9	Dave Bergman	.05	.04	.02
Panel		.60	.45	.25
10	Chet Lemon	.10	.08	.04

		MT	NR MT	EX
11	Dwight Lowry	.08	.06	.03
12	Dan Petry	.10	.08	.04
Panel		.80	.60	.30
13	Darrell Evans	.20	.15	.08
14	Darnell Coles	.10	.08	.04
15	Willie Hernandez	.10	.08	.04
Panel		1.00	.70	.40
16	Lou Whitaker	.30	.25	.12
17	Tom Brookens	.05	.04	.02
18	John Grubb	.05	.04	.02

1987 Coca-Cola White Sox

The Chicago White Sox Fan Club, in conjunction with Coca-Cola, offered members a set of 30 trading cards. For the $10 membership fee, fans received the set plus additional fan club gifts and privileges. The cards, which measure 2-5/8" by 4", feature full-color photos inside a blue and red border. The backs include the player's name, position, uniform number and statistics. The Coca-Cola logo is also included on the card backs.

		MT	NR MT	EX
Complete Set:		12.00	9.00	4.75
Common Player:		.25	.20	.10
1	Jerry Royster	.25	.20	.10
3	Harold Baines	.60	.45	.25
5	Ron Karkovice	.30	.25	.12
8	Daryl Boston	.25	.20	.10
10	Fred Manrique	.30	.25	.12
12	Steve Lyons	.25	.20	.10
13	Ozzie Guillen	.40	.30	.15
14	Russ Morman	.30	.25	.12
15	Donnie Hill	.25	.20	.10
16	Jim Fregosi	.30	.25	.12
17	Jerry Hairston	.25	.20	.10
19	Floyd Bannister	.35	.25	.14
21	Gary Redus	.25	.20	.10
22	Ivan Calderon	.40	.30	.15
25	Ron Hassey	.25	.20	.10
26	Jose DeLeon	.30	.25	.12
29	Greg Walker	.40	.30	.15
32	Tim Hulett	.25	.20	.10
33	Neil Allen	.25	.20	.10
34	Rich Dotson	.35	.25	.14
36	Ray Searage	.25	.20	.10
37	Bobby Thigpen	.40	.30	.15
40	Jim Winn	.25	.20	.10
43	Bob James	.25	.20	.10
50	Joel McKeon	.25	.20	.10
52	Joel Davis	.25	.20	.10
72	Carlton Fisk	.50	.40	.20
----	Ribbie & Roobarb (mascots)	.25	.20	.10
----	Nancy Faust (organist)	.25	.20	.10
----	Minnie Minoso	.30	.25	.12

1988 Coca-Cola Padres

A 20-card team set sponsored by Coca-Cola was designed as part of the San Diego Padres Junior Fan Club promotion for 1988. This set was distributed as a nine-card starter sheet, with 11 additional single

cards handed out during the team's home games. The standard-size cards feature full-color player photos framed by a black and orange border. The player's name is printed above the photo; uniform number and position appear lower right. A large Padres logo curves upward from the lower left corner. Card backs are brown on white and include the Padres logo upper left opposite the player's name and personal information. Career highlights and 1987 stats appear in the center of the card back above the Coca-Cola and Junior Padres Fan Club logos.

		MT	NR MT	EX
Complete Set:		35.00	25.00	13.00
Common Player:		.50	.40	.20
Panel		99.99	99.99	99.99
1	Garry Templeton	.75	.60	.30
5	Randy Ready	.50	.40	.20
10	Larry Bowa	.75	.60	.30
11	Tim Flannery	.50	.40	.20
35	Chris Brown	.75	.60	.30
45	Jimmy Jones	1.00	.70	.40
48	Mark Davis	.50	.40	.20
55	Mark Grant	.50	.40	.20
----	20th Anniversary Logo Card	.10	.08	.04
Singles		99.99	99.99	99.99
7	Keith Moreland	1.00	.70	.40
8	John Kruk	2.25	1.75	.90
9	Benito Santiago	3.25	2.50	1.25
14	Carmelo Martinez	1.00	.70	.40
15	Jack McKeon	1.00	.70	.40
19	Tony Gwynn	9.00	6.75	3.50
22	Stan Jefferson	1.00	.70	.40
27	Mark Parent	2.00	1.50	.80
30	Eric Show	1.50	1.25	.60
31	Ed Whitson	1.00	.70	.40
41	Lance McCullers	1.25	.90	.50
51	Greg Booker	1.00	.70	.40

1988 Coca-Cola White Sox

Part of a fan club membership package, this unnumbered 30-card set features full-color photos of 27 players, the team mascot, team organist and Comiskey Park. Cards have a bright red border, with the team logo in the lower left corner of the photo. A large player name fills the bottom border. Card backs are printed in black on grey and white and include player name, personal info and career summary. The set was included in the $10 membership package, with a portion of the cost going to the ChiSox Kids Charity.

		MT	NR MT	EX
Complete Set:		8.00	6.00	3.25
Common Player:		.20	.15	.08
(1)	Harold Baines	.50	.40	.20
(2)	Daryl Boston	.20	.15	.08
(3)	Ivan Calderon	.30	.25	.12
(4)	John Davis	.20	.15	.08
(5)	Jim Fregosi	.25	.20	.10
(6)	Carlton Fisk	.40	.30	.15
(7)	Ozzie Guillen	.30	.25	.12
(8)	Donnie Hill	.20	.15	.08
(9)	Rick Horton	.20	.15	.08
(10)	Lance Johnson	.30	.25	.12
(11)	Dave LaPoint	.20	.15	.08
(12)	Bill Long	.25	.20	.10
(13)	Steve Lyons	.20	.15	.08
(14)	Jack McDowell	.40	.30	.15
(15)	Fred Manrique	.20	.15	.08
(16)	Minnie Minoso	.25	.20	.10
(17)	Dan Pasqua	.30	.25	.12
(18)	John Pawlowski	.25	.20	.10
(19)	Melido Perez	.40	.30	.15
(20)	Billy Pierce	.25	.20	.10
(21)	Gary Redus	.20	.15	.08
(22)	Jerry Reuss	.25	.20	.10
(23)	Mark Salas	.20	.15	.08
(24)	Jose Segura	.30	.25	.12
(25)	Bobby Thigpen	.25	.20	.10
(26)	Greg Walker	.30	.25	.12
(27)	Kenny Williams	.30	.25	.12
(28)	Nancy Faust (organist)	.20	.15	.08
(29)	Ribbie & Roobarb (mascots)	.20	.15	.08
(30)	Comiskey Park	.40	.30	.15

1989 Coca-Cola Padres

This 20-card set is part of the Junior Padres Fan Club membership package. Members receive a 9-card starter set printed on one large perforated sheet. Additional cards are distributed to kids at specially designated games (free admission for kids). Card fronts feature an orange-and-brown double border, with a bright orange Padres logo printed lower left. Player uniform number and position are printed diagonally across the upper right corner, with the player's name in large block letters along the bottom border.

		MT	NR MT	EX
Complete Set:		30.00	22.00	12.00
Common Player:		.50	.40	.30
Panel		99.99	99.99	99.99
1	Garry Templeton	.70	.50	.30
5	Randy Ready	.50	.40	.20
12	Roberto Alomar	1.00	.70	.40
14	Carmelo Martinez	.50	.40	.20
15	Jack McKeon	.50	.40	.20

		MT	NR MT	EX
30	Eric Show	.50	.40	.20
31	Ed Whitson	.50	.40	.20
43	Dennis Rasmussen	.50	.40	.20
----	Logo Card	.10	.08	.04
Singles		99.99	99.99	99.99
6	Luis Salazar	1.00	.70	.40
9	Benito Santiago	3.00	2.25	1.25
10	Leon Roberts	1.00	.70	.40
11	Tim Flannery	1.00	.70	.40
18	Chris James	2.00	1.50	.80
19	Tony Gwynn	7.00	5.25	2.75
25	Jack Clark	3.00	2.25	1.25
27	Mark Parent	2.00	1.50	.80
35	Walt Terrell	1.00	.70	.40
47	Bruce Hurst	2.00	1.50	.80
48	Mark Davis	3.00	2.25	1.25
55	Mark Grant	1.00	.70	.30

1989 Coca-Cola White Sox

For the fifth straight year, Coca-Cola sponsored a set of cards featuring the Chicago White Sox. The 30-card set was distributed to fans attending a special promotional day at Comiskey Park and was also available by mail to members of the ChiSox fan club. The fronts of the cards feature a red, white and blue color scheme and include a pair of crossed bats. "White Sox" appears along the top, while the name and position are in the lower right, and a pennant proclaiming "Chicago's American Pastime" is just below the photo. The horizontal backs include player biographies, other data, special facts about Comiskey Park and the Coca-Cola logo.

		MT	NR MT	EX
Complete Set:		10.00	7.50	4.00
Common Player:		.20	.15	.08
1	New Comiskey Park, 1991	.40	.30	.15
2	Comiskey Park	.40	.30	.15
3	Jeff Torborg	.20	.15	.08
4	Coaching Staff	.20	.15	.08
5	Harold Baines	.50	.40	.20
6	Daryl Boston	.20	.15	.08
7	Ivan Calderon	.30	.25	.12
8	Carlton Fisk	.40	.30	.15
9	Dave Gallagher	.30	.25	.12
10	Ozzie Guillen	.30	.25	.12
11	Shawn Hillegas	.20	.15	.08
12	Barry Jones	.20	.15	.08
13	Ron Karkovice	.20	.15	.08
14	Eric King	.20	.15	.08
15	Ron Kittle	.30	.25	.12
16	Bill Long	.20	.15	.08
17	Steve Lyons	.20	.15	.08
18	Donn Pall	.20	.15	.08
19	Dan Pasqua	.30	.25	.12
20	Ken Patterson	.20	.15	.08
21	Melido Perez	.30	.25	.12
22	Jerry Reuss	.25	.20	.10
23	Billy Jo Robidoux	.20	.15	.08
24	Steve Rosenberg	.20	.15	.08
25	Jeff Schaefer	.25	.20	.10
26	Bobby Thigpen	.25	.20	.10
27	Greg Walker	.25	.20	.10
28	Eddie Williams	.25	.20	.10
29	Nancy Faust, organist	.20	.15	.08

		MT	NR MT	EX
30	Minnie Minoso	.20	.15	.08

1914 Cracker Jack

The 1914 Cracker Jack set, whose ACC designation is E145-1, is one of the most popular of the "E" card sets and features baseball stars from the American, National and Federal Leagues. The cards, which measure 2-1/4" by 3" and are printed on thin stock, were found in boxes of Cracker Jack. The 1914 issue consists of 144 cards with tinted color photographs on a red background. The numbered backs feature a short biography plus an advertisement. The advertising on the low-numbered cards in the set indicate that 10 million cards were issued, while the high-numbered cards boast that 15 million were printed.

		NR MT	EX	VG
	Complete Set:	20500.00	10250.00	6150.
	Common Player:	90.00	45.00	27.00
1	Otto Knabe	250.00	175.00	75.00
2	Home Run Baker	300.00	150.00	90.00
3	Joe Tinker	300.00	150.00	90.00
4	Larry Doyle	90.00	45.00	27.00
5	Ward Miller	90.00	45.00	27.00
6	Eddie Plank	350.00	175.00	100.00
7	Eddie Collins	300.00	150.00	90.00
8	Rube Oldring	90.00	45.00	27.00
9	Artie Hoffman (Hofman)	90.00	45.00	27.00
10	Stuffy McInnis	90.00	45.00	27.00
11	George Stovall	90.00	45.00	27.00
12	Connie Mack	350.00	175.00	100.00
13	Art Wilson	90.00	45.00	27.00
14	Sam Crawford	175.00	87.00	52.00
15	Reb Russell	90.00	45.00	27.00
16	Howie Camnitz	90.00	45.00	27.00
17a	Roger Bresnahan (no number on back)			
		300.00	150.00	90.00
17b	Roger Bresnahan (number on back)			
		300.00	150.00	90.00
18	Johnny Evers	275.00	150.00	80.00
19	Chief Bender	300.00	150.00	90.00
20	Cy Falkenberg	90.00	45.00	27.00
21	Heinie Zimmerman	90.00	45.00	27.00
22	Smoky Joe Wood	90.00	45.00	27.00
23	Charles Comiskey	300.00	150.00	90.00
24	George Mullen (Mullin)	90.00	45.00	27.00
25	Mike Simon	90.00	45.00	27.00
26	Jim Scott	90.00	45.00	27.00
27	Bill Carrigan	90.00	45.00	27.00
28	Jack Barry	90.00	45.00	27.00
29	Vean Gregg	90.00	45.00	27.00
30	Ty Cobb	2200.00	1000.00	625.00
31	Heinie Wagner	90.00	45.00	27.00
32	Mordecai Brown	175.00	87.00	52.00
33	Amos Strunk	90.00	45.00	27.00
34	Ira Thomas	90.00	45.00	27.00
35	Harry Hooper	275.00	150.00	80.00
36	Ed Walsh	300.00	150.00	90.00
37	Grover C. Alexander	400.00	160.00	100.00
38	Red Dooin	90.00	45.00	27.00
39	Chick Gandil	90.00	45.00	27.00
40	Jimmy Austin	90.00	45.00	27.00
41	Tommy Leach	90.00	45.00	27.00
42	Al Bridwell	90.00	45.00	27.00

		NR MT	EX	VG
43	Rube Marquard	275.00	150.00	80.00
44	Jeff Tesreau	90.00	45.00	27.00
45	Fred Luderus	90.00	45.00	27.00
46	Bob Groom	90.00	45.00	27.00
47	Josh Devore	90.00	45.00	27.00
48	Harry Lord	175.00	87.00	52.00
49	Dots Miller	90.00	45.00	27.00
50	John Hummell (Hummel)	90.00	45.00	27.00
51	Nap Rucker	90.00	45.00	27.00
52	Zach Wheat	275.00	150.00	80.00
53	Otto Miller	90.00	45.00	27.00
54	Marty O'Toole	90.00	45.00	27.00
55	Dick Hoblitzel (Hoblitzell)	90.00	45.00	27.00
56	Clyde Milan	90.00	45.00	27.00
57	Walter Johnson	875.00	425.00	250.00
58	Wally Schang	90.00	45.00	27.00
59	Doc Gessler	90.00	45.00	27.00
60	Rollie Zeider	250.00	125.00	75.00
61	Ray Schalk	200.00	100.00	60.00
62	Jay Cashion	250.00	125.00	75.00
63	Babe Adams	90.00	45.00	27.00
64	Jimmy Archer	90.00	45.00	27.00
65	Tris Speaker	425.00	170.00	106.00
66	Nap Lajoie	500.00	200.00	125.00
67	Doc Crandall	90.00	45.00	27.00
68	Honus Wagner	1000.00	500.00	300.00
69	John McGraw	400.00	200.00	125.00
70	Fred Clarke	200.00	100.00	60.00
71	Chief Meyers	90.00	45.00	27.00
72	Joe Boehling	90.00	45.00	27.00
73	Max Carey	200.00	100.00	60.00
74	Frank Owens	90.00	45.00	27.00
75	Miller Huggins	175.00	87.00	52.00
76	Claude Hendrix	90.00	45.00	27.00
77	Hughie Jennings	275.00	150.00	80.00
78	Fred Merkle	90.00	45.00	27.00
79	Ping Bodie	90.00	45.00	27.00
80	Ed Reulbach	90.00	45.00	27.00
81	Jim Delehanty (Delahanty)	90.00	45.00	27.00
82	Gavvy Cravath	90.00	45.00	27.00
83	Russ Ford	90.00	45.00	27.00
84	Elmer Knetzer	90.00	45.00	27.00
85	Buck Herzog	90.00	45.00	27.00
86	Burt Shotten	90.00	45.00	27.00
87	Hick Cady	90.00	45.00	27.00
88	Christy Mathewson	800.00	400.00	250.00
89	Larry Cheney	90.00	45.00	27.00
90	Frank Smith	90.00	45.00	27.00
91	Roger Peckinpaugh	90.00	45.00	27.00
92	Al Demaree	90.00	45.00	27.00
93	Del Pratt	300.00	120.00	75.00
94	Eddie Cicotte	90.00	45.00	27.00
95	Ray Keating	90.00	45.00	27.00
96	Beals Becker	90.00	45.00	27.00
97	Rube Benton	90.00	45.00	27.00
98	Frank Laporte (LaPorte)	90.00	45.00	27.00
99	Frank Chance	700.00	300.00	180.00
100	Tom Seaton	90.00	45.00	27.00
101	Wildfire Schulte	90.00	45.00	27.00
102	Ray Fisher	90.00	45.00	27.00
103	Shoeless Joe Jackson	2000.00	950.00	600.00
104	Vic Saier	90.00	45.00	27.00
105	Jimmy Lavender	90.00	45.00	27.00
106	Joe Birmingham	90.00	45.00	27.00
107	Tom Downey	90.00	45.00	27.00
108	Sherry Magee	90.00	45.00	27.00
109	Fred Blanding	90.00	45.00	27.00
110	Bob Bescher	90.00	45.00	27.00
111	Nixey Callahan	300.00	120.00	75.00
112	Jeff Sweeney	90.00	45.00	27.00
113	George Suggs	90.00	45.00	27.00
114	George Moriarity (Moriarty)	90.00	45.00	27.00
115	Ad Brennan	90.00	45.00	27.00
116	Rollie Zeider	90.00	45.00	27.00
117	Ted Easterly	90.00	45.00	27.00
118	Ed Konetchy	90.00	45.00	27.00
119	George Perring	90.00	45.00	27.00
120	Mickey Doolan	90.00	45.00	27.00
121	Hub Perdue	90.00	45.00	27.00
122	Donie Bush	90.00	45.00	27.00
123	Slim Sallee	90.00	45.00	27.00
124	Earle Moore (Earl)	90.00	45.00	27.00
125	Bert Niehoff	90.00	45.00	27.00
126	Walter Blair	90.00	45.00	27.00
127	Butch Schmidt	90.00	45.00	27.00
128	Steve Evans	90.00	45.00	27.00
129	Ray Caldwell	90.00	45.00	27.00
130	Ivy Wingo	90.00	45.00	27.00
131	George Baumgardner	90.00	45.00	27.00
132	Les Nunamaker	90.00	45.00	27.00
133	Branch Rickey	300.00	120.00	75.00

		NR MT	EX	VG
134	Armando Marsans	90.00	45.00	27.00
135	Bill Killifer (Killefer)	90.00	45.00	27.00
136	Rabbit Maranville	250.00	125.00	70.00
137	Bill Rariden	90.00	45.00	27.00
138	Hank Gowdy	90.00	45.00	27.00
139	Rebel Oakes	90.00	45.00	27.00
140	Danny Murphy	90.00	45.00	27.00
141	Cy Barger	90.00	45.00	27.00
142	Gene Packard	90.00	45.00	27.00
143	Jake Daubert	90.00	45.00	27.00
144	Jimmy Walsh	175.00	50.00	25.00

1915 Cracker Jack

The 1915 Cracker Jack set (E145-2) is a re-issue of the 1914 edition with some card additions and deletions, team designation changes, and new poses. A total of 176 cards comprise the set. The deletions involve card #'s 48, 60, 62, 99 and 111. Cards can be distinguished as either 1914 or 1915 by the backs. The advertising on the backs of the 1914 cards call the set complete at 144 pictures, while the 1915 version notes 176 pictures. A complete set and an album were available from the company.

		NR MT	EX	VG
Complete Set:		24000.00	12000.00	7000.
Common Player: 1-144		70.00	35.00	21.00
Common Player: 145-176		70.00	35.00	21.00
1	Otto Knabe	200.00	100.00	60.00
2	Home Run Baker	275.00	150.00	80.00
3	Joe Tinker	275.00	150.00	80.00
4	Larry Doyle	70.00	35.00	21.00
5	Ward Miller	70.00	35.00	21.00
6	Eddie Plank	325.00	175.00	100.00
7	Eddie Collins	275.00	150.00	80.00
8	Rube Oldring	70.00	35.00	21.00
9	Artie Hoffman (Hofman)	70.00	35.00	21.00
10	Stuffy McInnis	70.00	35.00	21.00
11	George Stovall	70.00	35.00	21.00
12	Connie Mack	300.00	120.00	75.00
13	Art Wilson	70.00	35.00	21.00
14	Sam Crawford	250.00	125.00	70.00
15	Reb Russell	70.00	35.00	21.00
16	Howie Camnitz	70.00	35.00	21.00
17	Roger Bresnahan	275.00	150.00	80.00
18	Johnny Evers	250.00	125.00	70.00
19	Chief Bender	165.00	82.00	49.00
20	Cy Falkenberg	70.00	35.00	21.00
21	Heinie Zimmerman	70.00	35.00	21.00
22	Smoky Joe Wood	70.00	35.00	21.00
23	Charles Comiskey	250.00	125.00	70.00
24	George Mullen (Mullin)	70.00	35.00	21.00
25	Mike Simon	70.00	35.00	21.00
26	Jim Scott	70.00	35.00	21.00
27	Bill Carrigan	70.00	35.00	21.00
28	Jack Barry	70.00	35.00	21.00
29	Vean Gregg	70.00	35.00	21.00
30	Ty Cobb	2000.00	900.00	525.00
31	Heinie Wagner	70.00	35.00	21.00
32	Mordecai Brown	140.00	70.00	42.00
33	Amos Strunk	70.00	35.00	21.00
34	Ira Thomas	70.00	35.00	21.00
35	Harry Hooper	250.00	125.00	70.00
36	Ed Walsh	250.00	125.00	70.00
37	Grover C. Alexander	375.00	150.00	94.00

		NR MT	EX	VG
38	Red Dooin	70.00	35.00	21.00
39	Chick Gandil	70.00	35.00	21.00
40	Jimmy Austin	70.00	35.00	21.00
41	Tommy Leach	70.00	35.00	21.00
42	Al Bridwell	70.00	35.00	21.00
43	Rube Marquard	250.00	125.00	70.00
44	Jeff Tesreau	70.00	35.00	21.00
45	Fred Luderus	70.00	35.00	21.00
46	Bob Groom	70.00	35.00	21.00
47	Josh Devore	70.00	35.00	21.00
48	Steve O'Neill	70.00	35.00	21.00
49	Dots Miller	70.00	35.00	21.00
50	John Hummell (Hummel)	70.00	35.00	21.00
51	Nap Rucker	70.00	35.00	21.00
52	Zach Wheat	250.00	125.00	70.00
53	Otto Miller	70.00	35.00	21.00
54	Marty O'Toole	70.00	35.00	21.00
55	Dick Hoblitzel (Hoblitzell)	70.00	35.00	21.00
56	Clyde Milan	70.00	35.00	21.00
57	Walter Johnson	700.00	300.00	180.00
58	Wally Schang	70.00	35.00	21.00
59	Doc Gessler	70.00	35.00	21.00
60	Oscar Dugey	70.00	35.00	21.00
61	Ray Schalk	200.00	100.00	60.00
62	Willie Mitchell	70.00	35.00	21.00
63	Babe Adams	70.00	35.00	21.00
64	Jimmy Archer	70.00	35.00	21.00
65	Tris Speaker	400.00	160.00	100.00
66	Nap Lajoie	500.00	200.00	125.00
67	Doc Crandall	70.00	35.00	21.00
68	Honus Wagner	900.00	450.00	275.00
69	John McGraw	350.00	175.00	100.00
70	Fred Clarke	200.00	100.00	60.00
71	Chief Meyers	70.00	35.00	21.00
72	Joe Boehling	70.00	35.00	21.00
73	Max Carey	200.00	100.00	60.00
74	Frank Owens	70.00	35.00	21.00
75	Miller Huggins	250.00	125.00	70.00
76	Claude Hendrix	70.00	35.00	21.00
77	Hughie Jennings	250.00	125.00	70.00
78	Fred Merkle	70.00	35.00	21.00
79	Ping Bodie	70.00	35.00	21.00
80	Ed Reulbach	70.00	35.00	21.00
81	Jim Delehanty (Delahanty)	70.00	35.00	21.00
82	Gavvy Cravath	70.00	35.00	21.00
83	Russ Ford	70.00	35.00	21.00
84	Elmer Knetzer	70.00	35.00	21.00
85	Buck Herzog	70.00	35.00	21.00
86	Burt Shotten	70.00	35.00	21.00
87	Hick Cady	70.00	35.00	21.00
88	Christy Mathewson	700.00	300.00	180.00
89	Larry Cheney	70.00	35.00	21.00
90	Frank Smith	70.00	35.00	21.00
91	Roger Peckinpaugh	70.00	35.00	21.00
92	Al Demaree	70.00	35.00	21.00
93	Del Pratt	70.00	35.00	21.00
94	Eddie Cicotte	70.00	35.00	21.00
95	Ray Keating	70.00	35.00	21.00
96	Beals Becker	70.00	35.00	21.00
97	Rube Benton	70.00	35.00	21.00
98	Frank Laporte (LaPorte)	70.00	35.00	21.00
99	Hal Chase	250.00	100.00	63.00
100	Tom Seaton	70.00	35.00	21.00
101	Wildfire Schulte	70.00	35.00	21.00
102	Ray Fisher	70.00	35.00	21.00
103	Shoeless Joe Jackson	2000.00	900.00	525.00
104	Vic Saier	70.00	35.00	21.00
105	Jimmy Lavender	70.00	35.00	21.00
106	Joe Birmingham	70.00	35.00	21.00
107	Tom Downey	70.00	35.00	21.00
108	Sherry Magee	70.00	35.00	21.00
109	Fred Blanding	70.00	35.00	21.00
110	Bob Bescher	70.00	35.00	21.00
111	Herbie Moran	70.00	35.00	21.00
112	Jeff Sweeney	70.00	35.00	21.00
113	George Suggs	70.00	35.00	21.00
114	George Moriarity (Moriarty)	70.00	35.00	21.00
115	Ad Brennan	70.00	35.00	21.00
116	Rollie Zeider	70.00	35.00	21.00
117	Ted Easterly	70.00	35.00	21.00
118	Ed Konetchy	70.00	35.00	21.00
119	George Perring	70.00	35.00	21.00
120	Mickey Doolan	70.00	35.00	21.00
121	Hub Perdue	70.00	35.00	21.00
122	Donie Bush	70.00	35.00	21.00
123	Slim Sallee	70.00	35.00	21.00
124	Earle Moore (Earl)	70.00	35.00	21.00
125	Bert Niehoff	70.00	35.00	21.00
126	Walter Blair	70.00	35.00	21.00
127	Butch Schmidt	70.00	35.00	21.00
128	Steve Evans	70.00	35.00	21.00

		NR MT	EX	VG
129	Ray Caldwell	70.00	35.00	21.00
130	Ivy Wingo	70.00	35.00	21.00
131	George Baumgardner	70.00	35.00	21.00
132	Les Nunamaker	70.00	35.00	21.00
133	Branch Rickey	300.00	120.00	75.00
134	Armando Marsans	70.00	35.00	21.00
135	Bill Killifer (Killefer)	70.00	35.00	21.00
136	Rabbit Maranville	200.00	100.00	60.00
137	Bill Rariden	70.00	35.00	21.00
138	Hank Gowdy	70.00	35.00	21.00
139	Rebel Oakes	70.00	35.00	21.00
140	Danny Murphy	70.00	35.00	21.00
141	Cy Barger	70.00	35.00	21.00
142	Gene Packard	70.00	35.00	21.00
143	Jake Daubert	70.00	35.00	21.00
144	Jimmy Walsh	70.00	35.00	21.00
145	Ted Cather	70.00	35.00	21.00
146	Lefty Tyler	70.00	35.00	21.00
147	Lee Magee	70.00	35.00	21.00
148	Owen Wilson	70.00	35.00	21.00
149	Hal Janvrin	70.00	35.00	21.00
150	Doc Johnston	70.00	35.00	21.00
151	Possum Whitted	70.00	35.00	21.00
152	George McQuillen (McQuillan)	70.00	35.00	21.00
153	Bill James	70.00	35.00	21.00
154	Dick Rudolph	70.00	35.00	21.00
155	Joe Connolly	70.00	35.00	21.00
156	Jean Dubuc	70.00	35.00	21.00
157	George Kaiserling	70.00	35.00	21.00
158	Fritz Maisel	70.00	35.00	21.00
159	Heinie Groh	70.00	35.00	21.00
160	Benny Kauff	70.00	35.00	21.00
161	Edd Rousch (Roush)	200.00	100.00	60.00
162	George Stallings	70.00	35.00	21.00
163	Bert Whaling	70.00	35.00	21.00
164	Bob Shawkey	70.00	35.00	21.00
165	Eddie Murphy	70.00	35.00	21.00
166	Bullet Joe Bush	100.00	50.00	30.00
167	Clark Griffith	250.00	125.00	70.00
168	Vin Campbell	70.00	35.00	21.00
169	Ray Collins	70.00	35.00	21.00
170	Hans Lobert	70.00	35.00	21.00
171	Earl Hamilton	70.00	35.00	21.00
172	Erskine Mayer	70.00	35.00	21.00
173	Tilly Walker	70.00	35.00	21.00
174	Bobby Veach	70.00	35.00	21.00
175	Joe Benz	100.00	45.00	27.00
176	Hippo Vaughn	200.00	80.00	50.00

1982 Cracker Jack

The Topps-produced 1982 Cracker Jack set was issued to promote the first "Old Timers Baseball Classic," held in Washington, D.C. Sixteen cards comprise the set which was issued in two sheets of eight cards, plus an advertising card located in the center. The individual cards are 2-1/2" by 3-1/2" in size with the complete sheets measuring 7-1/2" by 10-1/2". Card #'s 1-8 feature American League players with #'s 9-16 being former National League stars. The card fronts feature a full-color photo inside a Cracker Jack border. The backs contain the Cracker Jack logo plus a short player biography and his lifetime pitching or batting record. Complete sheets were available through a write-in offer.

		MT	NR MT	EX
Complete Panel Set:		8.00	6.00	3.25
Complete Singles Set:		3.50	2.75	1.50
Common Single Player:		.05	.04	.02
Panel		5.00	3.75	2.00
1	Larry Doby	.05	.04	.02
2	Bob Feller	.10	.08	.04
3	Whitey Ford	.10	.08	.04
4	Al Kaline	.10	.08	.04
5	Harmon Killebrew	.10	.08	.04
6	Mickey Mantle	1.00	.70	.40
7	Tony Oliva	.05	.04	.02
8	Brooks Robinson	.10	.08	.04
Panel		3.50	2.75	1.50
9	Hank Aaron	.20	.15	.08
10	Ernie Banks	.10	.08	.04
11	Ralph Kiner	.10	.08	.04
12	Eddie Mathews	.10	.08	.04
13	Willie Mays	.20	.15	.08
14	Robin Roberts	.10	.08	.04
15	Duke Snider	.10	.08	.04
16	Warren Spahn	.10	.08	.04
-----	Advertising Card	.02	.02	.01

1954 Dan-Dee Potato Chips

Issued in bags of potato chips, the cards in this 29-card set are commonly found with grease stains despite their waxed surface. The unnumbered cards, which measure 2-1/2" by 3-5/8", feature full-color photos. The card backs contain player statistical and biographical information. The set consists mostly of players from the Indians and Pirates. Photos of the Yankees players were also used for the Briggs Meats and Stahl-Meyer Franks sets. Cooper and Smith are the scarcest cards in the set.

		NR MT	EX	VG
Complete Set		4000.00	2000.00	1200.
Common Player		60.00	30.00	18.00
(1)	Bob Avila	60.00	30.00	18.00
(2)	Hank Bauer	80.00	40.00	24.00
(3)	Walker Cooper	350.00	175.00	105.00
(4)	Larry Doby	90.00	45.00	27.00
(5)	Luke Easter	60.00	30.00	18.00
(6)	Bob Feller	150.00	75.00	45.00
(7)	Bob Friend	60.00	30.00	18.00
(8)	Mike Garcia	60.00	30.00	18.00
(9)	Sid Gordon	60.00	30.00	18.00
(10)	Jim Hegan	60.00	30.00	18.00
(11)	Gil Hodges	150.00	75.00	45.00
(12)	Art Houtteman	60.00	30.00	18.00
(13)	Monte Irvin	90.00	45.00	27.00
(14)	Paul LaPalm (LaPalme)	60.00	30.00	18.00

		NR MT	EX	VG
(15)	Bob Lemon	110.00	55.00	33.00
(16)	Al Lopez	90.00	45.00	27.00
(17)	Mickey Mantle	1500.00	750.00	450.00
(18)	Dale Mitchell	60.00	30.00	18.00
(19)	Phil Rizzuto	125.00	62.00	37.00
(20)	Curtis Roberts	60.00	30.00	18.00
(21)	Al Rosen	80.00	40.00	24.00
(22)	Red Schoendienst	90.00	45.00	27.00
(23)	Paul Smith	450.00	225.00	135.00
(24)	Duke Snider	225.00	112.00	67.00
(25)	George Strickland	60.00	30.00	18.00
(26)	Max Surkont	60.00	30.00	18.00
(27)	Frank Thomas	125.00	62.00	37.00
(28)	Wally Westlake	60.00	30.00	18.00
(29)	Early Wynn	110.00	55.00	33.00

1987 David Berg Hot Dogs Cubs

Changing sponsors from Gatorade to David Berg Pure Beef Hot Dogs, the Chicago Cubs handed out a 26-card set of baseball cards to fans attending the July 29th game at Wrigley Field. The cards are printed in full-color on white stock and measure 2-7/8" by 4-1/4" in size. The set is numbered by the players' uniform numbers. The card backs contain player personal and statistical information, plus a full-color picture of a David Berg hot dog in a bun with all the garnishings. The set marked the sixth consecutive year the Cubs held a baseball card giveaway promotion.

		MT	NR MT	EX
Complete Set:		8.00	6.00	3.25
Common Player:		.10	.08	.04
1	Dave Martinez	.50	.40	.20
4	Gene Michael	.10	.08	.04
6	Keith Moreland	.30	.25	.12
7	Jody Davis	.30	.25	.12
8	Andre Dawson	1.00	.70	.40
10	Leon Durham	.30	.25	.12
11	Jim Sundberg	.10	.08	.04
12	Shawon Dunston	.60	.45	.25
19	Manny Trillo	.10	.08	.04
20	Bob Dernier	.10	.08	.04
21	Scott Sanderson	.10	.08	.04
22	Jerry Mumphrey	.10	.08	.04
23	Ryne Sandberg	2.00	1.50	.80
24	Brian Dayett	.10	.08	.04
29	Chico Walker	.10	.08	.04
31	Greg Maddux	.70	.50	.30
33	Frank DiPino	.10	.08	.04
34	Steve Trout	.20	.15	.08
36	Gary Matthews	.20	.15	.08
37	Ed Lynch	.10	.08	.04
39	Ron Davis	.10	.08	.04
40	Rick Sutcliffe	.70	.50	.30
46	Lee Smith	.30	.25	.12
47	Dickie Noles	.10	.08	.04
49	Jamie Moyer	.20	.15	.08
-----	The Coaching Staff (Johnny Oates, Jim Snyder, Herm Starrette, John Vukovich, Billy Williams)	.15	.11	.06

1988 David Berg Hot Dogs Cubs

This oversized (2-7/8" by 4-1/2") set of 26 cards was distributed to fans at Wrigley Field on August 24th. The set includes cards for the manager and coaching staff, as well as players. Full-color action photos are framed in red and blue on a white background. The backs feature small black and white player close-ups, colorful team logos, statistics and sponsor logos (David Berg Hot Dogs and Venture Store Restaurants). The numbers in the following checklist refer to players' uniforms.

		MT	NR MT	EX
Complete Set:		9.00	6.75	3.50
Common Player:		.10	.08	.04
2	Vance Law	.15	.11	.06
4	Don Zimmer	.15	.11	.06
7	Jody Davis	.30	.25	.12
8	Andre Dawson	1.00	.70	.40
9	Damon Berryhill	.80	.60	.30
12	Shawon Dunston	.60	.45	.25
17	Mark Grace	3.50	2.75	1.50
18	Angel Salazar	.10	.08	.04
19	Manny Trillo	.10	.08	.04
21	Scott Sanderson	.10	.08	.04
22	Jerry Mumphrey	.10	.08	.04
23	Ryne Sandberg	2.25	1.75	.90
24	Gary Varsho	.40	.30	.15
25	Rafael Palmeiro	1.25	.90	.50
28	Mitch Webster	.15	.11	.06
30	Darrin Jackson	.40	.30	.15
31	Greg Maddux	.70	.50	.30
32	Calvin Schiraldi	.20	.15	.08
33	Frank DiPino	.10	.08	.04
37	Pat Perry	.10	.08	.04
40	Rick Sutcliffe	.70	.50	.30
41	Jeff Pico	.50	.40	.20
45	Al Nipper	.10	.08	.04
49	Jamie Moyer	.20	.15	.08
50	Les Lancaster	.15	.11	.06
54	Rich Gossage	.70	.50	.30
-----	Joe Altobelli, Chuck Cottier, Larry Cox, Jose Martinez, Dick Pole	.10	.08	.04

1933 Delong

The DeLong Gum Company of Boston, Mass. was among the first to sell baseball cards with gum. It issued a set of 24 cards in 1933, the same year the Goudey Gum Co. issued its premiere set, making both companies pioneers in the field. The DeLong cards measure 2" by 3" and feature black and white player photos on a color background. The photos show the players in various action poses and position them in the middle of a miniature stadium setting so that they appear to be giant in size. Most of the cards in the set are vertically designed, but a few are horizontal. The backs of the cards, written by Austen Lake, editor of the Boston Transcript, contain a series of sports tips to help youngsters become better ballplayers. Lake later wrote the tips that appeared on the backs of the Diamond Stars cards issued by National Chicle from 1934-1936. The ACC designation for this set is R333. The checklist below gives the players' names exactly as they appear on the fronts of the cards.

		NR MT	EX	VG
Complete Set:		8000.00	4000.00	2500.
Common Player:		125.00	62.00	37.00
1	"Marty" McManus	150.00	75.00	45.00
2	Al Simmons	200.00	100.00	60.00
3	Oscar Melillo	125.00	62.00	37.00
4	William (Bill) Terry	250.00	125.00	75.00
5	Charlie Gehringer	250.00	125.00	75.00
6	Gordon (Mickey) Cochrane	250.00	125.00	75.00
7	Lou Gehrig	3000.00	1500.00	800.00
8	Hazen S. (Kiki) Cuyler	175.00	87.00	52.00
9	Bill Urbanski	125.00	62.00	37.00
10	Frank J. (Lefty) O'Doul	150.00	75.00	45.00
11	Freddie Lindstrom	175.00	87.00	52.00
12	Harold (Pie) Traynor	200.00	100.00	60.00
13	"Rabbit" Maranville	175.00	87.00	52.00
14	Vernon "Lefty" Gomez	250.00	125.00	75.00
15	Riggs Stephenson	125.00	62.00	37.00
16	Lon Warneke	125.00	62.00	37.00
17	Pepper Martin	150.00	75.00	45.00
18	Jimmy Dykes	125.00	62.00	37.00
19	Chick Hafey	175.00	87.00	52.00
20	Joe Vosmik	115.00	57.00	34.00
21	Jimmy Foxx	600.00	300.00	175.00
22	Charles (Chuck) Klein	175.00	87.00	52.00
23	Robert (Lefty) Grove	300.00	150.00	90.00
24	"Goose" Goslin	175.00	87.00	52.00

1900 Diamond Stars

Issued from 1934 through 1936, the Diamond Stars set (ACC designation R327) consists of 108 cards. Produced by National Chicle, the numbered cards measure 2-3/8" by 2-7/8" and are color art reproductions of actual photographs. The year of issue can be determined by the player's statistics found on the reverse of the card. The backs feature either a player biography or a baseball playing tip. Some cards can be found with either green or blue printing on the backs. Artwork for 12 cards that were never issued was uncovered several years ago and a set featuring those cards was subsequently made available to the collecting public. The complete set price does not include the higher priced variations.

		NR MT	EX	VG
Complete Set:		18000.00	9000.00	5500.00
Common Player: 1-31		90.00	45.00	27.00
Common Player: 32-72		70.00	35.00	21.00
Common Player: 73-84		75.00	38.00	23.00
Common Player: 85-96		125.00	62.00	37.00
Common Player: 97-108		300.00	150.00	90.00
1a	"Lefty" Grove (1934 green back)	1300.00	650.00	390.00
1b	"Lefty" Grove (1935 green back)	1300.00	650.00	390.00
2a	Al Simmons (1934 green back)	200.00	100.00	60.00
2b	Al Simmons (1935 green back)	200.00	100.00	60.00
2c	Al Simmons (1936 blue back)	225.00	112.00	67.00
3a	"Rabbit" Maranville (1934 green back)	70.00	35.00	21.00
3b	"Rabbit" Maranville (1935 green back)	70.00	35.00	21.00
4a	"Buddy" Myer (1934 green back)	90.00	45.00	27.00
4b	"Buddy" Myer (1935 green back)	90.00	45.00	27.00
4c	"Buddy" Myer (1936 blue back)	90.00	45.00	27.00
5a	Tom Bridges (1934 green back)	90.00	45.00	27.00
5b	Tom Bridges (1935 green back)	90.00	45.00	27.00
5c	Tom Bridges (1936 blue back)	90.00	45.00	27.00
6a	Max Bishop (1934 green back)	90.00	45.00	27.00
6b	Max Bishop (1935 green back)	90.00	45.00	27.00
7a	Lew Fonseca (1934 green back)	90.00	45.00	27.00
7b	Lew Fonseca (1935 green back)	90.00	45.00	27.00
8a	Joe Vosmik (1934 green back)	90.00	45.00	27.00
8b	Joe Vosmik (1935 green back)	90.00	45.00	27.00
8c	Joe Vosmik (1936 blue back)	90.00	45.00	27.00
9a	"Mickey" Cochrane (1934 green back)	225.00	112.00	67.00
9b	"Mickey" Cochrane (1935 green back)	225.00	112.00	67.00
9c	"Mickey" Cochrane (1936 blue back)	225.00	112.00	67.00
10a	Roy Mahaffey (1934 green back)	90.00	45.00	27.00
10b	Roy Mahaffey (1935 green back)	90.00	45.00	27.00
10c	Roy Mahaffey (1936 blue back)	90.00	45.00	27.00
11a	Bill Dickey (1934 green back)	275.00	137.00	82.00
11b	Bill Dickey (1935 green back)	275.00	137.00	82.00
12a	"Dixie" Walker (1934 green back)	90.00	45.00	27.00
12b	"Dixie" Walker (1935 green back)	90.00	45.00	27.00
12c	"Dixie" Walker (1936 blue back)	90.00	45.00	27.00
13a	George Blaeholder (1934 green back)	90.00	45.00	27.00
13b	George Blaeholder (1935 green back)	90.00	45.00	27.00
14a	Bill Terry (1934 green back)	110.00	55.00	33.00
14b	Bill Terry (1935 green back)	110.00	55.00	33.00
15a	Dick Bartell (1934 green back)	90.00	45.00	27.00
15b	Dick Bartell (1935 green back)	90.00	45.00	27.00
16a	Lloyd Waner (1934 green back)	125.00	62.00	37.00
16b	Lloyd Waner (1935 green back)	125.00	62.00	37.00
16c	Lloyd Waner (1936 blue back)	125.00	62.00	37.00
17a	Frankie Frisch (1934 green back)	110.00	55.00	33.00
17b	Frankie Frisch (1935 green back)	110.00	55.00	33.00
18a	"Chick" Hafey (1934 green back)	70.00	35.00	21.00
18b	"Chick" Hafey (1935 green back)	70.00	35.00	21.00
19a	Van Mungo (1934 green back)	90.00	45.00	27.00
19b	Van Mungo (1935 green back)	90.00	45.00	27.00
20a	"Shanty" Hogan (1934 green back)	90.00	45.00	27.00
20b	"Shanty" Hogan (1935 green back)	90.00	45.00	27.00
21a	Johnny Vergez (1934 green back)	90.00	45.00	27.00
21b	Johnny Vergez (1935 green back)	90.00	45.00	27.00
22a	Jimmy Wilson (1934 green back)	90.00	45.00	27.00
22b	Jimmy Wilson (1935 green back)	90.00	45.00	27.00
22c	Jimmy Wilson (1936 blue back)	90.00	45.00	27.00
23a	Bill Hallahan (1934 green back)	90.00	45.00	27.00
23b	Bill Hallahan (1935 green back)	90.00	45.00	27.00
24a	"Sparky" Adams (1934 green back)	90.00	45.00	27.00

		NR MT	EX	VG
24b	"Sparky" Adams (1935 green back)			
		90.00	45.00	27.00
25	Walter Berger	90.00	45.00	27.00
26a	"Pepper" Martin (1935 green back)			
		90.00	45.00	27.00
26b	"Pepper" Martin (1936 blue back)			
		90.00	45.00	27.00
27	"Pie" Traynor	225.00	112.00	67.00
28	"Al" Lopez	225.00	112.00	67.00
29	Robert Rolfe	90.00	45.00	27.00
30a	"Heinie" Manush (1935 green back)			
		125.00	62.00	37.00
30b	"Heinie" Manush (1936 blue back)			
		70.00	35.00	21.00
31a	"Kiki" Cuyler (1935 green back)			
		125.00	62.00	37.00
31b	"Kiki" Cuyler (1936 blue back)	125.00	62.00	37.00
32	Sam Rice	125.00	62.00	37.00
33	"Schoolboy" Rowe	90.00	45.00	27.00
34	Stanley Hack	90.00	45.00	27.00
35	Earle Averill	125.00	62.00	37.00
36a	Earnie Lombardi	125.00	62.00	37.00
36b	Ernie Lombardi	225.00	112.00	67.00
37	"Billie" Urbanski	70.00	35.00	21.00
38	Ben Chapman	90.00	45.00	27.00
39	Carl Hubbell	110.00	55.00	33.00
40	"Blondy" Ryan	70.00	35.00	21.00
41	Harvey Hendrick	70.00	35.00	21.00
42	Jimmy Dykes	90.00	45.00	27.00
43	Ted Lyons	65.00	32.00	19.50
44	Rogers Hornsby	250.00	125.00	75.00
45	"Jo Jo" White	70.00	35.00	21.00
46	"Red" Lucas	70.00	35.00	21.00
47	Cliff Bolton	70.00	35.00	21.00
48	"Rick" Ferrell	125.00	62.00	37.00
49	"Buck" Jordan	70.00	35.00	21.00
50	"Mel" Ott	275.00	137.00	82.00
51	John Whitehead	70.00	35.00	21.00
52	George Stainback	70.00	35.00	21.00
53	Oscar Melillo	70.00	35.00	21.00
54a	"Hank" Greenburg	200.00	150.00	80.00
54b	"Hank" Greenberg	250.00	125.00	75.00
55	Tony Cuccinello	70.00	35.00	21.00
56	"Gus" Suhr	70.00	35.00	21.00
57	"Cy" Blanton	70.00	35.00	21.00
58	Glenn Myatt	70.00	35.00	21.00
59	Jim Bottomley	125.00	62.00	37.00
60	Charley "Red" Ruffing	70.00	35.00	21.00
61	"Billie" Werber	70.00	35.00	21.00
62	Fred M. Frankhouse	70.00	35.00	21.00
63	"Stonewall" Jackson	125.00	62.00	37.00
64	Jimmie Foxx	250.00	200.00	100.00
65	"Zeke" Bonura	70.00	35.00	21.00
66	"Ducky" Medwick	70.00	35.00	21.00
67	Marvin Owen	70.00	35.00	21.00
68	"Sam" Leslie	70.00	35.00	21.00
69	Earl Grace	70.00	35.00	21.00
70	"Hal" Trosky	70.00	35.00	21.00
71	"Ossie" Bluege	70.00	35.00	21.00
72	"Tony" Piet	70.00	35.00	21.00
73a	"Fritz" Ostermueller (1935 green back)			
		75.00	38.00	23.00
73b	"Fritz" Ostermueller (1935 blue back)			
		75.00	38.00	23.00
73c	"Fritz" Ostermueller (1936 blue back)			
		75.00	38.00	23.00
74a	Tony Lazzeri (1935 green back)			
		125.00	62.00	37.00
74b	Tony Lazzeri (1935 blue back)	125.00	62.00	37.00
74c	Tony Lazzeri (1936 blue back)	125.00	62.00	37.00
75a	Irving Burns (1935 green back)	75.00	38.00	23.00
75b	Irving Burns (1935 blue back)	75.00	38.00	23.00
75c	Irving Burns (1936 blue back)	75.00	38.00	23.00
76a	Bill Rogell (1935 green back)	75.00	38.00	23.00
76b	Bill Rogell (1935 blue back)	75.00	38.00	23.00
76c	Bill Rogell (1936 blue back)	75.00	38.00	23.00
77a	Charlie Gehringer (1935 green back)			
		75.00	38.00	23.00
77b	Charlie Gehringer (1935 blue back)			
		75.00	38.00	23.00
77c	Charlie Gehringer (1936 blue back)			
		75.00	38.00	23.00
78a	Joe Kuhel (1935 green back)	75.00	38.00	23.00
78b	Joe Kuhel (1935 blue back)	75.00	38.00	23.00
78c	Joe Kuhel (1936 blue back)	75.00	38.00	23.00
79a	Willis Hudlin (1935 green back)	75.00	38.00	23.00
79b	Willis Hudlin (1935 blue back)	75.00	38.00	23.00
79c	Willis Hudlin (1936 blue back)	75.00	38.00	23.00
80a	Louis Chiozza (1935 green back)			
		75.00	38.00	23.00
80b	Louis Chiozza (1935 blue back)	75.00	38.00	23.00

		NR MT	EX	VG
80c	Louis Chiozza (1936 blue back)	75.00	38.00	23.00
81a	Bill DeLancey (1935 green back)	75.00	38.00	23.00
81b	Bill DeLancey (1935 blue back)	75.00	38.00	23.00
81c	Bill DeLancey (1936 blue back)	75.00	38.00	23.00
82a	John Babich (1935 green back)	75.00	38.00	23.00
82b	John Babich (1935 blue back)	75.00	38.00	23.00
82c	John Babich (1936 blue back)	75.00	38.00	23.00
83a	Paul Waner (1935 green back)	200.00	100.00	60.00
83b	Paul Waner (1935 blue back)	200.00	100.00	60.00
83c	Paul Waner (1936 blue back)	200.00	100.00	60.00
84a	Sam Byrd (1935 green back)	75.00	38.00	23.00
84b	Sam Byrd (1935 blue back)	75.00	38.00	23.00
84c	Sam Byrd (1936 blue back)	75.00	38.00	23.00
85	Julius Solters	125.00	62.00	37.00
86	Frank Crosetti	200.00	100.00	60.00
87	Steve O'Neil (O'Neill)	125.00	62.00	37.00
88	Geo. Selkirk	70.00	35.00	21.00
89	Joe Stripp	125.00	62.00	37.00
90	Ray Hayworth	125.00	62.00	37.00
91	Bucky Harris	70.00	35.00	21.00
92	Ethan Allen	125.00	62.00	37.00
93	Alvin Crowder	125.00	62.00	37.00
94	Wes Ferrell	125.00	62.00	37.00
95	Luke Appling	275.00	137.00	82.00
96	Lew Riggs	125.00	62.00	37.00
97	"Al" Lopez	225.00	112.00	67.00
98	"Schoolboy" Rowe	300.00	150.00	90.00
99	"Pie" Traynor	600.00	300.00	180.00
100	Earle Averill (Earl)	275.00	137.00	82.00
101	Dick Bartell	300.00	150.00	90.00
102	Van Mungo	300.00	150.00	90.00
103	Bill Dickey	475.00	225.00	140.00
104	Robert Rolfe	300.00	150.00	90.00
105	"Ernie" Lombardi	225.00	112.00	67.00
106	"Red" Lucas	300.00	150.00	90.00
107	Stanley Hack	300.00	150.00	90.00
108	Walter Berger	225.00	85.00	48.00

1988 Domino's Pizza Tigers

Domino's Pizza produced a 28-card set commemorating the 20th anniversary of the 1968 World Champion Detroit Tigers. The cards were given away at an Old Timers Game at Tiger Stadium in 1988. The cards, which measure 2-1/2" by 3-1/2", feature black and white photos semi-surrounded by a two-stripe band. The stripes on the card's left side are the same color (red and light blue) as the Domino's Pizza logo in the upper corner. The stripes on the card's right side match the colors of the Tigers logo (red and dark blue). The backs of all the cards (except for Ernie Harwell) contain a brief summary of the Tigers' 1968 season. Located at the bottom on the card backs are the players' major league records through 1968 plus their 1968 World Series statistics.

		MT	NR MT	EX
Complete Set:		11.00	8.25	4.50
Common Player:		.20	.15	.08
(1)	Gates Brown	.30	.25	.12
(2)	Norm Cash	.90	.70	.35
(3)	Wayne Comer	.20	.15	.08
(4)	Pat Dobson	.20	.15	.08
(5)	Bill Freehan	.60	.45	.25
(6)	John Hiller	.30	.25	.12
(7)	Ernie Harwell (announcer)	.20	.15	.08

		MT	NR MT	EX
(8)	Willie Horton	.60	.45	.25
(9)	Al Kaline	1.50	1.25	.60
(10)	Fred Lasher	.20	.15	.08
(11)	Mickey Lolich	.90	.70	.35
(12)	Tom Matchick	.20	.15	.08
(13)	Ed Mathews	.90	.70	.35
(14)	Dick McAuliff (McAuliffe)	.40	.30	.15
(15)	Denny McLain	1.00	.70	.40
(16)	Don McMahon	.20	.15	.08
(17)	Jim Northrup	.40	.30	.15
(18)	Ray Oyler	.20	.15	.08
(19)	Daryl Patterson	.20	.15	.08
(20)	Jim Price	.20	.15	.08
(21)	Joe Sparma	.20	.15	.08
(22)	Mickey Stanley	.40	.30	.15
(23)	Dick Tracewski	.20	.15	.08
(24)	Jon Warden	.20	.15	.08
(25)	Don Wert	.20	.15	.08
(26)	Earl Wilson	.20	.15	.08
(27)	Header Card	.20	.15	.08
(28)	Coupon Card	.20	.15	.08

1981 Donruss

TOM SEAVER PITCHER

The Donruss Co. of Memphis, Tenn., produced its premiere baseball card issue in 1981 in a set that consisted of 600 numbered cards and five unnumbered checklists. The cards, which measure 2-1/2" by 3-1/2", are printed on thin stock. The card fronts contain the Donruss logo plus the year of issue. The card backs are designed on a vertical format and have black print on red and white. The set, entitled "First Edition Collector Series," contains nearly 40 variations, those being first-printing errors that were corrected in a subsequent print run. The cards were issued in gum wax packs, with hobby dealer sales being coordinated by TCMA of Amawalk, N.Y. The complete set price does not include the higher priced variations.

		MT	NR MT	EX
Complete Set:		35.00	27.00	15.00
Common Player:		.06	.05	.02
1	Ozzie Smith	.50	.40	.20
2	Rollie Fingers	.25	.20	.10
3	Rick Wise	.08	.06	.03
4	Gene Richards	.06	.05	.02
5	Alan Trammell	.40	.30	.15
6	Tom Brookens	.08	.06	.03
7a	Duffy Dyer (1980 Avg. .185)	1.00	.70	.40
7b	Duffy Dyer (1980 Avg. 185)	.10	.08	.04
8	Mark Fidrych	.08	.06	.03
9	Dave Rozema	.06	.05	.02
10	Ricky Peters	.06	.05	.02
11	Mike Schmidt	1.50	1.25	.60
12	Willie Stargell	.40	.30	.15
13	Tim Foli	.06	.05	.02
14	Manny Sanguillen	.06	.05	.02
15	Grant Jackson	.06	.05	.02
16	Eddie Solomon	.06	.05	.02
17	Omar Moreno	.06	.05	.02
18	Joe Morgan	.60	.45	.25
19	Rafael Landestoy	.06	.05	.02
20	Bruce Bochy	.06	.05	.02

		MT	NR MT	EX
21	Joe Sambito	.06	.05	.02
22	Manny Trillo	.08	.06	.03
23a	*Dave Smith* (incomplete box around stats)			
		1.00	.70	.40
23b	*Dave Smith* (complete box around stats)			
		.30	.25	.12
24	Terry Puhl	.06	.05	.02
25	Bump Wills	.06	.05	.02
26a	John Ellis (Danny Walton photo - with bat)			
		1.25	.90	.50
26b	John Ellis (John Ellis photo - with glove)			
		.10	.08	.04
27	Jim Kern	.06	.05	.02
28	Richie Zisk	.08	.06	.03
29	John Mayberry	.08	.06	.03
30	Bob Davis	.06	.05	.02
31	Jackson Todd	.06	.05	.02
32	Al Woods	.06	.05	.02
33	Steve Carlton	.80	.60	.30
34	Lee Mazzilli	.08	.06	.03
35	John Stearns	.06	.05	.02
36	Roy Jackson	.06	.05	.02
37	Mike Scott	.70	.50	.30
38	Lamar Johnson	.06	.05	.02
39	Kevin Bell	.06	.05	.02
40	Ed Farmer	.06	.05	.02
41	Ross Baumgarten	.06	.05	.02
42	Leo Sutherland	.06	.05	.02
43	Dan Meyer	.06	.05	.02
44	Ron Reed	.06	.05	.02
45	Mario Mendoza	.06	.05	.02
46	Rick Honeycutt	.06	.05	.02
47	Glenn Abbott	.06	.05	.02
48	Leon Roberts	.06	.05	.02
49	Rod Carew	.60	.45	.25
50	Bert Campaneris	.10	.08	.04
51a	Tom Donahue (incorrect spelling)	1.00	.70	.40
51b	Tom Donohue (Donohue on front)	.10	.08	.04
52	Dave Frost	.06	.05	.02
53	Ed Halicki	.06	.05	.02
54	Dan Ford	.06	.05	.02
55	Garry Maddox	.10	.08	.04
56a	Steve Garvey ("Surpassed 25 HR..." on back)			
		1.75	1.25	.70
56b	Steve Garvey ("Surpassed 21 HR..." on back)			
		.60	.45	.25
57	Bill Russell	.08	.06	.03
58	Don Sutton	.30	.25	.12
59	Reggie Smith	.10	.08	.04
60	Rick Monday	.10	.08	.04
61	Ray Knight	.10	.08	.04
62	Johnny Bench	.80	.60	.30
63	Mario Soto	.08	.06	.03
64	Doug Bair	.06	.05	.02
65	George Foster	.20	.15	.08
66	Jeff Burroughs	.08	.06	.03
67	Keith Hernandez	.40	.30	.15
68	Tom Herr	.10	.08	.04
69	Bob Forsch	.08	.06	.03
70	John Fulgham	.06	.05	.02
71a	Bobby Bonds (lifetime HR 986)	1.00	.70	.40
71b	Bobby Bonds (lifetime HR 326)	.15	.11	.06
72a	Rennie Stennett ("...breaking broke leg..." on back)			
		1.00	.70	.40
72b	Rennie Stennett ("...breaking leg..." on back)			
		.10	.08	.04
73	Joe Strain	.06	.05	.02
74	Ed Whitson	.06	.05	.02
75	Tom Griffin	.06	.05	.02
76	Bill North	.06	.05	.02
77	Gene Garber	.06	.05	.02
78	Mike Hargrove	.06	.05	.02
79	Dave Rosello	.06	.05	.02
80	Ron Hassey	.06	.05	.02
81	Sid Monge	.06	.05	.02
82a	*Joe Charboneau* ("For some reason, Phillies..." on back)	1.00	.70	.40
82b	*Joe Charboneau* ("Phillies..." on back)			
		.12	.09	.05
83	Cecil Cooper	.15	.11	.06
84	Sal Bando	.10	.08	.04
85	Moose Haas	.06	.05	.02
86	Mike Caldwell	.06	.05	.02
87a	Larry Hisle ("...Twins with 28 RBI." on back)	1.00	.70	.40
87b	Larry Hisle ("...Twins with 28 HR" on back)			
		.10	.08	.04
88	Luis Gomez	.06	.05	.02
89	Larry Parrish	.10	.08	.04
90	Gary Carter	.40	.30	.15
91	*Bill Gullickson*	.15	.11	.06
92	Fred Norman	.06	.05	.02

		MT	NR MT	EX			MT	NR MT	EX
93	Tommy Hutton	.06	.05	.02	178	Bob Welch	.12	.09	.05
94	Carl Yastrzemski	.80	.60	.30	179	Dusty Baker	.10	.08	.04
95	Glenn Hoffman	.06	.05	.02	180	Rudy Law	.06	.05	.02
96	Dennis Eckersley	.12	.09	.05	181	Dave Concepcion	.15	.11	.06
97a	Tom Burgmeier (Throws: Right)	1.00	.70	.40	182	Johnny Bench	.50	.40	.20
97b	Tom Burgmeier (Throws: Left)	.10	.08	.04	183	Mike LaCoss	.06	.05	.02
98	Win Remmerswaal	.06	.05	.02	184	Ken Griffey	.12	.09	.05
99	Bob Horner	.12	.09	.05	185	Dave Collins	.08	.06	.03
100	George Brett	.80	.60	.30	186	Brian Asselstine	.06	.05	.02
101	Dave Chalk	.06	.05	.02	187	Garry Templeton	.10	.08	.04
102	Dennis Leonard	.08	.06	.03	188	Mike Phillips	.06	.05	.02
103	Renie Martin	.06	.05	.02	189	Pete Vukovich	.08	.06	.03
104	Amos Otis	.08	.06	.03	190	John Urrea	.06	.05	.02
105	Graig Nettles	.15	.11	.06	191	Tony Scott	.06	.05	.02
106	Eric Soderholm	.06	.05	.02	192	Darrell Evans	.12	.09	.05
107	Tommy John	.20	.15	.08	193	Milt May	.06	.05	.02
108	Tom Underwood	.06	.05	.02	194	Bob Knepper	.08	.06	.03
109	Lou Piniella	.12	.09	.05	195	Randy Moffitt	.06	.05	.02
110	Mickey Klutts	.06	.05	.02	196	Larry Herndon	.08	.06	.03
111	Bobby Murcer	.10	.08	.04	197	Rick Camp	.06	.05	.02
112	Eddie Murray	.70	.50	.30	198	Andre Thornton	.10	.08	.04
113	Rick Dempsey	.08	.06	.03	199	Tom Veryzer	.06	.05	.02
114	Scott McGregor	.08	.06	.03	200	Gary Alexander	.06	.05	.02
115	Ken Singleton	.10	.08	.04	201	Rick Waits	.06	.05	.02
116	Gary Roenicke	.06	.05	.02	202	Rick Manning	.06	.05	.02
117	Dave Revering	.06	.05	.02	203	Paul Molitor	.20	.15	.08
118	Mike Norris	.06	.05	.02	204	Jim Gantner	.08	.06	.03
119	Rickey Henderson	2.75	2.00	1.00	205	Paul Mitchell	.06	.05	.02
120	Mike Heath	.06	.05	.02	206	Reggie Cleveland	.06	.05	.02
121	Dave Cash	.06	.05	.02	207	Sixto Lezcano	.06	.05	.02
122	Randy Jones	.08	.06	.03	208	Bruce Benedict	.06	.05	.02
123	Eric Rasmussen	.06	.05	.02	209	Rodney Scott	.06	.05	.02
124	Jerry Mumphrey	.06	.05	.02	210	John Tamargo	.06	.05	.02
125	Richie Hebner	.06	.05	.02	211	Bill Lee	.08	.06	.03
126	Mark Wagner	.06	.05	.02	212	Andre Dawson	.50	.40	.20
127	Jack Morris	.30	.25	.12	213	Rowland Office	.06	.05	.02
128	Dan Petry	.08	.06	.03	214	Carl Yastrzemski	.80	.60	.30
129	Bruce Robbins	.06	.05	.02	215	Jerry Remy	.06	.05	.02
130	Champ Summers	.06	.05	.02	216	Mike Torrez	.08	.06	.03
131a	Pete Rose ("...see card 251." on back)				217	Skip Lockwood	.06	.05	.02
		2.25	1.75	.90	218	Fred Lynn	.20	.15	.08
131b	Pete Rose ("...see card 371." on back)				219	Chris Chambliss	.08	.06	.03
		1.25	.90	.50	220	Willie Aikens	.06	.05	.02
132	Willie Stargell	.40	.30	.15	221	John Wathan	.08	.06	.03
133	Ed Ott	.06	.05	.02	222	Dan Quisenberry	.15	.11	.06
134	Jim Bibby	.06	.05	.02	223	Willie Wilson	.15	.11	.06
135	Bert Blyleven	.12	.09	.05	224	Clint Hurdle	.06	.05	.02
136	Dave Parker	.30	.25	.12	225	Bob Watson	.08	.06	.03
137	Bill Robinson	.06	.05	.02	226	Jim Spencer	.06	.05	.02
138	Enos Cabell	.06	.05	.02	227	Ron Guidry	.25	.20	.10
139	Dave Bergman	.06	.05	.02	228	Reggie Jackson	.70	.50	.30
140	J R Richard	.10	.08	.04	229	Oscar Gamble	.08	.06	.03
141	Ken Forsch	.06	.05	.02	230	Jeff Cox	.06	.05	.02
142	Larry Bowa	.15	.11	.06	231	Luis Tiant	.12	.09	.05
143	Frank LaCorte (photo actually Randy				232	Rich Dauer	.06	.05	.02
	Niemann)	.06	.05	.02	233	Dan Graham	.06	.05	.02
144	Dennis Walling	.06	.05	.02	234	Mike Flanagan	.10	.08	.04
145	Buddy Bell	.12	.09	.05	235	John Lowenstein	.06	.05	.02
146	Ferguson Jenkins	.20	.15	.08	236	Benny Ayala	.06	.05	.02
147	Danny Darwin	.06	.05	.02	237	Wayne Gross	.06	.05	.02
148	John Grubb	.06	.05	.02	238	Rick Langford	.06	.05	.02
149	Alfredo Griffin	.08	.06	.03	239	Tony Armas	.10	.08	.04
150	Jerry Garvin	.06	.05	.02	240a	Bob Lacy (incorrect spelling)	1.00	.70	.40
151	*Paul Mirabella* (FC)	.10	.08	.04	240b	Bob Lacey (correct spelling)	.10	.08	.04
152	Rick Bosetti	.06	.05	.02	241	Gene Tenace	.08	.06	.03
153	Dick Ruthven	.06	.05	.02	242	Bob Shirley	.06	.05	.02
154	Frank Taveras	.06	.05	.02	243	Gary Lucas	.08	.06	.03
155	Craig Swan	.06	.05	.02	244	Jerry Turner	.06	.05	.02
156	*Jeff Reardon*	.70	.50	.30	245	John Wockenfuss	.06	.05	.02
157	Steve Henderson	.06	.05	.02	246	Stan Papi	.06	.05	.02
158	Jim Morrison	.06	.05	.02	247	Milt Wilcox	.06	.05	.02
159	Glenn Borgmann	.06	.05	.02	248	Dan Schatzeder	.06	.05	.02
160	*Lamarr Hoyt (LaMarr)*	.10	.08	.04	249	Steve Kemp	.08	.06	.03
161	Rich Wortham	.06	.05	.02	250	Jim Lentine	.06	.05	.02
162	Thad Bosley	.06	.05	.02	251	Pete Rose	1.00	.70	.40
163	Julio Cruz	.06	.05	.02	252	Bill Madlock	.12	.09	.05
164a	Del Unser (no 3B in stat heads)	1.00	.70	.40	253	Dale Berra	.06	.05	.02
164b	Del Unser (3B in stat heads)	.10	.08	.04	254	Kent Tekulve	.08	.06	.03
165	Jim Anderson	.06	.05	.02	255	Enrique Romo	.06	.05	.02
166	Jim Beattie	.06	.05	.02	256	Mike Easler	.08	.06	.03
167	Shane Rawley	.10	.08	.04	257	Chuck Tanner	.06	.05	.02
168	Joe Simpson	.06	.05	.02	258	Art Howe	.06	.05	.02
169	Rod Carew	.70	.50	.30	259	Alan Ashby	.06	.05	.02
170	Fred Patek	.06	.05	.02	260	Nolan Ryan	1.75	1.25	.70
171	Frank Tanana	.10	.08	.04	261a	Vern Ruhle (Ken Forsch photo - head			
172	Alfredo Martinez	.06	.05	.02		shot)	1.25	.90	.50
173	Chris Knapp	.06	.05	.02	261b	Vern Ruhle (Vern Ruhle photo - waist to			
174	Joe Rudi	.10	.08	.04		head shot)	.10	.08	.04
175	Greg Luzinski	.15	.11	.06	262	Bob Boone	.10	.08	.04
176	Steve Garvey	.50	.40	.20	263	Cesar Cedeno	.12	.09	.05
177	Joe Ferguson	.06	.05	.02	264	Jeff Leonard	.12	.09	.05

#	Name	MT	NR MT	EX
265	Pat Putnam	.06	.05	.02
266	Jon Matlack	.08	.06	.03
267	Dave Rajsich	.06	.05	.02
268	Billy Sample	.06	.05	.02
269	*Damaso Garcia*	.10	.08	.04
270	Tom Buskey	.06	.05	.02
271	Joey McLaughlin	.06	.05	.02
272	Barry Bonnell	.06	.05	.02
273	Tug McGraw	.10	.08	.04
274	Mike Jorgensen	.06	.05	.02
275	Pat Zachry	.06	.05	.02
276	Neil Allen	.08	.06	.03
277	Joel Youngblood	.06	.05	.02
278	Greg Pryor	.06	.05	.02
279	*Britt Burns*	.10	.08	.04
280	*Rich Dotson*	.35	.25	.14
281	Chet Lemon	.08	.06	.03
282	Rusty Kuntz	.06	.05	.02
283	Ted Cox	.06	.05	.02
284	Sparky Lyle	.10	.08	.04
285	Larry Cox	.06	.05	.02
286	Floyd Bannister	.10	.08	.04
287	Byron McLaughlin	.06	.05	.02
288	Rodney Craig	.06	.05	.02
289	Bobby Grich	.10	.08	.04
290	Dickie Thon	.08	.06	.03
291	Mark Clear	.06	.05	.02
292	Dave Lemanczyk	.06	.05	.02
293	Jason Thompson	.06	.05	.02
294	Rick Miller	.06	.05	.02
295	Lonnie Smith	.08	.06	.03
296	Ron Cey	.12	.09	.05
297	Steve Yeager	.06	.05	.02
298	Bobby Castillo	.06	.05	.02
299	Manny Mota	.08	.06	.03
300	Jay Johnstone	.08	.06	.03
301	Dan Driessen	.08	.06	.03
302	Joe Nolan	.06	.05	.02
303	Paul Householder	.06	.05	.02
304	Harry Spilman	.06	.05	.02
305	Cesar Geronimo	.06	.05	.02
306a	Gary Mathews (Mathews on front)	1.25	.90	.50
306b	Gary Matthews (Matthews on front)	.10	.08	.04
307	Ken Reitz	.06	.05	.02
308	Ted Simmons	.12	.09	.05
309	John Littlefield	.06	.05	.02
310	George Frazier	.06	.05	.02
311	Dane Iorg	.06	.05	.02
312	Mike Ivie	.06	.05	.02
313	Dennis Littlejohn	.06	.05	.02
314	Gary LaVelle (Lavelle)	.06	.05	.02
315	Jack Clark	.25	.20	.10
316	Jim Wohlford	.06	.05	.02
317	Rick Matula	.06	.05	.02
318	Toby Harrah	.08	.06	.03
319a	Dwane Kuiper (Dwane on front)	1.00	.70	.40
319b	Duane Kuiper (Duane on front)	.10	.08	.04
320	Len Barker	.08	.06	.03
321	Victor Cruz	.06	.05	.02
322	Dell Alston	.06	.05	.02
323	Robin Yount	.90	.70	.35
324	Charlie Moore	.06	.05	.02
325	Lary Sorensen	.06	.05	.02
326a	Gorman Thomas ("...30-HR mark 4th..." on back)	1.25	.90	.50
326b	Gorman Thomas ("...30-HR mark 3rd..." on back)	.10	.08	.04
327	Bob Rodgers	.08	.06	.03
328	Phil Niekro	.30	.25	.12
329	Chris Speier	.06	.05	.02
330a	Steve Rodgers (Rodgers on front)	1.00	.70	.40
330b	Steve Rogers (Rogers on front)	.10	.08	.04
331	Woodie Fryman	.08	.06	.03
332	Warren Cromartie	.06	.05	.02
333	Jerry White	.06	.05	.02
334	Tony Perez	.20	.15	.08
335	Carlton Fisk	.50	.40	.20
336	Dick Drago	.06	.05	.02
337	Steve Renko	.06	.05	.02
338	Jim Rice	.50	.40	.20
339	Jerry Royster	.06	.05	.02
340	Frank White	.10	.08	.04
341	Jamie Quirk	.06	.05	.02
342a	Paul Spittorff (Spittorff on front)	1.00	.70	.40
342b	Paul Splittorff (Splittorff on front)	.08	.06	.03
343	Marty Pattin	.06	.05	.02
344	Pete LaCock	.06	.05	.02
345	Willie Randolph	.10	.08	.04
346	Rick Cerone	.06	.05	.02
347	Rich Gossage	.20	.15	.08
348	Reggie Jackson	.70	.50	.30
349	Ruppert Jones	.06	.05	.02
350	Dave McKay	.06	.05	.02
351	Yogi Berra	.15	.11	.06
352	Doug Decinces (DeCinces)	.10	.08	.04
353	Jim Palmer	.40	.30	.15
354	Tippy Martinez	.06	.05	.02
355	Al Bumbry	.08	.06	.03
356	Earl Weaver	.10	.08	.04
357a	Bob Picciolo (Bob on front)	1.00	.70	.40
357b	Rob Picciolo (Rob on front)	.10	.08	.04
358	Matt Keough	.06	.05	.02
359	Dwayne Murphy	.08	.06	.03
360	Brian Kingman	.06	.05	.02
361	Bill Fahey	.06	.05	.02
362	Steve Mura	.06	.05	.02
363	Dennis Kinney	.06	.05	.02
364	Dave Winfield	.50	.40	.20
365	Lou Whitaker	.40	.30	.15
366	Lance Parrish	.35	.25	.14
367	Tim Corcoran	.06	.05	.02
368	Pat Underwood	.06	.05	.02
369	Al Cowens	.06	.05	.02
370	Sparky Anderson	.10	.08	.04
371	Pete Rose	1.00	.70	.40
372	Phil Garner	.08	.06	.03
373	Steve Nicosia	.06	.05	.02
374	John Candelaria	.10	.08	.04
375	Don Robinson	.08	.06	.03
376	Lee Lacy	.06	.05	.02
377	John Milner	.06	.05	.02
378	Craig Reynolds	.06	.05	.02
379a	Luis Pujois (Pujois on front)	1.00	.70	.40
379b	Luis Pujols (Pujols on front)	.10	.08	.04
380	Joe Niekro	.12	.09	.05
381	*Joaquin Andujar*	.10	.08	.04
382	*Keith Moreland*	.35	.25	.14
383	Jose Cruz	.12	.09	.05
384	Bill Virdon	.06	.05	.02
385	Jim Sundberg	.08	.06	.03
386	Doc Medich	.06	.05	.02
387	Al Oliver	.15	.11	.06
388	Jim Norris	.06	.05	.02
389	Bob Bailor	.06	.05	.02
390	Ernie Whitt	.08	.06	.03
391	Otto Velez	.06	.05	.02
392	Roy Howell	.06	.05	.02
393	*Bob Walk*	.25	.20	.10
394	Doug Flynn	.06	.05	.02
395	Pete Falcone	.06	.05	.02
396	Tom Hausman	.06	.05	.02
397	Elliott Maddox	.06	.05	.02
398	Mike Squires	.06	.05	.02
399	Marvis Foley	.06	.05	.02
400	Steve Trout	.06	.05	.02
401	Wayne Nordhagen	.06	.05	.02
402	Tony Larussa (LaRussa)	.08	.06	.03
403	Bruce Bochte	.06	.05	.02
404	Bake McBride	.06	.05	.02
405	Jerry Narron	.06	.05	.02
406	Rob Dressler	.06	.05	.02
407	Dave Heaverlo	.06	.05	.02
408	Tom Paciorek	.06	.05	.02
409	Carney Lansford	.10	.08	.04
410	Brian Downing	.10	.08	.04
411	Don Aase	.06	.05	.02
412	Jim Barr	.06	.05	.02
413	Don Baylor	.12	.09	.05
414	Jim Fregosi	.08	.06	.03
415	Dallas Green	.08	.06	.03
416	Dave Lopes	.10	.08	.04
417	Jerry Reuss	.10	.08	.04
418	Rick Sutcliffe	.20	.15	.08
419	Derrel Thomas	.06	.05	.02
420	Tommy LaSorda (Lasorda)	.10	.08	.04
421	*Charlie Leibrandt*	.30	.25	.12
422	Tom Seaver	.60	.45	.25
423	Ron Oester	.06	.05	.02
424	Junior Kennedy	.06	.05	.02
425	Tom Seaver	.60	.45	.25
426	Bobby Cox	.06	.05	.02
427	*Leon Durham*	.20	.15	.08
428	Terry Kennedy	.08	.06	.03
429	Silvio Martinez	.06	.05	.02
430	George Hendrick	.08	.06	.03
431	Red Schoendienst	.08	.06	.03
432	John LeMaster	.06	.05	.02
433	Vida Blue	.12	.09	.05
434	John Montefusco	.08	.06	.03
435	Terry Whitfield	.06	.05	.02

#	Player	MT	NR MT	EX
436	Dave Bristol	.06	.05	.02
437	Dale Murphy	.90	.70	.35
438	Jerry Dybzinski	.06	.05	.02
439	Jorge Orta	.06	.05	.02
440	Wayne Garland	.06	.05	.02
441	Miguel Dilone	.06	.05	.02
442	Dave Garcia	.06	.05	.02
443	Don Money	.06	.05	.02
444a	Buck Martinez (photo reversed)	1.00	.70	.40
444b	Buck Martinez (photo correct)	.10	.08	.04
445	Jerry Augustine	.06	.05	.02
446	Ben Oglivie	.08	.06	.03
447	Jim Slaton	.06	.05	.02
448	Doyle Alexander	.10	.08	.04
449	Tony Bernazard	.06	.05	.02
450	Scott Sanderson	.06	.05	.02
451	Dave Palmer	.06	.05	.02
452	Stan Bahnsen	.06	.05	.02
453	Dick Williams	.06	.05	.02
454	Rick Burleson	.08	.06	.03
455	Gary Allenson	.06	.05	.02
456	Bob Stanley	.06	.05	.02
457a	*John Tudor* (lifetime W/L 9.7)	1.50	1.25	.60
457b	*John Tudor* (lifetime W/L 9-7)	1.00	.70	.40
458	Dwight Evans	.15	.11	.06
459	Glenn Hubbard	.08	.06	.03
460	U L Washington	.06	.05	.02
461	Larry Gura	.06	.05	.02
462	Rich Gale	.06	.05	.02
463	Hal McRae	.10	.08	.04
464	Jim Frey	.06	.05	.02
465	Bucky Dent	.10	.08	.04
466	Dennis Werth	.06	.05	.02
467	Ron Davis	.08	.06	.03
468	Reggie Jackson	.70	.50	.30
469	Bobby Brown	.06	.05	.02
470	*Mike Davis*	.25	.20	.10
471	Gaylord Perry	.30	.25	.12
472	Mark Belanger	.08	.06	.03
473	Jim Palmer	.40	.30	.15
474	Sammy Stewart	.06	.05	.02
475	Tim Stoddard	.06	.05	.02
476	Steve Stone	.08	.06	.03
477	Jeff Newman	.06	.05	.02
478	Steve McCatty	.06	.05	.02
479	Billy Martin	.12	.09	.05
480	Mitchell Page	.06	.05	.02
481	Cy Young 1980 (Steve Carlton)	.35	.25	.14
482	Bill Buckner	.12	.09	.05
483a	Ivan DeJesus (lifetime hits 702)	1.00	.70	.40
483b	Ivan DeJesus (lifetime hits 642)	.10	.08	.04
484	Cliff Johnson	.06	.05	.02
485	Lenny Randle	.06	.05	.02
486	Larry Milbourne	.06	.05	.02
487	Roy Smalley	.06	.05	.02
488	John Castino	.06	.05	.02
489	Ron Jackson	.06	.05	.02
490a	Dave Roberts (1980 highlights begins "Showed pop...")	1.00	.70	.40
490b	Dave Roberts (1980 highlights begins "Declared himself...")	.10	.08	.04
491	MVP (George Brett)	.60	.45	.25
492	Mike Cubbage	.06	.05	.02
493	Rob Wilfong	.06	.05	.02
494	Danny Goodwin	.06	.05	.02
495	Jose Morales	.06	.05	.02
496	Mickey Rivers	.08	.06	.03
497	Mike Edwards	.06	.05	.02
498	Mike Sadek	.06	.05	.02
499	Lenn Sakata	.06	.05	.02
500	Gene Michael	.06	.05	.02
501	Dave Roberts	.06	.05	.02
502	Steve Dillard	.06	.05	.02
503	Jim Essian	.06	.05	.02
504	Rance Mulliniks	.06	.05	.02
505	Darrell Porter	.08	.06	.03
506	Joe Torre	.08	.06	.03
507	Terry Crowley	.06	.05	.02
508	Bill Travers	.06	.05	.02
509	Nelson Norman	.06	.05	.02
510	Bob McClure	.06	.05	.02
511	*Steve Howe*	.10	.08	.04
512	Dave Rader	.06	.05	.02
513	Mick Kelleher	.06	.05	.02
514	Kiko Garcia	.06	.05	.02
515	Larry Biittner	.06	.05	.02
516a	Willie Norwood (1980 highlights begins "Spent most...")	1.00	.70	.40
516b	Willie Norwood (1980 highlights begins "Traded to...")	.10	.08	.04
517	Bo Diaz	.08	.06	.03

#	Player	MT	NR MT	EX
518	Juan Beniquez	.06	.05	.02
519	Scot Thompson	.06	.05	.02
520	Jim Tracy	.06	.05	.02
521	Carlos Lezcano	.06	.05	.02
522	Joe Amalfitano	.06	.05	.02
523	Preston Hanna	.06	.05	.02
524a	Ray Burris (1980 highlights begins "Went on...")	1.00	.70	.40
524b	Ray Burris (1980 highlights begins "Drafted by...")	.10	.08	.04
525	Broderick Perkins	.06	.05	.02
526	Mickey Hatcher	.08	.06	.03
527	John Goryl	.06	.05	.02
528	Dick Davis	.06	.05	.02
529	Butch Wynegar	.06	.05	.02
530	Sal Butera	.06	.05	.02
531	Jerry Koosman	.10	.08	.04
532a	Jeff Zahn (Geoff) (1980 highlights begins "Was 2nd in...")	1.00	.70	.40
532b	Jeff Zahn (Geoff) (1980 highlights begins "Signed a 3 year...")	.10	.08	.04
533	Dennis Martinez	.08	.06	.03
534	Gary Thomasson	.06	.05	.02
535	Steve Macko	.06	.05	.02
536	Jim Kaat	.15	.11	.06
537	Best Hitters (George Brett, Rod Carew)	1.00	.70	.40
538	*Tim Raines*	5.00	3.75	2.00
539	Keith Smith	.06	.05	.02
540	Ken Macha	.06	.05	.02
541	Burt Hooton	.08	.06	.03
542	Butch Hobson	.06	.05	.02
543	Bill Stein	.06	.05	.02
544	Dave Stapleton	.06	.05	.02
545	Bob Pate	.06	.05	.02
546	Doug Corbett	.06	.05	.02
547	Darrell Jackson	.06	.05	.02
548	Pete Redfern	.06	.05	.02
549	Roger Erickson	.06	.05	.02
550	Al Hrabosky	.08	.06	.03
551	Dick Tidrow	.06	.05	.02
552	Dave Ford	.06	.05	.02
553	Dave Kingman	.15	.11	.06
554a	Mike Vail (1980 highlights begins "After...")	1.00	.70	.40
554b	Mike Vail (1980 highlights begins "Traded...")	.10	.08	.04
555a	Jerry Martin (1980 highlights begins "Overcame...")	1.00	.70	.40
555b	Jerry Martin (1980 highlights begins "Traded...")	.10	.08	.04
556a	Jesus Figueroa (1980 highlights begins "Had...")	1.00	.70	.40
556b	Jesus Figueroa (1980 highlights begins "Traded...")	.10	.08	.04
557	Don Stanhouse	.06	.05	.02
558	Barry Foote	.06	.05	.02
559	Tim Blackwell	.06	.05	.02
560	Bruce Sutter	.15	.11	.06
561	Rick Reuschel	.10	.08	.04
562	Lynn McGlothen	.06	.05	.02
563a	Bob Owchinko (1980 highlights begins "Traded...")	1.00	.70	.40
563b	Bob Owchinko (1980 highlights begins "Involved...")	.10	.08	.04
564	John Verhoeven	.06	.05	.02
565	Ken Landreaux	.06	.05	.02
566a	Glen Adams (Glen on front)	1.00	.70	.40
566b	Glenn Adams (Glenn on front)	.10	.08	.04
567	Hosken Powell	.06	.05	.02
568	Dick Noles	.06	.05	.02
569	*Danny Ainge*	.25	.20	.10
570	Bobby Mattick	.06	.05	.02
571	Joe LeFebvre (Lefebvre)	.06	.05	.02
572	Bobby Clark	.06	.05	.02
573	Dennis Lamp	.06	.05	.02
574	Randy Lerch	.06	.05	.02
575	Mookie Wilson	.60	.45	.25
576	Ron LeFlore	.08	.06	.03
577	Jim Dwyer	.06	.05	.02
578	Bill Castro	.06	.05	.02
579	Greg Minton	.06	.05	.02
580	Mark Littell	.06	.05	.02
581	Andy Hassler	.06	.05	.02
582	Dave Stieb	.20	.15	.08
583	Ken Oberkfell	.06	.05	.02
584	Larry Bradford	.06	.05	.02
585	Fred Stanley	.06	.05	.02
586	Bill Caudill	.06	.05	.02
587	Doug Capilla	.06	.05	.02
588	George Riley	.06	.05	.02

		MT	NR MT	EX
589	Willie Hernandez	.10	.08	.04
590	MVP (Mike Schmidt)	.80	.60	.30
591	Cy Young 1980 (Steve Stone)	.08	.06	.03
592	Rick Sofield	.06	.05	.02
593	Bombo Rivera	.06	.05	.02
594	Gary Ward	.08	.06	.03
595a	Dave Edwards (1980 highlights begins "Sidelined...")	1.00	.70	.40
595b	Dave Edwards (1980 highlights begins "Traded...")	.10	.08	.04
596	Mike Proly	.06	.05	.02
597	Tommy Boggs	.06	.05	.02
598	Greg Gross	.06	.05	.02
599	Elias Sosa	.06	.05	.02
600	Pat Kelly	.06	.05	.02
---a	Checklist 1-120 (51 Tom Donohue)	2.00	1.50	.80
---b	Checklist 1-120 (51 Tom Donahue)	.10	.08	.04
------	Checklist 121-240	.06	.05	.02
---a	Checklist 241-360 (306 Gary Mathews)	.70	.50	.30
---b	Checklist 241-360 (306 Gary Matthews)	.10	.08	.04
---a	Checklist 361-480 (379 Luis Pujois)	.70	.50	.30
---b	Checklist 361-480 (379 Luis Pujols)	.10	.08	.04
---a	Checklist 481-600 (566 Glen Adams)	.70	.50	.30
---b	Checklist 481-600 (566 Glenn Adams)	.10	.08	.04

1982 Donruss

Using card stock thicker than the previous year, Donruss issued a 660-card set which includes 653 numbered cards and seven unnumbered checklists. The cards, which measure 2-1/2" by 3-1/2", were sold with puzzle pieces rather than gum as a result of a lawsuit by Topps. The puzzle pieces (three pieces on one card per pack) feature Babe Ruth. The first 26 cards of the set, entitled Diamond Kings, showcase the artwork of Dick Perez of Perez-Steele Galleries. The card fronts display the Donruss logo and the year of issue. The card backs have black and blue ink on white stock and include the player's career highlights. The complete set price does not include the higher priced variations.

		MT	NR MT	EX
Complete Set:		35.00	27.00	15.00
Common Player:		.06	.05	.02
1	Pete Rose (DK)	1.25	.90	.50
2	Gary Carter (DK)	.50	.40	.20
3	Steve Garvey (DK)	.50	.40	.20
4	Vida Blue (DK)	.12	.09	.05
5a	Alan Trammel (DK) (name incorrect)	1.50	1.25	.60
5b	Alan Trammel (DK) (name correct)	.40	.30	.15
6	Len Barker (DK)	.08	.06	.03
7	Dwight Evans (DK)	.15	.11	.06
8	Rod Carew (DK)	.50	.40	.20
9	George Hendrick (DK)	.08	.06	.03
10	Phil Niekro (DK)	.30	.25	.12
11	Richie Zisk (DK)	.08	.06	.03

		MT	NR MT	EX
12	Dave Parker (DK)	.30	.25	.12
13	Nolan Ryan (DK)	.70	.50	.30
14	Ivan DeJesus (DK)	.08	.06	.03
15	George Brett (DK)	.70	.50	.30
16	Tom Seaver (DK)	.50	.40	.20
17	Dave Kingman (DK)	.15	.11	.06
18	Dave Winfield (DK)	.50	.40	.20
19	Mike Norris (DK)	.08	.06	.03
20	Carlton Fisk (DK)	.25	.20	.10
21	Ozzie Smith (DK)	.20	.15	.08
22	Roy Smalley (DK)	.08	.06	.03
23	Buddy Bell (DK)	.12	.09	.05
24	Ken Singleton (DK)	.10	.08	.04
25	John Mayberry (DK)	.08	.06	.03
26	Gorman Thomas (DK)	.10	.08	.04
27	Earl Weaver	.10	.08	.04
28	Rollie Fingers	.20	.15	.08
29	Sparky Anderson	.10	.08	.04
30	Dennis Eckersley	.12	.09	.05
31	Dave Winfield	.50	.40	.20
32	Burt Hooton	.08	.06	.03
33	Rick Waits	.06	.05	.02
34	George Brett	.70	.50	.30
35	Steve McCatty	.06	.05	.02
36	Steve Rogers	.08	.06	.03
37	Bill Stein	.06	.05	.02
38	Steve Renko	.06	.05	.02
39	Mike Squires	.06	.05	.02
40	George Hendrick	.08	.06	.03
41	Bob Knepper	.08	.06	.03
42	Steve Carlton	.50	.40	.20
43	Larry Biittner	.06	.05	.02
44	Chris Welsh	.06	.05	.02
45	Steve Nicosia	.06	.05	.02
46	Jack Clark	.25	.20	.10
47	Chris Chambliss	.08	.06	.03
48	Ivan DeJesus	.06	.05	.02
49	Lee Mazzilli	.08	.06	.03
50	Julio Cruz	.06	.05	.02
51	Pete Redfern	.06	.05	.02
52	Dave Stieb	.12	.09	.05
53	Doug Corbett	.06	.05	.02
54	Jorge Bell (FC)	7.00	5.25	2.75
55	Joe Simpson	.06	.05	.02
56	Rusty Staub	.10	.08	.04
57	Hector Cruz	.06	.05	.02
58	Claudell Washington (FC)	.10	.08	.04
59	Enrique Romo	.06	.05	.02
60	Gary Lavelle	.06	.05	.02
61	Tim Flannery	.06	.05	.02
62	Joe Nolan	.06	.05	.02
63	Larry Bowa	.15	.11	.06
64	Sixto Lezcano	.06	.05	.02
65	Joe Sambito	.06	.05	.02
66	Bruce Kison	.06	.05	.02
67	Wayne Nordhagen	.06	.05	.02
68	Woodie Fryman	.08	.06	.03
69	Billy Sample	.06	.05	.02
70	Amos Otis	.08	.06	.03
71	Matt Keough	.06	.05	.02
72	Toby Harrah	.08	.06	.03
73	Dave Righetti (FC)	2.00	1.50	.80
74	Carl Yastrzemski	.80	.60	.30
75	Bob Welch	.12	.09	.05
76a	Alan Trammel (name incorrect)	1.25	.90	.50
76b	Alan Trammell (name correct)	.40	.30	.15
77	Rick Dempsey	.08	.06	.03
78	Paul Molitor	.20	.15	.08
79	Dennis Martinez	.08	.06	.03
80	Jim Slaton	.06	.05	.02
81	Champ Summers	.06	.05	.02
82	Carney Lansford	.08	.06	.03
83	Barry Foote	.06	.05	.02
84	Steve Garvey	.50	.40	.20
85	Rick Manning	.06	.05	.02
86	John Wathan	.08	.06	.03
87	Brian Kingman	.06	.05	.02
88	Andre Dawson	.40	.30	.15
89	Jim Kern	.06	.05	.02
90	Bobby Grich	.10	.08	.04
91	Bob Forsch	.08	.06	.03
92	Art Howe	.06	.05	.02
93	Marty Bystrom	.06	.05	.02
94	Ozzie Smith	.20	.15	.08
95	Dave Parker	.30	.25	.12
96	Doyle Alexander	.10	.08	.04
97	Al Hrabosky	.08	.06	.03
98	Frank Taveras	.06	.05	.02
99	Tim Blackwell	.06	.05	.02
100	Floyd Bannister	.10	.08	.04
101	Alfredo Griffin	.08	.06	.03

		MT	NR MT	EX
102	Dave Engle	.06	.05	.02
103	Mario Soto	.08	.06	.03
104	Ross Baumgarten	.06	.05	.02
105	Ken Singleton	.10	.08	.04
106	Ted Simmons	.12	.09	.05
107	Jack Morris	.30	.25	.12
108	Bob Watson	.08	.06	.03
109	Dwight Evans	.15	.11	.06
110	Tom Lasorda	.10	.08	.04
111	Bert Blyleven	.12	.09	.05
112	Dan Quisenberry	.15	.11	.06
113	Rickey Henderson	1.00	.70	.40
114	Gary Carter	.35	.25	.14
115	Brian Downing	.10	.08	.04
116	Al Oliver	.15	.11	.06
117	LaMarr Hoyt	.06	.05	.02
118	Cesar Cedeno	.12	.09	.05
119	Keith Moreland	.10	.08	.04
120	Bob Shirley	.06	.05	.02
121	Terry Kennedy	.08	.06	.03
122	Frank Pastore	.06	.05	.02
123	Gene Garber	.06	.05	.02
124	Tony Pena(FC)	.25	.20	.10
125	Allen Ripley	.06	.05	.02
126	Randy Martz	.06	.05	.02
127	Richie Zisk	.08	.06	.03
128	Mike Scott	.15	.11	.06
129	Lloyd Moseby(FC)	.20	.15	.08
130	Rob Wilfong	.06	.05	.02
131	Tim Stoddard	.06	.05	.02
132	Gorman Thomas	.10	.08	.04
133	Dan Petry	.08	.06	.03
134	Bob Stanley	.06	.05	.02
135	Lou Piniella	.12	.09	.05
136	Pedro Guerrero(FC)	.70	.50	.30
137	Len Barker	.08	.06	.03
138	Richard Gale	.06	.05	.02
139	Wayne Gross	.06	.05	.02
140	*Tim Wallach*(FC)	1.50	1.25	.60
141	Gene Mauch	.08	.06	.03
142	Doc Medich	.06	.05	.02
143	Tony Bernazard	.06	.05	.02
144	Bill Virdon	.06	.05	.02
145	John Littlefield	.06	.05	.02
146	Dave Bergman	.06	.05	.02
147	Dick Davis	.06	.05	.02
148	Tom Seaver	.60	.45	.25
149	Matt Sinatro	.06	.05	.02
150	Chuck Tanner	.06	.05	.02
151	Leon Durham	.08	.06	.03
152	Gene Tenace	.08	.06	.03
153	Al Bumbry	.08	.06	.03
154	Mark Brouhard	.06	.05	.02
155	Rick Peters	.06	.05	.02
156	Jerry Remy	.06	.05	.02
157	Rick Reuschel	.10	.08	.04
158	Steve Howe	.08	.06	.03
159	Alan Bannister	.06	.05	.02
160	U L Washington	.06	.05	.02
161	Rick Langford	.06	.05	.02
162	Bill Gullickson	.08	.06	.03
163	Mark Wagner	.06	.05	.02
164	Geoff Zahn	.06	.05	.02
165	Ron LeFlore	.08	.06	.03
166	Dane Iorg	.06	.05	.02
167	Joe Niekro	.12	.09	.05
168	Pete Rose	1.00	.70	.40
169	Dave Collins	.08	.06	.03
170	Rick Wise	.08	.06	.03
171	Jim Bibby	.06	.05	.02
172	Larry Herndon	.08	.06	.03
173	Bob Horner	.12	.09	.05
174	Steve Dillard	.06	.05	.02
175	Mookie Wilson	.12	.09	.05
176	Dan Meyer	.06	.05	.02
177	Fernando Arroyo	.06	.05	.02
178	Jackson Todd	.06	.05	.02
179	Darrell Jackson	.06	.05	.02
180	Al Woods	.06	.05	.02
181	Jim Anderson	.06	.05	.02
182	Dave Kingman	.15	.11	.06
183	Steve Henderson	.06	.05	.02
184	Brian Asselstine	.06	.05	.02
185	Rod Scurry	.06	.05	.02
186	Fred Breining	.06	.05	.02
187	Danny Boone	.06	.05	.02
188	Junior Kennedy	.06	.05	.02
189	Sparky Lyle	.10	.08	.04
190	Whitey Herzog	.08	.06	.03
191	Dave Smith	.10	.08	.04
192	Ed Ott	.06	.05	.02
193	Greg Luzinski	.15	.11	.06
194	Bill Lee	.08	.06	.03
195	Don Zimmer	.06	.05	.02
196	Hal McRae	.12	.09	.05
197	Mike Norris	.06	.05	.02
198	Duane Kuiper	.06	.05	.02
199	Rick Cerone	.06	.05	.02
200	Jim Rice	.40	.30	.15
201	Steve Yeager	.06	.05	.02
202	Tom Brookens	.06	.05	.02
203	Jose Morales	.06	.05	.02
204	Roy Howell	.06	.05	.02
205	Tippy Martinez	.06	.05	.02
206	Moose Haas	.06	.05	.02
207	Al Cowens	.06	.05	.02
208	Dave Stapleton	.06	.05	.02
209	Bucky Dent	.10	.08	.04
210	Ron Cey	.12	.09	.05
211	Jorge Orta	.06	.05	.02
212	Jamie Quirk	.06	.05	.02
213	Jeff Jones	.06	.05	.02
214	Tim Raines	.90	.70	.35
215	Jon Matlack	.08	.06	.03
216	Rod Carew	.50	.40	.20
217	Jim Kaat	.15	.11	.06
218	Joe Pittman	.06	.05	.02
219	Larry Christenson	.06	.05	.02
220	Juan Bonilla	.06	.05	.02
221	Mike Easler	.08	.06	.03
222	Vida Blue	.12	.09	.05
223	Rick Camp	.06	.05	.02
224	Mike Jorgensen	.06	.05	.02
225	*Jody Davis*(FC)	.30	.25	.12
226	Mike Parrott	.06	.05	.02
227	Jim Clancy	.08	.06	.03
228	Hosken Powell	.06	.05	.02
229	Tom Hume	.06	.05	.02
230	Britt Burns	.06	.05	.02
231	Jim Palmer	.40	.30	.15
232	Bob Rodgers	.08	.06	.03
233	Milt Wilcox	.06	.05	.02
234	Dave Revering	.06	.05	.02
235	Mike Torrez	.08	.06	.03
236	Robert Castillo	.06	.05	.02
237	*Von Hayes*(FC)	.90	.70	.35
238	Renie Martin	.06	.05	.02
239	Dwayne Murphy	.08	.06	.03
240	Rodney Scott	.06	.05	.02
241	Fred Patek	.06	.05	.02
242	Mickey Rivers	.08	.06	.03
243	Steve Trout	.06	.05	.02
244	Jose Cruz	.12	.09	.05
245	Manny Trillo	.08	.06	.03
246	Lary Sorensen	.06	.05	.02
247	Dave Edwards	.06	.05	.02
248	Dan Driessen	.08	.06	.03
249	Tommy Boggs	.06	.05	.02
250	Dale Berra	.06	.05	.02
251	Ed Whitson	.06	.05	.02
252	*Lee Smith*(FC)	.60	.45	.25
253	Tom Paciorek	.06	.05	.02
254	Pat Zachry	.06	.05	.02
255	Luis Leal	.06	.05	.02
256	John Castino	.06	.05	.02
257	Rich Dauer	.06	.05	.02
258	Cecil Cooper	.15	.11	.06
259	Dave Rozema	.06	.05	.02
260	John Tudor	.15	.11	.06
261	Jerry Mumphrey	.06	.05	.02
262	Jay Johnstone	.08	.06	.03
263	Bo Diaz	.08	.06	.03
264	Dennis Leonard	.08	.06	.03
265	Jim Spencer	.06	.05	.02
266	John Milner	.06	.05	.02
267	Don Aase	.06	.05	.02
268	Jim Sundberg	.08	.06	.03
269	Lamar Johnson	.06	.05	.02
270	Frank LaCorte	.06	.05	.02
271	Barry Evans	.06	.05	.02
272	Enos Cabell	.06	.05	.02
273	Del Unser	.06	.05	.02
274	George Foster	.20	.15	.08
275	*Brett Butler*(FC)	.70	.50	.30
276	Ken Lacy	.06	.05	.02
277	Ken Reitz	.06	.05	.02
278	Keith Hernandez	.40	.30	.15
279	Doug DeCinces	.10	.08	.04
280	Charlie Moore	.06	.05	.02
281	Lance Parrish	.35	.25	.14
282	Ralph Houk	.08	.06	.03
283	Rich Gossage	.20	.15	.08

	MT	NR MT	EX			MT	NR MT	EX
284	Jerry Reuss	.10	.08	.04	372	Bruce Sutter	.15	.11	.06
285	Mike Stanton	.06	.05	.02	373	Joe Lefebvre	.06	.05	.02
286	Frank White	.10	.08	.04	374	Ray Knight	.10	.08	.04
287	Bob Owchinko	.06	.05	.02	375	Bruce Benedict	.06	.05	.02
288	Scott Sanderson	.06	.05	.02	376	Tim Foli	.06	.05	.02
289	Bump Wills	.06	.05	.02	377	Al Holland	.06	.05	.02
290	Dave Frost	.06	.05	.02	378	Ken Kravec	.06	.05	.02
291	Chet Lemon	.08	.06	.03	379	Jeff Burroughs	.08	.06	.03
292	Tito Landrum	.06	.05	.02	380	Pete Falcone	.06	.05	.02
293	Vern Ruhle	.06	.05	.02	381	Ernie Whitt	.08	.06	.03
294	Mike Schmidt	1.00	.90	.50	382	Brad Havens	.06	.05	.02
295	Sam Mejias	.06	.05	.02	383	Terry Crowley	.06	.05	.02
296	Gary Lucas	.06	.05	.02	384	Don Money	.06	.05	.02
297	John Candelaria	.10	.08	.04	385	Dan Schatzeder	.06	.05	.02
298	Jerry Martin	.06	.05	.02	386	Gary Allenson	.06	.05	.02
299	Dale Murphy	.90	.70	.35	387	Yogi Berra	.15	.11	.06
300	Mike Lum	.06	.05	.02	388	Ken Landreaux	.06	.05	.02
301	Tom Hausman	.06	.05	.02	389	Mike Hargrove	.06	.05	.02
302	Glenn Abbott	.06	.05	.02	390	Darryl Motley	.06	.05	.02
303	Roger Erickson	.06	.05	.02	391	Dave McKay	.06	.05	.02
304	Otto Velez	.06	.05	.02	392	Stan Bahnsen	.06	.05	.02
305	Danny Goodwin	.06	.05	.02	393	Ken Forsch	.06	.05	.02
306	John Mayberry	.08	.06	.03	394	Mario Mendoza	.06	.05	.02
307	Lenny Randle	.06	.05	.02	395	Jim Morrison	.06	.05	.02
308	Bob Bailor	.06	.05	.02	396	Mike Ivie	.06	.05	.02
309	Jerry Morales	.06	.05	.02	397	Broderick Perkins	.06	.05	.02
310	Rufino Linares	.06	.05	.02	398	Darrell Evans	.15	.11	.06
311	Kent Tekulve	.08	.06	.03	399	Ron Reed	.06	.05	.02
312	Joe Morgan	.40	.30	.15	400	Johnny Bench	.60	.45	.25
313	John Urrea	.06	.05	.02	401	*Steve Bedrosian*(FC)	.80	.60	.30
314	Paul Householder	.06	.05	.02	402	Bill Robinson	.06	.05	.02
315	Garry Maddox	.10	.08	.04	403	Bill Buckner	.12	.09	.05
316	Mike Ramsey	.06	.05	.02	404	Ken Oberkfell	.06	.05	.02
317	Alan Ashby	.06	.05	.02	405	*Cal Ripken, Jr.*(FC)	8.00	6.00	3.25
318	Bob Clark	.06	.05	.02	406	Jim Gantner	.08	.06	.03
319	Tony LaRussa	.08	.06	.03	407	Kirk Gibson(FC)	1.50	1.25	.60
320	Charlie Lea	.08	.06	.03	408	Tony Perez	.20	.15	.08
321	Danny Darwin	.06	.05	.02	409	Tommy John	.20	.15	.08
322	Cesar Geronimo	.06	.05	.02	410	*Dave Stewart*(FC)	3.00	2.25	1.25
323	Tom Underwood	.06	.05	.02	411	Dan Spillner	.06	.05	.02
324	Andre Thornton	.10	.08	.04	412	Willie Aikens	.06	.05	.02
325	Rudy May	.06	.05	.02	413	Mike Heath	.06	.05	.02
326	Frank Tanana	.10	.08	.04	414	Ray Burris	.06	.05	.02
327	Davey Lopes	.10	.08	.04	415	Leon Roberts	.06	.05	.02
328	Richie Hebner	.06	.05	.02	416	*Mike Witt*(FC)	.70	.50	.30
329	Mike Flanagan	.10	.08	.04	417	Bobby Molinaro	.06	.05	.02
330	Mike Caldwell	.06	.05	.02	418	Steve Braun	.06	.05	.02
331	Scott McGregor	.08	.06	.03	419	Nolan Ryan	1.00	.70	.40
332	Jerry Augustine	.06	.05	.02	420	Tug McGraw	.12	.09	.05
333	Stan Papi	.06	.05	.02	421	Dave Concepcion	.12	.09	.05
334	Rick Miller	.06	.05	.02	422a	Juan Eichelberger (Gary Lucas photo — white player)	1.25	.90	.50
335	Graig Nettles	.15	.11	.06	422b	Juan Eichelberger (correct photo - black player)	.08	.06	.03
336	Dusty Baker	.10	.08	.04	423	Rick Rhoden	.10	.08	.04
337	Dave Garcia	.06	.05	.02	424	Frank Robinson	.12	.09	.05
338	Larry Gura	.06	.05	.02	425	Eddie Miller	.06	.05	.02
339	Cliff Johnson	.06	.05	.02	426	Bill Caudill	.06	.05	.02
340	Warren Cromartie	.06	.05	.02	427	Doug Flynn	.06	.05	.02
341	Steve Comer	.06	.05	.02	428	Larry Anderson (Andersen)	.06	.05	.02
342	Rick Burleson	.08	.06	.03	429	Al Williams	.06	.05	.02
343	John Martin	.06	.05	.02	430	Jerry Garvin	.06	.05	.02
344	Craig Reynolds	.06	.05	.02	431	Glenn Adams	.06	.05	.02
345	Mike Proly	.06	.05	.02	432	Barry Bonnell	.06	.05	.02
346	Ruppert Jones	.06	.05	.02	433	Jerry Narron	.06	.05	.02
347	Omar Moreno	.06	.05	.02	434	John Stearns	.06	.05	.02
348	Greg Minton	.06	.05	.02	435	Mike Tyson	.06	.05	.02
349	*Rick Mahler*(FC)	.25	.20	.10	436	Glenn Hubbard	.08	.06	.03
350	Alex Trevino	.06	.05	.02	437	Eddie Solomon	.06	.05	.02
351	Mike Krukow	.08	.06	.03	438	Jeff Leonard	.10	.08	.04
352a	Shane Rawley (Jim Anderson photo — shaking hands)	1.25	.90	.50	439	Randy Bass	.06	.05	.02
352b	Shane Rawley (correct photo - kneeling)	.15	.11	.06	440	Mike LaCoss	.06	.05	.02
353	Garth Iorg	.06	.05	.02	441	Gary Matthews	.10	.08	.04
354	Pete Mackanin	.06	.05	.02	442	Mark Littell	.06	.05	.02
355	Paul Moskau	.06	.05	.02	443	Don Sutton	.30	.25	.12
356	Richard Dotson	.10	.08	.04	444	John Harris	.06	.05	.02
357	Steve Stone	.08	.06	.03	445	Vada Pinson	.08	.06	.03
358	Larry Hisle	.08	.06	.03	446	Elias Sosa	.06	.05	.02
359	Aurelio Lopez	.06	.05	.02	447	Charlie Hough	.10	.08	.04
360	Oscar Gamble	.08	.06	.03	448	Willie Wilson	.15	.11	.06
361	Tom Burgmeier	.06	.05	.02	449	Fred Stanley	.06	.05	.02
362	Terry Forster	.08	.06	.03	450	Tom Veryzer	.06	.05	.02
363	Joe Charboneau	.08	.06	.03	451	Ron Davis	.06	.05	.02
364	Ken Brett	.08	.06	.03	452	Mark Clear	.06	.05	.02
365	Tony Armas	.10	.08	.04	453	Bill Russell	.08	.06	.03
366	Chris Speier	.06	.05	.02	454	Lou Whitaker	.40	.30	.15
367	Fred Lynn	.20	.15	.08	455	Dan Graham	.06	.05	.02
368	Buddy Bell	.12	.09	.05	456	Reggie Cleveland	.06	.05	.02
369	Jim Essian	.06	.05	.02	457	Sammy Stewart	.06	.05	.02
370	Terry Puhl	.06	.05	.02	458	Pete Vuckovich	.08	.06	.03
371	Greg Gross	.06	.05	.02	459	John Wockenfuss	.06	.05	.02

		MT	NR MT	EX
460	Glenn Hoffman	.06	.05	.02
461	Willie Randolph	.10	.08	.04
462	Fernando Valenzuela(FC)	.80	.60	.30
463	Ron Hassey	.06	.05	.02
464	Paul Splittorff	.06	.05	.02
465	Rob Picciolo	.06	.05	.02
466	Larry Parrish	.10	.08	.04
467	Johnny Grubb	.06	.05	.02
468	Dan Ford	.06	.05	.02
469	Silvio Martinez	.06	.05	.02
470	Kiko Garcia	.06	.05	.02
471	Bob Boone	.10	.08	.04
472	Luis Salazar	.08	.06	.03
473	Randy Niemann	.06	.05	.02
474	Tom Griffin	.06	.05	.02
475	Phil Niekro	.30	.25	.12
476	Hubie Brooks(FC)	.25	.20	.10
477	Dick Tidrow	.06	.05	.02
478	Jim Beattie	.06	.05	.02
479	Damaso Garcia	.06	.05	.02
480	Mickey Hatcher	.08	.06	.03
481	Joe Price	.06	.05	.02
482	Ed Farmer	.06	.05	.02
483	Eddie Murray	.60	.45	.25
484	Ben Oglivie	.08	.06	.03
485	Kevin Saucier	.06	.05	.02
486	Bobby Murcer	.10	.08	.04
487	Bill Campbell	.06	.05	.02
488	Reggie Smith	.10	.08	.04
489	Wayne Garland	.06	.05	.02
490	Jim Wright	.06	.05	.02
491	Billy Martin	.12	.09	.05
492	Jim Fanning	.06	.05	.02
493	Don Baylor	.12	.09	.05
494	Rick Honeycutt	.06	.05	.02
495	Carlton Fisk	.50	.40	.20
496	Denny Walling	.06	.05	.02
497	Bake McBride	.06	.05	.02
498	Darrell Porter	.08	.06	.03
499	Gene Richards	.06	.05	.02
500	Ron Oester	.06	.05	.02
501	Ken Dayley(FC)	.20	.15	.08
502	Jason Thompson	.06	.05	.02
503	Milt May	.06	.05	.02
504	Doug Bird	.06	.05	.02
505	Bruce Bochte	.06	.05	.02
506	Neil Allen	.06	.05	.02
507	Joey McLaughlin	.06	.05	.02
508	Butch Wynegar	.06	.05	.02
509	Gary Roenicke	.06	.05	.02
510	Robin Yount	1.00	.70	.40
511	Dave Tobik	.06	.05	.02
512	Rich Gedman(FC)	.35	.25	.14
513	Gene Nelson(FC)	.12	.09	.05
514	Rick Monday	.10	.08	.04
515	Miguel Dilone	.06	.05	.02
516	Clint Hurdle	.06	.05	.02
517	Jeff Newman	.06	.05	.02
518	Grant Jackson	.06	.05	.02
519	Andy Hassler	.06	.05	.02
520	Pat Putnam	.06	.05	.02
521	Greg Pryor	.06	.05	.02
522	Tony Scott	.06	.05	.02
523	Steve Mura	.06	.05	.02
524	Johnnie LeMaster	.06	.05	.02
525	Dick Ruthven	.06	.05	.02
526	John McNamara	.06	.05	.02
527	Larry McWilliams	.06	.05	.02
528	Johnny Ray(FC)	.70	.50	.30
529	Pat Tabler(FC)	.60	.45	.25
530	Tom Herr	.10	.08	.04
531a	San Diego Chicken (trademark symbol on front)	1.25	.90	.50
531b	San Diego Chicken (no trademark symbol)	.50	.40	.20
532	Sal Butera	.06	.05	.02
533	Mike Griffin	.06	.05	.02
534	Kelvin Moore	.06	.05	.02
535	Reggie Jackson	.60	.45	.25
536	Ed Romero	.06	.05	.02
537	Derrel Thomas	.06	.05	.02
538	Mike O'Berry	.06	.05	.02
539	Jack O'Connor	.06	.05	.02
540	Bob Ojeda(FC)	.50	.40	.20
541	Roy Lee Jackson	.06	.05	.02
542	Lynn Jones	.06	.05	.02
543	Gaylord Perry	.30	.25	.12
544a	Phil Garner (photo reversed)	1.25	.90	.50
544b	Phil Garner (photo correct)	.10	.08	.04
545	Garry Templeton	.10	.08	.04
546	Rafael Ramirez(FC)	.10	.08	.04
547	Jeff Reardon	.20	.15	.08
548	Ron Guidry	.25	.20	.10
549	Tim Laudner(FC)	.25	.20	.10
550	John Henry Johnson	.06	.05	.02
551	Chris Bando	.06	.05	.02
552	Bobby Brown	.06	.05	.02
553	Larry Bradford	.06	.05	.02
554	Scott Fletcher(FC)	.30	.25	.12
555	Jerry Royster	.06	.05	.02
556	Shooty Babbitt	.06	.05	.02
557	Kent Hrbek(FC)	3.00	2.25	1.25
558	Yankee Winners (Ron Guidry, Tommy John)	.15	.11	.06
559	Mark Bomback	.06	.05	.02
560	Julio Valdez	.06	.05	.02
561	Buck Martinez	.06	.05	.02
562	Mike Marshall(FC)	1.00	.70	.40
563	Rennie Stennett	.06	.05	.02
564	Steve Crawford	.06	.05	.02
565	Bob Babcock	.06	.05	.02
566	Johnny Podres	.08	.06	.03
567	Paul Serna	.06	.05	.02
568	Harold Baines(FC)	.60	.45	.25
569	Dave LaRoche	.06	.05	.02
570	Lee May	.08	.06	.03
571	Gary Ward(FC)	.10	.08	.04
572	John Denny	.06	.05	.02
573	Roy Smalley	.06	.05	.02
574	Bob Brenly(FC)	.20	.15	.08
575	Bronx Bombers (Reggie Jackson, Dave Winfield)	.40	.30	.15
576	Luis Pujols	.06	.05	.02
577	Butch Hobson	.06	.05	.02
578	Harvey Kuenn	.08	.06	.03
579	Cal Ripken, Sr.	.08	.06	.03
580	Juan Berenguer	.08	.06	.03
581	Benny Ayala	.06	.05	.02
582	Vance Law(FC)	.15	.11	.06
583	Rick Leach(FC)	.12	.09	.05
584	George Frazier	.06	.05	.02
585	Phillies Finest (Pete Rose, Mike Schmidt)	.70	.50	.30
586	Joe Rudi	.10	.08	.04
587	Juan Beniquez	.06	.05	.02
588	Luis DeLeon(FC)	.08	.06	.03
589	Craig Swan	.06	.05	.02
590	Dave Chalk	.06	.05	.02
591	Billy Gardner	.06	.05	.02
592	Sal Bando	.08	.06	.03
593	Bert Campaneris	.10	.08	.04
594	Steve Kemp	.08	.06	.03
595a	Randy Lerch (Braves)	1.25	.90	.50
595b	Randy Lerch (Brewers)	.08	.06	.03
596	Bryan Clark	.06	.05	.02
597	Dave Ford	.06	.05	.02
598	Mike Scioscia(FC)	.20	.15	.08
599	John Lowenstein	.06	.05	.02
600	Rene Lachmann (Lachmann)	.06	.05	.02
601	Mick Kelleher	.06	.05	.02
602	Ron Jackson	.06	.05	.02
603	Jerry Koosman	.10	.08	.04
604	Dave Goltz	.08	.06	.03
605	Ellis Valentine	.06	.05	.02
606	Lonnie Smith	.08	.06	.03
607	Joaquin Andujar	.08	.06	.03
608	Garry Hancock	.06	.05	.02
609	Jerry Turner	.06	.05	.02
610	Bob Bonner	.06	.05	.02
611	Jim Dwyer	.06	.05	.02
612	Terry Bulling	.06	.05	.02
613	Joel Youngblood	.06	.05	.02
614	Larry Milbourne	.06	.05	.02
615	Phil Roof (Gene)	.06	.05	.02
616	Keith Drumright	.06	.05	.02
617	Dave Rosello	.06	.05	.02
618	Rickey Keeton	.06	.05	.02
619	Dennis Lamp	.06	.05	.02
620	Sid Monge	.06	.05	.02
621	Jerry White	.06	.05	.02
622	Luis Aguayo(FC)	.10	.08	.04
623	Jamie Easterly	.06	.05	.02
624	Steve Sax(FC)	2.75	2.00	1.00
625	Dave Roberts	.06	.05	.02
626	Rick Bosetti	.06	.05	.02
627	Terry Francona(FC)	.10	.08	.04
628	Pride of the Reds (Johnny Bench, Tom Seaver)	.35	.25	.14
629	Paul Mirabella	.06	.05	.02
630	Rance Mulliniks	.06	.05	.02
631	Kevin Hickey	.06	.05	.02
632	Reid Nichols	.06	.05	.02

		MT	NR MT	EX
633	Dave Geisel	.06	.05	.02
634	Ken Griffey	.12	.09	.05
635	Bob Lemon	.10	.08	.04
636	Orlando Sanchez	.06	.05	.02
637	Bill Almon	.06	.05	.02
638	Danny Ainge	.12	.09	.05
639	Willie Stargell	.40	.30	.15
640	Bob Sykes	.06	.05	.02
641	Ed Lynch	.06	.05	.02
642	John Ellis	.06	.05	.02
643	Fergie Jenkins	.15	.11	.06
644	Lenn Sakata	.06	.05	.02
645	Julio Gonzales	.06	.05	.02
646	Jesse Orosco(FC)	.15	.11	.06
647	Jerry Dybzinski	.06	.05	.02
648	Tommy Davis	.08	.06	.03
649	Ron Gardenhire	.06	.05	.02
650	Felipe Alou	.08	.06	.03
651	Harvey Haddix	.08	.06	.03
652	Willie Upshaw(FC)	.15	.11	.06
653	Bill Madlock	.12	.09	.05
---a	Checklist 1-26 DK (5 Trammel)	.70	.50	.30
---b	Checklist 1-26 DK (5 Trammell)	.08	.06	.03
----	Checklist 27-130	.06	.05	.02
----	Checklist 131-234	.06	.05	.02
----	Checklist 235-338	.06	.05	.02
----	Checklist 339-442	.06	.05	.02
----	Checklist 443-544	.06	.05	.02
----	Checklist 545-653	.06	.05	.02

1983 Donruss

 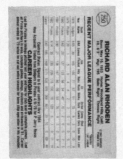

The 1983 Donruss set consists of 653 numbered cards plus seven unnumbered checklists. The cards, which measure 2-1/2" by 3-1/2", were issued with puzzle pieces (three pieces on one card per pack) that feature Ty Cobb. The first 26 cards in the set were once again the Diamond Kings series. The card fronts display the Donruss logo and the year of issue. The card backs have black print on yellow and white and include statistics, career highlights, and the player's contract status. (DK) in the checklist that follows indicates cards which belong to the Diamond Kings series.

		MT	NR MT	EX
Complete Set:		55.00	38.00	22.00
Common Player:		.06	.05	.02
1	Fernando Valenzuela (DK)	.40	.30	.15
2	Rollie Fingers (DK)	.20	.15	.08
3	Reggie Jackson (DK)	.50	.40	.20
4	Jim Palmer (DK)	.40	.30	.15
5	Jack Morris (DK)	.30	.25	.12
6	George Foster (DK)	.20	.15	.08
7	Jim Sundberg (DK)	.08	.06	.03
8	Willie Stargell (DK)	.40	.30	.15
9	Dave Stieb (DK)	.12	.09	.05
10	Joe Niekro (DK)	.12	.09	.05
11	Rickey Henderson (DK)	.60	.45	.25
12	Dale Murphy (DK)	.80	.60	.30
13	Toby Harrah (DK)	.08	.06	.03
14	Bill Buckner (DK)	.12	.09	.05
15	Willie Wilson (DK)	.15	.11	.06
16	Steve Carlton (DK)	.40	.30	.15
17	Ron Guidry (DK)	.25	.20	.10
18	Steve Rogers (DK)	.08	.06	.03

		MT	NR MT	EX
19	Kent Hrbek (DK)	.40	.30	.15
20	Keith Hernandez (DK)	.40	.30	.15
21	Floyd Bannister (DK)	.10	.08	.04
22	Johnny Bench (DK)	.40	.30	.15
23	Britt Burns (DK)	.08	.06	.03
24	Joe Morgan (DK)	.30	.25	.12
25	Carl Yastrzemski (DK)	.80	.60	.30
26	Terry Kennedy (DK)	.08	.06	.03
27	Gary Roenicke	.06	.05	.02
28	Dwight Bernard	.06	.05	.02
29	Pat Underwood	.06	.05	.02
30	Gary Allenson	.06	.05	.02
31	Ron Guidry	.25	.20	.10
32	Burt Hooton	.08	.06	.03
33	Chris Bando	.06	.05	.02
34	Vida Blue	.12	.09	.05
35	Rickey Henderson	.70	.50	.30
36	Ray Burris	.06	.05	.02
37	John Butcher	.06	.05	.02
38	Don Aase	.06	.05	.02
39	Jerry Koosman	.10	.08	.04
40	Bruce Sutter	.15	.11	.06
41	Jose Cruz	.12	.09	.05
42	Pete Rose	1.00	.70	.40
43	Cesar Cedeno	.12	.09	.05
44	Floyd Chiffer	.06	.05	.02
45	Larry McWilliams	.06	.05	.02
46	Alan Fowlkes	.06	.05	.02
47	Dale Murphy	.90	.70	.35
48	Doug Bird	.06	.05	.02
49	Hubie Brooks	.12	.09	.05
50	Floyd Bannister	.10	.08	.04
51	Jack O'Connor	.06	.05	.02
52	Steve Senteney	.06	.05	.02
53	Gary Gaetti(FC)	4.00	3.00	1.50
54	Damaso Garcia	.06	.05	.02
55	Gene Nelson	.06	.05	.02
56	Mookie Wilson	.10	.08	.04
57	Allen Ripley	.06	.05	.02
58	Bob Horner	.12	.09	.05
59	Tony Pena	.10	.08	.04
60	Gary Lavelle	.06	.05	.02
61	Tim Lollar	.06	.05	.02
62	Frank Pastore	.06	.05	.02
63	Garry Maddox	.10	.08	.04
64	Bob Forsch	.08	.06	.03
65	Harry Spilman	.06	.05	.02
66	Geoff Zahn	.06	.05	.02
67	Salome Barojas	.06	.05	.02
68	David Palmer	.06	.05	.02
69	Charlie Hough	.10	.08	.04
70	Dan Quisenberry	.15	.11	.06
71	Tony Armas	.10	.08	.04
72	Rick Sutcliffe	.12	.09	.05
73	Steve Balboni(FC)	.15	.11	.06
74	Jerry Remy	.06	.05	.02
75	Mike Scioscia	.08	.06	.03
76	John Wockenfuss	.06	.05	.02
77	Jim Palmer	.50	.40	.20
78	Rollie Fingers	.20	.15	.08
79	Joe Nolan	.06	.05	.02
80	Pete Vuckovich	.08	.06	.03
81	Rick Leach	.06	.05	.02
82	Rick Miller	.06	.05	.02
83	Graig Nettles	.15	.11	.06
84	Ron Cey	.12	.09	.05
85	Miguel Dilone	.06	.05	.02
86	John Wathan	.08	.06	.03
87	Kelvin Moore	.06	.05	.02
88a	Byrn Smith (first name incorrect)	.90	.70	.35
88b	Bryn Smith (first name correct)	.08	.06	.03
89	Dave Hostetler	.06	.05	.02
90	Rod Carew	.50	.40	.20
91	Lonnie Smith	.08	.06	.03
92	Bob Knepper	.08	.06	.03
93	Marty Bystrom	.06	.05	.02
94	Chris Welsh	.06	.05	.02
95	Jason Thompson	.06	.05	.02
96	Tom O'Malley	.06	.05	.02
97	Phil Niekro	.30	.25	.12
98	Neil Allen	.06	.05	.02
99	Bill Buckner	.12	.09	.05
100	Ed VandeBerg (Vande Berg)(FC)	.10	.08	.04
101	Jim Clancy	.08	.06	.03
102	Robert Castillo	.06	.05	.02
103	Bruce Berenyi	.06	.05	.02
104	Carlton Fisk	.40	.30	.15
105	Mike Flanagan	.10	.08	.04
106	Cecil Cooper	.15	.11	.06
107	Jack Morris	.30	.25	.12

		MT	NR MT	EX
108	Mike Morgan(FC)	.12	.09	.05
109	Luis Aponte	.06	.05	.02
110	Pedro Guerrero	.25	.20	.10
111	Len Barker	.08	.06	.03
112	Willie Wilson	.15	.11	.06
113	Dave Beard	.06	.05	.02
114	Mike Gates	.06	.05	.02
115	Reggie Jackson	.50	.40	.20
116	George Wright	.06	.05	.02
117	Vance Law	.08	.06	.03
118	Nolan Ryan	1.50	1.25	.60
119	Mike Krukow	.08	.06	.03
120	Ozzie Smith	.20	.15	.08
121	Broderick Perkins	.06	.05	.02
122	Tom Seaver	.50	.40	.20
123	Chris Chambliss	.08	.06	.03
124	Chuck Tanner	.06	.05	.02
125	Johnnie LeMaster	.06	.05	.02
126	Mel Hall(FC)	.50	.40	.20
127	Bruce Bochte	.06	.05	.02
128	Charlie Puleo(FC)	.12	.09	.05
129	Luis Leal	.06	.05	.02
130	John Pacella	.06	.05	.02
131	Glenn Gulliver	.06	.05	.02
132	Don Money	.06	.05	.02
133	Dave Rozema	.06	.05	.02
134	Bruce Hurst(FC)	.25	.20	.10
135	Rudy May	.06	.05	.02
136	Tom LaSorda (Lasorda)	.10	.08	.04
137	Dan Spillner (photo actually Ed Whitson)	.06	.05	.02
138	Jerry Martin	.06	.05	.02
139	Mike Norris	.06	.05	.02
140	Al Oliver	.15	.11	.06
141	Daryl Sconiers	.06	.05	.02
142	Lamar Johnson	.06	.05	.02
143	Harold Baines	.15	.11	.06
144	Alan Ashby	.06	.05	.02
145	Garry Templeton	.10	.08	.04
146	Al Holland	.06	.05	.02
147	Bo Diaz	.08	.06	.03
148	Dave Concepcion	.12	.09	.05
149	Rick Camp	.06	.05	.02
150	Jim Morrison	.06	.05	.02
151	Randy Martz	.06	.05	.02
152	Keith Hernandez	.40	.30	.15
153	John Lowenstein	.06	.05	.02
154	Mike Caldwell	.06	.05	.02
155	Milt Wilcox	.06	.05	.02
156	Rich Gedman	.08	.06	.03
157	Rich Gossage	.20	.15	.08
158	Jerry Reuss	.10	.08	.04
159	Ron Hassey	.06	.05	.02
160	Larry Gura	.06	.05	.02
161	Dwayne Murphy	.08	.06	.03
162	Woodie Fryman	.08	.06	.03
163	Steve Comer	.06	.05	.02
164	Ken Forsch	.06	.05	.02
165	Dennis Lamp	.06	.05	.02
166	David Green	.06	.05	.02
167	Terry Puhl	.06	.05	.02
168	Mike Schmidt	.80	.60	.30
169	Eddie Milner(FC)	.10	.08	.04
170	John Curtis	.06	.05	.02
171	Don Robinson	.08	.06	.03
172	Richard Gale	.06	.05	.02
173	Steve Bedrosian	.12	.09	.05
174	Willie Hernandez	.08	.06	.03
175	Ron Gardenhire	.06	.05	.02
176	Jim Beattie	.06	.05	.02
177	Tim Laudner	.08	.06	.03
178	Buck Martinez	.06	.05	.02
179	Kent Hrbek	.50	.40	.20
180	Alfredo Griffin	.08	.06	.03
181	Larry Andersen	.06	.05	.02
182	Pete Falcone	.06	.05	.02
183	Jody Davis	.10	.08	.04
184	Glenn Hubbard	.08	.06	.03
185	Dale Berra	.06	.05	.02
186	Greg Minton	.06	.05	.02
187	Gary Lucas	.06	.05	.02
188	Dave Van Gorder	.06	.05	.02
189	Bob Dernier(FC)	.10	.08	.04
190	Willie McGee(FC)	1.00	.70	.40
191	Dickie Thon	.08	.06	.03
192	Bob Boone	.10	.08	.04
193	Britt Burns	.06	.05	.02
194	Jeff Reardon	.12	.09	.05
195	Jon Matlack	.08	.06	.03
196	Don Slaught(FC)	.20	.15	.08
197	Fred Stanley	.06	.05	.02
198	Rick Manning	.06	.05	.02
199	Dave Righetti	.25	.20	.10
200	Dave Stapleton	.06	.05	.02
201	Steve Yeager	.06	.05	.02
202	Enos Cabell	.06	.05	.02
203	Sammy Stewart	.06	.05	.02
204	Moose Haas	.06	.05	.02
205	Lenn Sakata	.06	.05	.02
206	Charlie Moore	.06	.05	.02
207	Alan Trammell	.40	.30	.15
208	Jim Rice	.40	.30	.15
209	Roy Smalley	.06	.05	.02
210	Bill Russell	.08	.06	.03
211	Andre Thornton	.10	.08	.04
212	Willie Aikens	.06	.05	.02
213	Dave McKay	.06	.05	.02
214	Tim Blackwell	.06	.05	.02
215	Buddy Bell	.12	.09	.05
216	Doug DeCinces	.10	.08	.04
217	Tom Herr	.10	.08	.04
218	Frank LaCorte	.06	.05	.02
219	Steve Carlton	.50	.40	.20
220	Terry Kennedy	.08	.06	.03
221	Mike Easler	.08	.06	.03
222	Jack Clark	.25	.20	.10
223	Gene Garber	.06	.05	.02
224	Scott Holman	.06	.05	.02
225	Mike Proly	.06	.05	.02
226	Terry Bulling	.06	.05	.02
227	Jerry Garvin	.06	.05	.02
228	Ron Davis	.06	.05	.02
229	Tom Hume	.06	.05	.02
230	Marc Hill	.06	.05	.02
231	Dennis Martinez	.08	.06	.03
232	Jim Gantner	.08	.06	.03
233	Larry Pashnick	.06	.05	.02
234	Dave Collins	.08	.06	.03
235	Tom Burgmeier	.06	.05	.02
236	Ken Landreaux	.06	.05	.02
237	John Denny	.06	.05	.02
238	Hal McRae	.12	.09	.05
239	Matt Keough	.06	.05	.02
240	Doug Flynn	.06	.05	.02
241	Fred Lynn	.20	.15	.08
242	Billy Sample	.06	.05	.02
243	Tom Paciorek	.06	.05	.02
244	Joe Sambito	.06	.05	.02
245	Sid Monge	.06	.05	.02
246	Ken Oberkfell	.06	.05	.02
247	Joe Pittman (photo actually Juan Eichelberger)	.06	.05	.02
248	Mario Soto	.08	.06	.03
249	Claudell Washington	.08	.06	.03
250	Rick Rhoden	.10	.08	.04
251	Darrell Evans	.15	.11	.06
252	Steve Henderson	.06	.05	.02
253	Manny Castillo	.06	.05	.02
254	Craig Swan	.06	.05	.02
255	Joey McLaughlin	.06	.05	.02
256	Pete Redfern	.06	.05	.02
257	Ken Singleton	.10	.08	.04
258	Robin Yount	.60	.45	.25
259	Elias Sosa	.06	.05	.02
260	Bob Ojeda	.12	.09	.05
261	Bobby Murcer	.10	.08	.04
262	Candy Maldonado(FC)	.40	.30	.15
263	Rick Waits	.06	.05	.02
264	Greg Pryor	.06	.05	.02
265	Bob Owchinko	.06	.05	.02
266	Chris Speier	.06	.05	.02
267	Bruce Kison	.06	.05	.02
268	Mark Wagner	.06	.05	.02
269	Steve Kemp	.10	.08	.04
270	Phil Garner	.08	.06	.03
271	Gene Richards	.06	.05	.02
272	Renie Martin	.06	.05	.02
273	Dave Roberts	.06	.05	.02
274	Dan Driessen	.08	.06	.03
275	Rufino Linares	.06	.05	.02
276	Lee Lacy	.06	.05	.02
277	Ryne Sandberg(FC)	8.00	6.00	3.25
278	Darrell Porter	.08	.06	.03
279	Cal Ripken	1.00	.70	.40
280	Jamie Easterly	.06	.05	.02
281	Bill Fahey	.06	.05	.02
282	Glenn Hoffman	.06	.05	.02
283	Willie Randolph	.10	.08	.04
284	Fernando Valenzuela	.30	.25	.12
285	Alan Bannister	.06	.05	.02
286	Paul Splittorff	.06	.05	.02
287	Joe Rudi	.10	.08	.04

		MT	NR MT	EX			MT	NR MT	EX
288	Bill Gullickson	.06	.05	.02	376	Rod Scurry	.06	.05	.02
289	Danny Darwin	.06	.05	.02	377	Bob Brenly(FC)	.08	.06	.03
290	Andy Hassler	.06	.05	.02	378	Scot Thompson	.06	.05	.02
291	Ernesto Escarrega	.06	.05	.02	379	Julio Cruz	.06	.05	.02
292	Steve Mura	.06	.05	.02	380	John Stearns	.06	.05	.02
293	Tony Scott	.06	.05	.02	381	Dale Murray	.06	.05	.02
294	Manny Trillo	.08	.06	.03	382	*Frank Viola*(FC)	4.00	3.00	1.50
295	Greg Harris(FC)	.08	.06	.03	383	Al Bumbry	.08	.06	.03
296	Luis DeLeon	.06	.05	.02	384	Ben Oglivie	.08	.06	.03
297	Kent Tekulve	.08	.06	.03	385	Dave Tobik	.06	.05	.02
298	Atlee Hammaker(FC)	.12	.09	.05	386	Bob Stanley	.06	.05	.02
299	Bruce Benedict	.06	.05	.02	387	Andre Robertson	.06	.05	.02
300	Fergie Jenkins	.15	.11	.06	388	Jorge Orta	.06	.05	.02
301	Dave Kingman	.15	.11	.06	389	Ed Whitson	.06	.05	.02
302	Bill Caudill	.06	.05	.02	390	Don Hood	.06	.05	.02
303	John Castino	.06	.05	.02	391	Tim Underwood	.06	.05	.02
304	Ernie Whitt	.08	.06	.03	392	Tim Wallach	.20	.15	.08
305	Randy Johnson	.06	.05	.02	393	Steve Renko	.06	.05	.02
306	Garth Iorg	.06	.05	.02	394	Mickey Rivers	.08	.06	.03
307	Gaylord Perry	.30	.25	.12	395	Greg Luzinski	.12	.09	.05
308	Ed Lynch	.06	.05	.02	396	Art Howe	.06	.05	.02
309	Keith Moreland	.08	.06	.03	397	Alan Wiggins	.06	.05	.02
310	Rafael Ramirez	.06	.05	.02	398	Jim Barr	.06	.05	.02
311	Bill Madlock	.12	.09	.05	399	Ivan DeJesus	.06	.05	.02
312	Milt May	.06	.05	.02	400	*Tom Lawless*(FC)	.08	.06	.03
313	John Montefusco	.06	.05	.02	401	Bob Walk	.08	.06	.03
314	Wayne Krenchicki	.06	.05	.02	402	Jimmy Smith	.06	.05	.02
315	George Vukovich	.06	.05	.02	403	Lee Smith	.15	.11	.06
316	Joaquin Andujar	.08	.06	.03	404	George Hendrick	.08	.06	.03
317	Craig Reynolds	.06	.05	.02	405	Eddie Murray	.60	.45	.25
318	Rick Burleson	.08	.06	.03	406	Marshall Edwards	.06	.05	.02
319	Richard Dotson	.10	.08	.04	407	Lance Parrish	.35	.25	.14
320	Steve Rogers	.08	.06	.03	408	Carney Lansford	.08	.06	.03
321	Dave Schmidt(FC)	.10	.08	.04	409	Dave Winfield	.40	.30	.15
322	*Bud Black*(FC)	.20	.15	.08	410	Bob Welch	.12	.09	.05
323	Jeff Burroughs	.08	.06	.03	411	Larry Milbourne	.06	.05	.02
324	Von Hayes	.15	.11	.06	412	Dennis Leonard	.08	.06	.03
325	Butch Wynegar	.06	.05	.02	413	Dan Meyer	.06	.05	.02
326	Carl Yastrzemski	.70	.50	.30	414	Charlie Lea	.06	.05	.02
327	Ron Roenicke	.06	.05	.02	415	Rick Honeycutt	.06	.05	.02
328	*Howard Johnson*(FC)	8.00	6.00	3.25	416	Mike Witt	.15	.11	.06
329	Rick Dempsey	.08	.06	.03	417	Steve Trout	.06	.05	.02
330a	Jim Slaton (one yellow box on back)				418	Glenn Brummer	.06	.05	.02
		.70	.50	.30	419	Denny Walling	.06	.05	.02
330b	Jim Slaton (two yellow boxes on back)				420	Gary Matthews	.10	.08	.04
		.08	.06	.03	421	Charlie Liebrandt (Leibrandt)	.08	.06	.03
331	Benny Ayala	.06	.05	.02	422	Juan Eichelberger	.06	.05	.02
332	Ted Simmons	.12	.09	.05	423	*Matt Guante (Cecilio)*(FC)	.15	.11	.06
333	Lou Whitaker	.40	.30	.15	424	Bill Laskey	.06	.05	.02
334	Chuck Rainey	.06	.05	.02	425	Jerry Royster	.06	.05	.02
335	Lou Piniella	.12	.09	.05	426	Dickie Noles	.06	.05	.02
336	Steve Sax	.30	.25	.12	427	George Foster	.15	.11	.06
337	Toby Harrah	.08	.06	.03	428	*Mike Moore*(FC)	1.00	.70	.40
338	George Brett	.70	.50	.30	429	Gary Ward	.08	.06	.03
339	Davey Lopes	.10	.08	.04	430	Barry Bonnell	.06	.05	.02
340	Gary Carter	.40	.30	.15	431	Ron Washington	.06	.05	.02
341	John Grubb	.06	.05	.02	432	Rance Mulliniks	.06	.05	.02
342	Tim Foli	.06	.05	.02	433	Mike Stanton	.06	.05	.02
343	Jim Kaat	.15	.11	.06	434	Jesse Orosco	.10	.08	.04
344	Mike LaCoss	.06	.05	.02	435	Larry Bowa	.12	.09	.05
345	Larry Christenson	.06	.05	.02	436	Biff Pocoroba	.06	.05	.02
346	Juan Bonilla	.06	.05	.02	437	Johnny Ray	.12	.09	.05
347	Omar Moreno	.06	.05	.02	438	Joe Morgan	.30	.25	.12
348	Charles Davis(FC)	.20	.15	.08	439	*Eric Show*(FC)	.30	.25	.12
349	Tommy Boggs	.06	.05	.02	440	Larry Biittner	.06	.05	.02
350	Rusty Staub	.10	.08	.04	441	Greg Gross	.06	.05	.02
351	Bump Wills	.06	.05	.02	442	Gene Tenace	.08	.06	.03
352	Rick Sweet	.06	.05	.02	443	Danny Heep	.06	.05	.02
353	*Jim Gott*(FC)	.20	.15	.08	444	Bobby Clark	.06	.05	.02
354	Terry Felton	.06	.05	.02	445	Kevin Hickey	.06	.05	.02
355	Jim Kern	.06	.05	.02	446	Scott Sanderson	.06	.05	.02
356	Bill Almon	.06	.05	.02	447	Frank Tanana	.10	.08	.04
357	Tippy Martinez	.06	.05	.02	448	Cesar Geronimo	.06	.05	.02
358	Roy Howell	.06	.05	.02	449	Jimmy Sexton	.06	.05	.02
359	Dan Petry	.08	.06	.03	450	Mike Hargrove	.06	.05	.02
360	Jerry Mumphrey	.06	.05	.02	451	Doyle Alexander	.10	.08	.04
361	Mark Clear	.06	.05	.02	452	Dwight Evans	.15	.11	.06
362	Mike Marshall	.20	.15	.08	453	Terry Forster	.08	.06	.03
363	Lary Sorensen	.06	.05	.02	454	Tom Brookens	.06	.05	.02
364	Amos Otis	.08	.06	.03	455	Rich Dauer	.06	.05	.02
365	Rick Langford	.06	.05	.02	456	Rob Picciolo	.06	.05	.02
366	Brad Mills	.06	.05	.02	457	Terry Crowley	.06	.05	.02
367	Brian Downing	.10	.08	.04	458	Ned Yost	.06	.05	.02
368	Mike Richardt	.06	.05	.02	459	Kirk Gibson	.40	.30	.15
369	Aurelio Rodriguez	.08	.06	.03	460	Reid Nichols	.06	.05	.02
370	Dave Smith	.08	.06	.03	461	Oscar Gamble	.08	.06	.03
371	Tug McGraw	.12	.09	.05	462	Dusty Baker	.10	.08	.04
372	Doug Bair	.06	.05	.02	463	Jack Perconte	.06	.05	.02
373	Ruppert Jones	.06	.05	.02	464	Frank White	.10	.08	.04
374	Alex Trevino	.06	.05	.02	465	Mickey Klutts	.06	.05	.02
375	Ken Dayley	.06	.05	.02	466	Warren Cromartie	.06	.05	.02

		MT	NR MT	EX
467	Larry Parrish	.10	.08	.04
468	Bobby Grich	.10	.08	.04
469	Dane Iorg	.06	.05	.02
470	Joe Niekro	.12	.09	.05
471	Ed Farmer	.06	.05	.02
472	Tim Flannery	.06	.05	.02
473	Dave Parker	.30	.25	.12
474	Jeff Leonard	.10	.08	.04
475	Al Hrabosky	.08	.06	.03
476	Ron Hodges	.06	.05	.02
477	Leon Durham	.08	.06	.03
478	Jim Essian	.06	.05	.02
479	Roy Lee Jackson	.06	.05	.02
480	Brad Havens	.06	.05	.02
481	Joe Price	.06	.05	.02
482	Tony Bernazard	.06	.05	.02
483	Scott McGregor	.08	.06	.03
484	Paul Molitor	.20	.15	.08
485	Mike Ivie	.06	.05	.02
486	Ken Griffey	.12	.09	.05
487	Dennis Eckersley	.12	.09	.05
488	Steve Garvey	.40	.30	.15
489	Mike Fischlin	.06	.05	.02
490	U.L. Washington	.06	.05	.02
491	Steve McCatty	.06	.05	.02
492	Roy Johnson	.06	.05	.02
493	Don Baylor	.12	.09	.05
494	Bobby Johnson	.06	.05	.02
495	Mike Squires	.06	.05	.02
496	Bert Roberge	.06	.05	.02
497	Dick Ruthven	.06	.05	.02
498	Tito Landrum	.06	.05	.02
499	Sixto Lezcano	.06	.05	.02
500	Johnny Bench	.40	.30	.15
501	Larry Whisenton	.06	.05	.02
502	Manny Sarmiento	.06	.05	.02
503	Fred Breining	.06	.05	.02
504	Bill Campbell	.06	.05	.02
505	Todd Cruz	.06	.05	.02
506	Bob Bailor	.06	.05	.02
507	Dave Stieb	.12	.09	.05
508	Al Williams	.06	.05	.02
509	Dan Ford	.06	.05	.02
510	Gorman Thomas	.10	.08	.04
511	Chet Lemon	.08	.06	.03
512	Mike Torrez	.08	.06	.03
513	Shane Rawley	.10	.08	.04
514	Mark Belanger	.08	.06	.03
515	Rodney Craig	.06	.05	.02
516	Onix Concepcion	.06	.05	.02
517	Mike Heath	.06	.05	.02
518	Andre Dawson	.35	.25	.14
519	Luis Sanchez	.06	.05	.02
520	Terry Bogener	.06	.05	.02
521	Rudy Law	.06	.05	.02
522	Ray Knight	.10	.08	.04
523	Joe Lefebvre	.06	.05	.02
524	Jim Wohlford	.06	.05	.02
525	*Julio Franco*(FC)	4.00	3.00	1.50
526	Ron Oester	.06	.05	.02
527	Rick Mahler	.08	.06	.03
528	Steve Nicosia	.06	.05	.02
529	Junior Kennedy	.06	.05	.02
530a	Whitey Herzog (one yellow box on back)			
		.70	.50	.30
530b	Whitey Herzog (two yellow boxes on back)			
		.10	.08	.04
531a	Don Sutton (blue frame around photo)			
		1.00	.70	.40
531b	Don Sutton (green frame around photo)			
		.30	.25	.12
532	Mark Brouhard	.06	.05	.02
533a	Sparky Anderson (one yellow box on back)			
		.70	.50	.30
533b	Sparky Anderson (two yellow boxes on back)			
		.10	.08	.04
534	Roger LaFrancois	.06	.05	.02
535	George Frazier	.06	.05	.02
536	Tom Niedenfuer	.08	.06	.03
537	Ed Glynn	.06	.05	.02
538	Lee May	.08	.06	.03
539	Bob Kearney	.06	.05	.02
540	Tim Raines	.35	.25	.14
541	Paul Mirabella	.06	.05	.02
542	Luis Tiant	.12	.09	.05
543	Ron LeFlore	.08	.06	.03
544	*Dave LaPoint*(FC)	.30	.25	.12
545	Randy Moffitt	.06	.05	.02
546	Luis Aguayo	.06	.05	.02
547	Brad Lesley	.06	.05	.02
548	Luis Salazar	.06	.05	.02

		MT	NR MT	EX
549	John Candelaria	.10	.08	.04
550	Dave Bergman	.06	.05	.02
551	Bob Watson	.08	.06	.03
552	Pat Tabler	.10	.08	.04
553	Brent Gaff	.06	.05	.02
554	Al Cowens	.06	.05	.02
555	Tom Brunansky(FC)	.25	.20	.10
556	Lloyd Moseby	.12	.09	.05
557a	Pascual Perez (Twins)(FC)	.90	.70	.35
557b	Pascual Perez (Braves)(FC)	.15	.11	.06
558	Willie Upshaw	.08	.06	.03
559	Richie Zisk	.08	.06	.03
560	Pat Zachry	.06	.05	.02
561	Jay Johnstone	.08	.06	.03
562	Carlos Diaz	.06	.05	.02
563	John Tudor	.10	.08	.04
564	Frank Robinson	.12	.09	.05
565	Dave Edwards	.06	.05	.02
566	Paul Householder	.06	.05	.02
567	Ron Reed	.06	.05	.02
568	Mike Ramsey	.06	.05	.02
569	Kiko Garcia	.06	.05	.02
570	Tommy John	.20	.15	.08
571	Tony LaRussa	.08	.06	.03
572	Joel Youngblood	.06	.05	.02
573	*Wayne Tolleson*(FC)	.12	.09	.05
574	Keith Creel	.06	.05	.02
575	Billy Martin	.12	.09	.05
576	Jerry Dybzinski	.06	.05	.02
577	Rick Cerone	.06	.05	.02
578	Tony Perez	.20	.15	.08
579	*Greg Brock*(FC)	.35	.25	.14
580	*Glen Wilson (Glenn)*(FC)	.35	.25	.14
581	Tim Stoddard	.06	.05	.02
582	Bob McClure	.06	.05	.02
583	Jim Dwyer	.06	.05	.02
584	Ed Romero	.06	.05	.02
585	Larry Herndon	.08	.06	.03
586	*Wade Boggs*(FC)	18.00	13.50	7.25
587	Jay Howell(FC)	.15	.11	.06
588	Dave Stewart	.15	.11	.06
589	Bert Blyleven	.12	.09	.05
590	Dick Howser	.06	.05	.02
591	Wayne Gross	.06	.05	.02
592	Terry Francona	.06	.05	.02
593	Don Werner	.06	.05	.02
594	Bill Stein	.06	.05	.02
595	Jesse Barfield(FC)	.70	.50	.30
596	Bobby Molinaro	.06	.05	.02
597	Mike Vail	.06	.05	.02
598	*Tony Gwynn*(FC)	11.00	8.25	4.50
599	Gary Rajsich	.06	.05	.02
600	Jerry Ujdur	.06	.05	.02
601	Cliff Johnson	.06	.05	.02
602	Jerry White	.06	.05	.02
603	Bryan Clark	.06	.05	.02
604	Joe Ferguson	.06	.05	.02
605	Guy Sularz	.06	.05	.02
606a	Ozzie Virgil (green frame around photo)(FC)	.90	.70	.35
606b	Ozzie Virgil (orange frame around photo)(FC)	.08	.06	.03
607	Terry Harper(FC)	.06	.05	.02
608	Harvey Kuenn	.08	.06	.03
609	Jim Sundberg	.08	.06	.03
610	Willie Stargell	.40	.30	.15
611	Reggie Smith	.10	.08	.04
612	Rob Wilfong	.06	.05	.02
613	Niekro Brothers (Joe Niekro, Phil Niekro)	.15	.11	.06
614	Lee Elia	.06	.05	.02
615	Mickey Hatcher	.08	.06	.03
616	Jerry Hairston	.06	.05	.02
617	John Martin	.06	.05	.02
618	Wally Backman(FC)	.15	.11	.06
619	*Storm Davis*(FC)	.50	.40	.20
620	Alan Knicely	.06	.05	.02
621	John Stuper	.06	.05	.02
622	Matt Sinatro	.06	.05	.02
623	*Gene Petralli*(FC)	.15	.11	.06
624	Duane Walker	.06	.05	.02
625	Dick Williams	.06	.05	.02
626	Pat Corrales	.06	.05	.02
627	Vern Ruhle	.06	.05	.02
628	Joe Torre	.08	.06	.03
629	Anthony Johnson	.06	.05	.02
630	Steve Howe	.08	.06	.03
631	Gary Woods	.06	.05	.02
632	Lamarr Hoyt (LaMarr)	.06	.05	.02
633	Steve Swisher	.06	.05	.02
634	Terry Leach(FC)	.12	.09	.05

		MT	NR MT	EX
635	Jeff Newman	.06	.05	.02
636	Brett Butler	.10	.08	.04
637	Gary Gray	.06	.05	.02
638	Lee Mazzilli	.08	.06	.03
639a	Ron Jackson (A's)	18.00	13.50	7.25
639b	Ron Jackson (Angels - green frame around photo)	.90	.70	.35
639c	Ron Jackson (Angels - red frame around photo)	.20	.15	.08
640	Juan Beniquez	.06	.05	.02
641	Dave Rucker	.06	.05	.02
642	Luis Pujols	.06	.05	.02
643	Rick Monday	.10	.08	.04
644	Hosken Powell	.06	.05	.02
645	San Diego Chicken	.20	.15	.08
646	Dave Engle	.06	.05	.02
647	Dick Davis	.06	.05	.02
648	MVP's (Vida Blue, Joe Morgan, Frank Robinson)	.15	.11	.06
649	Al Chambers	.06	.05	.02
650	Jesus Vega	.06	.05	.02
651	Jeff Jones	.06	.05	.02
652	Marvis Foley	.06	.05	.02
653	Ty Cobb Puzzle	.06	.05	.02
---a	Dick Perez/DK Checklist (no word "Checklist" on back)	.70	.50	.30
---b	Dick Perez/DK Checklist (word "Checklist" on back)	.08	.06	.03
----	Checklist 27-130	.06	.05	.02
----	Checklist 131-234	.06	.05	.02
----	Checklist 235-338	.06	.05	.02
----	Checklist 339-442	.06	.05	.02
----	Checklist 443-546	.06	.05	.02
----	Checklist 547-653	.06	.05	.02

1983 Donruss Action All-Stars

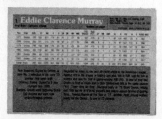

The cards in this 60-card set are designed on a horizontal format and contain a large close-up photo of the player on the left and a smaller action photo on the right. The cards, which measure 3-1/2" by 5", have deep red borders and contain the Donruss logo and the year of issue. The card backs have black print on red and white and contain various statistical and biographical information. The cards were sold with puzzle pieces (three pieces on one card per pack) that feature Mickey Mantle.

		MT	NR MT	EX
	Complete Set:	6.50	5.00	3.00
	Common Player:	.10	.08	.04
1	Eddie Murray	.30	.25	.12
2	Dwight Evans	.15	.11	.06
3a	Reggie Jackson (red covers part of statistics on back)	.35	.25	.14
3b	Reggie Jackson (red does not cover any statistics on back)	.35	.25	.14
4	Greg Luzinski	.12	.09	.05
5	Larry Herndon	.10	.08	.04

		MT	NR MT	EX
6	Al Oliver	.12	.09	.05
7	Bill Buckner	.10	.08	.04
8	Jason Thompson	.10	.08	.04
9	Andre Dawson	.20	.15	.08
10	Greg Minton	.10	.08	.04
11	Terry Kennedy	.10	.08	.04
12	Phil Niekro	.20	.15	.08
13	Willie Wilson	.12	.09	.05
14	Johnny Bench	.35	.25	.14
15	Ron Guidry	.15	.11	.06
16	Hal McRae	.10	.08	.04
17	Damaso Garcia	.10	.08	.04
18	Gary Ward	.10	.08	.04
19	Cecil Cooper	.12	.09	.05
20	Keith Hernandez	.25	.20	.10
21	Ron Cey	.12	.09	.05
22	Rickey Henderson	.50	.40	.20
23	Nolan Ryan	.50	.40	.20
24	Steve Carlton	.30	.25	.12
25	John Stearns	.10	.08	.04
26	Jim Sundberg	.10	.08	.04
27	Joaquin Andujar	.10	.08	.04
28	Gaylord Perry	.15	.11	.06
29	Jack Clark	.15	.11	.06
30	Bill Madlock	.12	.09	.05
31	Pete Rose	.35	.25	.14
32	Mookie Wilson	.10	.08	.04
33	Rollie Fingers	.15	.11	.06
34	Lonnie Smith	.10	.08	.04
35	Tony Pena	.10	.08	.04
36	Dave Winfield	.30	.25	.12
37	Tim Lollar	.10	.08	.04
38	Rod Carew	.30	.25	.12
39	Toby Harrah	.10	.08	.04
40	Buddy Bell	.10	.08	.04
41	Bruce Sutter	.12	.09	.05
42	George Brett	.40	.30	.15
43	Carlton Fisk	.35	.25	.14
44	Carl Yastrzemski	.40	.30	.15
45	Dale Murphy	.30	.25	.12
46	Bob Horner	.12	.09	.05
47	Dave Concepcion	.12	.09	.05
48	Dave Stieb	.12	.09	.05
49	Kent Hrbek	.20	.15	.08
50	Lance Parrish	.15	.11	.06
51	Joe Niekro	.12	.09	.05
52	Cal Ripken Jr.	.35	.25	.14
53	Fernando Valenzuela	.12	.09	.05
54	Rickie Zisk	.10	.08	.04
55	Leon Durham	.10	.08	.04
56	Robin Yount	.40	.30	.15
57	Mike Schmidt	.70	.50	.30
58	Gary Carter	.15	.11	.06
59	Fred Lynn	.15	.11	.06
60	Checklist	.10	.08	.04

1983 Donruss Hall Of Fame Heroes

The artwork of Dick Perez is featured in the 44-card Donruss Hall of Fame Heroes set issued in 1983. The standard-size cards (2-1/2" by 3-1/2") were available in wax packs that contained eight cards plus a Mickey Mantle puzzle piece card (three pieces on one card per pack). The backs, which display red and blue print on white stock, contain a short player biographical sketch derived from the Hall of Fame yearbook. The numbered set consists of 44 player cards, a Mantle puzzle card, and a checklist.

		MT	NR MT	EX
	Complete Set:	6.00	4.50	2.50
	Common Player:	.05	.04	.02
1	Ty Cobb	.50	.40	.20
2	Walter Johnson	.15	.11	.06
3	Christy Mathewson	.15	.11	.06
4	Josh Gibson	.10	.08	.04
5	Honus Wagner	.15	.11	.06
6	Jackie Robinson	.30	.25	.12
7	Mickey Mantle	1.00	.70	.40
8	Luke Appling	.05	.04	.02
9	Ted Williams	.50	.40	.20
10	Johnny Mize	.15	.11	.06
11	Satchel Paige	.15	.11	.06
12	Lou Boudreau	.15	.11	.06
13	Jimmie Foxx	.15	.11	.06
14	Duke Snider	.50	.40	.20
15	Monte Irvin	.15	.11	.06
16	Hank Greenberg	.15	.11	.06
17	Roberto Clemente	.20	.15	.08
18	Al Kaline	.30	.25	.12
19	Frank Robinson	.30	.25	.12
20	Joe Cronin	.09	.07	.04
21	Burleigh Grimes	.05	.04	.02
22	The Waner Brothers (Lloyd Waner, Paul Waner)	.09	.07	.04
23	Grover Alexander	.09	.07	.04
24	Yogi Berra	.30	.25	.12
25	James Bell	.05	.04	.02
26	Bill Dickey	.09	.07	.04
27	Cy Young	.15	.11	.06
28	Charlie Gehringer	.09	.07	.04
29	Dizzy Dean	.15	.11	.06
30	Bob Lemon	.15	.11	.06
31	Red Ruffing	.05	.04	.02
32	Stan Musial	.50	.40	.20
33	Carl Hubbell	.15	.11	.06
34	Hank Aaron	.50	.40	.20
35	John McGraw	.09	.07	.04
36	Bob Feller	.30	.25	.12
37	Casey Stengel	.15	.11	.06
38	Ralph Kiner	.15	.11	.06
39	Roy Campanella	.15	.11	.06
40	Mel Ott	.09	.07	.04
41	Robin Roberts	.15	.11	.06
42	Early Wynn	.15	.11	.06
43	Mickey Mantle Puzzle Card	.09	.07	.04
-----	Checklist	.09	.07	.04

1984 Donruss

The 1984 Donruss set consists of 651 numbered cards, seven unnumbered checklists and two "Living Legends" cards (designated A and B). The A and B cards were issued only in wax packs and not available to hobby dealers purchasing vending sets. The card fronts differ in style from the previous years, however the Donruss logo and year of issue are still included. The card backs have black print on green and white and are identical in format to the preceding year. The standard-size cards (2-1/2" by 3-1/2") were issued with a 63-piece puzzle of Duke Snider. A limited print run of the issue by Donruss has caused the set to

escalate in price in recent years. The complete set price in the checklist that follows does not include the higher priced variations. Cards marked with (DK) or (RR) in the checklist refer to the Diamond Kings and Rated Rookies subsets.

		MT	NR MT	EX
	Complete Set:	225.00	169.00	90.00
	Common Player:	.10	.08	.04
1a	Robin Yount (DK) (Perez-Steel on back)	.80	.60	.30
1b	Robin Yount (DK) (Perez-Steele on back)	1.50	1.25	.60
2a	Dave Concepcion (DK) (Perez-Steel on back)	.30	.25	.12
2b	Dave Concepcion (DK) (Perez-Steele on back)	.60	.45	.25
3a	Dwayne Murphy (DK) (Perez-Steel on back)	.25	.20	.10
3b	Dwayne Murphy (DK) (Perez-Steele on back)	.60	.45	.25
4a	John Castino (DK) (Perez-Steel on back)	.20	.15	.08
4b	John Castino (DK) (Perez-Steele on back)	.60	.45	.25
5a	Leon Durham (DK) (Perez-Steel on back)	.25	.20	.10
5b	Leon Durham (DK) (Perez-Steele on back)	.60	.45	.25
6a	Rusty Staub (DK) (Perez-Steel on back)	.30	.25	.12
6b	Rusty Staub (DK) (Perez-Steele on back)	.60	.45	.25
7a	Jack Clark (DK) (Perez-Steel on back)	.40	.30	.15
7b	Jack Clark (DK) (Perez-Steel on back)	.80	.60	.30
8a	Dave Dravecky (DK) (Perez-Steel on back)	.25	.20	.10
8b	Dave Dravecky (DK) (Perez-Steele on back)	.60	.45	.25
9a	Al Oliver (DK) (Perez-Steel on back)	.35	.25	.14
9b	Al Oliver (DK) (Perez-Steele on back)	.70	.50	.30
10a	Dave Righetti (DK) (Perez-Steel on back)	.40	.30	.15
10b	Dave Righetti (DK) (Perez-Steele on back)	.80	.60	.30
11a	Hal McRae (DK) (Perez-Steel on back)	.30	.25	.12
11b	Hal McRae (DK) (Perez-Steele on back)	.60	.45	.25
12a	Ray Knight (DK) (Perez-Steel on back)	.25	.20	.10
12b	Ray Knight (DK) (Perez-Steele on back)	.60	.45	.25
13a	Bruce Sutter (DK) (Perez-Steel on back)	.35	.25	.14
13b	Bruce Sutter (DK) (Perez-Steele on back)	.70	.50	.30
14a	Bob Horner (DK) (Perez-Steel on back)	.40	.30	.15
14b	Bob Horner (DK) (Perez-Steele on back)	.80	.60	.30
15a	Lance Parrish (DK) (Perez-Steel on back)	.60	.45	.25
15b	Lance Parrish (DK) (Perez-Steele on back)	1.25	.90	.50
16a	Matt Young (DK) (Perez-Steel on back)	.25	.20	.10
16b	Matt Young (DK) (Perez-Steele on back)	.60	.45	.25
17a	Fred Lynn (DK) (Perez-Steel on back)	.35	.25	.14
17b	Fred Lynn (DK) (Perez-Steele on back)	.70	.50	.30
18a	Ron Kittle (DK) (Perez-Steel on back)(FC)	.35	.25	.14
18b	Ron Kittle (DK) (Perez-Steele on back)(FC)	.70	.50	.30
19a	Jim Clancy (DK) (Perez-Steel on back)	.25	.20	.10
19b	Jim Clancy (DK) (Perez-Steele on back)	.60	.45	.25
20a	Bill Madlock (DK) (Perez-Steel on back)	.30	.25	.12
20b	Bill Madlock (DK) (Perez-Steele on back)	.60	.45	.25
21a	Larry Parrish (DK) (Perez-Steel on back)	.30	.25	.12

		MT	NR MT	EX
21b	Larry Parrish (DK) (Perez-Steele on back)			
		.60	.45	.25
22a	Eddie Murray (DK) (Perez-Steel on back)			
		1.25	.90	.50
22b	Eddie Murray (DK) (Perez-Steel on back)			
		2.50	2.00	1.00
23a	Mike Schmidt (DK) (Perez-Steel on back)			
		1.25	.90	.50
23b	Mike Schmidt (DK) (Perez-Steel on back)			
		2.50	2.00	1.00
24a	Pedro Guerrero (DK) (Perez-Steel on back)			
		.50	.40	.20
24b	Pedro Guerrero (DK) (Perez-Steele on back)			
		1.00	.70	.40
25a	Andre Thornton (DK) (Perez-Steel on back)			
		.30	.25	.12
25b	Andre Thornton (DK) (Perez-Steel on back)			
		.60	.45	.25
26a	Wade Boggs (DK) (Perez-Steel on back)			
		3.75	2.75	1.50
26b	Wade Boggs (DK) (Perez-Steel on back)			
		5.00	3.75	2.00
27	*Joel Skinner (RR)(FC)*	.20	.15	.08
28	Tom Dunbar (RR)	.10	.08	.04
29a	Mike Stenhouse (RR) (no number on back)			
		.15	.11	.06
29b	Mike Stenhouse (RR) (29 on back)			
		8.00	6.00	3.25
30a	*Ron Darling (no number on back)(FC)*			
		6.00	4.50	2.50
30b	*Ron Darling (30 on back)(FC)*	20.00	15.00	8.00
31	*Dion James (RR)(FC)*	.40	.30	.15
32	*Tony Fernandez (RR)(FC)*	7.00	5.25	2.75
33	Angel Salazar (RR)	.10	.08	.04
34	*Kevin McReynolds (RR)(FC)*	12.00	9.00	4.75
35	*Dick Schofield (RR)(FC)*	.40	.30	.15
36	*Brad Komminsk (RR)(FC)*	.15	.11	.06
37	*Tim Teufel (RR)(FC)*	.40	.30	.15
38	Doug Frobel (RR)	.10	.08	.04
39	*Greg Gagne (RR)(FC)*	.35	.25	.14
40	Mike Fuentes (RR)	.10	.08	.04
41	*Joe Carter (RR)(FC)*	15.00	11.00	6.00
42	Mike Brown (RR)	.10	.08	.04
43	Mike Jeffcoat (RR)	.10	.08	.04
44	*Sid Fernandez (RR)(FC)*	6.00	4.50	2.50
45	Brian Dayett (RR)	.10	.08	.04
46	Chris Smith (RR)	.10	.08	.04
47	Eddie Murray	1.25	.90	.50
48	Robin Yount	1.00	.70	.40
49	Lance Parrish	.50	.40	.20
50	Jim Rice	.90	.70	.35
51	Dave Winfield	.90	.70	.35
52	Fernando Valenzuela	.70	.50	.30
53	George Brett	1.50	1.25	.60
54	Rickey Henderson	1.75	1.25	.70
55	Gary Carter	.80	.60	.30
56	Buddy Bell	.20	.15	.08
57	Reggie Jackson	1.25	.90	.50
58	Harold Baines	.25	.20	.10
59	Ozzie Smith	.25	.20	.10
60	Nolan Ryan	1.25	.90	.50
61	Pete Rose	2.50	2.00	1.00
62	Ron Oester	.10	.08	.04
63	Steve Garvey	.90	.70	.35
64	Jason Thompson	.10	.08	.04
65	Jack Clark	.35	.25	.14
66	Dale Murphy	1.50	1.25	.60
67	Leon Durham	.12	.09	.05
68	*Darryl Strawberry(FC)*	35.00	27.00	15.00
69	Richie Zisk	.12	.09	.05
70	Kent Hrbek	.60	.45	.25
71	Dave Stieb	.25	.20	.10
72	Ken Schrom	.10	.08	.04
73	George Bell	1.75	1.25	.70
74	John Moses	.15	.11	.06
75	Ed Lynch	.10	.08	.04
76	Chuck Rainey	.10	.08	.04
77	Biff Pocoroba	.10	.08	.04
78	Cecilio Guante	.10	.08	.04
79	Jim Barr	.10	.08	.04
80	Kurt Bevacqua	.10	.08	.04
81	Tom Foley	.10	.08	.04
82	Joe Lefebvre	.10	.08	.04
83	*Andy Van Slyke(FC)*	3.50	2.75	1.50
84	Bob Lillis	.10	.08	.04
85	Rick Adams	.10	.08	.04
86	Jerry Hairston	.10	.08	.04
87	Bob James	.10	.08	.04
88	Joe Altobelli	.10	.08	.04
89	Ed Romero	.10	.08	.04
90	John Grubb	.10	.08	.04

		MT	NR MT	EX
91	John Henry Johnson	.10	.08	.04
92	Juan Espino	.10	.08	.04
93	Candy Maldonado	.20	.15	.08
94	Andre Thornton	.20	.15	.08
95	Onix Concepcion	.10	.08	.04
96	*Don Hill(FC)*	.20	.15	.08
97	Andre Dawson	.60	.45	.25
98	Frank Tanana	.15	.11	.06
99	*Curt Wilkerson(FC)*	.15	.11	.06
100	Larry Gura	.10	.08	.04
101	Dwayne Murphy	.12	.09	.05
102	Tom Brennan	.10	.08	.04
103	Dave Righetti	.40	.30	.15
104	Steve Sax	.30	.25	.12
105	Dan Petry	.12	.09	.05
106	Cal Ripken	1.25	.90	.50
107	Paul Molitor	.35	.25	.14
108	Fred Lynn	.35	.25	.14
109	Neil Allen	.10	.08	.04
110	Joe Niekro	.20	.15	.08
111	Steve Carlton	.90	.70	.35
112	Terry Kennedy	.15	.11	.06
113	Bill Madlock	.20	.15	.08
114	Chili Davis	.15	.11	.06
115	Jim Gantner	.12	.09	.05
116	Tom Seaver	1.00	.70	.40
117	Bill Buckner	.20	.15	.08
118	Bill Caudill	.10	.08	.04
119	Jim Clancy	.15	.11	.06
120	John Castino	.10	.08	.04
121	Dave Concepcion	.20	.15	.08
122	Greg Luzinski	.20	.15	.08
123	Mike Boddicker(FC)	.20	.15	.08
124	Pete Ladd	.10	.08	.04
125	Juan Berenguer	.10	.08	.04
126	John Montefusco	.10	.08	.04
127	Ed Jurak	.10	.08	.04
128	Tom Niedenfuer	.12	.09	.05
129	Bert Blyleven	.30	.25	.12
130	Bud Black	.12	.09	.05
131	Gorman Heimueller	.10	.08	.04
132	Dan Schatzeder	.10	.08	.04
133	Ron Jackson	.10	.08	.04
134	*Tom Henke(FC)*	.60	.45	.25
135	Kevin Hickey	.10	.08	.04
136	Mike Scott	.30	.25	.12
137	Bo Diaz	.12	.09	.05
138	Glenn Brummer	.10	.08	.04
139	Sid Monge	.10	.08	.04
140	Rich Gale	.10	.08	.04
141	Brett Butler	.15	.11	.06
142	Brian Harper	.10	.08	.04
143	John Rabb	.10	.08	.04
144	Gary Woods	.10	.08	.04
145	Pat Putnam	.10	.08	.04
146	*Jim Acker(FC)*	.15	.11	.06
147	Mickey Hatcher	.12	.09	.05
148	Todd Cruz	.10	.08	.04
149	Tom Tellmann	.10	.08	.04
150	John Wockenfuss	.10	.08	.04
151	Wade Boggs	10.00	7.50	4.00
152	Don Baylor	.20	.15	.08
153	Bob Welch	.20	.15	.08
154	Alan Bannister	.10	.08	.04
155	Willie Aikens	.10	.08	.04
156	Jeff Burroughs	.12	.09	.05
157	Bryan Little	.10	.08	.04
158	Bob Boone	.15	.11	.06
159	Dave Hostetler	.10	.08	.04
160	Jerry Dybzinski	.10	.08	.04
161	Mike Madden	.10	.08	.04
162	Luis DeLeon	.10	.08	.04
163	Willie Hernandez	.15	.11	.06
164	Frank Pastore	.10	.08	.04
165	Rick Camp	.10	.08	.04
166	Lee Mazzilli	.12	.09	.05
167	Scot Thompson	.10	.08	.04
168	Bob Forsch	.12	.09	.05
169	Mike Flanagan	.15	.11	.06
170	Rick Manning	.10	.08	.04
171	Chet Lemon	.12	.09	.05
172	Jerry Remy	.10	.08	.04
173	Ron Guidry	.35	.25	.14
174	Pedro Guerrero	.50	.40	.20
175	Willie Wilson	.25	.20	.10
176	Carney Lansford	.20	.15	.08
177	Al Oliver	.30	.25	.12
178	Jim Sundberg	.12	.09	.05
179	Bobby Grich	.20	.15	.08
180	Richard Dotson	.20	.15	.08
181	Joaquin Andujar	.12	.09	.05

		MT	NR MT	EX			MT	NR MT	EX
182	Jose Cruz	.20	.15	.08	273	Dave Stapleton	.10	.08	.04
183	Mike Schmidt	1.75	1.25	.70	274	Lou Piniella	.20	.15	.08
184	*Gary Redus*(FC)	.30	.25	.12	275	Jose Morales	.10	.08	.04
185	Garry Templeton	.15	.11	.06	276	Brod Perkins	.10	.08	.04
186	Tony Pena	.20	.15	.08	277	Butch Davis	.10	.08	.04
187	Greg Minton	.10	.08	.04	278	*Tony Phillips*(FC)	.20	.15	.08
188	Phil Niekro	.50	.40	.20	279	Jeff Reardon	.25	.20	.10
189	Ferguson Jenkins	.30	.25	.12	280	Ken Forsch	.10	.08	.04
190	Mookie Wilson	.15	.11	.06	281	*Pete O'Brien*(FC)	1.50	1.25	.60
191	Jim Beattie	.10	.08	.04	282	Tom Paciorek	.10	.08	.04
192	Gary Ward	.12	.09	.05	283	Frank LaCorte	.10	.08	.04
193	Jesse Barfield	.40	.30	.15	284	Tim Lollar	.10	.08	.04
194	Pete Filson	.10	.08	.04	285	Greg Gross	.10	.08	.04
195	Roy Lee Jackson	.10	.08	.04	286	Alex Trevino	.10	.08	.04
196	Rick Sweet	.10	.08	.04	287	Gene Garber	.10	.08	.04
197	Jesse Orosco	.15	.11	.06	288	Dave Parker	.50	.40	.20
198	*Steve Lake*(FC)	.12	.09	.05	289	Lee Smith	.20	.15	.08
199	Ken Dayley	.10	.08	.04	290	Dave LaPoint	.15	.11	.06
200	Manny Sarmiento	.10	.08	.04	291	*John Shelby*(FC)	.35	.25	.14
201	*Mark Davis*(FC)	.25	.20	.10	292	Charlie Moore	.10	.08	.04
202	Tim Flannery	.10	.08	.04	293	Alan Trammell	.60	.45	.25
203	Bill Scherrer	.10	.08	.04	294	Tony Armas	.20	.15	.08
204	Al Holland	.10	.08	.04	295	Shane Rawley	.20	.15	.08
205	David Von Ohlen	.10	.08	.04	296	Greg Brock	.15	.11	.06
206	Mike LaCoss	.10	.08	.04	297	Hal McRae	.20	.15	.08
207	Juan Beniquez	.10	.08	.04	298	Mike Davis	.12	.09	.05
208	*Juan Agosto*(FC)	.20	.15	.08	299	Tim Raines	.80	.60	.30
209	Bobby Ramos	.10	.08	.04	300	Bucky Dent	.15	.11	.06
210	Al Bumbry	.12	.09	.05	301	Tommy John	.35	.25	.14
211	Mark Brouhard	.10	.08	.04	302	Carlton Fisk	.50	.40	.20
212	Howard Bailey	.10	.08	.04	303	Darrell Porter	.12	.09	.05
213	Bruce Hurst	.20	.15	.08	304	Dickie Thon	.12	.09	.05
214	Bob Shirley	.10	.08	.04	305	Garry Maddox	.12	.09	.05
215	Pat Zachry	.10	.08	.04	306	Cesar Cedeno	.20	.15	.08
216	Julio Franco	.25	.20	.10	307	Gary Lucas	.10	.08	.04
217	Mike Armstrong	.10	.08	.04	308	Johnny Ray	.20	.15	.08
218	Dave Beard	.10	.08	.04	309	Andy McGaffigan	.10	.08	.04
219	Steve Rogers	.12	.09	.05	310	Claudell Washington	.12	.09	.05
220	John Butcher	.10	.08	.04	311	Ryne Sandberg	2.00	1.50	.80
221	*Mike Smithson*(FC)	.20	.15	.08	312	George Foster	.30	.25	.12
222	Frank White	.20	.15	.08	313	*Spike Owen*(FC)	.30	.25	.12
223	Mike Heath	.10	.08	.04	314	Gary Gaetti	.90	.70	.35
224	Chris Bando	.10	.08	.04	315	Willie Upshaw	.12	.09	.05
225	Roy Smalley	.10	.08	.04	316	Al Williams	.10	.08	.04
226	Dusty Baker	.20	.15	.08	317	Jorge Orta	.10	.08	.04
227	Lou Whitaker	.60	.45	.25	318	Orlando Mercado	.10	.08	.04
228	John Lowenstein	.10	.08	.04	319	*Junior Ortiz*(FC)	.12	.09	.05
229	Ben Oglivie	.12	.09	.05	320	Mike Proly	.10	.08	.04
230	Doug DeCinces	.15	.11	.06	321	Randy Johnson	.10	.08	.04
231	Lonnie Smith	.12	.09	.05	322	Jim Morrison	.10	.08	.04
232	Ray Knight	.15	.11	.06	323	Max Venable	.10	.08	.04
233	Gary Matthews	.20	.15	.08	324	Tony Gwynn	4.00	3.00	1.50
234	Juan Bonilla	.10	.08	.04	325	Duane Walker	.10	.08	.04
235	Rod Scurry	.10	.08	.04	326	Ozzie Virgil	.10	.08	.04
236	Atlee Hammaker	.10	.08	.04	327	Jeff Lahti	.10	.08	.04
237	Mike Caldwell	.10	.08	.04	328	*Bill Dawley*(FC)	.12	.09	.05
238	Keith Hernandez	.80	.60	.30	329	Rob Wilfong	.10	.08	.04
239	Larry Bowa	.25	.20	.10	330	Marc Hill	.10	.08	.04
240	Tony Bernazard	.10	.08	.04	331	Ray Burris	.10	.08	.04
241	Damaso Garcia	.10	.08	.04	332	Allan Ramirez	.10	.08	.04
242	Tom Brunansky	.35	.25	.14	333	Chuck Porter	.10	.08	.04
243	Dan Driessen	.12	.09	.05	334	Wayne Krenchicki	.10	.08	.04
244	Ron Kittle(FC)	.30	.25	.12	335	Gary Allenson	.10	.08	.04
245	Tim Stoddard	.10	.08	.04	336	*Bob Meacham*(FC)	.20	.15	.08
246	Bob Gibson	.10	.08	.04	337	Joe Beckwith	.10	.08	.04
247	Marty Castillo	.10	.08	.04	338	Rick Sutcliffe	.25	.20	.10
248	*Don Mattingly*(FC)	65.00	49.00	26.00	339	*Mark Huismann*(FC)	.15	.11	.06
249	Jeff Newman	.10	.08	.04	340	*Tim Conroy*(FC)	.15	.11	.06
250	*Alejandro Pena*(FC)	.40	.30	.15	341	Scott Sanderson	.10	.08	.04
251	Toby Harrah	.12	.09	.05	342	Larry Biittner	.10	.08	.04
252	Cesar Geronimo	.10	.08	.04	343	Dave Stewart	.20	.15	.08
253	Tom Underwood	.10	.08	.04	344	Darryl Motley	.10	.08	.04
254	Doug Flynn	.10	.08	.04	345	*Chris Codiroli*(FC)	.12	.09	.05
255	Andy Hassler	.10	.08	.04	346	Rick Behenna	.10	.08	.04
256	Odell Jones	.10	.08	.04	347	Andre Robertson	.10	.08	.04
257	Rudy Law	.10	.08	.04	348	Mike Marshall	.25	.20	.10
258	Harry Spilman	.10	.08	.04	349	Larry Herndon	.12	.09	.05
259	Marty Bystrom	.10	.08	.04	350	Rich Dauer	.10	.08	.04
260	Dave Rucker	.10	.08	.04	351	Cecil Cooper	.25	.20	.10
261	Ruppert Jones	.10	.08	.04	352	Rod Carew	.90	.70	.35
262	Jeff Jones	.10	.08	.04	353	Willie McGee	.40	.30	.15
263	*Gerald Perry*(FC)	1.50	1.25	.60	354	Phil Garner	.12	.09	.05
264	Gene Tenace	.12	.09	.05	355	Joe Morgan	.60	.45	.25
265	Brad Wellman	.10	.08	.04	356	Luis Salazar	.10	.08	.04
266	Dickie Noles	.10	.08	.04	357	John Candelaria	.20	.15	.08
267	Jamie Allen	.10	.08	.04	358	Bill Laskey	.10	.08	.04
268	Jim Gott	.15	.11	.06	359	Bob McClure	.10	.08	.04
269	Ron Davis	.10	.08	.04	360	Dave Kingman	.30	.25	.12
270	Benny Ayala	.10	.08	.04	361	Ron Cey	.20	.15	.08
271	Ned Yost	.10	.08	.04	362	*Matt Young*(FC)	.20	.15	.08
272	Dave Rozema	.10	.08	.04	363	Lloyd Moseby	.20	.15	.08

		MT	NR MT	EX			MT	NR MT	EX
364	Frank Viola	1.25	.90	.50	455	Rob Picciolo	.10	.08	.04
365	Eddie Milner	.10	.08	.04	456	Enos Cabell	.10	.08	.04
366	Floyd Bannister	.20	.15	.08	457	*Dennis "Oil Can" Boyd*(FC)	.50	.40	.20
367	Dan Ford	.10	.08	.04	458	Butch Wynegar	.10	.08	.04
368	Moose Haas	.10	.08	.04	459	Burt Hooton	.12	.09	.05
369	Doug Bair	.10	.08	.04	460	Ron Hassey	.10	.08	.04
370	*Ray Fontenot*(FC)	.12	.09	.05	461	*Danny Jackson*(FC)	2.50	2.00	1.00
371	Luis Aponte	.10	.08	.04	462	Bob Kearney	.10	.08	.04
372	Jack Fimple	.10	.08	.04	463	Terry Francona	.10	.08	.04
373	*Neal Heaton*(FC)	.20	.15	.08	464	Wayne Tolleson	.10	.08	.04
374	Greg Pryor	.10	.08	.04	465	Mickey Rivers	.12	.09	.05
375	Wayne Gross	.10	.08	.04	466	John Wathan	.12	.09	.05
376	Charlie Lea	.10	.08	.04	467	Bill Almon	.10	.08	.04
377	Steve Lubratich	.10	.08	.04	468	George Vukovich	.10	.08	.04
378	Jon Matlack	.12	.09	.05	469	Steve Kemp	.15	.11	.06
379	Julio Cruz	.10	.08	.04	470	Ken Landreaux	.10	.08	.04
380	John Mizerock	.10	.08	.04	471	Milt Wilcox	.10	.08	.04
381	*Kevin Gross*(FC)	.40	.30	.15	472	Tippy Martinez	.10	.08	.04
382	Mike Ramsey	.10	.08	.04	473	Ted Simmons	.20	.15	.08
383	Doug Gwosdz	.10	.08	.04	474	Tim Foli	.10	.08	.04
384	Kelly Paris	.10	.08	.04	475	George Hendrick	.12	.09	.05
385	Pete Falcone	.10	.08	.04	476	Terry Puhl	.10	.08	.04
386	Milt May	.10	.08	.04	477	Von Hayes	.25	.20	.10
387	Fred Breining	.10	.08	.04	478	Bobby Brown	.10	.08	.04
388	*Craig Lefferts*(FC)	.25	.20	.10	479	Lee Lacy	.10	.08	.04
389	Steve Henderson	.10	.08	.04	480	Joel Youngblood	.10	.08	.04
390	Randy Moffitt	.10	.08	.04	481	Jim Slaton	.10	.08	.04
391	Ron Washington	.10	.08	.04	482	*Mike Fitzgerald*(FC)	.20	.15	.08
392	Gary Roenicke	.10	.08	.04	483	Keith Moreland	.12	.09	.05
393	*Tom Candiotti*(FC)	.30	.25	.12	484	Ron Roenicke	.10	.08	.04
394	Larry Pashnick	.10	.08	.04	485	Luis Leal	.10	.08	.04
395	Dwight Evans	.30	.25	.12	486	Bryan Oelkers	.10	.08	.04
396	Goose Gossage	.40	.30	.15	487	Bruce Berenyi	.10	.08	.04
397	Derrel Thomas	.10	.08	.04	488	LaMarr Hoyt	.10	.08	.04
398	Juan Eichelberger	.10	.08	.04	489	Joe Nolan	.10	.08	.04
399	Leon Roberts	.10	.08	.04	490	Marshall Edwards	.10	.08	.04
400	Davey Lopes	.15	.11	.06	491	*Mike Laga*(FC)	.12	.09	.05
401	Bill Gullickson	.10	.08	.04	492	Rick Cerone	.10	.08	.04
402	Geoff Zahn	.10	.08	.04	493	Mike Miller (Rick)	.10	.08	.04
403	Billy Sample	.10	.08	.04	494	Rick Honeycutt	.10	.08	.04
404	Mike Squires	.10	.08	.04	495	Mike Hargrove	.10	.08	.04
405	Craig Reynolds	.10	.08	.04	496	Joe Simpson	.10	.08	.04
406	Eric Show	.15	.11	.06	497	*Keith Atherton*(FC)	.25	.20	.10
407	John Denny	.10	.08	.04	498	Chris Welsh	.10	.08	.04
408	Dann Bilardello	.10	.08	.04	499	Bruce Kison	.10	.08	.04
409	Bruce Benedict	.10	.08	.04	500	Bob Johnson	.10	.08	.04
410	Kent Tekulve	.12	.09	.05	501	Jerry Koosman	.15	.11	.06
411	Mel Hall	.20	.15	.08	502	Frank DiPino	.10	.08	.04
412	John Stuper	.10	.08	.04	503	Tony Perez	.40	.30	.15
413	Rick Dempsey	.12	.09	.05	504	Ken Oberkfell	.10	.08	.04
414	Don Sutton	.50	.40	.20	505	*Mark Thurmond*(FC)	.12	.09	.05
415	Jack Morris	.50	.40	.20	506	Joe Price	.10	.08	.04
416	John Tudor	.20	.15	.08	507	Pascual Perez	.15	.11	.06
417	Willie Randolph	.20	.15	.08	508	*Marvell Wynne*(FC)	.25	.20	.10
418	Jerry Reuss	.15	.11	.06	509	Mike Krukow	.12	.09	.05
419	Don Slaught	.10	.08	.04	510	Dick Ruthven	.10	.08	.04
420	Steve McCatty	.10	.08	.04	511	Al Cowens	.10	.08	.04
421	Tim Wallach	.25	.20	.10	512	Cliff Johnson	.10	.08	.04
422	Larry Parrish	.20	.15	.08	513	*Randy Bush*(FC)	.20	.15	.08
423	Brian Downing	.20	.15	.08	514	Sammy Stewart	.10	.08	.04
424	Britt Burns	.10	.08	.04	515	*Bill Schroeder*(FC)	.25	.20	.10
425	David Green	.10	.08	.04	516	Aurelio Lopez	.10	.08	.04
426	Jerry Mumphrey	.12	.09	.05	517	Mike Brown	.10	.08	.04
427	Ivan DeJesus	.10	.08	.04	518	Graig Nettles	.35	.25	.14
428	Mario Soto	.12	.09	.05	519	Dave Sax	.10	.08	.04
429	Gene Richards	.10	.08	.04	520	Gerry Willard	.10	.08	.04
430	Dale Berra	.10	.08	.04	521	Paul Splittorff	.10	.08	.04
431	Darrell Evans	.25	.20	.10	522	Tom Burgmeier	.10	.08	.04
432	Glenn Hubbard	.12	.09	.05	523	Chris Speier	.10	.08	.04
433	Jody Davis	.15	.11	.06	524	Bobby Clark	.10	.08	.04
434	Danny Heep	.10	.08	.04	525	George Wright	.10	.08	.04
435	*Ed Nunez*(FC)	.20	.15	.08	526	Dennis Lamp	.10	.08	.04
436	Bobby Castillo	.10	.08	.04	527	Tony Scott	.10	.08	.04
437	Ernie Whitt	.12	.09	.05	528	Ed Whitson	.10	.08	.04
438	Scott Ullger	.10	.08	.04	529	Ron Reed	.10	.08	.04
439	Doyle Alexander	.15	.11	.06	530	Charlie Puleo	.10	.08	.04
440	Domingo Ramos	.10	.08	.04	531	Jerry Royster	.10	.08	.04
441	Craig Swan	.10	.08	.04	532	Don Robinson	.12	.09	.05
442	Warren Brusstar	.10	.08	.04	533	Steve Trout	.10	.08	.04
443	Len Barker	.12	.09	.05	534	Bruce Sutter	.30	.25	.12
444	Mike Easler	.12	.09	.05	535	Bob Horner	.20	.15	.08
445	Renie Martin	.10	.08	.04	536	Pat Tabler	.15	.11	.06
446	*Dennis Rasmussen*(FC)	.70	.50	.30	537	Chris Chambliss	.12	.09	.05
447	Ted Power(FC)	.15	.11	.06	538	Bob Ojeda	.15	.11	.06
448	*Charlie Hudson*(FC)	.25	.20	.10	539	Alan Ashby	.10	.08	.04
449	*Danny Cox*(FC)	.70	.50	.30	540	Jay Johnstone	.12	.09	.05
450	Kevin Bass(FC)	.30	.25	.12	541	Bob Dernier	.10	.08	.04
451	Daryl Sconiers	.10	.08	.04	542	*Brook Jacoby*(FC)	1.25	.90	.50
452	Scott Fletcher	.12	.09	.05	543	U.L. Washington	.10	.08	.04
453	Bryn Smith	.10	.08	.04	544	Danny Darwin	.10	.08	.04
454	Jim Dwyer	.10	.08	.04	545	Kiko Garcia	.10	.08	.04

		MT	NR MT	EX
546	Vance Law	.12	.09	.05
547	Tug McGraw	.20	.15	.08
548	Dave Smith	.12	.09	.05
549	Len Matuszek	.10	.08	.04
550	Tom Hume	.10	.08	.04
551	Dave Dravecky	.15	.11	.06
552	Rick Rhoden	.15	.11	.06
553	Duane Kuiper	.10	.08	.04
554	Rusty Staub	.20	.15	.08
555	Bill Campbell	.10	.08	.04
556	Mike Torrez	.12	.09	.05
557	Dave Henderson(FC)	.25	.20	.10
558	Len Whitehouse	.10	.08	.04
559	Barry Bonnell	.10	.08	.04
560	Rick Lysander	.10	.08	.04
561	Garth Iorg	.10	.08	.04
562	Bryan Clark	.10	.08	.04
563	Brian Giles	.10	.08	.04
564	Vern Ruhle	.10	.08	.04
565	Steve Bedrosian	.20	.15	.08
566	Larry McWilliams	.10	.08	.04
567	Jeff Leonard	.15	.11	.06
568	Alan Wiggins	.10	.08	.04
569	Jeff Russell(FC)	.25	.20	.10
570	Salome Barojas	.10	.08	.04
571	Dane Iorg	.10	.08	.04
572	Bob Knepper	.15	.11	.06
573	Gary Lavelle	.10	.08	.04
574	Gorman Thomas	.15	.11	.06
575	Manny Trillo	.12	.09	.05
576	Jim Palmer	.70	.50	.30
577	Dale Murray	.10	.08	.04
578	Tom Brookens	.10	.08	.04
579	Rich Gedman	.15	.11	.06
580	Bill Doran(FC)	1.25	.90	.50
581	Steve Yeager	.10	.08	.04
582	Dan Spillner	.10	.08	.04
583	Dan Quisenberry	.15	.11	.06
584	Rance Mulliniks	.10	.08	.04
585	Storm Davis	.15	.11	.06
586	Dave Schmidt	.10	.08	.04
587	Bill Russell	.12	.09	.05
588	Pat Sheridan(FC)	.20	.15	.08
589	Rafael Ramirez	.10	.08	.04
590	Bud Anderson	.10	.08	.04
591	George Frazier	.10	.08	.04
592	Lee Tunnell(FC)	.12	.09	.05
593	Kirk Gibson	.60	.45	.25
594	Scott McGregor	.12	.09	.05
595	Bob Bailor	.10	.08	.04
596	Tom Herr	.20	.15	.08
597	Luis Sanchez	.10	.08	.04
598	Dave Engle	.10	.08	.04
599	Craig McMurtry(FC)	.15	.11	.06
600	Carlos Diaz	.10	.08	.04
601	Tom O'Malley	.10	.08	.04
602	Nick Esasky(FC)	2.25	1.75	.90
603	Ron Hodges	.10	.08	.04
604	Ed Vande Berg	.10	.08	.04
605	Alfredo Griffin	.12	.09	.05
606	Glenn Hoffman	.10	.08	.04
607	Hubie Brooks	.20	.15	.08
608	Richard Barnes (photo actually Neal Heaton)	.10	.08	.04
609	Greg Walker(FC)	.60	.45	.25
610	Ken Singleton	.20	.15	.08
611	Mark Clear	.10	.08	.04
612	Buck Martinez	.10	.08	.04
613	Ken Griffey	.15	.11	.06
614	Reid Nichols	.10	.08	.04
615	Doug Sisk(FC)	.12	.09	.05
616	Bob Brenly	.10	.08	.04
617	Joey McLaughlin	.10	.08	.04
618	Glenn Wilson	.12	.09	.05
619	Bob Stoddard	.10	.08	.04
620	Len Sakata (Lenn)	.10	.08	.04
621	Mike Young(FC)	.25	.20	.10
622	John Stefero	.10	.08	.04
623	Carmelo Martinez(FC)	.30	.25	.12
624	Dave Bergman	.10	.08	.04
625	Runnin' Reds (David Green, Willie McGee, Lonnie Smith, Ozzie Smith)	.30	.25	.12
626	Rudy May	.10	.08	.04
627	Matt Keough	.10	.08	.04
628	Jose DeLeon(FC)	.60	.45	.25
629	Jim Essian	.10	.08	.04
630	Darnell Coles(FC)	.35	.25	.14
631	Mike Warren	.10	.08	.04
632	Del Crandall	.10	.08	.04
633	Dennis Martinez	.12	.09	.05
634	Mike Moore	.12	.09	.05

		MT	NR MT	EX
635	Lary Sorensen	.10	.08	.04
636	Ricky Nelson	.10	.08	.04
637	Omar Moreno	.10	.08	.04
638	Charlie Hough	.15	.11	.06
639	Dennis Eckersley	.25	.20	.10
640	Walt Terrell(FC)	.40	.30	.15
641	Denny Walling	.10	.08	.04
642	Dave Anderson(FC)	.20	.15	.08
643	Jose Oquendo(FC)	.25	.20	.10
644	Bob Stanley	.10	.08	.04
645	Dave Geisel	.10	.08	.04
646	Scott Garrelts(FC)	.70	.50	.30
647	Gary Pettis(FC)	.30	.25	.12
648	Duke Snider Puzzle Card	.10	.08	.04
649	Johnnie LeMaster	.10	.08	.04
650	Dave Collins	.12	.09	.05
651	San Diego Chicken	.25	.20	.10
---a	Checklist 1-26 DK (Perez-Steel on back)	.12	.09	.05
---b	Checklist 1-26 DK (Perez-Steele on back)	.40	.30	.15
-----	Checklist 27-130	.10	.08	.04
-----	Checklist 131-234	.10	.08	.04
-----	Checklist 235-338	.10	.08	.04
-----	Checklist 339-442	.10	.08	.04
-----	Checklist 443-546	.10	.08	.04
-----	Checklist 547-651	.10	.08	.04
---A	Living Legends (Rollie Fingers, Gaylord Perry)	2.75	2.00	1.00
---B	Living Legends (Johnny Bench, Carl Yastrzemski)	5.00	3.75	2.00

1984 Donruss Action All-Stars

Full-color photos on the card fronts and backs make the 1984 Donruss Action All-Stars set somewhat unusual. The fronts contain a large action photo plus the Donruss logo and year of issue inside a deep red border. The top half of the card backs feature a close-up photo with the bottom portion containing biographical and statistical information. The cards, which measure 3-1/2" by 5", were sold with Ted Williams puzzle pieces.

		MT	NR MT	EX
	Complete Set:	7.00	5.25	2.75
	Common Player:	.09	.07	.04
1	Gary Lavelle	.09	.07	.04
2	Willie McGee	.15	.11	.06
3	Tony Pena	.09	.07	.04
4	Lou Whitaker	.15	.11	.06
5	Robin Yount	.35	.25	.14
6	Doug DeCinces	.09	.07	.04
7	John Castino	.09	.07	.04
8	Terry Kennedy	.09	.07	.04
9	Rickey Henderson	.50	.40	.20
10	Bob Horner	.12	.09	.05
11	Harold Baines	.15	.11	.06
12	Buddy Bell	.09	.07	.04
13	Fernando Valenzuela	.12	.09	.05
14	Nolan Ryan	.60	.45	.25
15	Andre Thornton	.09	.07	.04
16	Gary Redus	.09	.07	.04
17	Pedro Guerrero	.15	.11	.06

		MT	NR MT	EX				MT	NR MT	EX
18	Andre Dawson	.20	.15	.08		4	Jim Rice	.10	.08	.04
19	Dave Stieb	.12	.09	.05		5	Gorman Thomas	.10	.08	.04
20	Cal Ripken	.35	.25	.14		6	Ben Oglivie	.07	.05	.03
21	Ken Griffey	.12	.09	.05		7	Jeff Burroughs	.07	.05	.03
22	Wade Boggs	1.00	.70	.40		8	Hank Aaron	.35	.25	.14
23	Keith Hernandez	.25	.20	.10		9	Reggie Jackson	.30	.25	.12
24	Steve Carlton	.30	.25	.12		10	Carl Yastrzemski	.50	.40	.20
25	Hal McRae	.12	.09	.05		11	Mike Schmidt	.50	.40	.20
26	John Lowenstein	.09	.07	.04		12	Graig Nettles	.14	.11	.06
27	Fred Lynn	.15	.11	.06		13	Greg Luzinski	.10	.08	.04
28	Bill Buckner	.09	.07	.04		14	Ted Williams	1.00	.70	.40
29	Chris Chambliss	.09	.07	.04		15	George Brett	.35	.25	.14
30	Richie Zisk	.09	.07	.04		16	Wade Boggs	.50	.40	.20
31	Jack Clark	.15	.11	.06		17	Hal McRae	.10	.08	.04
32	George Hendrick	.09	.07	.04		18	Bill Buckner	.10	.08	.04
33	Bill Madlock	.12	.09	.05		19	Eddie Murray	.10	.08	.04
34	Lance Parrish	.15	.11	.06		20	Rogers Hornsby	.14	.11	.06
35	Paul Molitor	.15	.11	.06		21	Rod Carew	.20	.15	.08
36	Reggie Jackson	.35	.25	.14		22	Bill Madlock	.10	.08	.04
37	Kent Hrbek	.20	.15	.08		23	Lonnie Smith	.07	.05	.03
38	Steve Garvey	.20	.15	.08		24	Cecil Cooper	.10	.08	.04
39	Carney Lansford	.09	.07	.04		25	Ken Griffey	.10	.08	.04
40	Dale Murphy	.30	.25	.12		26	Ty Cobb	.40	.30	.15
41	Greg Luzinski	.12	.09	.05		27	Pete Rose	.40	.30	.15
42	Larry Parrish	.09	.07	.04		28	Rusty Staub	.10	.08	.04
43	Ryne Sandberg	.25	.20	.10		29	Tony Perez	.10	.08	.04
44	Dickie Thon	.09	.07	.04		30	Al Oliver	.10	.08	.04
45	Bert Blyleven	.12	.09	.05		31	Cy Young	.14	.11	.06
46	Ron Oester	.09	.07	.04		32	Gaylord Perry	.14	.11	.06
47	Dusty Baker	.09	.07	.04		33	Ferguson Jenkins	.10	.08	.04
48	Steve Rogers	.09	.07	.04		34	Phil Niekro	.14	.11	.06
49	Jim Clancy	.09	.07	.04		35	Jim Palmer	.30	.25	.12
50	Eddie Murray	.15	.11	.06		36	Tommy John	.10	.08	.04
51	Ron Guidry	.15	.11	.06		37	Walter Johnson	.20	.15	.08
52	Jim Rice	.15	.11	.06		38	Steve Carlton	.25	.20	.10
53	Tom Seaver	.30	.25	.12		39	Nolan Ryan	.50	.40	.20
54	Pete Rose	.30	.25	.12		40	Tom Seaver	.25	.20	.10
55	George Brett	.40	.30	.15		41	Don Sutton	.14	.11	.06
56	Dan Quisenberry	.09	.07	.04		42	Bert Blyleven	.10	.08	.04
57	Mike Schmidt	.60	.45	.25		43	Frank Robinson	.35	.25	.14
58	Ted Simmons	.12	.09	.05		44	Joe Morgan	.25	.20	.10
59	Dave Righetti	.15	.11	.06		45	Rollie Fingers	.14	.11	.06
60	Checklist	.09	.07	.04		46	Keith Hernandez	.10	.08	.04
						47	Robin Yount	.50	.40	.20
						48	Cal Ripken	.25	.20	.10
						49	Dale Murphy	.35	.25	.14
						50	Mickey Mantle	1.00	.70	.40
						51	Johnny Bench	.50	.40	.20
						52	Carlton Fisk	.30	.25	.12
						53	Tug McGraw	.10	.08	.04
						54	Paul Molitor	.10	.08	.04
						55	Carl Hubbell	.14	.11	.06
						56	Steve Garvey	.15	.11	.06
						57	Dave Parker	.14	.11	.06
						58	Gary Carter	.15	.11	.06
						59	Fred Lynn	.14	.11	.06
						60	Checklist	.10	.08	.04

1984 Donruss Champions

The 60-card Donruss Champions set includes ten Hall of Famers, forty-nine current players and one numbered checklist. The ten Hall of Famers' cards (called Grand Champions) feature the artwork of Dick Perez, while cards of the current players (called Champions) are color photos. The cards measure 3-1/2" by 5". The Grand Champions represent hallmarks of excellence in various statistical categories, while the Champions are the leaders among active players in each category. The ten Grand Champion cards are #'s 1, 8, 14, 20, 26, 31, 37, 43, 50 and 55. The cards were issued with Duke Snider puzzle pieces.

		MT	NR MT	EX
Complete Set:		6.50	5.00	3.00
Common Player:		.07	.05	.03
1	Babe Ruth	.60	.45	.25
2	George Foster	.10	.08	.04
3	Dave Kingman	.10	.08	.04

1985 Donruss

The black-bordered 1985 Donruss set includes 653 numbered cards and seven unnumbered checklists. Displaying the artwork of Dick Perez for the fourth consecutive year, card #'s 1-26 feature the Diamond Kings series. Donruss, realizing the hobby craze over rookie cards, included a Rated Rookies subset (card #'s 27-46). The cards, which are the standard size of 2-1/2" by 3-1/2", were issued with a Lou Gehrig puzzle. The backs of the cards have black print on yellow and white. The complete set price does not include the higher priced variations. (DK) and (RR) refer to the Diamond Kings and Rated Rookies subsets.

		MT	NR MT	EX
Complete Set:		130.00	97.00	52.00
Common Player:		.08	.06	.03
1	Ryne Sandberg (DK)	.60	.45	.25
2	Doug DeCinces (DK)	.10	.08	.04
3	Rich Dotson (DK)	.12	.09	.05
4	Bert Blyleven (DK)	.15	.11	.06
5	Lou Whitaker (DK)	.30	.25	.12
6	Dan Quisenberry (DK)	.15	.11	.06
7	Don Mattingly (DK)	6.00	4.50	2.50
8	Carney Lansford (DK)	.10	.08	.04
9	Frank Tanana (DK)	.12	.09	.05
10	Willie Upshaw (DK)	.10	.08	.04
11	Claudell Washington (DK)	.10	.08	.04
12	Mike Marshall (DK)	.20	.15	.08
13	Joaquin Andujar (DK)	.10	.08	.04
14	Cal Ripken, Jr. (DK)	.60	.45	.25
15	Jim Rice (DK)	.50	.40	.20
16	Don Sutton (DK)	.30	.25	.12
17	Frank Viola (DK)	.15	.11	.06
18	Alvin Davis (DK)(FC)	.60	.45	.25
19	Mario Soto (DK)	.10	.08	.04
20	Jose Cruz (DK)	.12	.09	.05
21	Charlie Lea (DK)	.10	.08	.04
22	Jesse Orosco (DK)	.10	.08	.04
23	Juan Samuel (DK)(FC)	.40	.30	.15
24	Tony Pena (DK)	.12	.09	.05
25	Tony Gwynn (DK)	.50	.40	.20
26	Bob Brenly (DK)	.10	.08	.04
27	*Danny Tartabull (RR)*(FC)	6.00	4.50	2.50
28	*Mike Bielecki (RR)*(FC)	.15	.11	.06
29	*Steve Lyons (RR)*(FC)	.20	.15	.08
30	*Jeff Reed (RR)*(FC)	.15	.11	.06
31	Tony Brewer (RR)	.08	.06	.03
32	*John Morris (RR)*(FC)	.15	.11	.06
33	*Daryl Boston (RR)*(FC)	.25	.20	.10
34	Alfonso Pulido (RR)	.08	.06	.03
35	*Steve Kiefer (RR)*(FC)	.10	.08	.04
36	*Larry Sheets (RR)*(FC)	.50	.40	.20
37	*Scott Bradley (RR)*(FC)	.25	.20	.10
38	*Calvin Schiraldi (RR)*(FC)	.30	.25	.12
39	*Shawon Dunston (RR)*(FC)	2.00	1.50	.80
40	Charlie Mitchell (RR)	.08	.06	.03
41	*Billy Hatcher (RR)*(FC)	.70	.50	.30
42	Russ Stephans (RR)	.08	.06	.03
43	Alejandro Sanchez (RR)	.08	.06	.03
44	*Steve Jeltz (RR)*(FC)	.15	.11	.06
45	*Jim Traber (RR)*(FC)	.30	.25	.12
46	Doug Loman (RR)	.08	.06	.03
47	Eddie Murray	.60	.45	.25
48	Robin Yount	.60	.45	.25
49	Lance Parrish	.30	.25	.12
50	Jim Rice	.50	.40	.20
51	Dave Winfield	.50	.40	.20
52	Fernando Valenzuela	.35	.25	.14
53	George Brett	.70	.50	.30
54	Dave Kingman	.15	.11	.06
55	Gary Carter	.40	.30	.15
56	Buddy Bell	.12	.09	.05
57	Reggie Jackson	.60	.45	.25
58	Harold Baines	.20	.15	.08
59	Ozzie Smith	.20	.15	.08
60	Nolan Ryan	.70	.50	.30
61	Mike Schmidt	.70	.50	.30
62	Dave Parker	.35	.25	.14
63	Tony Gwynn	1.00	.70	.40
64	Tony Pena	.12	.09	.05
65	Jack Clark	.25	.20	.10
66	Dale Murphy	.80	.60	.30
67	Ryne Sandberg	.50	.40	.20
68	Keith Hernandez	.40	.30	.15
69	*Alvin Davis*(FC)	3.75	2.75	1.50
70	Kent Hrbek	.30	.25	.12
71	Willie Upshaw	.10	.08	.04
72	Dave Engle	.08	.06	.03
73	Alfredo Griffin	.10	.08	.04
74a	Jack Perconte (last line of highlights begins "Batted .346...")	.10	.08	.04
74b	Jack Perconte (last line of highlights begins "Led the...")	1.25	.90	.50
75	Jesse Orosco	.10	.08	.04
76	Jody Davis	.12	.09	.05
77	Bob Horner	.12	.09	.05
78	Larry McWilliams	.08	.06	.03
79	Joel Youngblood	.08	.06	.03

		MT	NR MT	EX
80	Alan Wiggins	.08	.06	.03
81	Ron Oester	.08	.06	.03
82	Ozzie Virgil	.08	.06	.03
83	*Ricky Horton*(FC)	.35	.25	.14
84	Bill Doran	.12	.09	.05
85	Rod Carew	.50	.40	.20
86	LaMarr Hoyt	.08	.06	.03
87	Tim Wallach	.15	.11	.06
88	Mike Flanagan	.12	.09	.05
89	Jim Sundberg	.10	.08	.04
90	Chet Lemon	.10	.08	.04
91	Bob Stanley	.08	.06	.03
92	Willie Randolph	.12	.09	.05
93	Bill Russell	.10	.08	.04
94	Julio Franco	.15	.11	.06
95	Dan Quisenberry	.12	.09	.05
96	Bill Caudill	.08	.06	.03
97	Bill Gullickson	.08	.06	.03
98	Danny Darwin	.08	.06	.03
99	Curtis Wilkerson	.08	.06	.03
100	Bud Black	.08	.06	.03
101	Tony Phillips	.08	.06	.03
102	Tony Bernazard	.08	.06	.03
103	Jay Howell	.10	.08	.04
104	Burt Hooton	.10	.08	.04
105	Milt Wilcox	.08	.06	.03
106	Rich Dauer	.08	.06	.03
107	Don Sutton	.35	.25	.14
108	Mike Witt	.15	.11	.06
109	Bruce Sutter	.15	.11	.06
110	Enos Cabell	.08	.06	.03
111	John Denny	.08	.06	.03
112	Dave Dravecky	.10	.08	.04
113	Marvell Wynne	.08	.06	.03
114	Johnnie LeMaster	.08	.06	.03
115	Chuck Porter	.08	.06	.03
116	John Gibbons	.08	.06	.03
117	Keith Moreland	.10	.08	.04
118	Darnell Coles	.12	.09	.05
119	Dennis Lamp	.08	.06	.03
120	Ron Davis	.08	.06	.03
121	Nick Esasky	.10	.08	.04
122	Vance Law	.10	.08	.04
123	Gary Roenicke	.08	.06	.03
124	Bill Schroeder	.08	.06	.03
125	Dave Rozema	.08	.06	.03
126	Bobby Meacham	.08	.06	.03
127	Marty Barrett(FC)	.25	.20	.10
128	*R.J. Reynolds*(FC)	.30	.25	.12
129	Ernie Camacho	.08	.06	.03
130	Jorge Orta	.08	.06	.03
131	Lary Sorensen	.08	.06	.03
132	Terry Francona	.08	.06	.03
133	Fred Lynn	.25	.20	.10
134	Bobby Jones	.08	.06	.03
135	Jerry Hairston	.08	.06	.03
136	Kevin Bass	.12	.09	.05
137	Garry Maddox	.08	.06	.03
138	Dave LaPoint	.10	.08	.04
139	Kevin McReynolds	1.00	.70	.40
140	Wayne Krenchicki	.08	.06	.03
141	Rafael Ramirez	.08	.06	.03
142	Rod Scurry	.08	.06	.03
143	Greg Minton	.08	.06	.03
144	Tim Stoddard	.08	.06	.03
145	Steve Henderson	.08	.06	.03
146	George Bell	.50	.40	.20
147	Dave Meier	.08	.06	.03
148	Sammy Stewart	.08	.06	.03
149	Mark Brouhard	.08	.06	.03
150	Larry Herndon	.10	.08	.04
151	Oil Can Boyd	.10	.08	.04
152	Brian Dayett	.08	.06	.03
153	Tom Niedenfuer	.10	.08	.04
154	Brook Jacoby	.15	.11	.06
155	Onix Concepcion	.08	.06	.03
156	Tim Conroy	.08	.06	.03
157	*Joe Hesketh*(FC)	.15	.11	.06
158	Brian Downing	.12	.09	.05
159	Tommy Dunbar	.08	.06	.03
160	Marc Hill	.08	.06	.03
161	Phil Garner	.10	.08	.04
162	Jerry Davis	.08	.06	.03
163	Bill Campbell	.08	.06	.03
164	John Franco(FC)	1.25	.90	.50
165	Len Barker	.10	.08	.04
166	*Benny Distefano*(FC)	.10	.08	.04
167	George Frazier	.08	.06	.03
168	Tito Landrum	.08	.06	.03
169	Cal Ripken	.60	.45	.25
170	Cecil Cooper	.15	.11	.06

		MT	NR MT	EX			MT	NR MT	EX
171	Alan Trammell	.40	.30	.15	262	*Jay Tibbs*(FC)	.20	.15	.08
172	Wade Boggs	5.50	4.25	2.25	263	Bruce Benedict	.08	.06	.03
173	Don Baylor	.15	.11	.06	264	Don Robinson	.10	.08	.04
174	Pedro Guerrero	.30	.25	.12	265	Gary Lavelle	.08	.06	.03
175	Frank White	.12	.09	.05	266	Scott Sanderson	.08	.06	.03
176	Rickey Henderson	.60	.45	.25	267	Matt Young	.08	.06	.03
177	Charlie Lea	.08	.06	.03	268	Ernie Whitt	.10	.08	.04
178	Pete O'Brien	.20	.15	.08	269	Houston Jimenez	.08	.06	.03
179	Doug DeCinces	.12	.09	.05	270	*Ken Dixon*(FC)	.12	.09	.05
180	Ron Kittle	.12	.09	.05	271	Peter Ladd	.08	.06	.03
181	George Hendrick	.10	.08	.04	272	Juan Berenguer	.08	.06	.03
182	Joe Niekro	.12	.09	.05	273	*Roger Clemens*(FC)	14.00	10.50	5.50
183	Juan Samuel(FC)	.60	.45	.25	274	Rick Cerone	.08	.06	.03
184	Mario Soto	.10	.08	.04	275	Dave Anderson	.08	.06	.03
185	Goose Gossage	.25	.20	.10	276	George Vukovich	.08	.06	.03
186	Johnny Ray	.15	.11	.06	277	Greg Pryor	.08	.06	.03
187	Bob Brenly	.08	.06	.03	278	Mike Warren	.08	.06	.03
188	Craig McMurtry	.08	.06	.03	279	Bob James	.08	.06	.03
189	Leon Durham	.10	.08	.04	280	Bobby Grich	.12	.09	.05
190	*Dwight Gooden*(FC)	14.00	10.50	5.00	281	*Mike Mason*(FC)	.12	.09	.05
191	Barry Bonnell	.08	.06	.03	282	Ron Reed	.08	.06	.03
192	Tim Teufel	.12	.09	.05	283	Alan Ashby	.08	.06	.03
193	Dave Stieb	.15	.11	.06	284	Mark Thurmond	.08	.06	.03
194	Mickey Hatcher	.08	.06	.03	285	Joe Lefebvre	.08	.06	.03
195	Jesse Barfield	.25	.20	.10	286	Ted Power	.08	.06	.03
196	Al Cowens	.08	.06	.03	287	Chris Chambliss	.10	.08	.04
197	Hubie Brooks	.12	.09	.05	288	Lee Tunnell	.08	.06	.03
198	Steve Trout	.08	.06	.03	289	Rich Bordi	.08	.06	.03
199	Glenn Hubbard	.08	.06	.03	290	Glenn Brummer	.08	.06	.03
200	Bill Madlock	.15	.11	.06	291	Mike Boddicker	.12	.09	.05
201	*Jeff Robinson*(FC)	.35	.25	.14	292	Rollie Fingers	.25	.20	.10
202	Eric Show	.10	.08	.04	293	Lou Whitaker	.40	.30	.15
203	Dave Concepcion	.15	.11	.06	294	Dwight Evans	.15	.11	.06
204	Ivan DeJesus	.08	.06	.03	295	Don Mattingly	16.00	12.00	6.50
205	Neil Allen	.08	.06	.03	296	Mike Marshall	.15	.11	.06
206	Jerry Mumphrey	.08	.06	.03	297	Willie Wilson	.15	.11	.06
207	Mike Brown	.08	.06	.03	298	Mike Heath	.08	.06	.03
208	Carlton Fisk	.40	.30	.15	299	Tim Raines	.50	.40	.20
209	Bryn Smith	.08	.06	.03	300	Larry Parrish	.12	.09	.05
210	Tippy Martinez	.08	.06	.03	301	Geoff Zahn	.08	.06	.03
211	Dion James	.10	.08	.04	302	Rich Dotson	.12	.09	.05
212	Willie Hernandez	.10	.08	.04	303	David Green	.08	.06	.03
213	Mike Easler	.10	.08	.04	304	Jose Cruz	.12	.09	.05
214	Ron Guidry	.30	.25	.12	305	Steve Carlton	.50	.40	.20
215	Rick Honeycutt	.08	.06	.03	306	Gary Redus	.10	.08	.04
216	Brett Butler	.12	.09	.05	307	Steve Garvey	.50	.40	.20
217	Larry Gura	.08	.06	.03	308	Jose DeLeon	.10	.08	.04
218	Ray Burris	.08	.06	.03	309	Randy Lerch	.08	.06	.03
219	Steve Rogers	.10	.08	.04	310	Claudell Washington	.10	.08	.04
220	Frank Tanana	.12	.09	.05	311	Lee Smith	.12	.09	.05
221	Ned Yost	.08	.06	.03	312	Darryl Strawberry	4.00	3.00	1.50
222	*Bret Saberhagen*	8.00	6.00	3.25	313	Jim Beattie	.08	.06	.03
223	Mike Davis	.10	.08	.04	314	John Butcher	.08	.06	.03
224	Bert Blyleven	.15	.11	.06	315	Damaso Garcia	.10	.08	.04
225	Steve Kemp	.10	.08	.04	316	Mike Smithson	.08	.06	.03
226	Jerry Reuss	.10	.08	.04	317	Luis Leal	.08	.06	.03
227	Darrell Evans	.15	.11	.06	318	Ken Phelps(FC)	.25	.20	.10
228	Wayne Gross	.08	.06	.03	319	Wally Backman	.10	.08	.04
229	Jim Gantner	.10	.08	.04	320	Ron Cey	.12	.09	.05
230	Bob Boone	.10	.08	.04	321	Brad Komminsk	.08	.06	.03
231	Lonnie Smith	.10	.08	.04	322	Jason Thompson	.08	.06	.03
232	Frank DiPino	.08	.06	.03	323	*Frank Williams*(FC)	.20	.15	.08
233	Jerry Koosman	.12	.09	.05	324	Tim Lollar	.08	.06	.03
234	Graig Nettles	.20	.15	.08	325	*Eric Davis*(FC)	20.00	15.00	8.00
235	John Tudor	.12	.09	.05	326	Von Hayes	.12	.09	.05
236	John Rabb	.08	.06	.03	327	Andy Van Slyke	.40	.30	.15
237	Rick Manning	.08	.06	.03	328	Craig Reynolds	.08	.06	.03
238	Mike Fitzgerald	.08	.06	.03	329	Dick Schofield	.10	.08	.04
239	Gary Matthews	.12	.09	.05	330	Scott Fletcher	.10	.08	.04
240	*Jim Presley*(FC)	.80	.60	.30	331	Jeff Reardon	.15	.11	.06
241	Dave Collins	.10	.08	.04	332	Rick Dempsey	.10	.08	.04
242	Gary Gaetti	.30	.25	.12	333	Ben Oglivie	.10	.08	.04
243	Dann Bilardello	.08	.06	.03	334	Dan Petry	.10	.08	.04
244	Rudy Law	.08	.06	.03	335	Jackie Gutierrez	.08	.06	.03
245	John Lowenstein	.08	.06	.03	336	Dave Righetti	.25	.20	.10
246	Tom Tellmann	.08	.06	.03	337	Alejandro Pena	.10	.08	.04
247	Howard Johnson	.30	.25	.12	338	Mel Hall	.10	.08	.04
248	Ray Fontenot	.08	.06	.03	339	Pat Sheridan	.08	.06	.03
249	Tony Armas	.12	.09	.05	340	Keith Atherton	.08	.06	.03
250	Candy Maldonado	.12	.09	.05	341	David Palmer	.08	.06	.03
251	*Mike Jeffcoat*(FC)	.10	.08	.04	342	Gary Ward	.10	.08	.04
252	Dane Iorg	.08	.06	.03	343	Dave Stewart	.15	.11	.06
253	Bruce Bochte	.08	.06	.03	344	*Mark Gubicza*(FC)	1.00	.70	.40
254	Pete Rose	1.25	.90	.50	345	Carney Lansford	.12	.09	.05
255	Don Aase	.08	.06	.03	346	Jerry Willard	.08	.06	.03
256	George Wright	.08	.06	.03	347	Ken Griffey	.12	.09	.05
257	Britt Burns	.08	.06	.03	348	*Franklin Stubbs*(FC)	.30	.25	.12
258	Mike Scott	.20	.15	.08	349	Aurelio Lopez	.08	.06	.03
259	Len Matuszek	.08	.06	.03	350	Al Bumbry	.10	.08	.04
260	Dave Rucker	.08	.06	.03	351	Charlie Moore	.08	.06	.03
261	Craig Lefferts	.10	.08	.04	352	Luis Sanchez	.08	.06	.03

		MT	NR MT	EX			MT	NR MT	EX
353	Darrell Porter	.10	.08	.04	440	Mike Moore	.08	.06	.03
354	Bill Dawley	.08	.06	.03	441	Doug Sisk	.08	.06	.03
355	Charlie Hudson	.10	.08	.04	442	Dennis Eckersley	.15	.11	.06
356	Garry Templeton	.10	.08	.04	443	Gerald Perry	.25	.20	.10
357	Cecilio Guante	.08	.06	.03	444	Dale Berra	.08	.06	.03
358	Jeff Leonard	.12	.09	.05	445	Dusty Baker	.10	.08	.04
359	Paul Molitor	.20	.15	.08	446	Ed Whitson	.08	.06	.03
360	Ron Gardenhire	.08	.06	.03	447	Cesar Cedeno	.12	.09	.05
361	Larry Bowa	.12	.09	.05	448	*Rick Schu*(FC)	.20	.15	.08
362	Bob Kearney	.08	.06	.03	449	Joaquin Andujar	.10	.08	.04
363	Garth Iorg	.08	.06	.03	450	*Mark Bailey*(FC)	.12	.09	.05
364	Tom Brunansky	.15	.11	.06	451	*Ron Romanick*(FC)	.12	.09	.05
365	Brad Gulden	.08	.06	.03	452	Julio Cruz	.08	.06	.03
366	Greg Walker	.12	.09	.05	453	Miguel Dilone	.08	.06	.03
367	Mike Young	.10	.08	.04	454	Storm Davis	.12	.09	.05
368	Rick Waits	.08	.06	.03	455	Jaime Cocanower	.08	.06	.03
369	Doug Bair	.08	.06	.03	456	Barbaro Garbey	.12	.09	.05
370	Bob Shirley	.08	.06	.03	457	Rich Gedman	.12	.09	.05
371	Bob Ojeda	.12	.09	.05	458	Phil Niekro	.30	.25	.12
372	Bob Welch	.15	.11	.06	459	Mike Scioscia	.10	.08	.04
373	Neal Heaton	.08	.06	.03	460	Pat Tabler	.10	.08	.04
374	Danny Jackson (photo actually Steve Farr)	.80	.60	.30	461	Darryl Motley	.08	.06	.03
					462	Chris Codoroli (Codiroli)	.08	.06	.03
375	Donnie Hill	.08	.06	.03	463	Doug Flynn	.08	.06	.03
376	Mike Stenhouse	.08	.06	.03	464	Billy Sample	.08	.06	.03
377	Bruce Kison	.08	.06	.03	465	Mickey Rivers	.10	.08	.04
378	Wayne Tolleson	.08	.06	.03	466	John Wathan	.10	.08	.04
379	Floyd Bannister	.12	.09	.05	467	Bill Krueger	.08	.06	.03
380	Vern Ruhle	.08	.06	.03	468	Andre Thornton	.12	.09	.05
381	Tim Corcoran	.08	.06	.03	469	Rex Hudler	.12	.09	.05
382	Kurt Kepshire	.08	.06	.03	470	*Sid Bream*(FC)	.50	.40	.20
383	Bobby Brown	.08	.06	.03	471	Kirk Gibson	.40	.30	.15
384	Dave Van Gorder	.08	.06	.03	472	John Shelby	.10	.08	.04
385	Rick Mahler	.08	.06	.03	473	Moose Haas	.08	.06	.03
386	Lee Mazzilli	.10	.08	.04	474	Doug Corbett	.08	.06	.03
387	Bill Laskey	.08	.06	.03	475	Willie McGee	.35	.25	.14
388	Thad Bosley	.08	.06	.03	476	Bob Knepper	.10	.08	.04
389	Al Chambers	.08	.06	.03	477	Kevin Gross	.12	.09	.05
390	Tony Fernandez	.50	.40	.20	478	Carmelo Martinez	.10	.08	.04
391	Ron Washington	.08	.06	.03	479	Kent Tekulve	.10	.08	.04
392	Bill Swaggerty	.08	.06	.03	480	Chili Davis	.12	.09	.05
393	Bob Gibson	.08	.06	.03	481	Bobby Clark	.08	.06	.03
394	Marty Castillo	.08	.06	.03	482	Mookie Wilson	.12	.09	.05
395	Steve Crawford	.08	.06	.03	483	Dave Owen	.08	.06	.03
396	Clay Christiansen	.08	.06	.03	484	Ed Nunez	.08	.06	.03
397	Bob Bailor	.08	.06	.03	485	Rance Mulliniks	.08	.06	.03
398	Mike Hargrove	.08	.06	.03	486	Ken Schrom	.08	.06	.03
399	Charlie Leibrandt	.10	.08	.04	487	Jeff Russell	.08	.06	.03
400	Tom Burgmeier	.08	.06	.03	488	Tom Paciorek	.08	.06	.03
401	Razor Shines	.08	.06	.03	489	Dan Ford	.08	.06	.03
402	Rob Wilfong	.08	.06	.03	490	Mike Caldwell	.08	.06	.03
403	Tom Henke	.12	.09	.05	491	Scottie Earl	.08	.06	.03
404	Al Jones	.08	.06	.03	492	*Jose Rijo*(FC)	.70	.50	.30
405	Mike LaCoss	.08	.06	.03	493	Bruce Hurst	.15	.11	.06
406	Luis DeLeon	.08	.06	.03	494	Ken Landreaux	.08	.06	.03
407	Greg Gross	.08	.06	.03	495	Mike Fischlin	.08	.06	.03
408	Tom Hume	.08	.06	.03	496	Don Slaught	.08	.06	.03
409	Rick Camp	.08	.06	.03	497	Steve McCatty	.08	.06	.03
410	Milt May	.08	.06	.03	498	Gary Lucas	.08	.06	.03
411	*Henry Cotto*(FC)	.20	.15	.08	499	Gary Pettis	.10	.08	.04
412	Dave Von Ohlen	.08	.06	.03	500	Marvis Foley	.08	.06	.03
413	Scott McGregor	.10	.08	.04	501	Mike Squires	.08	.06	.03
414	Ted Simmons	.15	.11	.06	502	*Jim Pankovitz*(FC)	.15	.11	.06
415	Jack Morris	.30	.25	.12	503	Luis Aguayo	.08	.06	.03
416	Bill Buckner	.15	.11	.06	504	Ralph Citarella	.08	.06	.03
417	Butch Wynegar	.08	.06	.03	505	Bruce Bochy	.08	.06	.03
418	Steve Sax	.25	.20	.10	506	Bob Owchinko	.08	.06	.03
419	Steve Balboni	.10	.08	.04	507	Pascual Perez	.10	.08	.04
420	Dwayne Murphy	.10	.08	.04	508	Lee Lacy	.08	.06	.03
421	Andre Dawson	.30	.25	.12	509	Atlee Hammaker	.08	.06	.03
422	Charlie Hough	.10	.08	.04	510	Bob Dernier	.08	.06	.03
423	Tommy John	.25	.20	.10	511	Ed Vande Berg	.08	.06	.03
424a	Tom Seaver (Floyd Bannister photo — throwing left)	.80	.60	.30	512	Cliff Johnson	.08	.06	.03
424b	Tom Seaver (correct photo - throwing right)	5.00	3.75	2.00	513	Len Whitehouse	.08	.06	.03
					514	Dennis Martinez	.10	.08	.04
425	Tom Herr	.12	.09	.05	515	Ed Romero	.08	.06	.03
426	Terry Puhl	.08	.06	.03	516	Rusty Kuntz	.08	.06	.03
427	Al Holland	.08	.06	.03	517	Rick Miller	.08	.06	.03
428	Eddie Milner	.08	.06	.03	518	Dennis Rasmussen	.15	.11	.06
429	Terry Kennedy	.10	.08	.04	519	Steve Yeager	.08	.06	.03
430	John Candelaria	.12	.09	.05	520	Chris Bando	.08	.06	.03
431	Manny Trillo	.10	.08	.04	521	U.L. Washington	.08	.06	.03
432	Ken Oberkfell	.08	.06	.03	522	*Curt Young*(FC)	.40	.30	.15
433	Rick Sutcliffe	.15	.11	.06	523	Angel Salazar	.08	.06	.03
434	Ron Darling	.70	.50	.30	524	Curt Kaufman	.08	.06	.03
435	Spike Owen	.10	.08	.04	525	Odell Jones	.08	.06	.03
436	Frank Viola	.25	.20	.10	526	Juan Agosto	.08	.06	.03
437	Lloyd Moseby	.12	.09	.05	527	Denny Walling	.08	.06	.03
438	*Kirby Puckett*(FC)	18.00	13.50	7.25	528	Andy Hawkins(FC)	.20	.15	.08
439	Jim Clancy	.10	.08	.04	529	Sixto Lezcano	.08	.06	.03
					530	Skeeter Barnes	.08	.06	.03

	MT	NR MT	EX
531 Randy Johnson	.08	.06	.03
532 Jim Morrison	.08	.06	.03
533 Warren Brusstar	.08	.06	.03
534a *Jeff Pendleton* (first name incorrect)(FC)			
	.85	.60	.35
534b *Terry Pendleton* (first name correct)(FC)			
	2.50	2.00	1.00
535 Vic Rodriguez	.08	.06	.03
536 Bob McClure	.08	.06	.03
537 Dave Bergman	.08	.06	.03
538 Mark Clear	.08	.06	.03
539 *Mike Pagliarulo*(FC)	1.00	.70	.40
540 Terry Whitfield	.08	.06	.03
541 Joe Beckwith	.08	.06	.03
542 Jeff Burroughs	.10	.08	.04
543 Dan Schatzeder	.08	.06	.03
544 Donnie Scott	.08	.06	.03
545 Jim Slaton	.08	.06	.03
546 Greg Luzinski	.12	.09	.05
547 *Mark Salas*(FC)	.15	.11	.06
548 Dave Smith	.10	.08	.04
549 John Wockenfuss	.08	.06	.03
550 Frank Pastore	.08	.06	.03
551 Tim Flannery	.08	.06	.03
552 Rick Rhoden	.12	.09	.05
553 Mark Davis	.08	.06	.03
554 *Jeff Dedmon*(FC)	.15	.11	.06
555 Gary Woods	.08	.06	.03
556 Danny Heep	.08	.06	.03
557 *Mark Langston*(FC)	3.50	2.75	1.50
558 Darrell Brown	.08	.06	.03
559 *Jimmy Key*(FC)	1.50	1.25	.60
560 Rick Lysander	.08	.06	.03
561 Doyle Alexander	.12	.09	.05
562 Mike Stanton	.08	.06	.03
563 Sid Fernandez	.50	.40	.20
564 Richie Hebner	.08	.06	.03
565 Alex Trevino	.08	.06	.03
566 Brian Harper	.08	.06	.03
567 *Dan Gladden*(FC)	.40	.30	.15
568 Luis Salazar	.08	.06	.03
569 Tom Foley	.08	.06	.03
570 Larry Andersen	.08	.06	.03
571 Danny Cox	.12	.09	.05
572 Joe Sambito	.08	.06	.03
573 Juan Beniquez	.08	.06	.03
574 Joel Skinner	.08	.06	.03
575 *Randy St. Claire*(FC)	.15	.11	.06
576 Floyd Rayford	.08	.06	.03
577 Roy Howell	.08	.06	.03
578 John Grubb	.08	.06	.03
579 Ed Jurak	.08	.06	.03
580 John Montefusco	.08	.06	.03
581 *Orel Hershiser*(FC)	10.00	7.50	4.00
582 *Tom Waddell*(FC)	.08	.06	.03
583 Mark Huismann	.08	.06	.03
584 Joe Morgan	.30	.25	.12
585 Jim Wohlford	.08	.06	.03
586 Dave Schmidt	.08	.06	.03
587 *Jeff Kunkel*(FC)	.12	.09	.05
588 Hal McRae	.12	.09	.05
589 Bill Almon	.08	.06	.03
590 Carmen Castillo(FC)	.10	.08	.04
591 Omar Moreno	.08	.06	.03
592 *Ken Howell*(FC)	.20	.15	.08
593 Tom Brookens	.08	.06	.03
594 Joe Nolan	.08	.06	.03
595 Willie Lozado	.08	.06	.03
596 *Tom Nieto*(FC)	.12	.09	.05
597 Walt Terrell	.10	.08	.04
598 Al Oliver	.15	.11	.06
599 Shane Rawley	.12	.09	.05
600 *Denny Gonzalez*(FC)	.10	.08	.04
601 *Mark Grant*(FC)	.15	.11	.06
602 Mike Armstrong	.08	.06	.03
603 George Foster	.15	.11	.06
604 Davey Lopes	.10	.08	.04
605 Salome Barojas	.08	.06	.03
606 Roy Lee Jackson	.08	.06	.03
607 Pete Filson	.08	.06	.03
608 Duane Walker	.08	.06	.03
609 Glenn Wilson	.10	.08	.04
610 *Rafael Santana*(FC)	.20	.15	.08
611 Roy Smith	.08	.06	.03
612 Ruppert Jones	.08	.06	.03
613 Joe Cowley(FC)	.08	.06	.03
614 *Al Nipper* (photo actually Mike Brown)(FC)			
	.20	.15	.08
615 Gene Nelson	.08	.06	.03
616 Joe Carter	.50	.40	.20
617 Ray Knight	.12	.09	.05

	MT	NR MT	EX
618 Chuck Rainey	.08	.06	.03
619 Dan Driessen	.10	.08	.04
620 Daryl Sconiers	.08	.06	.03
621 Bill Stein	.08	.06	.03
622 Roy Smalley	.08	.06	.03
623 Ed Lynch	.08	.06	.03
624 *Jeff Stone*(FC)	.15	.11	.06
625 Bruce Berenyi	.08	.06	.03
626 Kelvin Chapman	.08	.06	.03
627 Joe Price	.08	.06	.03
628 Steve Bedrosian	.12	.09	.05
629 Vic Mata	.08	.06	.03
630 Mike Krukow	.10	.08	.04
631 *Phil Bradley*(FC)	.90	.70	.35
632 Jim Gott	.08	.06	.03
633 Randy Bush	.08	.06	.03
634 *Tom Browning*(FC)	2.00	1.50	.80
635 Lou Gehrig Puzzle Card	.08	.06	.03
636 Reid Nichols	.08	.06	.03
637 *Dan Pasqua*(FC)	.60	.45	.25
638 German Rivera	.08	.06	.03
639 *Don Schulze*(FC)	.10	.08	.04
640a Mike Jones (last line of highlights begins "Was 11-7...")	.10	.08	.04
640b Mike Jones (last line of highlights begins "Spent some ...")	1.25	.90	.50
641 Pete Rose	1.25	.90	.50
642 *Wade Rowdon*(FC)	.10	.08	.04
643 Jerry Narron	.08	.06	.03
644 *Darrell Miller*(FC)	.15	.11	.06
645 *Tim Hulett*(FC)	.15	.11	.06
646 Andy McGaffigan	.08	.06	.03
647 Kurt Bevacqua	.08	.06	.03
648 *John Russell*(FC)	.20	.15	.08
649 *Ron Robinson*(FC)	.25	.20	.10
650 Donnie Moore(FC)	.08	.06	.03
651a Two for the Title (Don Mattingly, Dave Winfield) (player names in yellow)	3.00	2.25	1.25
651b Two for the Title (Don Mattingly, Dave Winfield) (player names in white)	6.00	4.50	2.50
652 Tim Laudner	.08	.06	.03
653 *Steve Farr*(FC)	.35	.25	.14
----- Checklist 1-26 DK	.08	.06	.03
----- Checklist 27-130	.08	.06	.03
----- Checklist 131-234	.08	.06	.03
----- Checklist 235-338	.08	.06	.03
----- Checklist 339-442	.08	.06	.03
----- Checklist 443-546	.08	.06	.03
----- Checklist 547-653	.08	.06	.03

1985 Donruss Action All-Stars

In 1985, Donruss issued an Action All-Stars set for the third consecutive year. The card fronts feature an action photo with an inset head-shot of the player inside a black border with grey boxes through it. The card backs have black print on blue and white and include statistical and biographical information. The cards were issued with a Lou Gehrig puzzle.

	MT	NR MT	EX
Complete Set:	8.00	6.00	3.25
Common Player:	.09	.07	.04
1 Tim Raines	.35	.25	.14
2 Jim Gantner	.09	.07	.04
3 Mario Soto	.09	.07	.04
4 Spike Owen	.09	.07	.04

		MT	NR MT	EX
5	Lloyd Moseby	.12	.09	.05
6	Damaso Garcia	.09	.07	.04
7	Cal Ripken	.35	.25	.14
8	Dan Quisenberry	.09	.07	.04
9	Eddie Murray	.12	.09	.05
10	Tony Pena	.09	.07	.04
11	Buddy Bell	.09	.07	.04
12	Dave Winfield	.30	.25	.12
13	Ron Kittle	.12	.09	.05
14	Rich Gossage	.12	.09	.05
15	Dwight Evans	.15	.11	.06
16	Al Davis	.15	.11	.06
17	Mike Schmidt	.40	.30	.15
18	Pascual Perez	.09	.07	.04
19	Tony Gwynn	.30	.25	.12
20	Nolan Ryan	.50	.40	.20
21	Robin Yount	.50	.40	.20
22	Mike Marshall	.12	.09	.05
23	Brett Butler	.09	.07	.04
24	Ryne Sandberg	.25	.20	.10
25	Dale Murphy	.40	.30	.15
26	George Brett	.40	.30	.15
27	Jim Rice	.15	.11	.06
28	Ozzie Smith	.15	.11	.06
29	Larry Parrish	.09	.07	.04
30	Jack Clark	.15	.11	.06
31	Manny Trillo	.09	.07	.04
32	Dave Kingman	.12	.09	.05
33	Geoff Zahn	.09	.07	.04
34	Pedro Guerrero	.15	.11	.06
35	Dave Parker	.20	.15	.08
36	Rollie Fingers	.15	.11	.06
37	Fernando Valenzuela	.12	.09	.05
38	Wade Boggs	1.00	.70	.40
39	Reggie Jackson	.30	.25	.12
40	Kent Hrbek	.20	.15	.08
41	Keith Hernandez	.25	.20	.10
42	Lou Whitaker	.15	.11	.06
43	Tom Herr	.09	.07	.04
44	Alan Trammell	.20	.15	.08
45	Butch Wynegar	.09	.07	.04
46	Leon Durham	.09	.07	.04
47	Dwight Gooden	1.50	1.25	.60
48	Don Mattingly	2.00	1.50	.80
49	Phil Niekro	.20	.15	.08
50	Johnny Ray	.09	.07	.04
51	Doug DeCinces	.09	.07	.04
52	Willie Upshaw	.09	.07	.04
53	Lance Parrish	.15	.11	.06
54	Jody Davis	.09	.07	.04
55	Steve Carlton	.30	.25	.12
56	Juan Samuel	.09	.07	.04
57	Gary Carter	.12	.09	.05
58	Harold Baines	.15	.11	.06
59	Eric Show	.09	.07	.04
60	Checklist	.09	.07	.04

1985 Donruss Box Panels

In 1985, Donruss placed on the bottoms of their wax pack boxes a four-card panel which included three player cards and a Lou Gehrig puzzle card. The player cards, numbered PC 1 through PC 3, have backs identical to the regular 1985 Donruss issue. The card fronts are identical in design to the regular issue, but carry different picture poses.

		MT	NR MT	EX
Complete Panel Set:		6.50	5.00	3.00
Complete Singles Set:		4.50	3.50	1.50
Common Single Player:		.10	.08	.04
Panel		6.50	5.00	3.00
1	Dwight Gooden	4.00	3.00	1.50
2	Ryne Sanberg	.50	.40	.20
3	Ron Kittle	.10	.08	.04
----	Lou Gehrig Puzzle Card	.05	.04	.02

1985 Donruss Diamond Kings Supers

The 1985 Donruss Diamond Kings Supers are enlarged versions of the Diamond Kings card (#'s 1-26) in the regular 1985 Donruss set. The cards measure 4-15/16" by 6-3/4". The Diamond Kings series features the artwork of Dick Perez. Twenty-eight cards make up the set - 26 DK cards, an unnumbered checklist, and an unnumbered Dick Perez card. The back of the Perez card contains a brief history of Dick Perez and the Perez-Steele Galleries. The set could be obtained through a write-in offer found on the wrappers of the regular issue wax packs.

		MT	NR MT	EX
Complete Set:		11.00	8.25	4.50
Common Player:		.20	.15	.08
1	Ryne Sandberg	.60	.45	.25
2	Doug DeCinces	.20	.15	.08
3	Richard Dotson	.20	.15	.08
4	Bert Blyleven	.25	.20	.10
5	Lou Whitaker	.30	.25	.12
6	Dan Quisenberry	.20	.15	.08
7	Don Mattingly	4.50	3.25	1.75
8	Carney Lansford	.20	.15	.08
9	Frank Tanana	.20	.15	.08
10	Willie Upshaw	.20	.15	.08
11	Claudell Washington	.20	.15	.08
12	Mike Marshall	.25	.20	.10
13	Joaquin Andujar	.20	.15	.08
14	Cal Ripken, Jr.	.50	.40	.20
15	Jim Rice	.35	.25	.14
16	Don Sutton	.30	.25	.12
17	Frank Viola	.35	.25	.14
18	Alvin Davis	.30	.25	.12
19	Mario Soto	.20	.15	.08
20	Jose Cruz	.20	.15	.08
21	Charlie Lea	.20	.15	.08
22	Jesse Orosco	.20	.15	.08
23	Juan Samuel	.20	.15	.08
24	Tony Pena	.20	.15	.08
25	Tony Gwynn	.40	.30	.15
26	Bob Brenly	.20	.15	.08
----	Checklist	.12	.09	.05
----	Dick Perez (DK artist)	.12	.09	.05

NOTE: A card number in parentheses ( ) indicates the set is unnumbered.

1985 Donruss Highlights

Designed in the style of the regular 1985 Donruss set, this issue features the Player of the Month in the major leagues plus highlight cards of special baseball events and milestones that occurred during the 1985 season. Fifty-six cards, including an unnumbered checklist, comprise the set which was available only through hobby dealers. The cards measure 2-1/2" by 3-1/2" and have glossy fronts. The last two cards in the set feature Donruss' picks for the A.L. and N.L. Rookies of the Year. The set was issued in a specially designed box.

		MT	NR MT	EX
Complete Set:		24.00	18.00	9.50
Common Player:		.12	.09	.05
1	Sets Opening Day Record (Tom Seaver)			
		.40	.30	.15
2	Establishes A.L. Save Mark (Rollie Fingers)			
		.15	.11	.06
3	A.L. Player of the Month - April (Mike Davis)	.12	.09	.05
4	A.L. Pitcher of the Month - April (Charlie Leibrandt)	.12	.09	.05
5	N.L. Player of the Month - April (Dale Murphy)	.40	.30	.15
6	N.L. Pitcher of the Month - April (Fernando Valenzuela)	.12	.09	.05
7	N.L. Shortstop Record (Larry Bowa)			
		.12	.09	.05
8	Joins Reds 2000 Hit Club (Dave Concepcion)	.12	.09	.05
9	Eldest Grand Slammer (Tony Perez)			
		.15	.11	.06
10	N.L. Career Run Leader (Pete Rose)			
		.90	.70	.35
11	A.L. Player of the Month - May (George Brett)	.90	.70	.35
12	A.L. Pitcher of the Month - May (Dave Stieb)	.12	.09	.05
13	N.L. Player of the Month - May (Dave Parker)	.20	.15	.08
14	N.L. Pitcher of the Month - May (Andy Hawkins)	.12	.09	.05
15	Records 11th Straight Win (Andy Hawkins)	.12	.09	.05
16	Two Homers In First Inning (Von Hayes)			
		.15	.11	.06
17	A.L. Player of the Month - June (Rickey Henderson)	1.00	.70	.40
18	A.L. Pitcher of the Month - June (Jay Howell)	.12	.09	.05
19	N.L. Player of the Month - June (Pedro Guerrero)	.20	.15	.08
20	N.L. Pitcher of the Month - June (John Tudor)	.12	.09	.05
21	Marathon Game Iron Men (Gary Carter, Keith Hernandez)	.35	.25	.14
22	Records 4000th K (Nolan Ryan)	.75	.55	.30
23	All-Star Game MVP (LaMarr Hoyt)	.12	.09	.05
24	1st Ranger To Hit For Cycle (Oddibe McDowell)	.40	.30	.15
25	A.L. Player of the Month - July (George Brett)	.90	.70	.35
26	A.L. Pitcher of the Month - July (Bret Saberhagen)	1.50	1.25	.60
27	N.L. Player of the Month - July (Keith Hernandez)	.35	.25	.14

		MT	NR MT	EX
28	N.L. Pitcher of the Month - July (Fernando Valenzuela)	.12	.09	.05
29	Record Setting Base Stealers (Vince Coleman, Willie McGee)	.80	.60	.30
30	Notches 300th Career Win (Tom Seaver)	.35	.25	.14
31	Strokes 3000th Hit (Rod Carew)	.40	.30	.15
32	Establishes Met Record (Dwight Gooden)	2.25	1.75	.90
33	Achieves Strikeout Milestone (Dwight Gooden)	2.25	1.75	.90
34	Explodes For 9 RBI (Eddie Murray)	.70	.50	.30
35	A.L. Career Hbp Leader (Don Baylor)	.15	.11	.06
36	A.L. Player of the Month - August (Don Mattingly)	3.25	2.50	1.25
37	A.L. Pitcher of the Month - August (Dave Righetti)	.20	.15	.08
38	N.L. Player of the Month (Willie McGee)	.20	.15	.08
39	N.L. Pitcher of the Month - August (Shane Rawley)	.12	.09	.05
40	Ty-Breaking Hit (Pete Rose)	.90	.70	.35
41	Hits 3 Hrs Drives In 8 Runs (Andre Dawson)	.20	.15	.08
42	Sets Yankee Theft Mark (Rickey Henderson)	1.00	.70	.40
43	20 Wins In Rookie Season (Tom Browning)	.35	.25	.14
44	Yankee Milestone For Hits (Don Mattingly)	3.25	2.50	1.25
45	A.L. Player of the Month - September (Don Mattingly)	3.25	2.50	1.25
46	A.L. Pitcher of the Month - September (Charlie Leibrandt)	.12	.09	.05
47	N.L. Player of the Month - September (Gary Carter)	.12	.09	.05
48	N.L. Pitcher of the Month - September (Dwight Gooden)	2.25	1.75	.90
49	Major League Record Setter (Wade Boggs)	2.00	1.50	.80
50	Hurls Shutout For 300th Win (Phil Niekro)	.30	.25	.12
51	Venerable HR King (Darrell Evans)	.15	.11	.06
52	N.L. Switch-hitting Record (Willie McGee)	.20	.15	.08
53	Equals DiMaggio Feat (Dave Winfield)	.30	.25	.12
54	Donruss N.L. Rookie of the Year (Vince Coleman)	2.25	1.75	.90
55	Donruss A.L. Rookie of the Year (Ozzie Guillen)	.50	.40	.20
----	Checklist	.20	.15	.08

1985 Donruss Sluggers
of the Hall of Fame

In much the same manner as the first Bazooka

cards were issued in 1959, this eight-player set from Donruss consists of cards which formed the bottom panel of a box of bubble gum. When cut off the box, cards measure 3-1/2" by 6-1/2", with blank backs. Players are pictured on the cards in paintings done by Dick Perez.

		MT	NR MT	EX
	Complete Set:	8.00	6.00	3.25
	Common Player:	.60	.45	.25
1	Babe Ruth	1.50	1.25	.60
2	Ted Williams	1.00	.70	.40
3	Lou Gehrig	1.00	.70	.40
4	Johnny Mize	.60	.45	.25
5	Stan Musial	1.00	.70	.40
6	Mickey Mantle	3.00	2.25	1.25
7	Hank Aaron	1.00	.70	.40
8	Frank Robinson	.70	.50	.30

1986 Donruss

In 1986, Donruss issued a 660-card set which included 653 numbered cards and seven unnumbered checklists. The cards, which measure 2-1/2" by 3-1/2", have fronts that feature blue borders and backs that have black print on blue and white. For the fifth year in a row, the first 26 cards in the set are Diamond Kings. The Rated Rookies subset (card #'s 27-46) appears once again. The cards were distributed with a Hank Aaron puzzle. The complete set price does not include the higher priced variations. In the checklist that follows, (DK) and (RR) refer to the Diamond Kings and Rated Rookies series.

		MT	NR MT	EX
	Complete Set:	130.00	95.00	50.00
	Common Player:	.06	.05	.02
1	Kirk Gibson (DK)	.30	.25	.12
2	Goose Gossage (DK)	.20	.15	.08
3	Willie McGee (DK)	.15	.11	.06
4	George Bell (DK)	.30	.25	.12
5	Tony Armas (DK)	.10	.08	.04
6	Chili Davis (DK)	.10	.08	.04
7	Cecil Cooper (DK)	.12	.09	.05
8	Mike Boddicker (DK)	.10	.08	.04
9	Davey Lopes (DK)	.10	.08	.04
10	Bill Doran (DK)	.12	.09	.05
11	Bret Saberhagen (DK)	.25	.20	.10
12	Brett Butler (DK)	.10	.08	.04
13	Harold Baines (DK)	.15	.11	.06
14	Mike Davis (DK)	.10	.08	.04
15	Tony Perez (DK)	.15	.11	.06
16	Willie Randolph (DK)	.12	.09	.05
17	Bob Boone (DK)	.10	.08	.04
18	Orel Hershiser (DK)	1.00	.70	.40
19	Johnny Ray (DK)	.12	.09	.05
20	Gary Ward (DK)	.10	.08	.04
21	Rick Mahler (DK)	.08	.06	.03
22	Phil Bradley (DK)	.20	.15	.08
23	Jerry Koosman (DK)	.12	.09	.05
24	Tom Brunansky (DK)	.15	.11	.06
25	Andre Dawson (DK)	.30	.25	.12
26	Dwight Gooden (DK)	1.00	.70	.40

		MT	NR MT	EX
27	*Kal Daniels (RR)(FC)*	3.75	2.75	1.50
28	*Fred McGriff (RR)(FC)*	16.00	12.00	6.50
29	*Cory Snyder (RR)(FC)*	3.00	2.25	1.25
30	*Jose Guzman (RR)(FC)*	.30	.25	.12
31	*Ty Gainey (RR)(FC)*	.10	.08	.04
32	*Johnny Abrego (RR)(FC)*	.08	.06	.03
33a	*Andres Galarraga (RR) (no accent mark above "e" in Andres on back)(FC)*	4.00	3.00	1.50
33b	*Andres Galarraga (RR) (accent mark above "e" in Andres on back)(FC)*	5.00	3.75	2.00
34	*Dave Shipanoff (RR)(FC)*	.08	.06	.03
35	*Mark McLemore (RR)(FC)*	.20	.15	.08
36	*Marty Clary (RR)(FC)*	.08	.06	.03
37	*Paul O'Neill (RR)(FC)*	.80	.60	.30
38	*Danny Tartabull (RR)*	.80	.60	.30
39	*Jose Canseco (RR)(FC)*	55.00	41.00	22.00
40	*Juan Nieves (RR)(FC)*	.40	.30	.15
41	*Lance McCullers (RR)(FC)*	.35	.25	.14
42	*Rick Surhoff (RR)(FC)*	.08	.06	.03
43	*Todd Worrell (RR)(FC)*	1.00	.70	.40
44	*Bob Kipper (RR)(FC)*	.20	.15	.08
45	*John Habyan (RR)(FC)*	.15	.11	.06
46	*Mike Woodard (RR)(FC)*	.10	.08	.04
47	Mike Boddicker	.10	.08	.04
48	Robin Yount	.60	.45	.25
49	Lou Whitaker	.30	.25	.12
50	"Oil Can" Boyd	.08	.06	.03
51	Rickey Henderson	.60	.45	.25
52	Mike Marshall	.15	.11	.06
53	George Brett	.50	.40	.20
54	Dave Kingman	.15	.11	.06
55	Hubie Brooks	.10	.08	.04
56	*Oddibe McDowell(FC)*	.35	.25	.14
57	Doug DeCinces	.10	.08	.04
58	Britt Burns	.06	.05	.02
59	Ozzie Smith	.15	.11	.06
60	Jose Cruz	.10	.08	.04
61	Mike Schmidt	.50	.40	.20
62	Pete Rose	.80	.60	.30
63	Steve Garvey	.40	.30	.15
64	Tony Pena	.10	.08	.04
65	Chili Davis	.10	.08	.04
66	Dale Murphy	.60	.45	.25
67	Ryne Sandberg	.40	.30	.15
68	Gary Carter	.35	.25	.14
69	Alvin Davis	.30	.25	.12
70	Kent Hrbek	.25	.20	.10
71	George Bell	.30	.25	.12
72	Kirby Puckett	1.50	1.25	.60
73	Lloyd Moseby	.10	.08	.04
74	Bob Kearney	.06	.05	.02
75	Dwight Gooden	2.50	2.00	1.00
76	Gary Matthews	.10	.08	.04
77	Rick Mahler	.06	.05	.02
78	Benny Distefano	.06	.05	.02
79	Jeff Leonard	.08	.06	.03
80	Kevin McReynolds	.30	.25	.12
81	Ron Oester	.06	.05	.02
82	John Russell	.06	.05	.02
83	Tommy Herr	.10	.08	.04
84	Jerry Mumphrey	.06	.05	.02
85	Ron Romanick	.06	.05	.02
86	Daryl Boston	.08	.06	.03
87	Andre Dawson	.30	.25	.12
88	Eddie Murray	.40	.30	.15
89	Dion James	.08	.06	.03
90	Chet Lemon	.08	.06	.03
91	Bob Stanley	.06	.05	.02
92	Willie Randolph	.10	.08	.04
93	Mike Scioscia	.08	.06	.03
94	Tom Waddell	.06	.05	.02
95	Danny Jackson	.30	.25	.12
96	Mike Davis	.08	.06	.03
97	Mike Fitzgerald	.06	.05	.02
98	Gary Ward	.08	.06	.03
99	Pete O'Brien	.10	.08	.04
100	Bret Saberhagen	.40	.30	.15
101	Alfredo Griffin	.08	.06	.03
102	Brett Butler	.08	.06	.03
103	Ron Guidry	.20	.15	.08
104	Jerry Reuss	.08	.06	.03
105	Jack Morris	.30	.25	.12
106	Rick Dempsey	.08	.06	.03
107	Ray Burris	.06	.05	.02
108	Brian Downing	.10	.08	.04
109	Willie McGee	.15	.11	.06
110	Bill Doran	.10	.08	.04
111	Kent Tekulve	.08	.06	.03
112	Tony Gwynn	.40	.30	.15
113	Marvell Wynne	.06	.05	.02
114	David Green	.06	.05	.02
115	Jim Gantner	.08	.06	.03

		MT	NR MT	EX			MT	NR MT	EX
116	George Foster	.15	.11	.06	207	Bobby Grich	.10	.08	.04
117	Steve Trout	.06	.05	.02	208	Ozzie Guillen(FC)	.40	.30	.15
118	Mark Langston	.30	.25	.12	209	Jeff Reardon	.12	.09	.05
119	Tony Fernandez	.20	.15	.08	210	Cal Ripken Jr.	.50	.40	.20
120	John Butcher	.06	.05	.02	211	Bill Schroeder	.06	.05	.02
121	Ron Robinson	.08	.06	.03	212	Dan Petry	.08	.06	.03
122	Dan Spillner	.06	.05	.02	213	Jim Rice	.40	.30	.15
123	Mike Young	.06	.05	.02	214	Dave Righetti	.20	.15	.08
124	Paul Molitor	.15	.11	.06	215	Fernando Valenzuela	.35	.25	.14
125	Kirk Gibson	.35	.25	.14	216	Julio Franco	.12	.09	.05
126	Ken Griffey	.12	.09	.05	217	Darryl Motley	.06	.05	.02
127	Tony Armas	.08	.06	.03	218	Dave Collins	.08	.06	.03
128	Mariano Duncan(FC)	.15	.11	.06	219	Tim Wallach	.12	.09	.05
129	Mr. Clutch (Pat Tabler)	.08	.06	.03	220	George Wright	.06	.05	.02
130	Frank White	.10	.08	.04	221	Tommy Dunbar	.06	.05	.02
131	Carney Lansford	.10	.08	.04	222	Steve Balboni	.08	.06	.03
132	Vance Law	.08	.06	.03	223	Jay Howell	.08	.06	.03
133	Dick Schofield	.06	.05	.02	224	Joe Carter	.25	.20	.10
134	Wayne Tolleson	.06	.05	.02	225	Ed Whitson	.06	.05	.02
135	Greg Walker	.10	.08	.04	226	Orel Hershiser	1.25	.90	.50
136	Denny Walling	.06	.05	.02	227	Willie Hernandez	.08	.06	.03
137	Ozzie Virgil	.06	.05	.02	228	Lee Lacy	.06	.05	.02
138	Ricky Horton	.08	.06	.03	229	Rollie Fingers	.20	.15	.08
139	LaMarr Hoyt	.06	.05	.02	230	Bob Boone	.08	.06	.03
140	Wayne Krenchicki	.06	.05	.02	231	Joaquin Andujar	.08	.06	.03
141	Glenn Hubbard	.06	.05	.02	232	Craig Reynolds	.06	.05	.02
142	Cecilio Guante	.06	.05	.02	233	Shane Rawley	.10	.08	.04
143	Mike Krukow	.08	.06	.03	234	Eric Show	.08	.06	.03
144	Lee Smith	.10	.08	.04	235	Jose DeLeon	.08	.06	.03
145	Edwin Nunez	.06	.05	.02	236	Jose Uribe(FC)	.25	.20	.10
146	Dave Stieb	.12	.09	.05	237	Moose Haas	.06	.05	.02
147	Mike Smithson	.06	.05	.02	238	Wally Backman	.08	.06	.03
148	Ken Dixon	.06	.05	.02	239	Dennis Eckersley	.12	.09	.05
149	Danny Darwin	.06	.05	.02	240	Mike Moore	.06	.05	.02
150	Chris Pittaro	.06	.05	.02	241	Damaso Garcia	.06	.05	.02
151	Bill Buckner	.12	.09	.05	242	Tim Teufel	.06	.05	.02
152	Mike Pagliarulo	.20	.15	.08	243	Dave Concepcion	.12	.09	.05
153	Bill Russell	.08	.06	.03	244	Floyd Bannister	.10	.08	.04
154	Brook Jacoby	.10	.08	.04	245	Fred Lynn	.20	.15	.08
155	Pat Sheridan	.06	.05	.02	246	Charlie Moore	.06	.05	.02
156	Mike Gallego(FC)	.15	.11	.06	247	Walt Terrell	.08	.06	.03
157	Jim Wohlford	.06	.05	.02	248	Dave Winfield	.40	.30	.15
158	Gary Pettis	.06	.05	.02	249	Dwight Evans	.12	.09	.05
159	Toby Harrah	.08	.06	.03	250	Dennis Powell(FC)	.10	.08	.04
160	Richard Dotson	.10	.08	.04	251	Andre Thornton	.10	.08	.04
161	Bob Knepper	.08	.06	.03	252	Onix Concepcion	.06	.05	.02
162	Dave Dravecky	.08	.06	.03	253	Mike Heath	.06	.05	.02
163	Greg Gross	.06	.05	.02	254a	David Palmer (2B on front)	.06	.05	.02
164	Eric Davis	3.50	2.75	1.50	254b	David Palmer (P on front)	1.00	.70	.40
165	Gerald Perry	.15	.11	.06	255	Donnie Moore	.06	.05	.02
166	Rick Rhoden	.10	.08	.04	256	Curtis Wilkerson	.06	.05	.02
167	Keith Moreland	.08	.06	.03	257	Julio Cruz	.06	.05	.02
168	Jack Clark	.20	.15	.08	258	Nolan Ryan	.70	.50	.30
169	Storm Davis	.10	.08	.04	259	Jeff Stone	.06	.05	.02
170	Cecil Cooper	.12	.09	.05	260a	John Tudor (1981 Games is .18)	.10	.08	.04
171	Alan Trammell	.35	.25	.14	260b	John Tudor (1981 Games is 18)	1.00	.70	.40
172	Roger Clemens	4.00	3.00	1.50	261	Mark Thurmond	.06	.05	.02
173	Don Mattingly	6.00	4.50	2.50	262	Jay Tibbs	.06	.05	.02
174	Pedro Guerrero	.20	.15	.08	263	Rafael Ramirez	.06	.05	.02
175	Willie Wilson	.12	.09	.05	264	Larry McWilliams	.06	.05	.02
176	Dwayne Murphy	.08	.06	.03	265	Mark Davis	.06	.05	.02
177	Tim Raines	.40	.30	.15	266	Bob Dernier	.06	.05	.02
178	Larry Parrish	.10	.08	.04	267	Matt Young	.06	.05	.02
179	Mike Witt	.10	.08	.04	268	Jim Clancy	.08	.06	.03
180	Harold Baines	.15	.11	.06	269	Mickey Hatcher	.06	.05	.02
181	Vince Coleman(FC)	2.00	1.50	.80	270	Sammy Stewart	.06	.05	.02
182	Jeff Heathcock(FC)	.10	.08	.04	271	Bob Gibson	.06	.05	.02
183	Steve Carlton	.40	.30	.15	272	Nelson Simmons	.06	.05	.02
184	Mario Soto	.08	.06	.03	273	Rich Gedman	.10	.08	.04
185	Goose Gossage	.20	.15	.08	274	Butch Wynegar	.06	.05	.02
186	Johnny Ray	.12	.09	.05	275	Ken Howell	.06	.05	.02
187	Dan Gladden	.08	.06	.03	276	Mel Hall	.08	.06	.03
188	Bob Horner	.12	.09	.05	277	Jim Sundberg	.08	.06	.03
189	Rick Sutcliffe	.12	.09	.05	278	Chris Codiroli	.06	.05	.02
190	Keith Hernandez	.35	.25	.14	279	Herman Winningham(FC)	.15	.11	.06
191	Phil Bradley	.20	.15	.08	280	Rod Carew	.40	.30	.15
192	Tom Brunansky	.12	.09	.05	281	Don Slaught	.06	.05	.02
193	Jesse Barfield	.20	.15	.08	282	Scott Fletcher	.08	.06	.03
194	Frank Viola	.20	.15	.08	283	Bill Dawley	.06	.05	.02
195	Willie Upshaw	.08	.06	.03	284	Andy Hawkins	.06	.05	.02
196	Jim Beattie	.06	.05	.02	285	Glenn Wilson	.08	.06	.03
197	Darryl Strawberry	1.50	1.25	.60	286	Nick Esasky	.08	.06	.03
198	Ron Cey	.10	.08	.04	287	Claudell Washington	.08	.06	.03
199	Steve Bedrosian	.12	.09	.05	288	Lee Mazzilli	.08	.06	.03
200	Steve Kemp	.08	.06	.03	289	Jody Davis	.10	.08	.04
201	Manny Trillo	.08	.06	.03	290	Darrell Porter	.08	.06	.03
202	Garry Templeton	.08	.06	.03	291	Scott McGregor	.08	.06	.03
203	Dave Parker	.25	.20	.10	292	Ted Simmons	.12	.09	.05
204	John Denny	.06	.05	.02	293	Aurelio Lopez	.06	.05	.02
205	Terry Pendleton	.15	.11	.06	294	Marty Barrett	.10	.08	.04
206	Terry Puhl	.06	.05	.02	295	Dale Berra	.06	.05	.02

#	Name	MT	NR MT	EX
296	Greg Brock	.08	.06	.03
297	Charlie Leibrandt	.08	.06	.03
298	Bill Krueger	.06	.05	.02
299	Bryn Smith	.06	.05	.02
300	Burt Hooton	.08	.06	.03
301	Stu Cliburn(FC)	.12	.09	.05
302	Luis Salazar	.06	.05	.02
303	Ken Dayley	.06	.05	.02
304	Frank DiPino	.06	.05	.02
305	Von Hayes	.10	.08	.04
306a	Gary Redus (1983 2B is .20)	.08	.06	.03
306b	Gary Redus (1983 2B is 20)	1.00	.70	.40
307	Craig Lefferts	.06	.05	.02
308	Sam Khalifa	.06	.05	.02
309	Scott Garrelts	.06	.05	.02
310	Rick Cerone	.06	.05	.02
311	Shawon Dunston	.20	.15	.08
312	Howard Johnson	.12	.09	.05
313	Jim Presley	.15	.11	.06
314	Gary Gaetti	.25	.20	.10
315	Luis Leal	.06	.05	.02
316	Mark Salas	.06	.05	.02
317	Bill Caudill	.06	.05	.02
318	Dave Henderson	.10	.08	.04
319	Rafael Santana	.06	.05	.02
320	Leon Durham	.08	.06	.03
321	Bruce Sutter	.15	.11	.06
322	Jason Thompson	.06	.05	.02
323	Bob Brenly	.06	.05	.02
324	Carmelo Martinez	.08	.06	.03
325	Eddie Milner	.06	.05	.02
326	Juan Samuel	.15	.11	.06
327	Tom Nieto	.06	.05	.02
328	Dave Smith	.08	.06	.03
329	Urbano Lugo(FC)	.08	.06	.03
330	Joel Skinner	.06	.05	.02
331	Bill Gullickson	.06	.05	.02
332	Floyd Rayford	.06	.05	.02
333	Ben Oglivie	.08	.06	.03
334	Lance Parrish	.30	.25	.12
335	Jackie Gutierrez	.06	.05	.02
336	Dennis Rasmussen	.12	.09	.05
337	Terry Whitfield	.06	.05	.02
338	Neal Heaton	.06	.05	.02
339	Jorge Orta	.06	.05	.02
340	Donnie Hill	.06	.05	.02
341	Joe Hesketh	.06	.05	.02
342	Charlie Hough	.10	.08	.04
343	Dave Rozema	.06	.05	.02
344	Greg Pryor	.06	.05	.02
345	Mickey Tettleton(FC)	.70	.50	.30
346	George Vukovich	.06	.05	.02
347	Don Baylor	.12	.09	.05
348	Carlos Diaz	.06	.05	.02
349	Barbaro Garbey	.06	.05	.02
350	Larry Sheets	.12	.09	.05
351	Ted Higuera(FC)	1.25	.90	.50
352	Juan Beniquez	.06	.05	.02
353	Bob Forsch	.08	.06	.03
354	Mark Bailey	.06	.05	.02
355	Larry Andersen	.06	.05	.02
356	Terry Kennedy	.08	.06	.03
357	Don Robinson	.08	.06	.03
358	Jim Gott	.06	.05	.02
359	Earnest Riles(FC)	.20	.15	.08
360	John Christensen(FC)	.10	.08	.04
361	Ray Fontenot	.06	.05	.02
362	Spike Owen	.06	.05	.02
363	Jim Acker	.06	.05	.02
364a	Ron Davis (last line in highlights ends with "...in May.")	.08	.06	.03
364b	Ron Davis (last line in highlights ends with "...relievers (9).")	1.00	.70	.40
365	Tom Hume	.06	.05	.02
366	Carlton Fisk	.25	.20	.10
367	Nate Snell	.06	.05	.02
368	Rick Manning	.06	.05	.02
369	Darrell Evans	.15	.11	.06
370	Ron Hassey	.06	.05	.02
371	Wade Boggs	2.50	2.00	1.00
372	Rick Honeycutt	.06	.05	.02
373	Chris Bando	.06	.05	.02
374	Bud Black	.06	.05	.02
375	Steve Henderson	.06	.05	.02
376	Charlie Lea	.06	.05	.02
377	Reggie Jackson	.40	.30	.15
378	Dave Schmidt	.06	.05	.02
379	Bob James	.06	.05	.02
380	Glenn Davis(FC)	4.00	3.00	1.50
381	Tim Corcoran	.06	.05	.02
382	Danny Cox	.10	.08	.04
383	Tim Flannery	.06	.05	.02
384	Tom Browning	.20	.15	.08
385	Rick Camp	.06	.05	.02
386	Jim Morrison	.06	.05	.02
387	Dave LaPoint	.08	.06	.03
388	Davey Lopes	.08	.06	.03
389	Al Cowens	.06	.05	.02
390	Doyle Alexander	.10	.08	.04
391	Tim Laudner	.06	.05	.02
392	Don Aase	.06	.05	.02
393	Jaime Cocanower	.06	.05	.02
394	Randy O'Neal(FC)	.08	.06	.03
395	Mike Easler	.08	.06	.03
396	Scott Bradley	.06	.05	.02
397	Tom Niedenfuer	.08	.06	.03
398	Jerry Willard	.06	.05	.02
399	Lonnie Smith	.08	.06	.03
400	Bruce Bochte	.06	.05	.02
401	Terry Francona	.06	.05	.02
402	Jim Slaton	.06	.05	.02
403	Bill Stein	.06	.05	.02
404	Tim Hulett	.06	.05	.02
405	Alan Ashby	.06	.05	.02
406	Tim Stoddard	.06	.05	.02
407	Garry Maddox	.08	.06	.03
408	Ted Power	.06	.05	.02
409	Len Barker	.08	.06	.03
410	Denny Gonzalez	.06	.05	.02
411	George Frazier	.06	.05	.02
412	Andy Van Slyke	.15	.11	.06
413	Jim Dwyer	.06	.05	.02
414	Paul Householder	.06	.05	.02
415	Alejandro Sanchez	.06	.05	.02
416	Steve Crawford	.06	.05	.02
417	Dan Pasqua	.15	.11	.06
418	Enos Cabell	.06	.05	.02
419	Mike Jones	.06	.05	.02
420	Steve Kiefer	.06	.05	.02
421	Tim Burke(FC)	.30	.25	.12
422	Mike Mason	.06	.05	.02
423	Ruppert Jones	.06	.05	.02
424	Jerry Hairston	.06	.05	.02
425	Tito Landrum	.06	.05	.02
426	Jeff Calhoun	.06	.05	.02
427	Don Carman(FC)	.30	.25	.12
428	Tony Perez	.15	.11	.06
429	Jerry Davis	.06	.05	.02
430	Bob Walk	.06	.05	.02
431	Brad Wellman	.06	.05	.02
432	Terry Forster	.08	.06	.03
433	Billy Hatcher	.10	.08	.04
434	Clint Hurdle	.06	.05	.02
435	Ivan Calderon(FC)	.50	.40	.20
436	Pete Filson	.06	.05	.02
437	Tom Henke	.08	.06	.03
438	Dave Engle	.06	.05	.02
439	Tom Filer	.06	.05	.02
440	Gorman Thomas	.10	.08	.04
441	Rick Aguilera(FC)	.25	.20	.10
442	Scott Sanderson	.06	.05	.02
443	Jeff Dedmon	.06	.05	.02
444	Joe Orsulak(FC)	.15	.11	.06
445	Atlee Hammaker	.06	.05	.02
446	Jerry Royster	.06	.05	.02
447	Buddy Bell	.10	.08	.04
448	Dave Rucker	.06	.05	.02
449	Ivan DeJesus	.06	.05	.02
450	Jim Pankovits	.06	.05	.02
451	Jerry Narron	.06	.05	.02
452	Bryan Little	.06	.05	.02
453	Gary Lucas	.06	.05	.02
454	Dennis Martinez	.08	.06	.03
455	Ed Romero	.06	.05	.02
456	Bob Melvin(FC)	.12	.09	.05
457	Glenn Hoffman	.06	.05	.02
458	Bob Shirley	.06	.05	.02
459	Bob Welch	.12	.09	.05
460	Carmen Castillo	.06	.05	.02
461	Dave Leeper	.06	.05	.02
462	Tim Birtsas(FC)	.12	.09	.05
463	Randy St. Claire	.06	.05	.02
464	Chris Welsh	.06	.05	.02
465	Greg Harris	.06	.05	.02
466	Lynn Jones	.06	.05	.02
467	Dusty Baker	.08	.06	.03
468	Roy Smith	.06	.05	.02
469	Andre Robertson	.06	.05	.02
470	Ken Landreaux	.06	.05	.02
471	Dave Bergman	.06	.05	.02
472	Gary Roenicke	.06	.05	.02
473	Pete Vuckovich	.08	.06	.03

		MT	NR MT	EX
474	*Kirk McCaskill*(FC)	.35	.25	.14
475	Jeff Lahti	.06	.05	.02
476	Mike Scott	.20	.15	.08
477	*Darren Daulton*(FC)	.12	.09	.05
478	Graig Nettles	.15	.11	.06
479	Bill Almon	.06	.05	.02
480	Greg Minton	.06	.05	.02
481	Randy Ready(FC)	.10	.08	.04
482	*Lenny Dykstra*(FC)	.70	.50	.30
483	Thad Bosley	.06	.05	.02
484	*Harold Reynolds*(FC)	.60	.45	.25
485	Al Oliver	.12	.09	.05
486	Roy Smalley	.06	.05	.02
487	John Franco	.15	.11	.06
488	Juan Agosto	.06	.05	.02
489	Al Pardo	.06	.05	.02
490	*Bill Wegman*(FC)	.25	.20	.10
491	Frank Tanana	.10	.08	.04
492	*Brian Fisher*(FC)	.30	.25	.12
493	Mark Clear	.06	.05	.02
494	Len Matuszek	.06	.05	.02
495	Ramon Romero	.06	.05	.02
496	John Wathan	.08	.06	.03
497	Rob Picciolo	.06	.05	.02
498	U.L. Washington	.06	.05	.02
499	John Candelaria	.10	.08	.04
500	Duane Walker	.06	.05	.02
501	Gene Nelson	.06	.05	.02
502	John Mizerock	.06	.05	.02
503	Luis Aguayo	.06	.05	.02
504	Kurt Kepshire	.06	.05	.02
505	Ed Wojna	.06	.05	.02
506	Joe Price	.06	.05	.02
507	*Milt Thompson*(FC)	.30	.25	.12
508	Junior Ortiz	.06	.05	.02
509	Vida Blue	.10	.08	.04
510	Steve Engel	.06	.05	.02
511	Karl Best	.06	.05	.02
512	*Cecil Fielder*(FC)	.15	.11	.06
513	Frank Eufemia	.06	.05	.02
514	Tippy Martinez	.06	.05	.02
515	*Billy Robidoux*(FC)	.10	.08	.04
516	Bill Scherrer	.06	.05	.02
517	Bruce Hurst	.12	.09	.05
518	Rich Bordi	.06	.05	.02
519	Steve Yeager	.06	.05	.02
520	Tony Bernazard	.06	.05	.02
521	Hal McRae	.10	.08	.04
522	Jose Rijo	.10	.08	.04
523	*Mitch Webster*(FC)	.25	.20	.10
524	*Jack Howell*(FC)	.35	.25	.14
525	Alan Bannister	.06	.05	.02
526	Ron Kittle	.10	.08	.04
527	Phil Garner	.08	.06	.03
528	Kurt Bevacqua	.06	.05	.02
529	Kevin Gross	.08	.06	.03
530	Bo Diaz	.08	.06	.03
531	Ken Oberkfell	.06	.05	.02
532	Rick Reuschel	.10	.08	.04
533	Ron Meridith	.06	.05	.02
534	Steve Braun	.06	.05	.02
535	Wayne Gross	.06	.05	.02
536	Ray Searage	.06	.05	.02
537	Tom Brookens	.06	.05	.02
538	Al Nipper	.06	.05	.02
539	Billy Sample	.06	.05	.02
540	Steve Sax	.20	.15	.08
541	Dan Quisenberry	.10	.08	.04
542	Tony Phillips	.06	.05	.02
543	*Floyd Youmans*(FC)	.30	.25	.12
544	*Steve Buechele*(FC)	.25	.20	.10
545	Craig Gerber	.06	.05	.02
546	Joe DeSa	.06	.05	.02
547	Brian Harper	.06	.05	.02
548	Kevin Bass	.10	.08	.04
549	Tom Foley	.06	.05	.02
550	Dave Van Gorder	.06	.05	.02
551	Bruce Bochy	.06	.05	.02
552	R.J. Reynolds	.08	.06	.03
553	*Chris Brown*(FC)	.20	.15	.08
554	Bruce Benedict	.06	.05	.02
555	Warren Brusstar	.06	.05	.02
556	Danny Heep	.06	.05	.02
557	Darnell Coles	.08	.06	.03
558	Greg Gagne	.08	.06	.03
559	Ernie Whitt	.08	.06	.03
560	Ron Washington	.06	.05	.02
561	Jimmy Key	.15	.11	.06
562	Billy Swift(FC)	.15	.11	.06
563	Ron Darling	.15	.11	.06
564	Dick Ruthven	.06	.05	.02

		MT	NR MT	EX
565	Zane Smith(FC)	.15	.11	.06
566	Sid Bream	.10	.08	.04
567a	Joel Youngblood (P on front)	.08	.06	.03
567b	Joel Youngblood (IF on front)	1.00	.70	.40
568	Mario Ramirez	.06	.05	.02
569	Tom Runnells	.06	.05	.02
570	Rick Schu	.06	.05	.02
571	Bill Campbell	.06	.05	.02
572	Dickie Thon	.08	.06	.03
573	Al Holland	.06	.05	.02
574	Reid Nichols	.06	.05	.02
575	Bert Roberge	.06	.05	.02
576	Mike Flanagan	.10	.08	.04
577	Tim Leary(FC)	.35	.25	.14
578	Mike Laga	.06	.05	.02
579	Steve Lyons	.06	.05	.02
580	Phil Niekro	.30	.25	.12
581	Gilberto Reyes	.06	.05	.02
582	Jamie Easterly	.06	.05	.02
583	Mark Gubicza	.12	.09	.05
584	*Stan Javier*(FC)	.15	.11	.06
585	Bill Laskey	.06	.05	.02
586	Jeff Russell	.06	.05	.02
587	Dickie Noles	.06	.05	.02
588	Steve Farr	.08	.06	.03
589	*Steve Ontiveros*(FC)	.15	.11	.06
590	Mike Hargrove	.06	.05	.02
591	Marty Bystrom	.06	.05	.02
592	Franklin Stubbs	.08	.06	.03
593	Larry Herndon	.08	.06	.03
594	Bill Swaggerty	.06	.05	.02
595	Carlos Ponce	.06	.05	.02
596	*Pat Perry*(FC)	.12	.09	.05
597	Ray Knight	.08	.06	.03
598	*Steve Lombardozzi*(FC)	.15	.11	.06
599	Brad Havens	.06	.05	.02
600	*Pat Clements*(FC)	.12	.09	.05
601	Joe Niekro	.12	.09	.05
602	Hank Aaron Puzzle Card	.06	.05	.02
603	*Dwayne Henry*(FC)	.10	.08	.04
604	Mookie Wilson	.10	.08	.04
605	Buddy Biancalana	.06	.05	.02
606	Rance Mulliniks	.06	.05	.02
607	Alan Wiggins	.06	.05	.02
608	Joe Cowley	.06	.05	.02
609a	Tom Seaver (green stripes around name)	.40	.30	.15
609b	Tom Seaver (yellow stripes around name)	2.00	1.50	.80
610	Neil Allen	.06	.05	.02
611	Don Sutton	.30	.25	.12
612	*Fred Toliver*(FC)	.15	.11	.06
613	Jay Baller	.06	.05	.02
614	Marc Sullivan	.06	.05	.02
615	John Grubb	.06	.05	.02
616	Bruce Kison	.06	.05	.02
617	Bill Madlock	.12	.09	.05
618	Chris Chambliss	.08	.06	.03
619	Dave Stewart	.12	.09	.05
620	Tim Lollar	.06	.05	.02
621	Gary Lavelle	.06	.05	.02
622	Charles Hudson	.06	.05	.02
623	*Joel Davis*(FC)	.08	.06	.03
624	*Joe Johnson*(FC)	.08	.06	.03
625	Sid Fernandez	.12	.09	.05
626	Dennis Lamp	.06	.05	.02
627	Terry Harper	.06	.05	.02
628	Jack Lazorko	.06	.05	.02
629	*Roger McDowell*(FC)	.50	.40	.20
630	Mark Funderburk	.06	.05	.02
631	Ed Lynch	.06	.05	.02
632	Rudy Law	.06	.05	.02
633	*Roger Mason*(FC)	.08	.06	.03
634	*Mike Felder*(FC)	.15	.11	.06
635	Ken Schrom	.06	.05	.02
636	Bob Ojeda	.08	.06	.03
637	Ed Vande Berg	.06	.05	.02
638	Bobby Meacham	.06	.05	.02
639	Cliff Johnson	.06	.05	.02
640	Garth Iorg	.06	.05	.02
641	Dan Driessen	.08	.06	.03
642	Mike Brown	.06	.05	.02
643	John Shelby	.06	.05	.02
644	Ty-Breaking Hit (Pete Rose)	.50	.40	.20
645	Knuckle Brothers (Joe Niekro, Phil Niekro)	.15	.11	.06
646	Jesse Orosco	.08	.06	.03
647	*Billy Beane*(FC)	.06	.05	.02
648	Cesar Cedeno	.10	.08	.04
649	Bert Blyleven	.15	.11	.06
650	Max Venable	.06	.05	.02

		MT	NR MT	EX
651	Fleet Feet (Vince Coleman, Willie McGee)			
		.35	.25	.14
652	Calvin Schiraldi	.08	.06	.03
653	King of Kings (Pete Rose)	.70	.50	.30
——	Checklist 1-26 DK	.06	.05	.02
—a	Checklist 27-130 (45 is Beane)	.08	.06	.03
—b	Checklist 27-130 (45 is Habyan)	.60	.45	.25
——	Checklist 131-234	.06	.05	.02
——	Checklist 235-338	.06	.05	.02
——	Checklist 339-442	.06	.05	.02
——	Checklist 443-546	.06	.05	.02
——	Checklist 547-653	.06	.05	.02

1986 Donruss All-Stars

Issued in conjunction with the 1986 Donruss Pop-Ups set, the Donruss All-Stars set consists of 60 cards that measure 3-1/2" by 5". Fifty-nine players involved in the 1985 All-Star game plus an unnumbered checklist comprise the set. The card fronts have the same blue border found on the regular 1986 Donruss issue. Retail packs included one Pop-up card, three All-Star cards and one Hank Aaron puzzle card.

		MT	NR MT	EX
Complete Set:		6.00	4.50	2.50
Common Player:		.09	.07	.04
1	Tony Gwynn	.30	.25	.12
2	Tommy Herr	.09	.07	.04
3	Steve Garvey	.30	.25	.12
4	Dale Murphy	.40	.30	.15
5	Darryl Strawberry	.50	.40	.20
6	Graig Nettles	.12	.09	.05
7	Terry Kennedy	.09	.07	.04
8	Ozzie Smith	.15	.11	.06
9	LaMarr Hoyt	.09	.07	.04
10	Rickey Henderson	.50	.40	.20
11	Lou Whitaker	.15	.11	.06
12	George Brett	.40	.30	.15
13	Eddie Murray	.12	.09	.05
14	Cal Ripken, Jr.	.35	.25	.14
15	Dave Winfield	.25	.20	.10
16	Jim Rice	.12	.09	.05
17	Carlton Fisk	.15	.11	.06
18	Jack Morris	.15	.11	.06
19	Jose Cruz	.09	.07	.04
20	Tim Raines	.25	.20	.10
21	Nolan Ryan	.50	.40	.20
22	Tony Pena	.09	.07	.04
23	Jack Clark	.15	.11	.06
24	Dave Parker	.15	.11	.06
25	Tim Wallach	.12	.09	.05
26	Ozzie Virgil	.09	.07	.04
27	Fernando Valenzuela	.12	.09	.05
28	Dwight Gooden	.60	.45	.25
29	Glenn Wilson	.09	.07	.04
30	Garry Templeton	.09	.07	.04
31	Goose Gossage	.12	.09	.05
32	Ryne Sandberg	.25	.20	.10
33	Jeff Reardon	.12	.09	.05
34	Pete Rose	.35	.25	.14
35	Scott Garrelts	.09	.07	.04
36	Willie McGee	.12	.09	.05
37	Ron Darling	.12	.09	.05
38	Dick Williams	.09	.07	.04
39	Paul Molitor	.15	.11	.06

		MT	NR MT	EX
40	Damaso Garcia	.09	.07	.04
41	Phil Bradley	.12	.09	.05
42	Dan Petry	.09	.07	.04
43	Willie Hernandez	.09	.07	.04
44	Tom Brunansky	.12	.09	.05
45	Alan Trammell	.20	.15	.08
46	Donnie Moore	.09	.07	.04
47	Wade Boggs	.90	.70	.35
48	Ernie Whitt	.09	.07	.04
49	Harold Baines	.15	.11	.06
50	Don Mattingly	2.00	1.50	.80
51	Gary Ward	.09	.07	.04
52	Bert Blyleven	.12	.09	.05
53	Jimmy Key	.12	.09	.05
54	Cecil Cooper	.12	.09	.05
55	Dave Stieb	.12	.09	.05
56	Rich Gedman	.09	.07	.04
57	Jay Howell	.09	.07	.04
58	Sparky Anderson	.09	.07	.04
59	Minneapolis Metrodome	.09	.07	.04
——	Checklist	.09	.07	.04

1986 Donruss Box Panels

For the second year in a row, Donruss placed baseball cards on the bottom of their wax and cello pack boxes. The cards, which come four to a panel, are the standard 2-1/2" by 3-1/2" in size. With numbering that begins where Donruss left off in 1985, cards PC 4 through PC 6 were found on boxes of regular Donruss issue wax packs. Cards PC 7 through PC 9 were found on boxes of the 1986 All-Star/Pop-up packs. An unnumbered Hank Aaron puzzle card was included on each box.

		MT	NR MT	EX
Complete Panel Set:		6.00	4.50	2.50
Complete Singles Set:		3.00	2.25	1.25
Common Single Player:		.15	.11	.06
Panel		1.50	1.25	.60
4	Kirk Gibson	.35	.25	.14
5	Willie Hernandez	.15	.11	.06
6	Doug DeCinces	.15	.11	.06
——	Aaron Puzzle Card	.04	.03	.02
Panel		4.50	3.25	1.75
7	Wade Boggs	2.00	1.50	.80
8	Lee Smith	.15	.11	.06
9	Cecil Cooper	.20	.15	.08
——	Aaron Puzzle Card	.04	.03	.02

1986 Donruss Diamond Kings Supers

Donruss produced a set of giant-size Diamond Kings in 1986 for the second year in a row. The cards, which measure 4-11/6" by 6-3/4", are enlarged versions of the 26 Diamond Kings cards found in the regular 1986 Donruss set. Featuring the artwork of Dick Perez, the set consists of 28 cards - 26 DKs, an unnumbered checklist and an unnumbered Pete Rose "King of Kings" card.

		MT	NR MT	EX
Complete Set:		11.00	8.25	4.50
Common Player:		.20	.15	.08
1	Kirk Gibson	.50	.40	.20
2	Goose Gossage	.30	.25	.12
3	Willie McGee	.30	.25	.12
4	George Bell	.30	.25	.12
5	Tony Armas	.20	.15	.08
6	Chili Davis	.20	.15	.08
7	Cecil Cooper	.25	.20	.10
8	Mike Boddicker	.20	.15	.08
9	Davey Lopes	.20	.15	.08
10	Bill Doran	.25	.20	.10
11	Bret Saberhagen	.70	.50	.30
12	Brett Butler	.20	.15	.08
13	Harold Baines	.30	.25	.12
14	Mike Davis	.20	.15	.08
15	Tony Perez	.25	.20	.10
16	Willie Randolph	.25	.20	.10
18	Orel Hershiser	1.00	.70	.40
19	Johnny Ray	.25	.20	.10
20	Gary Ward	.20	.15	.08
21	Rick Mahler	.20	.15	.08
22	Phil Bradley	.30	.25	.12
23	Jerry Koosman	.20	.15	.08
24	Tom Brunansky	.25	.20	.10
25	Andre Dawson	.35	.25	.14
26	Dwight Gooden	1.50	1.25	.60
-----	Checklist	.15	.11	.06
-----	King of Kings (Pete Rose)	1.50	1.25	.60

1986 Donruss Highlights

Donruss, for the second year in a row, issued a 56-card highlights set which featured cards of the A.L. and N.L. Player of the Month plus significant events that took place during the 1986 season. The cards, which measure 2-1/2" by 3-1/2" in size, are similar in design to the regular 1986 Donruss set but have a gold border instead of blue. A "Highlights" logo appears in the lower left corner of each card front. The card backs are designed on a vertical format and feature black print on a yellow background. As in 1985, the set includes Donruss' picks for the Rookies of the Year awards. A new feature was three cards honoring the 1986 Hall of Fame inductees. The set,

available only through hobby dealers, was issued in a specially designed box.

		MT	NR MT	EX
Complete Set:		10.00	7.50	4.00
Common Player:		.10	.08	.04
1	Homers In First At-Bat (Will Clark)	2.00	1.50	.80
2	Oakland Milestone For Strikeouts (Jose Rijo)	.10	.08	.04
3	Royals' All-Time Hit Man (George Brett)	.20	.15	.08
4	Phillies RBI Leader (Mike Schmidt)	.30	.25	.12
5	KKKKKKKKKKKKKKKKKKKKK (Roger Clemens)	.75	.55	.20
6	A.L. Pitcher of the Month-April (Roger Clemens)	.50	.40	.20
7	A.L. Player of the Month-April (Kirby Puckett)	.50	.40	.20
8	N.L. Pitcher of the Month-April (Dwight Gooden)	.50	.40	.20
9	N.L. Player of the Month-April (Johnny Ray)	.10	.08	.04
10	Eclipses Mantle HR Record (Reggie Jackson)	.25	.20	.10
11	First Five Hit Game of Career (Wade Boggs)	.50	.40	.20
12	A.L. Pitcher of the Month-May (Don Aase)	.10	.08	.04
13	A.L. Player of the Month-May (Wade Boggs)	.50	.40	.20
14	N.L. Pitcher of the Month-May (Jeff Reardon)	.15	.11	.06
15	N.L. Player of the Month-May (Hubie Brooks)	.10	.08	.04
16	Notches 300th Career Win (Don Sutton)	.10	.08	.04
17	Starts Season 14-0 (Roger Clemens)	.50	.40	.20
18	A.L. Pitcher of the Month-June (Roger Clemens)	.50	.40	.20
19	A.L. Player of the Month-June (Kent Hrbek)	.10	.08	.04
20	N.L. Pitcher of the Month-June (Rick Rhoden)	.10	.08	.04
21	N.L. Player of the Month-June (Kevin Bass)	.10	.08	.04
22	Blasts 4 HRS in 1 Game (Bob Horner)	.10	.08	.04
23	Starting All Star Rookie (Wally Joyner)	.50	.40	.20
24	Starts 3rd Straight All Star Game (Darryl Strawberry)	.25	.20	.10
25	Ties All Star Game Record (Fernando Valenzuela)	.10	.08	.04
26	All Star Game MVP (Roger Clemens)	.50	.40	.20
27	A.L. Pitcher of the Month-July (Jack Morris)	.10	.08	.04
28	A.L. Player of the Month-July (Scott Fletcher)	.10	.08	.04
29	N.L. Pitcher of the Month-July (Todd Worrell)	.25	.20	.10
30	N.L. PLayer of the Month-July (Eric Davis)	.40	.30	.15
31	Records 3000th Strikeout (Bert Blyleven)	.15	.11	.06
32	1986 Hall of Fame Inductee (Bobby Doerr)	.15	.11	.06
33	1986 Hall of Fame Inductee (Ernie Lombardi)	.15	.11	.06
34	1986 Hall of Fame Inductee (Willie McCovey)	.20	.15	.08
35	Notches 4000th K (Steve Carlton)	.25	.20	.10
36	Surpasses DiMaggio Record (Mike Schmidt)	.40	.30	.15
37	Records 3rd "Quadruple Double" (Juan Samuel)	.10	.08	.04
38	A.L. Pitcher of the Month-August (Mike Witt)	.10	.08	.04
39	A.L. Player of the Month-August (Doug DeCinces)	.10	.08	.04
40	N.L. Pitcher of the Month-August (Bill Gullickson)	.10	.08	.04
41	N.L. Player of the Month-August (Dale Murphy)	.20	.15	.08
42	Sets Tribe Offensive Record (Joe Carter)	.25	.20	.10
43	Longest HR In Royals Stadium (Bo Jackson)	2.00	1.50	.80
44	Majors 1st No-Hitter In 2 Years (Joe Cowley)	.10	.08	.04

		MT	NR MT	EX
45	Sets M.L. Strikeout Record (Jim Deshaies)	.15	.11	.06
46	No Hitter Clinches Division (Mike Scott)	.10	.08	.04
47	A.L. Pitcher of the Month-September (Bruce Hurst)	.10	.08	.04
48	A.L. Player of the Month-September (Don Mattingly)	1.00	.70	.40
49	N.L. Pitcher of the Month-September (Mike Krukow)	.10	.08	.04
50	N.L. Player of the Month-September (Steve Sax)	.10	.08	.04
51	A.L. Record For Steals By A Rookie (John Cangelosi)	.10	.08	.04
52	Shatters M.L. Save Mark (Dave Righetti)	.10	.08	.04
53	Yankee Record For Hits & Doubles (Don Mattingly)	1.00	.70	.40
54	Donruss N.L. Rookie of the Year (Todd Worrell)	.25	.20	.10
55	Donruss A.L. Rookie of the Year (Jose Canseco)	3.00	2.25	1.25
56	Highlight Checklist	.10	.08	.04

1986 Donruss Pop-Ups

Issued in conjunction with the 1986 Donruss All-Stars set, the Donruss Pop-Ups (18 unnumbered cards) feature the 1985 All-Star Game starting lineups. The cards, which measure 2-1/2" by 5", are die-cut and fold out to form a three-dimensional stand-up card. The background for the cards is the Minneapolis Metrodome, site of the 1985 All-Star Game. Retail packs included one Pop-Up card, three All-Star cards and one Hank Aaron puzzle card.

		MT	NR MT	EX
	Complete Set:	5.00	3.75	2.00
	Common Player:	.20	.15	.08
(1)	George Brett	.60	.45	.25
(2)	Carlton Fisk	.30	.25	.12
(3)	Steve Garvey	.20	.15	.08
(4)	Tony Gwynn	.50	.40	.20
(5)	Rickey Henderson	.50	.40	.20
(6)	Tommy Herr	.20	.15	.08
(7)	LaMarr Hoyt	.20	.15	.08
(8)	Terry Kennedy	.20	.15	.08
(9)	Jack Morris	.20	.15	.08
(10)	Dale Murphy	.30	.25	.12
(11)	Eddie Murray	.20	.15	.08
(12)	Graig Nettles	.20	.15	.08
(13)	Jim Rice	.20	.15	.08
(14)	Cal Ripken Jr.	.50	.40	.20
(15)	Ozzie Smith	.30	.25	.12
(16)	Darryl Strawberry	.70	.50	.30
(17)	Lou Whitaker	.30	.25	.12
(18)	Dave Winfield	.30	.25	.12

1986 Donruss Rookies

Entitled "The Rookies," this 56-card set includes the top 55 rookies of 1986 plus an unnumbered checklist. The cards, which measure 2-1/2" by 3-1/2", are similar to the format used for the 1986 Donruss regular issue, except that the borders are green rather than blue. Several of the rookies who had cards in the regular 1986 Donruss set appear again in "The Rookies" set. The sets, which were only available through hobby dealers, came in a specially designed box.

		MT	NR MT	EX
	Complete Set:	50.00	37.00	20.00
	Common Player:	.15	.11	.06
1	Wally Joyner(FC)	3.50	2.75	1.50
2	Tracy Jones(FC)	.50	.40	.20
3	Allan Anderson(FC)	.40	.30	.15
4	Ed Correa(FC)	.25	.20	.10
5	Reggie Williams	.20	.15	.08
6	Charlie Kerfeld(FC)	.15	.11	.06
7	Andres Galarraga	.80	.60	.30
8	Bob Tewksbury(FC)	.15	.11	.06
9	Al Newman	.15	.11	.06
10	Andres Thomas(FC)	.40	.30	.15
11	Barry Bonds(FC)	1.50	1.25	.60
12	Juan Nieves	.15	.11	.06
13	Mark Eichhorn(FC)	.25	.20	.10
14	Dan Plesac(FC)	.40	.30	.15
15	Cory Snyder	1.75	1.25	.70
16	Kelly Gruber	.15	.11	.06
17	Kevin Mitchell(FC)	8.00	6.00	3.25
18	Steve Lombardozzi	.15	.11	.06
19	Mitch Williams	.60	.45	.25
20	John Cerutti(FC)	.25	.20	.10
21	Todd Worrell	.50	.40	.20
22	Jose Canseco	7.50	5.75	3.00
23	Pete Incaviglia(FC)	.80	.60	.30
24	Jose Guzman	.25	.20	.10
25	Scott Bailes(FC)	.25	.20	.10
26	Greg Mathews(FC)	.25	.20	.10
27	Eric King(FC)	.20	.15	.08
28	Paul Assenmacher	.20	.15	.08
29	Jeff Sellers	.25	.20	.10
30	Bobby Bonilla(FC)	1.25	.90	.50
31	Doug Drabek(FC)	.30	.25	.12
32	Will Clark(FC)	12.00	9.00	4.75
33	Bip Roberts	.15	.11	.06
34	Jim Deshaies(FC)	.25	.20	.10
35	Mike Lavalliere (LaValliere)(FC)	.30	.25	.12
36	Scott Bankhead(FC)	.20	.15	.08
37	Dale Sveum(FC)	.25	.20	.10
38	Bo Jackson(FC)	11.00	8.25	4.50
39	Rob Thompson(FC)	.50	.40	.20
40	Eric Plunk(FC)	.20	.15	.08
41	Bill Bathe	.15	.11	.06
42	John Kruk(FC)	.40	.30	.15
43	Andy Allanson(FC)	.20	.15	.08
44	Mark Portugal	.15	.11	.06
45	Danny Tartabull	1.00	.70	.40
46	Bob Kipper	.15	.11	.06
47	Gene Walter	.15	.11	.06
48	Rey Quinonez	.15	.11	.06
49	Bobby Witt(FC)	.40	.30	.15
50	Bill Mooneyham	.15	.11	.06
51	John Cangelosi(FC)	.20	.15	.08
52	Ruben Sierra(FC)	7.00	5.25	2.75

		MT	NR MT	EX
53	Rob Woodward	.15	.11	.06
54	Ed Hearn	.15	.11	.06
55	Joel McKeon	.15	.11	.06
56	Checklist 1-56	.05	.04	.02

1987 Donruss

The 1987 Donruss set consists of 660 numbered cards, each measuring 2-1/2" by 3-1/2" in size. Full color photos are surrounded by a bold black border separated by two narrow bands of yellow which enclose a brown area filled with baseballs. The player's name, team and team logo appear on the card fronts along with the words "Donruss '87." The card backs are designed on a horizontal format and contain black print on a yellow and white background. The backs are very similar to those in previous years' sets. Backs of cards issued in wax and rack packs face to the left when turned over, while those issued in vending sets face to the right.

		MT	NR MT	EX
Complete Set:		75.00	55.00	30.00
Common Player:		.05	.04	.02
1	Wally Joyner (DK)	1.25	.90	.50
2	Roger Clemens (DK)	.70	.50	.30
3	Dale Murphy (DK)	.40	.30	.15
4	Darryl Strawberry (DK)	.40	.30	.15
5	Ozzie Smith (DK)	.12	.09	.05
6	Jose Canseco (DK)	1.50	1.25	.60
7	Charlie Hough (DK)	.07	.05	.03
8	Brook Jacoby (DK)	.10	.08	.04
9	Fred Lynn (DK)	.12	.09	.05
10	Rick Rhoden (DK)	.10	.08	.04
11	Chris Brown (DK)	.10	.08	.04
12	Von Hayes (DK)	.10	.08	.04
13	Jack Morris (DK)	.20	.15	.08
14a	Kevin McReynolds (DK) ("Donruss Diamond Kings" in white band on back)	1.25	.90	.50
14b	Kevin McReynolds (DK) ("Donruss Diamond Kings" in yellow band on back)	.20	.15	.08
15	George Brett (DK)	.40	.30	.15
16	Ted Higuera (DK)	.20	.15	.08
17	Hubie Brooks (DK)	.10	.08	.04
18	Mike Scott (DK)	.12	.09	.05
19	Kirby Puckett (DK)	.25	.20	.10
20	Dave Winfield (DK)	.25	.20	.10
21	Lloyd Moseby (DK)	.10	.08	.04
22a	Eric Davis (DK) ("Donruss Diamond Kings" in white band on back)	3.00	2.25	1.25
22b	Eric Davis (DK) ("Donruss Diamond Kings" in yellow band on back)	1.00	.70	.40
23	Jim Presley (DK)	.12	.09	.05
24	Keith Moreland (DK)	.07	.05	.03
25a	Greg Walker (DK) ("Donruss Diamond Kings" in white band on back)	1.25	.90	.50
25b	Greg Walker (DK) ("Donruss Diamond Kings" in yellow band on back)	.10	.08	.04
26	Steve Sax (DK)	.12	.09	.05
27	Checklist 1-27	.05	.04	.02
28	B.J. Surhoff (RR)(FC)	.50	.40	.20
29	Randy Myers (RR)(FC)	.60	.45	.25
30	Ken Gerhart (RR)(FC)	.15	.11	.06
31	Benito Santiago (RR)(FC)	1.75	1.25	.70

		MT	NR MT	EX
32	Greg Swindell (RR)(FC)	1.25	.90	.50
33	Mike Birkbeck (RR)(FC)	.20	.15	.08
34	Terry Steinbach (RR)(FC)	1.00	.70	.40
35	Bo Jackson (RR)	7.00	5.25	2.75
36	Greg Maddux (RR)(FC)	1.25	.90	.50
37	Jim Lindeman (RR)(FC)	.15	.11	.06
38	Devon White (RR)(FC)	1.00	.70	.40
39	Eric Bell (RR)(FC)	.12	.09	.05
40	Will Fraser (RR)(FC)	.20	.15	.08
41	Jerry Browne (RR)(FC)	.35	.25	.14
42	Chris James (RR)(FC)	.70	.50	.30
43	Rafael Palmeiro (RR)(FC)	2.00	1.50	.80
44	Pat Dodson (RR)(FC)	.12	.09	.05
45	Duane Ward (RR)(FC)	.20	.15	.08
46	Mark McGwire (RR)(FC)	8.00	6.00	3.25
47	Bruce Fields (RR) (photo actually Darnell Coles)(FC)	.10	.08	.04
48	Eddie Murray	.35	.25	.14
49	Ted Higuera	.20	.15	.08
50	Kirk Gibson	.25	.20	.10
51	Oil Can Boyd	.07	.05	.03
52	Don Mattingly	2.50	2.00	1.00
53	Pedro Guerrero	.15	.11	.06
54	George Brett	.40	.30	.15
55	Jose Rijo	.07	.05	.03
56	Tim Raines	.30	.25	.12
57	Ed Correa	.15	.11	.06
58	Mike Witt	.10	.08	.04
59	Greg Walker	.10	.08	.04
60	Ozzie Smith	.15	.11	.06
61	Glenn Davis	.30	.25	.12
62	Glenn Wilson	.07	.05	.03
63	Tom Browning	.10	.08	.04
64	Tony Gwynn	.35	.25	.14
65	R.J. Reynolds	.07	.05	.03
66	Will Clark	12.00	9.00	4.75
67	Ozzie Virgil	.05	.04	.02
68	Rick Sutcliffe	.12	.09	.05
69	Gary Carter	.30	.25	.12
70	Mike Moore	.05	.04	.02
71	Bert Blyleven	.12	.09	.05
72	Tony Fernandez	.12	.09	.05
73	Kent Hrbek	.15	.11	.06
74	Lloyd Moseby	.10	.08	.04
75	Alvin Davis	.12	.09	.05
76	Keith Hernandez	.25	.20	.10
77	Ryne Sandberg	.35	.25	.14
78	Dale Murphy	.40	.30	.15
79	Sid Bream	.07	.05	.03
80	Chris Brown	.07	.05	.03
81	Steve Garvey	.25	.20	.10
82	Mario Soto	.07	.05	.03
83	Shane Rawley	.07	.05	.03
84	Willie McGee	.12	.09	.05
85	Jose Cruz	.10	.08	.04
86	Brian Downing	.07	.05	.03
87	Ozzie Guillen	.10	.08	.04
88	Hubie Brooks	.10	.08	.04
89	Cal Ripken	.35	.25	.14
90	Juan Nieves	.07	.05	.03
91	Lance Parrish	.20	.15	.08
92	Jim Rice	.30	.25	.12
93	Ron Guidry	.15	.11	.06
94	Fernando Valenzuela	.25	.20	.10
95	Andy Allanson	.15	.11	.06
96	Willie Wilson	.12	.09	.05
97	Jose Canseco	6.00	4.50	2.50
98	Jeff Reardon	.10	.08	.04
99	Bobby Witt	.35	.25	.14
100	Checklist 28-133	.05	.04	.02
101	Jose Guzman	.10	.08	.04
102	Steve Balboni	.07	.05	.03
103	Tony Phillips	.05	.04	.02
104	Brook Jacoby	.10	.08	.04
105	Dave Winfield	.30	.25	.12
106	Orel Hershiser	.40	.30	.15
107	Lou Whitaker	.25	.20	.10
108	Fred Lynn	.15	.11	.06
109	Bill Wegman	.07	.05	.03
110	Donnie Moore	.05	.04	.02
111	Jack Clark	.15	.11	.06
112	Bob Knepper	.07	.05	.03
113	Von Hayes	.10	.08	.04
114	Leon "Bip" Roberts	.05	.04	.02
115	Tony Pena	.08	.06	.03
116	Scott Garrelts	.05	.04	.02
117	Paul Molitor	.15	.11	.06
118	Darryl Strawberry	.60	.45	.25
119	Shawon Dunston	.10	.08	.04
120	Jim Presley	.10	.08	.04
121	Jesse Barfield	.20	.15	.08

		MT	NR MT	EX			MT	NR MT	EX
122	Gary Gaetti	.15	.11	.06	211	Floyd Bannister	.10	.08	.04
123	*Kurt Stillwell*	.25	.20	.10	212	Vance Law	.07	.05	.03
124	Joel Davis	.05	.04	.02	213	Rich Bordi	.05	.04	.02
125	Mike Boddicker	.07	.05	.03	214	*Dan Plesac*	.35	.25	.14
126	Robin Yount	.30	.25	.12	215	Dave Collins	.07	.05	.03
127	Alan Trammell	.25	.20	.10	216	Bob Stanley	.05	.04	.02
128	Dave Righetti	.15	.11	.06	217	Joe Niekro	.10	.08	.04
129	Dwight Evans	.12	.09	.05	218	Tom Niedenfuer	.07	.05	.03
130	Mike Scioscia	.07	.05	.03	219	Brett Butler	.07	.05	.03
131	Julio Franco	.10	.08	.04	220	Charlie Leibrandt	.07	.05	.03
132	Bret Saberhagen	.25	.20	.10	221	Steve Ontiveros	.05	.04	.02
133	Mike Davis	.07	.05	.03	222	Tim Burke	.05	.04	.02
134	Joe Hesketh	.05	.04	.02	223	Curtis Wilkerson	.05	.04	.02
135	*Wally Joyner*	1.75	1.25	.70	224	*Pete Incaviglia*	.60	.45	.25
136	Don Slaught	.05	.04	.02	225	Lonnie Smith	.07	.05	.03
137	Daryl Boston	.05	.04	.02	226	Chris Codiroli	.05	.04	.02
138	Nolan Ryan	.50	.40	.20	227	*Scott Bailes*	.20	.15	.08
139	Mike Schmidt	.50	.40	.20	228	Rickey Henderson	.35	.25	.14
140	Tommy Herr	.10	.08	.04	229	Ken Howell	.05	.04	.02
141	Garry Templeton	.07	.05	.03	230	Darnell Coles	.07	.05	.03
142	Kal Daniels	.80	.60	.30	231	Don Aase	.05	.04	.02
143	Billy Sample	.05	.04	.02	232	Tim Leary	.07	.05	.03
144	Johnny Ray	.10	.08	.04	233	Bob Boone	.07	.05	.03
145	*Rob Thompson*	.30	.25	.12	234	Ricky Horton	.07	.05	.03
146	Bob Dernier	.05	.04	.02	235	Mark Bailey	.05	.04	.02
147	Danny Tartabull	.25	.20	.10	236	Kevin Gross	.07	.05	.03
148	Ernie Whitt	.07	.05	.03	237	Lance McCullers	.07	.05	.03
149	Kirby Puckett	.35	.25	.14	238	Cecilio Guante	.05	.04	.02
150	Mike Young	.05	.04	.02	239	Bob Melvin	.05	.04	.02
151	Ernest Riles	.05	.04	.02	240	Billy Jo Robidoux	.05	.04	.02
152	Frank Tanana	.07	.05	.03	241	Roger McDowell	.12	.09	.05
153	Rich Gedman	.10	.08	.04	242	Leon Durham	.07	.05	.03
154	Willie Randolph	.10	.08	.04	243	Ed Nunez	.05	.04	.02
155a	Bill Madlock (name in brown band)	.12	.09	.05	244	Jimmy Key	.12	.09	.05
155b	Bill Madlock (name in red band)	.70	.50	.30	245	Mike Smithson	.05	.04	.02
156a	Joe Carter (name in brown band)	.15	.11	.06	246	Bo Diaz	.07	.05	.03
156b	Joe Carter (name in red band)	.70	.50	.30	247	Carlton Fisk	.20	.15	.08
157	Danny Jackson	.15	.11	.06	248	Larry Sheets	.08	.06	.03
158	Carney Lansford	.10	.08	.04	249	*Juan Castillo*(FC)	.10	.08	.04
159	Bryn Smith	.05	.04	.02	250	*Eric King*	.20	.15	.08
160	Gary Pettis	.05	.04	.02	251	*Doug Drabek*	.30	.25	.12
161	Oddibe McDowell	.10	.08	.04	252	Wade Boggs	1.50	1.25	.60
162	*John Cangelosi*	.12	.09	.05	253	Mariano Duncan	.05	.04	.02
163	Mike Scott	.15	.11	.06	254	Pat Tabler	.07	.05	.03
164	Eric Show	.07	.05	.03	255	Frank White	.10	.08	.04
165	Juan Samuel	.12	.09	.05	256	Alfredo Griffin	.07	.05	.03
166	Nick Esasky	.07	.05	.03	257	Floyd Youmans	.07	.05	.03
167	Zane Smith	.07	.05	.03	258	Rob Wilfong	.05	.04	.02
168	Mike Brown	.05	.04	.02	259	Pete O'Brien	.10	.08	.04
169	Keith Moreland	.07	.05	.03	260	Tim Hulett	.05	.04	.02
170	John Tudor	.10	.08	.04	261	Dickie Thon	.07	.05	.03
171	Ken Dixon	.05	.04	.02	262	Darren Daulton	.05	.04	.02
172	Jim Gantner	.07	.05	.03	263	Vince Coleman	.25	.20	.10
173	Jack Morris	.20	.15	.08	264	Andy Hawkins	.05	.04	.02
174	Bruce Hurst	.10	.08	.04	265	Eric Davis	1.25	.90	.50
175	Dennis Rasmussen	.10	.08	.04	266	*Andres Thomas*	.25	.20	.10
176	Mike Marshall	.12	.09	.05	267	*Mike Diaz*(FC)	.15	.11	.06
177	Dan Quisenberry	.07	.05	.03	268	Chili Davis	.07	.05	.03
178	Eric Plunk(FC)	.10	.08	.04	269	Jody Davis	.07	.05	.03
179	Tim Wallach	.12	.09	.05	270	Phil Bradley	.12	.09	.05
180	Steve Buechele	.07	.05	.03	271	George Bell	.25	.20	.10
181	Don Sutton	.20	.15	.08	272	Keith Atherton	.05	.04	.02
182	Dave Schmidt	.05	.04	.02	273	Storm Davis	.10	.08	.04
183	Terry Pendleton	.10	.08	.04	274	Rob Deer(FC)	.20	.15	.08
184	*Jim Deshaies*	.25	.20	.10	275	Walt Terrell	.07	.05	.03
185	Steve Bedrosian	.12	.09	.05	276	Roger Clemens	1.75	1.25	.70
186	Pete Rose	.60	.45	.25	277	Mike Easler	.07	.05	.03
187	Dave Dravecky	.07	.05	.03	278	Steve Sax	.15	.11	.06
188	Rick Reuschel	.10	.08	.04	279	Andre Thornton	.07	.05	.03
189	Dan Gladden	.05	.04	.02	280	Jim Sundberg	.07	.05	.03
190	Rick Mahler	.05	.04	.02	281	Bill Bathe	.05	.04	.02
191	Thad Bosley	.05	.04	.02	282	Jay Tibbs	.05	.04	.02
192	Ron Darling	.15	.11	.06	283	Dick Schofield	.05	.04	.02
193	Matt Young	.05	.04	.02	284	Mike Mason	.05	.04	.02
194	Tom Brunansky	.10	.08	.04	285	Jerry Hairston	.05	.04	.02
195	Dave Stieb	.12	.09	.05	286	Bill Doran	.10	.08	.04
196	Frank Viola	.15	.11	.06	287	Tim Flannery	.05	.04	.02
197	Tom Henke	.07	.05	.03	288	Gary Redus	.05	.04	.02
198	Karl Best	.05	.04	.02	289	John Franco	.10	.08	.04
199	Dwight Gooden	.90	.70	.35	290	*Paul Assenmacher*	.15	.11	.06
200	Checklist 134-239	.05	.04	.02	291	Joe Orsulak	.05	.04	.02
201	Steve Trout	.05	.04	.02	292	Lee Smith	.10	.08	.04
202	Rafael Ramirez	.05	.04	.02	293	Mike Laga	.05	.04	.02
203	Bob Walk	.05	.04	.02	294	Rick Dempsey	.07	.05	.03
204	Roger Mason	.05	.04	.02	295	Mike Felder	.05	.04	.02
205	Terry Kennedy	.07	.05	.03	296	Tom Brookens	.05	.04	.02
206	Ron Oester	.05	.04	.02	297	Al Nipper	.05	.04	.02
207	John Russell	.05	.04	.02	298	Mike Pagliarulo	.10	.08	.04
208	*Greg Mathews*	.20	.15	.08	299	Franklin Stubbs	.07	.05	.03
209	Charlie Kerfeld	.10	.08	.04	300	Checklist 240-345	.05	.04	.02
210	Reggie Jackson	.35	.25	.14	301	Steve Farr	.05	.04	.02

		MT	NR MT	EX			MT	NR MT	EX
302	*Bill Mooneyham*	.10	.08	.04	393	John Moses	.05	.04	.02
303	Andres Galarraga	.25	.20	.10	394	Garth Iorg	.05	.04	.02
304	Scott Fletcher	.07	.05	.03	395	Greg Gagne	.05	.04	.02
305	Jack Howell	.07	.05	.03	396	Nate Snell	.05	.04	.02
306	*Russ Morman*(FC)	.10	.08	.04	397	*Bryan Clutterbuck*(FC)	.10	.08	.04
307	Todd Worrell	.20	.15	.08	398	Darrell Evans	.12	.09	.05
308	Dave Smith	.07	.05	.03	399	Steve Crawford	.05	.04	.02
309	Jeff Stone	.05	.04	.02	400	Checklist 346-451	.05	.04	.02
310	Ron Robinson	.05	.04	.02	401	*Phil Lombardi*(FC)	.10	.08	.04
311	Bruce Bochy	.05	.04	.02	402	Rick Honeycutt	.05	.04	.02
312	Jim Winn	.05	.04	.02	403	Ken Schrom	.05	.04	.02
313	Mark Davis	.05	.04	.02	404	Bud Black	.05	.04	.02
314	Jeff Dedmon	.05	.04	.02	405	Donnie Hill	.05	.04	.02
315	*Jamie Moyer*(FC)	.20	.15	.08	406	Wayne Krenchicki	.05	.04	.02
316	Wally Backman	.07	.05	.03	407	*Chuck Finley*(FC)	.20	.15	.08
317	Ken Phelps	.07	.05	.03	408	Toby Harrah	.07	.05	.03
318	Steve Lombardozzi	.05	.04	.02	409	Steve Lyons	.05	.04	.02
319	Rance Mulliniks	.05	.04	.02	410	Kevin Bass	.10	.08	.04
320	Tim Laudner	.05	.04	.02	411	Marvell Wynne	.05	.04	.02
321	*Mark Eichhorn*	.15	.11	.06	412	Ron Roenicke	.05	.04	.02
322	*Lee Guetterman*	.15	.11	.06	413	*Tracy Jones*	.25	.20	.10
323	Sid Fernandez	.12	.09	.05	414	Gene Garber	.05	.04	.02
324	Jerry Mumphrey	.05	.04	.02	415	Mike Bielecki	.05	.04	.02
325	David Palmer	.05	.04	.02	416	Frank DiPino	.05	.04	.02
326	Bill Almon	.05	.04	.02	417	Andy Van Slyke	.12	.09	.05
327	Candy Maldonado	.07	.05	.03	418	Jim Dwyer	.05	.04	.02
328	*John Kruk*	.25	.20	.10	419	Ben Oglivie	.07	.05	.03
329	John Denny	.05	.04	.02	420	Dave Bergman	.05	.04	.02
330	Milt Thompson	.07	.05	.03	421	Joe Sambito	.05	.04	.02
331	*Mike LaValliere*	.25	.20	.10	422	*Bob Tewksbury*	.12	.09	.05
332	Alan Ashby	.05	.04	.02	423	Len Matuszek	.05	.04	.02
333	Doug Corbett	.05	.04	.02	424	*Mike Kingery*(FC)	.15	.11	.06
334	*Ron Karkovice*(FC)	.10	.08	.04	425	Dave Kingman	.12	.09	.05
335	Mitch Webster	.07	.05	.03	426	*Al Newman*	.07	.05	.03
336	Lee Lacy	.05	.04	.02	427	Gary Ward	.07	.05	.03
337	*Glenn Braggs*(FC)	.30	.25	.12	428	Ruppert Jones	.05	.04	.02
338	Dwight Lowry	.05	.04	.02	429	Harold Baines	.15	.11	.06
339	Don Baylor	.12	.09	.05	430	Pat Perry	.05	.04	.02
340	Brian Fisher	.07	.05	.03	431	Terry Puhl	.05	.04	.02
341	*Reggie Williams*	.10	.08	.04	432	Don Carman	.07	.05	.03
342	Tom Candiotti	.05	.04	.02	433	Eddie Milner	.05	.04	.02
343	Rudy Law	.05	.04	.02	434	LaMarr Hoyt	.05	.04	.02
344	Curt Young	.07	.05	.03	435	Rick Rhoden	.10	.08	.04
345	Mike Fitzgerald	.05	.04	.02	436	Jose Uribe	.07	.05	.03
346	*Ruben Sierra*	5.00	3.75	2.00	437	Ken Oberkfell	.05	.04	.02
347	*Mitch Williams*	.40	.30	.15	438	Ron Davis	.05	.04	.02
348	Jorge Orta	.05	.04	.02	439	Jesse Orosco	.07	.05	.03
349	Mickey Tettleton	.10	.08	.04	440	Scott Bradley	.05	.04	.02
350	Ernie Camacho	.05	.04	.02	441	Randy Bush	.05	.04	.02
351	Ron Kittle	.10	.08	.04	442	*John Cerutti*	.20	.15	.08
352	Ken Landreaux	.05	.04	.02	443	Roy Smalley	.05	.04	.02
353	Chet Lemon	.07	.05	.03	444	Kelly Gruber	.07	.05	.03
354	John Shelby	.05	.04	.02	445	Bob Kearney	.05	.04	.02
355	Mark Clear	.05	.04	.02	446	*Ed Hearn*	.10	.08	.04
356	Doug DeCinces	.07	.05	.03	447	Scott Sanderson	.05	.04	.02
357	Ken Dayley	.05	.04	.02	448	Bruce Benedict	.05	.04	.02
358	Phil Garner	.05	.04	.02	449	Junior Ortiz	.05	.04	.02
359	Steve Jeltz	.05	.04	.02	450	*Mike Aldrete*	.25	.20	.10
360	Ed Whitson	.05	.04	.02	451	Kevin McReynolds	.15	.11	.06
361	*Barry Bonds*	1.00	.70	.40	452	*Rob Murphy*(FC)	.20	.15	.08
362	Vida Blue	.10	.08	.04	453	Kent Tekulve	.07	.05	.03
363	Cecil Cooper	.12	.09	.05	454	Curt Ford(FC)	.07	.05	.03
364	Bob Ojeda	.07	.05	.03	455	Davey Lopes	.07	.05	.03
365	Dennis Eckersley	.12	.09	.05	456	Bobby Grich	.10	.08	.04
366	Mike Morgan	.05	.04	.02	457	Jose DeLeon	.07	.05	.03
367	Willie Upshaw	.07	.05	.03	458	Andre Dawson	.20	.15	.08
368	*Allan Anderson*(FC)	.25	.20	.10	459	Mike Flanagan	.07	.05	.03
369	Bill Gullickson	.07	.05	.03	460	*Joey Meyer*(FC)	.40	.30	.15
370	*Bobby Thigpen*(FC)	.30	.25	.12	461	*Chuck Cary*(FC)	.10	.08	.04
371	Juan Beniquez	.05	.04	.02	462	Bill Buckner	.10	.08	.04
372	Charlie Moore	.05	.04	.02	463	Bob Shirley	.05	.04	.02
373	Dan Petry	.07	.05	.03	464	*Jeff Hamilton*(FC)	.30	.25	.12
374	Rod Scurry	.05	.04	.02	465	Phil Niekro	.20	.15	.08
375	Tom Seaver	.40	.30	.15	466	Mark Gubicza	.12	.09	.05
376	Ed Vande Berg	.05	.04	.02	467	Jerry Willard	.05	.04	.02
377	Tony Bernazard	.05	.04	.02	468	*Bob Sebra*(FC)	.10	.08	.04
378	Greg Pryor	.05	.04	.02	469	Larry Parrish	.10	.08	.04
379	Dwayne Murphy	.07	.05	.03	470	Charlie Hough	.07	.05	.03
380	Andy McGaffigan	.05	.04	.02	471	Hal McRae	.10	.08	.04
381	Kirk McCaskill	.07	.05	.03	472	*Dave Leiper*(FC)	.10	.08	.04
382	Greg Harris	.05	.04	.02	473	Mel Hall	.07	.05	.03
383	Rich Dotson	.07	.05	.03	474	Dan Pasqua	.10	.08	.04
384	Craig Reynolds	.05	.04	.02	475	Bob Welch	.10	.08	.04
385	Greg Gross	.05	.04	.02	476	Johnny Grubb	.05	.04	.02
386	Tito Landrum	.05	.04	.02	477	Jim Traber	.07	.05	.03
387	Craig Lefferts	.05	.04	.02	478	*Chris Bosio*(FC)	.40	.30	.15
388	Dave Parker	.20	.15	.08	479	Mark McLemore	.07	.05	.03
389	Bob Horner	.10	.08	.04	480	John Morris	.05	.04	.02
390	Pat Clements	.05	.04	.02	481	Billy Hatcher	.07	.05	.03
391	Jeff Leonard	.07	.05	.03	482	Dan Schatzeder	.05	.04	.02
392	Chris Speier	.05	.04	.02	483	Rich Gossage	.15	.11	.06

		MT	NR MT	EX
484	Jim Morrison	.05	.04	.02
485	Bob Brenly	.05	.04	.02
486	Bill Schroeder	.05	.04	.02
487	Mookie Wilson	.10	.08	.04
488	*Dave Martinez*(FC)	.25	.20	.10
489	Harold Reynolds	.10	.08	.04
490	Jeff Hearron	.05	.04	.02
491	Mickey Hatcher	.05	.04	.02
492	*Barry Larkin*(FC)	2.25	1.75	.90
493	Bob James	.05	.04	.02
494	John Habyan	.05	.04	.02
495	*Jim Adduci*(FC)	.07	.05	.03
496	Mike Heath	.05	.04	.02
497	Tim Stoddard	.05	.04	.02
498	Tony Armas	.07	.05	.03
499	Dennis Powell	.05	.04	.02
500	Checklist 452-557	.05	.04	.02
501	Chris Bando	.05	.04	.02
502	*David Cone*(FC)	3.75	2.75	1.50
503	Jay Howell	.07	.05	.03
504	Tom Foley	.05	.04	.02
505	*Ray Chadwick*(FC)	.10	.08	.04
506	*Mike Loynd*(FC)	.15	.11	.06
507	Neil Allen	.05	.04	.02
508	Danny Darwin	.05	.04	.02
509	Rick Schu	.05	.04	.02
510	Jose Oquendo	.05	.04	.02
511	Gene Walter	.07	.05	.03
512	*Terry McGriff*(FC)	.12	.09	.05
513	Ken Griffey	.10	.08	.04
514	Benny Distefano	.05	.04	.02
515	*Terry Mulholland*(FC)	.12	.09	.05
516	Ed Lynch	.05	.04	.02
517	Bill Swift	.05	.04	.02
518	Manny Lee(FC)	.07	.05	.03
519	Andre David	.05	.04	.02
520	Scott McGregor	.07	.05	.03
521	Rick Manning	.05	.04	.02
522	Willie Hernandez	.07	.05	.03
523	Marty Barrett	.10	.08	.04
524	Wayne Tolleson	.05	.04	.02
525	*Jose Gonzalez*(FC)	.15	.11	.06
526	Cory Snyder	.70	.50	.30
527	Buddy Biancalana	.05	.04	.02
528	Moose Haas	.05	.04	.02
529	*Wilfredo Tejada*(FC)	.10	.08	.04
530	Stu Cliburn	.05	.04	.02
531	*Dale Mohorcic*(FC)	.20	.15	.08
532	Ron Hassey	.05	.04	.02
533	Ty Gainey	.05	.04	.02
534	Jerry Royster	.05	.04	.02
535	*Mike Maddux*(FC)	.20	.15	.08
536	Ted Power	.05	.04	.02
537	Ted Simmons	.12	.09	.05
538	*Rafael Belliard*(FC)	.12	.09	.05
539	Chico Walker	.05	.04	.02
540	Bob Forsch	.07	.05	.03
541	John Stefero	.05	.04	.02
542	*Dale Sveum*	.20	.15	.08
543	Mark Thurmond	.05	.04	.02
544	*Jeff Sellers*	.20	.15	.08
545	Joel Skinner	.05	.04	.02
546	Alex Trevino	.05	.04	.02
547	*Randy Kutcher*(FC)	.10	.08	.04
548	Joaquin Andujar	.07	.05	.03
549	*Casey Candaele*(FC)	.15	.11	.06
550	Jeff Russell	.05	.04	.02
551	John Candelaria	.10	.08	.04
552	Joe Cowley	.05	.04	.02
553	Danny Cox	.07	.05	.03
554	Denny Walling	.05	.04	.02
555	*Bruce Ruffin*(FC)	.20	.15	.08
556	Buddy Bell	.10	.08	.04
557	*Jimmy Jones*(FC)	.20	.15	.08
558	*Bobby Bonilla*	1.00	.70	.40
559	Jeff Robinson	.07	.05	.03
560	Ed Olwine	.05	.04	.02
561	*Glenallen Hill*(FC)	.12	.09	.05
562	Lee Mazzilli	.07	.05	.03
563	Mike Brown	.05	.04	.02
564	George Frazier	.05	.04	.02
565	*Mike Sharperson*(FC)	.10	.08	.04
566	*Mark Portugal*	.10	.08	.04
567	Rick Leach	.05	.04	.02
568	Mark Langston	.12	.09	.05
569	Rafael Santana	.05	.04	.02
570	Manny Trillo	.07	.05	.03
571	Cliff Speck	.05	.04	.02
572	Bob Kipper	.05	.04	.02
573	*Kelly Downs*(FC)	.30	.25	.12
574	*Randy Asadoor*(FC)	.10	.08	.04

		MT	NR MT	EX
575	*Dave Magadan*(FC)	.35	.25	.14
576	*Marvin Freeman*(FC)	.12	.09	.05
577	Jeff Lahti	.05	.04	.02
578	Jeff Calhoun	.05	.04	.02
579	Gus Polidor(FC)	.07	.05	.03
580	Gene Nelson	.05	.04	.02
581	Tim Teufel	.05	.04	.02
582	Odell Jones	.05	.04	.02
583	Mark Ryal	.05	.04	.02
584	Randy O'Neal	.05	.04	.02
585	*Mike Greenwell*(FC)	10.00	7.50	4.00
586	Ray Knight	.07	.05	.03
587	*Ralph Bryant*(FC)	.12	.09	.05
588	Carmen Castillo	.05	.04	.02
589	Ed Wojna	.05	.04	.02
590	Stan Javier	.05	.04	.02
591	*Jeff Musselman*(FC)	.20	.15	.08
592	*Mike Stanley*(FC)	.20	.15	.08
593	Darrell Porter	.07	.05	.03
594	*Drew Hall*(FC)	.20	.15	.08
595	*Rob Nelson*(FC)	.10	.08	.04
596	Bryan Oelkers	.05	.04	.02
597	*Scott Nielsen*(FC)	.10	.08	.04
598	*Brian Holton*(FC)	.20	.15	.08
599	*Kevin Mitchell*	5.00	3.75	2.00
600	Checklist 558-660	.05	.04	.02
601	Jackie Gutierrez	.05	.04	.02
602	*Barry Jones*(FC)	.12	.09	.05
603	Jerry Narron	.05	.04	.02
604	Steve Lake	.05	.04	.02
605	Jim Pankovits	.05	.04	.02
606	Ed Romero	.05	.04	.02
607	Dave LaPoint	.07	.05	.03
608	Don Robinson	.07	.05	.03
609	Mike Krukow	.07	.05	.03
610	*Dave Valle*(FC)	.12	.09	.05
611	Len Dykstra	.12	.09	.05
612	Roberto Clemente Puzzle Card	.05	.04	.02
613	Mike Trujillo(FC)	.05	.04	.02
614	Damaso Garcia	.05	.04	.02
615	Neal Heaton	.05	.04	.02
616	Juan Berenguer	.05	.04	.02
617	Steve Carlton	.25	.20	.10
618	Gary Lucas	.05	.04	.02
619	Geno Petralli	.05	.04	.02
620	Rick Aguilera	.07	.05	.03
621	Fred McGriff	2.75	2.00	1.00
622	Dave Henderson	.10	.08	.04
623	*Dave Clark*(FC)	.20	.15	.08
624	Angel Salazar	.05	.04	.02
625	Randy Hunt	.05	.04	.02
626	John Gibbons	.05	.04	.02
627	*Kevin Brown*(FC)	.07	.05	.03
628	Bill Dawley	.05	.04	.02
629	Aurelio Lopez	.05	.04	.02
630	Charlie Hudson	.05	.04	.02
631	Ray Soff	.05	.04	.02
632	*Ray Hayward*(FC)	.12	.09	.05
633	Spike Owen	.05	.04	.02
634	Glenn Hubbard	.05	.04	.02
635	*Kevin Elster*(FC)	.40	.30	.15
636	Mike LaCoss	.05	.04	.02
637	Dwayne Henry	.05	.04	.02
638	*Rey Quinones*	.15	.11	.06
639	Jim Clancy	.07	.05	.03
640	Larry Andersen	.05	.04	.02
641	Calvin Schiraldi	.05	.04	.02
642	*Stan Jefferson*(FC)	.20	.15	.08
643	Marc Sullivan	.05	.04	.02
644	Mark Grant	.05	.04	.02
645	Cliff Johnson	.05	.04	.02
646	Howard Johnson	.10	.08	.04
647	Dave Sax	.05	.04	.02
648	Dave Stewart	.12	.09	.05
649	Danny Heep	.05	.04	.02
650	Joe Johnson	.05	.04	.02
651	*Bob Brower*(FC)	.20	.15	.08
652	Rob Woodward	.07	.05	.03
653	John Mizerock	.05	.04	.02
654	*Tim Pyznarski*(FC)	.10	.08	.04
655	*Luis Aquino*(FC)	.10	.08	.04
656	Mickey Brantley(FC)	.10	.08	.04
657	Doyle Alexander	.07	.05	.03
658	Sammy Stewart	.05	.04	.02
659	Jim Acker	.05	.04	.02
660	Pete Ladd	.05	.04	.02

NOTE: A card number in parentheses ( ) indicates the set is unnumbered.

1987 Donruss All-Stars

Issued in conjunction with the Donruss Pop-Ups set for the second consecutive year, the 1987 Donruss All-Stars set consists of 59 players (plus a checklist) who were selected to the 1986 All-Star Game. Measuring 3-1/2" by 5" in size, the card fronts feature black borders and American or National League logos. Included on the backs are the player's career highlights and All-Star Game statistics. Retail packs included one pop-Up card, three All-Star cards and one Roberto Clemente puzzle.

		MT	NR MT	EX
Complete Set:		6.00	4.50	2.50
Common Player:		.09	.07	.04
1	Wally Joyner	1.00	.70	.40
2	Dave Winfield	.25	.20	.10
3	Lou Whitaker	.15	.11	.06
4	Kirby Puckett	.50	.40	.20
5	Cal Ripken, Jr.	.30	.25	.12
6	Rickey Henderson	.50	.40	.20
7	Wade Boggs	.80	.60	.30
8	Roger Clemens	.50	.40	.20
9	Lance Parrish	.09	.07	.04
10	Dick Howser	.09	.07	.04
11	Keith Hernandez	.10	.08	.04
12	Darryl Strawberry	.50	.40	.20
13	Ryne Sandberg	.25	.20	.10
14	Dale Murphy	.40	.30	.15
15	Ozzie Smith	.15	.11	.06
16	Tony Gwynn	.30	.25	.12
17	Mike Schmidt	.40	.30	.15
18	Dwight Gooden	.60	.45	.25
19	Gary Carter	.15	.11	.06
20	Whitey Herzog	.09	.07	.04
21	Jose Canseco	1.25	.90	.50
22	John Franco	.09	.07	.04
23	Jesse Barfield	.12	.09	.05
24	Rick Rhoden	.09	.07	.04
25	Harold Baines	.15	.11	.06
26	Sid Fernandez	.12	.09	.05
27	George Brett	.40	.30	.15
28	Steve Sax	.15	.11	.06
29	Jim Presley	.12	.09	.05
30	Dave Smith	.09	.07	.04
31	Eddie Murray	.10	.08	.04
32	Mike Scott	.12	.09	.05
33	Don Mattingly	2.00	1.50	.80
34	Dave Parker	.15	.11	.06
35	Tony Fernandez	.15	.11	.06
36	Tim Raines	.25	.20	.10
37	Brook Jacoby	.12	.09	.05
38	Chili Davis	.09	.07	.04
39	Rich Gedman	.09	.07	.04
40	Kevin Bass	.09	.07	.04
41	Frank White	.09	.07	.04
42	Glenn Davis	.15	.11	.06
43	Willie Hernandez	.09	.07	.04
44	Chris Brown	.09	.07	.04
45	Jim Rice	.10	.08	.04
46	Tony Pena	.09	.07	.04
47	Don Aase	.09	.07	.04
48	Hubie Brooks	.09	.07	.04
49	Charlie Hough	.09	.07	.04
50	Jody Davis	.09	.07	.04
51	Mike Witt	.09	.07	.04
52	Jeff Reardon	.12	.09	.05

		MT	NR MT	EX
53	Ken Schrom	.09	.07	.04
54	Fernando Valenzuela	.10	.08	.04
55	Dave Righetti	.15	.11	.06
56	Shane Rawley	.09	.07	.04
57	Ted Higuera	.12	.09	.05
58	Mike Krukow	.09	.07	.04
59	Lloyd Moseby	.09	.07	.04
60	Checklist	.09	.07	.04

1987 Donruss Box Panels

Continuing with an idea they initiated in 1985, Donruss once again placed baseball cards on the bottoms of their retail boxes. The cards, which are 2-1/2" by 3-1/2" in size, come four to a panel with each panel containing an unnumbered Roberto Clemente puzzle card. With numbering that begins where Donruss left off in 1986, cards PC 10 through PC 12 were found on boxes of Donruss regular issue wax packs. Cards PC 13 through PC 15 were located on boxes of the 1987 All-Star/Pop-Up packs.

		MT	NR MT	EX
Complete Panel Set:		6.00	4.50	2.50
Complete Singles Set:		3.00	2.25	1.25
Common Single Player:		.15	.11	.06
Panel		4.00	3.00	1.50
10	Dale Murphy	.50	.40	.20
11	Jeff Reardon	.20	.15	.08
12	Jose Canseco	2.00	1.50	.80
----	Roberto Clemente Puzzle Card	.04	.03	.02
Panel		2.25	1.75	.90
13	Mike Scott	.20	.15	.08
14	Roger Clemens	1.00	.70	.40
15	Mike Krukow	.15	.11	.06
----	Roberto Clemente Puzzle Card	.04	.03	.02

1987 Donruss Diamond Kings Supers

For a third straight baseball card season, Donruss produced a set of enlarged size Diamond Kings. The cards, which measure 4-11/16" by 6-3/4", are giant versions of the Diamond Kings subset found in the regular 1987 Donruss set. The 28-card set, which features the artwork of Dick Perez, contains 26 player cards, a checklist and a Roberto Clemente puzzle card. The set was available through a mail-in offer for $9.50 plus three wrappers.

		MT	NR MT	EX
	Complete Set:	10.00	7.50	4.00
	Common Player:	.20	.15	.08
1	Wally Joyner	1.25	.90	.50
2	Roger Clemens	1.00	.70	.40
3	Dale Murphy	.70	.50	.30
4	Darryl Strawberry	.90	.70	.35
5	Ozzie Smith	.30	.25	.12
6	Jose Canseco	2.00	1.50	.80
7	Charlie Hough	.20	.15	.08
8	Brook Jacoby	.20	.15	.08
9	Fred Lynn	.20	.15	.08
10	Rick Rhoden	.20	.15	.08
11	Chris Brown	.25	.20	.10
12	Von Hayes	.25	.20	.10
13	Jack Morris	.20	.15	.08
14	Kevin McReynolds	.35	.25	.14
15	George Brett	.70	.50	.30
16	Ted Higuera	.20	.15	.08
17	Hubie Brooks	.20	.15	.08
18	Mike Scott	.20	.15	.08
19	Kirby Puckett	.90	.70	.35
20	Dave Winfield	.30	.25	.12
21	Lloyd Moseby	.20	.15	.08
22	Eric Davis	.90	.70	.35
23	Jim Presley	.25	.20	.10
24	Keith Moreland	.20	.15	.08
25	Greg Walker	.20	.15	.08
26	Steve Sax	.30	.25	.12
27	Checklist	.15	.11	.06
-----	Roberto Clemente Puzzle Card	.15	.11	.06

1987 Donruss Highlights

NOLAN RYAN
Strikeout King—Again
October 4

NO. 53

For a third consecutive year, Donruss produced a 56-card set which highlighted the special events of the 1987 baseball season. The cards, which measure 2-1/2" by 3-1/2", have a front design similar to the regular 1987 Donruss set. A blue border and the "Highlights" logo are the significant differences. The card backs feature black print on a white background and include the date the event took place plus the particulars about it. As in the past, the set includes Donruss' picks for the A.L. and N.L. Rookies of the Year. The set was issued in a specially designed box and was available only through hobby dealers.

		MT	NR MT	EX
	Complete Set:	8.00	6.00	3.25
	Common Player:	.10	.08	.04
1	First No-Hitter For Brewers (Juan Nieves)	.15	.11	.06
2	Hits 500th Homer (Mike Schmidt)	.40	.30	.15
3	N.L. Player of the Month - April (Eric Davis)	.50	.40	.20
4	N.L. Pitcher of the Month - April (Sid Fernandez)	.10	.08	.04

		MT	NR MT	EX
5	A.L. Player of the Month - April (Brian Downing)	.10	.08	.04
6	A.L. Pitcher of the Month - April (Bret Saberhagen)	.30	.25	.12
7	Free Agent Holdout Returns (Tim Raines)	.25	.20	.10
8	N.L. Player of the Month - May (Eric Davis)	.50	.40	.20
9	N.L. Pitcher of the Month - May (Steve Bedrosian)	.15	.11	.06
10	A.L. Player of the Month - May (Larry Parrish)	.10	.08	.04
11	A.L. Pitcher of the Month - May (Jim Clancy)	.10	.08	.04
12	N.L. Player of the Month - June (Tony Gwynn)	.30	.25	.12
13	N.L. Pitcher of the Month - June (Orel Hershiser)	.25	.20	.10
14	A.L. Player of the Month - June (Wade Boggs)	.80	.60	.30
15	A.L. Pitcher of the Month - June (Steve Ontiveros)	.10	.08	.04
16	All Star Game Hero (Tim Raines)	.25	.20	.10
17	Consecutive Game Homer Streak (Don Mattingly)	1.00	.70	.40
18	1987 Hall of Fame Inductee (Jim "Catfish" Hunter)	.20	.15	.08
19	1987 Hall of Fame Inductee (Ray Dandridge)	.10	.08	.04
20	1987 Hall of Fame Inductee (Billy Williams)	.20	.15	.08
21	N.L. Player of the Month - July (Bo Diaz)	.10	.08	.04
22	N.L. Pitcher of the Month - July (Floyd Youmans)	.10	.08	.04
23	A.L. Player of the Month - July (Don Mattingly)	1.00	.70	.40
24	A.L. Pitcher of the Month - July (Frank Viola)	.20	.15	.08
25	Strikes Out 4 Batters In 1 Inning (Bobby Witt)	.15	.11	.06
26	Ties A.L. 9-Inning Game Hit Mark (Kevin Seitzer)	.50	.40	.20
27	Sets Rookie Home Run Record (Mark McGwire)	1.25	.90	.50
28	Sets Cubs' 1st Year Homer Mark (Andre Dawson)	.20	.15	.08
29	Hits In 39 Straight Games (Paul Molitor)	.15	.11	.06
30	Record Weekend (Kirby Puckett)	.50	.40	.20
31	N.L. Player of the Month - August (Andre Dawson)	.20	.15	.08
32	N.L. Pitcher of the Month - August (Doug Drabek)	.10	.08	.04
33	A.L. Player of the Month - August (Dwight Evans)	.15	.11	.06
34	A.L. Pitcher of the Month - August (Mark Langston)	.25	.20	.10
35	100 RBI In 1st 2 Major League Seasons (Wally Joyner)	.40	.30	.15
36	100 SB In 1st 3 Major League Seasons (Vince Coleman)	.20	.15	.08
37	Orioles' All Time Homer King (Eddie Murray)	.10	.08	.04
38	Ends Consecutive Innings Streak (Cal Ripken)	.30	.25	.12
39	Blue Jays Hit Record 10 Homers In 1 Gamelers. (Rob Ducey, Fred McGriff, Ernie Whitt)	.50	.40	.20
40	Equal A's RBI Marks (Jose Canseco, Mark McGwire)	2.50	2.00	1.00
41	Sets All-Time Catching Record (Bob Boone)	.10	.08	.04
42	Sets Mets' One-Season HR Mark (Darryl Strawberry)	.50	.40	.20
43	N.L.'s All-Time Switch Hit HR King (Howard Johnson)	.15	.11	.06
44	Five Straight 200-Hit Seasons (Wade Boggs)	.80	.60	.30
45	Eclipses Rookie Game Hitting Streak (Benito Santiago)	.40	.30	.15
46	Eclipses Jackson's A's HR Record (Mark McGwire)	1.25	.90	.50
47	13th Rookie To Collect 200 Hits (Kevin Seitzer)	.50	.40	.20
48	Sets Slam Record (Don Mattingly)	1.00	.70	.40
49	N.L. Player of the Month - September (Darryl Strawberry)	.50	.40	.20
50	N.L. Pitcher of the Month - September (Pascual Perez)	.10	.08	.04

		MT	NR MT	EX
51	A.L. Player of the Month - September (Alan Trammell)	.20	.15	.08
52	A.L. Pitcher of the Month - September (Doyle Alexander)	.10	.08	.04
53	Strikeout King - Again (Nolan Ryan)	.50	.40	.20
54	Donruss A.L. Rookie of the Year (Mark McGwire)	1.25	.90	.50
55	Donruss N.L. Rookie of the Year (Benito Santiago)	.40	.30	.15
56	Highlight Checklist	.10	.08	.04

1987 Donruss Opening Day

The Donruss Opening Day set includes all players in major league baseball's starting lineups on the opening day of the 1987 baseball season. Cards in the 272-piece set measure 2-1/2" by 3-1/2" and have a glossy coating. The card fronts are identical in design to the regular Donruss set, but new photos were utilized and the fronts contain maroon borders as opposed to black. The backs carry black printing on white and yellow and carry a brief player biography plus the player's career statistics. The set was packaged in a sturdy 15" by 5" by 2" box with a clear acetate lid.

	MT	NR MT	EX
Complete Set:	20.00	15.00	8.00
Common Player:	.05	.04	.02

		MT	NR MT	EX
1	Doug DeCinces	.07	.05	.03
2	Mike Witt	.12	.09	.05
3	George Hendrick	.07	.05	.03
4	Dick Schofield	.05	.04	.02
5	Devon White	.50	.40	.20
6	Butch Wynegar	.05	.04	.02
7	Wally Joyner	.75	.55	.30
8	Mark McLemore	.05	.04	.02
9	Brian Downing	.07	.05	.03
10	Gary Pettis	.05	.04	.02
11	Bill Doran	.07	.05	.03
12	Phil Garner	.05	.04	.02
13	Jose Cruz	.07	.05	.03
14	Kevin Bass	.07	.05	.03
15	Mike Scott	.12	.09	.05
16	Glenn Davis	.15	.11	.06
17	Alan Ashby	.05	.04	.02
18	Billy Hatcher	.07	.05	.03
19	Craig Reynolds	.05	.04	.02
20	Carney Lansford	.07	.05	.03
21	Mike Davis	.05	.04	.02
22	Reggie Jackson	.30	.25	.12
23	Mickey Tettleton	.07	.05	.03
24	Jose Canseco	1.75	1.25	.70
25	Rob Nelson	.05	.04	.02
26	Tony Phillips	.05	.04	.02
27	Dwayne Murphy	.05	.04	.02
28	Alfredo Griffin	.07	.05	.03
29	Curt Young	.05	.04	.02
30	Willie Upshaw	.05	.04	.02
31	Mike Sharperson	.05	.04	.02
32	Rance Mulliniks	.05	.04	.02
33	Ernie Whitt	.05	.04	.02
34	Jesse Barfield	.12	.09	.05
35	Tony Fernandez	.12	.09	.05
36	Lloyd Moseby	.07	.05	.03
37	Jimmy Key	.10	.08	.04

		MT	NR MT	EX
38	Fred McGriff	1.50	1.25	.60
39	George Bell	.25	.20	.10
40	Dale Murphy	.40	.30	.15
41	Rick Mahler	.05	.04	.02
42	Ken Griffey	.07	.05	.03
43	Andres Thomas	.10	.08	.04
44	Dion James	.05	.04	.02
45	Ozzie Virgil	.05	.04	.02
46	Ken Oberkfell	.05	.04	.02
47	Gary Roenicke	.05	.04	.02
48	Glenn Hubbard	.05	.04	.02
49	Bill Schroeder	.05	.04	.02
50	Greg Brock	.07	.05	.03
51	Billy Jo Robidoux	.05	.04	.02
52	Glenn Braggs	.12	.09	.05
53	Jim Gantner	.05	.04	.02
54	Paul Molitor	.15	.11	.06
55	Dale Sveum	.15	.11	.06
56	Ted Higuera	.12	.09	.05
57	Rob Deer	.07	.05	.02
58	Robin Yount	.35	.25	.14
59	Jim Lindeman	.10	.08	.04
60	Vince Coleman	.15	.11	.06
61	Tommy Herr	.07	.05	.03
62	Terry Pendleton	.07	.05	.03
63	John Tudor	.10	.08	.04
64	Tony Pena	.07	.05	.03
65	Ozzie Smith	.15	.11	.06
66	Tito Landrum	.05	.04	.02
67	Jack Clark	.15	.11	.06
68	Bob Dernier	.05	.04	.02
69	Rick Sutcliffe	.10	.08	.04
70	Andre Dawson	.20	.15	.08
71	Keith Moreland	.07	.05	.03
72	Jody Davis	.07	.05	.03
73	Brian Dayett	.05	.04	.02
74	Leon Durham	.07	.05	.03
75	Ryne Sandberg	.25	.20	.10
76	Shawon Dunston	.20	.15	.08
77	Mike Marshall	.10	.08	.04
78	Bill Madlock	.07	.05	.03
79	Orel Hershiser	.30	.25	.12
80	Mike Ramsey	.05	.04	.02
81	Ken Landreaux	.05	.04	.02
82	Mike Scioscia	.05	.04	.02
83	Franklin Stubbs	.07	.05	.03
84	Mariano Duncan	.05	.04	.02
85	Steve Sax	.15	.11	.06
86	Mitch Webster	.07	.05	.03
87	Reid Nichols	.05	.04	.02
88	Tim Wallach	.10	.08	.04
89	Floyd Youmans	.07	.05	.03
90	Andres Galarraga	.25	.20	.10
91	Hubie Brooks	.07	.05	.03
92	Jeff Reed	.05	.04	.02
93	Alonzo Powell	.05	.04	.02
94	Vance Law	.05	.04	.02
95	Bob Brenly	.05	.04	.02
96	Will Clark	2.00	1.50	.80
97	Chili Davis	.07	.05	.03
98	Mike Krukow	.05	.04	.02
99	Jose Uribe	.05	.04	.02
100	Chris Brown	.07	.05	.03
101	Rob Thompson	.10	.08	.04
102	Candy Maldonado	.07	.05	.03
103	Jeff Leonard	.07	.05	.03
104	Tom Candiotti	.05	.04	.02
105	Chris Bando	.05	.04	.02
106	Cory.Snyder	.30	.25	.12
107	Pat Tabler	.07	.05	.03
108	Andre Thornton	.07	.05	.03
109	Joe Carter	.25	.20	.10
110	Tony Bernazard	.05	.04	.02
111	Julio Franco	.10	.08	.04
112	Brook Jacoby	.10	.08	.04
113	Brett Butler	.07	.05	.03
114	Donnell Nixon	.05	.04	.02
115	Alvin Davis	.12	.09	.05
116	Mark Langston	.25	.20	.10
117	Harold Reynolds	.07	.05	.03
118	Ken Phelps	.05	.04	.02
119	Mike Kingery	.10	.08	.04
120	Dave Valle	.07	.05	.03
121	Rey Quinones	.07	.05	.03
122	Phil Bradley	.12	.09	.05
123	Jim Presley	.12	.09	.05
124	Keith Hernandez	.12	.09	.05
125	Kevin McReynolds	.12	.09	.05
126	Rafael Santana	.05	.04	.02
127	Bob Ojeda	.07	.05	.03
128	Darryl Strawberry	.60	.45	.25

		MT	NR MT	EX
129	Mookie Wilson	.07	.05	.03
130	Gary Carter	.15	.11	.06
131	Tim Teufel	.05	.04	.02
132	Howard Johnson	.20	.15	.08
133	Cal Ripken	.30	.25	.12
134	Rick Burleson	.05	.04	.02
135	Fred Lynn	.12	.09	.05
136	Eddie Murray	.15	.11	.06
137	Ray Knight	.07	.05	.03
138	Alan Wiggins	.05	.04	.02
139	John Shelby	.05	.04	.02
140	Mike Boddicker	.07	.05	.03
141	Ken Gerhart	.07	.05	.03
142	Terry Kennedy	.07	.05	.03
143	Steve Garvey	.30	.25	.12
144	Marvell Wynne	.05	.04	.02
145	Kevin Mitchell	1.50	1.25	.60
146	Tony Gwynn	.35	.25	.14
147	Joey Cora	.10	.08	.04
148	Benito Santiago	.60	.45	.25
149	Eric Show	.07	.05	.03
150	Garry Templeton	.07	.05	.03
151	Carmelo Martinez	.05	.04	.02
152	Von Hayes	.10	.08	.04
153	Lance Parrish	.10	.08	.04
154	Milt Thompson	.07	.05	.03
155	Mike Easler	.05	.04	.02
156	Juan Samuel	.10	.08	.04
157	Steve Jeltz	.05	.04	.02
158	Glenn Wilson	.05	.04	.02
159	Shane Rawley	.07	.05	.03
160	Mike Schmidt	.40	.30	.15
161	Andy Van Slyke	.10	.08	.04
162	Johnny Ray	.07	.05	.03
163a	Barry Bonds (dark jersey, photo actually Johnny Ray)	125.00	94.00	50.00
163b	Barry Bonds (white jersey, correct photo)	.15	.11	.06
164	Junior Ortiz	.05	.04	.02
165	Rafael Belliard	.05	.04	.02
166	Bob Patterson	.05	.04	.02
167	Bobby Bonilla	.15	.11	.06
168	Sid Bream	.07	.05	.03
169	Jim Morrison	.05	.04	.02
170	Jerry Browne	.10	.08	.04
171	Scott Fletcher	.05	.04	.02
172	Ruben Sierra	1.50	1.25	.60
173	Larry Parrish	.07	.05	.03
174	Pete O'Brien	.07	.05	.03
175	Pete Incaviglia	.35	.25	.14
176	Don Slaught	.05	.04	.02
177	Oddibe McDowell	.10	.08	.04
178	Charlie Hough	.07	.05	.03
179	Steve Buechele	.05	.04	.02
180	Bob Stanley	.05	.04	.02
181	Wade Boggs	1.00	.70	.40
182	Jim Rice	.10	.08	.04
183	Bill Buckner	.07	.05	.03
184	Dwight Evans	.10	.08	.04
185	Spike Owen	.05	.04	.02
186	Don Baylor	.10	.08	.04
187	Marc Sullivan	.05	.04	.02
188	Marty Barrett	.07	.05	.03
189	Dave Henderson	.07	.05	.03
190	Bo Diaz	.05	.04	.02
191	Barry Larkin	.90	.70	.35
192	Kal Daniels	.25	.20	.10
193	Terry Francona	.05	.04	.02
194	Tom Browning	.07	.05	.03
195	Ron Oester	.05	.04	.02
196	Buddy Bell	.07	.05	.03
197	Eric Davis	.60	.45	.25
198	Dave Parker	.15	.11	.06
199	Steve Balboni	.05	.04	.02
200	Danny Tartabull	.30	.25	.12
201	Ed Hearn	.05	.04	.02
202	Buddy Biancalana	.05	.04	.02
203	Danny Jackson	.05	.04	.02
204	Frank White	.08	.06	.03
205	Bo Jackson	2.00	1.50	.80
206	George Brett	.40	.30	.15
207	Kevin Seitzer	1.50	1.25	.60
208	Willie Wilson	.10	.08	.04
209	Orlando Mercado	.05	.04	.02
210	Darrell Evans	.07	.05	.03
211	Larry Herndon	.05	.04	.02
212	Jack Morris	.15	.11	.06
213	Chet Lemon	.07	.05	.03
214	Mike Heath	.05	.04	.02
215	Darnell Coles	.07	.05	.03
216	Alan Trammell	.20	.15	.08

		MT	NR MT	EX
217	Terry Harper	.05	.04	.02
218	Lou Whitaker	.15	.11	.06
219	Gary Gaetti	.15	.11	.06
220	Tom Nieto	.05	.04	.02
221	Kirby Puckett	.80	.60	.30
222	Tom Brunansky	.10	.08	.04
223	Greg Gagne	.05	.04	.02
224	Dan Gladden	.07	.05	.03
225	Mark Davidson	.07	.05	.03
226	Bert Blyleven	.10	.08	.04
227	Steve Lombardozzi	.05	.04	.02
228	Kent Hrbek	.15	.11	.06
229	Gary Redus	.05	.04	.02
230	Ivan Calderon	.10	.08	.04
231	Tim Hulett	.05	.04	.02
232	Carlton Fisk	.15	.11	.06
233	Greg Walker	.07	.05	.03
234	Ron Karkovice	.05	.04	.02
235	Ozzie Guillen	.07	.05	.03
236	Harold Baines	.12	.09	.05
237	Donnie Hill	.05	.04	.02
238	Rich Dotson	.07	.05	.03
239	Mike Pagliarulo	.10	.08	.04
240	Joel Skinner	.05	.04	.02
241	Don Mattingly	1.50	1.25	.60
242	Gary Ward	.05	.04	.02
243	Dave Winfield	.20	.15	.08
244	Dan Pasqua	.10	.08	.04
245	Wayne Tolleson	.05	.04	.02
246	Willie Randolph	.07	.05	.03
247	Dennis Rasmussen	.07	.05	.03
248	Rickey Henderson	.30	.25	.12
249	Angels Logo/Checklist	.05	.04	.02
250	Astros Logo/Checklist	.05	.04	.02
251	Athletics Logo/Checklist	.05	.04	.02
252	Blue Jays Logo/Checklist	.05	.04	.02
253	Braves Logo/Checklist	.05	.04	.02
254	Brewers Logo/Checklist	.05	.04	.02
255	Cardinals Logo/Checklist	.05	.04	.02
256	Dodgers Logo/Checklist	.05	.04	.02
257	Expos Logo/Checklist	.05	.04	.02
258	Giants Logo/Checklist	.05	.04	.02
259	Indians Logo/Checklist	.05	.04	.02
260	Mariners Logo/Checklist	.05	.04	.02
261	Orioles Logo/Checklist	.05	.04	.02
262	Padres Logo/Checklist	.05	.04	.02
263	Phillies Logo/Checklist	.05	.04	.02
264	Pirates Logo/Checklist	.05	.04	.02
265	Rangers Logo/Checklist	.05	.04	.02
266	Red Sox Logo/Checklist	.05	.04	.02
267	Reds Logo/Checklist	.05	.04	.02
268	Royals Logo/Checklist	.05	.04	.02
269	Tigers Logo/Checklist	.05	.04	.02
270	Twins Logo/Checklist	.05	.04	.02
271	White Sox-Cubs Logos/Checklist	.05	.04	.02
272	Yankees-Mets Logos/Checklist	.05	.04	.02

1987 Donruss Pop-Ups

For the second straight year, Donruss released in conjunction with its All-Stars issue a set of cards designed to fold out to form a three-dimensional stand-up card. Consisting of 20 cards, as opposed to the previous year's 18, the 1987 Donruss Pop-Ups set contains players selected to the 1986 All-Star Game. Background for the 2-1/2" by 5" cards is the Houston Astrodome, site of the 1986 mid-summer classic. Retail packs included one Pop-Up card, three All-Star cards and one Roberto Clemente puzzle card.

		MT	NR MT	EX
Complete Set:		5.00	3.75	2.00
Common Player:		.20	.15	.08
(1)	Wade Boggs	1.00	.70	.40
(2)	Gary Carter	.25	.20	.10
(3)	Roger Clemens	.80	.60	.30
(4)	Dwight Gooden	.80	.60	.30
(5)	Tony Gwynn	.50	.40	.20
(6)	Rickey Henderson	.75	.55	.30
(7)	Keith Hernandez	.25	.20	.10
(8)	Whitey Herzog	.20	.15	.08
(9)	Dick Howser	.20	.15	.08
(10)	Wally Joyner	.50	.40	.20
(11)	Dale Murphy	.60	.45	.25
(12)	Lance Parrish	.20	.15	.08
(13)	Kirby Puckett	.75	.55	.30
(14)	Cal Ripken	.50	.40	.20
(15)	Ryne Sandberg	.40	.30	.15
(16)	Mike Schmidt	.60	.45	.25
(17)	Ozzie Smith	.30	.25	.12
(18)	Darryl Strawberry	.50	.40	.20
(19)	Lou Whitaker	.20	.15	.08
(20)	Dave Winfield	.30	.25	.12

1987 Donruss Rookies

As they did in 1986, Donruss issued a 56-card set highlighting the major league's most promising rookies. The cards are the standard 2-1/2" by 3-1/2" size and are identical in design to the regular Donruss issue. The card fronts have green borders as opposed to the black found in the regular issue and carry the words "The Rookies" in the lower left portion of the card. The set came housed in a specially designed box and was available only through hobby dealers.

		MT	NR MT	EX
Complete Set:		15.00	11.00	6.00
Common Player:		.10	.08	.04
1	Mark McGwire	3.00	2.25	1.25
2	Eric Bell	.10	.08	.04
3	Mark Williamson(FC)	.15	.11	.06
4	Mike Greenwell	3.75	2.75	1.50
5	Ellis Burks(FC)	2.00	1.50	.80
6	DeWayne Buice(FC)	.20	.15	.08
7	Mark Mclemore (McLemore)	.10	.08	.04
8	Devon White	.50	.40	.20
9	Willie Fraser	.15	.11	.06
10	Lester Lancaster(FC)	.15	.11	.06

		MT	NR MT	EX
11	Ken Williams(FC)	.20	.15	.08
12	Matt Nokes(FC)	.70	.50	.30
13	Jeff Robinson(FC)	.40	.30	.15
14	Bo Jackson	4.00	3.00	1.50
15	Kevin Seitzer(FC)	1.50	1.25	.60
16	Billy Ripken(FC)	.25	.20	.10
17	B.J. Surhoff	.20	.15	.08
18	Chuck Crim(FC)	.15	.11	.06
19	Mike Birbeck	.10	.08	.04
20	Chris Bosio	.10	.08	.04
21	Les Straker(FC)	.20	.15	.08
22	Mark Davidson(FC)	.15	.11	.06
23	Gene Larkin(FC)	.25	.20	.10
24	Ken Gerhart	.15	.11	.06
25	Luis Polonia(FC)	.35	.25	.14
26	Terry Steinbach	.25	.20	.10
27	Mickey Brantley	.10	.08	.04
28	Mike Stanley	.20	.15	.08
29	Jerry Browne	.10	.08	.04
30	Todd Benzinger(FC)	.50	.40	.20
31	Fred McGriff	2.00	1.50	.80
32	Mike Henneman(FC)	.30	.25	.12
33	Casey Candaele	.10	.08	.04
34	Dave Magadan	.25	.20	.10
35	David Cone	1.25	.90	.50
36	Mike Jackson(FC)	.20	.15	.08
37	John Mitchell(FC)	.20	.15	.08
38	Mike Dunne(FC)	.25	.20	.10
39	John Smiley(FC)	.40	.30	.15
40	Joe Magrane(FC)	1.00	.70	.40
41	Jim Lindeman	.10	.08	.04
42	Shane Mack(FC)	.25	.20	.10
43	Stan Jefferson	.10	.08	.04
44	Benito Santiago	.60	.45	.25
45	Matt Williams(FC)	3.00	2.25	1.25
46	Dave Meads(FC)	.20	.15	.08
47	Rafael Palmeiro	.80	.60	.30
48	Bill Long(FC)	.20	.15	.08
49	Bob Brower	.10	.08	.04
50	James Steels(FC)	.15	.11	.06
51	Paul Noce(FC)	.15	.11	.06
52	Greg Maddux	.60	.45	.25
53	Jeff Musselman	.15	.11	.06
54	Brian Holton	.15	.11	.06
55	Chuck Jackson(FC)	.20	.15	.08
56	Checklist 1-56	.10	.08	.04

1988 Donruss

The 1988 Donruss set consists of 660 cards, each measuring 2-1/2" by 3-1/2" in size. The card fronts feature a full-color photo surrounded by a colorful border - alternating stripes of black, red, black, blue, black, blue, black, red and black (in that order), separated by soft-focus edges and airbrushed fades. The player's name and position appear in a red band at the bottom of the card. The Donruss logo is situated in the upper left corner of the card, while the team logo is located in the lower right corner. For the seventh consecutive season, Donruss included a subset of "Diamond Kings" cards (#'s 1-27) in the issue. And for the fifth straight year, Donruss incorporated their highly popular "Rated Rookies" (card #'s 28-47) with the set.

	MT	NR MT	EX
Complete Set:	28.00	21.00	12.00

		MT	NR MT	EX
	Common Player	.05	.04	.02
1	Mark McGwire (DK)	1.00	.70	.40
2	Tim Raines (DK)	.25	.20	.10
3	Benito Santiago (DK)	.30	.25	.12
4	Alan Trammell (DK)	.25	.20	.10
5	Danny Tartabull (DK)	.20	.15	.08
6	Ron Darling (DK)	.12	.09	.05
7	Paul Molitor (DK)	.12	.09	.05
8	Devon White (DK)	.20	.15	.08
9	Andre Dawson (DK)	.20	.15	.08
10	Julio Franco (DK)	.10	.08	.04
11	Scott Fletcher (DK)	.07	.05	.03
12	Tony Fernandez (DK)	.12	.09	.05
13	Shane Rawley (DK)	.07	.05	.03
14	Kal Daniels (DK)	.20	.15	.08
15	Jack Clark (DK)	.15	.11	.06
16	Dwight Evans (DK)	.12	.09	.05
17	Tommy John (DK)	.15	.11	.06
18,	Andy Van Slyke (DK)	.15	.11	.06
19	Gary Gaetti (DK)	.12	.09	.05
20	Mark Langston (DK)	.10	.08	.04
21	Will Clark (DK)	.80	.60	.30
22	Glenn Hubbard (DK)	.07	.05	.03
23	Billy Hatcher (DK)	.07	.05	.03
24	Bob Welch (DK)	.10	.08	.04
25	Ivan Calderon (DK)	.10	.08	.04
26	Cal Ripken, Jr. (DK)	.35	.25	.14
27	Checklist 1-27	.05	.04	.02
28	*Mackey Sasser* (RR)(FC)	.20	.15	.08
29	*Jeff Treadway* (RR)(FC)	.30	.25	.14
30	*Mike Campbell* (RR)(FC)	.25	.20	.10
31	*Lance Johnson* (RR)(FC)	.20	.15	.08
32	*Nelson Liriano* (RR)(FC)	.25	.20	.10
33	Shawn Abner (RR)(FC)	.20	.15	.08
34	*Roberto Alomar* (RR)(FC)	.70	.50	.30
35	*Shawn Hillegas* (RR)(FC)	.25	.20	.10
36	Joey Meyer (RR)	.20	.15	.08
37	Kevin Elster (RR)	.30	.25	.12
38	*Jose Lind* (RR)(FC)	.30	.25	.12
39	*Kirt Manwaring* (RR)(FC)	.35	.25	.14
40	*Mark Grace* (RR)(FC)	4.50	3.25	1.75
41	*Jody Reed* (RR)(FC)	.50	.40	.20
42	*John Farrell* (RR)(FC)	.35	.25	.14
43	*Al Leiter* (RR)(FC)	.70	.50	.30
44	*Gary Thurman* (RR)(FC)	.35	.25	.14
45	*Vicente Palacios* (RR)(FC)	.20	.15	.08
46	*Eddie Williams* (RR)(FC)	.25	.20	.10
47	*Jack McDowell* (RR)(FC)	.30	.25	.12
48	Ken Dixon	.05	.04	.02
49	Mike Birkbeck	.07	.05	.03
50	Eric King	.07	.05	.03
51	Roger Clemens	.60	.45	.25
52	Pat Clements	.05	.04	.02
53	Fernando Valenzuela	.25	.20	.10
54	Mark Gubicza	.12	.09	.05
55	Jay Howell	.07	.05	.03
56	Floyd Youmans	.05	.04	.02
57	Ed Correa	.05	.04	.02
58	*DeWayne Buice*	.15	.11	.06
59	Jose DeLeon	.07	.05	.03
60	Danny Cox	.07	.05	.03
61	Nolan Ryan	.50	.40	.20
62	Steve Bedrosian	.12	.09	.05
63	Tom Browning	.10	.08	.04
64	Mark Davis	.05	.04	.02
65	R.J. Reynolds	.05	.04	.02
66	Kevin Mitchell	.60	.45	.25
67	Ken Oberkfell	.05	.04	.02
68	Rick Sutcliffe	.10	.08	.04
69	Dwight Gooden	.60	.45	.25
70	Scott Bankhead	.07	.05	.03
71	Bert Blyleven	.12	.09	.05
72	Jimmy Key	.10	.08	.04
73	*Les Straker*	.15	.11	.06
74	Jim Clancy	.07	.05	.03
75	Mike Moore	.05	.04	.02
76	Ron Darling	.12	.09	.05
77	Ed Lynch	.05	.04	.02
78	Dale Murphy	.40	.30	.15
79	Doug Drabek	.07	.05	.03
80	Scott Garrelts	.05	.04	.02
81	Ed Whitson	.05	.04	.02
82	Rob Murphy	.07	.05	.03
83	Shane Rawley	.07	.05	.03
84	Greg Mathews	.07	.05	.03
85	Jim Deshaies	.07	.05	.03
86	Mike Witt	.07	.05	.03
87	Donnie Hill	.05	.04	.02
88	Jeff Reed	.05	.04	.02
89	Mike Boddicker	.07	.05	.03

		MT	NR MT	EX
90	Ted Higuera	.10	.08	.04
91	Walt Terrell	.07	.05	.03
92	Bob Stanley	.05	.04	.02
93	Dave Righetti	.15	.11	.06
94	Orel Hershiser	.25	.20	.10
95	Chris Bando	.05	.04	.02
96	Bret Saberhagen	.15	.11	.06
97	Curt Young	.07	.05	.03
98	Tim Burke	.05	.04	.02
99	Charlie Hough	.07	.05	.03
100a	Checklist 28-137	.05	.04	.02
100b	Checklist 28-133	.10	.08	.04
101	Bobby Witt	.10	.08	.04
102	George Brett	.40	.30	.15
103	Mickey Tettleton	.25	.20	.10
104	Scott Bailes	.07	.05	.03
105	Mike Pagliarulo	.10	.08	.04
106	Mike Scioscia	.07	.05	.03
107	Tom Brookens	.05	.04	.02
108	Ray Knight	.07	.05	.03
109	Dan Plesac	.10	.08	.04
110	Wally Joyner	.40	.30	.15
111	Bob Forsch	.07	.05	.03
112	Mike Scott	.12	.09	.05
113	Kevin Gross	.07	.05	.03
114	Benito Santiago	.35	.25	.14
115	Bob Kipper	.05	.04	.02
116	Mike Krukow	.07	.05	.03
117	Chris Bosio	.07	.05	.03
118	Sid Fernandez	.10	.08	.04
119	Jody Davis	.07	.05	.03
120	Mike Morgan	.05	.04	.02
121	Mark Eichhorn	.07	.05	.03
122	Jeff Reardon	.10	.08	.04
123	John Franco	.10	.08	.04
124	Richard Dotson	.07	.05	.03
125	Eric Bell	.05	.04	.02
126	Juan Nieves	.07	.05	.03
127	Jack Morris	.20	.15	.08
128	Rick Rhoden	.07	.05	.03
129	Rich Gedman	.07	.05	.03
130	Ken Howell	.05	.04	.02
131	Brook Jacoby	.10	.08	.04
132	Danny Jackson	.12	.09	.05
133	Gene Nelson	.05	.04	.02
134	Neal Heaton	.05	.04	.02
135	Willie Fraser	.05	.04	.02
136	Jose Guzman	.07	.05	.03
137	Ozzie Guillen	.07	.05	.03
138	Bob Knepper	.07	.05	.03
139	*Mike Jackson*	.20	.15	.08
140	*Joe Magrane*	.60	.45	.25
141	Jimmy Jones	.07	.05	.03
142	Ted Power	.05	.04	.02
143	Ozzie Virgil	.05	.04	.02
144	*Felix Fermin* (FC)	.15	.11	.06
145	Kelly Downs	.10	.08	.04
146	Shawon Dunston	.10	.08	.04
147	Scott Bradley	.05	.04	.02
148	Dave Stieb	.10	.08	.04
149	Frank Viola	.15	.11	.06
150	Terry Kennedy	.07	.05	.03
151	Bill Wegman	.05	.04	.02
152	*Matt Nokes*	.60	.45	.25
153	Wade Boggs	1.00	.70	.40
154	Wayne Tolleson	.05	.04	.02
155	Mariano Duncan	.05	.04	.02
156	Julio Franco	.10	.08	.04
157	Charlie Leibrandt	.07	.05	.03
158	Terry Steinbach	.10	.08	.04
159	Mike Fitzgerald	.05	.04	.02
160	Jack Lazorko	.05	.04	.02
161	Mitch Williams	.07	.05	.03
162	Greg Walker	.07	.05	.03
163	Alan Ashby	.05	.04	.02
164	Tony Gwynn	.35	.25	.14
165	Bruce Ruffin	.07	.05	.03
166	Ron Robinson	.05	.04	.02
167	Zane Smith	.07	.05	.03
168	Junior Ortiz	.05	.04	.02
169	Jamie Moyer	.07	.05	.03
170	Tony Pena	.07	.05	.03
171	Cal Ripken	.35	.25	.14
172	B.J. Surhoff	.12	.09	.05
173	Lou Whitaker	.25	.20	.10
174	*Ellis Burks*	1.75	1.25	.70
175	Ron Guidry	.15	.11	.06
176	Steve Sax	.15	.11	.06
177	Danny Tartabull	.20	.15	.08
178	Carney Lansford	.10	.08	.04
179	Casey Candaele	.05	.04	.02

		MT	NR MT	EX				MT	NR MT	EX
180	Scott Fletcher	.07	.05	.03		270	Lee Guetterman	.05	.04	.02
181	Mark McLemore	.05	.04	.02		271	Willie Upshaw	.07	.05	.03
182	Ivan Calderon	.10	.08	.04		272	Randy Bush	.05	.04	.02
183	Jack Clark	.15	.11	.06		273	Larry Sheets	.07	.05	.03
184	Glenn Davis	.15	.11	.06		274	Rob Deer	.07	.05	.03
185	Luis Aguayo	.05	.04	.02		275	Kirk Gibson	.20	.15	.08
186	Bo Diaz	.07	.05	.03		276	Marty Barrett	.07	.05	.03
187	Stan Jefferson	.07	.05	.03		277	Rickey Henderson	.35	.25	.14
188	Sid Bream	.07	.05	.03		278	Pedro Guerrero	.15	.11	.06
189	Bob Brenly	.05	.04	.02		279	Brett Butler	.07	.05	.03
190	Dion James	.07	.05	.03		280	Kevin Seitzer	.80	.60	.30
191	Leon Durham	.07	.05	.03		281	Mike Davis	.07	.05	.03
192	Jesse Orosco	.07	.05	.03		282	Andres Galarraga	.15	.11	.06
193	Alvin Davis	.12	.09	.05		283	Devon White	.30	.25	.12
194	Gary Gaetti	.12	.09	.05		284	Pete O'Brien	.07	.05	.03
195	Fred McGriff	.40	.30	.15		285	Jerry Hairston	.05	.04	.02
196	Steve Lombardozzi	.05	.04	.02		286	Kevin Bass	.07	.05	.03
197	Rance Mulliniks	.05	.04	.02		287	Carmelo Martinez	.07	.05	.03
198	Rey Quinones	.05	.04	.02		288	Juan Samuel	.12	.09	.05
199	Gary Carter	.25	.20	.10		289	Kal Daniels	.20	.15	.08
200a	Checklist 138-247	.05	.04	.02		290	Albert Hall	.05	.04	.02
200b	Checklist 134-239	.10	.08	.04		291	Andy Van Slyke	.12	.09	.05
201	Keith Moreland	.07	.05	.03		292	Lee Smith	.10	.08	.04
202	Ken Griffey	.07	.05	.03		293	Vince Coleman	.20	.15	.08
203	*Tommy Gregg*(FC)	.30	.25	.12		294	Tom Niedenfuer	.07	.05	.03
204	Will Clark	.80	.60	.30		295	Robin Yount	.30	.25	.12
205	John Kruk	.10	.08	.04		296	*Jeff Robinson*	.40	.30	.15
206	Buddy Bell	.07	.05	.03		297	*Todd Benzinger*	.40	.30	.15
207	Von Hayes	.07	.05	.03		298	Dave Winfield	.30	.25	.12
208	Tommy Herr	.07	.05	.03		299	Mickey Hatcher	.05	.04	.02
209	Craig Reynolds	.05	.04	.02		300a	Checklist 248-357	.05	.04	.02
210	Gary Pettis	.05	.04	.02		300b	Checklist 240-345	.10	.08	.04
211	Harold Baines	.12	.09	.05		301	Bud Black	.05	.04	.02
212	Vance Law	.07	.05	.03		302	Jose Canseco	1.50	1.25	.60
213	Ken Gerhart	.07	.05	.03		303	Tom Foley	.05	.04	.02
214	Jim Gantner	.05	.04	.02		304	Pete Incaviglia	.15	.11	.06
215	Chet Lemon	.07	.05	.03		305	Bob Boone	.07	.05	.03
216	Dwight Evans	.12	.09	.05		306	*Bill Long*	.20	.15	.08
217	Don Mattingly	1.50	1.25	.60		307	Willie McGee	.12	.09	.05
218	Franklin Stubbs	.07	.05	.03		308	*Ken Caminiti*(FC)	.25	.20	.10
219	Pat Tabler	.07	.05	.03		309	Darren Daulton	.05	.04	.02
220	Bo Jackson	1.00	.70	.40		310	Tracy Jones	.12	.09	.05
221	Tony Phillips	.05	.04	.02		311	Greg Booker	.07	.05	.03
222	Tim Wallach	.10	.08	.04		312	Mike LaValliere	.07	.05	.03
223	Ruben Sierra	.50	.40	.20		313	Chili Davis	.07	.05	.03
224	Steve Buechele	.05	.04	.02		314	Glenn Hubbard	.05	.04	.02
225	Frank White	.07	.05	.03		315	*Paul Noce*	.10	.08	.04
226	Alfredo Griffin	.07	.05	.03		316	Keith Hernandez	.20	.15	.08
227	Greg Swindell	.20	.15	.08		317	Mark Langston	.12	.09	.05
228	Willie Randolph	.07	.05	.03		318	Keith Atherton	.05	.04	.02
229	Mike Marshall	.12	.09	.05		319	Tony Fernandez	.12	.09	.05
230	Alan Trammell	.25	.20	.10		320	Kent Hrbek	.15	.11	.06
231	Eddie Murray	.35	.25	.14		321	John Cerutti	.07	.05	.03
232	Dale Sveum	.07	.05	.03		322	Mike Kingery	.05	.04	.02
233	Dick Schofield	.05	.04	.02		323	Dave Magadan	.12	.09	.05
234	Jose Oquendo	.05	.04	.02		324	Rafael Palmeiro	.40	.30	.15
235	Bill Doran	.07	.05	.03		325	Jeff Dedmon	.05	.04	.02
236	Milt Thompson	.05	.04	.02		326	Barry Bonds	.12	.09	.05
237	Marvell Wynne	.05	.04	.02		327	Jeffrey Leonard	.07	.05	.03
238	Bobby Bonilla	.15	.11	.06		328	Tim Flannery	.05	.04	.02
239	Chris Speier	.05	.04	.02		329	Dave Concepcion	.07	.05	.03
240	Glenn Braggs	.10	.08	.04		330	Mike Schmidt	.50	.40	.20
241	Wally Backman	.07	.05	.03		331	Bill Dawley	.05	.04	.02
242	Ryne Sandberg	.30	.25	.12		332	Larry Andersen	.05	.04	.02
243	Phil Bradley	.10	.08	.04		333	Jack Howell	.07	.05	.03
244	Kelly Gruber	.05	.04	.02		334	*Ken Williams*	.20	.15	.08
245	Tom Brunansky	.10	.08	.04		335	Bryn Smith	.05	.04	.02
246	Ron Oester	.05	.04	.02		336	*Billy Ripken*	.25	.20	.10
247	Bobby Thigpen	.10	.08	.04		337	Greg Brock	.07	.05	.03
248	Fred Lynn	.15	.11	.06		338	Mike Heath	.05	.04	.02
249	Paul Molitor	.12	.09	.05		339	Mike Greenwell	1.50	1.25	.60
250	Darrell Evans	.10	.08	.04		340	Claudell Washington	.07	.05	.03
251	Gary Ward	.07	.05	.03		341	Jose Gonzalez	.05	.04	.02
252	Bruce Hurst	.10	.08	.04		342	Mel Hall	.07	.05	.03
253	Bob Welch	.10	.08	.04		343	Jim Eisenreich	.07	.05	.03
254	Joe Carter	.12	.09	.05		344	Tony Bernazard	.05	.04	.02
255	Willie Wilson	.10	.08	.04		345	Tim Raines	.25	.20	.10
256	Mark McGwire	1.25	.90	.50		346	Bob Brower	.07	.05	.03
257	Mitch Webster	.07	.05	.03		347	Larry Parrish	.07	.05	.03
258	Brian Downing	.07	.05	.03		348	Thad Bosley	.05	.04	.02
259	Mike Stanley	.10	.08	.04		349	Dennis Eckersley	.12	.09	.05
260	Carlton Fisk	.20	.15	.08		350	Cory Snyder	.20	.15	.08
261	Billy Hatcher	.07	.05	.03		351	Rick Cerone	.05	.04	.02
262	Glenn Wilson	.07	.05	.03		352	John Shelby	.05	.04	.02
263	Ozzie Smith	.15	.11	.06		353	Larry Herndon	.05	.04	.02
264	Randy Ready	.05	.04	.02		354	John Habyan	.05	.04	.02
265	Kurt Stillwell	.10	.08	.04		355	*Chuck Crim*	.12	.09	.05
266	David Palmer	.05	.04	.02		356	Gus Polidor	.05	.04	.02
267	Mike Diaz	.07	.05	.03		357	Ken Dayley	.05	.04	.02
268	Rob Thompson	.07	.05	.03		358	Danny Darwin	.05	.04	.02
269	Andre Dawson	.20	.15	.08		359	Lance Parrish	.15	.11	.06

		MT	NR MT	EX
360	*James Steels*	.12	.09	.05
361	*Al Pedrique*(FC)	.15	.11	.06
362	Mike Aldrete	.07	.05	.03
363	Juan Castillo	.05	.04	.02
364	Len Dykstra	.10	.08	.04
365	Luis Quinones	.05	.04	.02
366	Jim Presley	.10	.08	.04
367	Lloyd Moseby	.07	.05	.03
368	Kirby Puckett	.50	.40	.25
369	Eric Davis	.80	.60	.30
370	Gary Redus	.05	.04	.02
371	Dave Schmidt	.05	.04	.02
372	Mark Clear	.05	.04	.02
373	Dave Bergman	.05	.04	.02
374	Charles Hudson	.05	.04	.02
375	Calvin Schiraldi	.05	.04	.02
376	Alex Trevino	.05	.04	.02
377	Tom Candiotti	.05	.04	.02
378	Steve Farr	.05	.04	.02
379	Mike Gallego	.05	.04	.02
380	Andy McGaffigan	.05	.04	.02
381	Kirk McCaskill	.07	.05	.03
382	Oddibe McDowell	.07	.05	.03
383	Floyd Bannister	.07	.05	.03
384	Denny Walling	.05	.04	.02
385	Don Carman	.07	.05	.03
386	Todd Worrell	.10	.08	.04
387	Eric Show	.07	.05	.03
388	Dave Parker	.20	.15	.08
389	Rick Mahler	.05	.04	.02
390	*Mike Dunne*	.25	.20	.08
391	Candy Maldonado	.07	.05	.03
392	Bob Dernier	.05	.04	.02
393	Dave Valle	.05	.04	.02
394	Ernie Whitt	.07	.05	.03
395	Juan Berenguer	.05	.04	.02
396	Mike Young	.05	.04	.02
397	Mike Felder	.05	.04	.02
398	Willie Hernandez	.07	.05	.03
399	Jim Rice	.30	.25	.12
400a	Checklist 358-467	.05	.04	.02
400b	Checklist 346-451	.10	.08	.04
401	Tommy John	.15	.11	.06
402	Brian Holton	.07	.05	.03
403	Carmen Castillo	.05	.04	.02
404	Jamie Quirk	.05	.04	.02
405	Dwayne Murphy	.07	.05	.03
406	*Jeff Parrett*(FC)	.25	.20	.10
407	Don Sutton	.20	.15	.08
408	Jerry Browne	.07	.05	.03
409	Jim Winn	.05	.04	.02
410	Dave Smith	.07	.05	.03
411	*Shane Mack*	.15	.11	.06
412	Greg Gross	.05	.04	.02
413	Nick Esasky	.07	.05	.03
414	Damaso Garcia	.05	.04	.02
415	Brian Fisher	.07	.05	.03
416	Brian Dayett	.05	.04	.02
417	Curt Ford	.05	.04	.02
418	*Mark Williamson*	.12	.09	.05
419	Bill Schroeder	.05	.04	.02
420	*Mike Henneman*	.25	.20	.10
421	*John Marzano*(FC)	.20	.15	.08
422	Ron Kittle	.07	.05	.03
423	Matt Young	.05	.04	.02
424	Steve Balboni	.07	.05	.03
425	*Luis Polonia*	.25	.20	.10
426	Randy St. Claire	.05	.04	.02
427	Greg Harris	.05	.04	.02
428	Johnny Ray	.07	.05	.03
429	Ray Searage	.05	.04	.02
430	Ricky Horton	.07	.05	.03
431	*Gerald Young*(FC)	.35	.25	.14
432	Rick Schu	.05	.04	.02
433	Paul O'Neill	.07	.05	.03
434	Rich Gossage	.15	.11	.06
435	John Cangelosi	.05	.04	.02
436	Mike LaCoss	.05	.04	.02
437	Gerald Perry	.10	.08	.04
438	Dave Martinez	.07	.05	.03
439	Darryl Strawberry	.35	.25	.14
440	John Moses	.05	.04	.02
441	Greg Gagne	.05	.04	.02
442	Jesse Barfield	.12	.09	.05
443	George Frazier	.05	.04	.02
444	Garth Iorg	.05	.04	.02
445	Ed Nunez	.05	.04	.02
446	Rick Aguilera	.05	.04	.02
447	Jerry Mumphrey	.05	.04	.02
448	Rafael Ramirez	.05	.04	.02
449	*John Smiley*	.35	.25	.14
450	Atlee Hammaker	.05	.04	.02
451	Lance McCullers	.07	.05	.03
452	Guy Hoffman(FC)	.07	.05	.03
453	Chris James	.12	.09	.05
454	Terry Pendleton	.07	.05	.03
455	*Dave Meads*	.15	.11	.06
456	Bill Buckner	.10	.08	.04
457	*John Pawlowski*(FC)	.10	.08	.04
458	Bob Sebra	.05	.04	.02
459	Jim Dwyer	.05	.04	.02
460	*Jay Aldrich*(FC)	.12	.09	.05
461	Frank Tanana	.07	.05	.03
462	Oil Can Boyd	.07	.05	.03
463	Dan Pasqua	.10	.08	.04
464	*Tim Crews*(FC)	.15	.11	.06
465	Andy Allanson	.07	.05	.03
466	*Bill Pecota*(FC)	.15	.11	.06
467	Steve Ontiveros	.05	.04	.02
468	Hubie Brooks	.10	.08	.04
469	*Paul Kilgus*(FC)	.20	.15	.08
470	Dale Mohorcic	.05	.04	.02
471	Dan Quisenberry	.07	.05	.03
472	Dave Stewart	.10	.08	.04
473	Dave Clark	.07	.05	.03
474	Joel Skinner	.05	.04	.02
475	Dave Anderson	.05	.04	.02
476	Dan Petry	.07	.05	.03
477	*Carl Nichols*(FC)	.12	.09	.05
478	Ernest Riles	.05	.04	.02
479	George Hendrick	.07	.05	.03
480	John Morris	.05	.04	.02
481	*Manny Hernandez*(FC)	.10	.08	.04
482	Jeff Stone	.05	.04	.02
483	Chris Brown	.07	.05	.03
484	Mike Bielecki	.05	.04	.02
485	Dave Dravecky	.07	.05	.03
486	Rick Manning	.05	.04	.02
487	Bill Almon	.05	.04	.02
488	Jim Sundberg	.07	.05	.03
489	Ken Phelps	.07	.05	.03
490	Tom Henke	.07	.05	.03
491	Dan Gladden	.05	.04	.02
492	Barry Larkin	.40	.30	.15
493	*Fred Manrique*(FC)	.15	.11	.06
494	Mike Griffin	.05	.04	.02
495	*Mark Knudson*(FC)	.10	.08	.04
496	Bill Madlock	.10	.08	.04
497	Tim Stoddard	.05	.04	.02
498	*Sam Horn*(FC)	.30	.25	.12
499	*Tracy Woodson*(FC)	.25	.20	.10
500a	Checklist 468-577	.05	.04	.02
500b	Checklist 452-557	.10	.08	.04
501	Ken Schrom	.05	.04	.02
502	Angel Salazar	.05	.04	.02
503	Eric Plunk	.05	.04	.02
504	Joe Hesketh	.05	.04	.02
505	Greg Minton	.05	.04	.02
506	Geno Petralli	.05	.04	.02
507	Bob James	.05	.04	.02
508	*Robbie Wine*(FC)	.12	.09	.05
509	Jeff Calhoun	.05	.04	.02
510	Steve Lake	.05	.04	.02
511	Mark Grant	.05	.04	.02
512	Frank Williams	.05	.04	.02
513	*Jeff Blauser*(FC)	.25	.20	.10
514	Bob Walk	.05	.04	.02
515	Craig Lefferts	.05	.04	.02
516	Manny Trillo	.07	.05	.03
517	Jerry Reed	.05	.04	.02
518	Rick Leach	.05	.04	.02
519	*Mark Davidson*	.12	.09	.05
520	*Jeff Ballard*(FC)	.35	.25	.14
521	*Dave Stapleton*(FC)	.10	.08	.04
522	Pat Sheridan	.05	.04	.02
523	Al Nipper	.05	.04	.02
524	Steve Trout	.05	.04	.02
525	Jeff Hamilton	.07	.05	.03
526	*Tommy Hinzo*(FC)	.15	.11	.06
527	Lonnie Smith	.07	.05	.03
528	*Greg Cadaret*(FC)	.20	.15	.08
529	Rob McClure (Bob)	.05	.04	.02
530	Chuck Finley	.10	.08	.04
531	Jeff Russell	.05	.04	.02
532	Steve Lyons	.05	.04	.02
533	Terry Puhl	.05	.04	.02
534	*Eric Nolte*(FC)	.15	.11	.06
535	Kent Tekulve	.07	.05	.03
536	*Pat Pacillo*(FC)	.15	.11	.06
537	Charlie Puleo	.05	.04	.02
538	*Tom Prince*(FC)	.15	.11	.06
539	Greg Maddux	.15	.11	.06

		MT	NR MT	EX
540	Jim Lindeman	.07	.05	.03
541	*Pete Stanicek*(FC)	.25	.20	.10
542	Steve Kiefer	.05	.04	.02
543	Jim Morrison	.05	.04	.02
544	Spike Owen	.05	.04	.02
545	*Jay Buhner*(FC)	.30	.25	.12
546	*Mike Devereaux*(FC)	.30	.25	.12
547	Jerry Don Gleaton	.05	.04	.02
548	Jose Rijo	.07	.05	.03
549	Dennis Martinez	.05	.04	.02
550	Mike Loynd	.05	.04	.02
551	Darrell Miller	.05	.04	.02
552	Dave LaPoint	.07	.05	.03
553	John Tudor	.10	.08	.04
554	*Rocky Childress*(FC)	.12	.09	.05
555	*Wally Ritchie*(FC)	.15	.11	.06
556	Terry McGriff	.05	.04	.02
557	Dave Leiper	.05	.04	.02
558	Jeff Robinson	.07	.05	.03
559	Jose Uribe	.05	.04	.02
560	Ted Simmons	.10	.08	.04
561	*Lester Lancaster*	.15	.11	.06
562	*Keith Miller*(FC)	.25	.20	.10
563	Harold Reynolds	.07	.05	.03
564	*Gene Larkin*	.20	.15	.08
565	Cecil Fielder	.05	.04	.02
566	Roy Smalley	.05	.04	.02
567	Duane Ward	.07	.05	.03
568	*Bill Wilkinson*(FC)	.15	.11	.06
569	Howard Johnson	.10	.08	.04
570	Frank DiPino	.05	.04	.02
571	*Pete Smith*(FC)	.20	.15	.08
572	Darnell Coles	.07	.05	.03
573	Don Robinson	.07	.05	.03
574	Rob Nelson	.05	.04	.02
575	Dennis Rasmussen	.10	.08	.04
576	Steve Jeltz (photo actually Juan Samuel)	.05	.04	.02
577	*Tom Pagnozzi*(FC)	.15	.11	.06
578	Ty Gainey	.05	.04	.02
579	Gary Lucas	.05	.04	.02
580	Ron Hassey	.05	.04	.02
581	Herm Winningham	.05	.04	.02
582	*Rene Gonzales*(FC)	.15	.11	.06
583	Brad Komminsk	.05	.04	.02
584	Doyle Alexander	.07	.05	.03
585	Jeff Sellers	.07	.05	.03
586	Bill Gullickson	.05	.04	.02
587	*Tim Belcher*(FC)	.50	.40	.20
588	*Doug Jones*(FC)	.35	.25	.14
589	*Melido Perez*(FC)	.30	.25	.12
590	Rick Honeycutt	.05	.04	.02
591	Pascual Perez	.07	.05	.03
592	Curt Wilkerson	.05	.04	.02
593	Steve Howe	.07	.05	.03
594	*John Davis*(FC)	.20	.15	.08
595	Storm Davis	.10	.08	.04
596	Sammy Stewart	.05	.04	.02
597	Neil Allen	.05	.04	.02
598	Alejandro Pena	.07	.05	.03
599	Mark Thurmond	.05	.04	.02
600a	Checklist 578-BC26	.05	.04	.02
600b	Checklist 558-660	.10	.08	.04
601	*Jose Mesa*(FC)	.20	.15	.08
602	*Don August*(FC)	.25	.20	.10
603	Terry Leach	.10	.08	.04
604	*Tom Newell*(FC)	.20	.15	.08
605	*Randall Byers*(FC)	.20	.15	.08
606	Jim Gott	.05	.04	.02
607	Harry Spilman	.05	.04	.02
608	John Candelaria	.07	.05	.03
609	*Mike Brumley*(FC)	.20	.15	.08
610	Mickey Brantley	.07	.05	.03
611	*Jose Nunez*(FC)	.25	.20	.10
612	Tom Nieto	.05	.04	.02
613	Rick Reuschel	.10	.08	.04
614	Lee Mazzilli	.12	.09	.05
615	*Scott Lusader*(FC)	.20	.15	.08
616	Bobby Meacham	.05	.04	.02
617	Kevin McReynolds	.15	.11	.06
618	Gene Garber	.05	.04	.02
619	*Barry Lyons*(FC)	.15	.11	.06
620	Randy Myers	.10	.08	.04
621	Donnie Moore	.05	.04	.02
622	Domingo Ramos	.05	.04	.02
623	Ed Romero	.05	.04	.02
624	*Greg Myers*(FC)	.20	.15	.08
625	Ripken Baseball Family (Billy Ripken, Cal Ripken, Jr., Cal Ripken, Sr.)	.15	.11	.06
626	Pat Perry	.05	.04	.02
627	Andres Thomas	.10	.08	.04

		MT	NR MT	EX
628	*Matt Williams*	.80	.60	.30
629	*Dave Hengel*(FC)	.20	.15	.08
630	Jeff Musselman	.07	.05	.03
631	Tim Laudner	.05	.04	.02
632	Bob Ojeda	.07	.05	.03
633	Rafael Santana	.05	.04	.02
634	*Wes Gardner*(FC)	.25	.20	.10
635	*Roberto Kelly*(FC)	1.00	.70	.40
636	Mike Flanagan	.12	.09	.05
637	*Jay Bell*(FC)	.20	.15	.08
638	Bob Melvin	.05	.04	.02
639	*Damon Berryhill*(FC)	.40	.30	.15
640	*David Wells*(FC)	.25	.20	.10
641	Stan Musial Puzzle Card	.05	.04	.02
642	Doug Sisk	.05	.04	.02
643	*Keith Hughes*(FC)	.20	.15	.08
644	*Tom Glavine*(FC)	.40	.30	.15
645	Al Newman	.05	.04	.02
646	Scott Sanderson	.05	.04	.02
647	Scott Terry	.10	.08	.04
648	Tim Teufel	.12	.09	.05
649	Garry Templeton	.12	.09	.05
650	Manny Lee	.05	.04	.02
651	Roger McDowell	.10	.08	.04
652	Mookie Wilson	.15	.11	.06
653	David Cone	.70	.50	.30
654	*Ron Gant*(FC)	.40	.30	.15
655	Joe Price	.12	.09	.05
656	George Bell	.25	.20	.10
657	*Gregg Jefferies*(FC)	5.00	3.75	2.00
658	*Todd Stottlemyre*(FC)	.50	.40	.20
659	*Geronimo Berroa*(FC)	.40	.30	.15
660	Jerry Royster	.12	.09	.05

1988 Donruss All-Stars

Keith Hernandez 1B

For the third consecutive year, this set of 64 cards featuring major league All-Stars was marketed in conjunction with Donruss Pop-Ups. The 1988 issue included a major change - the cards were reduced in size from 3-1/2" x 5" to a standard 2-1/2" x 3-1/2". The set features players from the 1987 All-Star Game starting lineup. Card fronts feature full-color photos, framed in blue, black and white, with a Donruss logo upper left. Player name and position appear in a red banner below the photo, along with the appropriate National or American League logo. All-Stars card backs include player stats and All-Star Game record. In 1988, All-Stars cards were distributed in individual packages containing three All-Stars, one Pop-Up and three Donruss puzzle pieces.

		MT	NR MT	EX
	Complete Set:	6.00	4.50	2.50
	Common Player:	.09	.07	.04
1	Don Mattingly	2.00	1.50	.80
2	Dave Winfield	.25	.20	.10
3	Willie Randolph	.09	.07	.04
4	Rickey Henderson	.50	.40	.20
5	Cal Ripken, Jr.	.30	.25	.12
6	George Bell	.20	.15	.08
7	Wade Boggs	.80	.60	.30
8	Bret Saberhagen	.15	.11	.06
9	Terry Kennedy	.09	.07	.04

		MT	NR MT	EX
10	John McNamara	.09	.07	.04
11	Jay Howell	.09	.07	.04
12	Harold Baines	.12	.09	.05
13	Harold Reynolds	.09	.07	.04
14	Bruce Hurst	.09	.07	.04
15	Kirby Puckett	.50	.40	.20
16	Matt Nokes	.20	.15	.08
17	Pat Tabler	.09	.07	.04
18	Dan Plesac	.12	.09	.05
19	Mark McGwire	1.00	.70	.40
20	Mike Witt	.09	.07	.04
21	Larry Parrish	.09	.07	.04
22	Alan Trammell	.20	.15	.08
23	Dwight Evans	.12	.09	.05
24	Jack Morris	.12	.09	.05
25	Tony Fernandez	.12	.09	.05
26	Mark Langston	.20	.15	.08
27	Kevin Seitzer	.40	.30	.15
28	Tom Henke	.09	.07	.04
29	Dave Righetti	.12	.09	.05
30	Oakland Coliseum	.09	.07	.04
31	Top Vote Getter (Wade Boggs)	.60	.45	.25
32	Checklist 1-32	.09	.07	.04
33	Jack Clark	.15	.11	.06
34	Darryl Strawberry	.40	.30	.15
35	Ryne Sandberg	.20	.15	.08
36	Andre Dawson	.20	.15	.08
37	Ozzie Smith	.15	.11	.06
38	Eric Davis	.50	.40	.20
39	Mike Schmidt	.40	.30	.15
40	Mike Scott	.12	.09	.05
41	Gary Carter	.12	.09	.05
42	Davey Johnson	.09	.07	.04
43	Rick Sutcliffe	.12	.09	.05
44	Willie McGee	.12	.09	.05
45	Hubie Brooks	.09	.07	.04
46	Dale Murphy	.40	.30	.15
47	Bo Diaz	.09	.07	.04
48	Pedro Guerrero	.15	.11	.06
49	Keith Hernandez	.15	.11	.06
50	Ozzie Virgil	.09	.07	.04
51	Tony Gwynn	.25	.20	.10
52	Rick Reuschel	.12	.09	.05
53	John Franco	.12	.09	.05
54	Jeffrey Leonard	.09	.07	.04
55	Juan Samuel	.15	.11	.06
56	Orel Hershiser	.20	.15	.08
57	Tim Raines	.20	.15	.08
58	Sid Fernandez	.12	.09	.05
59	Tim Wallach	.12	.09	.05
60	Lee Smith	.09	.07	.04
61	Steve Bedrosian	.12	.09	.05
62	MVP (Tim Raines)	.20	.15	.08
63	Top Vote Getter (Ozzie Smith)	.15	.11	.06
64	Checklist 33-64	.09	.07	.04

1988 Donruss Baseball's Best

The design of this 336-card set (2-1/2" by 3-1/2") is similar to the regular 1988 Donruss issue with the exception of the borders which are orange, instead of blue. Full-color player photos are framed by the Donruss logo upper left, team logo lower right and a bright red and white player name that spans the bottom margin. The backs are black and white, framed by a yellow border, and include personal information, year-by-year stats and major league totals. This set was packaged in a bright red cardboard box (10" x 11" x 12") that contained six individually shrink-wrapped packs of 56 cards. Donruss marketed the set via retail chain outlets including Walgreens, Venture, Wall-Mart, Ben Franklin, Shopko, Super X, Target, McCrory's, Osco, Woolworth and J.C. Murphy.

		MT	NR MT	EX
	Complete Set:	21.00	16.00	8.50
	Common Player:	.05	.04	.02
1	Don Mattingly	1.50	1.25	.60
2	Ron Gant	.10	.08	.04
3	Bob Boone	.05	.04	.02
4	Mark Grace	1.50	1.25	.60
5	Andy Allanson	.05	.04	.02
6	Kal Daniels	.12	.09	.05
7	Floyd Bannister	.07	.05	.03
8	Alan Ashby	.05	.04	.02
9	Marty Barrett	.07	.05	.03
10	Tim Belcher	.10	.08	.04
11	Harold Baines	.12	.09	.05
12	Hubie Brooks	.07	.05	.03
13	Doyle Alexander	.07	.05	.03
14	Gary Carter	.15	.11	.06
15	Glenn Braggs	.07	.05	.03
16	Steve Bedrosian	.07	.05	.03
17	Barry Bonds	.15	.11	.06
18	Bert Blyleven	.10	.08	.04
19	Tom Brunansky	.10	.08	.04
20	John Candelaria	.07	.05	.03
21	Shawn Abner	.15	.11	.06
22	Jose Canseco	1.25	.90	.50
23	Brett Butler	.07	.05	.03
24	Scott Bradley	.05	.04	.02
25	Ivan Calderon	.10	.08	.04
26	Rich Gossage	.10	.08	.04
27	Brian Downing	.07	.05	.03
28	Jim Rice	.10	.08	.04
29	Dion James	.05	.04	.02
30	Terry Kennedy	.07	.05	.03
31	George Bell	.10	.08	.04
32	Scott Fletcher	.05	.04	.02
33	Bobby Bonilla	.15	.11	.06
34	Tim Burke	.05	.04	.02
35	Darrell Evans	.07	.05	.03
36	Mike Davis	.05	.04	.02
37	Shawon Dunston	.15	.11	.06
38	Kevin Bass	.07	.05	.03
39	George Brett	.40	.30	.15
40	David Cone	.25	.20	.10
41	Ron Darling	.10	.08	.04
42	Roberto Alomar	.20	.15	.08
43	Dennis Eckersley	.10	.08	.04
44	Vince Coleman	.15	.11	.06
45	Sid Bream	.07	.05	.03
46	Gary Gaetti	.12	.09	.05
47	Phil Bradley	.12	.09	.05
48	Jim Clancy	.05	.04	.02
49	Jack Clark	.15	.11	.06
50	Mike Krukow	.05	.04	.02
51	Henry Cotto	.05	.04	.02
52	Rich Dotson	.07	.05	.03
53	Jim Gantner	.05	.04	.02
54	John Franco	.07	.05	.03
55	Pete Incaviglia	.12	.09	.05
56	Joe Carter	.20	.15	.08
57	Roger Clemens	.70	.50	.30
58	Gerald Perry	.10	.08	.04
59	Jack Howell	.05	.04	.02
60	Vance Law	.05	.04	.02
61	Jay Bell	.07	.05	.03
62	Eric Davis	.70	.50	.30
63	Gene Garber	.05	.04	.02
64	Glenn Davis	.12	.09	.05
65	Wade Boggs	1.00	.70	.40
66	Kirk Gibson	.20	.15	.08
67	Carlton Fisk	.15	.11	.06
68	Casey Candaele	.05	.04	.02
69	Mike Heath	.05	.04	.02
70	Kevin Elster	.15	.11	.06
71	Greg Brock	.07	.05	.03
72	Don Carman	.05	.04	.02
73	Doug Drabek	.07	.05	.03
74	Greg Gagne	.05	.04	.02
75	Danny Cox	.07	.05	.03
76	Rickey Henderson	.60	.45	.25
77	Chris Brown	.07	.05	.03
78	Terry Steinbach	.15	.11	.06
79	Will Clark	1.00	.70	.40

		MT	NR MT	EX
80	Mickey Brantley	.05	.04	.02
81	Ozzie Guillen	.07	.05	.03
82	Greg Maddux	.12	.09	.05
83	Kirk McCaskill	.05	.04	.02
84	Dwight Evans	.10	.08	.04
85	Ozzie Virgil	.05	.04	.02
86	Mike Morgan	.05	.04	.02
87	Tony Fernandez	.10	.08	.04
88	Jose Guzman	.05	.04	.02
89	Mike Dunne	.12	.09	.05
90	Andres Galarraga	.15	.11	.06
91	Mike Henneman	.10	.08	.04
92	Alfredo Griffin	.07	.05	.03
93	Rafael Palmeiro	.12	.09	.05
94	Jim Deshaies	.07	.05	.03
95	Mark Gubicza	.07	.05	.03
96	Dwight Gooden	.70	.50	.30
97	Howard Johnson	.25	.20	.10
98	Mark Davis	.05	.04	.02
99	Dave Stewart	.10	.08	.04
100	Joe Magrane	.12	.09	.05
101	Brian Fisher	.07	.05	.03
102	Kent Hrbek	.15	.11	.06
103	Kevin Gross	.05	.04	.02
104	Tom Henke	.07	.05	.03
105	Mike Pagliarulo	.10	.08	.04
106	Kelly Downs	.10	.08	.04
107	Alvin Davis	.12	.09	.05
108	Willie Randolph	.07	.05	.03
109	Rob Deer	.07	.05	.03
110	Bo Diaz	.05	.04	.02
111	Paul Kilgus	.10	.08	.04
112	Tom Candiotti	.05	.04	.02
113	Dale Murphy	.40	.30	.15
114	Rick Mahler	.05	.04	.02
115	Wally Joyner	.40	.30	.15
116	Ryne Sandberg	.25	.20	.10
117	John Farrell	.12	.09	.05
118	Nick Esasky	.05	.04	.02
119	Bo Jackson	.90	.70	.35
120	Bill Doran	.07	.05	.03
121	Ellis Burks	.70	.50	.30
122	Pedro Guerrero	.12	.09	.05
123	Dave LaPoint	.05	.04	.02
124	Neal Heaton	.05	.04	.02
125	Willie Hernandez	.05	.04	.02
126	Roger McDowell	.07	.05	.03
127	Ted Higuera	.10	.08	.04
128	Von Hayes	.10	.08	.04
129	Mike LaValliere	.07	.05	.03
130	Dan Gladden	.07	.05	.03
131	Willie McGee	.12	.09	.05
132	Al Lieter	.20	.15	.08
133	Mark Grant	.05	.04	.02
134	Bob Welch	.07	.05	.03
135	Dave Dravecky	.05	.04	.02
136	Mark Langston	.10	.08	.04
137	Dan Pasqua	.10	.08	.04
138	Rick Sutcliffe	.12	.09	.05
139	Dan Petry	.05	.04	.02
140	Rich Gedman	.07	.05	.03
141	Ken Griffey	.07	.05	.03
142	Eddie Murray	.10	.08	.04
143	Jimmy Key	.10	.08	.04
144	Dale Mohoric	.05	.04	.02
145	Jose Lind	.15	.11	.06
146	Dennis Martinez	.05	.04	.02
147	Chet Lemon	.07	.05	.03
148	Orel Hershiser	.20	.15	.08
149	Dave Martinez	.07	.05	.03
150	Billy Hatcher	.07	.05	.03
151	Charlie Leibrandt	.07	.05	.03
152	Keith Hernandez	.10	.08	.04
153	Kevin McReynolds	.12	.09	.05
154	Tony Gwynn	.30	.25	.12
155	Stan Javier	.05	.04	.02
156	Tony Pena	.07	.05	.03
157	Andy Van Slyke	.10	.08	.04
158	Gene Larkin	.07	.05	.03
159	Chris James	.10	.08	.04
160	Fred McGriff	.50	.40	.20
161	Rick Rhoden	.07	.05	.03
162	Scott Garrelts	.05	.04	.02
163	Mike Campbell	.12	.09	.05
164	Dave Righetti	.12	.09	.05
165	Paul Molitor	.15	.11	.06
166	Danny Jackson	.10	.08	.04
167	Pete O'Brien	.07	.05	.03
168	Julio Franco	.10	.08	.04
169	Mark McGwire	1.00	.70	.40
170	Zane Smith	.07	.05	.03
171	Johnny Ray	.07	.05	.03
172	Lester Lancaster	.07	.05	.03
173	Mel Hall	.05	.04	.02
174	Tracy Jones	.12	.09	.05
175	Kevin Seitzer	.35	.25	.14
176	Bob Knepper	.07	.05	.03
177	Mike Greenwell	.60	.45	.25
178	Mike Marshall	.10	.08	.04
179	Melido Perez	.15	.11	.06
180	Tim Raines	.30	.25	.12
181	Jack Morris	.12	.09	.05
182	Darryl Strawberry	.60	.45	.25
183	Robin Yount	.35	.25	.14
184	Lance Parrish	.15	.11	.06
185	Darnell Coles	.07	.05	.03
186	Kirby Puckett	.40	.30	.15
187	Terry Pendleton	.07	.05	.03
188	Don Slaught	.05	.04	.02
189	Jimmy Jones	.07	.05	.03
190	Dave Parker	.12	.09	.05
191	Mike Aldrete	.07	.05	.03
192	Mike Moore	.05	.04	.02
193	Greg Walker	.07	.05	.03
194	Calvin Schiraldi	.07	.05	.03
195	Dick Schofield	.05	.04	.02
196	Jody Reed	.25	.20	.10
197	Pete Smith	.10	.08	.04
198	Cal Ripken	.30	.25	.12
199	Lloyd Moseby	.07	.05	.03
200	Ruben Sierra	.25	.20	.10
201	R.J. Reynolds	.07	.05	.03
202	Bryn Smith	.05	.04	.02
203	Gary Pettis	.05	.04	.02
204	Steve Sax	.12	.09	.05
205	Frank DiPino	.05	.04	.02
206	Mike Scott	.12	.09	.05
207	Kurt Stillwell	.12	.09	.05
208	Mookie Wilson	.07	.05	.03
209	Lee Mazzilli	.05	.04	.02
210	Lance McCullers	.07	.05	.03
211	Rick Honeycutt	.05	.04	.02
212	John Tudor	.10	.08	.04
213	Jim Gott	.05	.04	.02
214	Frank Viola	.12	.09	.05
215	Juan Samuel	.10	.08	.04
216	Jesse Barfield	.12	.09	.05
217	Claudell Washington	.05	.04	.02
218	Rick Reuschel	.07	.05	.03
219	Jim Presley	.10	.08	.04
220	Tommy John	.12	.09	.05
221	Dan Plesac	.10	.08	.04
222	Barry Larkin	.20	.15	.08
223	Mike Stanley	.07	.05	.03
224	Cory Snyder	.25	.20	.10
225	Andre Dawson	.20	.15	.08
226	Ken Oberkfell	.05	.04	.02
227	Devon White	.20	.15	.08
228	Jamie Moyer	.05	.04	.02
229	Brook Jacoby	.10	.08	.04
230	Rob Murphy	.10	.08	.04
231	Bret Saberhagen	.20	.15	.08
232	Nolan Ryan	.50	.40	.20
233	Bruce Hurst	.10	.08	.04
234	Jesse Orosco	.07	.05	.03
235	Bobby Thigpen	.07	.05	.03
236	Pascual Perez	.05	.04	.02
237	Matt Nokes	.20	.15	.08
238	Bob Ojeda	.07	.05	.03
239	Joey Meyer	.07	.05	.03
240	Shane Rawley	.07	.05	.03
241	Jeff Robinson	.07	.05	.03
242	Jeff Reardon	.10	.08	.04
243	Ozzie Smith	.15	.11	.06
244	Dave Winfield	.30	.25	.12
245	John Kruk	.12	.09	.05
246	Carney Lansford	.07	.05	.03
247	Candy Maldonado	.07	.05	.03
248	Ken Phelps	.05	.04	.02
249	Ken Williams	.10	.08	.04
250	Al Nipper	.05	.04	.02
251	Mark McLemore	.05	.04	.02
252	Lee Smith	.07	.05	.03
253	Albert Hall	.05	.04	.02
254	Billy Ripken	.15	.11	.06
255	Kelly Gruber	.05	.04	.02
256	Charlie Hough	.07	.05	.03
257	John Smiley	.07	.05	.03
258	Tim Wallach	.10	.08	.04
259	Frank Tanana	.07	.05	.03
260	Mike Scioscia	.05	.04	.02
261	Damon Berryhill	.10	.08	.04

		MT	NR MT	EX
262	Dave Smith	.07	.05	.03
263	Willie Wilson	.10	.08	.04
264	Len Dykstra	.07	.05	.03
265	Randy Myers	.10	.08	.04
266	Keith Moreland	.07	.05	.03
267	Eric Plunk	.05	.04	.02
268	Todd Worrell	.10	.08	.04
269	Bob Walk	.05	.04	.02
270	Keith Atherton	.05	.04	.02
271	Mike Schmidt	.40	.30	.15
272	Mike Flanagan	.07	.05	.03
273	Rafael Santana	.05	.04	.02
274	Rob Thompson	.10	.08	.04
275	Rey Quinones	.05	.04	.02
276	Cecilio Guante	.05	.04	.02
277	B.J. Surhoff	.15	.11	.06
278	Chris Sabo	.80	.60	.30
279	Mitch Williams	.07	.05	.03
280	Greg Swindell	.10	.08	.04
281	Alan Trammell	.20	.15	.08
282	Storm Davis	.07	.05	.03
283	Chuck Finley	.05	.04	.02
284	Dave Stieb	.10	.08	.04
285	Scott Bailes	.05	.04	.02
286	Larry Sheets	.07	.05	.03
287	Danny Tartabull	.20	.15	.08
288	Checklist	.05	.04	.02
289	Todd Benzinger	.15	.11	.06
290	John Shelby	.05	.04	.02
291	Steve Lyons	.05	.04	.02
292	Mitch Webster	.05	.04	.02
293	Walt Terrell	.05	.04	.02
294	Pete Stanicek	.12	.09	.05
295	Chris Bosio	.05	.04	.02
296	Milt Thompson	.07	.05	.03
297	Fred Lynn	.12	.09	.05
298	Juan Berenguer	.05	.04	.02
299	Ken Dayley	.05	.04	.02
300	Joel Skinner	.05	.04	.02
301	Benito Santiago	.30	.25	.12
302	Ron Hassey	.05	.04	.02
303	Jose Uribe	.05	.04	.02
304	Harold Reynolds	.07	.05	.03
305	Dale Sveum	.07	.05	.03
306	Glenn Wilson	.05	.04	.02
307	Mike Witt	.07	.05	.03
308	Ron Robinson	.05	.04	.02
309	Denny Walling	.05	.04	.02
310	Joe Orsulak	.05	.04	.02
311	David Wells	.10	.08	.04
312	Steve Buechele	.05	.04	.02
313	Jose Oquendo	.05	.04	.02
314	Floyd Youmans	.07	.05	.03
315	Lou Whitaker	.12	.09	.05
316	Fernando Valenzuela	.12	.09	.05
317	Mike Boddicker	.07	.05	.03
318	Gerald Young	.15	.11	.06
319	Frank White	.07	.05	.03
320	Bill Wegman	.05	.04	.02
321	Tom Niedenfuer	.05	.04	.02
322	Ed Whitson	.05	.04	.02
323	Curt Young	.05	.04	.02
324	Greg Mathews	.10	.08	.04
325	Doug Jones	.07	.05	.03
326	Tommy Herr	.07	.05	.03
327	Kent Tekulve	.07	.05	.03
328	Rance Mulliniks	.05	.04	.02
329	Checklist	.05	.04	.02
330	Craig Lefferts	.05	.04	.02
331	Franklin Stubbs	.07	.05	.03
332	Rick Cerone	.05	.04	.02
333	Dave Schmidt	.05	.04	.02
334	Larry Parrish	.07	.05	.03
335	Tom Browning	.07	.05	.03
336	Checklist	.05	.04	.02

below. Each card features a large player closeup and a smaller full-figure inset on a split background that is white at the top and striped with multi-colors on the lower portion. Card backs are black and white with a blue border and contain the card number, DK logo, player name, team logo and a paragraph style career summary. A 12-piece Stan Musial puzzle was also included with the purchase of the super-size set which was marketed via a mail-in offer printed on Donruss wrappers.

		MT	NR MT	EX
Complete Set:		10.00	7.50	4.00
Common Player:		.20	.15	.08
1	Mark McGwire	1.25	.90	.50
2	Tim Raines	.30	.25	.12
3	Benito Santiago	.30	.25	.12
4	Alan Trammell	.30	.25	.12
5	Danny Tartabull	.35	.25	.14
6	Ron Darling	.30	.25	.12
7	Paul Molitor	.30	.25	.12
8	Devon White	.35	.25	.14
9	Andre Dawson	.30	.25	.12
10	Julio Franco	.25	.20	.10
11	Scott Fletcher	.20	.15	.08
12	Tony Fernandez	.30	.25	.12
13	Shane Rawley	.20	.15	.08
14	Kal Daniels	.30	.25	.12
15	Jack Clark	.30	.25	.12
16	Dwight Evans	.25	.20	.10
17	Tommy John	.25	.20	.10
18	Andy Van Slyke	.25	.20	.10
19	Gary Gaetti	.30	.25	.12
20	Mark Langston	.35	.25	.14
21	Will Clark	1.50	1.25	.60
22	Glenn Hubbard	.20	.15	.08
23	Billy Hatcher	.20	.15	.08
24	Bob Welch	.20	.15	.08
25	Ivan Calderon	.20	.15	.08
26	Cal Ripken, Jr.	.60	.45	.25
27	Checklist	.20	.15	.08
641	Stan Musial Puzzle Card	.20	.15	.08

1988 Donruss MVP

This 26-card set of standard-size player cards replaced the Donruss box-bottom cards in 1988.

1988 Donruss Diamond Kings Supers

This 28-card set (including the checklist) marks the fourth edition of Donruss' super-size (5"x7") set. These cards, exact duplicates of the 1988 Diamond Kings that feature player portraits by Dick Perez, have a red, blue and black striped border. A gold Diamond Kings banner curves above the player portrait and a matching oval name banner is printed

Instead of box-bottoms, the bonus cards (numbered BC-1 through BC-26) were randomly inserted in Donruss wax or rack packs. Cards feature the company's choice of Most Valuable Player for each major league team and are titled "Donruss MVP." The MVP cards were not included in the factory-collated sets. Card fronts carry the same basic red-blue-black flowing border design as the 1988 Donruss basic 660-card issue (with the exception of the Donruss MVP logo). Card backs are the same as the regular issue, except for the numbering system.

		MT	NR MT	EX
Complete Set:		5.00	3.75	2.00
Common Player:		.15	.11	.06
1	Cal Ripken	.30	.25	.12
2	Eric Davis	.50	.40	.20
3	Paul Molitor	.20	.15	.08
4	Mike Schmidt	.35	.25	.14
5	Ivan Calderon	.15	.11	.06
6	Tony Gwynn	.30	.25	.12
7	Wade Boggs	.75	.55	.30
8	Andy Van Slyke	.15	.11	.06
9	Joe Carter	.25	.20	.10
10	Andre Dawson	.25	.20	.10
11	Alan Trammell	.25	.20	.10
12	Mike Scott	.15	.11	.06
13	Wally Joyner	.25	.20	.10
14	Dale Murphy	.35	.25	.14
15	Kirby Puckett	.50	.40	.30
16	Pedro Guerrero	.20	.15	.08
17	Kevin Seitzer	.50	.40	.30
18	Tim Raines	.25	.20	.10
19	George Bell	.25	.20	.10
20	Darryl Strawberry	.50	.40	.30
21	Don Mattingly	1.50	1.25	.60
22	Ozzie Smith	.20	.15	.08
23	Mark McGwire	1.00	.70	.40
24	Will Clark	.90	.70	.35
25	Alvin Davis	.15	.11	.06
26	Ruben Sierra	.35	.25	.14

1988 Donruss Pop-Ups

Donruss introduced its Pop-Up cards in 1986. The first two annual issues featured 2-1/2" x 5" cards. In 1988, Donruss reduced the size of the Pop-Ups cards to a standard 2-1/2"x 3-1/2". The 1988 set includes 20 cards that fold out so that the upper portion of the player stands upright, giving a three-dimensional effect. Pop-ups feature players from the All-Star Game starting lineup. Card fronts feature full-color photos, with the player's name, team and position printed in black on a yellow banner near the bottom of the card front. As in previous issues, the card backs contain only the player's name, league and position. Pop-Ups were distributed in individual packages containing one Pop-Up, three puzzle pieces and three All-Star cards.

	MT	NR MT	EX
Complete Set:	4.00	3.00	1.50
Common Player:	.15	.11	.06

		MT	NR MT	EX
(1)	George Bell	.20	.15	.08
(2)	Wade Boggs	.75	.55	.30
(3)	Gary Carter	.20	.15	.08
(4)	Jack Clark	.20	.15	.08
(5)	Eric Davis	.50	.40	.20
(6)	Andre Dawson	.20	.15	.08
(7)	Rickey Henderson	.50	.40	.20
(8)	Davey Johnson	.15	.11	.06
(9)	Don Mattingly	1.00	.70	.40
(10)	Terry Kennedy	.15	.11	.06
(11)	John McNamara	.15	.11	.06
(12)	Willie Randolph	.15	.11	.06
(13)	Cal Ripken, Jr.	.50	.40	.20
(14)	Bret Saberhagen	.35	.25	.14
(15)	Ryne Sandberg	.40	.30	.15
(16)	Mike Schmidt	.60	.45	.25
(17)	Mike Scott	.15	.11	.06
(18)	Ozzie Smith	.20	.15	.08
(19)	Darryl Strawberry	.50	.40	.20
(20)	Dave Winfield	.25	.20	.10

1988 Donruss Rookies

For the third consecutive year, Donruss issued this 56-card boxed set highlighting current rookies. The complete set includes a checklist and a 15-piece Stan Musial Diamond Kings puzzle. As in previous years, the set is similar to the company's basic issue, with the exception of the logo and border color. Card fronts feature red, green and black-striped borders, with a red-and-white player name printed in the lower left corner beneath the full-color photo. "The Rookies" logo is printed in red, white and black in the lower right corner. The card backs are printed in black on bright aqua and include personal data, recent performance stats and major league totals, as well as 1984-88 year-by-year minor league stats. The cards are the standard 2-1/2" by 3-1/2" size.

		MT	NR MT	EX
Complete Set:		12.00	9.00	4.75
Common Player:		.10	.08	.04
1	Mark Grace	3.25	2.50	1.25
2	Mike Campbell	.10	.08	.04
3	Todd Frowirth(FC)	.20	.15	.08
4	Dave Stapleton	.10	.08	.04
5	Shawn Abner	.15	.11	.06
6	Jose Cecena(FC)	.25	.20	.10
7	Dave Gallagher(FC)	.25	.20	.10
8	Mark Parent(FC)	.25	.20	.10
9	Cecil Espy(FC)	.15	.11	.06
10	Pete Smith	.10	.08	.04
11	Jay Buhner	.20	.15	.08
12	Pat Borders(FC)	.30	.25	.12
13	Doug Jennings(FC)	.25	.20	.10
14	Brady Anderson(FC)	.40	.30	.15
15	Pete Stanicek	.15	.11	.06
16	Roberto Kelly	.30	.25	.12
17	Jeff Treadway	.15	.11	.06
18	Walt Weiss(FC)	.90	.70	.35
19	Paul Gibson(FC)	.20	.15	.08
20	Tim Crews	.10	.08	.04
21	Melido Perez	.15	.11	.06
22	Steve Peters(FC)	.20	.15	.08
23	Craig Worthington(FC)	.70	.50	.30
24	John Trautwein(FC)	.15	.11	.06

		MT	NR MT	EX
25	DeWayne Vaughn(FC)	.15	.11	.06
26	David Wells	.10	.08	.04
27	Al Leiter	.30	.25	.12
28	Tim Belcher	.20	.15	.08
29	Johnny Paredes(FC)	.20	.15	.08
30	Chris Sabo(FC)	.90	.70	.35
31	Damon Berryhill	.25	.20	.10
32	Randy Milligan(FC)	.20	.15	.08
33	Gary Thurman	.20	.15	.08
34	Kevin Elster	.20	.15	.08
35	Roberto Alomar	.30	.25	.12
36	Edgar Martinez(FC)	.25	.20	.10
37	Todd Stottlemyre	.15	.11	.06
38	Joey Meyer	.15	.11	.06
39	Carl Nichols	.10	.08	.04
40	Jack McDowell	.15	.11	.06
41	Jose Bautista(FC)	.20	.15	.08
42	Sil Campusano(FC)	.25	.20	.10
43	John Dopson(FC)	.20	.15	.08
44	Jody Reed	.35	.25	.14
45	Darrin Jackson(FC)	.20	.15	.08
46	Mike Capel(FC)	.20	.15	.08
47	Ron Gant	.20	.15	.08
48	John Davis	.10	.08	.04
49	Kevin Coffman(FC)	.15	.11	.06
50	Cris Carpenter(FC)	.35	.25	.14
51	Mackey Sasser	.10	.08	.04
52	Luis Alicea(FC)	.25	.20	.10
53	Bryan Harvey(FC)	.30	.25	.12
54	Steve Ellsworth(FC)	.15	.11	.06
55	Mike Macfarlane(FC)	.25	.20	.10
56	Checklist 1-56	.10	.08	.04

1989 Donruss

This basic annual issue consists of 660 standard-size (2-1/2" by 3-1/2") cards, including 26 Diamond Kings portrait cards and 20 Rated Rookies cards. Top and bottom borders of the cards are printed in a variety of colors that fade from dark to light (i.e. dark blue to light purple, bright red to pale yellow). A white-lettered player name is printed across the top margin. The team logo appears upper right and the Donruss logo lower left. A black stripe and thin white line make up the vertical side borders. The black outer stripe has a special varnish that gives a faintly visible filmstrip texture to the border. The backs (horizontal format) are printed in orange and black, similar to the 1988 design, with personal info, recent stats and major league totals. Team logo sticker cards (22 total) and Warren Spahn puzzle cards (63 total) are included in individual wax packs of cards.

		MT	NR MT	EX
Complete Set:		25.00	20.00	10.00
Common Player:		.04	.03	.02
1	Mike Greenwell (DK)	.60	.45	.25
2	Bobby Bonilla (DK)	.12	.09	.05
3	Pete Incaviglia (DK)	.12	.09	.05
4	Chris Sabo (DK)	.25	.20	.10
5	Robin Yount (DK)	.25	.20	.10
6	Tony Gwynn (DK)	.35	.25	.14
7	Carlton Fisk (DK)	.12	.09	.05
8	Cory Snyder (DK)	.15	.11	.06
9	David Cone (DK)	.35	.25	.14
10	Kevin Seitzer (DK)	.25	.20	.10

		MT	NR MT	EX
11	Rick Reuschel (DK)	.10	.08	.04
12	Johnny Ray (DK)	.10	.08	.04
13	Dave Schmidt (DK)	.08	.06	.03
14	Andres Galarraga (DK)	.15	.11	.06
15	Kirk Gibson (DK)	.20	.15	.08
16	Fred McGriff (DK)	.25	.20	.10
17	Mark Grace (DK)	1.25	.90	.50
18	Jeff Robinson (DK)	.12	.09	.05
19	Vince Coleman (DK)	.20	.15	.08
20	Dave Henderson (DK)	.10	.08	.04
21	Harold Reynolds (DK)	.08	.06	.03
22	Gerald Perry (DK)	.10	.08	.04
23	Frank Viola (DK)	.15	.11	.06
24	Steve Bedrosian (DK)	.10	.08	.04
25	Glenn Davis (DK)	.15	.11	.06
26	Don Mattingly (DK)	1.25	.90	.50
27	Checklist 1-27	.04	.03	.02
28	Sandy Alomar, Jr. (RR)(FC)	1.25	.90	.50
29	Steve Searcy (RR)(FC)	.30	.25	.12
30	Cameron Drew (RR)(FC)	.30	.25	.12
31	Gary Sheffield (RR)(FC)	1.75	1.25	.70
32	Erik Hanson (RR)(FC)	.35	.25	.14
33	Ken Griffey, Jr. (RR)(FC)	4.00	3.00	1.50
34	Greg Harris (RR)(FC)	.30	.25	.12
35	Gregg Jefferies (RR)	1.75	1.25	.70
36	Luis Medina (RR)(FC)	.40	.30	.15
37	Carlos Quintana (RR)	.30	.25	.12
38	Felix Jose (RR)(FC)	.25	.20	.10
39	Cris Carpenter (RR)(FC)	.35	.25	.14
40	Ron Jones (RR)(FC)	.35	.25	.14
41	Dave West (RR)(FC)	.60	.45	.25
42	Randy Johnson (RR)(FC)	.30	.25	.12
43	Mike Harkey (RR)(FC)	.30	.25	.12
44	Pete Harnisch (RR)(FC)	.30	.25	.12
45	Tom Gordon (RR)(FC)	2.50	2.00	1.00
46	Gregg Olson (RR)(FC)	1.50	1.25	.60
47	Alex Sanchez (RR)(FC)	.25	.20	.10
48	Ruben Sierra	.50	.40	.20
49	Rafael Palmeiro	.25	.20	.10
50	Ron Gant	.10	.08	.04
51	Cal Ripken, Jr.	.30	.25	.12
52	Wally Joyner	.20	.15	.08
53	Gary Carter	.20	.15	.08
54	Andy Van Slyke	.12	.09	.05
55	Robin Yount	.25	.20	.10
56	Pete Incaviglia	.10	.08	.04
57	Greg Brock	.06	.05	.02
58	Melido Perez	.08	.06	.03
59	Craig Lefferts	.04	.03	.02
60	Gary Pettis	.04	.03	.02
61	Danny Tartabull	.15	.11	.06
62	Guillermo Hernandez	.06	.05	.02
63	Ozzie Smith	.12	.09	.05
64	Gary Gaetti	.12	.09	.05
65	Mark Davis	.04	.03	.02
66	Lee Smith	.08	.06	.03
67	Dennis Eckersley	.10	.08	.04
68	Wade Boggs	.90	.70	.35
69	Mike Scott	.10	.08	.04
70	Fred McGriff	.50	.40	.20
71	Tom Browning	.08	.06	.03
72	Claudell Washington	.06	.05	.02
73	Mel Hall	.06	.05	.02
74	Don Mattingly	1.25	.90	.50
75	Steve Bedrosian	.08	.06	.03
76	Juan Samuel	.10	.08	.04
77	Mike Scioscia	.06	.05	.02
78	Dave Righetti	.12	.09	.05
79	Alfredo Griffin	.06	.05	.02
80	Eric Davis	.40	.30	.15
81	Juan Berenguer	.04	.03	.02
82	Todd Worrell	.08	.06	.03
83	Joe Carter	.12	.09	.05
84	Steve Sax	.12	.09	.05
85	Frank White	.06	.05	.02
86	John Kruk	.06	.05	.02
87	Rance Mulliniks	.04	.03	.02
88	Alan Ashby	.04	.03	.02
89	Charlie Leibrandt	.06	.05	.02
90	Frank Tanana	.06	.05	.02
91	Jose Canseco	1.25	.90	.50
92	Barry Bonds	.12	.09	.05
93	Harold Reynolds	.06	.05	.02
94	Mark McLemore	.04	.03	.02
95	Mark McGwire	.60	.45	.25
96	Eddie Murray	.25	.20	.10
97	Tim Raines	.25	.20	.10
98	Rob Thompson	.06	.05	.02
99	Kevin McReynolds	.12	.09	.05
100	Checklist 28-137	.04	.03	.02
101	Carlton Fisk	.20	.15	.08
102	Dave Martinez	.06	.05	.02

#	Player	MT	NR MT	EX
103	Glenn Braggs	.06	.05	.02
104	Dale Murphy	.30	.25	.12
105	Ryne Sandberg	.25	.20	.10
106	Dennis Martinez	.06	.05	.02
107	Pete O'Brien	.06	.05	.02
108	Dick Schofield	.04	.03	.02
109	Henry Cotto	.04	.03	.02
110	Mike Marshall	.12	.09	.05
111	Keith Moreland	.06	.05	.02
112	Tom Brunansky	.10	.08	.04
113	Kelly Gruber	.04	.03	.02
114	Brook Jacoby	.08	.06	.03
115	Keith Brown(FC)	.20	.15	.08
116	Matt Nokes	.15	.11	.06
117	Keith Hernandez	.20	.15	.08
118	Bob Forsch	.06	.05	.02
119	Bert Blyleven	.10	.08	.04
120	Willie Wilson	.08	.06	.03
121	Tommy Gregg	.08	.06	.03
122	Jim Rice	.25	.20	.10
123	Bob Knepper	.06	.05	.02
124	Danny Jackson	.12	.09	.05
125	Eric Plunk	.04	.03	.02
126	Brian Fisher	.06	.05	.02
127	Mike Pagliarulo	.08	.06	.03
128	Tony Gwynn	.30	.25	.12
129	Lance McCullers	.06	.05	.02
130	Andres Galarraga	.15	.11	.06
131	Jose Uribe	.04	.03	.02
132	Kirk Gibson	.20	.15	.08
133	David Palmer	.04	.03	.02
134	R.J. Reynolds	.04	.03	.02
135	Greg Walker	.06	.05	.02
136	Kirk McCaskill	.06	.05	.02
137	Shawon Dunston	.08	.06	.03
138	Andy Allanson	.04	.03	.02
139	Rob Murphy	.04	.03	.02
140	Mike Aldrete	.06	.05	.02
141	Terry Kennedy	.06	.05	.02
142	Scott Fletcher	.06	.05	.02
143	Steve Balboni	.06	.05	.02
144	Bret Saberhagen	.12	.09	.05
145	Ozzie Virgil	.04	.03	.02
146	Dale Sveum	.06	.05	.02
147	Darryl Strawberry	.35	.25	.14
148	Harold Baines	.10	.08	.04
149	George Bell	.25	.20	.10
150	Dave Parker	.12	.09	.05
151	Bobby Bonilla	.12	.09	.05
152	Mookie Wilson	.06	.05	.02
153	Ted Power	.04	.03	.02
154	Nolan Ryan	.35	.25	.14
155	Jeff Reardon	.08	.06	.03
156	Tim Wallach	.08	.06	.03
157	Jamie Moyer	.04	.03	.02
158	Rich Gossage	.10	.08	.04
159	Dave Winfield	.25	.20	.10
160	Von Hayes	.08	.06	.03
161	Willie McGee	.10	.08	.04
162	Rich Gedman	.06	.05	.02
163	Tony Pena	.06	.05	.02
164	Mike Morgan	.04	.03	.02
165	Charlie Hough	.06	.05	.02
166	Mike Stanley	.04	.03	.02
167	Andre Dawson	.20	.15	.08
168	Joe Boever(FC)	.04	.03	.02
169	Pete Stanicek	.08	.06	.03
170	Bob Boone	.06	.05	.02
171	Ron Darling	.10	.08	.04
172	Bob Walk	.04	.03	.02
173	Rob Deer	.06	.05	.02
174	Steve Buechele	.04	.03	.02
175	Ted Higuera	.08	.06	.03
176	Ozzie Guillen	.06	.05	.02
177	Candy Maldonado	.06	.05	.02
178	Doyle Alexander	.06	.05	.02
179	Mark Gubicza	.10	.08	.04
180	Alan Trammell	.15	.11	.06
181	Vince Coleman	.15	.11	.06
182	Kirby Puckett	.30	.25	.12
183	Chris Brown	.06	.05	.02
184	Marty Barrett	.06	.05	.02
185	Stan Javier	.04	.03	.02
186	Mike Greenwell	.60	.45	.25
187	Billy Hatcher	.06	.05	.02
188	Jimmy Key	.08	.06	.03
189	Nick Esasky	.06	.05	.02
190	Don Slaught	.04	.03	.02
191	Cory Snyder	.15	.11	.06
192	John Candelaria	.06	.05	.02
193	Mike Schmidt	.40	.30	.15
194	Kevin Gross	.06	.05	.02
195	John Tudor	.08	.06	.03
196	Neil Allen	.04	.03	.02
197	Orel Hershiser	.25	.20	.10
198	Kal Daniels	.15	.11	.06
199	Kent Hrbek	.15	.11	.06
200	Checklist 138-247	.04	.03	.02
201	Joe Magrane	.08	.06	.03
202	Scott Bailes	.04	.03	.02
203	Tim Belcher	.10	.08	.04
204	George Brett	.30	.25	.12
205	Benito Santiago	.12	.09	.05
206	Tony Fernandez	.10	.08	.04
207	Gerald Young	.10	.08	.04
208	Bo Jackson	.80	.60	.30
209	Chet Lemon	.06	.05	.02
210	Storm Davis	.08	.06	.03
211	Doug Drabek	.06	.05	.02
212	Mickey Brantley (photo actually Nelson Simmons)	.04	.03	.02
213	Devon White	.10	.08	.04
214	Dave Stewart	.08	.06	.03
215	Dave Schmidt	.04	.03	.02
216	Bryn Smith	.04	.03	.02
217	Brett Butler	.06	.05	.02
218	Bob Ojeda	.06	.05	.02
219	Steve Rosenberg(FC)	.20	.15	.08
220	Hubie Brooks	.08	.06	.03
221	B.J. Surhoff	.08	.06	.03
222	Rick Mahler	.04	.03	.02
223	Rick Sutcliffe	.08	.06	.03
224	Neal Heaton	.04	.03	.02
225	Mitch Williams	.06	.05	.02
226	Chuck Finley	.08	.06	.03
227	Mark Langston	.10	.08	.04
228	Jesse Orosco	.06	.05	.02
229	Ed Whitson	.04	.03	.02
230	Terry Pendleton	.08	.06	.03
231	Lloyd Moseby	.06	.05	.02
232	Greg Swindell	.10	.08	.04
233	John Franco	.08	.06	.03
234	Jack Morris	.15	.11	.06
235	Howard Johnson	.08	.06	.03
236	Glenn Davis	.12	.09	.05
237	Frank Viola	.12	.09	.05
238	Kevin Seitzer	.25	.20	.10
239	Gerald Perry	.08	.06	.03
240	Dwight Evans	.10	.08	.04
241	Jim Deshaies	.04	.03	.02
242	Bo Diaz	.06	.05	.02
243	Carney Lansford	.06	.05	.02
244	Mike LaValliere	.06	.05	.02
245	Rickey Henderson	.35	.25	.14
246	Roberto Alomar	.25	.20	.10
247	Jimmy Jones	.04	.03	.02
248	Pascual Perez	.06	.05	.02
249	Will Clark	.80	.60	.30
250	Fernando Valenzuela	.15	.11	.06
251	Shane Rawley	.06	.05	.02
252	Sid Bream	.06	.05	.02
253	Steve Lyons	.04	.03	.02
254	Brian Downing	.06	.05	.02
255	Mark Grace	1.50	1.25	.60
256	Tom Candiotti	.04	.03	.02
257	Barry Larkin	.20	.15	.08
258	Mike Krukow	.06	.05	.02
259	Billy Ripken	.06	.05	.02
260	Cecilio Guante	.04	.03	.02
261	Scott Bradley	.04	.03	.02
262	Floyd Bannister	.06	.05	.02
263	Pete Smith	.08	.06	.03
264	Jim Gantner	.04	.03	.02
265	Roger McDowell	.08	.06	.03
266	Bobby Thigpen	.08	.06	.03
267	Jim Clancy	.06	.05	.02
268	Terry Steinbach	.08	.06	.03
269	Mike Dunne	.08	.06	.03
270	Dwight Gooden	.50	.40	.20
271	Mike Heath	.04	.03	.02
272	Dave Smith	.06	.05	.02
273	Keith Atherton	.04	.03	.02
274	Tim Burke	.04	.03	.02
275	Damon Berryhill	.12	.09	.05
276	Vance Law	.06	.05	.02
277	Rich Dotson	.06	.05	.02
278	Lance Parrish	.15	.11	.06
279	Denny Walling	.04	.03	.02
280	Roger Clemens	.50	.40	.20
281	Greg Mathews	.06	.05	.02
282	Tom Niedenfuer	.06	.05	.02
283	Paul Kilgus	.10	.08	.04

		MT	NR MT	EX
284	Jose Guzman	.08	.06	.03
285	Calvin Schiraldi	.04	.03	.02
286	Charlie Puleo	.04	.03	.02
287	Joe Orsulak	.04	.03	.02
288	Jack Howell	.06	.05	.02
289	Kevin Elster	.08	.06	.03
290	Jose Lind	.10	.08	.04
291	Paul Molitor	.12	.09	.05
292	Cecil Espy	.08	.06	.03
293	Bill Wegman	.04	.03	.02
294	Dan Pasqua	.08	.06	.03
295	Scott Garrelts	.04	.03	.02
296	Walt Terrell	.06	.05	.02
297	Ed Hearn	.04	.03	.02
298	Lou Whitaker	.20	.15	.08
299	Ken Dayley	.04	.03	.02
300	Checklist 248-357	.04	.03	.02
301	Tommy Herr	.06	.05	.02
302	Mike Brumley	.06	.05	.02
303	Ellis Burks	.60	.45	.25
304	Curt Young	.06	.05	.02
305	Jody Reed	.10	.08	.04
306	Bill Doran	.06	.05	.02
307	David Wells	.06	.05	.02
308	Ron Robinson	.04	.03	.02
309	Rafael Santana	.04	.03	.02
310	Julio Franco	.10	.08	.04
311	Jack Clark	.15	.11	.06
312	Chris James	.08	.06	.03
313	Milt Thompson	.04	.03	.02
314	John Shelby	.04	.03	.02
315	Al Leiter	.15	.11	.06
316	Mike Davis	.06	.05	.02
317	*Chris Sabo*	.50	.40	.20
318	Greg Gagne	.04	.03	.02
319	Jose Oquendo	.04	.03	.02
320	John Farrell	.10	.08	.04
321	Franklin Stubbs	.04	.03	.02
322	Kurt Stillwell	.06	.05	.02
323	Shawn Abner	.10	.08	.04
324	Mike Flanagan	.06	.05	.02
325	Kevin Bass	.06	.05	.02
326	Pat Tabler	.06	.05	.02
327	Mike Henneman	.08	.06	.03
328	Rick Honeycutt	.04	.03	.02
329	John Smiley	.10	.08	.04
330	Rey Quinones	.04	.03	.02
331	Johnny Ray	.06	.05	.02
332	Bob Welch	.08	.06	.03
333	Larry Sheets	.06	.05	.02
334	Jeff Parrett	.08	.06	.03
335	Rick Reuschel	.08	.06	.03
336	Randy Myers	.10	.08	.04
337	Ken Williams	.06	.05	.02
338	Andy McGaffigan	.04	.03	.02
339	Joey Meyer	.08	.06	.03
340	Dion James	.04	.03	.02
341	Les Lancaster	.06	.05	.02
342	Tom Foley	.04	.03	.02
343	Geno Petralli	.04	.03	.02
344	Dan Petry	.06	.05	.02
345	Alvin Davis	.12	.09	.05
346	Mickey Hatcher	.04	.03	.02
347	Marvell Wynne	.04	.03	.02
348	Danny Cox	.06	.05	.02
349	Dave Stieb	.08	.06	.03
350	Jay Bell	.06	.05	.02
351	Jeff Treadway	.10	.08	.04
352	Luis Salazar	.04	.03	.02
353	Lenny Dykstra	.08	.06	.03
354	Juan Agosto	.04	.03	.02
355	Gene Larkin	.10	.08	.04
356	Steve Farr	.04	.03	.02
357	Paul Assenmacher	.04	.03	.02
358	Todd Benzinger	.12	.09	.05
359	Larry Andersen	.04	.03	.02
360	Paul O'Neill	.04	.03	.02
361	Ron Hassey	.04	.03	.02
362	Jim Gott	.04	.03	.02
363	Ken Phelps	.06	.05	.02
364	Tim Flannery	.04	.03	.02
365	Randy Ready	.04	.03	.02
366	*Nelson Santovenia*(FC)	.30	.25	.12
367	Kelly Downs	.08	.06	.03
368	Danny Heep	.04	.03	.02
369	Phil Bradley	.08	.06	.03
370	Jeff Robinson	.06	.05	.02
371	Ivan Calderon	.06	.05	.02
372	Mike Witt	.06	.05	.02
373	Greg Maddux	.10	.08	.04
374	Carmen Castillo	.04	.03	.02
375	Jose Rijo	.06	.05	.02
376	Joe Price	.04	.03	.02
377	R.C. Gonzalez	.04	.03	.02
378	Oddibe McDowell	.06	.05	.02
379	Jim Presley	.06	.05	.02
380	Brad Wellman	.04	.03	.02
381	Tom Glavine	.10	.08	.04
382	Dan Plesac	.08	.06	.03
383	Wally Backman	.06	.05	.02
384	*Dave Gallagher*	.25	.20	.10
385	Tom Henke	.06	.05	.02
386	Luis Polonia	.06	.05	.02
387	Junior Ortiz	.04	.03	.02
388	David Cone	.35	.25	.14
389	Dave Bergman	.04	.03	.02
390	Danny Darwin	.04	.03	.02
391	Dan Gladden	.04	.03	.02
392	*John Dopson*	.25	.20	.10
393	Frank DiPino	.04	.03	.02
394	Al Nipper	.04	.03	.02
395	Willie Randolph	.06	.05	.02
396	Don Carman	.06	.05	.02
397	Scott Terry	.06	.05	.02
398	Rick Cerone	.04	.03	.02
399	Tom Pagnozzi	.06	.05	.02
400	Checklist 358-467	.04	.03	.02
401	Mickey Tettleton	.08	.06	.03
402	Curtis Wilkerson	.04	.03	.02
403	Jeff Russell	.04	.03	.02
404	Pat Perry	.04	.03	.02
405	*Jose Alvarez*(FC)	.15	.11	.06
406	Rick Schu	.04	.03	.02
407	*Sherman Corbett*(FC)	.15	.11	.06
408	Dave Magadan	.10	.08	.04
409	Bob Kipper	.04	.03	.02
410	Don August	.08	.06	.03
411	Bob Brower	.04	.03	.02
412	Chris Bosio	.04	.03	.02
413	Jerry Reuss	.06	.05	.02
414	Atlee Hammaker	.04	.03	.02
415	Jim Walewander(FC)	.06	.05	.02
416	*Mike Macfarlane*	.20	.15	.08
417	Pat Sheridan	.04	.03	.02
418	Pedro Guerrero	.15	.11	.06
419	Allan Anderson	.06	.05	.02
420	*Mark Parent*	.20	.15	.08
421	Bob Stanley	.04	.03	.02
422	Mike Gallego	.04	.03	.02
423	Bruce Hurst	.08	.06	.03
424	Dave Meads	.04	.03	.02
425	Jesse Barfield	.10	.08	.04
426	*Rob Dibble*(FC)	.30	.25	.12
427	Joel Skinner	.04	.03	.02
428	Ron Kittle	.06	.05	.02
429	Rick Rhoden	.08	.06	.03
430	Bob Dernier	.04	.03	.02
431	Steve Jeltz	.04	.03	.02
432	Rick Dempsey	.06	.05	.02
433	Roberto Kelly	.10	.08	.04
434	Dave Anderson	.04	.03	.02
435	Herm Winningham	.04	.03	.02
436	Al Newman	.04	.03	.02
437	Jose DeLeon	.06	.05	.02
438	Doug Jones	.10	.08	.04
439	Brian Holton	.06	.05	.02
440	Jeff Montgomery(FC)	.06	.05	.02
441	Dickie Thon	.04	.03	.02
442	Cecil Fielder	.04	.03	.02
443	*John Fishel*(FC)	.20	.15	.08
444	Jerry Don Gleaton	.04	.03	.02
445	*Paul Gibson*	.15	.11	.06
446	Walt Weiss	.40	.30	.15
447	Glenn Wilson	.06	.05	.02
448	Mike Moore	.04	.03	.02
449	Chili Davis	.06	.05	.02
450	Dave Henderson	.08	.06	.03
451	*Jose Bautista*	.20	.15	.08
452	Rex Hudler	.04	.03	.02
453	Bob Brenly	.04	.03	.02
454	Mackey Sasser	.06	.05	.02
455	Daryl Boston	.04	.03	.02
456	Mike Fitzgerald	.04	.03	.02
457	Jeffery Leonard	.06	.05	.02
458	Bruce Sutter	.08	.06	.03
459	Mitch Webster	.06	.05	.02
460	Joe Hesketh	.04	.03	.02
461	Bobby Witt	.08	.06	.03
462	Stew Cliburn	.04	.03	.02
463	Scott Bankhead	.04	.03	.02
464	*Ramon Martinez*(FC)	.40	.30	.15
465	Dave Leiper	.04	.03	.02

		MT	NR MT	EX
466	*Luis Aliœa*	.20	.15	.08
467	John Cerutti	.06	.05	.02
468	Ron Washington	.04	.03	.02
469	Jeff Reed	.04	.03	.02
470	Jeff Robinson	.12	.09	.05
471	Sid Fernandez	.08	.06	.03
472	Terry Puhl	.04	.03	.02
473	Charlie Lea	.04	.03	.02
474	*Israel Sanchez*(FC)	.15	.11	.06
475	Bruce Benedict	.04	.03	.02
476	Oil Can Boyd	.06	.05	.02
477	Craig Reynolds	.04	.03	.02
478	Frank Williams	.04	.03	.02
479	Greg Cadaret	.10	.08	.04
480	*Randy Kramer*(FC)	.15	.11	.06
481	*Dave Eiland*(FC)	.20	.15	.08
482	Eric Show	.06	.05	.02
483	Garry Templeton	.06	.05	.02
484	Wallace Johnson(FC)	.04	.03	.02
485	Kevin Mitchell	.60	.45	.25
486	Tim Crews	.06	.05	.02
487	Mike Maddux	.04	.03	.02
488	Dave LaPoint	.06	.05	.02
489	Fred Manrique	.06	.05	.02
490	Greg Minton	.04	.03	.02
491	*Doug Dascenzo*(FC)	.25	.20	.10
492	Willie Upshaw	.06	.05	.02
493	*Jack Armstrong*(FC)	.20	.15	.08
494	Kirt Manwaring	.10	.08	.04
495	Jeff Ballard	.06	.05	.02
496	Jeff Kunkel	.04	.03	.02
497	Mike Campbell	.08	.06	.03
498	Gary Thurman	.10	.08	.04
499	Zane Smith	.06	.05	.02
500	Checklist 468-577	.04	.03	.02
501	Mike Birkbeck	.04	.03	.02
502	Terry Leach	.04	.03	.02
503	Shawn Hillegas	.06	.05	.02
504	Manny Lee	.04	.03	.02
505	*Doug Jennings*	.20	.15	.08
506	Ken Oberkfell	.04	.03	.02
507	Tim Teufel	.04	.03	.02
508	Tom Brookens	.04	.03	.02
509	Rafael Ramirez	.04	.03	.02
510	Fred Toliver	.04	.03	.02
511	*Brian Holman*(FC)	.20	.15	.08
512	Mike Bielecki	.04	.03	.02
513	*Jeff Pico*(FC)	.25	.20	.10
514	Charles Hudson	.04	.03	.02
515	Bruce Ruffin	.04	.03	.02
516	Larry McWilliams	.04	.03	.02
517	Jeff Sellers	.04	.03	.02
518	*John Costello*(FC)	.20	.15	.08
519	*Brady Anderson*	.35	.25	.14
520	Craig McMurtry	.04	.03	.02
521	Ray Hayward	.08	.06	.03
522	Drew Hall	.08	.06	.03
523	*Mark Lemke*(FC)	.20	.15	.08
524	*Oswald Peraza*(FC)	.20	.15	.08
525	*Bryan Harvey*	.25	.20	.10
526	Rick Aguilera	.04	.03	.02
527	Tom Prince	.06	.05	.02
528	Mark Clear	.04	.03	.02
529	Jerry Browne	.04	.03	.02
530	Juan Castillo	.04	.03	.02
531	Jack McDowell	.08	.06	.03
532	Chris Speier	.04	.03	.02
533	Darrell Evans	.08	.06	.03
534	Luis Aquino	.04	.03	.02
535	Eric King	.04	.03	.02
536	*Ken Hill*(FC)	.25	.20	.10
537	Randy Bush	.04	.03	.02
538	Shane Mack	.06	.05	.02
539	Tom Bolton(FC)	.06	.05	.02
540	Gene Nelson	.04	.03	.02
541	Wes Gardner	.06	.05	.02
542	Ken Caminiti	.06	.05	.02
543	Duane Ward	.04	.03	.02
544	*Norm Charlton*(FC)	.20	.15	.08
545	*Hal Morris*(FC)	.20	.15	.08
546	Rich Yett(FC)	.04	.03	.02
547	*Hensley Meulens*(FC)	.60	.45	.25
548	Greg Harris	.04	.03	.02
549	Darren Daulton	.04	.03	.02
550	Jeff Hamilton	.06	.05	.02
551	Luis Aguayo	.04	.03	.02
552	Tim Leary	.06	.05	.02
553	Ron Oester	.04	.03	.02
554	Steve Lombardozzi	.04	.03	.02
555	*Tim Jones*(FC)	.15	.11	.06
556	Bud Black	.04	.03	.02

		MT	NR MT	EX
557	Alejandro Pena	.04	.03	.02
558	*Jose DeJesus*(FC)	.15	.11	.06
559	Dennis Rasmussen	.08	.06	.03
560	*Pat Borders*	.20	.15	.08
561	*Craig Biggio*(FC)	.90	.70	.35
562	*Luis de los Santos*(FC)	.15	.11	.06
563	Fred Lynn	.10	.08	.04
564	*Todd Burns*(FC)	.30	.25	.12
565	Felix Fermin	.06	.05	.02
566	Darnell Coles	.06	.05	.02
567	Willie Fraser	.04	.03	.02
568	Glenn Hubbard	.04	.03	.02
569	*Craig Worthington*	.50	.40	.20
570	*Johnny Paredes*	.20	.15	.08
571	Don Robinson	.04	.03	.02
572	Barry Lyons	.04	.03	.02
573	Bill Long	.06	.05	.02
574	Tracy Jones	.10	.08	.04
575	Juan Nieves	.06	.05	.02
576	Andres Thomas	.06	.05	.02
577	*Rolando Roomes*(FC)	.35	.25	.14
578	Luis Rivera(FC)	.04	.03	.02
579	*Chad Kreuter*(FC)	.20	.15	.08
580	Tony Armas	.06	.05	.02
581	Jay Buhner	.10	.08	.04
582	Ricky Horton	.06	.05	.02
583	Andy Hawkins	.04	.03	.02
584	*Sil Campusano*	.20	.15	.08
585	Dave Clark	.06	.05	.02
586	*Van Snider*(FC)	.20	.15	.08
587	Todd Frohwirth(FC)	.06	.05	.02
588	Warren Spahn Puzzle Card	.04	.03	.02
589	*William Brennan*(FC)	.20	.15	.08
590	*German Gonzalez*(FC)	.20	.15	.08
591	Ernie Whitt	.06	.05	.02
592	Jeff Blauser	.08	.06	.03
593	Spike Owen	.04	.03	.02
594	Matt Williams	.10	.08	.04
595	Lloyd McClendon(FC)	.04	.03	.02
596	Steve Ontiveros	.04	.03	.02
597	*Scott Medvin*(FC)	.20	.15	.08
598	*Hipolito Pena*(FC)	.15	.11	.06
599	*Jerald Clark*(FC)	.25	.20	.10
600a	Checklist 578-BC26 (#635 is Kurt Schilling)	.15	.11	.06
600b	Checklist 578-BC26 (#635 is Curt Schilling)	.06	.05	.02
601	Carmelo Martinez	.04	.03	.02
602	Mike LaCoss	.04	.03	.02
603	Mike Devereaux	.15	.11	.06
604	*Alex Madrid*(FC)	.15	.11	.06
605	Gary Redus	.04	.03	.02
606	Lance Johnson	.06	.05	.02
607	*Terry Clark*(FC)	.15	.11	.06
608	Manny Trillo	.04	.03	.02
609	*Scott Jordan*(FC)	.15	.11	.06
610	Jay Howell	.06	.05	.02
611	*Francisco Melendez*(FC)	.25	.20	.10
612	Mike Boddicker	.06	.05	.02
613	Kevin Brown	.20	.15	.08
614	Dave Valle	.04	.03	.02
615	Tim Laudner	.04	.03	.02
616	*Andy Nezelek*(FC)	.20	.15	.08
617	Chuck Crim	.04	.03	.02
618	Jack Savage(FC)	.10	.08	.04
619	Adam Peterson(FC)	.10	.08	.04
620	Todd Stottlemyre	.10	.08	.04
621	*Lance Blankenship*(FC)	.25	.20	.10
622	*Miguel Garcia*(FC)	.15	.11	.06
623	Keith Miller	.06	.05	.02
624	*Ricky Jordan*(FC)	1.50	1.25	.60
625	Ernest Riles	.04	.03	.02
626	John Moses	.04	.03	.02
627	Nelson Liriano	.06	.05	.02
628	Mike Smithson	.04	.03	.02
629	Scott Sanderson	.04	.03	.02
630	Dale Mohorcic	.04	.03	.02
631	Marvin Freeman	.04	.03	.02
632	Mike Young	.04	.03	.02
633	Dennis Lamp	.04	.03	.02
634	*Dante Bichette*(FC)	.25	.20	.10
635	*Curt Schilling*(FC)	.15	.11	.06
636	*Scott May*(FC)	.15	.11	.06
637	*Mike Schooler*(FC)	.35	.25	.14
638	Rick Leach	.04	.03	.02
639	*Tom Lampkin*(FC)	.15	.11	.06
640	*Brian Meyer*(FC)	.15	.11	.06
641	Brian Harper	.04	.03	.02
642	*John Smoltz*(FC)	.60	.45	.25
643	40/40 Club (Jose Canseco)	.50	.40	.20
644	Bill Schroeder	.04	.03	.02

		MT	NR MT	EX
645	*Edgar Martinez*	.10	.08	.04
646	*Dennis Cook*(FC)	.35	.25	.14
647	Barry Jones	.04	.03	.02
648	59 and Counting (Orel Hershiser)	.15	.11	.06
649	*Rod Nichols*(FC)	.15	.11	.06
650	Jody Davis	.06	.05	.02
651	*Bob Milacki*(FC)	.25	.20	.10
652	Mike Jackson	.06	.05	.02
653	*Derek Lilliquist*(FC)	.35	.25	.14
654	Paul Mirabella	.04	.03	.02
655	Mike Diaz	.06	.05	.02
656	Jeff Musselman	.06	.05	.02
657	Jerry Reed	.04	.03	.02
658	*Kevin Blankenship*(FC)	.20	.15	.08
659	Wayne Tolleson	.04	.03	.02
660	*Eric Hetzel*(FC)	.20	.15	.08

		MT	NR MT	EX
39	Jamie Moyer	.06	.05	.02
40	Rick Rhoden	.08	.06	.03
41	Phil Bradley	.08	.06	.03
42	Paul Kilgus	.08	.06	.03
43	Milt Thompson	.06	.05	.02
44	Jerry Browne	.08	.06	.03
45	Bruce Hurst	.08	.06	.03
46	Claudell Washington	.08	.06	.03
47	Todd Benzinger	.12	.09	.05
48	Steve Balboni	.06	.05	.02
49	Oddibe McDowell	.08	.06	.03
50	Charles Hudson	.06	.05	.02
51	Ron Kittle	.08	.06	.03
52	Andy Hawkins	.06	.05	.02
53	Tom Brookens	.06	.05	.02
54	Tom Niedenfuer	.06	.05	.02
55	Jeff Parrett	.08	.06	.03
56	Checklist	.06	.05	.02

1989 Donruss Traded

Donruss issued its first "Traded" set in 1989, releasing a 56-card boxed set designed in the same style as the regular 1989 Donruss set. The set included a Stan Musial puzzle card and a checklist.

		MT	NR MT	EX
Complete Set:		6.00	4.50	2.50
Common Player:		.06	.05	.02
1	Jeffrey Leonard	.08	.06	.03
2	Jack Clark	.15	.11	.06
3	Kevin Gross	.06	.05	.02
4	Tommy Herr	.08	.06	.03
5	Bob Boone	.10	.08	.04
6	Rafael Palmeiro	.20	.15	.08
7	John Dopson	.15	.11	.06
8	Willie Randolph	.08	.06	.03
9	Chris Brown	.06	.05	.02
10	Wally Backman	.06	.05	.02
11	Steve Ontiveros	.06	.05	.02
12	Eddie Murray	.30	.25	.12
13	Lance McCullers	.08	.06	.03
14	Spike Owen	.06	.05	.02
15	Rob Murphy	.06	.05	.02
16	Pete O'Brien	.08	.06	.03
17	Ken Williams	.06	.05	.02
18	Nick Esasky	.06	.05	.02
19	Nolan Ryan	.50	.40	.20
20	Brian Holton	.06	.05	.02
21	Mike Moore	.08	.06	.03
22	Joel Skinner	.06	.05	.02
23	Steve Sax	.15	.11	.06
24	Rick Mahler	.06	.05	.02
25	Mike Aldrete	.06	.05	.02
26	Jesse Orosco	.08	.06	.03
27	Dave LaPoint	.06	.05	.02
28	Walt Terrell	.08	.06	.03
29	Eddie Williams	.08	.06	.03
30	Mike Devereaux	.10	.08	.04
31	Julio Franco	.15	.11	.06
32	Jim Clancy	.06	.05	.02
33	Felix Fermin	.06	.05	.02
34	Curtis Wilkerson	.06	.05	.02
35	Bert Blyleven	.12	.09	.05
36	Mel Hall	.08	.06	.03
37	Eric King	.06	.05	.02
38	Mitch Williams	.12	.09	.05

1989 Donruss Rookies

For the fourth straight year, Donruss issued a 56-card "Rookies" set in 1989. As in previous years, the set is similar in design to the regular Donruss set, except for a new "The Rookies" logo and a green and black border.

		MT	NR MT	EX
Complete Set:		25.00	20.00	10.00
Common Player:		.10	.08	.04
1	Gary Sheffield	.80	.60	.30
2	Gregg Jefferies	.80	.60	.30
3	Ken Griffey Jr.	2.50	2.00	1.00
4	Tom Gordon	1.50	1.25	.60
5	Billy Spiers(FC)	.35	.25	.14
6	Deion Sanders(FC)	1.50	1.25	.60
7	Donn Pall(FC)	.20	.15	.08
8	Steve Carter(FC)	.20	.15	.08
9	Francisco Oliveras(FC)	.15	.11	.06
10	Steve Wilson(FC)	.25	.20	.10
11	Bob Geren(FC)	.40	.30	.15
12	Tony Castillo(FC)	.15	.11	.06
13	Kenny Rogers(FC)	.20	.15	.08
14	Carlos Martinez(FC)	.20	.15	.08
15	Edgar Martinez	.10	.08	.04
16	Jim Abbott(FC)	3.00	2.25	1.25
17	Torey Lovullo(FC)	.20	.15	.08
18	Mark Carreon(FC)	.15	.11	.06
19	Geronimo Berroa	.10	.08	.04
20	Luis Medina	.10	.08	.04
21	Sandy Alomar Jr.	.40	.30	.15
22	Bob Milacki	.10	.08	.04
23	Joe Girardi(FC)	.25	.20	.10
24	German Gonzalez	.10	.08	.04
25	Craig Worthington	.15	.11	.06
26	Jerome Walton(FC)	5.00	3.75	2.00
27	Gary Wayne(FC)	.20	.15	.08
28	Tim Jones	.10	.08	.04
29	Dante Bichette	.10	.08	.04
30	Alexis Infante(FC)	.15	.11	.06
31	Ken Hill	.10	.08	.04
32	Dwight Smith(FC)	1.50	1.25	.60
33	Luis de los Santos	.10	.08	.04
34	Eric Yelding(FC)	.25	.20	.10
35	Gregg Olson	.70	.50	.30
36	Phil Stephenson(FC)	.15	.11	.06

		MT	NR MT	EX
37	Ken Patterson(FC)	.15	.11	.06
38	Rick Wrona(FC)	.25	.20	.10
39	Mike Brumley	.10	.08	.04
40	Cris Carpenter	.10	.08	.04
41	Jeff Brantley(FC)	.20	.15	.08
42	Ron Jones	.10	.08	.04
43	Randy Johnson	.10	.08	.04
44	Kevin Brown	.10	.08	.04
45	Ramon Martinez	.20	.15	.08
46	Greg Harris	.10	.08	.04
47	Steve Finley(FC)	.20	.15	.08
48	Randy Kramer	.10	.08	.04
49	Erik Hanson	.10	.08	.04
50	Matt Merullo(FC)	.15	.11	.06
51	Mike Devereaux	.10	.08	.04
52	Clay Parker(FC)	.15	.11	.06
53	Omar Vizquel(FC)	.20	.15	.08
54	Derek Lilliquist	.10	.08	.04
55	Junior Felix(FC)	1.25	.90	.50
56	Checklist	.10	.08	.04

1989 Donruss Pop-Ups

This set features the eighteen starters from the 1988 Major League All-Star game. The cards are designed with a perforated outline so each player can be popped out and made to stand upright. On the front side, each player's name, team, and position is featured in an orange-and-yellow rectangle below the borderless full-color photo. Each Pop-Up includes a unique double card, folded over and glued together on the back. The flip side features a red, white, and blue "Cincinnati Reds All-Star Game" logo at the top, a blue-lettered league designation, and the player's name and position in red. The lower portion of the flip side displays illustrated instructions for creating the base of the Pop-Up. The Pop-Ups were marketed in conjunction with All-Star and Warren Spahn Puzzle Cards.

		MT	NR MT	EX
	Complete Set:	6.00	4.50	2.50
	Common Player:	.20	.15	.08
(1)	Mark McGwire	.70	.50	.30
(2)	Jose Canseco	1.00	.70	.40
(3)	Paul Molitor	.30	.25	.12
(4)	Rickey Henderson	.50	.40	.20
(5)	Cal Ripken Jr.	.50	.40	.20
(6)	Dave Winfield	.40	.30	.15
(7)	Wade Boggs	1.00	.70	.40
(8)	Frank Viola	.30	.25	.12
(9)	Terry Steinbach	.20	.15	.08
(10)	Tom Kelly	.20	.15	.08
(11)	Will Clark	1.25	.90	.50
(12)	Darryl Strawberry	.70	.50	.30
(13)	Ryne Sandberg	.40	.30	.15
(14)	Andre Dawson	.35	.25	.14
(15)	Ozzie Smith	.30	.25	.12
(16)	Vince Coleman	.30	.25	.12
(17)	Bobby Bonilla	.30	.25	.12
(18)	Dwight Gooden	.50	.40	.20
(19)	Gary Carter	.20	.15	.08
(20)	Whitey Herzog	.20	.15	.08

1989 Donruss All-Stars

For the fourth consecutive year in conjunction with the Pop-Ups, Donruss featured a 64-card set with players from the 1988 All-Star Game. The card fronts include a red- to-gold fade or gold-to-red fade border and blue vertical side borders. The top border features the player's name and position along with the "Donruss 89" logo. Each full-color player photo is highlighted by a thin white line and includes a league logo in the lower right corner. Card backs reveal an orange-gold border and black and white printing. The player's ID and personal information is displayed with a gold star on both sides. The star in the left corner includes the card number. 1988 All-Star game statistics and run totals follow along with a career highlights feature surrounded by the team, All-Star Game MLB, MLBPA, and Leaf Inc. logos. The All-Stars were distributed in wax packages containing five All-Stars, one Pop-Up, and one three-piece Warren Spahn puzzle card.

		MT	NR MT	EX
	Complete Set:	5.00	3.75	2.00
	Common Player:	.09	.07	.04
1	Mark McGwire	.80	.60	.30
2	Jose Canseco	1.00	.70	.40
3	Paul Molitor	.12	.09	.05
4	Rickey Henderson	.30	.25	.12
5	Cal Ripken Jr.	.30	.25	.12
6	Dave Winfield	.20	.15	.08
7	Wade Boggs	.80	.60	.30
8	Frank Viola	.15	.11	.06
9	Terry Steinbach	.15	.11	.06
10	Tom Kelly	.09	.07	.04
11	George Brett	.12	.09	.05
12	Doyle Alexander	.09	.07	.04
13	Gary Gaetti	.12	.09	.05
14	Roger Clemens	.25	.20	.10
15	Mike Greenwell	.25	.20	.10
16	Dennis Eckersley	.12	.09	.05
17	Carney Lansford	.09	.07	.04
18	Mark Gubicza	.09	.07	.04
19	Tim Laudner	.09	.07	.04
20	Doug Jones	.09	.07	.04
21	Don Mattingly	1.50	1.25	.60
22	Dan Plesac	.12	.09	.05
23	Kirby Puckett	.30	.25	.12
24	Jeff Reardon	.09	.07	.04
25	Johnny Ray	.09	.07	.04
26	Jeff Russell	.09	.07	.04
27	Harold Reynolds	.09	.07	.04
28	Dave Stieb	.09	.07	.04
29	Kurt Stillwell	.09	.07	.04
30	Jose Canseco	1.25	.90	.50
31	Terry Steinbach	.15	.11	.06
32	AL Checklist	.09	.07	.05
33	Will Clark	1.25	.90	.50
34	Darryl Strawberry	.60	.45	.25
35	Ryne Sandberg	.20	.15	.08
36	Andre Dawson	.20	.15	.08
37	Ozzie Smith	.20	.15	.08
38	Vince Coleman	.15	.11	.06
39	Bobby Bonilla	.15	.11	.06
40	Dwight Gooden	.40	.30	.15
41	Gary Carter	.10	.08	.04
42	Whitey Herzog	.09	.07	.05
43	Shawon Dunston	.09	.07	.05
44	David Cone	.12	.09	.05

		MT	NR MT	EX
45	Andres Galarraga	.12	.09	.05
46	Mark Davis	.12	.09	.05
47	Barry Larkin	.12	.09	.05
48	Kevin Gross	.09	.07	.04
49	Vance Law	.09	.07	.04
50	Orel Hershiser	.20	.15	.08
51	Willie McGee	.09	.07	.04
52	Danny Jackson	.09	.07	.04
53	Rafael Palmeiro	.09	.07	.04
54	Bob Knepper	.09	.07	.04
55	Lance Parrish	.09	.07	.04
56	Greg Maddux	.20	.15	.08
57	Gerald Perry	.09	.07	.04
58	Bob Walk	.09	.07	.04
59	Chris Sabo	.12	.09	.04
60	Todd Worrell	.12	.09	.04
61	Andy Van Slyke	.12	.09	.04
62	Ozzie Smith	.20	.15	.08
63	Riverfront Stadium	.09	.07	.04
64	NL Checklist	.09	.07	.04

		MT	NR MT	EX
26	Ruben Sierra	.15	.11	.06

1989 Donruss Baseball's Best

For the second consecutive year, Donruss issued a "Baseball's Best" set in 1989 to highlight the game's top players. The special 336-card set was packaged in a special box and was sold at various retail chains nationwide following the conclusion of the 1989 baseball season. The cards are styled after the regular 1989 Donruss set with green borders and a glossy finish. The set included a Warren Spahn puzzle.

1989 Donruss MVP

This 26-card set, numbered BC-1 through BC-26, was randomly packed in Donruss wax packs, but were not included in factory sets or other card packs. Players highlighted in this set are selected by Donruss, one player per team. MVP cards feature a variation of the design in the basic Donruss issue, with multi-color upper and lower borders and black side borders. The player name and Donruss '89 logos appear in the upper margin with the team logo appearing lower right. The "MVP" designation in large, bright letters serves as a backdrop for the full-color player photo. The cards measure 2-1/2" by 3-1/2" in size.

		MT	NR MT	EX
	Complete Set:	4.00	3.00	1.50
	Common Player:	.15	.11	.06
1	Kirby Puckett	.50	.40	.20
2	Mike Scott	.15	.11	.06
3	Joe Carter	.20	.15	.08
4	Orel Hershiser	.25	.20	.10
5	Jose Canseco	.75	.55	.30
6	Darryl Strawberry	.60	.45	.25
7	George Brett	.35	.25	.14
8	Andre Dawson	.25	.20	.10
9	Paul Molitor	.20	.15	.08
10	Andy Van Slyke	.15	.11	.06
11	Dave Winfield	.20	.15	.08
12	Kevin Gross	.15	.11	.06
13	Mike Greenwell	.60	.45	.25
14	Ozzie Smith	.20	.15	.08
15	Cal Ripken	.30	.25	.12
16	Andres Galarraga	.20	.15	.08
17	Alan Trammell	.25	.20	.10
18	Kal Daniels	.20	.15	.08
19	Fred McGriff	.35	.25	.14
20	Tony Gwynn	.30	.25	.12
21	Wally Joyner	.30	.25	.12
22	Will Clark	.75	.55	.30
23	Ozzie Guillen	.15	.11	.06
24	Gerald Perry	.15	.11	.06
25	Alvin Davis	.15	.11	.06

		MT	NR MT	EX
	Complete Set:	15.00	11.00	6.00
	Common Player:	.05	.04	.02
1	Don Mattingly	2.00	1.50	.80
2	Tom Glavine	.08	.06	.03
3	Bert Blyleven	.08	.06	.03
4	Andre Dawson	.10	.08	.04
5	Pete O'Brien	.05	.04	.02
6	Eric Davis	.70	.50	.30
7	George Brett	.10	.08	.04
8	Glenn Davis	.10	.08	.04
9	Ellis Burks	.50	.40	.20
10	Kirk Gibson	.08	.06	.03
11	Carlton Fisk	.08	.06	.03
12	Andres Galarraga	.08	.06	.03
13	Alan Trammell	.06	.05	.02
14	Dwight Gooden	.60	.45	.25
15	Paul Molitor	.10	.08	.04
16	Roger McDowell	.05	.04	.02
17	Doug Drabek	.05	.04	.02
18	Kent Hrbek	.08	.06	.03
19	Vince Coleman	.08	.06	.03
20	Steve Sax	.08	.06	.03
21	Roberto Alomar	.30	.25	.12
22	Carney Lansford	.06	.05	.02
23	Will Clark	1.50	1.25	.60
24	Alvin Davis	.08	.06	.03
25	Bobby Thigpen	.08	.06	.03
26	Ryne Sandberg	.25	.20	.10
27	Devon White	.08	.06	.03
28	Mike Greenwell	.40	.30	.15
29	Dale Murphy	.10	.08	.04
30	Jeff Ballard	.10	.08	.04
31	Kelly Gruber	.08	.06	.03
32	Julio Franco	.07	.05	.03
33	Bobby Bonilla	.15	.11	.06
34	Tim Wallach	.05	.04	.02
35	Lou Whitaker	.07	.05	.03
36	Jay Howell	.07	.05	.03
37	Greg Maddux	.30	.25	.12
38	Bill Doran	.07	.05	.03
39	Danny Tartabull	.12	.09	.05
40	Darryl Strawberry	.50	.40	.20
41	Ron Darling	.10	.08	.06
42	Tony Gwynn	.30	.25	.12
43	Mark McGwire	.80	.60	.30
44	Ozzie Smith	.15	.11	.06
45	Andy Van Slyke	.12	.09	.05
46	Juan Berenguer	.05	.04	.02
47	Von Hayes	.08	.06	.03
48	Tony Fernandez	.12	.09	.05

		MT	NR MT	EX
49	Eric Plunk	.05	.04	.02
50	Ernest Riles	.05	.04	.02
51	Harold Reynolds	.07	.05	.03
52	Andy Hawkins	.06	.05	.02
53	Robin Yount	.35	.25	.14
54	Danny Jackson	.06	.05	.02
55	Nolan Ryan	.40	.30	.15
56	Joe Carter	.12	.09	.05
57	Jose Canseco	1.00	.70	.40
58	Jody Davis	.05	.04	.02
59	Lance Parrish	.06	.05	.02
60	Mitch Williams	.15	.11	.06
61	Brook Jacoby	.06	.05	.02
62	Tom Browning	.10	.08	.06
63	Kurt Stillwell	.06	.05	.02
64	Rafael Ramirez	.05	.04	.02
65	Roger Clemens	.50	.40	.20
66	Mike Scioscia	.07	.05	.02
67	Dave Gallagher	.07	.05	.02
68	Mark Langston	.15	.11	.06
69	Chet Lemon	.06	.05	.02
70	Kevin McReynolds	.25	.20	.10
71	Rob Deer	.06	.05	.02
72	Tommy Herr	.07	.05	.03
73	Barry Bonds	.12	.09	.05
74	Frank Viola	.15	.11	.06
75	Pedro Guerrero	.15	.11	.06
76	Dave Righetti	.07	.05	.03
77	Bruce Hurst	.08	.06	.03
78	Rickey Henderson	.40	.30	.15
79	Robby Thompson	.08	.06	.03
80	Randy Johnson	.25	.20	.10
81	Harold Baines	.12	.09	.05
82	Calvin Schiraldi	.05	.04	.02
83	Kirk McCaskill	.05	.04	.02
84	Lee Smith	.07	.05	.03
85	John Smoltz	.25	.20	.10
86	Mickey Tettleton	.20	.15	.08
87	Jimmy Key	.08	.06	.03
88	Rafael Palmeiro	.10	.08	.04
89	Sid Bream	.05	.04	.02
90	Dennis Martinez	.05	.04	.02
91	Frank Tanana	.05	.04	.02
92	Eddie Murray	.15	.11	.06
93	Shawon Dunston	.15	.11	.06
94	Mike Scott	.10	.08	.04
95	Bret Saberhagen	.25	.20	.10
96	David Cone	.20	.15	.08
97	Kevin Elster	.05	.04	.02
98	Jack Clark	.20	.15	.08
99	Dave Stewart	.20	.15	.08
100	Jose Oquendo	.06	.05	.02
101	Jose Lind	.05	.04	.02
102	Gary Gaetti	.12	.09	.05
103	Ricky Jordan	.25	.20	.10
104	Fred McGriff	.50	.40	.20
105	Don Slaught	.05	.04	.02
106	Jose Uribe	.05	.04	.02
107	Jeffrey Leonard	.07	.05	.02
108	Lee Guetterman	.05	.04	.02
109	Chris Bosio	.08	.06	.03
110	Barry Larkin	.15	.11	.06
111	Ruben Sierra	.30	.25	.12
112	Greg Swindell	.12	.09	.05
113	Gary Sheffield	.90	.70	.40
114	Lonnie Smith	.10	.08	.04
115	Chili Davis	.08	.06	.03
116	Damon Berryhill	.08	.06	.03
117	Tom Candiotti	.05	.04	.02
118	Kal Daniels	.10	.08	.04
119	Mark Gubicza	.10	.08	.04
120	Jim Deshaies	.08	.06	.03
121	Dwight Evans	.10	.08	.04
122	Mike Morgan	.05	.04	.02
123	Dan Pasqua	.05	.04	.02
124	Bryn Smith	.07	.05	.03
125	Doyle Alexander	.07	.05	.03
126	Howard Johnson	.25	.20	.10
127	Chuck Crim	.07	.05	.03
128	Darren Daulton	.05	.04	.02
129	**Jeff Robinson**	**.08**	**.06**	**.03**
130	**Kirby Puckett**	**.50**	**.40**	**.20**
131	**Joe Magrane**	**.10**	**.08**	**.04**
132	**Jesse Barfield**	**.07**	**.05**	**.03**
133	**Mark Davis ((Photo actually Dave Leiper))**			
		.25	.20	.10
134	Dennis Eckersley	.10	.08	.04
135	Mike Krukow	.05	.04	.02
136	Jay Buhner	.10	.08	.04
137	Ozzie Guillen	.08	.06	.03
138	Rick Sutcliffe	.12	.09	.05

		MT	NR MT	EX
139	Wally Joyner	.25	.20	.10
140	Wade Boggs	1.00	.70	.40
141	Jeff Treadway	.08	.06	.05
142	Cal Ripken	.30	.25	.12
143	Dave Steib	.10	.08	.04
144	Pete Incaviglia	.07	.05	.03
145	Bob Walk	.05	.04	.02
146	Nelson Santovenia	.10	.08	.04
147	Mike Heath	.05	.04	.02
148	Willie Randolph	.08	.06	.03
149	Paul Kilgus	.05	.04	.02
150	Billy Hatcher	.07	.05	.03
151	Steve Farr	.05	.04	.02
152	Gregg Jefferies	1.00	.70	.40
153	Randy Myers	.06	.05	.02
154	Garry Templeton	.06	.05	.02
155	Walt Weiss	.10	.08	.04
156	Terry Pendleton	.10	.08	.04
157	John Smiley	.08	.06	.03
158	Greg Gagne	.05	.04	.02
159	Lenny Dykstra	.08	.06	.03
160	Nelson Liriano	.05	.04	.02
161	Alvaro Espinosa	.70	.50	.30
162	Rick Reuschel	.08	.06	.03
163	Omar Vizquel	.35	.25	.14
164	Clay Parker	.15	.11	.06
165	Dan Plesac	.06	.05	.02
166	John Franco	.06	.05	.02
167	Scott Fletcher	.06	.05	.02
168	Cory Snyder	.12	.09	.05
169	Bo Jackson	1.00	.70	.40
170	Tommy Gregg	.08	.06	.03
171	**Jim Abbott**	**1.25**	**.90**	**.50**
172	**Jerome Walton**	**1.75**	**1.25**	**.70**
173	**Doug Jones**	**.06**	**.05**	**.02**
174	**Todd Benzinger**	**.08**	**.06**	**.03**
175	**Frank White**	**.08**	**.06**	**.03**
176	**Craig Biggio**	**.20**	**.15**	**.08**
177	**John Dopson**	**.10**	**.08**	**.06**
178	**Alfredo Griffin**	**.06**	**.05**	**.02**
179	**Melido Perez**	**.06**	**.05**	**.02**
180	**Tim Burke**	**.06**	**.05**	**.02**
181	Matt Nokes	.10	.08	.04
182	Gary Carter	.10	.08	.04
183	Ted Higuera	.08	.06	.03
184	Ken Howell	.05	.04	.02
185	Rey Quinones	.05	.04	.02
186	Wally Backman	.07	.05	.03
187	Tom Brunansky	.07	.05	.03
188	Steve Balboni	.05	.04	.02
189	Marvell Wynne	.05	.04	.02
190	Dave Henderson	.08	.06	.03
191	Don Robinson	.05	.04	.02
192	Ken Griffey Jr.	1.50	1.25	.60
193	Ivan Calderon	.05	.04	.02
194	Mike Bielecki	.07	.05	.03
195	Johnny Ray	.07	.05	.03
196	Rob Murphy	.05	.04	.02
197	Andres Thomas	.05	.04	.02
198	Phil Bradley	.06	.05	.02
199	Junior Felix	.70	.50	.30
200	Jeff Russell	.08	.06	.03
201	Mike LaValliere	.05	.04	.02
202	Kevin Gross	.06	.05	.02
203	Keith Moreland	.06	.05	.02
204	Mike Marshall	.06	.05	.02
205	Dwight Smith	.90	.70	.40
206	Jim Clancy	.05	.04	.02
207	Kevin Seitzer	.10	.08	.04
208	Keith Hernandez	.10	.08	.04
209	Bob Ojeda	.06	.05	.02
210	Ed Whitson	.06	.05	.02
211	Tony Phillips	.06	.05	.02
212	Milt Thompson	.05	.04	.02
213	Randy Kramer	.05	.04	.02
214	Randy Bush	.05	.04	.02
215	Randy Ready	.05	.04	.02
216	Duane Ward	.05	.04	.02
217	Jimmy Jones	.05	.04	.02
218	Scott Garrelts	.08	.06	.03
219	Scott Bankhead	.10	.08	.04
220	Lance McCullers	.06	.05	.02
221	B.J. Surhoff	.06	.05	.02
222	Chris Sabo	.06	.05	.02
223	Steve Buechele	.06	.05	.02
224	Joel Skinner	.05	.04	.02
225	Orel Hershiser	.15	.11	.06
226	Derek Lilliquist	.10	.08	.06
227	Claudell Washington	.08	.06	.05
228	Lloyd McClendon	.10	.08	.04
229	Felix Fermin	.05	.04	.02

		MT	NR MT	EX
230	Paul O'Neill	.08	.06	.03
231	Charlie Leibrandt	.05	.04	.02
232	Dave Smith	.06	.05	.02
233	Bob Stanley	.05	.04	.02
234	Tim Belcher	.15	.11	.06
235	Eric King	.05	.04	.02
236	Spike Owen	.05	.04	.02
237	Mike Henneman	.05	.04	.02
238	Juan Samuel	.06	.05	.02
239	Greg Brock	.06	.05	.02
240	John Kruk	.06	.05	.02
241	Glenn Wilson	.06	.05	.02
242	Jeff Reardon	.06	.05	.02
243	Todd Worrell	.08	.06	.03
244	Dave LaPoint	.05	.04	.02
245	Walt Terrell	.05	.04	.02
246	Mike Moore	.08	.06	.03
247	Kelly Downs	.05	.04	.02
248	Dave Valle	.05	.04	.02
249	Ron Kittle	.06	.05	.04
250	Steve Wilson	.10	.08	.04
251	Dick Schofield	.05	.04	.02
252	Marty Barrett	.06	.05	.02
253	Dion James	.06	.05	.02
254	Bob Milacki	.10	.08	.04
255	Ernie Whitt	.06	.05	.02
256	Kevin Brown	.08	.06	.03
257	R.J. Reynolds	.05	.04	.02
258	Tim Raines	.10	.08	.04
259	Frank Williams	.05	.04	.02
260	Jose Gonzalez	.05	.04	.02
261	Mitch Webster	.05	.04	.02
262	Ken Caminiti	.07	.05	.03
263	Bob Boone	.07	.05	.03
264	Dave Magadan	.07	.05	.03
265	Rick Aguilera	.05	.04	.02
266	Chris James	.05	.04	.02
267	Bob Welch	.07	.05	.03
268	Ken Dayley	.05	.04	.02
269	Junior Ortiz	.05	.04	.02
270	Allan Anderson	.08	.06	.03
271	Steve Jeltz	.05	.04	.02
272	George Bell	.10	.08	.04
273	Roberto Kelly	.10	.08	.04
274	Brett Butler	.07	.05	.03
275	Mike Schooler	.07	.05	.02
276	Ken Phelps	.05	.04	.02
277	Glenn Braggs	.06	.05	.02
278	Jose Rijo	.06	.05	.02
279	Bobby Witt	.06	.05	.02
280	Jerry Browne	.06	.05	.02
281	Kevin Mitchell	.70	.50	.30
282	Craig Worthington	.30	.25	.12
283	Greg Minton	.05	.04	.02
284	Nick Esasky	.07	.05	.03
285	John Farrell	.05	.04	.02
286	Rick Mahler	.05	.04	.02
287	Tom Gordon	.60	.45	.25
288	Gerald Young	.05	.04	.02
289	Jody Reed	.08	.06	.03
290	Jeff Hamilton	.05	.04	.02
291	Gerald Perry	.05	.04	.02
292	Hubie Brooks	.05	.04	.02
293	Bo Diaz	.05	.04	.02
294	Terry Puhl	.05	.04	.02
295	Jim Gantner	.05	.04	.02
296	Jeff Parrett	.05	.04	.02
297	Mike Boddicker	.05	.04	.02
298	Dan Gladden	.05	.04	.02
299	Tony Pena	.07	.05	.03
300	Checklist	.05	.04	.02
301	Tom Henke	.05	.04	.02
302	Pascual Perez	.05	.04	.02
303	Steve Bedrosian	.05	.04	.02
304	Ken Hill	.10	.08	.04
305	Jerry Reuss	.07	.05	.03
306	Jim Eisenreich	.05	.04	.02
307	Jack Howell	.05	.04	.02
308	Rick Cerone	.05	.04	.02
309	Tim Leary	.05	.04	.02
310	Joe Orsulak	.05	.04	.02
311	Jim Dwyer	.05	.04	.02
312	Geno Petralli	.05	.04	.02
313	Rick Honeycutt	.05	.04	.02
314	Tom Foley	.05	.04	.02
315	Kenny Rogers	.10	.08	.04
316	Mike Flanagan	.06	.05	.02
317	Bryan Harvey	.06	.05	.02
318	Billy Ripken	.05	.04	.02
319	Jeff Montgomery	.05	.04	.02
320	Erik Hanson	.12	.09	.05

		MT	NR MT	EX
321	Brian Downing	.06	.05	.02
322	Gregg Olson	.60	.45	.25
323	Terry Steinbach	.12	.09	.05
324	Sammy Sosa	.90	.70	.40
325	Gene Harris	.05	.04	.02
326	Mike Devereaux	.10	.08	.04
327	Dennis Cook	.12	.09	.05
.328	David Wells	.08	.06	.03
329	Checklist	.05	.04	.02
330	Kirt Manwaring	.10	.08	.04
331	Jim Presley	.05	.04	.02
332	Checklist	.05	.04	.02
333	Chuck Finley	.05	.04	.02
334	Rob Dibble	.08	.06	.03
335	Cecil Espy	.06	.05	.02
336	Dave Parker	.08	.06	.02

1990 Donruss MVP

This special 26-card set includes one player from each Major League team. Numbered BC-1 (the "BC" stands for "Bonus Card") through BC-26, the cards from this set were randomly packed in 1990 Donruss wax packs and were not available in factory sets or other types of packaging. The red-bordered cards are similar in design to the regular 1990 Donruss set, except the player photos are set against a special background made up of the "MVP" logo.

		MT	NR MT	EX
Complete Set:		2.50	2.00	1.00
Common Player:		.08	.06	.03
1	Bo Jackson	.30	.25	.12
2	Howard Johnson	.10	.08	.04
3	Dave Stewart	.08	.06	.03
4	Tony Gwynn	.15	.11	.06
5	Orel Hershiser	.10	.08	.04
6	Pedro Guerrero	.10	.08	.04
7	Tim Raines	.10	.08	.04
8	Kirby Puckett	.30	.25	.12
9	Alvin Davis	.08	.06	.03
10	Ryne Sandberg	.10	.08	.04
11	Kevin Mitchell	.20	.15	.08
12	John Smoltz	.40	.30	.15
13	George Bell	.10	.08	.04
14	Julio Franco	.10	.08	.04
15	Paul Molitor	.10	.08	.04
16	Bobby Bonilla	.12	.09	.05
17	Mike Greenwell	.30	.25	.12
18	Cal Ripken	.30	.25	.12
19	Carlton Fisk	.12	.09	.05
20	Chili Davis	.08	.06	.03
21	Glenn Davis	.10	.08	.04
22	Steve Sax	.10	.08	.04
23	Eric Davis	.30	.25	.12
24	Greg Swindell	.08	.06	.03
25	Von Hayes	.08	.06	.03
26	Alan Trammell	.10	.08	.04

NOTE: A card number in parentheses ( ) indicates the set is unnumbered.

1990 Donruss

Donruss celebrated its 10th anniversary in the baseball card hobby with a 715-card set in 1990, up from the 660-card sets of previous years. The standard-size cards feature bright red borders with the player's name in script along the top. The 1990 set included 26 "Diamond Kings" and 20 "Rated Rookies," along with a Carl Yastrzemski puzzle.

		MT	NR MT	EX
Complete Set:		25.00	18.50	10.00
Common Player:		.04	.03	.02
1	Bo Jackson (DK)	.40	.30	.15
2	Steve Sax (DK)	.12	.09	.05
3	Ruben Sierra (DK)	.30	.25	.12
4	Ken Griffey Jr. (DK)	.60	.45	.25
5	Mickey Tettleton (DK)	.12	.09	.05
6	Dave Stewart (DK)	.12	.09	.05
7	Jim DeShaies (DK)	.07	.05	.03
8	John Smoltz (DK)	.25	.20	.10
9	Mike Bielecki (DK)	.07	.05	.03
10	Brian Downing (DK)	.25	.20	.10
11	Kevin Mitchell (DK)	.35	.25	.14
12	Kelly Gruber (DK)	.08	.06	.03
13	Joe Magrane (DK)	.08	.06	.03
14	John Franco (DK)	.08	.06	.03
15	Ozzie Guillen (DK)	.08	.06	.03
16	Lou Whitaker (DK)	.08	.06	.03
17	John Smiley (DK)	.08	.06	.03
18	Howard Johnson (DK)	.30	.25	.12
19	Willie Randolph (DK)	.08	.06	.03
20	Chris Bosio (DK)	.07	.05	.03
21	Tommy Herr (DK)	.07	.05	.03
22	Dan Gladden (DK)	.07	.05	.03
23	Ellis Burks (DK)	.20	.15	.08
24	Pete O'Brien (DK)	.08	.06	.03
25	Bryn Smith (DK)	.07	.05	.03
26	Ed Whitson (DK)	.07	.05	.03
27	Checklist 1-27	.04	.03	.02
28	Robin Ventura (RR)(FC)	.35	.25	.14
29	*Todd Zeile* (RR)(FC)	1.50	1.25	.60
30	Sandy Alomar Jr. (RR)	.30	.25	.12
31	*Kent Mercker* (RR)(FC)	.30	.25	.12
32	*Ben McDonald* (RR)(FC)	1.75	1.25	.70
33	*Juan Gonzalez* (RR)(FC)	.40	.30	.15
34	*Eric Anthony* (RR)(FC)	1.50	1.25	.06
35	*Mike Fetters* (RR)(FC)	.20	.15	.08
36	*Marquis Grissom* (RR)(FC)	.70	.50	.30
37	*Greg Vaughn* (RR)(FC)	1.25	.90	.50
38	*Brian Dubois* (RR)(FC)	.25	.20	.10
39	Steve Avery (RR)(FC)	.40	.30	.15
40	*Mark Gardner* (RR)(FC)	.20	.15	.08
41	Andy Benes (RR)(FC)	.50	.40	.20
42	*Delino Deshields* (RR)(FC)	.25	.20	.10
43	*Scott Coolbaugh* (RR)(FC)	.70	.50	.30
44	*Pat Combs* (RR)(FC)	.40	.30	.15
45	Alex Sanchez (RR)	.15	.11	.06
46	*Kelly Mann* (RR)(FC)	.25	.20	.10
47	*Julio Machado* (RR)(FC)	.30	.25	.12
48	Pete Incaviglia	.05	.04	.02
49	Shawon Dunston	.07	.05	.03
50	Jeff Treadway	.05	.04	.02
51	Jeff Ballard	.10	.08	.04
52	Claudell Washington	.08	.06	.03
53	Juan Samuel	.10	.08	.04
54	John Smiley	.08	.06	.03
55	Rob Deer	.06	.05	.02
56	Geno Petralli	.04	.03	.02

		MT	NR MT	EX
57	Chris Bosio	.10	.08	.04
58	Carlton Fisk	.12	.09	.05
59	Kirt Manwaring	.10	.08	.04
60	Chet Lemon	.06	.05	.02
61	Bo Jackson	.40	.30	.15
62	Doyle Alexander	.05	.04	.02
63	Pedro Guerrero	.12	.09	.05
64	Allan Anderson	.07	.05	.03
65	Greg Harris	.07	.05	.03
66	Mike Greenwell	.25	.20	.10
67	Walt Weiss	.08	.06	.03
68	Wade Boggs	.30	.25	.12
69	Jim Clancy	.04	.03	.02
70	*Junior Felix*	.40	.30	.15
71	Barry Larkin	.12	.09	.05
72	Dave LaPoint	.05	.04	.02
73	Joel Skinner	.04	.03	.02
74	Jesse Barfield	.08	.06	.03
75	Tommy Herr	.08	.06	.03
76	Ricky Jordan	.20	.15	.08
77	Eddie Murray	.15	.11	.06
78	Steve Sax	.10	.08	.04
79	Tim Belcher	.10	.08	.04
80	Danny Jackson	.06	.05	.02
81	Kent Hrbek	.10	.08	.04
82	Milt Thompson	.05	.04	.02
83	Brook Jacoby	.07	.05	.03
84	Mike Marshall	.08	.06	.03
85	Kevin Seitzer	.12	.09	.05
86	Tony Gwynn	.15	.11	.06
87	Dave Steib	.08	.06	.03
88	Dave Smith	.06	.05	.02
89	Bret Saberhagen	.15	.11	.06
90	Alan Trammell	.10	.08	.04
91	Tony Phillips	.05	.04	.03
92	Doug Drabek	.05	.04	.03
93	Jeffrey Leonard	.09	.07	.04
94	Wally Joyner	.15	.11	.06
95	Carney Lansford	.09	.07	.04
96	Cal Ripken	.15	.11	.06
97	Andres Galarraga	.15	.11	.06
98	Kevin Mitchell	.30	.25	.12
99	Howard Johnson	.12	.09	.05
100	Checklist	.04	.03	.02
101	Melido Perez	.07	.05	.03
102	Spike Owen	.05	.04	.02
103	Paul Molitor	.10	.08	.04
104	Geronimo Berroa	.06	.05	.02
105	Ryne Sandberg	.15	.11	.06
106	Bryn Smith	.06	.05	.02
107	Steve Buechele	.04	.03	.02
108	Jim Abbott	.60	.45	.25
109	Alvin Davis	.10	.08	.04
110	Lee Smith	.05	.04	.02
111	Roberto Alomar	.09	.07	.04
112	Rick Reuschel	.09	.07	.04
113	Kelly Gruber	.09	.07	.04
114	Joe Carter	.09	.07	.04
115	Jose Rijo	.06	.05	.02
116	Greg Minton	.04	.03	.02
117	Bob Ojeda	.04	.03	.02
118	Glenn Davis	.08	.06	.03
119	Jeff Reardon	.05	.04	.02
120	**Kurt Stillwell**	.05	.04	.02
121	John Smoltz	.10	.08	.04
122	Dwight Evans	.08	.06	.03
123	**Eric Yelding**	.08	.06	.03
124	John Franco	.05	.04	.02
125	Jose Canseco	.40	.30	.15
126	Barry Bonds	.12	.09	.05
127	Lee Guetterman	.04	.03	.02
128	Jack Clark	.10	.08	.04
129	Dave Valle	.04	.03	.02
130	Hubie Brooks	.05	.04	.02
131	Ernest Riles	.04	.03	.02
132	Mike Morgan	.04	.03	.02
133	Steve Jeltz	.04	.03	.02
134	Jeff Robinson	.05	.04	.02
135	Ozzie Guillen	.05	.04	.02
136	Chili Davis	.06	.05	.02
137	Mitch Webster	.04	.03	.02
138	Jerry Browne	.06	.05	.02
139	Bo Diaz	.04	.03	.02
140	Robby Thompson	.07	.05	.03
141	Craig Worthington	.09	.07	.04
142	Julio Franco	.09	.07	.04
143	Brian Holman	.05	.04	.02
144	George Brett	.10	.08	.04
145	Tom Glavine	.10	.08	.04
146	Robin Yount	.20	.15	.08
147	Gary Carter	.06	.05	.02

		MT	NR MT	EX
148	Ron Kittle	.06	.05	.02
149	Tony Fernandez	.07	.05	.03
150	Dave Stewart	.07	.05	.03
151	Gary Gaetti	.07	.05	.03
152	Kevin Elster	.04	.03	.02
153	Gerald Perry	.05	.04	.02
154	Jesse Orosco	.05	.04	.02
155	Wally Backman	.05	.04	.02
156	Dennis Martinez	.05	.04	.02
157	Rick Sutcliffe	.08	.06	.03
158	Greg Maddux	.12	.09	.05
159	Andy Hawkins	.05	.04	.02
160	John Kruk	.05	.04	.02
161	Jose Oquendo	.05	.04	.02
162	John Dopson	.08	.06	.03
163	Joe Magrane	.08	.06	.03
164	Billy Ripken	.04	.03	.02
165	Fred Manrique	.04	.03	.02
166	Nolan Ryan	.25	.20	.10
167	Damon Berryhill	.06	.05	.02
168	Dale Murphy	.09	.07	.04
169	Mickey Tettleton	.08	.06	.03
170	Kirk McCaskill	.05	.04	.02
171	Dwight Gooden	.15	.11	.06
172	Jose Lind	.04	.03	.02
173	B.J. Surhoff	.07	.05	.03
174	Ruben Sierra	.12	.09	.05
175	Dan Plesac	.08	.06	.03
176	Dan Pasqua	.05	.04	.02
177	Kelly Downs	.05	.04	.02
178	Matt Nokes	.08	.06	.03
179	Luis Aquino	.04	.03	.02
180	Frank Tanana	.04	.03	.02
181	Tony Pena	.07	.05	.03
182	Dan Gladden	.05	.04	.02
183	Bruce Hurst	.05	.04	.02
184	Roger Clemens	.20	.15	.08
185	Mark McGwire	.30	.25	.12
186	Rob Murphy	.04	.03	.02
187	Jim Deshaies	.06	.05	.02
188	Fred McGriff	.20	.15	.08
189	Rob Dibble	.06	.05	.02
190	Don Mattingly	.90	.70	.35
191	Felix Fermin	.04	.03	.02
192	Roberto Kelly	.08	.06	.03
193	Dennis Cook	.08	.06	.03
194	Darren Daulton	.04	.03	.02
195	Alfredo Griffin	.05	.04	.02
196	Eric Plunk	.05	.04	.02
197	Orel Hershiser	.12	.09	.05
198	Paul O'Neil	.07	.05	.03
199	Randy Bush	.04	.03	.02
200	Checklist	.04	.03	.02
201	Ozzie Smith	.10	.08	.04
202	Pete O'Brien	.06	.05	.02
203	Jay Howell	.06	.05	.02
204	Mark Gibicza	.08	.06	.03
205	Ed Whitson	.04	.03	.02
206	George Bell	.09	.07	.04
207	Mike Scott	.09	.07	.04
208	Charlie Leibrandt	.04	.03	.02
209	Mike Heath	.04	.03	.02
210	Dennis Eckersley	.09	.07	.04
211	Mike LaValliere	.04	.03	.02
212	Darnell Coles	.04	.03	.02
213	Lance Parrish	.07	.05	.03
214	Mike Moore	.07	.05	.03
215	*Steve Finley*	.20	.15	.08
216	Tim Raines	.09	.07	.04
217	Scott Garrelts	.06	.05	.02
218	Kevin McReynolds	.09	.07	.04
219	Dave Gallagher	.08	.06	.03
220	Tim Wallach	.08	.06	.03
221	Chuck Crim	.04	.03	.02
222	Lonnie Smith	.08	.06	.03
223	Andre Dawson	.10	.08	.04
224	Nelson Santovenia	.07	.05	.03
225	Rafael Palmeiro	.07	.05	.03
226	Devon White	.07	.05	.03
227	Harold Reynolds	.07	.05	.03
228	Ellis Burks	.15	.11	.06
229	Mark Parent	.04	.03	.02
230	Will Clark	.60	.45	.25
231	Jimmy Key	.08	.06	.03
232	John Farrell	.04	.03	.02
233	Eric Davis	.30	.25	.12
234	Johnny Ray	.05	.04	.02
235	Darryl Strawberry	.30	.25	.12
236	Bill Doran	.05	.04	.02
237	Greg Gagne	.05	.04	.02
238	Jim Eisenreich	.04	.03	.02
239	Tommy Gregg	.06	.05	.02
240	Marty Barrett	.05	.04	.02
241	Rafael Ramirez	.05	.04	.02
242	Chris Sabo	.07	.05	.03
243	Dave Henderson	.07	.05	.03
244	Andy Van Slyke	.07	.05	.03
245	Alvaro Espinosa	.15	.11	.06
246	Garry Templeton	.06	.05	.02
247	Gene Harris	.04	.03	.02
248	Kevin Gross	.05	.04	.02
249	Brett Butler	.09	.07	.04
250	Willie Randolph	.07	.05	.03
251	Roger McDowell	.05	.04	.02
252	Rafael Belliard	.04	.03	.02
253	Steve Rosenberg	.04	.03	.02
254	Jack Howell	.04	.03	.02
255	Marvell Wynne	.04	.03	.02
256	Tom Candiotti	.05	.04	.02
257	Todd Benzinger	.05	.04	.02
258	Don Robinson	.04	.03	.02
259	Phil Bradley	.08	.06	.03
260	Cecil Espy	.05	.04	.02
261	Scott Bankhead	.05	.04	.02
262	Frank White	.07	.05	.03
263	Andres Thomas	.05	.04	.02
264	Glenn Braggs	.05	.04	.02
265	David Cone	.10	.08	.04
266	Bobby Thigpen	.07	.05	.03
267	Nelson Liriano	.04	.03	.02
268	Terry Steinbach	.09	.07	.04
269	Kirby Puckett	.30	.25	.12
270	Gregg Jefferies	.40	.30	.15
271	Jeff Blauser	.05	.04	.02
272	Cory Snyder	.07	.05	.03
273	Roy Smith	.05	.04	.02
274	Tom Foley	.04	.03	.02
275	Mitch Williams	.09	.07	.04
276	Paul Kilgus	.04	.03	.02
277	Don Slaught	.04	.03	.02
278	Von Hayes	.08	.06	.03
279	Vince Coleman	.10	.08	.04
280	Mike Boddicker	.05	.04	.02
281	Ken Dayley	.04	.03	.02
282	Mike Devereaux	.07	.05	.03
283	*Kenny Rogers*	.09	.07	.04
284	Jeff Russell	.07	.05	.04
285	*Jerome Walton*	1.75	1.25	.70
286	Derek Lilliquist	.08	.06	.03
287	Joe Orsulak	.04	.03	.02
288	Dick Schofield	.04	.03	.02
289	Ron Darling	.09	.07	.04
290	Bobby Bonilla	.12	.09	.05
291	Jim Gantner	.05	.04	.02
292	Bobby Witt	.05	.04	.02
293	Greg Brock	.05	.04	.02
294	Ivan Calderon	.05	.04	.02
295	Steve Bedrosian	.06	.05	.02
296	Mike Henneman	.06	.05	.02
297	Tom Gordon	.25	.20	.10
298	Lou Whitaker	.08	.06	.03
299	Terry Pendleton	.07	.05	.03
300	Checklist	.04	.03	.02
301	Juan Berenguer	.04	.03	.02
302	Mark Davis	.09	.07	.05
303	Nick Esasky	.09	.07	.05
304	Rickey Henderson	.15	.11	.06
305	Rick Cerone	.04	.03	.02
306	Craig Biggio	.15	.11	.06
307	Duane Ward	.04	.03	.02
308	Tom Browning	.07	.05	.03
309	Walt Terrell	.05	.04	.02
310	Greg Swindell	.10	.08	.04
311	Dave Righetti	.07	.05	.03
312	Mike Maddux	.04	.03	.02
313	Lenny Dykstra	.07	.05	.03
314	Jose Gonzalez	.08	.06	.03
315	Steve Balboni	.04	.03	.02
316	Mike Scioscia	.07	.05	.02
317	Ron Oester	.04	.03	.02
318	*Gary Wayne*	.09	.07	.04
319	Todd Worrell	.06	.05	.02
320	Doug Jones	.05	.04	.02
321	Jeff Hamilton	.05	.04	.02
322	Danny Tartabull	.09	.07	.04
323	Chris James	.05	.04	.02
324	Mike Flanagan	.05	.04	.02
325	Gerald Young	.05	.04	.02
326	Bob Boone	.09	.07	.04
327	Frank Williams	.04	.03	.02
328	Dave Parker	.09	.07	.04
329	Sid Bream	.04	.03	.02

		MT	NR MT	EX
330	Mike Schooler	.06	.05	.02
331	Bert Blyleven	.08	.06	.03
332	Bob Welch	.07	.05	.03
333	Bob Milacki	.06	.05	.02
334	Tim Burke	.05	.04	.02
335	Jose Uribe	.05	.04	.02
336	Randy Myers	.05	.04	.02
337	Eric King	.04	.03	.02
338	Mark Langston	.12	.09	.05
339	Ted Higuera	.08	.06	.03
340	Oddibe McDowell	.06	.05	.02
341	Lloyd McClendon	.07	.05	.03
342	Pascual Perez	.05	.04	.02
343	Kevin Brown	.08	.06	.03
344	Chuck Finley	.05	.04	.02
345	Erik Hanson	.09	.07	.05
346	Rich Gedman	.05	.04	.02
347	Bip Roberts	.10	.08	.04
348	Matt Williams	.20	.15	.08
349	Tom Henke	.05	.04	.02
350	Brad Kimminsk	.05	.04	.02
351	Jeff Reed	.04	.03	.02
352	Brian Downing	.05	.04	.02
353	Frank Viola	.09	.07	.04
354	Terry Puhl	.05	.04	.02
355	Brian Harper	.05	.04	.02
356	Steve Farr	.05	.04	.02
357	Joe Boever	.05	.04	.02
358	Danny Heep	.04	.03	.02
359	Larry Anderson	.04	.03	.02
360	Rolando Roomes	.10	.08	.04
361	Mike Gallego	.05	.04	.02
362	Bob Kipper	.04	.03	.02
363	Clay Parker	.07	.05	.03
364	Mike Pagliarulo	.05	.04	.02
365	Ken Griffey Jr.	1.00	.70	.40
366	Rex Hudler	.04	.03	.02
367	Pat Sheridan	.04	.03	.02
368	Kirk Gibson	.09	.07	.04
369	Jeff Parrett	.05	.04	.02
370	Bob Walk	.05	.04	.02
371	Ken Patterson	.04	.03	.02
372	Bryan Harvey	.05	.04	.02
373	Mike Bielecki	.07	.05	.03
374	*Tom Magrann*(FC)	.20	.15	.08
375	Rick Mahler	.05	.04	.02
376	Craig Lefferts	.05	.04	.02
377	Gregg Olson	.20	.15	.08
378	Jamie Moyer	.04	.03	.02
379	Randy Johnson	.09	.07	.04
380	Jeff Montgomery	.06	.05	.02
381	Marty Clary	.06	.05	.02
382	*Bill Spiers*	.15	.11	.06
383	Dave Magadan	.06	.05	.02
384	*Greg Hibbard*(FC)	.20	.15	.08
385	Ernie Whitt	.05	.04	.02
386	Rick Honeycutt	.04	.03	.02
387	Dave West	.08	.06	.03
388	Keith Hernandez	.07	.05	.03
389	Jose Alvarez	.04	.03	.02
390	*Joey Belle*(FC)	.90	.70	.35
391	Rick Aguilera	.05	.04	.02
392	Mike Fitzgerald	.04	.03	.02
393	*Dwight Smith*	.80	.60	.30
394	*Steve Wilson*	.09	.07	.04
395	*Bob Geren*	.20	.15	.08
396	Randy Ready	.04	.03	.02
397	Ken Hill	.07	.05	.03
398	Jody Reed	.05	.04	.02
399	Tom Brunansky	.07	.05	.03
400	Checklist	.04	.03	.02
401	Rene Gonzales	.04	.03	.02
402	Harold Baines	.09	.07	.04
403	Cecilio Guante	.04	.03	.02
404	Joe Girardi	.15	.11	.06
405	*Sergio Valdez*(FC)	.20	.15	.08
406	Mark Williamson	.04	.03	.02
407	Glenn Hoffman	.04	.03	.02
408	*Jeff Innis*(FC)	.10	.08	.04
409	Randy Kramer	.04	.03	.02
410	Charlie O'Brien(FC)	.04	.03	.02
411	Charlie Hough	.06	.05	.02
412	Gus Polidor	.04	.03	.02
413	Ron Karkovice	.04	.03	.02
414	Trevor Wilson(FC)	.07	.05	.03
415	*Kevin Ritz*(FC)	.20	.15	.08
416	Gary Thurman	.04	.03	.02
417	Jeff Robinson	.04	.03	.02
418	Scott Terry	.05	.04	.02
419	Tim Laudner	.04	.03	.02
420	Dennis Rasmussen	.04	.03	.02

		MT	NR MT	EX
421	Luis Rivera	.04	.03	.02
422	Jim Corsi(FC)	.07	.05	.03
423	Dennis Lamp	.04	.03	.02
424	Ken Caminiti	.06	.05	.02
425	David Wells	.06	.05	.02
426	Norm Charlton	.09	.07	.04
427	*Deion Sanders*	.70	.50	.30
428	Dion James	.05	.04	.02
429	Chuck Cary	.05	.04	.02
430	Ken Howell	.04	.03	.02
431	Steve Lake	.04	.03	.02
432	Kal Daniels	.09	.07	.04
433	Lance McCullers	.05	.04	.02
434	Lenny Harris(FC)	.10	.08	.04
435	*Scott Scudder*(FC)	.20	.15	.08
436	Gene Larkin	.04	.03	.02
437	Dan Quisenberry	.05	.04	.02
438	*Steve Olin*(FC)	.15	.11	.06
439	Mickey Hatcher	.05	.04	.02
440	Willie Wilson	.05	.04	.02
441	Mark Grant	.05	.04	.02
442	Mookie Wilson	.07	.05	.03
443	Alex Trevino	.04	.03	.02
444	Pat Tabler	.05	.04	.02
445	Dave Bergman	.04	.03	.02
446	Todd Burns	.05	.04	.02
447	R.J. Reynolds	.04	.03	.02
448	Jay Buhner	.08	.06	.03
449	*Lee Stevens*(FC)	.20	.15	.08
450	Ron Hassey	.04	.03	.02
451	Bob Melvin	.04	.03	.02
452	Dave Martinez	.05	.04	.02
453	*Greg Litton*(FC)	.25	.20	.10
454	Mark Carreon	.15	.11	.06
455	Scott Fletcher	.05	.04	.02
456	Otis Nixon	.04	.03	.02
457	*Tony Fossas*(FC)	.10	.08	.04
458	John Russell	.04	.03	.02
459	Paul Assenmacher	.04	.03	.02
460	Zane Smith	.04	.03	.02
461	Jack Daugherty	.20	.15	.08
462	*Rich Monteleone*(FC)	.15	.11	.06
463	Greg Briley(FC)	.25	.20	.10
464	Mike Smithson	.04	.03	.02
465	Benito Santiago	.09	.07	.04
466	*Jeff Brantley*	.10	.08	.04
467	Jose Nunez	.07	.05	.03
468	Scott Bailes	.04	.03	.02
469	Ken Griffey	.06	.05	.02
470	Bob McClure	.04	.03	.02
471	Mackey Sasser	.04	.03	.02
472	Glenn Wilson	.04	.03	.02
473	*Kevin Tapani*(FC)	.20	.15	.08
474	Bill Buckner	.05	.04	.02
475	Ron Gant	.05	.04	.02
476	Kevin Romine(FC)	.05	.04	.02
477	Juan Agosto	.04	.03	.02
478	Herm Winningham	.04	.03	.02
479	Storm Davis	.05	.04	.02
480	Jeff King(FC)	.09	.07	.04
481	*Kevin Mmahat*(FC)	.25	.20	.10
482	Carmelo Martinez	.05	.04	.02
483	*Omar Vizquel*	.10	.08	.04
484	Jim Dwyer	.04	.03	.02
485	Bob Knepper	.04	.03	.02
486	Dave Anderson	.04	.03	.02
487	Ron Jones	.09	.07	.04
488	Jay Bell	.05	.04	.02
489	*Sammy Sosa*(FC)	.60	.45	.25
490	*Kent Anderson*(FC)	.15	.11	.06
491	Domingo Ramos	.04	.03	.02
492	Dave Clark	.05	.04	.02
493	Tim Birtsas	.04	.03	.02
494	Ken Oberkfell	.04	.03	.02
495	Larry Sheets	.04	.03	.02
496	Jeff Kunkel	.04	.03	.02
497	Jim Presley	.04	.03	.02
498	Mike Macfarlane	.04	.03	.02
499	Pete Smith	.05	.04	.02
500	Checklist	.04	.03	.02
501	Gary Sheffield	.40	.30	.15
502	*Terry Bross*(FC)	.20	.15	.08
503	*Jerry Kutzler*(FC)	.20	.15	.08
504	Lloyd Moseby	.05	.04	.02
505	Curt Young	.04	.03	.02
506	Al Newman	.04	.03	.02
507	Keith Miller	.04	.03	.02
508	*Mike Stanton*(FC)	.20	.15	.08
509	Rich Yett	.04	.03	.02
510	*Tim Drummond*(FC)	.20	.15	.08
511	Joe Hesketh	.04	.03	.02

		MT	NR MT	EX
512	*Rick Wrona*	.10	.08	.04
513	Luis Salazar	.04	.03	.02
514	Hal Morris	.06	.05	.02
515	Terry Mullholland	.07	.05	.03
516	John Morris	.05	.04	.02
517	Carlos Quintana	.08	.06	.03
518	Frank DiPino	.04	.03	.02
519	Randy Milligan	.06	.05	.02
520	Chad Kreuter	.07	.05	.03
521	Mike Jeffcoat	.04	.03	.02
522	Mike Harkey	.10	.08	.04
523	Andy Nezelek	.07	.05	.03
524	Dave Schmidt	.04	.03	.02
525	Tony Armas	.04	.03	.02
526	Barry Lyons	.04	.03	.02
527	*Rick Reed*(FC)	.20	.15	.08
528	Jerry Reuss	.06	.05	.02
529	*Dean Palmer*(FC)	.70	.50	.30
530	*Jeff Petarek*(FC)	.20	.15	.08
531	*Carlos Martinez*	.20	.15	.08
532	Atlee Hammaker	.05	.04	.02
533	Mike Brumley	.04	.03	.02
534	Terry Leach	.04	.03	.02
535	*Doug Strange*(FC)	.20	.15	.08
536	Jose DeLeon	.05	.04	.02
537	Shane Rawley	.05	.04	.02
538	Joey Cora(FC)	.10	.08	.04
539	Eric Hetzel	.08	.06	.03
540	Gene Nelson	.04	.03	.02
541	Wes Gardner	.04	.03	.02
542	Mark Portugal	.04	.03	.02
543	Al Leiter	.05	.04	.02
544	Jack Armstrong	.04	.03	.02
545	**Greg Cadaret**	**.04**	**.03**	**.02**
546	**Rod Nichols**	**.04**	**.03**	**.02**
547	**Luis Polonia**	**.05**	**.04**	**.02**
548	**Charlie Hayes(FC)**	**.15**	**.11**	**.06**
549	**Dickie Thon**	**.04**	**.03**	**.02**
550	**Tim Crews**	**.04**	**.03**	**.02**
551	**Dave Winfield**	**.20**	**.15**	**.08**
552	**Mike Davis**	**.04**	**.03**	**.02**
553	**Ron Robinson**	**.04**	**.03**	**.02**
554	**Carmen Castillo**	**.04**	**.03**	**.02**
555	**John Costello**	**.04**	**.03**	**.02**
556	**Bud Black**	**.04**	**.03**	**.02**
557	**Rick Dempsey**	**.04**	**.03**	**.02**
558	Jim Acker	.04	.03	.02
559	Eric Show	.06	.05	.02
560	Pat Borders	.06	.05	.02
561	Danny Darwin	.04	.03	.02
562	*Rick Luecken*(FC)	.20	.15	.08
563	Edwin Nunez	.05	.04	.02
564	Felix Jose	.09	.07	.04
565	John Cangelosi	.04	.03	.02
566	Billy Swift	.04	.03	.02
567	Bill Schroeder	.04	.03	.02
568	Stan Javier	.04	.03	.02
569	Jim Traber	.04	.03	.02
570	Wallace Johnson	.04	.03	.02
571	Donnell Nixon	.04	.03	.02
572	Sid Fernandez	.08	.06	.03
573	Lance Johnson	.09	.07	.04
574	Andy McGaffigan	.04	.03	.02
575	Mark Knudson	.04	.03	.02
576	*Tommy Greene*(FC)	.25	.20	.10
577	Mark Grace	.25	.20	.10
578	*Larry Walker*(FC)	.25	.20	.10
579	Mike Stanley	.04	.03	.02
580	Mike Witt	.05	.04	.02
581	Scott Bradley	.04	.03	.02
582	Greg Harris	.07	.05	.03
583	Kevin Hickey	.04	.03	.02
584	Lee Mazzilli	.04	.03	.02
585	Jeff Pico	.04	.03	.02
586	*Joe Oliver*(FC)	.35	.25	.14
587	Willie Fraser	.04	.03	.02
588	Puzzle Card	.04	.03	.02
589	Kevin Bass	.06	.05	.03
590	John Moses	.04	.03	.02
591	Tom Pagnozzi	.04	.03	.02
592	*Tony Castillo*	.10	.08	.04
593	Jerald Clark	.06	.05	.03
594	Dan Schatzeder	.04	.03	.02
595	Luis Quinones	.04	.03	.02
596	Pete Harnisch	.08	.06	.03
597	**Gary Redus**	**.04**	**.03**	**.02**
598	**Mel Hall**	**.05**	**.04**	**.02**
599	**Rick Schu**	**.04**	**.03**	**.02**
600	**Checklist**	**.04**	**.03**	**.02**
601	**Mike Kingery**	**.04**	**.03**	**.02**
602	**Terry Kennedy**	**.04**	**.03**	**.02**

		MT	NR MT	EX
603	**Mike Sharperson**	**.06**	**.05**	**.02**
604	**Don Carman**	**.04**	**.03**	**.02**
605	**Jim Gott**	**.05**	**.04**	**.03**
606	**Donn Pall**	**.05**	**.04**	**.03**
607	**Rance Mulliniks**	**.04**	**.03**	**.02**
608	**Curt Wilkerson**	**.04**	**.03**	**.02**
609	**Mike Felder**	**.04**	**.03**	**.02**
610	**Guillermo Hernandez**	**.04**	**.03**	**.02**
611	Candy Maldonado	.05	.04	.02
612	Mark Thurmond	.04	.03	.02
613	Rick Leach	.04	.03	.02
614	Jerry Reed	.04	.03	.02
615	Franklin Stubbs	.05	.04	.02
616	Billy Hatcher	.05	.04	.02
617	Don August	.05	.04	.02
618	Tim Teufel	.04	.03	.02
619	Shawn Hillegas	.04	.03	.02
620	Manny Lee	.04	.03	.02
621	Gary Ward	.05	.04	.02
622	*Mark Guthrie*(FC)	.20	.15	.08
623	Jeff Musselman	.05	.04	.02
624	Mark Lemke	.07	.05	.03
625	Fernando Valenzuela	.07	.05	.03
626	*Paul Sorrento*(FC)	.20	.15	.08
627	Glenallen Hill	.20	.15	.08
628	Les Lancaster	.05	.04	.03
629	Vance Law	.04	.03	.02
630	Randy Velarde(FC)	.10	.08	.04
631	Todd Frohwirth	.04	.03	.02
632	Willie McGee	.06	.05	.02
633	Oil Can Boyd	.06	.05	.02
634	Cris Carpenter	.09	.07	.04
635	Brian Holton	.04	.03	.02
636	Tracy Jones	.05	.04	.02
637	Terry Steinbach (AS)	.09	.07	.04
638	Brady Anderson	.09	.07	.04
639	Jack Morris	.06	.05	.02
640	*Jaimie Navarro*(FC)	.20	.15	.08
641	Darrin Jackson	.05	.04	.02
642	*Mike Dyer*(FC)	.20	.15	.08
643	Mike Schmidt	.40	.30	.15
644	Henry Cotto	.04	.03	.02
645	John Cerutti	.05	.04	.02
646	*Francisco Cabera*(FC)	.40	.30	.15
647	Scott Sanderson	.05	.04	.02
648	Brian Meyer	.05	.04	.02
649	Ray Searage	.05	.04	.02
650	Bo Jackson (AS)	.50	.40	.20
651	Steve Lyons	.04	.03	.02
652	Mike LaCoss	.04	.03	.02
653	Ted Power	.04	.03	.02
654	Howard Johnson (AS)	.20	.15	.08
655	*Mauro Gozzo*(FC)	.15	.11	.06
656	*Mike Blowers*(FC)	.30	.25	.12
657	Paul Gibson	.05	.04	.02
658	Neal Heaton	.05	.04	.02
659	**Nolan Ryan (5000 K)**	**.30**	**.25**	**.12**
660	**Harold Baines (AS)**	**.09**	**.07**	**.04**
661	**Gary Pettis**	**.05**	**.04**	**.02**
662	***Clint Zavaras*(FC)**	**.20**	**.15**	**.08**
663	**Rick Reuschel**	**.08**	**.06**	**.03**
664	**Alejandro Pena**	**.05**	**.04**	**.02**
665	**Nolan Ryan**	**.15**	**.11**	**.06**
666	Ricky Horton	.04	.03	.02
667	Curt Schilling	.06	.05	.02
668	Bill Landrum(FC)	.05	.04	.02
669	Todd Stottlemyre	.05	.04	.02
670	Tim Leary	.05	.04	.02
671	*John Wetteland*(FC)	.25	.20	.10
672	Calvin Schiraldi	.04	.03	.02
673	Ruben Sierra (AS)	.09	.07	.04
674	Pedro Guerrero (AS)	.09	.07	.04
675	Ken Phelps	.04	.03	.02
676	Cal Ripken (AS)	.09	.07	.04
677	Denny Walling	.04	.03	.02
678	Goose Gossage	.04	.03	.02
679	*Gary Mielke*(FC)	.20	.15	.08
680	Bill Bathe	.04	.03	.02
681	Tom Lawless	.04	.03	.02
682	*Xavier Hernandez*(FC)	.20	.15	.08
683	Kirby Puckett (AS)	.09	.07	.04
684	Mariano Duncan	.05	.04	.02
685	Ramon Martinez	.10	.08	.04
686	Tim Jones	.05	.04	.02
687	Tom Filer	.04	.03	.02
688	Steve Lombardozzi	.04	.03	.02
689	*Bernie Williams*(FC)	.60	.45	.25
690	*Chip Hale*(FC)	.30	.25	.12
691	*Beau Allred*(FC)	.70	.50	.30
692	Ryne Sandberg (AS)	.09	.07	.04
693	*Jeff Huson*(FC)	.20	.15	.08

		MT	NR MT	EX
694	Curt Ford	.04	.03	.02
695	Eric Davis (AS)	.09	.07	.04
696	Scott Lusader	.05	.04	.02
697	Mark McGwire (AS)	.09	.07	.04
698	*Steve Cummings*(FC)	.20	.15	.08
699	*George Canale*(FC)	.20	.15	.08
700	Checklist	.04	.03	.02
701	Julio Franco (AS)	.09	.07	.04
702	*Dave Johnson*(FC)	.10	.08	.04
703	Dave Stewart (AS)	.08	.06	.03
704	*Dave Justice*(FC)	.20	.15	.08
705	Tony Gwynn (AS)	.09	.07	.04
706	Greg Myers	.06	.05	.02
707	Will Clark (AS)	.12	.09	.05
708	Benito Santiago (AS)	.08	.06	.03
709	Larry McWilliams	.04	.03	.02
710	Ozzie Smith (AS)	.08	.06	.03
711	*John Olerud*(FC)	2.00	1.50	.80
712	Wade Boggs (AS)	.09	.07	.04
713	*Gary Eave*(FC)	.15	.11	.06
714	Bob Tewksbury	.05	.04	.02
715	Kevin Mitchell (AS)	.09	.07	.04
716	A. Bartlett Giamatti	1.00	.70	.40

1986 Dorman's Cheese

DON MATTINGLY — NEW YORK YANKEES 1st BASE
RYNE SANDBERG — CHICAGO CUBS 2nd BASE

Found in specially-marked packages of Dorman's American Cheese Singles, the Dorman's set consists of ten two-card panels of baseball superstars. Labeled as a "Super Star Limited Edition" set, the panels measure 1-1/2" by 2" each and have a perforation line in the center. The fronts contain a color photo along with the Dorman's logo and the player's name, team and position. Due to a lack of proper licensing, all team insignias have been airbrushed from the players' caps. The backs of the cards contain brief player statistics.

		MT	NR MT	EX
Complete Panel Set:		30.00	22.00	12.00
Complete Singles Set:		12.00	9.00	4.75
Common Panel:		1.25	.90	.50
Common Single Player:		.15	.11	.06
Panel		2.00	1.50	.80
(1)	George Brett	.50	.40	.20
(2)	Jack Morris	.15	.11	.06
Panel		2.00	1.50	.80
(3)	Gary Carter	.30	.25	.12
(4)	Cal Ripken	.40	.30	.15
Panel		2.00	1.50	.80
(5)	Dwight Gooden	.60	.45	.25
(6)	Kent Hrbek	.20	.15	.08
Panel		3.00	1.50	.90
(7)	Rickey Henderson	.40	.30	.15
(8)	Mike Schmidt	.80	.60	.30
Panel		2.00	1.50	.80
(9)	Keith Hernandez	.30	.25	.12
(10)	Dale Murphy	.50	.40	.20
Panel		2.00	1.50	.80
(11)	Reggie Jackson	.40	.30	.15
(12)	Eddie Murray	.40	.30	.15

		MT	NR MT	EX
Panel		4.00	3.00	1.50
(13)	Don Mattingly	1.00	.70	.40
(14)	Ryne Sandberg	.30	.25	.12
Panel		1.25	.90	.50
(15)	Willie McGee	.15	.11	.06
(16)	Robin Yount	.30	.25	.12
Panel		2.25	1.75	.90
(17)	Rick Sutcliff (Sutcliffe)	.15	.11	.06
(18)	Wade Boggs	.80	.60	.30
Panel		1.50	1.25	.60
(19)	Dave Winfield	.40	.30	.15
(20)	Jim Rice	.20	.15	.10

1941 Double Play

Issued by Gum, Inc., this set includes 75 numbered cards (two consecutive numbers per card) featuring 150 baseball players. The cards, which are blank-backed and measure 2-1/2" by 3-1/8", contain sepia-tone photos of two players. Action and portrait poses are found in the set, with card designs on either a vertical or horizontal format. The last fifty cards are the scarcest of the set. Cards cut to form two single cards have little value.

		NR MT	EX	VG
Complete Set:		6500.00	3300.00	2000.
Common Player: 1-100		35.00	17.50	10.50
Common Player: 101-150		50.00	25.00	15.00
1	Larry French			
2	Vance Page	75.00	38.50	23.00
3	Billy Herman			
4	Stanley Hack	50.00	25.00	15.00
5	Linus Frey			
6	John Vander Meer	45.00	23.00	13.50
7	Paul Derringer			
8	Bucky Walters	35.00	17.50	10.50
9	Frank McCormick			
10	Bill Werber	35.00	17.50	10.50
11	Jimmy Ripple			
12	Ernie Lombardi	60.00	30.00	18.00
13	Alex Kampouris			
14	John Wyatt	35.00	17.50	10.50
15	Mickey Owen			
16	Paul Waner	60.00	30.00	18.00
17	Harry Lavagetto			
18	Harold Reiser	45.00	22.00	13.50
19	Jimmy Wasdell			
20	Dolph Camilli	45.00	22.00	13.50
21	Dixie Walker			
22	Ducky Medwick	60.00	30.00	18.00
23	Harold Reese			
24	Kirby Higbe	225.00	112.00	70.00
25	Harry Danning			
26	Cliff Melton	35.00	17.50	10.50
27	Harry Gumbert			
28	Burgess Whitehead	35.00	17.50	10.50
29	Joe Orengo			
30	Joe Moore	35.00	17.50	10.50
31	Mel Ott			
32	Babe Young	90.00	45.00	27.00
33	Lee Handley			
34	Arky Vaughan	60.00	30.00	18.00
35	Bob Klinger			
36	Stanley Brown	35.00	17.50	10.50
37	Terry Moore			
38	Gus Mancuso	35.00	17.50	10.50
39	Johnny Mize			
40	Enos Slaughter	100.00	50.00	30.00
41	John Cooney			

		NR MT	EX	VG
42	Sibby Sisti	35.00	17.50	10.50
43	Max West			
44	Carvel Rowell	35.00	17.50	10.50
45	Dan Litwhiler			
46	Merrill May	35.00	17.50	10.50
47	Frank Hayes			
48	Al Brancato	35.00	17.50	10.50
49	Bob Johnson			
50	Bill Nagel	35.00	17.50	10.50
51	Buck Newsom			
52	Hank Greenberg	90.00	45.00	27.00
53	Barney McCosky			
54	Charley Gehringer	90.00	45.00	27.00
55	Pinky Higgins			
56	Dick Bartell	35.00	17.50	10.50
57	Ted Williams			
58	Jim Tabor	550.00	280.00	165.00
59	Joe Cronin			
60	Jimmy Foxx	175.00	90.00	50.00
61	Lefty Gomez			
62	Phil Rizzuto	250.00	125.00	70.00
63	Joe DiMaggio			
64	Charley Keller	675.00	340.00	210.00
65	Red Rolfe			
66	Bill Dickey	125.00	62.00	37.00
67	Joe Gordon			
68	Red Ruffing	75.00	37.00	22.00
69	Mike Tresh			
70	Luke Appling	60.00	30.00	18.00
71	Moose Solters			
72	John Rigney	35.00	17.50	10.50
73	Buddy Meyer			
74	Ben Chapman	35.00	17.50	10.50
75	Cecil Travis			
76	George Case	35.00	17.50	10.50
77	Joe Krakauskas			
78	Bob Feller	150.00	75.00	45.00
79	Ken Keltner			
80	Hal Trosky	35.00	17.50	10.50
81	Ted Williams			
82	Joe Cronin	600.00	300.00	175.00
83	Joe Gordon			
84	Charley Keller	45.00	22.00	13.50
85	Hank Greenberg			
86	Red Ruffing	90.00	45.00	27.00
87	Hal Trosky			
88	George Case	35.00	17.50	10.50
89	Mel Ott			
90	Burgess Whitehead	90.00	45.00	27.00
91	Harry Danning			
92	Harry Gumbert	35.00	17.50	10.50
93	Babe Young			
94	Cliff Melton	35.00	17.50	10.50
95	Jimmy Ripple			
96	Bucky Walters	35.00	17.50	10.50
97	Stanley Hack			
98	Bob Klinger	35.00	17.50	10.50
99	Johnny Mize			
100	Dan Litwhiler	60.00	30.00	20.00
101	Dominic Dallessandro			
102	Augie Galan	50.00	25.00	15.00
103	Bill Lee			
104	Phil Cavarretta	50.00	25.00	15.00
105	Lefty Grove			
106	Bobby Doerr	150.00	70.00	45.00
107	Frank Pytlak			
108	Dom DiMaggio	60.00	30.00	20.00
109	Gerald Priddy			
110	John Murphy	60.00	30.00	20.00
111	Tommy Henrich			
112	Marius Russo	75.00	37.00	22.00
113	Frank Crosetti			
114	John Sturm	75.00	37.00	22.00
115	Ival Goodman			
116	Myron McCormick	50.00	25.00	15.00
117	Eddie Joost			
118	Ernest Koy	50.00	25.00	15.00
119	Lloyd Waner			
120	Henry Majeski	75.00	37.00	22.00
121	Buddy Hassett			
122	Eugene Moore	50.00	25.00	15.00
123	Nick Etten			
124	John Rizzo	50.00	25.00	15.00
125	Sam Chapman			
126	Wally Moses	50.00	25.00	15.00
127	John Babich			
128	Richard Siebert	50.00	25.00	15.00
129	Nelson Potter			
130	Benny McCoy	50.00	25.00	15.00
131	Clarence Campbell			
132	Louis Boudreau	75.00	37.00	22.00

		NR MT	EX	VG
133	Rolly Hemsley			
134	Mel Harder	50.00	25.00	15.00
135	Gerald Walker			
136	Joe Heving	50.00	25.00	15.00
137	John Rucker			
138	Ace Adams	50.00	25.00	15.00
139	Morris Arnovich			
140	Carl Hubbell	125.00	62.00	37.00
141	Lew Riggs			
142	Leo Durocher	75.00	37.00	22.00
143	Fred Fitzsimmons			
144	Joe Vosmik	50.00	25.00	15.00
145	Frank Crespi			
146	Jim Brown	50.00	25.00	15.00
147	Don Heffner			
148	Harland Clift (Harlond)	50.00	25.00	15.00
149	Debs Garms			
150	Elbert Fletcher	80.00	40.00	24.00

NOTE: A card number in parentheses ( ) indicates the set is unnumbered.

1950 Drake's

Entitled "TV Baseball Series", the 1950 Drake's Bakeries set pictures 36 different players on a television screen format. The cards, which measure 2-1/2" by 2-1/2", contain black and white photos surrounded by a black border. The card backs carry a player biography plus an advertisement advising collectors to look for the cards in packages of Oatmeal or Jumble cookies. The ACC designation for the set is D358.

		NR MT	EX	VG
Complete Set:		3800.00	1900.00	1140.
Common Player:		50.00	25.00	15.00
1	Elwin "Preacher" Roe	90.00	45.00	27.00
2	Clint Hartung	50.00	25.00	15.00
3	Earl Torgeson	50.00	25.00	15.00
4	Leland "Lou" Brissie	50.00	25.00	15.00
5	Edwin "Duke" Snider	300.00	150.00	90.00
6	Roy Campanella	325.00	162.00	97.00
7	Sheldon "Available" Jones	50.00	25.00	15.00
8	Carroll "Whitey" Lockman	50.00	25.00	15.00
9	Bobby Thomson	70.00	35.00	21.00
10	Dick Sisler	50.00	25.00	15.00
11	Gil Hodges	175.00	87.00	52.00
12	Eddie Waitkus	50.00	25.00	15.00
13	Bobby Doerr	125.00	62.00	37.00
14	Warren Spahn	200.00	100.00	60.00
15	John "Buddy" Kerr	50.00	25.00	15.00
16	Sid Gordon	50.00	25.00	15.00
17	Willard Marshall	50.00	25.00	15.00
18	Carl Furillo	80.00	40.00	24.00
19	Harold "Pee Wee" Reese	250.00	125.00	75.00
20	Alvin Dark	60.00	30.00	18.00
21	Del Ennis	50.00	25.00	15.00
22	Ed Stanky	60.00	30.00	18.00
23	Tommy "Old Reliable" Henrich	80.00	40.00	24.00
24	Larry "Yogi" Berra	325.00	162.00	97.00
25	Phil "Scooter" Rizzuto	200.00	100.00	60.00
26	Jerry Coleman	60.00	30.00	18.00
27	Joe Page	60.00	30.00	18.00
28	Allie Reynolds	80.00	40.00	24.00
29	Ray Scarborough	50.00	25.00	15.00
30	George "Birdie" Tebbetts	50.00	25.00	15.00
31	Maurice "Lefty" McDermott	50.00	25.00	15.00
32	Johnny Pesky	60.00	30.00	18.00
33	Dom "Little Professor" DiMaggio	70.00	35.00	21.00
34	Vern "Junior" Stephens	50.00	25.00	15.00

		NR MT	EX	VG
35	Bob Elliott	50.00	25.00	15.00
36	Enos "Country" Slaughter	175.00	87.00	52.00

1981 Drake's

Producing their first baseball card set since 1950, Drake Bakeries, in conjunction with Topps, issued a 33-card set entitled "Big Hitters." The cards, which are the standard 2-1/2" by 3-1/2" in size, feature 19 American League and 14 National League sluggers. Full-color photos, containing a facsimile autograph, are positioned in red frames for A.L. players and blue frames for N.L. hitters. The player's name, team, position, and the Drake's logo are also included on the card fronts. The card backs, which are similar to the regular 1981 Topps issue, contain the card number (1-33), statistical and biographical information, and the Drake's logo.

		MT	NR MT	EX
Complete Set:		7.00	5.25	2.75
Common Player:		.12	.09	.05
1	Carl Yastrzemski	.70	.50	.30
2	Rod Carew	.50	.40	.20
3	Pete Rose	1.00	.70	.40
4	Dave Parker	.25	.20	.10
5	George Brett	.70	.50	.30
6	Eddie Murray	.50	.40	.20
7	Mike Schmidt	.70	.50	.30
8	Jim Rice	.45	.35	.20
9	Fred Lynn	.25	.20	.10
10	Reggie Jackson	.60	.45	.25
11	Steve Garvey	.45	.35	.20
12	Ken Singleton	.12	.09	.05
13	Bill Buckner	.12	.09	.05
14	Dave Winfield	.50	.40	.20
15	Jack Clark	.30	.25	.12
16	Cecil Cooper	.20	.15	.08
17	Bob Horner	.20	.15	.08
18	George Foster	.20	.15	.08
19	Dave Kingman	.20	.15	.08
20	Cesar Cedeno	.12	.09	.05
21	Joe Charboneau	.12	.09	.05
22	George Hendrick	.12	.09	.05
23	Gary Carter	.45	.35	.20
24	Al Oliver	.20	.15	.08
25	Bruce Bochte	.12	.09	.05
26	Jerry Mumphrey	.12	.09	.05
27	Steve Kemp	.12	.09	.05
28	Bob Watson	.12	.09	.05
29	John Castino	.12	.09	.05
30	Tony Armas	.12	.09	.05
31	John Mayberry	.12	.09	.05
32	Carlton Fisk	.30	.25	.12
33	Lee Mazzilli	.12	.09	.05

1982 Drake's

Drake Bakeries produced, in conjunction with Topps, a "2nd Annual Collectors' Edition" in 1982. Thirty-three standard-size cards (2-1/2" by 3-1/2") make up the set. Like the previous year, the set is entitled "Big Hitters" and is comprised of 19

American League players and 14 from the National League. The card fronts have a mounted photo appearance and contain a facsimile autograph. The player's name, team, position, and the Drake's logo also are located on the fronts. The card backs, other than being numbered 1-33 and containing a Drake's copyright line, are identical to the regular 1982 Topps issue.

		MT	NR MT	EX
Complete Set:		9.00	6.75	3.50
Common Player:		.12	.09	.05
1	Tony Armas	.12	.09	.05
2	Buddy Bell	.20	.15	.08
3	Johnny Bench	.50	.40	.20
4	George Brett	.70	.50	.30
5	Bill Buckner	.12	.09	.05
6	Rod Carew	.50	.40	.20
7	Gary Carter	.45	.35	.20
8	Jack Clark	.30	.25	.12
9	Cecil Cooper	.20	.15	.08
10	Jose Cruz	.12	.09	.05
11	Dwight Evans	.20	.15	.08
12	Carlton Fisk	.30	.25	.12
13	George Foster	.20	.15	.08
14	Steve Garvey	.45	.35	.20
15	Kirk Gibson	.40	.30	.15
16	Mike Hargrove	.12	.09	.05
17	George Hendrick	.12	.09	.05
18	Bob Horner	.20	.15	.08
19	Reggie Jackson	.60	.45	.25
20	Terry Kennedy	.12	.09	.05
21	Dave Kingman	.20	.15	.08
22	Greg Luzinski	.20	.15	.08
23	Bill Madlock	.20	.15	.08
24	John Mayberry	.12	.09	.05
25	Eddie Murray	.50	.40	.20
26	Graig Nettles	.20	.15	.08
27	Jim Rice	.45	.35	.20
28	Pete Rose	1.00	.70	.30
29	Mike Schmidt	.70	.50	.30
30	Ken Singleton	.12	.09	.05
31	Dave Winfield	.50	.40	.20
32	Butch Wynegar	.12	.09	.05
33	Richie Zisk	.12	.09	.05

1983 Drake's

Seventeen American League and 16 National

League "Big Hitters" make up the 33-card "3rd Annual Collectors' Edition" set issued by Drake Bakeries in 1983. The Topps-produced set contains 33 cards which measure 2-1/2" by 3-1/2" in size. The card fronts are somewhat similar in design to the previous year's set. The backs are identical to the 1983 Topps regular issue except for being numbered 1-33 and containing a Drake's logo and copyright line.

		MT	NR MT	EX
Complete Set:		5.00	3.75	2.00
Common Player:		.12	.09	.05
1	Don Baylor	.20	.15	.08
2	Bill Buckner	.12	.09	.05
3	Rod Carew	.50	.40	.20
4	Gary Carter	.45	.35	.20
5	Jack Clark	.25	.20	.10
6	Cecil Cooper	.20	.15	.08
7	Dwight Evans	.20	.15	.08
8	George Foster	.20	.15	.08
9	Pedro Guerrero	.25	.20	.10
10	George Hendrick	.12	.09	.05
11	Bob Horner	.20	.15	.08
12	Reggie Jackson	.60	.45	.25
13	Steve Kemp	.12	.09	.05
14	Dave Kingman	.20	.15	.08
15	Bill Madlock	.20	.15	.08
16	Gary Matthews	.12	.09	.05
17	Hal McRae	.12	.09	.05
18	Dale Murphy	.70	.50	.30
19	Eddie Murray	.50	.40	.20
20	Ben Oglivie	.12	.09	.05
21	Al Oliver	.20	.15	.08
22	Jim Rice	.45	.35	.20
23	Cal Ripken	.60	.45	.25
24	Pete Rose	1.00	.70	.40
25	Mike Schmidt	.70	.50	.30
26	Ken Singleton	.12	.09	.05
27	Gorman Thomas	.12	.09	.05
28	Jason Thompson	.12	.09	.05
29	Mookie Wilson	.10	.08	.04
30	Willie Wilson	.20	.15	.08
31	Dave Winfield	.50	.40	.20
32	Carl Yastrzemski	.70	.50	.30
33	Robin Yount	.40	.30	.15

1984 Drake's

For the fourth year in a row, Drake Bakeries issued a 33-card "Big Hitters" set. The 1984 edition, produced again by Topps, includes 17 National League players and 16 from the American League. As in all previous years, the card fronts feature the player in a batting pose. The backs are identical to the 1984 Topps regular issue except for being numbered 1-33 and carrying the Drake's logo and copyright line. The cards are the standard size 2-1/2" by 3-1/2".

		MT	NR MT	EX
Complete Set:		5.00	3.75	2.00
Complete Set:		.12	.09	.05
1	Don Baylor	.20	.15	.08
2	Wade Boggs	1.25	.90	.50
3	George Brett	.70	.50	.30

		MT	NR MT	EX
4	Bill Buckner	.12	.09	.05
5	Rod Carew	.50	.40	.20
6	Gary Carter	.45	.35	.20
7	Ron Cey	.12	.09	.05
8	Cecil Cooper	.20	.15	.08
9	Andre Dawson	.35	.25	.14
10	Steve Garvey	.45	.35	.20
11	Pedro Guerrero	.25	.20	.10
12	George Hendrick	.12	.09	.05
13	Keith Hernandez	.40	.30	.15
14	Bob Horner	.20	.15	.08
15	Reggie Jackson	.60	.45	.25
16	Steve Kemp	.12	.09	.05
17	Ron Kittle	.20	.15	.08
18	Greg Luzinski	.20	.15	.08
19	Fred Lynn	.20	.15	.08
20	Bill Madlock	.20	.15	.08
21	Gary Matthews	.12	.09	.05
22	Dale Murphy	.70	.50	.30
23	Eddie Murray	.50	.40	.20
24	Al Oliver	.20	.15	.08
25	Jim Rice	.45	.35	.20
26	Cal Ripken	.60	.45	.25
27	Pete Rose	1.00	.70	.40
28	Mike Schmidt	.70	.50	.30
29	Darryl Strawberry	1.25	.90	.50
30	Alan Trammell	.30	.25	.12
31	Mookie Wilson	.12	.09	.05
32	Dave Winfield	.50	.40	.20
33	Robin Yount	.40	.30	.15

1985 Drake's

The "5th Annual Collectors' Edition" set produced by Topps for Drake Bakeries consists of 33 "Big Hitters" and 11 "Super Pitchers." The new "Super Pitchers" feature increased the set's size from the usual 33 cards to 44. The cards, which measure 2-1/2" by 3-1/2", show the player in either a batting or pitching pose. The backs differ only from the regular 1985 Topps issue in that they are numbered 1-44 and carry the Drake's logo.

		MT	NR MT	EX
Complete Set:		9.00	6.75	3.50
Commmon Player:		.12	.09	.05
1	Tony Armas	.12	.09	.05
2	Harold Baines	.20	.15	.08
3	Don Baylor	.20	.15	.08
4	George Brett	.70	.50	.30
5	Gary Carter	.45	.35	.20
6	Ron Cey	.12	.09	.05
7	Jose Cruz	.12	.09	.05
8	Alvin Davis	.25	.20	.10
9	Chili Davis	.12	.09	.05
10	Dwight Evans	.20	.15	.08
11	Steve Garvey	.45	.35	.20
12	Kirk Gibson	.35	.25	.14
13	Pedro Guerrero	.25	.20	.10
14	Tony Gwynn	.60	.45	.25
15	Keith Hernandez	.40	.30	.15
16	Kent Hrbek	.35	.25	.14
17	Reggie Jackson	.60	.45	.25
18	Gary Matthews	.12	.09	.05
19	Don Mattingly	2.25	1.75	.90
20	Dale Murphy	.70	.50	.30
21	Eddie Murray	.45	.35	.20

		MT	NR MT	EX
22	Dave Parker	.20	.15	.08
23	Lance Parrish	.25	.20	.10
24	Tim Raines	.45	.35	.20
25	Jim Rice	.45	.35	.20
26	Cal Ripken	.60	.45	.25
27	Juan Samuel	.25	.20	.10
28	Ryne Sandberg	.40	.30	.15
29	Mike Schmidt	.70	.50	.30
30	Darryl Strawberry	.90	.70	.35
31	Alan Trammell	.30	.25	.12
32	Dave Winfield	.50	.40	.20
33	Robin Yount	.40	.30	.15
34	Mike Boddicker	.12	.09	.05
35	Steve Carlton	.40	.30	.15
36	Dwight Gooden	1.50	1.25	.60
37	Willie Hernandez	.12	.09	.05
38	Mark Langston	.20	.15	.08
39	Dan Quisenberry	.12	.09	.05
40	Dave Righetti	.20	.15	.08
41	Tom Seaver	.40	.30	.15
42	Bob Stanley	.12	.09	.05
43	Rick Sutcliffe	.20	.15	.08
44	Bruce Sutter	.20	.15	.08

		MT	NR MT	EX
15	Tim Raines	.50	.40	.20
Panel		2.00	1.50	.80
16	Darryl Strawberry	.80	.60	.30
17	Bill Buckner	.20	.15	.08
Panel		2.75	2.00	1.00
18	Dave Winfield	.50	.40	.20
19	Ryne Sandberg	.40	.30	.15
20	Steve Balboni	.20	.15	.08
21	Tom Herr	.25	.20	.10
Panel		3.75	2.75	1.50
22	Pete Rose	.90	.70	.35
23	Willie McGee	.25	.20	.10
24	Harold Baines	.25	.20	.10
25	Eddie Murray	.50	.40	.20
Panel		4.00	3.00	1.50
26	Mike Schmidt	.60	.45	.25
27	Wade Boggs	1.25	.90	.50
28	Kirk Gibson	.35	.25	.14
Panel		2.00	1.50	.80
29	Bret Saberhagen	.35	.25	.14
30	John Tudor	.20	.15	.08
31	Orel Hershiser	.40	.30	.15
Panel		2.00	1.50	.80
32	Ron Guidry	.25	.20	.10
33	Nolan Ryan	.35	.25	.14
34	Dave Stieb	.25	.20	.10
Panel		2.75	2.00	1.00
35	Dwight Gooden	.80	.60	.30
36	Fernando Valenzuela	.35	.25	.14
37	Tom Browning	.25	.20	.10

1986 Drake's

For the sixth year in a row, Drake Bakeries issued a baseball card set. Produced for Drake's by Topps in the past, the 1986 set was not and was available only by buying the actual products the cards were printed on. The cards, which measure 2-1/2" by 3-1/2", were issued in either two-, three-, or four-card panels. Fourteen panels, consisting of 37 different players, comprise the set. The players who make up the set are tabbed as either "Big Hitters" or "Super Pitchers." Logos of various Drake's products can be found on the panel backs. The value of the set is higher when collected in either panel or complete box form.

		MT	NR MT	EX
Complete Panel Set:		40.00	30.00	16.00
Complete Singles Set:		25.00	18.50	10.00
Common Panel:		1.75	1.25	.70
Common Single Player:		.20	.15	.08
Panel		1.75	1.25	.70
1	Gary Carter	.50	.40	.20
2	Dwight Evans	.25	.20	.10
Panel		2.00	1.50	.80
3	Reggie Jackson	.60	.45	.25
4	Dave Parker	.25	.20	.10
Panel		2.00	1.50	.80
5	Rickey Henderson	.60	.45	.25
6	Pedro Guerrero	.30	.25	.12
Panel		5.00	3.75	2.00
7	Don Mattingly	2.00	1.50	.80
8	Mike Marshall	.25	.20	.10
9	Keith Moreland	.20	.15	.08
Panel		2.00	1.50	.80
10	Keith Hernandez	.40	.30	.15
11	Cal Ripken	.60	.45	.25
Panel		2.25	1.75	.90
12	Dale Murphy	.60	.45	.25
13	Jim Rice	.40	.30	.15
Panel		2.25	1.75	.90
14	George Brett	.60	.45	.25

1987 Drake's

For the seventh consecutive season, Drake Bakeries produced a baseball card set. The cards, which measure 2-1/2" by 3-1/2", were included in either two-, three-, or four-card panels on boxes of various Drake's products distributed in the eastern United States. The set is comprised of 33 cards, with 25 players branded as "Big Hitters" and 8 as "Super Pitchers". The card fronts carry a full-color photo and the Drake's logo surrounded by a brown and yellow border. The backs contain the player's complete major league record.

		MT	NR MT	EX
Complete Panel Set:		40.00	30.00	16.00
Complete Singles Set:		25.00	18.50	10.00
Common Panel:		1.75	1.25	.70
Common Single Player:		.20	.15	.08
Panel		4.00	3.00	1.50
1	Darryl Strawberry	.80	.60	.30
2	Wally Joyner	1.25	.90	.50
Panel		3.75	2.75	1.50
3	Von Hayes	.25	.20	.10
4	Jose Canseco	1.75	1.25	.70
Panel		2.00	1.50	.80
5	Dave Winfield	.50	.40	.20
6	Cal Ripken	.60	.45	.25
Panel		4.50	3.50	1.75
7	Keith Moreland	.20	.15	.08
8	Don Mattingly	2.00	1.50	.80
9	Willie McGee	.25	.20	.10
Panel		2.00	1.50	.80
10	Keith Hernandez	.40	.30	.15
11	Tony Gwynn	.60	.45	.25

	MT	NR MT	EX
Panel	4.25	3.25	1.75
12 Rickey Henderson	.50	.40	.20
13 Dale Murphy	.60	.45	.25
14 George Brett	.60	.45	.25
15 Jim Rice	.40	.30	.15
Panel	4.00	3.00	1.50
16 Wade Boggs	1.25	.90	.50
17 Kevin Bass	.20	.15	.08
18 Dave Parker	.25	.20	.10
19 Kirby Puckett	.50	.40	.20
Panel	2.00	1.50	.80
20 Gary Carter	.50	.40	.20
21 Ryne Sandberg	.40	.30	.15
22 Harold Baines	.25	.20	.10
Panel	2.75	2.00	1.00
23 Mike Schmidt	.60	.45	.25
24 Eddie Murray	.50	.40	.20
25 Steve Sax	.25	.20	.10
Panel	1.75	1.25	.70
26 Dwight Gooden	.80	.60	.30
27 Jack Morris	.25	.20	.10
Panel	1.75	1.25	.70
28 Ron Darling	.25	.20	.10
29 Fernando Valenzuela	.35	.25	.14
30 John Tudor	.20	.15	.08
Panel	2.50	2.00	1.00
31 Roger Clemens	.80	.60	.30
32 Nolan Ryan	.35	.25	.14
33 Mike Scott	.25	.20	.10

	MT	NR MT	EX
Panel	2.75	2.00	1.00
12 Dave Winfield	.50	.40	.20
13 Alan Trammell	.35	.25	.14
14 Tony Gwynn	.50	.40	.20
Panel	2.50	2.00	1.00
15 Dale Murphy	.60	.45	.25
16 Andre Dawson	.30	.25	.12
17 Von Hayes	.20	.15	.08
18 Willie Randolph	.20	.15	.08
Panel	2.00	1.50	.80
19 Kirby Puckett	.50	.40	.20
20 Juan Samuel	.25	.20	.10
21 Eddie Murray	.40	.30	.15
Panel	3.00	2.25	1.25
22 George Bell	.35	.25	.14
23 Larry Sheets	.20	.15	.08
24 Eric Davis	.70	.50	.30
Panel	2.25	1.75	.90
25 Cal Ripken	.60	.45	.25
26 Pedro Guerrero	.25	.20	.10
27 Will Clark	.50	.40	.20
Panel	2.00	1.50	.80
28 Dwight Gooden	.80	.60	.30
29 Frank Viola	.25	.20	.10
Panel	3.00	2.25	1.25
30 Roger Clemens	.80	.60	.30
31 Rick Sutcliffe	.20	.15	.08
32 Jack Morris	.25	.20	.10
33 John Tudor	.20	.15	.08

1988 Drake's

The 8th annual edition of this set includes 33 glossy full-color cards printed on cut-out panels of 2, 3 or 4 cards on Drake's dessert snack boxes. Card fronts have white borders with a large red and blue "Super Pitchers" (6 cards) or "Big Hitters" (27 cards) caption upper left, beside the "8th Annual Collector's Edition" label. The Drake logo, player name and team logo are printed in black and include the card number, personal data, batting/pitching record and sponsor logos. Sets were available exclusively on 12 different Drake's packages. To complete the set, collectors had to purchase all 12 products.

	MT	NR MT	EX
Complete Panel Set:	40.00	30.00	16.00
Complete Singles Set:	25.00	18.50	10.00
Common Panel:	1.75	1.25	.70
Common Single Player:	.20	.15	.08
Panel	4.25	3.25	1.75
1 Don Mattingly	2.00	1.50	.80
2 Tim Raines	.50	.40	.20
Panel	3.75	2.75	1.50
3 Darryl Strawberry	.80	.60	.30
4 Wade Boggs	1.25	.90	.50
Panel	3.25	2.50	1.25
5 Keith Hernandez	.40	.30	.15
6 Mark McGwire	1.25	.90	.50
Panel	2.75	2.00	1.00
7 Rickey Henderson	.50	.40	.20
8 Mike Schmidt	.60	.45	.25
9 Dwight Evans	.25	.20	.10
Panel	1.75	1.25	.70
10 Gary Carter	.50	.40	.20
11 Paul Molitor	.30	.25	.12

1909-11 E90-1 American Caramel

Davis, 1b Phila. Amer.

The E90-1 set was issued by the American Caramel Co. from 1909 through 1911, with the bulk of the set being produced in the first year. The cards, which measure 1-1/2" by 2-3/4" in size and were issued with sticks of caramel candy, are color reproductions of actual photographs. The card backs state that 100 subjects are included in the set though more actually do exist. There are several levels of scarcity in the set, those levels being mostly determined by the year the cards were issued. Mitchell (Cincinnati), Clarke (Pittsburg), Graham, and Sweeney (Boston) are the most difficult cards in the set to obtain. For the collector's convenience, the players' first names have been added in the checklist that follows. The complete set price includes all variations.

	NR MT	EX	VG
Complete Set:	17500.00	8750.00	5250.

		NR MT	EX	VG
Common Player:		40.00	20.00	12.00
(1)	Bill Bailey	40.00	20.00	12.00
(2)	Home Run Baker	110.00	55.00	33.00
(3)	Jack Barry	40.00	20.00	12.00
(4)	George Bell	40.00	20.00	12.00
(5)	Harry Bemis	80.00	40.00	24.00
(6)	Chief Bender	100.00	50.00	30.00
(7)	Bob Bescher	65.00	32.00	19.50
(8)	Cliff Blankenship	40.00	20.00	12.00
(9)	John Bliss	40.00	20.00	12.00
(10)	Bill Bradley	40.00	20.00	12.00
(11)	Kitty Bransfield ("P" on shirt)	40.00	20.00	12.00
(12)	Kitty Bransfield (no "P" on shirt)	65.00	32.00	19.50
(13)	Roger Bresnahan	100.00	50.00	30.00
(14)	Al Bridwell	40.00	20.00	12.00
(15)	Buster Brown (Boston)	40.00	20.00	12.00
(16)	Mordecai Brown (Chicago)	150.00	75.00	45.00
(17)	Donie Bush	40.00	20.00	12.00
(18)	John Butler	40.00	20.00	12.00
(19)	Howie Camnitz	40.00	20.00	12.00
(20)	Frank Chance	110.00	55.00	33.00
(21)	Hal Chase	55.00	27.00	16.50
(22a)	Fred Clarke (Philadelphia)	100.00	50.00	30.00
(22b)	Fred Clarke (Pittsburgh)	550.00	275.00	165.00
(23)	Wally Clement	65.00	32.00	19.50
(24)	Ty Cobb	900.00	450.00	270.00
(25)	Eddie Collins	110.00	55.00	33.00
(26)	Sam Crawford	100.00	50.00	30.00
(27)	Frank Corridon	40.00	20.00	12.00
(28)	Lou Criger	40.00	20.00	12.00
(29)	George Davis	40.00	20.00	12.00
(30)	Harry Davis	40.00	20.00	12.00
(31)	Ray Demmitt	100.00	50.00	30.00
(32)	Mike Donlin	40.00	20.00	12.00
(33)	Wild Bill Donovan	40.00	20.00	12.00
(34)	Red Dooin	40.00	20.00	12.00
(35)	Patsy Dougherty	80.00	40.00	24.00
(36)	Hugh Duffy	600.00	300.00	180.00
(37)	Jimmy Dygert	40.00	20.00	12.00
(38)	Rube Ellis	40.00	20.00	12.00
(39)	Clyde Engle	40.00	20.00	12.00
(40)	Art Fromme	90.00	45.00	27.00
(41)	George Gibson (back view)	150.00	75.00	45.00
(42)	George Gibson (front view)	40.00	20.00	12.00
(43)	Peaches Graham	800.00	400.00	240.00
(44)	Eddie Grant	40.00	20.00	12.00
(45)	Dolly Gray	40.00	20.00	12.00
(46)	Bob Groom	40.00	20.00	12.00
(47)	Charley Hall	40.00	20.00	12.00
(48)	Roy Hartzell (fielding)	40.00	20.00	12.00
(49)	Roy Hartzell (batting)	40.00	20.00	12.00
(50)	Heinie Heitmuller	40.00	20.00	12.00
(51)	Harry Howell (follow thru)	40.00	20.00	12.00
(52)	Harry Howell (windup)	65.00	32.00	19.50
(53)	Tex Irwin (Erwin)	40.00	20.00	12.00
(54)	Frank Isbell	40.00	20.00	12.00
(55)	Shoeless Joe Jackson	1000.00	500.00	300.00
(56)	Hughie Jennings	100.00	50.00	30.00
(57)	Buck Jordon (Jordan)	40.00	20.00	12.00
(58)	Addie Joss (portrait)	100.00	50.00	30.00
(59)	Addie Joss (pitching)	550.00	275.00	165.00
(60)	Ed Karger	550.00	275.00	165.00
(61a)	Willie Keeler (portrait, pink background)	100.00	50.00	30.00
(61b)	Willie Keeler (portrait, red background)	300.00	150.00	90.00
(62)	Willie Keeler (throwing)	600.00	300.00	180.00
(63)	John Knight	40.00	20.00	12.00
(64)	Harry Krause	40.00	20.00	12.00
(65)	Nap Lajoie	225.00	112.00	67.00
(66)	Tommy Leach (throwing)	40.00	20.00	12.00
(67)	Tommy Leach (batting)	40.00	20.00	12.00
(68)	Sam Leever	40.00	20.00	12.00
(69)	Hans Lobert	80.00	40.00	24.00
(70)	Harry Lumley	40.00	20.00	12.00
(71)	Rube Marquard	100.00	50.00	30.00
(72)	Christy Matthewson (Mathewson)	325.00	162.00	97.00
(73)	Stuffy McInnes (McInnis)	40.00	20.00	12.00
(74)	Harry McIntyre	40.00	20.00	12.00
(75)	Larry McLean	80.00	40.00	24.00
(76)	George McQuillan	40.00	20.00	12.00
(77)	Dots Miller	40.00	20.00	12.00
(78)	Fred Mitchell (New York)	40.00	20.00	12.00
(79)	Mike Mitchell (Cincinnati)	2200.00	1100.00	660.00
(80)	George Mullin	40.00	20.00	12.00
(81)	Rebel Oakes	40.00	20.00	12.00
(82)	Paddy O'Connor	40.00	20.00	12.00
(83)	Charley O'Leary	40.00	20.00	12.00
(84)	Orval Overall	65.00	32.00	19.50

		NR MT	EX	VG
(85)	Jim Pastorius	40.00	20.00	12.00
(86)	Ed Phelps	40.00	20.00	12.00
(87)	Eddie Plank	200.00	100.00	60.00
(88)	Lew Richie	40.00	20.00	12.00
(89)	Germany Schaefer	40.00	20.00	12.00
(90)	Biff Schlitzer	65.00	32.00	19.50
(91)	Johnny Seigle (Siegle)	80.00	40.00	24.00
(92)	Dave Shean	65.00	32.00	19.50
(93)	Jimmy Sheckard	65.00	32.00	19.50
(94)	Tris Speaker	500.00	250.00	150.00
(95)	Jake Stahl	550.00	275.00	165.00
(96)	Oscar Stanage	40.00	20.00	12.00
(97)	George Stone (no hands visible)	40.00	20.00	12.00
(98)	George Stone (left hand visible)	40.00	20.00	12.00
(99)	George Stovall	40.00	20.00	12.00
(100)	Ed Summers	40.00	20.00	12.00
(101)	Bill Sweeney (Boston)	800.00	400.00	240.00
(102)	Jeff Sweeney (New York)	40.00	20.00	12.00
(103)	Jesse Tannehill (Chicago A.L.)	40.00	20.00	12.00
(104)	Lee Tannehill (Chicago N.L.)	40.00	20.00	12.00
(105)	Fred Tenney	40.00	20.00	12.00
(106)	Ira Thomas (Philadelphia)	40.00	20.00	12.00
(107)	Roy Thomas (Boston)	40.00	20.00	12.00
(108)	Joe Tinker	100.00	50.00	30.00
(109)	Bob Unglaub	40.00	20.00	12.00
(110)	Jerry Upp	40.00	20.00	12.00
(111)	Honus Wagner (batting)	400.00	200.00	125.00
(112)	Honus Wagner (throwing)	400.00	200.00	125.00
(113)	Bobby Wallace	90.00	45.00	27.00
(114)	Ed Walsh	550.00	275.00	165.00
(115)	Vic Willis	40.00	20.00	12.00
(116)	Hooks Wiltse	80.00	40.00	24.00
(117)	Cy Young (Cleveland)	300.00	150.00	90.00
(118)	Cy Young (Boston)	200.00	100.00	60.00

1922 E120 American Caramel

One of the most popular of the "E" issues, the 1922 E120 set was produced by the American Caramel Co. in 1922 and distributed with sticks of caramel candy. The unnumbered cards measure 2" by 3-1/2" in size. Cards depicting players from the American League are printed in brown ink on yellow, while the National Leaguers are printed in green on a blue-green background. The card reverses carry team checklists Many of the E120 photos were used in other sets such as E121, W572, W573 and V61.

		NR MT	EX	VG
Complete Set:		10000.00	5000.00	3000.
Common Player:		30.00	15.00	9.00
(1)	Charles (Babe) Adams	30.00	15.00	9.00
(2)	Eddie Ainsmith	30.00	15.00	9.00
(3)	Vic Aldridge	30.00	15.00	9.00
(4)	Grover C. Alexander	70.00	35.00	21.00
(5)	Jim Bagby	30.00	15.00	9.00
(6)	Frank (Home Run) Baker	60.00	30.00	18.00
(7)	Dave (Beauty) Bancroft	60.00	30.00	18.00
(8)	Walt Barbare	30.00	15.00	9.00

		NR MT	EX	VG
(9)	Turner Barber	30.00	15.00	9.00
(10)	Jess Barnes	30.00	15.00	9.00
(11)	Clyde Barnhart	30.00	15.00	9.00
(12)	John Bassler	30.00	15.00	9.00
(13)	Will Bayne	30.00	15.00	9.00
(14)	Walter (Huck) Betts	30.00	15.00	9.00
(15)	Carson Bigbee	30.00	15.00	9.00
(16)	Lu Blue	30.00	15.00	9.00
(17)	Norman Boeckel	30.00	15.00	9.00
(18)	Sammy Bohne	30.00	15.00	9.00
(19)	George Burns	30.00	15.00	9.00
(20)	George Burns	30.00	15.00	9.00
(21)	"Bullet Joe" Bush	30.00	15.00	9.00
(22)	Leon Cadore	35.00	17.50	10.50
(23)	Marty Callaghan	30.00	15.00	9.00
(24)	Frank Calloway (Callaway)	30.00	15.00	9.00
(25)	Max Carey	60.00	30.00	18.00
(26)	Jimmy Caveney	30.00	15.00	9.00
(27)	Virgil Cheeves	30.00	15.00	9.00
(28)	Vern Clemons	30.00	15.00	9.00
(29)	Ty Cob (Cobb)	600.00	300.00	180.00
(30)	Bert Cole	30.00	15.00	9.00
(31)	Eddie Collins	75.00	37.00	22.00
(32)	John (Shano) Collins	30.00	15.00	9.00
(33)	T.P. (Pat) Collins	30.00	15.00	9.00
(34)	Wilbur Cooper	30.00	15.00	9.00
(35)	Harry Courtney	30.00	15.00	9.00
(36)	Stanley Coveleskie (Coveleski)	60.00	30.00	18.00
(37)	Elmer Cox	30.00	15.00	9.00
(38)	Sam Crane	30.00	15.00	9.00
(39)	Walton Cruise	30.00	15.00	9.00
(40)	Bill Cunningham	30.00	15.00	9.00
(41)	George Cutshaw	30.00	15.00	9.00
(42)	Dave Danforth	30.00	15.00	9.00
(43)	Jake Daubert	30.00	15.00	9.00
(44)	George Dauss	30.00	15.00	9.00
(45)	Frank (Dixie) Davis	30.00	15.00	9.00
(46)	Hank DeBerry	30.00	15.00	9.00
(47)	Albert (Lou) Devormer (DeVormer)	35.00	17.50	10.50
(48)	Bill Doak	30.00	15.00	9.00
(49)	Pete Donohue	30.00	15.00	9.00
(50)	"Shufflin" Phil Douglas	35.00	17.50	10.50
(51)	Joe Dugan	35.00	17.50	10.50
(52)	Louis (Pat) Duncan	30.00	15.00	9.00
(53)	Jimmy Dykes	35.00	17.50	10.50
(54)	Howard Ehmke	35.00	17.50	10.50
(55)	Frank Ellerbe	30.00	15.00	9.00
(56)	Urban (Red) Faber	60.00	30.00	18.00
(57)	Bib Falk (Bibb)	30.00	15.00	9.00
(58)	Dana Fillingim	30.00	15.00	9.00
(59)	Max Flack	30.00	15.00	9.00
(60)	Ira Flagstead	30.00	15.00	9.00
(61)	Art Fletcher	30.00	15.00	9.00
(62)	Horace Ford	30.00	15.00	9.00
(63)	Jack Fournier	30.00	15.00	9.00
(64)	Frank Frisch	70.00	35.00	21.00
(65)	Ollie Fuhrman	30.00	15.00	9.00
(66)	Clarance Galloway	30.00	15.00	9.00
(67)	Larry Gardner	30.00	15.00	9.00
(68)	Walter Gerber	30.00	15.00	9.00
(69)	Ed Gharrity	30.00	15.00	9.00
(70)	John Gillespie	30.00	15.00	9.00
(71)	Chas. (Whitey) Glazner	30.00	15.00	9.00
(72)	Johnny Gooch	30.00	15.00	9.00
(73)	Leon Goslin	60.00	30.00	18.00
(74)	Hank Gowdy	35.00	17.50	10.50
(75)	John Graney	30.00	15.00	9.00
(76)	Tom Griffith	30.00	15.00	9.00
(77)	Burleigh Grimes	60.00	30.00	18.00
(78)	Oscar Ray Grimes	30.00	15.00	9.00
(79)	Charlie Grimm	30.00	15.00	9.00
(80)	Heinie Groh	30.00	15.00	9.00
(81)	Jesse Haines	60.00	30.00	18.00
(82)	Earl Hamilton	30.00	15.00	9.00
(83)	Gene (Bubbles) Hargrave	30.00	15.00	9.00
(84)	Bryan Harris (Harriss)	30.00	15.00	9.00
(85)	Joe Harris	30.00	15.00	9.00
(86)	Stanley Harris	30.00	15.00	9.00
(87)	Chas. (Dowdy) Hartnett	60.00	30.00	18.00
(88)	Bob Hasty	30.00	15.00	9.00
(89)	Joe Hauser	30.00	15.00	9.00
(90)	Clif Heathcote (Cliff)	30.00	15.00	9.00
(91)	Harry Heilmann	60.00	30.00	18.00
(92)	Walter (Butch) Henline	30.00	15.00	9.00
(93)	Clarence (Shovel) Hodge	30.00	15.00	9.00
(94)	Walter Holke	30.00	15.00	9.00
(95)	Charles Hollocher	30.00	15.00	9.00
(96)	Harry Hooper	60.00	30.00	18.00
(97)	Rogers Hornsby	150.00	75.00	45.00
(98)	Waite Hoyt	60.00	30.00	18.00
(99)	Wilbur Hubbell (Wilbert)	30.00	15.00	9.00
(100)	Bernard (Bud) Hungling	30.00	15.00	9.00
(101)	Will Jacobson	30.00	15.00	9.00
(102)	Charlie Jamieson	30.00	15.00	9.00
(103)	Ernie Johnson	30.00	15.00	9.00
(104)	Sylvester Johnson	30.00	15.00	9.00
(105)	Walter Johnson	300.00	150.00	90.00
(106)	Jimmy Johnston	30.00	15.00	9.00
(107)	W.R. (Doc) Johnston	30.00	15.00	9.00
(108)	"Deacon" Sam Jones	35.00	17.50	10.50
(109)	Bob Jones	30.00	15.00	9.00
(110)	Percy Jones	30.00	15.00	9.00
(111)	Joe Judge	30.00	15.00	9.00
(112)	Ben Karr	30.00	15.00	9.00
(113)	Johnny Kelleher	30.00	15.00	9.00
(114)	George Kelly	60.00	30.00	18.00
(115)	Lee King	30.00	15.00	9.00
(116)	Wm (Larry) Kopff (Kopf)	30.00	15.00	9.00
(117)	Marty Krug	30.00	15.00	9.00
(118)	Johnny Lavan	30.00	15.00	9.00
(119)	Nemo Leibold	30.00	15.00	9.00
(120)	Roy Leslie	30.00	15.00	9.00
(121)	George Leverette (Leverett)	30.00	15.00	9.00
(122)	Adolfo Luque	30.00	15.00	9.00
(123)	Walter Mails	30.00	15.00	9.00
(124)	Al Mamaux	30.00	15.00	9.00
(125)	"Rabbit" Maranville	60.00	30.00	18.00
(126)	Cliff Markle	30.00	15.00	9.00
(127)	Richard (Rube) Marquard	60.00	30.00	18.00
(128)	Carl Mays	40.00	20.00	12.00
(129)	Hervey McClellan (Harvey)	30.00	15.00	9.00
(130)	Austin McHenry	30.00	15.00	9.00
(131)	"Stuffy" McInnis	35.00	17.50	10.50
(132)	Martin McManus	30.00	15.00	9.00
(133)	Mike McNally	35.00	17.50	10.50
(134)	Hugh McQuillan	30.00	15.00	9.00
(135)	Lee Meadows	30.00	15.00	9.00
(136)	Mike Menosky	30.00	15.00	9.00
(137)	Bob (Emil) Meusel	40.00	20.00	12.00
(138)	Emil (Irish) Meusel	30.00	15.00	9.00
(139)	Clyde Milan	30.00	15.00	9.00
(140)	Edmund (Bing) Miller	30.00	15.00	9.00
(141)	Elmer Miller	35.00	17.50	10.50
(142)	Lawrence (Hack) Miller	30.00	15.00	9.00
(143)	Clarence Mitchell	30.00	15.00	9.00
(144)	George Mogridge	30.00	15.00	9.00
(145)	Roy Moore	30.00	15.00	9.00
(146)	John L. Mokan	30.00	15.00	9.00
(147)	John Morrison	30.00	15.00	9.00
(148)	Johnny Mostil	30.00	15.00	9.00
(149)	Elmer Myers	30.00	15.00	9.00
(150)	Hy Myers	30.00	15.00	9.00
(151)	Roliene Naylor (Roleine)	30.00	15.00	9.00
(152)	Earl (Greasy) Neale	40.00	20.00	12.00
(153)	Art Nehf	30.00	15.00	9.00
(154)	Les Nunamaker	30.00	15.00	9.00
(155)	Joe Oeschger	35.00	17.50	10.50
(156)	Bob O'Farrell	30.00	15.00	9.00
(157)	Ivan Olson	30.00	15.00	9.00
(158)	George O'Neil	30.00	15.00	9.00
(159)	Steve O'Neill	30.00	15.00	9.00
(160)	Frank Parkinson	30.00	15.00	9.00
(161)	Roger Peckinpaugh	30.00	15.00	9.00
(162)	Herb Pennock	60.00	30.00	18.00
(163)	Ralph (Cy) Perkins	30.00	15.00	9.00
(164)	Will Pertica	30.00	15.00	9.00
(165)	Jack Peters	30.00	15.00	9.00
(166)	Tom Phillips	30.00	15.00	9.00
(167)	Val Picinich	30.00	15.00	9.00
(168)	Herman Pillette	30.00	15.00	9.00
(169)	Ralph Pinelli	35.00	17.50	10.50
(170)	Wallie Pipp	50.00	25.00	15.00
(171)	Clark Pittenger (Clarke)	30.00	15.00	9.00
(172)	Raymond Powell	30.00	15.00	9.00
(173)	Derrill Pratt	30.00	15.00	9.00
(174)	Jack Quinn	30.00	15.00	9.00
(175)	Joe (Goldie) Rapp	30.00	15.00	9.00
(176)	John Rawlings	30.00	15.00	9.00
(177)	Walter (Dutch) Reuther (Ruether)	30.00	15.00	9.00
(178)	Sam Rice	60.00	30.00	18.00
(179)	Emory Rigney	30.00	15.00	9.00
(180)	Jimmy Ring	30.00	15.00	9.00
(181)	Eppa Rixey	60.00	30.00	18.00
(182)	Charles Robertson	30.00	15.00	9.00
(183)	Ed Rommel	35.00	17.50	10.50
(184)	Eddie Roush	60.00	30.00	18.00
(185)	Harold (Muddy) Ruel (Herold)	30.00	15.00	9.00
(186)	Babe Ruth	900.00	450.00	275.00
(187)	Ray Schalk	60.00	30.00	18.00
(188)	Wallie Schang	35.00	17.50	10.50

	NR MT	EX	VG
(189) Ray Schmandt	30.00	15.00	9.00
(190) Walter Schmidt	30.00	15.00	9.00
(191) Joe Schultz	30.00	15.00	9.00
(192) Everett Scott	35.00	17.50	10.50
(193) Henry Severeid	30.00	15.00	9.00
(194) Joe Sewell	70.00	35.00	21.00
(195) Howard Shanks	30.00	15.00	9.00
(196) Bob Shawkey	30.00	15.00	9.00
(197) Earl Sheely	30.00	15.00	9.00
(198) Will Sherdel	30.00	15.00	9.00
(199) Ralph Shinners	30.00	15.00	9.00
(200) Urban Shocker	30.00	15.00	9.00
(201) Charles (Chick) Shorten	30.00	15.00	9.00
(202) George Sisler	70.00	35.00	21.00
(203) Earl Smith	30.00	15.00	9.00
(204) Earl Smith	30.00	15.00	9.00
(205) Elmer Smith	30.00	15.00	9.00
(206) Jack Smith	30.00	15.00	9.00
(207) Sherrod Smith	30.00	15.00	9.00
(208) Colonel Snover	30.00	15.00	9.00
(209) Frank Snyder	30.00	15.00	9.00
(210) Al Sothoron	30.00	15.00	9.00
(211) Bill Southworth	35.00	17.50	10.50
(212) Tris Speaker	150.00	75.00	45.00
(213) Arnold Statz	30.00	15.00	9.00
(214) Milton Stock	30.00	15.00	9.00
(215) Amos Strunk	30.00	15.00	9.00
(216) Jim Tierney	30.00	15.00	9.00
(217) John Tobin	30.00	15.00	9.00
(218) Fred Toney	30.00	15.00	9.00
(219) George Toporcer	30.00	15.00	9.00
(220) Harold (Pie) Traynor	60.00	30.00	18.00
(221) George Uhle	30.00	15.00	9.00
(222) Elam Vangilder	30.00	15.00	9.00
(223) Bob Veach	30.00	15.00	9.00
(224) Clarence (Tillie) Walker	30.00	15.00	9.00
(225) Curtis Walker	30.00	15.00	9.00
(226) Al Walters	30.00	15.00	9.00
(227) Bill Wambsganss	30.00	15.00	9.00
(228) Aaron (Erin) Ward	35.00	17.50	10.50
(229) John Watson	30.00	15.00	9.00
(230) Frank Welch	30.00	15.00	9.00
(231) Zach Wheat	60.00	30.00	18.00
(232) Fred (Cy) Williams	30.00	15.00	9.00
(233) Kenneth Williams	30.00	15.00	9.00
(234) Ivy Wingo	30.00	15.00	9.00
(235) Joe Wood	30.00	15.00	9.00
(236) Lawrence Woodall	30.00	15.00	9.00
(237) Russell Wrightstone	30.00	15.00	9.00
(238) Everett Yaryan	30.00	15.00	9.00
(239) Ross Young (Youngs)	60.00	30.00	18.00
(240) J.T. Zachary	30.00	15.00	9.00

1921 E121 American Caramel Series Of 80

DUFFY LEWIS
L. F. Washington Americans

THIS SET CONSISTS OF PICTURES OF EIGHTY OF THE leading BASE BALL STARS of the AMERICAN AND NATIONAL LEAGUES. Made only by— AMERICAN CARAMEL COMPANY, LANCASTER AND YORK, PENNA.

Issued circa 1921, the E121 Series of 80 is designated as such because of the card reverses which indicate the player pictured is just one of 80 baseball stars in the set. The figure of 80 supplied by the American Caramel Co. is incorrect as over 100

different pictures do exist. The unnumbered cards, which measure 2" by 3-1/2", feature black and white photos. Two different backs exist for the Series of 80. The common back variation has the first line ending with the word "the," while the scarcer version ends with the word "eighty." The complete set price does not include the variations.

	NR MT	EX	VG
Complete Set:	5700.00	2850.00	1710.
Commmon Player:	25.00	12.50	7.50
(1) G.C. Alexander (arms above head)	75.00	37.00	22.00
(2) Grover Alexander	60.00	30.00	18.00
(3) Jim Bagby	25.00	12.50	7.50
(4a) J. Franklin Baker	50.00	25.00	15.00
(4b) Frank Baker	50.00	25.00	15.00
(5) Dave Bancroft (batting)	50.00	25.00	15.00
(6) Dave Bancroft (leaping)	50.00	25.00	15.00
(7) Ping Bodie	25.00	12.50	7.50
(8) George Burns	25.00	12.50	7.50
(9) Geo. J. Burns	25.00	12.50	7.50
(10) Owen Bush	25.00	12.50	7.50
(11) Max Carey (batting)	50.00	25.00	15.00
(12) Max Carey (hands at hips)	50.00	25.00	15.00
(13) Cecil Causey	25.00	12.50	7.50
(14) Ty Cobb (throwing, looking front)	400.00	200.00	120.00
(15a) Ty Cobb (throwing, looking right, Mgr. on front)	400.00	200.00	120.00
(15b) Ty Cobb (throwing, looking right, Manager on front)	400.00	200.00	120.00
(16) Eddie Collins	70.00	35.00	21.00
(17) "Rip" Collins	25.00	12.50	7.50
(18) Jake Daubert	30.00	15.00	9.00
(19) George Dauss	25.00	12.50	7.50
(20) Charles Deal (dark uniform)	25.00	12.50	7.50
(21) Charles Deal (white uniform)	25.00	12.50	7.50
(22) William Doak	25.00	12.50	7.50
(23) Bill Donovan	25.00	12.50	7.50
(24) "Phil" Douglas	35.00	17.50	10.50
(25a) Johnny Evers (Manager)	50.00	25.00	15.00
(25b) Johnny Evers (Mgr.)	50.00	25.00	15.00
(26) Urban Faber (dark uniform)	50.00	25.00	15.00
(27) Urban Faber (white uniform)	50.00	25.00	15.00
(28) William Fewster (first name actually Wilson)	25.00	12.50	7.50
(29) Eddie Foster	25.00	12.50	7.50
(30) Frank Frisch	60.00	30.00	18.00
(31) W.L. Gardner	25.00	12.50	7.50
(32a) Alexander Gaston (no position on front)	25.00	12.50	7.50
(32b) Alexander Gaston (position on front)	25.00	12.50	7.50
(33) "Kid" Gleason	25.00	12.50	7.50
(34) "Mike" Gonzalez	25.00	12.50	7.50
(35) Hank Gowdy	25.00	12.50	7.50
(36) John Graney	25.00	12.50	7.50
(37) Tom Griffith	25.00	12.50	7.50
(38) Heinie Groh	30.00	15.00	9.00
(39) Harry Harper	25.00	12.50	7.50
(40) Harry Heilman (Heilmann)	50.00	25.00	15.00
(41) Walter Holke (portrait)	25.00	12.50	7.50
(42) Walter Holke (throwing)	25.00	12.50	7.50
(43) Charles Hollacher (Hollocher)	25.00	12.50	7.50
(44) Harry Hooper	50.00	25.00	15.00
(45) Rogers Hornsby	100.00	50.00	30.00
(46) Waite Hoyt	50.00	25.00	15.00
(47) Miller Huggins	50.00	25.00	15.00
(48) Wm. C. Jacobson	25.00	12.50	7.50
(49) Hugh Jennings	50.00	25.00	15.00
(50) Walter Johnson (throwing)	175.00	87.00	52.00
(51) Walter Johnson (hands at chest)	175.00	87.00	52.00
(52) James Johnston	25.00	12.50	7.50
(53) Joe Judge	25.00	12.50	7.50
(54) George Kelly	50.00	25.00	15.00
(55) Dick Kerr	25.00	12.50	7.50
(56) P.J. Kilduff	25.00	12.50	7.50
(57a) Bill Killifer (incorrect name)	35.00	17.50	10.50
(57b) Bill Killefer (correct name)	30.00	15.00	9.00
(58) John Lavan	25.00	12.50	7.50
(59) "Nemo" Leibold	25.00	12.50	7.50
(60) Duffy Lewis	30.00	15.00	9.00
(61) Al. Mamaux	25.00	12.50	7.50
(62) "Rabbit" Maranville	50.00	25.00	15.00
(63a) Carl May (incorrect name)	50.00	25.00	15.00
(63b) Carl Mays (correct name)	35.00	17.50	10.50
(64) John McGraw	70.00	35.00	21.00

		NR MT	EX	VG
(65)	Jack McInnis	25.00	12.50	7.50
(66)	M.J. McNally	25.00	12.50	7.50
(67)	Emil Muesel (Photo actually Lou DeVormer)	30.00	15.00	9.00
(68)	R. Meusel	40.00	20.00	12.00
(69)	Clyde Milan	25.00	12.50	7.50
(70)	Elmer Miller	25.00	12.50	7.50
(71)	Otto Miller	25.00	12.50	7.50
(72)	Guy Morton	25.00	12.50	7.50
(73)	Eddie Murphy	25.00	12.50	7.50
(74)	"Hy" Myers	25.00	12.50	7.50
(75)	Arthur Nehf	25.00	12.50	7.50
(76)	Steve O'Neill	25.00	12.50	7.50
(77a)	Roger Peckinbaugh (incorrect name)	30.00	15.00	9.00
(77b)	Roger Peckinpaugh (correct name)	35.00	17.50	10.50
(78a)	Jeff Pfeffer (Brooklyn)	25.00	12.50	7.50
(78b)	Jeff Pfeffer (St. Louis)	25.00	12.50	7.50
(79)	Walter Pipp	40.00	20.00	12.00
(80)	Jack Quinn	25.00	12.50	7.50
(81)	John Rawlings	25.00	12.50	7.50
(82)	E.C. Rice	50.00	25.00	15.00
(83)	Eppa Rixey, Jr.	50.00	25.00	15.00
(84)	Robert Roth	25.00	12.50	7.50
(85a)	Ed. Roush (C.F.)	50.00	25.00	15.00
(85b)	Ed. Roush (L.F.)	60.00	30.00	18.00
(86a)	Babe Ruth	600.00	300.00	180.00
(86b)	"Babe" Ruth	700.00	350.00	210.00
(86c)	George Ruth	700.00	350.00	210.00
(87)	"Bill" Ryan	25.00	12.50	7.50
(88)	"Slim" Sallee (glove showing)	25.00	12.50	7.50
(89)	"Slim" Sallee (no glove showing)	25.00	12.50	7.50
(90)	Ray Schalk	50.00	25.00	15.00
(91)	Walter Schang	25.00	12.50	7.50
(92a)	Fred Schupp (name incorrect)	35.00	17.50	10.50
(92b)	Ferd Schupp (name correct)	30.00	15.00	9.00
(93)	Everett Scott	25.00	12.50	7.50
(94)	Hank Severeid	25.00	12.50	7.50
(95)	Robert Shawkey	30.00	15.00	9.00
(96a)	Pat Shea	35.00	17.50	10.50
(96b)	"Pat" Shea	25.00	12.50	7.50
(97)	George Sisler (batting)	60.00	30.00	18.00
(98)	George Sisler (throwing)	60.00	30.00	18.00
(99)	Earl Smith	25.00	12.50	7.50
(100)	Frank Snyder	25.00	12.50	7.50
(101a)	Tris Speaker (Mgr.)	75.00	37.00	22.00
(101b)	Tris Speaker (Manager - large projection)	75.00	37.00	22.00
(101c)	Tris Speaker (Manager - small projection)	100.00	50.00	30.00
(102)	Milton Stock	25.00	12.50	7.50
(103)	Amos Strunk	25.00	12.50	7.50
(104)	Zeb Terry	25.00	12.50	7.50
(105)	Chester Thomas	25.00	12.50	7.50
(106)	Fred Toney (trees in background)	25.00	12.50	7.50
(107)	Fred Toney (no trees in background)	25.00	12.50	7.50
(108)	George Tyler	25.00	12.50	7.50
(109)	Jim Vaughn (dark hat)	25.00	12.50	7.50
(110)	Jim Vaughn (white hat)	25.00	12.50	7.50
(111)	Bob Veach (glove in air)	25.00	12.50	7.50
(112)	Bob Veach (arms crossed)	25.00	12.50	7.50
(113)	Oscar Vitt	25.00	12.50	7.50
(114)	W. Wambsganss (photo actually Fred Coumbe)	30.00	15.00	9.00
(115)	Aaron Ward	25.00	12.50	7.50
(116)	Zach Wheat	50.00	25.00	15.00
(117)	George Whitted	25.00	12.50	7.50
(118)	Fred Williams	30.00	15.00	9.00
(119)	Ivy B. Wingo	25.00	12.50	7.50
(120)	Joe Wood	30.00	15.00	9.00
(121)	"Pep" Young	25.00	12.50	7.50

1922 E121 American Caramel Series Of 120

Produced by the American Caramel Co. circa 1922, the E121 Series of 120 is labeled as such by the company's claim that the set contained 120 subjects. Identical in design to the E121 Series of 80 set except for the card backs, the cards measure 2" by 3-1/2" in size. Numerous variations are found in the set, most involving a change in the player's name, team or position. The complete set price does not include

ELMER SMITH
O. F.—Boston Americans

variations.

		NR MT	EX	VG
Complete Set:		7000.00	3500.00	2100.
Common Player:		25.00	12.50	7.50
(1)	Chas. "Babe" Adams	25.00	12.50	7.50
(2)	G.C. Alexander	60.00	30.00	18.00
(3)	Jim Bagby	25.00	12.50	7.50
(4)	Dave Bancroft	50.00	25.00	15.00
(5)	Turner Barber	25.00	12.50	7.50
(6a)	Carlson Bigbee (correct name Carson L. Bigbee)	35.00	17.50	10.50
(6b)	Carlson L. Bigbee	30.00	15.00	9.00
(6c)	Corson L. Bigbee	35.00	17.50	10.50
(6d)	L. Bigbee	30.00	15.00	9.00
(7)	"Bullet Joe" Bush	30.00	15.00	9.00
(8)	Max Carey	50.00	25.00	15.00
(9)	Cecil Causey	25.00	12.50	7.50
(10)	Ty Cobb (batting)	400.00	200.00	120.00
(11)	Ty Cobb (throwing)	400.00	200.00	120.00
(12)	Eddie Collins	60.00	30.00	18.00
(13)	A. Wilbur Cooper	25.00	12.50	7.50
(14)	Stanley Coveleskie (Coveleski)	50.00	25.00	15.00
(15)	Dave Danforth	25.00	12.50	7.50
(16)	Jake Daubert	30.00	15.00	9.00
(17)	George Dauss	25.00	12.50	7.50
(18)	"Dixie" Davis	25.00	12.50	7.50
(19)	Lou DeVormer	25.00	12.50	7.50
(20)	William Doak	25.00	12.50	7.50
(21)	Phil Douglas	25.00	12.50	7.50
(22)	Urban Faber	50.00	25.00	15.00
(23)	Bib Falk (Bibb)	25.00	12.50	7.50
(24)	Wm: Fewster (first name actually Wilson)	25.00	12.50	7.50
(25)	Max Flack	25.00	12.50	7.50
(26)	Ira Falgstead (Flagstead)	25.00	12.50	7.50
(27)	Frank Frisch	60.00	30.00	18.00
(28)	W.L. Gardner	25.00	12.50	7.50
(29)	Alexander Gaston	25.00	12.50	7.50
(30)	E.P. Gharrity	25.00	12.50	7.50
(31)	George Gibson	25.00	12.50	7.50
(32)	Chas. "Whitey" Glazner	25.00	12.50	7.50
(33)	"Kid" Gleason	25.00	12.50	7.50
(34)	Hank Gowdy	25.00	12.50	7.50
(35)	John Graney	25.00	12.50	7.50
(36)	Tom Griffith	25.00	12.50	7.50
(37)	Chas. Grimm	35.00	17.50	10.50
(38)	Heine Groh	30.00	15.00	9.00
(39)	Jess Haines	50.00	25.00	15.00
(40)	Harry Harper	25.00	12.50	7.50
(41a)	Harry Heilman (name incorrect)	60.00	30.00	18.00
(41b)	Harry Heilmann (name correct)	50.00	25.00	15.00
(42)	Clarence Hodge	25.00	12.50	7.50
(43)	Walter Holke (portrait)	35.00	17.50	10.50
(44)	Walter Holke (throwing)	25.00	12.50	7.50
(45)	Charles Hollocher	25.00	12.50	7.50
(46)	Harry Hooper	50.00	25.00	15.00
(47a)	Rogers Hornsby (2B.)	100.00	50.00	30.00
(47b)	Rogers Hornsby (O.F.)	150.00	75.00	45.00
(48)	Waite Hoyt	50.00	25.00	15.00
(49)	Miller Huggins	50.00	25.00	15.00
(50)	Walter Johnson	175.00	87.00	52.00
(51)	Joe Judge	25.00	12.50	7.50

		NR MT	EX	VG
(52)	George Kelly	50.00	25.00	15.00
(53)	Dick Kerr	25.00	12.50	7.50
(54)	P.J. Kilduff	25.00	12.50	7.50
(55)	Bill Killifer (Killefer) (batting)	25.00	12.50	7.50
(56)	Bill Killifer (Killefer) (throwing)	25.00	12.50	7.50
(57)	John Lavan	25.00	12.50	7.50
(58)	Walter Mails	25.00	12.50	7.50
(59)	"Rabbit" Maranville	50.00	25.00	15.00
(60)	Elwood Martin	25.00	12.50	7.50
(61)	Carl Mays	35.00	17.50	10.50
(62)	John J. McGraw	70.00	35.00	21.00
(63)	Jack McInnis	25.00	12.50	7.50
(64)	M.J. McNally	25.00	12.50	7.50
(65)	Emil Meusel (photo actually Lou DeVormer)	30.00	15.00	9.00
(66)	R. Meusel	40.00	20.00	12.00
(67)	Clyde Milan	25.00	12.50	7.50
(68)	Elmer Miller	25.00	12.50	7.50
(69)	Otto Miller	25.00	12.50	7.50
(70)	Johnny Mostil	25.00	12.50	7.50
(71)	Eddie Mulligan	25.00	12.50	7.50
(72a)	Hy Myers	25.00	12.50	7.50
(72b)	"Hy" Myers	35.00	17.50	10.50
(73)	Earl Neale	40.00	20.00	12.00
(74)	Arthur Nehf	25.00	12.50	7.50
(75)	Leslie Nunamaker	25.00	12.50	7.50
(76)	Joe Oeschger	25.00	12.50	7.50
(77)	Chas. O'Leary	35.00	17.50	10.50
(78)	Steve O'Neill	25.00	12.50	7.50
(79)	D.B. Pratt	25.00	12.50	7.50
(80a)	John Rawlings (2B.)	30.00	15.00	9.00
(80b)	John Rawlings (Utl.)	30.00	15.00	9.00
(81)	E.S. Rice (intials actually E.C.)	50.00	25.00	15.00
(82)	Eppa J. Rixey	50.00	25.00	15.00
(83)	Eppa Rixey, Jr.	50.00	25.00	15.00
(84)	Wilbert Robinson	50.00	25.00	15.00
(85)	Tom Rogers	25.00	12.50	7.50
(86a)	Ed Rounnel	30.00	15.00	9.00
(86b)	Ed. Rommel	30.00	15.00	9.00
(87)	Ed Roush	50.00	25.00	15.00
(88)	"Muddy" Ruel	25.00	12.50	7.50
(89)	Walter Ruether	25.00	12.50	7.50
(90a)	Babe Ruth (photo montage)	700.00	350.00	210.00
(90b)	"Babe" Ruth (photo montage)	600.00	300.00	180.00
(91a)	Babe Ruth (holding bird)	700.00	350.00	210.00
(91b)	"Babe" Ruth (holding bird)	600.00	300.00	180.00
(92)	"Babe" Ruth (holding ball)	600.00	300.00	180.00
(93)	Bill Ryan	25.00	12.50	7.50
(94)	Ray Schalk (catching)	50.00	25.00	15.00
(95)	Ray Schalk (batting)	50.00	25.00	15.00
(96)	Wally Schang	24.00	12.00	7.25
(97)	Ferd Schupp	35.00	17.50	10.50
(98)	Everett Scott	25.00	12.50	7.50
(99)	Joe Sewell	60.00	30.00	18.00
(100)	Robert Shawkey	30.00	15.00	9.00
(101)	Pat Shea	25.00	12.50	7.50
(102)	Earl Sheely	25.00	12.50	7.50
(103)	Urban Schocker	25.00	12.50	7.50
(104)	George Sisler (batting)	60.00	30.00	18.00
(105)	George Sisler (throwing)	75.00	37.00	22.00
(106)	Earl Smith	25.00	12.50	7.50
(107)	Elmer Smith	25.00	12.50	7.50
(108)	Frank Snyder	25.00	12.50	7.50
(109)	Bill Southworth	25.00	12.50	7.50
(110a)	Tris Speaker (large projection)	100.00	50.00	30.00
(110b)	Tris Speaker (small projection)	80.00	40.00	24.00
(111a)	Milton Stock	35.00	17.50	10.50
(111b)	Milton J. Stock	30.00	15.00	9.00
(112)	Amos Strunk	25.00	12.50	7.50
(113)	Zeb Terry	25.00	12.50	7.50
(114)	Fred Toney	25.00	12.50	7.50
(115)	George Topocer (Toporcer)	25.00	12.50	7.50
(116)	Bob Veach	25.00	12.50	7.50
(117)	Oscar Vitt	25.00	12.50	7.50
(118)	Curtis Walker	25.00	12.50	7.50
(119)	W. Wambsganss (photo actually Fred Coumbe)	30.00	15.00	9.00
(120)	Aaron Ward	25.00	12.50	7.50
(121)	Zach Wheat	40.00	20.00	12.00
(122a)	George Whitted (Pittsburgh)	30.00	15.00	9.00
(122b)	George Whitted (Brooklyn)	30.00	15.00	9.00
(123)	Fred Williams	30.00	15.00	9.00
(124)	Ivy B. Wingo	25.00	12.50	7.50
(125)	Ross Young (Youngs)	50.00	25.00	15.00

NOTE: A card number in parentheses ( ) indicates the set is unnumbered.

1966 East Hills Pirates

Stores in the East Hills Shopping Center, a large mall located in suburban Pittsburgh, distributed cards from this 25-card full-color set in 1966. The cards, which measure 3-1/4" by 4-1/4", are blank-backed and are numbered by the players' uniform numbers. The numbers appear in the lower right corners of the cards.

		NR MT	EX	VG
Complete Set:		30.00	15.00	9.00
Common Player:		.50	.25	.15
3	Harry Walker	.70	.35	.20
7	Bob Bailey	.50	.25	.15
8	Willie Stargell	6.00	3.00	1.75
9	Bill Mazeroski	1.50	.70	.45
10	Jim Pagliaroni	.50	.25	.15
11	Jose Pagan	.50	.25	.15
12	Jerry May	.50	.25	.15
14	Gene Alley	.60	.30	.20
15	Manny Mota	.80	.40	.25
16	Andy Rodgers	.50	.25	.15
17	Donn Clendenon	.60	.30	.20
18	Matty Alou	.80	.40	.25
19	Pete Mikkelsen	.50	.25	.15
20	Jesse Gonder	.50	.25	.15
21	Bob Clemente	10.00	5.00	3.00
22	Woody Fryman	.60	.30	.20
24	Jerry Lynch	.50	.25	.15
25	Tommie Sisk	.50	.25	.15
26	Roy Face	1.25	.60	.40
28	Steve Blass	.60	.30	.20
32	Vernon Law	1.25	.60	.40
34	Al McBean	.50	.25	.15
39	Bob Veale	.60	.30	.20
43	Don Cardwell	.50	.25	.15
45	Gene Michael	.60	.30	.20

1954 Esskay Hot Dogs Orioles

Measuring 2-1/4" by 3-1/2", the 1954 Esskay Hot Dogs set features the Baltimore Orioles. The unnumbered color cards were issued in panels of two on packages of hot dogs and are usually found with grease stains. The cards have waxed fronts with blank backs on a white stock. Complete boxes of Esskay Hot Dogs are scarce and command a price of 2-3 times greater than the single card values.

		NR MT	EX	VG
Complete Set:		3100.00	1550.00	930.00
Common Player:		90.00	45.00	27.00
(1)	Neil Berry	90.00	45.00	27.00
(2)	Michael Blyzka	90.00	45.00	27.00

VINICIO "CHICO" GARCIA, Infielder
Born December 13, 1928
Hometown: Mexico City, Mex.
Throws Right & Bats Right

		NR MT	EX	VG
'(3)	Harry Brecheen	90.00	45.00	27.00
(4)	Gil Coan	90.00	45.00	27.00
(5)	Joe Coleman	90.00	45.00	27.00
(6)	Clinton Courtney	90.00	45.00	27.00
(7)	Charles E. Diering	90.00	45.00	27.00
(8)	Jimmie Dykes	100.00	50.00	30.00
(9)	Frank J. Fanovich	90.00	45.00	27.00
(10)	Howard Fox	90.00	45.00	27.00
(11)	Jim Fridley	90.00	45.00	27.00
(12)	Vinicio "Chico" Garcia	90.00	45.00	27.00
(13)	Jehosie Heard	90.00	45.00	27.00
(14)	Darrell Johnson	90.00	45.00	27.00
(15)	Bob Kennedy	90.00	45.00	27.00
(16)	Dick Kokos	90.00	45.00	27.00
(17)	Dave Koslo	90.00	45.00	27.00
(18)	Lou Kretlow	90.00	45.00	27.00
(19)	Richard D. Kryhoski	90.00	45.00	27.00
(20)	Don Larsen	100.00	50.00	30.00
(21)	Donald E. Lenhardt	90.00	45.00	27.00
(22)	Richard Littlefield	90.00	45.00	27.00
(23)	Sam Mele	90.00	45.00	27.00
(24)	Les Moss	90.00	45.00	27.00
(25)	Ray L. Murray	90.00	45.00	27.00
(26a)	"Bobo" Newsom (no stadium lights in background)	125.00	62.00	37.00
(26b)	"Bobo" Newson (stadium lights in background)	125.00	62.00	37.00
(27)	Tom Oliver	90.00	45.00	27.00
(28)	Duane Pillette	90.00	45.00	27.00
(29)	Francis M. Skaff	90.00	45.00	27.00
(30)	Marlin Stuart	90.00	45.00	27.00
(31)	Robert L. Turley	150.00	75.00	45.00
(32)	Eddie Waitkus	90.00	45.00	27.00
(33)	Vic Wertz	110.00	55.00	33.00
(34)	Robert G. Young	90.00	45.00	27.00

1955 Esskay Hot Dogs Orioles

HARRY BYRD, Pitcher

For the second consecutive year, Esskay Meats placed two baseball cards of Orioles players on their boxes of hot dogs. The unnumbered, color cards measure 2-1/4" by 3-1/2" and can be distinguished from the previous year by unwaxed fronts and grey backs. Many of the same photos from 1954 were used with only minor picture-cropping differences.

		NR MT	EX	VG
Complete Set:		2300.00	1150.00	690.00
Common Player:		90.00	45.00	27.00
(1)	Cal Abrams	90.00	45.00	27.00
(2)	Robert S. Alexander	90.00	45.00	27.00
(3)	Harry Byrd	90.00	45.00	27.00
(4)	Gil Coan	90.00	45.00	27.00
(5)	Joseph P. Coleman	90.00	45.00	27.00
(6)	William R. Cox	90.00	45.00	27.00
(7)	Charles E. Diering	90.00	45.00	27.00
(8)	Walter A. Evers	90.00	45.00	27.00
(9)	Don Johnson	90.00	45.00	27.00
(10)	Robert D. Kennedy	90.00	45.00	27.00
(11)	Lou Kretlow	90.00	45.00	27.00
(12)	Robert L. Kuzava	90.00	45.00	27.00
(13)	Fred Marsh	90.00	45.00	27.00
(14)	Charles Maxwell	90.00	45.00	27.00
(15)	Jimmie McDonald	90.00	45.00	27.00
(16)	Bill Miller	90.00	45.00	27.00
(17)	Willy Miranda	90.00	45.00	27.00
(18)	Raymond L. Moore	90.00	45.00	27.00
(19)	John Lester Moss	90.00	45.00	27.00
(20)	"Bobo" Newsom	100.00	50.00	30.00
(21)	Duane Pillette	90.00	45.00	27.00
(22)	Edward S. Waitkus	90.00	45.00	27.00
(23)	Harold W. Smith	90.00	45.00	27.00
(24)	Gus Triandos	110.00	55.00	33.00
(25)	Eugene R. Woodling	110.00	55.00	33.00
(26)	Robert G. Young	90.00	45.00	27.00

1947-66 Exhibit Supply Co.

Referred to as "Exhibits" because they were issued by the Exhibit Supply Co. of Chicago, Ill., this group was produced over an 8-year span. They are frequently called "Salutations" because of the personalized greeting found on the card. The black and white cards, which measure 3-3/8" by 5-3/8", are unnumbered and blank-backed. Most exhibits were sold through vending machines for a penny. The complete set price includes all variations.

		NR MT	EX	VG
Complete Set:		3500.00	1750.00	1050.00
Common Player:		4.00	2.00	1.25
(1a)	Luke Appling ("Made In U.S.A." in left corner)	12.00	6.00	3.50
(1b)	Luke Appling ("Made In U.S.A." in right corner)	4.00	2.00	1.25

		NR MT	EX	VG
(2)	Earl Averill	375.00	175.00	100.00
(3)	Charles "Red" Barrett	4.00	2.00	1.25
(4)	Henry "Hank" Borowy	4.00	2.00	1.25
(5)	Lou Boudreau	8.00	4.00	2.50
(6)	Adolf Camilli	25.00	12.50	7.50
(7)	Phil Cavarretta	3.50	1.75	1.00
(8)	Harland Clift (Harlond)	12.00	6.00	3.50
(9)	Tony Cuccinello	25.00	12.50	7.50
(10)	Dizzy Dean	80.00	40.00	24.00
(11)	Paul Derringer	4.00	2.00	1.25
(12a)	Bill Dickey ("Made In U.S.A." in left corner)	25.00	12.50	7.50
(12b)	Bill Dickey ("Made In U.S.A." in right corner)	25.00	12.50	7.50
(13)	Joe DiMaggio	25.00	12.50	7.50
(14)	Bob Elliott	4.00	2.00	1.25
(15)	Bob Feller (portrait)	80.00	40.00	24.00
(16)	Bob Feller (pitching)	20.00	10.00	6.00
(17)	Dave Ferriss	4.00	2.00	1.25
(18)	Jimmy Foxx	80.00	40.00	24.00
(19)	Lou Gehrig	550.00	280.00	165.00
(20)	Charlie Gehringer	125.00	56.00	35.00
(21)	Vernon Gomez	180.00	90.00	55.00
(22a)	Joe Gordon (Cleveland)	25.00	12.50	7.50
(22b)	Joe Gordon (New York)	3.50	1.75	1.00
(23)	Hank Greenberg (Truly yours)	20.00	10.00	6.00
(24)	Hank Greenberg (Very truly yours)	80.00	40.00	24.00
(25)	Robert Grove	50.00	25.00	15.00
(26)	Gabby Hartnett	275.00	150.00	80.00
(27)	Buddy Hassett	15.00	7.50	4.50
(28a)	Jeff Heath (large projection)	25.00	12.50	7.50
(28b)	Jeff Heath (small projection)	4.00	2.00	1.25
(29)	Kirby Higbe	15.00	7.50	4.50
(30a)	Tommy Holmes (Yours truly)	4.00	2.00	1.25
(30b)	Tommy Holmes (Sincerely yours)	125.00	60.00	40.00
(31)	Carl Hubbell	25.00	12.50	7.50
(32)	Bob Johnson	15.00	7.50	4.50
(33)	Charles Keller	4.00	2.00	1.25
(34)	Ken Keltner	25.00	12.50	7.50
(35)	Chuck Klein	175.00	90.00	50.00
(36)	Mike Kreevich	80.00	40.00	24.00
(37)	Joe Kuhel	20.00	10.00	6.00
(38)	Bill Lee	20.00	10.00	6.00
(39)	Ernie Lombardi (Cordially)	200.00	100.00	60.00
(40)	Ernie Lombardi (Cordially yours)	8.00	4.00	2.50
(41a)	Martin Marion ("Made in U.S.A." in left corner)	4.00	2.00	1.25
(41b)	Martin Marion ("Made in U.S.A." in right corner)	4.00	2.00	1.25
(42)	Merrill May	20.00	10.00	6.00
(43a)	Frank McCormick ("Made In U.S.A." in left corner)	20.00	10.00	6.00
(43b)	Frank McCormick ("Made In U.S.A." in right corner)	3.50	1.75	1.00
(44a)	George McQuinn ("Made In U.S.A." in left corner)	20.00	10.00	6.00
(44b)	George McQuinn ("Made In U.S.A." in right corner)	3.50	1.75	1.00
(45)	Joe Medwick	20.00	10.00	6.00
(46a)	Johnny Mize ("Made In U.S.A." in left corner)	25.00	12.50	7.50
(46b)	Johnny Mize ("Made In U.S.A." in right corner)	15.00	7.50	4.50
(47)	Hugh Mulcahy	80.00	40.00	24.00
(48)	Hal Newhouser	4.00	2.00	1.25
(49)	Buck Newson (Newsom)	175.00	90.00	50.00
(50)	Louis (Buck) Newsom	4.00	2.00	1.25
(51a)	Mel Ott ("Made In U.S.A." in left corner)	40.00	20.00	12.00
(51b)	Mel Ott ("Made In U.S.A." in right corner)	20.00	10.00	6.00
(52a)	Andy Pafko ("C" on cap)	4.00	2.00	1.25
(52b)	Andy Pafko (plain cap)	4.00	2.00	1.25
(53)	Claude Passeau	3.50	1.75	1.00
(54a)	Howard Pollet ("Made In U.S.A." in left corner)	11.00	5.50	3.25
(54b)	Howard Pollet ("Made In U.S.A." in right corner)	4.00	2.00	1.25
(55a)	Pete Reiser ("Made In U.S.A." in left corner)	80.00	40.00	24.00
(55b)	Pete Reiser ("Made In U.S.A." in right corner)	4.00	2.00	1.25
(56)	Johnny Rizzo	90.00	45.00	27.00
(57)	Glenn Russell	90.00	45.00	27.00
(58)	George Stirnweiss	4.00	2.00	1.25
(59)	Cecil Travis	15.00	7.50	4.50
(60)	Paul Trout	4.00	2.00	1.25
(61)	Johnny Vander Meer	30.00	15.00	9.00
(62)	Arky Vaughn (Vaughan)	20.00	10.00	6.00

		NR MT	EX	VG
(63a)	Fred "Dixie" Walker ("D" on cap)	4.00	2.00	1.25
(63b)	Fred "Dixie" Walker ("D" blanked out)	25.00	12.50	7.50
(64)	"Bucky" Walters	4.00	2.00	1.25
(65)	Lon Warneke	6.50	3.25	2.00
(66)	Ted Williams (#9 shows)	250.00	125.00	75.00
(67)	Ted Williams (#9 not showing)	25.00	12.50	7.50
(68)	Rudy York	4.00	2.00	1.25

1900 Exhibits - 1947-1966

Called "Exhibits" as they were produced by the Exhibit Supply Co. of Chicago, Ill., this group covers a span of twenty years. Each unnumbered, black and white card, printed on heavy stock, measures 3-3/8" by 5-3/8" and is blank-backed. The Exhibit Supply Co. issued new sets each year, with many players being repeated year after year/ Other players appeared in only one or two years, thereby creating levels of scarcity. Many variations off the same basic pose are found in the group. Those cards are listed in the checklist that follows with an "a", "b", etc. following the assigned card number. The complete set includes all variations

		NR MT	EX	VG
	Complete Set:	3500.00	1750.00	1050.
	Common Player:	3.00	1.50	.90
(1)	Hank Aaron	12.00	6.00	3.50
(2a)	Joe Adcock (script signature)	3.00	1.50	.90
(2b)	Joe Adcock (plain signature)	5.00	2.50	1.50
(3)	Max Alvis	20.00	10.00	6.00
(4)	Johnny Antonelli (Braves)	3.00	1.50	.90
(5)	Johnny Antonelli (Giants)	5.00	2.50	1.50
(6)	Luis Aparicio (portrait)	7.00	3.50	2.00
(7)	Luis Aparicio (batting)	20.00	10.00	6.00
(8)	Luke Appling	7.00	3.50	2.00
(9a)	Ritchie Ashburn (Phillies, first name incorrect)	5.00	2.50	1.50
(9b)	Richie Ashburn (Phillies, first name correct)	7.00	3.50	2.00
(10)	Richie Ashburn (Cubs)	13.00	6.50	4.00
(11)	Bob Aspromonte	2.50	1.25	.70
(12)	Toby Atwell	2.50	1.25	.70
(13)	Ed Bailey (with cap)	3.50	1.75	1.00
(14)	Ed Bailey (no cap)	1.25	.60	.40
(15)	Gene Baker	1.25	.60	.40
(16a)	Ernie Banks (bat on shoulder. script signature)	10.00	5.00	3.00
(16b)	Ernie Banks (bat on shoulder. plain signature)	6.00	3.00	1.75
(17)	Ernie Banks (portrait)	12.00	6.00	3.50
(18)	Steve Barber	2.50	1.25	.70
(19)	Earl Battey	3.50	1.75	1.00
(20)	Matt Batts	2.50	1.25	.70
(21a)	Hank Bauer (N.Y. cap)	3.50	1.75	1.00
(21b)	Hank Bauer (plain cap)	5.00	2.50	1.50
(22)	Frank Baumholtz	2.50	1.25	.70
(23)	Gene Bearden	2.50	1.25	.70

		NR MT	EX	VG
(24)	Joe Beggs	12.00	6.00	3.50
(25)	Larry "Yogi" Berra	20.00	10.00	6.00
(26)	Yogi Berra	6.00	3.00	1.75
(27)	Steve Bilko	5.00	2.50	1.50
(28)	Ewell Blackwell (pitching)	7.00	3.50	2.00
(29)	Ewell Blackwell (portrait)	3.00	1.50	.90
(30a)	Don Blasingame (St. Louis cap)	3.00	1.50	.90
(30b)	Don Blasingame (plain cap)	6.00	3.00	1.75
(31)	Ken Boyer	7.00	3.50	2.00
(32)	Ralph Branca	7.00	3.50	2.00
(33)	Jackie Brandt	50.00	25.00	15.00
(34)	Harry Brecheen	3.00	1.50	.90
(35)	Tom Brewer	12.00	6.00	3.50
(36)	Lou Brissie	5.00	2.50	1.50
(37)	Bill Bruton	3.00	1.50	.90
(38)	Lew Burdette (pitching, side view)			
		3.00	1.50	.90
(39)	Lew Burdette (pitching, front view)			
		6.00	3.00	1.75
(40)	Johnny Callison	7.00	3.50	2.00
(41)	Roy Campanella	13.00	6.50	4.00
(42)	Chico Carrasquel (portrait)	13.00	6.50	4.00
(43)	Chico Carrasquel (leaping)	3.00	1.50	.90
(44)	George Case	12.00	6.00	3.50
(45)	Hugh Casey	5.00	2.50	1.50
(46)	Norm Cash	7.00	3.50	2.00
(47)	Orlando Cepeda (portrait)	7.00	3.50	2.00
(48)	Orlando Cepeda (batting)	7.00	3.50	2.00
(49a)	Bob Cerv (A's cap)	7.00	3.50	2.00
(49b)	Bob Cerv (plain cap)	16.00	8.00	4.75
(50)	Dean Chance	3.00	1.50	.90
(51)	Spud Chandler	12.00	6.00	3.50
(52)	Tom Cheney	3.00	1.50	.90
(53)	Bubba Church	5.00	2.50	1.50
(54)	Roberto Clemente	18.00	9.00	5.50
(55)	Rocky Colavito (portrait)	25.00	12.50	7.50
(56)	Rocky Colavito (batting)	7.00	3.50	2.00
(57)	Choo Choo Coleman	13.00	6.50	4.00
(58)	Gordy Coleman	20.00	10.00	6.00
(59)	Jerry Coleman	5.00	2.50	1.50
(60)	Mort Cooper	12.00	6.00	3.50
(61)	Walker Cooper	3.00	1.50	.90
(62)	Roger Craig	12.00	6.00	3.50
(63)	Delmar Crandall	3.00	1.50	.90
(64)	Joe Cunningham (batting)	25.00	12.50	7.50
(65)	Joe Cunningham (portrait)	7.00	3.50	2.00
(66)	Guy Curtwright (Curtright)	5.00	2.50	1.50
(67)	Bud Daley	35.00	17.50	10.50
(68a)	Alvin Dark (Braves)	7.00	3.50	2.00
(68b)	Alvin Dark (Giants)	5.00	2.50	1.50
(69)	Alvin Dark (Cubs)	7.00	3.50	2.00
(70)	Murray Dickson (Murry)	5.00	2.50	1.50
(71)	Bob Dillinger	7.00	3.50	2.00
(72)	Dom DiMaggio	18.00	9.00	5.50
(73)	Joe Dobson	7.00	3.50	2.00
(74)	Larry Doby	3.00	1.50	.90
(75)	Bobby Doerr	12.00	6.00	3.50
(76)	Dick Donovan (plain cap)	7.00	3.50	2.00
(77)	Dick Donovan (Sox cap)	4.00	2.00	1.25
(78)	Walter Dropo	3.00	1.50	.90
(79)	Don Drysdale (glove at waist)	25.00	12.50	7.50
(80)	Don Drysdale (portrait)	25.00	12.50	7.50
(81)	Luke Easter	5.00	2.50	1.50
(82)	Bruce Edwards	5.00	2.50	1.50
(83)	Del Ennis	3.00	1.50	.90
(84)	Al Evans	4.50	2.25	1.25
(85)	Walter Evers	3.00	1.50	.90
(86)	Ferris Fain (fielding)	7.00	3.50	2.00
(87)	Ferris Fain (portrait)	3.00	1.50	.90
(88)	Dick Farrell	3.00	1.50	.90
(89)	Ed "Whitey" Ford	13.00	6.50	4.00
(90)	Whitey Ford (pitching)	7.00	3.50	2.00
(91)	Whitey Ford (portrait)	60.00	30.00	17.50
(92)	Dick Fowler	7.00	3.50	2.00
(93)	Nelson Fox	5.00	2.50	1.50
(94)	Tito Francona	3.00	1.50	.90
(95)	Bob Friend	3.00	1.50	.90
(96)	Carl Furillo	7.00	3.50	2.00
(97)	Augie Galan	7.00	3.50	2.00
(98)	Jim Gentile	3.00	1.50	.90
(99)	Tony Gonzalez	3.00	1.50	.90
(100)	Billy Goodman (leaping)	3.00	1.50	.90
(101)	Billy Goodman (batting)	7.00	3.50	2.00
(102)	Ted Greengrass (Jim)	3.00	1.50	.90
(103)	Dick Groat	7.00	3.50	2.00
(104)	Steve Gromek	3.00	1.50	.90
(105)	Johnny Groth	3.00	1.50	.90
(106)	Orval Grove	13.00	6.50	4.00
(107a)	Frank Gustine (Pirates uniform)	5.00	2.50	1.50
(107b)	Frank Gustine (plain uniform)	5.00	2.50	1.50
(108)	Berthold Haas	13.00	6.50	4.00

		NR MT	EX	VG
(109)	Grady Hatton	5.00	2.50	1.50
(110)	Jim Hegan	3.00	1.50	.90
(111)	Tom Henrich	7.00	3.50	2.00
(112)	Ray Herbert	20.00	10.00	6.00
(113)	Gene Hermanski	4.50	2.25	1.25
(114)	Whitey Herzog	5.00	2.50	1.50
(115)	Kirby Higbe	13.00	6.50	4.00
(116)	Chuck Hinton	3.00	1.50	.90
(117)	Don Hoak	13.00	6.50	4.00
(118a)	Gil Hodges ("B" on cap)	7.00	3.50	2.00
(118b)	Gil Hodges ("LA" on cap)	7.00	3.50	2.00
(119)	Johnny Hopp	12.00	6.00	3.50
(120)	Elston Howard	3.00	1.50	.90
(121)	Frank Howard	7.00	3.50	2.00
(122)	Ken Hubbs	35.00	17.50	10.50
(123)	Tex Hughson	12.00	6.00	3.50
(124)	Fred Hutchinson	4.50	2.25	1.25
(125)	Monty Irvin	7.00	3.50	2.00
(126)	Joey Jay	3.00	1.50	.90
(127)	Jackie Jensen	25.00	12.50	7.50
(128)	Sam Jethroe	5.00	2.50	1.50
(129)	Bill Johnson	5.00	2.50	1.50
(130)	Walter Judnich	12.00	6.00	3.50
(131)	Al Kaline (kneeling)	18.00	9.00	5.50
(132)	Al Kaline (portrait)	18.00	9.00	5.50
(133)	George Kell	7.00	3.50	2.00
(134)	Charley Keller	4.50	2.25	1.25
(135)	Alex Kellner	3.00	1.50	.90
(136)	Kenn Keltner (Ken)	5.00	2.50	1.50
(137)	Harmon Killebrew (batting)	18.00	9.00	5.50
(138)	Harmon Killebrew (throwing)	18.00	9.00	5.50
(139)	Harmon Killibrew (Killebrew) (portrait)			
		25.00	12.50	7.50
(140)	Ellis Kinder	3.00	1.50	.90
(141)	Ralph Kiner	6.00	3.00	1.75
(142)	Billy Klaus	20.00	10.00	6.00
(143)	Ted Kluzewski (Kluszewski) (batting)			
		5.00	2.50	1.50
(144a)	Ted Kluzewski (Kluszewski) (Pirates uniform)	5.00	2.50	1.50
(144b)	Ted Kluzewski (Kluszewski) (plain uniform)	13.00	6.50	4.00
(145)	Don Kolloway	7.00	3.50	2.00
(146)	Jim Konstanty	5.00	2.50	1.50
(147)	Sandy Koufax	20.00	10.00	6.00
(148)	Ed Kranepool	50.00	25.00	15.00
(149a)	Tony Kubek (light background)	7.00	3.50	2.00
(149b)	Tony Kubek (dark background)	5.00	2.50	1.50
(150a)	Harvey Kuenn ("D" on cap)	12.00	6.00	3.50
(150b)	Harvey Kuenn (plain cap)	13.00	6.50	4.00
(151)	Harvey Kuenn ("SF" on cap)	7.00	3.50	2.00
(152)	Kurowski (Whitey)	4.50	2.25	1.25
(153)	Eddie Lake	5.00	2.50	1.50
(154)	Jim Landis	3.00	1.50	.90
(155)	Don Larsen	3.00	1.50	.90
(156)	Bob Lemon (glove not visible)	7.00	3.50	2.00
(157)	Bob Lemon (glove partially visible)			
		25.00	12.50	7.50
(158)	Buddy Lewis	12.00	6.00	3.50
(159)	Johnny Lindell	20.00	10.00	6.00
(160)	Phil Linz	20.00	10.00	6.00
(161)	Don Lock	20.00	10.00	6.00
(162)	Whitey Lockman	3.00	1.50	.90
(163)	Johnny Logan	3.00	1.50	.90
(164)	Dale Long ("P" on cap)	3.00	1.50	.90
(165)	Dale Long ("C" on cap)	7.00	3.50	2.00
(166)	Ed Lopat	5.00	2.50	1.50
(167a)	Harry Lowery (name misspelled)	5.00	2.50	1.50
(167b)	Harry Lowrey (name correct)	5.00	2.50	1.50
(168)	Sal Maglie	3.00	1.50	.90
(169)	Art Mahaffey	5.00	2.50	1.50
(170)	Hank Majeski	3.00	1.50	.90
(171)	Frank Malzone	3.00	1.50	.90
(172)	Mickey Mantle (batting, pinstriped uniform)	90.00	45.00	25.00
(173a)	Mickey Mantle (batting, no pinstripes, first name outlined in white)	40.00	20.00	12.00
173b	Mickey Mantle (batting, no pinstripes, first name not outlined in white)	40.00	20.00	12.00
(174)	Mickey Mantle (portrait)	175.00	87.00	52.00
(175)	Martin Marion	5.00	2.50	1.50
(176)	Roger Maris	15.00	7.50	4.50
(177)	Willard Marshall	3.50	1.75	1.00
(178a)	Eddie Matthews (name incorrect)	9.00	4.50	2.75
(178b)	Eddie Mathews (name correct)	10.00	5.00	3.00
(179)	Ed Mayo	3.50	1.75	1.00
(180)	Willie Mays (batting)	12.00	6.00	3.50
(181)	Willie Mays (portrait)	15.00	7.50	4.50
(182)	Bill Mazeroski (portrait)	5.00	2.50	1.50
(183)	Bill Mazeroski (batting)	5.00	2.50	1.50
(184)	Ken McBride	2.50	1.25	.70

	NR MT	EX	VG
(185a) Barney McCaskey (McCosky)	13.00	6.50	4.00
(185b) Barney McCoskey (McCosky)	90.00	45.00	27.00
(186) Lindy McDaniel	3.00	1.50	.90
(187) Gil McDougald	3.00	1.50	.90
(188) Albert Mele	13.00	6.50	4.00
(189) Sam Mele	5.00	2.50	1.50
(190) Orestes Minoso ("C" on cap)	7.00	3.50	2.00
(191) Orestes Minoso (Sox on cap)	3.00	1.50	.90
(192) Dale Mitchell	3.00	1.50	.90
(193) Wally Moon	7.00	3.50	2.00
(194) Don Mueller	5.00	2.50	1.50
(195) Stan Musial (kneeling)	12.00	6.00	3.50
(196) Stan Musial (batting)	35.00	17.50	10.50
(197) Charley Neal	18.00	9.00	5.50
(198) Don Newcombe (shaking hands)	7.00	3.50	2.00
(199a) Don Newcombe (Dodgers on jacket)			
	5.00	2.50	1.50
(199b) Don Newcombe (plain jacket)	5.00	2.50	1.50
(200) Hal Newhouser	3.00	1.50	.90
(201) Ron Northey	12.00	6.00	3.50
(202) Bill O'Dell	3.00	1.50	.90
(203) Joe Page	12.00	6.00	3.50
(204) Satchel Paige	35.00	17.50	10.50
(205) Milt Pappas	3.00	1.50	.90
(206) Camilo Pascual	3.00	1.50	.90
(207) Albie Pearson	20.00	10.00	6.00
(208) Johnny Pesky	3.00	1.50	.90
(209) Gary Peters	20.00	10.00	6.00
(210) Dave Philley	3.00	1.50	.90
(211) Billy Pierce	3.00	1.50	.90
(212) Jimmy Piersall	16.00	8.00	4.75
(213) Vada Pinson	7.00	3.50	2.00
(214) Bob Porterfield	3.00	1.50	.90
(215) John "Boog" Powell	35.00	17.50	10.50
(216) Vic Raschi	4.50	2.25	1.25
(217a) Harold "Peewee" Reese (fielding, ball partially visible)	6.00	3.00	1.75
(217b) Harold "Peewee" Reese (fielding, ball not visible)	6.00	3.00	1.75
(218) Del Rice	3.00	1.50	.90
(219) Bobby Richardson	55.00	28.00	16.50
(220) Phil Rizzuto	6.00	3.00	1.75
(221a) Robin Roberts (script signature)	12.00	6.00	3.50
(221b) Robin Roberts (plain signature)	6.00	3.00	1.75
(222) Brooks Robinson	25.00	12.50	7.50
(223) Eddie Robinson	3.00	1.50	.90
(224) Floyd Robinson	20.00	10.00	6.00
(225) Frankie Robinson	18.00	9.00	5.50
(226) Jackie Robinson	18.00	9.00	5.50
(227) Preacher Roe	4.50	2.25	1.25
(228) Bob Rogers (Rodgers)	20.00	10.00	6.00
(229) Richard Rollins	20.00	10.00	6.00
(230) Pete Runnels	12.00	6.00	3.50
(231) John Sain	5.00	2.50	1.50
(232) Ron Santo	6.00	3.00	1.75
(233) Henry Sauer	5.00	2.50	1.50
(234a) Carl Sawatski ("M" on cap)	3.00	1.50	.90
(234b) Carl Sawatski ("P" on cap)	3.00	1.50	.90
(234c) Carl Sawatski (plain cap)	13.00	6.50	4.00
(235) Johnny Schmitz	5.00	2.50	1.50
(236a) Red Schoendeinst (Schoendienst) (fielding, name in white)	5.00	2.50	1.50
(236b) Red Schoendeinst (Schoendienst) (fielding, name in red-brown)	7.00	3.50	2.00
(237) Red Schoendinst (Schoendienst) (batting)	3.00	1.50	.90
(238a) Herb Score ("C" on cap)	5.00	2.50	1.50
(238b) Herb Score (plain cap)	12.00	6.00	3.50
(239) Andy Seminick	3.00	1.50	.90
(240) Rip Sewell	7.00	3.50	2.00
(241) Norm Siebern	3.00	1.50	.90
(242) Roy Sievers (batting)	5.00	2.50	1.50
(243a) Roy Sievers (portrait, "W" on cap, light background)	7.00	3.50	2.00
(243b) Roy Sievers (portrait, "W" on cap, dark background)		2.50	1.50
(243c) Roy Sievers (portrait, plain cap)	4.50	2.25	1.25
(244) Curt Simmons	5.00	2.50	1.50
(245) Dick Sisler	5.00	2.50	1.50
(246) Bill Skowron	5.00	2.50	1.50
(247) Bill "Moose" Skowron	55.00	28.00	16.50
(248) Enos Slaughter	7.00	3.50	2.00
(249a) Duke Snider ("B" on cap)	8.50	4.25	2.50
(249b) Duke Snider ("LA" on cap)	18.00	9.00	5.50
(250a) Warren Spahn ("B" on cap)	6.00	3.00	1.75
(250b) Warren Spahn ("M" on cap)	8.50	4.25	2.50
(251) Stanley Spence	13.00	6.50	4.00
(252) Ed Stanky (plain uniform)	5.00	2.50	1.50
(253) Ed Stanky (Giants uniform)	5.00	2.50	1.50
(254) Vern Stephens (batting)	5.00	2.50	1.50
(255) Vern Stephens (portrait)	5.00	2.50	1.50

	NR MT	EX	VG
(256) Ed Stewart	5.00	2.50	1.50
(257) Snuffy Stirnweiss	13.00	6.50	4.00
(258) George "Birdie" Tebbetts	12.00	6.00	3.50
(259) Frankie Thomas (photo actually Bob Skinner)	25.00	12.50	7.50
(260) Frank Thomas (portrait)	13.00	6.50	4.00
(261) Lee Thomas	3.00	1.50	.90
(262) Bobby Thomson	7.00	3.50	2.00
(263a) Earl Torgeson (Braves uniform)	3.00	1.50	.90
(263b) Earl Torgeson (plain uniform)	5.00	2.50	1.50
(264) Gus Triandos	7.00	3.50	2.00
(265) Virgil Trucks	3.00	1.50	.90
(266) Johnny Vandermeer (VanderMeer)	13.00	6.50	4.00
(267) Emil Verban	7.00	3.50	2.00
(268) Mickey Vernon (throwing)	3.00	1.50	.90
(269) Mickey Vernon (batting)	3.00	1.50	.90
(270) Bill Voiselle	7.00	3.50	2.00
(271) Leon Wagner	3.00	1.50	.90
(272a) Eddie Waitkus (throwing, Chicago uniform)	7.00	3.50	2.00
(272b) Eddie Waitkus (throwing, plain uniform)	5.00	2.50	1.50
(273) Eddie Waitkus (portrait)	13.00	6.50	4.00
(274) Dick Wakefield	5.00	2.50	1.50
(275) Harry Walker	7.00	3.50	2.00
(276) Bucky Walters	4.50	2.25	1.25
(277) Pete Ward	25.00	12.50	7.50
(278) Herman Wehmeier	5.00	2.50	1.50
(279) Vic Wertz (batting)	3.00	1.50	.90
(280) Vic Wertz (portrait)	3.00	1.50	.90
(281) Wally Westlake	5.00	2.50	1.50
(282) Wes Westrum	13.00	6.50	4.00
(283) Billy Williams	13.00	6.50	4.00
(284) Maurice Wills	12.00	6.00	3.50
(285a) Gene Woodling (script signature)	3.00	1.50	.90
(285b) Gene Woodling (plain signature)	7.00	3.50	2.00
(286) Taffy Wright	5.00	2.50	1.50
(287) Carl Yastrazemski (Yastrzemski)	175.00	90.00	50.00
(288) Al Zarilla	5.00	2.50	1.50
(289a) Gus Zernial (script signature)	3.00	1.50	.90
(289b) Gus Zernial (plain signature)	7.00	3.50	2.00
(290) Braves Team - 1948	18.00	9.00	5.50
(291) Dodgers Team - 1949	20.00	10.00	6.00
(292) Dodgers Team - 1952	20.00	10.00	6.00
(293) Dodgers Team - 1955	20.00	10.00	6.00
(294) Dodgers Team - 1956	20.00	10.00	6.00
(295) Giants Team - 1951	18.00	9.00	5.50
(296) Giants Team - 1954	18.00	9.00	5.50
(297) Indians Team - 1948	18.00	9.00	5.50
(298) Indians Team - 1954	18.00	9.00	5.50
(299) Phillies Team - 1950	18.00	9.00	5.50
(300) Yankees Team - 1949	25.00	12.50	7.50
(301) Yankees Team - 1950	25.00	12.50	7.50
(302) Yankees Team - 1951	25.00	12.50	7.50
(303) Yankees Team - 1952	25.00	12.50	7.50
(304) Yankees Team - 1955	25.00	12.50	7.50
(305) Yankees Team - 1956	25.00	12.50	7.50

1962 Exhibit Supply Co. Statistic Backs

In 1962, the Exhibit Supply Co. added career

statistics to the yearly set they produced. The black and white, unnumbered cards measure 3-3/8" by 5-3/8". The statistics found on the back are printed in black or red. The red backs are three times greater in value. The set is comprised of 32 cards.

		NR MT	EX	VG
Complete Set:		275.00	150.00	80.00
Common Player:		3.00	1.50	.90
(1)	Hank Aaron	20.00	10.00	6.00
(2)	Luis Aparicio	4.00	2.00	1.25
(3)	Ernie Banks	7.00	3.50	2.00
(4)	Larry "Yogi" Berra	8.00	4.00	2.50
(5)	Ken Boyer	2.00	1.00	.60
(6)	Lew Burdette	1.50	.70	.45
(7)	Norm Cash	1.50	.70	.45
(8)	Orlando Cepeda	3.00	1.50	.90
(9)	Roberto Clemente	20.00	10.00	6.00
(10)	Rocky Colavito	2.00	1.00	.60
(11)	Ed "Whitey" Ford	7.00	3.50	2.00
(12)	Nelson Fox	3.00	1.50	.90
(13)	Tito Francona	3.00	1.50	.90
(14)	Jim Gentile	3.00	1.50	.90
(15)	Dick Groat	1.50	.70	.45
(16)	Don Hoak	1.50	.70	.45
(17)	Al Kaline	7.00	3.50	2.00
(18)	Harmon Killebrew	7.00	3.50	2.00
(19)	Sandy Koufax	18.00	9.00	5.50
(20)	Jim Landis	3.00	1.50	.90
(21)	Art Mahaffey	3.00	1.50	.90
(22)	Frank Malzone	3.00	1.50	.90
(23)	Mickey Mantle	50.00	25.00	15.00
(24)	Roger Maris	7.00	3.50	2.00
(25)	Eddie Mathews	5.00	2.50	1.50
(26)	Willie Mays	20.00	10.00	6.00
(27)	Wally Moon	1.50	.70	.45
(28)	Stan Musial	20.00	10.00	6.00
(29)	Milt Pappas	1.50	.70	.45
(30)	Vada Pinson	2.00	1.00	.60
(31)	Norm Siebern	3.00	1.50	.90
(32)	Warren Spahn	10.00	5.00	3.00

1963 Exhibit Supply Co.
Statistic Backs

The Exhibit Supply Co. issued a 64-card set with career statistics on the backs of the cards in 1963. The unnumbered, black and white cards are printed on thick cardboard and measure 3-3/8" by 5-3/8" in size. The statistics on the back are printed in black.

		NR MT	EX	VG
Complete Set:		325.00	175.00	100.00
Common Player:		3.00	1.50	.90
(1)	Hank Aaron	20.00	10.00	6.00
(2)	Luis Aparicio	4.00	2.00	1.25

		NR MT	EX	VG
(3)	Bob Aspromonte	3.00	1.50	.90
(4)	Ernie Banks	13.00	6.50	4.00
(5)	Steve Barber	3.00	1.50	.90
(6)	Earl Battey	3.00	1.50	.90
(7)	Larry "Yogi" Berra	8.00	4.00	2.50
(8)	Ken Boyer	2.00	1.00	.60
(9)	Lew Burdette	1.50	.70	.45
(10)	Johnny Callison	1.50	.70	.45
(11)	Norm Cash	1.50	.70	.45
(12)	Orlando Cepeda	3.00	1.50	.90
(13)	Dean Chance	3.00	1.50	.90
(14)	Tom Cheney	3.00	1.50	.90
(15)	Roberto Clemente	20.00	10.00	6.00
(16)	Rocky Colavito	2.00	1.00	.60
(17)	Choo Choo Coleman	3.00	1.50	.90
(18)	Roger Craig	1.50	.70	.45
(19)	Joe Cunningham	3.00	1.50	.90
(20)	Don Drysdale	5.00	2.50	1.50
(21)	Dick Farrell	3.00	1.50	.90
(22)	Ed "Whitey" Ford	13.00	6.50	4.00
(23)	Nelson Fox	3.00	1.50	.90
(24)	Tito Francona	3.00	1.50	.90
(25)	Jim Gentile	3.00	1.50	.90
(26)	Tony Gonzalez	3.00	1.50	.90
(27)	Dick Groat	1.50	.70	.45
(28)	Ray Herbert	3.00	1.50	.90
(29)	Chuck Hinton	3.00	1.50	.90
(30)	Don Hoak	1.50	.70	.45
(31)	Frank Howard	2.00	1.00	.60
(32)	Ken Hubbs	1.50	.70	.45
(33)	Joey Jay	3.00	1.50	.90
(34)	Al Kaline	13.00	6.50	4.00
(35)	Harmon Killebrew	13.00	6.50	4.00
(36)	Sandy Koufax	20.00	10.00	6.00
(37)	Harvey Kuenn	2.00	1.00	.60
(38)	Jim Landis	3.00	1.50	.90
(39)	Art Mahaffey	3.00	1.50	.90
(40)	Frank Malzone	3.00	1.50	.90
(41)	Mickey Mantle	90.00	45.00	27.50
(42)	Roger Maris	13.00	6.50	4.00
(43)	Eddie Mathews	5.00	2.50	1.50
(44)	Willie Mays	20.00	10.00	6.00
(45)	Bill Mazeroski	2.00	1.00	.60
(46)	Ken McBride	3.00	1.50	.90
(47)	Wally Moon	1.50	.70	.45
(48)	Stan Musial	20.00	10.00	6.00
(49)	Charlie Neal	3.00	1.50	.90
(50)	Bill O'Dell	3.00	1.50	.90
(51)	Milt Pappas	1.50	.70	.45
(52)	Camilo Pascual	1.50	.70	.45
(53)	Jimmy Piersall	2.00	1.00	.60
(54)	Vada Pinson	2.00	1.00	.60
(55)	Brooks Robinson	13.00	6.50	4.00
(56)	Frankie Robinson	13.00	6.50	4.00
(57)	Pete Runnels	1.50	.70	.45
(58)	Ron Santo	2.00	1.00	.60
(59)	Norm Siebern	3.00	1.50	.90
(60)	Warren Spahn	10.00	5.00	3.00
(61)	Lee Thomas	3.00	1.50	.90
(62)	Leon Wagner	3.00	1.50	.90
(63)	Billy Williams	4.00	2.00	1.25
(64)	Maurice Wills	3.00	1.50	.90

Definitions for grading conditions are located in the Introduction section at the front of this book.

A player's name in *italic* type indicates a rookie card. An (FC) indicates a player's first card for that particular card company.

1988 Fantastic Sam's

This set of 20 full-color player discs (2-1/2" diameter) was distributed during a Superstar Sweepstakes sponsored by Fantastic Sam's Family Haircutters' 1,800 stores nationwide. Each sweepstakes card consists of two connected discs (bright orange fronts, white backs) perforated for easy separation. One disc features the baseball player photo, the other carries the sweepstakes logo and a list of prizes. Player discs carry a Fantastic Sam's Baseball Superstars header curved above the photo, with his name, team and position printed in black. stats. The disc backs are black and white and include personal info, card number and 1987 player stats. Sweepstakes discs list contest prizes (Grand Prize was 4 tickets to a 1988 Championship game) on the front and an entry form on the flipside. Below the prize list is a silver scratch-off rectangle which may reveal an instant prize.

		MT	NR MT	EX
Complete Set:		10.00	7.50	4.00
Common Player:		.20	.15	.08
1	Kirby Puckett	.75	.60	.30
2	George Brett	1.00	.70	.40
3	Mark McGwire	1.75	1.25	.70
4	Wally Joyner	1.25	.90	.50
5	Paul Molitor	.20	.15	.08
6	Alan Trammell	.40	.30	.15
7	George Bell	.50	.40	.20
8	Wade Boggs	2.25	1.75	.90
9	Don Mattingly	3.50	2.75	1.50
10	Julio Franco	.20	.15	.08
11	Ozzie Smith	.20	.15	.08
12	Will Clark	.75	.60	.30
13	Dale Murphy	1.00	.70	.40
14	Eric Davis	1.50	1.25	.60
15	Andre Dawson	.50	.40	.20
16	Tim Raines	.60	.45	.25
17	Darryl Strawberry	1.25	.90	.50
18	Tony Gwynn	.75	.60	.30
19	Mike Schmidt	1.00	.70	.40
20	Pedro Guerrero	.20	.15	.08

1987 Farmland Dairies Mets

The New York Mets and Farmland Dairies produced a nine-card panel of baseball cards for members of the Junior Mets Club. Members of the club, kids 14 years of age and younger, received the perforated panel as part of a package featuring gifts and special privileges. The cards are the standard 2-1/2" by 3-1/2" with fronts containing a full-color photo encompassed by a blue border. The backs are designed on a vertical format and have player statistics and career highlights. The Farmland Dairies and Junior Mets Club logos are also carried on the cards backs.

		MT	NR MT	EX
Complete Panel Set:		12.00	9.00	4.75
Complete Singles Set:		4.00	3.00	1.50
Common Single Player:		.25	.20	.10
Panel		12.00	9.00	4.75
1	Mookie Wilson	.25	.20	.10
4	Len Dykstra	.30	.25	.12
8	Gary Carter	.70	.50	.30
12	Ron Darling	.40	.30	.15
18	Darryl Strawberry	.80	.60	.30
19	Bob Ojeda	.25	.20	.10
22	Kevin McReynolds	.40	.30	.15
42	Roger McDowell	.25	.20	.10
---	Team Card	.25	.20	.10

1988 Farmland Dairies Mets

Part of the Junior Mets Fan Club membership package, this set of 9 standard size cards was printed on a single panel. Card fronts feature full-color action shots framed in orange and blue. A white player name runs across the top border, with a large team logo, uniform number and position printed below the photo. Card backs are blue on brown and include personal data, stats and 1987 season highlights. The set was offered to fans 14 years and younger for a $6 fan club membership fee, with a $1 discount for those who sent in two proofs of purchase from Farmland Dairies milk cartons.

		MT	NR MT	EX
Complete Panel Set:		12.00	9.00	4.75
Complete Singles Set:		4.00	3.00	1.50
Common Single Player:		.25	.20	.10
Panel		12.00	9.00	4.75
8	Gary Carter	.70	.50	.30
16	Dwight Gooden	1.00	.70	.40
17	Keith Hernandez	.60	.45	.25
18	Darryl Strawberry	.80	.60	.30

		MT	NR MT	EX
20	Howard Johnson	.30	.25	.12
21	Kevin Elster	.35	.25	.14
42	Roger McDowell	.25	.20	.10
48	Randy Myers	.35	.25	.14

1959 Fleer Ted Williams

1938 – First Spring Training

This 80-card 1959 Fleer set tells of the life of baseball great Ted Williams, from his childhood years up to 1958. The full-color cards measure 2-1/2" by 3-1/2" in size and make use of both horizontal and vertical formats. The card backs, all designed horizontally, contain a continuing biography of Williams. Card #68 was withdrawn from the set early in production and is scarce. Counterfeit cards of #68 have been produced and can be distinguished by a cross-hatch pattern which appears over the photo on the card fronts.

		NR MT	EX	VG
Complete Set:		350.00	175.00	105.00
Common Player:		1.50	.70	.45

		NR MT	EX	VG
1	The Early Years	8.00	4.00	2.50
2	Ted's Idol - Babe Ruth	8.00	4.00	2.50
3	Practice Makes Perfect	1.50	.70	.45
4	1934 - Ted Learns The Fine Points	1.50	.70	.45
5	Ted's Fame Spreads - 1935-36	1.50	.70	.45
6	Ted Turns Professional	1.50	.70	.45
7	1936 - From Mound To Plate	1.50	.70	.45
8	1937 - First Full Season	1.50	.70	.45
9	1937 - First Step To The Majors	1.50	.70	.45
10	1938 - Gunning As A Pastime	1.50	.70	.45
11	1938 - First Spring Training	2.50	1.25	.70
12	1939 - Burning Up The Minors	1.50	.70	.45
13	1939 - Ted Shows He Will Stay	1.50	.70	.45
14	Outstanding Rookie of 1939	1.50	.70	.45
15	1940 - Williams Licks Sophomore Jinx	1.50	.70	.45
16	1941 - Williams' Greatest Year	1.50	.70	.45
17	1941 - How Ted Hit .400	1.50	.70	.45
18	1941 - All-Star Hero	1.50	.70	.45
19	1942 - Ted Wins Triple Crown	1.50	.70	.45
20	1942 - On To Naval Training	1.50	.70	.45
21	1943 - Honors For Williams	1.50	.70	.45
22	1944 - Ted Solos	1.50	.70	.45
23	1944 - Williams Wins His Wings	1.50	.70	.45
24	1945 - Sharpshooter	1.50	.70	.45
25	1945 - Ted Is Discharged	1.50	.70	.45
26	1946 - Off To A Flying Start	1.50	.70	.45
27	July 9, 1946 - One Man Show	1.50	.70	.45
28	July 14, 1946 - The Williams Shift	1.50	.70	.45
29	July 21, 1946, Ted Hits For The Cycle	1.50	.70	.45
30	1946 - Beating The Williams Shift	1.50	.70	.45
31	Oct. 1946 - Sox Lose The Series	1.50	.70	.45
32	1946 - Most Valuable Player	1.50	.70	.45
33	1947 - Another Triple Crown For Ted	1.50	.70	.45
34	1947 - Ted Sets Runs-Scored Record	1.50	.70	.45
35	1948 - The Sox Miss The Pennant	1.50	.70	.45
36	1948 - Banner Year For Ted	1.50	.70	.45
37	1949 - Sox Miss Out Again	1.50	.70	.45
38	1949 - Power Rampage	1.50	.70	.45
39	1950 - Great Start	1.75	.90	.50
40	July 11, 1950 - Ted Crashes Into Wall	1.50	.70	.45

		NR MT	EX	VG
41	1950 - Ted Recovers	1.50	.70	.45
42	1951 - Williams Slowed By Injury	1.50	.70	.45
43	1951 - Leads Outfielders In Double Plays	1.50	.70	.45
44	1952 - Back To The Marines	1.50	.70	.45
45	1952 - Farewell To Baseball?	1.50	.70	.45
46	1952 - Ready For Combat	1.50	.70	.45
47	1953 - Ted Crash Lands Jet	1.50	.70	.45
48	July 14, 1953 - Ted Returns	1.50	.70	.45
49	1953 - Smash Return	1.50	.70	.45
50	March 1954 - Spring Injury	1.50	.70	.45
51	May 16, 1954 - Ted Is Patched Up	1.50	.70	.45
52	1954 - Ted's Comeback	1.50	.70	.45
53	1954 - Ted's Comeback Is A Sucess	1.50	.70	.45
54	Dec. 1954, Fisherman Ted Hooks a Big One	1.50	.70	.45
55	1955 - Ted Decides Retirement Is "No Go"	1.50	.70	.45
56	1956 - Ted Reaches 400th Homer,	1.50	.70	.45
58	1957 - Williams Hits .388	1.50	.70	.45
59	1957 - Hot September For Ted	1.50	.70	.45
60	1957 - More Records For Ted	1.50	.70	.45
61	1957 - Outfielder Ted	1.50	.70	.45
62	1958 - 6th Batting Title For Ted	1.50	.70	.45
63	Ted's All-Star Record	1.50	.70	.45
64	1958 - Daughter And Famous Daddy	1.50	.70	.45
65	August 30, 1958	1.50	.70	.45
66	1958 - Powerhouse	1.50	.70	.45
67	Two Famous Fisherman	1.75	.90	.50
68	Jan. 23, 1959 - Ted Signs For 1959	200.00	100.00	60.00
69	A Future Ted Williams?	1.50	.70	.45
70	Ted Williams & Jim Thorpe	1.75	.90	.50
71	Ted's Hitting Fundamentals #1	1.50	.70	.45
72	Ted's Hitting Fundamentals #2	1.50	.70	.45
73	Ted's Hitting Fundamentals #3	1.50	.70	.45
74	Here's How!	1.50	.70	.45
75	Williams' Value To Red Sox	4.00	2.00	1.25
76	Ted's Remarkable "On Base" Record	1.50	.70	.45
77	Ted Relaxes	1.50	.70	.45
78	Honors For Williams	1.50	.70	.45
79	Where Ted Stands	1.50	.70	.45
80	Ted's Goals For 1959	3.00	1.50	.90

1960 Fleer

RABBIT MARANVILLE

The 1960 Fleer Baseball Greats set consists of 79 cards of the game's top players from the past. (The set does include a card of Ted Williams, who was in his final major league season). The cards are standard size (2-1/2" by 3-1/2") and feature color photos inside blue, green, red or yellow borders. The card backs carry a short player biography plus career hitting or pitching statistics. Cards with a Pepper Martin back (#80), but with another player pictured on the front are in existence.

		NR MT	EX	VG
Complete Set:		170.00	85.00	51.00
Common Player:		1.00	.50	.30

1	Nap Lajoie	4.00	2.00	1.25
2	Christy Mathewson	2.50	1.25	.70
3	Babe Ruth	25.00	12.50	7.50

		NR MT	EX	VG
4	Carl Hubbell	1.50	.70	.45
5	Grover Cleveland Alexander	2.00	1.00	.60
6	Walter Johnson	3.00	1.50	.90
7	Chief Bender	1.00	.50	.30
8	Roger Bresnahan	1.00	.50	.30
9	Mordecai Brown	1.00	.50	.30
10	Tris Speaker	1.50	.70	.45
11	Arky Vaughan	1.00	.50	.30
12	Zack Wheat	1.00	.50	.30
13	George Sisler	1.25	.60	.40
14	Connie Mack	2.00	1.00	.60
15	Clark Griffith	1.00	.50	.30
16	Lou Boudreau	1.00	.50	.30
17	Ernie Lombardi	1.00	.50	.30
18	Heinie Manush	1.00	.50	.30
19	Marty Marion	1.00	.50	.30
20	Eddie Collins	1.25	.60	.40
21	Rabbit Maranville	1.00	.50	.30
22	Joe Medwick	1.00	.50	.30
23	Ed Barrow	1.00	.50	.30
24	Mickey Cochrane	1.25	.60	.40
25	Jimmy Collins	1.00	.50	.30
26	Bob Feller	4.00	2.00	1.25
27	Luke Appling	1.00	.50	.30
28	Lou Gehrig	10.00	5.00	3.00
29	Gabby Hartnett	1.00	.50	.30
30	Chuck Klein	1.00	.50	.30
31	Tony Lazzeri	1.00	.50	.30
32	Al Simmons	1.00	.50	.30
33	Wilbert Robinson	1.00	.50	.30
34	Sam Rice	1.00	.50	.30
35	Herb Pennock	1.00	.50	.30
36	Mel Ott	1.50	.70	.45
37	Lefty O'Doul	1.00	.50	.30
38	Johnny Mize	1.25	.60	.40
39	Bing Miller	1.00	.50	.30
40	Joe Tinker	1.00	.50	.30
41	Frank Baker	1.00	.50	.30
42	Ty Cobb	10.00	5.00	3.00
43	Paul Derringer	1.00	.50	.30
44	Cap Anson	1.25	.60	.40
45	Jim Bottomley	1.00	.50	.30
46	Eddie Plank	1.00	.50	.30
47	Cy Young	2.50	1.25	.70
48	Hack Wilson	1.00	.50	.30
49	Ed Walsh	1.00	.50	.30
50	Frank Chance	1.00	.50	.30
51	Dazzy Vance	1.00	.50	.30
52	Bill Terry	1.25	.60	.40
53	Jimmy Foxx	2.00	1.00	.60
54	Lefty Gomez	1.25	.60	.40
55	Branch Rickey	1.00	.50	.30
56	Ray Schalk	1.00	.50	.30
57	Johnny Evers	1.00	.50	.30
58	Charlie Gehringer	1.25	.60	.40
59	Burleigh Grimes	1.00	.50	.30
60	Lefty Grove	1.50	.70	.45
61	Rube Waddell	1.00	.50	.30
62	Honus Wagner	3.00	1.50	.90
63	Red Ruffing	1.00	.50	.30
64	Judge Landis	1.00	.50	.30
65	Harry Heilmann	1.00	.50	.30
66	John McGraw	1.25	.60	.40
67	Hughie Jennings	1.00	.50	.30
68	Hal Newhouser	1.00	.50	.30
69	Waite Hoyt	1.00	.50	.30
70	Bobo Newsom	1.00	.50	.30
71	Earl Averill	1.00	.50	.30
72	Ted Williams	15.00	7.50	4.50
73	Warren Giles	1.00	.50	.30
74	Ford Frick	1.00	.50	.30
75	Ki Ki Cuyler	1.00	.50	.30
76	Paul Waner	1.00	.50	.30
77	Pie Traynor	1.00	.50	.30
78	Lloyd Waner	1.00	.50	.30
79	Ralph Kiner	3.00	1.50	.90

1961-62 Fleer

Over a two-year period, Fleer issued another set utilizing the Baseball Greats theme. The 154-card set was issued in two series and features a color player portrait against a color background. The player's name is located in a pennant set at the bottom of the card. The card backs feature orange and black on white stock and contain player biographical and statistical information. The cards measure 2-1/2" by

3-1/2" in size. The second series cards (#'s 89-154) were issued in 1962.

		NR MT	EX	VG
Complete Set:		425.00	212.00	127.00
Common Player: 1-88		1.00	.50	.30
Common Player: 89-154		3.00	1.50	.90
1	Baker, Cobb, Wheat/Checklist	10.00	5.00	3.00
2	G.C. Alexander	2.00	1.00	.60
3	Nick Altrock	1.00	.50	.30
4	Cap Anson	1.25	.60	.40
5	Earl Averill	1.00	.50	.30
6	Home Run Baker	1.00	.50	.30
7	Dave Bancroft	1.00	.50	.30
8	Chief Bender	1.00	.50	.30
9	Jim Bottomley	1.00	.50	.30
10	Roger Bresnahan	1.00	.50	.30
11	Mordecai Brown	1.00	.50	.30
12	Max Carey	1.00	.50	.30
13	Jack Chesbro	1.00	.50	.30
14	Ty Cobb	10.00	5.00	3.00
15	Mickey Cochrane	1.25	.60	.40
16	Eddie Collins	1.25	.60	.40
17	Earle Combs	1.00	.50	.30
18	Charles Comiskey	1.00	.50	.30
19	Ki Ki Cuyler	1.00	.50	.30
20	Paul Derringer	1.00	.50	.30
21	Howard Ehmke	1.00	.50	.30
22	Billy Evans	1.00	.50	.30
23	Johnny Evers	1.00	.50	.30
24	Red Faber	1.00	.50	.30
25	Bob Feller	4.00	2.00	1.25
26	Wes Ferrell	1.00	.50	.30
27	Lew Fonseca	1.00	.50	.30
28	Jimmy Foxx	2.00	1.00	.60
29	Ford Frick	1.00	.50	.30
30	Frankie Frisch	1.25	.60	.40
31	Lou Gehrig	10.00	5.00	3.00
32	Charlie Gehringer	1.25	.60	.40
33	Warren Giles	1.00	.50	.30
34	Lefty Gomez	1.25	.60	.40
35	Goose Goslin	1.00	.50	.30
36	Clark Griffith	1.00	.50	.30
37	Burleigh Grimes	1.00	.50	.30
38	Lefty Grove	1.50	.70	.45
39	Chick Hafey	1.00	.50	.30
40	Jesse Haines	1.00	.50	.30
41	Gabby Hartnett	1.00	.50	.30
42	Harry Heilmann	1.00	.50	.30
43	Rogers Hornsby	2.00	1.00	.60
44	Waite Hoyt	1.00	.50	.30
45	Carl Hubbell	1.50	.70	.45
46	Miller Huggins	1.00	.50	.30
47	Hughie Jennings	1.00	.50	.30
48	Ban Johnson	1.00	.50	.30
49	Walter Johnson	3.00	1.50	.90
50	Ralph Kiner	1.25	.60	.40
51	Chuck Klein	1.00	.50	.30
52	Johnny Kling	1.00	.50	.30
53	Judge Landis	1.00	.50	.30
54	Tony Lazzeri	1.00	.50	.30
55	Ernie Lombardi	1.00	.50	.30
56	Dolf Luque	1.00	.50	.30
57	Heinie Manush	1.00	.50	.30
58	Marty Marion	1.00	.50	.30
59	Christy Mathewson	2.50	1.25	.70
60	John McGraw	1.25	.60	.40
61	Joe Medwick	1.00	.50	.30
62	Bing Miller	1.00	.50	.30
63	Johnny Mize	1.25	.60	.40

		NR MT	EX	VG
64	Johnny Mostil	1.00	.50	.30
65	Art Nehf	1.00	.50	.30
66	Hal Newhouser	1.00	.50	.30
67	Bobo Newsom	1.00	.50	.30
68	Mel Ott	1.50	.70	.45
69	Allie Reynolds	1.00	.50	.30
70	Sam Rice	1.00	.50	.30
71	Eppa Rixey	1.00	.50	.30
72	Edd Roush	1.00	.50	.30
73	Schoolboy Rowe	1.00	.50	.30
74	Red Ruffing	1.00	.50	.30
75	Babe Ruth	25.00	12.50	7.50
76	Joe Sewell	1.00	.50	.30
77	Al Simmons	1.00	.50	.30
78	George Sisler	1.25	.60	.40
79	Tris Speaker	1.50	.70	.45
80	Fred Toney	1.00	.50	.30
81	Dazzy Vance	1.00	.50	.30
82	Jim Vaughn	1.00	.50	.30
83	Big Ed Walsh	1.00	.50	.30
84	Lloyd Waner	1.00	.50	.30
85	Paul Waner	1.00	.50	.30
86	Zach Wheat	1.00	.50	.30
87	Hack Wilson	1.00	.50	.30
88	Jimmy Wilson	1.00	.50	.30
89	Sisler & Traynor / Checklist	10.00	5.00	3.00
90	Babe Adams	3.00	1.50	.90
91	Dale Alexander	3.00	1.50	.90
92	Jim Bagby	3.00	1.50	.90
93	Ossie Bluege	3.00	1.50	.90
94	Lou Boudreau	4.00	2.00	1.25
95	Tommy Bridges	3.00	1.50	.90
96	Donnie Bush (Donie)	3.00	1.50	.90
97	Dolph Camilli	3.00	1.50	.90
98	Frank Chance	4.00	2.00	1.25
99	Jimmy Collins	3.00	1.50	.90
100	Stanley Coveleskie (Coveleski)	3.00	1.50	.90
101	Hughie Critz	3.00	1.50	.90
102	General Crowder	3.00	1.50	.90
103	Joe Dugan	3.00	1.50	.90
104	Bibb Falk	3.00	1.50	.90
105	Rick Ferrell	3.00	1.50	.90
106	Art Fletcher	3.00	1.50	.90
107	Dennis Galehouse	3.00	1.50	.90
108	Chick Galloway	3.00	1.50	.90
109	Mule Haas	3.00	1.50	.90
110	Stan Hack	3.00	1.50	.90
111	Bump Hadley	3.00	1.50	.90
112	Billy Hamilton	3.00	1.50	.90
113	Joe Hauser	3.00	1.50	.90
114	Babe Herman	3.00	1.50	.90
115	Travis Jackson	3.00	1.50	.90
116	Eddie Joost	3.00	1.50	.90
117	Addie Joss	3.00	1.50	.90
118	Joe Judge	3.00	1.50	.90
119	Joe Kuhel	3.00	1.50	.90
120	Nap Lajoie	6.00	3.00	1.75
121	Dutch Leonard	3.00	1.50	.90
122	Ted Lyons	3.00	1.50	.90
123	Connie Mack	6.00	3.00	1.75
124	Rabbit Maranville	3.00	1.50	.90
125	Fred Marberry	3.00	1.50	.90
126	Iron Man McGinnity	3.00	1.50	.90
127	Oscar Melillo	3.00	1.50	.90
128	Ray Mueller	3.00	1.50	.90
129	Kid Nichols	3.00	1.50	.90
130	Lefty O'Doul	3.00	1.50	.90
131	Bob O'Farrell	3.00	1.50	.90
132	Roger Peckinpaugh	3.00	1.50	.90
133	Herb Pennock	3.00	1.50	.90
134	George Pipgras	3.00	1.50	.90
135	Eddie Plank	3.00	1.50	.90
136	Ray Schalk	3.00	1.50	.90
137	Hal Schumacher	3.00	1.50	.90
138	Luke Sewell	3.00	1.50	.90
139	Bob Shawkey	3.00	1.50	.90
140	Riggs Stephenson	3.00	1.50	.90
141	Billy Sullivan	3.00	1.50	.90
142	Bill Terry	5.00	2.50	1.50
143	Joe Tinker	2.75	1.50	.80
144	Pie Traynor	4.00	2.00	1.25
145	George Uhle	3.00	1.50	.90
146	Hal Troskey (Trosky)	3.00	1.50	.90
147	Arky Vaughan	3.00	1.50	.90
148	Johnny Vander Meer	3.00	1.50	.90
149	Rube Waddell	3.00	1.50	.90
150	Honus Wagner	10.00	5.00	3.00
151	Dixie Walker	3.00	1.50	.90
152	Ted Williams	20.00	10.00	6.00
153	Cy Young	8.00	4.00	2.50
154	Ross Young (Youngs)	6.00	3.00	1.75

1963 Fleer

FRANK BOLLING
Milwaukee Braves—2nd Base

A lawsuit by Topps stopped Fleer's 1963 set at one series of 66 cards. Issued with a cookie rather than gum, the set features color photos of current players. The card backs include statistical information for 1962 and career plus a brief player biography. The cards, which measure 2-1/2" by 3-1/2", are numbered 1-66. An unnumbered checklist was issued with the set and is included in the complete set price in the checklist that follows. The checklist and #46 Adcock are scarce.

		NR MT	EX	VG
	Complete Set:	650.00	250.00	160.00
	Common Player:	2.00	1.00	.60
1	Steve Barber	4.00	2.00	1.25
2	Ron Hansen	2.00	1.00	.60
3	Milt Pappas	2.25	1.25	.70
4	Brooks Robinson	30.00	15.00	9.00
5	Willie Mays	50.00	30.00	15.00
6	Lou Clinton	2.00	1.00	.60
7	Bill Monbouquette	2.00	1.00	.60
8	Carl Yastrzemski	50.00	30.00	15.00
9	Ray Herbert	2.00	1.00	.60
10	Jim Landis	2.00	1.00	.60
11	Dick Donovan	2.00	1.00	.60
12	Tito Francona	2.00	1.00	.60
13	Jerry Kindall	2.00	1.00	.60
14	Frank Lary	2.25	1.25	.70
15	Dick Howser	2.50	1.25	.70
16	Jerry Lumpe	2.00	1.00	.60
17	Norm Siebern	2.00	1.00	.60
18	Don Lee	2.00	1.00	.60
19	Albie Pearson	2.00	1.00	.60
20	Bob Rodgers	2.25	1.25	.70
21	Leon Wagner	2.00	1.00	.60
22	Jim Kaat	6.00	3.00	1.75
23	Vic Power	2.00	1.00	.60
24	Rich Rollins	2.00	1.00	.60
25	Bobby Richardson	4.00	2.00	1.25
26	Ralph Terry	2.50	1.25	.70
27	Tom Cheney	2.25	1.25	.70
28	Chuck Cottier	2.00	1.00	.60
29	Jimmy Piersall	2.50	1.25	.70
30	Dave Stenhouse	2.00	1.00	.60
31	Glen Hobbie	2.00	1.00	.60
32	Ron Santo	3.00	1.50	.90
33	Gene Freese	2.00	1.00	.60
34	Vada Pinson	3.00	1.50	.90
35	Bob Purkey	2.00	1.00	.60
36	Joe Amalfitano	2.00	1.00	.60
37	Bob Aspromonte	2.00	1.00	.60
38	Dick Farrell	2.00	1.00	.60
39	Al Spangler	2.00	1.00	.60
40	Tommy Davis	2.50	1.25	.70
41	Don Drysdale	15.00	7.50	4.50
42	Sandy Koufax	80.00	40.00	24.00
43	Maury Wills	25.00	12.50	7.50
44	Frank Bolling	2.00	1.00	.60
45	Warren Spahn	20.00	10.00	6.00
46	Joe Adcock	85.00	42.00	25.00
47	Roger Craig	4.00	2.00	1.25
48	Al Jackson	2.25	1.25	.70
49	Rod Kanehl	2.25	1.25	.70
50	Ruben Amaro	2.00	1.00	.60

		NR MT	EX	VG
51	John Callison	2.25	1.25	.70
52	Clay Dalrymple	2.00	1.00	.60
53	Don Demeter	2.00	1.00	.60
54	Art Mahaffey	2.00	1.00	.60
55	"Smoky" Burgess	2.25	1.25	.70
56	Roberto Clemente	50.00	30.00	15.00
57	Elroy Face	2.25	1.25	.70
58	Vernon Law	2.25	1.25	.70
59	Bill Mazeroski	3.00	1.50	.90
60	Ken Boyer	3.00	1.50	.90
61	Bob Gibson	15.00	7.50	4.50
62	Gene Oliver	2.00	1.00	.60
63	Bill White	2.75	1.50	.80
64	Orlando Cepeda	5.00	2.50	1.50
65	Jimmy Davenport	2.00	1.00	.60
66	Billy O'Dell	3.00	1.50	.90
----	Checklist 1-66	325.00	130.00	81.00

1981 Fleer

For the first time in 18 years, Fleer issued a baseball card set featuring current players. Fleer's 660-card effort included numerous errors in the first printing run which were subsequently corrected in additional runs. The cards, which measure 2-1/2" by 3-1/2", are numbered alphabetically by team. The card fronts feature a full-color photo inside a border which is color-coded by team. The card backs have black, grey and yellow ink on white stock and carry player statistical information. The player's batting average or earned run average is located in a circle in the upper right corner of the card. The complete set price in the checklist that follows does not include the higher priced variations.

		MT	NR MT	EX
Complete Set:		35.00	27.00	15.00
Common Player:		.06	.05	.02
1	Pete Rose	1.75	1.25	.70
2	Larry Bowa	.15	.11	.06
3	Manny Trillo	.08	.06	.03
4	Bob Boone	.10	.08	.04
5a	Mike Schmidt (portrait)	1.00	.70	.40
5b	Mike Schmidt (batting)	.90	.70	.35
6a	Steve Carlton ("Lefty" on front)	.80	.60	.30
6b	Steve Carlton (Pitcher of the Year on front, date 1066 on back)	.60	.45	.25
6c	Steve Carlton (Pitcher of the Year on front, date 1966 on back)	2.00	1.50	.80
7a	Tug McGraw (Game Saver on front)	.50	.40	.20
7b	Tug McGraw (Pitcher on front)	.12	.09	.05
8	Larry Christenson	.06	.05	.02
9	Bake McBride	.06	.05	.02
10	Greg Luzinski	.15	.11	.06
11	Ron Reed	.06	.05	.02
12	Dickie Noles	.06	.05	.02
13	*Keith Moreland*	.35	.25	.14
14	*Bob Walk*	.25	.20	.10
15	Lonnie Smith	.08	.06	.03
16	Dick Ruthven	.06	.05	.02
17	Sparky Lyle	.10	.08	.04
18	Greg Gross	.06	.05	.02

		MT	NR MT	EX
19	Garry Maddox	.10	.08	.04
20	Nino Espinosa	.06	.05	.02
21	George Vukovich	.06	.05	.02
22	John Vukovich	.06	.05	.02
23	Ramon Aviles	.06	.05	.02
24a	Kevin Saucier (Ken Saucier on back)	.15	.11	.06
24b	Kevin Saucier (Kevin Saucier on back)	.70	.50	.30
25	Randy Lerch	.06	.05	.02
26	Del Unser	.06	.05	.02
27	Tim McCarver	.15	.11	.06
28a	George Brett (batting)	1.25	.90	.50
28b	George Brett (portrait)	.90	.70	.35
29a	Willie Wilson (portrait)	.60	.45	.25
29b	Willie Wilson (batting)	.15	.11	.06
30	Paul Splittorff	.06	.05	.02
31	Dan Quisenberry	.15	.11	.06
32a	Amos Otis (batting)	.50	.40	.20
32b	Amos Otis (portrait)	.10	.08	.04
33	Steve Busby	.08	.06	.03
34	U.L. Washington	.06	.05	.02
35	Dave Chalk	.06	.05	.02
36	Darrell Porter	.08	.06	.03
37	Marty Pattin	.06	.05	.02
38	Larry Gura	.06	.05	.02
39	Renie Martin	.06	.05	.02
40	Rich Gale	.06	.05	.02
41a	Hal McRae (dark blue "Royals" on front)	.40	.30	.15
41b	Hal McRae (light blue "Royals" on front)	.10	.08	.04
42	Dennis Leonard	.08	.06	.03
43	Willie Aikens	.06	.05	.02
44	Frank White	.10	.08	.04
45	Clint Hurdle	.06	.05	.02
46	John Wathan	.08	.06	.03
47	Pete LaCock	.06	.05	.02
48	Rance Mulliniks	.06	.05	.02
49	Jeff Twitty	.06	.05	.02
50	Jamie Quirk	.06	.05	.02
51	Art Howe	.06	.05	.02
52	Ken Forsch	.06	.05	.02
53	Vern Ruhle	.06	.05	.02
54	Joe Niekro	.12	.09	.05
55	Frank LaCorte	.06	.05	.02
56	J.R. Richard	.10	.08	.04
57	Nolan Ryan	1.75	1.25	.70
58	Enos Cabell	.06	.05	.02
59	Cesar Cedeno	.12	.09	.05
60	Jose Cruz	.12	.09	.05
61	Bill Virdon	.06	.05	.02
62	Terry Puhl	.06	.05	.02
63	Joaquin Andujar	.10	.08	.04
64	Alan Ashby	.06	.05	.02
65	Joe Sambito	.06	.05	.02
66	Denny Walling	.06	.05	.02
67	Jeff Leonard	.12	.09	.05
68	Luis Pujols	.06	.05	.02
69	Bruce Bochy	.06	.05	.02
70	Rafael Landestoy	.06	.05	.02
71	*Dave Smith*	.30	.25	.12
72	*Danny Heep*	.10	.08	.04
73	Julio Gonzalez	.06	.05	.02
74	Craig Reynolds	.06	.05	.02
75	Gary Woods	.06	.05	.02
76	Dave Bergman	.06	.05	.02
77	Randy Niemann	.06	.05	.02
78	Joe Morgan	.60	.45	.25
79a	Reggie Jackson (portrait)	1.00	.70	.40
79b	Reggie Jackson (batting)	.75	.60	.30
80	Bucky Dent	.10	.08	.04
81	Tommy John	.20	.15	.08
82	Luis Tiant	.12	.09	.05
83	Rick Cerone	.06	.05	.02
84	Dick Howser	.06	.05	.02
85	Lou Piniella	.12	.09	.05
86	Ron Davis	.08	.06	.03
87a	Graig Nettles (Craig on back)	12.00	9.00	4.75
87b	Graig Nettles (Graig on back)	.30	.25	.12
88	Ron Guidry	.25	.20	.10
89	Rich Gossage	.20	.15	.08
90	Rudy May	.06	.05	.02
91	Gaylord Perry	.30	.25	.12
92	Eric Soderholm	.06	.05	.02
93	Bob Watson	.08	.06	.03
94	Bobby Murcer	.10	.08	.04
95	Bobby Brown	.06	.05	.02
96	Jim Spencer	.06	.05	.02
97	Tom Underwood	.06	.05	.02
98	Oscar Gamble	.08	.06	.03

#	Name	MT	NR MT	EX
99	Johnny Oates	.06	.05	.02
100	Fred Stanley	.06	.05	.02
101	Ruppert Jones	.06	.05	.02
102	Dennis Werth	.06	.05	.02
103	Joe Lefebvre	.06	.05	.02
104	Brian Doyle	.06	.05	.02
105	Aurelio Rodriguez	.08	.06	.03
106	Doug Bird	.06	.05	.02
107	Mike Griffin	.06	.05	.02
108	Tim Lollar	.06	.05	.02
109	Willie Randolph	.10	.08	.04
110	Steve Garvey	.50	.40	.20
111	Reggie Smith	.10	.08	.04
112	Don Sutton	.30	.25	.12
113	Burt Hooton	.08	.06	.03
114a	Davy Lopes (Davey) (no finger on back)	.10	.08	.04
114b	Davy Lopes (Davey) (small finger on back)	1.00	.70	.40
115	Dusty Baker	.10	.08	.04
116	Tom Lasorda	.10	.08	.04
117	Bill Russell	.08	.06	.03
118	Jerry Reuss	.10	.08	.04
119	Terry Forster	.08	.06	.03
120a	Robert Welch (Bob Welch on back)	.20	.15	.08
120b	Robert Welch (Robert Welch on back)	1.00	.70	.40
121	Don Stanhouse	.06	.05	.02
122	Rick Monday	.10	.08	.04
123	Derrel Thomas	.06	.05	.02
124	Joe Ferguson	.06	.05	.02
125	Rick Sutcliffe	.20	.15	.08
126a	Ron Cey (no finger on back)	.12	.09	.05
126b	Ron Cey (small finger on back)	1.00	.70	.40
127	Dave Goltz	.08	.06	.03
128	Jay Johnstone	.08	.06	.03
129	Steve Yeager	.06	.05	.02
130	Gary Weiss	.06	.05	.02
131	*Mike Scioscia*	.60	.45	.25
132	Vic Davalillo	.08	.06	.03
133	Doug Rau	.06	.05	.02
134	Pepe Frias	.06	.05	.02
135	Mickey Hatcher	.08	.06	.03
136	*Steve Howe*	.10	.08	.04
137	Robert Castillo	.06	.05	.02
138	Gary Thomasson	.06	.05	.02
139	Rudy Law	.06	.05	.02
140	*Fernand Valenzuela (Fernando)*	4.00	3.00	1.50
141	Manny Mota	.08	.06	.03
142	Gary Carter	.40	.30	.15
143	Steve Rogers	.08	.06	.03
144	Warren Cromartie	.06	.05	.02
145	Andre Dawson	.40	.30	.15
146	Larry Parrish	.10	.08	.04
147	Rowland Office	.06	.05	.02
148	Ellis Valentine	.06	.05	.02
149	Dick Williams	.06	.05	.02
150	*Bill Gullickson*	.15	.11	.06
151	Elias Sosa	.06	.05	.02
152	John Tamargo	.06	.05	.02
153	Chris Speier	.06	.05	.02
154	Ron LeFlore	.08	.06	.03
155	Rodney Scott	.06	.05	.02
156	Stan Bahnsen	.06	.05	.02
157	Bill Lee	.08	.06	.03
158	Fred Norman	.06	.05	.02
159	Woodie Fryman	.08	.06	.03
160	Dave Palmer	.06	.05	.02
161	Jerry White	.06	.05	.02
162	Roberto Ramos	.06	.05	.02
163	John D'Acquisto	.06	.05	.02
164	Tommy Hutton	.06	.05	.02
165	*Charlie Lea*	.12	.09	.05
166	Scott Sanderson	.06	.05	.02
167	Ken Macha	.06	.05	.02
168	Tony Bernazard	.06	.05	.02
169	Jim Palmer	.40	.30	.15
170	Steve Stone	.08	.06	.03
171	Mike Flanagan	.10	.08	.04
172	Al Bumbry	.08	.06	.03
173	Doug DeCinces	.10	.08	.04
174	Scott McGregor	.08	.06	.03
175	Mark Belanger	.08	.06	.03
176	Tim Stoddard	.06	.05	.02
177a	Rick Dempsey (no finger on front)	.10	.08	.04
177b	Rick Dempsey (small finger on front)	1.00	.70	.40
178	Earl Weaver	.10	.08	.04
179	Tippy Martinez	.06	.05	.02
180	Dennis Martinez	.08	.06	.03
181	Sammy Stewart	.06	.05	.02
182	Rich Dauer	.06	.05	.02
183	Lee May	.08	.06	.03
184	Eddie Murray	.70	.50	.30
185	Benny Ayala	.06	.05	.02
186	John Lowenstein	.06	.05	.02
187	Gary Roenicke	.06	.05	.02
188	Ken Singleton	.10	.08	.04
189	Dan Graham	.06	.05	.02
190	Terry Crowley	.06	.05	.02
191	Kiko Garcia	.06	.05	.02
192	Dave Ford	.06	.05	.02
193	Mark Corey	.06	.05	.02
194	Lenn Sakata	.06	.05	.02
195	Doug DeCinces	.10	.08	.04
196	Johnny Bench	.60	.45	.25
197	Dave Concepcion	.15	.11	.06
198	Ray Knight	.10	.08	.04
199	Ken Griffey	.12	.09	.05
200	Tom Seaver	.60	.45	.25
201	Dave Collins	.08	.06	.03
202	George Foster	.20	.15	.08
203	Junior Kennedy	.06	.05	.02
204	Frank Pastore	.06	.05	.02
205	Dan Driessen	.08	.06	.03
206	Hector Cruz	.06	.05	.02
207	Paul Moskau	.06	.05	.02
208	*Charlie Leibrandt*	.30	.25	.12
209	Harry Spilman	.06	.05	.02
210	*Joe Price*	.12	.09	.05
211	Tom Hume	.06	.05	.02
212	Joe Nolan	.06	.05	.02
213	Doug Bair	.06	.05	.02
214	Mario Soto	.08	.06	.03
215a	Bill Bonham (no finger on back)	.08	.06	.03
215b	Bill Bonham (small finger on back)	1.00	.70	.40
216a	George Foster (Slugger on front)	.25	.20	.10
216b	George Foster (Outfield on front)	.20	.15	.08
217	Paul Householder	.06	.05	.02
218	Ron Oester	.06	.05	.02
219	Sam Mejias	.06	.05	.02
220	Sheldon Burnside	.06	.05	.02
221	Carl Yastrzemski	.80	.60	.30
222	Jim Rice	.50	.40	.20
223	Fred Lynn	.20	.15	.08
224	Carlton Fisk	.50	.40	.20
225	Rick Burleson	.08	.06	.03
226	Dennis Eckersley	.12	.09	.05
227	Butch Hobson	.06	.05	.02
228	Tom Burgmeier	.06	.05	.02
229	Garry Hancock	.06	.05	.02
230	Don Zimmer	.06	.05	.02
231	Steve Renko	.06	.05	.02
232	Dwight Evans	.15	.11	.06
233	Mike Torrez	.08	.06	.03
234	Bob Stanley	.06	.05	.02
235	Jim Dwyer	.06	.05	.02
236	Dave Stapleton	.06	.05	.02
237	Glenn Hoffman	.06	.05	.02
238	Jerry Remy	.06	.05	.02
239	Dick Drago	.06	.05	.02
240	Bill Campbell	.06	.05	.02
241	Tony Perez	.20	.15	.08
242	Phil Niekro	.30	.25	.12
243	Dale Murphy	.90	.70	.35
244	Bob Horner	.12	.09	.05
245	Jeff Burroughs	.08	.06	.03
246	Rick Camp	.06	.05	.02
247	Bob Cox	.06	.05	.02
248	Bruce Benedict	.06	.05	.02
249	Gene Garber	.06	.05	.02
250	Jerry Royster	.06	.05	.02
251a	Gary Matthews (no finger on back)	.12	.09	.05
251b	Gary Matthews (small finger on back)	1.00	.70	.40
252	Chris Chambliss	.08	.06	.03
253	Luis Gomez	.06	.05	.02
254	Bill Nahorodny	.06	.05	.02
255	Doyle Alexander	.10	.08	.04
256	Brian Asselstine	.06	.05	.02
257	Biff Pocoroba	.06	.05	.02
258	Mike Lum	.06	.05	.02
259	Charlie Spikes	.06	.05	.02
260	Glenn Hubbard	.08	.06	.03
261	Tommy Boggs	.06	.05	.02
262	Al Hrabosky	.08	.06	.03
263	Rick Matula	.06	.05	.02
264	Preston Hanna	.06	.05	.02
265	Larry Bradford	.06	.05	.02
266	*Rafael Ramirez*	.20	.15	.08
267	Larry McWilliams	.06	.05	.02

		MT	NR MT	EX
268	Rod Carew	.60	.45	.25
269	Bobby Grich	.10	.08	.04
270	Carney Lansford	.10	.08	.04
271	Don Baylor	.12	.09	.05
272	Joe Rudi	.10	.08	.04
273	Dan Ford	.06	.05	.02
274	Jim Fregosi	.08	.06	.03
275	Dave Frost	.06	.05	.02
276	Frank Tanana	.10	.08	.04
277	Dickie Thon	.08	.06	.03
278	Jason Thompson	.06	.05	.02
279	Rick Miller	.06	.05	.02
280	Bert Campaneris	.10	.08	.04
281	Tom Donohue	.06	.05	.02
282	Brian Downing	.10	.08	.04
283	Fred Patek	.06	.05	.02
284	Bruce Kison	.06	.05	.02
285	Dave LaRoche	.06	.05	.02
286	Don Aase	.06	.05	.02
287	Jim Barr	.06	.05	.02
288	Alfredo Martinez	.06	.05	.02
289	Larry Harlow	.06	.05	.02
290	Andy Hassler	.06	.05	.02
291	Dave Kingman	.15	.11	.06
292	Bill Buckner	.12	.09	.05
293	Rick Reuschel	.10	.08	.04
294	Bruce Sutter	.15	.11	.06
295	Jerry Martin	.06	.05	.02
296	Scot Thompson	.06	.05	.02
297	Ivan DeJesus	.06	.05	.02
298	Steve Dillard	.06	.05	.02
299	Dick Tidrow	.06	.05	.02
300	Randy Martz	.06	.05	.02
301	Lenny Randle	.06	.05	.02
302	Lynn McGlothen	.06	.05	.02
303	Cliff Johnson	.06	.05	.02
304	Tim Blackwell	.06	.05	.02
305	Dennis Lamp	.06	.05	.02
306	Bill Caudill	.06	.05	.02
307	Carlos Lezcano	.06	.05	.02
308	Jim Tracy	.06	.05	.02
309	Doug Capilla	.06	.05	.02
310	Willie Hernandez	.10	.08	.04
311	Mike Vail	.06	.05	.02
312	Mike Krukow	.08	.06	.03
313	Barry Foote	.06	.05	.02
314	Larry Biittner	.06	.05	.02
315	Mike Tyson	.06	.05	.02
316	Lee Mazzilli	.08	.06	.03
317	John Stearns	.06	.05	.02
318	Alex Trevino	.06	.05	.02
319	Craig Swan	.06	.05	.02
320	Frank Taveras	.06	.05	.02
321	Steve Henderson	.06	.05	.02
322	Neil Allen	.08	.06	.03
323	Mark Bomback	.06	.05	.02
324	Mike Jorgensen	.06	.05	.02
325	Joe Torre	.08	.06	.03
326	Elliott Maddox	.06	.05	.02
327	Pete Falcone	.06	.05	.02
328	Ray Burris	.06	.05	.02
329	Claudell Washington	.08	.06	.03
330	Doug Flynn	.06	.05	.02
331	Joel Youngblood	.06	.05	.02
332	Bill Almon	.06	.05	.02
333	Tom Hausman	.06	.05	.02
334	Pat Zachry	.06	.05	.02
335	*Jeff Reardon*	.70	.50	.30
336	*Wally Backman*	.35	.25	.14
337	Dan Norman	.06	.05	.02
338	Jerry Morales	.06	.05	.02
339	Ed Farmer	.06	.05	.02
340	Bob Molinaro	.06	.05	.02
341	Todd Cruz	.06	.05	.02
342a	*Britt Burns* (no finger on front)	.20	.15	.08
342b	*Britt Burns* (small finger on front)	1.00	.70	.40
343	Kevin Bell	.06	.05	.02
344	Tony LaRussa	.08	.06	.03
345	Steve Trout	.06	.05	.02
346	*Harold Baines*	2.00	1.50	.80
347	Richard Wortham	.06	.05	.02
348	Wayne Nordhagen	.06	.05	.02
349	Mike Squires	.06	.05	.02
350	Lamar Johnson	.06	.05	.02
351	Rickey Henderson	2.50	2.00	1.00
352	Francisco Barrios	.06	.05	.02
353	Thad Bosley	.06	.05	.02
354	Chet Lemon	.08	.06	.03
355	Bruce Kimm	.06	.05	.02
356	*Richard Dotson*	.35	.25	.14
357	Jim Morrison	.06	.05	.02

		MT	NR MT	EX
358	Mike Proly	.06	.05	.02
359	Greg Pryor	.06	.05	.02
360	Dave Parker	.30	.25	.12
361	Omar Moreno	.06	.05	.02
362a	Kent Tekulve (1071 Waterbury on back)	.15	.11	.06
362b	Kent Tekulve (1971 Waterbury on back)	.70	.50	.30
363	Willie Stargell	.40	.30	.15
364	Phil Garner	.08	.06	.03
365	Ed Ott	.06	.05	.02
366	Don Robinson	.08	.06	.03
367	Chuck Tanner	.06	.05	.02
368	Jim Rooker	.06	.05	.02
369	Dale Berra	.06	.05	.02
370	Jim Bibby	.06	.05	.02
371	Steve Nicosia	.06	.05	.02
372	Mike Easler	.08	.06	.03
373	Bill Robinson	.06	.05	.02
374	Lee Lacy	.06	.05	.02
375	John Candelaria	.10	.08	.04
376	Manny Sanguillen	.06	.05	.02
377	Rick Rhoden	.10	.08	.04
378	Grant Jackson	.06	.05	.02
379	Tim Foli	.06	.05	.02
380	*Rod Scurry*	.08	.06	.03
381	Bill Madlock	.12	.09	.05
382a	Kurt Bevacqua (photo reversed. backwards "P" on cap)	.15	.11	.06
382b	Kurt Bevacqua (correct photo)	.70	.50	.30
383	Bert Blyleven	.12	.09	.05
384	Eddie Solomon	.06	.05	.02
385	Enrique Romo	.06	.05	.02
386	John Milner	.06	.05	.02
387	Mike Hargrove	.06	.05	.02
388	Jorge Orta	.06	.05	.02
389	Toby Harrah	.08	.06	.03
390	Tom Veryzer	.06	.05	.02
391	Miguel Dilone	.06	.05	.02
392	Dan Spillner	.06	.05	.02
393	Jack Brohamer	.06	.05	.02
394	Wayne Garland	.06	.05	.02
395	Sid Monge	.06	.05	.02
396	Rick Waits	.06	.05	.02
397	*Joe Charboneau*	.10	.08	.04
398	Gary Alexander	.06	.05	.02
399	Jerry Dybzinski	.06	.05	.02
400	Mike Stanton	.06	.05	.02
401	Mike Paxton	.06	.05	.02
402	Gary Gray	.06	.05	.02
403	Rick Manning	.06	.05	.02
404	Bo Diaz	.08	.06	.03
405	Ron Hassey	.06	.05	.02
406	Ross Grimsley	.06	.05	.02
407	Victor Cruz	.06	.05	.02
408	Len Barker	.08	.06	.03
409	Bob Bailor	.06	.05	.02
410	Otto Velez	.06	.05	.02
411	Ernie Whitt	.08	.06	.03
412	Jim Clancy	.08	.06	.03
413	Barry Bonnell	.06	.05	.02
414	Dave Stieb	.20	.15	.08
415	*Damaso Garcia*	.10	.08	.04
416	John Mayberry	.08	.06	.03
417	Roy Howell	.06	.05	.02
418	*Dan Ainge*	.25	.20	.10
419a	Jesse Jefferson (Pirates on back)	.10	.08	.04
419b	Jesse Jefferson (Blue Jays on back)	.50	.40	.20
420	Joey McLaughlin	.06	.05	.02
421	*Lloyd Moseby*	.50	.40	.20
422	Al Woods	.06	.05	.02
423	Garth Iorg	.06	.05	.02
424	Doug Ault	.06	.05	.02
425	*Ken Schrom*	.06	.05	.02
426	Mike Willis	.06	.05	.02
427	Steve Braun	.06	.05	.02
428	Bob Davis	.06	.05	.02
429	Jerry Garvin	.06	.05	.02
430	Alfredo Griffin	.08	.06	.03
431	Bob Mattick	.06	.05	.02
432	Vida Blue	.12	.09	.05
433	Jack Clark	.25	.20	.10
434	Willie McCovey	.40	.30	.15
435	Mike Ivie	.06	.05	.02
436a	Darrel Evans (Darrel on front)	.15	.11	.06
436b	Darrel Evans (Darrell on front)	.70	.50	.30
437	Terry Whitfield	.06	.05	.02
438	Rennie Stennett	.06	.05	.02
439	John Montefusco	.08	.06	.03
440	Jim Wohlford	.06	.05	.02

		MT	NR MT	EX
441	Bill North	.06	.05	.02
442	Milt May	.06	.05	.02
443	Max Venable	.06	.05	.02
444	Ed Whitson	.06	.05	.02
445	*Al Holland*	.08	.06	.03
446	Randy Moffitt	.06	.05	.02
447	Bob Knepper	.08	.06	.03
448	Gary Lavelle	.06	.05	.02
449	Greg Minton	.06	.05	.02
450	Johnnie LeMaster	.06	.05	.02
451	Larry Herndon	.08	.06	.03
452	Rich Murray	.06	.05	.02
453	Joe Pettini	.06	.05	.02
454	Allen Ripley	.06	.05	.02
455	Dennis Littlejohn	.06	.05	.02
456	Tom Griffin	.06	.05	.02
457	Alan Hargesheimer	.06	.05	.02
458	Joe Strain	.06	.05	.02
459	Steve Kemp	.08	.06	.03
460	Sparky Anderson	.10	.08	.04
461	Alan Trammell	.40	.30	.15
462	Mark Fidrych	.08	.06	.03
463	Lou Whitaker	.40	.30	.15
464	Dave Rozema	.06	.05	.02
465	Milt Wilcox	.06	.05	.02
466	Champ Summers	.06	.05	.02
467	Lance Parrish	.35	.25	.14
468	Dan Petry	.08	.06	.03
469	Pat Underwood	.06	.05	.02
470	Rick Peters	.06	.05	.02
471	Al Cowens	.06	.05	.02
472	John Wockenfuss	.06	.05	.02
473	Tom Brookens	.08	.06	.03
474	Richie Hebner	.06	.05	.02
475	Jack Morris	.30	.25	.12
476	Jim Lentine	.06	.05	.02
477	Bruce Robbins	.06	.05	.02
478	Mark Wagner	.06	.05	.02
479	Tim Corcoran	.06	.05	.02
480a	Stan Papi (Pitcher on front)	.15	.11	.06
480b	Stan Papi (Shortstop on front)	.70	.50	.30
481	*Kirk Gibson*	3.75	2.75	1.50
482	Dan Schatzeder	.06	.05	.02
483	Amos Otis	.70	.50	.30
484	Dave Winfield	.50	.40	.20
485	Rollie Fingers	.25	.20	.10
486	Gene Richards	.06	.05	.02
487	Randy Jones	.08	.06	.03
488	Ozzie Smith	.40	.30	.15
489	Gene Tenace	.08	.06	.03
490	Bill Fahey	.06	.05	.02
491	John Curtis	.06	.05	.02
492	Dave Cash	.06	.05	.02
493a	Tim Flannery (photo reversed, batting righty)	.15	.11	.06
493b	Tim Flannery (photo correct, batting lefty)	.70	.50	.30
494	Jerry Mumphrey	.06	.05	.02
495	Bob Shirley	.06	.05	.02
496	Steve Mura	.06	.05	.02
497	Eric Rasmussen	.06	.05	.02
498	Broderick Perkins	.06	.05	.02
499	Barry Evans	.06	.05	.02
500	Chuck Baker	.06	.05	.02
501	*Luis Salazar*	.15	.11	.06
502	Gary Lucas	.08	.06	.03
503	Mike Armstrong	.06	.05	.02
504	Jerry Turner	.06	.05	.02
505	Dennis Kinney	.06	.05	.02
506	Willy Montanez (Willie)	.06	.05	.02
507	Gorman Thomas	.10	.08	.04
508	Ben Oglivie	.08	.06	.03
509	Larry Hisle	.08	.06	.03
510	Sal Bando	.10	.08	.04
511	Robin Yount	.90	.70	.35
512	Mike Caldwell	.06	.05	.02
513	Sixto Lezcano	.06	.05	.02
514a	Jerry Augustine (Billy Travers photo)	.15	.11	.06
514b	Billy Travers (correct name with photo)	.70	.50	.30
515	Paul Molitor	.20	.15	.08
516	Moose Haas	.06	.05	.02
517	Bill Castro	.06	.05	.02
518	Jim Slaton	.06	.05	.02
519	Lary Sorensen	.06	.05	.02
520	Bob McClure	.06	.05	.02
521	Charlie Moore	.06	.05	.02
522	Jim Gantner	.08	.06	.03
523	Reggie Cleveland	.06	.05	.02
524	Don Money	.06	.05	.02

		MT	NR MT	EX
525	Billy Travers	.06	.05	.02
526	Buck Martinez	.06	.05	.02
527	Dick Davis	.06	.05	.02
528	Ted Simmons	.12	.09	.05
529	Garry Templeton	.10	.08	.04
530	Ken Reitz	.06	.05	.02
531	Tony Scott	.06	.05	.02
532	Ken Oberkfell	.06	.05	.02
533	Bob Sykes	.06	.05	.02
534	Keith Smith	.06	.05	.02
535	John Littlefield	.06	.05	.02
536	Jim Kaat	.15	.11	.06
537	Bob Forsch	.08	.06	.03
538	Mike Phillips	.06	.05	.02
539	*Terry Landrum*	.10	.08	.04
540	*Leon Durham*	.20	.15	.08
541	Terry Kennedy	.08	.06	.03
542	George Hendrick	.08	.06	.03
543	Dane Iorg	.06	.05	.02
544	Mark Littell (photo actually Jeff Little)	.06	.05	.02
545	Keith Hernandez	.40	.30	.15
546	Silvio Martinez	.06	.05	.02
547a	Pete Vuckovich (photo actually Don Hood)	.15	.11	.06
547b	Don Hood (correct name with photo)	.70	.50	.30
548	Bobby Bonds	.10	.08	.04
549	Mike Ramsey	.06	.05	.02
550	Tom Herr	.10	.08	.04
551	Roy Smalley	.06	.05	.02
552	Jerry Koosman	.10	.08	.04
553	Ken Landreaux	.06	.05	.02
554	John Castino	.06	.05	.02
555	Doug Corbett	.06	.05	.02
556	Bombo Rivera	.06	.05	.02
557	Ron Jackson	.06	.05	.02
558	Butch Wynegar	.06	.05	.02
559	Hosken Powell	.06	.05	.02
560	Pete Redfern	.06	.05	.02
561	Roger Erickson	.06	.05	.02
562	Glenn Adams	.06	.05	.02
563	Rick Sofield	.06	.05	.02
564	Geoff Zahn	.06	.05	.02
565	Pete Mackanin	.06	.05	.02
566	Mike Cubbage	.06	.05	.02
567	Darrell Jackson	.06	.05	.02
568	Dave Edwards	.06	.05	.02
569	Rob Wilfong	.06	.05	.02
570	Sal Butera	.06	.05	.02
571	Jose Morales	.06	.05	.02
572	Rick Langford	.06	.05	.02
573	Mike Norris	.06	.05	.02
574	Rickey Henderson	1.25	.90	.50
575	Tony Armas	.10	.08	.04
576	Dave Revering	.06	.05	.02
577	Jeff Newman	.06	.05	.02
578	Bob Lacey	.06	.05	.02
579	Brian Kingman (photo actually Alan Wirth)	.06	.05	.02
580	Mitchell Page	.06	.05	.02
581	Billy Martin	.12	.09	.05
582	Rob Picciolo	.06	.05	.02
583	Mike Heath	.06	.05	.02
584	Mickey Klutts	.06	.05	.02
585	Orlando Gonzalez	.06	.05	.02
586	*Mike Davis*	.25	.20	.10
587	Wayne Gross	.06	.05	.02
588	Matt Keough	.06	.05	.02
589	Steve McCatty	.06	.05	.02
590	Dwayne Murphy	.08	.06	.03
591	Mario Guerrero	.06	.05	.02
592	Dave McKay	.06	.05	.02
593	Jim Essian	.06	.05	.02
594	Dave Heaverlo	.06	.05	.02
595	Maury Wills	.10	.08	.04
596	Juan Beniquez	.06	.05	.02
597	Rodney Craig	.06	.05	.02
598	Jim Anderson	.06	.05	.02
599	Floyd Bannister	.10	.08	.04
600	Bruce Bochte	.06	.05	.02
601	Julio Cruz	.06	.05	.02
602	Ted Cox	.06	.05	.02
603	Dan Meyer	.06	.05	.02
604	Larry Cox	.06	.05	.02
605	Bill Stein	.06	.05	.02
606	Steve Garvey	.50	.40	.20
607	Dave Roberts	.06	.05	.02
608	Leon Roberts	.06	.05	.02
609	Reggie Walton	.06	.05	.02
610	Dave Edler	.06	.05	.02

		MT	NR MT	EX
611	Larry Milbourne	.06	.05	.02
612	Kim Allen	.06	.05	.02
613	Mario Mendoza	.06	.05	.02
614	Tom Paciorek	.06	.05	.02
615	Glenn Abbott	.06	.05	.02
616	Joe Simpson	.06	.05	.02
617	Mickey Rivers	.08	.06	.03
618	Jim Kern	.06	.05	.02
619	Jim Sundberg	.08	.06	.03
620	Richie Zisk	.08	.06	.03
621	Jon Matlack	.08	.06	.03
622	Ferguson Jenkins	.20	.15	.08
623	Pat Corrales	.06	.05	.02
624	Ed Figueroa	.06	.05	.02
625	Buddy Bell	.12	.09	.05
626	Al Oliver	.15	.11	.06
627	Doc Medich	.06	.05	.02
628	Bump Wills	.06	.05	.02
629	Rusty Staub	.10	.08	.04
630	Pat Putnam	.06	.05	.02
631	John Grubb	.06	.05	.02
632	Danny Darwin	.06	.05	.02
633	Ken Clay	.06	.05	.02
634	Jim Norris	.06	.05	.02
635	John Butcher	.06	.05	.02
636	Dave Roberts	.06	.05	.02
637	Billy Sample	.06	.05	.02
638	Carl Yastrzemski	.80	.60	.30
639	Cecil Cooper	.15	.11	.06
640	Mike Schmidt	1.75	1.25	.70
641a	Checklist 1-50 (41 Hal McRae)	.10	.08	.04
641b	Checklist 1-50 (41 Hal McRae Double Threat)	.40	.30	.15
642	Checklist 51-109	.06	.05	.02
643	Checklist 110-168	.06	.05	.02
644a	Checklist 169-220 (202 George Foster)	.10	.08	.04
644b	Checklist 169-220 (202 George Foster "Slugger")	.40	.30	.15
645a	Triple Threat (Larry Bowa, Pete Rose, Mike Schmidt) (no number on back)	1.00	.70	.40
645b	Triple Threat (Larry Bowa, Pete Rose, Mike Schmidt) (645 on back)	2.00	1.50	.80
646	Checklist 221-267	.06	.05	.02
647	Checklist 268-315	.06	.05	.02
648	Checklist 316-359	.06	.05	.02
649	Checklist 360-408	.06	.05	.02
650	Reggie Jackson	1.50	1.25	.60
651	Checklist 409-458	.06	.05	.02
652a	Checklist 459-509 (483 Aurelio Lopez)	.10	.08	.04
652b	Checklist 459-506 (no 483)	.40	.30	.15
653	Willie Wilson	1.00	.70	.40
654a	Checklist 507-550 (514 Jerry Augustine)	.10	.08	.04
654b	Checklist 507-550 (514 Billy Travers)	.40	.30	.15
655	George Brett	2.00	1.50	.80
656	Checklist 551-593	.06	.05	.02
657	Tug McGraw	1.00	.70	.40
658	Checklist 594-637	.06	.05	.02
659a	Checklist 640-660 (last number on front is 551)	.10	.08	.04
659b	Checklist 640-660 (last number on front is 483)	.40	.30	.15
660a	Steve Carlton (date 1066 on back)	1.00	.70	.40
660b	Steve Carlton (date 1966 on back)	2.00	1.50	.80

1981 Fleer Star Stickers

The 128-card 1981 Fleer Star Sticker set was designed for the card fronts to be peeled away from the cardboard backs. The card obverses feature color photos with blue and yellow trim. The card backs are identical in design to the regular 1981 Fleer set except for color and numbering. The set contains three unnumbered checklist cards whose fronts depict Reggie Jackson (#'s 1-42), George Brett (#'s 43-83) and Mike Schmidt (#'s 84-125). The cards, which are the standard 2-1/2" by 3-1/2", were issued in gum wax packs.

		MT	NR MT	EX
	Complete Set	30.00	25.00	12.00
	Common Player	.10	.08	.04
1	Steve Garvey	.50	.40	.20
2	Ron LeFlore	.10	.08	.04
3	Ron Cey	.25	.20	.10
4	Dave Revering	.10	.08	.04
5	Tony Armas	.15	.11	.06
6	Mike Norris	.10	.08	.04
7	Steve Kemp	.15	.11	.06
8	Bruce Bochte	.10	.08	.04
9	Mike Schmidt	1.00	.70	.40
10	Scott McGregor	.10	.08	.04
11	Buddy Bell	.20	.15	.08
12	Carney Lansford	.20	.15	.08
13	Carl Yastrzemski	2.50	2.00	1.00
14	Ben Oglivie	.10	.08	.04
15	Willie Stargell	1.00	.70	.40
16	Cecil Cooper	.15	.11	.06
17	Gene Richards	.10	.08	.04
18	Jim Kern	.10	.08	.04
19	Jerry Koosman	.15	.11	.06
20	Larry Bowa	.20	.15	.08
21	Kent Tekulve	.15	.11	.06
22	Dan Driessen	.10	.08	.04
23	Phil Niekro	.50	.40	.20
24	Dan Quisenberry	.30	.25	.12
25	Dave Winfield	.50	.40	.20
26	Dave Parker	.50	.40	.20
27	Rick Langford	.10	.08	.04
28	Amos Otis	.15	.11	.06
29	Bill Buckner	.15	.11	.06
30	Al Bumbry	.10	.08	.04
31	Bake McBride	.10	.08	.04
32	Mickey Rivers	.10	.08	.04
33	Rick Burleson	.10	.08	.04
34	Dennis Eckersley	.25	.20	.10
35	Cesar Cedeno	.20	.15	.08
36	Enos Cabell	.10	.08	.04
37	Johnny Bench	1.50	1.25	.60
38	Robin Yount	1.00	.70	.40
39	Mark Belanger	.10	.08	.04
40	Rod Carew	.50	.40	.20
41	George Foster	.40	.30	.15
42	Lee Mazzilli	.15	.11	.06
43	Triple Threat (Larry Bowa, Pete Rose, Mike Schmidt)	2.00	1.50	.80
44	J.R. Richard	.15	.11	.06
45	Lou Piniella	.30	.25	.12
46	Ken Landreaux	.10	.08	.04
47	Rollie Fingers	.50	.40	.20
48	Joaquin Andujar	.10	.08	.04
49	Tom Seaver	1.50	1.25	.60
50	Bobby Grich	.20	.15	.08
51	Jon Matlack	.10	.08	.04
52	Jack Clark	.25	.20	.10
53	Jim Rice	.25	.20	.10
54	Rickey Henderson	1.50	1.25	.60
55	Roy Smalley	.10	.08	.04
56	Mike Flanagan	.15	.11	.06
57	Steve Rogers	.10	.08	.04
58	Carlton Fisk	.60	.45	.25
59	Don Sutton	.50	.40	.20
60	Ken Griffey	.20	.15	.08
61	Burt Hooton	.10	.08	.04
62	Dusty Baker	.20	.15	.08
63	Vida Blue	.25	.20	.10
64	Al Oliver	.30	.25	.12
65	Jim Bibby	.10	.08	.04
66	Tony Perez	.50	.40	.20
67	Davy Lopes (Davey)	.15	.11	.06
68	Bill Russell	.15	.11	.06
69	Larry Parrish	.20	.15	.08
70	Garry Maddox	.15	.11	.06
71	Phil Garner	.15	.11	.06
72	Graig Nettles	.35	.25	.14
73	Gary Carter	.50	.40	.20
74	Pete Rose	1.50	1.25	.60

		MT	NR MT	EX
75	Greg Luzinski	.30	.25	.12
76	Ron Guidry	.25	.20	.10
77	Gorman Thomas	.15	.11	.06
78	Jose Cruz	.20	.15	.08
79	Bob Boone	.15	.11	.06
80	Bruce Sutter	.35	.25	.14
81	Chris Chambliss	.15	.11	.06
82	Paul Molitor	.60	.45	.25
83	Tug McGraw	.25	.20	.10
84	Ferguson Jenkins	.40	.30	.15
85	Steve Carlton	1.25	.90	.50
86	Miguel Dilone	.10	.08	.04
87	Reggie Smith	.20	.15	.08
88	Rick Cerone	.10	.08	.04
89	Alan Trammell	.50	.40	.20
90	Doug DeCinces	.20	.15	.08
91	Sparky Lyle	.15	.11	.06
92	Warren Cromartie	.10	.08	.04
93	Rick Reuschel	.25	.20	.10
94	Larry Hisle	.10	.08	.04
95	Paul Splittorff	.10	.08	.04
96	Manny Trillo	.10	.08	.04
97	Frank White	.20	.15	.08
98	Fred Lynn	.25	.20	.10
99	Bob Horner	.15	.11	.06
100	Omar Moreno	.10	.08	.04
101	Dave Concepcion	.20	.15	.08
102	Larry Gura	.10	.08	.04
103	Ken Singleton	.20	.15	.08
104	Steve Stone	.15	.11	.06
105	Richie Zisk	.10	.08	.04
106	Willie Wilson	.40	.30	.15
107	Willie Randolph	.20	.15	.08
108	Nolan Ryan	1.25	.90	.50
109	Joe Morgan	.50	.40	.20
110	Bucky Dent	.20	.15	.08
111	Dave Kingman	.40	.30	.15
112	John Castino	.10	.08	.04
113	Joe Rudi	.20	.15	.08
114	Ed Farmer	.10	.08	.04
115	Reggie Jackson	1.00	.70	.40
116	George Brett	.50	.40	.20
117	Eddie Murray	.25	.20	.10
118	Rich Gossage	.25	.20	.10
119	Dale Murphy	.50	.40	.20
120	Ted Simmons	.15	.11	.06
121	Tommy John	.25	.20	.10
122	Don Baylor	.30	.25	.12
123	Andre Dawson	.50	.40	.20
124	Jim Palmer	1.00	.70	.40
125	Garry Templeton	.20	.15	.08
-----	Reggie Jackson/Checklist 1-42	1.50	1.25	.60
-----	George Brett/Checklist 43-83	1.75	1.25	.70
-----	Mike Schmidt/Checklist 84-125	1.75	1.25	.70

1982 Fleer

Fleer's 1982 set did not match the quality of the previous year's effort. Many of the photos in the set are blurred and have muddied backgrounds. The cards, which measure 2-1/2" by 3-1/2", feature color photos surrounded by a border frame which is color-coded by team. The card backs are blue, white, and yellow and contain the player's team logo plus the logos of Major League Baseball and the Major League Baseball Players Association. Due to a lawsuit by Topps, Fleer was forced to issue the set with team logo stickers rather than gum. The complete set price

does not include the higher priced variations.

		MT	NR MT	EX
	Complete Set:	35.00	27.00	15.00
	Common Player:	.06	.05	.02
1	Dusty Baker	.10	.08	.04
2	Robert Castillo	.06	.05	.02
3	Ron Cey	.12	.09	.05
4	Terry Forster	.08	.06	.03
5	Steve Garvey	.50	.40	.20
6	Dave Goltz	.08	.06	.03
7	Pedro Guerrero(FC)	.60	.45	.25
8	Burt Hooton	.08	.06	.03
9	Steve Howe	.08	.06	.03
10	Jay Johnstone	.08	.06	.03
11	Ken Landreaux	.06	.05	.02
12	Davey Lopes	.10	.08	.04
13	*Mike Marshall*(FC)	1.00	.70	.40
14	Bobby Mitchell	.06	.05	.02
15	Rick Monday	.10	.08	.04
16	*Tom Niedenfuer*(FC)	.30	.25	.12
17	*Ted Power*(FC)	.20	.15	.08
18	Jerry Reuss	.10	.08	.04
19	Ron Roenicke	.06	.05	.02
20	Bill Russell	.08	.06	.03
21	*Steve Sax*(FC)	2.75	2.00	1.00
22	Mike Scioscia	.08	.06	.03
23	Reggie Smith	.10	.08	.04
24	*Dave Stewart*(FC)	3.00	2.25	1.25
25	Rick Sutcliffe	.15	.11	.06
26	Derrel Thomas	.06	.05	.02
27	Fernando Valenzuela	.60	.45	.25
28	Bob Welch	.12	.09	.05
29	Steve Yeager	.06	.05	.02
30	Bobby Brown	.06	.05	.02
31	Rick Cerone	.06	.05	.02
32	Ron Davis	.06	.05	.02
33	Bucky Dent	.10	.08	.04
34	Barry Foote	.06	.05	.02
35	George Frazier	.06	.05	.02
36	Oscar Gamble	.08	.06	.03
37	Rich Gossage	.20	.15	.08
38	Ron Guidry	.25	.20	.10
39	Reggie Jackson	.60	.45	.25
40	Tommy John	.20	.15	.08
41	Rudy May	.06	.05	.02
42	Larry Milbourne	.06	.05	.02
43	Jerry Mumphrey	.06	.05	.02
44	Bobby Murcer	.10	.08	.04
45	*Gene Nelson*	.12	.09	.05
46	Graig Nettles	.15	.11	.06
47	Johnny Oates	.06	.05	.02
48	Lou Piniella	.12	.09	.05
49	Willie Randolph	.10	.08	.04
50	Rick Reuschel	.10	.08	.04
51	Dave Revering	.06	.05	.02
52	*Dave Righetti*(FC)	2.00	1.50	.80
53	Aurelio Rodriguez	.08	.06	.03
54	Bob Watson	.08	.06	.03
55	Dennis Werth	.06	.05	.02
56	Dave Winfield	.50	.40	.20
57	Johnny Bench	.60	.45	.25
58	Bruce Berenyi	.06	.05	.02
59	Larry Biittner	.06	.05	.02
60	Scott Brown	.06	.05	.02
61	Dave Collins	.08	.06	.03
62	Geoff Combe	.06	.05	.02
63	Dave Concepcion	.12	.09	.05
64	Dan Driessen	.08	.06	.03
65	Joe Edelen	.06	.05	.02
66	George Foster	.20	.15	.08
67	Ken Griffey	.12	.09	.05
68	Paul Householder	.06	.05	.02
69	Tom Hume	.06	.05	.02
70	Junior Kennedy	.06	.05	.02
71	Ray Knight	.10	.08	.04
72	Mike LaCoss	.06	.05	.02
73	Rafael Landestoy	.06	.05	.02
74	Charlie Leibrandt	.10	.08	.04
75	Sam Mejias	.06	.05	.02
76	Paul Moskau	.06	.05	.02
77	Joe Nolan	.06	.05	.02
78	Mike O'Berry	.06	.05	.02
79	Ron Oester	.06	.05	.02
80	Frank Pastore	.06	.05	.02
81	Joe Price	.06	.05	.02
82	Tom Seaver	.60	.45	.25
83	Mario Soto	.08	.06	.03
84	Mike Vail	.06	.05	.02
85	Tony Armas	.10	.08	.04

		MT	NR MT	EX
86	Shooty Babitt	.06	.05	.02
87	Dave Beard	.06	.05	.02
88	Rick Bosetti	.06	.05	.02
89	Keith Drumright	.06	.05	.02
90	Wayne Gross	.06	.05	.02
91	Mike Heath	.06	.05	.02
92	Rickey Henderson	.90	.70	.35
93	Cliff Johnson	.06	.05	.02
94	Jeff Jones	.06	.05	.02
95	Matt Keough	.06	.05	.02
96	Brian Kingman	.06	.05	.02
97	Mickey Klutts	.06	.05	.02
98	Rick Langford	.06	.05	.02
99	Steve McCatty	.06	.05	.02
100	Dave McKay	.06	.05	.02
101	Dwayne Murphy	.08	.06	.03
102	Jeff Newman	.06	.05	.02
103	Mike Norris	.06	.05	.02
104	Bob Owchinko	.06	.05	.02
105	Mitchell Page	.06	.05	.02
106	Rob Picciolo	.06	.05	.02
107	Jim Spencer	.06	.05	.02
108	Fred Stanley	.06	.05	.02
109	Tom Underwood	.06	.05	.02
110	Joaquin Andujar	.08	.06	.03
111	Steve Braun	.06	.05	.02
112	Bob Forsch	.08	.06	.03
113	George Hendrick	.08	.06	.03
114	Keith Hernandez	.40	.30	.15
115	Tom Herr	.10	.08	.04
116	Dane Iorg	.06	.05	.02
117	Jim Kaat	.15	.11	.06
118	Tito Landrum	.06	.05	.02
119	Sixto Lezcano	.06	.05	.02
120	Mark Littell	.06	.05	.02
121	John Martin	.06	.05	.02
122	Silvio Martinez	.06	.05	.02
123	Ken Oberkfell	.06	.05	.02
124	Darrell Porter	.08	.06	.03
125	Mike Ramsey	.06	.05	.02
126	Orlando Sanchez	.06	.05	.02
127	Bob Shirley	.06	.05	.02
128	Lary Sorensen	.06	.05	.02
129	Bruce Sutter	.15	.11	.06
130	Bob Sykes	.06	.05	.02
131	Garry Templeton	.10	.08	.04
132	Gene Tenace	.08	.06	.03
133	Jerry Augustine	.06	.05	.02
134	Sal Bando	.08	.06	.03
135	Mark Brouhard	.06	.05	.02
136	Mike Caldwell	.06	.05	.02
137	Reggie Cleveland	.06	.05	.02
138	Cecil Cooper	.15	.11	.06
139	Jamie Easterly	.06	.05	.02
140	Marshall Edwards	.06	.05	.02
141	Rollie Fingers	.20	.15	.08
142	Jim Gantner	.08	.06	.03
143	Moose Haas	.06	.05	.02
144	Larry Hisle	.08	.06	.03
145	Roy Howell	.06	.05	.02
146	Rickey Keeton	.06	.05	.02
147	Randy Lerch	.06	.05	.02
148	Paul Molitor	.20	.15	.08
149	Don Money	.06	.05	.02
150	Charlie Moore	.06	.05	.02
151	Ben Oglivie	.08	.06	.03
152	Ted Simmons	.12	.09	.05
153	Jim Slaton	.06	.05	.02
154	Gorman Thomas	.10	.08	.04
155	Robin Yount	.90	.70	.35
156	Pete Vukovich	.08	.06	.03
157	Benny Ayala	.06	.05	.02
158	Mark Belanger	.08	.06	.03
159	Al Bumbry	.08	.06	.03
160	Terry Crowley	.06	.05	.02
161	Rich Dauer	.06	.05	.02
162	Doug DeCinces	.10	.08	.04
163	Rick Dempsey	.08	.06	.03
164	Jim Dwyer	.06	.05	.02
165	Mike Flanagan	.10	.08	.04
166	Dave Ford	.06	.05	.02
167	Dan Graham	.06	.05	.02
168	Wayne Krenchicki	.06	.05	.02
169	John Lowenstein	.06	.05	.02
170	Dennis Martinez	.08	.06	.03
171	Tippy Martinez	.06	.05	.02
172	Scott McGregor	.08	.06	.03
173	Jose Morales	.06	.05	.02
174	Eddie Murray	.60	.45	.25
175	Jim Palmer	.40	.30	.15
176	*Cal Ripken, Jr.*(FC)	8.00	6.00	3.25

		MT	NR MT	EX
177	Gary Roenicke	.06	.05	.02
178	Lenn Sakata	.06	.05	.02
179	Ken Singleton	.10	.08	.04
180	Sammy Stewart	.06	.05	.02
181	Tim Stoddard	.06	.05	.02
182	Steve Stone	.08	.06	.03
183	Stan Bahnsen	.06	.05	.02
184	Ray Burris	.06	.05	.02
185	Gary Carter	.35	.25	.14
186	Warren Cromartie	.06	.05	.02
187	Andre Dawson	.40	.30	.15
188	*Terry Francona*(FC)	.10	.08	.04
189	Woodie Fryman	.08	.06	.03
190	Bill Gullickson	.08	.06	.03
191	Grant Jackson	.06	.05	.02
192	Wallace Johnson	.06	.05	.02
193	Charlie Lea	.06	.05	.02
194	Bill Lee	.08	.06	.03
195	Jerry Manuel	.06	.05	.02
196	Brad Mills	.06	.05	.02
197	John Milner	.06	.05	.02
198	Rowland Office	.06	.05	.02
199	David Palmer	.06	.05	.02
200	Larry Parrish	.10	.08	.04
201	Mike Phillips	.06	.05	.02
202	Tim Raines	.90	.70	.35
203	Bobby Ramos	.06	.05	.02
204	Jeff Reardon	.20	.15	.08
205	Steve Rogers	.08	.06	.03
206	Scott Sanderson	.06	.05	.02
207	Rodney Scott (photo actually Tim Raines)			
		.10	.08	.04
208	Elias Sosa	.06	.05	.02
209	Chris Speier	.06	.05	.02
210	*Tim Wallach*(FC)	1.50	1.25	.60
211	Jerry White	.06	.05	.02
212	Alan Ashby	.06	.05	.02
213	Cesar Cedeno	.12	.09	.05
214	Jose Cruz	.12	.09	.05
215	Kiko Garcia	.06	.05	.02
216	Phil Garner	.08	.06	.03
217	Danny Heep	.06	.05	.02
218	Art Howe	.06	.05	.02
219	Bob Knepper	.08	.06	.03
220	Frank LaCorte	.06	.05	.02
221	Joe Niekro	.12	.09	.05
222	Joe Pittman	.06	.05	.02
223	Terry Puhl	.06	.05	.02
224	Luis Pujols	.06	.05	.02
225	Craig Reynolds	.06	.05	.02
226	J.R. Richard	.10	.08	.04
227	Dave Roberts	.06	.05	.02
228	Vern Ruhle	.06	.05	.02
229	Nolan Ryan	1.00	.70	.40
230	Joe Sambito	.06	.05	.02
231	Tony Scott	.06	.05	.02
232	Dave Smith	.10	.08	.04
233	Harry Spilman	.06	.05	.02
234	Don Sutton	.30	.25	.12
235	Dickie Thon	.08	.06	.03
236	Denny Walling	.06	.05	.02
237	Gary Woods	.06	.05	.02
238	*Luis Aguayo*(FC)	.10	.08	.04
239	Ramon Aviles	.06	.05	.02
240	Bob Boone	.10	.08	.04
241	Larry Bowa	.15	.11	.06
242	Warren Brusstar	.06	.05	.02
243	Steve Carlton	.50	.40	.20
244	Larry Christenson	.06	.05	.02
245	Dick Davis	.06	.05	.02
246	Greg Gross	.06	.05	.02
247	Sparky Lyle	.10	.08	.04
248	Garry Maddox	.10	.08	.04
249	Gary Matthews	.10	.08	.04
250	Bake McBride	.06	.05	.02
251	Tug McGraw	.12	.09	.05
252	Keith Moreland	.10	.08	.04
253	Dickie Noles	.06	.05	.02
254	Mike Proly	.06	.05	.02
255	Ron Reed	.06	.05	.02
256	Pete Rose	1.00	.70	.40
257	Dick Ruthven	.06	.05	.02
258	Mike Schmidt	1.00	.70	.40
259	Lonnie Smith	.08	.06	.03
260	Manny Trillo	.08	.06	.03
261	Del Unser	.06	.05	.02
262	George Vukovich	.06	.05	.02
263	Tom Brookens	.06	.05	.02
264	George Cappuzzello	.06	.05	.02
265	Marty Castillo	.06	.05	.02
266	Al Cowens	.06	.05	.02

#	Player	MT	NR MT	EX
267	Kirk Gibson	.70	.50	.30
268	Richie Hebner	.06	.05	.02
269	Ron Jackson	.06	.05	.02
270	Lynn Jones	.06	.05	.02
271	Steve Kemp	.08	.06	.03
272	Rick Leach(FC)	.12	.09	.05
273	Aurelio Lopez	.06	.05	.02
274	Jack Morris	.30	.25	.12
275	Kevin Saucier	.06	.05	.02
276	Lance Parrish	.35	.25	.14
277	Rick Peters	.06	.05	.02
278	Dan Petry	.08	.06	.03
279	David Rozema	.06	.05	.02
280	Stan Papi	.06	.05	.02
281	Dan Schatzeder	.06	.05	.02
282	Champ Summers	.06	.05	.02
283	Alan Trammell	.40	.30	.15
284	Lou Whitaker	.40	.30	.15
285	Milt Wilcox	.06	.05	.02
286	John Wockenfuss	.06	.05	.02
287	Gary Allenson	.06	.05	.02
288	Tom Burgmeier	.06	.05	.02
289	Bill Campbell	.06	.05	.02
290	Mark Clear	.06	.05	.02
291	Steve Crawford	.06	.05	.02
292	Dennis Eckersley	.12	.09	.05
293	Dwight Evans	.15	.11	.06
294	Rich Gedman(FC)	.35	.25	.14
295	Garry Hancock	.06	.05	.02
296	Glenn Hoffman	.06	.05	.02
297	Bruce Hurst(FC)	.30	.25	.12
298	Carney Lansford	.08	.06	.03
299	Rick Miller	.06	.05	.02
300	Reid Nichols	.06	.05	.02
301	Bob Ojeda(FC)	.50	.40	.20
302	Tony Perez	.20	.15	.08
303	Chuck Rainey	.06	.05	.02
304	Jerry Remy	.06	.05	.02
305	Jim Rice	.40	.30	.15
306	Joe Rudi	.10	.08	.04
307	Bob Stanley	.06	.05	.02
308	Dave Stapleton	.06	.05	.02
309	Frank Tanana	.10	.08	.04
310	Mike Torrez	.08	.06	.03
311	John Tudor(FC)	.25	.20	.10
312	Carl Yastrzemski	.80	.60	.30
313	Buddy Bell	.12	.09	.05
314	Steve Comer	.06	.05	.02
315	Danny Darwin	.06	.05	.02
316	John Ellis	.06	.05	.02
317	John Grubb	.06	.05	.02
318	Rick Honeycutt	.06	.05	.02
319	Charlie Hough	.10	.08	.04
320	Ferguson Jenkins	.15	.11	.06
321	John Henry Johnson	.06	.05	.02
322	Jim Kern	.06	.05	.02
323	Jon Matlack	.08	.06	.03
324	Doc Medich	.06	.05	.02
325	Mario Mendoza	.06	.05	.02
326	Al Oliver	.15	.11	.06
327	Pat Putnam	.06	.05	.02
328	Mickey Rivers	.08	.06	.03
329	Leon Roberts	.06	.05	.02
330	Billy Sample	.06	.05	.02
331	Bill Stein	.06	.05	.02
332	Jim Sundberg	.08	.06	.03
333	Mark Wagner	.06	.05	.02
334	Bump Wills	.06	.05	.02
335	Bill Almon	.06	.05	.02
336	Harold Baines	.30	.25	.12
337	Ross Baumgarten	.06	.05	.02
338	Tony Bernazard	.06	.05	.02
339	Britt Burns	.06	.05	.02
340	Richard Dotson	.10	.08	.04
341	Jim Essian	.06	.05	.02
342	Ed Farmer	.06	.05	.02
343	Carlton Fisk	.50	.40	.20
344	Kevin Hickey	.06	.05	.02
345	Lamarr Hoyt (LaMarr)	.06	.05	.02
346	Lamar Johnson	.06	.05	.02
347	Jerry Koosman	.10	.08	.04
348	Rusty Kuntz	.06	.05	.02
349	Dennis Lamp	.06	.05	.02
350	Ron LeFlore	.08	.06	.03
351	Chet Lemon	.08	.06	.03
352	Greg Luzinski	.15	.11	.06
353	Bob Molinaro	.06	.05	.02
354	Jim Morrison	.06	.05	.02
355	Wayne Nordhagen	.06	.05	.02
356	Greg Pryor	.06	.05	.02
357	Mike Squires	.06	.05	.02
358	Steve Trout	.06	.05	.02
359	Alan Bannister	.06	.05	.02
360	Len Barker	.08	.06	.03
361	Bert Blyleven	.12	.09	.05
362	Joe Charboneau	.08	.06	.03
363	John Denny	.06	.05	.02
364	Bo Diaz	.08	.06	.03
365	Miguel Dilone	.06	.05	.02
366	Jerry Dybzinski	.06	.05	.02
367	Wayne Garland	.06	.05	.02
368	Mike Hargrove	.06	.05	.02
369	Toby Harrah	.08	.06	.03
370	Ron Hassey	.06	.05	.02
371	Von Hayes(FC)	.80	.60	.30
372	Pat Kelly	.06	.05	.02
373	Duane Kuiper	.06	.05	.02
374	Rick Manning	.06	.05	.02
375	Sid Monge	.06	.05	.02
376	Jorge Orta	.06	.05	.02
377	Dave Rosello	.06	.05	.02
378	Dan Spillner	.06	.05	.02
379	Mike Stanton	.06	.05	.02
380	Andre Thornton	.10	.08	.04
381	Tom Veryzer	.06	.05	.02
382	Rick Waits	.06	.05	.02
383	Doyle Alexander	.10	.08	.04
384	Vida Blue	.12	.09	.05
385	Fred Breining	.06	.05	.02
386	Enos Cabell	.06	.05	.02
387	Jack Clark	.25	.20	.10
388	Darrell Evans	.15	.11	.06
389	Tom Griffin	.06	.05	.02
390	Larry Herndon	.08	.06	.03
391	Al Holland	.06	.05	.02
392	Gary Lavelle	.06	.05	.02
393	Johnnie LeMaster	.06	.05	.02
394	Jerry Martin	.06	.05	.02
395	Milt May	.06	.05	.02
396	Greg Minton	.06	.05	.02
397	Joe Morgan	.50	.40	.20
398	Joe Pettini	.06	.05	.02
399	Alan Ripley	.06	.05	.02
400	Billy Smith	.06	.05	.02
401	Rennie Stennett	.06	.05	.02
402	Ed Whitson	.06	.05	.02
403	Jim Wohlford	.06	.05	.02
404	Willie Aikens	.06	.05	.02
405	George Brett	.70	.50	.30
406	Ken Brett	.08	.06	.03
407	Dave Chalk	.06	.05	.02
408	Rich Gale	.06	.05	.02
409	Cesar Geronimo	.06	.05	.02
410	Larry Gura	.06	.05	.02
411	Clint Hurdle	.06	.05	.02
412	Mike Jones	.06	.05	.02
413	Dennis Leonard	.08	.06	.03
414	Renie Martin	.06	.05	.02
415	Lee May	.08	.06	.03
416	Hal McRae	.12	.09	.05
417	Darryl Motley	.06	.05	.02
418	Rance Mulliniks	.06	.05	.02
419	Amos Otis	.08	.06	.03
420	Ken Phelps(FC)	.50	.40	.20
421	Jamie Quirk	.06	.05	.02
422	Dan Quisenberry	.15	.11	.06
423	Paul Splittorff	.06	.05	.02
424	U.L. Washington	.06	.05	.02
425	John Wathan	.08	.06	.03
426	Frank White	.10	.08	.04
427	Willie Wilson	.15	.11	.06
428	Brian Asselstine	.06	.05	.02
429	Bruce Benedict	.06	.05	.02
430	Tom Boggs	.06	.05	.02
431	Larry Bradford	.06	.05	.02
432	Rick Camp	.06	.05	.02
433	Chris Chambliss	.08	.06	.03
434	Gene Garber	.06	.05	.02
435	Preston Hanna	.06	.05	.02
436	Bob Horner	.12	.09	.05
437	Glenn Hubbard	.08	.06	.03
438a	Al Hrabosky (All Hrabosky. 5'1" on back)	20.00	15.00	8.00
438b	Al Hrabosky (Al Hrabosky. 5'1" on back)	1.25	.90	.50
438c	Al Hrabosky (Al Hrabosky. 5'10" on back)	.35	.25	.14
439	Rufino Linares	.06	.05	.02
440	Rick Mahler(FC)	.25	.20	.10
441	Ed Miller	.06	.05	.02
442	John Montefusco	.08	.06	.03
443	Dale Murphy	.90	.70	.35

	MT	NR MT	EX
444 Phil Niekro	.30	.25	.12
445 Gaylord Perry	.30	.25	.12
446 Biff Pocoroba	.06	.05	.02
447 Rafael Ramirez	.08	.06	.03
448 Jerry Royster	.06	.05	.02
449 Claudell Washington	.08	.06	.03
450 Don Aase	.06	.05	.02
451 Don Baylor	.12	.09	.05
452 Juan Beniquez	.06	.05	.02
453 Rick Burleson	.08	.06	.03
454 Bert Campaneris	.10	.08	.04
455 Rod Carew	.50	.40	.20
456 Bob Clark	.06	.05	.02
457 Brian Downing	.10	.08	.04
458 Dan Ford	.06	.05	.02
459 Ken Forsch	.06	.05	.02
460 Dave Frost	.06	.05	.02
461 Bobby Grich	.10	.08	.04
462 Larry Harlow	.06	.05	.02
463 John Harris	.06	.05	.02
464 Andy Hassler	.06	.05	.02
465 Butch Hobson	.06	.05	.02
466 Jesse Jefferson	.06	.05	.02
467 Bruce Kison	.06	.05	.02
468 Fred Lynn	.20	.15	.08
469 Angel Moreno	.06	.05	.02
470 Ed Ott	.06	.05	.02
471 Fred Patek	.06	.05	.02
472 Steve Renko	.06	.05	.02
473 *Mike Witt*(FC)	.70	.50	.30
474 Geoff Zahn	.06	.05	.02
475 Gary Alexander	.06	.05	.02
476 Dale Berra	.06	.05	.02
477 Kurt Bevacqua	.06	.05	.02
478 Jim Bibby	.06	.05	.02
479 John Candelaria	.10	.08	.04
480 Victor Cruz	.06	.05	.02
481 Mike Easler	.08	.06	.03
482 Tim Foli	.06	.05	.02
483 Lee Lacy	.06	.05	.02
484 Vance Law(FC)	.12	.09	.05
485 Bill Madlock	.12	.09	.05
486 Willie Montanez	.06	.05	.02
487 Omar Moreno	.06	.05	.02
488 Steve Nicosia	.06	.05	.02
489 Dave Parker	.30	.25	.12
490 Tony Pena(FC)	.25	.20	.10
491 Pascual Perez(FC)	.15	.11	.06
492 *Johnny Ray*(FC)	.70	.50	.30
493 Rick Rhoden	.10	.08	.04
494 Bill Robinson	.06	.05	.02
495 Don Robinson	.08	.06	.03
496 Enrique Romo	.06	.05	.02
497 Rod Scurry	.06	.05	.02
498 Eddie Solomon	.06	.05	.02
499 Willie Stargell	.40	.30	.15
500 Kent Tekulve	.08	.06	.03
501 Jason Thompson	.06	.05	.02
502 Glenn Abbott	.06	.05	.02
503 Jim Anderson	.06	.05	.02
504 Floyd Bannister	.10	.08	.04
505 Bruce Bochte	.06	.05	.02
506 Jeff Burroughs	.08	.06	.03
507 Bryan Clark	.06	.05	.02
508 Ken Clay	.06	.05	.02
509 Julio Cruz	.06	.05	.02
510 Dick Drago	.06	.05	.02
511 Gary Gray	.06	.05	.02
512 Dan Meyer	.06	.05	.02
513 Jerry Narron	.06	.05	.02
514 Tom Paciorek	.06	.05	.02
515 Casey Parsons	.06	.05	.02
516 Lenny Randle	.06	.05	.02
517 Shane Rawley	.10	.08	.04
518 Joe Simpson	.06	.05	.02
519 Richie Zisk	.08	.06	.03
520 Neil Allen	.06	.05	.02
521 Bob Bailor	.06	.05	.02
522 Hubie Brooks(FC)	.25	.20	.10
523 Mike Cubbage	.06	.05	.02
524 Pete Falcone	.06	.05	.02
525 Doug Flynn	.06	.05	.02
526 Tom Hausman	.06	.05	.02
527 Ron Hodges	.06	.05	.02
528 Randy Jones	.08	.06	.03
529 Mike Jorgensen	.06	.05	.02
530 Dave Kingman	.15	.11	.06
531 Ed Lynch	.06	.05	.02
532 Mike Marshall	.10	.08	.04
533 Lee Mazzilli	.08	.06	.03
534 Dyar Miller	.06	.05	.02
535 Mike Scott(FC)	.60	.45	.25
536 Rusty Staub	.10	.08	.04
537 John Stearns	.06	.05	.02
538 Craig Swan	.06	.05	.02
539 Frank Taveras	.06	.05	.02
540 Alex Trevino	.06	.05	.02
541 Ellis Valentine	.06	.05	.02
542 Mookie Wilson(FC)	.15	.11	.06
543 Joel Youngblood	.06	.05	.02
544 Pat Zachry	.06	.05	.02
545 Glenn Adams	.06	.05	.02
546 Fernando Arroyo	.06	.05	.02
547 John Verhoeven	.06	.05	.02
548 Sal Butera	.06	.05	.02
549 John Castino	.06	.05	.02
550 Don Cooper	.06	.05	.02
551 Doug Corbett	.06	.05	.02
552 Dave Engle	.06	.05	.02
553 Roger Erickson	.06	.05	.02
554 Danny Goodwin	.06	.05	.02
555a Darrell Jackson (black cap)	1.00	.70	.40
555b Darrell Jackson (red cap with emblem)	.10	.08	.04
555c Darrell Jackson (red cap, no emblem)	.25	.20	.10
556 Pete Mackanin	.06	.05	.02
557 Jack O'Connor	.06	.05	.02
558 Hosken Powell	.06	.05	.02
559 Pete Redfern	.06	.05	.02
560 Roy Smalley	.06	.05	.02
561 Chuck Baker	.06	.05	.02
562 Gary Ward	.08	.06	.03
563 Rob Wilfong	.06	.05	.02
564 Al Williams	.06	.05	.02
565 Butch Wynegar	.06	.05	.02
566 Randy Bass	.06	.05	.02
567 Juan Bonilla	.06	.05	.02
568 Danny Boone	.06	.05	.02
569 John Curtis	.06	.05	.02
570 Juan Eichelberger	.06	.05	.02
571 Barry Evans	.06	.05	.02
572 Tim Flannery	.06	.05	.02
573 Ruppert Jones	.06	.05	.02
574 Terry Kennedy	.08	.06	.03
575 Joe Lefebvre	.06	.05	.02
576a John Littlefield (pitching lefty)	150.00	105.00	60.00
576b John Littlefield (pitching righty)	.08	.06	.03
577 Gary Lucas	.06	.05	.02
578 Steve Mura	.06	.05	.02
579 Broderick Perkins	.06	.05	.02
580 Gene Richards	.06	.05	.02
581 Luis Salazar	.06	.05	.02
582 Ozzie Smith	.20	.15	.08
583 John Urrea	.06	.05	.02
584 Chris Welsh	.06	.05	.02
585 Rick Wise	.08	.06	.03
586 Doug Bird	.06	.05	.02
587 Tim Blackwell	.06	.05	.02
588 Bobby Bonds	.10	.08	.04
589 Bill Buckner	.12	.09	.05
590 Bill Caudill	.06	.05	.02
591 Hector Cruz	.06	.05	.02
592 *Jody Davis*(FC)	.30	.25	.12
593 Ivan DeJesus	.06	.05	.02
594 Steve Dillard	.06	.05	.02
595 Leon Durham	.08	.06	.03
596 Rawly Eastwick	.06	.05	.02
597 Steve Henderson	.06	.05	.02
598 Mike Krukow	.08	.06	.03
599 Mike Lum	.06	.05	.02
600 Randy Martz	.06	.05	.02
601 Jerry Morales	.06	.05	.02
602 Ken Reitz	.06	.05	.02
603a *Lee Smith* (Cubs logo reversed on back)(FC)	1.25	.90	.50
603b *Lee Smith* (Cubs logo correct)(FC)	.60	.45	.25
604 Dick Tidrow	.06	.05	.02
605 Jim Tracy	.06	.05	.02
606 Mike Tyson	.06	.05	.02
607 Ty Waller	.06	.05	.02
608 Danny Ainge	.12	.09	.05
609 *Jorge Bell*(FC)	7.00	5.25	2.75
610 Mark Bomback	.06	.05	.02
611 Barry Bonnell	.06	.05	.02
612 Jim Clancy	.08	.06	.03
613 Damaso Garcia	.06	.05	.02
614 Jerry Garvin	.06	.05	.02
615 Alfredo Griffin	.08	.06	.03
616 Garth Iorg	.06	.05	.02
617 Luis Leal	.06	.05	.02
618 Ken Macha	.06	.05	.02

		MT	NR MT	EX
619	John Mayberry	.08	.06	.03
620	Joey McLaughlin	.06	.05	.02
621	Lloyd Moseby	.12	.09	.05
622	Dave Stieb	.12	.09	.05
623	Jackson Todd	.06	.05	.02
624	Willie Upshaw(FC)	.15	.11	.06
625	Otto Velez	.06	.05	.02
626	Ernie Whitt	.08	.06	.03
627	Al Woods	.06	.05	.02
628	1981 All-Star Game	.08	.06	.03
629	All-Star Infielders (Bucky Dent, Frank White)	.10	.08	.04
630	Big Red Machine (Dave Concepcion, Dan Driessen, George Foster)	.15	.11	.06
631	Top N.L. Relief Pitcher (Bruce Sutter)	.15	.11	.06
632	Steve & Carlton (Steve Carlton, Carlton Fisk)	.25	.20	.10
633	3000th Game, May 25, 1981 (Carl Yastrzemski)	.35	.25	.14
634	Dynamic Duo (Johnny Bench, Tom Seaver)	.30	.25	.12
635	West Meets East (Gary Carter, Fernando Valenzuela)	.30	.25	.12
636a	N.L. Strikeout King (Fernando Valenzuela) ("...led he National League...")	1.00	.70	.40
636b	N.L. Strikeout King (Fernando Valenzuela) ("...led the National League...")	.50	.40	.20
637	1981 Home Run King (Mike Schmidt)	.40	.30	.15
638	N.L. All-Stars (Gary Carter, Dave Parker)	.25	.20	.10
639	Perfect Game! (Len Barker, Bo Diaz)	.08	.06	.03
640	Pete & Re-Pete (Pete Rose, Pete Rose, Jr.)	1.25	.90	.50
641	Phillies' Finest (Steve Carlton, Mike Schmidt, Lonnie Smith)	.50	.40	.20
642	Red Sox Reunion (Dwight Evans, Fred Lynn)	.15	.11	.06
643	1981 Most Hits, Most Runs (Rickey Henderson)	.35	.25	.14
644	Most Saves 1981 A.L. (Rollie Fingers)	.15	.11	.06
645	Most 1981 Wins (Tom Seaver)	.25	.20	.10
646a	Yankee Powerhouse (Reggie Jackson, Dave Winfield) (comma after "outfielder" on back)	1.25	.90	.50
646b	Yankee Powerhouse (Reggie Jackson, Dave Winfield) (no comma after "oufielder")	.60	.45	.25
647	Checklist 1-56	.06	.05	.02
648	Checklist 57-109	.06	.05	.02
649	Checklist 110-156	.06	.05	.02
650	Checklist 157-211	.06	.05	.02
651	Checklist 212-262	.06	.05	.02
652	Checklist 263-312	.06	.05	.02
653	Checklist 313-358	.06	.05	.02
654	Checklist 359-403	.06	.05	.02
655	Checklist 404-449	.06	.05	.02
656	Checklist 450-501	.06	.05	.02
657	Checklist 502-544	.06	.05	.02
658	Checklist 545-585	.06	.05	.02
659	Checklist 586-627	.06	.05	.02
660	Checklist 628-646	.06	.05	.02

1983 Fleer

The 1983 Fleer set features color photos set inside a light brown border. The cards are the standard size of 2-1/2" by 3-1/2". A team logo is located at the card bottom and the word "Fleer" is found at the top. The card backs are designed on a vertical format and include a small black and white photo of the player along with biographical and statistical information. The reverses are done in two shades of brown on white stock. The set was issued with team logo stickers.

		MT	NR MT	EX
	Complete Set:	60.00	40.00	25.00
	Common Player:	.06	.05	.02
1	Joaquin Andujar	.08	.06	.03
2	Doug Bair	.06	.05	.02
3	Steve Braun	.06	.05	.02
4	Glenn Brummer	.06	.05	.02
5	Bob Forsch	.08	.06	.03
6	David Green	.06	.05	.02
7	George Hendrick	.08	.06	.03
8	Keith Hernandez	.40	.30	.15
9	Tom Herr	.10	.08	.04
10	Dane Iorg	.06	.05	.02
11	Jim Kaat	.15	.11	.06
12	Jeff Lahti	.06	.05	.02
13	Tito Landrum	.06	.05	.02
14	*Dave LaPoint*(FC)	.30	.25	.12
15	*Willie McGee*(FC)	1.00	.70	.40
16	Steve Mura	.06	.05	.02
17	Ken Oberkfell	.06	.05	.02
18	Darrell Porter	.08	.06	.03
19	Mike Ramsey	.06	.05	.02
20	Gene Roof	.06	.05	.02
21	Lonnie Smith	.08	.06	.03
22	Ozzie Smith	.20	.15	.08
23	John Stuper	.06	.05	.02
24	Bruce Sutter	.15	.11	.06
25	Gene Tenace	.08	.06	.03
26	Jerry Augustine	.06	.05	.02
27	Dwight Bernard	.06	.05	.02
28	Mark Brouhard	.06	.05	.02
29	Mike Caldwell	.06	.05	.02
30	Cecil Cooper	.15	.11	.06
31	Jamie Easterly	.06	.05	.02
32	Marshall Edwards	.06	.05	.02
33	Rollie Fingers	.20	.15	.08
34	Jim Gantner	.08	.06	.03
35	Moose Haas	.06	.05	.02
36	Roy Howell	.06	.05	.02
37	Peter Ladd	.06	.05	.02
38	Bob McClure	.06	.05	.02
39	Doc Medich	.06	.05	.02
40	Paul Molitor	.20	.15	.08
41	Don Money	.06	.05	.02
42	Charlie Moore	.06	.05	.02
43	Ben Oglivie	.08	.06	.03
44	Ed Romero	.06	.05	.02
45	Ted Simmons	.12	.09	.05
46	Jim Slaton	.06	.05	.02
47	Don Sutton	.30	.25	.12
48	Gorman Thomas	.10	.08	.04
49	Pete Vuckovich	.08	.06	.03
50	Ned Yost	.06	.05	.02
51	Robin Yount	.60	.45	.25
52	Benny Ayala	.06	.05	.02
53	Bob Bonner	.06	.05	.02
54	Al Bumbry	.08	.06	.03
55	Terry Crowley	.06	.05	.02
56	*Storm Davis*(FC)	.50	.40	.20
57	Rich Dauer	.06	.05	.02
58	Rick Dempsey	.08	.06	.03
59	Jim Dwyer	.06	.05	.02
60	Mike Flanagan	.10	.08	.04
61	Dan Ford	.06	.05	.02
62	Glenn Gulliver	.06	.05	.02
63	John Lowenstein	.06	.05	.02
64	Dennis Martinez	.08	.06	.03
65	Tippy Martinez	.06	.05	.02
66	Scott McGregor	.08	.06	.03
67	Eddie Murray	.60	.45	.25
68	Joe Nolan	.06	.05	.02
69	Jim Palmer	.50	.40	.20
70	Cal Ripken, Jr.	1.00	.70	.40
71	Gary Roenicke	.06	.05	.02
72	Lenn Sakata	.06	.05	.02
73	Ken Singleton	.10	.08	.04
74	Sammy Stewart	.06	.05	.02
75	Tim Stoddard	.06	.05	.02
76	Don Aase	.06	.05	.02
77	Don Baylor	.12	.09	.05

		MT	NR MT	EX			MT	NR MT	EX
78	Juan Beniquez	.06	.05	.02	169	Ron Reed	.06	.05	.02
79	Bob Boone	.10	.08	.04	170	Bill Robinson	.06	.05	.02
80	Rick Burleson	.08	.06	.03	171	Pete Rose	1.00	.70	.40
81	Rod Carew	.50	.40	.20	172	Dick Ruthven	.06	.05	.02
82	Bobby Clark	.06	.05	.02	173	Mike Schmidt	.80	.60	.30
83	Doug Corbett	.06	.05	.02	174	Manny Trillo	.08	.06	.03
84	John Curtis	.06	.05	.02	175	Ozzie Virgil(FC)	.10	.08	.04
85	Doug DeCinces	.10	.08	.04	176	George Vukovich	.06	.05	.02
86	Brian Downing	.10	.08	.04	177	Gary Allenson	.06	.05	.02
87	Joe Ferguson	.06	.05	.02	178	Luis Aponte	.06	.05	.02
88	Tim Foli	.06	.05	.02	179	*Wade Boggs*(FC)	18.00	13.50	7.25
89	Ken Forsch	.06	.05	.02	180	Tom Burgmeier	.06	.05	.02
90	Dave Goltz	.08	.06	.03	181	Mark Clear	.06	.05	.02
91	Bobby Grich	.10	.08	.04	182	Dennis Eckersley	.12	.09	.05
92	Andy Hassler	.06	.05	.02	183	Dwight Evans	.15	.11	.06
93	Reggie Jackson	.50	.40	.20	184	Rich Gedman	.08	.06	.03
94	Ron Jackson	.06	.05	.02	185	Glenn Hoffman	.06	.05	.02
95	Tommy John	.20	.15	.08	186	Bruce Hurst	.10	.08	.04
96	Bruce Kison	.06	.05	.02	187	Carney Lansford	.08	.06	.03
97	Fred Lynn	.20	.15	.08	188	Rick Miller	.06	.05	.02
98	Ed Ott	.06	.05	.02	189	Reid Nichols	.06	.05	.02
99	Steve Renko	.06	.05	.02	190	Bob Ojeda	.12	.09	.05
100	Luis Sanchez	.06	.05	.02	191	Tony Perez	.20	.15	.08
101	Rob Wilfong	.06	.05	.02	192	Chuck Rainey	.06	.05	.02
102	Mike Witt	.15	.11	.06	193	Jerry Remy	.06	.05	.02
103	Geoff Zahn	.06	.05	.02	194	Jim Rice	.40	.30	.15
104	Willie Aikens	.06	.05	.02	195	Bob Stanley	.06	.05	.02
105	Mike Armstrong	.06	.05	.02	196	Dave Stapleton	.06	.05	.02
106	Vida Blue	.12	.09	.05	197	Mike Torrez	.08	.06	.03
107	*Bud Black*(FC)	.20	.15	.08	198	John Tudor	.10	.08	.04
108	George Brett	.70	.50	.30	199	Julio Valdez	.06	.05	.02
109	Bill Castro	.06	.05	.02	200	Carl Yastrzemski	.70	.50	.30
110	Onix Concepcion	.06	.05	.02	201	Dusty Baker	.10	.08	.04
111	Dave Frost	.06	.05	.02	202	Joe Beckwith	.06	.05	.02
112	Cesar Geronimo	.06	.05	.02	203	*Greg Brock*(FC)	.35	.25	.14
113	Larry Gura	.06	.05	.02	204	Ron Cey	.12	.09	.05
114	Steve Hammond	.06	.05	.02	205	Terry Forster	.08	.06	.03
115	Don Hood	.06	.05	.02	206	Steve Garvey	.40	.30	.15
116	Dennis Leonard	.08	.06	.03	207	Pedro Guerrero	.25	.20	.10
117	Jerry Martin	.06	.05	.02	208	Burt Hooton	.08	.06	.03
118	Lee May	.08	.06	.03	209	Steve Howe	.08	.06	.03
119	Hal McRae	.12	.09	.05	210	Ken Landreaux	.06	.05	.02
120	Amos Otis	.08	.06	.03	211	Mike Marshall	.20	.15	.08
121	Greg Pryor	.06	.05	.02	212	*Candy Maldonado*(FC)	.50	.40	.20
122	Dan Quisenberry	.15	.11	.06	213	Rick Monday	.10	.08	.04
123	*Don Slaught*(FC)	.20	.15	.08	214	Tom Niedenfuer	.10	.08	.04
124	Paul Splittorff	.06	.05	.02	215	Jorge Orta	.06	.05	.02
125	U.L. Washington	.06	.05	.02	216	Jerry Reuss	.10	.08	.04
126	John Wathan	.08	.06	.03	217	Ron Roenicke	.06	.05	.02
127	Frank White	.10	.08	.04	218	Vicente Romo	.06	.05	.02
128	Willie Wilson	.15	.11	.06	219	Bill Russell	.08	.06	.03
129	Steve Bedrosian(FC)	.35	.25	.14	220	Steve Sax	.30	.25	.12
130	Bruce Benedict	.06	.05	.02	221	Mike Scioscia	.08	.06	.03
131	Tommy Boggs	.06	.05	.02	222	Dave Stewart	.15	.11	.06
132	Brett Butler(FC)	.15	.11	.06	223	Derrel Thomas	.06	.05	.02
133	Rick Camp	.06	.05	.02	224	Fernando Valenzuela	.30	.25	.12
134	Chris Chambliss	.08	.06	.03	225	Bob Welch	.12	.09	.05
135	Ken Dayley(FC)	.10	.08	.04	226	Ricky Wright	.06	.05	.02
136	Gene Garber	.06	.05	.02	227	Steve Yeager	.06	.05	.02
137	Terry Harper	.06	.05	.02	228	Bill Almon	.06	.05	.02
138	Bob Horner	.12	.09	.05	229	Harold Baines	.15	.11	.06
139	Glenn Hubbard	.08	.06	.03	230	Salome Barojas	.06	.05	.02
140	Rufino Linares	.06	.05	.02	231	Tony Bernazard	.06	.05	.02
141	Rick Mahler	.08	.06	.03	232	Britt Burns	.06	.05	.02
142	Dale Murphy	.90	.70	.35	233	Richard Dotson	.10	.08	.04
143	Phil Niekro	.30	.25	.12	234	Ernesto Escarrega	.06	.05	.02
144	Pascual Perez	.08	.06	.03	235	Carlton Fisk	.30	.25	.12
145	Biff Pocoroba	.06	.05	.02	236	Jerry Hairston	.06	.05	.02
146	Rafael Ramirez	.06	.05	.02	237	Kevin Hickey	.06	.05	.02
147	Jerry Royster	.06	.05	.02	238	LaMarr Hoyt	.06	.05	.02
148	Ken Smith	.06	.05	.02	239	Steve Kemp	.10	.08	.04
149	Bob Walk	.08	.06	.03	240	Jim Kern	.06	.05	.02
150	Claudell Washington	.08	.06	.03	241	*Ron Kittle*(FC)	.70	.50	.30
151	Bob Watson	.08	.06	.03	242	Jerry Koosman	.10	.08	.04
152	Larry Whisenton	.06	.05	.02	243	Dennis Lamp	.06	.05	.02
153	Porfirio Altamirano	.06	.05	.02	244	Rudy Law	.06	.05	.02
154	Marty Bystrom	.06	.05	.02	245	Vance Law	.08	.06	.03
155	Steve Carlton	.50	.40	.20	246	Ron LeFlore	.08	.06	.03
156	Larry Christenson	.06	.05	.02	247	Greg Luzinski	.12	.09	.05
157	Ivan DeJesus	.06	.05	.02	248	Tom Paciorek	.06	.05	.02
158	John Denny	.06	.05	.02	249	Aurelio Rodriguez	.08	.06	.03
159	Bob Dernier(FC)	.10	.08	.04	250	Mike Squires	.06	.05	.02
160	Bo Diaz	.08	.06	.03	251	Steve Trout	.06	.05	.02
161	Ed Farmer	.06	.05	.02	252	Jim Barr	.06	.05	.02
162	Greg Gross	.06	.05	.02	253	Dave Bergman	.06	.05	.02
163	Mike Krukow	.08	.06	.03	254	Fred Breining	.06	.05	.02
164	Garry Maddox	.10	.08	.04	255	Bob Brenly(FC)	.08	.06	.03
165	Gary Matthews	.10	.08	.04	256	Jack Clark	.25	.20	.10
166	Tug McGraw	.12	.09	.05	257	Chili Davis(FC)	.20	.15	.08
167	Bob Molinaro	.06	.05	.02	258	Darrell Evans	.15	.11	.06
168	Sid Monge	.06	.05	.02	259	Alan Fowlkes	.06	.05	.02

		MT	NR MT	EX
260	Rich Gale	.06	.05	.02
261	Atlee Hammaker(FC)	.12	.09	.05
262	Al Holland	.06	.05	.02
263	Duane Kuiper	.06	.05	.02
264	Bill Laskey	.06	.05	.02
265	Gary Lavelle	.06	.05	.02
266	Johnnie LeMaster	.06	.05	.02
267	Renie Martin	.06	.05	.02
268	Milt May	.06	.05	.02
269	Greg Minton	.06	.05	.02
270	Joe Morgan	.40	.30	.15
271	Tom O'Malley	.06	.05	.02
272	Reggie Smith	.10	.08	.04
273	Guy Sularz	.06	.05	.02
274	Champ Summers	.06	.05	.02
275	Max Venable	.06	.05	.02
276	Jim Wohlford	.06	.05	.02
277	Ray Burris	.06	.05	.02
278	Gary Carter	.35	.25	.14
279	Warren Cromartie	.06	.05	.02
280	Andre Dawson	.35	.25	.14
281	Terry Francona	.06	.05	.02
282	Doug Flynn	.06	.05	.02
283	Woody Fryman	.08	.06	.03
284	Bill Gullickson	.06	.05	.02
285	Wallace Johnson	.06	.05	.02
286	Charlie Lea	.06	.05	.02
287	Randy Lerch	.06	.05	.02
288	Brad Mills	.06	.05	.02
289	Dan Norman	.06	.05	.02
290	Al Oliver	.15	.11	.06
291	David Palmer	.06	.05	.02
292	Tim Raines	.35	.25	.14
293	Jeff Reardon	.12	.09	.05
294	Steve Rogers	.08	.06	.03
295	Scott Sanderson	.06	.05	.02
296	Dan Schatzeder	.06	.05	.02
297	Bryn Smith	.08	.06	.03
298	Chris Speier	.06	.05	.02
299	Tim Wallach	.20	.15	.08
300	Jerry White	.06	.05	.02
301	Joel Youngblood	.06	.05	.02
302	Ross Baumgarten	.06	.05	.02
303	Dale Berra	.06	.05	.02
304	John Candelaria	.10	.08	.04
305	Dick Davis	.06	.05	.02
306	Mike Easler	.08	.06	.03
307	Richie Hebner	.06	.05	.02
308	Lee Lacy	.06	.05	.02
309	Bill Madlock	.12	.09	.05
310	Larry McWilliams	.06	.05	.02
311	John Milner	.06	.05	.02
312	Omar Moreno	.06	.05	.02
313	Jim Morrison	.06	.05	.02
314	Steve Nicosia	.06	.05	.02
315	Dave Parker	.30	.25	.12
316	Tony Pena	.10	.08	.04
317	Johnny Ray	.12	.09	.05
318	Rick Rhoden	.10	.08	.04
319	Don Robinson	.08	.06	.03
320	Enrique Romo	.06	.05	.02
321	Manny Sarmiento	.06	.05	.02
322	Rod Scurry	.06	.05	.02
323	Jim Smith	.06	.05	.02
324	Willie Stargell	.40	.30	.15
325	Jason Thompson	.06	.05	.02
326	Kent Tekulve	.08	.06	.03
327a	Tom Brookens (narrow (1/4") brown box at bottom on back)	.30	.25	.12
327b	Tom Brookens (wide (1 1/4") brown box at bottom on back)	.08	.06	.03
328	Enos Cabell	.06	.05	.02
329	Kirk Gibson	.40	.30	.15
330	Larry Herndon	.08	.06	.03
331	Mike Ivie	.06	.05	.02
332	Howard Johnson(FC)	8.00	6.00	3.25
333	Lynn Jones	.06	.05	.02
334	Rick Leach	.06	.05	.02
335	Chet Lemon	.08	.06	.03
336	Jack Morris	.30	.25	.12
337	Lance Parrish	.35	.25	.14
338	Larry Pashnick	.06	.05	.02
339	Dan Petry	.08	.06	.03
340	Dave Rozema	.06	.05	.02
341	Dave Rucker	.06	.05	.02
342	Elias Sosa	.06	.05	.02
343	Dave Tobik	.06	.05	.02
344	Alan Trammell	.40	.30	.15
345	Jerry Turner	.06	.05	.02
346	Jerry Ujdur	.06	.05	.02
347	Pat Underwood	.06	.05	.02
348	Lou Whitaker	.40	.30	.15
349	Milt Wilcox	.06	.05	.02
350	Glenn Wilson(FC)	.35	.25	.14
351	John Wockenfuss	.06	.05	.02
352	Kurt Bevacqua	.06	.05	.02
353	Juan Bonilla	.06	.05	.02
354	Floyd Chiffer	.06	.05	.02
355	Luis DeLeon	.06	.05	.02
356	Dave Dravecky(FC)	.50	.40	.20
357	Dave Edwards	.06	.05	.02
358	Juan Eichelberger	.06	.05	.02
359	Tim Flannery	.06	.05	.02
360	Tony Gwynn(FC)	12.00	9.00	4.75
361	Ruppert Jones	.06	.05	.02
362	Terry Kennedy	.08	.06	.03
363	Joe Lefebvre	.06	.05	.02
364	Sixto Lezcano	.06	.05	.02
365	Tim Lollar	.06	.05	.02
366	Gary Lucas	.06	.05	.02
367	John Montefusco	.06	.05	.02
368	Broderick Perkins	.06	.05	.02
369	Joe Pittman	.06	.05	.02
370	Gene Richards	.06	.05	.02
371	Luis Salazar	.06	.05	.02
372	Eric Show(FC)	.30	.25	.12
373	Garry Templeton	.10	.08	.04
374	Chris Welsh	.06	.05	.02
375	Alan Wiggins	.06	.05	.02
376	Rick Cerone	.06	.05	.02
377	Dave Collins	.08	.06	.03
378	Roger Erickson	.06	.05	.02
379	George Frazier	.06	.05	.02
380	Oscar Gamble	.08	.06	.03
381	Goose Gossage	.20	.15	.08
382	Ken Griffey	.12	.09	.05
383	Ron Guidry	.25	.20	.10
384	Dave LaRoche	.06	.05	.02
385	Rudy May	.06	.05	.02
386	John Mayberry	.08	.06	.03
387	Lee Mazzilli	.08	.06	.03
388	Mike Morgan(FC)	.12	.09	.05
389	Jerry Mumphrey	.06	.05	.02
390	Bobby Murcer	.10	.08	.04
391	Graig Nettles	.15	.11	.06
392	Lou Piniella	.12	.09	.05
393	Willie Randolph	.10	.08	.04
394	Shane Rawley	.10	.08	.04
395	Dave Righetti	.25	.20	.10
396	Andre Robertson	.06	.05	.02
397	Roy Smalley	.06	.05	.02
398	Dave Winfield	.40	.30	.15
399	Butch Wynegar	.06	.05	.02
400	Chris Bando	.06	.05	.02
401	Alan Bannister	.06	.05	.02
402	Len Barker	.08	.06	.03
403	Tom Brennan	.06	.05	.02
404	Carmelo Castillo(FC)	.12	.09	.05
405	Miguel Dilone	.06	.05	.02
406	Jerry Dybzinski	.06	.05	.02
407	Mike Fischlin	.06	.05	.02
408	Ed Glynn (photo actually Bud Anderson)	.06	.05	.02
409	Mike Hargrove	.06	.05	.02
410	Toby Harrah	.08	.06	.03
411	Ron Hassey	.06	.05	.02
412	Von Hayes	.15	.11	.06
413	Rick Manning	.06	.05	.02
414	Bake McBride	.06	.05	.02
415	Larry Milbourne	.06	.05	.02
416	Bill Nahorodny	.06	.05	.02
417	Jack Perconte	.06	.05	.02
418	Lary Sorensen	.06	.05	.02
419	Dan Spillner	.06	.05	.02
420	Rick Sutcliffe	.12	.09	.05
421	Andre Thornton	.10	.08	.04
422	Rick Waits	.06	.05	.02
423	Eddie Whitson	.06	.05	.02
424	Jesse Barfield(FC)	.60	.45	.25
425	Barry Bonnell	.06	.05	.02
426	Jim Clancy	.08	.06	.03
427	Damaso Garcia	.06	.05	.02
428	Jerry Garvin	.06	.05	.02
429	Alfredo Griffin	.08	.06	.03
430	Garth Iorg	.06	.05	.02
431	Roy Lee Jackson	.06	.05	.02
432	Luis Leal	.06	.05	.02
433	Buck Martinez	.06	.05	.02
434	Joey McLaughlin	.06	.05	.02
435	Lloyd Moseby	.12	.09	.05
436	Rance Mulliniks	.06	.05	.02
437	Dale Murray	.06	.05	.02

#	Player	MT	NR MT	EX
438	Wayne Nordhagen	.06	.05	.02
439	*Gene Petralli*(FC)	.15	.11	.06
440	Hosken Powell	.06	.05	.02
441	Dave Stieb	.12	.09	.05
442	Willie Upshaw	.08	.06	.03
443	Ernie Whitt	.08	.06	.03
444	Al Woods	.06	.05	.02
445	Alan Ashby	.06	.05	.02
446	Jose Cruz	.12	.09	.05
447	Kiko Garcia	.06	.05	.02
448	Phil Garner	.08	.06	.03
449	Danny Heep	.06	.05	.02
450	Art Howe	.06	.05	.02
451	Bob Knepper	.08	.06	.03
452	Alan Knicely	.06	.05	.02
453	Ray Knight	.10	.08	.04
454	Frank LaCorte	.06	.05	.02
455	Mike LaCoss	.06	.05	.02
456	Randy Moffitt	.06	.05	.02
457	Joe Niekro	.12	.09	.05
458	Terry Puhl	.06	.05	.02
459	Luis Pujols	.06	.05	.02
460	Craig Reynolds	.06	.05	.02
461	Bert Roberge	.06	.05	.02
462	Vern Ruhle	.06	.05	.02
463	Nolan Ryan	1.00	.70	.40
464	Joe Sambito	.06	.05	.02
465	Tony Scott	.06	.05	.02
466	Dave Smith	.08	.06	.03
467	Harry Spilman	.06	.05	.02
468	Dickie Thon	.08	.06	.03
469	Denny Walling	.06	.05	.02
470	Larry Andersen	.06	.05	.02
471	Floyd Bannister	.10	.08	.04
472	Jim Beattie	.06	.05	.02
473	Bruce Bochte	.06	.05	.02
474	Manny Castillo	.06	.05	.02
475	Bill Caudill	.06	.05	.02
476	Bryan Clark	.06	.05	.02
477	Al Cowens	.06	.05	.02
478	Julio Cruz	.06	.05	.02
479	Todd Cruz	.06	.05	.02
480	Gary Gray	.06	.05	.02
481	Dave Henderson(FC)	.20	.15	.08
482	*Mike Moore*(FC)	1.00	.70	.40
483	Gaylord Perry	.30	.25	.12
484	Dave Revering	.06	.05	.02
485	Joe Simpson	.06	.05	.02
486	Mike Stanton	.06	.05	.02
487	Rick Sweet	.06	.05	.02
488	*Ed Vande Berg*(FC)	.10	.08	.04
489	Richie Zisk	.08	.06	.03
490	Doug Bird	.06	.05	.02
491	Larry Bowa	.12	.09	.05
492	Bill Buckner	.12	.09	.05
493	Bill Campbell	.06	.05	.02
494	Jody Davis	.10	.08	.04
495	Leon Durham	.08	.06	.03
496	Steve Henderson	.06	.05	.02
497	Willie Hernandez	.08	.06	.03
498	Ferguson Jenkins	.15	.11	.06
499	Jay Johnstone	.08	.06	.03
500	Junior Kennedy	.06	.05	.02
501	Randy Martz	.06	.05	.02
502	Jerry Morales	.06	.05	.02
503	Keith Moreland	.08	.06	.03
504	Dickie Noles	.06	.05	.02
505	Mike Proly	.06	.05	.02
506	Allen Ripley	.06	.05	.02
507	*Ryne Sandberg*(FC)	8.00	6.00	3.25
508	Lee Smith	.15	.11	.06
509	Pat Tabler(FC)	.15	.11	.06
510	Dick Tidrow	.06	.05	.02
511	Bump Wills	.06	.05	.02
512	Gary Woods	.06	.05	.02
513	Tony Armas	.10	.08	.04
514	Dave Beard	.06	.05	.02
515	Jeff Burroughs	.08	.06	.03
516	John D'Acquisto	.06	.05	.02
517	Wayne Gross	.06	.05	.02
518	Mike Heath	.06	.05	.02
519	Rickey Henderson	.70	.50	.30
520	Cliff Johnson	.06	.05	.02
521	Matt Keough	.06	.05	.02
522	Brian Kingman	.06	.05	.02
523	Rick Langford	.06	.05	.02
524	Davey Lopes	.10	.08	.04
525	Steve McCatty	.06	.05	.02
526	Dave McKay	.06	.05	.02
527	Dan Meyer	.06	.05	.02
528	Dwayne Murphy	.08	.06	.03
529	Jeff Newman	.06	.05	.02
530	Mike Norris	.06	.05	.02
531	Bob Owchinko	.06	.05	.02
532	Joe Rudi	.10	.08	.04
533	Jimmy Sexton	.06	.05	.02
534	Fred Stanley	.06	.05	.02
535	Tom Underwood	.06	.05	.02
536	Neil Allen	.06	.05	.02
537	Wally Backman	.08	.06	.03
538	Bob Bailor	.06	.05	.02
539	Hubie Brooks	.12	.09	.05
540	Carlos Diaz	.06	.05	.02
541	Pete Falcone	.06	.05	.02
542	George Foster	.15	.11	.06
543	Ron Gardenhire	.06	.05	.02
544	Brian Giles	.06	.05	.02
545	Ron Hodges	.06	.05	.02
546	Randy Jones	.08	.06	.03
547	Mike Jorgensen	.06	.05	.02
548	Dave Kingman	.15	.11	.06
549	Ed Lynch	.06	.05	.02
550	Jesse Orosco(FC)	.15	.11	.06
551	Rick Ownbey	.06	.05	.02
552	*Charlie Puleo*(FC)	.12	.09	.05
553	Gary Rajsich	.06	.05	.02
554	Mike Scott	.15	.11	.06
555	Rusty Staub	.10	.08	.04
556	John Stearns	.06	.05	.02
557	Craig Swan	.06	.05	.02
558	Ellis Valentine	.06	.05	.02
559	Tom Veryzer	.06	.05	.02
560	Mookie Wilson	.10	.08	.04
561	Pat Zachry	.06	.05	.02
562	Buddy Bell	.12	.09	.05
563	John Butcher	.06	.05	.02
564	Steve Comer	.06	.05	.02
565	Danny Darwin	.06	.05	.02
566	Bucky Dent	.10	.08	.04
567	John Grubb	.06	.05	.02
568	Rick Honeycutt	.06	.05	.02
569	Dave Hostetler	.06	.05	.02
570	Charlie Hough	.10	.08	.04
571	Lamar Johnson	.06	.05	.02
572	Jon Matlack	.08	.06	.03
573	Paul Mirabella	.06	.05	.02
574	Larry Parrish	.10	.08	.04
575	Mike Richardt	.06	.05	.02
576	Mickey Rivers	.08	.06	.03
577	Billy Sample	.06	.05	.02
578	*Dave Schmidt*(FC)	.10	.08	.04
579	Bill Stein	.06	.05	.02
580	Jim Sundberg	.08	.06	.03
581	Frank Tanana	.10	.08	.04
582	Mark Wagner	.06	.05	.02
583	George Wright	.06	.05	.02
584	Johnny Bench	.40	.30	.15
585	Bruce Berenyi	.06	.05	.02
586	Larry Biittner	.06	.05	.02
587	Cesar Cedeno	.12	.09	.05
588	Dave Concepcion	.12	.09	.05
589	Dan Driessen	.08	.06	.03
590	Greg Harris(FC)	.08	.06	.03
591	Ben Hayes	.06	.05	.02
592	Paul Householder	.06	.05	.02
593	Tom Hume	.06	.05	.02
594	Wayne Krenchicki	.06	.05	.02
595	Rafael Landestoy	.06	.05	.02
596	Charlie Leibrandt	.08	.06	.03
597	*Eddie Milner*(FC)	.10	.08	.04
598	Ron Oester	.06	.05	.02
599	Frank Pastore	.06	.05	.02
600	Joe Price	.06	.05	.02
601	Tom Seaver	.50	.40	.20
602	Bob Shirley	.06	.05	.02
603	Mario Soto	.08	.06	.03
604	Alex Trevino	.06	.05	.02
605	Mike Vail	.06	.05	.02
606	Duane Walker	.06	.05	.02
607	Tom Brunansky(FC)	.25	.20	.10
608	Bobby Castillo	.06	.05	.02
609	John Castino	.06	.05	.02
610	Ron Davis	.06	.05	.02
611	Lenny Faedo	.06	.05	.02
612	Terry Felton	.06	.05	.02
613	*Gary Gaetti*(FC)	4.00	3.00	1.50
614	Mickey Hatcher	.08	.06	.03
615	Brad Havens	.06	.05	.02
616	Kent Hrbek(FC)	.80	.60	.30
617	Randy Johnson	.06	.05	.02
618	Tim Laudner(FC)	.12	.09	.05
619	Jeff Little	.06	.05	.02

		MT	NR MT	EX
620	Bob Mitchell	.06	.05	.02
621	Jack O'Connor	.06	.05	.02
622	John Pacella	.06	.05	.02
623	Pete Redfern	.06	.05	.02
624	Jesus Vega	.06	.05	.02
625	*Frank Viola*(FC)	4.00	3.00	1.50
626	Ron Washington	.06	.05	.02
627	Gary Ward	.08	.06	.03
628	Al Williams	.06	.05	.02
629	Red Sox All-Stars (Mark Clear, Dennis Eckersley, Carl Yastrzemski)	.25	.20	.10
630	300 Career Wins (Terry Bulling, Gaylord Perry)	.15	.11	.06
631	Pride of Venezuela (Dave Concepcion, Manny Trillo)	.10	.08	.04
632	All-Star Infielders (Buddy Bell, Robin Yount)	.15	.11	.06
633	Mr. Vet & Mr. Rookie (Kent Hrbek, Dave Winfield)	.25	.20	.10
634	Fountain of Youth (Pete Rose, Willie Stargell)	.40	.30	.15
635	Big Chiefs (Toby Harrah, Andre Thornton)	.08	.06	.03
636	"Smith Bros." (Lonnie Smith, Ozzie Smith)	.10	.08	.04
637	Base Stealers' Threat (Gary Carter, Bo Diaz)	.15	.11	.06
638	All-Star Catchers (Gary Carter, Carlton Fisk)	.20	.15	.08
639	The Silver Shoe (Rickey Henderson)	.30	.25	.12
640	Home Run Threats (Reggie Jackson, Ben Oglivie)	.25	.20	.10
641	Two Teams - Same Day (Joel Youngblood)	.08	.06	.03
642	Last Perfect Game (Len Barker, Ron Hassey)	.08	.06	.03
643	Blue (Vida Blue)	.10	.08	.04
644	Black & (Bud Black)	.10	.08	.04
645	Power (Reggie Jackson)	.30	.25	.12
646	Speed & (Rickey Henderson)	.30	.25	.12
647	Checklist 1-51	.06	.05	.02
648	Checklist 52-103	.06	.05	.02
649	Checklist 104-152	.06	.05	.02
650	Checklist 153-200	.06	.05	.02
651	Checklist 201-251	.06	.05	.02
652	Checklist 252-301	.06	.05	.02
653	Checklist 302-351	.06	.05	.02
654	Checklist 352-399	.06	.05	.02
655	Checklist 400-444	.06	.05	.02
656	Checklist 445-489	.06	.05	.02
657	Checklist 490-535	.06	.05	.02
658	Checklist 536-583	.06	.05	.02
659	Checklist 584-628	.06	.05	.02
660	Checklist 629-646	.06	.05	.02

1984 Fleer

The 1984 Fleer set contained 660 cards for the fourth consecutive year. The cards, which measure 2-1/2" by 3-1/2", feature a color photo surrounded by four white borders and two blue stripes. The top stripe contains the word "Fleer" with the lower carrying the player's name. The card backs contain a small black and white photo of the player and are done in blue ink on white stock. The set was issued with team logo stickers.

		MT	NR MT	EX
	Complete Set:	100.00	75.00	40.00
	Common Player:	.08	.06	.03
1	Mike Boddicker(FC)	.20	.15	.08
2	Al Bumbry	.10	.08	.04
3	Todd Cruz	.08	.06	.03
4	Rich Dauer	.08	.06	.03
5	Storm Davis	.12	.09	.05
6	Rick Dempsey	.10	.08	.04
7	Jim Dwyer	.08	.06	.03
8	Mike Flanagan	.12	.09	.05
9	Dan Ford	.08	.06	.03
10	John Lowenstein	.08	.06	.03
11	Dennis Martinez	.10	.08	.04
12	Tippy Martinez	.08	.06	.03
13	Scott McGregor	.10	.08	.04
14	Eddie Murray	.60	.45	.25
15	Joe Nolan	.08	.06	.03
16	Jim Palmer	.40	.30	.15
17	Cal Ripken, Jr.	.60	.45	.25
18	Gary Roenicke	.08	.06	.03
19	Lenn Sakata	.08	.06	.03
20	*John Shelby*(FC)	.25	.20	.10
21	Ken Singleton	.12	.09	.05
22	Sammy Stewart	.08	.06	.03
23	Tim Stoddard	.08	.06	.03
24	Marty Bystrom	.08	.06	.03
25	Steve Carlton	.50	.40	.20
26	Ivan DeJesus	.08	.06	.03
27	John Denny	.08	.06	.03
28	Bob Dernier	.08	.06	.03
29	Bo Diaz	.10	.08	.04
30	Kiko Garcia	.08	.06	.03
31	Greg Gross	.08	.06	.03
32	*Kevin Gross*(FC)	.35	.25	.14
33	Von Hayes	.15	.11	.06
34	Willie Hernandez	.12	.09	.05
35	Al Holland	.08	.06	.03
36	*Charles Hudson*(FC)	.20	.15	.08
37	Joe Lefebvre	.08	.06	.03
38	Sixto Lezcano	.08	.06	.03
39	Garry Maddox	.10	.08	.04
40	Gary Matthews	.12	.09	.05
41	Len Matuszek	.08	.06	.03
42	Tug McGraw	.12	.09	.05
43	Joe Morgan	.40	.30	.15
44	Tony Perez	.20	.15	.08
45	Ron Reed	.08	.06	.03
46	Pete Rose	1.00	.70	.40
47	*Juan Samuel*(FC)	3.50	2.75	1.50
48	Mike Schmidt	.80	.60	.30
49	Ozzie Virgil	.08	.06	.03
50	*Juan Agosto*(FC)	.15	.11	.06
51	Harold Baines	.25	.20	.10
52	Floyd Bannister	.12	.09	.05
53	Salome Barojas	.08	.06	.03
54	Britt Burns	.08	.06	.03
55	Julio Cruz	.08	.06	.03
56	Richard Dotson	.12	.09	.05
57	Jerry Dybzinski	.08	.06	.03
58	Carlton Fisk	.30	.25	.12
59	Scott Fletcher(FC)	.15	.11	.06
60	Jerry Hairston	.08	.06	.03
61	Kevin Hickey	.08	.06	.03
62	Marc Hill	.08	.06	.03
63	LaMarr Hoyt	.08	.06	.03
64	Ron Kittle	.15	.11	.06
65	Jerry Koosman	.12	.09	.05
66	Dennis Lamp	.08	.06	.03
67	Rudy Law	.08	.06	.03
68	Vance Law	.10	.08	.04
69	Greg Luzinski	.12	.09	.05
70	Tom Paciorek	.08	.06	.03
71	Mike Squires	.08	.06	.03
72	Dick Tidrow	.08	.06	.03
73	*Greg Walker*(FC)	.45	.35	.20
74	Glenn Abbott	.08	.06	.03
75	Howard Bailey	.08	.06	.03
76	Doug Bair	.08	.06	.03
77	Juan Berenguer	.08	.06	.03
78	Tom Brookens	.08	.06	.03
79	Enos Cabell	.08	.06	.03
80	Kirk Gibson	.40	.30	.15
81	John Grubb	.08	.06	.03
82	Larry Herndon	.10	.08	.04
83	Wayne Krenchicki	.08	.06	.03
84	Rick Leach	.08	.06	.03
85	Chet Lemon	.10	.08	.04
86	Aurelio Lopez	.08	.06	.03
87	Jack Morris	.30	.25	.12
88	Lance Parrish	.35	.25	.14

		MT	NR MT	EX			MT	NR MT	EX
89	Dan Petry	.10	.08	.04	180	Terry Harper	.08	.06	.03
90	Dave Rozema	.08	.06	.03	181	Bob Horner	.12	.09	.05
91	Alan Trammell	.40	.30	.15	182	Glenn Hubbard	.10	.08	.04
92	Lou Whitaker	.40	.30	.15	183	Randy Johnson	.08	.06	.03
93	Milt Wilcox	.08	.06	.03	184	*Craig McMurtry*(FC)	.12	.09	.05
94	Glenn Wilson	.10	.08	.04	185	Donnie Moore(FC)	.10	.08	.04
95	John Wockenfuss	.08	.06	.03	186	Dale Murphy	1.00	.70	.40
96	Dusty Baker	.12	.09	.05	187	Phil Niekro	.30	.25	.12
97	Joe Beckwith	.08	.06	.03	188	Pascual Perez	.10	.08	.04
98	Greg Brock	.12	.09	.05	189	Biff Pocoroba	.08	.06	.03
99	Jack Fimple	.08	.06	.03	190	Rafael Ramirez	.08	.06	.03
100	Pedro Guerrero	.35	.25	.14	191	Jerry Royster	.08	.06	.03
101	Rick Honeycutt	.08	.06	.03	192	Claudell Washington	.10	.08	.04
102	Burt Hooton	.10	.08	.04	193	Bob Watson	.10	.08	.04
103	Steve Howe	.12	.09	.05	194	Jerry Augustine	.08	.06	.03
104	Ken Landreaux	.08	.06	.03	195	Mark Brouhard	.08	.06	.03
105	Mike Marshall	.15	.11	.06	196	Mike Caldwell	.08	.06	.03
106	Rick Monday	.10	.08	.04	197	*Tom Candiotti*(FC)	.25	.20	.10
107	Jose Morales	.08	.06	.03	198	Cecil Cooper	.15	.11	.06
108	Tom Niedenfuer	.10	.08	.04	199	Rollie Fingers	.25	.20	.10
109	*Alejandro Pena*(FC)	.30	.25	.12	200	Jim Gantner	.10	.08	.04
110	Jerry Reuss	.12	.09	.05	201	Bob Gibson	.08	.06	.03
111	Bill Russell	.10	.08	.04	202	Moose Haas	.08	.06	.03
112	Steve Sax	.20	.15	.08	203	Roy Howell	.08	.06	.03
113	Mike Scioscia	.10	.08	.04	204	Pete Ladd	.08	.06	.03
114	Derrel Thomas	.08	.06	.03	205	Rick Manning	.08	.06	.03
115	Fernando Valenzuela	.40	.30	.15	206	Bob McClure	.08	.06	.03
116	Bob Welch	.15	.11	.06	207	Paul Molitor	.20	.15	.08
117	Steve Yeager	.08	.06	.03	208	Don Money	.08	.06	.03
118	Pat Zachry	.08	.06	.03	209	Charlie Moore	.08	.06	.03
119	Don Baylor	.15	.11	.06	210	Ben Oglivie	.10	.08	.04
120	Bert Campaneris	.12	.09	.05	211	Chuck Porter	.08	.06	.03
121	Rick Cerone	.08	.06	.03	212	Ed Romero	.08	.06	.03
122	*Ray Fontenot*(FC)	.10	.08	.04	213	Ted Simmons	.15	.11	.06
123	George Frazier	.08	.06	.03	214	Jim Slaton	.08	.06	.03
124	Oscar Gamble	.10	.08	.04	215	Don Sutton	.30	.25	.12
125	Goose Gossage	.25	.20	.10	216	Tom Tellmann	.08	.06	.03
126	Ken Griffey	.12	.09	.05	217	Pete Vuckovich	.10	.08	.04
127	Ron Guidry	.30	.25	.12	218	Ned Yost	.08	.06	.03
128	Jay Howell(FC)	.15	.11	.06	219	Robin Yount	.70	.50	.30
129	Steve Kemp	.10	.08	.04	220	Alan Ashby	.08	.06	.03
130	Matt Keough	.08	.06	.03	221	Kevin Bass(FC)	.20	.15	.08
131	*Don Mattingly*(FC)	35.00	27.50	15.00	222	Jose Cruz	.12	.09	.05
132	John Montefusco	.08	.06	.03	223	*Bill Dawley*(FC)	.10	.08	.04
133	Omar Moreno	.08	.06	.03	224	Frank DiPino	.08	.06	.03
134	Dale Murray	.08	.06	.03	225	*Bill Doran*(FC)	.70	.60	.30
135	Graig Nettles	.20	.15	.08	226	Phil Garner	.10	.08	.04
136	Lou Piniella	.15	.11	.06	227	Art Howe	.08	.06	.03
137	Willie Randolph	.12	.09	.05	228	Bob Knepper	.10	.08	.04
138	Shane Rawley	.12	.09	.05	229	Ray Knight	.12	.09	.05
139	Dave Righetti	.25	.20	.10	230	Frank LaCorte	.08	.06	.03
140	Andre Robertson	.08	.06	.03	231	Mike LaCoss	.08	.06	.03
141	Bob Shirley	.08	.06	.03	232	Mike Madden	.08	.06	.03
142	Roy Smalley	.08	.06	.03	233	Jerry Mumphrey	.08	.06	.03
143	Dave Winfield	.40	.30	.15	235	Terry Puhl	.08	.06	.03
144	Butch Wynegar	.08	.06	.03	236	Luis Pujols	.08	.06	.03
145	*Jim Acker*(FC)	.12	.09	.05	237	Craig Reynolds	.08	.06	.03
146	Doyle Alexander	.12	.09	.05	238	Vern Ruhle	.08	.06	.03
147	Jesse Barfield	.25	.20	.10	239	Nolan Ryan	1.75	1.25	.70
148	Jorge Bell	1.00	.70	.40	240	Mike Scott	.20	.15	.08
149	Barry Bonnell	.08	.06	.03	241	Tony Scott	.08	.06	.03
150	Jim Clancy	.10	.08	.04	242	Dave Smith	.10	.08	.04
151	Dave Collins	.10	.08	.04	243	Dickie Thon	.10	.08	.04
152	*Tony Fernandez*(FC)	5.00	3.75	2.00	244	Denny Walling	.08	.06	.03
153	Damaso Garcia	.08	.06	.03	245	Dale Berra	.08	.06	.03
154	Dave Geisel	.08	.06	.03	246	Jim Bibby	.08	.06	.03
155	Jim Gott(FC)	.10	.08	.04	247	John Candelaria	.12	.09	.05
156	Alfredo Griffin	.10	.08	.04	248	*Jose DeLeon*(FC)	.50	.40	.20
157	Garth Iorg	.08	.06	.03	249	Mike Easler	.10	.08	.04
158	Roy Lee Jackson	.08	.06	.03	250	Cecilio Guante(FC)	.10	.08	.04
159	Cliff Johnson	.08	.06	.03	251	Richie Hebner	.08	.06	.03
160	Luis Leal	.08	.06	.03	252	Lee Lacy	.08	.06	.03
161	Buck Martinez	.08	.06	.03	253	Bill Madlock	.12	.09	.05
162	Joey McLaughlin	.08	.06	.03	254	Milt May	.08	.06	.03
163	Randy Moffitt	.08	.06	.03	255	Lee Mazzilli	.10	.08	.04
164	Lloyd Moseby	.12	.09	.05	256	Larry McWilliams	.08	.06	.03
165	Rance Mulliniks	.08	.06	.03	257	Jim Morrison	.08	.06	.03
166	Jorge Orta	.08	.06	.03	258	Dave Parker	.30	.25	.12
167	Dave Stieb	.15	.11	.06	259	Tony Pena	.12	.09	.05
168	Willie Upshaw	.10	.08	.04	260	Johnny Ray	.12	.09	.05
169	Ernie Whitt	.10	.08	.04	261	Rick Rhoden	.12	.09	.05
170	Len Barker	.10	.08	.04	262	Don Robinson	.10	.08	.04
171	Steve Bedrosian	.12	.09	.05	263	Manny Sarmiento	.08	.06	.03
172	Bruce Benedict	.08	.06	.03	264	Rod Scurry	.08	.06	.03
173	Brett Butler	.10	.08	.04	265	Kent Tekulve	.10	.08	.04
174	Rick Camp	.08	.06	.03	266	Gene Tenace	.10	.08	.04
175	Chris Chambliss	.10	.08	.04	267	Jason Thompson	.08	.06	.03
176	Ken Dayley	.08	.06	.03	268	*Lee Tunnell*(FC)	.10	.08	.04
177	Pete Falcone	.08	.06	.03	269	*Marvell Wynne*(FC)	.20	.15	.08
178	Terry Forster	.10	.08	.04	270	Ray Burris	.08	.06	.03
179	Gene Garber	.08	.06	.03	271	Gary Carter	.40	.30	.15

#	Player	MT	NR MT	EX
272	Warren Cromartie	.08	.06	.03
273	Andre Dawson	.35	.25	.14
274	Doug Flynn	.08	.06	.03
275	Terry Francona	.08	.06	.03
276	Bill Gullickson	.08	.06	.03
277	Bob James	.08	.06	.03
278	Charlie Lea	.08	.06	.03
279	Bryan Little	.08	.06	.03
280	Al Oliver	.20	.15	.08
281	Tim Raines	.40	.30	.15
282	Bobby Ramos	.08	.06	.03
283	Jeff Reardon	.15	.11	.06
284	Steve Rogers	.10	.08	.04
285	Scott Sanderson	.08	.06	.03
286	Dan Schatzeder	.08	.06	.03
287	Bryn Smith	.08	.06	.03
288	Chris Speier	.08	.06	.03
289	Manny Trillo	.10	.08	.04
290	Mike Vail	.08	.06	.03
291	Tim Wallach	.15	.11	.06
292	Chris Welsh	.08	.06	.03
293	Jim Wohlford	.08	.06	.03
294	Kurt Bevacqua	.08	.06	.03
295	Juan Bonilla	.08	.06	.03
296	Bobby Brown	.08	.06	.03
297	Luis DeLeon	.08	.06	.03
298	Dave Dravecky	.10	.08	.04
299	Tim Flannery	.08	.06	.03
300	Steve Garvey	.50	.40	.20
301	Tony Gwynn	2.00	1.50	.80
302	Andy Hawkins(FC)	.40	.30	.15
303	Ruppert Jones	.08	.06	.03
304	Terry Kennedy	.10	.08	.04
305	Tim Lollar	.08	.06	.03
306	Gary Lucas	.08	.06	.03
307	Kevin McReynolds(FC)	7.00	5.25	2.75
308	Sid Monge	.08	.06	.03
309	Mario Ramirez	.08	.06	.03
310	Gene Richards	.08	.06	.03
311	Luis Salazar	.08	.06	.03
312	Eric Show	.12	.09	.05
313	Elias Sosa	.08	.06	.03
314	Garry Templeton	.12	.09	.05
315	Mark Thurmond(FC)	.10	.08	.04
316	Ed Whitson	.08	.06	.03
317	Alan Wiggins	.08	.06	.03
318	Neil Allen	.08	.06	.03
319	Joaquin Andujar	.10	.08	.04
320	Steve Braun	.08	.06	.03
321	Glenn Brummer	.08	.06	.03
322	Bob Forsch	.10	.08	.04
323	David Green	.08	.06	.03
324	George Hendrick	.10	.08	.04
325	Tom Herr	.12	.09	.05
326	Dane Iorg	.08	.06	.03
327	Jeff Lahti	.08	.06	.03
328	Dave LaPoint	.10	.08	.04
329	Willie McGee	.35	.25	.14
330	Ken Oberkfell	.08	.06	.03
331	Darrell Porter	.10	.08	.04
332	Jamie Quirk	.08	.06	.03
333	Mike Ramsey	.08	.06	.03
334	Floyd Rayford	.08	.06	.03
335	Lonnie Smith	.10	.08	.04
336	Ozzie Smith	.20	.15	.08
337	John Stuper	.08	.06	.03
338	Bruce Sutter	.20	.15	.08
339	Andy Van Slyke(FC)	2.50	2.00	1.00
340	Dave Von Ohlen	.08	.06	.03
341	Willie Aikens	.08	.06	.03
342	Mike Armstrong	.08	.06	.03
343	Bud Black	.10	.08	.04
344	George Brett	.70	.50	.30
345	Onix Concepcion	.08	.06	.03
346	Keith Creel	.08	.06	.03
347	Larry Gura	.08	.06	.03
348	Don Hood	.08	.06	.03
349	Dennis Leonard	.10	.08	.04
350	Hal McRae	.12	.09	.05
351	Amos Otis	.12	.09	.05
352	Gaylord Perry	.30	.25	.12
353	Greg Pryor	.08	.06	.03
354	Dan Quisenberry	.12	.09	.05
355	Steve Renko	.08	.06	.03
356	Leon Roberts	.08	.06	.03
357	Pat Sheridan(FC)	.15	.11	.06
358	Joe Simpson	.08	.06	.03
359	Don Slaught	.08	.06	.03
360	Paul Splittorff	.08	.06	.03
361	U.L. Washington	.08	.06	.03
362	John Wathan	.10	.08	.04
363	Frank White	.12	.09	.05
364	Willie Wilson	.15	.11	.06
365	Jim Barr	.08	.06	.03
366	Dave Bergman	.08	.06	.03
367	Fred Breining	.08	.06	.03
368	Bob Brenly	.08	.06	.03
369	Jack Clark	.25	.20	.10
370	Chili Davis	.12	.09	.05
371	Mark Davis(FC)	.20	.15	.08
372	Darrell Evans	.15	.11	.06
373	Atlee Hammaker	.08	.06	.03
374	Mike Krukow	.10	.08	.04
375	Duane Kuiper	.08	.06	.03
376	Bill Laskey	.08	.06	.03
377	Gary Lavelle	.08	.06	.03
378	Johnnie LeMaster	.08	.06	.03
379	Jeff Leonard	.12	.09	.05
380	Randy Lerch	.08	.06	.03
381	Renie Martin	.08	.06	.03
382	Andy McGaffigan	.08	.06	.03
383	Greg Minton	.08	.06	.03
384	Tom O'Malley	.08	.06	.03
385	Max Venable	.08	.06	.03
386	Brad Wellman	.08	.06	.03
387	Joel Youngblood	.08	.06	.03
388	Gary Allenson	.08	.06	.03
389	Luis Aponte	.08	.06	.03
390	Tony Armas	.12	.09	.05
391	Doug Bird	.08	.06	.03
392	Wade Boggs	7.00	5.25	2.75
393	Dennis Boyd(FC)	.35	.25	.14
394	Mike Brown	.08	.06	.03
395	Mark Clear	.08	.06	.03
396	Dennis Eckersley	.15	.11	.06
397	Dwight Evans	.20	.15	.08
398	Rich Gedman	.10	.08	.04
399	Glenn Hoffman	.08	.06	.03
400	Bruce Hurst	.15	.11	.06
401	John Henry Johnson	.08	.06	.03
402	Ed Jurak	.08	.06	.03
403	Rick Miller	.08	.06	.03
404	Jeff Newman	.08	.06	.03
405	Reid Nichols	.08	.06	.03
406	Bob Ojeda	.12	.09	.05
407	Jerry Remy	.08	.06	.03
408	Jim Rice	.40	.30	.15
409	Bob Stanley	.08	.06	.03
410	Dave Stapleton	.08	.06	.03
411	John Tudor	.12	.09	.05
412	Carl Yastrzemski	.80	.60	.30
413	Buddy Bell	.12	.09	.05
414	Larry Biittner	.08	.06	.03
415	John Butcher	.08	.06	.03
416	Danny Darwin	.08	.06	.03
417	Bucky Dent	.12	.09	.05
418	Dave Hostetler	.08	.06	.03
419	Charlie Hough	.12	.09	.05
420	Bobby Johnson	.08	.06	.03
421	Odell Jones	.08	.06	.03
422	Jon Matlack	.10	.08	.04
423	Pete O'Brien(FC)	1.00	.70	.40
424	Larry Parrish	.12	.09	.05
425	Mickey Rivers	.10	.08	.04
426	Billy Sample	.08	.06	.03
427	Dave Schmidt	.08	.06	.03
428	Mike Smithson(FC)	.15	.11	.06
429	Bill Stein	.08	.06	.03
430	Dave Stewart	.15	.11	.06
431	Jim Sundberg	.10	.08	.04
432	Frank Tanana	.12	.09	.05
433	Dave Tobik	.08	.06	.03
434	Wayne Tolleson(FC)	.10	.08	.04
435	George Wright	.08	.06	.03
436	Bill Almon	.08	.06	.03
437	Keith Atherton(FC)	.20	.15	.08
438	Dave Beard	.08	.06	.03
439	Tom Burgmeier	.08	.06	.03
440	Jeff Burroughs	.10	.08	.04
441	Chris Codiroli(FC)	.10	.08	.04
442	Tim Conroy(FC)	.12	.09	.05
443	Mike Davis	.10	.08	.04
444	Wayne Gross	.08	.06	.03
445	Garry Hancock	.08	.06	.03
446	Mike Heath	.08	.06	.03
447	Rickey Henderson	1.00	.70	.40
448	Don Hill(FC)	.15	.11	.06
449	Bob Kearney	.08	.06	.03
450	Bill Krueger	.08	.06	.03
451	Rick Langford	.08	.06	.03
452	Carney Lansford	.12	.09	.05
453	Davey Lopes	.10	.08	.04

		MT	NR MT	EX
454	Steve McCatty	.08	.06	.03
455	Dan Meyer	.08	.06	.03
456	Dwayne Murphy	.10	.08	.04
457	Mike Norris	.08	.06	.03
458	Ricky Peters	.08	.06	.03
459	*Tony Phillips*(FC)	.15	.11	.06
460	Tom Underwood	.08	.06	.03
461	Mike Warren	.08	.06	.03
462	Johnny Bench	.40	.30	.15
463	Bruce Berenyi	.08	.06	.03
464	Dann Bilardello	.08	.06	.03
465	Cesar Cedeno	.12	.09	.05
466	Dave Concepcion	.15	.11	.06
467	Dan Driessen	.10	.08	.04
468	*Nick Esasky*(FC)	2.00	1.50	.80
469	Rich Gale	.08	.06	.03
470	Ben Hayes	.08	.06	.03
471	Paul Householder	.08	.06	.03
472	Tom Hume	.08	.06	.03
473	Alan Knicely	.08	.06	.03
474	Eddie Milner	.08	.06	.03
475	Ron Oester	.08	.06	.03
476	Kelly Paris	.08	.06	.03
477	Frank Pastore	.08	.06	.03
478	Ted Power	.10	.08	.04
479	Joe Price	.08	.06	.03
480	Charlie Puleo	.08	.06	.03
481	*Gary Redus*(FC)	.25	.20	.10
482	Bill Scherrer	.08	.06	.03
483	Mario Soto	.10	.08	.04
484	Alex Trevino	.08	.06	.03
485	Duane Walker	.08	.06	.03
486	Larry Bowa	.15	.11	.06
487	Warren Brusstar	.08	.06	.03
488	Bill Buckner	.15	.11	.06
489	Bill Campbell	.08	.06	.03
490	Ron Cey	.12	.09	.05
491	Jody Davis	.10	.08	.04
492	Leon Durham	.10	.08	.04
493	Mel Hall(FC)	.20	.15	.08
494	Ferguson Jenkins	.20	.15	.08
495	Jay Johnstone	.10	.08	.04
496	*Craig Lefferts*(FC)	.20	.15	.08
497	*Carmelo Martinez*(FC)	.25	.20	.10
498	Jerry Morales	.08	.06	.03
499	Keith Moreland	.10	.08	.04
500	Dickie Noles	.08	.06	.03
501	Mike Proly	.08	.06	.03
502	Chuck Rainey	.08	.06	.03
503	Dick Ruthven	.08	.06	.03
504	Ryne Sandberg	2.00	1.50	.80
505	Lee Smith	.15	.11	.06
506	Steve Trout	.08	.06	.03
507	Gary Woods	.08	.06	.03
508	Juan Beniquez	.08	.06	.03
509	Bob Boone	.10	.08	.04
510	Rick Burleson	.10	.08	.04
511	Rod Carew	.50	.40	.20
512	Bobby Clark	.08	.06	.03
513	John Curtis	.08	.06	.03
514	Doug DeCinces	.12	.09	.05
515	Brian Downing	.12	.09	.05
516	Tim Foli	.08	.06	.03
517	Ken Forsch	.08	.06	.03
518	Bobby Grich	.12	.09	.05
519	Andy Hassler	.08	.06	.03
520	Reggie Jackson	.60	.45	.25
521	Ron Jackson	.08	.06	.03
522	Tommy John	.25	.20	.10
523	Bruce Kison	.08	.06	.03
524	Steve Lubratich	.08	.06	.03
525	Fred Lynn	.25	.20	.10
526	*Gary Pettis*(FC)	.25	.20	.10
527	Luis Sanchez	.08	.06	.03
528	Daryl Sconiers	.08	.06	.03
529	Ellis Valentine	.08	.06	.03
530	Rob Wilfong	.08	.06	.03
531	Mike Witt	.15	.11	.06
532	Geoff Zahn	.08	.06	.03
533	Bud Anderson	.08	.06	.03
534	Chris Bando	.08	.06	.03
535	Alan Bannister	.08	.06	.03
536	Bert Blyleven	.20	.15	.08
537	Tom Brennan	.08	.06	.03
538	Jamie Easterly	.08	.06	.03
539	Juan Eichelberger	.08	.06	.03
540	Jim Essian	.08	.06	.03
541	Mike Fischlin	.08	.06	.03
542	Julio Franco(FC)	1.25	.90	.50
543	Mike Hargrove	.08	.06	.03
544	Toby Harrah	.10	.08	.04
545	Ron Hassey	.08	.06	.03
546	*Neal Heaton*(FC)	.15	.11	.06
547	Bake McBride	.08	.06	.03
548	Broderick Perkins	.08	.06	.03
549	Lary Sorensen	.08	.06	.03
550	Dan Spillner	.08	.06	.03
551	Rick Sutcliffe	.15	.11	.06
552	Pat Tabler	.10	.08	.04
553	Gorman Thomas	.10	.08	.04
554	Andre Thornton	.12	.09	.05
555	George Vukovich	.08	.06	.03
556	Darrell Brown	.08	.06	.03
557	Tom Brunansky	.20	.15	.08
558	*Randy Bush*(FC)	.15	.11	.06
559	Bobby Castillo	.08	.06	.03
560	John Castino	.08	.06	.03
561	Ron Davis	.08	.06	.03
562	Dave Engle	.08	.06	.03
563	Lenny Faedo	.08	.06	.03
564	Pete Filson	.08	.06	.03
565	Gary Gaetti	.60	.45	.25
566	Mickey Hatcher	.10	.08	.04
567	Kent Hrbek	.40	.30	.15
568	Rusty Kuntz	.08	.06	.03
569	Tim Laudner	.08	.06	.03
570	Rick Lysander	.08	.06	.03
571	Bobby Mitchell	.08	.06	.03
572	Ken Schrom	.08	.06	.03
573	Ray Smith	.08	.06	.03
574	*Tim Teufel*(FC)	.30	.25	.12
575	Frank Viola	.80	.60	.30
576	Gary Ward	.10	.08	.04
577	Ron Washington	.08	.06	.03
578	Len Whitehouse	.08	.06	.03
579	Al Williams	.08	.06	.03
580	Bob Bailor	.08	.06	.03
581	Mark Bradley	.08	.06	.03
582	Hubie Brooks	.15	.11	.06
583	Carlos Diaz	.08	.06	.03
584	George Foster	.20	.15	.08
585	Brian Giles	.08	.06	.03
586	Danny Heep	.08	.06	.03
587	Keith Hernandez	.40	.30	.15
588	Ron Hodges	.08	.06	.03
589	Scott Holman	.08	.06	.03
590	Dave Kingman	.15	.11	.06
591	Ed Lynch	.08	.06	.03
592	*Jose Oquendo*(FC)	.15	.11	.06
593	Jesse Orosco	.10	.08	.04
594	*Junior Ortiz*(FC)	.10	.08	.04
595	Tom Seaver	.50	.40	.20
596	*Doug Sisk*(FC)	.10	.08	.04
597	Rusty Staub	.12	.09	.05
598	John Stearns	.08	.06	.03
599	*Darryl Strawberry*(FC)	20.00	15.00	8.00
600	Craig Swan	.08	.06	.03
601	*Walt Terrell*(FC)	.30	.25	.12
602	Mike Torrez	.10	.08	.04
603	Mookie Wilson	.12	.09	.05
604	Jamie Allen	.08	.06	.03
605	Jim Beattie	.08	.06	.03
606	Tony Bernazard	.08	.06	.03
607	Manny Castillo	.08	.06	.03
608	Bill Caudill	.08	.06	.03
609	Bryan Clark	.08	.06	.03
610	Al Cowens	.08	.06	.03
611	Dave Henderson	.12	.09	.05
612	Steve Henderson	.08	.06	.03
613	Orlando Mercado	.08	.06	.03
614	Mike Moore	.10	.08	.04
615	Ricky Nelson	.08	.06	.03
616	*Spike Owen*(FC)	.20	.15	.08
617	Pat Putnam	.08	.06	.03
618	Ron Roenicke	.08	.06	.03
619	Mike Stanton	.08	.06	.03
620	Bob Stoddard	.08	.06	.03
621	Rick Sweet	.08	.06	.03
622	Roy Thomas	.08	.06	.03
623	Ed Vande Berg	.08	.06	.03
624	*Matt Young*(FC)	.15	.11	.06
625	Richie Zisk	.10	.08	.04
626	'83 All-Star Game Record Breaker (Fred Lynn)	.12	.09	.05
627	'83 All-Star Game Record Breaker (Manny Trillo)	.10	.08	.04
628	N.L. Iron Man (Steve Garvey)	.20	.15	.08
629	A.L. Batting Runner-Up (Rod Carew)	.25	.20	.10
630	A.L. Batting Champion (Wade Boggs)	.60	.45	.25
631	Letting Go Of The Raines (Tim Raines)	.20	.15	.08

		MT	NR MT	EX
632	Double Trouble (Al Oliver)	.10	.08	.04
633	All-Star Second Base (Steve Sax)	.15	.11	.06
634	All-Star Shortstop (Dickie Thon)	.10	.08	.04
635	Ace Firemen (Tippy Martinez, Dan Quisenberry)	.10	.08	.04
636	Reds Reunited (Joe Morgan, Tony Perez, Pete Rose)	.50	.40	.20
637	Backstop Stars (Bob Boone, Lance Parrish)	.15	.11	.06
638	The Pine Tar Incident, 7/24/83 (George Brett, Gaylord Perry)	.30	.25	.12
639	1983 No-Hitters (Bob Forsch, Dave Righetti, Mike Warren)	.10	.08	.04
640	Retiring Superstars (Johnny Bench, Carl Yastrzemski)	.35	.25	.14
641	Going Out In Style (Gaylord Perry)	.15	.11	.06
642	300 Club & Strikeout Record (Steve Carlton)	.20	.15	.08
643	The Managers (Joe Altobelli, Paul Owens)	.10	.08	.04
644	The MVP (Rick Dempsey)	.10	.08	.04
645	The Rookie Winner (Mike Boddicker)(FC)	.12	.09	.05
646	The Clincher (Scott McGregor)	.10	.08	.04
647	Checklist: Orioles/Royals (Joe Altobelli)	.08	.06	.03
648	Checklist: Phillies/Giants (Paul Owens)	.08	.06	.03
649	Checklist: White Sox/Red Sox (Tony LaRussa)	.08	.06	.03
650	Checklist: Tigers/Rangers (Sparky Anderson)	.08	.06	.03
651	Checklist: Dodgers/A's (Tom Lasorda)	.08	.06	.03
652	Checklist: Yankees/Reds (Billy Martin)	.08	.06	.03
653	Checklist: Blue Jays/Cubs (Bobby Cox)	.08	.06	.03
654	Checklist: Braves/Angels (Joe Torre)	.08	.06	.03
655	Checklist: Brewers/Indians (Rene Lachemann)	.08	.06	.03
656	Checklist: Astros/Twins (Bob Lillis)	.08	.06	.03
657	Checklist: Pirates/Mets (Chuck Tanner)	.08	.06	.03
658	Checklist: Expos/Mariners (Bill Virdon)	.08	.06	.03
659	Checklist: Padres/Specials (Dick Williams)	.08	.06	.03
660	Checklist: Cardinals/Specials (Whitey Herzog)	.08	.06	.03

1984 Fleer Update

Following the lead of Topps, Fleer issued near the end of the baseball season a 132-card set to update player trades and include rookies not depicted in the regular issue. The cards, which measure 2-1/2" by 3-1/2", are identical in design to the regular issue but are numbered U-1 through U-132. Available to the collecting public only through hobby dealers, the set was printed in limited quantities and has escalated in price quite rapidly the past several years. The set was issued with team logo stickers in a specially designed box.

		MT	NR MT	EX
	Complete Set:	350.00	245.00	140.00
	Common Player:	.15	.11	.06
1	Willie Aikens	.15	.11	.06
2	Luis Aponte	.15	.11	.06
3	Mark Bailey(FC)	.20	.15	.08
4	Bob Bailor	.15	.11	.06
5	Dusty Baker	.30	.25	.12
6	Steve Balboni(FC)	.40	.30	.15
7	Alan Bannister	.15	.11	.06
8	Marty Barrett(FC)	2.50	2.00	1.00
9	Dave Beard	.15	.11	.06
10	Joe Beckwith	.15	.11	.06
11	Dave Bergman	.15	.11	.06
12	Tony Bernazard	.15	.11	.06
13	Bruce Bochte	.15	.11	.06
14	Barry Bonnell	.15	.11	.06
15	Phil Bradley(FC)	3.50	2.75	1.50
16	Fred Breining	.15	.11	.06
17	Mike Brown	.15	.11	.06
18	Bill Buckner	.50	.40	.20
19	Ray Burris	.15	.11	.06
20	John Butcher	.15	.11	.06
21	Brett Butler	.30	.25	.12
22	Enos Cabell	.15	.11	.06
23	Bill Campbell	.15	.11	.06
24	Bill Caudill	.15	.11	.06
25	Bobby Clark	.15	.11	.06
26	Bryan Clark	.15	.11	.06
27	Roger Clemens(FC)	85.00	64.00	34.00
28	Jaime Cocanower	.15	.11	.06
29	Ron Darling(FC)	12.00	9.00	4.75
30	Alvin Davis(FC)	10.00	7.50	4.00
31	Bob Dernier	.15	.11	.06
32	Carlos Diaz	.15	.11	.06
33	Mike Easler	.20	.15	.08
34	Dennis Eckersley	.80	.60	.30
35	Jim Essian	.15	.11	.06
36	Darrell Evans	.60	.45	.25
37	Mike Fitzgerald(FC)	.20	.15	.08
38	Tim Foli	.15	.11	.06
39	John Franco(FC)	5.00	3.75	2.00
40	George Frazier	.15	.11	.06
41	Rich Gale	.15	.11	.06
42	Barbaro Garbey	.20	.15	.08
43	Dwight Gooden(FC)	75.00	55.00	30.00
44	Goose Gossage	1.00	.70	.40
45	Wayne Gross	.15	.11	.06
46	Mark Gubicza(FC)	7.00	5.25	2.75
47	Jackie Gutierrez	.15	.11	.06
48	Toby Harrah	.20	.15	.08
49	Ron Hassey	.15	.11	.06
50	Richie Hebner	.15	.11	.06
51	Willie Hernandez	.40	.30	.15
52	Ed Hodge	.15	.11	.06
53	Ricky Horton(FC)	.70	.50	.30
54	Art Howe	.15	.11	.06
55	Dane Iorg	.15	.11	.06
56	Brook Jacoby(FC)	2.25	1.75	.90
57	Dion James(FC)	.40	.30	.15
58	Mike Jeffcoat(FC)	.20	.15	.08
59	Ruppert Jones	.15	.11	.06
60	Bob Kearney	.15	.11	.06
61	Jimmy Key(FC)	6.00	4.50	2.50
62	Dave Kingman	.70	.50	.30
63	Brad Komminsk(FC)	.20	.15	.08
64	Jerry Koosman	.50	.40	.20
65	Wayne Krenchicki	.15	.11	.06
66	Rusty Kuntz	.15	.11	.06
67	Frank LaCorte	.15	.11	.06
68	Dennis Lamp	.15	.11	.06
69	Tito Landrum	.15	.11	.06
70	Mark Langston(FC)	18.00	13.50	7.25
71	Rick Leach	.15	.11	.06
72	Craig Lefferts(FC)	.30	.25	.12
73	Gary Lucas	.15	.11	.06
74	Jerry Martin	.15	.11	.06
75	Carmelo Martinez	.30	.25	.12
76	Mike Mason(FC)	.20	.15	.08
77	Gary Matthews	.30	.25	.12
78	Andy McGaffigan	.15	.11	.06
79	Joey McLaughlin	.15	.11	.06
80	Joe Morgan	3.25	2.50	1.25
81	Darryl Motley	.15	.11	.06
82	Graig Nettles	1.50	1.25	.60
83	Phil Niekro	2.50	2.00	1.00
84	Ken Oberkfell	.15	.11	.06
85	Al Oliver	.80	.60	.30
86	Jorge Orta	.15	.11	.06
87	Amos Otis	.30	.25	.12
88	Bob Owchinko	.15	.11	.06

		MT	NR MT	EX
89	Dave Parker	2.00	1.50	.80
90	Jack Perconte	.15	.11	.06
91	Tony Perez	1.50	1.25	.60
92	Gerald Perry(FC)	2.25	1.75	.90
93	Kirby Puckett(FC)	85.00	65.00	35.00
94	Shane Rawley	.35	.30	.14
95	Floyd Rayford	.15	.11	.06
96	Ron Reed	.20	.15	.08
97	R.J. Reynolds(FC)	.90	.70	.35
98	Gene Richards	.15	.11	.06
99	Jose Rijo(FC)	2.50	2.00	1.00
100	Jeff Robinson(FC)	1.00	.70	.40
101	Ron Romanick(FC)	.20	.15	.08
102	Pete Rose	25.00	18.50	10.00
103	Bret Saberhagen(FC)	22.00	17.00	9.00
104	Scott Sanderson	.15	.11	.06
105	Dick Schofield(FC)	.40	.30	.15
106	Tom Seaver	7.00	5.25	2.75
107	Jim Slaton	.15	.11	.06
108	Mike Smithson	.20	.15	.08
109	Lary Sorensen	.15	.11	.06
110	Tim Stoddard	.15	.11	.06
111	Jeff Stone(FC)	.30	.25	.12
112	Champ Summers	.15	.11	.06
113	Jim Sundberg	.20	.15	.08
114	Rick Sutcliffe	.80	.60	.30
115	Craig Swan	.15	.11	.06
116	Derrel Thomas	.15	.11	.06
117	Gorman Thomas	.35	.30	.14
118	Alex Trevino	.15	.11	.06
119	Manny Trillo	.20	.15	.08
120	John Tudor	.60	.45	.25
121	Tom Underwood	.15	.11	.06
122	Mike Vail	.15	.11	.06
123	Tom Waddell(FC)	.15	.11	.06
124	Gary Ward	.20	.15	.08
125	Terry Whitfield	.15	.11	.06
126	Curtis Wilkerson	.15	.11	.06
127	Frank Williams(FC)	.35	.25	.14
128	Glenn Wilson	.25	.20	.10
129	John Wockenfuss	.15	.11	.06
130	Ned Yost	.15	.11	.06
131	Mike Young(FC)	.35	.25	.14
132	Checklist 1-132	.15	.11	.06

1985 Fleer

The 1985 Fleer set consists of 660 cards, each measuring 2-1/2" by 3-1/2" in size. The card fronts feature a color photo plus the player's team logo and the word "Fleer." The photos have a color-coded frame which corresponds to the player's team. A grey border surrounds the color-coded frame. The card backs are similar in design to the previous two years, but have two shades of red and black ink on white stock. For the fourth consecutive year, Fleer included special cards and team checklists in the set. Also incorporated in a set for the first time were ten "Major League Prospect" cards, each featuring two rookie hopefuls. The set was issued with team logo stickers.

		MT	NR MT	EX
Complete Set:		100.00	75.00	40.00
Common Player:		.06	.05	.02
1	Doug Bair	.06	.05	.02

		MT	NR MT	EX
2	Juan Berenguer	.06	.05	.02
3	Dave Bergman	.06	.05	.02
4	Tom Brookens	.06	.05	.02
5	Marty Castillo	.06	.05	.02
6	Darrell Evans	.12	.09	.05
7	Barbaro Garbey	.12	.09	.05
8	Kirk Gibson	.35	.25	.14
9	John Grubb	.06	.05	.02
10	Willie Hernandez	.08	.06	.03
11	Larry Herndon	.08	.06	.03
12	Howard Johnson	.30	.25	.12
13	Ruppert Jones	.06	.05	.02
14	Rusty Kuntz	.06	.05	.02
15	Chet Lemon	.08	.06	.03
16	Aurelio Lopez	.06	.05	.02
17	Sid Monge	.06	.05	.02
18	Jack Morris	.25	.20	.10
19	Lance Parrish	.30	.25	.12
20	Dan Petry	.08	.06	.03
21	Dave Rozema	.06	.05	.02
22	Bill Scherrer	.06	.05	.02
23	Alan Trammell	.35	.25	.14
24	Lou Whitaker	.35	.25	.14
25	Milt Wilcox	.06	.05	.02
26	Kurt Bevacqua	.06	.05	.02
27	*Greg Booker*(FC)	.15	.11	.06
28	Bobby Brown	.06	.05	.02
29	Luis DeLeon	.06	.05	.02
30	Dave Dravecky	.08	.06	.03
31	Tim Flannery	.06	.05	.02
32	Steve Garvey	.40	.30	.15
33	Goose Gossage	.20	.15	.08
34	Tony Gwynn	.90	.70	.35
35	Greg Harris	.06	.05	.02
36	Andy Hawkins	.08	.06	.03
37	Terry Kennedy	.08	.06	.03
38	Craig Lefferts	.08	.06	.03
39	Tim Lollar	.06	.05	.02
40	Carmelo Martinez	.08	.06	.03
41	Kevin McReynolds	1.00	.70	.40
42	Graig Nettles	.15	.11	.06
43	Luis Salazar	.06	.05	.02
44	Eric Show	.08	.06	.03
45	Garry Templeton	.08	.06	.03
46	Mark Thurmond	.06	.05	.02
47	Ed Whitson	.06	.05	.02
48	Alan Wiggins	.06	.05	.02
49	Rich Bordi	.06	.05	.02
50	Larry Bowa	.12	.09	.05
51	Warren Brusstar	.06	.05	.02
52	Ron Cey	.10	.08	.04
53	*Henry Cotto*(FC)	.15	.11	.06
54	Jody Davis	.10	.08	.04
55	Bob Dernier	.06	.05	.02
56	Leon Durham	.08	.06	.03
57	Dennis Eckersley	.12	.09	.05
58	George Frazier	.06	.05	.02
59	Richie Hebner	.06	.05	.02
60	Dave Lopes	.08	.06	.03
61	Gary Matthews	.10	.08	.04
62	Keith Moreland	.08	.06	.03
63	Rick Reuschel	.10	.08	.04
64	Dick Ruthven	.06	.05	.02
65	Ryne Sandberg	.50	.40	.20
66	Scott Sanderson	.06	.05	.02
67	Lee Smith	.10	.08	.04
68	Tim Stoddard	.06	.05	.02
69	Rick Sutcliffe	.12	.09	.05
70	Steve Trout	.06	.05	.02
71	Gary Woods	.06	.05	.02
72	Wally Backman	.08	.06	.03
73	Bruce Berenyi	.06	.05	.02
74	Hubie Brooks	.10	.08	.04
75	Kelvin Chapman	.06	.05	.02
76	Ron Darling	1.25	.90	.50
77	Sid Fernandez(FC)	.90	.70	.35
78	Mike Fitzgerald	.08	.06	.03
79	George Foster	.15	.11	.06
80	Brent Gaff	.06	.05	.02
81	Ron Gardenhire	.06	.05	.02
82	*Dwight Gooden*	10.00	7.50	4.00
83	Tom Gorman	.06	.05	.02
84	Danny Heep	.06	.05	.02
85	Keith Hernandez	.30	.25	.12
86	Ray Knight	.10	.08	.04
87	Ed Lynch	.06	.05	.02
88	Jose Oquendo	.08	.06	.03
89	Jesse Orosco	.08	.06	.03
90	*Rafael Santana*(FC)	.20	.15	.08
91	Doug Sisk	.06	.05	.02
92	Rusty Staub	.12	.09	.05

		MT	NR MT	EX				MT	NR MT	EX
93	Darryl Strawberry	4.00	3.00	1.50		184	Eddie Murray	.50	.40	.20
94	Walt Terrell	.08	.06	.03		185	Joe Nolan	.06	.05	.02
95	Mookie Wilson	.10	.08	.04		186	Floyd Rayford	.06	.05	.02
96	Jim Acker	.06	.05	.02		187	Cal Ripken, Jr.	.50	.40	.20
97	Willie Aikens	.06	.05	.02		188	Gary Roenicke	.06	.05	.02
98	Doyle Alexander	.10	.08	.04		189	Lenn Sakata	.06	.05	.02
99	Jesse Barfield	.25	.20	.10		190	John Shelby	.08	.06	.03
100	George Bell	.50	.40	.20		191	Ken Singleton	.08	.06	.03
101	Jim Clancy	.08	.06	.03		192	Sammy Stewart	.06	.05	.02
102	Dave Collins	.08	.06	.03		193	Bill Swaggerty	.06	.05	.02
103	Tony Fernandez	.35	.25	.14		194	Tom Underwood	.06	.05	.02
104	Damaso Garcia	.06	.05	.02		195	Mike Young	.12	.09	.05
105	Jim Gott	.06	.05	.02		196	Steve Balboni	.08	.06	.03
106	Alfredo Griffin	.08	.06	.03		197	Joe Beckwith	.06	.05	.02
107	Garth Iorg	.06	.05	.02		198	Bud Black	.06	.05	.02
108	Roy Lee Jackson	.06	.05	.02		199	George Brett	.50	.40	.20
109	Cliff Johnson	.06	.05	.02		200	Onix Concepcion	.06	.05	.02
110	Jimmy Key	1.00	.70	.40		201	Mark Gubicza	1.00	.70	.40
111	Dennis Lamp	.06	.05	.02		202	Larry Gura	.06	.05	.02
112	Rick Leach	.06	.05	.02		203	Mark Huismann(FC)	.06	.05	.02
113	Luis Leal	.06	.05	.02		204	Dane Iorg	.06	.05	.02
114	Buck Martinez	.06	.05	.02		205	Danny Jackson(FC)	1.00	.70	.40
115	Lloyd Moseby	.10	.08	.04		206	Charlie Leibrandt	.08	.06	.03
116	Rance Mulliniks	.06	.05	.02		207	Hal McRae	.10	.08	.04
117	Dave Stieb	.12	.09	.05		208	Darryl Motley	.06	.05	.02
118	Willie Upshaw	.08	.06	.03		209	Jorge Orta	.06	.05	.02
119	Ernie Whitt	.08	.06	.03		210	Greg Pryor	.06	.05	.02
120	Mike Armstrong	.06	.05	.02		211	Dan Quisenberry	.10	.08	.04
121	Don Baylor	.12	.09	.05		212	Bret Saberhagen	6.00	4.50	2.50
122	Marty Bystrom	.06	.05	.02		213	Pat Sheridan	.06	.05	.02
123	Rick Cerone	.06	.05	.02		214	Don Slaught	.06	.05	.02
124	Joe Cowley(FC)	.06	.05	.02		215	U.L. Washington	.06	.05	.02
125	Brian Dayett(FC)	.06	.05	.02		216	John Wathan	.08	.06	.03
126	Tim Foli	.06	.05	.02		217	Frank White	.10	.08	.04
127	Ray Fontenot	.06	.05	.02		218	Willie Wilson	.12	.09	.05
128	Ken Griffey	.10	.08	.04		219	Neil Allen	.06	.05	.02
129	Ron Guidry	.25	.20	.10		220	Joaquin Andujar	.08	.06	.03
130	Toby Harrah	.08	.06	.03		221	Steve Braun	.06	.05	.02
131	Jay Howell	.08	.06	.03		222	Danny Cox(FC)	.20	.20	.10
132	Steve Kemp	.08	.06	.03		223	Bob Forsch	.08	.06	.03
133	Don Mattingly	12.00	9.00	4.75		224	David Green	.06	.05	.02
134	Bobby Meacham	.06	.05	.02		225	George Hendrick	.08	.06	.03
135	John Montefusco	.06	.05	.02		226	Tom Herr	.10	.08	.04
136	Omar Moreno	.06	.05	.02		227	Ricky Horton	.30	.25	.12
137	Dale Murray	.06	.05	.02		228	Art Howe	.06	.05	.02
138	Phil Niekro	.25	.20	.10		229	Mike Jorgensen	.06	.05	.02
139	Mike Pagliarulo(FC)	.90	.70	.35		230	Kurt Kepshire	.06	.05	.02
140	Willie Randolph	.10	.08	.04		231	Jeff Lahti	.06	.05	.02
141	Dennis Rasmussen(FC)	.30	.25	.12		232	Tito Landrum	.06	.05	.02
142	Dave Righetti	.20	.15	.08		233	Dave LaPoint	.08	.06	.03
143	Jose Rijo	.50	.40	.20		234	Willie McGee	.30	.25	.12
144	Andre Robertson	.06	.05	.02		235	Tom Nieto(FC)	.10	.08	.04
145	Bob Shirley	.06	.05	.02		236	Terry Pendleton(FC)	.70	.50	.30
146	Dave Winfield	.35	.25	.14		237	Darrell Porter	.08	.06	.03
147	Butch Wynegar	.06	.05	.02		238	Dave Rucker	.06	.05	.02
148	Gary Allenson	.06	.05	.02		239	Lonnie Smith	.08	.06	.03
149	Tony Armas	.10	.08	.04		240	Ozzie Smith	.15	.11	.06
150	Marty Barrett	.20	.15	.08		241	Bruce Sutter	.12	.09	.05
151	Wade Boggs	3.75	2.75	1.50		242	Andy Van Slyke	.35	.25	.14
152	Dennis Boyd	.10	.08	.04		243	Dave Von Ohlen	.06	.05	.02
153	Bill Buckner	.12	.09	.05		244	Larry Andersen	.06	.05	.02
154	Mark Clear	.06	.05	.02		245	Bill Campbell	.06	.05	.02
155	Roger Clemens	10.00	7.50	4.00		246	Steve Carlton	.40	.30	.15
156	Steve Crawford	.06	.05	.02		247	Tim Corcoran	.06	.05	.02
157	Mike Easler	.08	.06	.03		248	Ivan DeJesus	.06	.05	.02
158	Dwight Evans	.12	.09	.05		249	John Denny	.06	.05	.02
159	Rich Gedman	.10	.08	.04		250	Bo Diaz	.08	.06	.03
160	Jackie Gutierrez	.06	.05	.02		251	Greg Gross	.06	.05	.02
161	Bruce Hurst	.12	.09	.05		252	Kevin Gross	.10	.08	.04
162	John Henry Johnson	.06	.05	.02		253	Von Hayes	.12	.09	.05
163	Rick Miller	.06	.05	.02		254	Al Holland	.06	.05	.02
164	Reid Nichols	.06	.05	.02		255	Charles Hudson	.08	.06	.03
165	Al Nipper(FC)	.15	.11	.06		256	Jerry Koosman	.10	.08	.04
166	Bob Ojeda	.10	.08	.04		257	Joe Lefebvre	.06	.05	.02
167	Jerry Remy	.06	.05	.02		258	Sixto Lezcano	.06	.05	.02
168	Jim Rice	.35	.25	.14		259	Garry Maddox	.10	.08	.04
169	Bob Stanley	.06	.05	.02		260	Len Matuszek	.06	.05	.02
170	Mike Boddicker	.10	.08	.04		261	Tug McGraw	.10	.08	.04
171	Al Bumbry	.08	.06	.03		262	Al Oliver	.12	.09	.05
172	Todd Cruz	.06	.05	.02		263	Shane Rawley	.10	.08	.04
173	Rich Dauer	.06	.05	.02		264	Juan Samuel	.30	.25	.12
174	Storm Davis	.10	.08	.04		265	Mike Schmidt	.60	.45	.25
175	Rick Dempsey	.08	.06	.03		266	Jeff Stone	.12	.09	.05
176	Jim Dwyer	.06	.05	.02		267	Ozzie Virgil	.06	.05	.02
177	Mike Flanagan	.10	.08	.04		268	Glenn Wilson	.08	.06	.03
178	Dan Ford	.06	.05	.02		269	John Wockenfuss	.06	.05	.02
179	Wayne Gross	.06	.05	.02		270	Darrell Brown	.06	.05	.02
180	John Lowenstein	.06	.05	.02		271	Tom Brunansky	.12	.09	.05
181	Dennis Martinez	.08	.06	.03		272	Randy Bush	.06	.05	.02
182	Tippy Martinez	.06	.05	.02		273	John Butcher	.06	.05	.02
183	Scott McGregor	.08	.06	.03		274	Bobby Castillo	.06	.05	.02

#	Player	MT	NR MT	EX	#	Player	MT	NR MT	EX
275	Ron Davis	.06	.05	.02	366	Dave Anderson	.06	.05	.02
276	Dave Engle	.06	.05	.02	367	Bob Bailor	.06	.05	.02
277	Pete Filson	.06	.05	.02	368	Greg Brock	.08	.06	.03
278	Gary Gaetti	.25	.20	.10	369	Carlos Diaz	.06	.05	.02
279	Mickey Hatcher	.06	.05	.02	370	Pedro Guerrero	.25	.20	.10
280	Ed Hodge	.06	.05	.02	371	*Orel Hershiser*(FC)	9.00	6.75	3.50
281	Kent Hrbek	.25	.20	.10	372	Rick Honeycutt	.06	.05	.02
282	Houston Jimenez	.06	.05	.02	373	Burt Hooton	.08	.06	.03
283	Tim Laudner	.06	.05	.02	374	*Ken Howell*(FC)	.15	.11	.06
284	Rick Lysander	.06	.05	.02	375	Ken Landreaux	.08	.06	.03
285	Dave Meier	.06	.05	.02	376	Candy Maldonado	.10	.08	.04
286	*Kirby Puckett*	15.00	11.00	6.00	377	Mike Marshall	.15	.11	.06
287	Pat Putnam	.06	.05	.02	378	Tom Niedenfuer	.08	.06	.03
288	Ken Schrom	.06	.05	.02	379	Alejandro Pena	.08	.06	.03
289	Mike Smithson	.06	.05	.02	380	Jerry Reuss	.08	.06	.03
290	Tim Teufel	.08	.06	.03	381	*R.J. Reynolds*	.25	.20	.10
291	Frank Viola	.20	.15	.08	382	German Rivera	.06	.05	.02
292	Ron Washington	.06	.05	.02	383	Bill Russell	.08	.06	.03
293	Don Aase	.06	.05	.02	384	Steve Sax	.20	.15	.08
294	Juan Beniquez	.06	.05	.02	385	Mike Scioscia	.08	.06	.03
295	Bob Boone	.08	.06	.03	386	*Franklin Stubbs*(FC)	.25	.20	.10
296	Mike Brown	.06	.05	.02	387	Fernando Valenzuela	.35	.25	.14
297	Rod Carew	.40	.30	.15	388	Bob Welch	.12	.09	.05
298	Doug Corbett	.06	.05	.02	389	Terry Whitfield	.06	.05	.02
299	Doug DeCinces	.10	.08	.04	390	Steve Yeager	.06	.05	.02
300	Brian Downing	.10	.08	.04	391	Pat Zachry	.06	.05	.02
301	Ken Forsch	.06	.05	.02	392	Fred Breining	.06	.05	.02
302	Bobby Grich	.10	.08	.04	393	Gary Carter	.35	.25	.14
303	Reggie Jackson	.40	.30	.15	394	Andre Dawson	.30	.25	.12
304	Tommy John	.20	.15	.08	395	Miguel Dilone	.06	.05	.02
305	Curt Kaufman	.06	.05	.02	396	Dan Driessen	.08	.06	.03
306	Bruce Kison	.06	.05	.02	397	Doug Flynn	.06	.05	.02
307	Fred Lynn	.20	.15	.08	398	Terry Francona	.06	.05	.02
308	Gary Pettis	.08	.06	.03	399	Bill Gullickson	.06	.05	.02
309	*Ron Romanick*	.10	.08	.04	400	Bob James	.06	.05	.02
310	Luis Sanchez	.06	.05	.02	401	Charlie Lea	.06	.05	.02
311	Dick Schofield	.12	.09	.05	402	Bryan Little	.06	.05	.02
312	Daryl Sconiers	.06	.05	.02	403	Gary Lucas	.06	.05	.02
313	Jim Slaton	.06	.05	.02	404	David Palmer	.06	.05	.02
314	Derrel Thomas	.06	.05	.02	405	Tim Raines	.35	.25	.14
315	Rob Wilfong	.06	.05	.02	406	Mike Ramsey	.06	.05	.02
316	Mike Witt	.12	.09	.05	407	Jeff Reardon	.12	.09	.05
317	Geoff Zahn	.06	.05	.02	408	Steve Rogers	.08	.06	.03
318	Len Barker	.08	.06	.03	409	Dan Schatzeder	.06	.05	.02
319	Steve Bedrosian	.12	.09	.05	410	Bryn Smith	.06	.05	.02
320	Bruce Benedict	.06	.05	.02	411	Mike Stenhouse	.06	.05	.02
321	Rick Camp	.06	.05	.02	412	Tim Wallach	.12	.09	.05
322	Chris Chambliss	.08	.06	.03	413	Jim Wohlford	.06	.05	.02
323	*Jeff Dedmon*(FC)	.12	.09	.05	414	Bill Almon	.06	.05	.02
324	Terry Forster	.08	.06	.03	415	Keith Atherton	.06	.05	.02
325	Gene Garber	.06	.05	.02	416	Bruce Bochte	.06	.05	.02
326	*Albert Hall*(FC)	.15	.11	.06	417	Tom Burgmeier	.06	.05	.02
327	Terry Harper	.06	.05	.02	418	Ray Burris	.06	.05	.02
328	Bob Horner	.12	.09	.05	419	Bill Caudill	.06	.05	.02
329	Glenn Hubbard	.06	.05	.02	420	Chris Codiroli	.06	.05	.02
330	Randy Johnson	.06	.05	.02	421	Tim Conroy	.06	.05	.02
331	Brad Komminsk	.06	.05	.02	422	Mike Davis	.08	.06	.03
332	Rick Mahler	.06	.05	.02	423	Jim Essian	.06	.05	.02
333	Craig McMurtry	.06	.05	.02	424	Mike Heath	.06	.05	.02
334	Donnie Moore	.06	.05	.02	425	Rickey Henderson	.50	.40	.20
335	Dale Murphy	.60	.45	.25	426	Donnie Hill	.06	.05	.02
336	Ken Oberkfell	.06	.05	.02	427	Dave Kingman	.15	.11	.06
337	Pascual Perez	.08	.06	.03	428	Bill Krueger	.06	.05	.02
338	Gerald Perry	.35	.25	.14	429	Carney Lansford	.10	.08	.04
339	Rafael Ramirez	.06	.05	.02	430	Steve McCatty	.06	.05	.02
340	Jerry Royster	.06	.05	.02	431	Joe Morgan	.30	.25	.12
341	Alex Trevino	.06	.05	.02	432	Dwayne Murphy	.08	.06	.03
342	Claudell Washington	.08	.06	.03	433	Tony Phillips	.06	.05	.02
343	Alan Ashby	.06	.05	.02	434	Lary Sorensen	.06	.05	.02
344	*Mark Bailey*	.10	.08	.04	435	Mike Warren	.06	.05	.02
345	Kevin Bass	.10	.08	.04	436	*Curt Young*(FC)	.35	.25	.14
346	Enos Cabell	.06	.05	.02	437	Luis Aponte	.06	.05	.02
347	Jose Cruz	.10	.08	.04	438	Chris Bando	.06	.05	.02
348	Bill Dawley	.06	.05	.02	439	Tony Bernazard	.06	.05	.02
349	Frank DiPino	.06	.05	.02	440	Bert Blyleven	.15	.11	.06
350	Bill Doran	.12	.09	.05	441	Brett Butler	.10	.08	.04
351	Phil Garner	.08	.06	.03	442	Ernie Camacho	.06	.05	.02
352	Bob Knepper	.08	.06	.03	443	*Joe Carter*(FC)	3.00	2.25	1.25
353	Mike LaCoss	.06	.05	.02	444	Carmelo Castillo	.06	.05	.02
354	Jerry Mumphrey	.06	.05	.02	445	Jamie Easterly	.06	.05	.02
355	Joe Niekro	.10	.08	.04	446	*Steve Farr*(FC)	.30	.25	.12
356	Terry Puhl	.06	.05	.02	447	Mike Fischlin	.06	.05	.02
357	Craig Reynolds	.06	.05	.02	448	Julio Franco	.12	.09	.05
358	Vern Ruhle	.06	.05	.02	449	Mel Hall	.08	.06	.03
359	Nolan Ryan	.60	.45	.25	450	Mike Hargrove	.06	.05	.02
360	Joe Sambito	.06	.05	.02	451	Neal Heaton	.06	.05	.02
361	Mike Scott	.15	.11	.06	452	Brook Jacoby	.30	.25	.12
362	Dave Smith	.08	.06	.03	453	*Mike Jeffcoat*	.08	.06	.03
363	*Julio Solano*(FC)	.08	.06	.03	454	*Don Schulze*(FC)	.08	.06	.03
364	Dickie Thon	.08	.06	.03	455	Roy Smith	.06	.05	.02
365	Denny Walling	.06	.05	.02	456	Pat Tabler	.08	.06	.03

	MT	NR MT	EX			MT	NR MT	EX
457	Andre Thornton	.10	.08	.04	548	Joe Price	.06	.05	.02
458	George Vukovich	.06	.05	.02	549	Gary Redus	.08	.06	.03
459	Tom Waddell	.06	.05	.02	550	Pete Rose	1.00	.70	.40
460	Jerry Willard	.06	.05	.02	551	Jeff Russell(FC)	.10	.08	.04
461	Dale Berra	.06	.05	.02	552	Mario Soto	.08	.06	.03
462	John Candelaria	.10	.08	.04	553	*Jay Tibbs*(FC)	.15	.11	.06
463	Jose DeLeon	.08	.06	.03	554	Duane Walker	.06	.05	.02
464	Doug Frobel	.06	.05	.02	555	Alan Bannister	.06	.05	.02
465	Cecilio Guante	.06	.05	.02	556	Buddy Bell	.12	.09	.05
466	Brian Harper	.06	.05	.02	557	Danny Darwin	.06	.05	.02
467	Lee Lacy	.06	.05	.02	558	Charlie Hough	.08	.06	.03
468	Bill Madlock	.12	.09	.05	559	Bobby Jones	.06	.05	.02
469	Lee Mazzilli	.08	.06	.03	560	Odell Jones	.06	.05	.02
470	Larry McWilliams	.06	.05	.02	561	*Jeff Kunkel*(FC)	.10	.08	.04
471	Jim Morrison	.06	.05	.02	562	*Mike Mason*	.10	.08	.04
472	Tony Pena	.10	.08	.04	563	Pete O'Brien	.12	.09	.05
473	Johnny Ray	.12	.09	.05	564	Larry Parrish	.10	.08	.04
474	Rick Rhoden	.10	.08	.04	565	Mickey Rivers	.08	.06	.03
475	Don Robinson	.08	.06	.03	566	Billy Sample	.06	.05	.02
476	Rod Scurry	.06	.05	.02	567	Dave Schmidt	.06	.05	.02
477	Kent Tekulve	.08	.06	.03	568	Donnie Scott	.06	.05	.02
478	Jason Thompson	.06	.05	.02	569	Dave Stewart	.12	.09	.05
479	John Tudor	.10	.08	.04	570	Frank Tanana	.10	.08	.04
480	Lee Tunnell	.06	.05	.02	571	Wayne Tolleson	.06	.05	.02
481	Marvell Wynne	.06	.05	.02	572	Gary Ward	.08	.06	.03
482	Salome Barojas	.06	.05	.02	573	Curtis Wilkerson	.08	.06	.03
483	Dave Beard	.06	.05	.02	574	George Wright	.06	.05	.02
484	Jim Beattie	.06	.05	.02	575	Ned Yost	.06	.05	.02
485	Barry Bonnell	.06	.05	.02	576	Mark Brouhard	.06	.05	.02
486	*Phil Bradley*	.90	.70	.35	577	Mike Caldwell	.06	.05	.02
487	Al Cowens	.06	.05	.02	578	Bobby Clark	.06	.05	.02
488	*Alvin Davis*	2.25	1.75	.90	579	Jaime Cocanower	.06	.05	.02
489	Dave Henderson	.10	.08	.04	580	Cecil Cooper	.15	.11	.06
490	Steve Henderson	.06	.05	.02	581	Rollie Fingers	.20	.15	.08
491	Bob Kearney	.06	.05	.02	582	Jim Gantner	.08	.06	.03
492	*Mark Langston*	2.75	2.00	1.00	583	Moose Haas	.06	.05	.02
493	Larry Milbourne	.06	.05	.02	584	Dion James	.12	.09	.05
494	Paul Mirabella	.06	.05	.02	585	Pete Ladd	.06	.05	.02
495	Mike Moore	.06	.05	.02	586	Rick Manning	.06	.05	.02
496	Edwin Nunez(FC)	.08	.06	.03	587	Bob McClure	.06	.05	.02
497	Spike Owen	.08	.06	.03	588	Paul Molitor	.15	.11	.06
498	Jack Perconte	.06	.05	.02	589	Charlie Moore	.06	.05	.02
499	Ken Phelps	.10	.08	.04	590	Ben Oglivie	.08	.06	.03
500	*Jim Presley*(FC)	.80	.60	.30	591	Chuck Porter	.06	.05	.02
501	Mike Stanton	.06	.05	.02	592	*Randy Ready*(FC)	.20	.15	.08
502	Bob Stoddard	.06	.05	.02	593	Ed Romero	.06	.05	.02
503	Gorman Thomas	.10	.08	.04	594	Bill Schroeder(FC)	.10	.08	.04
504	Ed Vande Berg	.06	.05	.02	595	Ray Searage	.06	.05	.02
505	Matt Young	.06	.05	.02	596	Ted Simmons	.12	.09	.05
506	Juan Agosto	.06	.05	.02	597	Jim Sundberg	.08	.06	.03
507	Harold Baines	.15	.11	.06	598	Don Sutton	.30	.25	.12
508	Floyd Bannister	.10	.08	.04	599	Tom Tellmann	.06	.05	.02
509	Britt Burns	.06	.05	.02	600	Rick Waits	.06	.05	.02
510	Julio Cruz	.06	.05	.02	601	Robin Yount	.50	.40	.20
511	Richard Dotson	.10	.08	.04	602	Dusty Baker	.08	.06	.03
512	Jerry Dybzinski	.06	.05	.02	603	Bob Brenly	.06	.05	.02
513	Carlton Fisk	.30	.25	.12	604	Jack Clark	.20	.15	.08
514	Scott Fletcher	.08	.06	.03	605	Chili Davis	.10	.08	.04
515	Jerry Hairston	.06	.05	.02	606	Mark Davis	.06	.05	.02
516	Marc Hill	.06	.05	.02	607	*Dan Gladden*(FC)	.30	.25	.12
517	LaMarr Hoyt	.06	.05	.02	608	Atlee Hammaker	.06	.05	.02
518	Ron Kittle	.10	.08	.04	609	Mike Krukow	.08	.06	.03
519	Rudy Law	.06	.05	.02	610	Duane Kuiper	.06	.05	.02
520	Vance Law	.08	.06	.03	611	Bob Lacey	.06	.05	.02
521	Greg Luzinski	.10	.08	.04	612	Bill Laskey	.06	.05	.02
522	Gene Nelson	.06	.05	.02	613	Gary Lavelle	.06	.05	.02
523	Tom Paciorek	.06	.05	.02	614	Johnnie LeMaster	.06	.05	.02
524	Ron Reed	.06	.05	.02	615	Jeff Leonard	.10	.08	.04
525	Bert Roberge	.06	.05	.02	616	Randy Lerch	.06	.05	.02
526	Tom Seaver	.40	.30	.15	617	Greg Minton	.06	.05	.02
527	Roy Smalley	.06	.05	.02	618	Steve Nicosia	.06	.05	.02
528	Dan Spillner	.06	.05	.02	619	Gene Richards	.06	.05	.02
529	Mike Squires	.06	.05	.02	620	*Jeff Robinson*	.30	.25	.12
530	Greg Walker	.12	.09	.05	621	Scot Thompson	.06	.05	.02
531	Cesar Cedeno	.10	.08	.04	622	Manny Trillo	.08	.06	.03
532	Dave Concepcion	.12	.09	.05	623	Brad Wellman	.06	.05	.02
533	*Eric Davis*(FC)	18.00	13.50	7.25	624	*Frank Williams*	.15	.11	.06
534	Nick Esasky	.08	.06	.03	625	Joel Youngblood	.06	.05	.02
535	Tom Foley	.06	.05	.02	626	Ripken-In-Action (Cal Ripken)	.30	.25	.12
536	*John Franco*	.80	.60	.30	627	Schmidt-In-Action (Mike Schmidt)	.30	.25	.12
537	Brad Gulden	.06	.05	.02	628	Giving the Signs (Sparky Anderson)	.08	.06	.03
538	Tom Hume	.06	.05	.02	629	A.L. Pitcher's Nightmare (Rickey			
539	Wayne Krenchicki	.06	.05	.02		Henderson, Dave Winfield)	.30	.25	.12
540	Andy McGaffigan	.06	.05	.02	630	N.L. Pitcher's Nightmare (Ryne Sandberg,			
541	Eddie Milner	.06	.05	.02		Mike Schmidt)	.30	.25	.12
542	Ron Oester	.06	.05	.02	631	N.L. All-Stars (Gary Carter, Steve Garvey,			
543	Bob Owchinko	.06	.05	.02		Ozzie Smith, Darryl Strawberry)	.30	.25	.12
544	Dave Parker	.25	.20	.10	632	All-Star Game Winning Battery (Gary			
545	Frank Pastore	.06	.05	.02		Carter, Charlie Lea)	.15	.11	.06
546	Tony Perez	.15	.11	.06	633	N.L. Pennant Clinchers (Steve Garvey,			
547	Ted Power	.06	.05	.02		Goose Gossage)	.20	.15	.08

		MT	NR MT	EX
634	N.L. Rookie Phenoms (Dwight Gooden, Juan Samuel)	1.00	.70	.40
635	Toronto's Big Guns (Willie Upshaw)	.08	.06	.03
636	Toronto's Big Guns (Lloyd Moseby)	.08	.06	.03
637	Holland (Al Holland)	.08	.06	.03
638	Tunnell (Lee Tunnell)	.08	.06	.03
639	500th Homer (Reggie Jackson)	.30	.25	.12
640	4,000th Hit (Pete Rose)	.50	.40	.20
641	Father & Son (Cal Ripken, Jr., Cal Ripken, Sr.)	.30	.25	.12
642	Cubs Team	.08	.06	.03
643	1984's Two Perfect Games & One No Hitter (Jack Morris, David Palmer, Mike Witt)	.15	.11	.06
644	Major League Prospect (Willie Lozado, Vic Mata)	.06	.05	.02
645	Major League Prospect (*Kelly Gruber, Randy O'Neal*)(FC)	1.00	.70	.40
646	Major League Prospect (*Jose Roman, Joel Skinner*)(FC)	.12	.09	.05
647	Major League Prospect (*Steve Kiefer, Danny Tartabull*)(FC)	5.00	3.75	2.00
648	Major League Prospect (*Rob Deer, Alejandro Sanchez*)(FC)	1.50	1.25	.60
649	Major League Prospect (*Shawon Dunston, Bill Hatcher*)(FC)	2.00	1.50	.80
650	Major League Prospect (*Mike Bielecki, Ron Robinson*)(FC)	.30	.25	.12
651	Major League Prospect (*Zane Smith, Paul Zuvella*)(FC)	.35	.25	.14
652	Major League Prospect (*Glenn Davis, Joe Hesketh*)(FC)	8.00	6.00	3.25
653	Major League Prospect (*Steve Jeltz, John Russell*)(FC)	.20	.15	.08
654	Checklist 1-95	.06	.05	.02
655	Checklist 96-195	.06	.05	.02
656	Checklist 196-292	.06	.05	.02
657	Checklist 293-391	.06	.05	.02
658	Checklist 392-481	.06	.05	.02
659	Checklist 482-575	.06	.05	.02
660	Checklist 576-660	.06	.05	.02

		MT	NR MT	EX
8	Andre Dawson	.15	.11	.06
9	Steve Garvey	.25	.20	.10
10	Goose Gossage	.12	.09	.05
11	Tony Gwynn	.40	.30	.15
12	Keith Hernandez	.20	.15	.08
13	Kent Hrbek	.15	.11	.06
14	Reggie Jackson	.30	.25	.12
15	Dave Kingman	.10	.08	.04
16	Ron Kittle	.07	.05	.03
17	Mark Langston	.25	.20	.10
18	Jeff Leonard	.05	.04	.02
19	Bill Madlock	.07	.05	.03
20	Don Mattingly	1.50	1.25	.60
21	Jack Morris	.15	.11	.06
22	Dale Murphy	.30	.25	.12
23	Eddie Murray	.25	.20	.10
24	Tony Pena	.07	.05	.03
25	Dan Quisenberry	.07	.05	.03
26	Tim Raines	.25	.20	.10
27	Jim Rice	.25	.20	.10
28	Cal Ripken, Jr.	.30	.25	.12
29	Pete Rose	.60	.45	.25
30	Nolan Ryan	.70	.50	.30
31	Ryne Sandberg	.20	.15	.08
32	Steve Sax	.15	.11	.06
33	Mike Schmidt	.50	.40	.20
34	Tom Seaver	.50	.40	.20
35	Ozzie Smith	.12	.09	.05
36	Mario Soto	.05	.04	.02
37	Dave Stieb	.10	.08	.04
38	Darryl Strawberry	.60	.45	.25
39	Rick Sutcliffe	.10	.08	.04
40	Alan Trammell	.20	.15	.08
41	Willie Upshaw	.05	.04	.02
42	Fernando Valenzuela	.20	.15	.08
43	Dave Winfield	.25	.20	.10
44	Robin Yount	.50	.40	.20

1985 Fleer Limited Edition

The 1985 Fleer Limited Edition 44-card set was distributed through McCrory's, J.J. Newbury, McClellan, Kress, YDC, and Green stores. The cards, which are the standard 2-1/2" by 3-1/2" size, have full-color photos inside a red and yellow frame. The card backs are set in black type against two different shades of yellow and contain the player's personal and statistical information. The set was issued in a specially designed box which carried the complete checklist for the set on the back. Six team logo stickers were also included with the set.

		MT	NR MT	EX
Complete Set:		8.00	6.00	3.25
Common Player:		.05	.04	.02
1	Buddy Bell	.07	.05	.03
2	Bert Blyleven	.10	.08	.04
3	Wade Boggs	.70	.50	.30
4	George Brett	.30	.25	.12
5	Rod Carew	.30	.25	.12
6	Steve Carlton	.25	.20	.10
7	Alvin Davis	.20	.15	.08

1985 Fleer Update

For the second straight year, Fleer issued a 132-card update set. The cards, which measure 2-1/2" by 3-1/2", portray players on their new teams and also includes rookies not depicted in the regular issue. The cards are identical in design to the 1985 Fleer set but are numbered U-1 through U-132. The set was issued with team logo stickers in a specially designed box and was available only through hobby dealers.

		MT	NR MT	EX
Complete Set:		16.00	12.00	6.50
Common Player:		.10	.08	.04
1	Don Aase	.15	.11	.06
2	Bill Almon	.10	.08	.04
3	Dusty Baker	.15	.11	.06
4	Dale Berra	.10	.08	.04
5	Karl Best(FC)	.10	.08	.04
6	Tim Birtsas(FC)	.20	.15	.08
7	Vida Blue	.20	.15	.08
8	Rich Bordi	.10	.08	.04
9	Daryl Boston(FC)	.20	.15	.08
10	Hubie Brooks	.20	.15	.08
11	Chris Brown(FC)	.25	.20	.10
12	Tom Browning(FC)	1.25	.90	.50
13	Al Bumbry	.10	.08	.04
14	Tim Burke(FC)	.50	.40	.20
15	Ray Burris	.10	.08	.04

		MT	NR MT	EX
16	Jeff Burroughs	.15	.11	.06
17	Ivan Calderon(FC)	.60	.45	.25
18	Jeff Calhoun	.10	.08	.04
19	Bill Campbell	.10	.08	.04
20	Don Carman(FC)	.40	.30	.15
21	Gary Carter	.80	.60	.30
22	Bobby Castillo	.10	.08	.04
23	Bill Caudill	.10	.08	.04
24	Rick Cerone	.10	.08	.04
25	Jack Clark	.35	.25	.14
26	Pat Clements(FC)	.20	.15	.08
27	Stewart Cliburn(FC)	.15	.11	.06
28	Vince Coleman(FC)	4.00	3.00	1.50
29	Dave Collins	.15	.11	.06
30	Fritz Connally	.10	.08	.04
31	Henry Cotto(FC)	.20	.15	.08
32	Danny Darwin	.15	.11	.06
33	Darren Daulton(FC)	.20	.15	.08
34	Jerry Davis	.10	.08	.04
35	Brian Dayett	.10	.08	.04
36	Ken Dixon(FC)	.10	.08	.04
37	Tommy Dunbar	.10	.08	.04
38	Mariano Duncan(FC)	.20	.15	.08
39	Bob Fallon	.10	.08	.04
40	Brian Fisher(FC)	.40	.30	.15
41	Mike Fitzgerald	.10	.08	.04
42	Ray Fontenot	.10	.08	.04
43	Greg Gagne(FC)	.35	.25	.14
44	Oscar Gamble	.15	.11	.06
45	Jim Gott	.10	.08	.04
46	David Green	.10	.08	.04
47	Alfredo Griffin	.15	.11	.06
48	Ozzie Guillen(FC)	.80	.60	.30
49	Toby Harrah	.15	.11	.06
50	Ron Hassey	.10	.08	.04
51	Rickey Henderson	1.25	.90	.50
52	Steve Henderson	.10	.08	.04
53	George Hendrick	.15	.11	.06
54	Teddy Higuera(FC)	2.25	1.75	.90
55	Al Holland	.10	.08	.04
56	Burt Hooton	.15	.11	.06
57	Jay Howell	.15	.11	.06
58	LaMarr Hoyt	.10	.08	.04
59	Tim Hulett(FC)	.20	.15	.08
60	Bob James	.10	.08	.04
61	Cliff Johnson	.10	.08	.04
62	Howard Johnson	1.50	1.25	.60
63	Ruppert Jones	.10	.08	.04
64	Steve Kemp	.15	.11	.06
65	Bruce Kison	.10	.08	.04
66	Mike LaCoss	.15	.11	.06
67	Lee Lacy	.15	.11	.06
68	Dave LaPoint	.20	.15	.08
69	Gary Lavelle	.10	.08	.04
70	Vance Law	.15	.11	.06
71	Manny Lee(FC)	.20	.15	.08
72	Sixto Lezcano	.10	.08	.04
73	Tim Lollar	.10	.08	.04
74	Urbano Lugo(FC)	.15	.11	.06
75	Fred Lynn	.30	.25	.12
76	Steve Lyons(FC)	.15	.11	.06
77	Mickey Mahler	.10	.08	.04
78	Ron Mathis(FC)	.10	.08	.04
79	Len Matuszek	.10	.08	.04
80	Oddibe McDowell(FC)	.70	.50	.30
81	Roger McDowell(FC)	.90	.70	.35
82	Donnie Moore	.10	.08	.04
83	Ron Musselman	.10	.08	.04
84	Al Oliver	.25	.20	.10
85	Joe Orsulak(FC)	.20	.15	.08
86	Dan Pasqua(FC)	.50	.40	.20
87	Chris Pittaro(FC)	.10	.08	.04
88	Rick Reuschel	.20	.15	.08
89	Earnie Riles(FC)	.20	.15	.08
90	Jerry Royster	.10	.08	.04
91	Dave Rozema	.10	.08	.04
92	Dave Rucker	.10	.08	.04
93	Vern Ruhle	.10	.08	.04
94	Mark Salas(FC)	.20	.15	.08
95	Luis Salazar	.10	.08	.04
96	Joe Sambito	.10	.08	.04
97	Billy Sample	.10	.08	.04
98	Alex Sanchez	.10	.08	.04
99	Calvin Schiraldi(FC)	.25	.20	.10
100	Rick Schu(FC)	.20	.15	.08
101	Larry Sheets(FC)	.50	.40	.20
102	Ron Shepherd	.10	.08	.04
103	Nelson Simmons(FC)	.10	.08	.04
104	Don Slaught	.10	.08	.04
105	Roy Smalley	.15	.11	.06
106	Lonnie Smith	.15	.11	.06

		MT	NR MT	EX
107	Nate Snell(FC)	.10	.08	.04
108	Lary Sorensen	.10	.08	.04
109	Chris Speier	.10	.08	.04
110	Mike Stenhouse	.10	.08	.04
111	Tim Stoddard	.10	.08	.04
112	John Stuper	.10	.08	.04
113	Jim Sundberg	.15	.11	.06
114	Bruce Sutter	.25	.20	.10
115	Don Sutton	.60	.45	.25
116	Bruce Tanner(FC)	.10	.08	.04
117	Kent Tekulve	.15	.11	.06
118	Walt Terrell	.15	.11	.06
119	Mickey Tettleton(FC)	1.00	.70	.40
120	Rich Thompson	.10	.08	.04
121	Louis Thornton(FC)	.10	.08	.04
122	Alex Trevino	.10	.08	.04
123	John Tudor	.30	.25	.12
124	Jose Uribe(FC)	.25	.20	.10
125	Dave Valle(FC)	.20	.15	.08
126	Dave Von Ohlen	.10	.08	.04
127	Curt Wardle	.10	.08	.04
128	U.L. Washington	.10	.08	.04
129	Ed Whitson	.10	.08	.04
130	Herm Winningham(FC)	.20	.15	.08
131	Rich Yett(FC)	.15	.11	.06
132	Checklist	.10	.08	.04

1986 Fleer

The 1986 Fleer set contains 660 color photos, with each card measuring 2-1/2" by 3-1/2" in size. The card fronts include the word "Fleer," the player's team logo, and a player picture enclosed by a dark blue border. The card reverses are minus the black and white photo that was included in past Fleer efforts. Player biographical and statistical information appear in black and yellow ink on white stock. As in 1985, Fleer devoted ten cards, entitled "Major League Prospects," to twenty promising rookie players. The 1986 set, as in the previous four years, was issued with team logo stickers.

		MT	NR MT	EX
Complete Set:		85.00	64.00	34.00
Common Player:		.06	.05	.02
1	Steve Balboni	.08	.06	.03
2	Joe Beckwith	.06	.05	.02
3	Buddy Biancalana	.06	.05	.02
4	Bud Black	.06	.05	.02
5	George Brett	.50	.40	.20
6	Onix Concepcion	.06	.05	.02
7	Steve Farr	.08	.06	.03
8	Mark Gubicza	.12	.09	.05
9	Dane Iorg	.06	.05	.02
10	Danny Jackson	.20	.15	.08
11	Lynn Jones	.06	.05	.02
12	Mike Jones	.06	.05	.02
13	Charlie Leibrandt	.08	.06	.03
14	Hal McRae	.10	.08	.04
15	Omar Moreno	.06	.05	.02
16	Darryl Motley	.06	.05	.02
17	Jorge Orta	.06	.05	.02
18	Dan Quisenberry	.08	.06	.03
19	Bret Saberhagen	1.00	.70	.40
20	Pat Sheridan	.06	.05	.02

		MT	NR MT	EX
21	Lonnie Smith	.08	.06	.03
22	Jim Sundberg	.08	.06	.03
23	John Wathan	.08	.06	.03
24	Frank White	.10	.08	.04
25	Willie Wilson	.12	.09	.05
26	Joaquin Andujar	.08	.06	.03
27	Steve Braun	.06	.05	.02
28	Bill Campbell	.06	.05	.02
29	Cesar Cedeno	.10	.08	.04
30	Jack Clark	.20	.15	.08
31	*Vince Coleman*	1.75	1.25	.70
32	Danny Cox	.10	.08	.04
33	Ken Dayley	.06	.05	.02
34	Ivan DeJesus	.06	.05	.02
35	Bob Forsch	.08	.06	.03
36	Brian Harper	.06	.05	.02
37	Tom Herr	.10	.08	.04
38	Ricky Horton	.08	.06	.03
39	Kurt Kepshire	.06	.05	.02
40	Jeff Lahti	.06	.05	.02
41	Tito Landrum	.06	.05	.02
42	Willie McGee	.15	.11	.06
43	Tom Nieto	.06	.05	.02
44	Terry Pendleton	.15	.11	.06
45	Darrell Porter	.08	.06	.03
46	Ozzie Smith	.15	.11	.06
47	John Tudor	.10	.08	.04
48	Andy Van Slyke	.15	.11	.06
49	*Todd Worrell*(FC)	.90	.70	.35
50	Jim Acker	.06	.05	.02
51	Doyle Alexander	.10	.08	.04
52	Jesse Barfield	.20	.15	.08
53	George Bell	.30	.25	.12
54	Jeff Burroughs	.08	.06	.03
55	Bill Caudill	.06	.05	.02
56	Jim Clancy	.08	.06	.03
57	Tony Fernandez	.20	.15	.08
58	Tom Filer	.06	.05	.02
59	Damaso Garcia	.06	.05	.02
60	Tom Henke(FC)	.15	.11	.06
61	Garth Iorg	.06	.05	.02
62	Cliff Johnson	.06	.05	.02
63	Jimmy Key	.15	.11	.06
64	Dennis Lamp	.06	.05	.02
65	Gary Lavelle	.06	.05	.02
66	Buck Martinez	.06	.05	.02
67	Lloyd Moseby	.10	.08	.04
68	Rance Mulliniks	.06	.05	.02
69	Al Oliver	.10	.08	.04
70	Dave Stieb	.12	.09	.05
71	Louis Thornton	.06	.05	.02
72	Willie Upshaw	.08	.06	.03
73	Ernie Whitt	.08	.06	.03
74	*Rick Aguilera*(FC)	.25	.20	.10
75	Wally Backman	.08	.06	.03
76	Gary Carter	.25	.20	.10
77	Ron Darling	.15	.11	.06
78	*Len Dykstra*(FC)	.60	.45	.25
79	Sid Fernandez	.12	.09	.05
80	George Foster	.15	.11	.06
81	Dwight Gooden	2.00	1.50	.80
82	Tom Gorman	.06	.05	.02
83	Danny Heep	.06	.05	.02
84	Keith Hernandez	.30	.25	.12
85	Howard Johnson	.12	.09	.05
86	Ray Knight	.08	.06	.03
87	Terry Leach	.08	.06	.03
88	Ed Lynch	.06	.05	.02
89	*Roger McDowell*(FC)	.40	.30	.15
90	Jesse Orosco	.08	.06	.03
91	Tom Paciorek	.06	.05	.02
92	Ronn Reynolds	.06	.05	.02
93	Rafael Santana	.06	.05	.02
94	Doug Sisk	.06	.05	.02
95	Rusty Staub	.10	.08	.04
96	Darryl Strawberry	1.75	1.25	.70
97	Mookie Wilson	.10	.08	.04
98	Neil Allen	.06	.05	.02
99	Don Baylor	.12	.09	.05
100	Dale Berra	.06	.05	.02
101	Rich Bordi	.06	.05	.02
102	Marty Bystrom	.06	.05	.02
103	Joe Cowley	.06	.05	.02
104	*Brian Fisher*	.30	.25	.12
105	Ken Griffey	.10	.08	.04
106	Ron Guidry	.20	.15	.08
107	Ron Hassey	.06	.05	.02
108	Rickey Henderson	.40	.30	.15
109	Don Mattingly	4.00	3.00	1.50
110	Bobby Meacham	.06	.05	.02
111	John Montefusco	.06	.05	.02
112	Phil Niekro	.25	.20	.10
113	Mike Pagliarulo	.20	.15	.08
114	Dan Pasqua	.20	.15	.08
115	Willie Randolph	.10	.08	.04
116	Dave Righetti	.20	.15	.08
117	Andre Robertson	.06	.05	.02
118	Billy Sample	.06	.05	.02
119	Bob Shirley	.06	.05	.02
120	Ed Whitson	.06	.05	.02
121	Dave Winfield	.30	.25	.12
122	Butch Wynegar	.06	.05	.02
123	Dave Anderson	.06	.05	.02
124	Bob Bailor	.06	.05	.02
125	Greg Brock	.08	.06	.03
126	Enos Cabell	.06	.05	.02
127	Bobby Castillo	.06	.05	.02
128	Carlos Diaz	.06	.05	.02
129	*Mariano Duncan*	.15	.11	.06
130	Pedro Guerrero	.20	.15	.08
131	Orel Hershiser	1.25	.90	.50
132	Rick Honeycutt	.06	.05	.02
133	Ken Howell	.06	.05	.02
134	Ken Landreaux	.06	.05	.02
135	Bill Madlock	.12	.09	.05
136	Candy Maldonado	.10	.08	.04
137	Mike Marshall	.15	.11	.06
138	Len Matuszek	.06	.05	.02
139	Tom Niedenfuer	.08	.06	.03
140	Alejandro Pena	.08	.06	.03
141	Jerry Reuss	.08	.06	.03
142	Bill Russell	.08	.06	.03
143	Steve Sax	.20	.15	.08
144	Mike Scioscia	.08	.06	.03
145	Fernando Valenzuela	.30	.25	.12
146	Bob Welch	.12	.09	.05
147	Terry Whitfield	.06	.05	.02
148	Juan Beniquez	.06	.05	.02
149	Bob Boone	.08	.06	.03
150	John Candelaria	.10	.08	.04
151	Rod Carew	.30	.25	.12
152	*Stewart Cliburn*(FC)	.12	.09	.05
153	Doug DeCinces	.10	.08	.04
154	Brian Downing	.08	.06	.03
155	Ken Forsch	.06	.05	.02
156	Craig Gerber	.06	.05	.02
157	Bobby Grich	.10	.08	.04
158	George Hendrick	.08	.06	.03
159	Al Holland	.06	.05	.02
160	Reggie Jackson	.35	.25	.14
161	Ruppert Jones	.06	.05	.02
162	*Urbano Lugo*	.08	.06	.03
163	*Kirk McCaskill*(FC)	.35	.25	.14
164	Donnie Moore	.06	.05	.02
165	Gary Pettis	.06	.05	.02
166	Ron Romanick	.06	.05	.02
167	Dick Schofield	.06	.05	.02
168	Daryl Sconiers	.06	.05	.02
169	Jim Slaton	.06	.05	.02
170	Don Sutton	.25	.20	.10
171	Mike Witt	.10	.08	.04
172	Buddy Bell	.10	.08	.04
173	Tom Browning	.30	.25	.12
174	Dave Concepcion	.12	.09	.05
175	Eric Davis	3.00	2.25	1.25
176	Bo Diaz	.08	.06	.03
177	Nick Esasky	.08	.06	.03
178	John Franco	.12	.09	.05
179	Tom Hume	.06	.05	.02
180	Wayne Krenchicki	.06	.05	.02
181	Andy McGaffigan	.06	.05	.02
182	Eddie Milner	.06	.05	.02
183	Ron Oester	.06	.05	.02
184	Dave Parker	.20	.15	.08
185	Frank Pastore	.06	.05	.02
186	Tony Perez	.15	.11	.06
187	Ted Power	.08	.06	.03
188	Joe Price	.06	.05	.02
189	Gary Redus	.06	.05	.02
190	Ron Robinson	.08	.06	.03
191	Pete Rose	.70	.50	.30
192	Mario Soto	.08	.06	.03
193	John Stuper	.06	.05	.02
194	Jay Tibbs	.06	.05	.02
195	Dave Van Gorder	.06	.05	.02
196	Max Venable	.06	.05	.02
197	Juan Agosto	.06	.05	.02
198	Harold Baines	.15	.11	.06
199	Floyd Bannister	.10	.08	.04
200	Britt Burns	.06	.05	.02
201	Julio Cruz	.06	.05	.02
202	*Joel Davis*(FC)	.08	.06	.03

		MT	NR MT	EX				MT	NR MT	EX
203	Richard Dotson	.10	.08	.04		294	Kevin Bass	.10	.08	.04
204	Carlton Fisk	.30	.25	.12		295	Jeff Calhoun	.06	.05	.02
205	Scott Fletcher	.08	.06	.03		296	Jose Cruz	.10	.08	.04
206	*Ozzie Guillen*	.40	.30	.15		297	Glenn Davis	.70	.50	.30
207	Jerry Hairston	.06	.05	.02		298	Bill Dawley	.06	.05	.02
208	Tim Hulett	.08	.06	.03		299	Frank DiPino	.06	.05	.02
209	Bob James	.06	.05	.02		300	Bill Doran	.10	.08	.04
210	Ron Kittle	.10	.08	.04		301	Phil Garner	.08	.06	.03
211	Rudy Law	.06	.05	.02		302	*Jeff Heathcock*(FC)	.10	.08	.04
212	Bryan Little	.06	.05	.02		303	*Charlie Kerfeld*(FC)	.15	.11	.06
213	Gene Nelson	.06	.05	.02		304	Bob Knepper	.08	.06	.03
214	Reid Nichols	.06	.05	.02		305	Ron Mathis	.06	.05	.02
215	Luis Salazar	.06	.05	.02		306	Jerry Mumphrey	.06	.05	.02
216	Tom Seaver	.40	.30	.15		307	Jim Pankovits	.06	.05	.02
217	Dan Spillner	.06	.05	.02		308	Terry Puhl	.06	.05	.02
218	Bruce Tanner	.06	.05	.02		309	Craig Reynolds	.06	.05	.02
219	Greg Walker	.10	.08	.04		310	Nolan Ryan	.50	.40	.20
220	Dave Wehrmeister	.06	.05	.02		311	Mike Scott	.15	.11	.06
221	Juan Berenguer	.06	.05	.02		312	Dave Smith	.08	.06	.03
222	Dave Bergman	.06	.05	.02		313	Dickie Thon	.08	.06	.03
223	Tom Brookens	.06	.05	.02		314	Denny Walling	.06	.05	.02
224	Darrell Evans	.12	.09	.05		315	Kurt Bevacqua	.06	.05	.02
225	Barbaro Garbey	.06	.05	.02		316	Al Bumbry	.06	.05	.02
226	Kirk Gibson	.30	.25	.12		317	Jerry Davis	.06	.05	.02
227	John Grubb	.06	.05	.02		318	Luis DeLeon	.06	.05	.02
228	Willie Hernandez	.08	.06	.03		319	Dave Dravecky	.08	.06	.03
229	Larry Herndon	.08	.06	.03		320	Tim Flannery	.06	.05	.02
230	Chet Lemon	.08	.06	.03		321	Steve Garvey	.30	.25	.12
231	Aurelio Lopez	.06	.05	.02		322	Goose Gossage	.20	.15	.08
232	Jack Morris	.20	.15	.08		323	Tony Gwynn	.40	.30	.15
233	Randy O'Neal	.06	.05	.02		324	Andy Hawkins	.06	.05	.02
234	Lance Parrish	.20	.15	.08		325	LaMarr Hoyt	.06	.05	.02
235	Dan Petry	.08	.06	.03		326	Roy Lee Jackson	.06	.05	.02
236	Alex Sanchez	.06	.05	.02		327	Terry Kennedy	.08	.06	.03
237	Bill Scherrer	.06	.05	.02		328	Craig Lefferts	.06	.05	.02
238	Nelson Simmons	.06	.05	.02		329	Carmelo Martinez	.08	.06	.03
239	Frank Tanana	.10	.08	.04		330	*Lance McCullers*(FC)	.25	.20	.10
240	Walt Terrell	.08	.06	.03		331	Kevin McReynolds	.30	.25	.12
241	Alan Trammell	.30	.25	.12		332	Graig Nettles	.15	.11	.06
242	Lou Whitaker	.30	.25	.12		333	Jerry Royster	.06	.05	.02
243	Milt Wilcox	.06	.05	.02		334	Eric Show	.08	.06	.03
244	Hubie Brooks	.10	.08	.04		335	Tim Stoddard	.06	.05	.02
245	*Tim Burke*(FC)	.30	.25	.12		336	Garry Templeton	.08	.06	.03
246	Andre Dawson	.20	.15	.08		337	Mark Thurmond	.06	.05	.02
247	Mike Fitzgerald	.06	.05	.02		338	Ed Wojna	.06	.05	.02
248	Terry Francona	.06	.05	.02		339	Tony Armas	.08	.06	.03
249	Bill Gullickson	.06	.05	.02		340	Marty Barrett	.10	.08	.04
250	Joe Hesketh	.06	.05	.02		341	Wade Boggs	2.25	1.75	.90
251	Bill Laskey	.06	.05	.02		342	Dennis Boyd	.08	.06	.03
252	Vance Law	.08	.06	.03		343	Bill Buckner	.12	.09	.05
253	Charlie Lea	.06	.05	.02		344	Mark Clear	.06	.05	.02
254	Gary Lucas	.06	.05	.02		345	Roger Clemens	3.00	2.25	1.25
255	David Palmer	.06	.05	.02		346	Steve Crawford	.06	.05	.02
256	Tim Raines	.30	.25	.12		347	Mike Easler	.08	.06	.03
257	Jeff Reardon	.12	.09	.05		348	Dwight Evans	.12	.09	.05
258	Bert Roberge	.06	.05	.02		349	Rich Gedman	.10	.08	.04
259	Dan Schatzeder	.06	.05	.02		350	Jackie Gutierrez	.06	.05	.02
260	Bryn Smith	.06	.05	.02		351	Glenn Hoffman	.06	.05	.02
261	Randy St. Claire(FC)	.08	.06	.03		352	Bruce Hurst	.12	.09	.05
262	Scot Thompson	.06	.05	.02		353	Bruce Kison	.06	.05	.02
263	Tim Wallach	.12	.09	.05		354	Tim Lollar	.06	.05	.02
264	U.L. Washington	.06	.05	.02		355	Steve Lyons	.08	.06	.03
265	*Mitch Webster*(FC)	.25	.20	.10		356	Al Nipper	.08	.06	.03
266	*Herm Winningham*	.15	.11	.06		357	Bob Ojeda	.08	.06	.03
267	*Floyd Youmans*(FC)	.30	.25	.12		358	Jim Rice	.30	.25	.12
268	Don Aase	.06	.05	.02		359	Bob Stanley	.06	.05	.02
269	Mike Boddicker	.08	.06	.03		360	Mike Trujillo	.06	.05	.02
270	Rich Dauer	.06	.05	.02		361	Thad Bosley	.06	.05	.02
271	Storm Davis	.10	.08	.04		362	Warren Brusstar	.06	.05	.02
272	Rick Dempsey	.08	.06	.03		363	Ron Cey	.10	.08	.04
273	Ken Dixon	.06	.05	.02		364	Jody Davis	.10	.08	.04
274	Jim Dwyer	.06	.05	.02		365	Bob Dernier	.06	.05	.02
275	Mike Flanagan	.10	.08	.04		366	Shawon Dunston	.15	.11	.06
276	Wayne Gross	.06	.05	.02		367	Leon Durham	.08	.06	.03
277	Lee Lacy	.06	.05	.02		368	Dennis Eckersley	.12	.09	.05
278	Fred Lynn	.20	.15	.08		369	Ray Fontenot	.06	.05	.02
279	Tippy Martinez	.06	.05	.02		370	George Frazier	.06	.05	.02
280	Dennis Martinez	.08	.06	.03		371	Bill Hatcher	.10	.08	.04
281	Scott McGregor	.08	.06	.03		372	Dave Lopes	.08	.06	.03
282	Eddie Murray	.40	.30	.15		373	Gary Matthews	.10	.08	.04
283	Floyd Rayford	.06	.05	.02		374	Ron Meredith	.06	.05	.02
284	Cal Ripken, Jr.	.40	.30	.15		375	Keith Moreland	.08	.06	.03
285	Gary Roenicke	.06	.05	.02		376	Reggie Patterson	.06	.05	.02
286	Larry Sheets	.20	.15	.08		377	Dick Ruthven	.06	.05	.02
287	John Shelby	.06	.05	.02		378	Ryne Sandberg	.40	.30	.15
288	Nate Snell	.06	.05	.02		379	Scott Sanderson	.06	.05	.02
289	Sammy Stewart	.06	.05	.02		380	Lee Smith	.10	.08	.04
290	Alan Wiggins	.06	.05	.02		381	Lary Sorensen	.06	.05	.02
291	Mike Young	.06	.05	.02		382	Chris Speier	.06	.05	.02
292	Alan Ashby	.06	.05	.02		383	Rick Sutcliffe	.12	.09	.05
293	Mark Bailey	.06	.05	.02		384	Steve Trout	.06	.05	.02

		MT	NR MT	EX				MT	NR MT	EX
385	Gary Woods	.06	.05	.02	476	Danny Tartabull	.50	.40	.20
386	Bert Blyleven	.15	.11	.06	477	Gorman Thomas	.10	.08	.04
387	Tom Brunansky	.12	.09	.05	478	Roy Thomas	.06	.05	.02
388	Randy Bush	.06	.05	.02	479	Ed Vande Berg	.06	.05	.02
389	John Butcher	.06	.05	.02	480	Frank Wills	.06	.05	.02
390	Ron Davis	.06	.05	.02	481	Matt Young	.06	.05	.02
391	Dave Engle	.06	.05	.02	482	Ray Burris	.06	.05	.02
392	Frank Eufemia	.06	.05	.02	483	Jaime Cocanower	.06	.05	.02
393	Pete Filson	.06	.05	.02	484	Cecil Cooper	.12	.09	.05
394	Gary Gaetti	.20	.15	.08	485	Danny Darwin	.06	.05	.02
395	Greg Gagne	.10	.08	.04	486	Rollie Fingers	.20	.15	.08
396	Mickey Hatcher	.06	.05	.02	487	Jim Gantner	.08	.06	.03
397	Kent Hrbek	.20	.15	.08	488	Bob Gibson	.06	.05	.02
398	Tim Laudner	.06	.05	.02	489	Moose Haas	.06	.05	.02
399	Rick Lysander	.06	.05	.02	490	*Teddy Higuera*	1.00	.70	.40
400	Dave Meier	.06	.05	.02	491	Paul Householder	.06	.05	.02
401	Kirby Puckett	1.25	.90	.50	492	Pete Ladd	.06	.05	.02
402	Mark Salas	.08	.06	.03	493	Rick Manning	.06	.05	.02
403	Ken Schrom	.06	.05	.02	494	Bob McClure	.06	.05	.02
404	Roy Smalley	.06	.05	.02	495	Paul Molitor	.15	.11	.06
405	Mike Smithson	.06	.05	.02	496	Charlie Moore	.06	.05	.02
406	Mike Stenhouse	.06	.05	.02	497	Ben Oglivie	.08	.06	.03
407	Tim Teufel	.06	.05	.02	498	Randy Ready	.06	.05	.02
408	Frank Viola	.15	.11	.06	499	*Earnie Riles*	.20	.15	.08
409	Ron Washington	.06	.05	.02	500	Ed Romero	.06	.05	.02
410	Keith Atherton	.06	.05	.02	501	Bill Schroeder	.06	.05	.02
411	Dusty Baker	.08	.06	.03	502	Ray Searage	.06	.05	.02
412	*Tim Birtsas*	.12	.09	.05	503	Ted Simmons	.12	.09	.05
413	Bruce Bochte	.06	.05	.02	504	Pete Vuckovich	.08	.06	.03
414	Chris Codiroli	.06	.05	.02	505	Rick Waits	.06	.05	.02
415	Dave Collins	.08	.06	.03	506	Robin Yount	.30	.25	.12
416	Mike Davis	.08	.06	.03	507	Len Barker	.08	.06	.03
417	Alfredo Griffin	.08	.06	.03	508	Steve Bedrosian	.12	.09	.05
418	Mike Heath	.06	.05	.02	509	Bruce Benedict	.06	.05	.02
419	Steve Henderson	.06	.05	.02	510	Rick Camp	.06	.05	.02
420	Donnie Hill	.06	.05	.02	511	Rick Cerone	.06	.05	.02
421	Jay Howell	.08	.06	.03	512	Chris Chambliss	.08	.06	.03
422	Tommy John	.20	.15	.08	513	Jeff Dedmon	.06	.05	.02
423	Dave Kingman	.15	.11	.06	514	Terry Forster	.08	.06	.03
424	Bill Krueger	.06	.05	.02	515	Gene Garber	.06	.05	.02
425	Rick Langford	.06	.05	.02	516	Terry Harper	.06	.05	.02
426	Carney Lansford	.10	.08	.04	517	Bob Horner	.12	.09	.05
427	Steve McCatty	.06	.05	.02	518	Glenn Hubbard	.06	.05	.02
428	Dwayne Murphy	.08	.06	.03	519	*Joe Johnson*(FC)	.08	.06	.03
429	*Steve Ontiveros*(FC)	.12	.09	.05	520	Brad Komminsk	.06	.05	.02
430	Tony Phillips	.06	.05	.02	521	Rick Mahler	.06	.05	.02
431	Jose Rijo	.10	.08	.04	522	Dale Murphy	.50	.40	.20
432	*Mickey Tettleton*	.90	.70	.35	523	Ken Oberkfell	.06	.05	.02
433	Luis Aguayo	.06	.05	.02	524	Pascual Perez	.08	.06	.03
434	Larry Andersen	.06	.05	.02	525	Gerald Perry	.12	.09	.05
435	Steve Carlton	.30	.25	.12	526	Rafael Ramirez	.06	.05	.02
436	*Don Carman*	.30	.25	.12	527	*Steve Shields*(FC)	.12	.09	.05
437	Tim Corcoran	.06	.05	.02	528	Zane Smith	.10	.08	.04
438	*Darren Daulton*	.12	.09	.05	529	Bruce Sutter	.12	.09	.05
439	John Denny	.06	.05	.02	530	*Milt Thompson*(FC)	.30	.25	.12
440	Tom Foley	.06	.05	.02	531	Claudell Washington	.08	.06	.03
441	Greg Gross	.06	.05	.02	532	Paul Zuvella	.06	.05	.02
442	Kevin Gross	.08	.06	.03	533	Vida Blue	.10	.08	.04
443	Von Hayes	.10	.08	.04	534	Bob Brenly	.06	.05	.02
444	Charles Hudson	.06	.05	.02	535	*Chris Brown*	.20	.15	.08
445	Garry Maddox	.08	.06	.03	536	Chili Davis	.10	.08	.04
446	Shane Rawley	.10	.08	.04	537	Mark Davis	.06	.05	.02
447	Dave Rucker	.06	.05	.02	538	Rob Deer	.12	.09	.05
448	John Russell	.06	.05	.02	539	Dan Driessen	.08	.06	.03
449	Juan Samuel	.12	.09	.05	540	Scott Garrelts	.08	.06	.03
450	Mike Schmidt	.50	.40	.20	541	Dan Gladden	.08	.06	.03
451	Rick Schu	.08	.06	.03	542	Jim Gott	.06	.05	.02
452	Dave Shipanoff	.06	.05	.02	543	David Green	.06	.05	.02
453	Dave Stewart	.12	.09	.05	544	Atlee Hammaker	.06	.05	.02
454	Jeff Stone	.06	.05	.02	545	Mike Jeffcoat	.06	.05	.02
455	Kent Tekulve	.08	.06	.03	546	Mike Krukow	.08	.06	.03
456	Ozzie Virgil	.06	.05	.02	547	Dave LaPoint	.08	.06	.03
457	Glenn Wilson	.08	.06	.03	548	Jeff Leonard	.08	.06	.03
458	Jim Beattie	.06	.05	.02	549	Greg Minton	.06	.05	.02
459	Karl Best	.06	.05	.02	550	Alex Trevino	.06	.05	.02
460	Barry Bonnell	.06	.05	.02	551	Manny Trillo	.08	.06	.03
461	Phil Bradley	.20	.15	.08	552	*Jose Uribe*	.20	.15	.08
462	*Ivan Calderon*	.40	.30	.15	553	Brad Wellman ●	.06	.05	.02
463	Al Cowens	.06	.05	.02	554	Frank Williams	.06	.05	.02
464	Alvin Davis	.30	.25	.12	555	Joel Youngblood	.06	.05	.02
465	Dave Henderson	.10	.08	.04	556	Alan Bannister	.06	.05	.02
466	Bob Kearney	.06	.05	.02	557	Glenn Brummer	.06	.05	.02
467	Mark Langston	.30	.25	.12	558	*Steve Buechele*(FC)	.20	.15	.08
468	Bob Long	.06	.05	.02	559	*Jose Guzman*(FC)	.30	.25	.12
469	Mike Moore	.06	.05	.02	560	Toby Harrah	.08	.06	.03
470	Edwin Nunez	.06	.05	.02	561	Greg Harris	.06	.05	.02
471	Spike Owen	.06	.05	.02	562	*Dwayne Henry*(FC)	.10	.08	.04
472	Jack Perconte	.06	.05	.02	563	Burt Hooton	.08	.06	.03
473	Jim Presley	.15	.11	.06	564	Charlie Hough	.08	.06	.03
474	Donnie Scott	.06	.05	.02	565	Mike Mason	.06	.05	.02
475	Bill Swift(FC)	.12	.09	.05	566	*Oddibe McDowell*	.30	.25	.12

		MT	NR MT	EX
567	Dickie Noles	.06	.05	.02
568	Pete O'Brien	.10	.08	.04
569	Larry Parrish	.10	.08	.04
570	Dave Rozema	.06	.05	.02
571	Dave Schmidt	.06	.05	.02
572	Don Slaught	.06	.05	.02
573	Wayne Tolleson	.06	.05	.02
574	Duane Walker	.06	.05	.02
575	Gary Ward	.08	.06	.03
576	Chris Welsh	.06	.05	.02
577	Curtis Wilkerson	.06	.05	.02
578	George Wright	.06	.05	.02
579	Chris Bando	.06	.05	.02
580	Tony Bernazard	.06	.05	.02
581	Brett Butler	.08	.06	.03
582	Ernie Camacho	.06	.05	.02
583	Joe Carter	.20	.15	.08
584	Carmello Castillo (Carmelo)	.06	.05	.02
585	Jamie Easterly	.06	.05	.02
586	Julio Franco	.10	.08	.04
587	Mel Hall	.08	.06	.03
588	Mike Hargrove	.06	.05	.02
589	Neal Heaton	.06	.05	.02
590	Brook Jacoby	.10	.08	.04
591	*Otis Nixon*(FC)	.12	.09	.05
592	Jerry Reed	.06	.05	.02
593	Vern Ruhle	.06	.05	.02
594	Pat Tabler	.08	.06	.03
595	Rich Thompson	.06	.05	.02
596	Andre Thornton	.08	.06	.03
597	Dave Von Ohlen	.06	.05	.02
598	George Vukovich	.06	.05	.02
599	Tom Waddell	.06	.05	.02
600	Curt Wardle	.06	.05	.02
601	Jerry Willard	.06	.05	.02
602	Bill Almon	.06	.05	.02
603	Mike Bielecki	.08	.06	.03
604	Sid Bream	.10	.08	.04
605	Mike Brown	.06	.05	.02
606	*Pat Clements*	.12	.09	.05
607	Jose DeLeon	.08	.06	.03
608	Denny Gonzalez	.06	.05	.02
609	Cecilio Guante	.06	.05	.02
610	Steve Kemp	.08	.06	.03
611	Sam Khalifa	.06	.05	.02
612	Lee Mazzilli	.08	.06	.03
613	Larry McWilliams	.06	.05	.02
614	Jim Morrison	.06	.05	.02
615	*Joe Orsulak*	.15	.11	.06
616	Tony Pena	.10	.08	.04
617	Johnny Ray	.10	.08	.04
618	Rick Reuschel	.10	.08	.04
619	R.J. Reynolds	.08	.06	.03
620	Rick Rhoden	.10	.08	.04
621	Don Robinson	.08	.06	.03
622	Jason Thompson	.06	.05	.02
623	Lee Tunnell	.06	.05	.02
624	Jim Winn	.06	.05	.02
625	Marvell Wynne	.06	.05	.02
626	Gooden In Action (Dwight Gooden)	.50	.40	.20
627	Mattingly In Action (Don Mattingly)	1.25	.90	.50
628	4,192! (Pete Rose)	.50	.40	.20
629	3,000 Career Hits (Rod Carew)	.20	.15	.08
630	300 Career Wins (Phil Niekro, Tom Seaver)	.20	.15	.08
631	Ouch! (Don Baylor)	.08	.06	.03
632	Instant Offense (Tim Raines, Darryl Strawberry)	.30	.25	.12
633	Shortstops Supreme (Cal Ripken, Jr., Alan Trammell)	.30	.25	.12
634	Boggs & "Hero" (Wade Boggs, George Brett)	.60	.45	.25
635	Braves Dynamic Duo (Bob Horner, Dale Murphy)	.30	.25	.12
636	Cardinal Ignitors (Vince Coleman, Willie McGee)	.35	.25	.14
637	Terror on the Basepaths (Vince Coleman)	.35	.25	.14
638	Charlie Hustle & Dr. K (Dwight Gooden, Pete Rose)	.70	.50	.30
639	1984 and 1985 A.L. Batting Champs (Wade Boggs, Don Mattingly)	1.75	1.25	.70
640	N.L. West Sluggers (Steve Garvey, Dale Murphy, Dave Parker)	.30	.25	.12
641	Staff Aces (Dwight Gooden, Fernando Valenzuela)	.40	.30	.15
642	Blue Jay Stoppers (Jimmy Key, Dave Stieb)	.10	.08	.04
643	A.L. All-Star Backstops (Carlton Fisk, Rich Gedman)	.10	.08	.04

		MT	NR MT	EX
644	Major League Prospect (*Benito Santiago, Gene Walter*)(FC)	5.00	3.75	2.00
645	Major League Prospect (*Colin Ward, Mike Woodard*)(FC)	.10	.08	.04
646	Major League Prospect (*Kal Daniels, Paul O'Neill*)(FC)	4.00	3.00	1.50
647	Major League Prospect (*Andres Galarraga, Fred Toliver*)(FC)	3.50	2.75	1.50
648	Major League Prospect (*Curt Ford, Bob Kipper*)(FC)	.25	.20	.10
649	Major League Prospect (*Jose Canseco, Eric Plunk*)(FC)	35.00	26.00	14.00
650	Major League Prospect (*Mark McLemore, Gus Polidor*)(FC)	.20	.15	.08
651	Major League Prospect (*Mickey Brantley, Rob Woodward*)(FC)	.35	.25	.14
652	Major League Prospect (*Mark Funderburk, Billy Joe Robidoux*)(FC)	.10	.08	.04
653	Major League Prospect (*Cecil Fielder, Cory Snyder*)(FC)	3.00	2.25	1.25
654	Checklist 1-97	.06	.05	.02
655	Checklist 98-196	.06	.05	.02
656	Checklist 197-291	.06	.05	.02
657	Checklist 292-385	.06	.05	.02
658	Checklist 386-482	.06	.05	.02
659	Checklist 483-578	.06	.05	.02
660	Checklist 579-660	.06	.05	.02

1986 Fleer All Star Team

Gary Carter
METS ● CATCHER

Fleer's choices for a major league All-Star team make up this 12-card set. The cards, which measure 2-1/2" by 3-1/2", were randomly inserted in 35¢ wax packs and 59¢ cello packs. The card fronts have a color photo set against a bright red background for A.L. players or a bright blue background for N.L. players. The card backs feature the player's career highlights set in white type against a red and blue background.

		MT	NR MT	EX
Complete Set:		20.00	15.00	8.00
Common Player:		.60	.45	.25
1	Don Mattingly	6.00	4.50	2.50
2	Tom Herr	.60	.45	.25
3	George Brett	2.00	1.50	.80
4	Gary Carter	1.00	.70	.40
5	Cal Ripken, Jr.	1.75	1.25	.70
6	Dave Parker	.75	.60	.30
7	Rickey Henderson	2.50	2.00	1.00
8	Pedro Guerrero	.75	.60	.30
9	Dan Quisenberry	.60	.45	.25
10	Dwight Gooden	4.00	3.00	1.50
11	Gorman Thomas	.60	.45	.25
12	John Tudor	.60	.45	.25

1986 Fleer Baseball's Best

The 1986 Fleer Baseball's Best set consists of 44 cards and was produced for the McCrory's store chain and their affiliated stores. Subtitled "Sluggers vs. Pitchers," the set contains 22 each of the game's best hitters and pitchers. The cards, which measure

2-1/2" by 3-1/2", have color photos depicting an action pose. The backs are done in blue and red ink on white stock and carry the player's personal and statistical information. The sets were issued in a specially designed box with six team logo stickers.

		MT	NR MT	EX
Complete Set:		7.00	5.25	2.75
Common Player:		.05	.04	.02
1	Bert Blyleven	.10	.08	.04
2	Wade Boggs	1.00	.70	.40
3	George Brett	.30	.25	.12
4	Tom Browning	.15	.11	.06
5	Jose Canseco	3.50	2.75	1.50
6	Will Clark	1.50	1.25	.60
7	Roger Clemens	.70	.50	.30
8	Alvin Davis	.10	.08	.04
9	Julio Franco	.10	.08	.04
10	Kirk Gibson	.20	.15	.08
11	Dwight Gooden	1.00	.70	.40
12	Goose Gossage	.12	.09	.05
13	Pedro Guerrero	.15	.11	.06
14	Ron Guidry	.12	.09	.05
15	Tony Gwynn	.25	.20	.10
16	Orel Hershiser	.20	.15	.08
17	Kent Hrbek	.15	.11	.06
18	Reggie Jackson	.25	.20	.10
19	Wally Joyner	.50	.40	.20
20	Charlie Leibrandt	.05	.04	.02
21	Don Mattingly	1.50	1.25	.60
22	Willie McGee	.12	.09	.05
23	Jack Morris	.15	.11	.06
24	Dale Murphy	.30	.25	.12
25	Eddie Murray	.25	.20	.10
26	Jeff Reardon	.07	.05	.03
27	Rick Reuschel	.07	.05	.03
28	Cal Ripken, Jr	.30	.25	.12
29	Pete Rose	.60	.45	.25
30	Nolan Ryan	.50	.40	.20
31	Bret Saberhagen	.15	.11	.06
32	Ryne Sandberg	.20	.15	.08
33	Mike Schmidt	.30	.25	.12
34	Tom Seaver	.25	.20	.10
35	Bryn Smith	.05	.04	.02
36	Mario Soto	.05	.04	.02
37	Dave Stieb	.10	.08	.04
38	Darryl Strawberry	.40	.30	.15
39	Rick Sutcliffe	.10	.08	.04
40	John Tudor	.10	.08	.04
41	Fernando Valenzuela	.20	.15	.08
42	Bobby Witt	.15	.11	.06
43	Mike Witt	.07	.05	.03
44	Robin Yount	.35	.25	.14

1986 Fleer Box Panels

Picking up on a Donruss idea, Fleer issued eight cards in panels of four on the bottoms of the wax and cello boxes. The cards are numbered C-1 through C-8 and are 2-1/2" by 3-1/2", with a complete panel measuring 5" by 7-1/8" in size. Included in the eight cards are six player cards and two team logo/checklist cards.

		MT	NR MT	EX
Complete Panel Set:		4.00	3.00	1.50
Complete Singles Set:		1.75	1.25	.70
Common Single Player:		.20	.15	.08
Panel		2.75	2.00	1.00
1	Royals Logo/Checklist	.05	.04	.02
2	George Brett	.60	.45	.25
3	Ozzie Guillen	.40	.30	.15
4	Dale Murphy	.60	.45	.25
Panel		1.50	1.25	.60
5	Cardinals Logo/Checklist	.05	.04	.02
6	Tom Browning	.20	.15	.08
7	Gary Carter	.35	.25	.14
8	Carlton Fisk	.20	.15	.08

1986 Fleer Future Hall Of Famers

The 1986 Fleer Future Hall of Famers set is comprised of six players Fleer felt would gain eventual entrance into the Baseball Hall of Fame. The cards are the standard 2-1/2" by 3-1/2" in size and were randomly inserted in three-pack cello packs. The card fronts feature a player photo set against a blue background with horizontal light blue stripes. The card backs are printed in black on a blue background and feature player highlights in paragraph form.

		MT	NR MT	EX
Complete Set:		10.00	7.50	4.00
Common Player:		1.50	1.25	.60
1	Pete Rose	1.50	1.25	.60
2	Steve Carlton	1.50	1.25	.60
3	Tom Seaver	1.50	1.25	.60
4	Rod Carew	1.50	1.25	.60
5	Nolan Ryan	2.00	1.50	.80
6	Reggie Jackson	1.50	1.25	.60

NOTE: A card number in parentheses ( ) indicates the set is unnumbered.

1986 Fleer League Leaders

Fleer's 1986 "League Leaders" set features 44 of the game's top players and was issued through the Walgreens drug store chain. The card fronts contain a color photo and feature the player's name, team and position in a blue band near the bottom of the card. The words "League Leaders" appear in a red band at the top of the card. The background for the card fronts is alternating blue and white stripes. The card backs are printed in blue, red and white and carry the player's statistical information and team logo. The cards are the standard 2-1/2" by 3-1/2" size. The set was issued in a special cardboard box, along with six team logo stickers.

		MT	NR MT	EX
Complete Set:		8.00	6.00	3.00
Common Player:		.05	.04	.02
1	Wade Boggs	1.00	.70	.40
2	George Brett	.30	.25	.12
3	Jose Canseco	3.50	2.75	1.50
4	Rod Carew	.30	.25	.12
5	Gary Carter	.25	.20	.10
6	Jack Clark	.12	.09	.05
7	Vince Coleman	.60	.45	.25
8	Jose Cruz	.05	.04	.02
9	Alvin Davis	.10	.08	.04
10	Mariano Duncan	.05	.04	.02
11	Leon Durham	.05	.04	.02
12	Carlton Fisk	.15	.11	.06
13	Julio Franco	.10	.08	.04
14	Scott Garrelts	.05	.04	.02
15	Steve Garvey	.25	.20	.10
16	Dwight Gooden	1.00	.70	.40
17	Ozzie Guillen	.10	.08	.04
18	Willie Hernandez	.05	.04	.02
19	Bob Horner	.07	.05	.03
20	Kent Hrbek	.15	.11	.06
21	Charlie Leibrandt	.05	.04	.02
22	Don Mattingly	1.50	1.25	.60
23	Oddibe McDowell	.12	.09	.05
24	Willie McGee	.10	.08	.04
25	Keith Moreland	.05	.04	.02
26	Lloyd Moseby	.07	.05	.03
27	Dale Murphy	.30	.25	.12
28	Phil Niekro	.15	.11	.06
29	Joe Orsulak	.05	.04	.02
30	Dave Parker	.12	.09	.05
31	Lance Parrish	.15	.11	.06
32	Kirby Puckett	.70	.50	.30
33	Tim Raines	.25	.20	.10
34	Earnie Riles	.07	.05	.03
35	Cal Ripken, Jr.	.30	.25	.12
36	Pete Rose	.60	.45	.25
37	Bret Saberhagen	.15	.11	.06
38	Juan Samuel	.10	.08	.04
39	Ryne Sandberg	.20	.15	.08
40	Tom Seaver	.25	.20	.10
41	Lee Smith	.07	.05	.03
42	Ozzie Smith	.12	.09	.05
43	Dave Stieb	.10	.08	.04
44	Robin Yount	.35	.25	.12

NOTE: A card number in parentheses ( ) indicates the set is unnumbered.

1986 Fleer Limited Edition

Produced for the McCrory's store chain and their affiliates for the second year in a row, the 1986 Fleer Limited Edition set contains 44 cards. The cards, which are the standard 2-1/2" by 3-1/2" size, have color photos enclosed by green, red and yellow trim. The card backs carry black print on two shades of red. The set was issued in a special cardboard box, along with six team logo stickers.

		MT	NR MT	EX
Complete Set:		7.00	5.25	2.75
Common Player:		.05	.04	.02
1	Doyle Alexander	.05	.04	.02
2	Joaquin Andujar	.05	.04	.02
3	Harold Baines	.12	.09	.05
4	Wade Boggs	1.00	.70	.40
5	Phil Bradley	.12	.09	.05
6	George Brett	.30	.25	.12
7	Hubie Brooks	.07	.05	.03
8	Chris Brown	.12	.09	.05
9	Tom Brunansky	.10	.08	.04
10	Gary Carter	.25	.20	.10
11	Vince Coleman	.60	.45	.25
12	Cecil Cooper	.07	.05	.03
13	Jose Cruz	.05	.04	.02
14	Mike Davis	.05	.04	.02
15	Carlton Fisk	.15	.11	.06
16	Julio Franco	.10	.08	.04
17	Damaso Garcia	.05	.04	.02
18	Rich Gedman	.05	.04	.02
19	Kirk Gibson	.20	.15	.08
20	Dwight Gooden	1.00	.70	.40
21	Pedro Guerrero	.15	.11	.06
22	Tony Gwynn	.25	.20	.10
23	Rickey Henderson	.50	.40	.20
24	Orel Hershiser	.20	.15	.08
25	LaMarr Hoyt	.05	.04	.02
26	Reggie Jackson	.30	.25	.12
27	Don Mattingly	1.50	1.25	.60
28	Oddibe McDowell	.12	.09	.05
29	Willie McGee	.10	.08	.04
30	Paul Molitor	.12	.09	.05
31	Dale Murphy	.30	.25	.12
32	Eddie Murray	.25	.20	.10
33	Dave Parker	.12	.09	.05
34	Tony Pena	.07	.05	.03
35	Jeff Reardon	.07	.05	.03
36	Cal Ripken, Jr.	.30	.25	.12
37	Pete Rose	.60	.45	.25
38	Bret Saberhagen	.15	.11	.06
39	Juan Samuel	.10	.08	.04
40	Ryne Sandberg	.20	.15	.08
41	Mike Schmidt	.30	.25	.12
42	Lee Smith	.07	.05	.03
43	Don Sutton	.12	.09	.05
44	Lou Whitaker	.15	.11	.06

1986 Fleer Mini

Fleer's 1986 "Classic Miniatures" set contains 120 cards that measure 1-13/16" by 2-9/16" in size. The design of the high-gloss cards is identical to the regular 1986 Fleer set but the player photos are entirely different. The set, which was issued in a specially designed box along with 18 team logo stickers, was available to the collecting public only through hobby dealers.

		MT	NR MT	EX
	Complete Set:	12.00	9.00	5.00
	Common Player:	.05	.04	.02
1	George Brett	.30	.25	.12
2	Dan Quisenberry	.07	.05	.03
3	Bret Saberhagen	.15	.11	.06
4	Lonnie Smith	.05	.04	.02
5	Willie Wilson	.10	.08	.04
6	Jack Clark	.12	.09	.05
7	Vince Coleman	.50	.40	.20
8	Tom Herr	.07	.05	.03
9	Willie McGee	.10	.08	.04
10	Ozzie Smith	.12	.09	.05
11	John Tudor	.07	.05	.03
12	Jesse Barfield	.12	.09	.05
13	George Bell	.20	.15	.08
14	Tony Fernandez	.10	.08	.04
15	Damaso Garcia	.05	.04	.02
16	Dave Stieb	.07	.05	.03
17	Gary Carter	.20	.15	.08
18	Ron Darling	.10	.08	.04
19	Dwight Gooden	.60	.45	.25
20	Keith Hernandez	.20	.15	.08
21	Darryl Strawberry	.50	.40	.20
22	Ron Guidry	.15	.11	.06
23	Rickey Henderson	.30	.25	.12
24	Don Mattingly	1.75	1.25	.70
25	Dave Righetti	.12	.09	.05
26	Dave Winfield	.20	.15	.08
27	Mariano Duncan	.07	.05	.03
28	Pedro Guerrero	.12	.09	.05
29	Bill Madlock	.10	.08	.04
30	Mike Marshall	.10	.08	.04
31	Fernando Valenzuela	.10	.08	.04
32	Reggie Jackson	.30	.25	.12
33	Gary Pettis	.05	.04	.02
34	Ron Romanick	.05	.04	.02
35	Don Sutton	.12	.09	.05
36	Mike Witt	.07	.05	.03
37	Buddy Bell	.07	.05	.03
38	Tom Browning	.10	.08	.04
39	Dave Parker	.12	.09	.05
40	Pete Rose	.60	.45	.25
41	Mario Soto	.05	.04	.02
42	Harold Baines	.12	.09	.05
43	Carlton Fisk	.15	.11	.06
44	Ozzie Guillen	.12	.09	.05
45	Ron Kittle	.07	.05	.03
46	Tom Seaver	.20	.15	.08
47	Kirk Gibson	.20	.15	.08
48	Jack Morris	.15	.11	.06
49	Lance Parrish	.15	.11	.06
50	Alan Trammell	.20	.15	.08
51	Lou Whitaker	.15	.11	.06
52	Hubie Brooks	.07	.05	.03
53	Andre Dawson	.15	.11	.06
54	Tim Raines	.20	.15	.08
55	Bryn Smith	.05	.04	.02
56	Tim Wallach	.10	.08	.04
57	Mike Boddicker	.05	.04	.02
58	Eddie Murray	.25	.20	.10
59	Cal Ripken	.30	.25	.12
60	John Shelby	.05	.04	.02
61	Mike Young	.05	.04	.02

		MT	NR MT	EX
62	Jose Cruz	.07	.05	.03
63	Glenn Davis	.15	.11	.06
64	Phil Garner	.05	.04	.02
65	Nolan Ryan	.50	.40	.20
66	Mike Scott	.12	.09	.05
67	Steve Garvey	.20	.15	.08
68	Goose Gossage	.12	.09	.05
69	Tony Gwynn	.25	.20	.10
70	Andy Hawkins	.05	.04	.02
71	Garry Templeton	.05	.04	.02
72	Wade Boggs	1.00	.70	.40
73	Roger Clemens	1.00	.70	.40
74	Dwight Evans	.12	.09	.05
75	Rich Gedman	.05	.04	.02
76	Jim Rice	.20	.15	.08
77	Shawon Dunston	.10	.08	.04
78	Leon Durham	.05	.04	.02
79	Keith Moreland	.05	.04	.02
80	Ryne Sandberg	.20	.15	.08
81	Rick Sutcliffe	.10	.08	.04
82	Bert Blyleven	.12	.09	.05
83	Tom Brunansky	.10	.08	.04
84	Kent Hrbek	.15	.11	.06
85	Kirby Puckett	.70	.50	.30
86	Bruce Bochte	.05	.04	.02
87	Jose Canseco	3.50	2.75	1.50
88	Mike Davis	.05	.04	.02
89	Jay Howell	.07	.05	.03
90	Dwayne Murphy	.05	.04	.02
91	Steve Carlton	.20	.15	.08
92	Von Hayes	.10	.08	.04
93	Juan Samuel	.12	.09	.05
94	Mike Schmidt	.30	.25	.12
95	Glenn Wilson	.05	.04	.02
96	Phil Bradley	.10	.08	.04
97	Alvin Davis	.10	.08	.04
98	Jim Presley	.10	.08	.04
99	Danny Tartabull	.15	.11	.06
100	Cecil Cooper	.10	.08	.04
101	Paul Molitor	.12	.09	.05
102	Earnie Riles	.07	.05	.03
103	Robin Yount	.30	.25	.12
104	Bob Horner	.10	.08	.04
105	Dale Murphy	.30	.25	.12
106	Bruce Sutter	.10	.08	.04
107	Claudell Washington	.05	.04	.02
108	Chris Brown	.12	.09	.05
109	Chili Davis	.05	.04	.02
110	Scott Garrelts	.05	.04	.02
111	Oddibe McDowell	.12	.09	.05
112	Pete O'Brien	.07	.05	.03
113	Gary Ward	.05	.04	.02
114	Brett Butler	.05	.04	.02
115	Julio Franco	.10	.08	.04
116	Brook Jacoby	.10	.08	.04
117	Mike Brown	.05	.04	.02
118	Joe Orsulak	.05	.04	.02
119	Tony Pena	.07	.05	.03
120	R.J. Reynolds	.05	.04	.02

1986 Fleer Star Stickers

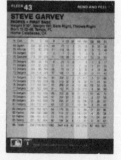

After a five-year layoff, Fleer once again produced a Star Sticker set. The cards, which measure 2-1/2" by 3-1/2", have color photos inside dark maroon borders. The card backs are identical to the 1986 regular issue except for the 1-132 numbering system and blue ink instead of yellow. The words "Bend and Peel" are found in the upper right corner of the card backs. Card #132 is a multi-player card featuring Dwight Gooden and Dale Murphy on the front and a complete checklist for the set on the reverse. The cards were sold in wax packs with team logo stickers.

		MT	NR MT	EX
	Complete Set	18.00	13.50	7.25
	Common Player	.05	.04	.02
1	Harold Baines	.20	.15	.08
2	Jesse Barfield	.20	.15	.08
3	Don Baylor	.12	.09	.05
4	Juan Beniquez	.05	.04	.02
5	Tim Birtsas	.08	.06	.03
6	Bert Blyleven	.15	.11	.06
7	Bruce Bochte	.05	.04	.02
8	Wade Boggs	1.00	.70	.40
9	Dennis Boyd	.12	.09	.05
10	Phil Bradley	.20	.15	.08
11	George Brett	.50	.40	.20
12	Hubie Brooks	.12	.09	.05
13	Chris Brown	.45	.35	.20
14	Tom Browning	.15	.11	.06
15	Tom Brunansky	.15	.11	.06
16	Bill Buckner	.10	.08	.04
17	Britt Burns	.05	.04	.02
18	Brett Butler	.08	.06	.03
19	Jose Canseco	3.50	2.75	1.50
20	Rod Carew	.40	.30	.15
21	Steve Carlton	.40	.30	.15
22	Don Carman	.20	.15	.08
23	Gary Carter	.40	.30	.15
24	Jack Clark	.20	.15	.08
25	Vince Coleman	.70	.50	.30
26	Cecil Cooper	.15	.11	.06
27	Jose Cruz	.10	.08	.04
28	Ron Darling	.20	.15	.08
29	Alvin Davis	.20	.15	.08
30	Jody Davis	.08	.06	.03
31	Mike Davis	.05	.04	.02
32	Andre Dawson	.25	.20	.10
33	Mariano Duncan	.10	.08	.04
34	Shawon Dunston	.15	.11	.06
35	Leon Durham	.08	.06	.03
36	Darrell Evans	.12	.09	.05
37	Tony Fernandez	.15	.11	.06
38	Carlton Fisk	.20	.15	.08
39	John Franco	.10	.08	.04
40	Julio Franco	.12	.09	.05
41	Damaso Garcia	.05	.04	.02
42	Scott Garrelts	.05	.04	.02
43	Steve Garvey	.25	.20	.10
44	Rich Gedman	.10	.08	.04
45	Kirk Gibson	.30	.25	.12
46	Dwight Gooden	.90	.70	.35
47	Pedro Guerrero	.20	.15	.08
48	Ron Guidry	.20	.15	.08
49	Ozzie Guillen	.30	.25	.12
50	Tony Gwynn	.40	.30	.15
51	Andy Hawkins	.08	.06	.03
52	Von Hayes	.12	.09	.05
53	Rickey Henderson	.70	.50	.30
54	Tom Henke	.12	.09	.05
55	Keith Hernandez	.35	.25	.14
56	Willie Hernandez	.05	.04	.02
57	Tom Herr	.10	.08	.04
58	Orel Hershiser	.30	.25	.12
59	Teddy Higuera	.60	.45	.25
60	Bob Horner	.12	.09	.05
61	Charlie Hough	.08	.06	.03
62	Jay Howell	.08	.06	.03
63	LaMarr Hoyt	.05	.04	.02
64	Kent Hrbek	.30	.25	.12
65	Reggie Jackson	.50	.40	.20
66	Bob James	.05	.04	.02
67	Dave Kingman	.12	.09	.05
68	Ron Kittle	.12	.09	.05
69	Charlie Leibrandt	.08	.06	.03
70	Fred Lynn	.25	.20	.10
71	Mike Marshall	.20	.15	.08
72	Don Mattingly	2.25	1.75	.90
73	Oddibe McDowell	.25	.20	.10
74	Willie McGee	.20	.15	.08
75	Scott McGregor	.05	.04	.02
76	Paul Molitor	.20	.15	.08
77	Donnie Moore	.05	.04	.02
78	Keith Moreland	.08	.06	.03
79	Jack Morris	.25	.20	.10
80	Dale Murphy	.40	.30	.15
81	Eddie Murray	.50	.40	.20
82	Phil Niekro	.25	.20	.10

		MT	NR MT	EX
83	Joe Orsulak	.10	.08	.04
84	Dave Parker	.25	.20	.10
85	Lance Parrish	.25	.20	.10
86	Larry Parrish	.08	.06	.03
87	Tony Pena	.10	.08	.04
88	Gary Pettis	.05	.04	.02
89	Jim Presley	.15	.11	.06
90	Kirby Puckett	.70	.50	.30
91	Dan Quisenberry	.12	.09	.05
92	Tim Raines	.35	.25	.14
93	Johnny Ray	.10	.08	.04
94	Jeff Reardon	.10	.08	.04
95	Rick Reuschel	.10	.08	.04
96	Jim Rice	.15	.11	.06
97	Dave Righetti	.20	.15	.08
98	Earnie Riles	.12	.09	.05
99	Cal Ripken, Jr.	.60	.45	.25
100	Ron Romanick	.05	.04	.02
101	Pete Rose	.50	.40	.20
102	Nolan Ryan	.50	.40	.20
103	Bret Saberhagen	.25	.20	.10
104	Mark Salas	.05	.04	.02
105	Juan Samuel	.15	.11	.06
106	Ryne Sandberg	.35	.25	.14
107	Mike Schmidt	.70	.50	.30
108	Mike Scott	.15	.11	.06
109	Tom Seaver	.30	.25	.12
110	Bryn Smith	.05	.04	.02
111	Dave Smith	.05	.04	.02
112	Lee Smith	.10	.08	.04
113	Ozzie Smith	.20	.15	.08
114	Mario Soto	.05	.04	.02
115	Dave Stieb	.12	.09	.05
116	Darryl Strawberry	.70	.50	.30
117	Bruce Sutter	.10	.08	.04
118	Garry Templeton	.08	.06	.03
119	Gorman Thomas	.08	.06	.03
120	Andre Thornton	.10	.08	.04
121	Allan Trammell	.20	.15	.08
122	John Tudor	.12	.09	.05
123	Fernando Valenzuela	.30	.25	.12
124	Frank Viola	.20	.15	.08
125	Gary Ward	.05	.04	.02
126	Lou Whitaker	.25	.20	.10
127	Frank White	.10	.08	.04
128	Glenn Wilson	.08	.06	.03
129	Willie Wilson	.15	.11	.06
130	Dave Winfield	.40	.30	.15
131	Robin Yount	.35	.25	.14
132	Dwight Gooden, Dale Murphy/Checklist	1.25	.90	.50

1986 Fleer
Star Stickers Box Panels

Four cards, numbered S-1 through S-4, were placed on the bottoms of 1986 Fleer Star Stickers wax pack boxes. The cards are nearly identical in format to the regular issue sticker cards. Individual cards measure 2-1/2" by 3-1/2" in size, while a complete panel of four measures 5" by 7-1/8".

	MT	NR MT	EX
Complete Panel Set:	3.00	2.25	1.25
Complete Singles Set:	1.50	1.25	.60
Common Single Player:	.30	.25	.12

	MT	NR MT	EX
Panel	3.00	2.25	1.25
1 Dodgers Logo	.05	.04	.02
2 Wade Boggs	1.00	.70	.40
3 Steve Garvey	.30	.25	.12
4 Dave Winfield	.30	.25	.12

1986 Fleer Update

Issued near the end of the baseball season, the 1986 Fleer Update set consists of 132 cards numbered U-1 through U-132. The cards, which measure 2-1/2" by 3-1/2" in size, are identical in design to the regular 1986 Fleer set. The purpose of the set is to update player trades and include new players not depicted in the regular issue. The set was issued with team logo stickers in a specially designed box and was available only through hobby dealers.

	MT	NR MT	EX
Complete Set:	30.00	22.00	12.00
Common Player:	.08	.06	.03

		MT	NR MT	EX
1	Mike Aldrete(FC)	.35	.25	.14
2	Andy Allanson(FC)	.20	.15	.08
3	Neil Allen	.08	.06	.03
4	Joaquin Andujar	.10	.08	.04
5	Paul Assenmacher(FC)	.20	.15	.08
6	Scott Bailes(FC)	.25	.20	.10
7	Jay Baller(FC)	.15	.11	.06
8	Scott Bankhead(FC)	.20	.15	.08
9	Bill Bathe(FC)	.08	.06	.03
10	Don Baylor	.15	.11	.06
11	Billy Beane(FC)	.08	.06	.03
12	Steve Bedrosian	.15	.11	.06
13	Juan Beniquez	.08	.06	.03
14	Barry Bonds(FC)	1.25	.90	.50
15	Bobby Bonilla(FC)	1.00	.70	.40
16	Rich Bordi	.08	.06	.03
17	Bill Campbell	.08	.06	.03
18	Tom Candiotti	.08	.06	.03
19	John Cangelosi(FC)	.20	.15	.08
20	Jose Canseco	7.00	5.25	2.75
21	Chuck Cary(FC)	.15	.11	.06
22	Juan Castillo(FC)	.10	.08	.04
23	Rick Cerone	.08	.06	.03
24	John Cerutti(FC)	.25	.20	.10
25	Will Clark(FC)	12.00	9.00	4.75
26	Mark Clear	.08	.06	.03
27	Darnell Coles(FC)	.15	.11	.06
28	Dave Collins	.10	.08	.04
29	Tim Conroy	.08	.06	.03
30	Ed Correa(FC)	.20	.15	.08
31	Joe Cowley	.08	.06	.03
32	Bill Dawley	.08	.06	.03
33	Rob Deer	.15	.11	.06
34	John Denny	.08	.06	.03
35	Jim DeShaies (Deshaies)(FC)	.25	.20	.10
36	Doug Drabek(FC)	.35	.25	.14
37	Mike Easler	.12	.09	.05
38	Mark Eichhorn(FC)	.20	.15	.08
39	Dave Engle	.08	.06	.03
40	Mike Fischlin	.08	.06	.03
41	Scott Fletcher	.15	.11	.06
42	Terry Forster	.12	.09	.05
43	Terry Francona	.08	.06	.03
44	Andres Galarraga	.90	.70	.35
45	Lee Guetterman(FC)	.20	.15	.08
46	Bill Gullickson	.08	.06	.03

		MT	NR MT	EX
47	Jackie Gutierrez	.08	.06	.03
48	Moose Haas	.08	.06	.03
49	Billy Hatcher	.15	.11	.06
50	Mike Heath	.08	.06	.03
51	Guy Hoffman(FC)	.10	.08	.04
52	Tom Hume	.08	.06	.03
53	Pete Incaviglia(FC)	.50	.40	.20
54	Dane Iorg	.08	.06	.03
55	Chris James(FC)	.60	.45	.25
56	Stan Javier(FC)	.25	.20	.10
57	Tommy John	.20	.15	.08
58	Tracy Jones(FC)	.40	.30	.15
59	Wally Joyner(FC)	2.50	2.00	1.00
60	Wayne Krenchicki	.08	.06	.03
61	John Kruk(FC)	.40	.30	.15
62	Mike LaCoss	.08	.06	.03
63	Pete Ladd	.08	.06	.03
64	Dave LaPoint	.15	.11	.06
65	Mike LaValliere(FC)	.30	.25	.12
66	Rudy Law	.08	.06	.03
67	Dennis Leonard	.10	.08	.04
68	Steve Lombardozzi(FC)	.20	.15	.08
69	Aurelio Lopez	.08	.06	.03
70	Mickey Mahler	.08	.06	.03
71	Candy Maldonado	.15	.11	.06
72	Roger Mason(FC)	.10	.08	.04
73	Greg Mathews(FC)	.25	.20	.10
74	Andy McGaffigan	.08	.06	.03
75	Joel McKeon(FC)	.12	.09	.05
76	Kevin Mitchell(FC)	7.00	5.25	2.75
77	Bill Mooneyham(FC)	.12	.09	.05
78	Omar Moreno	.08	.06	.03
79	Jerry Mumphrey	.08	.06	.03
80	Al Newman(FC)	.12	.09	.05
81	Phil Niekro	.40	.30	.15
82	Randy Niemann	.08	.06	.03
83	Juan Nieves(FC)	.20	.15	.08
84	Bob Ojeda	.12	.09	.05
85	Rick Ownbey	.08	.06	.03
86	Tom Paciorek	.08	.06	.03
87	David Palmer	.08	.06	.03
88	Jeff Parrett(FC)	.25	.20	.10
89	Pat Perry(FC)	.15	.11	.06
90	Dan Plesac(FC)	.35	.25	.14
91	Darrell Porter	.12	.09	.05
92	Luis Quinones(FC)	.12	.09	.05
93	Rey Quinonez(FC)	.20	.15	.08
94	Gary Redus	.10	.08	.04
95	Jeff Reed(FC)	.12	.09	.05
96	Bip Roberts(FC)	.08	.06	.03
97	Billy Joe Robidoux	.12	.09	.05
98	Gary Roenicke	.08	.06	.03
99	Ron Roenicke	.08	.06	.03
100	Angel Salazar	.08	.06	.03
101	Joe Sambito	.08	.06	.03
102	Billy Sample	.08	.06	.03
103	Dave Schmidt	.08	.06	.03
104	Ken Schrom	.08	.06	.03
105	Ruben Sierra(FC)	7.00	5.25	2.75
106	Ted Simmons	.20	.15	.08
107	Sammy Stewart	.08	.06	.03
108	Kurt Stillwell(FC)	.30	.25	.12
109	Dale Sveum(FC)	.25	.20	.10
110	Tim Teufel	.08	.06	.03
111	Bob Tewksbury(FC)	.12	.09	.05
112	Andres Thomas(FC)	.25	.20	.10
113	Jason Thompson	.08	.06	.03
114	Milt Thompson	.12	.09	.05
115	Rob Thompson(FC)	.40	.30	.15
116	Jay Tibbs	.08	.06	.03
117	Fred Toliver	.12	.09	.05
118	Wayne Tolleson	.08	.06	.03
119	Alex Trevino	.08	.06	.03
120	Manny Trillo	.10	.08	.04
121	Ed Vande Berg	.08	.06	.03
122	Ozzie Virgil	.08	.06	.03
123	Tony Walker(FC)	.08	.06	.03
124	Gene Walter	.12	.09	.05
125	Duane Ward(FC)	.20	.15	.08
126	Jerry Willard	.08	.06	.03
127	Mitch Williams(FC)	.60	.45	.25
128	Reggie Williams(FC)	.20	.15	.08
129	Bobby Witt(FC)	.50	.40	.20
130	Marvell Wynne	.08	.06	.03
131	Steve Yeager	.08	.06	.03
132	Checklist	.08	.06	.03

NOTE: A card number in parentheses ( ) indicates the set is unnumbered.

1987 Fleer

The 1987 Fleer set consists of 660 cards, each measuring 2-1/2" by 3-1/2". The card fronts feature an attractive blue and white border. The player's name and position appears in the upper left corner of the card. The player's team logo is located in the lower right corner. The card backs are done in blue, red and white and contain an innovative "Pro Scouts Report" feature which lists the hitter's or pitcher's batting and pitching strengths. For the third year in a row, Fleer included its "Major League Prospects" subset. Fleer produced a glossy-finish Collectors Edition set which came housed in a specially-designed tin box. It was speculated that 100,000 of the glossy sets were produced. After experiencing a dramatic deop in price during 1987, the glossy set now sells for only a few dollars more than the regular issue.

		MT	NR MT	EX
Complete Set:		90.00	67.00	36.00
Common Player:		.06	.05	.02
1	Rick Aguilera	.08	.06	.03
2	Richard Anderson	.06	.05	.02
3	Wally Backman	.08	.06	.03
4	Gary Carter	.25	.20	.10
5	Ron Darling	.15	.11	.06
6	Len Dykstra	.12	.09	.05
7	*Kevin Elster*(FC)	.50	.40	.20
8	Sid Fernandez	.12	.09	.05
9	Dwight Gooden	.90	.70	.35
10	*Ed Hearn*(FC)	.10	.08	.04
11	Danny Heep	.06	.05	.02
12	Keith Hernandez	.25	.20	.10
13	Howard Johnson	.10	.08	.04
14	Ray Knight	.08	.06	.03
15	Lee Mazzilli	.08	.06	.03
16	Roger McDowell	.12	.09	.05
17	*Kevin Mitchell*	8.00	6.00	3.25
18	Randy Niemann	.06	.05	.02
19	Bob Ojeda	.08	.06	.03
20	Jesse Orosco	.08	.06	.03
21	Rafael Santana	.06	.05	.02
22	Doug Sisk	.06	.05	.02
23	Darryl Strawberry	1.00	.70	.40
24	Tim Teufel	.06	.05	.02
25	Mookie Wilson	.10	.08	.04
26	Tony Armas	.08	.06	.03
27	Marty Barrett	.10	.08	.04
28	Don Baylor	.12	.09	.05
29	Wade Boggs	1.50	1.25	.60
30	Oil Can Boyd	.08	.06	.03
31	Bill Buckner	.10	.08	.04
32	Roger Clemens	1.25	.90	.50
33	Steve Crawford	.06	.05	.02
34	Dwight Evans	.12	.09	.05
35	Rich Gedman	.10	.08	.04
36	Dave Henderson	.10	.08	.04
37	Bruce Hurst	.10	.08	.04
38	Tim Lollar	.06	.05	.02
39	Al Nipper	.06	.05	.02
40	Spike Owen	.06	.05	.02
41	Jim Rice	.30	.25	.12
42	Ed Romero	.06	.05	.02
43	Joe Sambito	.06	.05	.02
44	Calvin Schiraldi	.10	.08	.04
45	Tom Seaver	.40	.30	.15

		MT	NR MT	EX
46	*Jeff Sellers*(FC)	.20	.15	.08
47	Bob Stanley	.06	.05	.02
48	Sammy Stewart	.06	.05	.02
49	Larry Andersen	.06	.05	.02
50	Alan Ashby	.06	.05	.02
51	Kevin Bass	.10	.08	.04
52	Jeff Calhoun	.06	.05	.02
53	Jose Cruz	.10	.08	.04
54	Danny Darwin	.06	.05	.02
55	Glenn Davis	.30	.25	.12
56	*Jim Deshaies*	.25	.20	.10
57	Bill Doran	.10	.08	.04
58	Phil Garner	.06	.05	.02
59	Billy Hatcher	.08	.06	.03
60	Charlie Kerfeld	.06	.05	.02
61	Bob Knepper	.08	.06	.03
62	Dave Lopes	.08	.06	.03
63	Aurelio Lopez	.06	.05	.02
64	Jim Pankovits	.06	.05	.02
65	Terry Puhl	.06	.05	.02
66	Craig Reynolds	.06	.05	.02
67	Nolan Ryan	.70	.50	.30
68	Mike Scott	.15	.11	.06
69	Dave Smith	.08	.06	.03
70	Dickie Thon	.08	.06	.03
71	Tony Walker	.06	.05	.02
72	Denny Walling	.06	.05	.02
73	Bob Boone	.08	.06	.03
74	Rick Burleson	.08	.06	.03
75	John Candelaria	.10	.08	.04
76	Doug Corbett	.06	.05	.02
77	Doug DeCinces	.08	.06	.03
78	Brian Downing	.08	.06	.03
79	*Chuck Finley*(FC)	.15	.11	.06
80	Terry Forster	.08	.06	.03
81	Bobby Grich	.10	.08	.04
82	George Hendrick	.08	.06	.03
83	Jack Howell(FC)	.10	.08	.04
84	Reggie Jackson	.35	.25	.14
85	Ruppert Jones	.06	.05	.02
86	*Wally Joyner*	1.75	1.25	.70
87	Gary Lucas	.06	.05	.02
88	Kirk McCaskill	.08	.06	.03
89	Donnie Moore	.06	.05	.02
90	Gary Pettis	.06	.05	.02
91	Vern Ruhle	.06	.05	.02
92	Dick Schofield	.06	.05	.02
93	Don Sutton	.20	.15	.08
94	Rob Wilfong	.06	.05	.02
95	Mike Witt	.10	.08	.04
96	*Doug Drabek*	.30	.25	.12
97	Mike Easler	.08	.06	.03
98	Mike Fischlin	.06	.05	.02
99	Brian Fisher	.08	.06	.03
100	Ron Guidry	.15	.11	.06
101	Rickey Henderson	.35	.25	.14
102	Tommy John	.20	.15	.08
103	Ron Kittle	.10	.08	.04
104	Don Mattingly	2.50	2.00	1.00
105	Bobby Meacham	.06	.05	.02
106	Joe Niekro	.10	.08	.04
107	Mike Pagliarulo	.10	.08	.04
108	Dan Pasqua	.10	.08	.04
109	Willie Randolph	.10	.08	.04
110	Dennis Rasmussen	.10	.08	.04
111	Dave Righetti	.15	.11	.06
112	Gary Roenicke	.06	.05	.02
113	Rod Scurry	.06	.05	.02
114	Bob Shirley	.06	.05	.02
115	Joel Skinner	.06	.05	.02
116	Tim Stoddard	.06	.05	.02
117	*Bob Tewksbury*	.12	.09	.05
118	Wayne Tolleson	.06	.05	.02
119	Claudell Washington	.08	.06	.03
120	Dave Winfield	.30	.25	.12
121	Steve Buechele	.08	.06	.03
122	*Ed Correa*	.15	.11	.06
123	Scott Fletcher	.08	.06	.03
124	Jose Guzman	.10	.08	.04
125	Toby Harrah	.08	.06	.03
126	Greg Harris	.06	.05	.02
127	Charlie Hough	.08	.06	.03
128	*Pete Incaviglia*	.60	.45	.25
129	Mike Mason	.06	.05	.02
130	Oddibe McDowell	.10	.08	.04
131	*Dale Mohorcic*(FC)	.20	.15	.08
132	Pete O'Brien	.10	.08	.04
133	Tom Paciorek	.06	.05	.02
134	Larry Parrish	.08	.06	.03
135	Geno Petralli	.06	.05	.02
136	Darrell Porter	.08	.06	.03

	MT	NR MT	EX			MT	NR MT	EX
137 Jeff Russell	.06	.05	.02	228 Tom Henke	.08	.06	.03
138 *Ruben Sierra*	7.00	5.25	2.75	229 Garth Iorg	.06	.05	.02
139 Don Slaught	.06	.05	.02	230 Cliff Johnson	.06	.05	.02
140 Gary Ward	.08	.06	.03	231 Joe Johnson	.06	.05	.02
141 Curtis Wilkerson	.06	.05	.02	232 Jimmy Key	.12	.09	.05
142 *Mitch Williams*	.40	.30	.15	233 Dennis Lamp	.06	.05	.02
143 *Bobby Witt*	.35	.25	.14	234 Rick Leach	.06	.05	.02
144 Dave Bergman	.06	.05	.02	235 Buck Martinez	.06	.05	.02
145 Tom Brookens	.06	.05	.02	236 Lloyd Moseby	.10	.08	.04
146 Bill Campbell	.06	.05	.02	237 Rance Mulliniks	.06	.05	.02
147 *Chuck Cary*	.10	.08	.04	238 Dave Stieb	.12	.09	.05
148 Darnell Coles	.08	.06	.03	239 Willie Upshaw	.08	.06	.03
149 Dave Collins	.08	.06	.03	240 Ernie Whitt	.08	.06	.03
150 Darrell Evans	.12	.09	.05	241 *Andy Allanson*	.15	.11	.06
151 Kirk Gibson	.25	.20	.10	242 *Scott Bailes*	.20	.15	.08
152 John Grubb	.06	.05	.02	243 Chris Bando	.06	.05	.02
153 Willie Hernandez	.08	.06	.03	244 Tony Bernazard	.06	.05	.02
154 Larry Herndon	.08	.06	.03	245 John Butcher	.06	.05	.02
155 *Eric King*	.20	.15	.08	246 Brett Butler	.08	.06	.03
156 Chet Lemon	.08	.06	.03	247 Ernie Camacho	.06	.05	.02
157 Dwight Lowry	.06	.05	.02	248 Tom Candiotti	.06	.05	.02
158 Jack Morris	.20	.15	.08	249 Joe Carter	.25	.20	.10
159 Randy O'Neal	.06	.05	.02	250 Carmen Castillo	.06	.05	.02
160 Lance Parrish	.20	.15	.08	251 Julio Franco	.10	.08	.04
161 Dan Petry	.08	.06	.03	252 Mel Hall	.08	.06	.03
162 Pat Sheridan	.06	.05	.02	253 Brook Jacoby	.10	.08	.04
163 Jim Slaton	.06	.05	.02	254 Phil Niekro	.20	.15	.08
164 Frank Tanana	.08	.06	.03	255 Otis Nixon	.06	.05	.02
165 Walt Terrell	.08	.06	.03	256 Dickie Noles	.06	.05	.02
166 Mark Thurmond	.06	.05	.02	257 Bryan Oelkers	.06	.05	.02
167 Alan Trammell	.25	.20	.10	258 Ken Schrom	.06	.05	.02
168 Lou Whitaker	.25	.20	.10	259 Don Schulze	.06	.05	.02
169 Luis Aguayo	.06	.05	.02	260 Cory Snyder	.70	.50	.30
170 Steve Bedrosian	.12	.09	.05	261 Pat Tabler	.08	.06	.03
171 Don Carman	.10	.08	.04	262 Andre Thornton	.08	.06	.03
172 Darren Daulton	.06	.05	.02	263 *Rich Yett*(FC)	.12	.09	.05
173 Greg Gross	.06	.05	.02	264 *Mike Aldrete*	.25	.20	.10
174 Kevin Gross	.08	.06	.03	265 Juan Berenguer	.06	.05	.02
175 Von Hayes	.10	.08	.04	266 Vida Blue	.10	.08	.04
176 Charles Hudson	.06	.05	.02	267 Bob Brenly	.06	.05	.02
177 Tom Hume	.06	.05	.02	268 Chris Brown	.08	.06	.03
178 Steve Jeltz	.06	.05	.02	269 *Will Clark*	35.00	27.00	15.00
179 *Mike Maddux*(FC)	.20	.15	.08	270 Chili Davis	.08	.06	.03
180 Shane Rawley	.08	.06	.03	271 Mark Davis	.06	.05	.02
181 Gary Redus	.06	.05	.02	272 *Kelly Downs*(FC)	.30	.25	.12
182 Ron Roenicke	.06	.05	.02	273 Scott Garrelts	.06	.05	.02
183 *Bruce Ruffin*(FC)	.20	.15	.08	274 Dan Gladden	.06	.05	.02
184 John Russell	.06	.05	.02	275 Mike Krukow	.08	.06	.03
185 Juan Samuel	.12	.09	.05	276 *Randy Kutcher*(FC)	.10	.08	.04
186 Dan Schatzeder	.06	.05	.02	277 Mike LaCoss	.06	.05	.02
187 Mike Schmidt	.60	.45	.25	278 Jeff Leonard	.08	.06	.03
188 Rick Schu	.06	.05	.02	279 Candy Maldonado	.08	.06	.03
189 Jeff Stone	.06	.05	.02	280 Roger Mason	.06	.05	.02
190 Kent Tekulve	.08	.06	.03	281 Bob Melvin(FC)	.08	.06	.03
191 Milt Thompson	.08	.06	.03	282 Greg Minton	.06	.05	.02
192 Glenn Wilson	.08	.06	.03	283 Jeff Robinson	.08	.06	.03
193 Buddy Bell	.10	.08	.04	284 Harry Spilman	.06	.05	.02
194 Tom Browning	.10	.08	.04	285 *Rob Thompson*	.35	.25	.14
195 Sal Butera	.06	.05	.02	286 Jose Uribe	.08	.06	.03
196 Dave Concepcion	.12	.09	.05	287 Frank Williams	.06	.05	.02
197 Kal Daniels	.80	.60	.30	288 Joel Youngblood	.06	.05	.02
198 Eric Davis	1.50	1.25	.60	289 Jack Clark	.15	.11	.06
199 John Denny	.06	.05	.02	290 Vince Coleman	.25	.20	.10
200 Bo Diaz	.08	.06	.03	291 Tim Conroy	.06	.05	.02
201 Nick Esasky	.08	.06	.03	292 Danny Cox	.08	.06	.03
202 John Franco	.10	.08	.04	293 Ken Dayley	.06	.05	.02
203 Bill Gullickson	.06	.05	.02	294 Curt Ford	.06	.05	.02
204 *Barry Larkin*(FC)	3.00	2.25	1.25	295 Bob Forsch	.08	.06	.03
205 Eddie Milner	.06	.05	.02	296 Tom Herr	.10	.08	.04
206 *Rob Murphy*(FC)	.20	.15	.08	297 Ricky Horton	.08	.06	.03
207 Ron Oester	.06	.05	.02	298 Clint Hurdle	.06	.05	.02
208 Dave Parker	.20	.15	.08	299 Jeff Lahti	.06	.05	.02
209 Tony Perez	.15	.11	.06	300 Steve Lake	.06	.05	.02
210 Ted Power	.06	.05	.02	301 Tito Landrum	.06	.05	.02
211 Joe Price	.06	.05	.02	302 *Mike LaValliere*	.25	.20	.10
212 Ron Robinson	.06	.05	.02	303 *Greg Mathews*(FC)	.20	.15	.08
213 Pete Rose	.60	.45	.25	304 Willie McGee	.12	.09	.05
214 Mario Soto	.08	.06	.03	305 Jose Oquendo	.06	.05	.02
215 *Kurt Stillwell*	.25	.20	.10	306 Terry Pendleton	.10	.08	.04
216 Max Venable	.06	.05	.02	307 Pat Perry	.08	.06	.03
217 Chris Welsh	.06	.05	.02	308 Ozzie Smith	.15	.11	.06
218 *Carl Willis*(FC)	.10	.08	.04	309 Ray Soff	.06	.05	.02
219 Jesse Barfield	.15	.11	.06	310 John Tudor	.10	.08	.04
220 George Bell	.25	.20	.10	311 Andy Van Slyke	.12	.09	.05
221 Bill Caudill	.06	.05	.02	312 Todd Worrell	.20	.15	.08
222 *John Cerutti*	.20	.15	.08	313 Dann Bilardello	.06	.05	.02
223 Jim Clancy	.08	.06	.03	314 Hubie Brooks	.10	.08	.04
224 *Mark Eichhorn*	.15	.11	.06	315 Tim Burke	.06	.05	.02
225 Tony Fernandez	.12	.09	.05	316 Andre Dawson	.20	.15	.08
226 Damaso Garcia	.06	.05	.02	317 Mike Fitzgerald	.06	.05	.02
227 Kelly Gruber	.06	.05	.02	318 Tom Foley	.06	.05	.02

		MT	NR MT	EX
319	Andres Galarraga	.40	.30	.15
320	Joe Hesketh	.06	.05	.02
321	Wallace Johnson	.06	.05	.02
322	Wayne Krenchicki	.06	.05	.02
323	Vance Law	.08	.06	.03
324	Dennis Martinez	.08	.06	.03
325	Bob McClure	.06	.05	.02
326	Andy McGaffigan	.06	.05	.02
327	*Al Newman*	.08	.06	.03
328	Tim Raines	.30	.25	.12
329	Jeff Reardon	.10	.08	.04
330	*Luis Rivera*(FC)	.10	.08	.04
331	*Bob Sebra*(FC)	.10	.08	.04
332	Bryn Smith	.06	.05	.02
333	Jay Tibbs	.06	.05	.02
334	Tim Wallach	.12	.09	.05
335	Mitch Webster	.08	.06	.03
336	Jim Wohlford	.06	.05	.02
337	Floyd Youmans	.08	.06	.03
338	*Chris Bosio*(FC)	.40	.30	.15
339	*Glenn Braggs*(FC)	.40	.30	.15
340	Rick Cerone	.06	.05	.02
341	Mark Clear	.06	.05	.02
342	*Bryan Clutterbuck*(FC)	.10	.08	.04
343	Cecil Cooper	.12	.09	.05
344	Rob Deer	.10	.08	.04
345	Jim Gantner	.08	.06	.03
346	Ted Higuera	.20	.15	.08
347	John Henry Johnson	.06	.05	.02
348	Tim Leary(FC)	.30	.25	.12
349	Rick Manning	.06	.05	.02
350	Paul Molitor	.15	.11	.06
351	Charlie Moore	.06	.05	.02
352	Juan Nieves	.10	.08	.04
353	Ben Oglivie	.08	.06	.03
354	*Dan Plesac*	.35	.25	.14
355	Ernest Riles	.06	.05	.02
356	Billy Joe Robidoux	.06	.05	.02
357	Bill Schroeder	.06	.05	.02
358	*Dale Sveum*	.20	.15	.08
359	Gorman Thomas	.10	.08	.04
360	Bill Wegman(FC)	.10	.08	.04
361	Robin Yount	.25	.20	.10
362	Steve Balboni	.08	.06	.03
363	*Scott Bankhead*	.30	.25	.12
364	Buddy Biancalana	.06	.05	.02
365	Bud Black	.06	.05	.02
366	George Brett	.40	.30	.15
367	Steve Farr	.06	.05	.02
368	Mark Gubicza	.12	.09	.05
369	*Bo Jackson*	15.00	11.00	6.00
370	Danny Jackson	.15	.11	.06
371	*Mike Kingery*	.15	.11	.06
372	Rudy Law	.06	.05	.02
373	Charlie Leibrandt	.08	.06	.03
374	Dennis Leonard	.08	.06	.03
375	Hal McRae	.10	.08	.04
376	Jorge Orta	.06	.05	.02
377	Jamie Quirk	.06	.05	.02
378	Dan Quisenberry	.08	.06	.03
379	Bret Saberhagen	.30	.25	.12
380	Angel Salazar	.06	.05	.02
381	Lonnie Smith	.08	.06	.03
382	Jim Sundberg	.08	.06	.03
383	Frank White	.10	.08	.04
384	Willie Wilson	.12	.09	.05
385	Joaquin Andujar	.08	.06	.03
386	Doug Bair	.06	.05	.02
387	Dusty Baker	.08	.06	.03
388	Bruce Bochte	.06	.05	.02
389	Jose Canseco	6.00	4.50	2.50
390	Chris Codiroli	.06	.05	.02
391	Mike Davis	.08	.06	.03
392	Alfredo Griffin	.08	.06	.03
393	Moose Haas	.06	.05	.02
394	Donnie Hill	.06	.05	.02
395	Jay Howell	.08	.06	.03
396	Dave Kingman	.12	.09	.05
397	Carney Lansford	.10	.08	.04
398	*David Leiper*(FC)	.12	.09	.05
399	*Bill Mooneyham*	.10	.08	.04
400	Dwayne Murphy	.08	.06	.03
401	Steve Ontiveros	.06	.05	.02
402	Tony Phillips	.06	.05	.02
403	Eric Plunk	.08	.06	.03
404	Jose Rijo	.08	.06	.03
405	*Terry Steinbach*(FC)	.90	.70	.35
406	Dave Stewart	.12	.09	.05
407	Mickey Tettleton	.06	.05	.02
408	Dave Von Ohlen	.06	.05	.02
409	Jerry Willard	.06	.05	.02

		MT	NR MT	EX
410	Curt Young	.08	.06	.03
411	Bruce Bochy	.06	.05	.02
412	Dave Dravecky	.08	.06	.03
413	Tim Flannery	.06	.05	.02
414	Steve Garvey	.25	.20	.10
415	Goose Gossage	.15	.11	.06
416	Tony Gwynn	.35	.25	.14
417	Andy Hawkins	.06	.05	.02
418	LaMarr Hoyt	.06	.05	.02
419	Terry Kennedy	.08	.06	.03
420	*John Kruk*	.25	.20	.10
421	Dave LaPoint	.08	.06	.03
422	Craig Lefferts	.06	.05	.02
423	Carmelo Martinez	.08	.06	.03
424	Lance McCullers	.08	.06	.03
425	Kevin McReynolds	.15	.11	.06
426	Graig Nettles	.12	.09	.05
427	Bip Roberts	.06	.05	.02
428	Jerry Royster	.06	.05	.02
429	Benito Santiago	.80	.60	.30
430	Eric Show	.08	.06	.03
431	Bob Stoddard	.06	.05	.02
432	Garry Templeton	.08	.06	.03
433	Gene Walter	.06	.05	.02
434	Ed Whitson	.06	.05	.02
435	Marvell Wynne	.06	.05	.02
436	Dave Anderson	.06	.05	.02
437	Greg Brock	.08	.06	.03
438	Enos Cabell	.06	.05	.02
439	Mariano Duncan	.06	.05	.02
440	Pedro Guerrero	.15	.11	.06
441	Orel Hershiser	.40	.30	.15
442	Rick Honeycutt	.06	.05	.02
443	Ken Howell	.06	.05	.02
444	Ken Landreaux	.06	.05	.02
445	Bill Madlock	.12	.09	.05
446	Mike Marshall	.12	.09	.05
447	Len Matuszek	.06	.05	.02
448	Tom Niedenfuer	.08	.06	.03
449	Alejandro Pena	.08	.06	.03
450	Dennis Powell(FC)	.08	.06	.03
451	Jerry Reuss	.08	.06	.03
452	Bill Russell	.08	.06	.03
453	Steve Sax	.15	.11	.06
454	Mike Scioscia	.08	.06	.03
455	Franklin Stubbs	.08	.06	.03
456	Alex Trevino	.06	.05	.02
457	Fernando Valenzuela	.25	.20	.10
458	Ed Vande Berg	.06	.05	.02
459	Bob Welch	.10	.08	.04
460	*Reggie Williams*	.10	.08	.04
461	Don Aase	.06	.05	.02
462	Juan Beniquez	.06	.05	.02
463	Mike Boddicker	.08	.06	.03
464	Juan Bonilla	.06	.05	.02
465	Rich Bordi	.06	.05	.02
466	Storm Davis	.10	.08	.04
467	Rick Dempsey	.08	.06	.03
468	Ken Dixon	.06	.05	.02
469	Jim Dwyer	.06	.05	.02
470	Mike Flanagan	.08	.06	.03
471	Jackie Gutierrez	.06	.05	.02
472	Brad Havens	.06	.05	.02
473	Lee Lacy	.06	.05	.02
474	Fred Lynn	.15	.11	.06
475	Scott McGregor	.08	.06	.03
476	Eddie Murray	.35	.25	.14
477	Tom O'Malley	.06	.05	.02
478	Cal Ripken, Jr.	.35	.25	.14
479	Larry Sheets	.08	.06	.03
480	John Shelby	.06	.05	.02
481	Nate Snell	.06	.05	.02
482	Jim Traber(FC)	.10	.08	.04
483	Mike Young	.06	.05	.02
484	Neil Allen	.06	.05	.02
485	Harold Baines	.15	.11	.06
486	Floyd Bannister	.10	.08	.04
487	Daryl Boston	.08	.06	.03
488	Ivan Calderon	.12	.09	.05
489	*John Cangelosi*	.12	.09	.05
490	Steve Carlton	.25	.20	.10
491	Joe Cowley	.06	.05	.02
492	Julio Cruz	.06	.05	.02
493	Bill Dawley	.06	.05	.02
494	Jose DeLeon	.08	.06	.03
495	Richard Dotson	.08	.06	.03
496	Carlton Fisk	.15	.11	.06
497	Ozzie Guillen	.10	.08	.04
498	Jerry Hairston	.06	.05	.02
499	Ron Hassey	.06	.05	.02
500	Tim Hulett	.06	.05	.02

#	Name	MT	NR MT	EX
501	Bob James	.06	.05	.02
502	Steve Lyons	.06	.05	.02
503	*Joel McKeon*	.10	.08	.04
504	Gene Nelson	.06	.05	.02
505	Dave Schmidt	.06	.05	.02
506	Ray Searage	.06	.05	.02
507	*Bobby Thigpen*(FC)	.35	.25	.14
508	Greg Walker	.10	.08	.04
509	Jim Acker	.06	.05	.02
510	Doyle Alexander	.08	.06	.03
511	*Paul Assenmacher*	.15	.11	.06
512	Bruce Benedict	.06	.05	.02
513	Chris Chambliss	.08	.06	.03
514	Jeff Dedmon	.06	.05	.02
515	Gene Garber	.06	.05	.02
516	Ken Griffey	.10	.08	.04
517	Terry Harper	.06	.05	.02
518	Bob Horner	.10	.08	.04
519	Glenn Hubbard	.06	.05	.02
520	Rick Mahler	.06	.05	.02
521	Omar Moreno	.06	.05	.02
522	Dale Murphy	.40	.30	.15
523	Ken Oberkfell	.06	.05	.02
524	Ed Olwine	.06	.05	.02
525	David Palmer	.06	.05	.02
526	Rafael Ramirez	.06	.05	.02
527	Billy Sample	.06	.05	.02
528	Ted Simmons	.12	.09	.05
529	Zane Smith	.08	.06	.03
530	Bruce Sutter	.12	.09	.05
531	*Andres Thomas*	.25	.20	.10
532	Ozzie Virgil	.06	.05	.02
533	*Allan Anderson*(FC)	.25	.20	.10
534	Keith Atherton	.06	.05	.02
535	Billy Beane	.06	.05	.02
536	Bert Blyleven	.12	.09	.05
537	Tom Brunansky	.10	.08	.04
538	Randy Bush	.06	.05	.02
539	George Frazier	.06	.05	.02
540	Gary Gaetti	.15	.11	.06
541	Greg Gagne	.06	.05	.02
542	Mickey Hatcher	.06	.05	.02
543	Neal Heaton	.06	.05	.02
544	Kent Hrbek	.15	.11	.06
545	Roy Lee Jackson	.06	.05	.02
546	Tim Laudner	.06	.05	.02
547	Steve Lombardozzi	.10	.08	.04
548	*Mark Portugal*(FC)	.10	.08	.04
549	Kirby Puckett	.90	.70	.35
550	Jeff Reed	.08	.06	.03
551	Mark Salas	.06	.05	.02
552	Roy Smalley	.06	.05	.02
553	Mike Smithson	.06	.05	.02
554	Frank Viola	.15	.11	.06
555	Thad Bosley	.06	.05	.02
556	Ron Cey	.10	.08	.04
557	Jody Davis	.08	.06	.03
558	Ron Davis	.06	.05	.02
559	Bob Dernier	.06	.05	.02
560	Frank DiPino	.06	.05	.02
561	Shawon Dunston	.10	.08	.04
562	Leon Durham	.08	.06	.03
563	Dennis Eckersley	.12	.09	.05
564	Terry Francona	.06	.05	.02
565	Dave Gumpert	.06	.05	.02
566	Guy Hoffman	.08	.06	.03
567	Ed Lynch	.06	.05	.02
568	Gary Matthews	.10	.08	.04
569	Keith Moreland	.08	.06	.03
570	*Jamie Moyer*(FC)	.20	.15	.08
571	Jerry Mumphrey	.06	.05	.02
572	Ryne Sandberg	.25	.20	.10
573	Scott Sanderson	.06	.05	.02
574	Lee Smith	.10	.08	.04
575	Chris Speier	.06	.05	.02
576	Rick Sutcliffe	.12	.09	.05
577	Manny Trillo	.08	.06	.03
578	Steve Trout	.06	.05	.02
579	Karl Best	.06	.05	.02
580	Scott Bradley(FC)	.08	.06	.03
581	Phil Bradley	.12	.09	.05
582	Mickey Brantley	.08	.06	.03
583	Mike Brown	.06	.05	.02
584	Alvin Davis	.12	.09	.05
585	*Lee Guetterman*(FC)	.15	.11	.06
586	Mark Huismann	.06	.05	.02
587	Bob Kearney	.06	.05	.02
588	Pete Ladd	.06	.05	.02
589	Mark Langston	.12	.09	.05
590	Mike Moore	.06	.05	.02
591	Mike Morgan	.06	.05	.02

#	Name	MT	NR MT	EX
592	John Moses	.06	.05	.02
593	Ken Phelps	.08	.06	.03
594	Jim Presley	.10	.08	.04
595	*Rey Quinonez (Quinones)*	.15	.11	.06
596	Harold Reynolds	.15	.11	.06
597	Billy Swift	.06	.05	.02
598	Danny Tartabull	.25	.20	.10
599	Steve Yeager	.06	.05	.02
600	Matt Young	.06	.05	.02
601	Bill Almon	.06	.05	.02
602	*Rafael Belliard*(FC)	.12	.09	.05
603	Mike Bielecki	.06	.05	.02
604	*Barry Bonds*	1.00	.70	.40
605	*Bobby Bonilla*	1.00	.70	.40
606	Sid Bream	.08	.06	.03
607	Mike Brown	.06	.05	.02
608	Pat Clements	.06	.05	.02
609	*Mike Diaz*(FC)	.15	.11	.06
610	Cecilio Guante	.06	.05	.02
611	*Barry Jones*(FC)	.12	.09	.05
612	Bob Kipper	.06	.05	.02
613	Larry McWilliams	.06	.05	.02
614	Jim Morrison	.06	.05	.02
615	Joe Orsulak	.06	.05	.02
616	Junior Ortiz	.06	.05	.02
617	Tony Pena	.08	.06	.03
618	Johnny Ray	.10	.08	.04
619	Rick Reuschel	.10	.08	.04
620	R.J. Reynolds	.06	.05	.02
621	Rick Rhoden	.10	.08	.04
622	Don Robinson	.08	.06	.03
623	Bob Walk	.06	.05	.02
624	Jim Winn	.06	.05	.02
625	Youthful Power (Jose Canseco, Pete Incaviglia)	.70	.50	.30
626	300 Game Winners (Phil Niekro, Don Sutton)	.12	.09	.05
627	A.L. Firemen (Don Aase, Dave Righetti)	.08	.06	.03
628	Rookie All-Stars (Jose Canseco, Wally Joyner)	2.00	1.50	.80
629	Magic Mets (Gary Carter, Sid Fernandez, Dwight Gooden, Keith Hernandez, Darryl Strawberry)	.60	.45	.25
630	N.L. Best Righties (Mike Krukow, Mike Scott)	.08	.06	.03
631	Sensational Southpaws (John Franco, Fernando Valenzuela)	.10	.08	.04
632	Count 'Em (Bob Horner)	.08	.06	.03
633	A.L. Pitcher's Nightmare (Jose Canseco, Kirby Puckett, Jim Rice)	1.50	1.25	.60
634	All Star Battery (Gary Carter, Roger Clemens)	.25	.20	.10
635	4,000 Strikeouts (Steve Carlton)	.12	.09	.05
636	Big Bats At First Sack (Glenn Davis, Eddie Murray)	.20	.15	.08
637	On Base (Wade Boggs, Keith Hernandez)	.35	.25	.14
638	Sluggers From Left Side (Don Mattingly, Darryl Strawberry)	.90	.70	.35
639	Former MVP's (Dave Parker, Ryne Sandberg)	.12	.09	.05
640	Dr. K. & Super K (Roger Clemens, Dwight Gooden)	.50	.40	.20
641	A.L. West Stoppers (Charlie Hough, Mike Witt)	.08	.06	.03
642	Doubles & Triples (Tim Raines, Juan Samuel)	.12	.09	.05
643	Outfielders With Punch (Harold Baines, Jesse Barfield)	.10	.08	.04
644	Major League Prospects *(Dave Clark, Greg Swindell)*(FC)	1.25	.90	.50
645	Major League Prospects *(Ron Karkovice, Russ Morman)*(FC)	.12	.09	.05
646	Major League Prospects *(Willie Fraser, Devon White)*(FC)	1.25	.90	.50
647	Major League Prospects *(Jerry Browne, Mike Stanley)*(FC)	.40	.30	.15
648	Major League Prospects *(Phil Lombardi, Dave Magadan)*(FC)	.50	.40	.20
649	Major League Prospects *(Ralph Bryant, Jose Gonzalez)*(FC)	.20	.15	.08
650	Major League Prospects *(Randy Asadoor, Jimmy Jones)*(FC)	.20	.15	.08
651	Major League Prospects *(Marvin Freeman, Tracy Jones)*	.25	.20	.10
652	Major League Prospects *(Kevin Seitzer, John Stefero)*(FC)	5.00	3.75	2.00
653	Major League Prospects *(Steve Fireovid, Rob Nelson)*(FC)	.10	.08	.04
654	Checklist 1-95	.06	.05	.02

		MT	NR MT	EX
655	Checklist 96-192	.06	.05	.02
656	Checklist 193-288	.06	.05	.02
657	Checklist 289-384	.06	.05	.02
658	Checklist 385-483	.06	.05	.02
659	Checklist 484-578	.06	.05	.02
660	Checklist 579-660	.06	.05	.02

1987 Fleer All Star Team

As in 1986, Fleer All Star Team cards were randomly inserted in Fleer wax and cello packs. Twelve cards, each measuring the standard 2-1/2" by 3-1/2", comprise the set. The card fronts feature a full-color player photo set against a gray background for American League players and a black background for National Leaguers. Card backs are printed in black, red and white and feature a lengthy player biography. Fleer's choices for a major league All-Star team is once again the theme for the set.

		MT	NR MT	EX
	Complete Set:	18.00	13.50	7.25
	Common Player:	.60	.45	.25
1	Don Mattingly	5.00	3.75	2.00
2	Gary Carter	1.00	.70	.40
3	Tony Fernandez	.75	.60	.30
4	Steve Sax	.75	.60	.30
5	Kirby Puckett	3.00	2.25	1.25
6	Mike Schmidt	2.00	1.50	.80
7	Mike Easler	.60	.45	.25
8	Todd Worrell	.75	.60	.30
9	George Bell	1.00	.70	.40
10	Fernando Valenzuela	1.00	.70	.40
11	Roger Clemens	2.25	1.75	.90
12	Tim Raines	1.25	.90	.50

1987 Fleer Award Winner

The 1987 Fleer Award Winners boxed set was prepared by Fleer for distribution by 7-Eleven stores. The cards, which measure 2-1/2" by 3-1/2", feature players who have won various major league awards during their careers. The card fronts contain full-color photos surrounded by a yellow border. The name of the award the player won is printed at the bottom of the card in an oval-shaped band designed to resemble a metal nameplate on a trophy. Card backs, printed in black, yellow and white, include lifetime major and minor league statistics along with typical personal information. Each boxed set contained six team logo stickers.

		MT	NR MT	EX
	Complete Set:	6.00	4.50	2.50
	Complete Set:	.05	.04	.02
1	Marty Barrett	.07	.05	.03
2	George Bell	.20	.15	.08
3	Bert Blyleven	.10	.08	.04
4	Bob Boone	.05	.04	.02
5	John Candelaria	.05	.04	.02
6	Jose Canseco	1.50	1.25	.60
7	Gary Carter	.25	.20	.10
8	Joe Carter	.25	.20	.10
9	Roger Clemens	.50	.40	.20
10	Cecil Cooper	.10	.08	.04
11	Eric Davis	.60	.45	.25
12	Tony Fernandez	.10	.08	.04
13	Scott Fletcher	.05	.04	.02
14	Bob Forsch	.05	.04	.02
15	Dwight Gooden	.50	.40	.20
16	Ron Guidry	.12	.09	.05
17	Ozzie Guillen	.07	.05	.03
18	Bill Gullickson	.05	.04	.02
19	Tony Gwynn	.25	.20	.10
20	Bob Knepper	.05	.04	.02
21	Ray Knight	.05	.04	.02
22	Mark Langston	.20	.15	.08
23	Candy Maldonado	.05	.04	.02
24	Don Mattingly	1.25	.90	.50
25	Roger McDowell	.07	.05	.03
26	Dale Murphy	.30	.25	.12
27	Dave Parker	.12	.09	.05
28	Lance Parrish	.15	.11	.06
29	Gary Pettis	.05	.04	.02
30	Kirby Puckett	.70	.50	.40
31	Johnny Ray	.07	.05	.03
32	Dave Righetti	.12	.09	.05
33	Cal Ripken, Jr.	.30	.25	.12
34	Bret Saberhagen	.15	.11	.06
35	Ryne Sandberg	.20	.15	.08
36	Mike Schmidt	.30	.25	.12
37	Mike Scott	.12	.09	.05
38	Ozzie Smith	.12	.09	.05
39	Robbie Thompson	.10	.08	.04
40	Fernando Valenzuela	.20	.15	.08
41	Mitch Webster	.05	.04	.02
42	Frank White	.07	.05	.03
43	Mike Witt	.07	.05	.03
44	Todd Worrell	.15	.11	.06

1987 Fleer Baseball All Stars

Produced by Fleer for exclusive distribution through Ben Franklin stores, the "Baseball All Stars" set is comprised of 44 cards which are the standard 2-1/2" by 3-1/2" size. The cards have full-color photos surrounded by a bright red border with white pinstripes at the top and bottom. The card backs are printed in blue, white and dark red and include complete major and minor league statistics. The set was issued in a special cardboard box.

		MT	NR MT	EX
Complete Set:		7.00	5.25	2.75
Common Player:		.05	.04	.02
1	Harold Baines	.10	.08	.04
2	Jesse Barfield	.12	.09	.05
3	Wade Boggs	1.00	.70	.40
4	Dennis "Oil Can" Boyd	.05	.04	.02
5	Scott Bradley	.05	.04	.02
6	Jose Canseco	1.50	1.25	.60
7	Gary Carter	.25	.20	.10
8	Joe Carter	.25	.20	.10
9	Mark Clear	.05	.04	.02
10	Roger Clemens	.50	.40	.20
11	Jose Cruz	.05	.04	.02
12	Chili Davis	.07	.05	.03
13	Jody Davis	.05	.04	.02
14	Rob Deer	.05	.04	.02
15	Brian Downing	.05	.04	.02
16	Sid Fernandez	.07	.05	.03
17	John Franco	.07	.05	.03
18	Andres Galarraga	.15	.11	.06
19	Dwight Gooden	.50	.40	.20
20	Tony Gwynn	.25	.20	.10
21	Charlie Hough	.05	.04	.02
22	Bruce Hurst	.10	.08	.04
23	Wally Joyner	.70	.50	.30
24	Carney Lansford	.05	.04	.02
25	Fred Lynn	.12	.09	.05
26	Don Mattingly	1.50	1.25	.60
27	Willie McGee	.10	.08	.04
28	Jack Morris	.15	.11	.06
29	Dale Murphy	.30	.25	.12
30	Bob Ojeda	.07	.05	.03
31	Tony Pena	.07	.05	.03
32	Kirby Puckett	.70	.50	.30
33	Dan Quisenberry	.07	.05	.03
34	Tim Raines	.25	.20	.10
35	Willie Randolph	.07	.05	.03
36	Cal Ripken, Jr.	.25	.20	.10
37	Pete Rose	.50	.40	.20
38	Nolan Ryan	.50	.40	.20
39	Juan Samuel	.10	.08	.04
40	Mike Schmidt	.30	.25	.12
41	Ozzie Smith	.12	.09	.05
42	Andres Thomas	.10	.08	.04
43	Fernando Valenzuela	.20	.15	.08
44	Mike Witt	.07	.05	.03

		MT	NR MT	EX
4	Wade Boggs	1.00	.70	.40
5	Sid Bream	.05	.04	.02
6	George Brett	.30	.25	.12
7	Ivan Calderon	.10	.08	.04
8	Jose Canseco	1.50	1.25	.60
9	Jack Clark	.12	.09	.05
10	Roger Clemens	.50	.40	.20
11	Eric Davis	.50	.40	.20
12	Andre Dawson	.15	.11	.06
13	Sid Fernandez	.07	.05	.03
14	John Franco	.07	.05	.03
15	Dwight Gooden	.50	.40	.20
16	Pedro Guerrero	.15	.11	.06
17	Tony Gwynn	.25	.20	.10
18	Rickey Henderson	.30	.25	.12
19	Tom Henke	.05	.04	.02
20	Ted Higuera	.10	.08	.04
21	Pete Incaviglia	.30	.25	.12
22	Wally Joyner	.50	.40	.20
23	Jeff Leonard	.05	.04	.02
24	Joe Magrane	.15	.11	.06
25	Don Mattingly	1.50	1.25	.60
26	Mark McGwire	1.50	1.25	.60
27	Jack Morris	.15	.11	.06
28	Dale Murphy	.30	.25	.12
29	Dave Parker	.12	.09	.05
30	Ken Phelps	.05	.04	.02
31	Kirby Puckett	.70	.50	.30
32	Tim Raines	.25	.20	.10
33	Jeff Reardon	.10	.08	.04
34	Dave Righetti	.12	.09	.05
35	Cal Ripken, Jr.	.30	.25	.12
36	Bret Saberhagen	.15	.11	.06
37	Mike Schmidt	.30	.25	.12
38	Mike Scott	.12	.09	.05
39	Kevin Seitzer	.50	.40	.20
40	Darryl Strawberry	.40	.30	.15
41	Rick Sutcliffe	.10	.08	.04
42	Pat Tabler	.05	.04	.02
43	Fernando Valenzuela	.10	.08	.04
44	Mike Witt	.07	.05	.03

1987 Fleer Baseball's Best

For a second straight baseball card season, Fleer produced for McCrory's stores and their affiliates a 44-card "Baseball's Best" set. Subtitled "Sluggers vs. Pitchers," 28 everyday players and 16 pitchers are featured. The card design is nearly identical to the previous year's effort. The cards, which measure 2-1/2" by 3-1/2", were housed in a specially designed box along with six team logo stickers.

		MT	NR MT	EX
Complete Set:		6.00	4.50	2.50
Common Player:		.05	.04	.02
1	Kevin Bass	.07	.05	.03
2	Jesse Barfield	.12	.09	.05
3	George Bell	.20	.15	.08

1987 Fleer Baseball's Exciting Stars

Another entry into the Fleer lineup of individual boxed sets, the "Baseball's Exciting Stars" set was produced by Fleer for Cumberland Farms stores. The card fronts feature a red, white and blue border with the words "Exciting Stars" printed in yellow at the top. The backs are printed in red and blue and carry complete major and minor league statistics. Included with the boxed set of 44 cards were six team logo stickers.

		MT	NR MT	EX
Complete Set:		7.00	5.25	2.75
Common Player:		.05	.04	.02
1	Don Aase	.05	.04	.02
2	Rick Aguilera	.07	.05	.03
3	Jesse Barfield	.12	.09	.05
4	Wade Boggs	1.00	.70	.40
5	Dennis "Oil Can" Boyd	.05	.04	.02
6	Sid Bream	.07	.05	.03
7	Jose Canseco	1.50	1.25	.60

		MT	NR MT	EX
8	Steve Carlton	.25	.20	.10
9	Gary Carter	.25	.20	.10
10	Will Clark	1.00	.70	.40
11	Roger Clemens	.40	.30	.15
12	Danny Cox	.07	.05	.03
13	Alvin Davis	.10	.08	.04
14	Eric Davis	.50	.40	.20
15	Rob Deer	.07	.05	.03
16	Brian Downing	.05	.04	.02
17	Gene Garber	.05	.04	.02
18	Steve Garvey	.25	.20	.10
19	Dwight Gooden	.50	.40	.20
20	Mark Gubicza	.10	.08	.04
21	Mel Hall	.05	.04	.02
22	Terry Harper	.05	.04	.02
23	Von Hayes	.10	.08	.04
24	Rickey Henderson	.60	.45	.25
25	Tom Henke	.05	.04	.02
26	Willie Hernandez	.05	.04	.02
27	Ted Higuera	.10	.08	.04
28	Rick Honeycutt	.05	.04	.02
29	Kent Hrbek	.15	.11	.06
30	Wally Joyner	.60	.45	.25
31	Charlie Kerfeld	.05	.04	.02
32	Fred Lynn	.12	.09	.05
33	Don Mattingly	1.50	1.25	.60
34	Tim Raines	.25	.20	.10
35	Dennis Rasmussen	.07	.05	.03
36	Johnny Ray	.07	.05	.03
37	Jim Rice	.20	.15	.08
38	Pete Rose	.50	.40	.20
39	Lee Smith	.07	.05	.03
40	Cory Snyder	.25	.20	.10
41	Darryl Strawberry	.40	.30	.15
42	Kent Tekulve	.05	.04	.02
43	Willie Wilson	.10	.08	.04
44	Bobby Witt	.12	.09	.05

		MT	NR MT	EX
11	Eric Davis	.50	.40	.20
12	Glenn Davis	.15	.11	.06
13	Shawon Dunston	.07	.05	.03
14	Mark Eichhorn	.10	.08	.04
15	Gary Gaetti	.12	.09	.05
16	Steve Garvey	.25	.20	.10
17	Kirk Gibson	.20	.15	.08
18	Dwight Gooden	.50	.40	.20
19	Von Hayes	.07	.05	.03
20	Willie Hernandez	.07	.05	.03
21	Ted Higuera	.10	.08	.04
22	Wally Joyner	.80	.60	.30
23	Bob Knepper	.05	.04	.02
24	Mike Krukow	.05	.04	.02
25	Jeff Leonard	.05	.04	.02
26	Don Mattingly	1.50	1.25	.60
27	Kirk McCaskill	.07	.05	.03
28	Kevin McReynolds	.12	.09	.05
29	Jim Morrison	.05	.04	.02
30	Dale Murphy	.30	.25	.12
31	Pete O'Brien	.07	.05	.03
32	Bob Ojeda	.07	.05	.03
33	Larry Parrish	.05	.04	.02
34	Ken Phelps	.05	.04	.02
35	Dennis Rasmussen	.07	.05	.03
36	Ernest Riles	.07	.05	.03
37	Cal Ripken, Jr.	.30	.25	.12
38	Ron Robinson	.05	.04	.02
39	Steve Sax	.15	.11	.06
40	Mike Schmidt	.30	.25	.12
41	John Tudor	.07	.05	.03
42	Fernando Valenzuela	.20	.15	.08
43	Mike Witt	.07	.05	.03
44	Curt Young	.05	.04	.02

1987 Fleer
Baseball's Game Winners

The 1987 Fleer "Baseball's Game Winners" boxed set of 44 cards was produced for distribution through Bi-Mart Discount Drug, Pay'n-Save, Mott's 5 & 10, M.E. Moses, and Winn's stores. The cards, which measure 2-1/2" by 3-1/2", have a light blue border with the player's name and game winning RBI or games won statistics in a yellow oval band at the top of the card. Below the full-color player photo is the name of the set in blue, yellow and red. Included in the boxed set were six team logo stickers.

		MT	NR MT	EX
Complete Set:		5.00	3.75	2.00
Common Player:		.05	.04	.02
1	Harold Baines	.10	.08	.04
2	Don Baylor	.10	.08	.04
3	George Bell	.20	.15	.08
4	Tony Bernazard	.05	.04	.02
5	Wade Boggs	1.00	.70	.40
6	George Brett	.40	.30	.15
7	Hubie Brooks	.07	.05	.03
8	Jose Canseco	1.00	.70	.40
9	Gary Carter	.20	.15	.08
10	Roger Clemens	.40	.30	.15

1987 Fleer
Baseball's Hottest Stars

The "Baseball's Hottest Stars" 44-card set was produced by Fleer for the Revco Drug Store chain. Measuring the standard 2-1/2" by 3-1/2", the cards feature full-color photos surrounded by a red, white and blue border. The player's name, position and team appear in a blue band at the bottom of the card. Card backs are printed in red, white and black and contain the player's lifetime professional statistics. The set was housed in a special cardboard box with six team logo stickers.

		MT	NR MT	EX
Complete Set:		7.00	5.25	2.75
Common Player:		.05	.04	.02
1	Joaquin Andujar	.05	.04	.02
2	Harold Baines	.10	.08	.04
3	Kevin Bass	.07	.05	.03
4	Don Baylor	.10	.08	.04
5	Barry Bonds	.20	.15	.08
6	George Brett	.30	.25	.12
7	Tom Brunansky	.10	.08	.04
8	Brett Butler	.05	.04	.02
9	Jose Canseco	1.50	1.25	.60
10	Roger Clemens	.50	.40	.20
11	Ron Darling	.10	.08	.04
12	Eric Davis	.50	.40	.20
13	Andre Dawson	.15	.11	.06

		MT	NR MT	EX
14	Doug DeCinces	.05	.04	.02
15	Leon Durham	.07	.05	.03
16	Mark Eichhorn	.10	.08	.04
17	Scott Garrelts	.05	.04	.02
18	Dwight Gooden	.50	.40	.20
19	Dave Henderson	.05	.04	.02
20	Rickey Henderson	.50	.40	.20
21	Keith Hernandez	.15	.11	.06
22	Ted Higuera	.10	.08	.04
23	Bob Horner	.07	.05	.03
24	Pete Incaviglia	.40	.30	.15
25	Wally Joyner	.50	.40	.20
26	Mark Langston	.07	.05	.03
27	Don Mattingly	1.75	1.25	.70
28	Dale Murphy	.30	.25	.12
29	Kirk McCaskill	.07	.05	.03
30	Willie McGee	.10	.08	.04
31	Dave Righetti	.12	.09	.05
32	Pete Rose	.40	.30	.15
33	Bruce Ruffin	.15	.11	.06
34	Steve Sax	.15	.11	.06
35	Mike Schmidt	.30	.25	.12
36	Larry Sheets	.10	.08	.04
37	Eric Show	.07	.05	.03
38	Dave Smith	.05	.04	.02
39	Cory Snyder	.25	.20	.10
40	Frank Tanana	.05	.04	.02
41	Alan Trammell	.20	.15	.08
42	Reggie Williams	.07	.05	.03
43	Mookie Wilson	.07	.05	.03
44	Todd Worrell	.15	.11	.06

1987 Fleer Box Panels

For the second straight year, Fleer produced a special set of cards designed to stimulate sales of their wax and cello pack boxes. In 1987, Fleer issued 16 cards in panels of four on the bottoms of retail boxes. The cards are numbered C-1 through C-16 and are 2-1/2" by 3-1/2" in size. The cards have the same design as the regular issue set with the player photos and card numbers being different.

		MT	NR MT	EX
Complete Panel Set:		8.00	6.00	3.25
Complete Singles Set:		3.50	2.75	1.50
Common Panel:		2.25	1.75	.90
Common Single Player:		.20	.15	.08
Panel		2.50	2.00	1.00
1	Mets Logo	.05	.04	.02
6	Keith Hernandez	.30	.25	.12
8	Dale Murphy	.60	.45	.25
14	Ryne Sandberg	.30	.25	.12
Panel		2.25	1.75	.90
2	Jesse Barfield	.20	.15	.08
3	George Brett	.60	.45	.25
5	Red Sox Logo	.05	.04	.02
11	Kirby Puckett	.30	.25	.12
Panel		2.75	2.00	1.00
4	Dwight Gooden	.80	.60	.30
9	Astros Logo	.05	.04	.02
10	Dave Parker	.25	.20	.10
15	Mike Schmidt	.60	.45	.25
Panel		2.75	2.00	1.00
7	Wally Joyner	1.00	.70	.40
12	Dave Righetti	.20	.15	.08
13	Angels Logo	.05	.04	.02

		MT	NR MT	EX
16	Robin Yount	.25	.20	.10

1987 Fleer '86 World Series

Fleer issued a set of 12 cards highlighting the 1986 World Series between the Boston Red Sox and New York Mets. The sets were available only with Fleer factory-packaged sets of 660 regular issue cards. The cards, which are the standard 2-1/2" by 3-1/2" size, have either horizontal or vertical formats. The fronts are bordered in red, white and blue stars and stripes with a thin gold frame around the photo. The backs are printed in red and blue ink on white stock and include information regarding the photo on the card fronts.

		MT	NR MT	EX
Complete Set:		6.00	4.50	2.50
Common Player:		.50	.40	.20
1	Left-Hand Finesse Beats Mets (Bruce Hurst)	.50	.40	.20
2	Hernandez And Boggs (Wade Boggs, Keith Hernandez)	1.00	.70	.40
3	Roger Clemens (Gary Carter)	.70	.50	.30
4	Clutch Hitting (Gary Carter)	.50	.40	.20
5	Darling Picks Up The Slack (Ron Darling)	.50	.40	.20
6	.433 Series Batting Average (Marty Barrett)	.50	.40	.20
7	Dwight Gooden	.70	.50	.30
8	Strategy At Work	.50	.40	.20
9	Dewey! (Dwight Evans)	.50	.40	.20
10	One Strike From Boston Victory (Dave Henderson, Spike Owen)	.50	.40	.20
11	Series Home Run Duo (Ray Knight, Darryl Strawberry)	.50	.40	.20
12	Series M.V.P. (Ray Knight)	.50	.40	.20

1987 Fleer Headliners

A continuation of the 1986 Future Hall of Famers idea, Fleer encountered legal problems with using the Hall of Fame name and abated them by entitling the set "Headliners." The cards, which are the standard

2-1/2" by 3-1/2" size, were randomly inserted in three-pack cello packs. Card fronts feature a player photo set against a beige background with bright red stripes. The card backs are printed in black, red and gray and offer a brief biography with an emphasis on the player's performance during the 1986 season.

		MT	NR MT	EX
	Complete Set:	10.00	7.50	4.00
	Common Player:	1.00	.70	.40
1	Wade Boggs	2.25	1.75	.90
2	Jose Canseco	3.00	2.25	1.25
3	Dwight Gooden	1.50	1.25	.60
4	Rickey Henderson	2.00	1.50	.80
5	Keith Hernandez	1.00	.70	.40
6	Jim Rice	1.00	.70	.40

1987 Fleer League Leaders

For the second year in a row, Fleer produced a 44-card "League Leaders" set for Walgreens. The card fronts feature a border style which is identical to that used in 1986. However, an elliptical shaped full-color player photo is placed diagonally on the front. "1987 Fleer League Leaders" appears in the upper left corner of the front although nowhere on the card does it state in which pitching, hitting or fielding department was the player a league leader. The card backs are printed in red and blue on white stock. The cards in the boxed set are the standard 2-1/2" by 3-1/2" size.

		MT	NR MT	EX
	Complete Set:	5.00	3.75	2.00
	Common Player:	.05	.04	.02
1	Jesse Barfield	.12	.09	.05
2	Mike Boddicker	.07	.05	.03
3	Wade Boggs	1.00	.70	.40
4	Phil Bradley	.10	.08	.04
5	George Brett	.30	.25	.12
6	Hubie Brooks	.07	.05	.03
7	Chris Brown	.07	.05	.03
8	Jose Canseco	.70	.50	.30
9	Joe Carter	.12	.09	.05
10	Roger Clemens	.40	.30	.15
11	Vince Coleman	.15	.11	.06
12	Joe Cowley	.05	.04	.02
13	Kal Daniels	.20	.15	.08
14	Glenn Davis	.15	.11	.06
15	Jody Davis	.07	.05	.03
16	Darrell Evans	.07	.05	.03
17	Dwight Evans	.10	.08	.04
18	John Franco	.07	.05	.03
19	Julio Franco	.10	.08	.04
20	Dwight Gooden	.40	.30	.15
21	Goose Gossage	.12	.09	.05
22	Tom Herr	.07	.05	.03
23	Ted Higuera	.10	.08	.04
24	Bob Horner	.07	.05	.03
25	Pete Incaviglia	.40	.30	.15
26	Wally Joyner	.40	.30	.15
27	Dave Kingman	.10	.08	.04
28	Don Mattingly	1.75	1.25	.70
29	Willie McGee	.10	.08	.04

		MT	NR MT	EX
30	Donnie Moore	.05	.04	.02
31	Keith Moreland	.05	.04	.02
32	Eddie Murray	.25	.20	.10
33	Mike Pagliarulo	.10	.08	.04
34	Larry Parrish	.05	.04	.02
35	Tony Pena	.07	.05	.03
36	Kirby Puckett	.50	.40	.20
37	Pete Rose	.50	.40	.20
38	Juan Samuel	.12	.09	.05
39	Ryne Sandberg	.20	.15	.08
40	Mike Schmidt	.30	.25	.12
41	Darryl Strawberry	.40	.30	.15
42	Greg Walker	.07	.05	.03
43	Bob Welch	.07	.05	.03
44	Todd Worrell	.12	.09	.05

1987 Fleer Limited Edition

For the third straight year, Fleer produced a Limited Edition set for the McCrory's store chain and their affiliates. The cards are the standard 2-1/2" by 3-1/2" size and feature light blue borders at the top and bottom and a diagonal red and white border running along both sides. The set was issued in a specially prepared cardboard box, along with six team logo stickers.

		MT	NR MT	EX
	Complete Set:	5.00	3.75	2.00
	Common Player:	.05	.04	.02
1	Floyd Bannister	.05	.04	.02
2	Marty Barrett	.07	.05	.03
3	Steve Bedrosian	.10	.08	.04
4	George Bell	.20	.15	.08
5	George Brett	.30	.25	.12
6	Jose Canseco	1.00	.70	.40
7	Joe Carter	.12	.09	.05
8	Will Clark	1.00	.70	.40
9	Roger Clemens	.40	.30	.15
10	Vince Coleman	.15	.11	.06
11	Glenn Davis	.15	.11	.06
12	Mike Davis	.05	.04	.02
13	Len Dykstra	.07	.05	.03
14	John Franco	.07	.05	.03
15	Julio Franco	.10	.08	.04
16	Steve Garvey	.25	.20	.10
17	Kirk Gibson	.20	.15	.08
18	Dwight Gooden	.40	.30	.15
19	Tony Gwynn	.25	.20	.10
20	Keith Hernandez	.20	.15	.08
21	Teddy Higuera	.10	.08	.04
22	Kent Hrbek	.15	.11	.06
23	Wally Joyner	.50	.40	.20
24	Mike Krukow	.05	.04	.02
25	Mike Marshall	.10	.08	.04
26	Don Mattingly	1.00	.70	.40
27	Oddibe McDowell	.10	.08	.04
28	Jack Morris	.15	.11	.06
29	Lloyd Moseby	.07	.05	.03
30	Dale Murphy	.30	.25	.12
31	Eddie Murray	.25	.20	.10
32	Tony Pena	.07	.05	.03
33	Jim Presley	.10	.08	.04
34	Jeff Reardon	.10	.08	.04
35	Jim Rice	.20	.15	.08
36	Pete Rose	.40	.30	.15
37	Mike Schmidt	.30	.25	.12

	MT	NR MT	EX
38 Mike Scott	.12	.09	.05
39 Lee Smith	.07	.05	.03
40 Lonnie Smith	.05	.04	.02
41 Gary Ward	.05	.04	.02
42 Dave Winfield	.25	.20	.10
43 Todd Worrell	.12	.09	.05
44 Robin Yount	.20	.15	.08

1987 Fleer Mini

Continuing with an idea originated the previous year, the Fleer "Classic Miniatures" set consists of 120 cards that measure 1-13/16" by 2-9/16" in size. The cards are identical in design to the regular issue set produced by Fleer, but use completely different photos. The set was issued in a specially prepared collectors box along with 18 team logo stickers. The Fleer Mini set was available only through hobby dealers.

	MT	NR MT	EX
Complete Set:	8.00	6.00	3.25
Common Player:	.05	.04	.02
1 Don Aase	.05	.04	.02
2 Joaquin Andujar	.05	.04	.02
3 Harold Baines	.12	.09	.05
4 Jesse Barfield	.12	.09	.05
5 Kevin Bass	.05	.04	.02
6 Don Baylor	.10	.08	.04
7 George Bell	.20	.15	.08
8 Tony Bernazard	.05	.04	.02
9 Bert Blyleven	.12	.09	.05
10 Wade Boggs	1.00	.70	.40
11 Phil Bradley	.10	.08	.04
12 Sid Bream	.05	.04	.02
13 George Brett	.30	.25	.12
14 Hubie Brooks	.07	.05	.03
15 Chris Brown	.07	.05	.03
16 Tom Candiotti	.05	.04	.02
17 Jose Canseco	1.50	1.25	.60
18 Gary Carter	.20	.15	.08
19 Joe Carter	.12	.09	.05
20 Roger Clemens	.60	.45	.25
21 Vince Coleman	.15	.11	.06
22 Cecil Cooper	.10	.08	.04
23 Ron Darling	.10	.08	.04
24 Alvin Davis	.10	.08	.04
25 Chili Davis	.05	.04	.02
26 Eric Davis	.80	.60	.30
27 Glenn Davis	.15	.11	.06
28 Mike Davis	.05	.04	.02
29 Doug DeCinces	.05	.04	.02
30 Rob Deer	.07	.05	.03
31 Jim Deshaies	.10	.08	.04
32 Bo Diaz	.05	.04	.02
33 Richard Dotson	.07	.05	.03
34 Brian Downing	.05	.04	.02
35 Shawon Dunston	.07	.05	.03
36 Mark Eichhorn	.10	.08	.04
37 Dwight Evans	.12	.09	.05
38 Tony Fernandez	.10	.08	.04
39 Julio Franco	.10	.08	.04
40 Gary Gaetti	.12	.09	.05
41 Andres Galarraga	.15	.11	.06
42 Scott Garrelts	.05	.04	.02
43 Steve Garvey	.20	.15	.08
44 Kirk Gibson	.20	.15	.08

	MT	NR MT	EX
45 Dwight Gooden	.60	.45	.25
46 Ken Griffey	.07	.05	.03
47 Mark Gubicza	.10	.08	.04
48 Ozzie Guillen	.07	.05	.03
49 Bill Gullickson	.05	.04	.02
50 Tony Gwynn	.25	.20	.10
51 Von Hayes	.10	.08	.04
52 Rickey Henderson	.50	.40	.20
53 Keith Hernandez	.15	.11	.06
54 Willie Hernandez	.05	.04	.02
55 Ted Higuera	.10	.08	.04
56 Charlie Hough	.05	.04	.02
57 Kent Hrbek	.15	.11	.06
58 Pete Incaviglia	.40	.30	.15
59 Wally Joyner	.80	.60	.30
60 Bob Knepper	.07	.05	.03
61 Mike Krukow	.05	.04	.02
62 Mark Langston	.10	.08	.04
63 Carney Lansford	.07	.05	.03
64 Jim Lindeman	.12	.09	.05
65 Bill Madlock	.10	.08	.04
66 Don Mattingly	1.75	1.25	.70
67 Kirk McCaskill	.05	.04	.02
68 Lance McCullers	.10	.08	.04
69 Keith Moreland	.05	.04	.02
70 Jack Morris	.15	.11	.06
71 Jim Morrison	.05	.04	.02
72 Lloyd Moseby	.07	.05	.03
73 Jerry Mumphrey	.05	.04	.02
74 Dale Murphy	.30	.25	.12
75 Eddie Murray	.25	.20	.10
76 Pete O'Brien	.07	.05	.03
77 Bob Ojeda	.07	.05	.03
78 Jesse Orosco	.05	.04	.02
79 Dan Pasqua	.10	.08	.04
80 Dave Parker	.12	.09	.05
81 Larry Parrish	.05	.04	.02
82 Jim Presley	.10	.08	.04
83 Kirby Puckett	.50	.40	.20
84 Dan Quisenberry	.07	.05	.03
85 Tim Raines	.20	.15	.08
86 Dennis Rasmussen	.07	.05	.03
87 Johnny Ray	.07	.05	.03
88 Jeff Reardon	.07	.05	.03
89 Jim Rice	.20	.15	.08
90 Dave Righetti	.12	.09	.05
91 Earnest Riles	.05	.04	.02
92 Cal Ripken, Jr.	.30	.25	.12
93 Ron Robinson	.05	.04	.02
94 Juan Samuel	.12	.09	.05
95 Ryne Sandberg	.20	.15	.08
96 Steve Sax	.15	.11	.06
97 Mike Schmidt	.30	.25	.12
98 Ken Schrom	.05	.04	.02
99 Mike Scott	.12	.09	.05
100 Ruben Sierra	1.50	1.25	.60
101 Lee Smith	.07	.05	.03
102 Ozzie Smith	.12	.09	.05
103 Cory Snyder	.20	.15	.08
104 Kent Tekulve	.05	.04	.02
105 Andres Thomas	.10	.08	.04
106 Rob Thompson	.10	.08	.04
107 Alan Trammell	.20	.15	.08
108 John Tudor	.07	.05	.03
109 Fernando Valenzuela	.20	.15	.08
110 Greg Walker	.07	.05	.03
111 Mitch Webster	.05	.04	.02
112 Lou Whitaker	.15	.11	.06
113 Frank White	.07	.05	.03
114 Reggie Williams	.10	.08	.04
115 Glenn Wilson	.05	.04	.02
116 Willie Wilson	.10	.08	.04
117 Dave Winfield	.20	.15	.08
118 Mike Witt	.07	.05	.03
119 Todd Worrell	.12	.09	.05
120 Floyd Youmans	.05	.04	.02

1987 Fleer Record Setters

Produced by Fleer for the Eckerd Drug chain, the 1987 Fleer Record Setters set contains 44 cards that measure the standard 2-1/2" by 3-1/2" size. Although the set is titled "Record Setters," the actual records the players have set is not specified anywhere on the cards. Given that several players included in the set were young prospects, a better title for those cards might have been "Possible

Record Setters." The set came housed in a special cardboard box with six team logo stickers.

		MT	NR MT	EX
Complete Set:		5.00	3.75	2.00
Common Player:		.05	.04	.02
1	George Brett	.30	.25	.12
2	Chris Brown	.07	.05	.03
3	Jose Canseco	1.00	.70	.40
4	Roger Clemens	.40	.30	.15
5	Alvin Davis	.10	.08	.04
6	Shawon Dunston	.07	.05	.03
7	Tony Fernandez	.10	.08	.04
8	Carlton Fisk	.12	.09	.05
9	Gary Gaetti	.10	.08	.04
10	Gene Garber	.05	.04	.02
11	Rich Gedman	.05	.04	.02
12	Dwight Gooden	.40	.30	.15
13	Ozzie Guillen	.07	.05	.03
14	Bill Gullickson	.05	.04	.02
15	Billy Hatcher	.07	.05	.03
16	Orel Hershiser	.20	.15	.08
17	Wally Joyner	.70	.50	.30
18	Ray Knight	.05	.04	.02
19	Craig Lefferts	.05	.04	.02
20	Don Mattingly	1.75	1.25	.70
21	Kevin Mitchell	.70	.50	.30
22	Lloyd Moseby	.07	.05	.03
23	Dale Murphy	.30	.25	.12
24	Eddie Murray	.25	.20	.10
25	Phil Niekro	.15	.11	.06
26	Ben Oglivie	.05	.04	.02
27	Jesse Orosco	.05	.04	.02
28	Joe Orsulak	.05	.04	.02
29	Larry Parrish	.05	.04	.02
30	Tim Raines	.25	.20	.10
31	Shane Rawley	.07	.05	.03
32	Dave Righetti	.12	.09	.05
33	Pete Rose	.40	.30	.15
34	Steve Sax	.15	.11	.06
35	Mike Schmidt	.30	.25	.12
36	Mike Scott	.12	.09	.05
37	Don Sutton	.12	.09	.05
38	Alan Trammell	.20	.15	.08
39	John Tudor	.10	.08	.04
40	Gary Ward	.05	.04	.02
41	Lou Whitaker	.15	.11	.06
42	Willie Wilson	.10	.08	.04
43	Todd Worrell	.15	.11	.06
44	Floyd Youmans	.10	.08	.04

1987 Fleer Star Stickers

The 1987 Fleer Star Stickers set contains 132 cards which become stickers if the back is bent and peeled off. As in the previous year, the card backs are identical, save the numbering system, to the regular issue cards. The cards measure 2-1/2" by 3-1/2" and were sold in wax packs with team logo stickers. The fronts have a green border with a red and white banner wrapped across the upper left corner and the sides. The backs are printed in green and yellow.

		MT	NR MT	EX
Complete Set:		18.00	13.50	7.25
Common Player:		.05	.04	.02
1	Don Aase	.05	.04	.02
2	Harold Baines	.20	.15	.08
3	Floyd Bannister	.08	.06	.03
4	Jesse Barfield	.20	.15	.08
5	Marty Barrett	.10	.08	.04
6	Kevin Bass	.10	.08	.04
7	Don Baylor	.12	.09	.05
8	Steve Bedrosian	.15	.11	.06
9	George Bell	.35	.25	.14
10	Bert Blyleven	.15	.11	.06
11	Mike Boddicker	.08	.06	.03
12	Wade Boggs	1.75	1.25	.70
13	Phil Bradley	.15	.11	.06
14	Sid Bream	.08	.06	.03
15	George Brett	.70	.50	.30
16	Hubie Brooks	.10	.08	.04
17	Tom Brunansky	.15	.11	.06
18	Tom Candiotti	.05	.04	.02
19	Jose Canseco	2.00	1.50	.80
20	Gary Carter	.40	.30	.15
21	Joe Carter	.20	.15	.08
22	Will Clark	2.00	1.50	.80
23	Mark Clear	.05	.04	.02
24	Roger Clemens	.90	.70	.35
25	Vince Coleman	.25	.20	.10
26	Jose Cruz	.10	.08	.04
27	Ron Darling	.20	.15	.08
28	Alvin Davis	.20	.15	.08
29	Chili Davis	.10	.08	.04
30	Eric Davis	1.00	.70	.40
31	Glenn Davis	.20	.15	.08
32	Mike Davis	.05	.04	.02
33	Andre Dawson	.25	.20	.10
34	Doug DeCinces	.08	.06	.03
35	Brian Downing	.08	.06	.03
36	Shawon Dunston	.12	.09	.05
37	Mark Eichhorn	.12	.09	.05
38	Dwight Evans	.15	.11	.06
39	Tony Fernandez	.15	.11	.06
40	Bob Forsch	.05	.04	.02
41	John Franco	.10	.08	.04
42	Julio Franco	.12	.09	.05
43	Gary Gaetti	.20	.15	.08
44	Gene Garber	.05	.04	.02
45	Scott Garrelts	.05	.04	.02
46	Steve Garvey	.40	.30	.15
47	Kirk Gibson	.30	.25	.12
48	Dwight Gooden	.90	.70	.35
49	Ken Griffey	.10	.08	.04
50	Ozzie Guillen	.10	.08	.04
51	Bill Gullickson	.05	.04	.02
52	Tony Gwynn	.40	.30	.15
53	Mel Hall	.08	.06	.03
54	Greg Harris	.05	.04	.02
55	Von Hayes	.12	.09	.05
56	Rickey Henderson	.70	.50	.30
57	Tom Henke	.10	.08	.04
58	Keith Hernandez	.35	.25	.14
59	Willie Hernandez	.05	.04	.02
60	Ted Higuera	.20	.15	.08
61	Bob Horner	.12	.09	.05
62	Charlie Hough	.08	.06	.03
63	Jay Howell	.08	.06	.03
64	Kent Hrbek	.30	.25	.12
65	Bruce Hurst	.12	.09	.05
66	Pete Incaviglia	.60	.45	.25
67	Bob James	.05	.04	.02
68	Wally Joyner	.50	.40	.20
69	Mike Krukow	.05	.04	.02
70	Mark Langston	.15	.11	.06

		MT	NR MT	EX
71	Carney Lansford	.08	.06	.03
72	Fred Lynn	.25	.20	.10
73	Bill Madlock	.12	.09	.05
74	Don Mattingly	2.00	1.50	.80
75	Kirk McCaskill	.05	.04	.02
76	Lance McCullers	.12	.09	.05
77	Oddibe McDowell	.15	.11	.06
78	Paul Molitor	.20	.15	.08
79	Keith Moreland	.08	.06	.03
80	Jack Morris	.25	.20	.10
81	Jim Morrison	.05	.04	.02
82	Jerry Mumphrey	.05	.04	.02
83	Dale Murphy	.70	.50	.30
84	Eddie Murray	.50	.40	.20
85	Ben Oglivie	.05	.04	.02
86	Bob Ojeda	.10	.08	.04
87	Jesse Orosco	.08	.06	.03
88	Dave Parker	.25	.20	.10
89	Larry Parrish	.08	.06	.03
90	Tony Pena	.10	.08	.04
91	Jim Presley	.15	.11	.06
92	Kirby Puckett	.70	.50	.30
93	Dan Quisenberry	.12	.09	.05
94	Tim Raines	.35	.25	.14
95	Dennis Rasmussen	.10	.08	.04
96	Shane Rawley	.08	.06	.03
97	Johnny Ray	.10	.08	.04
98	Jeff Reardon	.10	.08	.04
99	Jim Rice	.35	.25	.14
100	Dave Righetti	.20	.15	.08
101	Cal Ripken, Jr.	.60	.45	.25
102	Pete Rose	1.00	.70	.40
103	Nolan Ryan	.50	.40	.20
104	Juan Samuel	.15	.11	.06
105	Ryne Sandberg	.35	.25	.14
106	Steve Sax	.20	.15	.08
107	Mike Schmidt	.70	.50	.30
108	Mike Scott	.15	.11	.06
109	Dave Smith	.05	.04	.02
110	Lee Smith	.10	.08	.04
111	Lonnie Smith	.05	.04	.02
112	Ozzie Smith	.20	.15	.08
113	Cory Snyder	.50	.40	.20
114	Darryl Strawberry	.70	.50	.30
115	Don Sutton	.25	.20	.10
116	Kent Tekulve	.08	.06	.03
117	Gorman Thomas	.08	.06	.03
118	Alan Trammell	.30	.25	.12
119	John Tudor	.12	.09	.05
120	Fernando Valenzuela	.12	.09	.05
121	Bob Welch	.12	.09	.05
122	Lou Whitaker	.25	.20	.10
123	Frank White	.10	.08	.04
124	Reggie Williams	.12	.09	.05
125	Willie Wilson	.15	.11	.06
126	Dave Winfield	.40	.30	.15
127	Mike Witt	.10	.08	.04
128	Todd Worrell	.25	.20	.10
129	Curt Young	.08	.06	.03
130	Robin Yount	.30	.25	.12
131	Jose Canseco, Don Mattingly/Checklist	2.50	2.00	1.00
132	Eric Davis, Bo Jackson/Checklist	1.25	.90	.50

1987 Fleer
Star Sticker Box Panels

Fleer issued on the bottoms of their Fleer Star

Stickers wax pack boxes six player cards plus two team logo/checklist cards. The cards, which measure 2-1/2" by 3-1/2", are numbered S-1 through S-8. The cards are identical in design to the Star Stickers.

		MT	NR MT	EX
Complete Panel Set:		6.50	5.00	2.50
Complete Singles Set:		3.25	2.50	1.25
Common Single Player:		.15	.11	.06
Panel		5.75	4.25	2.25
2	Wade Boggs	1.00	.70	.40
3	Bert Blyleven	.20	.15	.08
6	Phillies Logo	.05	.04	.02
8	Don Mattingly	2.00	1.50	.80
Panel		1.00	.70	.40
1	Tigers Logo	.05	.04	.02
4	Jose Cruz	.15	.11	.06
5	Glenn Davis	.20	.15	.08
7	Bob Horner	.15	.11	.06

1987 Fleer Update

Fleer followed suit on a Topps idea in 1984 and began producing "Update" sets. The 1987 edition brings the regular Fleer set to date by including traded players and hot rookies. The cards measure 2-1/2" by 3-1/2" and are housed in a specially designed box with 25 team logo stickers. As a companion to the glossy-coated Fleer Collectors Edition set, Fleer produced a special edition Update set in its own tin box. Values of the glossy-coated cards are only a few dollars more than the regular Update cards.

		MT	NR MT	EX
Complete Set:		15.00	11.00	6.00
Common Player:		.06	.05	.02
1	Scott Bankhead	.08	.06	.03
2	Eric Bell(FC)	.15	.11	.06
3	Juan Beniquez	.06	.05	.02
4	Juan Berenguer	.06	.05	.02
5	Mike Birkbeck(FC)	.20	.15	.08
6	Randy Bockus(FC)	.15	.11	.06
7	Rod Booker(FC)	.15	.11	.06
8	Thad Bosley	.06	.05	.02
9	Greg Brock	.10	.08	.04
10	Bob Brower(FC)	.15	.11	.06
11	Chris Brown	.12	.09	.05
12	Jerry Browne	.15	.11	.06
13	Ralph Bryant	.10	.08	.04
14	DeWayne Buice(FC)	.20	.15	.08
15	Ellis Burks(FC)	2.00	1.50	.80
16	Casey Candaele(FC)	.15	.11	.06
17	Steve Carlton	.30	.25	.12
18	Juan Castillo	.08	.06	.03
19	Chuck Crim(FC)	.15	.11	.06
20	Mark Davidson(FC)	.20	.15	.08
21	Mark Davis	.06	.05	.02
22	Storm Davis	.12	.09	.05
23	Bill Dawley	.06	.05	.02
24	Andre Dawson	.40	.30	.15
25	Brian Dayett	.06	.05	.02
26	Rick Dempsey	.08	.06	.03
27	Ken Dowell(FC)	.15	.11	.06

		MT	NR MT	EX
28	Dave Dravecky	.10	.08	.04
29	Mike Dunne(FC)	.35	.25	.14
30	Dennis Eckersley	.20	.15	.08
31	Cecil Fielder	.06	.05	.02
32	Brian Fisher	.10	.08	.04
33	Willie Fraser	.10	.08	.04
34	Ken Gerhart(FC)	.15	.11	.06
35	Jim Gott	.06	.05	.02
36	Dan Gladden	.06	.05	.02
37	Mike Greenwell(FC)	4.00	3.00	1.50
38	Cecilio Guante	.06	.05	.02
39	Albert Hall	.06	.05	.02
40	Atlee Hammaker	.06	.05	.02
41	Mickey Hatcher	.06	.05	.02
42	Mike Heath	.06	.05	.02
43	Neal Heaton	.06	.05	.02
44	Mike Henneman(FC)	.30	.25	.12
45	Guy Hoffman	.06	.05	.02
46	Charles Hudson	.06	.05	.02
47	Chuck Jackson(FC)	.20	.15	.08
48	Mike Jackson(FC)	.20	.15	.08
49	Reggie Jackson	.40	.30	.15
50	Chris James	.35	.25	.14
51	Dion James	.12	.09	.05
52	Stan Javier	.06	.05	.02
53	Stan Jefferson(FC)	.20	.15	.08
54	Jimmy Jones	.10	.08	.04
55	Tracy Jones	.20	.15	.08
56	Terry Kennedy	.08	.06	.03
57	Mike Kingery	.08	.06	.03
58	Ray Knight	.10	.08	.04
59	Gene Larkin(FC)	.30	.25	.12
60	Mike LaValliere	.12	.09	.05
61	Jack Lazorko(FC)	.06	.05	.02
62	Terry Leach	.06	.05	.02
63	Rick Leach	.06	.05	.02
64	Craig Lefferts	.06	.05	.02
65	Jim Lindeman(FC)	.15	.11	.06
66	Bill Long(FC)	.20	.15	.08
67	Mike Loynd(FC)	.15	.11	.06
68	Greg Maddux(FC)	.90	.70	.35
69	Bill Madlock	.15	.11	.06
70	Dave Magadan	.25	.20	.10
71	Joe Magrane(FC)	1.00	.70	.40
72	Fred Manrique(FC)	.20	.15	.08
73	Mike Mason	.06	.05	.02
74	Lloyd McClendon(FC)	.15	.11	.06
75	Fred McGriff(FC)	2.50	2.00	1.00
76	Mark McGwire(FC)	3.50	2.75	1.50
77	Mark McLemore	.06	.05	.02
78	Kevin McReynolds	.30	.25	.12
79	Dave Meads(FC)	.15	.11	.06
80	Greg Minton	.06	.05	.02
81	John Mitchell(FC)	.15	.11	.06
82	Kevin Mitchell	2.00	1.50	.80
83	John Morris	.06	.05	.02
84	Jeff Musselman(FC)	.25	.20	.10
85	Randy Myers(FC)	.60	.45	.25
86	Gene Nelson	.06	.05	.02
87	Joe Niekro	.10	.08	.04
88	Tom Nieto	.06	.05	.02
89	Reid Nichols	.06	.05	.02
90	Matt Nokes(FC)	.70	.50	.30
91	Dickie Noles	.06	.05	.02
92	Edwin Nunez	.06	.05	.02
93	Jose Nunez(FC)	.25	.20	.10
94	Paul O'Neill	.10	.08	.04
95	Jim Paciorek(FC)	.06	.05	.02
96	Lance Parrish	.20	.15	.08
97	Bill Pecota(FC)	.20	.15	.08
98	Tony Pena	.12	.09	.05
99	Luis Polonia(FC)	.30	.25	.12
100	Randy Ready	.06	.05	.02
101	Jeff Reardon	.15	.11	.06
102	Gary Redus	.08	.06	.03
103	Rick Rhoden	.10	.08	.04
104	Wally Ritchie(FC)	.15	.11	.06
105	Jeff Robinson(FC)	.40	.30	.15
106	Mark Salas	.06	.05	.02
107	Dave Schmidt	.06	.05	.02
108	Kevin Seitzer	1.00	.70	.40
109	John Shelby	.06	.05	.02
110	John Smiley(FC)	.40	.30	.15
111	Lary Sorensen	.06	.05	.02
112	Chris Speier	.06	.05	.02
113	Randy St. Claire	.06	.05	.02
114	Jim Sundberg	.08	.06	.03
115	B.J. Surhoff(FC)	.40	.30	.15
116	Greg Swindell	.50	.40	.20
117	Danny Tartabull	.35	.25	.14
118	Dorn Taylor(FC)	.12	.09	.05
119	Lee Tunnell	.06	.05	.02

		MT	NR MT	EX
120	Ed Vande Berg	.06	.05	.02
121	Andy Van Slyke	.20	.15	.08
122	Gary Ward	.06	.05	.02
123	Devon White	.35	.25	.14
124	Alan Wiggins	.06	.05	.02
125	Bill Wilkinson(FC)	.15	.11	.06
126	Jim Winn	.06	.05	.02
127	Frank Williams	.06	.05	.02
128	Ken Williams(FC)	.20	.15	.08
129	Matt Williams(FC)	3.00	2.25	1.25
130	Herm Winningham	.06	.05	.02
131	Matt Young	.06	.05	.02
132	Checklist 1-132	.06	.05	.02

1988 Fleer

A clean, uncluttered look was the trademark of the 660-card 1988 Fleer set. The cards, which are the standard 2-1/2" by 3-1/2", feature blue and red diagonal lines set inside a white border. The player name and position are located on a slant in the upper left corner of the card. The player's team logo appears in the upper right corner. Below the player photo a blue and red band with the word "Fleer" appears. The backs of the cards include the card number, player personal information, and career statistics, plus a new feature called "At Their Best." This feature graphically shows a player's pitching or hitting statistics for home and road games and how he fared during day games as opposed to night contests. The set includes 19 special cards (#'s 622-640) and 12 "Major League Prospects" cards (#'s 641-653).

		MT	NR MT	EX
Complete Set:		28.00	21.00	11.00
Common Player:		.06	.05	.02
1	Keith Atherton	.06	.05	.02
2	Don Baylor	.10	.08	.04
3	Juan Berenguer	.06	.05	.02
4	Bert Blyleven	.12	.09	.05
5	Tom Brunansky	.10	.08	.04
6	Randy Bush	.06	.05	.02
7	Steve Carlton	.25	.20	.10
8	Mark Davidson(FC)	.12	.09	.05
9	George Frazier	.06	.05	.02
10	Gary Gaetti	.15	.11	.06
11	Greg Gagne	.06	.05	.02
12	Dan Gladden	.06	.05	.02
13	Kent Hrbek	.15	.11	.06
14	Gene Larkin	.20	.15	.08
15	Tim Laudner	.06	.05	.02
16	Steve Lombardozzi	.06	.05	.02
17	Al Newman	.06	.05	.02
18	Joe Niekro	.08	.06	.03
19	Kirby Puckett	.50	.40	.20
20	Jeff Reardon	.10	.08	.04
21a	Dan Schatzader (incorrect spelling)	.40	.30	.15
21b	Dan Schatzeder (correct spelling)	.06	.05	.02
22	Roy Smalley	.06	.05	.02
23	Mike Smithson	.06	.05	.02
24	Les Straker(FC)	.15	.11	.06

		MT	NR MT	EX
25	Frank Viola	.15	.11	.06
26	Jack Clark	.15	.11	.06
27	Vince Coleman	.20	.15	.08
28	Danny Cox	.08	.06	.03
29	Bill Dawley	.06	.05	.02
30	Ken Dayley	.06	.05	.02
31	Doug DeCinces	.08	.06	.03
32	Curt Ford	.06	.05	.02
33	Bob Forsch	.08	.06	.03
34	David Green	.06	.05	.02
35	Tom Herr	.08	.06	.03
36	Ricky Horton	.08	.06	.03
37	*Lance Johnson*(FC)	.20	.15	.08
38	Steve Lake	.06	.05	.02
39	Jim Lindeman	.10	.08	.04
40	*Joe Magrane*	.60	.45	.25
41	Greg Mathews	.08	.06	.03
42	Willie McGee	.12	.09	.05
43	John Morris	.06	.05	.02
44	Jose Oquendo	.06	.05	.02
45	Tony Pena	.08	.06	.03
46	Terry Pendleton	.08	.06	.03
47	Ozzie Smith	.15	.11	.06
48	John Tudor	.10	.08	.04
49	Lee Tunnell	.06	.05	.02
50	Todd Worrell	.10	.08	.04
51	Doyle Alexander	.08	.06	.03
52	Dave Bergman	.06	.05	.02
53	Tom Brookens	.06	.05	.02
54	Darrell Evans	.10	.08	.04
55	Kirk Gibson	.20	.15	.08
56	Mike Heath	.06	.05	.02
57	*Mike Henneman*	.25	.20	.10
58	Willie Hernandez	.08	.06	.03
59	Larry Herndon	.06	.05	.02
60	Eric King	.08	.06	.03
61	Chet Lemon	.08	.06	.03
62	*Scott Lusader*(FC)	.20	.15	.08
63	Bill Madlock	.10	.08	.04
64	Jack Morris	.20	.15	.08
65	Jim Morrison	.06	.05	.02
66	*Matt Nokes*	.50	.40	.20
67	Dan Petry	.08	.06	.03
68a	*Jeff Robinson* (Born 12-13-60 on back)			
		1.25	.90	.50
68b	*Jeff Robinson* (Born 12/14/61 on back)			
		.40	.30	.15
69	Pat Sheridan	.06	.05	.02
70	Nate Snell	.06	.05	.02
71	Frank Tanana	.08	.06	.03
72	Walt Terrell	.08	.06	.03
73	Mark Thurmond	.06	.05	.02
74	Alan Trammell	.25	.20	.10
75	Lou Whitaker	.25	.20	.10
76	Mike Aldrete	.08	.06	.03
77	Bob Brenly	.06	.05	.02
78	Will Clark	1.25	.90	.50
79	Chili Davis	.08	.06	.03
80	Kelly Downs	.10	.08	.04
81	Dave Dravecky	.08	.06	.03
82	Scott Garrelts	.06	.05	.02
83	Atlee Hammaker	.06	.05	.02
84	Dave Henderson	.10	.08	.04
85	Mike Krukow	.08	.06	.03
86	Mike LaCoss	.06	.05	.02
87	Craig Lefferts	.06	.05	.02
88	Jeff Leonard	.08	.06	.03
89	Candy Maldonado	.08	.06	.03
90	Ed Milner	.06	.05	.02
91	Bob Melvin	.06	.05	.02
92	Kevin Mitchell	.90	.70	.35
93	*Jon Perlman*(FC)	.12	.09	.05
94	Rick Reuschel	.10	.08	.04
95	Don Robinson	.08	.06	.03
96	Chris Speier	.06	.05	.02
97	Harry Spilman	.06	.05	.02
98	Robbie Thompson	.08	.06	.03
99	Jose Uribe	.06	.05	.02
100	*Mark Wasinger*(FC)	.15	.11	.06
101	*Matt Williams*	.60	.45	.25
102	Jesse Barfield	.15	.11	.06
103	George Bell	.25	.20	.10
104	Juan Beniquez	.06	.05	.02
105	John Cerutti	.08	.06	.03
106	Jim Clancy	.08	.06	.03
107	*Rob Ducey*(FC)	.15	.11	.06
108	Mark Eichhorn	.08	.06	.03
109	Tony Fernandez	.12	.09	.05
110	Cecil Fielder	.06	.05	.02
111	Kelly Gruber	.06	.05	.02
112	Tom Henke	.08	.06	.03
113	Garth Iorg (Iorg)	.06	.05	.02
114	Jimmy Key	.10	.08	.04
115	Rick Leach	.06	.05	.02
116	Manny Lee	.08	.06	.03
117	*Nelson Liriano*(FC)	.25	.20	.10
118	*Fred McGriff*	1.50	1.25	.60
119	Lloyd Moseby	.08	.06	.03
120	Rance Mulliniks	.06	.05	.02
121	Jeff Musselman	.10	.08	.04
122	*Jose Nunez*	.25	.20	.10
123	Dave Stieb	.10	.08	.04
124	Willie Upshaw	.08	.06	.03
125	Duane Ward(FC)	.08	.06	.03
126	Ernie Whitt	.08	.06	.03
127	Rick Aguilera	.06	.05	.02
128	Wally Backman	.08	.06	.03
129	*Mark Carreon*(FC)	.12	.09	.05
130	Gary Carter	.25	.20	.10
131	David Cone(FC)	1.25	.90	.50
132	Ron Darling	.12	.09	.05
133	Len Dykstra	.10	.08	.04
134	Sid Fernandez	.10	.08	.04
135	Dwight Gooden	.60	.45	.25
136	Keith Hernandez	.20	.15	.08
137	*Gregg Jefferies*(FC)	5.00	3.75	2.00
138	Howard Johnson	.10	.08	.04
139	Terry Leach	.06	.05	.02
140	*Barry Lyons*(FC)	.15	.11	.06
141	Dave Magadan	.12	.09	.05
142	Roger McDowell	.10	.08	.04
143	Kevin McReynolds	.15	.11	.06
144	*Keith Miller*(FC)	.25	.20	.10
145	*John Mitchell*(FC)	.20	.15	.08
146	Randy Myers	.15	.11	.06
147	Bob Ojeda	.08	.06	.03
148	Jesse Orosco	.08	.06	.03
149	Rafael Santana	.06	.05	.02
150	Doug Sisk	.06	.05	.02
151	Darryl Strawberry	.35	.25	.14
152	Tim Teufel	.06	.05	.02
153	Gene Walter	.06	.05	.02
154	Mookie Wilson	.08	.06	.03
155	*Jay Aldrich*(FC)	.12	.09	.05
156	Chris Bosio	.08	.06	.03
157	Glenn Braggs	.10	.08	.04
158	Greg Brock	.08	.06	.03
159	Juan Castillo	.06	.05	.02
160	Mark Clear	.06	.05	.02
161	Cecil Cooper	.10	.08	.04
162	*Chuck Crim*	.12	.09	.05
163	Rob Deer	.08	.06	.03
164	Mike Felder	.06	.05	.02
165	Jim Gantner	.06	.05	.02
166	Ted Higuera	.10	.08	.04
167	Steve Kiefer	.06	.05	.02
168	Rick Manning	.06	.05	.02
169	Paul Molitor	.12	.09	.05
170	Juan Nieves	.08	.06	.03
171	Dan Plesac	.10	.08	.04
172	Earnest Riles	.06	.05	.02
173	Bill Schroeder	.06	.05	.02
174	*Steve Stanicek*(FC)	.15	.11	.06
175	B.J. Surhoff	.20	.15	.08
176	Dale Sveum	.08	.06	.03
177	Bill Wegman	.06	.05	.02
178	Robin Yount	.30	.25	.12
179	Hubie Brooks	.10	.08	.04
180	Tim Burke	.06	.05	.02
181	Casey Candaele	.06	.05	.02
182	Mike Fitzgerald	.06	.05	.02
183	Tom Foley	.06	.05	.02
184	Andres Galarraga	.15	.11	.06
185	Neal Heaton	.06	.05	.02
186	Wallace Johnson	.06	.05	.02
187	Vance Law	.08	.06	.03
188	Dennis Martinez	.08	.06	.03
189	Bob McClure	.06	.05	.02
190	Andy McGaffigan	.06	.05	.02
191	Reid Nichols	.06	.05	.02
192	Pascual Perez	.08	.06	.03
193	Tim Raines	.25	.20	.10
194	Jeff Reed	.06	.05	.02
195	Bob Sebra	.06	.05	.02
196	Bryn Smith	.06	.05	.02
197	Randy St. Claire	.06	.05	.02
198	Tim Wallach	.10	.08	.04
199	Mitch Webster	.08	.06	.03
200	Herm Winningham	.06	.05	.02
201	Floyd Youmans	.06	.05	.02
202	*Brad Arnsberg*(FC)	.15	.11	.06
203	Rick Cerone	.06	.05	.02
204	Pat Clements	.06	.05	.02

		MT	NR MT	EX			MT	NR MT	EX
205	Henry Cotto	.06	.05	.02	296	Curt Young	.08	.06	.03
206	Mike Easler	.08	.06	.03	297	Luis Aguayo	.06	.05	.02
207	Ron Guidry	.15	.11	.06	298	Steve Bedrosian	.12	.09	.05
208	Bill Gullickson	.06	.05	.02	299	Jeff Calhoun	.06	.05	.02
209	Rickey Henderson	.35	.25	.14	300	Don Carman	.08	.06	.03
210	Charles Hudson	.06	.05	.02	301	Todd Frohwirth(FC)	.20	.15	.08
211	Tommy John	.15	.11	.06	302	Greg Gross	.06	.05	.02
212	Roberto Kelly(FC)	.90	.70	.35	303	Kevin Gross	.08	.06	.03
213	Ron Kittle	.08	.06	.03	304	Von Hayes	.08	.06	.03
214	Don Mattingly	1.50	1.25	.60	305	Keith Hughes(FC)	.20	.15	.08
215	Bobby Meacham	.06	.05	.02	306	Mike Jackson	.20	.15	.08
216	Mike Pagliarulo	.10	.08	.04	307	Chris James	.20	.15	.08
217	Dan Pasqua	.10	.08	.04	308	Steve Jeltz	.06	.05	.02
218	Willie Randolph	.08	.06	.03	309	Mike Maddux	.07	.05	.03
219	Rick Rhoden	.08	.06	.03	310	Lance Parrish	.15	.11	.06
220	Dave Righetti	.15	.11	.06	311	Shane Rawley	.08	.06	.03
221	Jerry Royster	.06	.05	.02	312	Wally Ritchie	.15	.11	.06
222	Tim Stoddard	.06	.05	.02	313	Bruce Ruffin	.08	.06	.03
223	Wayne Tolleson	.06	.05	.02	314	Juan Samuel	.12	.09	.05
224	Gary Ward	.08	.06	.03	315	Mike Schmidt	.50	.40	.20
225	Claudell Washington	.08	.06	.03	316	Rick Schu	.06	.05	.02
226	Dave Winfield	.30	.25	.12	317	Jeff Stone	.06	.05	.02
227	Buddy Bell	.08	.06	.03	318	Kent Tekulve	.08	.06	.03
228	Tom Browning	.10	.08	.04	319	Milt Thompson	.06	.05	.02
229	Dave Concepcion	.08	.06	.03	320	Glenn Wilson	.08	.06	.03
230	Kal Daniels	.20	.15	.08	321	Rafael Belliard	.06	.05	.02
231	Eric Davis	.80	.60	.30	322	Barry Bonds	.12	.09	.05
232	Bo Diaz	.08	.06	.03	323	Bobby Bonilla	.15	.11	.06
233	Nick Esasky	.08	.06	.03	324	Sid Bream	.08	.06	.03
234	John Franco	.10	.08	.04	325	John Cangelosi	.06	.05	.02
235	Guy Hoffman	.06	.05	.02	326	Mike Diaz	.08	.06	.03
236	Tom Hume	.06	.05	.02	327	Doug Drabek	.08	.06	.03
237	Tracy Jones	.12	.09	.05	328	Mike Dunne	.25	.20	.10
238	Bill Landrum(FC)	.10	.08	.04	329	Brian Fisher	.08	.06	.03
239	Barry Larkin	.40	.30	.15	330	Brett Gideon(FC)	.12	.09	.05
240	Terry McGriff(FC)	.06	.05	.02	331	Terry Harper	.06	.05	.02
241	Rob Murphy	.08	.06	.03	332	Bob Kipper	.06	.05	.02
242	Ron Oester	.06	.05	.02	333	Mike LaValliere	.08	.06	.03
243	Dave Parker	.20	.15	.08	334	Jose Lind(FC)	.30	.25	.12
244	Pat Perry	.06	.05	.02	335	Junior Ortiz	.06	.05	.02
245	Ted Power	.06	.05	.02	336	Vicente Palacios(FC)	.20	.15	.08
246	Dennis Rasmussen	.10	.08	.04	337	Bob Patterson(FC)	.12	.09	.05
247	Ron Robinson	.06	.05	.02	338	Al Pedrique(FC)	.15	.11	.06
248	Kurt Stillwell	.10	.08	.04	339	R.J. Reynolds	.06	.05	.02
249	Jeff Treadway(FC)	.25	.20	.10	340	John Smiley	.35	.25	.14
250	Frank Williams	.06	.05	.02	341	Andy Van Slyke	.12	.09	.05
251	Steve Balboni	.08	.06	.03	342	Bob Walk	.06	.05	.02
252	Bud Black	.06	.05	.02	343	Marty Barrett	.08	.06	.03
253	Thad Bosley	.06	.05	.02	344	Todd Benzinger(FC)	.40	.30	.15
254	George Brett	.40	.30	.15	345	Wade Boggs	1.00	.70	.40
255	John Davis(FC)	.20	.15	.08	346	Tom Bolton(FC)	.15	.11	.06
256	Steve Farr	.06	.05	.02	347	Oil Can Boyd	.08	.06	.03
257	Gene Garber	.06	.05	.02	348	Ellis Burks	1.75	1.25	.70
258	Jerry Gleaton	.06	.05	.02	349	Roger Clemens	.60	.45	.25
259	Mark Gubicza	.12	.09	.05	350	Steve Crawford	.06	.05	.02
260	Bo Jackson	1.50	1.25	.60	351	Dwight Evans	.12	.09	.05
261	Danny Jackson	.12	.09	.05	352	Wes Gardner(FC)	.25	.20	.10
262	Ross Jones(FC)	.12	.09	.05	353	Rich Gedman	.08	.06	.03
263	Charlie Leibrandt	.08	.06	.03	354	Mike Greenwell	2.00	1.50	.80
264	Bill Pecota	.15	.11	.06	355	Sam Horn(FC)	.30	.25	.12
265	Melido Perez(FC)	.30	.25	.12	356	Bruce Hurst	.10	.08	.04
266	Jamie Quirk	.06	.05	.02	357	John Marzano(FC)	.20	.15	.08
267	Dan Quisenberry	.08	.06	.03	358	Al Nipper	.06	.05	.02
268	Bret Saberhagen	.15	.11	.06	359	Spike Owen	.06	.05	.02
269	Angel Salazar	.06	.05	.02	360	Jody Reed(FC)	.50	.40	.20
270	Kevin Seitzer	.70	.50	.30	361	Jim Rice	.30	.25	.12
271	Danny Tartabull	.20	.15	.08	362	Ed Romero	.06	.05	.02
272	Gary Thurman(FC)	.20	.15	.08	363	Kevin Romine(FC)	.08	.06	.03
273	Frank White	.08	.06	.03	364	Joe Sambito	.06	.05	.02
274	Willie Wilson	.10	.08	.04	365	Calvin Schiraldi	.06	.05	.02
275	Tony Bernazard	.06	.05	.02	366	Jeff Sellers	.08	.06	.03
276	Jose Canseco	1.50	1.25	.60	367	Bob Stanley	.06	.05	.02
277	Mike Davis	.08	.06	.03	368	Scott Bankhead	.06	.05	.02
278	Storm Davis	.10	.08	.04	369	Phil Bradley	.10	.08	.04
279	Dennis Eckersley	.12	.09	.05	370	Scott Bradley	.06	.05	.02
280	Alfredo Griffin	.08	.06	.03	371	Mickey Brantley	.06	.05	.02
281	Rick Honeycutt	.06	.05	.02	372	Mike Campbell(FC)	.25	.20	.10
282	Jay Howell	.08	.06	.03	373	Alvin Davis	.12	.09	.05
283	Reggie Jackson	.35	.25	.14	374	Lee Guetterman	.06	.05	.02
284	Dennis Lamp	.06	.05	.02	375	Dave Hengel(FC)	.20	.15	.08
285	Carney Lansford	.10	.08	.04	376	Mike Kingery	.06	.05	.02
286	Mark McGwire	1.75	1.25	.70	377	Mark Langston	.12	.09	.05
287	Dwayne Murphy	.08	.06	.03	378	Edgar Martinez(FC)	.20	.15	.08
288	Gene Nelson	.06	.05	.02	379	Mike Moore	.06	.05	.02
289	Steve Ontiveros	.06	.05	.02	380	Mike Morgan	.06	.05	.02
290	Tony Phillips	.06	.05	.02	381	John Moses	.06	.05	.02
291	Eric Plunk	.06	.05	.02	382	Donnell Nixon(FC)	.20	.15	.08
292	Luis Polonia	.25	.20	.10	383	Edwin Nunez	.06	.05	.02
293	Rick Rodriguez(FC)	.12	.09	.05	384	Ken Phelps	.08	.06	.03
294	Terry Steinbach	.10	.08	.04	385	Jim Presley	.10	.08	.04
295	Dave Stewart	.10	.08	.04	386	Rey Quinones	.06	.05	.02

	MT	NR MT	EX
387 Jerry Reed	.06	.05	.02
388 Harold Reynolds	.08	.06	.03
389 Dave Valle	.08	.06	.03
390 *Bill Wilkinson*	.15	.11	.06
391 Harold Baines	.12	.09	.05
392 Floyd Bannister	.08	.06	.03
393 Daryl Boston	.06	.05	.02
394 Ivan Calderon	.10	.08	.04
395 Jose DeLeon	.08	.06	.03
396 Richard Dotson	.08	.06	.03
397 Carlton Fisk	.20	.15	.08
398 Ozzie Guillen	.08	.06	.03
399 Ron Hassey	.06	.05	.02
400 Donnie Hill	.06	.05	.02
401 Bob James	.06	.05	.02
402 Dave LaPoint	.08	.06	.03
403 *Bill Lindsey*(FC)	.12	.09	.05
404 *Bill Long*(FC)	.20	.15	.08
405 Steve Lyons	.06	.05	.02
406 *Fred Manrique*	.15	.11	.06
407 *Jack McDowell*(FC)	.25	.20	.10
408 Gary Redus	.06	.05	.02
409 Ray Searage	.06	.05	.02
410 Bobby Thigpen	.10	.08	.04
411 Greg Walker	.08	.06	.03
412 *Kenny Williams*	.20	.15	.08
413 Jim Winn	.06	.05	.02
414 Jody Davis	.08	.06	.03
415 Andre Dawson	.20	.15	.08
416 Brian Dayett	.06	.05	.02
417 Bob Dernier	.06	.05	.02
418 Frank DiPino	.06	.05	.02
419 Shawon Dunston	.10	.08	.04
420 Leon Durham	.08	.06	.03
421 *Les Lancaster*(FC)	.20	.15	.08
422 Ed Lynch	.06	.05	.02
423 Greg Maddux	.35	.25	.14
424 Dave Martinez(FC)	.07	.05	.03
425a Keith Moreland (bunting, photo actually Jody Davis)	3.50	2.75	1.50
425b Keith Moreland (standing upright, correct photo)	.08	.06	.03
426 Jamie Moyer	.08	.06	.03
427 Jerry Mumphrey	.06	.05	.02
428 *Paul Noce*(FC)	.10	.08	.04
429 Rafael Palmeiro(FC)	.70	.50	.30
430 Wade Rowdon(FC)	.08	.06	.03
431 Ryne Sandberg	.25	.20	.10
432 Scott Sanderson	.06	.05	.02
433 Lee Smith	.10	.08	.04
434 Jim Sundberg	.08	.06	.03
435 Rick Sutcliffe	.10	.08	.04
436 Manny Trillo	.08	.06	.03
437 Juan Agosto	.06	.05	.02
438 Larry Andersen	.06	.05	.02
439 Alan Ashby	.06	.05	.02
440 Kevin Bass	.08	.06	.03
441 *Ken Caminiti*(FC)	.25	.20	.10
442 *Rocky Childress*(FC)	.12	.09	.05
443 Jose Cruz	.08	.06	.03
444 Danny Darwin	.06	.05	.02
445 Glenn Davis	.15	.11	.06
446 Jim Deshaies	.08	.06	.03
447 Bill Doran	.08	.06	.03
448 Ty Gainey	.06	.05	.02
449 Billy Hatcher	.08	.06	.03
450 Jeff Heathcock	.06	.05	.02
451 Bob Knepper	.08	.06	.03
452 *Rob Mallicoat*(FC)	.12	.09	.05
453 *Dave Meads*	.15	.11	.06
454 Craig Reynolds	.06	.05	.02
455 Nolan Ryan	.50	.40	.20
456 Mike Scott	.12	.09	.05
457 Dave Smith	.08	.06	.03
458 Denny Walling	.06	.05	.02
459 *Robbie Wine*(FC)	.12	.09	.05
460 *Gerald Young*(FC)	.35	.25	.14
461 Bob Brower	.08	.06	.03
462a Jerry Browne (white player, photo actually Bob Brower)	3.50	2.75	1.50
462b Jerry Browne (black player, correct photo)	.08	.06	.03
463 Steve Buechele	.06	.05	.02
464 Edwin Correa	.06	.05	.02
465 *Cecil Espy*(FC)	.30	.25	.12
466 Scott Fletcher	.08	.06	.03
467 Jose Guzman	.08	.06	.03
468 Greg Harris	.06	.05	.02
469 Charlie Hough	.08	.06	.03
470 Pete Incaviglia	.15	.11	.06
471 *Paul Kilgus*(FC)	.20	.15	.08

	MT	NR MT	EX
472 Mike Loynd	.08	.06	.03
473 Oddibe McDowell	.08	.06	.03
474 Dale Mohorcic	.08	.06	.03
475 Pete O'Brien	.08	.06	.03
476 Larry Parrish	.08	.06	.03
477 Geno Petralli	.06	.05	.02
478 Jeff Russell	.06	.05	.02
479 Ruben Sierra	.70	.50	.30
480 Mike Stanley	.08	.06	.03
481 Curtis Wilkerson	.06	.05	.02
482 Mitch Williams	.08	.06	.03
483 Bobby Witt	.10	.08	.04
484 Tony Armas	.08	.06	.03
485 Bob Boone	.08	.06	.03
486 Bill Buckner	.10	.08	.04
487 *DeWayne Buice*	.15	.11	.06
488 Brian Downing	.08	.06	.03
489 Chuck Finley	.06	.05	.02
490 Willie Fraser	.06	.05	.02
491 Jack Howell	.08	.06	.03
492 Ruppert Jones	.06	.05	.02
493 Wally Joyner	.40	.30	.15
494 Jack Lazorko	.06	.05	.02
495 Gary Lucas	.06	.05	.02
496 Kirk McCaskill	.08	.06	.03
497 Mark McLemore	.06	.05	.02
498 Darrell Miller	.06	.05	.02
499 Greg Minton	.06	.05	.02
500 Donnie Moore	.06	.05	.02
501 Gus Polidor	.06	.05	.02
502 Johnny Ray	.08	.06	.03
503 Mark Ryal(FC)	.06	.05	.02
504 Dick Schofield	.06	.05	.02
505 Don Sutton	.20	.15	.08
506 Devon White	.25	.20	.10
507 Mike Witt	.08	.06	.03
508 Dave Anderson	.06	.05	.02
509 Tim Belcher(FC)	.60	.45	.25
510 Ralph Bryant	.06	.05	.02
511 *Tim Crews*(FC)	.15	.11	.06
512 *Mike Devereaux*(FC)	.30	.25	.12
513 Mariano Duncan	.06	.05	.02
514 Pedro Guerrero	.15	.11	.06
515 Jeff Hamilton(FC)	.12	.09	.05
516 Mickey Hatcher	.06	.05	.02
517 Brad Havens	.06	.05	.02
518 Orel Hershiser	.25	.20	.10
519 *Shawn Hillegas*(FC)	.20	.15	.08
520 Ken Howell	.06	.05	.02
521 Tim Leary	.08	.06	.03
522 Mike Marshall	.12	.09	.05
523 Steve Sax	.15	.11	.06
524 Mike Scioscia	.08	.06	.03
525 Mike Sharperson(FC)	.06	.05	.02
526 John Shelby	.06	.05	.02
527 Franklin Stubbs	.08	.06	.03
528 Fernando Valenzuela	.20	.15	.08
529 Bob Welch	.10	.08	.04
530 Matt Young	.06	.05	.02
531 Jim Acker	.06	.05	.02
532 Paul Assenmacher	.06	.05	.02
533 *Jeff Blauser*(FC)	.25	.20	.10
534 *Joe Boever*(FC)	.25	.20	.10
535 Martin Clary(FC)	.06	.05	.02
536 *Kevin Coffman*(FC)	.12	.09	.05
537 Jeff Dedmon	.06	.05	.02
538 *Ron Gant*(FC)	.40	.30	.15
539 *Tom Glavine*(FC)	.40	.30	.15
540 Ken Griffey	.08	.06	.03
541 Al Hall	.06	.05	.02
542 Glenn Hubbard	.06	.05	.02
543 Dion James	.08	.06	.03
544 Dale Murphy	.40	.30	.15
545 Ken Oberkfell	.06	.05	.02
546 David Palmer	.06	.05	.02
547 Gerald Perry	.10	.08	.04
548 Charlie Puleo	.06	.05	.02
549 Ted Simmons	.10	.08	.04
550 Zane Smith	.08	.06	.03
551 Andres Thomas	.08	.06	.03
552 Ozzie Virgil	.06	.05	.02
553 Don Aase	.06	.05	.02
554 *Jeff Ballard*(FC)	.35	.25	.14
555 Eric Bell	.08	.06	.03
556 Mike Boddicker	.08	.06	.03
557 Ken Dixon	.06	.05	.02
558 Jim Dwyer	.06	.05	.02
559 Ken Gerhart	.08	.06	.03
560 *Rene Gonzales*(FC)	.15	.11	.06
561 Mike Griffin	.06	.05	.02
562 John Hayban (Habyan)	.06	.05	.02

		MT	NR MT	EX
563	Terry Kennedy	.08	.06	.03
564	Ray Knight	.08	.06	.03
565	Lee Lacy	.06	.05	.02
566	Fred Lynn	.15	.11	.06
567	Eddie Murray	.35	.25	.14
568	Tom Niedenfuer	.08	.06	.03
569	*Bill Ripken*(FC)	.25	.20	.10
570	Cal Ripken, Jr.	.35	.25	.14
571	Dave Schmidt	.06	.05	.02
572	Larry Sheets	.08	.06	.03
573	*Pete Stanicek*(FC)	.15	.11	.06
574	*Mark Williamson*(FC)	.12	.09	.05
575	Mike Young	.06	.05	.02
576	Shawn Abner(FC)	.20	.15	.08
577	Greg Booker	.06	.05	.02
578	Chris Brown	.08	.06	.03
579	*Keith Comstock*(FC)	.12	.09	.05
580	*Joey Cora*(FC)	.12	.09	.05
581	Mark Davis	.06	.05	.02
582	Tim Flannery	.06	.05	.02
583	Goose Gossage	.15	.11	.06
584	Mark Grant	.06	.05	.02
585	Tony Gwynn	.35	.25	.14
586	Andy Hawkins	.06	.05	.02
587	Stan Jefferson	.10	.08	.04
588	Jimmy Jones	.08	.06	.03
589	John Kruk	.10	.08	.04
590	*Shane Mack*(FC)	.20	.15	.08
591	Carmelo Martinez	.08	.06	.03
592	Lance McCullers	.08	.06	.03
593	*Eric Nolte*(FC)	.15	.11	.06
594	Randy Ready	.06	.05	.02
595	Luis Salazar	.06	.05	.02
596	Benito Santiago	.35	.25	.14
597	Eric Show	.08	.06	.03
598	Garry Templeton	.08	.06	.03
599	Ed Whitson	.06	.05	.02
600	Scott Bailes	.08	.06	.03
601	Chris Bando	.06	.05	.02
602	*Jay Bell*(FC)	.20	.15	.08
603	Brett Butler	.08	.06	.03
604	Tom Candiotti	.06	.05	.02
605	Joe Carter	.12	.09	.05
606	Carmen Castillo	.06	.05	.02
607	*Brian Dorsett*(FC)	.15	.11	.06
608	*John Farrell*(FC)	.35	.25	.14
609	Julio Franco	.10	.08	.04
610	Mel Hall	.08	.06	.03
611	*Tommy Hinzo*(FC)	.15	.11	.06
612	Brook Jacoby	.10	.08	.04
613	*Doug Jones*(FC)	.35	.25	.14
614	Ken Schrom	.06	.05	.02
615	Cory Snyder	.20	.15	.08
616	Sammy Stewart	.06	.05	.02
617	Greg Swindell	.25	.20	.10
618	Pat Tabler	.08	.06	.03
619	Ed Vande Berg	.06	.05	.02
620	*Eddie Williams*(FC)	.20	.15	.08
621	Rich Yett	.06	.05	.02
622	Slugging Sophomores (Wally Joyner, Cory Snyder)	.35	.25	.14
623	Dominican Dynamite (George Bell, Pedro Guerrero)	.12	.09	.05
624	Oakland's Power Team (Jose Canseco, Mark McGwire)	1.25	.90	.50
625	Classic Relief (Dan Plesac, Dave Righetti)	.08	.06	.03
626	All Star Righties (Jack Morris, Bret Saberhagen, Mike Witt)	.10	.08	.04
627	Game Closers (Steve Bedrosian, John Franco)	.08	.06	.03
628	Masters of the Double Play (Ryne Sandberg, Ozzie Smith)	.12	.09	.05
629	Rookie Record Setter (Mark McGwire)	1.00	.70	.40
630	Changing the Guard in Boston (Todd Benzinger, Ellis Burks, Mike Greenwell)	1.00	.70	.40
631	N.L. Batting Champs (Tony Gwynn, Tim Raines)	.15	.11	.06
632	Pitching Magic (Orel Hershiser, Mike Scott)	.12	.09	.05
633	Big Bats At First (Mark McGwire, Pat Tabler)	.60	.45	.25
634	Hitting King and the Thief (Vince Coleman, Tony Gwynn)	.12	.09	.05
635	A.L. Slugging Shortstops (Tony Fernandez, Cal Ripken, Jr., Alan Trammell)	.15	.11	.06
636	Tried and True Sluggers (Gary Carter, Mike Schmidt)	.20	.15	.08

		MT	NR MT	EX
637	Crunch Time (Eric Davis, Darryl Strawberry)	.70	.50	.30
638	A.L. All Stars (Matt Nokes, Kirby Puckett)	.20	.15	.08
639	N.L. All Stars (Keith Hernandez, Dale Murphy)	.20	.15	.08
640	The "O's" Brothers (Bill Ripken, Cal Ripken, Jr.)	.12	.09	.05
641	Major League Prospects (*Mark Grace, Darrin Jackson*)(FC)	5.00	3.75	2.00
642	Major League Prospects (*Damon Berryhill, Jeff Montgomery*)(FC)	1.00	.70	.40
643	Major League Prospects (*Felix Fermin, Jessie Reid*)(FC)	.20	.15	.08
644	Major League Prospects (*Greg Myers, Greg Tabor*)(FC)	.20	.15	.08
645	Major League Prospects (*Jim Eppard, Joey Meyer*)(FC)	.25	.20	.10
646	Major League Prospects (*Adam Peterson, Randy Velarde*)(FC)	.30	.25	.12
647	Major League Prospects (*Chris Gwynn, Peter Smith*)(FC)	.40	.30	.15
648	Major League Prospects (*Greg Jelks, Tom Newell*)(FC)	.25	.20	.10
649	Major League Prospects (*Mario Diaz, Clay Parker*)(FC)	.25	.20	.10
650	Major League Prospects (*Jack Savage, Todd Simmons*)(FC)	.25	.20	.10
651	Major League Prospects (*John Burkett, Kirt Manwaring*)(FC)	.30	.25	.12
652	Major League Prospects (*Dave Otto, Walt Weiss*)(FC)	1.00	.70	.40
653	Major League Prospects (*Randell Byers (Randall), Jeff King*)(FC)	.25	.20	.10
654a	Checklist 1-101 (21 is Schatzader)	.10	.08	.04
654b	Checklist 1-101 (21 is Schatzeder)	.06	.05	.02
655	Checklist 102-201	.06	.05	.02
656	Checklist 202-296	.06	.05	.02
657	Checklist 297-390	.06	.05	.02
658	Checklist 391-483	.06	.05	.02
659	Checklist 484-575	.06	.05	.02
660	Checklist 576-660	.06	.05	.02

1988 Fleer All Star Team

For the third consecutive year, Fleer randomly inserted All Star cards in their wax and cello packs. Twelve cards make up the set, each card measuring 2-1/2" by 3-1/2" in size. Players chosen for the set are Fleer's choices for a major league All-Star team.

		MT	NR MT	EX
	Complete Set:	16.00	12.00	6.50
	Common Player:	.60	.45	.25
1	Matt Nokes	.75	.60	.30
2	Tom Henke	.60	.45	.25
3	Ted Higuera	.60	.45	.25
4	Roger Clemens	2.25	1.75	.90
5	George Bell	1.00	.70	.40
6	Andre Dawson	1.00	.70	.40
7	Eric Davis	2.25	1.75	.90
8	Wade Boggs	3.25	2.50	1.25
9	Alan Trammell	1.00	.70	.40
10	Juan Samuel	.75	.60	.30
11	Jack Clark	.75	.60	.30
12	Paul Molitor	.75	.60	.30

1988 Fleer Award Winners

This limited edition 44-card boxed set of 1987 award-winning player cards also includes six team logo sticker cards. Red, white, blue and yellow bands border the sharp, full-color player photos printed below a "Fleer Award Winners 1988" banner. The player's name and award are printed beneath the photo. Flip sides are red, white and blue and list personal information, career data, team logo and card number. This set was sold exclusively at 7-11 stores nationwide.

		MT	NR MT	EX
Complete Set:		7.00	5.25	2.75
Common Player:		.05	.04	.02
1	Steve Bedrosian	.10	.08	.04
2	George Bell	.20	.15	.08
3	Wade Boggs	1.25	.90	.50
4	Jose Canseco	1.25	.90	.50
5	Will Clark	.50	.40	.20
6	Roger Clemens	.40	.30	.15
7	Kal Daniels	.20	.15	.08
8	Eric Davis	.50	.40	.20
9	Andre Dawson	.15	.11	.06
10	Mike Dunne	.10	.08	.04
11	Dwight Evans	.10	.08	.04
12	Carlton Fisk	.15	.11	.06
13	Julio Franco	.07	.05	.03
14	Dwight Gooden	.40	.30	.15
15	Pedro Guerrero	.15	.11	.06
16	Tony Gwynn	.25	.20	.10
17	Orel Hershiser	.20	.15	.08
18	Tom Henke	.05	.04	.02
19	Ted Higuera	.10	.08	.04
20	Charlie Hough	.05	.04	.02
21	Wally Joyner	.30	.25	.12
22	Jimmy Key	.07	.05	.03
23	Don Mattingly	1.25	.90	.50
24	Mark McGwire	1.25	.90	.50
25	Paul Molitor	.12	.09	.05
26	Jack Morris	.12	.09	.05
27	Dale Murphy	.30	.25	.12
28	Terry Pendleton	.05	.04	.02
29	Kirby Puckett	.70	.50	.30
30	Tim Raines	.25	.20	.10
31	Jeff Reardon	.07	.05	.03
32	Harold Reynolds	.05	.04	.02
33	Dave Righetti	.12	.09	.05
34	Benito Santiago	.25	.20	.10
35	Mike Schmidt	.30	.25	.12
36	Mike Scott	.10	.08	.04
37	Kevin Seitzer	.60	.45	.25
38	Larry Sheets	.07	.05	.03
39	Ozzie Smith	.15	.11	.06
40	Darryl Strawberry	.40	.30	.15
41	Rick Sutcliffe	.10	.08	.04
42	Danny Tartabull	.12	.09	.05
43	Alan Trammell	.15	.11	.06
44	Tim Wallach	.10	.08	.04

A player's name in *italic* type indicates a rookie card. An (FC) indicates a player's first card for that particular card company.

1988 Fleer Baseball All Stars

This limited edition 44-card boxed set features excellent photography of major league All-Stars. The standard-size cards feature a sporty bright blue- and yellow-striped background. The player name is printed in white across the upper left front corner. "Fleer Baseball 88 All Stars" appears on a yellow band beneath the photo. Card backs feature a blue- and white-striped design with a yellow highlighted section at the top that contains the player name, card number, team, position and personal data, followed by lifetime career stats. Fleer All Stars are cello-wrapped in blue and yellow striped boxes with checklist backs. The set includes six team logo sticker cards that feature black and white aerial shots of major league ballparks. The set was marketed exclusively by Ben Franklin stores.

		MT	NR MT	EX
Complete Set:		6.00	4.50	2.50
Common Player:		.05	.04	.02
1	George Bell	.20	.15	.08
2	Wade Boggs	1.00	.70	.40
3	Bobby Bonilla	.12	.09	.05
4	George Brett	.30	.25	.12
5	Jose Canseco	1.00	.70	.40
6	Jack Clark	.15	.11	.06
7	Will Clark	1.00	.70	.40
8	Roger Clemens	.40	.30	.15
9	Eric Davis	.50	.40	.20
10	Andre Dawson	.15	.11	.06
11	Julio Franco	.07	.05	.03
12	Dwight Gooden	.40	.30	.15
13	Tony Gwynn	.25	.20	.10
14	Orel Hershiser	.20	.15	.08
15	Teddy Higuera	.10	.08	.04
16	Charlie Hough	.05	.04	.02
17	Kent Hrbek	.15	.11	.06
18	Bruce Hurst	.10	.08	.04
19	Wally Joyner	.30	.25	.12
20	Mark Langston	.10	.08	.04
21	Dave LaPoint	.05	.04	.02
22	Candy Maldonado	.05	.04	.02
23	Don Mattingly	1.00	.70	.40
24	Roger McDowell	.07	.05	.03
25	Mark McGwire	1.00	.70	.40
26	Jack Morris	.12	.09	.05
27	Dale Murphy	.30	.25	.12
28	Eddie Murray	.20	.15	.08
29	Matt Nokes	.30	.25	.12
30	Kirby Puckett	.70	.50	.30
31	Tim Raines	.25	.20	.10
32	Willie Randolph	.07	.05	.03
33	Jeff Reardon	.07	.05	.03
34	Nolan Ryan	.50	.40	.20
35	Juan Samuel	.10	.08	.04
36	Mike Schmidt	.30	.25	.12
37	Mike Scott	.10	.08	.04
38	Kevin Seitzer	.60	.45	.25
39	Ozzie Smith	.15	.11	.06
40	Darryl Strawberry	.40	.30	.15
41	Rick Sutcliffe	.10	.08	.04
42	Alan Trammell	.15	.11	.06
43	Tim Wallach	.10	.08	.04
44	Dave Winfield	.20	.15	.08

1988 Fleer Baseball MVP

1988 Fleer Baseball's Best

This boxed set of 44 standard-size cards and six team logo stickers was produced by Fleer for exclusive distribution at Toys "R" Us stores. This premiere edition features full-color player photos framed by a yellow and blue border. The player's name is printed in red below and to the left of the photo; team and position are printed in black in the lower right corner. The "Fleer Baseball MVP" logo appears bottom center. Card backs are yellow and blue on a white background. The player's team, position and personal data are followed by stats, logo and a blue banner bearing the player's name, team logo and card number. The six sticker cards feature black and white stadium photos on the backs.

This boxed set of 44 standard-size cards (2-1/2" by 3-1/2") and six team logo stickers is the third annual issue from Fleer highlighting the best major league sluggers and pitchers. Five additional player cards were printed on retail display box bottoms, along with a checklist logo card (numbered C-1 through C-6). Full-color player photos are framed by a green border that fades to yellow. A red (slugger) or blue (pitcher) player name is printed beneath the photo. The card backs are printed in green on a white background with yellow highlights. Card number, player name and personal info appear in a green vertical box on the left-hand side of the card back with a yellow cartoon-style team logo overprinted across a stats chart on the right. This set was produced by Fleer for exclusive distribution by McCrory's stores (McCrory, McClellan, J.J. Newberry, H.L. Green, TG&Y).

		MT	NR MT	EX
	Complete Set:	7.00	5.25	2.75
	Common Player:	.05	.04	.02
1	George Bell	.20	.15	.08
2	Wade Boggs	1.00	.70	.40
3	Jose Canseco	1.00	.70	.40
4	Ivan Calderon	.07	.05	.03
5	Will Clark	1.00	.70	.40
6	Roger Clemens	.40	.30	.15
7	Vince Coleman	.15	.11	.06
8	Eric Davis	.50	.40	.20
9	Andre Dawson	.15	.11	.06
10	Dave Dravecky	.05	.04	.02
11	Mike Dunne	.10	.08	.04
12	Dwight Evans	.10	.08	.04
13	Sid Fernandez	.07	.05	.03
14	Tony Fernandez	.10	.08	.04
15	Julio Franco	.07	.05	.03
16	Dwight Gooden	.40	.30	.15
17	Tony Gwynn	.25	.20	.10
18	Ted Higuera	.10	.08	.04
19	Charlie Hough	.05	.04	.02
20	Wally Joyner	.30	.25	.12
21	Mark Langston	.10	.08	.04
22	Don Mattingly	1.25	.90	.50
23	Mark McGwire	1.00	.70	.40
24	Jack Morris	.12	.09	.05
25	Dale Murphy	.30	.25	.12
26	Kirby Puckett	.50	.40	.20
27	Tim Raines	.25	.20	.10
28	Willie Randolph	.07	.05	.03
29	Ryne Sandberg	.20	.15	.08
30	Benito Santiago	.25	.20	.10
31	Mike Schmidt	.30	.25	.12
32	Mike Scott	.10	.08	.04
33	Kevin Seitzer	.60	.45	.25
34	Larry Sheets	.07	.05	.03
35	Ozzie Smith	.15	.11	.06
36	Dave Stewart	.10	.08	.04
37	Darryl Strawberry	.40	.30	.15
38	Rick Sutcliffe	.10	.08	.04
39	Alan Trammell	.15	.11	.06
40	Fernando Valenzuela	.20	.15	.08
41	Frank Viola	.12	.09	.05
42	Tim Wallach	.10	.08	.04
43	Dave Winfield	.20	.15	.08
44	Robin Yount	.25	.20	.10

		MT	NR MT	EX
	Complete Set:	5.00	3.75	2.00
	Common Player:	.05	.04	.02
1	George Bell	.20	.15	.08
2	Wade Boggs	1.00	.70	.40
3	Bobby Bonilla	.12	.09	.05
4	Tom Brunansky	.10	.08	.04
5	Ellis Burks	1.00	.70	.40
6	Jose Canseco	1.00	.70	.40
7	Joe Carter	.12	.09	.05
8	Will Clark	1.00	.70	.40
9	Roger Clemens	.40	.30	.15
10	Eric Davis	.50	.40	.20
11	Glenn Davis	.12	.09	.05
12	Andre Dawson	.15	.11	.06
13	Dennis Eckersley	.07	.05	.03
14	Andres Galarraga	.15	.11	.06
15	Dwight Gooden	.40	.30	.15
16	Pedro Guerrero	.15	.11	.06
17	Tony Gwynn	.25	.20	.10
18	Orel Hershiser	.20	.15	.08
19	Ted Higuera	.10	.08	.04
20	Pete Incaviglia	.12	.09	.05
21	Danny Jackson	.10	.08	.04
22	Doug Jennings	.07	.05	.03
23	Mark Langston	.10	.08	.04
24	Dave LaPoint	.05	.04	.02
25	Mike LaValliere	.07	.05	.03
26	Don Mattingly	1.00	.70	.40
27	Mark McGwire	1.00	.70	.40
28	Dale Murphy	.30	.25	.12
29	Ken Phelps	.05	.04	.02
30	Kirby Puckett	.50	.40	.20
31	Johnny Ray	.05	.04	.02
32	Jeff Reardon	.07	.05	.03
33	Dave Righetti	.12	.09	.05
34	Cal Ripkin, Jr. (Ripken)	.30	.25	.12
35	Chris Sabo	.90	.70	.35
36	Mike Schmidt	.30	.25	.12
37	Mike Scott	.10	.08	.04
38	Kevin Seitzer	.60	.45	.25
39	Dave Stewart	.10	.08	.04
40	Darryl Strawberry	.40	.30	.15
41	Greg Swindell	.10	.08	.04
42	Frank Tanana	.05	.04	.02
43	Dave Winfield	.20	.15	.08
44	Todd Worrell	.10	.08	.04

1988 Fleer Baseball's Best Box Panel

Six cards were placed on the bottoms of retail boxes of the Fleer 44-card Baseball's Best boxed sets in 1988. The cards, which measure 2-1/2" by 3-1/2", are identical in design to cards found in the 44-card set. The cards are numbered C-1 through C-6 and were produced by Fleer for distribution by McCrory stores and its affiliates.

	MT	NR MT	EX
Complete Panel Set:	1.50	1.25	.60
Complete Singles Set:	.90	.70	.35
Common Single Player:	.15	.11	.06
Panel	1.50	1.25	.60
1 Ron Darling	.20	.15	.08
2 Rickey Henderson	.40	.30	.15
3 Carney Lansford	.15	.11	.06
4 Rafael Palmeiro	.20	.15	.08
5 Frank Viola	.20	.15	.08
6 Twins Logo	.05	.04	.02

1988 Fleer Baseball's Exciting Stars

This 44-card limited-edition boxed set showcases star major leaguers. Player photos are slanted upwards to the right, framed by a blue border with a red and white bar stripe across the middle. The player's name is printed in white above the photo. "Baseball's Exciting Stars" is printed in red and yellow across the bottom margin, following the upward slant of the photo. Fleer's logo appears lower right intersecting a white baseball bearing the number "88." Card backs are numbered and printed in red, white and blue. The set was packaged in a checklist box, with six team logo sticker cards featuring black and white stadium photos on the flip sides. Exciting Stars was distributed via Cumberland Farm stores

throughout the northeastern U.S. and Florida.

		MT	NR MT	EX
Complete Set:		6.00	4.50	2.50
Common Player:		.05	.04	.02
1	Harold Baines	.10	.08	.04
2	Kevin Bass	.07	.05	.03
3	George Bell	.20	.15	.08
4	Wade Boggs	1.00	.70	.40
5	Mickey Brantley	.05	.04	.02
6	Sid Bream	.05	.04	.02
7	Jose Canseco	1.00	.70	.40
8	Jack Clark	.15	.11	.06
9	Will Clark	1.00	.70	.40
10	Roger Clemens	.40	.30	.15
11	Vince Coleman	.15	.11	.06
12	Eric Davis	.50	.40	.20
13	Andre Dawson	.15	.11	.06
14	Julio Franco	.07	.05	.03
15	Dwight Gooden	.40	.30	.15
16	Mike Greenwell	.70	.50	.30
17	Tony Gwynn	.25	.20	.10
18	Von Hayes	.07	.05	.03
19	Tom Henke	.05	.04	.02
20	Orel Hershiser	.20	.15	.08
21	Teddy Higuera	.10	.08	.04
22	Brook Jacoby	.07	.05	.03
23	Wally Joyner	.30	.25	.12
24	Jimmy Key	.07	.05	.03
25	Don Mattingly	1.00	.70	.40
26	Mark McGwire	1.00	.70	.40
27	Jack Morris	.12	.09	.05
28	Dale Murphy	.30	.25	.12
29	Matt Nokes	.30	.25	.12
30	Kirby Puckett	.50	.40	.20
31	Tim Raines	.25	.20	.10
32	Ryne Sandberg	.20	.15	.08
33	Benito Santiago	.25	.20	.10
34	Mike Schmidt	.30	.25	.12
35	Mike Scott	.10	.08	.04
36	Kevin Seitzer	.60	.45	.25
37	Larry Sheets	.07	.05	.03
38	Ruben Sierra	.12	.09	.05
39	Darryl Strawberry	.40	.30	.15
40	Ozzie Smith	.15	.11	.06
41	Danny Tartabull	.10	.08	.04
42	Alan Trammell	.15	.11	.06
43	Fernando Valenzuela	.20	.15	.08
44	Devon White	.20	.15	.08

1988 Fleer Baseball's Hottest Stars

This boxed set of 44 standard-size player cards and six team logo sticker cards was produced by Fleer for exclusive distribution at Revco drug stores nationwide. Card fronts feature full-color photos of players representing every major league team. Photos are framed in red, orange and yellow, with a blue and white player name printed across the bottom of the card front. A flaming baseball logo bearing the words "Hottest Stars" appears in the lower left corner of the player photo. Card backs are red, white and blue. The player's name, position, card number and team logo are printed across the top section, followed by a stats box, personal data, batting and throwing preferences. The set also includes six team logo sticker cards with flipside stadium photos in black and white.

		MT	NR MT	EX
Complete Set:		6.00	4.50	2.50
Common Player:		.05	.04	.02
1	George Bell	.20	.15	.08
2	Wade Boggs	1.00	.70	.40
3	Bobby Bonilla	.12	.09	.05
4	George Brett	.30	.25	.12
5	Jose Canseco	1.00	.70	.40
6	Will Clark	1.00	.70	.40
7	Roger Clemens	.40	.30	.15
8	Eric Davis	.50	.40	.20
9	Andre Dawson	.15	.11	.06
10	Tony Fernandez	.10	.08	.04
11	Julio Franco	.07	.05	.03
12	Gary Gaetti	.10	.08	.04
13	Dwight Gooden	.40	.30	.15
14	Mike Greenwell	.70	.50	.30
15	Tony Gwynn	.25	.20	.10
16	Rickey Henderson	.50	.40	.20
17	Keith Hernandez	.15	.11	.06
18	Tom Herr	.07	.05	.03
19	Orel Hershiser	.20	.15	.08
20	Ted Higuera	.10	.08	.04
21	Wally Joyner	.30	.25	.12
22	Jimmy Key	.07	.05	.03
23	Mark Langston	.10	.08	.04
24	Don Mattingly	1.25	.90	.50
25	Jack McDowell	.20	.15	.08
26	Mark McGwire	1.00	.70	.40
27	Kevin Mitchell	.50	.40	.20
28	Jack Morris	.12	.09	.05
29	Dale Murphy	.30	.25	.12
30	Kirby Puckett	.50	.40	.20
31	Tim Raines	.25	.20	.10
32	Shane Rawley	.05	.04	.02
33	Benito Santiago	.25	.20	.10
34	Mike Schmidt	.30	.25	.12
35	Mike Scott	.10	.08	.04
36	Kevin Seitzer	.60	.45	.25
37	Larry Sheets	.07	.05	.03
38	Ruben Sierra	.50	.40	.20
39	Dave Smith	.05	.04	.02
41	Darryl Strawberry	.40	.30	.15
42	Rick Sutcliffe	.10	.08	.04
43	Pat Tabler	.05	.04	.02
44	Alan Trammell	.15	.11	.06

1988 Fleer Box Panels

Fleer's third annual box-bottom issue once again included 16 full-color trading cards printed on the bottoms of four different wax and cello pack retail display boxes. Each box contains three player cards and one team logo card. Player cards follow the same design as the basic 1988 Fleer issue - full-color player photo, name upper left, team logo upper right, Fleer logo lower right. Card fronts feature a blue and red striped border, with a thin white line framing the photo. Card backs are printed in blue and red and include personal information and statistics. Standard-size, the cards are numbered C-1 through C-16.

		MT	NR MT	EX
Complete Panel Set:		6.25	4.75	2.50
Complete Singles Set:		2.50	2.00	1.00
Common Panel:		1.25	.90	.50
Common Single Player:		.15	.11	.06
Panel		2.00	1.50	.80
1	Cardinals Logo	.05	.04	.02
11	Mike Schmidt	.60	.45	.25
14	Dave Stewart	.15	.11	.06
15	Tim Wallach	.20	.15	.08
Panel		1.25	.90	.50
2	Dwight Evans	.15	.11	.06
8	Shane Rawley	.15	.11	.06
10	Ryne Sandberg	.30	.25	.12
13	Tigers Logo	.05	.04	.02
Panel		2.75	2.00	1.00
3	Andres Galarraga	.25	.20	.10*
6	Dale Murphy	.60	.45	.25
9	Giants Logo	.05	.04	.02
12	Kevin Seitzer	.80	.60	.30
Panel		2.25	1.75	.90
4	Wally Joyner	.60	.45	.25
5	Twins Logo	.05	.04	.02
7	Kirby Puckett	.40	.30	.15
16	Todd Worrell	.20	.15	.08

1988 Fleer '87 World Series

Highlights of the 1987 Series are captured in this full-color insert set found only in Fleer's regular 660-card factory sealed sets. This second World Series edition by Fleer features cards framed in red, with a blue and white starred bunting draped over the upper edges of the photo and a brief photo caption printed on a yellow band across the lower border. Numbered card backs are red, white and blue and include a description of the action pictured on the front, with stats for the Series.

		MT	NR MT	EX
Complete Set:		4.00	3.00	1.50
Common Player:		.30	.25	.12
1	"Grand" Hero In Game 1 (Dan Gladden)	.30	.25	.12
2	The Cardinals "Bush" Whacked (Randy Bush, Tony Pena)	.30	.25	.12
3	Masterful Performance Turns Momentum (John Tudor)	.30	.25	.12
4	The Wizard (Ozzie Smith)	.35	.25	.14
5	Throw Smoke! (Tony Pena, Todd Worrell)	.35	.25	.14
6	Cardinal Attack - Disruptive Speed (Vince Coleman)	.40	.30	.15
7	Herr's Wallop (Dan Driessen, Tom Herr)	.30	.25	.12
8	Kirby's Bat Comes Alive in Game 6 (Kirby Puckett)	1.00	.70	.40
9	Hrbek's Slam Forces Game 7 (Kent Hrbek)	.30	.25	.12
10	Herr, Out At First? (Rich Hacker (coach), Tom Herr, Lee Weyer (umpire))	.30	.25	.12
11	Game 7's Play At The Plate (Don Baylor, Dave Phillips (umpire))	.30	.25	.12
12	Series MVP with 16 K's (Frank Viola)	.35	.25	.14

1988 Fleer Headliners

This six-card special set was inserted in Fleer three-packs, sold by retail outlets and hobby dealers nationwide. The card fronts feature crisp full-color player cut-outs printed on a grey and white USA Today-style sports page. "Fleer Headliners 1988" is printed in black and red on a white banner across the top of the card, both front and back. A similar white banner across the card bottom bears the black and white National or American League logo and a red player/team name. Card backs are black on grey with red accents and include the card number and a three-paragraph career summary.

		MT	NR MT	EX
Complete Set:		8.00	6.00	3.25
Common Player:		1.00	.70	.40
1	Don Mattingly	3.00	2.25	1.25
2	Mark McGwire	2.00	1.50	.80
3	Jack Morris	1.00	.70	.40
4	Darryl Strawberry	1.50	1.25	.60
5	Dwight Gooden	1.50	1.25	.60
6	Tim Raines	1.25	.90	.50

1988 Fleer League Leaders

This 44-card boxed set is the third annual limited edition set from Fleer highlighting leading players. The 1988 edition contains the same type of information, front and back, as the previous sets, with a new color scheme and design. Card fronts have bright blue borders, solid on the lower portion, striped on the upper, with a gold bar separating the two sections. "Fleer's Baseball's League Leaders '88" headlines the card face. The full-color player photo is centered above a yellow player name banner. The numbered card backs are blue, pink and white, and contain player stats and personal notes. Six team logo sticker cards, with flipside black and white photos of ballparks, accompany this set which was marketed exclusively by Walgreen drug stores.

		MT	NR MT	EX
Complete Set:		6.00	4.50	2.50
Common Player:		.05	.04	.02
1	George Bell	.20	.15	.08
2	Wade Boggs	1.00	.70	.40
3	Ivan Calderon	.07	.05	.03
4	Jose Canseco	1.00	.70	.40
5	Will Clark	1.00	.70	.40
6	Roger Clemens	.40	.30	.15
7	Vince Coleman	.15	.11	.06
8	Eric Davis	.50	.40	.20
9	Andre Dawson	.15	.11	.06
10	Bill Doran	.07	.05	.03
11	Dwight Evans	.10	.08	.04
12	Julio Franco	.07	.05	.03
13	Gary Gaetti	.10	.08	.04
14	Andres Galarraga	.15	.11	.06
15	Dwight Gooden	.40	.30	.15
16	Tony Gwynn	.25	.20	.10
17	Tom Henke	.05	.04	.02
18	Keith Hernandez	.20	.15	.08
19	Orel Hershiser	.20	.15	.08
20	Ted Higuera	.10	.08	.04
21	Kent Hrbek	.15	.11	.06
22	Wally Joyner	.30	.25	.12
23	Jimmy Key	.07	.05	.03
24	Mark Langston	.10	.08	.04
25	Don Mattingly	1.00	.70	.40
26	Mark McGwire	1.00	.70	.40
27	Paul Molitor	.12	.09	.05
28	Jack Morris	.12	.09	.05
29	Dale Murphy	.30	.25	.12
30	Kirby Puckett	.50	.40	.20
31	Tim Raines	.25	.20	.10
32	Rick Rueschel	.07	.05	.03
33	Bret Saberhagen	.15	.11	.06
34	Benito Santiago	.25	.20	.10
35	Mike Schmidt	.30	.25	.12
36	Mike Scott	.10	.08	.04
37	Kevin Seitzer	.60	.45	.25
38	Larry Sheets	.07	.05	.03
39	Ruben Sierra	.50	.40	.20
40	Darryl Strawberry	.40	.30	.15
41	Rick Sutcliffe	.10	.08	.04
42	Alan Trammell	.15	.11	.06
43	Andy Van Slyke	.10	.08	.04
44	Todd Worrell	.10	.08	.04

1988 Fleer Mini

This third annual issue of miniatures (1-7/8" by 2-5/8") includes 120 high-gloss cards featuring new photos, not copies from the regular issue, although the card designs are identical. Card fronts have white borders, with red and blue striping and a bright color band beneath the photo leading to a blue Fleet logo lower right. The player name is printed upper left; the full-color team logo appears upper right. Card backs are red, white and blue and include personal data, yearly career stats and a stats breakdown of batting average, slugging percentage and on-base average, listed for day, night, home and road games. Card backs are numbered in alphabetical order by teams which are also listed alphabetically. The set includes 18 team logo stickers with black and white aerial stadium photos on the flip sides.

		MT	NR MT	EX
	Complete Set:	11.00	8.25	4.50
	Common Player:	.05	.04	.02
1	Eddie Murray	.25	.20	.10
2	Dave Schmidt	.05	.04	.02
3	Larry Sheets	.07	.05	.03
4	Wade Boggs	1.00	.70	.40
5	Roger Clemens	.60	.45	.25
6	Dwight Evans	.12	.09	.05
7	Mike Greenwell	1.00	.70	.40
8	Sam Horn	.20	.15	.08
9	Lee Smith	.07	.05	.03
10	Brian Downing	.05	.04	.02
11	Wally Joyner	.30	.25	.12
12	Devon White	.10	.08	.04
13	Mike Witt	.07	.05	.03
14	Ivan Calderon	.07	.05	.03
15	Ozzie Guillen	.07	.05	.03
16	Jack McDowell	.20	.15	.08
17	Kenny Williams	.12	.09	.05
18	Joe Carter	.20	.15	.08
19	Julio Franco	.10	.08	.04
20	Pat Tabler	.05	.04	.02
21	Doyle Alexander	.05	.04	.02
22	Jack Morris	.15	.11	.06
23	Matt Nokes	.30	.25	.12
24	Walt Terrell	.05	.04	.02
25	Alan Trammell	.20	.15	.08
26	Bret Saberhagen	.15	.11	.06
27	Kevin Seitzer	.60	.45	.25
28	Danny Tartabull	.15	.11	.06
29	Gary Thurman	.20	.15	.08
30	Ted Higuera	.10	.08	.04
31	Paul Molitor	.12	.09	.05
32	Dan Plesac	.10	.08	.04
33	Robin Yount	.25	.20	.10
34	Gary Gaetti	.12	.09	.05
35	Kent Hrbek	.15	.11	.06
36	Kirby Puckett	.50	.40	.20
37	Jeff Reardon	.07	.05	.03
38	Frank Viola	.12	.09	.05
39	Jack Clark	.12	.09	.05
40	Rickey Henderson	.50	.40	.20
41	Don Mattingly	1.75	1.25	.70
42	Willie Randolph	.05	.04	.02
43	Dave Righetti	.12	.09	.05
44	Dave Winfield	.20	.15	.08
45	Jose Canseco	1.50	1.25	.60
46	Mark McGwire	1.00	.70	.40
47	Dave Parker	.12	.09	.05
48	Dave Stewart	.07	.05	.03
49	Walt Weiss	.60	.45	.25
50	Bob Welch	.07	.05	.03
51	Mickey Brantley	.05	.04	.02
52	Mark Langston	.10	.08	.04
53	Harold Reynolds	.07	.05	.03
54	Scott Fletcher	.05	.04	.02
55	Charlie Hough	.05	.04	.02
56	Pete Incaviglia	.12	.09	.05
57	Larry Parrish	.05	.04	.02
58	Ruben Sierra	.35	.25	.14
59	George Bell	.20	.15	.08
60	Mark Eichhorn	.05	.04	.02
61	Tony Fernandez	.10	.08	.04
62	Tom Henke	.05	.04	.02
63	Jimmy Key	.07	.05	.03
64	Dion James	.05	.04	.02
65	Dale Murphy	.30	.25	.12
66	Zane Smith	.05	.04	.02
67	Andre Dawson	.15	.11	.06
68	Mark Grace	1.75	1.25	.70
69	Jerry Mumphrey	.05	.04	.02
70	Ryne Sandberg	.20	.15	.08
71	Rick Sutcliffe	.10	.08	.04
72	Kal Daniels	.12	.09	.05
73	Eric Davis	.70	.50	.30
74	John Franco	.07	.05	.03
75	Ron Robinson	.05	.04	.02
76	Jeff Treadway	.20	.15	.08
77	Kevin Bass	.07	.05	.03
78	Glenn Davis	.15	.11	.06
79	Nolan Ryan	.50	.40	.20
80	Mike Scott	.12	.09	.05
81	Dave Smith	.05	.04	.02
82	Kirk Gibson	.20	.15	.08
83	Pedro Guerrero	.12	.09	.05
84	Orel Hershiser	.20	.15	.08
85	Steve Sax	.15	.11	.06
86	Fernando Valenzuela	.15	.11	.06
87	Tim Burke	.05	.04	.02
88	Andres Galarraga	.15	.11	.06

		MT	NR MT	EX
89	Neal Heaton	.05	.04	.02
90	Tim Raines	.20	.15	.08
91	Tim Wallach	.10	.08	.04
92	Dwight Gooden	.60	.45	.25
93	Keith Hernandez	.15	.11	.06
94	Gregg Jefferies	2.00	1.50	.80
95	Howard Johnson	.10	.08	.04
96	Roger McDowell	.05	.04	.02
97	Darryl Strawberry	.50	.40	.20
98	Steve Bedrosian	.10	.08	.04
99	Von Hayes	.10	.08	.04
100	Shane Rawley	.05	.04	.02
101	Juan Samuel	.12	.09	.05
102	Mike Schmidt	.30	.25	.12
103	Bobby Bonilla	.15	.11	.06
104	Mike Dunne	.07	.05	.03
105	Andy Van Slyke	.10	.08	.04
106	Vince Coleman	.15	.11	.06
107	Bob Horner	.07	.05	.03
108	Willie McGee	.10	.08	.04
109	Ozzie Smith	.12	.09	.05
110	John Tudor	.07	.05	.03
111	Todd Worrell	.10	.08	.04
112	Tony Gwynn	.25	.20	.10
113	John Kruk	.12	.09	.05
114	Lance McCullers	.05	.04	.02
115	Benito Santiago	.15	.11	.06
116	Will Clark	.30	.25	.12
117	Jeff Leonard	.05	.04	.02
118	Candy Maldonado	.05	.04	.02
119	Rick Rueschel	.07	.05	.03
120	Don Robinson	.05	.04	.02

1988 Fleer Record Setters

For the second consecutive year, Fleer Corp. issued this special limited-edition 44-card set for exclusive distribution by Eckerd Drug stores. Cards are standard-size with red and blue borders framing the full-color player photos. A "1988 Fleer Record Setters" headline is printed on a yellow strip above the player's photo. The player's name, team and position appear beneath the pose. Card backs list personal information and career stats in red and blue ink on a white background. Each 44-card set comes cello-wrapped in a checklist box that contains six additional cards with peel-off team logo stickers. The sticker cards feature black and white aerial photos of major league ballparks, along with stadium statistics such as field size, seating capacity and date of the first game played.

		MT	NR MT	EX
	Complete Set:	5.00	3.75	2.00
	Common Player:	.05	.04	.02
1	Jesse Barfield	.10	.08	.04
2	George Bell	.20	.15	.08
3	Wade Boggs	1.00	.70	.40
4	Jose Canseco	1.00	.70	.40
5	Jack Clark	.15	.11	.06
6	Will Clark	1.00	.70	.40
7	Roger Clemens	.40	.30	.15
8	Alvin Davis	.10	.08	.04
9	Eric Davis	.50	.40	.20
10	Andre Dawson	.15	.11	.06

		MT	NR MT	EX
11	Mike Dunne	.10	.08	.04
12	John Franco	.07	.05	.03
13	Julio Franco	.07	.05	.03
14	Dwight Gooden	.40	.30	.15
15	Mark Gubicza	.07	.05	.03
16	Ozzie Guillen	.07	.05	.03
17	Tony Gwynn	.25	.20	.10
18	Orel Hershiser	.20	.15	.08
19	Teddy Higuera	.10	.08	.04
20	Howard Johnson	.07	.05	.03
21	Wally Joyner	.30	.25	.12
22	Jimmy Key	.07	.05	.03
23	Jeff Leonard	.05	.04	.02
24	Don Mattingly	1.25	.90	.50
25	Mark McGwire	1.00	.70	.40
26	Jack Morris	.12	.09	.05
27	Dale Murphy	.30	.25	.12
28	Larry Parrish	.05	.04	.02
29	Kirby Puckett	.50	.40	.20
30	Tim Raines	.25	.20	.10
31	Harold Reynolds	.07	.05	.03
32	Dave Righetti	.12	.09	.05
33	Cal Ripken, Jr.	.30	.25	.12
34	Benito Santiago	.25	.20	.10
35	Mike Schmidt	.30	.25	.12
36	Mike Scott	.10	.08	.04
37	Kevin Seitzer	.60	.45	.25
38	Ozzie Smith	.12	.09	.05
39	Darryl Strawberry	.40	.30	.15
40	Rick Sutcliffe	.10	.08	.04
41	Alan Trammell	.15	.11	.06
42	Frank Viola	.12	.09	.05
43	Mitch Williams	.05	.04	.02
44	Todd Worrell	.10	.08	.04

1988 Fleer Star Stickers

This set of 132 standard-size sticker cards (including a checklist card) features exclusive player photos, different from those in the Fleer regular issue. Card fronts have light gray borders sprinkled with multi-colored stars. The "Fleer Star Stickers" logo appears upper left, player names are printed beneath the photos. Card backs are printed in red, gray and black on white and include personal data and a breakdown of pitching and batting stats into day, night, home and road categories. Cards were marketed in two different display boxes that feature six players and two team logos from Fleer's 1988 Limited Edition box-bottom set.

		MT	NR MT	EX
Complete Set:		18.00	13.50	7.25
Common Player:		.05	.04	.02
1	Mike Boddicker	.08	.06	.03
2	Eddie Murray	.50	.40	.20
3	Cal Ripken, Jr.	.60	.45	.25
4	Larry Sheets	.15	.11	.06
5	Wade Boggs	1.75	1.25	.70
6	Ellis Burks	1.00	.70	.40
7	Roger Clemens	.90	.70	.35
8	Dwight Evans	.15	.11	.06
9	Mike Greenwell	1.00	.70	.40
10	Bruce Hurst	.12	.09	.05
11	Brian Downing	.08	.06	.03
12	Wally Joyner	.60	.45	.25

		MT	NR MT	EX
13	Mike Witt	.10	.08	.04
14	Ivan Calderon	.12	.09	.05
15	Jose DeLeon	.05	.04	.02
16	Ozzie Guillen	.15	.11	.06
17	Bobby Thigpen	.10	.08	.04
18	Joe Carter	.20	.15	.08
19	Julio Franco	.12	.09	.05
20	Brook Jacoby	.12	.09	.05
21	Cory Snyder	.40	.30	.15
22	Pat Tabler	.10	.08	.04
23	Doyle Alexander	.08	.06	.03
24	Kirk Gibson	.30	.25	.12
25	Mike Henneman	.20	.15	.08
26	Jack Morris	.25	.20	.10
27	Matt Nokes	.60	.45	.25
28	Walt Terrell	.05	.04	.02
29	Alan Trammell	.30	.25	.12
30	George Brett	.70	.50	.30
31	Charlie Leibrandt	.05	.04	.02
32	Bret Saberhagen	.25	.20	.10
33	Kevin Seitzer	.70	.50	.30
34	Danny Tartabull	.25	.20	.10
35	Frank White	.10	.08	.04
36	Rob Deer	.10	.08	.04
37	Ted Higuera	.15	.11	.06
38	Paul Molitor	.20	.15	.08
39	Dan Plesac	.12	.09	.05
40	Robin Yount	.30	.25	.12
41	Bert Blyleven	.15	.11	.06
42	Tom Brunansky	.15	.11	.06
43	Gary Gaetti	.20	.15	.08
44	Kent Hrbek	.30	.25	.12
45	Kirby Puckett	.50	.40	.20
46	Jeff Reardon	.10	.08	.04
47	Frank Viola	.15	.11	.06
48	Don Mattingly	2.00	1.50	.80
49	Mike Pagliarulo	.12	.09	.05
50	Willie Randolph	.08	.06	.03
51	Rick Rhoden	.08	.06	.03
52	Dave Righetti	.20	.15	.08
53	Dave Winfield	.40	.30	.15
54	Jose Canseco	2.00	1.50	.80
55	Carney Lansford	.08	.06	.03
56	Mark McGwire	1.25	.90	.50
57	Dave Stewart	.12	.09	.05
58	Curt Young	.08	.06	.03
59	Alvin Davis	.15	.11	.06
60	Mark Langston	.15	.11	.06
61	Ken Phelps	.05	.04	.02
62	Harold Reynolds	.10	.08	.04
63	Scott Fletcher	.05	.04	.02
64	Charlie Hough	.08	.06	.03
65	Pete Incaviglia	.25	.20	.10
66	Oddibe McDowell	.10	.08	.04
67	Pete O'Brien	.10	.08	.04
68	Larry Parrish	.08	.06	.03
69	Ruben Sierra	.25	.20	.10
70	Jesse Barfield	.12	.09	.05
71	George Bell	.25	.20	.10
72	Tony Fernandez	.12	.09	.05
73	Tom Henke	.10	.08	.04
74	Jimmy Key	.12	.09	.05
75	Lloyd Moseby	.10	.08	.04
76	Dion James	.05	.04	.02
77	Dale Murphy	.70	.50	.30
78	Zane Smith	.08	.06	.03
79	Andre Dawson	.25	.20	.10
80	Ryne Sandberg	.35	.25	.14
81	Rick Sutcliffe	.15	.11	.06
82	Kal Daniels	.25	.20	.10
83	Eric Davis	.80	.60	.30
84	John Franco	.10	.08	.04
85	Kevin Bass	.10	.08	.04
86	Glenn Davis	.20	.15	.08
87	Bill Doran	.10	.08	.04
88	Nolan Ryan	.50	.40	.20
89	Mike Scott	.15	.11	.06
90	Dave Smith	.05	.04	.02
91	Pedro Guerrero	.20	.15	.08
92	Orel Hershiser	.35	.25	.14
93	Steve Sax	.20	.15	.08
94	Fernando Valenzuela	.35	.25	.14
95	Tim Burke	.05	.04	.02
96	Andres Galarraga	.20	.15	.08
97	Tim Raines	.35	.25	.14
98	Tim Wallach	.12	.09	.05
99	Mitch Webster	.05	.04	.02
100	Ron Darling	.20	.15	.08
101	Sid Fernandez	.10	.08	.04
102	Dwight Gooden	.90	.70	.35
103	Keith Hernandez	.30	.25	.12

		MT	NR MT	EX
104	Howard Johnson	.12	.09	.05
105	Roger McDowell	.10	.08	.04
106	Darryl Strawberry	.70	.50	.30
107	Steve Bedrosian	.12	.09	.05
108	Von Hayes	.12	.09	.05
109	Shane Rawley	.08	.06	.03
110	Juan Samuel	.15	.11	.06
111	Mike Schmidt	.70	.50	.30
112	Milt Thompson	.05	.04	.02
113	Sid Bream	.08	.06	.03
114	Bobby Bonilla	.20	.15	.08
115	Mike Dunne	.15	.11	.06
116	Andy Van Slyke	.12	.09	.05
117	Vince Coleman	.25	.20	.10
118	Willie McGee	.15	.11	.06
119	Terry Pendleton	.10	.08	.04
120	Ozzie Smith	.20	.15	.08
121	John Tudor	.12	.09	.05
122	Todd Worrell	.20	.15	.08
123	Tony Gwynn	.40	.30	.15
124	John Kruk	.20	.15	.08
125	Benito Santiago	.30	.25	.12
126	Will Clark	1.00	.70	.40
127	Dave Dravecky	.05	.04	.02
128	Jeff Leonard	.05	.04	.02
129	Candy Maldonado	.05	.04	.02
130	Rick Rueschel	.10	.08	.04
131	Don Robinson	.05	.04	.02
132	Checklist	.05	.04	.02

1988 Fleer
Star Stickers Box Panels

RON GUIDRY

This set of eight box-bottom cards was printed on two different retail display boxes. Six players and two team logo sticker cards are included in the set, three player photos and one team photo per box. The full-color player photos are exclusively limited to the Fleer Star Sticker set. The cards, which measure 2-1/2" by 3-1/2", have a light gray border sprinkled with multi-color stars. The backs are printed in navy blue and red.

		MT	NR MT	EX
Complete Panel Set:		3.50	2.75	1.50
Complete Singles Set:		1.75	1.25	.70
Common Singles Player:		.15	.11	.06
Panel		2.50	2.00	1.00
1	Eric Davis, Mark McGwire	.70	.50	.30
3	Kevin Mitchell	.50	.40	.20
5	Rickey Henderson	.50	.40	.20
7	Tigers Logo	.05	.04	.02
Panel		1.25	.90	.50
2	Gary Carter	.35	.25	.14
4	Ron Guidry	.20	.15	.08
6	Don Baylor	.15	.11	.06
8	Giants Logo	.05	.04	.02

NOTE: A card number in parentheses ( ) indicates the set is unnumbered.

1988 Fleer Superstars

This is the fourth edition of Fleer's 44-card boxed set produced for distribution by McCrory's (1985-87 issues were simply titled "Fleer Limited Edition"). The Superstars standard-size card set features full-color player photos framed by red, white and blue striped top and bottom borders. "Fleer 1988" is printed in an elongated yellow oval banner above the photo. A pale yellow rectangle below the photo carries the player's name and team logo. Card fronts have a semi-glossy slightly textured finish. Card backs are red and blue on white and include card numbers, personal data and statistics. Six team logo sticker cards are also included in this set which was marketed in red, white and blue boxes with checklist backs. Boxed sets were sold exclusively at McCrory's stores and its affiliates.

		MT	NR MT	EX
Complete Set:		5.00	3.75	2.00
Common Player:		.05	.04	.02
1	Steve Bedrosian	.10	.08	.04
2	George Bell	.20	.15	.08
3	Wade Boggs	1.00	.70	.40
4	Barry Bonds	.12	.09	.05
5	Jose Canseco	1.00	.70	.40
6	Joe Carter	.12	.09	.05
7	Jack Clark	.15	.11	.06
8	Will Clark	1.00	.70	.40
9	Roger Clemens	.40	.30	.15
10	Alvin Davis	.10	.08	.04
11	Eric Davis	.50	.40	.20
12	Glenn Davis	.12	.09	.05
13	Andre Dawson	.15	.11	.06
14	Dwight Gooden	.40	.30	.15
15	Orel Hershiser	.20	.15	.08
16	Teddy Higuera	.10	.08	.04
17	Kent Hrbek	.15	.11	.06
18	Wally Joyner	.30	.25	.12
19	Jimmy Key	.07	.05	.03
20	John Kruk	.10	.08	.04
21	Jeff Leonard	.05	.04	.02
22	Don Mattingly	1.75	1.25	.70
23	Mark McGwire	1.00	.70	.40
24	Kevin McReynolds	.12	.09	.05
25	Dale Murphy	.30	.25	.12
26	Matt Nokes	.30	.25	.12
27	Terry Pendleton	.05	.04	.02
28	Kirby Puckett	.50	.40	.20
29	Tim Raines	.25	.20	.10
30	Rick Rhoden	.07	.05	.03
31	Cal Ripken, Jr.	.30	.25	.12
32	Benito Santiago	.25	.20	.10
33	Mike Schmidt	.30	.25	.12
34	Mike Scott	.10	.08	.04
35	Kevin Setizer	.60	.45	.25
36	Ruben Sierra	.25	.20	.10
37	Cory Snyder	.12	.09	.05
38	Darryl Strawberry	.40	.30	.15
39	Rick Sutcliffe	.10	.08	.04
40	Danny Tartabull	.12	.09	.05
41	Alan Trammell	.15	.11	.06
42	Ken Williams	.07	.05	.03
43	Mike Witt	.07	.05	.03
44	Robin Yount	.15	.11	.06

1988 Fleer Update

This 132-card update set (numbered U-1 through U-132 and 2-1/2" by 3-1/2") features traded veterans and rookies in a mixture of full-color action shots and close-ups, framed by white borders with red and blue stripes. Player name and position appear upper left, printed on an upward slant leading into the team logo, upper right. A bright stripe in a variety of colors (blue, red, green, yellow) edges the bottom of the photo and leads into the Fleer logo at lower right. The backs are red, white and blue-grey and include personal info, along with yearly and "At Their Best" (day, night, home, road) stats charts. The set was packaged in white cardboard boxes with red and blue stripes. A glossy-coated edition of the update set was issued in its own tin box and is valued at two times greater than the regular issue.

	MT	NR MT	EX
Complete Set:	12.00	9.00	4.75
Common Player:	.06	.05	.02

		MT	NR MT	EX
1	Jose Bautista(FC)	.20	.15	.08
2	Joe Orsulak	.06	.05	.02
3	Doug Sisk	.06	.05	.02
4	Craig Worthington(FC)	.50	.40	.20
5	Mike Boddicker	.08	.06	.03
6	Rick Cerone	.06	.05	.02
7	Larry Parrish	.08	.06	.03
8	Lee Smith	.10	.08	.04
9	Mike Smithson	.06	.05	.02
10	John Trautwein(FC)	.15	.11	.06
11	Sherman Corbett(FC)	.15	.11	.06
12	Chili Davis	.10	.08	.04
13	Jim Eppard	.08	.06	.03
14	Bryan Harvey(FC)	.30	.25	.12
15	John Davis	.08	.06	.03
16	Dave Gallagher(FC)	.25	.20	.10
17	Ricky Horton	.08	.06	.03
18	Dan Pasqua	.10	.08	.04
19	Melido Perez	.12	.09	.05
20	Jose Segura(FC)	.15	.11	.06
21	Andy Allanson	.08	.06	.03
22	Jon Perlman	.06	.05	.02
23	Domingo Ramos	.06	.05	.02
24	Rick Rodriguez	.08	.06	.03
25	Willie Upshaw	.10	.08	.04
26	Paul Gibson(FC)	.15	.11	.06
27	Don Heinkel(FC)	.15	.11	.06
28	Ray Knight	.08	.06	.03
29	Gary Pettis	.08	.06	.03
30	Luis Salazar	.06	.05	.02
31	Mike MacFarlane (Macfarlane)(FC)	.20	.15	.08
32	Jeff Montgomery	.08	.06	.03
33	Ted Power	.06	.05	.02
34	Israel Sanchez(FC)	.15	.11	.06
35	Kurt Stillwell	.10	.08	.04
36	Pat Tabler	.08	.06	.03
37	Don August(FC)	.20	.15	.08
38	Darryl Hamilton(FC)	.15	.11	.06
39	Jeff Leonard	.08	.06	.03
40	Joey Meyer	.15	.11	.06
41	Allan Anderson	.10	.08	.04
42	Brian Harper	.06	.05	.02
43	Tom Herr	.10	.08	.04
44	Charlie Lea	.06	.05	.02
45	John Moses	.06	.05	.02

		MT	NR MT	EX
46	John Candelaria	.10	.08	.04
47	Jack Clark	.15	.11	.06
48	Richard Dotson	.10	.08	.04
49	Al Leiter(FC)	.30	.25	.12
50	Rafael Santana	.06	.05	.02
51	Don Slaught	.06	.05	.02
52	Todd Burns(FC)	.25	.20	.10
53	Dave Henderson	.10	.08	.04
54	Doug Jennings(FC)	.15	.11	.06
55	Dave Parker	.12	.09	.05
56	Walt Weiss	.60	.45	.25
57	Bob Welch	.10	.08	.04
58	Henry Cotto	.06	.05	.02
59	Marion Diaz (Mario)	.08	.06	.03
60	Mike Jackson	.06	.05	.02
61	Bill Swift	.06	.05	.02
62	Jose Cecena(FC)	.15	.11	.06
63	Ray Hayward(FC)	.08	.06	.03
64	Jim Steels(FC)	.08	.06	.03
65	Pat Borders(FC)	.20	.15	.08
66	Sil Campusano(FC)	.25	.20	.10
67	Mike Flanagan	.10	.08	.04
68	Todd Stottlemyre(FC)	.25	.20	.10
69	David Wells(FC)	.08	.06	.03
70	Jose Alvarez(FC)	.15	.11	.06
71	Paul Runge	.06	.05	.02
72	Cesar Jimenez (German)(FC)	.15	.11	.06
73	Pete Smith	.08	.06	.03
74	John Smoltz(FC)	1.25	.90	.50
75	Damon Berryhill	.10	.08	.04
76	Goose Gossage	.15	.11	.06
77	Mark Grace	2.75	2.00	1.00
78	Darrin Jackson	.08	.06	.03
79	Vance Law	.08	.06	.03
80	Jeff Pico(FC)	.20	.15	.08
81	Gary Varsho(FC)	.20	.15	.08
82	Tim Birtsas	.06	.05	.02
83	Rob Dibble(FC)	.30	.25	.12
84	Danny Jackson	.15	.11	.06
85	Paul O'Neill	.08	.06	.03
86	Jose Rijo	.08	.06	.03
87	Chris Sabo(FC)	1.00	.70	.40
88	John Fishel(FC)	.15	.11	.06
89	Craig Biggio(FC)	1.25	.90	.50
90	Terry Puhl	.06	.05	.02
91	Rafael Ramirez	.06	.05	.02
92	Louie Meadows(FC)	.15	.11	.06
93	Kirk Gibson(FC)	.15	.11	.06
94	Alfredo Griffin	.08	.06	.03
95	Jay Howell	.08	.06	.03
96	Jesse Orosco	.08	.06	.03
97	Alejandro Pena	.08	.06	.03
98	Tracy Woodson(FC)	.10	.08	.04
99	John Dopson(FC)	.25	.20	.10
100	Brian Holman(FC)	.15	.11	.06
101	Rex Hudler(FC)	.08	.06	.03
102	Jeff Parrett(FC)	.10	.08	.04
103	Nelson Santovenia(FC)	.40	.30	.15
104	Kevin Elster	.12	.09	.05
105	Jeff Innis(FC)	.20	.15	.08
106	Mackey Sasser(FC)	.10	.08	.04
107	Phil Bradley	.10	.08	.04
108	Danny Clay(FC)	.15	.11	.06
109	Greg Harris	.06	.05	.02
110	Ricky Jordan(FC)	2.25	1.75	.90
111	David Palmer	.06	.05	.02
112	Jim Gott	.06	.05	.02
113	Tommy Gregg (photo actually Randy Milligan)(FC)	.10	.08	.04
114	Barry Jones	.06	.05	.02
115	Randy Miligan(FC)	.10	.08	.04
116	Luis Alicea(FC)	.15	.11	.06
117	Tom Brunansky	.12	.09	.05
118	John Costello(FC)	.15	.11	.06
119	Jose DeLeon	.08	.06	.03
120	Bob Horner	.10	.08	.04
121	Scott Terry(FC)	.10	.08	.04
122	Roberto Alomar(FC)	.50	.40	.20
123	Dave Leiper	.06	.05	.02
124	Keith Moreland	.08	.06	.03
125	Mark Parent(FC)	.20	.15	.08
126	Dennis Rasmussen	.10	.08	.04
127	Randy Bockus	.06	.05	.02
128	Brett Butler	.08	.06	.03
129	Donell Nixon	.06	.05	.02
130	Earnest Riles	.06	.05	.02
131	Roger Samuels(FC)	.15	.11	.06
132	Checklist	.06	.05	.02

1989 Fleer

This set includes 660 standard-size cards and was issued with 45 team logo stickers. Individual card fronts feature a grey and white striped background with full-color player photos framed by a bright line of color that slants upward to the right. The set also includes two subsets: 15 Major League Prospects and 12 SuperStar Specials. A special bonus set of 12 All-Star Team cards was randomly inserted in individual wax packs of 15 cards. The last seven cards in the set are checklists, with players listed alphabetically by teams.

		MT	NR MT	EX
	Complete Set:	28.00	21.00	12.00
	Common Player:	.05	.04	.02
1	Don Baylor	.10	.08	.04
2	Lance Blankenship(FC)	.25	.20	.10
3	Todd Burns	.30	.25	.12
4	Greg Cadaret(FC)	.07	.05	.03
5	Jose Canseco	1.25	.90	.50
6	Storm Davis	.10	.08	.04
7	Dennis Eckersley	.12	.09	.05
8	Mike Gallego(FC)	.05	.04	.02
9	Ron Hassey	.05	.04	.02
10	Dave Henderson	.10	.08	.04
11	Rick Honeycutt	.05	.04	.02
12	Glenn Hubbard	.05	.04	.02
13	Stan Javier	.05	.04	.02
14	Doug Jennings	.20	.15	.08
15	Felix Jose(FC)	.25	.20	.10
16	Carney Lansford	.07	.05	.03
17	Mark McGwire	.70	.50	.30
18	Gene Nelson	.05	.04	.02
19	Dave Parker	.12	.09	.05
20	Eric Plunk	.05	.04	.02
21	Luis Polonia	.07	.05	.03
22	Terry Steinbach	.10	.08	.04
23	Dave Stewart	.10	.08	.04
24	Walt Weiss	.30	.25	.12
25	Bob Welch	.10	.08	.04
26	Curt Young	.07	.05	.03
27	Rick Aguilera	.05	.04	.02
28	Wally Backman	.07	.05	.03
29	Mark Carreon	.07	.05	.03
30	Gary Carter	.20	.15	.08
31	David Cone	.40	.30	.15
32	Ron Darling	.12	.09	.05
33	Len Dykstra	.10	.08	.04
34	Kevin Elster	.10	.08	.04
35	Sid Fernandez	.10	.08	.04
36	Dwight Gooden	.50	.40	.20
37	Keith Hernandez	.25	.20	.10
38	Gregg Jefferies	2.00	1.50	.80
39	Howard Johnson	.10	.08	.04
40	Terry Leach	.05	.04	.02
41	Dave Magadan	.10	.08	.04
42	Bob McClure	.05	.04	.02
43	Roger McDowell	.10	.08	.04
44	Kevin McReynolds	.15	.11	.06
45	Keith Miller	.10	.08	.04
46	Randy Myers	.10	.08	.04
47	Bob Ojeda	.07	.05	.03
48	Mackey Sasser	.07	.05	.03
49	Darryl Strawberry	.40	.30	.15
50	Tim Teufel	.05	.04	.02

		MT	NR MT	EX
51	Dave West(FC)	.60	.45	.25
52	Mookie Wilson	.07	.05	.03
53	Dave Anderson	.05	.04	.02
54	Tim Belcher	.10	.08	.04
55	Mike Davis	.07	.05	.03
56	Mike Devereaux	.15	.11	.06
57	Kirk Gibson	.20	.15	.08
58	Alfredo Griffin	.07	.05	.03
59	Chris Gwynn	.12	.09	.05
60	Jeff Hamilton	.07	.05	.03
61a	Danny Heep (Home: San Antonio, TX)	1.00	.70	.40
61b	Danny Heep (Home: Lake Hills, TX)	.05	.04	.02
62	Orel Hershiser	.25	.20	.10
63	Brian Holton(FC)	.07	.05	.03
64	Jay Howell	.07	.05	.03
65	Tim Leary	.07	.05	.03
66	Mike Marshall	.12	.09	.05
67	Ramon Martinez(FC)	.40	.30	.15
68	Jesse Orosco	.07	.05	.03
69	Alejandro Pena	.07	.05	.03
70	Steve Sax	.15	.11	.06
71	Mike Scioscia	.07	.05	.03
72	Mike Sharperson	.05	.04	.02
73	John Shelby	.05	.04	.02
74	Franklin Stubbs	.05	.04	.02
75	John Tudor	.10	.08	.04
76	Fernando Valenzuela	.20	.15	.08
77	Tracy Woodson	.10	.08	.04
78	Marty Barrett	.07	.05	.03
79	Todd Benzinger	.12	.09	.05
80	Mike Boddicker	.07	.05	.03
81	Wade Boggs	1.00	.70	.40
82	"Oil Can" Boyd	.07	.05	.03
83	Ellis Burks	.60	.45	.25
84	Rick Cerone	.05	.04	.02
85	Roger Clemens	.50	.40	.20
86	Steve Curry(FC)	.20	.15	.08
87	Dwight Evans	.10	.08	.04
88	Wes Gardner	.07	.05	.03
89	Rich Gedman	.07	.05	.03
90	Mike Greenwell	.70	.50	.30
91	Bruce Hurst	.10	.08	.04
92	Dennis Lamp	.05	.04	.02
93	Spike Owen	.05	.04	.02
94	Larry Parrish	.07	.05	.03
95	Carlos Quintana(FC)	.30	.25	.12
96	Jody Reed	.12	.09	.05
97	Jim Rice	.25	.20	.10
98a	Kevin Romine (batting follow-thru, photo actually Randy Kutcher)	.50	.40	.20
98b	Kevin Romine (arms crossed on chest, correct photo)	.60	.45	.25
99	Lee Smith	.10	.08	.04
100	Mike Smithson	.05	.04	.02
101	Bob Stanley	.05	.04	.02
102	Allan Anderson	.07	.05	.03
103	Keith Atherton	.05	.04	.02
104	Juan Berenguer	.05	.04	.02
105	Bert Blyleven	.12	.09	.05
106	Eric Bullock(FC)	.15	.11	.06
107	Randy Bush	.05	.04	.02
108	John Christensen(FC)	.05	.04	.02
109	Mark Davidson	.07	.05	.03
110	Gary Gaetti	.15	.11	.06
111	Greg Gagne	.05	.04	.02
112	Dan Gladden	.05	.04	.02
113	German Gonzalez(FC)	.20	.15	.08
114	Brian Harper	.05	.04	.02
115	Tom Herr	.07	.05	.03
116	Kent Hrbek	.20	.15	.08
117	Gene Larkin	.10	.08	.04
118	Tim Laudner	.05	.04	.02
119	Charlie Lea	.05	.04	.02
120	Steve Lombardozzi	.05	.04	.02
121a	John Moses (Home: Phoenix, AZ)	1.00	.70	.40
121b	John Moses (Home: Tempe, AZ)	.05	.04	.02
122	Al Newman	.05	.04	.02
123	Mark Portugal	.05	.04	.02
124	Kirby Puckett	.35	.25	.14
125	Jeff Reardon	.10	.08	.04
126	Fred Toliver	.05	.04	.02
127	Frank Viola	.15	.11	.06
128	Doyle Alexander	.07	.05	.03
129	Dave Bergman	.05	.04	.02
130a	Tom Brookens (Mike Heath stats on back)	2.25	1.75	.90
130b	Tom Brookens (correct stats on back)	.30	.25	.12
131	Paul Gibson	.15	.11	.06
132a	Mike Heath (Tom Brookens stats on back)	2.25	1.75	.90

		MT	NR MT	EX
132b	Mike Heath (correct stats on back)	.30	.25	.12
133	*Don Heinkel*	.15	.11	.06
134	Mike Henneman	.10	.08	.04
135	Guillermo Hernandez	.07	.05	.03
136	Eric King	.05	.04	.02
137	Chet Lemon	.07	.05	.03
138	Fred Lynn	.10	.08	.04
139	Jack Morris	.15	.11	.06
140	Matt Nokes	.20	.15	.08
141	Gary Pettis	.05	.04	.02
142	Ted Power	.05	.04	.02
143	Jeff Robinson	.12	.09	.05
144	Luis Salazar	.05	.04	.02
145	*Steve Searcy*(FC)	.30	.25	.12
146	Pat Sheridan	.05	.04	.02
147	Frank Tanana	.07	.05	.03
148	Alan Trammell	.20	.15	.08
149	Walt Terrell	.07	.05	.03
150	Jim Walewander(FC)	.07	.05	.03
151	Lou Whitaker	.20	.15	.08
152	Tim Birtsas	.05	.04	.02
153	Tom Browning	.10	.08	.04
154	*Keith Brown*(FC)	.20	.15	.08
155	*Norm Charlton*(FC)	.20	.15	.08
156	Dave Concepcion	.10	.08	.04
157	Kal Daniels	.15	.11	.06
158	Eric Davis	.50	.40	.20
159	Bo Diaz	.07	.05	.03
160	*Rob Dibble*	.25	.20	.10
161	Nick Esasky	.07	.05	.03
162	John Franco	.10	.08	.04
163	Danny Jackson	.15	.11	.06
164	Barry Larkin	.25	.20	.10
165	Rob Murphy	.05	.04	.02
166	Paul O'Neill	.05	.04	.02
167	Jeff Reed	.05	.04	.02
168	Jose Rijo	.07	.05	.03
169	Ron Robinson	.05	.04	.02
170	*Chris Sabo*	.60	.45	.25
171	*Candy Sierra*(FC)	.15	.11	.06
172	*Van Snider*(FC)	.20	.15	.08
173	Jeff Treadway	.12	.09	.05
174	Frank Williams	.05	.04	.02
175	Herm Winningham	.05	.04	.02
176	Jim Adduci(FC)	.05	.04	.02
177	Don August	.10	.08	.04
178	Mike Birkbeck	.05	.04	.02
179	Chris Bosio	.05	.04	.02
180	Glenn Braggs	.07	.05	.03
181	Greg Brock	.07	.05	.03
182	Mark Clear	.05	.04	.02
183	Chuck Crim	.05	.04	.02
184	Rob Deer	.07	.05	.03
185	Tom Filer	.05	.04	.02
186	Jim Gantner	.05	.04	.02
187	*Darryl Hamilton*	.15	.11	.06
188	Ted Higuera	.10	.08	.04
189	Odell Jones	.05	.04	.02
190	Jeffrey Leonard	.07	.05	.03
191	Joey Meyer	.10	.08	.04
192	Paul Mirabella	.05	.04	.02
193	Paul Molitor	.15	.11	.06
194	Charlie O'Brien(FC)	.07	.05	.03
195	Dan Plesac	.10	.08	.04
196	*Gary Sheffield*(FC)	2.00	1.50	.80
197	B.J. Surhoff	.10	.08	.04
198	Dale Sveum	.07	.05	.03
199	Bill Wegman	.05	.04	.02
200	Robin Yount	.25	.20	.10
201	Rafael Belliard	.05	.04	.02
202	Barry Bonds	.12	.09	.05
203	Bobby Bonilla	.12	.09	.05
204	Sid Bream	.07	.05	.03
205	Benny Distefano(FC)	.05	.04	.02
206	Doug Drabek	.07	.05	.03
207	Mike Dunne	.10	.08	.04
208	Felix Fermin	.07	.05	.03
209	Brian Fisher	.07	.05	.03
210	Jim Gott	.05	.04	.02
211	Bob Kipper	.05	.04	.02
212	Dave LaPoint	.07	.05	.03
213	Mike LaValliere	.07	.05	.03
214	Jose Lind	.10	.08	.04
215	Junior Ortiz	.05	.04	.02
216	Vicente Palacios	.07	.05	.03
217	Tom Prince(FC)	.10	.08	.04
218	Gary Redus	.05	.04	.02
219	R.J. Reynolds	.05	.04	.02
220	Jeff Robinson	.07	.05	.03
221	John Smiley	.12	.09	.05
222	Andy Van Slyke	.12	.09	.05

		MT	NR MT	EX
223	Bob Walk	.05	.04	.02
224	Glenn Wilson	.07	.05	.03
225	Jesse Barfield	.10	.08	.04
226	George Bell	.25	.20	.10
227	*Pat Borders*	.25	.20	.10
228	John Cerutti	.07	.05	.03
229	Jim Clancy	.07	.05	.03
230	Mark Eichhorn	.07	.05	.03
231	Tony Fernandez	.12	.09	.05
232	Cecil Fielder	.05	.04	.02
233	Mike Flanagan	.07	.05	.03
234	Kelly Gruber	.05	.04	.02
235	Tom Henke	.07	.05	.03
236	Jimmy Key	.10	.08	.04
237	Rick Leach	.05	.04	.02
238	Manny Lee	.05	.04	.02
239	Nelson Liriano	.07	.05	.03
240	Fred McGriff	.50	.40	.20
241	Lloyd Moseby	.07	.05	.03
242	Rance Mulliniks	.05	.04	.02
243	Jeff Musselman	.07	.05	.03
244	Dave Stieb	.10	.08	.04
245	Todd Stottlemyre	.10	.08	.04
246	Duane Ward	.05	.04	.02
247	David Wells	.10	.08	.04
248	Ernie Whitt	.07	.05	.03
249	Luis Aguayo	.05	.04	.02
250a	Neil Allen (Home: Sarasota, FL)	1.50	1.25	.60
250b	Neil Allen (Home: Syosset, NY)	.05	.04	.02
251	John Candelaria	.07	.05	.03
252	Jack Clark	.15	.11	.06
253	Richard Dotson	.07	.05	.03
254	Rickey Henderson	.35	.25	.14
255	Tommy John	.12	.09	.05
256	Roberto Kelly	.20	.15	.08
257	Al Leiter	.15	.11	.06
258	Don Mattingly	1.50	1.25	.60
259	Dale Mohorcic	.05	.04	.02
260	*Hal Morris*(FC)	.20	.15	.08
261	Scott Nielsen(FC)	.10	.08	.04
262	Mike Pagliarulo	.10	.08	.04
263	*Hipolito Pena*(FC)	.15	.11	.06
264	Ken Phelps	.07	.05	.03
265	Willie Randolph	.07	.05	.03
266	Rick Rhoden	.07	.05	.03
267	Dave Righetti	.12	.09	.05
268	Rafael Santana	.05	.04	.02
269	Steve Shields(FC)	.07	.05	.03
270	Joel Skinner	.05	.04	.02
271	Don Slaught	.05	.04	.02
272	Claudell Washington	.07	.05	.03
273	Gary Ward	.07	.05	.03
274	Dave Winfield	.30	.25	.12
275	Luis Aquino(FC)	.05	.04	.02
276	Floyd Bannister	.07	.05	.03
277	George Brett	.35	.25	.14
278	Bill Buckner	.10	.08	.04
279	*Nick Capra*(FC)	.20	.15	.08
280	*Jose DeJesus*(FC)	.15	.11	.06
281	Steve Farr	.05	.04	.02
282	Jerry Gleaton	.05	.04	.02
283	Mark Gubicza	.10	.08	.04
284	*Tom Gordon*(FC)	3.75	2.00	1.25
285	Bo Jackson	.70	.50	.30
286	Charlie Leibrandt	.07	.05	.03
287	*Mike Macfarlane*	.20	.15	.08
288	Jeff Montgomery	.07	.05	.03
289	Bill Pecota	.07	.05	.03
290	Jamie Quirk	.05	.04	.02
291	Bret Saberhagen	.15	.11	.06
292	Kevin Seitzer	.30	.25	.12
293	Kurt Stillwell	.07	.05	.03
294	Pat Tabler	.07	.05	.03
295	Danny Tartabull	.20	.15	.08
296	Gary Thurman	.12	.09	.05
297	Frank White	.07	.05	.03
298	Willie Wilson	.10	.08	.04
299	Roberto Alomar	.50	.40	.20
300	*Sandy Alomar, Jr.*(FC)	1.25	.90	.50
301	Chris Brown	.07	.05	.03
302	Mike Brumley(FC)	.07	.05	.03
303	Mark Davis	.05	.04	.02
304	Mark Grant	.05	.04	.02
305	Tony Gwynn	.35	.25	.14
306	*Greg Harris*(FC)	.30	.25	.12
307	Andy Hawkins	.05	.04	.02
308	Jimmy Jones	.05	.04	.02
309	John Kruk	.07	.05	.03
310	Dave Leiper	.05	.04	.02
311	Carmelo Martinez	.05	.04	.02
312	Lance McCullers	.07	.05	.03

		MT	NR MT	EX
313	Keith Moreland	.07	.05	.03
314	Dennis Rasmussen	.10	.08	.04
315	Randy Ready	.05	.04	.02
316	Benito Santiago	.15	.11	.06
317	Eric Show	.07	.05	.03
318	Todd Simmons	.10	.08	.04
319	Garry Templeton	.07	.05	.03
320	Dickie Thon	.05	.04	.02
321	Ed Whitson	.05	.04	.02
322	Marvell Wynne	.05	.04	.02
323	Mike Aldrete	.07	.05	.03
324	Brett Butler	.07	.05	.03
325	Will Clark	.80	.60	.30
326	Kelly Downs	.10	.08	.04
327	Dave Dravecky	.07	.05	.03
328	Scott Garrelts	.05	.04	.02
329	Atlee Hammaker	.05	.04	.02
330	*Charlie Hayes*(FC)	.15	.11	.06
331	Mike Krukow	.07	.05	.03
332	Craig Lefferts	.05	.04	.02
333	Candy Maldonado	.07	.05	.03
334	Kirt Manwaring	.10	.08	.04
335	Bob Melvin	.05	.04	.02
336	Kevin Mitchell	.60	.45	.25
337	Donell Nixon	.05	.04	.02
338	*Tony Perezchica*(FC)	.15	.11	.06
339	Joe Price	.05	.04	.02
340	Rick Reuschel	.10	.08	.04
341	Earnest Riles	.05	.04	.02
342	Don Robinson	.05	.04	.02
343	Chris Speier	.05	.04	.02
344	Robby Thompson	.07	.05	.03
345	Jose Uribe	.05	.04	.02
346	Matt Williams	.12	.09	.05
347	*Trevor Wilson*(FC)	.15	.11	.06
348	Juan Agosto	.05	.04	.02
349	Larry Andersen	.05	.04	.02
350	Alan Ashby	.05	.04	.02
351	Kevin Bass	.07	.05	.03
352	Buddy Bell	.07	.05	.03
353	*Craig Biggio*	.60	.45	.25
354	Danny Darwin	.05	.04	.02
355	Glenn Davis	.25	.20	.10
356	Jim Deshaies	.05	.04	.02
357	Bill Doran	.07	.05	.03
358	*John Fishel*	.20	.15	.08
359	Billy Hatcher	.07	.05	.03
360	Bob Knepper	.07	.05	.03
361	*Louie Meadows*	.15	.11	.06
362	Dave Meads	.05	.04	.02
363	Jim Pankovits	.05	.04	.02
364	Terry Puhl	.05	.04	.02
365	Rafael Ramirez	.05	.04	.02
366	Craig Reynolds	.05	.04	.02
367	Mike Scott	.12	.09	.05
368	Nolan Ryan	.40	.30	.15
369	Dave Smith	.07	.05	.03
370	Gerald Young	.12	.09	.05
371	Hubie Brooks	.10	.08	.04
372	Tim Burke	.05	.04	.02
373	*John Dopson*	.25	.20	.10
374	Mike Fitzgerald	.05	.04	.02
375	Tom Foley	.05	.04	.02
376	Andres Galarraga	.15	.11	.06
377	Neal Heaton	.05	.04	.02
378	Joe Hesketh	.05	.04	.02
379	*Brian Holman*	.20	.15	.08
380	Rex Hudler	.05	.04	.02
381	*Randy Johnson*(FC)	.30	.25	.12
382	Wallace Johnson	.05	.04	.02
383	Tracy Jones	.10	.08	.04
384	Dave Martinez	.07	.05	.03
385	Dennis Martinez	.07	.05	.03
386	Andy McGaffigan	.05	.04	.02
387	Otis Nixon	.05	.04	.02
388	*Johnny Paredes*(FC)	.20	.15	.08
389	Jeff Parrett	.10	.08	.04
390	Pascual Perez	.07	.05	.03
391	Tim Raines	.25	.20	.10
392	Luis Rivera	.05	.04	.02
393	*Nelson Santovenia*	.25	.20	.10
394	Bryn Smith	.05	.04	.02
395	Tim Wallach	.10	.08	.04
396	Andy Allanson	.05	.04	.02
397	*Rod Allen*	.15	.11	.06
398	Scott Bailes	.05	.04	.02
399	Tom Candiotti	.05	.04	.02
400	Joe Carter	.12	.09	.05
401	Carmen Castillo	.05	.04	.02
402	Dave Clark	.07	.05	.03
403	John Farrell	.10	.08	.04
404	Julio Franco	.10	.08	.04
405	Don Gordon	.05	.04	.02
406	Mel Hall	.07	.05	.03
407	Brad Havens	.05	.04	.02
408	Brook Jacoby	.10	.08	.04
409	Doug Jones	.12	.09	.05
410	*Jeff Kaiser*(FC)	.15	.11	.06
411	*Luis Medina*(FC)	.40	.30	.15
412	Cory Snyder	.15	.11	.06
413	Greg Swindell	.12	.09	.05
414	*Ron Tingley*(FC)	.15	.11	.06
415	Willie Upshaw	.07	.05	.03
416	Ron Washington	.05	.04	.02
417	Rich Yett	.05	.04	.02
418	Damon Berryhill	.12	.09	.05
419	Mike Bielecki	.05	.04	.02
420	*Doug Dascenzo*(FC)	.30	.25	.12
421	Jody Davis	.07	.05	.03
422	Andre Dawson	.20	.15	.08
423	Frank DiPino	.05	.04	.02
424	Shawon Dunston	.10	.08	.04
425	"Goose" Gossage	.12	.09	.05
426	Mark Grace	1.50	1.25	.60
427	*Mike Harkey*(FC)	.30	.25	.12
428	Darrin Jackson	.07	.05	.03
429	Les Lancaster	.07	.05	.03
430	Vance Law	.07	.05	.03
431	Greg Maddux	.12	.09	.05
432	Jamie Moyer	.05	.04	.02
433	Al Nipper	.05	.04	.02
434	Rafael Palmeiro	.15	.11	.06
435	Pat Perry	.05	.04	.02
436	*Jeff Pico*	.25	.20	.10
437	Ryne Sandberg	.25	.20	.10
438	Calvin Schiraldi	.05	.04	.02
439	Rick Sutcliffe	.10	.08	.04
440	Manny Trillo	.05	.04	.02
441	*Gary Varsho*	.20	.15	.08
442	Mitch Webster	.07	.05	.03
443	*Luis Alicea*	.20	.15	.08
444	Tom Brunansky	.12	.09	.05
445	Vince Coleman	.15	.11	.06
446	*John Costello*	.20	.15	.08
447	Danny Cox	.07	.05	.03
448	Ken Dayley	.05	.04	.02
449	Jose DeLeon	.07	.05	.03
450	Curt Ford	.05	.04	.02
451	Pedro Guerrero	.15	.11	.06
452	Bob Horner	.10	.08	.04
453	*Tim Jones*(FC)	.15	.11	.06
454	Steve Lake	.05	.04	.02
455	Joe Magrane	.10	.08	.04
456	Greg Mathews	.07	.05	.03
457	Willie McGee	.12	.09	.05
458	Larry McWilliams	.05	.04	.02
459	Jose Oquendo	.05	.04	.02
460	Tony Pena	.07	.05	.03
461	Terry Pendleton	.10	.08	.04
462	*Steve Peters*(FC)	.15	.11	.06
463	Ozzie Smith	.15	.11	.06
464	Scott Terry	.08	.06	.03
465	Denny Walling	.05	.04	.02
466	Todd Worrell	.10	.08	.04
467	Tony Armas	.07	.05	.03
468	*Dante Bichette*(FC)	.25	.20	.10
469	Bob Boone	.07	.05	.03
470	*Terry Clark*(FC)	.15	.11	.06
471	Stew Cliburn(FC)	.05	.04	.02
472	*Mike Cook*(FC)	.15	.11	.06
473	*Sherman Corbett*	.15	.11	.06
474	Chili Davis	.07	.05	.03
475	Brian Downing	.07	.05	.03
476	Jim Eppard	.07	.05	.03
477	Chuck Finley	.05	.04	.02
478	Willie Fraser	.05	.04	.02
479	*Bryan Harvey*	.25	.20	.10
480	Jack Howell	.07	.05	.03
481	Wally Joyner	.25	.20	.10
482	Jack Lazorko	.05	.04	.02
483	Kirk McCaskill	.07	.05	.03
484	Mark McLemore	.05	.04	.02
485	Greg Minton	.05	.04	.02
486	Dan Petry	.07	.05	.03
487	Johnny Ray	.07	.05	.03
488	Dick Schofield	.05	.04	.02
489	Devon White	.12	.09	.05
490	Mike Witt	.07	.05	.03
491	Harold Baines	.12	.09	.05
492	Daryl Boston	.05	.04	.02
493	Ivan Calderon	.07	.05	.03
494	Mike Diaz	.07	.05	.03

		MT	NR MT	EX
495	Carlton Fisk	.20	.15	.08
496	*Dave Gallagher*	.25	.20	.10
497	Ozzie Guillen	.07	.05	.03
498	Shawn Hillegas	.07	.05	.03
499	Lance Johnson	.07	.05	.03
500	Barry Jones	.05	.04	.02
501	Bill Long	.07	.05	.03
502	Steve Lyons	.05	.04	.02
503	Fred Manrique	.07	.05	.03
504	Jack McDowell	.10	.08	.04
505	*Donn Pall*	.20	.15	.08
506	Kelly Paris	.05	.04	.02
507	Dan Pasqua	.10	.08	.04
508	*Ken Patterson*	.20	.15	.08
509	Melido Perez	.10	.08	.04
510	Jerry Reuss	.07	.05	.03
511	Mark Salas	.05	.04	.02
512	Bobby Thigpen	.10	.08	.04
513	Mike Woodard	.05	.04	.02
514	Bob Brower	.05	.04	.02
515	Steve Buechele	.05	.04	.02
516	*Jose Cecena*	.15	.11	.06
517	Cecil Espy	.07	.05	.03
518	Scott Fletcher	.07	.05	.03
519	Cecilio Guante	.05	.04	.02
520	Jose Guzman	.10	.08	.04
521	Ray Hayward	.05	.04	.02
522	Charlie Hough	.07	.05	.03
523	Pete Incaviglia	.12	.09	.05
524	Mike Jeffcoat	.05	.04	.02
525	Paul Kilgus	.10	.08	.04
526	*Chad Kreuter*(FC)	.20	.15	.08
527	Jeff Kunkel	.05	.04	.02
528	Oddibe McDowell	.07	.05	.03
529	Pete O'Brien	.07	.05	.03
530	Geno Petralli	.05	.04	.02
531	Jeff Russell	.05	.04	.02
532	Ruben Sierra	.50	.40	.20
533	Mike Stanley	.05	.04	.02
534	Ed Vande Berg	.05	.04	.02
535	Curtis Wilkerson	.05	.04	.02
536	Mitch Williams	.07	.05	.03
537	Bobby Witt	.10	.08	.04
538	Steve Balboni	.07	.05	.03
539	Scott Bankhead	.05	.04	.02
540	Scott Bradley	.05	.04	.02
541	Mickey Brantley	.05	.04	.02
542	Jay Buhner(FC)	.10	.08	.04
543	Mike Campbell	.10	.08	.04
544	Darnell Coles	.07	.05	.03
545	Henry Cotto	.05	.04	.02
546	Alvin Davis	.12	.09	.05
547	Mario Diaz	.07	.05	.03
548	Ken Griffey, Jr.(FC)	4.50	3.25	1.75
549	*Erik Hanson*(FC)	.30	.25	.12
550	Mike Jackson	.07	.05	.03
551	Mark Langston	.10	.08	.04
552	Edgar Martinez	.07	.05	.03
553	*Bill McGuire*(FC)	.15	.11	.06
554	Mike Moore	.05	.04	.02
555	Jim Presley	.07	.05	.03
556	Rey Quinones	.05	.04	.02
557	Jerry Reed	.05	.04	.02
558	Harold Reynolds	.07	.05	.03
559	*Mike Schooler*(FC)	.35	.25	.14
560	Bill Swift	.05	.04	.02
561	Dave Valle	.05	.04	.02
562	Steve Bedrosian	.10	.08	.04
563	Phil Bradley	.10	.08	.04
564	Don Carman	.07	.05	.03
565	Bob Dernier	.05	.04	.02
566	Marvin Freeman	.05	.04	.02
567	Todd Frohwirth	.07	.05	.03
568	Greg Gross	.05	.04	.02
569	Kevin Gross	.07	.05	.03
570	Greg Harris	.05	.04	.02
571	Von Hayes	.10	.08	.04
572	Chris James	.10	.08	.04
573	Steve Jeltz	.05	.04	.02
574	Ron Jones(FC)	.35	.25	.14
575	*Ricky Jordan*	1.50	1.25	.60
576	Mike Maddux	.05	.04	.02
577	David Palmer	.05	.04	.02
578	Lance Parrish	.15	.11	.06
579	Shane Rawley	.07	.05	.03
580	Bruce Ruffin	.05	.04	.02
581	Juan Samuel	.12	.09	.05
582	Mike Schmidt	.40	.30	.15
583	Kent Tekulve	.07	.05	.03
584	Milt Thompson	.05	.04	.02
585	*Jose Alvarez*	.15	.11	.06

		MT	NR MT	EX
586	Paul Assenmacher	.05	.04	.02
587	Bruce Benedict	.05	.04	.02
588	Jeff Blauser	.10	.08	.04
589	*Terry Blocker*(FC)	.15	.11	.06
590	Ron Gant	.12	.09	.05
591	Tom Glavine	.10	.08	.04
592	Tommy Gregg	.10	.08	.04
593	Albert Hall	.05	.04	.02
594	Dion James	.05	.04	.02
595	Rick Mahler	.05	.04	.02
596	Dale Murphy	.40	.30	.15
597	Gerald Perry	.10	.08	.04
598	Charlie Puleo	.05	.04	.02
599	Ted Simmons	.10	.08	.04
600	Pete Smith	.10	.08	.04
601	Zane Smith	.07	.05	.03
602	*John Smoltz*	.60	.45	.25
603	Bruce Sutter	.10	.08	.04
604	Andres Thomas	.07	.05	.03
605	Ozzie Virgil	.05	.04	.02
606	*Brady Anderson*(FC)	.35	.25	.14
607	Jeff Ballard	.07	.05	.03
608	*Jose Bautista*	.20	.15	.08
609	Ken Gerhart	.07	.05	.03
610	Terry Kennedy	.07	.05	.03
611	Eddie Murray	.30	.25	.12
612	Carl Nichols(FC)	.10	.08	.04
613	Tom Niedenfuer	.07	.05	.03
614	Joe Orsulak	.05	.04	.02
615	*Oswaldo Peraza (Oswald)*(FC)	.20	.15	.08
616a	Bill Ripken (obscenity on bat)	25.00	19.00	10.00
616b	Bill Ripken (obscenity on bat scrawled out in black)	20.00	15.00	8.00
616c	Bill Ripken (obscenity on bat blocked out in black)	1.00	.70	.40
616d	Bill Ripken (obscenity on bat whiteout)	35.00	27.50	15.00
617	Cal Ripken, Jr.	.35	.25	.14
618	Dave Schmidt	.05	.04	.02
619	Rick Schu	.05	.04	.02
620	Larry Sheets	.07	.05	.03
621	Doug Sisk	.05	.04	.02
622	Pete Stanicek	.10	.08	.04
623	Mickey Tettleton	.05	.04	.02
624	Jay Tibbs	.05	.04	.02
625	Jim Traber	.07	.05	.03
626	Mark Williamson	.07	.05	.03
627	*Craig Worthington*	.40	.30	.15
628	Speed and Power (Jose Canseco)	.60	.45	.25
629	Pitcher Perfect (Tom Browning)	.10	.08	.04
630	Like Father - Like Sons (Roberto Alomar, Sandy Alomar, Jr.)	.40	.30	.15
631	N.L. All-Stars (Will Clark, Rafael Palmeiro)	.40	.30	.15
632	Homeruns Coast to Coast (Will Clark, Darryl Strawberry)	.30	.25	.12
633	Hot Corner's - Hot Hitters (Wade Boggs, Carney Lansford)	.40	.30	.15
634	Triple A's (Jose Canseco, Mark McGwire, Terry Steinbach)	.60	.45	.25
635	Dual Heat (Mark Davis, Dwight Gooden)	.20	.15	.08
636	N.L. Pitching Power (David Cone, Danny Jackson)	.15	.11	.06
637	Cannon Arms (Bobby Bonilla, Chris Sabo)	.20	.15	.08
638	Double Trouble (Andres Galarraga, Gerald Perry)	.10	.08	.04
639	Power Center (Eric Davis, Kirby Puckett)	.30	.25	.12
640	Major League Prospects (*Cameron Drew, Steve Wilson*)(FC)	.25	.20	.10
641	Major League Prospects (*Kevin Brown, Kevin Reimer*)(FC)	.30	.25	.12
642	Major League Prospects (*Jerald Clark, Brad Pounders*)(FC)	.30	.25	.12
643	Major League Prospects (*Mike Capel, Drew Hall*)(FC)	.25	.20	.10
644	Major League Prospects (*Joe Girardi, Rolando Roomes*)(FC)	.50	.40	.20
645	Major League Prospects (*Marty Brown, Lenny Harris*)(FC)	.30	.25	.12
646	Major League Prospects (*Luis de los Santos, Jim Campbell*)(FC)	.25	.20	.10
647	Major League Prospects (*Miguel Garcia, Randy Kramer*)(FC)	.25	.20	.10
648	Major League Prospects (*Torey Lovullo, Robert Palacios*)(FC)	.25	.20	.10
649	Major League Prospects (*Jim Corsi, Bob Milacki*)(FC)	.25	.20	.10
650	Major League Prospects (*Grady Hall, Mike Rochford*)(FC)	.25	.20	.10

		MT	NR MT	EX
651	Major League Prospects (*Vance Lovelace,*			
	Terry Taylor)(FC)	.25	.20	.10
652	Major League Prospects (*Dennis Cook,*			
	Ken Hill)(FC)	.40	.30	.15
653	Major League Prospects (*Scott Service,*			
	Shane Turner)(FC)	.25	.20	.10
654	Checklist 1-101	.05	.04	.02
655	Checklist 102-200	.05	.04	.02
656	Checklist 201-298	.05	.04	.02
657	Checklist 299-395	.05	.04	.02
658	Checklist 396-490	.05	.04	.02
659	Checklist 491-584	.05	.04	.02
660	Checklist 585-660	.05	.04	.02

1989 Fleer All Star Team

This special 12-card set represents Fleer's choices for its 1989 Major League All-Star Team. For the fourth consecutive year, Fleer inserted the special cards randomly inside their regular 1989 wax and cello packs. The cards feature two player photos set against a green background with the "1989 Fleer All Star Team" logo bannered across the top, and the player's name, position and team in the lower left corner. The backs contain a several-paragraph player profile.

		MT	NR MT	EX
Complete Set:		13.00	9.75	5.25
Common Player:		.50	.40	.20
1	Bobby Bonilla	.60	.45	.25
2	Jose Canseco	2.00	1.50	.80
3	Will Clark	2.50	2.00	1.00
4	Dennis Eckersly	.50	.40	.20
5	Julio Franco	.60	.45	.25
6	Mike Greenwell	1.00	.70	.40
7	Orel Hershiser	1.00	.70	.40
8	Paul Molitor	.70	.50	.30
9	Mike Scioscia	.50	.40	.20
10	Darryl Strawberry	1.25	.90	.50
11	Alan Trammell	1.00	.70	.40
12	Frank Viola	.80	.60	.30

1989 Fleer's Baseball All Stars

This specially-boxed set was produced by Fleer for the Ben Franklin store chain. The full-color player photos are surrounded by a border of pink and yellow vertical bands. "Fleer Baseball All-Stars" appears along the top in red, white and blue. The set was sold in a box with a checklist on the back.

		MT	NR MT	EX
Complete Set:		4.00	3.00	1.50
Common Player:		.05	.04	.02
1	Doyle Alexander	.05	.04	.02
2	George Bell	.12	.09	.05
3	Wade Boggs	.70	.50	.30
4	Bobby Bonilla	.08	.06	.04

5	Jose Canseco	.80	.60	.30
6	Will Clark	.90	.70	.35
7	Roger Clemens	.30	.25	.12
8	Vince Coleman	.15	.11	.06
9	David Cone	.15	.11	.06
10	Mark Davis	.08	.06	.03
11	Andre Dawson	.10	.08	.04
12	Dennis Eckersley	.08	.06	.03
13	Andres Galarraga	.12	.09	.05
14	Kirk Gibson	.12	.09	.05
15	Dwight Gooden	.30	.25	.12
16	Mike Greenwell	.70	.50	.30
17	Mark Gubicza	.08	.06	.03
18	Ozzie Guillen	.05	.04	.02
19	Tony Gwynn	.20	.15	.08
20	Rickey Henderson	.15	.08	.04
21	Orel Hershiser	.20	.15	.08
22	Danny Jackson	.05	.04	.02
23	Doug Jones	.05	.04	.02
24	Ricky Jordan	.50	.40	.20
25	Bob Knepper	.05	.04	.02
26	Barry Larkin	.20	.15	.08
27	Vance Law	.05	.04	.02
28	Don Mattingly	1.00	.70	.40
29	Mark McGwire	.80	.60	.30
30	Paul Molitor	.08	.06	.02
31	Gerald Perry	.05	.04	.02
32	Kirby Puckett	.35	.25	.12
33	Johnny Ray	.05	.04	.02
34	Harold Reynolds	.08	.06	.03
35	Cal Ripken Jr.	.15	.11	.06
36	Don Robinson	.05	.04	.02
37	Ruben Sierra	.30	.25	.12
38	Dave Smith	.05	.04	.02
39	Darryl Strawberry	.35	.25	.14
40	Dave Steib	.08	.06	.03
41	Alan Trammell	.15	.11	.06
42	Andy Van Slyke	.10	.08	.04
43	Frank Viola	.15	.11	.06
44	Dave Winfield	.15	.11	.06

1989 Fleer Update

Fleer produced its sixth consecutive "Update" set in 1989 to supplement the company's regular set. As in the past, the set consisted of 132 cards (numbered U-1 through U-132) that were sold by hobby dealers in special collector's boxes.

		MT	NR MT	EX
	Complete Set:	18.00	13.50	7.25
	Common Player:	.06	.05	.02
1	Phil Bradley	.06	.05	.02
2	Mike Devereaux	.10	.08	.04
3	Steve Finley(FC)	.30	.25	.12
4	Kevin Hickey	.06	.05	.02
5	Brian Holton	.06	.05	.02
6	Bob Milacki	.20	.15	.08
7	Randy Milligan	.10	.08	.04
8	John Dopson	.15	.11	.06
9	Nick Esasky	.10	.08	.04
10	Rob Murphy	.06	.05	.02
11	Jim Abbott(FC)	2.75	2.00	1.00
12	Bert Blyleven	.06	.05	.02
13	Jeff Manto(FC)	.30	.25	.12
14	Bob McClure	.06	.05	.02
15	Lance Parrish	.06	.05	.02
16	Lee Stevens(FC)	.30	.25	.12
17	Claudell Washington	.06	.05	.02
18	Mark Davis	.06	.05	.02
19	Eric King	.06	.05	.02
20	Ron Kittle	.06	.05	.02
21	Matt Merullo(FC)	.25	.20	.10
22	Steve Rosenberg(FC)	.08	.06	.03
23	Robin Ventura(FC)	1.50	1.25	.60
24	Keith Atherton	.06	.05	.02
25	Joey Belle(FC)	1.50	1.25	.60
26	Jerry Browne	.06	.05	.02
27	Felix Fermin	.06	.05	.02
28	Brad Komminsk	.06	.05	.02
29	Pete O'Brien	.06	.05	.02
30	Mike Brumley	.06	.05	.02
31	Tracy Jones	.06	.05	.02
32	Mike Schwabe(FC)	.30	.25	.12
33	Gary Ward	.06	.05	.02
34	Frank Williams	.06	.05	.02
35	Kevin Appier(FC)	.20	.15	.08
36	Bob Boone	.06	.05	.02
37	Luis de los Santos	.10	.08	.04
38	Jim Eisenreich(FC)	.06	.05	.02
39	Jaime Navarro(FC)	.35	.25	.14
40	Bill Spiers(FC)	.40	.30	.15
41	Greg Vaughn(FC)	2.25	1.75	.90
42	Randy Veres(FC)	.20	.15	.08
43	Wally Backman	.06	.05	.02
44	Shane Rawley	.06	.05	.02
45	Steve Balboni	.06	.05	.02
46	Jesse Barfield	.06	.05	.02
47	Alvaro Espinosa(FC)	.30	.25	.12
48	Bob Geren(FC)	.40	.30	.15
49	Mel Hall	.06	.05	.02
50	Andy Hawkins	.06	.05	.02
51	Hensley Muelens(FC)	.50	.40	.20
52	Steve Sax	.15	.11	.06
53	Deion Sanders(FC)	1.25	.90	.50
54	Rickey Henderson	.30	.25	.12
55	Mike Moore	.10	.08	.04
56	Tony Phillips	.06	.05	.02
57	Greg Briley(FC)	1.00	.70	.40
58	Gene Harris	.10	.08	.04
59	Randy Johnson	.08	.06	.03
60	Jeffrey Leonard	.06	.05	.02
61	Dennis Powell	.06	.05	.02
62	Omar Vizquel(FC)	.30	.25	.12
63	Kevin Brown	.08	.06	.03
64	Julio Franco	.15	.11	.06
65	Jamie Moyer	.06	.05	.02
66	Rafael Palmeiro	.15	.11	.06
67	Nolan Ryan	1.00	.70	.40
68	Francisco Cabrera(FC)	.30	.25	.12
69	Junior Felix(FC)	1.25	.90	.50
70	Al Leiter	.06	.05	.02
71	Alex Sanchez(FC)	.20	.15	.08
72	Geronimo Berroa(FC)	.08	.06	.03
73	Derek Lilliquist(FC)	.20	.15	.08
74	Lonnie Smith	.10	.08	.04
75	Jeff Treadway	.06	.05	.02
76	Paul Kilgus	.06	.05	.02
77	Lloyd McClendon	.25	.20	.10
78	Scott Sanderson	.06	.05	.02
79	Dwight Smith(FC)	1.50	1.25	.60
80	Jerome Walton(FC)	4.50	3.50	1.75
81	Mitch Williams	.20	.15	.08
82	Steve Wilson	.25	.20	.10
83	Todd Benzinger	.06	.05	.02
84	Ken Griffey	.20	.15	.08
85	Rick Mahler	.06	.05	.02
86	Rolando Roomes	.20	.15	.08

		MT	NR MT	EX
87	Scott Scudder(FC)	.30	.25	.12
88	Jim Clancy	.06	.05	.02
89	Rick Rhoden	.06	.05	.02
90	Dan Schatzeder	.06	.05	.02
91	Mike Morgan	.06	.05	.02
92	Eddie Murray	.20	.15	.08
93	Willie Randolph	.06	.05	.02
94	Ray Searage	.06	.05	.02
95	Mike Aldrete	.06	.05	.02
96	Kevin Gross	.06	.05	.02
97	Mark Langston	.15	.11	.06
98	Spike Owen	.06	.05	.02
99	Zane Smith	.06	.05	.02
100	Don Aase	.06	.05	.02
101	Barry Lyons	.06	.05	.02
102	Juan Samuel	.06	.05	.02
103	Wally Whitehurst(FC)	.20	.15	.08
104	Dennis Cook	.20	.15	.08
105	Lenny Dykstra	.06	.05	.02
106	Charlie Hayes	.10	.08	.04
107	Tommy Herr	.06	.05	.02
108	Ken Howell	.06	.05	.02
109	John Kruk	.06	.05	.02
110	Roger McDowell	.06	.05	.02
111	Terry Mulholland(FC)	.06	.05	.02
112	Jeff Parrett	.06	.05	.02
113	Neal Heaton	.06	.05	.02
114	Jeff King	.10	.08	.04
115	Randy Kramer	.06	.05	.02
116	Bill Landrum	.06	.05	.02
117	Cris Carpenter(FC)	.25	.20	.10
118	Eric King	.06	.05	.02
119	Ken Hill	.15	.11	.06
120	Dan Quisenberry	.06	.05	.02
121	Milt Thompson	.06	.05	.02
122	Todd Zeile(FC)	3.25	2.50	1.25
123	Jack Clark	.10	.08	.04
124	Bruce Hurst	.06	.05	.02
125	Mark Parent	.06	.05	.02
126	Bip Roberts	.06	.05	.02
127	Jeff Brantley(FC)	.25	.20	.10
128	Terry Kennedy	.06	.05	.02
129	Mike LaCoss	.06	.05	.02
130	Greg Litton(FC)	.20	.15	.08
131	Mike Schmidt	1.00	.70	.40
132	Checklist	.06	.05	.02

1989 Fleer Baseball MVP

Filled with superstars, this 44-card boxed set was produced by Fleer in 1989 for the Toys 'R' Us chain. The fronts of the cards are designed in a yellow and green color scheme and include a "Fleer Baseball MVP" logo above the color player photo. The backs are printed in shades of green and yellow and include biographical notes and stats. The set was issued in a special box with a checklist on the back.

		MT	NR MT	EX
	Complete Set:	3.75	2.75	1.50
	Common Player:	.05	.04	.02
1	Steve Bedrosian	.05	.04	.02
2	George Bell	.12	.09	.05
3	Wade Boggs	.70	.50	.30
4	George Brett	.15	.11	.06

		MT	NR MT	EX
5	Hubie Brooks	.05	.04	.02
6	Jose Canseco	.90	.70	.35
7	Will Clark	.90	.70	.35
8	Roger Clemens	.30	.25	.12
9	Eric Davis	.20	.15	.08
10	Glenn Davis	.12	.09	.05
11	Andre Dawson	.12	.09	.05
12	Andres Galarraga	.12	.09	.05
13	Kirk Gibson	.15	.11	.06
14	Dwight Gooden	.30	.25	.12
15	Mark Grace	.25	.20	.10
16	Mike Greenwell	.50	.40	.20
17	Tony Gwynn	.20	.15	.08
18	Bryan Harvey	.05	.04	.02
19	Orel Hershiser	.25	.20	.10
20	Ted Higuera	.07	.05	.03
21	Danny Jackson	.05	.04	.02
22	Mike Jackson	.05	.04	.02
23	Doug Jones	.05	.04	.02
24	Greg Maddux	.07	.05	.03
25	Mike Marshall	.05	.04	.02
26	Don Mattingly	1.00	.70	.40
27	Fred McGriff	.30	.25	.12
28	Mark McGwire	.80	.60	.30
29	Kevin McReynolds	.15	.11	.06
30	Jack Morris	.05	.04	.02
31	Gerald Perry	.05	.04	.02
32	Kirby Puckett	.35	.25	.12
33	Chris Sabo	.20	.15	.08
34	Mike Scott	.12	.09	.05
35	Ruben Sierra	.25	.20	.10
36	Darryl Strawberry	.35	.25	.12
37	Danny Tartabull	.09	.07	.04
38	Bobby Thigpen	.09	.07	.04
39	Alan Trammell	.15	.11	.06
40	Andy Van Slyke	.12	.09	.05
41	Frank Viola	.12	.09	.05
42	Walt Weiss	.20	.15	.08
43	Dave Winfield	.15	.11	.06
44	Todd Worrell	.07	.05	.03

		MT	NR MT	EX
11	Andre Dawson	.12	.09	.05
12	Dwight Evans	.09	.07	.04
13	Andres Galarraga	.12	.09	.05
14	Kirk Gibson	.12	.09	.05
15	Dwight Gooden	.30	.25	.12
16	Jim Gott	.05	.04	.02
17	Mark Grace	.30	.25	.12
18	Mike Greenwell	.70	.50	.30
19	Mark Gibicza	.07	.05	.03
20	Tony Gwynn	.20	.15	.08
21	Rickey Henderson	.20	.15	.08
22	Tom Henke	.05	.04	.02
23	Mike Henneman	.05	.04	.02
24	Orel Hershiser	.25	.20	.10
25	Danny Jackson	.05	.04	.02
26	Gregg Jefferies	.80	.60	.30
27	Ricky Jordan	.60	.45	.25
28	Wally Joyner	.15	.11	.06
29	Mark Langston	.15	.11	.06
30	Tim Leary	.05	.04	.02
31	Don Mattingly	1.00	.70	.40
32	Mark McGwire	.80	.60	.30
33	Dale Murphy	.15	.11	.06
34	Kirby Puckett	.35	.25	.14
35	Chris Sabo	.30	.25	.12
36	Kevin Seitzer	.15	.11	.06
37	Ruben Sierra	.30	.25	.12
38	Ozzie Smith	.15	.11	.06
39	Dave Stewart	.07	.05	.03
40	Darryl Strawberry	.35	.25	.14
41	Alan Trammell	.15	.11	.06
42	Frank Viola	.15	.11	.06
43	Dave Winfield	.15	.11	.06
44			.15	.11

1989 Fleer 'Baseball's Exciting Stars'

Sold exclusively in Cumberland Farm stores, this 44-card boxed set pictures the game's top stars. The card fronts feature a color player photo surrounded by a blue border with "Baseball's Exciting Stars" along the top. The cards were were numbered alphabetically and packed in a special box with a complete checklist on the back.

		MT	NR MT	EX
Complete Set:		4.00	3.00	1.50
Common Player:		.05	.04	.02
1	Harold Baines	.07	.05	.03
2	Wade Boggs	.70	.50	.30
3	Jose Canseco	.90	.70	.35
4	Joe Carter	.12	.09	.05
5	Will Clark	.90	.70	.35
6	Roger Clemens	.30	.25	.12
7	Vince Coleman	.15	.11	.06
8	David Cone	.15	.11	.06
9	Eric Davis	.20	.15	.08
10	Glenn Davis	.15	.11	.06

1989 Fleer Heroes of Baseball

This 44-card boxed set was produced by Fleer for the Woolworth store chain. The fronts of the cards are designed in a red and blue color scheme and feature full-color photos that fade into a soft focus on all edges. "Fleer Heroes of Baseball" appears just above the player's name, team and position at the bottom of the card. The set is numbered alphabetically and was packaged in a special box with a checklist on the back.

		MT	NR MT	EX
Complete Set:		3.75	2.75	1.50
Common Player:		.05	.04	.02
1	George Bell	.12	.09	.05
2	Wade Boggs	.70	.50	.30
3	Barry Bonds	.12	.09	.05
4	Tom Brunansky	.08	.06	.03
5	Jose Canseco	.90	.70	.35
6	Joe Carter	.12	.09	.05
7	Will Clark	.90	.70	.35
8	Roger Clemens	.30	.25	.12
9	David Cone	.15	.11	.06
10	Eric Davis	.40	.30	.15
11	Glenn Davis	.12	.09	.05
12	Andre Dawson	.12	.09	.05
13	Dennis Eckersley	.07	.05	.03
14	John Franco	.05	.04	.02
15	Gary Gaetti	.12	.09	.05
16	Andres Galarraga	.15	.11	.06

		MT	NR MT	EX
17	Kirk Gibson	.12	.09	.05
18	Dwight Gooden	.30	.25	.12
19	Mike Greenwell	.50	.40	.20
20	Tony Gwynn	.25	.20	.10
21	Bryan Harvey	.05	.04	.02
22	Orel Hershiser	.20	.15	.08
23	Ted Higuera	.07	.05	.03
24	Danny Jackson	.05	.04	.02
25	Ricky Jordan	.40	.30	.15
26	Don Mattingly	1.00	.70	.40
27	Fred McGriff	.30	.25	.12
28	Mark McGwire	.60	.45	.25
29	Kevin McReynolds	.15	.11	.06
30	Gerald Perry	.05	.04	.02
31	Kirby Puckett	.30	.25	.12
32	Johnny Ray	.05	.04	.02
33	Harold Reynolds	.05	.04	.02
34	Cal Ripken Jr.	.15	.11	.06
35	Ryne Sandberg	.15	.11	.06
36	Kevin Seitzer	.15	.11	.06
37	Ruben Sierra	.30	.25	.12
38	Darryl Strawberry	.30	.25	.12
39	Bobby Thigpen	.05	.04	.02
40	Alan Trammell	.12	.09	.05
41	Andy Van Slyke	.10	.08	.04
42	Frank Viola	.15	.11	.06
43	Dave Winfield	.15	.11	.06
44	Robin Yount	.20	.15	.08

		MT	NR MT	EX
20	Orel Hershiser	.25	.20	.10
21	Pete Incaviglia	.05	.04	.02
22	Danny Jackson	.05	.04	.02
23	Gregg Jefferies	.90	.70	.35
24	Joe Magrane	.09	.07	.05
25	Don Mattingly	1.00	.70	.40
26	Fred McGriff	.30	.25	.12
27	Mark McGwire	.80	.60	.30
28	Dale Murphy	.15	.11	.06
29	Dan Plesac	.07	.05	.03
30	Kirby Puckett	.40	.30	.15
31	Harold Reynolds	.12	.09	.05
32	Cal Ripken Jr.	.15	.11	.06
33	Jeff Robinson	.05	.04	.02
34	Mike Scott	.12	.09	.05
35	Ozzie Smith	.15	.09	.05
36	Dave Stewart	.07	.05	.03
37	Darryl Strawberry	.30	.25	.12
38	Greg Swindell	.15	.11	.06
39	Bobby Thigpen	.08	.06	.03
40	Alan Trammell	.12	.09	.05
41	Andy Van Slyke	.12	.09	.05
42	Frank Viola	.12	.09	.05
43	Dave Winfield	.12	.09	.05
44	Robin Yount	.20	.15	.08

1989 Fleer Baseball Superstars

This 44-card boxed set was produced by Fleer for the McCrory store chain. The cards are the standard 2-1/2" by 3-1/2" and the full-color player photos are outlined in red with a tan-and-white striped border. The player's name, position and team logo appear at the bottom of the card. The backs carry yellow and white stripes and include the Fleer "SuperStars" logo, player stats and biographical information. The cards are numbered alphabetically and packaged in a special box that includes a checklist on the back.

1989 Fleer League Leaders

Eric Davis

Another of the various small, boxed sets issued by Fleer, the 44-card "League Leaders" set was produced for Walgreen stores. The standard-size cards feature color photos on the front surrounded by a red border with "Fleer League Leaders" across the top. The player's name, team and position appear in a yellow band at the bottom. The backs include player stats and data and the team logo. The cards are numbered alphabetically and packaged in a special box that includes the full checklist on the back.

		MT	NR MT	EX
Complete Set:		4.00	3.00	1.50
Common Player:		.05	.04	.02

		MT	NR MT	EX
1	Allan Anderson	.05	.04	.02
2	Wade Boggs	.70	.50	.30
3	Jose Canseco	.90	.70	.35
4	Will Clark	.90	.70	.35
5	Roger Clemens	.30	.25	.12
6	Vince Coleman	.15	.11	.06
7	David Cone	.15	.11	.06
8	Kal Daniels	.12	.09	.05
9	Chili Davis	.05	.04	.02
10	Eric Davis	.20	.15	.08
11	Glenn Davis	.15	.11	.06
12	Andre Dawson	.12	.09	.05
13	John Franco	.05	.04	.02
14	Andres Galarraga	.12	.09	.05
15	Kirk Gibson	.12	.09	.05
16	Dwight Gooden	.30	.25	.12
17	Mark Grace	.30	.25	.12
18	Mike Greenwell	.60	.45	.25
19	Tony Gwynn	.20	.15	.08

		MT	NR MT	EX
Complete Set:		4.00	3.00	1.50
Common Player:		.05	.04	.02

		MT	NR MT	EX
1	Roberto Alomar	.20	.15	.08
2	Harold Baines	.12	.09	.05
3	Tim Belcher	.12	.09	.05
4	Wade Boggs	.70	.50	.30
5	George Brett	.15	.11	.06
6	Jose Canseco	.90	.70	.35
7	Gary Carter	.05	.04	.02
8	Will Clark	.90	.70	.35
9	Roger Clemens	.30	.25	.12
10	Kal Daniels	.15	.11	.06
11	Eric Davis	.20	.15	.08
12	Andre Dawson	.12	.09	.05
13	Tony Fernandez	.12	.09	.05
14	Scott Fletcher	.05	.04	.02
15	Andres Galarraga	.15	.11	.06
16	Kirk Gibson	.15	.11	.06
17	Dwight Gooden	.30	.25	.12
18	Jim Gott	.05	.04	.02
19	Mark Grace	.30	.25	.12
20	Mike Greenwell	.50	.40	.20

NOTE: A card number in parentheses ( ) indicates the set is unnumbered.

		MT	NR MT	EX
21	Tony Gwynn	.20	.15	.08
22	Rickey Henderson	.20	.15	.08
23	Orel Hershiser	.20	.15	.08
24	Ted Higuera	.07	.05	.02
25	Gregg Jefferies	.90	.70	.35
26	Wally Joyner	.15	.11	.06
27	Mark Langston	.15	.11	.06
28	Greg Maddux	.15	.11	.06
29	Don Mattingly	1.00	.70	.40
30	Fred McGriff	.30	.25	.12
31	Mark McGwire	.80	.60	.30
32	Dan Plesac	.09	.07	.04
33	Kirby Puckett	.30	.25	.12
34	Jeff Reardon	.05	.04	.02
35	Chris Sabo	.12	.09	.05
36	Mike Schmidt	.25	.20	.10
37	Mike Scott	.10	.08	.04
38	Cory Snyder	.10	.08	.04
39	Darryl Strawberry	.30	.25	.12
40	Alan Trammell	.12	.09	.05
41	Frank Viola	.12	.09	.05
42	Walt Weiss	.12	.09	.05
43	Dave Winfield	.12	.09	.05
44	Todd Worrell	.05	.04	.02

		MT	NR MT	EX
24	Astros Logo	.05	.04	.02
25	Darryl Strawberry	.40	.30	.15
26	Alan Trammell	.20	.15	.08
27	Andy Van Slyke	.25	.20	.10
28	Frank Viola	.20	.15	.08

1989 Fleer For The Record

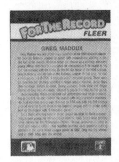

Fleers "For the Record" set features six players and their achievements from 1988. Fronts of the standard 2-1/2" by 3-1/2" cards feature a full color photo of the player set against a red background. The words "For the Record" appear in blue script at the top of the card and the players name on the bottom, printed in white type. Card backs are grey and describes individual accomplishments. The cards were distributed one per rack pack.

		MT	NR MT	EX
Complete Set:		5.00	3.75	2.00
			.80	.60
1	Wade Boggs	1.25	.90	.60
2	Roger Clemens	1.00	.70	.40
3	Andres Galarraga	.80	.60	.30
4	Kirk Gibson	.80	.60	.30
5	Greg Maddux	1.00	.70	.40
6	Don Mattingly	1.75	1.25	.80

1989 Fleer '88 World Series

This 12-card set, which depicts highlights of the 1988 World Series, was included as a special sub-set with the regular factory-collated Fleer set. It was not available as individual cards in wax packs, cello packs or any other form. Cards from this special six-card sub-set were inserted in 1989 Fleer three-packs and were not distributed in any other form. The red-bordered cards spotlight six of the game's top players. Fleer's "For the Record" banner is headlined along the top of each card. The player action photo is set against a "scoreboard" background, with the

1989 Fleer Box Panels

For the fourth consecutive year, Fleer issued a series of cards on the bottom panels of its regular 1989 wax pack boxes. The 28-card set includes 20 players and eight team logo cards, all designed in the identical style of the regular 1989 Fleer set. The box-bottom cards were randomly printed, four cards (three player cards and one team logo) on each bottom panel. The cards were numbered from C-1 to C-28.

		MT	NR MT	EX
Complete Panel Set:		6.00	4.50	2.50
Complete Singles Set:		3.00	2.25	1.25
Common Single Player:		.15	.11	.06
1	Mets Logo	5.00	.04	.02
2	Wade Boggs	.40	.30	.15
3	George Brett	.25	.20	.10
4	Jose Canseco	.50	.40	.20
5	A's Logo	.05	.04	.02
6	Will Clark	.50	.40	.20
7	David Cone	.50	.40	.20
8	Andres Galarraga	.25	.20	.10
9	Dodgers Logo	.05	.04	.02
10	Kirk Gibson	.15	.11	.06
11	Mike Greenwell	.25	.20	.10
12	Tony Gwynn	.25	.20	.10
13	Tigers Logo	.05	.04	.02
14	Orel Hershiser	.20	.15	.08
15	Danny Jackson	.15	.11	.06
16	Wally Joyner	.50	.40	.20
17	Red Sox Logo	.05	.04	.02
18	Yankees Logo	.05	.04	.02
19	Fred McGriff	.60	.45	.25
20	Kirby Puckett	.30	.25	.12
21	Chris Sabo	.15	.11	.06
22	Kevin Seitzer	.30	.25	.12
23	Pirates Logo	.05	.04	.02

player's name, team and position in a red band across the bottom. The backs include a several-paragraph player profile citing the player's 1988 season highlights.

	MT	NR MT	EX
Complete Set:	3.00	2.25	1.25
Common Player:	.25	.20	.10

		MT	NR MT	EX
1	Dodgers' Secret Weapon (Mickey Hatcher)	.25	.20	.10
2	Rookie Starts Series (Tim Belcher)	.35	.25	.14
3	Canseco Slams L.A. (Jose Canseco)	.40	.30	.20
4	Dramatic Comeback (Mike Scioscia)	.25	.20	.10
5	Gibson Steals The Show (Kirk Gibson)	.40	.30	.15
6	"Bulldog" (Orel Hershiser)	.30	.25	.12
7	One Swing, Three RBI's (Mike Marshall)	.25	.20	.10
8	Game-Winning Home Run (Mark McGwire)	.40	.30	.15
9	Sax's Speed Wins Game 4 (Steve Sax)	.25	.20	.10
10	Series Caps Award-Winning Year (Walt Weiss)	.25	.20	.10
11	The M.V.P. And His Shutout Magic (Orel Hershiser)	.35	.25	.14
12	Dodger Blue, World Champs	.25	.20	.10

1990 Fleer

Fleer's 1990 set, its 10th consecutive baseball card offering, again consisted of 660 cards numbered by team. The front of the cards feature mostly action photos surrounded by one of several different color bands and a white border. The "Fleer '90" logo appears in the upper left corner, while the team logo is the upper right. The player's name and position are printed in a flowing banner below the photo. The set includes various special cards, including a series of "Major League Prospects," Players of the Decade, team checklist cards and a series of multi-player cards. The backs include complete career stats, player data, and a special "Vital Signs" section showing on-base percentage, slugging percentage, etc. for batters; and strikeout and walk ratios, opposing batting averages, etc. for pitchers.

	MT	NR MT	EX
Complete Set:	22.00	16.50	8.75
Common Player:	.05	.04	.02

		MT	NR MT	EX
1	Lance Blankenship	.07	.05	.03
2	Todd Burns	.06	.05	.02
3	Jose Canseco	1.00	.70	.40
4	Jim Corsi	.09	.07	.04
5	Storm Davis	.06	.05	.02
6	Dennis Eckersley	.12	.09	.05
7	Mike Gallego	.06	.05	.02
8	Ron Hassey	.05	.04	.02
9	Dave Henderson	.10	.08	.06

		MT	NR MT	EX
10	Rickey Henderson	.30	.25	.12
11	Rick Honeycutt	.05	.04	.02
12	Stan Javier	.05	.04	.02
13	Flix Jose	.12	.09	.05
14	Carney Lansford	.07	.05	.03
15	Mark McGwire	.70	.50	.30
16	Mike Moore	.10	.08	.04
17	Gene Nelson	.05	.04	.02
18	Dave Parker	.12	.09	.05
19	Tony Phillips	.05	.04	.02
20	Terry Steinbach	.10	.08	.06
21	Dave Stewart	.10	.08	.06
22	Walt Weiss	.10	.08	.06
23	Bob Welch	.06	.05	.03
24	Curt Young	.05	.04	.02
25	Paul Assenmacher	.05	.04	.02
26	Damon Berryhill	.10	.08	.04
27	Mike Bielecki	.10	.08	.04
28	Kevin Blankenship	.07	.05	.03
29	Andre Dawson	.12	.09	.05
30	Shawon Dunston	.09	.07	.04
31	Joe Girardi	.20	.15	.08
32	Mark Grace	.25	.20	.10
33	Mike Harkey	.12	.09	.05
34	Paul Kilgus	.05	.04	.02
35	Les Lancaster	.06	.05	.02
36	Vance Law	.05	.04	.02
37	Greg Maddux	.10	.08	.04
38	Lloyd McClendon	.10	.08	.04
39	Jeff Pico	.05	.04	.02
40	Ryne Sandberg	.15	.11	.06
41	Scott Sanderson	.05	.04	.02
42	Dwight Smith	1.25	.90	.50
43	Rick Sutcliffe	.08	.06	.03
44	*Jerome Walton*	1.75	1.25	.70
45	Mitch Webster	.05	.04	.02
46	Curt Wilkerson	.05	.04	.02
47	*Dean Wilkins* (FC)	.25	.20	.10
48	Mitch Williams	.08	.06	.03
49	Steve Wilson	.15	.11	.06
50	Steve Bedrosian	.06	.05	.02
51	*Mike Benjamin* (FC)	.35	.25	.14
52	*Jeff Brantley*	.12	.09	.05
53	Brett Butler	.07	.05	.03
54	Will Clark	.50	.40	.20
55	Kelly Downs	.05	.04	.02
56	Scott Garrelts	.09	.07	.04
57	Atlee Hammaker	.05	.04	.02
58	Terry Kennedy	.05	.04	.02
59	Mike LaCoss	.05	.04	.02
60	Craig Lefferts	.06	.05	.02
61	*Greg Litton*	.25	.20	.10
62	Candy Maldonado	.06	.05	.02
63	Kirt Manwaring	.09	.07	.04
64	*Randy McCament* (FC)	.20	.15	.08
65	Kevin Mitchell	.30	.25	.12
66	Donnell Nixon	.05	.04	.02
67	Ken Oberkfell	.05	.04	.02
68	Rick Reuschel	.09	.07	.04
69	Ernest Riles	.05	.04	.02
70	Don Robinson	.05	.04	.02
71	Pat Sheridan	.05	.04	.02
72	Chris Speier	.05	.04	.02
73	Robby Thompson	.07	.05	.03
74	Jose Uribe	.06	.05	.02
75	Matt Williams	.20	.15	.08
76	George Bell	.10	.08	.04
77	Pat Borders	.07	.05	.03
78	John Cerutti	.05	.04	.02
79	*Junior Felix*	1.25	.90	.50
80	Tony Fernandez	.09	.07	.04
81	Mike Flanagan	.05	.04	.02
82	*Mauro Gozzo* (FC)	.20	.15	.08
83	Kelly Gruber	.07	.05	.03
84	Tom Henke	.05	.04	.02
85	Jimmy Key	.07	.05	.03
86	Manny Lee	.05	.04	.02
87	Nelson Liriano	.05	.04	.02
88	Lee Mazzilli	.05	.04	.02
89	Fred McGriff	.25	.20	.10
90	Lloyd Moseby	.06	.05	.02
91	Rance Mulliniks	.05	.04	.02
92	Alex Sanchez	.15	.11	.06
93	Dave Steib	.09	.07	.05
94	Todd Stottlemyre	.09	.07	.05
95	Duane Ward	.05	.04	.02
96	David Wells	.05	.04	.02
97	Ernie Whitt	.06	.05	.02
98	Frank Wills	.05	.04	.02
99	Mookie Wilson	.09	.07	.04
100	*Kevin Appier* (FC)	.25	.20	.10

#	Player	MT	NR MT	EX
101	Luis Aquino	.05	.04	.02
102	Bob Boone	.07	.05	.03
103	George Brett	.15	.11	.06
104	Jose DeJesus	.08	.06	.03
105	Luis de los Santos	.08	.06	.03
106	Jim Eisenreich	.05	.04	.02
107	Steve Farr	.05	.04	.02
108	Tom Gordon	.50	.40	.20
109	Mark Gubicza	.09	.07	.04
110	Bo Jackson	.35	.25	.14
111	Terry Leach	.05	.04	.02
112	Charlie Leibrandt	.05	.04	.02
113	*Rick Luecken*(FC)	.25	.20	.10
114	Mike Macfarlane	.05	.04	.02
115	Jeff Montgomery	.06	.05	.03
116	Bret Saberhagen	.10	.08	.04
117	Kevin Seitzer	.10	.08	.04
118	Kurt Stillwell	.06	.05	.02
119	Pat Tabler	.05	.04	.02
121	Gary Thurman	.05	.04	.02
122	Frank White	.07	.05	.03
123	Willie Wilson	.06	.05	.03
124	*Matt Winters*(FC)	.20	.15	.08
125	Jim Abbott	.70	.50	.30
126	Tony Armas	.05	.04	.02
127	Dante Bichette	.09	.07	.04
128	Bert Blyleven	.09	.07	.04
129	Chili Davis	.06	.05	.02
130	Brian Downing	.06	.05	.02
131	*Mike Fetters*(FC)	.35	.25	.12
132	Chuck Finley	.06	.05	.02
133	Willie Fraser	.05	.04	.02
134	Bryan Harvey	.05	.04	.02
135	Jack Howell	.05	.04	.02
136	Wally Joyner	.10	.08	.04
137	*Jeff Manto*	.20	.15	.08
138	Kirk McCaskill	.06	.05	.02
139	Bob McClure	.05	.04	.02
140	Greg Minton	.05	.04	.02
141	Lance Parrish	.07	.05	.02
142	Dan Petry	.05	.04	.02
143	Johnny Ray	.05	.04	.02
144	Dick Schofield	.06	.05	.02
145	*Lee Stevens*	.30	.25	.12
146	Claudell Washington	.06	.05	.02
147	Devon White	.08	.06	.03
148	Mike Witt	.06	.05	.02
149	Roberto Alomar	.10	.08	.04
150	Sandy Alomar Jr.	.40	.30	.15
151	Andy Benes(FC)	1.00	.70	.40
152	Jack Clark	.06	.05	.02
153	Pat Clements	.05	.04	.02
154	Joey Cora	.15	.11	.06
155	Mark Davis	.09	.07	.04
156	Mark Grant	.05	.04	.02
157	Tony Gwynn	.25	.20	.10
158	Greg Harris	.10	.08	.04
159	Bruce Hurst	.06	.05	.02
160	Darrin Jackson	.05	.04	.02
161	Chris James	.06	.05	.02
162	Carmelo Martinez	.06	.05	.02
163	Mike Pagliarulo	.06	.05	.02
164	Mark Parent	.05	.04	.02
165	Dennis Rasmussen	.05	.04	.02
166	Bip Roberts	.08	.06	.03
167	Benito Santiago	.12	.09	.05
168	Calvin Schiraldi	.05	.04	.02
169	Eric Show	.06	.05	.02
170	Garry Templeton	.06	.05	.02
171	Ed Whitson	.06	.05	.02
172	Brady Anderson	.07	.05	.03
173	Jeff Ballard	.07	.05	.03
174	Phil Bradley	.07	.05	.03
175	Mike Devereaux	.07	.05	.03
176	*Steve Finley*	.20	.15	.08
177	Pete Harnisch(FC)	.10	.08	.04
178	Kevin Hickey	.10	.08	.04
179	Brian Holton	.05	.04	.02
180	*Ben McDonald*(FC)	2.25	1.75	.90
181	Bob Melvin	.05	.04	.02
182	Bob Milacki	.07	.05	.03
183	Randy Milligan	.06	.05	.02
184	Gregg Olson(FC)	.60	.45	.25
185	Joe Orsulak	.05	.04	.02
186	Bill Ripken	.05	.04	.02
187	Cal Ripken Jr.	.15	.11	.06
188	Dave Schmidt	.05	.04	.02
189	Larry Sheets	.05	.04	.02
190	Mickey Tettleton	.08	.06	.03
191	Mark Thurmond	.05	.04	.02
192	Jay Tibbs	.05	.04	.02
193	Jim Traber	.05	.04	.02
194	Mark Williamson	.05	.04	.02
195	Craig Worthington	.15	.11	.06
196	Don Aase	.05	.04	.02
197	*Blaine Beatty*(FC)	.35	.25	.12
198	Mark Carreon	.10	.08	.04
199	Gary Carter	.06	.05	.02
200	David Cone	.10	.08	.04
201	Ron Darling	.07	.05	.03
202	Kevin Elster	.05	.04	.02
203	Sid Fernandez	.09	.07	.04
204	Dwight Gooden	.20	.15	.08
205	Keith Hernandez	.06	.05	.02
206	*Jeff Innis*	.15	.11	.06
207	Gregg Jefferies	.50	.40	.20
208	Howard Johnson	.10	.08	.04
209	Barry Lyons	.05	.04	.02
210	Dave Magadan	.06	.05	.02
211	Kevin McReynolds	.07	.05	.03
212	Jeff Musselman	.05	.04	.02
213	Randy Myers	.06	.05	.02
214	Bob Ojeda	.06	.05	.02
215	Juan Samuel	.06	.05	.02
216	Mackey Sasser	.05	.04	.02
217	Darryl Strawberry	.25	.20	.10
218	Tim Teufel	.05	.04	.02
219	Frank Viola	.10	.08	.04
220	Juan Agosto	.05	.04	.02
221	Larry Anderson	.05	.04	.02
222	*Eric Anthony*(FC)	2.25	1.75	.90
223	Kevin Bass	.08	.06	.03
224	Craig Biggio	.10	.08	.04
225	Ken Caminiti	.06	.05	.02
226	Jim Clancy	.05	.04	.02
227	Danny Darwin	.05	.04	.02
228	Glenn Davis	.09	.07	.04
229	Jim Deshaies	.07	.05	.02
230	Bill Doran	.06	.05	.02
231	Bob Forsch	.05	.04	.02
233	Terry Puhl	.05	.04	.02
234	Rafael Ramirez	.05	.04	.02
235	Rick Rhoden	.05	.04	.02
236	Dan Schatzeder	.05	.04	.02
237	Mike Scott	.08	.06	.03
238	Dave Smith	.06	.05	.02
239	Alex Trevino	.05	.04	.02
240	Glenn Wilson	.05	.04	.02
241	Gerald Young	.05	.04	.02
242	Tom Brunansky	.07	.05	.03
243	Cris Carpenter	.10	.08	.04
244	*Alex Cole*(FC)	.25	.20	.10
245	Vince Coleman	.10	.08	.04
246	John Costello	.05	.04	.02
247	Ken Dayley	.05	.04	.02
248	Jose DeLeon	.06	.05	.02
249	Frank DiPino	.05	.04	.02
250	Pedro Guerrero	.09	.07	.04
251	Ken Hill	.09	.07	.04
252	Joe Magrane	.09	.07	.04
253	Willie McGee	.06	.05	.02
254	John Morris	.05	.04	.02
255	Jose Oquendo	.06	.05	.02
256	Tony Pena	.06	.05	.02
257	Terry Pendleton	.06	.05	.02
258	Ted Power	.05	.04	.02
259	Dan Quisenberry	.05	.04	.02
260	Ozzie Smith	.09	.07	.04
261	Scott Terry	.06	.05	.02
262	Milt Thompson	.05	.04	.02
263	Denny Walling	.05	.04	.02
264	Todd Worrell	.06	.05	.02
265	*Todd Zeile*	2.00	1.50	.80
266	Marty Barrett	.05	.04	.02
267	Mike Boddicker	.05	.04	.02
268	Wade Boggs	.40	.30	.15
269	Ellis Burks	.35	.25	.12
270	Rick Cerone	.05	.04	.02
271	Roger Clemens	.25	.20	.10
272	John Dopson	.06	.05	.02
273	Nick Esasky	.07	.05	.03
274	Dwight Evans	.09	.07	.05
275	Wes Gardner	.05	.04	.02
276	Rich Gedman	.05	.04	.02
277	Mike Greenwell	.50	.40	.20
278	Danny Heep	.05	.04	.02
279	Eric Hetzel	.10	.08	.04
280	Dennis Lamp	.05	.04	.02
281	Rob Murphy	.05	.04	.02
282	Joe Price	.05	.04	.02
283	Carlos Quintana	.20	.15	.08
284	Jody Reed	.06	.05	.02

		MT	NR MT	EX
285	Luis Rivera	.05	.04	.02
286	Kevin Romine	.05	.04	.02
287	Lee Smith	.05	.04	.02
288	Mike Smithson	.05	.04	.02
289	Bob Stanley	.05	.04	.02
290	Harold Baines	.09	.07	.04
291	Kevin Brown	.09	.07	.04
292	Steve Buechele	.05	.04	.02
293	*Scott Coolbaugh*(FC)	.50	.40	.20
294	*Jack Daugherty*(FC)	.25	.20	.10
295	Cecil Espy	.06	.05	.02
296	Julio Franco	.07	.05	.03
297	*Juan Gonzalez*(FC)	.50	.40	.20
298	Cecilio Guante	.05	.04	.02
299	Drew Hall	.05	.04	.02
300	Charlie Hough	.06	.05	.02
301	Pete Incaviglia	.08	.06	.03
302	Mike Jeffcoat	.05	.04	.02
303	Chad Kreuter	.08	.06	.03
304	Jeff Kunkel	.05	.04	.02
305	Rick Leach	.05	.04	.02
306	Fred Manrique	.05	.04	.02
307	Jamie Moyer	.06	.05	.02
308	Rafael Palmeiro	.07	.05	.02
309	Geno Petralli	.05	.04	.02
310	Kevin Reimer	.10	.08	.06
311	*Kenny Rogers*	**.20**	**.15**	**.08**
312	Jeff Russell	.06	.05	.02
313	Nolan Ryan	.50	.40	.20
314	Ruben Sierra	.15	.11	.06
315	Bobby Witt	.05	.04	.02
316	Chris Bosio	.07	.05	.02
317	Glenn Braggs	.07	.05	.02
318	Greg Brock	.05	.04	.02
319	Chuck Crim	.05	.04	.02
320	Rob Deer	.06	.05	.02
321	Mike Felder	.05	.04	.02
322	Tom Filer	.05	.04	.02
323	*Tony Fossas*(FC)	.10	.08	.04
324	Jim Gantner	.06	.05	.02
325	Darryl Hamilton	.08	.06	.03
326	Ted Higuera	.08	.06	.03
327	Mark Knudson(FC)	.10	.08	.04
328	Bill Krueger	.05	.04	.02
329	*Tim McIntosh*(FC)	.25	.20	.10
330	Paul Molitor	.08	.06	.03
331	*Jaime Navarro*	.20	.15	.08
332	Charlie O'Brien	.05	.04	.02
333	*Jeff Peterek*(FC)	.25	.20	.10
334	Dan Plesac	.07	.05	.03
335	Jerry Reuss	.06	.05	.02
336	Gary Sheffield	.40	.30	.15
337	*Bill Spiers*	.35	.25	.12
338	B.J. Surhoff	.07	.05	.02
339	*Greg Vaughn*	2.00	1.50	.80
340	Robin Yount	.20	.15	.08
341	Hubie Brooks	.06	.05	.02
342	Tim Burke	.06	.05	.02
343	Mike Fitzgerald	.05	.04	.02
344	Tom Foley	.05	.04	.02
345	Andres Galarraga	.15	.11	.06
346	Damaso Garcia	.05	.04	.02
348	Kevin Gross	.06	.05	.02
349	Joe Hesketh	.05	.04	.02
350	*Jeff Huson*(FC)	.20	.15	.08
351	Wallace Johnson	.05	.04	.02
352	Mark Langston	.15	.11	.06
353	Dave Martinez	.06	.05	.02
354	Dennis Martinez	.06	.05	.02
355	Andy McGaffigan	.05	.04	.02
356	Otis Nixon	.05	.04	.02
357	Spike Owen	.05	.04	.02
358	Pascual Perez	.06	.05	.02
359	Tim Raines	.10	.08	.04
360	Nelson Santovenia	.10	.08	.04
361	Bryn Smith	.06	.05	.02
362	Zane Smith	.05	.04	.02
363	*Larry Walker*(FC)	.25	.20	.10
364	Tim Wallach	.06	.05	.02
365	Rick Aguilera	.05	.04	.02
366	Allan Anderson	.06	.05	.02
367	Wally Backman	.06	.05	.02
368	Doug Baker(FC)	.08	.06	.03
369	Juan Berenguer	.05	.04	.02
370	Randy Bush	.05	.04	.02
371	Carmen Castillo	.05	.04	.02
372	*Mike Dyer*(FC)	.15	.11	.06
373	Gary Gaetti	.07	.05	.03
374	Greg Gagne	.05	.04	.02
375	Dan Gladden	.05	.04	.02
376	German Gonzalez	.05	.04	.02

		MT	NR MT	EX
377	Brian Harper	.06	.05	.02
378	Kent Hrbek	.10	.08	.04
379	Gene Larkin	.05	.04	.02
380	Tim Laudner	.05	.04	.02
381	John Moses	.05	.04	.02
382	Al Newman	.05	.04	.02
383	Kirby Puckett	.40	.30	.15
384	Shane Rawley	.06	.05	.02
385	Jeff Reardon	.06	.05	.02
386	Roy Smith	.05	.04	.02
387	*Gary Wayne*(FC)	.15	.11	.06
388	Dave West	.25	.20	.10
389	Tim Belcher	.12	.09	.05
390	Tim Crews	.05	.04	.02
391	Mike Davis	.05	.04	.02
392	Rick Dempsey	.05	.04	.02
393	Kirk Gibson	.09	.07	.04
394	Jose Gonzalez	.05	.04	.02
395	Alfredo Griffin	.06	.05	.02
396	Jeff Hamilton	.06	.05	.02
397	Lenny Harris	.10	.08	.06
398	Mickey Hatcher	.05	.04	.02
399	Orel Hershiser	.12	.09	.05
400	Jay Howell	.06	.05	.02
401	Mike Marshall	.06	.05	.02
402	Ramon Martinez	.20	.15	.08
403	Mike Morgan	.05	.04	.02
404	Eddie Murray	.10	.08	.04
405	Alejandro Pena	.05	.04	.02
406	Willie Randolph	.08	.06	.03
407	Mike Scioscia	.06	.05	.02
408	Ray Searage	.05	.04	.02
409	Fernando Valenzuela	.07	.05	.03
410	*Jose Vizcaino*(FC)	.70	.50	.30
411	*John Wetteland*(FC)	.40	.30	.15
412	Jack Armstrong	.05	.04	.02
413	Todd Benzinger	.07	.05	.03
414	Tim Birtsas	.05	.04	.02
415	Tom Browning	.07	.05	.03
416	Norm Charlton	.08	.06	.03
417	Eric Davis	.20	.15	.08
418	Rob Dibble	.15	.11	.06
419	John Franco	.07	.05	.03
420	Ken Griffey Sr.	.07	.05	.03
421	*Chris Hammond*(FC)	.25	.20	.10
422	Danny Jackson	.06	.05	.02
423	Barry Larkin	.15	.11	.06
424	Tim Leary	.06	.05	.02
425	Rick Mahler	.05	.04	.02
426	*Joe Oliver*(FC)	.30	.25	.12
427	Paul O'Neil	.07	.05	.03
428	Luis Quinones	.05	.04	.02
429	Jeff Reed	.05	.04	.02
430	Jose Rijo	.07	.05	.03
431	Ron Robinson	.05	.04	.02
432	Rolando Roomes	.10	.08	.04
433	Chris Sabo	.15	.11	.06
434	*Scott Scudder*	.30	.25	.12
435	Herm Winningham	.05	.04	.02
436	Steve Balboni	.05	.04	.02
437	Jesse Barfield	.08	.06	.03
438	*Mike Blowers*(FC)	.25	.20	.10
439	Tom Brookens	.05	.04	.02
440	Greg Cadaret	.05	.04	.02
441	Alvaro Espinosa	.25	.20	.10
442	*Bob Geren*	.25	.20	.10
443	Lee Guetterman	.05	.04	.02
444	Mel Hall	.06	.05	.02
445	Andy Hawkins	.06	.05	.02
446	Roberto Kelly	.15	.11	.06
447	Don Mattingly	.80	.60	.30
448	Lance McCullers	.05	.04	.02
449	Hensley Muelens	.35	.25	.14
450	Dale Mohorcic	.05	.04	.02
451	Clay Parker	.20	.15	.08
452	Eric Plunk	.05	.04	.02
453	Dave Righetti	.07	.05	.03
454	*Deion Sanders*	1.00	.70	.40
455	Steve Sax	.07	.05	.03
456	Don Slaught	.05	.04	.02
457	Walt Terrell	.05	.04	.02
458	Dave Winfield	.15	.11	.06
459	Jay Bell	.05	.04	.02
460	Rafael Belliard	.05	.04	.02
461	Barry Bonds	.10	.08	.04
462	Bobby Bonilla	.10	.08	.04
463	Sid Bream	.05	.04	.02
464	Benny Distefano	.06	.05	.02
465	Doug Drabek	.06	.05	.02
466	Jim Gott	.06	.05	.02
467	Billy Hatcher	.06	.05	.02

		MT	NR MT	EX
468	Neal Heaton	.06	.05	.02
469	Jeff King	.20	.15	.08
470	Bob Kipper	.05	.04	.02
471	Randy Kramer	.05	.04	.02
472	Bill Landrum	.06	.05	.02
473	Mike LaValliere	.06	.05	.02
474	Jose Lind	.06	.05	.02
475	Junior Ortiz	.05	.04	.02
476	Gary Redus	.05	.04	.02
477	*Rick Reed*(FC)	.20	.15	.08
478	R.J. Reynolds	.05	.04	.02
479	Jeff Robinson	.05	.04	.02
480	John Smiley	.07	.05	.03
481	Andy Van Slyke	.09	.07	.04
482	Bob Walk	.06	.05	.04
483	Andy Allanson	.05	.04	.02
484	Scott Bailes	.05	.04	.02
485	*Joey Belle*	1.00	.70	.30
486	Bud Black	.05	.04	.02
487	Jerry Browne	.07	.05	.03
488	Tom Candiotti	.05	.04	.02
489	Joe Carter	.08	.06	.03
490	David Clark	.06	.05	.02
491	John Farrell	.06	.05	.02
492	Felix Fermin	.05	.04	.02
493	Brook Jacoby	.06	.05	.02
494	Dion James	.06	.05	.02
495	Doug Jones	.06	.05	.02
496	Brad Komminsk	.05	.04	.02
497	Rod Nichols	.05	.04	.02
498	Pete O'Brien	.07	.05	.03
499	*Steve Olin*(FC)	.35	.25	.12
500	Jesse Orosco	.05	.04	.02
501	Joel Skinner	.05	.04	.02
502	Cory Snyder	.09	.07	.04
503	Greg Swindell	.10	.08	.04
504	Rich Yett	.05	.04	.02
505	Scott Bankhead	.07	.05	.03
506	Scott Bradley	.05	.04	.02
507	Greg Briley	.25	.20	.10
508	Jay Buhner	.07	.05	.03
509	Darnell Coles	.05	.04	.02
510	Keith Comstock	.05	.04	.02
511	Henry Cotto	.05	.04	.02
512	Alvin Davis	.12	.09	.05
513	Ken Griffey Jr.	1.00	.70	.40
514	Erik Hanson	.20	.15	.08
515	Gene Harris	.15	.11	.06
516	Brian Holman	.07	.05	.03
517	Mike Jackson	.05	.04	.02
518	Randy Johnson	.15	.11	.06
519	Jeffrey Leonard	.08	.06	.03
520	Edgar Martinez	.10	.08	.04
521	Dennis Powell	.05	.04	.02
522	Jim Presley	.06	.05	.02
523	Jerry Reed	.05	.04	.02
524	Harold Reynolds	.07	.05	.03
525	Mike Schooler	.06	.05	.04
526	Bill Swift	.05	.04	.02
527	David Valle	.05	.04	.02
528	*Omar Vizquel*	.20	.15	.08
529	Ivan Calderon	.06	.05	.02
530	Carlton Fisk	.10	.08	.04
531	Scott Fletcher	.06	.05	.02
532	Dave Gallagher	.09	.07	.04
533	Ozzie Guillen	.07	.05	.03
534	*Greg Hibbard*(FC)	.15	.11	.06
535	Shawn Hillegas	.05	.04	.02
536	Lance Johnson	.07	.05	.03
537	Eric King	.05	.04	.02
538	Ron Kittle	.07	.05	.02
539	Steve Lyons	.05	.04	.02
540	Carlos Martinez	.15	.11	.06
541	*Tom McCarthy*(FC)	.20	.15	.08
542	*Matt Merullo*	.25	.20	.10
543	Donn Pall	.05	.04	.02
544	Dan Pasqua	.06	.05	.02
545	Ken Patterson	.06	.05	.02
546	Melido Perez	.07	.05	.03
547	Steve Rosenberg	.07	.05	.03
548	*Sammy Sosa*(FC)	.35	.30	.15
549	Bobby Thigpen	.07	.05	.03
550	Robin Ventura	1.50	1.25	.60
551	Greg Walker	.06	.05	.02
552	Don Carman	.05	.04	.02
553	*Pat Combs*(FC)	.70	.50	.30
554	Dennis Cook	.20	.15	.08
555	Darren Daulton	.05	.04	.02
556	Lenny Dykstra	.07	.05	.03
557	Curt Ford	.05	.04	.02
558	Charlie Hayes	.10	.08	.04
559	Von Hayes	.07	.05	.03
560	Tom Herr	.06	.05	.02
561	Ken Howell	.05	.04	.02
562	Steve Jeltz	.05	.04	.02
563	Ron Jones	.20	.15	.08
564	Ricky Jordan	.35	.25	.14
565	John Kruk	.07	.05	.03
566	Steve Lake	.05	.04	.02
567	Roger McDowell	.06	.05	.02
568	Terry Mulholland	.05	.04	.02
569	Dwayne Murphy	.05	.04	.02
570	Jeff Parrett	.06	.05	.02
571	Randy Ready	.05	.04	.02
572	Bruce Ruffin	.05	.04	.02
573	Dickie Thon	.05	.04	.02
574	Jose Alvarez	.05	.04	.02
575	Geronimo Berroa	.06	.05	.03
576	Jeff Blauser	.05	.04	.02
577	Joe Boever	.07	.05	.03
578	Marty Clary	.05	.04	.02
579	Jody Davis	.05	.04	.02
580	Mark Eichorn	.05	.04	.02
581	Darrell Evans	.06	.05	.02
582	Ron Gant	.06	.05	.02
583	Tom Glavine	.09	.07	.04
584	*Tommy Greene*(FC)	.25	.20	.10
585	Tommy Gregg	.20	.15	.08
586	*David Justice*(FC)	.35	.25	.14
587	Mark Lemke(FC)	.10	.08	.04
588	Derek Lilliquist	.10	.08	.04
589	Oddibe McDowell	.07	.05	.03
590	*Kent Mercker*(FC)	.40	.30	.15
591	Dale Murphy	.15	.11	.06
592	Gerald Perry	.06	.05	.02
593	Lonnie Smith	.06	.05	.02
594	Pete Smith	.07	.05	.03
595	John Smoltz	.15	.11	.06
596	*Mike Stanton*(FC)	.35	.25	.14
597	Andres Thomas	.06	.05	.02
598	Jeff Treadway	.06	.05	.02
599	Doyle Alexander	.06	.05	.02
600	Dave Bergman	.05	.04	.02
601	*Brian Dubois*(FC)	.35	.25	.14
602	Paul Gibson	.06	.05	.02
603	Mike Heath	.05	.04	.02
604	Mike Henneman	.07	.05	.03
605	Guillermo Hernandez	.05	.04	.02
606	*Shawn Holman*(FC)	.20	.15	.08
607	Tracy Jones	.09	.07	.04
608	Chet Lemon	.06	.05	.02
609	Fred Lynn	.06	.05	.02
610	Jack Morris	.07	.05	.02
611	Matt Nokes	.10	.08	.04
612	Gary Pettis	.05	.04	.02
613	*Kevin Ritz*(FC)	.15	.11	.06
614	Jeff Robinson	.07	.05	.03
615	Steve Searcy	.10	.08	.04
616	Frank Tanana	.06	.05	.02
617	Alan Trammell	.09	.07	.04
618	Gary Ward	.05	.04	.02
619	Lou Whitaker	.09	.07	.04
620	Frank Williams	.05	.04	.02
621	Players Of The Decade - 1980 (George Brett)	.25	.20	.10
622	Players Of The Decade - 1981 (Fernando Valenzuela)	.20	.15	.08
623	Players Of The Decade - 1982 (Dale Murphy)	.25	.20	.10
624	Players Of The Decade - 1983 (Cal Ripken Jr.)	.25	.20	.10
625	Players Of The Decade - 1984 (Ryne Sandberg)	.25	.20	.10
626	Players Of The Decade - 1985 (Don Mattingly)	.50	.40	.20
627	Players Of The Decade - 1986 (Roger Clemens)	.25	.20	.10
628	Players Of The Decade - 1987 (George Bell)	.20	.15	.08
629	Players Of The Decade - (Jose Canseco)	.60	.45	.25
630	Players Of The Decade - 1989 (Will Clark)	.60	.45	.25
631	Game Savers	.10	.08	.04
632	Boston Igniters	.10	.08	.04
633	The Starter & Stopper	.10	.08	.04
634	League's Best Shortstops	.10	.08	.04
635	Human Dynamos	.10	.08	.04
636	300 Strikeout Club	.10	.08	.04
637	The Dynamic Duo	.10	.08	.04
638	A.L. All Stars	.10	.08	.04
639	N.L. East Rivals	.10	.08	.04

		MT	NR MT	EX
640	R. Seanez, C. Charland(FC)	.20	.15	.08
641	George Canale, Kevin Maas(FC)			
		.20	.15	.08
642	Kelly Mann, D. Hansen(FC)	.30	.25	.12
643	G. Smith, S. Tate(FC)	.20	.15	.08
644	Tom Drees(FC)	.20	.15	.08
645	Mike Roesler, D. May(FC)	.25	.20	.10
646	S. Hemond, Mark Gardner(FC)	.25	.20	.10
647	J. Orlan, S. Lewis(FC)	.20	.15	.08
648	Rich Monteleone, D. Williams(FC)			
		.15	.11	.06
649	M. Huff, Steve Frey(FC)	.20	.15	.08
650	C. McElroy, Moises Alou(FC)	.40	.30	.15
651	B. Rose, M. Hartley(FC)	.25	.20	.10
652	M. Kinzer(FC)	.25	.20	.10
653	Delino Deshields, Jason Grimsley(FC)			
		.40	.30	.15
654	Athletics, Cubs, Giants & Blue Jays (Checklist)	.05	.04	.03
655	Royals, Angels, Padres & Orioles (Checklist)	.05	.04	.03
656	Mets, Astros, Cardinals & Red Sox (Checklist)	.05	.04	.03
657	Rangers, Brewers, Expos & Twins (Checklist)	.05	.04	.03
658	Dodgers, Reds, Yankees & Pirates (Checklist)	.05	.04	.03
659	Indians, Mariners, White Sox & Phillies (Checklist)	.05	.04	.03
660	Braves, Tigers & Special Cards (Checklist)			
		.05	.04	.03

1987 French/Bray Orioles

8 CAL RIPKEN, IF
Compliments of
FRENCH/BRAY, INC.

The Baltimore Orioles and French Bray, Inc. issued a baseball card set to be handed out to fans in attendance at Memorial Stadium on July 26th. Thirty perforated, detachable cards were printed within a three-panel fold-out piece measuring 9-1/2" by 11-1/4". The card fronts feature full-color player photos surrounded by an orange border. The French/Bray logo appears on the card front. The backs are of simple design, containing only the player's name, uniform number, position and professional record.

		MT	NR MT	EX
Complete Set:		10.00	7.50	4.00
Common Player:		.15	.11	.06
2	Alan Wiggins	.15	.11	.06
3	Bill Ripken	.80	.60	.30
6	Floyd Rayford	.15	.11	.06
7	Cal Ripken, Sr.	.15	.11	.06
8	Cal Ripken	1.75	1.25	.70
9	Jim Dwyer	.15	.11	.06
10	Terry Crowley	.15	.11	.06
15	Terry Kennedy	.20	.15	.08
16	Scott McGregor	.20	.15	.08
18	Larry Sheets	.50	.40	.20
19	Fred Lynn	.50	.40	.20
20	Frank Robinson	.40	.30	.15
24	Dave Schmidt	.15	.11	.06
25	Ray Knight	.20	.15	.08
27	Lee Lacy	.15	.11	.06
31	Mark Wiley	.15	.11	.06

		MT	NR MT	EX
32	Mark Williamson	.30	.25	.12
33	Eddie Murray	1.50	1.25	.60
38	Ken Gerhart	.50	.40	.20
39	Ken Dixon	.15	.11	.06
40	Jimmy Williams	.15	.11	.06
42	Mike Griffin	.15	.11	.06
43	Mike Young	.20	.15	.08
44	Elrod Hendricks	.15	.11	.06
45	Eric Bell	.30	.25	.12
46	Mike Flanagan	.25	.20	.10
49	Tom Niedenfuer	.20	.15	.08
52	Mike Boddicker	.25	.20	.10
54	John Habyan	.15	.11	.06
57	Tony Arnold	.15	.11	.06

1988 French/Bray Orioles

52 MIKE BODDICKER, RHS
Compliments of
FRENCH/BRAY, INC.

French-Bray sponsored a full-color brochure that was distributed to fans during an in-stadium promotion. A blue and orange front cover features inset photos of the Orioles in action on the upper left in a filmstrip motif. To the right is the Orioles logo and their 1988 slogan, "You Gotta Be There" above a baseball glove and ball. The 3-panel foldout measures approximately 9-1/2" by 11-1/4" and includes a team photo on the inside cover, with two perforated pages of individual cards featuring players, coaches and the team manager. Individual cards measure 2-1/4" by 3-1/8", with close-ups framed in white with an orange accent line. The player name and sponsor logo are printed beneath the photo. The black and white backs are numbered by player uniform and provide career stats. Additional copies of the brochure were made available from the Orioles Baseball Store following the free giveaway.

		MT	NR MT	EX
Complete Set:		8.00	6.00	3.25
Common Player:		.15	.11	.06
2	Don Buford	.15	.11	.06
6	Joe Orsulak	.15	.11	.06
7	Bill Ripken	.40	.30	.15
8	Cal Ripken	1.75	1.25	.70
9	Jim Dwyer	.15	.11	.06
10	Terry Crowley	.15	.11	.06
12	Mike Morgan	.15	.11	.06
14	Mickey Tettleton	.15	.11	.06
15	Terry Kennedy	.20	.15	.08
17	Pete Stanicek	.60	.45	.25
18	Larry Sheets	.40	.30	.15
19	Fred Lynn	.50	.40	.20
20	Frank Robinson	.40	.30	.15
23	Ozzie Peraza	.40	.30	.15
24	Dave Schmidt	.15	.11	.06
25	Rich Schu	.15	.11	.06
28	Jim Traber	.25	.20	.10
31	Herm Starrette	.15	.11	.06
33	Eddie Murray	1.50	1.25	.60
34	Jeff Ballard	.30	.25	.12
38	Ken Gerhart	.30	.25	.12
40	Minnie Mendoza	.15	.11	.06
41	Don Aase	.20	.15	.08
44	Elrod Hendricks	.15	.11	.06
47	John Hart	.15	.11	.06
48	Jose Bautista	.30	.25	.12

		MT	NR MT	EX
49	Tom Niedenfuer	.20	.15	.08
52	Mike Boddicker	.25	.20	.10
53	Jay Tibbs	.15	.11	.06
88	Rene Gonzales	.30	.25	.12

1989 French/Bray Orioles

16 PHIL BRADLEY, OF
Compliments of
French-Bray, Incorporated
Wilcox Walter Packing Paper Co.

This 32-card Baltimore Orioles team set was co-sponsored by French-Bray and the Wilcox Walter Furlong Paper Co., and was distributed as an in-stadium promotion to fans attending the May 12, 1989, Orioles game. Smaller than standard size, the cards measure 2-1/4" by 3" and feature a full-color player photo with number, name and position below. The backs, done in black and white, include brief player data and complete major and minor league stats.

		MT	NR MT	EX
	Complete Set:	8.00	6.00	3.25
	Common Player:	.15	.11	.06
3	Bill Ripken	.30	.25	.12
6	Joe Orsulak	.15	.11	.06
7	Cal Ripken, Sr.	.15	.11	.06
8	Cal Ripken, Jr.	1.75	1.25	.70
9	Brady Anderson	.20	.15	.08
10	Steve Finley	.80	.60	.30
11	Craig Worthington	.50	.40	.20
12	Mike Devereaux	.20	.15	.08
14	Mickey Tettleton	.20	.15	.08
15	Randy Milligan	.15	.11	.06
16	Phil Bradley	.20	.15	.08
18	Bob Milacki	.20	.15	.08
19	Larry Sheets	.15	.11	.06
20	Frank Robinson	.40	.30	.15
21	Mark Thurmond	.15	.11	.06
23	Kevin Hickey	.15	.11	.06
24	Dave Schmidt	.15	.11	.06
28	Jim Traber	.20	.15	.08
29	Jeff Ballard	.30	.25	.12
30	Gregg Olson	1.50	1.25	.60
31	Al Jackson	.15	.11	.06
32	Mark Williamson	.15	.11	.06
36	Bob Melvin	.15	.11	.06
37	Brian Holton	.15	.11	.06
40	Tom McCraw	.15	.11	.06
42	Pete Harnisch	.35	.25	.14
43	Fransisco Melendez	.20	.15	.08
44	Elrod Hendricks	.15	.11	.06
46	Johnny Oates	.15	.11	.06
48	Jose Bautista	.20	.15	.08
88	Rene Gonzales	.25	.20	.10

1928 Fro-joy

Capitalizing on the extreme popularity of Babe Ruth, this six-card set was given away with Fro-joy Cones during the August 6-11, 1928 Fro-joy Cone Week. The cards, which measure 2-1/16" by 4" in size, contain black and white photos designed on either a horizontal or vertical format. The card fronts

George Herman ("Babe") Ruth

"The Sultan of Swat," who holds the world's record for home-run hits in a single season with 60 circuit clouts during the regular playing season of 1927, topped by 2 more against Pittsburgh during the World's Series games last year.

Boys—Girls:
Fro-joy Ice Cream, in Fro-joy Cones, builds bone and strength. Eat one every day.

Chock-full of
"YOUTH UNITS"

PICTURE NO. 1

This is the first in a series of six pictures of "Babe" Ruth being given free with Fro-joy Cones during Fro-joy Cone Week, August 6th-11th, 1928. The complete set can be exchanged for a large reproduction of "Babe" Ruth's autographed photo. Ask your dealer for a FREE circular giving full details.

also contain a caption with a few sentences explaining the photo. The card backs contain advertising for Fro-joy Ice Cream and Cones.

		NR MT	EX	VG
	Complete Set:	850.00	425.00	255.00
	Common Player:	100.00	50.00	30.00
1	George Herman ("Babe") Ruth	150.00	75.00	45.00
2	Look Out, Mr. Pitcher!	150.00	75.00	45.00
3	"Babe" Ruth's Grip!	100.00	50.00	30.00
4	Ruth is a Crack Fielder	150.00	75.00	45.00
5	Bang! The Babe Lines Out!	150.00	75.00	45.00
6	When The "Babe" Comes Home	150.00	75.00	45.00

1983 Gardner's Brewers

PETE VUCKOVICH
BREWERS
P

Topps produced in 1983 for Gardner's Bakery of Madison, Wisconsin, a 22-card set featuring the American League champion Milwaukee Brewers. The cards, which measure 2-1/2" by 3-1/2", have colorful fronts which contain the player's name, team and position plus the Brewers and Gardner's logos. The card backs are identical to the regular Topps issue but are numbered 1-22. The cards were inserted in specially marked packages of Gardner's bread products and were susceptible to grease stains.

		MT	NR MT	EX
	Complete Set	25.00	18.50	10.00
	Common Player	.50	.40	.20
1	Harvey Kuenn	.70	.50	.30
2	Dwight Bernard	.50	.40	.20
3	Mark Brouhard	.50	.40	.20
4	Mike Caldwell	.50	.40	.20
5	Cecil Cooper	1.25	.90	.50
6	Marshall Edwards	.50	.40	.20
7	Rollie Fingers	1.50	1.25	.60
8	Jim Gantner	.70	.50	.30
9	Moose Haas	.50	.40	.20
10	Bob McClure	.50	.40	.20
11	Paul Molitor	2.00	1.50	.80
12	Don Money	.50	.40	.20
13	Charlie Moore	.50	.40	.20
14	Ben Oglivie	.60	.45	.25
15	Ed Romero	.50	.40	.20
16	Ted Simmons	.90	.70	.35
17	Jim Slaton	.50	.40	.20
18	Don Sutton	1.50	1.25	.60
19	Gorman Thomas	.70	.50	.30
20	Pete Vuckovich	.70	.50	.30
21	Ned Yost	.50	.40	.20
22	Robin Yount	2.50	2.00	1.00

1984 Gardner's Brewers

For the second straight year, Gardner's Bakery inserted baseball cards featuring the Milwaukee Brewers with their bread products. The 22-card set, entitled "1984 Series II," have multi-colored fronts that include the Brewers and Gardner's logos. The card backs are identical to the regular 1984 Topps issue except for the 1-22 numbering system. The Topps-produced cards are the standard 2-1/2" by 3-1/2" size. The cards are sometimes found with grease stains, resulting from contact with the bread.

		MT	NR MT	EX
	Complete Set:	20.00	15.00	8.00
	Common Player:	.50	.40	.20
1	Rene Lachemann	.50	.40	.20
2	Mark Brouhard	.50	.40	.20
3	Mike Caldwell	.50	.40	.20
4	Bobby Clark	.50	.40	.20
5	Cecil Cooper	1.00	.70	.40
6	Rollie Fingers	1.25	.90	.50
7	Jim Gantner	.70	.50	.30
8	Moose Haas	.50	.40	.20
9	Roy Howell	.50	.40	.20
10	Pete Ladd	.50	.40	.20
11	Rick Manning	.50	.40	.20

		MT	NR MT	EX
12	Bob McClure	.50	.40	.20
13	Paul Molitor	1.75	1.25	.70
14	Charlie Moore	.50	.40	.20
15	Ben Oglivie	.60	.45	.25
16	Ed Romero	.50	.40	.20
17	Ted Simmons	.80	.60	.30
18	Jim Sundberg	.50	.40	.20
19	Don Sutton	1.25	.90	.50
20	Tom Tellmann	.50	.40	.20
21	Pete Vuckovich	.60	.45	.25
22	Robin Yount	2.25	1.75	.90

1985 Gardner's Brewers

Gardner's Bakery issued a 22-card set featuring the Milwaukee Brewers for the third consecutive year in 1985. The set was produced by Topps and is designed in a horizontal format. The card fronts feature color photos inside blue, red and yellow frames. The player's name and position are placed in orange boxes to the right of the photo and are accompanied by the Brewers and Gardner's logos. The card backs are identical in design to the regular 1985 Topps set but are blue rather than green and are numbered 1- 22. The cards, which were inserted in specially marked bread products, are often found with grease stains.

		MT	NR MT	EX
	Complete Set:	15.00	11.00	6.00
	Common Player:	.35	.25	.14
1	George Bamberger	.35	.25	.14
2	Mark Brouhard	.35	.25	.14
3	Bob Clark	.35	.25	.14
4	Jaime Cocanower	.35	.25	.14
5	Cecil Cooper	.90	.70	.35
6	Rollie Fingers	1.25	.90	.50
7	Jim Gantner	.50	.40	.20
8	Moose Haas	.35	.25	.14
9	Dion James	.70	.50	.30
10	Pete Ladd	.35	.25	.14
11	Rick Manning	.35	.25	.14
12	Bob McClure	.35	.25	.14
13	Paul Molitor	1.50	1.25	.60
14	Charlie Moore	.35	.25	.14
15	Ben Oglivie	.50	.40	.20
16	Chuck Porter	.35	.25	.14
17	Ed Romero	.35	.25	.14
18	Bill Schroeder	.35	.25	.14
19	Ted Simmons	.70	.50	.30
20	Tom Tellmann	.35	.25	.14
21	Pete Vuckovich	.50	.40	.20
22	Robin Yount	2.00	1.50	.80

A player's name in *italic* type indicates a rookie card. An (FC) indicates a player's first card for that particular card company.

1989 Gardners Brewers

Returning after a three-year hiatus, Gardner's Bread of Madison, Wis., issued a 15-card Milwaukee Brewers set in 1989. The blue and white-bordered cards are the standard size and feature posed portrait photos with all Brewer logos airbrushed from the players' caps. The Gardner's logo appears at the top of the card, while the player's name is below the photo. The set, which was produced in conjunction with Mike Schechter Associates, was issued with loaves of bread or packages of buns, one card per package.

		MT	NR MT	EX
Complete Set:		4.00	3.00	1.50
Common Player:		.10	.08	.04
1	Paul Molitor	.35	.25	.12
2	Robin Yount	.50	.40	.20
3	Jim Gantner	.25	.20	.10
4	Rob Deer	.25	.20	.10
5	B.J. Surhoff	.25	.20	.10
6	Dale Sveum	.20	.15	.08
7	Ted Higuera	.25	.20	.10
8	Dan Plesac	.25	.20	.10
9	Bill Wegman	.15	.11	.06
10	Juan Nieves	.15	.11	.06
11	Greg Brock	.20	.15	.08
12	Glenn Braggs	.25	.20	.10
13	Joey Meyer	.15	.11	.06
14	Ernest Riles	.10	.08	.04
15	Don August	.15	.11	.06

1986 Gatorade Cubs

(19) MANNY TRILLO, IF

Gatorade sponsored this 28-card set which was given away at the July 17, 1986 Cubs game. The cards measure 2-7/8" by 4-1/4" and feature color photos set inside red and white frames. The Cubs logo appears at the top of the card in blue and red. The card backs include statistical information and the Gatorade logo. This set marked the fifth consecutive year the Cubs had held a baseball card giveaway promotion.

		MT	NR MT	EX
Complete Set:		9.00	6.75	3.50
Common Player:		.10	.08	.04
4	Gene Michael	.10	.08	.04
6	Keith Moreland	.30	.25	.12
7	Jody Davis	.30	.25	.12
10	Leon Durham	.30	.25	.12
11	Ron Cey	.30	.25	.12
12	Shawon Dunston	.80	.60	.30
15	Davey Lopes	.25	.20	.10
16	Terry Francona	.10	.08	.04
18	Steve Christmas	.10	.08	.04
19	Manny Trillo	.15	.11	.06
20	Bob Dernier	.10	.08	.04
21	Scott Sanderson	.10	.08	.04
22	Jerry Mumphrey	.10	.08	.04
23	Ryne Sandberg	2.00	1.50	.80
27	Thad Bosley	.10	.08	.04
28	Chris Speier	.10	.08	.04
29	Steve Lake	.10	.08	.04
31	Ray Fontenot	.10	.08	.04
34	Steve Trout	.20	.15	.08
36	Gary Matthews	.30	.25	.12
39	George Frazier	.10	.08	.04
40	Rick Sutcliffe	.70	.50	.30
43	Dennis Eckersley	.40	.30	.15
46	Lee Smith	.35	.25	.14
48	Jay Baller	.15	.11	.06
49	Jamie Moyer	.35	.25	.14
50	Guy Hoffman	.10	.08	.04
---	The Coaching Staff (Ruben Amaro, Billy Connors, Johnny Oates, John Vuckovich, Billy Williams)	.15	.11	.06

1987 Gatorade Indians

(28) CORY SNYDER, IF
COMPLIMENTS OF Gatorade

For the second year in a row, the Cleveland Indians gave out a perforated set of baseball cards to fans attending the Team Photo/Baseball Card Day promotion. Sponsored by Gatorade, the individual cards measure 2-1/2" by 3-1/8". The fronts contain a full-color photo surrounded by a red frame inside a white border. The player's name, uniform number and the Gatorade logo are also on the fronts. The card backs are printed in black, blue and red and carry a facsimile autograph and the player's playing record.

		MT	NR MT	EX
Complete Set:		8.00	5.00	2.50
Common Player:		.10	.05	.02
2	Brett Butler	.20	.25	.12
4	Tony Bernazard	.10	.09	.05
6	Andy Allanson	.15	.09	.05
7	Pat Corrales	.10	.09	.05
8	Carmen Castillo	.10	.05	.02
10	Pat Tabler	.20	.20	.10
11	Jamie Easterly	.10	.05	.02
12	Dave Clark	.20	.15	.08
13	Ernie Camacho	.10	.05	.02
14	Julio Franco	.40	.30	.15
17	Junior Noboa	.10	.15	.08
18	Ken Schrom	.10	.08	.04
20	Otis Nixon	.15	.05	.02

		MT	NR MT	EX
21	Greg Swindell	.80	.45	.25
22	Frank Wills	.10	.05	.02
23	Chris Bando	.10	.05	.02
24	Rick Dempsey	.15	.09	.05
26	Brook Jacoby	.60	.30	.15
27	Mel Hall	.30	.25	.12
28	Cory Snyder	.90	.70	.35
29	Andre Thornton	.30	.25	.12
30	Joe Carter	.80	.45	.25
35	Phil Niekro	.40	.30	.15
36	Ed Vande Berg	.10	.05	.02
42	Rich Yett	.10	.05	.02
43	Scott Bailes	.40	.30	.15
46	Doug Jones	.40	.15	.08
49	Tom Candiotti	.20	.09	.05
54	Tom Waddell	.10	.05	.02
---	Manager and Coaching Staff (Jack Aker, Bobby Bonds, Pat Corrales, Doc Edwards, Johnny Goryl)	.10	.05	.02

		MT	NR MT	EX
47	Jeff Kaiser	.10	.08	.04
49	Tom Candiotti	.20	.15	.08
50	Jeff Dedmon	.10	.08	.04
52	John Farrell	.40	.30	.15

1933 George C. Miller

The George C. Miller & Co. of Boston, Mass. issued a 32-card set in 1933. The set, which received limited distribution, consists of 16 National League and 16 American League players. The cards are color art reproductions of actual photographs and measure 2-3/8" by 2-7/8" in size. Two distinct variations can be found for each card in the set. Two different typefaces were used, one being much smaller than the other. The most substantial difference is "R" and "L" being used for the "Bats/Throws" information on one version, while the other spells out "Right" and "Left." Collectors were advised on the card backs to collect all 32 cards and return them for prizes. The cards, with a cancellation at the bottom, were returned to the collector with the prize. Two forms of cancellation were used; one involved the complete trimming of the bottom one-quarter of the card, the other a series of diamond-shaped punch holes. Cancelled cards have a significantly decreased value.

1988 Gatorade Indians

 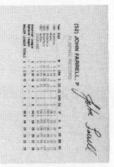

This 3-panel foldout was sponsored by Gatorade for distribution during an in-stadium giveaway. The white cover includes four game day photos. One panel of the 9-1/2" by 11-1/4" glossy full-color brochure features a team photo (with checklist), two panels consist of 30 perforated baseball cards (2-1/4" by 3") featuring team members. Posed close-up photos are framed in red on a white background. The player's name and uniform number are printed below the photo. The card backs are printed in red, blue and black on white. A facsimile autograph appears at the top right portion of the card back, opposite the player uniform number, name and position. Both major and minor league stats are listed.

		MT	NR MT	EX
	Complete Set:	8.00	6.00	3.25
	Common Player:	.10	.08	.04
2	Tom Spencer	.10	.08	.04
6	Andy Allanson	.15	.11	.06
7	Luis Issac	.10	.08	.04
8	Carmen Castillo	.10	.08	.04
9	Charlie Manuel	.10	.08	.04
10	Pat Tabler	.20	.15	.08
11	Doug Jones	.30	.25	.12
14	Julio Franco	.40	.30	.15
15	Ron Washington	.10	.08	.04
16	Jay Bell	.20	.15	.08
17	Bill Laskey	.10	.08	.04
20	Willie Upshaw	.20	.15	.08
21	Greg Swindell	.80	.60	.30
23	Chris Bando	.10	.08	.04
25	Dave Clark	.15	.11	.06
26	Brook Jacoby	.60	.45	.25
27	Mel Hall	.30	.25	.12
28	Cory Snyder	.80	.60	.30
30	Joe Carter	.80	.60	.30
31	Dan Schatzeder	.10	.08	.04
32	Doc Edwards	.10	.08	.04
33	Ron Kittle	.25	.20	.10
35	Mark Wiley	.10	.08	.04
42	Rich Yett	.10	.08	.04
43	Scott Bailes	.20	.15	.08
45	Johnny Goryl	.10	.08	.04

		NR MT	EX	VG
	Complete Set:	14500.00	7250.00	4350.
	Common Player:	250.00	125.00	75.00
(1)	Dale Alexander	250.00	125.00	75.00
(2)	"Ivy" Paul Andrews	2500.00	1250.00	750.00
(3)	Earl Averill	400.00	200.00	120.00
(4)	Dick Bartell	250.00	125.00	75.00
(5)	Walter Berger	250.00	125.00	75.00
(6)	Jim Bottomley	400.00	200.00	120.00
(7)	Joe Cronin	500.00	250.00	150.00
(8)	Jerome "Dizzy" Dean	800.00	400.00	240.00
(9)	William Dickey	600.00	300.00	180.00
(10)	Jimmy Dykes	250.00	125.00	75.00
(11)	Wesley Ferrell	250.00	125.00	75.00
(12)	Jimmy Foxx	600.00	300.00	180.00
(13)	Frank Frisch	450.00	225.00	135.00
(14)	Charlie Gehringer	450.00	225.00	135.00
(15)	Leon "Goose" Goslin	400.00	200.00	120.00
(16)	Charlie Grimm	250.00	125.00	75.00
(17)	Bob "Lefty" Grove	500.00	250.00	150.00
(18)	Charles "Chick" Hafey	400.00	200.00	120.00
(19)	Ray Hayworth	250.00	125.00	75.00
(20)	Charles "Chuck" Klein	400.00	200.00	120.00
(21)	Walter "Rabbit" Maranville	400.00	200.00	120.00
(22)	Oscar Melillo	250.00	125.00	75.00
(23)	Frank "Lefty" O'Doul	250.00	125.00	75.00
(24)	Melvin Ott	500.00	250.00	150.00
(25)	Carl Reynolds	250.00	125.00	75.00
(26)	Charles Ruffing	400.00	200.00	120.00
(27)	Al Simmons	400.00	200.00	120.00
(28)	Joe Stripp	250.00	125.00	75.00
(29)	Bill Terry	450.00	225.00	135.00
(30)	Lloyd Waner	400.00	200.00	120.00
(31)	Paul Waner	400.00	200.00	120.00
(32)	Lonnie Warneke	250.00	125.00	75.00

1953 Glendale Hot Dog Tigers

JOHN McGRAW
third base

Glendale Meats issued these unnumbered, full-color cards (2-5/8" by 3-3/4") in packages of hot dogs. Featuring Detroit Tigers players, the card fronts contain a player picture plus the player's name, a facsimile autograph, and the Tigers logo. The card reverses carry player statistical and biographical information plus an offer for a trip for two to the World Series. Collectors were advised to mail all the cards they had saved to Glendale Meats. The World Series trip plus 150 other prizes were to be given to the individuals sending in the most cards. As with most cards issued with food products, quality-condition cards are tough to find because of the cards' susceptibilty to stains. The Houtteman card is extremely scarce.

		NR MT	EX	VG
Complete Set:		5300.00	2650.00	1590.
Common Player:		100.00	50.00	30.00
(1)	Matt Batts	100.00	50.00	30.00
(2)	Johnny Bucha	100.00	50.00	30.00
(3)	Frank Carswell	100.00	50.00	30.00
(4)	Jim Delsing	100.00	50.00	30.00
(5)	Walt Dropo	100.00	50.00	30.00
(6)	Hal Erickson	100.00	50.00	30.00
(7)	Paul Foytack	100.00	50.00	30.00
(8)	Owen Friend	125.00	62.00	37.00
(9)	Ned Garver	100.00	50.00	30.00
(10)	Joe Ginsberg	350.00	175.00	105.00
(11)	Ted Gray	100.00	50.00	30.00
(12)	Fred Hatfield	100.00	50.00	30.00
(13)	Ray Herbert	125.00	62.00	37.00
(14)	Bill Hitchcock	100.00	50.00	30.00
(15)	Bill Hoeft	275.00	137.00	82.00
(16)	Art Houtteman	2000.00	1000.00	600.00
(17)	Milt Jordan	200.00	100.00	60.00
(18)	Harvey Kuenn	225.00	112.00	67.00
(19)	Don Lund	100.00	50.00	30.00
(20)	Dave Madison	100.00	50.00	30.00
(21)	Dick Marlowe	100.00	50.00	30.00
(22)	Pat Mullin	100.00	50.00	30.00
(23)	Bob Neiman	100.00	50.00	30.00
(24)	Johnny Pesky	125.00	62.00	37.00
(25)	Jerry Priddy	100.00	50.00	30.00
(26)	Steve Souchock	100.00	50.00	30.00
(27)	Russ Sullivan	100.00	50.00	30.00
(28)	Bill Wight	200.00	100.00	60.00

1961 Golden Press

The 1961 Golden Press set features 33 players, all enshrined in the Baseball Hall of Fame. The full color cards measure 2-1/2" by 3-1/2" and came in a booklet with perforations so that they could be easily removed. Full books with the cards intact would command a 50" premium over the set price in the checklist that follows. Card numbers 1-3 and 28-33 are slightly higher in price as they were located on the book's front and back covers, making them more

susceptible to scuffing and wear.

		NR MT	EX	VG
Complete Set:		50.00	25.00	15.00
Common Player:		.50	.25	.15
1	Mel Ott	1.50	.70	.45
2	Grover Cleveland Alexander	1.50	.70	.45
3	Babe Ruth	10.00	5.00	3.00
4	Hank Greenberg	.75	.40	.25
5	Bill Terry	.75	.40	.25
6	Carl Hubbell	.75	.40	.25
7	Rogers Hornsby	1.75	.90	.50
8	Dizzy Dean	3.00	1.50	.90
9	Joe DiMaggio	6.00	3.00	1.75
10	Charlie Gehringer	.75	.40	.25
11	Gabby Hartnett	.50	.25	.15
12	Mickey Cochrane	.75	.40	.25
13	George Sisler	.75	.40	.25
14	Joe Cronin	.75	.40	.25
15	Pie Traynor	.50	.25	.15
16	Lou Gehrig	6.00	3.00	1.75
17	Lefty Grove	.90	.45	.25
18	Chief Bender	.50	.25	.15
19	Frankie Frisch	.75	.40	.25
20	Al Simmons	.50	.25	.15
21	Home Run Baker	.50	.25	.15
22	Jimmy Foxx	1.75	.90	.50
23	John McGraw	.90	.45	.25
24	Christy Mathewson	2.50	1.25	.70
25	Ty Cobb	6.00	3.00	1.75
26	Dazzy Vance	.50	.25	.15
27	Bill Dickey	.90	.45	.25
28	Eddie Collins	.75	.40	.25
29	Walter Johnson	3.00	1.50	.90
30	Tris Speaker	1.50	.70	.45
31	Nap Lajoie	1.50	.70	.45
32	Honus Wagner	3.00	1.50	.90
33	Cy Young	3.00	1.50	.90

Definitions for grading conditions are located in the Introduction of this price guide.

NOTE: A card number in parentheses ( ) indicates the set is unnumbered.

A player's name in *italic* type indicates a rookie card. An (FC) indicates a player's first card for that particular card company.

1933 Goudey

Goudey Gum Co.'s first baseball card issue was their 240-card effort in 1933. The cards are color art reproductions of either portrait or action photos. The numbered cards measure 2-3/8" by 2-7/8" in size and carry a short player biography on the reverses. Card #106 (Napoleon Lajoie) is listed in the set not actually issued until 1934. The card is very scarce and is unique in that it carries a 1934 design obverse and a 1933 reverse. The ACC designation for the set is R319.

		NR MT	EX	VG
	Complete Set w/o Lajoie:	51000.00	25500.00	15300.
	Common Player: 1-40	75.00	37.00	22.00
	Common Player: 41-44	65.00	32.00	19.50
	Common Player: 45-52	75.00	37.00	22.00
	Common Player: 53-240	65.00	32.00	19.50
1	Benny Bengough	3500.00	1750.00	1050.
2	Arthur (Dazzy) Vance	150.00	75.00	45.00
3	Hugh Critz	75.00	37.00	22.00
4	Henry "Heinie" Schuble	75.00	37.00	22.00
5	Floyd (Babe) Herman	70.00	35.00	21.00
6a	Jimmy Dykes (age is 26 in bio)	90.00	45.00	27.00
6b	Jimmy Dykes (age is 36 in bio)	90.00	45.00	27.00
7	Ted Lyons	100.00	45.00	27.00
8	Roy Johnson	75.00	37.00	22.00
9	Dave Harris	75.00	37.00	22.00
10	Glenn Myatt	75.00	37.00	22.00
11	Billy Rogell	75.00	37.00	22.00
12	George Pipgras	90.00	45.00	27.00
13	Lafayette Thompson	55.00	27.00	16.50
14	Henry Johnson	75.00	37.00	22.00
15	Victor Sorrell	75.00	37.00	22.00
16	George Blaeholder	75.00	37.00	22.00
17	Watson Clark	75.00	37.00	22.00
18	Herold (Muddy) Ruel	75.00	37.00	22.00
19	Bill Dickey	300.00	150.00	90.00
20	Bill Terry	225.00	112.00	67.00
21	Phil Collins	75.00	37.00	22.00
22	Harold (Pie) Traynor	150.00	75.00	45.00
23	Hazen (Ki-Ki) Cuyler	150.00	75.00	45.00
24	Horace Ford	75.00	37.00	22.00
25	Paul Waner	150.00	75.00	45.00
26	Chalmer Cissell	75.00	37.00	22.00
27	George Connally	75.00	37.00	22.00
28	Dick Bartell	75.00	37.00	22.00
29	Jimmy Foxx	375.00	187.00	112.00
30	Frank Hogan	75.00	37.00	22.00
31	Tony Lazzeri	150.00	75.00	45.00
32	John (Bud) Clancy	75.00	37.00	22.00
33	Ralph Kress	75.00	37.00	22.00
34	Bob O'Farrell	75.00	37.00	22.00
35	Al Simmons	150.00	75.00	45.00
36	Tommy Thevenow	75.00	37.00	22.00
37	Jimmy Wilson	75.00	37.00	22.00
38	Fred Brickell	75.00	37.00	22.00
39	Mark Koenig	75.00	37.00	22.00
40	Taylor Douthit	75.00	37.00	22.00
41	Gus Mancuso	65.00	32.00	19.50
42	Eddie Collins	150.00	75.00	45.00
43	Lew Fonseca	75.00	37.00	22.00
44	Jim Bottomley	150.00	75.00	45.00
45	Larry Benton	75.00	37.00	22.00
46	Ethan Allen	75.00	37.00	22.00
47	Henry "Heinie" Manush	150.00	75.00	45.00
48	Marty McManus	75.00	37.00	22.00
49	Frank Frisch	225.00	112.00	67.00
50	Ed Brandt	75.00	37.00	22.00
51	Charlie Grimm	90.00	45.00	27.00
52	Andy Cohen	75.00	37.00	22.00
53	George Herman (Babe) Ruth	4000.00	2000.00	1200.
54	Ray Kremer	65.00	32.00	19.50
55	Perce (Pat) Malone	65.00	32.00	19.50
56	Charlie Ruffing	150.00	75.00	45.00
57	Earl Clark	65.00	32.00	19.50
58	Frank (Lefty) O'Doul	75.00	37.00	22.00
59	Edmund (Bing) Miller	65.00	32.00	19.50
60	Waite Hoyt	150.00	75.00	45.00
61	Max Bishop	65.00	32.00	19.50
62	"Pepper" Martin	75.00	37.00	22.00
63	Joe Cronin	150.00	75.00	45.00
64	Burleigh Grimes	150.00	75.00	45.00
65	Milton Gaston	65.00	32.00	19.50
66	George Grantham	65.00	32.00	19.50
67	Guy Bush	65.00	32.00	19.50
68	Horace Lisenbee	65.00	32.00	19.50
69	Randy Moore	65.00	32.00	19.50
70	Floyd (Pete) Scott	65.00	32.00	19.50
71	Robert J. Burke	65.00	32.00	19.50
72	Owen Carroll	65.00	32.00	19.50
73	Jesse Haines	150.00	75.00	45.00
74	Eppa Rixey	150.00	75.00	45.00
75	Willie Kamm	65.00	32.00	19.50
76	Gordon (Mickey) Cochrane	200.00	100.00	60.00
77	Adam Comorosky	65.00	32.00	19.50
78	Jack Quinn	65.00	32.00	19.50
79	Urban (Red) Faber	150.00	75.00	45.00
80	Clyde Manion	65.00	32.00	19.50
81	Sam Jones	65.00	32.00	19.50
82	Dibrell Williams	65.00	32.00	19.50
83	Pete Jablonowski	75.00	37.00	22.00
84	Glenn Spencer	65.00	32.00	19.50
85	John Henry "Heinie" Sand	65.00	32.00	19.50
86	Phil Todt	65.00	32.00	19.50
87	Frank O'Rourke	65.00	32.00	19.50
88	Russell Rollings	65.00	32.00	19.50
89	Tris Speaker	250.00	125.00	70.00
90	Jess Petty	65.00	32.00	19.50
91	Tom Zachary	65.00	32.00	19.50
92	Lou Gehrig	3500.00	1750.00	1050.
93	John Welch	65.00	32.00	19.50
94	Bill Walker	65.00	32.00	19.50
95	Alvin Crowder	65.00	32.00	19.50
96	Willis Hudlin	65.00	32.00	19.50
97	Joe Morrissey	65.00	32.00	19.50
98	Walter Berger	65.00	32.00	19.50
99	Tony Cuccinello	65.00	32.00	19.50
100	George Uhle	65.00	32.00	19.50
101	Richard Coffman	65.00	32.00	19.50
102	Travis C. Jackson	150.00	75.00	45.00
103	Earl Combs (Earle)	150.00	75.00	45.00
104	Fred Marberry	65.00	32.00	19.50
105	Bernie Friberg	65.00	32.00	19.50
106	Napoleon (Larry) Lajoie	25000.00	12500.00	7500.
107	Henry (Heinie) Manush	150.00	75.00	45.00
108	Joe Kuhel	65.00	32.00	19.50
109	Joe Cronin	150.00	75.00	45.00
110	Leon "Goose" Goslin	150.00	75.00	45.00
111	Monte Weaver	65.00	32.00	19.50
112	Fred Schulte	65.00	32.00	19.50
113	Oswald Bluege	65.00	32.00	19.50
114	Luke Sewell	65.00	32.00	19.50
115	Cliff Heathcote	65.00	32.00	19.50
116	Eddie Morgan	65.00	32.00	19.50
117	Walter (Rabbit) Maranville	150.00	75.00	45.00
118	Valentine J. (Val) Picinich	65.00	32.00	19.50
119	Rogers Hornsby	350.00	175.00	105.00
120	Carl Reynolds	65.00	32.00	19.50
121	Walter Stewart	65.00	32.00	19.50
122	Alvin Crowder	65.00	32.00	19.50
123	Jack Russell	65.00	32.00	19.50
124	Earl Whitehill	65.00	32.00	19.50
125	Bill Terry	200.00	100.00	60.00
126	Joe Moore	65.00	32.00	19.50
127	Melvin Ott	200.00	100.00	60.00
128	Charles (Chuck) Klein	150.00	75.00	45.00
129	Harold Schumacher	75.00	37.00	22.00
130	Fred Fitzsimmons	65.00	32.00	19.50
131	Fred Frankhouse	65.00	32.00	19.50
132	Jim Elliott	65.00	32.00	19.50
133	Fred Lindstrom	150.00	75.00	45.00
134	Edgar (Sam) Rice	150.00	75.00	45.00
135	Elwood (Woody) English	65.00	32.00	19.50
136	Flint Rhem	65.00	32.00	19.50
137	Fred (Red) Lucas	65.00	32.00	19.50
138	Herb Pennock	150.00	75.00	45.00
139	Ben Cantwell	65.00	32.00	19.50

		NR MT	EX	VG
140	Irving (Bump) Hadley	65.00	32.00	19.50
141	Ray Benge	65.00	32.00	19.50
142	Paul Richards	90.00	45.00	27.00
143	Glenn Wright	75.00	37.00	22.00
144	George Herman (Babe) Ruth	3500.00	1750.00	1050.
145	George Walberg	65.00	32.00	19.50
146	Walter Stewart	65.00	32.00	19.50
147	Leo Durocher	150.00	75.00	45.00
148	Eddie Farrell	65.00	32.00	19.50
149	George Herman (Babe) Ruth	4000.00	2000.00	1200.
150	Ray Kolp	65.00	32.00	19.50
151	D'Arcy (Jake) Flowers	65.00	32.00	19.50
152	James (Zack) Taylor	65.00	32.00	19.50
153	Charles (Buddy) Myer	65.00	32.00	19.50
154	Jimmy Foxx	210.00	105.00	63.00
155	Joe Judge	65.00	32.00	19.50
156	Danny Macfayden (MacFayden)	90.00	45.00	27.00
157	Sam Byrd	90.00	45.00	27.00
158	Morris (Moe) Berg	75.00	37.00	22.00
159	Oswald Bluege	65.00	32.00	19.50
160	Lou Gehrig	2500.00	1250.00	750.00
161	Al Spohrer	65.00	32.00	19.50
162	Leo Mangum	65.00	32.00	19.50
163	Luke Sewell	65.00	32.00	19.50
164	Lloyd Waner	150.00	75.00	45.00
165	Joe Sewell	150.00	75.00	45.00
166	Sam West	65.00	32.00	19.50
167	Jack Russell	65.00	32.00	19.50
168	Leon (Goose) Goslin	150.00	75.00	45.00
169	Al Thomas	65.00	32.00	19.50
170	Harry McCurdy	65.00	32.00	19.50
171	Charley Jamieson	65.00	32.00	19.50
172	Billy Hargrave	65.00	32.00	19.50
173	Roscoe Holm	65.00	32.00	19.50
174	Warren (Curley) Ogden	65.00	32.00	19.50
175	Dan Howley	65.00	32.00	19.50
176	John Ogden	65.00	32.00	19.50
177	Walter French	65.00	32.00	19.50
178	Jackie Warner	65.00	32.00	19.50
179	Fred Leach	65.00	32.00	19.50
180	Eddie Moore	65.00	32.00	19.50
181	George Herman (Babe) Ruth	3300.00	1650.00	990.00
182	Andy High	65.00	32.00	19.50
183	George Walberg	65.00	32.00	19.50
184	Charley Berry	65.00	32.00	19.50
185	Bob Smith	65.00	32.00	19.50
186	John Schulte	65.00	32.00	19.50
187	Henry (Heinie) Manush	150.00	75.00	45.00
188	Rogers Hornsby	350.00	175.00	105.00
189	Joe Cronin	150.00	75.00	45.00
190	Fred Schulte	65.00	32.00	19.50
191	Ben Chapman	90.00	45.00	27.00
192	Walter Brown	90.00	45.00	27.00
193	Lynford Lary	90.00	45.00	27.00
194	Earl Averill	150.00	75.00	45.00
195	Evar Swanson	65.00	32.00	19.50
196	Leroy Mahaffey	65.00	32.00	19.50
197	Richard (Rick) Ferrell	150.00	75.00	45.00
198	Irving (Jack) Burns	65.00	32.00	19.50
199	Tom Bridges	75.00	37.00	22.00
200	Bill Hallahan	65.00	32.00	19.50
201	Ernie Orsatti	65.00	32.00	19.50
202	Charles Leo (Gabby) Hartnett	150.00	75.00	45.00
203	Lonnie Warneke	65.00	32.00	19.50
204	Jackson Riggs Stephenson	90.00	45.00	27.00
205	Henry (Heinie) Meine	65.00	32.00	19.50
206	Gus Suhr	65.00	32.00	19.50
207	Melvin Ott	150.00	75.00	45.00
208	Byrne (Bernie) James	65.00	32.00	19.50
209	Adolfo Luque	65.00	32.00	19.50
210	Virgil Davis	65.00	32.00	19.50
211	Lewis (Hack) Wilson	150.00	75.00	45.00
212	Billy Urbanski	65.00	32.00	19.50
213	Earl Adams	65.00	32.00	19.50
214	John Kerr	65.00	32.00	19.50
215	Russell Van Atta	90.00	45.00	27.00
216	Vernon Gomez	150.00	75.00	45.00
217	Frank Crosetti	150.00	75.00	45.00
218	Wesley Ferrell	65.00	32.00	19.50
219	George (Mule) Haas	65.00	32.00	19.50
220	Robert (Lefty) Grove	350.00	175.00	105.00
221	Dale Alexander	65.00	32.00	19.50
222	Charley Gehringer	225.00	112.00	67.00
223	Jerome (Dizzy) Dean	750.00	375.00	225.00
224	Frank Demaree	65.00	32.00	19.50
225	Bill Jurges	65.00	32.00	19.50
226	Charley Root	65.00	32.00	19.50
227	Bill Herman	150.00	75.00	45.00
228	Tony Piet	65.00	32.00	19.50
229	Floyd Vaughan	150.00	75.00	45.00
230	Carl Hubbell	225.00	112.00	67.00

		NR MT	EX	VG
231	Joe Moore	65.00	32.00	19.50
232	Frank (Lefty) O'Doul	75.00	37.00	22.00
233	Johnny Vergez	65.00	32.00	19.50
234	Carl Hubbell	225.00	112.00	67.00
235	Fred Fitzsimmons	65.00	32.00	19.50
236	George Davis	65.00	32.00	19.50
237	Gus Mancuso	65.00	32.00	19.50
238	Hugh Critz	65.00	32.00	19.50
239	Leroy Parmelee	90.00	45.00	27.00
240	Harold Schumacher	275.00	30.00	15.00

1934 Goudey

The 1934 Goudey set contains 96 cards (2-3/8" by 2-7/8") that feature color art reproductions of actual photographs. The card fronts have two different designs; one featuring a small head-shot photo of Lou Gehrig with the words "Lou Gehrig says..." inside a blue band, while the other design carries a "Chuck Klein says..." and also has his photo. The card backs contain a short player biography that appears to have been written by Gehrig or Klein. The ACC designation for the set is R320.

		NR MT	EX	VG
Complete Set:		25000.00	12500.00	7500.
Common Player:		75.00	37.00	22.00
Common Player: 49-72		90.00	45.00	27.00
Common Player: 73-96		275.00	137.00	82.00
1	Jimmy Foxx	1000.00	500.00	300.00
2	Gordon (Mickey) Cochrane	250.00	125.00	75.00
3	Charlie Grimm	70.00	35.00	21.00
4	Elwood (Woody) English	75.00	37.00	22.00
5	Ed Brandt	75.00	37.00	22.00
6	Jerome (Dizzy) Dean	700.00	350.00	210.00
7	Leo Durocher	200.00	100.00	60.00
8	Tony Piet	75.00	37.00	22.00
9	Ben Chapman	90.00	45.00	27.00
10	Charles (Chuck) Klein	200.00	100.00	60.00
11	Paul Waner	200.00	100.00	60.00
12	Carl Hubbell	250.00	125.00	75.00
13	Frank Frisch	200.00	100.00	60.00
14	Willie Kamm	75.00	37.00	22.00
15	Alvin Crowder	75.00	37.00	22.00
16	Joe Kuhel	75.00	37.00	22.00
17	Hugh Critz	75.00	37.00	22.00
18	Henry (Heinie) Manush	200.00	100.00	60.00
19	Robert (Lefty) Grove	350.00	175.00	105.00
20	Frank Hogan	75.00	37.00	22.00
21	Bill Terry	250.00	125.00	75.00
22	Floyd Vaughan	200.00	100.00	60.00
23	Charley Gehringer	110.00	55.00	33.00
24	Ray Benge	75.00	37.00	22.00
25	Roger Cramer	75.00	37.00	22.00
26	Gerald Walker	75.00	37.00	22.00
27	Luke Appling	200.00	100.00	60.00
28	Ed. Coleman	75.00	37.00	22.00
29	Larry French	75.00	37.00	22.00
30	Julius Solters	75.00	37.00	22.00
31	Baxter Jordan	75.00	37.00	22.00
32	John (Blondy) Ryan	75.00	37.00	22.00
33	Frank (Don) Hurst	75.00	37.00	22.00
34	Charles (Chick) Hafey	200.00	100.00	60.00
35	Ernie Lombardi	200.00	100.00	60.00
36	Walter (Huck) Betts	75.00	37.00	22.00
37	Lou Gehrig	3100.00	1550.00	930.00

		NR MT	EX	VG
38	Oral Hildebrand	75.00	37.00	22.00
39	Fred Walker	75.00	37.00	22.00
40	John Stone	75.00	37.00	22.00
41	George Earnshaw	75.00	37.00	22.00
42	John Allen	90.00	45.00	27.00
43	Dick Porter	75.00	37.00	22.00
44	Tom Bridges	55.00	27.00	16.50
45	Oscar Melillo	75.00	37.00	22.00
46	Joe Stripp	75.00	37.00	22.00
47	John Frederick	75.00	37.00	22.00
48	James (Tex) Carleton	75.00	37.00	22.00
49	Sam Leslie	90.00	45.00	27.00
50	Walter Beck	90.00	45.00	27.00
51	Jim (Rip) Collins	90.00	45.00	27.00
52	Herman Bell	90.00	45.00	27.00
53	George Watkins	90.00	45.00	27.00
54	Wesley Schulmerich	90.00	45.00	27.00
55	Ed Holley	90.00	45.00	27.00
56	Mark Koenig	90.00	45.00	27.00
57	Bill Swift	90.00	45.00	27.00
58	Earl Grace	90.00	45.00	27.00
59	Joe Mowry	90.00	45.00	27.00
60	Lynn Nelson	90.00	45.00	27.00
61	Lou Gehrig	3100.00	1550.00	930.00
62	Henry Greenberg	350.00	175.00	105.00
63	Minter Hayes	90.00	45.00	27.00
64	Frank Grube	90.00	45.00	27.00
65	Cliff Bolton	90.00	45.00	27.00
66	Mel Harder	90.00	45.00	27.00
67	Bob Weiland	90.00	45.00	27.00
68	Bob Johnson	90.00	45.00	27.00
69	John Marcum	90.00	45.00	27.00
70	Ervin (Pete) Fox	90.00	45.00	27.00
71	Lyle Tinning	90.00	45.00	27.00
72	Arndt Jorgens	45.00	22.00	13.50
73	Ed Wells	275.00	137.00	82.00
74	Bob Boken	275.00	137.00	82.00
75	Bill Werber	275.00	137.00	82.00
76	Hal Trosky	275.00	137.00	82.00
77	Joe Vosmik	275.00	137.00	82.00
78	Frank (Pinkey) Higgins	275.00	137.00	82.00
79	Eddie Durham	275.00	137.00	82.00
80	Marty McManus	275.00	137.00	82.00
81	Bob Brown	275.00	137.00	82.00
82	Bill Hallahan	275.00	137.00	82.00
83	Jim Mooney	275.00	137.00	82.00
84	Paul Derringer	300.00	150.00	90.00
85	Adam Comorosky	275.00	137.00	82.00
86	Lloyd Johnson	275.00	137.00	82.00
87	George Darrow	275.00	137.00	82.00
88	Homer Peel	275.00	137.00	82.00
89	Linus Frey	275.00	137.00	82.00
90	Hazen (Ki-Ki) Cuyler	450.00	225.00	135.00
91	Dolph Camilli	275.00	137.00	82.00
92	Steve Larkin	275.00	137.00	82.00
93	Fred Ostermueller	275.00	137.00	82.00
94	Robert A. (Red) Rolfe	350.00	175.00	105.00
95	Myril Hoag	300.00	150.00	90.00
96	Jim DeShong	600.00	300.00	180.00

1935 Goudey

PICTURE 3 CARD F

The 1935 Goudey set features four players from the same team on one card. Thirty-six different cards make up the set with numerous front/back combinations existing. The card backs form nine different puzzles: 1) Tigers Team, 2) Chuck Klein, 3) Frankie Frisch, 4) Mickey Cochrane, 5) Joe Cronin, 6) Jimmy Foxx, 7) Al Simmons, 8) Indians Team, and 9)

Senators Team. The cards, which measure 2-3/8" by 2-7/8", have an ACC designation of R321.

	NR MT	EX	VG
Complete Set:	5200.00	2600.00	1350.
Common Player:	70.00	35.00	21.00

		NR MT	EX	VG
(1)	Sparky Adams, Jim Bottomley, Adam Comorosky, Tony Piet	100.00	50.00	30.00
(2)	Ethan Allen, Fred Brickell, Bubber Jonnard, Hack Wilson	100.00	50.00	30.00
(3)	Johnny Allen, Jimmie Deshong (DeShong), Red Rolfe, Dixie Walker	70.00	35.00	21.00
(4)	Luke Appling, Jimmie Dykes, George Earnshaw, Luke Sewell	100.00	50.00	30.00
(5)	Earl Averill, Oral Hildebrand, Willie Kamm, Hal Trosky	100.00	50.00	30.00
(6)	Dick Bartell, Hughie Critz, Gus Mancuso, Mel Ott	70.00	35.00	21.00
(7)	Ray Benge, Fred Fitzsimmons, Mark Koenig, Tom Zachary	70.00	35.00	21.00
(8)	Larry Benton, Ben Cantwell, Flint Rhem, Al Spohrer	70.00	35.00	21.00
(9)	Charlie Berry, Bobby Burke, Red Kress, Dazzy Vance	100.00	50.00	30.00
(10)	Max Bishop, Bill Cissell, Joe Cronin, Carl Reynolds	125.00	62.00	37.00
(11)	George Blaeholder, Dick Coffman, Oscar Melillo, Sammy West	70.00	35.00	21.00
(12)	Cy Blanton, Babe Herman, Tom Padden, Gus Suhr	70.00	35.00	21.00
(13)	Zeke Bonura, Mule Haas, Jackie Hayes, Ted Lyons	100.00	50.00	30.00
(14)	Jim Bottomley, Adam Comorosky, Willis Hudlin, Glenn Myatt	100.00	50.00	30.00
(15)	Ed Brandt, Fred Frankhouse, Shanty Hogan, Gene Moore	70.00	35.00	21.00
(16)	Ed Brandt, Rabbit Maranville, Marty McManus, Babe Ruth	1200.00	600.00	360.00
(17)	Tommy Bridges, Mickey Cochrane, Charlie Gehringer, Billy Rogell	175.00	87.00	52.00
(18)	Jack Burns, Frank Grube, Rollie Hemsley, Bob Weiland	70.00	35.00	21.00
(19)	Guy Bush, Waite Hoyt, Lloyd Waner, Paul Waner	150.00	75.00	45.00
(20)	Sammy Byrd, Danny MacFayden, Pepper Martin, Bob O'Farrell	70.00	35.00	21.00
(21)	Gilly Campbell, Ival Goodman, Alex Kampouris, Billy Meyers (Myers)	70.00	35.00	21.00
(22)	Tex Carleton, Dizzy Dean, Frankie Frisch, Ernie Orsatti	300.00	150.00	90.00
(23)	Watty Clark, Lonny Frey, Sam Leslie, Joe Stripp	70.00	35.00	21.00
(24)	Mickey Cochrane, Willie Kamm, Muddy Ruel, Al Simmons	150.00	75.00	45.00
(25)	Ed Coleman, Doc Cramer, Bob Johnson, Johnny Marcum	70.00	35.00	21.00
(26)	General Crowder, Goose Goslin, Firpo Marberry, Heinie Schuble	100.00	50.00	30.00
(27)	Kiki Cuyler, Woody English, Burleigh Grimes, Chuck Klein	70.00	35.00	21.00
(28)	Bill Dickey, Tony Lazzeri, Pat Malone, Red Ruffing	225.00	112.00	67.00
(29)	Rick Ferrell, Wes Ferrell, Fritz Ostermueller, Bill Werber	100.00	50.00	30.00
(30)	Pete Fox, Hank Greenberg, Schoolboy Rowe, Gee Walker	150.00	75.00	45.00
(31)	Jimmie Foxx, Pinky Higgins, Roy Mahaffey, Dib Williams	225.00	112.00	67.00
(32)	Bump Hadley, Lyn Lary, Heinie Manush, Monte Weaver	100.00	50.00	30.00
(33)	Mel Harder, Bill Knickerbocker, Lefty Stewart, Joe Vosmik	70.00	35.00	21.00
(34)	Travis Jackson, Gus Mancuso, Hal Schumacher, Bill Terry	175.00	87.00	52.00
(35)	Joe Kuhel, Buddy Meyer (Myer), John Stone, Earl Whitehill	70.00	35.00	21.00
(36)	Red Lucas, Tommy Thevenow, Pie Traynor, Glenn Wright	100.00	50.00	30.00

1936 Goudey

The 1936 Goudey set consists of 25 black and white cards, each measuring 2-3/8" by 2-7/8". A facsimile autograph is positioned on the card fronts. The card backs contain a brief player biography and were to be used by collectors to play a baseball game.

BALL

Too high and wide.

Over the press boxes.

Walter ('Wally') Berger — National League home run king in 1935 with 34 to his credit. He also led the league for most runs batted in. 130. One of the Game's top ranking stars since 1930.

FOUL

Different game situations (out, single, double, etc.) are given on each card. Numerous front/back exist in the set. The ACC designation for the set is R322.

	NR MT	EX	VG
Complete Set:	2500.00	1250.00	750.00
Common Player:	50.00	25.00	15.00
(1) Walter Berger	55.00	28.00	16.50
(2) Henry Bonura	50.00	25.00	15.00
(3) Stan Bordagaray	50.00	25.00	15.00
(4) Bill Brubaker	50.00	25.00	15.00
(5) Dolph Camilli	55.00	27.00	16.50
(6) Clydell Castleman	50.00	25.00	15.00
(7) "Mickey" Cochrane	200.00	100.00	60.00
(8) Joe Coscarart	50.00	25.00	15.00
(9) Frank Crosetti	100.00	50.00	30.00
(10) "Kiki" Cuyler	125.00	62.00	37.00
(11) Paul Derringer	55.00	27.00	16.50
(12) Jimmy Dykes	55.00	27.00	16.50
(13) "Rick" Ferrell	125.00	62.00	37.00
(14) "Lefty" Gomez	250.00	125.00	75.00
(15) Hank Greenberg	250.00	125.00	75.00
(16) "Bucky" Harris	125.00	62.00	37.00
(17) "Rolly" Hemsley	50.00	25.00	15.00
(18) Frank Higgins	50.00	25.00	15.00
(19) Oral Hildebrand	50.00	25.00	15.00
(20) "Chuck" Klein	150.00	75.00	45.00
(21) "Pepper" Martin	55.00	27.00	16.50
(22) "Buck" Newsom	55.00	27.00	16.50
(23) Joe Vosmik	50.00	25.00	15.00
(24) Paul Waner	150.00	75.00	45.00
(25) Bill Werber	50.00	25.00	15.00

1938 Goudey

JOE DI MAGGIO, Yankees

— No. 274 —
JOSEPH "JOE" DI MAGGIO
Born Martinez, Calif. Nov. 25, 1914
Bats Right   Throws Right
Height 6' 1½"   Weight 195 lbs.
Position   OUTFIELDER

"Joe" began his professional baseball career with the San Francisco Club in 1932. He entered the majors in 1936 with the New York Yankees to which team he is now playing.

His two year major league record is as follows:
Games ... 289   Runs ... 289   Hits ... 421
Total Bases ... 742   Runs Batted In ... 292
Stolen Bases ... 7   Batting Average ... .33

This is one of a series of 288 Baseball St.

BIG LEAGUE
CHEWING GUM
GOUDEY GUM CO.   BOSTON
Made by the originators of
INDIAN GUM

Sometimes referred to as the Goudey Heads-Up set, this issue begins numbering (#241) where the 1933 Goudey set left off. On the card fronts, a photo is used for the player's head with the body being a cartoon drawing. Twenty-four different players are pictured twice in the set. Card #'s 241-264 feature plain backgrounds on the card fronts. Card #'s 265-288 contain the same basic design and photo but include small drawings and comments within the background. The card backs contain player statistical

and biographical information. The ACC designation for the issue is R323.

	NR MT	EX	VG
Complete Set:	18000.00	9000.00	5500.
Common Player: 241-264	125.00	62.00	37.00
Common Player: 265-288	150.00	75.00	45.00
241 Charlie Gehringer	700.00	350.00	200.00
242 Ervin Fox	125.00	62.00	37.00
243 Joe Kuhel	125.00	62.00	37.00
244 Frank DeMaree	125.00	62.00	37.00
245 Frank Pytlak	125.00	62.00	37.00
246 Ernie Lombardi	200.00	100.00	60.00
247 Joe Vosmik	125.00	62.00	37.00
248 Dick Bartell	125.00	62.00	37.00
249 Jimmy Foxx	500.00	250.00	150.00
250 Joe DiMaggio	3500.00	1750.00	1000.
251 Bump Hadley	150.00	75.00	45.00
252 Zeke Bonura	125.00	62.00	37.00
253 Hank Greenberg	350.00	175.00	100.00
254 Van Lingle Mungo	150.00	75.00	45.00
255 Julius Solters	125.00	62.00	37.00
256 Vernon Kennedy	125.00	62.00	37.00
257 Al Lopez	135.00	67.00	40.00
258 Bobby Doerr	150.00	75.00	45.00
259 Bill Werber	125.00	62.00	37.00
260 Rudy York	150.00	75.00	45.00
261 Rip Radcliff	125.00	62.00	37.00
262 Joe Ducky Medwick	225.00	125.00	70.00
263 Marvin Owen	125.00	62.00	37.00
264 Bob Feller	550.00	280.00	165.00
265 Charlie Gehringer	400.00	200.00	125.00
266 Ervin Fox	150.00	75.00	45.00
267 Joe Kuhel	150.00	75.00	45.00
268 Frank DeMaree	150.00	75.00	45.00
269 Frank Pytlak	150.00	75.00	45.00
270 Ernie Lombardi	225.00	112.00	67.00
271 Joe Vosmik	150.00	75.00	45.00
272 Dick Bartell	150.00	75.00	45.00
273 Jimmy Foxx	550.00	280.00	165.00
274 Joe DiMaggio	3000.00	1500.00	900.00
275 Bump Hadley	150.00	75.00	45.00
276 Zeke Bonura	150.00	75.00	45.00
277 Hank Greenberg	400.00	200.00	125.00
278 Van Lingle Mungo	110.00	55.00	33.00
279 Julius Solters	150.00	75.00	45.00
280 Vernon Kennedy	150.00	75.00	45.00
281 Al Lopez	225.00	125.00	70.00
282 Bobby Doerr	225.00	125.00	70.00
283 Bill Werber	150.00	75.00	45.00
284 Rudy York	150.00	75.00	45.00
285 Rip Radcliff	150.00	75.00	45.00
286 Joe Ducky Medwick	250.00	125.00	70.00
287 Marvin Owen	150.00	75.00	45.00
288 Bob Feller	700.00	350.00	20.00

1941 Goudey

DARIO LODIGIANI
WHITE SOX—INFIELDER

Goudey Gum Co.'s last set was issued in 1941. The cards, which measure 2-3/8" by 2-7/8" in size, contain black and white photos set against blue, green, red or yellow backgrounds. The player's name, team and position plus the card number are situated in a box at the bottom of the card. The card reverses are blank. The ACC designation for the set is R324.

NOTE: A card number in parentheses ( ) indicates the set is unnumbered.

		NR MT	EX	VG
	Complete Set:	3200.00	1600.00	950.00
	Common Player:	50.00	25.00	15.00
1	Hugh Mulcahy	100.00	50.00	30.00
2	Harlond Clift	50.00	25.00	15.00
3	Louis Chiozza	50.00	25.00	15.00
4	Warren (Buddy) Rosar	36.00	18.00	11.00
5	George McQuinn	50.00	25.00	15.00
6	Emerson Dickman	50.00	25.00	15.00
7	Wayne Ambler	50.00	25.00	15.00
8	Bob Muncrief	50.00	25.00	15.00
9	Bill Dietrich	50.00	25.00	15.00
10	Taft Wright	50.00	25.00	15.00
11	Don Heffner	50.00	25.00	15.00
12	Fritz Ostermueller	50.00	25.00	15.00
13	Frank Hayes	50.00	25.00	15.00
14	John (Jack) Kramer	50.00	25.00	15.00
15	Dario Lodigiani	50.00	25.00	15.00
16	George Case	50.00	25.00	15.00
17	Vito Tamulis	50.00	25.00	15.00
18	Whitlow Wyatt	50.00	25.00	15.00
19	Bill Posedel	50.00	25.00	15.00
20	Carl Hubbell	175.00	90.00	50.00
21	Harold Warstler	175.00	90.00	50.00
22	Joe Sullivan	250.00	125.00	70.00
23	Norman (Babe) Young	175.00	90.00	50.00
24	Stanley Andrews	250.00	125.00	70.00
25	Morris Arnovich	175.00	90.00	50.00
26	Elburt Fletcher	50.00	25.00	15.00
27	Bill Crouch	60.00	30.00	18.00
28	Al Todd	50.00	25.00	15.00
29	Debs Garms	50.00	25.00	15.00
30	Jim Tobin	50.00	25.00	15.00
31	Chester Ross	50.00	25.00	15.00
32	George Coffman	60.00	30.00	18.00
33	Mel Ott	275.00	150.00	80.00

1981 Granny Goose
Potato Chips A's

The 1981 Granny Goose set features the Oakland A's. The cards, which measure 2-1/2" by 3-1/2" in size, were issued in bags of potato chips and are sometimes found with grease stains. The cards have full color fronts with the print done in the team's green and yellow colors. The backs contain the A's logo and a short player biography. The Revering card was withdrawn from the set shortly after he was traded and is in shorter supply than the rest of the cards in the set. The cards are numbered in the checklist that follows by the player's uniform number.

		MT	NR MT	EX
	Complete Set:	90.00	67.00	36.00
	Common Player:	2.00	1.50	.80
1	Billy Martin	10.00	7.50	4.00
2	Mike Heath	2.00	1.50	.80
5	Jeff Newman	2.00	1.50	.80
6	Mitchell Page	2.00	1.50	.80
8	Rob Picciolo	2.00	1.50	.80
10	Wayne Gross	5.00	3.75	2.00
13	Dave Revering	45.00	34.00	18.00
17	Mike Norris	2.00	1.50	.80
20	Tony Armas	4.00	3.00	1.50
21	Dwayne Murphy	3.00	2.25	1.25

		MT	NR MT	EX
22	Rick Langford	2.00	1.50	.80
27	Matt Keough	2.00	1.50	.80
35	Rickey Henderson	20.00	15.00	8.00
39	Dave McKay	2.00	1.50	.80
54	Steve McCatty	2.00	1.50	.80

1982 Granny Goose
Potato Chips A's

Granny Goose repeated its promotion from the previous year and issued another set featuring the Oakland A's. The cards, which measure 2-1/2" by 3-1/2", were distributed in two fashions - in bags of potato chips and at Fan Appreciation Day at Oakland-Alameda Coliseum. The cards are identical in design to the 1981 set and can be distinguished from it by the date on the copyright on the bottom of the card reverse. The cards are numbered in the checklist that follows by the player's uniform number.

		MT	NR MT	EX
	Complete Set:	15.00	11.00	6.00
	Common Player:	.40	.30	.15
1	Billy Martin	2.00	1.50	.80
2	Mike Heath	.40	.30	.15
5	Jeff Newman	.40	.30	.15
8	Rob Picciolo	.40	.30	.15
10	Wayne Gross	.40	.30	.15
11	Fred Stanley	.40	.30	.15
15	Davey Lopes	.80	.60	.30
17	Mike Norris	.40	.30	.15
20	Tony Armas	1.00	.70	.40
21	Dwayne Murphy	.60	.45	.25
22	Rick Langford	.40	.30	.15
27	Matt Keough	.40	.30	.15
35	Rickey Henderson	7.00	5.25	2.75
44	Cliff Johnson, Jr.	.40	.30	.15
54	Steve McCatty	.40	.30	.15

1983 Granny Goose
Potato Chips A's

For the third consecutive year, Granny Goose

issued a set of baseball cards featuring the Oakland A's. The cards were issued with or without a detachable coupon found at the bottom of each card. Issued in bags of potato chips were the coupon cards, which contain a scratch-off section offering prizes. The cards without the coupon section were given away to fans at Oakland-Alameda Coliseum on July 3, 1983. Cards with the detachable coupon command a 50 per cent premium over the coupon-less variety. The cards in the following checklist are numbered by the player's uniform number.

		MT	NR MT	EX
Complete Set		12.00	9.00	4.75
Common Player		.40	.30	.15
2	Mike Heath	.40	.30	.15
4	Carney Lansford	1.00	.70	.40
10	Wayne Gross	.40	.30	.15
14	Steve Boros	.40	.30	.15
15	Davey Lopes	.80	.60	.30
16	Mike Davis	.80	.60	.30
17	Mike Norris	.40	.30	.15
21	Dwayne Murphy	.60	.45	.25
22	Rick Langford	.40	.30	.15
27	Matt Keough	.40	.30	.15
31	Tom Underwood	.40	.30	.15
33	Dave Beard	.40	.30	.15
35	Rickey Henderson	7.00	5.25	2.75
39	Tom Burgmeier	.40	.30	.15
54	Steve McCatty	.40	.30	.15

1989 Hills Team MVP's

This high-gloss, 33-card boxed set of superstars was produced by Topps for the Hills department store chain. The words "Hills Team MVP's" appear above the player photos, while the player's name and team are printed below. The front of the card carries a red, white and blue color scheme with yellow and gold accents. The horizontal backs include player data set against a green playing field background.

		MT	NR MT	EX
Complete Set:		2.75	2.00	1.00
Common Player:		.05	.04	.02
1	Harold Baines	.05	.04	.02
2	Wade Boggs	.30	.25	.12
3	George Brett	.09	.07	.04
4	Tom Brunansky	.05	.04	.02
5	Jose Canseco	.35	.25	.14
6	Joe Carter	.05	.04	.02
7	Will Clark	.35	.25	.12

		MT	NR MT	EX
8	Roger Clemens	.10	.08	.04
9	Dave Cone	.05	.04	.02
10	Glenn Davis	.05	.04	.02
11	Andre Dawson	.09	.07	.04
12	Dennis Eckersley	.09	.07	.04
13	Andres Galarraga	.10	.08	.06
14	Kirk Gibson	.06	.05	.02
15	Mike Greenwell	.15	.11	.06
16	Tony Gwynn	.15	.11	.06
17	Orel Hershiser	.09	.07	.03
18	Danny Jackson	.05	.04	.02
19	Mark Langston	.09	.07	.04
20	Fred McGriff	.10	.08	.04
21	Dale Murphy	.06	.05	.04
22	Eddie Murray	.06	.05	.04
23	Kirby Puckett	.25	.20	.10
24	Johnny Ray	.05	.04	.02
25	Juan Samuel	.05	.04	.02
26	Ruben Sierra	.15	.11	.06
27	Dave Stewart	.05	.04	.02
28	Darryl Strawberry	.20	.15	.08
29	Allan Trammell	.06	.05	.02
30	Andy Van Slyke	.05	.04	.02
31	Frank Viola	.06	.05	.02
32	Dave Winfield	.06	.05	.02
33	Robin Yount	.09	.07	.03

1958 Hires Root Beer Test Set

PITCHER—SAN FRANCISCO GIANTS

Among the scarcest of the regional issues of the late 1950s is the eight-card test issue which preceded the Hires Root Beer set of 66 cards. Probably issued in a very limited area in the Northeast, the test cards differ from the regular issue in that they have sepia-toned, rather than color pictures, which are set against plain yellow or orange backgrounds (much like the 1958 Topps), instead of viewed through a knothole. Like the regular Hires cards, the 2-5/16" by 3-1/2" cards were issued with an attached wedge-shaped tab of like size. The tab offered membership in Hires baseball fan club, and served to hold the card into the carton of bottled root beer with which it was given away. Values quoted here are for cards with tabs. Cards without tabs would be valued approximately 50 per cent lower.

		NR MT	EX	VG
Complete Set:		1500.00	750.00	450.00
Common Player:		125.00	60.00	40.00
(1)	Johnny Antonelli	150.00	75.00	45.00
(2)	Jim Busby	125.00	60.00	40.00
(3)	Chico Fernandez	125.00	60.00	40.00
(4)	Bob Friend	150.00	75.00	45.00
(5)	Vern Law	150.00	75.00	45.00
(6)	Stan Lopata	125.00	60.00	40.00
(7)	Willie Mays	550.00	280.00	165.00
(8)	Al Pilarcik	125.00	60.00	40.00

Definitions for grading conditions are located in the Introduction of this price guide.

1958 Hires Root Beer

TED KLUSZEWSKI
INFIELD–PITTSBURGH PIRATES

Like most baseball cards issued with a tab in the 1950s, the Hires cards are extremely scarce today in their original form. The basic card was attached to a wedge-shaped tab that served the dual purpose of offering a fan club membership and of holding the card into the cardboard carton of soda bottles with which it was distributed. The card itself measures 2-5/16" by 3-1/2". The tab extends for another 3-1/2". Numbering of the Hires set begins at 10 and goes through 76, with card #69 never issued, making a set complete at 66 cards. Values given below are for cards with tabs. Cards without tabs would be valued approximately 50 per cent lower.

		NR MT	EX	VG
Complete Set:		2500.00	1250.00	700.00
Common Player:		25.00	12.50	7.50
10	Richie Ashburn	150.00	75.00	45.00
11	Chico Carrasquel	25.00	12.50	7.50
12	Dave Philley	25.00	12.50	7.50
13	Don Newcombe	28.00	14.00	8.50
14	Wally Post	25.00	12.50	7.50
15	Rip Repulski	25.00	12.50	7.50
16	Chico Fernandez	25.00	12.50	7.50
17	Larry Doby	28.00	14.00	8.50
18	Hector Brown	25.00	12.50	7.50
19	Danny O'Connell	25.00	12.50	7.50
20	Granny Hamner	25.00	12.50	7.50
21	Dick Groat	30.00	15.00	9.00
22	Ray Narleski	25.00	12.50	7.50
23	Pee Wee Reese	100.00	50.00	30.00
24	Bob Friend	30.00	15.00	9.00
25	Willie Mays	275.00	150.00	80.00
26	Bob Nieman	25.00	12.50	7.50
27	Frank Thomas	25.00	12.50	7.50
28	Curt Simmons	30.00	15.00	9.00
29	Stan Lopata	25.00	12.50	7.50
30	Bob Skinner	25.00	12.50	7.50
31	Ron Kline	25.00	12.50	7.50
32	Willie Miranda	25.00	12.50	7.50
33	Bob Avila	25.00	12.50	7.50
34	Clem Labine	30.00	15.00	9.00
35	Ray Jablonski	25.00	12.50	7.50
36	Bill Mazeroski	28.00	14.00	8.50
37	Billy Gardner	25.00	12.50	7.50
38	Pete Runnels	30.00	15.00	9.00
39	Jack Sanford	25.00	12.50	7.50
40	Dave Sisler	25.00	12.50	7.50
41	Don Zimmer	30.00	15.00	9.00
42	Johnny Podres	28.00	14.00	8.50
43	Dick Farrell	25.00	12.50	7.50
44	Hank Aaron	275.00	150.00	80.00
45	Bill Virdon	30.00	15.00	9.00
46	Bobby Thomson	30.00	15.00	9.00
47	Willard Nixon	25.00	12.50	7.50
48	Billy Loes	25.00	12.50	7.50
49	Hank Sauer	25.00	12.50	7.50
50	Johnny Antonelli	30.00	15.00	9.00
51	Daryl Spencer	25.00	12.50	7.50
52	Ken Lehman	25.00	12.50	7.50
53	Sammy White	25.00	12.50	7.50
54	Charley Neal	25.00	12.50	7.50
55	Don Drysdale	80.00	40.00	24.00
56	Jack Jensen	28.00	14.00	8.50
57	Ray Katt	25.00	12.50	7.50
58	Franklin Sullivan	25.00	12.50	7.50
59	Roy Face	30.00	15.00	9.00

		NR MT	EX	VG
60	Willie Jones	25.00	12.50	7.50
61	Duke Snider	125.00	62.00	37.00
62	Whitey Lockman	25.00	12.50	7.50
63	Gino Cimoli	30.00	15.00	9.00
64	Marv Grissom	25.00	12.50	7.50
65	Gene Baker	25.00	12.50	7.50
66	George Zuverink	25.00	12.50	7.50
67	Ted Kluszewski	28.00	14.00	8.50
68	Jim Busby	25.00	12.50	7.50
69	Not Issued			
70	Curt Barclay	25.00	12.50	7.50
71	Hank Foiles	25.00	12.50	7.50
72	Gene Stephens	25.00	12.50	7.50
73	Al Worthington	25.00	12.50	7.50
74	Al Walker	25.00	12.50	7.50
75	Bob Boyd	25.00	12.50	7.50
76	Al Pilarcik	30.00	15.00	9.00

1959 Home Run Derby

GIL HODGES
LOS ANGELES DODGERS

This 20-card unnumbered set was produced by American Motors to publicize the Home Run Derby television program. The cards measure approximately 3-1/4" by 5-1/4" and feature black and white player photos on black-backed white stock. The player name and team are printed beneath the photo. This set was reprinted (and marked as such) in 1988 by

		NR MT	EX	VG
Complete Set:		3500.00	1750.00	1050.
Common Player:		50.00	25.00	15.00
(1)	Hank Aaron	400.00	200.00	125.00
(2)	Bob Allison	60.00	30.00	18.00
(3)	Ernie Banks	250.00	125.00	70.00
(4)	Ken Boyer	100.00	50.00	30.00
(5)	Bob Cerv	60.00	30.00	18.00
(6)	Rocky Colavito	100.00	50.00	30.00
(7)	Gil Hodges	150.00	75.00	45.00
(8)	Jackie Jensen	100.00	50.00	30.00
(9)	Al Kaline	250.00	125.00	70.00
(10)	Harmon Killebrew	200.00	100.00	60.00
(11)	Jim Lemon	60.00	30.00	18.00
(12)	Mickey Mantle	1200.00	600.00	400.00
(13)	Ed Mathews	225.00	125.00	70.00
(14)	Willie Mays	450.00	225.00	112.00
(15)	Wally Post	60.00	30.00	18.00
(16)	Frank Robinson	225.00	125.00	70.00
(17)	Mark Scott (host)	100.00	50.00	30.00
(18)	Duke Snider	350.00	175.00	105.00
(19)	Dick Stuart	60.00	30.00	18.00
(20)	Gus Triandos	60.00	30.00	18.00

1947 Homogenized Bond Bread

Issued by Homogenized Bond Bread in 1947, this set consists of 48 unnumbered black and white cards, each measuring 2-1/4" by 3-1/2". Of the 48 cards, 44 are baseball players. The remaining four cards picture boxers. The cards are usually found with rounded corners, although cards with square corners are also known to exist. The set contains both portrait and action photos, and features the player's facsimile autograph on the front.

		NR MT	EX	VG
Complete Set:		400.00	200.00	120.00
Common Player:		4.00	2.00	1.25
(1)	Rex Barney	4.00	2.00	1.25
(2)	Larry Berra	30.00	15.00	9.00
(3)	Ewell Blackwell	4.00	2.00	1.25
(4)	Lou Boudreau	8.00	4.00	2.50
(5)	Ralph Branca	8.00	4.00	2.50
(6)	Harry Brecheen	4.00	2.00	1.25
(7)	Dom DiMaggio	8.00	4.00	2.50
(8)	Joe DiMaggio	75.00	37.00	22.00
(9)	Bobbie Doerr (Bobby)	8.00	4.00	2.50
(10)	Bruce Edwards	4.00	2.00	1.25
(11)	Bob Elliott	4.00	2.00	1.25
(12)	Del Ennis	4.00	2.00	1.25
(13)	Bob Feller	15.00	7.50	4.50
(14)	Carl Furillo	8.00	4.00	2.50
(15)	Cid Gordon (Sid)	4.00	2.00	1.25
(16)	Joe Gordon	4.00	2.00	1.25
(17)	Joe Hatten	4.00	2.00	1.25
(18)	Gil Hodges	15.00	7.50	4.50
(19)	Tommy Holmes	4.00	2.00	1.25
(20)	Larry Janson (Jansen)	4.00	2.00	1.25
(21)	Sheldon Jones	4.00	2.00	1.25
(22)	Edwin Joost	4.00	2.00	1.25
(23)	Charlie Keller	8.00	4.00	2.50
(24)	Ken Keltner	4.00	2.00	1.25
(25)	Buddy Kerr	4.00	2.00	1.25
(26)	Ralph Kiner	8.00	4.00	2.50
(27)	John Lindell	4.00	2.00	1.25
(28)	Whitey Lockman	4.00	2.00	1.25
(29)	Willard Marshall	4.00	2.00	1.25
(30)	Johnny Mize	8.00	4.00	2.50
(31)	Stan Musial	30.00	15.00	9.00
(32)	Andy Pafko	4.00	2.00	1.25
(33)	Johnny Pesky	4.00	2.00	1.25
(34)	Pee Wee Reese	25.00	12.50	7.50
(35)	Phil Rizzuto	15.00	7.50	4.50
(36)	Aaron Robinson	4.00	2.00	1.25
(37)	Jackie Robinson	30.00	15.00	9.00
(38)	John Sain	5.00	2.50	1.50
(39)	Enos Slaughter	8.00	4.00	2.50
(40)	Vern Stephens	4.00	2.00	1.25
(41)	George Tebbetts	4.00	2.00	1.25

		NR MT	EX	VG
(42)	Bob Thomson	8.00	4.00	2.50
(43)	Johnny Vandermeer (VanderMeer)			
		8.00	4.00	2.50
(44)	Ted Williams	30.00	15.00	9.00

1975 Hostess

The first of what would become five annual issues, the 1975 Hostess set consists of 50 three-card panels which formed the bottom of boxes of family-size snack cake products. Unlike many similar issues, the Hostess cards do not share common borders, so it was possible to cut them neatly and evenly from the box. Well-cut single cards measure 2-1/4" by 3-1/4", while a three-card panel measures 7-1/4" by 3-1/4". Because some of the panels were issued on packages of less popular snack cakes, they are somewhat scarcer today. Since the hobby was quite well- developed when the Hostess cards were first issued, there is no lack of complete panels. Even unused complete boxes are available today. Some of the photos in this issue also appear on Topps cards of the era.

		NR MT	EX	VG
Complete Panel Set:		350.00	175.00	105.00
Complete Singles Set:		150.00	75.00	45.00
Common Panel:		2.50	1.25	.70
Common Single Player:		.40	.20	.12
Panel 1		2.50	1.25	.70
1	Bobby Tolan	.40	.20	.12
2	Cookie Rojas	.40	.20	.12
3	Darrell Evans	.70	.35	.20
Panel 2		5.50	2.75	1.75
4	Sal Bando	.50	.25	.15
5	Joe Morgan	2.00	1.00	.60
6	Mickey Lolich	.60	.30	.20
Panel 3		4.00	2.00	1.25
7	Don Sutton	1.50	.70	.45
8	Bill Melton	.40	.20	.12
9	Tim Foli	.40	.20	.12
Panel 4		5.00	2.50	1.50
10	Joe Lahoud	.40	.20	.12
11a	Bert Hooten (incorrect spelling)	1.50	.70	.45
11b	Burt Hooton (correct spelling)	1.50	.70	.45
12	Paul Blair	.40	.20	.12
Panel 5		2.50	1.25	.70
13	Jim Barr	.40	.20	.12
14	Toby Harrah	.50	.25	.15
15	John Milner	.40	.20	.12
Panel 6		3.50	1.75	1.00
16	Ken Holtzman	.50	.25	.15
17	Cesar Cedeno	.50	.25	.15
18	Dwight Evans	.90	.45	.25
Panel 7		7.50	3.75	2.25
19	Willie McCovey	3.00	1.50	.90
20	Tony Oliva	.70	.35	.20
21	Manny Sanguillen	.40	.20	.12
Panel 8		8.00	4.00	2.50
22	Mickey Rivers	.50	.25	.15
23	Lou Brock	3.00	1.50	.90
24	Craig Nettles	.90	.45	.25
Panel 9		3.00	1.50	.90
25	Jimmy Wynn	.50	.25	.15

		NR MT	EX	VG
26	George Scott	.50	.25	.15
27	Greg Luzinski	.50	.25	.15
Panel 10		20.00	10.00	6.00
28	Bert Campaneris	.50	.25	.15
29	Pete Rose	8.00	4.00	2.50
30	Buddy Bell	.50	.25	.15
Panel 11		2.50	1.25	.70
31	Gary Matthews	.50	.25	.15
32	Fred Patek	.40	.20	.12
33	Mike Lum	.40	.20	.12
Panel 12		2.50	1.25	.70
34	Ellie Rodriguez	.40	.20	.12
35	Milt May	.40	.20	.12
36	Willie Horton	.50	.25	.15
Panel 13		10.00	5.00	3.00
37	Dave Winfield	4.50	2.25	1.25
38	Tom Grieve	.40	.20	.12
39	Barry Foote	.40	.20	.12
Panel 14		2.50	1.25	.70
40	Joe Rudi	.50	.25	.15
41	Bake McBride	.40	.20	.12
42	Mike Cuellar	.50	.25	.15
Panel 15		2.50	1.25	.70
43	Garry Maddox	.50	.25	.15
44	Carlos May	.40	.20	.12
45	Bud Harrelson	.40	.20	.12
Panel 16		15.00	7.50	4.50
46	Dave Chalk	.40	.20	.12
47	Dave Concepcion	.50	.25	.15
48	Carl Yastrzemski	6.50	3.25	2.00
Panel 17		9.00	4.50	2.75
49	Steve Garvey	4.00	2.00	1.25
50	Amos Otis	.50	.25	.15
51	Rickey Reuschel	.50	.25	.15
Panel 18		3.75	2.00	1.25
52	Rollie Fingers	1.25	.60	.40
53	Bob Watson	.40	.20	.12
54	John Ellis	.40	.20	.12
Panel 19		9.50	4.75	2.75
55	Bob Bailey	.40	.20	.12
56	Rod Carew	4.00	2.00	1.25
57	Richie Hebner	.40	.20	.12
Panel 20		10.00	5.00	3.00
58	Nolan Ryan	4.00	2.00	1.25
59	Reggie Smith	.50	.25	.15
60	Joe Coleman	.40	.20	.12
Panel 21		10.00	5.00	3.00
61	Ron Cey	.50	.25	.15
62	Darrell Porter	.50	.25	.15
63	Steve Carlton	4.00	2.00	1.25
Panel 22		2.50	1.25	.70
64	Gene Tenace	.40	.20	.12
65	Jose Cardenal	.40	.20	.12
66	Bill Lee	.40	.20	.12
Panel 23		2.50	1.25	.70
67	Dave Lopes	.50	.25	.15
68	Wilbur Wood	.50	.25	.15
69	Steve Renko	.40	.20	.12
Panel 24		3.00	1.50	.90
70	Joe Torre	.50	.25	.15
71	Ted Sizemore	.40	.20	.12
72	Bobby Grich	.50	.25	.15
Panel 25		11.00	5.50	3.25
73	Chris Speier	.40	.20	.12
74	Bert Blyleven	.70	.35	.20
75	Tom Seaver	4.50	2.25	1.25
Panel 26		2.50	1.25	.70
76	Nate Colbert	.40	.20	.12
77	Don Kessinger	.40	.20	.12
78	George Medich	.40	.20	.12
Panel 27		23.00	11.50	7.00
79	Andy Messersmith	.70	.35	.20
80	Robin Yount	9.00	4.50	2.75
81	Al Oliver	1.50	.70	.45
Panel 28		18.00	9.00	5.50
82	Bill Singer	.50	.25	.15
83	Johnny Bench	6.00	3.00	1.75
84	Gaylord Perry	3.00	1.50	.90
Panel 29		5.00	2.50	1.50
85	Dave Kingman	1.25	.60	.40
86	Ed Herrmann	.50	.25	.15
87	Ralph Garr	.60	.30	.20
Panel 30		23.00	11.50	7.00
88	Reggie Jackson	9.00	4.50	2.75
89a	Doug Radar (incorrect spelling)	2.00	1.00	.60
89b	Doug Rader (correct spelling)	2.00	1.00	.60
90	Elliott Maddox	.50	.25	.15
Panel 31		3.50	1.75	1.00
91	Bill Russell	.60	.30	.20
92	John Mayberry	.50	.25	.15
93	Dave Cash	.50	.25	.15

		NR MT	EX	VG
Panel 32		5.00	2.50	1.50
94	Jeff Burroughs	.60	.30	.20
95	Ted Simmons	1.25	.60	.40
96	Joe Decker	.50	.25	.15
Panel 33		10.00	5.00	3.00
97	Bill Buckner	1.00	.50	.30
98	Bobby Darwin	.50	.25	.15
99	Phil Niekro	3.50	1.75	1.00
Panel 34		3.00	1.50	.90
100	Mike Sundberg (Jim)	.50	.25	.15
101	Greg Gross	.40	.20	.12
102	Luis Tiant	.70	.35	.20
Panel 35		2.50	1.25	.70
103	Glenn Beckert	.40	.20	.12
104	Hal McRae	.50	.25	.15
105	Mike Jorgensen	.40	.20	.12
Panel 36		2.50	1.25	.70
106	Mike Hargrove	.40	.20	.12
107	Don Gullett	.40	.20	.12
108	Tito Fuentes	.40	.20	.12
Panel 37		3.50	1.75	1.00
109	John Grubb	.40	.20	.12
110	Jim Kaat	.90	.45	.25
111	Felix Millan	.40	.20	.12
Panel 38		2.50	1.25	.70
112	Don Money	.40	.20	.12
113	Rick Monday	.50	.25	.15
114	Dick Bosman	.40	.20	.12
Panel 39		3.50	1.75	1.00
115	Roger Metzger	.40	.20	.12
116	Fergie Jenkins	.90	.45	.25
117	Dusky Baker	.50	.25	.15
Panel 40		10.00	5.00	3.00
118	Billy Champion	.50	.25	.15
119	Bob Gibson	3.50	1.75	1.00
120	Bill Freehan	.80	.40	.25
Panel 41		2.50	1.25	.70
121	Cesar Geronimo	.40	.20	.12
122	Jorge Orta	.40	.20	.12
123	Cleon Jones	.40	.20	.12
Panel 42		10.50	5.25	3.25
124	Steve Busby	.40	.20	.12
125a	Bill Madlock (Pitcher)	2.00	1.00	.60
125b	Bill Madlock (Third Base)	2.00	1.00	.60
126	Jim Palmer	2.75	1.50	.80
Panel 43		4.25	2.25	1.25
127	Tony Perez	1.00	.50	.30
128	Larry Hisle	.40	.20	.12
129	Rusty Staub	.70	.35	.20
Panel 44		20.00	10.00	6.00
130	Hank Aaron	9.00	4.50	2.75
131	Rennie Stennett	.50	.25	.15
132	Rico Petrocelli	.70	.35	.20
Panel 45		16.00	8.00	4.75
133	Mike Schmidt	6.00	3.00	1.75
134	Sparky Lyle	.50	.25	.15
135	Willie Stargell	3.00	1.50	.90
Panel 46		7.00	3.50	2.00
136	Ken Henderson	.40	.20	.12
137	Willie Montanez	.40	.20	.12
138	Thurman Munson	2.50	1.25	.70
Panel 47		2.50	1.25	.70
139	Richie Zisk	.40	.20	.12
140	Geo. Hendricks (Hendrick)	.50	.25	.15
141	Bobby Murcer	.50	.25	.15
Panel 48		10.00	5.00	3.00
142	Lee May	.50	.25	.15
143	Carlton Fisk	1.00	.50	.30
144	Brooks Robinson	3.50	1.75	1.00
Panel 49		2.50	1.25	.70
145	Bobby Bonds	.50	.25	.15
146	Gary Sutherland	.40	.20	.12
147	Oscar Gamble	.40	.20	.12
Panel 50		6.00	3.00	1.75
148	Jim Hunter	2.50	1.25	.70
149	Tug McGraw	.50	.25	.15
150	Dave McNally	.50	.25	.15

1975 Hostess Twinkies

Believed to have been issued only in the Western states, and on a limited basis at that, the 1975 Hostess Twinkie set features 60 of the cards from the "regular" Hostess set of that year. The cards were issued one per pack with the popular snack cake. Card #'s 1-36 are a direct pick-up from the Hostess set, while the remaining 24 cards in the set were

		NR MT	EX	VG
122	Jorge Orta	.90	.45	.25
125	Bill Madlock	2.25	1.25	.70
130	Hank Aaron	15.00	7.50	4.50
136	Ken Henderson	.90	.45	.25

selected from the more popular names in the remainder of the Hostess issue - with an emphasis on West Coast players. Thus, after card #36, the '75 Twinkie cards are skip-numbered from 40-136. In identical 2-1/4" by 3-1/4" size, the Twinkie cards differ from the Hostess issue only in the presence of small black bars at top and bottom center of the back of the card. Values quoted are for full bottom panels.

		NR MT	EX	VG
Complete Set:		175.00	87.00	52.00
Common Player:		.90	.45	.25
1	Bobby Tolan	.90	.45	.25
2	Cookie Rojas	.90	.45	.25
3	Darrell Evans	2.00	1.00	.60
4	Sal Bando	1.25	.60	.40
5	Joe Morgan	5.00	2.50	1.50
6	Mickey Lolich	2.00	1.00	.60
7	Don Sutton	4.50	2.25	1.25
8	Bill Melton	.90	.45	.25
9	Tim Foli	.90	.45	.25
10	Joe Lahoud	.90	.45	.25
11	Bert Hooten (Burt Hooton)	1.25	.60	.40
12	Paul Blair	.90	.45	.25
13	Jim Barr	.90	.45	.25
14	Toby Harrah	.90	.45	.25
15	John Milner	.90	.45	.25
16	Ken Holtzman	1.00	.50	.30
17	Cesar Cedeno	1.25	.60	.40
18	Dwight Evans	3.00	1.50	.90
19	Willie McCovey	7.00	3.50	2.00
20	Tony Oliva	2.00	1.00	.60
21	Manny Sanguillen	.90	.45	.25
22	Mickey Rivers	.90	.45	.25
23	Lou Brock	6.50	3.25	2.00
24	Graig Nettles	3.00	1.50	.90
25	Jim Wynn	.90	.45	.25
26	George Scott	.90	.45	.25
27	Greg Luzinski	1.25	.60	.40
28	Bert Campaneris	1.25	.60	.40
29	Pete Rose	20.00	10.00	6.00
30	Buddy Bell	1.75	.90	.50
31	Gary Matthews	1.25	.60	.40
32	Fred Patek	.90	.45	.25
33	Mike Lum	.90	.45	.25
34	Ellie Rodriguez	.90	.45	.25
35	Milt May (photo actually Lee May)	1.25	.60	.40
36	Willie Horton	.90	.45	.25
40	Joe Rudi	1.25	.60	.40
43	Garry Maddox	.90	.45	.25
46	Dave Chalk	.90	.45	.25
49	Steve Garvey	10.00	5.00	3.00
52	Rollie Fingers	4.00	2.00	1.25
58	Nolan Ryan	10.00	5.00	3.00
61	Ron Cey	1.50	.70	.45
64	Gene Tenace	.90	.45	.25
65	Jose Cardenal	.90	.45	.25
67	Dave Lopes	1.25	.60	.40
68	Wilbur Wood	.90	.45	.25
73	Chris Speier	.90	.45	.25
77	Don Kessinger	.90	.45	.25
79	Andy Messersmith	.90	.45	.25
80	Robin Yount	15.00	7.50	4.50
82	Bill Singer	.90	.45	.25
103	Glenn Beckert	.90	.45	.25
110	Jim Kaat	2.50	1.25	.70
112	Don Money	.90	.45	.25
113	Rick Monday	1.25	.60	.40

1976 Hostess

GEORGE BRETT
Kansas City ROYALS
THIRD BASE

The second of five annual Hostess issues, the 1976 cards carried a "Bicentennial" color theme, with red, white and blue stripes at the bottom of the 2-1/4" by 3-1/4" cards. Like other Hostess issues, the cards were printed in panels of three as the bottom of family-size boxes of snack cake products. This leads to a degree of scarcity for some of the 150 cards in the set; those which were found on less-popular brands. A well-trimmed three-card panel measures 7-1/4" by 3-1/4" size. Some of the photos used in the 1976 Hostess set can also be found on Topps issues of the era.

		NR MT	EX	VG
Complete Panel Set:		350.00	175.00	105.00
Complete Singles Set:		175.00	87.00	52.00
Common Panel:		2.50	1.25	.70
Common Single Player:		.40	.20	.12
Panel 1		11.75	6.00	3.50
1	Fred Lynn	1.25	.60	.40
2	Joe Morgan	2.00	1.00	.60
3	Phil Niekro	2.25	1.25	.70
Panel 2		4.50	2.25	1.25
4	Gaylord Perry	1.75	.90	.50
5	Bob Watson	.40	.20	.12
6	Bill Freehan	.50	.25	.15
Panel 3		6.50	3.25	2.00
7	Lou Brock	3.00	1.50	.90
8	Al Fitzmorris	.40	.20	.12
9	Rennie Stennett	.40	.20	.12
Panel 4		9.00	4.50	2.75
10	Tony Oliva	.70	.35	.20
11	Robin Yount	4.00	2.00	1.25
12	Rick Manning	.40	.20	.12
Panel 5		3.50	1.75	1.00
13	Bobby Grich	.50	.25	.15
14	Terry Forster	.40	.20	.12
15	Dave Kingman	.70	.35	.20
Panel 6		7.00	3.50	2.00
16	Thurman Munson	2.50	1.25	.70
17	Rick Reuschel	.50	.25	.15
18	Bobby Bonds	.50	.25	.15
Panel 7		9.50	4.75	2.75
19	Steve Garvey	4.00	2.00	1.25
20	Vida Blue	.50	.25	.15
21	Dave Rader	.40	.20	.12
Panel 8		9.00	4.50	2.75
22	Johnny Bench	4.00	2.00	1.25
23	Luis Tiant	.50	.25	.15
24	Darrell Evans	.70	.35	.20
Panel 9		2.50	1.25	.70
25	Larry Dierker	.40	.20	.12
26	Willie Horton	.50	.25	.15
27	John Ellis	.40	.20	.12
Panel 10		3.00	1.50	.90
28	Al Cowens	.40	.20	.12
29	Jerry Reuss	.50	.25	.15
30	Reggie Smith	.50	.25	.15
Panel 11		13.00	6.50	4.00

		NR MT	EX	VG
31	Bobby Darwin	.50	.25	.15
32	Fritz Peterson	.50	.25	.15
33	Rod Carew	6.00	3.00	1.75
Panel 12		21.00	10.50	6.25
34	Carlos May	.50	.25	.15
35	Tom Seaver	6.00	3.00	1.75
36	Brooks Robinson	5.00	2.50	1.50
Panel 13		2.50	1.25	.70
37	Jose Cardenal	.40	.20	.12
38	Ron Blomberg	.40	.20	.12
39	Lee Stanton	.40	.20	.12
Panel 14		2.50	1.25	.70
40	Dave Cash	.40	.20	.12
41	John Montefusco	.40	.20	.12
42	Bob Tolan	.40	.20	.12
Panel 15		2.50	1.25	.70
43	Carl Morton	.40	.20	.12
44	Rick Burleson	.50	.25	.15
45	Don Gullett	.40	.20	.12
Panel 16		2.50	1.25	.70
46	Vern Ruhle	.40	.20	.12
47	Cesar Cedeno	.50	.25	.15
48	Toby Harrah	.50	.25	.15
Panel 17		6.00	3.00	1.75
49	Willie Stargell	3.00	1.50	.90
50	Al Hrabosky	.40	.20	.12
51	Amos Otis	.50	.25	.15
Panel 18		2.50	1.25	.70
52	Bud Harrelson	.50	.25	.15
53	Jim Hughes	.40	.20	.12
54	George Scott	.50	.25	.15
Panel 19		9.50	4.75	2.75
55	Mike Vail	.50	.25	.15
56	Jim Palmer	4.00	2.00	1.25
57	Jorge Orta	.80	.40	.25
Panel 20		3.50	1.75	1.00
58	Chris Chambliss	.80	.40	.25
59	Dave Chalk	.50	.25	.15
60	Ray Burris	.50	.25	.15
Panel 21		14.00	7.00	4.25
61	Bert Campaneris	.80	.40	.25
62	Gary Carter	6.00	3.00	1.75
63	Ron Cey	.90	.45	.25
Panel 22		28.00	14.00	8.50
64	Carlton Fisk	2.00	1.00	.60
65	Marty Perez	.50	.25	.15
66	Pete Rose	10.00	5.00	3.00
Panel 23		3.50	1.75	1.00
67	Roger Metzger	.50	.25	.15
68	Jim Sundberg	.60	.30	.20
69	Ron LeFlore	.60	.30	.20
Panel 24		3.50	1.75	1.00
70	Ted Sizemore	.50	.25	.15
71	Steve Busby	.50	.25	.15
72	Manny Sanguillen	.50	.25	.15
Panel 25		5.00	2.50	1.50
73	Larry Hisle	.60	.30	.20
74	Pete Broberg	.50	.25	.15
75	Boog Powell	1.25	.60	.40
Panel 26		6.50	3.25	2.00
76	Ken Singleton	.80	.40	.25
77	Rich Gossage	2.00	1.00	.60
78	Jerry Grote	.50	.25	.15
Panel 27		16.00	8.00	4.75
79	Nolan Ryan	6.00	3.00	1.75
80	Rick Monday	.70	.35	.20
81	Graig Nettles	1.25	.60	.40
Panel 28		18.00	9.00	5.50
82	Chris Speier	.40	.20	.12
83	Dave Winfield	4.00	2.00	1.25
84	Mike Schmidt	6.00	3.00	1.75
Panel 29		4.00	2.00	1.25
85	Buzz Capra	.40	.20	.12
86	Tony Perez	1.00	.50	.30
87	Dwight Evans	.90	.45	.25
Panel 30		2.50	1.25	.70
88	Mike Hargrove	.40	.20	.12
89	Joe Coleman	.40	.20	.12
90	Greg Gross	.40	.20	.12
Panel 31		2.50	1.25	.70
91	John Mayberry	.40	.20	.12
92	John Candelaria	.50	.25	.15
93	Bake McBride	.40	.20	.12
Panel 32		15.00	7.50	4.50
94	Hank Aaron	7.00	3.50	2.00
95	Buddy Bell	.50	.25	.15
96	Steve Braun	.40	.20	.12
Panel 33		2.50	1.25	.70
97	Jon Matlack	.40	.20	.12
98	Lee May	.50	.25	.15
99	Wilbur Wood	.50	.25	.15

		NR MT	EX	VG
Panel 34		4.00	2.00	1.25
100	Bill Madlock	.90	.45	.25
101	Frank Tanana	.50	.25	.15
102	Mickey Rivers	.50	.25	.15
Panel 35		3.75	2.00	1.25
103	Mike Ivie	.40	.20	.12
104	Rollie Fingers	1.25	.60	.40
105	Dave Lopes	.50	.25	.15
Panel 36		3.50	1.75	1.00
106	George Foster	.90	.45	.25
107	Denny Doyle	.40	.20	.12
108	Earl Williams	.40	.20	.12
Panel 37		2.50	1.25	.70
109	Tom Veryzer	.40	.20	.12
110	J.R. Richard	.50	.25	.15
111	Jeff Burroughs	.40	.20	.12
Panel 38		14.00	7.00	4.25
112	Al Oliver	.90	.45	.25
113	Ted Simmons	.80	.40	.25
114	Geroge Brett	5.00	2.50	1.50
Panel 39		3.00	1.50	.90
115	Frank Duffy	.40	.20	.12
116	Bert Blyleven	.80	.40	.25
117	Darrell Porter	.50	.25	.15
Panel 40		2.50	1.25	.70
118	Don Baylor	.70	.35	.20
119	Bucky Dent	.50	.25	.15
120	Felix Millan	.40	.20	.12
Panel 41		2.50	1.25	.70
121	Mike Cuellar	.50	.25	.15
122	Gene Tenace	.40	.20	.12
123	Bobby Murcer	.50	.25	.15
Panel 42		7.00	3.50	2.00
124	Willie McCovey	3.00	1.50	.90
125	Greg Luzinski	.50	.25	.15
126	Larry Parrish	.50	.25	.15
Panel 43		10.00	5.00	3.00
127	Jim Rice	4.00	2.00	1.25
128	Dave Concepcion	.50	.25	.15
129	Jim Wynn	.50	.25	.15
Panel 44		2.50	1.25	.70
130	Tom Grieve	.40	.20	.12
131	Mike Cosgrove	.40	.20	.12
132	Dan Meyer	.40	.20	.12
Panel 45		5.00	2.50	1.50
133	Dave Parker	1.50	.70	.45
134	Don Kessinger	.40	.20	.12
135	Hal McRae	.50	.25	.15
Panel 46		4.00	2.00	1.25
136	Don Money	.70	.35	.20
137	Dennis Eckersley	.90	.45	.25
138	Fergie Jenkins	.80	.40	.25
Panel 47		4.00	2.00	1.25
139	Mike Torrez	.40	.20	.12
140	Jerry Morales	.40	.20	.12
141	Jim Hunter	1.25	.60	.40
Panel 48		2.50	1.25	.70
142	Gary Matthews	.50	.25	.15
143	Randy Jones	.40	.20	.12
144	Mike Jorgensen	.40	.20	.12
Panel 49		13.00	6.50	4.00
145	Larry Bowa	.60	.30	.20
146	Reggie Jackson	5.00	2.50	1.50
147	Steve Yeager	.40	.20	.12
Panel 50		15.00	7.50	4.50
148	Dave May	.40	.20	.12
149	Carl Yastrzemski	6.50	3.25	2.00
150	Cesar Geronimo	.40	.20	.12

1976 Hostess Twinkies

The 60 cards in this regionally-issued (West Coast

only) set closely parallel the first 60 cards in the numerical sequence of the "regular" 1976 Hostess issue. The singular difference is the appearance on the back of a black band toward the center of the card at top and bottom. Also unlike the three-card panels of the regular Hostess issue, the 2-1/4" by 3-1/4" Twinkie cards were issued singly, as the cardboard stiffener for the cellophane-wrapped snack cakes. Values quoted are for complete bottom panels.

		NR MT	EX	VG
Complete Set:		175.00	87.00	52.00
Common Player:		.90	.45	.25
1	Fred Lynn	3.00	1.50	.90
2	Joe Morgan	5.00	2.50	1.50
3	Phil Niekro	4.50	2.25	1.25
4	Gaylord Perry	5.00	2.50	1.50
5	Bob Watson	.90	.45	.25
6	Bill Freehan	1.25	.60	.40
7	Lou Brock	7.00	3.50	2.00
8	Al Fitzmorris	.90	.45	.25
9	Rennie Stennett	.90	.45	.25
10	Tony Oliva	2.00	1.00	.60
11	Robin Yount	7.00	3.50	2.00
12	Rick Manning	.90	.45	.25
13	Bobby Grich	1.25	.60	.40
14	Terry Forster	.90	.45	.25
15	Dave Kingman	2.00	1.00	.60
16	Thurman Munson	6.50	3.25	2.00
17	Rick Reuschel	1.25	.60	.40
18	Bobby Bonds	1.25	.60	.40
19	Steve Garvey	10.00	5.00	3.00
20	Vida Blue	1.75	.90	.50
21	Dave Rader	.90	.45	.25
22	Johnny Bench	10.00	5.00	3.00
23	Luis Tiant	1.50	.70	.45
24	Darrell Evans	2.00	1.00	.60
25	Larry Dierker	.90	.45	.25
26	Willie Horton	.90	.45	.25
27	John Ellis	.90	.45	.25
28	Al Cowens	.90	.45	.25
29	Jerry Reuss	1.25	.60	.40
30	Reggie Smith	1.25	.60	.40
31	Bobby Darwin	.90	.45	.25
32	Fritz Peterson	.90	.45	.25
33	Rod Carew	10.00	5.00	3.00
34	Carlos May	.90	.45	.25
35	Tom Seaver	10.00	5.00	3.00
36	Brooks Robinson	9.00	4.50	2.75
37	Jose Cardenal	.90	.45	.25
38	Ron Blomberg	.90	.45	.25
39	Lee Stanton	.90	.45	.25
40	Dave Cash	.90	.45	.25
41	John Montefusco	.90	.45	.25
42	Bob Tolan	.90	.45	.25
43	Carl Morton	.90	.45	.25
44	Rick Burleson	.90	.45	.25
45	Don Gullett	.90	.45	.25
46	Vern Ruhle	.90	.45	.25
47	Cesar Cedeno	1.25	.60	.40
48	Toby Harrah	.90	.45	.25
49	Willie Stargell	7.00	3.50	2.00
50	Al Hrabosky	.90	.45	.25
51	Amos Otis	.90	.45	.25
52	Bud Harrelson	.90	.45	.25
53	Jim Hughes	.90	.45	.25
54	George Scott	.90	.45	.25
55	Mike Vail	.90	.45	.25
56	Jim Palmer	7.00	3.50	2.00
57	Jorge Orta	.90	.45	.25
58	Chris Chambliss	1.25	.60	.40
59	Dave Chalk	.90	.45	.25
60	Ray Burris	.90	.45	.25

1977 Hostess

The third of five consecutive annual issues, the 1977 Hostess cards retained the same card size 2-1/4" by 3-1/4", set size - 150 cards, and mode of issue - three cards on a 7-1/4" by 3-1/4" panel, as the previous two efforts. Because they were issued as the bottom panel of snack cake boxes, and because some brands of Hostess products were more popular than others, certain cards in the set are scarcer than others.

PETE ROSE
Cincinnati REDS
THIRD BASE

		NR MT	EX	VG
Complete Panel Set:		325.00	162.00	97.00
Complete Singles Set:		175.00	87.00	52.00
Common Panel:		2.50	1.25	.70
Common Single Player:		.40	.20	.12
Panel 1		18.00	9.00	5.50
1	Jim Palmer	2.75	1.50	.80
2	Joe Morgan	2.00	1.00	.60
3	Reggie Jackson	5.00	2.50	1.50
Panel 2		23.00	11.50	7.00
4	Carl Yastrzemski	6.00	3.00	1.75
5	Thurman Munson	2.50	1.25	.70
6	Johnny Bench	4.00	2.00	1.25
Panel 3		32.00	16.00	9.50
7	Tom Seaver	3.00	1.50	.90
8	Pete Rose	8.00	4.00	2.50
9	Rod Carew	4.00	2.00	1.25
Panel 4		2.50	1.25	.70
10	Luis Tiant	.60	.30	.20
11	Phil Garner	.50	.25	.15
12	Sixto Lezcano	.40	.20	.12
Panel 5		2.50	1.25	.70
13	Mike Torrez	.40	.20	.12
14	Dave Lopes	.50	.25	.15
15	Doug DeCinces	.50	.25	.15
Panel 6		2.50	1.25	.70
16	Jim Spencer	.40	.20	.12
17	Hal McRae	.50	.25	.15
18	Mike Hargrove	.40	.20	.12
Panel 7		4.50	2.25	1.25
19	Willie Montanez	.50	.25	.15
20	Roger Metzger	.50	.25	.15
21	Dwight Evans	1.50	.70	.45
Panel 8		10.00	5.00	3.00
22	Steve Rogers	.50	.25	.15
23	Jim Rice	4.00	2.00	1.25
24	Pete Falcone	.50	.25	.15
Panel 9		9.00	4.50	2.75
25	Greg Luzinski	.90	.45	.25
26	Randy Jones	.50	.25	.15
27	Willie Stargell	3.00	1.50	.90
Panel 10		3.50	1.75	1.00
28	John Hiller	.50	.25	.15
29	Bobby Murcer	.70	.35	.20
30	Rick Monday	.70	.35	.20
Panel 11		9.00	4.50	2.75
31	John Montefusco	.50	.25	.15
32	Lou Brock	4.00	2.00	1.25
33	Bill North	.50	.25	.15
Panel 12		32.00	16.00	9.50
34	Robin Yount	4.00	2.00	1.25
35	Steve Garvey	5.00	2.50	1.50
36	George Brett	8.00	4.00	2.50
Panel 13		3.50	1.75	1.00
37	Toby Harrah	.70	.35	.20
38	Jerry Royster	.50	.25	.15
39	Bob Watson	.60	.30	.20
Panel 14		9.50	4.75	2.75
40	George Foster	.90	.45	.25
41	Gary Carter	3.50	1.75	1.00
42	John Denny	.40	.20	.12
Panel 15		18.00	9.00	5.50
43	Mike Schmidt	5.00	2.50	1.50
44	Dave Winfield	3.75	2.00	1.25
45	Al Oliver	.90	.45	.25
Panel 16		3.00	1.50	.90
46	Mark Fidrych	.60	.30	.20
47	Larry Herndon	.50	.25	.15

		NR MT	EX	VG
48	Dave Goltz	.40	.20	.12
Panel 17		3.50	1.75	1.00
49	Jerry Morales	.40	.20	.12
50	Ron LeFlore	.50	.25	.15
51	Fred Lynn	.90	.45	.25
Panel 18		3.50	1.75	1.00
52	Vida Blue	.50	.25	.15
53	Rick Manning	.40	.20	.12
54	Bill Buckner	.70	.35	.20
Panel 19		2.50	1.25	.70
55	Lee May	.50	.25	.15
56	John Mayberry	.40	.20	.12
57	Darrel Chaney	.40	.20	.12
Panel 20		3.50	1.75	1.00
58	Cesar Cedeno	.50	.25	.15
59	Ken Griffey	.50	.25	.15
60	Dave Kingman	.80	.40	.25
Panel 21		3.50	1.75	1.00
61	Ted Simmons	.80	.40	.25
62	Larry Bowa	.50	.25	.15
63	Frank Tanana	.50	.25	.15
Panel 22		2.50	1.25	.70
64	Jason Thompson	.40	.20	.12
65	Ken Brett	.40	.20	.12
66	Roy Smalley	.40	.20	.12
Panel 23		2.50	1.25	.70
67	Ray Burris	.40	.20	.12
68	Rick Burleson	.40	.20	.12
69	Buddy Bell	.50	.25	.15
Panel 24		5.00	2.50	1.50
70	Don Sutton	2.00	1.00	.60
71	Mark Belanger	.40	.20	.12
72	Dennis Leonard	.40	.20	.12
Panel 25		5.00	2.50	1.50
73	Gaylord Perry	1.50	.70	.45
74	Dick Ruthven	.40	.20	.12
75	Jose Cruz	.50	.25	.15
Panel 26		4.25	2.25	1.25
76	Cesar Geronimo	.40	.20	.12
77	Jerry Koosman	.50	.25	.15
78	Garry Templeton	.80	.40	.25
Panel 27		10.00	5.00	3.00
79	Jim Hunter	1.25	.60	.40
80	John Candelaria	.50	.25	.15
81	Nolan Ryan	3.50	1.75	1.00
Panel 28		2.50	1.25	.70
82	Rusty Staub	.50	.25	.15
83	Jim Barr	.40	.20	.12
84	Butch Wynegar	.50	.25	.15
Panel 29		2.50	1.25	.70
85	Jose Cardenal	.40	.20	.12
86	Claudell Washington	.50	.25	.15
87	Bill Travers	.40	.20	.12
Panel 30		2.50	1.25	.70
88	Rick Waits	.40	.20	.12
89	Ron Cey	.50	.25	.15
90	Al Bumbry	.40	.20	.12
Panel 31		2.50	1.25	.70
91	Bucky Dent	.50	.25	.15
92	Amos Otis	.50	.25	.15
93	Tom Grieve	.40	.20	.12
Panel 32		2.50	1.25	.70
94	Enos Cabell	.40	.20	.12
95	Dave Concepcion	.50	.25	.15
96	Felix Millan	.40	.20	.12
Panel 33		2.50	1.25	.70
97	Bake McBride	.40	.20	.12
98	Chris Chambliss	.50	.25	.15
99	Butch Metzger	.40	.20	.12
Panel 34		2.50	1.25	.70
100	Rennie Stennett	.40	.20	.12
101	Dave Roberts	.40	.20	.12
102	Lyman Bostock	.50	.25	.15
Panel 35		3.50	1.75	1.00
103	Rick Reuschel	.50	.25	.15
104	Carlton Fisk	1.00	.50	.30
105	Jim Slaton	.40	.20	.12
Panel 36		2.50	1.25	.70
106	Dennis Eckersley	.60	.30	.20
107	Ken Singleton	.50	.25	.15
108	Ralph Garr	.40	.20	.12
Panel 37		8.00	4.00	2.50
109	Freddie Patek	.50	.25	.15
110	Jim Sundberg	.60	.30	.20
111	Phil Niekro	3.25	1.75	1.00
Panel 38		3.50	1.75	1.00
112	J.R. Richard	.70	.35	.20
113	Gary Nolan	.50	.25	.15
114	Jon Matlack	.60	.30	.20
Panel 39		20.00	10.00	6.00
115	Keith Hernandez	4.00	2.00	1.25

		NR MT	EX	VG
116	Graig Nettles	.70	.35	.20
117	Steve Carlton	4.50	2.25	1.25
Panel 40		6.50	3.25	2.00
118	Bill Madlock	1.50	.70	.45
119	Jerry Reuss	.80	.40	.25
120	Aurelio Rodriguez	.50	.25	.15
Panel 41		3.50	1.75	1.00
121	Dan Ford	.50	.25	.15
122	Ray Fosse	.50	.25	.15
123	George Hendrick	.70	.35	.20
Panel 42		2.50	1.25	.70
124	Alan Ashby	.40	.20	.12
125	Joe Lis	.40	.20	.12
126	Sal Bando	.50	.25	.15
Panel 43		4.00	2.00	1.25
127	Richie Zisk	.50	.25	.15
128	Rich Gossage	.90	.45	.25
129	Don Baylor	.60	.30	.20
Panel 44		2.50	1.25	.70
130	Dave McKay	.40	.20	.12
131	Bob Grich	.50	.25	.15
132	Dave Pagan	.40	.20	.12
Panel 45		2.50	1.25	.70
133	Dave Cash	.40	.20	.12
134	Steve Braun	.40	.20	.12
135	Dan Meyer	.40	.20	.12
Panel 46		4.25	2.25	1.25
136	Bill Stein	.40	.20	.12
137	Rollie Fingers	1.50	.70	.45
138	Brian Downing	.50	.25	.15
Panel 47		2.50	1.25	.70
139	Bill Singer	.40	.20	.12
140	Doyle Alexander	.50	.25	.15
141	Gene Tenace	.40	.20	.12
Panel 48		2.50	1.25	.70
142	Gary Matthews	.50	.25	.15
143	Don Gullett	.40	.20	.12
144	Wayne Garland	.40	.20	.12
Panel 49		2.50	1.25	.70
145	Pete Broberg	.40	.20	.12
146	Joe Rudi	.50	.25	.15
147	Glenn Abbott	.40	.20	.12
Panel 50		2.50	1.25	.70
148	George Scott	.50	.25	.15
149	Bert Campaneris	.50	.25	.15
150	Andy Messersmith	.50	.25	.15

1977 Hostess Twinkies

The 1977 Hostess Twinkie issue, at 150 different cards, is the largest of the single-panel Twinkie sets. It is also the most obscure. The cards, which measure 2-1/4" by 3-1/4", but are part of a larger panel, were found not only with Twinkies, but with Hostess Cupcakes as well. Card #'s 1-30 and 111-150 are Twinkies panels and #'s 31-135 are Cupcakes panels. Complete Cupcakes panels are approximately 2-1/4" by 4-1/2" in size, while complete Twinkies panels measure 3-1/8" by 4-1/4". The photos used in the set are identical to those in the 1977 Hostess three-card panel set. The main difference is the appearance of a black band at the center of the card back. The values quoted in the checklist that follows are for complete bottom panels.

	NR MT	EX	VG
Complete Set:	325.00	162.00	97.00

	Common Player:	NR MT .80	EX .40	VG .25
1	Jim Palmer	6.00	3.00	1.75
2	Joe Morgan	4.00	2.00	1.25
3	Reggie Jackson	10.00	5.00	3.00
4	Carl Yastrzemski	12.00	6.00	3.50
5	Thurman Munson	5.00	2.50	1.50
6	Johnny Bench	8.00	4.00	2.50
7	Tom Seaver	7.00	3.50	2.00
8	Pete Rose	15.00	7.50	4.50
9	Rod Carew	8.00	4.00	2.50
10	Luis Tiant	1.00	.50	.30
11	Phil Garner	.80	.40	.25
12	Sixto Lezcano	.80	.40	.25
13	Mike Torrez	.80	.40	.25
14	Dave Lopes	1.00	.50	.30
15	Doug DeCinces	1.00	.50	.30
16	Jim Spencer	.80	.40	.25
17	Hal McRae	1.00	.50	.30
18	Mike Hargrove	.80	.40	.25
19	Willie Montanez	.80	.40	.25
20	Roger Metzger	.80	.40	.25
21	Dwight Evans	2.00	1.00	.60
22	Steve Rogers	.80	.40	.25
23	Jim Rice	6.00	3.00	1.75
24	Pete Falcone	.80	.40	.25
25	Greg Luzinski	1.50	.70	.45
26	Randy Jones	.80	.40	.25
27	Willie Stargell	6.00	3.00	1.75
28	John Hiller	.80	.40	.25
29	Bobby Murcer	1.25	.60	.40
30	Rick Monday	1.00	.50	.30
31	John Montefusco	.80	.40	.25
32	Lou Brock	6.00	3.00	1.75
33	Bill North	.80	.40	.25
34	Robin Yount	6.00	3.00	1.75
35	Steve Garvey	7.00	3.50	2.00
36	George Brett	10.00	5.00	3.00
37	Toby Harrah	.80	.40	.25
38	Jerry Royster	.80	.40	.25
39	Bob Watson	1.00	.50	.30
40	George Foster	1.75	.90	.50
41	Gary Carter	7.00	3.50	2.00
42	John Denny	.80	.40	.25
43	Mike Schmidt	9.00	4.50	2.75
44	Dave Winfield	7.00	3.50	2.00
45	Al Oliver	1.75	.90	.50
46	Mark Fidrych	1.50	.70	.45
47	Larry Herndon	1.00	.50	.30
48	Dave Goltz	.80	.40	.25
49	Jerry Morales	.80	.40	.25
50	Ron LeFlore	1.00	.50	.30
51	Fred Lynn	1.75	.90	.50
52	Vida Blue	1.00	.50	.30
53	Rick Manning	.80	.40	.25
54	Bill Buckner	1.50	.70	.45
55	Lee May	1.00	.50	.30
56	John Mayberry	.80	.40	.25
57	Darrel Chaney	.80	.40	.25
58	Cesar Cedeno	1.25	.60	.40
59	Ken Griffey	1.25	.60	.40
60	Dave Kingman	1.75	.90	.50
61	Ted Simmons	1.50	.70	.45
62	Larry Bowa	1.25	.60	.40
63	Frank Tanana	1.00	.50	.30
64	Jason Thompson	.80	.40	.25
65	Ken Brett	.80	.40	.25
66	Roy Smalley	.80	.40	.25
67	Ray Burris	.80	.40	.25
68	Rick Burleson	.80	.40	.25
69	Buddy Bell	1.25	.60	.40
70	Don Sutton	3.50	1.75	1.00
71	Mark Belanger	.80	.40	.25
72	Dennis Leonard	.80	.40	.25
73	Gaylord Perry	4.00	2.00	1.25
74	Dick Ruthven	.80	.40	.25
75	Jose Cruz	1.25	.60	.40
76	Cesar Geronimo	.80	.40	.25
77	Jerry Koosman	1.25	.60	.40
78	Garry Templeton	2.50	1.25	.70
79	Jim Hunter	4.00	2.00	1.25
80	John Candelaria	1.00	.50	.30
81	Nolan Ryan	7.00	3.50	2.00
82	Rusty Staub	1.50	.70	.45
83	Jim Barr	.80	.40	.25
84	Butch Wynegar	1.00	.50	.30
85	Jose Cardenal	.80	.40	.25
86	Claudell Washington	1.00	.50	.30
87	Bill Travers	.80	.40	.25
88	Rick Waits	.80	.40	.25
89	Ron Cey	1.25	.60	.40

		NR MT	EX	VG
90	Al Bumbry	.80	.40	.25
91	Bucky Dent	1.00	.50	.30
92	Amos Otis	1.00	.50	.30
93	Tom Grieve	.80	.40	.25
94	Enos Cabell	.80	.40	.25
95	Dave Concepcion	1.25	.60	.40
96	Felix Millan	.80	.40	.25
97	Bake McBride	.80	.40	.25
98	Chris Chambliss	1.00	.50	.30
99	Butch Metzger	.80	.40	.25
100	Rennie Stennett	.80	.40	.25
101	Dave Roberts	.80	.40	.25
102	Lyman Bostock	1.00	.50	.30
103	Rick Reuschel	1.00	.50	.30
104	Carlton Fisk	2.25	1.25	.70
105	Jim Slaton	.80	.40	.25
106	Dennis Eckersley	1.25	.60	.40
107	Ken Singleton	1.00	.50	.30
108	Ralph Garr	.80	.40	.25
109	Freddie Patek	.80	.40	.25
110	Jim Sundberg	.80	.40	.25
111	Phil Niekro	3.50	1.75	1.00
112	J. R. Richard	1.00	.50	.30
113	Gary Nolan	.80	.40	.25
114	Jon Matlack	.80	.40	.25
115	Keith Hernandez	5.00	2.50	1.50
116	Graig Nettles	2.00	1.00	.60
117	Steve Carlton	7.00	3.50	2.00
118	Bill Madlock	1.50	.70	.45
119	Jerry Reuss	1.00	.50	.30
120	Aurelio Rodriguez	.80	.40	.25
121	Dan Ford	.80	.40	.25
122	Ray Fosse	.80	.40	.25
123	George Hendrick	1.00	.50	.30
124	Alan Ashby	.80	.40	.25
125	Joe Lis	.80	.40	.25
126	Sal Bando	1.00	.50	.30
127	Richie Zisk	1.00	.50	.30
128	Rich Gossage	1.75	.90	.50
129	Don Baylor	1.50	.70	.45
130	Dave McKay	.80	.40	.25
131	Bob Grich	1.00	.50	.30
132	Dave Pagan	.80	.40	.25
133	Dave Cash	.80	.40	.25
134	Steve Braun	.80	.40	.25
135	Dan Meyer	.80	.40	.25
136	Bill Stein	.80	.40	.25
137	Rollie Fingers	3.00	1.50	.90
138	Brian Downing	1.00	.50	.30
139	Bill Singer	.80	.40	.25
140	Doyle Alexander	1.00	.50	.30
141	Gene Tenace	1.00	.50	.30
142	Gary Matthews	1.00	.50	.30
143	Don Gullett	.80	.40	.25
144	Wayne Garland	.80	.40	.25
145	Pete Broberg	.80	.40	.25
146	Joe Rudi	1.00	.50	.30
147	Glenn Abbott	.80	.40	.25
148	George Scott	1.00	.50	.30
149	Bert Campaneris	1.25	.60	.40
150	Andy Messersmith	1.00	.50	.30

1978 Hostess

MICKEY RIVERS
NEW YORK YANKEES   cf

Other than the design on the front of the card, there was little different about the 1978 Hostess cards from the three years' issues which had preceded it, or the one which followed. The 2-1/4" by 3-1/4" cards were printed in panels of three

(7-1/4" by 3-1/4") as the bottom of family-sized boxes of snake cakes. The 1978 set was again complete at 150 cards. Like other years of Hostess issues, there are scarcities within the 1978 set that are the result of those panels having been issued with less-popular brands of snake cakes.

		NR MT	EX	VG
Complete Panel:		300.00	150.00	90.00
Complete Singles Set:		175.00	87.00	52.00
Common Panel:		2.50	1.25	.70
Common Single Player:		.40	.20	.12
Panel 1		4.00	2.00	1.25
1	Butch Hobson	.40	.20	.12
2	George Foster	.90	.45	.25
3	Bob Forsch	.50	.25	.15
Panel 2		5.00	2.50	1.50
4	Tony Perez	1.00	.50	.30
5	Bruce Sutter	.90	.45	.25
6	Hal McRae	.50	.25	.15
Panel 3		6.00	3.00	1.75
7	Tommy John	1.50	.70	.45
8	Greg Luzinski	.50	.25	.15
9	Enos Cabell	.40	.20	.12
Panel 4		7.00	3.50	2.00
10	Doug DeCinces	.50	.25	.15
11	Willie Stargell	3.00	1.50	.90
12	Ed Halicki	.40	.20	.12
Panel 5		2.50	1.25	.70
13	Larry Hisle	.40	.20	.12
14	Jim Slaton	.40	.20	.12
15	Buddy Bell	.50	.25	.15
Panel 6		2.50	1.25	.70
16	Earl Williams	.40	.20	.12
17	Glenn Abbott	.40	.20	.12
18	Dan Ford	.40	.20	.12
Panel 7		2.50	1.25	.70
19	Gary Mathews	.50	.25	.15
20	Eric Soderholm	.40	.20	.12
21	Bump Wills	.40	.20	.12
Panel 8		7.00	3.50	2.00
22	Keith Hernandez	2.50	1.25	.70
23	Dave Cash	.40	.20	.12
24	George Scott	.50	.25	.15
Panel 9		15.00	7.50	4.50
25	Ron Guidry	1.50	.70	.45
26	Dave Kingman	.80	.40	.25
27	George Brett	5.00	2.50	1.50
Panel 10		3.50	1.75	1.00
28	Bob Watson	.50	.25	.15
29	Bob Boone	.70	.35	.20
30	Reggie Smith	.70	.35	.20
Panel 11		20.00	10.00	6.00
31	Eddie Murray	10.00	5.00	3.00
32	Gary Lavelle	.50	.25	.15
33	Rennie Stennett	.50	.25	.15
Panel 12		3.50	1.75	1.00
34	Duane Kuiper	.50	.25	.15
35	Sixto Lezcano	.50	.25	.15
36	Dave Rozema	.50	.25	.15
Panel 13		3.50	1.75	1.00
37	Butch Wynegar	.50	.25	.15
38	Mitchell Page	.50	.25	.15
39	Bill Stein	.50	.25	.15
Panel 14		2.50	1.25	.70
40	Elliott Maddox	.40	.20	.12
41	Mike Hargrove	.40	.20	.12
42	Bobby Bonds	.50	.25	.15
Panel 15		15.00	7.50	4.50
43	Garry Templeton	.80	.40	.25
44	Johnny Bench	4.00	2.00	1.25
45	Jim Rice	4.00	2.00	1.25
Panel 16		13.00	6.50	4.00
46	Bill Buckner	.80	.40	.25
47	Reggie Jackson	5.00	2.50	1.50
48	Freddie Patek	.40	.20	.12
Panel 17		8.50	4.25	2.50
49	Steve Carlton	3.50	1.75	1.00
50	Cesar Cedeno	.50	.25	.15
51	Steve Yeager	.40	.20	.12
Panel 18		3.50	1.75	1.00
52	Phil Garner	.50	.25	.15
53	Lee May	.50	.25	.15
54	Darrell Evans	.70	.35	.20
Panel 19		2.50	1.25	.70
55	Steve Kemp	.50	.25	.15
56	Dusty Baker	.50	.25	.15
57	Ray Fosse	.40	.20	.12
Panel 20		2.50	1.25	.70

		NR MT	EX	VG
58	Manny Sanguillen	.40	.20	.12
59	Tom Johnson	.40	.20	.12
60	Lee Stanton	.40	.20	.12
Panel 21		10.00	5.00	3.00
61	Jeff Burroughs	.40	.20	.12
62	Bobby Grich	.50	.25	.15
63	Dave Winfield	4.00	2.00	1.25
Panel 22		3.50	1.75	1.00
64	Dan Driessen	.50	.25	.15
65	Ted Simmons	.80	.40	.25
66	Jerry Remy	.40	.20	.12
Panel 23		2.50	1.25	.70
67	Al Cowens	.40	.20	.12
68	Sparky Lyle	.50	.25	.15
69	Manny Trillo	.50	.25	.15
Panel 24		5.00	2.50	1.50
70	Don Sutton	1.50	.70	.45
71	Larry Bowa	.50	.25	.15
72	Jose Cruz	.50	.25	.15
Panel 25		8.00	4.00	2.50
73	Willie McCovey	3.00	1.50	.90
74	Bert Blyleven	.70	.35	.20
75	Ken Singleton	.50	.25	.15
Panel 26		2.50	1.25	.70
76	Bill North	.40	.20	.12
77	Jason Thompson	.40	.20	.12
78	Dennis Eckersley	.50	.25	.15
Panel 27		2.50	1.25	.70
79	Jim Sundberg	.50	.25	.15
80	Jerry Koosman	.50	.25	.15
81	Bruce Bochte	.40	.20	.12
Panel 28		8.50	4.25	2.50
82	George Hendrick	.50	.25	.15
83	Nolan Ryan	3.50	1.75	1.00
84	Roy Howell	.40	.20	.12
Panel 29		5.50	2.75	1.75
85	Butch Metzger	.40	.20	.12
86	George Medich	.40	.20	.12
87	Joe Morgan	2.00	1.00	.60
Panel 30		3.00	1.50	.90
88	Dennis Leonard	.50	.25	.15
89	Willie Randolph	.50	.25	.15
90	Bobby Murcer	.50	.25	.15
Panel 31		3.00	1.50	.90
91	Rick Manning	.40	.20	.12
92	J.R. Richard	.50	.25	.15
93	Ron Cey	.60	.30	.20
Panel 32		2.50	1.25	.70
94	Sal Bando	.50	.25	.15
95	Ron LeFlore	.50	.25	.15
96	Dave Goltz	.40	.20	.12
Panel 33		2.50	1.25	.70
97	Dan Meyer	.40	.20	.12
98	Chris Chambliss	.50	.25	.15
99	Biff Pocoroba	.40	.20	.12
Panel 34		2.50	1.25	.70
100	Oscar Gamble	.40	.20	.12
101	Frank Tanana	.50	.25	.15
102	Lenny Randle	.40	.20	.12
Panel 35		2.50	1.25	.70
103	Tommy Hutton	.40	.20	.12
104	John Candelaria	.50	.25	.15
105	Jorge Orta	.40	.20	.12
Panel 36		3.00	1.50	.90
106	Ken Reitz	.40	.20	.12
107	Bill Campbell	.40	.20	.12
108	Dave Concepcion	.70	.35	.20
Panel 37		2.50	1.25	.70
109	Joe Ferguson	.40	.20	.12
110	Mickey Rivers	.50	.25	.15
111	Paul Splittorff	.40	.20	.12
Panel 38		12.00	6.00	3.50
112	Davey Lopes	.50	.25	.15
113	Mike Schmidt	5.00	2.50	1.50
114	Joe Rudi	.50	.25	.15
Panel 39		7.00	3.50	2.00
115	Milt May	.40	.20	.12
116	Jim Palmer	3.00	1.50	.90
117	Bill Madlock	.70	.35	.20
Panel 40		2.50	1.25	.70
118	Roy Smalley	.40	.20	.12
119	Cecil Cooper	.50	.25	.15
120	Rick Langford	.40	.20	.12
Panel 41		5.75	3.00	1.75
121	Ruppert Jones	.40	.20	.12
122	Phil Niekro	2.25	1.25	.70
123	Toby Harrah	.50	.25	.15
Panel 42		2.50	1.25	.70
124	Chet Lemon	.50	.25	.15
125	Gene Tenace	.40	.20	.12
126	Steve Henderson	.40	.20	.12

	NR MT	EX	VG
Panel 43	20.00	10.00	6.00
127 Mike Torrez	.40	.20	.12
128 Pete Rose	8.00	4.00	2.50
129 John Denny	.50	.25	.15
Panel 44	4.00	2.00	1.25
130 Darrell Porter	.50	.25	.15
131 Rick Reuschel	.50	.25	.15
132 Graig Nettles	.90	.45	.25
Panel 45	4.50	2.25	1.25
133 Garry Maddox	.50	.25	.15
134 Mike Flanagan	.50	.25	.15
135 Dave Parker	1.25	.60	.40
Panel 46	7.50	3.75	2.25
136 Terry Whitfield	.40	.20	.12
137 Wayne Garland	.40	.20	.12
138 Robin Yount	3.00	1.50	.90
Panel 47	12.00	6.00	3.50
139 Gaylord Perry	2.50	1.25	.70
140 Rod Carew	4.00	2.00	1.25
141 Wayne Gross	.40	.20	.12
Panel 48	5.00	2.50	1.50
142 Barry Bonnell	.40	.20	.12
143 Willie Montanez	.40	.20	.12
144 Rollie Fingers	1.75	.90	.50
Panel 49	12.00	6.00	3.50
145 Bob Bailor	.40	.20	.12
146 Tom Seaver	3.50	1.75	1.00
147 Thurman Munson	2.50	1.25	.70
Panel 50	8.00	4.00	2.50
148 Lyman Bostock	.50	.25	.15
149 Gary Carter	3.50	1.75	1.00
150 Ron Blomberg	.40	.20	.12

1979 Hostess

The last of five consecutive annual issues, the 1979 Hostess set retained the 150-card set size, 2-1/4" by 3-1/4" single-card size and 7-1/4" by 3-1/4" three-card panel format from the previous years. The cards were printed as the bottom panel on family-size boxes of Hostess snack cakes. Some panels, which were printed on less-popular brands, are somewhat scarcer today than the rest of the set. Like all Hostess issues, because the hobby was in a well-developed state at the time of issue, the 1979s survive today in complete panels and complete unused boxes, for collectors who like original packaging.

	NR MT	EX	VG
Complete Panel Set:	325.00	162.00	97.00
Complete Singles Set:	175.00	87.00	52.00
Common Panel:	2.50	1.25	.70
Common Single Player:	.40	.20	.12
Panel 1	9.50	4.75	2.75
1 John Denny	.40	.20	.12
2 Jim Rice	4.00	2.00	1.25
3 Doug Bair	.40	.20	.12
Panel 2	2.50	1.25	.70
4 Darrell Porter	.50	.25	.15
5 Ross Grimsley	.40	.20	.12
6 Bobby Murcer	.50	.25	.15
Panel 3	18.00	9.00	5.50
7 Lee Mazzilli	.50	.25	.15
8 Steve Garvey	4.00	2.00	1.25
9 Mike Schmidt	5.00	2.50	1.50

	NR MT	EX	VG
Panel 4	6.50	3.25	2.00
10 Terry Whitfield	.40	.20	.12
11 Jim Palmer	3.00	1.50	.90
12 Omar Moreno	.40	.20	.12
Panel 5	2.50	1.25	.70
13 Duane Kuiper	.40	.20	.12
14 Mike Caldwell	.40	.20	.12
15 Steve Kemp	.50	.25	.15
Panel 6	2.50	1.25	.70
16 Dave Goltz	.40	.20	.12
17 Mitchell Page	.40	.20	.12
18 Bill Stein	.40	.20	.12
Panel 7	2.50	1.25	.70
19 Gene Tenace	.40	.20	.12
20 Jeff Burroughs	.40	.20	.12
21 Francisco Barrios	.40	.20	.12
Panel 8	8.00	4.00	2.50
22 Mike Torrez	.40	.20	.12
23 Ken Reitz	.40	.20	.12
24 Gary Carter	3.50	1.75	1.00
Panel 9	8.00	4.00	2.50
25 Al Hrabosky	.50	.25	.15
26 Thurman Munson	2.50	1.25	.70
27 Bill Buckner	.80	.40	.25
Panel 10	5.00	2.50	1.50
28 Ron Cey	.90	.45	.25
29 J.R. Richard	.70	.35	.20
30 Greg Luzinski	.90	.45	.25
Panel 11	5.00	2.50	1.50
31 Ed Ott	.50	.25	.15
32 Denny Martinez	.50	.25	.15
33 Darrell Evans	1.25	.60	.40
Panel 12	2.50	1.25	.70
34 Ron LeFlore	.50	.25	.15
35 Rick Waits	.40	.20	.12
36 Cecil Cooper	.50	.25	.15
Panel 13	9.50	4.75	2.75
37 Leon Roberts	.40	.20	.12
38 Rod Carew	4.00	2.00	1.25
39 John Henry Johnson	.40	.20	.12
Panel 14	2.50	1.25	.70
40 Chet Lemon	.50	.25	.15
41 Craig Swan	.40	.20	.12
42 Gary Matthews	.50	.25	.15
Panel 15	3.50	1.75	1.00
43 Lamar Johnson	.40	.20	.12
44 Ted Simmons	.80	.40	.25
45 Ken Griffey	.50	.25	.15
Panel 16	4.00	2.00	1.25
46 Freddie Patek	.40	.20	.12
47 Frank Tanana	.50	.25	.15
48 Rich Gossage	1.25	.60	.40
Panel 17	2.50	1.25	.70
49 Burt Hooton	.40	.20	.12
50 Ellis Valentine	.40	.20	.12
51 Ken Forsch	.40	.20	.12
Panel 18	5.00	2.50	1.50
52 Bob Knepper	.50	.25	.15
53 Dave Parker	1.50	.70	.45
54 Doug DeCinces	.50	.25	.15
Panel 19	8.00	4.00	2.50
55 Robin Yount	3.00	1.50	.90
56 Rusty Staub	.80	.40	.25
57 Gary Alexander	.40	.20	.12
Panel 20	2.50	1.25	.70
58 Julio Cruz	.40	.20	.12
59 Matt Keough	.40	.20	.12
60 Roy Smalley	.40	.20	.12
Panel 21	10.00	5.00	3.00
61 Joe Morgan	2.50	1.25	.70
62 Phil Niekro	2.50	1.25	.70
63 Don Baylor	.80	.40	.25
Panel 22	10.00	5.00	3.00
64 Dwight Evans	.90	.45	.25
65 Tom Seaver	4.00	2.00	1.25
66 George Hendrick	.50	.25	.15
Panel 23	14.00	7.00	4.25
67 Rick Reuschel	.50	.25	.15
68 Geroge Brett	6.00	3.00	1.75
69 Lou Piniella	.80	.40	.25
Panel 24	8.50	4.25	2.50
70 Enos Cabell	.40	.20	.12
71 Steve Carlton	3.50	1.75	1.00
72 Reggie Smith	.50	.25	.15
Panel 25	4.00	2.00	1.25
73 Rick Dempsey	.50	.25	.15
74 Vida Blue	.80	.40	.25
75 Phil Garner	.70	.35	.20
Panel 26	3.50	1.75	1.00
76 Rick Manning	.50	.25	.15
77 Mark Fidrych	.80	.40	.25

		NR MT	EX	VG
78	Mario Guerrero	.50	.25	.15
Panel 27		5.00	2.50	1.50
79	Bob Stinson	.50	.25	.15
80	Al Oliver	1.25	.60	.40
81	Doug Flynn	.50	.25	.15
Panel 28		6.00	3.00	1.75
82	John Mayberry	.40	.20	.12
83	Gaylord Perry	2.50	1.25	.70
84	Joe Rudi	.50	.25	.15
Panel 29		3.50	1.75	1.00
85	Dave Concepcion	.70	.35	.20
86	John Candelaria	.50	.25	.15
87	Pete Vuckovich	.50	.25	.15
Panel 30		5.00	2.50	1.50
88	Ivan DeJesus	.40	.20	.12
89	Ron Guidry	1.50	.70	.45
90	Hal McRae	.50	.25	.15
Panel 31		5.50	2.75	1.75
91	Cesar Cedeno	.50	.25	.15
92	Don Sutton	2.00	1.00	.60
93	Andre Thornton	.50	.25	.15
Panel 32		2.50	1.25	.70
94	Roger Erickson	.40	.20	.12
95	Larry Hisle	.40	.20	.12
96	Jason Thompson	.40	.20	.12
Panel 33		7.50	3.75	2.25
97	Jim Sundberg	.50	.25	.15
98	Bob Horner	3.00	1.50	.90
99	Ruppert Jones	.40	.20	.12
Panel 34		8.50	4.25	2.50
100	Willie Montanez	.40	.20	.12
101	Nolan Ryan	3.50	1.75	1.00
102	Ozzie Smith	.70	.35	.20
Panel 35		7.50	3.75	2.25
103	Eric Soderholm	.40	.20	.12
104	Willie Stargell	3.00	1.50	.90
105	Bob Bailor	.40	.20	.12
Panel 36		9.00	4.50	2.75
106	Carlton Fisk	1.25	.60	.40
107	George Foster	.90	.45	.25
108	Keith Hernandez	2.50	1.25	.70
Panel 37		4.00	2.00	1.25
109	Dennis Leonard	.50	.25	.15
110	Graig Nettles	.90	.45	.25
111	Jose Cruz	.50	.25	.15
Panel 38		3.50	1.75	1.00
112	Bobby Grich	.50	.25	.15
113	Bob Boone	.50	.25	.15
114	Dave Lopes	.50	.25	.15
Panel 39		15.00	7.50	4.50
115	Eddie Murray	4.50	2.25	1.25
116	Jack Clark	.90	.45	.25
117	Lou Whitaker	.50	.25	.15
Panel 40		10.00	5.00	3.00
118	Miguel Dilone	.40	.20	.12
119	Sal Bando	.50	.25	.15
120	Reggie Jackson	4.50	2.25	1.25
Panel 41		14.00	7.00	4.25
121	Dale Murphy	7.00	3.50	2.00
122	Jon Matlack	.40	.20	.12
123	Bruce Bochte	.40	.20	.12
Panel 42		9.00	4.50	2.75
124	John Stearns	.40	.20	.12
125	Dave Winfield	3.50	1.75	1.00
126	Jorge Orta	.40	.20	.12
Panel 43		9.00	4.50	2.75
127	Garry Templeton	.70	.35	.20
128	Johnny Bench	4.00	2.00	1.25
129	Butch Hobson	.40	.20	.12
Panel 44		4.50	2.25	1.25
130	Bruce Sutter	1.25	.60	.40
131	Bucky Dent	.50	.25	.15
132	Amos Otis	.50	.25	.15
Panel 45		3.50	1.75	1.00
133	Bert Blyleven	.70	.35	.20
134	Larry Bowa	.50	.25	.15
135	Ken Singleton	.50	.25	.15
Panel 46		3.50	1.75	1.00
136	Sixto Lezcano	.40	.20	.12
137	Roy Howell	.40	.20	.12
138	Bill Madlock	.80	.40	.25
Panel 47		2.50	1.25	.70
139	Dave Revering	.40	.20	.12
140	Richie Zisk	.50	.25	.15
141	Butch Wynegar	.50	.25	.15
Panel 48		18.00	9.00	5.50
142	Alan Ashby	.40	.20	.12
143	Sparky Lyle	.50	.25	.15
144	Pete Rose	8.00	4.00	2.50
Panel 49		4.00	2.00	1.25
145	Dennis Eckersley	.60	.30	.20

		NR MT	EX	VG
146	Dave Kingman	.80	.40	.25
147	Buddy Bell	.60	.30	.20
Panel 50		2.50	1.25	.70
148	Mike Hargrove	.40	.20	.12
149	Jerry Koosman	.50	.25	.15
150	Toby Harrah	.50	.25	.15

1985 Hostess Braves

After a five-year hiatus, Hostess returned to the production of baseball cards in 1985 with an Atlanta Braves team set. The 22 cards in the set were printed by Topps and inserted into packages of snack cake products, three cello-wrapped player cards and a header card per box. The 2-1/2" by 3-1/2" cards share a common back design with the regular-issue Topps cards of 1985.

		MT	NR MT	EX
Complete Set:		10.00	7.50	4.00
Common Player:		.35	.25	.14
1	Eddie Haas	.35	.25	.14
2	Len Barker	.35	.25	.14
3	Steve Bedrosian	.90	.70	.35
4	Bruce Benedict	.35	.25	.14
5	Rick Camp	.35	.25	.14
6	Rick Cerone	.35	.25	.14
7	Chris Chambliss	.40	.30	.15
8	Terry Forster	.35	.25	.14
9	Gene Garber	.35	.25	.14
10	Albert Hall	.50	.40	.20
11	Bob Horner	.70	.50	.30
12	Glenn Hubbard	.35	.25	.14
13	Brad Komminsk	.35	.25	.14
14	Rick Mahler	.40	.30	.15
15	Craig McMurtry	.35	.25	.14
16	Dale Murphy	2.00	1.50	.80
17	Ken Oberkfell	.40	.30	.15
18	Pascual Perez	.40	.30	.15
19	Gerald Perry	1.50	1.25	.60
20	Rafael Ramirez	.35	.25	.14
21	Bruce Sutter	.50	.40	.20
22	Claudell Washington	.40	.30	.15
----	Header Card	.10	.08	.04

1987 Hostess Stickers

Hostess of Canada issued a 30-card set of stickers

in specially marked bags of potato chips. One sticker, measuring 1-3/4" by 1-3/8" in size, was found in each bag. The stickers have full-color fronts with the player's name appearing in black type in a white band. The Hostess logo and the sticker number are also included on the fronts. The backs are written in both English and French and contain the player's name, position and team.

		MT	NR MT	EX
	Complete Set:	25.00	18.50	10.00
	Common Player:	.20	.15	.08
1	Jesse Barfield	.35	.25	.14
2	Ernie Whitt	.20	.15	.08
3	George Bell	1.00	.70	.40
4	Hubie Brooks	.20	.15	.08
5	Tim Wallach	.35	.25	.14
6	Floyd Youmans	.20	.15	.08
7	Dale Murphy	1.50	1.25	.60
8	Ryne Sandberg	1.00	.70	.40
9	Eric Davis	2.00	1.50	.80
10	Mike Scott	.35	.25	.14
11	Fernando Valenzuela	.75	.60	.30
12	Gary Carter	1.00	.70	.40
13	Mike Schmidt	1.50	1.25	.60
14	Tony Pena	.20	.15	.08
15	Ozzie Smith	.60	.45	.25
16	Tony Gwynn	1.25	.90	.50
17	Mike Krukow	.20	.15	.08
18	Eddie Murray	1.25	.90	.50
19	Wade Boggs	2.25	1.75	.90
20	Wally Joyner	2.00	1.50	.80
21	Harold Baines	.35	.25	.14
22	Brook Jacoby	.35	.25	.14
23	Lou Whitaker	.50	.40	.20
24	George Brett	1.50	1.25	.60
25	Robin Yount	.75	.60	.30
26	Kirby Puckett	1.25	.90	.50
27	Don Mattingly	3.50	2.75	1.50
28	Jose Canseco	3.00	2.25	1.25
29	Phil Bradley	.35	.25	.14
30	Pete O'Brien	.20	.15	.08

1988 Hostess Potato Chips Expos

The Expos and Blue Jays are showcased in this set of 24 discs (1-1/2" diameter). Full-color head shots are framed in white, surrounded by red stars. A yellow-banner "1988 Collectors Edition" label is printed (English and French) beneath the photo, followed by the player's name in black. Numbered disc backs are bilingual, blue and white, and include player name and stats. This set was distributed inside Hostess potato chip packages sold in Canada.

		MT	NR MT	EX
	Complete Panel Set:	12.00	9.00	4.75
	Complete Singles Set:	7.00	5.25	2.75
	Common Panel:	.75	.60	.30
	Common Single Player:	.25	.20	.10
	Panel	.90	.70	.35
1	Mitch Webster	.25	.20	.10

		MT	NR MT	EX
20	Lloyd Moseby	.40	.30	.15
	Panel	.90	.70	.35
2	Tim Burke	.25	.20	.10
23	Tom Henke	.40	.30	.15
	Panel	.80	.60	.30
3	Tom Foley	.25	.20	.10
13	Jim Clancy	.30	.25	.12
	Panel	.75	.60	.30
4	Herm Winningham	.25	.20	.10
14	Rance Mulliniks	.25	.20	.10
	Panel	1.25	.90	.50
5	Hubie Brooks	.40	.30	.15
24	Jimmy Key	.60	.45	.25
	Panel	1.00	.70	.40
6	Mike Fitzgerald	.25	.20	.10
17	Dave Stieb	.60	.45	.25
	Panel	2.25	1.75	.90
7	Tim Wallach	.70	.50	.30
15	Fred McGriff	1.00	.70	.40
	Panel	2.25	1.75	.90
8	Andres Galarraga	1.00	.70	.40
21	Tony Fernandez	.70	.50	.30
	Panel	.80	.60	.30
9	Floyd Youmans	.30	.25	.12
18	Mark Eichhorn	.30	.25	.12
	Panel	1.00	.70	.40
10	Neal Heaton	.25	.20	.10
19	Jesse Barfield	.70	.50	.30
	Panel	2.00	1.50	.80
11	Tim Raines	1.25	.90	.50
16	Ernie Whitt	.25	.20	.10
	Panel	1.75	1.25	.70
12	Casey Candaele	.25	.20	.10
22	George Bell	1.00	.70	.40

1953 Hunter Weiners Cardinals

From the great era of the regionally issued hot dog cards in the mid-1950s, the 1953 Hunter wieners set of St. Louis Cardinals is certainly among the rarest today. Originally issued in two-card panels, the cards are most often found as 2-1/4" by 3-1/4" singles today when they can be found at all. The cards feature a light blue facsimile autograph printed over the stat box at the bottom. They are blank-backed.

		NR MT	EX	VG
	Complete Set:	2300.00	1150.00	650.00
	Common Player:	60.00	30.00	18.00
(1)	Steve Bilko	60.00	30.00	18.00
(2)	Alpha Brazle	60.00	30.00	18.00
(3)	Cloyd Boyer	60.00	30.00	18.00
(4)	Cliff Chambers	60.00	30.00	18.00
(5)	Michael Clark	60.00	30.00	18.00
(6)	Jack Crimian	60.00	30.00	18.00
(7)	Lester Fusselman	60.00	30.00	18.00
(8)	Harvey Haddix	65.00	33.00	20.00
(9)	Solly Hemus	60.00	30.00	18.00
(10)	Ray Jablonski	60.00	30.00	18.00
(11)	William Johnson	60.00	30.00	18.00
(12)	Harry Lowrey	60.00	30.00	18.00
(13)	Lawrence Miggins	60.00	30.00	18.00
(14)	Stuart Miller	60.00	30.00	18.00
(15)	Wilmer Mizell	60.00	30.00	18.00

		NR MT	EX	VG
(16)	Stanley Musial	600.00	300.00	175.00
(17)	Joseph Presko	60.00	30.00	18.00
(18)	Delbert Rice	60.00	30.00	18.00
(19)	Harold Rice	60.00	30.00	18.00
(20)	Willard Schmidt	60.00	30.00	18.00
(21)	Albert Schoendienst	100.00	50.00	30.00
(22)	Richard Sisler	60.00	30.00	18.00
(23)	Enos Slaughter	150.00	75.00	45.00
(24)	Gerald Staley	60.00	30.00	18.00
(25)	Edward Stanky	70.00	35.00	21.00
(26)	John Yuhas	60.00	30.00	18.00

1954 Hunter Weiners Cardinals

A nearly impossible set to complete today by virtue of the method of its issue, the 1954 Hunter hot dog set essentially features what would traditionally be the front and back of a normal baseball card on two different cards. The "front," containing a color photo of one of 30 St. Louis Cardinals has a box at bottom challenging the collector to name him and quote his stats. The "back" features cartoon Cardinals in action, and contains the answers. However, because both parts were printed on a single panel, and because most of the back (non-picture) panels were thrown away years ago, it is an impossible challenge to complete a '54 Hunter set today. There is no back printing on the 2-1/4" by 3-1/2" cards.

		NR MT	EX	VG
Complete Set:		3900.00	1950.00	1170.
Common Player:		60.00	30.00	18.00
(1)	Tom Alston	60.00	30.00	18.00
(2)	Steve Bilko	60.00	30.00	18.00
(3)	Al Brazle	60.00	30.00	18.00
(4)	Tom Burgess	60.00	30.00	18.00
(5)	Cot Deal	60.00	30.00	18.00
(6)	Alex Grammas	60.00	30.00	18.00
(7)	Harvey Haddix	60.00	30.00	18.00
(8)	Solly Hemus	60.00	30.00	18.00
(9)	Ray Jablonski	60.00	30.00	18.00
(10)	Royce Lint	60.00	30.00	18.00
(11)	Peanuts Lowrey	60.00	30.00	18.00
(12)	Memo Luna	60.00	30.00	18.00
(13)	Stu Miller	60.00	30.00	18.00
(14)	Stan Musial	600.00	300.00	180.00
(15)	Tom Poholsky	60.00	30.00	18.00
(16)	Bill Posedel	60.00	30.00	18.00
(17)	Joe Presko	60.00	30.00	18.00
(18)	Vic Raschi	60.00	30.00	18.00
(19)	Dick Rand	60.00	30.00	18.00
(20)	Rip Repulski	60.00	30.00	18.00
(21)	Del Rice	60.00	30.00	18.00
(22)	John Riddle	60.00	30.00	18.00
(23)	Mike Ryba	60.00	30.00	18.00
(24)	Red Schoendienst	100.00	50.00	30.00
(25)	Dick Schofield	100.00	50.00	30.00
(26)	Eddie Stanky	110.00	55.00	33.00
(27)	Enos Slaughter	150.00	75.00	45.00
(28)	Gerry Staley	60.00	30.00	18.00
(29)	Ed Yuhas	60.00	30.00	18.00
(30)	Sal Yvars	60.00	30.00	18.00

1955 Hunter Weiners Cardinals

The 1955 team set of St. Louis Cardinals, included with packages of Hunter hot dogs, features the third format change in three years of issue. For 1955, the cards were printed in a tall, narrow 2" by 4-3/4" format, two to a panel. The cards featured both a posed action photo and a portrait photo, along with a facsimile autograph and brief biographical data on the front. There is no back printing, as the cards were part of the wrapping for packages of hot dogs.

		NR MT	EX	VG
Complete Set:		3200.00	1600.00	1500.
Common Player:		75.00	37.00	22.00
(1)	Thomas Edison Alston	75.00	37.00	22.00
(2)	Kenton Lloyd Boyer	225.00	112.00	67.00
(3)	Harry Lewis Elliott	75.00	37.00	22.00
(4)	John Edward Faszholz	75.00	37.00	22.00
(5)	Joseph Filmore Frazier	75.00	37.00	22.00
(6)	Alexander Pete Grammas	75.00	37.00	22.00
(7)	Harvey Haddix	125.00	62.00	37.00
(8)	Solly Joseph Hemus	75.00	37.00	22.00
(9)	Lawrence Curtis Jackson	75.00	37.00	22.00
(10)	Tony R. Jacobs	75.00	37.00	22.00
(11)	Gordon Bassett Jones	75.00	37.00	22.00
(12)	Paul Edmore LaPalme	75.00	37.00	22.00
(13)	Brooks Ulysses Lawrence	75.00	37.00	22.00
(14)	Wallace Wade Moon	125.00	62.00	37.00
(15)	Stanley Frank Musial	1000.00	500.00	300.00
(16)	Thomas George Poholsky	75.00	37.00	22.00
(17)	William John Posedel	75.00	37.00	22.00
(18)	Victor Angelo John Raschi	75.00	37.00	22.00
(19)	Eldon John Repulski	75.00	37.00	22.00
(20)	Delbert Rice	75.00	37.00	22.00
(21)	John Ludy Riddle	75.00	37.00	22.00
(22)	William F. Sarni	75.00	37.00	22.00
(23)	Albert Fred Schoendienst	175.00	87.00	52.00
(24)	Richard John Schofield (actually John Richard)	75.00	37.00	22.00
(25)	Frank Thomas Smith	75.00	37.00	22.00
(26)	Edward R. Stanky	125.00	62.00	37.00
(27)	Bobby Gene Tiefenauer	75.00	37.00	22.00
(28)	William Charles Virdon	175.00	87.00	52.00
(29)	Frederick E. Walker	75.00	37.00	22.00
(30)	Floyd Lewis Woolridge	75.00	37.00	22.00

Definitions for grading conditions are located in the Introduction of this price guide.

1982 Hygrade Expos

Gary Carter 8

BILLY SAMPLE OF

the Rangers

Billy Sample No. 5 OF

This 24-card Montreal Expos team set was the object of intense collector speculation when it was first issued. Single cello-wrapped cards were included in packages of Hygrade luncheon meat in the province of Quebec only. Until a mail-in offer for the complete set appeared later in the season, the set was selling for as high as $50. It remains a relatively scarce issue today. The 2" by 3" cards are printed on heavy paper, with round corners. Backs are printed only in French, and contain an offer for an album to house the set.

		MT	NR MT	EX
Complete Set:		40.00	30.00	16.00
Common Player:		1.00	.70	.40
Album:		6.00	4.50	2.50
0	Al Oliver	2.25	1.75	.90
4	Chris Speier	1.00	.70	.40
5	John Milner	1.00	.70	.40
6	Jim Fanning	1.00	.70	.40
8	Gary Carter	7.00	5.25	2.75
10	Andre Dawson	5.00	3.75	2.00
11	Frank Tavaras (Taveras)	1.00	.70	.40
16	Terry Francona	1.25	.90	.50
17	Tim Blackwell	1.00	.70	.40
18	Jerry White	1.00	.70	.40
20	Bob James	1.25	.90	.50
21	Scott Sanderson	1.00	.70	.40
24	Brad Mills	1.00	.70	.40
29	Tim Wallach	3.00	2.25	1.25
30	Tim Raines	7.00	5.25	2.75
34	Bill Gullickson	1.25	.90	.50
35	Woodie Fryman	1.00	.70	.40
38	Bryn Smith	1.50	1.25	.60
41	Jeff Reardon	2.00	1.50	.80
44	Dan Norman	1.00	.70	.40
45	Steve Rogers	1.25	.90	.50
48	Ray Burris	1.00	.70	.40
49	Warren Cromartie	1.00	.70	.40
53	Charlie Lea	1.00	.70	.40

1984 Jarvis Press Rangers

For its second annual "Baseball Card Day" game promotional set, the Rangers picked up a new sponsor, Jarvis Press of Dallas. The 30 cards in the set include 27 players, the manager, trainer and a group card of the coaches. Cards measure 2-3/8" by 3-1/2". Color game-action photos make up the card fronts. Backs, printed in black and white, include a portrait photo of the player. A source close to the promotion indicated 10,000 sets were produced.

		MT	NR MT	EX
Complete Set:		6.00	4.50	2.50
Common Player:		.12	.09	.05
1	Bill Stein	.12	.09	.05
2	Alan Bannister	.12	.09	.05
3	Wayne Tolleson	.12	.09	.05
5	Billy Sample	.12	.09	.05
6	Bobby Jones	.12	.09	.05
7	Ned Yost	.12	.09	.05
9	Pete O'Brien	.50	.40	.20
11	Doug Rader	.12	.09	.05
13	Tommy Dunbar	.12	.09	.05
14	Jim Anderson	.12	.09	.05
15	Larry Parrish	.30	.25	.12
16	Mike Mason	.12	.09	.05
17	Mickey Rivers	.20	.15	.08
19	Curtis Wilkerson	.12	.09	.05
20	Jeff Kunkel	.12	.09	.05
21	Odell Jones	.12	.09	.05
24	Dave Schmidt	.15	.11	.06
25	Buddy Bell	.50	.40	.20
26	George Wright	.12	.09	.05
28	Frank Tanana	.20	.15	.08
30	Marv Foley	.12	.09	.05
31	Dave Stewart	.40	.30	.15
32	Gary Ward	.20	.15	.08
36	Dickie Noles	.12	.09	.05
43	Donnie Scott	.12	.09	.05
44	Danny Darwin	.15	.11	.06
49	Charlie Hough	.30	.25	.12
53	Joey McLaughlin	.12	.09	.05
----	Coaching Staff (Rich Donnelly, Glenn Ezell, Merv Rettenmund, Dick Such, Wayne Terwilliger)	.12	.09	.05
----	Trainer (Bill Zeigler)	.12	.09	.05

1986 Jays Potato Chips

One of a handful of round baseball cards produced for inclusion in boxes of potato chips on a regional basis in 1986, the Jays set of 2-7/8" discs is believed to be the scarcest of the type. The 20 cards in the issue include the most popular Milwaukee Brewers and Chicago Cubs and White Sox players; the set having been distributed in the southern Wisconsin-northern Illinois area. Like many of the recent sets produced by Mike Schecter Associates, the '86 Jays cards feature player photos on which the team logos have been airbrushed off the caps.

		MT	NR MT	EX
	Complete Set:	25.00	18.50	10.00
	Common Player:	.60	.45	.25
(1)	Harold Baines	1.25	.90	.50
(2)	Cecil Cooper	1.00	.70	.40
(3)	Jody Davis	.75	.60	.30
(4)	Bob Dernier	.60	.45	.25
(5)	Richard Dotson	.75	.60	.30
(6)	Shawon Dunston	1.00	.70	.40
(7)	Carlton Fisk	1.50	1.25	.60
(8)	Jim Gantner	.60	.45	.25
(9)	Ozzie Guillen	.90	.70	.35
(10)	Teddy Higuera	1.75	1.25	.70
(11)	Ron Kittle	.75	.60	.30
(12)	Paul Molitor	1.50	1.25	.60
(13)	Keith Moreland	.75	.60	.30
(14)	Ernie Riles	.75	.60	.30
(15)	Ryne Sandberg	2.50	2.00	1.00
(16)	Tom Seaver	2.00	1.50	.80
(17)	Lee Smith	.90	.70	.35
(18)	Rick Sutcliffe	.90	.70	.35
(19)	Greg Walker	.90	.70	.35
(20)	Robin Yount	2.00	1.50	.80

1962 Jello

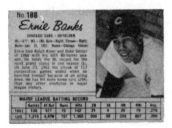

No. 188
Ernie Banks
CHICAGO CUBS – INFIELDER

Virtually identical in content to the 1962 Post cereal cards, the '62 Jell-O set of 197 was only issued in the Midwest. Players and card numbers are identical in the two sets, except Brooks Robinson (#29), Ted Kluszewski (#82) and Smoky Burgess (#176) were not issued in the Jell-O version. The Jell-O cards are easy to distinguish from the Post of that year by the absence of the red oval Post logo and red or blue border around the stat box. Cards which have been neatly trimmed from the box which they were printed will measure 3-1/2" by 2-1/2".

		NR MT	EX	VG
	Complete Set:	4300.00	2150.00	1290.
	Common Player:	6.00	3.00	1.75
1	Bill Skowron	20.00	10.00	6.00
2	Bobby Richardson	20.00	10.00	6.00
3	Cletis Boyer	10.00	5.00	3.00
4	Tony Kubek	15.00	7.50	4.50
5	Mickey Mantle	600.00	300.00	180.00
6	Roger Maris	100.00	50.00	30.00
7	Yogi Berra	60.00	30.00	18.00
8	Elston Howard	15.00	7.50	4.50
9	Whitey Ford	40.00	20.00	12.00
10	Ralph Terry	10.00	5.00	3.00
11	John Blanchard	7.00	3.50	2.00
12	Luis Arroyo	7.00	3.50	2.00
13	Bill Stafford	20.00	10.00	6.00
14	Norm Cash	10.00	5.00	3.00
15	Jake Wood	6.00	3.00	1.75
16	Steve Boros	6.00	3.00	1.75
17	Chico Fernandez	6.00	3.00	1.75
18	Billy Bruton	6.00	3.00	1.75
19	Ken Aspromonte	6.00	3.00	1.75
20	Al Kaline	40.00	20.00	12.00
21	Dick Brown	6.00	3.00	1.75
22	Frank Lary	7.00	3.50	2.00

		NR MT	EX	VG
23	Don Mossi	7.00	3.50	2.00
24	Phil Regan	6.00	3.00	1.75
25	Charley Maxwell	6.00	3.00	1.75
26	Jim Bunning	15.00	7.50	4.50
27	Jim Gentile	7.00	3.50	2.00
28	Marv Breeding	6.00	3.00	1.75
29	Not Issued			
30	Ron Hansen	6.00	3.00	1.75
31	Jackie Brandt	20.00	10.00	6.00
32	Dick Williams	7.00	3.50	2.00
33	Gus Triandos	7.00	3.50	2.00
34	Milt Pappas	7.00	3.50	2.00
35	Hoyt Wilhelm	25.00	12.50	7.50
36	Chuck Estrada	6.00	3.00	1.75
37	Vic Power	6.00	3.00	1.75
38	Johnny Temple	6.00	3.00	1.75
39	Bubba Phillips	20.00	10.00	6.00
40	Tito Francona	7.00	3.50	2.00
41	Willie Kirkland	6.00	3.00	1.75
42	John Romano	6.00	3.00	1.75
43	Jim Perry	10.00	5.00	3.00
44	Woodie Held	6.00	3.00	1.75
45	Chuck Essegian	6.00	3.00	1.75
46	Roy Sievers	7.00	3.50	2.00
47	Nellie Fox	15.00	7.50	4.50
48	Al Smith	6.00	3.00	1.75
49	Luis Aparicio	25.00	12.50	7.50
50	Jim Landis	6.00	3.00	1.75
51	Minnie Minoso	10.00	5.00	3.00
52	Andy Carey	20.00	10.00	6.00
53	Sherman Lollar	7.00	3.50	2.00
54	Bill Pierce	7.00	3.50	2.00
55	Early Wynn	25.00	12.50	7.50
56	Chuck Schilling	20.00	10.00	6.00
57	Pete Runnels	7.00	3.50	2.00
58	Frank Malzone	7.00	3.50	2.00
59	Don Buddin	10.00	5.00	3.00
60	Gary Geiger	6.00	3.00	1.75
61	Carl Yastrzemski	200.00	100.00	60.00
62	Jackie Jensen	20.00	10.00	6.00
63	Jim Pagliaroni	20.00	10.00	6.00
64	Don Schwall	6.00	3.00	1.75
65	Dale Long	7.00	3.50	2.00
66	Chuck Cottier	10.00	5.00	3.00
67	Billy Klaus	20.00	10.00	6.00
68	Coot Veal	6.00	3.00	1.75
69	Marty Keough	35.00	17.50	10.50
70	Willie Tasby	35.00	17.50	10.50
71	Gene Woodling	7.00	3.50	2.00
72	Gene Green	35.00	17.50	10.50
73	Dick Donovan	10.00	5.00	3.00
74	Steve Bilko	10.00	5.00	3.00
75	Rocky Bridges	20.00	10.00	6.00
76	Eddie Yost	10.00	5.00	3.00
77	Leon Wagner	10.00	5.00	3.00
78	Albie Pearson	10.00	5.00	3.00
79	Ken Hunt	10.00	5.00	3.00
80	Earl Averill	35.00	17.50	10.50
81	Ryne Duren	10.00	5.00	3.00
82	Not Issued			
83	Bob Allison	7.00	3.50	2.00
84	Billy Martin	15.00	7.50	4.50
85	Harmon Killebrew	35.00	17.50	10.50
86	Zorro Versalles	7.00	3.50	2.00
87	Lennie Green	20.00	10.00	6.00
88	Bill Tuttle	6.00	3.00	1.75
89	Jim Lemon	7.00	3.50	2.00
90	Earl Battey	20.00	10.00	6.00
91	Camilo Pascual	7.00	3.50	2.00
92	Norm Siebern	10.00	5.00	3.00
93	Jerry Lumpe	10.00	5.00	3.00
94	Dick Howser	10.00	5.00	3.00
95	Gene Stephens	35.00	17.50	10.50
96	Leo Posada	10.00	5.00	3.00
97	Joe Pignatano	10.00	5.00	3.00
98	Jim Archer	10.00	5.00	3.00
99	Haywood Sullivan	20.00	10.00	6.00
100	Art Ditmar	10.00	5.00	3.00
101	Gil Hodges	35.00	17.50	10.50
102	Charlie Neal	10.00	5.00	3.00
103	Daryl Spencer	10.00	5.00	3.00
104	Maury Wills	20.00	10.00	6.00
105	Tommy Davis	10.00	5.00	3.00
106	Willie Davis	10.00	5.00	3.00
107	John Roseboro	35.00	17.50	10.50
108	John Podres	10.00	5.00	3.00
109	Sandy Koufax	80.00	40.00	24.00
110	Don Drysdale	50.00	25.00	15.00
111	Larry Sherry	20.00	10.00	6.00
112	Jim Gilliam	20.00	10.00	6.00
113	Norm Larker	35.00	17.50	10.50

		NR MT	EX	VG
114	Duke Snider	70.00	35.00	21.00
115	Stan Williams	20.00	10.00	6.00
116	Gordon Coleman	70.00	35.00	21.00
117	Don Blasingame	20.00	10.00	6.00
118	Gene Freese	35.00	17.50	10.50
119	Ed Kasko	35.00	17.50	10.50
120	Gus Bell	20.00	10.00	6.00
121	Vada Pinson	10.00	5.00	3.00
122	Frank Robinson	35.00	17.50	10.50
123	Bob Purkey	10.00	5.00	3.00
124	Joey Jay	10.00	5.00	3.00
125	Jim Brosnan	10.00	5.00	3.00
126	Jim O'Toole	10.00	5.00	3.00
127	Jerry Lynch	10.00	5.00	3.00
128	Wally Post	10.00	5.00	3.00
129	Ken Hunt	10.00	5.00	3.00
130	Jerry Zimmerman	10.00	5.00	3.00
131	Willie McCovey	35.00	17.50	10.50
132	Jose Pagan	20.00	10.00	6.00
133	Felipe Alou	10.00	5.00	3.00
134	Jim Davenport	10.00	5.00	3.00
135	Harvey Kuenn	10.00	5.00	3.00
136	Orlando Cepeda	15.00	7.50	4.50
137	Ed Bailey	10.00	5.00	3.00
138	Sam Jones	10.00	5.00	3.00
139	Mike McCormick	10.00	5.00	3.00
140	Juan Marichal	40.00	20.00	12.00
141	Jack Sanford	10.00	5.00	3.00
142	Willie Mays	125.00	62.00	37.00
143	Stu Miller	70.00	35.00	21.00
144	Joe Amalfitano	10.00	5.00	3.00
145	Joe Adcock	10.00	5.00	3.00
146	Frank Bolling	6.00	3.00	1.75
147	Ed Mathews	35.00	17.50	10.50
148	Roy McMillan	7.00	3.50	2.00
149	Hank Aaron	125.00	62.00	37.00
150	Gino Cimoli	20.00	10.00	6.00
151	Frank Thomas	7.00	3.50	2.00
152	Joe Torre	10.00	5.00	3.00
153	Lou Burdette	10.00	5.00	3.00
154	Bob Buhl	7.00	3.50	2.00
155	Carlton Willey	6.00	3.00	1.75
156	Lee Maye	18.00	9.00	5.50
157	Al Spangler	35.00	17.50	10.50
158	Bill White	35.00	17.50	10.50
159	Ken Boyer	15.00	7.50	4.50
160	Joe Cunningham	10.00	5.00	3.00
161	Carl Warwick	10.00	5.00	3.00
162	Carl Sawatski	6.00	3.00	1.75
163	Lindy McDaniel	6.00	3.00	1.75
164	Ernie Broglio	10.00	5.00	3.00
165	Larry Jackson	6.00	3.00	1.75
166	Curt Flood	15.00	7.50	4.50
167	Curt Simmons	35.00	17.50	10.50
168	Alex Grammas	20.00	10.00	6.00
169	Dick Stuart	7.00	3.50	2.00
170	Bill Mazeroski	20.00	10.00	6.00
171	Don Hoak	10.00	5.00	3.00
172	Dick Groat	10.00	5.00	3.00
173	Roberto Clemente	125.00	62.00	37.00
174	Bob Skinner	20.00	10.00	6.00
175	Bill Virdon	35.00	17.50	10.50
176	Not Issued			
177	Elroy Face	10.00	5.00	3.00
178	Bob Friend	7.00	3.50	2.00
179	Vernon Law	20.00	10.00	6.00
180	Harvey Haddix	35.00	17.50	10.50
181	Hal Smith	20.00	10.00	6.00
182	Ed Bouchee	20.00	10.00	6.00
183	Don Zimmer	7.00	3.50	2.00
184	Ron Santo	10.00	5.00	3.00
185	Andre Rodgers	6.00	3.00	1.75
186	Richie Ashburn	15.00	7.50	4.50
187	George Altman	6.00	3.00	1.75
188	Ernie Banks	35.00	17.50	10.50
189	Sam Taylor	6.00	3.00	1.75
190	Don Elston	6.00	3.00	1.75
191	Jerry Kindall	20.00	10.00	6.00
192	Pancho Herrera	6.00	3.00	1.75
193	Tony Taylor	6.00	3.00	1.75
194	Ruben Amaro	20.00	10.00	6.00
195	Don Demeter	6.00	3.00	1.75
196	Bobby Gene Smith	6.00	3.00	1.75
197	Clay Dalrymple	6.00	3.00	1.75
198	Robin Roberts	25.00	12.50	7.50
199	Art Mahaffey	6.00	3.00	1.75
200	John Buzhardt	6.00	3.00	1.75

1963 Jello

Like the other Post and Jell-O issues of the era, the '63 Jell-O set includes many scarce cards; primarily those which were printed as the backs of less popular brands and sizes of the gelatin dessert. Slightly smaller than the virtually identical Post cereal cards of the same year, the 200 cards in the Jell-O issue measure 3-3/8" by 2-1/2". The easiest way to distinguish 1963 Jell-O cards from Post cards is by the red line that separates the 1962 stats from the lifetime stats. On Post cards, the line extends almost all the way to the side borders, on the Jell-O cards, the line begins and ends much closer to the stats.

		NR MT	EX	VG
	Complete Set:	2700.00	1350.00	810.00
	Common Player:	2.00	1.00	.60
1	Vic Power	2.50	1.25	.70
2	Bernie Allen	20.00	10.00	6.00
3	Zoilo Versalles	20.00	10.00	6.00
4	Rich Rollins	2.00	1.00	.60
5	Harmon Killebrew	8.00	4.00	2.50
6	Lenny Green	20.00	10.00	6.00
7	Bob Allison	3.00	1.50	.90
8	Earl Battey	15.00	7.50	4.50
9	Camilo Pascual	2.50	1.25	.70
10	Jim Kaat	35.00	17.50	10.50
11	Jack Kralick	2.00	1.00	.60
12	Bill Skowron	20.00	10.00	6.00
13	Bobby Richardson	5.00	2.50	1.50
14	Cletis Boyer	2.50	1.25	.70
15	Mickey Mantle	200.00	100.00	60.00
16	Roger Maris	20.00	10.00	6.00
17	Yogi Berra	20.00	10.00	6.00
18	Elston Howard	20.00	10.00	6.00
19	Whitey Ford	10.00	5.00	3.00
20	Ralph Terry	2.25	1.25	.70
21	John Blanchard	15.00	7.50	4.50
22	Bill Stafford	20.00	10.00	6.00
23	Tom Tresh	2.50	1.25	.70
24	Steve Bilko	2.00	1.00	.60
25	Bill Moran	2.00	1.00	.60
26	Joe Koppe	2.00	1.00	.60
27	Felix Torres	2.00	1.00	.60
28	Leon Wagner	2.50	1.25	.70
29	Albie Pearson	2.00	1.00	.60
30	Lee Thomas	2.00	1.00	.60
31	Bob Rodgers	20.00	10.00	6.00
32	Dean Chance	1.50	.70	.45
33	Ken McBride	20.00	10.00	6.00
34	George Thomas	20.00	10.00	6.00
35	Joe Cunningham	20.00	10.00	6.00
36	Nelson Fox	5.00	2.50	1.50
37	Luis Aparicio	6.00	3.00	1.75
38	Al Smith	2.00	1.00	.60
39	Floyd Robinson	2.00	1.00	.60
40	Jim Landis	2.00	1.00	.60
41	Charlie Maxwell	2.00	1.00	.60
42	Sherman Lollar	2.25	1.25	.70
43	Early Wynn	6.00	3.00	1.75
44	Juan Pizarro	20.00	10.00	6.00
45	Ray Herbert	20.00	10.00	6.00
46	Norm Cash	3.50	1.75	1.00
47	Steve Boros	20.00	10.00	6.00
48	Dick McAuliffe	2.25	1.25	.70
49	Bill Bruton	2.25	1.25	.70
50	Rocky Colavito	5.00	2.50	1.50

		NR MT	EX	VG
51	Al Kaline	12.00	6.00	3.50
52	Dick Brown	20.00	10.00	6.00
53	Jim Bunning	5.00	2.50	1.50
54	Hank Aguirre	2.00	1.00	.60
55	Frank Lary	20.00	10.00	6.00
56	Don Mossi	20.00	10.00	6.00
57	Jim Gentile	2.25	1.25	.70
58	Jackie Brandt	2.00	1.00	.60
59	Brooks Robinson	15.00	7.50	4.50
60	Ron Hansen	2.00	1.00	.60
61	Jerry Adair	55.00	27.00	16.50
62	John Powell	3.50	1.75	1.00
63	Russ Snyder	20.00	10.00	6.00
64	Steve Barber	2.00	1.00	.60
65	Milt Pappas	20.00	10.00	6.00
66	Robin Roberts	6.00	3.00	1.75
67	Tito Francona	2.25	1.25	.70
68	Jerry Kindall	20.00	10.00	6.00
69	Woodie Held	2.25	1.25	.70
70	Bubba Phillips	2.00	1.00	.60
71	Chuck Essegian	2.00	1.00	.60
72	Willie Kirkland	20.00	10.00	6.00
73	Al Luplow	2.00	1.00	.60
74	Ty Cline	20.00	10.00	6.00
75	Dick Donovan	2.00	1.00	.60
76	John Romano	2.00	1.00	.60
77	Pete Runnels	2.25	1.25	.70
78	Ed Bressoud	20.00	10.00	6.00
79	Frank Malzone	2.25	1.25	.70
80	Carl Yastrzemski	70.00	35.00	21.00
81	Gary Geiger	2.00	1.00	.60
82	Lou Clinton	20.00	10.00	6.00
83	Earl Wilson	2.50	1.25	.70
84	Bill Monbouquette	2.50	1.25	.70
85	Norm Siebern	2.50	1.25	.70
86	Jerry Lumpe	2.50	1.25	.70
87	Manny Jimenez	2.00	1.00	.60
88	Gino Cimoli	2.00	1.00	.60
89	Ed Charles	55.00	27.00	16.50
90	Ed Rakow	2.00	1.00	.60
91	Bob Del Greco	20.00	10.00	6.00
92	Haywood Sullivan	20.00	10.00	6.00
93	Chuck Hinton	2.00	1.00	.60
94	Ken Retzer	20.00	10.00	6.00
95	Harry Bright	20.00	10.00	6.00
96	Bob Johnson	2.00	1.00	.60
97	Dave Stenhouse	20.00	10.00	6.00
98	Chuck Cottier	2.25	1.25	.70
99	Tom Cheney	2.00	1.00	.60
100	Claude Osteen	20.00	10.00	6.00
101	Orlando Cepeda	5.00	2.50	1.50
102	Charley Hiller	20.00	10.00	6.00
103	Jose Pagan	20.00	10.00	6.00
104	Jim Davenport	2.00	1.00	.60
105	Harvey Kuenn	3.50	1.75	1.00
106	Willie Mays	60.00	30.00	18.00
107	Felipe Alou	3.00	1.50	.90
108	Tom Haller	2.25	1.25	.70
109	Juan Marichal	6.00	3.00	1.75
110	Jack Sanford	2.25	1.25	.70
111	Bill O'Dell	2.00	1.00	.60
112	Willie McCovey	90.00	45.00	27.00
113	Lee Walls	20.00	10.00	6.00
114	Jim Gilliam	20.00	10.00	6.00
115	Maury Wills	5.00	2.50	1.50
116	Ron Fairly	2.25	1.25	.70
117	Tommy Davis	3.00	1.50	.90
118	Duke Snider	9.00	4.50	2.75
119	Willie Davis	3.00	1.50	.90
120	John Roseboro	2.25	1.25	.70
121	Sandy Koufax	20.00	10.00	6.00
122	Stan Williams	20.00	10.00	6.00
123	Don Drysdale	9.00	4.50	2.75
124	Daryl Spencer	2.00	1.00	.60
125	Gordy Coleman	2.00	1.00	.60
126	Don Blasingame	20.00	10.00	6.00
127	Leo Cardenas	2.00	1.00	.60
128	Eddie Kasko	20.00	10.00	6.00
129	Jerry Lynch	2.00	1.00	.60
130	Vada Pinson	4.00	2.00	1.25
131	Frank Robinson	9.00	4.50	2.75
132	John Edwards	20.00	10.00	6.00
133	Joey Jay	2.00	1.00	.60
134	Bob Purkey	2.00	1.00	.60
135	Marty Keough	55.00	27.00	16.50
136	Jim O'Toole	20.00	10.00	6.00
137	Dick Stuart	2.25	1.25	.70
138	Bill Mazeroski	3.50	1.75	1.00
139	Dick Groat	3.00	1.50	.90
140	Don Hoak	2.25	1.25	.70
141	Bob Skinner	2.25	1.25	.70

		NR MT	EX	VG
142	Bill Virdon	3.00	1.50	.90
143	Roberto Clemente	60.00	30.00	18.00
144	Smoky Burgess	3.00	1.50	.90
145	Bob Friend	2.25	1.25	.70
146	Al McBean	20.00	10.00	6.00
147	ElRoy Face	3.00	1.50	.90
148	Joe Adcock	3.50	1.75	1.00
149	Frank Bolling	2.00	1.00	.60
150	Roy McMillan	2.00	1.00	.60
151	Eddie Mathews	8.00	4.00	2.50
152	Hank Aaron	60.00	30.00	18.00
153	Del Crandall	20.00	10.00	6.00
154	Bob Shaw	2.00	1.00	.60
155	Lew Burdette	3.50	1.75	1.00
156	Joe Torre	20.00	10.00	6.00
157	Tony Cloninger	35.00	17.50	10.50
158	Bill White	2.50	1.25	.70
159	Julian Javier	20.00	10.00	6.00
160	Ken Boyer	4.00	2.00	1.25
161	Julio Gotay	20.00	10.00	6.00
162	Curt Flood	3.00	1.50	.90
163	Charlie James	35.00	17.50	10.50
164	Gene Oliver	20.00	10.00	6.00
165	Ernie Broglio	2.00	1.00	.60
166	Bob Gibson	60.00	30.00	18.00
167	Lindy McDaniel	20.00	10.00	6.00
168	Ray Washburn	2.00	1.00	.60
169	Ernie Banks	12.00	6.00	3.50
170	Ron Santo	3.50	1.75	1.00
171	George Altman	2.00	1.00	.60
172	Billy Williams	60.00	30.00	18.00
173	Andre Rodgers	20.00	10.00	6.00
174	Ken Hubbs	3.00	1.50	.90
175	Don Landrum	20.00	10.00	6.00
176	Dick Bertell	20.00	10.00	6.00
177	Roy Sievers	2.50	1.25	.70
178	Tony Taylor	20.00	10.00	6.00
179	John Callison	2.50	1.25	.70
180	Don Demeter	2.00	1.00	.60
181	Tony Gonzalez	20.00	10.00	6.00
182	Wes Covington	20.00	10.00	6.00
183	Art Mahaffey	2.00	1.00	.60
184	Clay Dalrymple	2.00	1.00	.60
185	Al Spangler	2.00	1.00	.60
186	Roman Mejias	2.00	1.00	.60
187	Bob Aspromonte	50.00	25.00	15.00
188	Norm Larker	2.00	1.00	.60
189	Johnny Temple	2.00	1.00	.60
190	Carl Warwick	20.00	10.00	6.00
191	Bob Lillis	20.00	10.00	6.00
192	Dick Farrell	50.00	25.00	15.00
193	Gil Hodges	8.00	4.00	2.50
194	Marv Throneberry	3.00	1.50	.90
195	Charlie Neal	20.00	10.00	6.00
196	Frank Thomas	2.25	1.25	.70
197	Richie Ashburn	5.00	2.50	1.50
198	Felix Mantilla	20.00	10.00	6.00
199	Rod Kanehl	20.00	10.00	6.00
200	Roger Craig	20.00	10.00	6.00

1986 Jiffy Pop

One of the scarcer of the 1986 "regionals," the 20-card Jiffy Pop issue was inserted in packages of heat-and-eat popcorn. A production of Mike Schecter Associates, the 2-7/8" round discs feature 20 popular stars, many in the same pictures found in other '86 regionals. Like other MSA issues, caps have had the team logos erased, allowing Jiffy Pop to avoid having to pay a licensing fee to the teams.

		MT	NR MT	EX
	Complete Set:	40.00	30.00	16.00
	Common Player:	1.00	.70	.40
1	Jim Rice	1.75	1.25	.70
2	Wade Boggs	3.50	2.75	1.50
3	Lance Parrish	1.00	.70	.40
4	George Brett	2.50	2.00	1.00
5	Robin Yount	1.75	1.25	.70
6	Don Mattingly	6.00	4.50	2.50
7	Dave Winfield	2.00	1.50	.80
8	Reggie Jackson	2.25	1.75	.90
9	Cal Ripken	2.25	1.75	.90
10	Eddie Murray	2.00	1.50	.80
11	Pete Rose	3.50	2.75	1.50
12	Ryne Sandberg	1.75	1.25	.70
13	Nolan Ryan	1.50	1.25	.60
14	Fernando Valenzuela	1.25	.90	.50
15	Willie McGee	1.00	.70	.40
16	Dale Murphy	2.50	2.00	1.00
17	Mike Schmidt	2.50	2.00	1.00
18	Steve Garvey	2.00	1.50	.80
19	Gary Carter	2.00	1.50	.80
20	Dwight Gooden	3.00	2.25	1.25

1987 Jiffy Pop

For the second year in a row, Jiffy Pop inserted baseball discs in their packages of popcorn. The full-color discs measure 2-7/8" in diameter and were produced by Mike Schecter Associates of Cos Cob, Conn. Titled "2nd Annual Collectors' Edition," the card fronts feature player photos with all team insignias airbrushed away. Information on the backs of the discs are printed in bright red on white stock. Die-cut press sheets containing all 20 discs were available via a mail-in offer.

		MT	NR MT	EX
	Complete Set:	40.00	30.00	16.00
	Common Player:	1.00	.70	.40
1	Ryne Sandberg	1.75	1.25	.70
2	Dale Murphy	2.50	2.00	1.00
3	Jack Morris	1.00	.70	.40
4	Keith Hernandez	1.50	1.25	.60
5	George Brett	2.50	2.00	1.00
6	Don Mattingly	6.00	4.50	2.50
7	Ozzie Smith	1.00	.70	.40
8	Cal Ripken	2.25	1.75	.90
9	Dwight Gooden	3.00	2.25	1.25
10	Pedro Guerrero	1.00	.70	.40
11	Lou Whitaker	1.00	.70	.40
12	Roger Clemens	3.00	2.25	1.25
13	Lance Parrish	1.00	.70	.40
14	Rickey Henderson	2.25	1.75	.90
15	Fernando Valenzuela	1.25	.90	.50
16	Mike Schmidt	2.50	2.00	1.00
17	Darryl Strawberry	2.75	2.00	1.00
18	Mike Scott	1.00	.70	.40
19	Jim Rice	2.75	2.00	1.00
20	Wade Boggs	3.50	2.75	1.50

1988 Jiffy Pop

This 20-disc set is the third Jiffy Pop issue spotlighting leading players. Discs are 2-/12" in diameter, with a semi-gloss finish, and feature full-color closeups on white stock. Team logos have been airbrushed off the player's caps. The Jiffy Pop logo appears in red at the top of the dis; a banner running across the bottom encloses a "1988" and player name, also in red. The circular border is blue, with two large baseballs streaking toward the top logo. A third baseball appears lower right under the curved lavel "3rd Annual Collector's Edition." Dsic backs are white, with dark blue lettering, and contain player information and disc number.

		MT	NR MT	EX
	Complete Set:	25.00	18.50	10.00
	Common Player:	.75	.60	.30
1	Buddy Bell	.75	.60	.30
2	Wade Boggs	3.50	2.75	1.50
3	Gary Carter	1.50	1.25	.60
4	Jack Clark	1.00	.70	.40
5	Will Clark	1.50	1.25	.60
6	Roger Clemens	2.25	1.75	.90
7	Vince Coleman	1.00	.70	.40
8	Andre Dawson	1.25	.90	.50
9	Keith Hernandez	1.25	.90	.50
10	Kent Hrbek	1.25	.90	.50
11	Wally Joyner	1.50	1.25	.60
12	Paul Molitor	1.00	.70	.40
13	Eddie Murray	1.50	1.25	.60
14	Tim Raines	1.50	1.25	.60
15	Bret Saberhagen	1.25	.90	.50
16	Alan Trammell	1.25	.90	.50
17	Ozzie Virgil	.75	.60	.30
18	Tim Wallach	.75	.60	.30
19	Dave Winfield	1.50	1.25	.60
20	Robin Yount	1.25	.90	.50

1953 Johnston Cookies Braves

The first and most common of three annual issues, the '53 Johnston's were inserted into boxes of cookies on a regional basis. Complete sets were also available from the company, whose factory sits in the shadow of Milwaukee County Stadium. While at first glance appearing to be color photos, the pictures on the 25 cards in the set are actually well-done colorizations of black and white photos. Cards measure 2-9/16" by 3-5/8". Write-ups on the backs were "borrowed" from the Braves' 1953 yearbook.

		NR MT	EX	VG
Complete Set:		325.00	175.00	100.00
Common Player:		8.00	4.00	2.50
1	Charlie Grimm	10.00	5.00	3.00
2	John Antonelli	10.00	5.00	3.00
3	Vern Bickford	8.00	4.00	2.50
4	Bob Buhl	10.00	5.00	3.00
5	Lew Burdette	15.00	7.50	4.50
6	Dave Cole	8.00	4.00	2.50
7	Ernie Johnson	8.00	4.00	2.50
8	Dave Jolly	8.00	4.00	2.50
9	Don Liddle	8.00	4.00	2.50
10	Warren Spahn	45.00	23.00	13.50
11	Max Surkont	8.00	4.00	2.50
12	Jim Wilson	8.00	4.00	2.50
13	Sibby Sisti	8.00	4.00	2.50
14	Walker Cooper	8.00	4.00	2.50
15	Del Crandall	12.00	6.00	3.50
16	Ebba St. Claire	8.00	4.00	2.50
17	Joe Adcock	12.00	6.00	3.50
18	George Crowe	8.00	4.00	2.50
19	Jack Dittmer	8.00	4.00	2.50
20	Johnny Logan	10.00	5.00	3.00
21	Ed Mathews	45.00	23.00	13.50
22	Bill Bruton	10.00	5.00	3.00
23	Sid Gordon	8.00	4.00	2.50
24	Andy Pafko	10.00	5.00	3.00
25	Jim Pendleton	8.00	4.00	2.50

1954 Johnston Cookies Braves

HENRY AARON

In its second of three annual issues, Johnston's increased the number of cards in its 1954 Braves issue to 35, and switched to an unusual size, a narrow format, 2" by 3-7/8". Besides the players and managers, the '54 set also includes unnumbered cards of the team trainer and equipment manager. Other cards are numbered by uniform number. After his early-season injury (which gave Hank Aaron a chance to play regularly), Bobby Thomson's card was withdrawn, accounting for its scarcity and high value. A cardboard wall-hanging display into which cards could be inserted was available as a premium offer.

		NR MT	EX	VG
Complete Set:		800.00	400.00	240.00
Common Player:		10.00	5.00	3.00
1	Del Crandall	15.00	7.50	4.50
3	Jim Pendleton	10.00	5.00	3.00
4	Danny O'Connell	10.00	5.00	3.00
5	Henry Aaron	250.00	125.00	75.00
6	Jack Dittmer	10.00	5.00	3.00
9	Joe Adcock	15.00	7.50	4.50
10	Robert Buhl	15.00	7.50	4.50
11	Phillip Paine (Phillips)	10.00	5.00	3.00
12	Ben Johnson	10.00	5.00	3.00
13	Sibby Sisti	10.00	5.00	3.00

		NR MT	EX	VG
15	Charles Gorin	10.00	5.00	3.00
16	Chet Nichols	10.00	5.00	3.00
17	Dave Jolly	10.00	5.00	3.00
19	Jim Wilson	10.00	5.00	3.00
20	Ray Crone	10.00	5.00	3.00
21	Warren Spahn	55.00	28.00	16.50
22	Gene Conley	9.00	4.50	2.75
23	Johnny Logan	12.00	6.00	3.50
24	Charlie White	10.00	5.00	3.00
27	George Metkovich	10.00	5.00	3.00
28	John Cooney	10.00	5.00	3.00
29	Paul Burris	10.00	5.00	3.00
31	Wm. Walters	10.00	5.00	3.00
32	Ernest T. Johnson	10.00	5.00	3.00
33	Lew Burdette	18.00	9.00	5.50
34	Bob Thomson	175.00	87.00	52.00
35	Robert Keely	10.00	5.00	3.00
38	Billy Bruton	10.00	5.00	3.00
40	Charles Grimm	10.00	5.00	3.00
41	Ed Mathews	55.00	28.00	16.50
42	Sam Calderone	10.00	5.00	3.00
47	Joey Jay	10.00	5.00	3.00
48	Andy Pafko	12.00	6.00	3.50
----	Dr. Charles Lacks (trainer)	10.00	5.00	3.00
----	Joseph F. Taylor (asst. trainer)	10.00	5.00	3.00

1955 Johnston Cookies Braves

JIM PENDLETON

A third change in size and format was undertaken in the third and final year of Braves sets produced by Johnston's. The 35 cards in the 1955 set were issued in six fold-out panels of six cards each (Andy Pafko was double-printed). As in 1954, cards are numbered by uniform number, except those of the team equipment manager, trainer and road secretary (former Boston star Duffy Lewis). Single cards measure 2-7/8" by 4". Besides including panels in boxes of cookies, the '55 Johnston's could be ordered for 5¢ per panel by mail. The scarcest of the Johnston's issues, the 1955 set can be found today still in complete panels, or as single cards.

		NR MT	EX	VG
Complete Folder Set:		1200.00	600.00	350.00
Complete Singles Set:		750.00	375.00	225.00
Common Player:		15.00	7.50	4.50
Common Folder:		110.00	55.00	33.00
1	Del Crandall	20.00	10.00	6.00
3	Jim Pendleton	15.00	7.50	4.50
4	Danny O'Connell	15.00	7.50	4.50
6	Jack Dittmer	15.00	7.50	4.50
9	Joe Adcock	20.00	10.00	6.00
10	Bob Buhl	18.00	9.00	5.50
11	Phil Paine	15.00	7.50	4.50
12	Ray Crone	15.00	7.50	4.50
15	Charlie Gorin	15.00	7.50	4.50
16	Dave Jolly	15.00	7.50	4.50
17	Chet Nichols	15.00	7.50	4.50
18	Chuck Tanner	20.00	10.00	6.00
19	Jim Wilson	15.00	7.50	4.50
20	Dave Koslo	15.00	7.50	4.50
21	Warren Spahn	65.00	33.00	20.00
22	Gene Conley	18.00	9.00	5.50
23	John Logan	18.00	9.00	5.50
24	Charlie White	15.00	7.50	4.50
28	Johnny Cooney	15.00	7.50	4.50

		NR MT	EX	VG
30	Roy Smalley	15.00	7.50	4.50
31	Bucky Walters	15.00	7.50	4.50
32	Ernie Johnson	15.00	7.50	4.50
33	Lew Burdette	25.00	12.50	7.50
34	Bobby Thomson	20.00	10.00	6.00
35	Bob Keely	15.00	7.50	4.50
38	Billy Bruton	18.00	9.00	5.50
39	George Crowe	15.00	7.50	4.50
40	Charlie Grimm	18.00	9.00	5.50
41	Eddie Mathews	65.00	33.00	20.00
44	Hank Aaron	250.00	125.00	70.00
47	Joe Jay	15.00	7.50	4.50
48	Andy Pafko	18.00	9.00	5.50
----	Dr. Charles K. Lacks	15.00	7.50	4.50
----	Duffy Lewis	15.00	7.50	4.50
----	Joe Taylor	15.00	7.50	4.50
----	Series 1 Folder (Hank Aaron, Lew Burdette, Del Crandall, Charlie Gorin, Bob Keely, Danny O'Connell)	375.00	187.00	112.00
----	Series 2 Folder (Joe Adcock, Joe Jay, Dr. Charles K. Lacks, Chet Nichols, Andy Pafko, Charlie White)	125.00	62.00	37.00
----	Series 3 Folder (Gene Conley, George Crowe, Jim Pendleton, Roy Smalley, Warren Spahn, Joe Taylor)	175.00	87.00	52.00
----	Series 4 Folder (Billy Bruton, John Cooney, Dave Jolly, Dave Koslo, Johnny Logan, Andy Pafko)	125.00	62.00	37.00
----	Series 5 Folder (Ray Crone, Ernie Johnson, Duffy Lewis, Eddie Mathews, Phil Paine, Chuck Tanner)	200.00	100.00	60.00
----	Series 6 Folder (Bob Buhl, Jack Dittmer, Charlie Grimm, Bobby Thomson, Bucky Walters, Jim Wilson)	125.00	62.00	37.00

		MT	NR MT	EX
1	Mickey Mantle	.40	.30	.15
2	Maury Wills	.05	.04	.02
3	Elston Howard	.03	.02	.01
4	Sandy Koufax	.10	.08	.04
5	Brooks Robinson	.05	.04	.02
6	Ken Boyer	.03	.02	.01
7	Zoilo Versalles	.03	.02	.01
8	Willie Mays	.10	.08	.04
9	Frank Robinson	.05	.04	.02
10	Bob Clemente	.10	.08	.04
11	Carl Yastrzemski	.10	.08	.04
12	Orlando Cepeda	.03	.02	.01
13	Denny McLain	.03	.02	.01
14	Bob Gibson	.05	.04	.02
15	Harmon Killebrew	.05	.04	.02
16	Willie McCovey	.05	.04	.02
17	Boog Powell	.03	.02	.01
18	Johnny Bench	.07	.05	.03
19	Vida Blue	.03	.02	.01
20	Joe Torre	.03	.02	.01
21	Rich Allen	.03	.02	.01
22	Johnny Bench	.07	.05	.03
23	Reggie Jackson	.07	.05	.03
24	Pete Rose	.12	.09	.05
25	Jeff Burroughs	.03	.02	.01
26	Steve Garvey	.07	.05	.03
27	Fred Lynn	.03	.02	.01
28	Joe Morgan	.05	.04	.02
29	Thurman Munson	.05	.04	.02
30	Joe Morgan	.05	.04	.02
31	Rod Carew	.07	.05	.03
32	George Foster	.03	.02	.01
33	Jim Rice	.05	.04	.02
34	Dave Parker	.05	.04	.02
35	Don Baylor	.03	.02	.01
36	Keith Hernandez	.03	.02	.01
37	Willie Stargell	.05	.04	.02
38	George Brett	.07	.05	.03
39	Mike Schmidt	.07	.05	.03
40	Rollie Fingers	.05	.04	.02
41	Mike Schmidt	.07	.05	.03
42	Don Drysdale	.05	.04	.02
43	Hank Aaron	.10	.08	.04
44	Pete Rose	.12	.09	.05

1982 K-Mart

The first of what became dozens of boxed sets specially produced for retail chain stores by the major card producers, the 1982 K-Mart set has not enjoyed any collector popularity. The theme of the set is Most Valuable Players and selected record-breaking performances of the 1962-1981 seasons. The design used miniature reproductions of Topps cards of the era, except in a few cases where designs had to be created because original cards were never issued (1962 Maury Wills, 1975 Fred Lynn.) Originally sold for about $2 per boxed set of 44, large quantities were bought up by speculators who got burned when over-production and lack of demand caused the set to drop as low as 10¢. The 2-1/2" by 3-1/2" cards were printed by Topps.

	MT	NR MT	EX
Complete Set:	1.25	.90	.50
Common Player:	.03	.02	.01

1987 K-Mart

Produced by Topps for K-Mart, the 1987 K-Mart set was distributed by the department stores to celebrate their 25th anniversary. Entitled "Baseball's Stars of the Decades," the 33-card set was issued in a special cardboard box with one stick of bubblegum. The card fronts feature a full-color photo set diagonally against a red background. The backs contain career highlights plus pitching or batting statistics for the decade in which the player enjoyed his greatest success. Cards are the standard 2-1/2" by 3-1/2" by 3-1/2" size.

	MT	NR MT	EX
Complete Set:	5.00	3.75	2.00
Common Player:	.10	.08	.04
1 Hank Aaron	.50	.40	.20
2 Roberto Clemente	.40	.30	.15
3 Bob Gibson	.10	.08	.04
4 Harmon Killebrew	.10	.08	.04

		MT	NR MT	EX
5	Mickey Mantle	1.00	.70	.40
6	Juan Marichal	.10	.08	.04
7	Roger Maris	.30	.25	.12
8	Willie Mays	.50	.40	.20
9	Brooks Robinson	.30	.25	.12
10	Frank Robinson	.20	.15	.08
11	Carl Yastrzemski	.50	.40	.20
12	Johnny Bench	.30	.25	.12
13	Lou Brock	.20	.15	.08
14	Rod Carew	.30	.25	.12
15	Steve Carlton	.20	.15	.08
16	Reggie Jackson	.30	.25	.12
17	Jim Palmer	.10	.08	.04
18	Jim Rice	.10	.08	.04
19	Pete Rose	.60	.45	.25
20	Nolan Ryan	.20	.15	.08
21	Tom Seaver	.20	.15	.08
22	Willie Stargell	.10	.08	.04
23	Wade Boggs	.60	.45	.25
24	George Brett	.40	.30	.15
25	Gary Carter	.20	.15	.08
26	Dwight Gooden	.50	.40	.20
27	Rickey Henderson	.20	.15	.08
28	Don Mattingly	1.00	.70	.40
29	Dale Murphy	.40	.30	.15
30	Eddie Murray	.20	.15	.08
31	Mike Schmidt	.30	.25	.12
32	Darryl Strawberry	.40	.30	.15
33	Fernando Valenzuela	.10	.08	.04

		MT	NR MT	EX
19	Tim Raines	.20	.15	.08
20	Dave Righetti	.12	.09	.05
21	Cap Ripken	.25	.20	.10
22	Pete Rose	.50	.40	.20
23	Nolan Ryan	.15	.11	.06
24	Benny Santiago	.25	.20	.10
25	Mike Schmidt	.30	.25	.12
26	Mike Scott	.10	.08	.04
27	Kevin Seitzer	.60	.45	.25
28	Ozzie Smith	.15	.11	.06
29	Darryl Strawberry	.30	.25	.12
30	Rick Sutcliffe	.10	.08	.04
31	Fernando Valenzuela	.15	.11	.06
32	Todd Worrell	.10	.08	.04
33	Robin Yount	.15	.11	.06

1988 K-Mart

This 33-card boxed set, titled "Memorable Moments," was produced by Topps for distribution via K-Mart. Two previous Topps K-Mart sets were issued: a 44-card set in 1982 in honor of K-Mart's 20th anniversary and a 33-card set in 1987 for the company's 25th anniversary. The 1988 cards are standard-size with red, white and blue borders and a super glossy coating. Numbered card backs are printed in red and blue on white and highlight special events in the featured players' careers. The set was marketed in a bright yellow and green checklist box (gum included).

		MT	NR MT	EX
	Complete Set:	5.00	3.75	2.00
	Common Player:	.10	.08	.04
1	George Bell	.20	.15	.08
2	Wade Boggs	.80	.60	.30
3	George Brett	.30	.25	.12
4	Jose Canseco	.50	.40	.20
5	Jack Clark	.15	.11	.06
6	Will Clark	.25	.20	.10
7	Roger Clemens	.40	.30	.15
8	Vince Coleman	.15	.11	.06
9	Andre Dawson	.15	.11	.06
10	Dwight Gooden	.40	.30	.15
11	Pedro Guerrero	.15	.11	.06
12	Tony Gwynn	.25	.20	.10
13	Rickey Henderson	.25	.20	.10
14	Keith Hernandez	.15	.11	.06
15	Don Mattingly	1.50	1.25	.60
16	Mark McGwire	1.00	.70	.40
17	Paul Molitor	.12	.09	.05
18	Dale Murphy	.30	.25	.12

1955 Kahn's Wieners Reds

Compliments of Kahn's Wieners

"THE WIENER THE WORLD AWAITED"

The first of what would become 15 successive years of baseball card issues by the Kahn's meat company of Cincinnati is also the rarest. The set consists of six Cincinnati Redlegs player cards, 3-1/4" by 4". Printed in black and white, with blank backs, the '55 Kahn's cards were distributed at a one-day promotional event at a Cincinnati amusement park, where the featured players were on hand to sign autographs. Like the other Kahn's issues through 1963, the '55 cards have a 1/2" white panel containing an advertising message below the player photo. These cards are sometimes found with this portion cut off, greatly reducing the value of the card.

		NR MT	EX	VG
	Complete Set:	2200.00	1100.00	660.00
	Common Player:	300.00	150.00	90.00
(1)	Gus Bell	550.00	275.00	165.00
(2)	Ted Kluszewski	400.00	200.00	120.00
(3)	Roy McMillan	300.00	150.00	90.00
(4)	Joe Nuxhall	300.00	150.00	90.00
(5)	Wally Post	300.00	150.00	90.00
(6)	Johnny Temple	300.00	150.00	90.00

1956 Kahn's Wieners Reds

In 1956, Kahn's expanded its baseball card program to include 15 Redlegs players, and began issuing the cards one per pack in packages of hot dogs. Because the cards were packaged in direct contact with the meat, they are often found today in stained condition. In 3-1/4" by 4" format, black and white with blank backs, the '56 Kahn's cards can be distinguished from later issues by the presence of full stadium photographic backgrounds behind the player photos. Like all Kahn's issues, the 1956 set is unnumbered; the checklists are arranged alphabetically for convenience. The set features the first-ever baseball card of Hall of Famer Frank Robinson.

		NR MT	EX	VG
Complete Set:		1200.00	600.00	360.00
Common Player:		55.00	27.00	16.50
(1)	Ed Bailey	55.00	27.00	16.50
(2)	Gus Bell	60.00	30.00	18.00
(3)	Joe Black	60.00	30.00	18.00
(4)	"Smokey" Burgess	60.00	30.00	18.00
(5)	Art Fowler	55.00	27.00	16.50
(6)	Hershell Freeman	55.00	27.00	16.50
(7)	Ray Jablonski	55.00	27.00	16.50
(8)	John Klippstein	55.00	27.00	16.50
(9)	Ted Kluszewski	110.00	55.00	33.00
(10)	Brooks Lawrence	55.00	27.00	16.50
(11)	Roy McMillan	55.00	27.00	16.50
(12)	Joe Nuxhall	70.00	35.00	21.00
(13)	Wally Post	55.00	27.00	16.50
(14)	Frank Robinson	300.00	150.00	90.00
(15)	Johnny Temple	55.00	27.00	16.50

1957 Kahn's Wieners

In its third season of baseball card issue, Kahn's kept the basic 3-1/4" by 4" format, with black and white photos and blank backs. The issue was expanded to 28 players, all Pirates or Reds. The last of the blank-backed Kahn's sets, the 1957 Reds players can be distinguished from the 1956 issue by the general lack of background photo detail, in favor of a neutral light gray background. The Dick Groat card appears with two name variations, a facsimile autograph, "Richard Groat," and a printed "Dick Groat." Both Groat varieties are included in the complete set price.

	NR MT	EX	VG
Complete Set	2000.00	1000.00	600.00

		NR MT	EX	VG
Common Player		40.00	20.00	12.00
(1)	Tom Acker	40.00	20.00	12.00
(2)	Ed Bailey	40.00	20.00	12.00
(3)	Gus Bell	50.00	25.00	15.00
(4)	Smokey Burgess	50.00	25.00	15.00
(5)	Roberto Clemente	350.00	175.00	105.00
(6)	George Crowe	40.00	20.00	12.00
(7)	Elroy Face	50.00	25.00	15.00
(8)	Hershell Freeman	40.00	20.00	12.00
(9)	Robert Friend	50.00	25.00	15.00
(10)	Don Gross	40.00	20.00	12.00
(11a)	Dick Groat	60.00	30.00	18.00
(11b)	Richard Groat	175.00	87.00	52.00
(12)	Warren Hacker	40.00	20.00	12.00
(13)	Don Hoak	45.00	22.00	13.50
(14)	Hal Jeffcoat	40.00	20.00	12.00
(15)	Ron Kline	40.00	20.00	12.00
(16)	John Klippstein	40.00	20.00	12.00
(17)	Ted Kluszewski	75.00	37.00	22.00
(18)	Brooks Lawrence	40.00	20.00	12.00
(19)	Dale Long	40.00	20.00	12.00
(20)	Wm. Mazeroski	60.00	30.00	18.00
(21)	Roy McMillan	40.00	20.00	12.00
(22)	Joe Nuxhall	50.00	25.00	15.00
(23)	Wally Post	40.00	20.00	12.00
(24)	Frank Robinson	200.00	100.00	60.00
(25)	Johnny Temple	40.00	20.00	12.00
(26)	Frank Thomas	40.00	20.00	12.00
(27)	Bob Thurman	40.00	20.00	12.00
(28)	Lee Walls	40.00	20.00	12.00

1958 Kahn's Wieners

Long-time Cincinnati favorite Wally Post became the only Philadelphia Phillies ballplayer to appear in the 15-year run of Kahn's issues when he was traded in 1958, but included as part of the otherwise exclusively Pirates-Reds set. Like previous years, the '58 Kahn's were 3-1/4" by 4", with black and white player photos. Unlike previous years, however, the cards had printing on the back, a story by the pictured player, titled "My Greatest Thrill in Baseball." Quite similar to the 1959 issue, the '58 Kahn's can be distinguished by the fact that the top line of the advertising panel at bottom has the word "Wieners" in 1958, but not in 1959.

		NR MT	EX	VG
Complete Set:		2300.00	1150.00	690.00
Common Player:		40.00	20.00	12.00
(1)	Ed Bailey	40.00	20.00	12.00
(2)	Gene Baker	50.00	25.00	15.00
(3)	Gus Bell	50.00	25.00	15.00
(4)	Smokey Burgess	50.00	25.00	15.00
(5)	Roberto Clemente	350.00	175.00	105.00
(6)	George Crowe	40.00	20.00	12.00
(7)	Elroy Face	50.00	25.00	15.00
(8)	Henry Foiles	40.00	20.00	12.00
(9)	Dee Fondy	40.00	20.00	12.00
(10)	Robert Friend	50.00	25.00	15.00
(11)	Richard Groat	60.00	30.00	18.00
(12)	Harvey Haddix	50.00	25.00	15.00
(13)	Don Hoak	45.00	22.00	13.50
(14)	Hal Jeffcoat	50.00	25.00	15.00
(15)	Ronald L. Kline	50.00	25.00	15.00

		NR MT	EX	VG
(16)	Ted Kluszewski	75.00	37.00	22.00
(17)	Vernon Law	50.00	25.00	15.00
(18)	Brooks Lawrence	40.00	20.00	12.00
(19)	William Mazeroski	60.00	30.00	18.00
(20)	Roy McMillan	40.00	20.00	12.00
(21)	Joe Nuxhall	50.00	25.00	15.00
(22)	Wally Post	200.00	100.00	60.00
(23)	John Powers	40.00	20.00	12.00
(24)	Robert T. Purkey	40.00	20.00	12.00
(25)	Charles Rabe	200.00	100.00	60.00
(26)	Frank Robinson	175.00	87.00	52.00
(27)	Robert Skinner	40.00	20.00	12.00
(28)	Johnny Temple	40.00	20.00	12.00
(29)	Frank Thomas	200.00	100.00	60.00

		NR MT	EX	VG
(35)	Richard L. Stuart	45.00	22.00	13.50
(36)	John Temple	40.00	20.00	12.00
(37)	Frank Thomas	45.00	22.00	13.50
(38)	George A. Witt	40.00	20.00	12.00

1959 Kahn's Wieners

A third team was added to the Kahn's lineup in 1959, the Cleveland Indians joining the Pirates and Reds, bringing the number of cards in the set to 38. Again printed in black and white in the 3-1/4" by 4" size, the 1959 Kahn's cards can be differentiated from the previous issue by the lack of the word "Wieners" on the top line of the advertising panel at bottom. Backs again featured a story written by the pictured player, titled "The Toughest Play I Had to Make," "My Most Difficult Moment in Baseball," or "The Toughest Batters I Have to Face."

		NR MT	EX	VG
Complete Set:		3600.00	1800.00	1080.
Common Player:		40.00	20.00	12.00
(1)	Ed Bailey	40.00	20.00	12.00
(2)	Gary Bell	40.00	20.00	12.00
(3)	Gus Bell	50.00	25.00	15.00
(4)	Richard Brodowski	400.00	200.00	120.00
(5)	Forrest Burgess	50.00	25.00	15.00
(6)	Roberto Clemente	350.00	175.00	105.00
(7)	Rocky Colavito	75.00	37.00	22.00
(8)	ElRoy Face	50.00	25.00	15.00
(9)	Robert Friend	50.00	25.00	15.00
(10)	Joe Gordon	50.00	25.00	15.00
(11)	Jim Grant	40.00	20.00	12.00
(12)	Richard M. Groat	60.00	30.00	18.00
(13)	Harvey Haddix	350.00	175.00	105.00
(14)	Woodie Held	350.00	175.00	105.00
(15)	Don Hoak	45.00	22.00	13.50
(16)	Ronald Kline	40.00	20.00	12.00
(17)	Ted Kluszewski	75.00	37.00	22.00
(18)	Vernon Law	50.00	25.00	15.00
(19)	Jerry Lynch	40.00	20.00	12.00
(20)	Billy Martin	75.00	37.00	22.00
(21)	William Mazeroski	50.00	25.00	15.00
(22)	Cal McLish	350.00	175.00	105.00
(23)	Roy McMillan	40.00	20.00	12.00
(24)	Minnie Minoso	60.00	30.00	18.00
(25)	Russell Nixon	40.00	20.00	12.00
(26)	Joe Nuxhall	50.00	25.00	15.00
(27)	Jim Perry	50.00	25.00	15.00
(28)	Vada Pinson	60.00	30.00	18.00
(29)	Vic Power	40.00	20.00	12.00
(30)	Robert Purkey	40.00	20.00	12.00
(31)	Frank Robinson	175.00	87.00	52.00
(32)	Herb Score	50.00	25.00	15.00
(33)	Robert Skinner	40.00	20.00	12.00
(34)	George Strickland	40.00	20.00	12.00

1960 Kahn's Weiners

Compliments of Kahn's
"THE WIENER THE WORLD AWAITED"

Three more teams joined the Kahn's roster in 1960, the Chicago Cubs, Chicago White Sox and St. Louis Cardinals. A total of 42 different players are represented in the set. Again 3-1/4" by 4" and black and white photos, the 1960 Kahn's cards featured for the first time player stats and personal data on the back, except Harvey Kuenn, which was issued with blank back, probably because of the lateness of his trade to the Indians.

		NR MT	EX	VG
Complete Set:		1900.00	950.00	570.00
Common Player:		30.00	15.00	9.00
(1)	Ed Bailey	30.00	15.00	9.00
(2)	Gary Bell	30.00	15.00	9.00
(3)	Gus Bell	35.00	17.50	10.50
(4)	Forrest Burgess	35.00	17.50	10.50
(5)	Gino N. Cimoli	30.00	15.00	9.00
(6)	Roberto Clemente	175.00	87.00	52.00
(7)	ElRoy Face	35.00	17.50	10.50
(8)	Tito Francona	35.00	17.50	10.50
(9)	Robert Friend	35.00	17.50	10.50
(10)	Jim Grant	30.00	15.00	9.00
(11)	Richard Groat	40.00	20.00	12.00
(12)	Harvey Haddix	35.00	17.50	10.50
(13)	Woodie Held	30.00	15.00	9.00
(14)	Bill Henry	30.00	15.00	9.00
(15)	Don Hoak	35.00	17.50	10.50
(16)	Jay Hook	30.00	15.00	9.00
(17)	Eddie Kasko	30.00	15.00	9.00
(18)	Ronnie Kline	40.00	20.00	12.00
(19)	Ted Kluszewski	50.00	25.00	15.00
(20)	Harvey Kuenn	250.00	125.00	75.00
(21)	Vernon S. Law	35.00	17.50	10.50
(22)	Brooks Lawrence	30.00	15.00	9.00
(23)	Jerry Lynch	30.00	15.00	9.00
(24)	Billy Martin	60.00	30.00	18.00
(25)	William Mazeroski	40.00	20.00	12.00
(26)	Cal McLish	30.00	15.00	9.00
(27)	Roy McMillan	30.00	15.00	9.00
(28)	Don Newcombe	35.00	17.50	10.50
(29)	Russ Nixon	30.00	15.00	9.00
(30)	Joe Nuxhall	35.00	17.50	10.50
(31)	James J. O'Toole	30.00	15.00	9.00
(32)	Jim Perry	35.00	17.50	10.50
(33)	Vada Pinson	40.00	20.00	12.00
(34)	Vic Power	30.00	15.00	9.00
(35)	Robert T. Purkey	30.00	15.00	9.00
(36)	Frank Robinson	125.00	62.00	37.00
(37)	Herb Score	35.00	17.50	10.50
(38)	Robert R. Skinner	30.00	15.00	9.00
(39)	Richard L. Stuart	35.00	17.50	10.50
(40)	John Temple	30.00	15.00	9.00
(41)	Frank Thomas	40.00	20.00	12.00
(42)	Lee Walls	35.00	17.50	10.50

A player's name in *italic* type indicates a rookie card. An (FC) indicates a player's first card for that particular card company.

1961 Kahn's Weiners

Compliments of Kahn's
"THE WIENER THE WORLD AWAITED"

After a single season, the Chicago and St. Louis teams dropped out of the Kahn's program, but the 1961 set was larger than ever, at 43 cards. The same basic format - 3-1/4" by 4" size, black and white photos and statistical information on the back - was retained. For the first time in '61, the meat company made complete sets of the Kahn's cards available to collectors via a mail-in offer. This makes the 1961 and later Kahn's cards considerably easier to obtain than the earlier issues.

		NR MT	EX	VG
	Complete Set:	1200.00	600.00	360.00
	Common Player:	18.00	9.00	5.50
(1)	John A. Antonelli	20.00	10.00	6.00
(2)	Ed Bailey	18.00	9.00	5.50
(3)	Gary Bell	18.00	9.00	5.50
(4)	Gus Bell	20.00	10.00	6.00
(5)	James P. Brosnan	18.00	9.00	5.50
(6)	Forrest Burgess	20.00	10.00	6.00
(7)	Gino Cimoli	18.00	9.00	5.50
(8)	Roberto Clemente	175.00	87.00	52.00
(9)	Gordon Coleman	18.00	9.00	5.50
(10)	Jimmie Dykes	20.00	10.00	6.00
(11)	ElRoy Face	25.00	12.50	7.50
(12)	Tito Francona	20.00	10.00	6.00
(13)	Robert Friend	20.00	10.00	6.00
(14)	Gene L. Freese	18.00	9.00	5.50
(15)	Jim Grant	18.00	9.00	5.50
(16)	Richard M. Groat	30.00	15.00	9.00
(17)	Harvey Haddix	20.00	10.00	6.00
(18)	Woodie Held	18.00	9.00	5.50
(19)	Don Hoak	20.00	10.00	6.00
(20)	Jay Hook	18.00	9.00	5.50
(21)	Joe Jay	18.00	9.00	5.50
(22)	Eddie Kasko	18.00	9.00	5.50
(23)	Willie Kirkland	18.00	9.00	5.50
(24)	Vernon S. Law	25.00	12.50	7.50
(25)	Jerry Lynch	18.00	9.00	5.50
(26)	Jim Maloney	25.00	12.50	7.50
(27)	William Mazeroski	30.00	15.00	9.00
(28)	Wilmer D. Mizell	20.00	10.00	6.00
(29)	Glenn R. Nelson	18.00	9.00	5.50
(30)	James J. O'Toole	18.00	9.00	5.50
(31)	Jim Perry	20.00	10.00	6.00
(32)	John M. Phillips	18.00	9.00	5.50
(33)	Vada E. Pinson Jr.	30.00	15.00	9.00
(34)	Wally Post	18.00	9.00	5.50
(35)	Vic Power	18.00	9.00	5.50
(36)	Robert T. Purkey	18.00	9.00	5.50
(37)	Frank Robinson	125.00	62.00	37.00
(38)	John A. Romano Jr.	18.00	9.00	5.50
(39)	Dick Schofield	18.00	9.00	5.50
(40)	Robert Skinner	18.00	9.00	5.50
(41)	Hal Smith	18.00	9.00	5.50
(42)	Richard Stuart	20.00	10.00	6.00
(43)	John E. Temple	18.00	9.00	5.50

NOTE: A card number in parentheses ( ) indicates the set is unnumbered.

1962 Kahn's Weiners

Compliments of Kahn's
"THE WIENER THE WORLD AWAITED"

Besides the familiar Reds, Pirates and Indians players in the 1962 Kahn's set, a fourth team was added, the Minnesota Twins, though the overall size of the set was decreased from the previous year, to 38 players in 1962. The cards retained the 3-1/4" by 4" black and white format of previous years. The '62 Kahn's set is awash in variations. Besides the photo and front design variations on the Bell, Purkey and Power cards, each Cleveland player can be found with two back variations, listing the team either as "Cleveland" or "Cleveland Indians." The complete set values listed below include all variations.

		NR MT	EX	VG
	Complete Set:	2400.00	1200.00	720.00
	Common Player:	15.00	7.50	4.50
(1a)	Gary Bell (fat man in background)	150.00	75.00	45.00
(1b)	Gary Bell (no fat man)	40.00	20.00	12.00
(2)	James P. Brosnan	15.00	7.50	4.50
(3)	Forrest Burgess	20.00	10.00	6.00
(4)	Leonardo Cardenas	15.00	7.50	4.50
(5)	Roberto Clemente	125.00	62.00	37.00
(6a)	Ty Cline (Cleveland Indians back)	75.00	37.00	22.00
(6b)	Ty Cline (Cleveland back)	30.00	15.00	9.00
(7)	Gordon Coleman	15.00	7.50	4.50
(8)	Dick Donovan	30.00	15.00	9.00
(9)	John Edwards	15.00	7.50	4.50
(10a)	Tito Francona (Cleveland Indians back)	75.00	37.00	22.00
(10b)	Tito Francona (Cleveland back)	30.00	15.00	9.00
(11)	Gene Freese	15.00	7.50	4.50
(12)	Robert B. Friend	20.00	10.00	6.00
(13)	Joe Gibbon	90.00	45.00	27.00
(14a)	Jim Grant (Cleveland Indians back)	75.00	37.00	22.00
(14b)	Jim Grant (Cleveland back)	30.00	15.00	9.00
(15)	Richard M. Groat	25.00	12.50	7.50
(16)	Harvey Haddix	20.00	10.00	6.00
(17a)	Woodie Held (Cleveland Indians back)	90.00	45.00	27.00
(17b)	Woodie Held (Cleveland back)	30.00	15.00	9.00
(18)	Bill Henry	15.00	7.50	4.50
(19)	Don Hoak	20.00	10.00	6.00
(20)	Ken Hunt	15.00	7.50	4.50
(21)	Joseph R. Jay	15.00	7.50	4.50
(22)	Eddie Kasko	15.00	7.50	4.50
(23a)	Willie Kirkland (Cleveland Indians back)	75.00	37.00	22.00
(23b)	Willie Kirkland (Cleveland back)	30.00	15.00	9.00
(24a)	Barry Latman (Cleveland Indians back)	75.00	37.00	22.00
(24b)	Barry Latman (Cleveland back)	30.00	15.00	9.00
(25)	Jerry Lynch	15.00	7.50	4.50
(26)	Jim Maloney	20.00	10.00	6.00
(27)	William Mazeroski	25.00	12.50	7.50
(28)	Jim O'Toole	15.00	7.50	4.50
(29a)	Jim Perry (Cleveland Indians back)	90.00	45.00	27.00
(29b)	Jim Perry (Cleveland back)	30.00	15.00	9.00
(30a)	John M. Phillips (Cleveland Indians back)	75.00	37.00	22.00
(30b)	John M. Phillips (Cleveland back)	30.00	15.00	9.00
(31)	Vada E. Pinson	25.00	12.50	7.50
(32)	Wally Post	15.00	7.50	4.50
(33a)	Vic Power (Cleveland Indians back)	75.00	37.00	22.00
(33b)	Vic Power (Cleveland back)	30.00	15.00	9.00

	NR MT	EX	VG
(33c) Vic Power (Minnesota Twins back)			
	150.00	75.00	45.00
(34a) Robert T. Purkey (no autograph)			
	150.00	75.00	45.00
(34b) Robert T. Purkey (with autograph)			
	40.00	20.00	12.00
(35) Frank Robinson	80.00	40.00	24.00
(36a) John Romano (Cleveland Indians back)			
	75.00	37.00	22.00
(36b) John Romano (Cleveland back)	30.00	15.00	9.00
(37) Dick Stuart	20.00	10.00	6.00
(38) Bill Virdon	20.00	10.00	6.00

1963 Kahn's Weiners

Compliments of Kohn's
"THE WIENER THE WORLD AWAITED"

Compliments of Kahn's
"THE WIENER THE WORLD AWAITED"

In 1963, for the first time since Kahn's began issuing baseball cards in 1955, the design underwent a significant change, white borders were added to the top and sides of player photo. Also, the card size was changed to 3-3/16" by 4-1/4". Statistical and personal data continued to be printed on the card backs. Joining traditional Reds, Pirates and Indians personnel in the 30-card 1963 set were a handful of New York Yankees and Dick Groat, in his new identity as a St. Louis Cardinal.

	NR MT	EX	VG
Complete Set:	800.00	400.00	240.00
Common Player:	15.00	7.50	4.50
(1) Robert Bailey	15.00	7.50	4.50
(2) Don Blasingame	15.00	7.50	4.50
(3) Clete Boyer	25.00	12.50	7.50
(4) Forrest Burgess	20.00	10.00	6.00
(5) Leonardo Cardenas	15.00	7.50	4.50
(6) Roberto Clemente	125.00	62.00	37.00
(7) Don Clendennon (Donn Clendenon)			
	15.00	7.50	4.50
(8) Gordon Coleman	15.00	7.50	4.50
(9) John A. Edwards	15.00	7.50	4.50
(10) Gene Freese	15.00	7.50	4.50
(11) Robert B. Friend	20.00	10.00	6.00
(12) Joe Gibbon	15.00	7.50	4.50
(13) Dick Groat	25.00	12.50	7.50
(14) Harvey Haddix	20.00	10.00	6.00
(15) Elston Howard	30.00	15.00	9.00
(16) Joey Jay	15.00	7.50	4.50
(17) Eddie Kasko	15.00	7.50	4.50
(18) Tony Kubek	30.00	15.00	9.00
(19) Jerry Lynch	15.00	7.50	4.50
(20) Jim Maloney	20.00	10.00	6.00
(21) William Mazeroski	25.00	12.50	7.50
(22) Joe Nuxhall	20.00	10.00	6.00
(23) Jim O'Toole	15.00	7.50	4.50
(24) Vada E. Pinson	25.00	12.50	7.50
(25) Robert T. Purkey	15.00	7.50	4.50
(26) Bob Richardson	30.00	15.00	9.00
(27) Frank Robinson	70.00	35.00	21.00
(28) Bill Stafford	20.00	10.00	6.00
(29) Ralph W. Terry	25.00	12.50	7.50
(30) Bill Virdon	20.00	10.00	6.00

1964 Kahn's Weiners

After nearly a decade of virtually identical card issues, the 1964 Kahn's issue was an abrupt change. In a new size, 3" by 3-1/2", the nearly square cards featured a borderless color photo. The only other design element on the front of the card was a facsimile autograph. The advertising slogan which had traditionally appeared on the front of the card

was moved to the back, where it joined the player's stats and personal data. The teams in the 1964 issue once again reverted to the Reds, Pirates and Indians, for a total of 31 cards.

	NR MT	EX	VG
Complete Set:	925.00	462.00	277.00
Common Player:	9.00	4.50	2.75
(1) Max Alvis	9.00	4.50	2.75
(2) Bob Bailey	9.00	4.50	2.75
(3) Leonardo Cardenas	9.00	4.50	2.75
(4) Roberto Clemente	125.00	62.00	37.00
(5) Donn A. Clendenon	9.00	4.50	2.75
(6) Victor Davalillo	9.00	4.50	2.75
(7) Dick Donovan	9.00	4.50	2.75
(8) John A. Edwards	9.00	4.50	2.75
(9) Robert Friend	15.00	7.50	4.50
(10) Jim Grant	9.00	4.50	2.75
(11) Tommy Harper	9.00	4.50	2.75
(12) Woodie Held	9.00	4.50	2.75
(13) Joey Jay	9.00	4.50	2.75
(14) Jack Kralick	9.00	4.50	2.75
(15) Jerry Lynch	9.00	4.50	2.75
(16) Jim Maloney	15.00	7.50	4.50
(17) William S. Mazeroski	20.00	10.00	6.00
(18) Alvin McBean	9.00	4.50	2.75
(19) Joe Nuxhall	15.00	7.50	4.50
(20) Jim Pagliaroni	9.00	4.50	2.75
(21) Vada E. Pinson Jr.	20.00	10.00	6.00
(22) Robert T. Purkey	9.00	4.50	2.75
(23) Pedro Ramos	9.00	4.50	2.75
(24) Frank Robinson	70.00	35.00	21.00
(25) John Romano	9.00	4.50	2.75
(26) Pete Rose	400.00	200.00	120.00
(27) John Tsitouris	9.00	4.50	2.75
(28) Robert A. Veale Jr.	9.00	4.50	2.75
(29) Bill Virdon	15.00	7.50	4.50
(30) Leon Wagner	9.00	4.50	2.75
(31) Fred Whitfield	9.00	4.50	2.75

1965 Kahn's Weiners

There was little change for the Kahn's issue in 1965 beyond the addition of Milwaukee Braves players to the Reds, Pirates and Indians traditionally included in the set. At 45 players, the 1965 issue was the largest of the Kahn's sets. Once again in 3" by 3-1/2" size, the 1965s retained the borderless color photo design of the previous season. A look at the stats on the back will confirm the year of issue, however, since the last year of statistics is the year prior to the card's issue.

	NR MT	EX	VG
Complete Set:	1100.00	550.00	330.00
Common Player:	12.00	6.00	3.50
(1) Hank Aaron	125.00	62.00	37.00
(2) Max Alvis	12.00	6.00	3.50
(3) Jose Azcue	12.00	6.00	3.50
(4) Bob Bailey	12.00	6.00	3.50
(5) Frank Bolling	12.00	6.00	3.50
(6) Leonardo Cardenas	12.00	6.00	3.50
(7) Rico Ricardo Carty	15.00	7.50	4.50
(8) Donn A. Clendenon	12.00	6.00	3.50
(9) Tony Cloninger	12.00	6.00	3.50
(10) Gordon Coleman	12.00	6.00	3.50
(11) Victor Davalillo	12.00	6.00	3.50

1-3/8" advertising panel with a red rose logo and the word "Kahn's," separated from the player portion of the card by a black dotted line. Naturally, many of the cards are found today with the top portion cut off. Values listed here are for cards with the top portion intact. Players from the Cincinnati Reds, Pittsburgh Pirates, Cleveland Indians and Atlanta Braves were included in the set. Since the cards are blank-backed, collectors must learn to differentiate player poses to determine year of issue for some cards.

		NR MT	EX	VG
(12)	John A. Edwards	12.00	6.00	3.50
(13)	Sam Ellis	12.00	6.00	3.50
(14)	Robert Friend	15.00	7.50	4.50
(15)	Tommy Harper	12.00	6.00	3.50
(16)	Chuck Hinton	12.00	6.00	3.50
(17)	Dick Howser	15.00	7.50	4.50
(18)	Joey Jay	12.00	6.00	3.50
(19)	Deron Johnson	12.00	6.00	3.50
(20)	Jack Kralick	12.00	6.00	3.50
(21)	Denny Lemaster	12.00	6.00	3.50
(22)	Jerry Lynch	12.00	6.00	3.50
(23)	Jim Maloney	15.00	7.50	4.50
(24)	Lee Maye	12.00	6.00	3.50
(25)	William S. Mazeroski	20.00	10.00	6.00
(26)	Alvin McBean	12.00	6.00	3.50
(27)	Bill McCool	12.00	6.00	3.50
(28)	Sam McDowell	15.00	7.50	4.50
(29)	Donald McMahon	12.00	6.00	3.50
(30)	Denis Menke	12.00	6.00	3.50
(31)	Joe Nuxhall	15.00	7.50	4.50
(32)	Gene Oliver	12.00	6.00	3.50
(33)	Jim O'Toole	12.00	6.00	3.50
(34)	Jim Pagliaroni	12.00	6.00	3.50
(35)	Vada E. Pinson Jr.	20.00	10.00	6.00
(36)	Frank Robinson	70.00	35.00	21.00
(37)	Pete Rose	250.00	125.00	75.00
(38)	Willie Stargell	70.00	35.00	21.00
(39)	Ralph W. Terry	12.00	6.00	3.50
(40)	Luis Tiant	20.00	10.00	6.00
(41)	Joe Torre	25.00	12.50	7.50
(42)	John Tsitouris	12.00	6.00	3.50
(43)	Robert A. Veale Jr.	12.00	6.00	3.50
(44)	Bill Virdon	15.00	7.50	4.50
(45)	Leon Wagner	12.00	6.00	3.50

		NR MT	EX	VG
Complete Set:		1200.00	600.00	360.00
Common Player:		18.00	9.00	5.50
(1)	Henry Aaron	125.00	62.00	37.00
(2)	Felipe Alou	24.00	12.00	7.25
(3)	Max Alvis	18.00	9.00	5.50
(4)	Robert Bailey	18.00	9.00	5.50
(5)	Wade Blasingame	18.00	9.00	5.50
(6)	Frank Bolling	18.00	9.00	5.50
(7)	Leo Cardenas	18.00	9.00	5.50
(8)	Roberto Clemente	125.00	62.00	37.00
(9)	Tony Cloninger	18.00	9.00	5.50
(10)	Vic Davalillo	18.00	9.00	5.50
(11)	John Edwards	18.00	9.00	5.50
(12)	Sam Ellis	18.00	9.00	5.50
(13)	Pedro Gonzalez	18.00	9.00	5.50
(14)	Tommy Harper	18.00	9.00	5.50
(15)	Deron Johnson	18.00	9.00	5.50
(16)	Mack Jones	18.00	9.00	5.50
(17)	Denny Lemaster	18.00	9.00	5.50
(18)	Jim Maloney	24.00	12.00	7.25
(19)	William Mazeroski	28.00	14.00	8.50
(20)	Bill McCool	18.00	9.00	5.50
(21)	Sam McDowell	24.00	12.00	7.25
(22)	Denis Menke	18.00	9.00	5.50
(23)	Joe Nuxhall	24.00	12.00	7.25
(24)	Jim Pagliaroni	18.00	9.00	5.50
(25)	Milt Pappas	24.00	12.00	7.25
(26)	Vada Pinson	28.00	14.00	8.50
(27)	Pete Rose	250.00	125.00	75.00
(28)	Sonny Siebert	18.00	9.00	5.50
(29)	Willie Stargell	80.00	40.00	24.00
(30)	Joe Torre	28.00	14.00	8.50
(31)	Bob Veale	18.00	9.00	5.50
(32)	Fred Whitfield	18.00	9.00	5.50

1966 Kahn's Weiners

The fourth new format in five years greeted collector's with the introduction of Kahn's 1966 issue of 32 cards. The design consisted of a color photo bordered by white and yellow vertical stripes. The player's name was printed above the photo, and a facsimile autograph appeared across the photo. As printed, the cards were 2-13/16" by 4" in size. However, the top portion consisted of a 2-13/16" by

1967 Kahn's Weiners

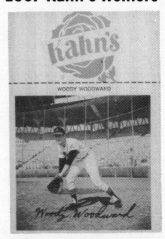

Retaining the basic format of the 1966 set (see listing for description), the '67 Kahn's set was expanded to 41 players through the addition of several New York Mets players to the previous season's lineup of Reds, Pirates, Indians and Braves. Making the 1967 set especially challenging for collectors is the fact that some cards are found in a smaller size and/or with different colored stripes bordering the color player photo. On the majority of cards, the size remained 2-13/16" by 4" (with ad at top; 2-13/16" by 2-5/8"without ad at top). However, because of packing in different products, the Ellis, Helms and Torre cards can be found in 2-13/16" by 3-1/4" size (with ad; 2-13/16" by 2-1/8" without ad). The handful of known border stripe variations are listed below. Values quoted are for cards with the top ad panel intact. All variation cards are included in the valuations given below for complete sets.

EARL WILSON

		NR MT	EX	VG
Complete Set:		1400.00	700.00	420.00
Common Player:		18.00	9.00	5.50
(1)	Henry Aaron	125.00	62.00	37.00
(2)	Gene Alley	18.00	9.00	5.50
(3)	Felipe Alou	24.00	12.00	7.25
(4a)	Matty Alou (yellow & white striped border)			
		24.00	12.00	7.25
(4b)	Matty Alou (red & white striped border)			
		28.00	14.00	8.50
(5)	Max Alvis	18.00	9.00	5.50
(6)	Ken Boyer	30.00	15.00	9.00
(7)	Leo Cardenas	18.00	9.00	5.50
(8)	Rico Carty	24.00	12.00	7.25
(9)	Tony Cloninger	18.00	9.00	5.50
(10)	Tommy Davis	24.00	12.00	7.25
(11)	John Edwards	18.00	9.00	5.50
(12a)	Sam Ellis (large size)	18.00	9.00	5.50
(12b)	Sam Ellis (small size)	28.00	14.00	8.50
(13)	Jack Fisher	18.00	9.00	5.50
(14)	Steve Hargan	18.00	9.00	5.50
(15)	Tom Harper	18.00	9.00	5.50
(16a)	Tom Helms (large size)	18.00	9.00	5.50
(16b)	Tom Helms (small size)	28.00	14.00	8.50
(17)	Deron Johnson	18.00	9.00	5.50
(18)	Ken Johnson	18.00	9.00	5.50
(19)	Cleon Jones	18.00	9.00	5.50
(20)	Ed Kranepool	18.00	9.00	5.50
(21a)	James Maloney (yellow & white striped border)			
		24.00	12.00	7.25
(21b)	James Maloney (red & white striped border)			
		28.00	14.00	8.50
(22)	Lee May	24.00	12.00	7.25
(23)	Wm. Mazeroski	28.00	14.00	8.50
(24)	Wm. McCool	18.00	9.00	5.50
(25)	Sam McDowell	24.00	12.00	7.25
(26)	Dennis Menke (Denis)	18.00	9.00	5.50
(27)	Jim Pagliaroni	18.00	9.00	5.50
(28)	Don Pavletich	18.00	9.00	5.50
(29)	Tony Perez	35.00	17.50	10.50
(30)	Vada Pinson	28.00	14.00	8.50
(31)	Dennis Ribant	18.00	9.00	5.50
(32)	Pete Rose	200.00	100.00	60.00
(33)	Art Shamsky	18.00	9.00	5.50
(34)	Bob Shaw	18.00	9.00	5.50
(35)	Sonny Siebert	18.00	9.00	5.50
(36)	Wm. Stargell (first name actually Wilver)			
		80.00	40.00	24.00
(37a)	Joe Torre (large size)	28.00	14.00	8.50
(37b)	Joe Torre (small size)	32.00	16.00	9.50
(38)	Bob Veale	18.00	9.00	5.50
(39)	Leon Wagner	18.00	9.00	5.50
(40)	Fred Whitfield	18.00	9.00	5.50
(41)	Woody Woodward	18.00	9.00	5.50

1968 Kahn's Weiners

The number of card size and stripe color variations increased with the 1968 Kahn's issue (see 1967 listing), though the basic card design was retained from the previous two seasons: 2-13/16" by 4" size (with ad panel at top; 2-13/16" by 2-5/8" with ad panel cut off), color photo bordered by yellow and white vertical stripes. In addition to the basic issue, a number of the cards appear in a smaller, 2-13/16" by 3-1/4", size, while some of them, and others, appear with variations in the color of border stripes. One card, Maloney, can be found with a top portion advertising Blue Mountain brand meats, as well as Kahn's. All in all, quite a challenge for the specialist. The 1968 set featured the largest number of teams represented in any Kahn's issue: Atlanta Braves, Chicago Cubs and White Sox, Cincinnati Reds,

Cleveland Indians, Detroit Tigers, New York Mets and Pittsburgh Pirates. Values quoted below are for cards with the ad panel at top; complete set prices include all variations.

		NR MT	EX	VG
Complete Set:		2000.00	1000.00	600.00
Common Player:		18.00	9.00	5.50
(1a)	Hank Aaron (large size)	125.00	62.00	37.00
(1b)	Hank Aaron (small size)	150.00	75.00	45.00
(2)	Tommy Agee	18.00	9.00	5.50
(3a)	Gene Alley (large size)	18.00	9.00	5.50
(3b)	Gene Alley (small size)	24.00	12.00	7.25
(4)	Felipe Alou	24.00	12.00	7.25
(5a)	Matty Alou (yellow striped border)			
		24.00	12.00	7.25
(5b)	Matty Alou (red striped border)	28.00	14.00	8.50
(6a)	Max Alvis (large size)	18.00	9.00	5.50
(6b)	Max Alvis (small size)	24.00	12.00	7.25
(7)	Gerry Arrigo	18.00	9.00	5.50
(8)	John Bench	450.00	225.00	135.00
(9a)	Clete Boyer (large size)	18.00	9.00	5.50
(9b)	Clete Boyer (small size)	24.00	12.00	7.25
(10)	Larry Brown	18.00	9.00	5.50
(11a)	Leo Cardenas (large size)	18.00	9.00	5.50
(11b)	Leo Cardenas (small size)	24.00	12.00	7.25
(12a)	Bill Freehan (large size)	24.00	12.00	7.25
(12b)	Bill Freehan (small size)	28.00	14.00	8.50
(13)	Steve Hargan	18.00	9.00	5.50
(14)	Joel Horlen	18.00	9.00	5.50
(15)	Tony Horton	24.00	12.00	7.25
(16)	Willie Horton	24.00	12.00	7.25
(17)	Ferguson Jenkins	32.00	16.00	9.50
(18)	Deron Johnson	18.00	9.00	5.50
(19)	Mack Jones	18.00	9.00	5.50
(20)	Bob Lee	18.00	9.00	5.50
(21a)	Jim Maloney (large size, rose logo)			
		24.00	12.00	7.25
(21b)	Jim Maloney (large size, blue mountain logo)	28.00	14.00	8.50
(21c)	Jim Maloney (small size, yellow & white striped border)	28.00	14.00	8.50
(21d)	Jim Maloney (small size, yellow, white & green striped border)	28.00	14.00	8.50
(22a)	Lee May (large size)	24.00	12.00	7.25
(22b)	Lee May (small size)	28.00	14.00	8.50
(23a)	Wm. Mazeroski (large size)	24.00	12.00	7.25
(23b)	Wm. Mazeroski (small size)	28.00	14.00	8.50
(24)	Dick McAuliffe	18.00	9.00	5.50
(25)	Bill McCool	18.00	9.00	5.50
(26a)	Sam McDowell (yellow striped border)			
		24.00	12.00	7.25
(26b)	Sam McDowell (red striped border)			
		28.00	14.00	8.50
(27a)	Tony Perez (yellow striped border)			
		35.00	17.50	10.50
(27b)	Tony Perez (red striped border)	40.00	20.00	12.00
(28)	Gary Peters	18.00	9.00	5.50
(29a)	Vada Pinson (large size)	24.00	12.00	7.25
(29b)	Vada Pinson (small size)	28.00	14.00	8.50
(30)	Chico Ruiz	18.00	9.00	5.50

		NR MT	EX	VG
(31a)	Ron Santo (yellow striped border)			
		24.00	12.00	7.25
(31b)	Ron Santo (red striped border)	28.00	14.00	8.50
(32)	Art Shamsky	18.00	9.00	5.50
(33)	Luis Tiant	24.00	12.00	7.25
(34a)	Joe Torre (large size)	28.00	14.00	8.50
(34b)	Joe Torre (small size)	32.00	16.00	9.50
(35a)	Bob Veale (large size)	18.00	9.00	5.50
(35b)	Bob Veale (small size)	24.00	12.00	7.25
(36)	Leon Wagner	18.00	9.00	5.50
(37)	Billy Williams	50.00	25.00	15.00
(38)	Earl Wilson	18.00	9.00	5.50

1969 Kahn's Weiners

In its 15th consecutive year of baseball card issuing, Kahn's continued the basic format adopted in 1966. The basic card issue of 22 players was printed in 2-13/16" by 4" size (with ad panel at top; 2-13/16" by 2-5/8" without panel) and are blanked-backed. Teams represented in the set included the Braves, Cubs, White Sox, Reds, Cardinals, Indians and Pirates. The cards featured a color photo and facsimile autograph bordered by yellow and white vertical stripes. At top was an ad panel consisting of the Kahn's red rose logo. However, because some cards were produced for inclusion in packages other than the standard hot dogs, a number of variations in card size and stripe color were created, as noted in the listings below. The smaller size cards, 2-13/16" by 3-1/4" with ad, 2-13/16" by 2-1/8" without ad, were created by more closely cropping the player photo at top and bottom. Values quoted below are for cards with the top logo panel intact. Complete set values include all the variations.

		NR MT	EX	VG
Complete Set:		1000.00	500.00	300.00
Common Player:		18.00	9.00	5.50
(1a)	Hank Aaron (large size)	125.00	62.00	37.00
(1b)	Hank Aaron (small size)	150.00	75.00	45.00
(2)	Matty Alou	24.00	12.00	7.25
(3)	Max Alvis	18.00	9.00	5.50
(4)	Gerry Arrigo	18.00	9.00	5.50
(5)	Steve Blass	18.00	9.00	5.50
(6)	Clay Carroll	18.00	9.00	5.50
(7)	Tony Cloninger	18.00	9.00	5.50
(8)	George Culver	18.00	9.00	5.50
(9)	Joel Horlen	18.00	9.00	5.50
(10)	Tony Horton	24.00	12.00	7.25
(11)	Alex Johnson	18.00	9.00	5.50
(12a)	Jim Maloney (large size)	24.00	12.00	7.25
(12b)	Jim Maloney (small size)	28.00	14.00	8.50
(13a)	Lee May (yellow striped border)	24.00	12.00	7.25
(13b)	Lee May (red striped border)	28.00	14.00	8.50
(14a)	Wm. Mazeroski (yellow striped border)			
		24.00	12.00	7.25

		NR MT	EX	VG
(14b)	Wm. Mazeroski (red striped border)			
		28.00	14.00	8.50
(15a)	Sam McDowell (yellow striped border)			
		24.00	12.00	7.25
(15b)	Sam McDowell (red striped border)			
		28.00	14.00	8.50
(16a)	Tony Perez (large size)	35.00	17.50	10.50
(16b)	Tony Perez (small size)	40.00	20.00	12.00
(17)	Gary Peters	18.00	9.00	5.50
(18a)	Ron Santo (yellow striped border)			
		24.00	12.00	7.25
(18b)	Ron Santo (red striped border)	28.00	14.00	8.50
(19)	Luis Tiant	24.00	12.00	7.25
(20)	Joe Torre	28.00	14.00	8.50
(21)	Bob Veale	18.00	9.00	5.50
(22)	Billy Williams	50.00	25.00	15.00

1987 Kahn's Wieners Reds

After a nearly 20-year layoff, Kahn's Wieners produced a baseball card set. Kahn's, who produced card sets between 1955 and 1968, sponsored a 28-card 9set that was distributed to fans attending the August 2nd game at Riverfront Stadium. The cards are the standard 2-1/2" by 3-1/2" size. The fronts offer a full-color player photo bordered in red and white. The backs carry the Kahn's logo and a head shot of the player.

		MT	NR MT	EX
Complete Set:		15.00	11.00	6.00
Common Player:		.20	.15	.08
6	Bo Diaz	.25	.20	.10
10	Terry Francona	.20	.15	.08
11	Kurt Stillwell	.70	.50	.30
12	Nick Esasky	.30	.25	.12
13	Dave Concepcion	.40	.30	.15
15	Barry Larkin	1.00	.70	.40
16	Ron Oester	.20	.15	.08
21	Paul O'Neill	.30	.25	.12
23	Lloyd McClendon	.20	.15	.08
25	Buddy Bell	.35	.25	.14
28	Kal Daniels	1.00	.70	.40
29	Tracy Jones	.70	.50	.30
30	Guy Hoffman	.20	.15	.08
31	John Franco	.50	.40	.20
32	Tom Browning	.50	.40	.20
33	Ron Robinson	.25	.20	.10
34	Bill Gullickson	.20	.15	.08
35	Pat Pacillo	.30	.25	.12
39	Dave Parker	.50	.40	.20
43	Bill Landrum	.20	.15	.08
44	Eric Davis	2.00	1.50	.80
46	Rob Murphy	.40	.30	.15
47	Frank Williams	.25	.20	.10
48	Ted Power	.20	.15	.08

NOTE: A card number in parentheses ( ) indicates the set is unnumbered.

1988 Kahn's Wieners Mets

Approximately 50,000 Mets fans received this complimentary card set during a ballpark promotion sponsored by Kahn's Wieners. Twenty-five players are featured in the set, along with manager Davey Johnson, four coaches and a team photo. Card fronts have a dark blue border with an orange rectangle framing the full-color player photo. Card numbers reflecting the players' uniform numbers, are printed in white in the upper right corner of the card face, beside the team logo. The player name appears upper left and the player position is centered in the bottom margin. The card backs are black and white with red line accents. In addition to player acquisition date, birthday and residence, a paragraph-style career summary is included. The cards measure 2-1/2" by 3-1/2".

		MT	NR MT	EX
Complete Set:		14.00	10.50	5.50
Common Player:		.20	.15	.08
1	Mookie Wilson	.35	.25	.14
2	Mackey Sasser	.30	.25	.12
3	Bud Harrelson	.20	.15	.08
4	Lenny Dykstra	.40	.30	.15
5	Davey Johnson	.30	.25	.12
6	Wally Backman	.20	.15	.08
8	Gary Carter	.80	.60	.30
11	Tim Teufel	.20	.15	.08
12	Ron Darling	.60	.45	.25
13	Lee Mazzilli	.20	.15	.08
15	Rick Aguilera	.20	.15	.08
16	Dwight Gooden	2.00	1.50	.80
17	Keith Hernandez	.80	.60	.30
18	Darryl Strawberry	1.50	1.25	.60
19	Bob Ojeda	.35	.25	.14
20	Howard Johnson	.80	.60	.30
21	Kevin Elster	.50	.40	.20
22	Kevin McReynolds	.60	.45	.25
26	Terry Leach	.20	.15	.08
28	Bill Robinson	.20	.15	.08
29	Dave Magadan	.40	.30	.15
30	Mel Stottlemyre	.20	.15	.08
31	Gene Walter	.20	.15	.08
33	Barry Lyons	.20	.15	.08
34	Sam Perlozzo	.20	.15	.08
42	Roger McDowell	.30	.25	.12
44	David Cone	.70	.50	.30
48	Randy Myers	.50	.40	.20
50	Sid Fernandez	.35	.25	.14
52	Greg Pavlick	.20	.15	.08
----	Team Photo	.20	.15	.08

1988 Kahn's Wieners Reds

This 26-card set was a one-time giveaway during the August 14th, 1988 Cincinnati Reds game. The glossy cards (2-1/2" by 3-1/2") feature full-color action photos inside red and white borders. The Reds logo, player uniform number, name and position are printed below the photo. The backs are black and white, with small player close-ups and career stats. A promotional 25-cent coupon for Kahn's Wieners was included with each set.

		MT	NR MT	EX
Complete Set:		12.00	9.00	4.75
Common Player:		.20	.15	.08
6	Bo Diaz	.25	.20	.10

		MT	NR MT	EX
8	Terry McGriff	.20	.15	.08
9	Eddie Milner	.20	.15	.08
10	Leon Durham	.30	.25	.12
11	Barry Larkin	.70	.50	.30
12	Nick Esasky	.30	.25	.12
13	Dave Concepcion	.40	.30	.15
14	Pete Rose	1.25	.90	.50
15	Jeff Treadway	.50	.40	.20
17	Chris Sabo	1.50	1.25	.60
20	Danny Jackson	.60	.45	.25
21	Paul O'Neill	.30	.25	.12
22	Dave Collins	.20	.15	.08
23	Jose Rijo	.35	.25	.14
28	Kal Daniels	.70	.50	.30
29	Tracy Jones	.50	.40	.20
30	Lloyd McClendon	.20	.15	.08
31	John Franco	.50	.40	.20
32	Tom Browning	.50	.40	.20
33	Ron Robinson	.25	.20	.10
40	Jack Armstrong	.25	.20	.10
44	Eric Davis	2.00	1.50	.80
46	Rob Murphy	.25	.20	.10
47	Frank Williams	.20	.15	.08
48	Tim Birtsas	.20	.15	.08
----	Coaches (Scott Breeden, Tommy Helms, Bruce Kimm, Jim Lett, Lee May, Tony Perez)			
		.20	.15	.08

1989 Kahn's Wieners Mets

This 30-card New York Mets team set was sponsored by Kahn's Wieners and was given to fans attending the July 6, 1989 Mets game at Shea Stadium. The standard-size cards feature a full-color photo surrounded by a blue and orange border with the player's name and uniform number across the top. The backs include the Kahn's logo, along with player information and complete Major League stats.

		MT	NR MT	EX
Complete Set:		18.00	13.50	7.25
Common Player:		.20	.15	.08
Team Card		.20	.15	.08
Jeff Innis, Keith Miller, Jeff Musselman, Frank Viola (Update Card)		1.50	1.25	.60
1	Mookie Wilson	.35	.25	.14
2	Mackey Sasser	.25	.20	.10
3	Bud Harrelson	.20	.15	.08
5	Davey Johnson	.25	.20	.10
7	Juan Samuel	.40	.30	.15
8	Gary Carter	.50	.40	.20
9	Gregg Jefferies	2.00	1.50	.80
12	Ron Darling	.50	.40	.20
13	Lee Mazzilli	.20	.15	.08

		MT	NR MT	EX
16	Dwight Gooden	1.75	1.50	.70
17	Keith Hernandez	.60	.45	.25
18	Darryl Strawberry	1.25	.90	.50
19	Bob Ojeda	.25	.20	.10
20	Howard Johnson	.70	.50	.30
21	Kevin Elster	.35	.25	.14
22	Kevin McReynolds	.50	.40	.20
28	Bill Robinson	.20	.15	.08
29	Dave Magadan	.30	.25	.12
30	Mel Stottlemyre	.20	.15	.08
32	Mark Carreon	.40	.30	.15
33	Barry Lyons	.20	.15	.08
34	Sam Perlozzo	.20	.15	.08
38	Rick Aguilera	.20	.15	.08
44	David Cone	.50	.40	.20
46	Dave West	.60	.45	.25
48	Randy Meyers	.35	.25	.14
50	Sid Fernandez	.35	.25	.14
51	Don Aase	.20	.15	.08
52	Greg Pavlick	.20	.15	.08

1989 Kahn's Wieners Reds

This 26-card Cincinnati Reds team set, sponsored by Kahn's Weiners, was distributed to fans attending the Aug. 6 Reds game at Riverfront Stadium. The standard-size, red-bordered cards feature action photos with the player's name in the upper left corner, his uniform number in the upper right and the Reds logo in the middle. The backs include a black-and-white head shot, player data and complete major and minor league stats. The Kahn's logo appears in the upper right corner of the back.

		MT	NR MT	EX
Complete Set:		10.00	7.50	4.00
Common Player:		.20	.15	.08
Coaches Card				
6	Bo Diaz			
7	Lenny Harris	.40	.30	.15
11	Barry Larkin	.50	.40	.20
12	Joel Youngblood	.20	.15	.08
14	Pete Rose	1.00	.70	.40
16	Ron Oester	.25	.20	.10
17	Chris Sabo	.40	.30	.15
20	Danny Jackson	.25	.20	.15
21	Paul O'Neill	.25	.20	.15
25	Todd Benzinger	.40	.30	.15
27	Jose Rijo	.25	.20	.10
28	Kal Daniels	.40	.30	.15
29	Herm Winningham	.20	.15	.08
30	Ken Griffey	.30	.25	.12
31	John Franco	.30	.25	.12
32	Tom Browning	.35	.25	.14
33	Ron Robinson	.20	.15	.08
34	Jeff Reed	.20	.15	.08
36	Rolando Roomes	.70	.50	.30
37	Norm Charlton	.50	.40	.20
42	Rick Mahler	.25	.20	.10
43	Kent Tekulve	.20	.15	.08
44	Eric Davis	2.00	1.50	.80
48	Tim Birtsas	.20	.15	.08
49	Rob Dibble	.60	.45	.25

1986 Kas Potato Chips Cardinals

One of a handful of 2-7/8" round baseball card "discs" created by Mike Schecter Associates for inclusion in boxes of potato chips, the 20-card Kas set features players of the defending National League Champion St. Louis Cardinals. Fronts feature color photo on which the team logos have been removed from the caps by airbrushing the photos, indicating Kas did not license with the Cardinals for use of its uniform logos. Card backs have minimal personal data and 1985 stats.

		MT	NR MT	EX
Complete Set:		18.00	13.50	7.25
Common Player:		.70	.50	.30
1	Vince Coleman	2.25	1.75	.90
2	Ken Dayley	.70	.50	.30
3	Tito Landrum	.70	.50	.30
4	Steve Braun	.70	.50	.30
5	Danny Cox	1.25	.90	.50
6	Bob Forsch	.80	.60	.30
7	Ozzie Smith	1.50	1.25	.60
8	Brian Harper	.70	.50	.30
9	Jack Clark	1.50	1.25	.60
10	Todd Worrell	2.25	1.75	.90
11	Joaquin Andujar	.70	.50	.30
12	Tom Nieto	.70	.50	.30
13	Kurt Kepshire	.70	.50	.30
14	Terry Pendleton	1.00	.70	.40
15	Tom Herr	1.00	.70	.40
16	Darrell Porter	.70	.50	.30
17	John Tudor	1.00	.70	.40
18	Jeff Lahti	.70	.50	.30
19	Andy Van Slyke	1.25	.90	.50
20	Willie McGee	1.50	1.25	.60

1986 Kay Bee

One of the most-widely distributed of the specialty boxed sets of 1986, the Kay Bee toy store chain sets of "Young Superstars of Baseball" was produced by Topps. The 2-1/2" by 3-1/2" cards are printed on white stock with a glossy surface finish. Backs, printed in red and black, are strongly reminiscent of the 1971 Topps cards. While the set concentrated on "young" stars of the game, few of the year's top rookies were included.

		MT	NR MT	EX
Complete Set:		5.00	3.75	2.00
Common Player:		.05	.04	.02
1	Rick Aguilera	.12	.09	.05
2	Chris Brown	.15	.11	.06
3	Tom Browning	.07	.05	.03
4	Tom Brunansky	.07	.05	.03
5	Vince Coleman	.50	.40	.20
6	Ron Darling	.10	.08	.04
7	Alvin Davis	.10	.08	.04
8	Mariano Duncan	.07	.05	.03
9	Shawon Dunston	.07	.05	.03
10	Sid Fernandez	.10	.08	.04
11	Tony Fernandez	.10	.08	.04
12	Brian Fisher	.10	.08	.04
13	John Franco	.07	.05	.03
14	Julio Franco	.10	.08	.04
15	Dwight Gooden	.50	.40	.20
16	Ozzie Guillen	.15	.11	.06
17	Tony Gwynn	.30	.25	.12
18	Jimmy Key	.10	.08	.04
19	Don Mattingly	1.75	1.25	.70
20	Oddibe McDowell	.15	.11	.06
21	Roger McDowell	.15	.11	.06
22	Dan Pasqua	.10	.08	.04
23	Terry Pendleton	.07	.05	.03
24	Jim Presley	.10	.08	.04
25	Kirby Puckett	.25	.20	.10
26	Earnie Riles	.07	.05	.03
27	Bret Saberhagen	.15	.11	.06
28	Mark Salas	.05	.04	.02
29	Juan Samuel	.12	.09	.05
30	Jeff Stone	.05	.04	.02
31	Darryl Strawberry	.40	.30	.15
32	Andy Van Slyke	.10	.08	.04
33	Frank Viola	.12	.09	.05

1987 Kay Bee

For a second straight year, Topps produced a 33-card set for the Kay Bee toy store chain. Called "Superstars of Baseball," the cards in the set measure the standard 2-1/2" by 3-1/2" size. The glossy-coated card fronts carry a full-color player photo plus the Kay Bee logo. The card backs, reminiscent of those found in the 1971 Topps set, offer a black and white head shot of the player along with his name, postion, personal information, playing record and a brief biography. The set was packaged in a specially designed box.

		MT	NR MT	EX
Complete Set:		5.00	3.75	2.00
Common Player:		.05	.04	.02
1	Harold Baines	.10	.08	.04
2	Jesse Barfield	.12	.09	.05
3	Don Baylor	.10	.08	.04
4	Wade Boggs	1.00	.70	.40
5	George Brett	.40	.30	.15
6	Hubie Brooks	.07	.05	.03

		MT	NR MT	EX
7	Jose Canseco	1.00	.70	.40
8	Gary Carter	.20	.15	.08
9	Joe Carter	.12	.09	.05
10	Roger Clemens	.40	.30	.15
11	Vince Coleman	.15	.11	.06
12	Glenn Davis	.15	.11	.06
13	Dwight Gooden	.40	.30	.15
14	Pedro Guerrero	.15	.11	.06
15	Tony Gwynn	.25	.20	.10
16	Rickey Henderson	.25	.20	.10
17	Keith Hernandez	.20	.15	.08
18	Wally Joyner	.50	.40	.20
19	Don Mattingly	1.75	1.25	.70
20	Jack Morris	.15	.11	.06
21	Dale Murphy	.30	.25	.12
22	Eddie Murray	.25	.20	.10
23	Dave Parker	.15	.11	.06
24	Kirby Puckett	.25	.20	.10
25	Tim Raines	.25	.20	.10
26	Jim Rice	.25	.20	.10
27	Dave Righetti	.12	.09	.05
28	Ryne Sandberg	.20	.15	.08
29	Mike Schmidt	.30	.25	.12
30	Mike Scott	.12	.09	.05
31	Darryl Strawberry	.40	.30	.15
32	Fernando Valenzuela	.20	.15	.08
33	Dave Winfield	.20	.15	.08

1988 Kay Bee
Superstars Of Baseball

This 33-card boxed set was produced by Topps for exclusive distribution via Kay Bee toy stores nationwide. Card fronts are super glossy and feature full-color player action photos below a bright red and yellow player name banner. Photos are framed in green above a large, cartoon-style Kay Bee logo. Card backs feature player closeups in a horizontal layout in blue ink on a green and white background. Card backs are numbered and carry a player name section that includes biographical information, career data and major league batting stats.

		MT	NR MT	EX
Complete Set:		5.00	3.75	2.00
Common Player:		.10	.08	.04
1	George Bell	.20	.15	.08
2	Wade Boggs	1.00	.70	.40
3	Jose Canseco	1.00	.70	.40
4	Joe Carter	.12	.09	.05
5	Jack Clark	.15	.11	.06
6	Alvin Davis	.10	.08	.04
7	Eric Davis	.80	.60	.30
8	Andre Dawson	.15	.11	.06
9	Darrell Evans	.10	.08	.04
10	Dwight Evans	.10	.08	.04
11	Gary Gaetti	.12	.09	.05
12	Pedro Guerrero	.15	.11	.06
13	Tony Gwynn	.25	.20	.10
14	Howard Johnson	.12	.09	.05
15	Wally Joyner	.30	.25	.12
16	Don Mattingly	1.75	1.25	.70
17	Willie McGee	.10	.08	.04
18	Mark McGwire	1.00	.70	.40
19	Paul Molitor	.12	.09	.05

		MT	NR MT	EX
20	Dale Murphy	.30	.25	.12
21	Dave Parker	.15	.11	.06
22	Lance Parrish	.15	.11	.06
23	Kirby Puckett	.25	.20	.10
24	Tim Raines	.25	.20	.10
25	Cal Ripken	.30	.25	.12
26	Juan Samuel	.12	.09	.05
27	Mike Schmidt	.30	.25	.12
28	Ruben Sierra	.12	.09	.05
29	Darryl Strawberry	.40	.30	.15
30	Danny Tartabull	.12	.09	.05
31	Alan Trammell	.15	.11	.06
32	Tim Wallach	.10	.08	.04
33	Dave Winfield	.20	.15	.08

		MT	NR MT	EX
29	Dave Righetti	.12	.09	.05
30	Cal Ripken, Jr.	.30	.25	.12
31	Don Robinson	.05	.04	.02
32	Bret Saberhagen	.15	.11	.06
33	Juan Samuel	.12	.09	.05
34	Mike Schmidt	.30	.25	.12
35	Mike Scott	.12	.09	.05
36	Kevin Seitzer	.60	.45	.25
37	Dave Smith	.05	.04	.02
38	Ozzie Smith	.15	.11	.06
39	Zane Smith	.05	.04	.02
40	Darryl Strawberry	.40	.30	.15
41	Rick Sutcliffe	.10	.08	.04
42	Bobby Thigpen	.07	.05	.03
43	Alan Trammell	.15	.11	.06
44	Andy Van Slyke	.10	.08	.04

1988 Kay Bee Team Leaders

This first-year boxed edition of 44 player and 6 team logo cards was produced by Fleer for distribution by Kay Bee toy stores nationwide. Full-color player photos are framed in black against a bright red border. Lettering is blue, yellow and black. The "Fleer Team Leaders 1988" logo is printed vertically along the left side of the card front; the Kay Bee logo appears in the lower right corner of the photo; player's name, team and position are centered in the bottom margin. Card backs (red, white and pink) repeat the Team Leaders logo, followed by stats, personal data, team and major league baseball logos. The player's name, card number and position are listed on the lower border. The set includes six team logo sticker cards that feature black and white stadium photos on the backs.

		MT	NR MT	EX
Complete Set:		5.00	3.75	2.00
Common Player:		.05	.04	.02
1	George Bell	.20	.15	.08
2	Wade Boggs	1.00	.70	.40
3	Jose Canseco	1.00	.70	.40
4	Will Clark	.25	.20	.10
5	Roger Clemens	.40	.30	.15
6	Eric Davis	.80	.60	.30
7	Andre Dawson	.15	.11	.06
8	Julio Franco	.07	.05	.03
9	Andres Galarraga	.15	.11	.06
10	Dwight Gooden	.40	.30	.15
11	Tony Gwynn	.25	.20	.10
12	Tom Henke	.05	.04	.02
13	Orel Hershiser	.10	.08	.04
14	Kent Hrbek	.15	.11	.06
15	Ted Higuera	.10	.08	.04
16	Wally Joyner	.30	.25	.12
17	Jimmy Key	.07	.05	.03
18	Mark Langston	.10	.08	.04
19	Don Mattingly	1.75	1.25	.70
20	Willie McGee	.10	.08	.04
21	Mark McGwire	1.00	.70	.40
22	Paul Molitor	.12	.09	.05
23	Jack Morris	.12	.09	.05
24	Dale Murphy	.30	.25	.12
25	Larry Parrish	.05	.04	.02
26	Kirby Puckett	.20	.15	.08
27	Tim Raines	.20	.15	.08
28	Jeff Reardon	.07	.05	.03

1989 Kay-Bee Superstars

The top stars of baseball were featured in this 33-card boxed set produced by Topps for the Kay-Bee Toy store chain. The glossy, standard-size cards display the Kee-Bee logo below the player photo on the front. The top of the card is headlined "Superstars of Baseball," with the player's name underneath. The backs of the cards include a small black-and-white player photo and personal data.

		MT	NR MT	EX
Complete Set:		5.00	3.75	2.00
Common Player:		.10	.08	.04
1	Wade Boggs	1.00	.70	.40
2	George Brett	.15	.11	.08
3	Jose Canseco	1.00	.70	.40
4	Gary Carter	.10	.08	.04
5	Jack Clark	.10	.08	.04
6	Will Clark	1.00	.70	.40
7	Roger Clemens	.25	.20	.10
8	Eric Davis	.60	.45	.25
9	Andre Dawson	.15	.11	.06
10	Dwight Evans	.10	.08	.04
11	Carlton Fisk	.10	.08	.04
12	Andres Galarraga	.10	.08	.04
13	Kirk Gibson	.10	.08	.04
14	Doc Gooden	.30	.25	.12
15	Mike Greenwell	.30	.25	.12
16	Pedro Guerrero	.15	.11	.08
17	Tony Gwynn	.25	.20	.10
18	Rickey Henderson	.25	.20	.10
19	Orel Hershiser	.15	.11	.06
20	Don Mattingly	1.25	.90	.50
21	Mark McGwire	.90	.70	.35
22	Dale Murphy	.20	.15	.08
23	Eddie Murray	.15	.11	.06
24	Kirby Puckett	.25	.20	.10
25	Rock Raines	.15	.11	.06
26	Ryne Sanberg	.15	.11	.06
27	Mike Schmidt	.30	.25	.12
28	Ozzie Smith	.10	.08	.04
29	Darryl Strawberry	.30	.25	.12
30	Alan Trammell	.12	.09	.05
31	Frank Viola	.12	.09	.05
32	Dave Winfield	.12	.09	.05

		MT	NR MT	EX
33	Robin Yount			

1970 Kellogg's

For 14 years in the 1970s and early 1980s, the Kellogg's cereal company provided Topps with virtually the only meaningful national competition in the baseball card market. Kellogg's kicked off its baseball card program in 1970 with a 75-player set of simulated 3-D cards. Single cards were available in selected brands of the company's cereal, while a mail-in program offered complete sets. The 3-D effect was achieved by the sandwiching of a clear color player photo between a purposely blurred stadium background scene and a layer of ribbed plastic. The relatively narrow dimension of the card, 2-1/4" by 3-1/2" and the nature of the plastic overlay seem to conspire to cause the cards to curl, often cracking the plastic layer, if not stored properly. Cards with major cracks in the plastic can be considered in Fair condition, at best.

		NR MT	EX	VG
Complete Set:		150.00	75.00	45.00
Common Player: 1-15		.80	.40	.25
Common Player: 16-30		.90	.45	.25
Common Player: 31-75		.80	.40	.25
1	Ed Kranepool	1.50	.70	.45
2	Pete Rose	20.00	10.00	6.00
3	Cleon Jones	.80	.40	.25
4	Willie McCovey	3.50	1.75	1.00
5	Mel Stottlemyre	1.00	.50	.30
6	Frank Howard	1.25	.60	.40
7	Tom Seaver	5.00	2.50	1.50
8	Don Sutton	2.50	1.25	.70
9	Jim Wynn	.80	.40	.25
10	Jim Maloney	.80	.40	.25
11	Tommie Agee	.80	.40	.25
12	Willie Mays	8.00	4.00	2.50
13	Juan Marichal	3.00	1.50	.90
14	Dave McNally	.90	.45	.25
15	Frank Robinson	3.50	1.75	1.00
16	Carlos May	1.00	.50	.30
17	Bill Singer	1.00	.50	.30
18	Rick Reichardt	1.00	.50	.30
19	Boog Powell	1.50	.70	.45
20	Gaylord Perry	3.50	1.75	1.00
21	Brooks Robinson	6.00	3.00	1.75
22	Luis Aparicio	3.50	1.75	1.00
23	Joel Horlen	1.00	.50	.30
24	Mike Epstein	1.00	.50	.30
25	Tom Haller	1.00	.50	.30
26	Willie Crawford	1.00	.50	.30
27	Roberto Clemente	10.00	5.00	3.00
28	Matty Alou	1.25	.60	.40
29	Willie Stargell	4.00	2.00	1.25
30	Tim Cullen	1.00	.50	.30
31	Randy Hundley	.80	.40	.25
32	Reggie Jackson	6.50	3.25	2.00
33	Rich Allen	1.25	.60	.40
34	Tim McCarver	1.00	.50	.30
35	Ray Culp	.80	.40	.25
36	Jim Fregosi	.90	.45	.25
37	Billy Williams	3.00	1.50	.90

		NR MT	EX	VG
38	Johnny Odom	.80	.40	.25
39	Bert Campaneris	.90	.45	.25
40	Ernie Banks	3.50	1.75	1.00
41	Chris Short	.80	.40	.25
42	Ron Santo	.90	.45	.25
43	Glenn Beckert	.80	.40	.25
44	Lou Brock	3.50	1.75	1.00
45	Larry Hisle	.80	.40	.25
46	Reggie Smith	.90	.45	.25
47	Rod Carew	4.00	2.00	1.25
48	Curt Flood	.90	.45	.25
49	Jim Lonborg	.80	.40	.25
50	Sam McDowell	.90	.45	.25
51	Sal Bando	.90	.45	.25
52	Al Kaline	4.00	2.00	1.25
53	Gary Nolan	.80	.40	.25
54	Rico Petrocelli	.80	.40	.25
55	Ollie Brown	.80	.40	.25
56	Luis Tiant	1.25	.60	.40
57	Bill Freehan	.90	.45	.25
58	Johnny Bench	5.00	2.50	1.50
59	Joe Pepitone	.90	.45	.25
60	Bobby Murcer	1.00	.50	.30
61	Harmon Killebrew	3.50	1.75	1.00
62	Don Wilson	.80	.40	.25
63	Tony Oliva	1.25	.60	.40
64	Jim Perry	.90	.45	.25
65	Mickey Lolich	1.25	.60	.40
66	Coco Laboy	.80	.40	.25
67	Dean Chance	.80	.40	.25
68	Ken Harrelson	.90	.45	.25
69	Willie Horton	.90	.45	.25
70	Wally Bunker	.80	.40	.25
71a	Bob Gibson (1959 IP blank)	5.00	2.50	1.50
71b	Bob Gibson (1959 IP 76)	3.00	1.50	.90
72	Joe Morgan	3.00	1.50	.90
73	Denny McLain	1.25	.60	.40
74	Tommy Harper	.80	.40	.25
75	Don Mincher	1.25	.60	.40

1971 Kellogg's

The scarcest and most valuable of the Kellogg's editions, the 75-card 1971 set was the only one not offered by the company on a mail-in basis; the only way to complete it was to buy ... and buy and buy ... boxes of cereal. Kellogg's again used the simulated 3-D effect in the cards' design, with the same result being many of the 2-1/4" by 3-1/2" cards are found today with cracks resulting from the cards' curling. A number of scarcer back variations are checklisted below. In addition, all 75 cards can be found with and without the 1970 date before the "Xograph" copyright line on the back; though there is no difference in value.

		NR MT	EX	VG
Complete Set:		800.00	400.00	240.00
Common Player:		8.00	4.00	2.50
1a	Wayne Simpson (SO 120)	12.00	6.00	3.50
1b	Wayne Simpson (SO 119)	15.00	7.50	4.50
2	Tom Seaver	30.00	15.00	9.00
3a	Jim Perry (IP 2238)	10.00	5.00	3.00
3b	Jim Perry (IP 2239)	15.00	7.50	4.50
4a	Bob Robertson (RBI 94)	8.00	4.00	2.50
4b	Bob Robertson (RBI 95)	12.00	6.00	3.50

		NR MT	EX	VG
5	Roberto Clemente	35.00	17.50	10.50
6a	Gaylord Perry (IP 2014)	15.00	7.50	4.50
6b	Gaylord Perry (IP 2015)	20.00	10.00	6.00
7a	Felipe Alou (1970 Oakland NL)	15.00	7.50	4.50
7b	Felipe Alou (1970 Oakland AL)	10.00	5.00	3.00
8	Denis Menke	8.00	4.00	2.50
9a	Don Kessinger (Hits 849)	10.00	5.00	3.00
9b	Don Kessinger (Hits 850)	15.00	7.50	4.50
10	Willie Mays	35.00	17.50	10.50
11	Jim Hickman	8.00	4.00	2.50
12	Tony Oliva	12.00	6.00	3.50
13	Manny Sanguillen	8.00	4.00	2.50
14a	Frank Howard (1968 Washington NL)			
		18.00	9.00	5.50
14b	Frank Howard (1968 Washington AL)			
		12.00	6.00	3.50
15	Frank Robinson	25.00	12.50	7.50
16	Willie Davis	10.00	5.00	3.00
17	Lou Brock	20.00	10.00	6.00
18	Cesar Tovar	8.00	4.00	2.50
19	Luis Aparicio	15.00	7.50	4.50
20	Boog Powell	12.00	6.00	3.50
21a	Dick Selma (SO 584)	8.00	4.00	2.50
21b	Dick Selma (SO 587)	12.00	6.00	3.50
22	Danny Walton	8.00	4.00	2.50
23	Carl Morton	8.00	4.00	2.50
24a	Sonny Siebert (SO 1054)	8.00	4.00	2.50
24b	Sonny Siebert (SO 1055)	12.00	6.00	3.50
25	Jim Merritt	8.00	4.00	2.50
26a	Jose Cardenal (Hits 828)	8.00	4.00	2.50
26b	Jose Cardenal (Hits 829)	12.00	6.00	3.50
27	Don Mincher	8.00	4.00	2.50
28a	Clyde Wright (California state logo)			
		8.00	4.00	2.50
28b	Clyde Wright (Angels crest logo)	12.00	6.00	3.50
29	Les Cain	8.00	4.00	2.50
30	Danny Cater	8.00	4.00	2.50
31	Don Sutton	15.00	7.50	4.50
32	Chuck Dobson	8.00	4.00	2.50
33	Willie McCovey	20.00	10.00	6.00
34	Mike Epstein	8.00	4.00	2.50
35a	Paul Blair (Runs 386)	8.00	4.00	2.50
35b	Paul Blair (Runs 385)	12.00	6.00	3.50
36a	Gary Nolan (SO 577)	8.00	4.00	2.50
36b	Gary Nolan (SO 581)	12.00	6.00	3.50
37	Sam McDowell	10.00	5.00	3.00
38	Amos Otis	10.00	5.00	3.00
39a	Ray Fosse (RBI 69)	8.00	4.00	2.50
39b	Ray Fosse (RBI 70)	12.00	6.00	3.50
40	Mel Stottlemyre	10.00	5.00	3.00
41	Cito Gaston	8.00	4.00	2.50
42	Dick Dietz	8.00	4.00	2.50
43	Roy White	10.00	5.00	3.00
44	Al Kaline	25.00	12.50	7.50
45	Carlos May	8.00	4.00	2.50
46a	Tommie Agee (RBI 313)	8.00	4.00	2.50
46b	Tommie Agee (RBI 314)	12.00	6.00	3.50
47	Tommy Harper	8.00	4.00	2.50
48	Larry Dierker	8.00	4.00	2.50
49	Mike Cuellar	10.00	5.00	3.00
50	Ernie Banks	25.00	12.50	7.50
51	Bob Gibson	20.00	10.00	6.00
52	Reggie Smith	10.00	5.00	3.00
53a	Matty Alou (RBI 273)	10.00	5.00	3.00
53b	Matty Alou (RBI 274)	15.00	7.50	4.50
54a	Alex Johnson (California state logo)			
		8.00	4.00	2.50
54b	Alex Johnson (Angels crest logo)	12.00	6.00	3.50
55	Harmon Killebrew	20.00	10.00	6.00
56	Billy Grabarkewitz	8.00	4.00	2.50
57	Rich Allen	12.00	6.00	3.50
58	Tony Perez	15.00	7.50	4.50
59a	Dave McNally (SO 1065)	10.00	5.00	3.00
59b	Dave McNally (SO 1067)	15.00	7.50	4.50
60a	Jim Palmer (SO 564)	15.00	7.50	4.50
60b	Jim Palmer (SO 567)	20.00	10.00	6.00
61	Billy Williams	15.00	7.50	4.50
62	Joe Torre	12.00	6.00	3.50
63a	Jim Northrup (AB 2773)	8.00	4.00	2.50
63b	Jim Northrup (AB 2772)	12.00	6.00	3.50
64a	Jim Fregosi (Calif. state logo - Hits 1326)			
		8.00	4.00	2.50
64b	Jim Fregosi (Calif. state logo - Hits 1327)			
		12.00	6.00	3.50
64c	Jim Fregosi (Angels crest logo)	12.00	6.00	3.50
65	Pete Rose	75.00	37.00	22.00
66a	Bud Harrelson (RBI 112)	8.00	4.00	2.50
66b	Bud Harrelson (RBI 113)	12.00	6.00	3.50
67	Tony Taylor	8.00	4.00	2.50
68	Willie Stargell	20.00	10.00	6.00
69	Tony Horton	8.50	4.25	2.50

		NR MT	EX	VG
70a	Claude Osteen (no number)	20.00	10.00	6.00
70b	Claude Osteen (#70 on back)	8.00	4.00	2.50
71	Glenn Beckert	10.00	5.00	3.00
72	Nate Colbert	8.00	4.00	2.50
73a	Rick Monday (AB 1705)	10.00	5.00	3.00
73b	Rick Monday (AB 1704)	15.00	7.50	4.50
74a	Tommy John (BB 444)	15.00	7.50	4.50
74b	Tommy John (BB 443)	20.00	10.00	6.00
75	Chris Short	12.00	6.00	3.50

1972 Kellogg's

For 1972, Kellogg's reduced both the number of cards in its set and the dimensions of each card, moving to a 2-1/8" by 3-1/4" size and fixing the set at 54 cards. Once again, the cards were produced to simulate a 3-D effect (see description for 1970 Kellogg's). The set was available via a mail-in offer. The checklist includes variations which resulted from the correction of erroneous statistics on the backs of some cards. The complete set values quoted do not include the scarcer variations.

		NR MT	EX	VG
Complete Set:		55.00	27.00	16.50
Common Player:		.70	.35	.20
1a	Tom Seaver (1970 ERA 2.85)	9.00	4.50	2.75
1b	Tom Seaver (1970 ERA 2.81)	6.50	3.25	2.00
2	Amos Otis	.80	.40	.25
3a	Willie Davis (Runs 842)	1.25	.60	.40
3b	Willie Davis (Runs 841)	.80	.40	.25
4	Wilbur Wood	.80	.40	.25
5	Bill Parsons	.70	.35	.20
6	Pete Rose	20.00	10.00	6.00
7a	Willie McCovey (HR 360)	5.00	2.50	1.50
7b	Willie McCovey (HR 370)	3.50	1.75	1.00
8	Fergie Jenkins	1.25	.60	.40
9a	Vida Blue (ERA 2.35)	1.50	.70	.45
9b	Vida Blue (ERA 2.31)	.90	.45	.25
10	Joe Torre	.90	.45	.25
11	Merv Rettenmund	.70	.35	.20
12	Bill Melton	.70	.35	.20
13a	Jim Palmer (Games 170)	4.75	2.50	1.50
13b	Jim Palmer (Games 168)	3.00	1.50	.90
14	Doug Rader	.70	.35	.20
15a	Dave Roberts (...Seaver, the NL leader...)			
		1.25	.60	.40
15b	Dave Roberts (...Seaver, the league leader...)			
		.70	.35	.20
16	Bobby Murcer	.80	.40	.25
17	Wes Parker	.70	.35	.20
18a	Joe Coleman (BB 394)	1.25	.60	.40
18b	Joe Coleman (BB 393)	.70	.35	.20
19	Manny Sanguillen	.70	.35	.20
20	Reggie Jackson	4.50	2.25	1.25
21	Ralph Garr	.70	.35	.20
22	Jim "Catfish" Hunter	2.50	1.25	.70
23	Rick Wise	.70	.35	.20
24	Glenn Beckert	.70	.35	.20
25	Tony Oliva	.90	.45	.25
26a	Bob Gibson (SO 2577)	4.75	2.50	1.50
26b	Bob Gibson (SO 2578)	3.00	1.50	.90
27a	Mike Cuellar (1971 ERA 3.80)	1.25	.60	.40
27b	Mike Cuellar (1971 ERA 3.08)	.80	.40	.25
28	Chris Speier	.70	.35	.20
29a	Dave McNally (ERA 3.18)	1.25	.60	.40

		NR MT	EX	VG
29b	Dave McNally (ERA 3.15)	.80	.40	.25
30	Chico Cardenas	.70	.35	.20
31a	Bill Freehan (AVG. .263)	1.25	.60	.40
31b	Bill Freehan (AVG. .262)	.80	.40	.25
32a	Bud Harrelson (Hits 634)	1.25	.60	.40
32b	Bud Harrelson (Hits 624)	.70	.35	.20
33a	Sam McDowell (...less than 200 innings...)	1.25	.60	.40
33b	Sam McDowell (...less than 225 innings...)	.80	.40	.25
34a	Claude Osteen (1971 ERA 3.25)	1.25	.60	.40
34b	Claude Osteen (1971 ERA 3.51)	.70	.35	.20
35	Reggie Smith	.80	.40	.25
36	Sonny Siebert	.70	.35	.20
37	Lee May	.80	.40	.25
38	Mickey Lolich	.90	.45	.25
39a	Cookie Rojas (2B 149)	1.25	.60	.40
39b	Cookie Rojas (2B 150)	.70	.35	.20
40	Dick Drago	.70	.35	.20
41	Nate Colbert	.70	.35	.20
42	Andy Messersmith	.70	.35	.20
43a	Dave Johnson (AVG. .262)	1.50	.70	.45
43b	Dave Johnson (AVG. .264)	.90	.45	.25
44	Steve Blass	.70	.35	.20
45	Bob Robertson	.70	.35	.20
46a	Billy Williams (...missed only one last season...)	5.00	2.50	1.50
46b	Billy Williams (phrase omitted)	3.00	1.50	.90
47	Juan Marichal	3.00	1.50	.90
48	Lou Brock	3.50	1.75	1.00
49	Roberto Clemente	7.00	3.50	2.00
50	Mel Stottlemyre	.80	.40	.25
51	Don Wilson	.70	.35	.20
52a	Sal Bando (RBI 355)	1.25	.60	.40
52b	Sal Bando (RBI 356)	.80	.40	.25
53a	Willie Stargell (2B 197)	5.00	2.50	1.50
53b	Willie Stargell (2B 196)	3.00	1.50	.90
54a	Willie Mays (RBI 1855)	12.00	6.00	3.50
54b	Willie Mays (RBI 1856)	8.50	4.25	2.50

		NR MT	EX	VG
9	Honus Wagner	1.00	.50	.30
10	Eddie Collins	.50	.25	.15
11	Tris Speaker	.70	.35	.20
12	Cy Young	.80	.40	.25
13	Lou Gehrig	2.00	1.00	.60
14	Babe Ruth	3.50	1.75	1.00
15	Ty Cobb	2.00	1.00	.60

1973 Kellogg's

The lone exception to Kellogg's long run of simulated 3-D effect cards came in 1973, when the cereal company's 54-card set was produced by "normal" printing methods. In 2'1/4" by 3-1/2" size, the design was otherwise quite compatible with the issues which preceded and succeeded it. Because it was available via a mail-in offer, it is not as scarce as some other Kellogg's issues.

		NR MT	EX	VG
Complete Set:		40.00	20.00	12.00
Common Player:		.50	.25	.15
1	Amos Otis	.60	.30	.20
2	Ellie Rodriguez	.50	.25	.15
3	Mickey Lolich	.80	.40	.25
4	Tony Oliva	.80	.40	.25
5	Don Sutton	1.25	.60	.40
6	Pete Rose	11.00	5.50	3.25
7	Steve Carlton	4.00	2.00	1.25
8	Bobby Bonds	.70	.35	.20
9	Wilbur Wood	.60	.30	.20
10	Billy Williams	2.50	1.25	.70
11	Steve Blass	.50	.25	.15
12	Jon Matlack	.50	.25	.15
13	Cesar Cedeno	.70	.35	.20
14	Bob Gibson	2.50	1.25	.70
15	Sparky Lyle	.60	.30	.20
16	Nolan Ryan	3.50	1.75	1.00
17	Jim Palmer	2.50	1.25	.70
18	Ray Fosse	.50	.25	.15
19	Bobby Murcer	.60	.30	.20
20	Jim "Catfish" Hunter	2.50	1.25	.70
21	Tug McGraw	.80	.40	.25
22	Reggie Jackson	4.50	2.25	1.25
23	Bill Stoneman	.50	.25	.15
24	Lou Piniella	.80	.40	.25
25	Willie Stargell	2.50	1.25	.70
26	Dick Allen	.90	.45	.25
27	Carlton Fisk	1.25	.60	.40
28	Fergie Jenkins	.90	.45	.25
29	Phil Niekro	1.50	.70	.45
30	Gary Nolan	.50	.25	.15
31	Joe Torre	.80	.40	.25
32	Bobby Tolan	.50	.25	.15
33	Nate Colbert	.50	.25	.15
34	Joe Morgan	2.50	1.25	.70
35	Bert Blyleven	.90	.45	.25
36	Joe Rudi	.60	.30	.20
37	Ralph Garr	.50	.25	.15
38	Gaylord Perry	2.00	1.00	.60
39	Bobby Grich	.60	.30	.20
40	Lou Brock	2.50	1.25	.70
41	Pete Broberg	.50	.25	.15
42	Manny Sanguillen	.50	.25	.15
43	Willie Davis	.60	.30	.20
44	Dave Kingman	.90	.45	.25
45	Carlos May	.50	.25	.15

1972 Kellogg's All-Time Baseball Greats

Kellogg's issued a second baseball card set in 1972, inserted into packages of breakfast rolls. The 2-1/4" by 3-1/2" cards also featured a simulated 3-D effect, but the 15 players in the set were "All-Time Baseball Greats", rather than current players. The set is virtually identical to a Rold Gold pretzel issue of 1970; the only difference being the 1972 copyright date on the back of the Kellog's cards, while the pretzel issue bears a 1970 date. The pretzel cards are considerably scarcer than the Kellogg's.

		NR MT	EX	VG
Complete Set:		15.00	7.50	4.50
Common Player:		.50	.25	.15
1	Walter Johnson	1.25	.60	.40
2	Rogers Hornsby	.80	.40	.25
3	John McGraw	.50	.25	.15
4	Mickey Cochrane	.50	.25	.15
5	George Sisler	.50	.25	.15
6	Babe Ruth	3.50	1.75	1.00
7	Robert "Lefty" Grove	.70	.35	.20
8	Harold "Pie" Traynor	.50	.25	.15

	NR MT	EX	VG
46 Tom Seaver	4.00	2.00	1.25
47 Mike Cuellar	.60	.30	.20
48 Joe Coleman	.50	.25	.15
49 Claude Osteen	.50	.25	.15
50 Steve Kline	.50	.25	.15
51 Rod Carew	4.00	2.00	1.25
52 Al Kaline	3.50	1.75	1.00
53 Larry Dierker	.50	.25	.15
54 Ron Santo	.70	.35	.20

	NR MT	EX	VG
44 Jim "Catfish" Hunter	2.50	1.25	.70
45 Willie Davis	.60	.30	.20
46 Bert Blyleven	.90	.45	.25
47 Pat Kelly	.50	.25	.15
48 Ken Singleton	.60	.30	.20
49 Manny Mota	.60	.30	.20
50 Dave Johnson	.90	.45	.25
51 Sal Bando	.60	.30	.20
52 Tom Seaver	3.50	1.75	1.00
53 Felix Millan	.50	.25	.15
54 Ron Blomberg	.80	.40	.25

1974 Kellogg's

For 1974, Kellogg's returned to the use of simulated 3-D for its 54-player baseball card issue (see 1970 Kellogg's listing for description). In 2-1/8" by 3-1/4" size, the cards were available as a complete set via a mail-in offer.

	NR MT	EX	VG
Complete Set:	40.00	20.00	12.00
Common Player:	.50	.25	.15

		NR MT	EX	VG
1	Bob Gibson	3.50	1.75	1.00
2	Rick Monday	.70	.35	.20
3	Joe Coleman	.50	.25	.15
4	Bert Campaneris	.70	.35	.20
5	Carlton Fisk	1.25	.60	.40
6	Jim Palmer	2.50	1.25	.70
7a	Ron Santo (Chicago Cubs)	1.50	.70	.45
7b	Ron Santo (Chicago White Sox)	.80	.40	.25
8	Nolan Ryan	3.50	1.75	1.00
9	Greg Luzinski	.80	.40	.25
10a	Buddy Bell (Runs 134)	1.50	.70	.45
10b	Buddy Bell (Runs 135)	.80	.40	.25
11	Bob Watson	.50	.25	.15
12	Bill Singer	.50	.25	.15
13	Dave May	.50	.25	.15
14	Jim Brewer	.50	.25	.15
15	Manny Sanguillen	.50	.25	.15
16	Jeff Burroughs	.50	.25	.15
17	Amos Otis	.50	.25	.15
18	Ed Goodson	.50	.25	.15
19	Nate Colbert	.50	.25	.15
20	Reggie Jackson	4.00	2.00	1.25
21	Ted Simmons	.90	.45	.25
22	Bobby Murcer	.60	.30	.20
23	Willie Horton	.60	.30	.20
24	Orlando Cepeda	1.25	.60	.40
25	Ron Hunt	.50	.25	.15
26	Wayne Twitchell	.50	.25	.15
27	Ron Fairly	.50	.25	.15
28	Johnny Bench	3.50	1.75	1.00
29	John Mayberry	.50	.25	.15
30	Rod Carew	3.50	1.75	1.00
31	Ken Holtzman	.50	.25	.15
32	Billy Williams	2.50	1.25	.70
33	Dick Allen	.80	.40	.25
34a	Wilbur Wood (SO 959)	1.25	.60	.40
34b	Wilbur Wood (SO 960)	.70	.35	.20
35	Danny Thompson	.50	.25	.15
36	Joe Morgan	2.50	1.25	.70
37	Willie Stargell	3.00	1.50	.90
38	Pete Rose	13.00	6.50	4.00
39	Bobby Bonds	.70	.35	.20
40	Chris Speier	.50	.25	.15
41	Sparky Lyle	.60	.30	.20
42	Cookie Rojas	.50	.25	.15
43	Tommy Davis	.60	.30	.20

1975 Kellogg's

While the card size remained the same at 2-1/8" by 3-1/4", the size of the 1975 Kellogg's "3-D" set was increased by three, to 57 cards. Despite the fact cards could be obtained by a mail-in offer, as well as in cereal boxes, the '75 Kellogg's are noticeably scarcer than the company's other issues, with the exception of the 1971 set. Also helping to raise the value of the cards is the presence of an unusually large number of current and future Hall of Famers.

	NR MT	EX	VG
Complete Set:	150.00	75.00	45.00
Common Player:	2.00	1.00	.60

		NR MT	EX	VG
1	Roy White	3.50	1.75	1.00
2	Ross Grimsley	2.00	1.00	.60
3	Reggie Smith	2.50	1.25	.70
4a	Bob Grich ("...1973 work..." in last line)	4.00	2.00	1.25
4b	Bob Grich (no "...1973 work...")	2.50	1.25	.70
5	Greg Gross	2.00	1.00	.60
6	Bob Watson	2.00	1.00	.60
7	Johnny Bench	11.00	5.50	3.25
8	Jeff Burroughs	2.00	1.00	.60
9	Elliott Maddox	2.00	1.00	.60
10	Jon Matlack	2.00	1.00	.60
11	Pete Rose	24.00	12.00	7.25
12	Leroy Stanton	2.00	1.00	.60
13	Bake McBride	2.00	1.00	.60
14	Jorge Orta	2.00	1.00	.60
15	Al Oliver	2.50	1.25	.70
16	John Briggs	2.00	1.00	.60
17	Steve Garvey	9.00	4.50	2.75
18	Brooks Robinson	10.00	5.00	3.00
19	John Hiller	2.00	1.00	.60
20	Lynn McGlothen	2.00	1.00	.60
21	Cleon Jones	2.00	1.00	.60
22	Fergie Jenkins	2.50	1.25	.70
23	Bill North	2.00	1.00	.60
24	Steve Busby	2.00	1.00	.60
25	Richie Zisk	2.00	1.00	.60
26	Nolan Ryan	10.00	5.00	3.00
27	Joe Morgan	6.50	3.25	2.00
28	Joe Rudi	2.50	1.25	.70
29	Jose Cardenal	2.00	1.00	.60
30	Andy Messersmith	2.00	1.00	.60
31	Willie Montanez	2.00	1.00	.60
32	Bill Buckner	2.50	1.25	.70
33	Rod Carew	10.00	5.00	3.00
34	Lou Piniella	2.50	1.25	.70
35	Ralph Garr	2.00	1.00	.60
36	Mike Marshall	2.00	1.00	.60
37	Garry Maddox	2.00	1.00	.60
38	Dwight Evans	3.00	1.50	.90

		NR MT	EX	VG
39	Lou Brock	9.00	4.50	2.75
40	Ken Singleton	2.50	1.25	.70
41	Steve Braun	2.00	1.00	.60
42	Dick Allen	2.50	1.25	.70
43	Johnny Grubb	2.00	1.00	.60
44a	Jim Hunter (Oakland)	12.00	6.00	3.50
44b	Jim Hunter (New York)	8.00	4.00	2.50
45	Gaylord Perry	6.50	3.25	2.00
46	George Hendrick	2.00	1.00	.60
47	Sparky Lyle	2.50	1.25	.70
48	Dave Cash	2.00	1.00	.60
49	Luis Tiant	2.50	1.25	.70
50	Cesar Geronimo	2.00	1.00	.60
51	Carl Yastrzemski	16.00	8.00	4.75
52	Ken Brett	2.00	1.00	.60
53	Hal McRae	2.50	1.25	.70
54	Reggie Jackson	12.00	6.00	3.50
55	Rollie Fingers	3.50	1.75	1.00
56	Mike Schmidt	14.00	7.00	4.25
57	Richie Hebner	2.50	1.25	.70

1976 Kellogg's

A sizeable list of corrected errors and other variation cards dots the checklist for the 57-card 1976 Kellogg's 3-D set. Again containing 57 cards, the first three cards in the set are found far less often than cards #4-57, indicating they were short-printed in relation to the rest of the set. The complete set values quoted below do not include the scarcer variation cards. Card size remained at 2-1/8" by 3-1/4".

		NR MT	EX	VG
	Complete Set:	65.00	32.00	19.50
	Common Player:	1.25	.60	.40
1	Steve Hargan	10.00	5.00	3.00
2	Claudell Washington	10.00	5.00	3.00
3	Don Gullett	10.00	5.00	3.00
4	Randy Jones	1.25	.60	.40
5	Jim "Catfish" Hunter	6.50	3.25	2.00
6a	Clay Carroll (Cincinnati)	3.00	1.50	.90
6b	Clay Carroll (Chicago)	1.50	.70	.45
7	Joe Rudi	1.50	.70	.45
8	Reggie Jackson	10.00	5.00	3.00
9	Felix Millan	1.25	.60	.40
10	Jim Rice	8.00	4.00	2.50
11	Bert Blyleven	2.50	1.25	.70
12	Ken Singleton	1.50	.70	.45
13	Don Sutton	2.50	1.25	.70
14	Joe Morgan	5.00	2.50	1.50
15	Dave Parker	4.00	2.00	1.25
16	Dave Cash	1.25	.60	.40
17	Ron LeFlore	1.25	.60	.40
18	Greg Luzinski	2.00	1.00	.60
19	Dennis Eckersley	2.25	1.25	.70
20	Bill Madlock	2.25	1.25	.70
21	George Scott	1.25	.60	.40
22	Willie Stargell	6.50	3.25	2.00
23	Al Hrabosky	1.25	.60	.40
24	Carl Yastrzemski	13.00	6.50	4.00
25	Jim Kaat	2.50	1.25	.70
26	Marty Perez	1.25	.60	.40
27	Bob Watson	1.25	.60	.40
28	Eric Soderholm	1.25	.60	.40
29	Bill Lee	1.25	.60	.40
30a	Frank Tanana (1975 ERA 2.63)	2.50	1.25	.70

		NR MT	EX	VG
30b	Frank Tanana (1975 ERA 2.62)	1.50	.70	.45
31	Fred Lynn	3.50	1.75	1.00
32a	Tom Seaver (1967 PCT. 552)	10.00	5.00	3.00
32b	Tom Seaver (1967 Pct. .552)	8.00	4.00	2.50
33	Steve Busby	1.25	.60	.40
34	Gary Carter	10.00	5.00	3.00
35	Rick Wise	1.25	.60	.40
36	Johnny Bench	10.00	5.00	3.00
37	Jim Palmer	8.00	4.00	2.50
38	Bobby Murcer	2.00	1.00	.60
39	Von Joshua	1.25	.60	.40
40	Lou Brock	8.00	4.00	2.50
41a	Mickey Rivers (last line begins "In three...")	2.75	1.50	.80
41b	Mickey Rivers (last line begins "The Yankees...")	1.25	.60	.40
42	Manny Sanguillen	1.50	.70	.45
43	Jerry Reuss	1.50	.70	.45
44	Ken Griffey	1.50	.70	.45
45a	Jorge Orta (AB 1616)	2.25	1.25	.70
45b	Jorge Orta (AB 1615)	1.25	.60	.40
46	John Mayberry	1.25	.60	.40
47a	Vida Blue (2nd line reads "...pitched more innings...")	3.00	1.50	.90
47b	Vida Blue (2nd line reads "...struck out more...")	2.00	1.00	.60
48	Rod Carew	10.00	5.00	3.00
49a	Jon Matlack (1975 ER 87)	2.25	1.25	.70
49b	Jon Matlack (1975 ER 86)	1.25	.60	.40
50	Boog Powell	2.50	1.25	.70
51a	Mike Hargrove (AB 935)	2.25	1.25	.70
51b	Mike Hargrove (AB 934)	1.25	.60	.40
52a	Paul Lindblad (1975 ERA 2.72)	2.25	1.25	.70
52b	Paul Lindblad (1975 ERA 2.73)	1.25	.60	.40
53	Thurman Munson	6.50	3.25	2.00
54	Steve Garvey	8.00	4.00	2.50
55	Pete Rose	18.00	9.00	5.50
56a	Greg Gross (Games 302)	2.25	1.25	.70
56b	Greg Gross (Games 334)	1.25	.60	.40
57	Ted Simmons	2.50	1.25	.70

1977 Kellogg's

Other than another innovative card design to complement the simulated 3-D effect, there was little change in the 1977 Kellogg's issue. Set size remained at 57 cards, the set remained in the 2-1/8" by 3-1/4" format, and the cards were available either individually in boxes of cereal, or as a complete set via a mail-in box top offer. The 1977 set is the last in which Kellogg's used a player portrait photo on the back of the card.

		NR MT	EX	VG
	Complete Set:	40.00	20.00	12.00
	Common Player:	.40	.20	.12
1	George Foster	.90	.45	.25
2	Bert Campaneris	.60	.30	.20
3	Fergie Jenkins	.90	.45	.25
4	Dock Ellis	.40	.20	.12
5	John Montefusco	.40	.20	.12
6	George Brett	8.50	4.25	2.50
7	John Candelaria	.50	.25	.15
8	Fred Norman	.40	.20	.12
9	Bill Travers	.40	.20	.12
10	Hal McRae	.60	.30	.20
11	Doug Rau	.40	.20	.12

		NR MT	EX	VG
12	Greg Luzinski	.70	.35	.20
13	Ralph Garr	.40	.20	.12
14	Steve Garvey	4.50	2.25	1.25
15	Rick Manning	.40	.20	.12
16	Lyman Bostock	.50	.25	.15
17	Randy Jones	.40	.20	.12
18a	Ron Cey (58 homers in first sentence)	1.00	.50	.30
18b	Ron Cey (48 homers in first sentence)	.60	.30	.20
19	Dave Parker	1.25	.60	.40
20	Pete Rose	11.00	5.50	3.25
21a	Wayne Garland (last line begins "Prior to...")	.90	.45	.25
21b	Wayne Garland (last line begins "There he...")	.40	.20	.12
22	Bill North	.40	.20	.12
23	Thurman Munson	2.50	1.25	.70
24	Tom Poquette	.40	.20	.12
25	Ron LeFlore	.50	.25	.15
26	Mark Fidrych	.50	.25	.15
27	Sixto Lezcano	.40	.20	.12
28	Dave Winfield	4.00	2.00	1.25
29	Jerry Koosman	.50	.25	.15
30	Mike Hargrove	.40	.20	.12
31	Willie Montanez	.40	.20	.12
32	Don Stanhouse	.40	.20	.12
33	Jay Johnstone	.50	.25	.15
34	Bake McBride	.40	.20	.12
35	Dave Kingman	.70	.35	.20
36	Freddie Patek	.40	.20	.12
37	Garry Maddox	.50	.25	.15
38a	Ken Reitz (last line begins "The previous...")	.90	.45	.25
38b	Ken Reitz (last line begins "In late...")	.40	.20	.12
39	Bobby Grich	.60	.30	.20
40	Cesar Geronimo	.40	.20	.12
41	Jim Lonborg	.40	.20	.12
42	Ed Figueroa	.40	.20	.12
43	Bill Madlock	.80	.40	.25
44	Jerry Remy	.40	.20	.12
45	Frank Tanana	.50	.25	.15
46	Al Oliver	.90	.45	.25
47	Charlie Hough	.50	.25	.15
48	Lou Piniella	.70	.35	.20
49	Ken Griffey	.60	.30	.20
50	Jose Cruz	.60	.30	.20
51	Rollie Fingers	1.25	.60	.40
52	Chris Chambliss	.50	.25	.15
53	Rod Carew	4.00	2.00	1.25
54	Andy Messersmith	.40	.20	.12
55	Mickey Rivers	.40	.20	.12
56	Butch Wynegar	.40	.20	.12
57	Steve Carlton	5.00	2.50	1.50

		NR MT	EX	VG
	Complete Set:	40.00	20.00	12.00
	Common Player:	.40	.20	.12
1	Steve Carlton	4.00	2.00	1.25
2	Bucky Dent	.50	.25	.15
3	Mike Schmidt	4.00	2.00	1.25
4	Ken Griffey	.50	.25	.15
5	Al Cowens	.40	.20	.12
6	George Brett	5.00	2.50	1.50
7	Lou Brock	3.00	1.50	.90
8	Rich Gossage	1.25	.60	.40
9	Tom Johnson	.40	.20	.12
10	George Foster	.70	.35	.20
11	Dave Winfield	3.50	1.75	1.00
12	Dan Meyer	.40	.20	.12
13	Chris Chambliss	.50	.25	.15
14	Paul Dade	.40	.20	.12
15	Jeff Burroughs	.40	.20	.12
16	Jose Cruz	.60	.30	.20
17	Mickey Rivers	.40	.20	.12
18	John Candelaria	.50	.25	.15
19	Ellis Valentine	.40	.20	.12
20	Hal McRae	.50	.25	.15
21	Dave Rozema	.40	.20	.12
22	Lenny Randle	.40	.20	.12
23	Willie McCovey	3.00	1.50	.90
24	Ron Cey	.70	.35	.20
25	Eddie Murray	10.00	5.00	3.00
26	Larry Bowa	.60	.30	.20
27	Tom Seaver	3.50	1.75	1.00
28	Garry Maddox	.50	.25	.15
29	Rod Carew	4.00	2.00	1.25
30	Thurman Munson	2.50	1.25	.70
31	Garry Templeton	.60	.30	.20
32	Eric Soderholm	.40	.20	.12
33	Greg Luzinski	.70	.35	.20
34	Reggie Smith	.50	.25	.15
35	Dave Goltz	.40	.20	.12
36	Tommy John	1.25	.60	.40
37	Ralph Garr	.40	.20	.12
38	Alan Bannister	.40	.20	.12
39	Bob Bailor	.40	.20	.12
40	Reggie Jackson	4.00	2.00	1.25
41	Cecil Cooper	.80	.40	.25
42	Burt Hooton	.40	.20	.12
43	Sparky Lyle	.50	.25	.15
44	Steve Ontiveros	.40	.20	.12
45	Rick Reuschel	.60	.30	.20
46	Lyman Bostock	.50	.25	.15
47	Mitchell Page	.40	.20	.12
48	Bruce Sutter	.70	.35	.20
49	Jim Rice	3.50	1.75	1.00
50	Bob Forsch	.40	.20	.12
51	Nolan Ryan	3.50	1.75	1.00
52	Dave Parker	1.25	.60	.40
53	Bert Blyleven	.90	.45	.25
54	Frank Tanana	.50	.25	.15
55	Ken Singleton	.50	.25	.15
56	Mike Hargrove	.40	.20	.12
57	Don Sutton	2.50	1.25	.70

1978 Kellogg's

Besides the substitution of a Tony the Tiger drawing for a player portrait photo on the back of the card, the 1978 Kellogg's set offered no major changes from the previous few years issues. Cards were once again in the 2-1/8" by 3-1/4" format, with 57 cards comprising a complete set. Single cards were available in selected brands of the company's cereal, while complete sets could be obtained by a mail-in offer.

1979 Kellogg's

For its 1979 3-D issue, Kellogg's increased the size of the set to 60 cards, but reduced the width of the cards to 1-15/16". Depth stayed the same as in previous years, 3-1/4". The narrower card format seems to have compounded the problem of curling and subsequent cracking of the ribbed plastic surface which helps give the card a 3-D effect. Cards with major cracks can be graded no higher than VG. The complete set price in the checklist that follows does not include the scarcer variations. Numerous minor variations featuring copyright and trademark logos can be found in the set.

		NR MT	EX	VG
	Complete Set:	30.00	15.00	9.00
	Common Player:	.30	.15	.09
1	Bruce Sutter	.80	.40	.25
2	Ted Simmons	.70	.35	.20
3	Ross Grimsley	.30	.15	.09
4	Wayne Nordhagen	.30	.15	.09
5a	Jim Palmer (PCT. .649)	2.25	1.25	.70
5b	Jim Palmer (PCT. .650)	1.50	.70	.45
6	John Henry Johnson	.30	.15	.09
7	Jason Thompson	.30	.15	.09
8	Pat Zachry	.30	.15	.09
9	Dennis Eckersley	.60	.30	.20
10a	Paul Splittorff (IP 1665)	.60	.30	.20
10b	Paul Splittorff (IP 1666)	.30	.15	.09
11a	Ron Guidry (Hits 397)	2.00	1.00	.60
11b	Ron Guidry (Hits 396)	1.25	.60	.40
12	Jeff Burroughs	.30	.15	.09
13	Rod Carew	2.50	1.25	.70
14a	Buddy Bell (no trade line in bio)	1.25	.60	.40
14b	Buddy Bell (trade line in bio)	.60	.30	.20
15	Jim Rice	2.50	1.25	.70
16	Garry Maddox	.50	.25	.15
17	Willie McCovey	2.50	1.25	.70
18	Steve Carlton	2.50	1.25	.70
19a	J. R. Richard (stats begin with 1972)	.60	.30	.20
19b	J. R. Richard (stats begin with 1971)	.30	.15	.09
20	Paul Molitor	.90	.45	.25
21a	Dave Parker (AVG. .281)	2.00	1.00	.60
21b	Dave Parker (AVG. .318)	1.00	.50	.30
22a	Pete Rose (1978 3B 3)	12.00	6.00	3.50
22b	Pete Rose (1978 3B 33)	8.00	4.00	2.50
23a	Vida Blue (Runs 819)	1.25	.60	.40
23b	Vida Blue (Runs 818)	.60	.30	.20
24	Richie Zisk	.30	.15	.09
25a	Darrell Porter (2B 101)	.80	.40	.25
25b	Darrell Porter (2B 111)	.40	.20	.12
26a	Dan Driessen (Games 642)	.80	.40	.25
26b	Dan Driessen (Games 742)	.40	.20	.12
27a	Geoff Zahn (1978 Minnesota)	.60	.30	.20
27b	Geoff Zahn (1978 Minnesota)	.30	.15	.09
28	Phil Niekro	1.25	.60	.40
29	Tom Seaver	2.50	1.25	.70
30	Fred Lynn	1.00	.50	.30
31	Bill Bonham	.30	.15	.09
32	George Foster	.70	.35	.20
33a	Terry Puhl (last line of bio begins "Terry...")	.60	.30	.20
33b	Terry Puhl (last line of bio begins "His...")	.30	.15	.09
34a	John Candelaria (age is 24)	.90	.45	.25
34b	John Candelaria (age is 25)	.50	.25	.15
35	Bob Knepper	.40	.20	.12
36	Freddie Patek	.30	.15	.09
37	Chris Chambliss	.40	.20	.12
38a	Bob Forsch (1977 Games 86)	.80	.40	.25
38b	Bob Forsch (1977 Games 35)	.40	.20	.12
39a	Ken Griffey (1978 AB 674)	.90	.45	.25
39b	Ken Griffey (1978 AB 614)	.50	.25	.15
40	Jack Clark	.90	.45	.25
41a	Dwight Evans (1978 Hits 13)	1.50	.70	.45
41b	Dwight Evans (1978 Hits 123)	.90	.45	.25
42	Lee Mazzilli	.40	.20	.12
43	Mario Guerrero	.30	.15	.09
44	Larry Bowa	.50	.25	.15
45a	Carl Yastrzemski (Games 9930)	6.00	3.00	1.75
45b	Carl Yastrzemski (Games 9929)	4.00	2.00	1.25
46a	Reggie Jackson (1978 Games 162)	5.00	2.50	1.50
46b	Reggie Jackson (1978 Games 139)	3.00	1.50	.90
47	Rick Reuschel	.60	.30	.20
48a	Mike Flanagan (1976 SO 57)	.90	.45	.25
48b	Mike Flanagan (1976 SO 56)	.50	.25	.15
49a	Gaylord Perry (1973 Hits 325)	2.00	1.00	.60
49b	Gaylord Perry (1973 Hits 315)	1.25	.60	.40
50	George Brett	3.50	1.75	1.00
51a	Craig Reynolds (last line of bio begins "He spent...")	.60	.30	.20
51b	Craig Reynolds (last line of bio begins "In those...")	.30	.15	.09

		NR MT	EX	VG
52	Davey Lopes	.40	.20	.12
53a	Bill Almon (2B 31)	.60	.30	.20
53b	Bill Almon (2B 41)	.30	.15	.09
54	Roy Howell	.30	.15	.09
55	Frank Tanana	.50	.25	.15
56a	Doug Rau (1978 PCT. .577)	.60	.30	.20
56b	Doug Rau (1978 PCT. .625)	.30	.15	.09
57a	Rick Monday (1976 Runs 197)	.90	.45	.25
57b	Rick Monday (1976 Runs 107)	.50	.25	.15
58	Jon Matlack	.30	.15	.09
59a	Ron Jackson (last line of bio begins "His best...")	.60	.30	.20
59b	Ron Jackson (last line of bio begins "The Twins...")	.30	.15	.09
60	Jim Sundberg	.50	.25	.15

1980 Kellogg's

The 1980 cereal company issue featured the narrowest format of any Kellogg's card, 1-7/8" by 3-1/4". For the second straight year, set size remained at 60 cards, available either singly in boxes of cereal, or as complete sets by a mail-in offer.

		NR MT	EX	VG
	Complete Set:	20.00	10.00	6.00
	Common Player:	.30	.15	.09
1	Ross Grimsley	.30	.15	.09
2	Mike Schmidt	3.00	1.50	.90
3	Mike Flanagan	.40	.20	.12
4	Ron Guidry	.90	.45	.25
5	Bert Blyleven	.80	.40	.25
6	Dave Kingman	.70	.35	.20
7	Jeff Newman	.30	.15	.09
8	Steve Rogers	.30	.15	.09
9	George Brett	3.00	1.50	.90
10	Bruce Sutter	.70	.35	.20
11	Gorman Thomas	.40	.20	.12
12	Darrell Porter	.30	.15	.09
13	Roy Smalley	.30	.15	.09
14	Steve Carlton	1.75	.90	.50
15	Jim Palmer	1.50	.70	.45
16	Bob Bailor	.30	.15	.09
17	Jason Thompson	.30	.15	.09
18	Graig Nettles	.80	.40	.25
19	Ron Cey	.50	.25	.15
20	Nolan Ryan	1.75	.90	.50
21	Ellis Valentine	.30	.15	.09
22	Larry Hisle	.30	.15	.09
23	Dave Parker	.90	.45	.25
24	Eddie Murray	2.50	1.25	.70
25	Willie Stargell	1.75	.90	.50
26	Reggie Jackson	2.50	1.25	.70
27	Carl Yastrzemski	3.50	1.75	1.00
28	Andre Thornton	.40	.20	.12
29	Davey Lopes	.40	.20	.12
30	Ken Singleton	.40	.20	.12
31	Steve Garvey	2.50	1.25	.70
32	Dave Winfield	2.50	1.25	.70
33	Steve Kemp	.40	.20	.12
34	Claudell Washington	.40	.20	.12
35	Pete Rose	6.50	3.25	2.00
36	Cesar Cedeno	.40	.20	.12
37	John Stearns	.30	.15	.09
38	Lee Mazzilli	.30	.15	.09
39	Larry Bowa	.40	.20	.12
40	Fred Lynn	.80	.40	.25

		NR MT	EX	VG
41	Carlton Fisk	.90	.45	.25
42	Vida Blue	.50	.25	.15
43	Keith Hernandez	1.25	.60	.40
44	Jim Rice	1.75	.90	.50
45	Ted Simmons	.80	.40	.25
46	Chet Lemon	.30	.15	.09
47	Fergie Jenkins	.50	.25	.15
48	Gary Matthews	.40	.20	.12
49	Tom Seaver	2.50	1.25	.70
50	George Foster	.70	.35	.20
51	Phil Niekro	1.25	.60	.40
52	Johnny Bench	2.50	1.25	.70
53	Buddy Bell	.50	.25	.15
54	Lance Parrish	.90	.45	.25
55	Joaquin Andujar	.30	.15	.09
56	Don Baylor	.50	.25	.15
57	Jack Clark	.80	.40	.25
58	J.R. Richard	.30	.15	.09
59	Bruce Bochte	.30	.15	.09
60	Rod Carew	2.50	1.25	.70

		MT	NR MT	EX
30	Ken Landreaux	.08	.04	.02
31	Keith Hernandez	.40	.20	.10
32	Cecil Cooper	.10	.05	.03
33	Rickey Henderson	.60	.30	.15
34	Frank White	.10	.05	.03
35	George Hendrick	.08	.04	.02
36	Reggie Smith	.10	.05	.03
37	Tug McGraw	.10	.05	.03
38	Tom Seaver	.50	.25	.13
39	Ken Singleton	.10	.05	.03
40	Fred Lynn	.20	.10	.05
41	Rich "Goose" Gossage	.20	.10	.05
42	Terry Puhl	.08	.04	.02
43	Larry Bowa	.10	.05	.03
44	Phil Garner	.08	.04	.02
45	Ron Guidry	.20	.10	.05
46	Lee Mazzilli	.08	.04	.02
47	Dave Kingman	.15	.08	.04
48	Carl Yastrzemski	.80	.40	.20
49	Rick Burleson	.08	.04	.02
50	Steve Carlton	.40	.20	.10
51	Alan Trammell	.30	.15	.08
52	Tommy John	.20	.10	.05
53	Paul Molitor	.20	.10	.05
54	Joe Charboneau	.08	.04	.02
55	Rick Langford	.08	.04	.02
56	Bruce Sutter	.10	.05	.03
57	Robin Yount	.35	.20	.09
58	Steve Stone	.08	.04	.02
59	Larry Gura	.08	.04	.02
60	Mike Flanagan	.10	.05	.03
61	Bob Horner	.15	.08	.04
62	Bruce Bochte	.08	.04	.02
63	Pete Rose	1.00	.50	.25
64	Buddy Bell	.15	.08	.04
65	Johnny Bench	.60	.30	.15
66	Mike Hargrove	.08	.04	.02

1981 Kellogg's

"Bigger" is the word to best describe Kellogg's 1981 card set. Not only were the cards themselves larger than ever before (or since) at 2-1/2" by 3-1/2", but the size of the set was increased to 66, the largest since the 75-card issues of 1970-1971. The '81 Kellogg's set was available only as complete sets by mail. It is thought that the wider format of the 1981s may help prevent the problems of curling and cracking from which other years of Kellogg's issues suffer.

		MT	NR MT	EX
Complete Set:		8.00	4.00	2.00
Common Player:		.08	.04	.02
1	George Foster	.15	.08	.04
2	Jim Palmer	.30	.15	.08
3	Reggie Jackson	.60	.30	.15
4	Al Oliver	.15	.08	.04
5	Mike Schmidt	.70	.35	.20
6	Nolan Ryan	.40	.20	.10
7	Bucky Dent	.10	.05	.03
8	George Brett	.70	.35	.20
9	Jim Rice	.35	.20	.09
10	Steve Garvey	.40	.20	.10
11	Willie Stargell	.30	.15	.08
12	Phil Niekro	.25	.13	.06
13	Dave Parker	.20	.10	.05
14	Cesar Cedeno	.10	.05	.03
15	Don Baylor	.10	.05	.03
16	J.R. Richard	.08	.04	.02
17	Tony Perez	.15	.08	.04
18	Eddie Murray	.60	.30	.15
19	Chet Lemon	.08	.04	.02
20	Ben Oglivie	.08	.04	.02
21	Dave Winfield	.50	.25	.13
22	Joe Morgan	.20	.10	.05
23	Vida Blue	.10	.05	.03
24	Willie Wilson	.15	.08	.04
25	Steve Henderson	.08	.04	.02
26	Rod Carew	.50	.25	.13
27	Garry Templeton	.08	.04	.02
28	Dave Concepcion	.10	.05	.03
29	Davey Lopes	.08	.04	.02

1982 Kellogg's

For the second straight year in 1982, Kellogg's cards were not inserted into cereal boxes, but had to be obtained by sending cash and box tops to the company for complete sets. The '82 cards were downsized both in number of cards in the set - 64 - and in physical dimensions, 2-1/8" by 3-1/4".

		MT	NR MT	EX
Complete Set:		12.00	6.00	3.00
Common Player:		.12	.06	.03
1	Richie Zisk	.12	.06	.03
2	Bill Buckner	.12	.06	.03
3	George Brett	.90	.45	.25
4	Rickey Henderson	.80	.40	.20
5	Jack Morris	.30	.15	.08
6	Ozzie Smith	.25	.13	.06
7	Rollie Fingers	.25	.13	.06
8	Tom Seaver	.50	.25	.13
9	Fernando Valenzuela	.60	.30	.15
10	Hubie Brooks	.12	.06	.03
11	Nolan Ryan	.50	.25	.13
12	Dave Winfield	.60	.30	.15
13	Bob Horner	.20	.10	.05
14	Reggie Jackson	.90	.45	.25
15	Burt Hooton	.12	.06	.03
16	Mike Schmidt	.90	.45	.25
17	Bruce Sutter	.20	.10	.05

		MT	NR MT	EX
18	Pete Rose	1.50	.70	.40
19	Dave Kingman	.20	.10	.05
20	Neil Allen	.12	.06	.03
21	Don Sutton	.25	.13	.06
22	Dave Concepcion	.20	.10	.05
23	Keith Hernandez	.50	.25	.13
24	Gary Carter	.70	.35	.20
25	Carlton Fisk	.30	.15	.08
26	Ron Guidry	.25	.13	.06
27	Steve Carlton	.50	.25	.13
28	Robin Yount	.40	.20	.10
29	John Castino	.12	.06	.03
30	Johnny Bench	.80	.40	.20
31	Bob Knepper	.12	.06	.03
32	Rich "Goose" Gossage	.20	.10	.05
33	Buddy Bell	.20	.10	.05
34	Art Howe	.12	.06	.03
35	Tony Armas	.12	.06	.03
36	Phil Niekro	.30	.15	.08
37	Len Barker	.12	.06	.03
38	Bobby Grich	.20	.10	.05
39	Steve Kemp	.12	.06	.03
40	Kirk Gibson	.35	.20	.09
41	Carney Lansford	.20	.10	.05
42	Jim Palmer	.40	.20	.10
43	Carl Yastrzemski	1.00	.50	.25
44	Rick Burleson	.12	.06	.03
45	Dwight Evans	.25	.13	.06
46	Ron Cey	.20	.10	.05
47	Steve Garvey	.70	.35	.20
48	Dave Parker	.30	.15	.08
49	Mike Easler	.12	.06	.03
50	Dusty Baker	.12	.06	.03
51	Rod Carew	.70	.35	.20
52	Chris Chambliss	.12	.06	.03
53	Tim Raines	.70	.35	.20
54	Chet Lemon	.12	.06	.03
55	Bill Madlock	.20	.10	.05
56	George Foster	.20	.10	.05
57	Dwayne Murphy	.12	.06	.03
58	Ken Singleton	.20	.10	.05
59	Mike Norris	.12	.06	.03
60	Cecil Cooper	.20	.10	.05
61	Al Oliver	.20	.10	.05
62	Willie Wilson	.25	.13	.06
63	Vida Blue	.20	.10	.05
64	Eddie Murray	.80	.40	.20

		MT	NR MT	EX
7	Fernando Valenzuela	.35	.25	.14
8	Rickey Henderson	.60	.45	.25
9	Carl Yastrzemski	.70	.50	.30
10	Rich "Goose" Gossage	.20	.15	.08
11	Eddie Murray	.50	.40	.20
12	Buddy Bell	.15	.11	.06
13	Jim Rice	.40	.30	.15
14	Robin Yount	.35	.25	.14
15	Dave Winfield	.50	.40	.20
16	Harold Baines	.20	.15	.08
17	Garry Templeton	.15	.11	.06
18	Bill Madlock	.25	.20	.10
19	Pete Vuckovich	.10	.08	.04
20	Pedro Guerrero	.25	.20	.10
21	Ozzie Smith	.20	.15	.08
22	George Foster	.20	.15	.08
23	Willie Wilson	.20	.15	.08
24	Johnny Ray	.15	.11	.06
25	George Hendrick	.10	.08	.04
26	Andre Thornton	.10	.08	.04
27	Leon Durham	.10	.08	.04
28	Cecil Cooper	.15	.11	.06
29	Don Baylor	.15	.11	.06
30	Lonnie Smith	.10	.08	.04
31	Nolan Ryan	.40	.30	.15
32	Dan Quisenberry (Quisenbery)	.15	.11	.06
33	Len Barker	.10	.08	.04
34	Neil Allen	.10	.08	.04
35	Jack Morris	.30	.25	.12
36	Dave Stieb	.15	.11	.06
37	Bruce Sutter	.15	.11	.06
38	Jim Sundberg	.10	.08	.04
39	Jim Palmer	.35	.25	.14
40	Lance Parrish	.30	.25	.12
41	Floyd Bannister	.15	.11	.06
42	Larry Gura	.10	.08	.04
43	Britt Burns	.10	.08	.04
44	Toby Harrah	.10	.08	.04
45	Steve Carlton	.40	.30	.15
46	Greg Minton	.10	.08	.04
47	Gorman Thomas	.15	.11	.06
48	Jack Clark	.25	.20	.10
49	Keith Hernandez	.40	.30	.15
50	Greg Luzinski	.15	.11	.06
51	Fred Lynn	.25	.20	.10
52	Dale Murphy	.70	.50	.30
53	Kent Hrbek	.35	.25	.14
54	Bob Horner	.15	.11	.06
55	Gary Carter	.50	.40	.20
56	Carlton Fisk	.25	.20	.10
57	Dave Concepcion	.15	.11	.06
58	Mike Schmidt	.70	.50	.30
59	Bill Buckner	.15	.11	.06
60	Bobby Grich	.15	.11	.06

1983 Kellogg's

In its 14th and final year of baseball card issue, Kellogg's returned to the policy of inserting single cards into cereal boxes, as well as offering complete sets by a mail-in box top redemption offer. The 3-D cards themselves returned to a narrow - 1-7/8" by 3-1/4" format, while the set size was reduced to 60 cards.

		MT	NR MT	EX
Complete Set:		12.00	9.00	4.75
Common Player:		.10	.08	.04

		MT	NR MT	EX
1	Rod Carew	.50	.40	.20
2	Rollie Fingers	.20	.15	.08
3	Reggie Jackson	.50	.40	.20
4	George Brett	.70	.50	.30
5	Hal McRae	.15	.11	.06
6	Pete Rose	1.25	.90	.50

1988 Kenner Starting Lineup

KIRBY PUCKETT 34

This massive three-sport set was distributed in conjunction with Kenner's Starting Lineup sports figurines, one card per statue. Cards were not sold separately. Baseball, football and basketball stars are included in the lineup of full-color figurines, with 123 cards devoted to baseball. Individual major league team assortments include one to seven players per team. The figurines are mildly reminiscent of the 1950s Hartland Statues, but Kenner's version features smaller (4" to 6") figures and a more extensive catalog which includes athletes other than baseball players. The Starting Lineup cards feature action photos framed in red and white, with the "Starting Lineup" logo in the upper left corner and the player's name printed along the bottom border. Colorful team logos are superimposed in the lower right corner of the player photos. As an added incentive to collectors, five UPC codes from the sport statue packages could be redeemed for an autographed baseball. The values in the checklist that follows include both the statue and card for the 123 baseball players in the set. Several players which were included in the package's checklist were pulled before production.

		MT	NR MT	EX
	Complete Set:	1300.00	975.00	520.00
	Common Player:	7.00	5.25	2.75
(1)	Alan Ashby	11.00	8.25	4.50
(2)	Harold Baines	8.00	6.00	3.25
(3)	Kevin Bass	11.00	8.25	4.50
(4)	Steve Bedrosian	8.00	6.00	3.25
(5)	Buddy Bell	8.00	6.00	3.25
(6)	George Bell	10.00	7.50	4.00
(7)	Mike Boddicker	8.00	6.00	3.25
(8)	Wade Boggs	11.00	8.25	4.50
(9)	Barry Bonds	11.00	8.25	4.50
(10)	Bobby Bonilla	11.00	8.25	4.50
(11)	Sid Bream	16.00	12.00	6.50
(12)	George Brett	10.00	7.50	4.00
(13)	Chris Brown	11.00	8.25	4.50
(14)	Tom Brunansky	10.00	7.50	4.00
(15)	Ellis Burks	25.00	18.50	10.00
(16)	Jose Canseco	40.00	30.00	16.00
(17)	Gary Carter	7.00	5.25	2.75
(18)	Joe Carter	10.00	7.50	4.00
(19)	Jack Clark	16.00	12.00	6.50
(20)	Will Clark	11.00	8.25	4.50
(21)	Roger Clemens	10.00	7.50	4.00
(22)	Vince Coleman	8.00	6.00	3.25
(23)	Kal Daniels	10.00	7.50	4.00
(24)	Alvin Davis	8.00	6.00	3.25
(25)	Eric Davis	10.00	7.50	4.00
(26)	Glenn Davis	11.00	8.25	4.50
(27)	Jody Davis	10.00	7.50	4.00
(28)	Andre Dawson	8.00	6.00	3.25
(29)	Rob Deer	8.00	6.00	3.25
(30)	Brian Downing	8.00	6.00	3.25
(31)	Mike Dunne	8.00	6.00	3.25
(32)	Shawon Dunston	16.00	12.00	6.50
(33)	Leon Durham	7.00	5.25	2.75
(34)	Len Dykstra	10.00	7.50	4.00
(35)	Dwight Evans	10.00	7.50	4.00
(36)	Carlton Fisk	10.00	7.50	4.00
(37)	John Franco	10.00	7.50	4.00
(38)	Julio Franco	10.00	7.50	4.00
(39)	Gary Gaetti	8.00	6.00	3.25
(40)	Dwight Gooden	10.00	7.50	4.00
(41)	Ken Griffey	10.00	7.50	4.00
(42)	Pedro Guerrero	8.00	6.00	3.25
(43)	Ozzie Guillen	10.00	7.50	4.00
(44)	Tony Gwynn	8.00	6.00	3.25
(45)	Mel Hall	10.00	7.50	4.00
(46)	Billy Hatcher	10.00	7.50	4.00
(47)	Von Hayes	11.00	8.25	4.50
(48)	Rickey Henderson	8.00	6.00	3.25
(49)	Keith Hernandez	10.00	7.50	4.00
(50)	Willie Hernandez	11.00	8.25	4.50
(51)	Tom Herr	10.00	7.50	4.00
(52)	Ted Higuera	11.00	8.25	4.50
(53)	Charlie Hough	10.00	7.50	4.00
(54)	Kent Hrbek	8.00	6.00	3.25
(55)	Pete Incaviglia	8.00	6.00	3.25
(56)	Howard Johnson	11.00	8.25	4.50
(57)	Wally Joyner	10.00	7.50	4.00
(58)	Terry Kennedy	10.00	7.50	4.00
(59)	John Kruk	11.00	8.25	4.50
(60)	Mark Langston	11.00	8.25	4.50
(61)	Carney Lansford	16.00	12.00	6.50
(62)	Jeffrey Leonard	7.00	5.25	2.75
(63)	Fred Lynn	8.00	6.00	3.25
(64)	Candy Maldonado	11.00	8.25	4.50
(65)	Mike Marshall	16.00	12.00	6.50
(66)	Don Mattingly	11.00	8.25	4.50
(67)	Willie McGee	8.00	6.00	3.25
(68)	Mark McGwire	20.00	15.00	8.00
(69)	Kevin McReynolds	11.00	8.25	4.50
(70)	Paul Molitor	8.00	6.00	3.25
(71)	Donnie Moore	11.00	8.25	4.50

		MT	NR MT	EX
(72)	Jack Morris	10.00	7.50	4.00
(73)	Dale Murphy	8.00	6.00	3.25
(74)	Eddie Murray	8.00	6.00	3.25
(75)	Matt Nokes	10.00	7.50	4.00
(76)	Pete O'Brien	10.00	7.50	4.00
(77)	Ken Oberkfell	10.00	7.50	4.00
(78)	Dave Parker	16.00	12.00	6.50
(79)	Larry Parrish	8.00	6.00	3.25
(80)	Ken Phelps	16.00	12.00	6.50
(81)	Jim Presley	8.00	6.00	3.25
(82)	Kirby Puckett	10.00	7.50	4.00
(83)	Dan Quisenberry	8.00	6.00	3.25
(84)	Tim Raines	10.00	7.50	4.00
(85)	Willie Randolph	8.00	6.00	3.25
(86)	Shane Rawley	10.00	7.50	4.00
(87)	Jeff Reardon	10.00	7.50	4.00
(88)	Gary Redus	11.00	8.25	4.50
(89)	Rick Reuschel	10.00	7.50	4.00
(90)	Jim Rice	8.00	6.00	3.25
(91)	Dave Righetti	8.00	6.00	3.25
(92)	Cal Ripken	10.00	7.50	4.00
(93)	Pete Rose	16.00	12.00	6.50
(94)	Nolan Ryan	20.00	15.00	8.00
(95)	Bret Saberhagen	8.00	6.00	3.25
(96)	Juan Samuel	8.00	6.00	3.25
(97)	Ryne Sandberg	8.00	6.00	3.25
(98)	Benito Santiago	10.00	7.50	4.00
(99)	Steve Sax	8.00	6.00	3.25
(100)	Mike Schmidt	10.00	7.50	4.00
(101)	Mike Scott	8.00	6.00	3.25
(102)	Kevin Seitzer	16.00	12.00	6.50
(103)	Ruben Sierra	11.00	8.25	4.50
(104)	Ozzie Smith	8.00	6.00	3.25
(105)	Zane Smith	10.00	7.50	4.00
(106)	Cory Snyder	10.00	7.50	4.00
(107)	Darryl Strawberry	8.00	6.00	3.25
(108)	Franklin Stubbs	16.00	12.00	6.50
(109)	B.J. Surhoff	10.00	7.50	4.00
(110)	Rick Sutcliffe	10.00	7.50	4.00
(111)	Pat Tabler	10.00	7.50	4.00
(112)	Danny Tartabull	10.00	7.50	4.00
(113)	Alan Trammell	10.00	7.50	4.00
(114)	Fernando Valenzuela	8.00	6.00	3.25
(115)	Andy Van Slyke	18.00	13.50	7.25
(116)	Frank Viola	10.00	7.50	4.00
(117)	Ozzie Virgil	8.00	6.00	3.25
(118)	Greg Walker	8.00	6.00	3.25
(119)	Lou Whitaker	8.00	6.00	3.25
(120)	Devon White	10.00	7.50	4.00
(121)	Dave Winfield	8.00	6.00	3.25
(122)	Mike Witt	8.00	6.00	3.25
(123)	Todd Worrell	11.00	8.25	4.50
(124)	Robin Yount	8.00	6.00	3.25

1989 Kenner Starting Lineup

Kenner returned in 1989 with another set of sports figurines and accompanying trading cards. As in the previous year, the figurines were sold individually with one card packaged with each figure. No cards were sold separately. The cards have the "Starting Lineup" logo in the upper left, while the words "1989 Edition" appear in the lower right corner. The values listed below include both the figure and the card. The values are based on relative scarcity, resulting in some minor stars and common players being priced higher than superstars, whose cards and figures were produced in much greater numbers.

		MT	NR MT	EX
	Complete Set:	1100.00	825.00	450.00
	Common Player:	4.00	3.00	1.50
(1)	Ozzie Smith	6.00	4.50	2.50
(2)	Tom Brunansky	7.00	5.25	2.75
(3)	Vince Coleman	6.00	4.50	2.50
(4)	Willie McGee	6.00	4.50	2.50
(5)	Todd Worrell	5.00	3.75	2.00
(6)	Tony Pena	7.00	5.25	2.75
(7)	Terry Pendleton	7.00	5.25	2.75
(8)	Pedro Guerrero	8.00	6.00	3.25
(9)	Mike Schmidt	8.00	6.00	3.25
(10)	Von Hayes	4.00	3.00	1.50
(11)	Juan Samuel	5.00	3.75	2.00
(12)	Steve Bedrosian	5.00	3.75	2.00
(13)	Milt Thompson	5.00	3.75	2.00
(14)	Phil Bradley	5.00	3.75	2.00
(15)	Chris James	6.00	4.50	2.50
(16)	Dale Murphy	8.00	6.00	3.25
(17)	Zane Smith	4.00	3.00	1.50
(18)	Gerald Perry	6.00	4.50	2.50
(19)	Dion James	6.00	4.50	2.50
(20)	Albert Hall	4.00	3.00	1.50
(21)	Bruce Sutter	5.00	3.75	2.00
(22)	Ron Gant	6.00	4.50	2.50
(23)	Tony Gwynn	7.00	5.25	2.75
(24)	Benito Santiago	6.00	4.50	2.50
(25)	John Kruk	5.00	3.75	2.00
(26)	Marvell Wynne	5.00	3.75	2.00
(27)	Roberto Alomar	7.00	5.25	2.75
(28)	Mark Davis	6.00	4.50	2.50
(29)	Ryne Sandberg	6.00	4.50	2.50
(30)	Andre Dawson	6.00	4.50	2.50
(31)	Greg Maddux	7.00	5.25	2.75
(32)	Rick Sutcliffe	5.00	3.75	2.00
(33)	Mark Grace	8.00	6.00	3.25
(34)	Shawon Dunston	4.00	3.00	1.50
(35)	Damon Berryhill	5.00	3.75	2.00
(36)	Barry Bonds	6.00	4.50	2.50
(37)	Andy Van Slyke	5.00	3.75	2.00
(38)	Bob Walk	5.00	3.75	2.00
(39)	Bobby Bonilla	5.00	3.75	2.00
(40)	Mike LaValliere	5.00	3.75	2.00
(41)	Doug Drabek	6.00	4.50	2.50
(42)	Jose Lind	6.00	4.50	2.50
(43)	Fernando Valenzuela	5.00	3.75	2.00
(44)	Mike Marshall	4.00	3.00	1.50
(45)	Orel Hershiser	8.00	6.00	3.25
(46)	John Shelby	4.00	3.00	1.50
(47)	Kirk Gibson	6.00	4.50	2.50
(48)	Mike Scioscia	5.00	3.75	2.00
(49)	Eric Davis	8.00	6.00	3.25
(50)	Kal Daniels	6.00	4.50	2.50
(51)	John Franco	6.00	4.50	2.50
(52)	Danny Jackson	5.00	3.75	2.00
(53)	Bo Diaz	5.00	3.75	2.00
(54)	Barry Larkin	7.00	5.25	2.75
(55)	Jeff Treadway	6.00	4.50	2.50
(56)	Chris Sabo	7.00	5.25	2.75
(57)	Darryl Strawberry	8.00	6.00	3.25
(58)	Keith Hernandez	6.00	4.50	2.50
(59)	Gary Carter	6.00	4.50	2.50
(60)	Dwight Gooden	9.00	6.75	3.50
(61)	Len Dykstra	4.00	3.00	1.50
(62)	David Cone	7.00	5.25	2.75
(63)	Kevin Elster	6.00	4.50	2.50
(64)	Kevin McReynolds	6.00	4.50	2.50
(65)	Randy Myers	6.00	4.50	2.50
(66)	Gregg Jefferies	15.00	11.00	6.00
(67)	Mike Scott	5.00	3.75	2.00
(68)	Glenn Davis	6.00	4.50	2.50
(69)	Kevin Bass	4.00	3.00	1.50
(70)	Dave Smith	4.00	3.00	1.50
(71)	Bill Doran	6.00	4.50	2.50
(72)	Gerald Young	4.00	3.00	1.50
(73)	Billy Hatcher	4.00	3.00	1.50
(74)	Will Clark	10.00	7.50	4.00
(75)	Candy Maldonado	4.00	3.00	1.50
(76)	Brett Butler	6.00	4.50	2.50
(77)	Kevin Mitchell	9.00	6.75	3.50
(78)	Jose Uribe	5.00	3.75	2.00
(79)	Robby Thompson	6.00	4.50	2.50
(80)	Tim Raines	7.00	5.25	2.75
(81)	Joe Carter	6.00	4.50	2.50
(82)	Mel Hall	5.00	3.75	2.00
(83)	Cory Snyder	6.00	4.50	2.50
(84)	Brook Jacoby	6.00	4.50	2.50
(85)	Greg Swindell	8.00	6.00	3.25

		MT	NR MT	EX
(86)	Doug Jones	6.00	4.50	2.50
(87)	Jack Morris	6.00	4.50	2.50
(88)	Alan Trammell	7.00	5.25	2.75
(89)	Matt Nokes	7.00	5.25	2.75
90	Luis Salazar	4.00	3.00	1.50
(91)	Chet Lemon	4.00	3.00	1.50
(92)	Lou Whitaker	6.00	4.50	2.50
(93)	Tom Brookens	4.00	3.00	1.50
(94)	Mike Henneman	6.00	4.50	2.50
(95)	Jose Canseco	15.00	11.00	6.00
(96)	Mark McGwire	10.00	7.50	4.00
(97)	Dave Parker	6.00	4.50	2.50
(98)	Dave Stewart	7.00	5.25	2.75
(99)	Bob Welch	6.00	4.50	2.50
(100)	Terry Steinbach	8.00	6.00	3.25
(101)	Carney Lansford	5.00	3.75	2.00
(102)	Dennis Eckersley	6.00	4.50	2.50
(103)	Walt Weiss	7.00	5.25	2.75
(104)	George Brett	8.00	6.00	3.25
105	Bret Saberhagen	8.00	6.00	3.25
(106)	Danny Tartabull	6.00	4.50	2.50
(107)	Kevin Seitzer	10.00	7.50	4.00
(108)	Bo Jackson	12.00	9.00	4.75
(109)	Kurt Stillwell	6.00	4.50	2.50
(110)	Pat Tabler	6.00	4.50	2.50
(111)	Mark Gubicza	7.00	5.25	2.75
(112)	Robin Yount	7.00	5.25	2.75
(113)	Rob Deer	5.00	3.75	2.00
(114)	Paul Molitor	6.00	4.50	2.50
(115)	Ted Higuera	6.00	4.50	2.50
(116)	B.J. Surhoff	6.00	4.50	2.50
(117)	Dan Plesac	6.00	4.50	2.50
(118)	Glenn Braggs	6.00	4.50	2.50
(119)	Wade Boggs	10.00	7.50	4.00
(120)	Roger Clemens	10.00	7.50	4.00
(121)	Jim Rice	6.00	4.50	2.50
(122)	Ellis Burks	8.00	6.00	3.25
(123)	Mike Greenwell	8.00	6.00	3.25
124	Lee Smith	5.00	3.75	2.00
(125)	Marty Barrett	5.00	3.75	2.00
(126)	Wally Joyner	8.00	6.00	3.25
(127)	Mike Witt	4.00	3.00	1.50
(128)	Devon White	6.00	4.50	2.50
(129)	Johnny Ray	5.00	3.75	2.00
(130)	Chili Davis	5.00	3.75	2.00
(131)	Jack Howell	5.00	3.75	2.00
(132)	Dick Schofield	5.00	3.75	2.00
(133)	Rickey Henderson	8.00	6.00	3.25
(134)	Don Mattingly	13.00	9.75	5.25
(135)	Dave Winfield	7.00	5.25	2.75
(136)	Dave Righetti	7.00	5.25	2.75
(137)	Mike Pagliarulo	5.00	3.75	2.00
(138)	Don Slaught	4.00	3.00	1.50
(139)	Al Leiter	4.00	3.00	1.50
(140)	George Bell	7.00	5.25	2.75
(141)	Brady Anderson	6.00	4.50	2.50
(142)	Cal Ripken	7.00	5.25	2.75
(143)	Larry Sheets	4.00	3.00	1.50
(144)	Pete Stanicek	4.00	3.00	1.50
(145)	Kirby Puckett	8.00	6.00	3.25
(146)	Kent Hrbek	6.00	4.50	2.50
(147)	Gary Gaetti	6.00	4.50	2.50
(148)	Jeff Reardon	5.00	3.75	2.00
(149)	Dan Gladden	5.00	3.75	2.00
(150)	Frank Viola	5.00	3.75	2.00
(151)	Tim Laudner	4.00	3.00	1.50
(152)	Alvin Davis	6.00	4.50	2.50
(153)	Mark Langston	6.00	4.50	2.50
(154)	Harold Reynolds	6.00	4.50	2.50
(155)	Rey Quinones	4.00	3.00	1.50
(156)	Harold Baines	6.00	4.50	2.50
(157)	Ozzie Guillen	4.00	3.00	1.50
(158)	Greg Walker	4.00	3.00	1.50
(159)	Ivan Calderon	5.00	3.75	2.00
(160)	Melido Perez	5.00	3.75	2.00
(161)	Bobby Thigpen	7.00	5.25	2.75
(162)	Dan Pasqua	6.00	4.50	2.50
(163)	Pete Incaviglia	6.00	4.50	2.50
(164)	Ruben Sierra	9.00	6.75	3.50
(165)	Scott Fletcher	4.00	3.00	1.50
(166)	Steve Buechele	4.00	3.00	1.50
(167)	Jeff Russell	5.00	3.75	2.00

NOTE: A card number in parentheses ( ) indicates the set is unnumbered.

1989 Kenner Starting Lineup Baseball Greats

The "Baseball Greats" series of figurines and trading cards was an addition to the Kenner "Starting Lineup" series for 1989. The series features baseball greats of the past, and were packaged two figurines and two collector cards per package. The collector cards that accompany the figures feature an original action photo of the player done in a sepia-tone to enhance the historic nature of the set. The Starting Lineup logo and "Baseball Greats" heading appear at the top of the card. The player's name and a descriptive nickname, such as "Sultan of Swat" appear below the photo. The backs of the cards carry a blue-and- white color scheme and include career stats. The values listed below include both the figure and the card.

		MT	NR MT	EX
Complete Set:		150.00	110.00	60.00
Common Player:		10.00	7.50	4.00
(1)	Willie Mays/ Willie McCovey	12.00	9.00	4.75
(2)	Johnny Bench/ Pete Rose	10.00	7.50	4.00
(3)	Ernie Banks/ Billy Williams	12.00	9.00	4.75
(4)	Stan Musial/ Bob Gibson	12.00	9.00	4.75
(5)	Roberto Clemente/ Willie Stargell	10.00	7.00	4.00
(6)	Babe Ruth/ Lou Gehrig	15.00	11.00	6.00
(7)	Hank Aaron/ Eddie Mathews	25.00	20.00	10.00
(8)	Mickey Mantle/ Joe DiMaggio	15.00	11.00	6.00
(9)	Don Drysdale/ Reggie Jackson	15.00	11.00	6.00
(10)	Carl Yastrzemski/ Hank Aaron	18.00	13.50	7.25

1988 King-B

Created by Mike Schechter Associates, the 1988 King-B set consists of 24 numbered discs that measure 2-3/4" in size. The cards were inserted in specially marked 7/16 ounce tubs of Jerky Stuff (shredded beef jerky). The card fronts feature full-color photos surrounded by a blue border. The King-B logo appears in the upper left portion of the

disc. The disc backs are printed in blue on white stock and carry player personal and playing information. Team insignias have been airbrushed from the players' caps and jerseys.

		MT	NR MT	EX
Complete Set:		30.00	22.00	12.00
Common Player:		.75	.60	.30
1	Mike Schmidt	1.75	1.25	.70
2	Dale Murphy	1.75	1.25	.70
3	Kirby Puckett	1.50	1.25	.60
4	Ozzie Smith	1.00	.70	.40
5	Tony Gwynn	1.50	1.25	.60
6	Mark McGwire	2.50	2.00	1.00
7	George Brett	1.75	1.25	.70
8	Darryl Strawberry	1.75	1.25	.70
9	Wally Joyner	1.50	1.25	.60
10	Cory Snyder	1.00	.70	.40
11	Barry Bonds	1.00	.70	.40
12	Darrell Evans	.75	.60	.30
13	Mike Scott	.75	.60	.30
14	Andre Dawson	1.25	.90	.50
15	Don Mattingly	5.00	3.75	2.00
16	Candy Maldonado	.75	.60	.30
17	Alvin Davis	1.00	.70	.40
18	Carlton Fisk	1.00	.70	.40
19	Fernando Valenzuela	1.00	.70	.40
20	Roger Clemens	2.00	1.50	.80
21	Larry Parrish	.75	.60	.30
22	Eric Davis	2.00	1.50	.80
23	Paul Molitor	1.00	.70	.40
24	Cal Ripken, Jr.	1.75	1.25	.70

1989 King-B

The second King-B baseball card set created by Mike Schechter Associates also consists of 24 circular baseball cards measuring 2-3/4" across. The cards were inserted into specially-marked tubs of "Jerky Stuff." The card fronts feature full-color photos bordered in red. The King-B logo appears in the upper left portion of the disc. Like the 1988 set, the team insignias have airbrushed from uniforms and caps. The backs are printed in red and display personal information and stats.

		MT	NR MT	EX
Complete Set:		30.00	22.00	12.00
Common Player:		.75	.60	.30
1	Kirk Gibson	1.00	.70	.40
2	Eddie Murray	1.00	.70	.40
3	Wade Boggs	2.25	1.75	.90
4	Mark McGwire	2.25	1.75	.90
5	Ryne Sandberg	1.75	1.25	.70
6	Ozzie Guillen	.75	.60	.30
7	Chris Sabo	1.25	.90	.50
8	Joe Carter	1.00	.70	.40
9	Alan Trammell	1.00	.70	.40
10	Nolan Ryan	2.50	2.00	1.00
11	Bo Jackson	2.50	2.00	1.00
12	Orel Hershiser	1.00	.70	.40
13	Robin Yount	1.50	1.25	.60
14	Frank Viola	1.00	.70	.40
15	Darryl Strawberry	1.50	1.25	.60
16	Dave Winfield	1.00	.70	.40

		MT	NR MT	EX
17	Jose Canseco	3.50	2.75	1.50
18	Von Hayes	.75	.60	.30
19	Andy Van Slyke	.75	.60	.30
20	Pedro Guerrero	1.00	.70	.40
21	Tony Gwynn	1.75	1.25	.70
22	Will Clark	2.50	2.00	1.00
23	Danny Jackson	.75	.60	.30
24	Pete Incaviglia	.75	.60	.30

1986 Kitty Clover
Potato Chips Royals

Twenty players of the 1985 World's Champion Kansas City Royals were featured in a round card set inserted into packages of potato chips in the K.C. area. The 2-7/8" discs were similar to a handful of snack issues produced by Mike Schecter Associates in that team logos have been airbrushed off the players' caps, and the photos of some of the players can be found on other regional issues of 1986.

		MT	NR MT	EX
Complete Set:		20.00	15.00	8.00
Common Player:		.70	.50	.30
1	Lonnie Smith	.70	.50	.30
2	Buddy Biancalana	.70	.50	.30
3	Bret Saberhagen	1.75	1.25	.70
4	Hal McRae	.90	.70	.35
5	Onix Concepcion	.70	.50	.30
6	Jorge Orta	.70	.50	.30
7	Bud Black	.70	.50	.30
8	Dan Quisenberry	1.00	.70	.40
9	Dane Iorg	.70	.50	.30
10	Charlie Leibrandt	.80	.60	.30
11	Pat Sheridan	.70	.50	.30
12	John Wathan	.80	.60	.30
13	Frank White	1.00	.70	.40
14	Darryl Motley	.70	.50	.30
15	Willie Wilson	1.25	.90	.50
16	Danny Jackson	1.25	.90	.50
17	Steve Balboni	.80	.60	.30
18	Jim Sundberg	.70	.50	.30
19	Mark Gubicza	1.25	.90	.50
20	George Brett	3.25	2.50	1.25

1987 Kraft

Kraft Foods, Inc. issued a 48-card set on specially marked packages of their Macaroni & Cheese Dinners. Titled "Home Plate Heroes," 24 two-card panels measuring 3-1/2" by 7-1/8" make up the set. Individual cards measure 2-1/4" by 3-1/2" and are numbered 1 through 48. The blank-backed cards feature fronts with full-color photos, although all team insignias have been erased. In conjunction with the card set, Kraft offered a contest to "Win A Day With A Major Leaguer." Mike Schecter Associates produced the set for Kraft. 120 different panel combinatons can be found.

		MT	NR MT	EX
Complete Set:		35.00	27.50	15.00
Common Player:		.20	.15	.08
1	Eddie Murray	.75	.60	.30
2	Dale Murphy	1.00	.70	.40
3	Cal Ripken	.75	.60	.30
4	Mike Scott	.35	.25	.14
5	Jim Rice	.50	.40	.20
6	Jody Davis	.20	.15	.08
7	Wade Boggs	1.50	1.25	.60
8	Ryne Sandberg	.50	.40	.20
9	Wally Joyner	1.50	1.25	.60
10	Eric Davis	1.25	.90	.50
11	Ozzie Guillen	.20	.15	.08
12	Tony Pena	.20	.15	.08
13	Harold Baines	.35	.25	.14
14	Johnny Ray	.20	.15	.08
15	Joe Carter	.35	.25	.14
16	Ozzie Smith	.35	.25	.14
17	Cory Snyder	.60	.45	.25
18	Vince Coleman	.35	.25	.14
19	Kirk Gibson	.50	.40	.20
20	Steve Garvey	.75	.60	.30
21	George Brett	1.00	.70	.40
22	John Tudor	.20	.15	.08
23	Robin Yount	.70	.50	.30
24	Von Hayes	.35	.25	.14
25	Kent Hrbek	.50	.40	.20
26	Darryl Strawberry	1.00	.70	.40
27	Kirby Puckett	.75	.60	.30
28	Ron Darling	.35	.25	.14
29	Don Mattingly	2.50	2.00	1.00
30	Mike Schmidt	1.00	.70	.40
31	Rickey Henderson	.75	.60	.30
32	Fernando Valenzuela	.50	.40	.20
33	Dave Winfield	.60	.45	.25
34	Pete Rose	1.25	.90	.50
35	Jose Canseco	2.00	1.50	.80
36	Glenn Davis	.35	.25	.14
37	Alvin Davis	.35	.25	.14
38	Steve Sax	.35	.25	.14
39	Pete Incaviglia	.70	.50	.30
40	Jeff Reardon	.35	.25	.14
41	Jesse Barfield	.35	.25	.14
42	Hubie Brooks	.20	.15	.08
43	George Bell	.50	.40	.20
44	Tony Gwynn	.75	.60	.30
45	Roger Clemens	1.00	.70	.40
46	Chili Davis	.20	.15	.08
47	Mike Witt	.20	.15	.08
48	Nolan Ryan	1.00	.70	.40

A player's name in _italic_ type indicates a rookie card. An (FC) indicates a player's first card for that particular card company.

Definitions for grading conditions are located in the Introduction section at the front of this book.

1986 Lite Beer Astros

This 22-card regional set of the Houston Astros was sponsored by Lite Beer and given away in a special stadium promotion. The large (4-1/2" by 6-3/4") cards featured full-color photos surrounded by a wide, white border. Diagonal color bands of yellow, orange, red and purple extend throught the upper right and lower left corners of the card, which also displays the Astros' 25th Anniversary logo and the Lite Beer logo in opposite corners. The backs include player information and statistics.

		MT	NR MT	EX
Complete Set:		60.00	45.00	24.00
Common Player:		1.50	1.25	.60
3	Phil Garner	1.50	1.25	.60
6	Mark Bailey	1.50	1.25	.60
10	Dickie Thon	2.00	1.50	.80
11	Frank DiPino	1.50	1.25	.60
12	Craig Reynolds	1.50	1.25	.60
14	Alan Ashby	1.50	1.25	.60
17	Kevin Bass	3.00	2.25	1.25
19	Bill Doran	3.00	2.25	1.25
20	Jim Pankovits	1.50	1.25	.60
21	Terry Puhl	1.50	1.25	.60
22	Hal Lanier	1.50	1.25	.60
25	Jose Cruz	3.00	2.25	1.25
27	Glenn Davis	7.00	5.25	2.75
28	Billy Hatcher	2.50	2.00	1.00
29	Denny Walling	1.50	1.25	.60
33	Mike Scott	4.00	3.00	1.50
34	Nolan Ryan	7.00	5.25	2.75
37	Charlie Kerfeld	2.00	1.50	.80
39	Bob Knepper	2.00	1.50	.80
43	Jim Deshaies	3.00	2.25	1.25
45	Dave Smith	2.00	1.50	.80
53	Mike Madden	1.50	1.25	.60

1960 Lake To Lake Dairy Braves

This 28-card set of unnumbered 2-1/2" by 3-1/4" cards offers a special challenge for the condition-conscious collector. Originally issued by being stapled to milk cartons, the cards were redeemable for prizes ranging from pen and pencil sets to Braves tickets. When sent in for redemption, the cards had a hole punched in the corner. Naturally, collectors most desire cards without the staple or punch holes. Cards are printed in blue ink on front, red ink on back. Because he was traded in May, and his card withdrawn, the Ray Boone card is scarce; the Billy Bruton card is unaccountably scarcer still.

		NR MT	EX	VG
Complete Set:		950.00	475.00	285.00
Common Player:		12.00	6.00	3.50
(1)	Henry Aaron	200.00	100.00	60.00
(2)	Joe Adcock	17.50	8.75	5.25
(3)	Ray Boone	125.00	62.00	37.00
(4)	Bill Bruton	200.00	100.00	60.00
(5)	Bob Buhl	17.50	8.75	5.25
(6)	Lou Burdette	20.00	10.00	6.00
(7)	Chuck Cottier	12.00	6.00	3.50
(8)	Wes Covington	15.00	7.50	4.50
(9)	Del Crandall	17.50	8.75	5.25
(10)	Charlie Dressen	15.00	7.50	4.50
(11)	Bob Giggie	12.00	6.00	3.50
(12)	Joey Jay	12.00	6.00	3.50
(13)	Johnny Logan	15.00	7.50	4.50
(14)	Felix Mantilla	12.00	6.00	3.50
(15)	Lee Maye	12.00	6.00	3.50
(16)	Don McMahon	12.00	6.00	3.50
(17)	George Myatt	12.00	6.00	3.50
(18)	Andy Pafko	15.00	7.50	4.50
(19)	Juan Pizarro	12.00	6.00	3.50
(20)	Mel Roach	12.00	6.00	3.50
(21)	Bob Rush	12.00	6.00	3.50
(22)	Bob Scheffing	12.00	6.00	3.50
(23)	Red Schoendienst	20.00	10.00	6.00
(24)	Warren Spahn	50.00	25.00	15.00
(25)	Al Spangler	12.00	6.00	3.50
(26)	Frank Torre	12.00	6.00	3.50
(27)	Carl Willey	12.00	6.00	3.50
(28)	Whitlow Wyatt	12.00	6.00	3.50

1948 Leaf

The first color baseball cards of the post-World War II era were the 98-card, 2-3/8" by 2-7/8", set produced by Chicago's Leaf Gum Company in 1948-1949. The color was crude, probably helping to make the set less popular than the Bowman issues of the same era. One of the toughest post-war sets to complete, exactly half of the Leaf issue - 49 of the cards - are significantly harder to find than the other 49. Probably intended to confound bubble gum buyers of the day, the set is skip-numbered between 1-168. Card backs contain offers of felt pennants, an album for the cards or 5-1/2" by 7-1/2" premium photos of Hall of Famers.

	NR MT	EX	VG
Complete Set:	14000.00	7000.00	4200.
Common Player:	15.00	7.50	4.50
Common Scarce Player:	200.00	100.00	60.00

		NR MT	EX	VG
1	Joe DiMaggio	600.00	250.00	150.00
3	Babe Ruth	750.00	375.00	225.00
4	Stan Musial	225.00	112.00	67.00
5	Virgil Trucks	200.00	100.00	60.00
8	Leroy Paige	1000.00	500.00	300.00
10	Paul Trout	15.00	7.50	4.50
11	Phil Rizzuto	75.00	37.00	22.00
13	Casimer Michaels	200.00	100.00	60.00
14	Billy Johnson	18.00	9.00	5.50
17	Frank Overmire	15.00	7.50	4.50
19	John Wyrostek	200.00	100.00	60.00
20	Hank Sauer	200.00	100.00	60.00
22	Al Evans	15.00	7.50	4.50
26	Sam Chapman	15.00	7.50	4.50
27	Mickey Harris	15.00	7.50	4.50
28	Jim Hegan	15.00	7.50	4.50
29	Elmer Valo	15.00	7.50	4.50
30	Bill Goodman	200.00	100.00	60.00
31	Lou Brissie	15.00	7.50	4.50
32	Warren Spahn	85.00	42.00	25.00
33	Harry Lowrey	200.00	100.00	60.00
36	Al Zarilla	200.00	100.00	60.00
38	Ted Kluszewski	30.00	15.00	9.00
39	Ewell Blackwell	18.00	9.00	5.50
42	Kent Peterson	15.00	7.50	4.50
43	Eddie Stevens	200.00	100.00	60.00
45	Ken Keltner	200.00	100.00	60.00
46	Johnny Mize	60.00	30.00	18.00
47	George Vico	15.00	7.50	4.50
48	Johnny Schmitz	200.00	100.00	60.00
49	Del Ennis	15.00	7.50	4.50
50	Dick Wakefield	15.00	7.50	4.50
51	Alvin Dark	250.00	125.00	75.00
53	John Vandermeer (Vander Meer)	18.00	9.00	5.50
54	Bobby Adams	200.00	100.00	60.00
55	Tommy Henrich	250.00	125.00	75.00
56	Larry Jensen (Jansen)	15.00	7.50	4.50
57	Bob McCall	15.00	7.50	4.50
59	Lucius Appling	50.00	25.00	15.00
61	Jake Early	15.00	7.50	4.50
62	Eddie Joost	200.00	100.00	60.00
63	Barney McCosky	200.00	100.00	60.00
65	Bob Elliot (Elliott)	15.00	7.50	4.50
66	Orval Grove	200.00	100.00	60.00
68	Ed Miller	200.00	100.00	60.00
70	John Wagner	160.00	80.00	48.00
72	Hank Edwards	15.00	7.50	4.50
73	Pat Seerey	15.00	7.50	4.50
75	Dom DiMaggio	225.00	112.00	67.00
76	Ted Williams	300.00	150.00	90.00
77	Roy Smalley	15.00	7.50	4.50
78	Walter Evers	200.00	100.00	60.00
79	Jackie Robinson	275.00	137.00	82.00
81	George Kurowski	200.00	100.00	60.00
82	Johnny Lindell	18.00	9.00	5.50
83	Bobby Doerr	50.00	25.00	15.00
84	Sid Hudson	15.00	7.50	4.50
85	Dave Philley	200.00	100.00	60.00
86	Ralph Weigel	15.00	7.50	4.50
88	Frank Gustine	200.00	100.00	60.00
91	Ralph Kiner	50.00	25.00	15.00
93	Bob Feller	700.00	350.00	210.00
95	George Stirnweiss	18.00	9.00	5.50
97	Martin Marion	18.00	9.00	5.50
98	Hal Newhouser	225.00	112.00	67.00
102a	Gene Hermansk (incorrect spelling)	200.00	100.00	60.00
102b	Gene Hermanski (correct spelling)	18.00	9.00	5.50
104	Edward Stewart	200.00	100.00	60.00
106	Lou Boudreau	45.00	22.00	13.50
108	Matthew Batts	200.00	100.00	60.00
111	Gerald Priddy	15.00	7.50	4.50
113	Emil Leonard	200.00	100.00	60.00
117	Joe Gordon	18.00	9.00	5.50
120	George Kell	400.00	200.00	120.00
121	John Pesky	200.00	100.00	60.00
123	Clifford Fannin	200.00	100.00	60.00
125	Andy Pafko	18.00	9.00	5.50
127	Enos Slaughter	400.00	200.00	120.00
128	Warren Rosar	15.00	7.50	4.50
129	Kirby Higbe	200.00	100.00	60.00
131	Sid Gordon	200.00	100.00	60.00
133	Tommy Holmes	200.00	100.00	60.00
136a	Cliff Aberson (full sleeve)	15.00	7.50	4.50
136b	Cliff Aberson (short sleeve)	80.00	40.00	24.00

		NR MT	EX	VG
137	Harry Walker	200.00	100.00	60.00
138	Larry Doby	275.00	137.00	82.00
139	Johnny Hopp	15.00	7.50	4.50
142	Danny Murtaugh	200.00	100.00	60.00
143	Dick Sisler	200.00	100.00	60.00
144	Bob Dillinger	200.00	100.00	60.00
146	Harold Reiser	225.00	112.00	67.00
149	Henry Majeski	200.00	100.00	60.00
153	Floyd Baker	200.00	100.00	60.00
158	Harry Brecheen	200.00	100.00	60.00
159	Mizell Platt	15.00	7.50	4.50
160	Bob Scheffing	200.00	100.00	60.00
161	Vernon Stephens	200.00	100.00	60.00
163	Freddy Hutchinson	225.00	112.00	67.00
165	Dale Mitchell	200.00	100.00	60.00
168	Phil Cavaretta (Cavarretta)	250.00	112.00	67.00

1960 Leaf

While known to the hobby as "Leaf" cards, this set of 144 cards carries the copyright of Sports Novelties Inc., Chicago. The 2-1/2" by 3-1/2" cards feature black and white player portrait photos, with background airbrushed away. Cards were sold in 5¢ wax packs with a marble, rather than a piece of bubble gum. The second half of the set, cards #73-144, are very scarce and make the set a real challenge for the collector. Card #25, Jim Grant, is found in two versions, with his own picture (black cap) and with a photo of Brooks Lawrence (white cap). Eight cards (#'s 1, 12, 17, 23, 35, 58, 61 and 72) exist with close-up photos that are much rarer than the normal cap to chest photos. It is believed the scarce "face only" cards are proof cards prepared by Leaf as only a handful are known to exist.

		NR MT	EX	VG
Complete Set:		1300.00	650.00	390.00
Common Player: 1-72		1.00	.50	.30
Common Player: 73-144		15.00	7.50	4.50
1	Luis Aparicio	9.00	3.50	2.00
2	Woody Held	1.00	.50	.30
3	Frank Lary	1.25	.60	.40
4	Camilo Pascual	1.25	.60	.40
5	Frank Herrera	1.00	.50	.30
6	Felipe Alou	1.25	.60	.40
7	Bennie Daniels	1.00	.50	.30
8	Roger Craig	1.25	.60	.40
9	Eddie Kasko	1.00	.50	.30
10	Bob Grim	1.00	.50	.30
11	Jim Busby	1.00	.50	.30
12	Ken Boyer	2.50	1.25	.70
13	Bob Boyd	1.00	.50	.30
14	Sam Jones	1.00	.50	.30
15	Larry Jackson	1.00	.50	.30
16	Roy Face	1.50	.70	.45
17	Walt Moryn	1.00	.50	.30
18	Jim Gilliam	2.50	1.25	.70
19	Don Newcombe	1.25	.60	.40
20	Glen Hobbie	1.00	.50	.30
21	Pedro Ramos	1.00	.50	.30
22	Ryne Duren	1.50	.70	.45
23	Joe Jay	1.00	.50	.30
24	Lou Berberet	1.00	.50	.30
25a	Jim Grant (white cap, photo actually Brooks Lawrence)	12.00	6.00	3.50

		NR MT	EX	VG
25b	Jim Grant (dark cap, correct photo)			
		30.00	15.00	9.00
26	Tom Borland	1.00	.50	.30
27	Brooks Robinson	15.00	7.50	4.50
28	Jerry Adair	1.25	.60	.40
29	Ron Jackson	1.00	.50	.30
30	George Strickland	1.00	.50	.30
31	Rocky Bridges	1.00	.50	.30
32	Bill Tuttle	1.00	.50	.30
33	Ken Hunt	1.25	.60	.40
34	Hal Griggs	1.00	.50	.30
35	Jim Coates	1.25	.60	.40
36	Brooks Lawrence	1.00	.50	.30
37	Duke Snider	15.00	7.50	4.50
38	Al Spangler	1.00	.50	.30
39	Jim Owens	1.00	.50	.30
40	Bill Virdon	1.50	.70	.45
41	Ernie Broglio	1.00	.50	.30
42	Andre Rodgers	1.00	.50	.30
43	Julio Becquer	1.00	.50	.30
44	Tony Taylor	1.00	.50	.30
45	Jerry Lynch	1.25	.60	.40
46	Cletis Boyer	1.50	.70	.45
47	Jerry Lumpe	1.25	.60	.40
48	Charlie Maxwell	1.00	.50	.30
49	Jim Perry	1.25	.60	.40
50	Danny McDevitt	1.00	.50	.30
51	Juan Pizarro	1.00	.50	.30
52	Dallas Green	1.50	.70	.45
53	Bob Friend	1.25	.60	.40
54	Jack Sanford	1.25	.60	.40
55	Jim Rivera	1.00	.50	.30
56	Ted Wills	1.00	.50	.30
57	Milt Pappas	1.25	.60	.40
58a	Hal Smith (team & position on back)			
		1.00	.50	.30
58b	Hal Smith (team blackened out on back)			
		35.00	17.50	10.50
58c	Hal Smith (team missing on back)			
		35.00	17.50	10.50
59	Bob Avila	1.00	.50	.30
60	Clem Labine	1.25	.60	.40
61	Vic Rehm	1.25	.60	.40
62	John Gabler	1.25	.60	.40
63	John Tsitouris	1.00	.50	.30
64	Dave Sisler	1.00	.50	.30
65	Vic Power	1.25	.60	.40
66	Earl Battey	1.25	.60	.40
67	Bob Purkey	1.25	.60	.40
68	Moe Drabowsky	1.00	.50	.30
69	Hoyt Wilhelm	6.00	3.00	1.75
70	Humberto Robinson	1.00	.50	.30
71	Whitey Herzog	2.00	1.00	.60
72	Dick Donovan	1.25	.60	.40
73	Gordon Jones	15.00	7.50	4.50
74	Joe Hicks	15.00	7.50	4.50
75	Ray Culp	18.00	9.00	5.50
76	Dick Drott	15.00	7.50	4.50
77	Bob Duliba	15.00	7.50	4.50
78	Art Ditmar	18.00	9.00	5.50
79	Steve Korcheck	15.00	7.50	4.50
80	Henry Mason	15.00	7.50	4.50
81	Harry Simpson	15.00	7.50	4.50
82	Gene Green	15.00	7.50	4.50
83	Bob Shaw	15.00	7.50	4.50
84	Howard Reed	15.00	7.50	4.50
85	Dick Stigman	15.00	7.50	4.50
86	Rip Repulski	15.00	7.50	4.50
87	Seth Morehead	15.00	7.50	4.50
88	Camilo Carreon	15.00	7.50	4.50
89	John Blanchard	18.00	9.00	5.50
90	Billy Hoeft	15.00	7.50	4.50
91	Fred Hopke	18.00	9.00	5.50
92	Joe Martin	15.00	7.50	4.50
93	Wally Shannon	18.00	9.00	5.50
94	Baseball's Two Hal Smiths (Harold Raymond Smith, Harold Wayne Smith)			
		20.00	10.00	6.00
95	Al Schroll	15.00	7.50	4.50
96	John Kucks	15.00	7.50	4.50
97	Tom Morgan	15.00	7.50	4.50
98	Willie Jones	15.00	7.50	4.50
99	Marshall Renfroe	18.00	9.00	5.50
100	Willie Tasby	15.00	7.50	4.50
101	Irv Noren	15.00	7.50	4.50
102	Russ Snyder	15.00	7.50	4.50
103	Bob Turley	20.00	10.00	6.00
104	Jim Woods	15.00	7.50	4.50
105	Ronnie Kline	15.00	7.50	4.50
106	Steve Bilko	15.00	7.50	4.50
107	Elmer Valo	18.00	9.00	5.50

		NR MT	EX	VG
108	Tom McAvoy	18.00	9.00	5.50
109	Stan Williams	15.00	7.50	4.50
110	Earl Averill	15.00	7.50	4.50
111	Lee Walls	15.00	7.50	4.50
112	Paul Richards	18.00	9.00	5.50
113	Ed Sadowski	15.00	7.50	4.50
114	Stover McIlwain	18.00	9.00	5.50
115	Chuck Tanner (photo actually Ken Kuhn)			
		20.00	10.00	6.00
116	Lou Klimchock	15.00	7.50	4.50
117	Neil Chrisley	15.00	7.50	4.50
118	John Callison	20.00	10.00	6.00
119	Hal Smith	15.00	7.50	4.50
120	Carl Sawatski	15.00	7.50	4.50
121	Frank Leja	18.00	9.00	5.50
122	Earl Torgeson	15.00	7.50	4.50
123	Art Schult	15.00	7.50	4.50
124	Jim Brosnan	18.00	9.00	5.50
125	George Anderson	25.00	12.50	7.50
126	Joe Pignatano	15.00	7.50	4.50
127	Rocky Nelson	15.00	7.50	4.50
128	Orlando Cepeda	35.00	17.50	10.50
129	Daryl Spencer	15.00	7.50	4.50
130	Ralph Lumenti	15.00	7.50	4.50
131	Sam Taylor	15.00	7.50	4.50
132	Harry Brecheen	18.00	9.00	5.50
133	Johnny Groth	15.00	7.50	4.50
134	Wayne Terwilliger	15.00	7.50	4.50
135	Kent Hadley	18.00	9.00	5.50
136	Faye Throneberry	15.00	7.50	4.50
137	Jack Meyer	15.00	7.50	4.50
138	Chuck Cottier	15.00	7.50	4.50
139	Joe DeMaestri	18.00	9.00	5.50
140	Gene Freese	15.00	7.50	4.50
141	Curt Flood	20.00	10.00	6.00
142	Gino Cimoli	15.00	7.50	4.50
143	Clay Dalrymple	15.00	7.50	4.50
144	Jim Bunning	60.00	15.00	9.00

1986 Lite Beer Rangers

#0 ODDIBE McDOWELL
Outfielder

This postcard-size (approximately 4" by 6") regional set of 28 Texas Rangers cards was sponsored by Lite Beer and was available by mail directly from the Rangers. The fronts featured full-color photos surrounded by a wide, white border with the player's name, uniform number and postion appearing below. The Rangers logo is displayed in the lower left corner, while the Lite Beer logo is in the lower right.

		MT	NR MT	EX
	Complete Set:	60.00	45.00	24.00
	Common Player:	1.50	1.25	.60
0	Oddibe McDowell	3.00	2.25	1.25
1	Scott Fletcher	2.00	1.50	.80
2	Bobby Valentine	2.00	1.50	.80
4	Don Slaught	1.50	1.25	.60
5	Pete Incaviglia	6.00	4.50	2.50
9	Pete O'Brien	3.00	2.25	1.25
10	Art Howe	1.50	1.25	.60
11	Toby Harrah	2.00	1.50	.80
12	Geno Petralli	1.50	1.25	.60
13	Joe Ferguson	1.50	1.25	.60
14	Tim Foli	1.50	1.25	.60
15	Larry Parrish	2.50	2.00	1.00
16	Mike Mason	1.50	1.25	.60

		MT	NR MT	EX
17	Darrell Porter	2.00	1.50	.80
18	Ed Correa	3.00	2.25	1.25
19	Curtis Wilkerson	1.50	1.25	.60
22	Steve Buechele	3.00	2.25	1.25
23	Jose Guzman	4.00	3.00	1.50
24	Ricky Wright	1.50	1.25	.60
27	Greg Harris	1.50	1.25	.60
31	Tom Robson	1.50	1.25	.60
32	Gary Ward	2.00	1.50	.80
35	Tom House	1.50	1.25	.60
44	Tom Paciorek	1.50	1.25	.60
45	Dwayne Henry	2.00	1.50	.80
48	Bobby Witt	5.00	3.75	2.00
49	Charlie Hough	3.00	2.25	1.25
----	Arlington Stadium	1.50	1.25	.60

1988 Louisville Slugger

Two more cards were added to the Hillerich & Bradsby hangtag collection in 1988. Hillerich & Bradsby, makers of Louisville Slugger bats and gloves, produced the cards to be attached to the company's baseball gloves. The 1988 Eric Davis and Mike Pagliarulo cards bring the total number of Hillerich & Bradsby hangtags issued since the first ones in 1981 (Graig Nettles and Steve Garvey) to 13. A small round hole is punched in the upper left corner of each standard-size card to enable them to be attached to the gloves, making it hard to find undamaged cards. The 1988 cards are numbered and follow the same basic design as previous issues - bright blue and green borders, player name and position above the full-color photo (with autograph overprint), yellow Louisville Slugger logo across the bottom border. Beneath the logo are the words "Member Louisville Slugger Bat & Glove Advisory Staff." The card backs are blue and green and include the player name, short biography and a list of personal records and information.

		MT	NR MT	EX
Complete Set:		160.00	120.00	64.00
Common Player:		5.00	3.75	2.00
(1)	Eric Davis (1988)	10.00	7.50	4.00
(2)	Steve Garvey (Dodgers - 1981)	25.00	18.50	10.00
(3)	Steve Garvey (Padres - 1985)	12.00	9.00	4.75
(4)	Pedro Guerrero (1982)	12.00	9.00	4.75
(5)	Orel Hershiser (1986)	20.00	15.00	8.00
(6)	Ray Knight (Astros - 1984)	15.00	11.00	6.00
(7)	Ray Knight (Mets - 1984)	10.00	7.50	4.00
(8)	Fred Lynn (1982)	5.00	3.75	2.00
(9)	Gary Matthews (1985)	15.00	11.00	6.00
(10)	Graig Nettles (Yankees - 1981)	12.00	9.00	4.75
(11)	Graig Nettles (Padres - 1984)	10.00	7.50	4.00
(12)	Mike Pagliarulo (1988)	5.00	3.75	2.00
(13)	Rick Rhoden (1985)	10.00	7.50	4.00

NOTE: A card number in parentheses ( ) indicates the set is unnumbered.

1987 M & M's

The M&M's "Star Lineup" set consists of 12 two card panels inserted in specially marked packages of large M&M's candy. The two-card panels measure 5" by 3-1/2" with individual cards measuring 2-1/2" by 3-1/2" in size. The full-color photos are enclosed by a wavy blue frame and a white border. Card backs are printed in red ink on white stock and carry the player's career statistics and highlights. All team insignias have been airbrushed away. The set was designed and produced by Mike Schechter and Associates.

		MT	NR MT	EX
Complete Panel Set:		18.00	13.50	7.25
Complete Singles Set:		8.00	6.00	3.25
Common Panel:		1.00	.70	.40
Common Single Player:		.10	.08	.04
Panel		1.50	1.25	.60
1	Wally Joyner	.50	.40	.20
2	Tony Pena	.10	.08	.04
Panel		1.50	1.25	.60
3	Mike Schmidt	.30	.25	.12
4	Ryne Sandberg	.20	.15	.08
Panel		2.25	1.75	.90
5	Wade Boggs	.70	.50	.30
6	Jack Morris	.20	.15	.08
Panel		1.25	.90	.50
7	Roger Clemens	.30	.25	.12
8	Harold Baines	.15	.11	.06
Panel		2.75	2.00	1.00
9	Dale Murphy	.30	.25	.12
10	Jose Canseco	1.00	.70	.40
Panel		3.25	2.50	1.25
11	Don Mattingly	1.25	.90	.50
12	Gary Carter	.20	.15	.08
Panel		1.50	1.25	.60
13	Cal Ripken, Jr.	.25	.20	.10
14	George Brett	.30	.25	.12
Panel		1.00	.70	.40
15	Kirby Puckett	.20	.15	.08
16	Joe Carter	.15	.11	.06
Panel		1.00	.70	.40
17	Mike Witt	.15	.11	.06
18	Mike Scott	.15	.11	.06
Panel		1.25	.90	.50
19	Fernando Valenzuela	.20	.15	.08
20	Steve Garvey	.20	.15	.08
Panel		1.00	.70	.40
21	Steve Sax	.15	.11	.06
22	Nolan Ryan	.20	.15	.08
Panel		1.25	.90	.50
23	Tony Gwynn	.25	.20	.10
24	Ozzie Smith	.15	.11	.06

1989 Marathon Cubs

This colorful 25-card Cubs team set was sponsored by Marathon and was distributed as a stadium promotion to fans attending the August 10, 1989, game at Chicago's Wrigley Field. The oversize (2-3/4" by 4-1/4") feature an action photo inside a diagonal box on the card front, with the Chicago Cubs logo at the top and the player's uniform number, name and position along the bottom. The backs include a small black-and-white photo, player data and the Cubs and Marathon logos.

		MT	NR MT	EX
Complete Set:		10.00	7.50	4.00
Common Player:		.10	.08	.04
Coaches Card		.10	.08	.04
2	Vance Law	.10	.08	.04
4	Don Zimmer	.15	.11	.06
7	Joe Girardi	.50	.40	.20
8	Andre Dawson	.70	.50	.30
9	Damon Berryhill	.40	.30	.15
10	Lloyd McClendon	.50	.40	.20
12	Shawon Dunston	.50	.40	.20
15	Domingo Ramos	.10	.08	.04
17	Mark Grace	2.25	1.75	.90
18	Dwight Smith	2.75	2.00	1.00
19	Curt Wilkerson	.10	.08	.04
20	Jerome Walton	3.50	2.75	1.50
21	Scott Sanderson	.10	.08	.04
23	Ryne Sandberg	2.00	1.50	.80
28	Mitch Williams	1.00	.70	.40
31	Greg Maddux	.70	.50	.30
32	Calvin Schiraldi	.10	.08	.04
33	Mitch Webster	.10	.08	.04
36	Mike Bielecki	.40	.30	.15
39	Paul Kilgus	.10	.08	.04
40	Rick Sutcliffe	.40	.30	.15
41	Jeff Pico	.25	.20	.10
44	Steve Wilson	.50	.40	.20
50	Les Lancaster	.15	.11	.06

1988 Master Bread Twins

This set of 12 cardboard discs (2-3/4" diameter) features full-color photos of Minnesota Twins team members. Disc fronts have a bright blue background with red, yellow and black printing. A thin white line frames the player photo which is centered beneath a "Master Is Good Bread" headliner and a vivid yellow player/team name banner. Disc backs are black and white with five stars printed above the player's name, team, personal data, disc number, stats and "1988 Collector's Edition" banner. The discs were printed in Canada and marketed exclusively in Minnesota in packages of Master Bread, one disc per loaf.

		MT	NR MT	EX
Complete Set:		10.00	7.50	4.00
Common Player:		.50	.40	.20
1	Bert Blyleven	1.00	.70	.40
2	Frank Viola	1.75	1.25	.70
3	Juan Berenguer	.50	.40	.20
4	Jeff Reardon	.80	.60	.30
5	Tim Laudner	.50	.40	.20
6	Steve Lombardozzi	.50	.40	.20
7	Randy Bush	.50	.40	.20
8	Kirby Puckett	2.00	1.50	.80
9	Gary Gaetti	1.75	1.25	.70
10	Kent Hrbek	1.75	1.25	.70
11	Greg Gagne	.50	.40	.20
12	Tom Brunansky	1.25	.90	.50

1986 Meadow Gold Blank Back Set Of 16

This was the second set to be distributed by Meadow Gold Dairy (Beatrice Foods) in 1986. It was issued on Double Play ice cream cartons, one card per package. Full-color player photos have team logos and insignias airbrushed away. This 16-card set is very similar to the Meadow Gold popsicle set, but the photos are different in some instances. The cards measure 2-3/8" by 3-1/2". The Willie McGee card is reportedly tougher to find than other cards in the set.

		MT	NR MT	EX
Complete Set:		100.00	75.00	40.00
Common Player:		4.00	3.00	1.50
(1)	George Brett	7.00	5.25	2.75
(2)	Wade Boggs	10.00	7.50	4.00
(3)	Carlton Fisk	4.00	3.00	1.50
(4)	Steve Garvey	6.00	4.50	2.50
(5)	Dwight Gooden	7.50	5.75	3.00
(6)	Pedro Guerrero	4.00	3.00	1.50
(7)	Reggie Jackson	6.50	5.00	2.50
(8)	Don Mattingly	15.00	11.00	6.00
(9)	Willie McGee	4.00	3.00	1.50
(10)	Dale Murphy	7.00	5.25	2.75
(11)	Cal Ripken	6.50	5.00	2.50
(12)	Pete Rose	8.00	6.00	3.25
(13)	Ryne Sandberg	6.00	4.50	2.50
(14)	Mike Schmidt	7.00	5.25	2.75
(15)	Fernando Valenzuela	5.00	3.75	2.00
(16)	Dave Winfield	6.50	5.00	2.50

1986 Meadow Gold Statistic Back Set Of 20

Beatrice Foods produced this set of 20 cards on specially marked boxes of Meadow Gold Double Play popsicles, fudgesicles and bubble gum coolers. They came in two-card panels and have full-color player pictures with player name, team and position printed below the photo. Card backs are printed in red ink and feature player career highlights. The cards measure 2-3/8" by 3-1/2" and were distributed in the West and Midwest. It is considered one of the toughest 1986 regional sets to complete.

	MT	NR MT	EX
Complete Panel Set:	35.00	26.00	14.00
Complete Singles Set:	18.00	13.50	7.25
Common Panel:	2.00	1.50	.80
Common Single Player:	.30	.25	.12
Panel 1	5.00	3.75	2.00
1 George Brett	1.50	1.25	.60
2 Fernando Valenzuela	.70	.50	.30
Panel 2	6.50	5.00	2.50
3 Dwight Gooden	2.00	1.50	.80
4 Dale Murphy	1.50	1.25	.60
Panel 3	10.00	7.50	4.00
5 Don Mattingly	5.00	3.75	2.00
6 Reggie Jackson	1.25	.90	.50
Panel 4	6.50	5.00	2.50
7 Dave Winfield	1.00	.70	.40
8 Pete Rose	2.00	1.50	.80
Panel 5	6.00	4.50	2.50
9 Wade Boggs	3.00	2.25	1.25
10 Willie McGee	.50	.40	.20
Panel 6	5.50	4.25	2.25
11 Cal Ripkin (Ripken)	1.25	.90	.50
12 Ryne Sandberg	1.00	.70	.40
Panel 7	5.00	3.75	2.00
13 Carlton Fisk	.50	.40	.20
14 Jim Rice	1.00	.70	.40
Panel 8	7.00	5.25	2.75
15 Steve Garvey	1.00	.70	.40
16 Mike Schmidt	2.00	1.50	.80
Panel 9	4.00	3.00	1.50
17 Bruce Sutter	.60	.45	.25
18 Pedro Guerrero	.60	.45	.25
Panel 10	4.00	3.00	1.50
19 Rick Sutcliff (Sutcliffe)	.60	.45	.25
20 Rich Gossage	.60	.45	.25

1986 Meadow Gold Milk

The third set from Meadow Gold from 1986 came on milk cartons; on pint, quart and half-gallon size containers. The cards measure 2-1/2" by 3-1/2" and feature drawings instead of photographs. Different dairies distributed the cards in various colors of ink. The cards can be found printed in red, brown or black ink. The crude drawings have prevented this rare set from being higher in price. It was believed that Don Mattingly and Fernando Valenzuela were part of the original set, but it has since been proven they were not.

not.

	MT	NR MT	EX
Complete Set:	50.00	37.00	20.00
Common Player:	2.00	1.50	.80
(1) Wade Boggs	10.00	7.50	4.00
(2) George Brett	5.00	3.75	2.00
(3) Steve Carlton	3.00	2.25	1.25
(4) Dwight Gooden	10.00	7.50	4.00
(5) Willie McGee	2.00	1.50	.80
(6) Dale Murphy	5.00	3.75	2.00
(7) Cal Ripken, Jr.	4.00	3.00	1.50
(8) Pete Rose	10.00	7.50	4.00
(9) Ryne Sandberg	3.00	2.25	1.25
(10) Mike Schmidt	5.00	3.75	2.00

1971 Milk Duds

These cards were issued on the backs of five-cent packages of Milk Duds candy. Most collectors prefer to collect complete boxes, rather than cut-out cards, which measure approximately 1-13/16" by 2-5/8" when trimmed tightly. Values quoted below are for complete boxes. The set includes 37 National League and 32 American League players. Card numbers appear on the box flap, with each number from 1 through 24 being shared by three different players. A suffix (a, b and c) has been added for the collector's convenience. Harmon Killebrew, Brooks Robinson and Pete Rose were double-printed.

	NR MT	EX	VG
Complete Set:	1100.00	550.00	330.00
Common Player:	7.00	3.50	2.00

		NR MT	EX	VG
1a	Frank Howard	11.00	5.50	3.25
1b	Fritz Peterson	7.00	3.50	2.00
1c	Pete Rose	80.00	40.00	24.00
2a	Johnny Bench	30.00	15.00	9.00
2b	Rico Carty	9.00	4.50	2.75
2c	Pete Rose	80.00	40.00	24.00
3a	Ken Holtzman	8.00	4.00	2.50
3b	Willie Mays	40.00	20.00	12.00
3c	Cesar Tovar	7.00	3.50	2.00
4a	Willie Davis	9.00	4.50	2.75
4b	Harmon Killebrew	20.00	10.00	6.00
4c	Felix Millan	7.00	3.50	2.00
5a	Billy Grabarkewitz	7.00	3.50	2.00
5b	Andy Messersmith	8.00	4.00	2.50
5c	Thurman Munson	20.00	10.00	6.00
6a	Luis Aparicio	18.00	9.00	5.50
6b	Lou Brock	25.00	12.50	7.50
6c	Bill Melton	7.00	3.50	2.00
7a	Ray Culp	7.00	3.50	2.00
7b	Willie McCovey	25.00	12.50	7.50
7c	Luke Walker	7.00	3.50	2.00
8a	Roberto Clemente	40.00	20.00	12.00
8b	Jim Merritt	7.00	3.50	2.00
8c	Claud Osteen (Claude)	8.00	4.00	2.50
9a	Stan Bahnsen	7.00	3.50	2.00
9b	Sam McDowell	9.00	4.50	2.75
9c	Billy Williams	18.00	9.00	5.50
10a	Jim Hickman	7.00	3.50	2.00
10b	Dave McNally	9.00	4.50	2.75
10c	Tony Perez	13.00	6.50	4.00
11a	Hank Aaron	40.00	20.00	12.00
11b	Glen Beckert (Glenn)	8.00	4.00	2.50
11c	Ray Fosse	7.00	3.50	2.00
12a	Alex Johnson	7.00	3.50	2.00
12b	Gaylord Perry	18.00	9.00	5.50
12c	Wayne Simpson	7.00	3.50	2.00
13a	Dave Johnson	9.00	4.50	2.75
13b	George Scott	8.00	4.00	2.50
13c	Tom Seaver	30.00	15.00	9.00
14a	Bill Freehan	9.00	4.50	2.75
14b	Bud Harrelson	8.00	4.00	2.50
14c	Manny Sanguillen	7.00	3.50	2.00
15a	Bob Gibson	25.00	12.50	7.50
15b	Rusty Staub	11.00	5.50	3.25
15c	Roy White	8.00	4.00	2.50
16a	Jim Fregosi	9.00	4.50	2.75
16b	Jim Hunter	18.00	9.00	5.50
16c	Mel Stottlemyer (Stottlemyre)	8.00	4.00	2.50
17a	Tommy Harper	7.00	3.50	2.00
17b	Frank Robinson	25.00	12.50	7.50
17c	Reggie Smith	9.00	4.50	2.75
18a	Orlando Cepeda	13.00	6.50	4.00
18b	Rico Petrocelli	8.00	4.00	2.50
18c	Brooks Robinson	25.00	12.50	7.50
19a	Tony Oliva	11.00	5.50	3.25
19b	Milt Pappas	8.00	4.00	2.50
19c	Bobby Tolan	7.00	3.50	2.00
20a	Ernie Banks	25.00	12.50	7.50
20b	Don Kessinger	8.00	4.00	2.50
20c	Joe Torre	9.00	4.50	2.75
21a	Fergie Jenkins	13.00	6.50	4.00
21b	Jim Palmer	18.00	9.00	5.50
21c	Ron Santo	9.00	4.50	2.75
22a	Randy Hundley	7.00	3.50	2.00
22b	Dennis Menke (Denis)	7.00	3.50	2.00
22c	Boog Powell	11.00	5.50	3.25
23a	Dick Dietz	7.00	3.50	2.00
23b	Tommy John	13.00	6.50	4.00
23c	Brooks Robinson	25.00	12.50	7.50
24a	Danny Cater	7.00	3.50	2.00
24b	Harmon Killebrew	18.00	9.00	5.50
24c	Jim Perry	8.00	4.00	2.50

		MT	NR MT	EX
	Complete Set:	10.00	7.50	4.00
	Common Player:	.25	.20	.10
(1)	Wade Boggs	1.50	1.25	.60
(2)	George Brett	.80	.60	.30
(3)	Rod Carew	.50	.40	.20
(4)	Steve Carlton	.40	.30	.15
(5)	Gary Carter	.50	.40	.20
(6)	Dave Concepcion	.25	.20	.10
(7)	Cecil Cooper	.25	.20	.10
(8)	Andre Dawson	.35	.25	.14
(9)	Carlton Fisk	.35	.25	.14
(10)	Steve Garvey	.50	.40	.20
(11)	Pedro Guerrero	.35	.25	.14
(12)	Ron Guidry	.25	.20	.10
(13)	Rickey Henderson	.60	.45	.25
(14)	Reggie Jackson	.50	.40	.20
(15)	Ron Kittle	.25	.20	.10
(16)	Bill Madlock	.25	.20	.10
(17)	Dale Murphy	.80	.60	.30
(18)	Al Oliver	.25	.20	.10
(19)	Darrell Porter	.25	.20	.10
(20)	Cal Ripken	.60	.45	.25
(21)	Pete Rose	1.25	.90	.50
(22)	Steve Sax	.35	.25	.14
(23)	Mike Schmidt	.80	.60	.30
(24)	Ted Simmons	.25	.20	.10
(25)	Ozzie Smith	.35	.25	.14
(26)	Dave Stieb	.25	.20	.10
(27)	Fernando Valenzuela	.35	.25	.14
(28)	Lou Whitaker	.35	.25	.14
(29)	Dave Winfield	.50	.40	.20
(30)	Robin Yount	.40	.30	.15

1986 Minnesota Twins Team Issue

This team-issued set contains 36 2-9/16" by 3-1/2" full-color cards. Fronts feature the Twins 25th anniversary logo and a jersey at the bottom of each card with the player's uniform number. All cards, except an action shot of Bert Blyleven, are posed photos, with a facsimile autograph on each. The set also includes a checklist and a team photo.

1984 Milton Bradley

In 1984 Milton Bradley printed their baseball game cards in full-color and adopted the standard baseball card size of 2-1/2" by 3-1/2". A total of 30 cards were in the set. The card fronts show the player photos with the team insignias and logos airbrushed away. The game is called Championship Baseball. Card backs varied in style; some had player statistics plus game information, and others only game information.

		MT	NR MT	EX
Complete Set:		6.00	4.50	2.50
Common Player:		.08	.06	.03
1	Christopher Francis Pittaro	.08	.06	.03
2	Stephen Paul Lombardozzi	.15	.11	.06
3	Roy Frederick Smalley, III	.10	.08	.04
4	Pedro Oliva, Jr.	.15	.11	.06
5	Gary Joseph Gaetti	.50	.40	.20
6	Michael Vaughn Hatcher	.08	.06	.03
7	Jeffrey Scott Reed	.08	.06	.03
8	Mark Bruce Salas	.08	.06	.03
9	Kent Alan Hrbek	.60	.45	.25
10	Timothy Jon Laudner	.15	.11	.06
11	Frank John Viola, Jr.	.50	.40	.20
12	Dennis Allen Burtt	.08	.06	.03
13	Alejandro Sanchez	.08	.06	.03
14	LeRoy Purdy Smith, III	.08	.06	.03
15	William Lamar Beane, III	.08	.06	.03
16	William Peter Filson	.08	.06	.03
17	Thomas Andrew Brunansky	.35	.25	.14
18	Robert Randall Bush	.08	.06	.03
19	Frank Anthony Eufemia, III	.08	.06	.03
20	John Mark Davidson	.15	.11	.06
21	Rik Aalbert Blyleven	.25	.20	.10
22	Gregory Carpenter Gagne	.15	.11	.06
23	John Daniel Butcher	.08	.06	.03
24	Kirby Puckett	.80	.60	.30
25	William Carol Latham, Jr.	.08	.06	.03
26	Ronald Washington	.08	.06	.03
27	Ronald Gene Davis	.08	.06	.03
28	Jay Thomas Kelly	.15	.11	.06
29	Richard Stanley Such	.08	.06	.03
30	Richard Francis Stelmaszek	.08	.06	.03
31	Raymond Robert Miller	.08	.06	.03
32	Willard Wayne Terwilliger	.08	.06	.03
33	Billy Mike Smithson	.08	.06	.03
34	Alvis Woods	.08	.06	.03
35	Team Photo	.08	.06	.03
36	Twins Logo/Checklist	.08	.06	.03

1987 Minnesota Twins Team Issue

The Minnesota Twins produced a 32-card set of 2-1/2" by 3-1/2" full-color baseball cards to be sold at the ballpark and through their souvenir catalog. The card fronts are borderless, containing only the player photo. The backs are printed in blue and red on white card stock and carry the player's personal data and career record. The Twins also produced a post card set which was similar in design to the standard-size card set, but utilized different photos.

		MT	NR MT	EX
Complete Set:		6.00	4.50	2.50
Common Player:		.08	.06	.03
1	Stephen Paul Lombardozzi	.15	.11	.06
2	Roy Frederick Smalley III	.10	.08	.04
3	Pedro Oliva, Jr.	.15	.11	.06
4	Gregory Carpenter Gagne	.15	.11	.06
5	Gary Joseph Gaetti	.50	.40	.20
6	Jay Thomas Kelly	.15	.11	.06
7	Thomas Andrew Nieto	.08	.06	.03
8	Mark Bruce Salas	.08	.06	.03
9	Kent Alan Hrbek	.60	.45	.25

		MT	NR MT	EX
10	Timothy Jon Laudner	.15	.11	.06
11	Frank John Viola, Jr.	.50	.40	.20
12	Lester Paul Straker	.25	.20	.10
13	George Allen Frazier	.08	.06	.03
14	Keith Rowe Atherton	.08	.06	.03
15	Thomas Andrew Brunansky	.35	.25	.14
16	Robert Randall Bush	.08	.06	.03
17	Albert Dwayne Newman	.08	.06	.03
18	John Mark Davidson	.08	.06	.03
19	Rik Aalbert Blyleven	.25	.20	.10
20	Clinton Daniel Gladden III	.15	.11	.06
21	Kirby Puckett	.80	.60	.30
22	Mark Steven Portugal	.08	.06	.03
23	Juan Bautista Berenguer	.08	.06	.03
24	Jeffrey James Reardon	.30	.25	.12
25	Richard Stanley Such	.08	.06	.03
26	Richard Francis Stelmaszek	.08	.06	.03
27	Warren Richard Renick	.08	.06	.03
28	Willard Wayne Terwilliger	.08	.06	.03
29	Joseph Charles Klink	.08	.06	.03
30	Billy Mike Smithson	.08	.06	.03
31	Team Photo	.08	.06	.03
32	Twins Logo/Checklist	.08	.06	.03

1988 Minnesota Twins Team Issue

The Twins issued this 33-card set (including checklist) to commemorate the team's 1987 Series victory. The slightly oversized cards (2-5/8" x 3-7/16") feature deluxe player photos printed on heavy stock with a gold-embossed "1987 World Champions" logo in the lower left corner. Many photos are duplicates of the regular season set but several new photos, including a group team shot, are included. Numbered card backs are red, white and blue and contain a player name, personal info and stats. A limited edition of 5000 sets were printed but only a few hundred were sold before the cards were taken off the market due to Major League Baseball licensing restrictions.

		MT	NR MT	EX
Complete Set:		8.00	6.00	3.25
Common Player:		.08	.06	.03
1	Stephen Paul Lombardozzi	.15	.11	.06
2	Roy Frederick Smalley, III	.10	.08	.04
3	Pedro Oliva, Jr.	.15	.11	.06
4	Gregory Carpenter Gagne	.15	.11	.06
5	Gary Joseph Gaetti	.60	.45	.25
6	Eugene Thomas Larkin	.25	.20	.10
7	Jay Thomas Kelly	.15	.11	.06
8	Kent Alan Hrbek	.70	.50	.30
9	Timothy Jon Laudner	.15	.11	.06
10	Frank John Viola, Jr.	.60	.45	.25
11	Lester Paul Straker	.25	.20	.10
12	Donald Edward Baylor	.30	.25	.12
13	George Allen Frazier	.08	.06	.03
14	Keith Rowe Atherton	.08	.06	.03
15	Thomas Andrew Brunansky	.40	.30	.15
16	Robert Randall Bush	.08	.06	.03
17	Albert Dwayne Newman	.08	.06	.03
18	John Mark Davidson	.08	.06	.03
19	Rik Aalbert Blyleven	.30	.25	.12

		MT	NR MT	EX
20	Daniel Ernest Schatzeder	.08	.06	.03
21	Clinton Daniel Gladden III	.20	.15	.08
22	Salvatore Philip Butera	.08	.06	.03
23	Kirby Puckett	1.00	.70	.40
24	Joseph Franklin Niekro	.25	.20	.10
25	Juan Bautista Berenguer	.08	.06	.03
26	Jeffrey James Reardon	.35	.25	.14
27	Richard Stanley Such	.08	.06	.03
28	Richard Francis Stelmaszek	.08	.06	.03
29	Warren Richard Renick	.08	.06	.03
30	Willard Wayne Terwilliger	.08	.06	.03
31	Team Photo	.08	.06	.03
32	World Champions Team Logo Card	.08	.06	.03
33	Team Logo Card/Checklist	.08	.06	.03

1959 Morrell Meats Dodgers

This popular set of Los Angeles Dodgers player cards was the first issue of a three-year run for the Southern California meat company. The 12 cards in this 2-1/2" by 3-1/2" set are unnumbered and feature fullframe, unbordered color photos. Card backs feature a company ad and list only the player's name, birthdate and birthplace. Two interesting errors exist in the set, as the cards for Clem Labine and Norm Larker show photos of Stan Williams and Joe Pignatano, respectively. Dodger greats Sandy Koufax and Duke Snider are key cards in the set.

		NR MT	EX	VG
	Complete Set:	1000.00	500.00	300.00
	Common Player:	50.00	25.00	15.00
(1)	Don Drysdale	100.00	50.00	30.00
(2)	Carl Furillo	65.00	32.00	19.50
(3)	Jim Gilliam	65.00	32.00	19.50
(4)	Gil Hodges	100.00	50.00	30.00
(5)	Sandy Koufax	175.00	87.00	52.00
(6)	Clem Labine (photo actually Stan Williams)	50.00	25.00	15.00
(7)	Norm Larker (photo actually Joe Pignatano)	50.00	25.00	15.00
(8)	Charlie Neal	50.00	25.00	15.00
(9)	Johnny Podres	65.00	32.00	19.50
(10)	John Roseboro	50.00	25.00	15.00
(11)	Duke Snider	125.00	62.00	37.00
(12)	Don Zimmer	50.00	25.00	15.00

1960 Morrell Meats Dodgers

This 12-card set is the same 2-1/2" by 3-1/2" size as the 1959 set, and again features unbordered color card fronts. Five of the players included are new to the Morrell's sets. Card backs in 1960 list player statistics and brief personal data on each player. Cards for Gil Hodges, Carl Furillo and Duke Snider are apparently more scarce than others in the set. The 1960 set is again unnumbered.

	NR MT	EX	VG
Complete Set:	525.00	262.00	157.00
Common Player:	15.00	7.50	4.50

		NR MT	EX	VG
(1)	Walt Alston	25.00	12.50	7.50
(2)	Roger Craig	15.00	7.50	4.50
(3)	Don Drysdale	40.00	20.00	12.00
(4)	Carl Furillo	70.00	35.00	21.00
(5)	Gil Hodges	100.00	50.00	30.00
(6)	Sandy Koufax	80.00	40.00	24.00
(7)	Wally Moon	15.00	7.50	4.50
(8)	Charlie Neal	15.00	7.50	4.50
(9)	Johnny Podres	20.00	10.00	6.00
(10)	John Roseboro	15.00	7.50	4.50
(11)	Larry Sherry	15.00	7.50	4.50
(12)	Duke Snider	125.00	62.00	37.00

1961 Morrell Meats Dodgers

The Morrell set shrunk to just six cards in 1961, with a format almost identical to the 1960 cards. Card fronts are again full-color, unbordered photos, with player statistics on the backs. The unnumbered cards measure a slightly smaller 2-1/4" by 3-1/4", and comparison of statistical information can also distinguish the cards from the 1960 version. Top cards in the set are Don Drysdale and Sandy Koufax, who are also the only two players to appear in all three years of the Morrell Meats sets.

		NR MT	EX	VG
	Complete Set:	200.00	100.00	60.00
	Common Player:	15.00	7.50	4.50
(1)	Tommy Davis	20.00	10.00	6.00
(2)	Don Drysdale	40.00	20.00	12.00
(3)	Frank Howard	20.00	10.00	6.00
(4)	Sandy Koufax	80.00	40.00	24.00
(5)	Norm Larker	15.00	7.50	4.50
(6)	Maury Wills	25.00	12.50	7.50

1983 Mother's Cookies Giants

After putting out Pacific Coast League sets in 1952 and 1953 Mother's Cookies distributed this full-color set of 20 San Francisco Giants cards three decades later. The 2-1/2" by 3-1/2" cards were produced by

Barry Colla and included the Giants logo and player's name on the attractive card fronts. Card backs are numbered and contain biographical information, the Mother's Cookies logo, and a space for the player's autograph. Fifteen cards were given to every fan at the August 7, 1983 Giants game, with each fan also receiving a coupon good for five additional cards.

		MT	NR MT	EX
Complete Set:		18.00	13.50	7.25
Common Player:		.50	.40	.20
1	Frank Robinson	1.50	1.25	.60
2	Jack Clark	2.50	2.00	1.00
3	Chili Davis	1.50	1.25	.60
4	Johnnie LeMaster	.50	.40	.20
5	Greg Minton	.50	.40	.20
6	Bob Brenly	.70	.50	.30
7	Fred Breining	.50	.40	.20
8	Jeff Leonard	1.00	.70	.40
9	Darrell Evans	1.50	1.25	.60
10	Tom O'Malley	.50	.40	.20
11	Duane Kuiper	.50	.40	.20
12	Mike Krukow	.70	.50	.30
13	Atlee Hammaker	.70	.50	.30
14	Gary Lavelle	.50	.40	.20
15	Bill Laskey	.50	.40	.20
16	Max Venable	.50	.40	.20
17	Joel Youngblood	.50	.40	.20
18	Dave Bergman	.50	.40	.20
19	Mike Vail	.50	.40	.20
20	Andy McGaffigan	.50	.40	.20

1984 Mother's Cookies A's

Following the success of their one set in 1983, Mother's Cookies issued five more team sets of cards in 1984. The A's set measures 2-1/2" by 3-1/2", and card fronts feature unbordered color photos with rounded corners. Card backs are quite similar in format to the 1983 Mother's Cookies Giants, with brief biographical information, card numbers, Mother's Cookies logo and space for player autograph. There are 28 cards in the A's set, with 20 of the cards distributed during a stadium promotion. Fans also received a coupon redeemable for eight additional cards. Since these additional cards do not

necessarily complete collectors' sets, Mother's Cookies cards become very popular among card traders. The A's set includes cards for the manager, coaches and a checklist.

		MT	NR MT	EX
Complete Set:		15.00	11.00	6.00
Common Player:		.50	.40	.20
1	Steve Boros	.50	.40	.20
2	Rickey Henderson	3.00	2.25	1.25
3	Joe Morgan	1.50	1.25	.60
4	Dwayne Murphy	.70	.50	.30
5	Mike Davis	.70	.50	.30
6	Bruce Bochte	.50	.40	.20
7	Carney Lansford	.80	.60	.30
8	Steve McCatty	.50	.40	.20
9	Mike Heath	.50	.40	.20
10	Chris Codiroli	.50	.40	.20
11	Bill Almon	.50	.40	.20
12	Bill Caudill	.50	.40	.20
13	Donnie Hill	.50	.40	.20
14	Lary Sorenson	.50	.40	.20
15	Dave Kingman	.80	.60	.30
16	Garry Hancock	.50	.40	.20
17	Jeff Burroughs	.60	.45	.25
18	Tom Burgmeier	.50	.40	.20
19	Jim Essian	.50	.40	.20
20	Mike Warren	.50	.40	.20
21	Davey Lopes	.60	.45	.25
22	Ray Burris	.50	.40	.20
23	Tony Phillips	.50	.40	.20
24	Tim Conroy	.50	.40	.20
25	Jeff Bettendorf	.50	.40	.20
26	Keith Atherton	.60	.45	.25
27	A's Coaches (Clete Boyer, Bob Didier, Jackie Moore, Ron Schueler, Billy Williams)			
		.50	.40	.20
28	Oakland Coliseum/Checklist	.50	.40	.20

1984 Mother's Cookies Astros

Mother's Cookies also issued a full-color team set for the Houston Astros in 1984. The Astros set measures 2-1/2" by 3-1/2", and card fronts feature unbordered color photos with rounded corners. Card backs are quite similar in format to the 1983 Mother's Cookies Giants, with brief biographical information, card numbers, Mother's Cookies logo and space for player autograph. There are 28 cards in the Astros set, with 20 of the cards distributed during a stadium promotion. Fans also received a coupon redeemable for eight additional cards. Since these additional cards do not necessarily complete collectors' sets, Mother's Cookies cards became very popular among card traders. The Astros set includes one card for the coaches and a checklist.

		MT	NR MT	EX
Complete Set:		15.00	11.00	6.00
Common Player:		.50	.40	.20
1	Nolan Ryan	2.50	2.00	1.00
2	Joe Niekro	.60	.45	.25
3	Alan Ashby	.50	.40	.20
4	Bill Doran	1.00	.70	.40

		MT	NR MT	EX
5	Phil Garner	.60	.45	.25
6	Ray Knight	.60	.45	.25
7	Dickie Thon	.60	.45	.25
8	Jose Cruz	.70	.50	.30
9	Jerry Mumphrey	.50	.40	.20
10	Terry Puhl	.50	.40	.20
11	Enos Cabell	.50	.40	.20
12	Harry Spilman	.50	.40	.20
13	Dave Smith	.60	.45	.25
14	Mike Scott	1.25	.90	.50
15	Bob Lillis	.50	.40	.20
16	Bob Knepper	.60	.45	.25
17	Frank DiPino	.50	.40	.20
18	Tom Wieghaus	.50	.40	.20
19	Denny Walling	.50	.40	.20
20	Tony Scott	.50	.40	.20
21	Alan Bannister	.50	.40	.20
22	Bill Dawley	.50	.40	.20
23	Vern Ruhle	.50	.40	.20
24	Mike LaCoss	.50	.40	.20
25	Mike Madden	.50	.40	.20
26	Craig Reynolds	.50	.40	.20
27	Astros Coaches (Cot Deal, Don Leppert, Denis Menke, Les Moss, Jerry Walker)	.50	.40	.20
28	Astros Logo/Checklist	.50	.40	.20

1984 Mother's Cookies Giants

Mother's Cookies issued a second annual full-color card set for the San Francisco Giants in 1984. The Giants set measures 2-1/2" by 3-1/2", and the round-cornered cards feature drawings of former Giant All-Star team selections. Card backs are quite similar in format to the 1983 Mother's Cookies Giants, with brief biographical information, card numbers and Mother's Cookies logo. No autograph space is included. There are 28 cards in the Giants set, with 20 of the cards distributed during a stadium promotion. Fans also received a coupon redeemable for eight additional cards. Since these additional cards do not necessarily complete collectors' sets, Mother's Cookies cards became very popular among card traders. Card number 28 is a checklist chart.

		MT	NR MT	EX
Complete Set:		18.00	13.50	7.25
Common Player:		.50	.40	.20
1	Willie Mays	2.50	2.00	1.00
2	Willie McCovey	2.00	1.50	.80
3	Juan Marichal	2.00	1.50	.80
4	Gaylord Perry	2.00	1.50	.80
5	Tom Haller	.60	.45	.25
6	Jim Davenport	.50	.40	.20
7	Jack Clark	1.25	.90	.50
8	Greg Minton	.50	.40	.20
9	Atlee Hammaker	.50	.40	.20
10	Gary Lavelle	.50	.40	.20
11	Orlando Cepeda	1.00	.70	.40
12	Bobby Bonds	.80	.60	.30
13	John Antonelli	.60	.45	.25
14	Bob Schmidt (photo actually Wes Westrum)	.50	.40	.20
15	Sam Jones	.50	.40	.20
16	Mike McCormick	.60	.45	.25
17	Ed Bailey	.50	.40	.20
18	Stu Miller	.50	.40	.20

		MT	NR MT	EX
19	Felipe Alou	.70	.50	.30
20	Jim Hart	.60	.45	.25
21	Dick Dietz	.50	.40	.20
22	Chris Speier	.50	.40	.20
23	Bobby Murcer	.70	.50	.30
24	John Montefusco	.50	.40	.20
25	Vida Blue	.70	.50	.30
26	Ed Whitson	.50	.40	.20
27	Darrell Evans	.70	.50	.30
28	All-Star Game Logo/Checklist	.50	.40	.20

1984 Mother's Cookies Mariners

Mother's Cookies also issued a full-color set for the Seattle Mariners in 1984. The Mariners set measures 2-1/2" by 3-1/2", and card fronts feature unbordered color photos with rounded corners. Card backs are quite similar in format to the 1983 Mother's Cookies Giants, with brief biographical information, card numbers, Mother's Cookies logo and space for player autograph. There are 28 cards in the Mariners set, with 20 of the cards distributed during a stadium promotion. Fans also received a coupon redeemable for eight additional cards. Since these additional cards do not necessarily complete collectors' sets, Mother's Cookies cards became very popular among card traders. The Mariners set includes one card each for the manager, coaches and a checklist.

		MT	NR MT	EX
Complete Set:		15.00	11.00	6.00
Common Player:		.50	.40	.20
1	Del Crandall	.60	.45	.25
2	Barry Bonnell	.50	.40	.20
3	Dave Henderson	.70	.50	.30
4	Bob Kearney	.50	.40	.20
5	Mike Moore	.50	.40	.20
6	Spike Owen	.70	.50	.30
7	Gorman Thomas	.70	.50	.30
8	Ed Vande Berg	.50	.40	.20
9	Matt Young	.60	.45	.25
10	Larry Milbourne	.50	.40	.20
11	Dave Beard	.50	.40	.20
12	Jim Beattie	.50	.40	.20
13	Mark Langston	1.50	1.25	.60
14	Orlando Mercado	.50	.40	.20
15	Jack Perconte	.50	.40	.20
16	Pat Putnam	.50	.40	.20
17	Paul Mirabella	.50	.40	.20
18	Domingo Ramos	.50	.40	.20
19	Al Cowens	.50	.40	.20
20	Mike Stanton	.50	.40	.20
21	Steve Henderson	.50	.40	.20
22	Bob Stoddard	.50	.40	.20
23	Alvin Davis	1.75	1.25	.70
24	Phil Bradley	1.50	1.25	.60
25	Roy Thomas	.50	.40	.20
26	Darnell Coles	.80	.60	.30
27	Mariners Coaches (Chuck Cottier, Frank Funk, Ben Hines, Phil Roof, Rick Sweet)	.50	.40	.20
28	Seattle Kingdome/Checklist	.50	.40	.20

1984 Mother's Cookies Padres

Mother's Cookies also issued a full-color set for the San Diego Padres in 1984. The Padres set measures 2-1/2" by 3-1/2", and card fronts feature unbordered color photos with rounded corners. Card backs are quite similar in format to the 1983 Mother's Cookies Giants, with brief biographical information, card numbers, Mother's Cookies logo and space for player autograph. There are 28 cards in the Padres set, with 20 of the cards distributed during a stadium promotion. Fans also received a coupon redeemable for eight additional cards. Since these additional cards do not necessarily complete collector's sets, Mother's Cookies cards became very popular among card traders. The Padres set includes one card each for the manager, coaches and a checklist.

		MT	NR MT	EX
Complete Set:		18.00	13.50	7.25
Common Player:		.50	.40	.20
1	Dick Williams	.50	.40	.20
2	Rich Gossage	1.00	.70	.40
3	Tim Lollar	.50	.40	.20
4	Eric Show	.70	.50	.30
5	Terry Kennedy	.60	.45	.25
6	Kurt Bevacqua	.50	.40	.20
7	Steve Garvey	2.00	1.50	.80
8	Garry Templeton	.70	.50	.30
9	Tony Gwynn	3.50	2.75	1.50
10	Alan Wiggins	.50	.40	.20
11	Dave Dravecky	.60	.45	.25
12	Tim Flannery	.50	.40	.20
13	Kevin McReynolds	2.25	1.75	.90
14	Bobby Brown	.50	.40	.20
15	Ed Whitson	.50	.40	.20
16	Doug Gwosdz	.50	.40	.20
17	Luis DeLeon	.50	.40	.20
18	Andy Hawkins	.60	.45	.25
19	Craig Lefferts	.50	.40	.20
20	Carmelo Martinez	.60	.45	.25
21	Sid Monge	.50	.40	.20
22	Graig Nettles	.80	.60	.30
23	Mario Ramirez	.50	.40	.20
24	Luis Salazar	.50	.40	.20
25	Champ Summers	.50	.40	.20
26	Mark Thurmond	.50	.40	.20
27	Padres Coaches (Harry Dunlop, Deacon Jones, Jack Krol, Norm Sherry, Ozzie Virgil)	.50	.40	.20
28	Jack Murphy Stadium/Checklist	.50	.40	.20

1985 Mother's Cookies A's

Mother's Cookies again issued five full-color sets for major league teams in 1985. The A's set measures 2-1/2" by 3-1/2", and card fronts feature unbordered color photos with rounded corners. Card backs are quite similar in format to the 1984 Mother's Cookies A's, with brief biographical information card numbers, Mother's Cookies logo

and space for player autograph. Card backs are dated 1985. There are 28 cards in the A's set, which was distributed in its entirety during a stadium promotion. The A's set includes one card each for the manager, coaches and a checklist.

		MT	NR MT	EX
Complete Set:		12.00	9.00	4.75
Common Player:		.40	.30	.15
1	Jackie Moore	.40	.30	.15
2	Dave Kingman	.70	.50	.30
3	Don Sutton	1.00	.70	.40
4	Mike Heath	.40	.30	.15
5	Alfredo Griffin	.60	.45	.25
6	Dwayne Murphy	.60	.45	.25
7	Mike Davis	.60	.45	.25
8	Carney Lansford	.70	.50	.30
9	Chris Codiroli	.40	.30	.15
10	Bruce Bochte	.40	.30	.15
11	Mickey Tettleton	.50	.40	.20
12	Donnie Hill	.40	.30	.15
13	Rob Picciolo	.40	.30	.15
14	Dave Collins	.50	.40	.20
15	Dusty Baker	.60	.45	.25
16	Tim Conroy	.40	.30	.15
17	Keith Atherton	.40	.30	.15
18	Jay Howell	.60	.45	.25
19	Mike Warren	.40	.30	.15
20	Steve McCatty	.40	.30	.15
21	Bill Krueger	.40	.30	.15
22	Curt Young	.70	.50	.30
23	Dan Meyer	.40	.30	.15
24	Mike Gallego	.50	.40	.20
25	Jeff Kaiser	.40	.30	.15
26	Steve Henderson	.40	.30	.15
27	A's Coaches (Clete Boyer, Bob Didier, Dave McKay, Wes Stock, Billy Williams)	.40	.30	.15
28	Oakland Coliseum/Checklist	.40	.30	.15

1985 Mother's Cookies Astros

Mother's Cookies issued a second annual full-color set for the Houston Astros in 1985. The Astros set measures 2-1/2" by 3-1/2", and card fronts feature unbordered color photos with rounded corners. Card backs are quite similar in format to the 1984

Mother's Cookies Astros, with brief biographical information, card number, Mother's Cookies logo and space for player autograph. Card backs are dated 1985. There are 28 cards in the Astros set, which was distributed in its entirety during a stadium promotion. The Astros set includes one card each for the manager, coaches and a checklist.

		MT	NR MT	EX
Complete Set:		12.00	9.00	4.75
Complete Player:		.40	.30	.15
1	Bob Lillis	.40	.30	.15
2	Nolan Ryan	2.00	1.50	.80
3	Phil Garner	.50	.40	.20
4	Jose Cruz	.60	.45	.25
5	Denny Walling	.40	.30	.15
6	Joe Niekro	.60	.45	.25
7	Terry Puhl	.40	.30	.15
8	Bill Doran	.60	.45	.25
9	Dickie Thon	.40	.30	.15
10	Enos Cabell	.40	.30	.15
11	Frank Dipino (DiPino)	.40	.30	.15
12	Julio Solano	.40	.30	.15
13	Alan Ashby	.40	.30	.15
14	Craig Reynolds	.40	.30	.15
15	Jerry Mumphrey	.40	.30	.15
16	Bill Dawley	.40	.30	.15
17	Mark Bailey	.40	.30	.15
18	Mike Scott	1.00	.70	.40
19	Harry Spilman	.40	.30	.15
20	Bob Knepper	.50	.40	.20
21	Dave Smith	.50	.40	.20
22	Kevin Bass	.60	.45	.25
23	Tim Tolman	.40	.30	.15
24	Jeff Calhoun	.40	.30	.15
25	Jim Pankovits	.40	.30	.15
26	Ron Mathis	.40	.30	.15
27	Astros Coaches (Cot Deal, Matt Galante, Don Leppert, Denis Menke, Jerry Walker)			
		.40	.30	.15
28	Astros Logo/Checklist	.40	.30	.15

1985 Mother's Cookies Giants

Mother's Cookies issued a third annual full-color set for the San Francisco Giants in 1985. The Giants set measures 2-1/2" by 3-1/2", and card fronts feature unbordered color photos of current players with rounded corners. Card backs are quite similar in format to the 1983 Mother's Cookies Giants, with brief biographical information, card numbers, Mother's Cookies logo and space for player autograph. Card backs are dated 1985. There are 28 cards in the Giants set, which was distributed in its entirety during a stadium promotion. The Giants set includes one card each for the manager, coaches and a checklist.

		MT	NR MT	EX
Complete Set:		12.00	9.00	4.75
Common Player:		.40	.30	.15
1	Jim Davenport	.40	.30	.15
2	Chili Davis	.60	.45	.25
3	Dan Gladden	.60	.45	.25

4	Jeff Leonard	.60	.45	.25
5	Manny Trillo	.50	.40	.20
6	Atlee Hammaker	.50	.40	.20
7	Bob Brenly	.50	.40	.20
8	Greg Minton	.40	.30	.15
9	Bill Laskey	.40	.30	.15
10	Vida Blue	.60	.45	.25
11	Mike Krukow	.50	.40	.20
12	Frank Williams	.60	.45	.25
13	Jose Uribe	.50	.40	.20
14	Johnnie LeMaster	.40	.30	.15
15	Scot Thompson	.40	.30	.15
16	Dave LaPoint	.50	.40	.20
17	David Green	.40	.30	.15
18	Chris Brown	1.00	.70	.40
19	Joel Youngblood	.40	.30	.15
20	Mark Davis	.40	.30	.15
21	Jim Gott	.40	.30	.15
22	Doug Gwosdz	.40	.30	.15
23	Scott Garrelts	.50	.40	.20
24	Gary Rajsich	.40	.30	.15
25	Rob Deer	1.00	.70	.40
26	Brad Wellman	.40	.30	.15
27	Coaches (Rocky Bridges, Chuck Hiller, Tom McCraw, Bob Miller, Jack Mull)	.40	.30	.15
28	Candlestick Park/Checklist	.40	.30	.15

1985 Mother's Cookies Mariners

Mother's Cookies issued a second annual full-color set for the Seattle Mariners in 1985. The Mariners set measures 2-1/2" by 3-1/2", and card fronts feature unbordered color photos with rounded corners. Card backs are quite similar in format to the 1984 Mother's Cookies Mariners, with brief biographical information, card numbers, Mother's Cookies logo and space for player autograph. Card backs are dated 1985. There are 28 cards in the Mariners set, which was distributed in its entirety during a stadium promotion. The Mariners set includes one card each for the coaches and a checklist.

		MT	NR MT	EX
Complete Set:		13.00	9.75	5.25
Common Player:		.40	.30	.15
1	Chuck Cottier	.40	.30	.15
2	Alvin Davis	1.25	.90	.50
3	Mark Langston	1.00	.70	.40
4	Dave Henderson	.40	.30	.15
5	Ed Vande Berg	.40	.30	.15
6	Al Cowens	.40	.30	.15
7	Spike Owen	.40	.30	.15
8	Mike Moore	.40	.30	.15
9	Gorman Thomas	.60	.45	.25
10	Barry Bonnell	.40	.30	.15
11	Jack Perconte	.40	.30	.15
12	Domingo Ramos	.40	.30	.15
13	Bob Kearney	.40	.30	.15
14	Matt Young	.40	.30	.15
15	Jim Beattie	.40	.30	.15
16	Mike Stanton	.40	.30	.15
17	David Valle	.50	.40	.20
18	Ken Phelps	.60	.45	.25
19	Salome Barojas	.40	.30	.15

		MT	NR MT	EX
20	Jim Presley	1.50	1.25	.60
21	Phil Bradley	1.00	.70	.40
22	Dave Geisel	.40	.30	.15
23	Harold Reynolds	.80	.60	.30
24	Edwin Nunez	.50	.40	.20
25	Mike Morgan	.40	.30	.15
26	Ivan Calderon	.80	.60	.30
27	Mariners Coaches (Deron Johnson, Jim Mahoney, Marty Martinez, Phil Regan, Phil Roof)	.40	.30	.15
28	Seattle Kingdome/Checklist	.40	.30	.15

1985 Mother's Cookies Padres

Mother's Cookies issued a second annual full-color set for the San Diego Padres in 1985. The Padres set measures 2-1/2" by 3-1/2", and card fronts feature unbordered color photos with rounded corners. Card backs are quite similar in format to the 1984 Mother's Cookies Padres, with brief biographical information, card numbers, Mother's Cookies logo and space for player autograph. Card backs are dated 1985. There are 28 cards in the Padres set, which was distributed in its entirety during a stadium promotion. The Padres set includes one card each for the manager, coaches and a checklist.

		MT	NR MT	EX
	Complete Set:	12.00	9.00	4.75
	Common Player:	.40	.30	.15
1	Dick Williams	.40	.30	.15
2	Tony Gwynn	3.00	2.25	1.25
3	Kevin McReynolds	1.50	1.25	.60
4	Graig Nettles	.70	.50	.30
5	Rich Gossage	.90	.70	.35
6	Steve Garvey	1.75	1.25	.70
7	Garry Templeton	.50	.40	.20
8	Dave Dravecky	.50	.40	.20
9	Eric Show	.60	.45	.25
10	Terry Kennedy	.50	.40	.20
11	Luis DeLeon	.40	.30	.15
12	Bruce Bochy	.40	.30	.15
13	Andy Hawkins	.50	.40	.20
14	Kurt Bevacqua	.40	.30	.15
15	Craig Lefferts	.40	.30	.15
16	Mario Ramirez	.40	.30	.15
17	LaMarr Hoyt	.40	.30	.15
18	Jerry Royster	.40	.30	.15
19	Tim Stoddard	.40	.30	.15
20	Tim Flannery	.40	.30	.15
21	Mark Thurmond	.40	.30	.15
22	Greg Booker	.50	.40	.20
23	Bobby Brown	.40	.30	.15
24	Carmelo Martinez	.50	.40	.20
25	Al Bumbry	.40	.30	.15
26	Jerry Davis	.40	.30	.15
27	Padres Coaches (Galen Cisco, Harry Dunlop, Deacon Jones, Jack Krol, Ozzie Virgil)	.40	.30	.15
28	Jack Murphy Stadium/Checklist	.40	.30	.15

NOTE: A card number in parentheses ( ) indicates the set is unnumbered.

1986 Mother's Cookies A's

Mother's Cookies produced four more full-color team card sets in 1986, with only the San Diego Padres not repeating from the 1985 group. The third annual set for the Oakland A's measures 2-1/2" by 3-1/2", and card fronts feature unbordered color photos with rounded corners. Card backs are quite similar in format to previous years, with brief biographical information, card numbers and the Mother's Cookies logo. Card backs are dated 1986. There are 28 cards in the A's set, with 20 of the cards distributed during a stadium promotion. Each fan also received a coupon redeemable for eight additional cards. The A's set includes one card each for the manager, coaches and a checklist.

		MT	NR MT	EX
	Complete Set:	22.00	16.50	8.75
	Common Player:	.30	.25	.12
1	Jackie Moore	.30	.25	.12
2	Dave Kingman	.60	.45	.25
3	Dusty Baker	.40	.30	.15
4	Joaquin Andujar	.40	.30	.15
5	Alfredo Griffin	.40	.30	.15
6	Dwayne Murphy	.40	.30	.15
7	Mike Davis	.40	.30	.15
8	Carney Lansford	.50	.40	.20
9	Jose Canseco	15.00	11.00	6.00
10	Bruce Bochte	.30	.25	.12
11	Mickey Tettleton	.30	.25	.12
12	Donnie Hill	.30	.25	.12
13	Jose Rijo	.60	.45	.25
14	Rick Langford	.30	.25	.12
15	Chris Codiroli	.30	.25	.12
16	Moose Haas	.30	.25	.12
17	Keith Atherton	.30	.25	.12
18	Jay Howell	.40	.30	.15
19	Tony Phillips	.30	.25	.12
20	Steve Henderson	.30	.25	.12
21	Bill Krueger	.30	.25	.12
22	Steve Ontiveros	.40	.30	.15
23	Bill Bathe	.30	.25	.12
24	Rickey Peters	.30	.25	.12
25	Tim Birtsas	.30	.25	.12
26	Trainers Card (Frank Ciensczyk, Larry Davis, Steve Vucinich, Barry Weinberg)	.30	.25	.12
27	Coaches Card (Bob Didier, Dave McKay, Jeff Newman, Ron Plaza, Wes Stock, Bob Watson)	.30	.25	.12
28	Oakland Coliseum/Checklist	.30	.25	.12

1986 Mother's Cookies Astros

Mother's Cookies produced a third annual set for the Houston Astros in 1985. The set measure 2-1/2" by 3-1/2", and card fronts feature unbordered color paintings of Houston's past All-Star Game performers. The round-cornered cards have backs quite similar in format to previous years, with brief biographical information, card numbers and the Mother's Cookies logo. Card backs are dated 1986.

There are 28 cards in the Astros set, with 20 of the cards distributed during a stadium promotion. Each fan also received a coupon redeemable for eight additional cards. The Astros set also includes a checklist card.

		MT	NR MT	EX
	Complete Set:	10.00	7.50	4.00
	Common Player:	.30	.25	.12
1	Dick Farrell	.30	.25	.12
2	Hal Woodeschick (Woodeschick)	.30	.25	.12
3	Joe Morgan	1.00	.70	.40
4	Claude Raymond	.30	.25	.12
5	Mike Cuellar	.40	.30	.15
6	Rusty Staub	.60	.45	.25
7	Jimmy Wynn	.40	.30	.15
8	Larry Dierker	.40	.30	.15
9	Denis Menke	.30	.25	.12
10	Don Wilson	.30	.25	.12
11	Cesar Cedeno	.50	.40	.20
12	Lee May	.40	.30	.15
13	Bob Watson	.40	.30	.15
14	Ken Forsch	.40	.30	.15
15	Joaquin Andujar	.40	.30	.15
16	Terry Puhl	.30	.25	.12
17	Joe Niekro	.40	.30	.15
18	Craig Reynolds	.30	.25	.12
19	Joe Sambito	.30	.25	.12
20	Jose Cruz	.60	.45	.25
21	J.R. Richard	.40	.30	.15
22	Bob Knepper	.40	.30	.15
23	Nolan Ryan	1.50	1.25	.60
24	Ray Knight	.40	.30	.15
25	Bill Dawley	.30	.25	.12
26	Dickie Thon	.40	.30	.15
27	Jerry Mumphrey	.30	.25	.12
28	Astros Logo/Checklist	.30	.25	.12

1986 Mother's Cookies Giants

Mother's Cookies produced a fourth annual set for the San Francisco Giants in 1985. Cards in the set measure 2-1/2" by 3-1/2", and the fronts feature unbordered color photos with rounded corners. Card backs are quite similar in format to previous years, with brief biographical information, card numbers, and the Mother's Cookies logo. Card backs are dated

1986. There are 28 cards in the Giants set, with 20 of the cards distributed during a stadium promotion. Each fan also received a coupon redeemable for eight additional cards. The Giants set also includes a card for the manager and a checklist.

		MT	NR MT	EX
	Complete Set:	15.00	11.00	6.00
	Common Player:	.30	.25	.12
1	Roger Craig	.40	.30	.15
2	Chili Davis	.60	.45	.25
3	Dan Gladden	.40	.30	.15
4	Jeff Leonard	.60	.45	.25
5	Bob Brenly	.40	.30	.15
6	Atlee Hammaker	.40	.30	.15
7	Will Clark	5.00	3.75	2.00
8	Greg Minton	.30	.25	.12
9	Candy Maldonado	.40	.30	.15
10	Vida Blue	.50	.40	.20
11	Mike Krukow	.40	.30	.15
12	Bob Melvin	.40	.30	.15
13	Jose Uribe	.40	.30	.15
14	Dan Driessen	.40	.30	.15
15	Jeff Robinson	.50	.40	.20
16	Rob Thompson	.80	.60	.30
17	Mike LaCoss	.30	.25	.12
18	Chris Brown	.60	.45	.25
19	Scott Garrelts	.50	.40	.20
20	Mark Davis	.50	.40	.20
21	Jim Gott	.30	.25	.12
22	Brad Wellman	.30	.25	.12
23	Roger Mason	.30	.25	.12
24	Bill Laskey	.30	.25	.12
25	Brad Gulden	.30	.25	.12
26	Joel Youngblood	.30	.25	.12
27	Juan Berenguer	.30	.25	.12
28	Coaches/Checklist (Bill Fahey, Bob Lillis, Gordy MacKenzie, Jose Morales, Norm Sherry)	.30	.25	.12

1986 Mother's Cookies Mariners

Mother's Cookies produced a third annual set for the Seattle Mariners in 1985. The set measures 2-1/2" by 3-1/2", and card fronts feature unbordered color photos with rounded corners. Card backs are quite similar in format to previous years, with brief biographical information, card numbers and the Mother's Cookies logo. Card backs are dated 1986. There are 28 cards in the Mariners set, with 20 of the cards distributed during a stadium promotion. Each fan also received a coupon redeemable for eight additional cards. The Mariners set also includes a card for the manager and a checklist.

		MT	NR MT	EX
	Complete Set:	12.00	9.00	4.75
	Common Player:	.30	.25	.12
1	Dick Williams	.30	.25	.12
2	Alvin Davis	1.00	.70	.40
3	Mark Langston	.80	.60	.30
4	Dave Henderson	.50	.40	.20

		MT	NR MT	EX
5	Steve Yeager	.30	.25	.12
6	Al Cowens	.30	.25	.12
7	Jim Presley	.70	.50	.30
8	Phil Bradley	.70	.50	.30
9	Gorman Thomas	.50	.40	.20
10	Barry Bonnell	.30	.25	.12
11	Milt Wilcox	.30	.25	.12
12	Domingo Ramos	.30	.25	.12
13	Paul Mirabella	.30	.25	.12
14	Matt Young	.30	.25	.12
15	Ivan Calderon	.60	.45	.25
16	Bill Swift	.40	.30	.15
17	Pete Ladd	.30	.25	.12
18	Ken Phelps	.40	.30	.15
19	Karl Best	.30	.25	.12
20	Spike Owen	.40	.30	.15
21	Mike Moore	.30	.25	.12
22	Danny Tartabull	1.75	1.25	.70
23	Bob Kearney	.30	.25	.12
24	Edwin Nunez	.30	.25	.12
25	Mike Morgan	.30	.25	.12
26	Roy Thomas	.30	.25	.12
27	Jim Beattie	.30	.25	.12
28	Coaches/Checklist (Deron Johnson, Marty Martinez, Phil Regan, Phil Roof, Ozzie Virgil)	.30	.25	.12

1987 Mother's Cookies A's

Continuing with a tradition of producing beautiful baseball cards, Mother's Cookies of Oakland, Calif. issued a 28-card set featuring every Oakland A's player to have been elected to the All-Star Game since 1968. The full-color photos came from the private collection of nationally known photographer Doug McWilliams. Twenty of the 28 cards were given out to fans attending the A's game of July 5th. An additional eight cards were available by redeeming a mail-in certificate. The cards, which measure 2-1/2" by 3-1/2", feature rounded corners. The card backs carry the player's All-Star Game statistics.

		MT	NR MT	EX
Complete Set:		16.00	12.00	6.50
Common Player:		.30	.25	.12
1	Bert Campaneris	.40	.30	.15
2	Rick Monday	.40	.30	.15
3	John Odom	.30	.25	.12
4	Sal Bando	.40	.30	.15
5	Reggie Jackson	1.50	1.25	.60
6	Jim Hunter	1.00	.70	.40
7	Vida Blue	.50	.40	.20
8	Dave Duncan	.30	.25	.12
9	Joe Rudi	.40	.30	.15
10	Rollie Fingers	.70	.50	.30
11	Ken Holtzman	.40	.30	.15
12	Dick Williams	.40	.30	.15
13	Alvin Dark	.30	.25	.12
14	Gene Tenace	.40	.30	.15
15	Claudell Washington	.40	.30	.15
16	Phil Garner	.30	.25	.12
17	Wayne Gross	.30	.25	.12
18	Matt Keough	.30	.25	.12
19	Jeff Newman	.30	.25	.12
20	Rickey Henderson	1.50	1.25	.60
21	Tony Armas	.40	.30	.15

		MT	NR MT	EX
22	Mike Norris	.30	.25	.12
23	Billy Martin	.50	.40	.20
24	Bill Caudill	.30	.25	.12
25	Jay Howell	.40	.30	.15
26	Jose Canseco	3.00	2.25	1.25
27	Jose and Reggie (Jose Canseco, Reggie Jackson)	2.00	1.50	.80
28	A's Logo/Checklist	.30	.25	.12

1987 Mother's Cookies Astros

Twenty of 28 cards featuring Astros players were given out to the first 25,000 fans attending the July 17th game at the Astrodome. An additional eight cards (though not necessarily the exact eight needed to complete a set) were available from the card producer, Mother's Cookies, by redeeming a mail-in certificate. The cards have rounded corners and measure the standard 2-1/2" by 3-1/2". The backs are printed in purple and orange and contain personal player information, the Mother's Cookies logo, the card number and a spot for the player's autograph.

		MT	NR MT	EX
Complete Set:		10.00	7.50	4.00
Common Player:		.30	.25	.12
1	Hal Lanier	.30	.25	.12
2	Mike Scott	1.00	.70	.40
3	Jose Cruz	.50	.40	.20
4	Bill Doran	.50	.40	.20
5	Bob Knepper	.40	.30	.15
6	Phil Garner	.40	.30	.15
7	Terry Puhl	.30	.25	.12
8	Nolan Ryan	2.00	1.50	.80
9	Kevin Bass	.50	.40	.20
10	Glenn Davis	1.00	.70	.40
11	Alan Ashby	.30	.25	.12
12	Charlie Kerfeld	.30	.25	.12
13	Denny Walling	.30	.25	.12
14	Danny Darwin	.30	.25	.12
15	Mark Bailey	.30	.25	.12
16	Davey Lopes	.40	.30	.15
17	Dave Meads	.40	.30	.15
18	Aurelio Lopez	.30	.25	.12
19	Craig Reynolds	.30	.25	.12
20	Dave Smith	.40	.30	.15
21	Larry Anderson (Andersen)	.30	.25	.12
22	Jim Pankovits	.30	.25	.12
23	Jim Deshaies	.50	.40	.20
24	Bert Pena	.30	.25	.12
25	Dickie Thon	.30	.25	.12
26	Billy Hatcher	.50	.40	.20
27	Astros Coaches (Yogi Berra, Matt Galante, Denis Menke, Les Moss, Gene Tenace)	.30	.25	.12
28	Houston Astrodome/Checklist	.30	.25	.12

NOTE: A card number in parentheses ( ) indicates the set is unnumbered.

1987 Mother's Cookies Dodgers

Mother's Cookies produced for the first time in 1987 a baseball card set featuring the Los Angeles Dodgers. Twenty of the 28 cards in the set were given out to youngsters 14 and under at Dodger Stadium on August 9th. An additional eight cards were available from Mother's Cookies via a mail-in coupon card. The borderless, full-color cards measure 2-1/2" by 3-1/2" and have rounded corners. A special album designed to house the set was available for $3.95 through a mail-in offer.

		MT	NR MT	EX
Complete Set:		10.00	7.50	4.00
Common Player:		.30	.25	.12
1	Tom Lasorda	.40	.30	.15
2	Pedro Guerrero	.80	.60	.30
3	Steve Sax	.80	.60	.30
4	Fernando Valenzuela	1.00	.70	.40
5	Mike Marshall	.70	.50	.30
6	Orel Hershiser	1.00	.70	.40
7	Mariano Duncan	.30	.25	.12
8	Bill Madlock	.40	.30	.15
9	Bob Welch	.40	.30	.15
10	Mike Scioscia	.40	.30	.15
11	Mike Ramsey	.30	.25	.12
12	Matt Young	.30	.25	.12
13	Franklin Stubbs	.40	.30	.15
14	Tom Niedenfuer	.40	.30	.15
15	Reggie Williams	.40	.30	.15
16	Rick Honeycutt	.30	.25	.12
17	Dave Anderson	.30	.25	.12
18	Alejandro Pena	.40	.30	.15
19	Ken Howell	.30	.25	.12
20	Len Matuszek	.30	.25	.12
21	Tim Leary	.40	.30	.15
22	Tracy Woodson	.40	.30	.15
23	Alex Trevino	.30	.25	.12
24	Ken Landreaux	.30	.25	.12
25	Mickey Hatcher	.30	.25	.12
26	Brian Holton	.40	.30	.15
27	Dodgers' Coaches (Joey Amalfitano, Mark Cresse, Don McMahon, Manny Mota, Ron Perranoski, Bill Russell)	.30	.25	.12
28	Dodger Stadium/Checklist	.30	.25	.12

1987 Mother's Cookies Giants

Distribution of the 1987 Mother's Cookies Giants, cards took place at Candlestick Park for the Giants' June 27th game. Twenty of the 28 cards in the set were given to the first 25,000 fans entering the park. The starter packet of 20 cards contained a mail-in coupon card which was good for an additional eight cards. The cards, which measure 2-1/2" by 3-1/2" in size have rounded corners. The card backs are printed in red and purple and contain personal and statistical information along with the Mother's Cookies logo.

		MT	NR MT	EX
Complete Set:		10.00	7.50	4.00
Common Player:		.30	.25	.12
1	Roger Craig	.40	.30	.15
2	Will Clark	1.50	1.25	.60
3	Chili Davis	.40	.30	.15
4	Bob Brenly	.30	.25	.12
5	Chris Brown	.50	.40	.20
6	Mike Krukow	.40	.30	.15
7	Candy Maldonado	.40	.30	.15
8	Jeffrey Leonard	.50	.40	.20
9	Greg Minton	.30	.25	.12
10	Robby Thompson	.40	.30	.15
11	Scott Garrelts	.30	.25	.12
12	Bob Melvin	.30	.25	.12
13	Jose Uribe	.30	.25	.12
14	Mark Davis	.30	.25	.12
15	Eddie Milner	.30	.25	.12
16	Harry Spilman	.30	.25	.12
17	Kelly Downs	.60	.45	.25
18	Chris Speier	.30	.25	.12
19	Jim Gott	.30	.25	.12
20	Joel Youngblood	.30	.25	.12
21	Mike LaCoss	.30	.25	.12
22	Matt Williams	.70	.50	.30
23	Roger Mason	.30	.25	.12
24	Mike Aldrete	.60	.45	.25
25	Jeff Robinson	.40	.30	.15
26	Mark Grant	.30	.25	.12
27	Coaches (Bill Fahey, Bob Lillis, Gordon MacKenzie, Jose Morales, Norm Sherry, Don Zimmer)	.30	.25	.12
28	Candlestick Park/Checklist	.30	.25	.12

1987 Mother's Cookies Mariners

For the fourth consecutive year, Mother's Cookies issued a baseball card set featuring the Seattle Mariners. Twenty of the 28 cards in the set were distributed to the first 20,000 fans entering the Kingdome on August 9th. An additional eight cards (though not necessarily the eight cards needed to complete the set) were available by redeeming a mail-in certificate. Collectors were encouraged to trade to complete a set. The 2-1/2" by 3-1/2" full-color cards feature glossy finishes and rounded corners. A specially designed album to house the set was available.

		MT	NR MT	EX
Complete Set:		8.00	6.00	3.25
Common Player:		.30	.25	.12
1	Dick Williams	.30	.25	.12
2	Alvin Davis	.80	.60	.30
3	Mike Moore	.30	.25	.12
4	Jim Presley	.60	.45	.25
5	Mark Langston	.70	.50	.30
6	Phil Bradley	.60	.45	.25
7	Ken Phelps	.40	.30	.15
8	Mike Morgan	.30	.25	.12
9	David Valle	.30	.25	.12
10	Harold Reynolds	.40	.30	.15
11	Edwin Nunez	.30	.25	.12
12	Bob Kearney	.30	.25	.12
13	Scott Bankhead	.40	.30	.15
14	Scott Bradley	.30	.25	.12
15	Mickey Brantley	.40	.30	.15
16	Mark Huismann	.30	.25	.12
17	Mike Kingery	.40	.30	.15
18	John Moses	.30	.25	.12
19	Donell Nixon	.40	.30	.15
20	Rey Quinones	.40	.30	.15
21	Domingo Ramos	.30	.25	.12
22	Jerry Reed	.30	.25	.12
23	Rich Renteria	.40	.30	.15
24	Rich Monteleone	.40	.30	.15
25	Mike Trujillo	.30	.25	.12
26	Bill Wilkinson	.40	.30	.15
27	John Christensen	.30	.25	.12
28	Coaches/Checklist (Billy Connors, Frank Howard, Phil Roof, Bobby Tolan, Ozzie Virgil)			
		.30	.25	.12

1987 Mother's Cookies Rangers

While Mother's Cookies of Oakland, Calif., had been producing high-quality baseball card sets of various teams, the Texas Rangers were highlighted for the first time in 1987. Twenty cards from the 28-card set were handed out to the first 25,000 fans entering Arlington Stadium on July 17th. An additional eight cards (though not necessarily the eight needed to complete a set) were available by redeeming a mail-in certificate. The cards, which measure 2-1/2" by 3-1/2", have rounded corners and glossy finishes like all Mother's Cookies issued in 1987.

		MT	NR MT	EX
Complete Set:		10.00	7.50	4.00
Complete Set:		.30	.25	.12
1	Bobby Valentine	.40	.30	.15
2	Pete Incaviglia	1.00	.70	.40
3	Charlie Hough	.40	.30	.15
4	Oddibe McDowell	.50	.40	.20
5	Larry Parrish	.50	.40	.20
6	Scott Fletcher	.40	.30	.15
7	Steve Buechele	.30	.25	.12
8	Tom Paciorek	.30	.25	.12
9	Pete O'Brien	.60	.45	.25

		MT	NR MT	EX
10	Darrell Porter	.30	.25	.12
11	Greg Harris	.30	.25	.12
12	Don Slaught	.30	.25	.12
13	Ruben Sierra	1.75	1.25	.70
14	Curtis Wilkerson	.30	.25	.12
15	Dale Mohorcic	.40	.30	.15
16	Ron Meredith	.30	.25	.12
17	Mitch Williams	.40	.30	.15
18	Bob Brower	.40	.30	.15
19	Edwin Correa	.30	.25	.12
20	Geno Petralli	.30	.25	.12
21	Mike Loynd	.40	.30	.15
22	Jerry Browne	.40	.30	.15
23	Jose Guzman	.50	.40	.20
24	Jeff Kunkel	.30	.25	.12
25	Bobby Witt	.60	.45	.25
26	Jeff Russell	.30	.25	.12
27	Trainers (Danny Wheat, Bill Zeigler)			
		.30	.25	.12
28	Rangers' Coaches/Checklist (Joe Ferguson, Tim Foli, Tom House, Art Howe, Dave Oliver, Tom Robson)	.30	.25	.12

1987 Mother's Cookies Mark McGwire

A four-card set featuring outstanding rookie Mark McGwire of the Oakland Athletics was produced by Mother's Cookies of Oakland, Calif. Cards are 2-1/2" by 3-1/2" and have rounded corners and glossy finishes like other Mother's issues. The four-card set was obtainable by two methods. A complete set could be received by sending in eight proof-of-purchase seals. Also, sets could be secured at the National Sports Collectors Convention held July 9-12 in San Francisco. Convention goers received one card as a bonus for each Mother's Cookies baseball card album purchased.

		MT	NR MT	EX
Complete Set:		20.00	15.00	8.00
Common Player:		4.00	3.00	1.50
1	Mark McGwire (portrait)	4.00	3.00	1.50
2	Mark McGwire (leaning on bat rack)			
		4.00	3.00	1.50
3	Mark McGwire (beginning batting swing)			
		4.00	3.00	1.50
4	Mark McGwire (batting follow-through)			
		4.00	3.00	1.50

1988 Mother's Cookies A's

Complete at 28 cards (including checklist), the 1988 Mother's Cookies A's set features full-color, borderless cards with rounded corners in the standard 2-1/2" by 3-1/2" size. The backs are printed in red and purple on white and include biographical information, the Mother's Cookies logo and card number. Starter sets of 20 cards were distributed at the stadium along with a promotional card redeemable for another eights cards (not necessarily those needed to complete the set). An album to house the cards was also available.

		MT	NR MT	EX
Complete Set:		16.00	12.00	6.50
Common Player:		.30	.25	.12
1	Tony LaRussa	.30	.25	.12
2	Mark McGwire	3.00	2.25	1.25
3	Dave Stewart	.50	.40	.20
4	Mickey Tettleton	.30	.25	.12
5	Dave Parker	.70	.50	.30
6	Carney Lansford	.50	.40	.20
7	Jose Canseco	3.00	2.25	1.25
8	Don Baylor	.50	.40	.20
9	Bob Welch	.40	.30	.15
10	Dennis Eckersley	.40	.30	.15
11	Walt Weiss	1.50	1.25	.60
12	Tony Phillips	.30	.25	.12
13	Steve Ontiveros	.30	.25	.12
14	Dave Henderson	.30	.25	.12
15	Stan Javier	.30	.25	.12
16	Ron Hassey	.30	.25	.12
17	Curt Young	.40	.30	.15
18	Glenn Hubbard	.30	.25	.12
19	Storm Davis	.30	.25	.12
20	Eric Plunk	.30	.25	.12
21	Matt Young	.30	.25	.12
22	Mike Gallego	.30	.25	.12
23	Rick Honeycutt	.30	.25	.12
24	Doug Jennings	.50	.40	.20
25	Gene Nelson	.30	.25	.12
26	Greg Cadaret	.40	.30	.15
27	A's Coaches (Dave Duncan, Rene Lachemann, Jim Lefebvre, Dave McKay, Mike Paul, Bob Watson)	.30	.25	.12
28	Jose Canseco, Mark McGwire	3.00	2.25	1.25

1988 Mother's Cookies Astros

One of six team sets issued by Mother's Cookies in 1988, the 28-card Houston Astros set is similar in design to other Mother's Cookies sets. The cards are the standard 2-1/2" by 3-1/2" size with rounded corners and feature full-color, borderless photos on the fronts with the player's name in an upper or lower corner. The backs feature red and purple printing on white and include brief biographical information, the

Mother's logo and card number. Twenty of the cards were distributed in a stadium promotion, along with a redemption card that could be exchanged for an additional eight cards (but not necessarily the eight needed to complete the set.) An album was also available to house the set.

		MT	NR MT	EX
Complete Set:		10.00	7.50	4.00
Common Player:		.30	.25	.12
1	Hal Lanier	.30	.25	.12
2	Mike Scott	.90	.70	.35
3	Gerald Young	.70	.50	.30
4	Bill Doran	.50	.40	.20
5	Bob Knepper	.40	.30	.15
6	Billy Hatcher	.50	.40	.20
7	Terry Puhl	.30	.25	.12
8	Nolan Ryan	1.50	1.25	.60
9	Kevin Bass	.50	.40	.20
10	Glenn Davis	.90	.70	.35
11	Alan Ashby	.30	.25	.12
12	Steve Henderson	.30	.25	.12
13	Denny Walling	.30	.25	.12
14	Danny Darwin	.30	.25	.12
15	Mark Bailey	.30	.25	.12
16	Ernie Camacho	.30	.25	.12
17	Rafael Ramirez	.30	.25	.12
18	Jeff Heathcock	.30	.25	.12
19	Craig Reynolds	.30	.25	.12
20	Dave Smith	.40	.30	.15
21	Larry Andersen	.30	.25	.12
22	Jim Pankovits	.30	.25	.12
23	Jim Deshaies	.40	.30	.15
24	Juan Agosto	.30	.25	.12
25	Chuck Jackson	.40	.30	.15
26	Joaquin Andujar	.40	.30	.15
27	Astros Coaches (Yogi Berra, Gene Clines, Matt Galante, Marc Hill, Denis Menke, Les Moss)	.30	.25	.12
28	Trainers Card/Checklist (Doc Ewell, Dave Labossiere, Dennis Liborio)	.30	.25	.12

1988 Mother's Cookies Dodgers

Similar in design to other Mother's Cookies sets, the 1988 Dodgers issue featured full-color, borderless photos with backs printed in red and purple. The 28 cards in the set measure the standard 2-1/2" by 3-1/2" with rounded corners. Starter packs of 20 cards were distributed at a ballpark promotion along with a coupon card that could be exchanged for an additional eight cards at a local card show or through the mail. The backs of the cards include brief player information, the Mother's Cookies logo and card number. The promotion also included a special album to house the set.

		MT	NR MT	EX
Complete Set:		10.00	7.50	4.00
Common Player:		.30	.25	.12
1	Tom Lasorda	.40	.30	.15
2	Pedro Guerrero	.80	.60	.30

		MT	NR MT	EX
3	Steve Sax	.80	.60	.30
4	Fernando Valenzuela	1.00	.70	.40
5	Mike Marshall	.70	.50	.30
6	Orel Hershiser	1.00	.70	.40
7	Alfredo Griffin	.30	.25	.12
8	Kirk Gibson	1.00	.70	.40
9	Don Sutton	.50	.40	.20
10	Mike Scioscia	.40	.30	.15
11	Franklin Stubbs	.40	.30	.15
12	Mike Davis	.40	.30	.15
13	Jesse Orosco	.40	.30	.15
14	John Shelby	.30	.25	.12
15	Rick Dempsey	.40	.30	.15
16	Jay Howell	.40	.30	.15
17	Dave Anderson	.30	.25	.12
18	Alejandro Pena	.40	.30	.15
19	Jeff Hamilton	.40	.30	.15
20	Danny Heep	.30	.25	.12
21	Tim Leary	.40	.30	.15
22	Brad Havens	.30	.25	.12
23	Tim Belcher	.60	.45	.25
24	Ken Howell	.30	.25	.12
25	Mickey Hatcher	.30	.25	.12
26	Brian Holton	.30	.25	.12
27	Mike Devereaux	.60	.45	.25
28	Dodgers Coaches/Checklist (Joe Amalfitano, Mark Cresse, Joe Ferguson, Ben Hines, Manny Mota, Ron Perranoski, Bill Russell)	.30	.25	.12

1988 Mother's Cookies Giants

One of six team sets issued in 1988 by Mother's Cookies, this 28-card Giants set featured full-color, borderless photos on a standard-size card with rounded corners. The backs, printed in red and purple, include brief player information, the Mother's Cookies logo and card number. Twenty different cards were distributed as a starter set at a stadium promotion along with a coupon card that could be redeemed for an additional eight cards (not necessarily those needed to complete the set). The redemption cards could be exchanged through the mail or redeemed at a local card show.

		MT	NR MT	EX
Complete Set:		10.00	7.50	4.00
Common Player:		.30	.25	.12
1	Roger Craig	.40	.30	.15
2	Will Clark	1.25	.90	.50
3	Kevin Mitchell	.40	.30	.15
4	Bob Brenly	.40	.30	.15
5	Mike Aldrete	.40	.30	.15
6	Mike Krukow	.40	.30	.15
7	Candy Maldonado	.40	.30	.15
8	Jeffrey Leonard	.40	.30	.15
9	Dave Dravecky	.40	.30	.15
10	Robby Thompson	.40	.30	.15
11	Scott Garrelts	.30	.25	.12
12	Bob Melvin	.30	.25	.12
13	Jose Uribe	.30	.25	.12
14	Brett Butler	.40	.30	.15
15	Rick Reuschel	.50	.40	.20
16	Harry Spilman	.30	.25	.12
17	Kelly Downs	.50	.40	.20
18	Chris Speier	.30	.25	.12

		MT	NR MT	EX
19	Atlee Hammaker	.30	.25	.12
20	Joel Youngblood	.30	.25	.12
21	Mike LaCoss	.30	.25	.12
22	Don Robinson	.30	.25	.12
23	Mark Wasinger	.40	.30	.15
24	Craig Lefferts	.30	.25	.12
25	Phil Garner	.30	.25	.12
26	Joe Price	.30	.25	.12
27	Giants Coaches (Dusty Baker, Bill Fahey, Bob Lillis, Gordie MacKenzie, Jose Morales, Norm Sherry)	.30	.25	.12
28	Logo Card/Checklist	.30	.25	.12

1988 Mother's Cookies Mariners

Similar in design to other Mother's Cookies sets, the 28-card Mariners issue featured full-color, borderless photos on a standard-size card with rounded corners. The backs, printed in red and purple, included brief biographical information, the Mother's Cookies logo and card number. Twenty-card starter packs were distributed at a stadium promotion, where fans also received a coupon card that could be exchanged for an additional eight cards (not necessarily those needed to complete the set). The coupon card could be redeemed through the mail or exchanged at a local baseball card show. As with the rest of the 1988 Mother's Cookies sets, an album was also available to house the cards.

		MT	NR MT	EX
Complete Set:		8.00	6.00	3.25
Common Player:		.30	.25	.12
1	Dick Williams	.30	.25	.12
2	Alvin Davis	.70	.50	.30
3	Mike Moore	.30	.25	.12
4	Jim Presley	.50	.40	.20
5	Mark Langston	.60	.45	.25
6	Henry Cotto	.30	.25	.12
7	Ken Phelps	.40	.30	.15
8	Steve Trout	.30	.25	.12
9	David Valle	.30	.25	.12
10	Harold Reynolds	.40	.30	.15
11	Edwin Nunez	.30	.25	.12
12	Glenn Wilson	.30	.25	.12
13	Scott Bankhead	.30	.25	.12
14	Scott Bradley	.30	.25	.12
15	Mickey Brantley	.30	.25	.12
16	Bruce Fields	.30	.25	.12
17	Mike Kingery	.30	.25	.12
18	Mike Campbell	.50	.40	.20
19	Mike Jackson	.40	.30	.15
20	Rey Quinones	.30	.25	.12
21	Mario Diaz	.30	.25	.12
22	Jerry Reed	.30	.25	.12
23	Rich Renteria	.30	.25	.12
24	Julio Solano	.30	.25	.12
25	Bill Swift	.30	.25	.12
26	Bill Wilkinson	.30	.25	.12
27	Mariners Coaches (Billy Connors, Frank Howard, Phil Roof, Jim Snyder, Ozzie Virgil)	.30	.25	.12
28	Trainers Card/Checklist (Henry Genzale, Rick Griffin)	.30	.25	.12

1988 Mother's Cookies Rangers

This 28-card set featuring the Texas Rangers was one of six team sets issued in 1988 by Mother's Cookies. Similar to other Mother's Cookies sets, the Rangers issue features full-color, borderless cards printed in the standard 2-1/2" by 3-1/2" format with rounded corners. The backs were printed in red and purple on white and included player information, the Mother's Cookies logo and card number. Twenty-card starter packs were distributed at a stadium promotion that included a redemption card good for another eight cards (not necessarily those needed to complete the set) either through the mail or at a local card show.

		MT	NR MT	EX
Complete Set:		8.00	6.00	3.25
Common Player:		.30	.25	.12
1	Bobby Valentine	.40	.30	.15
2	Pete Incaviglia	.70	.50	.30
3	Charlie Hough	.40	.30	.15
4	Oddibe McDowell	.50	.40	.20
5	Larry Parrish	.50	.40	.20
6	Scott Fletcher	.40	.30	.15
7	Steve Buechele	.40	.30	.15
8	Steve Kemp	.40	.30	.15
9	Pete O'Brien	.60	.45	.25
10	Ruben Sierra	.90	.70	.35
11	Mike Stanley	.50	.40	.20
12	Jose Cecena	.40	.30	.15
13	Cecil Espy	.40	.30	.15
14	Curtis Wilkerson	.30	.25	.12
15	Dale Mohorcic	.30	.25	.12
16	Ray Hayward	.30	.25	.12
17	Mitch Williams	.40	.30	.15
18	Bob Brower	.30	.25	.12
19	Paul Kilgus	.40	.30	.15
20	Geno Petralli	.30	.25	.12
21	James Steels	.30	.25	.12
22	Jerry Browne	.30	.25	.12
23	Jose Guzman	.40	.30	.15
24	DeWayne Vaughn	.40	.30	.15
25	Bobby Witt	.50	.40	.20
26	Jeff Russell	.30	.25	.12
27	Rangers Coaches (Richard Egan, Tom House, Art Howe, Davey Lopes, David Oliver, Tom Robson)	.30	.25	.12
28	Trainers Card/Checklist (Danny Wheat, Bill Zeigler)	.30	.25	.12

1988 Mother's Cookies Will Clark

In a baseball spring training-related promotion, Mother's Cookies of Oakland, Calif. produced a full-color four-card set featuring San Francisco Giants first baseman Will Clark. The cards, which have glossy finishes and rounded corners, came cellophane-wrapped in specially marked 18-ounce packages of Mother's Cookies products. The cards are identical in style to the regular Mother's Cookies issues.

		MT	NR MT	EX
Complete Set:		10.00	7.50	4.00
Common Player:		2.00	1.50	.80
1	Will Clark (bat on shoulder)	2.00	1.50	.80
2	Will Clark (kneeling)	2.00	1.50	.80
3	Will Clark (batting follow-thru)	2.00	1.50	.80
4	Will Clark (heading for first base)	2.00	1.50	.80

1988 Mother's Cookies Mark McGwire

For the second consecutive year, Mother's Cookies devoted a four-card set to Oakland A's slugger Mark McGwire. The full-color cards have rounded corners and measure 2-1/2" by 3-1/2" in size. The cards were in issued in specially marked 18-ounce packages of Mother's Cookies products in the northern California area. The cards are identical in design to the regular team issues produced by Mother's.

		MT	NR MT	EX
Complete Set:		15.00	11.00	6.00
Common Player:		3.00	2.25	1.25
1	Mark McGwire (holding oversized bat)	3.00	2.25	1.25
2	Mark McGwire (fielding)	3.00	2.25	1.25
3	Mark McGwire (kneeling)	3.00	2.25	1.25
4	Mark McGwire (bat in air)	3.00	2.25	1.25

NOTE: A card number in parentheses ( ) indicates the set is unnumbered.

1989 Mother's Cookies Athletics

The 1989 Mother's Cookies A's set consists of 28 cards designed in the tradional style: a glossy card with a borderless photo and rounded corners. A starter set of the cards was used as a stadium promotion and distributed to fans attending the July 30 Oakland game.

		MT	NR MT	EX
Complete Set:		12.00	9.00	4.75
Common Player:		.30	.25	.12
1	Tony LaRussa	.30	.25	.12
2	Mark McGwire	2.75	2.00	1.00
3	Terry Steinbach	.60	.45	.25
4	Dave Parker	.60	.45	.25
5	Carney Lansford	.50	.40	.20
6	Dave Stewart	.50	.40	.20
7	Jose Canseco	3.00	2.25	1.25
8	Walt Weiss	.50	.40	.20
9	Bob Welch	.40	.30	.15
10	Dennis Eckersley	.40	.30	.15
11	Tony Phillips	.30	.25	.12
12	Mike Moore	.50	.40	.20
13	Dave Henderson	.30	.25	.12
14	Curt Young	.30	.25	.12
15	Ron Hassey	.30	.25	.12
16	Eric Plunk	.30	.25	.12
17	Luis Polonia	.30	.25	.12
18	Storm Davis	.30	.25	.12
19	Glenn Hubbard	.30	.25	.12
20	Greg Cadaret	.30	.25	.12
21	Stan Javier	.30	.25	.12
22	Felix Jose	.40	.30	.15
23	Mike Gallego	.30	.25	.12
24	Todd Burns	.30	.25	.12
25	Rick Honeycutt	.30	.25	.12
26	Gene Nelson	.30	.25	.12
27	A's Coaches (Dave Duncan, Rene Lachemann, Art Kusnyer, Tommie Reynolds, Merv Rettenmund)	.30	.25	.12
28	Checklist (Photo of Weiss, McGwire & Canseco)	.30	.25	.12

1989 Mother's Cookies Astros

The 1989 Houston Astros team set issued by Mother's Cookies consisted of 28 cards designed in the traditional style of borderless photos and rounded corners. Partial sets were distributed to fans attending the July 22 Astros game at the Houston Astrodome. The cards feature the photography of Barry Colla and display the Mother's Cookies logo on the back.

		MT	NR MT	EX
Complete Set:		10.00	7.50	4.00
Common Player:		.30	.25	.12
1	Art Howe	.30	.25	.12

		MT	NR MT	EX
2	Mike Scott	.90	.70	.25
3	Gerald Young	.50	.40	.20
4	Bill Doran	.50	.40	.20
5	Billy Hatcher	.50	.40	.20
6	Terry Puhl	.30	.25	.12
7	Bob Knepper	.30	.25	.12
8	Kevin Bass	.50	.40	.20
9	Glenn Davis	.90	.70	.35
10	Alann Ashby	.30	.25	.12
11	Bob Forsch	.30	.25	.12
12	Greg Gross	.30	.25	.12
13	Danny Darwin	.30	.25	.12
14	Craig Biggio	1.00	.70	.40
15	Jim Clancy	.30	.25	.12
16	Rafael Ramirez	.30	.25	.12
17	Alex Trevino	.30	.25	.12
18	Craig Reynolds	.30	.25	.12
19	Dave Smith	.40	.30	.15
20	Larry Anderson	.30	.25	.12
21	Eric Yelding	.60	.45	.25
22	Jim Deshaies	.40	.30	.15
23	Juan Agosto	.30	.25	.12
24	Rick Rhoden	.30	.25	.12
25	Ken Caminiti	.60	.45	.25
26	Dave Meads	.30	.25	.12
27	Astro Coaches (Yogi Berra, Matt Galante, Phil Garner, Les Moss, Ed Napoleon, Ed Ott)	.30	.25	.12
28	Checklist (Trainers- Dave Labossiere, Doc Ewell Equip. Mgr.- Dennis Liborio)	.30	.25	.12

1989 Mother's Cookies Giants

The 1989 Mother's Cookies Giants set consists of 28 cards, all featuring borderless, color photos with rounded corners. Starter sets of the cards were distributed as a stadium promotion to fans attending the Aug. 6, 1989, Giants game at Candlestick Park.

		MT	NR MT	EX
Complete Set:		12.00	9.00	4.75
Common Player:		.30	.25	.12
1	Roger Craig	.40	.30	.15
2	Will Clark	1.25	.90	.50
3	Kevin Mitchell	1.00	.70	.40

		MT	NR MT	EX
4	Kelly Downs	.35	.25	.14
5	Brett Butler	.40	.30	.15
6	Mike Krukow	.30	.25	.12
7	Candy Maldonado	.30	.25	.12
8	Terry Kennedy	.30	.25	.12
9	Dave Dravecky	.40	.30	.15
10	Robby Thompson	.40	.30	.15
11	Scott Garrelts	.40	.30	.15
12	Matt Williams	.70	.50	.30
13	Jose Uribe	.30	.25	.12
14	Tracy Jones	.30	.25	.12
15	Rick Reuschel	.40	.30	.15
16	Ernest Riles	.30	.25	.12
17	Jeff Brantley	.50	.40	.20
18	Chris Speier	.30	.25	.12
19	Atlee Hammaker	.30	.25	.12
20	Ed Jurak	.30	.25	.12
21	Mike LaCoss	.30	.25	.12
22	Don Robinson	.30	.25	.12
23	Kirt Manwaring	.50	.40	.20
24	Craig Lefferts	.30	.25	.12
25	Donnell Nixon	.30	.25	.12
26	Joe Price	.30	.25	.12
27	Rich Gossage	.30	.25	.12
28	Checklist (Bill Fahey, Dusty Baker, Bob Lillis, Wendell Kim, Norm Sherry)	.30	.25	.12

		MT	NR MT	EX
26	Jeff Stone	.50	.40	.20
27	Rangers Coaches (Dick Egan, Tom Robson, Toby Harrah, Dave Oliver, Tom House, Dave Lopes)	.30	.25	.12
28	Checklist (Trainer Staff-Bill Ziegler, Danny Wheat)	.30	.25	.12

1989 Mother's Cookies
Jose Canseco

This special insert 4-card glossy set features Canseco in two posed (on standing, one kneeling) and two action (one batting, one running) shots. Full-color card fronts have rounded corners. Flip sides are numbered, printed in red and purple, and carry 1988 stats and career notes. Cards are individually cello-wrapped and inserted in Mother's Fudge 'N Chips, Oatmeal Raisin and Cocadas cookie bags.

		MT	NR MT	EX
Complete Set:		15.00	11.00	6.00
Common Player:		3.00	2.25	1.25
1	Jose Canseco (1 Of 4)	3.00	2.25	1.25
2	Jose Canseco (2 Of 4)	3.00	2.25	1.25
3	Jose Canseco (3 Of 4)	3.00	2.25	1.25
4	Jose Canseco (4 Of 4)	3.00	2.25	1.25

1989 Mother's Cookies
Rangers

The 1989 Mother's Cookies Rangers team set featured the traditional borderless photos and rounded corners. The standard-size set consisted of 28 cards featuring the photography of Barry Colla. Partial sets were distributed to fans attending the July 30, 1989 game at Arlington Stadium.

		MT	NR MT	EX
Complete Set:		9.00	6.75	3.50
Common Player:		.30	.25	.12
1	Bobby Valentine	.40	.30	.15
2	Nolan Ryan	1.50	1.25	.60
3	Julio Franco	.70	.50	.30
4	Charlie Hough	.40	.30	.15
5	Rafael Palmeiro	.70	.50	.30
6	Jeff Russell	.30	.25	.12
7	Ruben Sierra	.90	.70	.35
8	Steve Buechele	.30	.25	.12
9	Buddy Bell	.40	.30	.15
10	Pete Incaviglia	.40	.30	.15
11	Geno Petralli	.30	.25	.12
12	Cecil Espy	.40	.30	.15
13	Scott Fletcher	.30	.25	.12
14	Bobby Witt	.30	.25	.12
15	Brad Arnsberg	.40	.30	.15
16	Rick Leach	.30	.25	.12
17	Jamie Moyer	.40	.30	.15
18	Kevin Brown	.50	.40	.20
19	Jeff Kunkel	.30	.25	.12
20	Craig McMurtry	.30	.25	.12
21	Kenny Rogers	.50	.40	.20
22	Mike Stanley	.30	.25	.12
23	Cecilio Guante	.50	.40	.20
24	Jim Sundberg	.50	.40	.20
25	Jose Guzman	.50	.40	.20

1989 Mother's Cookies
Will Clark

Will Clark is featured on a special-edition glossy 4-card set inserted in Mother's big bag chocolate chip cookies. The standard-size (2-1/2" by 3-1/2") cards feature Clark in two posed (batting and catching) and two action (batting and running) shots. Purple and red backs (numbered) list 1986-88 stats.

		MT	NR MT	EX
Complete Set:		10.00	7.50	4.00
Common Player:		2.00	1.50	.80
1	Will Clark (1 Of 4)	2.00	1.50	.80
2	Will Clark (2 Of 4)	2.00	1.50	.80
3	Will Clark (3 Of 4)	2.00	1.50	.80
4	Will Clark (4 Of 4)	2.00	1.50	.80

1989 Mother's Cookies Ken Griffey, Jr.

This four-card set featuring Ken Griffey, Jr. was issued by Mother's Cookies and was available only in cookie packages in the states of WEashington and Oregon. The cards were also available at a Seattle Mariners Kingdome Baseball Card Show on Aug. 20, 1989, where the set was introduced. The cards were then packed inside specially- marked bags of cookies, one card per bag. The cards display the traditional Mother's Cookie's deign: glossy, borderless cards with rounded corners.

		MT	NR MT	EX
Complete Set:		16.00	12.00	6.50
Common Player:		3.50	2.75	1.50
1	Ken Griffey, Jr. (1 Of 4)	3.50	2.75	1.50
2	Ken Griffey, Jr. (2 Of 4)	3.50	2.75	1.50
3	Ken Griffey, Jr. (3 Of 4)	3.50	2.75	1.50
4	Ken Griffey, Jr. (4 Of 4)	3.50	2.75	1.50

1989 Mother's Cookies Mark McGwire

This special edition 4-card set features full-color glossy player photos by Barry Colla on standard-size (2-1/2" by 3-1/2") cards with rounded corners. Photos feature four different batting poses. Numbered flip sides, printed in purple and red, carry 1987 and 1988 statistics. Cards are individually cello-wrapped and inserted in Mother's Cookie Parade variety cookie bags.

		MT	NR MT	EX
Complete Set:		15.00	11.00	6.00
Common Player:		3.00	2.25	1.25
1	Mark McGwire (1 Of 4)	3.00	2.25	1.25
2	Mark McGwire (2 Of 4)	3.00	2.25	1.25
3	Mark McGwire (3 Of 4)	3.00	2.25	1.25
4	Mark McGwire (4 Of 4)	3.00	2.25	1.25

1969 Nabisco Team Flakes

Frank Robinson—OF
Baltimore Orioles

This set of cards is seen in two different sizes: 1-15/16" by 3" and 1-3/4" by 2-15/16". This is explained by the varying widths of the card borders on the backs of Nabisco cereal packages. Cards are action color photos bordered in yellow. Twenty-four of the top players in the game are included in the set, which was issued in three series of eight cards each. No team insignias are visible on any of the cards. Packages described the cards as "Mini Posters."

		NR MT	EX	VG
Complete Set:		400.00	200.00	120.00
Common Player:		4.00	2.00	1.25
(1)	Hank Aaron	45.00	22.00	13.50
(2)	Richie Allen	7.00	3.50	2.00
(3)	Lou Brock	25.00	12.50	7.50
(4)	Paul Casanova	4.00	2.00	1.25
(5)	Roberto Clemente	45.00	22.00	13.50
(6)	Al Ferrara	4.00	2.00	1.25
(7)	Bill Freehan	5.00	2.50	1.50
(8)	Jim Fregosi	5.00	2.50	1.50
(9)	Bob Gibson	20.00	10.00	6.00
(10)	Tony Horton	5.00	2.50	1.50
(11)	Tommy John	10.00	5.00	3.00
(12)	Al Kaline	25.00	12.50	7.50
(13)	Jim Lonborg	4.00	2.00	1.25
(14)	Juan Marichal	20.00	10.00	6.00
(15)	Willie Mays	45.00	22.00	13.50
(16)	Rick Monday	5.00	2.50	1.50
(17)	Tony Oliva	6.00	3.00	1.75
(18)	Brooks Robinson	30.00	15.00	9.00
(19)	Frank Robinson	25.00	12.50	7.50
(20)	Pete Rose	65.00	32.00	19.50
(21)	Ron Santo	6.00	3.00	1.75
(22)	Tom Seaver	35.00	17.50	10.50
(23)	Rusty Staub	6.00	3.00	1.75
(24)	Mel Stottlemyre	5.00	2.50	1.50

A player's name in *italic* type indicates a rookie card. An (FC) indicates a player's first card for that particular card company.

1986 National Photo Royals

(5) GEORGE BRETT, 3B

These 2-7/8" by 4-1/4" cards were a team issue produced in conjunction with National Photo. The 24- card set includes 21 players, manager Dick Howser, a card commemorating the Royals' 1985 World Championship and a discount offer card from National Photo. Card fronts feature full-color action photos with a blue "Kansas City Royals" at the top of each card. Each player's name, number and position are also included. Card backs list complete professional career statistics, along with the National Photo logo.

		MT	NR MT	EX
Complete Set:		10.00	7.50	4.00
Common Player:		.25	.20	.10
1	Buddy Biancalana	.25	.20	.10
3	Jorge Orta	.25	.20	.10
4	Greg Pryor	.25	.20	.10
5	George Brett	2.00	1.50	.80
6	Willie Wilson	.70	.50	.30
8	Jim Sundberg	.25	.20	.10
10	Dick Howser	.35	.25	.14
11	Hal McRae	.50	.40	.20
20	Frank White	.50	.40	.20
21	Lonnie Smith	.35	.25	.14
22	Dennis Leonard	.35	.25	.14
23	Mark Gubicza	.70	.50	.30
24	Darryl Motley	.25	.20	.10
25	Danny Jackson	.70	.50	.30
26	Steve Farr	.25	.20	.10
29	Dan Quisenberry	.50	.40	.20
31	Bret Saberhagen	1.00	.70	.40
35	Lynn Jones	.25	.20	.10
37	Charlie Leibrandt	.35	.25	.14
38	Mark Huismann	.25	.20	.10
40	Buddy Black	.35	.25	.14
45	Steve Balboni	.35	.25	.14
----	Header Card	.25	.20	.10
----	Discount Card	.25	.20	.10

1984 Nestle

The 792 cards in the 1984 Nestle set are identical to those in the 1984 Topps regular issue set except for the Nestle logo which replaces the Topps logo in the upper right corner of the card front. The set was issued by Nestle as six sheets (24" by 48" each) of 132 cards. A few enterprising dealers bought up the major portion of the 5,000 sheet sets that were supposedly issued and had them professionally cut into individual cards. Due to the ease in handling single cards, sets of individual cards have a greater value than complete sheet sets.

		MT	NR MT	EX
Complete Singles Set:		475.00	350.00	190.00
Common Single Player:		.20	.15	.08
Complete Sheet Set:		350.00	262.00	140.00
Sheet A:		200.00	150.00	80.00
Sheet B:		20.00	15.00	8.00
Sheet C:		20.00	15.00	8.00
Sheet D:		20.00	15.00	8.00
Sheet E:		20.00	15.00	8.00
Sheet F:		20.00	15.00	8.00
1	1983 Highlight (Steve Carlton)	1.75	1.25	.70
2	1983 Highlight (Rickey Henderson)	1.75	1.25	.70
3	1983 Highlight (Dan Quisenberry)	.30	.25	.12
4	1983 Highlight (Steve Carlton, Gaylord Perry, Nolan Ryan)	2.00	1.50	.80
5	1983 Highlight (Bob Forsch, Dave Righetti, Mike Warren)	.70	.50	.30
6	1983 Highlight (Johnny Bench, Gaylord Perry, Carl Yastrzemski)	2.00	1.50	.80
7	Gary Lucas	.20	.15	.08
8	Don Mattingly	275.00	200.00	100.00
9	Jim Gott	.20	.15	.08
10	Robin Yount	5.00	3.75	2.00
11	Twins Batting & Pitching Leaders (Kent Hrbek, Ken Schrom)	.70	.50	.30
12	Billy Sample	.20	.15	.08
13	Scott Holman	.20	.15	.08
14	Tom Brookens	.20	.15	.08
15	Burt Hooton	.30	.25	.12
16	Omar Moreno	.20	.15	.08
17	John Denny	.20	.15	.08
18	Dale Berra	.20	.15	.08
19	Ray Fontenot	.30	.25	.12
20	Greg Luzinski	.60	.45	.25
21	Joe Altobelli	.20	.15	.08
22	Bryan Clark	.20	.15	.08
23	Keith Moreland	.30	.25	.12
24	John Martin	.20	.15	.08
25	Glenn Hubbard	.30	.25	.12
26	Bud Black	.30	.25	.12
27	Daryl Sconiers	.20	.15	.08
28	Frank Viola	5.00	3.75	2.00
29	Danny Heep	.20	.15	.08
30	Wade Boggs	50.00	37.00	20.00
31	Andy McGaffigan	.20	.15	.08
32	Bobby Ramos	.20	.15	.08
33	Tom Burgmeier	.20	.15	.08
34	Eddie Milner	.20	.15	.08
35	Don Sutton	2.00	1.50	.80
36	Denny Walling	.20	.15	.08
37	Rangers Batting & Pitching Leaders (Buddy Bell, Rick Honeycutt)	.40	.30	.15
38	Luis DeLeon	.20	.15	.08
39	Garth Iorg	.20	.15	.08
40	Dusty Baker	.40	.30	.15
41	Tony Bernazard	.20	.15	.08
42	Johnny Grubb	.20	.15	.08
43	Ron Reed	.20	.15	.08
44	Jim Morrison	.20	.15	.08
45	Jerry Mumphrey	.20	.15	.08
46	Ray Smith	.20	.15	.08
47	Rudy Law	.20	.15	.08
48	Julio Franco	1.50	1.25	.60
49	John Stuper	.20	.15	.08
50	Chris Chambliss	.30	.25	.12
51	Jim Frey	.20	.15	.08
52	Paul Splittorff	.30	.25	.12
53	Juan Beniquez	.20	.15	.08
54	Jesse Orosco	.30	.25	.12
55	Dave Concepcion	.50	.40	.20
56	Gary Allenson	.20	.15	.08
57	Dan Schatzeder	.20	.15	.08
58	Max Venable	.20	.15	.08
59	Sammy Stewart	.20	.15	.08
60	Paul Molitor	1.25	.90	.50
61	Chris Codiroli	.30	.25	.12
62	Dave Hostetler	.20	.15	.08
63	Ed Vande Berg	.20	.15	.08

#	Player	MT	NR MT	EX
64	Mike Scioscia	.30	.25	.12
65	Kirk Gibson	4.00	3.00	1.50
66	Astros Batting & Pitching Leaders (Jose Cruz, Nolan Ryan)	1.00	.70	.40
67	Gary Ward	.30	.25	.12
68	Luis Salazar	.20	.15	.08
69	Rod Scurry	.20	.15	.08
70	Gary Matthews	.30	.25	.12
71	Leo Hernandez	.20	.15	.08
72	Mike Squires	.20	.15	.08
73	Jody Davis	.30	.25	.12
74	Jerry Martin	.20	.15	.08
75	Bob Forsch	.30	.25	.12
76	Alfredo Griffin	.30	.25	.12
77	Brett Butler	.30	.25	.12
78	Mike Torrez	.30	.25	.12
79	Rob Wilfong	.20	.15	.08
80	Steve Rogers	.30	.25	.12
81	Billy Martin	.50	.40	.20
82	Doug Bird	.20	.15	.08
83	Richie Zisk	.30	.25	.12
84	Lenny Faedo	.20	.15	.08
85	Atlee Hammaker	.20	.15	.08
86	John Shelby	1.00	.70	.40
87	Frank Pastore	.20	.15	.08
88	Rob Picciolo	.20	.15	.08
89	Mike Smithson	.20	.15	.08
90	Pedro Guerrero	3.50	2.75	1.50
91	Dan Spillner	.20	.15	.08
92	Lloyd Moseby	.40	.30	.15
93	Bob Knepper	.30	.25	.12
94	Mario Ramirez	.20	.15	.08
95	Aurelio Lopez	.20	.15	.08
96	Royals Batting & Pitching Leaders (Larry Gura, Hal McRae)	.40	.30	.15
97	LaMarr Hoyt	.20	.15	.08
98	Steve Nicosia	.20	.15	.08
99	Craig Lefferts	.70	.50	.30
100	Reggie Jackson	10.00	7.50	4.00
101	Porfirio Altamirano	.20	.15	.08
102	Ken Oberkfell	.20	.15	.08
103	Dwayne Murphy	.30	.25	.12
104	Ken Dayley	.30	.25	.12
105	Tony Armas	.30	.25	.12
106	Tim Stoddard	.20	.15	.08
107	Ned Yost	.20	.15	.08
108	Randy Moffitt	.20	.15	.08
109	Brad Wellman	.20	.15	.08
110	Ron Guidry	2.75	2.00	1.00
111	Bill Virdon	.30	.25	.12
112	Tom Niedenfuer	.30	.25	.12
113	Kelly Paris	.20	.15	.08
114	Checklist 1-132	.20	.15	.08
115	Andre Thornton	.30	.25	.12
116	George Bjorkman	.20	.15	.08
117	Tom Veryzer	.20	.15	.08
118	Charlie Hough	.30	.25	.12
119	Johnny Wockenfuss	.20	.15	.08
120	Keith Hernandez	5.00	3.75	2.00
121	Pat Sheridan	.70	.50	.30
122	Cecilio Guante	.30	.25	.12
123	Butch Wynegar	.30	.25	.12
124	Damaso Garcia	.20	.15	.08
125	Britt Burns	.20	.15	.08
126	Braves Batting & Pitching Leaders (Craig McMurtry, Dale Murphy)	1.25	.90	.50
127	Mike Madden	.20	.15	.08
128	Rick Manning	.20	.15	.08
129	Bill Laskey	.20	.15	.08
130	Ozzie Smith	2.00	1.50	.80
131	Batting Leaders (Wade Boggs, Bill Madlock)	2.50	2.00	1.00
132	Home Run Leaders (Jim Rice, Mike Schmidt)	2.00	1.50	.80
133	Runs Batted in Leaders (Cecil Cooper, Dale Murphy, Jim Rice)	2.00	1.50	.80
134	Stolen Base Leaders (Rickey Henderson, Tim Raines)	1.75	1.25	.70
135	Victory Leaders (John Denny, LaMarr Hoyt)	.30	.25	.12
136	Strikeout Leaders (Steve Carlton, Jack Morris)	1.00	.70	.40
137	Earned Run Average Leaders (Atlee Hammaker, Rick Honeycutt)	.30	.25	.12
138	Leading Firemen (Al Holland, Dan Quisenberry)	.30	.25	.12
139	Bert Campaneris	.40	.30	.15
140	Storm Davis	.50	.40	.20
141	Pat Corrales	.20	.15	.08
142	Rich Gale	.20	.15	.08
143	Jose Morales	.20	.15	.08
144	Brian Harper	.20	.15	.08
145	Gary Lavelle	.20	.15	.08
146	Ed Romero	.20	.15	.08
147	Dan Petry	.30	.25	.12
148	Joe Lefebvre	.20	.15	.08
149	Jon Matlack	.30	.25	.12
150	Dale Murphy	15.00	11.00	6.00
151	Steve Trout	.20	.15	.08
152	Glenn Brummer	.20	.15	.08
153	Dick Tidrow	.20	.15	.08
154	Dave Henderson	.40	.30	.15
155	Frank White	.40	.30	.15
156	Athletics Batting & Pitching Leaders (Tim Conroy, Rickey Henderson)	1.00	.70	.40
157	Gary Gaetti	2.50	2.00	1.00
158	John Curtis	.20	.15	.08
159	Darryl Cias	.20	.15	.08
160	Mario Soto	.30	.25	.12
161	Junior Ortiz	.20	.15	.08
162	Bob Ojeda	.40	.30	.15
163	Lorenzo Gray	.20	.15	.08
164	Scott Sanderson	.20	.15	.08
165	Ken Singleton	.40	.30	.15
166	Jamie Nelson	.20	.15	.08
167	Marshall Edwards	.20	.15	.08
168	Juan Bonilla	.20	.15	.08
169	Larry Parrish	.40	.30	.15
170	Jerry Reuss	.30	.25	.12
171	Frank Robinson	.40	.30	.15
172	Frank DiPino	.20	.15	.08
173	Marvell Wynne	.80	.60	.30
174	Juan Berenguer	.20	.15	.08
175	Graig Nettles	.80	.60	.30
176	Lee Smith	.60	.45	.25
177	Jerry Hairston	.20	.15	.08
178	Bill Krueger	.20	.15	.08
179	Buck Martinez	.20	.15	.08
180	Manny Trillo	.30	.25	.12
181	Roy Thomas	.20	.15	.08
182	Darryl Strawberry	60.00	45.00	24.00
183	Al Williams	.20	.15	.08
184	Mike O'Berry	.20	.15	.08
185	Sixto Lezcano	.20	.15	.08
186	Cardinals Batting & Pitching Leaders (Lonnie Smith, John Stuper)	.20	.15	.08
187	Luis Aponte	.20	.15	.08
188	Bryan Little	.20	.15	.08
189	Tim Conroy	.30	.25	.12
190	Ben Oglivie	.30	.25	.12
191	Mike Boddicker	.30	.25	.12
192	Nick Esasky	1.25	.90	.50
193	Darrell Brown	.20	.15	.08
194	Domingo Ramos	.20	.15	.08
195	Jack Morris	3.50	2.75	1.50
196	Don Slaught	.40	.30	.15
197	Gary Hancock	.20	.15	.08
198	Bill Doran	1.50	1.25	.60
199	Willie Hernandez	.30	.25	.12
200	Andre Dawson	4.50	3.50	1.75
201	Bruce Kison	.20	.15	.08
202	Bobby Cox	.20	.15	.08
203	Matt Keough	.20	.15	.08
204	Bobby Meacham	.40	.30	.15
205	Greg Minton	.20	.15	.08
206	Andy Van Slyke	5.00	3.75	2.00
207	Donnie Moore	.20	.15	.08
208	Jose Oquendo	.20	.15	.08
209	Manny Sarmiento	.20	.15	.08
210	Joe Morgan	3.00	2.25	1.25
211	Rick Sweet	.20	.15	.08
212	Broderick Perkins	.20	.15	.08
213	Bruce Hurst	.60	.45	.25
214	Paul Householder	.20	.15	.08
215	Tippy Martinez	.20	.15	.08
216	White Sox Batting & Pitching Leaders (Richard Dotson, Carlton Fisk)	.40	.30	.15
217	Alan Ashby	.20	.15	.08
218	Rick Waits	.20	.15	.08
219	Joe Simpson	.20	.15	.08
220	Fernando Valenzuela	5.00	3.75	2.00
221	Cliff Johnson	.20	.15	.08
222	Rick Honeycutt	.20	.15	.08
223	Wayne Krenchicki	.20	.15	.08
224	Sid Monge	.20	.15	.08
225	Lee Mazzilli	.30	.25	.12
226	Juan Eichelberger	.20	.15	.08
227	Steve Braun	.20	.15	.08
228	John Rabb	.20	.15	.08
229	Paul Owens	.20	.15	.08
230	Rickey Henderson	10.00	7.50	4.00
231	Gary Woods	.20	.15	.08

		MT	NR MT	EX
232	Tim Wallach	.70	.50	.30
233	Checklist 133-264	.20	.15	.08
234	Rafael Ramirez	.20	.15	.08
235	Matt Young	.40	.30	.15
236	Ellis Valentine	.20	.15	.08
237	John Castino	.20	.15	.08
238	Reid Nichols	.20	.15	.08
239	Jay Howell	.30	.25	.12
240	Eddie Murray	8.00	6.00	3.25
241	Billy Almon	.20	.15	.08
242	Alex Trevino	.20	.15	.08
243	Pete Ladd	.20	.15	.08
244	Candy Maldonado	.60	.45	.25
245	Rick Sutcliffe	.70	.50	.30
246	Mets Batting & Pitching Leaders (Tom Seaver, Mookie Wilson)	.70	.50	.30
247	Onix Concepcion	.20	.15	.08
248	Bill Dawley	.20	.15	.08
249	Jay Johnstone	.30	.25	.12
250	Bill Madlock	.60	.45	.25
251	Tony Gwynn	12.00	9.00	4.75
252	Larry Christenson	.20	.15	.08
253	Jim Wohlford	.20	.15	.08
254	Shane Rawley	.30	.25	.12
255	Bruce Benedict	.20	.15	.08
256	Dave Geisel	.20	.15	.08
257	Julio Cruz	.20	.15	.08
258	Luis Sanchez	.20	.15	.08
259	Sparky Anderson	.30	.25	.12
260	Scott McGregor	.30	.25	.12
261	Bobby Brown	.20	.15	.08
262	Tom Candiotti	.80	.60	.30
263	Jack Fimple	.20	.15	.08
264	Doug Frobel	.20	.15	.08
265	Donnie Hill	.20	.15	.08
266	Steve Lubratich	.20	.15	.08
267	Carmelo Martinez	.60	.45	.25
268	Jack O'Connor	.20	.15	.08
269	Aurelio Rodriguez	.30	.25	.12
270	Jeff Russell	.40	.30	.15
271	Moose Haas	.20	.15	.08
272	Rick Dempsey	.30	.25	.12
273	Charlie Puleo	.20	.15	.08
274	Rick Monday	.30	.25	.12
275	Len Matuszek	.20	.15	.08
276	Angels Batting & Pitching Leaders (Rod Carew, Geoff Zahn)	.70	.50	.30
277	Eddie Whitson	.20	.15	.08
278	Jorge Bell	6.00	4.50	2.50
279	Ivan DeJesus	.20	.15	.08
280	Floyd Bannister	.30	.25	.12
281	Larry Milbourne	.20	.15	.08
282	Jim Barr	.20	.15	.08
283	Larry Biittner	.20	.15	.08
284	Howard Bailey	.20	.15	.08
285	Darrell Porter	.30	.25	.12
286	Lary Sorensen	.20	.15	.08
287	Warren Cromartie	.20	.15	.08
288	Jim Beattie	.20	.15	.08
289	Randy Johnson	.20	.15	.08
290	Dave Dravecky	.30	.25	.12
291	Chuck Tanner	.30	.25	.12
292	Tony Scott	.20	.15	.08
293	Ed Lynch	.20	.15	.08
294	U.L. Washington	.20	.15	.08
295	Mike Flanagan	.30	.25	.12
296	Jeff Newman	.20	.15	.08
297	Bruce Berenyi	.20	.15	.08
298	Jim Gantner	.30	.25	.12
299	John Butcher	.20	.15	.08
300	Pete Rose	25.00	18.50	10.00
301	Frank LaCorte	.20	.15	.08
302	Barry Bonnell	.20	.15	.08
303	Marty Castillo	.20	.15	.08
304	Warren Brusstar	.20	.15	.08
305	Roy Smalley	.20	.15	.08
306	Dodgers Batting & Pitching Leaders (Pedro Guerrero, Bob Welch)	.60	.45	.25
307	Bobby Mitchell	.20	.15	.08
308	Ron Hassey	.20	.15	.08
309	Tony Phillips	.30	.25	.12
310	Willie McGee	3.00	2.25	1.25
311	Jerry Koosman	.40	.30	.15
312	Jorge Orta	.20	.15	.08
313	Mike Jorgensen	.20	.15	.08
314	Orlando Mercado	.20	.15	.08
315	Bob Grich	.30	.25	.12
316	Mark Bradley	.20	.15	.08
317	Greg Pryor	.20	.15	.08
318	Bill Gullickson	.20	.15	.08
319	Al Bumbry	.20	.15	.08

		MT	NR MT	EX
320	Bob Stanley	.20	.15	.08
321	Harvey Kuenn	.20	.15	.08
322	Ken Schrom	.20	.15	.08
323	Alan Knicely	.20	.15	.08
324	Alejandro Pena	.80	.60	.30
325	Darrell Evans	.40	.30	.15
326	Bob Kearney	.20	.15	.08
327	Ruppert Jones	.20	.15	.08
328	Vern Ruhle	.20	.15	.08
329	Pat Tabler	.50	.40	.20
330	John Candelaria	.40	.30	.15
331	Bucky Dent	.30	.25	.12
332	Kevin Gross	1.00	.70	.40
333	Larry Herndon	.20	.15	.08
334	Chuck Rainey	.20	.15	.08
335	Don Baylor	.50	.40	.20
336	Mariners Batting & Pitching Leaders (Pat Putnam, Matt Young)	.20	.15	.08
337	Kevin Hagen	.20	.15	.08
338	Mike Warren	.20	.15	.08
339	Roy Lee Jackson	.20	.15	.08
340	Hal McRae	.40	.30	.15
341	Dave Tobik	.20	.15	.08
342	Tim Foli	.20	.15	.08
343	Mark Davis	.20	.15	.08
344	Rick Miller	.20	.15	.08
345	Kent Hrbek	4.00	3.00	1.50
346	Kurt Bevacqua	.20	.15	.08
347	Allan Ramirez	.20	.15	.08
348	Toby Harrah	.30	.25	.12
349	Bob Gibson	.20	.15	.08
350	George Foster	.80	.60	.30
351	Russ Nixon	.20	.15	.08
352	Dave Stewart	.60	.45	.25
353	Jim Anderson	.20	.15	.08
354	Jeff Burroughs	.20	.15	.08
355	Jason Thompson	.20	.15	.08
356	Glenn Abbott	.20	.15	.08
357	Ron Cey	.40	.30	.15
358	Bob Dernier	.20	.15	.08
359	Jim Acker	.30	.25	.12
360	Willie Randolph	.50	.40	.20
361	Dave Smith	.30	.25	.12
362	David Green	.20	.15	.08
363	Tim Laudner	.20	.15	.08
364	Scott Fletcher	.40	.30	.15
365	Steve Bedrosian	.40	.30	.15
366	Padres Batting & Pitching Leaders (Dave Dravecky, Terry Kennedy)	.20	.15	.08
367	Jamie Easterly	.20	.15	.08
368	Hubie Brooks	.30	.25	.12
369	Steve McCatty	.20	.15	.08
370	Tim Raines	5.00	3.75	2.00
371	Dave Gumpert	.20	.15	.08
372	Gary Roenicke	.20	.15	.08
373	Bill Scherrer	.20	.15	.08
374	Don Money	.20	.15	.08
375	Dennis Leonard	.30	.25	.12
376	Dave Anderson	.30	.25	.12
377	Danny Darwin	.30	.25	.12
378	Bob Brenly	.20	.15	.08
379	Checklist 265-396	.20	.15	.08
380	Steve Garvey	8.00	6.00	3.25
381	Ralph Houk	.20	.15	.08
382	Chris Nyman	.20	.15	.08
383	Terry Puhl	.20	.15	.08
384	Lee Tunnell	.20	.15	.08
385	Tony Perez	1.00	.70	.40
386	George Hendrick AS	.30	.25	.12
387	Johnny Ray AS	.30	.25	.12
388	Mike Schmidt AS	3.00	2.25	1.25
389	Ozzie Smith AS	1.25	.90	.50
390	Tim Raines AS	2.00	1.50	.80
391	Dale Murphy AS	3.00	2.25	1.25
392	Andre Dawson AS	1.75	1.25	.70
393	Gary Carter AS	2.00	1.50	.80
394	Steve Rogers AS	.30	.25	.12
395	Steve Carlton AS	2.00	1.50	.80
396	Jesse Orosco AS	.30	.25	.12
397	Eddie Murray AS	2.50	2.00	1.00
398	Lou Whitaker AS	1.25	.90	.50
399	George Brett AS	3.00	2.25	1.25
400	Cal Ripken AS	2.75	2.00	1.00
401	Jim Rice AS	2.00	1.50	.80
402	Dave Winfield AS	2.50	2.00	1.00
403	Lloyd Moseby AS	.30	.25	.12
404	Ted Simmons AS	.40	.30	.15
405	LaMarr Hoyt AS	.30	.25	.12
406	Ron Guidry AS	1.25	.90	.50
407	Dan Quisenberry AS	.30	.25	.12
408	Lou Piniella	.80	.60	.30

	MT	NR MT	EX
409 Juan Agosto	.40	.30	.15
410 Claudell Washington	.30	.25	.12
411 Houston Jimenez	.20	.15	.08
412 Doug Rader	.20	.15	.08
413 Spike Owen	.30	.25	.12
414 Mitchell Page	.20	.15	.08
415 Tommy John	1.25	.90	.50
416 Dane Iorg	.20	.15	.08
417 Mike Armstrong	.20	.15	.08
418 Ron Hodges	.20	.15	.08
419 John Henry Johnson	.20	.15	.08
420 Cecil Cooper	.60	.45	.25
421 Charlie Lea	.20	.15	.08
422 Jose Cruz	.30	.25	.12
423 Mike Morgan	.20	.15	.08
424 Dann Bilardello	.20	.15	.08
425 Steve Howe	.30	.25	.12
426 Orioles Batting & Pitching Leaders (Mike Boddicker, Cal Ripken)	.90	.70	.35
427 Rick Leach	.20	.15	.08
428 Fred Breining	.20	.15	.08
429 Randy Bush	.20	.15	.08
430 Rusty Staub	.50	.40	.20
431 Chris Bando	.20	.15	.08
432 Charlie Hudson	.80	.60	.30
433 Rich Hebner	.20	.15	.08
434 Harold Baines	1.75	1.25	.70
435 Neil Allen	.20	.15	.08
436 Rick Peters	.20	.15	.08
437 Mike Proly	.20	.15	.08
438 Biff Pocoroba	.20	.15	.08
439 Bob Stoddard	.20	.15	.08
440 Steve Kemp	.30	.25	.12
441 Bob Lillis	.20	.15	.08
442 Byron McLaughlin	.20	.15	.08
443 Benny Ayala	.20	.15	.08
444 Steve Renko	.20	.15	.08
445 Jerry Remy	.20	.15	.08
446 Luis Pujols	.20	.15	.08
447 Tom Brunansky	1.25	.90	.50
448 Ben Hayes	.20	.15	.08
449 Joe Pettini	.20	.15	.08
450 Gary Carter	6.00	4.50	2.50
451 Bob Jones	.20	.15	.08
452 Chuck Porter	.20	.15	.08
453 Willie Upshaw	.30	.25	.12
454 Joe Beckwith	.20	.15	.08
455 Terry Kennedy	.30	.25	.12
456 Cubs Batting & Pitching Leaders (Keith Moreland, Fergie Jenkins)	.50	.40	.20
457 Dave Rozema	.20	.15	.08
458 Kiko Garcia	.20	.15	.08
459 Kevin Hickey	.20	.15	.08
460 Dave Winfield	6.00	4.50	2.50
461 Jim Maler	.20	.15	.08
462 Lee Lacy	.20	.15	.08
463 Dave Engle	.20	.15	.08
464 Jeff Jones	.20	.15	.08
465 Mookie Wilson	.30	.25	.12
466 Gene Garber	.20	.15	.08
467 Mike Ramsey	.20	.15	.08
468 Geoff Zahn	.20	.15	.08
469 Tom O'Malley	.20	.15	.08
470 Nolan Ryan	6.00	4.50	2.50
471 Dick Howser	.30	.25	.12
472 Mike Brown	.20	.15	.08
473 Jim Dwyer	.20	.15	.08
474 Greg Bargar	.20	.15	.08
475 Gary Redus	.80	.60	.30
476 Tom Tellmann	.20	.15	.08
477 Rafael Landestoy	.20	.15	.08
478 Alan Bannister	.20	.15	.08
479 Frank Tanana	.30	.25	.12
480 Ron Kittle	.80	.60	.30
481 Mark Thurmond	.30	.25	.12
482 Enos Cabell	.20	.15	.08
483 Fergie Jenkins	1.75	1.25	.70
484 Ozzie Virgil	.20	.15	.08
485 Rick Rhoden	.40	.30	.15
486 Yankees Batting & Pitching Leaders (Don Baylor, Ron Guidry)	.60	.45	.25
487 Ricky Adams	.20	.15	.08
488 Jesse Barfield	1.50	1.25	.60
489 Dave Von Ohien	.20	.15	.08
490 Cal Ripken	9.00	6.75	3.50
491 Bobby Castillo	.20	.15	.08
492 Tucker Ashford	.20	.15	.08
493 Mike Norris	.20	.15	.08
494 Chili Davis	.30	.25	.12
495 Rollie Fingers	2.50	2.00	1.00
496 Terry Francona	.20	.15	.08
497 Bud Anderson	.20	.15	.08
498 Rich Gedman	.30	.25	.12
499 Mike Witt	.70	.50	.30
500 George Brett	15.00	11.00	6.00
501 Steve Henderson	.20	.15	.08
502 Joe Torre	.30	.25	.12
503 Elias Sosa	.20	.15	.08
504 Mickey Rivers	.20	.15	.08
505 Pete Vuckovich	.20	.15	.08
506 Ernie Whitt	.20	.15	.08
507 Mike LaCoss	.20	.15	.08
508 Mel Hall	.30	.25	.12
509 Brad Havens	.20	.15	.08
510 Alan Trammell	5.00	3.75	2.00
511 Marty Bystrom	.20	.15	.08
512 Oscar Gamble	.20	.15	.08
513 Dave Beard	.20	.15	.08
514 Floyd Rayford	.20	.15	.08
515 Gorman Thomas	.30	.25	.12
516 Expos Batting & Pitching Leaders (Charlie Lea, Al Oliver)	.20	.15	.08
517 John Moses	.20	.15	.08
518 Greg Walker	1.25	.90	.50
519 Ron Davis	.20	.15	.08
520 Bob Boone	.30	.25	.12
521 Pete Falcone	.20	.15	.08
522 Dave Bergman	.20	.15	.08
523 Glenn Hoffman	.20	.15	.08
524 Carlos Diaz	.20	.15	.08
525 Willie Wilson	.60	.45	.25
526 Ron Oester	.20	.15	.08
527 Checklist 397-528	.20	.15	.08
528 Mark Brouhard	.20	.15	.08
529 Keith Atherton	.60	.45	.25
530 Dan Ford	.20	.15	.08
531 Steve Boros	.20	.15	.08
532 Eric Show	.40	.30	.15
533 Ken Landreaux	.20	.15	.08
534 Pete O'Brien	1.50	1.25	.60
535 Bo Diaz	.30	.25	.12
536 Doug Bair	.20	.15	.08
537 Johnny Ray	.40	.30	.15
538 Kevin Bass	.40	.30	.15
539 George Frazier	.20	.15	.08
540 George Hendrick	.30	.25	.12
541 Dennis Lamp	.20	.15	.08
542 Duane Kuiper	.20	.15	.08
543 Craig McMurtry	.40	.30	.15
544 Cesar Geronimo	.20	.15	.08
545 Bill Buckner	.60	.45	.25
546 Indians Batting & Pitching Leaders (Mike Hargrove, Lary Sorensen)	.20	.15	.08
547 Mike Moore	.20	.15	.08
548 Ron Jackson	.20	.15	.08
549 Walt Terrell	1.00	.70	.40
550 Jim Rice	6.00	4.50	2.50
551 Scott Ullger	.20	.15	.08
552 Ray Burris	.20	.15	.08
553 Joe Nolan	.20	.15	.08
554 Ted Power	.30	.25	.12
555 Greg Brock	.50	.40	.20
556 Joey McLaughlin	.20	.15	.08
557 Wayne Tolleson	.20	.15	.08
558 Mike Davis	.30	.25	.12
559 Mike Scott	1.50	1.25	.60
560 Carlton Fisk	2.00	1.50	.80
561 Whitey Herzog	.30	.25	.12
562 Manny Castillo	.20	.15	.08
563 Glenn Wilson	.30	.25	.12
564 Al Holland	.20	.15	.08
565 Leon Durham	.30	.25	.12
566 Jim Bibby	.20	.15	.08
567 Mike Heath	.20	.15	.08
568 Pete Filson	.20	.15	.08
569 Bake McBride	.20	.15	.08
570 Dan Quisenberry	.40	.30	.15
571 Bruce Bochy	.20	.15	.08
572 Jerry Royster	.20	.15	.08
573 Dave Kingman	.80	.60	.30
574 Brian Downing	.30	.25	.12
575 Jim Clancy	.30	.25	.12
576 Giants Batting & Pitching Leaders (Atlee Hammaker, Jeff Leonard)	.20	.15	.08
577 Mark Clear	.20	.15	.08
578 Lenn Sakata	.20	.15	.08
579 Bob James	.20	.15	.08
580 Lonnie Smith	.30	.25	.12
581 Jose DeLeon	1.00	.70	.40
582 Bob McClure	.20	.15	.08
583 Derrel Thomas	.20	.15	.08
584 Dave Schmidt	.20	.15	.08

No.	Name	MT	NR MT	EX
585	Dan Driessen	.30	.25	.12
586	Joe Niekro	.40	.30	.15
587	Von Hayes	.40	.30	.15
588	Milt Wilcox	.20	.15	.08
589	Mike Easler	.30	.25	.12
590	Dave Stieb	.50	.40	.20
591	Tony LaRussa	.30	.25	.12
592	Andre Robertson	.20	.15	.08
593	Jeff Lahti	.20	.15	.08
594	Gene Richards	.20	.15	.08
595	Jeff Reardon	.50	.40	.20
596	Ryne Sandberg	12.00	9.00	4.75
597	Rick Camp	.20	.15	.08
598	Rusty Kuntz	.20	.15	.08
599	Doug Sisk	.20	.15	.08
600	Rod Carew	7.00	5.25	2.75
601	John Tudor	.60	.45	.25
602	John Wathan	.30	.25	.12
603	Renie Martin	.20	.15	.08
604	John Lowenstein	.20	.15	.08
605	Mike Caldwell	.20	.15	.08
606	Blue Jays Batting & Pitching Leaders (Lloyd Moseby, Dave Stieb)	.40	.30	.15
607	Tom Hume	.20	.15	.08
608	Bobby Johnson	.20	.15	.08
609	Dan Meyer	.20	.15	.08
610	Steve Sax	2.50	2.00	1.00
611	Chet Lemon	.30	.25	.12
612	Harry Spilman	.20	.15	.08
613	Greg Gross	.20	.15	.08
614	Len Barker	.20	.15	.08
615	Garry Templeton	.30	.25	.12
616	Don Robinson	.20	.15	.08
617	Rick Cerone	.20	.15	.08
618	Dickie Noles	.20	.15	.08
619	Jerry Dybzinski	.20	.15	.08
620	Al Oliver	.70	.50	.30
621	Frank Howard	.30	.25	.12
622	Al Cowens	.20	.15	.08
623	Ron Washington	.20	.15	.08
624	Terry Harper	.20	.15	.08
625	Larry Gura	.20	.15	.08
626	Bob Clark	.20	.15	.08
627	Dave LaPoint	.40	.30	.15
628	Ed Jurak	.20	.15	.08
629	Rick Langford	.20	.15	.08
630	Ted Simmons	.80	.60	.30
631	Denny Martinez	.30	.25	.12
632	Tom Foley	.20	.15	.08
633	Mike Krukow	.30	.25	.12
634	Mike Marshall	1.50	1.25	.60
635	Dave Righetti	2.75	2.00	1.00
636	Pat Putnam	.20	.15	.08
637	Phillies Batting & Pitching Leaders (John Denny, Gary Matthews)	.20	.15	.08
638	George Vukovich	.20	.15	.08
639	Rick Lysander	.20	.15	.08
640	Lance Parrish	3.00	2.25	1.25
641	Mike Richardt	.20	.15	.08
642	Tom Underwood	.20	.15	.08
643	Mike Brown	.20	.15	.08
644	Tim Lollar	.20	.15	.08
645	Tony Pena	.40	.30	.15
646	Checklist 529-660	.20	.15	.08
647	Ron Roenicke	.20	.15	.08
648	Len Whitehouse	.20	.15	.08
649	Tom Herr	.40	.30	.15
650	Phil Niekro	2.75	2.00	1.00
651	John McNamara	.20	.15	.08
652	Rudy May	.20	.15	.08
653	Dave Stapleton	.20	.15	.08
654	Bob Bailor	.20	.15	.08
655	Amos Otis	.30	.25	.12
656	Bryn Smith	.20	.15	.08
657	Thad Bosley	.20	.15	.08
658	Jerry Augustine	.20	.15	.08
659	Duane Walker	.20	.15	.08
660	Ray Knight	.30	.25	.12
661	Steve Yeager	.20	.15	.08
662	Tom Brennan	.20	.15	.08
663	Johnnie LeMaster	.20	.15	.08
664	Dave Stegman	.20	.15	.08
665	Buddy Bell	.40	.30	.15
666	Tigers Batting & Pitching Leaders (Jack Morris, Lou Whitaker)	.70	.50	.30
667	Vance Law	.30	.25	.12
668	Larry McWilliams	.20	.15	.08
669	Dave Lopes	.20	.15	.08
670	Rich Gossage	2.00	1.50	.80
671	Jamie Quirk	.20	.15	.08
672	Ricky Nelson	.20	.15	.08
673	Mike Walters	.20	.15	.08
674	Tim Flannery	.20	.15	.08
675	Pascual Perez	.30	.25	.12
676	Brian Giles	.20	.15	.08
677	Doyle Alexander	.30	.25	.12
678	Chris Speier	.20	.15	.08
679	Art Howe	.20	.15	.08
680	Fred Lynn	2.25	1.75	.90
681	Tom Lasorda	.40	.30	.15
682	Dan Morogiello	.20	.15	.08
683	Marty Barrett	2.00	1.50	.80
684	Bob Shirley	.20	.15	.08
685	Willie Aikens	.20	.15	.08
686	Joe Price	.20	.15	.08
687	Roy Howell	.20	.15	.08
688	George Wright	.20	.15	.08
689	Mike Fischlin	.20	.15	.08
690	Jack Clark	3.50	2.75	1.50
691	Steve Lake	.20	.15	.08
692	Dickie Thon	.30	.25	.12
693	Alan Wiggins	.20	.15	.08
694	Mike Stanton	.20	.15	.08
695	Lou Whitaker	3.00	2.25	1.25
696	Pirates Batting & Pitching Leaders (Bill Madlock, Rick Rhoden)	.50	.40	.20
697	Dale Murray	.20	.15	.08
698	Marc Hill	.20	.15	.08
699	Dave Rucker	.20	.15	.08
700	Mike Schmidt	18.00	13.50	7.25
701	NL Active Career Batting Leaders (Bill Madlock, Dave Parker, Pete Rose)	2.00	1.50	.80
702	NL Active Career Hit Leaders (Tony Perez, Pete Rose, Rusty Staub)	2.00	1.50	.80
703	NL Active Career Home Run Leaders (Dave Kingman, Tony Perez, Mike Schmidt)	2.00	1.50	.80
704	NL Active Career RBI Leaders (Al Oliver, Tony Perez, Rusty Staub)	.60	.45	.25
705	NL Active Career Stolen Bases Leaders (Larry Bowa, Cesar Cedeno, Joe Morgan)	.70	.50	.30
706	NL Active Career Victory Leaders (Steve Carlton, Fergie Jenkins, Tom Seaver)	1.75	1.25	.70
707	NL Active Career Strikeout Leaders (Steve Carlton, Nolan Ryan, Tom Seaver)	2.00	1.50	.80
708	NL Active Career ERA Leaders (Steve Carlton, Steve Rogers, Tom Seaver)	1.75	1.25	.70
709	NL Active Career Save Leaders (Gene Garber, Tug McGraw, Bruce Sutter)	.50	.40	.20
710	AL Active Career Batting Leaders (George Brett, Rod Carew, Cecil Cooper)	2.00	1.50	.80
711	AL Active Career Hit Leaders (Bert Campaneris, Rod Carew, Reggie Jackson)	1.75	1.25	.70
712	AL Active Career Home Run Leaders (Reggie Jackson, Greg Luzinski, Graig Nettles)	1.50	1.25	.60
713	AL Active Career RBI Leaders (Reggie Jackson, Graig Nettles, Ted Simmons)	1.50	1.25	.60
714	AL Active Career Stolen Bases Leaders (Bert Campaneris, Dave Lopes, Omar Moreno)	.40	.30	.15
715	AL Active Career Victory Leaders (Tommy John, Jim Palmer, Don Sutton)	1.25	.90	.50
716	AL Active Career Strikeout Leaders (Bert Blyleven, Jerry Koosman, Don Sutton)	.70	.50	.30
717	AL Active Career ERA Leaders (Rollie Fingers, Ron Guidry, Jim Palmer)	1.25	.90	.50
718	AL Active Career Save Leaders (Rollie Fingers, Rich Gossage, Dan Quisenberry)	.90	.70	.35
719	Andy Hassler	.20	.15	.08
720	Dwight Evans	.80	.60	.30
721	Del Crandall	.20	.15	.08
722	Bob Welch	.40	.30	.15
723	Rich Dauer	.20	.15	.08
724	Eric Rasmussen	.20	.15	.08
725	Cesar Cedeno	.30	.25	.12
726	Brewers Batting & Pitching Leaders (Moose Haas, Ted Simmons)	.30	.25	.12
727	Joel Youngblood	.20	.15	.08
728	Tug McGraw	.30	.25	.12
729	Gene Tenace	.30	.25	.12
730	Bruce Sutter	1.25	.90	.50
731	Lynn Jones	.20	.15	.08
732	Terry Crowley	.20	.15	.08
733	Dave Collins	.30	.25	.12
734	Odell Jones	.20	.15	.08
735	Rick Burleson	.30	.25	.12

		MT	NR MT	EX
736	Dick Ruthven	.20	.15	.08
737	Jim Essian	.20	.15	.08
738	Bill Schroeder	.60	.45	.25
739	Bob Watson	.30	.25	.12
740	Tom Seaver	7.00	5.25	2.75
741	Wayne Gross	.20	.15	.08
742	Dick Williams	.20	.15	.08
743	Don Hood	.20	.15	.08
744	Jamie Allen	.20	.15	.08
745	Dennis Eckersley	.50	.40	.20
746	Mickey Hatcher	.20	.15	.08
747	Pat Zachry	.20	.15	.08
748	Jeff Leonard	.30	.25	.12
749	Doug Flynn	.20	.15	.08
750	Jim Palmer	5.00	3.75	2.00
751	Charlie Moore	.20	.15	.08
752	Phil Garner	.30	.25	.12
753	Doug Gwosdz	.20	.15	.08
754	Kent Tekulve	.30	.25	.12
755	Garry Maddox	.30	.25	.12
756	Reds Batting & Pitching Leaders (Ron Oester, Mario Soto)	.20	.15	.08
757	Larry Bowa	.40	.30	.15
758	Bill Stein	.20	.15	.08
759	Richard Dotson	.40	.30	.15
760	Bob Horner	.80	.60	.30
761	John Montefusco	.20	.15	.08
762	Rance Mulliniks	.20	.15	.08
763	Craig Swan	.20	.15	.08
764	Mike Hargrove	.20	.15	.08
765	Ken Forsch	.20	.15	.08
766	Mike Vail	.20	.15	.08
767	Carney Lansford	.40	.30	.15
768	Champ Summers	.20	.15	.08
769	Bill Caudill	.20	.15	.08
770	Ken Griffey	.30	.25	.12
771	Billy Gardner	.20	.15	.08
772	Jim Slaton	.20	.15	.08
773	Todd Cruz	.20	.15	.08
774	Tom Gorman	.20	.15	.08
775	Dave Parker	1.75	1.25	.70
776	Craig Reynolds	.20	.15	.08
777	Tom Paciorek	.20	.15	.08
778	Andy Hawkins	.80	.60	.30
779	Jim Sundberg	.20	.15	.08
780	Steve Carlton	6.00	4.50	2.50
781	Checklist 661-792	.20	.15	.08
782	Steve Balboni	.30	.25	.12
783	Luis Leal	.20	.15	.08
784	Leon Roberts	.20	.15	.08
785	Joaquin Andujar	.30	.25	.12
786	Red Sox Batting & Pitching Leaders (Wade Boggs, Bob Ojeda)	1.25	.90	.50
787	Bill Campbell	.20	.15	.08
788	Milt May	.20	.15	.08
789	Bert Blyleven	1.25	.90	.50
790	Doug DeCinces	.30	.25	.12
791	Terry Forster	.30	.25	.12
792	Bill Russell	.30	.25	.12

1984 Nestle Dream Team

This set was issued by the Nestle candy company in conjunction with Topps. Cards are in standard 2-1/2" by 3-1/2" size and feature the top 22 players of 1984, 11 from each league. This full-color "Dream Team" includes one player at each position, plus right- and left-handed starting pitchers and one reliever. Card fronts have a Nestle logo in the upper-right corner and card backs have the candy

company logo in the upper left. An unnumbered checklist was included with the set.

		MT	NR MT	EX
Complete Set:		20.00	15.00	8.00
Common Player:		.60	.45	.25
1	Eddie Murray	1.75	1.25	.70
2	Lou Whitaker	1.00	.70	.40
3	George Brett	2.25	1.75	.90
4	Cal Ripken	2.00	1.50	.80
5	Jim Rice	1.25	.90	.50
6	Dave Winfield	1.50	1.25	.60
7	Lloyd Moseby	.60	.45	.25
8	Lance Parrish	1.00	.70	.40
9	LaMarr Hoyt	.60	.45	.25
10	Ron Guidry	.80	.60	.30
11	Dan Quisenberry	.60	.45	.25
12	Steve Garvey	1.50	1.25	.60
13	Johnny Ray	.60	.45	.25
14	Mike Schmidt	2.25	1.75	.90
15	Ozzie Smith	.80	.60	.30
16	Andre Dawson	1.00	.70	.40
17	Tim Raines	1.50	1.25	.60
18	Dale Murphy	2.25	1.75	.90
19	Tony Pena	.60	.45	.25
20	John Denny	.60	.45	.25
21	Steve Carlton	1.25	.90	.50
22	Al Holland	.60	.45	.25
----	Checklist	.30	.25	.12

1987 Nestle

Nestle, in conjunction with Topps, issued a 33-card set in 1987. Card #'s 1-11 feature black and white photos of players from the "Golden Era." Cards #'s 12-33 features full-color photos of American (12-22.00 and National League (23-33.00 players from the "Modern Era" of baseball. Interestingly, the Feller card is not a photo but rather a color rendering of his 1953 Topps card. The cards measure 2-1/2" by 3-1/2" and have all team emblems airbrushed away. Three cards were inserted in specially marked six-packs of various Nestle candy bars. Two complete sets were available through a mail-in offer for $1.50 and three proof of purchase seals.

		MT	NR MT	EX
Complete Set:		8.00	6.00	3.25
Common Player:		.12	.09	.05
1	Lou Gehrig	.50	.40	.20
2	Rogers Hornsby	.25	.20	.10
3	Pie Traynor	.12	.09	.05
4	Honus Wagner	.30	.25	.12
5	Babe Ruth	.80	.60	.30
6	Tris Speaker	.20	.15	.08
7	Ty Cobb	.60	.45	.25
8	Mickey Cochrane	.12	.09	.05
9	Walter Johnson	.30	.25	.12
10	Carl Hubbell	.12	.09	.05
11	Jimmie Foxx	.25	.20	.10
12	Rod Carew	.30	.25	.12
13	Nellie Fox	.12	.09	.05
14	Brooks Robinson	.30	.25	.12
15	Luis Aparicio	.12	.09	.05

		MT	NR MT	EX
16	Frank Robinson	.20	.15	.08
17	Mickey Mantle	1.00	.70	.40
18	Ted Williams	.50	.40	.20
19	Yogi Berra	.30	.25	.12
20	Bob Feller	.25	.20	.10
21	Whitey Ford	.25	.20	.10
22	Harmon Killebrew	.20	.15	.08
23	Stan Musial	.50	.40	.20
24	Jackie Robinson	.40	.30	.15
25	Eddie Mathews	.20	.15	.08
26	Ernie Banks	.20	.15	.08
27	Roberto Clemente	.40	.30	.15
28	Willie Mays	.50	.40	.20
29	Hank Aaron	.50	.40	.20
30	Johnny Bench	.30	.25	.12
31	Bob Gibson	.20	.15	.08
32	Warren Spahn	.20	.15	.08
33	Duke Snider	.25	.20	.10

		MT	NR MT	EX
24	Pedro Guerrero	.35	.25	.14
25	Steve Bedrosian	.25	.20	.10
26	Gary Carter	.50	.40	.20
27	Jeff Reardon	.25	.20	.10
28	Dave Righetti	.35	.25	.14
29	Frank White	.25	.20	.10
30	Buddy Bell	.25	.20	.10
31	Tim Raines	.50	.40	.20
32	Wade Boggs	1.00	.70	.40
33	Dave Winfield	.50	.40	.20
34	George Bell	.40	.30	.15
35	Alan Trammell	.40	.30	.15
36	Joe Carter	.30	.25	.12
37	Jose Canseco	1.50	1.25	.60
38	Carlton Fisk	.40	.30	.15
39	Kirby Puckett	.50	.40	.20
40	Tony Gwynn	.50	.40	.20
41	Matt Nokes	.40	.30	.15
42	Keith Hernandez	.40	.30	.15
43	Nolan Ryan	.40	.30	.15
44	Wally Joyner	.50	.40	.20

1988 Nestle

This 44-card set was produced by Mike Schechter Associates for Nestle. "Dream Team" packets of 3 player cards and one checklist card were inserted in 6-packs of Nestle's chocolate candy bars. The 1988 issue, similar to the 33-card Nestle set produced by Topps, features current players divided into four Dream Teams (East and West teams for each league). The "1988 Nestle" header appears at the top of the red and yellow-bordered cards. Below the player closeup (in a plain airbrushed cap) is a blue oval player name banner. Card backs are red, white and blue with card numbers printed upper right above personal stats, career highlights and major league totals. The bright red, blue and yellow checklist card outlines two special offers; one for an uncut sheet of all 44 player cards and one for a 1988 replica autographed baseball.

		MT	NR MT	EX
Complete Set:		15.00	11.00	6.00
Common Player:		.25	.20	.10
1	Roger Clemens	.75	.60	.30
2	Dale Murphy	.60	.45	.25
3	Eric Davis	.60	.45	.25
4	Gary Gaetti	.30	.25	.12
5	Ozzie Smith	.35	.25	.14
6	Mike Schmidt	.60	.45	.25
7	Ozzie Guillen	.25	.20	.10
8	John Franco	.25	.20	.10
9	Andre Dawson	.40	.30	.15
10	Mark McGwire	1.00	.70	.40
11	Bret Saberhagen	.35	.25	.14
12	Benny Santiago	.35	.25	.14
13	Jose Uribe	.25	.20	.10
14	Will Clark	.50	.40	.20
15	Don Mattingly	1.75	1.25	.70
16	Juan Samuel	.30	.25	.12
17	Jack Clark	.35	.25	.14
18	Darryl Strawberry	.75	.60	.30
19	Bill Doran	.25	.20	.10
20	Pete Incaviglia	.30	.25	.12
21	Dwight Gooden	.75	.60	.30
22	Willie Randolph	.25	.20	.10
23	Tim Wallach	.25	.20	.10

1954 N.Y. Journal-American

Issued during the Golden Age of baseball in New York City, this 59-card set features only players from the three New York teams of the day - the Giants, Yankees and Dodgers. The 2" by 4" cards were issued at newsstands with the purchase of the now-extinct newspaper. Card fronts have promotional copy and a contest serial number in addition to the player's name and photo. Cards are black and white and unnumbered. Many of the game's top stars are included, such as Mickey Mantle, Willie Mays, Gil Hodges, Duke Snider, Jackie Robinson and Yogi Berra. Card backs featured team schedules. It has been theorized that a 60th Dodgers card should exist. Don Hoak and Bob Milliken have been suggested as the missing card, but the existence of either card has never been confirmed.

		NR MT	EX	VG
Complete Set:		1400.00	700.00	420.00
Common Player:		10.00	5.00	3.00
(1)	Johnny Antonelli	12.00	6.00	3.50
(2)	Hank Bauer	20.00	10.00	6.00
(3)	Yogi Berra	75.00	37.00	22.00
(4)	Joe Black	12.00	6.00	3.50
(5)	Harry Byrd	10.00	5.00	3.00
(6)	Roy Campanella	65.00	32.00	19.50
(7)	Andy Carey	10.00	5.00	3.00
(8)	Jerry Coleman	10.00	5.00	3.00
(9)	Joe Collins	10.00	5.00	3.00
(10)	Billy Cox	10.00	5.00	3.00
(11)	Al Dark	12.00	6.00	3.50
(12)	Carl Erskine	20.00	10.00	6.00

		NR MT	EX	VG
(13)	Whitey Ford	40.00	20.00	12.00
(14)	Carl Furillo	20.00	10.00	6.00
(15)	Junior Gilliam	20.00	10.00	6.00
(16)	Ruben Gomez	10.00	5.00	3.00
(17)	Marv Grissom	10.00	5.00	3.00
(18)	Jim Hearn	10.00	5.00	3.00
(19)	Gil Hodges	35.00	17.50	10.50
(20)	Bobby Hofman	10.00	5.00	3.00
(21)	Jim Hughes	10.00	5.00	3.00
(22)	Monte Irvin	25.00	12.50	7.50
(23)	Larry Jansen	10.00	5.00	3.00
(24)	Ray Katt	10.00	5.00	3.00
(25)	Steve Kraly	10.00	5.00	3.00
(26)	Bob Kuzava	10.00	5.00	3.00
(27)	Clem Labine	12.00	6.00	3.50
(28)	Frank Leja	10.00	5.00	3.00
(29)	Don Liddle	10.00	5.00	3.00
(30)	Whitey Lockman	10.00	5.00	3.00
(31)	Billy Loes	10.00	5.00	3.00
(32)	Eddie Lopat	20.00	10.00	6.00
(33)	Gil McDougald	20.00	10.00	6.00
(34)	Sal Maglie	12.00	6.00	3.50
(35)	Mickey Mantle	450.00	225.00	135.00
(36)	Willie Mays	175.00	87.00	52.00
(37)	Russ Meyer	10.00	5.00	3.00
(38)	Bill Miller	10.00	5.00	3.00
(39)	Tom Morgan	10.00	5.00	3.00
(40)	Don Mueller	10.00	5.00	3.00
(41)	Don Newcombe	20.00	10.00	6.00
(42)	Irv Noren	10.00	5.00	3.00
(43)	Erv Palica	10.00	5.00	3.00
(44)	PeeWee Reese	55.00	27.00	16.50
(45)	Allie Reynolds	20.00	10.00	6.00
(46)	Dusty Rhodes	10.00	5.00	3.00
(47)	Phil Rizzuto	35.00	17.50	10.50
(48)	Ed Robinson	10.00	5.00	3.00
(49)	Jackie Robinson	125.00	62.00	37.00
(50)	Preacher Roe	20.00	10.00	6.00
(51)	George Shuba	10.00	5.00	3.00
(52)	Duke Snider	90.00	45.00	27.00
(53)	Hank Thompson	10.00	5.00	3.00
(54)	Wes Westrum	10.00	5.00	3.00
(55)	Hoyt Wilhelm	30.00	15.00	9.00
(56)	Davey Williams	10.00	5.00	3.00
(57)	Dick Williams	12.00	6.00	3.50
(58)	Gene Woodling	12.00	6.00	3.50
(59)	Al Worthington	10.00	5.00	3.00

1986 N.Y. Mets Super Fan Club

This special nine-card panel was issued by the fan club of the 1986 World Champion New York Mets, along with other souvenir items gained with membership in the club. Included in the full-color set are eight top Mets players, with a promotional card in the center of the panel. Individual cards measure 2-1/2" by 3-1/2", and are perforated at the edges to facilitate separation. The full panel measures 70-1/2" by 10-1/2". Card fronts feature posed photos of each player, along with name, position and team logo. Backs feature career and personal data, and are printed in the team's blue and orange colors.

		MT	NR MT	EX
Complete Panel Set:		12.00	9.00	4.75
Complete Singles Set:		4.00	3.00	1.50
Common Single Player:		.15	.11	.06
Panel		12.00	9.00	4.75
1	Wally Backman	.15	.11	.06
2	Gary Carter	.70	.50	.30
3	Ron Darling	.40	.30	.15
4	Dwight Gooden	.90	.70	.35
5	Keith Hernandez	.60	.45	.25
6	Howard Johnson	.25	.20	.10
7	Roger McDowell	.40	.30	.15
8	Darryl Strawberry	.80	.60	.30
-—	Membership Card	.05	.04	.02

1960 Nu-Card

These large, 3-1/4" by 5-3/8" cards are printed in a mock newspaper format, with a headline, picture and story describing one of baseball's greatest events. There are 72 events featured in the set, which is printed in red and black. Each card is numbered in the upper left corner. The card backs offer a quiz question and answer. Certain cards in the set can be found with the fronts printed entirely in black. These cards may command a slight premium.

		NR MT	EX	VG
Complete Set:		125.00	62.00	37.00
Common Player:		.60	.30	.20
1	Babe Hits 3 Homers In A Series Game	10.00	5.00	3.00
2	Podres Pitching Wins Series	.75	.40	.25
3	Bevans Pitches No Hitter, Almost	.75	.40	.25
4	Box Score Devised By Reporter	.60	.30	.20
5	VanderMeer Pitches 2 No Hitters	1.00	.50	.30
6	Indians Take Bums	.60	.30	.20
7	DiMag Comes Thru	6.00	3.00	1.75
8	Mathewson Pitches 3 W.S. Shutouts	1.75	.90	.50
9	Haddix Pitches 12 Perfect Innings	.75	.40	.25
10	Thomson's Homer Sinks Dodgers	1.75	.90	.50
11	Hubbell Strikes Out 5 A.L. Stars	1.50	.70	.45
12	Pickoff Ends Series (Marty Marion)	.75	.40	.25
13	Cards Take Series From Yanks (Grover Cleveland Alexander)	1.50	.70	.45
14	Dizzy And Daffy Win Series	3.50	1.75	1.00
15	Owen Drops 3rd Strike	.75	.40	.25
16	Ruth Calls His Shot	8.00	4.00	2.50
17	Merkle Pulls Boner	.75	.40	.25
18	Larsen Hurls Perfect World Series Game	1.50	.70	.45
19	Bean Ball Ends Career Of Mickey Cochrane premium.	1.25	.60	.40
20	Banks Belts 47 Homers, Earns MVP Honors premium.	2.00	1.00	.60
21	Stan Musial Hits 5 Homers In 1 Day	3.50	1.75	1.00
22	Mickey Mantle Hits Longest Homer	12.00	6.00	3.50
23	Sievers Captures Home Run Title	.75	.40	.25
24	Gehrig Consecutive Game Record Ends	6.00	3.00	1.75
25	Red Schoendienst Key Player In Victory	.75	.40	.25
26	Midget Pinch-Hits For St. Louis Browns (Eddie Gaedel)	1.25	.60	.40

		NR MT	EX	VG
27	Willie Mays Makes Greatest Catch	4.00	2.00	1.25
28	Homer By Berra Puts Yanks In 1st Place	3.00	1.50	.90
29	Campy National League's MVP	3.00	1.50	.90
30	Bob Turley Hurls Yanks To Championship	.75	.40	.25
31	Dodgers Take Series From Sox In Six	.75	.40	.25
32	Furillo Hero As Dodgers Beat Chicago	.75	.40	.25
33	Adcock Gets Four Homers And A Double	.75	.40	.25
34	Dickey Chosen All Star Catcher	1.25	.60	.40
35	Burdette Beats Yanks In 3 Series Games	1.00	.50	.30
36	Umpires Clear White Sox Bench	.60	.30	.20
37	Reese Honored As Greatest Dodger S.S.	2.50	1.25	.70
38	Joe DiMaggio Hits In 56 Straight Games	6.00	3.00	1.75
39	Ted Williams Hits .406 For Season	5.00	2.50	1.50
40	Johnson Pitches 56 Scoreless Innings	2.25	1.25	.70
41	Hodges Hits 4 Home Runs In Nite Game	1.75	.90	.50
42	Greenberg Returns To Tigers From Army	1.25	.60	.40
43	Ty Cobb Named Best Player Of All Time	6.00	3.00	1.75
44	Robin Roberts Wins 28 Games	1.25	.60	.40
45	Rizzuto's 2 Runs Save 1st Place	1.50	.70	.45
46	Tigers Beat Out Senators For Pennant (Hal Newhouser)	.75	.40	.25
47	Babe Ruth Hits 60th Home Run	9.00	4.50	2.75
48	Cy Young Honored	1.75	.90	.50
49	Killebrew Starts Spring Training	1.75	.90	.50
50	Mantle Hits Longest Homer At Stadium	12.00	6.00	3.50
51	Braves Take Pennant (Hank Aaron)	3.50	1.75	1.00
52	Ted Williams Hero Of All Star Game	5.00	2.50	1.50
53	Robinson Saves Dodgers For Playoffs (Jackie Robinson)	3.50	1.75	1.00
54	Snodgrass Muffs A Fly Ball	.75	.40	.25
55	Snider Belts 2 Homers	2.25	1.25	.70
56	New York Giants Win 26 Straight Games (Christy Mathewson)	1.75	.90	.50
57	Ted Kluszewski Stars In 1st Game Win	.75	.40	.25
58	Ott Walks 5 Times In A Single Game (Mel Ott)	1.25	.60	.40
59	Harvey Kuenn Takes Batting Title	.75	.40	.25
60	Bob Feller Hurls 3rd No-Hitter Of Careerpremium.	2.25	1.25	.70
61	Yanks Champs Again! (Casey Stengel)	1.50	.70	.45
62	Aaron's Bat Beats Yankees In Series	4.00	2.00	1.25
63	Warren Spahn Beats Yanks in World Seriespremium.	1.50	.70	.45
64	Ump's Wrong Call Helps Dodgers	.75	.40	.25
65	Kaline Hits 3 Homers, 2 In Same Inning	2.00	1.00	.60
66	Bob Allison Named A.L. Rookie of Year	.75	.40	.25
67	McCovey Blasts Way Into Giant Lineup	1.75	.90	.50
68	Colavito Hits Four Homers In One Game	1.00	.50	.30
69	Erskine Sets Strike Out Record In W.S.	.75	.40	.25
70	Sal Maglie Pitches No-Hit Game	.75	.40	.25
71	Early Wynn Victory Crushes Yanks	1.25	.60	.40
72	Nellie Fox American League's M.V.P.	3.00	1.50	.90

1961 Nu-Card

Very similar in style to their set of the year before, the Nu-Card Baseball Scoops were issued in a smaller 2-1/2" by 3-1/2" size, but still featured the mock newspaper card front. This 80-card set is numbered from 401 to 480, with numbers shown on both the card front and back. These cards, which commemorate great moments in individual players' careers,

included only the headline and black and white photo on the fronts, with the descriptive story on the card backs. Cards are again printed in red and black. It appears the set may have been counterfeited, though when is not known. These cards can be determined by examining the card photo for unusual blurring and fuzziness.

		NR MT	EX	VG
Complete Set:		80.00	40.00	24.00
Common Player:		.30	.15	.09
401	Gentile Powers Birds Into 1st	1.00	.50	.30
402	Warren Spahn Hurls No-Hitter, Whiffs 15	1.00	.50	.30
403	Mazeroski's Homer Wins Series For Bucs	.75	.40	.25
404	Willie Mays' 3 Triples Paces Giants	2.50	1.25	.70
405	Woodie Held Slugs 2 Homers, 6 RBIs	.30	.15	.09
406	Vern Law Winner Of Cy Young Award	.40	.20	.12
407	Runnels Makes 9 Hits in Twin-Bill	.30	.15	.09
408	Braves' Lew Burdette Wins No-Hitter, 1-0	.70	.35	.20
409	Dick Stuart Hits 3 Homers, Single	.30	.15	.09
410	Don Cardwell Of Cubs Pitches No-Hit Game	.30	.15	.09
411	Camilo Pascual Strikes Out 15 Bosox	.30	.15	.09
412	Eddie Mathews Blasts 300th Big League HR	1.00	.50	.30
413	Groat, NL Bat King, Named Loop's MVP	.70	.35	.20
414	AL Votes To Expand To 10 Teams (Gene Autry)	1.25	.60	.40
415	Bobby Richardson Sets Series Mark	.75	.40	.25
416	Maris Nips Mantle For AL MVP Award	2.50	1.25	.70
417	Merkle Pulls Boner	.30	.15	.09
418	Larsen Hurls Perefect World Series Game	.75	.40	.25
419	Bean Ball Ends Career Of Mickey Cochrane	.70	.35	.20
420	Banks Belts 47 Homers, Earns MVP Award	1.50	.70	.45
421	Stan Musial Hits 5 Homers In 1 Day	2.50	1.25	.70
422	Mickey Mantle Hits Longest Homer	10.00	5.00	3.00
423	Sievers Captures Home Run Title	.30	.15	.09
424	Gehrig Consecutive Game Record Ends	5.00	2.50	1.50
425	Red Schoendienst Key Player In Victory	.70	.35	.20
426	Midget Pinch-Hits For St. Louis Browns (Eddie Gaedel)	.75	.40	.25
427	Willie Mays Makes Greatest Catch	2.50	1.25	.70
428	Robinson Saves Dodgers For Playoffs	2.50	1.25	.70
429	Campy Most Valuable Player	2.50	1.25	.70
430	Turley Hurls Yanks To Championship	.40	.20	.12
431	Dodgers Take Series From Sox In Six (Larry Sherry)	.30	.15	.09
432	Furillo Hero In 3rd World Series Game	.70	.35	.20
433	Adcock Gets Four Homers, Double	.70	.35	.20

	NR MT	EX	VG
434 Dickey Chosen All Star Catcher	1.00	.50	.30
435 Burdette Beats Yanks In 3 Series Games	.75	.40	.25
436 Umpires Clear White Sox Bench	.30	.15	.09
437 Reese Honored As Greatest Dodgers S.S.	1.50	.70	.45
438 Joe DiMaggio Hits In 56 Straight Games	5.00	2.50	1.50
439 Ted Williams Hits .406 For Season	4.00	2.00	1.25
440 Johnson Pitches 56 Scoreless Innings	2.50	1.25	.70
441 Hodges Hits 4 Home Runs In Nite Game	1.50	.70	.45
442 Greenberg Returns To Tigers From Army	1.00	.50	.30
443 Ty Cobb Named Best Player Of All Time	4.00	2.00	1.25
444 Robin Roberts Wins 28 Games	1.00	.50	.30
445 Rizzuto's 2 Runs Save 1st Place	1.25	.60	.40
446 Tigers Beat Out Senators For Pennant (Hal Newhouser)	.30	.15	.09
447 Babe Ruth Hits 60th Home Run	6.00	3.00	1.75
448 Cy Young Honored	1.50	.70	.45
449 Killebrew Starts Spring Training	1.25	.60	.40
450 Mantle Hits Longest Homer At Stadium	9.00	4.50	2.75
451 Braves Take Pennant	.30	.15	.09
452 Ted Williams Hero Of All Star Game	2.50	1.25	.70
453 Homer By Berra Puts Yanks In 1st Place	2.50	1.25	.70
454 Snodgrass Muffs A Fly Ball	.30	.15	.09
455 Babe Hits 3 Homers In A Series Game	5.00	2.50	1.50
456 New York Wins 26 Straight Games	.30	.15	.09
457 Ted Kluszewski Stars In 1st Series Win	.40	.20	.12
458 Ott Walks 5 Times In A Single Game	1.00	.50	.30
459 Harvey Kuenn Takes Batting Title	.40	.20	.12
460 Bob Feller Hurls 3rd No-Hitter Of Career	2.50	1.25	.70
461 Yanks Champs Again! (Casey Stengel)	1.50	.70	.45
462 Aaron's Bat Beats Yankees In Series	2.50	1.25	.70
463 Warren Spahn Beats Yanks In World Series	1.00	.50	.30
464 Ump's Wrong Call Helps Dodgers	.30	.15	.09
465 Kaline Hits 3 Homers, 2 In Same Inning	1.50	.70	.45
466 Bob Allison Named A.L. Rookie Of Year	.40	.20	.12
467 DiMag Comes Thru	5.00	2.50	1.50
468 Colavito Hits Four Homers In One Game	.70	.35	.20
469 Erskine Sets Strike Out Record In W.S.	.70	.35	.20
470 Sal Maglie Pitches No-Hit Game	.70	.35	.20
471 Early Wynn Victory Crushes Yanks	1.00	.50	.30
472 Nellie Fox American League's MVP	.75	.40	.25
473 Pickoff Ends Series (Marty Marion)	.40	.20	.12
474 Podres Pitching Wins Series	.80	.40	.25
475 Owen Drops 3rd Strike	.30	.15	.09
476 Dizzy And Daffy Win Series	2.50	1.25	.70
477 Mathewson Pitches 3 W.S. Shutouts	1.50	.70	.45
478 Haddix Pitches 12 Perfect Innings	.40	.20	.12
479 Hubbell Strike Out 5 A.L. Stars	1.00	.50	.30
480 Homer Sinks Dodgers (Bobby Thomson)	1.25	.60	.40

printed within a special three-panel, perforated fold-out piece which featured four action shots of the Indians on the cover. Unfolded, there are two panels containing the baseball cards and a third which contains a team photo. Cards measure 2-1/4" by 3-1/8" and are full-color studio portraits. Photos are framed in blue with a white border and list player name, number and position. Card fronts also include a picture of the sponsoring candy bar. Card backs include facsimile autograph and professional records. Each card is perforated for separation.

	MT	NR MT	EX
Complete Set:	8.00	6.00	3.25
Common Player:	.15	.11	.06
2 Brett Butler	.25	.20	.10
4 Tony Bernazard	.15	.11	.06
6 Andy Allanson	.25	.20	.10
7 Pat Corrales	.15	.11	.06
8 Carmen Castillo	.15	.11	.06
10 Pat Tabler	.30	.25	.12
13 Ernie Camacho	.15	.11	.06
14 Julio Franco	.40	.30	.15
15 Dan Rohn	.15	.11	.06
18 Ken Schrom	.15	.11	.06
20 Otis Nixon	.20	.15	.08
22 Fran Mullins	.15	.11	.06
23 Chris Bando	.15	.11	.06
24 Ed Williams	.35	.25	.14
26 Brook Jacoby	.50	.40	.20
27 Mel Hall	.30	.25	.12
29 Andre Thornton	.30	.25	.12
30 Joe Carter	.70	.50	.30
35 Phil Niekro	.50	.40	.20
36 Jamie Easterly	.15	.11	.06
37 Don Schulze	.15	.11	.06
42 Rich Yett	.20	.15	.08
43 Scott Bailes	.35	.25	.14
44 Neal Heaton	.15	.11	.06
46 Jim Kern	.15	.11	.06
48 Dickie Noles	.15	.11	.06
49 Tom Candiotti	.25	.20	.10
53 Reggie Ritter	.15	.11	.06
54 Tom Waddell	.15	.11	.06
---- Coaching Staff (Jack Aker, Bobby Bonds, Doc Edwards, Johnny Goryl)	.15	.11	.06

1986 Oh Henry Indians

This 30-card set of Cleveland Indians players was distributed by the team at a special Photo/Baseball Card Day at Municipal Stadium. The cards were

1988 Pacific Trading Cards Baseball Legends

Pacific Trading Cards rounded up 110 photos of the greatest baseball players from the past 40 years for its 1988 "Baseball Legends" set. All players featured in the set are (or were) members of the Major League Baseball Alumni Association. Card fronts feature silver outer borders and large, clear full-color player photos outlined in black against colorful banner-style inner borders of red, blue, green, orange or gold. The player's name and position are printed in white letters on the lower portion of the banner. Card backs are numbered and carry the Baseball Legends logo, player biography, major league career stats, and personal information. The cards were sold in boxed sets via candy wholesalers, with emphasis on Midwest and New England states. Complete collector sets in clear plastic boxes were made available via dealers or directly from Pacific Trading Cards.

		MT	NR MT	EX
Complete Set:		12.00	9.00	4.75
Common Player:		.06	.05	.02
1	Hank Aaron	.50	.40	.20
2	Red Shoendienst (Schoendienst)	.10	.08	.04
3	Brooks Robinson	.30	.25	.12
4	Luke Appling	.15	.11	.06
5	Gene Woodling	.06	.05	.02
6	Stan Musial	.50	.40	.20
7	Mickey Mantle	1.00	.70	.40
8	Richie Ashburn	.10	.08	.04
9	Ralph Kiner	.20	.15	.08
10	Phil Rizzuto	.20	.15	.08
11	Harvey Haddix	.06	.05	.02
12	Ken Boyer	.10	.08	.04
13	Clete Boyer	.06	.05	.02
14	Ken Harrelson	.06	.05	.02
15	Robin Roberts	.20	.15	.08
16	Catfish Hunter	.20	.15	.08
17	Frank Howard	.10	.08	.04
18	Jim Perry	.06	.05	.02
19	Elston Howard	.10	.08	.04
20	Jim Bouton	.10	.08	.04
21	Pee Wee Reese	.25	.20	.10
22	Mel Stottlemyer (Stottlemyre)	.10	.08	.04
23	Hank Sauer	.06	.05	.02
24	Willie Mays	.50	.40	.20
25	Tom Tresh	.06	.05	.02
26	Roy Sievers	.06	.05	.02
27	Leo Durocher	.15	.11	.06
28	Al Dark	.10	.08	.04
29	Tony Kubek	.15	.11	.06
30	Johnny Vander Meer	.10	.08	.04
31	Joe Adcock	.10	.08	.04
32	Bob Lemon	.20	.15	.08
33	Don Newcombe	.15	.11	.06
34	Thurman Munson	.20	.15	.08
35	Earl Battey	.06	.05	.02
36	Ernie Banks	.30	.25	.12
37	Matty Alou	.06	.05	.02
38	Dave McNally	.06	.05	.02
39	Mickey Lolich	.10	.08	.04
40	Jackie Robinson	.50	.40	.20
41	Allie Reynolds	.15	.11	.06
42	Don Larson (Larsen)	.10	.08	.04

		MT	NR MT	EX
43	Fergie Jenkins	.15	.11	.06
44	Jim Gilliam	.10	.08	.04
45	Bobby Thomson	.10	.08	.04
46	Sparky Anderson	.10	.08	.04
47	Roy Campanella	.30	.25	.12
48	Marv Throneberry	.10	.08	.04
49	Bill Virdon	.06	.05	.02
50	Ted Williams	.50	.40	.20
51	Minnie Minoso	.10	.08	.04
52	Bob Turley	.10	.08	.04
53	Yogi Berra	.30	.25	.12
54	Juan Marichal	.20	.15	.08
55	Duke Snider	.30	.25	.12
56	Harvey Kuenn	.10	.08	.04
57	Nellie Fox	.15	.11	.06
58	Felipe Alou	.06	.05	.02
59	Tony Oliva	.10	.08	.04
60	Bill Mazeroski	.10	.08	.04
61	Bobby Shantz	.10	.08	.04
62	Mark Fidrych	.06	.05	.02
63	Johnny Mize	.15	.11	.06
64	Ralph Terry	.06	.05	.02
65	Gus Bell	.06	.05	.02
66	Jerry Koosman	.10	.08	.04
67	Mike McCormick	.06	.05	.02
68	Lou Burdette	.10	.08	.04
69	George Kell	.15	.11	.06
70	Vic Raschi	.10	.08	.04
71	Chuck Connors	.20	.15	.08
72	Ted Kluszewski	.10	.08	.04
73	Bobby Doerr	.15	.11	.06
74	Bobby Richardson	.15	.11	.06
75	Carl Erskine	.15	.11	.06
76	Hoyt Wilhelm	.20	.15	.08
77	Bob Purkey	.06	.05	.02
78	Bob Friend	.06	.05	.02
79	Monte Irvin	.15	.11	.06
80	Jim Longborg (Lonborg)	.06	.05	.02
81	Wally Moon	.06	.05	.02
82	Moose Skowron	.10	.08	.04
83	Tommy Davis	.10	.08	.04
84	Enos Slaughter	.20	.15	.08
85	Sal Maglie	.10	.08	.04
86	Harmon Killebrew	.25	.20	.10
87	Gil Hodges	.25	.20	.10
88	Jim Kaat	.10	.08	.04
89	Roger Maris	.30	.25	.12
90	Billy Williams	.20	.15	.08
91	Luis Aparicio	.15	.11	.06
92	Jim Bunning	.15	.11	.06
93	Bill Freehan	.06	.05	.02
94	Orlando Cepeda	.10	.08	.04
95	Early Wynn	.20	.15	.08
96	Tug McGraw	.10	.08	.04
97	Ron Santo	.10	.08	.04
98	Del Crandall	.06	.05	.02
99	Sal Bando	.06	.05	.02
100	Joe DiMaggio	.70	.50	.30
101	Bob Feller	.30	.25	.12
102	Larry Doby	.15	.11	.06
103	Rollie Fingers	.15	.11	.06
104	Al Kaline	.30	.25	.12
105	Johnny Podres	.10	.08	.04
106	Lou Boudreau	.15	.11	.06
107	Zoilo Versalles	.06	.05	.02
108	Dick Groat	.06	.05	.02
109	Warren Spahn	.25	.20	.10
110	Johnny Bench	.40	.30	.15

1989 Pacific Trading Cards Legends II

Pacific Trading Cards issued its Baseball Legends II set as a carry over of its initial set. The photos are printed on silver background and have colorful inner borders of red, blue, orange or gold. Players' names and positions are printed in white letters below the photos. The card backs once again present the "Baseball Legends" logo, player biography, major league career statistics, and personal information. The Baseball Legends II are numbered 110-220 and were available in wax packs at a limited number of retail chains. The complete set was also made available via dealers or could be ordered directly from Pacific Trading Cards.

NOTE: A card number in parentheses ( ) indicates the set is unnumbered.

	MT	NR MT	EX
177 Joe Black	.10	.08	.04
178 Roy Face	.10	.08	.04
179 Earl Weaver	.06	.05	.02
180 Johnny Mize	.15	.11	.06
181 Roger Cramer	.06	.05	.02
182 Jim Piersall	.06	.05	.02
183 Ned Garver	.06	.05	.02
184 Billy Williams	.25	.20	.10
185 Lefty Grove	.15	.11	.06
186 Jim Grant	.06	.05	.02
187 Elmer Valo	.06	.05	.02
188 Ewell Blackwell	.10	.08	.04
189 Mel Ott	.20	.15	.08
190 Harry Walker	.06	.05	.02
191 Bill Campbell	.06	.05	.02
192 Walter Johnson	.30	.25	.12
193 Jim "Catfish" Hunter	.10	.08	.04
194 Charlie Keller	.10	.08	.04
195 Hank Greenberg	.15	.11	.06
196 Bobby Murcer	.06	.05	.02
197 Al Lopez	.06	.05	.02
198 Vida Blue	.10	.08	.04
199 Shag Crawford	.06	.05	.02
200 Arky Vaughan	.10	.08	.04
201 Smoky Burgess	.25	.20	.10
202 Rip Sewell	.06	.05	.02
203 Earl Averrill	.10	.08	.04
204 Milt Pappas	.06	.05	.02
205 Mel Harder	.06	.05	.02
206 Sam Jethroe	.06	.05	.02
207 Randy Hundley	.06	.05	.02
208 Jessie Haines	.10	.08	.04
209 Jack Brickhouse	.10	.08	.04
210 Whitey Ford	.20	.15	.08
211 Honus Wagner	1.00	.70	.40
212 Phil Niekro	.10	.08	.04
213 Gary Bell	.06	.05	.02
214 Jon Matlack	.06	.05	.02
215 Moe Drabowsky	.06	.05	.02
216 Edd Roush	.10	.08	.04
217 Joel Horlen	.06	.05	.02
218 Casey Stengel	.30	.25	.12
219 Burt Hooton	.06	.05	.02
220 Joe Jackson	.80	.60	.30

	MT	NR MT	EX
Complete Set:	9.00	6.75	3.50
Common Player:	.06	.05	.02
111 Reggie Jackson	.30	.25	.12
112 Rich Reese	.06	.05	.02
113 Frankie Frisch	.15	.11	.06
114 Ed Kranepool	.06	.05	.02
115 Al Hrabosky	.06	.05	.02
116 Eddie Mathews	.25	.20	.10
117 Ty Cobb	.50	.40	.20
118 Jim Davenport	.06	.05	.02
119 Buddy Lewis	.06	.05	.02
120 Virgil Trucks	.10	.08	.04
121 Del Ennis	.06	.05	.02
122 Dick Radatz	.06	.05	.02
123 Andy Pafko	.12	.09	.05
124 Wilbur Wood	.10	.08	.04
125 Joe Sewell	.15	.11	.06
126 Herb Score	.06	.05	.02
127 Paul Waner	.06	.05	.02
128 Lloyd Waner	.06	.05	.02
129 Brooks Robinson	.30	.25	.12
130 Bo Belinsky	.10	.08	.04
131 Phil Cavaretta	.06	.05	.02
132 Claude Osteen	.06	.05	.02
133 Tito Francona	.06	.05	.02
134 Billy Pierce	.06	.05	.02
135 Roberto Clemente	.50	.40	.20
136 Spud Chandler	.06	.05	.02
137 Enos Slaughter	.25	.20	.10
138 Ken Holtzman	.06	.05	.02
139 John Hopp	.06	.05	.02
140 Tony LaRussa	.06	.05	.02
141 Ryne Duren	.06	.05	.02
142 Glenn Beckert	.06	.05	.02
143 Ken Keltner	.06	.05	.02
144 Hank Bauer	.15	.11	.06
145 Roger Craig	.10	.08	.04
146 Frank Baker	.10	.08	.04
147 Jim O'Toole	.06	.05	.02
148 Rogers Hornsby	.30	.25	.12
149 Jose Cardenal	.06	.05	.02
150 Bobby Doerr	.10	.08	.04
151 Mickey Cochrane	.10	.08	.04
152 Gaylord Perry	.10	.08	.04
153 Frank Thomas	.06	.05	.02
154 Ted Williams	.40	.30	.15
155 Sam McDowell	.10	.08	.04
156 Bob Feller	.20	.15	.08
157 Bert Campaneris	.06	.05	.02
158 Thornton Lee	.06	.05	.02
159 Gary Peters	.06	.05	.02
160 Joe Medwick	.10	.08	.04
161 Joe Nuxhall	.10	.08	.04
162 Joe Schultz	.06	.05	.02
163 Harmon Killebrew	.25	.20	.10
164 Bucky Walters	.06	.05	.02
165 Bobby Allison	.10	.08	.04
166 Lou Boudreau	.15	.11	.08
167 Joe Cronin	.10	.08	.04
168 Mike Torrez	.10	.08	.04
169 Rich Rollins	.06	.05	.02
170 Tony Cuccinello	.06	.05	.02
171 Hoyt Wilhelm	.20	.15	.08
172 Ernie Harwell	.10	.08	.04
173 George Foster	.06	.05	.02
174 Lou Gehrig	.80	.60	.30
175 Dave Kingman	.06	.05	.02
176 Babe Ruth	1.00	.70	.40

1963 Pepsi-Cola Colt .45'S

This 16-card set was distributed regionally in Texas in bottled six-packs of Pepsi. The cards were issued on panels 2-3/8" by 9-1/8", which were fit in between the bottles in each carton. Values quoted in the checklist below are for complete panels. A standard 2-3/8" by 3-3/4" card was printed on each panel, which also included promos for Pepsi and the Colt .45's, as well as a team schedule. Card fronts were black and white posed action photos with blue and red trim. Player name and position and Pepsi logo are also included. Card backs offer player statistics and career highlights. The John Bateman card, which was apparently never distributed publicly, is among the rarest collectible baseball cards of the 1960s. The complete set price does not include the Bateman card.

	NR MT	EX	VG
Complete Set:	150.00	75.00	45.00
Common Player:	5.00	2.50	1.50
1 Bob Aspromonte	5.00	2.50	1.50
2 John Bateman	400.00	200.00	120.00
3 Bob Bruce	5.00	2.50	1.50
4 Jim Campbell	5.00	2.50	1.50
5 Dick Farrell	5.00	2.50	1.50
6 Ernie Fazio	5.00	2.50	1.50
7 Carroll Hardy	5.00	2.50	1.50
8 J.C. Hartman	5.00	2.50	1.50
9 Ken Johnson	5.00	2.50	1.50
10 Bob Lillis	5.00	2.50	1.50
11 Don McMahon	5.00	2.50	1.50
12 Pete Runnels	8.00	4.00	2.50
13 Al Spangler	5.00	2.50	1.50
14 Rusty Staub	15.00	7.50	4.50
15 Johnny Temple	5.00	2.50	1.50
16 Carl Warwick	60.00	30.00	18.00

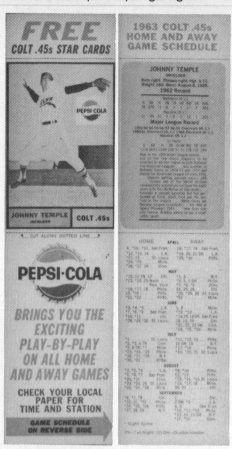

		MT	NR MT	EX
8	Mike Heath	.20	.15	.08
11	Sparky Anderson	.40	.30	.15
12	Luis Salazar	.20	.15	.08
14	Dave Bergman	.20	.15	.08
15	Pat Sheridan	.20	.15	.08
16	Tom Brookens	.20	.15	.08
19	Doyle Alexander	.25	.20	.10
21	Guillermo Hernandez	.25	.20	.10
22	Ray Knight	.25	.20	.10
24	Gary Pettis	.20	.15	.08
25	Eric King	.30	.25	.12
26	Frank Tanana	.30	.25	.12
31	Larry Herndon	.20	.15	.08
32	Jim Walewander	.25	.20	.10
33	Matt Nokes	.90	.70	.35
34	Chet Lemon	.25	.20	.10
35	Walt Terrell	.25	.20	.10
39	Mike Henneman	.40	.30	.15
41	Darrell Evans	.40	.30	.15
44	Jeff Robinson	.50	.40	.20
47	Jack Morris	.70	.50	.30
48	Paul Gibson	.30	.25	.12
-----	Coaches (Billy Consolo, Alex Grammas, Billy Muffett, Vada Pinson, Dick Tracewski)			
		.20	.15	.08

1985 Performance Printing Rangers

A local printing company sponsored this 28-card set of the Texas Rangers. The 2-3/8" by 3-1/2" cards are in full color and are numbered on the back by uniform number. Card fronts feature full-color, game-action photos. The 25 players on the Rangers' active roster at press time are included, along with manager Bobby Valentine and unnumbered coaches and trainer cards. The black and white card backs have a smaller portrait photo of each player, as well as biographical information and career statistics.

		MT	NR MT	EX
Complete Set:		6.00	4.50	2.50
Common Player:		.12	.09	.05
0	Oddibe McDowell	.80	.60	.30
1	Bill Stein	.12	.09	.05
2	Bobby Valentine	.15	.11	.06
3	Wayne Tolleson	.12	.09	.05
4	Don Slaught	.12	.09	.05
5	Alan Bannister	.12	.09	.05
6	Bobby Jones	.12	.09	.05
7	Glenn Brummer	.12	.09	.05
8	Luis Pujols	.12	.09	.05
9	Pete O'Brien	.50	.40	.20
11	Toby Harrah	.20	.15	.08
13	Tommy Dunbar	.12	.09	.05
15	Larry Parrish	.30	.25	.12
16	Mike Mason	.12	.09	.05
19	Curtis Wilkerson	.12	.09	.05
24	Dave Schmidt	.15	.11	.06
25	Buddy Bell	.50	.40	.20
27	Greg Harris	.15	.11	.06
30	Dave Rozema	.12	.09	.05
32	Gary Ward	.20	.15	.08
36	Dickie Noles	.12	.09	.05
41	Chris Welsh	.12	.09	.05

1988 Pepsi/Kroger Tigers

(41) DARRELL EVANS, IF

Approximately 38,000 sets of cards were given to fans at Tiger Stadium on July 30th, 1988. The set, sponsored by Pepsi-Cola and Kroger, includes 25 oversized (2-7/8" by 4-1/4") cards printed on glossy white stock with blue and orange borders. The card backs include small black and white close-up photos, the players' professional records and sponsor logos. The numbers in the following checklist refer to the players' uniform.

		MT	NR MT	EX
Complete Set:		9.00	6.75	3.50
Common Player:		.20	.15	.08
1	Lou Whitaker	.70	.50	.30
2	Alan Trammell	.90	.70	.35

		MT	NR MT	EX
44	Cliff Johnson	.12	.09	.05
46	Burt Hooton	.20	.15	.08
48	Dave Stewart	.40	.30	.15
49	Charlie Hough	.30	.25	.12
--—	Trainers (Danny Wheat, Bill Ziegler)			
		.12	.09	.05
--—	Rangers Coaches (Rich Donnelly, Glenn Ezell, Tom House, Art Howe, Wayne Terwilliger)			
		.12	.09	.05

1986 Performance Printing Rangers

For the second time, the Texas Rangers issued a full-color card set in conjunction with this local printing company. Fronts of the 28-card set include player name, position and team logo beneath the color photo. Backs of the 2-3/8" by 3-1/2" cards are in black and white, with a small portrait photo of each player along with personal and professional statistics. Cards were distributed at the August 23 Rangers home game, and the set includes all of the Rangers' fine rookies such as Bobby Witt, Pete Incaviglia, Edwin Correa and Ruben Sierra.

		MT	NR MT	EX
	Complete Set:	7.00	5.25	2.75
	Common Player:	.10	.08	.04
0	Oddibe McDowell	.50	.40	.20
1	Scott Fletcher	.20	.15	.08
2	Bobby Valentine	.15	.11	.06
3	Ruben Sierra	1.50	1.25	.60
4	Don Slaught	.10	.08	.04
9	Pete O'Brien	.40	.30	.15
11	Toby Harrah	.20	.15	.08
12	Geno Petralli	.10	.08	.04
15	Larry Parrish	.25	.20	.10
16	Mike Mason	.10	.08	.04
17	Darrell Porter	.15	.11	.06
18	Edwin Correa	.40	.30	.15
19	Curtis Wilkerson	.10	.08	.04
22	Steve Buechele	.30	.25	.12
23	Jose Guzman	.40	.30	.15
24	Ricky Wright	.10	.08	.04
27	Greg Harris	.15	.11	.06
28	Mitch Williams	.30	.25	.12
29	Pete Incaviglia	1.25	.90	.50
32	Gary Ward	.15	.11	.06
34	Dale Mohorcic	.30	.25	.12
40	Jeff Russell	.10	.08	.04
44	Tom Paciorek	.10	.08	.04
46	Mike Loynd	.30	.25	.12
48	Bobby Witt	.60	.45	.25
49	Charlie Hough	.25	.20	.10
--—	Coaching Staff (Joe Ferguson, Tim Foli, Tom House, Art Howe, Tom Robson)	.10	.08	.04
--—	Trainers (Danny Wheat, Bill Zeigler)			
		.10	.08	.04

1961 Peters Meats Twins

This set, featuring the first-year 1961 Minnesota Twins, is in a large, 4-5/8" by 3-1/2", format. Cards are on thick cardboard and heavily waxed, as they were used as partial packaging for the company's meat products. Card fronts feature full-color photos, team and Peters logos, and biographical information. The cards are blank-backed.

		NR MT	EX	VG
	Complete Set:	550.00	275.00	165.00
	Common Player:	12.00	6.00	3.50
1	Zoilo Versalles	18.00	9.00	5.50
2	Eddie Lopat	18.00	9.00	5.50
3	Pedro Ramos	12.00	6.00	3.50
4	Charles "Chuck" Stobbs	12.00	6.00	3.50
5	Don Mincher	18.00	9.00	5.50
6	Jack Kralick	12.00	6.00	3.50
7	Jim Kaat	40.00	20.00	12.00
8	Hal Naragon	12.00	6.00	3.50
9	Don Lee	12.00	6.00	3.50
10	Harry "Cookie" Lavagetto	14.00	7.00	4.25
11	Tom "Pete" Whisenant	12.00	6.00	3.50
12	Elmer Valo	12.00	6.00	3.50
13	Ray Moore	12.00	6.00	3.50
14	Billy Gardner	12.00	6.00	3.50
15	Lenny Green	12.00	6.00	3.50
16	Sam Mele	12.00	6.00	3.50
17	Jim Lemon	14.00	7.00	4.25
18	Harmon "Killer" Killebrew	125.00	62.00	37.00
19	Paul Giel	14.00	7.00	4.25
20	Reno Bertoia	12.00	6.00	3.50
21	Clyde McCullough	12.00	6.00	3.50
22	Earl Battey	18.00	9.00	5.50
23	Camilo Pascual	18.00	9.00	5.50
24	Dan Dobbek	12.00	6.00	3.50
25	Joe "Valvy" Valdivielso	12.00	6.00	3.50
26	Billy Consolo	12.00	6.00	3.50

1939 Play Ball

With the issuance of this card set by Gum Incorporated, a new era of baseball cards was born. Although the cards are black and white, the full-frame, actual photos on the card fronts are of better quality than previously seen, and the 2-1/2"

by 3-1/4" size was larger and more popular than the smaller tobacco and caramel cards of the early 20th Century. Card backs featured player names and extensive biographies. There are 162 cards in the set, including superstars Joe DiMaggio and Ted Williams. Card number 126 was never issued. The complete set price does not include all back variations found in the low-numbered series.

		NR MT	EX	VG
Complete Set:		13500.00	6750.00	4250.
Common Player: 1-115		20.00	10.00	6.00
Common Player: 116-162		115.00	57.00	34.00
1	Alvin Jacob Powell	150.00	75.00	45.00
2a	Lee Theo Grissom (name in upper case letters)	25.00	12.50	7.50
2b	Lee Theo Grissom (name in upper and lower case)	35.00	17.50	10.50
3a	Charles Herbert Ruffing (name in upper case letters)	125.00	62.00	37.00
3b	Charles Herbert Ruffing (name in upper and lower case)	135.00	67.00	40.00
4a	Eldon LeRoy Auker (name in upper case letters)	20.00	10.00	6.00
4b	Eldon LeRoy Auker (name in upper and lower case)	22.00	11.00	6.50
5a	James Luther Sewell (name in upper case letters)	22.00	11.00	6.50
5b	James Luther Sewell (name in upper and lower case)	24.00	12.00	7.25
6a	Leo Ernest Durocher (name in upper case letters)	100.00	50.00	30.00
6b	Leo Ernest Durocher (name in upper and lower case)	125.00	62.00	37.00
7a	Robert Pershing Doerr (name in upper case letters)	100.00	50.00	30.00
7b	Robert Pershing Doerr (name in upper and lower case)	100.00	50.00	30.00
8	Henry Pippen	20.00	10.00	6.00
9a	James Tobin (name in upper case letters)	20.00	10.00	6.00
9b	James Tobin (name in upper and lower case)	22.00	11.00	6.50
10	James Brooklyn DeShong	20.00	10.00	6.00
11	John Costa Rizzo	20.00	10.00	6.00
12	Hershel Ray Martin (Herschel)	20.00	10.00	6.00
13a	Luke Daniel Hamlin (name in upper case letters)	20.00	10.00	6.00
13b	Luke Daniel Hamlin (name in upper and lower case)	22.00	11.00	6.50
14a	James R. Tabor ("...Tabor batted .295,...")	20.00	10.00	6.00
14b	James R. Tabor ("...Tabor batted 295,...")	22.00	11.00	6.50
15a	Paul Derringer (name in upper case letters)	22.00	11.00	6.50
15b	Paul Derringer (name in upper and lower case)	24.00	12.00	7.25
16	John Peacock	20.00	10.00	6.00
17	Emerson Dickman	20.00	10.00	6.00
18a	Harry Danning (name in upper case letters)	20.00	10.00	6.00
18b	Harry Danning (name in upper and lower case)	22.00	11.00	6.50
19	Paul Dean	35.00	17.50	10.50
20	Joseph Heving	20.00	10.00	6.00
21a	Emil Leonard (name in upper case letters)	20.00	10.00	6.00
21b	Emil Leonard (name in upper and lower case)	22.00	11.00	6.50
22a	William Henry Walters (name in upper case letters)	22.00	11.00	6.50
22b	William Henry Walters (name in upper and lower case)	24.00	12.00	7.25
23	Burgess U. Whitehead	20.00	10.00	6.00
24a	Richard S. Coffman (S. Richard) ("...Senators the same year.")	20.00	10.00	6.00
24b	Richard S. Coffman (S. Richard) ("...Browns the same year.")	35.00	17.50	10.50
25a	George Alexander Selkirk (name in upper case letters)	35.00	17.50	10.50
25b	George Alexander Selkirk (name in upper and lower case)	40.00	20.00	12.00
26a	Joseph Paul DiMaggio ("...206 hits in 1938 games...")	1700.00	850.00	475.00
26b	Joseph Paul DiMaggio ("...206 hits in 138 games...")	1800.00	900.00	550.00
27a	Fred Ray Ostermueller (name in upper case letters)	20.00	10.00	6.00,

		NR MT	EX	VG
27b	Fred Ray Ostermueller (name in upper and lower case)	22.00	11.00	6.50
28	Sylvester Johnson	20.00	10.00	6.00
29a	John Francis Wilson (name in upper case letters)	20.00	10.00	6.00
29b	John Francis Wilson (name in upper and lower case)	22.00	11.00	6.50
30a	William Malcolm Dickey (name in upper case letters)	200.00	100.00	60.00
30b	William Malcolm Dickey (name in upper and lower case)	225.00	125.00	70.00
31a	Samuel West (name in upper case letters)	20.00	10.00	6.00
31b	Samuel West (name in upper and lower case)	22.00	11.00	6.50
32	Robert I. Seeds	20.00	10.00	6.00
33	Del Howard Young (name actually Del Edward)	20.00	10.00	6.00
34a	Frank Joseph Demaree (Joseph Franklin) (name in upper case letters)	20.00	10.00	6.00
34b	Frank Joseph Demaree (Joseph Franklin) (name in upper and lower case)	22.00	11.00	6.50
35a	William Frederick Jurges (name in upper case letters)	22.00	11.00	6.50
35b	William Frederick Jurges (name in upper and lower case)	24.00	12.00	7.25
36a	Frank Andrew McCormick (name in upper case letters)	20.00	10.00	6.00
36b	Frank Andrew McCormick (name in upper and lower case)	22.00	11.00	6.50
37	Virgil Lawrence Davis	20.00	10.00	6.00
38a	William Harrison Myers (name in upper case letters)	20.00	10.00	6.00
38b	William Harrison Myers (name in upper and lower case)	22.00	11.00	6.50
39a	Richard Benjamin Ferrell (name in upper case letters)	100.00	50.00	30.00
39b	Richard Benjamin Ferrell (name in upper and lower case)	125.00	62.00	37.00
40	James Charles Bagby Jr.	20.00	10.00	6.00
41a	Lonnie Warneke ("...the earned run department...")	20.00	10.00	6.00
41b	Lonnie Warneke ("...the earned-run department...")	22.00	11.00	6.50
42	Arndt Jorgens	24.00	12.00	7.25
43	Melo Almada	20.00	10.00	6.00
44	Donald Henry Heffner	20.00	10.00	6.00
45a	Merrill May (name in upper case letters)	20.00	10.00	6.00
45b	Merrill May (name in upper and lower case)	22.00	11.00	6.50
46a	Morris Arnovich (name in upper case letters)	20.00	10.00	6.00
46b	Morris Arnovich (name in upper and lower case)	22.00	11.00	6.50
47a	John Kelly Lewis, Jr. (name in upper case letters)	20.00	10.00	6.00
47b	John Kelly Lewis, Jr. (name in upper and lower case)	22.00	11.00	6.50
48a	Vernon Gomez (name in upper case letters)	200.00	100.00	60.00
48b	Vernon Gomez (name in upper and lower case)	225.00	125.00	70.00
49	Edward Miller	20.00	10.00	6.00
50a	Charles Len Gehringer (name actually Charles Leonard) (name in upper case letters)	200.00	100.00	60.00
50b	Charles Len Gehringer (name actually Charles Leonard) (name in upper & lower case)	225.00	125.00	70.00
51a	Melvin Thomas Ott (name in upper case)	200.00	100.00	60.00
51b	Melvin Thomas Ott (name in upper and lower case)	225.00	125.00	70.00
52a	Thomas D. Henrich (name in upper case letters)	40.00	20.00	12.00
52b	Thomas D. Henrich (name in upper and lower case)	45.00	22.00	13.50
53a	Carl Owen Hubbell (name in upper case letters)	200.00	100.00	60.00
53b	Carl Owen Hubbell (name in upper and lower case)	135.00	67.00	40.00
54a	Harry Edward Gumbert (name in upper case letters)	14.00	7.00	4.25
54b	Harry Edward Gumbert (name in upper and lower case)	16.00	8.00	4.75
55a	Floyd E. Vaughan (Joseph Floyd) (name in upper case letters)	75.00	37.00	22.00
55b	Floyd E. Vaughan (Joseph Floyd) (name in upper and lower case)	80.00	40.00	24.00
56a	Henry Greenberg (name in upper case letters)	150.00	75.00	45.00

	NR MT	EX	VG
56b Henry Greenberg (name in upper and lower case)	160.00	80.00	48.00
57a John A. Hassett (name in upper case letters)	20.00	10.00	6.00
57b John A. Hassett (name in upper and lower case)	22.00	11.00	6.50
58 Louis Peo Chiozza	20.00	10.00	6.00
59 Kendall Chase	20.00	10.00	6.00
60a Lynwood Thomas Rowe (name in upper case letters)	22.00	11.00	6.50
60b Lynwood Thomas Rowe (name in upper and lower case)	24.00	12.00	7.25
61a Anthony F. Cuccinello (name in upper case letters)	20.00	10.00	6.00
61b Anthony F. Cuccinello (name in upper and lower case)	22.00	11.00	6.50
62 Thomas Carey	20.00	10.00	6.00
63 Emmett Mueller	20.00	10.00	6.00
64a Wallace Moses, Jr. (name in upper case letters)	20.00	10.00	6.00
64b Wallace Moses, Jr. (name in upper and lower case)	22.00	11.00	6.50
65a Harry Francis Craft (name in upper case letters)	20.00	10.00	6.00
65b Harry Francis Craft (name in upper and lower case)	22.00	11.00	6.50
66 James A. Ripple	20.00	10.00	6.00
67 Edwin Joost	20.00	10.00	6.00
68 Fred Singleton	20.00	10.00	6.00
69 Elbert Preston Fletcher (Elburt)	20.00	10.00	6.00
70 Fred Maloy Frankhouse (Meloy)	20.00	10.00	6.00
71a Marcellus Monte Pearson (name actually Montgomery Marcellus) (name in upper case)	24.00	12.00	7.25
71b Marcellus Monte Pearson (name actually Montgomery Marcellus) (name in upper & lower)	35.00	17.50	10.50
72a Debs Garms (Born: Bango, Tex.)	20.00	10.00	6.00
72b Debs Garms (Born: Bangs, Tex.)	25.00	12.50	7.50
73a Harold H. Schumacher (Born: Dolgville, N.Y.)	22.00	11.00	6.50
73b Harold H. Schumacher (Born: Dolgville, N.Y.)	40.00	20.00	12.00
74a Harry A. Lavagetto (name in upper case letters)	24.00	12.00	7.25
74b Harry A. Lavagetto (name in upper and lower case)	15.00	7.50	4.50
75a Stanley Bordagaray (name in upper case letters)	20.00	10.00	6.00
75b Stanley Bordagaray (name in upper and lower case)	22.00	11.00	6.50
76 Goodwin George Rosen	20.00	10.00	6.00
77 Lewis Sidney Riggs	20.00	10.00	6.00
78a Julius Joseph Solters (name in upper case letters)	20.00	10.00	6.00
78b Julius Joseph Solters (name in upper and lower case)	22.00	11.00	6.50
79a Joseph Gregg Moore (given name is Joe) (Weight: 157 lbs.)	20.00	10.00	6.00
79b Joseph Gregg Moore (given name is Joe) (Weight: 175 lbs.)	25.00	12.50	7.50
80a Irwin Fox (Ervin) (Weight: 165 lbs.)	20.00	10.00	6.00
80b Irwin Fox (Ervin) (Weight: 157 lbs.)	25.00	12.50	7.50
81a Ellsworth Dahlgren (name in upper case letters)	24.00	12.00	7.25
81b Ellsworth Dahlgren (name in upper and lower case)	35.00	17.50	10.50
82a Charles Herbert Klein (name in upper case letters)	165.00	82.00	49.00
82b Charles Herbert Klein (name in upper and lower case)	175.00	87.00	52.00
83a August Richard Suhr (name in upper case letters)	20.00	10.00	6.00
83b August Richard Suhr (name in upper and lower case)	22.00	11.00	6.50
84 Lamar Newsome	20.00	10.00	6.00
85 John Walter Cooney	20.00	10.00	6.00
86a Adolph Camilli (Adolf) ("...start of the 1928 season,...")	22.00	11.00	6.50
86b Adolph Camilli (Adolf) ("...start of the 1938 season,...")	35.00	17.50	10.50
87 Milburn G. Shoffner (middle initial actually J.)	20.00	10.00	6.00
88 Charles Keller	50.00	25.00	15.00
89a Lloyd James Waner (name in upper case letters)	125.00	62.00	37.00
89b Lloyd James Waner (name in upper and lower case)	135.00	67.00	40.00
90a Robert H. Klinger (name in upper case letters)	20.00	10.00	6.00
90b Robert H. Klinger (name in upper and lower case)	22.00	11.00	6.50
91a John H. Knott (name in upper case letters)	20.00	10.00	6.00
91b John H. Knott (name in upper and lower case)	22.00	11.00	6.50
92a Ted Williams (name in upper case letters)	1500.00	750.00	450.00
92b Ted Williams (name in upper and lower case)	1800.00	900.00	550.00
93 Charles M. Gelbert	20.00	10.00	6.00
94 Henry E. Manush	115.00	57.00	34.00
95a Whitlow Wyatt (name in upper case letters)	22.00	11.00	6.50
95b Whitlow Wyatt (name in upper and lower case)	24.00	12.00	7.25
96a Ernest Gordon Phelps (name in upper case letters)	22.00	11.00	6.50
96b Ernest Gordon Phelps (name in upper and lower case)	24.00	12.00	7.25
97a Robert Lee Johnson (name in upper case letters)	20.00	10.00	6.00
97b Robert Lee Johnson (name in upper and lower case)	22.00	11.00	6.50
98 Arthur Carter Whitney	20.00	10.00	6.00
99a Walter Anton Berger (name in upper case letters)	22.00	11.00	6.50
99b Walter Anton Berger (name in upper and lower case)	24.00	12.00	7.25
100a Charles Solomon Myer (name in upper case letters)	20.00	10.00	6.00
100b Charles Solomon Myer (name in upper and lower case)	22.00	11.00	6.50
101a Roger M. Cramer ("...the Martinburg Club...")	20.00	10.00	6.00
101b Roger M. Cramer ("...the Martinsburg Club...")	25.00	12.50	7.50
102a Lemuel Floyd Young (name in upper case letters)	20.00	10.00	6.00
102b Lemuel Floyd Young (name in upper and lower case)	22.00	11.00	6.50
103 Morris Berg	22.00	11.00	6.50
104a Thomas Davis Bridges ("...280 games, winning 283,...")	22.00	11.00	6.50
104b Thomas Davis Bridges ("...280 games, winning 133,...")	35.00	17.50	10.50
105a Donald Eric McNair (name in upper case letters)	20.00	10.00	6.00
105b Donald Eric McNair (name in upper and lower case)	22.00	11.00	6.50
106 Albert Stark	20.00	10.00	6.00
107 Joseph Franklin Vosmik	20.00	10.00	6.00
108a Frank Witman Hayes (name in upper case letters)	20.00	10.00	6.00
108b Frank Witman Hayes (name in upper and lower case)	22.00	11.00	6.50
109a Myril Hoag (name in upper case letters)	20.00	10.00	6.00
109b Myril Hoag (name in upper and lower case)	22.00	11.00	6.50
110 Fred L. Fitzsimmons	22.00	11.00	6.50
111a Van Lingle Mungo (name in upper case letters)	35.00	17.50	10.50
111b Van Lingle Mungo (name in upper and lower case)	40.00	20.00	12.00
112a Paul Glee Waner ("...Waner, the older...")	125.00	62.00	37.00
112b Paul Glee Waner ("...Waner, the elder...")	150.00	75.00	45.00
113 Al Schacht	25.00	12.50	7.50
114a Cecil Travis (name in upper case letters)	20.00	10.00	6.00
114b Cecil Travis (name in upper and lower case)	22.00	11.00	6.50
115a Ralph Kress (name in upper case letters)	20.00	10.00	6.00
115b Ralph Kress (name in upper and lower case)	22.00	11.00	6.50
116 Eugene A. Desautels	75.00	37.00	22.00
117 Wayne Ambler	75.00	37.00	22.00
118 Lynn Nelson	75.00	37.00	22.00
119 Willard McKee Hershberger	75.00	37.00	22.00
120 Harold Benton Warstler (middle name actually Burton)	75.00	37.00	22.00
121 William J. Posedel	75.00	37.00	22.00
122 George Hartley McQuinn	75.00	37.00	22.00
123 Ray T. Davis	75.00	37.00	22.00
124 Walter George Brown	75.00	37.00	22.00
125 Clifford George Melton	75.00	37.00	22.00
126 Not Issued			
127 Gilbert Herman Brack	75.00	37.00	22.00

		NR MT	EX	VG
128	Joseph Emil Bowman	115.00	57.00	34.00
129	William Swift	115.00	57.00	34.00
130	Wilbur Lee Brubaker	115.00	57.00	34.00
131	Morton Cecil Cooper	115.00	57.00	34.00
132	James Roberson Brown	115.00	57.00	34.00
133	Lynn Myers	115.00	57.00	34.00
134	Forrest Pressnell	115.00	57.00	34.00
135	Arnold Malcolm Owen	115.00	57.00	34.00
136	Roy Chester Bell	115.00	57.00	34.00
137	Peter William Appleton	115.00	57.00	34.00
138	George Washington Case Jr.	115.00	57.00	34.00
139	Vitautas C. Tamulis	115.00	57.00	34.00
140	Raymond Hall Hayworth	115.00	57.00	34.00
141	Peter Coscarart	115.00	57.00	34.00
142	Ira Kendall Hutchinson	115.00	57.00	34.00
143	Howard Earl Averill	275.00	140.00	85.00
144	Henry J. Bonura	115.00	57.00	34.00
145	Hugh Noyes Mulcahy	115.00	57.00	34.00
146	Thomas Sunkel	115.00	57.00	34.00
147	George D. Coffman	115.00	57.00	34.00
148	William Trotter	115.00	57.00	34.00
149	Max Edward West	115.00	57.00	34.00
150	James Elton Walkup	115.00	57.00	34.00
151	Hugh Thomas Casey	125.00	62.00	37.00
152	Roy Weatherly	115.00	57.00	34.00
153	Paul H. Trout	125.00	62.00	37.00
154	John W. Hudson	115.00	57.00	34.00
155	James Paul Outlaw (middle name actually Paulus)	115.00	57.00	34.00
156	Raymond Berres	115.00	57.00	34.00
157	Donald Willard Padgett (middle name actually Wilson)	115.00	57.00	34.00
158	Luther Baxter Thomas	115.00	57.00	34.00
159	Russell E. Evans	115.00	57.00	34.00
160	Eugene Moore Jr.	115.00	57.00	34.00
161	Linus Reinhard Frey	135.00	67.00	40.00
162	Lloyd Albert Moore	250.00	125.00	70.00

1940 Play Ball

Following the success of their initial effort in 1939, Gum Incorporated issued a bigger and better set in 1940. The 240 black and white cards are once again in the 2-1/2" by 3-1/8" size, but the photos on the card fronts are enclosed by a frame which listed the player's name. Card backs again offer extensive biographies. Backs are also dated. A number of old-timers were issued along with the current day's players, and many Hall of Famers are included. The final 60 cards of the set are more difficult to obtain.

		NR MT	EX	VG
Complete Set:		20000.00	10000.00	6000.
Common Player: 1-120		22.00	11.00	6.50
Common Player: 121-180		25.00	12.50	7.50
Common Player: 181-240		80.00	40.00	24.00

		NR MT	EX	VG
1	Joe DiMaggio	2000.00	1000.00	600.00
2	"Art" Jorgens	25.00	9.00	5.50
3	"Babe" Dahlgren	25.00	12.50	7.50
4	"Tommy" Henrich	35.00	17.50	10.50
5	"Monte" Pearson	25.00	12.50	7.50
6	"Lefty" Gomez	200.00	100.00	60.00
7	"Bill" Dickey	200.00	100.00	60.00
8	"Twinkletoes" Selkirk	25.00	12.50	7.50
9	"Charley" Keller	35.00	17.50	10.50
10	"Red" Ruffing	75.00	37.00	22.00

		NR MT	EX	VG
11	"Jake" Powell	25.00	12.50	7.50
12	"Johnny" Schulte	25.00	12.50	7.50
13	"Jack" Knott	22.00	11.00	6.50
14	"Rabbit" McNair	22.00	11.00	6.50
15	George Case	22.00	11.00	6.50
16	Cecil Travis	22.00	11.00	6.50
17	"Buddy" Myer	22.00	11.00	6.50
18	"Charley" Gelbert	22.00	11.00	6.50
19	"Ken" Chase	22.00	11.00	6.50
20	"Buddy" Lewis	22.00	11.00	6.50
21	"Rick" Ferrell	65.00	32.00	19.50
22	"Sammy" West	22.00	11.00	6.50
23	"Dutch" Leonard	22.00	11.00	6.50
24	Frank "Blimp" Hayes	22.00	11.00	6.50
25	"Cherokee" Bob Johnson	22.00	11.00	6.50
26	"Wally" Moses	22.00	11.00	6.50
27	"Ted" Williams	1800.00	900.00	550.00
28	"Gene" Desautels	22.00	11.00	6.50
29	"Doc" Cramer	22.00	11.00	6.50
30	"Moe" Berg	25.00	12.50	7.50
31	"Jack" Wilson	22.00	11.00	6.50
32	"Jim" Bagby	22.00	11.00	6.50
33	"Fritz" Ostermueller	22.00	11.00	6.50
34	John Peacock	22.00	11.00	6.50
35	"Joe" Heving	22.00	11.00	6.50
36	"Jim" Tabor	22.00	11.00	6.50
37	Emerson Dickman	22.00	11.00	6.50
38	"Bobby" Doerr	100.00	50.00	30.00
39	"Tom" Carey	22.00	11.00	6.50
40	"Hank" Greenberg	250.00	125.00	75.00
41	"Charley" Gehringer	150.00	75.00	45.00
42	"Bud" Thomas	22.00	11.00	6.50
43	Pete Fox	22.00	11.00	6.50
44	"Dizzy" Trout	25.00	12.50	7.50
45	"Red" Kress	22.00	11.00	6.50
46	Earl Averill	100.00	50.00	30.00
47	"Old Os" Vitt	22.00	11.00	6.50
48	"Luke" Sewell	25.00	12.50	7.50
49	"Stormy Weather" Weatherly	22.00	11.00	6.50
50	"Hal" Trosky	22.00	11.00	6.50
51	"Don" Heffner	22.00	11.00	6.50
52	Myril Hoag	22.00	11.00	6.50
53	"Mac" McQuinn	22.00	11.00	6.50
54	"Bill" Trotter	22.00	11.00	6.50
55	"Slick" Coffman	22.00	11.00	6.50
56	"Eddie" Miller	22.00	11.00	6.50
57	Max West	22.00	11.00	6.50
58	"Bill" Posedel	22.00	11.00	6.50
59	"Rabbit" Warstler	22.00	11.00	6.50
60	John Cooney	22.00	11.00	6.50
61	"Tony" Cuccinello	22.00	11.00	6.50
62	"Buddy" Hassett	22.00	11.00	6.50
63	"Pete" Cascarart	22.00	11.00	6.50
64	"Van" Mungo	30.00	15.00	9.00
65	"Fitz" Fitzsimmons	25.00	12.50	7.50
66	"Babe" Phelps	25.00	12.50	7.50
67	"Whit" Wyatt	25.00	12.50	7.50
68	"Dolph" Camilli	25.00	12.50	7.50
69	"Cookie" Lavagetto	25.00	12.50	7.50
70	"Hot Potato" Hamlin	22.00	11.00	6.50
71	"Mel" Almada	22.00	11.00	6.50
72	"Chuck" Dressen	25.00	12.50	7.50
73	"Bucky" Walters	25.00	12.50	7.50
74	"Duke" Derringer	25.00	12.50	7.50
75	"Buck" McCormick	22.00	11.00	6.50
76	"Lonny" Frey	22.00	11.00	6.50
77	"Bill" Hershberger	22.00	11.00	6.50
78	"Lew" Riggs	22.00	11.00	6.50
79	"Wildfire" Craft	22.00	11.00	6.50
80	"Bill" Myers	22.00	11.00	6.50
81	"Wally" Berger	25.00	12.50	7.50
82	"Hank" Gowdy	22.00	11.00	6.50
83	"Cliff" Melton (Cliff)	22.00	11.00	6.50
84	"Jo-Jo" Moore	22.00	11.00	6.50
85	"Hal" Schumacher	25.00	12.50	7.50
86	Harry Gumbert	22.00	11.00	6.50
87	Carl Hubbell	200.00	100.00	60.00
88	"Mel" Ott	200.00	100.00	60.00
89	"Bill" Jurges	25.00	12.50	7.50
90	Frank Demaree	22.00	11.00	6.50
91	Bob "Suitcase" Seeds	22.00	11.00	6.50
92	"Whitey" Whitehead	22.00	11.00	6.50
93	Harry "The Horse" Danning	22.00	11.00	6.50
94	"Gus" Suhr	22.00	11.00	6.50
95	"Mul" Mulcahy	22.00	11.00	6.50
96	"Heinie" Mueller	22.00	11.00	6.50
97	"Morry" Arnovich	22.00	11.00	6.50
98	"Pinky" May	22.00	11.00	6.50
99	"Syl" Johnson	22.00	11.00	6.50
100	"Hersh" Martin	22.00	11.00	6.50
101	"Del" Young	22.00	11.00	6.50

		NR MT	EX	VG
102	"Chuck" Klein	100.00	50.00	30.00
103	"Elbie" Fletcher	14.00	7.00	4.25
104	"Big Poison" Waner	85.00	42.00	25.00
105	"Little Poison" Waner	85.00	42.00	25.00
106	"Pep" Young	14.00	7.00	4.25
107	"Arky" Vaughan	65.00	32.00	19.50
108	"Johnny" Rizzo	22.00	11.00	6.50
109	"Don" Padgett	22.00	11.00	6.50
110	"Tom" Sunkel	22.00	11.00	6.50
111	"Mickey" Owen	22.00	11.00	6.50
112	"Jimmy" Brown	22.00	11.00	6.50
113	"Mort" Cooper	22.00	11.00	6.50
114	"Lon" Warneke	22.00	11.00	6.50
115	"Mike" Gonzales (Gonzalez)	22.00	11.00	6.50
116	"Al" Schacht	25.00	12.50	7.50
117	"Dolly" Stark	22.00	11.00	6.50
118	"Schoolboy" Hoyt	100.00	50.00	30.00
119	"Ol Pete" Alexander	180.00	90.00	54.00
120	Walter "Big Train" Johnson	275.00	137.00	82.00
121	Atley Donald	25.00	12.50	7.50
122	"Sandy" Sundra	25.00	12.50	7.50
123	"Hildy" Hildebrand	25.00	12.50	7.50
124	"Colonel" Combs	135.00	67.00	40.00
125	"Art" Fletcher	25.00	12.50	7.50
126	"Jake" Solters	25.00	12.50	7.50
127	"Muddy" Ruel	25.00	12.50	7.50
128	"Pete" Appleton	25.00	12.50	7.50
129	"Bucky" Harris	100.00	50.00	30.00
130	"Deerfoot" Milan	25.00	12.50	7.50
131	"Zeke" Bonura	25.00	12.50	7.50
132	Connie Mack	225.00	112.00	67.00
133	"Jimmie" Foxx	275.00	137.00	82.00
134	"Joe" Cronin	150.00	75.00	45.00
135	"Line Drive" Nelson	25.00	12.50	7.50
136	"Cotton" Pippen	25.00	12.50	7.50
137	"Bing" Miller	25.00	12.50	7.50
138	"Beau" Bell	25.00	12.50	7.50
139	Elden Auker (Eldon)	25.00	12.50	7.50
140	"Dick" Coffman	25.00	12.50	7.50
141	"Casey" Stengel	200.00	100.00	60.00
142	"Highpockets" Kelly	100.00	50.00	30.00
143	"Gene" Moore	25.00	12.50	7.50
144	"Joe" Vosmik	25.00	12.50	7.50
145	"Vito" Tamulis	25.00	12.50	7.50
146	"Tot" Pressnell	25.00	12.50	7.50
147	"Johnny" Hudson	25.00	12.50	7.50
148	"Hugh" Casey	25.00	12.50	7.50
149	"Pinky" Shoffner	25.00	12.50	7.50
150	"Whitey" Moore	25.00	12.50	7.50
151	Edwin Joost	25.00	12.50	7.50
152	"Jimmy" Wilson	25.00	12.50	7.50
153	"Bill" McKechnie	100.00	50.00	30.00
154	"Jumbo" Brown	25.00	12.50	7.50
155	"Ray" Hayworth	25.00	12.50	7.50
156	"Daffy" Dean	30.00	15.00	9.00
157	"Lou" Chiozza	25.00	12.50	7.50
158	"Stonewall" Jackson	100.00	50.00	30.00
159	"Pancho" Snyder	25.00	12.50	7.50
160	"Hans" Lobert	25.00	12.50	7.50
161	"Debs" Garms	25.00	12.50	7.50
162	"Joe" Bowman	25.00	12.50	7.50
163	"Spud" Davis	25.00	12.50	7.50
164	"Ray" Berres	25.00	12.50	7.50
165	"Bob" Klinger	25.00	12.50	7.50
166	"Bill" Brubaker	25.00	12.50	7.50
167	"Frankie" Frisch	150.00	75.00	45.00
168	"Honus" Wagner	275.00	137.00	82.00
169	"Gabby" Street	25.00	12.50	7.50
170	"Tris" Speaker	250.00	125.00	75.00
171	Harry Heilmann	150.00	75.00	45.00
172	"Chief" Bender	150.00	75.00	45.00
173	"Larry" Lajoie	275.00	137.00	82.00
174	"Johnny" Evers	150.00	75.00	45.00
175	"Christy" Mathewson	275.00	137.00	82.00
176	"Heinie" Manush	150.00	75.00	45.00
177	Frank "Homerun" Baker	150.00	75.00	45.00
178	Max Carey	150.00	75.00	45.00
179	George Sisler	135.00	67.00	40.00
180	"Mickey" Cochrane	150.00	75.00	45.00
181	"Spud" Chandler	80.00	40.00	25.00
182	"Knick" Knickerbocker	80.00	40.00	25.00
183	Marvin Breuer	80.00	40.00	25.00
184	"Mule" Haas	80.00	40.00	24.00
185	"Joe" Kuhel	80.00	40.00	24.00
186	Taft Wright	80.00	40.00	24.00
187	"Jimmy" Dykes	60.00	30.00	18.00
188	"Joe" Krakauskas	80.00	40.00	24.00
189	"Jim" Bloodworth	80.00	40.00	24.00
190	"Charley" Berry	80.00	40.00	24.00
191	John Babich	80.00	40.00	24.00
192	"Dick" Siebert	80.00	40.00	24.00

		NR MT	EX	VG
193	"Chubby" Dean	80.00	40.00	24.00
194	"Sam" Chapman	80.00	40.00	24.00
195	"Dee" Miles	80.00	40.00	24.00
196	"Nonny" Nonnenkamp	80.00	40.00	24.00
197	"Lou" Finney	80.00	40.00	24.00
198	"Denny" Galehouse	80.00	40.00	24.00
199	"Pinky" Higgins	80.00	40.00	24.00
200	"Soupy" Campbell	80.00	40.00	24.00
201	Barney McCosky	80.00	40.00	24.00
202	"Al" Milnar	80.00	40.00	24.00
203	"Bad News" Hale	80.00	40.00	24.00
204	Harry Eisenstat	80.00	40.00	24.00
205	"Rollie" Hemsley	80.00	40.00	24.00
206	"Chet" Laabs	80.00	40.00	24.00
207	"Gus" Mancuso	80.00	40.00	24.00
208	Lee Gamble	80.00	40.00	24.00
209	"Hy" Vandenberg	80.00	40.00	24.00
210	"Bill" Lohrman	80.00	40.00	24.00
211	"Pop" Joiner	80.00	40.00	24.00
212	"Babe" Young	80.00	40.00	24.00
213	John Rucker	80.00	40.00	24.00
214	"Ken" O'Dea	80.00	40.00	24.00
215	"Johnnie" McCarthy	80.00	40.00	24.00
216	"Joe" Marty	80.00	40.00	24.00
217	Walter Beck	80.00	40.00	24.00
218	"Wally" Millies	80.00	40.00	24.00
219	"Russ" Bauers	80.00	40.00	24.00
220	Mace Brown	80.00	40.00	24.00
221	Lee Handley	80.00	40.00	24.00
222	"Max" Butcher	80.00	40.00	24.00
223	Hugh "Ee-Yah" Jennings	150.00	75.00	45.00
224	"Pie" Traynor	250.00	125.00	75.00
225	"Shoeless Joe" Jackson	1500.00	750.00	450.00
226	Harry Hooper	150.00	75.00	45.00
227	"Pop" Haines	150.00	75.00	45.00
228	"Charley" Grimm	80.00	40.00	25.00
229	"Buck" Herzog	80.00	40.00	24.00
230	"Red" Faber	150.00	75.00	45.00
231	"Dolf" Luque	80.00	40.00	24.00
232	"Goose" Goslin	150.00	75.00	45.00
233	"Moose" Earnshaw	80.00	40.00	24.00
234	Frank "Husk" Chance	200.00	100.00	60.00
235	John J. McGraw	250.00	125.00	75.00
236	"Sunny Jim" Bottomley	150.00	75.00	45.00
237	"Wee Willie" Keeler	225.00	112.00	67.00
238	"Poosh 'Em Up Tony" Lazzeri	100.00	50.00	30.00
239	George Uhle	70.00	30.00	18.00
240	"Bill" Atwood	200.00	100.00	60.00

1941 Play Ball

While the card backs are quite similar to the black and white cards Gum Incorporated issued in 1940, the card fronts in the 1941 set are printed in color. Many of the card photos, however, are just color versions of the player's 1940 card. The cards are still in the 2-1/2" by 3-1/8" size, but only 72 cards are included in the set. Joe DiMaggio and Ted Williams continue to be the key players in the set, while card numbers 49-72 are rarer than the lower-numbered cards. The cards were printed in sheets, and can still be found that way, or in paper strips, lacking the cardboard backing.

	NR MT	EX	VG
Complete Set:	7500.00	3750.00	2250.
Common Player: 1-48	45.00	22.00	13.50

Common Player: 49-72	NR MT 50.00	EX 25.00	VG 15.00
1 "Eddie" Miller	90.00	25.00	12.00
2 Max West	45.00	20.00	12.00
3 "Bucky" Walters	45.00	22.00	13.50
4 "Duke" Derringer	50.00	25.00	15.00
5 "Buck" McCormick	45.00	22.00	13.50
6 Carl Hubbell	135.00	67.00	40.00
7 "The Horse" Danning	45.00	22.00	13.50
8 "Mel" Ott	150.00	75.00	45.00
9 "Pinky" May	45.00	22.00	13.50
10 "Arky" Vaughan	50.00	25.00	15.00
11 Debs Garms	45.00	22.00	13.50
12 "Jimmy" Brown	45.00	22.00	13.50
13 "Jimmie" Foxx	200.00	100.00	60.00
14 "Ted" Williams	1100.00	550.00	330.00
15 "Joe" Cronin	90.00	45.00	27.00
16 "Hal" Trosky	45.00	22.00	13.50
17 "Stormy" Weatherly	45.00	22.00	13.50
18 "Hank" Greenberg	185.00	93.00	56.00
19 "Charley" Gehringer	135.00	67.00	40.00
20 "Red" Ruffing	90.00	45.00	27.00
21 "Charlie" Keller	50.00	25.00	15.00
22 "Indian Bob" Johnson	45.00	22.00	13.50
23 "Mac" McQuinn	45.00	22.00	13.50
24 "Dutch" Leonard	45.00	22.00	13.50
25 "Gene" Moore	45.00	22.00	13.50
26 Harry "Gunboat" Gumbert	45.00	22.00	13.50
27 "Babe" Young	45.00	22.00	13.50
28 "Joe" Marty	45.00	22.00	13.50
29 "Jack" Wilson	45.00	22.00	13.50
30 "Lou" Finney	45.00	22.00	13.50
31 "Joe" Kuhel	45.00	22.00	13.50
32 Taft Wright	45.00	22.00	13.50
33 "Happy" Milnar	45.00	22.00	13.50
34 "Rollie" Hemsley	45.00	22.00	13.50
35 "Pinky" Higgins	45.00	22.00	13.50
36 Barney McCosky	45.00	22.00	13.50
37 "Soupy" Campbell	45.00	22.00	13.50
38 Atley Donald	50.00	25.00	15.00
39 "Tommy" Henrich	50.00	25.00	15.00
40 "Johnny" Babich	45.00	22.00	13.50
41 Frank "Blimp" Hayes	45.00	22.00	13.50
42 "Wally" Moses	45.00	22.00	13.50
43 Albert "Bronk" Brancato	45.00	22.00	13.50
44 "Sam" Chapman	45.00	22.00	13.50
45 Elden Auker (Eldon)	45.00	22.00	13.50
46 "Sid" Hudson	45.00	22.00	13.50
47 "Buddy" Lewis	45.00	22.00	13.50
48 Cecil Travis	45.00	22.00	13.50
49 "Babe" Dahlgren	50.00	25.00	15.00
50 "Johnny" Cooney	50.00	25.00	15.00
51 "Dolph" Camilli	45.00	23.00	13.50
52 Kirby Higbe	50.00	25.00	15.00
53 Luke "Hot Potato" Hamlin	50.00	25.00	15.00
54 "Pee Wee" Reese	400.00	200.00	120.00
55 "Whit" Wyatt	50.00	25.00	15.00
56 "Vandy" Vander Meer	50.00	25.00	15.00
57 "Moe" Arnovich	50.00	25.00	15.00
58 "Frank" Demaree	50.00	25.00	15.00
59 "Bill" Jurges	50.00	25.00	15.00
60 "Chuck" Klein	120.00	60.00	36.00
61 "Vince" DiMaggio	120.00	60.00	36.00
62 "Elbie" Fletcher	50.00	25.00	15.00
63 "Dom" DiMaggio	120.00	60.00	36.00
64 "Bobby" Doerr	120.00	60.00	36.00
65 "Tommy" Bridges	45.00	23.00	13.50
66 Harland Clift (Harlond)	50.00	25.00	15.00
67 "Walt" Judnich	50.00	25.00	15.00
68 "Jack" Knott	50.00	25.00	15.00
69 George Case	50.00	25.00	15.00
70 "Bill" Dickey	350.00	175.00	105.00
71 "Joe" DiMaggio	1400.00	500.00	300.00
72 "Lefty" Gomez	450.00	175.00	105.00

1979 Police/Fire Safety Giants

Each of the full-color cards measures 2-5/8" by 4-1/8" and is numbered by player uniform number. The set includes 20 Giants players and coaches. The player's name, position and facsimile autograph are on the card fronts, along with the Giants logo. Card backs have a "Tip from the Giants" and sponsor logos for the Giants and radio station KNBR, all printed the Giants' orange and black colors. Half of the set

3 Mike Sadek
Catcher

Tips from
the Giants

was distributed at a ballpark promotion during the 1979 season, while the other cards were available only from police agencies in several San Francisco Bay area counties.

		NR MT	EX	VG
Complete Set:		20.00	10.00	6.00
Common Player:		.40	.20	.12
1	Dave Bristol	.40	.20	.12
2	Marc Hill	.40	.20	.12
3	Mike Sadek	.50	.25	.15
5	Tom Haller	.40	.20	.12
6	Joe Altobelli	.50	.25	.15
8	Larry Shepard	.50	.25	.15
9	Heity Cruz	.40	.20	.12
10	Johnnie LeMaster	.40	.20	.12
12	Jim Davenport	.40	.20	.12
14	Vida Blue	.80	.40	.25
15	Mike Ivie	.40	.20	.12
16	Roger Metzger	.40	.20	.12
17	Randy Moffitt	.40	.20	.12
18	Bill Madlock	1.25	.60	.40
21	Rob Andrews	.50	.25	.15
22	Jack Clark	2.50	1.25	.70
25	Dave Roberts	.30	.15	.09
26	John Montefusco	.50	.25	.15
28	Ed Halicki	.50	.25	.15
30	John Tamargo	.30	.15	.09
31	Larry Herndon	.40	.20	.12
36	Bill North	.50	.25	.15
39	Bob Knepper	.70	.35	.20
40	John Curtis	.50	.25	.15
41	Darrell Evans	1.25	.60	.40
43	Tom Griffin	.50	.25	.15
44	Willie McCovey	3.00	1.50	.90
46	Gary Lavelle	.50	.25	.15
49	Max Venable	.50	.25	.15

1980 Police/Fire Safety Dodgers

TIPS FROM THE DODGERS
FOUL...

STEVE GARVEY
No. 6 - Infielder

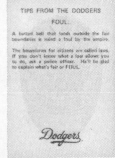

Dodgers

Producers of one of the most popular police and safety sets in baseball, the Los Angeles Dodgers began this successful promotion in 1980. The 2-13/16" by 4-1/8" cards feature attractive, full-color photos on the card fronts, along with brief personal statistics. Card backs include "Tips from the Dodgers" along with the team and Los Angeles Police Department logos. The 30 cards are numbered by player uniform number, with an unnumbered team card also included in the set.

		NR MT	EX	VG
Complete Set:		8.00	4.00	2.50
Common Player:		.30	.15	.09
5	Johnny Oates	.30	.15	.09
6	Steve Garvey	1.50	.70	.45
7	Steve Yeager	.30	.15	.09
8	Reggie Smith	.50	.25	.15
9	Gary Thomasson	.30	.15	.09
10	Ron Cey	.50	.25	.15
12	Dusty Baker	.40	.20	.12
13	Joe Ferguson	.30	.15	.09
15	Davey Lopes	.50	.25	.15
16	Rick Monday	.40	.20	.12
18	Bill Russell	.40	.20	.12
20	Don Sutton	.80	.40	.25
21	Jay Johnstone	.40	.20	.12
23	Teddy Martinez	.30	.15	.09
27	Joe Beckwith	.30	.15	.09
28	Pedro Guerrero	1.00	.50	.30
29	Don Stanhouse	.30	.15	.09
30	Derrel Thomas	.30	.15	.09
31	Doug Rau	.30	.15	.09
34	Ken Brett	.30	.15	.09
35	Bob Welch	.50	.25	.15
37	Robert Castillo	.30	.15	.09
38	Dave Goltz	.40	.20	.12
41	Jerry Reuss	.50	.25	.15
43	Rick Sutcliffe	.60	.30	.20
44	Mickey Hatcher	.40	.20	.12
46	Burt Hooton	.40	.20	.12
49	Charlie Hough	.40	.20	.12
51	Terry Forster	.40	.20	.12
----	Team Photo	.30	.15	.09

1980 Police/Fire Safety Giants

44 Willie McCovey
Infielder

The 1980 Giants police set is virtually identical in format to its 1979 forerunner. Card design and colors are the same on both front and back, with radio station KNBR and the San Francisco Police Department once again co-sponsors. The 2-5/8" by 4-1/8" cards once again feature fronts with full-color photos and facsimile autographs, while backs are in the team's orange and black colors. The set numbers 31 players and coaches, with each card numbered by uniform number. As in 1979, half the cards were distributed at a stadium promotion, with the remainder available only from police officers.

		NR MT	EX	VG
Complete Set:		11.00	5.50	3.25
Common Player:		.30	.15	.09
1	Dave Bristol	.30	.15	.09
2	Marc Hill	.30	.15	.09
3	Mike Sadek	.30	.15	.09
5	Jim Lefebvre	.30	.15	.09

		NR MT	EX	VG
6	Rennie Stennett	.30	.15	.09
7	Milt May	.30	.15	.09
8	Vern Benson	.30	.15	.09
9	Jim Wohlford	.30	.15	.09
10	Johnnie LeMaster	.30	.15	.09
12	Jim Davenport	.30	.15	.09
14	Vida Blue	.80	.40	.25
15	Mike Ivie	.30	.15	.09
16	Roger Metzger	.30	.15	.09
17	Randy Moffitt	.30	.15	.09
19	Al Holland	.30	.15	.09
20	Joe Strain	.30	.15	.09
22	Jack Clark	2.25	1.25	.70
26	John Montefusco	.40	.20	.12
28	Ed Halicki	.30	.15	.09
31	Larry Herndon	.40	.20	.12
32	Ed Whitson	.40	.20	.12
36	Bill North	.30	.15	.09
38	Greg Minton	.30	.15	.09
39	Bob Knepper	.50	.25	.15
41	Darrell Evans	.90	.45	.25
42	John Van Ornum	.30	.15	.09
43	Tom Griffin	.30	.15	.09
44	Willie McCovey	2.50	1.25	.70
45	Terry Whitfield	.30	.15	.09
46	Gary Lavelle	.30	.15	.09
47	Don McMahon	.30	.15	.09

1981 Police/Fire Safety Braves

 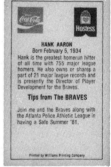

The first Atlanta Braves police set was a cooperative effort of the team, Hostess, Coca-Cola and the Atlanta Police Department. Card fronts feature full-color photos of 27 different Braves and manager Bobby Cox. Police and team logos are on the card backs. Card backs offer capsule biographies of the players, along with a tip for youngsters. The 2-5/8" by 4-1/8" cards are numbered by uniform number. Terry Harper (#19) appears to be somewhat scarcer than the other cards in the set. Reportedly, 33,000 sets were printed.

		MT	NR MT	EX
Complete Set:		12.00	9.00	4.75
Common Player:		.30	.25	.12
1	Jerry Royster	.30	.25	.12
3	Dale Murphy	2.50	2.00	1.00
4	Biff Pocoroba	.30	.25	.12
5	Bob Horner	1.00	.70	.40
6	Bob Cox	.30	.25	.12
9	Luis Gomez	.30	.25	.12
10	Chris Chambliss	.40	.30	.15
15	Bill Nahorodny	.30	.25	.12
16	Rafael Ramirez	.35	.25	.14
17	Glenn Hubbard	.35	.25	.14
18	Claudell Washington	.40	.30	.15
19	Terry Harper	.70	.50	.30
20	Bruce Benedict	.30	.25	.12
24	John Montefusco	.30	.25	.12
25	Rufino Linares	.30	.25	.12
26	Gene Garber	.30	.25	.12
30	Brian Asselstine	.30	.25	.12
34	Larry Bradford	.30	.25	.12
35	Phil Niekro	1.50	1.25	.60

		MT	NR MT	EX
37	Rick Camp	.30	.25	.12
39	Al Hrabosky	.35	.25	.14
40	Tommy Boggs	.30	.25	.12
42	Rick Mahler	.40	.30	.15
45	Ed Miller	.30	.25	.12
46	Gaylord Perry	1.50	1.25	.60
49	Preston Hanna	.30	.25	.12
-----	Hank Aaron	2.50	2.00	1.00

1981 Police/Fire Safety
Dodgers

A WORD FROM MANAGER
TOM LASORDA
"Here's the difference between a gang and a team. Gangs have no rules. They believe that anything goes. They rob, cripple and even kill just to get rid of the opposition. But teams thrive on opposition and every member plays by the rules. Gangs make cowards. Teams make heroes. Don't let anyone force you into a gang. Be good to yourself and join a team."

TOM LASORDA
No. 2 — Manager
LAPD SALUTES THE 1981
Dodgers

Very similar in format to their successful set of the year before, the Los Angeles Dodgers 1981 police set grew to 32 cards (from 30). This was due to the acquisitions of Ken Landreaux and Dave Stewart shortly before printing of the sets. These two cards may even have been added after the initial printing run, making them slightly more difficult to obtain. The full-color cards are again 2-13/16" by 4-1/8", with a safety tip on the card back. Each card front has the line "LAPD Salutes the 1981 Dodgers."

		MT	NR MT	EX
Complete Set:		10.00	7.50	4.00
Common Player:		.20	.15	.08
2	Tom Lasorda	.40	.30	.15
3	Rudy Law	.20	.15	.08
6	Steve Garvey	1.25	.90	.50
7	Steve Yeager	.20	.15	.08
8	Reggie Smith	.40	.30	.15
10	Ron Cey	.40	.30	.15
12	Dusty Baker	.30	.25	.12
13	Joe Ferguson	.20	.15	.08
14	Mike Scioscia	.30	.25	.12
15	Davey Lopes	.35	.25	.14
16	Rick Monday	.30	.25	.12
18	Bill Russell	.30	.25	.12
21	Jay Johnstone	.25	.20	.10
26	Don Stanhouse	.20	.15	.08
27	Joe Beckwith	.20	.15	.08
28	Pete Guerrero	.70	.50	.30
30	Derrel Thomas	.20	.15	.08
34	Fernando Valenzuela	2.00	1.50	.80
35	Bob Welch	.40	.30	.15
36	Pepe Frias	.20	.15	.08
37	Robert Castillo	.20	.15	.08
38	Dave Goltz	.25	.20	.10
41	Jerry Reuss	.35	.25	.14
43	Rick Sutcliffe	.50	.40	.20
44a	Mickey Hatcher	.25	.20	.10
44b	Ken Landreaux	.70	.50	.30
46	Burt Hooton	.25	.20	.10
48	Dave Stewart	1.50	1.25	.60
51	Terry Forster	.25	.20	.10
57	Steve Howe	.25	.20	.10
-----	Coaching Staff (Monty Basgall, Mark Cresse, Tom Lasorda, Manny Mota, Danny Ozark, Ron Perranoski)	.20	.15	.08
-----	Team Photo/Checklist	.20	.15	.08

1981 Police/Fire Safety
Mariners

FLOYD BANNISTER Pitcher
Seattle Mariners

TIPS from the MARINERS

TEAMWORK

Individual players working together in order to accomplish specific goals.

Crime prevention is a team effort — JOIN THE TEAM.

COURTESY OF THE FOLLOWING SPONSORS AND YOUR LOCAL LAW ENFORCEMENT AGENCY

These 2-5/8" by 4-1/8" cards were co-sponsored by the Washington State Crime Prevention Assoc., Coca-Cola, Kiawanis and Ernst Home Centers. There are 16 players featured in this full-color set with each card numbered in the lower left of the card back. Card fronts list player name and position and have a team logo. Card backs are printed in blue and red and offer a "Tip from the Mariners" along with the four sponsor logos.

		MT	NR MT	EX
Complete Set:		5.00	3.75	2.00
Common Player:		.25	.20	.10
1	Jeff Burroughs	.35	.25	.14
2	Floyd Bannister	.60	.45	.25
3	Glenn Abbott	.25	.20	.10
4	Jim Anderson	.25	.20	.10
5	Danny Meyer	.25	.20	.10
6	Dave Edler	.25	.20	.10
7	Julio Cruz	.25	.20	.10
8	Kenny Clay	.25	.20	.10
9	Lenny Randle	.25	.20	.10
10	Mike Parrott	.25	.20	.10
11	Tom Paciorek	.25	.20	.10
12	Jerry Narron	.25	.20	.10
13	Richie Zisk	.35	.25	.14
14	Maury Wills	.50	.40	.20
15	Joe Simpson	.25	.20	.10
16	Shane Rawley	.60	.45	.25

1981 Police/Fire Safety
Royals

CLINT HURDLE
Outfielder
6-3"
195 lbs.
Royals

Ten of the most popular 1981 Kansas City players are featured in this 2-1/2" by 4-1/8" card set. Card fronts feature full-color photos with player name, position, facsimile autograph and team logo. Backs include player statistics, a tip from the Royals and list the four sponsoring organizations. Surprisingly, the set was issued by the Ft. Myers, Fla., police department near the Royals' spring training headquarters.

	MT	NR MT	EX
Complete Set:	28.00	21.00	11.00
Common Player:	.35	.25	.14
(1) Willie Mays Aikens	.35	.25	.14
(2) George Brett	18.00	13.50	7.25
(3) Rich Gale	.35	.25	.14
(4) Clint Hurdle	.35	.25	.14
(5) Dennis Leonard	1.00	.70	.40
(6) Hal McRae	1.25	.90	.50
(7) Amos Otis	1.00	.70	.40
(8) U.L. Washington	.35	.25	.14
(9) Frank White	1.50	1.25	.60
(10) Willie Wilson	2.25	1.75	.90

1982 Police/Fire Safety Braves

Dale Murphy (3)
Outfield

After their successful debut in 1981, the Atlanta Braves, the Atlanta Police Department, Coca-Cola and Hostess issued another card set in '82. This 30-card set is extremely close in format to the 1981 set and again measures 2-5/8" by 4-1/8". The full-color player photos are outstanding, and each card front also bears a statement marking the 1982 Braves' record-breaking 13-game win streak at the season's beginning. Card backs offer short biographies and "Tips from the Braves." Sponsors logos are also included. Reportedly, only 8,000 of these sets were printed.

	MT	NR MT	EX
Complete Set:	20.00	15.00	8.00
Common Player:	.30	.25	.12
1 Jerry Royster	.30	.25	.12
3 Dale Murphy	3.50	2.75	1.50
4 Biff Pocoroba	.30	.25	.12
5 Bob Horner	1.25	.90	.50
6 Randy Johnson	.30	.25	.12
8 Bob Watson	2.00	1.50	.80
9 Joe Torre	.40	.30	.15
10 Chris Chambliss	.40	.30	.15
15 C. Washington	.40	.30	.15
16 Rafael Ramirez	.35	.25	.14
17 Glenn Hubbard	.35	.25	.14
20 Bruce Benedict	.30	.25	.12
22 Brett Butler	.70	.50	.30
23 Tommie Aaron	.40	.30	.15
25 Rufino Linares	.30	.25	.12
26 Gene Garber	.30	.25	.12
27 Larry McWilliams	.30	.25	.12
28 Larry Whisenton	.30	.25	.12
32 Steve Bedrosian	1.00	.70	.40
35 Phil Niekro	2.00	1.50	.80
37 Rick Camp	.30	.25	.12
38 Joe Cowley	.30	.25	.12
39 Al Hrabosky	.35	.25	.14
42 Rick Mahler	.40	.30	.15
43 Bob Walk	.35	.25	.14
45 Bob Gibson	1.50	1.25	.60
49 Preston Hanna	.30	.25	.12
52 Joe Pignatano	.30	.25	.12

	MT	NR MT	EX
53 Dal Maxvill	.30	.25	.12
54 Rube Walker	.30	.25	.12

1982 Police/Fire Safety Brewers

ROBIN YOUNT
No. 19 — Shortstop
New Berlin Police Department
Salutes The 1982
Milwaukee Brewers

The inaugural Milwaukee Brewers police set contains 30 cards in a 2-13/16" by 4-1/8" format. There are 26 players included in the set, which are numbered by player uniform number. Unnumbered cards were also issued for general manager Harry Dalton, manager Buck Rodgers, the coaches and a team card with checklist. The full-color photos are especially attractive, printed on the cards' crisp white stock. A number of Wisconsin law enforcement agencies distributed the cards and credit lines on the card fronts were changed accordingly.

	MT	NR MT	EX
Complete Set:	15.00	11.00	6.00
Common Player:	.30	.25	.12
4 Paul Molitor	1.00	.70	.40
5 Ned Yost	.30	.25	.12
7 Don Money	.25	.20	.10
9 Larry Hisle	.25	.20	.10
10 Bob McClure	.30	.25	.12
11 Ed Romero	.30	.25	.12
13 Roy Howell	.30	.25	.12
15 Cecil Cooper	.50	.40	.20
17 Jim Gantner	.30	.25	.12
19 Robin Yount	1.50	1.25	.60
20 Gorman Thomas	.40	.30	.15
22 Charlie Moore	.30	.25	.12
23 Ted Simmons	.50	.40	.20
24 Ben Oglivie	.30	.25	.12
26 Kevin Bass	.60	.45	.25
28 Jamie Easterly	.20	.15	.08
29 Mark Brouhard	.20	.15	.08
30 Moose Haas	.20	.15	.08
34 Rollie Fingers	.70	.50	.30
35 Randy Lerch	.20	.15	.08
37 Buck Rodgers	.20	.15	.08
41 Jim Slaton	.20	.15	.08
45 Doug Jones	.20	.15	.08
46 Jerry Augustine	.20	.15	.08
47 Dwight Bernard	.20	.15	.08
48 Mike Caldwell	.25	.20	.10
50 Pete Vuckovich	.30	.25	.12
----- Team Photo/Checklist	.20	.15	.08
----- Harry Dalton (general mgr.)	.20	.15	.08
----- Coaches Card (Pat Dobson, Larry Haney, Ron Hansen, Cal McLish, Buck Rodgers, Harry Warner)	.20	.15	.08

1982 Police/Fire Safety Dodgers

Again issued in the same 2-13/16" by 4-1/8" size of the '80 and '81 sets, the 1982 Los Angeles set commemorates the team's 1981 World Champion-

FERNANDO VALENZUELA
No. 34 – PITCHER
The Los Angeles Police Department
presents the World Champion
Dodgers

ship. In addition to the 26 cards numbered by uniform for players and manager Tom Lasorda, there are four unnumbered cards which feature the team winning the division, league and World Series titles, plus one of the World Series trophy. The full-color card photos are once again vivid portraits on a clean white card stock. Card backs offer brief biographies and stadium information in addition to a safety tip.

		MT	NR MT	EX
Complete Set:		6.00	4.50	2.50
Common Player:		.15	.11	.06
2	Tom Lasorda	.30	.25	.12
6	Steve Garvey	1.00	.70	.40
7	Steve Yeager	.15	.11	.06
8	Mark Belanger	.20	.15	.08
10	Ron Cey	.30	.25	.12
12	Dusty Baker	.25	.20	.10
14	Mike Scioscia	.25	.20	.10
16	Rick Monday	.25	.20	.10
18	Bill Russell	.20	.15	.08
21	Jay Johnstone	.20	.15	.08
26	Alejandro Pena	.60	.45	.25
28	Pedro Guerrero	.80	.60	.30
30	Derrel Thomas	.15	.11	.06
31	Jorge Orta	.15	.11	.06
34	Fernando Valenzuela	1.00	.70	.40
35	Bob Welch	.35	.25	.14
38	Dave Goltz	.15	.11	.06
40	Ron Roenicke	.15	.11	.06
41	Jerry Reuss	.25	.20	.10
44	Ken Landreaux	.15	.11	.06
46	Burt Hooton	.20	.15	.08
48	Dave Stewart	.30	.25	.12
49	Tom Niedenfuer	.35	.25	.14
51	Terry Forster	.20	.15	.08
52	Steve Sax	.90	.70	.35
57	Steve Howe	.20	.15	.08
-----	Division Championship	.15	.11	.06
-----	League Championship	.15	.11	.06
-----	World Series Championship	.15	.11	.06
-----	Trophy Card/Checklist	.15	.11	.06

1983 Police/Fire Safety Braves

Brett Butler (22)
Outfielder

An almost exact replica of their 1982 set, the 1983

Atlanta Braves police set includes 30 cards numbered by uniform. Sponsors Hostess, Coca-Cola and the Atlanta Police Department returned for the third year. The cards are again 2-5/8" by 4-1/8", with full-color photos and police and team logos on the card fronts. A statment noting the team's 1982 National League Western Division title in the upper right corner is the key difference on the card fronts. As in 1982, 8,000 sets were reportedly printed.

		MT	NR MT	EX
Complete Set:		15.00	11.00	6.00
Common Player:		.30	.25	.12
1	Jerry Royster	.30	.25	.12
3	Dale Murphy	3.50	2.75	1.50
4	Biff Pocoroba	.30	.25	.12
5	Bob Horner	1.00	.70	.40
6	Randy Johnson	.30	.25	.12
8	Bob Watson	.35	.25	.14
9	Joe Torre	.40	.30	.15
10	Chris Chambliss	.40	.30	.15
11	Ken Smith	.30	.25	.12
15	Claudell Washington	.40	.30	.15
16	Rafael Ramirez	.35	.25	.14
17	Glenn Hubbard	.35	.25	.14
19	Terry Harper	.30	.25	.12
20	Bruce Benedict	.30	.25	.12
22	Brett Butler	.40	.30	.15
24	Larry Owen	.30	.25	.12
26	Gene Garber	.30	.25	.12
27	Pascual Perez	.35	.25	.14
29	Craig McMurtry	.35	.25	.14
32	Steve Bedrosian	.60	.45	.25
33	Pete Falcone	.30	.25	.12
35	Phil Niekro	1.50	1.25	.60
36	Sonny Jackson	.30	.25	.12
37	Rick Camp	.30	.25	.12
45	Bob Gibson	1.25	.90	.50
49	Rick Behenna	.30	.25	.12
51	Terry Forster	.35	.25	.14
52	Joe Pignatano	.30	.25	.12
53	Dal Maxvill	.30	.25	.12
54	Rube Walker	.30	.25	.12

1983 Police/Fire Safety Brewers

16 MARSHALL EDWARDS — OF
The Milwaukee Police Department
Presents The 1983
Milwaukee Brewers

Similar to 1982, a number of issuer variations exist for the 1983 Brewers police set, as law enforcement agencies throughout the state distributed the set with their own credit lines on the cards. At least 28 variations are known to exist, with those issued by smaller agencies being scarcest. Prices quoted below are for the most common variations, generally the Milwaukee police department and a few small-town departments whose entire supply of police cards seem to have fallen into dealers' hands. Some specialists are willing to pay a premium for the scarcer departments' issues. The 30 2-13/16" 4-1/8" cards include 29 players and coaches, along with a team card (with a checklist back). The team card and group coaches' card are unnumbered, while the others are numbered by uniform number.

		MT	NR MT	EX
	Complete Set:	7.00	5.25	2.75
	Common Player:	.20	.15	.08
4	Paul Molitor	.90	.70	.35
5	Ned Yost	.20	.15	.08
7	Don Money	.25	.20	.10
8	Rob Picciolo	.20	.15	.08
10	Bob McClure	.20	.15	.08
11	Ed Romero	.20	.15	.08
13	Roy Howell	.20	.15	.08
15	Cecil Cooper	.50	.40	.20
16	Marshall Edwards	.20	.15	.08
17	Jim Gantner	.30	.25	.12
19	Robin Yount	1.25	.90	.50
20	Gorman Thomas	.40	.30	.15
21	Don Sutton	.60	.45	.25
22	Charlie Moore	.20	.15	.08
23	Ted Simmons	.50	.40	.20
24	Ben Oglivie	.30	.25	.12
26	Bob Skube	.20	.15	.08
27	Pete Ladd	.20	.15	.08
28	Jamie Easterly	.20	.15	.08
30	Moose Haas	.20	.15	.08
32	Harvey Kuenn	.30	.25	.12
34	Rollie Fingers	.70	.50	.30
40	Bob Gibson	.20	.15	.08
41	Jim Slaton	.20	.15	.08
42	Tom Tellmann	.20	.15	.08
46	Jerry Augustine	.20	.15	.08
48	Mike Caldwell	.25	.20	.10
50	Pete Vuckovich	.30	.25	.12
----	Team Photo/Checklist	.20	.15	.08
----	Coaches Card (Pat Dobson, Dave Garcia, Larry Haney, Ron Hansen)	.20	.15	.08

1983 Police/Fire Safety Dodgers

While these full-color cards remained 2-13/16" by 4-1/8" and card fronts were similar to those of previous years, the card backs are quite different. Card backs are in a horizontal design for the first time, and include a small head portrait photo of the player in the upper left corner. Fairly complete player statistics are included but there is no safety tip. The 30 cards are numbered by uniform number, with an unnumbered coaches card also included. Fronts include the year, team logo, player name and number.

		MT	NR MT	EX
	Complete Set:	6.00	4.50	2.50
	Common Player:	.15	.11	.06
2	Tom Lasorda	.30	.25	.12
3	Steve Sax	.60	.45	.25
5	Mike Marshall	.60	.45	.25
7	Steve Yeager	.15	.11	.06
12	Dusty Baker	.25	.20	.10
14	Mike Scioscia	.25	.20	.10
16	Rick Monday	.25	.20	.10
17	Greg Brock	.40	.30	.15
18	Bill Russell	.20	.15	.08
20	Candy Maldonado	.40	.30	.15
21	Ricky Wright	.15	.11	.06
22	Mark Bradley	.15	.11	.06

		MT	NR MT	EX
23	Dave Sax	.15	.11	.06
26	Alejandro Pena	.25	.20	.10
27	Joe Beckwith	.15	.11	.06
28	Pedro Guerrero	.60	.45	.25
30	Derrel Thomas	.15	.11	.06
34	Fernando Valenzuela	.70	.50	.30
35	Bob Welch	.30	.25	.12
38	Pat Zachry	.15	.11	.06
40	Ron Roenicke	.15	.11	.06
41	Jerry Reuss	.25	.20	.10
43	Jose Morales	.15	.11	.06
44	Ken Landreaux	.15	.11	.06
46	Burt Hooton	.20	.15	.08
47	Larry White	.15	.11	.06
48	Dave Stewart	.25	.20	.10
49	Tom Niedenfuer	.20	.15	.08
57	Steve Howe	.20	.15	.08
----	Coaches Card (Joe Amalfitano, Monty Basgall, Mark Cresse, Manny Mota, Ron Perranoski)	.15	.11	.06

1983 Police/Fire Safety Royals

After skipping the 1982 season, the Ft. Myers, Fla., police department issued a Royals safety set in 1983 that is almost identical to their set of 1981. The set is again 2-1/2" by 4-1/8" and numbers just 10 players. Cards are unnumbered, with vertical fronts and horizontal backs. Card fronts have team logos, player name and position and facsimile autographs. Backs list the four sponsoring organizations, a "Tip from the Royals" and a "Kids and Cops Fact" about each player.

		MT	NR MT	EX
	Complete Set:	28.00	21.00	11.00
	Common Player:	.35	.25	.14
(1)	Willie Mays Aikens	.35	.25	.14
(2)	George Brett	18.00	13.50	7.25
(3)	Dennis Leonard	1.00	.70	.40
(4)	Hal McRae	1.25	.90	.50
(5)	Amos Otis	1.00	.70	.40
(6)	Dan Quisenberry	1.75	1.25	.70
(7)	U.L. Washington	.35	.25	.14
(8)	John Wathan	.50	.40	.20
(9)	Frank White	1.50	1.25	.60
(10)	Willie Wilson	2.25	1.75	.90

1984 Police/Fire Safety Blue Jays

This 35-card set was issued in conjuction with the Toronto Sun newspaper and various Ontario area fire departments. The cards feature full-color action photos on the fronts, along with the player name, number and position. Rather than the customary wide white border on front, the Blue Jays fire safety set features bright blue borders. The card backs include brief player biographies and a fire safety tip.

The 2-1/2" by 3-1/2" cards were distributed five at a time at two-week intervals during the summer of 1984.

		MT	NR MT	EX
Complete Set:		10.00	7.50	4.00
Common Player:		.20	.15	.08
1	Tony Fernandez	1.00	.70	.40
3	Jimy Williams	.20	.15	.08
4	Alfredo Griffin	.30	.25	.12
5	Rance Mulliniks	.20	.15	.08
6	Bobby Cox	.20	.15	.08
7	Damaso Garcia	.30	.25	.12
8	John Sullivan	.20	.15	.08
9	Rick Leach	.20	.15	.08
10	Dave Collins	.25	.20	.10
11	George Bell	1.50	1.25	.60
12	Ernie Whitt	.30	.25	.12
13	Buck Martinez	.20	.15	.08
15	Lloyd Moseby	.50	.40	.20
16	Garth Iorg	.20	.15	.08
17	Kelly Gruber	.25	.20	.10
18	Jim Clancy	.30	.25	.12
23	Mitch Webster	.50	.40	.20
24	Willie Aikens	.20	.15	.08
25	Roy Lee Jackson	.20	.15	.08
26	Willie Upshaw	.30	.25	.12
27	Jimmy Key	1.00	.70	.40
29	Jesse Barfield	.80	.60	.30
31	Jim Acker	.20	.15	.08
33	Doyle Alexander	.30	.25	.12
34	Stan Clarke	.20	.15	.08
35	Bryan Clark	.20	.15	.08
37	Dave Stieb	.60	.45	.25
38	Jim Gott	.20	.15	.08
41	Al Widmar	.20	.15	.08
42	Billy Smith	.20	.15	.08
43	Cito Gaston	.20	.15	.08
44	Cliff Johnson	.20	.15	.08
48	Luis Leal	.20	.15	.08
53	Dennis Lamp	.20	.15	.08
-----	Team Logo/Checklist	.20	.15	.08

1984 Police/Fire Safety Braves

A fourth annual effort by the Braves, the Atlanta

Police Department, Coca-Cola and Hostess. This 30-card set continued to be printed in a 2-5/8" by 4-1/8" format, with full-color photos plus team and police logos on the card fronts. For the first time, the cards also have a large logo and date in the upper right corner. Hostess and Coke logos again are on the card backs, with brief player information and a safety tip. Two cards in the set (Pascual Perez and Rafael Ramirez) were issued in Spanish. Cards were distributed two per week by Atlanta police officers. As in 1982 and 1983, a reported 8,000 sets were printed.

		MT	NR MT	EX
Complete Set:		12.00	9.00	4.75
Common Player:		.25	.20	.10
1	Jerry Royster	.25	.20	.10
3	Dale Murphy	3.50	2.75	1.50
5	Bob Horner	1.00	.70	.40
6	Randy Johnson	.25	.20	.10
8	Bob Watson	.30	.25	.12
9	Joe Torre	.40	.30	.15
10	Chris Chambliss	.40	.30	.15
11	Mike Jorgensen	.25	.20	.10
15	Claudell Washington	.40	.30	.15
16	Rafael Ramirez	.30	.25	.12
17	Glenn Hubbard	.30	.25	.12
19	Terry Harper	.25	.20	.10
20	Bruce Benedict	.25	.20	.10
25	Alex Trevino	.25	.20	.10
26	Gene Garber	.25	.20	.10
27	Pascual Perez	.30	.25	.12
28	Gerald Perry	1.50	1.25	.60
29	Craig McMurtry	.25	.20	.10
31	Donnie Moore	.25	.20	.10
32	Steve Bedrosian	.60	.45	.25
33	Pete Falcone	.25	.20	.10
37	Rick Camp	.25	.20	.10
39	Len Barker	.25	.20	.10
42	Rick Mahler	.40	.30	.15
45	Bob Gibson	1.25	.90	.50
51	Terry Forster	.30	.25	.12
52	Joe Pignatano	.25	.20	.10
53	Dal Maxvill	.25	.20	.10
54	Rube Walker	.25	.20	.10
55	Luke Appling	.60	.45	.25

1984 Police/Fire Safety Brewers

The king of the variations again in 1984, the Milwaukee Brewers set has been found with more than 50 different police agencies' credit lines on the front of the cards. Once again, law enforcement agencies statewide participated in distributing the sets. Some departments also include a badge of the participating agency on the card backs. The full-color cards measure 2-13/16" by 4-1/8". There are 28 numbered player and manager cards, along with an unnumbered coaches card and a team card. Player names, uniform numbers and positions are listed on each card front. Prices listed are for the most common variety (Milwaukee police department); sets issued by smaller departments may be worth a premium to specialists.

		MT	NR MT	EX
	Complete Set:	6.00	4.50	2.50
	Common Player:	.15	.11	.06
2	Randy Ready	.30	.25	.12
4	Paul Molitor	.80	.60	.30
8	Jim Sundberg	.15	.11	.06
9	Rene Lachemann	.15	.11	.06
10	Bob McClure	.15	.11	.06
11	Ed Romero	.15	.11	.06
13	Roy Howell	.15	.11	.06
14	Dion James	.50	.40	.20
15	Cecil Cooper	.40	.30	.15
17	Jim Gantner	.25	.20	.10
19	Robin Yount	1.25	.90	.50
20	Don Sutton	.50	.40	.20
21	Bill Schroeder	.30	.25	.12
22	Charlie Moore	.15	.11	.06
23	Ted Simmons	.40	.30	.15
24	Ben Oglivie	.25	.20	.10
25	Bobby Clark	.15	.11	.06
27	Pete Ladd	.15	.11	.06
28	Rick Manning	.15	.11	.06
29	Mark Brouhard	.15	.11	.06
30	Moose Haas	.15	.11	.06
34	Rollie Fingers	.60	.45	.25
42	Tom Tellmann	.15	.11	.06
43	Chuck Porter	.15	.11	.06
46	Jerry Augustine	.15	.11	.06
47	Jaime Cocanower	.15	.11	.06
48	Mike Caldwell	.20	.15	.08
50	Pete Vuckovich	.25	.20	.10
----	Team Photo/Checklist	.15	.11	.06
----	Coaches Card (Pat Dobson, Dave Garcia, Larry Haney, Tom Trebelhorn)	.15	.11	.06

1984 Police/Fire Safety Dodgers

This was the fifth yearly effort of the Dodgers and the Los Angeles Police Department. There are 30 cards in the set, which remains 2-13/16" by 4-1/8". Card fronts are designed somewhat differently than previous years, with more posed photos, bolder player names and numbers and a different team logo. Card backs again feature a small portrait photo in the upper left corner, along with brief biographical information and an anti-drug tip. Card backs are in Dodger blue. Cards are numbered by uniform number, with an unnumbered coaches card also included.

		MT	NR MT	EX
	Complete Set:	8.00	6.00	3.25
	Common Player:	.15	.11	.06
2	Tom Lasorda	.30	.25	.12
3	Steve Sax	.60	.45	.25
5	Mike Marshall	.50	.40	.20
7	Steve Yeager	.15	.11	.06
9	Greg Brock	.30	.25	.12
10	Dave Anderson	.20	.15	.08
14	Mike Scioscia	.25	.20	.10
16	Rick Monday	.25	.20	.10

		MT	NR MT	EX
17	Rafael Landestoy	.15	.11	.06
18	Bill Russell	.20	.15	.08
20	Candy Maldonado	.25	.20	.10
21	Bob Bailor	.15	.11	.06
25	German Rivera	.15	.11	.06
26	Alejandro Pena	.25	.20	.10
27	Carlos Diaz	.15	.11	.06
28	Pedro Guerrero	.70	.50	.30
31	Jack Fimple	.15	.11	.06
34	Fernando Valenzuela	.70	.50	.30
35	Bob Welch	.30	.25	.12
38	Pat Zachry	.15	.11	.06
40	Rick Honeycutt	.15	.11	.06
41	Jerry Reuss	.25	.20	.10
43	Jose Morales	.15	.11	.06
44	Ken Landreaux	.15	.11	.06
45	Terry Whitfield	.15	.11	.06
46	Burt Hooton	.20	.15	.08
49	Tom Niedenfuer	.20	.15	.08
55	Orel Hershiser	2.50	2.00	1.00
56	Richard Rodas	.15	.11	.06
----	Coaches Card (Joe Amalfitano, Monty Basgall, Mark Cresse, Manny Mota, Ron Perranoski)	.15	.11	.06

1985 Police/Fire Safety Blue Jays

JESSE BARFIELD
29
outfielder

The Toronto Blue Jays issued a 35-card fire safety set for the second year in a row in 1985. Cards feature players, coaches, manager, checklist and team picture. The full-color photos are on the card fronts with a blue border. The backs feature player stats and a safety tip. The cards measure 2-1/2" by 3-1/2" and were distributed throughout the Province of Ontario, Canada.

		MT	NR MT	EX
	Complete Set:	8.00	6.00	3.25
	Common Player:	.20	.15	.08
1	Tony Fernandez	.70	.50	.30
3	Jimy Williams	.20	.15	.08
4	Manny Lee	.25	.20	.10
5	Rance Mulliniks	.20	.15	.08
6	Bobby Cox	.20	.15	.08
7	Damaso Garcia	.30	.25	.12
8	John Sullivan	.20	.15	.08
11	George Bell	1.25	.90	.50
12	Ernie Whitt	.30	.25	.12
13	Buck Martinez	.20	.15	.08
15	Lloyd Moseby	.40	.30	.15
16	Garth Iorg	.20	.15	.08
17	Kelly Gruber	.20	.15	.08
18	Jim Clancy	.30	.25	.12
22	Jimmy Key	.50	.40	.20
23	Mitch Webster	.25	.20	.10
24	Willie Aikens	.20	.15	.08
25	Len Matuszek	.20	.15	.08
26	Willie Upshaw	.30	.25	.12
28	Lou Thornton	.20	.15	.08
29	Jesse Barfield	.80	.60	.30
30	Ron Musselman	.20	.15	.08
31	Jim Acker	.20	.15	.08
33	Doyle Alexander	.30	.25	.12
36	Bill Caudill	.20	.15	.08

		MT	NR MT	EX
37	Dave Stieb	.50	.40	.20
41	Al Widmar	.20	.15	.08
42	Billy Smith	.20	.15	.08
43	Cito Gaston	.20	.15	.08
44	Jeff Burroughs	.20	.15	.08
46	Gary Lavelle	.20	.15	.08
48	Luis Leal	.20	.15	.08
50	Tom Henke	.40	.30	.15
53	Dennis Lamp	.20	.15	.08
----	Team Logo/Checklist	.20	.15	.08
----	Team Photo/Schedule	.20	.15	.08

1985 Police/Fire Safety
Braves

Dale Murphy (3)
Outfielder

There are again 30 full-color cards in this fifth annual set. Hostess, Coca-Cola and the Atlanta Police Department joined the team as sponsors again for the 2-5/8" by 4-1/8" set. Card backs are similar to previous years, with the only difference on the fronts being a swap in position for the year and team logo. The cards are checklisted by uniform number.

		MT	NR MT	EX
Complete Set:		12.00	9.00	4.75
Common Player:		.25	.20	.10
2	Albert Hall	.40	.30	.15
3	Dale Murphy	3.25	2.50	1.25
5	Rick Cerone	.25	.20	.10
7	Bobby Wine	.25	.20	.10
10	Chris Chambliss	.35	.25	.14
11	Bob Horner	1.00	.70	.40
12	Paul Runge	.30	.25	.12
15	Claudell Washington	.35	.25	.14
16	Rafael Ramirez	.30	.25	.12
17	Glenn Hubbard	.30	.25	.12
18	Paul Zuvella	.30	.25	.12
19	Terry Harper	.25	.20	.10
20	Bruce Benedict	.25	.20	.10
22	Eddie Haas	.25	.20	.10
24	Ken Oberkfell	.30	.25	.12
26	Gene Garber	.25	.20	.10
27	Pascual Perez	.30	.25	.12
28	Gerald Perry	1.00	.70	.40
29	Craig McMurtry	.25	.20	.10
32	Steve Bedrosian	.50	.40	.20
33	Johnny Sain	.35	.25	.14
34	Zane Smith	.60	.45	.25
36	Brad Komminsk	.25	.20	.10
37	Rick Camp	.25	.20	.10
39	Len Barker	.25	.20	.10
40	Bruce Sutter	.70	.50	.30
42	Rick Mahler	.35	.25	.14
51	Terry Forster	.30	.25	.12
52	Leo Mazzone	.25	.20	.10
53	Bobby Dews	.25	.20	.10

A player's name in *italic* type indicates a rookie card. An (FC) indicates a player's first card for that particular card company.

1985 Police/Fire Safety
Brewers

49   Ted Higuera   P
The Milwaukee Police Department
and The Milwaukee Journal
present the 1985
Milwaukee Brewers

Ted Higuera says:
When athletes graduate from high school, the best ones are drafted by the major-league teams. The rest pursue other careers.
It's important to learn a trade or profession. Be the best at what you do, and you'll be drafted for a good job when you graduate from school.
Watch the Thursday **Milwaukee Journal Sports Weekend** section for the 3 players featured on next week's baseball cards. You could win free tickets to a Brewer game!

The Brewers changed the size of their annual police set in 1985, but almost imperceptibly. The full-color cards are 2-3/4" by 4-1/8", a slight 1/16" narrower than the four previous efforts. Player and team name on the card fronts are much bolder than in previous years. Once again, numerous area police groups distributed the sets, leading to nearly 60 variations, as each agency put their own credit line on the cards. Card backs include the Brewers logo, a safety tip and, in some cases, a badge of the participating law enforcement group. There are 27 numbered player cards (by uniform number) and three unnumbered cards - team roster, coaches and a newspaper carrier card. Prices are for the most common departments.

		MT	NR MT	EX
Complete Set:		6.00	4.50	2.50
Common Player:		.15	.11	.06
2	Randy Ready	.15	.11	.06
4	Paul Molitor	.70	.50	.30
5	Doug Loman	.15	.11	.06
7	Paul Householder	.15	.11	.06
10	Bob McClure	.15	.11	.06
11	Ed Romero	.15	.11	.06
14	Dion James	.25	.20	.10
15	Cecil Cooper	.40	.30	.15
17	Jim Gantner	.25	.20	.10
18	Danny Darwin	.20	.15	.08
19	Robin Yount	1.00	.70	.40
21	Bill Schroeder	.20	.15	.08
22	Charlie Moore	.15	.11	.06
23	Ted Simmons	.40	.30	.15
24	Ben Oglivie	.25	.20	.10
26	Brian Giles	.15	.11	.06
27	Pete Ladd	.15	.11	.06
28	Rick Manning	.15	.11	.06
29	Mark Brouhard	.15	.11	.06
30	Moose Haas	.15	.11	.06
31	George Bamberger	.15	.11	.06
34	Rollie Fingers	.60	.45	.25
40	Bob Gibson	.15	.11	.06
41	Ray Searage	.15	.11	.06
47	Jaime Cocanower	.15	.11	.06
48	Ray Burris	.15	.11	.06
49	Ted Higuera	1.25	.90	.50
50	Pete Vuckovich	.25	.20	.10
----	Coaches Card (Andy Etchebarren, Larry Haney, Frank Howard, Tony Muser, Herm Starrette)	.15	.11	.06
----	Team Photo	.15	.11	.06

1985 Police/Fire Safety
Phillies

This is a brilliantly colored 2-5/8" by 4-1/8" set, co-sponsored by the Phillies and Cigna Corporation. Card fronts include the player name, number, position and team logo. The 16 cards are numbered

		MT	NR MT	EX
3	Mike Scott	.60	.45	.25
4	Kevin Bass	.40	.30	.15
5	Bill Doran	.40	.30	.15
6	Hal Lanier	.20	.15	.08
7	Denny Walling	.20	.15	.08
8	Alan Ashby	.20	.15	.08
9	Phil Garner	.25	.20	.10
10	Charlie Kerfeld	.25	.20	.10
11	Dave Smith	.30	.25	.12
12	Jose Cruz	.35	.25	.14
13	Craig Reynolds	.20	.15	.08
14	Mark Bailey	.20	.15	.08
15	Bob Knepper	.30	.25	.12
16	Julio Solano	.20	.15	.08
17	Dickie Thon	.25	.20	.10
18	Mike Madden	.20	.15	.08
19	Jeff Calhoun	.20	.15	.08
20	Tony Walker	.20	.15	.08
21	Terry Puhl	.20	.15	.08
22	Glenn Davis	1.00	.70	.40
23	Billy Hatcher	.40	.30	.15
24	Jim Deshaies	.40	.30	.15
25	Frank DiPino	.20	.15	.08
26	Coaching Staff (Yogi Berra, Matt Galante, Denis Menke, Les Moss, Gene Tenace)	.20	.15	.08

on the back and include biographical information and a safety tip. The cards were distributed by several Philadelphia area police departments.

		MT	NR MT	EX
Complete Set:		7.00	5.25	2.75
Common Player:		.15	.11	.06
1	Juan Samuel	.50	.40	.20
2	Von Hayes	.35	.25	.14
3	Ozzie Virgil	.20	.15	.08
4	Mike Schmidt	1.25	.90	.50
5	Greg Gross	.15	.11	.06
6	Tim Corcoran	.15	.11	.06
7	Jerry Koosman	.25	.20	.10
8	Jeff Stone	.20	.15	.08
9	Glenn Wilson	.25	.20	.10
10	Steve Jeltz	.20	.15	.08
11	Garry Maddox	.20	.15	.08
12	Steve Carlton	.90	.70	.35
13	John Denny	.15	.11	.06
14	Kevin Gross	.30	.25	.12
15	Shane Rawley	.30	.25	.12
16	Charlie Hudson	.25	.20	.10

1986 Police/Fire Safety
Astros

This full-color police safety set for the 1986 Houston Astros was issued by the Houston Police Department and sponsored by Kool-Aid. The 26-card set was distributed at the Astrodome on June 14, when 15,000 sets of the first 12 cards were given away. The balance of the set was distributed throughout the summer by the Houston police. The cards feature player photos on the fronts and a safety tip on the card backs. The cards measure 4-1/8" by 2-5/8".

		MT	NR MT	EX
Complete Set:		8.00	6.00	3.25
Common Player:		.20	.15	.08
1	Jim Pankovits	.20	.15	.08
2	Nolan Ryan	1.25	.90	.50

1986 Police/Fire Safety
Blue Jays

This was the third consecutive year the Toronto Blue Jays issued a fire safety set of 36 baseball cards. The cards were given out at many fire stations in Ontario, Canada. The cards are printed in full color and include players and other personnel. The set was co-sponsored by the local fire departments, Bubble Yum and the Toronto Star. The cards measure 2-1/2" by 3-1/2".

		MT	NR MT	EX
Complete Set:		8.00	6.00	3.25
Common Player:		.20	.15	.08
1	Tony Fernandez	.70	.50	.30
3	Jimy Williams	.20	.15	.08
5	Rance Mulliniks	.20	.15	.08
7	Damaso Garcia	.30	.25	.12
8	John Sullivan	.20	.15	.08
9	Rick Leach	.20	.15	.08
11	George Bell	1.25	.90	.50
12	Ernie Whitt	.30	.25	.12
13	Buck Martinez	.20	.15	.08
15	Lloyd Moseby	.40	.30	.15
16	Garth Iorg	.20	.15	.08
17	Kelly Gruber	.20	.15	.08
18	Jim Clancy	.30	.25	.12
22	Jimmy Key	.50	.40	.20
23	Cecil Fielder	.20	.15	.08
24	John McLaren	.20	.15	.08
25	Steve Davis	.20	.15	.08
26	Willie Upshaw	.30	.25	.12
29	Jesse Barfield	.80	.60	.30
31	Jim Acker	.20	.15	.08
33	Doyle Alexander	.30	.25	.12
36	Bill Caudill	.20	.15	.08
37	Dave Stieb	.50	.40	.20
38	Mark Eichhorn	.40	.30	.15

		MT	NR MT	EX
39	Don Gordon	.25	.20	.10
41	Al Widmar	.20	.15	.08
42	Billy Smith	.20	.15	.08
43	Cito Gaston	.20	.15	.08
44	Cliff Johnson	.20	.15	.08
46	Gary Lavelle	.20	.15	.08
49	Tom Filer	.20	.15	.08
50	Tom Henke	.40	.30	.15
53	Dennis Lamp	.20	.15	.08
54	Jeff Hearron	.20	.15	.08
----	Team Photo	.20	.15	.08
----	10th Anniversary Logo Card	.20	.15	.08

1986 Police/Fire Safety
Braves

Dale Murphy (3)
Outfield

The Police Athletic League of Atlanta issued a 30-card full-color set featuring the Atlanta Braves players and personnel. The cards measure 2-5/8" by 4-1/8". Card fronts include player photos with name, uniform number and position below the photo. The cards backs offer the 100th Anniversary Coca-Cola logo, player information, statistics and a safety related tip. This was the sixth consecutive year that the Braves issued a safety set. The cards were available from police officers in Atlanta.

		MT	NR MT	EX
	Complete Set:	11.00	8.25	4.50
	Common Player:	.25	.20	.10
2	Russ Nixon	.25	.20	.10
3	Dale Murphy	2.75	2.00	1.00
4	Bob Skinner	.25	.20	.10
5	Billy Sample	.25	.20	.10
7	Chuck Tanner	.35	.25	.14
8	Willie Stargell	.80	.60	.30
9	Ozzie Virgil	.35	.25	.14
10	Chris Chambliss	.35	.25	.14
11	Bob Horner	.80	.60	.30
14	Andres Thomas	.50	.40	.20
15	Claudell Washington	.35	.25	.14
16	Rafael Ramirez	.30	.25	.12
17	Glenn Hubbard	.30	.25	.12
18	Omar Moreno	.25	.20	.10
19	Terry Harper	.25	.20	.10
20	Bruce Benedict	.25	.20	.10
23	Ted Simmons	.50	.40	.20
24	Ken Oberkfell	.30	.25	.12
26	Gene Garber	.25	.20	.10
29	Craig McMurtry	.25	.20	.10
30	Paul Assenmacher	.40	.30	.15
33	Johnny Sain	.30	.25	.12
34	Zane Smith	.40	.30	.15
38	Joe Johnson	.25	.20	.10
40	Bruce Sutter	.60	.45	.25
42	Rick Mahler	.35	.25	.14
46	David Palmer	.25	.20	.10
48	Duane Ward	.30	.25	.12
49	Jeff Dedmon	.25	.20	.10
52	Al Monchak	.25	.20	.10

1986 Police/Fire Safety
Brewers

45   Rob Deer   *OF
The Fond du Lac Police Dept., KFIZ Radio,
and National Exchange Bank & Trust
present the 1986
Milwaukee Brewers

The Milwaukee Brewers, in conjunction with the Milwaukee Police Department, WTMJ Radio and Kinney Shoes, produced this attractive police safety set of 30 cards. The cards measure 2-13/16" by 4-1/2". A thin black border encloses a full-color Player photo on the front. The card backs give a safety tip and promos for the sponsor. The cards were distributed throughout the state of Wisconsin by numerous police departments; those of the smaller departments generally being scarcer than those issued in the big cities. Prices quoted below are for the most common departments' issues.

		MT	NR MT	EX
	Complete Set:	6.00	4.50	2.50
	Common Player:	.15	.11	.06
1	Ernest Riles	.30	.25	.12
2	Randy Ready	.15	.11	.06
3	Juan Castillo	.20	.15	.08
4	Paul Molitor	.70	.50	.30
7	Paul Householder	.15	.11	.06
10	Bob McClure	.15	.11	.06
11	Rick Cerone	.15	.11	.06
13	Billy Jo Robidoux	.30	.25	.12
15	Cecil Cooper	.40	.30	.15
16	Mike Felder	.30	.25	.12
17	Jim Gantner	.25	.20	.10
18	Danny Darwin	.20	.15	.08
19	Robin Yount	1.00	.70	.40
20	Juan Nieves	.40	.30	.15
21	Bill Schroeder	.15	.11	.06
22	Charlie Moore	.15	.11	.06
24	Ben Oglivie	.25	.20	.10
25	Mark Clear	.15	.11	.06
28	Rick Manning	.15	.11	.06
31	George Bamberger	.15	.11	.06
37	Dan Plesac	.60	.45	.25
39	Tim Leary	.15	.11	.06
41	Ray Searage	.15	.11	.06
43	Chuck Porter	.15	.11	.06
45	Rob Deer	.40	.30	.15
46	Bill Wegman	.30	.25	.12
47	Jamie Cocanower	.15	.11	.06
49	Ted Higuera	.50	.40	.20
----	Coaches Card (Andy Etchebarren, Larry Haney, Frank Howard, Tony Muser, Herm Starrette)	.15	.11	.06
----	Team Photo/Roster	.15	.11	.06

1986 Police/Fire Safety
Dodgers

After skipping the 1985 season, the Los Angeles Dodgers once again issued baseball cards related to police safety. The club had issued sets from 1980-84. The 1986 set features 30 full-color glossy cards measuring 2-1/4" by 4-1/8". The cards are numbered according to player uniforms. The backs

MIKE MARSHALL

feature brief player data and a safety tip from the Los Angeles Police Department. The sets were given away May 18 during Baseball Card Day at Dodger Stadium.

		MT	NR MT	EX
Complete Set:		6.50	5.00	2.50
Common Player:		.15	.11	.06
2	Tom Lasorda	.25	.20	.10
3	Steve Sax	.50	.40	.20
5	Mike Marshall	.40	.30	.15
9	Greg Brock	.25	.20	.10
10	Dave Anderson	.15	.11	.06
12	Bill Madlock	.30	.25	.12
14	Mike Scioscia	.25	.20	.10
17	Len Matuszek	.15	.11	.06
18	Bill Russell	.20	.15	.08
22	Franklin Stubbs	.25	.20	.10
23	Enos Cabell	.15	.11	.06
25	Mariano Duncan	.20	.15	.08
26	Alejandro Pena	.25	.20	.10
27	Carlos Diaz	.15	.11	.06
28	Pedro Guerrero	.60	.45	.25
29	Alex Trevino	.15	.11	.06
31	Ed Vande Berg	.15	.11	.06
34	Fernando Valenzuela	.60	.45	.25
35	Bob Welch	.30	.25	.12
40	Rick Honeycutt	.15	.11	.06
41	Jerry Reuss	.25	.20	.10
43	Ken Howell	.20	.15	.08
44	Ken Landreaux	.15	.11	.06
45	Terry Whitfield	.15	.11	.06
48	Dennis Powell	.20	.15	.08
49	Tom Niedenfuer	.20	.15	.08
51	Reggie Williams	.20	.15	.08
55	Orel Hershiser	1.00	.70	.40
-----	Team Photo/Checklist	.15	.11	.06
-----	Coaching Staff (Joe Amalfitano, Monty Basgall, Mark Cresse, Ben Hines, Don McMahon, Manny Mota, Ron Perranoski)			
		.15	.11	.06

1986 Police/Fire Safety Phillies

phillies #20 MIKE SCHMIDT 3RD BASE

For the second straight year, the Philadelphia Phillies issued a 16-card safety set. However, in 1986 the set was issued in conjunction with the

Philadelphia Fire Department rather than the police. Cigna Corporation remained a sponsor. The cards, which measure 2-5/8" by 4-1/8" in size, feature full color photos. Along with other pertinent information, the card backs contain a short player biography and a "Tips From The Dugout" fire safety hint.

		MT	NR MT	EX
Complete Set:		7.00	5.25	2.75
Common Player:		.15	.11	.06
1	Juan Samuel	.50	.40	.20
2	Don Carman	.35	.25	.14
3	Von Hayes	.30	.25	.12
4	Kent Tekulve	.20	.15	.08
5	Greg Gross	.15	.11	.06
6	Shane Rawley	.25	.20	.10
7	Darren Daulton	.20	.15	.08
8	Kevin Gross	.25	.20	.10
9	Steve Jeltz	.15	.11	.06
10	Mike Schmidt	1.25	.90	.50
11	Steve Bedrosian	.35	.25	.14
12	Gary Redus	.15	.11	.06
13	Charles Hudson	.15	.11	.06
14	John Russell	.20	.15	.08
15	Fred Toliver	.20	.15	.08
16	Glenn Wilson	.20	.15	.08

1987 Police/Fire Safety Astros

Astros #27 GLENN DAVIS INFIELDER

The 1987 Houston Astros safety set was produced through the combined efforts of the Astros, Deer Park Hospital and Sportsmedia Presentations. #'s 1-12 were handed out to youngsters 14 and under at the Astrodome on July 14th. The balance of the distribution was handled by Deer Park Hospital. The cards, which measure 2-5/8" by 4-1/8", contain full-color photos. The backs offer a brief team/player history and a "Tips From The Dugout" anti-drug message.

		MT	NR MT	EX
Complete Set:		8.00	6.00	3.25
Common Player:		.20	.15	.08
1	Larry Andersen	.20	.15	.08
2	Mark Bailey	.20	.15	.08
3	Jose Cruz	.35	.25	.14
4	Danny Darwin	.25	.20	.10
5	Bill Doran	.40	.30	.15
6	Billy Hatcher	.40	.30	.15
7	Hal Lanier	.20	.15	.08
8	Davey Lopes	.30	.25	.12
9	Dave Meads	.30	.25	.12
10	Craig Reynolds	.20	.15	.08
11	Mike Scott	.60	.45	.25
12	Denny Walling	.20	.15	.08
13	Aurelio Lopez	.20	.15	.08
14	Dickie Thon	.25	.20	.10
15	Terry Puhl	.20	.15	.08
16	Nolan Ryan	1.25	.90	.50
17	Dave Smith	.30	.25	.12
18	Julio Solano	.20	.15	.08
19	Jim Deshaies	.30	.25	.12

		MT	NR MT	EX
20	Bob Knepper	.30	.25	.12
21	Alan Ashby	.20	.15	.08
22	Kevin Bass	.40	.30	.15
23	Glenn Davis	1.00	.70	.40
24	Phil Garner	.25	.20	.10
25	Jim Pankovits	.20	.15	.08
26	Coaching Staff (Yogi Berra, Matt Galante, Denis Menke, Les Moss, Gene Tenace)	.20	.15	.08

1987 Police/Fire Safety
Blue Jays

JESSE BARFIELD
29
outfielder

For the fourth consecutive year, the Toronto Blue Jays issued a fire safety set of 36 cards. As in 1986, the set was sponsored by the local fire departments and governing agencies, Bubble Yum and the Toronto Star. The card fronts feature a full-color photo surrounded by a white border. The backs carry a fire safety tip and logos of all sponsors, plus player personal data and statistics. Produced on thin stock, cards in the set are the standard 2-1/2" by 3-1/2" size.

		MT	NR MT	EX
Complete Set:		9.00	6.75	3.50
Common Player:		.15	.11	.06
1	Tony Fernandez	.50	.40	.20
3	Jimy Williams	.15	.11	.06
5	Rance Mulliniks	.15	.11	.06
8	John Sullivan	.15	.11	.06
9	Rick Leach	.15	.11	.06
10	Mike Sharperson	.20	.15	.08
11	George Bell	1.00	.70	.40
12	Ernie Whitt	.25	.20	.10
15	Lloyd Moseby	.35	.25	.14
16	Garth Iorg	.15	.11	.06
17	Kelly Gruber	.15	.11	.06
18	Jim Clancy	.25	.20	.10
19	Fred McGriff	2.00	1.50	.80
22	Jimmy Key	.40	.30	.15
23	Cecil Fielder	.15	.11	.06
24	John McLaren	.15	.11	.06
26	Willie Upshaw	.25	.20	.10
29	Jesse Barfield	.60	.45	.25
31	Duane Ward	.15	.11	.06
33	Joe Johnson	.15	.11	.06
35	Jeff Musselman	.35	.25	.14
37	Dave Stieb	.40	.30	.15
38	Mark Eichhorn	.20	.15	.08
40	Rob Ducey	.20	.15	.08
41	Al Widmar	.15	.11	.06
42	Billy Smith	.15	.11	.06
43	Cito Gaston	.15	.11	.06
45	Jose Nunez	.35	.25	.14
46	Gary Lavelle	.15	.11	.06
47	Matt Stark	.15	.11	.06
48	Craig McMurtry	.15	.11	.06
50	Tom Henke	.30	.25	.12
54	Jeff Hearron	.15	.11	.06
55	John Cerutti	.20	.15	.08
-----	Logo/Won-Loss Record	.15	.11	.06
-----	Team Photo/Checklist	.15	.11	.06

1987 Police/Fire Safety
Brewers

Dan Plesac says:
"Major League Baseball selects their players by drafting athletes after they graduate from high school. Only a few make it in the big leagues, the rest pursue other careers.
Whatever career path you choose, if you study and work hard, you'll be the best at it, and you'll be drafted for a good job when you graduate. It's important to learn a trade or profession."

57   Dan Plesac   P
Iola, Manawa & Marion Police Departments and Wisconsin Power and Light present the 1987
Milwaukee Brewers

Listen to WTMJ Radio in Milwaukee or your local Brewers network station to learn who will be the 2 players featured on next weeks baseball cards.

The Milwaukee Brewers issued a safety set in 1987 for the sixth consecutive year. As in the past, many local police departments throughout Wisconsin participated in the giveaway program. The Milwaukee version was sponsored by Kinney Shoe Stores and WTMJ Radio and was handed out to youngsters attending the Baseball Card Day at County Stadium on May 9th. The cards, which measure 2-1/4" by 4-1/8", feature full-color photos plus a safety tip on the backs. Chris Bosio can be found with a uniform number of 26 or 29. The card was corrected to #29 in later printings.

		MT	NR MT	EX
Complete Set:		6.00	4.50	2.50
Common Player:		.15	.11	.06
1	Ernest Riles	.15	.11	.06
2	Edgar Diaz	.20	.15	.08
3	Juan Castillo	.15	.11	.06
4	Paul Molitor	.60	.45	.25
5	B.J. Surhoff	.60	.45	.25
7	Dale Sveum	.35	.25	.14
9	Greg Brock	.25	.20	.10
13	Billy Jo Robidoux	.15	.11	.06
14	Jim Paciorek	.15	.11	.06
15	Cecil Cooper	.30	.25	.12
16	Mike Felder	.15	.11	.06
17	Jim Gantner	.20	.15	.08
19	Robin Yount	1.00	.70	.40
20	Juan Nieves	.30	.25	.12
21	Bill Schroeder	.15	.11	.06
25	Mark Clear	.15	.11	.06
26a	Glenn Braggs	.60	.45	.25
26b	Chris Bosio	1.00	.70	.40
28	Rick Manning	.15	.11	.06
29	Chris Bosio	.30	.25	.12
32	Chuck Crim	.25	.20	.10
34	Mark Ciardi	.20	.15	.08
37	Dan Plesac	.40	.30	.15
38	John Henry Johnson	.15	.11	.06
40	Mike Birbeck	.25	.20	.10
42	Tom Trebelhorn	.20	.15	.08
45	Rob Deer	.30	.25	.12
46	Bill Wegman	.20	.15	.08
49	Ted Higuera	.40	.30	.15
-----	Coaches Card (Andy Etchebarren, Larry Haney, Chuck Hartenstein, Dave Hilton, Tony Muser)	.15	.11	.06
-----	Team Photo/Roster	.15	.11	.06

1987 Police/Fire Safety
Dodgers

Producing a police set for the seventh time in eight years, the 1987 edition contains 30 cards which measure 2-13/16" by 4-1/8". The set includes a special Dodger Stadium 25th Anniversary card. The card fronts contain a full-color photo plus the Dodger Stadium 25th Anniversay logo. The photos are a mix of action and posed shots. The backs contain personal player data plus a police safety tip. The cards were given out April 24th at Dodger Stadium and were distributed by the Los Angeles police department at a rate of two cards per week.

		MT	NR MT	EX
Complete Set:		6.00	4.50	2.50
Common Player:		.15	.11	.06
2	Tom Lasorda	.25	.20	.10
3	Steve Sax	.50	.40	.20
5	Mike Marshall	.40	.30	.15
10	Dave Anderson	.15	.11	.06
12	Bill Madlock	.30	.25	.12
14	Mike Scioscia	.25	.20	.10
15	Gilberto Reyes	.15	.11	.06
17	Len Matuszek	.15	.11	.06
21	Reggie Williams	.15	.11	.06
22	Franklin Stubbs	.25	.20	.10
23	Tim Leary	.15	.11	.06
25	Mariano Duncan	.15	.11	.06
26	Alejandro Pena	.25	.20	.10
28	Pedro Guerrero	.60	.45	.25
29	Alex Trevino	.15	.11	.06
33	Jeff Hamilton	.35	.25	.14
34	Fernando Valenzuela	.60	.45	.25
35	Bob Welch	.30	.25	.12
36	Matt Young	.15	.11	.06
40	Rick Honeycutt	.15	.11	.06
41	Jerry Reuss	.25	.20	.10
43	Ken Howell	.15	.11	.06
44	Ken Landreaux	.15	.11	.06
46	Ralph Bryant	.25	.20	.10
47	Jose Gonzalez	.30	.25	.12
49	Tom Niedenfuer	.20	.15	.08
51	Brian Holton	.30	.25	.12
55	Orel Hershiser	1.00	.70	.40
--—	Coaching Staff (Joe Amalfitano, Mark Cresse, Tom Lasorda, Don McMahon, Manny Mota, Ron Perranoski, Bill Russell)	.15	.11	.06
-——	Dodger Stadium/Checklist	.15	.11	.06

1988 Police/Fire Safety Astros

This set of 26 full-color cards highlighting the

Houston Astros was produced by the team, in conjunction with Deer Park Hospital and Sportsmedia Promotions for distribution to fans 14 years and younger at a ballpark giveaway. The 2-5/8" by 4-1/8" cards feature full-color player photos framed by a narrow blue border with an orange player/team name block below the photo. The blue and white card backs have orange borders and list card numbers, player information, career highlights and anti-drug tips.

		MT	NR MT	EX
Complete Set:		8.00	6.00	3.25
Common Player:		.20	.15	.08
1	Juan Agosto	.20	.15	.08
2	Larry Andersen	.20	.15	.08
3	Joaquin Andujar	.30	.25	.12
4	Alan Ashby	.20	.15	.08
5	Mark Bailey	.20	.15	.08
6	Kevin Bass	.40	.30	.15
7	Danny Darwin	.25	.20	.10
8	Glenn Davis	1.00	.70	.40
9	Jim Deshaies	.30	.25	.12
10	Bill Doran	.40	.30	.15
11	Billy Hatcher	.40	.30	.15
12	Jeff Heathcock	.20	.15	.08
13	Steve Henderson	.20	.15	.08
14	Chuck Jackson	.30	.25	.12
15	Bob Knepper	.30	.25	.12
16	Jim Pankovits	.20	.15	.08
17	Terry Puhl	.20	.15	.08
18	Rafael Ramirez	.20	.15	.08
19	Craig Reynolds	.20	.15	.08
20	Nolan Ryan	1.25	.90	.50
21	Mike Scott	.60	.45	.25
22	Dave Smith	.30	.25	.12
23	Denny Walling	.20	.15	.08
24	Gerald Young	.60	.45	.25
25	Hal Lanier	.20	.15	.08
26	Coaching Staff (Yogi Berra, Gene Clines, Matt Galante, Marc Hill, Denis Menke, Les Moss)	.20	.15	.08

1988 Police/Fire Safety Blue Jays

PAT BORDERS
catcher

This 36-card set features full-color action photos on 3-1/2" by 5" cards with white borders and a thin black line framing the photos. Card numbers (player's uniform #) appear lower left, team logo lower right; player's name and position are printed bottom center. Card backs are blue on white and include personal and career info, 1987 and career stats, sponsor logos and a fire safety tip. The set includes 34 player cards, a team photo checklist card and a team logo card with a year-by-year won/loss record. The set was sponsored by the Ontario Fire Chief Association, Ontario's Solicitor General, The Toronto Star and Bubble Yum and was distributed free as part of a community service project.

	MT	NR MT	EX
Complete Set:	7.00	5.25	2.75

		MT	NR MT	EX
Common Player:		.15	.11	.06
1	Tony Fernandez	.60	.45	.25
2	Nelson Liriano	.25	.20	.10
3	Jimy Williams	.15	.11	.06
4	Manny Lee	.15	.11	.06
5	Rance Mulliniks	.15	.11	.06
6	Silvestre Campusano	.40	.30	.15
7	John McLaren	.15	.11	.06
8	John Sullivan	.15	.11	.06
9	Rick Leach	.15	.11	.06
10	Pat Borders	.40	.30	.15
11	George Bell	1.00	.70	.40
12	Ernie Whitt	.25	.20	.10
13	Jeff Musselman	.20	.15	.08
15	Lloyd Moseby	.30	.25	.12
16	Todd Stottlemyre	.60	.45	.25
17	Kelly Gruber	.15	.11	.06
18	Jim Clancy	.25	.20	.10
19	Fred McGriff	1.00	.70	.40
21	Juan Beniquez	.15	.11	.06
22	Jimmy Key	.40	.30	.15
23	Cecil Fielder	.15	.11	.06
29	Jesse Barfield	.60	.45	.25
31	Duane Ward	.15	.11	.06
36	David Wells	.25	.20	.10
37	Dave Stieb	.40	.30	.15
38	Mark Eichhorn	.20	.15	.08
40	Rob Ducey	.15	.11	.06
41	Al Widmar	.15	.11	.06
42	Billy Smith	.15	.11	.06
43	Cito Gaston	.15	.11	.06
46	Mike Flanagan	.25	.20	.10
50	Tom Henke	.25	.20	.10
55	John Cerutti	.20	.15	.08
57	Winston Llenas	.15	.11	.06
----	Team Photo	.15	.11	.06
----	Team Logo	.15	.11	.06

		MT	NR MT	EX
11	Charlie O'Brien	.20	.15	.08
14	Jim Adduci	.15	.11	.06
16	Mike Felder	.15	.11	.06
17	Jim Gantner	.20	.15	.08
19	Robin Yount	1.00	.70	.40
20	Juan Nieves	.25	.20	.10
21	Bill Schroeder	.15	.11	.06
23	Joey Meyer	.35	.25	.14
25	Mark Clear	.15	.11	.06
26	Glenn Braggs	.30	.25	.12
28	Odell Jones	.15	.11	.06
29	Chris Bosio	.15	.11	.06
30	Steve Kiefer	.15	.11	.06
32	Chuck Crim	.15	.11	.06
33	Jay Aldrich	.15	.11	.06
37	Dan Plesac	.40	.30	.15
40	Mike Birkbeck	.20	.15	.08
42	Tom Trebelhorn	.15	.11	.06
43	Dave Stapleton	.25	.20	.10
45	Rob Deer	.30	.25	.12
46	Bill Wegman	.20	.15	.08
49	Ted Higuera	.40	.30	.15
----	Coaches Card (Andy Etchebarren, Larry Haney, Chuck Hartenstein, Dave Hilton, Tony Muser)	.15	.11	.06
----	Team Photo	.15	.11	.06

1988 Police/Fire Safety Dodgers

DON SUTTON 20

The Los Angeles police department sponsored this 30-card set (2-3/4" by 4-1/8") for use in a local crime prevention promotion. The sets include an unnumbered manager/coaches photo and three double-photo cards. The double cards feature posed closeups; the rest are action photos. The card fronts have white borders, with the team logo lower right and a bold black player name lower left. Card backs are black and white with a small closeup photo of the player, followed by personal and career info, a crime prevention tip and a LAPD badge logo. Card numbers refer to players' uniform numbers (the double-photo cards carry two numbers on both front and back).

		MT	NR MT	EX
Complete Set:		5.00	3.75	2.00
Common Player:		.15	.11	.06
2	Tom Lasorda	.25	.20	.10
3	Steve Sax	.50	.40	.20
5	Mike Marshall	.40	.30	.15
7	Alfredo Griffin	.20	.15	.08
9	Mickey Hatcher	.15	.11	.06
10	Dave Anderson	.15	.11	.06
12	Danny Heep	.15	.11	.06
14	Mike Scioscia	.20	.15	.08
17-21	Tito Landrum, Len Matuszek	.15	.11	.06
20	Don Sutton	.40	.30	.15
22	Franklin Stubbs	.20	.15	.08
23	Kirk Gibson	.60	.45	.25
25	Mariano Duncan	.15	.11	.06
26	Alejandro Pena	.20	.15	.08
27-52	Tim Crews, Mike Sharperson	.25	.20	.10
28	Pedro Guerrero	.50	.40	.20
29	Alex Trevino	.15	.11	.06
31	John Shelby	.15	.11	.06

1988 Police/Fire Safety Brewers

Juan Castillo says:
"A baseball player's day starts long before the game begins. We have to attend practice before each game and we must report on time unless we're properly excused. If we miss practice or arrive late, we can be fined or suspended and that hurts your career.

Protect your future and your career. Attend all your classes in school and on time. Don't miss school if you're really sick or have a good excuse. Practice good habits early in life and you will be on the right path to success."

Juan Castillo
1F
The Marathon County Sheriff's Dept. and Bradley Chrysler Center Inc.
2525 Grand Avenue, Wausau, WI 54401 present the 1988
Milwaukee Brewers

This 30-card set is the 7th annual issue sponsored by the Milwaukee Police Department for local distribution during a crime prevention promotion. The full-color card fronts (2-3/4" by 4-1/8") feature the same design as the 1987 set with white borders and a black frame outling the player photo and name. Sponsor credits and the team name are listed below the photo. The vertical card backs are blue on white with messages from the player and sponsors. Two group photos - one of the team's five coaches and one of the team (with a checklist back) - are unnumbered and printed horizontally. Card numbers refer to the players uniform numbers.

		MT	NR MT	EX
Complete Set:		6.00	4.50	2.50
Common Player:		.15	.11	.06
1	Ernest Riles	.15	.11	.06
3	Juan Castillo	.15	.11	.06
4	Paul Molitor	.60	.45	.25
5	B.J. Surhoff	.30	.25	.12
6	Dale Sveum	.20	.15	.08
9	Greg Brock	.20	.15	.08

		MT	NR MT	EX
33	Jeff Hamilton	.25	.20	.10
34	Fernando Valenzuela	.60	.45	.25
37	Mike Davis	.20	.15	.08
41	Brad Havens	.15	.11	.06
43	Ken Howell	.15	.11	.06
47	Jesse Orosco	.20	.15	.08
49-57	Tim Belcher, Shawn Hillegas	.30	.25	.12
50	Jay Howell	.20	.15	.08
51	Brian Holton	.20	.15	.08
54	Tim Leary	.25	.20	.10
55	Orel Hershiser	.80	.60	.30
----	Manager/Coaches (Joe Amalfitano, Steve Boros, Mark Cresse, Joe Ferguson, Tom Lasorda, Manny Mota, Ron Perranoski, Bill Russell)	.15	.11	.06

1988 Police/Fire Safety Tigers

This unnumbered issue, sponsored by the Michigan State Police features 13 players and manager Sparky Anderson in full-color standard-size (2-1/2" by 3-1/2") cards. Player photos are framed by a blue border, with the Detroit logo upper left and a large name block that lists the player's name, position batting/throwing preference, height, weight and birthday beneath the photo. The backs carry an anti-drug or anti-crime message.

		MT	NR MT	EX
Complete Set:		35.00	25.00	14.00
Common Player:		.50	.40	.20
(1)	Doyle Alexander	.50	.40	.20
(2)	Sparky Anderson	.50	.40	.20
(3)	Dave Bergman	.50	.40	.20
(4)	Tom Brookens	.50	.40	.20
(5)	Darrell Evans	.60	.45	.25
(6)	Larry Herndon	.50	.40	.20
(7)	Chet Lemon	.50	.40	.20
(8)	Jack Morris	.80	.60	.30
(9)	Matt Nokes	.80	.60	.30
(10)	Jeff Robinson	.60	.45	.25
(11)	Frank Tanana	.40	.30	.15
(12)	Walt Terrell	.50	.40	.20
(13)	Alan Trammell	1.00	.70	.40
(14)	Lou Whitaker	.80	.60	.30

1989 Police/Fire Safety Blue Jays

The 1989 Toronto Blue Jays safety set consisted of 34 standard-size cards co-sponsored by the Ontario Association of Fire Chiefs, Oh Henry! candy bars and A&P supermarkets. The card fronts feature color photos with the player's uniform number in large type in the upper left corner. His name and position are to the right above the photo. The Blue Jays "On the Move" logo is centered at the bottom. The backs of the cards include fire safety messages.

		MT	NR MT	EX
Complete Set:		6.00	4.50	2.50
Common Player:		.15	.11	.06
Team Photo		.15	.11	.06
Team Logo		.15	.11	.06
1	Tony Fernandez	.50	.40	.20
2	Nelson Liriano	.15	.11	.06

		MT	NR MT	EX
3	Jimy Williams	.15	.11	.06
4	Manny Lee	.15	.11	.06
5	Rance Mulliniks	.15	.11	.06
6	Silvestre Campusano	.20	.15	.08
7	John McLaren	.15	.11	.06
8	John Sullivan	.15	.11	.06
9	Bob Brenly	.15	.11	.06
10	Pat Borders	.30	.25	.12
11	George Bell	.90	.70	.35
12	Ernie Whitt	.25	.20	.10
13	Jeff Musselman	.15	.11	.06
15	Lloyd Moseby	.25	.20	.10
16	Greg Myers	.40	.30	.15
17	Kelly Gruber	.30	.25	.12
18	Tom Lawless	.15	.11	.06
19	Fred McGriff	1.00	.70	.40
22	Jimmy Key	.25	.20	.10
25	Mike Squires	.15	.11	.06
26	Sal Butera	.15	.11	.06
29	Jesse Barfield	.40	.30	.15
30	Todd Stottlemyre	.40	.30	.15
31	Duane Ward	.15	.11	.06
36	David Wells	.20	.15	.08
37	Dave Steib	.40	.30	.20
40	Rob Ducey	.15	.11	.06
41	Al Widman	.15	.11	.06
43	Cito Gaston	.20	.15	.08
44	Frank Wills	.15	.11	.06
45	Jose Nunez	.20	.15	.08
46	Mike Flanagan	.20	.15	.08
50	Tom Henke	.20	.15	.08
55	John Cerutti	.20	.15	.08

1989 Police/Fire Safety Brewers

The Milwaukee Brewers, in conjunction with various corporate and civic sponsors, issued a 30-card police set in 1989, the eighth consecutive police set issued by the club. Some 95 law enforcement agencies in Wisconsin participated in the program, each releasing their own version of the same set. The cards measure 2-13/16" by 4-1/8" and feature full-color action photos with the player's name, uniform number and position below, along with the sponsoring agencies. The backs include the traditional safety messages. The cards were distributed in complete sets at a stadium promotion and also handed out individually over the course of the summer by uniformed police officers in various Wisconsin cities and counties.

		MT	NR MT	EX
Complete Set:		7.00	5.25	2.75
Common Player:		.15	.11	.06
Team Photo		.15	.11	.06
Coaching Staff		.15	.11	.06
1	Gary Sheffield	1.00	.70	.40
4	Paul Molitor	.60	.45	.25
5	B.J. Surhoff	.30	.25	.12
6	Bill Spiers	.80	.60	.30
7	Dale Sveum	.20	.15	.08
9	Greg Brock	.20	.15	.08
14	Gus Polidor	.15	.11	.06
16	Mike Felder	.15	.11	.06
17	Jim Gantner	.20	.15	.08
19	Robin Yount	1.00	.70	.40
20	Juan Nieves	.20	.15	.08
22	Charlie O'Brien	.20	.15	.08
23	Joey Meyer	.15	.11	.06
25	Dave Engle	.15	.11	.06
26	Glenn Braggs	.25	.20	.10
27	Paul Mirabella	.15	.11	.06
29	Chris Bosio	.20	.15	.08
30	Terry Francona	.15	.11	.06
32	Chuck Crim	.15	.11	.06
37	Dan Plesac	.35	.25	.14
40	Mike Birkbeck	.15	.11	.06
41	Mark Knudson	.20	.15	.08
42	Tom Trebelhorn	.15	.11	.06
45	Rob Deer	.30	.25	.12
46	Bill Wegman	.15	.11	.06
48	Bryan Clutterbuck	.15	.11	.06
49	Teddy Higuera	.40	.30	.15

1989 Police/Fire Safety Dodgers

The Los Angeles Dodgers and the L.A. Police Department teamed up in 1989 to produce a 30-card police set. The cards, which measure 4-1/4" by 2-5/8", feature color action photos with the player's name and uniform number below. The Dodgers logo and "1989" appear in the upper left. The backs include player information plus a safety message.

		MT	NR MT	EX
Complete Set:		5.00	3.75	2.00
Common Player:		.15	.11	.06
Dodger Coaches		.15	.11	.06
2	Tom Lasorda	.25	.20	.10
3	Jeff Hamilton	.25	.20	.10
5	Mike Marshall	.30	.25	.12
7	Alfredo Griffin	.15	.11	.06
9	Mickey Hatcher	.15	.11	.06
10	Dave Anderson	.15	.11	.06
12	Willie Randolph	.25	.20	.10
14	Mike Scioscia	.20	.15	.08
17	Rick Dempsey	.15	.11	.06
20	Mike Davis	.15	.11	.06
21	Tracy Woodson	.25	.20	.10
22	Franklin Stubbs	.15	.11	.06
23	Kirk Gibson	.40	.30	.15
25	Mariano Duncan	.20	.15	.08
26	Alejandro Pena	.15	.11	.06
27	Mike Sharperson	.20	.15	.08
29	Ricky Horton	.15	.11	.06
30	John Tudor	.25	.20	.10
31	John Shelby	.15	.11	.06
33	Eddie Murray	.60	.45	.25

		MT	NR MT	EX
34	Fernando Valenzuela	.40	.30	.15
36	Mike Morgan	.15	.11	.06
48	Ramon Martinez	.60	.45	.25
50	Jay Howell	.20	.15	.08
52	Tim Crews	.15	.11	.06
54	Tim Leary	.20	.15	.08
55	Orel Hershiser	.80	.60	.30
57	Ray Searage	.15	.11	.06

1960 Post

These cards were issued on the backs of Grape Nuts cereal and measure an oversized 7" by 8-3/4". The nine cards in the set include five baseball players (Al Kaline, Mickey Mantle, Don Drysdale, Harmon Killebrew and Ed Mathews) as well as two football and two basketball players. The full-color photos were placed on a color background and bordered by a wood frame design. The cards covered the entire back of the cereal box and were blank backed. Card fronts also include the player's name and team and a facsimile autograph. A panel on the side of the box contains player biographical information. A scarce set, the cards are very difficult to obtain in mint condition.

		NR MT	EX	VG
Complete Set:		2600.00	1300.00	780.00
Common Player:		100.00	50.00	30.00
(1)	Bob Cousy	100.00	50.00	30.00
(2)	Don Drysdale	200.00	100.00	60.00
(3)	Frank Gifford	175.00	87.00	52.00
(4)	Al Kaline	250.00	125.00	75.00
(5)	Harmon Killebrew	200.00	100.00	60.00
(6)	Ed Mathews	200.00	100.00	60.00
(7)	Mickey Mantle	1200.00	600.00	360.00
(8)	Bob Pettit	100.00	50.00	30.00
(9)	John Unitas	175.00	87.00	52.00

1961 Post

Two hundred different players are included in this

set, but with variations the number of different cards exceeds 350. This was the first large-scale card set by the cereal company and it proved very popular with fans. Cards were issued both singly and in various panel sizes on the thick cardboard stock of cereal boxes, as well on thinner stock, in team sheets issued directly by Post via a mail-in offer. About 10 cards in the set were issued in significantly smaller quantities, making their prices much higher than other comparable players in the set. Individual cards measure a 3-1/2" by 2-1/2", and all cards are numbered in the upper left corner. Card fronts have full-color portait photos of the player, along with biographical information and 1960 and career statistics. Card backs are blank. The complete set price includes does not include the scarcer variations.

		NR MT	EX	VG
	Complete Set:	1175.00	587.00	352.00
	Common Player:	1.50	.70	.45
1a	Yogi Berra (box)	20.00	10.00	6.00
1b	Yogi Berra (company)	15.00	7.50	4.50
2a	Elston Howard (box)	5.00	2.50	1.50
2b	Elston Howard (company)	3.00	1.50	.90
3a	Bill Skowron (box)	2.50	1.25	.70
3b	Bill Skowron (company)	2.50	1.25	.70
4a	Mickey Mantle (box)	75.00	37.00	22.00
4b	Mickey Mantle (company)	75.00	37.00	22.00
5	Bob Turley (company)	12.00	6.00	3.50
6a	Whitey Ford (box)	8.00	4.00	2.50
6b	Whitey Ford (company)	8.00	4.00	2.50
7a	Roger Maris (box)	12.00	6.00	3.50
7b	Roger Maris (company)	12.00	6.00	3.50
8a	Bobby Richardson (box)	3.00	1.50	.90
8b	Bobby Richardson (company)	3.00	1.50	.90
9a	Tony Kubek (box)	3.00	1.50	.90
9b	Tony Kubek (company)	3.00	1.50	.90
10	Gil McDougald (box)	25.00	12.50	7.50
11	Cletis Boyer (box)	2.00	1.00	.60
12a	Hector Lopez (box)	2.00	1.00	.60
12b	Hector Lopez (company)	2.00	1.00	.60
13	Bob Cerv (box)	2.00	1.00	.60
14	Ryne Duren (box)	2.00	1.00	.60
15	Bobby Shantz (box)	2.00	1.00	.60
16	Art Ditmar (box)	2.00	1.00	.60
17	Jim Coates (box)	2.00	1.00	.60
18	John Blanchard (box)	2.00	1.00	.60
19a	Luis Aparicio (box)	5.00	2.50	1.50
19b	Luis Aparicio (company)	5.00	2.50	1.50
20a	Nelson Fox (box)	4.00	2.00	1.25
20b	Nelson Fox (company)	4.00	2.00	1.25
21a	Bill Pierce (box)	6.00	3.00	1.75
21b	Bill Pierce (company)	3.50	1.75	1.00
22a	Early Wynn (box)	7.00	3.50	2.00
22b	Early Wynn (company)	12.00	6.00	3.50
23	Bob Shaw (box)	75.00	37.00	22.00
24a	Al Smith (box)	3.00	1.50	.90
24b	Al Smith (company)	1.50	.70	.45
25a	Minnie Minoso (box)	2.50	1.25	.70
25b	Minnie Minoso (company)	2.50	1.25	.70
26a	Roy Sievers (box)	1.75	.90	.50
26b	Roy Sievers (company)	1.75	.90	.50
27a	Jim Landis (box)	2.00	1.00	.60
27b	Jim Landis (company)	1.50	.70	.45
28a	Sherman Lollar (box)	3.00	1.50	.90
28b	Sherman Lollar (company)	1.50	.70	.45
29	Gerry Staley (box)	1.50	.70	.45
30a	Gene Freese (box, White Sox)	1.50	.70	.45
30b	Gene Freese (company, Reds)	6.00	3.00	1.75
31	Ted Kluszewski (box)	3.00	1.50	.90
32	Turk Lown (box)	1.50	.70	.45
33a	Jim Rivera (box)	1.50	.70	.45
33b	Jim Rivera (company)	1.50	.70	.45
34	Frank Baumann (box)	1.50	.70	.45
35a	Al Kaline (box)	12.00	6.00	3.50
35b	Al Kaline (company)	10.00	5.00	3.00
36a	Rocky Colavito (box)	6.00	3.00	1.75
36b	Rocky Colavito (company)	3.50	1.75	1.00
37a	Charley Maxwell (box)	4.00	2.00	1.25
37b	Charley Maxwell (company)	1.50	.70	.45
38a	Frank Lary (box)	1.50	.70	.45
38b	Frank Lary (company)	1.50	.70	.45
39a	Jim Bunning (box)	4.00	2.00	1.25
39b	Jim Bunning (company)	4.00	2.00	1.25
40a	Norm Cash (box)	2.00	1.00	.60
40b	Norm Cash (company)	2.00	1.00	.60
41a	Frank Bolling (box, Tigers)	8.00	4.00	2.50
41b	Frank Bolling (company, Braves)	5.00	2.50	1.50

		NR MT	EX	VG
42a	Don Mossi (box)	1.50	.70	.45
42b	Don Mossi (company)	1.50	.70	.45
43a	Lou Berberet (box)	1.50	.70	.45
43b	Lou Berberet (company)	1.50	.70	.45
44	Dave Sisler (box)	1.50	.70	.45
45	Ed Yost (box)	1.50	.70	.45
46	Pete Burnside (box)	1.50	.70	.45
47a	Pete Runnels (box)	3.00	1.50	.90
47b	Pete Runnnels (company)	1.75	.90	.50
48a	Frank Malzone (box)	1.50	.70	.45
48b	Frank Malzone (company)	1.50	.70	.45
49a	Vic Wertz (box)	5.00	2.50	1.50
49b	Vic Wertz (company)	3.00	1.50	.90
50a	Tom Brewer (box)	2.50	1.25	.70
50b	Tom Brewer (company)	1.50	.70	.45
51a	Willie Tasby (box, no sold line)	8.00	4.00	2.50
51b	Willie Tasby (company, sold line)	1.50	.70	.45
52a	Russ Nixon (box)	1.50	.70	.45
52b	Russ Nixon (company)	1.50	.70	.45
53a	Don Buddin (box)	1.50	.70	.45
53b	Don Buddin (company)	1.50	.70	.45
54a	Bill Monbouquette (box)	1.50	.70	.45
54b	Bill Monbouquette (company)	1.50	.70	.45
55a	Frank Sullivan (box, Red Sox)	1.50	.70	.45
55b	Frank Sullivan (company, Phillies)	18.00	9.00	5.50
56a	Haywood Sullivan (box)	1.50	.70	.45
56b	Haywood Sullivan (company)	1.50	.70	.45
57a	Harvey Kuenn (box, Indians)	3.00	1.50	.90
57b	Harvey Kuenn (company, Giants)	6.00	3.00	1.75
58a	Gary Bell (box)	5.00	2.50	1.50
58b	Gary Bell (company)	1.75	.90	.50
59a	Jim Perry (box)	1.75	.90	.50
59b	Jim Perry (company)	1.75	.90	.50
60a	Jim Grant (box)	3.00	1.50	.90
60b	Jim Grant (company)	1.75	.90	.50
61a	Johnny Temple (box)	1.50	.70	.45
61b	Johnny Temple (company)	1.50	.70	.45
62a	Paul Foytack (box)	1.50	.70	.45
62b	Paul Foytack (company)	1.50	.70	.45
63a	Vic Power (box)	1.50	.70	.45
63b	Vic Power (company)	1.50	.70	.45
64a	Tito Francona (box)	1.50	.70	.45
64b	Tito Francona (company)	1.50	.70	.45
65a	Ken Aspromonte (box, no sold line)	6.00	3.00	1.75
65b	Ken Aspromonte (company, sold line)	6.00	3.00	1.75
66	Bob Wilson (box)	1.50	.70	.45
67a	John Romano (box)	1.50	.70	.45
67b	John Romano (company)	1.50	.70	.45
68a	Jim Gentile (box)	2.50	1.25	.70
68b	Jim Gentile (company)	1.50	.70	.45
69a	Gus Triandos (box)	3.00	1.50	.90
69b	Gus Triandos (company)	1.50	.70	.45
70	Gene Woodling (box)	15.00	7.50	4.50
71a	Milt Pappas (box)	3.00	1.50	.90
71b	Milt Pappas (company)	1.50	.70	.45
72a	Ron Hansen (box)	3.00	1.50	.90
72b	Ron Hansen (company)	1.50	.70	.45
73	Chuck Estrada (company)	75.00	37.00	22.00
74a	Steve Barber (box)	1.50	.70	.45
74b	Steve Barber (company)	1.50	.70	.45
75a	Brooks Robinson (box)	12.00	6.00	3.50
75b	Brooks Robinson (company)	10.00	5.00	3.00
76a	Jackie Brandt (box)	1.50	.70	.45
76b	Jackie Brandt (company)	1.50	.70	.45
77a	Marv Breeding (box)	1.50	.70	.45
77b	Marv Breedding (company)	1.50	.70	.45
78	Hal Brown (box)	1.50	.70	.45
79	Billy Klaus (box)	1.50	.70	.45
80a	Hoyt Wilhelm (box)	5.00	2.50	1.50
80b	Hoyt Wilhelm (company)	6.00	3.00	1.75
81a	Jerry Lumpe (box)	6.00	3.00	1.75
81b	Jerry Lumpe (company)	4.00	2.00	1.25
82a	Norm Siebern (box)	1.50	.70	.45
82b	Norm Siebern (company)	1.50	.70	.45
83a	Bud Daley (box)	1.75	.90	.50
83b	Bud Daley (company)	2.50	1.25	.70
84a	Bill Tuttle (box)	1.50	.70	.45
84b	Bill Tuttle (company)	1.50	.70	.45
85a	Marv Throneberry (box)	2.50	1.25	.70
85b	Marv Throneberry (company)	2.50	1.25	.70
86a	Dick Williams (box)	1.75	.90	.50
86b	Dick Williams (company)	2.00	1.00	.60
87a	Ray Herbert (box)	1.50	.70	.45
87b	Ray Herbert (company)	2.00	1.00	.60
88a	Whitey Herzog (box)	2.00	1.00	.60
88b	Whitey Herzog (company)	2.00	1.00	.60
89a	Ken Hamlin (box, no sold line)	1.50	.70	.45
89b	Ken Hamlin (company, sold line)	8.00	4.00	2.50

		NR MT	EX	VG
90a	Hank Bauer (box)	2.00	1.00	.60
90b	Hank Bauer (company)	2.00	1.00	.60
91a	Bob Allison (box, Minneapolis)	4.00	2.00	1.25
91b	Bob Allison (company, Minnesota)	5.00	2.50	1.50
92a	Harmon Killebrew (box, Minneapolis)	12.00	6.00	3.50
92b	Harmon Killebrew (company, Minnesota)	10.00	5.00	3.00
93a	Jim Lemon (box, Minneapolis)	40.00	20.00	12.00
93b	Jim Lemon (company, Minnesota)	5.00	2.50	1.50
94	Chuck Stobbs (company)	125.00	62.00	37.00
95a	Reno Bertoia (box, Minneapolis)	1.50	.70	.45
95b	Reno Bertoia (company, Minnesota)	4.00	2.00	1.25
96a	Billy Gardner (box, Minneapolis)	1.50	.70	.45
96b	Billy Gardner (company, Minnesota)	4.00	2.00	1.25
97a	Earl Battey (box, Minneapolis)	4.00	2.00	1.25
97b	Earl Battey (company, Minnesota)	4.00	2.00	1.25
98a	Pedro Ramos (box, Minneapolis)	1.50	.70	.45
98b	Pedro Ramos (company, Minnesota)	4.00	2.00	1.25
99a	Camilio Pascual (Camilo) (box, Minneapolis)	1.50	.70	.45
99b	Camilio Pascual (Camilo) (company, Minnesota)	4.00	2.00	1.25
100a	Billy Consolo (box, Minneapolis)	1.50	.70	.45
100b	Billy Consolo (company, Minnesota)	4.00	2.00	1.25
101a	Warren Spahn (box)	15.00	7.50	4.50
101b	Warren Spahn (company)	8.00	4.00	2.50
102a	Lew Burdette (box)	2.50	1.25	.70
102b	Lew Burdette (company)	2.50	1.25	.70
103a	Bob Buhl (box)	1.50	.70	.45
103b	Bob Buhl (company)	1.50	.70	.45
104a	Joe Adcock (box)	4.00	2.00	1.25
104b	Joe Adcock (company)	2.50	1.25	.70
105a	John Logan (box)	4.00	2.00	1.25
105b	John Logan (company)	1.75	.90	.50
106	Ed Mathews (company)	25.00	12.50	7.50
107a	Hank Aaron (box)	18.00	9.00	5.50
107b	Hank Aaron (company)	18.00	9.00	5.50
108a	Wes Covington (box)	1.50	.70	.45
108b	Wes Covington (company)	1.50	.70	.45
109a	Bill Bruton (box, Braves)	6.00	3.00	1.75
109b	Bill Bruton (company, Tigers)	8.00	4.00	2.50
110a	Del Crandall (box)	4.00	2.00	1.25
110b	Del Crandall (company)	1.75	.90	.50
111	Red Schoendienst (box)	5.00	2.50	1.50
112	Juan Pizarro (box)	1.50	.70	.45
113	Chuck Cottier (box)	8.00	4.00	2.50
114	Al Spangler (box)	1.50	.70	.45
115a	Dick Farrell (box)	6.00	3.00	1.75
115b	Dick Farrell (company)	4.00	2.00	1.25
116a	Jim Owens (box)	6.00	3.00	1.75
116b	Jim Owens (company)	4.00	2.00	1.25
117a	Robin Roberts (box)	6.00	3.00	1.75
117b	Robin Roberts (company)	6.00	3.00	1.75
118a	Tony Taylor (box)	1.50	.70	.45
118b	Tony Taylor (company)	1.50	.70	.45
119a	Lee Walls (box)	1.50	.70	.45
119b	Lee Walls (company)	1.50	.70	.45
120a	Tony Curry (box)	1.50	.70	.45
120b	Tony Curry (company)	1.50	.70	.45
121a	Pancho Herrera (box)	1.50	.70	.45
121b	Pancho Herrera (company)	1.50	.70	.45
122a	Ken Walters (box)	1.50	.70	.45
122b	Ken Walters (company)	1.50	.70	.45
123a	John Callison (box)	1.50	.70	.45
123b	John Callison (company)	1.50	.70	.45
124a	Gene Conley (box, Phillies)	1.50	.70	.45
124b	Gene Conley (company, Red Sox)	15.00	7.50	4.50
125a	Bob Friend (box)	4.00	2.00	1.25
125b	Bob Friend (company)	2.00	1.00	.60
126a	Vernon Law (box)	4.00	2.00	1.25
126b	Vernon Law (company)	2.00	1.00	.60
127a	Dick Stuart (box)	1.50	.70	.45
127b	Dick Stuart (company)	1.50	.70	.45
128a	Bill Mazeroski (box)	2.50	1.25	.70
128b	Bill Mazeroski (company)	2.50	1.25	.70
129a	Dick Groat (box)	3.00	1.50	.90
129b	Dick Groat (company)	2.00	1.00	.60
130a	Don Hoak (box)	1.50	.70	.45
130b	Don Hoak (company)	1.50	.70	.45
131a	Bob Skinner (box)	1.50	.70	.45
131b	Bob Skinner (company)	1.50	.70	.45
132a	Bob Clemente (box)	20.00	10.00	6.00

		NR MT	EX	VG
132b	Bob Clemente (company)	18.00	9.00	5.50
133	Roy Face (box)	3.00	1.50	.90
134	Harvey Haddix (box)	1.75	.90	.50
135	Bill Virdon (box)	25.00	12.50	7.50
136a	Gino Cimoli (box)	1.50	.70	.45
136b	Gino Cimoli (company)	1.50	.70	.45
137	Rocky Nelson (box)	1.50	.70	.45
138a	Smoky Burgess (box)	1.75	.90	.50
138b	Smoky Burgess (company)	1.75	.90	.50
139	Hal Smith (box)	1.50	.70	.45
140	Wilmer Mizell (box)	1.50	.70	.45
141a	Mike McCormick (box)	1.50	.70	.45
141b	Mike McCormick (company)	1.50	.70	.45
142a	John Antonelli (box, Giants)	3.00	1.50	.90
142b	John Antonelli (company, Indians)	4.00	2.00	1.25
143a	Sam Jones (box)	4.00	2.00	1.25
143b	Sam Jones (company)	2.00	1.00	.60
144a	Orlando Cepeda (box)	5.00	2.50	1.50
144b	Orlando Cepeda (company)	5.00	2.50	1.50
145a	Willie Mays (box)	18.00	9.00	5.50
145b	Willie Mays (company)	18.00	9.00	5.50
146a	Willie Kirkland (box, Giants)	5.00	2.50	1.50
146b	Willie Kirkland (company, Indians)	5.00	2.50	1.50
147a	Willie McCovey (box)	7.00	3.50	2.00
147b	Willie McCovey (company)	10.00	5.00	3.00
148a	Don Blasingame (box)	1.50	.70	.45
148b	Don Blasingame (company)	1.50	.70	.45
149a	Jim Davenport (box)	1.50	.70	.45
149b	Jim Davenport (company)	1.50	.70	.45
150a	Hobie Landrith (box)	1.50	.70	.45
150b	Hobie Landrith (company)	1.50	.70	.45
151	Bob Schmidt (box)	1.50	.70	.45
152a	Ed Bressoud (box)	1.50	.70	.45
152b	Ed Bressoud (company)	1.50	.70	.45
153a	Andre Rodgers (box, no traded line)	6.00	3.00	1.75
153b	Andre Rodgers (box, traded line)	1.50	.70	.45
154	Jack Sanford (box)	1.50	.70	.45
155	Billy O'Dell (box)	1.50	.70	.45
156a	Norm Larker (box)	2.50	1.25	.70
156b	Norm Larker (company)	2.50	1.25	.70
157a	Charlie Neal (box)	1.50	.70	.45
157b	Charlie Neal (company)	1.50	.70	.45
158a	Jim Gilliam (box)	4.00	2.00	1.25
158b	Jim Gilliam (company)	2.50	1.25	.70
159a	Wally Moon (box)	1.50	.70	.45
159b	Wally Moon (company)	1.50	.70	.45
160a	Don Drysdale (box)	7.00	3.50	2.00
160b	Don Drysdale (company)	8.00	4.00	2.50
161a	Larry Sherry (box)	1.50	.70	.45
161b	Larry Sherry (company)	1.50	.70	.45
162	Stan Williams (box)	5.00	2.50	1.50
163	Mel Roach (box)	40.00	20.00	12.00
164a	Maury Wills (box)	4.00	2.00	1.25
164b	Maury Wills (company)	4.00	2.00	1.25
165	Tom Davis (box)	2.00	1.00	.60
166a	John Roseboro (box)	1.50	.70	.45
166b	John Roseboro (company)	1.50	.70	.45
167a	Duke Snider (box)	8.00	4.00	2.50
167b	Duke Snider (company)	10.00	5.00	3.00
168a	Gil Hodges (box)	5.00	2.50	1.50
168b	Gil Hodges (company)	6.00	3.00	1.75
169	John Podres (box)	2.50	1.25	.70
170	Ed Roebuck (box)	1.50	.70	.45
171a	Ken Boyer (box)	6.00	3.00	1.75
171b	Ken Boyer (company)	4.00	2.00	1.25
172a	Joe Cunningham (box)	1.50	.70	.45
172b	Joe Cunningham (company)	1.50	.70	.45
173a	Daryl Spencer (box)	1.50	.70	.45
173b	Daryl Spencer (company)	1.50	.70	.45
174a	Larry Jackson (box)	1.50	.70	.45
174b	Larry Jackson (company)	1.50	.70	.45
175a	Lindy McDaniel (box)	1.50	.70	.45
175b	Lindy McDaniel (company)	1.50	.70	.45
176a	Bill White (box)	1.75	.90	.50
176b	Bill White (company)	1.75	.90	.50
177a	Alex Grammas (box)	1.50	.70	.45
177b	Alex Grammas (company)	1.50	.70	.45
178a	Curt Flood (box)	2.00	1.00	.60
178b	Curt Flood (company)	2.00	1.00	.60
179a	Ernie Broglio (box)	1.50	.70	.45
179b	Ernie Broglio (company)	1.50	.70	.45
180a	Hal Smith (box)	1.50	.70	.45
180b	Hal Smith (company)	1.50	.70	.45
181a	Vada Pinson (box)	2.50	1.25	.70
181b	Vada Pinson (company)	2.50	1.25	.70
182a	Frank Robinson (box)	12.00	6.00	3.50
182b	Frank Robinson (company)	18.00	9.00	5.50
183	Roy McMillan (box)	55.00	27.00	16.50
184a	Bob Purkey (box)	1.50	.70	.45

		NR MT	EX	VG
184b	Bob Purkey (company)	1.50	.70	.45
185a	Ed Kasko (box)	1.50	.70	.45
185b	Ed Kasko (company)	1.50	.70	.45
186a	Gus Bell (box)	1.50	.70	.45
186b	Gus Bell (company)	1.50	.70	.45
187a	Jerry Lynch (box)	1.50	.70	.45
187b	Jerry Lynch (company)	1.50	.70	.45
188a	Ed Bailey (box)	1.50	.70	.45
188b	Ed Bailey (company)	1.50	.70	.45
189a	Jim O'Toole (box)	1.50	.70	.45
189b	Jim O'Toole (company)	1.50	.70	.45
190a	Billy Martin (box, no sold line)	3.00	1.50	.90
190b	Billy Martin (company, sold line)	9.00	4.50	2.75
191a	Ernie Banks (box)	9.00	4.50	2.75
191b	Ernie Banks (company)	9.00	4.50	2.75
192a	Richie Ashburn (box)	3.00	1.50	.90
192b	Richie Ashburn (company)	3.00	1.50	.90
193a	Frank Thomas (box)	35.00	17.50	10.50
193b	Frank Thomas (company)	5.00	2.50	1.50
194a	Don Cardwell (box)	1.50	.70	.45
194b	Don Cardwell (company)	2.00	1.00	.60
195a	George Altman (box)	1.50	.70	.45
195b	George Altman (company)	2.00	1.00	.60
196a	Ron Santo (box)	3.00	1.50	.90
196b	Ron Santo (company)	3.00	1.50	.90
197a	Glen Hobbie (box)	1.50	.70	.45
197b	Glen Hobbie (company)	2.00	1.00	.60
198a	Sam Taylor (box)	1.50	.70	.45
198b	Sam Taylor (company)	2.00	1.00	.60
199a	Jerry Kindall (box)	1.50	.70	.45
199b	Jerry Kindall (company)	2.00	1.00	.60
200a	Don Elston (box)	3.00	1.50	.90
200b	Don Elston (company)	3.00	1.50	.90

1962 Post

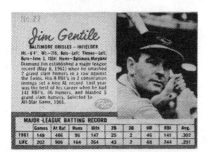

Like the 1961 Post set, there are 200 players pictured in the set of 3-1/2" by 2-1/2" cards. Differences include a Post logo on the card fronts and the player's name in script lettering. Cards are again blank backed and were issued in panels of five to seven cards on cereal boxes. American League players are numbered 1-100 and National League players 101-200. With variations there are 210 of the full-color cards known. A handful of the '62 cards were also issued in smaller quantities. The cards of Mickey Mantle and Roger Maris were reproduced in a special two-card panel for a Life magazine insert. the card stock for this insert is slightly thinner, with white margins. The 1962 Post Canadian and Jell-O sets have virtually the same checklist as this set. The complete set price does not include the scarcer variations.

		NR MT	EX	VG
Complete Set:		1100.00	550.00	330.00
Common Player:		1.50	.70	.45
1	Bill Skowron	4.00	2.00	1.25
2	Bobby Richardson	3.00	1.50	.90
3	Cletis Boyer	2.00	1.00	.60
4	Tony Kubek	3.00	1.50	.90
5a	Mickey Mantle (from box, no printing on back)	65.00	32.00	19.50
5b	Mickey Mantle (from ad, printing on back)	70.00	35.00	21.00

		NR MT	EX	VG
6a	Roger Maris (from box, no printing on back)	10.00	5.00	3.00
6b	Roger Maris (from ad, printing on back)	12.00	6.00	3.50
7	Yogi Berra	10.00	5.00	3.00
8	Elston Howard	3.00	1.50	.90
9	Whitey Ford	7.00	3.50	2.00
10	Ralph Terry	2.00	1.00	.60
11	John Blanchard	2.00	1.00	.60
12	Luis Arroyo	2.00	1.00	.60
13	Bill Stafford	2.00	1.00	.60
14a	Norm Cash (Throws: Right)	2.00	1.00	.60
14b	Norm Cash (Throws: Left)	5.00	2.50	1.50
15	Jake Wood	1.50	.70	.45
16	Steve Boros	1.50	.70	.45
17	Chico Fernandez	1.50	.70	.45
18	Bill Bruton	1.50	.70	.45
19	Rocky Colavito	3.00	1.50	.90
20	Al Kaline	8.00	4.00	2.50
21	Dick Brown	1.50	.70	.45
22	Frank Lary	1.50	.70	.45
23	Don Mossi	1.50	.70	.45
24	Phil Regan	1.50	.70	.45
25	Charley Maxwell	1.50	.70	.45
26	Jim Bunning	3.00	1.50	.90
27a	Jim Gentile (Home: Baltimore)	1.50	.70	.45
27b	Jim Gentile (Home: San Lorenzo)	5.00	2.50	1.50
28	Marv Breeding	1.50	.70	.45
29	Brooks Robinson	8.00	4.00	2.50
30	Ron Hansen	1.50	.70	.45
31	Jackie Brandt	1.50	.70	.45
32	Dick Williams	1.75	.90	.50
33	Gus Triandos	1.50	.70	.45
34	Milt Pappas	1.50	.70	.45
35	Hoyt Wilhelm	4.00	2.00	1.25
36	Chuck Estrada	5.00	2.50	1.50
37	Vic Power	1.50	.70	.45
38	Johnny Temple	1.50	.70	.45
39	Bubba Phillips	1.50	.70	.45
40	Tito Francona	1.50	.70	.45
41	Willie Kirkland	1.50	.70	.45
42	John Romano	1.50	.70	.45
43	Jim Perry	1.75	.90	.50
44	Woodie Held	1.50	.70	.45
45	Chuck Essegian	1.50	.70	.45
46	Roy Sievers	1.75	.90	.50
47	Nellie Fox	3.50	1.75	1.00
48	Al Smith	1.50	.70	.45
49	Luis Aparicio	4.00	2.00	1.25
50	Jim Landis	1.50	.70	.45
51	Minnie Minoso	2.00	1.00	.60
52	Andy Carey	1.50	.70	.45
53	Sherman Lollar	1.50	.70	.45
54	Bill Pierce	1.75	.90	.50
55	Early Wynn	25.00	12.50	7.50
56	Chuck Schilling	1.50	.70	.45
57	Pete Runnels	1.50	.70	.45
58	Frank Malzone	1.50	.70	.45
59	Don Buddin	1.50	.70	.45
60	Gary Geiger	1.50	.70	.45
61	Carl Yastrzemski	30.00	15.00	9.00
62	Jackie Jensen	2.00	1.00	.60
63	Jim Pagliaroni	1.50	.70	.45
64	Don Schwall	1.50	.70	.45
65	Dale Long	1.50	.70	.45
66	Chuck Cottier	1.50	.70	.45
67	Billy Klaus	1.50	.70	.45
68	Coot Veal	1.50	.70	.45
69	Marty Keough	25.00	12.50	7.50
70	Willie Tasby	1.50	.70	.45
71	Gene Woodling	1.50	.70	.45
72	Gene Green	1.50	.70	.45
73	Dick Donovan	1.50	.70	.45
74	Steve Bilko	1.50	.70	.45
75	Rocky Bridges	1.50	.70	.45
76	Eddie Yost	1.50	.70	.45
77	Leon Wagner	1.50	.70	.45
78	Albie Pearson	1.50	.70	.45
79	Ken Hunt	1.50	.70	.45
80	Earl Averill	1.50	.70	.45
81	Ryne Duren	1.50	.70	.45
82	Ted Kluszewski	2.50	1.25	.70
83	Bob Allison	20.00	10.00	6.00
84	Billy Martin	3.50	1.75	1.00
85	Harmon Killebrew	7.00	3.50	2.00
86	Zoilo Versalles	1.50	.70	.45
87	Lenny Green	1.50	.70	.45
88	Bill Tuttle	1.50	.70	.45
89	Jim Lemon	1.50	.70	.45
90	Earl Battey	1.50	.70	.45
91	Camilo Pascual	1.50	.70	.45

		NR MT	EX	VG
92	Norm Siebern	45.00	22.00	13.50
93	Jerry Lumpe	1.50	.70	.45
94	Dick Howser	2.00	1.00	.60
95a	Gene Stephens (Born: Jan. 5)	1.50	.70	.45
95b	Gene Stephens (Born: Jan. 20)	5.00	2.50	1.50
96	Leo Posada	1.50	.70	.45
97	Joe Pignatano	1.50	.70	.45
98	Jim Archer	1.50	.70	.45
99	Haywood Sullivan	1.50	.70	.45
100	Art Ditmar	1.50	.70	.45
101	Gil Hodges	50.00	25.00	15.00
102	Charlie Neal	1.50	.70	.45
103	Daryl Spencer	15.00	7.50	4.50
104	Maury Wills	4.00	2.00	1.25
105	Tommy Davis	2.00	1.00	.60
106	Willie Davis	1.75	.90	.50
107	John Roseboro	1.50	.70	.45
108	John Podres	2.50	1.25	.70
109a	Sandy Koufax (blue lines around stats)	25.00	12.50	7.50
109b	Sandy Koufax (red lines around stats)	15.00	7.50	4.50
110	Don Drysdale	7.00	3.50	2.00
111	Larry Sherry	1.50	.70	.45
112	Jim Gilliam	2.50	1.25	.70
113	Norm Larker	25.00	12.50	7.50
114	Duke Snider	8.00	4.00	2.50
115	Stan Williams	1.50	.70	.45
116	Gordy Coleman	60.00	30.00	18.00
117	Don Blasingame	1.50	.70	.45
118	Gene Freese	1.50	.70	.45
119	Ed Kasko	1.50	.70	.45
120	Gus Bell	1.50	.70	.45
121	Vada Pinson	2.50	1.25	.70
122	Frank Robinson	15.00	7.50	4.50
123	Bob Purkey	1.50	.70	.45
124a	Joey Jay (blue lines around stats)	8.00	4.00	2.50
124b	Joey Jay (red lines around stats)	1.50	.70	.45
125	Jim Brosnan	15.00	7.50	4.50
126	Jim O'Toole	1.50	.70	.45
127	Jerry Lynch	45.00	22.00	13.50
128	Wally Post	1.50	.70	.45
129	Ken Hunt	1.50	.70	.45
130	Jerry Zimmerman	1.50	.70	.45
131	Willie McCovey	60.00	30.00	18.00
132	Jose Pagan	1.50	.70	.45
133	Felipe Alou	1.75	.90	.50
134	Jim Davenport	1.50	.70	.45
135	Harvey Kuenn	2.00	1.00	.60
136	Orlando Cepeda	3.50	1.75	1.00
137	Ed Bailey	1.50	.70	.45
138	Sam Jones	1.50	.70	.45
139	Mike McCormick	1.50	.70	.45
140	Juan Marichal	60.00	30.00	18.00
141	Jack Sanford	1.50	.70	.45
142	Willie Mays	20.00	10.00	6.00
143	Stu Miller (photo actually Chuck Hiller)	6.00	3.00	1.75
144	Joe Amalfitano	10.00	5.00	3.00
145a	Joe Adock (name incorrect)	25.00	12.50	7.50
145b	Joe Adcock (name correct)	2.00	1.00	.60
146	Frank Bolling	1.50	.70	.45
147	Ed Mathews	7.00	3.50	2.00
148	Roy McMillan	1.50	.70	.45
149	Hank Aaron	20.00	10.00	6.00
150	Gino Cimoli	1.50	.70	.45
151	Frank Thomas	1.50	.70	.45
152	Joe Torre	3.00	1.50	.90
153	Lou Burdette	2.50	1.25	.70
154	Bob Buhl	1.50	.70	.45
155	Carlton Willey	1.50	.70	.45
156	Lee Maye	1.50	.70	.45
157	Al Spangler	1.50	.70	.45
158	Bill White	30.00	15.00	9.00
159	Ken Boyer	3.00	1.50	.90
160	Joe Cunningham	1.50	.70	.45
161	Carl Warwick	1.50	.70	.45
162	Carl Sawatski	1.50	.70	.45
163	Lindy McDaniel	1.50	.70	.45
164	Ernie Broglio	1.50	.70	.45
165	Larry Jackson	1.50	.70	.45
166	Curt Flood	2.00	1.00	.60
167	Curt Simmons	1.50	.70	.45
168	Alex Grammas	1.50	.70	.45
169	Dick Stuart	1.50	.70	.45
170	Bill Mazeroski	2.50	1.25	.70
171	Don Hoak	1.50	.70	.45
172	Dick Groat	2.00	1.00	.60
173a	Roberto Clemente (blue lines around stats)	25.00	12.50	7.50
173b	Roberto Clemente (red lines around stats)	15.00	7.50	4.50

		NR MT	EX	VG
174	Bob Skinner	1.50	.70	.45
175	Bill Virdon	1.75	.90	.50
176	Smoky Burgess	1.75	.90	.50
177	Elroy Face	1.75	.90	.50
178	Bob Friend	1.50	.70	.45
179	Vernon Law	1.50	.70	.45
180	Harvey Haddix	1.50	.70	.45
181	Hal Smith	1.50	.70	.45
182	Ed Bouchee	1.50	.70	.45
183	Don Zimmer	1.50	.70	.45
184	Ron Santo	2.50	1.25	.70
185	Andre Rodgers	1.50	.70	.45
186	Richie Ashburn	3.00	1.50	.90
187a	George Altman (last line is "...1955).)	1.50	.70	.45
187b	George Altman (last line is "...1955.")	3.00	1.50	.90
188	Ernie Banks	8.00	4.00	2.50
189	Sam Taylor	1.50	.70	.45
190	Don Elston	1.50	.70	.45
191	Jerry Kindall	1.50	.70	.45
192	Pancho Herrera	1.50	.70	.45
193	Tony Taylor	1.50	.70	.45
194	Ruben Amaro	1.50	.70	.45
195	Don Demeter	1.50	.70	.45
196	Bobby Gene Smith	1.50	.70	.45
197	Clay Dalrymple	1.50	.70	.45
198	Robin Roberts	5.00	2.50	1.50
199	Art Mahaffey	1.50	.70	.45
200	John Buzhardt	2.50	1.25	.70

1962 Post Cereal Canadian

This Canadian set of cards is scarce due to the much more limited distribution in Canada. The cards were printed on the back of the cereal box itself and contains a full-color player photo with biography and statistics given in both French and English. The card backs are blank. Cards measure 3-1/2" by 2-1/2". This 200-card set is very similar to the Post Cereal cards printed in the United States. the Post logo appears at the upper left corner in the Canadian issue. Several cards are scarce because of limited distribution and there are two Whitey Ford cards, the corrected version being the most scarce. The complete set price does not include the scarcer variations.

		NR MT	EX	VG
Complete Set:		2000.00	1000.00	600.00
Common Player:		2.50	1.25	.70
1	Bill Skowron	8.00	4.00	2.50
2	Bobby Richardson	6.00	3.00	1.75
3	Cletis Boyer	3.50	1.75	1.00
4	Tony Kubek	6.00	3.00	1.75
5a	Mickey Mantle (script name large)	150.00	75.00	45.00
5b	Mickey Mantle (script name small)	90.00	45.00	27.00
6	Roger Maris	15.00	7.50	4.50
7	Yogi Berra	15.00	7.50	4.50
8	Elston Howard	4.00	2.00	1.25
9a	Whitey Ford (Dodgers)	20.00	10.00	6.00
9b	Whitey Ford (Yankees)	35.00	17.50	10.50
10	Ralph Terry	25.00	12.50	7.50
11	John Blanchard	3.00	1.50	.90

		NR MT	EX	VG
12	Luis Arroyo	3.00	1.50	.90
13	Bill Stafford	3.00	1.50	.90
14	Norm Cash	4.00	2.00	1.25
15	Jake Wood	2.50	1.25	.70
16	Steve Boros	2.50	1.25	.70
17	Chico Fernandez	2.50	1.25	.70
18	Bill Bruton	2.50	1.25	.70
19a	Rocky Colavito (script name large)	7.00	3.50	2.00
19b	Rocky Colavito (script name small)	7.00	3.50	2.00
20	Al Kaline	15.00	7.50	4.50
21	Dick Brown	7.00	3.50	2.00
22a	Frank Lary (French bio variation)	7.00	3.50	2.00
22b	Frank Lary (French bio variation)	7.00	3.50	2.00
23	Don Mossi	2.50	1.25	.70
24	Phil Regan	2.50	1.25	.70
25	Charley Maxwell	2.50	1.25	.70
26	Jim Bunning	6.00	3.00	1.75
27a	Jim Gentile (French bio variation)	5.00	2.50	1.50
27b	Jim Gentile (French bio variation)	5.00	2.50	1.50
28	Marv Breeding	2.50	1.25	.70
29	Brooks Robinson	25.00	12.50	7.50
30	Ron Hansen	2.50	1.25	.70
31	Jackie Brandt	2.50	1.25	.70
32	Dick Williams	25.00	12.50	7.50
33	Gus Triandos	2.50	1.25	.70
34	Milt Pappas	3.00	1.50	.90
35	Hoyt Wilhelm	15.00	7.50	4.50
36	Chuck Estrada	2.50	1.25	.70
37	Vic Power	2.50	1.25	.70
38	Johnny Temple	2.50	1.25	.70
39	Bubba Phillips	25.00	12.50	7.50
40	Tito Francona	2.50	1.25	.70
41	Willie Kirkland	7.00	3.50	2.00
42	John Romano	7.00	3.50	2.00
43	Jim Perry	4.00	2.00	1.25
44	Woodie Held	2.50	1.25	.70
45	Chuck Essegian	2.50	1.25	.70
46	Roy Sievers	3.50	1.75	1.00
47	Nellie Fox	6.00	3.00	1.75
48	Al Smith	2.50	1.25	.70
49	Luis Aparicio	15.00	7.50	4.50
50	Jim Landis	2.50	1.25	.70
51	Minnie Minoso	25.00	12.50	7.50
52	Andy Carey	7.00	3.50	2.00
53	Sherman Lollar	2.50	1.25	.70
54	Bill Pierce	3.50	1.75	1.00
55	Early Wynn	12.00	6.00	3.50
56	Chuck Schilling	2.50	1.25	.70
57	Pete Runnels	3.00	1.50	.90
58	Frank Malzone	2.50	1.25	.70
59	Don Buddin	7.00	3.50	2.00
60	Gary Geiger	2.50	1.25	.70
61	Carl Yastrzemski	40.00	20.00	12.00
62	Jackie Jensen	9.00	4.50	2.75
63	Jim Pagliaroni	2.50	1.25	.70
64	Don Schwall	2.50	1.25	.70
65	Dale Long	2.50	1.25	.70
66	Chuck Cottier	2.50	1.25	.70
67	Billy Klaus	2.50	1.25	.70
68	Coot Veal	2.50	1.25	.70
69	Marty Keough	2.50	1.25	.70
70	Willie Tasby	25.00	12.50	7.50
71	Gene Woodling (photo reversed)	3.00	1.50	.90
72	Gene Green	2.50	1.25	.70
73	Dick Donovan	2.50	1.25	.70
74	Steve Bilko	2.50	1.25	.70
75	Rocky Bridges	6.00	3.00	1.75
76	Eddie Yost	2.50	1.25	.70
77	Leon Wagner	25.00	12.50	7.50
78	Albie Pearson	7.00	3.50	2.00
79	Ken Hunt	2.50	1.25	.70
80	Earl Averill	2.50	1.25	.70
81	Ryne Duren	4.00	2.00	1.25
82	Ted Kluszewski	4.00	2.00	1.25
83	Bob Allison	3.00	1.50	.90
84	Billy Martin	6.00	3.00	1.75
85	Harmon Killebrew	12.00	6.00	3.50
86	Zoilo Versalles	2.50	1.25	.70
87	Lenny Green	2.50	1.25	.70
88	Bill Tuttle	2.50	1.25	.70
89	Jim Lemon	2.50	1.25	.70
90	Earl Battey	2.50	1.25	.70
91	Camilo Pascual	3.00	1.50	.90
92	Norm Siebern	2.50	1.25	.70
93	Jerry Lumpe	2.50	1.25	.70
94	Dick Howser	25.00	12.50	7.50
95	Gene Stephens	2.50	1.25	.70
96	Leo Posada	2.50	1.25	.70
97	Joe Pignatano	2.50	1.25	.70
98	Jim Archer	2.50	1.25	.70
99	Haywood Sullivan	25.00	12.50	7.50
100	Art Ditmar	25.00	12.50	7.50
101	Gil Hodges	12.00	6.00	3.50
102	Charlie Neal	2.50	1.25	.70
103	Daryl Spencer	2.50	1.25	.70
104	Maury Wills	5.00	2.50	1.50
105	Tommy Davis	9.00	4.50	2.75
106	Willie Davis	4.00	2.00	1.25
107	John Roseboro	3.00	1.50	.90
108	John Podres	4.00	2.00	1.25
109	Sandy Koufax	30.00	15.00	9.00
110	Don Drysdale	15.00	7.50	4.50
111	Larry Sherry	25.00	12.50	7.50
112	Jim Gilliam	25.00	12.50	7.50
113	Norm Larker	2.50	1.25	.70
114	Duke Snider	25.00	12.50	7.50
115	Stan Williams	2.50	1.25	.70
116	Gordy Coleman	2.50	1.25	.70
117	Don Blasingame	25.00	12.50	7.50
118	Gene Freese	7.00	3.50	2.00
119	Ed Kasko	2.50	1.25	.70
120	Gus Bell	2.50	1.25	.70
121	Vada Pinson	5.00	2.50	1.50
122	Frank Robinson	15.00	7.50	4.50
123	Bob Purkey	25.00	12.50	7.50
124	Joey Jay	2.50	1.25	.70
125	Jim Brosnan	3.00	1.50	.90
126	Jim O'Toole	2.50	1.25	.70
127	Jerry Lynch	2.50	1.25	.70
128	Wally Post	55.00	27.00	16.50
129	Ken Hunt	2.50	1.25	.70
130	Jerry Zimmerman	2.50	1.25	.70
131	Willie McCovey	15.00	7.50	4.50
132	Jose Pagan	2.50	1.25	.70
133	Felipe Alou	3.50	1.75	1.00
134	Jim Davenport	2.50	1.25	.70
135	Harvey Kuenn	4.00	2.00	1.25
136	Orlando Cepeda	6.00	3.00	1.75
137	Ed Bailey	25.00	12.50	7.50
138	Sam Jones	25.00	12.50	7.50
139	Mike McCormick	2.50	1.25	.70
140	Juan Marichal	15.00	7.50	4.50
141	Jack Sanford	2.50	1.25	.70
142a	Willie Mays (big head)	35.00	17.50	10.50
142b	Willie Mays (small head)	50.00	25.00	15.00
143	Stu Miller	2.50	1.25	.70
144	Joe Amalfitano	25.00	12.50	7.50
145	Joe Adcock	4.00	2.00	1.25
146	Frank Bolling	2.50	1.25	.70
147	Ed Mathews	12.00	6.00	3.50
148	Roy McMillan	2.50	1.25	.70
149a	Hank Aaron (script name large)	35.00	17.50	10.50
149b	Hank Aaron (script name small)	35.00	17.50	10.50
150	Gino Cimoli	2.50	1.25	.70
151	Frank Thomas	2.50	1.25	.70
152	Joe Torre	5.00	2.50	1.50
153	Lou Burdette	5.00	2.50	1.50
154	Bob Buhl	3.00	1.50	.90
155	Carlton Willey	2.50	1.25	.70
156	Lee Maye	2.50	1.25	.70
157	Al Spangler	2.50	1.25	.70
158	Bill White	3.50	1.75	1.00
159	Ken Boyer	30.00	15.00	9.00
160	Joe Cunningham	2.50	1.25	.70
161	Carl Warwick	7.00	3.50	2.00
162	Carl Sawatski	2.50	1.25	.70
163	Lindy McDaniel	2.50	1.25	.70
164	Ernie Broglio	2.50	1.25	.70
165	Larry Jackson	2.50	1.25	.70
166	Curt Flood	4.00	2.00	1.25
167	Curt Simmons	8.00	4.00	2.50
168	Alex Grammas	2.50	1.25	.70
169	Dick Stuart	3.00	1.50	.90
170	Bill Mazeroski	25.00	12.50	7.50
171	Don Hoak	2.50	1.25	.70
172	Dick Groat	9.00	4.50	2.75
173	Roberto Clemente	30.00	15.00	9.00
174	Bob Skinner	2.50	1.25	.70
175	Bill Virdon	4.00	2.00	1.25
176	Smoky Burgess	8.00	4.00	2.50
177	Elroy Face	8.00	4.00	2.50
178	Bob Friend	3.00	1.50	.90
179	Vernon Law	3.50	1.75	1.00
180	Harvey Haddix	3.00	1.50	.90
181	Hal Smith	25.00	12.50	7.50
182	Ed Bouchee	2.50	1.25	.70
183	Don Zimmer	4.00	2.00	1.25
184	Ron Santo	5.00	2.50	1.50
185	Andre Rodgers	2.50	1.25	.70
186	Richie Ashburn	6.00	3.00	1.75

		NR MT	EX	VG
187	George Altman	2.50	1.25	.70
188	Ernie Banks	25.00	12.50	7.50
189	Sam Taylor	2.50	1.25	.70
190	Don Elston	2.50	1.25	.70
191	Jerry Kindall	2.50	1.25	.70
192	Pancho Herrera	2.50	1.25	.70
193	Tony Taylor	2.50	1.25	.70
194	Ruben Amaro	2.50	1.25	.70
195	Don Demeter	25.00	12.50	7.50
196	Bobby Gene Smith	2.50	1.25	.70
197	Clay Dalrymple	2.50	1.25	.70
198	Robin Roberts	12.00	6.00	3.50
199	Art Mahaffey	2.50	1.25	.70
200	John Buzhardt	5.00	2.50	1.50

1963 Post

Another 200-player, 3-1/2" by 2-1/2" set that, with variations, totals more than 205 cards. Numerous color variations also exist due to the different cereal boxes on which the cards were printed. As many as 25 cards in the set are considered scarce, making it much more difficult to complete than the other major Post sets. Star cards also command higher prices than in the '61 or '62 Post cards. The 1963 Post cards are almost identical to the '63 Jell-O set, which is a slight 1/4" narrower. Cards are still blank backed, with a color player photo, biographies and statistics on the numbered card fronts. No Post logo appears on the '63 cards. The complete set price does not include the scarcer variations.

		NR MT	EX	VG
Complete Set:		3250.00	1625.00	975.00
Common Player:		1.50	.70	.45
1	Vic Power	3.50	1.75	1.00
2	Bernie Allen	1.50	.70	.45
3	Zoilo Versalles	1.50	.70	.45
4	Rich Rollins	1.50	.70	.45
5	Harmon Killebrew	12.00	6.00	3.50
6	Lenny Green	35.00	17.50	10.50
7	Bob Allison	1.75	.90	.50
8	Earl Battey	1.50	.70	.45
9	Camilo Pascual	1.50	.70	.45
10	Jim Kaat	3.00	1.50	.90
11	Jack Kralick	1.50	.70	.45
12	Bill Skowron	2.00	1.00	.60
13	Bobby Richardson	3.00	1.50	.90
14	Cletis Boyer	2.00	1.00	.60
15	Mickey Mantle	325.00	162.00	97.00
16	Roger Maris	150.00	75.00	45.00
17	Yogi Berra	15.00	7.50	4.50
18	Elston Howard	3.00	1.50	.90
19	Whitey Ford	8.00	4.00	2.50
20	Ralph Terry	2.00	1.00	.60
21	John Blanchard	2.00	1.00	.60
22	Bill Stafford	2.00	1.00	.60
23	Tom Tresh	2.00	1.00	.60
24	Steve Bilko	1.50	.70	.45
25	Bill Moran	1.50	.70	.45
26a	Joe Koppe (1962 Avg. is .277)	1.50	.70	.45
26b	Joe Koppe (1962 Avg. is .227)	12.00	6.00	3.50
27	Felix Torres	1.50	.70	.45
28a	Leon Wagner (lifetime Avg. is .278)			
		1.50	.70	.45
28b	Leon Wagner (lifetime Avg. is .272)			
		12.00	6.00	3.50
29	Albie Pearson	1.50	.70	.45
30	Lee Thomas (photo actually George Thomas)	70.00	35.00	21.00
31	Bob Rodgers	1.50	.70	.45
32	Dean Chance	1.50	.70	.45
33	Ken McBride	1.50	.70	.45
34	George Thomas (photo actually Lee Thomas)	1.50	.70	.45
35	Joe Cunningham	1.50	.70	.45
36a	Nelson Fox (no bat showing)	3.50	1.75	1.00
36b	Nelson Fox (part of bat showing)	10.00	5.00	3.00
37	Luis Aparicio	4.00	2.00	1.25
38	Al Smith	25.00	12.50	7.50
39	Floyd Robinson	80.00	40.00	24.00
40	Jim Landis	1.50	.70	.45
41	Charlie Maxwell	1.50	.70	.45
42	Sherman Lollar	1.50	.70	.45
43	Early Wynn	6.00	3.00	1.75
44	Juan Pizarro	1.50	.70	.45
45	Ray Herbert	1.50	.70	.45
46	Norm Cash	2.00	1.00	.60
47	Steve Boros	1.50	.70	.45
48	Dick McAuliffe	25.00	12.50	7.50
49	Bill Bruton	1.50	.70	.45
50	Rocky Colavito	3.00	1.50	.90
51	Al Kaline	10.00	5.00	3.00
52	Dick Brown	1.50	.70	.45
53	Jim Bunning	90.00	45.00	27.00
54	Hank Aguirre	1.50	.70	.45
55	Frank Lary	1.50	.70	.45
56	Don Mossi	1.50	.70	.45
57	Jim Gentile	1.50	.70	.45
58	Jackie Brandt	1.50	.70	.45
59	Brooks Robinson	10.00	5.00	3.00
60	Ron Hansen	1.50	.70	.45
61	Jerry Adair	150.00	75.00	45.00
62	John Powell	3.00	1.50	.90
63	Russ Snyder	1.50	.70	.45
64	Steve Barber	1.50	.70	.45
65	Milt Pappas	1.50	.70	.45
66	Robin Roberts	4.00	2.00	1.25
67	Tito Francona	1.50	.70	.45
68	Jerry Kindall	1.50	.70	.45
69	Woodie Held	1.50	.70	.45
70	Bubba Phillips	15.00	7.50	4.50
71	Chuck Essegian	1.50	.70	.45
72	Willie Kirkland	1.50	.70	.45
73	Al Luplow	1.50	.70	.45
74	Ty Cline	1.50	.70	.45
75	Dick Donovan	1.50	.70	.45
76	John Romano	1.50	.70	.45
77	Pete Runnels	1.50	.70	.45
78	Ed Bressoud	1.50	.70	.45
79	Frank Malzone	1.50	.70	.45
80	Carl Yastrzemski	275.00	137.00	82.00
81	Gary Geiger	1.50	.70	.45
82	Lou Clinton	1.50	.70	.45
83	Earl Wilson	1.50	.70	.45
84	Bill Monbouquette	1.50	.70	.45
85	Norm Siebern	1.50	.70	.45
86	Jerry Lumpe	80.00	40.00	24.00
87	Manny Jimenez	80.00	40.00	24.00
88	Gino Cimoli	1.50	.70	.45
89	Ed Charles	1.50	.70	.45
90	Ed Rakow	1.50	.70	.45
91	Bob Del Greco	1.50	.70	.45
92	Haywood Sullivan	1.50	.70	.45
93	Chuck Hinton	1.50	.70	.45
94	Ken Retzer	1.50	.70	.45
95	Harry Bright	1.50	.70	.45
96	Bob Johnson	1.50	.70	.45
97	Dave Stenhouse	15.00	7.50	4.50
98	Chuck Cottier	25.00	12.50	7.50
99	Tom Cheney	1.50	.70	.45
100	Claude Osteen	15.00	7.50	4.50
101	Orlando Cepeda	3.00	1.50	.90
102	Charley Hiller	1.50	.70	.45
103	Jose Pagan	1.50	.70	.45
104	Jim Davenport	1.50	.70	.45
105	Harvey Kuenn	2.00	1.00	.60
106	Willie Mays	25.00	12.50	7.50
107	Felipe Alou	1.75	.90	.50
108	Tom Haller	90.00	45.00	27.00
109	Juan Marichal	6.00	3.00	1.75
110	Jack Sanford	1.50	.70	.45
111	Bill O'Dell	1.50	.70	.45
112	Willie McCovey	7.00	3.50	2.00
113	Lee Walls	1.50	.70	.45
114	Jim Gilliam	3.00	1.50	.90

		NR MT	EX	VG
115	Maury Wills	3.00	1.50	.90
116	Ron Fairly	1.50	.70	.45
117	Tommy Davis	2.00	1.00	.60
118	Duke Snider	8.00	4.00	2.50
119	Willie Davis	150.00	75.00	45.00
120	John Roseboro	1.50	.70	.45
121	Sandy Koufax	15.00	7.50	4.50
122	Stan Williams	1.50	.70	.45
123	Don Drysdale	7.00	3.50	2.00
124a	Daryl Spencer (no arm showing)	1.50	.70	.45
124b	Daryl Spencer (part of arm showing)	10.00	5.00	3.00
125	Gordy Coleman	1.50	.70	.45
126	Don Blasingame	1.50	.70	.45
127	Leo Cardenas	1.50	.70	.45
128	Eddie Kasko	150.00	75.00	45.00
129	Jerry Lynch	15.00	7.50	4.50
130	Vada Pinson	2.00	1.00	.60
131a	Frank Robinson (no stripes on hat)	8.00	4.00	2.50
131b	Frank Robinson (stripes on hat)	15.00	7.50	4.50
132	John Edwards	1.50	.70	.45
133	Joey Jay	1.50	.70	.45
134	Bob Purkey	1.50	.70	.45
135	Marty Keough	15.00	7.50	4.50
136	Jim O'Toole	1.50	.70	.45
137	Dick Stuart	1.50	.70	.45
138	Bill Mazeroski	2.00	1.00	.60
139	Dick Groat	2.00	1.00	.60
140	Don Hoak	30.00	15.00	9.00
141	Bob Skinner	15.00	7.50	4.50
142	Bill Virdon	2.00	1.00	.60
143	Roberto Clemente	20.00	10.00	6.00
144	Smoky Burgess	1.75	.90	.50
145	Bob Friend	1.50	.70	.45
146	Al McBean	1.50	.70	.45
147	El Roy Face (Elroy)	2.00	1.00	.60
148	Joe Adcock	2.00	1.00	.60
149	Frank Bolling	1.50	.70	.45
150	Roy McMillan	1.50	.70	.45
151	Eddie Mathews	6.00	3.00	1.75
152	Hank Aaron	70.00	35.00	21.00
153	Del Crandall	30.00	15.00	9.00
154a	Bob Shaw (third sentence has "In 1959" twice)	10.00	5.00	3.00
154b	Bob Shaw (third sentence has "In 1959" once)	1.50	.70	.45
155	Lew Burdette	2.00	1.00	.60
156	Joe Torre	3.00	1.50	.90
157	Tony Cloninger	1.50	.70	.45
158	Bill White	2.00	1.00	.60
159	Julian Javier	1.50	.70	.45
160	Ken Boyer	3.00	1.50	.90
161	Julio Gotay	1.50	.70	.45
162	Curt Flood	90.00	45.00	27.00
163	Charlie James	1.50	.70	.45
164	Gene Oliver	1.50	.70	.45
165	Ernie Broglio	1.50	.70	.45
166	Bob Gibson	7.00	3.50	2.00
167a	Lindy McDaniel (asterisk before trade line)	1.50	.70	.45
167b	Lindy McDaniel (no asterisk before trade line)	5.00	2.50	1.50
168	Ray Washburn	1.50	.70	.45
169	Ernie Banks	8.00	4.00	2.50
170	Ron Santo	2.00	1.00	.60
171	George Altman	1.50	.70	.45
172	Billy Williams	90.00	45.00	27.00
173	Andre Rodgers	6.00	3.00	1.75
174	Ken Hubbs	20.00	10.00	6.00
175	Don Landrum	1.50	.70	.45
176	Dick Bertell	15.00	7.50	4.50
177	Roy Sievers	1.75	.90	.50
178	Tony Taylor	1.50	.70	.45
179	John Callison	1.75	.90	.50
180	Don Demeter	1.50	.70	.45
181	Tony Gonzalez	1.50	.70	.45
182	Wes Covington	20.00	10.00	6.00
183	Art Mahaffey	1.50	.70	.45
184	Clay Dalrymple	1.50	.70	.45
185	Al Spangler	1.50	.70	.45
186	Roman Mejias	1.50	.70	.45
187	Bob Aspromonte	275.00	137.00	82.00
188	Norm Larker	30.00	15.00	9.00
189	Johnny Temple	1.50	.70	.45
190	Carl Warwick	1.50	.70	.45
191	Bob Lillis	1.50	.70	.45
192	Dick Farrell	1.50	.70	.45
193	Gil Hodges	7.00	3.50	2.00
194	Marv Throneberry	3.00	1.50	.90
195	Charlie Neal	10.00	5.00	3.00

		NR MT	EX	VG
196	Frank Thomas	150.00	75.00	45.00
197	Richie Ashburn	20.00	10.00	6.00
198	Felix Mantilla	1.50	.70	.45
199	Rod Kanehl	20.00	10.00	6.00
200	Roger Craig	3.00	1.50	.90

1986 Quaker Oats

The Quaker Company, in conjunction with Topps, produced this 33-card set of current baseball stars for packaging in groups of three in Chewy Granola Bars packages. The cards are noted as the "1st Annual Collectors Edition." They are numbered and measure 2-1/2" by 3-1/2". Card fronts feature full-color player photos with the product name at the top and the player name, team and position below the photo. The complete set was offered via mail order by the Quaker Company.

		MT	NR MT	EX
	Complete Set:	8.00	6.00	3.25
	Common Player:	.15	.11	.06
1	Willie McGee	.15	.11	.06
2	Dwight Gooden	.60	.45	.25
3	Vince Coleman	.30	.25	.12
4	Gary Carter	.25	.20	.10
5	Jack Clark	.15	.11	.06
6	Steve Garvey	.25	.20	.10
7	Tony Gwynn	.35	.25	.14
8	Dale Murphy	.40	.30	.15
9	Dave Parker	.15	.11	.06
10	Tim Raines	.25	.20	.10
11	Pete Rose	.60	.45	.25
12	Nolan Ryan	.25	.20	.10
13	Ryne Sandberg	.20	.15	.08
14	Mike Schmidt	.35	.25	.14
15	Ozzie Smith	.15	.11	.06
16	Darryl Strawberry	.40	.30	.15
17	Fernando Valenzuela	.20	.15	.08
18	Don Mattingly	1.50	1.25	.60
19	Bret Saberhagen	.20	.15	.08
20	Ozzie Guillen	.15	.11	.06
21	Bert Blyleven	.15	.11	.06
22	Wade Boggs	.80	.60	.30
23	George Brett	.40	.30	.15
24	Darrell Evans	.15	.11	.06
25	Rickey Henderson	.35	.25	.14
26	Reggie Jackson	.30	.25	.12
27	Eddie Murray	.30	.25	.12
28	Phil Niekro	.20	.15	.08
29	Dan Quisenberry	.15	.11	.06
30	Jim Rice	.25	.20	.10
31	Cal Ripken	.30	.25	.12
32	Tom Seaver	.25	.20	.10
33	Dave Winfield	.25	.20	.10
-----	Offer Card	.03	.02	.01

1984 Ralston Purina

This set, produced in conjunction with Topps, has 33 of the game's top players, and is titled "1st Annual Collector's Edition." The full-color photos on the 2-1/2" by 3-1/2" cards are all close-up poses. Topps' logo appears only on the card fronts, and the backs are completely different from Topps' regular issue of 1984. Card backs feature a checkerboard look, coinciding with the well-known Ralston Purina logo. Cards are numbered 1-33, with odd numbers for American Leaguers and even numbered cards for National League players. Four cards were packed in boxes of Cookie Crisp and Donkey Kong Junior brand cereals, and the complete set was available via a mail-in offer.

		MT	NR MT	EX
Complete Set:		4.00	3.00	1.50
Common Player:		.10	.08	.04
1	Eddie Murray	.30	.25	.12
2	Ozzie Smith	.10	.08	.04
3	Ted Simmons	.10	.08	.04
4	Pete Rose	.50	.40	.20
5	Greg Luzinski	.10	.08	.04
6	Andre Dawson	.15	.11	.06
7	Dave Winfield	.25	.20	.10
8	Tom Seaver	.25	.20	.10
9	Jim Rice	.25	.20	.10
10	Fernando Valenzuela	.20	.15	.08
11	Wade Boggs	.60	.45	.25
12	Dale Murphy	.35	.25	.14
13	George Brett	.35	.25	.14
14	Nolan Ryan	.20	.15	.08
15	Rickey Henderson	.30	.25	.12
16	Steve Carlton	.25	.20	.10
17	Rod Carew	.25	.20	.10
18	Steve Garvey	.25	.20	.10
19	Reggie Jackson	.25	.20	.10
20	Dave Concepcion	.10	.08	.04
21	Robin Yount	.20	.15	.08
22	Mike Schmidt	.35	.25	.14
23	Jim Palmer	.20	.15	.08
24	Bruce Sutter	.10	.08	.04
25	Dan Quisenberry	.10	.08	.04
26	Bill Madlock	.10	.08	.04
27	Cecil Cooper	.10	.08	.04
28	Gary Carter	.25	.20	.10
29	Fred Lynn	.15	.11	.06
30	Pedro Guerrero	.15	.11	.06
31	Ron Guidry	.15	.11	.06
32	Keith Hernandez	.20	.15	.08
33	Carlton Fisk	.15	.11	.06

1987 Ralston Purina

The Ralston Purina Company, in conjunction with Mike Schecter Associates, issued a 15-card set in specially marked boxes of Cookie Crisp and Honey Graham Chex brands of cereal. Three different cards, each measuring 2-1/2" by 3-1/2" and

wrapped in cellophane, were inserted in each box. The card fronts contain a full-color photo with the team insignia airbrushed away. Above the photo are two yellow crossed bats and a star, with the player's uniform number inside the star. The card backs are grey with red printing and contain the set name, card number, player's name, personal information and career major league statistics. As part of the Ralston Purina promotion, the company advertised an uncut sheet of cards which was available by finding an "instant-winner" game card or sending $1 plus two non-winning cards. Cards on the uncut sheet are identical in design to the single cards, save the omission of the words "1987 Collectors Edition" in the upper right corner. A complete uncut sheet in mint condition is valued at $10.

		MT	NR MT	EX
Complete Set:		15.00	11.00	6.00
Common Player:		1.00	.70	.40
1	Nolan Ryan	1.25	.90	.50
2	Steve Garvey	1.25	.90	.50
3	Wade Boggs	2.00	1.50	.80
4	Dave Winfield	1.25	.90	.50
5	Don Mattingly	3.00	2.25	1.25
6	Don Sutton	1.00	.70	.40
7	Dave Parker	1.00	.70	.40
8	Eddie Murray	1.25	.90	.50
9	Gary Carter	1.25	.90	.50
10	Roger Clemens	1.50	1.25	.60
11	Fernando Valenzuela	1.25	.90	.50
12	Cal Ripken Jr.	1.25	.90	.50
13	Ozzie Smith	1.00	.70	.40
14	Mike Schmidt	1.50	1.25	.60
15	Ryne Sandberg	1.25	.90	.50

1989 Ralston Purina

The Ralston Purina Co., in conjunction with Mike Schechter Associates, issued a 12-card "Superstars" set in 1989. As part of a late-spring and early-summer promotion, the standard-size cards were inserted, two per box, in specially-marked boxes of Crisp Crunch, Honey Nut O's, Fruit Rings and Frosted

Flakes in most parts of the country. Ads on cereal boxes also offered complete sets through a mail-in offer. The fronts of the cards feature full-color player photos flanked by stars in all four corners. "Super Stars" appears at the top; the player's name and position are at the bottom. The backs include player stats and data, the card number and copyright line.

		MT	NR MT	EX
Complete Set:		10.00	7.50	4.00
Common Player:		.80	.60	.30
1	Ozzie Smith	.80	.60	.30
2	Andre Dawson	.80	.60	.30
3	Darryl Strawberry	1.00	.70	.40
4	Mike Schmidt	1.25	.90	.50
5	Orel Hershiser	.90	.70	.35
6	Tim Raines	.80	.60	.30
7	Roger Clemens	1.25	.90	.50
8	Kirby Puckett	1.25	.90	.50
9	George Brett	1.00	.70	.40
10	Alan Trammell	.80	.60	.30
11	Don Mattingly	2.25	1.75	.90
12	Jose Canseco	2.00	1.50	.80

1954 Red Heart Dog Food

This set of 33 cards was issued in three color-coded series by the Red Heart Dog Food Co. Card fronts feature hand-colored photos on either a blue, green or red background. The 11 red-background cards are scarcer than the 11-card blue or green series. Backs of the 2-5/8" by 3-3/4" cards contain biographical and statistical information along with a Red Heart ad. Each 11-card series was available via a mail-in offer. As late as the early 1970s, the company was still sending cards to collectors who requested them.

		NR MT	EX	VG
Complete Set:		1600.00	800.00	480.00
Common Player:		20.00	10.00	6.00
(1)	Richie Ashburn	35.00	17.50	10.50
(2)	Frankie Baumholtz	25.00	12.50	7.50
(3)	Gus Bell	20.00	10.00	6.00
(4)	Billy Cox	25.00	12.50	7.50
(5)	Alvin Dark	25.00	12.50	7.50
(6)	Carl Erskine	30.00	15.00	9.00
(7)	Ferris Fain	20.00	10.00	6.00
(8)	Dee Fondy	20.00	10.00	6.00
(9)	Nelson Fox	30.00	15.00	9.00
(10)	Jim Gilliam	30.00	15.00	9.00
(11)	Jim Hegan	25.00	12.50	7.50
(12)	George Kell	30.00	15.00	9.00
(13)	Ted Kluszewski	30.00	15.00	9.00
(14)	Ralph Kiner	40.00	20.00	12.00
(15)	Harvey Kuenn	25.00	12.50	7.50
(16)	Bob Lemon	40.00	20.00	12.00
(17)	Sherman Lollar	20.00	10.00	6.00
(18)	Mickey Mantle	400.00	200.00	120.00
(19)	Billy Martin	40.00	20.00	12.00
(20)	Gil McDougald	30.00	15.00	9.00
(21)	Roy McMillan	20.00	10.00	6.00
(22)	Minnie Minoso	25.00	12.50	7.50
(23)	Stan Musial	225.00	112.00	67.00
(24)	Billy Pierce	25.00	12.50	7.50
(25)	Al Rosen	30.00	15.00	9.00

		NR MT	EX	VG
(26)	Hank Sauer	20.00	10.00	6.00
(27)	Red Schoendienst	30.00	15.00	9.00
(28)	Enos Slaughter	30.00	15.00	9.00
(29)	Duke Snider	75.00	37.00	22.00
(30)	Warren Spahn	50.00	25.00	15.00
(31)	Sammy White	20.00	10.00	6.00
(32)	Eddie Yost	20.00	10.00	6.00
(33)*	Gus Zernial	20.00	10.00	6.00

1982 Red Lobster Cubs

This 28-card set was co-sponsored by the team and a seafood restaurant chain for distribution at a 1982 Cubs promotional game. Card fronts are unbordered color photos, with player name, number, position and a superimposed facsimile autograph. The set includes 25 players on the 2-1/4" by 3-1/2" cards, along with a card for manager Lee Elia, an unnumbered card for the coaching staff and a team picture. Card backs have complete player statistics and a Red Lobster ad.

		MT	NR MT	EX
Complete Set:		12.00	9.00	4.75
Common Player:		.20	.15	.08
1	Larry Bowa	.40	.30	.15
4	Lee Elia	.20	.15	.08
6	Keith Moreland	.40	.30	.15
7	Jody Davis	.40	.30	.15
10	Leon Durham	.40	.30	.15
15	Junior Kennedy	.20	.15	.08
17	Bump Wills	.20	.15	.08
18	Scot Thompson	.20	.15	.08
21	Jay Johnstone	.25	.20	.10
22	Bill Buckner	.40	.30	.15
23	Ryne Sandberg	3.00	2.25	1.25
24	Jerry Morales	.20	.15	.08
25	Gary Woods	.20	.15	.08
28	Steve Henderson	.20	.15	.08
29	Bob Molinaro	.20	.15	.08
31	Fergie Jenkins	.70	.50	.30
33	Al Ripley	.20	.15	.08
34	Randy Martz	.20	.15	.08
36	Mike Proly	.20	.15	.08
37	Ken Kravec	.20	.15	.08
38	Willie Hernandez	.30	.25	.12
39	Bill Campbell	.20	.15	.08
41	Dick Tidrow	.20	.15	.08
46	Lee Smith	.50	.40	.20
47	Doug Bird	.20	.15	.08
48	Dickie Noles	.20	.15	.08
——	Team Photo	.20	.15	.08
——	Coaching Staff (Billy Connors, Tom Harmon, Gordy MacKenzie, John Vuckovich, Billy Williams)	.25	.20	.10

1952 Red Man

This was the first national set of tobacco cards produced since the golden days of tobacco sets in the early part of the century. There are 52 cards in the set, with 25 top players and one manager from each league. Player selection was made by editor J.G.

1953 Red Man

Taylor Spink of The Sporting News. Cards measure 3-1/2"by 4", including a 1/2" tab at the bottom of each card. These tabs were redeemable for a free baseball cap from Red Man. Cards are harder to find with tabs intact, and thus more valuable in that form. Values quoted here are for cards with tabs. Cards with the tabs removed would be valued about 35-40 percent of the quoted figures. Card fronts are full color paintings of each player with biographical information inset in the portrait area. Card backs contain company advertising. Cards are numbered and dated only on the tabs.

This was the chewing tobacco company's second annual set of 3-1/2" by 4" cards, including the tabs at the bottom of the cards. Formats for both the fronts and backs are similar to the '52 edition. The 1953 Red Man cards, however, include card numbers within the player biographical section, and the card backs are headlined "New for '53." Once again, cards with intact tabs (which were redeemable for a free cap) are more valuable. Prices below are for cards with tabs. Cards with tabs removed are worth about 35-40 percent of the stated values. Each league is represented by 25 players and a manager on the full-color cards, a total of 52.

		NR MT	EX	VG
Complete Set:		2100.00	1050.00	630.00
Common Player:		20.00	10.00	6.00
1A	Casey Stengel	55.00	27.00	16.50
1N	Leo Durocher	40.00	20.00	12.00
2A	Roberto Avila	20.00	10.00	6.00
2N	Richie Ashburn	35.00	17.50	10.50
3A	Larry "Yogi" Berra	80.00	40.00	24.00
3N	Ewell Blackwell	25.00	12.50	7.50
4A	Gil Coan	20.00	10.00	6.00
4N	Cliff Chambers	20.00	10.00	6.00
5A	Dom DiMaggio	30.00	15.00	9.00
5N	Murry Dickson	20.00	10.00	6.00
6A	Larry Doby	30.00	15.00	9.00
6N	Sid Gordon	20.00	10.00	6.00
7A	Ferris Fain	25.00	12.50	7.50
7N	Granny Hamner	20.00	10.00	6.00
8A	Bob Feller	80.00	40.00	24.00
8N	Jim Hearn	20.00	10.00	6.00
9A	Nelson Fox	35.00	17.50	10.50
9N	Monte Irvin	50.00	25.00	15.00
10A	Johnny Groth	20.00	10.00	6.00
10N	Larry Jansen	20.00	10.00	6.00
11A	Jim Hegan	20.00	10.00	6.00
11N	Willie Jones	20.00	10.00	6.00
12A	Eddie Joost	20.00	10.00	6.00
12N	Ralph Kiner	50.00	25.00	15.00
13A	George Kell	50.00	25.00	15.00
13N	Whitey Lockman	20.00	10.00	6.00
14A	Gil McDougald	30.00	15.00	9.00
14N	Sal Maglie	25.00	12.50	7.50
15A	Orestes Minoso	25.00	12.50	7.50
15N	Willie Mays	150.00	75.00	45.00
16A	Bill Pierce	25.00	12.50	7.50
16N	Stan Musial	150.00	75.00	45.00
17A	Bob Porterfield	20.00	10.00	6.00
17N	Pee Wee Reese	75.00	37.00	22.00
18A	Eddie Robinson	20.00	10.00	6.00
18N	Robin Roberts	50.00	25.00	15.00
19A	Saul Rogovin	20.00	10.00	6.00
19N	Al Schoendienst	30.00	15.00	9.00
20A	Bobby Shantz	25.00	12.50	7.50
20N	Enos Slaughter	50.00	25.00	15.00
21A	Vern Stephens	20.00	10.00	6.00
21N	Duke Snider	100.00	50.00	30.00
22A	Vic Wertz	20.00	10.00	6.00
22N	Warren Spahn	60.00	30.00	18.00
23A	Ted Williams	175.00	87.00	52.00
23N	Eddie Stanky	25.00	12.50	7.50
24A	Early Wynn	50.00	25.00	15.00
24N	Bobby Thomson	30.00	15.00	9.00
25A	Eddie Yost	20.00	10.00	6.00
25N	Earl Torgeson	20.00	10.00	6.00
26A	Gus Zernial	20.00	10.00	6.00
26N	Wes Westrum	20.00	10.00	6.00

		NR MT	EX	VG
Complete Set:		2350.00	1175.00	705.00
Common Player:		20.00	10.00	6.00
1A	Casey Stengel	55.00	27.00	16.50
1N	Charlie Dressen	25.00	12.50	7.50
2A	Hank Bauer	25.00	12.50	7.50
2N	Bobby Adams	20.00	10.00	6.00
3A	Larry "Yogi" Berra	80.00	40.00	24.00
3N	Richie Ashburn	35.00	17.50	10.50
4A	Walt Dropo	20.00	10.00	6.00
4N	Joe Black	25.00	12.50	7.50
5A	Nelson Fox	35.00	17.50	10.50
5N	Roy Campanella	80.00	40.00	24.00
6A	Jackie Jensen	25.00	12.50	7.50
6N	Ted Kluszewski	30.00	15.00	9.00
7A	Eddie Joost	20.00	10.00	6.00
7N	Whitey Lockman	20.00	10.00	6.00
8A	George Kell	50.00	25.00	15.00
8N	Sal Maglie	25.00	12.50	7.50
9A	Dale Mitchell	20.00	10.00	6.00
9N	Andy Pafko	25.00	12.50	7.50
10A	Phil Rizzuto	60.00	30.00	18.00
10N	Pee Wee Reese	75.00	37.00	22.00
11A	Eddie Robinson	20.00	10.00	6.00
11N	Robin Roberts	50.00	25.00	15.00
12A	Gene Woodling	25.00	12.50	7.50
12N	Al Schoendienst	30.00	15.00	9.00
13A	Gus Zernial	20.00	10.00	6.00
13N	Enos Slaughter	50.00	25.00	15.00
14A	Early Wynn	50.00	25.00	15.00
14N	Edwin "Duke" Snider	100.00	50.00	30.00
15A	Joe Dobson	20.00	10.00	6.00
15N	Ralph Kiner	50.00	25.00	15.00
16A	Billy Pierce	25.00	12.50	7.50
16N	Hank Sauer	20.00	10.00	6.00
17A	Bob Lemon	50.00	25.00	15.00
17N	Del Ennis	20.00	10.00	6.00
18A	Johnny Mize	50.00	25.00	15.00
18N	Granny Hamner	20.00	10.00	6.00
19A	Bob Porterfield	20.00	10.00	6.00
19N	Warren Spahn	60.00	30.00	18.00
20A	Bobby Shantz	25.00	12.50	7.50
20N	Wes Westrum	20.00	10.00	6.00
21A	"Mickey" Vernon	25.00	12.50	7.50
21N	Hoyt Wilhelm	50.00	25.00	15.00
22A	Dom DiMaggio	30.00	15.00	9.00
22N	Murry Dickson	20.00	10.00	6.00
23A	Gil McDougald	30.00	15.00	9.00
23N	Warren Hacker	20.00	10.00	6.00
24A	Al Rosen	30.00	15.00	9.00

		NR MT	EX	VG
24N	Gerry Staley	20.00	10.00	6.00
25A	Mel Parnell	20.00	10.00	6.00
25N	Bobby Thomson	25.00	12.50	7.50
26A	Roberto Avila	20.00	10.00	6.00
26N	Stan Musial	150.00	75.00	45.00

		NR MT	EX	VG
19Na	Enos Slaughter	90.00	45.00	27.00
19Nb	Gus Bell	90.00	45.00	27.00
20A	Larry "Yogi" Berra	80.00	40.00	24.00
20N	Johnny Logan	20.00	10.00	6.00
21A	Bob Lemon	50.00	25.00	15.00
21N	Johnny Antonelli	25.00	12.50	7.50
22A	Ferris Fain	25.00	12.50	7.50
22N	Gil Hodges	55.00	27.00	16.50
23A	Hank Bauer	25.00	12.50	7.50
23N	Eddie Mathews	55.00	27.00	16.50
24A	Jim Delsing	20.00	10.00	6.00
24N	Lew Burdette	30.00	15.00	9.00
25A	Gil McDougald	30.00	15.00	9.00
25N	Willie Mays	150.00	75.00	45.00

1954 Red Man

In 1954, the Red Man set eliminated managers from the set, and issued only 25 player cards for each league. There are, however, four variations which bring the total set size to 54 full-color cards. Two cards exist for Gus Bell and Enos Slaughter, while American Leaguers George Kell, Sam Mele and Dave Philley are each shown with two different teams. Complete set prices quoted below do not include the scarcer of the variation pairs. Cards still measure 3-1/2" by 4" with tabs intact. Cards without tabs are worth about 35-40 per cent of the values quoted below. Formats for the cards remain virtually unchanged, with card numbers included within the player information boxes as well as on the tabs.

		NR MT	EX	VG
Complete Set:		1950.00	975.00	585.00
Common Player:		20.00	10.00	6.00
1A	Bobby Avila	20.00	10.00	6.00
1N	Richie Ashburn	35.00	17.50	10.50
2A	Jim Busby	20.00	10.00	6.00
2N	Billy Cox	25.00	12.50	7.50
3A	Nelson Fox	35.00	17.50	10.50
3N	Del Crandall	25.00	12.50	7.50
4Aa	George Kell (Boston)	65.00	32.00	19.50
4Ab	George Kell (Chicago)	75.00	37.00	22.00
4N	Carl Erskine	30.00	15.00	9.00
5A	Sherman Lollar	20.00	10.00	6.00
5N	Monte Irvin	50.00	25.00	15.00
6Aa	Sam Mele (Baltimore)	50.00	25.00	15.00
6Ab	Sam Mele (Chicago)	75.00	37.00	22.00
6N	Ted Kluszewski	30.00	15.00	9.00
7A	Orestes Minoso	25.00	12.50	7.50
7N	Don Mueller	20.00	10.00	6.00
8A	Mel Parnell	20.00	10.00	6.00
8N	Andy Pafko	25.00	12.50	7.50
9Aa	Dave Philley (Cleveland)	50.00	25.00	15.00
9Ab	Dave Philley (Philadelphia)	75.00	37.00	22.00
9N	Del Rice	20.00	10.00	6.00
10A	Billy Pierce	25.00	12.50	7.50
10N	Al Schoendienst	30.00	15.00	9.00
11A	Jim Piersall	25.00	12.50	7.50
11N	Warren Spahn	60.00	30.00	18.00
12A	Al Rosen	30.00	15.00	9.00
12N	Curt Simmons	25.00	12.50	7.50
13A	"Mickey" Vernon	25.00	12.50	7.50
13N	Roy Campanella	80.00	40.00	24.00
14A	Sammy White	20.00	10.00	6.00
14N	Jim Gilliam	30.00	15.00	9.00
15A	Gene Woodling	25.00	12.50	7.50
15N	"Pee Wee" Reese	75.00	37.00	22.00
16A	Ed "Whitey" Ford	65.00	32.00	19.50
16N	Edwin "Duke" Snider	100.00	50.00	30.00
17A	Phil Rizzuto	60.00	30.00	18.00
17N	Rip Repulski	20.00	10.00	6.00
18A	Bob Porterfield	20.00	10.00	6.00
18N	Robin Roberts	50.00	25.00	15.00
19A	Al "Chico" Carrasquel	20.00	10.00	6.00

1955 Red Man

These 50 cards are quite similar to the 1954 edition, with card fronts virtually unchanged except for the data in the biographical box on the color picture area. This set of the 3-1/2" by 4" cards includes 25 players from each league, with no known variations. As with all Red Man sets, those cards complete with the redeemable tabs are more valuable. Values quoted below are for cards with tabs. Cards with the tabs removed are worth about 35-40 percent of those figures.

		NR MT	EX	VG
Complete Set:		1700.00	850.00	510.00
Common Player:		20.00	10.00	6.00
1A	Ray Boone	20.00	10.00	6.00
1N	Richie Ashburn	35.00	17.50	10.50
2A	Jim Busby	20.00	10.00	6.00
2N	Del Crandall	25.00	12.50	7.50
3A	Ed "Whitey" Ford	55.00	27.00	16.50
3N	Gil Hodges	65.00	32.00	19.50
4A	Nelson Fox	35.00	17.50	10.50
4N	Brooks Lawrence	20.00	10.00	6.00
5A	Bob Grim	20.00	10.00	6.00
5N	Johnny Logan	20.00	10.00	6.00
6A	Jack Harshman	20.00	10.00	6.00
6N	Sal Maglie	25.00	12.50	7.50
7A	Jim Hegan	20.00	10.00	6.00
7N	Willie Mays	150.00	75.00	45.00
8A	Bob Lemon	50.00	25.00	15.00
8N	Don Mueller	20.00	10.00	6.00
9A	Irv Noren	20.00	10.00	6.00
9N	Bill Sarni	20.00	10.00	6.00
10A	Bob Porterfield	20.00	10.00	6.00
10N	Warren Spahn	60.00	30.00	18.00
11A	Al Rosen	30.00	15.00	9.00
11N	Henry Thompson	20.00	10.00	6.00
12A	"Mickey" Vernon	25.00	12.50	7.50
12N	Hoyt Wilhelm	50.00	25.00	15.00
13A	Vic Wertz	20.00	10.00	6.00
13N	Johnny Antonelli	25.00	12.50	7.50
14A	Early Wynn	50.00	25.00	15.00
14N	Carl Erskine	30.00	15.00	9.00
15A	Bobby Avila	20.00	10.00	6.00
15N	Granny Hamner	20.00	10.00	6.00
16A	Larry "Yogi" Berra	80.00	40.00	24.00
16N	Ted Kluszewski	30.00	15.00	9.00
17A	Joe Coleman	20.00	10.00	6.00
17N	Pee Wee Reese	75.00	37.00	22.00
18A	Larry Doby	30.00	15.00	9.00

		NR MT	EX	VG
18N	Al Schoendienst	30.00	15.00	9.00
19A	Jackie Jensen	25.00	12.50	7.50
19N	Duke Snider	100.00	50.00	30.00
20A	Pete Runnels	20.00	10.00	6.00
20N	Frank Thomas	20.00	10.00	6.00
21A	Jim Piersall	25.00	12.50	7.50
21N	Ray Jablonski	20.00	10.00	6.00
22A	Hank Bauer	25.00	12.50	7.50
22N	James "Dusty" Rhodes	20.00	10.00	6.00
23A	"Chico" Carrasquel	20.00	10.00	6.00
23N	Gus Bell	20.00	10.00	6.00
24A	Orestes Minoso	25.00	12.50	7.50
24N	Curt Simmons	25.00	12.50	7.50
25A	Sandy Consuegra	20.00	10.00	6.00
25N	Marvin Grissom	20.00	10.00	6.00

1988 Revco

This super-glossy boxed set of 33 standard-size cards was produced by Topps for exclusive distribution by Revco stores east of the Mississippi River. Card fronts feature a large blue Revco logo in the upper left corner opposite a yellow and black boxed "Topps League Leader" label. Player photos are framed in black and orange with a diagonal player name banner in the lower right corner that lists the player's name, team and position on white, orange and gold stripes. The numbered card backs are horizontal, printed in red and black on white stock and include the player name, followed by personal biographical data, batting/pitching stats and a brief career summary.

		MT	NR MT	EX
	Complete Set:	5.00	3.75	2.00
	Common Player:	.05	.04	.02
1	Tony Gwynn	.25	.20	.10
2	Andre Dawson	.15	.11	.06
3	Vince Coleman	.15	.11	.06
4	Jack Clark	.15	.11	.06
5	Tim Raines	.25	.20	.10
6	Tim Wallach	.10	.08	.04
7	Juan Samuel	.10	.08	.04
8	Nolan Ryan	.15	.11	.06
9	Rick Sutcliffe	.10	.08	.04
10	Kent Tekulve	.05	.04	.02
11	Steve Bedrosian	.10	.08	.04
12	Orel Hershiser	.10	.08	.04
13	Rick Rueschel	.07	.05	.03
14	Fernando Valenzuela	.20	.15	.08
15	Bob Welch	.07	.05	.03
16	Wade Boggs	1.00	.70	.40
17	Mark McGwire	1.00	.70	.40
18	George Bell	.20	.15	.08
19	Harold Reynolds	.05	.04	.02
20	Paul Molitor	.12	.09	.05
21	Kirby Puckett	.25	.20	.10
22	Kevin Seitzer	.60	.45	.25
23	Brian Downing	.05	.04	.02
24	Dwight Evans	.10	.08	.04
25	Willie Wilson	.07	.05	.03
26	Danny Tartabull	.12	.09	.05
27	Jimmy Key	.07	.05	.03
28	Roger Clemens	.40	.30	.15
29	Dave Stewart	.10	.08	.04
30	Mark Eichhorn	.05	.04	.02

		MT	NR MT	EX
31	Tom Henke	.05	.04	.02
32	Charlie Hough	.05	.04	.02
33	Mark Langston	.10	.08	.04

1988 Rite Aid

This premiere edition was produced by Topps for distribution by Rite Aid drug and discount stores in the Eastern United States. The boxed set includes 33 standard-size full-color cards with at least one card for each major league team. Four cards in the set highlight MVP's from the 1987 season. Card fronts have white borders and carry a yellow "Team MVP's" header above the player photo which is outlined in red and blue. A large Rite Aid logo appears upper left; the players name appears bottom center. The numbered card backs are black on blue and white card stock in a horizontal layout containing the player name, biography and statistics.

		MT	NR MT	EX
	Complete Set:	5.00	3.75	2.00
	Common Player:	.05	.04	.02
1	Dale Murphy	.30	.25	.12
2	Andre Dawson	.15	.11	.06
3	Eric Davis	.50	.40	.20
4	Mike Scott	.10	.08	.04
5	Pedro Guerrero	.15	.11	.06
6	Tim Raines	.25	.20	.10
7	Darryl Strawberry	.40	.30	.15
8	Mike Schmidt	.30	.25	.12
9	Mike Dunne	.10	.08	.04
10	Jack Clark	.15	.11	.06
11	Tony Gwynn	.25	.20	.10
12	Will Clark	.30	.25	.12
13	Cal Ripken	.30	.25	.12
14	Wade Boggs	1.00	.70	.40
15	Wally Joyner	.30	.25	.12
16	Harold Baines	.12	.09	.05
17	Joe Carter	.12	.09	.05
18	Alan Trammell	.15	.11	.06
19	Kevin Seitzer	.60	.45	.25
20	Paul Molitor	.12	.09	.05
21	Kirby Puckett	.25	.20	.10
22	Don Mattingly	1.75	1.25	.70
23	Mark McGwire	1.00	.70	.40
24	Alvin Davis	.10	.08	.04
25	Ruben Sierra	.12	.09	.05
26	George Bell	.20	.15	.08
27	Jack Morris	.12	.09	.05
28	Jeff Reardon	.07	.05	.03
29	John Tudor	.07	.05	.03
30	Rick Rueschel	.07	.05	.03
31	Gary Gaetti	.12	.09	.05
32	Jeffrey Leonard	.05	.04	.02
33	Frank Viola	.12	.09	.05

1955 Rodeo Meats Athletics

This set of 2-1/2" by 3-1/2" color cards was issued by a local meat company to commemorate the first year of the Athletics in Kansas City. There are 38

Cloyd Boyer

1956 Rodeo Meats Athletics

Gus Zernial

different players included in the set, with nine players known to apppear in two different variations for a total of 47 cards in the set. Most variations are in background colors, although Bobby Shantz is also listed incorrectly as "Schantz" on one variation. The cards are unnumbered, with the Rodeo logo and player name on the fronts, and an ad for a scrapbook album listed on the backs.

Rodeo Meats issued another Kansas City Athletics set in 1956, but this one was a much smaller 13-card set. The 2-1/2" by 3-1/2" cards are again unnumbered, with the player name and Rodeo logo on the fronts. Card backs feature some of the same graphics and copy as the 1955 cards, but the album off is omitted. The full-color cards were only available in packages of Rodeo hot dogs.

		NR MT	EX	VG
Complete Set:		3400.00	1700.00	1020.
Common Player:		50.00	25.00	15.00
(1)	Joe Astroth	50.00	25.00	15.00
(2)	Harold Bevan	80.00	40.00	24.00
(3)	Charles Bishop	80.00	40.00	24.00
(4)	Don Bollweg	80.00	40.00	24.00
(5)	Lou Boudreau	125.00	62.00	37.00
(6)	Cloyd Boyer (blue background)	80.00	40.00	24.00
(7)	Cloyd Boyer (pink background)	50.00	25.00	15.00
(8)	Ed Burtschy	80.00	40.00	24.00
(9)	Art Ceccarelli	50.00	25.00	15.00
(10)	Joe DeMaestri (pea green background)	80.00	40.00	24.00
(11)	Joe DeMaestri (light green background)	50.00	25.00	15.00
(12)	Art Ditmar	50.00	25.00	15.00
(13)	John Dixon	80.00	40.00	24.00
(14)	Jim Finigan	50.00	25.00	15.00
(15)	Marion Fricano	80.00	40.00	24.00
(16)	John Gray	80.00	40.00	24.00
(17)	Tom Gorman	50.00	25.00	15.00
(18)	Ray Herbert	50.00	25.00	15.00
(19)	Forest "Spook" Jacobs (Forrest)	80.00	40.00	24.00
(20)	Alex Kellner	80.00	40.00	24.00
(21)	Harry Kraft (Craft)	50.00	25.00	15.00
(22)	Jack Littrell	50.00	25.00	15.00
(23)	Hector Lopez	60.00	30.00	18.00
(24)	Oscar Melillo	50.00	25.00	15.00
(25)	Arnold Portocarrero (purple background)	80.00	40.00	24.00
(26)	Arnold Portocarrero (grey background)	50.00	25.00	15.00
(27)	Vic Power (pink background)	90.00	45.00	27.00
(28)	Vic Power (yellow background)	60.00	30.00	18.00
(29)	Vic Raschi	80.00	40.00	24.00
(30)	Bill Renna (dark pink background)	80.00	40.00	24.00
(31)	Bill Renna (light pink background)	50.00	25.00	15.00
(32)	Al Robertson	80.00	40.00	24.00
(33)	Johnny Sain	90.00	45.00	27.00
(34a)	Bobby Schantz (incorrect spelling)	125.00	62.00	37.00
(34b)	Bobby Shantz (correct spelling)	90.00	45.00	27.00
(35)	Wilmer Shantz (orange background)	80.00	40.00	24.00
(36)	Wilmer Shantz (purple background)	50.00	25.00	15.00
(37)	Harry Simpson	50.00	25.00	15.00
(38)	Enos Slaughter	150.00	75.00	45.00
(39)	Lou Sleater	50.00	25.00	15.00
(40)	George Susce	50.00	25.00	15.00
(41)	Bob Trice	80.00	40.00	24.00
(42)	Elmer Valo (yellow background)	80.00	40.00	24.00
(43)	Elmer Valo (green background)	50.00	25.00	15.00
(44)	Bill Wilson (yellow background)	80.00	40.00	24.00
(45)	Bill Wilson (purple background)	50.00	25.00	15.00
(46)	Gus Zernial	60.00	30.00	18.00

		NR MT	EX	VG
Complete Set:		800.00	400.00	250.00
Common Player:		50.00	25.00	15.00
(1)	Joe Astroth	50.00	25.00	15.00
(2)	Lou Boudreau	125.00	62.00	37.00
(3)	Joe DeMaestri	50.00	25.00	15.00
(4)	Art Ditmar	50.00	25.00	15.00
(5)	Jim Finigan	50.00	25.00	15.00
(6)	Hector Lopez	60.00	30.00	18.00
(7)	Vic Power	60.00	30.00	18.00
(8)	Bobby Shantz	90.00	45.00	27.00
(9)	Harry Simpson	50.00	25.00	15.00
(10)	Enos Slaughter	125.00	62.00	37.00
(11)	Elmer Valo	50.00	25.00	15.00
(12)	Gus Zernial	60.00	30.00	18.00

1970 Rold Gold Pretzels

EDDIE COLLINS

The 1970 Rold Gold Pretzels set of 15 cards honors the "Greatest Players Ever" in the first 100 years of baseball as chosen by the Baseball Writers of America. The cards, which measure 2-1/4" by 3-1/2" in size, feature a simulated 3-D effect. The set was re-released in 1972 by Kellogg's in packages of Danish-Go-Rounds. Rold Gold cards can be differentiated from the Kellogg's cards of 1972 by the 1970 copyright date found on the card reverse.

		NR MT	EX	VG
Complete Set:		30.00	15.00	9.00
Common Player:		1.00	.50	.30
1	Walter Johnson	2.50	1.25	.70
2	Rogers Hornsby	1.50	.70	.45

		NR MT	EX	VG
3	John McGraw	1.00	.50	.30
4	Mickey Cochrane	1.00	.50	.30
5	George Sisler	1.00	.50	.30
6	Babe Ruth	7.00	3.50	2.00
7	Robert "Lefty" Grove	1.50	.70	.45
8	Harold "Pie" Traynor	1.00	.50	.30
9	Honus Wagner	1.75	.90	.50
10	Eddie Collins	1.00	.50	.30
11	Tris Speaker	1.50	.70	.45
12	Cy Young	1.00	.50	.30
13	Lou Gehrig	4.00	2.00	1.25
14	Babe Ruth	7.00	3.50	2.00
15	Ty Cobb	4.00	2.00	1.25

1950 Royal Desserts

This set of 24 cards was issued one per box on the backs of various Royal Dessert products over a period of three years. The basic set contains 24 players, however a number of variations create the much higher total for the set. In 1950, Royal issued cards with two different tints - black and white with red, or blue and white with red. Over the next two years, various sentences of the cards' biographies were updated up to three times in some cases. Some players from the set left the majors after 1950 and others were apparently never updated, but the 23 biography updates that do exist, added to the original 24 cards issued in 1950, give the set a total of 47 cards. The 2-1/2" by 3-1/2" cards are blank-backed with personal and playing biographies alongside the card front photos.

		NR MT	EX	VG
Complete Set:		900.00	450.00	270.00
Common Player:		20.00	10.00	6.00
1a	Stan Musial (2nd paragraph begins "Musial's 207...")	125.00	62.00	37.00
1b	Stan Musial (2nd paragraph begins "Musial batted...")	125.00	62.00	37.00
2a	Pee Wee Reese (2nd paragraph begins "Pee Wee's...")	70.00	35.00	21.00
2b	Pee Wee Reese (2nd paragraph begins "Captain...")	70.00	35.00	21.00
3a	George Kell (2nd paragraph ends "...in 1945, '46.")	35.00	17.50	10.50
3b	George Kell (2nd paragraph ends "...two base hits, 56.")	35.00	17.50	10.50
4a	Dom DiMaggio (2nd paragraph ends "...during 1947.")	30.00	15.00	9.00
4b	Dom DiMaggio (2nd paragraph ends "...with 11.")	30.00	15.00	9.00
5a	Warren Spahn (2nd paragraph ends "...shutouts 7.")	50.00	25.00	15.00
5b	Warren Spahn (2nd paragraph ends "...with 191.")	50.00	25.00	15.00
6a	Andy Pafko (2nd paragraph ends "...7 games.")	25.00	12.50	7.50
6b	Andy Pafko (2nd paragraph ends "...National League.")	25.00	12.50	7.50
6c	Andy Pafko (2nd paragraph ends "...weighs 190.")	25.00	12.50	7.50
7a	Andy Seminick (2nd paragraph ends "...as outfield.")	20.00	10.00	6.00
7b	Andy Seminick (2nd paragraph ends "...since 1916.")	20.00	10.00	6.00
7c	Andy Seminick (2nd paragraph ends "...in the outfield.")	20.00	10.00	6.00
7d	Andy Seminick (2nd paragraph ends "...right handed.")	20.00	10.00	6.00
8a	Lou Brissie (2nd paragraph ends "...when pitching.")	20.00	10.00	6.00
8b	Lou Brissie (2nd paragraph ends "...weighs 215.")	20.00	10.00	6.00
9a	Ewell Blackwell (2nd paragraph begins "Despite recent illness...")	25.00	12.50	7.50
9b	Ewell Blackwell (2nd paragraph begins "Blackwell's...")	25.00	12.50	7.50
10a	Bobby Thomson (2nd paragraph begins "In 1949...")	25.00	12.50	7.50
10b	Bobby Thomson (2nd paragraph begins "Thomson is...")	25.00	12.50	7.50
11a	Phil Rizzuto (2nd paragraph ends "...one 1942 game.")	60.00	30.00	18.00
11b	Phil Rizzuto (2nd paragraph ends "...Most Valuable Player.")	60.00	30.00	18.00
12	Tommy Henrich	30.00	15.00	9.00
13	Joe Gordon	25.00	12.50	7.50
14a	Ray Scarborough (Senators)	20.00	10.00	6.00
14b	Ray Scarborough (White Sox, 2nd paragraph ends "...military service.")	20.00	10.00	6.00
14c	Ray Scarborough (White Sox, 2nd paragraph ends "...the season.")	20.00	10.00	6.00
14d	Ray Scarborough (Red Sox)	20.00	10.00	6.00
15a	Stan Rojek (Pirates)	20.00	10.00	6.00
15b	Stan Rojek (Browns)	20.00	10.00	6.00
16	Luke Appling	30.00	15.00	9.00
17	Willard Marshall	20.00	10.00	6.00
18	Alvin Dark	30.00	15.00	9.00
19a	Dick Sisler (2nd paragraph ends "...service record.")	20.00	10.00	6.00
19b	Dick Sisler (2nd paragraph ends "...National League flag.")	20.00	10.00	6.00
19c	Dick Sisler (2nd paragraph ends "...Nov. 2, 1920.")	20.00	10.00	6.00
19d	Dick Sisler (2nd paragraph ends "...from '46 to '48.")	20.00	10.00	6.00
20	Johnny Ostrowski	20.00	10.00	6.00
21a	Virgil Trucks (2nd paragraph ends "...in military service.")	25.00	12.50	7.50
21b	Virgil Trucks (2nd paragraph ends "...that year.")	25.00	12.50	7.50
21c	Virgil Trucks (2nd paragraph ends "...for military service.")	25.00	12.50	7.50
22	Eddie Robinson	20.00	10.00	6.00
23	Nanny Fernandez	20.00	10.00	6.00
24	Ferris Fain	25.00	12.50	7.50

1952 Royal Desserts

This set, issued as a premium by Royal Desserts in 1952, consists of 16 unnumbered black and white cards, each measuring 5" by 7". The cards inlcude the inscription "To A Royal Fan" along with the player's facsimile autograph.

		NR MT	EX	VG
Complete Set:		375.00	187.00	112.00
Common Player:		15.00	7.50	4.50
(1)	Ewell Blackwell	18.00	9.00	5.50
(2)	Leland V. Brissie Jr.	15.00	7.50	4.50
(3)	Alvin Dark	18.00	9.00	5.50
(4)	Dom DiMaggio	20.00	10.00	6.00

		NR MT	EX	VG
(5)	Ferris Fain	15.00	7.50	4.50
(6)	George Kell	28.00	14.00	8.50
(7)	Stan Musial	60.00	30.00	18.00
(8)	Andy Pafko	18.00	9.00	5.50
(9)	Pee Wee Reese	35.00	17.50	10.50
(10)	Phil Rizzuto	35.00	17.50	10.50
(11)	Eddie Robinson	15.00	7.50	4.50
(12)	Ray Scarborough	15.00	7.50	4.50
(13)	Andy Seminick	15.00	7.50	4.50
(14)	Dick Sisler	15.00	7.50	4.50
(15)	Warren Spahn	30.00	15.00	9.00
(16)	Bobby Thomson	20.00	10.00	6.00

1988 Score

A fifth member joined the group of nationally distributed baseball cards in 1988. Titled "Score," the new cards are characterized by extremely sharp and excellent full-color photography and printing. Card backs are full-color also and carry a player head-shot, along with a brief biography and player personal and statistical information. The 660 cards in the set each measure 2-1/2" by 3-1/2" in size. The fronts come with one of six different border colors - blue, red, green, purple, orange and gold - which are equally divided at 110 cards per color. The Score set was produced by Major League Marketing, the same company that markets the "triple-action" Sportflics card sets.

		MT	NR MT	EX
Complete Set:		25.00	20.00	10.00
Common Player:		.04	.03	.02
1	Don Mattingly	1.50	1.25	.60
2	Wade Boggs	.80	.60	.30
3	Tim Raines	.20	.15	.08
4	Andre Dawson	.15	.11	.06
5	Mark McGwire	1.00	.70	.40
6	Kevin Seitzer	.60	.45	.25
7	Wally Joyner	.35	.25	.14
8	Jesse Barfield	.10	.08	.04
9	Pedro Guerrero	.15	.11	.06
10	Eric Davis	.60	.45	.25
11	George Brett	.30	.25	.12
12	Ozzie Smith	.12	.09	.05
13	Rickey Henderson	.25	.20	.10
14	Jim Rice	.20	.15	.08
15	*Matt Nokes*	.50	.40	.20
16	Mike Schmidt	.40	.30	.15
17	Dave Parker	.12	.09	.05
18	Eddie Murray	.25	.20	.10
19	Andres Galarraga	.12	.09	.05
20	Tony Fernandez	.10	.08	.04
21	Kevin McReynolds	.12	.09	.05
22	B.J. Surhoff	.10	.08	.04

		MT	NR MT	EX
23	Pat Tabler	.06	.05	.02
24	Kirby Puckett	.25	.20	.10
25	Benny Santiago	.35	.25	.14
26	Ryne Sandberg	.20	.15	.08
27	Kelly Downs	.08	.06	.03
28	Jose Cruz	.06	.05	.02
29	Pete O'Brien	.06	.05	.02
30	Mark Langston	.10	.08	.04
31	Lee Smith	.08	.06	.03
32	Juan Samuel	.10	.08	.04
33	Kevin Bass	.06	.05	.02
34	R.J. Reynolds	.04	.03	.02
35	Steve Sax	.12	.09	.05
36	John Kruk	.08	.06	.03
37	Alan Trammell	.15	.11	.06
38	Chris Bosio	.06	.05	.02
39	Brook Jacoby	.08	.06	.03
40	Willie McGee	.10	.08	.04
41	Dave Magadan	.10	.08	.04
42	Fred Lynn	.10	.08	.04
43	Kent Hrbek	.12	.09	.05
44	Brian Downing	.06	.05	.02
45	Jose Canseco	1.25	.90	.50
46	Jim Presley	.08	.06	.03
47	Mike Stanley	.06	.05	.02
48	Tony Pena	.06	.05	.02
49	David Cone	.80	.60	.30
50	Rick Sutcliffe	.08	.06	.03
51	Doug Drabek	.06	.05	.02
52	Bill Doran	.06	.05	.02
53	Mike Scioscia	.06	.05	.02
54	Candy Maldonado	.06	.05	.02
55	Dave Winfield	.20	.15	.08
56	Lou Whitaker	.20	.15	.08
57	Tom Henke	.06	.05	.02
58	Ken Gerhart	.06	.05	.02
59	Glenn Braggs	.08	.06	.03
60	Julio Franco	.08	.06	.03
61	Charlie Leibrandt	.06	.05	.02
62	Gary Gaetti	.10	.08	.04
63	Bob Boone	.06	.05	.02
64	*Luis Polonia*	.20	.15	.08
65	Dwight Evans	.10	.08	.04
66	Phil Bradley	.08	.06	.03
67	Mike Boddicker	.06	.05	.02
68	Vince Coleman	.15	.11	.06
69	Howard Johnson	.08	.06	.03
70	Tim Wallach	.08	.06	.03
71	Keith Moreland	.06	.05	.02
72	Barry Larkin	.20	.15	.08
73	Alan Ashby	.04	.03	.02
74	Rick Rhoden	.06	.05	.02
75	Darrell Evans	.08	.06	.03
76	Dave Stieb	.08	.06	.03
77	Dan Plesac	.08	.06	.03
78	Will Clark	1.00	.70	.40
79	Frank White	.06	.05	.02
80	Joe Carter	.10	.08	.04
81	Mike Witt	.06	.05	.02
82	Terry Steinbach	.10	.08	.04
83	Alvin Davis	.10	.08	.04
84	Tom Herr	.06	.05	.02
85	Vance Law	.06	.05	.02
86	Kal Daniels	.15	.11	.06
87	Rick Honeycutt	.04	.03	.02
88	Alfredo Griffin	.06	.05	.02
89	Bret Saberhagen	.20	.15	.08
90	Bert Blyleven	.10	.08	.04
91	Jeff Reardon	.08	.06	.03
92	Cory Snyder	.15	.11	.06
93	Greg Walker	.06	.05	.02
94	*Joe Magrane*	.40	.30	.15
95	Rob Deer	.06	.05	.02
96	Ray Knight	.06	.05	.02
97	Casey Candaele	.04	.03	.02
98	John Cerutti	.06	.05	.02
99	Buddy Bell	.08	.06	.03
100	Jack Clark	.12	.09	.05
101	Eric Bell	.06	.05	.02
102	Willie Wilson	.08	.06	.03
103	Dave Schmidt	.04	.03	.02
104	Dennis Eckersley	.10	.08	.04
105	Don Sutton	.12	.09	.05
106	Danny Tartabull	.15	.11	.06
107	Fred McGriff	1.00	.70	.40
108	*Les Straker*	.15	.11	.06
109	Lloyd Moseby	.06	.05	.02
110	Roger Clemens	.50	.40	.20
111	Glenn Hubbard	.04	.03	.02
112	*Ken Williams*	.20	.15	.08
113	Ruben Sierra	.35	.25	.14

#	Player	MT	NR MT	EX
114	Stan Jefferson	.06	.05	.02
115	Milt Thompson	.04	.03	.02
116	Bobby Bonilla	.12	.09	.05
117	Wayne Tolleson	.04	.03	.02
118	*Matt Williams*	.70	.50	.30
119	Chet Lemon	.06	.05	.02
120	Dale Sveum	.06	.05	.02
121	Dennis Boyd	.06	.05	.02
122	Brett Butler	.06	.05	.02
123	Terry Kennedy	.06	.05	.02
124	Jack Howell	.06	.05	.02
125	Curt Young	.06	.05	.02
126a	Dale Valle (first name incorrect)	.25	.20	.10
126b	Dave Valle (correct spelling)	.06	.05	.02
127	Curt Wilkerson	.04	.03	.02
128	Tim Teufel	.04	.03	.02
129	Ozzie Virgil	.04	.03	.02
130	Brian Fisher	.06	.05	.02
131	Lance Parrish	.12	.09	.05
132	Tom Browning	.08	.06	.03
133a	Larry Anderson (incorrect spelling)	.25	.20	.10
133b	Larry Andersen (correct spelling)	.06	.05	.02
134a	Bob Brenley (incorrect spelling)	.25	.20	.10
134b	Bob Brenly (correct spelling)	.06	.05	.02
135	Mike Marshall	.10	.08	.04
136	Gerald Perry	.08	.06	.03
137	Bobby Meacham	.04	.03	.02
138	Larry Herndon	.04	.03	.02
139	*Fred Manrique*	.12	.09	.05
140	Charlie Hough	.06	.05	.02
141	Ron Darling	.10	.08	.04
142	Herm Winningham	.04	.03	.02
143	Mike Diaz	.06	.05	.02
144	*Mike Jackson*	.15	.11	.06
145	Denny Walling	.04	.03	.02
146	Rob Thompson	.06	.05	.02
147	Franklin Stubbs	.06	.05	.02
148	Albert Hall	.04	.03	.02
149	Bobby Witt	.08	.06	.03
150	Lance McCullers	.06	.05	.02
151	Scott Bradley	.04	.03	.02
152	Mark McLemore	.04	.03	.02
153	Tim Laudner	.04	.03	.02
154	Greg Swindell	.15	.11	.06
155	Marty Barrett	.06	.05	.02
156	Mike Heath	.04	.03	.02
157	Gary Ward	.06	.05	.02
158a	Lee Mazilli (incorrect spelling)	.25	.20	.10
158b	Lee Mazzilli (correct spelling)	.08	.06	.03
159	Tom Foley	.04	.03	.02
160	Robin Yount	.20	.15	.08
161	Steve Bedrosian	.10	.08	.04
162	Bob Walk	.04	.03	.02
163	Nick Esasky	.06	.05	.02
164	*Ken Caminiti*	.25	.20	.10
165	Jose Uribe	.04	.03	.02
166	Dave Anderson	.04	.03	.02
167	Ed Whitson	.04	.03	.02
168	Ernie Whitt	.06	.05	.02
169	Cecil Cooper	.08	.06	.03
170	Mike Pagliarulo	.08	.06	.03
171	Pat Sheridan	.04	.03	.02
172	Chris Bando	.04	.03	.02
173	Lee Lacy	.04	.03	.02
174	Steve Lombardozzi	.04	.03	.02
175	Mike Greenwell	1.25	.90	.50
176	Greg Minton	.04	.03	.02
177	Moose Haas	.04	.03	.02
178	Mike Kingery	.04	.03	.02
179	Greg Harris	.04	.03	.02
180	Bo Jackson	.50	.40	.20
181	Carmelo Martinez	.06	.05	.02
182	Alex Trevino	.04	.03	.02
183	Ron Oester	.04	.03	.02
184	Danny Darwin	.04	.03	.02
185	Mike Krukow	.06	.05	.02
186	Rafael Palmeiro	.35	.25	.14
187	Tim Burke	.04	.03	.02
188	Roger McDowell	.08	.06	.03
189	Garry Templeton	.06	.05	.02
190	Terry Pendleton	.06	.05	.02
191	Larry Parrish	.06	.05	.02
192	Rey Quinones	.04	.03	.02
193	Joaquin Andujar	.06	.05	.02
194	Tom Brunansky	.08	.06	.03
195	Donnie Moore	.04	.03	.02
196	Dan Pasqua	.08	.06	.03
197	Jim Gantner	.04	.03	.02
198	Mark Eichhorn	.06	.05	.02
199	John Grubb	.04	.03	.02
200	*Bill Ripken*	.20	.15	.08
201	*Sam Horn*	.30	.25	.12
202	Todd Worrell	.08	.06	.03
203	Terry Leach	.04	.03	.02
204	Garth Iorg	.04	.03	.02
205	Brian Dayett	.04	.03	.02
206	Bo Diaz	.06	.05	.02
207	Craig Reynolds	.04	.03	.02
208	Brian Holton	.08	.06	.03
209	Marvelle Wynne (Marvell)	.04	.03	.02
210	Dave Concepcion	.06	.05	.02
211	Mike Davis	.06	.05	.02
212	Devon White	.15	.11	.06
213	Mickey Brantley	.04	.03	.02
214	Greg Gagne	.04	.03	.02
215	Oddibe McDowell	.06	.05	.02
216	Jimmy Key	.08	.06	.03
217	Dave Bergman	.04	.03	.02
218	Calvin Schiraldi	.04	.03	.02
219	Larry Sheets	.06	.05	.02
220	Mike Easler	.06	.05	.02
221	Kurt Stillwell	.08	.06	.03
222	*Chuck Jackson*	.15	.11	.06
223	Dave Martinez	.08	.06	.03
224	Tim Leary	.06	.05	.02
225	Steve Garvey	.20	.15	.08
226	Greg Mathews	.06	.05	.02
227	Doug Sisk	.04	.03	.02
228	Dave Henderson	.08	.06	.03
229	Jimmy Dwyer	.04	.03	.02
230	Larry Owen	.04	.03	.02
231	Andre Thornton	.06	.05	.02
232	Mark Salas	.04	.03	.02
233	Tom Brookens	.04	.03	.02
234	Greg Brock	.06	.05	.02
235	Rance Mulliniks	.04	.03	.02
236	Bob Brower	.06	.05	.02
237	Joe Niekro	.06	.05	.02
238	Scott Bankhead	.04	.03	.02
239	Doug DeCinces	.06	.05	.02
240	Tommy John	.12	.09	.05
241	Rich Gedman	.06	.05	.02
242	Ted Power	.04	.03	.02
243	*Dave Meads*	.12	.09	.05
244	Jim Sundberg	.06	.05	.02
245	Ken Oberkfell	.04	.03	.02
246	Jimmy Jones	.08	.06	.03
247	Ken Landreaux	.04	.03	.02
248	Jose Oquendo	.04	.03	.02
249	*John Mitchell*	.15	.11	.06
250	Don Baylor	.08	.06	.03
251	Scott Fletcher	.06	.05	.02
252	Al Newman	.04	.03	.02
253	Carney Lansford	.08	.06	.03
254	Johnny Ray	.06	.05	.02
255	Gary Pettis	.04	.03	.02
256	Ken Phelps	.06	.05	.02
257	Rick Leach	.04	.03	.02
258	Tim Stoddard	.04	.03	.02
259	Ed Romero	.04	.03	.02
260	Sid Bream	.06	.05	.02
261a	Tom Neidenfuer (incorrect spelling)	.25	.20	.10
261b	Tom Niedenfuer (correct spelling)	.06	.05	.02
262	Rick Dempsey	.06	.05	.02
263	Lonnie Smith	.06	.05	.02
264	Bob Forsch	.06	.05	.02
265	Barry Bonds	.10	.08	.04
266	Willie Randolph	.06	.05	.02
267	Mike Ramsey	.04	.03	.02
268	Don Slaught	.04	.03	.02
269	Mickey Tettleton	.04	.03	.02
270	Jerry Reuss	.06	.05	.02
271	Marc Sullivan	.04	.03	.02
272	Jim Morrison	.04	.03	.02
273	Steve Balboni	.06	.05	.02
274	Dick Schofield	.04	.03	.02
275	John Tudor	.08	.06	.03
276	*Gene Larkin*	.15	.11	.06
277	Harold Reynolds	.06	.05	.02
278	Jerry Browne	.06	.05	.02
279	Willie Upshaw	.06	.05	.02
280	Ted Higuera	.08	.06	.03
281	Terry McGriff	.04	.03	.02
282	Terry Puhl	.04	.03	.02
283	*Mark Wasinger*	.12	.09	.05
284	Luis Salazar	.04	.03	.02
285	Ted Simmons	.08	.06	.03
286	John Shelby	.04	.03	.02
287	*John Smiley*	.30	.25	.12
288	Curt Ford	.04	.03	.02
289	Steve Crawford	.04	.03	.02

		MT	NR MT	EX
290	Dan Quisenberry	.06	.05	.02
291	Alan Wiggins	.04	.03	.02
292	Randy Bush	.04	.03	.02
293	John Candelaria	.06	.05	.02
294	Tony Phillips	.04	.03	.02
295	Mike Morgan	.04	.03	.02
296	Bill Wegman	.04	.03	.02
297a	Terry Franconia (incorrect spelling)			
		.25	.20	.10
297b	Terry Francona (correct spelling)	.06	.05	.02
298	Mickey Hatcher	.04	.03	.02
299	Andres Thomas	.06	.05	.02
300	Bob Stanley	.04	.03	.02
301	*Alfredo Pedrique*	.12	.09	.05
302	Jim Lindeman	.06	.05	.02
303	Wally Backman	.06	.05	.02
304	Paul O'Neill	.06	.05	.02
305	Hubie Brooks	.08	.06	.03
306	Steve Buechele	.04	.03	.02
307	Bobby Thigpen	.08	.06	.03
308	George Hendrick	.06	.05	.02
309	John Moses	.04	.03	.02
310	Ron Guidry	.12	.09	.05
311	Bill Schroeder	.04	.03	.02
312	*Jose Nunez*	.20	.15	.08
313	Bud Black	.04	.03	.02
314	Joe Sambito	.04	.03	.02
315	Scott McGregor	.06	.05	.02
316	Rafael Santana	.04	.03	.02
317	Frank Williams	.04	.03	.02
318	Mike Fitzgerald	.04	.03	.02
319	Rick Mahler	.04	.03	.02
320	Jim Gott	.04	.03	.02
321	Mariano Duncan	.04	.03	.02
322	Jose Guzman	.06	.05	.02
323	Lee Guetterman	.04	.03	.02
324	Dan Gladden	.04	.03	.02
325	Gary Carter	.15	.11	.06
326	Tracy Jones	.10	.08	.04
327	Floyd Youmans	.04	.03	.02
328	Bill Dawley	.04	.03	.02
329	*Paul Noce*	.10	.08	.04
330	Angel Salazar	.04	.03	.02
331	Goose Gossage	.12	.09	.05
332	George Frazier	.04	.03	.02
333	Ruppert Jones	.04	.03	.02
334	Billy Jo Robidoux	.04	.03	.02
335	Mike Scott	.10	.08	.04
336	Randy Myers	.10	.08	.04
337	Bob Sebra	.04	.03	.02
338	Eric Show	.06	.05	.02
339	Mitch Williams	.06	.05	.02
340	Paul Molitor	.10	.08	.04
341	Gus Polidor	.04	.03	.02
342	Steve Trout	.04	.03	.02
343	Jerry Don Gleaton	.04	.03	.02
344	Bob Knepper	.06	.05	.02
345	Mitch Webster	.06	.05	.02
346	John Morris	.04	.03	.02
347	Andy Hawkins	.04	.03	.02
348	Dave Leiper	.04	.03	.02
349	Ernest Riles	.04	.03	.02
350	Dwight Gooden	.40	.30	.15
351	Dave Righetti	.12	.09	.05
352	Pat Dodson	.04	.03	.02
353	John Habyan	.04	.03	.02
354	Jim Deshaies	.06	.05	.02
355	Butch Wynegar	.04	.03	.02
356	Bryn Smith	.04	.03	.02
357	Matt Young	.04	.03	.02
358	*Tom Pagnozzi*	.12	.09	.05
359	Floyd Rayford	.04	.03	.02
360	Darryl Strawberry	.30	.25	.12
361	Sal Butera	.04	.03	.02
362	Domingo Ramos	.04	.03	.02
363	Chris Brown	.06	.05	.02
364	Jose Gonzalez	.04	.03	.02
365	Dave Smith	.06	.05	.02
366	Andy McGaffigan	.04	.03	.02
367	Stan Javier	.04	.03	.02
368	Henry Cotto	.04	.03	.02
369	Mike Birkbeck	.06	.05	.02
370	Len Dykstra	.08	.06	.03
371	Dave Collins	.06	.05	.02
372	Spike Owen	.04	.03	.02
373	Geno Petralli	.04	.03	.02
374	Ron Karkovice	.04	.03	.02
375	Shane Rawley	.06	.05	.02
376	*DeWayne Buice*	.15	.11	.06
377	*Bill Pecota*	.15	.11	.06
378	Leon Durham	.06	.05	.02

		MT	NR MT	EX
379	Ed Olwine	.04	.03	.02
380	Bruce Hurst	.08	.06	.03
381	Bob McClure	.04	.03	.02
382	Mark Thurmond	.04	.03	.02
383	Buddy Biancalana	.04	.03	.02
384	Tim Conroy	.04	.03	.02
385	Tony Gwynn	.25	.20	.10
386	Greg Gross	.04	.03	.02
387	*Barry Lyons*	.12	.09	.05
388	Mike Felder	.04	.03	.02
389	Pat Clements	.04	.03	.02
390	Ken Griffey	.06	.05	.02
391	Mark Davis	.04	.03	.02
392	Jose Rijo	.06	.05	.02
393	Mike Young	.04	.03	.02
394	Willie Fraser	.06	.05	.02
395	Dion James	.06	.05	.02
396	*Steve Shields*	.12	.09	.05
397	Randy St. Claire	.04	.03	.02
398	Danny Jackson	.12	.09	.05
399	Cecil Fielder	.06	.05	.02
400	Keith Hernandez	.15	.11	.06
401	Don Carman	.06	.05	.02
402	*Chuck Crim*	.12	.09	.05
403	Rob Woodward	.04	.03	.02
404	Junior Ortiz	.04	.03	.02
405	Glenn Wilson	.06	.05	.02
406	Ken Howell	.04	.03	.02
407	Jeff Kunkel	.04	.03	.02
408	Jeff Reed	.04	.03	.02
409	Chris James	.10	.08	.04
410	Zane Smith	.06	.05	.02
411	Ken Dixon	.04	.03	.02
412	Ricky Horton	.06	.05	.02
413	Frank DiPino	.04	.03	.02
414	*Shane Mack*	.15	.11	.06
415	Danny Cox	.06	.05	.02
416	Andy Van Slyke	.10	.08	.04
417	Danny Heep	.04	.03	.02
418	John Cangelosi	.04	.03	.02
419a	John Christiansen (incorrect spelling)			
		.25	.20	.10
419b	John Christensen (correct spelling)	.06	.05	.02
420	*Joey Cora*	.12	.09	.05
421	Mike LaValliere	.06	.05	.02
422	Kelly Gruber	.04	.03	.02
423	Bruce Benedict	.04	.03	.02
424	Len Matuszek	.04	.03	.02
425	Kent Tekulve	.06	.05	.02
426	Rafael Ramirez	.04	.03	.02
427	Mike Flanagan	.06	.05	.02
428	Mike Gallego	.04	.03	.02
429	Juan Castillo	.04	.03	.02
430	Neal Heaton	.04	.03	.02
431	Phil Garner	.04	.03	.02
432	*Mike Dunne*	.20	.15	.08
433	Wallace Johnson	.04	.03	.02
434	Jack O'Connor	.04	.03	.02
435	Steve Jeltz	.04	.03	.02
436	*Donnell Nixon*	.15	.11	.06
437	Jack Lazorko	.04	.03	.02
438	*Keith Comstock*	.12	.09	.05
439	Jeff Robinson	.04	.03	.02
440	Graig Nettles	.08	.06	.03
441	Mel Hall	.06	.05	.02
442	*Gerald Young*	.30	.25	.12
443	Gary Redus	.04	.03	.02
444	Charlie Moore	.04	.03	.02
445	Bill Madlock	.08	.06	.03
446	Mark Clear	.04	.03	.02
447	Greg Booker	.04	.03	.02
448	Rick Schu	.04	.03	.02
449	Ron Kittle	.06	.05	.02
450	Dale Murphy	.30	.25	.12
451	Bob Dernier	.04	.03	.02
452	Dale Mohorcic	.06	.05	.02
453	Rafael Belliard	.04	.03	.02
454	Charlie Puleo	.04	.03	.02
455	Dwayne Murphy	.06	.05	.02
456	Jim Eisenreich	.04	.03	.02
457	David Palmer	.04	.03	.02
458	Dave Stewart	.08	.06	.03
459	Pascual Perez	.06	.05	.02
460	Glenn Davis	.12	.09	.05
461	Dan Petry	.06	.05	.02
462	Jim Winn	.04	.03	.02
463	Darrell Miller	.04	.03	.02
464	Mike Moore	.04	.03	.02
465	Mike LaCoss	.04	.03	.02
466	Steve Farr	.04	.03	.02
467	Jerry Mumphrey	.04	.03	.02

#	Player	MT	NR MT	EX
468	Kevin Gross	.06	.05	.02
469	Bruce Bochy	.04	.03	.02
470	Orel Hershiser	.20	.15	.08
471	Eric King	.06	.05	.02
472	*Ellis Burks*	1.50	1.25	.60
473	Darren Daulton	.04	.03	.02
474	Mookie Wilson	.06	.05	.02
475	Frank Viola	.12	.09	.05
476	Ron Robinson	.04	.03	.02
477	Bob Melvin	.04	.03	.02
478	Jeff Musselman	.06	.05	.02
479	Charlie Kerfeld	.04	.03	.02
480	Richard Dotson	.06	.05	.02
481	Kevin Mitchell	.70	.50	.30
482	Gary Roenicke	.04	.03	.02
483	Tim Flannery	.04	.03	.02
484	Rich Yett	.04	.03	.02
485	Pete Incaviglia	.12	.09	.05
486	Rick Cerone	.04	.03	.02
487	Tony Armas	.06	.05	.02
488	Jerry Reed	.04	.03	.02
489	Davey Lopes	.06	.05	.02
490	Frank Tanana	.06	.05	.02
491	Mike Loynd	.04	.03	.02
492	Bruce Ruffin	.06	.05	.02
493	Chris Speier	.04	.03	.02
494	Tom Hume	.04	.03	.02
495	Jesse Orosco	.06	.05	.02
496	*Robby Wine, Jr.*	.12	.09	.05
497	*Jeff Montgomery*	.15	.11	.06
498	Jeff Dedmon	.04	.03	.02
499	Luis Aguayo	.04	.03	.02
500	Reggie Jackson (1968-75 Oakland Athletics)	.20	.15	.08
501	Reggie Jackson (1976 Baltimore Orioles)	.20	.15	.08
502	Reggie Jackson (1977-81 New York Yankees)	.20	.15	.08
503	Reggie Jackson (1982-86 California Angels)	.20	.15	.08
504	Reggie Jackson (1987 Oakland Athletics)	.20	.15	.08
505	Billy Hatcher	.06	.05	.02
506	Ed Lynch	.04	.03	.02
507	Willie Hernandez	.06	.05	.02
508	Jose DeLeon	.06	.05	.02
509	Joel Youngblood	.04	.03	.02
510	Bob Welch	.08	.06	.03
511	Steve Ontiveros	.04	.03	.02
512	Randy Ready	.04	.03	.02
513	Juan Nieves	.06	.05	.02
514	Jeff Russell	.04	.03	.02
515	Von Hayes	.06	.05	.02
516	Mark Gubicza	.10	.08	.04
517	Ken Dayley	.04	.03	.02
518	Don Aase	.04	.03	.02
519	Rick Reuschel	.08	.06	.03
520	*Mike Henneman*	.20	.15	.08
521	Rick Aguilera	.04	.03	.02
522	Jay Howell	.06	.05	.02
523	Ed Correa	.04	.03	.02
524	Manny Trillo	.06	.05	.02
525	Kirk Gibson	.15	.11	.06
526	*Wally Ritchie*	.12	.09	.05
527	Al Nipper	.04	.03	.02
528	Atlee Hammaker	.04	.03	.02
529	Shawon Dunston	.08	.06	.03
530	Jim Clancy	.06	.05	.02
531	Tom Paciorek	.04	.03	.02
532	Joel Skinner	.04	.03	.02
533	Scott Garrelts	.04	.03	.02
534	Tom O'Malley	.04	.03	.02
535	John Franco	.08	.06	.03
536	*Paul Kilgus*	.20	.15	.08
537	Darrell Porter	.06	.05	.02
538	Walt Terrell	.06	.05	.02
539	*Bill Long*	.15	.11	.06
540	George Bell	.20	.15	.08
541	Jeff Sellers	.06	.05	.02
542	*Joe Boever*	.12	.09	.05
543	Steve Howe	.06	.05	.02
544	Scott Sanderson	.04	.03	.02
545	Jack Morris	.15	.11	.06
546	*Todd Benzinger*	.30	.25	.12
547	Steve Henderson	.04	.03	.02
548	Eddie Milner	.04	.03	.02
549	*Jeff Robinson*	.35	.25	.14
550	Cal Ripken, Jr.	.25	.20	.10
551	Jody Davis	.06	.05	.02
552	Kirk McCaskill	.06	.05	.02
553	Craig Lefferts	.04	.03	.02
554	Darnell Coles	.06	.05	.02
555	Phil Niekro	.15	.11	.06
556	Mike Aldrete	.06	.05	.02
557	Pat Perry	.04	.03	.02
558	Juan Agosto	.04	.03	.02
559	Rob Murphy	.06	.05	.02
560	Dennis Rasmussen	.08	.06	.03
561	Manny Lee	.04	.03	.02
562	*Jeff Blauser*	.20	.15	.08
563	Bob Ojeda	.06	.05	.02
564	Dave Dravecky	.06	.05	.02
565	Gene Garber	.04	.03	.02
566	Ron Roenicke	.04	.03	.02
567	*Tommy Hinzo*	.12	.09	.05
568	*Eric Nolte*	.12	.09	.05
569	Ed Hearn	.04	.03	.02
570	*Mark Davidson*	.12	.09	.05
571	*Jim Walewander*	.12	.09	.05
572	Donnie Hill	.04	.03	.02
573	Jamie Moyer	.06	.05	.02
574	Ken Schrom	.04	.03	.02
575	Nolan Ryan	.30	.25	.12
576	Jim Acker	.04	.03	.02
577	Jamie Quirk	.04	.03	.02
578	*Jay Aldrich*	.10	.08	.04
579	Claudell Washington	.06	.05	.02
580	Jeff Leonard	.06	.05	.02
581	Carmen Castillo	.04	.03	.02
582	Daryl Boston	.04	.03	.02
583	*Jeff DeWillis*	.15	.11	.06
584	*John Marzano*	.20	.15	.08
585	Bill Gullickson	.06	.05	.02
586	Andy Allanson	.08	.06	.03
587	Lee Tunnell	.04	.03	.02
588	Gene Nelson	.04	.03	.02
589	Dave LaPoint	.06	.05	.02
590	Harold Baines	.10	.08	.04
591	Bill Buckner	.08	.06	.03
592	Carlton Fisk	.20	.15	.08
593	Rick Manning	.04	.03	.02
594	*Doug Jones*	.30	.25	.12
595	Tom Candiotti	.04	.03	.02
596	Steve Lake	.04	.03	.02
597	*Jose Lind*	.25	.20	.10
598	*Ross Jones*	.12	.09	.05
599	Gary Matthews	.06	.05	.02
600	Fernando Valezuela	.15	.11	.06
601	Dennis Martinez	.06	.05	.02
602	*Les Lancaster*	.15	.11	.06
603	Ozzie Guillen	.06	.05	.02
604	Tony Bernazard	.04	.03	.02
605	Chili Davis	.06	.05	.02
606	Roy Smalley	.04	.03	.02
607	Ivan Calderon	.08	.06	.03
608	Jay Tibbs	.04	.03	.02
609	Guy Hoffman	.04	.03	.02
610	Doyle Alexander	.06	.05	.02
611	Mike Bielecki	.04	.03	.02
612	*Shawn Hillegas*	.15	.11	.06
613	Keith Atherton	.04	.03	.02
614	Eric Plunk	.04	.03	.02
615	Sid Fernandez	.08	.06	.03
616	Dennis Lamp	.04	.03	.02
617	Dave Engle	.04	.03	.02
618	Harry Spilman	.04	.03	.02
619	Don Robinson	.06	.05	.02
620	*John Farrell*	.30	.25	.12
621	*Nelson Liriano*	.15	.11	.06
622	Floyd Bannister	.06	.05	.02
623	Rookie Prospect *(Randy Milligan)*	.25	.20	.10
624	Rookie Prospect *(Kevin Elster)*	.30	.25	.12
625	Rookie Prospect *(Jody Reed)*	.35	.25	.14
626	Rookie Prospect (Shawn Abner)	.20	.15	.08
627	Rookie Prospect *(Kirt Manwaring)*	.30	.25	.12
628	Rookie Prospect *(Pete Stanicek)*	.20	.15	.08
629	Rookie Prospect *(Rob Ducey)*	.12	.09	.05
630	Rookie Prospect *(Steve Kiefer)*	.04	.03	.02
631	Rookie Prospect *(Gary Thurman)*	.25	.20	.10
632	Rookie Prospect *(Darrel Akerfelds)*	.12	.09	.05
633	Rookie Prospect (Dave Clark)	.10	.08	.04
634	Rookie Prospect *(Roberto Kelly)*	.80	.60	.30
635	Rookie Prospect *(Keith Hughes)*	.15	.11	.06
636	Rookie Prospect *(John Davis)*	.15	.11	.06
637	Rookie Prospect *(Mike Devereaux)*	.30	.25	.12
638	Rookie Prospect *(Tom Glavine)*	.35	.25	.14
639	Rookie Prospect *(Keith Miller)*	.20	.15	.08
640	Rookie Prospect *(Chris Gwynn)*	.20	.15	.08
641	Rookie Prospect *(Tim Crews)*	.15	.11	.06
642	Rookie Prospect *(Mackey Sasser)*	.20	.15	.08
643	Rookie Prospect *(Vicente Palacios)*	.15	.11	.06
644	Rookie Prospect (Kevin Romine)	.06	.05	.02

		MT	NR MT	EX
645	Rookie Prospect *(Gregg Jefferies)*	3.50	2.75	1.50
646	Rookie Prospect *(Jeff Treadway)*	.20	.15	.08
647	Rookie Prospect *(Ronnie Gant)*	.30	.25	.12
648	Rookie Sluggers (Mark McGwire, Matt Nokes)	.30	.25	.12
649	Speed and Power (Eric Davis, Tim Raines)	.25	.20	.10
650	Game Breakers (Jack Clark, Don Mattingly)	.60	.45	.25
651	Super Shortstops (Tony Fernandez, Cal Ripken, Jr., Alan Trammell)	.15	.11	.06
652	1987 Highlights (Vince Coleman)	.08	.06	.03
653	1987 Highlights (Kirby Puckett)	.12	.09	.05
654	1987 Highlights (Benito Santiago)	.10	.08	.04
655	1987 Highlights (Juan Nieves)	.06	.05	.02
656	1987 Highlights (Steve Bedrosian)	.06	.05	.02
657	1987 Highlights (Mike Schmidt)	.15	.11	.06
658	1987 Highlights (Don Mattingly)	.60	.45	.25
659	1987 Highlights (Mark McGwire)	.40	.30	.15
660	1987 Highlights (Paul Molitor)	.08	.06	.03

1988 Score Box Panels

This 18-card set, produced by Major League Marketing and manufactured by Optigraphics, is the premiere box-bottom set issued under the Score trademark. The set features 1987 major league All-star players in full-color action poses, framed by a white border. A "1987 All-Star" banner (red or purple) curves above an orange player name block beneath the player photo. Card backs are printed in red, blue, gold and black and carry the card number, player name and position and league logo. Six colorful "Great Moments in Baseball" trivia cards are also invluded in this set. Each trivia card highlights an historical event at a famous ballpark.

		MT	NR MT	EX
Complete Panel Set:		8.00	6.00	3.25
Complete Singles Set:		3.00	2.25	1.25
Common Panel:		1.50	1.25	.60
Common Single Player:		.15	.11	.06
Panel		1.50	1.25	.60
1	Terry Kennedy	.15	.11	.06
3	Willie Randolph	.15	.11	.06
15	Eric Davis	.50	.40	.20
Panel		2.25	1.75	.90
3	Don Mattingly	.90	.70	.35
5	Cal Ripken, Jr.	.35	.25	.14
11	Jack Clark	.25	.20	.10
Panel		1.75	1.25	.70
4	Wade Boggs	.60	.45	.25
9	Bret Saberhagen	.20	.15	.08
12	Ryne Sandberg	.30	.25	.12
Panel		1.50	1.25	.60
6	George Bell	.25	.20	.10
13	Mike Schmidt	.35	.25	.14
18	Mike Scott	.15	.11	.06
Panel		1.75	1.25	.70
7	Rickey Henderson	.35	.25	.14
16	Andre Dawson	.25	.20	.10
17	Darryl Strawberry	.40	.30	.15
Panel		1.50	1.25	.60
8	Dave Winfield	.25	.20	.10
10	Gary Carter	.20	.15	.08
14	Ozzie Smith	.15	.11	.06

1988 Score Traded

veterans is similar in design to the 1988 Score set, except for a change in border color. Individual standard-size palyer cards (2-1/2" by 3-1/2") feature a bright orange border framing full-figure action photos highlighted by a thin white outline. The player name (in white) is centered in the bottom margin, flanked by three yellow stars lower left and a yellow Score logo lower right. The backs carry full-color player close-ups on a cream-colored background, followed by card number, team name and logo, player personal information and a purple stats chart that lists year-by-year and major league totals. A brief player profile follows the stats chart and on some cards, information is included about the players's trade or acquisition. The update is set also includes 10 Magic Motion 3-D trivia cards.

		MT	NR MT	EX
Complete Set:		35.00	27.50	15.00
Common Player:		.08	.06	.03
1T	Jack Clark	.20	.15	.08
2T	Danny Jackson	.20	.15	.08
3T	Brett Butler	.10	.08	.04
4T	Kurt Stillwell	.12	.09	.05
5T	Tom Brunansky	.15	.11	.06
6T	Dennis Lamp	.08	.06	.03
7T	Jose DeLeon	.10	.08	.04
8T	Tom Herr	.12	.09	.05
9T	Keith Moreland	.10	.08	.04
10T	Kirk Gibson	.20	.15	.08
11T	Bud Black	.08	.06	.03
12T	Rafael Ramirez	.08	.06	.03
13T	Luis Salazar	.08	.06	.03
14T	Goose Gossage	.15	.11	.06
15T	Bob Welch	.15	.11	.06
16T	Vance Law	.10	.08	.04
17T	Ray Knight	.10	.08	.04
18T	Dan Quisenberry	.10	.08	.04
19T	Don Slaught	.08	.06	.03
20T	Lee Smith	.12	.09	.05
21T	Rick Cerone	.08	.06	.03
22T	Pat Tabler	.10	.08	.04
23T	Larry McWilliams	.08	.06	.03
24T	Rick Horton	.10	.08	.04
25T	Graig Nettles	.12	.09	.05
26T	Dan Petry	.10	.08	.04
27T	Joe Rijo	.10	.08	.04
28T	Chili Davis	.10	.08	.04
29T	Dickie Thon	.10	.08	.04
30T	Mackey Sasser(FC)	.15	.11	.06
31T	Mickey Tettleton	.08	.06	.03
32T	Rick Dempsey	.08	.06	.03
33T	Ron Hassey	.08	.06	.03
34T	Phil Bradley	.12	.09	.05
35T	Jay Howell	.10	.08	.04
36T	Bill Buckner	.12	.09	.05
37T	Alfredo Griffin	.10	.08	.04
38T	Gary Pettis	.08	.06	.03
39T	Calvin Schiraldi	.08	.06	.03
40T	John Candelaria	.10	.08	.04
41T	Joe Orsulak	.08	.06	.03
42T	Willie Upshaw	.10	.08	.04
43T	Herm Winningham	.08	.06	.03

		MT	NR MT	EX
44T	Ron Kittle	.12	.09	.05
45T	Bob Dernier	.08	.06	.03
46T	Steve Balboni	.10	.08	.04
47T	Steve Shields	.08	.06	.03
48T	Henry Cotto	.08	.06	.03
49T	Dave Henderson	.10	.08	.04
50T	Dave Parker	.15	.11	.06
51T	Mike Young	.08	.06	.03
52T	Mark Salas	.08	.06	.03
53T	Mike Davis	.08	.06	.03
54T	Rafael Santana	.08	.06	.03
55T	Don Baylor	.15	.11	.06
56T	Dan Pasqua	.12	.09	.05
57T	Ernest Riles	.08	.06	.03
58T	Glenn Hubbard	.08	.06	.03
59T	Mike Smithson	.08	.06	.03
60T	Richard Dotson	.10	.08	.04
61T	Jerry Reuss	.10	.08	.04
62T	Mike Jackson	.10	.08	.04
63T	Floyd Bannister	.10	.08	.04
64T	Jesse Orosco	.10	.08	.04
65T	Larry Parrish	.10	.08	.04
66T	Jeff Bittiger(FC)	.20	.15	.08
67T	Ray Hayward(FC)	.10	.08	.04
68T	Ricky Jordan(FC)	2.75	2.00	1.00
69T	Tommy Gregg(FC)	.12	.09	.05
70T	Brady Anderson(FC)	.50	.40	.20
71T	Jeff Montgomery	.08	.06	.03
72T	Darryl Hamilton(FC)	.20	.15	.08
73T	Cecil Espy(FC)	.10	.08	.04
74T	Greg Briley(FC)	2.00	1.50	.80
75T	Joey Meyer(FC)	.20	.15	.08
76T	Mike Macfarlane(FC)	.25	.20	.10
77T	Oswald Peraza(FC)	.20	.15	.08
78T	Jack Armstrong(FC)	.20	.15	.08
79T	Don Heinkel(FC)	.20	.15	.08
80T	Mark Grace(FC)	4.00	3.00	1.50
81T	Steve Curry(FC)	.20	.15	.08
82T	Damon Berryhill(FC)	.40	.30	.15
83T	Steve Ellsworth(FC)	.20	.15	.08
84T	Pete Smith(FC)	.12	.09	.05
85T	Jack McDowell	.25	.20	.10
86T	Rob Dibble(FC)	.50	.40	.20
87T	Brian Harvey(FC)	.30	.25	.12
88T	John Dopson(FC)	.25	.20	.10
89T	Dave Gallagher(FC)	.25	.20	.10
90T	Todd Stottlemyre(FC)	.35	.25	.14
91T	Mike Schooler(FC)	.40	.30	.15
92T	Don Gordon(FC)	.08	.06	.03
93T	Sil Campusano(FC)	.25	.20	.10
94T	Jeff Pico(FC)	.25	.20	.10
95T	Jay Buhner(FC)	.30	.25	.12
96T	Nelson Santovenia(FC)	.35	.25	.14
97T	Al Leiter(FC)	.30	.25	.12
98T	Luis Alicea(FC)	.20	.15	.08
99T	Pat Borders(FC)	.25	.20	.10
100T	Chris Sabo(FC)	1.25	.90	.50
101T	Tim Belcher(FC)	.40	.30	.15
102T	Walt Weiss(FC)	.80	.60	.30
103T	Craig Biggio(FC)	1.50	1.25	.60
104T	Don August(FC)	.25	.20	.10
105T	Roberto Alomar(FC)	.70	.50	.30
106T	Todd Burns(FC)	.30	.25	.12
107T	John Costello(FC)	.20	.15	.08
108T	Melido Perez(FC)	.30	.25	.12
109T	Darrin Jackson(FC)	.12	.09	.05
110T	Orestes Destrade(FC)	.15	.11	.06

cards) from Optigraphics was divided into five separate 8-card sets. Similar to the company's regular issue, these cards are distinguished by excellent full-color photography on both front and back. The glossy player photos, with team logo in the lower right corner, are centered on a white background and framed by a vivid blue and green border. A player name banner beneath the photo includes the name, position and uniform number. The card backs feature ful-color player closeups beneath a hot pink player name/Score logo banner. Hot pink also frames the personal stats (in green), career stats (in black) and career biography (in blue). The backs also include quotes from well-known baseball authorities discussing player performance. This set was distributed via a write-in offer printed on 1988 Score 17-card package wrappers.

		MT	NR MT	EX
Complete Set:		9.00	6.75	3.50
Common Player:		.10	.08	.04
1	Mark McGwire	1.25	.90	.50
2	Benito Santiago	.30	.25	.12
3	Sam Horn	.25	.20	.10
4	Chris Bosio	.10	.08	.04
5	Matt Nokes	.40	.30	.15
6	Ken Williams	.15	.11	.06
7	Dion James	.10	.08	.04
8	B.J. Surhoff	.25	.20	.10
9	Joe Margrane	.20	.15	.08
10	Kevin Seitzer	.90	.70	.35
11	Stanley Jefferson	.10	.08	.04
12	Devon White	.30	.25	.12
13	Nelson Liriano	.15	.11	.06
14	Chris James	.25	.20	.10
15	Mike Henneman	.15	.11	.06
16	Terry Steinbach	.20	.15	.08
17	John Kruk	.25	.20	.10
18	Matt Williams	.30	.25	.12
19	Kelly Downs	.25	.20	.10
20	Bill Ripken	.15	.11	.06
21	Ozzie Guillen	.10	.08	.04
22	Luis Polonia	.15	.11	.06
23	Dave Magadan	.20	.15	.08
24	Mike Greenwell	1.00	.70	.40
25	Will Clark	.50	.40	.20
26	Mike Dunne	.20	.15	.08
27	Wally Joyner	.50	.40	.20
28	Robby Thompson	.10	.08	.04
29	Ken Caminiti	.20	.15	.08
30	Jose Canseco	1.75	1.25	.70
31	Todd Benzinger	.30	.25	.12
32	Pete Incaviglia	.20	.15	.08
33	John Farrell	.20	.15	.08
34	Casey Candaele	.10	.08	.04
35	Mike Aldrete	.10	.08	.04
36	Ruben Sierra	.40	.30	.15
37	Ellis Burks	1.00	.70	.40
38	Tracy Jones	.20	.15	.08
39	Kal Daniels	.30	.25	.12
40	Cory Snyder	.30	.25	.12

1988 Score
Young Superstar - Series I

This 40-card standard-size set (2-1/2" by 3-1/2"

1988 Score
Young Superstar - Series II

This set of 40 standard-size cards (2-1/2" by

3-1/2") and five Magic trivia cards is part of a double series issued by Score. Each series is divided into five smaller sets of eight baseball cards and one trivia card. The design on both series is similar, except for border color. Series I has blue and green borders. Series II has red and blue borders framing full-color player photos with the player name and team logo printed beneath the photo. The card backs carry full-color head shots and stats in a variety of colors. Young Superstar series were offered via a write-in offer on the backs of 1988 Score card package wrappers. For each 8-card subset, collectors were instructed to send two Score wrappers and $1. Complete sets were offered by a number of hobby dealers nationwide.

		MT	NR MT	EX
Complete Set:		9.00	6.75	3.50
Common Player:		.10	.08	.04
1	Don Mattingly	2.25	1.75	.90
2	Glenn Braggs	.15	.11	.06
3	Dwight Gooden	.70	.50	.30
4	Jose Lind	.25	.20	.10
5	Danny Tartabull	.30	.25	.12
6	Tony Fernandez	.15	.11	.06
7	Julio Franco	.15	.11	.06
8	Andres Galarraga	.30	.25	.12
9	Bobby Bonilla	.25	.20	.10
10	Eric Davis	.70	.50	.30
11	Gerald Young	.25	.20	.10
12	Barry Bonds	.25	.20	.10
13	Jerry Browne	.10	.08	.04
14	Jeff Blauser	.15	.11	.06
15	Mickey Brantley	.10	.08	.04
16	Floyd Youmans	.10	.08	.04
17	Bret Saberhagen	.25	.20	.10
18	Shawon Dunston	.15	.11	.06
19	Len Dykstra	.15	.11	.06
20	Darryl Strawberry	.70	.50	.30
21	Rick Aguilera	.10	.08	.04
22	Ivan Calderon	.10	.08	.04
23	Roger Clemens	.70	.50	.30
24	Vince Coleman	.30	.25	.12
25	Gary Thurman	.25	.20	.10
26	Jeff Treadway	.25	.20	.10
27	Oddibe McDowell	.10	.08	.04
28	Fred McGriff	.40	.30	.15
29	Mark McLemore	.10	.08	.04
30	Jeff Musselman	.10	.08	.04
31	Mitch Williams	.10	.08	.04
32	Dan Plesac	.15	.11	.06
33	Juan Nieves	.10	.08	.04
34	Barry Larkin	.30	.25	.12
35	Greg Mathews	.15	.11	.06
36	Shane Mack	.10	.08	.04
37	Scott Bankhead	.10	.08	.04
38	Eric Bell	.10	.08	.04
39	Greg Swindell	.25	.20	.10
40	Kevin Elster	.20	.15	.08

1989 Score

This set of 660 cards plus 56 Magic Motion trivia cards is the second annual basic issue from Score. Full-color player photos highlight 651 individual players and 9 season highlights, including the first

Wrigley Field night game. Action photos are framed by thin brightly colored borders (green, cyan blue, purple, orange, red, royal blue) with a baseball diamond logo/player name beneath the photo. Full-color player close-ups (1-5/16" by 1-5/8") are printed on the pastel-colored backs, along with the card number, personal information, stats and career highlights. The cards measure 2-1/2" by 3-1/2" in size.

		MT	NR MT	EX
Complete Set:		20.00	15.00	8.00
Common Player:		.03	.02	.01
1	Jose Canseco	1.00	.70	.40
2	Andre Dawson	.15	.11	.06
3	Mark McGwire	.60	.45	.25
4	Benny Santiago	.12	.09	.05
5	Rick Reuschel	.08	.06	.03
6	Fred McGriff	.35	.25	.14
7	Kal Daniels	.12	.09	.05
8	Gary Gaetti	.12	.09	.05
9	Ellis Burks	.50	.40	.20
10	Darryl Strawberry	.35	.25	.14
11	Julio Franco	.08	.06	.03
12	Lloyd Moseby	.06	.05	.02
13	*Jeff Pico*	.20	.15	.08
14	Johnny Ray	.06	.05	.02
15	Cal Ripken, Jr.	.30	.25	.12
16	Dick Schofield	.03	.02	.01
17	Mel Hall	.06	.05	.02
18	Bill Ripken	.06	.05	.02
19	Brook Jacoby	.08	.06	.03
20	Kirby Puckett	.35	.25	.14
21	Bill Doran	.06	.05	.02
22	Pete O'Brien	.06	.05	.02
23	Matt Nokes	.15	.11	.06
24	Brian Fisher	.06	.05	.02
25	Jack Clark	.12	.09	.05
26	Gary Pettis	.03	.02	.01
27	Dave Valle	.03	.02	.01
28	Willie Wilson	.08	.06	.03
29	Curt Young	.06	.05	.02
30	Dale Murphy	.30	.25	.12
31	Barry Larkin	.10	.08	.04
32	Dave Stewart	.08	.06	.03
33	Mike LaValliere	.06	.05	.02
34	Glen Hubbard	.03	.02	.01
35	Ryne Sandberg	.20	.15	.08
36	Tony Pena	.06	.05	.02
37	Greg Walker	.06	.05	.02
38	Von Hayes	.08	.06	.03
39	Kevin Mitchell	.40	.30	.15
40	Tim Raines	.25	.20	.10
41	Keith Hernandez	.20	.15	.08
42	Keith Moreland	.06	.05	.02
43	Ruben Sierra	.30	.25	.12
44	Chet Lemon	.06	.05	.02
45	Willie Randolph	.06	.05	.02
46	Andy Allanson	.03	.02	.01
47	Candy Maldonado	.06	.05	.02
48	Sid Bream	.06	.05	.02
49	Denny Walling	.03	.02	.01
50	Dave Winfield	.25	.20	.10
51	Alvin Davis	.10	.08	.04
52	Cory Snyder	.15	.11	.06
53	Hubie Brooks	.08	.06	.03
54	Chili Davis	.06	.05	.02
55	Kevin Seitzer	.25	.20	.10
56	Jose Uribe	.03	.02	.01
57	Tony Fernandez	.10	.08	.04
58	Tim Teufel	.03	.02	.01
59	Oddibe McDowell	.06	.05	.02
60	Les Lancaster	.06	.05	.02
61	Billy Hatcher	.06	.05	.02
62	Dan Gladden	.03	.02	.01
63	Marty Barrett	.06	.05	.02
64	Nick Esasky	.06	.05	.02
65	Wally Joyner	.20	.15	.08
66	Mike Greenwell	.60	.45	.25
67	Ken Williams	.06	.05	.02
68	Bob Horner	.08	.06	.03
69	Steve Sax	.12	.09	.05
70	Rickey Henderson	.30	.25	.12
71	Mitch Webster	.06	.05	.02
72	Rob Deer	.06	.05	.02
73	Jim Presley	.06	.05	.02
74	Albert Hall	.03	.02	.01
75a	George Brett ("...game's top hitters at 33..." on back)	.60	.45	.25

		MT	NR MT	EX
75b	George Brett ("...game's top hitters at 35..." on back)	.30	.25	.12
76	Brian Downing	.06	.05	.02
77	Dave Martinez	.06	.05	.02
78	Scott Fletcher	.06	.05	.02
79	Phil Bradley	.08	.06	.03
80	Ozzie Smith	.12	.09	.05
81	Larry Sheets	.06	.05	.02
82	Mike Aldrete	.06	.05	.02
83	Darnell Coles	.06	.05	.02
84	Len Dykstra	.08	.06	.03
85	Jim Rice	.20	.15	.08
86	Jeff Treadway	.10	.08	.04
87	Jose Lind	.08	.06	.03
88	Willie McGee	.10	.08	.04
89	Mickey Brantley	.03	.02	.01
90	Tony Gwynn	.30	.25	.12
91	R.J. Reynolds	.03	.02	.01
92	Milt Thompson	.03	.02	.01
93	Kevin McReynolds	.12	.09	.05
94	Eddie Murray	.25	.20	.10
95	Lance Parrish	.12	.09	.05
96	Ron Kittle	.06	.05	.02
97	Gerald Young	.10	.08	.04
98	Ernie Whitt	.06	.05	.02
99	Jeff Reed	.03	.02	.01
100	Don Mattingly	1.25	.90	.50
101	Gerald Perry	.08	.06	.03
102	Vance Law	.06	.05	.02
103	John Shelby	.03	.02	.01
104	Chris Sabo	.40	.30	.15
105	Danny Tartabull	.15	.11	.06
106	Glenn Wilson	.06	.05	.02
107	Mark Davidson	.06	.05	.02
108	Dave Parker	.10	.08	.04
109	Eric Davis	.35	.25	.14
110	Alan Trammell	.15	.11	.06
111	Ozzie Virgil	.03	.02	.01
112	Frank Tanana	.06	.05	.02
113	Rafael Ramirez	.03	.02	.01
114	Dennis Martinez	.06	.05	.02
115	Jose DeLeon	.06	.05	.02
116	Bob Ojeda	.06	.05	.02
117	Doug Drabek	.06	.05	.02
118	Andy Hawkins	.03	.02	.01
119	Greg Maddux(FC)	.10	.08	.04
120a	Cecil Fielder (photo on back reversed)	.20	.15	.08
120b	Cecil Fielder (correct photo)	.08	.06	.03
121	Mike Scioscia	.06	.05	.02
122	Dan Petry	.06	.05	.02
123	Terry Kennedy	.06	.05	.02
124	Kelly Downs	.08	.06	.03
125a	Greg Gross (first name incorrect on card back)	.20	.15	.08
125b	Greg Gross (first name correct on card back)	.08	.06	.03
126	Fred Lynn	.10	.08	.04
127	Barry Bonds	.10	.08	.04
128	Harold Baines	.10	.08	.04
129	Doyle Alexander	.06	.05	.02
130	Kevin Elster	.08	.06	.03
131	Mike Heath	.03	.02	.01
132	Teddy Higuera	.08	.06	.03
133	Charlie Leibrandt	.06	.05	.02
134	Tim Laudner	.03	.02	.01
135a	Ray Knight (photo reversed)	.25	.20	.09
135b	Ray Knight (correct photo)	.08	.06	.03
136	Howard Johnson	.08	.06	.03
137	Terry Pendleton	.08	.06	.03
138	Andy McGaffigan	.03	.02	.01
139	Ken Oberkfell	.03	.02	.01
140	Butch Wynegar	.03	.02	.01
141	Rob Murphy	.03	.02	.01
142	Rich Renteria(FC)	.12	.09	.05
143	Jose Guzman	.08	.06	.03
144	Andres Galarraga	.12	.09	.05
145	Rick Horton	.06	.05	.02
146	Frank DiPino	.03	.02	.01
147	Glenn Braggs	.06	.05	.02
148	John Kruk	.06	.05	.02
149	Mike Schmidt	.35	.25	.14
150	Lee Smith	.08	.06	.03
151	Robin Yount	.25	.20	.10
152	Mark Eichhorn	.06	.05	.02
153	DeWayne Buice	.04	.03	.02
154	B.J. Surhoff	.08	.06	.03
155	Vince Coleman	.12	.09	.05
156	Tony Phillips	.03	.02	.01
157	Willie Fraser	.03	.02	.01
158	Lance McCullers	.06	.05	.02
159	Greg Gagne	.03	.02	.01
160	Jesse Barfield	.08	.06	.03
161	Mark Langston	.08	.06	.03
162	Kurt Stillwell	.06	.05	.02
163	Dion James	.03	.02	.01
164	Glenn Davis	.12	.09	.05
165	Walt Weiss	.40	.30	.15
166	Dave Concepcion	.08	.06	.03
167	Alfredo Griffin	.06	.05	.02
168	Don Heinkel	.15	.11	.06
169	Luis Rivera(FC)	.03	.02	.01
170	Shane Rawley	.06	.05	.02
171	Darrell Evans	.08	.06	.03
172	Robby Thompson	.06	.05	.02
173	Jody Davis	.06	.05	.02
174	Andy Van Slyke	.12	.09	.05
175a	Wade Boggs ("And his .364 career BA..." on back)	1.25	.90	.50
175b	Wade Boggs ("And his .356 career BA..." on back)	.80	.60	.30
176	Garry Templeton	.06	.05	.02
177	Gary Redus	.03	.02	.01
178	Craig Lefferts	.03	.02	.01
179	Carney Lansford	.06	.05	.02
180	Ron Darling	.10	.08	.04
181	Kirk McCaskill	.06	.05	.02
182	Tony Armas	.06	.05	.02
183	Steve Farr	.03	.02	.01
184	Tom Brunansky	.10	.08	.04
185	Bryan Harvey	.20	.15	.08
186	Mike Marshall	.10	.08	.04
187	Bo Diaz	.06	.05	.02
188	Willie Upshaw	.06	.05	.02
189	Mike Pagliarulo	.08	.06	.03
190	Mike Krukow	.06	.05	.02
191	Tommy Herr	.06	.05	.02
192	Jim Pankovits	.03	.02	.01
193	Dwight Evans	.10	.08	.04
194	Kelly Gruber	.03	.02	.01
195	Bobby Bonilla	.10	.08	.04
196	Wallace Johnson	.03	.02	.01
197	Dave Stieb	.08	.06	.03
198	Pat Borders	.20	.15	.08
199	Rafael Palmeiro	.12	.09	.05
200	Doc Gooden	.40	.30	.15
201	Pete Incaviglia	.08	.06	.03
202	Chris James	.08	.06	.03
203	Marvell Wynne	.03	.02	.01
204	Pat Sheridan	.03	.02	.01
205	Don Baylor	.08	.06	.03
206	Paul O'Neill	.03	.02	.01
207	Pete Smith	.08	.06	.03
208	Mark McLemore	.03	.02	.01
209	Henry Cotto	.03	.02	.01
210	Kirk Gibson	.15	.11	.06
211	Claudell Washington	.06	.05	.02
212	Randy Bush	.03	.02	.01
213	Joe Carter	.10	.08	.04
214	Bill Buckner	.08	.06	.03
215a	Bert Blyleven (year of birth is 1957)	.25	.20	.10
215b	Bert Blyleven (year of birth is 1951)	.10	.08	.04
216	Brett Butler	.06	.05	.02
217	Lee Mazzilli	.06	.05	.02
218	Spike Owen	.03	.02	.01
219	Bill Swift	.03	.02	.01
220	Tim Wallach	.08	.06	.03
221	David Cone	.30	.25	.12
222	Don Carman	.06	.05	.02
223	Rich Gossage	.10	.08	.04
224	Bob Walk	.03	.02	.01
225	Dave Righetti	.10	.08	.04
226	Kevin Bass	.06	.05	.02
227	Kevin Gross	.06	.05	.02
228	Tim Burke	.03	.02	.01
229	Rick Mahler	.03	.02	.01
230	Lou Whitaker	.15	.11	.06
231	Luis Alicea	.15	.11	.06
232	Roberto Alomar	.40	.30	.15
233	Bob Boone	.06	.05	.02
234	Dickie Thon	.03	.02	.01
235	Shawon Dunston	.08	.06	.03
236	Pete Stanicek	.08	.06	.03
237	Craig Biggio	.40	.30	.15
238	Dennis Boyd	.05	.05	.02
239	Tom Candiotti	.03	.02	.01
240	Gary Carter	.15	.11	.06
241	Mike Stanley	.03	.02	.01
242	Ken Phelps	.06	.05	.02
243	Chris Bosio	.03	.02	.01

#	Player	MT	NR MT	EX
244	Les Straker	.06	.05	.02
245	Dave Smith	.06	.05	.02
246	John Candelaria	.06	.05	.02
247	Joe Orsulak	.03	.02	.01
248	Storm Davis	.08	.06	.03
249	Floyd Bannister	.06	.05	.02
250	Jack Morris	.12	.09	.05
251	Bret Saberhagen	.12	.09	.05
252	Tom Niedenfuer	.06	.05	.02
253	Neal Heaton	.03	.02	.01
254	Eric Show	.06	.05	.02
255	Juan Samuel	.10	.08	.04
256	Dale Sveum	.06	.05	.02
257	Jim Gott	.03	.02	.01
258	Scott Garrelts	.03	.02	.01
259	Larry McWilliams	.03	.02	.01
260	Steve Bedrosian	.08	.06	.03
261	Jack Howell	.06	.05	.02
262	Jay Tibbs	.03	.02	.01
263	Jamie Moyer	.03	.02	.01
264	Doug Sisk	.03	.02	.01
265	Todd Worrell	.08	.06	.03
266	John Farrell	.08	.06	.03
267	Dave Collins	.06	.05	.02
268	Sid Fernandez	.08	.06	.03
269	Tom Brookens	.03	.02	.01
270	Shane Mack	.06	.05	.02
271	Paul Kilgus	.08	.06	.03
272	Chuck Crim	.03	.02	.01
273	Bob Knepper	.06	.05	.02
274	Mike Moore	.03	.02	.01
275	Guillermo Hernandez	.06	.05	.02
276	Dennis Eckersley	.10	.08	.04
277	Graig Nettles	.10	.08	.04
278	Rich Dotson	.06	.05	.02
279	Larry Herndon	.03	.02	.01
280	Gene Larkin	.08	.06	.03
281	Roger McDowell	.08	.06	.03
282	Greg Swindell	.10	.08	.04
283	Juan Agosto	.03	.02	.01
284	Jeff Robinson	.06	.05	.02
285	Mike Dunne	.08	.06	.03
286	Greg Mathews	.06	.05	.02
287	Kent Tekulve	.06	.05	.02
288	Jerry Mumphrey	.03	.02	.01
289	Jack McDowell	.08	.06	.03
290	Frank Viola	.12	.09	.05
291	Mark Gubicza	.08	.06	.03
292	Dave Schmidt	.03	.02	.01
293	Mike Henneman	.08	.06	.03
294	Jimmy Jones	.03	.02	.01
295	Charlie Hough	.06	.05	.02
296	Rafael Santana	.03	.02	.01
297	Chris Speier	.03	.02	.01
298	Mike Witt	.06	.05	.02
299	Pascual Perez	.06	.05	.02
300	Nolan Ryan	.35	.25	.14
301	Mitch Williams	.06	.05	.02
302	Mookie Wilson	.06	.05	.02
303	Mackey Sasser	.06	.05	.02
304	John Cerutti	.06	.05	.02
305	Jeff Reardon	.08	.06	.03
306	Randy Myers	.08	.06	.03
307	Greg Brock	.06	.05	.02
308	Bob Welch	.08	.06	.03
309	Jeff Robinson	.12	.09	.05
310	Harold Reynolds	.06	.05	.02
311	Jim Walewander	.03	.02	.01
312	Dave Magadan	.08	.06	.03
313	Jim Gantner	.03	.02	.01
314	Walt Terrell	.06	.05	.02
315	Wally Backman	.06	.05	.02
316	Luis Salazar	.03	.02	.01
317	Rick Rhoden	.06	.05	.02
318	Tom Henke	.06	.05	.02
319	*Mike Macfarlane*	.20	.15	.08
320	Dan Plesac	.08	.06	.03
321	Calvin Schiraldi	.03	.02	.01
322	Stan Javier	.03	.02	.01
323	Devon White	.10	.08	.04
324	Scott Bradley	.03	.02	.01
325	Bruce Hurst	.08	.06	.03
326	Manny Lee	.03	.02	.01
327	Rick Aguilera	.03	.02	.01
328	Bruce Ruffin	.03	.02	.01
329	Ed Whitson	.03	.02	.01
330	Bo Jackson	.40	.30	.15
331	Ivan Calderon	.06	.05	.02
332	Mickey Hatcher	.03	.02	.01
333	Barry Jones(FC)	.03	.02	.01
334	Ron Hassey	.03	.02	.01

#	Player	MT	NR MT	EX
335	Bill Wegman	.03	.02	.01
336	Damon Berryhill	.15	.11	.06
337	Steve Ontiveros	.03	.02	.01
338	Dan Pasqua	.08	.06	.03
339	Bill Pecota	.06	.05	.02
340	Greg Cadaret	.06	.05	.02
341	Scott Bankhead	.03	.02	.01
342	Ron Guidry	.12	.09	.05
343	Danny Heep	.03	.02	.01
344	Bob Brower	.03	.02	.01
345	Rich Gedman	.06	.05	.02
346	*Nelson Santovenia*	.20	.15	.08
347	George Bell	.20	.15	.08
348	Ted Power	.03	.02	.01
349	Mark Grant	.03	.02	.01
350a	Roger Clemens (778 Wins)	1.00	.70	.40
350b	Roger Clemens (78 Wins)	.40	.30	.15
351	Bill Long	.06	.05	.02
352	Jay Bell(FC)	.06	.05	.02
353	Steve Balboni	.06	.05	.02
354	Bob Kipper	.03	.02	.01
355	Steve Jeltz	.03	.02	.01
356	Jesse Orosco	.06	.05	.02
357	Bob Dernier	.03	.02	.01
358	Mickey Tettleton	.03	.02	.01
359	Duane Ward(FC)	.03	.02	.01
360	Darrin Jackson(FC)	.08	.06	.03
361	Rey Quinones	.03	.02	.01
362	Mark Grace	1.75	1.25	.70
363	Steve Lake	.03	.02	.01
364	Pat Perry	.03	.02	.01
365	Terry Steinbach	.08	.06	.03
366	Alan Ashby	.03	.02	.01
367	Jeff Montgomery	.06	.05	.02
368	Steve Buechele	.03	.02	.01
369	Chris Brown	.06	.05	.02
370	Orel Hershiser	.20	.15	.08
371	Todd Benzinger	.10	.08	.04
372	Ron Gant	.15	.11	.06
373	Paul Assenmacher(FC)	.03	.02	.01
374	Joey Meyer	.08	.06	.03
375	Neil Allen	.03	.02	.01
376	Mike Davis	.06	.05	.02
377	Jeff Parrett(FC)	.08	.06	.03
378	Jay Howell	.06	.05	.02
379	Rafael Belliard	.03	.02	.01
380	Luis Polonia	.06	.05	.02
381	Keith Atherton	.03	.02	.01
382	Kent Hrbek	.15	.11	.06
383	Bob Stanley	.03	.02	.01
384	Dave LaPoint	.06	.05	.02
385	Rance Mulliniks	.03	.02	.01
386	Melido Perez	.08	.06	.03
387	Doug Jones	.10	.08	.04
388	Steve Lyons	.03	.02	.01
389	Alejandro Pena	.06	.05	.02
390	Frank White	.06	.05	.02
391	Pat Tabler	.06	.05	.02
392	Eric Plunk(FC)	.03	.02	.01
393	Mike Maddux(FC)	.03	.02	.01
394	Allan Anderson(FC)	.06	.05	.02
395	Bob Brenly	.03	.02	.01
396	Rick Cerone	.03	.02	.01
397	Scott Terry(FC)	.08	.06	.03
398	Mike Jackson	.06	.05	.02
399	Bobby Thigpen	.08	.06	.03
400	Don Sutton	.12	.09	.05
401	Cecil Espy	.06	.05	.02
402	Junior Ortiz	.03	.02	.01
403	Mike Smithson	.03	.02	.01
404	Bud Black	.03	.02	.01
405	Tom Foley	.03	.02	.01
406	Andres Thomas	.06	.05	.02
407	Rick Sutcliffe	.08	.06	.03
408	Brian Harper	.03	.02	.01
409	John Smiley	.10	.08	.04
410	Juan Nieves	.06	.05	.02
411	Shawn Abner	.08	.06	.03
412	Wes Gardner(FC)	.06	.05	.02
413	Darren Daulton	.03	.02	.01
414	Juan Berenguer	.03	.02	.01
415	Charles Hudson	.03	.02	.01
416	Rick Honeycutt	.03	.02	.01
417	Greg Booker	.03	.02	.01
418	Tim Belcher	.08	.06	.03
419	Don August	.08	.06	.03
420	Dale Mohorcic	.03	.02	.01
421	Steve Lombardozzi	.03	.02	.01
422	Atlee Hammaker	.03	.02	.01
423	Jerry Don Gleaton	.03	.02	.01
424	Scott Bailes(FC)	.03	.02	.01

#	Player	MT	NR MT	EX
425	Bruce Sutter	.08	.06	.03
426	Randy Ready	.03	.02	.01
427	Jerry Reed	.03	.02	.01
428	Bryn Smith	.03	.02	.01
429	Tim Leary	.06	.05	.02
430	Mark Clear	.03	.02	.01
431	Terry Leach	.03	.02	.01
432	John Moses	.03	.02	.01
433	Ozzie Guillen	.06	.05	.02
434	Gene Nelson	.03	.02	.01
435	Gary Ward	.06	.05	.02
436	Luis Aguayo	.03	.02	.01
437	Fernando Valenzuela	.15	.11	.06
438	Jeff Russell	.03	.02	.01
439	Cecilio Guante	.03	.02	.01
440	Don Robinson	.03	.02	.01
441	Rick Anderson(FC)	.03	.02	.01
442	Tom Glavine	.08	.06	.03
443	Daryl Boston	.03	.02	.01
444	Joe Price	.03	.02	.01
445	Stewart Cliburn	.03	.02	.01
446	Manny Trillo	.03	.02	.01
447	Joel Skinner	.03	.02	.01
448	Charlie Puleo	.03	.02	.01
449	Carlton Fisk	.12	.09	.05
450	Will Clark	.50	.40	.20
451	Otis Nixon	.03	.02	.01
452	Rick Schu	.03	.02	.01
453	Todd Stottlemyre	.15	.11	.06
454	Tim Birtsas	.03	.02	.01
455	*Dave Gallagher*	.20	.15	.08
456	Barry Lyons	.03	.02	.01
457	Fred Manrique	.06	.05	.02
458	Ernest Riles	.03	.02	.01
459	*Doug Jennings*(FC)	.20	.15	.08
460	Joe Magrane	.08	.06	.03
461	Jamie Quirk	.03	.02	.01
462	*Jack Armstrong*	.15	.11	.06
463	Bobby Witt	.08	.06	.03
464	Keith Miller	.06	.05	.02
465	*Todd Burns*	.30	.25	.12
466	*John Dopson*	.20	.15	.08
467	Rich Yett	.03	.02	.01
468	Craig Reynolds	.03	.02	.01
469	Dave Bergman	.03	.02	.01
470	Rex Hudler	.03	.02	.01
471	Eric King	.03	.02	.01
472	Joaquin Andujar	.06	.05	.02
473	*Sil Campusano*	.20	.15	.08
474	Terry Mulholland(FC)	.03	.02	.01
475	Mike Flanagan	.06	.05	.02
476	Greg Harris	.03	.02	.01
477	Tommy John	.10	.08	.04
478	Dave Anderson	.03	.02	.01
479	Fred Toliver	.03	.02	.01
480	Jimmy Key	.08	.06	.03
481	Donell Nixon	.03	.02	.01
482	Mark Portugal(FC)	.03	.02	.01
483	Tom Pagnozzi	.06	.05	.02
484	Jeff Kunkel	.03	.02	.01
485	Frank Williams	.03	.02	.01
486	Jody Reed	.10	.08	.04
487	Roberto Kelly	.25	.20	.10
488	Shawn Hillegas	.06	.05	.02
489	Jerry Reuss	.06	.05	.02
490	Mark Davis	.03	.02	.01
491	Jeff Sellers	.03	.02	.01
492	Zane Smith	.06	.05	.02
493	Al Newman(FC)	.03	.02	.01
494	Mike Young	.03	.02	.01
495	Larry Parrish	.06	.05	.02
496	Herm Winningham	.03	.02	.01
497	Carmen Castillo	.03	.02	.01
498	Joe Hesketh	.03	.02	.01
499	Darrell Miller	.03	.02	.01
500	Mike LaCoss	.03	.02	.01
501	Charlie Lea	.03	.02	.01
502	Bruce Benedict	.03	.02	.01
503	Chuck Finley(FC)	.03	.02	.01
504	Brad Wellman(FC)	.03	.02	.01
505	Tim Crews	.06	.05	.02
506	Ken Gerhart	.06	.05	.02
507a	Brian Holton (Born: Jan. 25, 1965 Denver, CO)	.20	.15	.08
507b	Brian Holton (Born: Nov. 29, 1959 McKeesport, PA)	.08	.06	.03
508	Dennis Lamp	.03	.02	.01
509	Bobby Meacham (1984 Games is 099)	.20	.15	.08
509b	Bobby Meacham (1984 Games is 99)	.08	.06	.03
510	Tracy Jones	.08	.06	.03
511	Mike Fitzgerald	.03	.02	.01
512	*Jeff Bittiger*	.12	.09	.05
513	Tim Flannery	.03	.02	.01
514	Ray Hayward(FC)	.03	.02	.01
515	Dave Leiper	.03	.02	.01
516	Rod Scurry	.03	.02	.01
517	Carmelo Martinez	.03	.02	.01
518	Curtis Wilkerson	.03	.02	.01
519	Stan Jefferson	.03	.02	.01
520	Dan Quisenberry	.06	.05	.02
521	Lloyd McClendon(FC)	.03	.02	.01
522	Steve Trout	.03	.02	.01
523	Larry Andersen	.03	.02	.01
524	Don Aase	.03	.02	.01
525	Bob Forsch	.06	.05	.02
526	Geno Petralli	.03	.02	.01
527	Angel Salazar	.03	.02	.01
528	*Mike Schooler*	.20	.15	.08
529	Jose Oquendo	.03	.02	.01
530	Jay Buhner	.10	.08	.04
531	Tom Bolton(FC)	.06	.05	.02
532	Al Nipper	.03	.02	.01
533	Dave Henderson	.08	.06	.03
534	*John Costello*(FC)	.20	.15	.08
535	Donnie Moore	.03	.02	.01
536	Mike Laga	.03	.02	.01
537	Mike Gallego	.03	.02	.01
538	Jim Clancy	.06	.05	.02
539	Joel Youngblood	.03	.02	.01
540	Rick Leach	.03	.02	.01
541	Kevin Romine	.03	.02	.01
542	Mark Salas	.03	.02	.01
543	Greg Minton	.03	.02	.01
544	Dave Palmer	.03	.02	.01
545	Dwayne Murphy	.06	.05	.02
546	Jim Deshaies	.03	.02	.01
547	Don Gordon(FC)	.03	.02	.01
548	*Ricky Jordan*	1.25	.90	.50
549	Mike Boddicker	.06	.05	.02
550	Mike Scott	.10	.08	.04
551	Jeff Ballard(FC)	.08	.06	.03
552a	Jose Rijo (uniform number #24 on card back)	.20	.15	.08
552b	Jose Rijo (uniform number #27 on card back)	.08	.06	.03
553	Danny Darwin	.03	.02	.01
554	Tom Browning	.08	.06	.03
555	Danny Jackson	.12	.09	.05
556	Rick Dempsey	.06	.05	.02
557	Jeffrey Leonard	.06	.05	.02
558	Jeff Musselman	.06	.05	.02
559	Ron Robinson	.03	.02	.01
560	John Tudor	.08	.06	.03
561	Don Slaught	.03	.02	.01
562	Dennis Rasmussen	.08	.06	.03
563	*Brady Anderson*	.30	.25	.12
564	Pedro Guerrero	.12	.09	.05
565	Paul Molitor	.12	.09	.05
566	*Terry Clark*(FC)	.15	.11	.06
567	Terry Puhl	.03	.02	.01
568	Mike Campbell(FC)	.08	.06	.03
569	Paul Mirabella	.03	.02	.01
570	Jeff Hamilton(FC)	.06	.05	.02
571	*Oswald Peraza*	.20	.15	.08
572	Bob McClure	.03	.02	.01
573	*Jose Bautista*(FC)	.15	.11	.06
574	Alex Trevino	.03	.02	.01
575	John Franco	.08	.06	.03
576	*Mark Parent*(FC)	.15	.11	.06
577	Nelson Liriano	.06	.05	.02
578	Steve Shields	.03	.02	.01
579	Odell Jones	.03	.02	.01
580	Al Leiter	.20	.15	.08
581	Dave Stapleton(FC)	.06	.05	.02
582	1988 World Series (Jose Canseco, Kirk Gibson, Orel Hershiser, Dave Stewart)	.20	.15	.08
583	Donnie Hill	.03	.02	.01
584	Chuck Jackson	.06	.05	.02
585	Rene Gonzales(FC)	.06	.05	.02
586	Tracy Woodson(FC)	.08	.06	.03
587	Jim Adduci(FC)	.03	.02	.01
588	Mario Soto	.06	.05	.02
589	Jeff Blauser	.08	.06	.03
590	Jim Traber	.06	.05	.02
591	Jon Perlman	.03	.02	.01
592	Mark Williamson(FC)	.06	.05	.02
593	Dave Meads	.03	.02	.01
594	Jim Eisenreich	.03	.02	.01
595	*Paul Gibson*(FC)	.15	.11	.06
596	Mike Birkbeck	.03	.02	.01

		MT	NR MT	EX
597	Terry Francona	.03	.02	.01
598	Paul Zuvella(FC)	.03	.02	.01
599	Franklin Stubbs	.03	.02	.01
600	Gregg Jefferies	1.50	1.25	.60
601	John Cangelosi	.03	.02	.01
602	Mike Sharperson(FC)	.03	.02	.01
603	Mike Diaz	.06	.05	.02
604	*Gary Varsho(FC)*	.20	.15	.08
605	*Terry Blocker(FC)*	.12	.09	.05
606	Charlie O'Brien(FC)	.03	.02	.01
607	Jim Eppard(FC)	.08	.06	.03
608	John Davis	.03	.02	.01
609	Ken Griffey, Sr.	.08	.06	.03
610	Buddy Bell	.06	.05	.02
611	Ted Simmons	.08	.06	.03
612	Matt Williams	.10	.08	.04
613	Danny Cox	.06	.05	.02
614	Al Pedrique	.03	.02	.01
615	Ron Oester	.03	.02	.01
616	*John Smoltz(FC)*	.50	.40	.20
617	Bob Melvin	.03	.02	.01
618	*Rob Dibble*	.20	.15	.08
619	Kirt Manwaring	.10	.08	.04
620	1989 Rookie (Felix Fermin)(FC)	.06	.05	.02
621	1989 Rookie *(Doug Dascenzo)(FC)*	.25	.20	.10
622	1989 Rookie *(Bill Brennan)(FC)*	.20	.15	.08
623	1989 Rookie *(Carlos Quintana)(FC)*	.35	.25	.14
624	1989 Rookie *(Mike Harkey)(FC)*	.30	.25	.12
625	1989 Rookie *(Gary Sheffield)(FC)*	1.25	.90	.50
626	1989 Rookie *(Tom Prince)(FC)*	.08	.06	.03
627	1989 Rookie *(Steve Searcy)(FC)*	.25	.20	.10
628	1989 Rookie *(Charlie Hayes)(FC)*	.15	.11	.06
629	1989 Rookie *(Felix Jose)(FC)*	.20	.15	.08
630	1989 Rookie *(Sandy Alomar)(FC)*	1.25	.90	.50
631	1989 Rookie *(Derek Lilliquist)(FC)*	.40	.30	.15
632	1989 Rookie (Geronimo Berroa)(FC)	.06	.05	.02
633	1989 Rookie *(Luis Medina)(FC)*	.35	.25	.14
634	1989 Rookie *(Tom Gordon)(FC)*	1.25	.90	.50
635	1989 Rookie *(Ramon Martinez)(FC)*	.35	.25	.14
636	1989 Rookie *(Craig Worthington)(FC)*	.50	.40	.20
637	1989 Rookie (Edgar Martinez)(FC)	.10	.08	.04
638	1989 Rookie *(Chad Krueter)(FC)*	.20	.15	.08
639	1989 Rookie *(Ron Jones)(FC)*	.30	.25	.12
640	1989 Rookie *(Van Snider)(FC)*	.20	.15	.08
641	1989 Rookie *(Lance Blankenship)(FC)*	.25	.20	.10
642	1989 Rookie *(Dwight Smith)(FC)*	3.00	2.25	1.25
643	1989 Rookie *(Cameron Drew)(FC)*	.20	.15	.08
644	1989 Rookie *(Jerald Clark)(FC)*	.20	.15	.08
645	1989 Rookie *(Randy Johnson)(FC)*	.25	.20	.10
646	1989 Rookie *(Norm Charlton)(FC)*	.20	.15	.08
647	1989 Rookie *(Todd Frohwirth)(FC)*	.08	.06	.03
648	1989 Rookie *(Luis de los Santos)(FC)*	.20	.15	.08
649	1989 Rookie *(Tim Jones)(FC)*	.15	.11	.06
650	1989 Rookie *(Dave West)(FC)*	.50	.40	.20
651	1989 Rookie *(Bob Milacki)(FC)*	.25	.20	.10
652	1988 Highlight (Wrigley Field)	.06	.05	.02
653	1988 Highlight (Orel Hershiser)	.10	.08	.04
654a	1988 Highlight (Wade Boggs) ("...sixth consecutive seaason..." on back)	1.00	.70	.40
654b	1988 Highlight (Wade Boggs) ("...sixth consecutive season..." on back)	.30	.25	.12
655	1988 Highlight (Jose Canseco)	.60	.45	.25
656	1988 Highlight (Doug Jones)	.06	.05	.02
657	1988 Highlight (Rickey Henderson)	.12	.09	.05
658	1988 Highlight (Tom Browning)	.06	.05	.02
659	1988 Highlight (Mike Greenwell)	.30	.25	.12
660	1988 Highlight (A.L. Win Streak)	.06	.05	.02

1989 Score Traded

Score issued its second consecutive traded set in 1989 to supplement and update its regular set. The 110-card traded set features the same basic card design as the regular 1989 Score set. The set consists of rookies and traded players pictured with correct teams. The set was sold by hobby dealers in a special box that included an assortment of "Magic Motion" trivia cards.

		MT	NR MT	EX
Complete Set:		15.00	11.00	6.00
Common Player:		.06	.05	.02
1T	Rafael Palmeiro	.10	.08	.04
2T	Nolan Ryan	1.50	1.25	.60
3T	Jack Clark	.10	.08	.04
4T	Dave LaPoint	.06	.05	.02
5T	Mike Moore	.08	.06	.03
6T	Pete O'Brien	.06	.05	.02
7T	Jeffrey Leonard	.06	.05	.02
8T	Rob Murphy	.06	.05	.02
9T	Tom Herr	.06	.05	.02
10T	Claudell Washington	.06	.05	.02
11T	Mike Pagliarulo	.06	.05	.02
12T	Steve Lake	.06	.05	.02
13T	Spike Owen	.06	.05	.02
14T	Andy Hawkins	.06	.05	.02
15T	Todd Benzinger	.06	.05	.02
16T	Mookie Wilson	.06	.05	.03
17T	Bert Blyleven	.08	.06	.03
18T	Jeff Treadway	.06	.05	.02
19T	Bruce Hurst	.08	.06	.03
20T	Steve Sax	.12	.09	.05
21T	Juan Samuel	.06	.05	.02
22T	Jesse Barfield	.06	.05	.02
23T	Carmelo Castillo	.06	.05	.02
24T	Terry Leach	.06	.05	.02
25T	Mark Langston	.12	.09	.05
26T	Eric King	.06	.05	.02
27T	Steve Balboni	.06	.05	.02
28T	Len Dykstra	.06	.05	.02
29T	Keith Moreland	.06	.05	.02
30T	Terry Kennedy	.06	.05	.02
31T	Eddie Murray	.12	.09	.05
32T	Mitch Williams	.10	.08	.04
33T	Jeff Parrett	.06	.05	.02
34T	Wally Backman	.06	.05	.02
35T	Julio Franco	.10	.08	.04
36T	Lance Parrish	.06	.05	.02
37T	Nick Esasky	.06	.05	.02
38T	Luis Polonia	.06	.05	.02
39T	Kevin Gross	.06	.05	.02
40T	John Dopson	.06	.05	.02
41T	Willie Randolph	.08	.06	.03
42T	Jim Clancy	.06	.05	.02
43T	Tracy Jones	.06	.05	.02
44T	Phil Bradley	.06	.05	.02
45T	Milt Thompson	.06	.05	.02
46T	Chris James	.06	.05	.02
47T	Scott Fletcher	.06	.05	.02
48T	Kal Daniels	.08	.06	.03
49T	Steve Bedrosian	.06	.05	.02
50T	Rickey Henderson	.40	.30	.15
51T	Dion James	.06	.05	.02
52T	Tim Leary	.06	.05	.02
53T	Roger McDowell	.06	.05	.02
54T	Mel Hall	.06	.05	.02
55T	Dickie Thon	.06	.05	.02
56T	Zane Smith	.06	.05	.02
57T	Danny Heep	.06	.05	.02
58T	Bob McClure	.06	.05	.02
59T	Brian Holton	.06	.05	.02
60T	Randy Ready	.06	.05	.02
61T	Bob Melvin	.06	.05	.02
62T	Harold Baines	.08	.06	.03
63T	Lance McCullers	.06	.05	.02
64T	Jody Davis	.06	.05	.02
65T	Darrell Evans	.06	.05	.02
66T	Joel Youngblood	.08	.06	.03
67T	Frank Viola	.08	.06	.03
68T	Mike Aldrete	.06	.05	.02

		MT	NR MT	EX
69T	Greg Cadaret	.06	.05	.02
70T	John Kruk	.06	.05	.02
71T	Pat Sheridan	.06	.05	.02
72T	Oddibe McDowell	.06	.05	.02
73T	Tom Brookens	.06	.05	.02
74T	Bob Boone	.08	.06	.03
75T	Walt Terrell	.06	.05	.02
76T	Joel Skinner	.06	.05	.02
77T	Randy Johnson	.10	.08	.04
78T	Felix Fermin	.06	.05	.03
79T	Rick Mahler	.06	.05	.03
80T	Rich Dotson	.06	.05	.03
81T	Cris Carpenter(FC)	.20	.15	.08
82T	Bill Spiers(FC)	.35	.25	.14
83T	Junior Felix(FC)	1.25	.90	.50
84T	Joe Girardi(FC)	.30	.25	.12
85T	Jerome Walton(FC)	4.00	3.00	1.50
86T	Greg Litton(FC)	.25	.20	.10
87T	Greg Harris(FC)	.20	.15	.08
88T	Jim Abbott(FC)	2.50	2.00	1.00
89T	Kevin Brown(FC)	.20	.15	.08
90T	John Wetteland(FC)	.50	.40	.20
91T	Gary Wayne(FC)	.20	.15	.08
92T	Rich Monteleone(FC)	.25	.20	.10
93T	Bob Geren(FC)	.50	.40	.20
94T	Clay Parker(FC)	.20	.15	.08
95T	Steve Finley(FC)	.35	.25	.14
96T	Gregg Olson(FC)	1.25	.90	.50
97T	Ken Patterson(FC)	.15	.11	.06
98T	Ken Hill(FC)	.20	.15	.08
99T	Scott Scudder(FC)	.35	.25	.14
100T	Ken Griffey, Jr.(FC)	3.50	2.75	1.50
101T	Jeff Brantley(FC)	.25	.20	.10
102T	Donn Pall(FC)	.15	.11	.06
103T	Carlos Martinez(FC)	.25	.20	.10
104T	Joe Oliver(FC)	.30	.25	.12
105T	Omar Vizquel(FC)	.25	.20	.10
106T	Joey Belle(FC)	1.25	.90	.50
107T	Kenny Rogers(FC)	.20	.15	.08
108T	Mark Carreon(FC)	.15	.11	.06
109T	Rolando Roomes(FC)	.30	.25	.12
110T	Pete Harnsisch(FC)	.20	.15	.08

1989 Score Young Superstar - Series I

This standard-size card set (2-1/2" by 3-1/2") displays full-color action photos with a high gloss finish. The card fronts feature a red and blue border surrounding the photo with the team logo in the lower right. A red band beneath the photo provided the setting for the player ID including name, position, and team number. The flip side features a red "Young Superstar" headline above a close-up photo. Above the headline, appears the player's personal information and statistics in orange and black ink respectively. The top of the flip side highlights the player's name and the Score logo in white within a purple band. To the right of the close-up photo a condensed scouting report and career highlights are revealed. The card number and related logos appear on the bottom portion. Five trivia cards featuring "A Year to Remember" accompanied the series. Each trivia card relates to a highlight from the past 56 years. This set was distributed via a write-in offer with Score card wrappers.

		MT	NR MT	EX
Complete Set:		8.00	6.00	3.25
Common Player:		.10	.08	.04
1	Gregg Jefferies	1.00	.70	.40
2	Jody Reed	.10	.08	.04
3	Mark Grace	.40	.30	.15
4	Dave Gallagher	.15	.11	.06
5	Bo Jackson	1.00	.70	.40
6	Jay Buhner	.10	.08	.04
7	Melido Perez	.10	.08	.04
8	Bobby Witt	.10	.08	.04
9	David Cone	.15	.11	.06
10	Chris Sabo	.15	.11	.06
11	Pat Borders	.10	.08	.04
12	Mark Grant	.10	.08	.04
13	Mike Macfarlane	.10	.08	.04
14	Mike Jackson	.10	.08	.04
15	Ricky Jordan	.30	.25	.12
16	Ron Gant	.10	.08	.04
17	Al Leiter	.10	.08	.04
18	Jeff Parrett	.10	.08	.04
19	Pete Smith	.10	.08	.04
20	Walt Weiss	.15	.11	.06
21	Doug Drabek	.12	.09	.05
22	Kirt Manwaring	.15	.11	.06
23	Keith Miller	.10	.08	.04
24	Damon Berryhill	.12	.09	.05
25	Gary Sheffield	1.00	.70	.40
26	Brady Anderson	.20	.15	.08
27	Mitch Williams	.15	.11	.06
28	Roberto Alomar	.30	.25	.12
29	Bobby Thigpen	.12	.09	.05
30	Bryan Harvey	.10	.08	.04
31	Jose Rijo	.15	.11	.06
32	Dave West	.35	.25	.12
33	Joey Meyer	.10	.08	.04
34	Allan Anderson	.12	.09	.05
35	Rafael Palmeiro	.20	.15	.08
36	Tim Belcher	.30	.25	.12
37	John Smiley	.15	.11	.06
38	Mackey Sasser	.10	.08	.04
39	Greg Maddux	.30	.25	.12
40	Ramon Martinez	.60	.45	.25
41	Randy Myers	.12	.09	.05
42	Scott Bankhead	.15	.11	.06

1989 Score Young Superstar - Series II

		MT	NR MT	EX
Complete Set:		7.00	5.25	2.75
Common Player:		.10	.08	.04
1	Sandy Alomar	.60	.45	.25
2	Tom Gordon, Tom Gordon	.60	.45	.25
3	Ron Jones, Ron Jones	.30	.25	.12
4	Todd Burns	.10	.08	.04
5	Paul O'Neill	.10	.08	.04
6	Gene Larkin	.10	.08	.04
7	Eric King	.10	.08	.04
8	Jeff Robinson	.10	.08	.04
9	Bill Wegman	.10	.08	.04
10	Cecil Espy	.12	.09	.05
11	Jose Guzman	.10	.08	.04
12	Kelly Gruber	.20	.15	.08
13	Duane Ward	.10	.08	.04
14	Mark Gubicza	.25	.20	.10
15	Norm Charlton	.20	.15	.08
16	Jose Oquendo	.10	.08	.04

		MT	NR MT	EX
17	Geronimo Berroa	.15	.11	.06
18	Dwight Smith	1.00	.70	.40
19	Lance McCullers	.10	.08	.04
20	Jimmy Jones	.10	.08	.04
21	Craig Worthington	.25	.20	.10
22	Mike Devereaux	.12	.09	.05
23	Bob Milacki	.15	.11	.06
24	Dale Sveum	.10	.08	.04
25	Carlos Quintana	.20	.15	.08
26	Luis Medina	.15	.11	.06
27	Steve Searcy	.15	.11	.06
28	Don August	.10	.08	.04
29	Shawn Hillegas	.10	.08	.04
30	Mike Campbell	.10	.08	.04
31	Mike Harkey	.25	.20	.10
32	Randy Johnson	.20	.15	.08
33	Craig Biggio	.35	.25	.12
34	Mike Schooler	.12	.09	.05
35	Andres Thomas	.10	.08	.04
36	Van Snider	.20	.15	.08
37	Cameron Drew	.15	.11	.06
38	Kevin Mitchell	.70	.50	.30
39	Lance Johnson	.15	.11	.06
40	Chad Kreuter	.20	.15	.08
41	Danny Jackson	.10	.08	.04
42	Kurt Stillwell	.10	.08	.04

1989 Score Rising Star

Similar in design to the Score Superstar set, this 100-card set showcased a host of rookies including Gary Sheffield and Gregg Jefferies. The full-color action photos are surrounded by a bright blue border with a green inner highlight line. The Score logo appears in the upper left in green and white. The player's name, position and team are found at the bottom. The flip sides display a full-color close-up of the player above his name and career highlights. The card number and player's rookie year are featured to the right. A "Rising Star" headline highlights the top border. Like the "Score Superstar" the Score "Rising Star" set was marketed as a combination with a related magazine. "1988-89 Baseball's 100 Hottest Rookies" accompanies the set which also includes six Magic Motion baseball trivia cards featuring "Rookies to Remember." The magazine/card sets were available at a select group of retailers.

		MT	NR MT	EX
Complete Set:		12.00	9.00	4.75
Common Player:		.07	.05	.03
1	Gregg Jefferies	.80	.60	.30
2	Vicente Palacios	.15	.11	.06
3	Cameron Drew	.25	.20	.10
4	Doug Dascenzo	.12	.09	.05
5	Luis Medina	.12	.09	.05
6	Craig Worthington	.20	.15	.08
7	Rob Ducey	.08	.06	.04
8	Hal Morris	.10	.08	.04
9	Bill Brennan	.07	.05	.03
10	Gary Sheffield	.80	.60	.30
11	Mike Devereaux	.10	.08	.04
12	Hensley Meulens	.40	.30	.15
13	Carlos Quintana	.20	.15	.08
14	Todd Frohwirth	.07	.05	.03
15	Scott Lusader	.09	.07	.04

		MT	NR MT	EX
16	Mark Carreon	.15	.11	.06
17	Torey Lovullo	.20	.15	.08
18	Randy Velarde	.12	.09	.05
19	Billy Bean	.09	.07	.04
20	Lance Blankenship	.15	.11	.06
21	Chris Gwynn	.15	.11	.06
22	Felix Jose	.20	.15	.08
23	Derek Lilliquist	.20	.15	.08
24	Gary Thurman	.07	.05	.03
25	Ron Jones	.20	.15	.08
26	Dave Justice	.40	.30	.15
27	Johnny Paredes	.08	.06	.03
28	Tim Jones	.10	.08	.04
29	Jose Gonzalez	.40	.30	.15
30	Geronimo Berroa	.15	.11	.06
31	Trevor Wilson	.12	.09	.05
32	Morris Madden	.30	.25	.12
33	Lance Johnson	.15	.11	.06
34	Marvin Freeman	.07	.05	.03
35	Jose Cecena	.07	.05	.03
36	Jim Corsi	.07	.05	.03
37	Rolando Roomes	.25	.20	.10
38	Scott Medvin	.07	.05	.03
39	Charlie Hayes	.20	.15	.08
40	Edgar Martinez	.15	.11	.06
41	Van Snider	.20	.15	.08
42	John Fishel	.07	.05	.02
43	Bruce Fields	.07	.05	.03
44	Darryl Hamilton	.09	.07	.04
45	Tom Prince	.09	.07	.03
46	Kirt Manwaring	.20	.15	.08
47	Steve Searcy	.12	.09	.05
48	Mike Harkey	.20	.15	.08
49	German Gonzalez	.07	.05	.03
50	Tony Perezchica	.07	.05	.03
51	Chad Kreuter	.15	.11	.06
52	Luis de los Santos	.10	.08	.04
53	Steve Curry	.07	.05	.03
54	Greg Bailey	.30	.25	.12
55	Ramon Martinez	.30	.25	.12
56	Ron Tingley	.07	.05	.03
57	Randy Kramer	.07	.05	.03
58	Alex Madrid	.07	.05	.03
59	Kevin Reimer	.15	.11	.06
60	Dave Otto	.07	.05	.03
61	Ken Patterson	.07	.05	.03
62	Keith Miller	.10	.08	.04
63	Randy Johnson	.10	.08	.04
64	Dwight Smith	1.00	.70	.40
65	Eric Yelding	.20	.15	.08
66	Bob Geren	.40	.30	.15
67	Shane Turner	.25	.20	.10
68	Tom Gordon	.70	.50	.30
69	Jeff Huson	.30	.25	.12
70	Marty Brown	.25	.20	.10
71	Nelson Santovenia	.20	.15	.08
72	Roberto Alomar	.20	.15	.08
73	Mike Schooler	.15	.11	.06
74	Pete Smith	.10	.08	.04
75	John Costello	.07	.05	.03
76	Chris Sabo	.20	.15	.08
77	Damon Berryhill	.09	.07	.04
78	Mark Grace	.60	.45	.25
79	Melido Perez	.07	.05	.03
80	Al Leiter	.07	.05	.03
81	Todd Stottlemyre	.20	.15	.08
82	Mackey Sasser	.07	.05	.03
83	Don August	.07	.05	.03
84	Jeff Treadway	.07	.05	.03
85	Jody Reed	.09	.07	.05
86	Mike Campbell	.07	.05	.03
87	Ron Gant	.09	.07	.04
88	Ricky Jordan	.30	.25	.12
89	Terry Clark	.07	.05	.03
90	Roberto Kelly	.20	.15	.08
91	Pat Borders	.20	.15	.08
92	Bryan Harvey	.20	.15	.08
93	Joey Meyer	.20	.15	.08
94	Tim Belcher	.25	.20	.10
95	Walt Weiss	.15	.11	.06
96	Dave Gallagher	.15	.11	.06
97	Mike Macfarlane	.07	.05	.03
98	Craig Biggio	.30	.25	.12
99	Jack Armstrong	.07	.05	.03
100	Todd Burns	.07	.05	.03

Definitions for grading conditions are located in the Introduction section at the front of this book.

1989 Score Superstar

This 100-card set features full-color action photos of baseball's superstars, and also includes six Magic Motion "Rookies to Remember" baseball trivia cards. The card fronts contain a bright red border with a blue line inside highlighting the photo. The score logo appears in the bottom left corner. The player ID is displayed in unique fashion using overlapping triangles in white, green, and yellow. The flip side features a full-color player close-up directly beneath a bright red "Superstar" headline. The set was marketed along with the magazine "1989 Baseball's 100 Hottest Players". The magazine/card set combo was available at select retailers.

		MT	NR MT	EX
Complete Set:		10.00	7.50	4.00
Common Player:		.06	.05	.02
1	Jose Canseco	1.00	.70	.40
2	David Cone	.15	.11	.06
3	Dave Winfield	.15	.11	.06
4	George Brett	.15	.11	.06
5	Frank Viola	.09	.07	.05
6	Cory Snyder	.06	.05	.02
7	Alan Trammell	.09	.07	.04
8	Dwight Evans	.09	.07	.04
9	Tim Leary	.06	.05	.03
10	Don Mattingly	1.25	.90	.50
11	Kirby Puckett	.30	.25	.12
12	Carney Lansford	.06	.05	.02
13	Dennis Martinez	.06	.05	.02
14	Kent Hrbek	.10	.08	.04
15	Doc Gooden	.30	.25	.12
16	Dennis Eckersley	.08	.06	.03
17	Kevin Seitzer	.08	.06	.03
18	Lee Smith	.06	.05	.02
19	Danny Tartabull	.15	.11	.06
20	Gerald Perry	.06	.05	.02
21	Gary Gaetti	.10	.08	.04
22	Rick Reuschel	.08	.06	.03
23	Keith Hernandez	.08	.06	.03
24	Jeff Reardon	.06	.05	.02
25	Mark McGwire	.80	.60	.30
26	Juan Samuel	.06	.05	.02
27	Jack Clark	.06	.05	.02
28	Robin Yount	.15	.11	.06
29	Steve Bedrosian	.06	.05	.02
30	Kirk Gibson	.08	.06	.03
31	Barry Bonds	.08	.06	.03
32	Dan Plesac	.06	.05	.02
33	Steve Sax	.06	.05	.02
34	Jeff Robinson	.06	.05	.02
35	Orel Hershiser	.10	.08	.04
36	Julio Franco	.08	.06	.03
37	Dave Righetti	.06	.05	.02
38	Bob Knepper	.06	.05	.02
39	Carlton Fisk	.08	.06	.03
41	Doug Jones	.06	.05	.02
42	Bobby Bonilla	.20	.15	.08
43	Ellis Burks	.30	.25	.12
44	Pedro Guerrero	.15	.11	.06
45	Rickey Henderson	.25	.20	.12
46	Glenn Davis	.10	.08	.04
47	Benny Santiago	.15	.11	.06
48	Greg Maddux	.20	.15	.08
49	Teddy Higuera	.06	.05	.02
50	Darryl Strawberry	.30	.25	.12
51	Mike Scott	.08	.06	.03

		MT	NR MT	EX
52	Mike Henneman	.06	.05	.02
53	Eric Davis	.35	.25	.12
54	Paul Molitor	.09	.07	.04
55	Rafael Palmeiro	.06	.05	.02
56	Joe Carter	.09	.07	.05
57	Ryne Sandberg	.15	.11	.06
58	Tony Fernandez	.08	.06	.03
59	Barry larkin	.10	.08	.04
60	Ozzie Guillen	.06	.05	.02
61	Tom Browning	.06	.05	.02
62	Mark Davis	.08	.06	.03
63	Tom Henke	.06	.05	.02
64	Nolan Ryan	.60	.45	.25
65	Fred McGriff	.30	.25	.12
66	Dale Murphy	.10	.08	.06
67	Mark Langston	.10	.08	.06
68	Bobby Thigpen	.06	.05	.02
69	Mark Gubicza	.08	.06	.03
70	Mike Greenwell	.50	.40	.20
71	Ron Darling	.06	.05	.02
72	Gerald Young	.06	.05	.02
73	Wally Joyner	.10	.08	.04
74	Andres Galarraga	.10	.08	.04
75	Danny Jackson	.06	.05	.02
76	Mike Schmidt	.25	.20	.10
77	Cal Ripken Jr.	.15	.11	.06
78	Alvin Davis	.08	.06	.03
79	Bruce Hurst	.06	.05	.02
80	Andre Dawson	.12	.09	.05
81	Bob Boone	.06	.05	.02
82	Harold Reynolds	.06	.05	.02
83	Eddie Murray	.06	.05	.02
84	Robby Thompson	.06	.05	.02
85	Will Clark	1.00	.70	.40
86	Vince Coleman	.09	.07	.04
87	Doug Drabek	.06	.05	.02
88	Ozzie Smith	.08	.06	.03
89	Bob Welch	.06	.05	.02
90	Roger Clemens	.25	.20	.10
91	George Bell	.08	.06	.03
92	Andy Van Slyke	.08	.06	.03
93	Willie McGee	.06	.05	.02
94	Todd Worrell	.06	.05	.02
95	Tim Raines	.06	.05	.02
96	Kevin McReynolds	.10	.08	.04
97	John Franco	.06	.05	.02
98	Jim Gott	.06	.05	.02
99	Johnny Ray	.06	.05	.02
100	Wade Boggs	.80	.60	.30

1989 Score Yankees

This 33-card New York Yankee team set was produced by Score as an in-stadium promotion in 1989 and was distributed to fans attending the July 29 game at Yankee Stadium. The standard-size cards include a full-color player photo with a line drawing of the famous Yankee Stadium facade running along the top of the card. The player's name, "New York Yankees" and position appear below the photo. A second full-color photo is included on the back of the card, along with stats, data and a brief player profile. The set includes a special Thurman Munson commemorative card.

	MT	NR MT	EX
Complete Set:	8.00	6.00	3.25

		MT	NR MT	EX
	Complete Set:	8.00	6.00	3.25
	Common Player:	.15	.11	.06
1	Don Mattingly	1.75	1.25	.70
2	Steve Sax	.30	.25	.12
3	Alvaro Espinoza	.40	.30	.15
4	Luis Polonia	.20	.15	.08
5	Jesse Barfield	.25	.20	.10
6	Dave Righetti	.25	.20	.10
7	Dave Winfield	.25	.20	.10
8	John Candelaria	.15	.11	.06
9	Wayne Tolleson	.15	.11	.06
10	Ken Phelps	.15	.11	.06
11	Rafael Santana	.15	.11	.06
12	Don Slaught	.15	.11	.06
13	Mike Pagliarulo	.20	.15	.08
14	Lance McCullers	.20	.15	.08
15	Dave LaPoint	.20	.15	.08
16	Dale Mohorcic	.15	.11	.06
17	Steve Balboni	.15	.11	.06
18	Roberto Kelly	.50	.40	.20
19	Andy Hawkins	.25	.20	.10
20	Mel Hall	.20	.15	.08
21	Tom Brookens	.15	.11	.06
22	Deion Sanders	1.00	.70	.40
23	Richard Dotson	.15	.11	.06
24	Lee Guetterman	.15	.11	.06
25	Bob Geren	.50	.40	.20
26	Jimmy Jones	.20	.15	.08
27	Chuck Cary	.20	.15	.08
28	Ron Guidry	.25	.20	.10
29	Hal Morris	.25	.20	.10
30	Clay Parker	.25	.20	.10
31	Dallas Green	.20	.15	.08
32	Thurman Munson (a Tribute)	.70	.50	.30
33	Sponsor Card	.15	.11	.06

		MT	NR MT	EX
	Complete Set:	22.00	16.50	8.75
	Common Player:	.04	.03	.02
1	Don Mattingly	1.50	1.25	.60
2	Cal Ripken Jr.	.25	.20	.10
3	Dwight Evans	.08	.06	.03
4	Barry Bonds	.12	.09	.05
5	Kevin McReynolds	.12	.09	.05
6	Ozzie Guillen	.05	.04	.02
7	Terry Kennedy	.04	.03	.02
8	Bryan Harvey	.06	.05	.02
9	Alan Trammell	.09	.07	.04
10	Cory Snyder	.09	.07	.04
11	Jody Reed	.05	.04	.02
12	Roberto Alomar	.20	.15	.08
13	Pedro Guerrero	.09	.07	.04
14	Gary Redus	.04	.03	.02
15	Marty Barrett	.05	.04	.02
16	Ricky Jordan	.35	.25	.12
17	Joe Magrane	.07	.05	.03
18	Sid Fernandez	.07	.05	.03
19	Rich Dotson	.04	.03	.02
20	Jack Clark	.09	.07	.04
21	Bob Walk	.05	.04	.02
22	Ron Karkovice	.04	.03	.02
23	Lenny Harris(FC)	.20	.15	.08
24	Phil Bradley	.06	.05	.02
25	Andres Galarraga	.15	.11	.06
26	Brian Downing	.06	.05	.02
27	Dave Martinez	.06	.05	.02
28	Eric King	.04	.03	.02
29	Barry Lyons	.04	.03	.02
30	Dave Schmidt	.04	.03	.02
31	Mike Boddicker	.06	.05	.04
32	Tom Foley	.04	.03	.02
33	Brady Anderson	.07	.05	.03
34	Jim Presley	.05	.04	.02
35	Lance Parrish	.06	.05	.02
36	Von Hayes	.09	.07	.03
37	Lee Smith	.06	.05	.02
38	Herm Winningham	.04	.03	.02
39	Alejandro Pena	.04	.03	.02
40	Mike Scott	.09	.07	.04
41	Joe Orsulak	.04	.03	.02
42	Rafael Ramirez	.05	.04	.02
43	Gerald Young	.05	.04	.02
44	Dick Schofield	.05	.04	.02
45	Dave Smith	.06	.05	.02
46	Dave Magadan	.07	.05	.03
47	Dennis Martinez	.06	.05	.02
48	Greg Minton	.04	.03	.02
49	Milt Thompson	.04	.03	.02
50	Orel Hershiser	.12	.09	.05
51	Bip Roberts(FC)	.09	.07	.04
52	Jerry Browne	.09	.07	.04
53	Bob Ojeda	.05	.04	.02
54	Fernando Valenzuela	.09	.07	.04
55	Matt Nokes	.09	.07	.04
56	Brook Jacoby	.08	.06	.03
57	Frank Tanana	.05	.04	.02
58	Scott Fletcher	.05	.04	.02
59	Ron Oester	.05	.04	.02
60	Bob Boone	.08	.06	.03
61	Dan Gladden	.08	.06	.03
62	Darnell Coles	.04	.03	.02
63	Gregg Olson	.60	.45	.25
64	Todd Burns	.05	.04	.02
65	Todd Benzinger	.07	.05	.03
66	Dale Murphy	.12	.09	.05
67	Mike Flanagan	.06	.05	.02
68	Jose Oquendo	.06	.05	.02
69	Cecil Espy	.08	.06	.03
70	Chris Sabo	.20	.15	.08
71	Shane Rawley	.05	.04	.02
72	Tom Brunansky	.08	.06	.03
73	Vance Law	.05	.04	.02
74	B.J. Surhoff	.08	.06	.03
75	Lou Whitaker	.09	.07	.04
76	Ken Caminiti	.09	.07	.04
77	Nelson Liriano	.04	.03	.02
78	Tommy Gregg	.09	.07	.04
79	Don Slaught	.05	.04	.02
80	Eddie Murray	.12	.09	.05
81	Joe Boever	.08	.06	.02
82	Charlie Leibrandt	.06	.05	.02
83	Jose Lind	.06	.05	.02
84	Tony Phillips	.05	.04	.02
85	Mitch Webster	.04	.03	.02
86	Dan Plesac	.07	.05	.02
87	Rick Mahler	.05	.04	.02
88	Steve Lyons	.05	.04	.02

1990 Score

The regular Score set increased to 704 cards in 1990. Included were a series of cards picturing first-round draft picks, an expanded subset of rookie cards, four World Series specials, five Highlight cards, and a 13-card "Dream Team" series featuring the game's top players pictured on old tobacco-style cards. For the first time in a Score set, team logos are displayed on the card fronts in the lower right corner. Card backs again include a full-color portrait photo with player data. A one-paragraph write-up of each player was again provide by former Sports Illustrated editor Les Woodcock. The Score set was again distributed with "Magic Motion" triva cards, this year using "Baseball's Most Valuable Players" as its theme. Following the pattern established for its premiere set in 1989, Upper Deck again issued a 700-card set before the start of the 1990 season and announced plans to release a final 100-card series in late summer. The set again features full-color glossy photos on both front and back. There are 26 special "Star Rookie" cards, along with a pair of specials highlighting Will Clark and Bo Jackson, the top vote-getters in the 1989 All-Star Game balloting. Special cards also pay tribute to Nolan Ryan and Mike Schmidt. The team checklist cards feature the artwork of Vernon Wells.

#	Player	MT	NR MT	EX
89	Tony Fernandez	.09	.07	.04
90	Ryne Sandberg	.20	.15	.08
91	Nick Esasky	.09	.07	.04
92	Luis Salazar	.04	.03	.02
93	Pete Incaviglia	.08	.06	.03
94	Ivan Calderon	.06	.05	.02
95	Jeff Treadway	.06	.05	.02
96	Kurt Stillwell	.06	.05	.02
97	Gary Sheffield	.50	.40	.20
98	Jeffrey Leonard	.07	.05	.03
99	Andres Thomas	.05	.04	.02
100	Roberto Kelly	.15	.11	.06
101	*Alvaro Espinosa*(FC)	.25	.20	.10
102	Greg Gagne	.05	.04	.02
103	John Farrell	.05	.04	.02
104	Willie Wilson	.05	.04	.02
105	Glenn Braggs	.08	.06	.03
106	Chet Lemon	.06	.05	.02
107	Jamie Moyer	.06	.05	.02
108	Chuck Crim	.04	.03	.02
109	Dave Valle	.04	.03	.02
110	Walt Weiss	.15	.11	.06
111	Larry Sheets	.04	.03	.02
112	Don Robinson	.05	.04	.02
113	Danny Heep	.04	.03	.02
114	Carmelo Martinez	.06	.05	.02
115	Dave Gallagher	.08	.06	.03
116	Mike LaValliere	.05	.04	.02
117	Bob McClure	.04	.03	.02
118	Rene Gonzales	.04	.03	.02
119	Mark Parent	.05	.04	.02
120	Wally Joyner	.15	.11	.06
121	Mark Gubicza	.09	.07	.04
122	Tony Pena	.08	.06	.03
123	Carmen Castillo	.04	.03	.02
124	Howard Johnson	.20	.15	.08
125	Steve Sax	.10	.08	.04
126	Tim Belcher	.10	.08	.04
127	Tim Burke	.06	.05	.02
128	Al Newman	.04	.03	.02
129	Dennis Rasmussen	.05	.04	.02
130	Doug Jones	.06	.05	.02
131	Fred Lynn	.09	.07	.04
132	Jeff Hamilton	.06	.05	.02
133	German Gonzalez	.05	.04	.02
134	John Morris	.05	.04	.02
135	Dave Parker	.10	.08	.04
136	Gary Pettis	.05	.04	.02
137	Dennis Boyd	.07	.05	.02
138	Candy Maldonado	.06	.05	.02
139	Rick Cerone	.04	.03	.02
140	George Brett	.15	.11	.06
141	Dave Clark	.05	.04	.02
142	Dickie Thon	.05	.04	.02
143	Junior Ortiz	.04	.03	.02
144	Don August	.06	.05	.02
145	Gary Gaetti	.10	.08	.04
146	Kirt Manwaring	.12	.09	.05
147	Jeff Reed	.04	.03	.02
148	Jose Alvarez(FC)	.08	.06	.03
149	Mike Schooler	.08	.06	.03
150	Mark Grace	.50	.40	.20
151	Geronimo Berroa	.08	.06	.03
152	Barry Jones	.04	.03	.02
153	Geno Petralli	.05	.04	.02
154	Jim Deshaies	.08	.06	.03
155	Barry Larkin	.15	.11	.06
156	Alfredo Griffin	.05	.04	.02
157	Tom Henke	.06	.05	.02
158	Mike Jeffcoat(FC)	.05	.04	.02
159	Bob Welch	.09	.07	.04
160	Julio Franco	.10	.08	.04
161	Henry Cotto	.04	.03	.02
162	Terry Steinbach	.10	.08	.04
163	Damon Berryhill	.08	.06	.03
164	Tim Crews	.04	.03	.02
165	Tom Browning	.09	.07	.04
166	Frd Manrique	.04	.03	.02
167	Harold Reynolds	.09	.07	.04
168	Ron Hassey	.05	.04	.02
169	Shawon Dunston	.08	.06	.03
170	Bobby Bonilla	.15	.11	.06
171	Tom Herr	.07	.05	.03
172	Mike Heath	.04	.03	.02
173	Rich Gedman	.05	.04	.02
174	Bill Ripken	.05	.04	.02
175	Pete O'Brien	.07	.05	.03
176a	Lloyd McClendon (Uniform number 1 on back)	2.00	1.50	.80
176b	Lloyd McClendon (Uniform number 10 on back)	.20	.15	.08

#	Player	MT	NR MT	EX
177	Brian Holton	.05	.04	.02
178	Jeff Blauser	.05	.04	.02
179	Jim Eisenreich	.05	.04	.02
180	Bert Blyleven	.09	.07	.04
181	Rob Murphy	.05	.04	.02
182	Bill Doran	.07	.05	.03
183	Curt Ford	.04	.03	.02
184	Mike Henneman	.06	.05	.02
185	Eric Davis	.30	.25	.12
186	Lance McCullers	.06	.05	.03
187	*Steve Davis*(FC)	.25	.20	.10
188	Bill Wegman	.05	.04	.02
189	Brian Harper	.06	.05	.02
190	Mike Moore	.09	.07	.04
191	Dale Mohorcic	.04	.03	.02
192	Tim Wallach	.09	.07	.04
193	Keith Hernandez	.09	.07	.04
194	Dave Righetti	.07	.05	.03
195	Bret Saberhagen	.20	.15	.08
196	Paul Kilgus	.04	.03	.02
197	Bud Black	.05	.04	.02
198	Juan Samuel	.09	.07	.04
199	Kevin Seitzer	.15	.11	.06
200	Darryl Strawberry	.30	.25	.12
201	Dave Steib	.09	.07	.04
202	Charlie Hough	.06	.05	.02
203	Jack Morris	.08	.06	.03
204	Rance Mulliniks	.04	.03	.02
205	Alvin Davis	.10	.08	.04
206	Jack Howell	.06	.05	.02
207	Ken Patterson(FC)	.06	.05	.02
208	Terry Pendleton	.09	.07	.03
209	Craig Lefferts	.06	.05	.02
210	Kevin Brown(FC)	.10	.08	.04
211	Dan Petry	.04	.03	.02
212	Dave Leiper	.06	.05	.02
213	Daryl Boston	.04	.03	.02
214	Kevin Hickey(FC)	.08	.06	.03
215	Mike Krukow	.06	.05	.02
216	Terry Francona	.04	.03	.02
217	Kirk McCaskill	.08	.06	.03
218	Scott Bailes	.05	.04	.02
219	Bob Forsch	.04	.03	.02
220	Mike Aldrete	.05	.04	.02
221	Steve Buechele	.06	.05	.02
222	Jesse Barfield	.09	.07	.05
223	Juan Berenguer	.06	.05	.02
224	Andy McGaffigan	.06	.05	.02
225	Pete Smith	.09	.07	.04
226	Mike Witt	.06	.05	.02
227	Jay Howell	.08	.06	.03
228	Scott Bradley	.05	.04	.02
229	*Jerome Walton*	2.25	1.75	.90
230	Greg Swindell	.15	.11	.06
231	Atlee Hammaker	.04	.03	.02
232	Mike Devereaux	.09	.07	.04
233	Ken Hill	.09	.07	.04
234	Craig Worthington	.20	.15	.08
235	Scott Terry	.08	.06	.03
236	Brett Butler	.09	.07	.04
237	Doyle Alexander	.07	.05	.03
238	Dave Anderson	.04	.03	.02
239	Bob Milacki	.10	.08	.04
240	Dwight Smith	1.25	.90	.50
250	Nolan Ryan	.50	.40	.20
251	Kevin Gross	.07	.05	.03
252	Randy Milligan	.07	.05	.03
253	Mike LaCoss	.05	.04	.02
254	Dave Bergman	.04	.03	.02
255	Tony Gwynn	.35	.25	.12
256	Felix Fermin	.04	.03	.02
257	Greg Harris	.10	.08	.04
258	*Junior Felix*	1.25	.90	.50
259	Mark Davis	.09	.07	.04
260	Vince Coleman	.15	.11	.06
261	Paul Gibson	.10	.08	.04
262	Mitch Williams	.10	.08	.04
263	Jeff Russell	.08	.06	.03
264	*Omar Vizquel*	.20	.15	.08
265	Andre Dawson	.12	.09	.05
266	Storm Davis	.08	.06	.03
267	Guillermo Hernandez	.04	.03	.02
268	Mike Felder	.05	.04	.02
269	Tom Candiotti	.05	.04	.02
270	Bruce Hurst	.09	.07	.04
271	Fred McGriff	.30	.25	.12
272	Glenn Davis	.15	.11	.60
273	John Franco	.09	.07	.04
274	Rich Yett	.04	.03	.02
275	Craig Biggio	.15	.11	.06
276	Gene Larkin	.05	.04	.02

#	Player	MT	NR MT	EX		#	Player	MT	NR MT	EX
277	Rob Dibble	.20	.15	.08		365	Jeff Montgomery	.06	.05	.02
278	Randy Bush	.05	.04	.02		366	Bill Krueger(FC)	.04	.03	.02
279	Kevin Bass	.08	.06	.03		367	John Cangelosi	.04	.03	.02
280	Bo Jackson	.50	.40	.20		368	Jose Gonzalez	.10	.08	.04
281	Wally Backman	.06	.05	.02		369	*Greg Hibbard*(FC)	.20	.15	.08
282	Larry Anderson	.04	.03	.02		370	John Smoltz	.20	.15	.08
283	Chris Bosio	.09	.07	.04		371	*Jeff Brantley*	.15	.11	.06
284	Juan Agosto	.04	.03	.02		372	Frank White	.08	.06	.03
285	Ozzie Smith	.10	.08	.04		373	Ed Whitson	.06	.05	.02
286	George Bell	.10	.08	.04		374	Willie McGee	.09	.07	.04
287	Rex Hudler	.05	.04	.02		375	Jose Canseco	.70	.50	.30
288	Pat Borders	.10	.08	.04		376	Randy Ready	.04	.03	.02
289	Danny Jackson	.07	.05	.03		377	Don Aase	.04	.03	.02
290	Carlton Fisk	.09	.07	.04		378	Tony Armas	.05	.04	.02
291	Tracy Jones	.05	.04	.02		379	Steve Bedrosian	.07	.05	.03
292	Alan Anderson	.07	.05	.03		380	Chuck Finley	.07	.05	.03
293	Johnny Ray	.07	.05	.03		381	Kent Hrbek	.12	.09	.05
294	Lee Guetterman	.04	.03	.02		382	Jim Gantner	.06	.05	.02
295	Paul O'Neill	.09	.07	.05		383	Mel Hall	.06	.05	.02
296	Carney Lansford	.08	.06	.03		384	Mike Marshall	.07	.05	.03
297	Tom Brookens	.04	.03	.02		385	Mark McGwire	.70	.50	.30
298	Claudell Washington	.08	.06	.03		386	Wayne Tolleson	.04	.03	.02
299	Hubie Brooks	.08	.06	.03		387	Brian Holton	.05	.04	.02
300	Will Clark	.80	.60	.30		388	*John Wetteland*	.30	.25	.12
301	*Kenny Rogers*	.20	.15	.08		389	Darren Daulton	.04	.03	.02
302	Darrell Evans	.07	.05	.03		390	Rob Deer	.07	.05	.03
303	Greg Briley	.25	.20	.10		391	John Moses	.04	.03	.02
304	Donn Pall	.09	.07	.04		392	Todd Worrell	.07	.05	.03
305	Teddy Higuera	.09	.07	.04		393	Chuck Cary(FC)	.10	.08	.04
306	Dan Pasqua	.07	.05	.02		394	Stan Javier	.05	.04	.02
307	Dave Winfield	.15	.11	.06		395	Willie Randolph	.09	.07	.04
308	Dennis Powell	.04	.03	.02		396	Bill Buckner	.06	.05	.02
309	Jose DeLeon	.08	.06	.03		397	Robby Thompson	.07	.05	.02
310	Roger Clemens	.25	.20	.10		398	Mike Scioscia	.07	.05	.03
311	Melido Perez	.09	.07	.04		399	Lonnie Smith	.09	.07	.04
312	Devon White	.09	.07	.04		400	Kirby Puckett	.40	.30	.15
313	Doc Gooden	.25	.20	.10		401	Mark Langston	.15	.11	.06
314	*Carlos Martinez*	.20	.15	.08		402	Danny Darwin	.04	.03	.02
315	Dennis Eckersley	.10	.08	.04		403	Greg Maddux	.15	.11	.06
316	Clay Parker	.12	.09	.05		404	Lloyd Moseby	.07	.05	.02
317	Rick Honeycutt	.05	.04	.02		405	Rafael Palmeiro	.09	.07	.04
318	Tim Laudner	.05	.04	.02		406	Chad Kreuter	.10	.08	.04
319	Joe Carter	.10	.08	.04		407	Jimmy Key	.09	.07	.05
320	Robin Yount	.20	.15	.08		408	Tim Birtsas	.04	.03	.02
321	Felix Jose	.15	.11	.06		409	Tim Raines	.10	.08	.04
322	Mickey Tettleton	.09	.07	.04		410	Dave Stewart	.09	.07	.04
323	Mike Gallego	.04	.03	.02		411	*Eric Yelding*(FC)	.20	.15	.08
324	Edgar Martinez	.09	.07	.04		412	*Kent Anderson*(FC)	.20	.15	.08
325	Dave Henderson	.09	.07	.04		413	Les Lancaster	.05	.04	.02
326	Chili Davis	.09	.07	.04		414	Rick Dempsey	.04	.03	.02
327	Steve Balboni	.05	.04	.02		415	Randy Johnson	.10	.08	.04
328	Jody Davis	.04	.03	.02		416	Gary Carter	.07	.05	.03
329	Shawn Hillegas	.04	.03	.02		417	Rolando Roomes	.15	.11	.06
330	Jim Abbott	.70	.50	.30		418	Dan Schatzeder	.04	.03	.02
331	John Dopson	.10	.08	.04		419	Bryn Smith	.07	.05	.03
332	Mark Williamson	.04	.03	.02		420	Ruben Sierra	.20	.15	.08
333	Jeff Robinson	.08	.06	.03		421	Steve Jeltz	.04	.03	.02
334	John Smiley	.09	.07	.04		422	Ken Oberkfell	.04	.03	.02
335	Bobby Thigpen	.07	.05	.03		423	Sid Bream	.04	.03	.02
336	Garry Templeton	.05	.04	.02		424	Jom Clancy	.04	.03	.02
337	Marvell Wynne	.05	.04	.02		425	Kelly Gruber	.09	.07	.04
338a	Ken Griffey Sr. (Uniform number 25 on card back)	2.00	1.50	.80		426	Rick Leach	.04	.03	.02
						427	Lenny Dykstra	.07	.05	.03
338b	Ken Griffey Sr. (Uniform number 30 on card back)	.15	.11	.06		428	Jeff Pico	.06	.05	.02
						429	John Cerutti	.06	.05	.02
339	*Steve Finley*	.25	.20	.10		430	David Cone	.15	.11	.06
340	Ellis Burks	.25	.20	.10		431	Jeff Kunkel	.04	.03	.02
341	Frank Williams	.04	.03	.02		432	Luis Aquino	.05	.04	.02
342	Mike Morgan	.05	.04	.02		433	Ernie Whitt	.05	.04	.02
343	Kevin Mitchell	.35	.25	.12		434	Bo Diaz	.05	.04	.02
344	Joel Youngblood	.04	.03	.02		435	Steve Lake	.04	.03	.02
345	Mike Greenwell	.50	.40	.20		436	Pat Perry	.04	.03	.02
346	Glenn Wilson	.05	.04	.02		437	Mike Davis	.05	.04	.02
347	john Costello	.05	.04	.02		438	Cecilio Guante	.04	.03	.02
348	Wes Gardner	.04	.03	.02		439	Duane Ward	.04	.03	.02
349	Jeff Ballard	.09	.07	.04		440	Andy Van Slyke	.10	.08	.04
350	Mark Thurmond	.04	.03	.02		441	Gene Nelson	.04	.03	.02
351	Randy Myers	.07	.05	.03		442	Luis Polonia	.06	.05	.02
352	Shawn Abner	.07	.05	.03		443	Kevin Elster	.06	.05	.02
353	Jesse Orosco	.04	.03	.02		444	Keith Moreland	.06	.05	.02
354	Greg Walker	.05	.04	.02		445	Roger McDowell	.06	.05	.02
355	Pete Harnisch	.15	.11	.06		446	Ron Darling	.08	.06	.03
356	Steve Farr	.05	.04	.02		447	Ernest Riles	.04	.03	.02
357	Dave LaPoint	.05	.04	.02		448	Mookie Wilson	.08	.06	.03
358	Willie Fraser	.05	.04	.02		449a	*Bill Spiers* (66 missing for year of birth)	20.00	15.00	8.00
359	Mickey Hatcher	.04	.03	.02						
360	Rickey Henderson	.30	.25	.12		449b	*Bill Spiers* (1966 for birth year)	.25	.20	.10
361	Mike Fitzgerald	.04	.03	.02		450	Rick Sutcliffe	.07	.05	.03
362	Bill Schroeder	.04	.03	.02		451	Nelson Santovenia	.10	.08	.04
363	Mark Carreon	.10	.08	.04		452	Andy Allanson	.04	.03	.02
364	Ron Jones	.10	.08	.04		453	Bob Melvin	.04	.03	.02

#	Player	MT	NR MT	EX
454	Benny Santiago	.12	.09	.05
455	Jose Uribe	.05	.04	.02
456	Bill Landrum(FC)	.08	.06	.03
457	Bobby Witt	.07	.05	.03
458	Kevin Romine	.07	.05	.03
459	Lee Mazzilli	.04	.03	.02
460	Paul Molitor	.10	.08	.04
461	Ramon Martinez(FC)	.20	.15	.08
462	Frank DiPino	.04	.03	.02
463	Walt Terrell	.06	.05	.02
464	*Bob Geren*	.30	.25	.12
465	Rick Reuchel	.09	.07	.04
466	Mark Grant	.06	.05	.02
467	John Kruk	.07	.05	.03
468	Gregg Jefferies	.80	.60	.30
469	R.J. Reynolds	.04	.03	.02
470	Harold Baines	.09	.07	.04
471	Dennis Lamp	.04	.03	.02
472	Tom Gordon	.60	.45	.25
473	Terry Puhl	.04	.03	.02
474	Curtis Wilkerson	.04	.03	.02
475	Dan Quisenberry	.05	.04	.02
476	Oddibe McDowell	.07	.05	.03
477	Zane Smith	.04	.03	.02
478	Franklin Stubbs	.04	.03	.02
479	Wallace Johnson	.04	.03	.02
480	Jay Tibbs	.04	.03	.02
481	Tom Glavine	.09	.07	.03
482	Manny Lee	.05	.04	.02
483	Joe Hesketh	.04	.03	.02
484	Mike Bielecki	.07	.05	.03
485	Greg Brock	.06	.05	.02
486	Pascual Perez	.06	.05	.02
487	Kirk Gibson	.09	.07	.04
488	Scott Sanderson	.05	.04	.02
489	Domingo Ramos	.04	.03	.02
490	Kal Daniels	.10	.08	.04
491	David Wells	.05	.04	.02
492	Jerry Reed	.04	.03	.02
493	Eric Show	.06	.05	.02
494	Mike Pagliarulo	.06	.05	.02
495	Ron Robinson	.05	.04	.02
496	Brad Komminsk	.04	.03	.02
497	*Greg Litton*	.25	.20	.10
498	Chris James	.07	.05	.02
499	Luis Quinines(FC)	.05	.04	.02
500	Frank Viola	.10	.08	.04
501	Tim Teufel	.05	.04	.02
502	Terry Leach	.04	.03	.02
503	Matt Williams	.20	.15	.08
504	Tim Leary	.06	.05	.02
505	Doug Drabek	.06	.05	.02
506	Mariano Duncan	.06	.05	.02
507	Charlie Hayes	.10	.08	.04
508	*Joey Belle*	1.00	.70	.40
509	Pat Sheridan	.05	.04	.02
510	Mackey Sasser	.05	.04	.02
511	Jose Rijo	.09	.07	.04
512	Mike Smithson	.04	.03	.02
513	Gary Ward	.04	.03	.02
514	Dion James	.06	.05	.02
515	Jim Gott	.06	.05	.02
516	Drew Hall(FC)	.07	.05	.03
517	Doug Bair	.04	.03	.02
518	*Scott Scudder*	.20	.15	.08
519	Rick Auilera	.06	.05	.02
520	Rafael Belliard	.05	.04	.02
521	Jay Buhner	.10	.08	.04
522	Jeff Reardon	.06	.05	.02
523	Steve Rosenberg(FC)	.09	.07	.04
524	Randy Velarde(FC)	.09	.07	.04
525	Jeff Musselman	.09	.07	.04
526	Bill Long	.06	.05	.02
527	*Gary Wayne*	.10	.08	.04
528	*Dave Johnson*(FC)	.15	.11	.06
529	Ron Kittle	.08	.06	.03
530	Erik Hanson(FC)	.20	.15	.08
531	Steve Wilson(FC)	.20	.15	.08
532	Joey Meyer	.04	.03	.02
533	Curt Young	.04	.03	.02
534	Kelly Downs	.06	.05	.02
535	Joe Girardi	.20	.15	.08
536	Lance Blankenship	.09	.07	.04
537	Greg Mathews	.05	.04	.02
538	Donell Nixon	.04	.03	.02
539	Mark Knudson(FC)	.09	.07	.04
540	*Jeff Wetherby*(FC)	.30	.25	.12
541	Darrin Jackson	.04	.03	.02
542	Terry Mulholland	.09	.07	.03
543	Eric Hetzel(FC)	.15	.11	.06
544	*Rick Reed*(FC)	.25	.20	.10
545	Dennis Cook(FC)	.15	.11	.06
546	Mike Jackson	.05	.04	.02
547	Brian Fisher	.06	.05	.02
548	*Gene Harris*(FC)	.20	.15	.08
549	Jeff King(FC)	.20	.15	.08
550	Dave Dravecky (Salute)	.10	.08	.04
551	Randy Kutcher(FC)	.08	.06	.03
552	Mark Portugal	.06	.05	.02
553	*Jim Corsi*(FC)	.12	.09	.05
554	Todd Stottlemyre	.12	.09	.05
555	Scott Bankhead	.09	.07	.04
556	Ken Dayley	.05	.04	.02
557	*Rick Wrona*(FC)	.25	.20	.10
558	*Sammy Sosa*(FC)	.35	.25	.14
559	Keith Miller	.08	.06	.03
560	Ken Griffey Jr.	1.25	.90	.50
561a	Ryne Sandberg (No Errors- 3B Position designation)	60.00	45.00	25.00
561b	Ryne Sandberg (No Errors- 2B position designation)	.25	.20	.10
562	Billy Hatcher	.06	.05	.02
563	Jay Bell(FC)	.09	.07	.04
564	*Jack Daugherty*(FC)	.30	.25	.12
565	*Rich Monteleone*	.20	.15	.08
566	Bo Jackson (NIKE)	1.00	.70	.40
567	*Tony Fossas*(FC)	.10	.08	.04
568	*Roy Smith*(FC)	.15	.11	.06
569	Jaime Navarro(FC)	.35	.25	.14
570	Lance Johnson(FC)	.15	.11	.06
571	*Mike Dyer*(FC)	.25	.20	.10
572	Kevin Ritz(FC)	.20	.15	.08
573	Dave West	.15	.11	.06
574	*Gary Mielke*(FC)	.25	.20	.10
575	Scott Lusader(FC)	.09	.07	.04
576	*Joe Oliver*	.25	.20	.10
577	Sandy Alomar Jr.	.60	.45	.25
578	Andy Benes(FC)	1.25	.90	.50
579	Tim Jones	.07	.05	.03
580	*Randy McCament*(FC)	.25	.20	10.00
581	Curt Schilling(FC)	.15	.11	.06
582	John Orton(FC)	.25	.20	.10
583a	Milt Cuyler (Pitched in 989 games)(FC)	3.00	2.25	1.25
583b	Milt Cuyler (pitched in 98 games)(FC)	.40	.30	.15
584	Eric Anthony(FC)	2.50	2.00	1.00
585	*Greg Vaughn*(FC)	2.00	1.50	.80
586	Deion Sanders(FC)	.80	.60	.30
587	Jose Dejesus(FC)	.15	.11	.06
588	Chip Hale(FC)	.30	.25	.12
589	John Olerud(FC)	2.50	2.00	1.00
590	Steve Olin(FC)	.35	.25	.12
591	*Marquis Grissom*(FC)	1.25	.90	.50
592	Moises Alou(FC)	.50	.40	.20
593	Mark Lemke(FC)	.10	.08	.04
594	*Dean Palmer*(FC)	.30	.25	.12
595	*Robin Ventura*(FC)	1.50	1.25	.60
596	*Tino Martinez*(FC)	.50	.40	.20
597	*Mike Huff*(FC)	.25	.20	.10
598	Scott Hemond(FC)	.25	.20	.10
599	*Wally Whitehurst*(FC)	.20	.15	.08
600	Todd Zeile(FC)	2.00	1.50	.80
601	Glenallen Hill(FC)	.25	.20	.10
602	Hal Morris(FC)	.15	.11	.06
603	Juan Bell(FC)	.15	.11	.06
604	*Bobby Rose*(FC)	.25	.20	.10
605	Matt Merullo(FC)	.20	.15	.08
606	Kevin Maas(FC)	.20	.15	.08
607	Randy Nosek(FC)	.25	.20	.10
608	*Billy Bates*(FC)	.20	.15	.08
609	*Mike Stanton*(FC)	.25	.20	.10
610	Goose Gozzo(FC)	.30	.25	.12
611	*Charles Nagy*(FC)	.25	.20	.10
612	*Scott Coolbaugh*(FC)	.50	.40	.20
613	Jose Vizcaino(FC)	.35	.25	.12
614	Greg Smith(FC)	.20	.15	.08
615	*Jeff Huson*(FC)	.20	.15	.08
616	*Mickey Weston*(FC)	.20	.15	.08
617	*John Pawlowski*(FC)	.20	.15	.08
618	*Joe Skalski*(FC)	.20	.15	.08
619	Bernie Williams(FC)	.90	.70	.35
620	*Shawn Holman*(FC)	.25	.20	.10
621	Gary Eave(FC)	.25	.20	.10
622	Darrin Fletcher(FC)	.25	.20	.10
623	Pat Combs(FC)	.90	.70	.35
624	Mike Blowers(FC)	.30	.25	.12
625	Kevin Appier(FC)	.30	.25	.12
626	Pat Austin(FC)	.30	.25	.12
627	Kelly Mann(FC)	.40	.30	.15
628	Matt Kinzer(FC)	.25	.20	.10
629	Chris Hammond(FC)	.25	.20	.10

		MT	NR MT	EX
630	*Dean Wilkins*(FC)	.25	.20	.10
631	*Larry Walker*(FC)	.25	.20	.10
632	*Blaine Beatty*(FC)	.40	.30	.15
633	*Tom Barrett*(FC)	.12	.09	.05
634	*Stan Belinda*(FC)	.25	.20	.10
635	*Tex Smith*(FC)	.25	.20	.10
636	*Hensley Meulens*(FC)	.40	.30	.15
637	*Juan Gonzalez*(FC)	.60	.45	.25
638	*Lenny Webster*(FC)	.25	.20	.10
639	*Mark Gardner*(FC)	.25	.20	.10
640	*Tommy Greene*(FC)	.25	.20	.10
641	*Mike Hartley*(FC)	.25	.20	.10
642	*Phil Stephenson*(FC)	.15	.11	.06
643	*Kevin Mmahat*(FC)	.15	.11	.06
644	*Ed Whited*(FC)	.15	.11	.06
645	*Delino DeShields*(FC)	.50	.40	.20
646	*Kevin Blankenship*(FC)	.15	.11	.06
647	*Paul Sorrento*(FC)	.40	.30	.15
648	*Mike Roesler*(FC)	.25	.20	.12
649	*Jason Grimsley*(FC)	.25	.20	.10
650	*Dave Justice*(FC)	.50	.40	.20
651	*Scott Cooper*(FC)	.25	.20	.10
652	Dave Eiland(FC)	.15	.11	.06
653	*Mike Munoz*(FC)	.25	.20	.10
654	*Jeff Fischer*(FC)	.25	.20	.10
655	*Terry Jorgenson*(FC)	.20	.15	.08
656	*George Canale*(FC)	.40	.30	.15
657	*Brian Dubois*(FC)	.40	.30	.15
658	Carlos Quintana	.10	.08	.04
659	Luis De Los Santos	.10	.08	.04
660	Jerald Clark	.10	.08	.04
661	*Donald Harris (#1 Draft Pick)(FC)*	.30	.25	.12
662	*Paul Coleman (#1 Draft Pick)(FC)*	.40	.30	.15
663	*Frank Thomas (#1 Draft Pick)(FC)*	.60	.45	.25
664	*Brent Mayne (#1 Draft Pick)(FC)*	.20	.15	.08
665	*Eddie Zosky (#1 Draft Pick)(FC)*	.20	.15	.08
666	*Steve Hosey (#1 Draft Pick)(FC)*	.20	.15	.08
667	*Scott Bryant (#1 Draft Pick)(FC)*	.20	.15	.08
668	*Tom Goodwin (#1 Draft Pick)(FC)*	.20	.15	.08
669	*Cal Eldred (#1 Draft Pick)(FC)*	.20	.15	.08
670	*Earl Cunningham (#1 Draft Pick)(FC)*	.50	.40	.20
671	*Alan Zinter (#1 Draft Pick)(FC)*	.25	.20	.10
672	*Chuck Knoblauch (#1 Draft Pick)(FC)*	.25	.20	.10
673	*Kyle Abbott (#1 Draft Pick)(FC)*	.25	.20	.10
674	*Roger Salkeld (#1 Draft Pick)(FC)*	.30	.25	.12
675	*Maurice Vaughn (#1 Draft Pick)(FC)*	.30	.25	.12
676	*Kiki Jones (#1 Draft Pick)(FC)*	.25	.20	.10
677	*Tyler Houston (#1 Draft Pick)(FC)*	.40	.30	.15
678	*Jeff Jackson (#1 Draft Pick)(FC)*	.40	.30	.15
679	*Greg Gohr (#1 Draft Pick)(FC)*	.25	.20	.10
680	*Ben McDonald (#1 Draft Pick)(FC)*	2.50	2.00	1.00
681	*Greg Blosser (#1 Draft Pick)(FC)*	.30	.25	.12
682	*Willie Green (#1 Draft Pick)(FC)*	.25	.20	.10
683	Wade Boggs (Dream Team)	.20	.15	.08
684	Will Clark (Dream Team)	.20	.15	.08
685	Tony Gwynn (Dream Team)	.20	.15	.08
686	Rickey Henderson (Dream Team)	.20	.15	.08
687	Bo Jackson (Dream Team)	.20	.15	.11
688	Mark Langston (Dream Team)	.20	.15	.11
689	Barry Larkin (Dream Team)	.20	.15	.11
690	Kirby Puckett (Dream Team)	.20	.15	.11
691	Ryne Sanberg (Dream Team)	.20	.15	.11
692	Mike Scott (Dream Team)	.20	.15	.11
693	Terry Steinbach (Dream Team)	.20	.15	.11
694	Bobby Thigpen (Dream Team)	.20	.15	.11
695	Mitch Williams (Dream Team)	.20	.15	.11
696	Nolan Ryan (5000 K)	.50	.40	.20
697	Bo Jackson (All Star MVP)	.35	.25	.14
698	Rickey Henderson (ALCS MVP)	.25	.20	.10
699	Will Clark (NLCS MVP)	.35	.25	.14
700	World Series 1,2	.30	.25	.12
701	Candlestick	.30	.25	.12
702	World Series Game 3	.30	.25	.12
703	World Series Wrap-up	.30	.25	.12
704	Wade Boggs (200 Hit)	.25	.20	.10

1989 Scoremasters

This unique 42-card boxed set from Score was reproduced from original artwork done by sports artist Jeffrey Rubin. The paitings are reproduced on a standard-size, white, glossy stock, and the set includes the top stars of the game, including four key rookies (Walton, Gordon, Jefferies and Griffey Jr.).

		MT	NR MT	EX
	Complete Set:	13.00	9.75	5.25
	Common Player:	.20	.15	.08
1	Bo Jackson	.70	.50	.30
2	Jerome Walton	1.50	1.25	.60
3	Cal Ripken Jr.	.35	.25	.12
4	Mike Scott	.20	.15	.08
5	Nolan Ryan	.80	.60	.30
6	Don Mattingly	1.25	.90	.50
7	Tom Gordon	1.00	.70	.40
8	Jack Morris	.20	.15	.08
9	Carlton Fisk	.30	.25	.12
10	Will Clark	1.00	.70	.40
11	George Brett	.40	.30	.15
12	Kevin Mitchell	.40	.30	.15
13	Mark Langston	.30	.25	.12
14	Dave Stewart	.20	.15	.08
15	Dale Murphy	.25	.20	.10
16	Gary Gaetti	.20	.15	.08
17	Wade Boggs	.50	.40	.20
18	Eric Davis	.70	.50	.30
19	Kirby Puckett	.70	.50	.30
20	Roger Clemens	.50	.40	.20
21	Orel Hershiser	.30	.25	.12
22	Mark Grace	.50	.40	.20
23	Ryne Sandberg	.35	.25	.12
24	Barry Larkin	.20	.15	.08
25	Ellis Burks	.40	.30	.15
26	Doc Gooden	.40	.30	.15
27	Ozzie Smith	.25	.20	.10
28	Andre Dawson	.20	.15	.08
29	Julio Franco	.20	.15	.08
30	Ken Griffey Jr.	1.50	1.25	.60
31	Ruben Sierra	.30	.25	.12
32	Mark McGwire	.80	.60	.30
33	Andres Galarraga	.20	.15	.08
34	Joe Carter	.30	.25	.12
35	Vince Coleman	.20	.15	.08
36	Mike Greenwell	.50	.40	.20
37	Tony Gwynn	.40	.30	.15
38	Andy Van Slyke	.20	.15	.08
39	Gregg Jefferies	1.00	.70	.40
40	Jose Canseco	1.00	.70	.40
41	Dave Winfield	.20	.15	.08
42	Darryl Strawberry	.40	.30	.15

1985 7-11 Twins

The Minnesota Twins, in co-operation with 7-Eleven and the Fire Marshall's Association, issued this set of 13 baseball fire safety cards. The card fronts feature full-color pictures of Twins players. A fire safety tip and short player history appear on the back. The cards were given out at all 7-Eleven stores in the state and at the Twins June 3 baseball game. Each fan received one baseball card with a poster which told how to collect the other cards in the set. Twelve cards feature players and the 13th card has an artist's rendering of Twins players on the front and a checklist of the set on the back. A group of 50,000 cards was distributed to fifth graders throughout the state by the fire departments.

		MT	NR MT	EX
	Complete Set:	6.00	4.50	2.50
	Common Player:	.20	.15	.08
1	Kirby Puckett	2.00	1.50	.80
2	Frank Viola	1.00	.70	.40
3	Mickey Hatcher	.20	.15	.08
4	Kent Hrbek	1.25	.90	.50
5	John Butcher	.20	.15	.08
6	Roy Smalley	.20	.15	.08
7	Tom Brunansky	.80	.60	.30
8	Ron Davis	.20	.15	.08
9	Gary Gaetti	1.00	.70	.40
10	Tim Teufel	.30	.25	.12
11	Mike Smithson	.20	.15	.08
12	Tim Laudner	.30	.25	.12
----	Checklist	.10	.08	.04

1984 7-Up Cubs

The Chicago Cubs and 7-Up issued this 28-card set featuring full-color game-action photos on a 2-1/4" by 3-1/2" borderless front. The backs have the player's stats and personal information. This was the third consecutive year the Cubs issued this type of set as a giveaway at a "Baseball Card Day" promotional game.

		MT	NR MT	EX
	Complete Set:	12.00	9.00	4.75
	Common Player:	.20	.15	.08
1	Larry Bowa	.40	.30	.15
6	Keith Moreland	.40	.30	.15
7	Jody Davis	.40	.30	.15
10	Leon Durham	.40	.30	.15
11	Ron Cey	.40	.30	.15
15	Ron Hassey	.20	.15	.08
18	Richie Hebner	.20	.15	.08
19	Dave Owen	.20	.15	.08
20	Bob Dernier	.20	.15	.08
21	Jay Johnstone	.25	.20	.10
23	Ryne Sandberg	3.00	2.25	1.25
24	Scott Sanderson	.25	.20	.10
25	Gary Woods	.20	.15	.08
27	Thad Bosley	.20	.15	.08
28	Henry Cotto	.30	.25	.12
34	Steve Trout	.25	.20	.10
36	Gary Matthews	.40	.30	.15
39	George Frazier	.20	.15	.08
40	Rick Sutcliffe	.80	.60	.30
41	Warren Brusstar	.20	.15	.08
42	Rich Bordi	.20	.15	.08
43	Dennis Eckersley	.50	.40	.20
44	Dick Ruthven	.20	.15	.08
46	Lee Smith	.50	.40	.20
47	Rick Reuschel	.50	.40	.20
49	Tim Stoddard	.20	.15	.08
----	Jim Frey	.20	.15	.08
----	Cubs Coaches (Ruben Amaro, Billy			

		MT	NR MT	EX
	Connors, Johnny Oates, John Vukovich, Don			
	Zimmer)	.20	.15	.08

1985 7-Up Cubs

(10) LEON DURHAM IF

This was the second year a Chicago Cubs card set was released with 7-Up as the sponsor. The set has 28 unnumbered cards in the standard 2-1/2" by 3-1/2" size. They were distributed to fans attending the Cubs game on August 14 at Wrigley Field. They feature full-color game-action photos of the players. Card backs contain the player's professional stats.

		MT	NR MT	EX
	Complete Set:	7.00	5.25	2.75
	Common Player:	.10	.08	.04
1	Larry Bowa	.25	.20	.10
6	Keith Moreland	.30	.25	.12
7	Jody Davis	.30	.25	.12
10	Leon Durham	.30	.25	.12
11	Ron Cey	.30	.25	.12
15	Davey Lopes	.25	.20	.10
16	Steve Lake	.10	.08	.04
18	Richie Hebner	.10	.08	.04
20	Bob Dernier	.10	.08	.04
21	Scott Sanderson	.15	.11	.06
22	Billy Hatcher	.30	.25	.12
23	Ryne Sandberg	2.00	1.50	.80
24	Brian Dayett	.10	.08	.04
25	Gary Woods	.10	.08	.04
27	Thad Bosley	.10	.08	.04
28	Chris Speier	.10	.08	.04
31	Ray Fontenot	.10	.08	.04
34	Steve Trout	.20	.15	.08
36	Gary Matthews	.30	.25	.12
39	George Frazier	.10	.08	.04
40	Rick Sutcliffe	.70	.50	.30
41	Warren Brusstar	.10	.08	.04
42	Lary Sorensen	.10	.08	.04
43	Dennis Eckersley	.40	.30	.15
44	Dick Ruthven	.10	.08	.04
46	Lee Smith	.35	.25	.14
----	Jim Frey	.10	.08	.04
----	Coaching Staff (Ruben Amaro, Billy			
	Connors, Johnny Oates, John Vukovich, Don			
	Zimmer)	.10	.08	.04

1984 Smokey Bear Angels

This 32-card set was distributed at a June home

game to fans 14 and under. Cards measure 2-1/2" by 3-1/2". The full-color card fronts list the player name along with the team logo and Forestry service logos commemorating the 40th birthday of Smokey the the Bear. The black and white card backs list tips for preventing forest fires.

		MT	NR MT	EX
Complete Set:		8.00	6.00	3.25
Common Player:		.20	.15	.08
(1)	Don Aase	.20	.15	.08
(2)	Juan Beniquez	.20	.15	.08
(3)	Bob Boone	.30	.25	.12
(4)	Rick Burleson	.30	.25	.12
(5)	Rod Carew	1.00	.70	.40
(6)	John Curtis	.20	.15	.08
(7)	Doug DeCinces	.30	.25	.12
(8)	Brian Downing	.30	.25	.12
(9)	Ken Forsch	.20	.15	.08
(10)	Bobby Grich	.30	.25	.12
(11)	Reggie Jackson	1.25	.90	.50
(12)	Ron Jackson	.20	.15	.08
(13)	Tommy John	.60	.45	.25
(14)	Curt Kaufman	.20	.15	.08
(15)	Bruce Kison	.20	.15	.08
(16)	Frank LaCorte	.20	.15	.08
(17)	Fred Lynn	.60	.45	.25
(18)	John McNamara	.20	.15	.08
(19)	Jerry Narron	.20	.15	.08
(20)	Gary Pettis	.40	.30	.15
(21)	Robert Picciolo	.20	.15	.08
(22)	Ron Romanick	.20	.15	.08
(23)	Luis Sanchez	.20	.15	.08
(24)	Dick Schofield	.30	.25	.12
(25)	Daryl Sconiers	.20	.15	.08
(26)	Jim Slaton	.20	.15	.08
(27)	Ellis Valentine	.20	.15	.08
(28)	Robert Wilfong	.20	.15	.08
(29)	Mike Witt	.50	.40	.20
(30)	Geoff Zahn	.20	.15	.08
----	Forestry Dept. Logo Card	.10	.08	.04
----	Smokey Logo Card	.10	.08	.04

1984 Smokey Bear Dodgers

Unlike the California Angels and San Diego Padres sets issued in conjunction with the Forestry Service in 1984, the Los Angeles Dodgers set contains only three players, pictured on much larger 5" by 7" cards. Ken Landreaux, Tom Niedenfuer and Steve Sax (plus a Smokey the Bear card) are pictured on the cards. Each player is pictured in a forest scene on the full-color fronts. Backs of the unnumbered cards have brief biographical information and lifetime statistics. The cards were distributed at a Dodgers home game.

		MT	NR MT	EX
Complete Set:		10.00	7.50	4.00
Common Player:		2.50	2.00	1.00
(1)	Ken Landreaux	2.50	2.00	1.00
(2)	Tom Niedenfuer	2.50	2.00	1.00
(3)	Steve Sax	5.00	3.75	2.00
(4)	Smokey Bear	.50	.40	.20

1984 Smokey Bear Jackson Mets In Majors

This set, issued in conjunction with the Mississippi Forestry Commission, features big leaguers who played for the Mets' Double-A farm club. The fifteen 3" by 4" cards have a black and white portrait photo on the front with the name, position and major league team shown in blue. A Smokey the Bear logo is also included. Card backs feature player information and career highlights.

		MT	NR MT	EX
Complete Set:		60.00	45.00	25.00
Common Player:		1.00	.70	.40
(1)	Neil Allen	1.00	.70	.40
(2)	Wally Backman	2.00	1.50	.80
(3)	Hubie Brooks	3.00	2.25	1.25
(4)	Jody Davis	2.00	1.50	.80
(5)	Brian Giles	1.00	.70	.40
(6)	Dave Johnson	2.00	1.50	.80
(7)	Tim Leary	2.00	1.50	.80
(8)	Lee Mazzilli	2.00	1.50	.80
(9)	Jesse Orosco	2.00	1.50	.80
(10)	Jeff Reardon	3.00	2.25	1.25
(11)	Doug Sisk	1.00	.70	.40
(12)	Darryl Strawberry	20.00	15.00	8.00
(13)	Mookie Wilson	4.00	3.00	1.50
(14)	Marvel Wynne (Marvell)	2.00	1.50	.80
(15)	Ned Yost	1.00	.70	.40

1984 Smokey Bear Padres

This set of 28 full-color cards is very similar in format to the Angels set of the same year. San Diego Padres players are posed in photos with Smokey the Bear. Forestry Department and team logos are also pictured on the card fronts. The Padres cards feature players, coaches, broadcasters and the Famous Chicken, all posing with Smokey. The backs of the cards which were distributed at a Padres home game, offer brief player information and a fire prevention tip.

		MT	NR MT	EX
	Complete Set:	10.00	7.50	4.00
	Common Player:	.25	.20	.10
1	Garry Templeton	.40	.30	.15
2	Alan Wiggins	.25	.20	.10
4	Luis Salazar	.25	.20	.10
6	Steve Garvey	1.25	.90	.50
7	Kurt Bevacqua	.25	.20	.10
10	Doug Gwosdz	.25	.20	.10
11	Tim Flannery	.25	.20	.10
16	Terry Kennedy	.40	.30	.15
18	Kevin McReynolds	1.25	.90	.50
19	Tony Gwynn	1.50	1.25	.60
20	Bobby Brown	.25	.20	.10
30	Eric Show	.50	.40	.20
31	Ed Whitson	.25	.20	.10
35	Luis DeLeon	.25	.20	.10
38	Mark Thurmond	.25	.20	.10
42	Sid Monge	.25	.20	.10
43	Dave Dravecky	.40	.30	.15
48	Tim Lollar	.25	.20	.10
----	Smokey Logo Card	.25	.20	.10
----	The Chicken (mascot)	.40	.30	.15
----	Dave Campbell (broadcaster)	.25	.20	.10
----	Jerry Coleman (broadcaster)	.25	.20	.10
----	Harry Dunlop (coach)	.25	.20	.10
----	Harold (Doug) Harvey (umpire)	.25	.20	.10
----	Jack Krol (coach)	.25	.20	.10
----	Jack McKeon (vice-president)	.25	.20	.10
----	Norm Sherry (coach)	.25	.20	.10
----	Ozzie Virgil (coach)	.25	.20	.10
----	Dick Williams (manager)	.25	.20	.10

1985 Smokey Bear Angels

The California Forestry Service and the California Angels gave this full-color set of oversized baseball cards to fans attending the July 14 game at Anaheim Stadium. The 24 cards feature player photos on the fronts with their last name at the top of the cards above the picture. On the card bottoms are the logos for Smokey Bear, the Angels, the State Forestry Service and the U.S. Forestry Service. The cards measure 4-1/4" by 6". On the card backs, printed in black and white, are personal data, limited playing stats and a wildfire safety tip from Smokey the Bear.

		MT	NR MT	EX
	Complete Set:	7.00	5.25	2.75
	Complete Set:	.20	.15	.08
1	Mike Witt	.50	.40	.20
2	Reggie Jackson	1.25	.90	.50
3	Bob Boone	.30	.25	.12
4	Mike Brown	.20	.15	.08
5	Rod Carew	1.00	.70	.40
6	Doug DeCinces	.30	.25	.12
7	Brian Downing	.30	.25	.12
8	Ken Forsch	.20	.15	.08
9	Gary Pettis	.20	.15	.08
10	Jerry Narron	.20	.15	.08
11	Ron Romanick	.20	.15	.08
12	Bobby Grich	.30	.25	.12
13	Dick Schofield	.30	.25	.12
14	Juan Beniquez	.20	.15	.08
15	Geoff Zahn	.20	.15	.08
16	Luis Sanchez	.20	.15	.08
17	Jim Slaton	.20	.15	.08
18	Doug Corbett	.20	.15	.08
19	Ruppert Jones	.20	.15	.08
20	Rob Wilfong	.20	.15	.08

		MT	NR MT	EX
21	Donnie Moore	.20	.15	.08
22	Pat Clements	.20	.15	.08
23	Tommy John	.60	.45	.25
24	Gene Mauch	.30	.25	.12

1986 Smokey Bear Angels

The California Angels, in conjuction with the Forestry Service, issued this 24-card set of Wildfire Prevention baseball cards. The cards measure 4-1/4" by 6" and offer a full-color front with the player's picture placed in an oval frame. The card backs have player stats with a drawing and slogan for fire prevention. The sets were given out on August 9th at the Angles game in Anaheim Stadium.

		MT	NR MT	EX
	Complete Set:	8.00	6.00	3.25
	Common Player:	.20	.15	.08
1	Mike Witt	.50	.40	.20
2	Reggie Jackson	1.25	.90	.50
3	Bob Boone	.30	.25	.12
4	Don Sutton	.60	.45	.25
5	Kirk McCaskill	.50	.40	.20
6	Doug DeCinces	.30	.25	.12
7	Brian Downing	.30	.25	.12
8	Doug Corbett	.20	.15	.08
9	Gary Pettis	.20	.15	.08
10	Jerry Narron	.20	.15	.08
11	Ron Romanick	.20	.15	.08
12	Bobby Grich	.30	.25	.12
13	Dick Schofield	.30	.25	.12
14	George Hendrick	.30	.25	.12
15	Rick Burleson	.30	.25	.12
16	John Candelaria	.30	.25	.12
17	Jim Slaton	.20	.15	.08
18	Darrell Miller	.30	.25	.12
19	Ruppert Jones	.20	.15	.08
20	Rob Wilfong	.20	.15	.08
21	Donnie Moore	.20	.15	.08
22	Wally Joyner	2.50	2.00	1.00
23	Terry Forster	.30	.25	.12
24	Gene Mauch	.30	.25	.12

1987 Smokey Bear

The U.S. Forestry Service and Major League Baseball united in an effort to promote National Smokey the Bear Day. Two perforated sheets of baseball cards, one each for the American and

National Leagues, were produced by the Forestry Service. The sheet of American Leaguers measures 18" by 24" and contains 16 full-color cards. The National League sheet measures 20" by 18" and contains 15 cards. Each individual card is 4" by 6" and contains a fire prevention tip on the back. An average number of 25,000 sets was sent to all teams.

		MT	NR MT	EX
Complete Set:		8.00	6.00	3.25
Common Player:		.20	.15	.08
1A	Jose Canseco	1.50	1.25	.60
1N	Steve Sax	.40	.30	.15
2A	Dennis "Oil Can" Boyd	.20	.15	.08
2Na	Dale Murphy (shirttail out)	5.00	3.75	2.00
2Nb	Dale Murphy (shirttail in)	.80	.60	.30
3A	John Candelaria	.20	.15	.08
3Na	Jody Davis (standing)	3.50	2.75	1.50
3Nb	Jody Davis (kneeling)	.25	.20	.10
4A	Harold Baines	.30	.25	.12
4N	Bill Gullickson	.20	.15	.08
5A	Joe Carter	.30	.25	.12
5N	Mike Scott	.30	.25	.12
6A	Jack Morris	.40	.30	.15
6N	Roger McDowell	.25	.20	.10
7A	Buddy Biancalana	.20	.15	.08
7N	Steve Bedrosian	.30	.25	.12
8A	Kirby Puckett	.70	.50	.30
8N	Johnny Ray	.25	.20	.10
9A	Mike Pagliarulo	.25	.20	.10
9N	Ozzie Smith	.30	.25	.12
10A	Larry Sheets	.25	.20	.10
10N	Steve Garvey	.60	.45	.25
11A	Mike Moore	.20	.15	.08
11N	Smokey Bear Logo Card	.05	.04	.02
12A	Charlie Hough	.20	.15	.08
12N	Mike Krukow	.20	.15	.08
13A	Smokey Bear Logo Card	.05	.04	.02
13N	Smokey Bear	.05	.04	.02
14A	Tom Henke	.20	.15	.08
14N	Mike Fitzgerald	.20	.15	.08
15A	Jim Gantner	.20	.15	.08
15N	National League Logo Card	.05	.04	.02
16A	American League Logo Card	.05	.04	.02

1987 Smokey Bear A's

The 1987 Smokey Bear A's set is not comparable to any other Smokey Bear issue produced in 1987 or before. The 12 cards in the set are bound together in a book titled "Smokey Bear's Fire Prevention Color-Grams." The Color-Gram cards feature two cards in one. A near-standard size (2-1/2" by 3-3/4") black and white card is attached to a large perforated (3-3/4" by 6") card, also black and white. The large card, which has a postcard back, features a caricature photo of the player and is intended to be colored and then mailed. The card backs contain personal and statistical information and carry a Smokey the Bear cartoon message. The books were distributed at an Oakland A's game during the 1987 season.

		MT	NR MT	EX
Complete Book:		6.00	4.50	2.50
Complete Singles Set:		3.00	2.25	1.25
Common Single Player:		.15	.11	.06
(1)	Joaquin Andujar	.20	.15	.08
(2)	Jose Canseco	1.50	1.25	.60
(3)	Mike Davis	.25	.20	.10

		MT	NR MT	EX
(4)	Alfredo Griffin	.25	.20	.10
(5)	Moose Haas	.15	.11	.06
(6)	Jay Howell	.25	.20	.10
(7)	Reggie Jackson	.80	.60	.30
(8)	Carney Lansford	.30	.25	.12
(9)	Dwayne Murphy	.25	.20	.10
(10)	Tony Phillips	.15	.11	.06
(11)	Dave Stewart	.40	.30	.15
(12)	Curt Young	.30	.25	.12

1987 Smokey Bear Angels

A 24-card set featuring the California Angels and produced by the U.S. Forestry Service was distributed to 25,000 fans in attendance at Anaheim Stadium on August 1st. The full-color cards measure 4" x 6". The card fronts carry a unique design with baseballs and bats framing the player photo. Only the player's last name is given on the card fronts. The backs contain the player's name, position and personal statistics along with a Smokey Bear cartoon and a fire prevention tip.

		MT	NR MT	EX
Complete Set:		8.00	6.00	3.25
Common Player:		.20	.15	.08
1	John Candelaria	.30	.25	.12
2	Don Sutton	.60	.45	.25
3	Mike Witt	.50	.40	.20
4	Gary Lucas	.20	.15	.08
5	Kirk McCaskill	.30	.25	.12
6	Chuck Finley	.30	.25	.12
7	Willie Fraser	.30	.25	.12
8	Donnie Moore	.20	.15	.08
9	Urbano Lugo	.20	.15	.08
10	Butch Wynegar	.25	.20	.10
11	Darrell Miller	.20	.15	.08
12	Wally Joyner	2.00	1.50	.80
13	Mark McLemore	.20	.15	.08
14	Mark Ryal	.20	.15	.08
15	Dick Schofield	.25	.20	.10
16	Jack Howell	.30	.25	.12
17	Doug DeCinces	.30	.25	.12
18	Gus Polidor	.20	.15	.08
19	Brian Downing	.30	.25	.12
20	Gary Pettis	.20	.15	.08
21	Ruppert Jones	.20	.15	.08
22	George Hendrick	.25	.20	.10
23	Devon White	1.25	.90	.50
-----	Smokey Bear Logo Card/Checklist	.10	.08	.04

1987 Smokey Bear Braves

Cards from the 1987 Smokey Bear Atlanta Braves set were given out at several different Braves games, with about 25,000 sets in all being distributed. The 4" by 6" cards feature Atlanta players in an oval frame, bordered in red, white and blue. Only the player's last name is listed on the card fronts. Card backs contain the player's name, position and personal data plus a Smokey Bear cartoon with a fire safety message.

		MT	NR MT	EX
Complete Set:		8.00	6.00	3.25
Common Player:		.20	.15	.08
1	Zane Smith	.40	.30	.15
2	Charlie Puleo	.20	.15	.08

		MT	NR MT	EX
3	Randy O'Neal	.20	.15	.08
4	David Palmer	.20	.15	.08
5	Rick Mahler	.30	.25	.12
6	Ed Olwine	.20	.15	.08
7	Jeff Dedmon	.20	.15	.08
8	Paul Assenmacher	.30	.25	.12
9	Gene Garber	.20	.15	.08
10	Jim Acker	.20	.15	.08
11	Bruce Benedict	.20	.15	.08
12	Ozzie Virgil	.20	.15	.08
13	Ted Simmons	.40	.30	.15
14	Dale Murphy	1.25	.90	.50
15	Graig Nettles	.40	.30	.15
16	Ken Oberkfell	.20	.15	.08
17	Gerald Perry	.60	.45	.25
18	Rafael Ramirez	.20	.15	.08
19	Ken Griffey	.30	.25	.12
20	Andres Thomas	.30	.25	.12
21	Glenn Hubbard	.20	.15	.08
22	Damaso Garcia	.20	.15	.08
23	Gary Roenicke	.20	.15	.08
24	Dion James	.30	.25	.12
25	Albert Hall	.20	.15	.08
26	Chuck Tanner	.20	.15	.08
——	Smokey Bear Logo Card/Checklist	.10	.08	.04

1987 Smokey Bear Cardinals

Approximately 25,000 fans in attendance at Busch Stadium on August 24th received a 25-card set featuring the St. Louis Cardinals. Produced by the U.S. Forestry Service, the cards measure 4" by 6". The card fronts feature a full-color photo set inside an oval frame. Only the player's last name appears on the front. The card reverse carries the player's name, position and personal data plus a Smokey Bear cartoon with a fire prevention message.

		MT	NR MT	EX
Complete Set:		8.00	6.00	3.25
Common Player:		.20	.15	.08
1	Ray Soff	.20	.15	.08
2	Todd Worrell	.50	.40	.20
3	John Tudor	.35	.25	.14
4	Pat Perry	.20	.15	.08
5	Rick Horton	.20	.15	.08
6	Dan Cox	.30	.25	.12
7	Bob Forsch	.30	.25	.12
8	Greg Mathews	.40	.30	.15
9	Bill Dawley	.20	.15	.08
10	Steve Lake	.20	.15	.08

		MT	NR MT	EX
11	Tony Pena	.30	.25	.12
12	Tom Pagnozzi	.30	.25	.12
13	Jack Clark	.80	.60	.30
14	Jim Lindeman	.35	.25	.14
15	Mike Laga	.20	.15	.08
16	Terry Pendleton	.40	.30	.15
17	Ozzie Smith	.80	.60	.30
18	Jose Oquendo	.20	.15	.08
19	Tom Lawless	.20	.15	.08
20	Tom Herr	.30	.25	.12
21	Curt Ford	.20	.15	.08
22	Willie McGee	.70	.50	.30
23	Tito Landrum	.20	.15	.08
24	Vince Coleman	.80	.60	.30
25	Whitey Herzog	.30	.25	.12

1987 Smokey Bear Dodgers

The 40-card Smokey Bear Dodgers set features "25 Years of Dodger All-Stars." The cards, which measure 2-1/2" by 3-3/4", were given out to fans 14 years of age and younger at the September 18th game at Dodgers Stadium. The card fronts contain full-color photos set in the shape of Dodger Stadium and have attractive silver borders. The backs carry the player's All-Star Game record plus a fire prevention message. Many of the photos used in the set were from team-issued picture packs sold by the Dodgers in the past.

		MT	NR MT	EX
Complete Set:		10.00	7.50	4.00
Common Player:		.20	.15	.08
(1)	Walt Alston	.40	.30	.15
(2)	Dusty Baker	.25	.20	.10
(3)	Jim Brewer	.20	.15	.08
(4)	Ron Cey	.30	.25	.12
(5)	Tommy Davis	.25	.20	.10
(6)	Willie Davis	.25	.20	.10
(7)	Don Drysdale	.80	.60	.30
(8)	Steve Garvey	.80	.60	.30
(9)	Bill Grabarkewitz	.20	.15	.08
(10)	Pedro Guerrero	.50	.40	.20
(11)	Tom Haller	.20	.15	.08
(12)	Orel Hershiser	.60	.45	.25
(13)	Burt Hooton	.20	.15	.08
(14)	Steve Howe	.20	.15	.08
(15)	Tommy John	.50	.40	.20
(16)	Sandy Koufax	1.25	.90	.50
(17)	Tom Lasorda	.30	.25	.12
(18)	Jim Lefebvre	.20	.15	.08
(19)	Davey Lopes	.25	.20	.10
(20)	Mike Marshall (outfielder)	.40	.30	.15
(21)	Mike Marshall (pitcher)	.25	.20	.10
(22)	Andy Messersmith	.20	.15	.08
(23)	Rick Monday	.25	.20	.10
(24)	Manny Mota	.25	.20	.10
(25)	Claude Osteen	.20	.15	.08
(26)	Johnny Podres	.30	.25	.12
(27)	Phil Regan	.20	.15	.08
(28)	Jerry Reuss	.25	.20	.10
(29)	Rick Rhoden	.25	.20	.10
(30)	John Roseboro	.25	.20	.10
(31)	Bill Russell	.25	.20	.10
(32)	Steve Sax	.40	.30	.15
(33)	Bill Singer	.20	.15	.08
(34)	Reggie Smith	.25	.20	.10

		MT	NR MT	EX
(35)	Don Sutton	.60	.45	.25
(36)	Fernando Valenzuela	.70	.50	.30
(37)	Bob Welch	.30	.25	.12
(38)	Maury Wills	.40	.30	.15
(39)	Jim Wynn	.20	.15	.08
(40)	Logo Card/Checklist	.10	.08	.04

1987 Smokey Bear Rangers

The 1987 Smokey Bear Rangers set is made up of 32 full-color cards. Co-sponsored by the Texas Rangers, U.S. Forest Service and Texas Forest Service, the set was given out to fans at special promotions at Arlington Stadium. The cards measure 4-1/4" by 6" and feature full-color photos on the fronts. The backs contain brief player personal information, along with the card number and a Smokey the Bear message. Cards of Mike Mason and Tom Paciorek were withdrawn from the sets given out by the Rangers and are quite scarce.

		MT	NR MT	EX
	Complete Set:	55.00	41.00	22.00
	Common Player:	.30	.25	.12
1	Charlie Hough	.60	.45	.25
2	Greg Harris	.30	.25	.12
3	Jose Guzman	.60	.45	.25
4	Mike Mason	20.00	15.00	8.00
5	Dale Mohorcic	.50	.40	.20
6	Bobby Witt	.80	.60	.30
7	Mitch Williams	.50	.40	.20
8	Geno Petralli	.30	.25	.12
9	Don Slaught	.30	.25	.12
10	Darrell Porter	.30	.25	.12
11	Steve Beuchele	.40	.30	.15
12	Pete O'Brien	.60	.45	.25
13	Scott Fletcher	.40	.30	.15
14	Tom Paciorek	20.00	15.00	8.00
15	Pete Incaviglia	1.00	.70	.40
16	Oddibe McDowell	.60	.45	.25
17	Ruben Sierra	1.50	1.25	.60
18	Larry Parrish	.50	.40	.20
19	Bobby Valentine	.40	.30	.15
20	Tom House	.30	.25	.12
21	Tom Robson	.30	.25	.12
22	Edwin Correa	.40	.30	.15
23	Mike Stanley	.60	.45	.25
24	Joe Ferguson	.30	.25	,12
25	Art Howe	.30	.25	.12
26	Bob Brower	.50	.40	.20
27	Mike Loynd	.50	.40	.20
28	Curtis Wilkerson	.30	.25	.12
29	Tim Foli	.30	.25	.12
30	Dave Oliver	.30	.25	.12
31	Jerry Browne	.50	.40	.20
32	Jeff Russell	.30	.25	.12

1988 Smokey Bear Angels

This set includes 25 borderless full-color cards (2-1/2" by 3-1/2") that are highlighted by a thin white inset outline on the card fronts. The player name, team logo and a Smokey Bear picture logo appear in the lower right corner. The backs are black and white and include personal information and a large cartoon-style fire prevention logo. The set also includes a team logo checklist card. Part of the U.S. Forest Service fire prevention campaign, the cards were distributed in three separate in-stadium giveaways during August and September, 1988 games.

		MT	NR MT	EX
	Complete Set:	10.00	7.50	4.00
	Common Player:	.30	.25	.12
1	Cookie Rojas	.30	.25	.12
2	Johnny Ray	.40	.30	.15
3	Jack Howell	.40	.30	.15
4	Mike Witt	.50	.40	.20
5	Tony Armas	.40	.30	.15
6	Gus Polidor	.30	.25	.12
7	DeWayne Buice	.40	.30	.15
8	Dan Petry	.40	.30	.15
9	Bob Boone	.40	.30	.15
10	Chili Davis	.40	.30	.15
11	Greg Minton	.30	.25	.12
12	Kirk McCaskill	.40	.30	.15
13	Devon White	.80	.60	.30
14	Willie Fraser	.30	.25	.12
15	Chuck Finley	.30	.25	.12
16	Dick Schofield	.30	.25	.12
17	Wally Joyner	1.50	1.25	.60
18	Brian Downing	.40	.30	.15
19	Stewart Cliburn	.30	.25	.12
20	Dónnie Moore	.30	.25	.12
21	Bryan Harvey	.40	.30	.15
22	Mark McLemore	.30	.25	.12
23	Butch Wynegar	.30	.25	.12
24	George Hendrick	.40	.30	.15
----	Team Logo/Checklist	.30	.25	.12

1988 Smokey Bear Cardinals

This set of 25 oversized (3" by 5") cards features full-color action photos that fill the entire card fronts. A thin white line frames the player photo. The player name, team logo and Smokey Bear picture logo are printed in the lower right corner. The black and white cards backs contain player information and a Smokey Bear fire prevention cartoon. The card sets were distributed to young St. Louis fans as part of a Forest Service fire prevention campaign. The National Association of State Foresters co-sponsored this set.

		MT	NR MT	EX
	Complete Set:	10.00	7.50	4.00
	Common Player:	.20	.15	.08
1	Whitey Herzog	.30	.25	.12
2	Danny Cox	.30	.25	.12

		MT	NR MT	EX
3	Ken Dayley	.20	.15	.08
4	Jose DeLeon	.30	.25	.12
5	Bob Forsch	.30	.25	.12
6	Joe Magrane	.50	.40	.20
7	Greg Mathews	.30	.25	.12
8	Scott Terry	.20	.15	.08
9	John Tudor	.35	.25	.14
10	Todd Worrell	.50	.40	.20
11	Steve Lake	.20	.15	.08
12	Tom Pagnozzi	.20	.15	.08
13	Tony Pena	.30	.25	.12
14	Bob Horner	.35	.25	.14
15	Tom Lawless	.20	.15	.08
16	Jose Oquendo	.20	.15	.08
17	Terry Pendleton	.40	.30	.15
18	Ozzie Smith	.80	.60	.30
19	Vince Coleman	.80	.60	.30
20	Curt Ford	.20	.15	.08
21	Willie McGee	.70	.50	.30
22	Larry McWilliams	.20	.15	.08
23	Steve Peters	.30	.25	.12
24	Luis Alicea	.30	.25	.12
25	Tom Brunansky	.50	.40	.20

		MT	NR MT	EX
22	Dusty Baker	.25	.20	.10
23	Tom Lasorda	.30	.25	.12
24	Fernando Valenzuela	.70	.50	.30
25	Steve Sax	.40	.30	.15
26	Dodger Stadium	.20	.15	.08
27	Ron Cey	.30	.25	.12
28	Pedro Guerrero	.50	.40	.20
29	Mike Marshall (outfielder)	.40	.30	.15
30	Don Sutton	.60	.45	.25
-----	Logo Card/Checklist	.20	.15	.08
-----	Smokey Bear	.20	.15	.08

1988 Smokey Bear Dodgers

Record-breaking Dodgers from the past three decades are featured on this 32-card perforated sheet. Individual cards measure 2-1/2" by 4" and are printed on a light blue background in a design similar to the 1987 Smokey Bear Dodgers All-Star set. The black and white card backs contain the player name, a brief summary of the player's record-breaking performance and a reproduction of one of a number of Smokey Bear fire prevention posters printed during the 1950s through the 1980s. The sheets were distributed to fans of Dodger Stadium. Sponsors include the Forest Service, California Dept. of Forestry and the Bureau of Land Management.

		MT	NR MT	EX
	Complete Set:	10.00	7.50	4.00
	Common Player:	.20	.15	.08
1	Walter Alston	.40	.30	.15
2	John Roseboro	.25	.20	.10
3	Frank Howard	.40	.30	.15
4	Sandy Koufax	1.25	.90	.50
5	Manny Mota	.25	.20	.10
6	Record Pitchers (Sandy Koufax, Jerry Reuss, Bill Singer)	.70	.50	.30
7	Maury Wills	.40	.30	.15
8	Tommy Davis	.25	.20	.10
9	Phil Regan	.20	.15	.08
10	Wes Parker	.20	.15	.08
11	Don Drysdale	.80	.60	.30
12	Willie Davis	.25	.20	.10
13	Bill Russell	.25	.20	.10
14	Jim Brewer	.20	.15	.08
15	Record Fielders (Ron Cey, Steve Garvey, Davey Lopes, Bill Russell)	.50	.40	.20
16	Mike Marshall (pitcher)	.25	.20	.10
17	Steve Garvey	.80	.60	.30
18	Davey Lopes	.25	.20	.10
19	Burt Hooton	.20	.15	.08
20	Jim Wynn	.20	.15	.08
21	Record Hitters (Dusty Baker, Ron Cey, Steve Garvey, Reggie Smith)	.50	.40	.20

1988 Smokey Bear Padres

This 33-card oversized (3" by 5") set was produced in conjunction with the U.S. Forest Service as a fire prevention campaign promotion. A full-color player photo, framed by a thin white line, fills the card face. The player number and position and Smokey Bear logo appear lower right. The black and white card backs are printed in horizontal postcard format, with player info and a Smokey Bear cartoon on the left half of the card back. The set was available for purchase at the Padres Gift Shop. Cards of Candy Sierra and Larry Bowa were not released by the Padres and are quite rare. The complete set price does not include the two rare cards.

		MT	NR MT	EX
	Complete Set:	12.00	9.00	4.75
	Common Player:	.30	.25	.12
(1)	Shawn Abner	.50	.40	.20
(2)	Roberto Alomar	1.25	.90	.50
(3)	Sandy Alomar	.30	.25	.12
(4)	Greg Booker	.30	.25	.12
(5)	Larry Bowa	10.00	7.50	4.00
(6)	Chris Brown	.40	.30	.15
(7)	Mark Davis	.30	.25	.12
(8)	Pat Dobson	.30	.25	.12
(9)	Tim Flannery	.30	.25	.12
(10)	Mark Grant	.30	.25	.12
(11)	Tony Gwynn	1.50	1.25	.60
(12)	Andy Hawkins	.50	.40	.20
(13)	Stan Jefferson	.30	.25	.12
(14)	Jimmy Jones	.30	.25	.12
(15)	John Kruk	.80	.60	.30
(16)	Dave Leiper	.30	.25	.12
(17)	Shane Mack	.40	.30	.15
(18)	Carmelo Martinez	.40	.30	.15
(19)	Lance McCullers	.40	.30	.15
(20)	Keith Moreland	.40	.30	.15
(21)	Eric Nolte	.40	.30	.15
(22)	Amos Otis	.30	.25	.12
(23)	Mark Parent	.40	.30	.15
(24)	Randy Ready	.30	.25	.12
(25)	Greg Riddoch	.30	.25	.12
(26)	Benito Santiago	.80	.60	.30
(27)	Eric Show	.50	.40	.20
(28)	Candy Sierra	10.00	7.50	4.00
(29)	Denny Sommers	.30	.25	.12
(30)	Garry Templeton	.40	.30	.15
(31)	Dickie Thon	.40	.30	.15
(32)	Ed Whitson	.30	.25	.12
(33)	Marvell Wynne	.30	.25	.12

1988 Smokey Bear Rangers

This 21-card oversized (3-1/2" by 5") set was distributed to Rangers' fans at Smokey Bear Game Day on August 7th. The card fronts feature full-color action photos framed in an oval blue and red border on a white background. A nameplate above the photo identifies the player and a "Wildfire Prevention" logo is printed beneath the photo. Rangers (left) and Smokey (right) logos fill the upper corners of the card face. The card backs are black and white and include player info. U.S. and Texas Forest Service logos, and fire prevention tips.

		MT	NR MT	EX
Complete Set:		9.00	6.75	3.50
Common Player:		.30	.25	.12
1	Tom O'Malley	.30	.25	.12
2	Pete O'Brien	.50	.40	.20
3	Geno Petralli	.30	.25	.12
4	Pete Incaviglia	.70	.50	.30
5	Oddibe McDowell	.50	.40	.20
6	Dale Mohorcic	.30	.25	.12
7	Bobby Witt	.60	.45	.25
8	Bobby Valentine	.40	.30	.15
9	Ruben Sierra	1.00	.70	.40
10	Scott Fletcher	.40	.30	.15
11	Mike Stanley	.40	.30	.15
12	Steve Buechele	.40	.30	.15
13	Charlie Hough	.50	.40	.20
14	Larry Parrish	.40	.30	.15
15	Jerry Browne	.30	.25	.12
16	Bob Brower	.30	.25	.12
17	Jeff Russell	.30	.25	.12
18	Edwin Correa	.30	.25	.12
19	Mitch Williams	.40	.30	.15
20	Jose Guzman	.40	.30	.15
21	Curtis Wilkerson	.30	.25	.12

1988 Smokey Bear Royals

This 28-card set featuring full-color player caricatures by K.K. Goodale was produced for an in-stadium promotion on August 14, 1988. The 3" by 5" cards depict players, manager and coaches in action poses against a white background with a

Royals logo upper left, opposite the Smokey Bear logo. The backs are black and white and contain brief player data and a Smokey cartoon.

		MT	NR MT	EX
Complete Set:		12.00	9.00	4.75
Common Player:		.20	.15	.08
1	John Wathan	.30	.25	.12
2	Royals Coaches (Frank Funk, Adrian Garrett, Mike Lum, Ed Napolean, Bob Schaefer, Jim Schaefer)	.20	.15	.08
3	Willie Wilson	.40	.30	.15
4	Danny Tartabull	.70	.50	.30
5	Bo Jackson	1.50	1.25	.60
6	Gary Thurman	.40	.30	.15
7	Jerry Don Gleaton	.20	.15	.08
8	Floyd Bannister	.30	.25	.12
9	Buddy Black	.20	.15	.08
10	Steve Farr	.20	.15	.08
11	Gene Garber	.20	.15	.08
12	Mark Gubicza	.50	.40	.20
13	Charlie Liebrandt	.30	.25	.12
14	Ted Power	.20	.15	.08
15	Dan Quisenberry	.30	.25	.12
16	Bret Saberhagen	.70	.50	.30
17	Mike Macfarlane	.30	.25	.12
18	Scotti Madison	.30	.25	.12
19	Jamie Quirk	.20	.15	.08
20	George Brett	1.25	.90	.50
21	Kevin Seitzer	.80	.60	.30
22	Bill Pecota	.20	.15	.08
23	Kurt Stillwell	.35	.25	.14
24	Brad Wellman	.20	.15	.08
25	Frank White	.30	.25	.12
26	Jim Eisenreich	.20	.15	.08
27	Smokey Bear	.20	.15	.08
----	Checklist	.20	.15	.08

1988 Smokey Bear Twins

This 8-1/4" by 3-3/4" booklet contains a dozen postcards called Color-Grams featuring caricatures (suitable for coloring) of star players from the Minnesota Twins. Postcards are attached along a perforated edge to a baseball card-size stub with a black and white photo of the featured player. The backs of the postcards include the player name and personal information. The card stubs include the same information, along with a fire prevention tip. Twins Color-Grams were produced as a public service by the U.S. Forest Service and Dept. of Agriculture and were distributed to fans at the Metrodome.

		MT	NR MT	EX
Complete Set:		12.00	.50	.30
Common Player:		.70	.50	.30
(1)	Bert Blyleven	1.00	.50	.30
(2)	Randy Bush	.70	.50	.30
(3)	Gary Gaetti	1.50	.50	.30
(4)	Greg Gagne	.70	.50	.30
(5)	Dan Gladden	.70	.50	.30
(6)	Kent Hrbek	1.75	.50	.30
(7)	Gene Larkin	.70	.50	.30
(8)	Tim Laudner	.70	.50	.30
(9)	Al Newman	.70	.50	.30
(10)	Kirby Puckett	2.00	.50	.30
(11)	Jeff Reardon	1.00	.50	.30
(12)	Frank Viola	1.75	.50	.30

1989 Smokey Bear Angels All-Stars

The U.S. Forest Service, in conjunction with the California Angels, issued a 20-card set of "Angels All-Stars" in 1989. The standard-size cards are printed on a silver background and the player photos are bordered in red. Beneath the photo a banner stretches across homeplate, reading "Angels All-Stars," along with the player's name and position, which are flanked by Smokey Bear on the left and the Angels 1989 All-Star Game logo on the right. Card backs highlight the player's career with the Angels and include an illustrated fire prevention tip. The set features the top players in the club's history. issued by the U.S. Forest Service in conjunction with the Houston Astros. The posed player photos are set against a blue background. The player's name, team logo and a small picture of Smokey Bear appear along the bottom. The backs include fire safety messages.

		MT	NR MT	EX
Complete Set:		6.00	4.50	2.50
Common Player:		.20	.15	.08
1	Bill Rigney	.20	.15	.08
2	Dean Chance	.20	.15	.08
3	Jim Fregosi	.40	.30	.15
4	Bobby Knoop	.40	.30	.15
5	Don Mincher	.20	.15	.08
6	Clyde Wright	.20	.15	.08
7	Nolan Ryan	1.00	.70	.40
8	Frank Robinson	.80	.60	.30
9	Frank Tanana	.20	.15	.08
10	Rod Carew	.50	.40	.20
11	Bobby Grich	.20	.15	.08
12	Brian Downing	.20	.15	.08
13	Don Baylor	.35	.25	.14
14	Fred Lynn	.20	.15	.08
15	Reggie Jackson	.70	.50	.30
16	Doug DeCinces	.20	.15	.08
17	Bob Boone	.20	.15	.08
18	Wally Joyner	.60	.45	.25
19	Mike Witt	.20	.15	.08
20	Johnny Ray	.20	.15	.08

1989 Smokey Bear Cardinals

This 25-card set featuring action player photos was issued by the U.S. Forest Service to promote fire safety. The cards measure 4" by 6" and include the player's name, team logo and a small picture of Smokey Bear beneath the player photo.

		MT	NR MT	EX
Complete Set:		10.00	7.50	4.00
Common Player:		.20	.15	.08
(1)	Tom Brunansky	.50	.40	.20
(2)	Cris Carpenter	.50	.40	.20
(3)	Vince Coleman	.80	.60	.30
(4)	John Costello	.30	.25	.12
(5)	Ken Dayley	.20	.15	.08
(6)	Jose DeLeon	.35	.25	.14
(7)	Frank DiPino	.20	.15	.08
(8)	Whitey Herzog	.30	.25	.12

(9)	Ken Hill	.80	.60	.30
(10)	Pedro Guerrero	.80	.60	.30
(11)	Tim Jones	.30	.25	.12
(12)	Jim Lindeman	.20	.15	.08
(13)	Joe Magrane	.50	.40	.20
(14)	Willie McGee	.50	.40	.20
(15)	John Morris	.30	.25	.12
(16)	Jose Oquendo	.30	.25	.12
(17)	Tom Pagnozzi	.20	.15	.08
(18)	Tony Pena	.30	.25	.12
(19)	Terry Pendleton	.30	.25	.12
(20)	Dan Quisenberry	.20	.15	.08
(21)	Ozzie Smith	.80	.60	.30
(22)	Scott Terry	.30	.25	.12
(23)	Milt Thompson	.30	.25	.12
(24)	Denny Walling	.20	.15	.11
(25)	Todd Worrell	.50	.40	.20

1986 Sportflics

The premiere issue from Sportflics was distributed nationally by Amurol Division of Wrigley Gum Company. These high quality, three-phase "Magic Motion" cards depict three different photos per card, with each visible separately as the card is tilted. The 1986 issue features 200 full-color baseball cards plus 133 trivia cards. The cards come in the standard 2-1/2" by 3-1/2" size with the backs containing player stats and personal information. There are three different types of picture cards: 1) Tri-Star cards - 50 cards feature three players on one card; 2) Big Six cards - 10 cards which have six players in special categories; and 3) the Big Twelve card of 12 World Series players from the Kansas City Royals. The trivia cards are 1-3/4" by 2" and do not have player photos.

		MT	NR MT	EX
Complete Set:		40.00	30.00	16.00
Common Player:		.10	.08	.04
1	George Brett	1.00	.70	.40
2	Don Mattingly	4.00	3.00	1.50
3	Wade Boggs	2.00	1.50	.80
4	Eddie Murray	.60	.45	.25
5	Dale Murphy	1.00	.70	.40
6	Rickey Henderson	.70	.50	.30
7	Harold Baines	.20	.15	.08
8	Cal Ripken, Jr.	.60	.45	.25
9	Orel Hershiser	.40	.30	.15
10	Bret Saberhagen	.30	.25	.12
11	Tim Raines	.40	.30	.15
12	Fernando Valenzuela	.30	.25	.12
13	Tony Gwynn	.60	.45	.25
14	Pedro Guerrero	.25	.20	.10

#	Player/Subject	MT	NR MT	EX
15	Keith Hernandez	.35	.25	.14
16	Ernest Riles	.20	.15	.08
17	Jim Rice	.40	.30	.15
18	Ron Guidry	.25	.20	.10
19	Willie McGee	.25	.20	.10
20	Ryne Sandberg	.40	.30	.15
21	Kirk Gibson	.35	.25	.14
22	Ozzie Guillen	.30	.25	.12
23	Dave Parker	.25	.20	.10
24	Vince Coleman	2.00	1.50	.80
25	Tom Seaver	.40	.30	.15
26	Brett Butler	.10	.08	.04
27	Steve Carlton	.40	.30	.15
28	Gary Carter	.35	.25	.14
29	Cecil Cooper	.15	.11	.06
30	Jose Cruz	.10	.08	.04
31	Alvin Davis	.20	.15	.08
32	Dwight Evans	.15	.11	.06
33	Julio Franco	.15	.11	.06
34	Damaso Garcia	.10	.08	.04
35	Steve Garvey	.40	.30	.15
36	Kent Hrbek	.25	.20	.10
37	Reggie Jackson	.50	.40	.20
38	Fred Lynn	.20	.15	.08
39	Paul Molitor	.15	.11	.06
40	Jim Presley	.15	.11	.06
41	Dave Righetti	.20	.15	.08
42a	Robin Yount (Yankees logo on back)	2.00	1.50	.80
42b	Robin Yount (Brewers logo on back)	.60	.45	.25
43	Nolan Ryan	.60	.45	.25
44	Mike Schmidt	1.00	.70	.40
45	Lee Smith	.10	.08	.04
46	Rick Sutcliffe	.15	.11	.06
47	Bruce Sutter	.15	.11	.06
48	Lou Whitaker	.20	.15	.08
49	Dave Winfield	.50	.40	.20
50	Pete Rose	1.50	1.25	.60
51	National League MVPs (Steve Garvey, Pete Rose, Ryne Sandberg)	.70	.50	.30
52	Slugging Stars (Harold Baines, George Brett, Jim Rice)	.35	.25	.14
53	No-Hitters (Phil Niekro, Jerry Reuss, Mike Witt)	.15	.11	.06
54	Big Hitters (Don Mattingly, Cal Ripken, Jr., Robin Yount)	1.25	.90	.50
55	Bullpen Aces (Goose Gossage, Dan Quisenberry, Lee Smith)	.10	.08	.04
56	Rookies of the Year (Pete Rose, Steve Sax, Darryl Strawberry)	.80	.60	.30
57	American League MVPs (Don Baylor, Reggie Jackson, Cal Ripken, Jr.)	.35	.25	.14
58	Repeat Batting Champs (Bill Madlock, Dave Parker, Pete Rose)	.60	.45	.25
59	Cy Young Winners (Mike Flanagan, Ron Guidry, LaMarr Hoyt)	.10	.08	.04
60	Double Award Winners (Tom Seaver, Rick Sutcliffe, Fernando Valenzuela)	.20	.15	.08
61	Home Run Champs (Tony Armas, Reggie Jackson, Jim Rice)	.25	.20	.10
62	National League MVPs (Keith Hernandez, Dale Murphy, Mike Schmidt)	.50	.40	.20
63	American League MVPs (George Brett, Fred Lynn, Robin Yount)	.30	.25	.12
64	Comeback Players (Bert Blyleven, John Denny, Jerry Koosman)	.10	.08	.04
65	Cy Young Relievers (Rollie Fingers, Willie Hernandez, Bruce Sutter)	.15	.11	.06
66	Rookies Of The Year (Andre Dawson, Bob Horner, Gary Matthews)	.15	.11	.06
67	Rookies Of The Year (Carlton Fisk, Ron Kittle, Tom Seaver)	.15	.11	.06
68	Home Run Champs (George Foster, Dave Kingman, Mike Schmidt)	.30	.25	.12
69	Double Award Winners (Rod Carew, Cal Ripken, Jr., Pete Rose)	.70	.50	.30
70	Cy Young Winners (Steve Carlton, Tom Seaver, Rick Sutcliffe)	.25	.20	.10
71	Top Sluggers (Reggie Jackson, Fred Lynn, Robin Yount)	.30	.25	.12
72	Rookies of the Year (Dave Righetti, Rick Sutcliffe, Fernando Valenzuela)	.15	.11	.06
73	Rookies Of The Year (Fred Lynn, Eddie Murray, Cal Ripken, Jr.)	.25	.20	.10
74	Rookies Of The Year (Rod Carew, Alvin Davis, Lou Whitaker)	.20	.15	.08
75	Batting Champs (Wade Boggs, Carney Lansford, Don Mattingly)	1.50	1.25	.60
76	Jesse Barfield	.20	.15	.08
77	Phil Bradley	.15	.11	.06
78	Chris Brown	.25	.20	.10
79	Tom Browning	.30	.25	.12
80	Tom Brunansky	.15	.11	.06
81	Bill Buckner	.10	.08	.04
82	Chili Davis	.10	.08	.04
83	Mike Davis	.10	.08	.04
84	Rich Gedman	.10	.08	.04
85	Willie Hernandez	.10	.08	.04
86	Ron Kittle	.10	.08	.04
87	Lee Lacy	.10	.08	.04
88	Bill Madlock	.15	.11	.06
89	Mike Marshall	.15	.11	.06
90	Keith Moreland	.10	.08	.04
91	Graig Nettles	.15	.11	.06
92	Lance Parrish	.20	.15	.08
93	Kirby Puckett	.40	.30	.15
94	Juan Samuel	.20	.15	.08
95	Steve Sax	.20	.15	.08
96	Dave Stieb	.10	.08	.04
97	Darryl Strawberry	.80	.60	.30
98	Willie Upshaw	.10	.08	.04
99	Frank Viola	.20	.15	.08
100	Dwight Gooden	1.50	1.25	.60
101	Joaquin Andujar	.10	.08	.04
102	George Bell	.40	.30	.15
103	Bert Blyleven	.15	.11	.06
104	Mike Boddicker	.10	.08	.04
105	Britt Burns	.10	.08	.04
106	Rod Carew	.40	.30	.15
107	Jack Clark	.25	.20	.10
108	Danny Cox	.10	.08	.04
109	Ron Darling	.15	.11	.06
110	Andre Dawson	.25	.20	.10
111	Leon Durham	.10	.08	.04
112	Tony Fernandez	.15	.11	.06
113	Tom Herr	.10	.08	.04
114	Teddy Higuera	.80	.60	.30
115	Bob Horner	.15	.11	.06
116	Dave Kingman	.15	.11	.06
117	Jack Morris	.20	.15	.08
118	Dan Quisenberry	.10	.08	.04
119	Jeff Reardon	.15	.11	.06
120	Bryn Smith	.10	.08	.04
121	Ozzie Smith	.25	.20	.10
122	John Tudor	.15	.11	.06
123	Tim Wallach	.15	.11	.06
124	Willie Wilson	.15	.11	.06
125	Carlton Fisk	.25	.20	.10
126	RBI Sluggers (Gary Carter, George Foster, Al Oliver)	.15	.11	.06
127	Run Scorers (Keith Hernandez, Tim Raines, Ryne Sandberg)	.25	.20	.10
128	Run Scorers (Paul Molitor, Cal Ripken, Jr., Willie Wilson)	.20	.15	.08
129	No-Hitters (John Candelaria, Dennis Eckersley, Bob Forsch)	.10	.08	.04
130	World Series MVPs (Ron Cey, Rollie Fingers, Pete Rose)	.50	.40	.20
131	All-Star Game MVPs (Dave Concepcion, George Foster, Bill Madlock)	.10	.08	.04
132	Cy Young Winners (Vida Blue, John Denny, Fernando Valenzuela)	.15	.11	.06
133	Comeback Players (Doyle Alexander, Joaquin Andujar, Richard Dotson)	.10	.08	.04
134	Big Winners (John Denny, Tom Seaver, Rick Sutcliffe)	.15	.11	.06
135	Veteran Pitchers (Phil Niekro, Tom Seaver, Don Sutton)	.25	.20	.10
136	Rookies Of The Year (Vince Coleman, Dwight Gooden, Alfredo Griffin)	.80	.60	.30
137	All-Star Game MVPs (Gary Carter, Steve Garvey, Fred Lynn)	.20	.15	.08
138	Veteran Hitters (Tony Perez, Pete Rose, Rusty Staub)	.50	.40	.20
139	Power Hitters (George Foster, Jim Rice, Mike Schmidt)	.30	.25	.12
140	Batting Champs (Bill Buckner, Tony Gwynn, Al Oliver)	.20	.15	.08
141	No-Hitters (Jack Morris, Dave Righetti, Nolan Ryan)	.20	.15	.08
142	No-Hitters (Vida Blue, Bert Blyleven, Tom Seaver)	.15	.11	.06
143	Strikeout Kings (Dwight Gooden, Nolan Ryan, Fernando Valenzuela)	.80	.60	.30
144	Base Stealers (Dave Lopes, Tim Raines, Willie Wilson)	.15	.11	.06
145	RBI Sluggers (Tony Armas, Cecil Cooper, Eddie Murray)	.15	.11	.06
146	American League MVPs (Rod Carew, Rollie Fingers, Jim Rice)	.25	.20	.10
147	World Series MVPs (Rick Dempsey, Reggie Jackson, Alan Trammell)	.25	.20	.10

		MT	NR MT	EX
148	World Series MVPs (Pedro Guerrero, Darrell Porter, Mike Schmidt)	.20	.15	.08
149	ERA Leaders (Mike Boddicker, Ron Guidry, Rick Sutcliffe)	.10	.08	.04
150	Comeback Players (Reggie Jackson, Dave Kingman, Fred Lynn)	.20	.15	.08
151	Buddy Bell	.15	.11	.06
152	Dennis Boyd	.10	.08	.04
153	Dave Concepcion	.15	.11	.06
154	Brian Downing	.10	.08	.04
155	Shawon Dunston	.15	.11	.06
156	John Franco	.15	.11	.06
157	Scott Garrelts	.10	.08	.04
158	Bob James	.10	.08	.04
159	Charlie Leibrandt	.10	.08	.04
160	Oddibe McDowell	.30	.25	.12
161	Roger McDowell	.50	.40	.20
162	Mike Moore	.10	.08	.04
163	Phil Niekro	.25	.20	.10
164	Al Oliver	.15	.11	.06
165	Tony Pena	.10	.08	.04
166	Ted Power	.10	.08	.04
167	Mike Scioscia	.10	.08	.04
168	Mario Soto	.10	.08	.04
169	Bob Stanley	.10	.08	.04
170	Garry Templeton	.10	.08	.04
171	Andre Thornton	.10	.08	.04
172	Alan Trammell	.30	.25	.12
173	Doug DeCinces	.10	.08	.04
174	Greg Walker	.10	.08	.04
175	Don Sutton	.25	.20	.10
176	1985 Award Winners (Vince Coleman, Dwight Gooden, Ozzie Guillen, Don Mattingly, Wille McGee, Bret Saberhagen)	1.25	.90	.50
177	1985 Hot Rookies (Stewart Cliburn, Brian Fisher, Joe Hesketh, Joe Orsulak, Mark Salas, Larry Sheets)	.40	.30	.15
178	Future Stars (Jose Canseco, Mark Funderburk, Mike Greenwell, Steve Lombardozzi, Billy Joe Robidoux, Dan Tartabull)	20.00	15.00	8.00
179	1985 Gold Glovers (George Brett, Ron Guidry, Keith Hernandez, Don Mattingly, Willie McGee, Dale Murphy)	1.25	.90	.50
180	Active .300 Hitters (Wade Boggs, George Brett, Rod Carew, Cecil Cooper, Don Mattingly, Willie Wilson)	1.25	.90	.50
181	Active .300 Hitters (Pedro Guerrero, Tony Gwynn, Keith Hernandez, Bill Madlock, Dave Parker, Pete Rose)	.70	.50	.30
182	1985 Milestones (Rod Carew, Phil Niekro, Pete Rose, Nolan Ryan, Tom Seaver, Matt Tallman)	1.25	.90	.50
183	1985 Triple Crown (Wade Boggs, Darrell Evans, Don Mattingly, Willie McGee, Dale Murphy, Dave Parker)	1.25	.90	.50
184	1985 Highlights (Wade Boggs, Dwight Gooden, Rickey Henderson, Don Mattingly, Willie McGee, John Tudor)	1.50	1.25	.60
185	1985 20-Game Winners (Joaquin Andujar, Tom Browning, Dwight Gooden, Ron Guidry, Bret Saberhagen, John Tudor)	.60	.45	.25
186	Kansas City Royals (Steve Balboni, George Brett, Dane Iorg, Danny Jackson, Charlie Leibrandt, Darryl Motley, Dan Quisenberry, Bret Saberhagen, Lonnie Smith, Jim Sundberg, Frank White, Willie Wilson)	.40	.30	.15
187	Hubie Brooks	.10	.08	.04
188	Glenn Davis	.60	.45	.25
189	Darrell Evans	.10	.08	.04
190	Rich Gossage	.15	.11	.06
191	Andy Hawkins	.10	.08	.04
192	Jay Howell	.10	.08	.04
193	LaMarr Hoyt	.10	.08	.04
194	Davey Lopes	.10	.08	.04
195	Mike Scott	.20	.15	.08
196	Ted Simmons	.15	.11	.06
197	Gary Ward	.10	.08	.04
198	Bob Welch	.15	.11	.06
199	Mike Young	.10	.08	.04
200	Buddy Biancalana	.10	.08	.04

NOTE: A card number in parentheses ( ) indicates the card set is unnumbered.

1986 Sportflics Decade Greats

This set, produced by Sportflics, features outstanding players, by position, from the 1930s to the 1980s by decades. The card fronts are printed in sepia-toned photos or full-color with the Sportflics three-phase "Magic Motion" animation. The complete set contains 75 cards with 59 single player cards and 16 multi-player cards. Bigraphies appear on the card backs which are printed in full-color and color-coded by decade. The set was distributed only through hobby dealers and is in the popular 2-1/2" by 3-1/2" size.

		MT	NR MT	EX
	Complete Set:	14.00	10.50	5.50
	Common Player:	.15	.11	.06
1	Babe Ruth	2.50	2.00	1.00
2	Jimmie Foxx	.40	.30	.15
3	Lefty Grove	.30	.25	.12
4	Hank Greenberg	.30	.25	.12
5	Al Simmons	.15	.11	.06
6	Carl Hubbell	.30	.25	.12
7	Joe Cronin	.25	.20	.10
8	Mel Ott	.30	.25	.12
9	Lefty Gomez	.30	.25	.12
10	Lou Gehrig	1.50	1.25	.60
11	Pie Traynor	.15	.11	.06
12	Charlie Gehringer	.30	.25	.12
13	Catchers (Mickey Cochrane, Bill Dickey, Gabby Hartnett)	.30	.25	.12
14	Pitchers (Dizzy Dean, Paul Derringer, Red Ruffing)	.30	.25	.12
15	Outfielders (Earl Averill, Joe Medwick, Paul Waner)	.15	.11	.06
16	Bob Feller	.60	.45	.25
17	Lou Boudreau	.15	.11	.06
18	Enos Slaughter	.25	.20	.10
19	Hal Newhouser	.15	.11	.06
20	Joe DiMaggio	1.50	1.25	.60
21	Pee Wee Reese	.40	.30	.15
22	Phil Rizzuto	.30	.25	.12
23	Ernie Lombardi	.15	.11	.06
24	Infielders (Joe Cronin, George Kell, Johnny Mize)	.15	.11	.06
25	Ted Williams	1.25	.90	.50
26	Mickey Mantle	3.00	2.25	1.25
27	Warren Spahn	.30	.25	.12
28	Jackie Robinson	1.00	.70	.40
29	Ernie Banks	.30	.25	.12
30	Stan Musial	1.00	.70	.40
31	Yogi Berra	.60	.45	.25
32	Duke Snider	.70	.50	.30
33	Roy Campanella	.70	.50	.30
34	Eddie Mathews	.30	.25	.12
35	Ralph Kiner	.30	.25	.12
36	Early Wynn	.25	.20	.10
37	Double Play Duo (Luis Aparicio, Nellie Fox)	.25	.20	.10
38	First Basemen (Gil Hodges, Ted Kluszewski, Mickey Vernon)	.25	.20	.10
40	Henry Aaron	1.00	.70	.40
41	Frank Robinson	.30	.25	.12
42	Bob Gibson	.30	.25	.12
43	Roberto Clemente	1.00	.70	.40
44	Whitey Ford	.40	.30	.15
45	Brooks Robinson	.50	.40	.20
46	Juan Marichal	.25	.20	.10

		MT	NR MT	EX
47	Carl Yastrzemski	1.00	.70	.40
48	First Basemen (Orlando Cepeda, Harmon Killebrew, Willie McCovey)	.30	.25	.12
49	Catchers (Bill Freehan, Elston Howard, Joe Torre)	.15	.11	.06
50	Willie Mays	1.00	.70	.40
51	Outfielders (Al Kaline, Tony Oliva, Billy Williams)	.30	.25	.12
52	Tom Seaver	.60	.45	.25
53	Reggie Jackson	.70	.50	.30
54	Steve Carlton	.40	.30	.15
55	Mike Schmidt	.70	.50	.30
56	Joe Morgan	.25	.20	.10
57	Jim Rice	.40	.30	.15
58	Jim Palmer	.30	.25	.12
59	Lou Brock	.30	.25	.12
60	Pete Rose	1.25	.90	.50
61	Steve Garvey	.40	.30	.15
62	Catchers (Carlton Fisk, Thurman Munson, Ted Simmons)	.25	.20	.10
63	Pitchers (Vida Blue, Catfish Hunter, Nolan Ryan)	.30	.25	.12
64	George Brett	.80	.60	.30
65	Don Mattingly	2.25	1.75	.90
66	Fernando Valenzuela	.30	.25	.12
67	Dale Murphy	.80	.60	.30
68	Wade Boggs	1.50	1.25	.60
69	Rickey Henderson	.60	.45	.25
70	Eddie Murray	.60	.45	.25
71	Ron Guidry	.25	.20	.10
72	Catchers (Gary Carter, Lance Parrish, Tony Pena)	.30	.25	.12
73	Infielders (Cal Ripken, Jr., Lou Whitaker, Robin Yount)	.30	.25	.12
74	Outfielders (Pedro Guerrero, Tim Raines, Dave Winfield)	.30	.25	.12
75	Dwight Gooden	1.00	.70	.40

		MT	NR MT	EX
12	Bobby Witt	.40	.30	.15
13	Barry Bonds	.70	.50	.30
14	Andres Thomas	.20	.15	.08
15	Jim Deshaies	.30	.25	.12
16	Ruben Sierra	2.00	1.50	.80
17	Steve Lombardozzi	.20	.15	.08
18	Cory Snyder	.50	.40	.20
19	Reggie Williams	.20	.15	.08
20	Mitch Williams	.20	.15	.08
21	Glenn Braggs	.30	.25	.12
22	Danny Tartabull	.80	.60	.30
23	Charlie Kerfeld	.20	.15	.08
24	Paul Assenmacher	.20	.15	.08
25	Robby Thompson	.30	.25	.12
26	Bobby Bonilla	.70	.50	.30
27	Andres Galarraga	.70	.50	.30
28	Billy Jo Robidoux	.20	.15	.08
29	Bruce Ruffin	.30	.25	.12
30	Greg Swindell	.60	.45	.25
31	John Cangelosi	.20	.15	.08
32	Jim Traber	.20	.15	.08
33	Russ Morman	.20	.15	.08
34	Barry Larkin	.60	.45	.25
35	Todd Worrell	.50	.40	.20
36	John Cerutti	.20	.15	.08
37	Mike Kingery	.20	.15	.08
38	Mark Eichhorn	.20	.15	.08
39	Scott Bankhead	.20	.15	.08
40	Bo Jackson	2.00	1.50	.80
41	Greg Mathews	.30	.25	.12
42	Eric King	.20	.15	.08
43	Kal Daniels	.80	.60	.30
44	Calvin Schiraldi	.20	.15	.08
45	Mickey Brantley	.20	.15	.08
46	Outstanding Rookie Seasons (Fred Lynn, Willie Mays, Pete Rose)	.80	.60	.30
47	Outstanding Rookie Seasons (Dwight Gooden, Tom Seaver, Fernando Valenzuela)	.80	.60	.30
48	Outstanding Rookie Seasons (Eddie Murray, Dave Righetti, Cal Ripken, Jr., Steve Sax, Darryl Strawberry, Lou Whitaker)	.60	.45	.25
49	Kevin Mitchell	2.00	1.50	.80
50	Mike Diaz	.20	.15	.08

1986 Sportflics Rookies

The 1986 Rookies set issued by Sportflics offers 50 cards and features 47 individual rookie players. In addition, there are two Tri-Star cards; one highlights former Rookies of the Year and the other features three prominent players. There is one "Big Six" card featuring six superstars. The full-color photos on the 2-1/2" by 3-1/2" cards use Sportflics three-phase "Magic Motion" animation. The set was packaged in an attractive collector box which also contained 34 trivia cards that measure 1-3/4" by 2". The set was distributed only by hobby dealers.

		MT	NR MT	EX
	Complete Set:	20.00	15.00	8.00
	Common Player:	.20	.15	.08
1	John Kruk	.80	.60	.30
2	Edwin Correa	.20	.15	.08
3	Pete Incaviglia	.50	.40	.20
4	Dale Sveum	.30	.25	.12
5	Juan Nieves	.30	.25	.12
6	Will Clark	3.50	2.75	1.50
7	Wally Joyner	2.50	2.00	1.00
8	Lance McCullers	.20	.15	.08
9	Scott Bailes	.20	.15	.08
10	Dan Plesac	.40	.30	.15
11	Jose Canseco	4.00	3.00	1.50

1987 Sportflics

For its second season in the national baseball card market, Sportflics' basic issue was again a 200-card set of 2-1/2" by 3-1/2" "Magic Motion" cards, which offer three different photos on the same card, each visible in turn as the card is moved from top to bottom or side to side. Besides single-player cards, the '87 Sportflics set includes several three- and six-player cards, though not as many as in the 1986 set. The card backs feature a small player portrait photo on the single-player cards, an innovation for 1987.

		MT	NR MT	EX
	Complete Set:	35.00	27.50	15.00
	Common Player:	.10	.08	.04
1	Don Mattingly	3.50	2.75	1.50
2	Wade Boggs	2.00	1.50	.80
3	Dale Murphy	.70	.50	.30
4	Rickey Henderson	.60	.45	.25

#	Player	MT	NR MT	EX
5	George Brett	.70	.50	.30
6	Eddie Murray	.50	.40	.20
7	Kirby Puckett	.40	.30	.15
8	Ryne Sandberg	.30	.25	.12
9	Cal Ripken Jr.	.50	.40	.20
10	Roger Clemens	.80	.60	.30
11	Ted Higuera	.15	.11	.06
12	Steve Sax	.20	.15	.08
13	Chris Brown	.10	.08	.04
14	Jesse Barfield	.15	.11	.06
15	Kent Hrbek	.20	.15	.08
16	Robin Yount	.30	.25	.12
17	Glenn Davis	.25	.20	.10
18	Hubie Brooks	.10	.08	.04
19	Mike Scott	.15	.11	.06
20	Darryl Strawberry	.70	.50	.30
21	Alvin Davis	.15	.11	.06
22	Eric Davis	.80	.60	.30
23	Danny Tartabull	.30	.25	.12
24a	Cory Snyder (Pat Tabler photo on back (facing front), 3/4 swing on front)	1.50	1.25	.60
24b	Cory Snyder (Pat Tabler photo on back (facing front), 1/4 swing on front)	1.50	1.25	.60
24c	Cory Snyder (Snyder photo on back (facing to side))	1.00	.70	.40
25	Pete Rose	1.25	.90	.50
26	Wally Joyner	1.50	1.25	.60
27	Pedro Guerrero	.20	.15	.08
28	Tom Seaver	.30	.25	.12
29	Bob Knepper	.10	.08	.04
30	Mike Schmidt	.60	.45	.25
31	Tony Gwynn	.50	.40	.20
32	Don Slaught	.10	.08	.04
33	Todd Worrell	.30	.25	.12
34	Tim Raines	.40	.30	.15
35	Dave Parker	.20	.15	.08
36	Bob Ojeda	.10	.08	.04
37	Pete Incaviglia	.50	.40	.20
38	Bruce Hurst	.15	.11	.06
39	Bobby Witt	.40	.30	.15
40	Steve Garvey	.40	.30	.15
41	Dave Winfield	.40	.30	.15
42	Jose Cruz	.10	.08	.04
43	Orel Hershiser	.40	.30	.15
44	Reggie Jackson	.50	.40	.20
45	Chili Davis	.10	.08	.04
46	Robby Thompson	.30	.25	.12
47	Dennis Boyd	.10	.08	.04
48	Kirk Gibson	.30	.25	.12
49	Fred Lynn	.20	.15	.08
50	Gary Carter	.30	.25	.12
51	George Bell	.40	.30	.15
52	Pete O'Brien	.10	.08	.04
53	Ron Darling	.15	.11	.06
54	Paul Molitor	.15	.11	.06
55	Mike Pagliarulo	.15	.11	.06
56	Mike Boddicker	.10	.08	.04
57	Dave Righetti	.20	.15	.08
58	Len Dykstra(FC)	.15	.11	.06
59	Mike Witt	.10	.08	.04
60	Tony Bernazard	.10	.08	.04
61	John Kruk	.30	.25	.12
62	Mike Krukow	.10	.08	.04
63	Sid Fernandez	.15	.11	.06
64	Gary Gaetti	.20	.15	.08
65	Vince Coleman	.30	.25	.12
66	Pat Tabler	.10	.08	.04
67	Mike Scioscia	.10	.08	.04
68	Scott Garrelts	.10	.08	.04
69	Brett Butler	.10	.08	.04
70	Bill Buckner	.10	.08	.04
71a	Dennis Rasmussen (John Montefusco photo on back)	.25	.20	.10
71b	Dennis Rasmussen (Rasmussen photo on back)	.15	.11	.06
72	Tim Wallach	.15	.11	.06
73	Bob Horner	.15	.11	.06
74	Willie McGee	.15	.11	.06
75	American League First Basemen (Wally Joyner, Don Mattingly, Eddie Murray)	1.50	1.25	.60
76	Jesse Orosco	.10	.08	.04
77	National League Relief Pitchers (Jeff Reardon, Dave Smith, Todd Worrell)	.15	.11	.06
78	Candy Maldonado	.10	.08	.04
79	National League Shortstops (Hubie Brooks, Shawon Dunston, Ozzie Smith)	.15	.11	.06
80	American League Left Fielders (George Bell, Jose Canseco, Jim Rice)	1.50	1.25	.60
81	Bert Blyleven	.15	.11	.06
82	Mike Marshall	.15	.11	.06
83	Ron Guidry	.20	.15	.08
84	Julio Franco	.15	.11	.06
85	Willie Wilson	.15	.11	.06
86	Lee Lacy	.10	.08	.04
87	Jack Morris	.20	.15	.08
88	Ray Knight	.10	.08	.04
89	Phil Bradley	.15	.11	.06
90	Jose Canseco	3.00	2.25	1.25
91	Gary Ward	.10	.08	.04
92	Mike Easler	.10	.08	.04
93	Tony Pena	.10	.08	.04
94	Dave Smith	.10	.08	.04
95	Will Clark	5.00	3.75	2.00
96	Lloyd Moseby	.10	.08	.04
97	Jim Rice	.40	.30	.15
98	Shawon Dunston	.15	.11	.06
99	Don Sutton	.25	.20	.10
100	Dwight Gooden	1.00	.70	.40
101	Lance Parrish	.20	.15	.08
102	Mark Langston	.15	.11	.06
103	Floyd Youmans	.10	.08	.04
104	Lee Smith	.10	.08	.04
105	Willie Hernandez	.10	.08	.04
106	Doug DeCinces	.10	.08	.04
107	Ken Schrom	.10	.08	.04
108	Don Carman	.10	.08	.04
109	Brook Jacoby	.15	.11	.06
110	Steve Bedrosian	.15	.11	.06
111	American League Pitchers (Roger Clemens, Teddy Higuera, Jack Morris)	.50	.40	.20
112	American League Second Basemen (Marty Barrett, Tony Bernazard, Lou Whitaker)	.10	.08	.04
113	American League Shortstops (Tony Fernandez, Scott Fletcher, Cal Ripken)	.25	.20	.10
114	American League Third Basemen (Wade Boggs, George Brett, Gary Gaetti)	.80	.60	.30
115	National League Third Basemen (Chris Brown, Mike Schmidt, Tim Wallach)	.35	.25	.14
116	National League Second Basemen (Bill Doran, Johnny Ray, Ryne Sandberg)	.15	.11	.06
117	National League Right Fielders (Kevin Bass, Tony Gwynn, Dave Parker)	.25	.20	.10
118	Hot Rookie Prospects (David Clark, Pat Dodson, Ty Gainey, Phil Lombardi, Benito Santiago, Terry Steinbach)	1.75	1.25	.70
119	1986 Season Highlights (Dave Righetti, Mike Scott, Fernando Valenzuela)	.15	.11	.06
120	National League Pitchers (Dwight Gooden, Mike Scott, Fernando Valenzuela)	.40	.30	.15
121	Johnny Ray	.10	.08	.04
122	Keith Moreland	.10	.08	.04
123	Juan Samuel	.15	.11	.06
124	Wally Backman	.10	.08	.04
125	Nolan Ryan	1.00	.70	.40
126	Greg Harris	.10	.08	.04
127	Kirk McCaskill	.10	.08	.04
128	Dwight Evans	.15	.11	.06
129	Rick Rhoden	.10	.08	.04
130	Bill Madlock	.15	.11	.06
131	Oddibe McDowell	.10	.08	.04
132	Darrell Evans	.10	.08	.04
133	Keith Hernandez	.30	.25	.12
134	Tom Brunansky	.15	.11	.06
135	Kevin McReynolds	.20	.15	.08
136	Scott Fletcher	.10	.08	.04
137	Lou Whitaker	.20	.15	.08
138	Carney Lansford	.10	.08	.04
139	Andre Dawson	.25	.20	.10
140	Carlton Fisk	.20	.15	.08
141	Buddy Bell	.15	.11	.06
142	Ozzie Smith	.20	.15	.08
143	Dan Pasqua	.15	.11	.06
144	Kevin Mitchell	1.50	1.25	.60
145	Bret Saberhagen	.25	.20	.10
146	Charlie Kerfeld	.10	.08	.04
147	Phil Niekro	.25	.20	.10
148	John Candelaria	.10	.08	.04
149	Rich Gedman	.10	.08	.04
150	Fernando Valenzuela	.30	.25	.12
151	National League Catchers (Gary Carter, Tony Pena, Mike Scioscia)	.15	.11	.06
152	National League Left Fielders (Vince Coleman, Jose Cruz, Tim Raines)	.20	.15	.08
153	American League Right Fielders (Harold Baines, Jesse Barfield, Dave Winfield)	.25	.20	.10
154	American League Catchers (Rich Gedman, Lance Parrish, Don Slaught)	.10	.08	.04

		MT	NR MT	EX
155	National League Center Fielders (Eric Davis, Kevin McReynolds, Dale Murphy)	.70	.50	.30
156	1986 Season Highlights (Jim Deshaies, Mike Schmidt, Don Sutton)	.30	.25	.12
157	American League Speedburners (John Cangelosi, Rickey Henderson, Gary Pettis)	.25	.20	.10
158	Hot Rookie Prospects (Randy Asadoor, Casey Candaele, Dave Cochrane, Rafael Palmeiro, Tim Pyznarski, Kevin Seitzer)	2.50	2.00	1.00
159	The Best of the Best (Roger Clemens, Dwight Gooden, Rickey Henderson, Don Mattingly, Dale Murphy, Eddie Murray)	1.25	.90	.50
160	Roger McDowell	.15	.11	.06
161	Brian Downing	.10	.08	.04
162	Bill Doran	.10	.08	.04
163	Don Baylor	.15	.11	.06
164	Alfredo Griffin	.10	.08	.04
165	Don Aase	.10	.08	.04
166	Glenn Wilson	.10	.08	.04
167	Dan Quisenberry	.10	.08	.04
168	Frank White	.10	.08	.04
169	Cecil Cooper	.15	.11	.06
170	Jody Davis	.10	.08	.04
171	Harold Baines	.20	.15	.08
172	Rob Deer	.10	.08	.04
173	John Tudor	.15	.11	.06
174	Larry Parrish	.10	.08	.04
175	Kevin Bass	.10	.08	.04
176	Joe Carter	.15	.11	.06
177	Mitch Webster	.10	.08	.04
178	Dave Kingman	.15	.11	.06
179	Jim Presley	.15	.11	.06
180	Mel Hall	.10	.08	.04
181	Shane Rawley	.10	.08	.04
182	Marty Barrett	.10	.08	.04
183	Damaso Garcia	.10	.08	.04
184	Bobby Grich	.10	.08	.04
185	Leon Durham	.10	.08	.04
186	Ozzie Guillen	.10	.08	.04
187	Tony Fernandez	.15	.11	.06
188	Alan Trammell	.30	.25	.12
189	Jim Clancy	.10	.08	.04
190	Bo Jackson	3.00	2.25	1.25
191	Bob Forsch	.10	.08	.04
192	John Franco	.10	.08	.04
193	Von Hayes	.10	.08	.04
194	American League Relief Pitchers (Don Aase, Mark Eichhorn, Dave Righetti)	.10	.08	.04
195	National League First Basemen (Will Clark, Glenn Davis, Keith Hernandez)	1.00	.70	.40
196	1986 Season Highlights (Roger Clemens, Joe Cowley, Bob Horner)	.35	.25	.14
197	The Best of the Best (Wade Boggs, George Brett, Hubie Brooks, Tony Gwynn, Tim Raines, Ryne Sandberg)	.80	.60	.30
198	American League Center Fielders (Rickey Henderson, Fred Lynn, Kirby Puckett)	.25	.20	.10
199	National League Speedburners (Vince Coleman, Eric Davis, Tim Raines)	.50	.40	.20
200	Steve Carlton	.40	.30	.15

1987 Sportflics Rookie Discs

The 1987 Sportflics Rookie Discs set consists of seven discs which measure 4" in diameter. The front of the discs offer three "Magic Motion" photos in full

color, encompassed by a blue border. The disc backs are printed in red, blue, yellow and green and include the team logo, player statistics, player biography and the disc number. The set was issued with Cooperstown Timeless Trivia Cards.

		MT	NR MT	EX
	Complete Set:	20.00	15.00	8.00
	Common Player:	1.00	.70	.40
1	Casey Candaele	1.00	.70	.40
2	Mark McGwire	4.00	3.00	1.50
3	Kevin Seitzer	3.00	2.25	1.25
4	Joe Magrane	2.00	1.50	.80
5	Benito Santiago	2.50	2.00	1.00
6	Dave Magadan	2.00	1.50	.80
7	Devon White	2.50	2.00	1.00

1987 Sportflics Rookie Prospects

The 1987 Sportflics Rookie Prospects set consists of 10 cards that are the standard 2-1/2" by 3-1/2" size. The card fronts feature Sportflics' "Magic Motion" process. Card backs contain a player photo plus a short biography and player personal and statistical information. The set was offered in two separately wrapped mylar packs of five cards to hobby dealers purchasing cases of Sportflics' Team Preview set. Twenty-four packs of "Rookie Prospects" cards were included with each case.

		MT	NR MT	EX
	Complete Set:	10.00	7.50	4.00
	Common Player:	.50	.40	.20
1	Terry Steinbach	1.00	.70	.40
2	Rafael Palmeiro	1.50	1.25	.60
3	Dave Magadan	1.00	.70	.40
4	Marvin Freeman	.50	.40	.20
5	Brick Smith	.50	.40	.20
6	B.J. Surhoff	1.25	.90	.50
7	John Smiley	.50	.40	.20
8	Alonzo Powell	.50	.40	.20
9	Benny Santiago	1.50	1.25	.60
10	Devon White	1.50	1.25	.60

1987 Sportflics Rookies

The 1987 Sportflics Rookies set was issued in two series of 25 cards. The first was released in July with the second series following in October. The cards, which are the standard 2-1/2" by 3-1/2", feature Sportflics' special "Magic Motion" process. The card fronts contain a full-color photo and present three different pictures, depending on how the card is held. The backs also contain a full-color photo along with player statistics and a biography.

		MT	NR MT	EX
	Complete Set:	15.00	11.00	6.00
	Common Player:	.20	.15	.08

		MT	NR MT	EX
1	Eric Bell	.20	.15	.08
2	Chris Bosio	.20	.15	.08
3	Bob Brower	.20	.15	.08
4	Jerry Browne	.20	.15	.08
5	Ellis Burks	1.50	1.25	.60
6	Casey Candaele	.20	.15	.08
7	Joey Cora	.20	.15	.08
8	Ken Gerhart	.30	.25	.12
9	Mike Greenwell	2.00	1.50	.80
10	Stan Jefferson	.20	.15	.08
11	Dave Magadan	.40	.30	.15
12	Joe Magrane	.40	.30	.15
13	Fred McGriff	.80	.60	.30
14	Mark McGwire	2.00	1.50	.80
15	Mark McLemore	.20	.15	.08
16	Jeff Musselman	.20	.15	.08
17	Matt Nokes	.70	.50	.30
18	Paul O'Neill	.20	.15	.08
19	Luis Polonia	.20	.15	.08
20	Benny Santiago	.80	.60	.30
21	Kevin Seitzer	1.00	.70	.40
22	Terry Steinbach	.30	.25	.12
23	B.J. Surhoff	.70	.50	.30
24	Devon White	1.00	.70	.40
25	Matt Williams	.40	.30	.15
26	DeWayne Buice	.20	.15	.08
27	Willie Fraser	.20	.15	.08
28	Bill Ripken	.30	.25	.12
29	Mike Henneman	.30	.25	.12
30	Shawn Hillegas	.20	.15	.08
31	Shane Mack	.20	.15	.08
32	Rafael Palmeiro	.70	.50	.30
33	Mike Jackson	.20	.15	.08
34	Gene Larkin	.20	.15	.08
35	Jimmy Jones	.20	.15	.08
36	Gerald Young	.40	.30	.15
37	Ken Caminiti	.20	.15	.08
38	Sam Horn	.60	.45	.25
39	David Cone	1.00	.70	.40
40	Mike Dunne	.50	.40	.20
41	Ken Williams	.30	.25	.12
42	John Morris	.20	.15	.08
43	Jim Lindeman	.30	.25	.12
44	Todd Benzinger	.70	.50	.30
45	Mike Stanley	.30	.25	.12
46	Les Straker	.20	.15	.08
47	Jeff Robinson	.50	.40	.20
48	Jeff Blauser	.30	.25	.12
49	John Marzano	.30	.25	.12
50	Keith Miller	.30	.25	.12

1987 Sportflics Superstar Discs

Released in three series of six discs and numbered 1 through 18, the 1987 Sportflics Superstar Disc set features the special "Magic Motion" process. Each disc, which measures 4-1/2" in diameter, contains three different player photos, depending which way it is tilted. A red border, containing eleven stars, the player's name and uniform number, surrounds the photo. The backs have a turquoise border which carries the words "Superstar Disc Collector Series." The backs also include the team logo, player statistics, player biography and the disc number. The discs were issued with eighteen 1-3/4" by 2-1/2" Cooperstown Timeless Trivia Cards.

		MT	NR MT	EX
Complete Set:		65.00	49.00	26.00
Common Player:		2.00	1.50	.80
1	Jose Canseco	6.00	4.50	2.50
2	Mike Scott	2.00	1.50	.80
3	Ryne Sandberg	2.50	2.00	1.00
4	Mike Schmidt	3.75	2.75	1.50
5	Dale Murphy	3.75	2.75	1.50
6	Fernando Valenzuela	2.50	2.00	1.00
7	Tony Gwynn	3.50	2.75	1.50
8	Cal Ripken	3.50	2.75	1.50
9	Gary Carter	2.75	2.00	1.00
10	Cory Snyder	2.75	2.00	1.00
11	Kirby Puckett	3.00	2.25	1.25
12	George Brett	3.75	2.75	1.50
13	Keith Hernandez	2.50	2.00	1.00
14	Rickey Henderson	3.50	2.75	1.50
15	Tim Raines	2.75	2.00	1.00
16	Bo Jackson	3.50	2.75	1.50
17	Pete Rose	4.00	3.00	1.50
18	Eric Davis	3.75	2.75	1.50

1987 Sportflics Team Preview

The 1987 Sportflics Team Preview set appeared to be a good idea, but never caught on with collectors. The intent of the set is to provide a pre-season look at each of the 26 major league clubs. The card backs contain three categories of the team preview Outlook, Newcomers to Watch and Summary. Using the "Magic Motion" process, 12 different players are featured on the card fronts. Four of the different player photos can be made visible at once. The cards, which measure 2-1/2" by 3-1/2", were issued with team logo/trivia cards in a specially designed box.

		MT	NR MT	EX
Complete Set:		10.00	7.50	4.00
Common Team:		.40	.30	.15
1	Texas Rangers (Scott Fletcher, Greg Harris, Charlie Hough, Pete Incaviglia, Mike Loynd, Oddibe McDowell, Pete O'Brien, Larry Parrish, Ruben Sierra, Don Slaught, Mitch Williams, Bobby Witt)	.50	.40	.20
2	New York Mets (Wally Backman, Gary Carter, Ron Darling, Lenny Dykstra, Sid Fernandez, Dwight Gooden, Keith Hernandez, Dave Magadan, Kevin McReynolds, Randy Myers, Bob Ojeda, Darryl Strawberry)	.70	.50	.30
3	Cleveland Indians (Tony Bernazard, Brett Butler, Tom Candiotti, Joe Carter, Julio Franco, Mel Hall, Brook Jacoby, Phil Niekro, Ken Schrom, Cory Snyder, Greg Swindell, Pat Tabler)	.50	.40	.20
4	Cincinnati Reds (Buddy Bell, Tom Browning, Kal Daniels, Eric Davis, John Franco, Bill Gullickson, Tracy Jones, Barry Larkin, Rob Murphy, Paul O'Neill, Dave Parker, Pete Rose)	.60	.45	.25

		MT	NR MT	EX
5	Toronto Blue Jays (Jesse Barfield, George Bell, John Cerutti, Mark Eichhorn, Tony Fernandez, Tom Henke, Glenallen Hill, Jimmy Key, Fred McGriff, Lloyd Moseby, Dave Stieb, Willie Upshaw)	.50	.40	.20
6	Philadelphia Phillies (Steve Bedrosian, Don Carman, Marvin Freeman, Kevin Gross, Von Hayes, Shane Rawley, Bruce Ruffin, Juan Samuel, Mike Schmidt, Kent Tekulve, Milt Thompson, Glenn Wilson)	.50	.40	.20
7	New York Yankees (Rickey Henderson, Phil Lombardi, Don Mattingly, Mike Pagliarulo, Dan Pasqua, Willie Randolph, Dennis Rasmussen, Rick Rhoden, Dave Righetti, Joel Skinner, Bob Tewksbury, Dave Winfield)	.80	.60	.30
8	Houston Astros (Kevin Bass, Jose Cruz, Glenn Davis, Jim Deshaies, Bill Doran, Ty Gainey, Charlie Kerfeld, Bob Knepper, Nolan Ryan, Mike Scott, Dave Smith, Robby Wine)	.40	.30	.15
9	Boston Red Sox (Marty Barrett, Don Baylor, Wade Boggs, Dennis Boyd, Roger Clemens, Pat Dodson, Dwight Evans, Mike Greenwell, Dave Henderson, Bruce Hurst, Jim Rice, Calvin Schiraldi)	.60	.45	.25
10	San Francisco Giants (Bob Brenly, Chris Brown, Will Clark, Chili Davis, Kelly Downs, Scott Garrelts, Mark Grant, Mike Krukow, Jeff Leonard, Candy Maldonado, Terry Mulholland, Robby Thompson)	.50	.40	.20
11	California Angels (John Candelaria, Doug DeCinces, Brian Downing, Ruppert Jones, Wally Joyner, Kirk McCaskill, Darrell Miller, Donnie Moore, Gary Pettis, Don Sutton, Devon White, Mike Witt)	.50	.40	.20
12	St. Louis Cardinals (Jack Clark, Vince Coleman, Danny Cox, Bob Forsch, Tom Herr, Joe Magrane, Willie McGee, Terry Pendleton, Ozzie Smith, John Tudor, Andy Van Slyke, Todd Worrell)	.60	.45	.25
13	Kansas City Royals (George Brett, Mark Gubicza, Bo Jackson, Charlie Leibrandt, Hal McRae, Dan Quisenberry, Bret Saberhagen, Kevin Seitzer, Lonnie Smith, Danny Tartabull, Frank White, Willie Wilson)	.50	.40	.20
14	Los Angeles Dodgers (Ralph Bryant, Mariano Duncan, Jose Gonzalez, Pedro Guerrero, Orel Hershiser, Mike Marshall, Steve Sax, Mike Scioscia, Franklin Stubbs, Fernando Valenzuela, Reggie Williams, Matt Young)	.50	.40	.20
15	Detroit Tigers (Darnell Coles, Darrell Evans, Kirk Gibson, Willie Hernandez, Eric King, Chet Lemon, Dwight Lowry, Jack Morris, Dan Petry, Frank Tanana, Alan Trammell, Lou Whitaker)	.60	.45	.25
16	San Diego Padres (Randy Asadoor, Steve Garvey, Tony Gwynn, Andy Hawkins, Jim Jones, John Kruk, Craig Lefferts, Shane Mack, Lance McCullers, Kevin Mitchell, Benny Santiago, Ed Wojna)	.50	.40	.20
17	Minnesota Twins (Bert Blyleven, Tom Brunansky, Gary Gaetti, Greg Gagne, Kent Hrbek, Joe Klink, Steve Lombardozzi, Kirby Puckett, Jeff Reardon, Mark Salas, Roy Smalley, Frank Viola)	.60	.45	.25
18	Pittsburgh Pirates (Barry Bonds, Bobby Bonilla, Sid Bream, Mike Diaz, Brian Fisher, Jim Morrison, Joe Orsulak, Bob Patterson, Tony Pena, Johnny Ray, R.J. Reynolds, John Smiley)	.50	.40	.20
19	Milwaukee Brewers (Glenn Braggs, Rob Deer, Teddy Higuera, Paul Molitor, Juan Nieves, Dan Plesac, Tim Pyznarski, Ernest Riles, Billy Jo Robidoux, B.J. Surhoff, Dale Sveum, Robin Yount)	.50	.40	.20
20	Montreal Expos (Hubie Brooks, Tim Burke, Casey Candaele, Dave Collins, Mike Fitzgerald, Andres Galarraga, Billy Moore, Alonzo Powell, Randy St. Claire, Tim Wallach, Mitch Webster, Floyd Youmans)	.50	.40	.20
21	Baltimore Orioles (Don Aase, Eric Bell, Mike Boddicker, Ken Gerhardt, Terry Kennedy, Ray Knight, Lee Lacy, Fred Lynn, Eddie Murray, Cal Ripken, Jr., Larry Sheets, Jim Traber)	.50	.40	.20
22	Chicago Cubs (Jody Davis, Shawon Dunston, Leon Durham, Dennis Eckersley, Greg Maddux, Dave Martinez, Keith Moreland, Jerry Mumphrey, Rafael Palmeiro, Ryne Sandberg, Scott Sanderson, Lee Smith)	.40	.30	.15
23	Oakland Athletics (Jose Canseco, Mike Davis, Alfredo Griffin, Reggie Jackson, Carney Lansford, Mark McGwire, Dwayne Murphy, Rob Nelson, Tony Phillips, Jose Rijo, Terry Steinbach, Curt Young)	.70	.50	.30
24	Atlanta Braves (Paul Assenmacher, Gene Garber, Tom Glavine, Ken Griffey, Glenn Hubbard, Dion James, Rick Mahler, Dale Murphy, Ken Oberkfell, David Palmer, Zane Smith, Andres Thomas)	.50	.40	.20
25	Seattle Mariners (Scott Bankhead, Phil Bradley, Scott Bradley, Mickey Brantley, Alvin Davis, Steve Fireovid, Mark Langston, Mike Moore, Donell Nixon, Ken Phelps, Jim Presley, Dave Valle)	.40	.30	.15
26	Chicago White Sox (Harold Baines, John Cangelosi, Dave Cochrane, Joe Cowley, Carlton Fisk, Ozzie Guillen, Ron Hassey, Bob James, Ron Karkovice, Russ Mormon, Bobby Thigpen, Greg Walker)	.40	.30	.15

1988 Sportflics

The design of the 1988 Sportflics set differs greatly from the previous two years. Besides increasing the number of cards in the set to 225, Sportflics included the player name, team and uniform number on the card front. The triple-action color photos are surrounded by a red border. The backs are re-designed, also. Full-color action photos, plus extensive statistics and informative biographies are utilized. Three highlights cards and three rookie prospects card are included in the set. The cards are the standard 2-1/2" by 3-1/2".

		MT	NR MT	EX
Complete Set:		35.00	27.50	15.00
Common Player:		.10	.08	.04
1	Don Mattingly	3.00	2.25	1.25
2	Tim Raines	.35	.25	.14
3	Andre Dawson	.25	.20	.10
4	George Bell	.30	.25	.12
5	Joe Carter	.15	.11	.06
6	Matt Nokes	.50	.40	.20
7	Dave Winfield	.35	.25	.14
8	Kirby Puckett	.35	.25	.14
9	Will Clark	.80	.60	.30
10	Eric Davis	.70	.50	.30
11	Rickey Henderson	.50	.40	.20
12	Ryne Sandberg	.25	.20	.10
13	Jesse Barfield	.15	.11	.06
14	Ozzie Guillen	.10	.08	.04
15	Bret Saberhagen	.20	.15	.08
16	Tony Gwynn	.40	.30	.15
17	Kevin Seitzer	.50	.40	.20
18	Jack Clark	.20	.15	.08
19	Danny Tartabull	.30	.25	.12
20	Ted Higuera	.15	.11	.06
21	Charlie Leibrandt, Jr.	.10	.08	.04
22	Benny Santiago	.50	.40	.20
23	Fred Lynn	.15	.11	.06
24	Rob Thompson	.10	.08	.04
25	Alan Trammell	.25	.20	.10
26	Tony Fernandez	.15	.11	.06
27	Rick Sutcliffe	.15	.11	.06
28	Gary Carter	.25	.20	.10

		MT	NR MT	EX				MT	NR MT	EX
29	Cory Snyder	.30	.25	.12		120	Reggie Jackson	.40	.30	.15
30	Lou Whitaker	.20	.15	.08		121	Mike Pagliarulo	.15	.11	.06
31	Keith Hernandez	.25	.20	.10		122	Tommy John	.20	.15	.08
32	Mike Witt	.10	.08	.04		123	Bill Madlock	.15	.11	.06
33	Harold Baines	.15	.11	.06		124	Ken Caminiti	.30	.25	.12
34	Robin Yount	.25	.20	.10		125	Gary Ward	.10	.08	.04
35	Mike Schmidt	.60	.45	.25		126	Candy Maldonado	.10	.08	.04
36	Dion James	.10	.08	.04		127	Harold Reynolds	.10	.08	.04
37	Tom Candiotti	.10	.08	.04		128	Joe Magrane	.30	.25	.12
38	Tracy Jones	.15	.11	.06		129	Mike Henneman	.25	.20	.10
39	Nolan Ryan	.60	.45	.25		130	Jim Gantner	.10	.08	.04
40	Fernando Valenzuela	.25	.20	.10		131	Bobby Bonilla	.15	.11	.06
41	Vance Law	.10	.08	.04		132	John Farrell	.30	.25	.12
42	Roger McDowell	.10	.08	.04		133	Frank Tanana	.10	.08	.04
43	Carlton Fisk	.15	.11	.06		134	Zane Smith	.10	.08	.04
44	Scott Garrelts	.10	.08	.04		135	Dave Righetti	.20	.15	.08
45	Lee Guetterman	.10	.08	.04		136	Rick Reuschel	.10	.08	.04
46	Mark Langston	.15	.11	.06		137	Dwight Evans	.15	.11	.06
47	Willie Randolph	.10	.08	.04		138	Howard Johnson	.10	.08	.04
48	Bill Doran	.10	.08	.04		139	Terry Leach	.10	.08	.04
49	Larry Parrish	.10	.08	.04		140	Casey Candaele	.10	.08	.04
50	Wade Boggs	1.75	1.25	.70		141	Tom Herr	.10	.08	.04
51	Shane Rawley	.10	.08	.04		142	Tony Pena	.10	.08	.04
52	Alvin Davis	.15	.11	.06		143	Lance Parrish	.20	.15	.08
53	Jeff Reardon	.15	.11	.06		144	Ellis Burks	1.75	1.25	.70
54	Jim Presley	.10	.08	.04		145	Pete O'Brien	.10	.08	.04
55	Kevin Bass	.10	.08	.04		146	Mike Boddicker	.10	.08	.04
56	Kevin McReynolds	.20	.15	.08		147	Buddy Bell	.10	.08	.04
57	B.J. Surhoff	.15	.11	.06		148	Bo Jackson	.60	.45	.25
58	Julio Franco	.15	.11	.06		149	Frank White	.10	.08	.04
59	Eddie Murray	.40	.30	.15		150	George Brett	.60	.45	.25
60	Jody Davis	.10	.08	.04		151	Tim Wallach	.10	.08	.04
61	Todd Worrell	.15	.11	.06		152	Cal Ripken, Jr.	.40	.30	.15
62	Von Hayes	.10	.08	.04		153	Brett Butler	.10	.08	.04
63	Billy Hatcher	.10	.08	.04		154	Gary Gaetti	.15	.11	.06
64	John Kruk	.15	.11	.06		155	Darryl Strawberry	.60	.45	.25
65	Tom Henke	.10	.08	.04		156	Alfredo Griffin	.10	.08	.04
66	Mike Scott	.15	.11	.06		157	Marty Barrett	.10	.08	.04
67	Vince Coleman	.20	.15	.08		158	Jim Rice	.30	.25	.12
68	Ozzie Smith	.20	.15	.08		159	Terry Pendleton	.10	.08	.04
69	Ken Williams	.20	.15	.08		160	Orel Hershiser	.35	.25	.14
70	Steve Bedrosian	.15	.11	.06		161	Larry Sheets	.10	.08	.04
71	Luis Polonia	.20	.15	.08		162	Dave Stewart	.10	.08	.04
72	Brook Jacoby	.15	.11	.06		163	Shawon Dunston	.15	.11	.06
73	Ron Darling	.15	.11	.06		164	Keith Moreland	.10	.08	.04
74	Lloyd Moseby	.10	.08	.04		165	Ken Oberkfell	.10	.08	.04
75	Wally Joyner	.40	.30	.15		166	Ivan Calderon	.10	.08	.04
76	Dan Quisenberry	.10	.08	.04		167	Bob Welch	.15	.11	.06
77	Scott Fletcher	.10	.08	.04		168	Fred McGriff	.40	.30	.15
78	Kirk McCaskill	.10	.08	.04		169	Pete Incaviglia	.15	.11	.06
79	Paul Molitor	.15	.11	.06		170	Dale Murphy	.60	.45	.25
80	Mike Aldrete	.10	.08	.04		171	Mike Dunne	.25	.20	.10
81	Neal Heaton	.10	.08	.04		172	Chili Davis	.10	.08	.04
82	Jeffrey Leonard	.10	.08	.04		173	Milt Thompson	.10	.08	.04
83	Dave Magadan	.15	.11	.06		174	Terry Steinbach	.15	.11	.06
84	Danny Cox	.10	.08	.04		175	Oddibe McDowell	.10	.08	.04
85	Lance McCullers	.10	.08	.04		176	Jack Morris	.20	.15	.08
86	Jay Howell	.10	.08	.04		177	Sid Fernandez	.15	.11	.06
87	Charlie Hough	.10	.08	.04		178	Ken Griffey	.10	.08	.04
88	Gene Garber	.10	.08	.04		179	Lee Smith	.10	.08	.04
89	Jesse Orosco	.10	.08	.04		180	1987 Highlights (Juan Nieves, Kirby			
90	Don Robinson	.10	.08	.04			Puckett, Mike Schmidt)	.25	.20	.10
91	Willie McGee	.15	.11	.06		181	Brian Downing	.10	.08	.04
92	Bert Blyleven	.15	.11	.06		182	Andres Galarraga	.20	.15	.08
93	Phil Bradley	.15	.11	.06		183	Rob Deer	.10	.08	.04
94	Terry Kennedy	.10	.08	.04		184	Greg Brock	.10	.08	.04
95	Kent Hrbek	.20	.15	.08		185	Doug DeCinces	.10	.08	.04
96	Juan Samuel	.15	.11	.06		186	Johnny Ray	.10	.08	.04
97	Pedro Guerrero	.20	.15	.08		187	Hubie Brooks	.10	.08	.04
98	Sid Bream	.10	.08	.04		188	Darrell Evans	.10	.08	.04
99	Devon White	.30	.25	.12		189	Mel Hall	.10	.08	.04
100	Mark McGwire	1.25	.90	.50		190	Jim Deshaies	.10	.08	.04
101	Dave Parker	.15	.11	.06		191	Dan Plesac	.15	.11	.06
102	Glenn Davis	.20	.15	.08		192	Willie Wilson	.15	.11	.06
103	Greg Walker	.10	.08	.04		193	Mike LaValliere	.10	.08	.04
104	Rick Rhoden	.10	.08	.04		194	Tom Brunansky	.15	.11	.06
105	Mitch Webster	.10	.08	.04		195	John Franco	.15	.11	.06
106	Lenny Dykstra	.10	.08	.04		196	Frank Viola	.20	.15	.08
107	Gene Larkin	.15	.11	.06		197	Bruce Hurst	.10	.08	.04
108	Floyd Youmans	.10	.08	.04		198	John Tudor	.10	.08	.04
109	Andy Van Slyke	.15	.11	.06		199	Bob Forsch	.10	.08	.04
110	Mike Scioscia	.10	.08	.04		200	Dwight Gooden	.60	.45	.25
111	Kirk Gibson	.25	.20	.10		201	Jose Canseco	1.75	1.25	.70
112	Kal Daniels	.30	.25	.12		202	Carney Lansford	.10	.08	.04
113	Ruben Sierra	.50	.40	.20		203	Kelly Downs	.10	.08	.04
114	Sam Horn	.30	.25	.12		204	Glenn Wilson	.10	.08	.04
115	Ray Knight	.10	.08	.04		205	Pat Tabler	.10	.08	.04
116	Jimmy Key	.10	.08	.04		206	Mike Davis	.10	.08	.04
117	Bo Diaz	.10	.08	.04		207	Roger Clemens	.60	.45	.25
118	Mike Greenwell	1.50	1.25	.60		208	Dave Smith	.10	.08	.04
119	Barry Bonds	.20	.15	.08		209	Curt Young	.10	.08	.04

		MT	NR MT	EX
210	Mark Eichhorn	.10	.08	.04
211	Juan Nieves	.10	.08	.04
212	Bob Boone	.10	.08	.04
213	Don Sutton	.20	.15	.08
214	Willie Upshaw	.10	.08	.04
215	Jim Clancy	.10	.08	.04
216	Bill Ripken	.25	.20	.10
217	Ozzie Virgil	.10	.08	.04
218	Dave Concepcion	.10	.08	.04
219	Alan Ashby	.10	.08	.04
220	Mike Marshall	.15	.11	.06
221	1987 Highlights (Vince Coleman, Mark McGwire, Paul Molitor)	.50	.40	.20
222	1987 Highlights (Steve Bedrosian, Don Mattingly, Benito Santiago)	.80	.60	.30
223	Hot Rookie Prospects (Shawn Abner, Jay Buhner, Gary Thurman)	.40	.30	.15
224	Hot Rookie Prospects (Tim Crews, John Davis, Vincente Palacios)	.30	.25	.12
225	Hot Rookie Prospects (Keith Miller, Jody Reed, Jeff Treadway)	.50	.40	.20

1988 Sportflics Gamewinners

This set of 25 standard-size cards (2-1/2" by 3-1/2"), featuring star players in the Sportflics patented 3-D Magic Motion design, was issued by Weiser Card Co. of Plainsboro, N.J., for use as a youth organizational fundraiser. (Weiser's president is former Yankees outfielder Bobby Murcer.) A limited number of sets was produced for test marketing in the Northwestern U.S., with plans for a 1989 set to be marketed nationwide. A green- and-yellow Gamewinners logo banner spans the upper border of the cards face, with a matching player name (with uniform number and position) below the full-color triple photo. The card backs carry large full-color player photos (1-3/4" by 1-3/4"), along with stats, personal information and career high- lights.

		MT	NR MT	EX
	Complete Set:	10.00	7.50	4.00
	Common Player:	.20	.15	.08
1	Don Mattingly	2.50	2.00	1.00
2	Mark McGwire	1.00	.70	.40
3	Wade Boggs	1.50	1.25	.60
4	Will Clark	.60	.45	.25
5	Eric Davis	.80	.60	.30
6	Willie Randolph	.20	.15	.08
7	Dave Winfield	.50	.40	.20
8	Rickey Henderson	.60	.45	.25
9	Dwight Gooden	.80	.60	.30
10	Benny Santiago	.40	.30	.15
11	Keith Hernandez	.40	.30	.15
12	Juan Samuel	.30	.25	.12
13	Kevin Seitzer	.60	.45	.25
14	Gary Carter	.50	.40	.20
15	Darryl Strawberry	.80	.60	.30
16	Rick Rhoden	.20	.15	.08
17	Howard Johnson	.20	.15	.08
18	Matt Nokes	.50	.40	.20
19	Dave Righetti	.30	.25	.12
20	Roger Clemens	.80	.60	.30
21	Mike Schmidt	.70	.50	.30

		MT	NR MT	EX
22	Kevin McReynolds	.30	.25	.12
23	Mike Pagliarulo	.20	.15	.08
24	Kevin Elster	.20	.15	.08
25	Jack Clark	.30	.25	.12

1989 Sportflics

This basic issue includes 225 standard-size player cards (2-1/2" by 3-1/2") and 153 trivia cards, all featuring the patented Magic Motion design. A 5-card sub-set of triple photo cards called "Tri-Star" features a mix of veterans and rookies. The card fronts feature a white outer border and double color inner border in one of six color schemes (i.e. red, blue, purple). The inner border color changes when the card is tilted and the bottom border carries a double stripe of colors. The player names appears in the top border, player postition and uniform number appear, alternately, in the bottom border. The card backs contain crisp 1-7/8" by 1-3/4" player action shots, along with personal information, stats and career highlights. "The Unforgettables" trivia cards in this set salute members of the Hall of Fame, with each /
/

		MT	NR MT	EX
	Complete Set:	40.00	30.00	15.00
	Common Player:	.10	.08	.04
1	Jose Canseco	1.75	1.25	.70
2	Wally Joyner	.40	.30	.15
3	Roger Clemens	.60	.45	.25
4	Greg Swindell	.15	.11	.06
5	Jack Morris	.20	.15	.08
6	Mickey Brantley	.10	.08	.04
7	Jim Presley	.15	.11	.06
8	Pete O'Brien	.10	.08	.04
9	Jesse Barfield	.15	.11	.06
10	Frank Viola	.20	.15	.08
11	Kevin Bass	.10	.08	.04
12	Glenn Wilson	.10	.08	.04
13	Chris Sabo	1.00	.70	.40
14	Fred McGriff	.50	.40	.20
15	Mark Grace	1.25	.90	.50
16	Devon White	.20	.15	.08
17	Juan Samuel	.15	.11	.06
18	Lou Whitaker	.25	.20	.10
19	Greg Walker	.10	.08	.04
20	Roberto Alomar	.50	.40	.20
21	Mike Schmidt	.60	.45	.25
22	Benny Santiago	.25	.20	.10
23	Dave Stewart	.10	.08	.04
24	Dave Winfield	.35	.25	.14
25	George Bell	.30	.25	.12
26	Jack Clark	.20	.15	.08
27	Doug Drabek	.10	.08	.04
28	Ron Gant	.15	.11	.06
29	Glenn Braggs	.10	.08	.04
30	Rafael Palmeiro	.20	.15	.08
31	Brett Butler	.10	.08	.04
32	Ron Darling	.15	.11	.06
33	Alvin Davis	.15	.11	.06
34	Bob Walk	.10	.08	.04
35	Dave Stieb	.15	.11	.06
36	Orel Hershiser	.40	.30	.15

		MT	NR MT	EX			MT	NR MT	EX
37	John Farrell	.15	.11	.06	128	Dan Plesac	.15	.11	.06
38	Doug Jones	.10	.08	.04	129	Chili Davis	.10	.08	.04
39	Kelly Downs	.10	.08	.04	130	Bryan Harvey	.25	.20	.10
40	Bob Boone	.10	.08	.04	131	Don August	.15	.11	.06
41	Gary Sheffield	2.25	1.75	.90	132	Mike Harkey	.50	.40	.20
42	Doug Dascenzo	.30	.25	.12	133	Luis Polonia	.10	.08	.04
43	Chad Krueter	.20	.15	.08	134	Craig Worthington	.35	.25	.14
44	Ricky Jordan	1.75	1.25	.70	135	Joey Meyer	.15	.11	.06
45	Dave West	.70	.50	.30	136	Barry Larkin	.25	.20	.10
46	Danny Tartabull	.30	.25	.12	137	Glenn Davis	.20	.15	.08
47	Teddy Higuera	.15	.11	.06	138	Mike Scioscia	.10	.08	.04
48	Gary Gaetti	.15	.11	.06	139	Andres Galarraga	.20	.15	.08
49	Dave Parker	.15	.11	.06	140	Doc Gooden	.60	.45	.25
50	Don Mattingly	3.00	2.25	1.25	141	Keith Moreland	.10	.08	.04
51	David Cone	.25	.20	.10	142	Kevin Mitchell	.10	.08	.04
52	Kal Daniels	.25	.20	.10	143	Mike Greenwell	.80	.60	.30
53	Carney Lansford	.10	.08	.04	144	Mel Hall	.10	.08	.04
54	Mike Marshall	.15	.11	.06	145	Rickey Henderson	.50	.40	.20
55	Kevin Seitzer	.30	.25	.12	146	Barry Bonds	.20	.15	.08
56	Mike Henneman	.10	.08	.04	147	Eddie Murray	.40	.30	.15
57	Bill Doran	.10	.08	.04	148	Lee Smith	.10	.08	.04
58	Steve Sax	.20	.15	.08	149	Julio Franco	.15	.11	.06
59	Lance Parrish	.15	.11	.06	150	Tim Raines	.35	.25	.14
60	Keith Hernandez	.25	.20	.10	151	Mitch Williams	.10	.08	.04
61	Jose Uribe	.10	.08	.04	152	Tim Laudner	.10	.08	.04
62	Jose Lind	.15	.11	.06	153	Mike Pagliarulo	.15	.11	.06
63	Steve Bedrosian	.15	.11	.06	154	Floyd Bannister	.10	.08	.04
64	George Brett	.60	.45	.25	155	Gary Carter	.25	.20	.10
65	Kirk Gibson	.25	.20	.10	156	Kirby Puckett	.40	.30	.15
66	Cal Ripken, Jr.	.50	.40	.20	157	Harold Baines	.20	.15	.08
67	Mitch Webster	.10	.08	.04	158	Dave Righetti	.20	.15	.08
68	Fred Lynn	.15	.11	.06	159	Mark Langston	.15	.11	.06
69	Eric Davis	.60	.45	.25	160	Tony Gwynn	.50	.40	.20
70	Bo Jackson	.70	.50	.30	161	Tom Brunansky	.15	.11	.06
71	Kevin Elster	.15	.11	.06	162	Vance Law	.10	.08	.04
72	Rick Reuschel	.10	.08	.04	163	Kelly Gruber	.10	.08	.04
73	Tim Burke	.10	.08	.04	164	Gerald Perry	.15	.11	.06
74	Mark Davis	.10	.08	.04	165	Harold Reynolds	.10	.08	.04
75	Claudell Washington	.10	.08	.04	166	Andy Van Slyke	.15	.11	.06
76	Lance McCullers	.10	.08	.04	167	Jimmy Key	.15	.11	.06
77	Mike Moore	.10	.08	.04	168	Jeff Reardon	.15	.11	.06
78	Robby Thompson	.10	.08	.04	169	Milt Thompson	.10	.08	.04
79	Roger McDowell	.10	.08	.04	170	Will Clark	.80	.60	.30
80	Danny Jackson	.15	.11	.06	171	Chet Lemon	.10	.08	.04
81	Tim Leary	.10	.08	.04	172	Pat Tabler	.10	.08	.04
82	Bobby Witt	.15	.11	.06	173	Jim Rice	.30	.25	.12
83	Jim Gott	.10	.08	.04	174	Billy Hatcher	.10	.08	.04
84	Andy Hawkins	.10	.08	.04	175	Bruce Hurst	.15	.11	.06
85	Ozzie Guillen	.10	.08	.04	176	John Franco	.15	.11	.06
86	John Tudor	.15	.11	.06	177	Van Snider	.25	.20	.10
87	Todd Burns	.25	.20	.10	178	Ron Jones	.35	.25	.14
88	Dave Gallagher	.25	.20	.10	179	Jerald Clark	.30	.25	.12
89	Jay Buhner	.15	.11	.06	180	Tom Browning	.15	.11	.06
90	Gregg Jefferies	2.00	1.50	.80	181	Von Hayes	.10	.08	.04
91	Bob Welch	.15	.11	.06	182	Bobby Bonilla	.15	.11	.06
92	Charlie Hough	.10	.08	.04	183	Todd Worrell	.15	.11	.06
93	Tony Fernandez	.15	.11	.06	184	John Kruk	.15	.11	.06
94	Ozzie Virgil	.10	.08	.04	185	Scott Fletcher	.10	.08	.04
95	Andre Dawson	.25	.20	.10	186	Willie Wilson	.15	.11	.06
96	Hubie Brooks	.10	.08	.04	187	Jody Davis	.10	.08	.04
97	Kevin McReynolds	.20	.15	.08	188	Kent Hrbek	.20	.15	.08
98	Mike LaValliere	.10	.08	.04	189	Ruben Sierra	.35	.25	.14
99	Terry Pendleton	.10	.08	.04	190	Shawon Dunston	.15	.11	.06
100	Wade Boggs	1.75	1.25	.70	191	Ellis Burks	.70	.50	.30
101	Dennis Eckersley	.15	.11	.06	192	Brook Jacoby	.15	.11	.06
102	Mark Gubicza	.15	.11	.06	193	Jeff Robinson	.15	.11	.06
103	Frank Tanana	.10	.08	.04	194	Rich Dotson	.10	.08	.04
104	Joe Carter	.15	.11	.06	195	Johnny Ray	.10	.08	.04
105	Ozzie Smith	.20	.15	.08	196	Cory Snyder	.25	.20	.10
106	Dennis Martinez	.10	.08	.04	197	Mike Witt	.10	.08	.04
107	Jeff Treadway	.15	.11	.06	198	Marty Barrett	.10	.08	.04
108	Greg Maddux	.15	.11	.06	199	Robin Yount	.30	.25	.12
109	Bret Saberhagen	.20	.15	.08	200	Mark McGwire	1.00	.70	.40
110	Dale Murphy	.60	.45	.25	201	Ryne Sandberg	.30	.25	.12
111	Rob Deer	.10	.08	.04	202	John Candelaria	.10	.08	.04
112	Pete Incaviglia	.15	.11	.06	203	Matt Nokes	.20	.15	.08
113	Vince Coleman	.20	.15	.08	204	Dwight Evans	.15	.11	.06
114	Tim Wallach	.15	.11	.06	205	Darryl Strawberry	.60	.45	.25
115	Nolan Ryan	.60	.45	.25	206	Willie McGee	.15	.11	.06
116	Walt Weiss	.35	.25	.14	207	Bobby Thigpen	.15	.11	.06
117	Brian Downing	.10	.08	.04	208	B.J. Surhoff	.15	.11	.06
118	Melido Perez	.15	.11	.06	209	Paul Molitor	.15	.11	.06
119	Terry Steinbach	.15	.11	.06	210	Jody Reed	.15	.11	.06
120	Mike Scott	.15	.11	.06	211	Doyle Alexander	.10	.08	.04
121	Tim Belcher	.15	.11	.06	212	Dennis Rasmussen	.15	.11	.06
122	Mike Boddicker	.10	.08	.04	213	Kevin Gross	.10	.08	.04
123	Len Dykstra	.10	.08	.04	214	Kirk McCaskill	.10	.08	.04
124	Fernando Valenzuela	.25	.20	.10	215	Alan Trammell	.30	.25	.12
125	Gerald Young	.15	.11	.06	216	Damon Berryhill	.15	.11	.06
126	Tom Henke	.10	.08	.04	217	Rick Sutcliffe	.15	.11	.06
127	Dave Henderson	.10	.08	.04	218	Don Slaught	.10	.08	.04

		MT	NR MT	EX
219	Carlton Fisk	.30	.25	.12
220	Allan Anderson	.10	.08	.04
221	1988 Highlights (Wade Boggs, Jose Canseco, Mike Greenwell)	1.50	1.25	.60
222	1988 Highlights (Tom Browning, Dennis Eckersley, Orel Hershiser)	.25	.20	.10
223	Hot Rookie Prospects (Sandy Alomar, Gregg Jefferies, Gary Sheffield)	2.00	1.50	.80
224	Hot Rookie Prospects (Randy Johnson, Ramon Martinez, Bob Milacki)	.60	.45	.25
225	Hot Rookie Prospects (Geronimo Berroa, Cameron Drew, Ron Jones)	.35	.25	.14

1990 Sportflics

The Sportflics set for 1990 again contained 225 cards. The cards feature the unique "Magic Motion" effect which displays either of two different photos depending on how the card is tilted. (Previous year's sets had used three photos per card.) The two-photo "Magic Motion" sequence is designed to depict sequential game-action, showing a batter following through on his swing, a pitcher completed his motion, etc. Sportflics also added a moving red and yellow "marquee" border on the cards to complement the animation effect. The player's name, which appears below the animation, remains stationary. The set includes 19 special rookie cards. The backs contain a color player photo, team logo, player information and stats. The cards were distributed in non-transparent mylar packs with small MVP trivia cards.

		MT	NR MT	EX
	Complete Set:	32.00	24.00	13.00
	Common Player:	.10	.08	.04
1	Kevin Mitchell	.40	.30	.15
2	Wade Boggs	1.00	.70	.40
3	Cory Snyder	.10	.08	.04
4	Paul O'Neill	.10	.08	.04
5	Will Clark	1.00	.70	.40
6	Tony Fernandez	.10	.08	.04
7	Ken Griffey Jr.	1.25	.90	.50
8	Nolan Ryan	.60	.45	.25
9	Rafael Palmeiro	.10	.08	.04
10	Jesse Barfield	.10	.08	.04
11	Kirby Puckett	.40	.30	.15
12	Steve Sax	.10	.08	.04
13	Fred McGriff	.40	.30	.15
14	Gregg Jefferies	1.50	1.25	.06
15	Mark Grace	.90	.70	.35
16	Devon White	.10	.08	.04
17	Juan Samuel	.15	.11	.06
18	Robin Yount	.25	.20	.10
19	Glenn Davis	.10	.08	.04
20	Jeffrey Leonard	.10	.08	.04
21	Chili Davis	.10	.08	.04
22	Craig Biggio	.70	.50	.30
23	Jose Canseco	1.50	1.25	.70
24	Derek Lilliquist	.30	.25	.12
25	Chris Bosio	.10	.08	.04
26	Dave Steib	.10	.08	.04
27	Bobby Thigpen	.10	.08	.04
28	Jack Clark	.10	.08	.04
29	Kevin Ritz	.30	.25	.12

		MT	NR MT	EX
30	Tom Gordon	.80	.60	.30
31	Bryan Harvey	.10	.08	.04
32	Jim Deshaies	.10	.08	.04
33	Terry Steinbach	.15	.11	.06
34	Tom Glavine	.15	.11	.06
35	Bob Welch	.10	.08	.04
36	Charlie Hayes	.20	.15	.08
37	Jeff Reardon	.10	.08	.04
38	Joe Orsulak	.10	.08	.04
39	Scott Garrelts	.10	.08	.04
40	Bob Boone	.10	.08	.04
41	Scott Bankhead	.10	.08	.04
42	Tom Henke	.10	.08	.04
43	Greg Briley	.40	.30	.15
44	Teddy Higuera	.10	.08	.04
45	Pat Borders	.10	.08	.04
46	Kevin Seitzer	.15	.11	.06
47	Bruce Hurst	.15	.11	.06
48	Ozzie Guillen	.10	.08	.04
49	Wally Joyner	.50	.40	.20
50	Mike Greenwell	.70	.50	.30
51	Gary Gaetti	.12	.09	.05
52	Gary Sheffield	1.25	.90	.50
53	Dennis Martinez	.10	.08	.04
54	Ryne Sanberg	.20	.15	.08
55	Mike Scott	.12	.09	.05
56	Todd Benzinger	.10	.08	.04
57	Kelly Gruber	.15	.11	.06
58	Jose Lind	.10	.08	.04
59	Allan Anderson	.10	.08	.04
60	Robby Thompson	.10	.08	.04
61	John Smoltz	.30	.25	.12
62	Mark Davis	.12	.09	.05
63	Tom Herr	.10	.08	.06
64	Randy Johnson	.20	.15	.08
65	Lonnie Smith	.10	.08	.04
66	Pedro Guerrero	.15	.11	.06
67	Jerome Walton	1.50	1.25	.60
68	Ramon Martinez	.40	.30	.15
69	Tim Raines	.12	.09	.05
70	Matt Williams	.20	.15	.08
71	Joe Oliver	.35	.25	.12
72	Nick Esasky	.12	.09	:05
73	Kevin Brown	.25	.20	.10
74	Walt Weiss	.12	.09	.05
75	Roger McDowell	.10	.08	.04
76	Jose DeLeon	.10	.08	.04
77	Brian Downing	.10	.08	.04
78	Jay Howell	.10	.08	.04
79	Jose Uribe	.10	.08	.04
80	Ellis Burks	.50	.40	.20
81	Sammy Sosa	.50	.40	.20
82	Johnny Ray	.50	.40	.20
83	Danny Darwin	.10	.08	.04
84	Carney Lansford	.12	.09	.05
85	Jose Oquendo	.10	.08	.04
86	John Cerutti	.10	.08	.04
87	Dave Winfield	.15	.11	.08
88	Dave Righetti	.10	.08	.04
89	Danny Jackson	.10	.08	.04
90	Andy Benes	1.50	1.25	.60
91	Tom Browning	.10	.08	.04
92	Pete O'Brien	.10	.08	.04
93	Roberto Alomar	.15	.11	.06
94	Bret Saberhagen	.15	.11	.06
95	Phil Bradley	.10	.08	.04
96	Doug Jones	.10	.08	.04
97	Eric Davis	.80	.60	.30
98	Tony Gwynn	.40	.30	.15
99	Jim Abbott	1.50	1.25	.60
100	Cal Ripken Jr.	.15	.11	.06
101	Andy Van Slyke	.12	.09	.05
102	Dan Plesac	.10	.08	.04
103	Lou Whitaker	.10	.08	.04
104	Steve Bedrosian	.10	.08	.04
105	Dave Gallagher	.10	.08	.04
106	Keith Hernandez	.10	.08	.04
107	Duane Ward	.10	.08	.04
108	Andre Dawson	.15	.11	.08
109	Howard Johnson	.20	.15	.08
110	Mark Langston	.12	.09	.05
111	Jerry Browne	.10	.08	.04
112	Alvin Davis	.10	.08	.04
113	Sid Fernandez	.10	.08	.04
114	Mike Devereaux	.10	.08	.04
115	Benny Santiago	.12	.09	.05
116	Bip Roberts	.10	.08	.04
117	Craig Worthington	.15	.11	.06
118	Kevin Elster	.10	.08	.04
119	Harold Reynolds	.10	.08	.04
120	Joe Carter	.15	.11	.06

		MT	NR MT	EX
121	Brian Harper	.10	.08	.04
122	Frank Viola	.15	.11	.06
123	Jeff Ballard	.10	.08	.04
124	John Kruk	.10	.08	.04
125	Harold Baines	.10	.08	.04
126	Tom Candiotti	.10	.08	.04
127	Kevin McReynolds	.15	.11	.06
128	Mookie Wilson	.10	.08	.04
129	Danny Tartabull	.12	.09	.05
130	Craig Lefferts	.10	.08	.04
131	Jose DeJesus	.15	.11	.06
132	John Orton	.30	.20	.10
133	Curt Schilling	.20	.15	.08
134	Marquis Grissom	1.25	.90	.50
135	Greg Vaughn	1.25	.90	.50
136	Brett Butler	.10	.08	.04
137	Rob Deer	.10	.08	.04
138	John Franco	.10	.08	.04
139	Keith Moreland	.10	.08	.04
140	Dave Smith	.10	.08	.04
141	Mark McGwire	1.00	.70	.40
142	Vince Coleman	.15	.11	.06
143	Barry Bonds	.15	.11	.06
144	Mike Henneman	.10	.08	.04
145	Doc Gooden	.30	.25	.12
146	Darryl Strawberry	.30	.25	.12
147	Von Hayes	.10	.08	.04
148	Andres Galarraga	.12	.09	.05
149	Roger Clemens	.25	.20	.10
150	Don Mattingly	1.50	1.25	.60
151	Joe Magrane	.10	.08	.04
152	Dwight Smith	1.25	.90	.50
153	Ricky Jordan	.30	.25	.12
154	Alan Trammell	.10	.08	.04
155	Brook Jacoby	.10	.08	.04
156	Lenny Dykstra	.10	.08	.04
157	Mike LaValliere	.10	.08	.04
158	Julio Franco	.12	.09	.05
159	Joey Belle	1.00	.70	.40
160	Barry Larkin	.15	.11	.06
161	Rick Reuschel	.10	.08	.04
162	Nelson Santovenia	.10	.08	.04
163	Mike Scioscia	.10	.08	.04
164	Damon Berryhill			
165	Todd Worrell			
166	Jim Eisenreich			
167	Ivan Calderon			
168	Goose Gozzo	.25	.20	.10
169	Kirk McCaskill	.10	.08	.04
170	Dennis Eckersley	.10	.08	.04
171	Mickey Tettleton	.12	.09	.05
172	Chuck Finley	.10	.08	.04
173	Dave Magadan	.10	.08	.04
174	Terry Pendleton	.10	.08	.04
175	Willie Randolph	.10	.08	.04
176	Jeff Huson	.25	.20	.10
177	Todd Zeile	2.00	1.50	.80
178	Steve Olin	.40	.30	.15
179	Eric Anthony	2.00	1.50	.80
180	Scott Coolbaugh	.50	.40	.20
181	Rick Sutcliffe	.10	.08	.04
182	Tim Wallach	.10	.08	.04
183	Paul Molitor	.12	.09	.05
184	Roberto Kelly	.12	.09	.05
185	Mike Moore	.10	.08	.04
186	Junior Felix	1.00	.70	.40
187	Mike Schooler	.10	.08	.04
188	Ruben Sierra	.20	.15	.08
189	Dale Murphy	.12	.09	.05
190	Dan Gladden	.10	.08	.04
191	John Smiley	.10	.08	.04
192	Jeff Russell	.10	.08	.04
193	Bert Blyleven	.10	.08	.04
194	Dave Stewart	.12	.09	.05
195	Bobby Bonilla	.12	.09	.05
196	Mitch Williams	.10	.08	.04
197	Orel Hershiser	.20	.15	.08
198	Kevin Bass	.10	.08	.04
199	Tim Burke	.10	.08	.04
200	Bo Jackson	.50	.40	.20
201	David Cone	.12	.09	.05
202	Gary Pettis	.10	.08	.04
203	Kent Hrbek	.10	.08	.04
204	Carlton Fisk	.10	.08	.04
205	Bob Geren	.30	.25	.12
206	Bill Spiers	.40	.30	.15
207	Oddibe McDowell	.10	.08	.04
208	Rickey Henderson	.30	.25	.12
209	Ken Caminiti	.10	.08	.04
210	Devon White	.10	.08	.04
211	Greg Maddux	.15	.11	.06

		MT	NR MT	EX
212	Ed Whitson	.10	.08	.04
213	Carlos Martinez	.25	.20	.10
214	George Brett	.25	.20	.10
215	Gregg Olson	.50	.40	.20
216	Kenny Rogers	.20	.15	.08
217	Dwight Evans	.10	.08	.04
218	Pat Tabler	.10	.08	.04
219	Jeff Treadway	.10	.08	.04
220	Scott Fletcher	.10	.08	.04
221	Deion Sanders	1.00	.70	.40
222	Robin Ventura	1.00	.70	.40
223	Chip Hale	.50	.40	.20
224	Tommy Greene	.40	.30	.15
225	Dean Palmer	.40	.30	.15

1953 Stahl-Meyer Franks

These nine cards, issued in packages of hot dogs by a New York area meat company, feature three players from each of the New York teams of the day - Dodgers Giants and Yankees. Cards in the set measure 3-1/4" by 4-1/2". The card fronts in this unnumbered set feature color photos with player name and facsimile autograph. The backs list both biographical and statistical information on half the card and a ticket offer promotion on the other half. The card corners are cut diagonally, although some cards (apparantly cut from sheets) with square corners have been seen. Cards are white-bordered.

		NR MT	EX	VG
Complete Set:		4000.00	2000.00	1200.
Common Player:		125.00	62.00	37.00
(1)	Hank Bauer	150.00	75.00	45.00
(2)	Roy Campanella	500.00	250.00	150.00
(3)	Gil Hodges	275.00	137.00	82.00
(4)	Monte Irvin	200.00	100.00	60.00
(5)	Whitey Lockman	125.00	62.00	37.00
(6)	Mickey Mantle	1800.00	900.00	540.00
(7)	Phil Rizzuto	275.00	137.00	82.00
(8)	Duke Snider	500.00	250.00	150.00
(9)	Bobby Thompson	150.00	75.00	45.00

1954 Stahl-Meyer Franks

The 1954 set of Stahl-Meyer Franks was increased to 12 cards which retained the 3-1/4" by 4-1/2" size. The most prominent addition to the '54 set was New Giants slugger Willie Mays. The card fronts are identical in format to the previous year's set. However, the backs are different as they are designed on a vertical format. The backs also contain an advertisement for a "Johnny Stahl-Meyer Baseball Kit." The cards in the set are unnumbered.

	NR MT	EX	VG
Complete Set:	5200.00	2600.00	1560.
Common Player:	125.00	62.00	37.00

		NR MT	EX	VG
(1)	Hank Bauer	150.00	75.00	45.00
(2)	Carl Erskine	150.00	75.00	45.00
(3)	Gil Hodges	300.00	150.00	90.00
(4)	Monte Irvin	225.00	112.00	67.00
(5)	Whitey Lockman	125.00	62.00	37.00
(6)	Gil McDougald	150.00	75.00	45.00
(7)	Mickey Mantle	2000.00	1000.00	600.00
(8)	Willie Mays	1000.00	500.00	300.00
(9)	Don Mueller	125.00	62.00	37.00
(10)	Don Newcombe	150.00	75.00	45.00
(11)	Phil Rizzuto	300.00	150.00	90.00
(12)	Duke Snider	525.00	262.00	157.00

1955 Stahl-Meyer Franks

Eleven of the 12 players in the 1955 set are the same as those featured in 1954. The exception is the New York Giants Dusty Rhodes, who replaced Willie Mays on the 3-1/4" by 4-1/2" cards. The card fronts are again full-color photos bordered in yellow with diagonal corners, and four players from each of the three New York teams are featured. The backs offer a new promotion, with a drawing of Mickey Mantle and advertisements selling pennants and caps. Player statistics are still included on the vertical card backs. The cards in the set are unnumbered.

		NR MT	EX	VG
Complete Set:		4300.00	2150.00	1290.
Common Player:		125.00	62.00	37.00
(1)	Hank Bauer	150.00	75.00	45.00
(2)	Carl Erskine	150.00	75.00	45.00
(3)	Gil Hodges	300.00	150.00	90.00
(4)	Monte Irvin	200.00	100.00	60.00
(5)	Whitey Lockman	125.00	62.00	37.00
(6)	Mickey Mantle	2000.00	1000.00	600.00
(7)	Gil McDougald	150.00	75.00	45.00
(8)	Don Mueller	125.00	62.00	37.00
(9)	Don Newcombe	150.00	75.00	45.00
(10)	Jim Rhodes	125.00	62.00	37.00
(11)	Phil Rizzuto	300.00	150.00	90.00
(12)	Duke Snider	525.00	262.00	157.00

1983 Stuart Expos

This set of Montreal Expos players and coaches was issued by a Montreal area baking company for inclusion in packages of snack cakes. The 30 cards feature full-color player photos, with the player name, number and team logo also on the card fronts. The backs list brief player biographies in both English and French. Twenty-five players are pictured on the 2-1/2" by 3-1/2" cards.

		MT	NR MT	EX
Complete Set:		8.00	6.00	3.25
Common Player:		.20	.15	.08
1	Bill Virdon	.25	.20	.10
2	Woodie Fryman	.25	.20	.10
3	Vern Rapp	.20	.15	.08
4	Andre Dawson	1.00	.70	.40
5	Jeff Reardon	.40	.30	.15
6	Al Oliver	.35	.25	.14
7	Doug Flynn	.20	.15	.08
8	Gary Carter	1.00	.70	.40
9	Tim Raines	1.50	1.25	.60
10	Steve Rogers	.30	.25	.12
11	Billy DeMars	.20	.15	.08
12	Tim Wallach	.60	.45	.25
13	Galen Cisco	.20	.15	.08
14	Terry Francona	.20	.15	.08
15	Bill Gullickson	.20	.15	.08
16	Ray Burris	.20	.15	.08
17	Scott Sanderson	.20	.15	.08
18	Warren Cromartie	.20	.15	.08
19	Jerry White	.20	.15	.08
20	Bobby Ramos	.20	.15	.08
21	Jim Wolhford	.20	.15	.08
22	Dan Schatzeder	.20	.15	.08
23	Charlie Lea	.20	.15	.08
24	Bryan Little	.20	.15	.08
25	Mel Wright	.20	.15	.08
26	Tim Blackwell	.20	.15	.08
27	Chris Speier	.20	.15	.08
28	Randy Lerch	.20	.15	.08
29	Bryn Smith	.30	.25	.12
30	Brad Mills	.20	.15	.08

1984 Stuart Expos

For the second year in a row, Stuart Cakes issued a

full-color card set of the Montreal Expos. The 2-1/2" by 3-1/2" cards again list the player name and number along with the team and company logos on the card fronts. The backs are bilingual with biographical information in both English and French. The 40-card set was issued in two series. Card numbers 21-40, issued late in the summer, are more difficult to find than the first 20 cards. The 40 cards include players, the manager, coaches and team mascot.

	MT	NR MT	EX
Complete Set:	32.00	24.00	13.00
Common Player: 1-20	.20	.15	.08
Common Player: 21-40	.40	.30	.15
1 Youppi! (mascot)	.20	.15	.08
2 Bill Virdon	.25	.20	.10
3 Billy DeMars	.20	.15	.08
4 Galen Cisco	.20	.15	.08
5 Russ Nixon	.20	.15	.08
6 Felipe Alou	.25	.20	.10
7 Dan Schatzeder	.20	.15	.08
8 Charlie Lea	.20	.15	.08
9 Bobby Ramos	.20	.15	.08
10 Bob James	.20	.15	.08
11 Andre Dawson	1.25	.90	.50
12 Gary Lucas	.20	.15	.08
13 Jeff Reardon	.50	.40	.20
14 Tim Wallach	.70	.50	.30
15 Gary Carter	1.25	.90	.50
16 Bill Gullickson	.20	.15	.08
17 Pete Rose	2.25	1.75	.90
18 Terry Francona	.20	.15	.08
19 Steve Rogers	.30	.25	.12
20 Tim Raines	1.50	1.25	.60
21 Bryn Smith	.50	.40	.20
22 Greg Harris	.40	.30	.15
23 David Palmer	.40	.30	.15
24 Jim Wohlford	.40	.30	.15
25 Miguel Dilone	.40	.30	.15
26 Mike Stenhouse	.40	.30	.15
27 Chris Speier	.40	.30	.15
28 Derrel Thomas	.40	.30	.15
29 Doug Flynn	.40	.30	.15
30 Bryan Little	.40	.30	.15
31 Argenis Salazar	.40	.30	.15
32 Mike Fuentes	.40	.30	.15
33 Joe Kerrigan	.40	.30	.15
34 Andy McGaffigan	.45	.35	.20
35 Fred Breining	.40	.30	.15
36 Expos 1983 All-Stars (Gary Carter, Andre Dawson, Tim Raines, Steve Rogers)	1.50	1.25	.60
37 Co-Players Of The Year (Andre Dawson, Tim Raines)	1.50	1.25	.60
38 Expos' Coaching Staff (Felipe Alou, Galen Cisco, Billy DeMars, Joe Kerrigan, Russ Nixon, Bill Virdon)	.40	.30	.15
39 Team Photo	.40	.30	.15
40 Checklist	.40	.30	.15

1987 Stuart

Twenty-eight four-part folding panels make up the 1987 Stuart Super Stars set, which was issued only in Canada. Three player cards and a sweepstakes entry form card comprise each panel. All 26 major league teams are included with the Montreal Expos and

Toronto Blue Jays being represented twice. The cards, which are full color and measure 2-1/2" by 3-1/2", are written in both English and French. The card backs contain the player's previous year's statistics. All team insignias have been airbrushed away.

	MT	NR MT	EX
Complete Panel Set:	50.00	37.00	20.00
Complete Singles Set:	20.00	15.00	8.00
Common Panel:	.80	.60	.30
Common Single Player:	.10	.08	.04
Panel (New York Mets)	4.00	3.00	1.50
1a Gary Carter	.50	.40	.20
1b Keith Hernandez	.40	.30	.15
1c Darryl Strawberry	.60	.45	.25
Panel (Atlanta Braves)	2.25	1.75	.90
2a Bruce Benedict	.10	.08	.04
2b Ken Griffey	.15	.11	.06
2c Dale Murphy	.60	.45	.25
Panel (Chicago Cubs)	1.50	1.25	.60
3a Jody Davis	.15	.11	.06
3b Andre Dawson	.30	.25	.12
3c Leon Durham	.15	.11	.06
Panel (Cincinnati Reds)	2.50	2.00	1.00
4a Buddy Bell	.15	.11	.06
4b Eric Davis	.60	.45	.25
4c Dave Parker	.25	.20	.10
Panel (Houston Astros)	2.25	1.75	.90
5a Glenn Davis	.25	.20	.10
5b Nolan Ryan	.40	.30	.15
5c Mike Scott	.25	.20	.10
Panel (Los Angeles Dodgers)	2.25	1.75	.90
6a Pedro Guerrero	.25	.20	.10
6b Mike Marshall	.20	.15	.08
6c Fernando Valenzuela	.40	.30	.15
Panel (Montreal Expos)	1.75	1.25	.70
7a Tim Raines	.40	.30	.15
7b Tim Wallach	.20	.15	.08
7c Mitch Webster	.10	.08	.04
Panel (Montreal Expos)	.80	.60	.30
8a Hubie Brooks	.15	.11	.06
8b Bryn Smith	.10	.08	.04
8c Floyd Youmans	.10	.08	.04
Panel (Philadelphia Phillies)	2.25	1.75	.90
9a Shane Rawley	.10	.08	.04
9b Juan Samuel	.20	.15	.08
9c Mike Schmidt	.60	.45	.25
Panel (Pittsburgh Pirates)	.80	.60	.30
10a Jim Morrison	.10	.08	.04
10b Johnny Ray	.15	.11	.06
10c R.J. Reynolds	.10	.08	.04
Panel (St. Louis Cardinals)	2.00	1.50	.80
11a Jack Clark	.25	.20	.10
11b Vince Coleman	.30	.25	.12
11c Ozzie Smith	.25	.20	.10
Panel (San Diego Padres)	3.00	2.25	1.25
12a Steve Garvey	.50	.40	.20
12b Tony Gwynn	.50	.40	.20
12c John Kruk	.20	.15	.08
Panel (San Francisco Giants)	.80	.60	.30
13a Chili Davis	.10	.08	.04
13b Jeffrey Leonard	.10	.08	.04
13c Robbie Thompson	.10	.08	.04
Panel (Baltimore Orioles)	3.00	2.25	1.25
14a Fred Lynn	.25	.20	.10
14b Eddie Murray	.50	.40	.20
14c Cal Ripken	.50	.40	.20
Panel (Boston Red Sox)	4.00	3.00	1.50
15a Don Baylor	.15	.11	.06
15b Wade Boggs	.80	.60	.30
15c Roger Clemens	.60	.45	.25
Panel	2.50	2.00	1.00
16a Doug DeCinces	.10	.08	.04
16b Wally Joyner	.80	.60	.30
16c Mike Witt	.10	.08	.04
Panel (Chicago White Sox)	1.50	1.25	.60
17a Harold Baines	.20	.15	.08
17b Carlton Fisk	.25	.20	.10
17c Ozzie Guillen	.15	.11	.06
Panel (Cleveland Indians)	1.00	.70	.40
18a Joe Carter	.20	.15	.08
18b Julio Franco	.15	.11	.06
18c Pat Tabler	.10	.08	.04
Panel (Detroit Tigers)	2.50	2.00	1.00
19a Kirk Gibson	.40	.30	.15
19b Jack Morris	.25	.20	.10
19c Alan Trammell	.40	.30	.15
Panel (Kansas City Royals)	2.50	2.00	1.00

		MT	NR MT	EX
20a	George Brett	.60	.45	.25
20b	Bret Saberhagen	.30	.25	.12
20c	Willie Wilson	.15	.11	.06
Panel (Milwaukee Brewers)		2.00	1.50	.80
21a	Cecil Cooper	.15	.11	.06
21b	Paul Molitor	.20	.15	.08
21c	Robin Yount	.40	.30	.15
Panel (Minnesota Twins)		2.50	2.00	1.00
22a	Tom Brunansky	.20	.15	.08
22b	Kent Hrbek	.30	.25	.12
22c	Kirby Puckett	.50	.40	.20
Panel (New York Yankees)		5.00	3.75	2.00
23a	Rickey Henderson	.50	.40	.20
23b	Don Mattingly	1.00	.70	.40
23c	Dave Winfield	.50	.40	.20
Panel (Oakland A's)		2.75	2.00	1.00
24a	Jose Canseco	.90	.70	.35
24b	Alfredo Griffin	.10	.08	.04
24c	Carney Lansford	.10	.08	.04
Panel 25 (Seattle Mariners)		1.25	.90	.50
25a	Phil Bradley	.15	.11	.06
25b	Alvin Davis	.20	.15	.08
25c	Mark Langston	.20	.15	.08
Panel (Texas Rangers)		1.25	.90	.50
26a	Pete Incaviglia	.30	.25	.12
26b	Pete O'Brien	.10	.08	.04
26c	Larry Parrish	.10	.08	.04
Panel (Toronto Blue Jays)		2.25	1.75	.90
27a	Jesse Barfield	.20	.15	.08
27b	George Bell	.40	.30	.15
27c	Tony Fernandez	.20	.15	.08
Panel (Toronto Blue Jays)		.80	.60	.30
28a	Lloyd Moseby	.10	.08	.04
28b	Dave Stieb	.15	.11	.06
28c	Ernie Whitt	.10	.08	.04

		NR MT	EX	VG
D	Dick Stuart	55.00	27.00	16.50
1	Barry Latman	40.00	20.00	12.00
2	Gary Bell	45.00	22.00	13.50
3	Dick Donovan	40.00	20.00	12.00
4	Frank Funk	40.00	20.00	12.00
5	Jim Perry	60.00	30.00	18.00
6	Not issued			
7	Johnny Romano	40.00	20.00	12.00
8	Ty Cline	40.00	20.00	12.00
9	Tito Francona	45.00	22.00	13.50
10	Bob Nieman	300.00	150.00	90.00
11	Willie Kirkland	40.00	20.00	12.00
12	Woodie Held	45.00	22.00	13.50
13	Jerry Kindall	40.00	20.00	12.00
14	Bubba Phillips	40.00	20.00	12.00
15	Mel Harder	45.00	22.00	13.50
16	Salty Parker	40.00	20.00	12.00
17	Ray Katt	40.00	20.00	12.00
18	Mel McGaha	40.00	20.00	12.00
19	Pedro Ramos	40.00	20.00	12.00

1963 Sugardale Weiners

Sugardale Meats again featured Cleveland and Pittsburgh players in its 1963 set, which grew to 31 cards. The black and white cards again measure 5-1/8" by 3-3/4", and consist of 28 Indians and five Pirates players. Card formats are virtually identical to the 1962 cards, with the only real difference being the information included in the player biographies. The cards are numbered 1-38, with numbers 6, 21, 22 and 29-32 not issued. Cards for Bob Skinner (#35) and Jim Perry (#5) are scarce as these two players were traded during the season and their cards withdrawn from distribution. The red card backs again offer playing tips.

		NR MT	EX	VG
Complete Set:		1300.00	650.00	390.00
A	Don Cardwell	40.00	20.00	12.00
B	Robert R. Skinner	125.00	62.00	37.00
C	Donald B. Schwall	40.00	20.00	12.00
D	Jim Pagliaroni	40.00	20.00	12.00
E	Dick Schofield	45.00	22.00	13.50
1	Barry Latman	40.00	20.00	12.00
2	Gary Bell	45.00	22.00	13.50
3	Dick Donovan	40.00	20.00	12.00
4	Joe Adcock	60.00	30.00	18.00
5	Jim Perry	150.00	75.00	45.00
6	Not issued			
7	Johnny Romano	40.00	20.00	12.00
8	Mike De La Hoz	40.00	20.00	12.00
9	Tito Francona	45.00	22.00	13.50
10	Gene Green	40.00	20.00	12.00
11	Willie Kirkland	40.00	20.00	12.00
12	Woodie Held	45.00	22.00	13.50
13	Jerry Kindall	40.00	20.00	12.00

1962 Sugardale Weiners

The Sugardale Meats set of black and white cards measure 5-1/8" by 3-3/4". The 22-card set includes 18 Cleveland Indians and four Pittsburgh Pirates players. The Indians cards are numbered from 1-19 with card number 6 not issued. The Pirates cards are lettered from A to D. The card fronts contain a relatively small player photo, with biographical information and Sugardale logo. The backs are printed in red and offer playing tips and another company logo. Card number 10 (Bob Nieman) is considerably more scarce than other cards in the set.

		NR MT	EX	VG
Complete Set:		1500.00	750.00	450.00
Common Player:		40.00	20.00	12.00
A	Dick Groat	70.00	35.00	21.00
B	Roberto Clemente	500.00	300.00	150.00
C	Don Hoak	55.00	27.00	16.50

		NR MT	EX	VG
14	Max Alvis	45.00	22.00	13.50
15	Mel Harder	45.00	22.00	13.50
16	George Strickland	40.00	20.00	12.00
17	Elmer Valo	40.00	20.00	12.00
18	Birdie Tebbetts	45.00	22.00	13.50
19	Pedro Ramos	40.00	20.00	12.00
20	Al Luplow	40.00	20.00	12.00
21	Not issued			
22	Not issued			
23	Jim Grant	45.00	22.00	13.50
24	Victor Davalillo	45.00	22.00	13.50
25	Jerry Walker	40.00	20.00	12.00
26	Sam McDowell	60.00	30.00	18.00
27	Fred Whitfield	40.00	20.00	12.00
28	Jack Kralick	40.00	20.00	12.00
29	Not issued			
30	Not issued			
31	Not issued			
32	Not issued			
33	Bob Allen	40.00	20.00	12.00

1911 T3 Turkey Reds

Turkey Reds are the only cabinet cards the average collector can have a realistic chance to complete. Obtained by mailing in coupons found in Turkey Red, Fez and Old Mill brand cigarettes, the Turkey Reds measure 5 3/4" by 8", a size known to collectors as "cabinet cards." Turkey Reds feature full color lithograph fronts with wide gray frames. Backs carried either a numbered ordering list or an ad for Turkey Red cigarettes. The Turkey Red series consists of 25 boxers and 100 baseball players. Despite their cost, Turkey Reds remain very popular today as the most attractive of the cabinet sets.

		NR MT	EX	VG
Complete Set:		32000.00	16000.00	9600.
Common Player: 1-50		250.00	125.00	75.00
Common Player: 77-126		275.00	137.00	82.00
1	Mordecai Brown	450.00	225.00	135.00
2	Bill Bergen	250.00	125.00	75.00
3	Tommy Leach	250.00	125.00	75.00
4	Roger Bresnahan	450.00	225.00	135.00
5	Sam Crawford	400.00	200.00	125.00
6	Hal Chase	300.00	150.00	90.00
7	Howie Camnitz	250.00	125.00	75.00
8	Fred Clarke	400.00	200.00	125.00

		NR MT	EX	VG
9	Ty Cobb	4000.00	2000.00	1250.
10	Art Devlin	250.00	125.00	75.00
11	Bill Dahlen	250.00	125.00	75.00
12	Wil Bill Donovan	250.00	125.00	75.00
13	Larry Doyle	250.00	125.00	75.00
14	Red Dooin	250.00	125.00	75.00
15	Kid Elberfeld	250.00	125.00	75.00
16	Johnny Evers	400.00	200.00	125.00
17	Clark Griffith	400.00	200.00	125.00
18	Hughie Jennings	400.00	200.00	125.00
19	Addie Joss	400.00	200.00	125.00
20	Tim Jordan	250.00	125.00	75.00
21	Red Kleinow	250.00	125.00	75.00
22	Harry Krause	250.00	125.00	75.00
23	Nap Lajoie	800.00	400.00	240.00
24	Mike Mitchell	250.00	125.00	75.00
25	Matty McIntyre	250.00	125.00	75.00
26	John McGraw	700.00	350.00	200.00
27	Christy Mathewson	1200.00	600.00	350.00
28a	Harry McIntyre (Brooklyn)	250.00	125.00	75.00
28b	Harry McIntyre (Brooklyn and Chicago)	350.00	175.00	105.00
29	Amby McConnell	250.00	125.00	75.00
30	George Mullin	250.00	125.00	75.00
31	Sherry Magee	250.00	125.00	75.00
32	Orval Overall	250.00	125.00	75.00
33	Jake Pfeister	250.00	125.00	75.00
34	Nap Rucker	250.00	125.00	75.00
35	Joe Tinker	400.00	200.00	125.00
36	Tris Speaker	800.00	400.00	250.00
37	Slim Sallee	250.00	125.00	75.00
38	Jake Stahl	250.00	125.00	75.00
39	Rube Waddell	400.00	200.00	125.00
40a	Vic Willis (Pittsburg)	250.00	125.00	82.00
40b	Vic Willis (Pittsburg and St. Louis)	350.00	175.00	105.00
41	Hooks Wiltse	250.00	125.00	82.00
42	Cy Young	1000.00	500.00	300.00
43	Out At Third	150.00	75.00	45.00
44	Trying To Catch Him Napping	150.00	75.00	45.00
45	Jordan & Herzog At First	150.00	75.00	45.00
46	Safe At Third	150.00	75.00	45.00
47	Frank Chance At Bat	450.00	225.00	135.00
48	Jack Murray At Bat	150.00	75.00	45.00
49	A Close Play At Second	150.00	75.00	45.00
50	Chief Myers At Bat	150.00	75.00	45.00
77	Red Ames	275.00	150.00	80.00
78	Home Run Baker	400.00	200.00	120.00
79	George Bell	275.00	150.00	80.00
80	Chief Bender	500.00	250.00	150.00
81	Bob Bescher	275.00	150.00	80.00
82	Kitty Bransfield	275.00	150.00	80.00
83	Al Bridwell	275.00	150.00	80.00
84	George Browne	275.00	150.00	80.00
85	Bill Burns	275.00	150.00	80.00
86	Bill Carrigan	275.00	150.00	80.00
87	Eddie Collins	500.00	250.00	150.00
88	Harry Coveleski	275.00	150.00	80.00
89	Lou Criger	275.00	150.00	80.00
90a	Mickey Doolin (name incorrect)	375.00	187.00	112.00
90b	Mickey Doolan (name correct)	275.00	150.00	80.00
91	Tom Downey	275.00	150.00	80.00
92	Jimmy Dygert	275.00	150.00	80.00
93	Art Fromme	275.00	150.00	80.00
94	George Gibson	275.00	150.00	80.00
95	Peaches Graham	275.00	150.00	80.00
96	Bob Groom	275.00	150.00	80.00
97	Dick Hoblitzell	275.00	150.00	80.00
98	Solly Hofman	275.00	150.00	80.00
99	Walter Johnson	1500.00	750.00	450.00
100	Davy Jones	275.00	150.00	80.00
101	Wee Willie Keeler	450.00	225.00	135.00
102	Johnny Kling	275.00	150.00	80.00
103	Ed Konetchy	275.00	150.00	80.00
104	Ed Lennox	275.00	150.00	80.00
105	Hans Lobert	275.00	150.00	80.00
106	Harry Lord	275.00	150.00	80.00
107	Rube Manning	275.00	150.00	80.00
108	Fred Merkle	275.00	150.00	80.00
109	Pat Moran	275.00	150.00	80.00
110	George McBride	275.00	150.00	80.00
111	Harry Niles	275.00	150.00	80.00
112a	Dode Paskert (Cincinnati)	350.00	175.00	105.00
112b	Dode Paskert (Cincinnati and Philadelphia)	275.00	150.00	80.00
113	Bugs Raymond	275.00	150.00	80.00
114	Bob Rhoades (Rhoads)	350.00	175.00	105.00
115	Admiral Schlei	275.00	150.00	80.00
116	Boss Schmidt	275.00	150.00	80.00
117	Wildfire Schulte	275.00	150.00	80.00

		NR MT	EX	VG
118	Frank Smith	275.00	150.00	80.00
119	George Stone	275.00	150.00	80.00
120	Gabby Street	275.00	150.00	80.00
121	Billy Sullivan	275.00	150.00	80.00
122a	Fred Tenney (New York)	350.00	175.00	105.00
122b	Fred Tenney (New York and Boston)			
		275.00	150.00	80.00
123	Ira Thomas	275.00	150.00	80.00
124	Bobby Wallace	400.00	200.00	125.00
125	Ed Walsh	500.00	250.00	150.00
126	Owen Wilson	275.00	150.00	80.00

1911 T201
Mecca Double Folders

These cards found in packages of Mecca cigarettes feature one player when the card is open, and another when the card is folded; two players sharing the same pair of legs. Mecca Double Folders measure 2-1/4" by 4-11/16." The fronts are color lithographs with the player's name appearing in black script in the upper left. The backs are printed in red and contain an innovation in the form of player statistics. The 50-card set contains 100 different players including a number of Hall of Famers. The Mecca Double Folders, with two players (Topps "borrowed" the idea in 1955) and statistics, were one of the most innovative series of the tobacco card era.

		NR MT	EX	VG
Complete Set:		4000.00	2000.00	1200.
Common Player:		40.00	20.00	12.00
(1)	Abstein, Butler	40.00	20.00	12.00
(2)	Baker, Collins	80.00	40.00	24.00
(3)	Baker, Downie (Downey)	40.00	20.00	12.00
(4)	Barrett, McGlynn	40.00	20.00	12.00
(5)	Barry, Lapp	40.00	20.00	12.00
(6)	Bender, Oldring	80.00	40.00	24.00
(7)	Bergen, Wheat	80.00	40.00	24.00
(8)	Blair, Hartzell	40.00	20.00	12.00
(9)	Bresnahan, Huggins	125.00	62.00	37.00
(10)	Bridwell, Matthewson (Mathewson)			
		300.00	150.00	90.00
(11)	Brown, Hofman	80.00	40.00	24.00
(12)	Byrne, Clarke	60.00	30.00	18.00
(13)	Chance, Evers	100.00	50.00	30.00
(14)	Chase, Sweeney	50.00	25.00	15.00
(15)	Cicotte, Thoney	45.00	22.00	13.50
(16)	Clarke, Gaspar	40.00	20.00	12.00
(17)	Cobb, Crawford	750.00	375.00	225.00
(18)	Cole, Kling	40.00	20.00	12.00
(19)	Coombs, Thomas	40.00	20.00	12.00
(20)	Daubert, Rucker	45.00	22.00	13.50
(21)	Donovan, Stroud	40.00	20.00	12.00
(22)	Dooin, Titus	40.00	20.00	12.00
(23)	Dougherty, Lord	300.00	150.00	90.00
(24)	Downs, Odwell	40.00	20.00	12.00

		NR MT	EX	VG
(25)	Doyle, Meyers	40.00	20.00	12.00
(26)	Dygert, Seymour	40.00	20.00	12.00
(27)	Elberfeld, McBride	40.00	20.00	12.00
(28)	Falkenberg, Lajoie	150.00	75.00	45.00
(29)	Fitzpatrick, Killian	40.00	20.00	12.00
(30)	Ford, Johnson	40.00	20.00	12.00
(31)	Foster, Ward	40.00	20.00	12.00
(32)	Gardner, Speaker	150.00	75.00	45.00
(33)	Gibson, Leach	40.00	20.00	12.00
(34)	Graham, Mattern	40.00	20.00	12.00
(35)	Grant, McLean	40.00	20.00	12.00
(36)	Hauser, Lush	40.00	20.00	12.00
(37)	Herzog, Miller	40.00	20.00	12.00
(38)	Hickman, Hinchman	40.00	20.00	12.00
(39)	Jennings, Summers	75.00	37.00	22.00
(40)	Johnson, Street	300.00	150.00	90.00
(41)	LaPorte, Stephens	40.00	20.00	12.00
(42)	Lake, Wallace	60.00	30.00	18.00
(43)	Leifield, Simon	40.00	20.00	12.00
(44)	Lobert, Moore	40.00	20.00	12.00
(45)	McCabe, Starr	40.00	20.00	12.00
(46)	McCarty, McGinnity	60.00	30.00	18.00
(47)	Merkle, Wiltse	45.00	22.00	13.50
(48)	Payne, Walsh	75.00	37.00	22.00
(49)	Stovall, Turner	40.00	20.00	12.00
(50)	Williams, Woodruff	40.00	20.00	12.00

1912 T202
Hassan Triple Folders

Measuring 5-1/2" by 2-1/4", Hassan cigarette cards carried the concept of multiple-player cards even furher than the innovative Mecca set of the previous year. Scored so that the two end cards - which are full-color and very close to exact duplicates of T205 "Gold Borders" - can fold over the black and white center panel, the Hassan Triple Folder appears like a booklet when closed. The two end cards are individual player cards, while the larger center panel contains an action scene. Usually the two player cards are not related to the action scene. The unique Hassan Triple Folders feature player biographies on the back of the two individual cards with a description of the action on the back of the center panel. Values depend on the player featured in the center panel, as well as the players featured on the end cards.

		NR MT	EX	VG
Complete Set of 132:		25000.00	12500.00	7500.
Common Player:		100.00	50.00	30.00
(1a)	A Close Play At The Home Plate (LaPorte, Wallace)	150.00	75.00	45.00
(1b)	A Close Play At The Home Plate (Pelty, Wallace)	150.00	75.00	45.00
(2)	A Desperate Slide For Third (Ty Cobb, O'Leary)	1200.00	600.00	360.00
(3a)	A Great Batsman (Barger, Bergen)	100.00	50.00	30.00
(3b)	A Great Batsman (Bergen, Rucker)	100.00	50.00	30.00
(4)	Ambrose McConnell At Bat (Blair, Quinn)	100.00	50.00	30.00

		NR MT	EX	VG
(5)	A Wide Throw Saves Crawford (Mullin, Stanage)	100.00	50.00	30.00
(6)	Baker Gets His Man (Baker, Collins)	350.00	175.00	105.00
(7)	Birmingham Gets To Third (Johnson, Street)	475.00	237.00	142.00
(8)	Birmingham's Home Run (Birmingham, Turner)	500.00	250.00	150.00
(9)	Bush Just Misses Austin (Magee, Moran)	100.00	50.00	30.00
(10a)	Carrigan Blocks His Man (Gaspar, McLean)	100.00	50.00	30.00
(10b)	Carrigan Blocks His Man (Carrigan, Wagner)	100.00	50.00	30.00
(11)	Catching Him Napping (Bresnahan, Oakes)	150.00	75.00	45.00
(12)	Caught Asleep Off First (Bresnahan, Harmon)	150.00	75.00	45.00
(13a)	Chance Beats Out A Hit (Chance, Foxen)	250.00	125.00	75.00
(13b)	Chance Beats Out A Hit (Archer, McIntyre)	100.00	50.00	30.00
(13c)	Chance Beats Out A Hit (Archer, Overall)	100.00	50.00	30.00
(13d)	Chance Beats Out A Hit (Archer, Rowan)	100.00	50.00	30.00
(13e)	Chance Beats Out A Hit (Chance, Shean)	250.00	125.00	75.00
(14a)	Chase Dives Into Third (Chase, Wolter)	100.00	50.00	30.00
(14b)	Chase Dives Into Third (Clarke, Gibson)	150.00	75.00	45.00
(14c)	Chase Dives Into Third (Gibson, Phillippe)	100.00	50.00	30.00
(15a)	Chase Gets Ball Too Late (Egan, Mitchell)	100.00	50.00	30.00
(15b)	Chase Gets Ball Too Late (Chase, Wolter)	100.00	50.00	30.00
(16a)	Chase Guarding First (Chase, Wolter)	100.00	50.00	30.00
(16b)	Chase Guarding First (Clarke, Gibson)	150.00	75.00	45.00
(16c)	Chase Guarding First (Gibson, Leifield)	100.00	50.00	30.00
(17)	Chase Ready For The Squeeze Play (Magee, Paskert)	100.00	50.00	30.00
(18)	Chase Safe At Third (Baker, Barry)	150.00	75.00	45.00
(19)	Chief Bender Waiting For A Good One (Bender, Thomas)	150.00	75.00	45.00
(20)	Clarke Hikes For Home (Bridwell, Kling)	100.00	50.00	30.00
(21)	Close At First (Ball, Stovall)	100.00	50.00	30.00
(22a)	Close At The Plate (Payne, Walsh)	150.00	75.00	45.00
(22b)	Close At The Plate (Payne, White)	100.00	50.00	30.00
(23)	Close At Third - Speaker (Speaker, Wood)	275.00	137.00	82.00
(24)	Close At Third - Wagner (Carrigan, Wagner)	100.00	50.00	30.00
(25a)	Collins Easily Safe (Byrne, Clarke)	150.00	75.00	45.00
(25b)	Collins Easily Safe (Baker, Collins)	300.00	150.00	90.00
(25c)	Collins Easily Safe (Collins, Murphy)	150.00	75.00	45.00
(26)	Crawford About To Smash One (Stanage, Summers)	100.00	50.00	30.00
(27)	Cree Rolls Home (Daubert, Hummel)	100.00	50.00	30.00
(28)	Davy Jones' Great Slide (Delahanty, Jones)	100.00	50.00	30.00
(29a)	Devlin Gets His Man (Devlin (Giants), Mathewson)	500.00	250.00	150.00
(29b)	Devlin Gets His Man (Devlin (Rustlers), Mathewson)	300.00	150.00	90.00
(29c)	Devlin Gets His Man (Fletcher, Mathewson)	275.00	137.00	82.00
(29d)	Devlin Gets His Man (Mathewson, Meyers)	275.00	137.00	82.00
(30a)	Donlin Out At First (Camnitz, Gibson)	100.00	50.00	30.00
(30b)	Donlin Out At First (Doyle, Merkle)	100.00	50.00	30.00
(30c)	Donlin Out At First (Leach, Wilson)	100.00	50.00	30.00
(30d)	Donlin Out At First (Dooin, Magee)	100.00	50.00	30.00
(30e)	Donlin Out At First (Gibson, Phillippe)	100.00	50.00	30.00

		NR MT	EX	VG
(31a)	Dooin Gets His Man (Dooin, Doolan)	100.00	50.00	30.00
(31b)	Dooin Gets His Man (Dooin, Lobert)	100.00	50.00	30.00
(31c)	Dooin Gets His Man (Dooin, Titus)	100.00	50.00	30.00
(32)	Easy For Larry (Doyle, Merkle)	100.00	50.00	30.00
(33)	Elberfeld Beats The Throw (Elberfeld, Milan)	100.00	50.00	30.00
(34)	Elberfeld Gets His Man (Elberfeld, Milan)	100.00	50.00	30.00
(35)	Engle In A Close Play (Engle, Speaker)	275.00	137.00	82.00
(36a)	Evers Makes A Safe Slide (Archer, Evers)	150.00	75.00	45.00
(36b)	Evers Makes A Safe Slide (Chance, Evers)	150.00	75.00	45.00
(36c)	Evers Makes A Safe Slide (Archer, Overall)	100.00	50.00	30.00
(36d)	Evers Makes A Safe Slide (Archer, Reulbach)	100.00	50.00	30.00
(36e)	Evers Makes A Safe Slide (Chance, Tinker)	150.00	75.00	45.00
(37)	Fast Work At Third (Cobb, O'Leary)	1200.00	600.00	360.00
(38a)	Ford Putting Over A Spitter (Ford, Vaughn)	100.00	50.00	30.00
(38b)	Ford Putting Over A Spitter (Sweeney)	100.00	50.00	30.00
(39)	Good Play At Third (Cobb, Moriarity)	1200.00	600.00	360.00
(40)	Grant Gets His Man (Grant, Hoblitzell)	100.00	50.00	30.00
(41a)	Hal Chase Too Late (McConnell, McIntyre)	100.00	50.00	30.00
(41b)	Hal Chase Too Late (McLean, Suggs)	100.00	50.00	30.00
(42)	Harry Lord At Third (Lennox, Tinker)	150.00	75.00	45.00
(43)	Hartzell Covering Third (Dahlen, Scanlan)	100.00	50.00	30.00
(44)	Hartsel Strikes Out (Gray, Groom)	100.00	50.00	30.00
(45)	Held At Third (Lord, Tannehill)	100.00	50.00	30.00
(46)	Jake Stahl Guarding First (Cicotte, Stahl)	100.00	50.00	30.00
(47)	Jim Delahanty At Bat (Delahanty, Jones)	100.00	50.00	30.00
(48a)	Just Before The Battle (Ames, Meyers)	100.00	50.00	30.00
(48b)	Just Before The Battle (Bresnahan, McGraw)	250.00	125.00	75.00
(48c)	Just Before The Battle (Crandall, Meyers)	100.00	50.00	30.00
(48d)	Just Before The Battle (Becker, Devore)	100.00	50.00	30.00
(48e)	Just Before The Battle (Fletcher, Mathewson)	250.00	125.00	75.00
(48f)	Just Before The Battle (Marquard, Meyers)	100.00	50.00	30.00
(48g)	Just Before The Battle (Jennings, McGraw)	250.00	125.00	75.00
(48h)	Just Before The Battle (Mathewson, Meyers)	250.00	125.00	75.00
(48i)	Just Before The Battle (Murray, Snodgrass)	100.00	50.00	30.00
(48j)	Just Before The Battle (Meyers, Wiltse)	100.00	50.00	30.00
(49)	Knight Catches A Runner (Johnson, Knight)	300.00	150.00	90.00
(50a)	Lobert Almost Caught (Bridwell, Kling)	100.00	50.00	30.00
(50b)	Lobert Almost Caught (Kling, Young)	275.00	137.00	82.00
(50c)	Lobert Almost Caught (Kling, Mattern)	100.00	50.00	30.00
(50d)	Lobert Almost Caught (Kling, Steinfeldt)	100.00	50.00	30.00
(51)	Lobert Gets Tenney (Dooin, Lobert)	100.00	50.00	30.00
(52)	Lord Catches His Man (Lord, Tannehil)	100.00	50.00	30.00
(53)	McConnell Caught (Needham, Richie)	100.00	50.00	30.00
(54)	McIntyre At Bat (McConnell, McIntyre)	100.00	50.00	30.00
(55)	Moriarty Spiked (Stanage, Willett)	100.00	50.00	30.00
(56)	Nearly Caught (Bates, Bescher)	100.00	50.00	30.00

		NR MT	EX	VG
(57)	Oldring Almost Home (Lord, Oldring)	100.00	50.00	30.00
(58)	Schaefer On First (McBride, Milan)	100.00	50.00	30.00
(59)	Schaefer Steals Second (Clark Griffith, McBride)	150.00	75.00	45.00
(60)	Scoring From Second (Lord, Oldring)	100.00	50.00	30.00
(61a)	Scrambling Back To First (Barger, Bergen)	100.00	50.00	30.00
(61b)	Scrambling Back To First (Chase, Wolter)	100.00	50.00	30.00
(62)	Speaker Almost Caught (Clarke, Miller)	150.00	75.00	45.00
(63)	Speaker Rounding Third (Speaker, Wood)	275.00	137.00	82.00
(64)	Speaker Scores (Engle, Speaker)	275.00	137.00	82.00
(65)	Stahl Safe (Austin, Stovall)	100.00	50.00	30.00
(66)	Stone About To Swing (Schulte, Sheckard)	100.00	50.00	30.00
(67a)	Sullivan Puts Up A High One (Evans, Huggins)	150.00	75.00	45.00
(67b)	Sullivan Puts Up A High One (Gray, Groom)	100.00	50.00	30.00
(68a)	Sweeney Gets Stahl (Ford, Vaughn)	100.00	50.00	30.00
(68b)	Sweeney Gets Stahl (Ford, Sweeney)	100.00	50.00	30.00
(69)	Tenney Lands Safely (Latham, Raymond)	100.00	50.00	30.00
(70a)	The Athletic Infield (Baker, Barry)	100.00	50.00	30.00
(70b)	The Athletic Infield (Brown, Graham)	150.00	75.00	45.00
(70c)	The Athletic Infield (Hauser, Konetchy)	150.00	75.00	45.00
(70d)	The Athletic Infield (Krause, Thomas)	100.00	50.00	30.00
(71)	The Pinch Hitter (Egan, Hoblitzell)	100.00	50.00	30.00
(72)	The Scissors Slide (Birmingham, Turner)	100.00	50.00	30.00
(73a)	Tom Jones At Bat (Fromme, McLean)	100.00	50.00	30.00
(73b)	Tom Jones At Bat (Gaspar, McLean)	100.00	50.00	30.00
(74a)	Too Late For Devlin (Ames, Meyers)	100.00	50.00	30.00
(74b)	Too Late For Devlin (Crandall, Meyers)	100.00	50.00	30.00
(74c)	Too Late For Devlin (Devlin (Giants), Mathewson)	375.00	187.00	112.00
(74d)	Too Late For Devlin (Devlin (Rustlers), Mathewson)	300.00	150.00	90.00
(74e)	Too Late For Devlin (Marquard, Meyers)	150.00	75.00	45.00
(74f)	Too Late For Devlin (Meyers, Wiltse)	100.00	50.00	30.00
(75a)	Ty Cobb Steals Third (Cobb, Jennings)	1400.00	700.00	425.00
(75b)	Ty Cobb Steals Third (Cobb, Moriarty)	1200.00	600.00	360.00
(75c)	Ty Cobb Steals Third (Austin, Stovall)	1100.00	550.00	330.00
(76)	Wheat Strikes Out (Dahlen, Wheat)	150.00	75.00	45.00

1911 T205 Gold Border

Taking their hobby nickname from their border color, these cards were issued in a number of different cigarette brands. The cards measure 1-1/2" by 2-5/8". American League cards feature a color lithograph of the player inside a stylized baseball diamond. National League cards have head-and-shoulders portraits and a plain background, plus the first ever use of a facsimile autograph in a major card set. The 12 minor league players in the set feature three-quarter length portraits or action pictures in an elaborate frame of columns and other devices. Card backs of the major leaguers carry the player's full name (a first) and statistics. Card backs of the minor leaguers lack the statistics. The complete set price does not include the scarcer variations.

		NR MT	EX	VG
	Complete Set:	50000.00	25000.00	15000.
	Common Player:	100.00	50.00	30.00
(1)	Edward J. Abbaticchio	100.00	50.00	30.00
(2)	Doc Adkins	300.00	150.00	90.00
(3)	Leon K. Ames	100.00	50.00	30.00
(4)	Jas. P. Archer	100.00	50.00	30.00
(5)	Jimmy Austin	100.00	50.00	30.00
(6)	Bill Bailey	100.00	50.00	30.00
(7)	Home Run Baker	500.00	250.00	150.00
(8)	Neal Ball	100.00	50.00	30.00
(9)	E.B. Barger (full "B" on cap)	100.00	50.00	30.00
(10)	E.B. Barger (partial "B" on cap)	350.00	175.00	105.00
(11)	Jack Barry	100.00	50.00	30.00
(12)	Emil Batch	300.00	150.00	90.00
(13)	John W. Bates	100.00	50.00	30.00
(14)	Fred Beck	100.00	50.00	30.00
(15)	B. Becker	100.00	50.00	30.00
(16)	George G. Bell	100.00	50.00	30.00
(17)	Chas. Bender	500.00	250.00	150.00
(18)	William Bergen	100.00	50.00	30.00
(19)	Bob Bescher	100.00	50.00	30.00
(20)	Joe Birmingham	100.00	50.00	30.00
(21)	Lena Blackburne	100.00	50.00	30.00
(22)	William E. Bransfield	100.00	50.00	30.00
(23)	Roger P. Bresnahan (mouth closed)	500.00	250.00	150.00
(24)	Roger P. Bresnahan (mouth open)	600.00	300.00	180.00
(25)	A.H. Bridwell	100.00	50.00	30.00
(26)	Mordecai Brown	500.00	250.00	150.00
(27)	Robert Byrne	100.00	50.00	30.00
(28)	Hick Cady	300.00	150.00	90.00
(29)	H. Camnitz	100.00	50.00	30.00
(30)	Bill Carrigan	100.00	50.00	30.00
(31)	Frank J. Chance	500.00	250.00	150.00
(32a)	Hal Chase (both ears show, gold diamond frame extends below shoulders)	200.00	100.00	60.00
(32b)	Hal Chase (both ears show, gold diamond frame ends at shoulders)	200.00	100.00	60.00
(33)	Hal Chase (only left ear shows)	550.00	275.00	165.00
(34)	Ed Cicotte	100.00	50.00	30.00
(35)	Fred C. Clarke	275.00	137.00	82.00
(36)	Ty Cobb	3500.00	1725.00	625.00
(37)	Eddie Collins (mouth closed)	350.00	175.00	105.00
(38)	Eddie Collins (mouth open)	500.00	250.00	150.00
(39)	Jimmy Collins	500.00	250.00	150.00
(40)	Frank J. Corridon	100.00	50.00	30.00
(41a)	Otis Crandall ("t" not crossed in name)	100.00	50.00	30.00
(41b)	Otis Crandall ("t" crossed in name)	100.00	50.00	30.00
(42)	Lou Criger	100.00	50.00	30.00
(43)	W.F. Dahlen	275.00	137.00	82.00
(44)	Jake Daubert	110.00	55.00	33.00
(45)	Jim Delahanty	100.00	50.00	30.00
(46)	Arthur Devlin	100.00	50.00	30.00
(47)	Josh Devore	100.00	50.00	30.00
(48)	W.R. Dickson	100.00	50.00	30.00
(49)	Jiggs Donohue (Donahue)	500.00	250.00	150.00
(50)	Chas. S. Dooin	100.00	50.00	30.00
(51)	Michael J. Doolan	100.00	50.00	30.00
(52a)	Patsy Dougherty (red sock for team emblem)	100.00	50.00	30.00

		NR MT	EX	VG
(52b)	Patsy Dougherty (white sock for team emblem)	275.00	137.00	82.00
(53)	Thomas Downey	100.00	50.00	30.00
(54)	Larry Doyle	100.00	50.00	30.00
(55)	Hugh Duffy	500.00	250.00	150.00
(56)	Jack Dunn	300.00	150.00	90.00
(57)	Jimmy Dygert	100.00	50.00	30.00
(58)	R. Egan	100.00	50.00	30.00
(59)	Kid Elberfeld	100.00	50.00	30.00
(60)	Clyde Engle	100.00	50.00	30.00
(61)	Louis Evans	100.00	50.00	30.00
(62)	John J. Evers	400.00	200.00	120.00
(63)	Robert Ewing	100.00	50.00	30.00
(64)	G.C. Ferguson	100.00	50.00	30.00
(65)	Ray Fisher	350.00	175.00	105.00
(66)	Arthur Fletcher	100.00	50.00	30.00
(67)	John A. Flynn	100.00	50.00	30.00
(68)	Russ Ford (black cap)	100.00	50.00	30.00
(69)	Russ Ford (white cap)	350.00	175.00	105.00
(70)	Wm. A. Foxen	100.00	50.00	30.00
(71)	Jimmy Frick	300.00	150.00	90.00
(72)	Arthur Fromme	100.00	50.00	30.00
(73)	Earl Gardner	100.00	50.00	30.00
(74)	H.L. Gaspar	100.00	50.00	30.00
(75)	George Gibson	100.00	50.00	30.00
(76)	Wilbur Goode	100.00	50.00	30.00
(77)	George F. Graham (Rustlers)	100.00	50.00	30.00
(78)	George F. Graham (Cubs)	500.00	250.00	150.00
(79)	Edward L. Grant	400.00	200.00	120.00
(80a)	Dolly Gray (no stats on back)	100.00	50.00	30.00
(80b)	Dolly Gray (stats on back)	275.00	137.00	82.00
(81)	Clark Griffith	500.00	250.00	150.00
(82)	Bob Groom	100.00	50.00	30.00
(83)	Charlie Hanford	300.00	150.00	90.00
(84)	Bob Harmon (both ears show)	100.00	50.00	30.00
(85)	Bob Harmon (only left ear shows)	500.00	250.00	150.00
(86)	Topsy Hartsel	100.00	50.00	30.00
(87)	Arnold J. Hauser	100.00	50.00	30.00
(88)	Charlie Hemphill	100.00	50.00	30.00
(89)	C.L. Herzog	100.00	50.00	30.00
(90a)	R. Hoblitzell (no stats on back)	600.00	300.00	180.00
(90b)	R. Hoblitzel ("Cin." after 2nd 1908 in stats)	300.00	150.00	90.00
(90c)	R. Hoblitzel (name incorrect, no "Cin." after 1908 in stats)	100.00	50.00	30.00
(90d)	R. Hoblitzel (name correct, no "Cin." after 1908 in stats)	300.00	150.00	90.00
(91)	Danny Hoffman	100.00	50.00	30.00
(92)	Miller J. Huggins	350.00	175.00	105.00
(93)	John E. Hummel	100.00	50.00	30.00
(94)	Fred Jacklitsch	100.00	50.00	30.00
(95)	Hughie Jennings	500.00	250.00	150.00
(96)	Walter Johnson	1000.00	500.00	150.00
(97)	D. Jones	100.00	50.00	30.00
(98)	Tom Jones	100.00	50.00	30.00
(99)	Addie Joss	600.00	300.00	180.00
(100)	Ed Karger	275.00	137.00	82.00
(101)	Ed Killian	100.00	50.00	30.00
(102)	Red Kleinow	275.00	137.00	82.00
(103)	John G. Kling	100.00	50.00	30.00
(104)	Jack Knight	100.00	50.00	30.00
(105)	Ed Konetchy	100.00	50.00	30.00
(106)	Harry Krause	100.00	50.00	30.00
(107)	Floyd M. Kroh	100.00	50.00	30.00
(108)	Frank LaPorte	100.00	50.00	30.00
(109)	Frank Lang (Lange)	100.00	50.00	30.00
(110a)	A. Latham (A. Latham on back)	100.00	50.00	30.00
(110b)	A. Latham (W.A. Latham on back)	100.00	50.00	30.00
(111)	Thomas W. Leach	100.00	50.00	30.00
(112)	Watty Lee	300.00	150.00	90.00
(113)	Sam Leever	100.00	50.00	30.00
(114a)	A. Leifield (initial "A." on front)	100.00	50.00	30.00
(114b)	A.P. Leifield (initials "A.P." on front)	100.00	50.00	30.00
(115)	Edgar Lennox	100.00	50.00	30.00
(116)	Paddy Livingston	100.00	50.00	30.00
(117)	John B. Lobert	100.00	50.00	30.00
(118)	Bris Lord (Athletics)	100.00	50.00	30.00
(119)	Harry Lord (White Sox)	100.00	50.00	30.00
(120)	Jno. C. Lush	100.00	50.00	30.00
(121)	Nick Maddox	100.00	50.00	30.00
(122)	Sherwood R. Magee	110.00	55.00	33.00
(123)	R.W. Marquard	400.00	200.00	120.00
(124)	C. Mathewson	800.00	400.00	137.00
(125)	A.A. Mattern	100.00	50.00	30.00
(126)	Sport McAllister	300.00	150.00	90.00
(127)	George McBride	100.00	50.00	30.00
(128)	Amby McConnell	100.00	50.00	30.00
(129)	P.M. McElveen	100.00	50.00	30.00
(130)	J.J. McGraw	500.00	250.00	150.00
(131)	Harry McIntyre (Cubs)	100.00	50.00	30.00
(132)	Matty McIntyre (White Sox)	100.00	50.00	30.00
(133)	M.A. McLean (initials actually J.B.)	100.00	50.00	30.00
(134)	Fred Merkle	110.00	55.00	33.00
(135)	George Merritt	300.00	150.00	90.00
(136)	J.T. Meyers	100.00	50.00	30.00
(137)	Clyde Milan	100.00	50.00	30.00
(138)	J.D. Miller	100.00	50.00	30.00
(139)	M.F. Mitchell	100.00	50.00	30.00
(140a)	P.J. Moran (stray line of type below stats)	100.00	50.00	30.00
(140b)	P.J. Moran (no stray line)	100.00	50.00	30.00
(141)	George Moriarty	100.00	50.00	30.00
(142)	George Mullin	100.00	50.00	30.00
(143)	Danny Murphy	100.00	50.00	30.00
(144)	Jack Murray	100.00	50.00	30.00
(145)	John Nee	300.00	150.00	90.00
(146)	Thomas J. Needham	100.00	50.00	30.00
(147)	Rebel Oakes	100.00	50.00	30.00
(148)	Rube Oldring	100.00	50.00	30.00
(149)	Charley O'Leary	100.00	50.00	30.00
(150)	Fred Olmstead	100.00	50.00	30.00
(151)	Orval Overall	100.00	50.00	30.00
(152)	Freddy Parent	100.00	50.00	30.00
(153)	George Paskert	100.00	50.00	30.00
(154)	Billy Payne	100.00	50.00	30.00
(155)	Barney Pelty	100.00	50.00	30.00
(156)	John Pfeister	100.00	50.00	30.00
(157)	Jimmy Phelan	300.00	150.00	90.00
(158)	E.J. Phelps	100.00	50.00	30.00
(159)	C. Phillippe	100.00	50.00	30.00
(160)	Jack Quinn	100.00	50.00	30.00
(161)	A.L. Raymond	500.00	250.00	150.00
(162)	E.M. Reulbach	100.00	50.00	30.00
(163)	Lewis Richie	100.00	50.00	30.00
(164)	John A. Rowan	400.00	200.00	120.00
(165)	George N. Rucker	100.00	50.00	30.00
(166)	W.D. Scanlan	350.00	175.00	105.00
(167)	Germany Schaefer	100.00	50.00	30.00
(168)	George Schlei	100.00	50.00	30.00
(169)	Boss Schmidt	100.00	50.00	30.00
(170)	F.M. Schulte	100.00	50.00	30.00
(171)	Jim Scott	100.00	50.00	30.00
(172)	B.H. Sharpe	100.00	50.00	30.00
(173)	David Shean (Rustlers)	100.00	50.00	30.00
(174)	David Shean (Cubs)	500.00	250.00	150.00
(175)	Jas. T. Sheckard	100.00	50.00	30.00
(176)	Hack Simmons	100.00	50.00	30.00
(177)	Tony Smith	100.00	50.00	30.00
(178)	Fred C. Snodgrass	100.00	50.00	30.00
(179)	Tris Speaker	600.00	300.00	180.00
(180)	Jake Stahl	100.00	50.00	30.00
(181)	Oscar Stanage	100.00	50.00	30.00
(182)	Harry Steinfeldt	110.00	55.00	33.00
(183)	George Stone	100.00	50.00	30.00
(184)	George Stovall	100.00	50.00	30.00
(185)	Gabby Street	100.00	50.00	30.00
(186)	George F. Suggs	500.00	250.00	150.00
(187)	Ed Summers	100.00	50.00	30.00
(188)	Jeff Sweeney	350.00	175.00	105.00
(189)	Lee Tannehill	100.00	50.00	30.00
(190)	Ira Thomas	100.00	50.00	30.00
(191)	Joe Tinker	500.00	250.00	150.00
(192)	John Titus	100.00	50.00	30.00
(193)	Terry Turner	500.00	250.00	150.00
(194)	James Vaughn	100.00	50.00	30.00
(195)	Heinie Wagner	350.00	175.00	105.00
(196)	Bobby Wallace (with cap)	350.00	175.00	105.00
(197a)	Bobby Wallace (no cap, one line of 1910 stats)	500.00	250.00	150.00
(197b)	Bobby Wallace (no cap, two lines of 1910 stats)	550.00	275.00	165.00
(198)	Ed Walsh	500.00	250.00	150.00
(199)	Z.D. Wheat	400.00	200.00	120.00
(200)	Doc White (White Sox)	100.00	50.00	30.00
(201)	Kirb. White (Pirates)	400.00	200.00	120.00
(202)	Irvin K. Wilhelm	500.00	250.00	150.00
(203)	Ed Willett	100.00	50.00	30.00
(204)	J. Owen Wilson	100.00	50.00	30.00
(205)	George R. Wiltse (both ears show)	100.00	50.00	30.00
(206)	George R. Wiltse (only right ear shows)	500.00	250.00	150.00
(207)	Harry Wolter	100.00	50.00	30.00
(208)	Cy Young	600.00	270.00	112.00

NOTE: A card number in parentheses ( ) indicates the set is unnumbered.

1909-11 T206 White Border

The nearly 525 cards which make up the T206 set are the most popular of the early tobacco card issues Players are depicted in a color lithograph against a variety of colorful backgrounds, surrounded by a white border. The player names on the 1-1/2" by 2-5/8" cards appear at the bottom with the city and league, when a city had more than one team. Backs contain an ad for one of 16 brands of cigarettes. There are 389 major leaguer cards and 134 minor leaguer cards in the set, but with front/back varieties the number of potentially different cards runs into the thousands. The set features many expensive cards including a number of pose and/or team variations, along with the very scarce Eddie Plank card and the "King of Baseball Cards," the T206 Honus Wagner, the most avidly sought of all baseball cards. The complete set price does not include the Doyle (N.Y. Natl.), Magie, Plank and Wagner cards.

		NR MT	EX	VG
Complete Set:		88000.00	44000.00	26500.
Common Player:		80.00	40.00	25.00
Common Minor Leaguer:		85.00	42.50	27.00
Common Southern Leaguer:		200.00	100.00	60.00
(1)	Ed Abbaticchio (blue sleeves)	95.00	47.00	28.00
(2)	Ed Abbaticchio (brown sleeves)	80.00	40.00	24.00
(3)	Fred Abbott	85.00	42.00	25.00
(4)	Bill Abstein	80.00	40.00	24.00
(5)	Doc Adkins	85.00	42.00	25.00
(6)	Whitey Alperman	95.00	47.00	28.00
(7)	Red Ames (hands at chest)	95.00	47.00	28.00
(8)	Red Ames (hands above head)	95.00	47.00	28.00
(9)	Red Ames (portrait)	80.00	40.00	24.00
(10)	John Anderson	85.00	42.00	25.00
(11)	Frank Arellanes	80.00	40.00	24.00
(12)	Herman Armbruster	85.00	42.00	25.00
(13)	Harry Arndt	85.00	42.00	25.00
(14)	Jake Atz	80.00	40.00	24.00
(15)	Home Run Baker	300.00	150.00	90.00
(16)	Neal Ball (New York)	95.00	47.00	28.00
(17)	Neal Ball (Cleveland)	80.00	40.00	24.00
(18)	Jap Barbeau	95.00	47.00	28.00
(19)	Cy Barger	85.00	42.00	25.00
(20)	Jack Barry (Philadelphia)	80.00	40.00	24.00
(21)	Shad Barry (Milwaukee)	85.00	42.00	25.00
(22)	Jack Bastian	200.00	100.00	60.00
(23)	Emil Batch	85.00	42.00	25.00
(24)	Johnny Bates	95.00	47.00	28.00
(25)	Harry Bay	200.00	100.00	60.00
(26)	Ginger Beaumont	95.00	47.00	28.00
(27)	Fred Beck	80.00	40.00	24.00
(28)	Beals Becker	80.00	40.00	24.00
(29)	Jake Beckley	300.00	150.00	90.00
(30)	George Bell (hands above head)	95.00	47.00	28.00
(31)	George Bell (pitching follow thru)			
		80.00	40.00	24.00

		NR MT	EX	VG
(32)	Chief Bender (pitching, no trees in background)	275.00	137.00	82.00
(33)	Chief Bender (pitching, trees in background)	275.00	137.00	82.00
(34)	Chief Bender (portrait)	300.00	150.00	90.00
(35)	Bill Bergen (batting)	95.00	47.00	28.00
(36)	Bill Bergen (catching)	85.00	42.00	25.00
(37)	Heinie Berger	80.00	40.00	24.00
(38)	Bill Bernhard	200.00	100.00	60.00
(39)	Bob Bescher (hands in air)	80.00	40.00	24.00
(40)	Bob Bescher (portrait)	80.00	40.00	24.00
(41)	Joe Birmingham	95.00	47.00	28.00
(42)	Lena Blackburne	85.00	42.00	25.00
(43)	Jack Bliss	80.00	40.00	24.00
(44)	Frank Bowerman	95.00	47.00	28.00
(45)	Bill Bradley (portrait)	95.00	47.00	28.00
(46)	Bill Bradley (with bat)	80.00	40.00	24.00
(47)	Dave Brain	85.00	42.00	25.00
(48)	Kitty Bransfield	95.00	47.00	28.00
(49)	Roy Brashear	85.00	42.00	25.00
(50)	Ted Breitenstein	200.00	100.00	60.00
(51)	Roger Bresnahan (portrait)	350.00	175.00	105.00
(52)	Roger Bresnahan (with bat)	275.00	137.00	82.00
(53)	Al Bridwell (portrait, no cap)	80.00	40.00	24.00
(54)	Al Bridwell (portrait, with cap)	95.00	47.00	28.00
(55a)	George Brown (Browne) (Chicago)	95.00	47.00	28.00
(55b)	George Brown (Browne) (Washington)	600.00	300.00	180.00
(56)	Mordecai Brown (Chicago on shirt)	275.00	137.00	82.00
(57)	Mordecai Brown (Cubs on shirt)	350.00	175.00	105.00
(58)	Mordecai Brown (portrait)	300.00	150.00	90.00
(59)	Al Burch (batting)	180.00	90.00	54.00
(60)	Al Burch (fielding)	80.00	40.00	24.00
(61)	Fred Burchell	85.00	42.00	25.00
(62)	Jimmy Burke	85.00	42.00	25.00
(63)	Bill Burns	80.00	40.00	24.00
(64)	Donie Bush	80.00	40.00	24.00
(65)	John Butler	85.00	42.00	25.00
(66)	Bobby Byrne	80.00	40.00	24.00
(67)	Howie Camnitz (arm at side)	80.00	40.00	24.00
(68)	Howie Camnitz (arms folded)	95.00	47.00	28.00
(69)	Howie Camnitz (hands above head)	80.00	40.00	24.00
(70)	Billy Campbell	80.00	40.00	24.00
(71)	Scoops Carey	200.00	100.00	60.00
(72)	Charley Carr	85.00	42.00	25.00
(73)	Bill Carrigan	80.00	40.00	24.00
(74)	Doc Casey	85.00	42.00	25.00
(75)	Peter Cassidy	85.00	42.00	25.00
(76)	Frank Chance (batting)	300.00	150.00	90.00
(77)	Frank Chance (portrait, red background)	350.00	175.00	105.00
(78)	Frank Chance (portrait, yellow background)	300.00	150.00	90.00
(79)	Bill Chappelle	85.00	42.00	25.00
(80)	Chappie Charles	80.00	40.00	24.00
(81)	Hal Chase (holding trophy)	100.00	50.00	30.00
(82)	Hal Chase (portrait, blue background)	100.00	50.00	30.00
(83)	Hal Chase (portrait, pink background)	180.00	90.00	54.00
(84)	Hal Chase (throwing, dark cap)	100.00	50.00	30.00
(85)	Hal Chase (throwing, white cap)	300.00	150.00	90.00
(86)	Jack Chesbro	350.00	175.00	105.00
(87)	Ed Cicotte	100.00	50.00	30.00
(88)	Bill Clancy (Clancey)	85.00	42.00	25.00
(89)	Josh Clark (Clarke) (Columbus)	85.00	42.00	25.00
(90)	Fred Clarke (Pittsburg, holding bat)	300.00	150.00	90.00
(91)	Fred Clarke (Pittsburg, portrait)	300.00	150.00	90.00
(92)	Nig Clarke (Cleveland)	95.00	47.00	28.00
(93)	Bill Clymer	85.00	42.00	25.00
(94)	Ty Cobb (portrait, green background)	1800.00	900.00	550.00
(95)	Ty Cobb (portrait, red background)	2000.00	1000.00	600.00
(96)	Ty Cobb (with bat off shoulder)	2500.00	1250.00	750.00
(97)	Ty Cobb (with bat on shoulder)	1800.00	900.00	550.00
(98)	Cad Coles	200.00	100.00	60.00
(99)	Eddie Collins (Philadelphia)	100.00	50.00	30.00
(100)	Jimmy Collins (Minneapolis)	100.00	50.00	30.00
(101)	Bunk Congalton	85.00	42.00	25.00
(102)	Wid Conroy (fielding)	95.00	47.00	28.00
(103)	Wid Conroy (with bat)	80.00	40.00	24.00
(104)	Harry Covaleski (Coveleski)	95.00	47.00	28.00
(105)	Doc Crandall (portrait, no cap)	95.00	47.00	28.00

	NR MT	EX	VG
(106) Doc Crandall (portrait, with cap)	80.00	40.00	24.00
(107) Bill Cranston	200.00	100.00	60.00
(108) Gavvy Cravath	100.00	50.00	30.00
(109) Sam Crawford (throwing)	350.00	175.00	105.00
(110) Sam Crawford (with bat)	300.00	150.00	90.00
(111) Birdie Cree	80.00	40.00	24.00
(112) Lou Criger	95.00	47.00	28.00
(113) Dode Criss	95.00	47.00	28.00
(114) Monte Cross	85.00	42.00	25.00
(115a)Bill Dahlen (Boston)	95.00	47.00	28.00
(115b)Bill Dahlen (Brooklyn)	300.00	150.00	90.00
(116) Paul Davidson	85.00	42.00	25.00
(117) George Davis (Chicago)	95.00	47.00	28.00
(118) Harry Davis (Philadelphia, Davis on front)	80.00	40.00	24.00
(119) Harry Davis (Philadelphia, H. Davis on front)	95.00	47.00	28.00
(120) Frank Delehanty (Delahanty) (Louisville)	85.00	42.00	25.00
(121) Jim Delehanty (Delahanty) (Washington)	95.00	47.00	28.00
(122a)Ray Demmitt (New York)	80.00	40.00	24.00
(122b)Ray Demmitt (St. Louis)	2800.00	1400.00	800.00
(123) Rube Dessau	85.00	42.00	25.00
(124) Art Devlin	95.00	47.00	28.00
(125) Josh Devore	80.00	40.00	24.00
(126) Bill Dineen (Dinneen)	80.00	40.00	24.00
(127) Mike Donlin (fielding)	180.00	90.00	54.00
(128) Mike Donlin (seated)	95.00	47.00	28.00
(129) Mike Donlin (with bat)	80.00	40.00	24.00
(130) Jiggs Donohue (Donahue)	95.00	47.00	28.00
(131) Wild Bill Donovan (portrait)	95.00	47.00	28.00
(132) Wild Bill Donovan (throwing)	80.00	40.00	24.00
(133) Red Dooin	95.00	47.00	28.00
(134) Mickey Doolan (batting)	80.00	40.00	24.00
(135) Mickey Doolan (fielding)	80.00	40.00	24.00
(136) Mickey Doolin (Doolan)	95.00	47.00	28.00
(137) Gus Dorner	85.00	42.00	25.00
(138) Patsy Dougherty (arm in air)	80.00	40.00	24.00
(139) Patsy Dougherty (portrait)	95.00	47.00	28.00
(140) Tom Downey (batting)	80.00	40.00	24.00
(141) Tom Downey (fielding)	80.00	40.00	24.00
(142) Jerry Downs	85.00	42.00	25.00
(143a)Joe Doyle (N.Y. Natl., hands above head)	17000.00	8500.00	5000.
(143b)Joe Doyle (N.Y., hands above head)	80.00	40.00	24.00
(144) Larry Doyle (N.Y. Nat'l., portrait)	95.00	47.00	28.00
(145) Larry Doyle (N.Y. Nat'l., throwing)	100.00	50.00	30.00
(146) Larry Doyle (N.Y. Nat'l., with bat)	95.00	47.00	28.00
(147) Jean Dubuc	80.00	40.00	24.00
(148) Hugh Duffy	275.00	137.00	82.00
(149) Jack Dunn (Baltimore)	85.00	42.00	25.00
(150) Joe Dunn (Brooklyn)	85.00	42.00	25.00
(151) Bull Durham	95.00	47.00	28.00
(152) Jimmy Dygert	80.00	40.00	24.00
(153) Ted Easterly	80.00	40.00	24.00
(154) Dick Egan	80.00	40.00	24.00
(155a)Kid Elberfeld (New York)	95.00	47.00	28.00
(155b)Kid Elberfeld (Washington, portrait)	1500.00	750.00	450.00
(156) Kid Elberfeld (Washington, fielding)	80.00	40.00	24.00
(157) Roy Ellam	200.00	100.00	60.00
(158) Clyde Engle	80.00	40.00	24.00
(159) Steve Evans	80.00	40.00	24.00
(160) Johnny Evers (portrait)	400.00	200.00	120.00
(161) Johnny Evers (with bat, Chicago on shirt)	275.00	137.00	82.00
(162) Johnny Evers (with bat, Cubs on shirt)	350.00	175.00	105.00
(163) Bob Ewing	95.00	47.00	28.00
(164) Cecil Ferguson	80.00	40.00	24.00
(165) Hobe Ferris	95.00	47.00	28.00
(166) Lou Fiene (portrait)	80.00	40.00	24.00
(167) Lou Fiene (throwing)	80.00	40.00	24.00
(168) Steamer Flanagan	85.00	42.00	25.00
(169) Art Fletcher	80.00	40.00	24.00
(170) Elmer Flick	300.00	150.00	90.00
(171) Russ Ford	80.00	40.00	24.00
(172) Ed Foster	200.00	100.00	60.00
(173) Jerry Freeman	85.00	42.00	25.00
(174) John Frill	80.00	40.00	24.00
(175) Charlie Fritz	200.00	100.00	60.00
(176) Art Fromme	80.00	40.00	24.00
(177) Chick Gandil	95.00	47.00	28.00
(178) Bob Ganley	95.00	47.00	28.00
(179) John Ganzel	85.00	42.00	25.00

	NR MT	EX	VG
(180) Harry Gasper	80.00	40.00	24.00
(181) Rube Geyer	80.00	40.00	24.00
(182) George Gibson	95.00	47.00	28.00
(183) Billy Gilbert	95.00	47.00	28.00
(184) Wilbur Goode (Good)	95.00	47.00	28.00
(185) Bill Graham (St. Louis)	80.00	40.00	24.00
(186) Peaches Graham (Boston)	80.00	40.00	24.00
(187) Dolly Gray	80.00	40.00	24.00
(188) Ed Greminger	200.00	100.00	60.00
(189) Clark Griffith (batting)	300.00	150.00	90.00
(190) Clark Griffith (portrait)	350.00	175.00	105.00
(191) Moose Grimshaw	85.00	42.00	25.00
(192) Bob Groom	80.00	40.00	24.00
(193) Guiheen	200.00	100.00	60.00
(194) Ed Hahn	95.00	47.00	28.00
(195) Bob Hall	85.00	42.00	25.00
(196) Bill Hallman	85.00	42.00	25.00
(197) Jack Hannifan (Hannifin)	85.00	42.00	25.00
(198) Bill Hart (Little Rock)	200.00	100.00	60.00
(199) Jimmy Hart (Montgomery)	200.00	100.00	60.00
(200) Topsy Hartsel	80.00	40.00	24.00
(201) Jack Hayden	85.00	42.00	25.00
(202) J. Ross Helm	200.00	100.00	60.00
(203) Charlie Hemphill	95.00	47.00	28.00
(204) Buck Herzog (Boston)	80.00	40.00	24.00
(205) Buck Herzog (New York)	95.00	47.00	28.00
(206) Gordon Hickman	200.00	100.00	60.00
(207) Bill Hinchman (Cleveland)	95.00	47.00	28.00
(208) Harry Hinchman (Toledo)	85.00	42.00	25.00
(209) Dick Hoblitzell	80.00	40.00	24.00
(210) Danny Hoffman (St. Louis)	80.00	40.00	24.00
(211) Izzy Hoffman (Providence)	85.00	42.00	25.00
(212) Solly Hofman	80.00	40.00	24.00
(213) Bock Hooker	200.00	100.00	60.00
(214) Del Howard (Chicago)	80.00	40.00	24.00
(215) Ernie Howard (Savannah)	200.00	100.00	60.00
(216) Harry Howell (hand at waist)	80.00	40.00	24.00
(217) Harry Howell (portrait)	80.00	40.00	24.00
(218) Miller Huggins (hands at mouth)	275.00	137.00	82.00
(219) Miller Huggins (portrait)	300.00	150.00	90.00
(220) Rudy Hulswitt	80.00	40.00	24.00
(221) John Hummel	80.00	40.00	24.00
(222) George Hunter	80.00	40.00	24.00
(223) Frank Isbell	95.00	47.00	28.00
(224) Fred Jacklitsch	95.00	47.00	28.00
(225) Jimmy Jackson	85.00	42.00	25.00
(226) Hughie Jennings (one hand showing)	275.00	137.00	82.00
(227) Hughie Jennings (both hands showing)	275.00	137.00	82.00
(228) Hughie Jennings (portrait)	300.00	150.00	90.00
(229) Walter Johnson (hands at chest)	600.00	300.00	112.00
(230) Walter Johnson (portrait)	650.00	325.00	120.00
(231) Fielder Jones (Chicago, hands at hips)	95.00	47.00	28.00
(232) Fielder Jones (Chicago, portrait)	95.00	47.00	28.00
(233) Davy Jones (Detroit)	80.00	40.00	24.00
(234) Tom Jones (St. Louis)	95.00	47.00	28.00
(235) Dutch Jordan (Atlanta)	200.00	100.00	60.00
(236) Tim Jordan (Brooklyn, batting)	80.00	40.00	24.00
(237) Tim Jordan (Brooklyn, portrait)	95.00	47.00	28.00
(238) Addie Joss (hands at chest)	300.00	150.00	90.00
(239) Addie Joss (portrait)	350.00	175.00	105.00
(240) Ed Karger	95.00	47.00	28.00
(241) Willie Keeler (portrait)	400.00	200.00	120.00
(242) Willie Keeler (with bat)	400.00	200.00	120.00
(243) Joe Kelley	275.00	137.00	82.00
(244) J.F. Kiernan	200.00	100.00	60.00
(245) Ed Killian (hands at chest)	80.00	40.00	24.00
(246) Ed Killian (portrait)	95.00	47.00	28.00
(247) Frank King	200.00	100.00	60.00
(248) Rube Kisinger (Kissinger)	85.00	42.00	25.00
(249a)Red Kleinow (Boston)	525.00	262.00	157.00
(249b)Red Kleinow (New York, catching)	80.00	40.00	24.00
(250) Red Kleinow (New York, with bat)	95.00	47.00	28.00
(251) Johnny Kling	95.00	47.00	28.00
(252) Otto Knabe	80.00	40.00	24.00
(253) Jack Knight (portrait)	80.00	40.00	24.00
(254) Jack Knight (with bat)	80.00	40.00	24.00
(255) Ed Konetchy (glove above head)	95.00	47.00	28.00
(256) Ed Konetchy (glove near ground)	80.00	40.00	24.00
(257) Harry Krause (pitching)	80.00	40.00	24.00
(258) Harry Krause (portrait)	80.00	40.00	24.00
(259) Rube Kroh	80.00	40.00	24.00
(260) Otto Kruger (Krueger)	85.00	42.00	25.00
(261) James Lafitte	200.00	100.00	60.00

	NR MT	EX	VG
(262) Nap Lajoie (portrait)	600.00	300.00	180.00
(263) Nap Lajoie (throwing)	525.00	262.00	157.00
(264) Nap Lajoie (with bat)	525.00	262.00	157.00
(265) Joe Lake (New York)	95.00	47.00	28.00
(266) Joe Lake (St. Louis, ball in hand)	80.00	40.00	24.00
(267) Joe Lake (St. Louis, no ball in hand)			
	80.00	40.00	24.00
(268) Frank LaPorte	80.00	40.00	24.00
(269) Arlie Latham	80.00	40.00	24.00
(270) Bill Lattimore	85.00	42.00	25.00
(271) Jimmy Lavender	85.00	42.00	25.00
(272) Tommy Leach (bending over)	80.00	40.00	24.00
(273) Tommy Leach (portrait)	95.00	47.00	28.00
(274) Lefty Leifield (batting)	80.00	40.00	24.00
(275) Lefty Leifield (pitching)	95.00	47.00	28.00
(276) Ed Lennox	80.00	40.00	24.00
(277) Harry Lentz (Sentz)	200.00	100.00	60.00
(278) Glenn Liebhardt	95.00	47.00	28.00
(279) Vive Lindaman	95.00	47.00	28.00
(280) Perry Lipe	200.00	100.00	60.00
(281) Paddy Livingstone (Livingston)	80.00	40.00	24.00
(282) Hans Lobert	95.00	47.00	28.00
(283) Harry Lord	80.00	40.00	24.00
(284) Harry Lumley	95.00	47.00	28.00
(285a) Carl Lundgren (Chicago)	300.00	150.00	90.00
(285b) Carl Lundgren (Kansas City)	85.00	42.00	25.00
(286) Nick Maddox	80.00	40.00	24.00
(287a) Sherry Magie (Magee)	10000.00	5000.00	3000.
(287b) Sherry Magee (portrait)	100.00	50.00	30.00
(288) Sherry Magee (with bat)	95.00	47.00	28.00
(289) Bill Malarkey	85.00	42.00	25.00
(290) Billy Maloney	85.00	42.00	25.00
(291) George Manion	200.00	100.00	60.00
(292) Rube Manning (batting)	95.00	47.00	28.00
(293) Rube Manning (pitching)	80.00	40.00	24.00
(294) Rube Marquard (hands at thighs)			
	350.00	175.00	105.00
(295) Rube Marquard (pitching follow thru)			
	300.00	150.00	90.00
(296) Rube Marquard (portrait)	300.00	150.00	90.00
(297) Doc Marshall	80.00	40.00	24.00
(298) Christy Mathewson (dark cap)	550.00	275.00	120.00
(299) Christy Mathewson (portrait)	600.00	300.00	127.00
(300) Christy Mathewson (white cap)	600.00	300.00	127.00
(301) Al Mattern	80.00	40.00	24.00
(302) John McAleese	80.00	40.00	24.00
(303) George McBride	80.00	40.00	24.00
(304) Pat McCauley	200.00	100.00	60.00
(305) Moose McCormick	80.00	40.00	24.00
(306) Pryor McElveen	80.00	40.00	24.00
(307) Dan McGann	85.00	42.00	25.00
(308) Jim McGinley	85.00	42.00	25.00
(309) Iron Man McGinnity	300.00	150.00	90.00
(310) Stoney McGlynn	85.00	42.00	25.00
(311) John McGraw (finger in air)	350.00	175.00	105.00
(312) John McGraw (glove at hip)	300.00	150.00	90.00
(313) John McGraw (portrait, no cap)			
	350.00	175.00	105.00
(314) John McGraw (portrait, with cap)			
	300.00	150.00	90.00
(315) Harry McIntyre (Brooklyn)	95.00	47.00	28.00
(316) Harry McIntyre (Brooklyn & Chicago)			
	80.00	40.00	24.00
(317) Matty McIntyre (Detroit)	80.00	40.00	24.00
(318) Larry McLean	80.00	40.00	24.00
(319) George McQuillan (ball in hand)	95.00	47.00	28.00
(320) George McQuillan (with bat)	80.00	40.00	24.00
(321) Fred Merkle (portrait)	100.00	50.00	30.00
(322) Fred Merkle (throwing)	95.00	47.00	28.00
(323) George Merritt	85.00	42.00	25.00
(324) Chief Meyers	80.00	40.00	24.00
(325) Clyde Milan	80.00	40.00	24.00
(326) Dots Miller (Pittsburg)	80.00	40.00	24.00
(327) Molly Miller (Dallas)	200.00	100.00	60.00
(328) Bill Milligan	85.00	42.00	25.00
(329) Fred Mitchell (Toronto)	85.00	42.00	25.00
(330) Mike Mitchell (Cincinnati)	80.00	40.00	24.00
(331) Dan Moeller	85.00	42.00	25.00
(332) Carlton Molesworth	200.00	100.00	60.00
(333) Herbie Moran (Providence)	85.00	42.00	25.00
(334) Pat Moran (Chicago)	80.00	40.00	24.00
(335) George Moriarty	80.00	40.00	24.00
(336) Mike Mowrey	80.00	40.00	24.00
(337) Dom Mullaney	200.00	100.00	60.00
(338) George Mullen (Mullin)	80.00	40.00	24.00
(339) George Mullin (throwing)	95.00	47.00	28.00
(340) George Mullin (with bat)	80.00	40.00	24.00
(341) Danny Murphy (batting)	80.00	40.00	24.00
(342) Danny Murphy (throwing)	95.00	47.00	28.00
(343) Red Murray (batting)	80.00	40.00	24.00
(344) Red Murray (portrait)	80.00	40.00	24.00

	NR MT	EX	VG
(345) Chief Myers (Meyers) (batting)	80.00	40.00	24.00
(346) Chief Myers (Meyers) (fielding)	80.00	40.00	24.00
(347) Billy Nattress	85.00	42.00	25.00
(348) Tom Needham	80.00	40.00	24.00
(349) Simon Nicholls (hands on knees)	95.00	47.00	28.00
(350) Simon Nichols (Nicholls) (batting)			
	80.00	40.00	24.00
(351) Harry Niles	95.00	47.00	28.00
(352) Rebel Oakes	80.00	40.00	24.00
(353) Frank Oberlin	85.00	42.00	25.00
(354) Peter O'Brien	85.00	42.00	25.00
(355a) Bill O'Hara (New York)	80.00	40.00	24.00
(355b) Bill O'Hara (St. Louis)	2400.00	1200.00	540.00
(356) Rube Oldring (batting)	80.00	40.00	24.00
(357) Rube Oldring (fielding)	95.00	47.00	28.00
(358) Charley O'Leary (hands on knees)			
	80.00	40.00	24.00
(359) Charley O'Leary (portrait)	95.00	47.00	28.00
(360) William J. O'Neil	85.00	42.00	25.00
(361) Al Orth	200.00	100.00	60.00
(362) William Otey	200.00	100.00	60.00
(363) Orval Overall (hand face level)	80.00	40.00	24.00
(364) Orval Overall (hands waist level)	80.00	40.00	24.00
(365) Orval Overall (portrait)	95.00	47.00	28.00
(366) Frank Owen	95.00	47.00	28.00
(367) George Paige	200.00	100.00	60.00
(368) Fred Parent	95.00	47.00	28.00
(369) Dode Paskert	80.00	40.00	24.00
(370) Jim Pastorius	95.00	47.00	28.00
(371) Harry Pattee	180.00	90.00	54.00
(372) Billy Payne	80.00	40.00	24.00
(373) Barney Pelty (horizontal photo)			
	180.00	90.00	54.00
(374) Barney Pelty (vertical photo)	80.00	40.00	24.00
(375) Hub Perdue	200.00	100.00	60.00
(376) George Perring	80.00	40.00	24.00
(377) Arch Persons	200.00	100.00	60.00
(378) Francis (Big Jeff) Pfeffer	80.00	40.00	24.00
(379) Jake Pfeister (Pfiester) (seated)	80.00	40.00	24.00
(380) Jake Pfeister (Pfiester) (throwing)			
	80.00	40.00	24.00
(381) Jimmy Phelan	85.00	42.00	25.00
(382) Eddie Phelps	80.00	40.00	24.00
(383) Deacon Phillippe	80.00	40.00	24.00
(384) Ollie Pickering	85.00	42.00	25.00
(385) Eddie Plank	14000.00	7500.00	3750.
(386) Phil Poland	85.00	42.00	25.00
(387) Jack Powell	95.00	47.00	28.00
(388) Mike Powers	180.00	90.00	54.00
(389) Billy Purtell	80.00	40.00	24.00
(390) Ambrose Puttman (Puttmann)	85.00	42.00	25.00
(391) Lee Quillen (Quillin)	85.00	42.00	25.00
(392) Jack Quinn	80.00	40.00	24.00
(393) Newt Randall	85.00	42.00	25.00
(394) Bugs Raymond	80.00	40.00	24.00
(395) Ed Reagan	200.00	100.00	60.00
(396) Ed Reulbach (glove showing)	180.00	90.00	54.00
(397) Ed Reulbach (no glove showing)	80.00	40.00	24.00
(398) Dutch Revelle	200.00	100.00	60.00
(399) Bob Rhoades (Rhoads) (hands at chest)			
	80.00	40.00	24.00
(400) Bob Rhoades (Rhoads) (right arm extended)	80.00	40.00	24.00
(401) Charlie Rhodes	80.00	40.00	24.00
(402) Claude Ritchey	95.00	47.00	28.00
(403) Lou Ritter	85.00	42.00	25.00
(404) Ike Rockenfeld	200.00	100.00	60.00
(405) Claude Rossman	80.00	40.00	24.00
(406) Nap Rucker (portrait)	95.00	47.00	28.00
(407) Nap Rucker (throwing)	80.00	40.00	24.00
(408) Dick Rudolph	85.00	42.00	25.00
(409) Ray Ryan	200.00	100.00	60.00
(410) Germany Schaefer (Detroit)	95.00	47.00	28.00
(411) Germany Schaefer (Washington)			
	80.00	40.00	24.00
(412) George Schirm	85.00	42.00	25.00
(413) Larry Schlafly	85.00	42.00	25.00
(414) Admiral Schlei (batting)	80.00	40.00	24.00
(415) Admiral Schlei (catching)	95.00	47.00	28.00
(416) Admiral Schlei (portrait)	80.00	40.00	24.00
(417) Boss Schmidt (portrait)	80.00	40.00	24.00
(418) Boss Schmidt (throwing)	95.00	47.00	28.00
(419) Ossee Schreck (Schreckengost)	85.00	42.00	25.00
(420) Wildfire Schulte (front view)	95.00	47.00	28.00
(421) Wildfire Schulte (back view)	80.00	40.00	24.00
(422) Jim Scott	80.00	40.00	24.00
(423) Charles Seitz	200.00	100.00	60.00
(424) Cy Seymour (batting)	95.00	47.00	28.00
(425) Cy Seymour (portrait)	80.00	40.00	24.00
(426) Cy Seymour (throwing)	80.00	40.00	24.00
(427) Spike Shannon	85.00	42.00	25.00

	NR MT	EX	VG
(428) Bud Sharpe	85.00	42.00	25.00
(429) Shag Shaughnessy	200.00	100.00	60.00
(430) Al Shaw (St. Louis)	95.00	47.00	28.00
(431) Hunky Shaw (Providence)	85.00	42.00	25.00
(432) Jimmy Sheckard (glove showing)	80.00	40.00	24.00
(433) Jimmy Sheckard (no glove showing)	95.00	47.00	28.00
(434) Bill Shipke	95.00	47.00	28.00
(435) Jimmy Slagle	85.00	42.00	25.00
(436) Carlos Smith (Shreveport)	200.00	100.00	60.00
(437) Frank Smith (Chicago, F. Smith on front)	200.00	100.00	60.00
(438a) Frank Smith (Chicago, white cap)	80.00	40.00	24.00
(438b) Frank Smith (Chicago & Boston)	600.00	300.00	180.00
(439) "Happy" Smith (Brooklyn)	80.00	40.00	24.00
(440) Heinie Smith (Buffalo)	85.00	42.00	25.00
(441) Sid Smith (Atlanta)	200.00	100.00	60.00
(442) Fred Snodgrass (batting)	95.00	47.00	28.00
(443) Fred Snodgrass (catching)	95.00	47.00	28.00
(444) Bob Spade	80.00	40.00	24.00
(445) Tris Speaker	300.00	150.00	75.00
(446) Tubby Spencer	95.00	47.00	28.00
(447) Jake Stahl (glove shows)	80.00	40.00	24.00
(448) Jake Stahl (no glove shows)	95.00	47.00	28.00
(449) Oscar Stanage	80.00	40.00	24.00
(450) Dolly Stark	200.00	100.00	60.00
(451) Charlie Starr	80.00	40.00	24.00
(452) Harry Steinfeldt (portrait)	40.00	20.00	12.00
(453) Harry Steinfeldt (with bat)	95.00	47.00	28.00
(454) Jim Stephens	80.00	40.00	24.00
(455) George Stone	95.00	47.00	28.00
(456) George Stovall (batting)	80.00	40.00	24.00
(457) George Stovall (portrait)	95.00	47.00	28.00
(458) Sam Strang	85.00	42.00	25.00
(459) Gabby Street (catching)	80.00	40.00	24.00
(460) Gabby Street (portrait)	80.00	40.00	24.00
(461) Billy Sullivan	95.00	47.00	28.00
(462) Ed Summers	80.00	40.00	24.00
(463) Bill Sweeney (Boston)	80.00	40.00	24.00
(464) Jeff Sweeney (New York)	80.00	40.00	24.00
(465) Jesse Tannehill (Washington)	80.00	40.00	24.00
(466) Lee Tannehill (Chicago, L. Tannehill on front)	95.00	47.00	28.00
(467) Lee Tannehill (Chicago, Tannehill on front)	80.00	40.00	24.00
(468) Dummy Taylor	85.00	42.00	25.00
(469) Fred Tenney	95.00	47.00	28.00
(470) Tony Thebo	200.00	100.00	60.00
(471) Jake Thielman	85.00	42.00	25.00
(472) Ira Thomas	80.00	40.00	24.00
(473) Woodie Thornton	200.00	100.00	60.00
(474) Joe Tinker (bat off shoulder)	300.00	150.00	90.00
(475) Joe Tinker (bat on shoulder)	300.00	150.00	90.00
(476) Joe Tinker (hands on knees)	350.00	175.00	105.00
(477) Joe Tinker (portrait)	350.00	175.00	105.00
(478) John Titus	80.00	40.00	24.00
(479) Terry Turner	95.00	47.00	28.00
(480) Bob Unglaub	80.00	40.00	24.00
(481) Juan Violat (Viola)	200.00	100.00	60.00
(482) Rube Waddell (portrait)	350.00	175.00	105.00
(483) Rube Waddell (throwing)	350.00	175.00	105.00
(484) Heinie Wagner (bat on left shoulder)	90.00	45.00	27.00
(485) Heinie Wagner (bat on right shoulder)	80.00	40.00	24.00
(486) Honus Wagner	99000.00	50000.00	30000.
(487) Bobby Wallace	100.00	50.00	30.00
(488) Ed Walsh	100.00	50.00	30.00
(489) Jack Warhop	80.00	40.00	24.00
(490) Jake Weimer	95.00	47.00	28.00
(491) James Westlake	200.00	100.00	60.00
(492) Zack Wheat	275.00	137.00	82.00
(493) Doc White (Chicago, pitching)	80.00	40.00	24.00
(494) Doc White (Chicago, portrait)	95.00	47.00	28.00
(495) Foley White (Houston)	200.00	100.00	60.00
(496) Jack White (Buffalo)	85.00	42.00	25.00
(497) Kaiser Wilhelm (hands at chest)	95.00	47.00	28.00
(498) Kaiser Wilhelm (with bat)	80.00	40.00	24.00
(499) Ed Willett	80.00	40.00	24.00
(500) Ed Willetts (Willett)	80.00	40.00	24.00
(501) Jimmy Williams	95.00	47.00	28.00
(502) Vic Willis (Pittsburg)	90.00	45.00	27.00
(503) Vic Willis (St. Louis, throwing)	80.00	40.00	24.00
(504) Vic Willis (St. Louis, with bat)	80.00	40.00	24.00
(505) Owen Wilson	80.00	40.00	24.00
(506) Hooks Wiltse (pitching)	85.00	42.00	25.00
(507) Hooks Wiltse (portrait, no cap)	95.00	47.00	28.00
(508) Hooks Wiltse (portrait, with cap)	80.00	40.00	24.00

	NR MT	EX	VG
(509) Lucky Wright	85.00	42.00	25.00
(510) Cy Young (Cleveland, glove shows)	400.00	200.00	125.00
(511) Cy Young (Cleveland, bare hand shows)	400.00	200.00	125.00
(512) Cy Young (Cleveland, portrait)	400.00	200.00	125.00
(513) Irv Young (Minneapolis)	85.00	42.00	25.00
(514) Heinie Zimmerman	80.00	40.00	24.00

1912 T207 Brown Background

Harry Lord

Harry Lord, the brilliant White Sox third baseman, came to Chicago in one of the queerest baseball deals ever recorded. Lord first achieved success in the New England League, where, in 1908, he was lifted to the Boston Americans. Although rated as a wonderful ball player, he fell out with the club management and was traded to Comiskey, who secured a star. Lord played wonderful ball in 1911 and is rated by many as the greatest third baseman now playing—a worthy successor to Bradley and Collins. Last season he batted .321, fielded .941 and led his club with stolen bases.

RECRUIT LITTLE CIGARS

LORD-CHICAGO-AMER.

These 1-1/2" by 2-5/8" cards take their name from the background color which frames the rather drab sepia and white player drawings. They have tan borders making them less colorful than the more popular issues of their era. Player pictures are also on the dull side, with a white strip containing the player's last name, team and league. The card backs have the player's full name, a baseball biography and an ad for one of several brands of cigarettes. The set features 200 players including stars and three classic rarities: Irving Lewis (Boston-Nat.), Ward Miller (Chicago-Nat.) and Louis Lowdermilk (St. Louis-Nat.). There are a number of other scarce cards in the set, including a higher than usual number of obscure players.

	NR MT	EX	VG
Complete Set:	35000.00	17500.00	1000.
Common Player:	75.00	37.00	22.00
(1) John B. Adams	150.00	75.00	45.00
(2) Edward Ainsmith	75.00	37.00	22.00
(3) Rafael Almeida	150.00	75.00	45.00
(4a) James Austin (insignia on shirt)	100.00	50.00	30.00
(4b) James Austin (no insignia on shirt)	150.00	75.00	45.00
(5) Neal Ball	75.00	37.00	22.00
(6) Eros Barger	75.00	37.00	22.00
(7) Jack Barry	75.00	37.00	22.00
(8) Charles Bauman	150.00	75.00	45.00
(9) Beals Becker	75.00	37.00	22.00
(10) Chief (Albert) Bender	275.00	137.00	82.00
(11) Joseph Benz	150.00	75.00	45.00
(12) Robert Bescher	75.00	37.00	22.00
(13) Joe Birmingham	150.00	75.00	45.00
(14) Russell Blackburne	150.00	75.00	45.00
(15) Fred Blanding	150.00	75.00	45.00
(16) Jimmy Block	75.00	37.00	22.00
(17) Ping Bodie	75.00	37.00	22.00
(18) Hugh Bradley	75.00	37.00	22.00
(19) Roger Bresnahan	175.00	87.00	52.00
(20) J.F. Bushelman	150.00	75.00	45.00
(21) Henry (Hank) Butcher	150.00	75.00	45.00
(22) Robert M. Byrne	75.00	37.00	22.00
(23) John James Callahan	75.00	37.00	22.00
(24) Howard Camnitz	75.00	37.00	22.00
(25) Max Carey	175.00	87.00	52.00
(26) William Carrigan	75.00	37.00	22.00
(27) George Chalmers	75.00	37.00	22.00

		NR MT	EX	VG
(28)	Frank Leroy Chance	200.00	100.00	60.00
(29)	Edward Cicotte	85.00	42.00	25.00
(30)	Tom Clarke	75.00	37.00	22.00
(31)	Leonard Cole	75.00	37.00	22.00
(32)	John Collins	125.00	62.00	37.00
(33)	Robert Coulson	75.00	37.00	22.00
(34)	Tex Covington	75.00	37.00	22.00
(35)	Otis Crandall	75.00	37.00	22.00
(36)	William Cunningham	150.00	75.00	45.00
(37)	Dave Danforth	75.00	37.00	22.00
(38)	Bert Daniels	75.00	37.00	22.00
(39)	John Daubert	85.00	42.00	25.00
(40a)	Harry Davis (brown "C" on cap)	100.00	50.00	30.00
(40b)	Harry Davis (blue "C" on cap)	100.00	50.00	30.00
(41)	Jim Delehanty	75.00	37.00	22.00
(42)	Claude Derrick	75.00	37.00	22.00
(43)	Arthur Devlin	75.00	37.00	22.00
(44)	Joshua Devore	75.00	37.00	22.00
(45)	Mike Donlin	150.00	75.00	45.00
(46)	Edward Donnelly	150.00	75.00	45.00
(47)	Charles Dooin	75.00	37.00	22.00
(48)	Tom Downey	150.00	75.00	45.00
(49)	Lawrence Doyle	75.00	37.00	22.00
(50)	Del Drake	75.00	37.00	22.00
(51)	Ted Easterly	75.00	37.00	22.00
(52)	George Ellis	75.00	37.00	22.00
(53)	Clyde Engle	75.00	37.00	22.00
(54)	R.E. Erwin	75.00	37.00	22.00
(55)	Louis Evans	75.00	37.00	22.00
(56)	John Ferry	75.00	37.00	22.00
(57a)	Ray Fisher (blue cap)	100.00	50.00	30.00
(57b)	Ray Fisher (white cap)	100.00	50.00	30.00
(58)	Arthur Fletcher	75.00	37.00	22.00
(59)	Jacques Fournier	150.00	75.00	45.00
(60)	Arthur Fromme	75.00	37.00	22.00
(61)	Del Gainor	75.00	37.00	22.00
(62)	William Lawrence Gardner	75.00	37.00	22.00
(63)	Lefty George	75.00	37.00	22.00
(64)	Roy Golden	75.00	37.00	22.00
(65)	Harry Gowdy	75.00	37.00	22.00
(66)	George Graham	125.00	62.00	37.00
(67)	J.G. Graney	75.00	37.00	22.00
(68)	Vean Gregg	150.00	75.00	45.00
(69)	Casey Hageman	75.00	37.00	22.00
(70)	Charlie Hall	75.00	37.00	22.00
(71)	E.S. Hallinan	75.00	37.00	22.00
(72)	Earl Hamilton	75.00	37.00	22.00
(73)	Robert Harmon	75.00	37.00	22.00
(74)	Grover Hartley	150.00	75.00	45.00
(75)	Olaf Henriksen	75.00	37.00	22.00
(76)	John Henry	125.00	62.00	37.00
(77)	Charles Herzog	150.00	75.00	45.00
(78)	Robert Higgins	75.00	37.00	22.00
(79)	Chester Hoff	150.00	75.00	45.00
(80)	William Hogan	75.00	37.00	22.00
(81)	Harry Hooper	325.00	162.00	97.00
(82)	Ben Houser	150.00	75.00	45.00
(83)	Hamilton Hyatt	150.00	75.00	45.00
(84)	Walter Johnson	900.00	450.00	270.00
(85)	George Kaler	75.00	37.00	22.00
(86)	William Kelly	150.00	75.00	45.00
(87)	Jay Kirke	150.00	75.00	45.00
(88)	John Kling	75.00	37.00	22.00
(89)	Otto Knabe	75.00	37.00	22.00
(90)	Elmer Knetzer	75.00	37.00	22.00
(91)	Edward Konetchy	75.00	37.00	22.00
(92)	Harry Krause	75.00	37.00	22.00
(93)	"Red" Kuhn	150.00	75.00	45.00
(94)	Joseph Kutina	150.00	75.00	45.00
(95)	F.H. (Bill) Lange	150.00	75.00	45.00
(96)	Jack Lapp	75.00	37.00	22.00
(97)	W. Arlington Latham	75.00	37.00	22.00
(98)	Thomas W. Leach	75.00	37.00	22.00
(99)	Albert Leifield	75.00	37.00	22.00
(100)	Edgar Lennox	75.00	37.00	22.00
(101)	Duffy Lewis	75.00	37.00	22.00
(102a)	Irving Lewis (no emblem on sleeve)	3500.00	1750.00	1000.
(102b)	Irving Lewis (emblem on sleeve)	3200.00	1600.00	950.00
(103)	Jack Lively	75.00	37.00	22.00
(104a)	Paddy Livingston ("A" on shirt)	275.00	137.00	82.00
(104b)	Paddy Livingston (big "C" on shirt)	275.00	137.00	82.00
(104c)	Paddy Livingston (little "C" on shirt)	100.00	50.00	30.00
(105)	Briscoe Lord (Philadelphia)	75.00	37.00	22.00
(106)	Harry Lord (Chicago)	75.00	37.00	22.00
(107)	Louis Lowdermilk	2800.00	1400.00	840.00
(108)	Richard Marquard	275.00	137.00	82.00

		NR MT	EX	VG
(110)	George McBride	75.00	37.00	22.00
(111)	Alexander McCarthy	175.00	87.00	52.00
(112)	Edward McDonald	75.00	37.00	22.00
(113)	John J. McGraw	325.00	162.00	97.00
(114)	Harry McIntire (McIntyre)	75.00	37.00	22.00
(115)	Matthew McIntyre	75.00	37.00	22.00
(116)	William McKechnie	300.00	150.00	90.00
(117)	Larry McLean	75.00	37.00	22.00
(118)	Clyde Milan	75.00	37.00	22.00
(119)	John B. Miller (Pittsburg)	75.00	37.00	22.00
(120)	Otto Miller (Brooklyn)	150.00	75.00	45.00
(121)	Roy Miller (Boston)	150.00	75.00	45.00
(122)	Ward Miller (Chicago)	3500.00	1750.00	1000.
(123)	Mike Mitchell (Cleveland, front depicts Willie Mitchell)	125.00	62.00	37.00
(124)	Mike Mitchell (Cincinnati)	75.00	37.00	22.00
(125)	Geo. Mogridge	150.00	75.00	45.00
(126)	Earl Moore	150.00	75.00	45.00
(127)	Patrick J. Moran	75.00	37.00	22.00
(128)	Cy Morgan (Philadelphia)	75.00	37.00	22.00
(129)	Ray Morgan (Washington)	75.00	37.00	22.00
(130)	George Moriarty	150.00	75.00	45.00
(131a)	George Mullin ("D" on cap)	100.00	50.00	30.00
(131b)	George Mullin (no "D" on cap)	100.00	50.00	30.00
(132)	Thomas Needham	75.00	37.00	22.00
(133)	Red Nelson	150.00	75.00	45.00
(134)	Herbert Northen	75.00	37.00	22.00
(135)	Leslie Nunamaker	75.00	37.00	22.00
(136)	Rebel Oakes	75.00	37.00	22.00
(137)	Buck O'Brien	75.00	37.00	22.00
(138)	Rube Oldring	75.00	37.00	22.00
(139)	Ivan Olson	75.00	37.00	22.00
(140)	Martin J. O'Toole	75.00	37.00	22.00
(141)	George Paskart (Paskert)	75.00	37.00	22.00
(142)	Barney Pelty	150.00	75.00	45.00
(143)	Herbert Perdue	75.00	37.00	22.00
(144)	O.C. Peters	150.00	75.00	45.00
(145)	Arthur Phelan	150.00	75.00	45.00
(146)	Jack Quinn	75.00	37.00	22.00
(147)	Don Carlos Ragan	475.00	237.00	142.00
(148)	Arthur Rasmussen	500.00	250.00	150.00
(149)	Morris Rath	150.00	75.00	45.00
(150)	Edward Reulbach	75.00	37.00	22.00
(151)	Napoleon Rucker	75.00	37.00	22.00
(152)	J.B. Ryan	150.00	75.00	45.00
(153)	Victor Saier	900.00	450.00	270.00
(154)	William Scanlon	75.00	37.00	22.00
(155)	Germany Schaefer	75.00	37.00	22.00
(156)	Wilbur Schardt	75.00	37.00	22.00
(157)	Frank Schulte	75.00	37.00	22.00
(158)	Jim Scott	75.00	37.00	22.00
(159)	Henry Severoid (Severeid)	75.00	37.00	22.00
(160)	Mike Simon	75.00	37.00	22.00
(161)	Frank E. Smith (Cincinnati)	75.00	37.00	22.00
(162)	Wallace Smith (St. Louis)	75.00	37.00	22.00
(163)	Fred Snodgrass	75.00	37.00	22.00
(164)	Tristam Speaker	900.00	450.00	270.00
(165)	Harry Lee Spratt	75.00	37.00	22.00
(166)	Edward Stack	75.00	37.00	22.00
(167)	Oscar Stanage	75.00	37.00	22.00
(168)	William Steele	75.00	37.00	22.00
(169)	Harry Steinfeldt	75.00	37.00	22.00
(170)	George Stovall	75.00	37.00	22.00
(171)	Charles (Gabby) Street	75.00	37.00	22.00
(172)	Amos Strunk	75.00	37.00	22.00
(173)	William Sullivan	75.00	37.00	22.00
(174)	William J. Sweeney	150.00	75.00	45.00
(175)	Leeford Tannehill	75.00	37.00	22.00
(176)	C.D. Thomas	75.00	37.00	22.00
(177)	Joseph Tinker	275.00	137.00	82.00
(178)	Bert Tooley	75.00	37.00	22.00
(179)	Terence Turner (Terrence)	75.00	37.00	22.00
(180)	George Tyler	550.00	275.00	165.00
(181)	Jim Vaughn	75.00	37.00	22.00
(182)	Chas. (Heinie) Wagner	75.00	37.00	22.00
(183)	Ed (Dixie) Walker	75.00	37.00	22.00
(184)	Robert Wallace	175.00	87.00	52.00
(185)	John Warhop	75.00	37.00	22.00
(186)	George Weaver	150.00	75.00	45.00
(187)	Zach Wheat	175.00	87.00	52.00
(188)	G. Harris White	150.00	75.00	45.00
(189)	Ernest Wilie	150.00	75.00	45.00
(190)	Bob Williams	75.00	37.00	22.00
(191)	Arthur Wilson (New York)	150.00	75.00	45.00
(192)	Owen Wilson (Pittsburg)	75.00	37.00	22.00
(193)	George Wiltse	75.00	37.00	22.00
(194)	Ivey Wingo	75.00	37.00	22.00
(195)	Harry Wolverton	75.00	37.00	22.00
(196)	Joe Wood	125.00	62.00	37.00
(197)	Eugene Woodburn	150.00	75.00	45.00
(198)	Ralph Works	450.00	225.00	135.00

	NR MT	EX	VG
(199) Stanley Yerkes	75.00	37.00	22.00
(200) Rollie Zeider	125.00	62.00	37.00

	MT	NR MT	EX
—— The 1915 Phillies	.15	.11	.06
—— The 1950 Phillies	.15	.11	.06
—— The 1980 Phillies	.15	.11	.06
—— The 1983 Phillies	.15	.11	.06
—— June 11, 1985 - A Night To Remember			
	.15	.11	.06

1986 Tastykake Phillies

#26   CHRIS JAMES   OF   TASTYKAKE.

The 1986 Tastykake Phillies set consists of 49 cards that measure 3-1/2" by 5-1/4" in size. The cards were given away at the Phillies' annual baseball card day promotion. The card fronts feature a full-color photo along with the player's name, uniform number and position. The card backs are printed in red and black and carry a brief player biography. Five cards commemorating past Phillies' pennants were included in the set.

	MT	NR MT	EX
Complete Set:	12.00	9.00	4.75
Common Player:	.15	.11	.06
2 Jim Davenport	.15	.11	.06
3 Claude Osteen	.15	.11	.06
4 Lee Elia	.15	.11	.06
5 Mike Ryan	.15	.11	.06
6 John Russell	.20	.15	.08
7 John Felske	.15	.11	.06
8 Juan Samuel	.50	.40	.20
9 Von Hayes	.35	.25	.14
10 Darren Daulton	.15	.11	.06
11 Tom Foley	.15	.11	.06
12 Glenn Wilson	.20	.15	.08
14 Jeff Stone	.15	.11	.06
15 Rick Schu	.20	.15	.08
16 Luis Aguayo	.15	.11	.06
20 Mike Schmidt	1.00	.70	.40
21 Greg Gross	.15	.11	.06
22 Gary Redus	.15	.11	.06
23 Joe Lefebvre	.15	.11	.06
24 Milt Thompson	.30	.25	.12
25 Del Unser	.15	.11	.06
26 Chris James	1.00	.70	.40
27 Kent Tekulve	.20	.15	.08
28 Shane Rawley	.25	.20	.10
29 Ronn Reynolds	.15	.11	.06
30 Steve Jeltz	.15	.11	.06
31 Garry Maddox	.25	.20	.10
32 Steve Carlton	.70	.50	.30
33 Dave Shipanoff	.15	.11	.06
35 Randy Lerch	.15	.11	.06
36 Robin Roberts	.60	.45	.25
39 Dave Rucker	.15	.11	.06
40 Steve Bedrosian	.40	.30	.15
41 Tom Hume	.15	.11	.06
42 Don Carman	.50	.40	.20
43 Fred Toliver	.20	.15	.08
46 Kevin Gross	.30	.25	.12
47 Larry Andersen	.15	.11	.06
48 Dave Stewart	.30	.25	.12
49 Charles Hudson	.20	.15	.08
50 Rocky Childress	.20	.15	.08
—— Future Phillies (Ramon Caraballo, Joe Cipolloni)	.20	.15	.08
—— Future Phillies (Arturo Gonzalez, Mike Maddux)	.40	.30	.15
—— Future Phillies (Ricky Jordan, Francisco Melendez)	3.00	2.25	1.25
—— Future Phillies (Randy Day, Kevin Ward)	.20	.15	.08

1987 Tastykake Phillies

#20   MIKE SCHMIDT   3B   TASTYKAKE.

A 46-card set featuring the Philadelphia Phillies and sponsored by Tastykake was given out to fans present at Veterans Stadium for the Phillies' April 12th baseball card day promotion. The cards measure 3-1/2" by 5-1/4" with fronts that feature a full-color player photo framed with a white border. The player's number, name and position appear below the photo. Card backs are printed in red and black and contain a brief biography. The set was available for $4 via a mail-in offer to the Phillies ball club.

	MT	NR MT	EX
Complete Set:	10.00	7.50	4.00
Common Player:	.15	.11	.06
6 John Russell	.15	.11	.06
7 John Felske	.15	.11	.06
8 Juan Samuel	.50	.40	.20
10 Darren Daulton	.15	.11	.06
11 Greg Legg	.20	.15	.08
12 Glenn Wilson	.20	.15	.08
13 Lance Parrish	.50	.40	.20
14 Jeff Stone	.15	.11	.06
15 Rick Schu	.15	.11	.06
16 Luis Aguayo	.15	.11	.06
17 Ron Roenicke	.15	.11	.06
18 Chris James	1.00	.70	.40
20 Mike Schmidt	1.00	.70	.40
21 Greg Gross	.15	.11	.06
23 Joe Cipolloni	.20	.15	.08
24 Milt Thompson	.20	.15	.08
27 Kent Tekulve	.20	.15	.08
28 Shane Rawley	.25	.20	.10
29 Ronn Reynolds	.15	.11	.06
30 Steve Jeltz	.15	.11	.06
33 Mike Jackson	.40	.30	.15
34 Mike Easler	.20	.15	.08
35 Dan Schatzeder	.15	.11	.06
37 Ken Dowell	.20	.15	.08
38 Jim Olander	.20	.15	.08
39a Joe Cowley	.15	.11	.06
39b Bob Scanlan	.20	.15	.08
40 Steve Bedrosian	.40	.30	.15
41 Tom Hume	.15	.11	.06
42 Don Carman	.30	.25	.12
43 Freddie Toliver	.15	.11	.06
44 Mike Maddux	.30	.25	.12
45 Greg Jelks	.40	.30	.15
46 Kevin Gross	.25	.20	.10
47 Bruce Ruffin	.40	.30	.15
48 Marvin Freeman	.30	.25	.12
49 Len Watts	.20	.15	.08
50 Tom Newell	.20	.15	.08
51 Ken Jackson	.30	.25	.12
52 Todd Frohwirth	.30	.25	.12
58 Doug Bair	.15	.11	.06
—— Shawn Burton, Rick Lundblade	.20	.15	.08

		MT	NR MT	EX
----	Jeff Kaye, Darren Loy	.20	.15	.08
----	Phillies Coaches (Jim Davenport, Lee Elia, Claude Osteen, Mike Ryan, Del Unser)	.15	.11	.06
----	Phillie Phanatic	.15	.11	.06
----	Team Photo	.15	.11	.06

		MT	NR MT	EX
----	Phillie Phanatic	.15	.11	.06
----	Team Photo	.15	.11	.06
----	Broadcasters (Richie Ashburn, Harry Kalas, Garry Maddox, Andy Musser, Chris Wheeler)	.15	.11	.06

1988 Tastykake Phillies

This 39-card set was co-produced by Tastykake and the Phillies. The semi-glossy oversize cards, 4-7/8" by 6-1/4", feature full-color action photos with white borders. The coaching staff, young player prospects, the team mascot and a full team photo are included in the set. The card backs carry personal data and career stats in black letters, with the Phillies and Tastykake logos in red. Card numbers correspond to player uniform numbers. The cards were available upon request from individual players and were not made available as a set. Nine cards (#'s 4, 6, 7, 11, 15 Gutierrez, 16 Bowa, 17, 33 and Broadcasters) were added later in the year. These cards have blank backs.

		MT	NR MT	EX
	Complete Set:	12.00	9.00	4.75
	Common Player:	.15	.11	.06
4a	Lee Elia (vertical format)	.15	.11	.06
4b	Lee Elia (horizontal format)	.15	.11	.06
6	John Russell	.15	.11	.06
7	John Vukovich	.15	.11	.06
8	Juan Samuel	.50	.40	.20
9	Von Hayes	.35	.25	.14
10	Darren Daulton	.15	.11	.06
11	Keith Miller	.40	.30	.15
13	Lance Parrish	.50	.40	.20
15a	Bill Almon	.15	.11	.06
15b	Jackie Gutierrez	.15	.11	.06
16a	Luis Aguayo	.15	.11	.06
16b	Larry Bowa	.20	.15	.08
17	Ricky Jordan	2.00	1.50	.80
18	Chris James	.40	.30	.15
19	Mike Young	.15	.11	.06
20	Mike Schmidt	1.00	.70	.40
21	Greg Gross	.15	.11	.06
22	Bob Dernier	.15	.11	.06
24	Milt Thompson	.20	.15	.08
27	Kent Tekulve	.25	.20	.10
28	Shane Rawley	.25	.20	.10
29	Phil Bradley	.50	.40	.20
30	Steve Jeltz	.15	.11	.06
31	Jeff Calhoun	.15	.11	.06
33	Greg Harris	.15	.11	.06
38	Wally Ritchie	.25	.20	.10
40	Steve Bedrosian	.35	.25	.14
42	Don Carman	.25	.20	.10
44	Mike Maddux	.25	.20	.10
45	David Palmer	.15	.11	.06
46	Kevin Gross	.25	.20	.10
47	Bruce Ruffin	.20	.15	.08
52	Todd Frohwirth	.20	.15	.08
----	Coaching Staff (Dave Bristol, Claude Osteen, Mike Ryan, Tony Taylor, Del Unser, John Vukovich)	.15	.11	.06
----	Phillies Prospects (Tom Barrett, Brad Brink, Steve DeAngelis, Ron Jones, Keith Miller, Brad Moore, Howard Nichols, Shane Turner)	.40	.30	.15

1989 Tastykake Phillies

These oversize (approximately 4" by 6") cards feature very nice borderless action photos of the Philadelphia Phillies. The 36-card set was sponsored by Tastykake (whose logo appears on the bottom of the card backs) and was given to fans attending the May 13 Phillies game as a stadium promotion. The backs include player information and complete stats.

		MT	NR MT	EX
	Complete Set:	15.00	11.00	6.00
	Common Player:	.15	.11	.06
2	Larry Bowa	.15	.11	.06
3	Darold Knowles	.15	.11	.06
4	Denis Menke	.15	.11	.06
4a	Lenny Dykstra (Update Card)	.25	.20	.10
5	Mike Ryan	.15	.11	.06
6	Dwayne Murphy	.15	.11	.06
7	John Vuckovich	.15	.11	.06
8	Juan Samuel	.50	.40	.20
8a	Charlie Hayes (Update Card)	.25	.20	.10
9	Von Hayes	.35	.25	.12
10	Darren Daulton	.15	.11	.06
12	Tony Taylor	.15	.11	.06
15	Floyd Youmans	.15	.11	.06
16	Nick Leyva	.20	.15	.08
17	Rickey Jordan	1.00	.70	.40
19	Tom Nieto	.15	.11	.06
20	Mike Schmidt	1.00	.70	.40
21	Dickie Thon	.15	.11	.06
22	Bob Dernier	.15	.11	.06
24	Curt Ford	.15	.11	.06
25	Steve Lake	.15	.11	.06
26	Chris James	.80	.60	.30
27	Randy O'Neal	.15	.11	.06
28	Tom Herr	.30	.25	.12
30	Steve Jeltz	.15	.11	.06
31	Mark Ryal	.25	.20	.15
33	Greg Harris	.15	.11	.06
34	Alex Madrid	.20	.15	.08
40	Steve Bedrosian	.35	.25	.12
41	Steve Ontiveros	.20	.15	.08
42	Don Carman	.20	.15	.08
43	Ken Howell	.15	.11	.06
44	Mike Maddux	.25	.20	.10
46	Larry McWilliams	.15	.11	.06
47	Bruce Ruffin	.30	.25	.12
49	Jeff Parrett	.30	.25	.12
52	Todd Frohwirth	.20	.15	.08
----	Sponsor Card	.15	.11	.06

NOTE: A card number in parentheses ( ) indicates the set is unnumbered.

1933 Tattoo Orbit

IRVING D. HADLEY

Pitcher
St. Louis "Browns"
Born July 5, 1904
Height, 5 ft. 10½ in.
Weight, 190 lbs.

Found in 1¢ packages of Tattoo gum, these 2" by 2-1/4" cards were produced by the Orbit Gum Company of Chicago, Illinois. The fronts feature a photograph which is tinted to give skin some color. Stylized baseball park backgrounds are separated from the photograph by a black line. The rest of the background is printed in vivid red, yellow and green. Card backs have the player's name, team, position, birth date, height and weight. The 60-card set is not common, but their interesting format does not seem to have struck a responsive chord in today's of Bump Hadley and George Blaeholder are the most elusive, followed by those of Ivy Andrews and Rogers Hornsby.

		NR MT	EX	VG
Complete Set:		2800.00	1400.00	840.00
Common Player:		35.00	17.50	10.50
(1)	Dale Alexander	35.00	17.50	10.50
(2)	Ivy Paul Andrews	100.00	50.00	30.00
(3)	Earl Averill	55.00	27.00	16.50
(4)	Richard Bartell	35.00	17.50	10.50
(5)	Walter Berger	35.00	17.50	10.50
(6)	George F. Blaeholder	125.00	62.00	37.00
(7)	Irving J. Burns	35.00	17.50	10.50
(8)	Guy T. Bush	35.00	17.50	10.50
(9)	Bruce D. Campbell	35.00	17.50	10.50
(10)	William Cissell	35.00	17.50	10.50
(11)	Lefty Clark	35.00	17.50	10.50
(12)	Mickey Cochrane	65.00	32.00	19.50
(13)	Phil Collins	35.00	17.50	10.50
(14)	Hazen Kiki Cuyler	55.00	27.00	16.50
(15)	Dizzy Dean	150.00	75.00	45.00
(16)	Jimmy Dykes	40.00	20.00	12.00
(17)	George L. Earnshaw	35.00	17.50	10.50
(18)	Woody English	35.00	17.50	10.50
(19)	Lewis A. Fonseca	40.00	20.00	12.00
(20)	Jimmy Foxx	100.00	50.00	30.00
(21)	Burleigh A. Grimes	55.00	27.00	16.50
(22)	Charles John Grimm	40.00	20.00	12.00
(23)	Robert M. Grove	65.00	32.00	19.50
(24)	Frank Grube	35.00	17.50	10.50
(25)	George W. Haas	35.00	17.50	10.50
(26)	Irving D. Hadley	125.00	62.00	37.00
(27)	Chick Hafey	55.00	27.00	16.50
(28)	Jesse Joseph Haines	55.00	27.00	16.50
(29)	William Hallahan	35.00	17.50	10.50
(30)	Melvin Harder	35.00	17.50	10.50
(31)	Gabby Hartnett	55.00	27.00	16.50
(32)	Babe Herman	40.00	20.00	12.00
(33)	William Herman	55.00	27.00	16.50
(34)	Rogers Hornsby	150.00	75.00	45.00
(35)	Roy C. Johnson	35.00	17.50	10.50
(36)	J. Smead Jolley	35.00	17.50	10.50
(37)	William Jurges	35.00	17.50	10.50
(38)	William Kamm	35.00	17.50	10.50
(39)	Mark A. Koenig	35.00	17.50	10.50
(40)	James J. Levey	35.00	17.50	10.50
(41)	Ernie Lombardi	55.00	27.00	16.50
(42)	Red Lucas	35.00	17.50	10.50
(43)	Ted Lyons	55.00	27.00	16.50
(44)	Connie Mack	75.00	37.00	22.00
(45)	Pat Malone	35.00	17.50	10.50
(46)	Pepper Martin	40.00	20.00	12.00
(47)	Marty McManus	35.00	17.50	10.50
(48)	Frank J. O'Doul	40.00	20.00	12.00

		NR MT	EX	VG
(49)	Richard Porter	35.00	17.50	10.50
(50)	Carl N. Reynolds	35.00	17.50	10.50
(51)	Charles Henry Root	35.00	17.50	10.50
(52)	Robert Seeds	35.00	17.50	10.50
(53)	Al H. Simmons	55.00	27.00	16.50
(54)	Jackson Riggs Stepheson	40.00	20.00	12.00
(55)	Bud Tinning	35.00	17.50	10.50
(56)	Joe Vosmik	35.00	17.50	10.50
(57)	Rube Walberg	35.00	17.50	10.50
(58)	Paul Waner	55.00	27.00	16.50
(59)	Lonnie Warneke	35.00	17.50	10.50
(60)	Arthur C. Whitney	35.00	17.50	10.50

1986 Texas Gold Ice Cream Reds

(14) PETE ROSE MANAGER

One of the last regional baseball card sets produced during the 1986 season was a 28-card team set sponsored by a Cincinnati-area ice cream company and given to fans attending a September 19th game. Photos on the 2-1/2" by 3-1/2" cards are game-action shots, and include three different cards of playing manager Pete Rose. The set is also notable for the inclusion of first cards of some of the Reds' young stars.

		MT	NR MT	EX
Complete Set:		20.00	15.00	8.00
Common Player:		.25	.20	.10
6	Bo Diaz	.35	.25	.14
9	Max Venable	.25	.20	.10
11	Kurt Stillwell	.80	.60	.30
12	Nick Esasky	.35	.25	.14
13	Dave Concepcion	.50	.40	.20
14a	Pete Rose (commemorative)	1.25	.90	.50
14b	Pete Rose (infield)	1.50	1.25	.60
14c	Pete Rose (manager)	1.50	1.25	.60
16	Ron Oester	.25	.20	.10
20	Eddie Milner	.25	.20	.10
22	Sal Butera	.25	.20	.10
24	Tony Perez	.70	.50	.30
25	Buddy Bell	.35	.25	.14
28	Kal Daniels	1.50	1.25	.60
29	Tracy Jones	.80	.60	.30
31	John Franco	.60	.45	.25
32	Tom Browning	.60	.45	.25
33	Ron Robinson	.35	.25	.14
34	Bill Gullickson	.25	.20	.10
36	Mario Soto	.35	.25	.14
39	Dave Parker	.80	.60	.30
40	John Denny	.25	.20	.10
44	Eric Davis	2.50	2.00	1.00
45	Chris Welsh	.25	.20	.10
48	Ted Power	.25	.20	.10
49	Joe Price	.25	.20	.10
----	Coaches Card (Scott Breeden, Billy DeMars, Tommy Helms, Bruce Kimm, Jim Lett, George Scherger)	.25	.20	.10
----	Logo/Coupon Card	.10	.08	.04

A player's name in *italic* type indicates a rookie card. An (FC) indicates a player's first card for that particular card company.

1983 Thorn Apple Valley Cubs

This set of 27 cards was issued in conjuction with a "Baseball Card Day" promotion at Wrigley Field in 1983. Thorn Apple Valley was the meat company which produced the hot dogs sold at the ballpark. The cards feature borderless color photos with the player's name, uniform number (also the card's number in the checklist) and an abbreviation for their position. Card backs feature annual statistics. Of the 27 cards, which measure 2-1/4" by 3-1/2", 25 feature players, one is a team card, and one features the manager and coaches.

		MT	NR MT	EX
Complete Set:		12.00	9.00	4.75
Common Player:		.20	.15	.08
1	Larry Bowa	.40	.30	.15
6	Keith Moreland	.40	.30	.15
7	Jody Davis	.40	.30	.15
10	Leon Durham	.40	.30	.15
11	Ron Cey	.40	.30	.15
16	Steve Lake	.20	.15	.08
20	Thad Bosley	.20	.15	.08
21	Jay Johnstone	.25	.20	.10
22	Bill Buckner	.40	.30	.15
23	Ryne Sandberg	3.00	2.25	1.25
24	Jerry Morales	.20	.15	.08
25	Gary Woods	.20	.15	.08
27	Mel Hall	.30	.25	.12
29	Tom Veryzer	.20	.15	.08
30	Chuck Rainey	.20	.15	.08
31	Fergie Jenkins	.70	.50	.30
32	Craig Lefferts	.30	.25	.12
33	Joe Carter	2.50	2.00	1.00
34	Steve Trout	.25	.20	.10
36	Mike Proly	.20	.15	.08
39	Bill Campbell	.20	.15	.08
41	Warren Brusstar	.20	.15	.08
44	Dick Ruthven	.20	.15	.08
46	Lee Smith	.50	.40	.20
48	Dickie Noles	.20	.15	.08
----	Coaching Staff (Ruben Amaro, Billy Connors, Duffy Dyer, Lee Elia, Fred Koenig, John Vukovich)	.20	.15	.08
----	Team Photo	.20	.15	.08

1947 Tip Top Bread

This 163-card set actually consists of a group of regional issues, some of which are more scarce then others. The 2-1/4" by 3" cards are borderless with a black and white player photo below which is a white strip containing the player's name, position, city name and league. Backs carry an advertisement. The set is known for a quantity of obscure players, many of whom played during the talent-lean World War II seasons. Overall it is a scarce set, with a number of interesting cards including first-issues of Yogi Berra and Joe Garagiola.

		NR MT	EX	VG
Complete Set:		9000.00	4500.00	2700.
Common Player:		35.00	17.50	10.50
(1)	Bill Ayers	35.00	17.50	10.50
(2)	Floyd Baker	50.00	25.00	15.00
(3)	Charles Barrett	50.00	25.00	15.00
(4)	Eddie Basinski	35.00	17.50	10.50
(5)	John Berardino	50.00	25.00	15.00
(6)	Larry Berra	175.00	87.00	52.00
(7)	Bill Bevens	50.00	25.00	15.00
(8)	Robert Blattner	35.00	17.50	10.50
(9)	Ernie Bonham	35.00	17.50	10.50
(10)	Bob Bragan	45.00	22.00	13.50
(11)	Ralph Branca	70.00	35.00	21.00
(12)	Alpha Brazle	35.00	17.50	10.50
(13)	Bobbie Brown	60.00	30.00	18.00
(14)	Mike Budnick	35.00	17.50	10.50
(15)	Ken Burkhart	35.00	17.50	10.50
(16)	Thomas Byrne	50.00	25.00	15.00
(17)	Earl Caldwell	50.00	25.00	15.00
(18)	"Hank" Camelli	50.00	25.00	15.00
(19)	Hugh Casey	45.00	22.00	13.50
(20)	Phil Cavarretta	65.00	32.00	19.50
(21)	Bob Chipman	50.00	25.00	15.00
(22)	Lloyd Christopher	50.00	25.00	15.00
(23)	Bill Cox	35.00	17.50	10.50
(24)	Bernard Creger	35.00	17.50	10.50
(25)	Frank Crosetti	65.00	32.00	19.50
(26)	Joffre Cross	35.00	17.50	10.50
(27)	Leon Culberson	50.00	25.00	15.00
(28)	Dick Culler	50.00	25.00	15.00
(29)	Dom DiMaggio	100.00	50.00	30.00
(30)	George Dickey	60.00	30.00	18.00
(31)	Chas. E. Diering	35.00	17.50	10.50
(32)	Joseph Dobson	50.00	25.00	15.00
(33)	Bob Doerr	150.00	75.00	45.00
(34)	Ervin Dusak	35.00	17.50	10.50
(35)	Bruce Edwards	40.00	20.00	12.00
(36)	Walter "Hoot" Evers	50.00	25.00	15.00
(37)	Clifford Fannin	35.00	17.50	10.50
(38)	"Nanny" Fernandez	50.00	25.00	15.00
(39)	Dave "Boo" Ferriss	50.00	25.00	15.00
(40)	Elbie Fletcher	35.00	17.50	10.50
(41)	Dennis Galehouse	35.00	17.50	10.50
(42)	Joe Garagiola	100.00	50.00	30.00
(43)	Sid Gordon	35.00	17.50	10.50
(44)	John Gorsica	50.00	25.00	15.00
(45)	Hal Gregg	40.00	20.00	12.00
(46)	Frank Gustine	35.00	17.50	10.50
(47)	Stanley Hack	65.00	32.00	19.50
(48)	Mickey Harris	50.00	25.00	15.00
(49)	Clinton Hartung	35.00	17.50	10.50
(50)	Joe Hatten	40.00	20.00	12.00
(51)	Frank Hayes	50.00	25.00	15.00
(52)	"Jeff" Heath	35.00	17.50	10.50
(53)	Tom Henrich	70.00	35.00	21.00
(54)	Gene Hermanski	40.00	20.00	12.00
(55)	Kirby Higbe	35.00	17.50	10.50
(56)	Ralph Hodgin	50.00	25.00	15.00
(57)	Tex Hughson	50.00	25.00	15.00
(58)	Fred Hutchinson	70.00	35.00	21.00
(59)	LeRoy Jarvis	35.00	17.50	10.50
(60)	"Si" Johnson	50.00	25.00	15.00
(61)	Don Johnson	50.00	25.00	15.00
(62)	Earl Johnson	50.00	25.00	15.00
(63)	John Jorgensen	40.00	20.00	12.00
(64)	Walter Judnick (Judnich)	35.00	17.50	10.50
(65)	Tony Kaufmann	35.00	17.50	10.50
(66)	George Kell	175.00	87.00	52.00
(67)	Charlie Keller	65.00	32.00	19.50
(68)	Bob Kennedy	50.00	25.00	15.00
(69)	Montia Kennedy	35.00	17.50	10.50
(70)	Ralph Kiner	80.00	40.00	24.00
(71)	Dave Koslo	35.00	17.50	10.50
(72)	Jack Kramer	35.00	17.50	10.50
(73)	Joe Kuhel	50.00	25.00	15.00
(74)	George Kurowski	35.00	17.50	10.50

		NR MT	EX	VG
(75)	Emil Kush	50.00	25.00	15.00
(76)	"Eddie" Lake	50.00	25.00	15.00
(77)	Harry Lavagetto	45.00	22.00	13.50
(78)	Bill Lee	50.00	25.00	15.00
(79)	Thornton Lee	50.00	25.00	15.00
(80)	Paul Lehner	35.00	17.50	10.50
(81)	John Lindell	50.00	25.00	15.00
(82)	Danny Litwhiler	50.00	25.00	15.00
(83)	"Mickey" Livingston	50.00	25.00	15.00
(84)	Carroll Lockman	35.00	17.50	10.50
(85)	Jack Lohrke	35.00	17.50	10.50
(86)	Ernie Lombardi	80.00	40.00	24.00
(87)	Vic Lombardi	40.00	20.00	12.00
(88)	Edmund Lopat	65.00	32.00	19.50
(89)	Harry Lowrey	50.00	25.00	15.00
(90)	Marty Marion	50.00	25.00	15.00
(91)	Willard Marshall	35.00	17.50	10.50
(92)	Phil Masi	50.00	25.00	15.00
(93)	Edward J. Mayo	50.00	25.00	15.00
(94)	Clyde McCullough	50.00	25.00	15.00
(95)	Frank Melton	40.00	20.00	12.00
(96)	Cass Michaels	50.00	25.00	15.00
(97)	Ed Miksis	40.00	20.00	12.00
(98)	Arthur Mills	50.00	25.00	15.00
(99)	Johnny Mize	80.00	40.00	24.00
(100)	Lester Moss	35.00	17.50	10.50
(101)	"Pat" Mullin	50.00	25.00	15.00
(102)	"Bob" Muncrief	35.00	17.50	10.50
(103)	George Munger	35.00	17.50	10.50
(104)	Fritz Ostermueller	35.00	17.50	10.50
(105)	James P. Outlaw	50.00	25.00	15.00
(106)	Frank "Stub" Overmire	50.00	25.00	15.00
(107)	Andy Pafko	60.00	30.00	18.00
(108)	Joe Page	50.00	25.00	15.00
(109)	Roy Partee	50.00	25.00	15.00
(110)	Johnny Pesky	60.00	30.00	18.00
(111)	Nelson Potter	35.00	17.50	10.50
(112)	Mel Queen	50.00	25.00	15.00
(113)	Marion Rackley	40.00	20.00	12.00
(114)	Al Reynolds	70.00	35.00	21.00
(115)	Del Rice	35.00	17.50	10.50
(116)	Marv Rickert	50.00	25.00	15.00
(117)	John Rigney	50.00	25.00	15.00
(118)	Aaron Robinson	50.00	25.00	15.00
(119)	"Preacher" Roe	45.00	22.00	13.50
(120)	Carvel Rowell	50.00	25.00	15.00
(121)	Jim Russell	35.00	17.50	10.50
(122)	Rip Russell	50.00	25.00	15.00
(123)	Phil Rizzuto	100.00	50.00	30.00
(124)	Connie Ryan	50.00	25.00	15.00
(125)	John Sain	90.00	45.00	27.00
(126)	Ray Sanders	50.00	25.00	15.00
(127)	Fred Sanford	35.00	17.50	10.50
(128)	Johnny Schmitz	50.00	25.00	15.00
(129)	Joe Schultz	35.00	17.50	10.50
(130)	"Rip" Sewell	35.00	17.50	10.50
(131)	Dick Sisler	35.00	17.50	10.50
(132)	"Sibby" Sisti	50.00	25.00	15.00
(133)	Enos Slaughter	80.00	40.00	24.00
(134)	"Billy" Southworth	50.00	25.00	15.00
(135)	Warren Spahn	175.00	87.00	52.00
(136)	Verne Stephens (Vern)	35.00	17.50	10.50
(137)	George Sternweiss (Stirnweiss)	50.00	25.00	15.00
(138)	Ed Stevens	40.00	20.00	12.00
(139)	Nick Strincevich	35.00	17.50	10.50
(140)	"Bobby" Sturgeon	50.00	25.00	15.00
(141)	Robt. "Bob" Swift	50.00	25.00	15.00
(142)	Geo. "Birdie" Tibbetts (Tebbetts)	55.00	27.00	16.50
(143)	"Mike" Tresh	55.00	27.00	16.50
(144)	Ken Trinkle	35.00	17.50	10.50
(145)	Paul "Diz" Trout	55.00	27.00	16.50
(146)	Virgil "Fire" Trucks	55.00	27.00	16.50
(147)	Thurman Tucker	50.00	25.00	15.00
(148)	Bill Voiselle	35.00	17.50	10.50
(149)	Hal Wagner	50.00	25.00	15.00
(150)	Honus Wagner	100.00	50.00	30.00
(151)	Eddy Waitkus	50.00	25.00	15.00
(152)	Richard "Dick" Wakefield	50.00	25.00	15.00
(153)	Jack Wallaesa	50.00	25.00	15.00
(154)	Charles Wensloff	50.00	25.00	15.00
(155)	Ted Wilks	35.00	17.50	10.50
(156)	Mickey Witek	35.00	17.50	10.50
(157)	"Jerry" Witte	35.00	17.50	10.50
(158)	Ed Wright	50.00	25.00	15.00
(159)	Taft Wright	50.00	25.00	15.00
(160)	Henry Wyse	50.00	25.00	15.00
(161)	"Rudy" York	55.00	27.00	16.50
(162)	Al Zarilla	35.00	17.50	10.50
(163)	Bill Zuber	50.00	25.00	15.00

1948 Topps Magic Photos

The first Topps baseball cards appeared as a subset of 19 cards from an issue of 252 "Magic Photos." The set takes its name from the self-developing nature of the cards. The cards were blank on the front when first taken from the wrapper. By spitting on the wrapper and holding it to the card while exposing it to light the black and white photo appeared. Measuring 7/8" by 1-1/2," the cards are very similar to Topps 1956 "Hocus Focus" issue.

		NR MT	EX	VG
Complete Set:		700.00	350.00	210.00
Common Player:		10.00	5.00	3.00
1	Lou Boudreau	20.00	10.00	6.00
2	Cleveland Indians	10.00	5.00	3.00
3	Bob Eliott	15.00	7.50	4.50
4	Cleveland Indians 4-3	10.00	5.00	3.00
5	Cleveland Indians 4-1 (Lou Boudreau Scoring)	20.00	10.00	6.00
6	"Babe" Ruth 714	150.00	75.00	45.00
7	Tris Speaker 793	25.00	12.50	7.50
8	Rogers Hornsby	35.00	17.50	10.50
9	Connie Mack	30.00	15.00	9.00
10	Christy Mathewson	40.00	20.00	12.00
11	Hans Wagner	40.00	20.00	12.00
12	Grover Alexander	30.00	15.00	9.00
13	Ty Cobb	100.00	50.00	30.00
14	Lou Gehrig	100.00	50.00	30.00
15	Walter Johnson	40.00	20.00	12.00
16	Cy Young	30.00	15.00	9.00
17	George Sisler 257	20.00	10.00	6.00
18	Tinker and Evers	20.00	10.00	6.00
19	Third Base Cleveland Indians	10.00	5.00	3.00

1951 Topps Blue Backs

Sold two cards in a package with a piece of candy for 1¢, the Topps Blue Backs are more scarce then their Red Back counterparts. The 2" by 2-5/8" cards carry a black and white player photograph on a red, white, yellow and green background along with the player's name and other information including their 1950 record on the front. The back is printed in blue on a white background. The 52-card set has varied baseball situations on them, making the playing of a rather elementary game of baseball possible. Although scarce, Blue Backs were printed on thick cardboard and have survived quite well over the years. There are, however, few stars (Johnny Mize and Enos Slaughter are two) in the set. Despite being a Topps product, Blue Backs do not currently enjoy great popularity.

		NR MT	EX	VG
	Complete Set:	1900.00	950.00	575.00
	Common Player:	30.00	15.00	9.00
1	Eddie Yost	30.00	15.00	9.00
2	Henry (Hank) Majeski	30.00	15.00	9.00
3	Richie Ashburn	50.00	25.00	15.00
4	Del Ennis	30.00	15.00	9.00
5	Johnny Pesky	25.00	12.50	7.50
6	Albert (Red) Schoendienst	35.00	17.50	10.50
7	Gerald Staley	30.00	15.00	9.00
8	Dick Sisler	30.00	15.00	9.00
9	Johnny Sain	35.00	17.50	10.50
10	Joe Page	30.00	15.00	9.00
11	Johnny Groth	30.00	15.00	9.00
12	Sam Jethroe	30.00	15.00	9.00
13	James (Mickey) Vernon	25.00	12.50	7.50
14	George Munger	30.00	15.00	9.00
15	Eddie Joost	30.00	15.00	9.00
16	Murry Dickson	30.00	15.00	9.00
17	Roy Smalley	30.00	15.00	9.00
18	Ned Garver	30.00	15.00	9.00
19	Phil Masi	30.00	15.00	9.00
20	Ralph Branca	30.00	15.00	9.00
21	Billy Johnson	30.00	15.00	9.00
22	Bob Kuzava	30.00	15.00	9.00
23	Paul (Dizzy) Trout	30.00	15.00	9.00
24	Sherman Lollar	30.00	15.00	9.00
25	Sam Mele	30.00	15.00	9.00
26	Chico Carresquel (Carrasquel)	30.00	15.00	9.00
27	Andy Pafko	25.00	12.50	7.50
28	Harry (The Cat) Brecheen	30.00	15.00	9.00
29	Granville Hamner	30.00	15.00	9.00
30	Enos (Country) Slaughter	60.00	30.00	18.00
31	Lou Brissie	30.00	15.00	9.00
32	Bob Elliott	30.00	15.00	9.00
33	Don Lenhardt	30.00	15.00	9.00
34	Earl Torgeson	30.00	15.00	9.00
35	Tommy Byrne	30.00	15.00	9.00
36	Cliff Fannin	30.00	15.00	9.00
37	Bobby Doerr	55.00	27.00	16.50
38	Irv Noren	30.00	15.00	9.00
39	Ed Lopat	30.00	15.00	9.00
40	Vic Wertz	25.00	12.50	7.50
41	Johnny Schmitz	30.00	15.00	9.00
42	Bruce Edwards	30.00	15.00	9.00
43	Willie (Puddin' Head) Jones	30.00	15.00	9.00
44	Johnny Wyrostek	30.00	15.00	9.00
45	Bill Pierce	25.00	12.50	7.50
46	Gerry Priddy	30.00	15.00	9.00
47	Herman Wehmeier	30.00	15.00	9.00
48	Billy Cox	30.00	15.00	9.00
49	Henry (Hank) Sauer	30.00	15.00	9.00
50	Johnny Mize	60.00	30.00	18.00
51	Eddie Waitkus	30.00	15.00	9.00
52	Sam Chapman	30.00	15.00	9.00

1951 Topps Red Backs

Like the Blue Backs, the Topps Red Backs which

were sold at the same time, came two to a package for 1¢. Their black and white photographs appear on a red, white, blue and yellow background. The back printing is red on white. Their 2" by 2-5/8" size is the same as Blue Backs. Also identical is the set size (52 cards) and the game situations to be found on the fronts of the cards, for use in playing a card game of baseball. Red Backs are more common than the Blue Backs by virtue of a recent discovery of a large hoard of unopened boxes.

		NR MT	EX	VG
	Complete Set:	750.00	375.00	230.00
	Common Player:	9.00	4.50	2.75
1	Larry (Yogi) Berra	75.00	38.00	23.50
2	Sid Gordon	5.00	2.50	1.50
3	Ferris Fain	9.00	4.50	2.75
4	Verne Stephens (Vern)	9.00	4.50	2.75
5	Phil Rizzuto	25.00	12.50	7.50
6	Allie Reynolds	10.00	5.00	3.00
7	Howie Pollet	5.00	2.50	1.50
8	Early Wynn	25.00	12.50	7.50
9	Roy Sievers	9.00	4.50	2.75
10	Mel Parnell	9.00	4.50	2.75
11	Gene Hermanski	5.00	2.50	1.50
12	Jim Hegan	5.00	2.50	1.50
13	Dale Mitchell	5.00	2.50	1.50
14	Wayne Terwilliger	5.00	2.50	1.50
15	Ralph Kiner	25.00	12.50	7.50
16	Preacher Roe	8.00	4.00	2.50
17	Dave Bell	8.00	4.00	2.50
18	Gerry Coleman	8.00	4.00	2.50
19	Dick Kokos	5.00	2.50	1.50
20	Dominick DiMaggio (Dominic)	10.00	5.00	3.00
21	Larry Jansen	5.00	2.50	1.50
22	Bob Feller	25.00	12.50	7.50
23	Ray Boone	9.00	4.50	2.75
24	Hank Bauer	10.00	5.00	3.00
25	Cliff Chambers	5.00	2.50	1.50
26	Luke Easter	9.00	4.50	2.75
27	Wally Westlake	5.00	2.50	1.50
28	Elmer Valo	5.00	2.50	1.50
29	Bob Kennedy	5.00	2.50	1.50
30	Warren Spahn	25.00	12.50	7.50
31	Gil Hodges	25.00	12.50	7.50
32	Henry Thompson	5.00	2.50	1.50
33	William Werle	5.00	2.50	1.50
34	Grady Hatton	5.00	2.50	1.50
35	Al Rosen	10.00	5.00	3.00
36a	Gus Zernial (Chicago in bio)	20.00	10.00	6.00
36b	Gus Zernial (Philadelphia in bio)	12.00	6.00	3.50
37	Wes Westrum	9.00	4.50	2.75
38	Ed (Duke) Snider	60.00	30.00	17.50
39	Ted Kluszewski	10.00	5.00	3.00
40	Mike Garcia	9.00	4.50	2.75
41	Whitey Lockman	5.00	2.50	1.50
42	Ray Scarborough	5.00	2.50	1.50
43	Maurice McDermott	5.00	2.50	1.50
44	Sid Hudson	5.00	2.50	1.50
45	Andy Seminick	5.00	2.50	1.50
46	Billy Goodman	5.00	2.50	1.50
47	Tommy Glaviano	5.00	2.50	1.50
48	Eddie Stanky	9.00	4.50	2.75
49	Al Zarilla	5.00	2.50	1.50
50	Monte Irvin	25.00	12.50	7.50
51	Eddie Robinson	5.00	2.50	1.50
52a	Tommy Holmes (Boston in bio)	20.00	10.00	6.00
52b	Tommy Holmes (Hartford in bio)	20.00	10.00	6.00

1951 Topps Connie Mack's All-Stars

A set of die-cut, 2-1/16" by 5-1/4" cards, all eleven players are Hall of Famers. The cards feature a black and white photograph of the player printed on a red background with a red, white, blue, yellow and black plaque underneath. Like the "Current All-Stars," with which they were issued, the background could be removed making it possible for the card to stand up. This practice, however, resulted in the card's mutilation and lowers its condition in the eyes of today's collectors. Connie Mack All-Stars are scarce today and, despite being relatively expensive, retain a certain popularity as one of Topps first issues.

	NR MT	EX	VG
Complete Set:	6000.00	3000.00	1750.
Common Player:	200.00	100.00	60.00

(1)	Grover Cleveland Alexander	300.00	150.00	90.00
(2)	Gordon Stanley Cochrane	225.00	112.00	67.00
(3)	Edward Trowbridge Collins	200.00	100.00	60.00
(4)	James J. Collins	200.00	100.00	60.00
(5)	Henry Louis Gehrig	1200.00	600.00	350.00
(6)	Walter Johnson	500.00	250.00	150.00
(7)	Connie Mack	225.00	112.00	67.00
(8)	Christopher Mathewson	450.00	225.00	135.00
(9)	George Herman Ruth	1500.00	750.00	450.00
(10)	Tristram Speaker	200.00	100.00	60.00
(11)	John Peter Wagner	450.00	225.00	135.00

1951 Topps Current All-Stars

The Topps Current All-Stars are very similar to the Connie Mack All-Stars of the same year. The 2-1/16 by 5-1/4" cards have a black and white photograph on a red die-cut background. Most of the background could be folded over or removed so that the card would stand up. A plaque at the base carries brief biographical information. The set was to contain 11 cards, but only eight were actually issued in gum packs. Those of Jim Konstanty, Robin Roberts and Eddie Stanky were not released and are very rare. A big problem with the set is that if the card was used as it was intended it was folded and, thus, damaged from a collector's viewpoint. That makes top quality examples of any players difficult to find and quite expensive.

		NR MT	EX	VG
Complete Set:		20000.00	10000.00	6000.
Common Player:		175.00	87.00	52.00
(1)	Lawrence (Yogi) Berra	650.00	325.00	195.00
(2)	Lawrence Eugene Doby	250.00	125.00	75.00
(3)	Walter Dropo	250.00	125.00	75.00
(4)	Walter (Hoot) Evers	175.00	87.00	52.00
(5)	George Clyde Kell	400.00	200.00	120.00
(6)	Ralph McPherran Kiner	425.00	212.00	127.00
(7)	James Casimir Konstanty	5500.00	2750.00	1650.
(8)	Robert G. Lemon	425.00	212.00	127.00
(9)	Phillip Rizzuto	450.00	225.00	135.00
(10)	Robin Evan Roberts	5500.00	2750.00	1650.
(11)	Edward Raymond Stanky	5500.00	2750.00	1650.

1951 Topps Teams

An innovative issue for 1951, the Topps team cards were a nine-card set, 5-1/4" by 2-1/16," which carried a black and white picture of a major league team surrounded by a yellow border on the front. The back identifies team members with red printing on white cardboard. There are two versions of each card, with and without the date "1950" in the banner that carries the team name. Undated versions are valued slightly higher than the cards with dates. Strangely only nine teams were issued. Scarcity varies, with the Cardinals and Red Sox being the most difficult to obtain. The complete set price does not include the scarcer variations.

		NR MT	EX	VG
Complete Set:		1250.00	625.00	375.00
Common Team:		90.00	45.00	27.00
(1a)	Boston Red Sox (1950)	150.00	75.00	45.00
(1b)	Boston Red Sox (without 1950)	175.00	87.00	52.00
(2a)	Brooklyn Dodgers (1950)	175.00	87.00	52.00
(2b)	Brooklyn Dodgers (without 1950)	200.00	100.00	60.00
(3a)	Chicago White Sox (1950)	90.00	45.00	27.00
(3b)	Chicago White Sox (without 1950)	120.00	60.00	36.00
(4a)	Cincinnati Reds (1950)	90.00	45.00	27.00
(4b)	Cincinnati Reds (without 1950)	120.00	60.00	36.00
(5a)	New York Giants (1950)	150.00	75.00	45.00
(5b)	New York Giants (without 1950)	175.00	87.00	52.00
(6a)	Philadelphia Athletics (1950)	90.00	45.00	27.00
(6b)	Philadelphia Athletics (without 1950)	120.00	60.00	36.00
(7a)	Philadelphia Phillies (1950)	90.00	45.00	27.00
(7b)	Philadelphia Phillies (without 1950)	120.00	60.00	36.00
(8a)	St. Louis Cardinals (1950)	90.00	45.00	27.00
(8b)	St. Louis Cardinals (without 1950)	120.00	60.00	36.00
(9a)	Washington Senators (1950)	90.00	45.00	27.00
(9b)	Washington Senators (without 1950)	120.00	60.00	36.00

1952 Topps

At 407 cards, the 1952 Topps set was the largest

set of its day, both in number of cards and physical
dimensions of the cards. Cards are 2-5/8" by 3-3/4"
with a hand-colored black and white photo on front.
Major baseball card innovations presented in the set
include the first-ever use of color team logos as part
of the design, and the inclusion of stats for the
previous season and overall career on the backs. A
major variety in the set is that first 80 cards can be
found with backs printed entirely in black or black and
red. Backs entirely in black command a $10-15
premium. Card numbers 311-407 were printed in
limited supplies and are extremely rare.

	NR MT	EX	VG
Complete Set:	38000.00	3300.00	7600.
Common Player: 1-80	50.00	30.00	15.00
Common Player: 81-250	20.00	7.50	3.00
Common Player: 251-280	40.00	16.00	6.00
Common Player: 281-300	45.00	23.00	13.50
Common Player: 301-310	40.00	12.00	6.00
Common Player: 311-407	150.00	75.00	45.00

#	Name	NR MT	EX	VG
1	Andy Pafko	1000.00	100.00	12.00
2	James E. Runnels	80.00	20.00	6.00
3	Hank Thompson	55.00	15.00	5.50
4	Don Lenhardt	55.00	15.00	5.50
5	Larry Jansen	55.00	15.00	5.50
6	Grady Hatton	55.00	15.00	5.50
7	Wayne Terwilliger	60.00	16.00	6.00
8	Fred Marsh	55.00	15.00	5.50
9	Bobby Hogue	65.00	18.00	6.50
10	Al Rosen	80.00	24.00	8.00
11	Phil Rizzuto	175.00	45.00	15.00
12	Monty Basgall	55.00	15.00	5.50
13	Johnny Wyrostek	55.00	15.00	5.50
14	Bob Elliott	55.00	15.00	5.50
15	Johnny Pesky	60.00	16.00	6.00
16	Gene Hermanski	55.00	15.00	5.50
17	Jim Hegan	55.00	15.00	5.50
18	Merrill Combs	55.00	15.00	5.50
19	Johnny Bucha	55.00	15.00	5.50
20	Billy Loes	125.00	56.00	35.00
21	Ferris Fain	60.00	16.00	6.00
22	Dom DiMaggio	80.00	20.00	8.00
23	Billy Goodman	55.00	15.00	5.50
24	Luke Easter	60.00	16.00	6.00
25	Johnny Groth	55.00	15.00	5.50
26	Monty Irvin	90.00	27.00	9.00
27	Sam Jethroe	55.00	15.00	5.50
28	Jerry Priddy	55.00	15.00	5.50
29	Ted Kluszewski	80.00	24.00	8.00
30	Mel Parnell	60.00	16.00	6.00
31	Gus Zernial	60.00	16.00	6.00
32	Eddie Robinson	55.00	15.00	5.50
33	Warren Spahn	200.00	80.00	50.00
34	Elmer Valo	55.00	15.00	5.50
35	Hank Sauer	60.00	16.00	6.00
36	Gil Hodges	150.00	75.00	45.00
37	Duke Snider	250.00	100.00	63.00
38	Wally Westlake	55.00	15.00	5.50
39	"Dizzy" Trout	60.00	16.00	6.00
40	Irv Noren	55.00	15.00	5.50
41	Bob Wellman	55.00	15.00	5.50
42	Lou Kretlow	55.00	15.00	5.50
43	Ray Scarborough	55.00	15.00	5.50
44	Con Dempsey	55.00	15.00	5.50
45	Eddie Joost	55.00	15.00	5.50
46	Gordon Goldsberry	55.00	15.00	5.50
47	Willie Jones	55.00	15.00	5.50
48a	Joe Page (Johnny Sain bio)	225.00	68.00	23.00
48b	Joe Page (correct bio)	80.00	24.00	8.00
49a	Johnny Sain (Joe Page bio)	225.00	68.00	23.00
49b	Johnny Sain (correct bio)	80.00	24.00	8.00
50	Marv Rickert	55.00	15.00	5.50
51	Jim Russell	60.00	16.00	6.00
52	Don Mueller	55.00	15.00	5.50
53	Chris Van Cuyk	60.00	16.00	6.00
54	Leo Kiely	55.00	15.00	5.50
55	Ray Boone	60.00	16.00	6.00
56	Tommy Glaviano	55.00	15.00	5.50
57	Ed Lopat	80.00	24.00	8.00
58	Bob Mahoney	55.00	15.00	5.50
59	Robin Roberts	125.00	38.00	12.50
60	Sid Hudson	55.00	15.00	5.50
61	"Tookie" Gilbert	55.00	15.00	5.50
62	Chuck Stobbs	55.00	15.00	5.50
63	Howie Pollet	55.00	15.00	5.50
64	Roy Sievers	65.00	18.00	6.50
65	Enos Slaughter	125.00	56.00	35.00
66	"Preacher" Roe	80.00	24.00	8.00
67	Allie Reynolds	80.00	24.00	8.00
68	Cliff Chambers	55.00	15.00	5.50
69	Virgil Stallcup	55.00	15.00	5.50
70	Al Zarilla	55.00	15.00	5.50
71	Tom Upton	55.00	15.00	5.50
72	Karl Olson	55.00	15.00	5.50
73	William Werle	55.00	15.00	5.50
74	Andy Hansen	55.00	15.00	5.50
75	Wes Westrum	60.00	16.00	6.00
76	Eddie Stanky	65.00	18.00	6.50
77	Bob Kennedy	55.00	15.00	5.50
78	Ellis Kinder	55.00	15.00	5.50
79	Gerald Staley	55.00	15.00	5.50
80	Herman Wehmeier	55.00	15.00	5.50
81	Vernon Law	25.00	11.00	6.25
82	Duane Pillette	20.00	9.00	5.00
83	Billy Johnson	20.00	9.00	5.00
84	Vern Stephens	20.00	9.00	5.00
85	Bob Kuzava	30.00	13.50	7.50
86	Ted Gray	20.00	9.00	5.00
87	Dale Coogan	20.00	9.00	5.00
88	Bob Feller	125.00	56.00	35.00
89	Johnny Lipon	20.00	9.00	5.00
90	Mickey Grasso	20.00	9.00	5.00
91	Al Schoendienst	60.00	30.00	18.00
92	Dale Mitchell	20.00	9.00	5.00
93	Al Sima	20.00	9.00	5.00
94	Sam Mele	20.00	9.00	5.00
95	Ken Holcombe	20.00	9.00	5.00
96	Willard Marshall	20.00	9.00	5.00
97	Earl Torgeson	20.00	9.00	5.00
98	Bill Pierce	25.00	11.00	6.25
99	Gene Woodling	40.00	18.00	10.00
100	Del Rice	20.00	9.00	5.00
101	Max Lanier	20.00	9.00	5.00
102	Bill Kennedy	20.00	9.00	5.00
103	Cliff Mapes	20.00	9.00	5.00
104	Don Kolloway	20.00	9.00	5.00
105	John Pramesa	20.00	9.00	5.00
106	Mickey Vernon	25.00	11.00	6.25
107	Connie Ryan	20.00	9.00	5.00
108	Jim Konstanty	25.00	11.00	6.25
109	Ted Wilks	20.00	9.00	5.00
110	Dutch Leonard	20.00	9.00	5.00
111	Harry Lowrey	20.00	9.00	5.00
112	Henry Majeski	20.00	9.00	5.00
113	Dick Sisler	20.00	9.00	5.00
114	Willard Ramsdell	20.00	9.00	5.00
115	George Munger	20.00	9.00	5.00
116	Carl Scheib	20.00	9.00	5.00
117	Sherman Lollar	25.00	11.00	6.25
118	Ken Raffensberger	20.00	9.00	5.00
119	Maurice McDermott	20.00	9.00	5.00
120	Bob Chakales	20.00	9.00	5.00
121	Gus Niarhos	20.00	9.00	5.00
122	Jack Jensen	70.00	35.00	21.00
123	Eddie Yost	25.00	11.00	6.25
124	Monte Kennedy	20.00	9.00	5.00
125	Bill Rigney	25.00	11.00	6.25
126	Fred Hutchinson	25.00	11.00	6.25
127	Paul Minner	20.00	9.00	5.00
128	Don Bollweg	30.00	13.50	7.50
129	Johnny Mize	70.00	35.00	21.00
130	Sheldon Jones	20.00	9.00	5.00
131	Morrie Martin	20.00	9.00	5.00
132	Clyde Kluttz	20.00	9.00	5.00
133	Al Widmar	20.00	9.00	5.00
134	Joe Tipton	20.00	9.00	5.00
135	Dixie Howell	20.00	9.00	5.00
136	Johnny Schmitz	25.00	11.00	6.25
137	Roy McMillan	25.00	11.00	6.25
138	Bill MacDonald	20.00	9.00	5.00
139	Ken Wood	20.00	9.00	5.00
140	John Antonelli	25.00	11.00	6.25
141	Clint Hartung	20.00	9.00	5.00
142	Harry Perkowski	20.00	9.00	5.00
143	Les Moss	20.00	9.00	5.00
144	Ed Blake	20.00	9.00	5.00
145	Joe Haynes	20.00	9.00	5.00
146	Frank House	20.00	9.00	5.00
147	Bob Young	20.00	9.00	5.00
148	Johnny Klippstein	20.00	9.00	5.00
149	Dick Kryhoski	20.00	9.00	5.00
150	Ted Beard	20.00	9.00	5.00
151	Wally Post	20.00	9.00	5.00
152	Al Evans	20.00	9.00	5.00
153	Bob Rush	20.00	9.00	5.00
154	Joe Muir	20.00	9.00	5.00
155	Frank Overmire	30.00	13.50	7.50
156	Frank Hiller	20.00	9.00	5.00
157	Bob Usher	20.00	9.00	5.00

		NR MT	EX	VG			NR MT	EX	VG
158	Eddie Waitkus	20.00	9.00	5.00	249	Bobby Adams	20.00	9.00	5.00
159	Saul Rogovin	20.00	9.00	5.00	250	Carl Erskine	50.00	30.00	15.00
160	Owen Friend	20.00	9.00	5.00	251	Chico Carrasquel	40.00	16.00	6.00
161	Bud Byerly	20.00	9.00	5.00	252	Vern Bickford	40.00	16.00	6.00
162	Del Crandall	25.00	11.00	6.25	253	Johnny Berardino	50.00	18.00	7.50
163	Stan Rojek	20.00	9.00	5.00	254	Joe Dobson	40.00	16.00	6.00
164	Walt Dubiel	20.00	9.00	5.00	255	Clyde Vollmer	40.00	16.00	6.00
165	Eddie Kazak	20.00	9.00	5.00	256	Pete Suder	40.00	16.00	6.00
166	Paul LaPalme	20.00	9.00	5.00	257	Bobby Avila	40.00	16.00	6.00
167	Bill Howerton	20.00	9.00	5.00	258	Steve Gromek	40.00	16.00	6.00
168	Charlie Silvera	30.00	13.50	7.50	259	Bob Addis	40.00	16.00	6.00
169	Howie Judson	20.00	9.00	5.00	260	Pete Castiglione	40.00	16.00	6.00
170	Gus Bell	25.00	11.00	6.25	261	Willie Mays	950.00	325.00	125.00
171	Ed Erautt	20.00	9.00	5.00	262	Virgil Trucks	45.00	18.00	6.75
172	Eddie Miksis	20.00	9.00	5.00	263	Harry Brecheen	45.00	18.00	6.75
173	Roy Smalley	20.00	9.00	5.00	264	Roy Hartsfield	40.00	16.00	6.00
174	Clarence Marshall	20.00	9.00	5.00	265	Chuck Diering	40.00	16.00	6.00
175	*Billy Martin*	250.00	100.00	63.00	266	Murry Dickson	40.00	16.00	6.00
176	Hank Edwards	20.00	9.00	5.00	267	Sid Gordon	40.00	16.00	6.00
177	Bill Wight	20.00	9.00	5.00	268	Bob Lemon	150.00	75.00	45.00
178	Cass Michaels	20.00	9.00	5.00	269	Willard Nixon	40.00	16.00	6.00
179	Frank Smith	20.00	9.00	5.00	270	Lou Brissie	40.00	16.00	6.00
180	*Charley Maxwell*	25.00	11.00	6.25	271	Jim Delsing	40.00	16.00	6.00
181	Bob Swift	20.00	9.00	5.00	272	Mike Garcia	45.00	18.00	6.75
182	Billy Hitchcock	20.00	9.00	5.00	273	Erv Palica	45.00	18.00	6.75
183	Erv Dusak	20.00	9.00	5.00	274	Ralph Branca	60.00	25.00	9.00
184	Bob Ramazzotti	20.00	9.00	5.00	275	Pat Mullin	40.00	16.00	6.00
185	Bill Nicholson	20.00	9.00	5.00	276	Jim Wilson	40.00	16.00	6.00
186	Walt Masterson	20.00	9.00	5.00	277	Early Wynn	150.00	75.00	45.00
187	Bob Miller	20.00	9.00	5.00	278	Al Clark	40.00	16.00	6.00
188	Clarence Podbielan	25.00	11.00	6.25	279	Ed Stewart	40.00	16.00	6.00
189	Pete Reiser	25.00	11.00	6.25	280	Cloyd Boyer	40.00	16.00	6.00
190	Don Johnson	20.00	9.00	5.00	281	Tommy Brown	50.00	20.00	7.50
191	Yogi Berra	325.00	120.00	60.00	282	Birdie Tebbetts	50.00	20.00	7.50
192	Myron Ginsberg	20.00	9.00	5.00	283	Phil Masi	50.00	20.00	7.50
193	Harry Simpson	20.00	9.00	5.00	284	Hank Arft	50.00	20.00	7.50
194	Joe Hatten	20.00	9.00	5.00	285	Cliff Fannin	50.00	20.00	7.50
195	*Orestes Minoso*	60.00	30.00	18.00	286	Joe DeMaestri	50.00	20.00	7.50
196	Solly Hemus	20.00	9.00	5.00	287	Steve Bilko	50.00	20.00	7.50
197	George Strickland	20.00	9.00	5.00	288	Chet Nichols	50.00	20.00	7.50
198	Phil Haugstad	25.00	11.00	6.25	289	Tommy Holmes	55.00	25.00	8.25
199	George Zuverink	20.00	9.00	5.00	290	Joe Astroth	50.00	20.00	7.50
200	Ralph Houk	50.00	23.00	12.50	291	Gil Coan	50.00	20.00	7.50
201	Alex Kellner	20.00	9.00	5.00	292	Floyd Baker	50.00	20.00	7.50
202	Joe Collins	30.00	13.50	7.50	293	Sibby Sisti	50.00	20.00	7.50
203	Curt Simmons	25.00	11.00	6.25	294	Walker Cooper	50.00	20.00	7.50
204	Ron Northey	20.00	9.00	5.00	295	Phil Cavarretta	55.00	22.00	8.25
205	Clyde King	25.00	11.00	6.25	296	"Red" Rolfe	50.00	20.00	7.50
206	Joe Ostrowski	30.00	13.50	7.50	297	Andy Seminick	50.00	20.00	7.50
207	Mickey Harris	20.00	9.00	5.00	298	Bob Ross	50.00	20.00	7.50
208	Marlin Stuart	20.00	9.00	5.00	299	Ray Murray	50.00	20.00	7.50
209	Howie Fox	20.00	9.00	5.00	300	Barney McCosky	50.00	20.00	7.50
210	Dick Fowler	20.00	9.00	5.00	301	Bob Porterfield	40.00	16.00	6.00
211	Ray Coleman	20.00	9.00	5.00	302	Max Surkont	40.00	16.00	6.00
212	Ned Garver	20.00	9.00	5.00	303	Harry Dorish	40.00	16.00	6.00
213	Nippy Jones	20.00	9.00	5.00	304	Sam Dente	40.00	16.00	6.00
214	Johnny Hopp	30.00	13.50	7.50	305	Paul Richards	45.00	18.00	6.75
215	Hank Bauer	40.00	18.00	10.00	306	Lou Sleator	40.00	16.00	6.00
216	Richie Ashburn	60.00	30.00	18.00	307	Frank Campos	40.00	16.00	6.00
217	George Stirnweiss	20.00	9.00	5.00	308	Luis Aloma	40.00	16.00	6.00
218	Clyde McCullough	20.00	9.00	5.00	309	Jim Busby	40.00	16.00	6.00
219	Bobby Shantz	25.00	11.00	6.25	310	George Metkovich	40.00	16.00	6.00
220	Joe Presko	20.00	9.00	5.00	311	Mickey Mantle	6500.00	2325.00	1300.
221	Granny Hamner	20.00	9.00	5.00	312	Jackie Robinson	800.00	400.00	225.00
222	"Hoot" Evers	20.00	9.00	5.00	313	Bobby Thomson	175.00	90.00	48.00
223	Del Ennis	25.00	11.00	6.25	314	Roy Campanella	1200.00	500.00	232.00
224	Bruce Edwards	20.00	9.00	5.00	315	Leo Durocher	225.00	100.00	60.00
225	Frank Baumholtz	20.00	9.00	5.00	316	Davey Williams	150.00	75.00	45.00
226	Dave Philley	25.00	11.00	6.25	317	Connie Marrero	150.00	75.00	45.00
227	Joe Garagiola	60.00	27.00	12.00	318	Hal Gregg	150.00	75.00	45.00
228	Al Brazle	20.00	9.00	5.00	319	Al Walker	150.00	75.00	45.00
229	Gene Bearden	20.00	9.00	5.00	320	John Rutherford	150.00	75.00	45.00
230	Matt Batts	20.00	9.00	5.00	321	*Joe Black*	225.00	90.00	56.00
231	Sam Zoldak	20.00	9.00	5.00	322	Randy Jackson	150.00	75.00	45.00
232	Billy Cox	30.00	13.50	7.50	323	Bubba Church	150.00	75.00	45.00
233	*Bob Friend*	25.00	11.00	6.25	324	Warren Hacker	150.00	75.00	45.00
234	Steve Souchock	20.00	9.00	5.00	325	Bill Serena	150.00	75.00	45.00
235	Walt Dropo	25.00	11.00	6.25	326	George Shuba	150.00	75.00	45.00
236	Ed Fitz Gerald	20.00	9.00	5.00	327	Archie Wilson	150.00	75.00	45.00
237	Jerry Coleman	30.00	13.50	7.50	328	Bob Borkowski	150.00	75.00	45.00
238	Art Houtteman	20.00	9.00	5.00	329	Ivan Delock	150.00	75.00	45.00
239	Rocky Bridges	25.00	11.00	6.25	330	Turk Lown	150.00	75.00	45.00
240	Jack Phillips	20.00	9.00	5.00	331	Tom Morgan	160.00	80.00	48.00
241	Tommy Byrne	20.00	9.00	5.00	332	Tony Bartirome	150.00	75.00	45.00
242	Tom Poholsky	20.00	9.00	5.00	333	Pee Wee Reese	500.00	225.00	135.00
243	Larry Doby	30.00	13.50	7.50	334	Wilmer Mizell	150.00	75.00	45.00
244	Vic Wertz	25.00	11.00	6.25	335	Ted Lepcio	150.00	75.00	45.00
245	Sherry Robertson	20.00	9.00	5.00	336	Dave Koslo	150.00	75.00	45.00
246	George Kell	50.00	23.00	12.50	337	Jim Hearn	150.00	75.00	45.00
247	Randy Gumpert	20.00	9.00	5.00	338	Sal Yvars	150.00	75.00	45.00
248	Frank Shea	20.00	9.00	5.00	339	Russ Meyer	150.00	75.00	45.00

		NR MT	EX	VG
340	Bob Hooper	150.00	75.00	45.00
341	Hal Jeffcoat	150.00	75.00	45.00
342	*Clem Labine*	200.00	90.00	52.00
343	Dick Gernert	150.00	75.00	45.00
344	Ewell Blackwell	160.00	80.00	48.00
345	Sam White	150.00	75.00	45.00
346	George Spencer	150.00	75.00	45.00
347	Joe Adcock	175.00	90.00	48.00
348	Bob Kelly	150.00	75.00	45.00
349	Bob Cain	150.00	75.00	45.00
350	Cal Abrams	150.00	75.00	45.00
351	Al Dark	200.00	90.00	52.00
352	Karl Drews	150.00	75.00	45.00
353	Bob Del Greco	150.00	75.00	45.00
354	Fred Hatfield	150.00	75.00	45.00
355	Bobby Morgan	150.00	75.00	45.00
356	Toby Atwell	150.00	75.00	45.00
357	Smoky Burgess	175.00	90.00	48.00
358	John Kucab	150.00	75.00	45.00
359	Dee Fondy	150.00	75.00	45.00
360	George Crowe	150.00	75.00	45.00
361	Bill Posedel	150.00	75.00	45.00
362	Ken Heintzelman	150.00	75.00	45.00
363	Dick Rozek	150.00	75.00	45.00
364	Clyde Sukeforth	150.00	75.00	45.00
365	"Cookie" Lavagetto	150.00	75.00	45.00
366	Dave Madison	150.00	75.00	45.00
367	Bob Thorpe	150.00	75.00	45.00
368	Ed Wright	150.00	75.00	45.00
369	*Dick Groat*	250.00	125.00	60.00
370	Billy Hoeft	150.00	75.00	45.00
371	Bob Hofman	150.00	75.00	45.00
372	*Gil McDougald*	250.00	120.00	67.00
373	Jim Turner	160.00	80.00	48.00
374	Al Benton	150.00	75.00	45.00
375	Jack Merson	150.00	75.00	45.00
376	Faye Throneberry	150.00	75.00	45.00
377	Chuck Dressen	175.00	90.00	52.00
378	Les Fusselman	150.00	75.00	45.00
379	Joe Rossi	150.00	75.00	45.00
380	Clem Koshorek	150.00	75.00	45.00
381	Milton Stock	150.00	75.00	45.00
382	Sam Jones	150.00	75.00	45.00
383	Del Wilber	150.00	75.00	45.00
384	Frank Crosetti	250.00	125.00	67.00
385	Herman Franks	150.00	75.00	45.00
386	Eddie Yuhas	150.00	75.00	45.00
387	Billy Meyer	150.00	75.00	45.00
388	Bob Chipman	150.00	75.00	45.00
389	Ben Wade	150.00	75.00	45.00
390	Glenn Nelson	150.00	75.00	45.00
391	Ben Chapman (photo actually Sam Chapman)	150.00	75.00	45.00
392	*Hoyt Wilhelm*	400.00	190.00	112.00
393	Ebba St. Claire	150.00	75.00	45.00
394	Billy Herman	200.00	90.00	52.00
395	Jake Pitler	150.00	75.00	45.00
396	*Dick Williams*	175.00	90.00	52.00
397	Forrest Main	150.00	75.00	45.00
398	Hal Rice	150.00	75.00	45.00
399	Jim Fridley	150.00	75.00	45.00
400	Bill Dickey	500.00	225.00	135.00
401	Bob Schultz	150.00	75.00	45.00
402	Earl Harrist	150.00	75.00	45.00
403	Bill Miller	160.00	80.00	48.00
404	Dick Brodowski	150.00	75.00	45.00
405	Eddie Pellagrini	150.00	75.00	45.00
406	*Joe Nuxhall*	175.00	87.00	52.00
407	*Ed Mathews*	1800.00	400.00	135.00

1953 Topps

The 1953 Topps set reflects the company's

continuing legal battles with Bowman. The set, originally intended to consist of 280 cards, is lacking six numbers (#'s 253, 261, 267, 268, 271 and 275) which probably represent players whose contracts were lost to the competition. The 2-5/8" by 3-3/4" cards feature painted player pictures. A color team logo appears at a bottom panel (red for American Leauge and black for National.) Card backs contain the first baseball trivia questions along with brief statistics and player biographies. In the red panel at the top which lists the player's personal data, cards from the 2nd Series (#'s 86-165 plus 10, 44, 61, 72 and 81) can be found with that data printed in either black or white, black being the scarcer variety. Card numbers 221-280 are the scarce high numbers.

		NR MT	EX	VG
Complete Set:		12000.00	6000.00	3600.
Common Player Singleprint: 1-165		25.00	12.50	7.50
Common Player: 1-165		20.00	10.00	6.00
Common Player: 166-220		18.00	9.00	5.50
Common Player Singleprint: 221-280		90.00	45.00	27.00
Common Player: 221-280		45.00	23.00	13.50
1	Jackie Robinson	600.00	240.00	150.00
2	Luke Easter	25.00	12.50	7.50
3	George Crowe	25.00	12.50	7.50
4	Ben Wade	25.00	12.50	7.50
5	Joe Dobson	25.00	12.50	7.50
6	Sam Jones	25.00	12.50	7.50
7	Bob Borkowski	20.00	10.00	6.00
8	Clem Koshorek	20.00	10.00	6.00
9	Joe Collins	30.00	15.00	9.00
10	Smoky Burgess	30.00	15.00	9.00
11	Sal Yvars	25.00	12.50	7.50
12	Howie Judson	20.00	10.00	6.00
13	Connie Marrero	20.00	10.00	6.00
14	Clem Labine	25.00	12.50	7.50
15	Bobo Newsom	25.00	12.50	7.50
16	Harry Lowrey	20.00	10.00	6.00
17	Billy Hitchcock	25.00	12.50	7.50
18	Ted Lepcio	20.00	10.00	6.00
19	Mel Parnell	20.00	10.00	6.00
20	Hank Thompson	25.00	12.50	7.50
21	Billy Johnson	25.00	12.50	7.50
22	Howie Fox	25.00	12.50	7.50
23	Toby Atwell	20.00	10.00	6.00
24	Ferris Fain	25.00	12.50	7.50
25	Ray Boone	25.00	12.50	7.50
26	Dale Mitchell	20.00	10.00	6.00
27	Roy Campanella	200.00	80.00	50.00
28	Eddie Pellagrini	25.00	12.50	7.50
29	Hal Jeffcoat	25.00	12.50	7.50
30	Willard Nixon	25.00	12.50	7.50
31	Ewell Blackwell	40.00	20.00	12.00
32	Clyde Vollmer	25.00	12.50	7.50
33	Bob Kennedy	20.00	10.00	6.00
34	George Shuba	25.00	12.50	7.50
35	Irv Noren	25.00	12.50	7.50
36	Johnny Groth	20.00	10.00	6.00
37	Ed Mathews	90.00	45.00	27.00
38	Jim Hearn	20.00	10.00	6.00
39	Eddie Miksis	25.00	12.50	7.50
40	John Lipon	25.00	12.50	7.50
41	Enos Slaughter	70.00	35.00	21.00
42	Gus Zernial	20.00	10.00	6.00
43	Gil McDougald	50.00	25.00	15.00
44	Ellis Kinder	30.00	15.00	9.00
45	Grady Hatton	20.00	10.00	6.00
46	Johnny Klippstein	20.00	10.00	6.00
47	Bubba Church	20.00	10.00	6.00
48	Bob Del Greco	20.00	10.00	6.00
49	Faye Throneberry	20.00	10.00	6.00
50	Chuck Dressen	25.00	12.50	7.50
51	Frank Campos	20.00	10.00	6.00
52	Ted Gray	20.00	10.00	6.00
53	Sherman Lollar	20.00	10.00	6.00
54	Bob Feller	85.00	42.00	25.00
55	Maurice McDermott	20.00	10.00	6.00
56	Gerald Staley	20.00	10.00	6.00
57	Carl Scheib	25.00	12.50	7.50
58	George Metkovich	25.00	12.50	7.50
59	Karl Drews	20.00	10.00	6.00
60	Cloyd Boyer	20.00	10.00	6.00
61	Early Wynn	85.00	42.00	25.00
62	Monte Irvin	35.00	17.50	10.50
63	Gus Niarhos	20.00	10.00	6.00
64	Dave Philley	25.00	12.50	7.50
65	Earl Harrist	25.00	12.50	7.50

		NR MT	EX	VG			NR MT	EX	VG
66	Orestes Minoso	30.00	15.00	9.00	157	Bob Addis	20.00	10.00	6.00
67	Roy Sievers	25.00	12.50	7.50	158	*John Logan*	25.00	12.50	7.50
68	Del Rice	25.00	12.50	7.50	159	Wayne Terwilliger	20.00	10.00	6.00
69	Dick Brodowski	25.00	12.50	7.50	160	Bob Young	20.00	10.00	6.00
70	Ed Yuhas	25.00	12.50	7.50	161	Vern Bickford	20.00	10.00	6.00
71	Tony Bartirome	25.00	12.50	7.50	162	Ted Kluszewski	30.00	15.00	9.00
72	Fred Hutchinson	25.00	12.50	7.50	163	Fred Hatfield	20.00	10.00	6.00
73	Eddie Robinson	25.00	12.50	7.50	164	Frank Shea	20.00	10.00	6.00
74	Joe Rossi	25.00	12.50	7.50	165	Billy Hoeft	20.00	10.00	6.00
75	Mike Garcia	25.00	12.50	7.50	166	Bill Hunter	18.00	9.00	5.50
76	Pee Wee Reese	100.00	45.00	27.00	167	Art Schult	20.00	10.00	6.00
77	John Mize	75.00	37.00	22.00	168	Willard Schmidt	18.00	9.00	5.50
78	Al Schoendienst	50.00	30.00	15.00	169	Dizzy Trout	20.00	10.00	6.00
79	Johnny Wyrostek	25.00	12.50	7.50	170	Bill Werle	18.00	9.00	5.50
80	Jim Hegan	25.00	12.50	7.50	171	Bill Glynn	18.00	9.00	5.50
81	Joe Black	40.00	20.00	12.00	172	Rip Repulski	18.00	9.00	5.50
82	Mickey Mantle	1900.00	750.00	375.00	173	Preston Ward	18.00	9.00	5.50
83	Howie Pollet	25.00	12.50	7.50	174	Billy Loes	20.00	10.00	6.00
84	Bob Hooper	20.00	10.00	6.00	175	Ron Kline	18.00	9.00	5.50
85	Bobby Morgan	25.00	12.50	7.50	176	*Don Hoak*	20.00	10.00	5.50
86	Billy Martin	65.00	32.00	19.50	177	Jim Dyck	18.00	9.00	5.50
87	Ed Lopat	35.00	17.50	10.50	178	Jim Waugh	18.00	9.00	5.50
88	Willie Jones	20.00	10.00	6.00	179	Gene Hermanski	18.00	9.00	5.50
89	Chuck Stobbs	20.00	10.00	6.00	180	Virgil Stallcup	18.00	9.00	5.50
90	Hank Edwards	20.00	10.00	6.00	181	Al Zarilla	18.00	9.00	5.50
91	Ebba St. Claire	20.00	10.00	6.00	182	Bob Hofman	18.00	9.00	5.50
92	Paul Minner	20.00	10.00	6.00	183	*Stu Miller*	20.00	10.00	6.00
93	Hal Rice	20.00	10.00	6.00	184	*Hal Brown*	20.00	10.00	6.00
94	William Kennedy	20.00	10.00	6.00	185	Jim Pendleton	18.00	9.00	5.50
95	Willard Marshall	20.00	10.00	6.00	186	Charlie Bishop	18.00	9.00	5.50
96	Virgil Trucks	25.00	12.50	7.50	187	Jim Fridley	18.00	9.00	5.50
97	Don Kolloway	20.00	10.00	6.00	188	*Andy Carey*	20.00	10.00	6.00
98	Cal Abrams	20.00	10.00	6.00	189	Ray Jablonski	18.00	9.00	5.50
99	Dave Madison	20.00	10.00	6.00	190	Dixie Walker	20.00	10.00	6.00
100	Bill Miller	25.00	12.50	7.50	191	Ralph Kiner	50.00	25.00	15.00
101	Ted Wilks	20.00	10.00	6.00	192	Wally Westlake	18.00	9.00	5.50
102	Connie Ryan	20.00	10.00	6.00	193	Mike Clark	18.00	9.00	5.50
103	Joe Astroth	20.00	10.00	6.00	194	Eddie Kazak	18.00	9.00	5.50
104	Yogi Berra	175.00	70.00	44.00	195	Ed McGhee	18.00	9.00	5.50
105	Joe Nuxhall	25.00	12.50	7.50	196	Bob Keegan	18.00	9.00	5.50
106	Johnny Antonelli	25.00	12.50	7.50	197	Del Crandall	20.00	10.00	6.00
107	Danny O'Connell	20.00	10.00	6.00	198	Forrest Main	18.00	9.00	5.50
108	Bob Porterfield	20.00	10.00	6.00	199	Marion Fricano	18.00	9.00	5.50
109	Alvin Dark	25.00	12.50	7.50	200	Gordon Goldsberry	18.00	9.00	5.50
110	Herman Wehmeier	20.00	10.00	6.00	201	Paul LaPalme	18.00	9.00	5.50
111	Hank Sauer	16.00	8.00	4.75	202	Carl Sawatski	18.00	9.00	5.50
112	Ned Garver	20.00	10.00	6.00	203	Cliff Fannin	18.00	9.00	5.50
113	Jerry Priddy	20.00	10.00	6.00	204	Dick Bokelmann	18.00	9.00	5.50
114	Phil Rizzuto	75.00	37.00	22.00	205	Vern Benson	18.00	9.00	5.50
115	George Spencer	20.00	10.00	6.00	206	*Ed Bailey*	20.00	10.00	6.00
116	Frank Smith	20.00	10.00	6.00	207	Whitey Ford	90.00	45.00	27.00
117	Sid Gordon	20.00	10.00	6.00	208	Jim Wilson	18.00	9.00	5.50
118	Gus Bell	16.00	8.00	4.75	209	Jim Greengrass	18.00	9.00	5.50
119	John Sain	35.00	17.50	10.50	210	*Bob Cerv*	20.00	10.00	6.00
120	Davey Williams	20.00	10.00	6.00	211	J.W. Porter	18.00	9.00	5.50
121	Walt Dropo	20.00	10.00	6.00	212	Jack Dittmer	18.00	9.00	5.50
122	Elmer Valo	20.00	10.00	6.00	213	Ray Scarborough	20.00	10.00	6.00
123	Tommy Byrne	20.00	10.00	6.00	214	*Bill Bruton*	20.00	10.00	6.00
124	Sibby Sisti	20.00	10.00	6.00	215	*Gene Conley*	20.00	10.00	6.00
125	Dick Williams	25.00	12.50	7.50	216	Jim Hughes	20.00	10.00	6.00
126	Bill Connelly	20.00	10.00	6.00	217	Murray Wall	18.00	9.00	5.50
127	Clint Courtney	20.00	10.00	6.00	218	Les Fusselman	18.00	9.00	5.50
128	Wilmer Mizell	20.00	10.00	6.00	219	Pete Runnels (photo actually Don			
129	Keith Thomas	20.00	10.00	6.00		Johnson)	20.00	10.00	6.00
130	Turk Lown	20.00	10.00	6.00	220	Satchell Paige	325.00	130.00	81.00
131	Harry Byrd	20.00	10.00	6.00	221	Bob Milliken	90.00	45.00	27.00
132	Tom Morgan	25.00	12.50	7.50	222	Vic Janowicz	45.00	23.00	13.50
133	Gil Coan	20.00	10.00	6.00	223	John O'Brien	45.00	23.00	13.50
134	Rube Walker	25.00	12.50	7.50	224	Lou Sleater	45.00	23.00	13.50
135	Al Rosen	30.00	15.00	9.00	225	Bobby Shantz	60.00	30.00	18.00
136	Ken Heintzelman	20.00	10.00	6.00	226	Ed Erautt	90.00	45.00	27.00
137	John Rutherford	25.00	12.50	7.50	227	Morris Martin	45.00	23.00	13.50
138	George Kell	60.00	30.00	18.00	228	Hal Newhouser	100.00	45.00	27.00
139	Sammy White	20.00	10.00	6.00	229	Rocky Krsnich	90.00	45.00	27.00
140	Tommy Glaviano	20.00	10.00	6.00	230	Johnny Lindell	45.00	23.00	13.50
141	Allie Reynolds	35.00	17.50	10.50	231	Solly Hemus	45.00	23.00	13.50
142	Vic Wertz	25.00	12.50	7.50	232	Dick Kokos	90.00	45.00	27.00
143	Billy Pierce	25.00	12.50	7.50	233	Al Aber	90.00	45.00	27.00
144	Bob Schultz	20.00	10.00	6.00	234	Ray Murray	45.00	23.00	13.50
145	Harry Dorish	20.00	10.00	6.00	235	John Hetki	45.00	23.00	13.50
146	Granville Hamner	20.00	10.00	6.00	236	Harry Perkowski	90.00	45.00	27.00
147	Warren Spahn	110.00	50.00	28.00	237	Clarence Podbielan	45.00	23.00	13.50
148	Mickey Grasso	20.00	10.00	6.00	238	Cal Hogue	45.00	23.00	13.50
149	Dom DiMaggio	25.00	12.50	7.50	239	Jim Delsing	90.00	45.00	27.00
150	Harry Simpson	20.00	10.00	6.00	240	Freddie Marsh	45.00	23.00	13.50
151	Hoyt Wilhelm	50.00	30.00	15.00	241	Al Sima	45.00	23.00	13.50
152	Bob Adams	20.00	10.00	6.00	242	Charlie Silvera	90.00	45.00	27.00
153	Andy Seminick	20.00	10.00	6.00	243	Carlos Bernier	45.00	23.00	13.50
154	Dick Groat	25.00	12.50	7.50	244	Willie Mays	1400.00	560.00	350.00
155	Dutch Leonard	20.00	10.00	6.00	245	Bill Norman	90.00	45.00	27.00
156	Jim Rivera	20.00	10.00	6.00	246	*Roy Face*	90.00	45.00	27.00

		NR MT	EX	VG
247	Mike Sandlock	45.00	23.00	13.50
248	Gene Stephens	45.00	23.00	13.50
249	Ed O'Brien	45.00	23.00	13.50
250	Bob Wilson	90.00	45.00	27.00
251	Sid Hudson	90.00	45.00	27.00
252	Henry Foiles	90.00	45.00	27.00
253	Not Issued			
254	Preacher Roe	80.00	40.00	24.00
255	Dixie Howell	90.00	45.00	27.00
256	Les Peden	90.00	45.00	27.00
257	Bob Boyd	90.00	45.00	27.00
258	*Jim Gilliam*	275.00	110.00	69.00
259	Roy McMillan	90.00	45.00	27.00
260	Sam Calderone	90.00	45.00	27.00
261	Not Issued			
262	Bob Oldis	90.00	45.00	27.00
263	*John Podres*	250.00	100.00	63.00
264	Gene Woodling	75.00	38.00	23.00
265	Jackie Jensen	125.00	56.00	35.00
266	Bob Cain	90.00	45.00	27.00
267	Not Issued			
268	Not Issued			
269	Duane Pillette	90.00	45.00	27.00
270	Vern Stephens	90.00	45.00	27.00
271	Not Issued			
272	Bill Antonello	90.00	45.00	27.00
273	*Harvey Haddix*	90.00	45.00	27.00
274	John Riddle	90.00	45.00	27.00
275	Not Issued			
276	Ken Raffensberger	45.00	23.00	13.50
277	Don Lund	90.00	45.00	27.00
278	Willie Miranda	90.00	45.00	27.00
279	Joe Coleman	45.00	23.00	13.50
280	Milt Bolling	300.00	45.00	27.00

1954 Topps

The first issue to use two player pictures on the front, the 1954 Topps set is very popular today. Solid color backgrounds frame both color head- and-shoulders and black and white action pictures of the player. The player's name, position, team and team logo appear at the top. Backs include an "Inside Baseball" cartoon regarding the player as well as statistics and biography. The 250-card, 2-5/8" by 3-3/4", set includes manager and coaches cards, and the first use of two players together on a modern card; the players were, appropriately, the O'Brien twins.

		NR MT	EX	VG
Complete Set:		6500.00	3250.00	1950.
Common Player: 1-50		10.00	5.00	3.00
Common Player: 51-75		20.00	10.00	6.00
Common Player: 76-250		12.00	6.00	3.50
1	Ted Williams	550.00	100.00	45.00
2	Gus Zernial	12.00	6.00	3.50
3	Monte Irvin	25.00	12.50	7.50
4	Hank Sauer	10.00	5.00	3.00
5	Ed Lopat	25.00	12.50	7.50
6	Pete Runnels	11.00	5.50	3.25
7	Ted Kluszewski	15.00	7.50	4.50
8	Bobby Young	10.00	5.00	3.00
9	Harvey Haddix	11.00	5.50	3.25
10	Jackie Robinson	225.00	90.00	56.00
11	Paul Smith	10.00	5.00	3.00

		NR MT	EX	VG
12	Del Crandall	11.00	5.50	3.25
13	Billy Martin	60.00	30.00	18.00
14	Preacher Roe	18.00	9.00	5.50
15	Al Rosen	15.00	7.50	4.50
16	Vic Janowicz	10.00	5.00	3.00
17	Phil Rizzuto	70.00	35.00	21.00
18	Walt Dropo	10.00	5.00	3.00
19	Johnny Lipon	10.00	5.00	3.00
20	Warren Spahn	80.00	40.00	24.00
21	Bobby Shantz	12.00	6.00	3.50
22	Jim Greengrass	10.00	5.00	3.00
23	Luke Easter	11.00	5.50	3.25
24	Granny Hamner	10.00	5.00	3.00
25	*Harvey Kuenn*	25.00	12.50	7.50
26	Ray Jablonski	10.00	5.00	3.00
27	Ferris Fain	11.00	5.50	3.25
28	Paul Minner	10.00	5.00	3.00
29	Jim Hegan	10.00	5.00	3.00
30	Ed Mathews	70.00	35.00	21.00
31	Johnny Klippstein	10.00	5.00	3.00
32	Duke Snider	125.00	56.00	35.00
33	Johnny Schmitz	10.00	5.00	3.00
34	Jim Rivera	10.00	5.00	3.00
35	Junior Gilliam	20.00	10.00	6.00
36	Hoyt Wilhelm	30.00	15.00	9.00
37	Whitey Ford	75.00	37.00	22.00
38	Eddie Stanky	11.00	5.50	3.25
39	Sherm Lollar	11.00	5.50	3.25
40	Mel Parnell	11.00	5.50	3.25
41	Willie Jones	10.00	5.00	3.00
42	Don Mueller	10.00	5.00	3.00
43	Dick Groat	12.00	6.00	3.50
44	Ned Garver	10.00	5.00	3.00
45	Richie Ashburn	25.00	12.50	7.50
46	Ken Raffensberger	10.00	5.00	3.00
47	Ellis Kinder	10.00	5.00	3.00
48	Billy Hunter	10.00	5.00	3.00
49	Ray Murray	10.00	5.00	3.00
50	Yogi Berra	200.00	80.00	50.00
51	Johnny Lindell	20.00	10.00	6.00
52	Vic Power	20.00	10.00	6.00
53	Jack Dittmer	20.00	10.00	6.00
54	Vern Stephens	20.00	10.00	6.00
55	Phil Cavarretta	22.00	11.00	6.50
56	Willie Miranda	25.00	12.50	7.50
57	Luis Aloma	20.00	10.00	6.00
58	Bob Wilson	20.00	10.00	6.00
59	Gene Conley	22.00	11.00	6.50
60	Frank Baumholtz	20.00	10.00	6.00
61	Bob Cain	20.00	10.00	6.00
62	Eddie Robinson	25.00	12.50	7.50
63	Johnny Pesky	22.00	11.00	6.50
64	Hank Thompson	20.00	10.00	6.00
65	Bob Swift	20.00	10.00	6.00
66	Ted Lepcio	20.00	10.00	6.00
67	Jim Willis	20.00	10.00	6.00
68	Sammy Calderone	20.00	10.00	6.00
69	Bud Podbielan	20.00	10.00	6.00
70	Larry Doby	45.00	23.00	13.50
71	Frank Smith	20.00	10.00	6.00
72	Preston Ward	20.00	10.00	6.00
73	Wayne Terwilliger	20.00	10.00	6.00
74	Bill Taylor	20.00	10.00	6.00
75	Fred Haney	20.00	10.00	6.00
76	Bob Scheffing	12.00	6.00	3.50
77	Ray Boone	13.00	6.50	4.00
78	Ted Kazanski	12.00	6.00	3.50
79	Andy Pafko	13.00	6.50	4.00
80	Jackie Jensen	15.00	7.50	4.50
81	Dave Hoskins	12.00	6.00	3.50
82	Milt Bolling	12.00	6.00	3.50
83	Joe Collins	15.00	7.50	4.50
84	Dick Cole	12.00	6.00	3.50
85	*Bob Turley*	15.00	7.50	4.50
86	Billy Herman	20.00	10.00	6.00
87	Roy Face	15.00	7.50	4.50
88	Matt Batts	12.00	6.00	3.50
89	Howie Pollet	12.00	6.00	3.50
90	Willie Mays	325.00	130.00	81.00
91	Bob Oldis	12.00	6.00	3.50
92	Wally Westlake	12.00	6.00	3.50
93	Sid Hudson	12.00	6.00	3.50
94	*Ernie Banks*	600.00	250.00	150.00
95	Hal Rice	12.00	6.00	3.50
96	Charlie Silvera	15.00	7.50	4.50
97	Jerry Lane	12.00	6.00	3.50
98	Joe Black	15.00	7.50	4.50
99	Bob Hofman	12.00	6.00	3.50
100	Bob Keegan	12.00	6.00	3.50
101	Gene Woodling	20.00	10.00	6.00
102	Gil Hodges	60.00	30.00	18.00

		NR MT	EX	VG
103	*Jim Lemon*	13.00	6.50	4.00
104	Mike Sandlock	12.00	6.00	3.50
105	Andy Carey	15.00	7.50	4.50
106	Dick Kokos	12.00	6.00	3.50
107	Duane Pillette	12.00	6.00	3.50
108	Thornton Kipper	12.00	6.00	3.50
109	Bill Bruton	13.00	6.50	4.00
110	Harry Dorish	12.00	6.00	3.50
111	Jim Delsing	12.00	6.00	3.50
112	Bill Renna	12.00	6.00	3.50
113	Bob Boyd	12.00	6.00	3.50
114	Dean Stone	12.00	6.00	3.50
115	"Rip" Repulski	12.00	6.00	3.50
116	Steve Bilko	12.00	6.00	3.50
117	Solly Hemus	12.00	6.00	3.50
118	Carl Scheib	12.00	6.00	3.50
119	Johnny Antonelli	13.00	6.50	4.00
120	Roy McMillan	12.00	6.00	3.50
121	Clem Labine	13.00	6.50	4.00
122	Johnny Logan	13.00	6.50	4.00
123	Bobby Adams	12.00	6.00	3.50
124	Marion Fricano	12.00	6.00	3.50
125	Harry Perkowski	12.00	6.00	3.50
126	Ben Wade	13.00	6.50	4.00
127	Steve O'Neill	12.00	6.00	3.50
128	*Henry Aaron*	1000.00	450.00	225.00
129	Forrest Jacobs	12.00	6.00	3.50
130	Hank Bauer	20.00	10.00	6.00
131	Reno Bertoia	12.00	6.00	3.50
132	*Tom Lasorda*	125.00	56.00	35.00
133	Del Baker	12.00	6.00	3.50
134	Cal Hogue	12.00	6.00	3.50
135	Joe Presko	12.00	6.00	3.50
136	Connie Ryan	12.00	6.00	3.50
137	*Wally Moon*	15.00	7.50	4.50
138	Bob Borkowski	12.00	6.00	3.50
139	Ed & Johnny O'Brien	25.00	12.50	7.50
140	Tom Wright	12.00	6.00	3.50
141	*Joe Jay*	13.00	6.50	4.00
142	Tom Poholsky	12.00	6.00	3.50
143	Rollie Hemsley	12.00	6.00	3.50
144	Bill Werle	12.00	6.00	3.50
145	Elmer Valo	12.00	6.00	3.50
146	Don Johnson	12.00	6.00	3.50
147	John Riddle	12.00	6.00	3.50
148	Bob Trice	12.00	6.00	3.50
149	Jim Robertson	12.00	6.00	3.50
150	Dick Kryhoski	12.00	6.00	3.50
151	Alex Grammas	12.00	6.00	3.50
152	Mike Blyzka	12.00	6.00	3.50
153	"Rube" Walker	13.00	6.50	4.00
154	Mike Fornieles	12.00	6.00	3.50
155	Bob Kennedy	12.00	6.00	3.50
156	Joe Coleman	12.00	6.00	3.50
157	Don Lenhardt	12.00	6.00	3.50
158	"Peanuts" Lowrey	12.00	6.00	3.50
159	Dave Philley	12.00	6.00	3.50
160	"Red" Kress	12.00	6.00	3.50
161	John Hetki	12.00	6.00	3.50
162	Herman Wehmeier	12.00	6.00	3.50
163	Frank House	12.00	6.00	3.50
164	Stu Miller	12.00	6.00	3.50
165	Jim Pendleton	12.00	6.00	3.50
166	Johnny Podres	25.00	12.50	7.50
167	Don Lund	12.00	6.00	3.50
168	Morrie Martin	12.00	6.00	3.50
169	Jim Hughes	13.00	6.50	4.00
170	*Jim Rhodes*	13.00	6.50	4.00
171	Leo Kiely	12.00	6.00	3.50
172	Hal Brown	12.00	6.00	3.50
173	Jack Harshman	12.00	6.00	3.50
174	Tom Qualters	12.00	6.00	3.50
175	Frank Leja	15.00	7.50	4.50
176	Bob Keely	12.00	6.00	3.50
177	Bob Milliken	13.00	6.50	4.00
178	Bill Glynn (Glynn)	12.00	6.00	3.50
179	Gair Allie	12.00	6.00	3.50
180	Wes Westrum	13.00	6.50	4.00
181	Mel Roach	12.00	6.00	3.50
182	Chuck Harmon	12.00	6.00	3.50
183	Earle Combs	20.00	10.00	6.00
184	Ed Bailey	12.00	6.00	3.50
185	Chuck Stobbs	12.00	6.00	3.50
186	Karl Olson	12.00	6.00	3.50
187	"Heinie" Manush	20.00	10.00	6.00
188	Dave Jolly	12.00	6.00	3.50
189	Bob Ross	12.00	6.00	3.50
190	Ray Herbert	12.00	6.00	3.50
191	*Dick Schofield*	13.00	6.50	4.00
192	"Cot" Deal	12.00	6.00	3.50
193	Johnny Hopp	12.00	6.00	3.50

		NR MT	EX	VG
194	Bill Sarni	12.00	6.00	3.50
195	Bill Consolo	12.00	6.00	3.50
196	Stan Jok	12.00	6.00	3.50
197	"Schoolboy" Rowe	13.00	6.50	4.00
198	Carl Sawatski	12.00	6.00	3.50
199	"Rocky" Nelson	12.00	6.00	3.50
200	Larry Jansen	12.00	6.00	3.50
201	*Al Kaline*	600.00	240.00	150.00
202	*Bob Purkey*	13.00	6.50	4.00
203	Harry Brecheen	13.00	6.50	4.00
204	Angel Scull	12.00	6.00	3.50
205	Johnny Sain	20.00	10.00	6.00
206	Ray Crone	12.00	6.00	3.50
207	Tom Oliver	12.00	6.00	3.50
208	Grady Hatton	12.00	6.00	3.50
209	Charlie Thompson	13.00	6.50	4.00
210	*Bob Buhl*	13.00	6.50	4.00
211	Don Hoak	13.00	6.50	4.00
212	Mickey Micelotta	12.00	6.00	3.50
213	John Fitzpatrick	12.00	6.00	3.50
214	Arnold Portocarrero	12.00	6.00	3.50
215	Ed McGhee	12.00	6.00	3.50
216	Al Sima	12.00	6.00	3.50
217	Paul Schreiber	12.00	6.00	3.50
218	Fred Marsh	12.00	6.00	3.50
219	Charlie Kress	12.00	6.00	3.50
220	Ruben Gomez	12.00	6.00	3.50
221	Dick Brodowski	12.00	6.00	3.50
222	Bill Wilson	12.00	6.00	3.50
223	Joe Haynes	12.00	6.00	3.50
224	Dick Weik	12.00	6.00	3.50
225	Don Liddle	12.00	6.00	3.50
226	Jehosie Heard	12.00	6.00	3.50
227	Buster Mills	12.00	6.00	3.50
228	Gene Hermanski	12.00	6.00	3.50
229	Bob Talbot	12.00	6.00	3.50
230	Bob Kuzava	15.00	7.50	4.50
231	Roy Smalley	12.00	6.00	3.50
232	Lou Limmer	12.00	6.00	3.50
233	Augie Galan	12.00	6.00	3.50
234	*Jerry Lynch*	13.00	6.50	4.00
235	Vern Law	13.00	6.50	4.00
236	Paul Penson	12.00	6.00	3.50
237	Mike Ryba	12.00	6.00	3.50
238	Al Aber	12.00	6.00	3.50
239	*Bill Skowron*	45.00	23.00	13.50
240	Sam Mele	12.00	6.00	3.50
241	Bob Miller	12.00	6.00	3.50
242	Curt Roberts	12.00	6.00	3.50
243	Ray Blades	12.00	6.00	3.50
244	Leroy Wheat	12.00	6.00	3.50
245	Roy Sievers	13.00	6.50	4.00
246	Howie Fox	12.00	6.00	3.50
247	Eddie Mayo	12.00	6.00	3.50
248	*Al Smith*	13.00	6.50	4.00
249	Wilmer Mizell	12.00	6.00	3.50
250	Ted Williams	550.00	100.00	45.00

1955 Topps

The 1955 Topps set is numerically the smallest of the regular issue Topps sets. The 3-3/4" by 2-5/8" cards mark the first time that Topps used a horizontal format. While that format was new, the design was not; they are very similar to the 1954 cards to the point many pictures appeared in both years. Although it was slated for a 210-card set, the 1955 Topps set turned out to be only 206 cards with numbers 175, 186, 203 and 209 never being released. The scarce high numbers in this set begin with #161.

		NR MT	EX	VG
Complete Set:		4900.00	2450.00	1470.
Common Player: 1-150		5.00	2.50	1.50
Common Player: 151-160		7.00	3.50	2.00
Common Player: 161-210		15.00	7.50	4.50
1	"Dusty" Rhodes	30.00	15.00	9.00
2	Ted Williams	325.00	90.00	44.00
3	Art Fowler	5.00	2.50	1.50
4	Al Kaline	125.00	56.00	35.00
5	Jim Gilliam	10.00	5.00	3.00
6	Stan Hack	6.00	3.00	1.75
7	Jim Hegan	5.00	2.50	1.50
8	Hal Smith	5.00	2.50	1.50

		NR MT	EX	VG
68	Jim Davis	5.00	2.50	1.50
69	Ed Bailey	5.00	2.50	1.50
70	Al Rosen	12.00	6.00	3.50
71	Ruben Gomez	5.00	2.50	1.50
72	Karl Olson	5.00	2.50	1.50
73	Jack Shepard	5.00	2.50	1.50
74	Bob Borkowski	5.00	2.50	1.50
75	Sandy Amoros	6.00	3.00	1.75
76	Howie Pollet	5.00	2.50	1.50
77	Arnold Portocarrero	5.00	2.50	1.50
78	Gordon Jones	5.00	2.50	1.50
79	Danny Schell	5.00	2.50	1.50
80	Bob Grim	9.00	4.50	2.75
81	Gene Conley	6.00	3.00	1.75
82	Chuck Harmon	5.00	2.50	1.50
83	Tom Brewer	5.00	2.50	1.50
84	*Camilo Pascual*	7.00	3.50	2.00
85	*Don Mossi*	7.00	3.50	2.00
86	Bill Wilson	5.00	2.50	1.50
87	Frank House	5.00	2.50	1.50
88	*Bob Skinner*	7.00	3.50	2.00
89	Joe Frazier	5.00	2.50	1.50
90	Karl Spooner	9.00	4.50	2.75
91	Milt Bolling	5.00	2.50	1.50
92	*Don Zimmer*	18.00	9.00	5.50
93	Steve Bilko	5.00	2.50	1.50
94	Reno Bertoia	5.00	2.50	1.50
95	Preston Ward	5.00	2.50	1.50
96	Charlie Bishop	5.00	2.50	1.50
97	Carlos Paula	5.00	2.50	1.50
98	Johnny Riddle	5.00	2.50	1.50
99	Frank Leja	9.00	4.50	2.75
100	Monte Irvin	20.00	10.00	6.00
101	Johnny Gray	5.00	2.50	1.50
102	Wally Westlake	5.00	2.50	1.50
103	Charlie White	5.00	2.50	1.50
104	Jack Harshman	5.00	2.50	1.50
105	Chuck Diering	5.00	2.50	1.50
106	*Frank Sullivan*	6.00	3.00	1.75
107	Curt Roberts	5.00	2.50	1.50
108	"Rube" Walker	6.00	3.00	1.75
109	Ed Lopat	12.00	6.00	3.50
110	Gus Zernial	6.00	3.00	1.75
111	Bob Milliken	6.00	3.00	1.75
112	Nelson King	5.00	2.50	1.50
113	Harry Brecheen	6.00	3.00	1.75
114	Lou Ortiz	5.00	2.50	1.50
115	Ellis Kinder	5.00	2.50	1.50
116	Tom Hurd	5.00	2.50	1.50
117	Mel Roach	5.00	2.50	1.50
118	Bob Purkey	5.00	2.50	1.50
119	Bob Lennon	5.00	2.50	1.50
120	Ted Kluszewski	15.00	7.50	4.50
121	Bill Renna	5.00	2.50	1.50
122	Carl Sawatski	5.00	2.50	1.50
123	*Sandy Koufax*	600.00	240.00	150.00
124	*Harmon Killebrew*	250.00	100.00	63.00
125	*Ken Boyer*	35.00	17.50	10.50
126	*Dick Hall*	6.00	3.00	1.75
127	*Dale Long*	6.00	3.00	1.75
128	Ted Lepcio	5.00	2.50	1.50
129	Elvin Tappe	5.00	2.50	1.50
130	Mayo Smith	5.00	2.50	1.50
131	Grady Hatton	5.00	2.50	1.50
132	Bob Trice	5.00	2.50	1.50
133	Dave Hoskins	5.00	2.50	1.50
134	Joe Jay	5.00	2.50	1.50
135	Johnny O'Brien	5.00	2.50	1.50
136	"Bunky" Stewart	5.00	2.50	1.50
137	Harry Elliott	5.00	2.50	1.50
138	Ray Herbert	5.00	2.50	1.50
139	Steve Kraly	9.00	4.50	2.75
140	Mel Parnell	6.00	3.00	1.75
141	Tom Wright	5.00	2.50	1.50
142	Jerry Lynch	5.00	2.50	1.50
143	Dick Schofield	5.00	2.50	1.50
144	Joe Amalfitano	5.00	2.50	1.50
145	Elmer Valo	5.00	2.50	1.50
146	*Dick Donovan*	6.00	3.00	1.75
147	Laurin Pepper	5.00	2.50	1.50
148	Hal Brown	5.00	2.50	1.50
149	Ray Crone	5.00	2.50	1.50
150	Mike Higgins	5.00	2.50	1.50
151	"Red" Kress	7.00	3.50	2.00
152	*Harry Agganis*	75.00	38.00	23.00
153	"Bud" Podbielan	7.00	3.50	2.00
154	Willie Miranda	7.00	3.50	2.00
155	Ed Mathews	80.00	40.00	24.00
156	Joe Black	20.00	10.00	6.00
157	Bob Miller	7.00	3.50	2.00
158	Tom Carroll	15.00	7.50	4.50

		NR MT	EX	VG
9	Bob Miller	5.00	2.50	1.50
10	Bob Keegan	5.00	2.50	1.50
11	Ferris Fain	6.00	3.00	1.75
12	"Jake" Thies	5.00	2.50	1.50
13	Fred Marsh	5.00	2.50	1.50
14	Jim Finigan	5.00	2.50	1.50
15	Jim Pendleton	5.00	2.50	1.50
16	Roy Sievers	7.00	3.50	2.00
17	Bobby Hofman	5.00	2.50	1.50
18	Russ Kemmerer	5.00	2.50	1.50
19	Billy Herman	10.00	5.00	3.00
20	Andy Carey	9.00	4.50	2.75
21	Alex Grammas	5.00	2.50	1.50
22	Bill Skowron	12.00	6.00	3.50
23	Jack Parks	5.00	2.50	1.50
24	Hal Newhouser	6.00	3.00	1.75
25	Johnny Podres	15.00	7.50	4.50
26	Dick Groat	7.00	3.50	2.00
27	Billy Gardner	5.00	2.50	1.50
28	Ernie Banks	100.00	45.00	27.00
29	Herman Wehmeier	5.00	2.50	1.50
30	Vic Power	5.00	2.50	1.50
31	Warren Spahn	60.00	30.00	18.00
32	Ed McGhee	5.00	2.50	1.50
33	Tom Qualters	5.00	2.50	1.50
34	Wayne Terwilliger	5.00	2.50	1.50
35	Dave Jolly	5.00	2.50	1.50
36	Leo Kiely	5.00	2.50	1.50
37	*Joe Cunningham*	7.00	3.50	2.00
38	Bob Turley	12.00	6.00	3.50
39	Bill Glynn	5.00	2.50	1.50
40	Don Hoak	7.00	3.50	2.00
41	Chuck Stobbs	5.00	2.50	1.50
42	"Windy" McCall	5.00	2.50	1.50
43	Harvey Haddix	6.00	3.00	1.75
44	"Corky" Valentine	5.00	2.50	1.50
45	Hank Sauer	5.00	2.50	1.50
46	Ted Kazanski	5.00	2.50	1.50
47	Hank Aaron	250.00	100.00	63.00
48	Bob Kennedy	5.00	2.50	1.50
49	J.W. Porter	5.00	2.50	1.50
50	Jackie Robinson	175.00	70.00	44.00
51	Jim Hughes	6.00	3.00	1.75
52	Bill Tremel	5.00	2.50	1.50
53	Bill Taylor	5.00	2.50	1.50
54	Lou Limmer	5.00	2.50	1.50
55	"Rip" Repulski	5.00	2.50	1.50
56	Ray Jablonski	5.00	2.50	1.50
57	*Billy O'Dell*	6.00	3.00	1.75
58	Jim Rivera	5.00	2.50	1.50
59	Gair Allie	5.00	2.50	1.50
60	Dean Stone	5.00	2.50	1.50
61	"Spook" Jacobs	5.00	2.50	1.50
62	Thornton Kipper	5.00	2.50	1.50
63	Joe Collins	9.00	4.50	2.75
64	*Gus Triandos*	7.00	3.50	2.00
65	Ray Boone	6.00	3.00	1.75
66	Ron Jackson	5.00	2.50	1.50
67	Wally Moon	6.00	3.00	1.75

		NR MT	EX	VG
159	Johnny Schmitz	7.00	3.50	2.00
160	Ray Narleski	7.00	3.50	2.00
161	*Chuck Tanner*	25.00	12.50	7.50
162	Joe Coleman	15.00	7.50	4.50
163	Faye Throneberry	15.00	7.50	4.50
164	*Roberto Clemente*	900.00	360.00	220.00
165	Don Johnson	15.00	7.50	4.50
166	Hank Bauer	30.00	15.00	9.00
167	Tom Casagrande	15.00	7.50	4.50
168	Duane Pillette	15.00	7.50	4.50
169	Bob Oldis	15.00	7.50	4.50
170	Jim Pearce	15.00	7.50	4.50
171	Dick Brodowski	15.00	7.50	4.50
172	Frank Baumholtz	15.00	7.50	4.50
173	Bob Kline	15.00	7.50	4.50
174	Rudy Minarcin	15.00	7.50	4.50
175	Not Issued			
176	Norm Zauchin	15.00	7.50	4.50
177	Jim Robertson	15.00	7.50	4.50
178	Bobby Adams	15.00	7.50	4.50
179	Jim Bolger	15.00	7.50	4.50
180	Clem Labine	18.00	9.00	5.50
181	Roy McMillan	15.00	7.50	4.50
182	Humberto Robinson	15.00	7.50	4.50
183	Tony Jacobs	15.00	7.50	4.50
184	Harry Perkowski	15.00	7.50	4.50
185	Don Ferrarese	15.00	7.50	4.50
186	Not Issued			
187	Gil Hodges	110.00	50.00	28.00
188	Charlie Silvera	18.00	9.00	5.50
189	Phil Rizzuto	125.00	56.00	35.00
190	Gene Woodling	20.00	10.00	6.00
191	Ed Stanky	18.00	9.00	5.50
192	Jim Delsing	15.00	7.50	4.50
193	Johnny Sain	35.00	17.50	10.50
194	Willie Mays	400.00	160.00	100.00
195	Ed Roebuck	18.00	9.00	5.50
196	Gale Wade	15.00	7.50	4.50
197	Al Smith	15.00	7.50	4.50
198	Yogi Berra	225.00	90.00	56.00
199	Bert Hamric	18.00	9.00	5.50
200	Jack Jensen	35.00	17.50	10.50
201	Sherm Lollar	18.00	9.00	5.50
202	Jim Owens	15.00	7.50	4.50
203	Not Issued			
204	Frank Smith	15.00	7.50	4.50
205	Gene Freese	15.00	7.50	4.50
206	Pete Daley	15.00	7.50	4.50
207	Bill Consolo	15.00	7.50	4.50
208	Ray Moore	15.00	7.50	4.50
209	Not Issued			
210	Duke Snider	400.00	95.00	50.00

1955 Topps Doubleheaders

This set is a throwback to the 1911 T201 Mecca Double Folders. The cards were perforated allowing them to be folded. Open, there is a color painting of a player set against a ballpark background. When folded, a different stadium and player appears, although both share the same lower legs and feet. Back gives abbreviated career histories. Placed side by side in reverse numerical order, the backgrounds form a continuous stadium scene. When open, the cards measure 2-1/16" by 4-7/8." The 66 cards in the set mean 132 total players, all of whom also appeared in the lower number regular 1955 Topps set.

		NR MT	EX	VG
	Complete Set:	3500.00	1750.00	1050.
	Common Player:	25.00	12.50	7.50
1	Al Rosen			
2	Chuck Diering	25.00	12.50	7.50
3	Monte Irvin			
4	Russ Kemmerer	25.00	12.50	7.50
5	Ted Kazanski			
6	Gordon Jones	25.00	12.50	7.50
7	Bill Taylor			
8	Billy O'Dell	25.00	12.50	7.50
9	J.W. Porter			
10	Thornton Kipper	25.00	12.50	7.50
11	Curt Roberts			
12	Arnie Portocarrero	25.00	12.50	7.50
13	Wally Westlake			
14	Frank House	25.00	12.50	7.50
15	"Rube" Walker			
16	Lou Limmer	25.00	12.50	7.50
17	Dean Stone			
18	Charlie White	25.00	12.50	7.50
19	Karl Spooner			
20	Jim Hughes	25.00	12.50	7.50
21	Bill Skowron			
22	Frank Sullivan	25.00	12.50	7.50
23	Jack Shepard			
24	Stan Hack	25.00	12.50	7.50
25	Jackie Robinson			
26	Don Hoak	275.00	137.00	80.00
27	"Dusty" Rhodes			
28	Jim Davis	25.00	12.50	7.50
29	Vic Power			
30	Ed Bailey	25.00	12.50	7.50
31	Howie Pollet			
32	Ernie Banks	150.00	75.00	45.00
33	Jim Pendleton			
34	Gene Conley	25.00	12.50	7.50
35	Karl Olson	25.00	12.50	7.50
36	Andy Carey	25.00	12.50	7.50
37	Wally Moon	25.00	12.50	7.50
38	Joe Cunningham	25.00	12.50	7.50
39	Fred Marsh			
40	"Jake" Thies	25.00	12.50	7.50
41	Ed Lopat			
42	Harvey Haddix	25.00	12.50	7.50
43	Leo Kiely			
44	Chuck Stobbs	25.00	12.50	7.50
45	Al Kaline			
46	"Corky" Valentine	200.00	100.00	60.00
47	"Spook" Jacobs			
48	Johnny Gray	25.00	12.50	7.50
49	Ron Jackson			
50	Jim Finigan	25.00	12.50	7.50
51	Ray Jablonski			
52	Bob Keegan	25.00	12.50	7.50
53	Billy Herman			
54	Sandy Amoros	25.00	12.50	7.50
55	Chuck Harmon			
56	Bob Skinner	25.00	12.50	7.50
57	Dick Hall			
58	Bob Grim	25.00	12.50	7.50
59	Billy Glynn			
60	Bob Miller	25.00	12.50	7.50
61	Billy Gardner			
62	John Hetki	25.00	12.50	7.50
63	Bob Borkowski			
64	Bob Turley	25.00	12.50	7.50
65	Joe Collins			
66	Jack Harshman	25.00	12.50	7.50
67	Jim Hegan			
68	Jack Parks	25.00	12.50	7.50
69	Ted Williams			
70	Hal Smith	300.00	150.00	90.00
71	Gair Allie			
72	Grady Hatton	25.00	12.50	7.50
73	Jerry Lynch			
74	Harry Brecheen	25.00	12.50	7.50

		NR MT	EX	VG
75	Tom Wright			
76	"Bunky" Stewart	25.00	12.50	7.50
77	Dave Hoskins			
78	Ed McGhee	25.00	12.50	7.50
79	Roy Sievers			
80	Art Fowler	25.00	12.50	7.50
81	Danny Schell			
82	Gus Triandos	25.00	12.50	7.50
83	Joe Frazier			
84	Don Mossi	25.00	12.50	7.50
85	Elmer Valo			
86	Hal Brown	25.00	12.50	7.50
87	Bob Kennedy			
88	"Windy" McCall	25.00	12.50	7.50
89	Ruben Gomez			
90	Jim Rivera	25.00	12.50	7.50
91	Lou Ortiz			
92	Milt Bolling	25.00	12.50	7.50
93	Carl Sawatski			
94	Elvin Tappe	25.00	12.50	7.50
95	Dave Jolly			
96	Bobby Hofman	25.00	12.50	7.50
97	Preston Ward			
98	Don Zimmer	25.00	12.50	7.50
99	Bill Renna			
100	Dick Groat	25.00	12.50	7.50
101	Bill Wilson			
102	Bill Tremel	25.00	12.50	7.50
103	Hank Sauer			
104	Camilo Pascual	25.00	12.50	7.50
105	Hank Aaron			
106	Ray Herbert	300.00	150.00	90.00
107	Alex Grammas			
108	Tom Qualters	25.00	12.50	7.50
109	Hal Newhouser			
110	Charlie Bishop	25.00	12.50	7.50
111	Harmon Killebrew			
112	John Podres	110.00	55.00	33.00
113	Ray Boone			
114	Bob Purkey	25.00	12.50	7.50
115	Dale Long			
116	Ferris Fain	25.00	12.50	7.50
117	Steve Bilko			
118	Bob Milliken	25.00	12.50	7.50
119	Mel Parnell			
120	Tom Hurd	25.00	12.50	7.50
121	Ted Kluszewski			
122	Jim Owens	25.00	12.50	7.50
123	Gus Zernial			
124	Bob Trice	25.00	12.50	7.50
125	"Rip" Repulski			
126	Ted Lepcio	25.00	12.50	7.50
127	Warren Spahn			
128	Tom Brewer	200.00	100.00	60.00
129	Jim Gilliam			
130	Ellis Kinder	25.00	12.50	7.50
131	Herm Wehmeier			
132	Wayne Terwilliger	25.00	12.50	7.50

1956 Topps

This 340-card set is quite similar in design to the 1955 Topps set, again using both a portrait and an "action" picture. Some portraits are the same as those used in 1955 (and even 1954). Innovations found in the 1956 Topps set of 2-5/8" by 3-3/4" cards include team cards introduced as part of a regular set. Additionally, there are two unnumbered checklist cards (the complete set price quoted below does not include the checklist cards). Finally, there are cards of the two league presidents, William Harridge and Warren Giles. On the backs, a three-panel cartoon depicts big moments from the player's career while biographical information appears above the cartoon and the statistics below. Card backs for numbers 1-180 can be found with either white or grey cardboard. Some dealers charge a premium for grey backs (#'s 1-100) and white hacks (#'s 101-180).

		NR MT	EX	VG
Complete Set:		5000.00	2500.00	1500.
Common Player: 1-100		5.00	2.50	1.50
Common Player: 101-180		7.50	3.75	2.25
Common Player: 181-260		10.00	5.00	3.00
Common Player: 261-340		7.50	3.75	2.25
1	William Harridge	125.00	15.00	1.75
2	Warren Giles	9.00	3.00	1.75
3	Elmer Valo	5.00	2.50	1.50
4	Carlos Paula	5.00	2.50	1.50
5	Ted Williams	200.00	80.00	50.00
6	Ray Boone	6.00	3.00	1.75
7	Ron Negray	5.00	2.50	1.50
8	Walter Alston	25.00	12.50	7.50
9	Ruben Gomez	5.00	2.50	1.50
10	Warren Spahn	35.00	17.50	10.50
11a	Cubs Team (with date)	40.00	20.00	12.00
11b	Cubs Team (no date, name centered)			
		9.00	4.50	2.75
11c	Cubs Team (no date, name at left)			
		12.00	6.00	3.50
12	Andy Carey	7.50	3.75	2.25
13	Roy Face	7.50	3.75	2.25
14	Ken Boyer	9.00	4.50	2.75
15	Ernie Banks	50.00	25.00	15.00
16	*Hector Lopez*	7.50	3.75	2.25
17	Gene Conley	6.00	3.00	1.75
18	Dick Donovan	5.00	2.50	1.50
19	Chuck Diering	5.00	2.50	1.50
20	Al Kaline	60.00	30.00	18.00
21	Joe Collins	7.50	3.75	2.25
22	Jim Finigan	5.00	2.50	1.50
23	Freddie Marsh	5.00	2.50	1.50
24	Dick Groat	7.50	3.75	2.25
25	Ted Kluszewski	9.00	4.50	2.75
26	Grady Hatton	5.00	2.50	1.50
27	Nelson Burbrink	5.00	2.50	1.50
28	Bobby Hofman	5.00	2.50	1.50
29	Jack Harshman	5.00	2.50	1.50
30	Jackie Robinson	150.00	60.00	38.00
31	Hank Aaron	175.00	70.00	44.00
32	Frank House	5.00	2.50	1.50
33	Roberto Clemente	225.00	90.00	56.00
34	Tom Brewer	5.00	2.50	1.50
35	Al Rosen	9.00	4.50	2.75
36	Rudy Minarcin	5.00	2.50	1.50
37	Alex Grammas	5.00	2.50	1.50
38	Bob Kennedy	5.00	2.50	1.50
39	Don Mossi	6.00	3.00	1.75
40	Bob Turley	9.00	4.50	2.75
41	Hank Sauer	5.00	2.50	1.50
42	Sandy Amoros	6.00	3.00	1.75
43	Ray Moore	5.00	2.50	1.50
44	"Windy" McCall	5.00	2.50	1.50
45	Gus Zernial	6.00	3.00	1.75
46	Gene Freese	5.00	2.50	1.50
47	Art Fowler	5.00	2.50	1.50
48	Jim Hegan	5.00	2.50	1.50
49	*Pedro Ramos*	6.00	3.00	1.75
50	"Dusty" Rhodes	6.00	3.00	1.75
51	Ernie Oravetz	5.00	2.50	1.50
52	Bob Grim	7.50	3.75	2.25
53	Arnold Portocarrero	5.00	2.50	1.50
54	Bob Keegan	5.00	2.50	1.50
55	Wally Moon	6.00	3.00	1.75
56	Dale Long	6.00	3.00	1.75
57	"Duke" Maas	5.00	2.50	1.50
58	Ed Roebuck	6.00	3.00	1.75
59	Jose Santiago	5.00	2.50	1.50

		NR MT	EX	VG			NR MT	EX	VG
60	Mayo Smith	5.00	2.50	1.50	131	Bob Roselli	7.50	3.75	2.25
61	Bill Skowron	9.00	4.50	2.75	132	Bobby Avila	7.50	3.75	2.25
62	Hal Smith	5.00	2.50	1.50	133	Ray Narleski	7.50	3.75	2.25
63	*Roger Craig*	18.00	9.00	5.50	134	Cardinals Team	9.00	4.50	2.75
64	Luis Arroyo	5.00	2.50	1.50	135	Mickey Mantle	650.00	250.00	175.00
65	Johnny O'Brien	5.00	2.50	1.50	136	Johnny Logan	8.00	4.00	2.50
66	Bob Speake	5.00	2.50	1.50	137	Al Silvera	7.50	3.75	2.25
67	Vic Power	5.00	2.50	1.50	138	Johnny Antonelli	8.00	4.00	2.50
68	Chuck Stobbs	5.00	2.50	1.50	139	Tommy Carroll	10.00	5.00	3.00
69	Chuck Tanner	7.50	3.75	2.25	140	*Herb Score*	15.00	7.50	4.50
70	Jim Rivera	5.00	2.50	1.50	141	Joe Frazier	7.50	3.75	2.25
71	Frank Sullivan	5.00	2.50	1.50	142	Gene Baker	7.50	3.75	2.25
72a	Phillies Team (with date)	40.00	20.00	12.00	143	Jim Piersall	10.00	5.00	3.00
72b	Phillies Team (no date, name centered)				144	Leroy Powell	7.50	3.75	2.25
		9.00	4.50	2.75	145	Gil Hodges	35.00	17.50	10.50
72c	Philadelphia Phillies (no date, name at left)				146	Senators Team	9.00	4.50	2.75
		12.00	6.00	3.50	147	Earl Torgeson	7.50	3.75	2.25
73	Wayne Terwilliger	5.00	2.50	1.50	148	Alvin Dark	10.00	5.00	3.00
74	Jim King	5.00	2.50	1.50	149	"Dixie" Howell	7.50	3.75	2.25
75	Roy Sievers	6.00	3.00	1.75	150	"Duke" Snider	100.00	45.00	27.00
76	Ray Crone	5.00	2.50	1.50	151	"Spook" Jacobs	7.50	3.75	2.25
77	Harvey Haddix	6.00	3.00	1.75	152	Billy Hoeft	7.50	3.75	2.25
78	Herman Wehmeier	5.00	2.50	1.50	153	Frank Thomas	7.50	3.75	2.25
79	Sandy Koufax	225.00	90.00	56.00	154	Dave Pope	7.50	3.75	2.25
80	Gus Triandos	6.00	3.00	1.75	155	Harvey Kuenn	9.00	4.50	2.75
81	Wally Westlake	5.00	2.50	1.50	156	Wes Westrum	8.00	4.00	2.50
82	Bill Renna	5.00	2.50	1.50	157	Dick Brodowski	7.50	3.75	2.25
83	Karl Spooner	6.00	3.00	1.75	158	Wally Post	7.50	3.75	2.25
84	"Babe" Birrer	5.00	2.50	1.50	159	Clint Courtney	7.50	3.75	2.25
85a	Indians Team (with date)	40.00	20.00	12.00	160	Billy Pierce	9.00	4.50	2.75
85b	Indians Team (no date, name centered)				161	Joe DeMaestri	7.50	3.75	2.25
		9.00	4.50	2.75	162	"Gus" Bell	8.00	4.00	2.50
85c	Indians Team (no date, name at left)				163	Gene Woodling	8.00	4.00	2.50
		12.00	6.00	3.50	164	Harmon Killebrew	60.00	30.00	18.00
86	Ray Jablonski	5.00	2.50	1.50	165	"Red" Schoendienst	25.00	12.50	7.50
87	Dean Stone	5.00	2.50	1.50	166	Dodgers Team	125.00	56.00	35.00
88	Johnny Kucks	7.50	3.75	2.25	167	Harry Dorish	7.50	3.75	2.25
89	Norm Zauchin	5.00	2.50	1.50	168	Sammy White	7.50	3.75	2.25
90a	Redlegs Team (with date)	40.00	20.00	12.00	169	Bob Nelson	7.50	3.75	2.25
90b	Redlegs Team (no date, name centered)				170	Bill Virdon	9.00	4.50	2.75
		9.00	4.50	2.75	171	Jim Wilson	7.50	3.75	2.25
90c	Redlegs Team (no date, name at left)				172	*Frank Torre*	8.00	4.00	2.50
		12.00	6.00	3.50	173	Johnny Podres	15.00	7.50	4.50
91	Gail Harris	5.00	2.50	1.50	174	Glen Gorbous	7.50	3.75	2.25
92	"Red" Wilson	5.00	2.50	1.50	175	Del Crandall	9.00	4.50	2.75
93	George Susce, Jr.	5.00	2.50	1.50	176	Alex Kellner	7.50	3.75	2.25
94	Ronnie Kline	5.00	2.50	1.50	177	Hank Bauer	15.00	7.50	4.50
95a	Braves Team (with date)	40.00	20.00	12.00	178	Joe Black	8.00	4.00	2.50
95b	Braves Team (no date, name centered)				179	Harry Chiti	7.50	3.75	2.25
		9.00	4.50	2.75	180	Robin Roberts	25.00	12.50	7.50
95c	Braves Team (no date, name at left)				181	Billy Martin	45.00	22.00	13.50
		12.00	6.00	3.50	182	Paul Minner	10.00	5.00	3.00
96	Bill Tremel	5.00	2.50	1.50	183	Stan Lopata	10.00	5.00	3.00
97	Jerry Lynch	5.00	2.50	1.50	184	Don Bessent	11.00	5.50	3.25
98	Camilo Pascual	6.00	3.00	1.75	185	Bill Bruton	11.00	5.50	3.25
99	Don Zimmer	9.00	4.50	2.75	186	Ron Jackson	10.00	5.00	3.00
100a	Orioles Team (with date)	40.00	20.00	12.00	187	Early Wynn	30.00	15.00	9.00
100b	Orioles Team (no date, name centered)				188	White Sox Team	12.00	6.00	3.50
		9.00	4.50	2.75	189	Ned Garver	10.00	5.00	3.00
100c	Orioles Team (no date, name at left)				190	Carl Furillo	18.00	9.00	5.50
		12.00	6.00	3.50	191	Frank Lary	11.00	5.50	3.25
101	Roy Campanella	100.00	45.00	27.00	192	"Smoky" Burgess	11.00	5.50	3.25
102	Jim Davis	7.50	3.75	2.25	193	Wilmer Mizell	10.00	5.00	3.00
103	Willie Miranda	7.50	3.75	2.25	194	Monte Irvin	25.00	12.50	7.50
104	Bob Lennon	7.50	3.75	2.25	195	George Kell	25.00	12.50	7.50
105	Al Smith	7.50	3.75	2.25	196	Tom Poholsky	10.00	5.00	3.00
106	Joe Astroth	7.50	3.75	2.25	197	Granny Hamner	10.00	5.00	3.00
107	Ed Mathews	35.00	17.50	10.50	198	Ed Fitzgerald (Fitz Gerald)	10.00	5.00	3.00
108	Laurin Pepper	7.50	3.75	2.25	199	Hank Thompson	10.00	5.00	3.00
109	Enos Slaughter	25.00	12.50	7.50	200	Bob Feller	75.00	37.00	22.00
110	Yogi Berra	100.00	45.00	27.00	201	"Rip" Repulski	10.00	5.00	3.00
111	Red Sox Team	10.00	5.00	3.00	202	Jim Hearn	10.00	5.00	3.00
112	Dee Fondy	7.50	3.75	2.25	203	Bill Tuttle	10.00	5.00	3.00
113	Phil Rizzuto	45.00	23.00	13.50	204	Art Swanson	10.00	5.00	3.00
114	Jim Owens	7.50	3.75	2.25	205	"Whitey" Lockman	10.00	5.00	3.00
115	Jackie Jensen	10.00	5.00	3.00	206	Erv Palica	10.00	5.00	3.00
116	Eddie O'Brien	7.50	3.75	2.25	207	Jim Small	10.00	5.00	3.00
117	Virgil Trucks	8.00	4.00	2.50	208	Elston Howard	25.00	12.50	7.50
118	"Nellie" Fox	18.00	9.00	5.50	209	Max Surkont	10.00	5.00	3.00
119	*Larry Jackson*	8.00	4.00	2.50	210	Mike Garcia	11.00	5.50	3.25
120	Richie Ashburn	18.00	9.00	5.50	211	Murry Dickson	10.00	5.00	3.00
121	Pirates Team	9.00	4.50	2.75	212	Johnny Temple	10.00	5.00	3.00
122	Willard Nixon	7.50	3.75	2.25	213	Tigers Team	18.00	9.00	5.00
123	Roy McMillan	7.50	3.75	2.25	214	Bob Rush	10.00	5.00	3.00
124	Don Kaiser	7.50	3.75	2.25	215	Tommy Byrne	15.00	7.50	4.50
125	"Minnie" Minoso	10.00	5.00	3.00	216	Jerry Schoonmaker	10.00	5.00	3.00
126	Jim Brady	7.50	3.75	2.25	217	Billy Klaus	10.00	5.00	3.00
127	Willie Jones	7.50	3.75	2.25	218	Joe Nuxall (Nuxhall)	11.00	5.50	3.25
128	Eddie Yost	7.50	3.75	2.25	219	Lew Burdette	12.00	6.00	3.50
129	"Jake" Martin	7.50	3.75	2.25	220	Del Ennis	11.00	5.50	3.25
130	Willie Mays	200.00	80.00	50.00	221	Bob Friend	11.00	5.50	3.25

		NR MT	EX	VG
222	Dave Philley	10.00	5.00	3.00
223	Randy Jackson	11.00	5.50	3.25
224	"Bud" Podbielan	10.00	5.00	3.00
225	Gil McDougald	20.00	10.00	6.00
226	Giants Team	40.00	20.00	12.00
227	Russ Meyer	10.00	5.00	3.00
228	"Mickey" Vernon	11.00	5.50	3.25
229	Harry Brecheen	11.00	5.50	3.25
230	"Chico" Carrasquel	10.00	5.00	3.00
231	Bob Hale	10.00	5.00	3.00
232	"Toby" Atwell	10.00	5.00	3.00
233	Carl Erskine	20.00	10.00	6.00
234	"Pete" Runnels	11.00	5.50	3.25
235	Don Newcombe	18.00	9.00	5.50
236	Athletics Team	12.00	6.00	3.50
237	Jose Valdivielso	10.00	5.00	3.00
238	Walt Dropo	11.00	5.50	3.25
239	Harry Simpson	10.00	5.00	3.00
240	"Whitey" Ford	70.00	35.00	21.00
241	Don Mueller	10.00	5.00	3.00
242	Hershell Freeman	10.00	5.00	3.00
243	Sherm Lollar	11.00	5.50	3.25
244	Bob Buhl	11.00	5.50	3.25
245	Billy Goodman	10.00	5.00	3.00
246	Tom Gorman	10.00	5.00	3.00
247	Bill Sarni	10.00	5.00	3.00
248	Bob Porterfield	10.00	5.00	3.00
249	Johnny Klippstein	10.00	5.00	3.00
250	Larry Doby	15.00	7.50	4.50
251	Yankees Team	150.00	60.00	38.00
252	Vernon Law	11.00	5.50	3.25
253	Irv Noren	15.00	7.50	4.50
254	George Crowe	10.00	5.00	3.00
255	Bob Lemon	25.00	12.50	7.50
256	Tom Hurd	10.00	5.00	3.00
257	Bobby Thomson	12.00	6.00	3.50
258	Art Ditmar	10.00	5.00	3.00
259	Sam Jones	10.00	5.00	3.00
260	"Pee Wee" Reese	90.00	45.00	27.00
261	Bobby Shantz	8.00	4.00	2.50
262	Howie Pollet	6.00	3.00	1.75
263	Bob Miller	6.00	3.00	1.75
264	Ray Monzant	6.00	3.00	1.75
265	Sandy Consuegra	6.00	3.00	1.75
266	Don Ferrarese	6.00	3.00	1.75
267	Bob Nieman	7.50	3.75	2.25
268	Dale Mitchell	6.00	3.00	1.75
269	Jack Meyer	6.00	3.00	1.75
270	Billy Loes	8.00	4.00	2.50
271	Foster Castleman	6.00	3.00	1.75
272	Danny O'Connell	6.00	3.00	1.75
273	Walker Cooper	6.00	3.00	1.75
274	Frank Baumholtz	6.00	3.00	1.75
275	Jim Greengrass	6.00	3.00	1.75
276	George Zuverink	6.00	3.00	1.75
277	Daryl Spencer	6.00	3.00	1.75
278	Chet Nichols	6.00	3.00	1.75
279	Johnny Groth	6.00	3.00	1.75
280	Jim Gilliam	10.00	5.00	3.00
281	Art Houtteman	6.00	3.00	1.75
282	Warren Hacker	6.00	3.00	1.75
283	Hal Smith	6.00	3.00	1.75
284	Ike Delock	6.00	3.00	1.75
285	Eddie Miksis	6.00	3.00	1.75
286	Bill Wight	6.00	3.00	1.75
287	Bobby Adams	6.00	3.00	1.75
288	Bob Cerv	15.00	7.50	4.50
289	Hal Jeffcoat	6.00	3.00	1.75
290	Curt Simmons	7.50	3.75	2.25
291	Frank Kellert	6.00	3.00	1.75
292	*Luis Aparicio*	90.00	45.00	27.00
293	Stu Miller	6.00	3.00	1.75
294	Ernie Johnson	6.00	3.00	1.75
295	Clem Labine	8.00	4.00	2.50
296	Andy Seminick	6.00	3.00	1.75
297	Bob Skinner	7.50	3.75	2.25
298	Johnny Schmitz	6.00	3.00	1.75
299	Charley Neal	15.00	7.50	4.50
300	Vic Wertz	7.50	3.75	2.25
301	Marv Grissom	6.00	3.00	1.75
302	Eddie Robinson	9.00	4.50	2.75
303	Jim Dyck	6.00	3.00	1.75
304	Frank Malzone	7.50	3.75	2.25
305	Brooks Lawrence	6.00	3.00	1.75
306	Curt Roberts	6.00	3.00	1.75
307	Hoyt Wilhelm	25.00	12.50	7.50
308	"Chuck" Harmon	6.00	3.00	1.75
309	*Don Blasingame*	7.50	3.75	2.25
310	Steve Gromek	6.00	3.00	1.75
311	Hal Naragon	6.00	3.00	1.75
312	Andy Pafko	8.00	4.00	2.50

		NR MT	EX	VG
313	Gene Stephens	6.00	3.00	1.75
314	Hobie Landrith	6.00	3.00	1.75
315	Milt Bolling	6.00	3.00	1.75
316	Jerry Coleman	10.00	5.00	3.00
317	Al Aber	6.00	3.00	1.75
318	Fred Hatfield	6.00	3.00	1.75
319	Jack Crimian	6.00	3.00	1.75
320	Joe Adcock	8.00	4.00	2.50
321	Jim Konstanty	9.00	4.50	2.75
322	Karl Olson	6.00	3.00	1.75
323	Willard Schmidt	6.00	3.00	1.75
324	"Rocky" Bridges	6.00	3.00	1.75
325	Don Liddle	6.00	3.00	1.75
326	Connie Johnson	6.00	3.00	1.75
327	Bob Wiesler	6.00	3.00	1.75
328	Preston Ward	6.00	3.00	1.75
329	Lou Berberet	6.00	3.00	1.75
330	Jim Busby	6.00	3.00	1.75
331	Dick Hall	6.00	3.00	1.75
332	Don Larsen	20.00	10.00	6.00
333	Rube Walker	7.50	3.75	2.25
334	Bob Miller	6.00	3.00	1.75
335	Don Hoak	7.50	3.75	2.25
336	Ellis Kinder	6.00	3.00	1.75
337	Bobby Morgan	6.00	3.00	1.75
338	Jim Delsing	6.00	3.00	1.75
339	Rance Pless	6.00	3.00	1.75
340	Mickey McDermott	20.00	4.00	2.50
----	Checklist 1/3	225.00	90.00	56.00
----	Checklist 2/4	225.00	90.00	56.00

1956 Topps Hocus Focus Large

These sets are a direct descendant of the 1948 Topps Magic Photo" issue. Again, the baseball players were part of a larger overall series covering several topical areas. There are two distinct issues of Hocus Focus cards in 1956. The "large" cards, measuring 1" by 1-5/8," consists of 18 players. The "small" cards, 7/8 by 1-3/8," state on the back that they are a series of 23, though only 13 are known. Besides players on the cards themselves, the easiest way to distinguish Hocus Focus cards of 1956 from the Magic Photos series of 1948 is to remember that the 1956 cards actually have the words "Hocus Focus" on the back. The photos on these cards were developed by wetting the cards surface and exposing to light. Prices below are for cards with well-developed pictures. Cards with poorly developed photos are worth significantly less.

		NR MT	EX	VG
	Complete Set:	525.00	262.00	157.00
	Common Player:	10.00	5.00	3.00
1	Dick Groat	25.00	12.50	7.50
2	Ed Lopat	25.00	12.50	7.50
3	Hank Sauer	10.00	5.00	3.00
4	"Dusty" Rhodes	10.00	5.00	3.00
5	Ted Williams	125.00	62.00	37.00
6	Harvey Haddix	10.00	5.00	3.00
7	Ray Boone	10.00	5.00	3.00
8	Al Rosen	25.00	12.50	7.50
9	Mayo Smith	10.00	5.00	3.00
10	Warren Spahn	70.00	35.00	21.00
11	Jim Rivera	10.00	5.00	3.00

		NR MT	EX	VG
12	Ted Kluszewski	25.00	12.50	7.50
13	Gus Zernial	10.00	5.00	3.00
14	Jackie Robinson	100.00	50.00	30.00
15	Hal Smith	10.00	5.00	3.00
16	Johnny Schmitz	10.00	5.00	3.00
17	"Spook" Jacobs	10.00	5.00	3.00
18	Mel Parnell	10.00	5.00	3.00

1956 Topps Pins

One of Topps first specialty issues, the 60-pin set of ballplayers issued in 1956 contains a high percentage of big-name stars which, combined with the scarcity of the pins, makes collecting a complete set extremely challenging. Compounding the situation is the fact that some pins are seen far less often than others, though the reason is unknown. Chuck Stobbs, Hector Lopez and Chuck Diering are unaccountably scarce. Measuring 1-1/8" in diameter, the pins utilize the same portraits found on 1956 Topps baseball cards. The photos are set against a solid color background.

		NR MT	EX	VG
Complete Set:		2500.00	1250.00	750.00
Common Player:		15.00	7.50	4.50
(1)	Hank Aaron	90.00	45.00	27.00
(2)	Sandy Amoros	15.00	7.50	4.50
(3)	Luis Arroyo	15.00	7.50	4.50
(4)	Ernie Banks	50.00	25.00	15.00
(5)	Yogi Berra	70.00	35.00	21.00
(6)	Joe Black	15.00	7.50	4.50
(7)	Ray Boone	15.00	7.50	4.50
(8)	Ken Boyer	20.00	10.00	6.00
(9)	Joe Collins	15.00	7.50	4.50
(10)	Gene Conley	15.00	7.50	4.50
(11)	Chuck Diering	225.00	112.00	67.00
(12)	Dick Donovan	15.00	7.50	4.50
(13)	Jim Finigan	15.00	7.50	4.50
(14)	Art Fowler	15.00	7.50	4.50
(15)	Ruben Gomez	15.00	7.50	4.50
(16)	Dick Groat	20.00	10.00	6.00
(17)	Harvey Haddix	15.00	7.50	4.50
(18)	Jack Harshman	15.00	7.50	4.50
(19)	Grady Hatton	15.00	7.50	4.50
(20)	Jim Hegan	15.00	7.50	4.50
(21)	Gil Hodges	40.00	20.00	12.00
(22)	Bobby Hofman	15.00	7.50	4.50
(23)	Frank House	15.00	7.50	4.50
(24)	Jackie Jensen	20.00	10.00	6.00
(25)	Al Kaline	60.00	30.00	18.00
(26)	Bob Kennedy	15.00	7.50	4.50
(27)	Ted Kluszewski	25.00	12.50	7.50
(28)	Dale Long	15.00	7.50	4.50
(29)	Hector Lopez	200.00	100.00	60.00
(30)	Ed Mathews	40.00	20.00	12.00
(31)	Willie Mays	90.00	45.00	27.00
(32)	Roy McMillan	15.00	7.50	4.50
(33)	Willie Miranda	15.00	7.50	4.50
(34)	Wally Moon	15.00	7.50	4.50
(35)	Don Mossi	15.00	7.50	4.50
(36)	Ron Negray	15.00	7.50	4.50
(37)	Johnny O'Brien	15.00	7.50	4.50
(38)	Carlos Paula	15.00	7.50	4.50
(39)	Vic Power	15.00	7.50	4.50
(40)	Jim Rivera	15.00	7.50	4.50

		NR MT	EX	VG
(41)	Phil Rizzuto	40.00	20.00	12.00
(42)	Jackie Robinson	90.00	45.00	27.00
(43)	Al Rosen	25.00	12.50	7.50
(44)	Hank Sauer	15.00	7.50	4.50
(45)	Roy Sievers	15.00	7.50	4.50
(46)	Bill Skowron	20.00	10.00	6.00
(47)	Al Smith	15.00	7.50	4.50
(48)	Hal Smith	15.00	7.50	4.50
(49)	Mayo Smith	15.00	7.50	4.50
(50)	Duke Snider	70.00	35.00	21.00
(51)	Warren Spahn	50.00	25.00	15.00
(52)	Karl Spooner	15.00	7.50	4.50
(53)	Chuck Stobbs	175.00	87.00	52.00
(54)	Frank Sullivan	15.00	7.50	4.50
(55)	Bill Tremel	15.00	7.50	4.50
(56)	Gus Triandos	15.00	7.50	4.50
(57)	Bob Turley	20.00	10.00	6.00
(58)	Herman Wehmeier	15.00	7.50	4.50
(59)	Ted Williams	110.00	55.00	33.00
(60)	Gus Zernial	15.00	7.50	4.50

1957 Topps

For 1957, Topps reduced the size of its cards to the now-standard 2-1/2" by 3-1/2." Set size was increased to 407 cards. Another change came in the form of the use of real color photographs as opposed to the hand-colored black and whites of previous years. For the first time since 1954, there were also cards with more than one player. The two, "Dodger Sluggers" and "Yankees' Power Hitters" began a trend toward the increased use of muliltple-player cards. Another first-time innovation, found on the backs, is complete players statistics. The scarce cards in the set are not the highest numbers, but rather numbers 265-352. Four unnumbered checklist cards were issued along with the set. They are quite expensive and are not included in the complete set prices quoted below.

	NR MT	EX	VG
Complete Set:	6500.00	3250.00	1950.
Common Player: 1-264	5.00	2.50	1.50
Common Player: 265-352	15.00	7.50	4.50
Common Player: 353-407	5.00	2.50	1.50

		NR MT	EX	VG
1	Ted Williams	425.00	100.00	38.00
2	Yogi Berra	125.00	56.00	35.00
3	Dale Long	5.00	2.50	1.50
4	Johnny Logan	5.00	2.50	1.50
5	Sal Maglie	8.00	4.00	2.50
6	Hector Lopez	5.00	2.50	1.50
7	Luis Aparicio	20.00	10.00	6.00
8	Don Mossi	5.00	2.50	1.50
9	Johnny Temple	5.00	2.50	1.50
10	Willie Mays	200.00	80.00	50.00
11	George Zuverink	5.00	2.50	1.50
12	Dick Groat	6.00	3.00	1.75
13	Wally Burnette	5.00	2.50	1.50
14	Bob Nieman	5.00	2.50	1.50
15	Robin Roberts	20.00	10.00	6.00
16	Walt Moryn	5.00	2.50	1.50
17	Billy Gardner	5.00	2.50	1.50
18	*Don Drysdale*	170.00	65.00	40.00
19	Bob Wilson	5.00	2.50	1.50
20	Hank Aaron (photo reversed)	200.00	80.00	50.00

		NR MT	EX	VG			NR MT	EX	VG
21	Frank Sullivan	5.00	2.50	1.50	110	Bill Virdon	6.00	3.00	1.75
22	Jerry Snyder (photo actually Ed Fitz Gerald)		2.50	1.50	111	Hal Smith	5.00	2.50	1.50
23	Sherm Lollar	5.00	2.50	1.50	112	Tom Brewer	5.00	2.50	1.50
24	*Bill Mazeroski*	20.00	10.00	6.00	113	Wilmer Mizell	5.00	2.50	1.50
25	Whitey Ford	45.00	22.00	13.50	114	Braves Team	10.00	5.00	3.00
26	Bob Boyd	5.00	2.50	1.50	115	Jim Gilliam	8.00	4.00	2.50
27	Ted Kazanski	5.00	2.50	1.50	116	Mike Fornieles	5.00	2.50	1.50
28	Gene Conley	5.00	2.50	1.50	117	Joe Adcock	6.00	3.00	1.75
29	*Whitey Herzog*	18.00	9.00	5.50	118	Bob Porterfield	5.00	2.50	1.50
30	Pee Wee Reese	50.00	30.00	15.00	119	Stan Lopata	5.00	2.50	1.50
31	Ron Northey	5.00	2.50	1.50	120	Bob Lemon	18.00	9.00	5.50
32	Hersh Freeman	5.00	2.50	1.50	121	*Cletis Boyer*	10.00	5.00	3.00
33	Jim Small	5.00	2.50	1.50	122	Ken Boyer	8.00	4.00	2.50
34	Tom Sturdivant	6.00	3.00	1.75	123	Steve Ridzik	5.00	2.50	1.50
35	*Frank Robinson*	175.00	70.00	44.00	124	Dave Philley	5.00	2.50	1.50
36	Bob Grim	6.00	3.00	1.75	125	Al Kaline	60.00	30.00	18.00
37	Frank Torre	5.00	2.50	1.50	126	Bob Wiesler	5.00	2.50	1.50
38	Nellie Fox	12.00	6.00	3.50	127	Bob Buhl	5.00	2.50	1.50
39	Al Worthington	5.00	2.50	1.50	128	Ed Bailey	5.00	2.50	1.50
40	Early Wynn	18.00	9.00	5.50	129	Saul Rogovin	5.00	2.50	1.50
41	Hal Smith	5.00	2.50	1.50	130	Don Newcombe	10.00	5.00	3.00
42	Dee Fondy	5.00	2.50	1.50	131	Milt Bolling	5.00	2.50	1.50
43	Connie Johnson	5.00	2.50	1.50	132	Art Ditmar	6.00	3.00	1.75
44	Joe DeMaestri	5.00	2.50	1.50	133	Del Crandall	6.00	3.00	1.75
45	Carl Furillo	9.00	4.50	2.75	134	Don Kaiser	5.00	2.50	1.50
46	Bob Miller	5.00	2.50	1.50	135	Bill Skowron	12.00	6.00	3.50
47	Don Blasingame	5.00	2.50	1.50	136	Jim Hegan	5.00	2.50	1.50
48	Bill Bruton	5.00	2.50	1.50	137	Bob Rush	5.00	2.50	1.50
49	Daryl Spencer	5.00	2.50	1.50	138	Minnie Minoso	8.00	4.00	2.50
50	Herb Score	6.00	3.00	1.75	139	Lou Kretlow	5.00	2.50	1.50
51	Clint Courtney	5.00	2.50	1.50	140	Frank Thomas	5.00	2.50	1.50
52	Lee Walls	5.00	2.50	1.50	141	Al Aber	5.00	2.50	1.50
53	Clem Labine	6.00	3.00	1.75	142	Charley Thompson	5.00	2.50	1.50
54	Elmer Valo	5.00	2.50	1.50	143	Andy Pafko	6.00	3.00	1.75
55	Ernie Banks	70.00	35.00	21.00	144	Ray Narleski	5.00	2.50	1.50
56	Dave Sisler	5.00	2.50	1.50	145	Al Smith	5.00	2.50	1.50
57	Jim Lemon	5.00	2.50	1.50	146	Don Ferrarese	5.00	2.50	1.50
58	Ruben Gomez	5.00	2.50	1.50	147	Al Walker	6.00	3.00	1.75
59	Dick Williams	6.00	3.00	1.75	148	Don Mueller	5.00	2.50	1.50
60	Billy Hoeft	5.00	2.50	1.50	149	Bob Kennedy	5.00	2.50	1.50
61	Dusty Rhodes	5.00	2.50	1.50	150	Bob Friend	6.00	3.00	1.75
62	Billy Martin	40.00	20.00	12.00	151	Willie Miranda	5.00	2.50	1.50
63	Ike Delock	5.00	2.50	1.50	152	Jack Harshman	5.00	2.50	1.50
64	Pete Runnels	6.00	3.00	1.75	153	Karl Olson	5.00	2.50	1.50
65	Wally Moon	5.00	2.50	1.50	154	Red Schoendienst	20.00	10.00	6.00
66	Brooks Lawrence	5.00	2.50	1.50	155	Jim Brosnan	5.00	2.50	1.50
67	Chico Carrasquel	5.00	2.50	1.50	156	Gus Triandos	5.00	2.50	1.50
68	Ray Crone	5.00	2.50	1.50	157	Wally Post	5.00	2.50	1.50
69	Roy McMillan	5.00	2.50	1.50	158	Curt Simmons	6.00	3.00	1.75
70	Richie Ashburn	15.00	7.50	4.50	159	Solly Drake	5.00	2.50	1.50
71	Murry Dickson	5.00	2.50	1.50	160	Billy Pierce	6.00	3.00	1.75
72	Bill Tuttle	5.00	2.50	1.50	161	Pirates Team	8.00	4.00	2.50
73	George Crowe	5.00	2.50	1.50	162	Jack Meyer	5.00	2.50	1.50
74	Vito Valentinetti	5.00	2.50	1.50	163	Sammy White	5.00	2.50	1.50
75	Jim Piersall	6.00	3.00	1.75	164	Tommy Carroll	6.00	3.00	1.75
76	Bob Clemente	125.00	56.00	35.00	165	Ted Kluszewski	18.00	9.00	5.50
77	Paul Foytack	5.00	2.50	1.50	166	Roy Face	6.00	3.00	1.75
78	Vic Wertz	6.00	3.00	1.75	167	Vic Power	5.00	2.50	1.50
79	*Lindy McDaniel*	6.00	3.00	1.75	168	Frank Lary	6.00	3.00	1.75
80	Gil Hodges	50.00	30.00	15.00	169	Herb Plews	5.00	2.50	1.50
81	Herm Wehmeier	5.00	2.50	1.50	170	Duke Snider	85.00	42.00	25.00
82	Elston Howard	10.00	5.00	3.00	171	Red Sox Team	9.00	4.50	2.75
83	Lou Skizas	5.00	2.50	1.50	172	Gene Woodling	6.00	3.00	1.75
84	Moe Drabowsky	5.00	2.50	1.50	173	Roger Craig	8.00	4.00	2.50
85	Larry Doby	8.00	4.00	2.50	174	Willie Jones	5.00	2.50	1.50
86	Bill Sarni	5.00	2.50	1.50	175	Don Larsen	8.00	4.00	2.50
87	Tom Gorman	5.00	2.50	1.50	176	Gene Baker	5.00	2.50	1.50
88	Harvey Kuenn	6.00	3.00	1.75	177	Eddie Yost	5.00	2.50	1.50
89	Roy Sievers	5.00	2.50	1.50	178	Don Bessent	5.00	2.50	1.50
90	Warren Spahn	50.00	30.00	15.00	179	Ernie Oravetz	5.00	2.50	1.50
91	Mack Burk	5.00	2.50	1.50	180	Gus Bell	5.00	2.50	1.50
92	Mickey Vernon	6.00	3.00	1.75	181	Dick Donovan	5.00	2.50	1.50
93	Hal Jeffcoat	5.00	2.50	1.50	182	Hobie Landrith	5.00	2.50	1.50
94	Bobby Del Greco	5.00	2.50	1.50	183	Cubs Team	8.00	4.00	2.50
95	Mickey Mantle	650.00	250.00	175.00	184	*Tito Francona*	6.00	3.00	1.75
96	*Hank Aguirre*	6.00	3.00	1.75	185	Johnny Kucks	6.00	3.00	1.75
97	Yankees Team	30.00	15.00	9.00	186	Jim King	5.00	2.50	1.50
98	Al Dark	8.00	4.00	2.50	187	Virgil Trucks	5.00	2.50	1.50
99	Bob Keegan	5.00	2.50	1.50	188	Felix Mantilla	5.00	2.50	1.50
100	League Presidents (Warren Giles, William Harridge)	6.00	3.00	1.75	189	Willard Nixon	5.00	2.50	1.50
101	Chuck Stobbs	5.00	2.50	1.50	190	Randy Jackson	5.00	2.50	1.50
102	Ray Boone	5.00	2.50	1.50	191	Joe Margoneri	5.00	2.50	1.50
103	Joe Nuxhall	6.00	3.00	1.75	192	Jerry Coleman	6.00	3.00	1.75
104	Hank Foiles	5.00	2.50	1.50	193	Del Rice	5.00	2.50	1.50
105	Johnny Antonelli	5.00	2.50	1.50	194	Hal Brown	5.00	2.50	1.50
106	Ray Moore	5.00	2.50	1.50	195	Bobby Avila	5.00	2.50	1.50
107	Jim Rivera	5.00	2.50	1.50	196	Larry Jackson	5.00	2.50	1.50
108	Tommy Byrne	6.00	3.00	1.75	197	Hank Sauer	5.00	2.50	1.50
109	Hank Thompson	5.00	2.50	1.50	198	Tigers Team	9.00	4.50	2.75
					199	Vernon Law	6.00	3.00	1.75
					200	Gil McDougald	12.00	6.00	3.50

#	Name	NR MT	EX	VG		#	Name	NR MT	EX	VG
201	Sandy Amoros	5.00	2.50	1.50		292	Billy Klaus	15.00	7.50	4.50
202	Dick Gernert	5.00	2.50	1.50		293	Ted Abernathy	15.00	7.50	4.50
203	Hoyt Wilhelm	18.00	9.00	5.50		294	Rocky Bridges	15.00	7.50	4.50
204	Athletics Team	8.00	4.00	2.50		295	Joe Collins	18.00	9.00	5.50
205	Charley Maxwell	5.00	2.50	1.50		296	Johnny Klippstein	15.00	7.50	4.50
206	Willard Schmidt	5.00	2.50	1.50		297	Jack Crimian	15.00	7.50	4.50
207	Billy Hunter	5.00	2.50	1.50		298	Irv Noren	15.00	7.50	4.50
208	Lew Burdette	6.00	3.00	1.75		299	Chuck Harmon	15.00	7.50	4.50
209	Bob Skinner	5.00	2.50	1.50		300	Mike Garcia	18.00	9.00	5.50
210	Roy Campanella	80.00	40.00	24.00		301	Sam Esposito	15.00	7.50	4.50
211	Camilo Pascual	5.00	2.50	1.50		302	Sandy Koufax	300.00	120.00	75.00
212	*Rocco Colavito*	35.00	17.50	10.50		303	Billy Goodman	15.00	7.50	4.50
213	Les Moss	5.00	2.50	1.50		304	Joe Cunningham	18.00	9.00	5.50
214	Phillies Team	8.00	4.00	2.50		305	Chico Fernandez	15.00	7.50	4.50
215	Enos Slaughter	20.00	10.00	6.00		306	Darrell Johnson	18.00	9.00	5.50
216	Marv Grissom	5.00	2.50	1.50		307	Jack Phillips	15.00	7.50	4.50
217	Gene Stephens	5.00	2.50	1.50		308	Dick Hall	15.00	7.50	4.50
218	Ray Jablonski	5.00	2.50	1.50		309	Jim Busby	15.00	7.50	4.50
219	Tom Acker	5.00	2.50	1.50		310	Max Surkont	15.00	7.50	4.50
220	Jackie Jensen	6.00	3.00	1.75		311	Al Pilarcik	15.00	7.50	4.50
221	Dixie Howell	5.00	2.50	1.50		312	*Tony Kubek*	100.00	45.00	27.00
222	Alex Grammas	5.00	2.50	1.50		313	Mel Parnell	18.00	9.00	5.50
223	Frank House	5.00	2.50	1.50		314	Ed Bouchee	15.00	7.50	4.50
224	Marv Blaylock	5.00	2.50	1.50		315	Lou Berberet	15.00	7.50	4.50
225	Harry Simpson	5.00	2.50	1.50		316	Billy O'Dell	15.00	7.50	4.50
226	Preston Ward	5.00	2.50	1.50		317	Giants Team	40.00	20.00	12.00
227	Jerry Staley	5.00	2.50	1.50		318	Mickey McDermott	15.00	7.50	4.50
228	Smoky Burgess	6.00	3.00	1.75		319	Gino Cimoli	18.00	9.00	5.50
229	George Susce	5.00	2.50	1.50		320	Neil Chrisley	15.00	7.50	4.50
230	George Kell	18.00	9.00	5.50		321	Red Murff	15.00	7.50	4.50
231	Solly Hemus	5.00	2.50	1.50		322	Redlegs Team	40.00	20.00	12.00
232	Whitey Lockman	5.00	2.50	1.50		323	Wes Westrum	18.00	9.00	5.50
233	Art Fowler	5.00	2.50	1.50		324	Dodgers Team	90.00	45.00	27.00
234	Dick Cole	5.00	2.50	1.50		325	Frank Bolling	15.00	7.50	4.50
235	Tom Poholsky	5.00	2.50	1.50		326	Pedro Ramos	15.00	7.50	4.50
236	Joe Ginsberg	5.00	2.50	1.50		327	Jim Pendleton	15.00	7.50	4.50
237	Foster Castleman	5.00	2.50	1.50		328	*Brooks Robinson*	300.00	120.00	75.00
238	Eddie Robinson	5.00	2.50	1.50		329	White Sox Team	25.00	12.50	7.50
239	Tom Morgan	5.00	2.50	1.50		330	Jim Wilson	15.00	7.50	4.50
240	Hank Bauer	10.00	5.00	3.00		331	Ray Katt	15.00	7.50	4.50
241	Joe Lonnett	5.00	2.50	1.50		332	Bob Bowman	15.00	7.50	4.50
242	Charley Neal	5.00	2.50	1.50		333	Ernie Johnson	15.00	7.50	4.50
243	Cardinals Team	8.00	4.00	2.50		334	Jerry Schoonmaker	15.00	7.50	4.50
244	Billy Loes	5.00	2.50	1.50		335	Granny Hamner	15.00	7.50	4.50
245	Rip Repulski	5.00	2.50	1.50		336	*Haywood Sullivan*	18.00	9.00	5.50
246	Jose Valdivielso	5.00	2.50	1.50		337	Rene Valdes	18.00	9.00	5.50
247	Turk Lown	5.00	2.50	1.50		338	*Jim Bunning*	90.00	45.00	27.00
248	Jim Finigan	5.00	2.50	1.50		339	Bob Speake	15.00	7.50	4.50
249	Dave Pope	5.00	2.50	1.50		340	Bill Wight	15.00	7.50	4.50
250	Ed Mathews	25.00	12.50	7.50		341	Don Gross	15.00	7.50	4.50
251	Orioles Team	8.00	4.00	2.50		342	Gene Mauch	20.00	10.00	6.00
252	Carl Erskine	10.00	5.00	3.00		343	Taylor Phillips	15.00	7.50	4.50
253	Gus Zernial	5.00	2.50	1.50		344	Paul LaPalme	15.00	7.50	4.50
254	Ron Negray	5.00	2.50	1.50		345	Paul Smith	15.00	7.50	4.50
255	Charlie Silvera	5.00	2.50	1.50		346	Dick Littlefield	15.00	7.50	4.50
256	Ronnie Kline	5.00	2.50	1.50		347	Hal Naragon	15.00	7.50	4.50
257	Walt Dropo	5.00	2.50	1.50		348	Jim Hearn	15.00	7.50	4.50
258	Steve Gromek	5.00	2.50	1.50		349	Nelson King	15.00	7.50	4.50
259	Eddie O'Brien	5.00	2.50	1.50		350	Eddie Miksis	15.00	7.50	4.50
260	Del Ennis	5.00	2.50	1.50		351	Dave Hillman	15.00	7.50	4.50
261	Bob Chakales	5.00	2.50	1.50		352	Ellis Kinder	15.00	7.50	4.50
262	Bobby Thomson	6.00	3.00	1.75		353	Cal Neeman	5.00	2.50	1.50
263	George Strickland	5.00	2.50	1.50		354	Rip Coleman	5.00	2.50	1.50
264	Bob Turley	8.00	4.00	2.50		355	Frank Malzone	5.00	2.50	1.50
265	Harvey Haddix	20.00	10.00	6.00		356	Faye Throneberry	5.00	2.50	1.50
266	Ken Kuhn	15.00	7.50	4.50		357	Earl Torgeson	5.00	2.50	1.50
267	Danny Kravitz	15.00	7.50	4.50		358	Jerry Lynch	5.00	2.50	1.50
268	Jackie Collum	15.00	7.50	4.50		359	Tom Cheney	5.00	2.50	1.50
269	Bob Cerv	15.00	7.50	4.50		360	Johnny Groth	5.00	2.50	1.50
270	Senators Team	25.00	12.50	7.50		361	Curt Barclay	5.00	2.50	1.50
271	Danny O'Connell	15.00	7.50	4.50		362	Roman Mejias	5.00	2.50	1.50
272	Bobby Shantz	25.00	12.50	7.50		363	Eddie Kasko	5.00	2.50	1.50
273	Jim Davis	15.00	7.50	4.50		364	Cal McLish	5.00	2.50	1.50
274	Don Hoak	18.00	9.00	5.50		365	Ossie Virgil	5.00	2.50	1.50
275	Indians Team	25.00	12.50	7.50		366	Ken Lehman	5.00	2.50	1.50
276	Jim Pyburn	15.00	7.50	4.50		367	Ed Fitz Gerald	5.00	2.50	1.50
277	Johnny Podres	60.00	30.00	18.00		368	Bob Purkey	5.00	2.50	1.50
278	Fred Hatfield	15.00	7.50	4.50		369	Milt Graff	5.00	2.50	1.50
279	Bob Thurman	15.00	7.50	4.50		370	Warren Hacker	5.00	2.50	1.50
280	Alex Kellner	15.00	7.50	4.50		371	Bob Lennon	5.00	2.50	1.50
281	Gail Harris	15.00	7.50	4.50		372	Norm Zauchin	5.00	2.50	1.50
282	Jack Dittmer	15.00	7.50	4.50		373	Pete Whisenant	5.00	2.50	1.50
283	*Wes Covington*	18.00	9.00	5.50		374	Don Cardwell	5.00	2.50	1.50
284	Don Zimmer	20.00	10.00	6.00		375	*Jim Landis*	6.00	3.00	1.75
285	Ned Garver	15.00	7.50	4.50		376	Don Elston	5.00	2.50	1.50
286	*Bobby Richardson*	90.00	45.00	27.00		377	Andre Rodgers	5.00	2.50	1.50
287	Sam Jones	15.00	7.50	4.50		378	Elmer Singleton	5.00	2.50	1.50
288	Ted Lepcio	15.00	7.50	4.50		379	Don Lee	5.00	2.50	1.50
289	Jim Bolger	15.00	7.50	4.50		380	Walker Cooper	5.00	2.50	1.50
290	Andy Carey	18.00	9.00	5.50		381	Dean Stone	5.00	2.50	1.50
291	Windy McCall	15.00	7.50	4.50		382	Jim Brideweser	5.00	2.50	1.50

		NR MT	EX	VG
383	*Juan Pizarro*	6.00	3.00	1.75
384	Bobby Gene Smith	5.00	2.50	1.50
385	Art Houtteman	5.00	2.50	1.50
386	Lyle Luttrell	5.00	2.50	1.50
387	*Jack Sanford*	6.00	3.00	1.75
388	Pete Daley	5.00	2.50	1.50
389	Dave Jolly	5.00	2.50	1.50
390	Reno Bertoia	5.00	2.50	1.50
391	*Ralph Terry*	8.00	4.00	2.50
392	Chuck Tanner	6.00	3.00	1.75
393	Raul Sanchez	5.00	2.50	1.50
394	Luis Arroyo	5.00	2.50	1.50
395	Bubba Phillips	5.00	2.50	1.50
396	Casey Wise	5.00	2.50	1.50
397	Roy Smalley	5.00	2.50	1.50
398	Al Cicotte	6.00	3.00	1.75
399	Billy Consolo	5.00	2.50	1.50
400	Dodgers' Sluggers (Roy Campanella, Carl Furillo, Gil Hodges, Duke Snider)	150.00	60.00	38.00
401	*Earl Battey*	6.00	3.00	1.75
402	Jim Pisoni	5.00	2.50	1.50
403	Dick Hyde	5.00	2.50	1.50
404	Harry Anderson	5.00	2.50	1.50
405	Duke Maas	5.00	2.50	1.50
406	Bob Hale	5.00	2.50	1.50
407	Yankees' Power Hitters (Yogi Berra, Mickey Mantle)	275.00	110.00	69.00
---a	Checklist Series 1-2 (Big Blony ad on back)	125.00	56.00	35.00
---b	Checklist Series 1-2 (Bazooka ad on back)	125.00	56.00	35.00
---a	Checklist Series 2-3 (Big Blony ad on back)	175.00	70.00	44.00
---b	Checklist Series 2-3 (Bazooka ad on back)	175.00	70.00	44.00
---a	Checklist Series 3-4 (Big Blony ad on back)	350.00	140.00	88.00
---b	Checklist Series 3-4 (Bazooka ad on back)	350.00	140.00	88.00
---a	Checklist Series 4-5 (Big Blony ad on back)	400.00	160.00	100.00
---b	Checklist Series 4-5 (Bazooka ad on back)	400.00	160.00	100.00
——	Contest Card (Saturday, May 4th)	15.00	7.50	4.50
——	Contest Card (Saturday, May 25th)	15.00	7.50	4.50
——	Contest Card (Saturday, June 22nd)	15.00	7.50	4.50
——	Contest Card (Friday, July 19)	15.00	7.50	4.50
——	Lucky Penny Insert Card	15.00	7.50	4.50

1958 Topps

Topps continued to expand its set size in 1958 with the release of a 494-card set. One card (#145) was not issued after Ed Bouchee was suspended from baseball. Cards retained the 2-1/2" by 3-1/2" size. There are a number of variations, including yellow or white lettering on 33 cards between numbers 2-108 (higher priced yellow letter variations checklisted below are not included in the complete set prices). The number of multiple-player cards was increased. A major innovation is the addition of 20 "All-Star" cards. For the first time, checklists were incorporated into the numbered series, as the backs of team cards.

		NR MT	EX	VG
	Complete Set:	3700.00	1850.00	1110.
	Common Player: 1-110	5.00	2.50	1.50
	Common Player: 111-440	2.50	1.25	.70
	Common Player: 441-495	2.00	1.00	.60
1	Ted Williams	375.00	80.00	35.00
2a	Bob Lemon (yellow team letters)	35.00	17.50	10.50
2b	Bob Lemon (white team letters)	15.00	7.50	4.50
3	Alex Kellner	5.00	2.50	1.50
4	Hank Foiles	5.00	2.50	1.50
5	Willie Mays	125.00	56.00	35.00
6	George Zuverink	5.00	2.50	1.50
7	Dale Long	5.00	2.50	1.50
8a	Eddie Kasko (yellow name letters)	20.00	10.00	6.00
8b	Eddie Kasko (white name letters)	5.00	2.50	1.50
9	Hank Bauer	9.00	4.50	2.75
10	Lou Burdette	8.00	4.00	2.50
11a	Jim Rivera (yellow team letters)	20.00	10.00	6.00
11b	Jim Rivera (white team letters)	5.00	2.50	1.50
12	George Crowe	5.00	2.50	1.50
13a	Billy Hoeft (yellow team letters)	20.00	10.00	6.00
13b	Billy Hoeft (white name, orange triangle by foot)	6.00	3.00	1.75
13c	Billy Hoeft (white name, red triangle by foot)	5.00	2.50	1.50
14	Rip Repulski	5.00	2.50	1.50
15	Jim Lemon	5.00	2.50	1.50
16	Charley Neal	5.00	2.50	1.50
17	Felix Mantilla	5.00	2.50	1.50
18	Frank Sullivan	5.00	2.50	1.50
19	Giants Team/Checklist 1-88	10.00	5.00	3.00
20a	Gil McDougald (yellow name letters)	25.00	12.50	7.50
20b	Gil McDougald (white name letters)	9.00	4.50	2.75
21	Curt Barclay	5.00	2.50	1.50
22	Hal Naragon	5.00	2.50	1.50
23a	Bill Tuttle (yellow name letters)	20.00	10.00	6.00
23b	Bill Tuttle (white name letters)	5.00	2.50	1.50
24a	Hobie Landrith (yellow name letters)	20.00	10.00	6.00
24b	Hobie Landrith (white name letters)	5.00	2.50	1.50
25	Don Drysdale	30.00	15.00	9.00
26	Ron Jackson	5.00	2.50	1.50
27	Bud Freeman	5.00	2.50	1.50
28	Jim Busby	5.00	2.50	1.50
29	Ted Lepcio	5.00	2.50	1.50
30a	Hank Aaron (yellow name letters)	200.00	80.00	50.00
30b	Hank Aaron (white name letters)	125.00	56.00	35.00
31	Tex Clevenger	5.00	2.50	1.50
32a	J.W. Porter (yellow name letters)	20.00	10.00	6.00
32b	J.W. Porter (white name letters)	5.00	2.50	1.50
33a	Cal Neeman (yellow team letters)	20.00	10.00	6.00
33b	Cal Neeman (white team letters)	5.00	2.50	1.50
34	Bob Thurman	5.00	2.50	1.50
35a	Don Mossi (yellow team letters)	20.00	10.00	6.00
35b	Don Mossi (white team letters)	5.00	2.50	1.50
36	Ted Kazanski	5.00	2.50	1.50
37	*Mike McCormick* (photo actually Ray Monzant)	6.00	3.00	1.75
38	Dick Gernert	5.00	2.50	1.50
39	Bob Martyn	5.00	2.50	1.50
40	George Kell	12.00	6.00	3.50
41	Dave Hillman	5.00	2.50	1.50
42	*John Roseboro*	6.00	3.00	1.75
43	Sal Maglie	8.00	4.00	2.50
44	Senators Team/Checklist 1-88	10.00	5.00	3.00
45	Dick Groat	6.00	3.00	1.75
46a	Lou Sleater (yellow name letters)	20.00	10.00	6.00
46b	Lou Sleater (white name letters)	5.00	2.50	1.50
47	*Roger Maris*	300.00	110.00	70.00
48	Chuck Harmon	5.00	2.50	1.50
49	Smoky Burgess	6.00	3.00	1.75
50a	Billy Pierce (yellow team letters)	20.00	10.00	6.00
50b	Billy Pierce (white team letters)	6.00	3.00	1.75
51	Del Rice	5.00	2.50	1.50
52a	Bob Clemente (yellow team letters)	125.00	56.00	35.00
52b	Bob Clemente (white team letters)	70.00	35.00	21.00
53a	Morrie Martin (yellow name letters)	20.00	10.00	6.00
53b	Morrie Martin (white name letters)	5.00	2.50	1.50

		NR MT	EX	VG
54	*Norm Siebern*	7.00	3.50	2.00
55	Chico Carrasquel	5.00	2.50	1.50
56	Bill Fischer	5.00	2.50	1.50
57a	Tim Thompson (yellow name letters)			
		20.00	10.00	6.00
57b	Tim Thompson (white name letters)			
		5.00	2.50	1.50
58a	Art Schult (yellow team letters)	20.00	10.00	6.00
58b	Art Schult (white team letters)	5.00	2.50	1.50
59	Dave Sisler	5.00	2.50	1.50
60a	Del Ennis (yellow name letters)	20.00	10.00	6.00
60b	Del Ennis (white name letters)	5.00	2.50	1.50
61a	Darrell Johnson (yellow name letters)			
		20.00	10.00	6.00
61b	Darrell Johnson (white name letters)			
		6.00	3.00	1.75
62	Joe DeMaestri	5.00	2.50	1.50
63	Joe Nuxhall	6.00	3.00	1.75
64	Joe Lonnett	5.00	2.50	1.50
65a	Von McDaniel (yellow name letters)			
		20.00	10.00	6.00
65b	Von McDaniel (white name letters)			
		5.00	2.50	1.50
66	Lee Walls	5.00	2.50	1.50
67	Joe Ginsberg	5.00	2.50	1.50
68	Daryl Spencer	5.00	2.50	1.50
69	Wally Burnette	5.00	2.50	1.50
70a	Al Kaline (yellow name letters)	90.00	45.00	27.00
70b	Al Kaline (white name letters)	55.00	27.00	16.50
71	Dodgers Team/Checklist 1-88	15.00	7.50	4.50
72	Bud Byerly	5.00	2.50	1.50
73	Pete Daley	5.00	2.50	1.50
74	Roy Face	6.00	3.00	1.75
75	Gus Bell	5.00	2.50	1.50
76a	Dick Farrell (yellow team letters)			
		20.00	10.00	6.00
76b	Dick Farrell (white team letters)	5.00	2.50	1.50
77a	Don Zimmer (yellow team letters)			
		20.00	10.00	6.00
77b	Don Zimmer (white team letters)	6.00	3.00	1.75
78a	Ernie Johnson (yellow team letters)			
		20.00	10.00	6.00
78b	Ernie Johnson (white team letters)			
		5.00	2.50	1.50
79a	Dick Williams (yellow team letters)			
		20.00	10.00	6.00
79b	Dick Williams (white team letters)	6.00	3.00	1.75
80	Dick Drott	5.00	2.50	1.50
81a	*Steve Boros* (yellow team letters)			
		20.00	10.00	6.00
81b	*Steve Boros* (white team letters)	5.00	2.50	1.50
82	Ronnie Kline	5.00	2.50	1.50
83	Bob Hazle	5.00	2.50	1.50
84	Billy O'Dell	5.00	2.50	1.50
85a	Luis Aparicio (yellow team letters)			
		30.00	15.00	9.00
85b	Luis Aparicio (white team letters)			
		12.00	6.00	3.50
86	Valmy Thomas	5.00	2.50	1.50
87	Johnny Kucks	6.00	3.00	1.75
88	Duke Snider	40.00	20.00	12.00
89	Billy Klaus	5.00	2.50	1.50
90	Robin Roberts	15.00	7.50	4.50
91	Chuck Tanner	6.00	3.00	1.75
92a	Clint Courtney (yellow name letters)			
		20.00	10.00	6.00
92b	Clint Courtney (white name letters)			
		5.00	2.50	1.50
93	Sandy Amoros	5.00	2.50	1.50
94	Bob Skinner	5.00	2.50	1.50
95	Frank Bolling	5.00	2.50	1.50
96	Joe Durham	5.00	2.50	1.50
97a	Larry Jackson (yellow name letters)			
		20.00	10.00	6.00
97b	Larry Jackson (white name letters)			
		5.00	2.50	1.50
98a	Billy Hunter (yellow name letters)			
		20.00	10.00	6.00
98b	Billy Hunter (white name letters)	5.00	2.50	1.50
99	Bobby Adams	5.00	2.50	1.50
100a	Early Wynn (yellow team letters)	30.00	15.00	9.00
100b	Early Wynn (white team letters)	15.00	7.50	4.50
101a	Bobby Richardson (yellow name letters)			
		30.00	15.00	9.00
101b	Bobby Richardson (white name letters)			
		10.00	5.00	3.00
102	George Strickland	5.00	2.50	1.50
103	Jerry Lynch	5.00	2.50	1.50
104	Jim Pendleton	5.00	2.50	1.50
105	Billy Gardner	5.00	2.50	1.50
106	Dick Schofield	5.00	2.50	1.50
107	Ossie Virgil	5.00	2.50	1.50
108a	Jim Landis (yellow team letters)	20.00	10.00	6.00
108b	Jim Landis (white team letters)	5.00	2.50	1.50
109	Herb Plews	5.00	2.50	1.50
110	Johnny Logan	5.00	2.50	1.50
111	Stu Miller	2.50	1.25	.70
112	Gus Zernial	2.75	1.50	.80
113	Jerry Walker	2.50	1.25	.70
114	Irv Noren	2.50	1.25	.70
115	Jim Bunning	10.00	5.00	3.00
116	Dave Philley	2.75	1.50	.80
117	Frank Torre	2.50	1.25	.70
118	Harvey Haddix	2.50	1.25	.70
119	Harry Chiti	2.50	1.25	.70
120	Johnny Podres	5.00	2.50	1.50
121	Eddie Miksis	2.50	1.25	.70
122	Walt Moryn	2.50	1.25	.70
123	Dick Tomanek	2.50	1.25	.70
124	Bobby Usher	2.50	1.25	.70
125	Al Dark	3.75	2.00	1.25
126	Stan Palys	2.50	1.25	.70
127	Tom Sturdivant	3.75	2.00	1.25
128	*Willie Kirkland*	2.75	1.50	.80
129	Jim Derrington	2.50	1.25	.70
130	Jackie Jensen	3.75	2.00	1.25
131	Bob Henrich	2.50	1.25	.70
132	Vernon Law	3.25	1.75	1.00
133	Russ Nixon	2.50	1.25	.70
134	Phillies Team/Checklist 89-176	8.00	4.00	2.50
135	Mike Drabowsky	2.50	1.25	.70
136	Jim Finnigan	2.50	1.25	.70
137	Russ Kemmerer	2.50	1.25	.70
138	Earl Torgeson	2.50	1.25	.70
139	George Brunet	2.50	1.25	.70
140	Wes Covington	2.75	1.50	.80
141	Ken Lehman	2.50	1.25	.70
142	Enos Slaughter	18.00	9.00	5.50
143	Billy Muffett	2.50	1.25	.70
144	Bobby Morgan	2.50	1.25	.70
145	Not Issued			
146	Dick Gray	2.50	1.25	.70
147	*Don McMahon*	3.25	1.75	1.00
148	Billy Consolo	2.50	1.25	.70
149	Tom Acker	2.50	1.25	.70
150	Mickey Mantle	475.00	200.00	120.00
151	Buddy Pritchard	2.50	1.25	.70
152	Johnny Antonelli	3.25	1.75	1.00
153	Les Moss	2.50	1.25	.70
154	Harry Byrd	2.50	1.25	.70
155	Hector Lopez	2.50	1.25	.70
156	Dick Hyde	2.50	1.25	.70
157	Dee Fondy	2.50	1.25	.70
158	Indians Team/Checklist 177-264	7.00	3.50	2.00
159	Taylor Phillips	2.50	1.25	.70
160	Don Hoak	2.75	1.50	.80
161	Don Larsen	6.00	3.00	1.75
162	Gil Hodges	18.00	9.00	5.50
163	Jim Wilson	2.50	1.25	.70
164	Bob Taylor	2.50	1.25	.70
165	Bob Nieman	2.50	1.25	.70
166	Danny O'Connell	2.50	1.25	.70
167	Frank Baumann	2.50	1.25	.70
168	Joe Cunningham	2.75	1.50	.80
169	Ralph Terry	2.75	1.50	.80
170	Vic Wertz	3.25	1.75	1.00
171	Harry Anderson	2.50	1.25	.70
172	Don Gross	2.50	1.25	.70
173	Eddie Yost	2.75	1.50	.80
174	A's Team/Checklist 89-176	8.00	4.00	2.50
175	*Marv Throneberry*	8.00	4.00	2.50
176	Bob Buhl	2.75	1.50	.80
177	Al Smith	2.50	1.25	.70
178	Ted Kluszewski	5.00	2.50	1.50
179	Willy Miranda	2.50	1.25	.70
180	Lindy McDaniel	2.50	1.25	.70
181	Willie Jones	2.50	1.25	.70
182	Joe Caffie	2.50	1.25	.70
183	Dave Jolly	2.50	1.25	.70
184	Elvin Tappe	2.50	1.25	.70
185	Ray Boone	2.75	1.50	.80
186	Jack Meyer	2.50	1.25	.70
187	Sandy Koufax	100.00	45.00	27.00
188	Milt Bolling (photo actually Lou Berberet)			
		2.50	1.25	.70
189	George Susce	2.50	1.25	.70
190	Red Schoendienst	15.00	7.50	4.50
191	Art Ceccarelli	2.50	1.25	.70
192	Milt Graff	2.50	1.25	.70
193	*Jerry Lumpe*	5.00	2.50	1.50
194	Roger Craig	3.25	1.75	1.00
195	Whitey Lockman	2.50	1.25	.70

		NR MT	EX	VG
196	Mike Garcia	2.75	1.50	.80
197	Haywood Sullivan	2.75	1.50	.80
198	Bill Virdon	3.25	1.75	1.00
199	Don Blasingame	2.50	1.25	.70
200	Bob Keegan	2.50	1.25	.70
201	Jim Bolger	2.50	1.25	.70
202	*Woody Held*	3.25	1.75	1.00
203	Al Walker	2.50	1.25	.70
204	Leo Kiely	2.50	1.25	.70
205	Johnny Temple	2.50	1.25	.70
206	Bob Shaw	3.25	1.75	1.00
207	Solly Hemus	2.50	1.25	.70
208	Cal McLish	2.50	1.25	.70
209	Bob Anderson	2.50	1.25	.70
210	Wally Moon	2.75	1.50	.80
211	Pete Burnside	2.50	1.25	.70
212	Bubba Phillips	2.50	1.25	.70
213	Red Wilson	2.50	1.25	.70
214	Willard Schmidt	2.50	1.25	.70
215	Jim Gilliam	5.00	2.50	1.50
216	Cards Team/Checklist 177-264	7.00	3.50	2.00
217	Jack Harshman	2.50	1.25	.70
218	Dick Rand	2.50	1.25	.70
219	Camilo Pascual	2.75	1.50	.80
220	Tom Brewer	2.50	1.25	.70
221	Jerry Kindall	2.50	1.25	.70
222	Bud Daley	2.50	1.25	.70
223	Andy Pafko	3.25	1.75	1.00
224	Bob Grim	3.75	2.00	1.25
225	Billy Goodman	2.50	1.25	.70
226	Bob Smith (photo actually Bobby Gene Smith)	2.50	1.25	.70
227	Gene Stephens	2.50	1.25	.70
228	Duke Maas	2.50	1.25	.70
229	Frank Zupo	2.50	1.25	.70
230	Richie Ashburn	8.00	4.00	2.50
231	Lloyd Merritt	2.50	1.25	.70
232	Reno Bertoia	2.50	1.25	.70
233	Mickey Vernon	2.75	1.50	.80
234	Carl Sawatski	2.50	1.25	.70
235	Tom Gorman	2.50	1.25	.70
236	Ed Fitz Gerald	2.50	1.25	.70
237	Bill Wight	2.50	1.25	.70
238	Bill Mazeroski	7.00	3.50	2.00
239	Chuck Stobbs	2.50	1.25	.70
240	Moose Skowron	7.00	3.50	2.00
241	Dick Littlefield	2.50	1.25	.70
242	Johnny Klippstein	2.50	1.25	.70
243	Larry Raines	2.50	1.25	.70
244	*Don Demeter*	2.75	1.50	.80
245	*Frank Lary*	2.75	1.50	.80
246	Yankees Team/Checklist 177-264	30.00	15.00	9.00
247	Casey Wise	2.50	1.25	.70
248	Herm Wehmeier	2.50	1.25	.70
249	Ray Moore	2.50	1.25	.70
250	Roy Sievers	3.25	1.75	1.00
251	Warren Hacker	2.50	1.25	.70
252	Bob Trowbridge	2.50	1.25	.70
253	Don Mueller	2.50	1.25	.70
254	Alex Grammas	2.50	1.25	.70
255	Bob Turley	5.00	2.50	1.50
256	White Sox Team/Checklist 265-352	8.00	4.00	2.50
257	Hal Smith	2.50	1.25	.70
258	Carl Erskine	5.00	2.50	1.50
259	Al Pilarcik	2.50	1.25	.70
260	Frank Malzone	2.75	1.50	.80
261	Turk Lown	2.50	1.25	.70
262	Johnny Groth	2.50	1.25	.70
263	Eddie Bressoud	2.75	1.50	.80
264	Jack Sanford	2.75	1.50	.80
265	Pete Runnels	2.75	1.50	.80
266	Connie Johnson	2.50	1.25	.70
267	Sherm Lollar	2.75	1.50	.80
268	Granny Hamner	2.50	1.25	.70
269	Paul Smith	2.50	1.25	.70
270	Warren Spahn	35.00	17.50	10.50
271	Billy Martin	10.00	5.00	3.00
272	Ray Crone	2.50	1.25	.70
273	Hal Smith	2.50	1.25	.70
274	Rocky Bridges	2.50	1.25	.70
275	Elston Howard	8.00	4.00	2.50
276	Bobby Avila	2.50	1.25	.70
277	Virgil Trucks	2.75	1.50	.80
278	Mack Burk	2.50	1.25	.70
279	Bob Boyd	2.50	1.25	.70
280	Jim Piersall	3.25	1.75	1.00
281	Sam Taylor	2.50	1.25	.70
282	Paul Foytack	2.50	1.25	.70
283	Ray Shearer	2.50	1.25	.70

		NR MT	EX	VG
284	Ray Katt	2.50	1.25	.70
285	Frank Robinson	55.00	28.00	16.50
286	Gino Cimoli	2.50	1.25	.70
287	Sam Jones	2.50	1.25	.70
288	Harmon Killebrew	50.00	30.00	15.00
289	Series Hurling Rivals (Lou Burdette, Bobby Shantz)	4.00	2.00	1.25
290	Dick Donovan	2.50	1.25	.70
291	Don Landrum	2.50	1.25	.70
292	Ned Garver	2.50	1.25	.70
293	Gene Freese	2.50	1.25	.70
294	Hal Jeffcoat	2.50	1.25	.70
295	Minnie Minoso	4.00	2.00	1.25
296	*Ryne Duren*	6.00	3.00	1.75
297	Don Buddin	2.50	1.25	.70
298	Jim Hearn	2.50	1.25	.70
299	Harry Simpson	3.75	2.00	1.25
300	League Presidents (Warren Giles, William Harridge)	3.75	2.00	1.25
301	Randy Jackson	2.50	1.25	.70
302	Mike Baxes	2.50	1.25	.70
303	Neil Chrisley	2.50	1.25	.70
304	Tigers' Big Bats (Al Kaline, Harvey Kuenn)	8.00	4.00	2.50
305	Clem Labine	2.75	1.50	.80
306	Whammy Douglas	2.50	1.25	.70
307	Brooks Robinson	45.00	22.00	13.50
308	Paul Giel	2.50	1.25	.70
309	Gail Harris	2.50	1.25	.70
310	Ernie Banks	40.00	20.00	12.00
311	Bob Purkey	2.50	1.25	.70
312	Red Sox Team/Checklist 353-440	8.00	4.00	2.50
313	Bob Rush	2.50	1.25	.70
314	Dodgers' Boss & Power (Walter Alston, Duke Snider)	15.00	7.50	4.50
315	Bob Friend	3.25	1.75	1.00
316	Tito Francona	2.75	1.50	.80
317	*Albie Pearson*	3.25	1.75	1.00
318	Frank House	2.50	1.25	.70
319	Lou Skizas	2.50	1.25	.70
320	Whitey Ford	35.00	17.50	10.50
321	Sluggers Supreme (Ted Kluszewski, Ted Williams)	15.00	7.50	4.50
322	Harding Peterson	2.50	1.25	.70
323	Elmer Valo	2.50	1.25	.70
324	Hoyt Wilhelm	15.00	7.50	4.50
325	Joe Adcock	3.25	1.75	1.00
326	Bob Miller	2.50	1.25	.70
327	Cubs Team/Checklist 265-352	8.00	4.00	2.50
328	Ike Delock	2.50	1.25	.70
329	Bob Cerv	2.50	1.25	.70
330	Ed Bailey	2.50	1.25	.70
331	Pedro Ramos	2.50	1.25	.70
332	Jim King	2.50	1.25	.70
333	Andy Carey	3.75	2.00	1.25
334	Mound Aces (Bob Friend, Billy Pierce)	3.25	1.75	1.00
335	Ruben Gomez	2.50	1.25	.70
336	Bert Hamric	2.50	1.25	.70
337	Hank Aguirre	2.50	1.25	.70
338	Walt Dropo	2.75	1.50	.80
339	Fred Hatfield	2.50	1.25	.70
340	Don Newcombe	6.00	3.00	1.75
341	Pirates Team/Checklist 265-352	8.00	4.00	2.50
342	Jim Brosnan	2.75	1.50	.80
343	*Orlando Cepeda*	40.00	20.00	12.00
344	Bob Porterfield	2.50	1.25	.70
345	Jim Hegan	2.50	1.25	.70
346	Steve Bilko	2.50	1.25	.70
347	Don Rudolph	2.50	1.25	.70
348	Chico Fernandez	2.50	1.25	.70
349	Murry Dickson	2.50	1.25	.70
350	Ken Boyer	5.00	2.50	1.50
351	Braves' Fence Busters (Hank Aaron, Joe Adcock, Del Crandall, Ed Mathews)	20.00	10.00	6.00
352	Herb Score	3.75	2.00	1.25
353	Stan Lopata	2.50	1.25	.70
354	Art Ditmar	3.75	2.00	1.25
355	Bill Bruton	2.75	1.50	.80
356	Bob Malkmus	2.50	1.25	.70
357	Danny McDevitt	2.50	1.25	.70
358	Gene Baker	2.50	1.25	.70
359	Billy Loes	2.50	1.25	.70
360	Roy McMillan	2.50	1.25	.70
361	Mike Fornieles	2.50	1.25	.70
362	Ray Jablonski	2.50	1.25	.70
363	Don Elston	2.50	1.25	.70
364	Earl Battey	2.75	1.50	.80
365	Tom Morgan	2.50	1.25	.70
366	Gene Green	2.50	1.25	.70

		NR MT	EX	VG
367	Jack Urban	2.50	1.25	.70
368	Rocky Colavito	10.00	5.00	3.00
369	Ralph Lumenti	2.50	1.25	.70
370	Yogi Berra	70.00	35.00	21.00
371	Marty Keough	2.50	1.25	.70
372	Don Cardwell	2.50	1.25	.70
373	Joe Pignatano	2.50	1.25	.70
374	Brooks Lawrence	2.50	1.25	.70
375	Pee Wee Reese	50.00	30.00	15.00
376	Charley Rabe	2.50	1.25	.70
377a	Braves Team (alphabetical checklist on back)	9.00	4.50	2.75
377b	Braves Team (numerical checklist on back)	60.00	30.00	18.00
378	Hank Sauer	2.75	1.50	.80
379	Ray Herbert	2.50	1.25	.70
380	Charley Maxwell	2.50	1.25	.70
381	Hal Brown	2.50	1.25	.70
382	Al Cicotte	3.75	2.00	1.25
383	Lou Berberet	2.50	1.25	.70
384	John Goryl	2.50	1.25	.70
385	Wilmer Mizell	2.50	1.25	.70
386	Birdie's Young Sluggers (Ed Bailey, Frank Robinson, Birdie Tebbetts)	7.00	3.50	2.00
387	Wally Post	2.50	1.25	.70
388	Billy Moran	2.50	1.25	.70
389	Bill Taylor	2.50	1.25	.70
390	Del Crandall	3.25	1.75	1.00
391	Dave Melton	2.50	1.25	.70
392	Bennie Daniels	2.50	1.25	.70
393	Tony Kubek	12.00	6.00	3.50
394	*Jim Grant*	3.25	1.75	1.00
395	Willard Nixon	2.50	1.25	.70
396	Dutch Dotterer	2.50	1.25	.70
397a	Tigers Team (alphabetical checklist on back)	9.00	4.50	2.75
397b	Tigers Team (numerical checklist on back)	60.00	30.00	18.00
398	Gene Woodling	2.75	1.50	.80
399	Marv Grissom	2.50	1.25	.70
400	Nellie Fox	8.00	4.00	2.50
401	Don Bessent	2.50	1.25	.70
402	Bobby Gene Smith	2.50	1.25	.70
403	Steve Korcheck	2.50	1.25	.70
404	Curt Simmons	3.25	1.75	1.00
405	Ken Aspromonte	2.50	1.25	.70
406	Vic Power	2.50	1.25	.70
407	Carlton Willey	2.50	1.25	.70
408a	Orioles Team (alphabetical checklist on back)	8.00	4.00	2.50
408b	Orioles Team (numerical checklist on back)	60.00	30.00	18.00
409	Frank Thomas	2.50	1.25	.70
410	Murray Wall	2.50	1.25	.70
411	*Tony Taylor*	2.75	1.50	.80
412	Jerry Staley	2.50	1.25	.70
413	*Jim Davenport*	2.75	1.50	.80
414	Sammy White	2.50	1.25	.70
415	Bob Bowman	2.50	1.25	.70
416	Foster Castleman	2.50	1.25	.70
417	Carl Furillo	6.00	3.00	1.75
418	World Series Batting Foes (Hank Aaron, Mickey Mantle)	100.00	45.00	27.00
419	Bobby Shantz	4.50	2.25	1.25
420	*Vada Pinson*	15.00	7.50	4.50
421	Dixie Howell	2.50	1.25	.70
422	Norm Zauchin	2.50	1.25	.70
423	Phil Clark	2.50	1.25	.70
424	Larry Doby	4.00	2.00	1.25
425	Sam Esposito	2.50	1.25	.70
426	Johnny O'Brien	2.50	1.25	.70
427	Al Worthington	2.50	1.25	.70
428a	Redlegs Team (alphabetical checklist on back)	8.00	4.00	2.50
428b	Redlegs Team (numerical checklist on back)	50.00	25.00	15.00
429	Gus Triandos	2.75	1.50	.80
430	Bobby Thomson	3.25	1.75	1.00
431	Gene Conley	2.75	1.50	.80
432	John Powers	2.50	1.25	.70
433	Pancho Herrera	2.50	1.25	.70
434	Harvey Kuenn	3.25	1.75	1.00
435	Ed Roebuck	2.50	1.25	.70
436	Rival Fence Busters (Willie Mays, Duke Snider)	35.00	17.50	10.50
437	Bob Speake	2.50	1.25	.70
438	Whitey Herzog	3.75	2.00	1.25
439	Ray Narleski	2.50	1.25	.70
440	Ed Mathews	20.00	10.00	6.00
441	Jim Marshall	2.00	1.00	.60
442	Phil Paine	2.00	1.00	.60

		NR MT	EX	VG
443	Billy Harrell	4.50	2.25	1.25
444	Danny Kravitz	2.00	1.00	.60
445	Bob Smith	2.00	1.00	.60
446	Carroll Hardy	4.50	2.25	1.25
447	Ray Monzant	2.00	1.00	.60
448	*Charlie Lau*	2.75	1.50	.80
449	Gene Fodge	2.00	1.00	.60
450	Preston Ward	4.50	2.25	1.25
451	Joe Taylor	2.00	1.00	.60
452	Roman Mejias	2.00	1.00	.60
453	Tom Qualters	2.00	1.00	.60
454	Harry Hanebrink	2.00	1.00	.60
455	Hal Griggs	2.00	1.00	.60
456	Dick Brown	2.00	1.00	.60
457	*Milt Pappas*	2.75	1.50	.80
458	Julio Becquer	2.00	1.00	.60
459	Ron Blackburn	2.00	1.00	.60
460	Chuck Essegian	2.00	1.00	.60
461	Ed Mayer	2.00	1.00	.60
462	Gary Geiger	4.50	2.25	1.25
463	Vito Valentinetti	2.00	1.00	.60
464	*Curt Flood*	10.00	5.00	3.00
465	Arnie Portocarrero	2.00	1.00	.60
466	Pete Whisenant	2.00	1.00	.60
467	Glen Hobbie	2.00	1.00	.60
468	Bob Schmidt	2.00	1.00	.60
469	Don Ferrarese	2.00	1.00	.60
470	R.C. Stevens	2.00	1.00	.60
471	Lenny Green	2.00	1.00	.60
472	Joe Jay	2.00	1.00	.60
473	Bill Renna	2.00	1.00	.60
474	Roman Semproch	2.00	1.00	.60
475	All-Star Managers (Fred Haney, Casey Stengel)	15.00	7.50	4.50
476	Stan Musial AS	25.00	12.50	7.50
477	Bill Skowron AS	4.00	2.00	1.25
478	Johnny Temple AS	2.50	1.25	.70
479	Nellie Fox AS	5.00	2.50	1.50
480	Eddie Mathews AS	10.00	5.00	3.00
481	Frank Malzone AS	2.50	1.25	.70
482	Ernie Banks AS	15.00	7.50	4.50
483	Luis Aparicio AS	8.00	4.00	2.50
484	Frank Robinson AS	12.00	6.00	3.50
485	Ted Williams AS	40.00	20.00	12.00
486	Willie Mays AS	30.00	15.00	9.00
487	Mickey Mantle AS	50.00	30.00	15.00
488	Hank Aaron AS	25.00	12.50	7.50
489	Jackie Jensen AS	3.25	1.75	1.00
490	Ed Bailey AS	2.50	1.25	.70
491	Sherm Lollar AS	2.50	1.25	.70
492	Bob Friend AS	3.25	1.75	1.00
493	Bob Turley AS	3.75	2.00	1.25
494	Warren Spahn AS	15.00	7.50	4.50
495	Herb Score AS	6.00	2.00	1.00
———	Contest Card (All-Star Game, July 8)	15.00	7.50	4.50
———	Felt Emblems Insert Card	15.00	7.50	4.50

1959 Topps

These 2-1/2" by 3-1/2" cards have a round photograph at the center of the front with a solid-color background and white border. A facsimile autograph is found across the photo. The 572-card set marks the largest set issued to that time. Card numbers below 507 have red and green printing with the card number in white in a green box. On high number cards beginning with #507, the printing is black and red and the card number is in a black box.

Specialty cards include multiple-player cards, team cards with checklists, "All-Star" cards, highlights from previous season, and 31 "Rookie Stars." There is also a card of the commissioner, Ford Frick, and one Roy Campanella in a wheelchair. A handful of cards can be found with and without lines added to the biographies on back indicating trades or demotions; those without the added lines are considerably more rare and valuable aand are not included in the complete set price. Card numbers 199-286 can be found with either white or grey backs, with the grey stock being the less common.

		NR MT	EX	VG
Complete Set:		4000.00	2000.00	1200.
Common Player: 1-110		4.00	2.00	1.25
Common Player: 111-506		2.50	1.25	.70
Common Player: 507-572		10.00	5.00	3.00
1	Ford Frick	75.00	3.75	1.50
2	Eddie Yost	5.00	2.00	1.25
3	Don McMahon	4.00	2.00	1.25
4	Albie Pearson	4.00	2.00	1.25
5	Dick Donovan	4.00	2.00	1.25
6	Alex Grammas	4.00	2.00	1.25
7	Al Pilarcik	4.00	2.00	1.25
8	Phillies Team/Checklist 1-88	12.00	6.00	3.50
9	Paul Giel	4.00	2.00	1.25
10	Mickey Mantle	350.00	140.00	88.00
11	Billy Hunter	4.00	2.00	1.25
12	Vern Law	5.00	2.50	1.50
13	Dick Gernert	4.00	2.00	1.25
14	Pete Whisenant	4.00	2.00	1.25
15	Dick Drott	4.00	2.00	1.25
16	Joe Pignatano	4.00	2.00	1.25
17	Danny's All-Stars (Ted Kluszewski, Danny Murtaugh, Frank Thomas)	5.00	2.50	1.50
18	Jack Urban	4.00	2.00	1.25
19	Ed Bressoud	4.00	2.00	1.25
20	Duke Snider	40.00	20.00	12.00
21	Connie Johnson	4.00	2.00	1.25
22	Al Smith	4.00	2.00	1.25
23	Murry Dickson	5.00	2.50	1.50
24	Red Wilson	4.00	2.00	1.25
25	Don Hoak	4.50	2.25	1.25
26	Chuck Stobbs	4.00	2.00	1.25
27	Andy Pafko	4.50	2.25	1.25
28	Red Worthington	4.00	2.00	1.25
29	Jim Bolger	4.00	2.00	1.25
30	Nellie Fox	10.00	5.00	3.00
31	Ken Lehman	4.00	2.00	1.25
32	Don Buddin	4.00	2.00	1.25
33	Ed Fitz Gerald	4.00	2.00	1.25
34	Pitchers Beware (Al Kaline, Charlie Maxwell)	9.00	4.50	2.75
35	Ted Kluszewski	7.00	3.50	2.00
36	Hank Aguirre	4.00	2.00	1.25
37	Gene Green	4.00	2.00	1.25
38	Morrie Martin	4.00	2.00	1.25
39	Ed Bouchee	4.00	2.00	1.25
40	Warren Spahn	40.00	20.00	12.00
41	Bob Martyn	4.00	2.00	1.25
42	Murray Wall	4.00	2.00	1.25
43	Steve Bilko	4.00	2.00	1.25
44	Vito Valentinetti	4.00	2.00	1.25
45	Andy Carey	5.00	2.50	1.50
46	Bill Henry	4.00	2.00	1.25
47	Jim Finigan	4.00	2.00	1.25
48	Orioles Team/Checklist 1-88	10.00	5.00	3.00
49	Bill Hall	4.00	2.00	1.25
50	Willie Mays	100.00	45.00	27.00
51	Rip Coleman	4.00	2.00	1.25
52	Coot Veal	4.00	2.00	1.25
53	Stan Williams	4.00	2.00	1.25
54	Mel Roach	4.00	2.00	1.25
55	Tom Brewer	4.00	2.00	1.25
56	Carl Sawatski	4.00	2.00	1.25
57	Al Cicotte	4.00	2.00	1.25
58	Eddie Miksis	4.00	2.00	1.25
59	Irv Noren	4.00	2.00	1.25
60	Bob Turley	6.00	3.00	1.75
61	Dick Brown	4.00	2.00	1.25
62	Tony Taylor	4.00	2.00	1.25
63	Jim Hearn	4.00	2.00	1.25
64	Joe DeMaestri	4.00	2.00	1.25
65	Frank Torre	4.00	2.00	1.25
66	Joe Ginsberg	4.00	2.00	1.25
67	Brooks Lawrence	4.00	2.00	1.25
68	Dick Schofield	4.00	2.00	1.25
69	Giants Team/Checklist 89-176	12.00	6.00	3.50
70	Harvey Kuenn	5.00	2.50	1.50
71	Don Bessent	4.00	2.00	1.25
72	Bill Renna	4.00	2.00	1.25
73	Ron Jackson	4.00	2.00	1.25
74	Directing the Power (Cookie Lavagetto, Jim Lemon, Roy Sievers)	4.50	2.25	1.25
75	Sam Jones	4.00	2.00	1.25
76	Bobby Richardson	9.00	4.50	2.75
77	John Goryl	4.00	2.00	1.25
78	Pedro Ramos	4.00	2.00	1.25
79	Harry Chiti	4.00	2.00	1.25
80	Minnie Minoso	5.00	2.50	1.50
81	Hal Jeffcoat	4.00	2.00	1.25
82	Bob Boyd	4.00	2.00	1.25
83	Bob Smith	4.00	2.00	1.25
84	Reno Bertoia	4.00	2.00	1.25
85	Harry Anderson	4.00	2.00	1.25
86	Bob Keegan	4.00	2.00	1.25
87	Danny O'Connell	4.00	2.00	1.25
88	Herb Score	4.50	2.25	1.25
89	Billy Gardner	4.00	2.00	1.25
90	Bill Skowron	8.00	4.00	2.50
91	Herb Moford	4.00	2.00	1.25
92	Dave Philley	4.00	2.00	1.25
93	Julio Becquer	4.00	2.00	1.25
94	W. Sox Team/Checklist 89-176	15.00	7.50	4.50
95	Carl Willey	4.00	2.00	1.25
96	Lou Berberet	4.00	2.00	1.25
97	Jerry Lynch	4.00	2.00	1.25
98	Arnie Portocarrero	4.00	2.00	1.25
99	Ted Kazanski	4.00	2.00	1.25
100	Bob Cerv	4.00	2.00	1.25
101	Alex Kellner	4.00	2.00	1.25
102	*Felipe Alou*	6.00	3.00	1.75
103	Billy Goodman	4.00	2.00	1.25
104	Del Rice	4.00	2.00	1.25
105	Lee Walls	4.00	2.00	1.25
106	Hal Woodeshick	4.00	2.00	1.25
107	Norm Larker	4.00	2.00	1.25
108	Zack Monroe	5.00	2.50	1.50
109	Bob Schmidt	4.00	2.00	1.25
110	George Witt	4.00	2.00	1.25
111	Redlegs Team/Checklist 89-176	8.00	4.00	2.50
112	Billy Consolo	2.50	1.25	.70
113	Taylor Phillips	2.50	1.25	.70
114	Earl Battey	2.75	1.50	.80
115	Mickey Vernon	2.75	1.50	.80
116	Bob Allison	4.00	2.00	1.25
117	*John Blanchard*	3.25	1.75	1.00
118	John Buzhardt	2.50	1.25	.70
119	*John Callison*	4.00	2.00	1.25
120	Chuck Coles	2.50	1.25	.70
121	Bob Conley	2.50	1.25	.70
122	Bennie Daniels	2.50	1.25	.70
123	Don Dillard	2.50	1.25	.70
124	Dan Dobbek	2.50	1.25	.70
125	*Ron Fairly*	3.50	1.75	1.00
126	Eddie Haas	2.50	1.25	.70
127	Kent Hadley	2.50	1.25	.70
128	Bob Hartman	2.50	1.25	.70
129	Frank Herrera	2.50	1.25	.70
130	Lou Jackson	2.50	1.25	.70
131	*Deron Johnson*	3.25	1.75	1.00
132	Don Lee	2.50	1.25	.70
133	*Bob Lillis*	2.75	1.50	.80
134	Jim McDaniel	2.50	1.25	.70
135	Gene Oliver	2.50	1.25	.70
136	*Jim O'Toole*	2.75	1.50	.80
137	Dick Ricketts	2.50	1.25	.70
138	John Romano	2.50	1.25	.70
139	Ed Sadowski	2.50	1.25	.70
140	Charlie Secrest	2.50	1.25	.70
141	Joe Shipley	2.50	1.25	.70
142	Dick Stigman	2.50	1.25	.70
143	Willie Tasby	2.50	1.25	.70
144	Jerry Walker	2.50	1.25	.70
145	Dom Zanni	2.50	1.25	.70
146	Jerry Zimmerman	2.50	1.25	.70
147	Cub's Clubbers (Ernie Banks, Dale Long, Walt Moryn)	9.00	4.50	2.75
148	Mike McCormick	2.75	1.50	.80
149	Jim Bunning	8.00	4.00	2.50
150	Stan Musial	100.00	45.00	27.00
151	Bob Malkmus	2.50	1.25	.70
152	Johnny Klippstein	2.50	1.25	.70
153	Jim Marshall	2.50	1.25	.70
154	Ray Herbert	2.50	1.25	.70
155	Enos Slaughter	15.00	7.50	4.50
156	Ace Hurlers (Billy Pierce, Robin Roberts)	3.50	1.75	1.00
157	Felix Mantilla	2.50	1.25	.70

		NR MT	EX	VG
158	Walt Dropo	2.75	1.50	.80
159	Bob Shaw	2.50	1.25	.70
160	Dick Groat	3.00	1.50	.90
161	Frank Baumann	2.50	1.25	.70
162	Bobby G. Smith	2.50	1.25	.70
163	Sandy Koufax	80.00	40.00	24.00
164	Johnny Groth	2.50	1.25	.70
165	Bill Bruton	2.75	1.50	.80
166	Destruction Crew (Rocky Colavito, Larry Doby, Minnie Minoso)	3.25	1.75	1.00
167	Duke Maas	3.00	1.50	.90
168	Carroll Hardy	2.50	1.25	.70
169	Ted Abernathy	2.50	1.25	.70
170	Gene Woodling	2.75	1.50	.80
171	Willard Schmidt	2.50	1.25	.70
172	A's Team/Checklist 177-242	7.00	3.50	2.00
173	Bill Monbouquette	2.75	1.50	.80
174	Jim Pendleton	2.50	1.25	.70
175	Dick Farrell	2.50	1.25	.70
176	Preston Ward	2.50	1.25	.70
177	Johnny Briggs	2.50	1.25	.70
178	Ruben Amaro	2.50	1.25	.70
179	Don Rudolph	2.50	1.25	.70
180	Yogi Berra	60.00	30.00	18.00
181	Bob Porterfield	2.50	1.25	.70
182	Milt Graff	2.50	1.25	.70
183	Stu Miller	2.50	1.25	.70
184	Harvey Haddix	2.75	1.50	.80
185	Jim Busby	2.50	1.25	.70
186	Mudcat Grant	2.75	1.50	.80
187	Bubba Phillips	2.50	1.25	.70
188	Juan Pizarro	2.50	1.25	.70
189	Neil Chrisley	2.50	1.25	.70
190	Bill Virdon	2.75	1.50	.80
191	Russ Kemmerer	2.50	1.25	.70
192	Charley Beamon	2.50	1.25	.70
193	Sammy Taylor	2.50	1.25	.70
194	Jim Brosnan	2.75	1.50	.80
195	Rip Repulski	2.50	1.25	.70
196	Billy Moran	2.50	1.25	.70
197	Ray Semproch	2.50	1.25	.70
198	Jim Davenport	2.50	1.25	.70
199	Leo Kiely	2.50	1.25	.70
200	Warren Giles	2.75	1.50	.80
201	Tom Acker	2.50	1.25	.70
202	Roger Maris	125.00	56.00	35.00
203	Ozzie Virgil	2.50	1.25	.70
204	Casey Wise	2.50	1.25	.70
205	Don Larsen	7.00	3.50	2.00
206	Carl Furillo	5.00	2.50	1.50
207	George Strickland	2.50	1.25	.70
208	Willie Jones	2.50	1.25	.70
209	Lenny Green	2.50	1.25	.70
210	Ed Bailey	2.50	1.25	.70
211	Bob Blaylock	2.50	1.25	.70
212	Fence Busters (Hank Aaron, Eddie Mathews)	18.00	9.00	5.50
213	Jim Rivera	2.50	1.25	.70
214	Marcelino Solis	2.50	1.25	.70
215	Jim Lemon	2.50	1.25	.70
216	Andre Rodgers	2.50	1.25	.70
217	Carl Erskine	4.00	2.00	1.25
218	Roman Mejias	2.50	1.25	.70
219	George Zuverink	2.50	1.25	.70
220	Frank Malzone	2.75	1.50	.80
221	Bob Bowman	2.50	1.25	.70
222	Bobby Shantz	3.50	1.75	1.00
223	Cards Team/Checklist 265-352	7.00	3.50	2.00
224	Claude Osteen	3.00	1.50	.90
225	Johnny Logan	2.75	1.50	.80
226	Art Ceccarelli	2.50	1.25	.70
227	Hal Smith	2.50	1.25	.70
228	Don Gross	2.50	1.25	.70
229	Vic Power	2.50	1.25	.70
230	Bill Fischer	2.50	1.25	.70
231	Ellis Burton	2.50	1.25	.70
232	Eddie Kasko	2.50	1.25	.70
233	Paul Foytack	2.50	1.25	.70
234	Chuck Tanner	3.00	1.50	.90
235	Valmy Thomas	2.50	1.25	.70
236	Ted Bowsfield	2.50	1.25	.70
237	Run Preventers (Gil McDougald, Bobby Richardson, Bob Turley)	4.00	2.00	1.25
238	Gene Baker	2.50	1.25	.70
239	Bob Trowbridge	2.50	1.25	.70
240	Hank Bauer	7.00	3.50	2.00
241	Billy Muffett	2.50	1.25	.70
242	Ron Samford	2.50	1.25	.70
243	Marv Grissom	2.50	1.25	.70
244	Dick Gray	2.50	1.25	.70
245	Ned Garver	2.50	1.25	.70
246	J.W. Porter	2.50	1.25	.70
247	Don Ferrarese	2.50	1.25	.70
248	Red Sox Team/Checklist 177-264	8.00	4.00	2.50
249	Bobby Adams	2.50	1.25	.70
250	Billy O'Dell	2.50	1.25	.70
251	Cletis Boyer	4.50	2.25	1.25
252	Ray Boone	2.75	1.50	.80
253	Seth Morehead	2.50	1.25	.70
254	Zeke Bella	2.50	1.25	.70
255	Del Ennis	2.75	1.50	.80
256	Jerry Davie	2.50	1.25	.70
257	Leon Wagner	3.00	1.50	.90
258	Fred Kipp	2.50	1.25	.70
259	Jim Pisoni	2.50	1.25	.70
260	Early Wynn	15.00	7.50	4.50
261	Gene Stephens	2.50	1.25	.70
262	Hitters' Foes (Don Drysdale, Clem Labine, Johnny Podres)	8.00	4.00	2.50
263	Buddy Daley	2.50	1.25	.70
264	Chico Carrasquel	2.50	1.25	.70
265	Ron Kline	2.50	1.25	.70
266	Woody Held	2.75	1.50	.80
267	John Romonosky	2.50	1.25	.70
268	Tito Francona	2.75	1.50	.80
269	Jack Meyer	2.50	1.25	.70
270	Gil Hodges	18.00	9.00	5.50
271	Orlando Pena	2.75	1.50	.80
272	Jerry Lumpe	3.25	1.75	1.00
273	Joe Jay	2.50	1.25	.70
274	Jerry Kindall	2.50	1.25	.70
275	Jack Sanford	2.50	1.25	.70
276	Pete Daley	2.50	1.25	.70
277	Turk Lown	2.50	1.25	.70
278	Chuck Essegian	2.50	1.25	.70
279	Ernie Johnson	2.50	1.25	.70
280	Frank Bolling	2.50	1.25	.70
281	Walt Craddock	2.50	1.25	.70
282	R.C. Stevens	2.50	1.25	.70
283	Russ Heman	2.50	1.25	.70
284	Steve Korcheck	2.50	1.25	.70
285	Joe Cunningham	2.75	1.50	.80
286	Dean Stone	2.50	1.25	.70
287	Don Zimmer	2.75	1.50	.80
288	Dutch Dotterer	2.50	1.25	.70
289	Johnny Kucks	3.00	1.50	.90
290	Wes Covington	2.75	1.50	.80
291	Pitching Partners (Camilo Pascual, Pedro Ramos)	2.75	1.50	.80
292	Dick Williams	2.75	1.50	.80
293	Ray Moore	2.50	1.25	.70
294	Hank Foiles	2.50	1.25	.70
295	Billy Martin	9.00	4.50	2.75
296	Ernie Broglio	2.75	1.50	.80
297	Jackie Brandt	2.75	1.50	.80
298	Tex Clevenger	2.50	1.25	.70
299	Billy Klaus	2.50	1.25	.70
300	Richie Ashburn	9.00	4.50	2.75
301	Earl Averill	2.50	1.25	.70
302	Don Mossi	2.75	1.50	.80
303	Marty Keough	2.50	1.25	.70
304	Cubs Team/Checklist 265-352	7.00	3.50	2.00
305	Curt Raydon	2.50	1.25	.70
306	Jim Gilliam	5.00	2.50	1.50
307	Curt Barclay	2.50	1.25	.70
308	Norm Siebern	3.50	1.75	1.00
309	Sal Maglie	3.00	1.50	.90
310	Luis Aparicio	15.00	7.50	4.50
311	Norm Zauchin	2.50	1.25	.70
312	Don Newcombe	4.50	2.25	1.25
313	Frank House	2.50	1.25	.70
314	Don Cardwell	2.50	1.25	.70
315	Joe Adcock	3.00	1.50	.90
316a	Ralph Lumenti (without option statement)	80.00	40.00	24.00
316b	Ralph Lumenti (with option statement)	2.50	1.25	.70
317	N.L. Hitting Kings (Richie Ashburn, Willie Mays)	15.00	7.50	4.50
318	Rocky Bridges	2.50	1.25	.70
319	Dave Hillman	2.50	1.25	.70
320	Bob Skinner	2.75	1.50	.80
321a	Bob Giallombardo (without option statement)	80.00	40.00	24.00
321b	Bob Giallombardo (with option statement)	2.50	1.25	.70
322a	Harry Hanebrink (without trade statement)	65.00	33.00	18.00
322b	Harry Hanebrink (with trade statement)	2.50	1.25	.70
323	Frank Sullivan	2.50	1.25	.70

		NR MT	EX	VG
324	Don Demeter	2.50	1.25	.70
325	Ken Boyer	5.00	2.50	1.50
326	Marv Throneberry	4.00	2.00	1.25
327	*Gary Bell*	2.75	1.50	.80
328	Lou Skizas	2.50	1.25	.70
329	Tigers Team/Checklist 353-429	8.00	4.00	2.50
330	Gus Triandos	2.75	1.50	.80
331	Steve Boros	2.75	1.50	.80
332	Ray Monzant	2.50	1.25	.70
333	Harry Simpson	2.50	1.25	.70
334	Glen Hobbie	2.50	1.25	.70
335	Johnny Temple	2.50	1.25	.70
336a	Billy Loes (without trade statement)			
		65.00	33.00	18.00
336b	Billy Loes (with trade statement)	2.50	1.25	.70
337	George Crowe	2.50	1.25	.70
338	*George Anderson*	12.00	6.00	3.50
339	Roy Face	3.00	1.50	.90
340	Roy Sievers	2.75	1.50	.80
341	Tom Qualters	2.50	1.25	.70
342	Ray Jablonski	2.50	1.25	.70
343	Billy Hoeft	2.50	1.25	.70
344	Russ Nixon	2.50	1.25	.70
345	Gil McDougald	8.00	4.00	2.50
346	Batter Bafflers (Tom Brewer, Dave Sisler)			
		2.75	1.50	.80
347	Bob Buhl	2.75	1.50	.80
348	Ted Lepcio	2.50	1.25	.70
349	Hoyt Wilhelm	15.00	7.50	4.50
350	Ernie Banks	50.00	25.00	15.00
351	Earl Torgeson	2.50	1.25	.70
352	Robin Roberts	15.00	7.50	4.50
353	Curt Flood	3.00	1.50	.90
354	Pete Burnside	2.50	1.25	.70
355	Jim Piersall	3.00	1.50	.90
356	Bob Mabe	2.50	1.25	.70
357	*Dick Stuart*	4.50	2.25	1.25
358	Ralph Terry	2.75	1.50	.80
359	*Bill White*	15.00	7.50	4.50
360	Al Kaline	50.00	25.00	15.00
361	Willard Nixon	2.50	1.25	.70
362a	Dolan Nichols (without option statement)			
		80.00	40.00	24.00
362b	Dolan Nichols (with option statement)			
		2.50	1.25	.70
363	Bobby Avila	2.50	1.25	.70
364	Danny McDevitt	2.50	1.25	.70
365	Gus Bell	2.75	1.50	.80
366	Humberto Robinson	2.50	1.25	.70
367	Cal Neeman	2.50	1.25	.70
368	Don Mueller	2.50	1.25	.70
369	Dick Tomanek	2.50	1.25	.70
370	Pete Runnels	2.75	1.50	.80
371	Dick Brodowski	2.50	1.25	.70
372	Jim Hegan	2.50	1.25	.70
373	Herb Plews	2.50	1.25	.70
374	Art Ditmar	3.00	1.50	.90
375	Bob Nieman	2.50	1.25	.70
376	Hal Naragon	2.50	1.25	.70
377	Johnny Antonelli	2.75	1.50	.80
378	Gail Harris	2.50	1.25	.70
379	Bob Miller	2.50	1.25	.70
380	Hank Aaron	100.00	45.00	27.00
381	Mike Baxes	2.50	1.25	.70
382	Curt Simmons	2.75	1.50	.80
383	Words of Wisdom (Don Larsen, Casey Stengel)	5.00	2.50	1.50
384	Dave Sisler	2.50	1.25	.70
385	Sherm Lollar	2.75	1.50	.80
386	Jim Delsing	2.50	1.25	.70
387	Don Drysdale	20.00	10.00	6.00
388	Bob Will	2.50	1.25	.70
389	Joe Nuxhall	2.75	1.50	.80
390	Orlando Cepeda	9.00	4.50	2.75
391	Milt Pappas	2.75	1.50	.80
392	Whitey Herzog	4.50	2.25	1.25
393	Frank Lary	2.75	1.50	.80
394	Randy Jackson	2.50	1.25	.70
395	Elston Howard	7.00	3.50	2.00
396	Bob Rush	2.50	1.25	.70
397	Senators Team/Checklist 430-495			
		7.00	3.50	2.00
398	Wally Post	2.50	1.25	.70
399	Larry Jackson	2.50	1.25	.70
400	Jackie Jensen	4.00	2.00	1.25
401	Ron Blackburn	2.50	1.25	.70
402	Hector Lopez	2.50	1.25	.70
403	Clem Labine	2.75	1.50	.80
404	Hank Sauer	2.75	1.50	.80
405	Roy McMillan	2.50	1.25	.70
406	Solly Drake	2.50	1.25	.70

		NR MT	EX	VG
407	Moe Drabowsky	2.50	1.25	.70
408	Keystone Combo (Luis Aparicio, Nellie Fox)	7.00	3.50	2.00
409	Gus Zernial	2.75	1.50	.80
410	Billy Pierce	2.75	1.50	.80
411	Whitey Lockman	2.50	1.25	.70
412	Stan Lopata	2.50	1.25	.70
413	Camillo Pascual (Camilo)	2.75	1.50	.80
414	Dale Long	2.75	1.50	.80
415	Bill Mazeroski	3.50	1.75	1.00
416	Haywood Sullivan	2.50	1.25	.70
417	Virgil Trucks	3.00	1.50	.90
418	Gino Cimoli	2.50	1.25	.70
419	Braves Team/Checklist 353-429	8.00	4.00	2.50
420	Rocco Colavito	4.50	2.25	1.25
421	Herm Wehmeier	2.50	1.25	.70
422	Hobie Landrith	2.50	1.25	.70
423	Bob Grim	2.50	1.25	.70
424	Ken Aspromonte	2.50	1.25	.70
425	Del Crandall	2.75	1.50	.80
426	Jerry Staley	2.50	1.25	.70
427	Charlie Neal	2.50	1.25	.70
428	Buc Hill Aces (Roy Face, Bob Friend, Ron Kline, Vern Law)	3.25	1.75	1.00
429	Bobby Thomson	2.75	1.50	.80
430	Whitey Ford	25.00	12.50	7.50
431	Whammy Douglas	2.50	1.25	.70
432	Smoky Burgess	3.00	1.50	.90
433	Billy Harrell	2.50	1.25	.70
434	Hal Griggs	2.50	1.25	.70
435	Frank Robinson	35.00	17.50	10.50
436	Granny Hamner	2.50	1.25	.70
437	Ike Delock	2.50	1.25	.70
438	Sam Esposito	2.50	1.25	.70
439	Brooks Robinson	30.00	15.00	9.00
440	Lou Burdette	8.00	4.00	2.50
441	John Roseboro	2.75	1.50	.80
442	Ray Narleski	2.50	1.25	.70
443	Daryl Spencer	2.50	1.25	.70
444	*Ronnie Hansen*	2.75	1.50	.80
445	Cal McLish	2.50	1.25	.70
446	Rocky Nelson	2.50	1.25	.70
447	Bob Anderson	2.50	1.25	.70
448	Vada Pinson	4.00	2.00	1.25
449	Tom Gorman	2.50	1.25	.70
450	Ed Mathews	20.00	10.00	6.00
451	Jimmy Constable	2.50	1.25	.70
452	Chico Fernandez	2.50	1.25	.70
453	Les Moss	2.50	1.25	.70
454	Phil Clark	2.50	1.25	.70
455	Larry Doby	3.25	1.75	1.00
456	Jerry Casale	2.50	1.25	.70
457	Dodgers Team/Checklist 430-495			
		12.00	6.00	3.50
458	Gordon Jones	2.50	1.25	.70
459	Bill Tuttle	2.50	1.25	.70
460	Bob Friend	2.75	1.50	.80
461	Mantle Hits 42nd Homer For Crown			
		25.00	12.50	7.50
462	Colavito's Great Catch Saves Game			
		3.00	1.50	.90
463	Kaline Becomes Youngest Bat Champ			
		8.00	4.00	2.50
464	Mays' Catch Makes Series History			
		15.00	7.50	4.50
465	Sievers Sets Homer Mark	2.75	1.50	.80
466	Pierce All Star Starter	2.75	1.50	.80
467	Aaron Clubs World Series Homer	15.00	7.50	4.50
468	Snider's Play Brings L.A. Victory	9.00	4.50	2.75
469	Hustler Banks Wins M.V.P. Award	8.00	4.00	2.50
470	Musial Raps Out 3,000th Hit	12.00	6.00	3.50
471	Tom Sturdivant	3.00	1.50	.90
472	Gene Freese	2.50	1.25	.70
473	Mike Fornieles	2.50	1.25	.70
474	Moe Thacker	2.50	1.25	.70
475	Jack Harshman	2.50	1.25	.70
476	Indians Team/Checklist 496-572	7.00	3.50	2.00
477	Barry Latman	2.50	1.25	.70
478	Bob Clemente	70.00	35.00	21.00
479	Lindy McDaniel	2.50	1.25	.70
480	Red Schoendienst	12.00	6.00	3.50
481	Charley Maxwell	2.50	1.25	.70
482	Russ Meyer	2.50	1.25	.70
483	Clint Courtney	2.50	1.25	.70
484	Willie Kirkland	2.50	1.25	.70
485	Ryne Duren	3.50	1.75	1.00
486	Sammy White	2.50	1.25	.70
487	Hal Brown	2.50	1.25	.70
488	Walt Moryn	2.50	1.25	.70
489	John C. Powers	2.50	1.25	.70
490	Frank Thomas	2.50	1.25	.70

		NR MT	EX	VG
491	Don Blasingame	2.50	1.25	.70
492	Gene Conley	2.75	1.50	.80
493	Jim Landis	2.50	1.25	.70
494	Don Pavletich	2.50	1.25	.70
495	Johnny Podres	4.00	2.00	1.25
496	Wayne Terwilliger	2.50	1.25	.70
497	Hal R. Smith	2.50	1.25	.70
498	Dick Hyde	2.50	1.25	.70
499	Johnny O'Brien	2.50	1.25	.70
500	Vic Wertz	2.75	1.50	.80
501	Bobby Tiefenauer	2.50	1.25	.70
502	Al Dark	3.25	1.75	1.00
503	Jim Owens	2.50	1.25	.70
504	Ossie Alvarez	2.50	1.25	.70
505	Tony Kubek	8.00	4.00	2.50
506	Bob Purkey	2.50	1.25	.70
507	Bob Hale	10.00	5.00	3.00
508	Art Fowler	10.00	5.00	3.00
509	*Norm Cash*	25.00	12.50	7.50
510	Yankees Team/Checklist 496-572			
		45.00	22.00	13.50
511	George Susce	10.00	5.00	3.00
512	George Altman	10.00	5.00	3.00
513	Tom Carroll	10.00	5.00	3.00
514	*Bob Gibson*	300.00	120.00	75.00
515	Harmon Killebrew	75.00	38.00	23.00
516	Mike Garcia	11.00	5.50	3.25
517	Joe Koppe	10.00	5.00	3.00
518	*Mike Cueller (Cuellar)*	15.00	7.50	4.50
519	Infield Power (Dick Gernert, Frank Malzone, Pete Runnels)	12.00	6.00	3.50
520	Don Elston	10.00	5.00	3.00
521	Gary Geiger	10.00	5.00	3.00
522	Gene Snyder	10.00	5.00	3.00
523	Harry Bright	10.00	5.00	3.00
524	Larry Osborne	10.00	5.00	3.00
525	Jim Coates	11.00	5.50	3.25
526	Bob Speake	10.00	5.00	3.00
527	Solly Hemus	10.00	5.00	3.00
528	Pirates Team/Checklist 496-572			
		25.00	12.50	7.50
529	*George Bamberger*	11.00	5.50	3.25
530	Wally Moon	11.00	5.50	3.25
531	Ray Webster	10.00	5.00	3.00
532	Mark Freeman	10.00	5.00	3.00
533	Darrell Johnson	11.00	5.50	3.25
534	Faye Throneberry	10.00	5.00	3.00
535	Ruben Gomez	10.00	5.00	3.00
536	Dan Kravitz	10.00	5.00	3.00
537	Rodolfo Arias	10.00	5.00	3.00
538	Chick King	10.00	5.00	3.00
539	Gary Blaylock	10.00	5.00	3.00
540	Willy Miranda	10.00	5.00	3.00
541	Bob Thurman	10.00	5.00	3.00
542	*Jim Perry*	15.00	7.50	4.50
543	Corsair Outfield Trio (Bob Clemente, Bob Skinner, Bill Virdon)	35.00	17.50	10.50
544	Lee Tate	10.00	5.00	3.00
545	Tom Morgan	10.00	5.00	3.00
546	Al Schroll	10.00	5.00	3.00
547	Jim Baxes	10.00	5.00	3.00
548	Elmer Singleton	10.00	5.00	3.00
549	Howie Nunn	10.00	5.00	3.00
550	Roy Campanella	100.00	45.00	27.00
551	Fred Haney AS	11.00	5.50	3.25
552	Casey Stengel AS	30.00	15.00	9.00
553	Orlando Cepeda AS	12.00	6.00	3.50
554	Bill Skowron AS	12.00	6.00	3.50
555	Bill Mazeroski AS	12.00	6.00	3.50
556	Nellie Fox AS	15.00	7.50	4.50
557	Ken Boyer AS	12.00	6.00	3.50
558	Frank Malzone AS	11.00	5.50	3.25
559	Ernie Banks AS	25.00	12.50	7.50
560	Luis Aparicio AS	20.00	10.00	6.00
561	Hank Aaron AS	65.00	32.00	19.50
562	Al Kaline AS	30.00	15.00	9.00
563	Willie Mays AS	65.00	32.00	19.50
564	Mickey Mantle AS	150.00	60.00	38.00
565	Wes Covington AS	11.00	5.50	3.25
566	Roy Sievers AS	11.00	5.50	3.25
567	Del Crandall AS	11.00	5.50	3.25
568	Gus Triandos AS	11.00	5.50	3.25
569	Bob Friend AS	11.00	5.50	3.25
570	Bob Turley AS	11.00	5.50	3.25
571	Warren Spahn AS	30.00	15.00	9.00
572	Billy Pierce AS	15.00	6.00	3.25
-----	Elect Your Favorite Rookie Insert (paper stock, September 29 date on back)	15.00	7.50	4.50
-----	Felt Pennants Insert (paper stock)	15.00	7.50	4.50

1960 Topps

In 1960, Topps returned to a horizontal format (3-1/2" by 2-1/2") with a color portrait and a black and white "action" photograph on the front. The Backs returned to the use of just the previous year and lifetime statistics along with a cartoon and short career summary or previous season highlights. Specialty cards in the 572-card set are multi-player cards, managers and coaches cards, and highlights of the 1959 World Series. Two groups of rookie cards are included. The first are numbers 117-148, which are the Sport Magazine rookies. The second group is called "Topps All-Star Rookies." Finally, there is a continuation of the All-Star cards to close out the set in the scarcer high numbers. Card #'s 375-440 can be found with backs printed on either white or grey cardboard, with the white stock being the less common.

		NR MT	EX	VG
Complete Set:		3400.00	1700.00	1020.
Common Player: 1-286		1.50	.70	.45
Common Player: 287-440		1.75	.90	.50
Common Player: 441-506		3.50	1.75	1.00
Common Player: 507-572		8.00	4.00	2.50
1	Early Wynn	35.00	10.00	5.00
2	Roman Mejias	2.25	.70	.45
3	Joe Adcock	2.25	1.25	.70
4	Bob Purkey	1.50	.70	.45
5	Wally Moon	1.75	.90	.50
6	Lou Berberet	1.50	.70	.45
7	Master & Mentor (Willie Mays, Bill Rigney)	8.00	4.00	2.50
8	Bud Daley	1.50	.70	.45
9	Faye Throneberry	1.50	.70	.45
10	Ernie Banks	30.00	15.00	9.00
11	Norm Siebern	1.75	.90	.50
12	Milt Pappas	1.75	.90	.50
13	Wally Post	1.50	.70	.45
14	Jim Grant	1.50	.70	.45
15	Pete Runnels	1.75	.90	.50
16	Ernie Broglio	1.50	.70	.45
17	Johnny Callison	1.75	.90	.50
18	Dodgers Team/Checklist 1-88	10.00	5.00	3.00
19	Felix Mantilla	1.50	.70	.45
20	Roy Face	2.00	1.00	.60
21	Dutch Dotterer	1.50	.70	.45
22	Rocky Bridges	1.50	.70	.45
23	Eddie Fisher	1.50	.70	.45
24	Dick Gray	1.50	.70	.45
25	Roy Sievers	3.50	1.75	1.00
26	Wayne Terwilliger	1.50	.70	.45
27	Dick Drott	1.50	.70	.45
28	Brooks Robinson	30.00	15.00	9.00
29	Clem Labine	1.75	.90	.50
30	Tito Francona	1.75	.90	.50

#	Player	NR MT	EX	VG
31	Sammy Esposito	1.50	.70	.45
32	Sophomore Stalwarts (Jim O'Toole, Vada Pinson)	3.50	1.75	1.00
33	Tom Morgan	1.50	.70	.45
34	George Anderson	2.50	1.25	.70
35	Whitey Ford	25.00	12.50	7.50
36	Russ Nixon	1.50	.70	.45
37	Bill Bruton	1.75	.90	.50
38	Jerry Casale	1.50	.70	.45
39	Earl Averill	1.50	.70	.45
40	Joe Cunningham	1.75	.90	.50
41	Barry Latman	1.50	.70	.45
42	Hobie Landrith	1.50	.70	.45
43	Senators Team/Checklist 1-88	6.00	3.00	1.75
44	Bobby Locke	1.50	.70	.45
45	Roy McMillan	1.50	.70	.45
46	Jack Fisher	1.50	.70	.45
47	Don Zimmer	2.25	1.25	.70
48	Hal Smith	1.50	.70	.45
49	Curt Raydon	1.50	.70	.45
50	Al Kaline	25.00	12.50	7.50
51	Jim Coates	2.00	1.00	.60
52	Dave Philley	1.50	.70	.45
53	Jackie Brandt	1.50	.70	.45
54	Mike Fornieles	1.50	.70	.45
55	Bill Mazeroski	3.00	1.50	.90
56	Steve Korcheck	1.50	.70	.45
57	Win - Savers (Turk Lown, Gerry Staley)	1.75	.90	.50
58	Gino Cimoli	1.50	.70	.45
59	Juan Pizarro	1.50	.70	.45
60	Gus Triandos	1.75	.90	.50
61	Eddie Kasko	1.50	.70	.45
62	Roger Craig	2.25	1.25	.70
63	George Strickland	1.50	.70	.45
64	Jack Meyer	1.50	.70	.45
65	Elston Howard	6.00	3.00	1.75
66	Bob Trowbridge	1.50	.70	.45
67	Jose Pagan	1.75	.90	.50
68	Dave Hillman	1.50	.70	.45
69	Billy Goodman	1.50	.70	.45
70	Lou Burdette	3.25	1.75	1.00
71	Marty Keough	1.50	.70	.45
72	Tigers Team/Checklist 89-176	8.00	4.00	2.50
73	Bob Gibson	25.00	12.50	7.50
74	Walt Moryn	1.50	.70	.45
75	Vic Power	1.50	.70	.45
76	Bill Fischer	1.50	.70	.45
77	Hank Foiles	1.50	.70	.45
78	Bob Grim	1.50	.70	.45
79	Walt Dropo	1.75	.90	.50
80	Johnny Antonelli	2.00	1.00	.60
81	Russ Snyder	1.50	.70	.45
82	Ruben Gomez	1.50	.70	.45
83	Tony Kubek	4.50	2.25	1.25
84	Hal Smith	1.50	.70	.45
85	Frank Lary	1.75	.90	.50
86	Dick Gernert	1.50	.70	.45
87	John Romonosky	1.50	.70	.45
88	John Roseboro	1.75	.90	.50
89	Hal Brown	1.50	.70	.45
90	Bobby Avila	1.50	.70	.45
91	Bennie Daniels	1.50	.70	.45
92	Whitey Herzog	3.25	1.75	1.00
93	Art Schult	1.50	.70	.45
94	Leo Kiely	1.50	.70	.45
95	Frank Thomas	1.50	.70	.45
96	Ralph Terry	2.50	1.25	.70
97	Ted Lepcio	1.50	.70	.45
98	Gordon Jones	1.50	.70	.45
99	Lenny Green	1.50	.70	.45
100	Nellie Fox	7.00	3.50	2.00
101	Bob Miller	1.50	.70	.45
102	Kent Hadley	2.00	1.00	.60
103	Dick Farrell	1.50	.70	.45
104	Dick Schofield	1.50	.70	.45
105	Larry Sherry	1.50	.70	.45
106	Billy Gardner	1.50	.70	.45
107	Carl Willey	1.50	.70	.45
108	Pete Daley	1.50	.70	.45
109	Cletis Boyer	3.00	1.50	.90
110	Cal McLish	1.50	.70	.45
111	Vic Wertz	1.75	.90	.50
112	Jack Harshman	1.50	.70	.45
113	Bob Skinner	1.50	.70	.45
114	Ken Aspromonte	1.50	.70	.45
115	Fork & Knuckler (Roy Face, Hoyt Wilhelm)	4.00	2.00	1.25
116	Jim Rivera	1.50	.70	.45
117	Tom Borland	1.50	.70	.45
118	Bob Bruce	1.50	.70	.45
119	Chico Cardenas	1.75	.90	.50
120	Duke Carmel	1.50	.70	.45
121	Camilo Carreon	1.50	.70	.45
122	Don Dillard	1.50	.70	.45
123	Dan Dobbek	1.50	.70	.45
124	Jim Donohue	1.50	.70	.45
125	Dick Ellsworth	1.75	.90	.50
126	Chuck Estrada	1.75	.90	.50
127	Ronnie Hansen	1.50	.70	.45
128	Bill Harris	1.50	.70	.45
129	Bob Hartman	1.50	.70	.45
130	Frank Herrera	1.50	.70	.45
131	Ed Hobaugh	1.50	.70	.45
132	Frank Howard	10.00	5.00	3.00
133	Manuel Javier	2.00	1.00	.60
134	Deron Johnson	2.00	1.00	.60
135	Ken Johnson	1.50	.70	.45
136	Jim Kaat	25.00	12.50	7.50
137	Lou Klimchock	1.50	.70	.45
138	Art Mahaffey	1.75	.90	.50
139	Carl Mathias	1.50	.70	.45
140	Julio Navarro	1.50	.70	.45
141	Jim Proctor	1.50	.70	.45
142	Bill Short	2.00	1.00	.60
143	Al Spangler	1.50	.70	.45
144	Al Stieglitz	1.50	.70	.45
145	Jim Umbricht	1.50	.70	.45
146	Ted Wieand	1.50	.70	.45
147	Bob Will	1.50	.70	.45
148	Carl Yastrzemski	350.00	140.00	88.00
149	Bob Nieman	1.50	.70	.45
150	Billy Pierce	2.25	1.25	.70
151	Giants Team/Checklist 177-264	6.00	3.00	1.75
152	Gail Harris	1.50	.70	.45
153	Bobby Thomson	2.00	1.00	.60
154	Jim Davenport	1.50	.70	.45
155	Charlie Neal	1.50	.70	.45
156	Art Ceccarelli	1.50	.70	.45
157	Rocky Nelson	1.50	.70	.45
158	Wes Covington	1.50	.70	.45
159	Jim Piersall	2.00	1.00	.60
160	Rival All Stars (Ken Boyer, Mickey Mantle)	30.00	15.00	9.00
161	Ray Narleski	1.50	.70	.45
162	Sammy Taylor	1.50	.70	.45
163	Hector Lopez	2.00	1.00	.60
164	Reds Team/Checklist 89-176	7.00	3.50	2.00
165	Jack Sanford	1.50	.70	.45
166	Chuck Essegian	1.50	.70	.45
167	Valmy Thomas	1.50	.70	.45
168	Alex Grammas	1.50	.70	.45
169	Jake Striker	1.50	.70	.45
170	Del Crandall	2.00	1.00	.60
171	Johnny Groth	1.50	.70	.45
172	Willie Kirkland	1.50	.70	.45
173	Billy Martin	7.00	3.50	2.00
174	Indians Team/Checklist 89-176	6.00	3.00	1.75
175	Pedro Ramos	1.50	.70	.45
176	Vada Pinson	3.25	1.75	1.00
177	Johnny Kucks	1.50	.70	.45
178	Woody Held	1.50	.70	.45
179	Rip Coleman	1.50	.70	.45
180	Harry Simpson	1.50	.70	.45
181	Billy Loes	1.50	.70	.45
182	Glen Hobbie	1.50	.70	.45
183	Eli Grba	2.00	1.00	.60
184	Gary Geiger	1.50	.70	.45
185	Jim Owens	1.50	.70	.45
186	Dave Sisler	1.50	.70	.45
187	Jay Hook	1.50	.70	.45
188	Dick Williams	2.00	1.00	.60
189	Don McMahon	1.50	.70	.45
190	Gene Woodling	1.75	.90	.50
191	Johnny Klippstein	1.50	.70	.45
192	Danny O'Connell	1.50	.70	.45
193	Dick Hyde	1.50	.70	.45
194	Bobby Gene Smith	1.50	.70	.45
195	Lindy McDaniel	1.50	.70	.45
196	Andy Carey	2.00	1.00	.60
197	Ron Kline	1.50	.70	.45
198	Jerry Lynch	1.50	.70	.45
199	Dick Donovan	1.50	.70	.45
200	Willie Mays	80.00	40.00	24.00
201	Larry Osborne	1.50	.70	.45
202	Fred Kipp	1.50	.70	.45
203	Sammy White	1.50	.70	.45
204	Ryne Duren	2.50	1.25	.70
205	Johnny Logan	1.75	.90	.50
206	Claude Osteen	1.75	.90	.50
207	Bob Boyd	1.50	.70	.45
208	White Sox Team/Checklist 177-264	6.00	3.00	1.75

		NR MT	EX	VG
209	Ron Blackburn	1.50	.70	.45
210	Harmon Killebrew	20.00	10.00	6.00
211	Taylor Phillips	1.50	.70	.45
212	Walt Alston	6.00	3.00	1.75
213	Chuck Dressen	1.75	.90	.50
214	Jimmie Dykes	1.50	.70	.45
215	Bob Elliott	1.50	.70	.45
216	Joe Gordon	1.75	.90	.50
217	Charley Grimm	1.75	.90	.50
218	Solly Hemus	1.50	.70	.45
219	Fred Hutchinson	1.75	.90	.50
220	Billy Jurges	1.50	.70	.45
221	Cookie Lavagetto	1.50	.70	.45
222	Al Lopez	5.00	2.50	1.50
223	Danny Murtaugh	1.75	.90	.50
224	Paul Richards	1.75	.90	.50
225	Bill Rigney	1.50	.70	.45
226	Eddie Sawyer	1.50	.70	.45
227	Casey Stengel	18.00	9.00	5.50
228	Ernie Johnson	1.50	.70	.45
229	Joe Morgan	1.50	.70	.45
230	Mound Magicians (Bob Buhl, Lou Burdette, Warren Spahn)	6.00	3.00	1.75
231	Hal Naragon	1.50	.70	.45
232	Jim Busby	1.50	.70	.45
233	Don Elston	1.50	.70	.45
234	Don Demeter	1.50	.70	.45
235	Gus Bell	1.75	.90	.50
236	Dick Ricketts	1.50	.70	.45
237	Elmer Valo	2.00	1.00	.60
238	Danny Kravitz	1.50	.70	.45
239	Joe Shipley	1.50	.70	.45
240	Luis Aparicio	10.00	5.00	3.00
241	Albie Pearson	1.50	.70	.45
242	Cards Team/Checklist 265-352	6.00	3.00	1.75
243	Bubba Phillips	1.50	.70	.45
244	Hal Griggs	1.50	.70	.45
245	Eddie Yost	1.75	.90	.50
246	Lee Maye	1.50	.70	.45
247	Gil McDougald	4.50	2.25	1.25
248	Del Rice	1.50	.70	.45
249	Earl Wilson	1.75	.90	.50
250	Stan Musial	70.00	35.00	21.00
251	Bobby Malkmus	1.50	.70	.45
252	Ray Herbert	1.50	.70	.45
253	Eddie Bressoud	1.50	.70	.45
254	Arnie Portocarrero	1.50	.70	.45
255	Jim Gilliam	3.25	1.75	1.00
256	Dick Brown	1.50	.70	.45
257	Gordy Coleman	1.50	.70	.45
258	Dick Groat	4.00	2.00	1.25
259	George Altman	1.50	.70	.45
260	Power Plus (Rocky Colavito, Tito Francona)	3.00	1.50	.90
261	Pete Burnside	1.50	.70	.45
262	Hank Bauer	2.00	1.00	.60
263	Darrell Johnson	1.50	.70	.45
264	Robin Roberts	15.00	7.50	4.50
265	Rip Repulski	1.50	.70	.45
266	Joe Jay	1.50	.70	.45
267	Jim Marshall	1.50	.70	.45
268	Al Worthington	1.50	.70	.45
269	Gene Green	1.50	.70	.45
270	Bob Turley	3.25	1.75	1.00
271	Julio Becquer	1.50	.70	.45
272	Fred Green	1.50	.70	.45
273	Neil Chrisley	1.50	.70	.45
274	Tom Acker	1.50	.70	.45
275	Curt Flood	3.00	1.50	.90
276	Ken McBride	1.50	.70	.45
277	Harry Bright	1.50	.70	.45
278	Stan Williams	1.50	.70	.45
279	Chuck Tanner	2.50	1.25	.70
280	Frank Sullivan	1.50	.70	.45
281	Ray Boone	1.75	.90	.50
282	Joe Nuxhall	2.00	1.00	.60
283	John Blanchard	2.75	1.50	.80
284	Don Gross	1.50	.70	.45
285	Harry Anderson	1.50	.70	.45
286	Ray Semproch	1.50	.70	.45
287	Felipe Alou	2.50	1.25	.70
288	Bob Mabe	1.75	.90	.50
289	Willie Jones	1.75	.90	.50
290	Jerry Lumpe	2.00	1.00	.60
291	Bob Keegan	1.75	.90	.50
292	Dodger Backstops (Joe Pignatano, John Roseboro)	2.00	1.00	.60
293	Gene Conley	2.00	1.00	.60
294	Tony Taylor	1.50	.70	.45
295	Gil Hodges	18.00	9.00	5.50
296	Nelson Chittum	1.75	.90	.50
297	Reno Bertoia	1.75	.90	.50
298	George Witt	1.75	.90	.50
299	Earl Torgeson	1.75	.90	.50
300	Hank Aaron	80.00	40.00	24.00
301	Jerry Davie	1.75	.90	.50
302	Phillies Team/Checklist 353-429	7.00	3.50	2.00
303	Billy O'Dell	1.75	.90	.50
304	Joe Ginsberg	1.75	.90	.50
305	Richie Ashburn	7.00	3.50	2.00
306	Frank Baumann	1.75	.90	.50
307	Gene Oliver	1.75	.90	.50
308	Dick Hall	1.75	.90	.50
309	Bob Hale	1.75	.90	.50
310	Frank Malzone	2.00	1.00	.60
311	Raul Sanchez	1.75	.90	.50
312	Charlie Lau	2.00	1.00	.60
313	Turk Lown	1.75	.90	.50
314	Chico Fernandez	1.75	.90	.50
315	Bobby Shantz	3.25	1.75	1.00
316	Willie McCovey	125.00	56.00	35.00
317	Pumpsie Green	1.75	.90	.50
318	Jim Baxes	1.75	.90	.50
319	Joe Koppe	1.75	.90	.50
320	Bob Allison	2.25	1.25	.70
321	Ron Fairly	2.00	1.00	.60
322	Willie Tasby	1.75	.90	.50
323	Johnny Romano	1.75	.90	.50
324	Jim Perry	2.50	1.25	.70
325	Jim O'Toole	2.00	1.00	.60
326	Bob Clemente	75.00	37.00	22.00
327	Ray Sadecki	2.25	1.25	.70
328	Earl Battey	2.00	1.00	.60
329	Zack Monroe	2.25	1.25	.70
330	Harvey Kuenn	3.00	1.50	.90
331	Henry Mason	1.75	.90	.50
332	Yankees Team/Checklist 265-352	20.00	10.00	6.00
333	Danny McDevitt	1.75	.90	.50
334	Ted Abernathy	1.75	.90	.50
335	Red Schoendienst	10.00	5.00	3.00
336	Ike Delock	1.75	.90	.50
337	Cal Neeman	1.75	.90	.50
338	Ray Monzant	1.75	.90	.50
339	Harry Chiti	1.75	.90	.50
340	Harvey Haddix	2.25	1.25	.70
341	Carroll Hardy	1.75	.90	.50
342	Casey Wise	1.75	.90	.50
343	Sandy Koufax	70.00	35.00	21.00
344	Clint Courtney	1.75	.90	.50
345	Don Newcombe	2.50	1.25	.70
346	J.C. Martin (photo actually Gary Peters)	1.75	.90	.50
347	Ed Bouchee	1.75	.90	.50
348	Barry Shetrone	1.75	.90	.50
349	Moe Drabowsky	1.75	.90	.50
350	Mickey Mantle	275.00	110.00	69.00
351	Don Nottebart	1.75	.90	.50
352	Cincy Clouters (Gus Bell, Jerry Lynch, Frank Robinson)	5.00	2.50	1.50
353	Don Larsen	2.25	1.25	.70
354	Bob Lillis	1.75	.90	.50
355	Bill White	3.00	1.50	.90
356	Joe Amalfitano	1.75	.90	.50
357	Al Schroll	1.75	.90	.50
358	Joe DeMaestri	2.25	1.25	.70
359	Buddy Gilbert	1.75	.90	.50
360	Herb Score	2.50	1.25	.70
361	Bob Oldis	1.75	.90	.50
362	Russ Kemmerer	1.75	.90	.50
363	Gene Stephens	1.75	.90	.50
364	Paul Foytack	1.75	.90	.50
365	Minnie Minoso	3.00	1.50	.90
366	Dallas Green	3.25	1.75	1.00
367	Bill Tuttle	1.75	.90	.50
368	Daryl Spencer	1.75	.90	.50
369	Billy Hoeft	1.75	.90	.50
370	Bill Skowron	6.00	3.00	1.75
371	Bud Byerly	1.75	.90	.50
372	Frank House	1.75	.90	.50
373	Don Hoak	2.00	1.00	.60
374	Bob Buhl	2.00	1.00	.60
375	Dale Long	2.00	1.00	.60
376	Johnny Briggs	1.75	.90	.50
377	Roger Maris	90.00	45.00	27.00
378	Stu Miller	1.75	.90	.50
379	Red Wilson	1.75	.90	.50
380	Bob Shaw	1.75	.90	.50
381	Braves Team/Checklist 353-429	7.00	3.50	2.00
382	Ted Bowsfield	1.75	.90	.50
383	Leon Wagner	1.75	.90	.50
384	Don Cardwell	1.75	.90	.50

		NR MT	EX	VG
385	World Series Game 1 (Neal Steals Second)	3.50	1.75	1.00
386	World Series Game 2 (Neal Belts 2nd Homer)	3.50	1.75	1.00
387	World Series Game 3 (Furillo Breaks Up Game)	3.50	1.75	1.00
388	World Series Game 4 (Hodges' Winning Homer)	3.75	2.00	1.25
389	World Series Game 5 (Luis Swipes Base)	3.75	2.00	1.25
390	World Series Game 6 (Scrambling After Ball)	3.50	1.75	1.00
391	World Series Summary (The Champs Celebrate)	3.50	1.75	1.00
392	Tex Clevenger	1.75	.90	.50
393	Smoky Burgess	2.50	1.25	.70
394	Norm Larker	1.75	.90	.50
395	Hoyt Wilhelm	15.00	7.50	4.50
396	Steve Bilko	1.75	.90	.50
397	Don Blasingame	1.75	.90	.50
398	Mike Cuellar	2.25	1.25	.70
399	Young Hill Stars (Jack Fisher, Milt Pappas, Jerry Walker)	2.25	1.25	.70
400	Rocky Colavito	5.00	2.50	1.50
401	Bob Duliba	1.75	.90	.50
402	Dick Stuart	2.00	1.00	.60
403	Ed Sadowski	1.75	.90	.50
404	Bob Rush	1.75	.90	.50
405	Bobby Richardson	6.00	3.00	1.75
406	Billy Klaus	1.75	.90	.50
407	*Gary Peters* (photo actually J.C. Martin)	2.25	1.25	.70
408	Carl Furillo	4.00	2.00	1.25
409	Ron Samford	1.75	.90	.50
410	Sam Jones	1.75	.90	.50
411	Ed Bailey	1.75	.90	.50
412	Bob Anderson	1.75	.90	.50
413	A's Team/Checklist 430-495	7.00	3.50	2.00
414	Don Williams	1.75	.90	.50
415	Bob Cerv	1.75	.90	.50
416	Humberto Robinson	1.75	.90	.50
417	Chuck Cottier	1.75	.90	.50
418	Don Mossi	2.00	1.00	.60
419	George Crowe	1.75	.90	.50
420	Ed Mathews	25.00	12.50	7.50
421	Duke Maas	2.25	1.25	.70
422	Johnny Powers	1.75	.90	.50
423	Ed Fitz Gerald	1.75	.90	.50
424	Pete Whisenant	1.75	.90	.50
425	Johnny Podres	3.00	1.50	.90
426	Ron Jackson	1.75	.90	.50
427	Al Grunwald	1.75	.90	.50
428	Al Smith	1.75	.90	.50
429	American League Kings (Nellie Fox, Harvey Kuenn)	2.25	1.25	.70
430	Art Ditmar	2.00	1.00	.60
431	Andre Rodgers	1.75	.90	.50
432	Chuck Stobbs	1.75	.90	.50
433	Irv Noren	1.75	.90	.50
434	Brooks Lawrence	1.75	.90	.50
435	Gene Freese	1.75	.90	.50
436	Marv Throneberry	2.25	1.25	.70
437	Bob Friend	2.50	1.25	.70
438	Jim Coker	1.75	.90	.50
439	Tom Brewer	1.75	.90	.50
440	Jim Lemon	2.00	1.00	.60
441	Gary Bell	3.50	1.75	1.00
442	Joe Pignatano	3.50	1.75	1.00
443	Charlie Maxwell	3.50	1.75	1.00
444	Jerry Kindall	3.50	1.75	1.00
445	Warren Spahn	30.00	15.00	9.00
446	Ellis Burton	3.50	1.75	1.00
447	Ray Moore	3.50	1.75	1.00
448	*Jim Gentile*	4.00	2.00	1.25
449	Jim Brosnan	3.75	2.00	1.25
450	Orlando Cepeda	8.00	4.00	2.50
451	Curt Simmons	4.00	2.00	1.25
452	Ray Webster	3.50	1.75	1.00
453	Vern Law	4.50	2.25	1.25
454	Hal Woodeshick	3.50	1.75	1.00
455	Orioles Coaches (Harry Brecheen, Lum Harris, Eddie Robinson)	3.75	2.00	1.25
456	Red Sox Coaches (Del Baker, Billy Herman, Sal Maglie, Rudy York)	4.00	2.00	1.25
457	Cubs Coaches (Lou Klein, Charlie Root, Elvin Tappe)	3.75	2.00	1.25
458	White Sox Coaches (Ray Berres, Johnny Cooney, Tony Cuccinello, Don Gutteridge)	3.75	2.00	1.25
459	Reds Coaches (Cot Deal, Wally Moses, Reggie Otero)	3.75	2.00	1.25

		NR MT	EX	VG
460	Indians Coaches (Mel Harder, Red Kress, Bob Lemon, Jo-Jo White)	4.00	2.00	1.25
461	Tigers Coaches (Luke Appling, Tom Ferrick, Billy Hitchcock)	4.00	2.00	1.25
462	A's Coaches (Walker Cooper, Fred Fitzsimmons, Don Heffner)	3.75	2.00	1.25
463	Dodgers Coaches (Joe Becker, Bobby Bragan, Greg Mulleavy, Pete Reiser)	4.00	2.00	1.25
464	Braves Coaches (George Myatt, Andy Pafko, Bob Scheffing, Whitlow Wyatt)	3.75	2.00	1.25
465	Yankees Coaches (Frank Crosetti, Bill Dickey, Ralph Houk, Ed Lopat)	7.00	3.50	2.00
466	Phillies Coaches (Dick Carter, Andy Cohen, Ken Silvestri)	3.75	2.00	1.25
467	Pirates Coaches (Bill Burwell, Sam Narron, Frank Oceak, Mickey Vernon)	4.00	2.00	1.25
468	Cardinals Coaches (Ray Katt, Johnny Keane, Howie Pollet, Harry Walker)	3.75	2.00	1.25
469	Giants Coaches (Salty Parker, Bill Posedel, Wes Westrum)	3.75	2.00	1.25
470	Senators Coaches (Ellis Clary, Sam Mele, Bob Swift)	3.75	2.00	1.25
471	Ned Garver	3.50	1.75	1.00
472	Al Dark	4.50	2.25	1.25
473	Al Cicotte	3.50	1.75	1.00
474	Haywood Sullivan	3.75	2.00	1.25
475	Don Drysdale	25.00	12.50	7.50
476	Lou Johnson	3.50	1.75	1.00
477	Don Ferrarese	3.50	1.75	1.00
478	Frank Torre	3.50	1.75	1.00
479	Georges Maranda	3.50	1.75	1.00
480	Yogi Berra	40.00	20.00	12.00
481	Wes Stock	3.50	1.75	1.00
482	Frank Bolling	3.50	1.75	1.00
483	Camilo Pascual	3.75	2.00	1.25
484	Pirates Team/Checklist 430-495	15.00	7.50	4.50
485	Ken Boyer	4.50	2.25	1.25
486	Bobby Del Greco	3.50	1.75	1.00
487	Tom Sturdivant	3.50	1.75	1.00
488	Norm Cash	5.00	2.50	1.50
489	Steve Ridzik	3.50	1.75	1.00
490	Frank Robinson	30.00	15.00	9.00
491	Mel Roach	3.50	1.75	1.00
492	Larry Jackson	3.50	1.75	1.00
493	Duke Snider	40.00	20.00	12.00
494	Orioles Team/Checklist 496-572	7.00	3.50	2.00
495	Sherm Lollar	2.00	1.00	.60
496	Bill Virdon	4.00	2.00	1.25
497	John Tsitouris	3.50	1.75	1.00
498	Al Pilarcik	3.50	1.75	1.00
499	Johnny James	4.00	2.00	1.25
500	Johnny Temple	3.50	1.75	1.00
501	Bob Schmidt	3.50	1.75	1.00
502	Jim Bunning	8.00	4.00	2.50
503	Don Lee	3.50	1.75	1.00
504	Seth Morehead	3.50	1.75	1.00
505	Ted Kluszewski	5.00	2.50	1.50
506	Lee Walls	3.50	1.75	1.00
507	Dick Stigman	8.00	4.00	2.50
508	Billy Consolo	8.00	4.00	2.50
509	*Tommy Davis*	18.00	9.00	5.50
510	Jerry Staley	8.00	4.00	2.50
511	Ken Walters	8.00	4.00	2.50
512	Joe Gibbon	8.00	4.00	2.50
513	Cubs Team/Checklist 496-572	20.00	10.00	6.00
514	*Steve Barber*	9.00	4.50	2.75
515	Stan Lopata	8.00	4.00	2.50
516	Marty Kutyna	8.00	4.00	2.50
517	Charley James	8.00	4.00	2.50
518	*Tony Gonzalez*	9.00	4.50	2.75
519	Ed Roebuck	8.00	4.00	2.50
520	Don Buddin	8.00	4.00	2.50
521	Mike Lee	8.00	4.00	2.50
522	Ken Hunt	9.00	4.50	2.75
523	*Clay Dalrymple*	9.00	4.50	2.75
524	Bill Henry	8.00	4.00	2.50
525	Marv Breeding	8.00	4.00	2.50
526	Paul Giel	8.00	4.00	2.50
527	Jose Valdivielso	8.00	4.00	2.50
528	Ben Johnson	8.00	4.00	2.50
529	Norm Sherry	8.00	4.00	2.50
530	Mike McCormick	9.00	4.50	2.75
531	Sandy Amoros	8.00	4.00	2.50
532	Mike Garcia	10.00	5.00	3.00
533	Lu Clinton	8.00	4.00	2.50
534	Ken MacKenzie	8.00	4.00	2.50
535	Whitey Lockman	8.00	4.00	2.50
536	Wynn Hawkins	8.00	4.00	2.50
537	Red Sox Team/Checklist 496-572	20.00	10.00	6.00

		NR MT	EX	VG
538	Frank Barnes	8.00	4.00	2.50
539	Gene Baker	8.00	4.00	2.50
540	Jerry Walker	8.00	4.00	2.50
541	Tony Curry	8.00	4.00	2.50
542	Ken Hamlin	8.00	4.00	2.50
543	Elio Chacon	8.00	4.00	2.50
544	Bill Monbouquette	9.00	4.50	2.75
545	Carl Sawatski	8.00	4.00	2.50
546	Hank Aguirre	8.00	4.00	2.50
547	*Bob Aspromonte*	9.00	4.50	2.75
548	*Don Mincher*	9.00	4.50	2.75
549	John Buzhardt	8.00	4.00	2.50
550	Jim Landis	8.00	4.00	2.50
551	Ed Rakow	8.00	4.00	2.50
552	Walt Bond	8.00	4.00	2.50
553	Bill Skowron AS	12.00	6.00	3.50
554	Willie McCovey AS	45.00	22.00	13.50
555	Nellie Fox AS	15.00	7.50	4.50
556	Charlie Neal AS	9.00	4.50	2.75
557	Frank Malzone AS	9.00	4.50	2.75
558	Eddie Mathews AS	25.00	12.50	7.50
559	Luis Aparicio AS	18.00	9.00	5.50
560	Ernie Banks AS	35.00	17.50	10.50
561	Al Kaline AS	35.00	17.50	10.50
562	Joe Cunningham AS	9.00	4.50	2.75
563	Mickey Mantle AS	150.00	60.00	38.00
564	Willie Mays AS	85.00	42.00	25.00
565	Roger Maris AS	85.00	42.00	25.00
566	Hank Aaron AS	85.00	42.00	25.00
567	Sherm Lollar AS	9.00	4.50	2.75
568	Del Crandall AS	9.00	4.50	2.75
569	Camilo Pascual AS	9.00	4.50	2.75
570	Don Drysdale AS	25.00	12.50	7.50
571	Billy Pierce AS	9.00	4.50	2.75
572	Johnny Antonelli AS	15.00	5.00	2.75
---	Elect Your Favorite Rookie Insert (paper stock, no date on back)	15.00	7.50	4.50
---	Hot Iron Transfer Insert (paper stock)	15.00	7.50	4.50

1960 Topps Baseball Tattoos

Probably the least popular of all Topps products among parents and teachers, the Topps Tattoos were delightful little items on the reverse of the wrappers of Topps "Tattoo Bubble Gum." The entire wrapper was 1-9/16" by 3-1/2." The happy owner simply moistened his skin and applied the back of the wrapper to the wet spot. Presto, out came a "tattoo" in color (although often blurred by running colors). The set offered 96 tattoo possibilities of which 55 were players, 16 teams, 15 action shots and 10 autographed balls. Surviving specimens are very rare today.

	NR MT	EX	VG
Complete Set:	625.00	312.00	187.00

		NR MT	EX	VG
Common Player:		2.50	1.25	.70
(1)	Hank Aaron	25.00	12.50	7.50
(2)	Bob Allison	5.00	2.50	1.50
(3)	John Antonelli	5.00	2.50	1.50
(4)	Richie Ashburn	7.00	3.50	2.00
(5)	Ernie Banks	15.00	7.50	4.50
(6)	Yogi Berra	18.00	9.00	5.50
(7)	Lew Burdette	6.00	3.00	1.75
(8)	Orlando Cepeda	7.00	3.50	2.00
(9)	Rocky Colavito	6.00	3.00	1.75
(10)	Joe Cunningham	2.50	1.25	.70
(11)	Buddy Daley	2.50	1.25	.70
(12)	Don Drysdale	12.00	6.00	3.50
(13)	Ryne Duren	5.00	2.50	1.50
(14)	Roy Face	5.00	2.50	1.50
(15)	Whitey Ford	15.00	7.50	4.50
(16)	Nellie Fox	7.00	3.50	2.00
(17)	Tito Francona	2.50	1.25	.70
(18)	Gene Freese	2.50	1.25	.70
(19)	Jim Gilliam	6.00	3.00	1.75
(20)	Dick Groat	6.00	3.00	1.75
(21)	Ray Herbert	2.50	1.25	.70
(22)	Glen Hobbie	2.50	1.25	.70
(23)	Jackie Jensen	6.00	3.00	1.75
(24)	Sam Jones	2.50	1.25	.70
(25)	Al Kaline	15.00	7.50	4.50
(26)	Harmon Killebrew	12.00	6.00	3.50
(27)	Harvy Kuenn (Harvey)	6.00	3.00	1.75
(28)	Frank Lary	2.50	1.25	.70
(29)	Vernon Law	5.00	2.50	1.50
(30)	Frank Malzone	2.50	1.25	.70
(31)	Mickey Mantle	75.00	37.00	22.00
(32)	Roger Maris	15.00	7.50	4.50
(33)	Ed Mathews	12.00	6.00	3.50
(34)	Willie Mays	25.00	12.50	7.50
(35)	Cal Mclish	2.50	1.25	.70
(36)	Wally Moon	5.00	2.50	1.50
(37)	Walt Moryn	2.50	1.25	.70
(38)	Don Mossi	2.50	1.25	.70
(39)	Stan Musial	25.00	12.50	7.50
(40)	Charlie Neal	2.50	1.25	.70
(41)	Don Newcombe	5.00	2.50	1.50
(42)	Milt Pappas	5.00	2.50	1.50
(43)	Camilo Pascual	5.00	2.50	1.50
(44)	Billie Pierce (Billy)	5.00	2.50	1.50
(45)	Robin Roberts	12.00	6.00	3.50
(46)	Frank Robinson	15.00	7.50	4.50
(47)	Pete Runnels	5.00	2.50	1.50
(48)	Herb Score	5.00	2.50	1.50
(49)	Warren Spahn	12.00	6.00	3.50
(50)	Johnny Temple	2.50	1.25	.70
(51)	Gus Triandos	2.50	1.25	.70
(52)	Jerry Walker	2.50	1.25	.70
(53)	Bill White	5.00	2.50	1.50
(54)	Gene Woodling	5.00	2.50	1.50
(55)	Early Wynn	12.00	6.00	3.50
(56)	Chicago Cubs Logo	2.50	1.25	.70
(57)	Cincinnati Reds Logo	2.50	1.25	.70
(58)	Los Angeles Dodgers Logo	2.50	1.25	.70
(59)	Milwaukee Braves Logo	2.50	1.25	.70
(60)	Philadelphia Phillies Logo	2.50	1.25	.70
(61)	Pittsburgh Pirates Logo	5.00	2.50	1.50
(62)	San Francisco Giants Logo	2.50	1.25	.70
(63)	St. Louis Cardinals Logo	2.50	1.25	.70
(64)	Baltimore Orioles Logo	2.50	1.25	.70
(65)	Boston Red Sox Logo	2.50	1.25	.70
(66)	Chicago White Sox Logo	2.50	1.25	.70
(67)	Cleveland Indians Logo	2.50	1.25	.70
(68)	Detroit Tigers Logo	2.50	1.25	.70
(69)	Kansas City Athletics Logo	2.50	1.25	.70
(70)	New York Yankees Logo	6.00	3.00	1.75
(71)	Washington Senators Logo	2.50	1.25	.70
(72)	Autograph (Richie Ashburn)	2.50	1.25	.70
(73)	Autograph (Rocky Colavito)	2.50	1.25	.70
(74)	Autograph (Roy Face)	2.50	1.25	.70
(75)	Autograph (Jackie Jensen)	2.50	1.25	.70
(76)	Autograph (Harmon Killebrew)	5.00	2.50	1.50
(77)	Autograph (Mickey Mantle)	25.00	12.50	7.50
(78)	Autograph (Willie Mays)	10.00	5.00	3.00
(79)	Autograph (Stan Musial)	10.00	5.00	3.00
(80)	Autograph (Billy Pierce)	2.50	1.25	.70
(81)	Autograph (Jerry Walker)	2.50	1.25	.70
(82)	Run-Down	2.50	1.25	.70
(83)	Out At First	2.50	1.25	.70
(84)	The Final Word	2.50	1.25	.70
(85)	Twisting Foul	2.50	1.25	.70
(86)	Out At Home	2.50	1.25	.70
(87)	Circus Catch	2.50	1.25	.70
(88)	Great Catch	2.50	1.25	.70
(89)	Stolen Base	2.50	1.25	.70

		NR MT	EX	VG
(90)	Grand Slam Homer	2.50	1.25	.70
(91)	Double Play	2.50	1.25	.70
(92)	Right-Handed Follow-Thru (no caption)			
		2.50	1.25	.70
(93)	Right-Handed High Leg Kick (no caption)			
		2.50	1.25	.70
(94)	Left-Handed Pitcher (no caption)	2.50	1.25	.70
(95)	Right-Handed Batter (no caption)	2.50	1.25	.70
(96)	Left-Handed Batter (no caption)	2.50	1.25	.70

1961 Topps

Except for some of the specialty cards, Topps returned to a vertical format with their 1961 cards. The set is numbered through 598, however only 587 cards were printed. No numbers 426, 587 and 588 were issued. Two cards numbered 463 exist (one a Braves team card and one a player card of Jack Fisher). Actually, the Braves team card is checklisted as #426. Designs for 1961 are basically large color portraits; the backs return to extensive statistics. A three-panel cartoon highlighting the player's career appears on the card backs. Innovations include numbered checklists, cards for statistical leaders, and 10 "Baseball Thrills" cards. The scarce high numbers are card numbers 523-589.

		NR MT	EX	VG
Complete Set:		4400.00	2200.00	1320.
Common Player: 1-370		1.00	.50	.30
Common Player: 371-522		1.50	.70	.45
Common Player: 523-589		20.00	10.00	6.00
1	Dick Groat	12.00	2.00	.70
2	Roger Maris	110.00	50.00	28.00
3	John Buzhardt	1.00	.50	.30
4	Lenny Green	1.00	.50	.30
5	Johnny Romano	1.00	.50	.30
6	Ed Roebuck	1.00	.50	.30
7	White Sox Team	2.50	1.25	.70
8	Dick Williams	1.50	.70	.45
9	Bob Purkey	1.00	.50	.30
10	Brooks Robinson	25.00	12.50	7.50
11	Curt Simmons	1.25	.60	.40
12	Moe Thacker	1.00	.50	.30
13	Chuck Cottier	1.00	.50	.30
14	Don Mossi	1.25	.60	.40
15	Willie Kirkland	1.00	.50	.30
16	Billy Muffett	1.00	.50	.30
17	Checklist 1-88	5.00	2.50	1.50
18	Jim Grant	1.00	.50	.30
19	Cletis Boyer	2.25	1.25	.70
20	Robin Roberts	10.00	5.00	3.00
21	*Zorro Versalles*	2.00	1.00	.60
22	Clem Labine	1.25	.60	.40
23	Don Demeter	1.00	.50	.30
24	Ken Johnson	1.00	.50	.30
25	Red's Heavy Artillery (Gus Bell, Vada Pinson, Frank Robinson)	5.00	2.50	1.50
26	Wes Stock	1.00	.50	.30
27	Jerry Kindall	1.00	.50	.30
28	Hector Lopez	1.50	.70	.45
29	Don Nottebart	1.00	.50	.30
30	Nellie Fox	6.00	3.00	1.75
31	Bob Schmidt	1.00	.50	.30
32	Ray Sadecki	1.00	.50	.30

		NR MT	EX	VG
33	Gary Geiger	1.00	.50	.30
34	Wynn Hawkins	1.00	.50	.30
35	*Ron Santo*	10.00	5.00	3.00
36	Jack Kralick	1.00	.50	.30
37	Charlie Maxwell	1.00	.50	.30
38	Bob Lillis	1.00	.50	.30
39	Leo Posada	1.00	.50	.30
40	Bob Turley	2.50	1.25	.70
41	N.L. Batting Leaders (Bob Clemente, Dick Groat, Norm Larker, Willie Mays)	4.00	2.00	1.25
42	A.L. Batting Leaders (Minnie Minoso, Pete Runnels, Bill Skowron, Al Smith)	2.50	1.25	.70
43	N.L. Home Run Leaders (Hank Aaron, Ernie Banks, Ken Boyer, Eddie Mathews)	4.00	2.00	1.25
44	A.L. Home Run Leaders (Rocky Colavito, Jim Lemon, Mickey Mantle, Roger Maris)	15.00	7.50	4.50
45	N.L. E.R.A. Leaders (Ernie Broglio, Don Drysdale, Bob Friend, Mike McCormick, Stan Williams)	3.25	1.75	1.00
46	A.L. E.R.A. Leaders (Frank Baumann, Hal Brown, Jim Bunning, Art Ditmar)	2.50	1.25	.70
47	N.L. Pitching Leaders (Ernie Broglio, Lou Burdette, Vern Law, Warren Spahn)	3.25	1.75	1.00
48	A.L. Pitching Leaders (Bud Daley, Art Ditmar, Chuck Estrada, Frank Lary, Milt Pappas, Jim Perry)	2.50	1.25	.70
49	N.L. Strikeout Leaders (Ernie Broglio, Don Drysdale, Sam Jones, Sandy Koufax)	4.00	2.00	1.25
50	A.L. Strikeout Leaders (Jim Bunning, Frank Lary, Pedro Ramos, Early Wynn)	3.00	1.50	.90
51	Tigers Team	3.50	1.75	1.00
52	George Crowe	1.00	.50	.30
53	Russ Nixon	1.00	.50	.30
54	Earl Francis	1.00	.50	.30
55	Jim Davenport	1.00	.50	.30
56	Russ Kemmerer	1.00	.50	.30
57	Marv Throneberry	1.75	.90	.50
58	Joe Schaffernoth	1.00	.50	.30
59	Jim Woods	1.00	.50	.30
60	Woodie Held	1.00	.50	.30
61	Ron Piche	1.00	.50	.30
62	Al Pilarcik	1.00	.50	.30
63	Jim Kaat	8.00	4.00	2.50
64	Alex Grammas	1.00	.50	.30
65	Ted Kluszewski	4.00	2.00	1.25
66	Bill Henry	1.00	.50	.30
67	Ossie Virgil	1.00	.50	.30
68	Deron Johnson	1.50	.70	.45
69	Earl Wilson	1.00	.50	.30
70	Bill Virdon	2.00	1.00	.60
71	Jerry Adair	1.25	.60	.40
72	Stu Miller	1.00	.50	.30
73	Al Spangler	1.00	.50	.30
74	Joe Pignatano	1.00	.50	.30
75	Lindy Shows Larry (Larry Jackson, Lindy McDaniel)	1.50	.70	.45
76	Harry Anderson	1.00	.50	.30
77	Dick Stigman	1.00	.50	.30
78	Lee Walls	1.00	.50	.30
79	Joe Ginsberg	1.00	.50	.30
80	Harmon Killebrew	18.00	9.00	5.50
81	Tracy Stallard	1.00	.50	.30
82	Joe Christopher	1.00	.50	.30
83	Bob Bruce	1.00	.50	.30
84	Lee Maye	1.00	.50	.30
85	Jerry Walker	1.00	.50	.30
86	Dodgers Team	3.50	1.75	1.00
87	Joe Amalfitano	1.00	.50	.30
88	Richie Ashburn	6.00	3.00	1.75
89	Billy Martin	6.00	3.00	1.75
90	Jerry Staley	1.00	.50	.30
91	Walt Moryn	1.00	.50	.30
92	Hal Naragon	1.00	.50	.30
93	Tony Gonzalez	1.00	.50	.30
94	Johnny Kucks	1.00	.50	.30
95	Norm Cash	3.50	1.75	1.00
96	Billy O'Dell	1.00	.50	.30
97	Jerry Lynch	1.00	.50	.30
98a	Checklist 89-176 (word "Checklist" in red on front)	7.00	3.50	2.00
98b	Checklist 89-176 ("Checklist" in yellow, 98 on back in black)	5.00	2.50	1.50
98c	Checklist 89-176 ("Checklist" in yellow, 98 on back in white)	7.00	3.50	2.00
99	Don Buddin	1.00	.50	.30
100	Harvey Haddix	1.50	.70	.45
101	Bubba Phillips	1.00	.50	.30
102	Gene Stephens	1.00	.50	.30

		NR MT	EX	VG			NR MT	EX	VG
103	Ruben Amaro	1.00	.50	.30	191	Mike de la Hoz	1.00	.50	.30
104	John Blanchard	1.50	.70	.45	192	Dick Brown	1.00	.50	.30
105	Carl Willey	1.00	.50	.30	193	Gene Conley	1.25	.60	.40
106	Whitey Herzog	2.25	1.25	.70	194	Gordy Coleman	1.00	.50	.30
107	Seth Morehead	1.00	.50	.30	195	Jerry Casale	1.00	.50	.30
108	Dan Dobbek	1.00	.50	.30	196	Ed Bouchee	1.00	.50	.30
109	Johnny Podres	2.25	1.25	.70	197	Dick Hall	1.00	.50	.30
110	Vada Pinson	3.00	1.50	.90	198	Carl Sawatski	1.00	.50	.30
111	Jack Meyer	1.00	.50	.30	199	Bob Boyd	1.00	.50	.30
112	Chico Fernandez	1.00	.50	.30	200	Warren Spahn	25.00	12.50	7.50
113	Mike Fornieles	1.00	.50	.30	201	Pete Whisenant	1.00	.50	.30
114	Hobie Landrith	1.00	.50	.30	202	Al Neiger	1.00	.50	.30
115	Johnny Antonelli	1.25	.60	.40	203	Eddie Bressoud	1.00	.50	.30
116	Joe DeMaestri	1.50	.70	.45	204	Bob Skinner	1.25	.60	.40
117	Dale Long	1.25	.60	.40	205	Bill Pierce	1.75	.90	.50
118	Chris Cannizzaro	1.00	.50	.30	206	Gene Green	1.00	.50	.30
119	A's Big Armor (Hank Bauer, Jerry Lumpe, Norm Siebern)	1.50	.70	.45	207	Dodger Southpaws (Sandy Koufax, Johnny Podres)	15.00	7.50	4.50
120	Ed Mathews	15.00	7.50	4.50	208	Larry Osborne	1.00	.50	.30
121	Eli Grba	1.00	.50	.30	209	Ken McBride	1.00	.50	.30
122	Cubs Team	2.50	1.25	.70	210	Pete Runnels	1.25	.60	.40
123	Billy Gardner	1.00	.50	.30	211	Bob Gibson	20.00	10.00	6.00
124	J.C. Martin	1.00	.50	.30	212	Haywood Sullivan	1.25	.60	.40
125	Steve Barber	1.00	.50	.30	213	*Bill Stafford*	2.00	1.00	.60
126	Dick Stuart	1.25	.60	.40	214	Danny Murphy	1.00	.50	.30
127	Ron Kline	1.00	.50	.30	215	Gus Bell	1.25	.60	.40
128	Rip Repulski	1.00	.50	.30	216	Ted Bowsfield	1.00	.50	.30
129	Ed Hobaugh	1.00	.50	.30	217	Mel Roach	1.00	.50	.30
130	Norm Larker	1.00	.50	.30	218	Hal Brown	1.00	.50	.30
131	Paul Richards	1.25	.60	.40	219	Gene Mauch	2.50	1.25	.70
132	Al Lopez	3.00	1.50	.90	220	Al Dark	1.25	.60	.40
133	Ralph Houk	3.00	1.50	.90	221	Mike Higgins	1.00	.50	.30
134	Mickey Vernon	1.25	.60	.40	222	Jimmie Dykes	1.00	.50	.30
135	Fred Hutchinson	1.25	.60	.40	223	Bob Scheffing	1.00	.50	.30
136	Walt Alston	4.00	2.00	1.25	224	Joe Gordon	1.25	.60	.40
137	Chuck Dressen	1.25	.60	.40	225	Bill Rigney	1.00	.50	.30
138	Danny Murtaugh	1.25	.60	.40	226	Harry Lavagetto	1.00	.50	.30
139	Solly Hemus	1.00	.50	.30	227	Juan Pizarro	1.00	.50	.30
140	Gus Triandos	1.25	.60	.40	228	Yankees Team	10.00	5.00	3.00
141	*Billy Williams*	70.00	35.00	21.00	229	Rudy Hernandez	1.00	.50	.30
142	Luis Arroyo	1.50	.70	.45	230	Don Hoak	1.25	.60	.40
143	Russ Snyder	1.00	.50	.30	231	Dick Drott	1.00	.50	.30
144	Jim Coker	1.00	.50	.30	232	Bill White	1.50	.70	.45
145	Bob Buhl	1.25	.60	.40	233	Joe Jay	1.00	.50	.30
146	Marty Keough	1.00	.50	.30	234	Ted Lepcio	1.00	.50	.30
147	Ed Rakow	1.00	.50	.30	235	Camilo Pascual	1.25	.60	.40
148	Julian Javier	1.25	.60	.40	236	Don Gile	1.00	.50	.30
149	Bob Oldis	1.00	.50	.30	237	Billy Loes	1.00	.50	.30
150	Willie Mays	70.00	35.00	21.00	238	Jim Gilliam	2.50	1.25	.70
151	Jim Donohue	1.00	.50	.30	239	Dave Sisler	1.00	.50	.30
152	Earl Torgeson	1.00	.50	.30	240	Ron Hansen	1.00	.50	.30
153	Don Lee	1.00	.50	.30	241	Al Cicotte	1.00	.50	.30
154	Bobby Del Greco	1.00	.50	.30	242	Hal W. Smith	1.00	.50	.30
155	Johnny Temple	1.25	.60	.40	243	Frank Lary	1.25	.60	.40
156	Ken Hunt	1.00	.50	.30	244	Chico Cardenas	1.25	.60	.40
157	Cal McLish	1.00	.50	.30	245	Joe Adcock	2.00	1.00	.60
158	Pete Daley	1.00	.50	.30	246	Bob Davis	1.00	.50	.30
159	Orioles Team	2.50	1.25	.70	247	Billy Goodman	1.00	.50	.30
160	Whitey Ford	20.00	10.00	6.00	248	Ed Keegan	1.00	.50	.30
161	Sherman Jones (photo actually Eddie Fisher)	1.00	.50	.30	249	Reds Team	4.00	2.00	1.25
162	Jay Hook	1.00	.50	.30	250	Buc Hill Aces (Roy Face, Vern Law)	2.00	1.00	.60
163	Ed Sadowski	1.00	.50	.30	251	Bill Bruton	1.00	.50	.30
164	Felix Mantilla	1.00	.50	.30	252	Bill Short	1.50	.70	.45
165	Gino Cimoli	1.00	.50	.30	253	Sammy Taylor	1.00	.50	.30
166	Danny Kravitz	1.00	.50	.30	254	Ted Sadowski	1.00	.50	.30
167	Giants Team	2.50	1.25	.70	255	Vic Power	1.00	.50	.30
168	Tommy Davis	3.00	1.50	.90	256	Billy Hoeft	1.00	.50	.30
169	Don Elston	1.00	.50	.30	257	Carroll Hardy	1.00	.50	.30
170	Al Smith	1.00	.50	.30	258	Jack Sanford	1.00	.50	.30
171	Paul Foytack	1.00	.50	.30	259	John Schaive	1.00	.50	.30
172	Don Dillard	1.00	.50	.30	260	Don Drysdale	15.00	7.50	4.50
173	Beantown Bombers (Jackie Jensen, Frank Malzone, Vic Wertz)	2.00	1.00	.60	261	Charlie Lau	1.25	.60	.40
174	Ray Semproch	1.00	.50	.30	262	Tony Curry	1.00	.50	.30
175	Gene Freese	1.00	.50	.30	263	Ken Hamlin	1.00	.50	.30
176	Ken Aspromonte	1.00	.50	.30	264	Glen Hobbie	1.00	.50	.30
177	Don Larsen	1.50	.70	.45	265	Tony Kubek	5.00	2.50	1.50
178	Bob Nieman	1.00	.50	.30	266	Lindy McDaniel	1.00	.50	.30
179	Joe Koppe	1.00	.50	.30	267	Norm Siebern	1.25	.60	.40
180	Bobby Richardson	5.00	2.50	1.50	268	Ike DeLock (Delock)	1.00	.50	.30
181	Fred Green	1.00	.50	.30	269	Harry Chiti	1.00	.50	.30
182	Dave Nicholson	1.00	.50	.30	270	Bob Friend	1.50	.70	.45
183	Andre Rodgers	1.00	.50	.30	271	Jim Landis	1.00	.50	.30
184	Steve Bilko	1.00	.50	.30	272	Tom Morgan	1.00	.50	.30
185	Herb Score	1.50	.70	.45	273	Checklist 265-352	5.00	2.50	1.50
186	Elmer Valo	1.00	.50	.30	274	Gary Bell	1.00	.50	.30
187	Billy Klaus	1.00	.50	.30	275	Gene Woodling	1.25	.60	.40
188	Jim Marshall	1.00	.50	.30	276	Ray Rippelmeyer	1.00	.50	.30
189	Checklist 177-264	5.00	2.50	1.50	277	Hank Foiles	1.00	.50	.30
190	Stan Williams	1.00	.50	.30	278	Don McMahon	1.00	.50	.30
					279	Jose Pagan	1.00	.50	.30

		NR MT	EX	VG
280	Frank Howard	2.50	1.25	.70
281	Frank Sullivan	1.00	.50	.30
282	Faye Throneberry	1.00	.50	.30
283	Bob Anderson	1.00	.50	.30
284	Dick Gernert	1.00	.50	.30
285	Sherm Lollar	1.25	.60	.40
286	George Witt	1.00	.50	.30
287	Carl Yastrzemski	125.00	56.00	35.00
288	Albie Pearson	1.00	.50	.30
289	Ray Moore	1.00	.50	.30
290	Stan Musial	65.00	33.00	20.00
291	Tex Clevenger	1.00	.50	.30
292	Jim Baumer	1.00	.50	.30
293	Tom Sturdivant	1.00	.50	.30
294	Don Blasingame	1.00	.50	.30
295	Milt Pappas	1.25	.60	.40
296	Wes Covington	1.00	.50	.30
297	Athletics Team	2.50	1.25	.70
298	Jim Golden	1.00	.50	.30
299	Clay Dalrymple	1.00	.50	.30
300	Mickey Mantle	275.00	110.00	69.00
301	Chet Nichols	1.00	.50	.30
302	Al Heist	1.00	.50	.30
303	Gary Peters	1.25	.60	.40
304	Rocky Nelson	1.00	.50	.30
305	Mike McCormick	1.25	.60	.40
306	World Series Game 1 (Virdon Saves Game)	3.50	1.75	1.00
307	World Series Game 2 (Mantle Slams 2 Homers)	20.00	10.00	6.00
308	World Series Game 3 (Richardson Is Hero)	4.00	2.00	1.25
309	World Series Game 4 (Cimoli Is Safe In Crucial Play)	3.00	1.50	.90
310	World Series Game 5 (Face Saves the Day)	3.50	1.75	1.00
311	World Series Game 6 (Ford Pitches Second Shutout)	5.00	2.50	1.50
312	World Series Game 7 (Mazeroski's Homer Wins It!)	5.00	2.50	1.50
313	World Series Summary (The Winners Celebrate)	3.00	1.50	.90
314	Bob Miller	1.00	.50	.30
315	Earl Battey	1.25	.60	.40
316	Bobby Gene Smith	1.00	.50	.30
317	*Jim Brewer*	1.25	.60	.40
318	Danny O'Connell	1.00	.50	.30
319	Valmy Thomas	1.00	.50	.30
320	Lou Burdette	2.50	1.25	.70
321	Marv Breeding	1.00	.50	.30
322	Bill Kunkel	1.00	.50	.30
323	Sammy Esposito	1.00	.50	.30
324	Hank Aguirre	1.00	.50	.30
325	Wally Moon	1.25	.60	.40
326	Dave Hillman	1.00	.50	.30
327	*Matty Alou*	4.00	2.00	1.25
328	Jim O'Toole	1.00	.50	.30
329	Julio Becquer	1.00	.50	.30
330	Rocky Colavito	3.00	1.50	.90
331	Ned Garver	1.00	.50	.30
332	Dutch Dotterer (photo actually Tommy Dotterer)	1.00	.50	.30
333	Fritz Brickell	1.50	.70	.45
334	Walt Bond	1.00	.50	.30
335	Frank Bolling	1.00	.50	.30
336	Don Mincher	1.25	.60	.40
337	Al's Aces (Al Lopez, Herb Score, Early Wynn)	3.50	1.75	1.00
338	Don Landrum	1.00	.50	.30
339	Gene Baker	1.00	.50	.30
340	Vic Wertz	1.25	.60	.40
341	Jim Owens	1.00	.50	.30
342	Clint Courtney	1.00	.50	.30
343	Earl Robinson	1.00	.50	.30
344	Sandy Koufax	80.00	40.00	24.00
345	Jim Piersall	2.00	1.00	.60
346	Howie Nunn	1.00	.50	.30
347	Cardinals Team	2.50	1.25	.70
348	Steve Boros	1.00	.50	.30
349	Danny McDevitt	1.50	.70	.45
350	Ernie Banks	25.00	12.50	7.50
351	Jim King	1.00	.50	.30
352	Bob Shaw	1.00	.50	.30
353	Howie Bedell	1.00	.50	.30
354	Billy Harrell	1.00	.50	.30
355	Bob Allison	1.25	.60	.40
356	Ryne Duren	2.25	1.25	.70
357	Daryl Spencer	1.00	.50	.30
358	Earl Averill	1.00	.50	.30
359	Dallas Green	1.25	.60	.40
360	Frank Robinson	20.00	10.00	6.00

		NR MT	EX	VG
361a	Checklist 353-429 ("Topps Baseball" in black on front)	5.00	2.50	1.50
361b	Checklist 353-429 ("Topps Baseball" in yellow)	6.00	3.00	1.75
362	Frank Funk	1.00	.50	.30
363	John Roseboro	1.25	.60	.40
364	Moe Drabowsky	1.00	.50	.30
365	Jerry Lumpe	1.25	.60	.40
366	Eddie Fisher	1.00	.50	.30
367	Jim Rivera	1.00	.50	.30
368	Bennie Daniels	1.00	.50	.30
369	Dave Philley	1.25	.60	.40
370	Roy Face	2.00	1.00	.60
371	Bill Skowron	5.00	2.50	1.50
372	Bob Hendley	1.50	.70	.45
373	Red Sox Team	5.00	2.50	1.50
374	Paul Giel	1.50	.70	.45
375	Ken Boyer	4.00	2.00	1.25
376	Mike Roarke	1.50	.70	.45
377	Ruben Gomez	1.50	.70	.45
378	Wally Post	1.50	.70	.45
379	Bobby Shantz	2.50	1.25	.70
380	Minnie Minoso	3.00	1.50	.90
381	Dave Wickersham	1.50	.70	.45
382	Frank Thomas	1.50	.70	.45
383	Frisco First Liners (Mike McCormick, Billy O'Dell, Jack Sanford)	2.00	1.00	.60
384	Chuck Essegian	1.50	.70	.45
385	Jim Perry	2.50	1.25	.70
386	Joe Hicks	1.50	.70	.45
387	Duke Maas	2.50	1.25	.70
388	Bob Clemente	70.00	35.00	21.00
389	Ralph Terry	3.00	1.50	.90
390	Del Crandall	2.50	1.25	.70
391	Winston Brown	1.50	.70	.45
392	Reno Bertoia	1.50	.70	.45
393	Batter Bafflers (Don Cardwell, Glen Hobbie)	1.75	.90	.50
394	Ken Walters	1.50	.70	.45
395	Chuck Estrada	1.50	.70	.45
396	Bob Aspromonte	1.50	.70	.45
397	Hal Woodeshick	1.50	.70	.45
398	Hank Bauer	2.50	1.25	.70
399	Cliff Cook	1.50	.70	.45
400	Vern Law	2.50	1.25	.70
401	Babe Ruth Hits 60th Homer	15.00	7.50	4.50
402	Larsen Pitches Perfect Game	10.00	5.00	3.00
403	Brooklyn-Boston Play 26-Inning Tie	2.00	1.00	.60
404	Hornsby Tops N.L. With .424 Average	3.50	1.75	1.00
405	Gehrig Benched After 2,130 Games	12.00	6.00	3.50
406	Mantle Blasts 565 ft. Home Run	30.00	15.00	9.00
407	Jack Chesbro Wins 41st Game	2.50	1.25	.70
408	Mathewson Strikes Out 267 Batters	3.50	1.75	1.00
409	Johnson Hurls 3rd Shutout in 4 Days	4.00	2.00	1.25
410	Haddix Pitches 12 Perfect Innings	2.50	1.25	.70
411	Tony Taylor	1.50	.70	.45
412	Larry Sherry	1.50	.70	.45
413	Eddie Yost	1.75	.90	.50
414	Dick Donovan	1.50	.70	.45
415	Hank Aaron	80.00	40.00	24.00
416	*Dick Howser*	5.00	2.50	1.50
417	*Juan Marichal*	80.00	40.00	24.00
418	Ed Bailey	1.50	.70	.45
419	Tom Borland	1.50	.70	.45
420	Ernie Broglio	1.50	.70	.45
421	Ty Cline	1.50	.70	.45
422	Bud Daley	1.50	.70	.45
423	Charlie Neal	1.50	.70	.45
424	Turk Lown	1.50	.70	.45
425	Yogi Berra	60.00	30.00	18.00
426	Not Issued			
427	Dick Ellsworth	1.50	.70	.45
428	Ray Barker	1.50	.70	.45
429	Al Kaline	35.00	17.50	10.50
430	Bill Mazeroski	3.50	1.75	1.00
431	Chuck Stobbs	1.50	.70	.45
432	Coot Veal	1.50	.70	.45
433	Art Mahaffey	1.50	.70	.45
434	Tom Brewer	1.50	.70	.45
435	Orlando Cepeda	7.00	3.50	2.00
436	*Jim Maloney*	2.50	1.25	.70
437a	Checklist 430-506 (#440 is Louis Aparicio)	6.00	3.00	1.75
437b	Checklist 430-506 (#440 is Luis Aparicio)	6.50	3.25	2.00
438	Curt Flood	2.50	1.25	.70

		NR MT	EX	VG
439	*Phil Regan*	1.75	.90	.50
440	Luis Aparicio	12.00	6.00	3.50
441	Dick Bertell	1.50	.70	.45
442	Gordon Jones	1.50	.70	.45
443	Duke Snider	35.00	17.50	10.50
444	Joe Nuxhall	1.75	.90	.50
445	Frank Malzone	1.75	.90	.50
446	Bob "Hawk" Taylor	1.50	.70	.45
447	Harry Bright	1.50	.70	.45
448	Del Rice	1.50	.70	.45
449	*Bobby Bolin*	1.75	.90	.50
450	Jim Lemon	1.50	.70	.45
451	Power For Ernie (Ernie Broglio, Daryl Spencer, Bill White)	1.75	.90	.50
452	Bob Allen	1.50	.70	.45
453	Dick Schofield	1.50	.70	.45
454	Pumpsie Green	1.50	.70	.45
455	Early Wynn	15.00	7.50	4.50
456	Hal Bevan	1.50	.70	.45
457	Johnny James	1.50	.70	.45
458	Willie Tasby	1.50	.70	.45
459	Terry Fox	1.50	.70	.45
460	Gil Hodges	18.00	9.00	5.50
461	Smoky Burgess	2.50	1.25	.70
462	Lou Klimchock	1.50	.70	.45
463a	Braves Team (should be card #426)	4.00	2.00	1.25
463b	Jack Fisher	1.75	.90	.50
464	*Leroy Thomas*	1.50	.70	.45
465	Roy McMillan	1.50	.70	.45
466	Ron Moeller	1.50	.70	.45
467	Indians Team	3.50	1.75	1.00
468	Johnny Callison	1.75	.90	.50
469	Ralph Lumenti	1.50	.70	.45
470	Roy Sievers	1.75	.90	.50
471	Phil Rizzuto MVP	8.00	4.00	2.50
472	Yogi Berra MVP	25.00	12.50	7.50
473	Bobby Shantz MVP	3.50	1.75	1.00
474	Al Rosen MVP	3.50	1.75	1.00
475	Mickey Mantle MVP	65.00	32.00	19.50
476	Jackie Jensen MVP	3.50	1.75	1.00
477	Nellie Fox MVP	4.00	2.00	1.25
478	Roger Maris MVP	30.00	15.00	9.00
479	Jim Konstanty MVP	2.50	1.25	.70
480	Roy Campanella MVP	20.00	10.00	6.00
481	Hank Sauer MVP	2.50	1.25	.70
482	Willie Mays MVP	25.00	12.50	7.50
483	Don Newcombe MVP	3.50	1.75	1.00
484	Hank Aaron MVP	25.00	12.50	7.50
485	Ernie Banks MVP	15.00	7.50	4.50
486	Dick Groat MVP	3.50	1.75	1.00
487	Gene Oliver	1.50	.70	.45
488	Joe McClain	1.50	.70	.45
489	Walt Dropo	1.75	.90	.50
490	Jim Bunning	8.00	4.00	2.50
491	Phillies Team	3.50	1.75	1.00
492	Ron Fairly	1.75	.90	.50
493	Don Zimmer	2.00	1.00	.60
494	Tom Cheney	1.50	.70	.45
495	Elston Howard	6.00	3.00	1.75
496	Ken MacKenzie	1.50	.70	.45
497	Willie Jones	1.50	.70	.45
498	Ray Herbert	1.50	.70	.45
499	Chuck Schilling	1.50	.70	.45
500	Harvey Kuenn	3.00	1.50	.90
501	John DeMerit	1.50	.70	.45
502	Clarence Coleman	1.50	.70	.45
503	Tito Francona	1.75	.90	.50
504	Billy Consolo	1.50	.70	.45
505	Red Schoendienst	8.00	4.00	2.50
506	*Willie Davis*	7.00	3.50	2.00
507	Pete Burnside	1.50	.70	.45
508	Rocky Bridges	1.50	.70	.45
509	Camilo Carreon	1.50	.70	.45
510	Art Ditmar	2.50	1.25	.70
511	Joe Morgan	1.50	.70	.45
512	Bob Will	1.50	.70	.45
513	Jim Brosnan	1.75	.90	.50
514	Jake Wood	1.50	.70	.45
515	Jackie Brandt	1.50	.70	.45
516	Checklist 507-587	6.00	3.00	1.75
517	Willie McCovey	40.00	20.00	12.00
518	Andy Carey	1.50	.70	.45
519	Jim Pagliaroni	1.50	.70	.45
520	Joe Cunningham	1.75	.90	.50
521	Brother Battery (Larry Sherry, Norm Sherry)	2.00	1.00	.60
522	Dick Farrell	1.50	.70	.45
523	Joe Gibbon	20.00	10.00	6.00
524	Johnny Logan	22.00	11.00	6.50
525	*Ron Perranoski*	22.00	11.00	6.50

		NR MT	EX	VG
526	R.C. Stevens	20.00	10.00	6.00
527	Gene Leek	20.00	10.00	6.00
528	Pedro Ramos	20.00	10.00	6.00
529	Bob Roselli	20.00	10.00	6.00
530	Bobby Malkmus	20.00	10.00	6.00
531	Jim Coates	22.00	11.00	6.50
532	Bob Hale	20.00	10.00	6.00
533	Jack Curtis	20.00	10.00	6.00
534	Eddie Kasko	20.00	10.00	6.00
535	Larry Jackson	20.00	10.00	6.00
536	Bill Tuttle	20.00	10.00	6.00
537	Bobby Locke	20.00	10.00	6.00
538	Chuck Hiller	20.00	10.00	6.00
539	Johnny Klippstein	20.00	10.00	6.00
540	Jackie Jensen	30.00	15.00	9.00
541	Roland Sheldon	22.00	11.00	6.50
542	Twins Team	40.00	20.00	12.00
543	Roger Craig	35.00	17.50	10.50
544	George Thomas	20.00	10.00	6.00
545	Hoyt Wilhelm	55.00	28.00	16.50
546	Marty Kutyna	20.00	10.00	6.00
547	Leon Wagner	22.00	11.00	6.50
548	Ted Wills	20.00	10.00	6.00
549	Hal R. Smith	20.00	10.00	6.00
550	Frank Baumann	20.00	10.00	6.00
551	George Altman	20.00	10.00	6.00
552	Jim Archer	20.00	10.00	6.00
553	Bill Fischer	20.00	10.00	6.00
554	Pirates Team	35.00	17.50	10.50
555	Sam Jones	20.00	10.00	6.00
556	Ken R. Hunt	20.00	10.00	6.00
557	Jose Valdivielso	20.00	10.00	6.00
558	Don Ferrarese	20.00	10.00	6.00
559	Jim Gentile	22.00	11.00	6.50
560	Barry Latman	20.00	10.00	6.00
561	Charley James	20.00	10.00	6.00
562	Bill Monbouquette	22.00	11.00	6.50
563	Bob Cerv	22.00	11.00	6.50
564	Don Cardwell	20.00	10.00	6.00
565	Felipe Alou	25.00	12.50	7.50
566	Paul Richards AS	25.00	12.50	7.50
567	Danny Murtaugh AS	25.00	12.50	7.50
568	Bill Skowron AS	35.00	17.50	10.50
569	Frank Herrera AS	25.00	12.50	7.50
570	Nellie Fox AS	40.00	20.00	12.00
571	Bill Mazeroski AS	35.00	17.50	10.50
572	Brooks Robinson AS	80.00	40.00	24.00
573	Ken Boyer AS	35.00	17.50	10.50
574	Luis Aparicio AS	45.00	23.00	13.50
575	Ernie Banks AS	75.00	38.00	23.00
576	Roger Maris AS	90.00	45.00	27.00
577	Hank Aaron AS	125.00	56.00	35.00
578	Mickey Mantle AS	300.00	120.00	75.00
579	Willie Mays AS	125.00	56.00	35.00
580	Al Kaline AS	75.00	38.00	23.00
581	Frank Robinson AS	75.00	38.00	23.00
582	Earl Battey AS	25.00	12.50	7.50
583	Del Crandall AS	30.00	15.00	9.00
584	Jim Perry AS	30.00	15.00	9.00
585	Bob Friend AS	30.00	15.00	9.00
586	Whitey Ford AS	75.00	38.00	23.00
587	Not Issued			
588	Not Issued			
589	Warren Spahn AS	125.00	56.00	35.00

1961 Topps Dice Game

One of the more obscure Topps test issues that may have never actually been issued is the 1961 Topps Dice Game. Eighteen black and white cards, each measuring 2-1/2" by 3-1/2" in size, comprise the set. Interestingly, there are no identifying marks, such as copyrights or trademarks, to indicate the set was produced by Topps. The card backs contain various baseball plays that occur when a certain pitch is called and a specific number of the dice is rolled.

		NR MT	EX	VG
	Complete Set:	7200.00	3600.00	2150.
	Common Player:	100.00	50.00	30.00
(1)	Earl Battey	100.00	50.00	30.00
(2)	Del Crandall	100.00	50.00	30.00
(3)	Jim Davenport	100.00	50.00	30.00
(4)	Don Drysdale	300.00	150.00	90.00
(5)	Dick Groat	150.00	75.00	45.00
(6)	Al Kaline	600.00	300.00	175.00
(7)	Tony Kubek	150.00	75.00	45.00
(8)	Mickey Mantle	2500.00	1250.00	750.00
(9)	Willie Mays	1000.00	500.00	300.00
(10)	Bill Mazeroski	150.00	75.00	45.00
(11)	Stan Musial	800.00	400.00	240.00
(12)	Camilo Pascual	100.00	50.00	30.00
(13)	Bobby Richardson	150.00	75.00	45.00
(14)	Brooks Robinson	400.00	200.00	120.00
(15)	Frank Robinson	300.00	150.00	90.00
(16)	Norm Siebern	100.00	50.00	30.00
(17)	Leon Wagner	100.00	50.00	30.00
(18)	Bill White	100.00	50.00	30.00

1961 Topps Magic Rub-Offs

Not too different in concept from the tattoos of the previous year, the Topps Magic Rub-Off was designed to leave impressions of team themes or individual players when properly applied. Measuring 2-1/16" by 3-1/16," the Magic Rub-Off was not designed specifically for application to the owner's skin. The set of 36 Rub-Offs seems to almost be a tongue-in-cheek product as the team themes were a far cry from official logos, and the players seem to have been included for their nicknames. Among the players (one representing each team) the best known and most valuable are Yogi Berra and Ernie Banks.

		NR MT	EX	VG
	Complete Set:	85.00	42.00	25.00
	Common Player:	1.00	.50	.30
(1)	Baltimore Orioles Pennant	1.00	.50	.30
(2)	Ernie "Bingo" Banks	12.00	6.00	3.50
(3)	Yogi Berra	20.00	10.00	6.00
(4)	Boston Red Sox Pennant	1.00	.50	.30
(5)	Jackie "Ozark" Brandt	1.25	.60	.40
(6)	Jim "Professor" Brosnan	1.25	.60	.40
(7)	Chicago Cubs Pennant	1.00	.50	.30
(8)	Chicago White Sox Pennant	1.00	.50	.30
(9)	Cincinnati Red Legs Pennant	1.00	.50	.30
(10)	Cleveland Indians Pennant	1.00	.50	.30
(11)	Detroit Tigers Pennant	1.25	.60	.40
(12)	Henry "Dutch" Dotterer	1.25	.60	.40
(13)	Joe "Flash" Gordon	1.50	.70	.45
(14)	Harvey "The Kitten" Haddix	1.50	.70	.45
(15)	Frank "Pancho" Hererra	1.25	.60	.40
(16)	Frank "Tower" Howard	3.50	1.75	1.00
(17)	"Sad" Sam Jones	1.25	.60	.40

		NR MT	EX	VG
(18)	Kansas City Athletics Pennant	1.00	.50	.30
(19)	Los Angeles Angels Pennant	1.00	.50	.30
(20)	Los Angeles Dodgers Pennant	1.25	.60	.40
(21)	Omar "Turk" Lown	1.25	.60	.40
(22)	Billy "The Kid" Martin	6.00	3.00	1.75
(23)	Duane "Duke" Mass (Maas)	1.25	.60	.40
(24)	Charlie "Paw Paw" Maxwell	1.25	.60	.40
(25)	Milwaukee Braves Pennant	1.00	.50	.30
(26)	Minnesota Twins Pennant	1.00	.50	.30
(27)	"Farmer" Ray Moore	1.00	.50	.30
(28)	Walt "Moose" Moryn	1.00	.50	.30
(29)	New York Yankees Pennant	2.50	1.25	.70
(30)	Philadelphia Phillies Pennant	1.00	.50	.30
(31)	Pittsburgh Pirates Pennant	1.00	.50	.30
(32)	John "Honey" Romano	1.25	.60	.40
(33)	"Pistol Pete" Runnels	1.50	.70	.45
(34)	St. Louis Cardinals Pennant	1.00	.50	.30
(35)	San Francisco Giants Pennant	1.00	.50	.30
(36)	Washington Senators Pennant	1.00	.50	.30

1961 Topps Stamps

Issued as an added insert to 1961 Topps wax packes these 1-3/8" by 1-3/16" stamps were designd to be collected and be placed in an album which could be bought for an additional 10¢. Packs of cards contained two stamps. There are 208 stamps in a complete set which depict 207 different players (Al Kaline appears twice). There are 104 players on brown stamps and 104 on green. While there are many Hall of Famers on the stamps, prices remain low because there is relatively little interest in what is a non-card set.

		NR MT	EX	VG
	Complete Set:	225.00	112.00	70.00
	Stamp Album:	35.00	17.50	10.50
	Common Player:	.40	.20	.12
(1)	Hank Aaron	10.00	5.00	3.00
(2)	Joe Adcock	.35	.20	.11
(3)	Hank Aguirre	.40	.20	.12
(4)	Bob Allison	.30	.15	.09
(5)	George Altman	.40	.20	.12
(6)	Bob Anderson	.40	.20	.12
(7)	Johnny Antonelli	.30	.15	.09
(8)	Luis Aparicio	1.50	.70	.45
(9)	Luis Arroyo	.35	.20	.11
(10)	Richie Ashburn	.80	.40	.25
(11)	Ken Aspromonte	.40	.20	.12
(12)	Ed Bailey	.40	.20	.12
(13)	Ernie Banks	6.00	3.00	1.75
(14)	Steve Barber	.40	.20	.12
(15)	Earl Battey	.30	.15	.09
(16)	Hank Bauer	.50	.25	.15
(17)	Gus Bell	.30	.15	.09
(18)	Yogi Berra	5.00	2.50	1.50
(19)	Reno Bertoia	.40	.20	.12
(20)	John Blanchard	.35	.20	.11
(21)	Don Blasingame	.40	.20	.12
(22)	Frank Bolling	.40	.20	.12
(23)	Steve Boros	.40	.20	.12
(24)	Ed Bouchee	.40	.20	.12
(25)	Bob Boyd	.40	.20	.12
(26)	Cletis Boyer	.35	.20	.11
(27)	Ken Boyer	.50	.25	.15
(28)	Jackie Brandt	.40	.20	.12

Johnny Callison caption: JOHNNY CALLISON PHILA PHILLIES OUTFIELD

		NR MT	EX	VG
(29)	Marv Breeding	.40	.20	.12
(30)	Eddie Bressoud	.40	.20	.12
(31)	Jim Brewer	.40	.20	.12
(32)	Tom Brewer	.40	.20	.12
(33)	Jim Brosnan	.30	.15	.09
(34)	Bill Bruton	.40	.20	.12
(35)	Bob Buhl	.30	.15	.09
(36)	Jim Bunning	1.00	.50	.30
(37)	Smoky Burgess	.30	.15	.09
(38)	John Buzhardt	.40	.20	.12
(39)	Johnny Callison	.30	.15	.09
(40)	Chico Cardenas	.40	.20	.12
(41)	Andy Carey	.40	.20	.12
(42)	Jerry Casale	.40	.20	.12
(43)	Norm Cash	.50	.25	.15
(44)	Orlando Cepeda	1.25	.60	.40
(45)	Bob Cerv	.40	.20	.12
(46)	Harry Chiti	.40	.20	.12
(47)	Gene Conley	.30	.15	.09
(48)	Wes Covington	.40	.20	.12
(49)	Del Crandall	.35	.20	.11
(50)	Tony Curry	.40	.20	.12
(51)	Bud Daley	.40	.20	.12
(52)	Pete Daley	.40	.20	.12
(53)	Clay Dalrymple	.40	.20	.12
(54)	Jim Davenport	.40	.20	.12
(55)	Tommy Davis	.35	.20	.11
(56)	Bobby Del Greco	.40	.20	.12
(57)	Ike Delock	.40	.20	.12
(58)	Art Ditmar	.35	.20	.11
(59)	Dick Donovan	.40	.20	.12
(60)	Don Drysdale	6.00	3.00	1.75
(61)	Dick Ellsworth	.40	.20	.12
(62)	Don Elston	.40	.20	.12
(63)	Chuck Estrada	.40	.20	.12
(64)	Roy Face	.35	.20	.11
(65)	Dick Farrell	.40	.20	.12
(66)	Chico Fernandez	.40	.20	.12
(67)	Curt Flood	.35	.20	.11
(68)	Whitey Ford	4.00	2.00	1.25
(69)	Tito Francona	.40	.20	.12
(70)	Gene Freese	.40	.20	.12
(71)	Bob Friend	.35	.20	.11
(72)	Billy Gardner	.40	.20	.12
(73)	Ned Garver	.40	.20	.12
(74)	Gary Geiger	.40	.20	.12
(75)	Jim Gentile	.40	.20	.12
(76)	Dick Gernert	.40	.20	.12
(77)	Tony Gonzalez	.40	.20	.12
(78)	Alex Grammas	.40	.20	.12
(79)	Jim Grant	.40	.20	.12
(80)	Dick Groat	.35	.20	.11
(81)	Dick Hall	.40	.20	.12
(82)	Ron Hansen	.40	.20	.12
(83)	Bob Hartman	.40	.20	.12
(84)	Woodie Held	.40	.20	.12
(85)	Ray Herbert	.40	.20	.12
(86)	Frank Herrera	.40	.20	.12
(87)	Whitey Herzog	.50	.25	.15
(88)	Don Hoak	.30	.15	.09
(89)	Elston Howard	.80	.40	.25
(90)	Frank Howard	.50	.25	.15
(91)	Ken Hunt	.40	.20	.12
(92)	Larry Jackson	.40	.20	.12
(93)	Julian Javier	.40	.20	.12
(94)	Joe Jay	.40	.20	.12
(95)	Jackie Jensen	.50	.25	.15
(96)	Jim Kaat	1.00	.50	.30
(97a)	Al Kaline (green)	7.00	3.50	2.00
(97b)	Al Kaline (brown)	7.00	3.50	2.00
(98)	Eddie Kasko	.40	.20	.12
(99)	Russ Kemmerer	.40	.20	.12
(100)	Harmon Killebrew	5.00	2.50	1.50
(101)	Billy Klaus	.40	.20	.12
(102)	Ron Kline	.40	.20	.12
(103)	Johnny Klippstein	.40	.20	.12
(104)	Ted Kluszewski	.40	.20	.12
(105)	Tony Kubek	.80	.40	.25
(106)	Harvey Kuenn	.50	.25	.15
(107)	Jim Landis	.40	.20	.12
(108)	Hobie Landrith	.40	.20	.12
(109)	Norm Larker	.40	.20	.12
(110)	Frank Lary	.40	.20	.12
(111)	Barry Latman	.40	.20	.12
(112)	Vern Law	.30	.15	.09
(113)	Jim Lemon	.40	.20	.12
(114)	Sherm Lollar	.30	.15	.09
(115)	Dale Long	.30	.15	.09
(116)	Jerry Lumpe	.40	.20	.12
(117)	Jerry Lynch	.40	.20	.12
(118)	Art Mahaffey	.40	.20	.12

		NR MT	EX	VG
(119)	Frank Malzone	.40	.20	.12
(120)	Felix Mantilla	.40	.20	.12
(121)	Mickey Mantle	50.00	25.00	15.00
(122)	Juan Marichal	5.00	2.50	1.50
(123)	Roger Maris	12.00	6.00	3.50
(124)	Billy Martin	1.00	.50	.30
(125)	J.C. Martin	.40	.20	.12
(126)	Ed Mathews	3.00	1.50	.90
(127)	Charlie Maxwell	.40	.20	.12
(128)	Willie Mays	7.00	3.50	2.00
(129)	Bill Mazeroski	.50	.25	.15
(130)	Mike McCormick	.40	.20	.12
(131)	Willie McCovey	3.00	1.50	.90
(132)	Lindy McDaniel	.40	.20	.12
(133)	Roy McMillan	.40	.20	.12
(134)	Minnie Minoso	.50	.25	.15
(135)	Bill Monbouquette	.40	.20	.12
(136)	Wally Moon	.30	.15	.09
(137)	Stan Musial	7.00	3.50	2.00
(138)	Charlie Neal	.40	.20	.12
(139)	Rocky Nelson	.40	.20	.12
(140)	Russ Nixon	.40	.20	.12
(141)	Billy O'Dell	.40	.20	.12
(142)	Jim O'Toole	.40	.20	.12
(143)	Milt Pappas	.30	.15	.09
(144)	Camilo Pascual	.30	.15	.09
(145)	Jim Perry	.35	.20	.11
(146)	Bubba Phillips	.40	.20	.12
(147)	Bill Pierce	.35	.20	.11
(148)	Jim Piersall	.35	.20	.11
(149)	Vada Pinson	.50	.25	.15
(150)	Johnny Podres	.35	.20	.11
(151)	Wally Post	.40	.20	.12
(152)	Vic Powers (Power)	.40	.20	.12
(153)	Pedro Ramos	.40	.20	.12
(154)	Robin Roberts	1.50	.70	.45
(155)	Brooks Robinson	3.75	2.00	1.25
(156)	Frank Robinson	3.50	1.75	1.00
(157)	Ed Roebuck	.40	.20	.12
(158)	John Romano	.40	.20	.12
(159)	John Roseboro	.30	.15	.09
(160)	Pete Runnels	.30	.15	.09
(161)	Ed Sadowski	.40	.20	.12
(162)	Jack Sanford	.40	.20	.12
(163)	Ron Santo	.35	.20	.11
(164)	Ray Semproch	.40	.20	.12
(165)	Bobby Shantz	.50	.25	.15
(166)	Bob Shaw	.40	.20	.12
(167)	Larry Sherry	.40	.20	.12
(168)	Norm Siebern	.40	.20	.12
(169)	Roy Sievers	.35	.20	.11
(170)	Curt Simmons	.30	.15	.09
(171)	Dave Sisler	.40	.20	.12
(172)	Bob Skinner	.40	.20	.12
(173)	Al Smith	.40	.20	.12
(174)	Hal Smith	.40	.20	.12
(175)	Hal Smith	.40	.20	.12
(176)	Duke Snider	3.75	2.00	1.25
(177)	Warren Spahn	3.00	1.50	.90
(178)	Daryl Spencer	.40	.20	.12
(179)	Bill Stafford	.35	.20	.11
(180)	Jerry Staley	.40	.20	.12
(181)	Gene Stephens	.40	.20	.12
(182)	Chuck Stobbs	.40	.20	.12
(183)	Dick Stuart	.30	.15	.09
(184)	Willie Tasby	.40	.20	.12
(185)	Sammy Taylor	.40	.20	.12
(186)	Tony Taylor	.40	.20	.12
(187)	Johnny Temple	.40	.20	.12
(188)	Marv Throneberry	.50	.25	.15
(189)	Gus Triandos	.30	.15	.09
(190)	Bob Turley	.35	.20	.11
(191)	Bill Tuttle	.40	.20	.12
(192)	Zorro Versalles	.40	.20	.12
(193)	Bill Virdon	.35	.20	.11
(194)	Lee Walls	.40	.20	.12
(195)	Vic Wertz	.30	.15	.09
(196)	Pete Whisenant	.40	.20	.12
(197)	Bill White	.30	.15	.09
(198)	Hoyt Wilhelm	1.50	.70	.45
(199)	Bob Will	.40	.20	.12
(200)	Carl Willey	.40	.20	.12
(201)	Billy Williams	2.50	1.25	.70
(202)	Dick Williams	.50	.25	.15
(203)	Stan Williams	.40	.20	.12
(204)	Gene Woodling	.35	.20	.11
(205)	Early Wynn	2.00	1.00	.60
(206)	Carl Yastrzemski	12.00	6.00	3.50
(207)	Eddie Yost	.40	.20	.12

1962 Topps

The 1962 Topps set established another plateau for set size with 598 cards. The 2-1/2" by 3-1/2" cards feature a photograph set against a woodgrain background. The lower righthand corner has been made to look like it is curling away. Many established specialty cards dot the set including statistical leaders, multi-player cards, team cards, checklists, World Series cards and All-Stars. Of note is that 1962 was the first year of the multi-player rookie card. There is a 9-card "In Action" subset and a 10-card run of special Babe Ruth cards. Photo variations of several cards in the 2nd Series (#'s 110-196) exist. All cards in the 2nd Series can be found with two distinct printing variations, an early printing with the cards containing a very noticeable greenish tint, having been corrected to clear photos in subsequent print runs. The complete set price in the checklist that follows does not include the higher-priced variations.

		NR MT	EX	VG
Complete Set:		4000.00	1800.00	1000.
Common Player: 1-370		1.50	.70	.40
Common Player: 371-522		2.50	1.25	.60
Common Player: 523-598		12.00	5.50	3.00
1	Roger Maris	175.00	18.00	10.00
2	Jim Brosnan	1.75	.60	.30
3	Pete Runnels	1.50	.70	.40
4	John DeMerit	2.00	.90	.50
5	Sandy Koufax	80.00	40.00	24.00
6	Marv Breeding	1.50	.70	.40
7	Frank Thomas	2.00	.90	.50
8	Ray Herbert	1.50	.70	.40
9	Jim Davenport	1.50	.70	.40
10	Bob Clemente	70.00	35.00	21.00
11	Tom Morgan	1.50	.70	.40
12	Harry Craft	1.50	.70	.40
13	Dick Howser	1.75	.80	.45
14	Bill White	1.50	.70	.40
15	Dick Donovan	1.50	.70	.40
16	Darrell Johnson	1.50	.70	.40
17	Johnny Callison	1.75	.80	.45
18	Managers' Dream (Mickey Mantle, Willie Mays)	80.00	36.00	20.00
19	*Ray Washburn*	1.50	.70	.40
20	Rocky Colavito	3.00	1.25	.70
21	Jim Kaat	4.00	1.75	1.00
22a	Checklist 1-88 (numbers 121 - 176 on back)	5.00	2.25	1.25
22b	Checklist 1-88 (numbers 33-88 on back)	4.00	1.75	1.00
23	Norm Larker	1.50	.70	.40
24	Tigers Team	3.50	1.50	.90
25	Ernie Banks	25.00	12.50	7.50
26	Chris Cannizzaro	2.00	.90	.50
27	Chuck Cottier	1.50	.70	.40
28	Minnie Minoso	2.50	1.25	.60
29	Casey Stengel	15.00	6.75	3.75
30	Ed Mathews	12.00	5.50	3.00
31	*Tom Tresh*	7.00	3.25	1.75
32	John Roseboro	1.75	.80	.45
33	Don Larsen	1.75	.80	.45
34	Johnny Temple	1.50	.70	.40
35	*Don Schwall*	1.75	.80	.45
36	Don Leppert	1.50	.70	.40

		NR MT	EX	VG
37	Tribe Hill Trio (Barry Latman, Jim Perry, Dick Stigman)	1.75	.80	.45
38	Gene Stephens	1.50	.70	.40
39	Joe Koppe	1.50	.70	.40
40	Orlando Cepeda	5.00	2.25	1.25
41	Cliff Cook	1.50	.70	.40
42	Jim King	1.50	.70	.40
43	Dodgers Team	3.50	1.50	.90
44	Don Taussig	1.50	.70	.40
45	Brooks Robinson	20.00	9.00	5.00
46	*Jack Baldschun*	1.50	.70	.40
47	Bob Will	1.50	.70	.40
48	Ralph Terry	2.50	1.25	.60
49	Hal Jones	1.50	.70	.40
50	Stan Musial	65.00	29.00	16.00
51	A.L. Batting Leaders (Norm Cash, Elston Howard, Al Kaline, Jim Piersall)	3.00	1.25	.70
52	N.L. Batting Leaders (Ken Boyer, Bob Clemente, Wally Moon, Vada Pinson)	3.50	1.50	.90
53	A.L. Home Run Leaders (Jim Gentile, Harmon Killebrew, Mickey Mantle, Roger Maris)	15.00	7.50	3.50
54	N.L. Home Run Leaders (Orlando Cepeda, Willie Mays, Frank Robinson)	3.50	1.50	.90
55	A.L. E.R.A. Leaders (Dick Donovan, Don Mossi, Milt Pappas, Bill Stafford)	2.50	1.25	.60
56	N.L. E.R.A. Leaders (Mike McCormick, Jim O'Toole, Curt Simmons, Warren Spahn)	3.00	1.25	.70
57	A.L. Win Leaders (Steve Barber, Jim Bunning, Whitey Ford, Frank Lary)	3.00	1.25	.70
58	N.L. Win Leaders (Joe Jay, Jim O'Toole, Warren Spahn)	3.00	1.25	.70
59	A.L. Strikeout Leaders (Jim Bunning, Whitey Ford, Camilo Pascual, Juan Pizzaro)	3.00	1.25	.70
60	N.L. Strikeout Leaders (Don Drysdale, Sandy Koufax, Jim O'Toole, Stan Williams)	3.50	1.50	.90
61	Cardinals Team	2.50	1.25	.60
62	Steve Boros	1.50	.70	.40
63	*Tony Cloninger*	2.00	.90	.50
64	Russ Snyder	1.50	.70	.40
65	Bobby Richardson	6.00	2.75	1.50
66	Cuno Barragon (Barragan)	1.50	.70	.40
67	Harvey Haddix	1.75	.80	.45
68	Ken L. Hunt	1.50	.70	.40
69	Phil Ortega	1.50	.70	.40
70	Harmon Killebrew	15.00	6.75	3.75
71	Dick LeMay	1.50	.70	.40
72	Bob's Pupils (Steve Boros, Bob Scheffing, Jake Wood)	1.75	.80	.45
73	Nellie Fox	7.00	3.25	1.75
74	Bob Lillis	1.50	.70	.40
75	Milt Pappas	1.75	.80	.45
76	Howie Bedell	1.50	.70	.40
77	Tony Taylor	1.50	.70	.40
78	Gene Green	1.50	.70	.40
79	Ed Hobaugh	1.50	.70	.40
80	Vada Pinson	2.50	1.25	.60
81	Jim Pagliaroni	1.50	.70	.40
82	Deron Johnson	1.50	.70	.40
83	Larry Jackson	1.50	.70	.40
84	Lenny Green	1.50	.70	.40
85	Gil Hodges	12.00	6.00	3.50
86	*Donn Clendenon*	1.75	.80	.45
87	Mike Roarke	1.50	.70	.40
88	Ralph Houk	2.50	1.25	.60
89	Barney Schultz	1.50	.70	.40
90	Jim Piersall	2.00	.90	.50
91	J.C. Martin	1.50	.70	.40
92	Sam Jones	1.50	.70	.40
93	John Blanchard	2.00	.90	.50
94	Jay Hook	2.00	.90	.50
95	Don Hoak	1.75	.80	.45
96	Eli Grba	1.50	.70	.40
97	Tito Francona	1.50	.70	.40
98	Checklist 89-176	4.00	1.75	1.00
99	*John Powell*	10.00	5.00	3.00
100	Warren Spahn	25.00	12.50	7.50
101	Carroll Hardy	1.50	.70	.40
102	Al Schroll	1.50	.70	.40
103	Don Blasingame	1.50	.70	.40
104	Ted Savage	1.50	.70	.40
105	Don Mossi	1.50	.70	.40
106	Carl Sawatski	1.50	.70	.40
107	Mike McCormick	1.50	.70	.40
108	Willie Davis	2.50	1.25	.60
109	Bob Shaw	1.50	.70	.40
110	Bill Skowron	5.00	2.25	1.25
111	Dallas Green	1.75	.80	.45

		NR MT	EX	VG
112	Hank Foiles	1.50	.70	.40
113	White Sox Team	2.50	1.25	.60
114	Howie Koplitz	1.50	.70	.40
115	Bob Skinner	1.50	.70	.40
116	Herb Score	2.00	.90	.50
117	Gary Geiger	1.50	.70	.40
118	Julian Javier	1.50	.70	.40
119	Danny Murphy	1.50	.70	.40
120	Bob Purkey	1.50	.70	.40
121	Billy Hitchcock	1.50	.70	.40
122	Norm Bass	1.50	.70	.40
123	Mike de la Hoz	1.50	.70	.40
124	Bill Pleis	1.50	.70	.40
125	Gene Woodling	1.75	.80	.45
126	Al Cicotte	1.50	.70	.40
127	Pride of the A's (Hank Bauer, Jerry Lumpe, Norm Siebern)	1.75	.80	.45
128	Art Fowler	1.50	.70	.40
129a	Lee Walls (facing left)	15.00	7.50	4.50
129b	Lee Walls (facing right)	1.50	.70	.40
130	Frank Bolling	1.50	.70	.40
131	Pete Richert	1.75	.80	.45
132a	Angels Team (with inset photos)	10.00	4.50	2.50
132b	Angels Team (without inset photos)	3.00	1.25	.70
133	Felipe Alou	1.75	.80	.45
134a	Billy Hoeft (green sky in background)	15.00	7.50	4.50
134b	Billy Hoeft (blue sky in background)	1.50	.70	.40
135	Babe As A Boy	7.00	3.25	1.75
136	Babe Joins Yanks	7.00	3.25	1.75
137	Babe and Mgr. Huggins	7.00	3.25	1.75
138	The Famous Slugger	7.00	3.25	1.75
139a	Hal Reniff (pitching)	40.00	20.00	12.00
139b	Hal Reniff (portrait)	18.00	9.00	5.50
139c	Babe Hits 60	7.00	3.25	1.75
140	Gehrig and Ruth	9.00	4.00	2.25
141	Twilight Years	7.00	3.25	1.75
142	Coaching for the Dodgers	7.00	3.25	1.75
143	Greatest Sports Hero	7.00	3.25	1.75
144	Farewell Speech	7.00	3.25	1.75
145	Barry Latman	1.50	.70	.40
146	Don Demeter	1.50	.70	.40
147a	Bill Kunkel (pitching)	15.00	7.50	4.50
147b	Bill Kunkel (portrait)	1.50	.70	.40
148	Wally Post	1.50	.70	.40
149	Bob Duliba	1.50	.70	.40
150	Al Kaline	20.00	9.00	5.00
151	Johnny Klippstein	1.50	.70	.40
152	Mickey Vernon	1.50	.70	.40
153	Pumpsie Green	1.50	.70	.40
154	Lee Thomas	1.50	.70	.40
155	Stu Miller	1.50	.70	.40
156	Merritt Ranew	1.50	.70	.40
157	Wes Covington	1.50	.70	.40
158	Braves Team	3.00	1.25	.70
159	Hal Reniff	2.00	.90	.50
160	Dick Stuart	1.50	.70	.40
161	Frank Baumann	1.50	.70	.40
162	Sammy Drake	2.00	.90	.50
163	Hot Corner Guardians (Cletis Boyer, Billy Gardner)	3.00	1.25	.70
164	Hal Naragon	1.50	.70	.40
165	Jackie Brandt	1.50	.70	.40
166	Don Lee	1.50	.70	.40
167	Tim McCarver	12.00	6.00	3.50
168	Leo Posada	1.50	.70	.40
169	Bob Cerv	2.00	.90	.50
170	Ron Santo	3.50	1.50	.90
171	Dave Sisler	1.50	.70	.40
172	Fred Hutchinson	1.50	.70	.40
173	Chico Fernandez	1.50	.70	.40
174a	Carl Willey (with cap)	15.00	7.50	4.50
174b	Carl Willey (no cap)	1.50	.70	.40
175	Frank Howard	3.00	1.25	.70
176a	Eddie Yost (batting)	15.00	7.50	4.50
176b	Eddie Yost (portrait)	1.50	.70	.40
177	Bobby Shantz	1.75	.80	.45
178	Camilo Carreon	1.50	.70	.40
179	Tom Sturdivant	1.50	.70	.40
180	Bob Allison	1.75	.80	.45
181	Paul Brown	1.50	.70	.40
182	Bob Nieman	1.50	.70	.40
183	Roger Craig	3.00	1.25	.70
184	Haywood Sullivan	1.50	.70	.40
185	Roland Sheldon	2.00	.90	.50
186	Mack Jones	1.50	.70	.40
187	Gene Conley	1.50	.70	.40
188	Chuck Hiller	1.50	.70	.40
189	Dick Hall	1.50	.70	.40

		NR MT	EX	VG
190a	Wally Moon (with cap)	9.00	4.00	2.25
190b	Wally Moon (no cap)	1.75	.80	.45
191	Jim Brewer	1.50	.70	.40
192a	Checklist 177-264 (192 is Check List, 3)	6.00	2.75	1.50
192b	Checklist 177-264 (192 is Check List 3)	4.00	1.75	1.00
193	Eddie Kasko	1.50	.70	.40
194	Dean Chance	3.00	1.25	.70
195	Joe Cunningham	1.50	.70	.40
196	Terry Fox	1.50	.70	.40
197	Daryl Spencer	1.50	.70	.40
198	Johnny Keane	1.50	.70	.40
199	Gaylord Perry	75.00	34.00	18.50
200	Mickey Mantle	350.00	120.00	75.00
201	Ike Delock	1.50	.70	.40
202	Carl Warwick	1.50	.70	.40
203	Jack Fisher	1.50	.70	.40
204	Johnny Weekly	1.50	.70	.40
205	Gene Freese	1.50	.70	.40
206	Senators Team	2.50	1.25	.60
207	Pete Burnside	1.50	.70	.40
208	Billy Martin	6.00	2.75	1.50
209	Jim Fregosi	5.00	2.25	1.25
210	Roy Face	2.00	.90	.50
211	Midway Masters (Frank Bolling, Roy McMillan)	1.75	.80	.45
212	Jim Owens	1.50	.70	.40
213	Richie Ashburn	6.00	2.75	1.50
214	Dom Zanni	1.50	.70	.40
215	Woody Held	1.50	.70	.40
216	Ron Kline	1.50	.70	.40
217	Walt Alston	4.00	1.75	1.00
218	Joe Torre	10.00	4.50	2.50
219	Al Downing	4.00	1.75	1.00
220	Roy Sievers	1.75	.80	.45
221	Bill Short	1.50	.70	.40
222	Jerry Zimmerman	1.50	.70	.40
223	Alex Grammas	1.50	.70	.40
224	Don Rudolph	1.50	.70	.40
225	Frank Malzone	1.50	.70	.40
226	Giants Team	4.00	1.75	1.00
227	Bobby Tiefenauer	1.50	.70	.40
228	Dale Long	1.50	.70	.40
229	Jesus McFarlane	1.50	.70	.40
230	Camilo Pascual	1.75	.80	.45
231	Ernie Bowman	1.50	.70	.40
232	World Series Game 1 (Yanks Win Opener)	3.00	1.25	.70
233	World Series Game 2 (Jay Ties It Up)	3.00	1.25	.70
234	World Series Game 3 (Maris Wins It In The 9th)	8.00	3.50	2.00
235	World Series Game 4 (Ford Sets New Mark)	7.00	3.25	1.75
236	World Series Game 5 (Yanks Crush Reds In Finale)	3.00	1.25	.70
237	World Series Summary (The Winners Celebrate)	3.00	1.25	.70
238	Norm Sherry	1.50	.70	.40
239	Cecil Butler	1.50	.70	.40
240	George Altman	1.50	.70	.40
241	Johnny Kucks	1.50	.70	.40
242	Mel McGaha	1.50	.70	.40
243	Robin Roberts	12.00	5.50	3.00
244	Don Gile	1.50	.70	.40
245	Ron Hansen	1.50	.70	.40
246	Art Ditmar	1.50	.70	.40
247	Joe Pignatano	1.50	.70	.40
248	Bob Aspromonte	1.50	.70	.40
249	Ed Keegan	1.50	.70	.40
250	Norm Cash	3.00	1.25	.70
251	Yankees Team	8.00	3.50	2.00
252	Earl Francis	1.50	.70	.40
253	Harry Chiti	1.50	.70	.40
254	Gordon Windhorn	1.50	.70	.40
255	Juan Pizarro	1.50	.70	.40
256	Elio Chacon	2.00	.90	.50
257	Jack Spring	1.50	.70	.40
258	Marty Keough	1.50	.70	.40
259	Lou Klimchock	1.50	.70	.40
260	Bill Pierce	2.00	.90	.50
261	George Alusik	1.50	.70	.40
262	Bob Schmidt	1.50	.70	.40
263	The Right Pitch (Joe Jay, Bob Purkey, Jim Turner)	1.75	.80	.45
264	Dick Ellsworth	1.50	.70	.40
265	Joe Adcock	2.00	.90	.50
266	John Anderson	1.50	.70	.40
267	Dan Dobbek	1.50	.70	.40
268	Ken McBride	1.50	.70	.40

		NR MT	EX	VG
269	Bob Oldis	1.50	.70	.40
270	Dick Groat	2.00	.90	.50
271	Ray Rippelmeyer	1.50	.70	.40
272	Earl Robinson	1.50	.70	.40
273	Gary Bell	1.50	.70	.40
274	Sammy Taylor	1.50	.70	.40
275	Norm Siebern	1.50	.70	.40
276	Hal Kostad	1.50	.70	.40
277	Checklist 265-352	4.00	1.75	1.00
278	Ken Johnson	1.50	.70	.40
279	Hobie Landrith	2.00	.90	.50
280	Johnny Podres	2.50	1.25	.60
281	*Jake Gibbs*	2.25	1.00	.60
282	Dave Hillman	1.50	.70	.40
283	Charlie Smith	1.50	.70	.40
284	Ruben Amaro	1.50	.70	.40
285	Curt Simmons	2.00	.90	.50
286	Al Lopez	3.00	1.25	.70
287	George Witt	1.50	.70	.40
288	Billy Williams	20.00	10.00	6.00
289	Mike Krsnich	1.50	.70	.40
290	Jim Gentile	1.50	.70	.40
291	Hal Stowe	2.00	.90	.50
292	Jerry Kindall	1.50	.70	.40
293	Bob Miller	2.00	.90	.50
294	Phillies Team	2.50	1.25	.60
295	Vern Law	2.00	.90	.50
296	Ken Hamlin	1.50	.70	.40
297	Ron Perranoski	1.50	.70	.40
298	Bill Tuttle	1.50	.70	.40
299	*Don Wert*	1.50	.70	.40
300	Willie Mays	100.00	45.00	33.00
301	Galen Cisco	1.50	.70	.40
302	*John Edwards*	1.50	.70	.40
303	Frank Torre	1.50	.70	.40
304	Dick Farrell	1.50	.70	.40
305	Jerry Lumpe	1.50	.70	.40
306	Redbird Rippers (Larry Jackson, Lindy McDaniel)	1.75	.80	.45
307	Jim Grant	1.50	.70	.40
308	Neil Chrisley	2.00	.90	.50
309	Moe Morhardt	1.50	.70	.40
310	Whitey Ford	25.00	12.50	7.50
311	Kubek Makes The Double Play	3.50	1.50	.90
312	Spahn Shows No-Hit Form	7.00	3.50	2.00
313	Maris Blasts 61st	15.00	6.75	3.75
314	Colavito's Power	3.50	1.50	.90
315	Ford Tosses A Curve	6.00	2.75	1.50
316	Killebrew Sends One Into Orbit	5.00	2.25	1.25
317	Musial Plays 21st Season	12.00	5.50	3.00
318	The Switch Hitter Connects (Mickey Mantle)	30.00	13.50	7.50
319	McCormick Shows His Stuff	1.75	.80	.45
320	Hank Aaron	100.00	45.00	33.00
321	Lee Stange	1.50	.70	.40
322	Al Dark	1.75	.80	.45
323	Don Landrum	1.50	.70	.40
324	Joe McClain	1.50	.70	.40
325	Luis Aparicio	15.00	7.50	4.50
326	Tom Parsons	1.50	.70	.40
327	Ozzie Virgil	1.50	.70	.40
328	Ken Walters	1.50	.70	.40
329	Bob Bolin	1.50	.70	.40
330	Johnny Romano	1.50	.70	.40
331	Moe Drabowsky	1.50	.70	.40
332	Don Buddin	1.50	.70	.40
333	Frank Cipriani	1.50	.70	.40
334	Red Sox Team	3.50	1.50	.90
335	Bill Bruton	1.50	.70	.40
336	Billy Muffett	1.50	.70	.40
337	Jim Marshall	2.00	.90	.50
338	Billy Gardner	2.25	1.00	.60
339	Jose Valdivielso	1.50	.70	.40
340	Don Drysdale	25.00	11.00	6.25
341	Mike Hershberger	1.50	.70	.40
342	Ed Rakow	1.50	.70	.40
343	Albie Pearson	1.50	.70	.40
344	Ed Bauta	1.50	.70	.40
345	Chuck Schilling	1.50	.70	.40
346	Jack Kralick	1.50	.70	.40
347	Chuck Hinton	1.50	.70	.40
348	Larry Burright	1.50	.70	.40
349	Paul Foytack	1.50	.70	.40
350	Frank Robinson	25.00	11.00	6.25
351	Braves' Backstops (Del Crandall, Joe Torre)	3.00	1.25	.70
352	Frank Sullivan	1.50	.70	.40
353	Bill Mazeroski	3.50	1.50	.90
354	Roman Mejias	1.50	.70	.40
355	Steve Barber	1.50	.70	.40
356	Tom Haller	1.75	.80	.45
357	Jerry Walker	1.50	.70	.40
358	Tommy Davis	2.50	1.25	.60
359	Bobby Locke	1.50	.70	.40
360	Yogi Berra	60.00	30.00	18.00
361	Bob Hendley	1.50	.70	.40
362	Ty Cline	1.50	.70	.40
363	Bob Roselli	1.50	.70	.40
364	Ken Hunt	1.50	.70	.40
365	Charley Neal	2.00	.90	.50
366	Phil Regan	1.50	.70	.40
367	Checklist 353-429	4.00	1.75	1.00
368	Bob Tillman	1.50	.70	.40
369	Ted Bowsfield	1.50	.70	.40
370	Ken Boyer	4.00	1.75	1.00
371	Earl Battey	2.75	1.25	.70
372	Jack Curtis	2.50	1.25	.60
373	Al Heist	2.50	1.25	.60
374	Gene Mauch	2.75	1.25	.70
375	Ron Fairly	2.75	1.25	.70
376	Bud Daley	3.00	1.25	.70
377	Johnny Orsino	2.50	1.25	.60
378	Bennie Daniels	2.50	1.25	.60
379	Chuck Essegian	2.50	1.25	.60
380	Lou Burdette	4.00	1.75	1.00
381	Chico Cardenas	2.50	1.25	.60
382	Dick Williams	3.50	1.50	.90
383	Ray Sadecki	2.50	1.25	.60
384	Athletics Team	3.50	1.50	.90
385	Early Wynn	20.00	10.00	6.00
386	Don Mincher	2.50	1.25	.60
387	Lou Brock	90.00	41.00	33.00
388	Ryne Duren	2.75	1.25	.70
389	Smoky Burgess	3.00	1.25	.70
390	Orlando Cepeda AS	5.00	2.25	1.25
391	Bill Mazeroski AS	3.50	1.50	.90
392	Ken Boyer AS	3.50	1.50	.90
393	Roy McMillan AS	2.75	1.25	.70
394	Hank Aaron AS	30.00	15.00	9.00
395	Willie Mays AS	25.00	11.00	6.25
396	Frank Robinson AS	12.00	5.50	3.00
397	John Roseboro AS	2.75	1.25	.70
398	Don Drysdale AS	10.00	4.50	2.50
399	Warren Spahn AS	10.00	4.50	2.50
400	Elston Howard	7.00	3.25	1.75
401	AL & NL Homer Kings (Orlando Cepeda, Roger Maris)	20.00	9.00	5.00
402	Gino Cimoli	2.50	1.25	.60
403	Chet Nichols	2.50	1.25	.60
404	Tim Harkness	2.50	1.25	.60
405	Jim Perry	3.00	1.25	.70
406	Bob Taylor	2.50	1.25	.60
407	Hank Aguirre	2.50	1.25	.60
408	Gus Bell	3.00	1.25	.70
409	Pirates Team	3.50	1.50	.90
410	Al Smith	2.50	1.25	.60
411	Danny O'Connell	2.50	1.25	.60
412	Charlie James	2.50	1.25	.60
413	Matty Alou	3.50	1.50	.90
414	Joe Gaines	2.50	1.25	.60
415	Bill Virdon	3.50	1.50	.90
416	Bob Scheffing	2.50	1.25	.60
417	Joe Azcue	2.50	1.25	.60
418	Andy Carey	2.50	1.25	.60
419	Bob Bruce	2.50	1.25	.60
420	Gus Triandos	2.75	1.25	.70
421	Ken MacKenzie	3.00	1.25	.70
422	Steve Bilko	2.50	1.25	.60
423	Rival League Relief Aces (Roy Face, Hoyt Wilhelm)	5.00	2.25	1.25
424	Al McBean	2.50	1.25	.60
425	Carl Yastrzemski	150.00	68.00	38.00
426	Bob Farley	2.50	1.25	.60
427	Jake Wood	2.50	1.25	.60
428	Joe Hicks	2.50	1.25	.60
429	Bill O'Dell	2.50	1.25	.60
430	Tony Kubek	7.00	3.25	1.75
431	*Bob Rodgers*	3.00	1.25	.70
432	Jim Pendleton	2.50	1.25	.60
433	Jim Archer	2.50	1.25	.60
434	Clay Dalrymple	2.50	1.25	.60
435	Larry Sherry	2.50	1.25	.60
436	Felix Mantilla	3.00	1.25	.70
437	Ray Moore	2.50	1.25	.60
438	Dick Brown	2.50	1.25	.60
439	Jerry Buchek	2.50	1.25	.60
440	Joe Jay	2.50	1.25	.60
441	Checklist 430-506	5.00	2.25	1.25
442	Wes Stock	2.50	1.25	.60
443	Del Crandall	3.50	1.50	.90
444	Ted Wills	2.50	1.25	.60
445	Vic Power	2.50	1.25	.60

		NR MT	EX	VG
446	Don Elston	2.50	1.25	.60
447	Willie Kirkland	2.50	1.25	.60
448	Joe Gibbon	2.50	1.25	.60
449	Jerry Adair	2.50	1.25	.60
450	Jim O'Toole	2.50	1.25	.60
451	*Jose Tartabull*	2.75	1.25	.70
452	Earl Averill	2.50	1.25	.60
453	Cal McLish	2.50	1.25	.60
454	Floyd Robinson	2.50	1.25	.60
455	Luis Arroyo	3.00	1.25	.70
456	Joe Amalfitano	2.50	1.25	.60
457	Lou Clinton	2.50	1.25	.60
458a	Bob Buhl ("M" on cap)	2.75	1.25	.70
458b	Bob Buhl (plain cap)	60.00	30.00	18.00
459	Ed Bailey	2.50	1.25	.60
460	Jim Bunning	8.00	3.50	2.00
461	*Ken Hubbs*	8.00	3.50	2.00
462a	Willie Tasby ("W" on cap)	2.50	1.25	.60
462b	Willie Tasby (plain cap)	60.00	30.00	18.00
463	Hank Bauer	3.00	1.25	.70
464	*Al Jackson*	3.50	1.50	.90
465	Reds Team	4.00	1.75	1.00
466	Norm Cash AS	4.00	1.75	1.00
467	Chuck Schilling AS	3.00	1.25	.70
468	Brooks Robinson AS	12.00	5.50	3.00
469	Luis Aparicio AS	8.00	3.50	2.00
470	Al Kaline AS	10.00	4.50	2.50
471	Mickey Mantle AS	65.00	29.00	16.00
472	Rocky Colavito AS	5.00	2.25	1.25
473	Elston Howard AS	5.00	2.25	1.25
474	Frank Lary AS	3.00	1.25	.70
475	Whitey Ford AS	10.00	4.50	2.50
476	Orioles Team	3.50	1.50	.90
477	Andre Rodgers	2.50	1.25	.60
478	Don Zimmer	3.50	1.50	.90
479	*Joel Horlen*	2.75	1.25	.70
480	Harvey Kuenn	3.50	1.50	.90
481	Vic Wertz	2.75	1.25	.70
482	Sam Mele	2.50	1.25	.60
483	Don McMahon	2.50	1.25	.60
484	Dick Schofield	2.50	1.25	.60
485	Pedro Ramos	2.50	1.25	.60
486	Jim Gilliam	4.00	1.75	1.00
487	Jerry Lynch	2.50	1.25	.60
488	Hal Brown	2.50	1.25	.60
489	Julio Gotay	2.50	1.25	.60
490	Clete Boyer	4.00	1.75	1.00
491	Leon Wagner	2.50	1.25	.60
492	Hal Smith	2.50	1.25	.60
493	Danny McDevitt	2.50	1.25	.60
494	Sammy White	2.50	1.25	.60
495	Don Cardwell	2.50	1.25	.60
496	Wayne Causey	2.50	1.25	.60
497	Ed Bouchee	3.00	1.25	.70
498	Jim Donohue	2.50	1.25	.60
499	Zoilo Versalles	2.75	1.25	.70
500	Duke Snider	30.00	13.50	7.50
501	Claude Osteen	2.75	1.25	.70
502	Hector Lopez	3.00	1.25	.70
503	Danny Murtaugh	2.75	1.25	.70
504	Eddie Bressoud	2.50	1.25	.60
505	Juan Marichal	25.00	11.00	6.25
506	Charley Maxwell	2.50	1.25	.60
507	Ernie Broglio	2.50	1.25	.60
508	Gordy Coleman	2.50	1.25	.60
509	*Dave Giusti*	2.75	1.25	.70
510	Jim Lemon	2.50	1.25	.60
511	Bubba Phillips	2.50	1.25	.60
512	Mike Fornieles	2.50	1.25	.60
513	Whitey Herzog	4.00	1.75	1.00
514	Sherm Lollar	2.75	1.25	.70
515	Stan Williams	2.50	1.25	.60
516	Checklist 507-598	8.00	3.50	2.00
517	Dave Wickersham	2.50	1.25	.60
518	Lee Maye	2.50	1.25	.60
519	Bob Johnson	2.50	1.25	.60
520	Bob Friend	3.00	1.25	.70
521	Jacke Davis	2.50	1.25	.60
522	Lindy McDaniel	2.50	1.25	.60
523	Russ Nixon	12.00	5.50	3.00
524	Howie Nunn	12.00	5.50	3.00
525	George Thomas	12.00	5.50	3.00
526	Hal Woodeshick	12.00	5.50	3.00
527	*Dick McAuliffe*	15.00	5.00	2.75
528	Turk Lown	12.00	5.50	3.00
529	John Schaive	12.00	5.50	3.00
530	Bob Gibson	90.00	41.00	33.00
531	Bobby G. Smith	12.00	5.50	3.00
532	Dick Stigman	12.00	5.50	3.00
533	Charley Lau	13.00	5.75	3.25
534	Tony Gonzalez	12.00	5.50	3.00

		NR MT	EX	VG
535	Ed Roebuck	12.00	5.50	3.00
536	Dick Gernert	12.00	5.50	3.00
537	Indians Team	15.00	6.75	3.75
538	Jack Sanford	12.00	5.50	3.00
539	Billy Moran	12.00	5.50	3.00
540	Jim Landis	12.00	5.50	3.00
541	Don Nottebart	12.00	5.50	3.00
542	Dave Philley	12.00	5.50	3.00
543	Bob Allen	12.00	5.50	3.00
544	Willie McCovey	90.00	41.00	33.00
545	Hoyt Wilhelm	55.00	25.00	14.00
546	Moe Thacker	12.00	5.50	3.00
547	Don Ferrarese	12.00	5.50	3.00
548	Bobby Del Greco	12.00	5.50	3.00
549	Bill Rigney	12.00	5.50	3.00
550	Art Mahaffey	12.00	5.50	3.00
551	Harry Bright	12.00	5.50	3.00
552	Cubs Team	15.00	6.75	3.75
553	Jim Coates	15.00	6.75	3.75
554	Bubba Morton	12.00	5.50	3.00
555	John Buzhardt	12.00	5.50	3.00
556	Al Spangler	12.00	5.50	3.00
557	Bob Anderson	12.00	5.50	3.00
558	John Goryl	12.00	5.50	3.00
559	Mike Higgins	12.00	5.50	3.00
560	Chuck Estrada	12.00	5.50	3.00
561	Gene Oliver	12.00	5.50	3.00
562	Bill Henry	12.00	5.50	3.00
563	Ken Aspromonte	12.00	5.50	3.00
564	Bob Grim	12.00	5.50	3.00
565	Jose Pagan	12.00	5.50	3.00
566	Marty Kutyna	12.00	5.50	3.00
567	Tracy Stallard	12.00	5.50	3.00
568	Jim Golden	12.00	5.50	3.00
569	Ed Sadowski	12.00	5.50	3.00
570	Bill Stafford	15.00	6.75	3.75
571	Billy Klaus	12.00	5.50	3.00
572	Bob Miller	13.00	5.75	3.25
573	Johnny Logan	13.00	5.75	3.25
574	Dean Stone	12.00	5.50	3.00
575	Red Schoendienst	25.00	11.25	6.25
576	Russ Kemmerer	12.00	5.50	3.00
577	Dave Nicholson	12.00	5.50	3.00
578	Jim Duffalo	12.00	5.50	3.00
579	Jim Schaffer	12.00	5.50	3.00
580	Bill Monbouquette	13.00	5.75	3.25
581	Mel Roach	12.00	5.50	3.00
582	Ron Piche	12.00	5.50	3.00
583	Larry Osborne	12.00	5.50	3.00
584	Twins Team	15.00	6.75	3.75
585	Glen Hobbie	12.00	5.50	3.00
586	Sammy Esposito	12.00	5.50	3.00
587	Frank Funk	12.00	5.50	3.00
588	Birdie Tebbetts	12.00	5.50	3.00
589	Bob Turley	18.00	8.00	4.50
590	Curt Flood	18.00	8.00	4.50
591	Rookie Parade Pitchers (*Sam McDowell,* Ron Nischwitz, Art Quirk, *Dick Radatz, Ron Taylor*)	35.00	15.50	8.75
592	Rookie Parade Pitchers (*Bo Belinsky,* Joe Bonikowski, *Jim Bouton,* Dan Pfister, Dave Stenhouse)	45.00	20.00	11.25
593	Rookie Parade Pitchers (Craig Anderson, *Jack Hamilton,* Jack Lamabe, Bob Moorhead, *Bob Veale*)	25.00	11.25	6.25
594	Rookie Parade Catchers (Doug Camilli, *Doc Edwards,* Don Pavletich, Ken Retzer, *Bob Uecker*)	125.00	56.00	35.00
595	Rookie Parade Infielders (*Ed Charles,* Marlin Coughtry, Bob Sadowski, Felix Torres)	25.00	11.25	6.25
596	Rookie Parade Infielders (*Bernie Allen,* Phil Linz, Joe Pepitone, Rich Rollins)	40.00	18.00	10.00
597	Rookie Parade Infielders (Rod Kanehl, Jim McKnight, *Denis Menke,* Amado Samuel)	25.00	11.25	6.25
598	Rookie Parade Outfielders (Howie Goss, *Jim Hickman,* Manny Jimenez, Al Luplow, Ed Olivares)	60.00	30.00	18.00

1962 Topps Baseball Bucks

Issued in their own 1¢ package, the 1962 Topps "Baseball Bucks" were another in the growing list of specialty Topps items. The 96 Baseball Bucks in the set measure 4-1/8" by 1-3/4," and were designed to look vaguely like dollar bills. The center player portrait has a banner underneath with the player's name. His home park is shown on the right and there is some biographical information on the left. The back features a large denomination, with the player's league and team logo on either side.

		NR MT	EX	VG
Complete Set:		650.00	325.00	190.00
Common Player:		2.00	1.00	.60
(1)	Hank Aaron	30.00	15.00	9.00
(2)	Joe Adcock	3.00	1.50	.90
(3)	George Altman	2.00	1.00	.60
(4)	Jim Archer	2.00	1.00	.60
(5)	Richie Ashburn	5.00	2.50	1.50
(6)	Ernie Banks	20.00	10.00	8.00
(7)	Earl Battey	2.50	1.25	.70
(8)	Gus Bell	2.50	1.25	.70
(9)	Yogi Berra	18.00	9.00	5.50
(10)	Ken Boyer	3.00	1.50	.90
(11)	Jackie Brandt	2.00	1.00	.60
(12)	Jim Bunning	4.00	2.00	1.25
(13)	Lou Burdette	3.00	1.50	.90
(14)	Don Cardwell	2.00	1.00	.60
(15)	Norm Cash	3.00	1.50	.90
(16)	Orlando Cepeda	4.50	2.25	1.25
(17)	Bob Clemente	40.00	20.00	12.50
(18)	Rocky Colavito	3.00	1.50	.90
(19)	Chuck Cottier	2.00	1.00	.60
(20)	Roger Craig	2.50	1.25	.70
(21)	Bennie Daniels	2.00	1.00	.60
(22)	Don Demeter	2.00	1.00	.60
(23)	Don Drysdale	15.00	7.50	4.50
(24)	Chuck Estrada	2.00	1.00	.60
(25)	Dick Farrell	2.00	1.00	.60
(26)	Whitey Ford	12.00	6.00	3.50
(27)	Nellie Fox	4.00	2.00	1.25
(28)	Tito Francona	2.00	1.00	.60
(29)	Bob Friend	2.50	1.25	.70
(30)	Jim Gentile	2.00	1.00	.60
(31)	Dick Gernert	2.00	1.00	.60
(32)	Lenny Green	2.00	1.00	.60
(33)	Dick Groat	3.00	1.50	.90
(34)	Woody Held	2.00	1.00	.60
(35)	Don Hoak	2.50	1.25	.70
(36)	Gil Hodges	10.00	5.00	3.00
(37)	Frank Howard	3.00	1.50	.90
(38)	Elston Howard	4.00	2.00	1.25
(39)	Dick Howser	3.00	1.50	.90
(40)	Ken Hunt	2.00	1.00	.60
(41)	Larry Jackson	2.00	1.00	.60
(42)	Joe Jay	4.00	2.00	1.25
(43)	Al Kaline	12.00	6.00	3.50
(44)	Harmon Killebrew	12.00	6.00	3.50
(45)	Sandy Koufax	35.00	17.50	10.50
(46)	Harvey Kuenn	4.00	2.00	1.25
(47)	Jim Landis	2.00	1.00	.60
(48)	Norm Larker	2.00	1.00	.60
(49)	Frank Lary	2.00	1.00	.60
(50)	Jerry Lumpe	2.00	1.00	.60
(51)	Art Mahaffey	2.00	1.00	.60
(52)	Frank Malzone	2.00	1.00	.60
(53)	Felix Mantilla	2.50	1.25	.70
(54)	Mickey Mantle	125.00	62.00	37.00
(55)	Roger Maris	12.00	6.00	3.50
(56)	Ed Mathews	10.00	5.00	3.00
(57)	Willie Mays	35.00	17.50	10.50
(58)	Ken McBride	2.00	1.00	.60
(59)	Mike McCormick	2.00	1.00	.60
(60)	Minnie Minoso	4.00	2.00	1.25

		NR MT	EX	VG
(61)	Wally Moon	2.50	1.25	.70
(62)	Stu Miller	2.00	1.00	.60
(63)	Stan Musial	30.00	15.00	9.00
(64)	Danny O'Connell	2.00	1.00	.60
(65)	Jim O'Toole	4.00	2.00	1.25
(66)	Camilo Pascual	2.50	1.25	.70
(67)	Jim Perry	3.00	1.50	.90
(68)	Jimmy Piersall	4.00	2.00	1.25
(69)	Vada Pinson	6.00	3.00	1.75
(70)	Juan Pizarro	2.00	1.00	.60
(71)	Johnny Podres	3.00	1.50	.90
(72)	Vic Power	2.00	1.00	.60
(73)	Bob Purkey	12.00	6.00	3.50
(74)	Pedro Ramos	2.00	1.00	.60
(75)	Brooks Robinson	15.00	7.50	4.50
(76)	Floyd Robinson	2.00	1.00	.60
(77)	Frank Robinson	15.00	7.50	4.50
(78)	Johnny Romano	2.00	1.00	.60
(79)	Pete Runnels	2.50	1.25	.70
(80)	Don Schwall	2.00	1.00	.60
(81)	Bobby Shantz	3.00	1.50	.90
(82)	Norm Siebern	2.00	1.00	.60
(83)	Roy Sievers	2.50	1.25	.70
(84)	Hal (W.) Smith	2.00	1.00	.60
(85)	Warren Spahn	10.00	5.00	3.00
(86)	Dick Stuart	2.50	1.25	.70
(87)	Tony Taylor	2.00	1.00	.60
(88)	Lee Thomas	2.00	1.00	.60
(89)	Gus Triandos	2.50	1.25	.70
(90)	Leon Wagner	2.00	1.00	.60
(91)	Jerry Walker	2.00	1.00	.60
(92)	Bill White	2.50	1.25	.70
(93)	Billy Williams	9.00	4.50	2.75
(94)	Gene Woodling	2.50	1.25	.70
(95)	Early Wynn	9.00	4.50	2.75
(96)	Carl Yastrzemski	30.00	15.00	9.00

1962 Topps Stamps

An artistic improvement over the somewhat drab Topps stamps of the previous year, the 1962 stamps, 1-3/8" by 1-7/8," had color player photographs set on red or yellow backgrounds. As in 1961, they were issued in two-stamp panels as insert with Topps baseball cards. A change from 1961 was the inclusion of team emblems in the set. A complete set consists of 201 stamps; Roy Sievers was originally portrayed on the wrong team - Athletics - and was later corrected to the Phillies.

		NR MT	EX	VG
Complete Set:		220.00	110.00	67.00
Stamp Album:		35.00	17.50	10.50
Common Player:		.25	.13	.08
(1)	Hank Aaron	10.00	5.00	3.00
(2)	Jerry Adair	.25	.13	.08
(3)	Joe Adcock	.35	.20	.11
(4)	Bob Allison	.30	.15	.09
(5)	Felipe Alou	.35	.20	.11
(6)	George Altman	.25	.13	.08
(7)	Joe Amalfitano	.25	.13	.08
(8)	Ruben Amaro	.25	.13	.08
(9)	Luis Aparicio	1.50	.70	.45
(10)	Jim Archer	.25	.13	.08
(11)	Bob Aspromonte	.25	.13	.08
(12)	Ed Bailey	.25	.13	.08

		NR MT	EX	VG			NR MT	EX	VG
(13)	Jack Baldschun	.25	.13	.08	(104)	Willie Mays	7.00	3.50	2.00
(14)	Ernie Banks	6.00	3.00	1.75	(105)	Bill Mazeroski	.50	.25	.15
(15)	Earl Battey	.30	.15	.09	(106)	Ken McBride	.25	.13	.08
(16)	Gus Bell	.35	.20	.11	(107)	Tim McCarver	.50	.25	.15
(17)	Yogi Berra	5.00	2.50	1.50	(108)	Joe McClain	.25	.13	.08
(18)	Dick Bertell	.25	.13	.08	(109)	Mike McCormick	.25	.13	.08
(19)	Steve Bilko	.25	.13	.08	(110)	Lindy McDaniel	.25	.13	.08
(20)	Frank Bolling	.25	.13	.08	(111)	Roy McMillan	.25	.13	.08
(21)	Steve Boros	.25	.13	.08	(112)	Bob L. Miller	.35	.20	.11
(22)	Ted Bowsfield	.25	.13	.08	(113)	Stu Miller	.25	.13	.08
(23)	Clete Boyer	.35	.20	.11	(114)	Minnie Minoso	.50	.25	.15
(24)	Ken Boyer	.50	.25	.15	(115)	Bill Monbouquette	.25	.13	.08
(25)	Jackie Brandt	.25	.13	.08	(116)	Wally Moon	.30	.15	.09
(26)	Bill Bruton	.25	.13	.08	(117)	Don Mossi	.30	.15	.09
(27)	Jim Bunning	1.00	.50	.30	(118)	Stan Musial	7.00	3.50	2.00
(28)	Lou Burdette	.35	.20	.11	(119)	Russ Nixon	.25	.13	.08
(29)	Smoky Burgess	.30	.15	.09	(120)	Danny O'Connell	.25	.13	.08
(30)	Johnny Callizon (Callison)	.30	.15	.09	(121)	Jim O'Toole	.25	.13	.08
(31)	Don Cardwell	.25	.13	.08	(122)	Milt Pappas	.30	.15	.09
(32)	Camilo Carreon	.25	.13	.08	(123)	Camilo Pascual	.30	.15	.09
(33)	Norm Cash	.50	.25	.15	(124)	Albie Pearson	.25	.13	.08
(34)	Orlando Cepeda	1.00	.50	.30	(125)	Jim Perry	.35	.20	.11
(35)	Bob Clemente	15.00	7.50	4.50	(126)	Bubba Phillips	.25	.13	.08
(36)	Ty Cline	.25	.13	.08	(127)	Jimmy Piersall	.35	.20	.11
(37)	Rocky Colavito	.80	.40	.25	(128)	Vada Pinson	.50	.25	.15
(38)	Gordon Coleman	.25	.13	.08	(129)	Juan Pizarro	.25	.13	.08
(39)	Chuck Cottier	.25	.13	.08	(130)	Johnny Podres	.35	.20	.11
(40)	Roger Craig	.35	.20	.11	(131)	Leo Posada	.25	.13	.08
(41)	Del Crandall	.35	.20	.11	(132)	Vic Power	.25	.13	.08
(42)	Pete Daley	.25	.13	.08	(133)	Bob Purkey	.25	.13	.08
(43)	Clay Dalrymple	.25	.13	.08	(134)	Pedro Ramos	.25	.13	.08
(44)	Bennie Daniels	.25	.13	.08	(135)	Bobby Richardson	.80	.40	.25
(45)	Jim Davenport	.25	.13	.08	(136)	Brooks Robinson	3.75	2.00	1.25
(46)	Don Demeter	.25	.13	.08	(137)	Floyd Robinson	.25	.13	.08
(47)	Dick Donovan	.25	.13	.08	(138)	Frank Robinson	3.50	1.75	1.00
(48)	Don Drysdale	7.00	3.50	2.00	(139)	Bob Rodgers	.30	.15	.09
(49)	John Edwards	.25	.13	.08	(140)	Johnny Romano	.25	.13	.08
(50)	Dick Ellsworth	.25	.13	.08	(141)	John Roseboro	.30	.15	.09
(51)	Chuck Estrada	.25	.13	.08	(142)	Pete Runnels	.30	.15	.09
(52)	Roy Face	.35	.20	.11	(143)	Ray Sadecki	.25	.13	.08
(53)	Ron Fairly	.30	.15	.09	(144)	Ron Santo	.35	.20	.11
(54)	Dick Farrell	.25	.13	.08	(145)	Chuck Schilling	.25	.13	.08
(55)	Whitey Ford	5.00	2.50	1.50	(146)	Barney Schultz	.25	.13	.08
(56)	Mike Fornieles	.25	.13	.08	(147)	Don Schwall	.25	.13	.08
(57)	Nellie Fox	.80	.40	.25	(148)	Bobby Shantz	.35	.20	.11
(58)	Tito Francona	.25	.13	.08	(149)	Bob Shaw	.25	.13	.08
(59)	Gene Freese	.25	.13	.08	(150)	Norm Siebern	.25	.13	.08
(60)	Bob Friend	.35	.20	.11	(151a)	Roy Sievers (Kansas City)	1.00	.50	.30
(61)	Gary Geiger	.25	.13	.08	(151b)	Roy Sievers (Philadelphia)	.30	.15	.09
(62)	Jim Gentile	.25	.13	.08	(152)	Bill Skowron	.50	.25	.15
(63)	Tony Gonzalez	.25	.13	.08	(153)	Hal (W.) Smith	.25	.13	.08
(64)	Lenny Green	.25	.13	.08	(154)	Duke Snider	3.75	2.00	1.25
(65)	Dick Groat	.35	.20	.11	(155)	Warren Spahn	3.00	1.50	.90
(66)	Ron Hansen	.25	.13	.08	(156)	Al Spangler	.25	.13	.08
(67)	Al Heist	.25	.13	.08	(157)	Daryl Spencer	.25	.13	.08
(68)	Woody Held	.25	.13	.08	(158)	Gene Stephens	.25	.13	.08
(69)	Ray Herbert	.25	.13	.08	(159)	Dick Stuart	.30	.15	.09
(70)	Chuck Hinton	.25	.13	.08	(160)	Haywood Sullivan	.25	.13	.08
(71)	Don Hoak	.30	.15	.09	(161)	Tony Taylor	.25	.13	.08
(72)	Glen Hobbie	.25	.13	.08	(162)	George Thomas	.25	.13	.08
(73)	Gil Hodges	5.00	2.50	1.50	(163)	Lee Thomas	.25	.13	.08
(74)	Jay Hook	.35	.20	.11	(164)	Bob Tiefenauer	.25	.13	.08
(75)	Elston Howard	.80	.40	.25	(165)	Joe Torre	.50	.25	.15
(76)	Frank Howard	.50	.25	.15	(166)	Gus Triandos	.30	.15	.09
(77)	Dick Howser	.35	.20	.11	(167)	Bill Tuttle	.25	.13	.08
(78)	Ken Hunt	.25	.13	.08	(168)	Zoilo Versalles	.25	.13	.08
(79)	Larry Jackson	.25	.13	.08	(169)	Bill Virdon	.35	.20	.11
(80)	Julian Javier	.25	.13	.08	(170)	Leon Wagner	.25	.13	.08
(81)	Joe Jay	.25	.13	.08	(171)	Jerry Walker	.25	.13	.08
(82)	Bob Johnson	.25	.13	.08	(172)	Lee Walls	.25	.13	.08
(83)	Sam Jones	.25	.13	.08	(173)	Bill White	.30	.15	.09
(84)	Al Kaline	7.00	3.50	2.00	(174)	Hoyt Wilhelm	1.50	.70	.45
(85)	Eddie Kasko	.25	.13	.08	(175)	Billy Williams	2.00	1.00	.60
(86)	Harmon Killebrew	5.00	2.50	1.50	(176)	Jake Wood	.25	.13	.08
(87)	Sandy Koufax	10.00	5.00	3.00	(177)	Gene Woodling	.35	.20	.11
(88)	Jack Kralick	.25	.13	.08	(178)	Early Wynn	2.00	1.00	.60
(89)	Tony Kubek	.80	.40	.25	(179)	Carl Yastrzemski	12.00	6.00	3.50
(90)	Harvey Kuenn	.50	.25	.15	(180)	Don Zimmer	.35	.20	.11
(91)	Jim Landis	.25	.13	.08	(181)	Baltimore Orioles Logo	.25	.13	.08
(92)	Hobie Landrith	.35	.20	.11	(182)	Boston Red Sox Logo	.25	.13	.08
(93)	Frank Lary	.25	.13	.08	(183)	Chicago Cubs Logo	.25	.13	.08
(94)	Barry Latman	.25	.13	.08	(184)	Chicago White Sox Logo	.25	.13	.08
(95)	Jerry Lumpe	.25	.13	.08	(185)	Cincinnati Reds Logo	.25	.13	.08
(96)	Art Mahaffey	.25	.13	.08	(186)	Cleveland Indians Logo	.25	.13	.08
(97)	Frank Malzone	.25	.13	.08	(187)	Detroit Tigers Logo	.25	.13	.08
(98)	Felix Mantilla	.35	.20	.11	(188)	Houston Colts Logo	.25	.13	.08
(99)	Mickey Mantle	45.00	22.00	13.50	(189)	Kansas City Athletics Logo	.25	.13	.08
(100)	Juan Marichal	2.00	1.00	.60	(190)	Los Angeles Angels Logo	.25	.13	.08
(101)	Roger Maris	5.00	2.50	1.50	(191)	Los Angeles Dodgers Logo	.25	.13	.08
(102)	J.C. Martin	.25	.13	.08	(192)	Milwaukee Braves Logo	.25	.13	.08
(103)	Ed Mathews	3.00	1.50	.90	(193)	Minnesota Twins Logo	.25	.13	.08

		NR MT	EX	VG
(194)	New York Mets Logo	.35	.20	.11
(195)	New York Yankees Logo	.35	.20	.11
(196)	Philadelphia Phillies Logo	.25	.13	.08
(197)	Pittsburgh Pirates Logo	.25	.13	.08
(198)	St. Louis Cardinals Logo	.25	.13	.08
(199)	San Francisco Giants Logo	.25	.13	.08
(200)	Washington Senators Logo	.25	.13	.08

1963 Topps

Although the number of cards dropped to 576, the 1963 Topps set is among the most popular of the 1960s. A color photo dominates the 2-1/2" by 3-1/2" card, but a colored circle at the bottom carries a black and white portrait as well. A colored band gives the player's name, team and position. The backs again feature career statistics and a cartoon, career summary and brief biographical details. The set is somewhat unlike those immediately preceding it in that there are fewer specialty cards. The major groupings are statistical leaders, World Series highlights and rookies. It is one rookie which makes the set special - Pete Rose. As one of most avidly sought cards in history and a high-numbered card at that, the Rose rookie card accounts for much of the value of a complete set.

		NR MT	EX	VG
Complete Set:		3600.00	1800.00	1080.
Common Player: 1-283		.70	.35	.20
Common Player: 284-446		2.00	1.00	.60
Common Player: 447-506		8.00	4.00	2.50
Common Player: 507-576		5.00	2.50	1.50
1	N.L. Batting Leaders (Hank Aaron, Tommy Davis, Stan Musial, Frank Robinson, Bill White)	20.00	4.00	2.50
2	A.L. Batting Leaders (Chuck Hinton, Mickey Mantle, Floyd Robinson, Pete Runnels, Norm Siebern)	15.00	7.50	4.50
3	N.L. Home Run Leaders (Hank Aaron, Ernie Banks, Orlando Cepeda, Willie Mays, Frank Robinson)	8.00	4.00	2.50
4	A.L. Home Run Leaders (Norm Cash, Rocky Colavito, Jim Gentile, Harmon Killebrew, Roger Maris, Leon Wagner)	4.00	2.00	1.25
5	N.L. E.R.A. Leaders (Don Drysdale, Bob Gibson, Sandy Koufax, Bob Purkey, Bob Shaw)	4.00	2.00	1.25
6	A.L. E.R.A. Leaders (Hank Aguirre, Dean Chance, Eddie Fisher, Whitey Ford, Robin Roberts)	3.50	1.75	1.00
7	N.L. Pitching Leaders (Don Drysdale, Joe Jay, Art Mahaffey, Billy O'Dell, Bob Purkey, Jack Sanford)	3.50	1.75	1.00
8	A.L. Pitching Leaders (Jim Bunning, Dick Donovan, Ray Herbert, Camilo Pascual, Ralph Terry)	3.00	1.50	.90
9	N.L. Strikeout Leaders (Don Drysdale, Dick Farrell, Bob Gibson, Sandy Koufax, Billy O'Dell)	4.00	2.00	1.25
10	A.L. Strikeout Leaders (Jim Bunning, Jim Kaat, Camilo Pascual, Juan Pizarro, Ralph Terry)	3.00	1.50	.90
11	Lee Walls	.70	.35	.20

		NR MT	EX	VG
12	Steve Barber	.70	.35	.20
13	Phillies Team	2.25	1.25	.70
14	Pedro Ramos	.70	.35	.20
15	Ken Hubbs	2.00	1.00	.60
16	Al Smith	.70	.35	.20
17	Ryne Duren	1.00	.50	.30
18	Buc Blasters (Smoky Burgess, Bob Clemente, Bob Skinner, Dick Stuart)	8.00	4.00	2.50
19	Pete Burnside	.70	.35	.20
20	Tony Kubek	4.00	2.00	1.25
21	Marty Keough	.70	.35	.20
22	Curt Simmons	1.00	.50	.30
23	Ed Lopat	1.25	.60	.40
24	Bob Bruce	.70	.35	.20
25	Al Kaline	25.00	12.50	7.50
26	Ray Moore	.70	.35	.20
27	Choo Choo Coleman	1.25	.60	.40
28	Mike Fornieles	.70	.35	.20
29a	1962 Rookie Stars (John Boozer, *Ray Culp, Sammy Ellis*, Jesse Gonder)	5.00	2.50	1.50
29b	1963 Rookie Stars (John Boozer, *Ray Culp, Sammy Ellis*, Jesse Gonder)	1.25	.60	.40
30	Harvey Kuenn	1.50	.70	.45
31	Cal Koonce	.70	.35	.20
32	Tony Gonzalez	.70	.35	.20
33	Bo Belinsky	2.00	1.00	.60
34	Dick Schofield	.70	.35	.20
35	John Buzhardt	.70	.35	.20
36	Jerry Kindall	.70	.35	.20
37	Jerry Lynch	.70	.35	.20
38	Bud Daley	1.25	.60	.40
39	Angels Team	2.25	1.25	.70
40	Vic Power	.70	.35	.20
41	Charlie Lau	1.00	.50	.30
42	Stan Williams	1.25	.60	.40
43	Veteran Masters (Casey Stengel, Gene Woodling)	4.00	2.00	1.25
44	Terry Fox	.70	.35	.20
45	Bob Aspromonte	.70	.35	.20
46	*Tommie Aaron*	1.25	.60	.40
47	Don Lock	.70	.35	.20
48	Birdie Tebbetts	.70	.35	.20
49	*Dal Maxvill*	1.25	.60	.40
50	Bill Pierce	1.25	.60	.40
51	George Alusik	.70	.35	.20
52	Chuck Schilling	.70	.35	.20
53	Joe Moeller	.70	.35	.20
54a	1962 Rookie Stars (Jack Cullen, *Dave DeBusschere*, Harry Fanok, Nelson Mathews)	6.50	3.25	2.00
54b	1963 Rookie Stars (Jack Cullen, *Dave DeBusschere*, Harry Fanok, Nelson Mathews)	3.00	1.50	.90
55	Bill Virdon	1.50	.70	.45
56	Dennis Bennett	.70	.35	.20
57	Billy Moran	.70	.35	.20
58	Bob Will	.70	.35	.20
59	Craig Anderson	1.00	.50	.30
60	Elston Howard	6.00	3.00	1.75
61	Ernie Bowman	.70	.35	.20
62	Bob Hendley	.70	.35	.20
63	Reds Team	2.50	1.25	.70
64	Dick McAuliffe	.90	.45	.25
65	Jackie Brandt	.70	.35	.20
66	Mike Joyce	.70	.35	.20
67	Ed Charles	.70	.35	.20
68	Friendly Foes (Gil Hodges, Duke Snider)	6.50	3.25	2.00
69	Bud Zipfel	.70	.35	.20
70	Jim O'Toole	.70	.35	.20
71	*Bobby Wine*	.90	.45	.25
72	Johnny Romano	.70	.35	.20
73	Bobby Bragan	.90	.45	.25
74	*Denver Lemaster*	.90	.45	.25
75	Bob Allison	1.25	.60	.40
76	Earl Wilson	.70	.35	.20
77	Al Spangler	.70	.35	.20
78	Marv Throneberry	3.50	1.75	1.00
79	Checklist 1-88	2.50	1.25	.70
80	Jim Gilliam	3.00	1.50	.90
81	Jimmie Schaffer	.70	.35	.20
82	Ed Rakow	.70	.35	.20
83	Charley James	.70	.35	.20
84	Ron Kline	.70	.35	.20
85	Tom Haller	.90	.45	.25
86	Charley Maxwell	.70	.35	.20
87	Bob Veale	.90	.45	.25
88	Ron Hansen	.70	.35	.20
89	Dick Stigman	.70	.35	.20
90	Gordy Coleman	.70	.35	.20
91	Dallas Green	.90	.45	.25

#	Player	NR MT	EX	VG
92	Hector Lopez	1.25	.60	.40
93	Galen Cisco	.90	.45	.25
94	Bob Schmidt	.70	.35	.20
95	Larry Jackson	.70	.35	.20
96	Lou Clinton	.70	.35	.20
97	Bob Duliba	.70	.35	.20
98	George Thomas	.70	.35	.20
99	Jim Umbricht	.70	.35	.20
100	Joe Cunningham	.90	.45	.25
101	Joe Gibbon	.70	.35	.20
102a	Checklist 89-176 ("Checklist" in red on front)	3.00	1.50	.90
102b	Checklist 89-176 ("Checklist" in white)	6.00	3.00	1.75
103	Chuck Essegian	.70	.35	.20
104	Lew Krausse	.70	.35	.20
105	Ron Fairly	.90	.45	.25
106	Bob Bolin	.70	.35	.20
107	Jim Hickman	1.00	.50	.30
108	Hoyt Wilhelm	9.00	4.50	2.75
109	Lee Maye	.70	.35	.20
110	Rich Rollins	.90	.45	.25
111	Al Jackson	1.00	.50	.30
112	Dick Brown	.70	.35	.20
113	Don Landrum (photo actally Ron Santo)	.90	.45	.25
114	Dan Osinski	.70	.35	.20
115	Carl Yastrzemski	70.00	35.00	21.00
116	Jim Brosnan	.90	.45	.25
117	Jacke Davis	.70	.35	.20
118	Sherm Lollar	.90	.45	.25
119	Bob Lillis	.70	.35	.20
120	Roger Maris	40.00	20.00	12.00
121	Jim Hannan	.70	.35	.20
122	Julio Gotay	.70	.35	.20
123	Frank Howard	2.50	1.25	.70
124	Dick Howser	1.50	.70	.45
125	Robin Roberts	6.00	3.00	1.75
126	Bob Uecker	25.00	12.50	7.50
127	Bill Tuttle	.70	.35	.20
128	Matty Alou	.90	.45	.25
129	Gary Bell	.70	.35	.20
130	Dick Groat	1.50	.70	.45
131	Senators Team	2.25	1.25	.70
132	Jack Hamilton	.70	.35	.20
133	Gene Freese	.70	.35	.20
134	Bob Scheffing	.70	.35	.20
135	Richie Ashburn	4.50	2.25	1.25
136	Ike Delock	.70	.35	.20
137	Mack Jones	.70	.35	.20
138	Pride of N.L. (Willie Mays, Stan Musial)	25.00	12.50	7.50
139	Earl Averill	.70	.35	.20
140	Frank Lary	.90	.45	.25
141	Manny Mota	4.00	2.00	1.25
142	World Series Game 1 (Yanks' Ford Wins Series Opener)	3.50	1.75	1.00
143	World Series Game 2 (Sanford Flashes Shutout Magic)	2.25	1.25	.70
144	World Series Game 3 (Maris Sparks Yankee Rally)	4.00	2.00	1.25
145	World Series Game 4 (Hiller Blasts Grand Slammer)	2.25	1.25	.70
146	World Series Game 5 (Tresh's Homer Defeats Giants)	3.00	1.50	.90
147	World Series Game 6 (Pierce Stars In 3 Hit Victory)	3.00	1.50	.90
148	World Series Game 7 (Yanks Celebrate As Terry Wins)	3.00	1.50	.90
149	Marv Breeding	.70	.35	.20
150	Johnny Podres	2.00	1.00	.60
151	Pirates Team	2.25	1.25	.70
152	Ron Nischwitz	.70	.35	.20
153	Hal Smith	.70	.35	.20
154	Walt Alston	3.00	1.50	.90
155	Bill Stafford	1.25	.60	.40
156	Roy McMillan	.70	.35	.20
157	Diego Segui	.90	.45	.25
158	1963 Rookie Stars (Rogelio Alvarez, Tommy Harper, Dave Roberts, Bob Saverine)	.90	.45	.25
159	Jim Pagliaroni	.70	.35	.20
160	Juan Pizarro	.70	.35	.20
161	Frank Torre	.70	.35	.20
162	Twins Team	2.25	1.25	.70
163	Don Larsen	1.25	.60	.40
164	Bubba Morton	.70	.35	.20
165	Jim Kaat	5.00	2.50	1.50
166	Johnny Keane	.70	.35	.20
167	Jim Fregosi	1.50	.70	.45
168	Russ Nixon	.70	.35	.20
169	1963 Rookie Stars (Dick Egan, Julio Navarro, Gaylord Perry, Tommie Sisk)	18.00	9.00	5.50
170	Joe Adcock	1.50	.70	.45
171	Steve Hamilton	.70	.35	.20
172	Gene Oliver	.70	.35	.20
173	Bomber's Best (Mickey Mantle, Bobby Richardson, Tom Tresh)	35.00	17.50	10.50
174	Larry Burright	1.00	.50	.30
175	Bob Buhl	.90	.45	.25
176	Jim King	.70	.35	.20
177	Bubba Phillips	.70	.35	.20
178	Johnny Edwards	.70	.35	.20
179	Ron Piche	.70	.35	.20
180	Bill Skowron	1.50	.70	.45
181	Sammy Esposito	.70	.35	.20
182	Albie Pearson	.70	.35	.20
183	Joe Pepitone	4.00	2.00	1.25
184	Vern Law	1.25	.60	.40
185	Chuck Hiller	.70	.35	.20
186	Jerry Zimmerman	.70	.35	.20
187	Willie Kirkland	.70	.35	.20
188	Eddie Bressoud	.70	.35	.20
189	Dave Giusti	.70	.35	.20
190	Minnie Minoso	1.50	.70	.45
191	Checklist 177-264	3.00	1.50	.90
192	Clay Dalrymple	.70	.35	.20
193	Andre Rodgers	.70	.35	.20
194	Joe Nuxhall	.90	.45	.25
195	Manny Jimenez	.70	.35	.20
196	Doug Camilli	.70	.35	.20
197	Roger Craig	2.00	1.00	.60
198	Lenny Green	.70	.35	.20
199	Joe Amalfitano	.70	.35	.20
200	Mickey Mantle	275.00	110.00	69.00
201	Cecil Butler	.70	.35	.20
202	Red Sox Team	2.50	1.25	.70
203	Chico Cardenas	.70	.35	.20
204	Don Nottebart	.70	.35	.20
205	Luis Aparicio	10.00	5.00	3.00
206	Ray Washburn	.70	.35	.20
207	Ken Hunt	.70	.35	.20
208	1963 Rookie Stars (Ron Herbel, John Miller, Ron Taylor, Wally Wolf)	.70	.35	.20
209	Hobie Landrith	.70	.35	.20
210	Sandy Koufax	80.00	40.00	24.00
211	Fred Whitfield	.70	.35	.20
212	Glen Hobbie	.70	.35	.20
213	Billy Hitchcock	.70	.35	.20
214	Orlando Pena	.70	.35	.20
215	Bob Skinner	.90	.45	.25
216	Gene Conley	.90	.45	.25
217	Joe Christopher	1.00	.50	.30
218	Tiger Twirlers (Jim Bunning, Frank Lary, Don Mossi)	2.00	1.00	.60
219	Chuck Cottier	.70	.35	.20
220	Camilo Pascual	.90	.45	.25
221	Cookie Rojas	.90	.45	.25
222	Cubs Team	2.25	1.25	.70
223	Eddie Fisher	.70	.35	.20
224	Mike Roarke	.70	.35	.20
225	Joe Jay	.70	.35	.20
226	Julian Javier	.90	.45	.25
227	Jim Grant	.70	.35	.20
228	1963 Rookie Stars (Max Alvis, Bob Bailey, Ed Kranepool, Pedro Oliva)	25.00	12.50	7.50
229	Willie Davis	1.50	.70	.45
230	Pete Runnels	.90	.45	.25
231	Eli Grba (photo actually Ryne Duren)	.90	.45	.25
232	Frank Malzone	.90	.45	.25
233	Casey Stengel	12.00	6.00	3.50
234	Dave Nicholson	.70	.35	.20
235	Billy O'Dell	.70	.35	.20
236	Bill Bryan	.70	.35	.20
237	Jim Coates	1.25	.60	.40
238	Lou Johnson	.70	.35	.20
239	Harvey Haddix	.90	.45	.25
240	Rocky Colavito	3.00	1.50	.90
241	Billy Smith	.70	.35	.20
242	Power Plus (Hank Aaron, Ernie Banks)	15.00	7.50	4.50
243	Don Leppert	.70	.35	.20
244	John Tsitouris	.70	.35	.20
245	Gil Hodges	12.00	6.00	3.50
246	Lee Stange	.70	.35	.20
247	Yankees Team	8.00	4.00	2.50
248	Tito Francona	.90	.45	.25
249	Leo Burke	.70	.35	.20
250	Stan Musial	80.00	40.00	24.00
251	Jack Lamabe	.70	.35	.20

		NR MT	EX	VG
252	Ron Santo	2.00	1.00	.60
253	1963 Rookie Stars (Len Gabrielson, Pete Jernigan, Deacon Jones, John Wojcik)	.70	.35	.20
254	Mike Hershberger	.70	.35	.20
255	Bob Shaw	.70	.35	.20
256	Jerry Lumpe	.90	.45	.25
257	Hank Aguirre	.70	.35	.20
258	Alvin Dark	.90	.45	.25
259	Johnny Logan	.90	.45	.25
260	Jim Gentile	.90	.45	.25
261	Bob Miller	.70	.35	.20
262	Ellis Burton	.70	.35	.20
263	Dave Stenhouse	.70	.35	.20
264	Phil Linz	1.50	.70	.45
265	Vada Pinson	2.50	1.25	.70
266	Bob Allen	.70	.35	.20
267	Carl Sawatski	.70	.35	.20
268	Don Demeter	.70	.35	.20
269	Don Mincher	.90	.45	.25
270	Felipe Alou	.90	.45	.25
271	Dean Stone	.70	.35	.20
272	Danny Murphy	.70	.35	.20
273	Sammy Taylor	1.00	.50	.30
274	Checklist 265-352	3.00	1.50	.90
275	Ed Mathews	12.00	6.00	3.50
276	Barry Shetrone	.70	.35	.20
277	Dick Farrell	.70	.35	.20
278	Chico Fernandez	.70	.35	.20
279	Wally Moon	.90	.45	.25
280	Bob Rodgers	.90	.45	.25
281	Tom Sturdivant	.70	.35	.20
282	Bob Del Greco	.70	.35	.20
283	Roy Sievers	.90	.45	.25
284	Dave Sisler	2.00	1.00	.60
285	Dick Stuart	2.25	1.25	.70
286	Stu Miller	2.00	1.00	.60
287	Dick Bertell	2.00	1.00	.60
288	White Sox Team	3.50	1.75	1.00
289	Hal Brown	2.75	1.50	.80
290	Bill White	2.25	1.25	.70
291	Don Rudolph	2.00	1.00	.60
292	Pumpsie Green	2.25	1.25	.70
293	Bill Pleis	2.00	1.00	.60
294	Bill Rigney	2.00	1.00	.60
295	Ed Roebuck	2.00	1.00	.60
296	Doc Edwards	2.25	1.25	.70
297	Jim Golden	2.00	1.00	.60
298	Don Dillard	2.00	1.00	.60
299	1963 Rookie Stars (Tom Butters, Bob Dustal, Dave Morehead, Dan Schneider)	2.00	1.00	.60
300	Willie Mays	90.00	45.00	27.00
301	Bill Fischer	2.00	1.00	.60
302	Whitey Herzog	3.50	1.75	1.00
303	Earl Francis	2.00	1.00	.60
304	Harry Bright	2.00	1.00	.60
305	Don Hoak	2.25	1.25	.70
306	Star Receivers (Earl Battey, Elston Howard)	3.50	1.75	1.00
307	Chet Nichols	2.00	1.00	.60
308	Camilo Carreon	2.00	1.00	.60
309	Jim Brewer	2.00	1.00	.60
310	Tommy Davis	3.00	1.50	.90
311	Joe McClain	2.00	1.00	.60
312	Colt .45s Team	7.00	3.50	2.00
313	Ernie Broglio	2.00	1.00	.60
314	John Goryl	2.00	1.00	.60
315	Ralph Terry	3.00	1.50	.90
316	Norm Sherry	1.25	.60	.40
317	Sam McDowell	3.00	1.50	.90
318	Gene Mauch	2.25	1.25	.70
319	Joe Gaines	2.00	1.00	.60
320	Warren Spahn	25.00	12.50	7.50
321	Gino Cimoli	2.00	1.00	.60
322	Bob Turley	2.25	1.25	.70
323	Bill Mazeroski	3.50	1.75	1.00
324	1963 Rookie Stars (Vic Davalillo, Phil Roof, Pete Ward, George Williams)	2.50	1.25	.70
325	Jack Sanford	2.00	1.00	.60
326	Hank Foiles	2.00	1.00	.60
327	Paul Foytack	2.00	1.00	.60
328	Dick Williams	2.75	1.50	.80
329	Lindy McDaniel	2.00	1.00	.60
330	Chuck Hinton	2.00	1.00	.60
331	Series Foes (Bill Pierce, Bill Stafford)	3.00	1.50	.90
332	Joel Horlen	2.00	1.00	.60
333	Carl Warwick	2.00	1.00	.60
334	Wynn Hawkins	2.25	1.25	.70
335	Leon Wagner	2.25	1.25	.70
336	Ed Bauta	2.00	1.00	.60

		NR MT	EX	VG
337	Dodgers Team	8.00	4.00	2.50
338	Russ Kemmerer	2.00	1.00	.60
339	Ted Bowsfield	2.00	1.00	.60
340	Yogi Berra	60.00	30.00	18.00
341	Jack Baldschun	2.00	1.00	.60
342	Gene Woodling	2.50	1.25	.70
343	Johnny Pesky	2.25	1.25	.70
344	Don Schwall	2.00	1.00	.60
345	Brooks Robinson	30.00	15.00	9.00
346	Billy Hoeft	2.00	1.00	.60
347	Joe Torre	4.50	2.25	1.25
348	Vic Wertz	2.25	1.25	.70
349	Zoilo Versalles	2.25	1.25	.70
350	Bob Purkey	2.00	1.00	.60
351	Al Luplow	2.00	1.00	.60
352	Ken Johnson	2.00	1.00	.60
353	Billy Williams	20.00	10.00	6.00
354	Dom Zanni	2.00	1.00	.60
355	Dean Chance	2.25	1.25	.70
356	John Schaive	2.00	1.00	.60
357	George Altman	2.00	1.00	.60
358	Milt Pappas	2.25	1.25	.70
359	Haywood Sullivan	2.25	1.25	.70
360	Don Drysdale	20.00	10.00	6.00
361	Clete Boyer	3.50	1.75	1.00
362	Checklist 353-429	4.00	2.00	1.25
363	Dick Radatz	2.25	1.25	.70
364	Howie Goss	2.00	1.00	.60
365	Jim Bunning	8.00	4.00	2.50
366	Tony Taylor	2.00	1.00	.60
367	Tony Cloninger	2.25	1.25	.70
368	Ed Bailey	2.00	1.00	.60
369	Jim Lemon	2.00	1.00	.60
370	Dick Donovan	2.00	1.00	.60
371	Rod Kanehl	2.25	1.25	.70
372	Don Lee	2.00	1.00	.60
373	Jim Campbell	2.00	1.00	.60
374	Claude Osteen	2.25	1.25	.70
375	Ken Boyer	4.00	2.00	1.25
376	Johnnie Wyatt	2.00	1.00	.60
377	Orioles Team	3.50	1.75	1.00
378	Bill Henry	2.00	1.00	.60
379	Bob Anderson	2.00	1.00	.60
380	Ernie Banks	30.00	15.00	9.00
381	Frank Baumann	2.00	1.00	.60
382	Ralph Houk	3.50	1.75	1.00
383	Pete Richert	2.00	1.00	.60
384	Bob Tillman	2.00	1.00	.60
385	Art Mahaffey	2.00	1.00	.60
386	1963 Rookie Stars (John Bateman, Larry Bearnarth, Ed Kirkpatrick, Garry Roggenburk)	2.25	1.25	.70
387	Al McBean	2.00	1.00	.60
388	Jim Davenport	2.00	1.00	.60
389	Frank Sullivan	2.00	1.00	.60
390	Hank Aaron	100.00	45.00	27.00
391	Bill Dailey	2.00	1.00	.60
392	Tribe Thumpers (Tito Francona, Johnny Romano)	2.25	1.25	.70
393	Ken MacKenzie	2.25	1.25	.70
394	Tim McCarver	4.00	2.00	1.25
395	Don McMahon	2.00	1.00	.60
396	Joe Koppe	2.00	1.00	.60
397	Athletics Team	3.50	1.75	1.00
398	Boog Powell	4.50	2.25	1.25
399	Dick Ellsworth	2.00	1.00	.60
400	Frank Robinson	35.00	17.50	10.50
401	Jim Bouton	8.00	4.00	2.50
402	Mickey Vernon	2.25	1.25	.70
403	Ron Perranoski	2.25	1.25	.70
404	Bob Oldis	2.00	1.00	.60
405	Floyd Robinson	2.00	1.00	.60
406	Howie Koplitz	2.00	1.00	.60
407	1963 Rookie Stars (Larry Elliot, Frank Kostro, Chico Ruiz, Dick Simpson)	2.00	1.00	.60
408	Billy Gardner	2.00	1.00	.60
409	Roy Face	2.75	1.50	.80
410	Earl Battey	2.25	1.25	.70
411	Jim Constable	2.00	1.00	.60
412	Dodgers' Big Three (Don Drysdale, Sandy Koufax, Johnny Podres)	25.00	12.50	7.50
413	Jerry Walker	2.00	1.00	.60
414	Ty Cline	2.00	1.00	.60
415	Bob Gibson	30.00	15.00	9.00
416	Alex Grammas	2.00	1.00	.60
417	Giants Team	3.50	1.75	1.00
418	Johnny Orsino	2.00	1.00	.60
419	Tracy Stallard	2.25	1.25	.70
420	Bobby Richardson	8.00	4.00	2.50
421	Tom Morgan	2.00	1.00	.60
422	Fred Hutchinson	2.25	1.25	.70

		NR MT	EX	VG
423	Ed Hobaugh	2.00	1.00	.60
424	Charley Smith	2.00	1.00	.60
425	Smoky Burgess	2.50	1.25	.70
426	Barry Latman	2.00	1.00	.60
427	Bernie Allen	2.00	1.00	.60
428	Carl Boles	2.00	1.00	.60
429	Lou Burdette	3.00	1.50	.90
430	Norm Siebern	2.25	1.25	.70
431a	Checklist 430-506 ("Checklist" in black on front)	4.50	2.25	1.25
431b	Checklist 430-506 ("Checklist" in white)	7.00	3.50	2.00
432	Roman Mejias	2.00	1.00	.60
433	Denis Menke	2.25	1.25	.70
434	Johnny Callison	2.50	1.25	.70
435	Woody Held	2.00	1.00	.60
436	Tim Harkness	2.25	1.25	.70
437	Bill Bruton	2.00	1.00	.60
438	Wes Stock	2.00	1.00	.60
439	Don Zimmer	2.75	1.50	.80
440	Juan Marichal	20.00	10.00	6.00
441	Lee Thomas	2.00	1.00	.60
442	J.C. Hartman	2.00	1.00	.60
443	Jim Piersall	2.75	1.50	.80
444	Jim Maloney	2.25	1.25	.70
445	Norm Cash	3.00	1.50	.90
446	Whitey Ford	30.00	15.00	9.00
447	Felix Mantilla	8.00	4.00	2.50
448	Jack Kralick	8.00	4.00	2.50
449	Jose Tartabull	8.00	4.00	2.50
450	Bob Friend	9.00	4.50	2.75
451	Indians Team	10.00	5.00	3.00
452	Barney Schultz	8.00	4.00	2.50
453	Jake Wood	8.00	4.00	2.50
454a	Art Fowler (card # on orange background)	10.00	5.00	3.00
454b	Art Fowler (card # on white background)	8.00	4.00	2.50
455	Ruben Amaro	8.00	4.00	2.50
456	Jim Coker	8.00	4.00	2.50
457	Tex Clevenger	9.00	4.50	2.75
458	Al Lopez	11.00	5.50	3.25
459	Dick LeMay	8.00	4.00	2.50
460	Del Crandall	9.00	4.50	2.75
461	Norm Bass	8.00	4.00	2.50
462	Wally Post	8.00	4.00	2.50
463	Joe Schaffernoth	8.00	4.00	2.50
464	Ken Aspromonte	8.00	4.00	2.50
465	Chuck Estrada	8.00	4.00	2.50
466	1963 Rookie Stars (Bill Freehan, Tony Martinez, Nate Oliver, Jerry Robinson)	25.00	12.50	7.50
467	Phil Ortega	8.00	4.00	2.50
468	Carroll Hardy	8.00	4.00	2.50
469	Jay Hook	9.00	4.50	2.75
470	Tom Tresh	20.00	10.00	6.00
471	Ken Retzer	8.00	4.00	2.50
472	Lou Brock	80.00	40.00	24.00
473	Mets Team	30.00	15.00	9.00
474	Jack Fisher	8.00	4.00	2.50
475	Gus Triandos	8.00	4.00	2.50
476	Frank Funk	8.00	4.00	2.50
477	Donn Clendenon	9.00	4.50	2.75
478	Paul Brown	8.00	4.00	2.50
479	*Ed Brinkman*	9.00	4.50	2.75
480	Bill Monbouquette	9.00	4.50	2.75
481	Bob Taylor	8.00	4.00	2.50
482	Felix Torres	8.00	4.00	2.50
483	Jim Owens	8.00	4.00	2.50
484	Dale Long	9.00	4.50	2.75
485	Jim Landis	8.00	4.00	2.50
486	Ray Sadecki	8.00	4.00	2.50
487	John Roseboro	9.00	4.50	2.75
488	Jerry Adair	8.00	4.00	2.50
489	Paul Toth	8.00	4.00	2.50
490	Willie McCovey	70.00	35.00	21.00
491	Harry Craft	8.00	4.00	2.50
492	Dave Wickersham	8.00	4.00	2.50
493	Walt Bond	8.00	4.00	2.50
494	Phil Regan	8.00	4.00	2.50
495	Frank Thomas	9.00	4.50	2.75
496	1963 Rookie Stars (Carl Bouldin, *Steve Dalkowski*, Fred Newman, Jack Smith)	9.00	4.50	2.75
497	Bennie Daniels	8.00	4.00	2.50
498	Eddie Kasko	8.00	4.00	2.50
499	J.C. Martin	8.00	4.00	2.50
500	Harmon Killebrew	50.00	25.00	15.00
501	Joe Azcue	8.00	4.00	2.50
502	Daryl Spencer	8.00	4.00	2.50
503	Braves Team	10.00	5.00	3.00

		NR MT	EX	VG
504	Bob Johnson	8.00	4.00	2.50
505	Curt Flood	12.00	6.00	3.50
506	Gene Green	9.00	4.50	2.75
507	Roland Sheldon	6.00	3.00	1.75
508	Ted Savage	5.00	2.50	1.50
509a	Checklist 507-576 (copyright centered)	15.00	7.50	4.50
509b	Checklist 509-576 (copyright to right)	12.00	6.00	3.50
510	Ken McBride	5.00	2.50	1.50
511	Charlie Neal	5.50	2.75	1.75
512	Cal McLish	5.00	2.50	1.50
513	Gary Geiger	5.00	2.50	1.50
514	Larry Osborne	5.00	2.50	1.50
515	Don Elston	5.00	2.50	1.50
516	Purnal Goldy	5.00	2.50	1.50
517	Hal Woodeshick	5.00	2.50	1.50
518	Don Blasingame	5.00	2.50	1.50
519	Claude Raymond	5.00	2.50	1.50
520	Orlando Cepeda	15.00	7.50	4.50
521	Dan Pfister	5.00	2.50	1.50
522	1963 Rookie Stars (Mel Nelson, Gary Peters, Art Quirk, Jim Roland)	5.50	2.75	1.75
523	Bill Kunkel	6.00	3.00	1.75
524	Cardinals Team	8.00	4.00	2.50
525	Nellie Fox	12.00	6.00	3.50
526	Dick Hall	5.00	2.50	1.50
527	Ed Sadowski	5.00	2.50	1.50
528	Carl Willey	5.50	2.75	1.75
529	Wes Covington	5.00	2.50	1.50
530	Don Mossi	5.50	2.75	1.75
531	Sam Mele	5.00	2.50	1.50
532	Steve Boros	5.00	2.50	1.50
533	Bobby Shantz	6.00	3.00	1.75
534	Ken Walters	5.00	2.50	1.50
535	Jim Perry	6.00	3.00	1.75
536	Norm Larker	5.00	2.50	1.50
537	1963 Rookie Stars (Pedro Gonzalez, *Ken McMullen, Pete Rose, Al Weis*)	600.00	240.00	150.00
538	George Brunet	5.00	2.50	1.50
539	Wayne Causey	5.00	2.50	1.50
540	Bob Clemente	125.00	56.00	35.00
541	Ron Moeller	5.00	2.50	1.50
542	Lou Klimchock	5.00	2.50	1.50
543	Russ Snyder	5.00	2.50	1.50
544	1963 Rookie Stars (Duke Carmel, Bill Haas, Dick Phillips, *Rusty Staub*)	25.00	12.50	7.50
545	Jose Pagan	5.00	2.50	1.50
546	Hal Reniff	6.00	3.00	1.75
547	Gus Bell	5.50	2.75	1.75
548	Tom Satriano	5.00	2.50	1.50
549	1963 Rookie Stars (*Marcelino Lopez*, Pete Lovrich, Elmo Plaskett, Paul Ratliff)	5.50	2.75	1.75
550	Duke Snider	50.00	25.00	15.00
551	Billy Klaus	5.00	2.50	1.50
552	Tigers Team	12.00	6.00	3.50
553	1963 Rookie Stars (Brock Davis, Jim Gosger, John Herrnstein, *Willie Stargell*)	200.00	80.00	50.00
554	Hank Fischer	5.00	2.50	1.50
555	John Blanchard	6.00	3.00	1.75
556	Al Worthington	5.00	2.50	1.50
557	Cuno Barragan	5.00	2.50	1.50
558	1963 Rookie Stars (Bill Faul, *Ron Hunt*, Bob Lipski, Al Moran)	6.00	3.00	1.75
559	Danny Murtaugh	5.50	2.75	1.75
560	Ray Herbert	5.00	2.50	1.50
561	Mike de la Hoz	5.00	2.50	1.50
562	1963 Rookie Stars (Randy Cardinal, *Dave McNally*, Don Rowe, Ken Rowe)	9.00	4.50	2.75
563	Mike McCormick	5.50	2.75	1.75
564	George Banks	5.00	2.50	1.50
565	Larry Sherry	5.00	2.50	1.50
566	Cliff Cook	5.50	2.75	1.75
567	Jim Duffalo	5.00	2.50	1.50
568	Bob Sadowski	5.00	2.50	1.50
569	Luis Arroyo	6.00	3.00	1.75
570	Frank Bolling	5.00	2.50	1.50
571	Johnny Klippstein	5.00	2.50	1.50
572	Jack Spring	5.00	2.50	1.50
573	Coot Veal	5.00	2.50	1.50
574	Hal Kolstad	5.00	2.50	1.50
575	Don Cardwell	5.50	2.75	1.50
576	Johnny Temple	8.00	2.50	1.25

A player's name in *italic* type indicates a rookie card. An (FC) indicates a player's first card for that particular card company.

1963 Topps Peel-Offs

   Measuring 1-1/4" by 2-3/4," Topps Peel-Offs were an insert with 1963 Topps baseball cards. There are 46 players in the unnumbered set, each pictured in a color photo inside an oval with the player's name, team and position in a band below. The back of the Peel-Off is removable, leaving a sticky surface that made the Peel-Off a popular decorative item among youngsters of the day. Naturally, that makes them quite scarce today, but as a non-card Topps issue, demand is not particularly strong.

		NR MT	EX	VG
Complete Set:		175.00	87.00	52.00
Common Player:		1.00	.50	.30
(1)	Hank Aaron	10.00	5.00	3.00
(2)	Luis Aparicio	3.00	1.50	.90
(3)	Richie Ashburn	2.00	1.00	.60
(4)	Bob Aspromonte	1.00	.50	.30
(5)	Ernie Banks	5.00	2.50	1.50
(6)	Ken Boyer	1.50	.70	.45
(7)	Jim Bunning	1.75	.90	.50
(8)	Johnny Callison	1.25	.60	.40
(9)	Orlando Cepeda	1.75	.90	.50
(10)	Bob Clemente	8.00	4.00	2.50
(11)	Rocky Colavito	1.75	.90	.50
(12)	Tommy Davis	1.50	.70	.45
(13)	Dick Donovan	1.00	.50	.30
(14)	Don Drysdale	4.00	2.00	1.25
(15)	Dick Farrell	1.00	.50	.30
(16)	Jim Gentile	1.00	.50	.30
(17)	Ray Herbert	1.00	.50	.30
(18)	Chuck Hinton	1.00	.50	.30
(19)	Ken Hubbs	1.50	.70	.45
(20)	Al Jackson	1.00	.50	.30
(21)	Al Kaline	5.00	2.50	1.50
(22)	Harmon Killebrew	5.00	2.50	1.50
(23)	Sandy Koufax	8.00	4.00	2.50
(24)	Jerry Lumpe	1.00	.50	.30
(25)	Art Mahaffey	1.00	.50	.30
(26)	Mickey Mantle	50.00	25.00	15.00
(27)	Willie Mays	10.00	5.00	3.00
(28)	Bill Mazeroski	1.50	.70	.45
(29)	Bill Monbouquette	1.00	.50	.30
(30)	Stan Musial	10.00	5.00	3.00
(31)	Camilo Pascual	1.25	.60	.40
(32)	Bob Purkey	1.00	.50	.30
(33)	Bobby Richardson	1.75	.90	.50
(34)	Brooks Robinson	6.00	3.00	1.75
(35)	Floyd Robinson	1.00	.50	.30
(36)	Frank Robinson	5.00	2.50	1.50
(37)	Bob Rodgers	1.00	.50	.30
(38)	Johnny Romano	1.00	.50	.30
(39)	Jack Sanford	1.00	.50	.30
(40)	Norm Siebern	1.00	.50	.30
(41)	Warren Spahn	5.00	2.50	1.50
(42)	Dave Stenhouse	1.00	.50	.30
(43)	Ralph Terry	1.25	.60	.40
(44)	Lee Thomas	1.00	.50	.30
(45)	Bill White	1.25	.60	.40
(46)	Carl Yastrzemski	12.00	6.00	3.50

A player's name in _italic_ type indicates a rookie card. An (FC) indicates a player's first card for that particular card company.

1964 Topps

   The 1964 Topps set is a 587-card issue of 2-1/2" by 3-1/2" cards which is considered by many as being among the company's best efforts. Card fronts feature a large color photo which blends into a top panel which contains the team name, while a panel below the picture carries the player's name and position. An interesting innovation on the back is a baseball quiz question which required the rubbing of a white panel to reveal the answer. As in 1963, specialty cards remained modest in number with a 12-card set of statistical leaders, a few multi-player cards, rookies and World Series highlights. An interesting card is an "In Memoriam" card for Ken Hubbs who was killed in an airplane crash.

		NR MT	EX	VG
Complete Set:		2200.00	1100.00	650.00
Common Player: 1-370		.70	.35	.20
Common Player: 371-522		1.00	.50	.30
Common Player: 523-587		4.00	2.00	1.25
1	N.L. E.R.A. Leaders (Dick Ellsworth, Bob Friend, Sandy Koufax)	10.00	3.00	1.50
2	A.L. E.R.A. Leaders (Camilo Pascual, Gary Peters, Juan Pizarro)	3.00	1.50	.90
3	N.L. Pitching Leaders (Sandy Koufax, Jim Maloney, Juan Marichal, Warren Spahn)	5.00	2.50	1.50
4a	A.L. Pitching Leaders (Jim Bouton, Whitey Ford, Camilo Pascual) (apostrophe after "Pitching" on back)	5.00	2.50	1.50
4b	A.L. Pitching Leaders (Jim Bouton, Whitey Ford, Camilo Pascual) (no apostrophe)	3.50	1.75	1.00
5	N.L. Strikeout Leaders (Don Drysdale, Sandy Koufax, Jim Maloney)	4.00	2.00	1.25
6	A.L. Strikeout Leaders (Jim Bunning, Camilo Pascual, Dick Stigman)	3.00	1.50	.90
7	N.L. Batting Leaders (Hank Aaron, Bob Clemente, Tommy Davis, Dick Groat)	5.00	2.50	1.50
8	A.L. Batting Leaders (Al Kaline, Rich Rollins, Carl Yastrzemski)	5.00	2.50	1.50
9	N.L. Home Run Leaders (Hank Aaron, Orlando Cepeda, Willie Mays, Willie McCovey)	5.00	2.50	1.50
10	A.L. Home Run Leaders (Bob Allison, Harmon Killebrew, Dick Stuart)	3.50	1.75	1.00
11	N.L. R.B.I. Leaders (Hank Aaron, Ken Boyer, Bill White)	4.50	2.25	1.25
12	A.L. R.B.I. Leaders (Al Kaline, Harmon Killebrew, Dick Stuart)	4.50	2.25	1.25
13	Hoyt Wilhelm	8.00	4.00	2.50
14	Dodgers Rookies (Dick Nen, Nick Willhite)	.70	.35	.20
15	Zoilo Versalles	.80	.40	.25
16	John Boozer	.70	.35	.20
17	Willie Kirkland	.70	.35	.20
18	Billy O'Dell	.70	.35	.20
19	Don Wert	.70	.35	.20
20	Bob Friend	1.25	.60	.40
21	Yogi Berra	30.00	15.00	9.00
22	Jerry Adair	.70	.35	.20
23	Chris Zachary	.70	.35	.20
24	Carl Sawatski	.70	.35	.20
25	Bill Monbouquette	.80	.40	.25
26	Gino Cimoli	.70	.35	.20
27	Mets Team	3.50	1.75	1.00

		NR MT	EX	VG
28	Claude Osteen	.80	.40	.25
29	Lou Brock	25.00	12.50	7.50
30	Ron Perranoski	.80	.40	.25
31	Dave Nicholson	.70	.35	.20
32	Dean Chance	1.25	.60	.40
33	Reds Rookies (Sammy Ellis, Mel Queen)	.80	.40	.25
34	Jim Perry	1.25	.60	.40
35	Ed Mathews	12.00	6.00	3.50
36	Hal Reniff	1.00	.50	.30
37	Smoky Burgess	1.25	.60	.40
38	*Jim Wynn*	1.50	.70	.45
39	Hank Aguirre	.70	.35	.20
40	Dick Groat	1.50	.70	.45
41	Friendly Foes (Willie McCovey, Leon Wagner)	3.00	1.50	.90
42	Moe Drabowsky	.70	.35	.20
43	Roy Sievers	.90	.45	.25
44	Duke Carmel	.80	.40	.25
45	Milt Pappas	.90	.45	.25
46	Ed Brinkman	.80	.40	.25
47	Giants Rookies (*Jesus Alou*, Ron Herbel)	1.25	.60	.40
48	Bob Perry	.70	.35	.20
49	Bill Henry	.70	.35	.20
50	Mickey Mantle	200.00	80.00	50.00
51	Pete Richert	.70	.35	.20
52	Chuck Hinton	.70	.35	.20
53	Denis Menke	.70	.35	.20
54	Sam Mele	.70	.35	.20
55	Ernie Banks	20.00	10.00	6.00
56	Hal Brown	.70	.35	.20
57	Tim Harkness	.80	.40	.25
58	Don Demeter	.70	.35	.20
59	Ernie Broglio	.70	.35	.20
60	Frank Malzone	.80	.40	.25
61	Angel Backstops (Bob Rodgers, Ed Sadowski)	.80	.40	.25
62	Ted Savage	.70	.35	.20
63	Johnny Orsino	.70	.35	.20
64	Ted Abernathy	.70	.35	.20
65	Felipe Alou	1.25	.60	.40
66	Eddie Fisher	.70	.35	.20
67	Tigers Team	3.50	1.75	1.00
68	Willie Davis	1.50	.70	.45
69	Clete Boyer	1.50	.70	.45
70	Joe Torre	2.50	1.25	.70
71	Jack Spring	.70	.35	.20
72	Chico Cardenas	.70	.35	.20
73	*Jimmie Hall*	.80	.40	.25
74	Pirates Rookies (Tom Butters, Bob Priddy)	.70	.35	.20
75	Wayne Causey	.70	.35	.20
76	Checklist 1-88	3.00	1.50	.90
77	Jerry Walker	.70	.35	.20
78	Merritt Ranew	.70	.35	.20
79	Bob Heffner	.70	.35	.20
80	Vada Pinson	2.50	1.25	.70
81	All-Star Vets (Nellie Fox, Harmon Killebrew)	4.00	2.00	1.25
82	Jim Davenport	.70	.35	.20
83	Gus Triandos	.80	.40	.25
84	Carl Willey	.80	.40	.25
85	Pete Ward	.80	.40	.25
86	Al Downing	1.50	.70	.45
87	Cardinals Team	4.00	2.00	1.25
88	John Roseboro	.80	.40	.25
89	Boog Powell	2.50	1.25	.70
90	Earl Battey	.80	.40	.25
91	Bob Bailey	.80	.40	.25
92	Steve Ridzik	.70	.35	.20
93	Gary Geiger	.70	.35	.20
94	Braves Rookies (Jim Britton, Larry Maxie)	.70	.35	.20
95	George Altman	.80	.40	.25
96	Bob Buhl	.80	.40	.25
97	Jim Fregosi	1.25	.60	.40
98	Bill Bruton	.70	.35	.20
99	Al Stanek	.70	.35	.20
100	Elston Howard	5.00	2.50	1.50
101	Walt Alston	3.00	1.50	.90
102	Checklist 89-176	3.00	1.50	.90
103	Curt Flood	2.00	1.00	.60
104	Art Mahaffey	.70	.35	.20
105	Woody Held	.70	.35	.20
106	Joe Nuxhall	.80	.40	.25
107	White Sox Rookies (Bruce Howard, Frank Kreutzer)	.70	.35	.20
108	John Wyatt	.70	.35	.20
109	Rusty Staub	5.00	2.50	1.50
110	Albie Pearson	.70	.35	.20

		NR MT	EX	VG
111	Don Elston	.70	.35	.20
112	Bob Tillman	.70	.35	.20
113	Grover Powell	.80	.40	.25
114	Don Lock	.70	.35	.20
115	Frank Bolling	.70	.35	.20
116	Twins Rookies (Tony Oliva, Jay Ward)	4.00	2.00	1.25
117	Earl Francis	.70	.35	.20
118	John Blanchard	1.00	.50	.30
119	Gary Kolb	.70	.35	.20
120	Don Drysdale	15.00	7.50	4.50
121	Pete Runnels	.80	.40	.25
122	Don McMahon	.70	.35	.20
123	Jose Pagan	.70	.35	.20
124	Orlando Pena	.70	.35	.20
125	Pete Rose	125.00	56.00	35.00
126	Russ Snyder	.70	.35	.20
127	Angels Rookies (Aubrey Gatewood, Dick Simpson)	.70	.35	.20
128	*Mickey Lolich*	8.00	4.00	2.50
129	Amado Samuel	.80	.40	.25
130	Gary Peters	.80	.40	.25
131	Steve Boros	.80	.40	.25
132	Braves Team	2.25	1.25	.70
133	Jim Grant	.70	.35	.20
134	Don Zimmer	1.50	.70	.45
135	Johnny Callison	1.50	.70	.45
136	World Series Game 1 (Koufax Strikes Out 15)	5.00	2.50	1.50
137	World Series Game 2 (Davis Sparks Rally)	2.50	1.25	.70
138	World Series Game 3 (L.A. Takes 3rd Straight)	2.50	1.25	.70
139	World Series Game 4 (Sealing Yanks' Doom)	2.50	1.25	.70
140	World Series Summary (The Dodgers Celebrate)	2.50	1.25	.70
141	Danny Murtaugh	.80	.40	.25
142	John Bateman	.70	.35	.20
143	Bubba Phillips	.70	.35	.20
144	Al Worthington	.70	.35	.20
145	Norm Siebern	.80	.40	.25
146	Indians Rookies (Bob Chance, *Tommy John*)	25.00	12.50	7.50
147	Ray Sadecki	.70	.35	.20
148	J.C. Martin	.70	.35	.20
149	Paul Foytack	.70	.35	.20
150	Willie Mays	65.00	33.00	20.00
151	Athletics Team	2.25	1.25	.70
152	Denver Lemaster	.70	.35	.20
153	Dick Williams	1.50	.70	.45
154	Dick Tracewski	.70	.35	.20
155	Duke Snider	18.00	9.00	5.50
156	Bill Dailey	.70	.35	.20
157	Gene Mauch	.90	.45	.25
158	Ken Johnson	.70	.35	.20
159	Charlie Dees	.70	.35	.20
160	Ken Boyer	4.00	2.00	1.25
161	Dave McNally	1.25	.60	.40
162	Hitting Area (Vada Pinson, Dick Sisler)	.80	.40	.25
163	Donn Clendenon	1.00	.50	.30
164	Bud Daley	1.00	.50	.30
165	Jerry Lumpe	.80	.40	.25
166	Marty Keough	.70	.35	.20
167	Senators Rookies (Mike Brumley, *Lou Piniella*)	12.00	6.00	3.50
168	Al Weis	.70	.35	.20
169	Del Crandall	1.25	.60	.40
170	Dick Radatz	.80	.40	.25
171	Ty Cline	.70	.35	.20
172	Indians Team	2.25	1.25	.70
173	Ryne Duren	.90	.45	.25
174	Doc Edwards	.80	.40	.25
175	Billy Williams	8.00	4.00	2.50
176	Tracy Stallard	.80	.40	.25
177	Harmon Killebrew	12.00	6.00	3.50
178	Hank Bauer	.90	.45	.25
179	Carl Warwick	.70	.35	.20
180	Tommy Davis	1.50	.70	.45
181	Dave Wickersham	.70	.35	.20
182	Sox Sockers (Chuck Schilling, Carl Yastrzemski)	7.00	3.50	2.00
183	Ron Taylor	.70	.35	.20
184	Al Luplow	.70	.35	.20
185	Jim O'Toole	.70	.35	.20
186	Roman Mejias	.70	.35	.20
187	Ed Roebuck	.70	.35	.20
188	Checklist 177-264	3.00	1.50	.90
189	Bob Hendley	.70	.35	.20
190	Bobby Richardson	4.50	2.25	1.25

#	Player	NR MT	EX	VG
191	Clay Dalrymple	.70	.35	.20
192	Cubs Rookies (John Boccabella, Billy Cowan)	.70	.35	.20
193	Jerry Lynch	.70	.35	.20
194	John Goryl	.70	.35	.20
195	Floyd Robinson	.70	.35	.20
196	Jim Gentile	.80	.40	.25
197	Frank Lary	.80	.40	.25
198	Len Gabrielson	.70	.35	.20
199	Joe Azcue	.70	.35	.20
200	Sandy Koufax	60.00	30.00	18.00
201	Orioles Rookies (Sam Bowens, Wally Bunker)	.80	.40	.25
202	Galen Cisco	.80	.40	.25
203	John Kennedy	.70	.35	.20
204	Matty Alou	.90	.45	.25
205	Nellie Fox	4.00	2.00	1.25
206	Steve Hamilton	1.00	.50	.30
207	Fred Hutchinson	.80	.40	.25
208	Wes Covington	.70	.35	.20
209	Bob Allen	.70	.35	.20
210	Carl Yastrzemski	70.00	35.00	21.00
211	Jim Coker	.70	.35	.20
212	Pete Lovrich	.70	.35	.20
213	Angels Team	2.25	1.25	.70
214	Ken McMullen	.80	.40	.25
215	Ray Herbert	.70	.35	.20
216	Mike de la Hoz	.70	.35	.20
217	Jim King	.70	.35	.20
218	Hank Fischer	.70	.35	.20
219	Young Aces (Jim Bouton, Al Downing)	2.00	1.00	.60
220	Dick Ellsworth	.70	.35	.20
221	Bob Saverine	.70	.35	.20
222	Bill Pierce	.90	.45	.25
223	George Banks	.70	.35	.20
224	Tommie Sisk	.70	.35	.20
225	Roger Maris	45.00	23.00	13.50
226	Colts Rookies (Gerald Grote, Larry Yellen)	1.25	.60	.40
227	Barry Latman	.70	.35	.20
228	Felix Mantilla	.70	.35	.20
229	Charley Lau	.80	.40	.25
230	Brooks Robinson	20.00	10.00	6.00
231	Dick Calmus	.70	.35	.20
232	Al Lopez	3.00	1.50	.90
233	Hal Smith	.70	.35	.20
234	Gary Bell	.70	.35	.20
235	Ron Hunt	.80	.40	.25
236	Bill Faul	.70	.35	.20
237	Cubs Team	2.25	1.25	.70
238	Roy McMillan	.70	.35	.20
239	Herm Starrette	.70	.35	.20
240	Bill White	1.50	.70	.45
241	Jim Owens	.70	.35	.20
242	Harvey Kuenn	1.50	.70	.45
243	Phillies Rookies (Richie Allen, John Herrnstein)	8.00	4.00	2.50
244	Tony LaRussa	2.50	1.25	.70
245	Dick Stigman	.70	.35	.20
246	Manny Mota	1.25	.60	.40
247	Dave DeBusschere	2.00	1.00	.60
248	Johnny Pesky	.80	.40	.25
249	Doug Camilli	.70	.35	.20
250	Al Kaline	18.00	9.00	5.50
251	Choo Choo Coleman	.80	.40	.25
252	Ken Aspromonte	.70	.35	.20
253	Wally Post	.70	.35	.20
254	Don Hoak	.80	.40	.25
255	Lee Thomas	.70	.35	.20
256	Johnny Weekly	.70	.35	.20
257	Giants Team	2.25	1.25	.70
258	Garry Roggenburk	.70	.35	.20
259	Harry Bright	1.00	.50	.30
260	Frank Robinson	18.00	9.00	5.50
261	Jim Hannan	.70	.35	.20
262	Cardinals Rookie Stars (Harry Fanok, Mike Shannon)	1.50	.70	.45
263	Chuck Estrada	.70	.35	.20
264	Jim Landis	.70	.35	.20
265	Jim Bunning	5.00	2.50	1.50
266	Gene Freese	.70	.35	.20
267	Wilbur Wood	1.50	.70	.45
268	Bill's Got It (Danny Murtaugh, Bill Virdon)	.90	.45	.25
269	Ellis Burton	.70	.35	.20
270	Rich Rollins	.70	.35	.20
271	Bob Sadowski	.70	.35	.20
272	Jake Wood	.70	.35	.20
273	Mel Nelson	.70	.35	.20
274	Checklist 265-352	3.00	1.50	.90
275	John Tsitouris	.70	.35	.20
276	Jose Tartabull	.70	.35	.20
277	Ken Retzer	.70	.35	.20
278	Bobby Shantz	1.50	.70	.45
279	Joe Koppe	.70	.35	.20
280	Juan Marichal	10.00	5.00	3.00
281	Yankees Rookies (Jake Gibbs, Tom Metcalf)	1.00	.50	.30
282	Bob Bruce	.70	.35	.20
283	Tommy McCraw	.80	.40	.25
284	Dick Schofield	.70	.35	.20
285	Robin Roberts	10.00	5.00	3.00
286	Don Landrum	.70	.35	.20
287	Red Sox Rookies (Tony Conigliaro, Bill Spanswick)	4.00	2.00	1.25
288	Al Moran	.80	.40	.25
289	Frank Funk	.70	.35	.20
290	Bob Allison	.90	.45	.25
291	Phil Ortega	.70	.35	.20
292	Mike Roarke	.70	.35	.20
293	Phillies Team	2.25	1.25	.70
294	Ken Hunt	.70	.35	.20
295	Roger Craig	1.50	.70	.45
296	Ed Kirkpatrick	.70	.35	.20
297	Ken MacKenzie	.70	.35	.20
298	Harry Craft	.70	.35	.20
299	Bill Stafford	1.00	.50	.30
300	Hank Aaron	65.00	33.00	20.00
301	Larry Brown	.70	.35	.20
302	Dan Pfister	.70	.35	.20
303	Jim Campbell	.70	.35	.20
304	Bob Johnson	.70	.35	.20
305	Jack Lamabe	.70	.35	.20
306	Giant Gunners (Orlando Cepeda, Willie Mays)	12.00	6.00	3.50
307	Joe Gibbon	.70	.35	.20
308	Gene Stephens	.70	.35	.20
309	Paul Toth	.70	.35	.20
310	Jim Gilliam	3.00	1.50	.90
311	Tom Brown	.70	.35	.20
312	Tigers Rookies (Fritz Fisher, Fred Gladding)	.70	.35	.20
313	Chuck Hiller	.70	.35	.20
314	Jerry Buchek	.70	.35	.20
315	Bo Belinsky	.90	.45	.25
316	Gene Oliver	.70	.35	.20
317	Al Smith	.70	.35	.20
318	Twins Team	2.25	1.25	.70
319	Paul Brown	.70	.35	.20
320	Rocky Colavito	3.00	1.50	.90
321	Bob Lillis	.70	.35	.20
322	George Brunet	.70	.35	.20
323	John Buzhardt	.70	.35	.20
324	Casey Stengel	12.00	6.00	3.50
325	Hector Lopez	1.00	.50	.30
326	Ron Brand	.70	.35	.20
327	Don Blasingame	.70	.35	.20
328	Bob Shaw	.70	.35	.20
329	Russ Nixon	.70	.35	.20
330	Tommy Harper	.80	.40	.25
331	A.L. Bombers (Norm Cash, Al Kaline, Mickey Mantle, Roger Maris)	55.00	27.00	16.50
332	Ray Washburn	.70	.35	.20
333	Billy Moran	.70	.35	.20
334	Lew Krausse	.70	.35	.20
335	Don Mossi	.80	.40	.25
336	Andre Rodgers	.70	.35	.20
337	Dodgers Rookies (Al Ferrara, Jeff Torborg)	.80	.40	.25
338	Jack Kralick	.70	.35	.20
339	Walt Bond	.70	.35	.20
340	Joe Cunningham	.80	.40	.25
341	Jim Roland	.70	.35	.20
342	Willie Stargell	25.00	12.50	7.50
343	Senators Team	2.25	1.25	.70
344	Phil Linz	1.00	.50	.30
345	Frank Thomas	.80	.40	.25
346	Joe Jay	.70	.35	.20
347	Bobby Wine	.80	.40	.25
348	Ed Lopat	.90	.45	.25
349	Art Fowler	.70	.35	.20
350	Willie McCovey	20.00	10.00	6.00
351	Dan Schneider	.70	.35	.20
352	Eddie Bressoud	.70	.35	.20
353	Wally Moon	.90	.45	.25
354	Dave Giusti	.70	.35	.20
355	Vic Power	.70	.35	.20
356	Reds Rookies (Bill McCool, Chico Ruiz)	.70	.35	.20
357	Charley James	.70	.35	.20
358	Ron Kline	.70	.35	.20

	NR MT	EX	VG
359 Jim Schaffer	.70	.35	.20
360 Joe Pepitone	2.50	1.25	.70
361 Jay Hook	.80	.40	.25
362 Checklist 353-429	3.00	1.50	.90
363 Dick McAuliffe	.80	.40	.25
364 Joe Gaines	.70	.35	.20
365 Cal McLish	.70	.35	.20
366 Nelson Mathews	.70	.35	.20
367 Fred Whitfield	.70	.35	.20
368 White Sox Rookies (Fritz Ackley, Don Buford)	.90	.45	.25
369 Jerry Zimmerman	.70	.35	.20
370 Hal Woodeshick	.70	.35	.20
371 Frank Howard	3.00	1.50	.90
372 Howie Koplitz	1.00	.50	.30
373 Pirates Team	3.00	1.50	.90
374 Bobby Bolin	1.00	.50	.30
375 Ron Santo	2.50	1.25	.70
376 Dave Morehead	1.00	.50	.30
377 Bob Skinner	1.00	.50	.30
378 Braves Rookies (Jack Smith, Woody Woodward)	1.25	.60	.40
379 Tony Gonzalez	1.00	.50	.30
380 Whitey Ford	25.00	12.50	7.50
381 Bob Taylor	1.25	.60	.40
382 Wes Stock	1.00	.50	.30
383 Bill Rigney	1.00	.50	.30
384 Ron Hansen	1.00	.50	.30
385 Curt Simmons	1.25	.60	.40
386 Lenny Green	1.00	.50	.30
387 Terry Fox	1.00	.50	.30
388 Athletics Rookies (John O'Donoghue, George Williams)	1.00	.50	.30
389 Jim Umbricht	1.00	.50	.30
390 Orlando Cepeda	4.50	2.25	1.25
391 Sam McDowell	1.25	.60	.40
392 Jim Pagliaroni	1.00	.50	.30
393 Casey Teaches (Ed Kranepool, Casey Stengel)	3.00	1.50	.90
394 Bob Miller	1.00	.50	.30
395 Tom Tresh	3.00	1.50	.90
396 Dennis Bennett	1.00	.50	.30
397 Chuck Cottier	1.00	.50	.30
398 Mets Rookies (Bill Haas, Dick Smith)	1.25	.60	.40
399 Jackie Brandt	1.00	.50	.30
400 Warren Spahn	20.00	10.00	6.00
401 Charlie Maxwell	1.00	.50	.30
402 Tom Sturdivant	1.00	.50	.30
403 Reds Team	3.50	1.75	1.00
404 Tony Martinez	1.00	.50	.30
405 Ken McBride	1.00	.50	.30
406 Al Spangler	1.00	.50	.30
407 Bill Freehan	2.00	1.00	.60
408 Cubs Rookies (Fred Burdette, Jim Stewart)	1.00	.50	.30
409 Bill Fischer	1.00	.50	.30
410 Dick Stuart	1.25	.60	.40
411 Lee Walls	1.00	.50	.30
412 Ray Culp	1.00	.50	.30
413 Johnny Keane	1.00	.50	.30
414 Jack Sanford	1.00	.50	.30
415 Tony Kubek	5.00	2.50	1.50
416 Lee Maye	1.00	.50	.30
417 Don Cardwell	1.00	.50	.30
418 Orioles Rookies (Darold Knowles, Les Narum)	1.25	.60	.40
419 Ken Harrelson	3.00	1.50	.90
420 Jim Maloney	1.25	.60	.40
421 Camilo Carreon	1.00	.50	.30
422 Jack Fisher	1.25	.60	.40
423 Tops In NL (Hank Aaron, Willie Mays)	50.00	30.00	15.00
424 Dick Bertell	1.00	.50	.30
425 Norm Cash	2.50	1.25	.70
426 Bob Rodgers	1.25	.60	.40
427 Don Rudolph	1.00	.50	.30
428 Red Sox Rookies (Archie Skeen, Pete Smith)	1.00	.50	.30
429 Tim McCarver	3.00	1.50	.90
430 Juan Pizarro	1.00	.50	.30
431 George Alusik	1.00	.50	.30
432 Ruben Amaro	1.00	.50	.30
433 Yankees Team	8.00	4.00	2.50
434 Don Nottebart	1.00	.50	.30
435 Vic Davalillo	1.00	.50	.30
436 Charlie Neal	1.00	.50	.30
437 Ed Bailey	1.00	.50	.30
438 Checklist 430-506	4.00	2.00	1.25
439 Harvey Haddix	1.50	.70	.45
440 Bob Clemente	65.00	32.00	19.50
441 Bob Duliba	1.00	.50	.30
442 Pumpsie Green	1.25	.60	.40
443 Chuck Dressen	1.25	.60	.40
444 Larry Jackson	1.00	.50	.30
445 Bill Skowron	2.50	1.25	.70
446 Julian Javier	1.25	.60	.40
447 Ted Bowsfield	1.00	.50	.30
448 Cookie Rojas	1.25	.60	.40
449 Deron Johnson	1.00	.50	.30
450 Steve Barber	1.00	.50	.30
451 Joe Amalfitano	1.00	.50	.30
452 Giants Rookies (Gil Garrido, Jim Hart)	1.25	.60	.40
453 Frank Baumann	1.00	.50	.30
454 Tommie Aaron	1.25	.60	.40
455 Bernie Allen	1.00	.50	.30
456 Dodgers Rookies (Wes Parker, John Werhas)	2.00	1.00	.60
457 Jesse Gonder	1.25	.60	.40
458 Ralph Terry	2.00	1.00	.60
459 Red Sox Rookies (Pete Charton, Dalton Jones)	1.00	.50	.30
460 Bob Gibson	15.00	7.50	4.50
461 George Thomas	1.00	.50	.30
462 Birdie Tebbetts	1.00	.50	.30
463 Don Leppert	1.00	.50	.30
464 Dallas Green	1.25	.60	.40
465 Mike Hershberger	1.00	.50	.30
466 Athletics Rookies (Dick Green, Aurelio Monteagudo)	1.25	.60	.40
467 Bob Aspromonte	1.00	.50	.30
468 Gaylord Perry	25.00	12.50	7.50
469 Cubs Rookies (Fred Norman, Sterling Slaughter)	1.00	.50	.30
470 Jim Bouton	3.00	1.50	.90
471 Gates Brown	1.25	.60	.40
472 Vern Law	1.50	.70	.45
473 Orioles Team	3.00	1.50	.90
474 Larry Sherry	1.00	.50	.30
475 Ed Charles	1.00	.50	.30
476 Braves Rookies (Rico Carty, Dick Kelley)	1.25	.60	.40
477 Mike Joyce	.90	.45	.25
478 Dick Howser	2.00	1.00	.60
479 Cardinals Rookies (Dave Bakenhaster, Johnny Lewis)	1.00	.50	.30
480 Bob Purkey	1.00	.50	.30
481 Chuck Schilling	1.00	.50	.30
482 Phillies Rookies (John Briggs, Danny Cater)	1.25	.60	.40
483 Fred Valentine	1.00	.50	.30
484 Bill Pleis	1.00	.50	.30
485 Tom Haller	1.25	.60	.40
486 Bob Kennedy	1.00	.50	.30
487 Mike McCormick	1.25	.60	.40
488 Yankees Rookies (Bob Meyer, Pete Mikkelsen)	1.50	.70	.45
489 Julio Navarro	1.00	.50	.30
490 Ron Fairly	1.50	.70	.45
491 Ed Rakow	1.00	.50	.30
492 Colts Rookies (Jim Beauchamp, Mike White)	1.00	.50	.30
493 Don Lee	1.00	.50	.30
494 Al Jackson	1.25	.60	.40
495 Bill Virdon	2.00	1.00	.60
496 White Sox Team	3.00	1.50	.90
497 Jeoff Long	1.00	.50	.30
498 Dave Stenhouse	1.00	.50	.30
499 Indians Rookies (Chico Salmon, Gordon Seyfried)	1.00	.50	.30
500 Camilo Pascual	1.25	.60	.40
501 Bob Veale	1.25	.60	.40
502 Angels Rookies (Bobby Knoop, Bob Lee)	1.25	.60	.40
503 Earl Wilson	1.00	.50	.30
504 Claude Raymond	1.00	.50	.30
505 Stan Williams	1.50	.70	.45
506 Bobby Bragan	1.25	.60	.40
507 John Edwards	1.00	.50	.30
508 Diego Segui	1.00	.50	.30
509 Pirates Rookies (Gene Alley, Orlando McFarlane)	1.25	.60	.40
510 Lindy McDaniel	1.00	.50	.30
511 Lou Jackson	1.00	.50	.30
512 Tigers Rookies (Willie Horton, Joe Sparma)	3.00	1.50	.90
513 Don Larsen	1.50	.70	.45
514 Jim Hickman	1.25	.60	.40
515 Johnny Romano	1.00	.50	.30
516 Twins Rookies (Jerry Arrigo, Dwight Siebler)	1.00	.50	.30

		NR MT	EX	VG
517a	Checklist 507-587 (wrong numbering on			
	back)	7.00	3.50	2.00
517b	Checklist 507-587 (correct numbering on			
	back)	4.50	2.25	1.25
518	Carl Bouldin	1.00	.50	.30
519	Charlie Smith	1.25	.60	.40
520	Jack Baldschun	1.00	.50	.30
521	Tom Satriano	1.00	.50	.30
522	Bobby Tiefenauer	1.00	.50	.30
523	Lou Burdette	6.00	3.00	1.75
524	Reds Rookies (Jim Dickson, Bobby Klaus)			
		4.00	2.00	1.25
525	Al McBean	4.00	2.00	1.25
526	Lou Clinton	4.00	2.00	1.25
527	Larry Bearnarth	4.50	2.25	1.25
528	Athletics Rookies (Dave Duncan, Tom			
	Reynolds)	4.50	2.25	1.25
529	Al Dark	4.50	2.25	1.25
530	Leon Wagner	4.50	2.25	1.25
531	Dodgers Team	8.00	4.00	2.50
532	Twins Rookies (Bud Bloomfield, Joe			
	Nossek)	4.00	2.00	1.25
533	Johnny Klippstein	4.00	2.00	1.25
534	Gus Bell	4.50	2.25	1.25
535	Phil Regan	4.00	2.00	1.25
536	Mets Rookies (Larry Elliot, John			
	Stephenson)	4.50	2.25	1.25
537	Dan Osinski	4.00	2.00	1.25
538	Minnie Minoso	6.00	3.00	1.75
539	Roy Face	5.00	2.50	1.50
540	Luis Aparicio	15.00	7.50	4.50
541	Braves Rookies (Phil Niekro, Phil Roof)			
		90.00	45.00	27.00
542	Don Mincher	4.50	2.25	1.25
543	Bob Uecker	40.00	20.00	12.00
544	Colts Rookies (Steve Hertz, Joe Hoerner)			
		4.00	2.00	1.25
545	Max Alvis	4.50	2.25	1.25
546	Joe Christopher	4.50	2.25	1.25
547	Gil Hodges	12.00	6.00	3.50
548	N.L. Rookies (Wayne Schurr, Paul			
	Speckenbach)	4.00	2.00	1.25
549	Joe Moeller	4.00	2.00	1.25
550	Ken Hubbs	10.00	5.00	3.00
551	Billy Hoeft	4.00	2.00	1.25
552	Indians Rookies (Tom Kelley, Sonny			
	Siebert)	4.50	2.25	1.25
553	Jim Brewer	4.00	2.00	1.25
554	Hank Foiles	4.00	2.00	1.25
555	Lee Stange	4.00	2.00	1.25
556	Mets Rookies (Steve Dillon, Ron Locke)			
		4.50	2.25	1.25
557	Leo Burke	4.00	2.00	1.25
558	Don Schwall	4.00	2.00	1.25
559	Dick Phillips	4.00	2.00	1.25
560	Dick Farrell	4.00	2.00	1.25
561	Phillies Rookies (Dave Bennett, Rick Wise)			
		4.50	2.25	1.25
562	Pedro Ramos	4.00	2.00	1.25
563	Dal Maxvill	4.50	2.25	1.25
564	A.L. Rookies (Joe McCabe, Jerry			
	McNertney)	4.00	2.00	1.25
565	Stu Miller	4.00	2.00	1.25
566	Ed Kranepool	5.00	2.50	1.50
567	Jim Kaat	8.00	4.00	2.50
568	N.L. Rookies (Phil Gagliano, Cap			
	Peterson)	4.00	2.00	1.25
569	Fred Newman	4.00	2.00	1.25
570	Bill Mazeroski	6.00	3.00	1.75
571	Gene Conley	3.50	1.75	1.00
572	A.L. Rookies (Dick Egan, Dave Gray)			
		4.00	2.00	1.25
573	Jim Duffalo	4.00	2.00	1.25
574	Manny Jimenez	4.00	2.00	1.25
575	Tony Cloninger	4.50	2.25	1.25
576	Mets Rookies (Jerry Hinsley, Bill			
	Wakefield)	4.50	2.25	1.25
577	Gordy Coleman	4.00	2.00	1.25
578	Glen Hobbie	4.00	2.00	1.25
579	Red Sox Team	6.00	3.00	1.75
580	Johnny Podres	6.00	3.00	1.75
581	Yankees Rookies (Pedro Gonzalez, Archie			
	Moore)	5.00	2.50	1.50
582	Rod Kanehl	4.50	2.25	1.25
583	Tito Francona	4.50	2.25	1.25
584	Joel Horlen	4.00	2.00	1.25
585	Tony Taylor	4.00	2.00	1.25
586	Jim Piersall	6.00	3.00	1.75
587	Bennie Daniels	8.00	2.50	1.25

1964 Topps Coins

The 164 metal coins in this set were issued by Topps as inserts in the company's baseball card wax packs. The series is divided into two principal types, 120 "regular" coins and 44 All-Star coins. The 1-1/2" diameter coins feature a full-color background for the player photos in the "regular" series, while the players in the All-Star series are featured against plain red or blue backgrounds. There are two variations each of the Mantle, Causey and Hinton coins among the All-Star subset.

		NR MT	EX	VG
Complete Set:		650.00	325.00	200.00
Common Player:		1.00	.50	.30
1	Don Zimmer	1.00	.50	.30
2	Jim Wynn	1.00	.50	.30
3	Johnny Orsino	1.00	.50	.30
4	Jim Bouton	1.25	.60	.40
5	Dick Groat	1.25	.60	.40
6	Leon Wagner	1.00	.50	.30
7	Frank Malzone	1.00	.50	.30
8	Steve Barber	1.00	.50	.30
9	Johnny Romano	1.00	.50	.30
10	Tom Tresh	1.25	.60	.40
11	Felipe Alou	1.00	.50	.30
12	Dick Stuart	1.00	.50	.30
13	Claude Osteen	1.00	.50	.30
14	Juan Pizarro	1.00	.50	.30
15	Donn Clendenon	1.00	.50	.30
16	Jimmie Hall	1.00	.50	.30
17	Larry Jackson	1.00	.50	.30
18	Brooks Robinson	12.00	6.00	3.50
19	Bob Allison	1.00	.50	.30
20	Ed Roebuck	1.00	.50	.30
21	Pete Ward	1.00	.50	.30
22	Willie McCovey	8.00	4.00	2.50
23	Elston Howard	1.50	.70	.45
24	Diego Segui	1.00	.50	.30
25	Ken Boyer	1.50	.70	.45
26	Carl Yastrzemski	20.00	10.00	6.00
27	Bill Mazeroski	1.50	.70	.45
28	Jerry Lumpe	1.00	.50	.30
29	Woody Held	1.00	.50	.30
30	Dick Radatz	1.00	.50	.30
31	Luis Aparicio	5.00	2.50	1.50
32	Dave Nicholson	1.00	.50	.30
33	Ed Mathews	8.00	4.00	2.50
34	Don Drysdale	10.00	5.00	3.00
35	Ray Culp	1.00	.50	.30
36	Juan Marichal	8.00	4.00	2.50
37	Frank Robinson	8.00	4.00	2.50
38	Chuck Hinton	1.00	.50	.30
39	Floyd Robinson	1.00	.50	.30
40	Tommy Harper	1.00	.50	.30
41	Ron Hansen	1.00	.50	.30
42	Ernie Banks	10.00	5.00	3.00
43	Jesse Gonder	1.00	.50	.30
44	Billy Williams	7.00	3.50	2.00
45	Vada Pinson	1.50	.70	.45
46	Rocky Colavito	1.50	.70	.45
47	Bill Monbouquette	1.00	.50	.30
48	Max Alvis	1.00	.50	.30
49	Norm Siebern	1.00	.50	.30
50	John Callison	1.00	.50	.30
51	Rich Rollins	1.00	.50	.30
52	Ken McBride	1.00	.50	.30

		NR MT	EX	VG
53	Don Lock	1.00	.50	.30
54	Ron Fairly	1.00	.50	.30
55	Bob Clemente	20.00	10.00	6.00
56	Dick Ellsworth	1.00	.50	.30
57	Tommy Davis	1.25	.60	.40
58	Tony Gonzalez	1.00	.50	.30
59	Bob Gibson	10.00	5.00	3.00
60	Jim Maloney	1.00	.50	.30
61	Frank Howard	1.50	.70	.45
62	Jim Pagliaroni	1.00	.50	.30
63	Orlando Cepeda	2.00	1.00	.60
64	Ron Perranoski	1.00	.50	.30
65	Curt Flood	1.25	.60	.40
66	Al McBean	1.00	.50	.30
67	Dean Chance	1.00	.50	.30
68	Ron Santo	1.25	.60	.40
69	Jack Baldschun	1.00	.50	.30
70	Milt Pappas	1.00	.50	.30
71	Gary Peters	1.00	.50	.30
72	Bobby Richardson	1.50	.70	.45
73	Lee Thomas	1.00	.50	.30
74	Hank Aguirre	1.00	.50	.30
75	Carl Willey	1.00	.50	.30
76	Camilo Pascual	1.00	.50	.30
77	Bob Friend	1.00	.50	.30
78	Bill White	1.00	.50	.30
79	Norm Cash	1.25	.60	.40
80	Willie Mays	18.00	9.00	5.50
81	Duke Carmel	1.00	.50	.30
82	Pete Rose	25.00	12.50	7.50
83	Hank Aaron	20.00	10.00	6.00
84	Bob Aspromonte	1.00	.50	.30
85	Jim O'Toole	1.00	.50	.30
86	Vic Davalillo	1.00	.50	.30
87	Bill Freehan	1.00	.50	.30
88	Warren Spahn	8.00	4.00	2.50
89	Ron Hunt	1.00	.50	.30
90	Denis Menke	1.00	.50	.30
91	Turk Farrell	1.00	.50	.30
92	Jim Hickman	1.00	.50	.30
93	Jim Bunning	2.00	1.00	.60
94	Bob Hendley	1.00	.50	.30
95	Ernie Broglio	1.00	.50	.30
96	Rusty Staub	1.50	.70	.45
97	Lou Brock	8.00	4.00	2.50
98	Jim Fregosi	1.00	.50	.30
99	Jim Grant	1.00	.50	.30
100	Al Kaline	15.00	7.50	4.50
101	Earl Battey	1.00	.50	.30
102	Wayne Causey	1.00	.50	.30
103	Chuck Schilling	1.00	.50	.30
104	Boog Powell	1.50	.70	.45
105	Dave Wickersham	1.00	.50	.30
106	Sandy Koufax	15.00	7.50	4.50
107	John Bateman	1.00	.50	.30
108	Ed Brinkman	1.00	.50	.30
109	Al Downing	1.00	.50	.30
110	Joe Azcue	1.00	.50	.30
111	Albie Pearson	1.00	.50	.30
112	Harmon Killebrew	10.00	5.00	3.00
113	Tony Taylor	1.00	.50	.30
114	Alvin Jackson	1.00	.50	.30
115	Billy O'Dell	1.00	.50	.30
116	Don Demeter	1.00	.50	.30
117	Ed Charles	1.00	.50	.30
118	Joe Torre	1.50	.70	.45
119	Don Nottebart	1.00	.50	.30
120	Mickey Mantle	40.00	20.00	12.00
121	Joe Pepitone	1.25	.60	.40
122	Dick Stuart	1.00	.50	.30
123	Bobby Richardson	1.50	.70	.45
124	Jerry Lumpe	1.00	.50	.30
125	Brooks Robinson	10.00	5.00	3.00
126	Frank Malzone	1.00	.50	.30
127	Luis Aparicio	5.00	2.50	1.50
128	Jim Fregosi	1.00	.50	.30
129	Al Kaline	15.00	7.50	4.50
130	Leon Wagner	1.00	.50	.30
131a	Mickey Mantle (batting lefthanded)			
		45.00	23.00	13.50
131b	Mickey Mantle (batting righthanded)			
		45.00	23.00	13.50
132	Albie Pearson	1.00	.50	.30
133	Harmon Killebrew	10.00	5.00	3.00
134	Carl Yastrzemski	20.00	10.00	6.00
135	Elston Howard	1.50	.70	.45
136	Earl Battey	1.00	.50	.30
137	Camilo Pascual	1.00	.50	.30
138	Jim Bouton	1.25	.60	.40
139	Whitey Ford	8.00	4.00	2.50
140	Gary Peters	1.00	.50	.30

		NR MT	EX	VG
141	Bill White	1.00	.50	.30
142	Orlando Cepeda	2.00	1.00	.60
143	Bill Mazeroski	1.50	.70	.45
144	Tony Taylor	1.00	.50	.30
145	Ken Boyer	1.50	.70	.45
146	Ron Santo	1.25	.60	.40
147	Dick Groat	1.25	.60	.40
148	Roy McMillan	1.00	.50	.30
149	Hank Aaron	18.00	9.00	4.50
150	Bob Clemente	20.00	10.00	6.00
151	Willie Mays	18.00	9.00	5.50
152	Vada Pinson	1.50	.70	.45
153	Tommy Davis	1.25	.60	.40
154	Frank Robinson	8.00	4.00	2.50
155	Joe Torre	1.50	.70	.45
156	Tim McCarver	1.25	.60	.40
157	Juan Marichal	7.00	3.50	2.00
158	Jim Maloney	1.00	.50	.30
159	Sandy Koufax	15.00	7.50	4.50
160	Warren Spahn	8.00	4.00	2.50
161a	Wayne Causey (N.L. on back)	15.00	7.50	4.50
161b	Wayne Causey (A.L. on back)	1.00	.50	.30
162a	Chuck Hinton (N.L. on back)	15.00	7.50	4.50
162b	Chuck Hinton (A.L. on back)	1.00	.50	.30
163	Bob Aspromonte	1.00	.50	.30
164	Ron Hunt	1.00	.50	.30

1964 Topps Giants

Measuring 3-1/8" by 5-1/4" the Topps Giants were the company's first postcard-size issue. The cards feature large color photographs surrounded by white borders with a white baseball containing the player's name, position and team. Card backs carry another photo of the player surrounded by a newspaper-style explanation of the depicted career highlight. The 60-card set contains primarily stars which means it's an excellent place to find inexpensive cards of Hall of Famers. The '64 Giants were not printed in equal quantity and seven of the cards, including Sandy Koufax and Willie Mays, are significantly scarcer than the remainder of the set.

		NR MT	EX	VG
	Complete Set:	75.00	38.00	23.00
	Common Player:	.12	.06	.04
1	Gary Peters	.12	.06	.04
2	Ken Johnson	.12	.06	.04
3	Sandy Koufax	15.00	7.50	4.50
4	Bob Bailey	.12	.06	.04
5	Milt Pappas	.25	.13	.08
6	Ron Hunt	.12	.06	.04
7	Whitey Ford	1.75	.90	.50
8	Roy McMillan	.12	.06	.04
9	Rocky Colavito	.40	.20	.12
10	Jim Bunning	.50	.25	.15
11	Bob Clemente	5.00	2.50	1.50
12	Al Kaline	3.00	1.50	.90
13	Nellie Fox	.60	.30	.20
14	Tony Gonzalez	.12	.06	.04
15	Jim Gentile	.12	.06	.04
16	Dean Chance	.12	.06	.04
17	Dick Ellsworth	.12	.06	.04
18	Jim Fregosi	.25	.13	.08
19	Dick Groat	.40	.20	.12
20	Chuck Hinton	.12	.06	.04

		NR MT	EX	VG
21	Elston Howard	.50	.25	.15
22	Dick Farrell	.12	.06	.04
23	Albie Pearson	.12	.06	.04
24	Frank Howard	.50	.25	.15
25	Mickey Mantle	15.00	7.50	4.50
26	Joe Torre	.40	.20	.12
27	Ed Brinkman	.12	.06	.04
28	Bob Friend	2.50	1.25	.70
29	Frank Robinson	1.75	.90	.50
30	Bill Freehan	.25	.13	.08
31	Warren Spahn	1.25	.60	.40
32	Camilo Pascual	.12	.06	.04
33	Pete Ward	.12	.06	.04
34	Jim Maloney	.12	.06	.04
35	Dave Wickersham	.12	.06	.04
36	Johnny Callison	.25	.13	.08
37	Juan Marichal	2.00	1.00	.60
38	Harmon Killebrew	2.00	1.00	.60
39	Luis Aparicio	1.25	.60	.40
40	Dick Radatz	.12	.06	.04
41	Bob Gibson	3.00	1.50	.90
42	Dick Stuart	2.50	1.25	.70
43	Tommy Davis	.40	.20	.12
44	Tony Oliva	.50	.25	.15
45	Wayne Causey	2.50	1.25	.70
46	Max Alvis	.12	.06	.04
47	Galen Cisco	2.50	1.25	.70
48	Carl Yastrzemski	3.00	1.50	.90
49	Hank Aaron	5.00	2.50	1.50
50	Brooks Robinson	2.00	1.00	.60
51	Willie Mays	15.00	7.50	4.50
52	Billy Williams	1.25	.60	.40
53	Juan Pizarro	.12	.06	.04
54	Leon Wagner	.12	.06	.04
55	Orlando Cepeda	.70	.35	.20
56	Vada Pinson	.50	.25	.15
57	Ken Boyer	.60	.30	.20
58	Ron Santo	.40	.20	.12
59	John Romano	.12	.06	.04
60	Bill Skowron	2.50	1.25	.70

1964 Topps Photo Tatoos

Apparently not content to leave the skin of American children without adornment, Topps jumped back into the tattoo field in 1964 with the release of a new series. Measuring 1-9/16" by 3-1/2," there were 75 tattoos in a complete set. The picture side for the 20 team tattoos gives the team logo and name. For the player tattoos, the picture side has the player's face, name and team.

		NR MT	EX	VG
Complete Set:		600.00	300.00	180.00
Common Player:		3.00	1.50	.90
(1)	Hank Aaron	40.00	20.00	12.50

		NR MT	EX	VG
(2)	H. Aguirre	3.00	1.50	.90
(3)	Max Alvis	3.00	1.50	.90
(4)	Ernie Banks	25.00	12.50	7.50
(5)	S. Barber	3.00	1.50	.90
(6)	K. Boyer	5.00	2.50	1.50
(7)	J. Callison	4.00	2.00	1.25
(8)	Norm Cash	5.00	2.50	1.50
(9)	W. Causey	3.00	1.50	.90
(10)	O. Cepeda	7.00	3.50	2.00
(11)	R. Colavito	7.00	3.50	2.00
(12)	Ray Culp	3.00	1.50	.90
(13)	Davalillo	3.00	1.50	.90
(14)	Drabowsky	3.00	1.50	.90
(15)	Ellsworth	3.00	1.50	.90
(16)	Curt Flood	5.00	2.50	1.50
(17)	B. Freehan	4.00	2.00	1.25
(18)	J. Fregosi	4.00	2.00	1.25
(19)	Bob Friend	4.00	2.00	1.25
(20)	D. Groat	4.00	2.00	1.25
(21)	Woody Held	3.00	1.50	.90
(22)	F. Howard	5.00	2.50	1.50
(23)	Al Jackson	3.00	1.50	.90
(24)	L. Jackson	3.00	1.50	.90
(25)	K. Johnson	3.00	1.50	.90
(26)	Al Kaline	25.00	12.50	7.50
(27a)	Killebrew (green background)	25.00	12.50	7.50
(27b)	Killebrew (red background)	25.00	12.50	7.50
(28)	S. Koufax	35.00	17.50	10.50
(29)	Lock	3.00	1.50	.90
(30)	F. Malzone	3.00	1.50	.90
(31)	M. Mantle	100.00	45.00	27.00
(32)	E. Mathews	15.00	7.50	4.50
(33a)	Willie Mays (yellow background encompasses entire head)	40.00	20.00	12.50
(33b)	Willie Mays (yellow background covers one-half of head)	40.00	20.00	12.50
(34)	Mazeroski	5.00	2.50	1.50
(35)	K. McBride	3.00	1.50	.90
(36)	Monbouquette	3.00	1.50	.90
(37)	Nicholson	3.00	1.50	.90
(38)	C. Osteen	4.00	2.00	1.25
(39)	M. Pappas	4.00	2.00	1.25
(40)	C. Pascual	4.00	2.00	1.25
(41)	A. Pearson	3.00	1.50	.90
(42)	Perranoski	3.00	1.50	.90
(43)	G. Peters	3.00	1.50	.90
(44)	B. Powell	5.00	2.50	1.50
(45)	F. Robinson	20.00	10.00	6.00
(46)	J. Romano	3.00	1.50	.90
(47)	N. Siebern	3.00	1.50	.90
(48)	W. Spahn	15.00	7.50	4.50
(49)	D. Stuart	4.00	2.00	1.25
(50)	Lee Thomas	3.00	1.50	.90
(51)	Joe Torre	5.00	2.50	1.50
(52)	Pete Ward	3.00	1.50	.90
(53)	C. Willey	3.00	1.50	.90
(54)	B. Williams	25.00	12.50	7.50
(55)	Yastrzemski	50.00	25.00	15.00
(56)	Baltimore Orioles Logo	3.00	1.50	.90
(57)	Boston Red Sox Logo	3.00	1.50	.90
(58)	Chicago Cubs Logo	3.00	1.50	.90
(59)	Chicago White Sox Logo	3.00	1.50	.90
(60)	Cincinnati Reds Logo	3.00	1.50	.90
(61)	Cleveland Indians Logo	3.00	1.50	.90
(62)	Detroit Tigers Logo	2.50	1.25	.70
(63)	Houston Colts Logo	3.00	1.50	.90
(64)	Kansas City Athletics Logo	3.00	1.50	.90
(65)	Los Angeles Angels Logo	3.00	1.50	.90
(66)	Los Angeles Dodgers Logo	2.50	1.25	.70
(67)	Milwaukee Braves Logo	3.00	1.50	.90
(68)	Minnesota Twins Logo	3.00	1.50	.90
(69)	New York Mets Logo	2.50	1.25	.70
(70)	New York Yankees Logo	4.00	2.00	1.25
(71)	Philadelphia Phillies Logo	3.00	1.50	.90
(72)	Pittsburgh Pirates Logo	3.00	1.50	.90
(73)	St. Louis Cardinals Logo	2.50	1.25	.70
(74)	San Francisco Giants Logo	3.00	1.50	.90
(75)	Washington Senators Logo	3.00	1.50	.90

1964 Topps Stand-Ups

These 2-1/2" by 3-1/2" cards were the first since the All-Star sets of 1951 to be die-cut. This made it possible for a folded card to stand on display. The 77-cards in the set feature color photographs of the player with yellow and green backgrounds. Directions for folding are on the yellow top background, and when folded only the green background remains. Of the 77 cards, 55 were double-printed while 22 were single-printed, making them twice as scarce. Included in the single-printed group are Warren Spahn, Don Drysdale, Juan Marichal, Willie McCovey and Carl Yastrzemski.

		NR MT	EX	VG
Complete Set:		1600.00	800.00	480.00
Common Player:		2.50	1.25	.70
(1)	Hank Aaron	60.00	30.00	18.00
(2)	Hank Aguirre	2.50	1.25	.70
(3)	George Altman	2.50	1.25	.70
(4)	Max Alvis	2.50	1.25	.70
(5)	Bob Aspromonte	2.50	1.25	.70
(6)	Jack Baldschun	15.00	7.50	4.50
(7)	Ernie Banks	25.00	12.50	7.50
(8)	Steve Barber	2.50	1.25	.70
(9)	Earl Battey	2.50	1.25	.70
(10)	Ken Boyer	6.00	3.00	1.75
(11)	Ernie Broglio	2.50	1.25	.70
(12)	Johnny Callison	4.00	2.00	1.25
(13)	Norm Cash	18.00	9.00	5.50
(14)	Wayne Causey	2.50	1.25	.70
(15)	Orlando Cepeda	8.00	4.00	2.50
(16)	Ed Charles	2.50	1.25	.70
(17)	Bob Clemente	55.00	27.00	16.50
(18)	Donn Clendenon	15.00	7.50	4.50
(19)	Rocky Colavito	6.00	3.00	1.75
(20)	Ray Culp	15.00	7.50	4.50
(21)	Tommy Davis	6.00	3.00	1.75
(22)	Don Drysdale	70.00	35.00	21.00
(23)	Dick Ellsworth	2.50	1.25	.70
(24)	Dick Farrell	2.50	1.25	.70
(25)	Jim Fregosi	4.00	2.00	1.25
(26)	Bob Friend	4.00	2.00	1.25
(27)	Jim Gentile	2.50	1.25	.70
(28)	Jesse Gonder	15.00	7.50	4.50
(29)	Tony Gonzalez	15.00	7.50	4.50
(30)	Dick Groat	6.00	3.00	1.75
(31)	Woody Held	2.50	1.25	.70
(32)	Chuck Hinton	2.50	1.25	.70
(33)	Elston Howard	7.00	3.50	2.00
(34)	Frank Howard	18.00	9.00	5.50
(35)	Ron Hunt	2.50	1.25	.70
(36)	Al Jackson	2.50	1.25	.70
(37)	Ken Johnson	2.50	1.25	.70
(38)	Al Kaline	25.00	12.50	7.50
(39)	Harmon Killebrew	25.00	12.50	7.50
(40)	Sandy Koufax	40.00	20.00	12.00
(41)	Don Lock	15.00	7.50	4.50
(42)	Jerry Lumpe	15.00	7.50	4.50
(43)	Jim Maloney	2.50	1.25	.70
(44)	Frank Malzone	2.50	1.25	.70
(45)	Mickey Mantle	250.00	125.00	75.00
(46)	Juan Marichal	70.00	35.00	21.00
(47)	Ed Mathews	70.00	35.00	21.00
(48)	Willie Mays	60.00	30.00	18.00
(49)	Bill Mazeroski	6.00	3.00	1.75
(50)	Ken McBride	2.50	1.25	.70
(51)	Willie McCovey	70.00	35.00	21.00
(52)	Claude Osteen	2.50	1.25	.70
(53)	Jim O'Toole	2.50	1.25	.70
(54)	Camilo Pascual	2.50	1.25	.70
(55)	Albie Pearson	15.00	7.50	4.50
(56)	Gary Peters	2.50	1.25	.70
(57)	Vada Pinson	6.00	3.00	1.75
(58)	Juan Pizarro	2.50	1.25	.70
(59)	Boog Powell	6.00	3.00	1.75
(60)	Bobby Richardson	7.00	3.50	2.00
(61)	Brooks Robinson	30.00	15.00	9.00
(62)	Floyd Robinson	2.50	1.25	.70
(63)	Frank Robinson	25.00	12.50	7.50
(64)	Ed Roebuck	15.00	7.50	4.50
(65)	Rich Rollins	2.50	1.25	.70
(66)	Johnny Romano	2.50	1.25	.70
(67)	Ron Santo	18.00	9.00	5.50
(68)	Norm Siebern	2.50	1.25	.70
(69)	Warren Spahn	70.00	35.00	21.00
(70)	Dick Stuart	15.00	7.50	4.50
(71)	Lee Thomas	2.50	1.25	.70
(72)	Joe Torre	7.00	3.50	2.00
(73)	Pete Ward	2.50	1.25	.70
(74)	Bill White	15.00	7.50	4.50
(75)	Billy Williams	70.00	35.00	21.00
(76)	Hal Woodeshick	15.00	7.50	4.50
(77)	Carl Yastrzemski	275.00	137.00	82.00

1965 Topps

The 1965 Topps set features a large color photograph of the player which was surrounded by a colored, round-cornered frame and a white border. the bottom of the 2-1/2" by 3-1/2" cards include a pennant with a color team logo and name over the left side of a rectangle which features the player's name and position. Backs feature statistics and, if space allowed, a cartoon and headline about the player. There are no multi-player cards in the 1965 set other than the usual team cards and World Series highlights. Rookie cards include team, as well as league groupings of from two to four players per card. Also present in the 598-card set are statistical leaders.

		NR MT	EX	VG
Complete Set:		2500.00	1250.00	750.00
Common Player: 1-198		.70	.35	.20
Common Player: 199-446		.90	.45	.25
Common Player: 447-522		1.25	.60	.40
Common Player: 523-598		4.00	2.00	1.25
1	A.L. Batting Leaders (Elston Howard, Tony Oliva, Brooks Robinson)	8.00	3.00	1.25
2	N.L. Batting Leaders (Hank Aaron, Rico Carty, Bob Clemente)	5.00	2.50	1.50
3	A.L. Home Run Leaders (Harmon Killebrew, Mickey Mantle, Boog Powell)	15.00	7.50	4.50
4	N.L. Home Run Leaders (Johnny Callison, Orlando Cepeda, Jim Hart, Willie Mays, Billy Williams)	4.50	2.25	1.25
5	A.L. RBI Leaders (Harmon Killebrew, Mickey Mantle, Brooks Robinson, Dick Stuart)	15.00	7.50	4.50
6	N.L. RBI Leaders (Ken Boyer, Willie Mays, Ron Santo)	4.50	2.25	1.25
7	A.L. ERA Leaders (Dean Chance, Joel Horlen)	2.50	1.25	.70
8	N.L. ERA Leaders (Don Drysdale, Sandy Koufax)	4.50	2.25	1.25
9	A.L. Pitching Leaders (Wally Bunker, Dean Chance, Gary Peters, Juan Pizarro, Dave Wickersham)	4.00	2.00	1.25
10	N.L. Pitching Leaders (Larry Jackson, Juan Marichal, Ray Sadecki)	3.50	1.75	1.00

	NR MT	EX	VG
11 A.L. Strikeout Leaders (Dean Chance, Al Downing, Camilo Pascual)	2.50	1.25	.70
12 N.L. Strikeout Leaders (Don Drysdale, Bob Gibson, Bob Veale)	3.50	1.75	1.00
13 Pedro Ramos	1.00	.50	.30
14 Len Gabrielson	.70	.35	.20
15 Robin Roberts	8.00	4.00	2.50
16 Astros Rookies (*Sonny Jackson, Joe Morgan*)	80.00	40.00	24.00
17 Johnny Romano	.70	.35	.20
18 Bill McCool	.70	.35	.20
19 Gates Brown	.80	.40	.25
20 Jim Bunning	4.00	2.00	1.25
21 Don Blasingame	.70	.35	.20
22 Charlie Smith	.80	.40	.25
23 Bob Tiefenauer	.70	.35	.20
24 Twins Team	4.00	2.00	1.25
25 Al McBean	.70	.35	.20
26 Bobby Knoop	.70	.35	.20
27 Dick Bertell	.70	.35	.20
28 Barney Schultz	.70	.35	.20
29 Felix Mantilla	.70	.35	.20
30 Jim Bouton	2.50	1.25	.70
31 Mike White	.70	.35	.20
32 Herman Franks	.70	.35	.20
33 Jackie Brandt	.70	.35	.20
34 Cal Koonce	.70	.35	.20
35 Ed Charles	.70	.35	.20
36 Bobby Wine	.80	.40	.25
37 Fred Gladding	.70	.35	.20
38 Jim King	.70	.35	.20
39 Gerry Arrigo	.70	.35	.20
40 Frank Howard	2.50	1.25	.70
41 White Sox Rookies (Bruce Howard, Marv Staehle)	.70	.35	.20
42 Earl Wilson	.70	.35	.20
43 Mike Shannon	.80	.40	.25
44 Wade Blasingame	.70	.35	.20
45 Roy McMillan	.80	.40	.25
46 Bob Lee	.70	.35	.20
47 Tommy Harper	.80	.40	.25
48 Claude Raymond	.80	.40	.25
49 Orioles Rookies (*Curt Blefary*, John Miller)	.90	.45	.25
50 Juan Marichal	8.00	4.00	2.50
51 Billy Bryan	.70	.35	.20
52 Ed Roebuck	.70	.35	.20
53 Dick McAuliffe	.80	.40	.25
54 Joe Gibbon	.70	.35	.20
55 Tony Conigliaro	2.50	1.25	.70
56 Ron Kline	.70	.35	.20
57 Cardinals Team	2.25	1.25	.70
58 Fred Talbot	.70	.35	.20
59 Nate Oliver	.70	.35	.20
60 Jim O'Toole	.70	.35	.20
61 Chris Cannizzaro	.80	.40	.25
62 Jim Katt (Kaat)	5.00	2.50	1.50
63 Ty Cline	.70	.35	.20
64 Lou Burdette	2.00	1.00	.60
65 Tony Kubek	4.50	2.25	1.25
66 Bill Rigney	.70	.35	.20
67 Harvey Haddix	.90	.45	.25
68 Del Crandall	.90	.45	.25
69 Bill Virdon	1.25	.60	.40
70 Bill Skowron	1.25	.60	.40
71 John O'Donoghue	.70	.35	.20
72 Tony Gonzalez	.70	.35	.20
73 Dennis Ribant	.80	.40	.25
74 Red Sox Rookies (*Rico Petrocelli*, Jerry Stephenson)	2.50	1.25	.70
75 Deron Johnson	.70	.35	.20
76 Sam McDowell	.90	.45	.25
77 Doug Camilli	.70	.35	.20
78 Dal Maxvill	.80	.40	.25
79a Checklist 1-88 (61 is C. Cannizzaro)	3.00	1.50	.90
79b Checklist 1-88 (61 is Cannizzaro)	5.00	2.50	1.50
80 Turk Farrell	.70	.35	.20
81 Don Buford	.80	.40	.25
82 Braves Rookies (*Santos Alomar*, John Braun)	.80	.40	.25
83 George Thomas	.70	.35	.20
84 Ron Herbel	.70	.35	.20
85 Willie Smith	.70	.35	.20
86 Les Narum	.70	.35	.20
87 Nelson Mathews	.70	.35	.20
88 Jack Lamabe	.70	.35	.20
89 Mike Hershberger	.70	.35	.20
90 Rich Rollins	.70	.35	.20
91 Cubs Team	2.25	1.25	.70
92 Dick Howser	1.25	.60	.40

	NR MT	EX	VG
93 Jack Fisher	.80	.40	.25
94 Charlie Lau	.90	.45	.25
95 Bill Mazeroski	2.50	1.25	.70
96 Sonny Siebert	.80	.40	.25
97 Pedro Gonzalez	1.00	.50	.30
98 Bob Miller	.70	.35	.20
99 Gil Hodges	6.00	3.00	1.75
100 Ken Boyer	2.50	1.25	.70
101 Fred Newman	.70	.35	.20
102 Steve Boros	.80	.40	.25
103 Harvey Kuenn	1.25	.60	.40
104 Checklist 89-176	3.00	1.50	.90
105 Chico Salmon	.70	.35	.20
106 Gene Oliver	.70	.35	.20
107 Phillies Rookies (*Pat Corrales*, Costen Shockley)	2.00	1.00	.60
108 Don Mincher	.80	.40	.25
109 Walt Bond	.70	.35	.20
110 Ron Santo	1.50	.70	.45
111 Lee Thomas	.70	.35	.20
112 Derrell Griffith	.70	.35	.20
113 Steve Barber	.70	.35	.20
114 Jim Hickman	.90	.45	.25
115 Bobby Richardson	4.50	2.25	1.25
116 Cardinals Rookies (Dave Dowling, *Bob Tolan*)	1.25	.60	.40
117 Wes Stock	.70	.35	.20
118 *Hal Lanier*	1.50	.70	.45
119 John Kennedy	.70	.35	.20
120 Frank Robinson	15.00	7.50	4.50
121 Gene Alley	.80	.40	.25
122 Bill Pleis	.70	.35	.20
123 Frank Thomas	.70	.35	.20
124 Tom Satriano	.70	.35	.20
125 Juan Pizarro	.70	.35	.20
126 Dodgers Team	4.00	2.00	1.25
127 Frank Lary	.80	.40	.25
128 Vic Davalillo	.80	.40	.25
129 Bennie Daniels	.70	.35	.20
130 Al Kaline	20.00	10.00	6.00
131 Johnny Keane	1.50	.70	.45
132 World Series Game 1 (Cards Take Opener)	2.50	1.25	.70
133 World Series Game 2 (Stottlemyre Wins)	3.00	1.50	.90
134 World Series Game 3 (Mantle's Clutch HR)	18.00	9.00	5.50
135 World Series Game 4 (Boyer's Grand Slam)	2.50	1.25	.70
136 World Series Game 5 (10th Inning Triumph)	2.50	1.25	.70
137 World Series Game 6 (Bouton Wins Again)	3.00	1.50	.90
138 World Series Game 7 (Gibson Wins Finale)	3.50	1.75	1.00
139 World Series Summary (The Cards Celebrate)	2.50	1.25	.70
140 Dean Chance	.80	.40	.25
141 Charlie James	.70	.35	.20
142 Bill Monbouquette	.80	.40	.25
143 Pirates Rookies (John Gelnar, Jerry May)	.70	.35	.20
144 Ed Kranepool	.90	.45	.25
145 *Luis Tiant*	7.00	3.50	2.00
146 Ron Hansen	.70	.35	.20
147 Dennis Bennett	.70	.35	.20
148 Willie Kirkland	.70	.35	.20
149 Wayne Schurr	.70	.35	.20
150 Brooks Robinson	20.00	10.00	6.00
151 Athletics Team	2.25	1.25	.70
152 Phil Ortega	.70	.35	.20
153 Norm Cash	2.00	1.00	.60
154 Bob Humphreys	.70	.35	.20
155 Roger Maris	40.00	20.00	12.00
156 Bob Sadowski	.70	.35	.20
157 Zoilo Versalles	1.50	.70	.45
158 Dick Sisler	.70	.35	.20
159 Jim Duffalo	.70	.35	.20
160 Bob Clemente	65.00	33.00	20.00
161 Frank Baumann	.70	.35	.20
162 Russ Nixon	.70	.35	.20
163 John Briggs	.70	.35	.20
164 Al Spangler	.70	.35	.20
165 Dick Ellsworth	.70	.35	.20
166 Indians Rookies (*Tommie Agee*, George Culver)	1.50	.70	.45
167 Bill Wakefield	.80	.40	.25
168 Dick Green	.80	.40	.25
169 Dave Vineyard	.70	.35	.20
170 Hank Aaron	60.00	30.00	18.00
171 Jim Roland	.70	.35	.20

#	Player	NR MT	EX	VG
172	Jim Piersall	1.50	.70	.45
173	Tigers Team	3.25	1.75	1.00
174	Joe Jay	.70	.35	.20
175	Bob Aspromonte	.70	.35	.20
176	Willie McCovey	18.00	9.00	5.50
177	Pete Mikkelsen	1.00	.50	.30
178	Dalton Jones	.70	.35	.20
179	Hal Woodeshick	.70	.35	.20
180	Bob Allison	1.25	.60	.40
181	Senators Rookies (Don Loun, Joe McCabe)	.70	.35	.20
182	Mike de la Hoz	.70	.35	.20
183	Dave Nicholson	.70	.35	.20
184	John Boozer	.70	.35	.20
185	Max Alvis	.70	.35	.20
186	Billy Cowan	.70	.35	.20
187	Casey Stengel	18.00	9.00	5.00
188	Sam Bowens	.70	.35	.20
189	Checklist 177-264	3.00	1.50	.90
190	Bill White	1.25	.60	.40
191	Phil Regan	.70	.35	.20
192	Jim Coker	.70	.35	.20
193	Gaylord Perry	12.00	6.00	3.50
194	Angels Rookies (Bill Kelso, *Rick Reichardt*)	.80	.40	.25
195	Bob Veale	.80	.40	.25
196	Ron Fairly	.80	.40	.25
197	Diego Segui	.70	.35	.20
198	Smoky Burgess	1.25	.60	.40
199	Bob Heffner	.90	.45	.25
200	Joe Torre	2.50	1.25	.70
201	Twins Rookies (*Cesar Tovar*, Sandy Valdespino)	1.00	.50	.30
202	Leo Burke	.90	.45	.25
203	Dallas Green	1.25	.60	.40
204	Russ Snyder	.90	.45	.25
205	Warren Spahn	20.00	10.00	6.00
206	Willie Horton	1.25	.60	.40
207	Pete Rose	150.00	60.00	38.00
208	Tommy John	10.00	5.00	3.00
209	Pirates Team	2.50	1.25	.70
210	Jim Fregosi	1.50	.70	.45
211	Steve Ridzik	.90	.45	.25
212	Ron Brand	.90	.45	.25
213	Jim Davenport	.90	.45	.25
214	Bob Purkey	.90	.45	.25
215	Pete Ward	.90	.45	.25
216	Al Worthington	.90	.45	.25
217	Walt Alston	3.50	1.75	1.00
218	Dick Schofield	.90	.45	.25
219	Bob Meyer	.90	.45	.25
220	Billy Williams	10.00	5.00	3.00
221	John Tsitouris	.90	.45	.25
222	Bob Tillman	.90	.45	.25
223	Dan Osinski	.90	.45	.25
224	Bob Chance	.90	.45	.25
225	Bo Belinsky	1.00	.50	.30
226	Yankees Rookies (Jake Gibbs, Elvio Jimenez)	1.50	.70	.45
227	Bobby Klaus	1.00	.50	.30
228	Jack Sanford	.90	.45	.25
229	Lou Clinton	.90	.45	.25
230	Ray Sadecki	.90	.45	.25
231	Jerry Adair	.90	.45	.25
232	*Steve Blass*	1.00	.50	.30
233	Don Zimmer	1.50	.70	.45
234	White Sox Team	4.00	2.00	1.25
235	Chuck Hinton	.90	.45	.25
236	*Dennis McLain*	12.00	6.00	3.50
237	Bernie Allen	.90	.45	.25
238	Joe Moeller	.90	.45	.25
239	Doc Edwards	1.00	.50	.30
240	Bob Bruce	.90	.45	.25
241	Mack Jones	.90	.45	.25
242	George Brunet	.90	.45	.25
243	Reds Rookies (Ted Davidson, *Tommy Helms*)	1.00	.50	.30
244	Lindy McDaniel	.90	.45	.25
245	Joe Pepitone	3.00	1.50	.90
246	Tom Butters	.90	.45	.25
247	Wally Moon	1.00	.50	.30
248	Gus Triandos	1.00	.50	.30
249	Dave McNally	1.25	.60	.40
250	Willie Mays	65.00	32.00	19.50
251	Billy Herman	2.00	1.00	.60
252	Pete Richert	.90	.45	.25
253	Danny Cater	1.00	.50	.30
254	Roland Sheldon	1.50	.70	.45
255	Camilo Pascual	1.00	.50	.30
256	Tito Francona	1.00	.50	.30
257	Jim Wynn	1.25	.60	.40
258	Larry Bearnarth	1.00	.50	.30
259	Tigers Rookies (*Jim Northrup, Ray Oyler*)	1.25	.60	.40
260	Don Drysdale	15.00	7.50	4.50
261	Duke Carmel	1.50	.70	.45
262	Bud Daley	.90	.45	.25
263	Marty Keough	.90	.45	.25
264	Bob Buhl	1.00	.50	.30
265	Jim Pagliaroni	.90	.45	.25
266	*Bert Campaneris*	3.00	1.50	.90
267	Senators Team	2.50	1.25	.70
268	Ken McBride	.90	.45	.25
269	Frank Bolling	.90	.45	.25
270	Milt Pappas	1.00	.50	.30
271	Don Wert	.90	.45	.25
272	Chuck Schilling	.90	.45	.25
273	Checklist 265-352	3.25	1.75	1.00
274	Lum Harris	.90	.45	.25
275	Dick Groat	1.75	.90	.50
276	Hoyt Wilhelm	10.00	5.00	3.00
277	Johnny Lewis	1.00	.50	.30
278	Ken Retzer	.90	.45	.25
279	Dick Tracewski	.90	.45	.25
280	Dick Stuart	1.00	.50	.30
281	Bill Stafford	1.50	.70	.45
282	Giants Rookies (Dick Estelle, *Masanori Murakami*)	1.25	.60	.40
283	Fred Whitfield	.90	.45	.25
284	Nick Willhite	.90	.45	.25
285	Ron Hunt	1.00	.50	.30
286	Athletics Rookies (Jim Dickson, Aurelio Monteagudo)	.90	.45	.25
287	Gary Kolb	.90	.45	.25
288	Jack Hamilton	.90	.45	.25
289	Gordy Coleman	.90	.45	.25
290	Wally Bunker	.90	.45	.25
291	Jerry Lynch	.90	.45	.25
292	Larry Yellen	.90	.45	.25
293	Angels Team	2.50	1.25	.70
294	Tim McCarver	2.75	1.50	.80
295	Dick Radatz	1.00	.50	.30
296	Tony Taylor	.90	.45	.25
297	Dave DeBusschere	3.50	1.75	1.00
298	Jim Stewart	.90	.45	.25
299	Jerry Zimmerman	.90	.45	.25
300	Sandy Koufax	70.00	35.00	21.00
301	Birdie Tebbetts	.90	.45	.25
302	Al Stanek	.90	.45	.25
303	Johnny Orsino	.90	.45	.25
304	Dave Stenhouse	.90	.45	.25
305	Rico Carty	1.50	.70	.45
306	Bubba Phillips	.90	.45	.25
307	Barry Latman	.90	.45	.25
308	Mets Rookies (*Cleon Jones*, Tom Parsons)	1.25	.60	.40
309	Steve Hamilton	1.50	.70	.45
310	Johnny Callison	1.25	.60	.40
311	Orlando Pena	.90	.45	.25
312	Joe Nuxhall	1.00	.50	.30
313	Jimmie Schaffer	.90	.45	.25
314	Sterling Slaughter	.90	.45	.25
315	Frank Malzone	1.00	.50	.30
316	Reds Team	2.75	1.50	.80
317	Don McMahon	.90	.45	.25
318	Matty Alou	1.00	.50	.30
319	Ken McMullen	.90	.45	.25
320	Bob Gibson	18.00	9.00	5.50
321	Rusty Staub	3.50	1.75	1.00
322	Rick Wise	1.00	.50	.30
323	Hank Bauer	1.00	.50	.30
324	Bobby Locke	.90	.45	.25
325	Donn Clendenon	1.00	.50	.30
326	Dwight Siebler	.90	.45	.25
327	Denis Menke	.90	.45	.25
328	Eddie Fisher	.90	.45	.25
329	Hawk Taylor	1.00	.50	.30
330	Whitey Ford	18.00	9.00	5.50
331	Dodgers Rookies (Al Ferrara, John Purdin)	1.00	.50	.30
332	Ted Abernathy	.90	.45	.25
333	Tommie Reynolds	.90	.45	.25
334	Vic Roznovsky	.90	.45	.25
335	Mickey Lolich	3.50	1.75	1.00
336	Woody Held	.90	.45	.25
337	Mike Cuellar	1.50	.70	.45
338	Phillies Team	2.50	1.25	.70
339	Ryne Duren	1.00	.50	.30
340	Tony Oliva	3.50	1.75	1.00
341	Bobby Bolin	.90	.45	.25
342	Bob Rodgers	1.00	.50	.30
343	Mike McCormick	1.00	.50	.30

	NR MT	EX	VG
344 Wes Parker	1.00	.50	.30
345 Floyd Robinson	.90	.45	.25
346 Bobby Bragan	1.00	.50	.30
347 Roy Face	1.50	.70	.45
348 George Banks	.90	.45	.25
349 Larry Miller	1.00	.50	.30
350 Mickey Mantle	350.00	140.00	88.00
351 Jim Perry	1.25	.60	.40
352 *Alex Johnson*	1.00	.50	.30
353 Jerry Lumpe	1.00	.50	.30
354 Cubs Rookies (Billy Ott, Jack Warner)			
	.90	.45	.25
355 Vada Pinson	2.50	1.25	.70
356 Bill Spanswick	.90	.45	.25
357 Carl Warwick	.90	.45	.25
358 Albie Pearson	.90	.45	.25
359 Ken Johnson	.90	.45	.25
360 Orlando Cepeda	5.00	2.50	1.50
361 Checklist 353-429	3.25	1.75	1.00
362 Don Schwall	.90	.45	.25
363 Bob Johnson	.90	.45	.25
364 Galen Cisco	1.00	.50	.30
365 Jim Gentile	1.00	.50	.30
366 Dan Schneider	.90	.45	.25
367 Leon Wagner	1.00	.50	.30
368 White Sox Rookies (*Ken Berry*, Joel Gibson)			
	1.00	.50	.30
369 Phil Linz	1.50	.70	.45
370 Tommy Davis	1.50	.70	.45
371 Frank Kreutzer	.90	.45	.25
372 Clay Dalrymple	.90	.45	.25
373 Curt Simmons	1.00	.50	.30
374 Angels Rookies (*Jose Cardenal*, Dick Simpson)			
	1.00	.50	.30
375 Dave Wickersham	.90	.45	.25
376 Jim Landis	.90	.45	.25
377 Willie Stargell	20.00	10.00	6.00
378 Chuck Estrada	.90	.45	.25
379 Giants Team	2.50	1.25	.70
380 Rocky Colavito	3.00	1.50	.90
381 Al Jackson	1.00	.50	.30
382 J.C. Martin	.90	.45	.25
383 Felipe Alou	1.00	.50	.30
384 Johnny Klippstein	.90	.45	.25
385 Carl Yastrzemski	75.00	38.00	23.00
386 Cubs Rookies (Paul Jaeckel, Fred Norman)			
	.90	.45	.25
387 Johnny Podres	2.00	1.00	.60
388 John Blanchard	1.50	.70	.45
389 Don Larsen	1.25	.60	.40
390 Bill Freehan	1.25	.60	.40
391 Mel McGaha	.90	.45	.25
392 Bob Friend	1.50	.70	.45
393 Ed Kirkpatrick	.90	.45	.25
394 Jim Hannan	.90	.45	.25
395 Jim Hart	1.00	.50	.30
396 Frank Bertaina	.90	.45	.25
397 Jerry Buchek	.90	.45	.25
398 Reds Rookies (Dan Neville, *Art Shamsky*)			
	1.00	.50	.30
399 Ray Herbert	.90	.45	.25
400 Harmon Killebrew	15.00	7.50	4.50
401 Carl Willey	1.00	.50	.30
402 Joe Amalfitano	.90	.45	.25
403 Red Sox Team	3.00	1.50	.90
404 Stan Williams	.90	.45	.25
405 John Roseboro	1.00	.50	.30
406 Ralph Terry	1.00	.50	.30
407 Lee Maye	.90	.45	.25
408 Larry Sherry	.90	.45	.25
409 Astros Rookies (Jim Beauchamp, *Larry Dierker*)			
	1.00	.50	.30
410 Luis Aparicio	9.00	4.50	2.75
411 Roger Craig	2.00	1.00	.60
412 Bob Bailey	.90	.45	.25
413 Hal Reniff	1.50	.70	.45
414 Al Lopez	3.00	1.50	.90
415 Curt Flood	1.50	.70	.45
416 Jim Brewer	.90	.45	.25
417 Ed Brinkman	1.00	.50	.30
418 Johnny Edwards	.90	.45	.25
419 Ruben Amaro	.90	.45	.25
420 Larry Jackson	.90	.45	.25
421 Twins Rookies (Gary Dotter, Jay Ward)			
	.90	.45	.25
422 Aubrey Gatewood	.90	.45	.25
423 Jesse Gonder	1.00	.50	.30
424 Gary Bell	.90	.45	.25
425 Wayne Causey	.90	.45	.25
426 Braves Team	2.50	1.25	.70
427 Bob Saverine	.90	.45	.25
428 Bob Shaw	.90	.45	.25
429 Don Demeter	.90	.45	.25
430 Gary Peters	1.00	.50	.30
431 Cardinals Rookies (Nelson Briles, Wayne Spiezio)			
	1.00	.50	.30
432 Jim Grant	1.00	.50	.30
433 John Bateman	.90	.45	.25
434 Dave Morehead	.90	.45	.25
435 Willie Davis	1.50	.70	.45
436 Don Elston	.90	.45	.25
437 Chico Cardenas	.90	.45	.25
438 Harry Walker	1.00	.50	.30
439 Moe Drabowsky	.90	.45	.25
440 Tom Tresh	2.50	1.25	.70
441 Denver Lemaster	.90	.45	.25
442 Vic Power	.90	.45	.25
443 Checklist 430-506	3.25	1.75	1.00
444 Bob Hendley	.90	.45	.25
445 Don Lock	.90	.45	.25
446 Art Mahaffey	.90	.45	.25
447 Julian Javier	1.25	.60	.40
448 Lee Stange	1.25	.60	.40
449 Mets Rookies (Jerry Hinsley, Gary Kroll)			
	1.50	.70	.45
450 Elston Howard	5.00	2.50	1.50
451 Jim Owens	1.25	.60	.40
452 Gary Geiger	1.25	.60	.40
453 Dodgers Rookies (*Willie Crawford*, John Werhas)			
	1.50	.70	.45
454 Ed Rakow	1.25	.60	.40
455 Norm Siebern	1.50	.70	.45
456 Bill Henry	1.25	.60	.40
457 Bob Kennedy	1.25	.60	.40
458 John Buzhardt	1.25	.60	.40
459 Frank Kostro	1.25	.60	.40
460 Richie Allen	6.00	3.00	1.75
461 Braves Rookies (*Clay Carroll*, Phil Niekro)			
	35.00	17.50	10.50
462 Lew Krausse (photo actually Pete Lovrich)			
	1.25	.60	.40
463 Manny Mota	1.50	.70	.45
464 Ron Piche	1.25	.60	.40
465 Tom Haller	1.25	.60	.40
466 Senators Rookies (Pete Craig, Dick Nen)			
	1.25	.60	.40
467 Ray Washburn	1.25	.60	.40
468 Larry Brown	1.25	.60	.40
469 Don Nottebart	1.25	.60	.40
470 Yogi Berra	50.00	30.00	15.00
471 Billy Hoeft	1.25	.60	.40
472 Don Pavletich	1.25	.60	.40
473 Orioles Rookies (*Paul Blair, Dave Johnson*)			
	9.00	4.50	2.75
474 Cookie Rojas	1.25	.60	.40
475 Clete Boyer	3.00	1.50	.90
476 Billy O'Dell	1.25	.60	.40
477 Cardinals Rookies (Fritz Ackley, *Steve Carlton*)			
	200.00	80.00	50.00
478 Wilbur Wood	1.00	.50	.30
479 Ken Harrelson	2.50	1.25	.70
480 Joel Horlen	1.25	.60	.40
481 Indians Team	3.00	1.50	.90
482 Bob Priddy	1.25	.60	.40
483 George Smith	1.25	.60	.40
484 Ron Perranoski	1.50	.70	.45
485 Nellie Fox	6.00	3.00	1.75
486 Angels Rookies (Tom Egan, Pat Rogan)			
	1.25	.60	.40
487 Woody Woodward	1.50	.70	.45
488 Ted Wills	1.25	.60	.40
489 Gene Mauch	1.50	.70	.45
490 Earl Battey	1.50	.70	.45
491 Tracy Stallard	1.25	.60	.40
492 Gene Freese	1.25	.60	.40
493 Tigers Rookies (Bruce Brubaker, Bill Roman)			
	1.25	.60	.40
494 Jay Ritchie	1.25	.60	.40
495 Joe Christopher	1.50	.70	.45
496 Joe Cunningham	1.25	.60	.40
497 Giants Rookies (*Ken Henderson*, Jack Hiatt)			
	1.50	.70	.45
498 Gene Stephens	1.25	.60	.40
499 Stu Miller	1.25	.60	.40
500 Ed Mathews	18.00	9.00	5.50
501 Indians Rookies (Ralph Gagliano, Jim Rittwage)			
	1.25	.60	.40
502 Don Cardwell	1.25	.60	.40
503 Phil Gagliano	1.25	.60	.40
504 Jerry Grote	1.50	.70	.45
505 Ray Culp	1.25	.60	.40
506 Sam Mele	1.25	.60	.40

		NR MT	EX	VG
507	Sammy Ellis	1.25	.60	.40
508a	Checklist 507-598 (large print on front)	6.00	3.00	1.75
508b	Checklist 507-598 (small print on front)	4.00	2.00	1.25
509	Red Sox Rookies (Bob Guindon, Gerry Vezendy)	1.25	.60	.40
510	Ernie Banks	40.00	20.00	12.00
511	Ron Locke	1.50	.70	.45
512	Cap Peterson	1.25	.60	.40
513	Yankees Team	9.00	4.50	2.75
514	Joe Azcue	1.25	.60	.40
515	Vern Law	2.00	1.00	.60
516	Al Weis	1.25	.60	.40
517	Angels Rookies (Paul Schaal, Jack Warner)	1.25	.60	.40
518	Ken Rowe	1.25	.60	.40
519	Bob Uecker	45.00	22.00	13.50
520	Tony Cloninger	1.50	.70	.45
521	Phillies Rookies (Dave Bennett, Morrie Stevens)	1.25	.60	.40
522	Hank Aguirre	1.25	.60	.40
523	Mike Brumley	4.00	2.00	1.25
524	Dave Giusti	4.00	2.00	1.25
525	Eddie Bressoud	4.00	2.00	1.25
526	Athletics Rookies (*Jim Hunter, Rene Lachemann, Skip Lockwood, Johnny Odom*)	90.00	45.00	27.00
527	Jeff Torborg	4.50	2.25	1.25
528	George Altman	4.00	2.00	1.25
529	Jerry Fosnow	4.00	2.00	1.25
530	Jim Maloney	4.50	2.25	1.25
531	Chuck Hiller	4.00	2.00	1.25
532	Hector Lopez	5.00	2.50	1.50
533	Mets Rookies (Jim Bethke, *Tug McGraw*, Dan Napolean, *Ron Swoboda*)	12.00	6.00	3.50
534	John Herrnstein	4.00	2.00	1.25
535	Jack Kralick	4.00	2.00	1.25
536	Andre Rodgers	4.00	2.00	1.25
537	Angels Rookies (Marcelino Lopez, *Rudy May*, Phil Roof)	5.00	2.50	1.50
538	Chuck Dressen	4.50	2.25	1.25
539	Herm Starrette	4.00	2.00	1.25
540	Lou Brock	40.00	20.00	12.00
541	White Sox Rookies (Greg Bollo, Bob Locker)	4.00	2.00	1.25
542	Lou Klimchock	4.00	2.00	1.25
543	Ed Connolly	4.00	2.00	1.25
544	Howie Reed	4.00	2.00	1.25
545	Jesus Alou	4.50	2.25	1.25
546	Indians Rookies (Ray Barker, Bill Davis, Mike Hedlund, Floyd Weaver)	4.00	2.00	1.25
547	Jake Wood	4.00	2.00	1.25
548	Dick Stigman	4.00	2.00	1.25
549	Cubs Rookies (*Glenn Beckert*, Roberto Pena)	5.00	2.50	1.50
550	*Mel Stottlemyre*	15.00	7.50	4.50
551	Mets Team	12.00	6.00	3.50
552	Julio Gotay	4.00	2.00	1.25
553	Astros Rookies (Dan Coombs, Jack McClure, Gene Ratliff)	4.00	2.00	1.25
554	Chico Ruiz	4.00	2.00	1.25
555	Jack Baldschun	4.00	2.00	1.25
556	Red Schoendienst	7.00	3.50	2.00
557	Jose Santiago	4.00	2.00	1.25
558	Tommie Sisk	4.00	2.00	1.25
559	Ed Bailey	4.00	2.00	1.25
560	Boog Powell	6.00	3.00	1.75
561	Dodgers Rookies (Dennis Daboll, *Mike Kekich, Jim Lefebvre*, Hector Valle)	6.00	3.00	1.75
562	Billy Moran	4.00	2.00	1.25
563	Julio Navarro	4.00	2.00	1.25
564	Mel Nelson	4.00	2.00	1.25
565	Ernie Broglio	4.00	2.00	1.25
566	Yankees Rookies (Gil Blanco, Art Lopez, Ross Moschitto)	5.00	2.50	1.50
567	Tommie Aaron	4.50	2.25	1.25
568	Ron Taylor	4.00	2.00	1.25
569	Gino Cimoli	4.00	2.00	1.25
570	Claude Osteen	4.50	2.25	1.25
571	Ossie Virgil	4.00	2.00	1.25
572	Orioles Team	6.00	3.00	1.75
573	Red Sox Rookies (*Jim Lonborg*, Gerry Moses, Mike Ryan, Bill Schlesinger)	8.00	4.00	2.50
574	Roy Sievers	4.50	2.25	1.25
575	Jose Pagan	4.00	2.00	1.25
576	Terry Fox	4.00	2.00	1.25
577	A.L. Rookies (Jim Buschhorn, Darold Knowles, Richie Scheinblum)	4.00	2.00	1.25
578	Camilo Carreon	4.00	2.00	1.25
579	Dick Smith	4.00	2.00	1.25

		NR MT	EX	VG
580	Jimmie Hall	4.00	2.00	1.25
581	N.L. Rookies (Kevin Collins, *Tony Perez*, Dave Ricketts)	50.00	30.00	15.00
582	Bob Schmidt	5.00	2.50	1.50
583	Wes Covington	4.00	2.00	1.25
584	Harry Bright	4.00	2.00	1.25
585	Hank Fischer	4.00	2.00	1.25
586	Tommy McCraw	4.00	2.00	1.25
587	Joe Sparma	4.00	2.00	1.25
588	Lenny Green	4.00	2.00	1.25
589	Giants Rookies (Frank Linzy, Bob Schroder)	4.00	2.00	1.25
590	Johnnie Wyatt	4.00	2.00	1.25
591	Bob Skinner	4.50	2.25	1.25
592	Frank Bork	4.00	2.00	1.25
593	Tigers Rookies (Jackie Moore, John Sullivan)	4.00	2.00	1.25
594	Joe Gaines	4.00	2.00	1.25
595	Don Lee	4.00	2.00	1.25
596	Don Landrum	4.00	2.00	1.25
597	Twins Rookies (Joe Nossek, Dick Reese, John Sevcik)	4.50	2.00	1.25
598	Al Downing	10.00	3.00	1.75

1965 Topps Embossed

Inserted in regular packs, the 2-1/8" by 3-1/2" Topps Embossed cards are one of the more fascinating issues of the company. The fronts feature an embossed profile portrait on gold foil-like cardboard (some collectors report finding the cards with silver cardboard). The player's name, team and position are below the portrait - which is good, because most of the embossed portraits are otherwise unrecognizeable. There is a gold border with American players framed in blue and National Leaguers in red. The set contains 72 cards divided equally bewteen the leagues. The set provides an inexpensive way to add some interesting cards to a collection. Being special cards, many stars appear in the set.

		NR MT	EX	VG
Complete Set:		70.00	35.00	21.00
Common Player:		.50	.25	.15
1	Carl Yastrzemski	5.00	2.50	1.50
2	Ron Fairly	.50	.25	.15
3	Max Alvis	.50	.25	.15
4	Jim Ray Hart	.50	.25	.15
5	Bill Skowron	.60	.30	.20
6	Ed Kranepool	.50	.25	.15
7	Tim McCarver	.60	.30	.20
8	Sandy Koufax	5.00	2.50	1.50
9	Donn Clendenon	.50	.25	.15
10	John Romano	.50	.25	.15
11	Mickey Mantle	15.00	7.50	4.50
12	Joe Torre	.70	.35	.20
13	Al Kaline	5.00	2.50	1.50
14	Al McBean	.50	.25	.15
15	Don Drysdale	1.50	.70	.45
16	Brooks Robinson	2.00	1.00	.60
17	Jim Bunning	1.00	.50	.30
18	Gary Peters	.50	.25	.15
19	Bob Clemente	5.00	2.50	1.50
20	Milt Pappas	.50	.25	.15
21	Wayne Causey	.50	.25	.15

		NR MT	EX	VG
22	Frank Robinson	2.00	1.00	.60
23	Bill Mazeroski	.60	.30	.20
24	Diego Segui	.50	.25	.15
25	Jim Bouton	.60	.30	.20
26	Ed Mathews	1.50	.70	.45
27	Willie Mays	6.00	3.00	1.75
28	Ron Santo	.60	.30	.20
29	Boog Powell	.60	.30	.20
30	Ken McBride	.50	.25	.15
31	Leon Wagner	.50	.25	.15
32	John Callison	.50	.25	.15
33	Zoilo Versalles	.50	.25	.15
34	Jack Baldschun	.50	.25	.15
35	Ron Hunt	.50	.25	.15
36	Richie Allen	.70	.35	.20
37	Frank Malzone	.50	.25	.15
38	Bob Allison	.50	.25	.15
39	Jim Fregosi	.60	.30	.20
40	Billy Williams	1.50	.70	.45
41	Bill Freehan	.50	.25	.15
42	Vada Pinson	.70	.35	.20
43	Bill White	.50	.25	.15
44	Roy McMillan	.50	.25	.15
45	Orlando Cepeda	1.00	.50	.30
46	Rocky Colavito	.70	.35	.20
47	Ken Boyer	.70	.35	.20
48	Dick Radatz	.50	.25	.15
49	Tommy Davis	.60	.30	.20
50	Walt Bond	.50	.25	.15
51	John Orsino	.50	.25	.15
52	Joe Christopher	.50	.25	.15
53	Al Spangler	.50	.25	.15
54	Jim King	.50	.25	.15
55	Mickey Lolich	.70	.35	.20
56	Harmon Killebrew	2.00	1.00	.60
57	Bob Shaw	.50	.25	.15
58	Ernie Banks	4.00	2.00	1.25
59	Hank Aaron	5.00	2.50	1.50
60	Chuck Hinton	.50	.25	.15
61	Bob Aspromonte	.50	.25	.15
62	Lee Maye	.50	.25	.15
63	Joe Cunningham	.50	.25	.15
64	Pete Ward	.50	.25	.15
65	Bobby Richardson	1.00	.50	.30
66	Dean Chance	.50	.25	.15
67	Dick Ellsworth	.50	.25	.15
68	Jim Maloney	.50	.25	.15
69	Bob Gibson	1.50	.70	.45
70	Earl Battey	.50	.25	.15
71	Tony Kubek	1.00	.50	.30
72	Jack Kralick	.50	.25	.15

1965 Topps Transfers

Issued as strips of three players each as inserts in 1965, the Topps Transfers were 2" by 3" portraits of players. The transfers have blue or red bands at the top and bottom with the team name and position in the top band and the player's name in the bottom. As is so often the case, the superstars in the transfer set can be quite expensive, but like many of Topps non-card products, the transfers are neither terribly expensive or popular today.

		NR MT	EX	VG
Complete Set:		200.00	100.00	60.00
Common Player:		.60	.30	.20
(1)	Hank Aaron	15.00	7.50	4.50
(2)	Richie Allen	.80	.40	.25

		NR MT	EX	VG
(3)	Bob Allison	.70	.35	.20
(4)	Max Alvis	.60	.30	.20
(5)	Luis Aparicio	2.50	1.25	.70
(6)	Bob Aspromonte	.60	.30	.20
(7)	Walt Bond	.60	.30	.20
(8)	Jim Bouton	.80	.40	.25
(9)	Ken Boyer	.80	.40	.25
(10)	Jim Bunning	1.00	.50	.30
(11)	John Callison	.70	.35	.20
(12)	Rico Carty	.70	.35	.20
(13)	Wayne Causey	.60	.30	.20
(14)	Orlando Cepeda	1.00	.50	.30
(15)	Bob Chance	.60	.30	.20
(16)	Dean Chance	.60	.30	.20
(17)	Joe Christopher	.60	.30	.20
(18)	Bob Clemente	15.00	7.50	4.50
(19)	Rocky Colavito	.80	.40	.25
(20)	Tony Conigliaro	.70	.35	.20
(21)	Tommy Davis	.80	.40	.25
(22)	Don Drysdale	4.00	2.00	1.25
(23)	Bill Freehan	.70	.35	.20
(24)	Jim Fregosi	.70	.35	.20
(25)	Bob Gibson	4.00	2.00	1.25
(26)	Dick Groat	.70	.35	.20
(27)	Tom Haller	.60	.30	.20
(28)	Chuck Hinton	.60	.30	.20
(29)	Elston Howard	1.00	.50	.30
(30)	Ron Hunt	.60	.30	.20
(31)	Al Jackson	.60	.30	.20
(32)	Al Kaline	5.00	2.50	1.50
(33)	Harmon Killebrew	5.00	2.50	1.50
(34)	Jim King	.60	.30	.20
(35)	Ron Kline	.60	.30	.20
(36)	Bobby Knoop	.60	.30	.20
(37)	Sandy Koufax	10.00	5.00	3.00
(38)	Ed Kranepool	.60	.30	.20
(39)	Jim Maloney	.60	.30	.20
(40)	Mickey Mantle	60.00	30.00	18.00
(41)	Juan Marichal	4.00	2.00	1.25
(42)	Lee Maye	.60	.30	.20
(43)	Willie Mays	15.00	7.50	4.50
(44)	Bill Mazeroski	.80	.40	.25
(45)	Tony Oliva	.80	.40	.25
(46)	Jim O'Toole	.60	.30	.20
(47)	Milt Pappas	.70	.35	.20
(48)	Camilo Pascual	.70	.35	.20
(49)	Gary Peters	.60	.30	.20
(50)	Vada Pinson	.80	.40	.25
(51)	Juan Pizarro	.60	.30	.20
(52)	Boog Powell	.80	.40	.25
(53)	Dick Radatz	.60	.30	.20
(54)	Bobby Richardson	1.00	.50	.30
(55)	Brooks Robinson	6.00	3.00	1.75
(56)	Frank Robinson	5.00	2.50	1.50
(57)	Bob Rodgers	.70	.35	.20
(58)	John Roseboro	.70	.35	.20
(59)	Ron Santo	.80	.40	.25
(60)	Diego Segui	.60	.30	.20
(61)	Bill Skowron	.70	.35	.20
(62)	Al Spangler	.60	.30	.20
(63)	Dick Stuart	.70	.35	.20
(64)	Luis Tiant	.80	.40	.25
(65)	Joe Torre	.80	.40	.25
(66)	Bob Veale	.60	.30	.20
(67)	Leon Wagner	.60	.30	.20
(68)	Pete Ward	.60	.30	.20
(69)	Bill White	.70	.35	.20
(70)	Dave Wickersham	.60	.30	.20
(71)	Billy Williams	3.00	1.50	.90
(72)	Carl Yastrzemski	25.00	12.50	7.50

1966 Topps

In 1966, Topps produced another 598-card set. The 2-1/2" by 3-1/2" cards feature the almost traditional color photograph with a diagonal strip in the upper left-hand corner carrying the team name. A band at the bottom carries the player's name and position. Multi-player cards returned in 1966 after having had a year's hiatus. The statistical leader cards feature the categorical leader and two runners-up. Most team managers have cards as well. The 1966 set features a handful of cards found with without a notice of the player's sale or trade to another team. Cards without the notice bring higher higher prices not included in the complete set prices below.

		NR MT	EX	VG
	Complete Set:	3200.00	1600.00	960.00
	Common Player: 1-110	.60	.30	.20
	Common Player: 111-446	.70	.35	.20
	Common Player: 447-522	3.50	1.75	1.00
	Common Player Singleprint: 523-598	20.00	10.00	6.00
	Common Player: 523-598	15.00	7.50	4.50
1	Willie Mays	110.00	25.00	12.00
2	Ted Abernathy	.80	.30	.20
3	Sam Mele	.60	.30	.20
4	Ray Culp	.60	.30	.20
5	Jim Fregosi	1.00	.50	.30
6	Chuck Schilling	.60	.30	.20
7	Tracy Stallard	.60	.30	.20
8	Floyd Robinson	.60	.30	.20
9	Clete Boyer	1.50	.70	.45
10	Tony Cloninger	.70	.35	.20
11	Senators Rookies (Brant Alyea, Pete Craig)	.60	.30	.20
12	John Tsitouris	.60	.30	.20
13	Lou Johnson	.60	.30	.20
14	Norm Siebern	.70	.35	.20
15	Vern Law	1.00	.50	.30
16	Larry Brown	.70	.35	.20
17	Johnny Stephenson	.70	.35	.20
18	Roland Sheldon	.60	.30	.20
19	Giants Team	2.00	1.00	.60
20	Willie Horton	.80	.40	.25
21	Don Nottebart	.60	.30	.20
22	Joe Nossek	.60	.30	.20
23	Jack Sanford	.60	.30	.20
24	*Don Kessinger*	1.25	.60	.40
25	Pete Ward	.60	.30	.20
26	Ray Sadecki	.60	.30	.20
27	Orioles Rookies (*Andy Etchebarren,* Darold Knowles)	.70	.35	.20
28	Phil Niekro	10.00	5.00	3.00
29	Mike Brumley	.60	.30	.20
30	Pete Rose	60.00	30.00	18.00
31	Jack Cullen	.80	.40	.25
32	Adolfo Phillips	.60	.30	.20
33	Jim Pagliaroni	.60	.30	.20
34	Checklist 1-88	2.00	1.00	.60
35	Ron Swoboda	.80	.40	.25
36	Jim Hunter	25.00	12.50	7.50
37	Billy Herman	1.50	.70	.45
38	Ron Nischwitz	.60	.30	.20
39	Ken Henderson	.60	.30	.20
40	Jim Grant	.60	.30	.20
41	Don LeJohn	.60	.30	.20
42	Aubrey Gatewood	.60	.30	.20
43	Don Landrum	.60	.30	.20
44	Indians Rookies (Bill Davis, Tom Kelley)	.60	.30	.20
45	Jim Gentile	.70	.35	.20
46	Howie Koplitz	.60	.30	.20
47	J.C. Martin	.60	.30	.20
48	Paul Blair	.80	.40	.25
49	Woody Woodward	.70	.35	.20
50	Mickey Mantle	175.00	70.00	44.00
51	Gordon Richardson	.70	.35	.20
52	Power Plus (Johnny Callison, Wes Covington)	1.00	.50	.30
53	Bob Duliba	.60	.30	.20
54	Jose Pagan	.60	.30	.20
55	Ken Harrelson	1.50	.70	.45
56	Sandy Valdespino	.60	.30	.20
57	Jim Lefebvre	.70	.35	.20
58	Dave Wickersham	.60	.30	.20
59	Reds Team	2.25	1.25	.70
60	Curt Flood	1.50	.70	.45
61	Bob Bolin	.60	.30	.20
62a	Merritt Ranew (no sold statement)	15.00	7.50	4.50

		NR MT	EX	VG
62b	Merritt Ranew (with sold statement)	.60	.30	.20
63	Jim Stewart	.60	.30	.20
64	Bob Bruce	.60	.30	.20
65	Leon Wagner	.70	.35	.20
66	Al Weis	.60	.30	.20
67	Mets Rookies (Cleon Jones, Dick Selma)	.80	.40	.25
68	Hal Reniff	.80	.40	.25
69	Ken Hamlin	.60	.30	.20
70	Carl Yastrzemski	60.00	30.00	18.00
71	Frank Carpin	.60	.30	.20
72	Tony Perez	8.00	4.00	2.50
73	Jerry Zimmerman	.60	.30	.20
74	Don Mossi	.70	.35	.20
75	Tommy Davis	1.50	.70	.45
76	Red Schoendienst	1.50	.70	.45
77	Johnny Orsino	.60	.30	.20
78	Frank Linzy	.60	.30	.20
79	Joe Pepitone	2.00	1.00	.60
80	Richie Allen	2.50	1.25	.70
81	Ray Oyler	.60	.30	.20
82	Bob Hendley	.60	.30	.20
83	Albie Pearson	.60	.30	.20
84	Braves Rookies (Jim Beauchamp, Dick Kelley)	.60	.30	.20
85	Eddie Fisher	.60	.30	.20
86	John Bateman	.60	.30	.20
87	Dan Napoleon	.70	.35	.20
88	Fred Whitfield	.60	.30	.20
89	Ted Davidson	.60	.30	.20
90	Luis Aparicio	9.00	4.50	2.75
91a	Bob Uecker (no trade statement)	55.00	28.00	16.50
91b	Bob Uecker (with trade statement)	15.00	7.50	4.50
92	Yankees Team	4.00	2.00	1.25
93	Jim Lonborg	1.00	.50	.30
94	Matty Alou	1.00	.50	.30
95	Pete Richert	.60	.30	.20
96	Felipe Alou	1.00	.50	.30
97	Jim Merritt	.60	.30	.20
98	Don Demeter	.60	.30	.20
99	Buc Belters (Donn Clendenon, Willie Stargell)	3.50	1.75	1.00
100	Sandy Koufax	50.00	30.00	15.00
101a	Checklist 89-176 (115 is Spahn)	7.00	3.50	2.00
101b	Checklist 89-176 (115 is Henry)	3.00	1.50	.90
102	Ed Kirkpatrick	.60	.30	.20
103a	Dick Groat (no trade statement)	20.00	10.00	6.00
103b	Dick Groat (with trade statement)	1.50	.70	.45
104a	Alex Johnson (no trade statement)	15.00	7.50	4.50
104b	Alex Johnson (with trade statement)	.70	.35	.20
105	Milt Pappas	.70	.35	.20
106	Rusty Staub	2.50	1.25	.70
107	Athletics Rookies (Larry Stahl, Ron Tompkins)	.60	.30	.20
108	Bobby Klaus	.70	.35	.20
109	Ralph Terry	.70	.35	.20
110	Ernie Banks	18.00	9.00	5.50
111	Gary Peters	.80	.40	.25
112	Manny Mota	.90	.45	.25
113	Hank Aguirre	.70	.35	.20
114	Jim Gosger	.70	.35	.20
115	Bill Henry	.70	.35	.20
116	Walt Alston	2.50	1.25	.70
117	Jake Gibbs	1.00	.50	.30
118	Mike McCormick	.80	.40	.25
119	Art Shamsky	.70	.35	.20
120	Harmon Killebrew	15.00	7.50	4.50
121	Ray Herbert	.70	.35	.20
122	Joe Gaines	.70	.35	.20
123	Pirates Rookies (Frank Bork, Jerry May)	.70	.35	.20
124	Tug McGraw	3.00	1.50	.90
125	Lou Brock	20.00	10.00	6.00
126	*Jim Palmer*	150.00	60.00	38.00
127	Ken Berry	.70	.35	.20
128	Jim Landis	.70	.35	.20
129	Jack Kralick	.70	.35	.20
130	Joe Torre	2.25	1.25	.70
131	Angels Team	2.25	1.25	.70
132	Orlando Cepeda	3.50	1.75	1.00
133	Don McMahon	.70	.35	.20
134	Wes Parker	.80	.40	.25
135	Dave Morehead	.70	.35	.20
136	Woody Held	.70	.35	.20
137	Pat Corrales	1.00	.50	.30
138	Roger Repoz	1.00	.50	.30

		NR MT	EX	VG
139	Cubs Rookies (Byron Browne, Don Young)			
		.70	.35	.20
140	Jim Maloney	.80	.40	.25
141	Tom McCraw	.70	.35	.20
142	Don Dennis	.70	.35	.20
143	Jose Tartabull	.70	.35	.20
144	Don Schwall	.70	.35	.20
145	Bill Freehan	.90	.45	.25
146	George Altman	.70	.35	.20
147	Lum Harris	.70	.35	.20
148	Bob Johnson	.70	.35	.20
149	Dick Nen	.70	.35	.20
150	Rocky Colavito	2.50	1.25	.70
151	Gary Wagner	.70	.35	.20
152	Frank Malzone	.80	.40	.25
153	Rico Carty	1.50	.70	.45
154	Chuck Hiller	.80	.40	.25
155	Marcelino Lopez	.70	.35	.20
156	DP Combo (Hal Lanier, Dick Schofield)			
		1.00	.50	.30
157	Rene Lachemann	.80	.40	.25
158	Jim Brewer	.70	.35	.20
159	Chico Ruiz	.70	.35	.20
160	Whitey Ford	20.00	10.00	6.00
161	Jerry Lumpe	.80	.40	.25
162	Lee Maye	.70	.35	.20
163	Tito Francona	.80	.40	.25
164	White Sox Rookies (Tommie Agee, Marv Staehle)			
		.90	.45	.25
165	Don Lock	.70	.35	.20
166	Chris Krug	.70	.35	.20
167	Boog Powell	2.50	1.25	.70
168	Dan Osinski	.70	.35	.20
169	Duke Sims	.70	.35	.20
170	Cookie Rojas	.70	.35	.20
171	Nick Willhite	.70	.35	.20
172	Mets Team	3.00	1.50	.90
173	Al Spangler	.70	.35	.20
174	Ron Taylor	.70	.35	.20
175	Bert Campaneris	1.50	.70	.45
176	Jim Davenport	.70	.35	.20
177	Hector Lopez	1.00	.50	.30
178	Bob Tillman	.70	.35	.20
179	Cardinals Rookies (Dennis Aust, Bob Tolan)			
		.80	.40	.25
180	Vada Pinson	2.50	1.25	.70
181	Al Worthington	.70	.35	.20
182	Jerry Lynch	.70	.35	.20
183a	Checklist 177-264 (large print on front)			
		2.50	1.25	.70
183b	Checklist 177-264 (small print on front)			
		4.00	2.00	1.25
184	Denis Menke	.70	.35	.20
185	Bob Buhl	.80	.40	.25
186	Ruben Amaro	1.00	.50	.30
187	Chuck Dressen	.80	.40	.25
188	Al Luplow	.80	.40	.25
189	John Roseboro	.90	.45	.25
190	Jimmie Hall	.70	.35	.20
191	Darrell Sutherland	.80	.40	.25
192	Vic Power	.70	.35	.20
193	Dave McNally	1.00	.50	.30
194	Senators Team	2.25	1.25	.70
195	Joe Morgan	18.00	9.00	5.50
196	Don Pavletich	.70	.35	.20
197	Sonny Siebert	.80	.40	.25
198	*Mickey Stanley*	1.00	.50	.30
199	Chisox Clubbers (Floyd Robinson, Johnny Romano, Bill Skowron)			
		1.00	.50	.30
200	Ed Mathews	8.00	4.00	2.50
201	Jim Dickson	.70	.35	.20
202	Clay Dalrymple	.70	.35	.20
203	Jose Santiago	.70	.35	.20
204	Cubs Team	2.25	1.25	.70
205	Tom Tresh	2.00	1.00	.60
206	Alvin Jackson	.70	.35	.20
207	Frank Quilici	.70	.35	.20
208	Bob Miller	.70	.35	.20
209	Tigers Rookies (Fritz Fisher, *John Hiller*)			
		1.25	.60	.40
210	Bill Mazeroski	2.50	1.25	.70
211	Frank Kreutzer	.70	.35	.20
212	Ed Kranepool	1.00	.50	.30
213	Fred Newman	.70	.35	.20
214	Tommy Harper	.80	.40	.25
215	N.L. Batting Leaders (Hank Aaron, Bob Clemente, Willie Mays)			
		8.00	4.00	2.50
216	A.L. Batting Leaders (Vic Davalillo, Tony Oliva, Carl Yastrzemski)			
		4.00	2.00	1.25
217	N.L. Home Run Leaders (Willie Mays, Willie McCovey, Billy Williams)			
		5.00	2.50	1.50
218	A.L. Home Run Leaders (Norm Cash, Tony Conigliaro, Willie Horton)			
		2.50	1.25	.70
219	N.L. RBI Leaders (Deron Johnson, Willie Mays, Frank Robinson)			
		4.00	2.00	1.25
220	A.L. RBI Leaders (Rocky Colavito, Willie Horton, Tony Oliva)			
		2.50	1.25	.70
221	N.L. ERA Leaders (Sandy Koufax, Vern Law, Juan Marichal)			
		4.00	2.00	1.25
222	A.L. ERA Leaders (Eddie Fisher, Sam McDowell, Sonny Siebert)			
		2.50	1.25	.70
223	N.L. Pitching Leaders (Tony Cloninger, Don Drysdale, Sandy Koufax)			
		4.00	2.00	1.25
224	A.L. Pitching Leaders (Jim Grant, Jim Kaat, Mel Stottlemyre)			
		3.00	1.50	.90
225	N.L. Strikeout Leaders (Bob Gibson, Sandy Koufax, Bob Veale)			
		4.00	2.00	1.25
226	A.L. Strikeout Leaders (Mickey Lolich, Sam McDowell, Denny McLain, Sonny Siebert)			
		2.50	1.25	.70
227	Russ Nixon	.70	.35	.20
228	Larry Dierker	.80	.40	.25
229	Hank Bauer	.80	.40	.25
230	Johnny Callison	1.25	.60	.40
231	Floyd Weaver	.70	.35	.20
232	Glenn Beckert	1.00	.50	.30
233	Dom Zanni	.70	.35	.20
234	Yankees Rookies (Rich Beck, *Roy White*)			
		3.50	1.75	1.00
235	Don Cardwell	.70	.35	.20
236	Mike Hershberger	.70	.35	.20
237	Billy O'Dell	.70	.35	.20
238	Dodgers Team	3.50	1.75	1.00
239	Orlando Pena	.70	.35	.20
240	Earl Battey	.80	.40	.25
241	Dennis Ribant	.80	.40	.25
242	Jesus Alou	.80	.40	.25
243	Nelson Briles	.80	.40	.25
244	Astros Rookies (Chuck Harrison, Sonny Jackson)			
		.70	.35	.20
245	John Buzhardt	.70	.35	.20
246	Ed Bailey	.70	.35	.20
247	Carl Warwick	.70	.35	.20
248	Pete Mikkelsen	.70	.35	.20
249	Bill Rigney	.70	.35	.20
250	Sam Ellis	.70	.35	.20
251	Ed Brinkman	.80	.40	.25
252	Denver Lemaster	.70	.35	.20
253	Don Wert	.70	.35	.20
254	Phillies Rookies (*Ferguson Jenkins*, Bill Sorrell)			
		30.00	15.00	9.00
255	Willie Stargell	15.00	7.50	4.50
256	Lew Krausse	.70	.35	.20
257	Jeff Torborg	.80	.40	.25
258	Dave Giusti	.70	.35	.20
259	Red Sox Team	2.50	1.25	.70
260	Bob Shaw	.70	.35	.20
261	Ron Hansen	.70	.35	.20
262	Jack Hamilton	.80	.40	.25
263	Tom Egan	.70	.35	.20
264	Twins Rookies (Andy Kosco, Ted Uhlaender)			
		.70	.35	.20
265	Stu Miller	.70	.35	.20
266	Pedro Gonzalez	.70	.35	.20
267	Joe Sparma	.70	.35	.20
268	John Blanchard	.70	.35	.20
269	Don Heffner	.70	.35	.20
270	Claude Osteen	.90	.45	.25
271	Hal Lanier	1.00	.50	.30
272	Jack Baldschun	.70	.35	.20
273	Astro Aces (Bob Aspromonte, Rusty Staub)			
		1.50	.70	.45
274	Buster Narum	.70	.35	.20
275	Tim McCarver	2.50	1.25	.70
276	Jim Bouton	2.50	1.25	.70
277	George Thomas	.70	.35	.20
278	Calvin Koonce	.70	.35	.20
279a	Checklist 265-352 (player's cap black)			
		4.00	2.00	1.25
279b	Checklist 265-352 (player's cap red)			
		3.00	1.50	.90
280	Bobby Knoop	.70	.35	.20
281	Bruce Howard	.70	.35	.20
282	Johnny Lewis	.80	.40	.25
283	Jim Perry	1.00	.50	.30
284	Bobby Wine	.80	.40	.25
285	Luis Tiant	2.50	1.25	.70
286	Gary Geiger	.70	.35	.20
287	Jack Aker	.70	.35	.20
288	Dodgers Rookies (*Bill Singer, Don Sutton*)			
		70.00	35.00	21.00
289	Larry Sherry	.80	.40	.25

	NR MT	EX	VG			NR MT	EX	VG
290	Ron Santo	2.00	1.00	.60	377	Turk Farrell	.70	.35	.20
291	Moe Drabowsky	.70	.35	.20	378	Dick Tracewski	.70	.35	.20
292	Jim Coker	.70	.35	.20	379	Cardinals Team	2.25	1.25	.70
293	Mike Shannon	.80	.40	.25	380	Tony Conigliaro	2.00	1.00	.60
294	Steve Ridzik	.70	.35	.20	381	Hank Fischer	.70	.35	.20
295	Jim Hart	.80	.40	.25	382	Phil Roof	.70	.35	.20
296	Johnny Keane	1.25	.60	.40	383	Jackie Brandt	.70	.35	.20
297	Jim Owens	.70	.35	.20	384	Al Downing	1.50	.70	.45
298	Rico Petrocelli	1.25	.60	.40	385	Ken Boyer	2.50	1.25	.70
299	Lou Burdette	2.00	1.00	.60	386	Gil Hodges	5.00	2.50	1.50
300	Bob Clemente	55.00	27.00	16.50	387	Howie Reed	.70	.35	.20
301	Greg Bollo	.70	.35	.20	388	Don Mincher	.80	.40	.25
302	Ernie Bowman	.80	.40	.25	389	Jim O'Toole	.70	.35	.20
303	Indians Team	2.25	1.25	.70	390	Brooks Robinson	15.00	7.50	4.50
304	John Herrnstein	.70	.35	.20	391	Chuck Hinton	.70	.35	.20
305	Camilo Pascual	.90	.45	.25	392	Cubs Rookies (Bill Hands, Randy Hundley)			
306	Ty Cline	.70	.35	.20			.90	.45	.25
307	Clay Carroll	.80	.40	.25	393	George Brunet	.70	.35	.20
308	Tom Haller	.80	.40	.25	394	Ron Brand	.70	.35	.20
309	Diego Segui	.70	.35	.20	395	Len Gabrielson	.70	.35	.20
310	Frank Robinson	20.00	10.00	6.00	396	Jerry Stephenson	.70	.35	.20
311	Reds Rookies (Tommy Helms, Dick Simpson)				397	Bill White	1.00	.50	.30
		.90	.45	.25	398	Danny Cater	.70	.35	.20
312	Bob Saverine	.70	.35	.20	399	Ray Washburn	.70	.35	.20
313	Chris Zachary	.70	.35	.20	400	Zoilo Versalles	.80	.40	.25
314	Hector Valle	.70	.35	.20	401	Ken McMullen	.70	.35	.20
315	Norm Cash	2.00	1.00	.60	402	Jim Hickman	.90	.45	.25
316	Jack Fisher	.80	.40	.25	403	Fred Talbot	.70	.35	.20
317	Dalton Jones	.70	.35	.20	404	Pirates Team	2.25	1.25	.70
318	Harry Walker	.80	.40	.25	405	Elston Howard	4.00	2.00	1.25
319	Gene Freese	.70	.35	.20	406	Joe Jay	.70	.35	.20
320	Bob Gibson	15.00	7.50	4.50	407	John Kennedy	.70	.35	.20
321	Rick Reichardt	.70	.35	.20	408	Lee Thomas	.70	.35	.20
322	Bill Faul	.70	.35	.20	409	Billy Hoeft	.70	.35	.20
323	Ray Barker	1.00	.50	.30	410	Al Kaline	18.00	9.00	5.50
324	John Boozer	.70	.35	.20	411	Gene Mauch	.90	.45	.25
325	Vic Davalillo	.80	.40	.25	412	Sam Bowens	.70	.35	.20
326	Braves Team	2.25	1.25	.70	413	John Romano	.70	.35	.20
327	Bernie Allen	.70	.35	.20	414	Dan Coombs	.70	.35	.20
328	Jerry Grote	.90	.45	.25	415	Max Alvis	.70	.35	.20
329	Pete Charton	.70	.35	.20	416	Phil Ortega	.70	.35	.20
330	Ron Fairly	.90	.45	.25	417	Angels Rookies (Jim McGlothlin, Ed Sukla)			
331	Ron Herbel	.70	.35	.20			.70	.35	.20
332	Billy Bryan	.70	.35	.20	418	Phil Gagliano	.70	.35	.20
333	Senators Rookies (Joe Coleman, Jim French)				419	Mike Ryan	.70	.35	.20
		.90	.45	.25	420	Juan Marichal	8.00	4.00	2.50
334	Marty Keough	.70	.35	.20	421	Roy McMillan	.80	.40	.25
335	Juan Pizarro	.70	.35	.20	422	Ed Charles	.70	.35	.20
336	Gene Alley	.80	.40	.25	423	Ernie Broglio	.70	.35	.20
337	Fred Gladding	.70	.35	.20	424	Reds Rookies (Lee May, Darrell Osteen)			
338	Dal Maxvill	.80	.40	.25			2.25	1.25	.70
339	Del Crandall	1.00	.50	.30	425	Bob Veale	.80	.40	.25
340	Dean Chance	.80	.40	.25	426	White Sox Team	2.25	1.25	.70
341	Wes Westrum	.90	.45	.25	427	John Miller	.70	.35	.20
342	Bob Humphreys	.70	.35	.20	428	Sandy Alomar	.70	.35	.20
343	Joe Christopher	.70	.35	.20	429	Bill Monbouquette	.80	.40	.25
344	Steve Blass	.80	.40	.25	430	Don Drysdale	12.00	6.00	3.50
345	Bob Allison	1.00	.50	.30	431	Walt Bond	.70	.35	.20
346	Mike de la Hoz	.70	.35	.20	432	Bob Heffner	.70	.35	.20
347	Phil Regan	.70	.35	.20	433	Alvin Dark	.80	.40	.25
348	Orioles Team	3.50	1.75	1.00	434	Willie Kirkland	.70	.35	.20
349	Cap Peterson	.70	.35	.20	435	Jim Bunning	6.00	3.00	1.75
350	Mel Stottlemyre	3.00	1.50	.90	436	Julian Javier	.70	.35	.20
351	Fred Valentine	.70	.35	.20	437	Al Stanek	.70	.35	.20
352	Bob Aspromonte	.70	.35	.20	438	Willie Smith	.70	.35	.20
353	Al McBean	.70	.35	.20	439	Pedro Ramos	1.00	.50	.30
354	Smoky Burgess	1.00	.50	.30	440	Deron Johnson	.70	.35	.20
355	Wade Blasingame	.70	.35	.20	441	Tommie Sisk	.70	.35	.20
356	Red Sox Rookies (Owen Johnson, Ken Sanders)				442	Orioles Rookies (Ed Barnowski, Eddie Watt)			
		.70	.35	.20			.70	.35	.20
357	Gerry Arrigo	.70	.35	.20	443	Bill Wakefield	.80	.40	.25
358	Charlie Smith	.70	.35	.20	444a	Checklist 430-506 (456 is R. Sox Rookies)			
359	Johnny Briggs	.70	.35	.20			3.00	1.50	.90
360	Ron Hunt	.90	.45	.25	444b	Checklist 430-506 (456 is Red Sox Rookies)			
361	Tom Satriano	.70	.35	.20			5.00	2.50	1.50
362	Gates Brown	.70	.35	.20	445	Jim Kaat	4.00	2.00	1.25
363	Checklist 353-429	3.00	1.50	.90	446	Mack Jones	.70	.35	.20
364	Nate Oliver	.70	.35	.20	447	Dick Ellsworth (photo actually Ken Hubbs)			
365	Roger Maris	55.00	28.00	16.50			3.50	1.75	1.00
366	Wayne Causey	.70	.35	.20	448	Eddie Stanky	3.75	2.00	1.25
367	Mel Nelson	.70	.35	.20	449	Joe Moeller	3.50	1.75	1.00
368	Charlie Lau	.90	.45	.25	450	Tony Oliva	7.00	3.50	2.00
369	Jim King	.70	.35	.20	451	Barry Latman	3.50	1.75	1.00
370	Chico Cardenas	.70	.35	.20	452	Joe Azcue	3.50	1.75	1.00
371	Lee Stange	.70	.35	.20	453	Ron Kline	3.50	1.75	1.00
372	Harvey Kuenn	1.50	.70	.45	454	Jerry Buchek	3.50	1.75	1.00
373	Giants Rookies (Dick Estelle, Jack Hiatt)				455	Mickey Lolich	6.00	3.00	1.75
		.70	.35	.20	456	Red Sox Rookies (Darrell Brandon, Joe Foy)			
374	Bob Locker	.70	.35	.20			3.50	1.75	1.00
375	Donn Clendenon	.80	.40	.25	457	Joe Gibbon	3.50	1.75	1.00
376	Paul Schaal	.70	.35	.20	458	Manny Jiminez (Jimenez)	3.50	1.75	1.00

		NR MT	EX	VG
459	Bill McCool	3.50	1.75	1.00
460	Curt Blefary	3.50	1.75	1.00
461	Roy Face	6.00	3.00	1.75
462	Bob Rodgers	2.50	1.25	.70
463	Phillies Team	6.00	3.00	1.75
464	Larry Bearnarth	3.75	2.00	1.25
465	Don Buford	3.75	2.00	1.25
466	Ken Johnson	3.50	1.75	1.00
467	Vic Roznovsky	3.50	1.75	1.00
468	Johnny Podres	6.00	3.00	1.75
469	Yankees Rookies (Bobby Murcer, Dooley Womack)	9.00	4.50	2.75
470	Sam McDowell	4.00	2.00	1.25
471	Bob Skinner	3.50	1.75	1.00
472	Terry Fox	3.50	1.75	1.00
473	Rich Rollins	3.50	1.75	1.00
474	Dick Schofield	3.50	1.75	1.00
475	Dick Radatz	3.75	2.00	1.25
476	Bobby Bragan	3.75	2.00	1.25
477	Steve Barber	3.50	1.75	1.00
478	Tony Gonzalez	3.50	1.75	1.00
479	Jim Hannan	3.50	1.75	1.00
480	Dick Stuart	3.75	2.00	1.25
481	Bob Lee	3.50	1.75	1.00
482	Cubs Rookies (John Boccabella, Dave Dowling)	3.50	1.75	1.00
483	Joe Nuxhall	3.75	2.00	1.25
484	Wes Covington	3.50	1.75	1.00
485	Bob Bailey	3.50	1.75	1.00
486	Tommy John	15.00	7.50	4.50
487	Al Ferrara	3.50	1.75	1.00
488	George Banks	3.50	1.75	1.00
489	Curt Simmons	3.75	2.00	1.25
490	Bobby Richardson	12.00	6.00	3.50
491	Dennis Bennett	3.50	1.75	1.00
492	Athletics Team	5.00	2.50	1.50
493	Johnny Klippstein	3.50	1.75	1.00
494	Gordon Coleman	3.50	1.75	1.00
495	Dick McAuliffe	3.75	2.00	1.25
496	Lindy McDaniel	3.50	1.75	1.00
497	Chris Cannizzaro	3.50	1.75	1.00
498	Pirates Rookies (Woody Fryman, Luke Walker)	4.00	2.00	1.25
499	Wally Bunker	3.50	1.75	1.00
500	Hank Aaron	70.00	35.00	21.00
501	John O'Donoghue	3.50	1.75	1.00
502	Lenny Green	3.50	1.75	1.00
503	Steve Hamilton	3.75	2.00	1.25
504	Grady Hatton	3.50	1.75	1.00
505	Jose Cardenal	3.50	1.75	1.00
506	Bo Belinsky	3.75	2.00	1.25
507	John Edwards	3.50	1.75	1.00
508	Steve Hargan	3.75	2.00	1.25
509	Jake Wood	3.50	1.75	1.00
510	Hoyt Wilhelm	15.00	7.50	4.50
511	Giants Rookies (Bob Barton, Tito Fuentes)	3.75	2.00	1.25
512	Dick Stigman	3.50	1.75	1.00
513	Camilo Carreon	3.50	1.75	1.00
514	Hal Woodeshick	3.50	1.75	1.00
515	Frank Howard	7.00	3.50	2.00
516	Eddie Bressoud	2.00	1.00	.60
517a	Checklist 507-598 (529 is W. Sox Rookies)	7.00	3.50	2.00
517b	Checklist 506-598 (529 is White Sox Rookies)	8.00	4.00	2.50
518	Braves Rookies (Herb Hippauf, Arnie Umbach)	3.50	1.75	1.00
519	Bob Friend	6.00	3.00	1.75
520	Jim Wynn	4.00	2.00	1.25
521	John Wyatt	3.50	1.75	1.00
522	Phil Linz	3.50	1.75	1.00
523	Bob Sadowski	15.00	7.50	4.50
524	Giants Rookies (Ollie Brown, Don Mason)	20.00	10.00	6.00
525	Gary Bell	15.00	7.50	4.50
526	Twins Team	50.00	25.00	15.00
527	Julio Navarro	15.00	7.50	4.50
528	Jesse Gonder	20.00	10.00	6.00
529	White Sox Rookies (Lee Elia, Dennis Higgins, Bill Voss)	18.00	9.00	5.50
530	Robin Roberts	30.00	15.00	9.00
531	Joe Cunningham	15.00	7.50	4.50
532	Aurelio Monteagudo	15.00	7.50	4.50
533	Jerry Adair	15.00	7.50	4.50
534	Mets Rookies (Dave Eilers, Rob Gardner)	18.00	9.00	5.50
535	Willie Davis	25.00	12.50	7.50
536	Dick Egan	15.00	7.50	4.50
537	Herman Franks	15.00	7.50	4.50
538	Bob Allen	15.00	7.50	4.50

		NR MT	EX	VG
539	Astros Rookies (Bill Heath, Carroll Sembera)	15.00	7.50	4.50
540	Denny McLain	35.00	17.50	10.50
541	Gene Oliver	15.00	7.50	4.50
542	George Smith	15.00	7.50	4.50
543	Roger Craig	20.00	10.00	6.00
544	Cardinals Rookies (Joe Hoerner, George Kernek, Jimmy Williams)	20.00	10.00	6.00
545	Dick Green	20.00	10.00	6.00
546	Dwight Siebler	15.00	7.50	4.50
547	Horace Clarke	20.00	10.00	6.00
548	Gary Kroll	20.00	10.00	6.00
549	Senators Rookies (Al Closter, Casey Cox)	15.00	7.50	4.50
550	Willie McCovey	95.00	45.00	27.00
551	Bob Purkey	20.00	10.00	6.00
552	Birdie Tebbetts	15.00	7.50	4.50
553	Major League Rookies (Pat Garrett, Jackie Warner)	15.00	7.50	4.50
554	Jim Northrup	18.00	9.00	5.50
555	Ron Perranoski	18.00	9.00	5.50
556	Mel Queen	20.00	10.00	6.00
557	Felix Mantilla	15.00	7.50	4.50
558	Red Sox Rookies (Guido Grilli, Pete Magrini, George Scott)	18.00	9.00	5.50
559	Roberto Pena	15.00	7.50	4.50
560	Joel Horlen	15.00	7.50	4.50
561	Choo Choo Coleman	20.00	10.00	6.00
562	Russ Snyder	15.00	7.50	4.50
563	Twins Rookies (Pete Cimino, Cesar Tovar)	18.00	9.00	5.50
564	Bob Chance	15.00	7.50	4.50
565	Jimmy Piersall	30.00	15.00	9.00
566	Mike Cuellar	18.00	9.00	5.50
567	Dick Howser	20.00	10.00	6.00
568	Athletics Rookies (Paul Lindblad, Ron Stone)	15.00	7.50	4.50
569	Orlando McFarlane	15.00	7.50	4.50
570	Art Mahaffey	20.00	10.00	6.00
571	Dave Roberts	15.00	7.50	4.50
572	Bob Priddy	15.00	7.50	4.50
573	Derrell Griffith	15.00	7.50	4.50
574	Mets Rookies (Bill Hepler, Bill Murphy)	18.00	9.00	5.50
575	Earl Wilson	15.00	7.50	4.50
576	Dave Nicholson	20.00	10.00	6.00
577	Jack Lamabe	15.00	7.50	4.50
578	Chi Chi Olivo	15.00	7.50	4.50
579	Orioles Rookies (Frank Bertaina, Gene Brabender, Dave Johnson)	20.00	10.00	6.00
580	Billy Williams	55.00	27.00	16.50
581	Tony Martinez	15.00	7.50	4.50
582	Garry Roggenburk	15.00	7.50	4.50
583	Tigers Team	85.00	42.00	25.00
584	Yankees Rookies (Frank Fernandez, Fritz Peterson)	18.00	9.00	5.50
585	Tony Taylor	15.00	7.50	4.50
586	Claude Raymond	15.00	7.50	4.50
587	Dick Bertell	15.00	7.50	4.50
588	Athletics Rookies (Chuck Dobson, Ken Suarez)	15.00	7.50	4.50
589	Lou Klimchock	18.00	9.00	5.50
590	Bill Skowron	30.00	15.00	9.00
591	N.L. Rookies (Grant Jackson, Bart Shirley)	20.00	10.00	6.00
592	Andre Rodgers	15.00	7.50	4.50
593	Doug Camilli	20.00	10.00	6.00
594	Chico Salmon	15.00	7.50	4.50
595	Larry Jackson	15.00	7.50	4.50
596	Astros Rookies (Nate Colbert, Greg Sims)	18.00	9.00	5.50
597	John Sullivan	15.00	7.50	4.50
598	Gaylord Perry	225.00	50.00	28.00

1966 Topps Rub-Offs

Returning to a concept last tried in 1961, Topps tried an expanded version of Rub-Offs in 1966. Measuring 2-1/16" by 3," the Rub-Offs are in vertical format for the 100 players and horizontal for the 20 team pennants. The player Rub-Offs feature a color photo.

	NR MT	EX	VG
Complete Set:	225.00	112.00	67.00
Common Player:	.60	.30	.20

		NR MT	EX	VG
(73)	Johnny Orsino	.60	.30	.20
(74)	Phil Ortega	.60	.30	.20
(75)	Milt Pappas	.70	.35	.20
(76)	Dick Radatz	.60	.30	.20
(77)	Bobby Richardson	1.50	.70	.45
(78)	Pete Richert	.60	.30	.20
(79)	Brooks Robinson	4.00	2.00	1.25
(80)	Floyd Robinson	.60	.30	.20
(81)	Frank Robinson	3.50	1.75	1.00
(82)	Cookie Rojas	.60	.30	.20
(83)	Pete Rose	20.00	10.00	6.00
(84)	John Roseboro	.60	.30	.20
(85)	Ron Santo	1.00	.50	.30
(86)	Bill Skowron	.70	.35	.20
(87)	Willie Stargell	3.00	1.50	.90
(88)	Mel Stottlemyre	.70	.35	.20
(89)	Dick Stuart	.60	.30	.20
(90)	Ron Swoboda	.60	.30	.20
(91)	Fred Talbot	.60	.30	.20
(92)	Ralph Terry	.60	.30	.20
(93)	Joe Torre	1.00	.50	.30
(94)	Tom Tresh	.70	.35	.20
(95)	Bob Veale	.60	.30	.20
(96)	Pete Ward	.60	.30	.20
(97)	Bill White	.70	.35	.20
(98)	Billy Williams	2.00	1.00	.60
(99)	Jim Wynn	.70	.35	.20
(100)	Carl Yastrzemski	12.00	6.00	3.50
(101)	Angels Pennant	.60	.30	.20
(102)	Astros Pennant	.60	.30	.20
(103)	Athletics Pennant	.60	.30	.20
(104)	Braves Pennant	.60	.30	.20
(105)	Cards Pennant	.60	.30	.20
(106)	Cubs Pennant	.60	.30	.20
(107)	Dodgers Pennant	.60	.30	.20
(108)	Giants Pennant	.60	.30	.20
(109)	Indians Pennant	.60	.30	.20
(110)	Mets Pennant	.60	.30	.20
(111)	Orioles Pennant	.60	.30	.20
(112)	Phillies Pennant	.60	.30	.20
(113)	Pirates Pennant	.60	.30	.20
(114)	Red Sox Pennant	.60	.30	.20
(115)	Reds Pennant	.60	.30	.20
(116)	Senators Pennant	.60	.30	.20
(117)	Tigers Pennant	.60	.30	.20
(118)	Twins Pennant	.60	.30	.20
(119)	White Sox Pennant	.60	.30	.20
(120)	Yankees Pennant	.60	.30	.20

(1)	Hank Aaron	8.00	4.00	2.50
(2)	Jerry Adair	.60	.30	.20
(3)	Richie Allen	1.00	.50	.30
(4)	Jesus Alou	.60	.30	.20
(5)	Max Alvis	.60	.30	.20
(6)	Bob Aspromonte	.60	.30	.20
(7)	Ernie Banks	3.50	1.75	1.00
(8)	Earl Battey	.70	.35	.20
(9)	Curt Blefary	.60	.30	.20
(10)	Ken Boyer	1.00	.50	.30
(11)	Bob Bruce	.60	.30	.20
(12)	Jim Bunning	1.50	.70	.45
(13)	Johnny Callison	.70	.35	.20
(14)	Bert Campaneris	.70	.35	.20
(15)	Jose Cardenal	.60	.30	.20
(16)	Dean Chance	.60	.30	.20
(17)	Ed Charles	.60	.30	.20
(18)	Bob Clemente	7.00	3.50	2.00
(19)	Tony Cloninger	.60	.30	.20
(20)	Rocky Colavito	1.00	.50	.30
(21)	Tony Conigliaro	1.00	.50	.30
(22)	Vic Davalillo	.60	.30	.20
(23)	Willie Davis	.70	.35	.20
(24)	Don Drysdale	3.00	1.50	.90
(25)	Sammy Ellis	.60	.30	.20
(26)	Dick Ellsworth	.60	.30	.20
(27)	Ron Fairly	.70	.35	.20
(28)	Dick Farrell	.60	.30	.20
(29)	Eddie Fisher	.60	.30	.20
(30)	Jack Fisher	.60	.30	.20
(31)	Curt Flood	.70	.35	.20
(32)	Whitey Ford	3.50	1.75	1.00
(33)	Bill Freehan	.70	.35	.20
(34)	Jim Fregosi	.70	.35	.20
(35)	Bob Gibson	3.00	1.50	.90
(36)	Jim Grant	.60	.30	.20
(37)	Jimmie Hall	.60	.30	.20
(38)	Ken Harrelson	.70	.35	.20
(39)	Jim Hart	.60	.30	.20
(40)	Joel Horlen	.60	.30	.20
(41)	Willie Horton	.70	.35	.20
(42)	Frank Howard	1.00	.50	.30
(43)	Deron Johnson	.60	.30	.20
(44)	Al Kaline	4.00	2.00	1.25
(45)	Harmon Killebrew	4.00	2.00	1.25
(46)	Bobby Knoop	.60	.30	.20
(47)	Sandy Koufax	7.00	3.50	2.00
(48)	Ed Kranepool	.60	.30	.20
(49)	Gary Kroll	.60	.30	.20
(50)	Don Landrum	.60	.30	.20
(51)	Vernon Law	.70	.35	.20
(52)	Johnny Lewis	.60	.30	.20
(53)	Don Lock	.60	.30	.20
(54)	Mickey Lolich	1.00	.50	.30
(55)	Jim Maloney	.60	.30	.20
(56)	Felix Mantilla	.60	.30	.20
(57)	Mickey Mantle	40.00	20.00	12.00
(58)	Juan Marichal	3.00	1.50	.90
(59)	Ed Mathews	3.00	1.50	.90
(60)	Willie Mays	8.00	4.00	2.50
(61)	Bill Mazeroski	1.00	.50	.30
(62)	Dick McAuliffe	.60	.30	.20
(63)	Tim McCarver	.70	.35	.20
(64)	Willie McCovey	3.00	1.50	.90
(65)	Sammy McDowell	.70	.35	.20
(66)	Ken McMullen	.60	.30	.20
(67)	Denis Menke	.60	.30	.20
(68)	Bill Monbouquette	.60	.30	.20
(69)	Joe Morgan	2.00	1.00	.60
(70)	Fred Newman	.60	.30	.20
(71)	John O'Donoghue	.60	.30	.20
(72)	Tony Oliva	1.00	.50	.30

1967 Topps

This 609-card set of 2-1/2" by 3-1/2" cards marked the largest set up to that time for Topps. Card fronts feature large color photographs bordered by white. The player's name and position are printed at the top along with the team at the bottom. Across the front of the card with the exception of #254 (Milt Pappas) there is a facsimile autograph. The backs were the first to be done vertically, although they continued to carry familiar statistical and biographical information. The only subsets are statistical leaders and World Series highlights. Rookie cards are done by team or league with two players per card. The high numbers (#'s 534-609) in '67 are quite scarce, and while it is known that some are even scarcer, by virtue of having been short-printed in relation to the rest of the series, there is no general agreement on which cards are involved.

		NR MT	EX	VG
	Complete Set:	3300.00	1650.00	1000.
	Common Player: 1-110	.60	.30	.20
	Common Player: 111-370	.70	.35	.20
	Common Player: 371-457	.80	.40	.25
	Common Player: 458-533	3.00	1.50	.90
	Common Player: 534-609	5.00	2.50	1.50
1	The Champs (Hank Bauer, Brooks Robinson, Frank Robinson)	8.00	4.00	2.50
2	Jack Hamilton	.80	.40	.25
3	Duke Sims	.60	.30	.20
4	Hal Lanier	.80	.40	.25
5	Whitey Ford	12.00	6.00	3.50
6	Dick Simpson	.60	.30	.20
7	Don McMahon	.60	.30	.20
8	Chuck Harrison	.60	.30	.20
9	Ron Hansen	.60	.30	.20
10	Matty Alou	.80	.40	.25
11	Barry Moore	.60	.30	.20
12	Dodgers Rookies (Jimmy Campanis, Bill Singer)	.70	.35	.20
13	Joe Sparma	.60	.30	.20
14	Phil Linz	.60	.30	.20
15	Earl Battey	.70	.35	.20
16	Bill Hands	.60	.30	.20
17	Jim Gosger	.60	.30	.20
18	Gene Oliver	.60	.30	.20
19	Jim McGlothlin	.60	.30	.20
20	Orlando Cepeda	4.00	2.00	1.25
21	Dave Bristol	.60	.30	.20
22	Gene Brabender	.60	.30	.20
23	Larry Elliot	.70	.35	.20
24	Bob Allen	.60	.30	.20
25	Elston Howard	3.00	1.50	.90
26a	Bob Priddy (no trade statement)	8.00	4.00	2.50
26b	Bob Priddy (with trade statement)	.60	.30	.20
27	Bob Saverine	.60	.30	.20
28	Barry Latman	.60	.30	.20
29	Tommy McCraw	.60	.30	.20
30	Al Kaline	15.00	7.50	4.50
31	Jim Brewer	.60	.30	.20
32	Bob Bailey	.60	.30	.20
33	Athletics Rookies (Sal Bando, Randy Schwartz)	1.75	.90	.50
34	Pete Cimino	.60	.30	.20
35	Rico Carty	1.00	.50	.30
36	Bob Tillman	.60	.30	.20
37	Rick Wise	.70	.35	.20
38	Bob Johnson	.60	.30	.20
39	Curt Simmons	.80	.40	.25
40	Rick Reichardt	.60	.30	.20
41	Joe Hoerner	.60	.30	.20
42	Mets Team	3.00	1.50	.90
43	Chico Salmon	.60	.30	.20
44	Joe Nuxhall	.80	.40	.25
45	Roger Maris	25.00	12.50	7.50
46	Lindy McDaniel	.60	.30	.20
47	Ken McMullen	.60	.30	.20
48	Bill Freehan	.80	.40	.25
49	Roy Face	1.25	.60	.40
50	Tony Oliva	2.50	1.25	.70
51	Astros Rookies (Dave Adlesh, Wes Bales)	.60	.30	.20
52	Dennis Higgins	.60	.30	.20
53	Clay Dalrymple	.60	.30	.20
54	Dick Green	.60	.30	.20
55	Don Drysdale	12.00	6.00	3.50
56	Jose Tartabull	.60	.30	.20
57	Pat Jarvis	.70	.35	.20
58	Paul Schaal	.60	.30	.20
59	Ralph Terry	.80	.40	.25
60	Luis Aparicio	5.00	2.50	1.50
61	Gordy Coleman	.60	.30	.20
62	Checklist 1-109 (Frank Robinson)	3.00	1.50	.90
63	Cards' Clubbers (Lou Brock, Curt Flood)	4.50	2.25	1.25
64	Fred Valentine	.60	.30	.20
65	Tom Haller	.70	.35	.20
66	Manny Mota	.80	.40	.25
67	Ken Berry	.60	.30	.20
68	Bob Buhl	.70	.35	.20
69	Vic Davalillo	.70	.35	.20
70	Ron Santo	1.75	.90	.50
71	Camilo Pascual	.70	.35	.20
72	Tigers Rookies (George Korince, John Matchick)	.60	.30	.20
73	Rusty Staub	2.50	1.25	.70
74	Wes Stock	.60	.30	.20

		NR MT	EX	VG
75	George Scott	1.00	.50	.30
76	Jim Barbieri	.60	.30	.20
77	Dooley Womack	.80	.40	.25
78	Pat Corrales	1.00	.50	.30
79	Bubba Morton	.60	.30	.20
80	Jim Maloney	.70	.35	.20
81	Eddie Stanky	.70	.35	.20
82	Steve Barber	.60	.30	.20
83	Ollie Brown	.60	.30	.20
84	Tommie Sisk	.60	.30	.20
85	Johnny Callison	1.00	.50	.30
86a	Mike McCormick (no trade statement)	9.00	4.50	2.75
86b	Mike McCormick (with trade statement)	.70	.35	.20
87	George Altman	.60	.30	.20
88	Mickey Lolich	2.25	1.25	.70
89	Felix Millan	.80	.40	.25
90	Jim Nash	.60	.30	.20
91	Johnny Lewis	.70	.35	.20
92	Ray Washburn	.60	.30	.20
93	Yankees Rookies (Stan Bahnsen, Bobby Murcer)	2.50	1.25	.70
94	Ron Fairly	.80	.40	.25
95	Sonny Siebert	.70	.35	.20
96	Art Shamsky	.60	.30	.20
97	Mike Cuellar	.80	.40	.25
98	Rich Rollins	.60	.30	.20
99	Lee Stange	.60	.30	.20
100	Frank Robinson	10.00	5.00	3.00
101	Ken Johnson	.60	.30	.20
102	Phillies Team	2.00	1.00	.60
103a	Checklist 110-196 (Mickey Mantle) (170 is D McAuliffe)	8.00	4.00	2.50
103b	Checklist 110-196 (Mickey Mantle) (170 is D. McAuliffe)	6.00	3.00	1.75
104	Minnie Rojas	.60	.30	.20
105	Ken Boyer	2.00	1.00	.60
106	Randy Hundley	.70	.35	.20
107	Joel Horlen	.60	.30	.20
108	Alex Johnson	.60	.30	.20
109	Tribe Thumpers (Rocky Colavito, Leon Wagner)	1.50	.70	.45
110	Jack Aker	.60	.30	.20
111	John Kennedy	.70	.35	.20
112	Dave Wickersham	.70	.35	.20
113	Dave Nicholson	.70	.35	.20
114	Jack Baldschun	.70	.35	.20
115	Paul Casanova	.70	.35	.20
116	Herman Franks	.70	.35	.20
117	Darrell Brandon	.70	.35	.20
118	Bernie Allen	.70	.35	.20
119	Wade Blasingame	.70	.35	.20
120	Floyd Robinson	.70	.35	.20
121	Ed Bressoud	.80	.40	.25
122	George Brunet	.70	.35	.20
123	Pirates Rookies (Jim Price, Luke Walker)	.70	.35	.20
124	Jim Stewart	.70	.35	.20
125	Moe Drabowsky	.70	.35	.20
126	Tony Taylor	.70	.35	.20
127	John O'Donoghue	.70	.35	.20
128	Ed Spiezio	.70	.35	.20
129	Phil Roof	.70	.35	.20
130	Phil Regan	.70	.35	.20
131	Yankees Team	4.00	2.00	1.25
132	Ozzie Virgil	.70	.35	.20
133	Ron Kline	.70	.35	.20
134	Gates Brown	.70	.35	.20
135	Deron Johnson	.70	.35	.20
136	Carroll Sembera	.70	.35	.20
137	Twins Rookies (Ron Clark, Jim Ollom)	.70	.35	.20
138	Dick Kelley	.70	.35	.20
139	Dalton Jones	.70	.35	.20
140	Willie Stargell	15.00	7.50	4.50
141	John Miller	.70	.35	.20
142	Jackie Brandt	.70	.35	.20
143	Sox Sockers (Don Buford, Pete Ward)	.80	.40	.25
144	Bill Hepler	.80	.40	.25
145	Larry Brown	.70	.35	.20
146	Steve Carlton	60.00	30.00	18.00
147	Tom Egan	.70	.35	.20
148	Adolfo Phillips	.70	.35	.20
149	Joe Moeller	.70	.35	.20
150	Mickey Mantle	200.00	80.00	50.00
151	World Series Game 1 (Moe Mows Down 11)	2.00	1.00	.60
152	World Series Game 2 (Palmer Blanks Dodgers)	3.50	1.75	1.00

		NR MT	EX	VG
153	World Series Game 3 (Blair's Homer Defeats L.A.)	2.00	1.00	.60
154	World Series Game 4 (Orioles Win 4th Straight)	2.00	1.00	.60
155	World Series Summary (The Winners Celebrate)	2.00	1.00	.60
156	Ron Herbel	.70	.35	.20
157	Danny Cater	.70	.35	.20
158	Jimmy Coker	.70	.35	.20
159	Bruce Howard	.70	.35	.20
160	Willie Davis	1.25	.60	.40
161	Dick Williams	1.25	.60	.40
162	Billy O'Dell	.70	.35	.20
163	Vic Roznovsky	.70	.35	.20
164	Dwight Siebler	.70	.35	.20
165	Cleon Jones	.80	.40	.25
166	Ed Mathews	8.00	4.00	2.50
167	Senators Rookies (Joe Coleman, Tim Cullen)	.80	.40	.25
168	Ray Culp	.70	.35	.20
169	Horace Clarke	1.00	.50	.30
170	Dick McAuliffe	.80	.40	.25
171	Calvin Koonce	.70	.35	.20
172	Bill Heath	.70	.35	.20
173	Cardinals Team	2.00	1.00	.60
174	Dick Radatz	.80	.40	.25
175	Bobby Knoop	.70	.35	.20
176	Sammy Ellis	.70	.35	.20
177	Tito Fuentes	.70	.35	.20
178	John Buzhardt	.70	.35	.20
179	Braves Rookies (Cecil Upshaw, Chas. Vaughn)	.70	.35	.20
180	Curt Blefary	.70	.35	.20
181	Terry Fox	.70	.35	.20
182	Ed Charles	.70	.35	.20
183	Jim Pagliaroni	.70	.35	.20
184	George Thomas	.70	.35	.20
185	Ken Holtzman	2.75	1.50	.80
186	Mets Maulers (Ed Kranepool, Ron Swoboda)	1.50	.70	.45
187	Pedro Ramos	.70	.35	.20
188	Ken Harrelson	1.50	.70	.45
189	Chuck Hinton	.70	.35	.20
190	Turk Farrell	.70	.35	.20
191a	Checklist 197-283 (Willie Mays) (214 is Dick Kelley)	5.00	2.50	1.50
191b	Checklist 197-283 (Willie Mays) (214 is Tom Kelley)	4.00	2.00	1.25
192	Fred Gladding	.70	.35	.20
193	Jose Cardenal	.80	.40	.25
194	Bob Allison	.90	.45	.25
195	Al Jackson	.70	.35	.20
196	Johnny Romano	.70	.35	.20
197	Ron Perranoski	.80	.40	.25
198	Chuck Hiller	.80	.40	.25
199	Billy Hitchcock	.70	.35	.20
200	Willie Mays	55.00	28.00	16.50
201	Hal Reniff	1.00	.50	.30
202	Johnny Edwards	.70	.35	.20
203	Al McBean	.70	.35	.20
204	Orioles Rookies (*Mike Epstein*, Tom Phoebus)	.90	.45	.25
205	Dick Groat	1.50	.70	.45
206	Dennis Bennett	.70	.35	.20
207	John Orsino	.70	.35	.20
208	Jack Lamabe	.70	.35	.20
209	Joe Nossek	.70	.35	.20
210	Bob Gibson	10.00	5.00	3.00
211	Twins Team	2.00	1.00	.60
212	Chris Zachary	.70	.35	.20
213	*Jay Johnstone*	1.75	.90	.50
214	Tom Kelley	.70	.35	.20
215	Ernie Banks	15.00	7.50	4.50
216	Bengal Belters (Norm Cash, Al Kaline)	3.50	1.75	1.00
217	Rob Gardner	.80	.40	.25
218	Wes Parker	.80	.40	.25
219	Clay Carroll	.80	.40	.25
220	Jim Hart	.80	.40	.25
221	Woody Fryman	.80	.40	.25
222	Reds Rookies (Lee May, Darrell Osteen)	1.00	.50	.30
223	Mike Ryan	.70	.35	.20
224	Walt Bond	.70	.35	.20
225	Mel Stottlemyre	2.25	1.25	.70
226	Julian Javier	.80	.40	.25
227	Paul Lindblad	.70	.35	.20
228	Gil Hodges	5.00	2.50	1.50
229	Larry Jackson	.70	.35	.20
230	Boog Powell	2.50	1.25	.70
231	John Bateman	.70	.35	.20
232	Don Buford	.80	.40	.25
233	A.L. ERA Leaders (Steve Hargan, Joel Horlen, Gary Peters)	2.00	1.00	.60
234	N.L. ERA Leaders (Mike Cuellar, Sandy Koufax, Juan Marichal)	4.00	2.00	1.25
235	A.L. Pitching Leaders (Jim Kaat, Denny McLain, Earl Wilson)	2.50	1.25	.70
236	N.L. Pitching Leaders (Bob Gibson, Sandy Koufax, Juan Marichal, Gaylord Perry)	5.00	2.50	1.50
237	A.L. Strikeout Leaders (Jim Kaat, Sam McDowell, Earl Wilson)	2.50	1.25	.70
238	N.L. Strikeout Leaders (Jim Bunning, Sandy Koufax, Bob Veale)	4.00	2.00	1.25
239	AL 1966 Batting Leaders (Al Kaline, Tony Oliva, Frank Robinson)	4.00	2.00	1.25
240	N.L. Batting Leaders (Felipe Alou, Matty Alou, Rico Carty)	2.00	1.00	.60
241	A.L. RBI Leaders (Harmon Killebrew, Boog Powell, Frank Robinson)	3.50	1.75	1.00
242	N.L. RBI Leaders (Hank Aaron, Richie Allen, Bob Clemente)	5.00	2.50	1.50
243	A.L. Home Run Leaders (Harmon Killebrew, Boog Powell, Frank Robinson)	3.50	1.75	1.00
244	N.L. Home Run Leaders (Hank Aaron, Richie Allen, Willie Mays)	5.00	2.50	1.50
245	Curt Flood	1.50	.70	.45
246	Jim Perry	1.00	.50	.30
247	Jerry Lumpe	.80	.40	.25
248	Gene Mauch	.80	.40	.25
249	Nick Willhite	.70	.35	.20
250	Hank Aaron	60.00	30.00	18.00
251	Woody Held	.70	.35	.20
252	Bob Bolin	.70	.35	.20
253	Indians Rookies (Bill Davis, Gus Gil)	.70	.35	.20
254	Milt Pappas	.80	.40	.25
255	Frank Howard	2.50	1.25	.70
256	Bob Hendley	.70	.35	.20
257	Charley Smith	1.00	.50	.30
258	Lee Maye	.70	.35	.20
259	Don Dennis	.70	.35	.20
260	Jim Lefebvre	.80	.40	.25
261	John Wyatt	.70	.35	.20
262	Athletics Team	2.00	1.00	.60
263	Hank Aguirre	.70	.35	.20
264	Ron Swoboda	.80	.40	.25
265	Lou Burdette	1.50	.70	.45
266	Pitt Power (Donn Clendenon, Willie Stargell)	3.50	1.75	1.00
267	Don Schwall	.70	.35	.20
268	John Briggs	.70	.35	.20
269	Don Nottebart	.70	.35	.20
270	Zoilo Versalles	.80	.40	.25
271	Eddie Watt	.70	.35	.20
272	Cubs Rookies (Bill Connors, Dave Dowling)	.70	.35	.20
273	Dick Lines	.70	.35	.20
274	Bob Aspromonte	.70	.35	.20
275	Fred Whitfield	.70	.35	.20
276	Bruce Brubaker	.70	.35	.20
277	Steve Whitaker	1.00	.50	.30
278	Checklist 284-370 (Jim Kaat)	3.00	1.50	.90
279	Frank Linzy	.70	.35	.20
280	Tony Conigliaro	2.00	1.00	.60
281	Bob Rodgers	.70	.35	.20
282	Johnny Odom	.80	.40	.25
283	Gene Alley	.80	.40	.25
284	Johnny Podres	3.00	1.50	.90
285	Lou Brock	15.00	7.50	4.50
286	Wayne Causey	.70	.35	.20
287	Mets Rookies (Greg Goossen, Bart Shirley)	.80	.40	.25
288	Denver Lemaster	.70	.35	.20
289	Tom Tresh	1.75	.90	.50
290	Bill White	1.00	.50	.30
291	Jim Hannan	.70	.35	.20
292	Don Pavletich	.70	.35	.20
293	Ed Kirkpatrick	.70	.35	.20
294	Walt Alston	3.25	1.75	1.00
295	Sam McDowell	1.00	.50	.30
296	Glenn Beckert	.80	.40	.25
297	Dave Morehead	.70	.35	.20
298	Ron Davis	.70	.35	.20
299	Norm Siebern	.80	.40	.25
300	Jim Kaat	4.50	2.25	1.25
301	Jesse Gonder	.70	.35	.20
302	Orioles Team	2.00	1.00	.60
303	Gil Blanco	.70	.35	.20
304	Phil Gagliano	.70	.35	.20
305	Earl Wilson	.70	.35	.20

	NR MT	EX	VG
306 *Bud Harrelson*	1.75	.90	.50
307 Jim Beauchamp	.70	.35	.20
308 Al Downing	1.25	.60	.40
309 Hurlers Beware (Richie Allen, Johnny Callison)	2.00	1.00	.60
310 Gary Peters	.80	.40	.25
311 Ed Brinkman	.80	.40	.25
312 Don Mincher	.80	.40	.25
313 Bob Lee	.70	.35	.20
314 Red Sox Rookies (*Mike Andrews, Reggie Smith*)	3.00	1.50	.90
315 Billy Williams	8.00	4.00	2.50
316 Jack Kralick	.70	.35	.20
317 Cesar Tovar	.70	.35	.20
318 Dave Giusti	.70	.35	.20
319 Paul Blair	.80	.40	.25
320 Gaylord Perry	8.00	4.00	2.50
321 Mayo Smith	.70	.35	.20
322 Jose Pagan	.70	.35	.20
323 Mike Hershberger	.70	.35	.20
324 Hal Woodeshick	.70	.35	.20
325 Chico Cardenas	.70	.35	.20
326 Bob Uecker	20.00	10.00	6.00
327 Angels Team	2.00	1.00	.60
328 Clete Boyer	.90	.45	.25
329 Charlie Lau	.80	.40	.25
330 Claude Osteen	.80	.40	.25
331 Joe Foy	.70	.35	.20
332 Jesus Alou	.70	.35	.20
333 Ferguson Jenkins	5.00	2.50	1.50
334 Twin Terrors (Bob Allison, Harmon Killebrew)	3.50	1.75	1.00
335 Bob Veale	.80	.40	.25
336 Joe Azcue	.70	.35	.20
337 Joe Morgan	10.00	5.00	3.00
338 Bob Locker	.70	.35	.20
339 Chico Ruiz	.70	.35	.20
340 Joe Pepitone	2.00	1.00	.60
341 Giants Rookies (*Dick Dietz*, Bill Sorrell)	.80	.40	.25
342 Hank Fischer	.70	.35	.20
343 Tom Satriano	.70	.35	.20
344 Ossie Chavarria	.70	.35	.20
345 Stu Miller	.70	.35	.20
346 Jim Hickman	.80	.40	.25
347 Grady Hatton	.70	.35	.20
348 Tug McGraw	2.25	1.25	.70
349 Bob Chance	.70	.35	.20
350 Joe Torre	2.00	1.00	.60
351 Vern Law	1.25	.60	.40
352 Ray Oyler	.70	.35	.20
353 Bill McCool	.70	.35	.20
354 Cubs Team	2.00	1.00	.60
355 Carl Yastrzemski	90.00	45.00	27.00
356 Larry Jaster	.70	.35	.20
357 Bill Skowron	1.50	.70	.45
358 Ruben Amaro	1.00	.50	.30
359 Dick Ellsworth	.70	.35	.20
360 Leon Wagner	.80	.40	.25
361 Checklist 371-457 (Bob Clemente)	4.50	2.25	1.25
362 Darold Knowles	.70	.35	.20
363 Dave Johnson	2.00	1.00	.60
364 Claude Raymond	.70	.35	.20
365 John Roseboro	.80	.40	.25
366 Andy Kosco	.70	.35	.20
367 Angels Rookies (Bill Kelso, Don Wallace)	.70	.35	.20
368 Jack Hiatt	.70	.35	.20
369 Jim Hunter	8.00	4.00	2.50
370 Tommy Davis	1.50	.70	.45
371 Jim Lonborg	1.50	.70	.45
372 Mike de la Hoz	.80	.40	.25
373 White Sox Rookies (Duane Josephson, Fred Klages)	.80	.40	.25
374 Mel Queen	.80	.40	.25
375 Jake Gibbs	1.00	.50	.30
376 Don Lock	.80	.40	.25
377 Luis Tiant	2.25	1.25	.70
378 Tigers Team	3.00	1.50	.90
379 Jerry May	.80	.40	.25
380 Dean Chance	.90	.45	.25
381 Dick Schofield	.80	.40	.25
382 Dave McNally	1.00	.50	.30
383 Ken Henderson	.80	.40	.25
384 Cardinals Rookies (Jim Cosman, Dick Hughes)	.80	.40	.25
385 Jim Fregosi	1.25	.60	.40
386 Dick Selma	.90	.45	.25
387 Cap Peterson	.80	.40	.25
388 Arnold Earley	.80	.40	.25
389 Al Dark	.90	.45	.25
390 Jim Wynn	1.00	.50	.30
391 Wilbur Wood	.90	.45	.25
392 Tommy Harper	.90	.45	.25
393 Jim Bouton	2.25	1.25	.70
394 Jake Wood	.80	.40	.25
395 Chris Short	1.00	.50	.30
396 Atlanta Aces (Tony Cloninger, Denis Menke)	1.00	.50	.30
397 Willie Smith	.80	.40	.25
398 Jeff Torborg	.90	.45	.25
399 Al Worthington	.80	.40	.25
400 Bob Clemente	55.00	28.00	16.50
401 Jim Coates	.80	.40	.25
402 Phillies Rookies (Grant Jackson, Billy Wilson)	.80	.40	.25
403 Dick Nen	.80	.40	.25
404 Nelson Briles	.90	.45	.25
405 Russ Snyder	.80	.40	.25
406 Lee Elia	.90	.45	.25
407 Reds Team	2.50	1.25	.70
408 Jim Northrup	.90	.45	.25
409 Ray Sadecki	.80	.40	.25
410 Lou Johnson	.80	.40	.25
411 Dick Howser	1.50	.70	.45
412 Astros Rookies (Norm Miller, *Doug Rader*)	1.00	.50	.30
413 Jerry Grote	.90	.45	.25
414 Casey Cox	.80	.40	.25
415 Sonny Jackson	.80	.40	.25
416 Roger Repoz	.80	.40	.25
417 Bob Bruce	.80	.40	.25
418 Sam Mele	.80	.40	.25
419 Don Kessinger	.90	.45	.25
420 Denny McLain	3.00	1.50	.90
421 Dal Maxvill	.90	.45	.25
422 Hoyt Wilhelm	8.00	4.00	2.50
423 Fence Busters (Willie Mays, Willie McCovey)	12.00	6.00	3.50
424 Pedro Gonzalez	.80	.40	.25
425 Pete Mikkelsen	.80	.40	.25
426 Lou Clinton	1.00	.50	.30
427 Ruben Gomez	.80	.40	.25
428 Dodgers Rookies (Tom Hutton, *Gene Michael*)	1.00	.50	.30
429 Garry Roggenburk	.80	.40	.25
430 Pete Rose	75.00	37.00	22.00
431 Ted Uhlaender	.80	.40	.25
432 Jimmie Hall	.80	.40	.25
433 Al Luplow	.90	.45	.25
434 Eddie Fisher	.80	.40	.25
435 Mack Jones	.80	.40	.25
436 Pete Ward	.80	.40	.25
437 Senators Team	2.25	1.25	.70
438 Chuck Dobson	.80	.40	.25
439 Byron Browne	.80	.40	.25
440 Steve Hargan	.80	.40	.25
441 Jim Davenport	.80	.40	.25
442 Yankees Rookies (*Bill Robinson*, Joe Verbanic)	1.25	.60	.40
443 Tito Francona	.90	.45	.25
444 George Smith	.80	.40	.25
445 Don Sutton	15.00	7.50	4.50
446 Russ Nixon	.80	.40	.25
447 Bo Belinsky	1.00	.50	.30
448 Harry Walker	.90	.45	.25
449 Orlando Pena	.80	.40	.25
450 Richie Allen	3.00	1.50	.90
451 Fred Newman	.80	.40	.25
452 Ed Kranepool	1.00	.50	.30
453 Aurelio Monteagudo	.80	.40	.25
454a Checklist 458-533 (Juan Marichal) (left ear shows)	5.00	2.50	1.50
454b Checklist 458-533 (Juan Marichal) (no left ear)	4.00	2.00	1.25
455 Tommie Agee	.70	.35	.20
456 Phil Niekro	7.00	3.50	2.00
457 Andy Etchebarren	.80	.40	.25
458 Lee Thomas	3.00	1.50	.90
459 Senators Rookies (*Dick Bosman*, Pete Craig)	3.75	2.00	1.25
460 Harmon Killebrew	30.00	15.00	9.00
461 Bob Miller	3.00	1.50	.90
462 Bob Barton	3.00	1.50	.90
463 Tribe Hill Aces (Sam McDowell, Sonny Siebert)	4.00	2.00	1.25
464 Dan Coombs	3.00	1.50	.90
465 Willie Horton	3.75	2.00	1.25
466 Bobby Wine	3.00	1.50	.90
467 Jim O'Toole	3.00	1.50	.90
468 Ralph Houk	4.50	2.25	1.25

		NR MT	EX	VG
469	Len Gabrielson	3.00	1.50	.90
470	Bob Shaw	3.00	1.50	.90
471	Rene Lachemann	3.00	1.50	.90
472	Pirates Rookies (John Gelnar, George Spriggs)	3.00	1.50	.90
473	Jose Santiago	3.00	1.50	.90
474	Bob Tolan	3.75	2.00	1.25
475	Jim Palmer	40.00	20.00	12.00
476	Tony Perez	50.00	30.00	15.00
477	Braves Team	4.75	2.50	1.50
478	Bob Humphreys	3.00	1.50	.90
479	Gary Bell	3.00	1.50	.90
480	Willie McCovey	15.00	7.50	4.50
481	Leo Durocher	4.50	2.25	1.25
482	Bill Monbouquette	3.75	2.00	1.25
483	Jim Landis	3.00	1.50	.90
484	Jerry Adair	3.00	1.50	.90
485	Tim McCarver	4.50	2.25	1.25
486	Twins Rookies (Rich Reese, Bill Whitby)	3.00	1.50	.90
487	Tom Reynolds	3.00	1.50	.90
488	Gerry Arrigo	3.00	1.50	.90
489	Doug Clemens	3.00	1.50	.90
490	Tony Cloninger	3.75	2.00	1.25
491	Sam Bowens	3.00	1.50	.90
492	Pirates Team	4.75	2.50	1.50
493	Phil Ortega	3.00	1.50	.90
494	Bill Rigney	3.00	1.50	.90
495	Fritz Peterson	4.00	2.00	1.25
496	Orlando McFarlane	3.00	1.50	.90
497	Ron Campbell	3.00	1.50	.90
498	Larry Dierker	3.75	2.00	1.25
499	Indians Rookies (George Culver, Jose Vidal)	3.00	1.50	.90
500	Juan Marichal	15.00	7.50	4.50
501	Jerry Zimmerman	3.00	1.50	.90
502	Derrell Griffith	3.00	1.50	.90
503	Dodgers Team	5.00	2.50	1.50
504	Orlando Martinez	3.00	1.50	.90
505	Tommy Helms	3.00	1.50	.90
506	Smoky Burgess	4.00	2.00	1.25
507	Orioles Rookies (Ed Barnowski, Larry Haney)	3.00	1.50	.90
508	Dick Hall	3.00	1.50	.90
509	Jim King	3.00	1.50	.90
510	Bill Mazeroski	4.50	2.25	1.25
511	Don Wert	3.00	1.50	.90
512	Red Schoendienst	6.00	3.00	1.75
513	Marcelino Lopez	3.00	1.50	.90
514	John Werhas	3.00	1.50	.90
515	Bert Campaneris	4.00	2.00	1.25
516	Giants Team	4.75	2.50	1.50
517	Fred Talbot	3.75	2.00	1.25
518	Denis Menke	3.00	1.50	.90
519	Ted Davidson	3.00	1.50	.90
520	Max Alvis	3.00	1.50	.90
521	Bird Bombers (Curt Blefary, Boog Powell)	4.50	2.25	1.25
522	John Stephenson	3.00	1.50	.90
523	Jim Merritt	3.00	1.50	.90
524	Felix Mantilla	3.00	1.50	.90
525	Ron Hunt	3.75	2.00	1.25
526	Tigers Rookies (Pat Dobson, George Korince)	3.75	2.00	1.25
527	Dennis Ribant	3.00	1.50	.90
528	Rico Petrocelli	3.75	2.00	1.25
529	Gary Wagner	3.00	1.50	.90
530	Felipe Alou	4.00	2.00	1.25
531	Checklist 534-609 (Brooks Robinson)	5.00	2.50	1.50
532	Jim Hicks	3.00	1.50	.90
533	Jack Fisher	3.00	1.50	.90
534	Hank Bauer	8.00	4.00	2.50
535	Donn Clendenon	6.00	3.00	1.75
536	Cubs Rookies (Joe Niekro, Paul Popovich)	25.00	12.50	7.50
537	Chuck Estrada	5.00	2.50	1.50
538	J.C. Martin	8.00	4.00	2.50
539	Dick Egan	5.00	2.50	1.50
540	Norm Cash	25.00	12.50	7.50
541	Joe Gibbon	8.00	4.00	2.50
542	Athletics Rookies (Rick Monday, Tony Pierce)	12.00	6.00	3.50
543	Dan Schneider	8.00	4.00	2.50
544	Indians Team	12.00	6.00	3.50
545	Jim Grant	8.00	4.00	2.50
546	Woody Woodward	8.00	4.00	2.50
547	Red Sox Rookies (Russ Gibson, Bill Rohr)	8.00	4.00	2.50
548	Tony Gonzalez	5.00	2.50	1.50
549	Jack Sanford	12.00	6.00	3.50
550	Vada Pinson	6.00	3.00	1.75
551	Doug Camilli	5.00	2.50	1.50
552	Ted Savage	5.00	2.50	1.50
553	Yankees Rookies (Mike Hegan, Thad Tillotson)	15.00	7.50	4.50
554	Andre Rodgers	5.00	2.50	1.50
555	Don Cardwell	8.00	4.00	2.50
556	Al Weis	5.00	2.50	1.50
557	Al Ferrara	12.00	6.00	3.50
558	Orioles Rookies (*Mark Belanger*, Bill Dillman)	18.00	9.00	5.50
559	Dick Tracewski	5.00	2.50	1.50
560	Jim Bunning	40.00	20.00	12.00
561	Sandy Alomar	8.00	4.00	2.50
562	Steve Blass	6.00	3.00	1.75
563	Joe Adcock	18.00	9.00	5.50
564	Astros Rookies (Alonzo Harris, Aaron Pointer)	8.00	4.00	2.50
565	Lew Krausse	8.00	4.00	2.50
566	Gary Geiger	5.00	2.50	1.50
567	Steve Hamilton	8.00	4.00	2.50
568	John Sullivan	8.00	4.00	2.50
569	A.L. Rookies (Hank Allen, *Rod Carew*)	250.00	100.00	63.00
570	Maury Wills	75.00	37.00	22.00
571	Larry Sherry	12.00	6.00	3.50
572	Don Demeter	12.00	6.00	3.50
573	White Sox Team	15.00	7.50	4.50
574	Jerry Buchek	12.00	6.00	3.50
575	*Dave Boswell*	12.00	6.00	3.50
576	N.L. Rookies (Norm Gigon, Ramon Hernandez)	18.00	9.00	5.50
577	Bill Short	8.00	4.00	2.50
578	John Boccabella	8.00	4.00	2.50
579	Bill Henry	8.00	4.00	2.50
580	Rocky Colavito	35.00	17.50	10.50
581	Mets Rookies (Bill Denehy, *Tom Seaver*)	875.00	350.00	219.00
582	Jim Owens	5.00	2.50	1.50
583	Ray Barker	8.00	4.00	2.50
584	Jim Piersall	18.00	9.00	5.50
585	Wally Bunker	8.00	4.00	2.50
586	Manny Jimenez	8.00	4.00	2.50
587	N.L. Rookies (Don Shaw, Gary Sutherland)	15.00	7.50	4.50
588	Johnny Klippstein	5.00	2.50	1.50
589	Dave Ricketts	5.00	2.50	1.50
590	Pete Richert	8.00	4.00	2.50
591	Ty Cline	5.00	2.50	1.50
592	N.L. Rookies (Jim Shellenback, Ron Willis)	7.00	3.50	2.00
593	Wes Westrum	8.00	4.00	2.50
594	Dan Osinski	8.00	4.00	2.50
595	Cookie Rojas	5.00	2.50	1.50
596	Galen Cisco	5.00	2.50	1.50
597	Ted Abernathy	5.00	2.50	1.50
598	White Sox Rookies (Ed Stroud, Walt Williams)	7.00	3.50	2.00
599	Bob Duliba	5.00	2.50	1.50
600	Brooks Robinson	175.00	70.00	44.00
601	Bill Bryan	8.00	4.00	2.50
602	Juan Pizarro	8.00	4.00	2.50
603	Athletics Rookies (Tim Talton, Ramon Webster)	8.00	4.00	2.50
604	Red Sox Team	75.00	38.00	23.00
605	Mike Shannon	6.00	3.00	1.75
606	Ron Taylor	8.00	4.00	2.50
607	Mickey Stanley	6.00	3.00	1.75
608	Cubs Rookies (Rich Nye, John Upham)	6.00	3.00	1.75
609	Tommy John	90.00	30.00	16.50

1967 Topps Pin-Ups

The 5" by 7" "All Star Pin-ups" were inserts to regular 1967 Topps baseball cards. They feature a full color picture with the player's name, position and team in a circle on the lower left side of the front. The numbered set consists of 32 players (generally big names). Even so, they are rather inexpensive. Because the large paper pin-ups had to be folded several times to fit into the wax packs, they are almost never found in true "Mint" condition.

		NR MT	EX	VG
Complete Set:		40.00	20.00	12.00
Common Player:		.25	.13	.08
1	Boog Powell	.40	.20	.12
2	Bert Campaneris	.30	.15	.09

		NR MT	EX	VG
	Complete Set:	6500.00	3300.00	2000.
	Common Player:	65.00	32.00	19.50
1	Pete Rose	700.00	350.00	210.00
2	Gary Peters	65.00	32.00	19.50
3	Frank Robinson	200.00	100.00	60.00
4	Jim Lonborg	65.00	32.00	19.50
5	Ron Swoboda	65.00	32.00	19.50
6	Harmon Killebrew	200.00	100.00	60.00
7	Bob Clemente	800.00	400.00	240.00
8	Mickey Mantle	1500.00	750.00	450.00
9	Jim Fregosi	75.00	37.00	22.00
10	Al Kaline	300.00	150.00	90.00
11	Don Drysdale	250.00	125.00	75.00
12	Dean Chance	65.00	32.00	19.50
13	Orlando Cepeda	75.00	37.00	22.00
14	Tim McCarver	75.00	37.00	22.00
15	Frank Howard	75.00	37.00	22.00
16	Max Alvis	65.00	32.00	19.50
17	Rusty Staub	75.00	37.00	22.00
18	Richie Allen	75.00	37.00	22.00
19	Willie Mays	600.00	300.00	175.00
20	Hank Aaron	600.00	300.00	175.00
21	Carl Yastrzemski	600.00	300.00	180.00
22	Ron Santo	75.00	37.00	22.00
23	Jim Hunter	200.00	100.00	60.00
24	Jim Wynn	65.00	32.00	19.50

3	Brooks Robinson	3.00	1.50	.90
4	Tommie Agee	.25	.13	.08
5	Carl Yastrzemski	3.50	1.75	1.00
6	Mickey Mantle	12.00	6.00	3.50
7	Frank Howard	.50	.25	.15
8	Sam McDowell	.25	.13	.08
9	Orlando Cepeda	.60	.30	.20
10	Chico Cardenas	.25	.13	.08
11	Bob Clemente	5.00	2.50	1.50
12	Willie Mays	5.00	2.50	1.50
13	Cleon Jones	.25	.13	.08
14	John Callison	.25	.13	.08
15	Hank Aaron	5.00	2.50	1.50
16	Don Drysdale	3.00	1.50	.90
17	Bobby Knoop	.25	.13	.08
18	Tony Oliva	.50	.25	.15
19	Frank Robinson	2.00	1.00	.60
20	Denny McLain	.50	.25	.15
21	Al Kaline	5.00	2.50	1.50
22	Joe Pepitone	.40	.20	.12
23	Harmon Killebrew	5.00	2.50	1.50
24	Leon Wagner	.25	.13	.08
25	Joe Morgan	5.00	2.50	1.50
26	Ron Santo	.40	.20	.12
27	Joe Torre	.60	.30	.20
28	Juan Marichal	2.00	1.00	.60
29	Matty Alou	.25	.13	.08
30	Felipe Alou	.25	.13	.08
31	Ron Hunt	.25	.13	.08
32	Willie McCovey	2.00	1.00	.60

1967 Topps Stickers Pirates

Considered a "test" issue, this 33-sticker set of 1/2" by 3-1/2" stickers is very similar to the Red Sox stickers which were produced the same year. Player stickers have a color picture (often just the player's head) and the player's name in large "comic book" letters. Besides the players, there are other topics such as "I Love the Pirates," "Bob Clemente for Mayor," and a number of similar sentiments. The stickers have blank backs and are rather scarce.

1967 Topps Stand-Ups

WILLIE MAYS

Never actually issued, no more than a handful of each of these rare test issues has made their way into the hobby market. Designed so that the color photo of the player's head could be popped out of the black background, and the top folded over to create a stand-up display, examples of these 3-1/8" by 5-1/4" cards can be found either die-cut around the portrait or without the cutting. Blank-backed, there are 24 cards in the set, numbered on the front at bottom left. The cards are popular with advanced superstar collectors.

		NR MT	EX	VG
	Complete Set:	200.00	100.00	60.00
	Common Player:	3.00	1.50	.90
1	Gene Alley	5.00	2.50	1.50
2	Matty Alou	7.00	3.50	2.00
3	Dennis Ribant	3.00	1.50	.90
4	Steve Blass	5.00	2.50	1.50
5	Juan Pizarro	3.00	1.50	.90
6	Bob Clemente	75.00	38.00	23.00
7	Donn Clendenon	5.00	2.50	1.50
8	Roy Face	7.00	3.50	2.00
9	Woody Fryman	3.00	1.50	.90
10	Jesse Gonder	3.00	1.50	.90
11	Vern Law	7.00	3.50	2.00
12	Al McBean	3.00	1.50	.90
13	Jerry May	3.00	1.50	.90
14	Bill Mazeroski	12.00	6.00	3.50
15	Pete Mikkelsen	3.00	1.50	.90
16	Manny Mota	5.00	2.50	1.50
17	Billy O'Dell	3.00	1.50	.90
18	Jose Pagan	3.00	1.50	.90
19	Jim Pagliaroni	3.00	1.50	.90
20	Johnny Pesky	3.00	1.50	.90
21	Tommie Sisk	3.00	1.50	.90
22	Willie Stargell	40.00	20.00	12.50

		NR MT	EX	VG
23	Bob Veale	5.00	2.50	1.50
24	Harry Walker	3.00	1.50	.90
25	I Love The Pirates	3.00	1.50	.90
26	Let's Go Pirates	3.00	1.50	.90
27	Bob Clemente For Mayor	35.00	17.50	10.50
28	National League Batting Champion (Matty Alou)	4.00	2.00	1.25
29	Happiness Is A Pirate Win	3.00	1.50	.90
30	Donn Clendenon Is My Hero	4.00	2.00	1.25
31	Pirates' Home Run Champion (Willie Stargell)	15.00	7.50	4.50
32	Pirates Logo	3.00	1.50	.90
33	Pirates Pennant	3.00	1.50	.90

1967 Topps Stickers Red Sox

Like the 1967 Pirates Stickers, the Red Sox Stickers were part of the same test procedure. The Red Sox Stickers have the same 2-1/2" by 3-1/2" dimensions color picture and large player's name on the front. A set is complete at 33 stickers. The majority are players, but themes such as "Let's Go Red Sox" are also included.

		NR MT	EX	VG
Complete Set:		200.00	100.00	60.00
Common Player:		3.00	1.50	.90
1	Dennis Bennett	3.00	1.50	.90
2	Darrell Brandon	3.00	1.50	.90
3	Tony Conigliaro	10.00	5.00	3.00
4	Don Demeter	3.00	1.50	.90
5	Hank Fischer	3.00	1.50	.90
6	Joe Foy	3.00	1.50	.90
7	Mike Andrews	3.00	1.50	.90
8	Dalton Jones	3.00	1.50	.90
9	Jim Lonborg	9.00	4.50	2.75
10	Don McMahon	3.00	1.50	.90
11	Dave Morehead	3.00	1.50	.90
12	George Smith	3.00	1.50	.90
13	Rico Petrocelli	6.00	3.00	1.75
14	Mike Ryan	3.00	1.50	.90
15	Jose Santiago	3.00	1.50	.90
16	George Scott	6.00	3.00	1.75
17	Sal Maglie	5.00	2.50	1.50
18	Reggie Smith	10.00	5.00	3.00
19	Lee Stange	3.00	1.50	.90
20	Jerry Stephenson	3.00	1.50	.90
21	Jose Tartabull	3.00	1.50	.90
22	George Thomas	3.00	1.50	.90
23	Bob Tillman	3.00	1.50	.90
24	Johnnie Wyatt	3.00	1.50	.90
25	Carl Yastrzemski	75.00	37.00	22.00
26	Dick Williams	6.00	3.00	1.75
27	I Love The Red Sox	3.00	1.50	.90
28	Let's Go Red Sox	3.00	1.50	.90
29	Carl Yastrzemski For Mayor	35.00	17.50	10.50
30	Tony Conigliaro Is My Hero	7.00	3.50	2.00
31	Happiness Is A Boston Win	3.00	1.50	.90
32	Red Sox Logo	3.00	1.50	.90
33	Red Sox Pennant	3.00	1.50	.90

A player's name in *italic* type indicates a rookie card. An (FC) indicates a player's first card for that particular card company.

1968 Topps

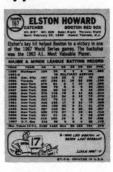

In 1968, Topps returned to a 598-card set of 2-1/2" by 3-1/2" cards. It is not, however, more of the same by way of appearance as the cards feature a color photograph on a background of what appears to be a burlap fabric. The player's name is below the photo but on the unusual background. A colored circle on the lower right carries the team and position. Backs were also changed. While retaining the vertical format introduced the previous year, with stats in the middle and cartoon at the bottom. The set features many of the old favorite subsets, including statistical leaders, World Series highlights, multi-player cards, checklists, rookie cards and the return of All-Star cards.

		NR MT	EX	VG
Complete Set:		1700.00	850.00	500.00
Common Player: 1-533		.60	.30	.20
Common Player: 534-598		1.00	.50	.30
1	N.L. Batting Leaders (Matty Alou, Bob Clemente, Tony Gonzalez)	8.00	2.00	1.00
2	A.L. Batting Leaders (Al Kaline, Frank Robinson, Carl Yastrzemski)	4.00	2.00	1.25
3	N.L. RBI Leaders (Hank Aaron, Orlando Cepeda, Bob Clemente)	4.00	2.00	1.25
4	A.L. RBI Leaders (Harmon Killebrew, Frank Robinson, Carl Yastrzemski)	4.00	2.00	1.25
5	N.L. Home Run Leaders (Hank Aaron, Willie McCovey, Ron Santo, Jim Wynn)	4.00	2.00	1.25
6	A.L. Home Run Leaders (Frank Howard, Harmon Killebrew, Carl Yastrzemski)	4.00	2.00	1.25
7	N.L. ERA Leaders (Jim Bunning, Phil Niekro, Chris Short)	2.50	1.25	.70
8	A.L. ERA Leaders (Joe Horlen, Gary Peters, Sonny Siebert)	1.50	.70	.45
9	N.L. Pitching Leaders (Jim Bunning, Ferguson Jenkins, Mike McCormick, Claude Osteen)	2.50	1.25	.70
10a	A.L. Pitching Leaders (Dean Chance, Jim Lonborg, Earl Wilson) ("Lonberg" on back)	3.50	1.75	1.00
10b	A.L. Pitching Leaders (Dean Chance, Jim Lonborg, Earl Wilson) ("Lonborg" on back)	1.50	.70	.45
11	N.L. Strikeout Leaders (Jim Bunning, Ferguson Jenkins, Gaylord Perry)	3.00	1.50	.90
12	A.L. Strikeout Leaders (Dean Chance, Jim Lonborg, Sam McDowell)	1.50	.70	.45
13	Chuck Hartenstein	.60	.30	.20
14	Jerry McNertney	.60	.30	.20
15	Ron Hunt	.70	.35	.20
16	Indians Rookies (Lou Piniella, Richie Scheinblum)	2.50	1.25	.70
17	Dick Hall	.60	.30	.20
18	Mike Hershberger	.60	.30	.20
19	Juan Pizarro	.60	.30	.20
20	Brooks Robinson	12.00	6.00	3.50
21	Ron Davis	.60	.30	.20
22	Pat Dobson	.70	.35	.20
23	Chico Cardenas	.60	.30	.20
24	Bobby Locke	.60	.30	.20
25	Julian Javier	.70	.35	.20
26	Darrell Brandon	.60	.30	.20
27	Gil Hodges	6.00	3.00	1.75
28	Ted Uhlaender	.60	.30	.20

		NR MT	EX	VG
29	Joe Verbanic	.90	.45	.25
30	Joe Torre	2.00	1.00	.60
31	Ed Stroud	.60	.30	.20
32	Joe Gibbon	.60	.30	.20
33	Pete Ward	.60	.30	.20
34	Al Ferrara	.60	.30	.20
35	Steve Hargan	.60	.30	.20
36	Pirates Rookies (Bob Moose, *Bob Robertson*)	.90	.45	.25
37	Billy Williams	7.00	3.50	2.00
38	Tony Pierce	.60	.30	.20
39	Cookie Rojas	.60	.30	.20
40	Denny McLain	3.75	2.00	1.25
41	Julio Gotay	.60	.30	.20
42	Larry Haney	.60	.30	.20
43	Gary Bell	.60	.30	.20
44	Frank Kostro	.60	.30	.20
45	Tom Seaver	90.00	45.00	27.00
46	Dave Ricketts	.60	.30	.20
47	Ralph Houk	1.75	.90	.50
48	Ted Davidson	.60	.30	.20
49a	Ed Brinkman (yellow team letters)	60.00	30.00	18.00
49b	Ed Brinkman (white team letters)	.70	.35	.20
50	Willie Mays	40.00	20.00	12.00
51	Bob Locker	.60	.30	.20
52	Hawk Taylor	.60	.30	.20
53	Gene Alley	.70	.35	.20
54	Stan Williams	.60	.30	.20
55	Felipe Alou	1.00	.50	.30
56	Orioles Rookies (Dave Leonhard, Dave May)	.60	.30	.20
57	Dan Schneider	.60	.30	.20
58	Ed Mathews	7.00	3.50	2.00
59	Don Lock	.60	.30	.20
60	Ken Holtzman	1.00	.50	.30
61	Reggie Smith	1.50	.70	.45
62	Chuck Dobson	.60	.30	.20
63	Dick Kenworthy	.70	.35	.20
64	Jim Merritt	.60	.30	.20
65	John Roseboro	.90	.45	.25
66a	Casey Cox (yellow team letters)	60.00	30.00	18.00
66b	Casey Cox (white team letters)	.60	.30	.20
67	Checklist 1-109 (Jim Kaat)	3.00	1.50	.90
68	Ron Willis	.60	.30	.20
69	Tom Tresh	1.75	.90	.50
70	Bob Veale	.70	.35	.20
71	Vern Fuller	.60	.30	.20
72	Tommy John	5.00	2.50	1.50
73	Jim Hart	.70	.35	.20
74	Milt Pappas	.90	.45	.25
75	Don Mincher	.70	.35	.20
76	Braves Rookies (Jim Britton, Ron Reed)	1.00	.50	.30
77	*Don Wilson*	.90	.45	.25
78	Jim Northrup	.70	.35	.20
79	Ted Kubiak	.60	.30	.20
80	Rod Carew	70.00	35.00	21.00
81	Larry Jackson	.60	.30	.20
82	Sam Bowens	.60	.30	.20
83	John Stephenson	.60	.30	.20
84	Bob Tolan	.70	.35	.20
85	Gaylord Perry	6.00	3.00	1.75
86	Willie Stargell	8.00	4.00	2.50
87	Dick Williams	1.00	.50	.30
88	Phil Regan	.60	.30	.20
89	Jake Gibbs	.90	.45	.25
90	Vada Pinson	2.00	1.00	.60
91	Jim Ollom	.60	.30	.20
92	Ed Kranepool	.90	.45	.25
93	Tony Cloninger	.70	.35	.20
94	Lee Maye	.60	.30	.20
95	Bob Aspromonte	.60	.30	.20
96	Senators Rookies (Frank Coggins, Dick Nold)	.60	.30	.20
97	Tom Phoebus	.60	.30	.20
98	Gary Sutherland	.60	.30	.20
99	Rocky Colavito	2.25	1.25	.70
100	Bob Gibson	10.00	5.00	3.00
101	Glenn Beckert	.90	.45	.25
102	Jose Cardenal	.70	.35	.20
103	Don Sutton	6.00	3.00	1.75
104	Dick Dietz	.60	.30	.20
105	Al Downing	1.25	.60	.40
106	Dalton Jones	.60	.30	.20
107	Checklist 110-196 (Juan Marichal)	3.50	1.75	1.00
108	Don Pavletich	.60	.30	.20
109	Bert Campaneris	1.00	.50	.30
110	Hank Aaron	40.00	20.00	12.00
111	Rich Reese	.60	.30	.20
112	Woody Fryman	.70	.35	.20
113	Tigers Rookies (Tom Matchick, Daryl Patterson)	.60	.30	.20
114	Ron Swoboda	.90	.45	.25
115	Sam McDowell	.90	.45	.25
116	Ken McMullen	.60	.30	.20
117	Larry Jaster	.60	.30	.20
118	Mark Belanger	1.00	.50	.30
119	Ted Savage	.60	.30	.20
120	Mel Stottlemyre	2.00	1.00	.60
121	Jimmie Hall	.60	.30	.20
122	Gene Mauch	.90	.45	.25
123	Jose Santiago	.60	.30	.20
124	Nate Oliver	.60	.30	.20
125	Joe Horlen	.60	.30	.20
126	Bobby Etheridge	.60	.30	.20
127	Paul Lindblad	.60	.30	.20
128	Astros Rookies (Tom Dukes, Alonzo Harris)	.60	.30	.20
129	Mickey Stanley	.70	.35	.20
130	Tony Perez	5.00	2.50	1.50
131	Frank Bertaina	.60	.30	.20
132	Bud Harrelson	1.00	.50	.30
133	Fred Whitfield	.60	.30	.20
134	Pat Jarvis	.60	.30	.20
135	Paul Blair	.70	.35	.20
136	Randy Hundley	.60	.30	.20
137	Twins Team	2.00	1.00	.60
138	Ruben Amaro	.90	.45	.25
139	Chris Short	.90	.45	.25
140	Tony Conigliaro	1.50	.70	.45
141	Dal Maxvill	.70	.35	.20
142	White Sox Rookies (Buddy Bradford, Bill Voss)	.60	.30	.20
143	Pete Cimino	.60	.30	.20
144	Joe Morgan	7.00	3.50	2.00
145	Don Drysdale	8.00	4.00	2.50
146	Sal Bando	1.00	.50	.30
147	Frank Linzy	.60	.30	.20
148	Dave Bristol	.60	.30	.20
149	Bob Saverine	.60	.30	.20
150	Bob Clemente	40.00	20.00	12.00
151	World Series Game 1 (Brock Socks 4-Hits In Opener)	3.50	1.75	1.00
152	World Series Game 2 (Yaz Smashes Two Homers)	5.00	2.50	1.50
153	World Series Game 3 (Briles Cools Off Boston)	2.00	1.00	.60
154	World Series Game 4 (Gibson Hurls Shutout!)	3.50	1.75	1.00
155	World Series Game 5 (Lonborg Wins Again!)	2.50	1.25	.70
156	World Series Game 6 (Petrocelli Socks Two Homers)	2.50	1.25	.70
157	World Series Game 7 (St. Louis Wins It!)	2.00	1.00	.60
158	World Series Summary (The Cardinals Celebrate!)	2.00	1.00	.60
159	Don Kessinger	.90	.45	.25
160	Earl Wilson	.70	.35	.20
161	Norm Miller	.60	.30	.20
162	Cardinals Rookies (Hal Gilson, *Mike Torrez*)	1.00	.50	.30
163	Gene Brabender	.60	.30	.20
164	Ramon Webster	.60	.30	.20
165	Tony Oliva	2.50	1.25	.70
166	Claude Raymond	.60	.30	.20
167	Elston Howard	3.00	1.50	.90
168	Dodgers Team	2.50	1.25	.70
169	Bob Bolin	.60	.30	.20
170	Jim Fregosi	1.00	.50	.30
171	Don Nottebart	.60	.30	.20
172	Walt Williams	.60	.30	.20
173	John Boozer	.60	.30	.20
174	Bob Tillman	.60	.30	.20
175	Maury Wills	3.50	1.75	1.00
176	Bob Allen	.60	.30	.20
177	Mets Rookies (*Jerry Koosman, Nolan Ryan*)	875.00	350.00	219.00
178	Don Wert	.70	.35	.20
179	Bill Stoneman	.60	.30	.20
180	Curt Flood	1.50	.70	.45
181	Jerry Zimmerman	.60	.30	.20
182	Dave Giusti	.60	.30	.20
183	Bob Kennedy	.60	.30	.20
184	Lou Johnson	.60	.30	.20
185	Tom Haller	.70	.35	.20
186	Eddie Watt	.60	.30	.20
187	Sonny Jackson	.60	.30	.20
188	Cap Peterson	.60	.30	.20
189	Bill Landis	.60	.30	.20

		NR MT	EX	VG
190	Bill White	1.00	.50	.30
191	Dan Frisella	.70	.35	.20
192a	Checklist 197-283 (Carl Yastrzemski) ("To increase the..." on back)	4.50	2.25	1.25
192b	Checklist 197-283 (Carl Yastrzemski) ("To increase your..." on back)	6.00	3.00	1.75
193	Jack Hamilton	.60	.30	.20
194	Don Buford	.70	.35	.20
195	Joe Pepitone	2.00	1.00	.60
196	Gary Nolan	.60	.30	.20
197	Larry Brown	.60	.30	.20
198	Roy Face	1.25	.60	.40
199	A's Rookies (Darrell Osteen, Roberto Rodriguez)	.60	.30	.20
200	Orlando Cepeda	4.00	2.00	1.25
201	*Mike Marshall*	1.75	.90	.50
202	Adolfo Phillips	.60	.30	.20
203	Dick Kelley	.60	.30	.20
204	Andy Etchebarren	.60	.30	.20
205	Juan Marichal	8.00	4.00	2.50
206	Cal Ermer	.60	.30	.20
207	Carroll Sembera	.60	.30	.20
208	Willie Davis	1.00	.50	.30
209	Tim Cullen	.60	.30	.20
210	Gary Peters	.70	.35	.20
211	J.C. Martin	.70	.35	.20
212	Dave Morehead	.60	.30	.20
213	Chico Ruiz	.60	.30	.20
214	Yankees Rookies (Stan Bahnsen, Frank Fernandez)	1.00	.50	.30
215	Jim Bunning	4.50	2.25	1.25
216	Bubba Morton	.60	.30	.20
217	Turk Farrell	.60	.30	.20
218	Ken Suarez	.60	.30	.20
219	Rob Gardner	.60	.30	.20
220	Harmon Killebrew	9.00	4.50	2.75
221	Braves Team	2.00	1.00	.60
222	Jim Hardin	.60	.30	.20
223	Ollie Brown	.60	.30	.20
224	Jack Aker	.60	.30	.20
225	Richie Allen	2.25	1.25	.70
226	Jimmie Price	.60	.30	.20
227	Joe Hoerner	.60	.30	.20
228	Dodgers Rookies (*Jack Billingham*, Jim Fairey)	.80	.40	.25
229	Fred Klages	.60	.30	.20
230	Pete Rose	50.00	25.00	15.00
231	Dave Baldwin	.60	.30	.20
232	Denis Menke	.60	.30	.20
233	George Scott	.90	.45	.25
234	Bill Monbouquette	.90	.45	.25
235	Ron Santo	1.50	.70	.45
236	Tug McGraw	1.75	.90	.50
237	Alvin Dark	.90	.45	.25
238	Tom Satriano	.60	.30	.20
239	Bill Henry	.60	.30	.20
240	Al Kaline	10.00	5.00	3.00
241	Felix Millan	.70	.35	.20
242	Moe Drabowsky	.60	.30	.20
243	Rich Rollins	.60	.30	.20
244	John Donaldson	.60	.30	.20
245	Tony Gonzalez	.60	.30	.20
246	Fritz Peterson	1.00	.50	.30
247	Red Rookies (*Johnny Bench*, Ron Tompkins)	300.00	120.00	75.00
248	Fred Valentine	.60	.30	.20
249	Bill Singer	.80	.40	.25
250	Carl Yastrzemski	30.00	15.00	9.00
251	*Manny Sanguillen*	1.25	.60	.40
252	Angels Team	2.00	1.00	.60
253	Dick Hughes	.60	.30	.20
254	Cleon Jones	.90	.45	.25
255	Dean Chance	.70	.35	.20
256	Norm Cash	2.00	1.00	.60
257	Phil Niekro	5.00	2.50	1.50
258	Cubs Rookies (Jose Arcia, Bill Schlesinger)	.60	.30	.20
259	Ken Boyer	1.75	.90	.50
260	Jim Wynn	.90	.45	.25
261	Dave Duncan	.60	.30	.20
262	Rick Wise	.70	.35	.20
263	Horace Clarke	.90	.45	.25
264	Ted Abernathy	.60	.30	.20
265	Tommy Davis	1.50	.70	.45
266	Paul Popovich	.60	.30	.20
267	Herman Franks	.60	.30	.20
268	Bob Humphreys	.60	.30	.20
269	Bob Tiefenauer	.60	.30	.20
270	Matty Alou	1.00	.50	.30
271	Bobby Knoop	.60	.30	.20
272	Ray Culp	.60	.30	.20

		NR MT	EX	VG
273	Dave Johnson	1.75	.90	.50
274	Mike Cuellar	.90	.45	.25
275	Tim McCarver	1.75	.90	.50
276	Jim Roland	.60	.30	.20
277	Jerry Buchek	.70	.35	.20
278a	Checklist 284-370 (Orlando Cepeda) (copyright at right)	3.00	1.50	.90
278b	Checklist 284-370 (Orlando Cepeda) (copyright at left)	5.00	2.50	1.50
279	Bill Hands	.60	.30	.20
280	Mickey Mantle	150.00	60.00	38.00
281	Jim Campanis	.60	.30	.20
282	Rick Monday	1.25	.60	.40
283	Mel Queen	.60	.30	.20
284	John Briggs	.60	.30	.20
285	Dick McAuliffe	.80	.40	.25
286	Cecil Upshaw	.60	.30	.20
287	White Sox Rookies (Mickey Abarbanel, Cisco Carlos)	.60	.30	.20
288	Dave Wickersham	.60	.30	.20
289	Woody Held	.60	.30	.20
290	Willie McCovey	8.00	4.00	2.50
291	Dick Lines	.60	.30	.20
292	Art Shamsky	.80	.40	.25
293	Bruce Howard	.60	.30	.20
294	Red Schoendienst	1.50	.70	.45
295	Sonny Siebert	.60	.30	.20
296	Byron Browne	.60	.30	.20
297	Russ Gibson	.60	.30	.20
298	Jim Brewer	.60	.30	.20
299	Gene Michael	1.00	.50	.30
300	Rusty Staub	2.00	1.00	.60
301	Twins Rookies (George Mitterwald, Rick Renick)	.60	.30	.20
302	Gerry Arrigo	.60	.30	.20
303	Dick Green	.60	.30	.20
304	Sandy Valdespino	.60	.30	.20
305	Minnie Rojas	.60	.30	.20
306	Mike Ryan	.60	.30	.20
307	John Hiller	.90	.45	.25
308	Pirates Team	2.00	1.00	.60
309	Ken Henderson	.60	.30	.20
310	Luis Aparicio	5.00	2.50	1.50
311	Jack Lamabe	.60	.30	.20
312	Curt Blefary	.60	.30	.20
313	Al Weis	.70	.35	.20
314	Red Sox Rookies (Bill Rohr, George Spriggs)	.60	.30	.20
315	Zoilo Versalles	.70	.35	.20
316	Steve Barber	.90	.45	.25
317	Ron Brand	.60	.30	.20
318	Chico Salmon	.60	.30	.20
319	George Culver	.60	.30	.20
320	Frank Howard	2.00	1.00	.60
321	Leo Durocher	2.25	1.25	.70
322	Dave Boswell	.70	.35	.20
323	Deron Johnson	.60	.30	.20
324	Jim Nash	.60	.30	.20
325	Manny Mota	.90	.45	.25
326	Dennis Ribant	.60	.30	.20
327	Tony Taylor	.60	.30	.20
328	Angels Rookies (Chuck Vinson, Jim Weaver)	.60	.30	.20
329	Duane Josephson	.60	.30	.20
330	Roger Maris	25.00	12.50	7.50
331	Dan Osinski	.60	.30	.20
332	Doug Rader	.70	.35	.20
333	Ron Herbel	.60	.30	.20
334	Orioles Team	2.00	1.00	.60
335	Bob Allison	1.00	.50	.30
336	John Purdin	.60	.30	.20
337	Bill Robinson	.90	.45	.25
338	Bob Johnson	.60	.30	.20
339	Rich Nye	.60	.30	.20
340	Max Alvis	.60	.30	.20
341	Jim Lemon	.60	.30	.20
342	Ken Johnson	.60	.30	.20
343	Jim Gosger	.60	.30	.20
344	Donn Clendenon	.70	.35	.20
345	Bob Hendley	.70	.35	.20
346	Jerry Adair	.60	.30	.20
347	George Brunet	.60	.30	.20
348	Phillies Rookies (Larry Colton, Dick Thoenen)	.60	.30	.20
349	Ed Spiezio	.60	.30	.20
350	Hoyt Wilhelm	6.00	3.00	1.75
351	Bob Barton	.60	.30	.20
352	Jackie Hernandez	.60	.30	.20
353	Mack Jones	.60	.30	.20
354	Pete Richert	.60	.30	.20
355	Ernie Banks	10.00	5.00	3.00

		NR MT	EX	VG
356	Checklist 371-457 (Ken Holtzman)			
		2.50	1.25	.70
357	Len Gabrielson	.60	.30	.20
358	Mike Epstein	.70	.35	.20
359	Joe Moeller	.60	.30	.20
360	Willie Horton	.90	.45	.25
361	Harmon Killebrew AS	5.00	2.50	1.50
362	Orlando Cepeda AS	2.75	1.50	.80
363	Rod Carew AS	8.00	4.00	2.50
364	Joe Morgan AS	3.00	1.50	.90
365	Brooks Robinson AS	6.00	3.00	1.75
366	Ron Santo AS	1.75	.90	.50
367	Jim Fregosi AS	1.00	.50	.30
368	Gene Alley AS	1.00	.50	.30
369	Carl Yastrzemski AS	15.00	7.50	4.50
370	Hank Aaron AS	15.00	7.50	4.50
371	Tony Oliva AS	2.00	1.00	.60
372	Lou Brock AS	5.00	2.50	1.50
373	Frank Robinson AS	5.00	2.50	1.50
374	Bob Clemente AS	15.00	7.50	4.50
375	Bill Freehan AS	1.00	.50	.30
376	Tim McCarver AS	1.50	.70	.45
377	Joe Horlen AS	1.00	.50	.30
378	Bob Gibson AS	5.00	2.50	1.50
379	Gary Peters AS	1.00	.50	.30
380	Ken Holtzman AS	1.00	.50	.30
381	Boog Powell	2.50	1.25	.70
382	Ramon Hernandez	.60	.30	.20
383	Steve Whitaker	.90	.45	.25
384	Reds Rookies (Bill Henry, *Hal McRae*)			
		6.00	3.00	1.75
385	Jim Hunter	5.00	2.50	1.50
386	Greg Goossen	.70	.35	.20
387	Joe Foy	.60	.30	.20
388	Ray Washburn	.60	.30	.20
389	Jay Johnstone	.90	.45	.25
390	Bill Mazeroski	1.75	.90	.50
391	Bob Priddy	.60	.30	.20
392	Grady Hatton	.60	.30	.20
393	Jim Perry	1.00	.50	.30
394	Tommie Aaron	.90	.45	.25
395	Camilo Pascual	.90	.45	.25
396	Bobby Wine	.60	.30	.20
397	Vic Davalillo	.70	.35	.20
398	Jim Grant	.60	.30	.20
399	Ray Oyler	.70	.35	.20
400a	Mike McCormick (white team letters)			
		40.00	20.00	12.00
400b	Mike McCormick (yellow team letters)			
		.70	.35	.20
401	Mets Team	3.25	1.75	1.00
402	Mike Hegan	1.00	.50	.30
403	John Buzhardt	.60	.30	.20
404	Floyd Robinson	.60	.30	.20
405	Tommy Helms	.70	.35	.20
406	Dick Ellsworth	.60	.30	.20
407	Gary Kolb	.60	.30	.20
408	Steve Carlton	40.00	20.00	12.00
409	Orioles Rookies (Frank Peters, Ron Stone)			
		.60	.30	.20
410	Ferguson Jenkins	3.50	1.75	1.00
411	Ron Hansen	.60	.30	.20
412	Clay Carroll	.70	.35	.20
413	Tommy McCraw	.60	.30	.20
414	Mickey Lolich	2.75	1.50	.80
415	Johnny Callison	1.00	.50	.30
416	Bill Rigney	.60	.30	.20
417	Willie Crawford	.60	.30	.20
418	Eddie Fisher	.60	.30	.20
419	Jack Hiatt	.60	.30	.20
420	Cesar Tovar	.60	.30	.20
421	Ron Taylor	.70	.35	.20
422	Rene Lachemann	.60	.30	.20
423	Fred Gladding	.60	.30	.20
424	White Sox Team	2.00	1.00	.60
425	Jim Maloney	.70	.35	.20
426	Hank Allen	.60	.30	.20
427	Dick Calmus	.60	.30	.20
428	Vic Roznovsky	.60	.30	.20
429	Tommie Sisk	.60	.30	.20
430	Rico Petrocelli	.90	.45	.25
431	Dooley Womack	.90	.45	.25
432	Indians Rookies (Bill Davis, Jose Vidal)			
		.60	.30	.20
433	Bob Rodgers	.90	.45	.25
434	Ricardo Joseph	.60	.30	.20
435	Ron Perranoski	.70	.35	.20
436	Hal Lanier	.90	.45	.25
437	Don Cardwell	.70	.35	.20
438	Lee Thomas	.60	.30	.20
439	Luman Harris	.60	.30	.20

		NR MT	EX	VG
440	Claude Osteen	.90	.45	.25
441	Alex Johnson	.60	.30	.20
442	Dick Bosman	.60	.30	.20
443	Joe Azcue	.60	.30	.20
444	Jack Fisher	.60	.30	.20
445	Mike Shannon	.70	.35	.20
446	Ron Kline	.60	.30	.20
447	Tigers Rookies (George Korince, Fred Lasher)			
		.60	.30	.20
448	Gary Wagner	.60	.30	.20
449	Gene Oliver	.60	.30	.20
450	Jim Kaat	4.00	2.00	1.25
451	Al Spangler	.60	.30	.20
452	Jesus Alou	.70	.35	.20
453	Sammy Ellis	.60	.30	.20
454	Checklist 458-533 (Frank Robinson)			
		4.00	2.00	1.25
455	Rico Carty	1.00	.50	.30
456	John O'Donoghue	.60	.30	.20
457	Jim Lefebvre	.70	.35	.20
458	Lew Krausse	.60	.30	.20
459	Dick Simpson	.60	.30	.20
460	Jim Lonborg	1.00	.50	.30
461	Chuck Hiller	.60	.30	.20
462	Barry Moore	.60	.30	.20
463	Jimmie Schaffer	.60	.30	.20
464	Don McMahon	.60	.30	.20
465	Tommie Agee	.90	.45	.25
466	Bill Dillman	.60	.30	.20
467	Dick Howser	1.50	.70	.45
468	Larry Sherry	.60	.30	.20
469	Ty Cline	.60	.30	.20
470	Bill Freehan	1.00	.50	.30
471	Orlando Pena	.60	.30	.20
472	Walt Alston	2.50	1.25	.70
473	Al Worthington	.60	.30	.20
474	Paul Schaal	.60	.30	.20
475	Joe Niekro	2.25	1.25	.70
476	Woody Woodward	.70	.35	.20
477	Phillies Team	2.00	1.00	.60
478	Dave McNally	1.00	.50	.30
479	Phil Gagliano	.60	.30	.20
480	Manager's Dream (Chico Cardenas, Bob Clemente, Tony Oliva)	15.00	7.50	4.50
481	John Wyatt	.60	.30	.20
482	Jose Pagan	.60	.30	.20
483	Darold Knowles	.60	.30	.20
484	Phil Roof	.60	.30	.20
485	Ken Berry	.60	.30	.20
486	Cal Koonce	.70	.35	.20
487	Lee May	1.25	.60	.40
488	Dick Tracewski	.60	.30	.20
489	Wally Bunker	.60	.30	.20
490	Super Stars (Harmon Killebrew, Mickey Mantle, Willie Mays)	50.00	30.00	15.00
491	Denny Lemaster	.60	.30	.20
492	Jeff Torborg	.70	.35	.20
493	Jim McGlothlin	.60	.30	.20
494	Ray Sadecki	.60	.30	.20
495	Leon Wagner	.70	.35	.20
496	Steve Hamilton	.90	.45	.25
497	Cards Team	3.50	1.75	1.00
498	Bill Bryan	.60	.30	.20
499	Steve Blass	.70	.35	.20
500	Frank Robinson	10.00	5.00	3.00
501	John Odom	.70	.35	.20
502	Mike Andrews	.60	.30	.20
503	Al Jackson	.70	.35	.20
504	Russ Snyder	.60	.30	.20
505	Joe Sparma	.70	.35	.20
506	Clarence Jones	.60	.30	.20
507	Wade Blasingame	.60	.30	.20
508	Duke Sims	.60	.30	.20
509	Dennis Higgins	.60	.30	.20
510	Ron Fairly	.90	.45	.25
511	Bill Kelso	.60	.30	.20
512	Grant Jackson	.60	.30	.20
513	Hank Bauer	.90	.45	.25
514	Al McBean	.60	.30	.20
515	Russ Nixon	.60	.30	.20
516	Pete Mikkelsen	.60	.30	.20
517	Diego Segui	.60	.30	.20
518a	Checklist 534-598 (Clete Boyer) (539 is Maj. L. Rookies)	3.00	1.50	.90
518b	Checklist 534-598 (Clete Boyer) (539 is Amer. L. Rookies)	5.00	2.50	1.50
519	Jerry Stephenson	.60	.30	.20
520	Lou Brock	12.00	6.00	3.50
521	Don Shaw	.70	.35	.20
522	Wayne Causey	.60	.30	.20
523	John Tsitouris	.60	.30	.20

		NR MT	EX	VG
524	Andy Kosco	.90	.45	.25
525	Jim Davenport	.60	.30	.20
526	Bill Denehy	.60	.30	.20
527	Tito Francona	.70	.35	.20
528	Tigers Team	8.00	4.00	2.50
529	Bruce Von Hoff	.60	.30	.20
530	Bird Belters (Brooks Robinson, Frank			
	Robinson)	7.00	3.50	2.00
531	Chuck Hinton	.60	.30	.20
532	Luis Tiant	1.75	.90	.50
533	Wes Parker	.90	.45	.25
534	Bob Miller	1.00	.50	.30
535	Danny Cater	1.00	.50	.30
536	Bill Short	1.25	.60	.40
537	Norm Siebern	1.00	.50	.30
538	Manny Jimenez	1.00	.50	.30
539	Major League Rookies (Mike Ferraro, Jim			
	Ray)	1.25	.60	.40
540	Nelson Briles	1.00	.50	.30
541	Sandy Alomar	1.00	.50	.30
542	John Boccabella	1.00	.50	.30
543	Bob Lee	1.00	.50	.30
544	Mayo Smith	1.25	.60	.40
545	Lindy McDaniel	1.00	.50	.30
546	Roy White	2.50	1.25	.70
547	Dan Coombs	1.00	.50	.30
548	Bernie Allen	1.00	.50	.30
549	Orioles Rookies (Curt Motton, Roger			
	Nelson)	1.00	.50	.30
550	Clete Boyer	1.25	.60	.40
551	Darrell Sutherland	1.00	.50	.30
552	Ed Kirkpatrick	1.00	.50	.30
553	Hank Aguirre	1.00	.50	.30
554	A's Team	3.00	1.50	.90
555	Jose Tartabull	1.00	.50	.30
556	Dick Selma	1.25	.60	.40
557	Frank Quilici	1.00	.50	.30
558	John Edwards	1.00	.50	.30
559	Pirates Rookies (Carl Taylor, Luke Walker)			
		1.00	.50	.30
560	Paul Casanova	1.00	.50	.30
561	Lee Elia	1.00	.50	.30
562	Jim Bouton	2.50	1.25	.70
563	Ed Charles	1.25	.60	.40
564	Eddie Stanky	1.25	.60	.40
565	Larry Dierker	1.25	.60	.40
566	Ken Harrelson	2.00	1.00	.60
567	Clay Dalrymple	1.00	.50	.30
568	Willie Smith	1.00	.50	.30
569	N.L. Rookies (Ivan Murrell, Les Rohr)			
		1.25	.60	.40
570	Rick Reichardt	1.00	.50	.30
571	Tony LaRussa	1.75	.90	.50
572	Don Bosch	1.25	.60	.40
573	Joe Coleman	1.25	.60	.40
574	Reds Team	3.00	1.50	.90
575	Jim Palmer	20.00	10.00	6.00
576	Dave Adlesh	1.00	.50	.30
577	Fred Talbot	1.25	.60	.40
578	Orlando Martinez	1.00	.50	.30
579	N.L. Rookies (*Larry Hisle*, *Mike Lum*)			
		1.75	.90	.50
580	Bob Bailey	1.00	.50	.30
581	Garry Roggenburk	1.00	.50	.30
582	Jerry Grote	1.25	.60	.40
583	Gates Brown	1.25	.60	.40
584	Larry Shepard	1.00	.50	.30
585	Wilbur Wood	1.25	.60	.40
586	Jim Pagliaroni	1.00	.50	.30
587	Roger Repoz	1.00	.50	.30
588	Dick Schofield	1.00	.50	.30
589	Twins Rookies (Ron Clark, Moe Ogier)			
		1.00	.50	.30
590	Tommy Harper	1.25	.60	.40
591	Dick Nen	1.00	.50	.30
592	John Bateman	1.00	.50	.30
593	Lee Stange	1.00	.50	.30
594	Phil Linz	1.25	.60	.40
595	Phil Ortega	1.00	.50	.30
596	Charlie Smith	1.25	.60	.40
597	Bill McCool	1.00	.50	.30
598	Jerry May	2.00	.60	.30

A player's name in *italic* type indicates a rookie card. An (FC) indicates a player's first card for that particular card company.

1968 Topps
Action All-Star Stickers

Still another of the many Topps test issues of the late 1960s, the Action All-Star stickers were sold in a strip of three, with bubblegum, for 10¢. The strip is comprised of three 3-1/4" by 5-1/4" panels, perforated at the joints for separation. The central panel which is numbered, contains a large color picture of a star player. The top and bottom panels contains smaller pictures of three players each. While there are 16 numbered center panels, only 12 of them are different; panels 13-16 show players previously used. Similarly, the triple-player panels at top and bottom of stickers 13-16 repeat panels from #'s 1-4. Prices below are for stickers which have all three panels still joined. Individual panels are priced signicantly lower.

	NR MT	EX	VG
Complete Set:	1300.00	650.00	390.00
Common Player:	18.00	9.00	5.50

		NR MT	EX	VG
1	Orlando Cepeda, Joe Horlen, Al Kaline, Bill Mazeroski, Claude Osteen, Mel Stottlemyre, Carl Yastrzemski	100.00	50.00	30.00
2	Don Drysdale, Harmon Killebrew, Mike McCormick, Tom Phoebus, George Scott, Ron Swoboda, Pete Ward	30.00	15.00	9.00
3	Hank Aaron, Paul Casanova, Jim Maloney, Joe Pepitone, Rick Reichardt, Frank Robinson, Tom Seaver	35.00	17.50	10.50
4	Bob Aspromonte, Johnny Callison, Dean Chance, Jim Lefebvre, Jim Lonborg, Frank Robinson, Ron Santo	25.00	12.50	7.50
5	Bert Campaneris, Al Downing, Willie Horton, Ed Kranepool, Willie Mays, Pete Rose, Ron Santo	200.00	100.00	60.00
6	Max Alvis, Ernie Banks, Al Kaline, Tim McCarver, Rusty Staub, Walt Williams, Carl Yastrzemski	70.00	35.00	21.00
7	Rod Carew, Tony Gonzalez, Steve Hargan, Mickey Mantle, Willie McCovey, Rick Monday, Billy Williams	300.00	150.00	90.00
8	Clete Boyer, Jim Bunning, Tony Conigliaro, Mike Cuellar, Joe Horlen, Ken McMullen, Don Mincher	18.00	9.00	5.50
9	Orlando Cepeda, Bob Clemente, Jim Fregosi, Harmon Killebrew, Willie Mays, Chris Short, Earl Wilson	40.00	20.00	12.00
10	Hank Aaron, Bob Gibson, Bud Harrelson, Jim Hunter, Mickey Mantle, Gary Peters, Vada Pinson	100.00	50.00	30.00
11	Don Drysdale, Bill Freehan, Frank Howard, Ferguson Jenkins, Tony Oliva, Bob Veale, Jim Wynn	30.00	15.00	9.00
12	Richie Allen, Bob Clemente, Sam McDowell, Jim McGlothlin, Tony Perez, Brooks Robinson, Joe Torre	100.00	50.00	30.00
13	Dean Chance, Don Drysdale, Jim Lefebvre, Tom Phoebus, Frank Robinson, George Scott, Carl Yastrzemski	100.00	50.00	30.00
14	Paul Casanova, Orlando Cepeda, Joe Horlen, Harmon Killebrew, Bill Mazeroski, Rick Reichardt, Tom Seaver	35.00	17.50	10.50
15	Bob Aspromonte, Johnny Callison, Jim Lonborg, Mike McCormick, Frank Robinson, Ron Swoboda, Pete Ward	30.00	15.00	9.00
16	Hank Aaron, Al Kaline, Jim Maloney, Claude Osteen, Joe Pepitone, Ron Santo, Mel Stottlemyre	30.00	15.00	9.00

1968 Topps Discs

One of the scarcest of all Topps collectibles, this 28-player set was apparently a never-completed test issue. These full-color, cardboard discs, which measure approximately 2-1/8" in diameter, were apparantly intended to be made into a "pin" set, but for some reason, production was never completed and no actual "pins" are known to exist. Uncut sheets of the player discs have been found, however. The discs includea player portrait photo with the name beneath and the city and team nickname along the sides. The set includes eight Hall of Famers.

	NR MT	EX	VG
Complete Set:	3500.00	1750.00	1050.
Common Player:	35.00	17.50	10.50

		NR MT	EX	VG
(1)	Hank Aaron	250.00	125.00	75.00
(2)	Richie Allen	60.00	30.00	18.00
(3)	Gene Alley	35.00	17.50	10.50
(4)	Rod Carew	300.00	150.00	90.00
(5)	Orlando Cepeda	60.00	30.00	18.00
(6)	Dean Chance	35.00	17.50	10.50
(7)	Bob Clemente	350.00	175.00	100.00
(8)	Tommy Davis	35.00	17.50	10.50
(9)	Bill Freehan	35.00	17.50	10.50
(10)	Jim Fregosi	35.00	17.50	10.50
(11)	Steve Hargan	35.00	17.50	10.50
(12)	Frank Howard	60.00	30.00	18.00
(13)	Al Kaline	200.00	100.00	60.00
(14)	Harmon Killebrew	150.00	75.00	45.00
(15)	Mickey Mantle	600.00	300.00	175.00
(16)	Willie Mays	300.00	150.00	90.00
(17)	Mike McCormick	35.00	17.50	10.50
(18)	Rick Monday	35.00	17.50	10.50
(19)	Claude Osteen	35.00	17.50	10.50
(20)	Gary Peters	35.00	17.50	10.50
(21)	Brooks Robinson	200.00	100.00	60.00
(22)	Frank Robinson	150.00	75.00	45.00
(23)	Pete Rose	400.00	200.00	125.00
(24)	Ron Santo	60.00	30.00	18.00
(25)	Rusty Staub	60.00	30.00	18.00
(26)	Joe Torre	60.00	30.00	18.00
(27)	Carl Yastrzemski	150.00	75.00	45.00
(28)	Bob Veale	35.00	17.50	10.50

1968 Topps Game

A throwback to the Red and Blue Back sets of 1951, the 33-cards in the 1968 Topps Game set, inserted into packs of regular '68 Topps cards or purchases as a complete boxed set, enable the owner to play a game of baseball based on the game situations on each card. Also on the 2-1/4" by 3-1/4" cards were a color photograph of a player and his facsimile autograph. One redeeming social value of the set (assuming you're not mesmerized by the game) is that it affords an inexpensive way to get big-name cards as the set is loaded with stars, but not at all popular with collectors.

		NR MT	EX	VG
Complete Set:		50.00	25.00	15.00
Common Player:		.30	.15	.09
1	Mateo Alou	.50	.25	.15
2	Mickey Mantle	15.00	7.50	4.50
3	Carl Yastrzemski	3.25	1.75	1.00
4	Henry Aaron	3.00	1.50	.90
5	Harmon Killebrew	1.75	.90	.50
6	Roberto Clemente	3.00	1.50	.90
7	Frank Robinson	1.75	.90	.50
8	Willie Mays	3.00	1.50	.90
9	Brooks Robinson	2.00	1.00	.60
10	Tommy Davis	.50	.25	.15
11	Bill Freehan	.50	.25	.15
12	Claude Osteen	.40	.20	.12
13	Gary Peters	.30	.15	.09
14	Jim Lonborg	.40	.20	.12
15	Steve Hargan	.30	.15	.09
16	Dean Chance	.40	.20	.12

		NR MT	EX	VG
17	Mike McCormick	.30	.15	.09
18	Tim McCarver	.60	.30	.20
19	Ron Santo	.60	.30	.20
20	Tony Gonzalez	.30	.15	.09
21	Frank Howard	.70	.35	.20
22	George Scott	.40	.20	.12
23	Rich Allen	.70	.35	.20
24	Jim Wynn	.40	.20	.12
25	Gene Alley	.40	.20	.12
26	Rick Monday	.40	.20	.12
27	Al Kaline	2.00	1.00	.60
28	Rusty Staub	.70	.35	.20
29	Rod Carew	2.75	1.50	.80
30	Pete Rose	7.50	3.75	2.25
31	Joe Torre	.70	.35	.20
32	Orlando Cepeda	1.00	.50	.30
33	Jim Fregosi	.50	.25	.15

1968 Topps Plaks

Among the scarcest of the Topps test issues of the late 1960s, the "All Star Baseball Plaks" were plastic busts of two dozen stars of the era which came packaged like model airplane parts. The busts had to be snapped off a sprue and could be inserted into a base which carried the player's name. Packed with the plastic plaks was one of two checklist cards which featured six color photos per side. The 2-1/8" by 4" checklist cards are popular with superstar collectors and are considerably easier to find today than the actual plaks.

		NR MT	EX	VG
Complete Set:		2500.00	1250.00	750.00
Common Player:		20.00	10.00	6.00
1	Max Alvis	20.00	10.00	6.00
2	Frank Howard	30.00	15.00	9.00
3	Dean Chance	20.00	10.00	6.00

		NR MT	EX	VG
4	Jim Hunter	50.00	25.00	15.00
5	Jim Fregosi	25.00	12.50	7.50
6	Al Kaline	60.00	30.00	18.00
7	Harmon Killebrew	60.00	30.00	18.00
8	Gary Peters	20.00	10.00	6.00
9	Jim Lonborg	20.00	10.00	6.00
10	Frank Robinson	60.00	30.00	18.00
11	Mickey Mantle	800.00	400.00	240.00
12	Carl Yastrzemski	175.00	87.00	52.00
13	Hank Aaron	100.00	50.00	30.00
14	Bob Clemente	100.00	50.00	30.00
15	Richie Allen	30.00	15.00	9.00
16	Tommy Davis	25.00	12.50	7.50
17	Orlando Cepeda	30.00	15.00	9.00
18	Don Drysdale	50.00	25.00	15.00
19	Willie Mays	100.00	50.00	30.00
20	Rusty Staub	30.00	15.00	9.00
21	Tim McCarver	30.00	15.00	9.00
22	Pete Rose	250.00	125.00	75.00
23	Ron Santo	30.00	15.00	9.00
24	Jim Wynn	20.00	10.00	6.00
--——	Checklist Card 1-12	250.00	125.00	75.00
--——	Checklist Card 13-24	250.00	125.00	75.00

1968 Topps Posters

Yet another innovation from the creative minds at Topps appeared in 1968; a set of color player posters. Measuring 9-3/4" by 18-1/8," each poster was sold separately with its own piece of gum, rather than as an insert. The posters feature a large color photograph with a star at the bottom containing the player's name, position and team. There are 24 different posters which were folded numerous times to fit into the package they were sold in.

		NR MT	EX	VG
Complete Set:		300.00	150.00	90.00
Common Player:		3.00	1.50	.90
1	Dean Chance	3.00	1.50	.90
2	Max Alvis	3.00	1.50	.90
3	Frank Howard	8.00	4.00	2.50
4	Jim Fregosi	7.00	3.50	2.00
5	Jim Hunter	12.00	6.00	3.50
6	Bob Clemente	25.00	12.50	7.50
7	Don Drysdale	12.00	6.00	3.50
8	Jim Wynn	3.00	1.50	.90
9	Al Kaline	25.00	12.50	7.50
10	Harmon Killebrew	20.00	10.00	6.00
11	Jim Lonborg	3.00	1.50	.90
12	Orlando Cepeda	8.00	4.00	2.50

		NR MT	EX	VG
13	Gary Peters	3.00	1.50	.90
14	Hank Aaron	25.00	12.50	7.50
15	Richie Allen	8.00	4.00	2.50
16	Carl Yastrzemski	20.00	10.00	6.00
17	Ron Swoboda	3.00	1.50	.90
18	Mickey Mantle	50.00	25.00	15.00
19	Tim McCarver	7.00	3.50	2.00
20	Willie Mays	25.00	12.50	7.50
21	Ron Santo	7.00	3.50	2.00
22	Rusty Staub	7.00	3.50	2.00
23	Pete Rose	40.00	20.00	12.00
24	Frank Robinson	15.00	7.50	4.50

1968 Topps 3-D

These are very rare pioneer issues on the part of Topps. The cards measure 2-1/4" by 3-1/2" and were specially printed to simulate a three-dimensional effect. Backgrounds are a purposely blurred stadium scene, in front of which was a normally sharp color player photograph. The outer layer is a thin coating of ribbed plastic. The special process gives the picture the illusion of depth when the card is moved or tilted. As this was done two years before Kellogg's began its 3-D cards, this 12-card test issue really was breaking new ground. Unfortunately, production and distribution were limited making the cards very tough to find.

		NR MT	EX	VG
	Complete Set:	7000.00	3500.00	2100.
	Common Player:	350.00	175.00	105.00
(1)	Bob Clemente	1400.00	700.00	420.00
(2)	Willie Davis	400.00	200.00	125.00
(3)	Ron Fairly	400.00	200.00	125.00
(4)	Curt Flood	400.00	200.00	125.00
(5)	Jim Lonborg	400.00	200.00	125.00
(6)	Jim Maloney	350.00	175.00	105.00
(7)	Tony Perez	500.00	250.00	150.00
(8)	Boog Powell	450.00	230.00	135.00
(9)	Bill Robinson	350.00	175.00	105.00
(10)	Rusty Staub	450.00	230.00	135.00
(11)	Mel Stottlemyre	400.00	200.00	120.00
(12)	Ron Swoboda	350.00	175.00	105.00

1969 Topps

The 1969 Topps set broke yet another record for quantity as the issue is officially a whopping 664 cards. With substantial numbers of variations, the number of possible cards runs closer to 700. The design of the 2-1/2" by 3-1/2" cards in the set feature a color photo with the team name printed in block letters underneath. A circle contains the player's name and position. Card backs returned to a horizontal format. Despite the size of the set, it contains no teamcards. It does, however, have multi-player cards, All-Stars, statistical leaders, and World Series highlights. Most significant among the

varieties are white and yellow letter cards from the run of #'s 440-511. The complete set prices below do not include the scarcer and more expensive "white letter" variations.

		NR MT	EX	VG
	Complete Set:	1600.00	800.00	450.00
	Common Player: 1-218	.40	.20	.12
	Common Player: 219-327	.90	.45	.25
	Common Player: 328-512	.40	.20	.12
	Common Player: 513-664	.70	.35	.20
1	A.L. Batting Leaders (Danny Cater, Tony Oliva, Carl Yastrzemski)	7.00	2.00	1.00
2	N.L. Batting Leaders (Felipe Alou, Matty Alou, Pete Rose)	4.00	2.00	1.25
3	A.L. RBI Leaders (Ken Harrelson, Frank Howard, Jim Northrup)	2.00	1.00	.60
4	N.L. RBI Leaders (Willie McCovey, Ron Santo, Billy Williams)	3.50	1.75	1.00
5	A.L. Home Run Leaders (Ken Harrelson, Willie Horton, Frank Howard)	2.00	1.00	.60
6	N.L. Home Run Leaders (Richie Allen, Ernie Banks, Willie McCovey)	3.50	1.75	1.00
7	A.L. ERA Leaders (Sam McDowell, Dave McNally, Luis Tiant)	2.00	1.00	.60
8	N.L. ERA Leaders (Bobby Bolin, Bob Gibson, Bob Veale)	3.00	1.50	.90
9	A.L. Pitching Leaders (Denny McLain, Dave McNally, Mel Stottlemyre, Luis Tiant)	2.00	1.00	.60
10	N.L. Pitching Leaders (Bob Gibson, Fergie Jenkins, Juan Marichal)	3.50	1.75	1.00
11	A.L. Strikeout Leaders (Sam McDowell, Denny McLain, Luis Tiant)	2.00	1.00	.60
12	N.L. Strikeout Leaders (Bob Gibson, Fergie Jenkins, Bill Singer)	3.00	1.50	.90
13	Mickey Stanley	.50	.25	.15
14	Al McBean	.40	.20	.12
15	Boog Powell	2.50	1.25	.70
16	Giants Rookies (Cesar Gutierrez, Rich Robertson)	.40	.20	.12
17	Mike Marshall	1.25	.60	.40
18	Dick Schofield	.40	.20	.12
19	Ken Suarez	.40	.20	.12
20	Ernie Banks	10.00	5.00	3.00
21	Jose Santiago	.40	.20	.12
22	Jesus Alou	.50	.25	.15
23	Lew Krausse	.40	.20	.12
24	Walt Alston	3.00	1.50	.90
25	Roy White	1.25	.60	.40
26	Clay Carroll	.50	.25	.15
27	Bernie Allen	.40	.20	.12
28	Mike Ryan	.40	.20	.12
29	Dave Morehead	.40	.20	.12
30	Bob Allison	1.00	.50	.30
31	Mets Rookies (Gary Gentry, Amos Otis)	1.25	.60	.40
32	Sammy Ellis	.40	.20	.12
33	Wayne Causey	.40	.20	.12
34	Gary Peters	.50	.25	.15
35	Joe Morgan	6.00	3.00	1.75
36	Luke Walker	.40	.20	.12
37	Curt Motton	.40	.20	.12
38	Zoilo Versalles	.50	.25	.15
39	Dick Hughes	.40	.20	.12
40	Mayo Smith	.40	.20	.12
41	Bob Barton	.40	.20	.12
42	Tommy Harper	1.00	.50	.30
43	Joe Niekro	1.25	.60	.40

		NR MT	EX	VG
44	Danny Cater	.40	.20	.12
45	Maury Wills	2.50	1.25	.70
46	Fritz Peterson	1.00	.50	.30
47a	Paul Popovich (emblem visible thru airbrush)	4.00	2.00	1.25
47b	Paul Popovich (helmet emblem completely airbrushed)	.40	.20	.12
48	Brant Alyea	.40	.20	.12
49a	Royals Rookies (Steve Jones, Eliseo Rodriguez) (Rodriguez on front)	6.00	3.00	1.75
49b	Royals Rookies (Steve Jones, Eliseo Rodriguez) (Rodriguez on front)	.40	.20	.12
50	Bob Clemente	30.00	15.00	9.00
51	Woody Fryman	.50	.25	.15
52	Mike Andrews	.40	.20	.12
53	Sonny Jackson	.40	.20	.12
54	Cisco Carlos	.40	.20	.12
55	Jerry Grote	1.00	.50	.30
56	Rich Reese	.40	.20	.12
57	Checklist 1-109 (Denny McLain)	3.00	1.50	.90
58	Fred Gladding	.40	.20	.12
59	Jay Johnstone	.70	.35	.20
60	Nelson Briles	.40	.20	.12
61	Jimmie Hall	.40	.20	.12
62	Chico Salmon	.80	.40	.25
63	Jim Hickman	.50	.25	.15
64	Bill Monbouquette	.50	.25	.15
65	Willie Davis	1.00	.50	.30
66	Orioles Rookies (Mike Adamson, *Merv Rettenmund*)	.70	.35	.20
67	Bill Stoneman	.40	.20	.12
68	Dave Duncan	.40	.20	.12
69	Steve Hamilton	.70	.35	.20
70	Tommy Helms	.50	.25	.15
71	Steve Whitaker	.40	.20	.12
72	Ron Taylor	.60	.30	.20
73	Johnny Briggs	.40	.20	.12
74	Preston Gomez	.40	.20	.12
75	Luis Aparicio	5.00	2.50	1.50
76	Norm Miller	.40	.20	.12
77a	Ron Perranoski (LA visible thru airbrush)	4.50	2.25	1.25
77b	Ron Perranoski (cap emblem completely airbrushed)	.50	.25	.15
78	Tom Satriano	.40	.20	.12
79	Milt Pappas	.70	.35	.20
80	Norm Cash	1.75	.90	.50
81	Mel Queen	.40	.20	.12
82	Pirates Rookies (*Rich Hebner, Al Oliver*)	9.00	4.50	2.75
83	Mike Ferraro	.80	.40	.25
84	Bob Humphreys	.40	.20	.12
85	Lou Brock	8.00	4.00	2.50
86	Pete Richert	.40	.20	.12
87	Horace Clarke	.70	.35	.20
88	Rich Nye	.40	.20	.12
89	Russ Gibson	.40	.20	.12
90	Jerry Koosman	2.50	1.25	.70
91	Al Dark	.70	.35	.20
92	Jack Billingham	.50	.25	.15
93	Joe Foy	.40	.20	.12
94	Hank Aguirre	.40	.20	.12
95	Johnny Bench	110.00	50.00	28.00
96	Denver Lemaster	.40	.20	.12
97	Buddy Bradford	.40	.20	.12
98	Dave Giusti	.40	.20	.12
99a	Twins Rookies (Danny Morris, *Graig Nettles*) (black loop above "Twins")	20.00	10.00	6.00
99b	Twins Rookies (Danny Morris, *Graig Nettles*) (no black loop)	12.00	6.00	3.50
100	Hank Aaron	40.00	20.00	12.00
101	Daryl Patterson	.40	.20	.12
102	Jim Davenport	.40	.20	.12
103	Roger Repoz	.40	.20	.12
104	Steve Blass	.50	.25	.15
105	Rick Monday	.80	.40	.25
106	Jim Hannan	.40	.20	.12
107a	Checklist 110-218 (Bob Gibson) (161 is Jim Purdin)	3.00	1.50	.90
107b	Checklist 110-218 (Bob Gibson) (161 is John Purdin)	6.00	3.00	1.75
108	Tony Taylor	.40	.20	.12
109	Jim Lonborg	.80	.40	.25
110	Mike Shannon	.50	.25	.15
111	Johnny Morris	.80	.40	.25
112	J.C. Martin	.70	.35	.20
113	Dave May	.40	.20	.12
114	Yankees Rookies (Alan Closter, John Cumberland)	.70	.35	.20
115	Bill Hands	.40	.20	.12
116	Chuck Harrison	.40	.20	.12
117	Jim Fairey	.40	.20	.12
118	Stan Williams	.40	.20	.12
119	Doug Rader	.50	.25	.15
120	Pete Rose	35.00	17.50	10.50
121	Joe Grzenda	.40	.20	.12
122	Ron Fairly	.80	.40	.25
123	Wilbur Wood	.80	.40	.25
124	Hank Bauer	.80	.40	.25
125	Ray Sadecki	.40	.20	.12
126	Dick Tracewski	.40	.20	.12
127	Kevin Collins	.60	.30	.20
128	Tommie Aaron	.70	.35	.20
129	Bill McCool	.40	.20	.12
130	Carl Yastrzemski	25.00	12.50	7.50
131	Chris Cannizzaro	.40	.20	.12
132	Dave Baldwin	.40	.20	.12
133	Johnny Callison	1.00	.50	.30
134	Jim Weaver	.40	.20	.12
135	Tommy Davis	1.50	.70	.45
136	Cards Rookies (Steve Huntz, Mike Torrez)	.50	.25	.15
137	Wally Bunker	.40	.20	.12
138	John Bateman	.40	.20	.12
139	Andy Kosco	.40	.20	.12
140	Jim Lefebvre	.50	.25	.15
141	Bill Dillman	.40	.20	.12
142	Woody Woodward	.50	.25	.15
143	Joe Nossek	.40	.20	.12
144	Bob Hendley	.60	.30	.20
145	Max Alvis	.50	.25	.15
146	Jim Perry	1.00	.50	.30
147	Leo Durocher	2.25	1.25	.70
148	Lee Stange	.40	.20	.12
149	Ollie Brown	.40	.20	.12
150	Denny McLain	3.00	1.50	.90
151a	Clay Dalrymple (Phillies)	7.00	3.50	2.00
151b	Clay Dalrymple (Orioles)	.40	.20	.12
152	Tommie Sisk	.40	.20	.12
153	Ed Brinkman	.50	.25	.15
154	Jim Britton	.40	.20	.12
155	Pete Ward	.40	.20	.12
156	Astros Rookies (Hal Gilson, Leon McFadden)	.40	.20	.12
157	Bob Rodgers	.70	.35	.20
158	Joe Gibbon	.40	.20	.12
159	Jerry Adair	.40	.20	.12
160	Vada Pinson	2.00	1.00	.60
161	John Purdin	.40	.20	.12
162	World Series Game 1 (Gibson Fans 17; Sets New Record)	3.50	1.75	1.00
163	World Series Game 2 (Tiger Homers Deck The Cards)	2.50	1.25	.70
164	World Series Game 3 (McCarver's Homer Puts St. Louis Ahead)	2.50	1.25	.70
165	World Series Game 4 (Brock's Lead-Off Homer Starts Cards' Romp)	3.50	1.75	1.00
166	World Series Game 5 (Kaline's Key Hit Sparks Tiger Rally)	3.50	1.75	1.00
167	World Series Game 6 (Tiger 10-Run Inning Ties Mark)	2.50	1.25	.70
168	World Series Game 7 (Lolich Series Hero, Outduels Gibson)	2.75	1.50	.80
169	World Series Summary (Tigers Celebrate Their Victory)	2.50	1.25	.70
170	Frank Howard	2.00	1.00	.60
171	Glenn Beckert	.80	.40	.25
172	Jerry Stephenson	.40	.20	.12
173	White Sox Rookies (Bob Christian, Gerry Nyman)	.40	.20	.12
174	Grant Jackson	.40	.20	.12
175	Jim Bunning	4.00	2.00	1.25
176	Joe Azcue	.40	.20	.12
177	Ron Reed	.50	.25	.15
178	Ray Oyler	.80	.40	.25
179	Don Pavletich	.40	.20	.12
180	Willie Horton	.80	.40	.25
181	Mel Nelson	.40	.20	.12
182	Bill Rigney	.40	.20	.12
183	Don Shaw	.40	.20	.12
184	Roberto Pena	.40	.20	.12
185	Tom Phoebus	.40	.20	.12
186	John Edwards	.40	.20	.12
187	Leon Wagner	.50	.25	.15
188	Rick Wise	.50	.25	.15
189	Red Sox Rookies (Joe Lahoud, John Thibdeau)	.40	.20	.12
190	Willie Mays	40.00	20.00	12.00
191	Lindy McDaniel	.70	.35	.20
192	Jose Pagan	.40	.20	.12
193	Don Cardwell	.70	.35	.20
194	Ted Uhlaender	.40	.20	.12

		NR MT	EX	VG
195	John Odom	.50	.25	.15
196	Lum Harris	.40	.20	.12
197	Dick Selma	.40	.20	.12
198	Willie Smith	.40	.20	.12
199	Jim French	.40	.20	.12
200	Bob Gibson	12.00	6.00	3.50
201	Russ Snyder	.40	.20	.12
202	Don Wilson	.40	.20	.12
203	Dave Johnson	1.50	.70	.45
204	Jack Hiatt	.40	.20	.12
205	Rick Reichardt	.40	.20	.12
206	Phillies Rookies (Larry Hisle, Barry Lersch)	.80	.40	.25
207	Roy Face	1.25	.60	.40
208a	Donn Clendenon (Expos)	7.00	3.50	2.00
208b	Donn Clendenon (Houston)	.50	.25	.15
209	Larry Haney (photo reversed)	.80	.40	.25
210	Felix Millan	.40	.20	.12
211	Galen Cisco	.40	.20	.12
212	Tom Tresh	1.25	.60	.40
213	Gerry Arrigo	.40	.20	.12
214	Checklist 219-327	2.50	1.25	.70
215	Rico Petrocelli	.80	.40	.25
216	Don Sutton	4.00	2.00	1.25
217	John Donaldson	.40	.20	.12
218	John Roseboro	.60	.30	.20
219	*Freddie Patek*	1.25	.60	.40
220	Sam McDowell	1.25	.60	.40
221	Art Shamsky	1.00	.50	.30
222	Duane Josephson	.90	.45	.25
223	Tom Dukes	.90	.45	.25
224	Angels Rookies (Bill Harrelson, Steve Kealey)	.90	.45	.25
225	Don Kessinger	1.00	.50	.30
226	Bruce Howard	.90	.45	.25
227	Frank Johnson	.90	.45	.25
228	Dave Leonhard	.90	.45	.25
229	Don Lock	.90	.45	.25
230	Rusty Staub	2.50	1.25	.70
231	Pat Dobson	1.00	.50	.30
232	Dave Ricketts	.90	.45	.25
233	Steve Barber	1.00	.50	.30
234	Dave Bristol	.90	.45	.25
235	Jim Hunter	7.00	3.50	2.00
236	Manny Mota	1.00	.50	.30
237	*Bobby Cox*	1.50	.70	.45
238	Ken Johnson	.90	.45	.25
239	Bob Taylor	.90	.45	.25
240	Ken Harrelson	2.00	1.00	.60
241	Jim Brewer	.90	.45	.25
242	Frank Kostro	.90	.45	.25
243	Ron Kline	.90	.45	.25
244	Indians Rookies (*Ray Fosse*, George Woodson)	1.25	.60	.40
245	Ed Charles	1.00	.50	.30
246	Joe Coleman	1.00	.50	.30
247	Gene Oliver	.90	.45	.25
248	Bob Priddy	.90	.45	.25
249	Ed Spiezio	.90	.45	.25
250	Frank Robinson	12.00	6.00	3.50
251	Ron Herbel	.90	.45	.25
252	Chuck Cottier	.90	.45	.25
253	Jerry Johnson	.90	.45	.25
254	Joe Schultz	1.00	.50	.30
255	Steve Carlton	30.00	15.00	9.00
256	Gates Brown	.90	.45	.25
257	Jim Ray	.90	.45	.25
258	Jackie Hernandez	.90	.45	.25
259	Bill Short	.90	.45	.25
260	*Reggie Jackson*	300.00	120.00	75.00
261	Bob Johnson	.90	.45	.25
262	Mike Kekich	1.00	.50	.30
263	Jerry May	.90	.45	.25
264	Bill Landis	.90	.45	.25
265	Chico Cardenas	.90	.45	.25
266	Dodgers Rookies (Alan Foster, Tom Hutton)	.90	.45	.25
267	Vicente Romo	.90	.45	.25
268	Al Spangler	.90	.45	.25
269	Al Weis	1.00	.50	.30
270	Mickey Lolich	3.50	1.75	1.00
271	Larry Stahl	.90	.45	.25
272	Ed Stroud	.90	.45	.25
273	Ron Willis	.90	.45	.25
274	Clyde King	.90	.45	.25
275	Vic Davalillo	.90	.45	.25
276	Gary Wagner	.90	.45	.25
277	*Rod Hendricks*	.90	.45	.25
278	Gary Geiger	.90	.45	.25
279	Roger Nelson	.90	.45	.25
280	Alex Johnson	.90	.45	.25

		NR MT	EX	VG
281	Ted Kubiak	.90	.45	.25
282	Pat Jarvis	.90	.45	.25
283	Sandy Alomar	.90	.45	.25
284	Expos Rookies (Jerry Robertson, Mike Wegener)	.90	.45	.25
285	Don Mincher	1.00	.50	.30
286	*Dock Ellis*	1.25	.60	.40
287	Jose Tartabull	.90	.45	.25
288	Ken Holtzman	1.00	.50	.30
289	Bart Shirley	.90	.45	.25
290	Jim Kaat	4.50	2.25	1.25
291	Vern Fuller	.90	.45	.25
292	Al Downing	1.25	.60	.40
293	Dick Dietz	.90	.45	.25
294	Jim Lemon	.90	.45	.25
295	Tony Perez	4.50	2.25	1.25
296	*Andy Messersmith*	1.25	.60	.40
297	Deron Johnson	.90	.45	.25
298	Dave Nicholson	.90	.45	.25
299	Mark Belanger	1.00	.50	.30
300	Felipe Alou	1.25	.60	.40
301	Darrell Brandon	.90	.45	.25
302	Jim Pagliaroni	.90	.45	.25
303	Cal Koonce	1.00	.50	.30
304	Padres Rookies (Bill Davis, *Clarence Gaston*)	1.00	.50	.30
305	Dick McAuliffe	1.00	.50	.30
306	Jim Grant	.90	.45	.25
307	Gary Kolb	.90	.45	.25
308	Wade Blasingame	.90	.45	.25
309	Walt Williams	.90	.45	.25
310	Tom Haller	1.00	.50	.30
311	*Sparky Lyle*	2.00	1.00	.60
312	Lee Elia	.90	.45	.25
313	Bill Robinson	1.00	.50	.30
314	Checklist 328-425 (Don Drysdale)	3.50	1.75	1.00
315	Eddie Fisher	.90	.45	.25
316	Hal Lanier	1.00	.50	.30
317	Bruce Look	.90	.45	.25
318	Jack Fisher	.90	.45	.25
319	Ken McMullen	.90	.45	.25
320	Dal Maxvill	1.00	.50	.30
321	Jim McAndrew	1.00	.50	.30
322	Jose Vidal	1.00	.50	.30
323	Larry Miller	.90	.45	.25
324	Tigers Rookies (Les Cain, Dave Campbell)	.90	.45	.25
325	Jose Cardenal	1.00	.50	.30
326	Gary Sutherland	.90	.45	.25
327	Willie Crawford	.90	.45	.25
328	Joe Horlen	.40	.20	.12
329	Rick Joseph	.40	.20	.12
330	Tony Conigliaro	1.50	.70	.45
331	Braves Rookies (Gil Garrido, *Tom House*)	.50	.25	.15
332	Fred Talbot	.80	.40	.25
333	Ivan Murrell	.40	.20	.12
334	Phil Roof	.40	.20	.12
335	Bill Mazeroski	1.75	.90	.50
336	Jim Roland	.40	.20	.12
337	Marty Martinez	.40	.20	.12
338	*Del Unser*	.50	.25	.15
339	Reds Rookies (Steve Mingori, Jose Pena)	.40	.20	.12
340	Dave McNally	.80	.40	.25
341	Dave Adlesh	.40	.20	.12
342	Bubba Morton	.40	.20	.12
343	Dan Frisella	.70	.35	.20
344	Tom Matchick	.40	.20	.12
345	Frank Linzy	.40	.20	.12
346	Wayne Comer	.80	.40	.25
347	Randy Hundley	.40	.20	.12
348	Steve Hargan	.40	.20	.12
349	Dick Williams	.80	.40	.25
350	Richie Allen	2.00	1.00	.60
351	Carroll Sembera	.40	.20	.12
352	Paul Schaal	.40	.20	.12
353	Jeff Torborg	.50	.25	.15
354	Nate Oliver	.80	.40	.25
355	Phil Niekro	5.00	2.50	1.50
356	Frank Quilici	.40	.20	.12
357	Carl Taylor	.40	.20	.12
358	Athletics Rookies (George Lauzerique, Roberto Rodriguez)	.40	.20	.12
359	Dick Kelley	.40	.20	.12
360	Jim Wynn	.80	.40	.25
361	Gary Holman	.40	.20	.12
362	Jim Maloney	.50	.25	.15
363	Russ Nixon	.40	.20	.12
364	Tommie Agee	.80	.40	.25
365	Jim Fregosi	1.00	.50	.30

		NR MT	EX	VG
366	Bo Belinsky	1.00	.50	.30
367	Lou Johnson	.40	.20	.12
368	Vic Roznovsky	.40	.20	.12
369	Bob Skinner	.40	.20	.12
370	Juan Marichal	7.00	3.50	2.00
371	Sal Bando	.80	.40	.25
372	Adolfo Phillips	.40	.20	.12
373	Fred Lasher	.40	.20	.12
374	Bob Tillman	.40	.20	.12
375	Harmon Killebrew	12.00	6.00	3.50
376	Royals Rookies (Mike Fiore, *Jim Rooker*)	.50	.25	.15
377	Gary Bell	.80	.40	.25
378	Jose Herrera	.40	.20	.12
379	Ken Boyer	1.75	.90	.50
380	Stan Bahnsen	.80	.40	.25
381	Ed Kranepool	.80	.40	.25
382	Pat Corrales	.80	.40	.25
383	Casey Cox	.40	.20	.12
384	Larry Shepard	.40	.20	.12
385	Orlando Cepeda	3.50	1.75	1.00
386	Jim McGlothlin	.40	.20	.12
387	Bobby Klaus	.40	.20	.12
388	Tom McCraw	.40	.20	.12
389	Dan Coombs	.40	.20	.12
390	Bill Freehan	.70	.35	.20
391	Ray Culp	.40	.20	.12
392	Bob Burda	.40	.20	.12
393	Gene Brabender	.40	.20	.12
394	Pilots Rookies (Lou Piniella, Marv Staehle)	2.25	1.25	.70
395	Chris Short	.60	.30	.20
396	Jim Campanis	.40	.20	.12
397	Chuck Dobson	.40	.20	.12
398	Tito Francona	.50	.25	.15
399	Bob Bailey	.40	.20	.12
400	Don Drysdale	8.00	4.00	2.50
401	Jake Gibbs	.80	.40	.25
402	Ken Boswell	.70	.35	.20
403	Bob Miller	.40	.20	.12
404	Cubs Rookies (Vic LaRose, Gary Ross)	.40	.20	.12
405	Lee May	1.00	.50	.30
406	Phil Ortega	.40	.20	.12
407	Tom Egan	.40	.20	.12
408	Nate Colbert	.40	.20	.12
409	Bob Moose	.40	.20	.12
410	Al Kaline	10.00	5.00	3.00
411	Larry Dierker	.50	.25	.15
412	Checklist 426-512 (Mickey Mantle)	7.00	3.50	2.00
413	Roland Sheldon	.80	.40	.25
414	Duke Sims	.40	.20	.12
415	Ray Washburn	.40	.20	.12
416	Willie McCovey AS	3.50	1.75	1.00
417	Ken Harrelson AS	1.00	.50	.30
418	Tommy Helms AS	.70	.35	.20
419	Rod Carew AS	4.50	2.25	1.25
420	Ron Santo AS	1.00	.50	.30
421	Brooks Robinson AS	4.00	2.00	1.25
422	Don Kessinger AS	.70	.35	.20
423	Bert Campaneris AS	.80	.40	.25
424	Pete Rose AS	12.00	6.00	3.50
425	Carl Yastrzemski AS	6.00	3.00	1.75
426	Curt Flood AS	1.00	.50	.30
427	Tony Oliva AS	1.50	.70	.45
428	Lou Brock AS	3.50	1.75	1.00
429	Willie Horton AS	.80	.40	.25
430	Johnny Bench AS	10.00	5.00	3.00
431	Bill Freehan AS	.70	.35	.20
432	Bob Gibson AS	3.50	1.75	1.00
433	Denny McLain AS	1.50	.70	.45
434	Jerry Koosman AS	1.00	.50	.30
435	Sam McDowell AS	.80	.40	.25
436	Gene Alley	.70	.35	.20
437	Luis Alcaraz	.40	.20	.12
438	Gary Waslewski	.40	.20	.12
439	White Sox Rookies (Ed Herrmann, Dan Lazar)	.40	.20	.12
440a	Willie McCovey (last name in white)	90.00	45.00	27.00
440b	Willie McCovey (last name in yellow)	20.00	10.00	6.00
441a	Dennis Higgins (last name in white)	10.00	5.00	3.00
441b	Dennis Higgins (last name in yellow)	.40	.20	.12
442	Ty Cline	.40	.20	.12
443	Don Wert	.40	.20	.12
444a	Joe Moeller (last name in white)	10.00	5.00	3.00
444b	Joe Moeller (last name in yellow)	.40	.20	.12
445	Bobby Knoop	.40	.20	.12
446	Claude Raymond	.40	.20	.12
447a	Ralph Houk (last name in white)	15.00	7.50	4.50
447b	Ralph Houk (last name in yellow)	1.50	.70	.45
448	Bob Tolan	.50	.25	.15
449	Paul Lindblad	.40	.20	.12
450	Billy Williams	6.00	3.00	1.75
451a	Rich Rollins (first name in white)	10.00	5.00	3.00
451b	Rich Rollins (first name in yellow)	.80	.40	.25
452a	Al Ferrara (first name in white)	10.00	5.00	3.00
452b	Al Ferrara (first name in yellow)	.40	.20	.12
453	Mike Cuellar	.80	.40	.25
454a	Phillies Rookies (Larry Colton, *Don Money*) (names in white)	10.00	5.00	3.00
454b	Phillies Rookies (Larry Colton, *Don Money*) (names in yellow)	.80	.40	.25
455	Sonny Siebert	.40	.20	.12
456	Bud Harrelson	1.00	.50	.30
457	Dalton Jones	.40	.20	.12
458	Curt Blefary	.40	.20	.12
459	Dave Boswell	.40	.20	.12
460	Joe Torre	1.75	.90	.50
461a	Mike Epstein (last name in white)	10.00	5.00	3.00
461b	Mike Epstein (last name in yellow)	.50	.25	.15
462	Red Schoendienst	1.50	.70	.45
463	Dennis Ribant	.40	.20	.12
464a	Dave Marshall (last name in white)	10.00	5.00	3.00
464b	Dave Marshall (last name in yellow)	.40	.20	.12
465	Tommy John	4.50	2.25	1.25
466	John Boccabella	.40	.20	.12
467	Tom Reynolds	.40	.20	.12
468a	Pirates Rookies (Bruce Dal Canton, Bob Robertson) (names in white)	10.00	5.00	3.00
468b	Pirates Rookies (Bruce Dal Canton, Bob Robertson) (names in yellow)	.50	.25	.15
469	Chico Ruiz	.40	.20	.12
470a	Mel Stottlemyre (last name in white)	15.00	7.50	4.50
470b	Mel Stottlemyre (last name in yellow)	1.50	.70	.45
471a	Ted Savage (last name in white)	10.00	5.00	3.00
471b	Ted Savage (last name in yellow)	.40	.20	.12
472	Jim Price	.40	.20	.12
473a	Jose Arcia (first name in white)	10.00	5.00	3.00
473b	Jose Arcia (first name in yellow)	.40	.20	.12
474	Tom Murphy	.40	.20	.12
475	Tim McCarver	1.50	.70	.45
476a	Red Sox Rookies (*Ken Brett*, Gerry Moses) (names in white)	10.00	5.00	3.00
476b	Red Sox Rookies (*Ken Brett*, Gerry Moses) (names in yellow)	.50	.25	.15
477	Jeff James	.40	.20	.12
478	Don Buford	.60	.30	.20
479	Richie Scheinblum	.40	.20	.12
480	Tom Seaver	60.00	30.00	18.00
481	*Bill Melton*	.80	.40	.25
482a	Jim Gosger (first name in white)	10.00	5.00	3.00
482b	Jim Gosger (first name in yellow)	.80	.40	.25
483	Ted Abernathy	.40	.20	.12
484	Joe Gordon	.50	.25	.15
485a	Gaylord Perry (last name in white)	60.00	30.00	18.00
485b	Gaylord Perry (last name in yellow)	10.00	5.00	3.00
486a	Paul Casanova (last name in white)	10.00	5.00	3.00
486b	Paul Casanova (last name in yellow)	.40	.20	.12
487	Denis Menke	.40	.20	.12
488	Joe Sparma	.40	.20	.12
489	Clete Boyer	.80	.40	.25
490	Matty Alou	1.00	.50	.30
491a	Twins Rookies (Jerry Crider, George Mitterwald) (names in white)	10.00	5.00	3.00
491b	Twins Rookies (Jerry Crider, George Mitterwald) (names in yellow)	.40	.20	.12
492	Tony Cloninger	.50	.25	.15
493a	Wes Parker (last name in white)	10.00	5.00	3.00
493b	Wes Parker (last name in yellow)	.70	.35	.20
494	Ken Berry	.40	.20	.12
495	Bert Campaneris	1.25	.60	.40
496	Larry Jaster	.40	.20	.12
497	Julian Javier	.40	.20	.12
498	Juan Pizarro	.40	.20	.12
499	Astros Rookies (Don Bryant, Steve Shea)	.40	.20	.12
500a	Mickey Mantle (last name in white)	475.00	190.00	119.00
500b	Mickey Mantle (last name in yellow)	175.00	70.00	44.00

		NR MT	EX	VG
501a	Tony Gonzalez (first name in white)			
		10.00	5.00	3.00
501b	Tony Gonzalez (first name in yellow)			
		.40	.20	.12
502	Minnie Rojas	.40	.20	.12
503	Larry Brown	.40	.20	.12
504	Checklist 513-588 (Brooks Robinson)			
		4.00	2.00	1.25
505a	Bobby Bolin (last name in white)	10.00	5.00	3.00
505b	Bobby Bolin (last name in yellow)	.40	.20	.12
506	Paul Blair	.50	.25	.15
507	Cookie Rojas	.40	.20	.12
508	Moe Drabowsky	.40	.20	.12
509	Manny Sanguillen	.50	.25	.15
510	Rod Carew	25.00	12.50	7.50
511a	Diego Segui (first name in white)	10.00	5.00	3.00
511b	Diego Segui (first name in yellow)	.80	.40	.25
512	Cleon Jones	.80	.40	.25
513	Camilo Pascual	.90	.45	.25
514	Mike Lum	.70	.35	.20
515	Dick Green	.70	.35	.20
516	Earl Weaver	3.50	1.75	1.00
517	Mike McCormick	.80	.40	.25
518	Fred Whitfield	.70	.35	.20
519	Yankees Rookies (Len Boehmer, Gerry Kenney)	1.00	.50	.30
520	Bob Veale	.80	.40	.25
521	George Thomas	.70	.35	.20
522	Joe Hoerner	.70	.35	.20
523	Bob Chance	.70	.35	.20
524	Expos Rookies (Jose Laboy, Floyd Wicker)			
		.70	.35	.20
525	Earl Wilson	.70	.35	.20
526	Hector Torres	.70	.35	.20
527	Al Lopez	3.00	1.50	.90
528	Claude Osteen	.90	.45	.25
529	Ed Kirkpatrick	.70	.35	.20
530	Cesar Tovar	.70	.35	.20
531	Dick Farrell	.70	.35	.20
532	Bird Hill Aces (Mike Cuellar, Jim Hardin, Dave McNally, Tom Phoebus)	1.50	.70	.45
533	Nolan Ryan	225.00	90.00	56.00
534	Jerry McNertney	.90	.45	.25
535	Phil Regan	.70	.35	.20
536	Padres Rookies (Danny Breeden, *Dave Roberts*)	.80	.40	.25
537	Mike Paul	.70	.35	.20
538	Charlie Smith	.70	.35	.20
539	Ted Shows How (Mike Epstein, Ted Williams)	3.25	1.75	1.00
540	Curt Flood	1.50	.70	.45
541	Joe Verbanic	1.00	.50	.30
542	Bob Aspromonte	.70	.35	.20
543	Fred Newman	.70	.35	.20
544	Tigers Rookies (Mike Kilkenny, Ron Woods)	.70	.35	.20
545	Willie Stargell	10.00	5.00	3.00
546	Jim Nash	.70	.35	.20
547	Billy Martin	3.25	1.75	1.00
548	Bob Locker	.70	.35	.20
549	Ron Brand	.70	.35	.20
550	Brooks Robinson	12.00	6.00	3.50
551	Wayne Granger	.70	.35	.20
552	Dodgers Rookies (*Ted Sizemore, Bill Sudakis*)	.80	.40	.25
553	Ron Davis	.70	.35	.20
554	Frank Bertaina	.70	.35	.20
555	Jim Hart	.80	.40	.25
556	A's Stars (Sal Bando, Bert Campaneris, Danny Cater)	1.50	.70	.45
557	Frank Fernandez	1.00	.50	.30
558	*Tom Burgmeier*	.80	.40	.25
559	Cards Rookies (Joe Hague, Jim Hicks)			
		.70	.35	.20
560	Luis Tiant	1.50	.70	.45
561	Ron Clark	.70	.35	.20
562	*Bob Watson*	1.00	.50	.30
563	Marty Pattin	.90	.45	.25
564	Gil Hodges	6.00	3.00	1.75
565	Hoyt Wilhelm	6.00	3.00	1.75
566	Ron Hansen	.70	.35	.20
567	Pirates Rookies (Elvio Jimenez, Jim Shellenback)	.70	.35	.20
568	Cecil Upshaw	.70	.35	.20
569	Billy Harris	.70	.35	.20
570	Ron Santo	1.75	.90	.50
571	Cap Peterson	.70	.35	.20
572	Giants Heroes (Juan Marichal, Willie McCovey)	7.00	3.50	2.00
573	Jim Palmer	15.00	7.50	4.50
574	George Scott	.90	.45	.25

		NR MT	EX	VG
575	Bill Singer	.80	.40	.25
576	Phillies Rookies (Ron Stone, Bill Wilson)			
		.70	.35	.20
577	Mike Hegan	1.00	.50	.30
578	Don Bosch	.70	.35	.20
579	*Dave Nelson*	.80	.40	.25
580	Jim Northrup	.80	.40	.25
581	Gary Nolan	.70	.35	.20
582a	Checklist 589-664 (Tony Oliva) (red circle on back)	3.50	1.75	1.00
582b	Checklist 589-664 (Tony Oliva) (white circle on back)	2.50	1.25	.70
583	*Clyde Wright*	.80	.40	.25
584	Don Mason	.70	.35	.20
585	Ron Swoboda	.90	.45	.25
586	Tim Cullen	.70	.35	.20
587	*Joe Rudi*	1.75	.90	.50
588	Bill White	1.00	.50	.30
589	Joe Pepitone	2.00	1.00	.60
590	Rico Carty	1.00	.50	.30
591	Mike Hedlund	.70	.35	.20
592	Padres Rookies (Rafael Robles, Al Santorini)	.70	.35	.20
593	Don Nottebart	.70	.35	.20
594	Dooley Womack	.70	.35	.20
595	Lee Maye	.70	.35	.20
596	Chuck Hartenstein	.70	.35	.20
597	A.L. Rookies (Larry Burchart, *Rollie Fingers*, Bob Floyd)	35.00	17.50	10.50
598	Ruben Amaro	.70	.35	.20
599	John Boozer	.70	.35	.20
600	Tony Oliva	2.25	1.25	.70
601	Tug McGraw	2.00	1.00	.60
602	Cubs Rookies (Alec Distaso, Jim Qualls, Don Young)	.70	.35	.20
603	Joe Keough	.70	.35	.20
604	Bobby Etheridge	.70	.35	.20
605	Dick Ellsworth	.70	.35	.20
606	Gene Mauch	.90	.45	.25
607	Dick Bosman	.70	.35	.20
608	Dick Simpson	1.00	.50	.30
609	Phil Gagliano	.70	.35	.20
610	Jim Hardin	.70	.35	.20
611	Braves Rookies (Bob Didier, Walt Hriniak, Gary Neibauer)	.70	.35	.20
612	Jack Aker	1.00	.50	.30
613	Jim Beauchamp	.70	.35	.20
614	Astros Rookies (Tom Griffin, Skip Guinn)			
		.70	.35	.20
615	Len Gabrielson	.70	.35	.20
616	Don McMahon	.70	.35	.20
617	Jesse Gonder	.70	.35	.20
618	Ramon Webster	.70	.35	.20
619	Royals Rookies (Bill Butler, *Pat Kelly*, Juan Rios)	.80	.40	.25
620	Dean Chance	.80	.40	.25
621	Bill Voss	.70	.35	.20
622	Dan Osinski	.70	.35	.20
623	Hank Allen	.70	.35	.20
624	N.L. Rookies (Darrel Chaney, Duffy Dyer, Terry Harmon)	.80	.40	.25
625	Mack Jones	.70	.35	.20
626	Gene Michael	1.00	.50	.30
627	George Stone	.70	.35	.20
628	Red Sox Rookies (*Bill Conigliaro*, Syd O'Brien, Fred Wenz)	.90	.45	.25
629	Jack Hamilton	.70	.35	.20
630	*Bobby Bonds*	9.00	4.50	2.75
631	John Kennedy	.90	.45	.25
632	Jon Warden	.70	.35	.20
633	Harry Walker	.80	.40	.25
634	Andy Etchebarren	.70	.35	.20
635	George Culver	.70	.35	.20
636	Woodie Held	.70	.35	.20
637	Padres Rookies (Jerry DaVanon, *Clay Kirby*, Frank Reberger)	.80	.40	.25
638	Ed Sprague	.70	.35	.20
639	Barry Moore	.70	.35	.20
640	Fergie Jenkins	3.50	1.75	1.00
641	N.L. Rookies (Bobby Darwin, Tommy Dean, John Miller)	.70	.35	.20
642	John Hiller	.80	.40	.25
643	Billy Cowan	1.00	.50	.30
644	Chuck Hinton	.70	.35	.20
645	George Brunet	.70	.35	.20
646	Expos Rookies (Dan McGinn, *Carl Morton*)	.90	.45	.25
647	Dave Wickersham	.70	.35	.20
648	Bobby Wine	.70	.35	.20
649	Al Jackson	.90	.45	.25
650	Ted Williams	7.00	3.50	2.00

		NR MT	EX	VG
651	Gus Gil	.90	.45	.25
652	Eddie Watt	.70	.35	.20
653	*Aurelio Rodriguez* (photo actually batboy			
	Leonard Garcia)	1.50	.70	.45
654	White Sox Rookies *(Carlos May, Rich*			
	Morales, Don Secrist)	.90	.45	.25
655	Mike Hershberger	.70	.35	.20
656	Dan Schneider	.70	.35	.20
657	Bobby Murcer	2.25	1.25	.70
658	A.L. Rookies (Bill Burbach, Tom Hall, Jim			
	Miles)	1.00	.50	.30
659	Johnny Podres	1.75	.90	.50
660	Reggie Smith	1.75	.90	.50
661	Jim Merritt	.70	.35	.20
662	Royals Rookies (Dick Drago, Bob Oliver,			
	George Spriggs)	.80	.40	.25
663	Dick Radatz	.90	.45	.25
664	Ron Hunt	2.00	.50	.25

1969 Topps Decals

Designed as an insert for 1969 regular issue card packs, these decals are virtually identical in format to the '69 cards. The 48 decals in the set measure 1" by 2-1/2," although they are mounted on white paper backing which measures 1-3/4" by 2-1/8."

		NR MT	EX	VG
Complete Set:		150.00	75.00	45.00
Common Player:		1.00	.50	.30
(1)	Hank Aaron	15.00	7.50	4.50
(2)	Richie Allen	2.50	1.25	.70
(3)	Felipe Alou	1.75	.90	.50
(4)	Matty Alou	1.75	.90	.50
(5)	Luis Aparicio	4.50	2.25	1.25
(6)	Bob Clemente	15.00	7.50	4.50
(7)	Donn Clendenon	1.00	.50	.30
(8)	Tommy Davis	1.75	.90	.50
(9)	Don Drysdale	7.00	3.50	2.00
(10)	Joe Foy	1.00	.50	.30
(11)	Jim Fregosi	1.75	.90	.50
(12)	Bob Gibson	7.00	3.50	2.00
(13)	Tony Gonzalez	1.00	.50	.30
(14)	Tom Haller	1.00	.50	.30
(15)	Ken Harrelson	1.75	.90	.50
(16)	Tommy Helms	1.00	.50	.30
(17)	Willie Horton	1.75	.90	.50
(18)	Frank Howard	2.50	1.25	.70
(19)	Reggie Jackson	25.00	12.50	7.50
(20)	Fergie Jenkins	3.50	1.75	1.00
(21)	Harmon Killebrew	6.00	3.00	1.75
(22)	Jerry Koosman	1.75	.90	.50
(23)	Mickey Mantle	35.00	17.50	10.50
(24)	Willie Mays	15.00	7.50	4.50
(25)	Tim McCarver	1.75	.90	.50
(26)	Willie McCovey	7.00	3.50	2.00
(27)	Sam McDowell	1.75	.90	.50
(28)	Denny McLain	1.75	.90	.50
(29)	Dave McNally	1.75	.90	.50
(30)	Don Mincher	1.00	.50	.30
(31)	Rick Monday	1.75	.90	.50
(32)	Tony Oliva	3.00	1.50	.90
(33)	Camilo Pascual	1.00	.50	.30
(34)	Rick Reichardt	1.00	.50	.30
(35)	Pete Rose	20.00	10.00	6.00
(36)	Frank Robinson	7.00	3.50	2.00
(37)	Ron Santo	1.75	.90	.50

		NR MT	EX	VG
(38)	Dick Selma	1.00	.50	.30
(39)	Tom Seaver	20.00	10.00	6.00
(40)	Chris Short	1.00	.50	.30
(41)	Rusty Staub	1.75	.90	.50
(42)	Mel Stottlemyre	1.75	.90	.50
(43)	Luis Tiant	1.75	.90	.50
(44)	Pete Ward	1.00	.50	.30
(45)	Hoyt Wilhelm	6.00	3.00	1.75
(46)	Maury Wills	2.50	1.25	.70
(47)	Jim Wynn	1.75	.90	.50
(48)	Carl Yastrzemski	15.00	7.50	4.50

1969 Topps Deckle Edge

These 2-1/4" by 3-1/4" inch cards take their name from their interesting borders which have a scalloped effect. The fronts have a black and white picture of the player along with a blue facsimile autograph. Backs have the player's name and the card number in light blue ink in a small box at the bottom of the card. Technically, there are only 33 numbered cards, but there are actually 35 possible players; both Jim Wynn and Hoyt Wilhelm cards are found as #11 while cards of Joe Foy and Rusty Staub can be found as #22. Many of the players in the set are stars.

		NR MT	EX	VG
Complete Set:		60.00	30.00	17.50
Common Player:		.30	.15	.09
1	Brooks Robinson	2.50	1.25	.70
2	Boog Powell	.50	.25	.15
3	Ken Harrelson	.40	.20	.12
4	Carl Yastrzemski	5.00	2.50	1.50
5	Jim Fregosi	.40	.20	.12
6	Luis Aparicio	1.25	.60	.40
7	Luis Tiant	.40	.20	.12
8	Denny McLain	.40	.20	.12
9	Willie Horton	.40	.20	.12
10	Bill Freehan	.40	.20	.12
11a	Hoyt Wilhelm	3.25	1.75	1.00
11b	Jim Wynn	5.00	2.50	1.50
12	Rod Carew	6.00	3.00	1.75
13	Mel Stottlemyre	.40	.20	.12
14	Rick Monday	.40	.20	.12
15	Tommy Davis	.40	.20	.12
16	Frank Howard	.50	.25	.15
17	Felipe Alou	.40	.20	.12
18	Don Kessinger	.40	.20	.12
19	Ron Santo	.50	.25	.15
20	Tommy Helms	.30	.15	.09
21	Pete Rose	7.00	3.50	2.00
22a	Rusty Staub	2.25	1.25	.70
22b	Joe Foy	7.00	3.50	2.00
23	Tom Haller	.30	.15	.09
24	Maury Wills	.50	.25	.15
25	Jerry Koosman	.40	.20	.12
26	Richie Allen	.50	.25	.15
27	Bob Clemente	6.00	3.00	1.75
28	Curt Flood	.40	.20	.12
29	Bob Gibson	3.00	1.50	.90
30	Al Ferrara	.30	.15	.09
31	Willie McCovey	3.00	1.50	.90
32	Juan Marichal	3.00	1.50	.90
33	Willie Mays	5.00	2.50	1.50

1969 Topps
4-On-1 Mini Stickers

Another in the long line of Topps test issues, the 4-on-1s are 2-1/2" by 3-1/2" cards with blank backs featuring a quartet of miniature stickers in the design of the same cards from the 1969 Topps regular set. There are 25 different cards, for a total of 100 different stickers. As they are not common, Mint cards bring fairly strong prices on today's market. As the set was drawn from the 3rd Series of the regular cards, it includes some rookie stickers and World Series highlight stickers.

	NR MT	EX	VG
Complete Set:	950.00	475.00	285.00
Common Player:	15.00	7.50	4.50
(1) Jerry Adair, Willie Mays, Johnny Morris, Don Wilson	100.00	50.00	30.00
(2) Tommie Aaron, Jim Britton, Donn Clendenon, Woody Woodward	15.00	7.50	4.50
(3) World Series Game 4, Tommy Davis, Don Pavletich, Vada Pinson	20.00	10.00	6.00
(4) Max Alvis, Glenn Beckert, Ron Fairly, Rick Wise	15.00	7.50	4.50
(5) Johnny Callison, Jim French, Lum Harris, Dick Selma	15.00	7.50	4.50
(6) World Series Game 3, Bob Gibson, Larry Haney, Rick Reichardt	40.00	20.00	12.00
(7) Houston Rookie Stars, Wally Bunker, Don Cardwell, Joe Gibbon	15.00	7.50	4.50
(8) Ollie Brown, Jim Bunning, Andy Kosco, Ron Reed	20.00	10.00	6.00
(9) Bill Dillman, Jim Lefebvre, John Purdin, John Roseboro	15.00	7.50	4.50
(10) Bill Hands, Chuck Harrison, Lindy McDaniel, Felix Millan	15.00	7.50	4.50
(11) Jack Hiatt, Dave Johnson, Mel Nelson, Tommie Sisk	18.00	9.00	5.50
(12) Clay Dalrymple, Leo Durocher, John Odom, Wilbur Wood	18.00	9.00	5.50
(13) Hank Bauer, Kevin Collins, Ray Oyler, Russ Snyder	15.00	7.50	4.50
(14) Red Sox Rookie Stars, World Series Game 7, Gerry Arrigo, Jim Perry	18.00	9.00	5.50
(15) World Series Game 2, Bill McCool, Roberto Pena, Doug Rader	15.00	7.50	4.50
(16) Ed Brinkman, Roy Face, Willie Horton, Bob Rodgers	18.00	9.00	5.50
(17) Dave Baldwin, J.C. Martin, Dave May, Ray Sadecki	15.00	7.50	4.50
(18) World Series Game 1, Jose Pagan, Tom Phoebus, Mike Shannon	15.00	7.50	4.50
(19) Pete Rose, Lee Stange, Don Sutton, Ted Uhlaender	275.00	137.00	82.00
(20) Joe Grzenda, Frank Howard, Dick Tracewski, Jim Weaver	20.00	10.00	6.00
(21) White Sox Rookie Stars, Joe Azcue, Grant Jackson, Denny McLain	20.00	10.00	6.00
(22) John Edwards, Jim Fairey, Phillies Rookies, Stan Williams	15.00	7.50	4.50
(23) World Series Summary, John Bateman, Willie Smith, Leon Wagner	15.00	7.50	4.50
(24) World Series Game 5, Yankees Rookies, Chris Cannizzaro, Bob Hendley	15.00	7.50	4.50
(25) Cardinals Rookie Stars, Joe Nossek, Rico Petrocelli, Carl Yastrzemski	175.00	87.00	52.00

1969 Topps Stamps

Topps continued to refine its efforts at baseball stamps in 1969 with the release of 240 player stamps, each measuring 1" by 1-7/16." Each stamp jsd s color photo along with the player's name, position and team. Unlike prior stamp issues, the 1969 stamps have 24 separate albums (one per team). The stamps were issued in strips of 12.

	NR MT	EX	VG
Complete Sheet Set:	110.00	55.00	33.00
Common Sheet:	1.25	.60	.40
Complete Stamp Album Set:	14.00	7.00	4.25
Single Stamp Album:	.50	.25	.15
(1) Tommie Agee, Sandy Alomar, Jose Cardenal, Dean Chance, Joe Foy, Jim Grant, Don Kessinger, Mickey Mantle, Jerry May, Bob Rodgers, Cookie Rojas, Gary Sutherland	18.00	9.00	5.50
(2) Jesus Alou, Mike Andrews, Larry Brown, Moe Drabowsky, Alex Johnson, Lew Krausse, Jim Lefebvre, Dal Maxvill, John Odom, Claude Osteen, Rick Reichardt, Luis Tiant	1.50	.70	.45
(3) Hank Aaron, Matty Alou, Max Alvis, Nelson Briles, Eddie Fisher, Bud Harrelson, Willie Horton, Randy Hundley, Larry Jaster, Jim Kaat, Gary Peters, Pete Ward	7.00	3.50	2.00
(4) Don Buford, John Callison, Tommy Davis, Jackie Hernandez, Fergie Jenkins, Lee May, Denny McLain, Bob Oliver, Roberto Pena, Tony Perez, Joe Torre, Tom Tresh	3.00	1.50	.90
(5) Jim Bunning, Dean Chance, Joe Foy, Sonny Jackson, Don Kessinger, Rick Monday, Gaylord Perry, Roger Repoz, Cookie Rojas, Mel Stottlemyre, Leon Wagner, Jim Wynn	3.00	1.50	.90
(6) Felipe Alou, Gerry Arrigo, Bob Aspromonte, Gary Bell, Clay Dalrymple, Jim Fregosi, Tony Gonzalez, Duane Josephson, Dick McAuliffe, Tony Oliva, Brooks Robinson, Willie Stargell	6.00	3.00	1.75
(7) Steve Barber, Donn Clendenon, Joe Coleman, Vic Davalillo, Russ Gibson, Jerry Grote, Tom Haller, Andy Kosco, Willie McCovey, Don Mincher, Joe Morgan, Don Wilson	4.00	2.00	1.25
(8) George Brunet, Don Buford, John Callison, Danny Cater, Tommy Davis, Willie Davis, John Edwards, Jim Hart, Mickey Lolich, Willie Mays, Roberto Pena, Mickey Stanley	7.00	3.50	2.00
(9) Ernie Banks, Glenn Beckert, Ken Berry, Horace Clarke, Bob Clemente, Larry Dierker, Len Gabrielson, Jake Gibbs, Jerry Koosman, Sam McDowell, Tom Satriano, Bill Singer	3.50	1.75	1.00
(10) Gene Alley, Lou Brock, Larry Brown, Moe Drabowsky, Frank Howard, Tommie John, Roger Nelson, Claude Osteen, Phil Regan, Rick Reichardt, Tony Taylor, Roy White	4.00	2.00	1.25
(11) Bob Allison, John Bateman, Don Drysdale, Dave Johnson, Harmon Killebrew, Jim Maloney, Bill Mazeroski, Gerry McNertney, Ron Perranoski, Rico Petrocelli, Pete Rose, Billy Williams	18.00	9.00	5.50

		NR MT	EX	VG
(12)	Bernie Allen, Jose Arcia, Stan Bahnsen, Sal Bando, Jim Davenport, Tito Francona, Dick Green, Ron Hunt, Mack Jones, Vada Pinson, George Scott, Don Wert 1.50		.70	.45
(13)	Gerry Arrigo, Bob Aspromonte, Joe Azcue, Curt Blefary, Orlando Cepeda, Bill Freehan, Jim Fregosi, Dave Giusti, Duane Josephson, Tim McCarver, Jose Santiago, Bob Tolan 2.00		1.00	.60
(14)	Jerry Adair, Johnny Bench, Clete Boyer, John Briggs, Bert Campaneris, Woody Fryman, Ron Kline, Bobby Knoop, Ken McMullen, Adolfo Phillips, John Roseboro, Tom Seaver 7.00		3.50	2.00
(15)	Norm Cash, Ron Fairly, Bob Gibson, Bill Hands, Cleon Jones, Al Kaline, Paul Schaal, Mike Shannon, Duke Sims, Reggie Smith, Steve Whitaker, Carl Yastrzemski 12.00		6.00	3.50
(16)	Steve Barber, Paul Casanova, Dick Dietz, Russ Gibson, Jerry Grote, Tom Haller, Ed Kranepool, Juan Marichal, Denis Menke, Jim Nash, Bill Robinson, Frank Robinson 4.00		2.00	1.25
(17)	Bobby Bolin, Ollie Brown, Rod Carew, Mike Epstein, Bud Harrelson, Larry Jaster, Dave McNally, Willie Norton, Milt Pappas, Gary Peters, Paul Popovich, Stan Williams 6.00		3.00	1.75
(18)	Ted Abernathy, Bob Allison, Ed Brinkman, Don Drysdale, Jim Hardin, Julian Javier, Hal Lanier, Jim McGlothlin, Ron Perranoski, Rich Rollins, Ron Santo, Billy Williams 3.00		1.50	.90
(19)	Richie Allen, Luis Aparicio, Wally Bunker, Curt Flood, Ken Harrelson, Jim Hunter, Denver Lemaster, Felix Millan, Jim Northrop (Northrup), Art Shamsky, Larry Stahl, Ted Uhlaender 3.00		1.50	.90
(20)	Bob Bailey, Johnny Bench, Woody Fryman, Jim Hannan, Ron Kline, Al McBean, Camilo Pascual, Joe Pepitone, Doug Rader, Ron Reed, John Roseboro, Sonny Siebert 3.00		1.50	.90
(21)	Jack Aker, Tommy Harper, Tommy Helms, Dennis Higgins, Jim Hunter, Don Lock, Lee Maye, Felix Millan, Jim Northrop (Northrup), Larry Stahl, Don Sutton, Zoilo Versalles 3.00		1.50	.90
(22)	Norm Cash, Ed Charles, Joe Horlen, Pat Jarvis, Jim Lonborg, Manny Mota, Boog Powell, Dick Selma, Mike Shannon, Duke Sims, Steve Whitaker, Hoyt Wilhelm 3.00		1.50	.90
(23)	Bernie Allen, Ray Culp, Al Ferrara, Tito Francona, Dick Green, Ron Hunt, Ray Oyler, Tom Phoebus, Rusty Staub, Bob Veale, Maury Wills, Wilbur Wood 2.00		1.00	.60
(24)	Ernie Banks, Mark Belanger, Steve Blass, Horace Clarke, Bob Clemente, Larry Dierker, Dave Duncan, Chico Salmon, Chris Short, Ron Swoboda, Cesar Tovar, Rick Wise 3.50		1.75	1.00

the bottom which carries the player's name, team, position, a copyright line and the card number. Another unusual feature is that the cards have rounded corners. The 66-card set saw limited production, meaning supplies are tight today. Considering the quality of the cards and the fact that many big names are represented, it's easy to understand why the set is quite expensive and desirable.

		NR MT	EX	VG
	Complete Set:	3600.00	1800.00	1080.
	Common Player:	10.00	5.00	3.00
1	Dave McNally	15.00	7.50	4.50
2	Frank Robinson	100.00	50.00	30.00
3	Brooks Robinson	100.00	50.00	30.00
4	Ken Harrelson	15.00	7.50	4.50
5	Carl Yastrzemski	300.00	150.00	90.00
6	Ray Culp	10.00	5.00	3.00
7	James Fregosi	12.00	6.00	3.50
8	Rick Reichardt	10.00	5.00	3.00
9	V. Davalillo	10.00	5.00	3.00
10	Luis Aparicio	35.00	17.50	10.50
11	Pete Ward	10.00	5.00	3.00
12	Joe Horlen	10.00	5.00	3.00
13	Luis Tiant	15.00	7.50	4.50
14	Sam McDowell	12.00	6.00	3.50
15	Jose Cardenal	10.00	5.00	3.00
16	Willie Horton	12.00	6.00	3.50
17	Denny McLain	15.00	7.50	4.50
18	Bill Freehan	12.00	6.00	3.50
19	Harmon Killebrew	75.00	38.00	23.00
20	Tony Oliva	20.00	10.00	6.00
21	Dean Chance	10.00	5.00	3.00
22	Joe Foy	10.00	5.00	3.00
23	Roger Nelson	10.00	5.00	3.00
24	Mickey Mantle	600.00	300.00	175.00
25	Mel Stottlemyre	12.00	6.00	3.50
26	Roy White	12.00	6.00	3.50
27	Rick Monday	12.00	6.00	3.50
28	Reginald Jackson	450.00	225.00	135.00
29	Dagoberto Campaneris	12.00	6.00	3.50
30	Frank Howard	20.00	10.00	6.00
31	Camilo Pascual	12.00	6.00	3.50
32	Tommy Davis	15.00	7.50	4.50
33	Don Mincher	10.00	5.00	3.00
34	Henry Aaron	200.00	100.00	60.00
35	Felipe Rojas Alou	12.00	6.00	3.50
36	Joseph Torre	15.00	7.50	4.50
37	Fergie Jenkins	15.00	7.50	4.50
38	Ronald Santo	15.00	7.50	4.50
39	Billy Williams	40.00	20.00	12.00
40	Tommy Helms	10.00	5.00	3.00
41	Pete Rose	400.00	200.00	120.00
42	Joe Morgan	75.00	38.00	23.00
43	Jim Wynn	12.00	6.00	3.50
44	Curt Blefary	10.00	5.00	3.00
45	Willie Davis	12.00	6.00	3.50
46	Donald Drysdale	50.00	25.00	15.00
47	Tom Haller	10.00	5.00	3.00
48	Rusty Staub	20.00	10.00	6.00
49	Maurice Wills	20.00	10.00	6.00
50	Cleon Jones	10.00	5.00	3.00
51	Jerry Koosman	15.00	7.50	4.50
52	Tom Seaver	150.00	75.00	45.00
53	Rich Allen	15.00	7.50	4.50
54	Chris Short	10.00	5.00	3.00
55	Cookie Rojas	10.00	5.00	3.00
56	Mateo Alou	12.00	6.00	3.50
57	Steve Blass	10.00	5.00	3.00
58	Roberto Clemente	250.00	125.00	70.00
59	Curt Flood	15.00	7.50	4.50
60	Robert Gibson	75.00	38.00	23.00
61	Tim McCarver	15.00	7.50	4.50
62	Dick Selma	10.00	5.00	3.00
63	Ollie Brown	10.00	5.00	3.00
64	Juan Marichal	60.00	30.00	18.00
65	Willie Mays	200.00	100.00	60.00
66	Willie McCovey	60.00	30.00	18.00

1969 Topps Super

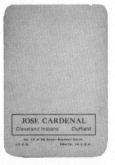

JOSE CARDENAL
Cleveland Indians   Outfield

These 2-1/4" by 3-1/4" cards are not the bigger "Super" cards which would be seen in following years. Rather, what enabled Topps to dub them "Super Baseball Cards" is their high-gloss finish which enhances the bright color photograph used on their fronts. The only other design element on the front is a facsimile autograph. The backs contain a box at the

1969 Topps Team Posters

Picking up where the 1968 posters left off, the 1969 poster is larger at about 12" by 20." The posters, 24 in number like the previous year, are very different in style. Each has a team focus with a large pennant carrying the team name, along with nine or ten photos of players. Each of the photos carries a name and a facsimile autograph. Unfortunately, the bigger size of 1969 posters meant they had to be folded to fit in their packages as was the case in 1968. That means that collectors today will have a tough job finding them without fairly heavy creases from the folding.

	NR MT	EX	VG
Complete Set:	800.00	400.00	240.00
Common Poster:	17.00	8.50	5.00

1 Detroit Tigers (Norm Cash, Bill Freehan, Willie Horton, Al Kaline, Mickey Lolich, Dick McAuliffe, Denny McLain, Jim Northrup, Mickey Stanley, Don Wert, Earl Wilson)
40.00 20.00 12.00

2 Atlanta Braves (Hank Aaron, Felipe Alou, Clete Boyer, Rico Carty, Tito Francona, Sonny Jackson, Pat Jarvis, Felix Millan, Phil Niekro, Milt Pappas, Joe Torre) 40.00 20.00 12.00

3 Boston Red Sox (Mike Andrews, Tony Conigliaro, Ray Culp, Russ Gibson, Ken Harrelson, Jim Lonborg, Rico Petrocelli, Jose Santiago, George Scott, Reggie Smith, Carl Yastrzemski) 60.00 30.00 18.00

4 Chicago Cubs (Ernie Banks, Glenn Beckert, Bill Hands, Jim Hickman, Ken Holtzman, Randy Hundley, Fergie Jenkins, Don Kessinger, Adolfo Phillips, Ron Santo, Billy Williams) 35.00 17.50 10.50

5 Baltimore Orioles (Mark Belanger, Paul Blair, Don Buford, Andy Etchebarren, Jim Hardin, Dave Johnson, Dave McNally, Tom Phoebus, Boog Powell, Brooks Robinson, Frank Robinson) 50.00 25.00 15.00

6 Houston Astros (Curt Blefary, Donn Clendenon, Larry Dierker, John Edwards, Denny Lemaster, Denis Menke, Norm Miller, Joe Morgan, Doug Rader, Don Wilson, Jim Wynn) 17.00 8.50 5.00

7 Kansas City Royals (Jerry Adair, Wally Bunker, Mike Fiore, Joe Foy, Jackie Hernandez, Pat Kelly, Dave Morehead, Roger Nelson, Dave Nicholson, Eliseo Rodriguez, Steve Whitaker) 17.00 8.50 5.00

8 Philadelphia Phillies (Richie Allen, Johnny Callison, Woody Fryman, Larry Hisle, Don Money, Cookie Rojas, Mike Ryan, Chris Short, Tony Taylor, Bill White, Rick Wise)
17.00 8.50 5.00

9 Seattle Pilots (Jack Aker, Steve Barber, Gary Bell, Tommy Davis, Jim Gosger, Tommy Harper, Gerry McNertney, Don Mincher, Ray Oyler, Rich Rollins, Chico Salmon) 35.00 17.50 10.50

10 Montreal Expos (Bob Bailey, John Bateman, Jack Billingham, Jim Grant, Larry Jaster, Mack Jones, Manny Mota, Rusty Staub, Gary Sutherland, Jim Williams, Maury Wills) 17.00 8.50 5.00

11 Chicago White Sox (Sandy Alomar, Luis Aparicio, Ken Berry, Buddy Bradford, Joe Horlen, Tommy John, Duane Josephson, Tom McCraw, Bill Melton, Pete Ward, Wilbur Wood) 17.00 8.50 5.00

12 San Diego Padres (Jose Arcia, Danny Breeden, Ollie Brown, Bill Davis, Ron Davis, Tony Gonzalez, Dick Kelley, Al McBean, Roberto Pena, Dick Selma, Ed Spiezio)
17.00 8.50 5.00

	NR MT	EX	VG

13 Cleveland Indians (Max Alvis, Joe Azcue, Jose Cardenal, Vern Fuller, Lou Johnson, Sam McDowell, Sonny Siebert, Duke Sims, Russ Snyder, Luis Tiant, Zoilo Versalles)
17.00 8.50 5.00

14 San Francisco Giants (Bobby Bolin, Jim Davenport, Dick Dietz, Jim Hart, Ron Hunt, Hal Lanier, Juan Marichal, Willie Mays, Willie McCovey, Gaylord Perry, Charlie Smith)
40.00 20.00 12.00

15 Minnesota Twins (Bob Allison, Chico Cardenas, Rod Carew, Dean Chance, Jim Kaat, Harmon Killebrew, Tony Oliva, Jim Perry, John Roseboro, Cesar Tovar, Ted Uhlaender) 40.00 20.00 12.00

16 Pittsburgh Pirates (Gene Alley, Matty Alou, Steve Blass, Jim Bunning, Bob Clemente, Rich Hebner, Jerry May, Bill Mazeroski, Bob Robertson, Willie Stargell, Bob Veale) 40.00 20.00 12.00

17 California Angels (Ruben Amaro, George Brunet, Bob Chance, Vic Davalillo, Jim Fregosi, Bobby Knoop, Jim McGlothlin, Rick Reichardt, Roger Repoz, Bob Rodgers, Hoyt Wilhelm) 20.00 10.00 6.00

18 St. Louis Cardinals (Nelson Briles, Lou Brock, Orlando Cepeda, Curt Flood, Bob Gibson, Julian Javier, Dal Maxvill, Tim McCarver, Vada Pinson, Mike Shannon, Ray Washburn) 35.00 17.50 10.50

19 New York Yankees (Stan Bahnsen, Horace Clarke, Bobby Cox, Jake Gibbs, Mickey Mantle, Joe Pepitone, Fritz Peterson, Bill Robinson, Mel Stottlemyre, Tom Tresh, Roy White) 90.00 45.00 27.00

20 Cincinnati Reds (Gerry Arrigo, Johnny Bench, Tommy Helms, Alex Johnson, Jim Maloney, Lee May, Gary Nolan, Tony Perez, Pete Rose, Bob Tolan, Woody Woodward)
90.00 45.00 27.00

21 Oakland Athletics (Sal Bando, Bert Campaneris, Danny Cater, Dick Green, Mike Hershberger, Jim Hunter, Reggie Jackson, Rick Monday, Jim Nash, John Odom, Jim Pagliaroni) 60.00 30.00 18.00

22 Los Angeles Dodgers (Willie Crawford, Willie Davis, Don Drysdale, Ron Fairly, Tom Haller, Andy Kosco, Jim Lefebvre, Claude Osteen, Paul Popovich, Bill Singer, Bill Sudakis) 35.00 17.50 10.50

23 Washington Senators (Bernie Allen, Brant Alyea, Ed Brinkman, Paul Casanova, Joe Coleman, Mike Epstein, Jim Hannan, Frank Howard, Ken McMullen, Camilo Pascual, Del Unser) 17.00 8.50 5.00

24 New York Mets (Tommie Agee, Ken Boswell, Ed Charles, Jerry Grote, Bud Harrelson, Cleon Jones, Jerry Koosman, Ed Kranepool, Jim McAndrew, Tom Seaver, Ron Swoboda) 100.00 50.00 30.00

1970 Topps

Topps established another set size record by coming out with 720 cards in 1970. The 2-1/2" by 3-1/2" cards have a color photo with a thin white frame. The photo have the player's team overprinted at the top, while the player's name in script and his position are at the bottom. A gray border surrounds the front.   Card backs follows the normal design pattern, although they are more readable than some issues of the past.   Team cards returned and were joined with many of the usual specialty cards.   The World Series highlights were joined by cards with playoff highlights. Statistical leaders and All-Stars are also included in the set.   High-numbered cards provide the most expensive cards in the set.

		NR MT	EX	VG
Complete Set:		1450.00	725.00	420.00
Common Player: 1-546		.30	.15	.09
Common Player: 547-633		.80	.40	.25
Common Player: 634-720		2.00	1.00	.60
1	World Champions (Mets Team)	10.00	3.00	1.00
2	Diego Segui	.60	.30	.20
3	Darrel Chaney	.30	.15	.09
4	Tom Egan	.30	.15	.09
5	Wes Parker	.40	.20	.12
6	Grant Jackson	.30	.15	.09
7	Indians Rookies (Gary Boyd, Russ Nagelson)	.30	.15	.09
8	Jose Martinez	.30	.15	.09
9	Checklist 1-132	2.50	1.25	.70
10	Carl Yastrzemski	25.00	12.50	7.50
11	Nate Colbert	.30	.15	.09
12	John Hiller	.40	.20	.12
13	Jack Hiatt	.30	.15	.09
14	Hank Allen	.30	.15	.09
15	Larry Dierker	.40	.20	.12
16	Charlie Metro	.30	.15	.09
17	Hoyt Wilhelm	4.00	2.00	1.25
18	Carlos May	.50	.25	.15
19	John Boccabella	.30	.15	.09
20	Dave McNally	.60	.30	.20
21	Athletics Rookies (Vida Blue, Gene Tenace)	2.00	1.00	.60
22	Ray Washburn	.30	.15	.09
23	Bill Robinson	.50	.25	.15
24	Dick Selma	.30	.15	.09
25	Cesar Tovar	.30	.15	.09
26	Tug McGraw	1.25	.60	.40
27	Chuck Hinton	.30	.15	.09
28	Billy Wilson	.30	.15	.09
29	Sandy Alomar	.30	.15	.09
30	Matty Alou	.80	.40	.25
31	Marty Pattin	.50	.25	.15
32	Harry Walker	.40	.20	.12
33	Don Wert	.30	.15	.09
34	Willie Crawford	.30	.15	.09
35	Joe Horlen	.30	.15	.09
36	Reds Rookies (Danny Breeden, Bernie Carbo)	.50	.25	.15
37	Dick Drago	.30	.15	.09
38	Mack Jones	.30	.15	.09
39	Mike Nagy	.30	.15	.09
40	Rich Allen	1.50	.70	.45
41	George Lauzerique	.30	.15	.09
42	Tito Fuentes	.30	.15	.09
43	Jack Aker	.50	.25	.15
44	Roberto Pena	.30	.15	.09
45	Dave Johnson	1.00	.50	.30
46	Ken Rudolph	.30	.15	.09
47	Bob Miller	.30	.15	.09
48	Gill Garrido (Gil)	.30	.15	.09
49	Tim Cullen	.30	.15	.09
50	Tommie Agee	.40	.20	.12
51	Bob Christian	.30	.15	.09
52	Bruce Dal Canton	.30	.15	.09
53	John Kennedy	.50	.25	.15
54	Jeff Torborg	.40	.20	.12
55	John Odom	.40	.20	.12
56	Phillies Rookies (Joe Lis, Scott Reid)	.30	.15	.09
57	Pat Kelly	.30	.15	.09
58	Dave Marshall	.30	.15	.09
59	Dick Ellsworth	.30	.15	.09
60	Jim Wynn	.60	.30	.20
61	N.L. Batting Leaders (Bob Clemente, Cleon Jones, Pete Rose)	5.00	2.50	1.50
62	A.L. Batting Leaders (Rod Carew, Tony Oliva, Reggie Smith)	2.50	1.25	.70
63	N.L. RBI Leaders (Willie McCovey, Tony Perez, Ron Santo)	2.50	1.25	.70
64	A.L. RBI Leaders (Reggie Jackson, Harmon Killebrew, Boog Powell)	2.50	1.25	.70
65	N.L. Home Run Leaders (Hank Aaron, Lee May, Willie McCovey)	3.00	1.50	.90
66	A.L. Home Run Leaders (Frank Howard, Reggie Jackson, Harmon Killebrew)	2.50	1.25	.70

		NR MT	EX	VG
67	N.L. ERA Leaders (Steve Carlton, Bob Gibson, Juan Marichal)	3.00	1.50	.90
68	A.L. ERA Leaders (Dick Bosman, Mike Cuellar, Jim Palmer)	2.00	1.00	.60
69	N.L. Pitching Leaders (Fergie Jenkins, Juan Marichal, Phil Niekro, Tom Seaver)	2.50	1.25	.70
70	A.L. Pitching Leaders (Dave Boswell, Mike Cuellar, Dennis McLain, Dave McNally, Jim Perry, Mel Stottlemyre)	2.00	1.00	.60
71	N.L. Strikeout Leaders (Bob Gibson, Fergie Jenkins, Bill Singer)	2.50	1.25	.70
72	A.L. Strikeout Leaders (Mickey Lolich, Sam McDowell, Andy Messersmith)	2.00	1.00	.60
73	Wayne Granger	.30	.15	.09
74	Angels Rookies (Greg Washburn, Wally Wolf)	.30	.15	.09
75	Jim Kaat	2.50	1.25	.70
76	Carl Taylor	.30	.15	.09
77	Frank Linzy	.30	.15	.09
78	Joe Lahoud	.30	.15	.09
79	Clay Kirby	.30	.15	.09
80	Don Kessinger	.40	.20	.12
81	Dave May	.30	.15	.09
82	Frank Fernandez	.50	.25	.15
83	Don Cardwell	.30	.15	.09
84	Paul Casanova	.30	.15	.09
85	Max Alvis	.30	.15	.09
86	Lum Harris	.30	.15	.09
87	Steve Renko	.30	.15	.09
88	Pilots Rookies (Dick Baney, Miguel Fuentes)	.50	.25	.15
89	Juan Rios	.30	.15	.09
90	Tim McCarver	1.00	.50	.30
91	Rich Morales	.30	.15	.09
92	George Culver	.30	.15	.09
93	Rick Renick	.30	.15	.09
94	Fred Patek	.40	.20	.12
95	Earl Wilson	.30	.15	.09
96	Cards Rookies (Leron Lee, Jerry Reuss)	1.75	.90	.50
97	Joe Moeller	.30	.15	.09
98	Gates Brown	.30	.15	.09
99	Bobby Pfeil	.30	.15	.09
100	Mel Stottlemyre	1.00	.50	.30
101	Bobby Floyd	.30	.15	.09
102	Joe Rudi	.80	.40	.25
103	Frank Reberger	.30	.15	.09
104	Gerry Moses	.30	.15	.09
105	Tony Gonzalez	.30	.15	.09
106	Darold Knowles	.30	.15	.09
107	Bobby Etheridge	.30	.15	.09
108	Tom Burgmeier	.40	.20	.12
109	Expos Rookies (Garry Jestadt, Carl Morton)	.40	.20	.12
110	Bob Moose	.30	.15	.09
111	Mike Hegan	.50	.25	.15
112	Dave Nelson	.30	.15	.09
113	Jim Ray	.30	.15	.09
114	Gene Michael	.60	.30	.20
115	Alex Johnson	.40	.20	.12
116	Sparky Lyle	1.00	.50	.30
117	Don Young	.30	.15	.09
118	George Mitterwald	.30	.15	.09
119	Chuck Taylor	.30	.15	.09
120	Sal Bando	.80	.40	.25
121	Orioles Rookies (Fred Beene, Terry Crowley)	.40	.20	.12
122	George Stone	.30	.15	.09
123	Don Gutteridge	.30	.15	.09
124	Larry Jaster	.30	.15	.09
125	Deron Johnson	.30	.15	.09
126	Marty Martinez	.30	.15	.09
127	Joe Coleman	.40	.20	.12
128a	Checklist 133-263 (226 is R Perranoski)	3.00	1.50	.90
128b	Checklist 133-263 (226 is R. Perranoski)	2.50	1.25	.70
129	Jimmie Price	.30	.15	.09
130	Ollie Brown	.30	.15	.09
131	Dodgers Rookies (Ray Lamb, Bob Stinson)	.30	.15	.09
132	Jim McGlothlin	.30	.15	.09
133	Clay Carroll	.40	.20	.12
134	Danny Walton	.50	.25	.15
135	Dick Dietz	.30	.15	.09
136	Steve Hargan	.30	.15	.09
137	Art Shamsky	.30	.15	.09
138	Joe Foy	.30	.15	.09
139	Rich Nye	.30	.15	.09
140	Reggie Jackson	60.00	30.00	18.00

		NR MT	EX	VG
141	Pirates Rookies *(Dave Cash*, Johnny Jeter)	.50	.25	.15
142	Fritz Peterson	.50	.25	.15
143	Phil Gagliano	.30	.15	.09
144	Ray Culp	.30	.15	.09
145	Rico Carty	.80	.40	.25
146	Danny Murphy	.30	.15	.09
147	Angel Hermoso	.30	.15	.09
148	Earl Weaver	1.25	.60	.40
149	Billy Champion	.30	.15	.09
150	Harmon Killebrew	6.00	3.00	1.75
151	Dave Roberts	.30	.15	.09
152	Ike Brown	.30	.15	.09
153	Gary Gentry	.30	.15	.09
154	Senators Rookies (Jan Dukes, Jim Miles)	.30	.15	.09
155	Denis Menke	.30	.15	.09
156	Eddie Fisher	.30	.15	.09
157	Manny Mota	.50	.25	.15
158	Jerry McNertney	.50	.25	.15
159	Tommy Helms	.40	.20	.12
160	Phil Niekro	3.50	1.75	1.00
161	Richie Scheinblum	.30	.15	.09
162	Jerry Johnson	.30	.15	.09
163	Syd O'Brien	.30	.15	.09
164	Ty Cline	.30	.15	.09
165	Ed Kirkpatrick	.30	.15	.09
166	Al Oliver	2.00	1.00	.60
167	Bill Burbach	.50	.25	.15
168	Dave Watkins	.30	.15	.09
169	Tom Hall	.30	.15	.09
170	Billy Williams	4.50	2.25	1.25
171	Jim Nash	.30	.15	.09
172	Braves Rookies *(Ralph Garr*, Garry Hill)	1.00	.50	.30
173	Jim Hicks	.30	.15	.09
174	Ted Sizemore	.30	.15	.09
175	Dick Bosman	.30	.15	.09
176	Jim Hart	.40	.20	.12
177	Jim Northrup	.40	.20	.12
178	Denny Lemaster	.30	.15	.09
179	Ivan Murrell	.30	.15	.09
180	Tommy John	2.75	1.50	.80
181	Sparky Anderson	1.25	.60	.40
182	Dick Hall	.30	.15	.09
183	Jerry Grote	.40	.20	.12
184	Ray Fosse	.40	.20	.12
185	Don Mincher	.50	.25	.15
186	Rick Joseph	.30	.15	.09
187	Mike Hedlund	.30	.15	.09
188	Manny Sanguillen	.40	.20	.12
189	Yankees Rookies (Dave McDonald, *Thurman Munson*)	60.00	30.00	18.00
190	Joe Torre	1.25	.60	.40
191	Vicente Romo	.30	.15	.09
192	Jim Qualls	.30	.15	.09
193	Mike Wegener	.30	.15	.09
194	Chuck Manuel	.30	.15	.09
195	N.L. Playoff Game 1 (Seaver Wins Opener!)	3.00	1.50	.90
196	N.L. Playoff Game 2 (Mets Show Muscle!)	1.75	.90	.50
197	N.L. Playoff Game 3 (Ryan Saves The Day!)	6.00	3.00	1.75
198	N.L. Playoffs Summary (We're Number One!)	1.75	.90	.50
199	A.L. Playoff Game 1 (Orioles Win A Squeaker!)	1.50	.70	.45
200	A.L. Playoff Game 2 (Powell Scores Winning Run!)	1.75	.90	.50
201	A.L. Playoff Game 3 (Birds Wrap It Up!)	1.50	.70	.45
202	A.L. Playoffs Summary (Sweep Twins In Three!)	1.50	.70	.45
203	Rudy May	.40	.20	.12
204	Len Gabrielson	.30	.15	.09
205	Bert Campaneris	.80	.40	.25
206	Clete Boyer	.40	.20	.12
207	Tigers Rookies (Norman McRae, Bob Reed)	.30	.15	.09
208	Fred Gladding	.30	.15	.09
209	Ken Suarez	.30	.15	.09
210	Juan Marichal	8.00	4.00	2.50
211	Ted Williams	7.00	3.50	2.00
212	Al Santorini	.30	.15	.09
213	Andy Etchebarren	.30	.15	.09
214	Ken Boswell	.30	.15	.09
215	Reggie Smith	.60	.30	.20
216	Chuck Hartenstein	.30	.15	.09
217	Ron Hansen	.30	.15	.09
218	Ron Stone	.30	.15	.09

		NR MT	EX	VG
219	Jerry Kenney	.50	.25	.15
220	Steve Carlton	15.00	7.50	4.50
221	Ron Brand	.30	.15	.09
222	Jim Rooker	.30	.15	.09
223	Nate Oliver	.30	.15	.09
224	Steve Barber	.50	.25	.15
225	Lee May	.60	.30	.20
226	Ron Perranoski	.40	.20	.12
227	Astros Rookies *(John Mayberry*, Bob Watkins)	1.00	.50	.30
228	Aurelio Rodriguez	.40	.20	.12
229	Rich Robertson	.30	.15	.09
230	Brooks Robinson	10.00	5.00	3.00
231	Luis Tiant	1.25	.60	.40
232	Bob Didier	.30	.15	.09
233	Lew Krausse	.30	.15	.09
234	Tommy Dean	.30	.15	.09
235	Mike Epstein	.40	.20	.12
236	Bob Veale	.40	.20	.12
237	Russ Gibson	.30	.15	.09
238	Jose Laboy	.30	.15	.09
239	Ken Berry	.30	.15	.09
240	Fergie Jenkins	2.50	1.25	.70
241	Royals Rookies (Al Fitzmorris, Scott Northey)	.30	.15	.09
242	Walter Alston	1.75	.90	.50
243	Joe Sparma	.30	.15	.09
244a	Checklist 264-372 (red bat on front)	3.00	1.50	.90
244b	Checklist 264-372 (brown bat on front)	2.50	1.25	.70
245	Leo Cardenas	.30	.15	.09
246	Jim McAndrew	.30	.15	.09
247	Lou Klimchock	.30	.15	.09
248	Jesus Alou	.40	.20	.12
249	Bob Locker	.50	.25	.15
250	Willie McCovey	6.00	3.00	1.75
251	Dick Schofield	.30	.15	.09
252	Lowell Palmer	.30	.15	.09
253	Ron Woods	.50	.25	.15
254	Camilo Pascual	.50	.25	.15
255	*Jim Spencer*	.50	.25	.15
256	Vic Davalillo	.40	.20	.12
257	Dennis Higgins	.30	.15	.09
258	Paul Popovich	.30	.15	.09
259	Tommie Reynolds	.30	.15	.09
260	Claude Osteen	.50	.25	.15
261	Curt Motton	.30	.15	.09
262	Padres Rookies (Jerry Morales, Jim Williams)	.30	.15	.09
263	Duane Josephson	.30	.15	.09
264	Rich Hebner	.40	.20	.12
265	Randy Hundley	.30	.15	.09
266	Wally Bunker	.30	.15	.09
267	Twins Rookies (Herman Hill, Paul Ratliff)	.30	.15	.09
268	Claude Raymond	.30	.15	.09
269	Cesar Gutierrez	.30	.15	.09
270	Chris Short	.40	.20	.12
271	Greg Goossen	.50	.25	.15
272	Hector Torres	.30	.15	.09
273	Ralph Houk	1.00	.50	.30
274	Gerry Arrigo	.30	.15	.09
275	Duke Sims	.30	.15	.09
276	Ron Hunt	.40	.20	.12
277	Paul Doyle	.30	.15	.09
278	Tommie Aaron	.50	.25	.15
279	*Bill Lee*	.50	.25	.15
280	Donn Clendenon	.40	.20	.12
281	Casey Cox	.30	.15	.09
282	Steve Huntz	.30	.15	.09
283	Angel Bravo	.30	.15	.09
284	Jack Baldschun	.30	.15	.09
285	Paul Blair	.40	.20	.12
286	Dodgers Rookies *(Bill Buckner*, Jack Jenkins)	5.00	2.50	1.50
287	Fred Talbot	.30	.15	.09
288	Larry Hisle	.40	.20	.12
289	Gene Brabender	.50	.25	.15
290	Rod Carew	15.00	7.50	4.50
291	Leo Durocher	1.25	.60	.40
292	Eddie Leon	.30	.15	.09
293	Bob Bailey	.30	.15	.09
294	Jose Azcue	.30	.15	.09
295	Cecil Upshaw	.30	.15	.09
296	Woody Woodward	.40	.20	.12
297	Curt Blefary	.50	.25	.15
298	Ken Henderson	.30	.15	.09
299	Buddy Bradford	.30	.15	.09
300	Tom Seaver	40.00	20.00	12.00
301	Chico Salmon	.30	.15	.09

	NR MT	EX	VG
302 Jeff James	.30	.15	.09
303 Brant Alyea	.30	.15	.09
304 *Bill Russell*	1.50	.70	.45
305 World Series Game 1 (Buford Belts Leadoff Homer!)	1.75	.90	.50
306 World Series Game 2 (Clendenon's Homer Breaks Ice!)	1.75	.90	.50
307 World Series Game 3 (Agee's Catch Saves The Day!)	1.75	.90	.50
308 World Series Game 4 (Martin's Bunt Ends Deadlock!)	1.75	.90	.50
309 World Series Game 5 (Koosman Shuts The Door!)	1.75	.90	.50
310 World Series Summary (Mets Whoop It Up!)	1.75	.90	.50
311 Dick Green	.30	.15	.09
312 Mike Torrez	.40	.20	.12
313 Mayo Smith	.30	.15	.09
314 Bill McCool	.30	.15	.09
315 Luis Aparicio	4.50	2.25	1.25
316 Skip Guinn	.30	.15	.09
317 Red Sox Rookies (Luis Alvarado, Billy Conigliaro)	.40	.20	.12
318 Willie Smith	.30	.15	.09
319 Clayton Dalrymple	.30	.15	.09
320 Jim Maloney	.40	.20	.12
321 Lou Piniella	1.50	.70	.45
322 Luke Walker	.30	.15	.09
323 Wayne Comer	.50	.25	.15
324 Tony Taylor	.30	.15	.09
325 Dave Boswell	.30	.15	.09
326 Bill Voss	.30	.15	.09
327 Hal King	.30	.15	.09
328 George Brunet	.30	.15	.09
329 Chris Cannizzaro	.30	.15	.09
330 Lou Brock	6.00	3.00	1.75
331 Chuck Dobson	.30	.15	.09
332 Bobby Wine	.30	.15	.09
333 Bobby Murcer	1.25	.60	.40
334 Phil Regan	.30	.15	.09
335 Bill Freehan	.40	.20	.12
336 Del Unser	.30	.15	.09
337 Mike McCormick	.40	.20	.12
338 Paul Schaal	.30	.15	.09
339 Johnny Edwards	.30	.15	.09
340 Tony Conigliaro	1.25	.60	.40
341 Bill Sudakis	.30	.15	.09
342 Wilbur Wood	.40	.20	.12
343a Checklist 373-459 (red bat on front)	3.50	1.75	1.00
343b Checklist 373-459 (brown bat on front)	3.00	1.50	.90
344 Marcelino Lopez	.30	.15	.09
345 Al Ferrara	.30	.15	.09
346 Red Schoendienst	1.25	.60	.40
347 Russ Snyder	.30	.15	.09
348 Mets Rookies (Jesse Hudson, Mike Jorgensen)	.40	.20	.12
349 Steve Hamilton	.50	.25	.15
350 Roberto Clemente	35.00	17.50	10.50
351 Tom Murphy	.30	.15	.09
352 Bob Barton	.30	.15	.09
353 Stan Williams	.30	.15	.09
354 Amos Otis	.50	.25	.15
355 Doug Rader	.30	.15	.09
356 Fred Lasher	.30	.15	.09
357 Bob Burda	.30	.15	.09
358 *Pedro Borbon*	.40	.20	.12
359 Phil Flood	.50	.25	.15
360 Curt Flood	1.00	.50	.30
361 Ray Jarvis	.30	.15	.09
362 Joe Hague	.30	.15	.09
363 Tom Shopay	.30	.15	.09
364 Dan McGinn	.30	.15	.09
365 Zoilo Versalles	.40	.20	.12
366 Barry Moore	.30	.15	.09
367 Mike Lum	.30	.15	.09
368 Ed Herrmann	.30	.15	.09
369 Alan Foster	.30	.15	.09
370 Tommy Harper	.70	.35	.20
371 Rod Gaspar	.30	.15	.09
372 Dave Giusti	.30	.15	.09
373 Roy White	1.00	.50	.30
374 Tommie Sisk	.30	.15	.09
375 Johnny Callison	.80	.40	.25
376 Lefty Phillips	.30	.15	.09
377 Bill Butler	.30	.15	.09
378 Jim Davenport	.30	.15	.09
379 Tom Tischinski	.30	.15	.09
380 Tony Perez	3.00	1.50	.90
381 Athletics Rookies (Bobby Brooks, Mike Olivo)	.30	.15	.09
382 Jack DiLauro	.30	.15	.09
383 Mickey Stanley	.40	.20	.12
384 Gary Neibauer	.30	.15	.09
385 George Scott	.40	.20	.12
386 Bill Dillman	.30	.15	.09
387 Orioles Team	1.50	.70	.45
388 Byron Browne	.30	.15	.09
389 Jim Shellenback	.30	.15	.09
390 Willie Davis	.80	.40	.25
391 Larry Brown	.30	.15	.09
392 Walt Hriniak	.30	.15	.09
393 John Gelnar	.50	.25	.15
394 Gil Hodges	4.00	2.00	1.25
395 Walt Williams	.30	.15	.09
396 Steve Blass	.40	.20	.12
397 Roger Repoz	.30	.15	.09
398 Bill Stoneman	.30	.15	.09
399 Yankees Team	2.00	1.00	.60
400 Denny McLain	1.50	.70	.45
401 Giants Rookies (John Harrell, Bernie Williams)	.30	.15	.09
402 Ellie Rodriguez	.30	.15	.09
403 Jim Bunning	3.25	1.75	1.00
404 Rich Reese	.30	.15	.09
405 Bill Hands	.30	.15	.09
406 Mike Andrews	.30	.15	.09
407 Bob Watson	.40	.20	.12
408 Paul Lindblad	.30	.15	.09
409 Bob Tolan	.40	.20	.12
410 Boog Powell	2.00	1.00	.60
411 Dodgers Team	1.50	.70	.45
412 Larry Burchart	.30	.15	.09
413 Sonny Jackson	.30	.15	.09
414 Paul Edmondson	.30	.15	.09
415 Julian Javier	.30	.15	.09
416 Joe Verbanic	.50	.25	.15
417 John Bateman	.30	.15	.09
418 John Donaldson	.50	.25	.15
419 Ron Taylor	.30	.15	.09
420 Ken McMullen	.30	.15	.09
421 Pat Dobson	.40	.20	.12
422 Royals Team	1.25	.60	.40
423 Jerry May	.30	.15	.09
424 Mike Kilkenny	.30	.15	.09
425 Bobby Bonds	1.25	.60	.40
426 Bill Rigney	.30	.15	.09
427 Fred Norman	.30	.15	.09
428 Don Buford	.40	.20	.12
429 Cubs Rookies (Randy Bobb, Jim Cosman)	.30	.15	.09
430 Andy Messersmith	.50	.25	.15
431 Ron Swoboda	.40	.20	.12
432a Checklist 460-546 ("Baseball" on front in yellow)	4.00	2.00	1.25
432b Checklist 460-546 ("Baseball" on front in white)	2.50	1.25	.70
433 Ron Bryant	.30	.15	.09
434 Felipe Alou	.70	.35	.20
435 Nelson Briles	.30	.15	.09
436 Phillies Team	1.25	.60	.40
437 Danny Cater	.50	.25	.15
438 Pat Jarvis	.30	.15	.09
439 Lee Maye	.30	.15	.09
440 Bill Mazeroski	1.00	.50	.30
441 John O'Donoghue	.50	.25	.15
442 Gene Mauch	.70	.35	.20
443 Al Jackson	.30	.15	.09
444 White Sox Rookies (Bill Farmer, John Matias)	.30	.15	.09
445 Vada Pinson	1.25	.60	.40
446 *Billy Grabarkewitz*	.40	.20	.12
447 Lee Stange	.30	.15	.09
448 Astros Team	1.25	.60	.40
449 Jim Palmer	10.00	5.00	3.00
450 Willie McCovey AS	3.50	1.75	1.00
451 Boog Powell AS	1.00	.50	.30
452 Felix Millan AS	.50	.25	.15
453 Rod Carew AS	4.00	2.00	1.25
454 Ron Santo AS	.80	.40	.25
455 Brooks Robinson AS	3.50	1.75	1.00
456 Don Kessinger AS	.50	.25	.15
457 Rico Petrocelli AS	.50	.25	.15
458 Pete Rose AS	8.00	4.00	2.50
459 Reggie Jackson AS	8.00	4.00	2.50
460 Matty Alou AS	.70	.35	.20
461 Carl Yastrzemski AS	5.00	2.50	1.50
462 Hank Aaron AS	5.50	2.75	1.75
463 Frank Robinson AS	3.50	1.75	1.00
464 Johnny Bench AS	5.00	2.50	1.50
465 Bill Freehan AS	.50	.25	.15
466 Juan Marichal AS	2.75	1.50	.80

		NR MT	EX	VG
467	Denny McLain AS	.80	.40	.25
468	Jerry Koosman AS	.60	.30	.20
469	Sam McDowell AS	.60	.30	.20
470	Willie Stargell	7.00	3.50	2.00
471	Chris Zachary	.30	.15	.09
472	Braves Team	1.25	.60	.40
473	Don Bryant	.50	.25	.15
474	Dick Kelley	.30	.15	.09
475	Dick McAuliffe	.40	.20	.12
476	Don Shaw	.30	.15	.09
477	Orioles Rookies (Roger Freed, Al Severinsen)	.30	.15	.09
478	Bob Heise	.30	.15	.09
479	Dick Woodson	.30	.15	.09
480	Glenn Beckert	.40	.20	.12
481	Jose Tartabull	.30	.15	.09
482	Tom Hilgendorf	.30	.15	.09
483	Gail Hopkins	.30	.15	.09
484	Gary Nolan	.30	.15	.09
485	Jay Johnstone	.50	.25	.15
486	Terry Harmon	.30	.15	.09
487	Cisco Carlos	.30	.15	.09
488	J.C. Martin	.30	.15	.09
489	Eddie Kasko	.30	.15	.09
490	Bill Singer	.40	.20	.12
491	Graig Nettles	4.00	2.00	1.25
492	Astros Rookies (Keith Lampard, Scipio Spinks)	.30	.15	.09
493	Lindy McDaniel	.50	.25	.15
494	Larry Stahl	.30	.15	.09
495	Dave Morehead	.30	.15	.09
496	Steve Whitaker	.30	.15	.09
497	Eddie Watt	.30	.15	.09
498	Al Weis	.30	.15	.09
499	Skip Lockwood	.50	.25	.15
500	Hank Aaron	25.00	12.50	7.50
501	White Sox Team	1.25	.60	.40
502	Rollie Fingers	4.00	2.00	1.25
503	Dal Maxvill	.40	.20	.12
504	Don Pavletich	.30	.15	.09
505	Ken Holtzman	.40	.20	.12
506	Ed Stroud	.30	.15	.09
507	Pat Corrales	.50	.25	.15
508	Joe Niekro	.70	.35	.20
509	Expos Team	1.25	.60	.40
510	Tony Oliva	1.75	.90	.50
511	Joe Hoerner	.30	.15	.09
512	Billy Harris	.30	.15	.09
513	Preston Gomez	.30	.15	.09
514	Steve Hovley	.50	.25	.15
515	Don Wilson	.30	.15	.09
516	Yankees Rookies (John Ellis, Jim Lyttle)	.50	.25	.15
517	Joe Gibbon	.30	.15	.09
518	Bill Melton	.40	.20	.12
519	Don McMahon	.30	.15	.09
520	Willie Horton	.70	.35	.20
521	Cal Koonce	.30	.15	.09
522	Angels Team	1.25	.60	.40
523	Jose Pena	.30	.15	.09
524	Alvin Dark	.60	.30	.20
525	Jerry Adair	.30	.15	.09
526	Ron Herbel	.30	.15	.09
527	Don Bosch	.30	.15	.09
528	Elrod Hendricks	.30	.15	.09
529	Bob Aspromonte	.30	.15	.09
530	Bob Gibson	8.00	4.00	2.50
531	Ron Clark	.30	.15	.09
532	Danny Murtaugh	.50	.25	.15
533	Buzz Stephen	.50	.25	.15
534	Twins Team	1.50	.70	.45
535	Andy Kosco	.30	.15	.09
536	Mike Kekich	.50	.25	.15
537	Joe Morgan	5.00	2.50	1.50
538	Bob Humphreys	.30	.15	.09
539	Phillies Rookies (*Larry Bowa*, Dennis Doyle)	3.00	1.50	.90
540	Gary Peters	.40	.20	.12
541	Bill Heath	.30	.15	.09
542a	Checklist 547-633 (grey bat on front)	3.50	1.75	1.00
542b	Checklist 547-633 (brown bat on front)	2.50	1.25	.70
543	Clyde Wright	.30	.15	.09
544	Reds Team	1.25	.60	.40
545	Ken Harrelson	1.25	.60	.40
546	Ron Reed	.40	.20	.12
547	Rick Monday	1.00	.50	.30
548	Howie Reed	.80	.40	.25
549	Cardinals Team	1.75	.90	.50
550	Frank Howard	2.25	1.25	.70

		NR MT	EX	VG
551	Dock Ellis	.90	.45	.25
552	Royals Rookies (Don O'Riley, Dennis Paepke, Fred Rico)	.80	.40	.25
553	Jim Lefebvre	.90	.45	.25
554	Tom Timmermann	.80	.40	.25
555	Orlando Cepeda	3.25	1.75	1.00
556	Dave Bristol	.90	.45	.25
557	Ed Kranepool	1.00	.50	.30
558	Vern Fuller	.80	.40	.25
559	Tommy Davis	1.25	.60	.40
560	Gaylord Perry	7.00	3.50	2.00
561	Tom McCraw	.80	.40	.25
562	Ted Abernathy	.80	.40	.25
563	Red Sox Team	2.00	1.00	.60
564	Johnny Briggs	.80	.40	.25
565	Jim Hunter	7.00	3.50	2.00
566	Gene Alley	.90	.45	.25
567	Bob Oliver	.80	.40	.25
568	Stan Bahnsen	.90	.45	.25
569	Cookie Rojas	.80	.40	.25
570	Jim Fregosi	1.00	.50	.30
571	Jim Brewer	.80	.40	.25
572	Frank Quilici	.80	.40	.25
573	Padres Rookies (Mike Corkins, Rafael Robles, Ron Slocum)	.80	.40	.25
574	Bobby Bolin	.90	.45	.25
575	Cleon Jones	.90	.45	.25
576	Milt Pappas	.90	.45	.25
577	Bernie Allen	.80	.40	.25
578	Tom Griffin	.80	.40	.25
579	Tigers Team	2.25	1.25	.70
580	Pete Rose	75.00	37.00	22.00
581	Tom Satriano	.80	.40	.25
582	Mike Paul	.80	.40	.25
583	Hal Lanier	.90	.45	.25
584	Al Downing	.90	.45	.25
585	Rusty Staub	2.00	1.00	.60
586	Rickey Clark	.80	.40	.25
587	Jose Arcia	.80	.40	.25
588a	Checklist 634-720 (666 is Adolpho Phillips)	4.50	2.25	1.25
588b	Checklist 634-720 (666 is Adolfo Phillips)	3.00	1.50	.90
589	Joe Keough	.80	.40	.25
590	Mike Cuellar	.90	.45	.25
591	Mike Ryan	.80	.40	.25
592	Daryl Patterson	.80	.40	.25
593	Cubs Team	1.75	.90	.50
594	Jake Gibbs	.90	.45	.25
595	Maury Wills	2.50	1.25	.70
596	Mike Hershberger	.90	.45	.25
597	Sonny Siebert	.80	.40	.25
598	Joe Pepitone	1.25	.60	.40
599	Senators Rookies (Gene Martin, Dick Stelmaszek, Dick Such)	.80	.40	.25
600	Willie Mays	45.00	23.00	13.50
601	Pete Richert	.80	.40	.25
602	Ted Savage	.80	.40	.25
603	Ray Oyler	.80	.40	.25
604	Clarence Gaston	.80	.40	.25
605	Rick Wise	.90	.45	.25
606	Chico Ruiz	.80	.40	.25
607	Gary Waslewski	.80	.40	.25
608	Pirates Team	1.75	.90	.50
609	*Buck Martinez*	.90	.45	.25
610	Jerry Koosman	1.25	.60	.40
611	Norm Cash	1.50	.70	.45
612	Jim Hickman	.90	.45	.25
613	Dave Baldwin	.90	.45	.25
614	Mike Shannon	.90	.45	.25
615	Mark Belanger	.90	.45	.25
616	Jim Merritt	.80	.40	.25
617	Jim French	.80	.40	.25
618	Billy Wynne	.80	.40	.25
619	Norm Miller	.80	.40	.25
620	Jim Perry	1.00	.50	.30
621	Braves Rookies (*Darrell Evans*, Rick Kester, Mike McQueen)	7.00	3.50	2.00
622	Don Sutton	4.50	2.25	1.25
623	Horace Clarke	.90	.45	.25
624	Clyde King	.80	.40	.25
625	Dean Chance	.90	.45	.25
626	Dave Ricketts	.80	.40	.25
627	Gary Wagner	.80	.40	.25
628	Wayne Garrett	.80	.40	.25
629	Merv Rettenmund	.80	.40	.25
630	Ernie Banks	15.00	7.50	4.50
631	Athletics Team	1.75	.90	.50
632	Gary Sutherland	.80	.40	.25
633	Roger Nelson	.80	.40	.25
634	Bud Harrelson	2.25	1.25	.70

	NR MT	EX	VG
635 Bob Allison	2.25	1.25	.70
636 Jim Stewart	2.00	1.00	.60
637 Indians Team	3.00	1.50	.90
638 Frank Bertaina	2.00	1.00	.60
639 Dave Campbell	2.00	1.00	.60
640 Al Kaline	25.00	12.50	7.50
641 Al McBean	2.00	1.00	.60
642 Angels Rookies (Greg Garrett, Gordon Lund, Jarvis Tatum)	2.00	1.00	.60
643 Jose Pagan	2.00	1.00	.60
644 Gerry Nyman	2.00	1.00	.60
645 Don Money	2.00	1.00	.60
646 Jim Britton	2.00	1.00	.60
647 Tom Matchick	2.00	1.00	.60
648 Larry Haney	2.00	1.00	.60
649 Jimmie Hall	2.00	1.00	.60
650 Sam McDowell	2.50	1.25	.70
651 Jim Gosger	2.00	1.00	.60
652 Rich Rollins	2.25	1.25	.70
653 Moe Drabowsky	2.00	1.00	.60
654 N.L. Rookies (Boots Day, Oscar Gamble, Angel Mangual)	2.50	1.25	.70
655 John Roseboro	2.25	1.25	.70
656 Jim Hardin	2.00	1.00	.60
657 Padres Team	4.00	2.00	1.25
658 Ken Tatum	2.00	1.00	.60
659 Pete Ward	2.25	1.25	.70
660 Johnny Bench	125.00	56.00	35.00
661 Jerry Robertson	2.00	1.00	.60
662 Frank Lucchesi	2.00	1.00	.60
663 Tito Francona	2.25	1.25	.70
664 Bob Robertson	2.00	1.00	.60
665 Jim Lonborg	2.25	1.25	.70
666 Adolfo Phillips	2.00	1.00	.60
667 Bob Meyer	2.25	1.25	.70
668 Bob Tillman	2.00	1.00	.60
669 White Sox Rookies (Bart Johnson, Dan Lazar, Mickey Scott)	2.00	1.00	.60
670 Ron Santo	3.25	1.75	1.00
671 Jim Campanis	2.00	1.00	.60
672 Leon McFadden	2.00	1.00	.60
673 Ted Uhlaender	2.00	1.00	.60
674 Dave Leonhard	2.00	1.00	.60
675 Jose Cardenal	2.25	1.25	.70
676 Senators Team	3.25	1.75	1.00
677 Woodie Fryman	2.25	1.25	.70
678 Dave Duncan	2.00	1.00	.60
679 Ray Sadecki	2.00	1.00	.60
680 Rico Petrocelli	2.25	1.25	.70
681 Bob Garibaldi	2.00	1.00	.60
682 Dalton Jones	2.00	1.00	.60
683 Reds Rookies (Vern Geishert, Hal McRae, Wayne Simpson)	2.75	1.50	.80
684 Jack Fisher	2.00	1.00	.60
685 Tom Haller	2.25	1.25	.70
686 Jackie Hernandez	2.00	1.00	.60
687 Bob Priddy	2.00	1.00	.60
688 Ted Kubiak	2.25	1.25	.70
689 Frank Tepedino	2.25	1.25	.70
690 Ron Fairly	2.25	1.25	.70
691 Joe Grzenda	2.00	1.00	.60
692 Duffy Dyer	2.00	1.00	.60
693 Bob Johnson	2.00	1.00	.60
694 Gary Ross	2.00	1.00	.60
695 Bobby Knoop	2.00	1.00	.60
696 Giants Team	3.25	1.75	1.00
697 Jim Hannan	2.00	1.00	.60
698 Tom Tresh	2.75	1.50	.80
699 Hank Aguirre	2.00	1.00	.60
700 Frank Robinson	25.00	12.50	7.50
701 Jack Billingham	2.00	1.00	.60
702 A.L. Rookies (Bob Johnson, Ron Klimkowski, Bill Zepp)	2.25	1.25	.70
703 Lou Marone	2.00	1.00	.60
704 Frank Baker	2.00	1.00	.60
705 Tony Cloninger	2.25	1.25	.70
706 John McNamara	2.50	1.25	.70
707 Kevin Collins	2.00	1.00	.60
708 Jose Santiago	2.00	1.00	.60
709 Mike Fiore	2.00	1.00	.60
710 Felix Millan	2.00	1.00	.60
711 Ed Brinkman	2.25	1.25	.70
712 Nolan Ryan	200.00	80.00	50.00
713 Pilots Team	10.00	5.00	3.00
714 Al Spangler	2.00	1.00	.60
715 Mickey Lolich	5.00	2.50	1.50
716 Cards Rookies (Sal Campisi, Reggie Cleveland, Santiago Guzman)	2.25	1.25	.70
717 Tom Phoebus	2.00	1.00	.60
718 Ed Spiezio	2.00	1.00	.60
719 Jim Roland	2.25	.90	.50

	NR MT	EX	VG
720 Rick Reichardt	4.00	1.00	.50

1970 Topps Candy Lids

The 1970 Topps Candy Lids are a test issue that was utilized again in 1973. The set is made up of 24 lids that measure 1-7/8" in diameter and were the tops of small 1.1 oz. tubs of "Baseball Stars Candy." Unlike the 1973 versions, the 1970 lids have no border surrounding the full-color photos. Frank Howard, Tom Seaver and Carl Yastrzemski photos are found on the bottom (inside) of the candy lid.

		NR MT	EX	VG
Complete Set:		2000.00	1000.00	600.00
Common Player:		30.00	15.00	9.00
(1)	Hank Aaron	200.00	100.00	60.00
(2)	Rich Allen	50.00	25.00	15.00
(3)	Luis Aparicio	80.00	40.00	24.00
(4)	Johnny Bench	200.00	100.00	60.00
(5)	Ollie Brown	30.00	15.00	9.00
(6)	Willie Davis	30.00	15.00	9.00
(7)	Jim Fregosi	30.00	15.00	9.00
(8)	Mike Hegan	30.00	15.00	9.00
(9)	Frank Howard	50.00	25.00	15.00
(10)	Reggie Jackson	200.00	100.00	60.00
(11)	Fergie Jenkins	60.00	30.00	18.00
(12)	Harmon Killebrew	100.00	50.00	30.00
(13)	Juan Marichal	100.00	50.00	30.00
(14)	Bill Mazeroski	50.00	25.00	15.00
(15)	Tim McCarver	50.00	25.00	15.00
(16)	Sam McDowell	30.00	15.00	9.00
(17)	Denny McLain	50.00	25.00	15.00
(18)	Lou Piniella	50.00	25.00	15.00
(19)	Frank Robinson	100.00	50.00	30.00
(20)	Tom Seaver	175.00	87.00	52.00
(21)	Rusty Staub	50.00	25.00	15.00
(22)	Mel Stottlemyre	50.00	25.00	15.00
(23)	Jim Wynn	30.00	15.00	9.00
(24)	Carl Yastrzemski	150.00	75.00	45.00

1970 Topps Posters

Helping to ease a price increase, Topps included extremely fragile 8-11/16" by 9-5/8" posters in packs of regular cards. The posters feature color portraits and a smaller black and white "action" pose as well as the player's name, team and position at the top. Although there are Hall of Famers in the 24-poster set, all the top names are not represented. Once again, due to folding, heavy creases are a fact of life for today's collector.

		NR MT	EX	VG
Complete Set:		25.00	12.50	7.50
Common Player:		.40	.20	.12
1	Joe Horlen	.40	.20	.12
2	Phil Niekro	1.50	.70	.45
3	Willie Davis	.50	.25	.15
4	Lou Brock	2.00	1.00	.60
5	Ron Santo	.60	.30	.20
6	Ken Harrelson	.50	.25	.15
7	Willie McCovey	2.00	1.00	.60
8	Rick Wise	.40	.20	.12
9	Andy Messersmith	.40	.20	.12
10	Ron Fairly	.50	.25	.15
11	Johnny Bench	3.25	1.75	1.00
12	Frank Robinson	2.50	1.25	.70
13	Tommie Agee	.40	.20	.12
14	Roy White	.50	.25	.15
15	Larry Dierker	.40	.20	.12
16	Rod Carew	3.00	1.50	.90
17	Don Mincher	.40	.20	.12
18	Ollie Brown	.40	.20	.12
19	Ed Kirkpatrick	.40	.20	.12
20	Reggie Smith	.50	.25	.15
21	Bob Clemente	5.00	2.50	1.50
22	Frank Howard	.60	.30	.20
23	Bert Campaneris	.50	.25	.15
24	Denny McLain	.60	.30	.20

1970 Topps Scratch-Offs

Needing inserts, and having not given up on the idea of a game which could be played with baseball cards, Topps provided a new game - the baseball scratch-off. The set consists of 24 cards. Unfolded, they measure 3-3/8" by 5," and reveal a baseball game of sorts which was played by rubbing the black ink off playing squares which then determined the "action." Fronts of the cards have a player picture as "captain," while backs have instructions and a scoreboard. Inserts with white centers are from 1970 while those with red centers are from 1971.

		NR MT	EX	VG
Complete Set:		20.00	10.00	6.00
Common Player:		.30	.15	.09
(1)	Hank Aaron	2.00	1.00	.60
(2)	Rich Allen	.50	.25	.15
(3)	Luis Aparicio	1.00	.50	.30
(4)	Sal Bando	.30	.15	.09
(5)	Glenn Beckert	.30	.15	.09
(6)	Dick Bosman	.30	.15	.09
(7)	Nate Colbert	.30	.15	.09
(8)	Mike Hegan	.30	.15	.09
(9)	Mack Jones	.30	.15	.09
(10)	Al Kaline	1.50	.70	.45
(11)	Harmon Killebrew	1.50	.70	.45

		NR MT	EX	VG
(12)	Juan Marichal	1.25	.60	.40
(13)	Tim McCarver	.40	.20	.12
(14)	Sam McDowell	.30	.15	.09
(15)	Claude Osteen	.30	.15	.09
(16)	Tony Perez	.60	.30	.20
(17)	Lou Piniella	.40	.20	.12
(18)	Boog Powell	.50	.25	.15
(19)	Tom Seaver	2.00	1.00	.60
(20)	Jim Spencer	.30	.15	.09
(21)	Willie Stargell	1.25	.60	.40
(22)	Mel Stottlemyre	.30	.15	.09
(23)	Jim Wynn	.30	.15	.09
(24)	Carl Yastrzemski	2.25	1.25	.70

1970 Topps Story Booklets

Measuring 2-1/2" by 3-7/16," the Topps Story Booklet was a 1970 regular pack insert. The booklet feature a photo, title and booklet number on the "cover." Inside are six pages of comic book story. The backs give a checklist of other available booklets. Not every star had a booklet as the set is only 24 in number.

		NR MT	EX	VG
Complete Set:		25.00	12.50	7.50
Common Player:		.30	.15	.09
1	Mike Cuellar	.40	.20	.12
2	Rico Petrocelli	.40	.20	.12
3	Jay Johnstone	.40	.20	.12
4	Walt Williams	.30	.15	.09
5	Vada Pinson	.50	.25	.15
6	Bill Freehan	.40	.20	.12
7	Wally Bunker	.30	.15	.09
8	Tony Oliva	.50	.25	.15
9	Bobby Murcer	.40	.20	.12
10	Reggie Jackson	5.00	2.50	1.50
11	Tommy Harper	.30	.15	.09
12	Mike Epstein	.30	.15	.09
13	Orlando Cepeda	.80	.40	.25
14	Ernie Banks	3.00	1.50	.90
15	Pete Rose	8.00	4.00	2.50
16	Denis Menke	.30	.15	.09
17	Bill Singer	.30	.15	.09
18	Rusty Staub	.50	.25	.15
19	Cleon Jones	.30	.15	.09
20	Deron Johnson	.30	.15	.09
21	Bob Moose	.30	.15	.09
22	Bob Gibson	4.00	2.00	1.25
23	Al Ferrara	.30	.15	.09
24	Willie Mays	7.00	3.50	2.00

1970 Topps Super

Representing a refinement of the concept begun in 1969, the 1970 Topps Supers had a new 3-1/8" by 5-1/4 postcard size. Printed on heavy stock with rounded corners, card fronts feature a borderless color photograph and facsimile autograph. Card backs are simply an enlarged back from the player's regular 1970 Topps card. The Topps Supers set numbers 42 cards. Probably due to the press sheet configuration eight of the 42 had smaller printings.

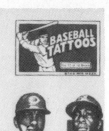

The most elusive is card #38 (Boog Powell). The set was more widely produced than was the case in 1969, meaning collectors stand a much better chance of affording it.

		NR MT	EX	VG
Complete Set:		200.00	100.00	60.00
Common Player:		.75	.40	.25
1	Claude Osteen	3.00	1.50	.90
2	Sal Bando	3.50	1.75	1.00
3	Luis Aparicio	2.50	1.25	.70
4	Harmon Killebrew	4.00	2.00	1.25
5	Tom Seaver	25.00	12.50	7.50
6	Larry Dierker	.80	.40	.25
7	Bill Freehan	1.00	.50	.30
8	Johnny Bench	15.00	7.50	4.50
9	Tommy Harper	.80	.40	.25
10	Sam McDowell	1.00	.50	.30
11	Louis Brock	4.00	2.00	1.25
12	Roberto Clemente	15.00	7.50	4.50
13	Willie McCovey	4.00	2.00	1.25
14	Rico Petrocelli	.80	.40	.25
15	Philip Niekro	2.25	1.25	.70
16	Frank Howard	1.50	.70	.45
17	Denny McLain	1.25	.60	.40
18	Willie Mays	15.00	7.50	4.50
19	Wilver Stargell	3.50	1.75	1.00
20	Joe Horlen	.80	.40	.25
21	Ronald Santo	1.00	.50	.30
22	Dick Bosman	.80	.40	.25
23	Tim McCarver	1.00	.50	.30
24	Henry Aaron	15.00	7.50	4.50
25	Andy Messersmith	.80	.40	.25
26	Tony Oliva	1.25	.60	.40
27	Mel Stottlemyre	1.00	.50	.30
28	Reginald M. Jackson	18.00	9.00	5.50
29	Carl Yastrzemski	12.00	6.00	3.50
30	James Fregosi	1.00	.50	.30
31	Vada Pinson	1.25	.60	.40
32	Lou Piniella	1.25	.60	.40
33	Robert Gibson	4.00	2.00	1.25
34	Pete Rose	25.00	12.50	7.50
35	Jim Wynn	1.00	.50	.30
36	Ollie Brown	3.00	1.50	.90
37	Frank Robinson	18.00	9.00	5.50
38	John "Boog" Powell	60.00	30.00	18.00
39	Willie Davis	3.50	1.75	1.00
40	Billy Williams	12.00	6.00	3.50
41	Rusty Staub	1.25	.60	.40
42	Tommie Agee	.80	.40	.25

1971 Topps Baseball Tattoos

Topps once again produced baseball tattoos in 1971. This time, the tattoos came in a variety of sizes, shapes and themes. The sheets of tattoos measure 3-1/2" by 14-1/4." Each sheet contains an assortment of tattoos in two sizes, 1-3/4" by 2-3/8," or 1-3/16" by 1-3/4." There are players, facsimile autographed baseballs, team pennants and assorted baseball cartoon figures carried on the 16 different sheets. Listings below are for complete sheets; with the exception of the biggest-name stars, individual tattoos have little or no collector value.

		NR MT	EX	VG
Complete Sheet Set:		175.00	87.00	52.00
Common Sheet:		4.00	2.00	1.25
1	Brooks Robinson Autograph, Montreal Expos Pennant, San Francisco Giants Pennant, Sal Bando, Dick Bosman, Nate Colbert, Cleon Jones, Juan Marichal, B. Robinson	10.00	5.00	3.00
2	Boston Red Sox Pennant, Carl Yastrzemski Autograph, New York Mets Pennant, Glenn Beckert, Tommy Harper, Ken Henderson, Fritz Peterson, Bob Robertson, C. Yastrzemski	18.00	9.00	5.50
3	Jim Fregosi Autograph, New York Yankees Pennant, Philadelphia Phillies Pennant ector value., Orlando Cepeda, Jim Fregosi, Randy Hundley, Reggie Jackson, Jerry Koosman, Jim Palmer	15.00	7.50	4.50
4	Kansas City Royals Pennant, Oakland Athletics Pennant, Sam McDowell Autograph, Dick Dietz, C. Gaston, Dave Johnson, Sam McDowell, Gary Nolan, Amos Otis	3.50	1.75	1.00
5	Al Kaline Autograph, Atlanta Braves Pennant, L.A. Dodgers Pennant, B. Grabarkewitz, Al Kaline, Lee May, Tom Murphy, Vada Pinson, M. Sanguillen	10.00	5.00	3.00
6	Chicago Cubs Pennant, Cincinnati Reds Pennant, Harmon Killebrew Autograph, Luis Aparicio, Paul Blair, C. Cannizzaro, D. Clendenon, Larry Dieker, H. Killebrew	10.00	5.00	3.00
7	Boog Powell Autograph, Cleveland Indians Pennant, Milwaukee Brewers Pennant, Rich Allen, B. Campaneris, Don Money, Boog Powell, Ted Savage, Rusty Staub	5.00	2.50	1.50
8	Chicago White Sox Pennant, Frank Howard Autograph, San Diego Padres Pennant, Leo Cardenas, Bill Hands, Frank Howard, Wes Parker, Reggie Smith, W. Stargell	5.00	2.50	1.50
9	Detroit Tigers Pennant, Henry Aaron Autograph, Hank Aaron, Tommy Agee, Jim Hunter, Dick McAuliffe, Tony Perez, Lou Piniella	15.00	7.50	4.50
10	Baltimore Orioles Pennant, Fergie Jenkins Autograph, R. Clemente, T. Conigliaro, Fergie Jenkins, T. Munson, Gary Peters, Joe Torre	12.00	6.00	3.50
11	Johnny Bench Autograph, Washington Senators Pennant, Johnny Bench, Rico Carty, B. Mazeroski, Bob Oliver, R. Petrocelli, F. Robinson	10.00	5.00	3.00
12	Billy Williams Autograph, Houston Astros Pennant, Bill Freehan, Dave McNally, Felix Millan, M. Stottlemyre, Bob Tolan, Billy Williams	6.00	3.00	1.75
13	Pittsburgh Pirates Pennant, Willie McCovey Autograph, Ray Culp, Bud Harrelson, Mickey Lolich, W. McCovey, Ron Santo, Roy White	9.00	4.50	2.75
14	Minnesota Twins Pennant, Tom Seaver Autograph, Bill Melton, Jim Perry, Pete Rose, Tom Seaver, Maury Wills, Clyde Wright	25.00	12.50	7.50
15	Robert Gibson Autograph, St. Louis Cardinals Pennant, Rod Carew, Bob Gibson, Alex Johnson, Don Kessinger, Jim Merritt, Rick Monday	9.00	4.50	2.75
16	California Angels Pennant, Willie Mays Autograph, Larry Bowa, Mike Cuellar, Ray Fosse, Willie Mays, Carl Morton, Tony Oliva	15.00	7.50	4.50

1971 Topps

In 1971, Topps again increased the size of its set to 752 cards. These well-liked cards, measuring 2-1/2" by 3-1/2," feature a large color photo which has a thin white frame. Above the picture, in the card's overall black border, is the player's name, team and position. A facsimile autograph completes the front. Backs feature a major change as a black and white "snapshot" of the player appears. Abbreviated statistics, a line giving the player's first pro and major league games and a short biography complete the back of these innovative cards. Specialty cards in this issue are limited. There are statistical leaders as well as World Series and playoff highlights. High numbered cards #644-752 are scarce.

		NR MT	EX	VG
	Complete Set:	1500.00	750.00	425.00
	Common Player: 1-523	.35	.20	.11
	Common Player: 524-643	.80	.40	.25
	Common Player: 644-752	2.25	1.25	.70
1	World Champions (Orioles Team)	5.00	1.25	.60
2	Dock Ellis	.50	.20	.12
3	Dick McAuliffe	.40	.20	.12
4	Vic Davalillo	.40	.20	.12
5	Thurman Munson	20.00	10.00	6.00
6	Ed Spiezio	.35	.20	.11
7	Jim Holt	.35	.20	.11
8	Mike McQueen	.35	.20	.11
9	George Scott	.50	.25	.15
10	Claude Osteen	.50	.25	.15
11	*Elliott Maddox*	.50	.25	.15
12	Johnny Callison	.60	.30	.20
13	White Sox Rookies (Charlie Brinkman, Dick Moloney)	.35	.20	.11
14	*Dave Concepcion*	5.00	2.50	1.50
15	Andy Messersmith	.40	.20	.12
16	*Ken Singleton*	1.75	.90	.50
17	Billy Sorrell	.35	.20	.11
18	Norm Miller	.35	.20	.11
19	Skip Pitlock	.35	.20	.11
20	Reggie Jackson	30.00	15.00	9.00
21	Dan McGinn	.35	.20	.11
22	Phil Roof	.35	.20	.11
23	Oscar Gamble	.40	.20	.12
24	Rich Hand	.35	.20	.11
25	Clarence Gaston	.35	.20	.11
26	*Bert Blyleven*	20.00	10.00	6.00
27	Pirates Rookies (Fred Cambria, Gene Clines)	.35	.20	.11
28	Ron Klimkowski	.40	.20	.12
29	Don Buford	.40	.20	.12
30	Phil Niekro	3.25	1.75	1.00
31	Eddie Kasko	.35	.20	.11
32	Jerry DaVanon	.35	.20	.11
33	Del Unser	.35	.20	.11
34	Sandy Vance	.35	.20	.11
35	Lou Piniella	1.25	.60	.40
36	Dean Chance	.40	.20	.12
37	Rich McKinney	.35	.20	.11
38	*Jim Colborn*	.40	.20	.12
39	Tigers Rookies (Gene Lamont, *Lerrin LaGrow*)	.40	.20	.12
40	Lee May	.60	.30	.20
41	Rick Austin	.35	.20	.11

		NR MT	EX	VG
42	Boots Day	.35	.20	.11
43	Steve Kealey	.35	.20	.11
44	Johnny Edwards	.35	.20	.11
45	Jim Hunter	3.75	2.00	1.25
46	Dave Campbell	.35	.20	.11
47	Johnny Jeter	.35	.20	.11
48	Dave Baldwin	.35	.20	.11
49	Don Money	.40	.20	.12
50	Willie McCovey	6.00	3.00	1.75
51	Steve Kline	.40	.20	.12
52	Braves Rookies (Oscar Brown, *Earl Williams*)	.40	.20	.12
53	Paul Blair	.40	.20	.12
54	Checklist 1-132	2.50	1.25	.70
55	Steve Carlton	15.00	7.50	4.50
56	Duane Josephson	.35	.20	.11
57	Von Joshua	.35	.20	.11
58	Bill Lee	.40	.20	.12
59	Gene Mauch	.60	.30	.20
60	Dick Bosman	.35	.20	.11
61	A.L. Batting Leaders (Alex Johnson, Tony Oliva, Carl Yastrzemski)	2.25	1.25	.70
62	N.L. Batting Leaders (Rico Carty, Manny Sanguillen, Joe Torre)	1.25	.60	.40
63	A.L. RBI Leaders (Tony Conigliaro, Frank Howard, Boog Powell)	1.25	.60	.40
64	N.L. RBI Leaders (Johnny Bench, Tony Perez, Billy Williams)	2.25	1.25	.70
65	A.L. Home Run Leaders (Frank Howard, Harmon Killebrew, Carl Yastrzemski)	2.25	1.25	.70
66	N.L. Home Run Leaders (Johnny Bench, Tony Perez, Billy Williams)	2.25	1.25	.70
67	A.L. ERA Leaders (Jim Palmer, Diego Segui, Clyde Wright)	1.25	.60	.40
68	N.L. ERA Leaders (Tom Seaver, Wayne Simpson, Luke Walker)	1.50	.70	.45
69	A.L. Pitching Leaders (Mike Cuellar, Dave McNally, Jim Perry)	1.25	.60	.40
70	N.L. Pitching Leaders (Bob Gibson, Fergie Jenkins, Gaylord Perry)	2.00	1.00	.60
71	A.L. Strikeout Leaders (Bob Johnson, Mickey Lolich, Sam McDowell)	1.25	.60	.40
72	N.L. Strikeout Leaders (Bob Gibson, Fergie Jenkins, Tom Seaver)	2.25	1.25	.70
73	George Brunet	.35	.20	.11
74	Twins Rookies (Pete Hamm, Jim Nettles)	.35	.20	.11
75	Gary Nolan	.35	.20	.11
76	Ted Savage	.35	.20	.11
77	Mike Compton	.35	.20	.11
78	Jim Spencer	.40	.20	.12
79	Wade Blasingame	.35	.20	.11
80	Bill Melton	.40	.20	.12
81	Felix Millan	.35	.20	.11
82	Casey Cox	.35	.20	.11
83	Mets Rookies (Randy Bobb, *Tim Foli*)	.50	.25	.15
84	Marcel Lachemann	.35	.20	.11
85	Billy Grabarkewitz	.35	.20	.11
86	Mike Kilkenny	.35	.20	.11
87	Jack Heidemann	.35	.20	.11
88	Hal King	.35	.20	.11
89	Ken Brett	.35	.20	.11
90	Joe Pepitone	.70	.35	.20
91	Bob Lemon	1.25	.60	.40
92	Fred Wenz	.35	.20	.11
93	Senators Rookies (Norm McRae, Denny Riddleberger)	.35	.20	.11
94	Don Hahn	.35	.20	.11
95	Luis Tiant	1.50	.70	.45
96	Joe Hague	.35	.20	.11
97	Floyd Wicker	.35	.20	.11
98	Joe Decker	.35	.20	.11
99	Mark Belanger	.40	.20	.12
100	Pete Rose	45.00	23.00	13.50
101	Les Cain	.35	.20	.11
102	Astros Rookies (*Ken Forsch*, Larry Howard)	.50	.25	.15
103	Rich Severson	.35	.20	.11
104	Dan Frisella	.35	.20	.11
105	Tony Conigliaro	1.25	.60	.40
106	Tom Dukes	.35	.20	.11
107	Roy Foster	.35	.20	.11
108	John Cumberland	.35	.20	.11
109	Steve Hovley	.35	.20	.11
110	Bill Mazeroski	1.25	.60	.40
111	Yankees Rookies (Loyd Colson, Bobby Mitchell)	.40	.20	.12
112	Manny Mota	.60	.30	.20
113	Jerry Crider	.35	.20	.11
114	Billy Conigliaro	.40	.20	.12

		NR MT	EX	VG
115	Donn Clendenon	.40	.20	.12
116	Ken Sanders	.35	.20	.11
117	*Ted Simmons*	8.00	4.00	2.50
118	Cookie Rojas	.35	.20	.11
119	Frank Lucchesi	.35	.20	.11
120	Willie Horton	.60	.30	.20
121	1971 Rookie Stars (Jim Dunegan, Roe Skidmore)	.35	.20	.11
122	Eddie Watt	.35	.20	.11
123a	Checklist 133-263 (card # on right, orange helmet)	2.50	1.25	.70
123b	Checklist 133-263 (card # on right, red helmet)	2.50	1.25	.70
123c	Checklist 133-263 (card # centered)	3.50	1.75	1.00
124	*Don Gullett*	.70	.35	.20
125	Ray Fosse	.35	.20	.11
126	Danny Coombs	.35	.20	.11
127	*Danny Thompson*	.40	.20	.12
128	Frank Johnson	.35	.20	.11
129	Aurelio Monteagudo	.35	.20	.11
130	Denis Menke	.35	.20	.11
131	Curt Blefary	.40	.20	.12
132	Jose Laboy	.35	.20	.11
133	Mickey Lolich	1.25	.60	.40
134	Jose Arcia	.35	.20	.11
135	Rick Monday	.50	.25	.15
136	Duffy Dyer	.35	.20	.11
137	Marcelino Lopez	.35	.20	.11
138	Phillies Rookies (Joe Lis, *Willie Montanez*)	.50	.25	.15
139	Paul Casanova	.35	.20	.11
140	Gaylord Perry	4.00	2.00	1.25
141	Frank Quilici	.35	.20	.11
142	Mack Jones	.35	.20	.11
143	Steve Blass	.40	.20	.12
144	Jackie Hernandez	.35	.20	.11
145	Bill Singer	.40	.20	.12
146	Ralph Houk	.80	.40	.25
147	Bob Priddy	.35	.20	.11
148	John Mayberry	.50	.25	.15
149	Mike Hershberger	.35	.20	.11
150	Sam McDowell	.70	.35	.20
151	Tommy Davis	.70	.35	.20
152	Angels Rookies (Lloyd Allen, Winston Llenas)	.35	.20	.11
153	Gary Ross	.35	.20	.11
154	Cesar Gutierrez	.35	.20	.11
155	Ken Henderson	.35	.20	.11
156	Bart Johnson	.35	.20	.11
157	Bob Bailey	.35	.20	.11
158	Jerry Reuss	1.00	.50	.30
159	Jarvis Tatum	.35	.20	.11
160	Tom Seaver	25.00	12.50	7.50
161	Coins Checklist	2.50	1.25	.70
162	Jack Billingham	.35	.20	.11
163	Buck Martinez	.35	.20	.11
164	Reds Rookies (Frank Duffy, *Milt Wilcox*)	.60	.30	.20
165	Cesar Tovar	.35	.20	.11
166	Joe Hoerner	.35	.20	.11
167	Tom Grieve	.35	.20	.11
168	Bruce Dal Canton	.35	.20	.11
169	Ed Herrmann	.35	.20	.11
170	Mike Cuellar	.60	.30	.20
171	Bobby Wine	.35	.20	.11
172	Duke Sims	.35	.20	.11
173	Gil Garrido	.35	.20	.11
174	*Dave LaRoche*	.50	.25	.15
175	Jim Hickman	.40	.20	.12
176	Red Sox Rookies (Doug Griffin, Bob Montgomery)	.35	.20	.11
177	Hal McRae	.70	.35	.20
178	Dave Duncan	.35	.20	.11
179	Mike Corkins	.35	.20	.11
180	Al Kaline	12.00	6.00	3.50
181	Hal Lanier	.60	.30	.20
182	Al Downing	.40	.20	.12
183	Gil Hodges	4.00	2.00	1.25
184	Stan Bahnsen	.50	.25	.15
185	Julian Javier	.40	.20	.12
186	Bob Spence	.35	.20	.11
187	Ted Abernathy	.35	.20	.11
188	Dodgers Rookies (Mike Strahler, *Bob Valentine*)	1.75	.90	.50
189	George Mitterwald	.35	.20	.11
190	Bob Tolan	.40	.20	.12
191	Mike Andrews	.35	.20	.11
192	Billy Wilson	.35	.20	.11
193	*Bob Grich*	1.75	.90	.50
194	Mike Lum	.35	.20	.11
195	A.L. Playoff Game 1 (Powell Muscles Twins!)	1.25	.60	.40
196	A.L. Playoff Game 2 (McNally Makes It Two Straight!)	1.25	.60	.40
197	A.L. Playoff Game 3 (Palmer Mows 'Em Down!)	1.75	.90	.50
198	A.L. Playoffs Summary (A Team Effort!)	1.25	.60	.40
199	N.L. Playoff Game 1 (Cline Pinch-Triple Decides It!)	1.25	.60	.40
200	N.L. Playoff Game 2 (Tolan Scores For Third Time!)	1.25	.60	.40
201	N.L. Playoff Game 3 (Cline Scores Winning Run!)	1.25	.60	.40
202	N.L. Playoffs Summary (World Series Bound!)	1.25	.60	.40
203	*Larry Gura*	.70	.35	.20
204	Brewers Rookies (George Kopacz, Bernie Smith)	.35	.20	.11
205	Gerry Moses	.35	.20	.11
206a	Checklist 264-393 (orange helmet)	2.50	1.25	.70
206b	Checklist 264-393 (red helmet)	2.50	1.25	.70
207	Alan Foster	.35	.20	.11
208	Billy Martin	1.75	.90	.50
209	Steve Renko	.35	.20	.11
210	Rod Carew	18.00	9.00	5.50
211	Phil Hennigan	.35	.20	.11
212	Rich Hebner	.40	.20	.12
213	Frank Baker	.40	.20	.12
214	Al Ferrara	.35	.20	.11
215	Diego Segui	.35	.20	.11
216	Cards Rookies (Reggie Cleveland, Luis Melendez)	.35	.20	.11
217	Ed Stroud	.35	.20	.11
218	Tony Cloninger	.40	.20	.12
219	Elrod Hendricks	.35	.20	.11
220	Ron Santo	.80	.40	.25
221	Dave Morehead	.35	.20	.11
222	Bob Watson	.40	.20	.12
223	Cecil Upshaw	.35	.20	.11
224	Alan Gallagher	.35	.20	.11
225	Gary Peters	.40	.20	.12
226	Bill Russell	.60	.30	.20
227	Floyd Weaver	.35	.20	.11
228	Wayne Garrett	.35	.20	.11
229	Jim Hannan	.35	.20	.11
230	Willie Stargell	6.00	3.00	1.75
231	Indians Rookies (Vince Colbert, *John Lowenstein*)	.50	.25	.15
232	John Strohmayer	.35	.20	.11
233	Larry Bowa	1.75	.90	.50
234	Jim Lyttle	.40	.20	.12
235	Nate Colbert	.35	.20	.11
236	Bob Humphreys	.35	.20	.11
237	*Cesar Cedeno*	1.50	.70	.45
238	Chuck Dobson	.35	.20	.11
239	Red Schoendienst	1.00	.50	.30
240	Clyde Wright	.35	.20	.11
241	Dave Nelson	.35	.20	.11
242	Jim Ray	.35	.20	.11
243	Carlos May	.40	.20	.12
244	Bob Tillman	.35	.20	.11
245	Jim Kaat	2.50	1.25	.70
246	Tony Taylor	.35	.20	.11
247	Royals Rookies (Jerry Cram, *Paul Splittorff*)	.70	.35	.20
248	Hoyt Wilhelm	3.75	2.00	1.25
249	Chico Salmon	.35	.20	.11
250	Johnny Bench	35.00	17.50	10.50
251	Frank Reberger	.35	.20	.11
252	Eddie Leon	.35	.20	.11
253	Bill Sudakis	.35	.20	.11
254	Cal Koonce	.35	.20	.11
255	Bob Robertson	.35	.20	.11
256	Tony Gonzalez	.35	.20	.11
257	Nelson Briles	.35	.20	.11
258	Dick Green	.35	.20	.11
259	Dave Marshall	.35	.20	.11
260	Tommy Harper	.40	.20	.12
261	Darold Knowles	.35	.20	.11
262	Padres Rookies (Dave Robinson, Jim Williams)	.35	.20	.11
263	John Ellis	.40	.20	.12
264	Joe Morgan	5.00	2.50	1.50
265	Jim Northrup	.40	.20	.12
266	Bill Stoneman	.35	.20	.11
267	Rich Morales	.35	.20	.11
268	Phillies Team	1.25	.60	.40
269	Gail Hopkins	.35	.20	.11
270	Rico Carty	.70	.35	.20

	NR MT	EX	VG
271 Bill Zepp	.35	.20	.11
272 Tommy Helms	.40	.20	.12
273 Pete Richert	.35	.20	.11
274 Ron Slocum	.35	.20	.11
275 Vada Pinson	1.25	.60	.40
276 Giants Rookies (Mike Davison, *George Foster*)	4.00	2.00	1.25
277 Gary Waslewski	.40	.20	.12
278 Jerry Grote	.50	.25	.15
279 Lefty Phillips	.35	.20	.11
280 Fergie Jenkins	3.00	1.50	.90
281 Danny Walton	.35	.20	.11
282 Jose Pagan	.35	.20	.11
283 Dick Such	.35	.20	.11
284 Jim Gosger	.35	.20	.11
285 Sal Bando	.60	.30	.20
286 Jerry McNertney	.35	.20	.11
287 Mike Fiore	.35	.20	.11
288 Joe Moeller	.35	.20	.11
289 White Sox Team	1.25	.60	.40
290 Tony Oliva	1.50	.70	.45
291 George Culver	.35	.20	.11
292 Jay Johnstone	.60	.30	.20
293 Pat Corrales	.50	.25	.15
294 Steve Dunning	.35	.20	.11
295 Bobby Bonds	1.25	.60	.40
296 Tom Timmermann	.35	.20	.11
297 Johnny Briggs	.35	.20	.11
298 Jim Nelson	.35	.20	.11
299 Ed Kirkpatrick	.35	.20	.11
300 Brooks Robinson	9.00	4.50	2.75
301 Earl Wilson	.35	.20	.11
302 Phil Gagliano	.35	.20	.11
303 Lindy McDaniel	.40	.20	.12
304 Ron Brand	.35	.20	.11
305 Reggie Smith	.60	.30	.20
306 Jim Nash	.35	.20	.11
307 Don Wert	.35	.20	.11
308 Cards Team	1.25	.60	.40
309 Dick Ellsworth	.35	.20	.11
310 Tommie Agee	.40	.20	.12
311 Lee Stange	.35	.20	.11
312 Harry Walker	.40	.20	.12
313 Tom Hall	.35	.20	.11
314 Jeff Torborg	.40	.20	.12
315 Ron Fairly	.50	.25	.15
316 Fred Scherman	.35	.20	.11
317 Athletics Rookies (Jim Driscoll, Angel Mangual)	.35	.20	.11
318 Rudy May	.40	.20	.12
319 Ty Cline	.35	.20	.11
320 Dave McNally	.50	.25	.15
321 Tom Matchick	.35	.20	.11
322 Jim Beauchamp	.35	.20	.11
323 Billy Champion	.35	.20	.11
324 Graig Nettles	2.50	1.25	.70
325 Juan Marichal	5.00	2.50	1.50
326 Richie Scheinblum	.35	.20	.11
327 World Series Game 1 (Powell Homers To Opposite Field!)	1.25	.60	.40
328 World Series Game 2 (Buford Goes 2-For 4!)	1.25	.60	.40
329 World Series Game 3 (F. Robinson Shows Muscle!)	2.00	1.00	.60
330 World Series Game 4 (Reds Stay Alive!)	1.25	.60	.40
331 World Series Game 5 (B. Robinson Commits Robbery!)	2.00	1.00	.60
332 World Series Summary (Clinching Performance!)	1.25	.60	.40
333 Clay Kirby	.35	.20	.11
334 Roberto Pena	.35	.20	.11
335 Jerry Koosman	1.00	.50	.30
336 Tigers Team	1.75	.90	.50
337 Jesus Alou	.40	.20	.12
338 Gene Tenace	.50	.25	.15
339 Wayne Simpson	.35	.20	.11
340 Rico Petrocelli	.50	.25	.15
341 *Steve Garvey*	65.00	33.00	20.00
342 Frank Tepedino	.40	.20	.12
343 Pirates Rookies (Ed Acosta, *Milt May*)	.40	.20	.12
344 Ellie Rodriguez	.35	.20	.11
345 Joe Horlen	.35	.20	.11
346 Lum Harris	.35	.20	.11
347 Ted Uhlaender	.35	.20	.11
348 Fred Norman	.35	.20	.11
349 Rich Reese	.35	.20	.11
350 Billy Williams	4.50	2.25	1.25
351 Jim Shellenback	.35	.20	.11
352 Denny Doyle	.35	.20	.11
353 Carl Taylor	.35	.20	.11
354 Don McMahon	.35	.20	.11
355 Bud Harrelson	.40	.20	.12
356 Bob Locker	.35	.20	.11
357 Reds Team	1.25	.60	.40
358 Danny Cater	.40	.20	.12
359 Ron Reed	.40	.20	.12
360 Jim Fregosi	.80	.40	.25
361 Don Sutton	3.50	1.75	1.00
362 Orioles Rookies (Mike Adamson, Roger Freed)	.35	.20	.11
363 Mike Nagy	.35	.20	.11
364 Tommy Dean	.35	.20	.11
365 Bob Johnson	.35	.20	.11
366 Ron Stone	.35	.20	.11
367 Dalton Jones	.35	.20	.11
368 Bob Veale	.40	.20	.12
369a Checklist 394-523 (orange helmet)	2.50	1.25	.70
369b Checklist 394-523 (red helmet, black line above ear)	2.50	1.25	.70
369c Checklist 394-523 (red helmet, no line)	2.50	1.25	.70
370 Joe Torre	2.25	1.25	.70
371 Jack Hiatt	.35	.20	.11
372 Lew Krausse	.35	.20	.11
373 Tom McCraw	.35	.20	.11
374 Clete Boyer	.50	.25	.15
375 Steve Hargan	.35	.20	.11
376 Expos Rookies (Clyde Mashore, Ernie McAnally)	.35	.20	.11
377 Greg Garrett	.35	.20	.11
378 Tito Fuentes	.35	.20	.11
379 Wayne Granger	.35	.20	.11
380 Ted Williams	5.00	2.50	1.50
381 Fred Gladding	.35	.20	.11
382 Jake Gibbs	.40	.20	.12
383 Rod Gaspar	.35	.20	.11
384 Rollie Fingers	2.50	1.25	.70
385 Maury Wills	1.25	.60	.40
386 Red Sox Team	1.50	.70	.45
387 Ron Herbel	.35	.20	.11
388 Al Oliver	1.75	.90	.50
389 Ed Brinkman	.40	.20	.12
390 Glenn Beckert	.50	.25	.15
391 Twins Rookies (Steve Brye, Cotton Nash)	.35	.20	.11
392 Grant Jackson	.35	.20	.11
393 Merv Rettenmund	.40	.20	.12
394 Clay Carroll	.40	.20	.12
395 Roy White	.70	.35	.20
396 Dick Schofield	.35	.20	.11
397 Alvin Dark	.50	.25	.15
398 Howie Reed	.35	.20	.11
399 Jim French	.35	.20	.11
400 Hank Aaron	25.00	12.50	7.50
401 Tom Murphy	.35	.20	.11
402 Dodgers Team	1.50	.70	.45
403 Joe Coleman	.40	.20	.12
404 Astros Rookies (Buddy Harris, Roger Metzger)	.35	.20	.11
405 Leo Cardenas	.35	.20	.11
406 Ray Sadecki	.35	.20	.11
407 Joe Rudi	.60	.30	.20
408 Rafael Robles	.35	.20	.11
409 Don Pavletich	.35	.20	.11
410 Ken Holtzman	.40	.20	.12
411 George Spriggs	.35	.20	.11
412 Jerry Johnson	.35	.20	.11
413 Pat Kelly	.35	.20	.11
414 Woodie Fryman	.40	.20	.12
415 Mike Hegan	.35	.20	.11
416 Gene Alley	.40	.20	.12
417 Dick Hall	.35	.20	.11
418 Adolfo Phillips	.35	.20	.11
419 Ron Hansen	.40	.20	.12
420 Jim Merritt	.35	.20	.11
421 John Stephenson	.35	.20	.11
422 Frank Bertaina	.35	.20	.11
423 Tigers Rookies (Tim Marting, Dennis Saunders)	.35	.20	.11
424 Roberto Rodriguez (Rodriguez)	.35	.20	.11
425 Doug Rader	.35	.20	.11
426 Chris Cannizzaro	.35	.20	.11
427 Bernie Allen	.35	.20	.11
428 Jim McAndrew	.35	.20	.11
429 Chuck Hinton	.35	.20	.11
430 Wes Parker	.40	.20	.12
431 Tom Burgmeier	.35	.20	.11
432 Bob Didier	.35	.20	.11
433 Skip Lockwood	.35	.20	.11

		NR MT	EX	VG
434	Gary Sutherland	.35	.20	.11
435	Jose Cardenal	.40	.20	.12
436	Wilbur Wood	.50	.25	.15
437	Danny Murtaugh	.40	.20	.12
438	Mike McCormick	.50	.25	.15
439	Phillies Rookies (*Greg Luzinski*, Scott Reid)	2.00	1.00	.60
440	Bert Campaneris	.70	.35	.20
441	Milt Pappas	.40	.20	.12
442	Angels Team	1.25	.60	.40
443	Rich Robertson	.35	.20	.11
444	Jimmie Price	.35	.20	.11
445	Art Shamsky	.35	.20	.11
446	Bobby Bolin	.35	.20	.11
447	*Cesar Geronimo*	.60	.30	.20
448	Dave Roberts	.35	.20	.11
449	Brant Alyea	.35	.20	.11
450	Bob Gibson	8.00	4.00	2.50
451	Joe Keough	.35	.20	.11
452	John Boccabella	.35	.20	.11
453	Terry Crowley	.35	.20	.11
454	Mike Paul	.35	.20	.11
455	Don Kessinger	.40	.20	.12
456	Bob Meyer	.35	.20	.11
457	Willie Smith	.35	.20	.11
458	White Sox Rookies (Dave Lemonds, Ron Lolich)	.35	.20	.11
459	Jim Lefebvre	.40	.20	.12
460	Fritz Peterson	.50	.25	.15
461	Jim Hart	.40	.20	.12
462	Senators Team	1.50	.70	.45
463	Tom Kelley	.35	.20	.11
464	Aurelio Rodriguez	.40	.20	.12
465	Tim McCarver	.80	.40	.25
466	Ken Berry	.35	.20	.11
467	Al Santorini	.35	.20	.11
468	Frank Fernandez	.35	.20	.11
469	Bob Aspromonte	.35	.20	.11
470	Bob Oliver	.35	.20	.11
471	Tom Griffin	.35	.20	.11
472	Ken Rudolph	.35	.20	.11
473	Gary Wagner	.35	.20	.11
474	Jim Fairey	.35	.20	.11
475	Ron Perranoski	.40	.20	.12
476	Dal Maxvill	.40	.20	.12
477	Earl Weaver	1.00	.50	.30
478	Bernie Carbo	.40	.20	.12
479	Dennis Higgins	.35	.20	.11
480	Manny Sanguillen	.40	.20	.12
481	Daryl Patterson	.35	.20	.11
482	Padres Team	1.25	.60	.40
483	Gene Michael	.50	.25	.15
484	Don Wilson	.35	.20	.11
485	Ken McMullen	.35	.20	.11
486	Steve Huntz	.35	.20	.11
487	Paul Schaal	.35	.20	.11
488	Jerry Stephenson	.35	.20	.11
489	Luis Alvarado	.35	.20	.11
490	Deron Johnson	.35	.20	.11
491	Jim Hardin	.35	.20	.11
492	Ken Boswell	.35	.20	.11
493	Dave May	.35	.20	.11
494	Braves Rookies (Ralph Garr, Rick Kester)	.50	.25	.15
495	Felipe Alou	.60	.30	.20
496	Woody Woodward	.40	.20	.12
497	Horacio Pina	.35	.20	.11
498	John Kennedy	.35	.20	.11
499	Checklist 524-643	2.50	1.25	.70
500	Jim Perry	.60	.30	.20
501	Andy Etchebarren	.35	.20	.11
502	Cubs Team	1.25	.60	.40
503	Gates Brown	.35	.20	.11
504	Ken Wright	.35	.20	.11
505	Ollie Brown	.35	.20	.11
506	Bobby Knoop	.35	.20	.11
507	George Stone	.35	.20	.11
508	Roger Repoz	.35	.20	.11
509	Jim Grant	.35	.20	.11
510	Ken Harrelson	1.25	.60	.40
511	Chris Short	.40	.20	.12
512	Red Sox Rookies (Mike Garman, Dick Mills)	.35	.20	.11
513	Nolan Ryan	75.00	38.00	23.00
514	Ron Woods	.40	.20	.12
515	Carl Morton	.35	.20	.11
516	Ted Kubiak	.35	.20	.11
517	Charlie Fox	.35	.20	.11
518	Joe Grzenda	.35	.20	.11
519	Willie Crawford	.35	.20	.11
520	Tommy John	3.00	1.50	.90
521	Leron Lee	.35	.20	.11
522	Twins Team	1.25	.60	.40
523	John Odom	.40	.20	.12
524	Mickey Stanley	.90	.45	.25
525	Ernie Banks	12.00	6.00	3.50
526	Ray Jarvis	.80	.40	.25
527	Cleon Jones	.90	.45	.25
528	Wally Bunker	.80	.40	.25
529	N.L. Rookies (Bill Buckner, Enzo Hernandez, Marty Perez)	2.50	1.25	.70
530	Carl Yastrzemski	30.00	15.00	9.00
531	Mike Torrez	.90	.45	.25
532	Bill Rigney	.80	.40	.25
533	Mike Ryan	.80	.40	.25
534	Luke Walker	.80	.40	.25
535	Curt Flood	1.75	.90	.50
536	Claude Raymond	.80	.40	.25
537	Tom Egan	.80	.40	.25
538	Angel Bravo	.80	.40	.25
539	Larry Brown	.80	.40	.25
540	Larry Dierker	.90	.45	.25
541	Bob Burda	.80	.40	.25
542	Bob Miller	.80	.40	.25
543	Yankees Team	2.75	1.50	.80
544	Vida Blue	2.50	1.25	.70
545	Dick Dietz	.80	.40	.25
546	John Matias	.80	.40	.25
547	Pat Dobson	.90	.45	.25
548	Don Mason	.80	.40	.25
549	Jim Brewer	.80	.40	.25
550	Harmon Killebrew	12.00	6.00	3.50
551	Frank Linzy	.80	.40	.25
552	Buddy Bradford	.80	.40	.25
553	Kevin Collins	.80	.40	.25
554	Lowell Palmer	.80	.40	.25
555	Walt Williams	.80	.40	.25
556	Jim McGlothlin	.80	.40	.25
557	Tom Satriano	.80	.40	.25
558	Hector Torres	.80	.40	.25
559	A.L. Rookies (Terry Cox, Bill Gogolewski, Gary Jones)	.90	.45	.25
560	Rusty Staub	2.25	1.25	.70
561	Syd O'Brien	.80	.40	.25
562	Dave Giusti	.80	.40	.25
563	Giants Team	2.00	1.00	.60
564	Al Fitzmorris	.80	.40	.25
565	Jim Wynn	1.00	.50	.30
566	Tim Cullen	.80	.40	.25
567	Walt Alston	2.50	1.25	.70
568	Sal Campisi	.80	.40	.25
569	Ivan Murrell	.80	.40	.25
570	Jim Palmer	10.00	5.00	3.00
571	Ted Sizemore	.80	.40	.25
572	Jerry Kenney	.90	.45	.25
573	Ed Kranepool	1.00	.50	.30
574	Jim Bunning	4.00	2.00	1.25
575	Bill Freehan	1.00	.50	.30
576	Cubs Rookies (Brock Davis, Adrian Garrett, Garry Jestadt)	.80	.40	.25
577	Jim Lonborg	1.00	.50	.30
578	Ron Hunt	.90	.45	.25
579	Marty Pattin	.80	.40	.25
580	Tony Perez	4.00	2.00	1.25
581	Roger Nelson	.80	.40	.25
582	Dave Cash	.80	.40	.25
583	Ron Cook	.80	.40	.25
584	Indians Team	2.00	1.00	.60
585	Willie Davis	2.25	1.25	.70
586	Dick Woodson	.80	.40	.25
587	Sonny Jackson	.80	.40	.25
588	Tom Bradley	.80	.40	.25
589	Bob Barton	.80	.40	.25
590	Alex Johnson	.80	.40	.25
591	Jackie Brown	.80	.40	.25
592	Randy Hundley	.80	.40	.25
593	Jack Aker	.90	.45	.25
594	Cards Rookies (Bob Chlupsa, *Al Hrabosky*, Bob Stinson)	2.25	1.25	.70
595	Dave Johnson	1.75	.90	.50
596	Mike Jorgensen	.80	.40	.25
597	Ken Suarez	.80	.40	.25
598	Rick Wise	.90	.45	.25
599	Norm Cash	2.00	1.00	.60
600	Willie Mays	35.00	17.50	10.50
601	Ken Tatum	.80	.40	.25
602	Marty Martinez	.80	.40	.25
603	Pirates Team	3.00	1.50	.90
604	John Gelnar	.80	.40	.25
605	Orlando Cepeda	3.25	1.75	1.00
606	Chuck Taylor	.80	.40	.25
607	Paul Ratliff	.80	.40	.25

		NR MT	EX	VG
608	Mike Wegener	.80	.40	.25
609	Leo Durocher	2.25	1.25	.70
610	Amos Otis	1.00	.50	.30
611	Tom Phoebus	.80	.40	.25
612	Indians Rookies (Lou Camilli, Ted Ford, Steve Mingori)	.80	.40	.25
613	Pedro Borbon	.90	.45	.25
614	Billy Cowan	.80	.40	.25
615	Mel Stottlemyre	1.75	.90	.50
616	Larry Hisle	.90	.45	.25
617	Clay Dalrymple	.80	.40	.25
618	Tug McGraw	2.25	1.25	.70
619a	Checklist 644-752 (no copyright on back)	4.50	2.25	1.25
619b	Checklist 644-752 (with copyright, no wavy line on helmet brim)	3.00	1.50	.90
619c	Checklist 644-752 (with copyright, wavy line on helmet brim)	3.00	1.50	.90
620	Frank Howard	2.25	1.25	.70
621	Ron Bryant	.80	.40	.25
622	Joe Lahoud	.80	.40	.25
623	Pat Jarvis	.80	.40	.25
624	Athletics Team	2.00	1.00	.60
625	Lou Brock	10.00	5.00	3.00
626	Freddie Patek	.90	.45	.25
627	Steve Hamilton	.80	.40	.25
628	John Bateman	.80	.40	.25
629	John Hiller	.90	.45	.25
630	Roberto Clemente	25.00	12.50	7.50
631	Eddie Fisher	.80	.40	.25
632	Darrel Chaney	.80	.40	.25
633	A.L. Rookies (Bobby Brooks, Pete Koegel, Scott Northey)	.80	.40	.25
634	Phil Regan	.80	.40	.25
635	Bobby Murcer	2.00	1.00	.60
636	Denny Lemaster	.80	.40	.25
637	Dave Bristol	.80	.40	.25
638	Stan Williams	.80	.40	.25
639	Tom Haller	.90	.45	.25
640	Frank Robinson	15.00	7.50	4.50
641	Mets Team	3.50	1.75	1.00
642	Jim Roland	.80	.40	.25
643	Rick Reichardt	.80	.40	.25
644	Jim Stewart	2.25	1.25	.70
645	Jim Maloney	2.50	1.25	.70
646	Bobby Floyd	2.25	1.25	.70
647	Juan Pizarro	2.25	1.25	.70
648	Mets Rookies (Rich Folkers, Ted Martinez, Jon Matlack)	3.50	1.75	1.00
649	Sparky Lyle	3.00	1.50	.90
650	Rich Allen	6.00	3.00	1.75
651	Jerry Robertson	2.25	1.25	.70
652	Braves Team	3.25	1.75	1.00
653	Russ Snyder	2.25	1.25	.70
654	Don Shaw	2.25	1.25	.70
655	Mike Epstein	2.50	1.25	.70
656	Gerry Nyman	2.25	1.25	.70
657	Jose Azcue	2.25	1.25	.70
658	Paul Lindblad	2.25	1.25	.70
659	Byron Browne	2.25	1.25	.70
660	Ray Culp	2.25	1.25	.70
661	Chuck Tanner	3.00	1.50	.90
662	Mike Hedlund	2.25	1.25	.70
663	Marv Staehle	2.25	1.25	.70
664	Major League Rookies (Archie Reynolds, Bob Reynolds, Ken Reynolds)	2.25	1.25	.70
665	Ron Swoboda	2.25	1.25	.70
666	Gene Brabender	2.25	1.25	.70
667	Pete Ward	2.50	1.25	.70
668	Gary Neibauer	2.25	1.25	.70
669	Ike Brown	2.25	1.25	.70
670	Bill Hands	2.25	1.25	.70
671	Bill Voss	2.25	1.25	.70
672	Ed Crosby	2.25	1.25	.70
673	Gerry Janeski	2.25	1.25	.70
674	Expos Team	3.25	1.75	1.00
675	Dave Boswell	2.25	1.25	.70
676	Tommie Reynolds	2.25	1.25	.70
677	Jack DiLauro	2.25	1.25	.70
678	George Thomas	2.25	1.25	.70
679	Don O'Riley	2.25	1.25	.70
680	Don Mincher	2.50	1.25	.70
681	Bill Butler	2.25	1.25	.70
682	Terry Harmon	2.25	1.25	.70
683	Bill Burbach	2.50	1.25	.70
684	Curt Motton	2.25	1.25	.70
685	Moe Drabowsky	2.25	1.25	.70
686	Chico Ruiz	2.25	1.25	.70
687	Ron Taylor	2.25	1.25	.70
688	Sparky Anderson	3.50	1.75	1.00
689	Frank Baker	2.25	1.25	.70

		NR MT	EX	VG
690	Bob Moose	2.25	1.25	.70
691	Bob Heise	2.25	1.25	.70
692	A.L. Rookies (Hal Haydel, Rogelio Moret, Wayne Twitchell)	2.25	1.25	.70
693	Jose Pena	2.25	1.25	.70
694	Rick Renick	2.25	1.25	.70
695	Joe Niekro	3.25	1.75	1.00
696	Jerry Morales	2.25	1.25	.70
697	Rickey Clark	2.25	1.25	.70
698	Brewers Team	3.50	1.75	1.00
699	Jim Britton	2.25	1.25	.70
700	Boog Powell	4.00	2.00	1.25
701	Bob Garibaldi	2.25	1.25	.70
702	Milt Ramirez	2.25	1.25	.70
703	Mike Kekich	2.50	1.25	.70
704	J.C. Martin	2.25	1.25	.70
705	Dick Selma	2.25	1.25	.70
706	Joe Foy	2.25	1.25	.70
707	Fred Lasher	2.25	1.25	.70
708	Russ Nagelson	2.25	1.25	.70
709	Major League Rookies (Dusty Baker, Don Baylor, Tom Paciorek)	30.00	15.00	9.00
710	Sonny Siebert	2.25	1.25	.70
711	Larry Stahl	2.25	1.25	.70
712	Jose Martinez	2.25	1.25	.70
713	Mike Marshall	2.75	1.50	.80
714	Dick Williams	2.75	1.50	.80
715	Horace Clarke	2.50	1.25	.70
716	Dave Leonhard	2.25	1.25	.70
717	Tommie Aaron	2.50	1.25	.70
718	Billy Wynne	2.25	1.25	.70
719	Jerry May	2.25	1.25	.70
720	Matty Alou	2.75	1.50	.80
721	John Morris	2.25	1.25	.70
722	Astros Team	3.25	1.75	1.00
723	Vicente Romo	2.25	1.25	.70
724	Tom Tischinski	2.25	1.25	.70
725	Gary Gentry	2.25	1.25	.70
726	Paul Popovich	2.25	1.25	.70
727	Ray Lamb	2.25	1.25	.70
728	N.L. Rookies (Keith Lampard, Wayne Redmond, Bernie Williams)	2.25	1.25	.70
729	Dick Billings	2.25	1.25	.70
730	Jim Rooker	2.25	1.25	.70
731	Jim Qualls	2.25	1.25	.70
732	Bob Reed	2.25	1.25	.70
733	Lee Maye	2.25	1.25	.70
734	Rob Gardner	2.50	1.25	.70
735	Mike Shannon	2.50	1.25	.70
736	Mel Queen	2.25	1.25	.70
737	Preston Gomez	2.25	1.25	.70
738	Russ Gibson	2.25	1.25	.70
739	Barry Lersch	2.25	1.25	.70
740	Luis Aparicio	15.00	7.50	4.50
741	Skip Guinn	2.25	1.25	.70
742	Royals Team	3.25	1.75	1.00
743	John O'Donoghue	2.25	1.25	.70
744	Chuck Manuel	2.25	1.25	.70
745	Sandy Alomar	2.25	1.25	.70
746	Andy Kosco	2.25	1.25	.70
747	N.L. Rookies (Balor Moore, Al Severinsen, Scipio Spinks)	2.25	1.25	.70
748	John Purdin	2.25	1.25	.70
749	Ken Szotkiewicz	2.25	1.25	.70
750	Denny McLain	6.00	3.00	1.75
751	Al Weis	2.50	1.25	.70
752	Dick Drago	3.75	1.25	.70

1971 Topps Coins

Measuring 1-1/2" in diameter, the latest edition of

the Topps coins was a 153-piece set. The coins feature a color photograph surrounded by a colored band on the front. The band carries the player's name, team, position and several stars. Backs have a short biography, the coin number and encouragement to collect the entire set. Back colors differ, with #'s 1-51 having a brass back, #'s 52-102 chrome backs, and the rest have blue backs. Most of the stars of the period are included in the set/

		NR MT	EX	VG
	Complete Set:	400.00	200.00	120.00
	Common Player:	.90	.45	.25
1	Clarence Gaston	.90	.45	.25
2	Dave Johnson	1.25	.60	.40
3	Jim Bunning	2.00	1.00	.60
4	Jim Spencer	.90	.45	.25
5	Felix Millan	.90	.45	.25
6	Gerry Moses	.90	.45	.25
7	Fergie Jenkins	2.00	1.00	.60
8	Felipe Alou	1.00	.50	.30
9	Jim McGlothlin	.90	.45	.25
10	Dick McAuliffe	.90	.45	.25
11	Joe Torre	1.50	.70	.45
12	Jim Perry	1.25	.60	.40
13	Bobby Bonds	1.25	.60	.40
14	Danny Cater	.90	.45	.25
15	Bill Mazeroski	1.50	.70	.45
16	Luis Aparicio	5.00	2.50	1.50
17	Doug Rader	.90	.45	.25
18	Vada Pinson	1.50	.70	.45
19	John Bateman	.90	.45	.25
20	Lew Krausse	.90	.45	.25
21	Billy Grabarkewitz	.90	.45	.25
22	Frank Howard	1.50	.70	.45
23	Jerry Koosman	1.25	.60	.40
24	Rod Carew	8.00	4.00	2.50
25	Al Ferrara	.90	.45	.25
26	Dave McNally	1.00	.50	.30
27	Jim Hickman	.90	.45	.25
28	Sandy Alomar	.90	.45	.25
29	Lee May	1.00	.50	.30
30	Rico Petrocelli	1.00	.50	.30
31	Don Money	.90	.45	.25
32	Jim Rooker	.90	.45	.25
33	Dick Dietz	.90	.45	.25
34	Roy White	1.00	.50	.30
35	Carl Morton	.90	.45	.25
36	Walt Williams	.90	.45	.25
37	Phil Niekro	3.25	1.75	1.00
38	Bill Freehan	1.00	.50	.30
39	Julian Javier	.90	.45	.25
40	Rick Monday	1.00	.50	.30
41	Don Wilson	.90	.45	.25
42	Ray Fosse	.90	.45	.25
43	Art Shamsky	.90	.45	.25
44	Ted Savage	.90	.45	.25
45	Claude Osteen	1.00	.50	.30
46	Ed Brinkman	.90	.45	.25
47	Matty Alou	1.00	.50	.30
48	Bob Oliver	.90	.45	.25
49	Danny Coombs	.90	.45	.25
50	Frank Robinson	7.00	3.50	2.00
51	Randy Hundley	.90	.45	.25
52	Cesar Tovar	.90	.45	.25
53	Wayne Simpson	.90	.45	.25
54	Bobby Murcer	1.25	.60	.40
55	Tony Taylor	.90	.45	.25
56	Tommy John	2.50	1.25	.70
57	Willie McCovey	7.00	3.50	2.00
58	Carl Yastrzemski	15.00	7.50	4.50
59	Bob Bailey	.90	.45	.25
60	Clyde Wright	.90	.45	.25
61	Orlando Cepeda	2.00	1.00	.60
62	Al Kaline	7.00	3.50	2.00
63	Bob Gibson	7.00	3.50	2.00
64	Bert Campaneris	1.25	.60	.40
65	Ted Sizemore	.90	.45	.25
66	Duke Sims	.90	.45	.25
67	Bud Harrelson	.90	.45	.25
68	Jerry McNertney	.90	.45	.25
69	Jim Wynn	1.00	.50	.30
70	Dick Bosman	.90	.45	.25
71	Roberto Clemente	15.00	7.50	4.50
72	Rich Reese	.90	.45	.25
73	Gaylord Perry	4.00	2.00	1.25
74	Boog Powell	1.50	.70	.45
75	Billy Williams	5.00	2.50	1.50
76	Bill Melton	.90	.45	.25
77	Nate Colbert	.90	.45	.25
78	Reggie Smith	1.25	.60	.40
79	Deron Johnson	.90	.45	.25
80	Jim Hunter	5.00	2.50	1.50
81	Bob Tolan	.90	.45	.25
82	Jim Northrup	.90	.45	.25
83	Ron Fairly	1.00	.50	.30
84	Alex Johnson	.90	.45	.25
85	Pat Jarvis	.90	.45	.25
86	Sam McDowell	1.00	.50	.30
87	Lou Brock	7.00	3.50	2.00
88	Danny Walton	.90	.45	.25
89	Denis Menke	.90	.45	.25
90	Jim Palmer	7.00	3.50	2.00
91	Tommie Agee	.90	.45	.25
92	Duane Josephson	.90	.45	.25
93	Willie Davis	1.00	.50	.30
94	Mel Stottlemyre	1.00	.50	.30
95	Ron Santo	1.25	.60	.40
96	Amos Otis	1.00	.50	.30
97	Ken Henderson	.90	.45	.25
98	George Scott	1.00	.50	.30
99	Dock Ellis	.90	.45	.25
100	Harmon Killebrew	7.00	3.50	2.00
101	Pete Rose	30.00	15.00	9.00
102	Rick Reichardt	.90	.45	.25
103	Cleon Jones	.90	.45	.25
104	Ron Perranoski	.90	.45	.25
105	Tony Perez	2.50	1.25	.70
106	Mickey Lolich	1.25	.60	.40
107	Tim McCarver	1.25	.60	.40
108	Reggie Jackson	12.00	6.00	3.50
109	Chris Cannizzaro	.90	.45	.25
110	Steve Hargan	.90	.45	.25
111	Rusty Staub	2.50	1.25	.70
112	Andy Messersmith	1.00	.50	.30
113	Rico Carty	1.25	.60	.40
114	Brooks Robinson	7.00	3.50	2.00
115	Steve Carlton	7.00	3.50	2.00
116	Mike Hegan	.90	.45	.25
117	Joe Morgan	4.50	2.25	1.25
118	Thurman Munson	5.00	2.50	1.50
119	Don Kessinger	1.00	.50	.30
120	Joe Horlen	.90	.45	.25
121	Wes Parker	1.00	.50	.30
122	Sonny Siebert	.90	.45	.25
123	Willie Stargell	5.00	2.50	1.50
124	Ellie Rodriguez	.90	.45	.25
125	Juan Marichal	5.00	2.50	1.50
126	Mike Epstein	.90	.45	.25
127	Tom Seaver	8.00	4.00	2.50
128	Tony Oliva	2.50	1.25	.70
129	Jim Merritt	.90	.45	.25
130	Willie Horton	1.00	.50	.30
131	Rick Wise	.90	.45	.25
132	Sal Bando	1.00	.50	.30
133	Ollie Brown	.90	.45	.25
134	Ken Harrelson	1.00	.50	.30
135	Mack Jones	.90	.45	.25
136	Jim Fregosi	1.00	.50	.30
137	Hank Aaron	15.00	7.50	4.50
138	Fritz Peterson	.90	.45	.25
139	Joe Hague	.90	.45	.25
140	Tommy Harper	.90	.45	.25
141	Larry Dierker	.90	.45	.25
142	Tony Conigliaro	1.50	.70	.45
143	Glenn Beckert	1.00	.50	.30
144	Carlos May	.90	.45	.25
145	Don Sutton	3.25	1.75	1.00
146	Paul Casanova	.90	.45	.25
147	Bob Moose	.90	.45	.25
148	Leo Cardenas	.90	.45	.25
149	Johnny Bench	8.00	4.00	2.50
150	Mike Cuellar	1.00	.50	.30
151	Donn Clendenon	.90	.45	.25
152	Lou Piniella	1.25	.60	.40
153	Willie Mays	15.00	7.50	4.50

1971 Topps Greatest Moments

This 55-card set features a great moment from the careers of top players at the time. The front of the 2-1/2" by 4-3/4" cards features a portrait photo of the player at the left and deckle-edge action photo at the right. There is a small headline on the white border of the action photo. The player's name and "One of Baseball's Greatest Moments" along with a black border complete the front. The back features a detail from the front photo and the story of the event. The newspaper style presentation includes the name of real newspapers. Relatively scarce, virtually every card in this set is a star or at least an above-average player.

1971 Topps Super

Topps continued to produce its special oversized cards in 1971. The cards, measuring 3-1/8" by 5-1/4," carry a large color photograph with a facsimile autograph on the front. Backs are basically enlargements of the player's regular Topps card. The set size ged to 63 cards in 1971, so there are no short-printed cards as in 1970. Again, Topps included almost every major star who was active at the time, so the set of oversized cards with rounded corners remains an interesting source for those seeking the big names of the era.

		NR MT	EX	VG
Complete Set:		1600.00	800.00	480.00
Common Player:		4.00	2.00	1.25
1	Thurman Munson	60.00	30.00	18.00
2	Hoyt Wilhelm	30.00	15.00	9.00
3	Rico Carty	15.00	7.50	4.50
4	Carl Morton	4.00	2.00	1.25
5	Sal Bando	5.00	2.50	1.50
6	Bert Campaneris	5.00	2.50	1.50
7	Jim Kaat	20.00	10.00	6.00
8	Harmon Killebrew	60.00	30.00	18.00
9	Brooks Robinson	75.00	37.00	22.00
10	Jim Perry	15.00	7.50	4.50
11	Tony Oliva	20.00	10.00	6.00
12	Vada Pinson	20.00	10.00	6.00
13	Johnny Bench	175.00	87.00	52.00
14	Tony Perez	25.00	12.50	7.50
15	Pete Rose	90.00	45.00	27.00
16	Jim Fregosi	4.00	2.00	1.25
17	Alex Johnson	4.00	2.00	1.25
18	Clyde Wright	4.00	2.00	1.25
19	Al Kaline	25.00	12.50	7.50
20	Denny McLain	20.00	10.00	6.00
21	Jim Northrup	15.00	7.50	4.50
22	Bill Freehan	15.00	7.50	4.50
23	Mickey Lolich	20.00	10.00	6.00
24	Bob Gibson	18.00	9.00	5.50
25	Tim McCarver	5.00	2.50	1.50
26	Orlando Cepeda	7.00	3.50	2.00
27	Lou Brock	18.00	9.00	5.50
28	Nate Colbert	4.00	2.00	1.25
29	Maury Wills	20.00	10.00	6.00
30	Wes Parker	15.00	7.50	4.50
31	Jim Wynn	15.00	7.50	4.50
32	Larry Dierker	15.00	7.50	4.50
33	Bill Melton	15.00	7.50	4.50
34	Joe Morgan	40.00	20.00	12.00
35	Rusty Staub	20.00	10.00	6.00
36	Ernie Banks	25.00	12.50	7.50
37	Billy Williams	50.00	25.00	15.00
38	Lou Piniella	20.00	10.00	6.00
39	Rico Petrocelli	4.00	2.00	1.25
40	Carl Yastrzemski	60.00	30.00	18.00
41	Willie Mays	45.00	22.00	13.50
42	Tommy Harper	15.00	7.50	4.50
43	Jim Bunning	7.00	3.50	2.00
44	Fritz Peterson	15.00	7.50	4.50
45	Roy White	15.00	7.50	4.50
46	Bobby Murcer	15.00	7.50	4.50
47	Reggie Jackson	250.00	125.00	75.00
48	Frank Howard	20.00	10.00	6.00
49	Dick Bosman	15.00	7.50	4.50
50	Sam McDowell	4.00	2.00	1.25
51	Luis Aparicio	12.00	6.00	3.50
52	Willie McCovey	15.00	7.50	4.50
53	Joe Pepitone	15.00	7.50	4.50
54	Jerry Grote	15.00	7.50	4.50
55	Bud Harrelson	15.00	7.50	4.50

		NR MT	EX	VG
Complete Set:		175.00	87.00	52.00
Common Player:		.70	.35	.20
1	Reggie Smith	1.00	.50	.30
2	Gaylord Perry	3.00	1.50	.90
3	Ted Savage	.70	.35	.20
4	Donn Clendenon	.70	.35	.20
5	John "Boog" Powell	1.25	.60	.40
6	Tony Perez	1.75	.90	.50
7	Dick Bosman	.70	.35	.20
8	Alex Johnson	.70	.35	.20
9	Rusty Staub	1.25	.60	.40
10	Mel Stottlemyre	1.00	.50	.30
11	Tony Oliva	1.50	.70	.45
12	Bill Freehan	1.00	.50	.30
13	Fritz Peterson	.70	.35	.20
14	Wes Parker	.70	.35	.20
15	Cesar Cedeno	1.25	.60	.40
16	Sam McDowell	1.00	.50	.30
17	Frank Howard	1.50	.70	.45
18	Dave McNally	1.00	.50	.30
19	Rico Petrocelli	.70	.35	.20
20	Pete Rose	25.00	12.50	7.50
21	Luke Walker	.70	.35	.20
22	Nate Colbert	.70	.35	.20
23	Luis Aparicio	2.50	1.25	.70
24	Jim Perry	1.00	.50	.30
25	Louis Brock	4.50	2.25	1.25
26	Roy White	1.00	.50	.30
27	Claude Osteen	.70	.35	.20
28	Carl W. Morton	.70	.35	.20
29	Ricardo A. Jacabo Carty	1.00	.50	.30
30	Larry Dierker	.70	.35	.20
31	Dagoberto Campaneris	1.00	.50	.30
32	Johnny Bench	8.00	4.00	2.50
33	Felix Millan	.70	.35	.20
34	Tim McCarver	1.25	.60	.40
35	Ronald Santo	1.25	.60	.40
36	Tommie Agee	.70	.35	.20
37	Roberto Clemente	10.00	5.00	3.00
38	Reggie Jackson	15.00	7.50	4.50
39	Clyde Wright	.70	.35	.20
40	Rich Allen	1.50	.70	.45
41	Curt Flood	1.25	.60	.40
42	Fergie Jenkins	1.75	.90	.50
43	Willie Stargell	3.00	1.50	.90
44	Henry Aaron	10.00	5.00	3.00
45	Amos Otis	1.00	.50	.30
46	Willie McCovey	4.50	2.25	1.25
47	William Melton	.70	.35	.20
48	Robert Gibson	3.50	1.75	1.00
49	Carl Yastrzemski	15.00	7.50	4.50
50	Glenn Beckert	1.00	.50	.30
51	Ray Fosse	.70	.35	.20

		NR MT	EX	VG
52	Clarence Gaston	.70	.35	.20
53	Tom Seaver	8.00	4.00	2.50
54	Al Kaline	6.00	3.00	1.75
55	Jim Northrup	.70	.35	.20
56	Willie Mays	10.00	5.00	3.00
57	Sal Bando	1.00	.50	.30
58	Deron Johnson	.70	.35	.20
59	Brooks Robinson	7.00	3.50	2.00
60	Harmon Killebrew	6.00	3.00	1.75
61	Joseph Torre	1.75	.90	.50
62	Lou Piniella	1.25	.60	.40
63	Tommy Harper	.70	.35	.20

1972 Topps

The largest Topps issue of its time appeared in 1972, with the set size reaching the 787 mark. The 2-1/2" by 3-1/2" cards are something special as well. Their fronts have a color photo which is shaped into an arch and surrounded by two different color borders, all of which is inside the overall white border. The player's name is in a white panel below the picture while the team name is above the picture in what might best be described as "superhero" type in a variety of colors. No mention of the player's position appears on the front. Cards backs are tame by comparison, featuring statistics and a trivia question. The set features a record number of specialty card including more than six dozen "In Action" (shown as "IA" in checklists below) cards featuring action shots of popular players. There are the usual statistical leaders, playoff and World Series highlights. Other innovations are 16 "Boyhood Photo" cards which depict scrapbook black and white photos of 1972's top players, and a group of cards depicting the trophies which comprise baseball's major awards. Finally, a group of seven "Traded" cards was included which feature a large "Traded" across the front of the card.

		NR MT	EX	VG
Complete Set:		1300.00	650.00	390.00
Common Player: 1-394		.25	.13	.08
Common Player: 395-525		.30	.15	.09
Common Player: 526-656		.70	.35	.20
Common Player: 657-787		2.25	1.25	.70

1	World Champions (Pirates Team)	4.00	.75	.45
2	Ray Culp	.25	.13	.08
3	Bob Tolan	.30	.15	.09
4	Checklist 1-132	2.25	1.25	.70
5	John Bateman	.25	.13	.08
6	Fred Scherman	.25	.13	.08
7	Enzo Hernandez	.25	.13	.08
8	Ron Swoboda	.30	.15	.09
9	Stan Williams	.25	.13	.08
10	Amos Otis	.40	.20	.12
11	Bobby Valentine	.60	.30	.20
12	Jose Cardenal	.30	.15	.09
13	Joe Grzenda	.25	.13	.08
14	Phillies Rookiess (Mike Anderson, Pete Koegel, Wayne Twitchell)	.25	.13	.08
15	Walt Williams	.25	.13	.08
16	Mike Jorgensen	.25	.13	.08
17	Dave Duncan	.25	.13	.08

		NR MT	EX	VG
18a	Juan Pizarro (green under "C" and "S")	3.50	1.75	1.00
18b	Juan Pizarro (yellow under "C" and "S")	.25	.13	.08
19	Billy Cowan	.25	.13	.08
20	Don Wilson	.25	.13	.08
21	Braves Team	.90	.45	.25
22	Rob Gardner	.30	.15	.09
23	Ted Kubiak	.25	.13	.08
24	Ted Ford	.25	.13	.08
25	Bill Singer	.30	.15	.09
26	Andy Etchebarren	.25	.13	.08
27	Bob Johnson	.25	.13	.08
28	Twins Rookies (Steve Brye, Bob Gebhard, Hal Haydel)	.25	.13	.08
29a	Bill Bonham (green under "C" and "S")	3.50	1.75	1.00
29b	Bill Bonham (yellow under "C" and "S")	.30	.15	.09
30	Rico Petrocelli	.50	.25	.15
31	Cleon Jones	.30	.15	.09
32	Cleon Jones IA	.30	.15	.09
33	Billy Martin	1.50	.70	.45
34	Billy Martin IA	.80	.40	.25
35	Jerry Johnson	.25	.13	.08
36	Jerry Johnson IA	.25	.13	.08
37	Carl Yastrzemski	12.00	6.00	3.50
38	Carl Yastrzemski IA	8.00	4.00	2.50
39	Bob Barton	.25	.13	.08
40	Bob Barton IA	.25	.13	.08
41	Tommy Davis	.60	.30	.20
42	Tommy Davis IA	.30	.15	.09
43	Rick Wise	.30	.15	.09
44	Rick Wise IA	.25	.13	.08
45a	Glenn Beckert (green under "C" and "S")	3.50	1.75	1.00
45b	Glenn Beckert (yellow under "C" and "S")	.40	.20	.12
46	Glenn Beckert IA	.30	.15	.09
47	John Ellis	.30	.15	.09
48	John Ellis IA	.30	.15	.09
49	Willie Mays	18.00	9.00	5.50
50	Willie Mays IA	9.00	4.50	2.75
51	Harmon Killebrew	4.00	2.00	1.25
52	Harmon Killebrew IA	2.00	1.00	.60
53	Bud Harrelson	.40	.20	.12
54	Bud Harrelson IA	.30	.15	.09
55	Clyde Wright	.25	.13	.08
56	Rich Chiles	.25	.13	.08
57	Bob Oliver	.25	.13	.08
58	Ernie McAnally	.25	.13	.08
59	*Fred Stanley*	.40	.20	.12
60	Manny Sanguillen	.30	.15	.09
61	Cubs Rookies (Gene Hiser, *Burt Hooton*, Earl Stephenson)	1.00	.50	.30
62	Angel Mangual	.25	.13	.08
63	Duke Sims	.25	.13	.08
64	Pete Broberg	.25	.13	.08
65	Cesar Cedeno	.80	.40	.25
66	Ray Corbin	.25	.13	.08
67	Red Schoendienst	.80	.40	.25
68	Jim York	.25	.13	.08
69	Roger Freed	.25	.13	.08
70	Mike Cuellar	.50	.25	.15
71	Angels Team	.90	.45	.25
72	*Bruce Kison*	.80	.40	.25
73	Steve Huntz	.25	.13	.08
74	Cecil Upshaw	.25	.13	.08
75	Bert Campaneris	.60	.30	.20
76	Don Carrithers	.25	.13	.08
77	Ron Theobald	.25	.13	.08
78	Steve Arlin	.25	.13	.08
79	Red Sox Rookies (*Cecil Cooper, Carlton Fisk*, Mike Garman)	60.00	30.00	18.00
80	Tony Perez	2.00	1.00	.60
81	Mike Hedlund	.25	.13	.08
82	Ron Woods	.25	.13	.08
83	Dalton Jones	.25	.13	.08
84	Vince Colbert	.25	.13	.08
85	N.L. Batting Leaders (Glenn Beckert, Ralph Garr, Joe Torre)	1.25	.60	.40
86	A.L. Batting Leaders (Bobby Murcer, Tony Oliva, Merv Rettenmund)	1.25	.60	.40
87	N.L. RBI Leaders (Hank Aaron, Willie Stargell, Joe Torre)	2.25	1.25	.70
88	A.L. RBI Leaders (Harmon Killebrew, Frank Robinson, Reggie Smith)	2.25	1.25	.70
89	N.L. Home Run Leaders (Hank Aaron, Lee May, Willie Stargell)	2.25	1.25	.70
90	A.L. Home Run Leaders (Norm Cash, Reggie Jackson, Bill Melton)	1.75	.90	.50

		NR MT	EX	VG
91	N.L. ERA Leaders (Dave Roberts, Tom Seaver, Don Wilson)	1.75	.90	.50
92	A.L. ERA Leaders (Vida Blue, Jim Palmer, Wilbur Wood)	1.50	.70	.45
93	N.L. Pitching Leaders (Steve Carlton, Al Downing, Fergie Jenkins, Tom Seaver)	2.00	1.00	.60
94	A.L. Pitching Leaders (Vida Blue, Mickey Lolich, Wilbur Wood)	1.25	.60	.40
95	N.L. Strikeout Leaders (Fergie Jenkins, Tom Seaver, Bill Stoneman)	1.75	.90	.50
96	A.L. Strikeout Leaders (Vida Blue, Joe Coleman, Mickey Lolich)	1.25	.60	.40
97	Tom Kelley	.25	.13	.08
98	Chuck Tanner	.50	.25	.15
99	*Ross Grimsley*	.60	.30	.20
100	Frank Robinson	4.00	2.00	1.25
101	Astros Rookies (Ray Busse, Bill Grief, *J.R. Richard*)	1.00	.50	.30
102	Lloyd Allen	.25	.13	.08
103	Checklist 133-263	2.25	1.25	.70
104	*Toby Harrah*	1.00	.50	.30
105	Gary Gentry	.25	.13	.08
106	Brewers Team	.90	.45	.25
107	*Jose Cruz*	1.75	.90	.50
108	Gary Waslewski	.30	.15	.09
109	Jerry May	.25	.13	.08
110	Ron Hunt	.30	.15	.09
111	Jim Grant	.25	.13	.08
112	Greg Luzinski	.80	.40	.25
113	Rogelio Moret	.25	.13	.08
114	Bill Buckner	1.25	.60	.40
115	Jim Fregosi	.70	.35	.20
116	*Ed Farmer*	.30	.15	.09
117a	Cleo James (green under "C" and "S")	3.50	1.75	1.00
117b	Cleo James (yellow under "C" and "S")	.25	.13	.08
118	Skip Lockwood	.25	.13	.08
119	Marty Perez	.25	.13	.08
120	Bill Freehan	.60	.30	.20
121	Ed Sprague	.25	.13	.08
122	Larry Biittner	.25	.13	.08
123	Ed Acosta	.25	.13	.08
124	Yankees (Alan Closter, Roger Hambright, Rusty Torres)	.30	.15	.09
125	Dave Cash	.25	.13	.08
126	Bart Johnson	.25	.13	.08
127	Duffy Dyer	.25	.13	.08
128	Eddie Watt	.25	.13	.08
129	Charlie Fox	.25	.13	.08
130	Bob Gibson	5.00	2.50	1.50
131	Jim Nettles	.25	.13	.08
132	Joe Morgan	4.00	2.00	1.25
133	Joe Keough	.25	.13	.08
134	Carl Morton	.25	.13	.08
135	Vada Pinson	.80	.40	.25
136	Darrel Chaney	.25	.13	.08
137	Dick Williams	.50	.25	.15
138	Mike Kekich	.30	.15	.09
139	Tim McCarver	.80	.40	.25
140	Pat Dobson	.30	.15	.09
141	Mets Rookies (Buzz Capra, Jon Matlack, Leroy Stanton)	.40	.20	.12
142	*Chris Chambliss*	1.25	.60	.40
143	Garry Jestadt	.25	.13	.08
144	Marty Pattin	.25	.13	.08
145	Don Kessinger	.40	.20	.12
146	Steve Kealey	.25	.13	.08
147	*Dave Kingman*	3.50	1.75	1.00
148	Dick Billings	.25	.13	.08
149	Gary Neibauer	.25	.13	.08
150	Norm Cash	.70	.35	.20
151	Jim Brewer	.25	.13	.08
152	Gene Clines	.25	.13	.08
153	Rick Auerbach	.25	.13	.08
154	Ted Simmons	1.50	.70	.45
155	Larry Dierker	.30	.15	.09
156	Twins Team	.90	.45	.25
157	Don Gullett	.40	.20	.12
158	Jerry Kenney	.30	.15	.09
159	John Boccabella	.25	.13	.08
160	Andy Messersmith	.40	.20	.12
161	Brock Davis	.25	.13	.08
162	Brewers Rookies (Jerry Bell, *Darrell Porter*, Bob Reynolds) (Bell & Porter photos transposed)	1.00	.50	.30
163	Tug McGraw	.80	.40	.25
164	Tug McGraw IA	.40	.20	.12
165	*Chris Speier*	.80	.40	.25
166	Chris Speier IA	.40	.20	.12
167	Deron Johnson	.25	.13	.08
168	Deron Johnson IA	.25	.13	.08
169	Vida Blue	.80	.40	.25
170	Vida Blue IA	.40	.20	.12
171	Darrell Evans	1.50	.70	.45
172	Darrell Evans IA	.80	.40	.25
173	Clay Kirby	.25	.13	.08
174	Clay Kirby IA	.25	.13	.08
175	Tom Haller	.30	.15	.09
176	Tom Haller IA	.25	.13	.08
177	Paul Schaal	.25	.13	.08
178	Paul Schaal IA	.25	.13	.08
179	Dock Ellis	.30	.15	.09
180	Dock Ellis IA	.25	.13	.08
181	Ed Kranepool	.40	.20	.12
182	Ed Kranepool IA	.30	.15	.09
183	Bill Melton	.30	.15	.09
184	Bill Melton IA	.25	.13	.08
185	Ron Bryant	.25	.13	.08
186	Ron Bryant IA	.25	.13	.08
187	Gates Brown	.25	.13	.08
188	Frank Lucchesi	.25	.13	.08
189	Gene Tenace	.40	.20	.12
190	Dave Giusti	.25	.13	.08
191	*Jeff Burroughs*	.80	.40	.25
192	Cubs Team	.90	.45	.25
193	*Kurt Bevacqua*	.40	.20	.12
194	Fred Norman	.25	.13	.08
195	Orlando Cepeda	2.00	1.00	.60
196	Mel Queen	.25	.13	.08
197	Johnny Briggs	.25	.13	.08
198	Dodgers Rookies (*Charlie Hough*, Bob O'Brien, Mike Strahler)	2.25	1.25	.70
199	Mike Fiore	.25	.13	.08
200	Lou Brock	4.00	2.00	1.25
201	Phil Roof	.25	.13	.08
202	Scipio Spinks	.25	.13	.08
203	*Ron Blomberg*	.50	.25	.15
204	Tommy Helms	.25	.13	.08
205	Dick Drago	.25	.13	.08
206	Dal Maxvill	.30	.15	.09
207	Tom Egan	.25	.13	.08
208	Milt Pappas	.40	.20	.12
209	Joe Rudi	.60	.30	.20
210	Denny McLain	1.25	.60	.40
211	Gary Sutherland	.25	.13	.08
212	Grant Jackson	.25	.13	.08
213	Angels Rookies (Art Kusnyer, Billy Parker, Tom Silverio)	.25	.13	.08
214	Mike McQueen	.25	.13	.08
215	Alex Johnson	.25	.13	.08
216	Joe Niekro	.50	.25	.15
217	Roger Metzger	.25	.13	.08
218	Eddie Kasko	.25	.13	.08
219	*Rennie Stennett*	.40	.20	.12
220	Jim Perry	.60	.30	.20
221	N.L. Playoffs (Bucs Champs!)	1.25	.60	.40
222	A.L. Playoffs (Orioles Champs!)	1.25	.60	.40
223	World Series Game 1	1.25	.60	.40
224	World Series Game 2	1.25	.60	.40
225	World Series Game 3	1.25	.60	.40
226	World Series Game 4	1.50	.70	.45
227	World Series Game 5	1.25	.60	.40
228	World Series Game 6	1.25	.60	.40
229	World Series Game 7	1.25	.60	.40
230	World Series Summary (Series Celebration)	1.25	.60	.40
231	Casey Cox	.25	.13	.08
232	Giants Rookies (Chris Arnold, Jim Barr, Dave Rader)	.30	.15	.09
233	Jay Johnstone	.40	.20	.12
234	Ron Taylor	.25	.13	.08
235	Merv Rettenmund	.30	.15	.09
236	Jim McGlothlin	.25	.13	.08
237	Yankees Team	1.25	.60	.40
238	Leron Lee	.25	.13	.08
239	Tom Timmermann	.25	.13	.08
240	Rich Allen	1.75	.90	.50
241	Rollie Fingers	2.50	1.25	.70
242	Don Mincher	.30	.15	.09
243	Frank Linzy	.25	.13	.08
244	Steve Braun	.25	.13	.08
245	Tommie Agee	.30	.15	.09
246	Tom Burgmeier	.25	.13	.08
247	Milt May	.25	.13	.08
248	Tom Bradley	.25	.13	.08
249	Harry Walker	.30	.15	.09
250	Boog Powell	1.25	.60	.40
251a	Checklist 264-394 (small print on front)	2.25	1.25	.70
251b	Checklist 264-394 (large print on front)	2.25	1.25	.70

		NR MT	EX	VG
252	Ken Reynolds	.25	.13	.08
253	Sandy Alomar	.25	.13	.08
254	Boots Day	.25	.13	.08
255	Jim Lonborg	.40	.20	.12
256	George Foster	1.50	.70	.45
257	Tigers Rookies (Jim Foor, Tim Hosley, Paul Jata)	.25	.13	.08
258	Randy Hundley	.25	.13	.08
259	Sparky Lyle	.70	.35	.20
260	Ralph Garr	.40	.20	.12
261	Steve Mingori	.25	.13	.08
262	Padres Team	.90	.45	.25
263	Felipe Alou	.50	.25	.15
264	Tommy John	2.00	1.00	.60
265	Wes Parker	.30	.15	.09
266	Bobby Bolin	.25	.13	.08
267	Dave Concepcion	1.75	.90	.50
268	A's Rookies (Dwain Anderson, Chris Floethe)	.25	.13	.08
269	Don Hahn	.25	.13	.08
270	Jim Palmer	5.00	2.50	1.50
271	Ken Rudolph	.25	.13	.08
272	*Mickey Rivers*	1.00	.50	.30
273	Bobby Floyd	.25	.13	.08
274	Al Severinsen	.25	.13	.08
275	Cesar Tovar	.25	.13	.08
276	Gene Mauch	.50	.25	.15
277	Elliott Maddox	.30	.15	.09
278	Dennis Higgins	.25	.13	.08
279	Larry Brown	.25	.13	.08
280	Willie McCovey	4.00	2.00	1.25
281	Bill Parsons	.25	.13	.08
282	Astros Team	.90	.45	.25
283	Darrell Brandon	.25	.13	.08
284	Ike Brown	.25	.13	.08
285	Gaylord Perry	4.00	2.00	1.25
286	Gene Alley	.30	.15	.09
287	Jim Hardin	.30	.15	.09
288	Johnny Jeter	.25	.13	.08
289	Syd O'Brien	.25	.13	.08
290	Sonny Siebert	.25	.13	.08
291	Hal McRae	.60	.30	.20
292	Hal McRae IA	.30	.15	.09
293	Danny Frisella	.25	.13	.08
294	Danny Frisella IA	.25	.13	.08
295	Dick Dietz	.25	.13	.08
296	Dick Dietz IA	.25	.13	.08
297	Claude Osteen	.40	.20	.12
298	Claude Osteen IA	.30	.15	.09
299	Hank Aaron	18.00	9.00	5.50
300	Hank Aaron IA	8.00	4.00	2.50
301	George Mitterwald	.25	.13	.08
302	George Mitterwald IA	.25	.13	.08
303	Joe Pepitone	.50	.25	.15
304	Joe Pepitone IA	.30	.15	.09
305	Ken Boswell	.25	.13	.08
306	Ken Boswell IA	.25	.13	.08
307	Steve Renko	.25	.13	.08
308	Steve Renko IA	.25	.13	.08
309	Roberto Clemente	18.00	9.00	5.50
310	Roberto Clemente IA	6.00	3.00	1.75
311	Clay Carroll	.30	.15	.09
312	Clay Carroll IA	.25	.13	.08
313	Luis Aparicio	3.00	1.50	.90
314	Luis Aparicio IA	1.50	.70	.45
315	Paul Splittorff	.30	.15	.09
316	Cardinals Rookies (*Jim Bibby*, Santiago Guzman, Jorge Roque)	.50	.25	.15
317	Rich Hand	.25	.13	.08
318	Sonny Jackson	.25	.13	.08
319	Aurelio Rodriguez	.30	.15	.09
320	Steve Blass	.30	.15	.09
321	Joe Lahoud	.25	.13	.08
322	Jose Pena	.25	.13	.08
323	Earl Weaver	.80	.40	.25
324	Mike Ryan	.25	.13	.08
325	Mel Stottlemyre	.80	.40	.25
326	Pat Kelly	.25	.13	.08
327	*Steve Stone*	1.00	.50	.30
328	Red Sox Team	1.00	.50	.30
329	Roy Foster	.25	.13	.08
330	Jim Hunter	3.50	1.75	1.00
331	Stan Swanson	.25	.13	.08
332	Buck Martinez	.25	.13	.08
333	Steve Barber	.25	.13	.08
334	Rangers Rookies (Bill Fahey, Jim Mason, Tom Ragland)	.25	.13	.08
335	Bill Hands	.25	.13	.08
336	Marty Martinez	.25	.13	.08
337	Mike Kilkenny	.25	.13	.08
338	Bob Grich	.70	.35	.20
339	Ron Cook	.25	.13	.08
340	Roy White	.70	.35	.20
341	Boyhood Photo (Joe Torre)	.50	.25	.15
342	Boyhood Photo (Wilbur Wood)	.40	.20	.12
343	Boyhood Photo (Willie Stargell)	1.50	.70	.45
344	Boyhood Photo (Dave McNally)	.40	.20	.12
345	Boyhood Photo (Rick Wise)	.30	.15	.09
346	Boyhood Photo (Jim Fregosi)	.40	.20	.12
347	Boyhood Photo (Tom Seaver)	2.00	1.00	.60
348	Boyhood Photo (Sal Bando)	.40	.20	.12
349	Al Fitzmorris	.25	.13	.08
350	Frank Howard	1.25	.60	.40
351	Braves Rookies (Jimmy Britton, Tom House, Rick Kester)	.25	.13	.08
352	Dave LaRoche	.30	.15	.09
353	Art Shamsky	.25	.13	.08
354	Tom Murphy	.25	.13	.08
355	Bob Watson	.30	.15	.09
356	Gerry Moses	.25	.13	.08
357	Woodie Fryman	.30	.15	.09
358	Sparky Anderson	.70	.35	.20
359	Don Pavletich	.25	.13	.08
360	Dave Roberts	.25	.13	.08
361	Mike Andrews	.25	.13	.08
362	Mets Team	1.25	.60	.40
363	Ron Klimkowski	.25	.13	.08
364	Johnny Callison	.50	.25	.15
365	Dick Bosman	.25	.13	.08
366	Jimmy Rosario	.25	.13	.08
367	Ron Perranoski	.30	.15	.09
368	Danny Thompson	.30	.15	.09
369	Jim Lefebvre	.30	.15	.09
370	Don Buford	.30	.15	.09
371	Denny Lemaster	.25	.13	.08
372	Royals Rookies (Lance Clemons, Monty Montgomery)	.25	.13	.08
373	John Mayberry	.40	.20	.12
374	Jack Heidemann	.25	.13	.08
375	Reggie Cleveland	.25	.13	.08
376	Andy Kosco	.25	.13	.08
377	Terry Harmon	.25	.13	.08
378	Checklist 395-525	2.25	1.25	.70
379	Ken Berry	.25	.13	.08
380	Earl Williams	.30	.15	.09
381	White Sox Team	.90	.45	.25
382	Joe Gibbon	.25	.13	.08
383	Brant Alyea	.25	.13	.08
384	Dave Campbell	.25	.13	.08
385	Mickey Stanley	.30	.15	.09
386	Jim Colborn	.25	.13	.08
387	Horace Clarke	.30	.15	.09
388	Charlie Williams	.25	.13	.08
389	Bill Rigney	.25	.13	.08
390	Willie Davis	.50	.25	.15
391	Ken Sanders	.25	.13	.08
392	Pirates Rookies (Fred Cambria, *Richie Zisk*)	.70	.35	.20
393	Curt Motton	.25	.13	.08
394	Ken Forsch	.30	.15	.09
395	Matty Alou	.60	.30	.20
396	Paul Lindblad	.30	.15	.09
397	Phillies Team	.90	.45	.25
398	Larry Hisle	.40	.20	.12
399	Milt Wilcox	.40	.20	.12
400	Tony Oliva	1.50	.70	.45
401	Jim Nash	.30	.15	.09
402	Bobby Heise	.30	.15	.09
403	John Cumberland	.30	.15	.09
404	Jeff Torborg	.40	.20	.12
405	Ron Fairly	.50	.25	.15
406	*George Hendrick*	1.00	.50	.30
407	Chuck Taylor	.30	.15	.09
408	Jim Northrup	.40	.20	.12
409	Frank Baker	.40	.20	.12
410	Fergie Jenkins	2.00	1.00	.60
411	Bob Montgomery	.30	.15	.09
412	Dick Kelley	.30	.15	.09
413	White Sox Rookies (Don Eddy, Dave Lemonds)	.30	.15	.09
414	Bob Miller	.30	.15	.09
415	Cookie Rojas	.30	.15	.09
416	Johnny Edwards	.30	.15	.09
417	Tom Hall	.30	.15	.09
418	Tom Shopay	.30	.15	.09
419	Jim Spencer	.30	.15	.09
420	Steve Carlton	15.00	7.50	4.50
421	Ellie Rodriguez	.30	.15	.09
422	Ray Lamb	.30	.15	.09
423	Oscar Gamble	.40	.20	.12
424	Bill Gogolewski	.30	.15	.09
425	Ken Singleton	.70	.35	.20

		NR MT	EX	VG
426	Ken Singleton IA	.40	.20	.12
427	Tito Fuentes	.30	.15	.09
428	Tito Fuentes IA	.30	.15	.09
429	Bob Robertson	.30	.15	.09
430	Bob Robertson IA	.30	.15	.09
431	Clarence Gaston	.30	.15	.09
432	Clarence Gaston IA	.30	.15	.09
433	Johnny Bench	25.00	12.50	7.50
434	Johnny Bench IA	10.00	5.00	3.00
435	Reggie Jackson	18.00	9.00	5.50
436	Reggie Jackson IA	10.00	5.00	3.00
437	Maury Wills	1.50	.70	.45
438	Maury Wills IA	.70	.35	.20
439	Billy Williams	3.50	1.75	1.00
440	Billy Williams IA	1.75	.90	.50
441	Thurman Munson	15.00	7.50	4.50
442	Thurman Munson IA	8.00	4.00	2.50
443	Ken Henderson	.30	.15	.09
444	Ken Henderson IA	.30	.15	.09
445	Tom Seaver	15.00	7.50	4.50
446	Tom Seaver IA	9.00	4.50	2.75
447	Willie Stargell	4.00	2.00	1.25
448	Willie Stargell IA	2.00	1.00	.60
449	Bob Lemon	.90	.45	.25
450	Mickey Lolich	1.25	.60	.40
451	Tony LaRussa	.60	.30	.20
452	Ed Herrmann	.30	.15	.09
453	Barry Lersch	.30	.15	.09
454	A's Team	2.00	1.00	.60
455	Tommy Harper	.40	.20	.12
456	Mark Belanger	.40	.20	.12
457	Padres Rookies (Darcy Fast, Mike Ivie, Derrel Thomas)	.40	.20	.12
458	Aurelio Monteagudo	.30	.15	.09
459	Rick Renick	.30	.15	.09
460	Al Downing	.40	.20	.12
461	Tim Cullen	.30	.15	.09
462	Rickey Clark	.30	.15	.09
463	Bernie Carbo	.30	.15	.09
464	Jim Roland	.30	.15	.09
465	Gil Hodges	3.00	1.50	.90
466	Norm Miller	.30	.15	.09
467	Steve Kline	.40	.20	.12
468	Richie Scheinblum	.30	.15	.09
469	Ron Herbel	.30	.15	.09
470	Ray Fosse	.30	.15	.09
471	Luke Walker	.30	.15	.09
472	Phil Gagliano	.30	.15	.09
473	Dan McGinn	.30	.15	.09
474	Orioles Rookies (Don Baylor, Roric Harrison, Johnny Oates)	2.50	1.25	.70
475	Gary Nolan	.30	.15	.09
476	Lee Richard	.30	.15	.09
477	Tom Phoebus	.30	.15	.09
478a	Checklist 526-656 (small print on front)	2.25	1.25	.70
478b	Checklist 526-656 (large printing on front)	2.25	1.25	.70
479	Don Shaw	.30	.15	.09
480	Lee May	.60	.30	.20
481	Billy Conigliaro	.30	.15	.09
482	Joe Hoerner	.30	.15	.09
483	Ken Suarez	.30	.15	.09
484	Lum Harris	.30	.15	.09
485	Phil Regan	.30	.15	.09
486	John Lowenstein	.30	.15	.09
487	Tigers Team	1.50	.70	.45
488	Mike Nagy	.30	.15	.09
489	Expos Rookies (Terry Humphrey, Keith Lampard)	.30	.15	.09
490	Dave McNally	.50	.25	.15
491	Boyhood Photo (Lou Piniella)	.60	.30	.20
492	Boyhood Photo (Mel Stottlemyre)	.40	.20	.12
493	Boyhood Photo (Bob Bailey)	.30	.15	.09
494	Boyhood Photo (Willie Horton)	.40	.20	.12
495	Boyhood Photo (Bill Melton)	.30	.15	.09
496	Boyhood Photo (Bud Harrelson)	.40	.20	.12
497	Boyhood Photo (Jim Perry)	.40	.20	.12
498	Boyhood Photo (Brooks Robinson)	2.00	1.00	.60
499	Vicente Romo	.30	.15	.09
500	Joe Torre	1.25	.60	.40
501	Pete Hamm	.30	.15	.09
502	Jackie Hernandez	.30	.15	.09
503	Gary Peters	.30	.15	.09
504	Ed Spiezio	.30	.15	.09
505	Mike Marshall	.50	.25	.15
506	Indians Rookies (Terry Ley, Jim Moyer, Dick Tidrow)	.60	.30	.20
507	Fred Gladding	.30	.15	.09
508	Ellie Hendricks	.30	.15	.09

		NR MT	EX	VG
509	Don McMahon	.30	.15	.09
510	Ted Williams	5.00	2.50	1.50
511	Tony Taylor	.30	.15	.09
512	Paul Popovich	.30	.15	.09
513	Lindy McDaniel	.40	.20	.12
514	Ted Sizemore	.30	.15	.09
515	Bert Blyleven	3.25	1.75	1.00
516	Oscar Brown	.30	.15	.09
517	Ken Brett	.40	.20	.12
518	Wayne Garrett	.30	.15	.09
519	Ted Abernathy	.30	.15	.09
520	Larry Bowa	1.25	.60	.40
521	Alan Foster	.30	.15	.09
522	Dodgers Team	1.25	.60	.40
523	Chuck Dobson	.30	.15	.09
524	Reds Rookies (Ed Armbrister, Mel Behney)	.30	.15	.09
525	Carlos May	.40	.20	.12
526	Bob Bailey	.70	.35	.20
527	Dave Leonhard	.70	.35	.20
528	Ron Stone	.70	.35	.20
529	Dave Nelson	.70	.35	.20
530	Don Sutton	3.50	1.75	1.00
531	Freddie Patek	.70	.35	.20
532	Fred Kendall	.70	.35	.20
533	Ralph Houk	1.25	.60	.40
534	Jim Hickman	.80	.40	.25
535	Ed Brinkman	.80	.40	.25
536	Doug Rader	.70	.35	.20
537	Bob Locker	.70	.35	.20
538	Charlie Sands	.70	.35	.20
539	*Terry Forster*	1.25	.60	.40
540	Felix Millan	.70	.35	.20
541	Roger Repoz	.70	.35	.20
542	Jack Billingham	.70	.35	.20
543	Duane Josephson	.70	.35	.20
544	Ted Martinez	.70	.35	.20
545	Wayne Granger	.70	.35	.20
546	Joe Hague	.70	.35	.20
547	Indians Team	1.50	.70	.45
548	Frank Reberger	.70	.35	.20
549	Dave May	.70	.35	.20
550	Brooks Robinson	12.00	6.00	3.50
551	Ollie Brown	.70	.35	.20
552	Ollie Brown IA	.70	.35	.20
553	Wilbur Wood	.90	.45	.25
554	Wilbur Wood IA	.80	.40	.25
555	Ron Santo	1.50	.70	.45
556	Ron Santo IA	.80	.40	.25
557	John Odom	.70	.35	.20
558	John Odom IA	.70	.35	.20
559	Pete Rose	60.00	30.00	18.00
560	Pete Rose IA	30.00	15.00	9.00
561	Leo Cardenas	.70	.35	.20
562	Leo Cardenas IA	.70	.35	.20
563	Ray Sadecki	.70	.35	.20
564	Ray Sadecki IA	.70	.35	.20
565	Reggie Smith	.90	.45	.25
566	Reggie Smith IA	.80	.40	.25
567	Juan Marichal	6.00	3.00	1.75
568	Juan Marichal IA	3.00	1.50	.90
569	Ed Kirkpatrick	.70	.35	.20
570	Ed Kirkpatrick IA	.70	.35	.20
571	Nate Colbert	.70	.35	.20
572	Nate Colbert IA	.70	.35	.20
573	Fritz Peterson	.80	.40	.25
574	Fritz Peterson IA	.80	.40	.25
575	Al Oliver	2.00	1.00	.60
576	Leo Durocher	1.25	.60	.40
577	Mike Paul	.70	.35	.20
578	Billy Grabarkewitz	.70	.35	.20
579	*Doyle Alexander*	2.75	1.50	.80
580	Lou Piniella	1.75	.90	.50
581	Wade Blasingame	.70	.35	.20
582	Expos Team	2.25	1.25	.70
583	Darold Knowles	.70	.35	.20
584	Jerry McNertney	.70	.35	.20
585	George Scott	.80	.40	.25
586	Denis Menke	.70	.35	.20
587	Billy Wilson	.70	.35	.20
588	Jim Holt	.70	.35	.20
589	Hal Lanier	1.00	.50	.30
590	Graig Nettles	2.50	1.25	.70
591	Paul Casanova	.70	.35	.20
592	Lew Krausse	.70	.35	.20
593	Rich Morales	.70	.35	.20
594	Jim Beauchamp	.70	.35	.20
595	Nolan Ryan	60.00	30.00	18.00
596	Manny Mota	.90	.45	.25
597	Jim Magnuson	.80	.40	.25
598	Hal King	.70	.35	.20

#	Name	NR MT	EX	VG
599	Billy Champion	.70	.35	.20
600	Al Kaline	12.00	6.00	3.50
601	George Stone	.70	.35	.20
602	Dave Bristol	.70	.35	.20
603	Jim Ray	.70	.35	.20
604a	Checklist 657-787 (copyright on right)	3.50	1.75	1.00
604b	Checklist 657-787 (copyright on left)	5.00	2.50	1.50
605	Nelson Briles	.70	.35	.20
606	Luis Melendez	.70	.35	.20
607	Frank Duffy	.70	.35	.20
608	Mike Corkins	.70	.35	.20
609	Tom Grieve	.70	.35	.20
610	Bill Stoneman	.70	.35	.20
611	Rich Reese	.70	.35	.20
612	Joe Decker	.70	.35	.20
613	Mike Ferraro	.70	.35	.20
614	Ted Uhlaender	.70	.35	.20
615	Steve Hargan	.70	.35	.20
616	*Joe Ferguson*	.80	.40	.25
617	Royals Team	2.25	1.25	.70
618	Rich Robertson	.70	.35	.20
619	Rich McKinney	.80	.40	.25
620	Phil Niekro	4.50	2.25	1.25
621	Commissioners Award	.90	.45	.25
622	MVP Award	.90	.45	.25
623	Cy Young Award	.90	.45	.25
624	Minor League Player Of The Year Award	.90	.45	.25
625	Rookie Of The Year Award	.90	.45	.25
626	Babe Ruth Award	1.00	.50	.30
627	Moe Drabowsky	.70	.35	.20
628	Terry Crowley	.70	.35	.20
629	Paul Doyle	.70	.35	.20
630	Rich Hebner	.80	.40	.25
631	John Strohmayer	.70	.35	.20
632	Mike Hegan	.70	.35	.20
633	Jack Hiatt	.70	.35	.20
634	Dick Woodson	.70	.35	.20
635	Don Money	.80	.40	.25
636	Bill Lee	.90	.45	.25
637	Preston Gomez	.70	.35	.20
638	Ken Wright	.70	.35	.20
639	J.C. Martin	.70	.35	.20
640	Joe Coleman	.80	.40	.25
641	Mike Lum	.70	.35	.20
642	Denny Riddleberger	.70	.35	.20
643	Russ Gibson	.70	.35	.20
644	Bernie Allen	.80	.40	.25
645	Jim Maloney	.80	.40	.25
646	Chico Salmon	.70	.35	.20
647	Bob Moose	.70	.35	.20
648	Jim Lyttle	.70	.35	.20
649	Pete Richert	.70	.35	.20
650	Sal Bando	1.00	.50	.30
651	Reds Team	2.00	1.00	.60
652	Marcelino Lopez	.70	.35	.20
653	Jim Fairey	.70	.35	.20
654	Horacio Pina	.70	.35	.20
655	Jerry Grote	.80	.40	.25
656	Rudy May	.80	.40	.25
657	Bobby Wine	2.25	1.25	.70
658	Steve Dunning	2.25	1.25	.70
659	Bob Aspromonte	2.25	1.25	.70
660	Paul Blair	2.50	1.25	.70
661	Bill Virdon	2.50	1.25	.70
662	Stan Bahnsen	2.50	1.25	.70
663	Fran Healy	2.25	1.25	.70
664	Bobby Knoop	2.25	1.25	.70
665	Chris Short	2.50	1.25	.70
666	Hector Torres	2.25	1.25	.70
667	Ray Newman	2.25	1.25	.70
668	Rangers Team	3.25	1.75	1.00
669	Willie Crawford	2.25	1.25	.70
670	Ken Holtzman	2.75	1.50	.80
671	Donn Clendenon	2.50	1.25	.70
672	Archie Reynolds	2.25	1.25	.70
673	Dave Marshall	2.25	1.25	.70
674	John Kennedy	2.25	1.25	.70
675	Pat Jarvis	2.25	1.25	.70
676	Danny Cater	2.25	1.25	.70
677	Ivan Murrell	2.25	1.25	.70
678	Steve Luebber	2.25	1.25	.70
679	Astros Rookies (Bob Fenwick, Bob Stinson)	2.25	1.25	.70
680	Dave Johnson	3.50	1.75	1.00
681	Bobby Pfeil	2.25	1.25	.70
682	Mike McCormick	2.50	1.25	.70
683	Steve Hovley	2.25	1.25	.70
684	Hal Breeden	2.25	1.25	.70
685	Joe Horlen	2.25	1.25	.70
686	Steve Garvey	55.00	28.00	16.50
687	Del Unser	2.25	1.25	.70
688	Cardinals Team	3.25	1.75	1.00
689	Eddie Fisher	2.25	1.25	.70
690	Willie Montanez	2.50	1.25	.70
691	Curt Blefary	2.25	1.25	.70
692	Curt Blefary IA	2.25	1.25	.70
693	Alan Gallagher	2.25	1.25	.70
694	Alan Gallagher IA	2.25	1.25	.70
695	Rod Carew	70.00	35.00	21.00
696	Rod Carew IA	25.00	12.50	7.50
697	Jerry Koosman	4.50	2.25	1.25
698	Jerry Koosman IA	2.50	1.25	.70
699	Bobby Murcer	4.00	2.00	1.25
700	Bobby Murcer IA	2.50	1.25	.70
701	Jose Pagan	2.25	1.25	.70
702	Jose Pagan IA	2.25	1.25	.70
703	Doug Griffin	2.25	1.25	.70
704	Doug Griffin IA	2.25	1.25	.70
705	Pat Corrales	2.50	1.25	.70
706	Pat Corrales IA	2.25	1.25	.70
707	Tim Foli	2.25	1.25	.70
708	Tim Foli IA	2.25	1.25	.70
709	Jim Kaat	6.50	3.25	2.00
710	Jim Kaat IA	3.25	1.75	1.00
711	Bobby Bonds	3.75	2.00	1.25
712	Bobby Bonds IA	2.50	1.25	.70
713	Gene Michael	2.50	1.25	.70
714	Gene Michael IA	2.50	1.25	.70
715	Mike Epstein	2.50	1.25	.70
716	Jesus Alou	2.50	1.25	.70
717	Bruce Dal Canton	2.25	1.25	.70
718	Del Rice	2.25	1.25	.70
719	Cesar Geronimo	2.50	1.25	.70
720	Sam McDowell	3.00	1.50	.90
721	Eddie Leon	2.25	1.25	.70
722	Bill Sudakis	2.25	1.25	.70
723	Al Santorini	2.25	1.25	.70
724	A.L. Rookies (John Curtis, Rich Hinton, Mickey Scott)	2.50	1.25	.70
725	Dick McAuliffe	2.50	1.25	.70
726	Dick Selma	2.25	1.25	.70
727	Jose Laboy	2.25	1.25	.70
728	Gail Hopkins	2.25	1.25	.70
729	Bob Veale	2.50	1.25	.70
730	Rick Monday	2.75	1.50	.80
731	Orioles Team	3.25	1.75	1.00
732	George Culver	2.25	1.25	.70
733	Jim Hart	2.50	1.25	.70
734	Bob Burda	2.25	1.25	.70
735	Diego Segui	2.25	1.25	.70
736	Bill Russell	3.00	1.50	.90
737	*Lenny Randle*	2.50	1.25	.70
738	Jim Merritt	2.25	1.25	.70
739	Don Mason	2.25	1.25	.70
740	Rico Carty	3.25	1.75	1.00
741	Major League Rookies (Tom Hutton, *Rick Miller, John Milner*)	2.50	1.25	.70
742	Jim Rooker	2.25	1.25	.70
743	Cesar Gutierrez	2.25	1.25	.70
744	*Jim Slaton*	2.50	1.25	.70
745	Julian Javier	2.25	1.25	.70
746	Lowell Palmer	2.25	1.25	.70
747	Jim Stewart	2.25	1.25	.70
748	Phil Hennigan	2.25	1.25	.70
749	Walter Alston	5.00	2.50	1.50
750	Willie Horton	2.75	1.50	.80
751	Steve Carlton Traded	30.00	15.00	9.00
752	Joe Morgan Traded	18.00	9.00	5.50
753	Denny McLain Traded	6.00	3.00	1.75
754	Frank Robinson Traded	18.00	9.00	5.50
755	Jim Fregosi Traded	2.75	1.50	.80
756	Rick Wise Traded	2.50	1.25	.70
757	Jose Cardenal Traded	2.50	1.25	.70
758	Gil Garrido	2.25	1.25	.70
759	Chris Cannizzaro	2.25	1.25	.70
760	Bill Mazeroski	3.75	2.00	1.25
761	Major League Rookies (*Ron Cey, Ben Oglivie, Bernie Williams*)	12.00	6.00	3.50
762	Wayne Simpson	2.25	1.25	.70
763	Ron Hansen	2.25	1.25	.70
764	Dusty Baker	3.00	1.50	.90
765	Ken McMullen	2.25	1.25	.70
766	Steve Hamilton	2.25	1.25	.70
767	Tom McCraw	2.25	1.25	.70
768	Denny Doyle	2.25	1.25	.70
769	Jack Aker	2.50	1.25	.70
770	Jim Wynn	2.75	1.50	.80
771	Giants Team	3.25	1.75	1.00
772	Ken Tatum	2.25	1.25	.70

		NR MT	EX	VG
773	Ron Brand	2.25	1.25	.70
774	Luis Alvarado	2.25	1.25	.70
775	Jerry Reuss	3.50	1.75	1.00
776	Bill Voss	2.25	1.25	.70
777	Hoyt Wilhelm	10.00	5.00	3.00
778	Twins Rookies (Vic Albury, *Rick Dempsey*, Jim Strickland)	3.25	1.75	1.00
779	Tony Cloninger	2.50	1.25	.70
780	Dick Green	2.25	1.25	.70
781	Jim McAndrew	2.25	1.25	.70
782	Larry Stahl	2.25	1.25	.70
783	Les Cain	2.25	1.25	.70
784	Ken Aspromonte	2.25	1.25	.70
785	Vic Davalillo	2.25	1.25	.70
786	Chuck Brinkman	2.50	1.25	.70
787	Ron Reed	4.50	1.25	.70

1972 Topps Cloth Stickers

Despite the fact they were never actually issued, examples of this test issue can readily be found within the hobby. The set of 33 contains stickers with designs identical to cards found in three contiguous rows of a regular Topps card sheet that year; thus the inclusion of a meaningless checklist card. Sometimes found in complete 33-sticker strips, individual stickers nominally measure 2-1/2" by 3-1/2," though dimensions vary according to the care with which they were cut. Stickers are unnumbered and blank-backed, and do not contain glue.

		NR MT	EX	VG
	Complete Set:	175.00	87.00	52.00
	Common Player:	3.00	1.50	.90
(1)	Hank Aaron	50.00	25.00	15.00
(2)	Luis Aparicio IA	10.00	5.00	3.00
(3)	Ike Brown	3.00	1.50	.90
(4)	Johnny Callison	5.00	2.50	1.50
(5)	Checklist 264-319	3.00	1.50	.90
(6)	Roberto Clemente IA	25.00	12.50	7.50
(7)	Dave Concepcion	8.00	4.00	2.50
(8)	Ron Cook	3.00	1.50	.90
(9)	Willie Davis	5.00	2.50	1.50
(10)	Al Fitzmorris	3.00	1.50	.90
(11)	Bobby Floyd	3.00	1.50	.90
(12)	Roy Foster	3.00	1.50	.90
(13)	Jim Fregosi Boyhood Photo	4.00	2.00	1.25
(14)	Danny Frisella IA	3.00	1.50	.90
(15)	Woody Fryman	3.50	1.75	1.00
(16)	Terry Harmon	3.00	1.50	.90
(17)	Frank Howard	7.00	3.50	2.00
(18)	Ron Klimkowski	3.00	1.50	.90
(19)	Joe Lahoud	3.00	1.50	.90
(20)	Jim Lefebvre	3.50	1.75	1.00
(21)	Elliott Maddox	3.00	1.50	.90
(22)	Marty Martinez	3.00	1.50	.90
(23)	Willie McCovey	25.00	12.50	7.50
(24)	Hal McRae	6.00	3.00	1.75
(25)	Syd O'Brien	3.00	1.50	.90
(26)	Red Sox Team	4.00	2.00	1.25
(27)	Aurelio Rodriguez	3.50	1.75	1.00
(28)	Al Severinsen	3.00	1.50	.90
(29)	Art Shamsky	3.00	1.50	.90
(30)	Steve Stone	4.00	2.00	1.25
(31)	Stan Swanson	3.00	1.50	.90
(32)	Bob Watson	3.50	1.75	1.00

		NR MT	EX	VG
(33)	Roy White	6.00	3.00	1.75

1972 Topps Posters

Issued as a separate set, rather than as a wax pack insert, the twenty-four 9-7/16" by 18" posters of 1972 feature a borderless full-color picture on the front with the player's name, team and position. Printed on very thin paper, the posters, as happened with earlier issues, were folded for packaging, causing large creases which cannot be removed. Even so, they are good display items for they feature many of stars of the period.

		NR MT	EX	VG
	Complete Set:	300.00	150.00	90.00
	Common Player:	5.00	2.50	1.50
1	Dave McNally	5.00	2.50	1.50
2	Carl Yastrzemski	30.00	15.00	9.00
3	Bill Melton	5.00	2.50	1.50
4	Ray Fosse	5.00	2.50	1.50
5	Mickey Lolich	6.00	3.00	1.75
6	Amos Otis	5.00	2.50	1.50
7	Tony Oliva	6.00	3.00	1.75
8	Vida Blue	6.00	3.00	1.75
9	Hank Aaron	20.00	10.00	6.00
10	Fergie Jenkins	8.00	4.00	2.50
11	Pete Rose	50.00	25.00	15.00
12	Willie Davis	6.00	3.00	1.75
13	Tom Seaver	20.00	10.00	6.00
14	Rick Wise	5.00	2.50	1.50
15	Willie Stargell	12.00	6.00	3.50
16	Joe Torre	7.00	3.50	2.00
17	Willie Mays	20.00	10.00	6.00
18	Andy Messersmith	5.00	2.50	1.50
19	Wilbur Wood	5.00	2.50	1.50
20	Harmon Killebrew	15.00	7.50	4.50
21	Billy Williams	12.00	6.00	3.50
22	Bud Harrelson	5.00	2.50	1.50
23	Roberto Clemente	20.00	10.00	6.00
24	Willie McCovey	15.00	7.50	4.50

A player's name in *italic* type indicates a rookie card. An (FC) indicates a player's first card for that particular card company.

1973 Topps

Topps cut back to 660 cards in 1973. The set is interesting for it marks the last time cards were issued by series, a procedure which had produced many a scarce high number card over the years. These 2-1/2" by 3-1/2" cards have a color photo, accented by a silhouette of a player on the front, indicative of his position. Card backs are vertical for the first time since 1968, with the usual statistical and biographical information. Specialty cards begin with card number 1, which depicted Ruth, Mays and Aaron as the all-time home run leaders. It was followed by statistical leaders, although there also were additional all-time leader cards. Also present are playoff and World Series highlights. From the age-and-youth department, the 1973 Topps set has coaches and managers as well as more "Boyhood Photos."

		NR MT	EX	VG
Complete Set:		675.00	325.00	200.00
Common Player: 1-396		.25	.13	.08
Common Player: 397-528		.40	.20	.12
Common Player: 529-660		1.25	.60	.40
1	All Time Home Run Leaders (Hank Aaron, Willie Mays, Babe Ruth)	15.00	7.50	4.50
2	Rich Hebner	.30	.15	.09
3	Jim Lonborg	.40	.20	.12
4	John Milner	.25	.13	.08
5	Ed Brinkman	.30	.15	.09
6	Mac Scarce	.25	.13	.08
7	Rangers Team	.90	.45	.25
8	Tom Hall	.25	.13	.08
9	Johnny Oates	.25	.13	.08
10	Don Sutton	2.00	1.00	.60
11	Chris Chambliss	.70	.35	.20
12a	Padres Mgr./Coaches (Dave Garcia, Johnny Podres, Bob Skinner, Whitey Wietelmann, Don Zimmer) (Coaches background brown)	.50	.25	.15
12b	Padres Mgr./Coaches (Dave Garcia, Johnny Podres, Bob Skinner, Whitey Wietelmann, Don Zimmer) (Coaches background orange)	.40	.20	.12
13	George Hendrick	.70	.35	.20
14	Sonny Siebert	.25	.13	.08
15	Ralph Garr	.30	.15	.09
16	Steve Braun	.25	.13	.08
17	Fred Gladding	.25	.13	.08
18	Leroy Stanton	.25	.13	.08
19	Tim Foli	.25	.13	.08
20a	Stan Bahnsen (small gap in left border)	.50	.25	.15
20b	Stan Bahnsen (no gap)	.25	.13	.08
21	Randy Hundley	.25	.13	.08
22	Ted Abernathy	.25	.13	.08
23	Dave Kingman	1.25	.60	.40
24	Al Santorini	.25	.13	.08
25	Roy White	.40	.20	.12
26	Pirates Team	.90	.45	.25
27	Bill Gogolewski	.25	.13	.08
28	Hal McRae	.50	.25	.15
29	Tony Taylor	.25	.13	.08
30	Tug McGraw	.60	.30	.20
31	Buddy Bell	3.25	1.75	1.00
32	Fred Norman	.25	.13	.08
33	Jim Breazeale	.25	.13	.08
34	Pat Dobson	.30	.15	.09
35	Willie Davis	.50	.25	.15
36	Steve Barber	.25	.13	.08
37	Bill Robinson	.25	.13	.08
38	Mike Epstein	.30	.15	.09
39	Dave Roberts	.25	.13	.08
40	Reggie Smith	.50	.25	.15
41	Tom Walker	.25	.13	.08
42	Mike Andrews	.25	.13	.08
43	Randy Moffitt	.30	.15	.09
44	Rick Monday	.40	.20	.12
45	Ellie Rodriguez (photo actually Paul Ratliff)	.25	.13	.08
46	Lindy McDaniel	.30	.15	.09
47	Luis Melendez	.25	.13	.08
48	Paul Splittorff	.30	.15	.09
49a	Twins Mgr./Coaches (Vern Morgan, Frank Quilici, Bob Rodgers, Ralph Rowe, Al Worthington) (Coaches background brown)	.50	.25	.15
49b	Twins Mgr./Coaches (Vern Morgan, Frank Quilici, Bob Rodgers, Ralph Rowe, Al Worthington) (Coaches background orange)	.30	.15	.09
50	Roberto Clemente	15.00	7.50	4.50
51	Chuck Seelbach	.25	.13	.08
52	Denis Menke	.25	.13	.08
53	Steve Dunning	.25	.13	.08
54	Checklist 1-132	2.00	1.00	.60
55	Jon Matlack	.40	.20	.12
56	Merv Rettenmund	.30	.15	.09
57	Derrel Thomas	.25	.13	.08
58	Mike Paul	.25	.13	.08
59	Steve Yeager	.60	.30	.20
60	Ken Holtzman	.40	.20	.12
61	Batting Leaders (Rod Carew, Billy Williams)	1.75	.90	.50
62	Home Run Leaders (Dick Allen, Johnny Bench)	1.50	.70	.45
63	Runs Batted In Leaders (Dick Allen, Johnny Bench)	1.50	.70	.45
64	Stolen Base Leaders (Lou Brock, Bert Campaneris)	1.25	.60	.40
65	Earned Run Average Leaders (Steve Carlton, Luis Tiant)	1.25	.60	.40
66	Victory Leaders (Steve Carlton, Gaylord Perry, Wilbur Wood)	1.25	.60	.40
67	Strikeout Leaders (Steve Carlton, Nolan Ryan)	2.50	1.25	.70
68	Leading Firemen (Clay Carroll, Sparky Lyle)	.80	.40	.25
69	Phil Gagliano	.25	.13	.08
70	Milt Pappas	.40	.20	.12
71	Johnny Briggs	.25	.13	.08
72	Ron Reed	.30	.15	.09
73	Ed Herrmann	.25	.13	.08
74	Billy Champion	.25	.13	.08
75	Vada Pinson	.80	.40	.25
76	Doug Rader	.25	.13	.08
77	Mike Torrez	.30	.15	.09
78	Richie Scheinblum	.25	.13	.08
79	Jim Willoughby	.25	.13	.08
80	Tony Oliva	1.25	.60	.40
81a	Cubs Mgr./Coaches (Hank Aguirre, Ernie Banks, Larry Jansen, Whitey Lockman, Pete Reiser) (trees in Coaches background)	.70	.35	.20
81b	Cubs Mgr./Coaches (Hank Aguirre, Ernie Banks, Larry Jansen, Whitey Lockman, Pete Reiser) (orange, solid background)	.50	.25	.15
82	Fritz Peterson	.30	.15	.09
83	Leron Lee	.25	.13	.08
84	Rollie Fingers	1.50	.70	.45
85	Ted Simmons	1.25	.60	.40
86	Tom McCraw	.25	.13	.08
87	Ken Boswell	.25	.13	.08
88	Mickey Stanley	.30	.15	.09
89	Jack Billingham	.25	.13	.08
90	Brooks Robinson	5.00	2.50	1.50
91	Dodgers Team	1.00	.50	.30
92	Jerry Bell	.25	.13	.08
93	Jesus Alou	.30	.15	.09
94	Dick Billings	.25	.13	.08
95	Steve Blass	.30	.15	.09
96	Doug Griffin	.25	.13	.08
97	Willie Montanez	.30	.15	.09
98	Dick Woodson	.25	.13	.08
99	Carl Taylor	.25	.13	.08
100	Hank Aaron	15.00	7.50	4.50
101	Ken Henderson	.25	.13	.08
102	Rudy May	.30	.15	.09

		NR MT	EX	VG
103	Celerino Sanchez	.30	.15	.09
104	Reggie Cleveland	.25	.13	.08
105	Carlos May	.30	.15	.09
106	Terry Humphrey	.25	.13	.08
107	Phil Hennigan	.25	.13	.08
108	Bill Russell	.40	.20	.12
109	Doyle Alexander	1.00	.50	.30
110	Bob Watson	.30	.15	.09
111	Dave Nelson	.25	.13	.08
112	Gary Ross	.25	.13	.08
113	Jerry Grote	.30	.15	.09
114	Lynn McGlothen	.25	.13	.08
115	Ron Santo	.80	.40	.25
116a	Yankees Mgr./Coaches (Jim Hegan, Ralph Houk, Elston Howard, Dick Howser, Jim Turner) (Coaches background brown)	1.00	.50	.30
116b	Yankees Mgr./Coaches (Jim Hegan, Ralph Houk, Elston Howard, Dick Howser, Jim Turner) (Coaches background orange)	.70	.35	.20
117	Ramon Hernandez	.25	.13	.08
118	John Mayberry	.40	.20	.12
119	Larry Bowa	.80	.40	.25
120	Joe Coleman	.30	.15	.09
121	Dave Rader	.25	.13	.08
122	Jim Strickland	.25	.13	.08
123	Sandy Alomar	.25	.13	.08
124	Jim Hardin	.25	.13	.08
125	Ron Fairly	.40	.20	.12
126	Jim Brewer	.25	.13	.08
127	Brewers Team	.90	.45	.25
128	Ted Sizemore	.25	.13	.08
129	Terry Forster	.40	.20	.12
130	Pete Rose	20.00	10.00	6.00
131a	Red Sox Mgr./Coaches (Doug Camilli, Eddie Kasko, Don Lenhardt, Eddie Popowski, Lee Stange) (Coaches background brown)	.50	.25	.15
131b	Red Sox Mgr./Coaches (Doug Camilli, Eddie Kasko, Don Lenhardt, Eddie Popowski, Lee Stange) (Coaches background orange)	.30	.15	.09
132	Matty Alou	.60	.30	.20
133	Dave Roberts	.25	.13	.08
134	Milt Wilcox	.30	.15	.09
135	Lee May	.50	.25	.15
136a	Orioles Mgr./Coaches (George Bamberger, Jim Frey, Billy Hunter, George Staller, Earl Weaver) (Coaches background brown)	1.00	.50	.30
136b	Orioles Mgr./Coaches (George Bamberger, Jim Frey, Billy Hunter, George Staller, Earl Weaver) (Coaches background orange)	.70	.35	.20
137	Jim Beauchamp	.25	.13	.08
138	Horacio Pina	.25	.13	.08
139	Carmen Fanzone	.25	.13	.08
140	Lou Piniella	.80	.40	.25
141	Bruce Kison	.30	.15	.09
142	Thurman Munson	6.00	3.00	1.75
143	John Curtis	.25	.13	.08
144	Marty Perez	.25	.13	.08
145	Bobby Bonds	.70	.35	.20
146	Woodie Fryman	.30	.15	.09
147	Mike Anderson	.25	.13	.08
148	*Dave Goltz*	.60	.30	.20
149	Ron Hunt	.30	.15	.09
150	Wilbur Wood	.40	.20	.12
151	Wes Parker	.30	.15	.09
152	Dave May	.25	.13	.08
153	Al Hrabosky	.40	.20	.12
154	Jeff Torborg	.30	.15	.09
155	Sal Bando	.70	.35	.20
156	Cesar Geronimo	.30	.15	.09
157	Denny Riddleberger	.25	.13	.08
158	Astros Team	.90	.45	.25
159	Clarence Gaston	.25	.13	.08
160	Jim Palmer	5.00	2.50	1.50
161	Ted Martinez	.25	.13	.08
162	Pete Broberg	.25	.13	.08
163	Vic Davalillo	.30	.15	.09
164	Monty Montgomery	.25	.13	.08
165	Luis Aparicio	2.75	1.50	.80
166	Terry Harmon	.25	.13	.08
167	Steve Stone	.50	.25	.15
168	Jim Northrup	.30	.15	.09
169	Ron Schueler	.25	.13	.08
170	Harmon Killebrew	3.50	1.75	1.00
171	Bernie Carbo	.25	.13	.08
172	Steve Kline	.30	.15	.09
173	Hal Breeden	.25	.13	.08
174	*Rich Gossage*	5.00	2.50	1.50
175	Frank Robinson	5.00	2.50	1.50
176	Chuck Taylor	.25	.13	.08
177	Bill Plummer	.25	.13	.08
178	Don Rose	.25	.13	.08
179a	A's Mgr./Coaches (Jerry Adair, Vern Hoscheit, Irv Noren, Wes Stock, Dick Williams) (Coaches background brown)	.80	.40	.25
179b	A's Mgr./Coaches (Jerry Adair, Vern Hoscheit, Irv Noren, Wes Stock, Dick Williams) (Coaches background orange)	.50	.25	.15
180	Fergie Jenkins	1.50	.70	.45
181	Jack Brohamer	.25	.13	.08
182	*Mike Caldwell*	.50	.25	.15
183	Don Buford	.30	.15	.09
184	Jerry Koosman	.50	.25	.15
185	Jim Wynn	.40	.20	.12
186	Bill Fahey	.25	.13	.08
187	Luke Walker	.25	.13	.08
188	Cookie Rojas	.25	.13	.08
189	Greg Luzinski	.70	.35	.20
190	Bob Gibson	3.50	1.75	1.00
191	Tigers Team	1.25	.60	.40
192	Pat Jarvis	.25	.13	.08
193	Carlton Fisk	6.00	3.00	1.75
194	*Jorge Orta*	.50	.25	.15
195	Clay Carroll	.30	.15	.09
196	Ken McMullen	.25	.13	.08
197	Ed Goodson	.25	.13	.08
198	Horace Clarke	.30	.15	.09
199	Bert Blyleven	1.50	.70	.45
200	Billy Williams	2.75	1.50	.80
201	A.L. Playoffs (Hendrick Scores Winning Run.)	1.00	.50	.30
202	N.L. Playoffs (Foster's Run Decides It.)	1.00	.50	.30
203	World Series Game 1 (Tenace The Menace.)	1.00	.50	.30
204	World Series Game 2 (A's Make It Two Straight.)	1.00	.50	.30
205	World Series Game 3 (Reds Win Squeeker.)	1.00	.50	.30
206	World Series Game 4 (Tenace Singles In Ninth.)	1.00	.50	.30
207	World Series Game 5 (Odom Out At Plate.)	1.00	.50	.30
208	World Series Game 6 (Reds' Slugging Ties Series.)	1.00	.50	.30
209	World Series Game 7 (Campy Starts Winning Rally.)	1.00	.50	.30
210	World Series Summary (World Champions.)	1.00	.50	.30
211	Balor Moore	.25	.13	.08
212	Joe Lahoud	.25	.13	.08
213	Steve Garvey	10.00	5.00	3.00
214	Dave Hamilton	.25	.13	.08
215	Dusty Baker	.50	.25	.15
216	Toby Harrah	.40	.20	.12
217	Don Wilson	.25	.13	.08
218	Aurelio Rodriguez	.30	.15	.09
219	Cardinals Team	.90	.45	.25
220	Nolan Ryan	35.00	17.50	10.50
221	Fred Kendall	.25	.13	.08
222	Rob Gardner	.25	.13	.08
223	Bud Harrelson	.30	.15	.09
224	Bill Lee	.30	.15	.09
225	Al Oliver	1.25	.60	.40
226	Ray Fosse	.25	.13	.08
227	Wayne Twitchell	.25	.13	.08
228	Bobby Darwin	.25	.13	.08
229	Roric Harrison	.25	.13	.08
230	Joe Morgan	3.00	1.50	.90
231	Bill Parsons	.25	.13	.08
232	Ken Singleton	.40	.20	.12
233	Ed Kirkpatrick	.25	.13	.08
234	*Bill North*	.50	.25	.15
235	Jim Hunter	3.00	1.50	.90
236	Tito Fuentes	.25	.13	.08
237a	Braves Mgr./Coaches (Lew Burdette, Jim Busby, Roy Hartsfield, Eddie Mathews, Ken Silvestri) (Coaches background brown)	1.25	.60	.40
237b	Braves Mgr./Coaches (Lew Burdette, Jim Busby, Roy Hartsfield, Eddie Mathews, Ken Silvestri) (Coaches background orange)	1.00	.50	.30
238	Tony Muser	.25	.13	.08
239	Pete Richert	.25	.13	.08

#	Player	NR MT	EX	VG
240	Bobby Murcer	.60	.30	.20
241	Dwain Anderson	.25	.13	.08
242	George Culver	.25	.13	.08
243	Angels Team	.90	.45	.25
244	Ed Acosta	.25	.13	.08
245	Carl Yastrzemski	10.00	5.00	3.00
246	Ken Sanders	.25	.13	.08
247	Del Unser	.25	.13	.08
248	Jerry Johnson	.25	.13	.08
249	Larry Biittner	.25	.13	.08
250	Manny Sanguillen	.30	.15	.09
251	Roger Nelson	.25	.13	.08
252a	Giants Mgr./Coaches (Joe Amalfitano, Charlie Fox, Andy Gilbert, Don McMahon, John McNamara) (Coaches background brown)	.50	.25	.15
252b	Giants Mgr./Coaches (Joe Amalfitano, Charlie Fox, Andy Gilbert, Don McMahon, John McNamara) (Coaches background orange)	.30	.15	.09
253	Mark Belanger	.30	.15	.09
254	Bill Stoneman	.25	.13	.08
255	Reggie Jackson	15.00	7.50	4.50
256	Chris Zachary	.25	.13	.08
257a	Mets Mgr./Coaches (Yogi Berra, Roy McMillan, Joe Pignatano, Rube Walker, Eddie Yost) (Coaches background brown)	1.50	.70	.45
257b	Mets Mgr./Coaches (Yogi Berra, Roy McMillan, Joe Pignatano, Rube Walker, Eddie Yost) (Coaches background orange)	1.25	.60	.40
258	Tommy John	1.75	.90	.50
259	Jim Holt	.25	.13	.08
260	Gary Nolan	.25	.13	.08
261	Pat Kelly	.25	.13	.08
262	Jack Aker	.25	.13	.08
263	George Scott	.30	.15	.09
264	Checklist 133-264	2.00	1.00	.60
265	Gene Michael	.40	.20	.12
266	Mike Lum	.25	.13	.08
267	Lloyd Allen	.25	.13	.08
268	Jerry Morales	.25	.13	.08
269	Tim McCarver	.70	.35	.20
270	Luis Tiant	.80	.40	.25
271	Tom Hutton	.25	.13	.08
272	Ed Farmer	.25	.13	.08
273	Chris Speier	.30	.15	.09
274	Darold Knowles	.25	.13	.08
275	Tony Perez	1.25	.60	.40
276	Joe Lovitto	.25	.13	.08
277	Bob Miller	.25	.13	.08
278	Orioles Team	.90	.45	.25
279	Mike Strahler	.25	.13	.08
280	Al Kaline	4.50	2.25	1.25
281	Mike Jorgensen	.25	.13	.08
282	Steve Hovley	.25	.13	.08
283	Ray Sadecki	.25	.13	.08
284	Glenn Borgmann	.25	.13	.08
285	Don Kessinger	.30	.15	.09
286	Frank Linzy	.25	.13	.08
287	Eddie Leon	.25	.13	.08
288	Gary Gentry	.25	.13	.08
289	Bob Oliver	.25	.13	.08
290	Cesar Cedeno	.40	.20	.12
291	Rogelio Moret	.25	.13	.08
292	Jose Cruz	.80	.40	.25
293	Bernie Allen	.30	.15	.09
294	Steve Arlin	.25	.13	.08
295	Bert Campaneris	.60	.30	.20
296	Reds Mgr./Coaches (Sparky Anderson, Alex Grammas, Ted Kluszewski, George Scherger, Larry Shepard)	.70	.35	.20
297	Walt Williams	.25	.13	.08
298	Ron Bryant	.25	.13	.08
299	Ted Ford	.25	.13	.08
300	Steve Carlton	10.00	5.00	3.00
301	Billy Grabarkewitz	.25	.13	.08
302	Terry Crowley	.25	.13	.08
303	Nelson Briles	.25	.13	.08
304	Duke Sims	.25	.13	.08
305	Willie Mays	20.00	10.00	6.00
306	Tom Burgmeier	.25	.13	.08
307	Boots Day	.25	.13	.08
308	Skip Lockwood	.25	.13	.08
309	Paul Popovich	.25	.13	.08
310	Dick Allen	.80	.40	.25
311	Joe Decker	.25	.13	.08
312	Oscar Brown	.25	.13	.08
313	Jim Ray	.25	.13	.08
314	Ron Swoboda	.30	.15	.09
315	John Odom	.30	.15	.09
316	Padres Team	.90	.45	.25
317	Danny Cater	.25	.13	.08
318	Jim McGlothlin	.25	.13	.08
319	Jim Spencer	.25	.13	.08
320	Lou Brock	3.50	1.75	1.00
321	Rich Hinton	.25	.13	.08
322	*Garry Maddox*	.80	.40	.25
323	Tigers Mgr./Coaches (Art Fowler, Billy Martin, Joe Schultz, Charlie Silvera, Dick Tracewski)	1.00	.50	.30
324	Al Downing	.30	.15	.09
325	Boog Powell	1.00	.50	.30
326	Darrell Brandon	.25	.13	.08
327	John Lowenstein	.25	.13	.08
328	Bill Bonham	.25	.13	.08
329	Ed Kranepool	.30	.15	.09
330	Rod Carew	10.00	5.00	3.00
331	Carl Morton	.25	.13	.08
332	*John Felske*	.30	.15	.09
333	Gene Clines	.25	.13	.08
334	Freddie Patek	.25	.13	.08
335	Bob Tolan	.30	.15	.09
336	Tom Bradley	.25	.13	.08
337	Dave Duncan	.25	.13	.08
338	Checklist 265-396	2.00	1.00	.60
339	Dick Tidrow	.30	.15	.09
340	Nate Colbert	.30	.15	.09
341	Boyhood Photo (Jim Palmer)	1.25	.60	.40
342	Boyhood Photo (Sam McDowell)	.40	.20	.12
343	Boyhood Photo (Bobby Murcer)	.40	.20	.12
344	Boyhood Photo (Jim Hunter)	1.25	.60	.40
345	Boyhood Photo (Chris Speier)	.30	.15	.09
346	Boyhood Photo (Gaylord Perry)	1.25	.60	.40
347	Royals Team	.90	.45	.25
348	Rennie Stennett	.30	.15	.09
349	Dick McAuliffe	.30	.15	.09
350	Tom Seaver	15.00	7.50	4.50
351	Jimmy Stewart	.25	.13	.08
352	*Don Stanhouse*	.40	.20	.12
353	Steve Brye	.25	.13	.08
354	Billy Parker	.25	.13	.08
355	Mike Marshall	.40	.20	.12
356	White Sox Mgr./Coaches (Joe Lonnett, Jim Mahoney, Al Monchak, Johnny Sain, Chuck Tanner)	.50	.25	.15
357	Ross Grimsley	.30	.15	.09
358	Jim Nettles	.25	.13	.08
359	Cecil Upshaw	.25	.13	.08
360	Joe Rudi (photo actually Gene Tenace)	.40	.20	.12
361	Fran Healy	.25	.13	.08
362	Eddie Watt	.25	.13	.08
363	Jackie Hernandez	.25	.13	.08
364	Rick Wise	.30	.15	.09
365	Rico Petrocelli	.40	.20	.12
366	Brock Davis	.25	.13	.08
367	Burt Hooton	.40	.20	.12
368	Bill Buckner	.70	.35	.20
369	Lerrin LaGrow	.25	.13	.08
370	Willie Stargell	3.50	1.75	1.00
371	Mike Kekich	.30	.15	.09
372	Oscar Gamble	.30	.15	.09
373	Clyde Wright	.25	.13	.08
374	Darrell Evans	.70	.35	.20
375	Larry Dierker	.30	.15	.09
376	Frank Duffy	.25	.13	.08
377	Expos Mgr./Coaches (Dave Bristol, Larry Doby, Gene Mauch, Cal McLish, Jerry Zimmerman)	.50	.25	.15
378	Lenny Randle	.25	.13	.08
379	Cy Acosta	.25	.13	.08
380	Johnny Bench	15.00	7.50	4.50
381	Vicente Romo	.25	.13	.08
382	Mike Hegan	.25	.13	.08
383	Diego Segui	.25	.13	.08
384	Don Baylor	1.00	.50	.30
385	Jim Perry	.50	.25	.15
386	Don Money	.30	.15	.09
387	Jim Barr	.25	.13	.08
388	Ben Oglivie	.50	.25	.15
389	Mets Team	1.75	.90	.50
390	Mickey Lolich	.70	.35	.20
391	*Lee Lacy*	.80	.40	.25
392	Dick Drago	.25	.13	.08
393	Jose Cardenal	.30	.15	.09
394	Sparky Lyle	.70	.35	.20
395	Roger Metzger	.25	.13	.08
396	Grant Jackson	.25	.13	.08
397	Dave Cash	.40	.20	.12
398	Rich Hand	.40	.20	.12
399	George Foster	1.50	.70	.45
400	Gaylord Perry	3.00	1.50	.90

		NR MT	EX	VG
401	Clyde Mashore	.40	.20	.12
402	Jack Hiatt	.40	.20	.12
403	Sonny Jackson	.40	.20	.12
404	Chuck Brinkman	.40	.20	.12
405	Cesar Tovar	.40	.20	.12
406	Paul Lindblad	.40	.20	.12
407	Felix Millan	.40	.20	.12
408	Jim Colborn	.40	.20	.12
409	Ivan Murrell	.40	.20	.12
410	Willie McCovey	3.50	1.75	1.00
411	Ray Corbin	.40	.20	.12
412	Manny Mota	.60	.30	.20
413	Tom Timmermann	.40	.20	.12
414	Ken Rudolph	.40	.20	.12
415	Marty Pattin	.40	.20	.12
416	Paul Schaal	.40	.20	.12
417	Scipio Spinks	.40	.20	.12
418	Bobby Grich	.60	.30	.20
419	Casey Cox	.50	.25	.15
420	Tommie Agee	.50	.25	.15
421	Angels Mgr./Coaches (Tom Morgan, Salty Parker, Jimmie Reese, John Roseboro, Bobby Winkles)	.40	.20	.12
422	Bob Robertson	.40	.20	.12
423	Johnny Jeter	.40	.20	.12
424	Denny Doyle	.40	.20	.12
425	Alex Johnson	.40	.20	.12
426	Dave LaRoche	.40	.20	.12
427	Rick Auerbach	.40	.20	.12
428	Wayne Simpson	.40	.20	.12
429	Jim Fairey	.40	.20	.12
430	Vida Blue	.80	.40	.25
431	Gerry Moses	.50	.25	.15
432	Dan Frisella	.40	.20	.12
433	Willie Horton	.60	.30	.20
434	Giants Team	1.00	.50	.30
435	Rico Carty	.60	.30	.20
436	Jim McAndrew	.40	.20	.12
437	John Kennedy	.40	.20	.12
438	Enzo Hernandez	.40	.20	.12
439	Eddie Fisher	.40	.20	.12
440	Glenn Beckert	.50	.25	.15
441	Gail Hopkins	.40	.20	.12
442	Dick Dietz	.40	.20	.12
443	Danny Thompson	.50	.25	.15
444	Ken Brett	.50	.25	.15
445	Ken Berry	.40	.20	.12
446	Jerry Reuss	.60	.30	.20
447	Joe Hague	.40	.20	.12
448	John Hiller	.50	.25	.15
449a	Indians Mgr./Coaches (Ken Aspromonte, Rocky Colavito, Joe Lutz, Warren Spahn) (Spahn's ear pointed)	.50	.25	.15
449b	Indians Mgr./Coaches (Ken Aspromonte, Rocky Colavito, Joe Lutz, Warren Spahn) (Spahn's ear round)	.80	.40	.25
450	Joe Torre	1.00	.50	.30
451	John Vukovich	.40	.20	.12
452	Paul Casanova	.40	.20	.12
453	Checklist 397-528	2.25	1.25	.70
454	Tom Haller	.50	.25	.15
455	Bill Melton	.50	.25	.15
456	Dick Green	.40	.20	.12
457	John Strohmayer	.40	.20	.12
458	Jim Mason	.40	.20	.12
459	Jimmy Howarth	.40	.20	.12
460	Bill Freehan	.60	.30	.20
461	Mike Corkins	.40	.20	.12
462	Ron Blomberg	.50	.25	.15
463	Ken Tatum	.40	.20	.12
464	Cubs Team	1.00	.50	.30
465	Dave Giusti	.40	.20	.12
466	Jose Arcia	.40	.20	.12
467	Mike Ryan	.40	.20	.12
468	Tom Griffin	.40	.20	.12
469	Dan Monzon	.40	.20	.12
470	Mike Cuellar	.60	.30	.20
471	Hit Leader (Ty Cobb)	3.00	1.50	.90
472	Grand Slam Leader (Lou Gehrig)	3.00	1.50	.90
473	Total Base Leader (Hank Aaron)	3.00	1.50	.90
474	R.B.I. Leader (Babe Ruth)	5.00	2.50	1.50
475	Batting Leader (Ty Cobb)	3.00	1.50	.90
476	Shutout Leader (Walter Johnson)	1.25	.60	.40
477	Victory Leader (Cy Young)	1.25	.60	.40
478	Strikeout Leader (Walter Johnson)	1.25	.60	.40
479	Hal Lanier	.60	.30	.20
480	Juan Marichal	3.50	1.75	1.00
481	White Sox Team	1.25	.60	.40
482	*Rick Reuschel*	6.00	3.00	1.75
483	Dal Maxvill	.50	.25	.15

		NR MT	EX	VG
484	Ernie McAnally	.40	.20	.12
485	Norm Cash	.80	.40	.25
486a	Phillies Mgr./Coaches (Carroll Berringer, Billy DeMars, Danny Ozark, Ray Rippelmeyer, Bobby Wine) (Coaches background brown red)	.70	.35	.20
486b	Phillies Mgr./Coaches (Carroll Beringer, Billy DeMars, Danny Ozark, Ray Rippelmeyer, Bobby Wine) (Coaches background orange)	.50	.25	.15
487	Bruce Dal Canton	.40	.20	.12
488	Dave Campbell	.40	.20	.12
489	Jeff Burroughs	.60	.30	.20
490	Claude Osteen	.60	.30	.20
491	Bob Montgomery	.40	.20	.12
492	Pedro Borbon	.40	.20	.12
493	Duffy Dyer	.40	.20	.12
494	Rich Morales	.40	.20	.12
495	Tommy Helms	.40	.20	.12
496	Ray Lamb	.40	.20	.12
497	Cardinals Mgr./Coaches (Vern Benson, George Kissell, Red Schoendienst, Barney Schultz)	.90	.45	.25
498	Graig Nettles	2.50	1.25	.70
499	Bob Moose	.40	.20	.12
500	A's Team	1.75	.90	.50
501	Larry Gura	.50	.25	.15
502	Bobby Valentine	.60	.30	.20
503	Phil Niekro	3.00	1.50	.90
504	Earl Williams	.40	.20	.12
505	Bob Bailey	.40	.20	.12
506	Bart Johnson	.40	.20	.12
507	Darrel Chaney	.40	.20	.12
508	Gates Brown	.40	.20	.12
509	Jim Nash	.40	.20	.12
510	Amos Otis	.60	.30	.20
511	Sam McDowell	.60	.30	.20
512	Dalton Jones	.40	.20	.12
513	Dave Marshall	.40	.20	.12
514	Jerry Kenney	.40	.20	.12
515	Andy Messersmith	.50	.25	.15
516	Danny Walton	.40	.20	.12
517a	Pirates Mgr./Coaches (Don Leppert, Bill Mazeroski, Dave Ricketts, Bill Virdon, Mel Wright) (Coaches background brown)	1.00	.50	.30
517b	Pirates Mgr./Coaches (Don Leppert, Bill Mazeroski, Dave Ricketts, Bill Virdon, Mel Wright) (Coaches background orange)	.50	.25	.15
518	Bob Veale	.50	.25	.15
519	John Edwards	.40	.20	.12
520	Mel Stottlemyre	.60	.30	.20
521	Braves Team	1.00	.50	.30
522	Leo Cardenas	.40	.20	.12
523	Wayne Granger	.40	.20	.12
524	Gene Tenace	.40	.20	.12
525	Jim Fregosi	.70	.35	.20
526	Ollie Brown	.40	.20	.12
527	Dan McGinn	.40	.20	.12
528	Paul Blair	.50	.25	.15
529	Milt May	1.25	.60	.40
530	Jim Kaat	3.25	1.75	1.00
531	Ron Woods	1.25	.60	.40
532	Steve Mingori	1.25	.60	.40
533	Larry Stahl	1.25	.60	.40
534	Dave Lemonds	1.25	.60	.40
535	John Callison	1.50	.70	.45
536	Phillies Team	2.50	1.25	.70
537	Bill Slayback	1.25	.60	.40
538	Jim Hart	1.50	.70	.45
539	Tom Murphy	1.25	.60	.40
540	Cleon Jones	1.50	.70	.45
541	Bob Bolin	1.25	.60	.40
542	Pat Corrales	1.50	.70	.45
543	Alan Foster	1.25	.60	.40
544	Von Joshua	1.25	.60	.40
545	Orlando Cepeda	3.25	1.75	1.00
546	Jim York	1.25	.60	.40
547	Bobby Heise	1.25	.60	.40
548	Don Durham	1.25	.60	.40
549	Rangers Mgr./Coaches (Chuck Estrada, Whitey Herzog, Chuck Hiller, Jackie Moore)	2.00	1.00	.60
550	Dave Johnson	2.75	1.50	.80
551	Mike Kilkenny	1.25	.60	.40
552	J.C. Martin	1.25	.60	.40
553	Mickey Scott	1.25	.60	.40
554	Dave Concepcion	2.50	1.25	.70
555	Bill Hands	1.25	.60	.40
556	Yankees Team	4.00	2.00	1.25
557	Bernie Williams	1.25	.60	.40

		NR MT	EX	VG
558	Jerry May	1.25	.60	.40
559	Barry Lersch	1.25	.60	.40
560	Frank Howard	2.25	1.25	.70
561	Jim Geddes	1.25	.60	.40
562	Wayne Garrett	1.25	.60	.40
563	Larry Haney	1.25	.60	.40
564	Mike Thompson	1.25	.60	.40
565	Jim Hickman	1.50	.70	.45
566	Lew Krausse	1.25	.60	.40
567	Bob Fenwick	1.25	.60	.40
568	Ray Newman	1.25	.60	.40
569	Dodgers Mgr./Coaches (Red Adams, Walt Alston, Monty Basgall, Jim Gillam, Tom Lasorda)	3.00	1.50	.90
570	Bill Singer	1.50	.70	.45
571	Rusty Torres	1.25	.60	.40
572	Gary Sutherland	1.25	.60	.40
573	Fred Beene	1.50	.70	.45
574	Bob Didier	1.25	.60	.40
575	Dock Ellis	1.50	.70	.45
576	Expos Team	2.50	1.25	.70
577	*Eric Soderholm*	1.50	.70	.45
578	Ken Wright	1.25	.60	.40
579	Tom Grieve	1.25	.60	.40
580	Joe Pepitone	2.00	1.00	.60
581	Steve Kealey	1.25	.60	.40
582	Darrell Porter	1.75	.90	.50
583	Bill Greif	1.25	.60	.40
584	Chris Arnold	1.25	.60	.40
585	Joe Niekro	2.00	1.00	.60
586	Bill Sudakis	1.50	.70	.45
587	Rich McKinney	1.25	.60	.40
588	Checklist 529-660	10.00	5.00	3.00
589	Ken Forsch	1.50	.70	.45
590	Deron Johnson	1.25	.60	.40
591	Mike Hedlund	1.25	.60	.40
592	John Boccabella	1.25	.60	.40
593	Royals Mgr./Coaches (Galen Cisco, Harry Dunlop, Charlie Lau, Jack McKeon)	1.50	.70	.45
594	Vic Harris	1.25	.60	.40
595	Don Gullett	1.50	.70	.45
596	Red Sox Team	2.75	1.50	.80
597	Mickey Rivers	1.75	.90	.50
598	Phil Roof	1.25	.60	.40
599	Ed Crosby	1.25	.60	.40
600	Dave McNally	1.75	.90	.50
601	Rookie Catchers (George Pena, Sergio Robles, Rick Stelmaszek)	1.25	.60	.40
602	Rookie Pitchers (Mel Behney, Ralph Garcia, *Doug Rau*)	1.50	.70	.45
603	Rookie Third Basemen (Terry Hughes, Bill McNulty, *Ken Reitz*)	1.50	.70	.45
604	Rookie Pitchers (Jesse Jefferson, Dennis O'Toole, Bob Strampe)	1.25	.60	.40
605	Rookie First Basemen (Pat Bourque, *Enos Cabell*, Gonzalo Marquez)	1.75	.90	.50
606	Rookie Outfielders (*Gary Matthews*, Tom Paciorek, Jorge Roque)	2.25	1.25	.70
607	Rookie Shortstops (Ray Busse, Pepe Frias, Mario Guerrero)	1.25	.60	.40
608	Rookie Pitchers (*Steve Busby*, Dick Colpaert, *George Medich*)	1.50	.70	.45
609	Rookie Second Basemen (Larvell Blanks, Pedro Garcia, *Dave Lopes*)	3.00	1.50	.90
610	Rookie Pitchers (Jimmy Freeman, Charlie Hough, Hank Webb)	1.75	.90	.50
611	Rookie Outfielders (Rich Coggins, Jim Wohlford, Richie Zisk)	1.50	.70	.45
612	Rookie Pitchers (Steve Lawson, Bob Reynolds, Brent Strom)	1.25	.60	.40
613	Rookie Catchers (*Bob Boone*, Mike Ivie, Skip Jutze)	25.00	12.50	7.50
614	Rookie Outfielders (*Alonza Bumbry, Dwight Evans*, Charlie Spikes)	50.00	30.00	15.00
615	Rookie Third Basemen (Ron Cey, John Hilton, *Mike Schmidt*)	300.00	120.00	75.00
616	Rookie Pitchers (Norm Angelini, Steve Blateric, Mike Garman)	1.50	.70	.45
617	Rich Chiles	1.25	.60	.40
618	Andy Etchebarren	1.25	.60	.40
619	Billy Wilson	1.25	.60	.40
620	Tommy Harper	1.50	.70	.45
621	Joe Ferguson	1.25	.60	.40
622	Larry Hisle	1.50	.70	.45
623	Steve Renko	1.25	.60	.40
624	Astros Mgr./Coaches (Leo Durocher, Preston Gomez, Grady Hatton, Hub Kittle, Jim Owens)	2.25	1.25	.70
625	Angel Mangual	1.25	.60	.40
626	Bob Barton	1.25	.60	.40
627	Luis Alvarado	1.25	.60	.40

		NR MT	EX	VG
628	Jim Slaton	1.50	.70	.45
629	Indians Team	2.50	1.25	.70
630	Denny McLain	3.00	1.50	.90
631	Tom Matchick	1.25	.60	.40
632	Dick Selma	1.25	.60	.40
633	Ike Brown	1.25	.60	.40
634	Alan Closter	1.50	.70	.45
635	Gene Alley	1.50	.70	.45
636	Rick Clark	1.25	.60	.40
637	Norm Niller	1.25	.60	.40
638	Ken Reynolds	1.25	.60	.40
639	Willie Crawford	1.25	.60	.40
640	Dick Bosman	1.25	.60	.40
641	Reds Team	2.75	1.50	.80
642	Jose Laboy	1.25	.60	.40
643	Al Fitzmorris	1.25	.60	.40
644	Jack Heidemann	1.25	.60	.40
645	Bob Locker	1.25	.60	.40
646	Brewers Mgr./Coaches (Del Crandall, Harvey Kuenn, Joe Nossek, Bob Shaw, Jim Walton)	1.75	.90	.50
647	George Stone	1.25	.60	.40
648	Tom Egan	1.25	.60	.40
649	Rich Folkers	1.25	.60	.40
650	Felipe Alou	1.75	.90	.50
651	Don Carrithers	1.25	.60	.40
652	Ted Kubiak	1.25	.60	.40
653	Joe Hoerner	1.25	.60	.40
654	Twins Team	2.50	1.25	.70
655	Clay Kirby	1.25	.60	.40
656	John Ellis	1.25	.60	.40
657	Bob Johnson	1.25	.60	.40
658	Elliott Maddox	1.50	.70	.45
659	Jose Pagan	1.50	.70	.45
660	Fred Scherman	2.25	.70	.45

1973 Topps Candy Lids

A bit out of the ordinary, the Topps Candy Lids were the top of a product called "Baseball Stars Bubble Gum." The bottom (inside) of the lids carry a color photo of a player with a ribbon which contains the name, position and team. The lids are 1-7/8" in diameter. A total of 55 different lids were made, featuring most of the stars of the day.

		NR MT	EX	VG
Complete Set:		400.00	200.00	120.00
Common Player:		2.00	1.00	.60
(1)	Hank Aaron	30.00	15.00	9.00
(2)	Dick Allen	4.00	2.00	1.25
(3)	Dusty Baker	2.00	1.00	.60
(4)	Sal Bando	3.00	1.50	.90
(5)	Johnny Bench	20.00	10.00	6.00
(6)	Bobby Bonds	3.00	1.50	.90
(7)	Dick Bosman	2.00	1.00	.60
(8)	Lou Brock	15.00	7.50	4.50
(9)	Rod Carew	20.00	10.00	6.00
(10)	Steve Carlton	20.00	10.00	6.00
(11)	Nate Colbert	2.00	1.00	.60
(12)	Willie Davis	3.00	1.50	.90
(13)	Larry Dierker	2.00	1.00	.60
(14)	Mike Epstein	2.00	1.00	.60
(15)	Carlton Fisk	7.00	3.50	2.00
(16)	Tim Foli	2.00	1.00	.60
(17)	Ray Fosse	2.00	1.00	.60
(18)	Bill Freehan	3.00	1.50	.90

		NR MT	EX	VG
(19)	Bob Gibson	15.00	7.50	4.50
(20)	Bud Harrelson	2.00	1.00	.60
(21)	Jim Hunter	12.00	6.00	3.50
(22)	Reggie Jackson	25.00	12.50	7.50
(23)	Fergie Jenkins	7.00	3.50	2.00
(24)	Al Kaline	15.00	7.50	4.50
(25)	Harmon Killebrew	15.00	7.50	4.50
(26)	Clay Kirby	2.00	1.00	.60
(27)	Mickey Lolich	4.00	2.00	1.25
(28)	Greg Luzinski	3.00	1.50	.90
(29)	Mike Marshall	2.00	1.00	.60
(30)	Lee May	2.00	1.00	.60
(31)	John Mayberry	2.00	1.00	.60
(32)	Willie Mays	30.00	15.00	9.00
(33)	Willie McCovey	15.00	7.50	4.50
(34)	Thurman Munson	15.00	7.50	4.50
(35)	Bobby Murcer	3.00	1.50	.90
(36)	Gary Nolan	2.00	1.00	.60
(37)	Amos Otis	2.00	1.00	.60
(38)	Jim Palmer	12.00	6.00	3.50
(39)	Gaylord Perry	12.00	6.00	3.50
(40)	Lou Piniella	3.00	1.50	.90
(41)	Brooks Robinson	18.00	9.00	5.50
(42)	Frank Robinson	15.00	7.50	4.50
(43)	Ellie Rodriguez	2.00	1.00	.60
(44)	Pete Rose	65.00	32.00	19.50
(45)	Nolan Ryan	18.00	9.00	5.50
(46)	Manny Sanguillen	2.00	1.00	.60
(47)	George Scott	2.00	1.00	.60
(48)	Tom Seaver	20.00	10.00	6.00
(49)	Chris Speier	2.00	1.00	.60
(50)	Willie Stargell	15.00	7.50	4.50
(51)	Don Sutton	12.00	6.00	3.50
(52)	Joe Torre	4.00	2.00	1.25
(53)	Billy Williams	12.00	6.00	3.50
(54)	Wilbur Wood	2.00	1.00	.60
(55)	Carl Yastrzemski	25.00	12.50	7.50

1973 Topps Comics

Strictly a test issue, if ever publicly distributed at all (most are found without any folding which would have occurred had they actually been used to wrap a piece of bubblegum), the 24 players in the 1973 Topps Comics issue appear on 4-5/8" by 3-7/16" waxed paper wrappers. The inside of the wrapper combines a color photo and facsimile autograph with a comic-style presentation of the player's career highlights. The Comics share a checklist with the 1973 Topps Pin-Ups, virtually all star players.

		NR MT	EX	VG
Complete Set:		1400.00	700.00	420.00
Common Player:		35.00	17.50	10.50
(1)	Hank Aaron	100.00	50.00	30.00

		NR MT	EX	VG
(2)	Dick Allen	40.00	20.00	12.00
(3)	Johnny Bench	80.00	40.00	24.00
(4)	Steve Carlton	65.00	32.00	19.50
(5)	Nate Colbert	35.00	17.50	10.50
(6)	Willie Davis	40.00	20.00	12.00
(7)	Mike Epstein	35.00	17.50	10.50
(8)	Reggie Jackson	100.00	50.00	30.00
(9)	Harmon Killebrew	60.00	30.00	18.00
(10)	Mickey Lolich	40.00	20.00	12.00
(11)	Mike Marshall	35.00	17.50	10.50
(12)	Lee May	35.00	17.50	10.50
(13)	Willie McCovey	60.00	30.00	18.00
(14)	Bobby Murcer	40.00	20.00	12.00
(15)	Gaylord Perry	50.00	25.00	15.00
(16)	Lou Piniella	40.00	20.00	12.00
(17)	Brooks Robinson	60.00	30.00	18.00
(18)	Nolan Ryan	60.00	30.00	18.00
(19)	George Scott	35.00	17.50	10.50
(20)	Tom Seaver	80.00	40.00	24.00
(21)	Willie Stargell	50.00	25.00	15.00
(22)	Joe Torre	40.00	20.00	12.00
(23)	Billy Williams	50.00	25.00	15.00
(24)	Carl Yastrzemski	125.00	62.00	37.00

1973 Topps Pin-Ups

Another test issue of 1973, the 24 Topps Pin-Ups include the same basic format and the same checklist of star-caliber players as the Comics test issue of the same year. The 3-7/16" by 4-5/8" Pin-Ups are actually the inside of a wrapper for a piece of bubblegum. The color player photo features a decorative lozenge inserted at bottom with the player's name, team and position. There is also a facsimile autograph. Curiously, neither the Pin-Ups nor the Comics of 1973 bear team logos on the players' caps.

		NR MT	EX	VG
Complete Set:		1250.00	625.00	375.00
Common Player:		30.00	15.00	9.00
(1)	Hank Aaron	90.00	45.00	27.00
(2)	Dick Allen	35.00	17.50	10.50
(3)	Johnny Bench	70.00	35.00	21.00
(4)	Steve Carlton	60.00	30.00	18.00
(5)	Nate Colbert	30.00	15.00	9.00
(6)	Willie Davis	35.00	17.50	10.50
(7)	Mike Epstein	30.00	15.00	9.00
(8)	Reggie Jackson	90.00	45.00	27.00
(9)	Harmon Killebrew	50.00	25.00	15.00
(10)	Mickey Lolich	35.00	17.50	10.50
(11)	Mike Marshall	30.00	15.00	9.00
(12)	Lee May	30.00	15.00	9.00
(13)	Willie McCovey	50.00	25.00	15.00
(14)	Bobby Murcer	35.00	17.50	10.50
(15)	Gaylord Perry	45.00	22.00	13.50
(16)	Lou Piniella	35.00	17.50	10.50
(17)	Brooks Robinson	55.00	27.00	16.50
(18)	Nolan Ryan	55.00	27.00	16.50
(19)	George Scott	30.00	15.00	9.00
(20)	Tom Seaver	75.00	37.00	22.00
(21)	Willie Stargell	45.00	22.00	13.50
(22)	Joe Torre	35.00	17.50	10.50
(23)	Billy Williams	45.00	22.00	13.50
(24)	Carl Yastrzemski	110.00	55.00	33.00

1973 Topps Team Checklists

This is a 24-card unnumbered set of 2-1/2" by 3-1/2" cards that is generally believed to have been included with the high-numbered series in 1973, while also being made available in a mail-in offer. The front of the cards have the team name at the top and a white panel with various facsimile autographs takes up the rest of the space except for a blue border. Backs feature the team name and checklist. Relatively scarce, these somewhat mysterious cards are not included by many in their collections despite their obvious relationship to the regular set.

		NR MT	EX	VG
Complete Set:		70.00	35.00	21.00
Common Checklist:		2.50	1.25	.70
(1)	Atlanta Braves	3.00	1.50	.90
(2)	Baltimore Orioles	3.00	1.50	.90
(3)	Boston Red Sox	3.00	1.50	.90
(4)	California Angels	3.00	1.50	.90
(5)	Chicago Cubs	3.00	1.50	.90
(6)	Chicago White Sox	3.00	1.50	.90
(7)	Cincinnati Reds	3.00	1.50	.90
(8)	Cleveland Indians	3.00	1.50	.90
(9)	Detroit Tigers	3.50	1.75	1.00
(10)	Houston Astros	3.00	1.50	.90
(11)	Kansas City Royals	3.00	1.50	.90
(12)	Los Angeles Dodgers	3.00	1.50	.90
(13)	Milwaukee Brewers	3.00	1.50	.90
(14)	Minnesota Twins	3.00	1.50	.90
(15)	Montreal Expos	3.00	1.50	.90
(16)	New York Mets	3.50	1.75	1.00
(17)	New York Yankees	3.50	1.75	1.00
(18)	Oakland A's	3.50	1.75	1.00
(19)	Philadelphia Phillies	3.00	1.50	.90
(20)	Pittsburgh Pirates	3.00	1.50	.90
(21)	St. Louis Cardinals	3.00	1.50	.90
(22)	San Diego Padres	3.00	1.50	.90
(23)	San Francisco Giants	3.00	1.50	.90
(24)	Texas Rangers	3.00	1.50	.90

1974 Topps

Issued all at once at the beginning of the year, rather than by series throughout the baseball season

as had been done since 1952, this 660-card '74 Topps set features a famous group of error cards. At the time the cards were printed, it was uncertain whether the San Diego Padres would move to Washington, D.C., and by the time a decision was made some Padres cards had appeared with a "Washington, Nat'l League" designation on the front. A total of 15 cards were affected, and those with the Washington designation bring prices well in excess of regular cards of the same players (the Washington variations are not included in the complete set prices quoted below). The 2-1/2" by 3-1/2" cards feature color photos (frequently game-action shots) along with the player's name, team and position. Specialty cards abound, starting with a Hank Aaron tribute and running through the usual managers, statistical leaders, playoff and World Series highlights, multi-player rookie cards and All-Stars.

		NR MT	EX	VG
Complete Set:		350.00	175.00	105.00
Common Player:		.20	.10	.06
1	Hank Aaron	20.00	10.00	6.00
2	Aaron Special 1954-57	3.00	1.50	.90
3	Aaron Special 1958-61	3.00	1.50	.90
4	Aaron Special 1962-65	3.00	1.50	.90
5	Aaron Special 1966-69	3.00	1.50	.90
6	Aaron Special 1970-73	3.00	1.50	.90
7	Jim Hunter	3.00	1.50	.90
8	George Theodore	.20	.10	.06
9	Mickey Lolich	.60	.30	.20
10	Johnny Bench	12.00	6.00	3.50
11	Jim Bibby	.25	.13	.08
12	Dave May	.20	.10	.06
13	Tom Hilgendorf	.20	.10	.06
14	Paul Popovich	.20	.10	.06
15	Joe Torre	.80	.40	.25
16	Orioles Team	.80	.40	.25
17	Doug Bird	.20	.10	.06
18	Gary Thomasson	.20	.10	.06
19	Gerry Moses	.25	.13	.08
20	Nolan Ryan	25.00	12.50	7.50
21	Bob Gallagher	.20	.10	.06
22	Cy Acosta	.20	.10	.06
23	Craig Robinson	.20	.10	.06
24	John Hiller	.25	.13	.08
25	Ken Singleton	.30	.15	.09
26	Bill Campbell	.40	.20	.12
27	George Scott	.30	.15	.09
28	Manny Sanguillen	.25	.13	.08
29	Phil Niekro	2.00	1.00	.60
30	Bobby Bonds	.50	.25	.15
31	Astros Mgr./Coaches (Roger Craig, Preston Gomez, Grady Hatton, Hub Kittle, Bob Lillis)	.20	.10	.06
32a	John Grubb (Washington)	3.50	1.75	1.00
32b	John Grubb (San Diego)	.25	.13	.08
33	Don Newhauser	.20	.10	.06
34	Andy Kosco	.20	.10	.06
35	Gaylord Perry	2.25	1.25	.70
36	Cardinals Team	.80	.40	.25
37	Dave Sells	.20	.10	.06
38	Don Kessinger	.25	.13	.08
39	Ken Suarez	.20	.10	.06
40	Jim Palmer	4.00	2.00	1.25
41	Bobby Floyd	.20	.10	.06
42	Claude Osteen	.30	.15	.09
43	Jim Wynn	.30	.15	.09
44	Mel Stottlemyre	.40	.20	.12
45	Dave Johnson	.70	.35	.20
46	Pat Kelly	.20	.10	.06
47	Dick Ruthven	.25	.13	.08
48	Dick Sharon	.20	.10	.06
49	Steve Renko	.20	.10	.06
50	Rod Carew	5.50	2.75	1.75
51	Bobby Heise	.20	.10	.06
52	Al Oliver	1.00	.50	.30
53a	Fred Kendall (Washington)	3.50	1.75	1.00
53b	Fred Kendall (San Diego)	.25	.13	.08
54	Elias Sosa	.25	.13	.08
55	Frank Robinson	3.50	1.75	1.00
56	Mets Team	1.00	.50	.30
57	Darold Knowles	.20	.10	.06
58	Charlie Spikes	.20	.10	.06
59	Ross Grimsley	.25	.13	.08
60	Lou Brock	3.50	1.75	1.00

		NR MT	EX	VG
61	Luis Aparicio	2.50	1.25	.70
62	Bob Locker	.20	.10	.06
63	Bill Sudakis	.20	.10	.06
64	Doug Rau	.20	.10	.06
65	Amos Otis	.30	.15	.09
66	Sparky Lyle	.50	.25	.15
67	Tommy Helms	.20	.10	.06
68	Grant Jackson	.20	.10	.06
69	Del Unser	.20	.10	.06
70	Dick Allen	.80	.40	.25
71	Danny Frisella	.20	.10	.06
72	Aurleio Rodriguez	.25	.13	.08
73	Mike Marshall	.70	.35	.20
74	Twins Team	.80	.40	.25
75	Jim Colborn	.20	.10	.06
76	Mickey Rivers	.30	.15	.09
77a	Rich Troedson (Washington)	3.50	1.75	1.00
77b	Rich Troedson (San Diego)	.25	.13	.08
78	Giants Mgr./Coaches (Joe Amalfitano, Charlie Fox, Andy Gilbert, Don McMahon, John McNamara)	.20	.10	.06
79	Gene Tenace	.30	.15	.09
80	Tom Seaver	7.00	3.50	2.00
81	Frank Duffy	.20	.10	.06
82	Dave Giusti	.20	.10	.06
83	Orlando Cepeda	1.00	.50	.30
84	Rick Wise	.25	.13	.08
85	Joe Morgan	2.75	1.50	.80
86	Joe Ferguson	.20	.10	.06
87	Fergie Jenkins	1.25	.60	.40
88	Freddie Patek	.20	.10	.06
89	Jackie Brown	.20	.10	.06
90	Bobby Murcer	.40	.20	.12
91	Ken Forsch	.25	.13	.08
92	Paul Blair	.25	.13	.08
93	Rod Gilbreath	.20	.10	.06
94	Tigers Team	.90	.45	.25
95	Steve Carlton	7.00	3.50	2.00
96	*Jerry Hairston*	.40	.20	.12
97	Bob Bailey	.20	.10	.06
98	Bert Blyleven	1.00	.50	.30
99	Brewers Mgr./Coaches (Del Crandall, Harvey Kuenn, Joe Nossek, Jim Walton, Al Widmar)	.25	.13	.08
100	Willie Stargell	3.00	1.50	.90
101	Bobby Valentine	.30	.15	.09
102a	Bill Greif (Washington)	3.50	1.75	1.00
102b	Bill Greif (San Diego)	.25	.13	.08
103	Sal Bando	.40	.20	.12
104	Ron Bryant	.20	.10	.06
105	Carlton Fisk	2.00	1.00	.60
106	Harry Parker	.20	.10	.06
107	Alex Johnson	.20	.10	.06
108	Al Hrabosky	.25	.13	.08
109	Bob Grich	.40	.20	.12
110	Billy Williams	2.75	1.50	.80
111	Clay Carroll	.25	.13	.08
112	Dave Lopes	.40	.20	.12
113	Dick Drago	.20	.10	.06
114	Angels Team	.80	.40	.25
115	Willie Horton	.30	.15	.09
116	Jerry Reuss	.30	.15	.09
117	Ron Blomberg	.25	.13	.08
118	Bill Lee	.25	.13	.08
119	Phillies Mgr./Coaches (Carroll Beringer, Bill DeMars, Danny Ozark, Ray Ripplemeyer, Bobby Wine)	.25	.13	.08
120	Wilbur Wood	.30	.15	.09
121	Larry Lintz	.20	.10	.06
122	Jim Holt	.20	.10	.06
123	Nelson Briles	.20	.10	.06
124	Bob Coluccio	.20	.10	.06
125a	Nate Colbert (Washington)	3.50	1.75	1.00
125b	Nate Colbert (San Diego)	.30	.15	.09
126	Checklist 1-132	1.50	.70	.45
127	Tom Paciorek	.25	.13	.08
128	John Ellis	.20	.10	.06
129	Chris Speier	.25	.13	.08
130	Reggie Jackson	10.00	5.00	3.00
131	Bob Boone	.50	.25	.15
132	Felix Millan	.20	.10	.06
133	*David Clyde*	.30	.15	.09
134	Denis Menke	.20	.10	.06
135	Roy White	.40	.20	.12
136	Rick Reuschel	.80	.40	.25
137	Al Bumbry	.25	.13	.08
138	Ed Brinkman	.25	.13	.08
139	Aurelio Monteagudo	.20	.10	.06
140	Darrell Evans	.60	.30	.20
141	Pat Bourque	.20	.10	.06
142	Pedro Garcia	.20	.10	.06
143	Dick Woodson	.20	.10	.06
144	Dodgers Mgr./Coaches (Red Adams, Walter Alston, Monty Basgall, Jim Gilliam, Tom Lasorda)	1.25	.60	.40
145	Dock Ellis	.25	.13	.08
146	Ron Fairly	.30	.15	.09
147	Bart Johnson	.20	.10	.06
148a	Dave Hilton (Washington)	3.50	1.75	1.00
148b	Dave Hilton (San Diego)	.25	.13	.08
149	Mac Scarce	.20	.10	.06
150	John Mayberry	.30	.15	.09
151	Diego Segui	.20	.10	.06
152	Oscar Gamble	.30	.15	.09
153	Jon Matlack	.30	.15	.09
154	Astros Team	.80	.40	.25
155	Bert Campaneris	.40	.20	.12
156	Randy Moffitt	.20	.10	.06
157	Vic Harris	.20	.10	.06
158	Jack Billingham	.20	.10	.06
159	Jim Ray Hart	.25	.13	.08
160	Brooks Robinson	3.50	1.75	1.00
161	*Ray Burris*	.40	.20	.12
162	Bill Freehan	.40	.20	.12
163	Ken Berry	.20	.10	.06
164	Tom House	.20	.10	.06
165	Willie Davis	.40	.20	.12
166	Royals Mgr./Coaches (Galen Cisco, Harry Dunlop, Charlie Lau, Jack McKeon)	.25	.13	.08
167	Luis Tiant	.50	.25	.15
168	Danny Thompson	.25	.13	.08
169	*Steve Rogers*	.70	.35	.20
170	Bill Melton	.25	.13	.08
171	Eduardo Rodriguez	.20	.10	.06
172	Gene Clines	.20	.10	.06
173a	*Randy Jones* (Washington)	4.00	2.00	1.25
173b	*Randy Jones* (San Diego)	.40	.20	.12
174	Bill Robinson	.20	.10	.06
175	Reggie Cleveland	.20	.10	.06
176	John Lowenstein	.20	.10	.06
177	Dave Roberts	.20	.10	.06
178	Garry Maddox	.40	.20	.12
179	Mets Mgr./Coaches (Yogi Berra, Roy McMillan, Joe Pignatano, Rube Walker, Eddie Yost)	1.25	.60	.40
180	Ken Holtzman	.30	.15	.09
181	Cesar Geronimo	.25	.13	.08
182	Lindy McDaniel	.25	.13	.08
183	Johnny Oates	.20	.10	.06
184	Rangers Team	.80	.40	.25
185	Jose Cardenal	.25	.13	.08
186	Fred Scherman	.20	.10	.06
187	Don Baylor	.70	.35	.20
188	Rudy Meoli	.20	.10	.06
189	Jim Brewer	.20	.10	.06
190	Tony Oliva	.80	.40	.25
191	Al Fitzmorris	.20	.10	.06
192	Mario Guerrero	.20	.10	.06
193	Tom Walker	.20	.10	.06
194	Darrell Porter	.30	.15	.09
195	Carlos May	.25	.13	.08
196	Jim Fregosi	.40	.20	.12
197a	Vicente Romo (Washington)	3.50	1.75	1.00
197b	Vicente Romo (San Diego)	.25	.13	.08
198	Dave Cash	.20	.10	.06
199	Mike Kekich	.20	.10	.06
200	Cesar Cedeno	.40	.20	.12
201	Batting Leaders (Rod Carew, Pete Rose)	3.00	1.50	.90
202	Home Run Leaders (Reggie Jackson, Willie Stargell)	2.00	1.00	.60
203	Runs Batted In Leaders (Reggie Jackson, Willie Stargell)	2.00	1.00	.60
204	Stolen Base Leaders (Lou Brock, Tommy Harper)	1.25	.60	.40
205	Victory Leaders (Ron Bryant, Wilbur Wood)	.50	.25	.15
206	Earned Run Average Leaders (Jim Palmer, Tom Seaver)	2.00	1.00	.60
207	Strikeout Leaders (Nolan Ryan, Tom Seaver)	2.00	1.00	.60
208	Leading Firemen (John Hiller, Mike Marshall)	.50	.25	.15
209	Ted Sizemore	.20	.10	.06
210	Bill Singer	.25	.13	.08
211	Cubs Team	.80	.40	.25
212	Rollie Fingers	1.50	.70	.45
213	Dave Rader	.20	.10	.06
214	Billy Grabarkewitz	.20	.10	.06
215	Al Kaline	3.50	1.75	1.00
216	Ray Sadecki	.20	.10	.06
217	Tim Foli	.20	.10	.06

	NR MT	EX	VG
218 Johnny Briggs	.20	.10	.06
219 Doug Griffin	.20	.10	.06
220 Don Sutton	2.00	1.00	.60
221 White Sox Mgr./Coaches (Joe Lonnett, Jim Mahoney, Alex Monchak, Johnny Sain, Chuck Tanner)	.30	.15	.09
222 Ramon Hernandez	.20	.10	.06
223 Jeff Burroughs	.50	.25	.15
224 Roger Metzger	.20	.10	.06
225 Paul Splittorff	.25	.13	.08
226a Washington Nat'l. Team	6.00	3.00	1.75
226b Padres Team	1.00	.50	.30
227 Mike Lum	.20	.10	.06
228 Ted Kubiak	.20	.10	.06
229 Fritz Peterson	.30	.15	.09
230 Tony Perez	1.25	.60	.40
231 Dick Tidrow	.20	.10	.06
232 Steve Brye	.20	.10	.06
233 Jim Barr	.20	.10	.06
234 John Milner	.20	.10	.06
235 Dave McNally	.30	.15	.09
236 Cardinals Mgr./Coaches (Vern Benson, George Kissell, Johnny Lewis, Red Schoendienst, Barney Schultz)	.40	.20	.12
237 Ken Brett	.25	.13	.08
238 Fran Healy	.20	.10	.06
239 Bill Russell	.30	.15	.09
240 Joe Coleman	.25	.13	.08
241a Glenn Beckert (Washington)	4.00	2.00	1.25
241b Glenn Beckert (San Diego)	.30	.15	.09
242 Bill Gogolewski	.20	.10	.06
243 Bob Oliver	.20	.10	.06
244 Carl Morton	.20	.10	.06
245 Cleon Jones	.25	.13	.08
246 A's Team	1.25	.60	.40
247 Rick Miller	.20	.10	.06
248 Tom Hall	.20	.10	.06
249 George Mitterwald	.20	.10	.06
250a Willie McCovey (Washington)	25.00	12.50	7.50
250b Willie McCovey (San Diego)	4.00	2.00	1.25
251 Graig Nettles	1.50	.70	.45
252 Dave Parker	25.00	12.50	7.50
253 John Boccabella	.20	.10	.06
254 Stan Bahnsen	.20	.10	.06
255 Larry Bowa	.40	.20	.12
256 Tom Griffin	.20	.10	.06
257 Buddy Bell	1.25	.60	.40
258 Jerry Morales	.20	.10	.06
259 Bob Reynolds	.20	.10	.06
260 Ted Simmons	.80	.40	.25
261 Jerry Bell	.20	.10	.06
262 Ed Kirkpatrick	.20	.10	.06
263 Checklist 133-264	1.50	.70	.45
264 Joe Rudi	.40	.20	.12
265 Tug McGraw	.60	.30	.20
266 Jim Northrup	.25	.13	.08
267 Andy Messersmith	.30	.15	.09
268 Tom Grieve	.20	.10	.06
269 Bob Johnson	.20	.10	.06
270 Ron Santo	.50	.25	.15
271 Bill Hands	.20	.10	.06
272 Paul Casanova	.20	.10	.06
273 Checklist 265-396	1.50	.70	.45
274 Fred Beene	.25	.13	.08
275 Ron Hunt	.25	.13	.08
276 Angels Mgr./Coaches (Tom Morgan, Salty Parker, Jimmie Reese, John Roseboro, Bobby Winkles)	.20	.10	.06
277 Gary Nolan	.20	.10	.06
278 Cookie Rojas	.20	.10	.06
279 Jim Crawford	.20	.10	.06
280 Carl Yastrzemski	9.00	4.50	2.75
281 Giants Team	.80	.40	.25
282 Doyle Alexander	.40	.20	.12
283 Mike Schmidt	55.00	28.00	16.50
284 Dave Duncan	.20	.10	.06
285 Reggie Smith	.40	.20	.12
286 Tony Muser	.20	.10	.06
287 Clay Kirby	.20	.10	.06
288 Gorman Thomas	1.50	.70	.45
289 Rick Auerbach	.20	.10	.06
290 Vida Blue	.60	.30	.20
291 Don Hahn	.20	.10	.06
292 Chuck Seelbach	.20	.10	.06
293 Milt May	.20	.10	.06
294 Steve Foucault	.20	.10	.06
295 Rick Monday	.30	.15	.09
296 Ray Corbin	.20	.10	.06
297 Hal Breeden	.20	.10	.06
298 Roric Harrison	.20	.10	.06
299 Gene Michael	.30	.15	.09

	NR MT	EX	VG
300 Pete Rose	15.00	7.50	4.50
301 Bob Montgomery	.20	.10	.06
302 Rudy May	.25	.13	.08
303 George Hendrick	.30	.15	.09
304 Don Wilson	.20	.10	.06
305 Tito Fuentes	.20	.10	.06
306 Orioles Mgr./Coaches (George Bamberger, Jim Frey, Billy Hunter, George Staller, Earl Weaver)	.70	.35	.20
307 Luis Melendez	.20	.10	.06
308 Bruce Dal Canton	.20	.10	.06
309a Dave Roberts (Washington)	3.50	1.75	1.00
309b Dave Roberts (San Diego)	.25	.13	.08
310 Terry Forster	.30	.15	.09
311 Jerry Grote	.25	.13	.08
312 Deron Johnson	.20	.10	.06
313 Berry Lersch	.20	.10	.06
314 Brewers Team	.80	.40	.25
315 Ron Cey	.60	.30	.20
316 Jim Perry	.40	.20	.12
317 Richie Zisk	.30	.15	.09
318 Jim Merritt	.20	.10	.06
319 Randy Hundley	.20	.10	.06
320 Dusty Baker	.40	.20	.12
321 Steve Braun	.20	.10	.06
322 Ernie McAnally	.20	.10	.06
323 Richie Scheinblum	.20	.10	.06
324 Steve Kline	.25	.13	.08
325 Tommy Harper	.25	.13	.08
326 Reds Mgr./Coaches (Sparky Anderson, Alex Grammas, Ted Kluszewski, George Scherger, Larry Shepard)	.50	.25	.15
327 Tom Timmermann	.20	.10	.06
328 Skip Jutze	.20	.10	.06
329 Mark Belanger	.30	.15	.09
330 Juan Marichal	2.75	1.50	.80
331 All Star Catchers (Johnny Bench, Carlton Fisk)	2.00	1.00	.60
332 All Star First Basemen (Hank Aaron, Dick Allen)	2.00	1.00	.60
333 All Star Second Basemen (Rod Carew, Joe Morgan)	2.00	1.00	.60
334 All Star Third Basemen (Brooks Robinson, Ron Santo)	1.25	.60	.40
335 All Star Shortstops (Bert Campaneris, Chris Speier)	.40	.20	.12
336 All Star Left Fielders (Bobby Murcer, Pete Rose)	2.50	1.25	.70
337 All Star Center Fielders (Cesar Cedeno, Amos Otis)	.40	.20	.12
338 All Star Right Fielders (Reggie Jackson, Billy Williams)	2.00	1.00	.60
339 All Star Pitchers (Jim Hunter, Rick Wise)	.80	.40	.25
340 Thurman Munson	4.00	2.00	1.25
341 Dan Driessen	.80	.40	.25
342 Jim Lonborg	.30	.15	.09
343 Royals Team	.80	.40	.25
344 Mike Caldwell	.25	.13	.08
345 Bill North	.25	.13	.08
346 Ron Reed	.25	.13	.08
347 Sandy Alomar	.20	.10	.06
348 Pete Richert	.20	.10	.06
349 John Vukovich	.20	.10	.06
350 Bob Gibson	2.75	1.50	.80
351 Dwight Evans	3.50	1.75	1.00
352 Bill Stoneman	.20	.10	.06
353 Rich Coggins	.20	.10	.06
354 Cubs Mgr./Coaches (Hank Aguirre, Whitey Lockman, Jim Marshall, J.C. Martin, Al Spangler)	.20	.10	.06
355 Dave Nelson	.20	.10	.06
356 Jerry Koosman	.40	.20	.12
357 Buddy Bradford	.20	.10	.06
358 Dal Maxvill	.25	.13	.08
359 Brent Strom	.20	.10	.06
360 Greg Luzinski	.70	.35	.20
361 Don Carrithers	.20	.10	.06
362 Hal King	.20	.10	.06
363 Yankees Team	1.25	.60	.40
364a Clarence Gaston (Washington)	3.50	1.75	1.00
364b Clarence Gaston (San Diego)	.25	.13	.08
365 Steve Busby	.25	.13	.08
366 Larry Hisle	.25	.13	.08
367 Norm Cash	.50	.25	.15
368 Manny Mota	.40	.20	.12
369 Paul Lindblad	.20	.10	.06
370 Bob Watson	.25	.13	.08
371 Jim Slaton	.20	.10	.06
372 Ken Reitz	.20	.10	.06
373 John Curtis	.20	.10	.06

		NR MT	EX	VG
374	Marty Perez	.20	.10	.06
375	Earl Williams	.20	.10	.06
376	Jorge Orta	.25	.13	.08
377	Ron Woods	.20	.10	.06
378	Burt Hooton	.30	.15	.09
379	Rangers Mgr./Coaches (Art Fowler, Frank Lucchesi, Billy Martin, Jackie Moore, Charlie Silvera)	.80	.40	.25
380	Bud Harrelson	.25	.13	.08
381	Charlie Sands	.20	.10	.06
382	Bob Moose	.20	.10	.06
383	Phillies Team	.80	.40	.25
384	Chris Chambliss	.40	.20	.12
385	Don Gullett	.25	.13	.08
386	Gary Matthews	.60	.30	.20
387a	Rich Morales (Washington)	3.50	1.75	1.00
387b	Rich Morales (San Diego)	.25	.13	.08
388	Phil Roof	.20	.10	.06
389	Gates Brown	.20	.10	.06
390	Lou Piniella	.70	.35	.20
391	Billy Champion	.20	.10	.06
392	Dick Green	.20	.10	.06
393	Orlando Pena	.20	.10	.06
394	Ken Henderson	.20	.10	.06
395	Doug Rader	.20	.10	.06
396	Tommy Davis	.40	.20	.12
397	George Stone	.20	.10	.06
398	Duke Sims	.25	.13	.08
399	Mike Paul	.20	.10	.06
400	Harmon Killebrew	3.00	1.50	.90
401	Elliott Maddox	.20	.10	.06
402	Jim Rooker	.20	.10	.06
403	Red Sox Mgr./Coaches (Don Bryant, Darrell Johnson, Eddie Popowski, Lee Stange, Don Zimmer)	.25	.13	.08
404	Jim Howarth	.20	.10	.06
405	Ellie Rodriguez	.20	.10	.06
406	Steve Arlin	.20	.10	.06
407	Jim Wohlford	.20	.10	.06
408	Charlie Hough	.40	.20	.12
409	Ike Brown	.20	.10	.06
410	Pedro Borbon	.20	.10	.06
411	Frank Baker	.20	.10	.06
412	Chuck Taylor	.20	.10	.06
413	Don Money	.25	.13	.08
414	Checklist 397-528	1.50	.70	.45
415	Gary Gentry	.20	.10	.06
416	White Sox Team	.80	.40	.25
417	Rich Folkers	.20	.10	.06
418	Walt Williams	.20	.10	.06
419	Wayne Twitchell	.20	.10	.06
420	Ray Fosse	.20	.10	.06
421	Dan Fife	.20	.10	.06
422	Gonzalo Marquez	.20	.10	.06
423	Fred Stanley	.25	.13	.08
424	Jim Beauchamp	.20	.10	.06
425	Pete Broberg	.20	.10	.06
426	Rennie Stennett	.20	.10	.06
427	Bobby Bolin	.20	.10	.06
428	Gary Sutherland	.20	.10	.06
429	Dick Lange	.20	.10	.06
430	Matty Alou	.40	.20	.12
431	*Gene Garber*	.50	.25	.15
432	Chris Arnold	.20	.10	.06
433	Lerrin LaGrow	.20	.10	.06
434	Ken McMullen	.20	.10	.06
435	Dave Concepcion	.70	.35	.20
436	Don Hood	.20	.10	.06
437	Jim Lyttle	.20	.10	.06
438	Ed Herrmann	.20	.10	.06
439	Norm Miller	.20	.10	.06
440	Jim Kaat	1.25	.60	.40
441	Tom Ragland	.20	.10	.06
442	Alan Foster	.20	.10	.06
443	Tom Hutton	.20	.10	.06
444	Vic Davalillo	.25	.13	.08
445	George Medich	.30	.15	.09
446	Len Randle	.20	.10	.06
447	Twins Mgr./Coaches (Vern Morgan, Frank Quilici, Bob Rodgers, Ralph Rowe)	.20	.10	.06
448	Ron Hodges	.20	.10	.06
449	Tom McCraw	.20	.10	.06
450	Rich Hebner	.25	.13	.08
451	Tommy John	1.50	.70	.45
452	Gene Hiser	.20	.10	.06
453	Balor Moore	.20	.10	.06
454	Kurt Bevacqua	.20	.10	.06
455	Tom Bradley	.20	.10	.06
456	*Dave Winfield*	50.00	30.00	15.00
457	Chuck Goggin	.20	.10	.06
458	Jim Ray	.20	.10	.06
459	Reds Team	.90	.45	.25
460	Boog Powell	.90	.45	.25
461	John Odom	.25	.13	.08
462	Luis Alvarado	.20	.10	.06
463	Pat Dobson	.30	.15	.09
464	Jose Cruz	.80	.40	.25
465	Dick Bosman	.20	.10	.06
466	Dick Billings	.20	.10	.06
467	Winston Llenas	.20	.10	.06
468	Pepe Frias	.20	.10	.06
469	Joe Decker	.20	.10	.06
470	A.L. Playoffs	2.00	1.00	.60
471	N.L. Playoffs	.80	.40	.25
472	World Series Game 1	.80	.40	.25
473	World Series Game 2	2.00	1.00	.60
474	World Series Game 3	.80	.40	.25
475	World Series Game 4	.80	.40	.25
476	World Series Game 5	.80	.40	.25
477	World Series Game 6	2.00	1.00	.60
478	World Series Game 7	.80	.40	.25
479	World Series Summary	.80	.40	.25
480	Willie Crawford	.20	.10	.06
481	Jerry Terrell	.20	.10	.06
482	Bob Didier	.20	.10	.06
483	Braves Team	.80	.40	.25
484	Carmen Fanzone	.20	.10	.06
485	Felipe Alou	.40	.20	.12
486	Steve Stone	.40	.20	.12
487	Ted Martinez	.20	.10	.06
488	Andy Etchebarren	.20	.10	.06
489	Pirates Mgr./Coaches (Don Leppert, Bill Mazeroski, Danny Murtaugh, Don Osborn, Bob Skinner)	.30	.15	.09
490	Vada Pinson	.70	.35	.20
491	Roger Nelson	.20	.10	.06
492	Mike Rogodzinski	.20	.10	.06
493	Joe Hoerner	.20	.10	.06
494	Ed Goodson	.20	.10	.06
495	Dick McAuliffe	.25	.13	.08
496	Tom Murphy	.20	.10	.06
497	Bobby Mitchell	.20	.10	.06
498	Pat Corrales	.40	.20	.12
499	Rusty Torres	.20	.10	.06
500	Lee May	.40	.20	.12
501	Eddie Leon	.20	.10	.06
502	Dave LaRoche	.20	.10	.06
503	Eric Soderholm	.20	.10	.06
504	Joe Niekro	.40	.20	.12
505	Bill Buckner	.50	.25	.15
506	Ed Farmer	.20	.10	.06
507	Larry Stahl	.20	.10	.06
508	Expos Team	.80	.40	.25
509	Jesse Jefferson	.20	.10	.06
510	Wayne Garrett	.20	.10	.06
511	Toby Harrah	.30	.15	.09
512	Joe Lahoud	.20	.10	.06
513	Jim Campanis	.20	.10	.06
514	Paul Schaal	.20	.10	.06
515	Willie Montanez	.25	.13	.08
516	Horacio Pina	.20	.10	.06
517	Mike Hegan	.25	.13	.08
518	Derrel Thomas	.20	.10	.06
519	Bill Sharp	.20	.10	.06
520	Tim McCarver	.60	.30	.20
521	Indians Mgr./Coaches (Ken Aspromonte, Clay Bryant, Tony Pacheco)	.20	.10	.06
522	J.R. Richard	.30	.15	.09
523	Cecil Cooper	1.50	.70	.45
524	Bill Plummer	.20	.10	.06
525	Clyde Wright	.20	.10	.06
526	Frank Tepedino	.20	.10	.06
527	Bobby Darwin	.20	.10	.06
528	Bill Bonham	.20	.10	.06
529	Horace Clarke	.25	.13	.08
530	Mickey Stanley	.25	.13	.08
531	Expos Mgr./Coaches (Dave Bristol, Larry Doby, Gene Mauch, Cal McLish, Jerry Zimmerman)	.40	.20	.12
532	Skip Lockwood	.20	.10	.06
533	Mike Phillips	.20	.10	.06
534	Eddie Watt	.20	.10	.06
535	Bob Tolan	.25	.13	.08
536	Duffy Dyer	.20	.10	.06
537	Steve Mingori	.20	.10	.06
538	Cesar Tovar	.20	.10	.06
539	Lloyd Allen	.20	.10	.06
540	Bob Robertson	.20	.10	.06
541	Indians Team	.80	.40	.25
542	Rich Gossage	2.00	1.00	.60
543	Danny Cater	.20	.10	.06
544	Ron Schueler	.20	.10	.06

	NR MT	EX	VG
545 Billy Conigliaro	.20	.10	.06
546 Mike Corkins	.20	.10	.06
547 Glenn Borgmann	.20	.10	.06
548 Sonny Siebert	.20	.10	.06
549 Mike Jorgensen	.20	.10	.06
550 Sam McDowell	.40	.20	.12
551 Von Joshua	.20	.10	.06
552 Denny Doyle	.20	.10	.06
553 Jim Willoughby	.20	.10	.06
554 Tim Johnson	.20	.10	.06
555 Woodie Fryman	.25	.13	.08
556 Dave Campbell	.20	.10	.06
557 Jim McGlothlin	.20	.10	.06
558 Bill Fahey	.20	.10	.06
559 Darrel Chaney	.20	.10	.06
560 Mike Cuellar	.40	.20	.12
561 Ed Kranepool	.30	.15	.09
562 Jack Aker	.20	.10	.06
563 Hal McRae	.40	.20	.12
564 Mike Ryan	.20	.10	.06
565 Milt Wilcox	.25	.13	.08
566 Jackie Hernandez	.20	.10	.06
567 Red Sox Team	.90	.45	.25
568 Mike Torrez	.25	.13	.08
569 Rick Dempsey	.40	.20	.12
570 Ralph Garr	.30	.15	.09
571 Rich Hand	.20	.10	.06
572 Enzo Hernandez	.20	.10	.06
573 Mike Adams	.20	.10	.06
574 Bill Parsons	.20	.10	.06
575 Steve Garvey	9.00	4.50	2.75
576 Scipio Spinks	.20	.10	.06
577 Mike Sadek	.20	.10	.06
578 Ralph Houk	.40	.20	.12
579 Cecil Upshaw	.20	.10	.06
580 Jim Spencer	.20	.10	.06
581 Fred Norman	.20	.10	.06
582 *Bucky Dent*	.90	.45	.25
583 Marty Pattin	.20	.10	.06
584 Ken Rudolph	.20	.10	.06
585 Merv Rettenmund	.25	.13	.08
586 Jack Brohamer	.20	.10	.06
587 *Larry Christenson*	.25	.13	.08
588 Hal Lanier	.40	.20	.12
589 Boots Day	.20	.10	.06
590 Rogelio Moret	.20	.10	.06
591 Sonny Jackson	.20	.10	.06
592 Ed Bane	.20	.10	.06
593 Steve Yeager	.25	.13	.08
594 Leroy Stanton	.20	.10	.06
595 Steve Blass	.25	.13	.08
596 Rookie Pitchers (Wayne Garland, Fred Holdsworth, *Mark Littell*, Dick Pole)	.30	.15	.09
597 Rookie Shortstops (Dave Chalk, John Gamble, Pete Mackanin, *Manny Trillo*) .80	.40	.25
598 Rookie Outfielders (Dave Augustine, *Ken Griffey*, Steve Ontiveros, Jim Tyrone) 4.00	2.00	1.25
599a Rookie Pitchers (Ron Diorio, Dave Freisleben, Frank Riccelli, Greg Shanahan) (Freisleben- Washington) .80	.40	.25
599b Rookie Pitchers (Ron Diorio, Dave Freisleben, Frank Riccelli, Greg Shanahan) (Freisleben- San Diego large print) 3.50	1.75	1.00
599c Rookie Pitchers (Ron Diorio, Dave Freisleben, Frank Riccelli, Greg Shanahan) (Freisleben- San Diego small print) 6.00	3.00	1.75
600 Rookie Infielders (Ron Cash, Jim Cox, *Bill Madlock*, Reggie Sanders) 2.25	1.25	.70
601 Rookie Outfielders (Ed Armbrister, Rich Bladt, *Brian Downing, Bake McBride*) 2.00	1.00	.60
602 Rookie Pitchers (Glenn Abbott, Rick Henninger, Craig Swan, Dan Vossler) .20	.10	.06
603 Rookie Catchers (Barry Foote, Tom Lundstedt, *Charlie Moore*, Sergio Robles) .30	.15	.09
604 Rookie Infielders (Terry Hughes, John Knox, *Andy Thornton, Frank White*) 3.00	1.50	.90
605 Rookie Pitchers (Vic Albury, Ken Frailing, Kevin Kobel, *Frank Tanana*) 1.50	.70	.45
606 Rookie Outfielders (Jim Fuller, Wilbur Howard, Tommy Smith, Otto Velez) .25	.13	.08
607 Rookie Shortstops (Leo Foster, Tom Heintzelman, Dave Rosello, *Frank Taveras*) .25	.13	.08
608a Rookie Pitchers (Bob Apodaco, Dick Baney, John D'Acquisto, Mike Wallace) 2.50	1.25	.70
608b Rookie Pitchers (Bob Apodaca, Dick Baney, John D'Acquisto, Mike Wallace) .25	.13	.08
609 Rico Petrocelli	.30	.15	.09

	NR MT	EX	VG
610 Dave Kingman	.90	.45	.25
611 Rick Stelmaszek	.20	.10	.06
612 Luke Walker	.20	.10	.06
613 Dan Monzon	.20	.10	.06
614 Adrian Devine	.20	.10	.06
615 Johnny Jeter	.20	.10	.06
616 Larry Gura	.25	.13	.08
617 Ted Ford	.20	.10	.06
618 Jim Mason	.20	.10	.06
619 Mike Anderson	.20	.10	.06
620 Al Downing	.25	.13	.08
621 Bernie Carbo	.20	.10	.06
622 Phil Gagliano	.20	.10	.06
623 Celerino Sanchez	.25	.13	.08
624 Bob Miller	.20	.10	.06
625 Ollie Brown	.20	.10	.06
626 Pirates Team	.80	.40	.25
627 Carl Taylor	.20	.10	.06
628 Ivan Murrell	.20	.10	.06
629 Rusty Staub	.70	.35	.20
630 Tommie Agee	.25	.13	.08
631 Steve Barber	.20	.10	.06
632 George Culver	.20	.10	.06
633 Dave Hamilton	.20	.10	.06
634 Braves Mgr./Coaches (Jim Busby, Eddie Mathews, Connie Ryan, Ken Silvestri, Herm Starrette)	.90	.45	.25
635 John Edwards	.20	.10	.06
636 Dave Goltz	.25	.13	.08
637 Checklist 529-660	1.50	.70	.45
638 Ken Sanders	.20	.10	.06
639 Joe Lovitto	.20	.10	.06
640 Milt Pappas	.40	.20	.12
641 Chuck Brinkman	.20	.10	.06
642 Terry Harmon	.20	.10	.06
643 Dodgers Team	.90	.45	.25
644 Wayne Granger	.25	.13	.08
645 Ken Boswell	.20	.10	.06
646 George Foster	1.25	.60	.40
647 *Juan Beniquez*	.70	.35	.20
648 Terry Crowley	.20	.10	.06
649 Fernando Gonzalez	.20	.10	.06
650 Mike Epstein	.20	.10	.06
651 Leron Lee	.20	.10	.06
652 Gail Hopkins	.20	.10	.06
653 Bob Stinson	.20	.10	.06
654a Jesus Alou (no position listed)	5.00	2.50	1.50
654b Jesus Alou (Outfield)	.40	.20	.12
655 Mike Tyson	.20	.10	.06
656 Adrian Garrett	.20	.10	.06
657 Jim Shellenback	.20	.10	.06
658 Lee Lacy	.30	.15	.09
659 Joe Lis	.20	.10	.06
660 Larry Dierker	.50	.15	.09

1974 Topps Deckle Edge

These borderless 2-7/8" by 5" cards feature a black and white photograph with a facsimile autograph on the front. The backs have in handwritten script the player's name, team, position and the date and location of the picture. Below is a mock newspaper clipping providing a detail from the player's career. The cards take their names from their specially cut edges which give them a scalloped appearance. The 72-card set was a test issue and received rather limited distribution.

	NR MT	EX	VG
Complete Set:	2000.00	1000.00	600.00
Common Player:	10.00	5.00	3.00

		NR MT	EX	VG
1	Amos Otis	10.00	5.00	3.00
2	Darrell Evans	15.00	7.50	4.50
3	Robert Gibson	50.00	25.00	15.00
4	David Nelson	10.00	5.00	3.00
5	Steven N. Carlton	80.00	40.00	25.00
6	Jim "Catfish" Hunter	40.00	20.00	12.00
7	Thurman Munson	50.00	25.00	15.00
8	Bob Grich	15.00	7.50	4.50
9	Tom Seaver	100.00	50.00	30.00
10	Ted L. Simmons	20.00	10.00	6.00
11	Robert J. Valentine	10.00	5.00	3.00
12	Don Sutton	25.00	12.50	7.50
13	Wilbur Wood	10.00	5.00	3.00
14	Douglas Lee Rader	10.00	5.00	3.00
15	Chris Chambliss	10.00	5.00	3.00
16	Pete Rose	200.00	100.00	60.00
17	John F. Hiller	10.00	5.00	3.00
18	Burt Hooton	10.00	5.00	3.00
19	Tim Foli	10.00	5.00	3.00
20	Louis Brock	60.00	30.00	20.00
21	Ron Bryant	10.00	5.00	3.00
22	Manuel Sanguillen	10.00	5.00	3.00
23	Bobby Tolan	10.00	5.00	3.00
24	Greg Luzinski	15.00	7.50	4.50
25	Brooks Robinson	60.00	30.00	18.00
26	Felix Millan	10.00	5.00	3.00
27	Luis Tiant	15.00	7.50	4.50
28	Willie McCovey	60.00	30.00	20.00
29	Chris Speier	10.00	5.00	3.00
30	George Scott	10.00	5.00	3.00
31	Willie Stargell	50.00	25.00	15.00
32	Rod Carew	100.00	50.00	30.00
33	Leslie Charles Spikes	10.00	5.00	3.00
34	Nate Colbert	10.00	5.00	3.00
35	Richie Hebner	10.00	5.00	3.00
36	Bobby Lee Bonds	15.00	7.50	4.50
37	Buddy Bell	15.00	7.50	4.50
38	Claude Osteen	10.00	5.00	3.00
39	Richard A. Allen	15.00	7.50	4.50
40	Bill Russell	10.00	5.00	3.00
41	Nolan Ryan	175.00	87.00	52.00
42	Willie Davis	15.00	7.50	4.50
43	Carl Yastrzemski	125.00	62.00	37.00
44	Jonathon T. Matlack	10.00	5.00	3.00
45	Jim Palmer	30.00	15.00	9.00
46	Dagoberto Campaneris	15.00	7.50	4.50
47	Bert Blyleven	20.00	10.00	6.00
48	Jeff Burroughs	10.00	5.00	3.00
49	James W. Colborn	10.00	5.00	3.00
50	Dave Johnson	15.00	7.50	4.50
51	John Mayberry	10.00	5.00	3.00
52	Don Kessinger	10.00	5.00	3.00
53	Joseph H. Coleman	10.00	5.00	3.00
54	Tony Perez	20.00	10.00	6.00
55	Jose Cardenal	10.00	5.00	3.00
56	Paul Splittorff	10.00	5.00	3.00
57	Henry Aaron	150.00	75.00	45.00
58	David May	10.00	5.00	3.00
59	Fergie Jenkins	30.00	15.00	9.00
60	Ron Blomberg	10.00	5.00	3.00
61	Reggie Jackson	150.00	75.00	45.00
62	Tony Oliva	15.00	7.50	4.50
63	Bobby Ray Murcer	15.00	7.50	4.50
64	Carlton Fisk	20.00	10.00	6.00
65	Stephen Rogers	10.00	5.00	3.00
66	Frank Robinson	40.00	20.00	12.00
67	Joe Ferguson	10.00	5.00	3.00
68	Bill Melton	10.00	5.00	3.00
69	Robert Watson	10.00	5.00	3.00
70	Larry Bowa	15.00	7.50	4.50
71	Johnny Bench	90.00	45.00	27.00
72	Willie Horton	10.00	5.00	3.00

1974 Topps Puzzles

One of many test issues by Topps in the mid-1970s, the 12-player jigsaw puzzle set was an innovation which never caught on with collectors. The 40-piece puzzles (4-3/4" by 7-1/2") feature color photos with a decorative lozenge at bottom naming the player, team and position. The puzzles came in individual wrappers.

	NR MT	EX	VG
Complete Set:	600.00	300.00	200.00
Common Player:	12.00	6.00	3.50

		NR MT	EX	VG
(1)	Hank Aaron	80.00	40.00	25.00
(2)	Dick Allen	12.00	6.00	3.50
(3)	Johnny Bench	75.00	38.00	23.00
(4)	Bobby Bonds	12.00	6.00	3.50
(5)	Bob Gibson	35.00	17.50	10.50
(6)	Reggie Jackson	60.00	30.00	18.00
(7)	Bobby Murcer	12.00	6.00	3.50
(8)	Jim Palmer	50.00	25.00	15.00
(9)	Nolan Ryan	80.00	40.00	24.00
(10)	Tom Seaver	80.00	40.00	24.00
(11)	Willie Stargell	30.00	15.00	9.00
(12)	Carl Yastrzemski	70.00	35.00	21.00

1974 Topps Stamps

Topps continued to market baseball stamps in 1974 through the release of 240 unnumbered stamps featuring color player portraits. The player's name, team and position are found in an oval at the bottom of the 1" by 1-1/2" stamps. The stamps, sold separately rather than issued as an insert, came in strips of six which were then pasted in an appropriate team album designed to hold 10 stamps.

	NR MT	EX	VG
Complete Sheet Set:	100.00	50.00	30.00
Common Sheet:	1.00	.50	.30
Complete Stamp Album Set:	75.00	37.00	22.00
Single Stamp Album:	2.50	1.25	.70

		NR MT	EX	VG
(1)	Hank Aaron, Luis Aparicio, Bob Bailey, Johnny Bench, Ron Blomberg, Bob Boone, Lou Brock, Bud Harrelson, Randy Jones, Dave Rader, Nolan Ryan, Joe Torre	6.00	3.00	1.75
(2)	Buddy Bell, Steve Braun, Jerry Grote, Tommy Helms, Bill Lee, Mike Lum, Dave May, Brooks Robinson, Bill Russell, Del Unser, Wilbur Wood, Carl Yastrzemski	10.00	5.00	3.00
(3)	Jerry Bell, Jerry Bell, Jim Colborn, Toby Harrah, Ken Henderson, John Hiller, Randy Hundley, Don Kessinger, Jerry Koosman, Dave Lopes, Felix Millan, Thurman Munson, Ted Simmons	3.50	1.75	1.00
(4)	Jerry Bell, Bill Buckner, Jim Colborn, Ken Henderson, Don Kessinger, Felix Millan, George Mitterwald, Dave Roberts, Ted Simmons, Jim Slaton, Charlie Spikes, Paul			

	NR MT	EX	VG
Splittorff	1.00	.50	.30

(5)   Glenn Beckert, Jim Bibby, Bill Buckner, Jim Lonborg, George Mitterwald, Dave Parker, Dave Roberts, Jim Slaton, Reggie Smith, Charlie Spikes, Paul Splittorff, Bob Watson   3.50   1.75   1.00

(6)   Paul Blair, Bobby Bonds, Ed Brinkman, Norm Cash, Mike Epstein, Tommy Harper, Mike Marshall, Phil Niekro, Cookie Rojas, George Scott, Mel Stottlemyre, Jim Wynn   3.50   1.75   1.00

(7)   Jack Billingham, Reggie Cleveland, Bobby Darwin, Dave Duncan, Tim Foli, Ed Goodson, Cleon Jones, Mickey Lolich, George Medich, John Milner, Rick Monday, Bobby Murcer   1.00   .50   .30

(8)   Steve Carlton, Orlando Cepeda, Joe Decker, Reggie Jackson, Dave Johnson, John Mayberry, Bill Melton, Roger Metzger, Dave Nelson, Jerry Reuss, Jim Spencer, Bobby Valentine   6.00   3.00   1.75

(9)   Dan Driessen, Pedro Garcia, Grant Jackson, Al Kaline, Clay Kirby, Carlos May, Willie Montanez, Rogelio Moret, Jim Palmer, Doug Rader, J. R. Richard, Frank Robinson   3.50   1.75   1.00

(10)   Pedro Garcia, Ralph Garr, Wayne Garrett, Ron Hunt, Al Kaline, Fred Kendall, Carlos May, Jim Palmer, Doug Rader, Frank Robinson, Rick Wise, Richie Zisk   3.50   1.75   1.00

(11)   Dusty Baker, Larry Bowa, Steve Busby, Chris Chambliss, Dock Ellis, Cesar Geronimo, Fran Healy, Deron Johnson, Jorge Orta, Joe Rudi, Mickey Stanley, Rennie Stennett   3.50   1.75   1.00

(12)   Bob Coluccio, Ray Corbin, John Ellis, Oscar Gamble, Dave Giusti, Bill Greif, Alex Johnson, Mike Jorgensen, Andy Messersmith, Elias Sosa, Willie Stargell   3.50   1.75   1.00

(13)   Ron Bryant, Nate Colbert, Jose Cruz, Dan Driessen, Billy Grabarkewitz, Don Gullett, Willie Horton, Grant Jackson, Clay Kirby, Willie Montanez, Rogelio Moret, J. R. Richard   1.00   .50   .30

(14)   Carlton Fisk, Bill Freehan, Bobby Grich, Vic Harris, George Hendrick, Ed Herrmann, Jim Holt, Ken Holtzman, Fergie Jenkins, Lou Piniella, Steve Rogers, Ken Singleton   3.50   1.75   1.00

(15)   Stan Bahnsen, Sal Bando, Mark Belanger, David Clyde, Willie Crawford, Burt Hooton, Jon Matlack, Tim McCarver, Joe Morgan, Gene Tenace, Dick Tidrow, Dave Winfield   5.00   2.50   1.50

(16)   Hank Aaron, Stan Bahnsen, Bob Bailey, Johnny Bench, Bob Boone, Joe Matlack, Tim McCarver, Joe Morgan, Dave Rader, Gene Tenace, Dick Tidrow, Joe Torre   5.00   2.50   1.50

(17)   John Boccabella, Frank Duffy, Darrell Evans, Sparky Lyle, Lee May, Don Money, Bill North, Ted Sizemore, Chris Speier, Wayne Twitchell, Billy Williams, Earl Williams   1.00   .50   .30

(18)   John Boccabella, Bobby Darwin, Frank Duffy, Dave Duncan, Tim Foli, Cleon Jones, Mickey Lolich, Sparky Lyle, Lee May, Rick Monday, Bill North, Billy Williams   1.00   .50   .30

(19)   Don Baylor, Vida Blue, Tom Bradley, Jose Cardenal, Ron Cey, Greg Luzinski, Johnny Oates, Tony Oliva, Al Oliver, Tony Perez, Darrell Porter, Roy White   3.50   1.75   1.00

(20)   Pedro Borbon, Rod Carew, Roric Harrison, Jim Hunter, Ed Kirkpatrick, Garry Maddox, Gene Michael, Rick Miller, Claude Osteen, Amos Otis, Rich Reuschel, Mike Tyson   5.00   2.50   1.50

(21)   Sandy Alomar, Bert Campaneris, Tommy Davis, Joe Ferguson, Tito Fuentes, Jerry Morales, Carl Morton, Gaylord Perry, Vada Pinson, Dave Roberts, Ellie Rodriguez   3.50   1.75   1.00

(22)   Dick Allen, Jeff Burroughs, Joe Coleman, Terry Forster, Bob Gibson, Harmon Killebrew, Tug McGraw, Bob Oliver, Steve Renko, Pete Rose, Luis Tiant, Otto Velez   13.00   6.50   4.00

(23)   Johnny Briggs, Willie Davis, Jim Fregosi, Rich Hebner, Pat Kelly, Dave Kingman, Willie McCovey, Graig Nettles, Freddie Patek, Marty Pattin, Manny Sanguillen, Richie Scheinblum   5.00   2.50   1.50

(24)   Bert Blyleven, Nelson Briles, Cesar Cedeno, Ron Fairly, Johnny Grubb, Dave McNally, Aurelio Rodriguez, Ron Santo, Tom Seaver, Bill Singer, Bill Sudakis, Don Sutton   6.00   3.00   1.75

1974 Topps Team Checklists

This set is a repeat of the 1973 mystery set in the form of 24 unnumbered 2-1/2" by 3-1/2" checklist cards. As with the 1973 set, the 1974s feature a team name on the front at the top with a white panel and a number of facsimile autographs below. Backs feature the team name and a checklist. The big difference between the 1973 and 1974 checklists is that the 1973s have blue borders while the 1974s have a red border. The 1974s were inserted into packages of the regular issue Topps cards.

		NR MT	EX	VG
Complete Set:		10.00	5.00	3.00
Common Checklist:		.50	.25	.15
(1)	Atlanta Braves	.50	.25	.15
(2)	Baltimore Orioles	.50	.25	.15
(3)	Boston Red Sox	.50	.25	.15
(4)	California Angels	.50	.25	.15
(5)	Chicago Cubs	.50	.25	.15
(6)	Chicago White Sox	.50	.25	.15
(7)	Cincinnati Reds	.50	.25	.15
(8)	Cleveland Indians	.50	.25	.15
(9)	Detroit Tigers	.50	.25	.15
(10)	Houston Astros	.50	.25	.15
(11)	Kansas City Royals	.50	.25	.15
(12)	Los Angeles Dodgers	.50	.25	.15
(13)	Milwaukee Brewers	.50	.25	.15
(14)	Minnesota Twins	.50	.25	.15
(15)	Montreal Expos	.50	.25	.15
(16)	New York Mets	.50	.25	.15
(17)	New York Yankees	.50	.25	.15
(18)	Oakland A's	.50	.25	.15
(19)	Philadelphia Phillies	.50	.25	.15
(20)	Pittsburgh Pirates	.50	.25	.15
(21)	St. Louis Cardinals	.50	.25	.15
(22)	San Diego Padres	.50	.25	.15
(23)	San Francisco Giants	.50	.25	.15
(24)	Texas Rangers	.50	.25	.15

1974 Topps Traded

Appearing late in the season, these 2-1/2" by 3-1/2" cards are basically the same as the regular issue Topps cards. The major change was that a big red panel with the word "Traded" was added below the player photo. Backs feature a "Baseball News" newspaper which contains the details of the trade. Card numbers correspond to the player's regular card number in 1974 except that the suffix "T" is added after the number. The set consists of 43 player cards and a checklist. In most cases, Topps did not obtain pictures of the players in their new uniforms. Instead the Topps artists simply provided the needed changes to existing photos.

		NR MT	EX	VG
	Complete Set:	7.00	3.50	2.00
	Common Player:	.12	.06	.04
23T	Craig Robinson	.12	.06	.04
42T	Claude Osteen	.15	.08	.05
43T	Jim Wynn	.20	.10	.06
51T	Bobby Heise	.12	.06	.04
59T	Ross Grimsley	.15	.08	.05
62T	Bob Locker	.12	.06	.04
63T	Bill Sudakis	.12	.06	.04
73T	Mike Marshall	.20	.10	.06
123T	Nelson Briles	.12	.06	.04
139T	Aurelio Monteagudo	.12	.06	.04
151T	Diego Segui	.12	.06	.04
165T	Willie Davis	.20	.10	.06
175T	Reggie Cleveland	.12	.06	.04
182T	Lindy McDaniel	.12	.06	.04
186T	Fred Scherman	.12	.06	.04
249T	George Mitterwald	.12	.06	.04
262T	Ed Kirkpatrick	.12	.06	.04
269T	Bob Johnson	.12	.06	.04
270T	Ron Santo	.30	.15	.09
313T	Barry Lersch	.12	.06	.04
319T	Randy Hundley	.12	.06	.04
330T	Juan Marichal	1.25	.60	.40
348T	Pete Richert	.12	.06	.04
373T	John Curtis	.12	.06	.04
390T	Lou Piniella	.50	.25	.15
428T	Gary Sutherland	.12	.06	.04
454T	Kurt Bevacqua	.12	.06	.04
458T	Jim Ray	.12	.06	.04
485T	Felipe Alou	.20	.10	.06
486T	Steve Stone	.20	.10	.06
496T	Tom Murphy	.12	.06	.04
516T	Horacio Pina	.12	.06	.04
534T	Eddie Watt	.12	.06	.04
538T	Cesar Tovar	.12	.06	.04
544T	Ron Schueler	.12	.06	.04
579T	Cecil Upshaw	.12	.06	.04
585T	Merv Rettenmund	.15	.08	.05
612T	Luke Walker	.12	.06	.04
616T	Larry Gura	.15	.08	.05
618T	Jim Mason	.12	.06	.04
630T	Tommie Agee	.15	.08	.05
648T	Terry Crowley	.12	.06	.04
649T	Fernando Gonzalez	.12	.06	.04
----	Traded Checklist	.70	.35	.20

1975 Topps

MANNY MOTA

This year Topps produced another 660-card set, one which collectors either seem to like or despise. The 2-1/2" by 3-1/2" cards have a color photo which is framed by a round-cornered white frame. Around that is an eye-catching two-color border in bright

colors. The team name appears at the top in bright letters while the player name is at the bottom and his position a baseball at the lower right. A facsimile autograph runs across the picture. The card backs are vertical feature normal statistical and biographica information along with a trivia quiz. Specialty cards include a new 24-card series on MVP winners going back to 1951. Other specialty cards include statistical leaders and post-season highlights. The real highlight of the set, however, are the rookie cards which include their numbers such names as George Brett, Gary Carter, Robin Yount, Jim Rice, Keith Hernandez and Fred Lynn. While the set was released at one time, card numbers 1-132 were printed in somewhat shorter supply than the remainder of the issue.

		NR MT	EX	VG
	Complete Set:	550.00	275.00	165.00
	Common Player: 1-132	.30	.15	.09
	Common Player: 133-660	.20	.10	.06
	Complete Mini Set:	850.00	425.00	255.00
	Common Mini Player:	.40	.20	.12
1	'74 Highlights (Hank Aaron)	15.00	7.50	4.50
2	'74 Highlights (Lou Brock)	2.00	1.00	.60
3	'74 Highlights (Bob Gibson)	1.75	.90	.50
4	'74 Highlights (Al Kaline)	1.75	.90	.50
5	'74 Highlights (Nolan Ryan)	3.00	1.50	.90
6	'74 Highlights (Mike Marshall)	.40	.20	.12
7	'74 Highlights (Dick Bosman, Steve Busby, Nolan Ryan)	1.00	.50	.30
8	Rogelio Moret	.30	.15	.09
9	Frank Tepedino	.30	.15	.09
10	Willie Davis	.35	.20	.11
11	Bill Melton	.35	.20	.11
12	David Clyde	.35	.20	.11
13	Gene Locklear	.30	.15	.09
14	Milt Wilcox	.35	.20	.11
15	Jose Cardenal	.35	.20	.11
16	Frank Tanana	.40	.20	.12
17	Dave Concepcion	.60	.30	.20
18	Tigers Team (Ralph Houk)	.90	.45	.25
19	Jerry Koosman	.40	.20	.12
20	Thurman Munson	6.00	3.00	1.75
21	Rollie Fingers	1.50	.70	.45
22	Dave Cash	.30	.15	.09
23	Bill Russell	.35	.20	.11
24	Al Fitzmorris	.30	.15	.09
25	Lee May	.40	.20	.12
26	Dave McNally	.35	.20	.11
27	Ken Reitz	.30	.15	.09
28	Tom Murphy	.30	.15	.09
29	Dave Parker	5.00	2.50	1.50
30	Bert Blyleven	1.00	.50	.30
31	Dave Rader	.30	.15	.09
32	Reggie Cleveland	.30	.15	.09
33	Dusty Baker	.40	.20	.12
34	Steve Renko	.30	.15	.09
35	Ron Santo	.50	.25	.15
36	Joe Lovitto	.30	.15	.09
37	Dave Freisleben	.30	.15	.09
38	Buddy Bell	.80	.40	.25
39	Andy Thornton	.70	.35	.20
40	Bill Singer	.35	.20	.11
41	Cesar Geronimo	.35	.20	.11
42	Joe Coleman	.35	.20	.11
43	Cleon Jones	.35	.20	.11
44	Pat Dobson	.35	.20	.11
45	Joe Rudi	.40	.20	.12
46	Phillies Team (Danny Ozark)	.80	.40	.25
47	Tommy John	1.25	.60	.40
48	Freddie Patek	.30	.15	.09
49	Larry Dierker	.30	.15	.09
50	Brooks Robinson	3.50	1.75	1.00
51	*Bob Forsch*	.80	.40	.25
52	Darrell Porter	.35	.20	.11
53	Dave Giusti	.30	.15	.09
54	Eric Soderholm	.30	.15	.09
55	Bobby Bonds	.50	.25	.15
56	Rick Wise	.35	.20	.11
57	Dave Johnson	.80	.40	.25
58	Chuck Taylor	.30	.15	.09
59	Ken Henderson	.30	.15	.09
60	Fergie Jenkins	1.25	.60	.40
61	Dave Winfield	12.00	6.00	3.50
62	Fritz Peterson	.30	.15	.09
63	Steve Swisher	.30	.15	.09
64	Dave Chalk	.30	.15	.09

	NR MT	EX	VG
65 Don Gullett	.35	.20	.11
66 Willie Horton	.35	.20	.11
67 Tug McGraw	.50	.25	.15
68 Ron Blomberg	.35	.20	.11
69 John Odom	.35	.20	.11
70 Mike Schmidt	30.00	15.00	9.00
71 Charlie Hough	.35	.20	.11
72 Royals Team (Jack McKeon)	.80	.40	.25
73 J.R. Richard	.35	.20	.11
74 Mark Belanger	.35	.20	.11
75 Ted Simmons	.70	.35	.20
76 Ed Sprague	.30	.15	.09
77 Richie Zisk	.35	.20	.11
78 Ray Corbin	.30	.15	.09
79 Gary Matthews	.40	.20	.12
80 Carlton Fisk	2.00	1.00	.60
81 Ron Reed	.35	.20	.11
82 Pat Kelly	.30	.15	.09
83 Jim Merritt	.30	.15	.09
84 Enzo Hernandez	.30	.15	.09
85 Bill Bonham	.30	.15	.09
86 Joe Lis	.30	.15	.09
87 George Foster	1.25	.60	.40
88 Tom Egan	.30	.15	.09
89 Jim Ray	.30	.15	.09
90 Rusty Staub	.60	.30	.20
91 Dick Green	.30	.15	.09
92 Cecil Upshaw	.35	.20	.11
93 Dave Lopes	.40	.20	.12
94 Jim Lonborg	.35	.20	.11
95 John Mayberry	.35	.20	.11
96 Mike Cosgrove	.30	.15	.09
97 Earl Williams	.30	.15	.09
98 Rich Folkers	.30	.15	.09
99 Mike Hegan	.30	.15	.09
100 Willie Stargell	2.50	1.25	.70
101 Expos Team (Gene Mauch)	.80	.40	.25
102 Joe Decker	.30	.15	.09
103 Rick Miller	.30	.15	.09
104 Bill Madlock	1.25	.60	.40
105 Buzz Capra	.30	.15	.09
106 *Mike Hargrove*	.40	.20	.12
107 Jim Barr	.30	.15	.09
108 Tom Hall	.30	.15	.09
109 George Hendrick	.35	.20	.11
110 Wilbur Wood	.35	.20	.11
111 Wayne Garrett	.30	.15	.09
112 Larry Hardy	.30	.15	.09
113 Elliott Maddox	.35	.20	.11
114 Dick Lange	.30	.15	.09
115 Joe Ferguson	.30	.15	.09
116 Lerrin LaGrow	.30	.15	.09
117 Orioles Team (Earl Weaver)	.90	.45	.25
118 Mike Anderson	.30	.15	.09
119 Tommy Helms	.30	.15	.09
120 Steve Busby (photo actually Fran Healy)	.35	.20	.11
121 Bill North	.30	.15	.09
122 Al Hrabosky	.35	.20	.11
123 Johnny Briggs	.30	.15	.09
124 Jerry Reuss	.40	.20	.12
125 Ken Singleton	.40	.20	.12
126 Checklist 1-132	1.50	.70	.45
127 Glen Borgmann	.30	.15	.09
128 Bill Lee	.35	.20	.11
129 Rick Monday	.35	.20	.11
130 Phil Niekro	2.00	1.00	.60
131 Toby Harrah	.35	.20	.11
132 Randy Moffitt	.30	.15	.09
133 Dan Driessen	.30	.15	.09
134 Ron Hodges	.20	.10	.06
135 Charlie Spikes	.20	.10	.06
136 Jim Mason	.25	.13	.08
137 Terry Forster	.30	.15	.09
138 Del Unser	.20	.10	.06
139 Horacio Pina	.20	.10	.06
140 Steve Garvey	6.00	3.00	1.75
141 Mickey Stanley	.25	.13	.08
142 Bob Reynolds	.20	.10	.06
143 *Cliff Johnson*	.40	.20	.12
144 Jim Wohlford	.20	.10	.06
145 Ken Holtzman	.30	.15	.09
146 Padres Team (John McNamara)	.80	.40	.25
147 Pedro Garcia	.20	.10	.06
148 Jim Rooker	.20	.10	.06
149 Tim Foli	.20	.10	.06
150 Bob Gibson	2.50	1.25	.70
151 Steve Brye	.20	.10	.06
152 Mario Guerrero	.20	.10	.06
153 Rick Reuschel	.40	.20	.12
154 Mike Lum	.20	.10	.06

	NR MT	EX	VG
155 Jim Bibby	.20	.10	.06
156 Dave Kingman	.90	.45	.25
157 Pedro Borbon	.20	.10	.06
158 Jerry Grote	.25	.13	.08
159 Steve Arlin	.20	.10	.06
160 Graig Nettles	1.50	.70	.45
161 Stan Bahnsen	.20	.10	.06
162 Willie Montanez	.20	.10	.06
163 Jim Brewer	.20	.10	.06
164 Mickey Rivers	.25	.13	.08
165 Doug Rader	.20	.10	.06
166 Woodie Fryman	.25	.13	.08
167 Rich Coggins	.20	.10	.06
168 Bill Greif	.20	.10	.06
169 Cookie Rojas	.20	.10	.06
170 Bert Campaneris	.40	.20	.12
171 Ed Kirkpatrick	.20	.10	.06
172 Red Sox Team (Darrell Johnson)	1.25	.60	.40
173 Steve Rogers	.30	.15	.09
174 Bake McBride	.25	.13	.08
175 Don Money	.25	.13	.08
176 Burt Hooton	.30	.15	.09
177 Vic Correll	.20	.10	.06
178 Cesar Tovar	.20	.10	.06
179 Tom Bradley	.20	.10	.06
180 Joe Morgan	3.00	1.50	.90
181 Fred Beene	.20	.10	.06
182 Don Hahn	.20	.10	.06
183 Mel Stottlemyre	.40	.20	.12
184 Jorge Orta	.20	.10	.06
185 Steve Carlton	6.00	3.00	1.75
186 Willie Crawford	.20	.10	.06
187 Denny Doyle	.20	.10	.06
188 Tom Griffin	.20	.10	.06
189 1951 - MVPs (Larry (Yogi) Berra, Roy Campanella)	1.50	.70	.45
190 1952 - MVPs (Hank Sauer, Bobby Shantz)	.40	.20	.12
191 1953 - MVPs (Roy Campanella, Al Rosen)	.90	.45	.25
192 1954 - MVPs (Yogi Berra, Willie Mays)	1.50	.70	.45
193 1955 - MVPs (Yogi Berra, Roy Campanella)	1.50	.70	.45
194 1956 - MVPs (Mickey Mantle, Don Newcombe)	6.00	3.00	1.75
195 1957 - MVPs (Hank Aaron, Mickey Mantle)	7.00	3.50	2.00
196 1958 - MVPs (Ernie Banks, Jackie Jensen)	.90	.45	.25
197 1959 - MVPs (Ernie Banks, Nellie Fox)	.90	.45	.25
198 1960 - MVPs (Dick Groat, Roger Maris)	1.25	.60	.40
199 1961 - MVPs (Roger Maris, Frank Robinson)	1.50	.70	.45
200 1962 - MVPs (Mickey Mantle, Maury Wills)	5.00	2.50	1.50
201 1963 - MVPs (Elston Howard, Sandy Koufax)	1.50	.70	.45
202 1964 - MVPs (Ken Boyer, Brooks Robinson)	1.25	.60	.40
203 1965 - MVPs (Willie Mays, Zoilo Versalles)	1.25	.60	.40
204 1966 - MVPs (Bob Clemente, Frank Robinson)	1.50	.70	.45
205 1967 - MVPs (Orlando Cepeda, Carl Yastrzemski)	1.25	.60	.40
206 1968 - MVPs (Bob Gibson, Denny McLain)	1.25	.60	.40
207 1969 - MVPs (Harmon Killebrew, Willie McCovey)	1.50	.70	.45
208 1970 - MVPs (Johnny Bench, Boog Powell)	1.25	.60	.40
209 1971 - MVPs (Vida Blue, Joe Torre)	.50	.25	.15
210 1972 - MVPs (Rich Allen, Johnny Bench)	1.25	.60	.40
211 1973 - MVPs (Reggie Jackson, Pete Rose)	4.00	2.00	1.25
212 1974 - MVPs (Jeff Burroughs, Steve Garvey)	.90	.45	.25
213 Oscar Gamble	.25	.13	.08
214 Harry Parker	.20	.10	.06
215 Bobby Valentine	.30	.15	.09
216 Giants Team (Wes Westrum)	.80	.40	.25
217 Lou Piniella	.70	.35	.20
218 Jerry Johnson	.20	.10	.06
219 Ed Herrmann	.20	.10	.06
220 Don Sutton	1.50	.70	.45
221 Aurelio Rodriguez (Rodriquez)	.25	.13	.08
222 Dan Spillner	.20	.10	.06

	NR MT	EX	VG
223 Robin Yount	100.00	45.00	27.00
224 Ramon Hernandez	.20	.10	.06
225 Bob Grich	.40	.20	.12
226 Bill Campbell	.25	.13	.08
227 Bob Watson	.25	.13	.08
228 George Brett	90.00	45.00	27.00
229 Barry Foote	.20	.10	.06
230 Jim Hunter	2.00	1.00	.60
231 Mike Tyson	.20	.10	.06
232 Diego Segui	.20	.10	.06
233 Billy Grabarkewitz	.20	.10	.06
234 Tom Grieve	.20	.10	.06
235 Jack Billingham	.20	.10	.06
236 Angels Team (Dick Williams)	.80	.40	.25
237 Carl Morton	.20	.10	.06
238 Dave Duncan	.20	.10	.06
239 George Stone	.20	.10	.06
240 Garry Maddox	.25	.13	.08
241 Dick Tidrow	.25	.13	.08
242 Jay Johnstone	.25	.13	.08
243 Jim Kaat	1.25	.60	.40
244 Bill Buckner	.50	.25	.15
245 Mickey Lolich	.50	.25	.15
246 Cardinals Team (Red Schoendienst)	.80	.40	.25
247 Enos Cabell	.25	.13	.08
248 Randy Jones	.25	.13	.08
249 Danny Thompson	.25	.13	.08
250 Ken Brett	.25	.13	.08
251 Fran Healy	.20	.10	.06
252 Fred Scherman	.20	.10	.06
253 Jesus Alou	.25	.13	.08
254 Mike Torrez	.25	.13	.08
255 Dwight Evans	1.50	.70	.45
256 Billy Champion	.20	.10	.06
257 Checklist 133-264	1.50	.70	.45
258 Dave LaRoche	.20	.10	.06
259 Len Randle	.20	.10	.06
260 Johnny Bench	7.00	3.50	2.00
261 Andy Hassler	.20	.10	.06
262 Rowland Office	.20	.10	.06
263 Jim Perry	.40	.20	.12
264 John Milner	.20	.10	.06
265 Ron Bryant	.20	.10	.06
266 Sandy Alomar	.25	.13	.08
267 Dick Ruthven	.20	.10	.06
268 Hal McRae	.40	.20	.12
269 Doug Rau	.20	.10	.06
270 Ron Fairly	.30	.15	.09
271 Jerry Moses	.20	.10	.06
272 Lynn McGlothen	.20	.10	.06
273 Steve Braun	.20	.10	.06
274 Vicente Romo	.20	.10	.06
275 Paul Blair	.25	.13	.08
276 White Sox Team (Chuck Tanner)	.80	.40	.25
277 Frank Taveras	.20	.10	.06
278 Paul Lindblad	.20	.10	.06
279 Milt May	.20	.10	.06
280 Carl Yastrzemski	7.00	3.50	2.00
281 Jim Slaton	.20	.10	.06
282 Jerry Morales	.20	.10	.06
283 Steve Foucault	.20	.10	.06
284 Ken Griffey	.70	.35	.20
285 Ellie Rodriguez	.20	.10	.06
286 Mike Jorgensen	.20	.10	.06
287 Roric Harrison	.20	.10	.06
288 Bruce Ellingsen	.20	.10	.06
289 Ken Rudolph	.20	.10	.06
290 Jon Matlack	.25	.13	.08
291 Bill Sudakis	.25	.13	.08
292 Ron Schueler	.20	.10	.06
293 Dick Sharon	.20	.10	.06
294 Geoff Zahn	.40	.20	.12
295 Vada Pinson	.60	.30	.20
296 Alan Foster	.20	.10	.06
297 Craig Kusick	.20	.10	.06
298 Johnny Grubb	.20	.10	.06
299 Bucky Dent	.40	.20	.12
300 Reggie Jackson	10.00	5.00	3.00
301 Dave Roberts	.20	.10	.06
302 Rick Burleson	.50	.25	.15
303 Grant Jackson	.20	.10	.06
304 Pirates Team (Danny Murtaugh)	.80	.40	.25
305 Jim Colborn	.20	.10	.06
306 Batting Leaders (Rod Carew, Ralph Garr)	.80	.40	.25
307 Home Run Leaders (Dick Allen, Mike Schmidt)	.90	.45	.25
308 Runs Batted In Leaders (Johnny Bench, Jeff Burroughs)	.90	.45	.25
309 Stolen Base Leaders (Lou Brock, Bill North)	.80	.40	.25
310 Victory Leaders (Jim Hunter, Fergie Jenkins, Andy Messersmith, Phil Niekro)	.80	.40	.25
311 Earned Run Average Leaders (Buzz Capra, Jim Hunter)	.50	.25	.15
312 Strikeout Leaders (Steve Carlton, Nolan Ryan)	1.75	.90	.50
313 Leading Firemen (Terry Forster, Mike Marshall)	.50	.25	.15
314 Buck Martinez	.20	.10	.06
315 Don Kessinger	.25	.13	.08
316 Jackie Brown	.20	.10	.06
317 Joe Lahoud	.20	.10	.06
318 Ernie McAnally	.20	.10	.06
319 Johnny Oates	.20	.10	.06
320 Pete Rose	18.00	9.00	5.50
321 Rudy May	.25	.13	.08
322 Ed Goodson	.20	.10	.06
323 Fred Holdsworth	.20	.10	.06
324 Ed Kranepool	.30	.15	.09
325 Tony Oliva	.80	.40	.25
326 Wayne Twitchell	.20	.10	.06
327 Jerry Hairston	.20	.10	.06
328 Sonny Siebert	.20	.10	.06
329 Ted Kubiak	.20	.10	.06
330 Mike Marshall	.30	.15	.09
331 Indians Team (Frank Robinson)	.90	.45	.25
332 Fred Kendall	.20	.10	.06
333 Dick Drago	.20	.10	.06
334 Greg Gross	.30	.15	.09
335 Jim Palmer	3.50	1.75	1.00
336 Rennie Stennett	.20	.10	.06
337 Kevin Kobel	.20	.10	.06
338 Rick Stelmaszek	.20	.10	.06
339 Jim Fregosi	.40	.20	.12
340 Paul Splittorff	.25	.13	.08
341 Hal Breeden	.20	.10	.06
342 Leroy Stanton	.20	.10	.06
343 Danny Frisella	.20	.10	.06
344 Ben Oglivie	.30	.15	.09
345 Clay Carroll	.25	.13	.08
346 Bobby Darwin	.20	.10	.06
347 Mike Caldwell	.20	.10	.06
348 Tony Muser	.20	.10	.06
349 Ray Sadecki	.20	.10	.06
350 Bobby Murcer	.40	.20	.12
351 Bob Boone	.40	.20	.12
352 Darold Knowles	.20	.10	.06
353 Luis Melendez	.20	.10	.06
354 Dick Bosman	.20	.10	.06
355 Chris Cannizzaro	.20	.10	.06
356 Rico Petrocelli	.30	.15	.09
357 Ken Forsch	.25	.13	.08
358 Al Bumbry	.25	.13	.08
359 Paul Popovich	.20	.10	.06
360 George Scott	.30	.15	.09
361 Dodgers Team (Walter Alston)	1.00	.50	.30
362 Steve Hargan	.20	.10	.06
363 Carmen Fanzone	.20	.10	.06
364 Doug Bird	.20	.10	.06
365 Bob Bailey	.20	.10	.06
366 Ken Sanders	.20	.10	.06
367 Craig Robinson	.20	.10	.06
368 Vic Albury	.20	.10	.06
369 Merv Rettenmund	.20	.10	.06
370 Tom Seaver	7.00	3.50	1.00
371 Gates Brown	.20	.10	.06
372 John D'Acquisto	.20	.10	.06
373 Bill Sharp	.20	.10	.06
374 Eddie Watt	.20	.10	.06
375 Roy White	.40	.20	.12
376 Steve Yeager	.20	.10	.06
377 Tom Hilgendorf	.20	.10	.06
378 Derrel Thomas	.20	.10	.06
379 Bernie Carbo	.20	.10	.06
380 Sal Bando	.40	.20	.12
381 John Curtis	.20	.10	.06
382 Don Baylor	.60	.30	.20
383 Jim York	.20	.10	.06
384 Brewers Team (Del Crandall)	.80	.40	.25
385 Dock Ellis	.25	.13	.08
386 Checklist 265-396	1.50	.70	.45
387 Jim Spencer	.20	.10	.06
388 Steve Stone	.30	.15	.09
389 Tony Solaita	.20	.10	.06
390 Ron Cey	.40	.20	.12
391 Don DeMola	.20	.10	.06
392 Bruce Bochte	.40	.20	.12
393 Gary Gentry	.20	.10	.06
394 Larvell Blanks	.20	.10	.06
395 Bud Harrelson	.25	.13	.08

		NR MT	EX	VG			NR MT	EX	VG
396	Fred Norman	.20	.10	.06	487	Astros Team (Preston Gomez)	.80	.40	.25
397	Bill Freehan	.40	.20	.12	488	Bill Travers	.20	.10	.06
398	Elias Sosa	.20	.10	.06	489	Cecil Cooper	1.00	.50	.30
399	Terry Harmon	.20	.10	.06	490	Reggie Smith	.30	.15	.09
400	Dick Allen	.80	.40	.25	491	Doyle Alexander	.40	.20	.12
401	Mike Wallace	.25	.13	.08	492	Rich Hebner	.25	.13	.08
402	Bob Tolan	.25	.13	.08	493	Don Stanhouse	.20	.10	.06
403	Tom Buskey	.20	.10	.06	494	*Pete LaCock*	.25	.13	.08
404	Ted Sizemore	.20	.10	.06	495	Nelson Briles	.20	.10	.06
405	John Montague	.20	.10	.06	496	Pepe Frias	.20	.10	.06
406	Bob Gallagher	.20	.10	.06	497	Jim Nettles	.20	.10	.06
407	*Herb Washington*	.30	.15	.09	498	Al Downing	.25	.13	.08
408	Clyde Wright	.20	.10	.06	499	Marty Perez	.20	.10	.06
409	Bob Robertson	.20	.10	.06	500	Nolan Ryan	15.00	7.50	4.50
410	Mike Cueller (Cuellar)	.40	.20	.12	501	Bill Robinson	.20	.10	.06
411	George Mitterwald	.20	.10	.06	502	Pat Bourque	.20	.10	.06
412	Bill Hands	.20	.10	.06	503	Fred Stanley	.25	.13	.08
413	Marty Pattin	.20	.10	.06	504	Buddy Bradford	.20	.10	.06
414	Manny Mota	.30	.15	.09	505	Chris Speier	.25	.13	.08
415	John Hiller	.25	.13	.08	506	Leron Lee	.20	.10	.06
416	Larry Lintz	.20	.10	.06	507	Tom Carroll	.20	.10	.06
417	Skip Lockwood	.20	.10	.06	508	Bob Hansen	.20	.10	.06
418	Leo Foster	.20	.10	.06	509	Dave Hilton	.20	.10	.06
419	Dave Goltz	.25	.13	.08	510	Vida Blue	.50	.25	.15
420	Larry Bowa	.40	.20	.12	511	Rangers Team (Billy Martin)	.90	.45	.25
421	Mets Team (Yogi Berra)	1.00	.50	.30	512	Larry Milbourne	.20	.10	.06
422	Brian Downing	.30	.15	.09	513	Dick Pole	.20	.10	.06
423	Clay Kirby	.20	.10	.06	514	Jose Cruz	.50	.25	.15
424	John Lowenstein	.20	.10	.06	515	Manny Sanguillen	.25	.13	.08
425	Tito Fuentes	.20	.10	.06	516	Don Hood	.20	.10	.06
426	George Medich	.25	.13	.08	517	Checklist 397-528	1.25	.60	.40
427	Clarence Gaston	.20	.10	.06	518	Leo Cardenas	.20	.10	.06
428	Dave Hamilton	.20	.10	.06	519	Jim Todd	.20	.10	.06
429	*Jim Dwyer*	.30	.15	.09	520	Amos Otis	.30	.15	.09
430	Luis Tiant	.50	.25	.15	521	Dennis Blair	.20	.10	.06
431	Rod Gilbreath	.20	.10	.06	522	Gary Sutherland	.20	.10	.06
432	Ken Berry	.20	.10	.06	523	Tom Paciorek	.25	.13	.08
433	Larry Demery	.20	.10	.06	524	John Doherty	.20	.10	.06
434	Bob Locker	.20	.10	.06	525	Tom House	.20	.10	.06
435	Dave Nelson	.20	.10	.06	526	Larry Hisle	.25	.13	.08
436	Ken Frailing	.20	.10	.06	527	Mac Scarce	.20	.10	.06
437	*Al Cowens*	.40	.20	.12	528	Eddie Leon	.20	.10	.06
438	Don Carrithers	.20	.10	.06	529	Gary Thomasson	.20	.10	.06
439	Ed Brinkman	.25	.13	.08	530	Gaylord Perry	2.25	1.25	.70
440	Andy Messersmith	.30	.15	.09	531	Reds Team (Sparky Anderson)	.90	.45	.25
441	Bobby Heise	.20	.10	.06	532	Gorman Thomas	.60	.30	.20
442	Maximino Leon	.20	.10	.06	533	Rudy Meoli	.20	.10	.06
443	Twins Team (Frank Quilici)	.80	.40	.25	534	Alex Johnson	.25	.13	.08
444	Gene Garber	.25	.13	.08	535	Gene Tenace	.25	.13	.08
445	Felix Millan	.20	.10	.06	536	Bob Moose	.20	.10	.06
446	Bart Johnson	.20	.10	.06	537	Tommy Harper	.25	.13	.08
447	Terry Crowley	.20	.10	.06	538	Duffy Dyer	.20	.10	.06
448	Frank Duffy	.20	.10	.06	539	Jesse Jefferson	.20	.10	.06
449	Charlie Williams	.20	.10	.06	540	Lou Brock	3.00	1.50	.90
450	Willie McCovey	3.00	1.50	.90	541	Roger Metzger	.20	.10	.06
451	Rick Dempsey	.40	.20	.12	542	Pete Broberg	.20	.10	.06
452	Angel Mangual	.20	.10	.06	543	Larry Biittner	.20	.10	.06
453	Claude Osteen	.30	.15	.09	544	Steve Mingori	.20	.10	.06
454	Doug Griffin	.20	.10	.06	545	Billy Williams	2.25	1.25	.70
455	Don Wilson	.20	.10	.06	546	John Knox	.20	.10	.06
456	Bob Coluccio	.20	.10	.06	547	Von Joshua	.20	.10	.06
457	Mario Mendoza	.20	.10	.06	548	Charlie Sands	.20	.10	.06
458	Ross Grimsley	.25	.13	.08	549	Bill Butler	.20	.10	.06
459	A.L. Championships	.80	.40	.25	550	Ralph Garr	.25	.13	.08
460	N.L. Championships	.80	.40	.25	551	Larry Christenson	.20	.10	.06
461	World Series Game 1	1.50	.70	.45	552	Jack Brohamer	.20	.10	.06
462	World Series Game 2	.80	.40	.25	553	John Boccabella	.20	.10	.06
463	World Series Game 3	1.00	.50	.30	554	Rich Gossage	1.25	.60	.40
464	World Series Game 4	.80	.40	.25	555	Al Oliver	.80	.40	.25
465	World Series Game 5	.80	.40	.25	556	Tim Johnson	.20	.10	.06
466	World Series Summary	.80	.40	.25	557	Larry Gura	.25	.13	.08
467	Ed Halicki	.20	.10	.06	558	Dave Roberts	.20	.10	.06
468	Bobby Mitchell	.20	.10	.06	559	Bob Montgomery	.20	.10	.06
469	Tom Dettore	.20	.10	.06	560	Tony Perez	1.00	.50	.30
470	Jeff Burroughs	.30	.15	.09	561	A's Team (Alvin Dark)	.90	.45	.25
471	Bob Stinson	.20	.10	.06	562	Gary Nolan	.20	.10	.06
472	Bruce Dal Canton	.20	.10	.06	563	Wilbur Howard	.20	.10	.06
473	Ken McMullen	.20	.10	.06	564	Tommy Davis	.40	.20	.12
474	Luke Walker	.20	.10	.06	565	Joe Torre	.70	.35	.20
475	Darrell Evans	.60	.30	.20	566	Ray Burris	.20	.10	.06
476	*Ed Figueroa*	.30	.15	.09	567	*Jim Sundberg*	.70	.35	.20
477	Tom Hutton	.20	.10	.06	568	Dale Murray	.20	.10	.06
478	Tom Burgmeier	.20	.10	.06	569	Frank White	.40	.20	.12
479	Ken Boswell	.20	.10	.06	570	Jim Wynn	.30	.15	.09
480	Carlos May	.25	.13	.08	571	Dave Lemanczyk	.20	.10	.06
481	*Will McEnaney*	.30	.15	.09	572	Roger Nelson	.20	.10	.06
482	Tom McCraw	.20	.10	.06	573	Orlando Pena	.20	.10	.06
483	Steve Ontiveros	.20	.10	.06	574	Tony Taylor	.20	.10	.06
484	Glenn Beckert	.30	.15	.09	575	Gene Clines	.20	.10	.06
485	Sparky Lyle	.40	.20	.12	576	Phil Roof	.20	.10	.06
486	Ray Fosse	.20	.10	.06	577	John Morris	.20	.10	.06

		NR MT	EX	VG
578	Dave Tomlin	.20	.10	.06
579	Skip Pitlock	.20	.10	.06
580	Frank Robinson	3.00	1.50	.90
581	Darrel Chaney	.20	.10	.06
582	Eduardo Rodriguez	.20	.10	.06
583	Andy Etchebarren	.20	.10	.06
584	Mike Garman	.20	.10	.06
585	Chris Chambliss	.40	.20	.12
586	Tim McCarver	.60	.30	.20
587	Chris Ward	.20	.10	.06
588	Rick Auerbach	.20	.10	.06
589	Braves Team (Clyde King)	.80	.40	.25
590	Cesar Cedeno	.40	.20	.12
591	Glenn Abbott	.20	.10	.06
592	Balor Moore	.20	.10	.06
593	Gene Lamont	.20	.10	.06
594	Jim Fuller	.20	.10	.06
595	Joe Niekro	.40	.20	.12
596	Ollie Brown	.20	.10	.06
597	Winston Llenas	.20	.10	.06
598	Bruce Kison	.20	.10	.06
599	Nate Colbert	.20	.10	.06
600	Rod Carew	5.00	2.50	1.50
601	Juan Beniquez	.30	.15	.09
602	John Vukovich	.20	.10	.06
603	Lew Krausse	.20	.10	.06
604	Oscar Zamora	.20	.10	.06
605	John Ellis	.20	.10	.06
606	Bruce Miller	.20	.10	.06
607	Jim Holt	.20	.10	.06
608	Gene Michael	.30	.15	.09
609	Ellie Hendricks	.20	.10	.06
610	Ron Hunt	.25	.13	.08
611	Yankees Team (Bill Virdon)	1.25	.60	.40
612	Terry Hughes	.20	.10	.06
613	Bill Parsons	.20	.10	.06
614	Rookie Pitchers (Jack Kucek, Dyar Miller, Vern Ruhle, Paul Siebert)	.20	.10	.06
615	Rookie Pitchers (Pat Darcy, *Dennis Leonard*, Tom Underwood, Hank Webb)	.60	.30	.20
616	Rookie Outfielders (Dave Augustine, Pepe Mangual, *Jim Rice*, John Scott)	30.00	15.00	9.00
617	Rookie Infielders (Mike Cubbage, *Doug DeCinces*, Reggie Sanders, Manny Trillo)	1.25	.60	.40
618	Rookie Pitchers (*Jamie Easterly*, Tom Johnson, *Scott McGregor*, Rick Rhoden)	2.25	1.25	.70
619	Rookie Outfielders (Benny Ayala, Nyls Nyman, Tommy Smith, Jerry Turner)	.20	.10	.06
620	Rookie Catchers-Outfielders (*Gary Carter*, Marc Hill, Danny Meyer, Leon Roberts)	35.00	17.50	10.50
621	Rookie Pitchers (*John Denny*, Rawly Eastwick, *Jim Kern*, Juan Veintidos)	.60	.30	.20
622	Rookie Outfielders (Ed Armbrister, *Fred Lynn*, Tom Poquette, Terry Whitfield)	12.00	6.00	3.50
623	Rookie Infielders (*Phil Garner*, Keith Hernandez, Bob Sheldon, Tom Veryzer)	20.00	10.00	6.00
624	Rookie Pitchers (Doug Konieczny, *Gary Lavelle*, Jim Otten, Eddie Solomon)	.30	.15	.09
625	Boog Powell	.70	.35	.20
626	Larry Haney	.20	.10	.06
627	Tom Walker	.20	.10	.06
628	*Ron LeFlore*	.80	.40	.25
629	Joe Hoerner	.20	.10	.06
630	Greg Luzinski	.70	.35	.20
631	Lee Lacy	.25	.13	.08
632	Morris Nettles	.20	.10	.06
633	Paul Casanova	.20	.10	.06
634	Cy Acosta	.20	.10	.06
635	Chuck Dobson	.20	.10	.06
636	Charlie Moore	.25	.13	.08
637	Ted Martinez	.20	.10	.06
638	Cubs Team (Jim Marshall)	.80	.40	.25
639	Steve Kline	.20	.10	.06
640	Harmon Killebrew	2.50	1.25	.70
641	Jim Northrup	.25	.13	.08
642	Mike Phillips	.20	.10	.06
643	Brent Strom	.20	.10	.06
644	Bill Fahey	.20	.10	.06
645	Danny Cater	.20	.10	.06
646	Checklist 529-660	1.50	.70	.45
647	*Claudell Washington*	2.50	1.25	.70
648	Dave Pagan	.25	.13	.08
649	Jack Heidemann	.20	.10	.06
650	Dave May	.20	.10	.06
651	John Morlan	.20	.10	.06

		NR MT	EX	VG
652	Lindy McDaniel	.20	.10	.06
653	Lee Richards	.20	.10	.06
654	Jerry Terrell	.20	.10	.06
655	Rico Carty	.40	.20	.12
656	Bill Plummer	.20	.10	.06
657	Bob Oliver	.20	.10	.06
658	Vic Harris	.20	.10	.06
659	Bob Apodaca	.20	.10	.06
660	Hank Aaron	20.00	10.00	6.00

1975 Topps Mini

RON CEY

One of the most popular Topps sets of the 1970s is really a test issue. The Topps Minis measure 2-1/4" by 3-1/8," exactly 20% smaller than the regular card size. Other than their size, the Minis are in every way the same as the regular cards. The experiment primarily took place in parts of Michigan and the West Coast, where the Minis were snapped up quickly by collectors.

		NR MT	EX	VG
	Complete Set:	11000.00	550.00	325.00
	Common Player:	.40	.20	.12
1	'74 Highlights (Hank Aaron)	25.00	12.50	7.50
2	'74 Highlights (Lou Brock)	3.50	1.75	1.00
3	'74 Highlights (Bob Gibson)	3.25	1.75	1.00
4	'74 Highlights (Al Kaline)	3.25	1.75	1.00
5	'74 Highlights (Nolan Ryan)	3.25	1.75	1.00
6	'74 Highlights (Mike Marshall)	.60	.30	.20
7	'74 Highlights (Dick Bosman, Steve Busby, Nolan Ryan)	1.50	.70	.45
8	Rogelio Moret	.40	.20	.12
9	Frank Tepedino	.40	.20	.12
10	Willie Davis	.60	.30	.20
11	Bill Melton	.40	.20	.12
12	David Clyde	.40	.20	.12
13	Gene Locklear	.40	.20	.12
14	Milt Wilcox	.40	.20	.12
15	Jose Cardenal	.40	.20	.12
16	Frank Tanana	.60	.30	.20
17	Dave Concepcion	.90	.45	.25
18	Tigers Team (Ralph Houk)	1.25	.60	.40
19	Jerry Koosman	.40	.20	.12
20	Thurman Munson	10.00	5.00	3.00
21	Rollie Fingers	3.00	1.50	.90
22	Dave Cash	.40	.20	.12
23	Bill Russell	.60	.30	.20
24	Al Fitzmorris	.40	.20	.12
25	Lee May	.60	.30	.20
26	Dave McNally	.60	.30	.20
27	Ken Reitz	.40	.20	.12
28	Tom Murphy	.40	.20	.12
29	Dave Parker	10.00	5.00	3.00
30	Bert Blyleven	2.00	1.00	.60
31	Dave Rader	.40	.20	.12
32	Reggie Cleveland	.40	.20	.12
33	Dusty Baker	.60	.30	.20
34	Steve Renko	.40	.20	.12
35	Ron Santo	.80	.40	.25
36	Joe Lovitto	.40	.20	.12
37	Dave Freisleben	.40	.20	.12
38	Buddy Bell	1.50	.70	.45
39	Andy Thornton	1.00	.50	.30
40	Bill Singer	.40	.20	.12
41	Cesar Geronimo	.40	.20	.12
42	Joe Coleman	.40	.20	.12

		NR MT	EX	VG
43	Cleon Jones	.40	.20	.12
44	Pat Dobson	.40	.20	.12
45	Joe Rudi	.60	.30	.20
46	Phillies Team (Danny Ozark)	1.25	.60	.40
47	Tommy John	2.50	1.25	.70
48	Freddie Patek	.40	.20	.12
49	Larry Dierker	.40	.20	.12
50	Brooks Robinson	7.00	3.50	2.00
51	Bob Forsch	1.25	.60	.40
52	Darrell Porter	.60	.30	.20
53	Dave Giusti	.40	.20	.12
54	Eric Soderholm	.40	.20	.12
55	Bobby Bonds	.80	.40	.25
56	Rick Wise	.60	.30	.20
57	Dave Johnson	1.25	.60	.40
58	Chuck Taylor	.40	.20	.12
59	Ken Henderson	.40	.20	.12
60	Fergie Jenkins	1.75	.90	.50
61	Dave Winfield	20.00	10.00	6.00
62	Fritz Peterson	.40	.20	.12
63	Steve Swisher	.40	.20	.12
64	Dave Chalk	.40	.20	.12
65	Don Gullett	.40	.20	.12
66	Willie Horton	.60	.30	.20
67	Tug McGraw	.80	.40	.25
68	Ron Blomberg	.40	.20	.12
69	John Odom	.40	.20	.12
70	Mike Schmidt	75.00	38.00	23.00
71	Charlie Hough	.60	.30	.20
72	Royals Team (Jack McKeon)	1.25	.60	.40
73	J.R. Richard	.60	.30	.20
74	Mark Belanger	.60	.30	.20
75	Ted Simmons	1.00	.50	.30
76	Ed Sprague	.40	.20	.12
77	Richie Zisk	.60	.30	.20
78	Ray Corbin	.40	.20	.12
79	Gary Matthews	.60	.30	.20
80	Carlton Fisk	7.00	3.50	2.00
81	Ron Reed	.40	.20	.12
82	Pat Kelly	.40	.20	.12
83	Jim Merritt	.40	.20	.12
84	Enzo Hernandez	.40	.20	.12
85	Bill Bonham	.40	.20	.12
86	Joe Lis	.40	.20	.12
87	George Foster	1.75	.90	.50
88	Tom Egan	.40	.20	.12
89	Jim Ray	.40	.20	.12
90	Rusty Staub	.90	.45	.25
91	Dick Green	.40	.20	.12
92	Cecil Upshaw	.40	.20	.12
93	Dave Lopes	.60	.30	.20
94	Jim Lonborg	.40	.20	.12
95	John Mayberry	.40	.20	.12
96	Mike Cosgrove	.40	.20	.12
97	Earl Williams	.40	.20	.12
98	Rich Folkers	.40	.20	.12
99	Mike Hegan	.40	.20	.12
100	Willie Stargell	7.00	3.50	2.00
101	Expos Team (Gene Mauch)	1.25	.60	.40
102	Joe Decker	.40	.20	.12
103	Rick Miller	.40	.20	.12
104	Bill Madlock	2.00	1.00	.60
105	Buzz Capra	.40	.20	.12
106	Mike Hargrove	.60	.30	.20
107	Jim Barr	.40	.20	.12
108	Tom Hall	.40	.20	.12
109	George Hendrick	.40	.20	.12
110	Wilbur Wood	.40	.20	.12
111	Wayne Garrett	.40	.20	.12
112	Larry Hardy	.40	.20	.12
113	Elliott Maddox	.40	.20	.12
114	Dick Lange	.40	.20	.12
115	Joe Ferguson	.40	.20	.12
116	Lerrin LaGrow	.40	.20	.12
117	Orioles Team (Earl Weaver)	1.25	.60	.40
118	Mike Anderson	.40	.20	.12
119	Tommy Helms	.40	.20	.12
120	Steve Busby (photo actually Fran Healy)			
		.40	.20	.12
121	Bill North	.40	.20	.12
122	Al Hrabosky	.40	.20	.12
123	Johnny Briggs	.40	.20	.12
124	Jerry Reuss	.60	.30	.20
125	Ken Singleton	.60	.30	.20
126	Checklist 1-132	2.25	1.25	.70
127	Glen Borgmann	.40	.20	.12
128	Bill Lee	.60	.30	.20
129	Rick Monday	.60	.30	.20
130	Phil Niekro	4.00	2.00	1.25
131	Toby Harrah	.40	.20	.12
132	Randy Moffitt	.40	.20	.12

		NR MT	EX	VG
133	Dan Driessen	.60	.30	.20
134	Ron Hodges	.40	.20	.12
135	Charlie Spikes	.40	.20	.12
136	Jim Mason	.40	.20	.12
137	Terry Forster	.40	.20	.12
138	Del Unser	.40	.20	.12
139	Horacio Pina	.40	.20	.12
140	Steve Garvey	12.00	6.00	3.50
141	Mickey Stanley	.40	.20	.12
142	Bob Reynolds	.40	.20	.12
143	Cliff Johnson	.40	.20	.12
144	Jim Wohlford	.40	.20	.12
145	Ken Holtzman	.60	.30	.20
146	Padres Team (John McNamara)	1.25	.60	.40
147	Pedro Garcia	.40	.20	.12
148	Jim Rooker	.40	.20	.12
149	Tim Foli	.40	.20	.12
150	Bob Gibson	7.00	3.50	2.00
151	Steve Brye	.40	.20	.12
152	Mario Guerrero	.40	.20	.12
153	Rick Reuschel	.60	.30	.20
154	Mike Lum	.40	.20	.12
155	Jim Bibby	.40	.20	.12
156	Dave Kingman	1.50	.70	.45
157	Pedro Borbon	.40	.20	.12
158	Jerry Grote	.40	.20	.12
159	Steve Arlin	.40	.20	.12
160	Graig Nettles	2.25	1.25	.70
161	Stan Bahnsen	.40	.20	.12
162	Willie Montanez	.40	.20	.12
163	Jim Brewer	.40	.20	.12
164	Mickey Rivers	.60	.30	.20
165	Doug Rader	.40	.20	.12
166	Woodie Fryman	.40	.20	.12
167	Rich Coggins	.40	.20	.12
168	Bill Greif	.40	.20	.12
169	Cookie Rojas	.40	.20	.12
170	Bert Campaneris	.60	.30	.20
171	Ed Kirkpatrick	.40	.20	.12
172	Red Sox Team (Darrell Johnson)	1.25	.60	.40
173	Steve Rogers	.40	.20	.12
174	Bake McBride	.40	.20	.12
175	Don Money	.40	.20	.12
176	Burt Hooton	.40	.20	.12
177	Vic Correll	.40	.20	.12
178	Cesar Tovar	.40	.20	.12
179	Tom Bradley	.40	.20	.12
180	Joe Morgan	10.00	5.00	3.00
181	Fred Beene	.40	.20	.12
182	Don Hahn	.40	.20	.12
183	Mel Stottlemyre	.60	.30	.20
184	Jorge Orta	.40	.20	.12
185	Steve Carlton	20.00	10.00	6.00
186	Willie Crawford	.40	.20	.12
187	Denny Doyle	.40	.20	.12
188	Tom Griffin	.40	.20	.12
189	1951-MVPs (Larry (Yogi) Berra, Roy Campanella)	2.25	1.25	.70
190	1952-MVPs (Hank Sauer, Bobby Shantz)	.60	.30	.20
191	1953-MVPs (Roy Campanella, Al Rosen)	1.25	.60	.40
192	1954-MVPs (Yogi Berra, Willie Mays)	2.25	1.25	.70
193	1955-MVPs (Yogi Berra, Roy Campanella)	2.25	1.25	.70
194	1956-MVPs (Mickey Mantle, Don Newcombe)	9.00	4.50	2.75
195	1957-MVPs (Hank Aaron, Mickey Mantle)	10.00	5.00	3.00
196	1958-MVPs (Ernie Banks, Jackie Jensen)	1.25	.60	.40
197	1959-MVPs (Ernie Banks, Nellie Fox)	1.25	.60	.40
198	1960-MVPs (Dick Groat, Roger Maris)	1.75	.90	.50
199	1961-MVPs (Roger Maris, Frank Robinson)	2.25	1.25	.70
200	1962-MVPs (Mickey Mantle, Maury Wills)	9.00	4.50	2.75
201	1963-MVPs (Elston Howard, Sandy Koufax)	2.25	1.25	.70
202	1964-MVPs (Ken Boyer, Brooks Robinson)	1.75	.90	.50
203	1965-MVPs (Willie Mays, Zoilo Versalles)	1.75	.90	.50
204	1966-MVPs (Bob Clemente, Frank Robinson)	2.25	1.25	.70
205	1967-MVPs (Orlando Cepeda, Carl Yastrzemski)	1.75	.90	.50
206	1968-MVPs (Bob Gibson, Denny McLain)	1.75	.90	.50

#	Player	NR MT	EX	VG
207	1969-MVPs (Harmon Killebrew, Willie McCovey)	2.25	1.25	.70
208	1970-MVPs (Johnny Bench, Boog Powell)	1.75	.90	.50
209	1971-MVPs (Vida Blue, Joe Torre)	.80	.40	.25
210	1972-MVPs (Rich Allen, Johnny Bench)	1.75	.90	.50
211	1973-MVPs (Reggie Jackson, Pete Rose)	7.00	3.50	2.00
212	1974-MVPs (Jeff Burroughs, Steve Garvey)	1.25	.60	.40
213	Oscar Gamble	.40	.20	.12
214	Harry Parker	.40	.20	.12
215	Bobby Valentine	.40	.20	.12
216	Giants Team (Wes Westrum)	1.25	.60	.40
217	Lou Piniella	.80	.40	.25
218	Jerry Johnson	.40	.20	.12
219	Ed Herrmann	.40	.20	.12
220	Don Sutton	3.00	1.50	.90
221	Aurelio Rodriquez (Rodriguez)	.40	.20	.12
222	Dan Spillner	.40	.20	.12
223	Robin Yount	200.00	100.00	60.00
224	Ramon Hernandez	.40	.20	.12
225	Bob Grich	.60	.30	.20
226	Bill Campbell	.40	.20	.12
227	Bob Watson	.40	.20	.12
228	George Brett	150.00	75.00	45.00
229	Barry Foote	.40	.20	.12
230	Jim Hunter	4.00	2.00	1.25
231	Mike Tyson	.40	.20	.12
232	Diego Segui	.40	.20	.12
233	Billy Grabarkewitz	.40	.20	.12
234	Tom Grieve	.40	.20	.12
235	Jack Billingham	.40	.20	.12
236	Angels Team (Dick Williams)	1.25	.60	.40
237	Carl Morton	.40	.20	.12
238	Dave Duncan	.40	.20	.12
239	George Stone	.40	.20	.12
240	Garry Maddox	.60	.30	.20
241	Dick Tidrow	.40	.20	.12
242	Jay Johnstone	.60	.30	.20
243	Jim Kaat	2.00	1.00	.60
244	Bill Buckner	.80	.40	.25
245	Mickey Lolich	.80	.40	.25
246	Cardinals Team (Red Schoendienst)	1.25	.60	.40
247	Enos Cabell	.40	.20	.12
248	Randy Jones	.40	.20	.12
249	Danny Thompson	.40	.20	.12
250	Ken Brett	.40	.20	.12
251	Fran Healy	.40	.20	.12
252	Fred Scherman	.40	.20	.12
253	Jesus Alou	.40	.20	.12
254	Mike Torrez	.40	.20	.12
255	Dwight Evans	2.25	1.25	.70
256	Billy Champion	.40	.20	.12
257	Checklist 133-264	2.25	1.25	.70
258	Dave LaRoche	.40	.20	.12
259	Len Randle	.40	.20	.12
260	Johnny Bench	15.00	7.50	4.50
261	Andy Hassler	.40	.20	.12
262	Rowland Office	.40	.20	.12
263	Jim Perry	.60	.30	.20
264	John Milner	.40	.20	.12
265	Ron Bryant	.40	.20	.12
266	Sandy Alomar	.40	.20	.12
267	Dick Ruthven	.40	.20	.12
268	Hal McRae	.60	.30	.20
269	Doug Rau	.40	.20	.12
270	Ron Fairly	.60	.30	.20
271	Jerry Moses	.40	.20	.12
272	Lynn McGlothen	.40	.20	.12
273	Steve Braun	.40	.20	.12
274	Vicente Romo	.40	.20	.12
275	Paul Blair	.60	.30	.20
276	White Sox Team (Chuck Tanner)	1.25	.60	.40
277	Frank Taveras	.40	.20	.12
278	Paul Lindblad	.40	.20	.12
279	Milt May	.40	.20	.12
280	Carl Yastrzemski	15.00	7.50	4.50
281	Jim Slaton	.40	.20	.12
282	Jerry Morales	.40	.20	.12
283	Steve Foucault	.40	.20	.12
284	Ken Griffey	1.00	.50	.30
285	Ellie Rodriguez	.40	.20	.12
286	Mike Jorgensen	.40	.20	.12
287	Roric Harrison	.40	.20	.12
288	Bruce Ellingsen	.40	.20	.12
289	Ken Rudolph	.40	.20	.12
290	Jon Matlack	.40	.20	.12
291	Bill Sudakis	.40	.20	.12
292	Ron Schueler	.40	.20	.12
293	Dick Sharon	.40	.20	.12
294	Geoff Zahn	.40	.20	.12
295	Vada Pinson	.90	.45	.25
296	Alan Foster	.40	.20	.12
297	Craig Kusick	.40	.20	.12
298	Johnny Grubb	.40	.20	.12
299	Bucky Dent	.60	.30	.20
300	Reggie Jackson	20.00	10.00	6.00
301	Dave Roberts	.40	.20	.12
302	Rick Burleson	.80	.40	.25
303	Grant Jackson	.40	.20	.12
304	Pirates Team (Danny Murtaugh)	1.25	.60	.40
305	Jim Colborn	.40	.20	.12
306	Batting Leaders (Rod Carew, Ralph Garr)	1.25	.60	.40
307	Home Run Leaders (Dick Allen, Mike Schmidt)	1.25	.60	.40
308	Runs Batted In Leaders (Johnny Bench, Jeff Burroughs)	1.25	.60	.40
309	Stole Base Leaders (Lou Brock, Bill North)	1.25	.60	.40
310	Victory Leaders (Jim Hunter, Fergie Jenkins, Andy Messersmith, Phil Niekro)	1.25	.60	.40
311	Earned Run Average Leaders (Buzz Capra, Jim Hunter)	.80	.40	.25
312	Strikeout Leaders (Steve Carlton, Nolan Ryan)	2.50	1.25	.70
313	Leading Firemen (Terry Forster, Mike Marshall)	.80	.40	.25
314	Buck Martinez	.40	.20	.12
315	Don Kessinger	.40	.20	.12
316	Jackie Brown	.40	.20	.12
317	Joe Lahoud	.40	.20	.12
318	Ernie McAnally	.40	.20	.12
319	Johnny Oates	.40	.20	.12
320	Pete Rose	40.00	20.00	12.00
321	Rudy May	.40	.20	.12
322	Ed Goodson	.40	.20	.12
323	Fred Holdsworth	.40	.20	.12
324	Ed Kranepool	.40	.20	.12
325	Tony Oliva	1.25	.60	.40
326	Wayne Twitchell	.40	.20	.12
327	Jerry Hairston	.40	.20	.12
328	Sonny Siebert	.40	.20	.12
329	Ted Kubiak	.40	.20	.12
330	Mike Marshall	.60	.30	.20
331	Indians Team (Frank Robinson)	1.25	.60	.40
332	Fred Kendall	.40	.20	.12
333	Dick Drago	.40	.20	.12
334	Greg Gross	.40	.20	.12
335	Jim Palmer	15.00	7.50	4.50
336	Rennie Stennett	.40	.20	.12
337	Kevin Kobel	.40	.20	.12
338	Rick Stelmaszek	.40	.20	.12
339	Jim Fregosi	.60	.30	.20
340	Paul Splittorff	.40	.20	.12
341	Hal Breeden	.40	.20	.12
342	Leroy Stanton	.40	.20	.12
343	Danny Frisella	.40	.20	.12
344	Ben Oglivie	.60	.30	.20
345	Clay Carroll	.40	.20	.12
346	Bobby Darwin	.40	.20	.12
347	Mike Caldwell	.40	.20	.12
348	Tony Muser	.40	.20	.12
349	Ray Sadecki	.40	.20	.12
350	Bobby Murcer	.60	.30	.20
351	Bob Boone	.60	.30	.20
352	Darold Knowles	.40	.20	.12
353	Luis Melendez	.40	.20	.12
354	Dick Bosman	.40	.20	.12
355	Chris Cannizzaro	.40	.20	.12
356	Rico Petrocelli	.40	.20	.12
357	Ken Forsch	.40	.20	.12
358	Al Bumbry	.40	.20	.12
359	Paul Popovich	.40	.20	.12
360	George Scott	.40	.20	.12
361	Dodgers Team (Walter Alston)	1.50	.70	.45
362	Steve Hargan	.40	.20	.12
363	Carmen Fanzone	.40	.20	.12
364	Doug Bird	.40	.20	.12
365	Bob Bailey	.40	.20	.12
366	Ken Sanders	.40	.20	.12
367	Craig Robinson	.40	.20	.12
368	Vic Albury	.40	.20	.12
369	Merv Rettenmund	.40	.20	.12
370	Tom Seaver	25.00	12.50	7.50
371	Gates Brown	.40	.20	.12
372	John D'Acquisto	.40	.20	.12
373	Bill Sharp	.40	.20	.12

		NR MT	EX	VG				NR MT	EX	VG
374	Eddie Watt	.40	.20	.12		465	World Series Game 5	1.25	.60	.40
375	Roy White	.60	.30	.20		466	World Series Summary	1.25	.60	.40
376	Steve Yeager	.40	.20	.12		467	Ed Halicki	.40	.20	.12
377	Tom Hilgendorf	.40	.20	.12		468	Bobby Mitchell	.40	.20	.12
378	Derrel Thomas	.40	.20	.12		469	Tom Dettore	.40	.20	.12
379	Bernie Carbo	.40	.20	.12		470	Jeff Burroughs	.40	.20	.12
380	Sal Bando	.60	.30	.20		471	Bob Stinson	.40	.20	.12
381	John Curtis	.40	.20	.12		472	Bruce Dal Canton	.40	.20	.12
382	Don Baylor	.90	.45	.25		473	Ken McMullen	.40	.20	.12
383	Jim York	.40	.20	.12		474	Luke Walker	.40	.20	.12
384	Brewers Team (Del Crandall)	1.25	.60	.40		475	Darrell Evans	.90	.45	.25
385	Dock Ellis	.40	.20	.12		476	Ed Figueroa	.40	.20	.12
386	Checklist 265-396	2.25	1.25	.70		477	Tom Hutton	.40	.20	.12
387	Jim Spencer	.40	.20	.12		478	Tom Burgmeier	.40	.20	.12
388	Steve Stone	.60	.30	.20		479	Ken Boswell	.40	.20	.12
389	Tony Solaita	.40	.20	.12		480	Carlos May	.40	.20	.12
390	Ron Cey	.60	.30	.20		481	Will McEnaney	.40	.20	.12
391	Don DeMola	.40	.20	.12		482	Tom McCraw	.40	.20	.12
392	Bruce Bochte	.40	.20	.12		483	Steve Ontiveros	.40	.20	.12
393	Gary Gentry	.40	.20	.12		484	Glenn Beckert	.40	.20	.12
394	Larvell Blanks	.40	.20	.12		485	Sparky Lyle	.60	.30	.20
395	Bud Harrelson	.40	.20	.12		486	Ray Fosse	.40	.20	.12
396	Fred Norman	.40	.20	.12		487	Astros Team (Preston Gomez)	1.25	.60	.40
397	Bill Freehan	.60	.30	.20		488	Bill Travers	.40	.20	.12
398	Elias Sosa	.40	.20	.12		489	Cecil Cooper	1.50	.70	.45
399	Terry Harmon	.40	.20	.12		490	Reggie Smith	.60	.30	.20
400	Dick Allen	1.25	.60	.40		491	Doyle Alexander	.60	.30	.20
401	Mike Wallace	.40	.20	.12		492	Rich Hebner	.40	.20	.12
402	Bob Tolan	.40	.20	.12		493	Doug Stanhouse	.40	.20	.12
403	Tom Buskey	.40	.20	.12		494	Pete LaCock	.40	.20	.12
404	Ted Sizemore	.40	.20	.12		495	Nelson Briles	.40	.20	.12
405	John Montague	.40	.20	.12		496	Pepe Frias	.40	.20	.12
406	Bob Gallagher	.40	.20	.12		497	Jim Nettles	.40	.20	.12
407	Herb Washington	.40	.20	.12		498	Al Downing	.40	.20	.12
408	Clyde Wright	.40	.20	.12		499	Marty Perez	.40	.20	.12
409	Bob Robertson	.40	.20	.12		500	Nolan Ryan	40.00	20.00	12.00
410	Mike Cueller (Cuellar)	.60	.30	.20		501	Bill Robinson	.40	.20	.12
411	George Mitterwald	.40	.20	.12		502	Pat Bourque	.40	.20	.12
412	Bill Hands	.40	.20	.12		503	Fred Stanley	.40	.20	.12
413	Marty Pattin	.40	.20	.12		504	Buddy Bradford	.40	.20	.12
414	Manny Mota	.60	.30	.20		505	Chris Speier	.40	.20	.12
415	John Hiller	.40	.20	.12		506	Leron Lee	.40	.20	.12
416	Larry Lintz	.40	.20	.12		507	Tom Carroll	.40	.20	.12
417	Skip Lockwood	.40	.20	.12		508	Bob Hansen	.40	.20	.12
418	Leo Foster	.40	.20	.12		509	Dave Hilton	.40	.20	.12
419	Dave Goltz	.40	.20	.12		510	Vida Blue	.80	.40	.25
420	Larry Bowa	.60	.30	.20		511	Rangers Team (Billy Martin)	1.25	.60	.40
421	Mets Team (Yogi Berra)	1.50	.70	.45		512	Larry Milbourne	.40	.20	.12
422	Brian Downing	.60	.30	.20		513	Dick Pole	.40	.20	.12
423	Clay Kirby	.40	.20	.12		514	Jose Cruz	.80	.40	.25
424	John Lowenstein	.40	.20	.12		515	Manny Sanguillen	.40	.20	.12
425	Tito Fuentes	.40	.20	.12		516	Don Hood	.40	.20	.12
426	George Medich	.40	.20	.12		517	Checklist 397-528	2.25	1.25	.70
427	Clarence Gaston	.40	.20	.12		518	Leo Cardenas	.40	.20	.12
428	Dave Hamilton	.40	.20	.12		519	Jim Todd	.40	.20	.12
429	Jim Dwyer	.40	.20	.12		520	Amos Otis	.40	.20	.12
430	Luis Tiant	.80	.40	.25		521	Dennis Blair	.40	.20	.12
431	Rod Gilbreath	.40	.20	.12		522	Gary Sutherland	.40	.20	.12
432	Ken Berry	.40	.20	.12		523	Tom Paciorek	.40	.20	.12
433	Larry Demery	.40	.20	.12		524	John Doherty	.40	.20	.12
434	Bob Locker	.40	.20	.12		525	Tom House	.40	.20	.12
435	Dave Nelson	.40	.20	.12		526	Larry Hisle	.40	.20	.12
436	Ken Frailing	.40	.20	.12		527	Mac Scarce	.40	.20	.12
437	Al Cowens	.40	.20	.12		528	Eddie Leon	.40	.20	.12
438	Don Carrithers	.40	.20	.12		529	Gary Thomasson	.40	.20	.12
439	Ed Brinkman	.40	.20	.12		530	Gaylord Perry	6.00	3.00	1.75
440	Andy Messersmith	.60	.30	.20		531	Reds Team (Sparky Anderson)	1.25	.60	.40
441	Bobby Heise	.40	.20	.12		532	Gorman Thomas	.80	.40	.25
442	Maximino Leon	.40	.20	.12		533	Rudy Meoli	.40	.20	.12
443	Twins Team (Frank Quilici)	1.25	.60	.40		534	Alex Johnson	.40	.20	.12
444	Gene Garber	.40	.20	.12		535	Gene Tenace	.40	.20	.12
445	Felix Millan	.40	.20	.12		536	Bob Moose	.40	.20	.12
446	Bart Johnson	.40	.20	.12		537	Tommy Harper	.40	.20	.12
447	Terry Crowley	.40	.20	.12		538	Duffy Dyer	.40	.20	.12
448	Frank Duffy	.40	.20	.12		539	Jesse Jefferson	.40	.20	.12
449	Charlie Williams	.40	.20	.12		540	Lou Brock	7.00	3.50	2.00
450	Willie McCovey	7.00	3.50	2.00		541	Roger Metzger	.40	.20	.12
451	Rick Dempsey	.60	.30	.20		542	Pete Broberg	.40	.20	.12
452	Angel Mangual	.40	.20	.12		543	Larry Biittner	.40	.20	.12
453	Claude Osteen	.40	.20	.12		544	Steve Mingori	.40	.20	.12
454	Doug Griffin	.40	.20	.12		545	Billy Williams	6.00	3.00	1.75
455	Don Wilson	.40	.20	.12		546	John Knox	.40	.20	.12
456	Bob Coluccio	.40	.20	.12		547	Von Joshua	.40	.20	.12
457	Mario Mendoza	.40	.20	.12		548	Charlie Sands	.40	.20	.12
458	Ross Grimsley	.40	.20	.12		549	Bill Butler	.40	.20	.12
459	A.L. Championships	1.25	.60	.40		550	Ralph Garr	.40	.20	.12
460	N.L. Championships	1.25	.60	.40		551	Larry Christenson	.40	.20	.12
461	World Series Game 1	2.25	1.25	.70		552	Jack Brohamer	.40	.20	.12
462	World Series Game 2	1.50	.70	.45		553	John Boccabella	.40	.20	.12
463	World Series Game 3	1.50	.70	.45		554	Rich Gossage	1.75	.90	.50
464	World Series Game 4	1.25	.60	.40		555	Al Oliver	1.25	.60	.40

		NR MT	EX	VG
556	Tim Johnson	.40	.20	.12
557	Larry Gura	.40	.20	.12
558	Dave Roberts	.40	.20	.12
559	Bob Montgomery	.40	.20	.12
560	Tony Perez	1.25	.60	.40
561	A's Team (Alvin Dark)	1.25	.60	.40
562	Gary Nolan	.40	.20	.12
563	Wilbur Howard	.40	.20	.12
564	Tommy Davis	.60	.30	.20
565	Joe Torre	1.00	.50	.30
566	Ray Burris	.40	.20	.12
567	Jim Sundberg	1.00	.50	.30
568	Dale Murray	.40	.20	.12
569	Frank White	.60	.30	.20
570	Jim Wynn	.60	.30	.20
571	Dave Lemanczyk	.40	.20	.12
572	Roger Nelson	.40	.20	.12
573	Orlando Pena	.40	.20	.12
574	Tony Taylor	.40	.20	.12
575	Gene Clines	.40	.20	.12
576	Phil Roof	.40	.20	.12
577	John Morris	.40	.20	.12
578	Dave Tomlin	.40	.20	.12
579	Skip Pitlock	.40	.20	.12
580	Frank Robinson	7.00	3.50	2.00
581	Darrel Chaney	.40	.20	.12
582	Eduardo Rodriguez	.40	.20	.12
583	Andy Etchebarren	.40	.20	.12
584	Mike Garman	.40	.20	.12
585	Chris Chambliss	.60	.30	.20
586	Tim McCarver	.90	.45	.25
587	Chris Ward	.40	.20	.12
588	Rick Auerbach	.40	.20	.12
589	Braves Team (Clyde King)	1.25	.60	.40
590	Cesar Cedeno	.60	.30	.20
591	Glenn Abbott	.40	.20	.12
592	Balor Moore	.40	.20	.12
593	Gene Lamont	.40	.20	.12
594	Jim Fuller	.40	.20	.12
595	Joe Niekro	.60	.30	.20
596	Ollie Brown	.40	.20	.12
597	Winston Llenas	.40	.20	.12
598	Bruce Kison	.40	.20	.12
599	Nate Colbert	.40	.20	.12
600	Rod Carew	18.00	9.00	5.50
601	Juan Beniquez	.40	.20	.12
602	John Vukovich	.40	.20	.12
603	Lew Krausse	.40	.20	.12
604	Oscar Zamora	.40	.20	.12
605	John Ellis	.40	.20	.12
606	Bruce Miller	.40	.20	.12
607	Jim Holt	.40	.20	.12
608	Gene Michael	.40	.20	.12
609	Ellie Hendricks	.40	.20	.12
610	Ron Hunt	.40	.20	.12
611	Yankees Team (Bill Virdon)	1.75	.90	.50
612	Terry Hughes	.40	.20	.12
613	Bill Parsons	.40	.20	.12
614	Rookie Pitchers (Jack Kucek, Dyar Miller, Vern Ruhle, Paul Siebert)	.40	.20	.12
615	Rookie Pitchers (Pat Darcy, Dennis Leonard, Tom Underwood, Hank Webb)	.90	.45	.25
616	Rookie Outfielders (Dave Augustine, Pepe Mangual, Jim Rice, John Scott)	50.00	25.00	15.00
617	Rookie Infielders (Mike Cubbage, Doug DeCinces, Reggie Sanders, Manny Trillo)	2.50	1.25	.70
618	Rookie Pitchers (Jamie Easterly, Tom Johnson, Scott McGregor, Rick Rhoden)	5.00	2.50	1.50
619	Rookie Outfielders (Benny Ayala, Nyls Nyman, Tommy Smith, Jerry Turner)	.40	.20	.12
620	Rookie Catchers-Outfielders (Gary Carter, Marc Hill, Danny Meyer, Leon Roberts)	50.00	25.00	15.00
621	Rookie Pitchers (John Denny, Rawly Eastwick, Jim Kern, Juan Veintidos)	.90	.45	.25
622	Rookie Outfielders (Ed Armbrister, Fred Lynn, Tom Poquette, Terry Whitfield)	15.00	7.50	4.50
623	Rookie Infielders (Phil Garner, Keith Hernandez, Bob Sheldon, Tom Veryzer)	40.00	20.00	12.00
624	Rookie Pitchers (Doug Konieczny, Gary Lavelle, Jim Otten, Eddie Solomon)	.40	.20	.12
625	Boog Powell	1.00	.50	.30
626	Larry Haney	.40	.20	.12
627	Tom Walker	.40	.20	.12
628	Ron LeFlore	1.25	.60	.40
629	Joe Hoerner	.40	.20	.12

		NR MT	EX	VG
630	Greg Luzinski	1.00	.50	.30
631	Lee Lacy	.40	.20	.12
632	Morris Nettles	.40	.20	.12
633	Paul Casanova	.40	.20	.12
634	Cy Acosta	.40	.20	.12
635	Chuck Dobson	.40	.20	.12
636	Charlie Moore	.40	.20	.12
637	Ted Martinez	.40	.20	.12
638	Cubs Team (Jim Marshall)	1.25	.60	.40
639	Steve Kline	.40	.20	.12
640	Harmon Killebrew	6.00	3.00	1.75
641	Jim Northrup	.40	.20	.12
642	Mike Phillips	.40	.20	.12
643	Brent Strom	.40	.20	.12
644	Bill Fahey	.40	.20	.12
645	Danny Cater	.40	.20	.12
646	Checklist 529-660	2.25	1.25	.70
647	Claudell Washington	2.50	1.25	.70
648	Dave Pagan	.40	.20	.12
649	Jack Heidemann	.40	.20	.12
650	Dave May	.40	.20	.12
651	John Morlan	.40	.20	.12
652	Lindy McDaniel	.40	.20	.12
653	Lee Richards	.40	.20	.12
654	Jerry Terrell	.40	.20	.12
655	Rico Carty	.60	.30	.20
656	Bill Plummer	.40	.20	.12
657	Bob Oliver	.40	.20	.12
658	Vic Harris	.40	.20	.12
659	Bob Apodaca	.40	.20	.12
660	Hank Aaron	35.00	17.50	10.50

1976 Topps

These 2-1/2" by 3-1/2" cards begin a design trend for Topps. The focus was more on the photo quality than in past years with a corresponding trend toward simplicity in the borders. The front of the cards has the player's name and team in two strips while his position is in the lower left corner under a drawing of a player representing that position. The backs have a bat and ball with the card number on the left; statistics and personal information and career highlights on the right. The 660-card set features a number of specialty sets including record-setting performances, statistical leaders, playoff and World Series highlights, the Sporting News All-Time All-Stars and father and son combinations.

		NR MT	EX	VG
	Complete Set:	275.00	138.00	83.00
	Commmon Player:	.15	.08	.05
1	'75 Record Breaker (Hank Aaron)	12.00	6.00	3.50
2	'75 Record Breaker (Bobby Bonds)	.40	.20	.12
3	'75 Record Breaker (Mickey Lolich)	.35	.20	.11
4	'75 Record Breaker (Dave Lopes)	.35	.20	.11
5	'75 Record Breaker (Tom Seaver)	1.50	.70	.45
6	'75 Record Breaker (Rennie Stennett)	.30	.15	.09
7	Jim Umbarger	.15	.08	.05
8	Tito Fuentes	.15	.08	.05
9	Paul Lindblad	.15	.08	.05
10	Lou Brock	2.50	1.25	.70
11	Jim Hughes	.15	.08	.05

		NR MT	EX	VG
12	Richie Zisk	.20	.10	.06
13	Johnny Wockenfuss	.15	.08	.05
14	Gene Garber	.20	.10	.06
15	George Scott	.25	.13	.08
16	Bob Apodaca	.15	.08	.05
17	Yankees Team (Billy Martin)	1.25	.60	.40
18	Dale Murray	.15	.08	.05
19	George Brett	18.00	9.00	5.50
20	Bob Watson	.20	.10	.06
21	Dave LaRoche	.15	.08	.05
22	Bill Russell	.20	.10	.06
23	Brian Downing	.25	.13	.08
24	Cesar Geronimo	.20	.10	.06
25	Mike Torrez	.20	.10	.06
26	Andy Thornton	.25	.13	.08
27	Ed Figueroa	.15	.08	.05
28	Dusty Baker	.25	.13	.08
29	Rick Burleson	.30	.15	.09
30	*John Montefusco*	.35	.20	.11
31	Len Randle	.15	.08	.05
32	Danny Frisella	.15	.08	.05
33	Bill North	.15	.08	.05
34	Mike Garman	.15	.08	.05
35	Tony Oliva	.60	.30	.20
36	Frank Taveras	.15	.08	.05
37	John Hiller	.20	.10	.06
38	Garry Maddox	.20	.10	.06
39	Pete Broberg	.15	.08	.05
40	Dave Kingman	.80	.40	.25
41	*Tippy Martinez*	.40	.20	.12
42	Barry Foote	.15	.08	.05
43	Paul Splittorff	.20	.10	.06
44	Doug Rader	.15	.08	.05
45	Boog Powell	.60	.30	.20
46	Dodgers Team (Walter Alston)	1.00	.50	.30
47	Jesse Jefferson	.15	.08	.05
48	Dave Concepcion	.40	.20	.12
49	Dave Duncan	.15	.08	.05
50	Fred Lynn	2.00	1.00	.60
51	Ray Burris	.15	.08	.05
52	Dave Chalk	.15	.08	.05
53	Mike Beard	.15	.08	.05
54	Dave Rader	.15	.08	.05
55	Gaylord Perry	2.00	1.00	.60
56	Bob Tolan	.20	.10	.06
57	Phil Garner	.30	.15	.09
58	Ron Reed	.20	.10	.06
59	Larry Hisle	.20	.10	.06
60	Jerry Reuss	.30	.15	.09
61	Ron LeFlore	.30	.15	.09
62	Johnny Oates	.15	.08	.05
63	Bobby Darwin	.15	.08	.05
64	Jerry Koosman	.30	.15	.09
65	Chris Chambliss	.30	.15	.09
66	Father & Son (Buddy Bell, Gus Bell)	.50	.25	.15
67	Father & Son (Bob Boone, Ray Boone)	.40	.20	.12
68	Father & Son (Joe Coleman, Joe Coleman, Jr.)	.20	.10	.06
69	Father & Son (Jim Hegan, Mike Hegan)	.20	.10	.06
70	Father & Son (Roy Smalley, Roy Smalley, Jr.)	.25	.13	.08
71	Steve Rogers	.20	.10	.06
72	Hal McRae	.25	.13	.08
73	Orioles Team (Earl Weaver)	.80	.40	.25
74	Oscar Gamble	.20	.10	.06
75	Larry Dierker	.20	.10	.06
76	Willie Crawford	.15	.08	.05
77	Pedro Borbon	.15	.08	.05
78	Cecil Cooper	1.00	.50	.30
79	Jerry Morales	.15	.08	.05
80	Jim Kaat	.90	.45	.25
81	Darrell Evans	.50	.25	.15
82	Von Joshua	.15	.08	.05
83	Jim Spencer	.15	.08	.05
84	Brent Strom	.15	.08	.05
85	Mickey Rivers	.25	.13	.08
86	Mike Tyson	.15	.08	.05
87	Tom Burgmeier	.15	.08	.05
88	Duffy Dyer	.15	.08	.05
89	Vern Ruhle	.15	.08	.05
90	Sal Bando	.30	.15	.09
91	Tom Hutton	.15	.08	.05
92	Eduardo Rodriguez	.15	.08	.05
93	Mike Phillips	.15	.08	.05
94	Jim Dwyer	.30	.15	.09
95	Brooks Robinson	2.75	1.50	.80
96	Doug Bird	.15	.08	.05
97	Wilbur Howard	.15	.08	.05

		NR MT	EX	VG
98	*Dennis Eckersley*	5.00	2.50	1.50
99	Lee Lacy	.20	.10	.06
100	Jim Hunter	2.00	1.00	.60
101	Pete LaCock	.15	.08	.05
102	Jim Willoughby	.15	.08	.05
103	Biff Pocoroba	.15	.08	.05
104	Reds Team (Sparky Anderson)	.90	.45	.25
105	Gary Lavelle	.15	.08	.05
106	Tom Grieve	.15	.08	.05
107	Dave Roberts	.15	.08	.05
108	Don Kirkwood	.15	.08	.05
109	Larry Lintz	.15	.08	.05
110	Carlos May	.20	.10	.06
111	Danny Thompson	.20	.10	.06
112	*Kent Tekulve*	.80	.40	.25
113	Gary Sutherland	.15	.08	.05
114	Jay Johnstone	.25	.13	.08
115	Ken Holtzman	.25	.13	.08
116	Charlie Moore	.15	.08	.05
117	Mike Jorgensen	.15	.08	.05
118	Red Sox Team (Darrell Johnson)	.90	.45	.25
119	Checklist 1-132	1.25	.60	.40
120	Rusty Staub	.35	.20	.11
121	Tony Solaita	.15	.08	.05
122	Mike Cosgrove	.15	.08	.05
123	Walt Williams	.20	.10	.06
124	Doug Rau	.15	.08	.05
125	Don Baylor	.50	.25	.15
126	Tom Dettore	.15	.08	.05
127	Larvell Blanks	.15	.08	.05
128	Ken Griffey	.35	.20	.11
129	Andy Etchebarren	.15	.08	.05
130	Luis Tiant	.40	.20	.12
131	Bill Stein	.25	.13	.08
132	Don Hood	.15	.08	.05
133	Gary Matthews	.25	.13	.08
134	Mike Ivie	.15	.08	.05
135	Bake McBride	.20	.10	.06
136	Dave Goltz	.20	.10	.06
137	Bill Robinson	.15	.08	.05
138	Lerrin LaGrow	.15	.08	.05
139	Gorman Thomas	.35	.20	.11
140	Vida Blue	.40	.20	.12
141	*Larry Parrish*	.80	.40	.25
142	Dick Drago	.15	.08	.05
143	Jerry Grote	.20	.10	.06
144	Al Fitzmorris	.15	.08	.05
145	Larry Bowa	.35	.20	.11
146	George Medich	.20	.10	.06
147	Astros Team (Bill Virdon)	.80	.40	.25
148	Stan Thomas	.15	.08	.05
149	Tommy Davis	.30	.15	.09
150	Steve Garvey	4.50	2.25	1.25
151	Bill Bonham	.15	.08	.05
152	Leroy Stanton	.15	.08	.05
153	Buzz Capra	.15	.08	.05
154	Bucky Dent	.30	.15	.09
155	Jack Billingham	.15	.08	.05
156	Rico Carty	.25	.13	.08
157	Mike Caldwell	.15	.08	.05
158	Ken Reitz	.15	.08	.05
159	Jerry Terrell	.15	.08	.05
160	Dave Winfield	6.00	3.00	1.75
161	Bruce Kison	.15	.08	.05
162	Jack Pierce	.15	.08	.05
163	Jim Slaton	.15	.08	.05
164	Pepe Mangual	.15	.08	.05
165	Gene Tenace	.20	.10	.06
166	Skip Lockwood	.15	.08	.05
167	Freddie Patek	.15	.08	.05
168	Tom Hilgendorf	.15	.08	.05
169	Graig Nettles	1.00	.50	.30
170	Rick Wise	.20	.10	.06
171	Greg Gross	.15	.08	.05
172	Rangers Team (Frank Lucchesi)	.80	.40	.25
173	Steve Swisher	.15	.08	.05
174	Charlie Hough	.25	.13	.08
175	Ken Singleton	.30	.15	.09
176	Dick Lange	.15	.08	.05
177	Marty Perez	.15	.08	.05
178	Tom Buskey	.15	.08	.05
179	George Foster	1.00	.50	.30
180	Rich Gossage	1.25	.60	.40
181	Willie Montanez	.20	.10	.06
182	Harry Rasmussen	.15	.08	.05
183	Steve Braun	.15	.08	.05
184	Bill Greif	.15	.08	.05
185	Dave Parker	3.75	1.75	1.00
186	Tom Walker	.15	.08	.05
187	Pedro Garcia	.15	.08	.05
188	Fred Scherman	.15	.08	.05

		NR MT	EX	VG
189	Claudell Washington	.40	.20	.12
190	Jon Matlack	.25	.13	.08
191	N.L. Batting Leaders (Bill Madlock, Manny Sanguillen, Ted Simmons)	.60	.30	.20
192	A.L. Batting Leaders (Rod Carew, Fred Lynn, Thurman Munson)	1.50	.70	.45
193	N.L. Home Run Leaders (Dave Kingman, Greg Luzinski, Mike Schmidt)	1.25	.60	.40
194	A.L. Home Run Leaders (Reggie Jackson, John Mayberry, George Scott)	1.25	.60	.40
195	N.L. Runs Batted In Ldrs. (Johnny Bench, Greg Luzinski, Tony Perez)	1.25	.60	.40
196	A.L. Runs Batted In Ldrs. (Fred Lynn, John Mayberry, George Scott)	.60	.30	.20
197	N.L. Stolen Base Leaders (Lou Brock, Dave Lopes, Joe Morgan)	.90	.45	.25
198	A.L. Stolen Base Leaders (Amos Otis, Mickey Rivers, Claudell Washington)	.50	.25	.15
199	N.L. Victory Leaders (Randy Jones, Andy Messersmith, Tom Seaver)	.80	.40	.25
200	A.L. Victory Leaders (Vida Blue, Jim Hunter, Jim Palmer)	.90	.45	.25
201	N.L. Earned Run Avg. Ldrs. (Randy Jones, Andy Messersmith, Tom Seaver)	.80	.40	.25
202	A.L. Earned Run Avg. Ldrs. (Dennis Eckersley, Jim Hunter, Jim Palmer)	.90	.45	.25
203	N.L. Strikeout Leaders (Andy Messersmith, John Montefusco, Tom Seaver)	.80	.40	.25
204	A.L. Strikeout Leaders (Bert Blyleven, Gaylord Perry, Frank Tanana)	.70	.35	.20
205	Major League Leading Firemen (Rich Gossage, Al Hrabosky)	.50	.25	.15
206	Manny Trillo	.20	.10	.06
207	Andy Hassler	.15	.08	.05
208	Mike Lum	.15	.08	.05
209	Alan Ashby	.35	.20	.11
210	Lee May	.25	.13	.08
211	Clay Carroll	.20	.10	.06
212	Pat Kelly	.15	.08	.05
213	Dave Heaverlo	.15	.08	.05
214	Eric Soderholm	.15	.08	.05
215	Reggie Smith	.25	.13	.08
216	Expos Team (Karl Kuehl)	.80	.40	.25
217	Dave Freisleben	.15	.08	.05
218	John Knox	.15	.08	.05
219	Tom Murphy	.15	.08	.05
220	Manny Sanguillen	.20	.10	.06
221	Jim Todd	.15	.08	.05
222	Wayne Garrett	.15	.08	.05
223	Ollie Brown	.15	.08	.05
224	Jim York	.15	.08	.05
225	Roy White	.25	.13	.08
226	Jim Sundberg	.25	.13	.08
227	Oscar Zamora	.15	.08	.05
228	John Hale	.15	.08	.05
229	*Jerry Remy*	.30	.15	.09
230	Carl Yastrzemski	7.00	3.50	2.00
231	Tom House	.15	.08	.05
232	Frank Duffy	.15	.08	.05
233	Grant Jackson	.15	.08	.05
234	Mike Sadek	.15	.08	.05
235	Bert Blyleven	1.00	.50	.30
236	Royals Team (Whitey Herzog)	.80	.40	.25
237	Dave Hamilton	.15	.08	.05
238	Larry Biittner	.15	.08	.05
239	John Curtis	.15	.08	.05
240	Pete Rose	15.00	7.50	4.50
241	Hector Torres	.15	.08	.05
242	Dan Meyer	.15	.08	.05
243	Jim Rooker	.15	.08	.05
244	Bill Sharp	.15	.08	.05
245	Felix Millan	.15	.08	.05
246	Cesar Tovar	.15	.08	.05
247	Terry Harmon	.15	.08	.05
248	Dick Tidrow	.20	.10	.06
249	Cliff Johnson	.20	.10	.06
250	Fergie Jenkins	1.00	.50	.30
251	Rick Monday	.30	.15	.09
252	Tim Nordbrook	.15	.08	.05
253	Bill Buckner	.50	.25	.15
254	Rudy Meoli	.15	.08	.05
255	Fritz Peterson	.15	.08	.05
256	Rowland Office	.15	.08	.05
257	Ross Grimsley	.20	.10	.06
258	Nyls Nyman	.15	.08	.05
259	Darrel Chaney	.15	.08	.05
260	Steve Busby	.20	.10	.06
261	Gary Thomasson	.15	.08	.05
262	Checklist 133-264	1.50	.70	.45
263	*Lyman Bostock*	.80	.40	.25

		NR MT	EX	VG
264	Steve Renko	.15	.08	.05
265	Willie Davis	.30	.15	.09
266	Alan Foster	.15	.08	.05
267	Aurelio Rodriguez	.20	.10	.06
268	Del Unser	.15	.08	.05
269	Rick Austin	.15	.08	.05
270	Willie Stargell	3.00	1.50	.90
271	Jim Lonborg	.20	.10	.06
272	Rick Dempsey	.25	.13	.08
273	Joe Niekro	.30	.15	.09
274	Tommy Harper	.20	.10	.06
275	*Rick Manning*	.40	.20	.12
276	Mickey Scott	.15	.08	.05
277	Cubs Team (Jim Marshall)	.80	.40	.25
278	Bernie Carbo	.15	.08	.05
279	Roy Howell	.15	.08	.05
280	Burt Hooton	.20	.10	.06
281	Dave May	.15	.08	.05
282	Dan Osborn	.15	.08	.05
283	Merv Rettenmund	.15	.08	.05
284	Steve Ontiveros	.15	.08	.05
285	Mike Cuellar	.25	.13	.08
286	Jim Wohlford	.15	.08	.05
287	Pete Mackanin	.15	.08	.05
288	Bill Campbell	.15	.08	.05
289	Enzo Hernandez	.15	.08	.05
290	Ted Simmons	.60	.30	.20
291	Ken Sanders	.15	.08	.05
292	Leon Roberts	.15	.08	.05
293	Bill Castro	.15	.08	.05
294	Ed Kirkpatrick	.15	.08	.05
295	Dave Cash	.15	.08	.05
296	Pat Dobson	.20	.10	.06
297	Roger Metzger	.15	.08	.05
298	Dick Bosman	.15	.08	.05
299	Champ Summers	.15	.08	.05
300	Johnny Bench	6.00	3.00	1.75
301	Jackie Brown	.15	.08	.05
302	Rick Miller	.15	.08	.05
303	Steve Foucault	.15	.08	.05
304	Angels Team (Dick Williams)	.80	.40	.25
305	Andy Messersmith	.25	.13	.08
306	Rod Gilbreath	.15	.08	.05
307	Al Bumbry	.20	.10	.06
308	Jim Barr	.15	.08	.05
309	Bill Melton	.20	.10	.06
310	Randy Jones	.30	.15	.09
311	Cookie Rojas	.15	.08	.05
312	Don Carrithers	.15	.08	.05
313	*Dan Ford*	.25	.13	.08
314	Ed Kranepool	.25	.13	.08
315	Al Hrabosky	.20	.10	.06
316	Robin Yount	20.00	10.00	6.00
317	*John Candelaria*	1.75	.90	.50
318	Bob Boone	.30	.15	.09
319	Larry Gura	.20	.10	.06
320	Willie Horton	.25	.13	.08
321	Jose Cruz	.35	.20	.11
322	Glenn Abbott	.15	.08	.05
323	Rob Sperring	.15	.08	.05
324	Jim Bibby	.15	.08	.05
325	Tony Perez	.80	.40	.25
326	Dick Pole	.15	.08	.05
327	Dave Moates	.15	.08	.05
328	Carl Morton	.15	.08	.05
329	Joe Ferguson	.15	.08	.05
330	Nolan Ryan	15.00	7.50	4.50
331	Padres Team (John McNamara)	.80	.40	.25
332	Charlie Williams	.15	.08	.05
333	Bob Coluccio	.15	.08	.05
334	Dennis Leonard	.25	.13	.08
335	Bob Grich	.25	.13	.08
336	Vic Albury	.15	.08	.05
337	Bud Harrelson	.20	.10	.06
338	Bob Bailey	.15	.08	.05
339	John Denny	.25	.13	.08
340	Jim Rice	8.00	4.00	2.50
341	All Time All-Stars (Lou Gehrig)	3.00	1.50	.90
342	All Time All-Stars (Rogers Hornsby)	1.25	.60	.40
343	All Time All-Stars (Pie Traynor)	.80	.40	.25
344	All Time All-Stars (Honus Wagner)	1.25	.60	.40
345	All Time All-Stars (Babe Ruth)	5.00	2.50	1.50
346	All Time All-Stars (Ty Cobb)	3.00	1.50	.90
347	All Time All-Stars (Ted Williams)	3.00	1.50	.90
348	All Time All-Stars (Mickey Cochrane)	.80	.40	.25
349	All Time All-Stars (Walter Johnson)	1.25	.60	.40
350	All Time All-Stars (Lefty Grove)	1.00	.50	.30
351	Randy Hundley	.15	.08	.05

		NR MT	EX	VG			NR MT	EX	VG
352	Dave Giusti	.15	.08	.05	443	Giants Team	.80	.40	.25
353	*Sixto Lezcano*	.30	.15	.09	444	Gary Nolan	.15	.08	.05
354	Ron Blomberg	.20	.10	.06	445	Rico Petrocelli	.25	.13	.08
355	Steve Carlton	5.00	2.50	1.50	446	Larry Haney	.15	.08	.05
356	Ted Martinez	.15	.08	.05	447	Gene Locklear	.15	.08	.05
357	Ken Forsch	.20	.10	.06	448	Tom Johnson	.15	.08	.05
358	Buddy Bell	.50	.25	.15	449	Bob Robertson	.15	.08	.05
359	Rick Reuschel	.30	.15	.09	450	Jim Palmer	4.00	2.00	1.25
360	Jeff Burroughs	.20	.10	.06	451	Buddy Bradford	.15	.08	.05
361	Tigers Team (Ralph Houk)	1.00	.50	.30	452	Tom Hausman	.15	.08	.05
362	Will McEnaney	.15	.08	.05	453	Lou Piniella	.60	.30	.20
363	*Dave Collins*	.40	.20	.12	454	Tom Griffin	.15	.08	.05
364	Elias Sosa	.15	.08	.05	455	Dick Allen	.50	.25	.15
365	Carlton Fisk	2.00	1.00	.60	456	Joe Coleman	.20	.10	.06
366	Bobby Valentine	.30	.15	.09	457	Ed Crosby	.15	.08	.05
367	Bruce Miller	.15	.08	.05	458	Earl Williams	.15	.08	.05
368	Wilbur Wood	.25	.13	.08	459	Jim Brewer	.15	.08	.05
369	Frank White	.30	.15	.09	460	Cesar Cedeno	.30	.15	.09
370	Ron Cey	.40	.20	.12	461	NL & AL Championships	.80	.40	.25
371	Ellie Hendricks	.15	.08	.05	462	1975 World Series	.80	.40	.25
372	Rick Baldwin	.15	.08	.05	463	Steve Hargan	.15	.08	.05
373	Johnny Briggs	.15	.08	.05	464	Ken Henderson	.15	.08	.05
374	Dan Warthen	.15	.08	.05	465	Mike Marshall	.30	.15	.09
375	Ron Fairly	.25	.13	.08	466	Bob Stinson	.15	.08	.05
376	Rich Hebner	.20	.10	.06	467	Woodie Fryman	.20	.10	.06
377	Mike Hegan	.15	.08	.05	468	Jesus Alou	.20	.10	.06
378	Steve Stone	.25	.13	.08	469	Rawly Eastwick	.15	.08	.05
379	Ken Boswell	.15	.08	.05	470	Bobby Murcer	.35	.20	.11
380	Bobby Bonds	.35	.20	.11	471	Jim Burton	.15	.08	.05
381	Denny Doyle	.15	.08	.05	472	Bob Davis	.15	.08	.05
382	Matt Alexander	.15	.08	.05	473	Paul Blair	.20	.10	.06
383	John Ellis	.15	.08	.05	474	Ray Corbin	.15	.08	.05
384	Phillies Team (Danny Ozark)	.80	.40	.25	475	Joe Rudi	.30	.15	.09
385	Mickey Lolich	.40	.20	.12	476	Bob Moose	.15	.08	.05
386	Ed Goodson	.15	.08	.05	477	Indians Team (Frank Robinson)	.80	.40	.25
387	Mike Miley	.15	.08	.05	478	Lynn McGlothen	.15	.08	.05
388	Stan Perzanowski	.15	.08	.05	479	Bobby Mitchell	.15	.08	.05
389	Glenn Adams	.15	.08	.05	480	Mike Schmidt	20.00	10.00	6.00
390	Don Gullett	.20	.10	.06	481	Rudy May	.20	.10	.06
391	Jerry Hairston	.15	.08	.05	482	Tim Hosley	.15	.08	.05
392	Checklist 265-396	1.50	.70	.45	483	Mickey Stanley	.20	.10	.06
393	Paul Mitchell	.15	.08	.05	484	Eric Raich	.15	.08	.05
394	Fran Healy	.15	.08	.05	485	Mike Hargrove	.20	.10	.06
395	Jim Wynn	.30	.15	.09	486	Bruce Dal Canton	.15	.08	.05
396	Bill Lee	.20	.10	.06	487	Leron Lee	.15	.08	.05
397	Tim Foli	.15	.08	.05	488	Claude Osteen	.20	.10	.06
398	Dave Tomlin	.15	.08	.05	489	Skip Jutze	.15	.08	.05
399	Luis Melendez	.15	.08	.05	490	Frank Tanana	.30	.15	.09
400	Rod Carew	4.25	2.25	1.25	491	Terry Crowley	.15	.08	.05
401	Ken Brett	.20	.10	.06	492	Marty Pattin	.15	.08	.05
402	Don Money	.20	.10	.06	493	Derrel Thomas	.15	.08	.05
403	Geoff Zahn	.20	.10	.06	494	Craig Swan	.15	.08	.05
404	Enos Cabell	.20	.10	.06	495	Nate Colbert	.15	.08	.05
405	Rollie Fingers	1.25	.60	.40	496	Juan Beniquez	.20	.10	.06
406	Ed Herrmann	.20	.10	.06	497	Joe McIntosh	.15	.08	.05
407	Tom Underwood	.15	.08	.05	498	Glenn Borgmann	.15	.08	.05
408	Charlie Spikes	.15	.08	.05	499	Mario Guerrero	.15	.08	.05
409	Dave Lemanczyk	.15	.08	.05	500	Reggie Jackson	9.00	4.50	2.75
410	Ralph Garr	.20	.10	.06	501	Billy Champion	.15	.08	.05
411	Bill Singer	.20	.10	.06	502	Tim McCarver	.50	.25	.15
412	Toby Harrah	.25	.13	.08	503	Elliott Maddox	.20	.10	.06
413	Pete Varney	.15	.08	.05	504	Pirates Team (Danny Murtaugh)	.80	.40	.25
414	Wayne Garland	.15	.08	.05	505	Mark Belanger	.20	.10	.06
415	Vada Pinson	.50	.25	.15	506	George Mitterwald	.15	.08	.05
416	Tommy John	1.25	.60	.40	507	Ray Bare	.15	.08	.05
417	Gene Clines	.15	.08	.05	508	*Duane Kuiper*	.20	.10	.06
418	Jose Morales	.15	.08	.05	509	Bill Hands	.15	.08	.05
419	Reggie Cleveland	.15	.08	.05	510	Amos Otis	.25	.13	.08
420	Joe Morgan	4.00	2.00	1.25	511	Jamie Easterly	.15	.08	.05
421	A's Team	.80	.40	.25	512	Ellie Rodriguez	.15	.08	.05
422	Johnny Grubb	.15	.08	.05	513	Bart Johnson	.15	.08	.05
423	Ed Halicki	.15	.08	.05	514	Dan Driessen	.30	.15	.09
424	Phil Roof	.15	.08	.05	515	Steve Yeager	.15	.08	.05
425	Rennie Stennett	.15	.08	.05	516	Wayne Granger	.15	.08	.05
426	Bob Forsch	.25	.13	.08	517	John Milner	.15	.08	.05
427	Kurt Bevacqua	.15	.08	.05	518	*Doug Flynn*	.20	.10	.06
428	Jim Crawford	.15	.08	.05	519	Steve Brye	.15	.08	.05
429	Fred Stanley	.20	.10	.06	520	Willie McCovey	2.50	1.25	.70
430	Jose Cardenal	.20	.10	.06	521	Jim Colborn	.15	.08	.05
431	Dick Ruthven	.15	.08	.05	522	Ted Sizemore	.15	.08	.05
432	Tom Veryzer	.15	.08	.05	523	Bob Montgomery	.15	.08	.05
433	Rick Waits	.15	.08	.05	524	Pete Falcone	.15	.08	.05
434	Morris Nettles	.15	.08	.05	525	Billy Williams	2.25	1.25	.70
435	Phil Niekro	2.00	1.00	.60	526	Checklist 397-528	1.50	.70	.45
436	Bill Fahey	.15	.08	.05	527	Mike Anderson	.15	.08	.05
437	Terry Forster	.25	.13	.08	528	Dock Ellis	.20	.10	.06
438	Doug DeCinces	.50	.25	.15	529	Deron Johnson	.15	.08	.05
439	Rick Rhoden	.60	.30	.20	530	Don Sutton	1.50	.70	.45
440	John Mayberry	.25	.13	.08	531	Mets Team (Joe Frazier)	.90	.45	.25
441	Gary Carter	10.00	5.00	3.00	532	Milt May	.15	.08	.05
442	Hank Webb	.15	.08	.05	533	Lee Richard	.15	.08	.05

		NR MT	EX	VG
534	Stan Bahnsen	.15	.08	.05
535	Dave Nelson	.15	.08	.05
536	Mike Thompson	.15	.08	.05
537	Tony Muser	.15	.08	.05
538	Pat Darcy	.15	.08	.05
539	John Balaz	.15	.08	.05
540	Bill Freehan	.25	.13	.08
541	Steve Mingori	.15	.08	.05
542	Keith Hernandez	6.00	3.00	1.75
543	Wayne Twitchell	.15	.08	.05
544	Pepe Frias	.15	.08	.05
545	Sparky Lyle	.35	.20	.11
546	Dave Rosello	.15	.08	.05
547	Roric Harrison	.15	.08	.05
548	Manny Mota	.25	.13	.08
549	Randy Tate	.15	.08	.05
550	Hank Aaron	10.00	5.00	3.00
551	Jerry DaVanon	.15	.08	.05
552	Terry Humphrey	.15	.08	.05
553	Randy Moffitt	.15	.08	.05
554	Ray Fosse	.15	.08	.05
555	Dyar Miller	.15	.08	.05
556	Twins Team (Gene Mauch)	.80	.40	.25
557	Dan Spillner	.15	.08	.05
558	Clarence Gaston	.15	.08	.05
559	Clyde Wright	.15	.08	.05
560	Jorge Orta	.15	.08	.05
561	Tom Carroll	.15	.08	.05
562	Adrian Garrett	.15	.08	.05
563	Larry Demery	.15	.08	.05
564	Bubble Gum Blowing Champ (Kurt Bevacqua)	.30	.15	.09
565	Tug McGraw	.35	.20	.11
566	Ken McMullen	.15	.08	.05
567	George Stone	.15	.08	.05
568	Rob Andrews	.15	.08	.05
569	Nelson Briles	.15	.08	.05
570	George Hendrick	.20	.10	.06
571	Don DeMola	.15	.08	.05
572	Rich Coggins	.20	.10	.06
573	Bill Travers	.15	.08	.05
574	Don Kessinger	.20	.10	.06
575	Dwight Evans	1.00	.50	.30
576	Maximino Leon	.15	.08	.05
577	Marc Hill	.15	.08	.05
578	Ted Kubiak	.15	.08	.05
579	Clay Kirby	.15	.08	.05
580	Bert Campaneris	.30	.15	.09
581	Cardinals Team (Red Schoendienst)	.80	.40	.25
582	Mike Kekich	.15	.08	.05
583	Tommy Helms	.15	.08	.05
584	Stan Wall	.15	.08	.05
585	Joe Torre	.50	.25	.15
586	Ron Schueler	.15	.08	.05
587	Leo Cardenas	.15	.08	.05
588	Kevin Kobel	.15	.08	.05
589	Rookie Pitchers (Santo Alcala, *Mike Flanagan*, Joe Pactwa, Pablo Torrealba)	1.00	.50	.30
590	Rookie Outfielders (Henry Cruz, *Chet Lemon, Ellis Valentine*, Terry Whitfield)	1.00	.50	.30
591	Rookie Pitchers (Steve Grilli, Craig Mitchell, Jose Sosa, George Throop)	.15	.08	.05
592	Rookie Infielders (Dave McKay, *Willie Randolph, Jerry Royster*, Roy Staiger)	5.00	2.50	1.50
593	Rookie Pitchers (Larry Anderson, Ken Crosby, Mark Littell, *Butch Metzger*)	.25	.13	.08
594	Rookie Catchers & Outfielders (Andy Merchant, Ed Ott, Royle Stillman, Jerry White)	.15	.08	.05
595	Rookie Pitchers (Steve Barr, Art DeFilippis, Randy Lerch, Sid Monge)	.15	.08	.05
596	Rookie Infielders (Lamar Johnson, *Johnny LeMaster*, Jerry Manuel, *Craig Reynolds*)	.35	.20	.11
597	Rookie Pitchers (*Don Aase*, Jack Kucek, Frank LaCorte, Mike Pazik)	.50	.25	.15
598	Rookie Outfielders (Hector Cruz, *Jamie Quirk*, Jerry Turner, Joe Wallis)	.20	.10	.06
599	Rookie Pitchers (Rob Dressler, *Ron Guidry*, Bob McClure, Pat Zachry)	10.00	5.00	3.00
600	Tom Seaver	6.00	3.00	1.75
601	Ken Rudolph	.15	.08	.05
602	Doug Konieczny	.15	.08	.05
603	Jim Holt	.15	.08	.05
604	Joe Lovitto	.15	.08	.05
605	Al Downing	.20	.10	.06
606	Brewers Team (Alex Grammas)	.80	.40	.25

		NR MT	EX	VG
607	Rich Hinton	.15	.08	.05
608	Vic Correll	.15	.08	.05
609	Fred Norman	.15	.08	.05
610	Greg Luzinski	.40	.20	.12
611	Rich Folkers	.15	.08	.05
612	Joe Lahoud	.15	.08	.05
613	Tim Johnson	.15	.08	.05
614	Fernando Arroyo	.15	.08	.05
615	Mike Cubbage	.15	.08	.05
616	Buck Martinez	.15	.08	.05
617	Darold Knowles	.15	.08	.05
618	Jack Brohamer	.15	.08	.05
619	Bill Butler	.15	.08	.05
620	Al Oliver	.70	.35	.20
621	Tom Hall	.15	.08	.05
622	Rick Auerbach	.15	.08	.05
623	Bob Allietta	.15	.08	.05
624	Tony Taylor	.15	.08	.05
625	J.R. Richard	.25	.13	.08
626	Bob Sheldon	.15	.08	.05
627	Bill Plummer	.15	.08	.05
628	John D'Acquisto	.15	.08	.05
629	Sandy Alomar	.20	.10	.06
630	Chris Speier	.20	.10	.06
631	Braves Team (Dave Bristol)	.80	.40	.25
632	Rogelio Moret	.15	.08	.05
633	*John Stearns*	.30	.15	.09
634	Larry Christenson	.15	.08	.05
635	Jim Fregosi	.25	.13	.08
636	Joe Decker	.15	.08	.05
637	Bruce Bochte	.20	.10	.06
638	Doyle Alexander	.30	.15	.09
639	Fred Kendall	.15	.08	.05
640	Bill Madlock	1.00	.50	.30
641	Tom Paciorek	.20	.10	.06
642	Dennis Blair	.15	.08	.05
643	Checklist 529-660	1.50	.70	.45
644	Tom Bradley	.15	.08	.05
645	Darrell Porter	.20	.10	.06
646	John Lowenstein	.15	.08	.05
647	Al Cowens	.20	.10	.06
648	Dave Roberts	.15	.08	.05
649	Thurman Munson	4.50	2.25	1.25
650	John Odom	.20	.10	.06
651	Ed Armbrister	.15	.08	.05
652	*Mike Norris*	.30	.15	.09
653	Doug Griffin	.15	.08	.05
654	Mike Vail	.15	.08	.05
655	White Sox Team (Chuck Tanner)	.80	.40	.25
656	*Roy Smalley*	.40	.20	.12
657	Jerry Johnson	.15	.08	.05
658	Ben Oglivie	.25	.13	.08
659	Dave Lopes	.60	.13	.08

1976 Topps Traded

Similar to the Topps Traded set of 1974, the 2-1/2" by 3-1/2" cards feature photos of players traded after the printing deadline. The style of the cards is essentially the same as the regular issue but with a large "Sports Extra" headline announcing the trade and its date. The backs continue in newspaper style to detail the specifics of the trade. There are 43 player cards and one checklist in the set. Numbers reamin the same as the player's regular card, with the addition of a "T" suffix.

		NR MT	EX	VG
Complete Set:		8.00	4.00	2.50
Common Player:		.15	.08	.05
27T	Ed Figueroa	.20	.10	.06
28T	Dusty Baker	.35	.20	.11
44T	Doug Rader	.15	.08	.05
58T	Ron Reed	.20	.10	.06
74T	Oscar Gamble	.25	.13	.08
80T	Jim Kaat	.60	.30	.20
83T	Jim Spencer	.15	.08	.05
85T	Mickey Rivers	.30	.15	.09
99T	Lee Lacy	.20	.10	.06
120T	Rusty Staub	.50	.25	.15
127T	Larvell Blanks	.15	.08	.05
146T	George Medich	.15	.08	.05
158T	Ken Reitz	.15	.08	.05
208T	Mike Lum	.15	.08	.05
211T	Clay Carroll	.20	.10	.06
231T	Tom House	.15	.08	.05
250T	Fergie Jenkins	.70	.35	.20
259T	Darrel Chaney	.15	.08	.05
292T	Leon Roberts	.15	.08	.05
296T	Pat Dobson	.20	.10	.06
309T	Bill Melton	.20	.10	.06
338T	Bob Bailey	.15	.08	.05
380T	Bobby Bonds	.35	.20	.11
383T	John Ellis	.15	.08	.05
385T	Mickey Lolich	.50	.25	.15
401T	Ken Brett	.20	.10	.06
410T	Ralph Garr	.20	.10	.06
411T	Bill Singer	.20	.10	.06
428T	Jim Crawford	.15	.08	.05
434T	Morris Nettles	.15	.08	.05
464T	Ken Henderson	.15	.08	.05
497T	Joe McIntosh	.15	.08	.05
524T	Pete Falcone	.15	.08	.05
527T	Mike Anderson	.15	.08	.05
528T	Dock Ellis	.20	.10	.06
532T	Milt May	.15	.08	.05
554T	Ray Fosse	.15	.08	.05
579T	Clay Kirby	.15	.08	.05
583T	Tommy Helms	.15	.08	.05
592T	Willie Randolph	1.00	.50	.30
618T	Jack Brohamer	.15	.08	.05
632T	Rogelio Moret	.15	.08	.05
649T	Dave Roberts	.15	.08	.05
----	Traded Checklist	.80	.40	.25

1977 Topps

The 1977 Topps Set is a 660-card effort featuring front designs dominated by a color photograph on which there is a facsimile autograph. Above the picture are the player's name, team and position. The backs of the 2-1/2" by 3-1/2" cards include personal and career statistics along with newspaper-style highlights and a cartoon. Specialty cards include statistical leaders, record performances, a new "Turn Back The Clock" feature which highlighted great past moments and a "Big League Brothers" feature.

	NR MT	EX	VG
Complete Set:	275.00	138.00	83.00
Common Player:	.15	.08	.05

		NR MT	EX	VG
1	Batting Leaders (George Brett, Bill Madlock)	2.50	.70	.45
2	Home Run Leaders (Graig Nettles, Mike Schmidt)	1.25	.60	.40
3	Runs Batted In Leaders (George Foster, Lee May)	.50	.25	.15
4	Stolen Base Leaders (Dave Lopes, Bill North)	.30	.15	.09
5	Victory Leaders (Randy Jones, Jim Palmer)	.80	.40	.25
6	Strikeout Leaders (Nolan Ryan, Tom Seaver)	2.00	1.00	.60
7	Earned Run Avg. Ldrs. (John Denny, Mark Fidrych)	.30	.15	.09
8	Leading Firemen (Bill Campbell, Rawly Eastwick)	.30	.15	.09
9	Doug Rader	.15	.08	.05
10	Reggie Jackson	7.00	3.50	2.00
11	Rob Dressler	.15	.08	.05
12	Larry Haney	.15	.08	.05
13	Luis Gomez	.15	.08	.05
14	Tommy Smith	.15	.08	.05
15	Don Gullett	.20	.10	.06
16	Bob Jones	.15	.08	.05
17	Steve Stone	.25	.13	.08
18	Indians Team (Frank Robinson)	.80	.40	.25
19	John D'Acquisto	.15	.08	.05
20	Graig Nettles	.90	.45	.25
21	Ken Forsch	.20	.10	.06
22	Bill Freehan	.25	.13	.08
23	Dan Driessen	.25	.13	.08
24	Carl Morton	.15	.08	.05
25	Dwight Evans	1.75	.90	.50
26	Ray Sadecki	.15	.08	.05
27	Bill Buckner	.35	.20	.11
28	Woodie Fryman	.20	.10	.06
29	Bucky Dent	.25	.13	.08
30	Greg Luzinski	.40	.20	.12
31	Jim Todd	.15	.08	.05
32	Checklist 1-132	1.25	.60	.40
33	Wayne Garland	.15	.08	.05
34	Angels Team (Norm Sherry)	.70	.35	.20
35	Rennie Stennett	.15	.08	.05
36	John Ellis	.15	.08	.05
37	Steve Hargan	.15	.08	.05
38	Craig Kusick	.15	.08	.05
39	Tom Griffin	.15	.08	.05
40	Bobby Murcer	.30	.15	.09
41	Jim Kern	.15	.08	.05
42	Jose Cruz	.30	.15	.09
43	Ray Bare	.15	.08	.05
44	Bud Harrelson	.20	.10	.06
45	Rawly Eastwick	.15	.08	.05
46	Buck Martinez	.15	.08	.05
47	Lynn McGlothen	.15	.08	.05
48	Tom Paciorek	.15	.08	.05
49	Grant Jackson	.15	.08	.05
50	Ron Cey	.35	.20	.11
51	Brewers Team (Alex Grammas)	.70	.35	.20
52	Ellis Valentine	.20	.10	.06
53	Paul Mitchell	.15	.08	.05
54	Sandy Alomar	.20	.10	.06
55	Jeff Burroughs	.25	.13	.08
56	Rudy May	.20	.10	.06
57	Marc Hill	.15	.08	.05
58	Chet Lemon	.30	.15	.09
59	Larry Christenson	.15	.08	.05
60	Jim Rice	4.50	2.25	1.25
61	Manny Sanguillen	.15	.08	.05
62	Eric Raich	.15	.08	.05
63	Tito Fuentes	.15	.08	.05
64	Larry Biittner	.15	.08	.05
65	Skip Lockwood	.15	.08	.05
66	Roy Smalley	.20	.10	.06
67	Joaquin Andujar	.60	.30	.20
68	Bruce Bochte	.20	.10	.06
69	Jim Crawford	.15	.08	.05
70	Johnny Bench	5.50	2.75	1.50
71	Dock Ellis	.20	.10	.06
72	Mike Anderson	.15	.08	.05
73	Charlie Williams	.15	.08	.05
74	A's Team (Jack McKeon)	.70	.35	.20
75	Dennis Leonard	.20	.10	.06
76	Tim Foli	.15	.08	.05
77	Dyar Miller	.15	.08	.05
78	Bob Davis	.15	.08	.05
79	Don Money	.15	.08	.05
80	Andy Messersmith	.25	.13	.08
81	Juan Beniquez	.20	.10	.06
82	Jim Rooker	.15	.08	.05
83	Kevin Bell	.15	.08	.05
84	Ollie Brown	.15	.08	.05
85	Duane Kuiper	.15	.08	.05

		NR MT	EX	VG
86	Pat Zachry	.15	.08	.05
87	Glenn Borgmann	.15	.08	.05
88	Stan Wall	.15	.08	.05
89	*Butch Hobson*	.20	.10	.06
90	Cesar Cedeno	.30	.15	.09
91	John Verhoeven	.15	.08	.05
92	Dave Rosello	.15	.08	.05
93	Tom Poquette	.15	.08	.05
94	Craig Swan	.15	.08	.05
95	Keith Hernandez	3.00	1.50	.90
96	Lou Piniella	.40	.20	.12
97	Dave Heaverlo	.15	.08	.05
98	Milt May	.15	.08	.05
99	Tom Hausman	.15	.08	.05
100	Joe Morgan	2.25	1.25	.70
101	Dick Bosman	.15	.08	.05
102	Jose Morales	.15	.08	.05
103	Mike Bacsik	.15	.08	.05
104	*Omar Moreno*	.25	.13	.08
105	Steve Yeager	.15	.08	.05
106	Mike Flanagan	.35	.20	.11
107	Bill Melton	.20	.10	.06
108	Alan Foster	.15	.08	.05
109	Jorge Orta	.15	.08	.05
110	Steve Carlton	4.50	2.25	1.25
111	Rico Petrocelli	.25	.13	.08
112	Bill Greif	.15	.08	.05
113	Blue Jays Mgr./Coaches (Roy Hartsfield, Don Leppert, Bob Miller, Jackie Moore, Harry Warner)	.25	.13	.08
114	Bruce Dal Canton	.15	.08	.05
115	Rick Manning	.20	.10	.06
116	Joe Niekro	.30	.15	.09
117	Frank White	.25	.13	.08
118	Rick Jones	.15	.08	.05
119	John Stearns	.20	.10	.06
120	Rod Carew	4.00	2.00	1.25
121	Gary Nolan	.15	.08	.05
122	Ben Oglivie	.20	.10	.06
123	Fred Stanley	.20	.10	.06
124	George Mitterwald	.15	.08	.05
125	Bill Travers	.15	.08	.05
126	Rod Gilbreath	.15	.08	.05
127	Ron Fairly	.25	.13	.08
128	Tommy John	1.25	.60	.40
129	Mike Sadek	.15	.08	.05
130	Al Oliver	.60	.30	.20
131	Orlando Ramirez	.15	.08	.05
132	Chip Lang	.15	.08	.05
133	Ralph Garr	.20	.10	.06
134	Padres Team (John McNamara)	.70	.35	.20
135	Mark Belanger	.20	.10	.06
136	*Jerry Mumphrey*	.40	.20	.12
137	Jeff Terpko	.15	.08	.05
138	Bob Stinson	.15	.08	.05
139	Fred Norman	.15	.08	.05
140	Mike Schmidt	15.00	7.50	4.50
141	Mark Littell	.15	.08	.05
142	Steve Dillard	.15	.08	.05
143	Ed Herrmann	.15	.08	.05
144	*Bruce Sutter*	2.00	1.00	.70
145	Tom Veryzer	.15	.08	.05
146	Dusty Baker	.25	.13	.08
147	Jackie Brown	.15	.08	.05
148	Fran Healy	.20	.10	.06
149	Mike Cubbage	.15	.08	.05
150	Tom Seaver	4.50	2.25	1.25
151	Johnnie LeMaster	.15	.08	.05
152	Gaylord Perry	1.75	.90	.50
153	Ron Jackson	.15	.08	.05
154	Dave Giusti	.15	.08	.05
155	Joe Rudi	.25	.13	.08
156	Pete Mackanin	.15	.08	.05
157	Ken Brett	.20	.10	.06
158	Ted Kubiak	.15	.08	.05
159	Bernie Carbo	.15	.08	.05
160	Will McEnaney	.15	.08	.05
161	*Garry Templeton*	.80	.40	.25
162	Mike Cuellar	.25	.13	.08
163	Dave Hilton	.15	.08	.05
164	Tug McGraw	.35	.20	.11
165	Jim Wynn	.25	.13	.08
166	Bill Campbell	.15	.08	.05
167	Rich Hebner	.15	.08	.05
168	Charlie Spikes	.15	.08	.05
169	Darold Knowles	.15	.08	.05
170	Thurman Munson	4.50	2.25	1.25
171	Ken Sanders	.15	.08	.05
172	John Milner	.15	.08	.05
173	Chuck Scrivener	.15	.08	.05
174	Nelson Briles	.15	.08	.05

		NR MT	EX	VG
175	*Butch Wynegar*	.40	.20	.12
176	Bob Robertson	.15	.08	.05
177	Bart Johnson	.15	.08	.05
178	Bombo Rivera	.15	.08	.05
179	Paul Hartzell	.15	.08	.05
180	Dave Lopes	.25	.13	.08
181	Ken McMullen	.15	.08	.05
182	Dan Spillner	.15	.08	.05
183	Cardinals Team (Vern Rapp)	.70	.35	.20
184	Bo McLaughlin	.15	.08	.05
185	Sixto Lezcano	.20	.10	.06
186	Doug Flynn	.15	.08	.05
187	Dick Pole	.15	.08	.05
188	Bob Tolan	.20	.10	.06
189	Rick Dempsey	.20	.10	.06
190	Ray Burris	.15	.08	.05
191	Doug Griffin	.15	.08	.05
192	Clarence Gaston	.15	.08	.05
193	Larry Gura	.15	.08	.05
194	Gary Matthews	.25	.13	.08
195	Ed Figueroa	.20	.10	.06
196	Len Randle	.15	.08	.05
197	Ed Ott	.15	.08	.05
198	Wilbur Wood	.20	.10	.06
199	Pepe Frias	.15	.08	.05
200	Frank Tanana	.30	.15	.09
201	Ed Kranepool	.25	.13	.08
202	Tom Johnson	.15	.08	.05
203	Ed Armbrister	.15	.08	.05
204	Jeff Newman	.15	.08	.05
205	Pete Falcone	.15	.08	.05
206	Boog Powell	.50	.25	.15
207	Glenn Abbott	.15	.08	.05
208	Checklist 133-264	1.25	.60	.40
209	Rob Andrews	.15	.08	.05
210	Fred Lynn	1.50	.70	.45
211	Giants Team (Joe Altobelli)	.70	.35	.20
212	Jim Mason	.15	.08	.05
213	Maximino Leon	.15	.08	.05
214	Darrell Porter	.20	.10	.06
215	Butch Metzger	.15	.08	.05
216	Doug DeCinces	.25	.13	.08
217	Tom Underwood	.15	.08	.05
218	*John Wathan*	.60	.30	.20
219	Joe Coleman	.20	.10	.06
220	Chris Chambliss	.30	.15	.09
221	Bob Bailey	.15	.08	.05
222	Francisco Barrios	.15	.08	.05
223	Earl Williams	.15	.08	.05
224	Rusty Torres	.15	.08	.05
225	Bob Apodaca	.15	.08	.05
226	Leroy Stanton	.15	.08	.05
227	*Joe Sambito*	.25	.13	.08
228	Twins Team (Gene Mauch)	.80	.40	.25
229	Don Kessinger	.20	.10	.06
230	Vida Blue	.40	.20	.12
231	Record Breaker (George Brett)	2.00	1.00	.60
232	Record Breaker (Minnie Minoso)	.35	.20	.11
233	Record Breaker (Jose Morales)	.20	.10	.06
234	Record Breaker (Nolan Ryan)	1.50	.70	.45
235	Cecil Cooper	.60	.30	.20
236	Tom Buskey	.15	.08	.05
237	Gene Clines	.15	.08	.05
238	Tippy Martinez	.15	.08	.05
239	Bill Plummer	.15	.08	.05
240	Ron LeFlore	.25	.13	.08
241	Dave Tomlin	.15	.08	.05
242	Ken Henderson	.15	.08	.05
243	Ron Reed	.20	.10	.06
244	John Mayberry	.20	.10	.06
245	Rick Rhoden	.30	.15	.09
246	Mike Vail	.15	.08	.05
247	Chris Knapp	.15	.08	.05
248	Wilbur Howard	.15	.08	.05
249	Pete Redfern	.15	.08	.05
250	Bill Madlock	.40	.20	.12
251	Tony Muser	.15	.08	.05
252	Dale Murray	.15	.08	.05
253	John Hale	.15	.08	.05
254	Doyle Alexander	.30	.15	.09
255	George Scott	.20	.10	.06
256	Joe Hoerner	.15	.08	.05
257	Mike Miley	.15	.08	.05
258	Luis Tiant	.35	.20	.11
259	Mets Team (Joe Frazier)	.80	.40	.25
260	J.R. Richard	.25	.13	.08
261	Phil Garner	.20	.10	.06
262	Al Cowens	.15	.08	.05
263	Mike Marshall	.25	.13	.08
264	Tom Hutton	.15	.08	.05
265	*Mark Fidrych*	.70	.35	.20

		NR MT	EX	VG			NR MT	EX	VG
266	Derrel Thomas	.15	.08	.05	355	Lou Brock	2.25	1.25	.70
267	Ray Fosse	.15	.08	.05	356	Checklist 265-396	1.25	.60	.40
268	Rick Sawyer	.15	.08	.05	357	Tim McCarver	.40	.20	.12
269	Joe Lis	.15	.08	.05	358	Tom House	.15	.08	.05
270	Dave Parker	2.50	1.25	.70	359	Willie Randolph	.80	.40	.25
271	Terry Forster	.20	.10	.06	360	Rick Monday	.25	.13	.08
272	Lee Lacy	.15	.08	.05	361	Eduardo Rodriguez	.15	.08	.05
273	Eric Soderholm	.15	.08	.05	362	Tommy Davis	.30	.15	.09
274	Don Stanhouse	.15	.08	.05	363	Dave Roberts	.15	.08	.05
275	Mike Hargrove	.20	.10	.06	364	Vic Correll	.15	.08	.05
276	A.L. Championship (Chambliss' Dramatic				365	Mike Torrez	.20	.10	.06
	Homer Decides It)	.70	.35	.20	366	Ted Sizemore	.15	.08	.05
277	N.L. Championship (Reds Sweep Phillies 3				367	Dave Hamilton	.15	.08	.05
	In Row)	.70	.35	.20	368	Mike Jorgensen	.15	.08	.05
278	Danny Frisella	.15	.08	.05	369	Terry Humphrey	.15	.08	.05
279	Joe Wallis	.15	.08	.05	370	John Montefusco	.20	.10	.06
280	Jim Hunter	2.00	1.00	.60	371	Royals Team (Whitey Herzog)	.80	.40	.25
281	Roy Staiger	.15	.08	.05	372	Rich Folkers	.15	.08	.05
282	Sid Monge	.15	.08	.05	373	Bert Campaneris	.30	.15	.09
283	Jerry DaVanon	.15	.08	.05	374	Kent Tekulve	.30	.15	.09
284	Mike Norris	.20	.10	.06	375	Larry Hisle	.20	.10	.06
285	Brooks Robinson	2.50	1.25	.70	376	Nino Espinosa	.15	.08	.05
286	Johnny Grubb	.15	.08	.05	377	Dave McKay	.15	.08	.05
287	Reds Team (Sparky Anderson)	.80	.40	.25	378	Jim Umbarger	.15	.08	.05
288	Bob Montgomery	.15	.08	.05	379	Larry Cox	.15	.08	.05
289	Gene Garber	.20	.10	.06	380	Lee May	.25	.13	.08
290	Amos Otis	.20	.10	.06	381	Bob Forsch	.20	.10	.06
291	*Jason Thompson*	.35	.20	.11	382	Charlie Moore	.15	.08	.05
292	Rogelio Moret	.15	.08	.05	383	Stan Bahnsen	.15	.08	.05
293	Jack Brohamer	.15	.08	.05	384	Darrel Chaney	.15	.08	.05
294	George Medich	.15	.08	.05	385	Dave LaRoche	.15	.08	.05
295	Gary Carter	6.00	3.00	1.75	386	Manny Mota	.25	.13	.08
296	Don Hood	.15	.08	.05	387	Yankees Team (Billy Martin)	1.25	.60	.40
297	Ken Reitz	.15	.08	.05	388	Terry Harmon	.15	.08	.05
298	Charlie Hough	.25	.13	.08	389	Ken Kravec	.15	.08	.05
299	Otto Velez	.15	.08	.05	390	Dave Winfield	4.00	2.00	1.25
300	Jerry Koosman	.30	.15	.09	391	Dan Warthen	.15	.08	.05
301	Toby Harrah	.20	.10	.06	392	Phil Roof	.15	.08	.05
302	Mike Garman	.15	.08	.05	393	John Lowenstein	.15	.08	.05
303	Gene Tenace	.20	.10	.06	394	Bill Laxton	.15	.08	.05
304	Jim Hughes	.15	.08	.05	395	Manny Trillo	.20	.10	.06
305	Mickey Rivers	.25	.13	.08	396	Tom Murphy	.15	.08	.05
306	Rick Waits	.15	.08	.05	397	*Larry Herndon*	.40	.20	.12
307	Gary Sutherland	.15	.08	.05	398	Tom Burgmeier	.15	.08	.05
308	Gene Pentz	.15	.08	.05	399	Bruce Boisclair	.15	.08	.05
309	Red Sox Team (Don Zimmer)	.80	.40	.25	400	Steve Garvey	3.25	1.75	1.00
310	Larry Bowa	.30	.15	.09	401	Mickey Scott	.15	.08	.05
311	Vern Ruhle	.15	.08	.05	402	Tommy Helms	.15	.08	.05
312	Rob Belloir	.15	.08	.05	403	Tom Grieve	.15	.08	.05
313	Paul Blair	.20	.10	.06	404	Eric Rasmussen	.15	.08	.05
314	Steve Mingori	.15	.08	.05	405	Claudell Washington	.25	.13	.08
315	Dave Chalk	.15	.08	.05	406	Tim Johnson	.15	.08	.05
316	Steve Rogers	.20	.10	.06	407	Dave Freisleben	.15	.08	.05
317	Kurt Bevacqua	.15	.08	.05	408	Cesar Tovar	.15	.08	.05
318	Duffy Dyer	.15	.08	.05	409	Pete Broberg	.15	.08	.05
319	Rich Gossage	.90	.45	.25	410	Willie Montanez	.15	.08	.05
320	Ken Griffey	.30	.15	.09	411	World Series Games 1 & 2	.70	.35	.20
321	Dave Goltz	.20	.10	.06	412	World Series Games 3 & 4	.70	.35	.20
322	Bill Russell	.20	.10	.06	413	World Series Summary	.70	.35	.20
323	Larry Lintz	.15	.08	.05	414	Tommy Harper	.20	.10	.06
324	John Curtis	.15	.08	.05	415	Jay Johnstone	.20	.10	.06
325	Mike Ivie	.15	.08	.05	416	Chuck Hartenstein	.15	.08	.05
326	Jesse Jefferson	.15	.08	.05	417	Wayne Garrett	.15	.08	.05
327	Astros Team (Bill Virdon)	.70	.35	.20	418	White Sox Team (Bob Lemon)	.80	.40	.25
328	Tommy Boggs	.15	.08	.05	419	Steve Swisher	.15	.08	.05
329	Ron Hodges	.15	.08	.05	420	Rusty Staub	.35	.20	.11
330	George Hendrick	.20	.10	.06	421	Doug Rau	.15	.08	.05
331	Jim Colborn	.15	.08	.05	422	Freddie Patek	.15	.08	.05
332	Elliott Maddox	.20	.10	.06	423	Gary Lavelle	.15	.08	.05
333	Paul Reuschel	.15	.08	.05	424	Steve Brye	.15	.08	.05
334	Bill Stein	.15	.08	.05	425	Joe Torre	.40	.20	.12
335	Bill Robinson	.15	.08	.05	426	Dick Drago	.15	.08	.05
336	Denny Doyle	.15	.08	.05	427	Dave Rader	.15	.08	.05
337	Ron Schueler	.15	.08	.05	428	Rangers Team (Frank Lucchesi)	.70	.35	.20
338	Dave Duncan	.15	.08	.05	429	Ken Boswell	.15	.08	.05
339	Adrian Devine	.15	.08	.05	430	Fergie Jenkins	.80	.40	.25
340	Hal McRae	.30	.15	.09	431	Dave Collins	.25	.13	.08
341	Joe Kerrigan	.15	.08	.05	432	Buzz Capra	.15	.08	.05
342	Jerry Remy	.15	.08	.05	433	Turn Back The Clock (Nate Colbert)			
343	Ed Halicki	.15	.08	.05			.20	.10	.06
344	Brian Downing	.25	.13	.08	434	Turn Back The Clock (Carl Yastrzemski)			
345	Reggie Smith	.25	.13	.08			2.00	1.00	.60
346	Bill Singer	.20	.10	.06	435	Turn Back The Clock (Maury Wills)	.35	.20	.11
347	George Foster	1.25	.60	.40	436	Turn Back The Clock (Bob Keegan)	.20	.10	.06
348	Brent Strom	.15	.08	.05	437	Turn Back The Clock (Ralph Kiner)	.50	.25	.15
349	Jim Holt	.15	.08	.05	438	Marty Perez	.15	.08	.05
350	Larry Dierker	.20	.10	.06	439	Gorman Thomas	.30	.15	.09
351	Jim Sundberg	.20	.10	.06	440	Jon Matlack	.20	.10	.06
352	Mike Phillips	.15	.08	.05	441	Larvell Blanks	.15	.08	.05
353	Stan Thomas	.15	.08	.05	442	Braves Team (Dave Bristol)	.70	.35	.20
354	Pirates Team (Chuck Tanner)	.80	.40	.25	443	Lamar Johnson	.15	.08	.05

#	Player	NR MT	EX	VG
444	Wayne Twitchell	.15	.08	.05
445	Ken Singleton	.25	.13	.08
446	Bill Bonham	.15	.08	.05
447	Jerry Turner	.15	.08	.05
448	Ellie Rodriguez	.15	.08	.05
449	Al Fitzmorris	.15	.08	.05
450	Pete Rose	9.00	4.50	2.75
451	Checklist 397-528	1.25	.60	.40
452	Mike Caldwell	.15	.08	.05
453	Pedro Garcia	.15	.08	.05
454	Andy Etchebarren	.15	.08	.05
455	Rick Wise	.20	.10	.06
456	Leon Roberts	.15	.08	.05
457	Steve Luebber	.15	.08	.05
458	Leo Foster	.15	.08	.05
459	Steve Foucault	.15	.08	.05
460	Willie Stargell	2.50	1.25	.70
461	Dick Tidrow	.20	.10	.06
462	Don Baylor	.35	.20	.11
463	Jamie Quirk	.15	.08	.05
464	Randy Moffitt	.15	.08	.05
465	Rico Carty	.25	.13	.08
466	Fred Holdsworth	.15	.08	.05
467	Phillies Team (Danny Ozark)	.70	.35	.20
468	Ramon Hernandez	.15	.08	.05
469	Pat Kelly	.15	.08	.05
470	Ted Simmons	.60	.30	.20
471	Del Unser	.15	.08	.05
472	Rookie Pitchers (Don Aase, Bob McClure, Gil Patterson, Dave Wehrmeister)	.25	.13	.08
473	Rookie Outfielders (Andre Dawson, Gene Richards, John Scott, Denny Walling)	35.00	17.50	10.50
474	Rookie Shortstops (Bob Bailor, Kiko Garcia, Craig Reynolds, Alex Taveras)	.15	.08	.05
475	Rookie Pitchers (Chris Batton, Rick Camp, Scott McGregor, Manny Sarmiento)	.30	.15	.09
476	Rookie Catchers (Gary Alexander, Rick Cerone, Dale Murphy, Kevin Pasley)	60.00	30.00	18.00
477	Rookie Infielders (Doug Ault, Rich Dauer, Orlando Gonzalez, Phil Mankowski)	.25	.13	.08
478	Rookie Pitchers (Jim Gideon, Leon Hooten, Dave Johnson, Mark Lemongello)	.15	.08	.05
479	Rookie Outfielders (Brian Asselstine, Wayne Gross, Sam Mejias, Alvis Woods)	.25	.13	.08
480	Carl Yastrzemski	5.00	2.50	1.50
481	Roger Metzger	.15	.08	.05
482	Tony Solaita	.15	.08	.05
483	Richie Zisk	.20	.10	.06
484	Burt Hooton	.20	.10	.06
485	Roy White	.30	.15	.09
486	Ed Bane	.15	.08	.05
487	Rookie Pitchers (Larry Anderson, Ed Glynn, Joe Henderson, Greg Terlecky)	.15	.08	.05
488	Rookie Outfielders (Jack Clark, Ruppert Jones, Lee Mazzilli, Dan Thomas)	25.00	12.50	7.50
489	Rookie Pitchers (Len Barker, Randy Lerch, Greg Minton, Mike Overy)	.40	.20	.12
490	Rookie Shortstops (Billy Almon, Mickey Klutts, Tommy McMillan, Mark Wagner)	.25	.13	.08
491	Rookie Pitchers (Mike Dupree, Denny Martinez, Craig Mitchell, Bob Sykes)	1.50	.70	.45
492	Rookie Outfielders (Tony Armas, Steve Kemp, Carlos Lopez, Gary Woods)	1.00	.50	.30
493	Rookie Pitchers (Mike Krukow, Jim Otten, Gary Wheelock, Mike Willis)	.70	.35	.20
494	Rookie Infielders (Juan Bernhardt, Mike Champion, Jim Gantner, Bump Wills)	.50	.25	.15
495	Al Hrabosky	.20	.10	.06
496	Gary Thomasson	.15	.08	.05
497	Clay Carroll	.20	.10	.06
498	Sal Bando	.25	.13	.08
499	Pablo Torrealba	.15	.08	.05
500	Dave Kingman	.60	.30	.20
501	Jim Bibby	.15	.08	.05
502	Randy Hundley	.15	.08	.05
503	Bill Lee	.20	.10	.06
504	Dodgers Team (Tom Lasorda)	1.00	.50	.30
505	Oscar Gamble	.20	.10	.06
506	Steve Grilli	.15	.08	.05
507	Mike Hegan	.15	.08	.05
508	Dave Pagan	.15	.08	.05
509	Cookie Rojas	.15	.08	.05
510	John Candelaria	.80	.40	.25
511	Bill Fahey	.15	.08	.05
512	Jack Billingham	.15	.08	.05

#	Player	NR MT	EX	VG
513	Jerry Terrell	.15	.08	.05
514	Cliff Johnson	.15	.08	.05
515	Chris Speier	.15	.08	.05
516	Bake McBride	.15	.08	.05
517	Pete Vuckovich	.50	.25	.15
518	Cubs Team (Herman Franks)	.70	.35	.20
519	Don Kirkwood	.15	.08	.05
520	Garry Maddox	.20	.10	.06
521	Bob Grich	.25	.13	.08
522	Enzo Hernandez	.15	.08	.05
523	Rollie Fingers	1.25	.60	.40
524	Rowland Office	.15	.08	.05
525	Dennis Eckersley	1.25	.60	.40
526	Larry Parrish	.35	.20	.11
527	Dan Meyer	.15	.08	.05
528	Bill Castro	.15	.08	.05
529	Jim Essian	.15	.08	.05
530	Rick Reuschel	.30	.15	.09
531	Lyman Bostock	.25	.13	.08
532	Jim Willoughby	.15	.08	.05
533	Mickey Stanley	.20	.10	.06
534	Paul Splittorff	.20	.10	.06
535	Cesar Geronimo	.20	.10	.06
536	Vic Albury	.15	.08	.05
537	Dave Roberts	.15	.08	.05
538	Frank Taveras	.15	.08	.05
539	Mike Wallace	.15	.08	.05
540	Bob Watson	.20	.10	.06
541	John Denny	.15	.08	.05
542	Frank Duffy	.15	.08	.05
543	Ron Blomberg	.20	.10	.06
544	Gary Ross	.15	.08	.05
545	Bob Boone	.25	.13	.08
546	Orioles Team (Earl Weaver)	.80	.40	.25
547	Willie McCovey	2.00	1.00	.60
548	Joel Youngblood	.30	.15	.09
549	Jerry Royster	.15	.08	.05
550	Randy Jones	.20	.10	.06
551	Bill North	.15	.08	.05
552	Pepe Mangual	.15	.08	.05
553	Jack Heidemann	.15	.08	.05
554	Bruce Kimm	.15	.08	.05
555	Dan Ford	.20	.10	.06
556	Doug Bird	.15	.08	.05
557	Jerry White	.15	.08	.05
558	Elias Sosa	.15	.08	.05
559	Alan Bannister	.15	.08	.05
560	Dave Concepcion	.35	.20	.11
561	Pete LaCock	.15	.08	.05
562	Checklist 529-660	1.25	.60	.40
563	Bruce Kison	.15	.08	.05
564	Alan Ashby	.20	.10	.06
565	Mickey Lolich	.50	.25	.15
566	Rick Miller	.15	.08	.05
567	Enos Cabell	.20	.10	.06
568	Carlos May	.20	.10	.06
569	Jim Lonborg	.20	.10	.06
570	Bobby Bonds	.35	.20	.11
571	Darrell Evans	.40	.20	.12
572	Ross Grimsley	.20	.10	.06
573	Joe Ferguson	.15	.08	.05
574	Aurelio Rodriguez	.20	.10	.06
575	Dick Ruthven	.15	.08	.05
576	Fred Kendall	.15	.08	.05
577	Jerry Augustine	.15	.08	.05
578	Bob Randall	.15	.08	.05
579	Don Carrithers	.15	.08	.05
580	George Brett	8.00	4.00	2.50
581	Pedro Borbon	.15	.08	.05
582	Ed Kirkpatrick	.15	.08	.05
583	Paul Lindblad	.15	.08	.05
584	Ed Goodson	.15	.08	.05
585	Rick Burleson	.20	.10	.06
586	Steve Renko	.15	.08	.05
587	Rick Baldwin	.15	.08	.05
588	Dave Moates	.15	.08	.05
589	Mike Cosgrove	.15	.08	.05
590	Buddy Bell	.30	.15	.09
591	Chris Arnold	.15	.08	.05
592	Dan Briggs	.15	.08	.05
593	Dennis Blair	.15	.08	.05
594	Biff Pocoroba	.15	.08	.05
595	John Hiller	.20	.10	.06
596	Jerry Martin	.25	.13	.08
597	Mariners Mgr./Coaches (Don Bryant, Jim Busby, Darrell Johnson, Vada Pinson, Wes Stock)	.25	.13	.08
598	Sparky Lyle	.35	.20	.11
599	Mike Tyson	.15	.08	.05
600	Jim Palmer	2.50	1.25	.70
601	Mike Lum	.15	.08	.05

		NR MT	EX	VG
602	Andy Hassler	.15	.08	.05
603	Willie Davis	.25	.13	.08
604	Jim Slaton	.15	.08	.05
605	Felix Millan	.15	.08	.05
606	Steve Braun	.15	.08	.05
607	Larry Demery	.15	.08	.05
608	Roy Howell	.15	.08	.05
609	Jim Barr	.15	.08	.05
610	Jose Cardenal	.20	.10	.06
611	Dave Lemanczyk	.15	.08	.05
612	Barry Foote	.15	.08	.05
613	Reggie Cleveland	.15	.08	.05
614	Greg Gross	.15	.08	.05
615	Phil Niekro	1.50	.70	.45
616	Tommy Sandt	.15	.08	.05
617	Bobby Darwin	.15	.08	.05
618	Pat Dobson	.20	.10	.06
619	Johnny Oates	.15	.08	.05
620	Don Sutton	1.50	.70	.45
621	Tigers Team (Ralph Houk)	.80	.40	.25
622	Jim Wohlford	.15	.08	.05
623	Jack Kucek	.15	.08	.05
624	Hector Cruz	.15	.08	.05
625	Ken Holtzman	.25	.13	.08
626	Al Bumbry	.20	.10	.06
627	Bob Myrick	.15	.08	.05
628	Mario Guerrero	.15	.08	.05
629	Bobby Valentine	.25	.13	.08
630	Bert Blyleven	.80	.40	.25
631	Big League Brothers (George Brett, Ken Brett)	1.75	.90	.50
632	Big League Brothers (Bob Forsch, Ken Forsch)	.30	.15	.09
633	Big League Brothers (Carlos May, Lee May)	.30	.15	.09
634	Big League Brothers (Paul Reuschel, Rick Reuschel) (names switched)	.30	.15	.09
635	Robin Yount	10.00	5.00	3.00
636	Santo Alcala	.15	.08	.05
637	Alex Johnson	.15	.08	.05
638	Jim Kaat	.80	.40	.25
639	Jerry Morales	.15	.08	.05
640	Carlton Fisk	1.75	.90	.50
641	Dan Larson	.15	.08	.05
642	Willie Crawford	.15	.08	.05
643	Mike Pazik	.15	.08	.05
644	Matt Alexander	.15	.08	.05
645	Jerry Reuss	.25	.13	.08
646	Andres Mora	.15	.08	.05
647	Expos Team (Dick Williams)	.80	.40	.25
648	Jim Spencer	.15	.08	.05
649	Dave Cash	.15	.08	.05
650	Nolan Ryan	10.00	5.00	3.00
651	Von Joshua	.15	.08	.05
652	Tom Walker	.15	.08	.05
653	Diego Segui	.15	.08	.05
654	Ron Pruitt	.15	.08	.05
655	Tony Perez	.80	.40	.25
656	Ron Guidry	2.75	1.50	.80
657	Mick Kelleher	.15	.08	.05
658	Marty Pattin	.15	.08	.05
659	Merv Rettenmund	.15	.08	.05
660	Willie Horton	.40	.13	.08

which could be joined to form a photo of the American League or National League All-Star teams. Issued as a separate issue, the 2-1/2" by 3-1/2" stickers have a paper backing which could be removed to allow the cloth to be adhered to a jacket, adhered to a jacket, notebook, etc.

		NR MT	EX	VG
Complete Set:		100.00	50.00	30.00
Common Player:		.20	.10	.06
1	Alan Ashby	.20	.10	.06
2	Buddy Bell	1.00	.50	.30
3	Johnny Bench	5.00	2.50	1.50
4	Vida Blue	.50	.25	.15
5	Bert Blyleven	1.00	.50	.30
6	Steve Braun	.50	.25	.15
7	George Brett	7.00	3.50	2.00
8	Lou Brock	3.00	1.50	.90
9	Jose Cardenal	.20	.10	.06
10	Rod Carew	8.00	4.00	2.50
11	Steve Carlton	6.00	3.00	1.75
12	Dave Cash	.20	.10	.06
13	Cesar Cedeno	1.00	.50	.30
14	Ron Cey	.50	.25	.15
15	Mark Fidrych	.50	.25	.15
16	Dan Ford	.20	.10	.06
17	Wayne Garland	.20	.10	.06
18	Ralph Garr	.20	.10	.06
19	Steve Garvey	4.00	2.00	1.25
20	Mike Hargrove	.20	.10	.06
21	Jim Hunter	3.00	1.50	.90
22	Reggie Jackson	6.00	3.00	1.75
23	Randy Jones	.20	.10	.06
24	Dave Kingman	1.00	.50	.30
25	Bill Madlock	.70	.35	.20
26	Lee May	.50	.25	.15
27	John Mayberry	.20	.10	.06
28	Andy Messersmith	.20	.10	.06
29	Willie Montanez	.20	.10	.06
30	John Montefusco	.50	.25	.15
31	Joe Morgan	3.00	1.50	.90
32	Thurman Munson	3.00	1.50	.90
33	Bobby Murcer	.50	.25	.15
34	Al Oliver	1.25	.60	.40
35	Dave Pagan	.20	.10	.06
36	Jim Palmer	8.00	4.00	2.50
37	Tony Perez	.70	.35	.20
38	Pete Rose	12.00	6.00	3.50
39	Joe Rudi	.50	.25	.15
40	Nolan Ryan	15.00	7.50	4.50
41	Mike Schmidt	12.00	6.00	3.50
42	Tom Seaver	10.00	5.00	3.00
43	Ted Simmons	.70	.35	.20
44	Bill Singer	.20	.10	.06
45	Willie Stargell	1.50	.70	.45
46	Rusty Staub	.50	.25	.15
47	Don Sutton	1.25	.60	.40
48	Luis Tiant	.70	.35	.20
49	Bill Travers	.20	.10	.06
50	Claudell Washington	.50	.25	.15
51	Bob Watson	.20	.10	.06
52	Dave Winfield	3.00	1.50	.90
53	Carl Yastrzemski	4.50	2.25	1.25
54	Robin Yount	10.00	5.00	3.00
55	Richie Zisk	.20	.10	.06

1977 Topps Cloth Stickers

One of the few Topps specialty issues of the late 1970s, the 73-piece set of cloth stickers issued in 1977 includes 55 player stickers and 18 puzzle cards

1978 Topps

JACK CLARK

At 726 cards, this was the largest issue from Topps

since 1972. In design, the color player photo is slightly larger than usual, with the player's name and team at the bottom. In the upper right-hand corner of the 2-1/2" by 3-1/2" cards there is a small white baseball with the player's position. Most of the starting All-Stars from the previous year had a red, white and blue shield instead of the baseball. Backs feature statistics and a baseball situation which made a card game of baseball possible. Specialty cards include baseball records, statistical leaders and the World Series and playoffs. As one row of cards per sheet had to be double-printed to accommodate the 726-card set size, some cards are more common, yet that seems to have no serious impact on their prices.

		NR MT	EX	VG
Complete Set:		225.00	110.00	70.00
Common Player:		.12	.06	.04
1	Record Breaker (Lou Brock)	2.00	.45	.25
2	Record Breaker (Sparky Lyle)	.25	.13	.08
3	Record Breaker (Willie McCovey)	.70	.35	.20
4	Record Breaker (Brooks Robinson)	.90	.45	.25
5	Record Breaker (Pete Rose)	2.00	1.00	.60
6	Record Breaker (Nolan Ryan)	1.25	.60	.40
7	Record Breaker (Reggie Jackson)	1.50	.70	.45
8	Mike Sadek	.12	.06	.04
9	Doug DeCinces	.25	.13	.08
10	Phil Niekro	1.25	.60	.40
11	Rick Manning	.12	.06	.04
12	Don Aase	.20	.10	.06
13	Art Howe	.12	.06	.04
14	Lerrin LaGrow	.12	.06	.04
15	Tony Perez	.25	.13	.08
16	Roy White	.25	.13	.08
17	Mike Krukow	.25	.13	.08
18	Bob Grich	.25	.13	.08
19	Darrell Porter	.20	.10	.06
20	Pete Rose	3.50	1.75	1.00
21	Steve Kemp	.25	.13	.08
22	Charlie Hough	.20	.10	.06
23	Bump Wills	.12	.06	.04
24	Don Money	.12	.06	.04
25	Jon Matlack	.20	.10	.06
26	Rich Hebner	.12	.06	.04
27	Geoff Zahn	.12	.06	.04
28	Ed Ott	.12	.06	.04
29	Bob Lacey	.12	.06	.04
30	George Hendrick	.20	.10	.06
31	Glenn Abbott	.12	.06	.04
32	Garry Templeton	.30	.15	.09
33	Dave Lemanczyk	.12	.06	.04
34	Willie McCovey	2.00	1.00	.60
35	Sparky Lyle	.30	.15	.09
36	*Eddie Murray*	30.00	15.00	9.00
37	Rick Waits	.12	.06	.04
38	Willie Montanez	.12	.06	.04
39	*Floyd Bannister*	1.00	.50	.30
40	Carl Yastrzemski	3.00	1.50	.90
41	Burt Hooton	.20	.10	.06
42	Jorge Orta	.12	.06	.04
43	Bill Atkinson	.12	.06	.04
44	Toby Harrah	.20	.10	.06
45	Mark Fidrych	.25	.13	.08
46	Al Cowens	.12	.06	.04
47	Jack Billingham	.12	.06	.04
48	Don Baylor	.35	.20	.11
49	Ed Kranepool	.20	.10	.06
50	Rick Reuschel	.40	.20	.12
51	Charlie Moore	.12	.06	.04
52	Jim Lonborg	.20	.10	.06
53	Phil Garner	.12	.06	.04
54	Tom Johnson	.12	.06	.04
55	Mitchell Page	.12	.06	.04
56	Randy Jones	.20	.10	.06
57	Dan Meyer	.12	.06	.04
58	Bob Forsch	.20	.10	.06
59	Otto Velez	.12	.06	.04
60	Thurman Munson	2.75	1.50	.80
61	Larvell Blanks	.12	.06	.04
62	Jim Barr	.12	.06	.04
63	Don Zimmer	.20	.10	.06
64	Gene Pentz	.12	.06	.04
65	Ken Singleton	.25	.13	.08
66	White Sox Team	.50	.25	.15
67	Claudell Washington	.25	.13	.08
68	Steve Foucault	.12	.06	.04
69	Mike Vail	.12	.06	.04

		NR MT	EX	VG
70	Rich Gossage	.70	.35	.20
71	Terry Humphrey	.12	.06	.04
72	Andre Dawson	5.00	2.50	1.50
73	Andy Hassler	.12	.06	.04
74	Checklist 1-121	.90	.45	.25
75	Dick Ruthven	.12	.06	.04
76	Steve Ontiveros	.12	.06	.04
77	Ed Kirkpatrick	.12	.06	.04
78	Pablo Torrealba	.12	.06	.04
79	Darrell Johnson	.12	.06	.04
80	Ken Griffey	.25	.13	.08
81	Pete Redfern	.12	.06	.04
82	Giants Team	.50	.25	.15
83	Bob Montgomery	.12	.06	.04
84	Kent Tekulve	.25	.13	.08
85	Ron Fairly	.20	.10	.06
86	Dave Tomlin	.12	.06	.04
87	John Lowenstein	.12	.06	.04
88	Mike Phillips	.12	.06	.04
89	Ken Clay	.20	.10	.06
90	Larry Bowa	.30	.15	.09
91	Oscar Zamora	.12	.06	.04
92	Adrian Devine	.12	.06	.04
93	Bobby Cox	.12	.06	.04
94	Chuck Scrivener	.12	.06	.04
95	Jamie Quirk	.12	.06	.04
96	Orioles Team	.50	.25	.15
97	Stan Bahnsen	.12	.06	.04
98	Jim Essian	.12	.06	.04
99	*Willie Hernandez*	.70	.35	.20
100	George Brett	4.00	2.00	1.25
101	Sid Monge	.12	.06	.04
102	Matt Alexander	.12	.06	.04
103	Tom Murphy	.12	.06	.04
104	Lee Lacy	.12	.06	.04
105	Reggie Cleveland	.12	.06	.04
106	Bill Plummer	.12	.06	.04
107	Ed Halicki	.12	.06	.04
108	Von Joshua	.12	.06	.04
109	Joe Torre	.30	.15	.09
110	Richie Zisk	.20	.10	.06
111	Mike Tyson	.12	.06	.04
112	Astros Team	.50	.25	.15
113	Don Carrithers	.12	.06	.04
114	Paul Blair	.20	.10	.06
115	Gary Nolan	.12	.06	.04
116	Tucker Ashford	.12	.06	.04
117	John Montague	.12	.06	.04
118	Terry Harmon	.12	.06	.04
119	Denny Martinez	.25	.13	.08
120	Gary Carter	3.00	1.50	.90
121	Alvis Woods	.12	.06	.04
122	Dennis Eckersley	.70	.35	.20
123	Manny Trillo	.20	.10	.06
124	*Dave Rozema*	.25	.13	.08
125	George Scott	.20	.10	.06
126	Paul Moskau	.12	.06	.04
127	Chet Lemon	.20	.10	.06
128	Bill Russell	.20	.10	.06
129	Jim Colborn	.12	.06	.04
130	Jeff Burroughs	.20	.10	.06
131	Bert Blyleven	.60	.30	.20
132	Enos Cabell	.20	.10	.06
133	Jerry Augustine	.12	.06	.04
134	*Steve Henderson*	.25	.13	.08
135	Ron Guidry	.70	.35	.20
136	Ted Sizemore	.12	.06	.04
137	Craig Kusick	.12	.06	.04
138	Larry Demery	.12	.06	.04
139	Wayne Gross	.12	.06	.04
140	Rollie Fingers	.70	.35	.20
141	Ruppert Jones	.20	.10	.06
142	John Montefusco	.20	.10	.06
143	Keith Hernandez	2.50	1.25	.70
144	Jesse Jefferson	.12	.06	.04
145	Rick Monday	.20	.10	.06
146	Doyle Alexander	.30	.15	.09
147	Lee Mazzilli	.25	.13	.08
148	Andre Thornton	.25	.13	.08
149	Dale Murray	.12	.06	.04
150	Bobby Bonds	.35	.20	.11
151	Milt Wilcox	.12	.06	.04
152	*Ivan DeJesus*	.20	.10	.06
153	Steve Stone	.25	.13	.08
154	Cecil Cooper	.20	.10	.06
155	Butch Hobson	.12	.06	.04
156	Andy Messersmith	.20	.10	.06
157	Pete LaCock	.12	.06	.04
158	Joaquin Andujar	.25	.13	.08
159	Lou Piniella	.35	.20	.11
160	Jim Palmer	2.00	1.00	.60

	NR MT	EX	VG
161 Bob Boone	.25	.13	.08
162 Paul Thormodsgard	.12	.06	.04
163 Bill North	.12	.06	.04
164 Bob Owchinko	.12	.06	.04
165 Rennie Stennett	.12	.06	.04
166 Carlos Lopez	.12	.06	.04
167 Tim Foli	.12	.06	.04
168 Reggie Smith	.25	.13	.08
169 Jerry Johnson	.12	.06	.04
170 Lou Brock	2.00	1.00	.60
171 Pat Zachry	.12	.06	.04
172 Mike Hargrove	.20	.10	.06
173 Robin Yount	5.00	2.50	1.50
174 Wayne Garland	.12	.06	.04
175 Jerry Morales	.12	.06	.04
176 Milt May	.12	.06	.04
177 Gene Garber	.12	.06	.04
178 Dave Chalk	.12	.06	.04
179 Dick Tidrow	.20	.10	.06
180 Dave Concepcion	.35	.20	.11
181 Ken Forsch	.20	.10	.06
182 Jim Spencer	.12	.06	.04
183 Doug Bird	.12	.06	.04
184 Checklist 122-242	.90	.45	.25
185 Ellis Valentine	.20	.10	.06
186 *Bob Stanley*	.25	.13	.08
187 Jerry Royster	.12	.06	.04
188 Al Bumbry	.20	.10	.06
189 Tom Lasorda	.30	.15	.09
190 John Candelaria	.25	.13	.08
191 Rodney Scott	.12	.06	.04
192 Padres Team	.50	.25	.15
193 Rich Chiles	.12	.06	.04
194 Derrel Thomas	.12	.06	.04
195 Larry Dierker	.20	.10	.06
196 Bob Bailor	.12	.06	.04
197 Nino Espinosa	.12	.06	.04
198 Ron Pruitt	.12	.06	.04
199 Craig Reynolds	.12	.06	.04
200 Reggie Jackson	3.50	1.75	1.00
201 Batting Leaders (Rod Carew, Dave Parker)	.80	.40	.25
202 Home Run Leaders (George Foster, Jim Rice)	.25	.13	.08
203 Runs Batted In Ldrs. (George Foster, Larry Hisle)	.25	.13	.08
204 Stolen Base Leaders (Freddie Patek, Frank Taveras)	.12	.06	.04
205 Victory Leaders (Steve Carlton, Dave Goltz, Dennis Leonard, Jim Palmer)	.60	.30	.20
206 Strikeout Leaders (Phil Niekro, Nolan Ryan)	.35	.20	.11
207 Earned Run Avg. Ldrs. (John Candelaria, Frank Tanana)	.12	.06	.04
208 Leading Firemen (Bill Campbell, Rollie Fingers)	.35	.20	.11
209 Dock Ellis	.12	.06	.04
210 Jose Cardenal	.12	.06	.04
211 Earl Weaver	.20	.10	.06
212 Mike Caldwell	.12	.06	.04
213 Alan Bannister	.12	.06	.04
214 Angels Team	.50	.25	.15
215 Darrell Evans	.35	.20	.11
216 Mike Paxton	.12	.06	.04
217 Rod Gilbreath	.12	.06	.04
218 Marty Pattin	.12	.06	.04
219 Mike Cubbage	.12	.06	.04
220 Pedro Borbon	.12	.06	.04
221 Chris Speier	.20	.10	.06
222 Jerry Martin	.12	.06	.04
223 Bruce Kison	.12	.06	.04
224 Jerry Tabb	.12	.06	.04
225 Don Gullett	.12	.06	.04
226 Joe Ferguson	.12	.06	.04
227 Al Fitzmorris	.12	.06	.04
228 Manny Mota	.12	.06	.04
229 Leo Foster	.12	.06	.04
230 Al Hrabosky	.20	.10	.06
231 Wayne Nordhagen	.12	.06	.04
232 Mickey Stanley	.20	.10	.06
233 Dick Pole	.12	.06	.04
234 Herman Franks	.12	.06	.04
235 Tim McCarver	.35	.20	.11
236 Terry Whitfield	.12	.06	.04
237 Rich Dauer	.12	.06	.04
238 Juan Beniquez	.20	.10	.06
239 Dyar Miller	.12	.06	.04
240 Gene Tenace	.20	.10	.06
241 Pete Vuckovich	.20	.10	.06
242 Barry Bonnell	.12	.06	.04
243 Bob McClure	.12	.06	.04
244 Expos Team	.20	.10	.06
245 Rick Burleson	.20	.10	.06
246 Dan Driessen	.20	.10	.06
247 Larry Christenson	.12	.06	.04
248 Frank White	.12	.06	.04
249 Dave Goltz	.12	.06	.04
250 Graig Nettles	.30	.15	.09
251 Don Kirkwood	.12	.06	.04
252 Steve Swisher	.12	.06	.04
253 Jim Kern	.12	.06	.04
254 Dave Collins	.20	.10	.06
255 Jerry Reuss	.20	.10	.06
256 Joe Altobelli	.12	.06	.04
257 Hector Cruz	.12	.06	.04
258 John Hiller	.20	.10	.06
259 Dodgers Team	.80	.40	.25
260 Bert Campaneris	.25	.13	.08
261 Tim Hosley	.12	.06	.04
262 Rudy May	.12	.06	.04
263 Danny Walton	.12	.06	.04
264 Jamie Easterly	.12	.06	.04
265 Sal Bando	.12	.06	.04
266 *Bob Shirley*	.20	.10	.06
267 Doug Ault	.12	.06	.04
268 Gil Flores	.12	.06	.04
269 Wayne Twitchell	.12	.06	.04
270 Carlton Fisk	1.75	.90	.50
271 Randy Lerch	.12	.06	.04
272 Royle Stillman	.12	.06	.04
273 Fred Norman	.12	.06	.04
274 Freddie Patek	.12	.06	.04
275 Dan Ford	.12	.06	.04
276 Bill Bonham	.12	.06	.04
277 Bruce Boisclair	.12	.06	.04
278 Enrique Romo	.12	.06	.04
279 Bill Virdon	.20	.10	.06
280 Buddy Bell	.30	.15	.09
281 Eric Rasmussen	.12	.06	.04
282 Yankees Team	1.00	.50	.30
283 Omar Moreno	.12	.06	.04
284 Randy Moffitt	.12	.06	.04
285 Steve Yeager	.12	.06	.04
286 Ben Oglivie	.20	.10	.06
287 Kiko Garcia	.12	.06	.04
288 Dave Hamilton	.12	.06	.04
289 Checklist 243-363	.90	.45	.25
290 Willie Horton	.20	.10	.06
291 Gary Ross	.12	.06	.04
292 Gene Richard	.12	.06	.04
293 Mike Willis	.12	.06	.04
294 Larry Parrish	.25	.13	.08
295 Bill Lee	.20	.10	.06
296 Biff Pocoroba	.12	.06	.04
297 Warren Brusstar	.12	.06	.04
298 Tony Armas	.25	.13	.08
299 Whitey Herzog	.30	.15	.09
300 Joe Morgan	2.00	1.00	.60
301 Buddy Schultz	.12	.06	.04
302 Cubs Team	.50	.25	.15
303 Sam Hinds	.12	.06	.04
304 John Milner	.12	.06	.04
305 Rico Carty	.20	.10	.06
306 Joe Niekro	.25	.13	.08
307 Glenn Borgmann	.12	.06	.04
308 Jim Rooker	.12	.06	.04
309 Cliff Johnson	.20	.10	.06
310 Don Sutton	1.25	.60	.40
311 Jose Baez	.12	.06	.04
312 Greg Minton	.12	.06	.04
313 Andy Etchebarren	.12	.06	.04
314 Paul Lindblad	.12	.06	.04
315 Mark Belanger	.20	.10	.06
316 Henry Cruz	.12	.06	.04
317 Dave Johnson	.30	.15	.09
318 Tom Griffin	.12	.06	.04
319 Alan Ashby	.12	.06	.04
320 Fred Lynn	.90	.45	.25
321 Santo Alcala	.12	.06	.04
322 Tom Paciorek	.12	.06	.04
323 Jim Fregosi	.12	.06	.04
324 Vern Rapp	.12	.06	.04
325 Bruce Sutter	.50	.25	.15
326 Mike Lum	.12	.06	.04
327 Rick Langford	.12	.06	.04
328 Brewers Team	.50	.25	.15
329 John Verhoeven	.12	.06	.04
330 Bob Watson	.20	.10	.06
331 Mark Littell	.12	.06	.04
332 Duane Kuiper	.12	.06	.04
333 Jim Todd	.12	.06	.04
334 John Stearns	.12	.06	.04

#	Player	NR MT	EX	VG
335	Bucky Dent	.30	.15	.09
336	Steve Busby	.20	.10	.06
337	Tom Grieve	.12	.06	.04
338	Dave Heaverlo	.12	.06	.04
339	Mario Guerrero	.12	.06	.04
340	Bake McBride	.12	.06	.04
341	Mike Flanagan	.25	.13	.08
342	Aurelio Rodriguez	.20	.10	.06
343	John Wathan	.12	.06	.04
344	Sam Ewing	.12	.06	.04
345	Luis Tiant	.35	.20	.11
346	Larry Biittner	.12	.06	.04
347	Terry Forster	.20	.10	.06
348	Del Unser	.12	.06	.04
349	Rick Camp	.12	.06	.04
350	Steve Garvey	2.75	1.50	.80
351	Jeff Torborg	.20	.10	.06
352	Tony Scott	.12	.06	.04
353	Doug Bair	.12	.06	.04
354	Cesar Geronimo	.20	.10	.06
355	Bill Travers	.12	.06	.04
356	Mets Team	.70	.35	.20
357	Tom Poquette	.12	.06	.04
358	Mark Lemongello	.12	.06	.04
359	Marc Hill	.12	.06	.04
360	Mike Schmidt	6.00	3.00	1.75
361	Chris Knapp	.12	.06	.04
362	Dave May	.12	.06	.04
363	Bob Randall	.12	.06	.04
364	Jerry Turner	.12	.06	.04
365	Ed Figueroa	.20	.10	.06
366	Larry Milbourne	.12	.06	.04
367	Rick Dempsey	.20	.10	.06
368	Balor Moore	.12	.06	.04
369	Tim Nordbrook	.12	.06	.04
370	Rusty Staub	.30	.15	.09
371	Ray Burris	.12	.06	.04
372	Brian Asselstine	.12	.06	.04
373	Jim Willoughby	.12	.06	.04
374	Jose Morales	.12	.06	.04
375	Tommy John	.90	.45	.25
376	Jim Wohlford	.12	.06	.04
377	Manny Sarmiento	.12	.06	.04
378	Bobby Winkles	.12	.06	.04
379	Skip Lockwood	.12	.06	.04
380	Ted Simmons	.40	.20	.12
381	Phillies Team	.70	.35	.20
382	Joe Lahoud	.12	.06	.04
383	Mario Mendoza	.12	.06	.04
384	Jack Clark	3.25	1.75	1.00
385	Tito Fuentes	.12	.06	.04
386	Bob Gorinski	.12	.06	.04
387	Ken Holtzman	.25	.13	.08
388	Bill Fahey	.12	.06	.04
389	Julio Gonzalez	.12	.06	.04
390	Oscar Gamble	.20	.10	.06
391	Larry Haney	.12	.06	.04
392	Billy Almon	.12	.06	.04
393	Tippy Martinez	.12	.06	.04
394	Roy Howell	.12	.06	.04
395	Jim Hughes	.12	.06	.04
396	Bob Stinson	.12	.06	.04
397	Greg Gross	.12	.06	.04
398	Don Hood	.12	.06	.04
399	Pete Mackanin	.12	.06	.04
400	Nolan Ryan	7.00	3.50	2.00
401	Sparky Anderson	.30	.15	.09
402	Dave Campbell	.12	.06	.04
403	Bud Harrelson	.20	.10	.06
404	Tigers Team	.60	.30	.20
405	Rawly Eastwick	.12	.06	.04
406	Mike Jorgensen	.12	.06	.04
407	Odell Jones	.12	.06	.04
408	Joe Zdeb	.12	.06	.04
409	Ron Schueler	.12	.06	.04
410	Bill Madlock	.50	.25	.15
411	A.L. Championships (Yankees Rally To Defeat Royals)	.70	.35	.20
412	N.L. Championships (Dodgers Overpower Phillies In Four)	.50	.25	.15
413	World Series (Reggie & Yankees Reign Supreme)	1.25	.60	.40
414	Darold Knowles	.12	.06	.04
415	Ray Fosse	.12	.06	.04
416	Jack Brohamer	.12	.06	.04
417	Mike Garman	.12	.06	.04
418	Tony Muser	.12	.06	.04
419	Jerry Garvin	.12	.06	.04
420	Greg Luzinski	.35	.20	.11
421	Junior Moore	.12	.06	.04
422	Steve Braun	.12	.06	.04
423	Dave Rosello	.12	.06	.04
424	Red Sox Team	.70	.35	.20
425	Steve Rogers	.12	.06	.04
426	Fred Kendall	.12	.06	.04
427	*Mario Soto*	.40	.20	.12
428	Joel Youngblood	.20	.10	.06
429	Mike Barlow	.12	.06	.04
430	Al Oliver	.40	.20	.12
431	Butch Metzger	.12	.06	.04
432	Terry Bulling	.12	.06	.04
433	Fernando Gonzalez	.12	.06	.04
434	Mike Norris	.12	.06	.04
435	Checklist 364-484	.90	.45	.25
436	Vic Harris	.12	.06	.04
437	Bo McLaughlin	.12	.06	.04
438	John Ellis	.12	.06	.04
439	Ken Kravec	.12	.06	.04
440	Dave Lopes	.25	.13	.08
441	Larry Gura	.12	.06	.04
442	Elliott Maddox	.12	.06	.04
443	Darrel Chaney	.12	.06	.04
444	Roy Hartsfield	.12	.06	.04
445	Mike Ivie	.12	.06	.04
446	Tug McGraw	.35	.20	.11
447	Leroy Stanton	.12	.06	.04
448	Bill Castro	.12	.06	.04
449	Tim Blackwell	.12	.06	.04
450	Tom Seaver	3.00	1.50	.90
451	Twins Team	.50	.25	.15
452	Jerry Mumphrey	.20	.10	.06
453	Doug Flynn	.12	.06	.04
454	Dave LaRoche	.12	.06	.04
455	Bill Robinson	.12	.06	.04
456	Vern Ruhle	.12	.06	.04
457	Bob Bailey	.12	.06	.04
458	Jeff Newman	.12	.06	.04
459	Charlie Spikes	.12	.06	.04
460	Jim Hunter	1.75	.90	.50
461	Rob Andrews	.12	.06	.04
462	Rogelio Moret	.12	.06	.04
463	Kevin Bell	.12	.06	.04
464	Jerry Grote	.20	.10	.06
465	Hal McRae	.30	.15	.09
466	Dennis Blair	.12	.06	.04
467	Alvin Dark	.20	.10	.06
468	*Warren Cromartie*	.20	.10	.06
469	Rick Cerone	.20	.10	.06
470	J.R. Richard	.25	.13	.08
471	Roy Smalley	.20	.10	.06
472	Ron Reed	.20	.10	.06
473	Bill Buckner	.30	.15	.09
474	Jim Slaton	.12	.06	.04
475	Gary Matthews	.20	.10	.06
476	Bill Stein	.12	.06	.04
477	Doug Capilla	.12	.06	.04
478	Jerry Remy	.12	.06	.04
479	Cardinals Team	.50	.25	.15
480	Ron LeFlore	.25	.13	.08
481	Jackson Todd	.12	.06	.04
482	Rick Miller	.12	.06	.04
483	Ken Macha	.12	.06	.04
484	Jim Norris	.12	.06	.04
485	Chris Chambliss	.30	.15	.09
486	John Curtis	.12	.06	.04
487	Jim Tyrone	.12	.06	.04
488	Dan Spillner	.12	.06	.04
489	Rudy Meoli	.12	.06	.04
490	Amos Otis	.20	.10	.06
491	Scott McGregor	.20	.10	.06
492	Jim Sundberg	.20	.10	.06
493	Steve Renko	.12	.06	.04
494	Chuck Tanner	.20	.10	.06
495	Dave Cash	.12	.06	.04
496	*Jim Clancy*	.30	.15	.09
497	Glenn Adams	.12	.06	.04
498	Joe Sambito	.12	.06	.04
499	Mariners Team	.50	.25	.15
500	George Foster	.70	.35	.20
501	Dave Roberts	.12	.06	.04
502	Pat Rockett	.12	.06	.04
503	Ike Hampton	.12	.06	.04
504	Roger Freed	.12	.06	.04
505	Felix Millan	.12	.06	.04
506	Ron Blomberg	.12	.06	.04
507	Willie Crawford	.12	.06	.04
508	Johnny Oates	.12	.06	.04
509	Brent Strom	.12	.06	.04
510	Willie Stargell	2.00	1.00	.60
511	Frank Duffy	.12	.06	.04
512	Larry Herndon	.20	.10	.06
513	Barry Foote	.12	.06	.04

		NR MT	EX	VG
514	Rob Sperring	.12	.06	.04
515	Tim Corcoran	.12	.06	.04
516	Gary Beare	.12	.06	.04
517	Andres Mora	.12	.06	.04
518	Tommy Boggs	.12	.06	.04
519	Brian Downing	.25	.13	.08
520	Larry Hisle	.20	.10	.06
521	Steve Staggs	.12	.06	.04
522	Dick Williams	.20	.10	.06
523	*Donnie Moore*	.25	.13	.08
524	Bernie Carbo	.12	.06	.04
525	Jerry Terrell	.12	.06	.04
526	Reds Team	.60	.30	.20
527	Vic Correll	.12	.06	.04
528	Rob Picciolo	.12	.06	.04
529	Paul Hartzell	.12	.06	.04
530	Dave Winfield	2.50	1.25	.70
531	Tom Underwood	.12	.06	.04
532	Skip Jutze	.12	.06	.04
533	Sandy Alomar	.12	.06	.04
534	Wilbur Howard	.12	.06	.04
535	Checklist 485-605	.90	.45	.25
536	Roric Harrison	.12	.06	.04
537	Bruce Bochte	.20	.10	.06
538	Johnnie LeMaster	.12	.06	.04
539	Vic Davalillo	.12	.06	.04
540	Steve Carlton	2.75	1.50	.80
541	Larry Cox	.12	.06	.04
542	Tim Johnson	.12	.06	.04
543	Larry Harlow	.12	.06	.04
544	Len Randle	.12	.06	.04
545	Bill Campbell	.12	.06	.04
546	Ted Martinez	.12	.06	.04
547	John Scott	.12	.06	.04
548	Billy Hunter	.12	.06	.04
549	Joe Kerrigan	.12	.06	.04
550	John Mayberry	.20	.10	.06
551	Braves Team	.50	.25	.15
552	Francisco Barrios	.12	.06	.04
553	*Terry Puhl*	.35	.20	.11
554	Joe Coleman	.20	.10	.06
555	Butch Wynegar	.20	.10	.06
556	Ed Armbrister	.12	.06	.04
557	Tony Solaita	.12	.06	.04
558	Paul Mitchell	.12	.06	.04
559	Phil Mankowski	.12	.06	.04
560	Dave Parker	2.25	1.25	.70
561	Charlie Williams	.12	.06	.04
562	Glenn Burke	.12	.06	.04
563	Dave Rader	.12	.06	.04
564	Mick Kelleher	.12	.06	.04
565	Jerry Koosman	.25	.13	.08
566	Merv Rettenmund	.12	.06	.04
567	Dick Drago	.12	.06	.04
568	Tom Hutton	.12	.06	.04
569	*Lary Sorensen*	.20	.10	.06
570	Dave Kingman	.60	.30	.20
571	Buck Martinez	.12	.06	.04
572	Rick Wise	.20	.10	.06
573	Luis Gomez	.12	.06	.04
574	Bob Lemon	.30	.15	.09
575	Pat Dobson	.20	.10	.06
576	Sam Mejias	.12	.06	.04
577	A's Team	.50	.25	.15
578	Buzz Capra	.12	.06	.04
579	*Rance Mulliniks*	.35	.20	.11
580	Rod Carew	2.75	1.50	.80
581	Lynn McGlothen	.12	.06	.04
582	Fran Healy	.20	.10	.06
583	George Medich	.12	.06	.04
584	John Hale	.12	.06	.04
585	Woodie Fryman	.12	.06	.04
586	Ed Goodson	.12	.06	.04
587	John Urrea	.12	.06	.04
588	Jim Mason	.12	.06	.04
589	*Bob Knepper*	1.00	.50	.30
590	Bobby Murcer	.30	.15	.09
591	George Zeber	.20	.10	.06
592	Bob Apodaca	.12	.06	.04
593	Dave Skaggs	.12	.06	.04
594	Dave Freisleben	.12	.06	.04
595	Sixto Lezcano	.12	.06	.04
596	Gary Wheelock	.12	.06	.04
597	Steve Dillard	.12	.06	.04
598	Eddie Solomon	.12	.06	.04
599	Gary Woods	.12	.06	.04
600	Frank Tanana	.25	.13	.08
601	Gene Mauch	.25	.13	.08
602	Eric Soderholm	.12	.06	.04
603	Will McEnaney	.12	.06	.04
604	Earl Williams	.12	.06	.04
605	Rick Rhoden	.25	.13	.08
606	Pirates Team	.50	.25	.15
607	Fernando Arroyo	.12	.06	.04
608	Johnny Grubb	.12	.06	.04
609	John Denny	.12	.06	.04
610	Garry Maddox	.20	.10	.06
611	Pat Scanlon	.12	.06	.04
612	Ken Henderson	.12	.06	.04
613	Marty Perez	.12	.06	.04
614	Joe Wallis	.12	.06	.04
615	Clay Carroll	.20	.10	.06
616	Pat Kelly	.12	.06	.04
617	Joe Nolan	.12	.06	.04
618	Tommy Helms	.12	.06	.04
619	*Thad Bosley*	.20	.10	.06
620	Willie Randolph	.30	.15	.09
621	Craig Swan	.12	.06	.04
622	Champ Summers	.12	.06	.04
623	Eduardo Rodriguez	.12	.06	.04
624	Gary Alexander	.12	.06	.04
625	Jose Cruz	.25	.13	.08
626	Blue Jays Team	.25	.13	.08
627	Dave Johnson	.12	.06	.04
628	Ralph Garr	.20	.10	.06
629	Don Stanhouse	.12	.06	.04
630	Ron Cey	.25	.13	.08
631	Danny Ozark	.20	.10	.06
632	Rowland Office	.12	.06	.04
633	Tom Veryzer	.12	.06	.04
634	Len Barker	.20	.10	.06
635	Joe Rudi	.25	.13	.08
636	Jim Bibby	.12	.06	.04
637	Duffy Dyer	.12	.06	.04
638	Paul Splittorff	.20	.10	.06
639	Gene Clines	.12	.06	.04
640	Lee May	.12	.06	.04
641	Doug Rau	.12	.06	.04
642	Denny Doyle	.12	.06	.04
643	Tom House	.12	.06	.04
644	Jim Dwyer	.12	.06	.04
645	Mike Torrez	.20	.10	.06
646	Rick Auerbach	.12	.06	.04
647	Steve Dunning	.12	.06	.04
648	Gary Thomasson	.12	.06	.04
649	*Moose Haas*	.25	.13	.08
650	Cesar Cedeno	.25	.13	.08
651	Doug Rader	.12	.06	.04
652	Checklist 606-726	.90	.45	.25
653	Ron Hodges	.12	.06	.04
654	Pepe Frias	.12	.06	.04
655	Lyman Bostock	.20	.10	.06
656	Dave Garcia	.12	.06	.04
657	Bombo Rivera	.12	.06	.04
658	Manny Sanguillen	.12	.06	.04
659	Rangers Team	.50	.25	.15
660	Jason Thompson	.20	.10	.06
661	Grant Jackson	.12	.06	.04
662	Paul Dade	.12	.06	.04
663	Paul Reuschel	.12	.06	.04
664	Fred Stanley	.20	.10	.06
665	Dennis Leonard	.20	.10	.06
666	Billy Smith	.12	.06	.04
667	Jeff Byrd	.12	.06	.04
668	Dusty Baker	.25	.13	.08
669	Pete Falcone	.12	.06	.04
670	Jim Rice	3.50	1.75	1.00
671	Gary Lavelle	.12	.06	.04
672	Don Kessinger	.20	.10	.06
673	Steve Brye	.12	.06	.04
674	*Ray Knight*	.60	.30	.20
675	Jay Johnstone	.20	.10	.06
676	Bob Myrick	.12	.06	.04
677	Ed Herrmann	.12	.06	.04
678	Tom Burgmeier	.12	.06	.04
679	Wayne Garrett	.12	.06	.04
680	Vida Blue	.30	.15	.09
681	Rob Belloir	.12	.06	.04
682	Ken Brett	.20	.10	.06
683	Mike Champion	.12	.06	.04
684	Ralph Houk	.20	.10	.06
685	Frank Taveras	.12	.06	.04
686	Gaylord Perry	1.75	.90	.50
687	*Julio Cruz*	.25	.13	.08
688	George Mitterwald	.12	.06	.04
689	Indians Team	.50	.25	.15
690	Mickey Rivers	.25	.13	.08
691	Ross Grimsley	.20	.10	.06
692	Ken Reitz	.12	.06	.04
693	Lamar Johnson	.12	.06	.04
694	Elias Sosa	.12	.06	.04
695	Dwight Evans	1.50	.70	.45

		NR MT	EX	VG
696	Steve Mingori	.12	.06	.04
697	Roger Metzger	.12	.06	.04
698	Juan Bernhardt	.12	.06	.04
699	Jackie Brown	.12	.06	.04
700	Johnny Bench	3.50	1.75	1.00
701	Rookie Pitchers (*Tom Hume*, Larry Landreth, *Steve McCatty*, Bruce Taylor)	.25	.13	.08
702	Rookie Catchers (Bill Nahorodny, Kevin Pasley, Rick Sweet, Don Werner)	.12	.06	.04
703	Rookie Pitchers (*Larry Andersen*, Tim Jones, Mickey Mahler, *Jack Morris*)	5.00	2.50	1.50
704	Rookie 2nd Basemen (*Garth Iorg*, Dave Oliver, Sam Perlozzo, *Lou Whitaker*)	12.00	6.00	3.50
705	Rookie Outfielders (*Dave Bergman*, Miguel Dilone, Clint Hurdle, Willie Norwood)	.25	.13	.08
706	Rookie 1st Basemen (Wayne Cage, Ted Cox, *Pat Putnam, Dave Revering*)	.20	.10	.06
707	Rookie Shortstops (Mickey Klutts, *Paul Molitor, Alan Trammell, U.L. Washington*)	45.00	23.00	13.50
708	Rookie Catchers (*Bo Diaz*, Dale Murphy, *Lance Parrish, Ernie Whitt*)	25.00	12.50	7.50
709	Rookie Pitchers (Steve Burke, *Matt Keough*, Lance Rautzhan, *Dan Schatzeder*)	.20	.10	.06
710	Rookie Outfielders (Dell Alston, Rick Bosetti, *Mike Easler*, Keith Smith)	.50	.25	.15
711	Rookie Pitchers (Cardell Camper, Dennis Lamp, Craig Mitchell, Roy Thomas)	.12	.06	.04
712	Bobby Valentine	.25	.13	.08
713	Bob Davis	.12	.06	.04
714	Mike Anderson	.12	.06	.04
715	Jim Kaat	.60	.30	.20
716	Clarence Gaston	.12	.06	.04
717	Nelson Briles	.12	.06	.04
718	Ron Jackson	.12	.06	.04
719	Randy Elliott	.12	.06	.04
720	Fergie Jenkins	.60	.30	.20
721	Billy Martin	.70	.35	.20
722	Pete Broberg	.12	.06	.04
723	Johnny Wockenfuss	.12	.06	.04
724	Royals Team	.70	.35	.20
725	Kurt Bevacqua	.12	.06	.04
726	Wilbur Wood	.40	.10	.06

1979 Topps

WILLIE McCOVEY 1B
GIANTS

The size of this issue remained the same as in 1978 with 726 cards making their appearance. Actually, the 2-1/2" by 3-1/2" cards have a relatively minor design change from the previous year. The large color photo still dominates the front, with the player's name, team and position below it. The baseball with the player's position was moved to the lower left and the position replaced by a Topps logo. On the back, the printing color was changed and the game situation was replaced by a quiz called "Baseball Dates". Specialty cards include statistical leaders, major league records set during the season and eight cards devoted to career records. For the first time, rookies were arranged by teams under the heading of "Prospects."

	NR MT	EX	VG
Complete Set:	140.00	70.00	42.00

		NR MT	EX	VG
Common Player:		.12	.06	.04
1	Batting Leaders (Rod Carew, Dave Parker)	1.50	.40	.25
2	Home Run Leaders (George Foster, Jim Rice)	.50	.25	.15
3	Runs Batted In Leaders (George Foster, Jim Rice)	.50	.25	.15
4	Stolen Base Leaders (Ron LeFlore, Omar Moreno)	.25	.13	.08
5	Victory Leaders (Ron Guidry, Gaylord Perry)	.50	.25	.15
6	Strikeout Leaders (J.R. Richard, Nolan Ryan)	.50	.25	.15
7	Earned Run Avg. Leaders (Ron Guidry, Craig Swan)	.25	.13	.08
8	Leading Firemen (Rollie Fingers, Rich Gossage)	.40	.20	.12
9	Dave Campbell	.12	.06	.04
10	Lee May	.20	.10	.06
11	Marc Hill	.12	.06	.04
12	Dick Drago	.12	.06	.04
13	Paul Dade	.12	.06	.04
14	Rafael Landestoy	.12	.06	.04
15	Ross Grimsley	.20	.10	.06
16	Fred Stanley	.20	.10	.06
17	Donnie Moore	.20	.10	.06
18	Tony Solaita	.12	.06	.04
19	Larry Gura	.12	.06	.04
20	Joe Morgan	.40	.20	.12
21	Kevin Kobel	.12	.06	.04
22	Mike Jorgensen	.12	.06	.04
23	Terry Forster	.20	.10	.06
24	Paul Molitor	4.00	2.00	1.25
25	Steve Carlton	2.75	1.50	.80
26	Jamie Quirk	.12	.06	.04
27	Dave Goltz	.20	.10	.06
28	Steve Brye	.12	.06	.04
29	Rick Langford	.12	.06	.04
30	Dave Winfield	2.50	1.25	.70
31	Tom House	.12	.06	.04
32	Jerry Mumphrey	.12	.06	.04
33	Dave Rozema	.12	.06	.04
34	Rob Andrews	.12	.06	.04
35	Ed Figueroa	.20	.10	.06
36	Alan Ashby	.12	.06	.04
37	Joe Kerrigan	.12	.06	.04
38	Bernie Carbo	.12	.06	.04
39	Dale Murphy	8.00	4.00	2.50
40	Dennis Eckersley	.35	.20	.11
41	Twins Team (Gene Mauch)	.50	.25	.15
42	Ron Blomberg	.12	.06	.04
43	Wayne Twitchell	.12	.06	.04
44	Kurt Bevacqua	.12	.06	.04
45	Al Hrabosky	.20	.10	.06
46	Ron Hodges	.12	.06	.04
47	Fred Norman	.12	.06	.04
48	Merv Rettenmund	.12	.06	.04
49	Vern Ruhle	.12	.06	.04
50	Steve Garvey	1.25	.60	.40
51	Ray Fosse	.12	.06	.04
52	Randy Lerch	.12	.06	.04
53	Mick Kelleher	.12	.06	.04
54	Dell Alston	.12	.06	.04
55	Willie Stargell	2.00	1.00	.60
56	John Hale	.12	.06	.04
57	Eric Rasmussen	.12	.06	.04
58	Bob Randall	.12	.06	.04
59	John Denny	.12	.06	.04
60	Mickey Rivers	.20	.10	.06
61	Bo Diaz	.20	.10	.06
62	Randy Moffitt	.12	.06	.04
63	Jack Brohamer	.12	.06	.04
64	Tom Underwood	.12	.06	.04
65	Mark Belanger	.20	.10	.06
66	Tigers Team (Les Moss)	.60	.30	.20
67	Jim Mason	.12	.06	.04
68	Joe Niekro	.12	.06	.04
69	Elliott Maddox	.12	.06	.04
70	John Candelaria	.25	.13	.08
71	Brian Downing	.20	.10	.06
72	Steve Mingori	.12	.06	.04
73	Ken Henderson	.12	.06	.04
74	*Shane Rawley*	.70	.35	.20
75	Steve Yeager	.12	.06	.04
76	Warren Cromartie	.12	.06	.04
77	Dan Briggs	.12	.06	.04
78	Elias Sosa	.12	.06	.04
79	Ted Cox	.12	.06	.04
80	Jason Thompson	.20	.10	.06
81	Roger Erickson	.12	.06	.04

		NR MT	EX	VG			NR MT	EX	VG
82	Mets Team (Joe Torre)	.60	.30	.20	173	John Lowenstein	.12	.06	.04
83	Fred Kendall	.12	.06	.04	174	Rick Auerbach	.12	.06	.04
84	Greg Minton	.12	.06	.04	175	George Hendrick	.20	.10	.06
85	Gary Matthews	.20	.10	.06	176	Aurelio Rodriguez	.20	.10	.06
86	Rodney Scott	.12	.06	.04	177	Ron Reed	.20	.10	.06
87	Pete Falcone	.12	.06	.04	178	Alvis Woods	.12	.06	.04
88	Bob Molinaro	.12	.06	.04	179	Jim Beattie	.12	.06	.04
89	Dick Tidrow	.20	.10	.06	180	Larry Hisle	.20	.10	.06
90	Bob Boone	.25	.13	.08	181	Mike Garman	.12	.06	.04
91	Terry Crowley	.12	.06	.04	182	Tim Johnson	.12	.06	.04
92	Jim Bibby	.12	.06	.04	183	Paul Splittorff	.20	.10	.06
93	Phil Mankowski	.12	.06	.04	184	Darrel Chaney	.12	.06	.04
94	Len Barker	.12	.06	.04	185	Mike Torrez	.20	.10	.06
95	Robin Yount	4.25	2.25	1.25	186	Eric Soderholm	.12	.06	.04
96	Indians Team (Jeff Torborg)	.50	.25	.15	187	Mark Lemongello	.12	.06	.04
97	Sam Mejias	.12	.06	.04	188	Pat Kelly	.12	.06	.04
98	Ray Burris	.12	.06	.04	189	*Eddie Whitson*	.50	.25	.15
99	John Wathan	.20	.10	.06	190	Ron Cey	.25	.13	.08
100	Tom Seaver	1.75	.90	.50	191	Mike Norris	.12	.06	.04
101	Roy Howell	.12	.06	.04	192	Cardinals Team (Ken Boyer)	.50	.25	.15
102	Mike Anderson	.12	.06	.04	193	Glenn Adams	.12	.06	.04
103	Jim Todd	.12	.06	.04	194	Randy Jones	.20	.10	.06
104	Johnny Oates	.12	.06	.04	195	Bill Madlock	.40	.20	.12
105	Rick Camp	.12	.06	.04	196	Steve Kemp	.12	.06	.04
106	Frank Duffy	.12	.06	.04	197	Bob Apodaca	.12	.06	.04
107	Jesus Alou	.20	.10	.06	198	Johnny Grubb	.12	.06	.04
108	Eduardo Rodriguez	.12	.06	.04	199	Larry Milbourne	.12	.06	.04
109	Joel Youngblood	.12	.06	.04	200	Johnny Bench	1.50	.70	.45
110	Vida Blue	.30	.15	.09	201	Record Breaker (Mike Edwards)	.12	.06	.04
111	Roger Freed	.12	.06	.04	202	Record Breaker (Ron Guidry)	.35	.20	.11
112	Phillies Team (Danny Ozark)	.50	.25	.15	203	Record Breaker (J.R. Richard)	.20	.10	.06
113	Pete Redfern	.12	.06	.04	204	Record Breaker (Pete Rose)	1.50	.70	.45
114	Cliff Johnson	.20	.10	.06	205	Record Breaker (John Stearns)	.12	.06	.04
115	Nolan Ryan	6.00	3.00	1.75	206	Record Breaker (Sammy Stewart)	.12	.06	.04
116	*Ozzie Smith*	20.00	10.00	6.00	207	Dave Lemanczyk	.12	.06	.04
117	Grant Jackson	.12	.06	.04	208	Clarence Gaston	.12	.06	.04
118	Bud Harrelson	.20	.10	.06	209	Reggie Cleveland	.12	.06	.04
119	Don Stanhouse	.12	.06	.04	210	Larry Bowa	.30	.15	.09
120	Jim Sundberg	.20	.10	.06	211	Denny Martinez	.20	.10	.06
121	Checklist 1-121	.25	.13	.08	212	*Carney Lansford*	5.00	2.50	1.50
122	Mike Paxton	.12	.06	.04	213	Bill Travers	.12	.06	.04
123	Lou Whitaker	2.25	1.25	.70	214	Red Sox Team (Don Zimmer)	.60	.30	.20
124	Dan Schatzeder	.12	.06	.04	215	Willie McCovey	1.50	.70	.45
125	Rick Burleson	.20	.10	.06	216	Wilbur Wood	.20	.10	.06
126	Doug Bair	.12	.06	.04	217	Steve Dillard	.12	.06	.04
127	Thad Bosley	.12	.06	.04	218	Dennis Leonard	.20	.10	.06
128	Ted Martinez	.12	.06	.04	219	Roy Smalley	.20	.10	.06
129	Marty Pattin	.12	.06	.04	220	Cesar Geronimo	.20	.10	.06
130	Bob Watson	.12	.06	.04	221	Jesse Jefferson	.12	.06	.04
131	Jim Clancy	.25	.13	.08	222	Bob Beall	.12	.06	.04
132	Rowland Office	.12	.06	.04	223	Kent Tekulve	.25	.13	.08
133	Bill Castro	.12	.06	.04	224	Dave Revering	.12	.06	.04
134	Alan Bannister	.12	.06	.04	225	Rich Gossage	.70	.35	.20
135	Bobby Murcer	.25	.13	.08	226	Ron Pruitt	.12	.06	.04
136	Jim Kaat	.60	.30	.20	227	Steve Stone	.20	.10	.06
137	Larry Wolfe	.12	.06	.04	228	Vic Davalillo	.12	.06	.04
138	Mark Lee	.12	.06	.04	229	Doug Flynn	.12	.06	.04
139	Luis Pujols	.12	.06	.04	230	Bob Forsch	.20	.10	.06
140	Don Gullett	.20	.10	.06	231	Johnny Wockenfuss	.12	.06	.04
141	Tom Paciorek	.12	.06	.04	232	Jimmy Sexton	.12	.06	.04
142	Charlie Williams	.12	.06	.04	233	Paul Mitchell	.12	.06	.04
143	Tony Scott	.12	.06	.04	234	Toby Harrah	.20	.10	.06
144	Sandy Alomar	.12	.06	.04	235	Steve Rogers	.20	.10	.06
145	Rick Rhoden	.25	.13	.08	236	Jim Dwyer	.12	.06	.04
146	Duane Kuiper	.12	.06	.04	237	Billy Smith	.12	.06	.04
147	Dave Hamilton	.12	.06	.04	238	Balor Moore	.12	.06	.04
148	Bruce Boisclair	.12	.06	.04	239	Willie Horton	.20	.10	.06
149	Manny Sarmiento	.12	.06	.04	240	Rick Reuschel	.25	.13	.08
150	Wayne Cage	.12	.06	.04	241	Checklist 122-242	.25	.13	.08
151	John Hiller	.20	.10	.06	242	Pablo Torrealba	.12	.06	.04
152	Rick Cerone	.20	.10	.06	243	Buck Martinez	.12	.06	.04
153	Dennis Lamp	.12	.06	.04	244	Pirates Team (Chuck Tanner)	.80	.40	.25
154	Jim Gantner	.12	.06	.04	245	Jeff Burroughs	.20	.10	.06
155	Dwight Evans	1.00	.50	.30	246	Darrell Jackson	.12	.06	.04
156	Buddy Solomon	.12	.06	.04	247	Tucker Ashford	.12	.06	.04
157	U.L. Washington	.12	.06	.04	248	Pete LaCock	.12	.06	.04
158	Joe Sambito	.12	.06	.04	249	Paul Thormodsgard	.12	.06	.04
159	Roy White	.25	.13	.08	250	Willie Randolph	.30	.15	.09
160	Mike Flanagan	.30	.15	.09	251	Jack Morris	2.00	1.00	.60
161	Barry Foote	.12	.06	.04	252	Bob Stinson	.12	.06	.04
162	Tom Johnson	.12	.06	.04	253	Rick Wise	.20	.10	.06
163	Glenn Burke	.12	.06	.04	254	Luis Gomez	.12	.06	.04
164	Mickey Lolich	.40	.20	.12	255	Tommy John	.80	.40	.25
165	Frank Taveras	.12	.06	.04	256	Mike Sadek	.12	.06	.04
166	Leon Roberts	.12	.06	.04	257	Adrian Devine	.12	.06	.04
167	Roger Metzger	.12	.06	.04	258	Mike Phillips	.12	.06	.04
168	Dave Freisleben	.12	.06	.04	259	Reds Team (Sparky Anderson)	.60	.30	.20
169	Bill Nahorodny	.12	.06	.04	260	Richie Zisk	.20	.10	.06
170	Don Sutton	1.25	.60	.40	261	Mario Guerrero	.12	.06	.04
171	Gene Clines	.12	.06	.04	262	Nelson Briles	.12	.06	.04
172	Mike Bruhert	.12	.06	.04	263	Oscar Gamble	.20	.10	.06

#	Name	NR MT	EX	VG
264	*Don Robinson*	.50	.25	.15
265	Don Money	.12	.06	.04
266	Jim Willoughby	.12	.06	.04
267	Joe Rudi	.20	.10	.06
268	Julio Gonzalez	.12	.06	.04
269	Woodie Fryman	.20	.10	.06
270	Butch Hobson	.12	.06	.04
271	Rawly Eastwick	.12	.06	.04
272	Tim Corcoran	.12	.06	.04
273	Jerry Terrell	.12	.06	.04
274	Willie Norwood	.12	.06	.04
275	Junior Moore	.12	.06	.04
276	Jim Colborn	.12	.06	.04
277	Tom Grieve	.12	.06	.04
278	Andy Messersmith	.25	.13	.08
279	Jerry Grote	.12	.06	.04
280	Andre Thornton	.25	.13	.08
281	Vic Correll	.12	.06	.04
282	Blue Jays Team (Roy Hartsfield)	.50	.25	.15
283	Ken Kravec	.12	.06	.04
284	Johnnie LeMaster	.12	.06	.04
285	Bobby Bonds	.30	.15	.09
286	Duffy Dyer	.12	.06	.04
287	Andres Mora	.12	.06	.04
288	Milt Wilcox	.20	.10	.06
289	Jose Cruz	.25	.13	.08
290	Dave Lopes	.25	.13	.08
291	Tom Griffin	.12	.06	.04
292	Don Reynolds	.12	.06	.04
293	Jerry Garvin	.12	.06	.04
294	Pepe Frias	.12	.06	.04
295	Mitchell Page	.12	.06	.04
296	Preston Hanna	.12	.06	.04
297	Ted Sizemore	.12	.06	.04
298	Rich Gale	.12	.06	.04
299	Steve Ontiveros	.12	.06	.04
300	Rod Carew	2.25	1.25	.70
301	Tom Hume	.12	.06	.04
302	Braves Team (Bobby Cox)	.50	.25	.15
303	Lary Sorensen	.12	.06	.04
304	Steve Swisher	.12	.06	.04
305	Willie Montanez	.12	.06	.04
306	Floyd Bannister	.30	.15	.09
307	Larvell Blanks	.12	.06	.04
308	Bert Blyleven	.60	.30	.20
309	Ralph Garr	.20	.10	.06
310	Thurman Munson	2.25	1.25	.70
311	Gary Lavelle	.12	.06	.04
312	Bob Robertson	.12	.06	.04
313	Dyar Miller	.12	.06	.04
314	Larry Harlow	.12	.06	.04
315	Jon Matlack	.20	.10	.06
316	Milt May	.12	.06	.04
317	Jose Cardenal	.12	.06	.04
318	*Bob Welch*	2.50	1.25	.70
319	Wayne Garrett	.12	.06	.04
320	Carl Yastrzemski	2.50	1.25	.70
321	Gaylord Perry	1.50	.70	.45
322	Danny Goodwin	.12	.06	.04
323	Lynn McGlothen	.12	.06	.04
324	Mike Tyson	.12	.06	.04
325	Cecil Cooper	.40	.20	.12
326	Pedro Borbon	.12	.06	.04
327	Art Howe	.12	.06	.04
328	A's Team (Jack McKeon)	.50	.25	.15
329	Joe Coleman	.20	.10	.06
330	George Brett	3.00	1.50	.90
331	Mickey Mahler	.12	.06	.04
332	Gary Alexander	.12	.06	.04
333	Chet Lemon	.20	.10	.06
334	Craig Swan	.12	.06	.04
335	Chris Chambliss	.25	.13	.08
336	Bobby Thompson	.12	.06	.04
337	John Montague	.12	.06	.04
338	Vic Harris	.12	.06	.04
339	Ron Jackson	.12	.06	.04
340	Jim Palmer	1.50	.70	.45
341	*Willie Upshaw*	.40	.20	.12
342	Dave Roberts	.12	.06	.04
343	Ed Glynn	.12	.06	.04
344	Jerry Royster	.12	.06	.04
345	Tug McGraw	.30	.15	.09
346	Bill Buckner	.30	.15	.09
347	Doug Rau	.12	.06	.04
348	Andre Dawson	4.00	2.00	1.25
349	Jim Wright	.12	.06	.04
350	Garry Templeton	.20	.10	.06
351	Wayne Nordhagen	.12	.06	.04
352	Steve Renko	.12	.06	.04
353	Checklist 243-363	.60	.30	.20
354	Bill Bonham	.12	.06	.04

#	Name	NR MT	EX	VG
355	Lee Mazzilli	.20	.10	.06
356	Giants Team (Joe Altobelli)	.50	.25	.15
357	Jerry Augustine	.12	.06	.04
358	Alan Trammell	4.00	2.00	1.25
359	Dan Spillner	.12	.06	.04
360	Amos Otis	.20	.10	.06
361	Tom Dixon	.12	.06	.04
362	Mike Cubbage	.12	.06	.04
363	Craig Skok	.12	.06	.04
364	Gene Richards	.12	.06	.04
365	Sparky Lyle	.30	.15	.09
366	Juan Bernhardt	.12	.06	.04
367	Dave Skaggs	.12	.06	.04
368	Don Aase	.20	.10	.06
369a	Bump Wills (Blue Jays)	3.00	1.50	.90
369b	Bump Wills (Rangers)	3.50	1.75	1.00
370	Dave Kingman	.35	.20	.11
371	Jeff Holly	.12	.06	.04
372	Lamar Johnson	.12	.06	.04
373	Lance Rautzhan	.12	.06	.04
374	Ed Herrmann	.12	.06	.04
375	Bill Campbell	.12	.06	.04
376	Gorman Thomas	.25	.13	.08
377	Paul Moskau	.12	.06	.04
378	Rob Picciolo	.12	.06	.04
379	Dale Murray	.12	.06	.04
380	John Mayberry	.20	.10	.06
381	Astros Team (Bill Virdon)	.50	.25	.15
382	Jerry Martin	.12	.06	.04
383	Phil Garner	.20	.10	.06
384	Tommy Boggs	.12	.06	.04
385	Dan Ford	.12	.06	.04
386	Francisco Barrios	.12	.06	.04
387	Gary Thomasson	.12	.06	.04
388	Jack Billingham	.12	.06	.04
389	Joe Zdeb	.12	.06	.04
390	Rollie Fingers	.70	.35	.20
391	Al Oliver	.40	.20	.12
392	Doug Ault	.12	.06	.04
393	Scott McGregor	.20	.10	.06
394	Randy Stein	.12	.06	.04
395	Dave Cash	.12	.06	.04
396	Bill Plummer	.12	.06	.04
397	Sergio Ferrer	.12	.06	.04
398	Ivan DeJesus	.12	.06	.04
399	David Clyde	.12	.06	.04
400	Jim Rice	2.50	1.25	.70
401	Ray Knight	.25	.13	.08
402	Paul Hartzell	.12	.06	.04
403	Tim Foli	.12	.06	.04
404	White Sox Team (Don Kessinger)	.50	.25	.15
405	Butch Wynegar	.20	.10	.06
406	Joe Wallis	.12	.06	.04
407	Pete Vuckovich	.20	.10	.06
408	Charlie Moore	.12	.06	.04
409	*Willie Wilson*	1.25	.60	.40
410	Darrell Evans	.30	.15	.09
411	Hits Record Holders (Ty Cobb, George Sisler)	.70	.35	.20
412	Runs Batted In Record Holders (Hank Aaron, Hack Wilson)	.70	.35	.20
413	Home Run Record Holders (Hank Aaron, Roger Maris)	1.00	.50	.30
414	Batting Avg. Record Holders (Ty Cobb, Roger Hornsby)	.70	.35	.20
415	Stolen Bases Record Holders (Lou Brock)	.70	.35	.20
416	Wins Record Holders (Jack Chesbro, Cy Young)	.40	.20	.12
417	Strikeouts Record Holders (Walter Johnson, Nolan Ryan)	.40	.20	.12
418	Earned Run Avg. Record Holders (Walter Johnson, Dutch Leonard)	.20	.10	.06
419	Dick Ruthven	.12	.06	.04
420	Ken Griffey	.25	.13	.08
421	Doug DeCinces	.25	.13	.08
422	Ruppert Jones	.12	.06	.04
423	Bob Montgomery	.12	.06	.04
424	Angels Team (Jim Fregosi)	.60	.30	.20
425	Rick Manning	.12	.06	.04
426	Chris Speier	.20	.10	.06
427	Andy Replogle	.12	.06	.04
428	Bobby Valentine	.25	.13	.08
429	John Urrea	.12	.06	.04
430	Dave Parker	1.50	.70	.45
431	Glenn Borgmann	.12	.06	.04
432	Dave Heaverlo	.12	.06	.04
433	Larry Biittner	.12	.06	.04
434	Ken Clay	.20	.10	.06
435	Gene Tenace	.20	.10	.06
436	Hector Cruz	.12	.06	.04

	NR MT	EX	VG			NR MT	EX	VG
437	Rick Williams	.12	.06	.04	527	Lerrin LaGrow	.12	.06	.04
438	Horace Speed	.12	.06	.04	528	Wayne Gross	.12	.06	.04
439	Frank White	.25	.13	.08	529	Brian Asselstine	.12	.06	.04
440	Rusty Staub	.30	.15	.09	530	Frank Tanana	.25	.13	.08
441	Lee Lacy	.12	.06	.04	531	Fernando Gonzalez	.12	.06	.04
442	Doyle Alexander	.25	.13	.08	532	Buddy Schultz	.12	.06	.04
443	Bruce Bochte	.12	.06	.04	533	Leroy Stanton	.12	.06	.04
444	*Aurelio Lopez*	.20	.10	.06	534	Ken Forsch	.12	.06	.04
445	Steve Henderson	.12	.06	.04	535	Ellis Valentine	.12	.06	.04
446	Jim Lonborg	.20	.10	.06	536	Jerry Reuss	.20	.10	.06
447	Manny Sanguillen	.12	.06	.04	537	Tom Veryzer	.12	.06	.04
448	Moose Haas	.12	.06	.04	538	Mike Ivie	.12	.06	.04
449	Bombo Rivera	.12	.06	.04	539	John Ellis	.12	.06	.04
450	Dave Concepcion	.30	.15	.09	540	Greg Luzinski	.30	.15	.09
451	Royals Team (Whitey Herzog)	.50	.25	.15	541	Jim Slaton	.12	.06	.04
452	Jerry Morales	.12	.06	.04	542	Rick Bosetti	.12	.06	.04
453	Chris Knapp	.12	.06	.04	543	Kiko Garcia	.12	.06	.04
454	Len Randle	.12	.06	.04	544	Fergie Jenkins	.40	.20	.12
455	Bill Lee	.12	.06	.04	545	John Stearns	.12	.06	.04
456	Chuck Baker	.12	.06	.04	546	Bill Russell	.20	.10	.06
457	Bruce Sutter	.50	.25	.15	547	Clint Hurdle	.12	.06	.04
458	Jim Essian	.12	.06	.04	548	Enrique Romo	.12	.06	.04
459	Sid Monge	.12	.06	.04	549	Bob Bailey	.12	.06	.04
460	Graig Nettles	.50	.25	.15	550	Sal Bando	.20	.10	.06
461	Jim Barr	.12	.06	.04	551	Cubs Team (Herman Franks)	.50	.25	.15
462	Otto Velez	.12	.06	.04	552	Jose Morales	.12	.06	.04
463	Steve Comer	.12	.06	.04	553	Denny Walling	.12	.06	.04
464	Joe Nolan	.12	.06	.04	554	Matt Keough	.12	.06	.04
465	Reggie Smith	.25	.13	.08	555	Biff Pocoroba	.12	.06	.04
466	Mark Littell	.12	.06	.04	556	Mike Lum	.12	.06	.04
467	Don Kessinger	.12	.06	.04	557	Ken Brett	.20	.10	.06
468	Stan Bahnsen	.12	.06	.04	558	Jay Johnstone	.20	.10	.06
469	Lance Parrish	3.00	1.50	.90	559	Greg Pryor	.12	.06	.04
470	Garry Maddox	.12	.06	.04	560	John Montefusco	.12	.06	.04
471	Joaquin Andujar	.20	.10	.06	561	Ed Ott	.12	.06	.04
472	Craig Kusick	.12	.06	.04	562	Dusty Baker	.25	.13	.08
473	Dave Roberts	.12	.06	.04	563	Roy Thomas	.12	.06	.04
474	Dick Davis	.12	.06	.04	564	Jerry Turner	.12	.06	.04
475	Dan Driessen	.20	.10	.06	565	Rico Carty	.25	.13	.08
476	Tom Poquette	.12	.06	.04	566	Nino Espinosa	.12	.06	.04
477	Bob Grich	.25	.13	.08	567	Rich Hebner	.12	.06	.04
478	Juan Beniquez	.12	.06	.04	568	Carlos Lopez	.12	.06	.04
479	Padres Team (Roger Craig)	.50	.25	.15	569	Bob Sykes	.12	.06	.04
480	Fred Lynn	.70	.35	.20	570	Cesar Cedeno	.25	.13	.08
481	Skip Lockwood	.12	.06	.04	571	Darrell Porter	.20	.10	.06
482	Craig Reynolds	.12	.06	.04	572	Rod Gilbreath	.12	.06	.04
483	Checklist 364-484	.25	.13	.08	573	Jim Kern	.12	.06	.04
484	Rick Waits	.12	.06	.04	574	Claudell Washington	.20	.10	.06
485	Bucky Dent	.25	.13	.08	575	Luis Tiant	.30	.15	.09
486	Bob Knepper	.25	.13	.08	576	Mike Parrott	.12	.06	.04
487	Miguel Dilone	.12	.06	.04	577	Brewers Team (George Bamberger)			
488	Bob Owchinko	.12	.06	.04			.50	.25	.15
489	Larry Cox (photo actually Dave Rader)				578	Pete Broberg	.12	.06	.04
		.12	.06	.04	579	Greg Gross	.12	.06	.04
490	Al Cowens	.12	.06	.04	580	Ron Fairly	.20	.10	.06
491	Tippy Martinez	.12	.06	.04	581	Darold Knowles	.12	.06	.04
492	Bob Bailor	.12	.06	.04	582	Paul Blair	.20	.10	.06
493	Larry Christenson	.12	.06	.04	583	Julio Cruz	.12	.06	.04
494	Jerry White	.12	.06	.04	584	Jim Rooker	.12	.06	.04
495	Tony Perez	.60	.30	.20	585	Hal McRae	.25	.13	.08
496	Barry Bonnell	.12	.06	.04	586	*Bob Horner*	1.25	.60	.40
497	Glenn Abbott	.12	.06	.04	587	Ken Reitz	.12	.06	.04
498	Rich Chiles	.12	.06	.04	588	Tom Murphy	.12	.06	.04
499	Rangers Team (Pat Corrales)	.50	.25	.15	589	Terry Whitfield	.12	.06	.04
500	Ron Guidry	.90	.45	.25	590	J.R. Richard	.20	.10	.06
501	Junior Kennedy	.12	.06	.04	591	Mike Hargrove	.20	.10	.06
502	Steve Braun	.12	.06	.04	592	Mike Krukow	.20	.10	.06
503	Terry Humphrey	.12	.06	.04	593	Rick Dempsey	.20	.10	.06
504	*Larry McWilliams*	.20	.10	.06	594	Bob Shirley	.12	.06	.04
505	Ed Kranepool	.20	.10	.06	595	Phil Niekro	1.25	.60	.40
506	John D'Acquisto	.12	.06	.04	596	Jim Wohlford	.12	.06	.04
507	Tony Armas	.20	.10	.06	597	Bob Stanley	.20	.10	.06
508	Charlie Hough	.20	.10	.06	598	Mark Wagner	.12	.06	.04
509	Mario Mendoza	.12	.06	.04	599	Jim Spencer	.20	.10	.06
510	Ted Simmons	.40	.20	.12	600	George Foster	.60	.30	.20
511	Paul Reuschel	.12	.06	.04	601	Dave LaRoche	.12	.06	.04
512	Jack Clark	1.50	.70	.45	602	Checklist 485-605	.60	.30	.20
513	Dave Johnson	.30	.15	.09	603	Rudy May	.12	.06	.04
514	Mike Proly	.12	.06	.04	604	Jeff Newman	.12	.06	.04
515	Enos Cabell	.12	.06	.04	605	Rick Monday	.12	.06	.04
516	Champ Summers	.12	.06	.04	606	Expos Team (Dick Williams)	.50	.25	.15
517	Al Bumbry	.20	.10	.06	607	Omar Moreno	.12	.06	.04
518	Jim Umbarger	.12	.06	.04	608	Dave McKay	.12	.06	.04
519	Ben Oglivie	.20	.10	.06	609	Silvio Martinez	.12	.06	.04
520	Gary Carter	2.50	1.25	.70	610	Mike Schmidt	6.00	3.00	1.75
521	Sam Ewing	.12	.06	.04	611	Jim Norris	.12	.06	.04
522	Ken Holtzman	.20	.10	.06	612	*Rick Honeycutt*	.30	.15	.09
523	John Milner	.12	.06	.04	613	Mike Edwards	.12	.06	.04
524	Tom Burgmeier	.12	.06	.04	614	Willie Hernandez	.20	.10	.06
525	Freddie Patek	.12	.06	.04	615	Ken Singleton	.20	.10	.06
526	Dodgers Team (Tom Lasorda)	.60	.30	.20	616	Billy Almon	.12	.06	.04

		NR MT	EX	VG
617	Terry Puhl	.12	.06	.04
618	Jerry Remy	.12	.06	.04
619	*Ken Landreaux*	.25	.13	.08
620	Bert Campaneris	.25	.13	.08
621	Pat Zachry	.12	.06	.04
622	Dave Collins	.20	.10	.06
623	Bob McClure	.12	.06	.04
624	Larry Herndon	.20	.10	.06
625	Mark Fidrych	.25	.13	.08
626	Yankees Team (Bob Lemon)	.80	.40	.25
627	Gary Serum	.12	.06	.04
628	Del Unser	.12	.06	.04
629	Gene Garber	.12	.06	.04
630	Bake McBride	.12	.06	.04
631	Jorge Orta	.12	.06	.04
632	Don Kirkwood	.12	.06	.04
633	Rob Wilfong	.12	.06	.04
634	Paul Lindblad	.20	.10	.06
635	Don Baylor	.50	.25	.15
636	Wayne Garland	.12	.06	.04
637	Bill Robinson	.12	.06	.04
638	Al Fitzmorris	.12	.06	.04
639	Manny Trillo	.20	.10	.06
640	Eddie Murray	5.00	2.50	1.50
641	*Bobby Castillo*	.12	.06	.04
642	Wilbur Howard	.12	.06	.04
643	Tom Hausman	.12	.06	.04
644	Manny Mota	.20	.10	.06
645	George Scott	.12	.06	.04
646	Rick Sweet	.12	.06	.04
647	Bob Lacey	.12	.06	.04
648	Lou Piniella	.35	.20	.11
649	John Curtis	.12	.06	.04
650	Pete Rose	4.50	2.25	1.25
651	Mike Caldwell	.12	.06	.04
652	Stan Papi	.12	.06	.04
653	Warren Brusstar	.12	.06	.04
654	Rick Miller	.12	.06	.04
655	Jerry Koosman	.30	.15	.09
656	Hosken Powell	.12	.06	.04
657	George Medich	.12	.06	.04
658	Taylor Duncan	.12	.06	.04
659	Mariners Team (Darrell Johnson)	.50	.25	.15
660	Ron LeFlore	.12	.06	.04
661	Bruce Kison	.12	.06	.04
662	Kevin Bell	.12	.06	.04
663	Mike Vail	.12	.06	.04
664	Doug Bird	.12	.06	.04
665	Lou Brock	1.50	.70	.45
666	Rich Dauer	.12	.06	.04
667	Don Hood	.12	.06	.04
668	Bill North	.12	.06	.04
669	Checklist 606-726	.60	.30	.20
670	Jim Hunter	.70	.35	.20
671	Joe Ferguson	.12	.06	.04
672	Ed Halicki	.12	.06	.04
673	Tom Hutton	.12	.06	.04
674	Dave Tomlin	.12	.06	.04
675	Tim McCarver	.30	.15	.09
676	Johnny Sutton	.12	.06	.04
677	Larry Parrish	.25	.13	.08
678	Geoff Zahn	.12	.06	.04
679	Derrel Thomas	.12	.06	.04
680	Carlton Fisk	1.25	.60	.40
681	*John Henry Johnson*	.12	.06	.04
682	Dave Chalk	.12	.06	.04
683	Dan Meyer	.12	.06	.04
684	Jamie Easterly	.12	.06	.04
685	Sixto Lezcano	.12	.06	.04
686	Ron Schueler	.12	.06	.04
687	Rennie Stennett	.12	.06	.04
688	Mike Willis	.12	.06	.04
689	Orioles Team (Earl Weaver)	.70	.35	.20
690	Buddy Bell	.12	.06	.04
691	Dock Ellis	.12	.06	.04
692	Mickey Stanley	.20	.10	.06
693	Dave Rader	.12	.06	.04
694	Burt Hooton	.20	.10	.06
695	Keith Hernandez	2.00	1.00	.60
696	Andy Hassler	.12	.06	.04
697	Dave Bergman	.12	.06	.04
698	Bill Stein	.12	.06	.04
699	Hal Dues	.12	.06	.04
700	Reggie Jackson	1.50	.70	.45
701	Orioles Prospects (Mark Corey, John Flinn, *Sammy Stewart*)	.20	.10	.06
702	Red Sox Prospects (Joel Finch, Garry Hancock, Allen Ripley)	.12	.06	.04
703	Angels Prospects (Jim Anderson, Dave Frost, Bob Slater)	.12	.06	.04
704	White Sox Prospects (Ross Baumgarten, Mike Colbern, *Mike Squires*)	.20	.10	.06

		NR MT	EX	VG
705	Indians Prospects (*Alfredo Griffin*, Tim Norrid, Dave Oliver)	.70	.35	.20
706	Tigers Prospects (Dave Stegman, Dave Tobik, Kip Young)	.12	.06	.04
707	Royals Prospects (Randy Bass, Jim Gaudet, Randy McGilberry)	.12	.06	.04
708	Brewers Prospects (*Kevin Bass, Eddie Romero*, Ned Yost)	1.00	.50	.30
709	Twins Prospects (Sam Perlozzo, Rick Sofield, Kevin Stanfield)	.12	.06	.04
710	Yankees Prospects (Brian Doyle, *Mike Heath*, Dave Rajsich)	.30	.15	.09
711	A's Prospects (*Dwayne Murphy*, Bruce Robinson, Alan Wirth)	.50	.25	.15
712	Mariners Prospects (Bud Anderson, Greg Biercevicz, Byron McLaughlin)	.12	.06	.04
713	Rangers Prospects (*Danny Darwin*, Pat Putnam, *Billy Sample*)	.40	.20	.12
714	Blue Jays Prospects (Victor Cruz, Pat Kelly, Ernie Whitt)	.20	.10	.06
715	Braves Prospects (*Bruce Benedict, Glenn Hubbard*, Larry Whisenton)	.40	.20	.12
716	Cubs Prospects (Dave Geisel, Karl Pagel, *Scot Thompson*)	.12	.06	.04
717	Reds Prospects (*Mike LaCoss, Ron Oester, Harry Spilman*)	.40	.20	.12
718	Astros Prospects (Bruce Bochy, Mike Fischlin, Don Pisker)	.12	.06	.04
719	Dodgers Prospects (*Pedro Guerrero, Rudy Law*, Joe Simpson)	10.00	5.00	3.00
720	Expos Prospects (Jerry Fry, Jerry Pirtle, *Scott Sanderson*)	.30	.15	.09
721	Mets Prospects (*Juan Berenguer*, Dwight Bernard, Dan Norman)	.30	.15	.09
722	Phillies Prospects (*Jim Morrison, Lonnie Smith*, Jim Wright)	2.00	1.00	.60
723	Pirates Prospects (*Dale Berra*, Eugenio Cotes, Ben Wiltbank)	.20	.10	.06
724	Cardinals Prospects (Tom Bruno, *George Frazier, Terry Kennedy*)	.50	.25	.15
725	Padres Prospects (Jim Beswick, Steve Mura, Broderick Perkins)	.12	.06	.04
726	Giants Prospects (Greg Johnston, Joe Strain, John Tamargo)	.25	.06	.04

1979 Topps Comics

Issued as the 3" by 3-3/4" wax wrapper for a piece of bubblegum, this "test" issue was bought up in great quantities by speculators and remains rather common. It is also inexpensive, because the comic-style player representations were not popular with collectors. The set is complete at 33 pieces.

		NR MT	EX	VG
Complete Set:		6.50	3.25	2.00
Common Player:		.10	.05	.03
1	Eddie Murray	.40	.20	.12
2	Jim Rice	.30	.15	.09
3	Carl Yastrzemski	.60	.30	.20
4	Nolan Ryan	.30	.15	.09
5	Chet Lemon	.10	.05	.03
6	Andre Thornton	.10	.05	.03
7	Rusty Staub	.15	.08	.05
8	Ron LeFlore	.10	.05	.03
9	George Brett	.50	.25	.15
10	Larry Hisle	.10	.05	.03

		NR MT	EX	VG
11	Rod Carew	.35	.20	.11
12	Reggie Jackson	.40	.20	.12
13	Ron Guidry	.20	.10	.06
14	Mitchell Page	.10	.05	.03
15	Leon Roberts	.10	.05	.03
16	Al Oliver	.15	.08	.05
17	John Mayberry	.10	.05	.03
18	Bob Horner	.20	.10	.06
19	Phil Niekro	.25	.13	.08
20	Dave Kingman	.15	.08	.05
21	John Bench	.40	.20	.12
22	Tom Seaver	.40	.20	.12
23	J.R. Richard	.10	.05	.03
24	Steve Garvey	.35	.20	.11
25	Reggie Smith	.15	.08	.05
26	Ross Grimsley	.10	.05	.03
27	Craig Swan	.10	.05	.03
28	Pete Rose	.90	.45	.25
29	Dave Parker	.20	.10	.06
30	Ted Simmons	.15	.08	.05
31	Dave Winfield	.30	.15	.09
32	Jack Clark	.20	.10	.06
33	Vida Blue	.15	.08	.05

1980 Topps

Again numbering 726 cards measuring 2-1/2" by 3-1/2", Topps did make some design changes in 1980. Fronts have the usual color picture with a facsimile autograph. The player's name appears above the picture, while his position is on a pennant at the upper left and his team on another pennant in the lower right. Backs no longer feature games, returning instead to statistics, personal information, a few headlines and a cartoon about the player. Specialty cards include statistical leaders, and previous season highlights. Many rookies again appear in team threesomes.

		NR MT	EX	VG
Complete Set:		140.00	70.00	42.00
Common Player:		.12	.06	.04
1	1979 Highlights (Lou Brock, Carl Yastrzemski)	1.50	.70	.45
2	1979 Highlights (Willie McCovey)	.80	.40	.25
3	1979 Highlights (Manny Mota)	.20	.10	.06
4	1979 Highlights (Pete Rose)	2.00	1.00	.60
5	1979 Highlights (Garry Templeton)	.20	.10	.06
6	1979 Highlights (Del Unser)	.12	.06	.04
7	Mike Lum	.12	.06	.04
8	Craig Swan	.12	.06	.04
9	Steve Braun	.12	.06	.04
10	Denny Martinez	.20	.10	.06
11	Jimmy Sexton	.12	.06	.04
12	John Curtis	.12	.06	.04
13	Ron Pruitt	.12	.06	.04
14	Dave Cash	.12	.06	.04
15	Bill Campbell	.12	.06	.04
16	Jerry Narron	.20	.10	.06
17	Bruce Sutter	.35	.25	.14
18	Ron Jackson	.12	.06	.04
19	Balor Moore	.12	.06	.04
20	Dan Ford	.12	.06	.04
21	Manny Sarmiento	.12	.06	.04
22	Pat Putnam	.12	.06	.04
23	Derrel Thomas	.12	.06	.04

		NR MT	EX	VG
24	Jim Slaton	.12	.06	.04
25	Lee Mazzilli	.20	.10	.06
26	Marty Pattin	.12	.06	.04
27	Del Unser	.12	.06	.04
28	Bruce Kison	.12	.06	.04
29	Mark Wagner	.12	.06	.04
30	Vida Blue	.30	.15	.09
31	Jay Johnstone	.20	.10	.06
32	Julio Cruz	.12	.06	.04
33	Tony Scott	.12	.06	.04
34	Jeff Newman	.12	.06	.04
35	Luis Tiant	.30	.15	.09
36	Rusty Torres	.12	.06	.04
37	Kiko Garcia	.12	.06	.04
38	Dan Spillner	.12	.06	.04
39	Rowland Office	.12	.06	.04
40	Carlton Fisk	1.00	.50	.30
41	Rangers Team (Pat Corrales)	.50	.25	.15
42	*Dave Palmer*	.40	.20	.12
43	Bombo Rivera	.12	.06	.04
44	Bill Fahey	.12	.06	.04
45	Frank White	.25	.13	.08
46	Rico Carty	.20	.10	.06
47	Bill Bonham	.12	.06	.04
48	Rick Miller	.12	.06	.04
49	Mario Guerrero	.12	.06	.04
50	J.R. Richard	.20	.10	.06
51	Joe Ferguson	.12	.06	.04
52	Warren Brusstar	.12	.06	.04
53	Ben Oglivie	.20	.10	.06
54	Dennis Lamp	.12	.06	.04
55	Bill Madlock	.40	.20	.12
56	Bobby Valentine	.20	.10	.06
57	Pete Vuckovich	.20	.10	.06
58	Doug Flynn	.12	.06	.04
59	Eddy Putman	.12	.06	.04
60	Bucky Dent	.25	.13	.08
61	Gary Serum	.12	.06	.04
62	Mike Ivie	.12	.06	.04
63	Bob Stanley	.20	.10	.06
64	Joe Nolan	.12	.06	.04
65	Al Bumbry	.20	.10	.06
66	Royals Team (Jim Frey)	.60	.30	.20
67	Doyle Alexander	.25	.13	.08
68	Larry Harlow	.12	.06	.04
69	Rick Williams	.12	.06	.04
70	Gary Carter	2.00	1.00	.60
71	John Milner	.12	.06	.04
72	Fred Howard	.12	.06	.04
73	Dave Collins	.20	.10	.06
74	Sid Monge	.12	.06	.04
75	Bill Russell	.20	.10	.06
76	John Stearns	.12	.06	.04
77	*Dave Stieb*	3.25	1.75	1.00
78	Ruppert Jones	.12	.06	.04
79	Bob Owchinko	.12	.06	.04
80	Ron LeFlore	.20	.10	.06
81	Ted Sizemore	.12	.06	.04
82	Astros Team (Bill Virdon)	.50	.25	.15
83	*Steve Trout*	.30	.15	.09
84	Gary Lavelle	.12	.06	.04
85	Ted Simmons	.40	.20	.12
86	Dave Hamilton	.12	.06	.04
87	Pepe Frias	.12	.06	.04
88	Ken Landreaux	.20	.10	.06
89	Don Hood	.20	.10	.06
90	Manny Trillo	.20	.10	.06
91	Rick Dempsey	.20	.10	.06
92	Rick Rhoden	.25	.13	.08
93	Dave Roberts	.12	.06	.04
94	*Neil Allen*	.30	.15	.09
95	Cecil Cooper	.35	.20	.11
96	A's Team (Jim Marshall)	.50	.25	.15
97	Bill Lee	.20	.10	.06
98	Jerry Terrell	.12	.06	.04
99	Victor Cruz	.12	.06	.04
100	Johnny Bench	2.50	1.25	.70
101	Aurelio Lopez	.12	.06	.04
102	Rich Dauer	.12	.06	.04
103	*Bill Caudill*	.20	.10	.06
104	Manny Mota	.20	.10	.06
105	Frank Tanana	.20	.10	.06
106	*Jeff Leonard*	1.00	.50	.30
107	Francisco Barrios	.12	.06	.04
108	Bob Horner	.40	.30	.15
109	Bill Travers	.12	.06	.04
110	Fred Lynn	.35	.20	.11
111	Bob Knepper	.20	.10	.06
112	White Sox Team (Tony LaRussa)	.50	.25	.15
113	Geoff Zahn	.12	.06	.04
114	Juan Beniquez	.12	.06	.04

		NR MT	EX	VG
115	Sparky Lyle	.25	.13	.08
116	Larry Cox	.12	.06	.04
117	Dock Ellis	.12	.06	.04
118	Phil Garner	.20	.10	.06
119	Sammy Stewart	.12	.06	.04
120	Greg Luzinski	.30	.15	.09
121	Checklist 1-121	.50	.25	.15
122	Dave Rosello	.12	.06	.04
123	Lynn Jones	.12	.06	.04
124	Dave Lemanczyk	.12	.06	.04
125	Tony Perez	.50	.25	.15
126	Dave Tomlin	.12	.06	.04
127	Gary Thomasson	.12	.06	.04
128	Tom Burgmeier	.12	.06	.04
129	Craig Reynolds	.12	.06	.04
130	Amos Otis	.20	.10	.06
131	Paul Mitchell	.12	.06	.04
132	Biff Pocoroba	.12	.06	.04
133	Jerry Turner	.12	.06	.04
134	Matt Keough	.12	.06	.04
135	Bill Buckner	.30	.15	.09
136	Dick Ruthven	.12	.06	.04
137	*John Castino*	.20	.10	.06
138	Ross Baumgarten	.12	.06	.04
139	*Dane Iorg*	.20	.10	.06
140	Rich Gossage	.60	.30	.20
141	Gary Alexander	.12	.06	.04
142	Phil Huffman	.12	.06	.04
143	Bruce Bochte	.12	.06	.04
144	Steve Comer	.12	.06	.04
145	Darrell Evans	.30	.15	.09
146	Bob Welch	.60	.30	.20
147	Terry Puhl	.12	.06	.04
148	Manny Sanguillen	.12	.06	.04
149	Tom Hume	.12	.06	.04
150	Jason Thompson	.20	.10	.06
151	Tom Hausman	.12	.06	.04
152	John Fulgham	.12	.06	.04
153	Tim Blackwell	.12	.06	.04
154	Lary Sorensen	.12	.06	.04
155	Jerry Remy	.12	.06	.04
156	Tony Brizzolara	.12	.06	.04
157	Willie Wilson	.20	.10	.06
158	Rob Picciolo	.12	.06	.04
159	Ken Clay	.20	.10	.06
160	Eddie Murray	3.00	1.50	.90
161	Larry Christenson	.12	.06	.04
162	Bob Randall	.12	.06	.04
163	Steve Swisher	.12	.06	.04
164	Greg Pryor	.12	.06	.04
165	Omar Moreno	.12	.06	.04
166	Glenn Abbott	.12	.06	.04
167	Jack Clark	1.00	.50	.30
168	Rick Waits	.12	.06	.04
169	Luis Gomez	.12	.06	.04
170	Burt Hooton	.20	.10	.06
171	Fernando Gonzalez	.12	.06	.04
172	Ron Hodges	.12	.06	.04
173	John Henry Johnson	.12	.06	.04
174	Ray Knight	.20	.10	.06
175	Rick Reuschel	.25	.13	.08
176	Champ Summers	.12	.06	.04
177	Dave Heaverlo	.12	.06	.04
178	Tim McCarver	.30	.15	.09
179	*Ron Davis*	.20	.10	.06
180	Warren Cromartie	.12	.06	.04
181	Moose Haas	.12	.06	.04
182	Ken Reitz	.12	.06	.04
183	Jim Anderson	.12	.06	.04
184	Steve Renko	.12	.06	.04
185	Hal McRae	.25	.13	.08
186	Junior Moore	.12	.06	.04
187	Alan Ashby	.12	.06	.04
188	Terry Crowley	.12	.06	.04
189	Kevin Kobel	.12	.06	.04
190	Buddy Bell	.25	.13	.08
191	Ted Martinez	.12	.06	.04
192	Braves Team (Bobby Cox)	.50	.25	.15
193	Dave Goltz	.20	.10	.06
194	Mike Easler	.20	.10	.06
195	John Montefusco	.20	.10	.06
196	Lance Parrish	1.50	.70	.45
197	Byron McLaughlin	.12	.06	.04
198	Dell Alston	.12	.06	.04
199	Mike LaCoss	.20	.10	.06
200	Jim Rice	2.00	1.00	.60
201	Batting Leaders (Keith Hernandez, Fred Lynn)	.50	.25	.15
202	Home Run Leaders (Dave Kingman, Gorman Thomas)	.25	.13	.08
203	Runs Batted In Leaders (Don Baylor, Dave Winfield)	.50	.25	.15

		NR MT	EX	VG
204	Stolen Base Leaders (Omar Moreno, Willie Wilson)	.20	.10	.06
205	Victory Leaders (Mike Flanagan, Joe Niekro, Phil Niekro)	.40	.20	.12
206	Strikeout Leaders (J.R. Richard, Nolan Ryan)	.50	.25	.15
207	Earned Run Avg. Leaders (Ron Guidry, J.R. Richard)	.25	.13	.08
208	Wayne Cage	.12	.06	.04
209	Von Joshua	.12	.06	.04
210	Steve Carlton	2.50	1.25	.70
211	Dave Skaggs	.12	.06	.04
212	Dave Roberts	.12	.06	.04
213	Mike Jorgensen	.12	.06	.04
214	Angels Team (Jim Fregosi)	.50	.25	.15
215	Sixto Lezcano	.12	.06	.04
216	Phil Mankowski	.12	.06	.04
217	Ed Halicki	.12	.06	.04
218	Jose Morales	.12	.06	.04
219	Steve Mingori	.12	.06	.04
220	Dave Concepcion	.30	.15	.09
221	Joe Cannon	.12	.06	.04
222	*Ron Hassey*	.35	.20	.11
223	Bob Sykes	.12	.06	.04
224	Willie Montanez	.12	.06	.04
225	Lou Piniella	.30	.15	.09
226	Bill Stein	.12	.06	.04
227	Len Barker	.12	.06	.04
228	Johnny Oates	.12	.06	.04
229	Jim Bibby	.12	.06	.04
230	Dave Winfield	2.00	1.00	.60
231	Steve McCatty	.12	.06	.04
232	Alan Trammell	2.00	1.00	.60
233	LaRue Washington	.12	.06	.04
234	Vern Ruhle	.12	.06	.04
235	Andre Dawson	2.75	1.50	.80
236	Marc Hill	.12	.06	.04
237	Scott McGregor	.20	.10	.06
238	Rob Wilfong	.12	.06	.04
239	Don Aase	.12	.06	.04
240	Dave Kingman	.40	.20	.12
241	Checklist 122-242	.50	.25	.15
242	Lamar Johnson	.12	.06	.04
243	Jerry Augustine	.12	.06	.04
244	Cardinals Team (Ken Boyer)	.50	.25	.15
245	Phil Niekro	.90	.45	.25
246	Tim Foli	.12	.06	.04
247	Frank Riccelli	.12	.06	.04
248	Jamie Quirk	.12	.06	.04
249	Jim Clancy	.20	.10	.06
250	Jim Kaat	.50	.25	.15
251	Kip Young	.12	.06	.04
252	Ted Cox	.12	.06	.04
253	John Montague	.12	.06	.04
254	Paul Dade	.12	.06	.04
255	Dusty Baker	.12	.06	.04
256	Roger Erickson	.12	.06	.04
257	Larry Herndon	.20	.10	.06
258	Paul Moskau	.12	.06	.04
259	Mets Team (Joe Torre)	.60	.30	.20
260	Al Oliver	.35	.20	.11
261	Dave Chalk	.12	.06	.04
262	Benny Ayala	.12	.06	.04
263	Dave LaRoche	.12	.06	.04
264	Bill Robinson	.12	.06	.04
265	Robin Yount	3.25	1.75	1.00
266	Bernie Carbo	.12	.06	.04
267	Dan Schatzeder	.12	.06	.04
268	Rafael Landestoy	.12	.06	.04
269	Dave Tobik	.12	.06	.04
270	Mike Schmidt	2.00	1.00	.60
271	Dick Drago	.12	.06	.04
272	Ralph Garr	.20	.10	.06
273	Eduardo Rodriguez	.12	.06	.04
274	Dale Murphy	5.50	2.75	1.75
275	Jerry Koosman	.25	.13	.08
276	Tom Veryzer	.12	.06	.04
277	Rick Bosetti	.12	.06	.04
278	Jim Spencer	.20	.10	.06
279	Rob Andrews	.12	.06	.04
280	Gaylord Perry	.90	.45	.25
281	Paul Blair	.20	.10	.06
282	Mariners Team (Darrell Johnson)	.50	.25	.15
283	John Ellis	.12	.06	.04
284	Larry Murray	.12	.06	.04
285	Don Baylor	.35	.20	.11
286	Darold Knowles	.12	.06	.04
287	John Lowenstein	.12	.06	.04
288	Dave Rozema	.12	.06	.04
289	Bruce Bochy	.12	.06	.04
290	Steve Garvey	2.00	1.00	.60

	NR MT	EX	VG			NR MT	EX	VG
291 Randy Scarbery	.12	.06	.04		382 Dave Freisleben	.12	.06	.04
292 Dale Berra	.12	.06	.04		383 Ed Ott	.12	.06	.04
293 Elias Sosa	.12	.06	.04		384 Joey McLaughlin	.12	.06	.04
294 Charlie Spikes	.12	.06	.04		385 Enos Cabell	.12	.06	.04
295 Larry Gura	.12	.06	.04		386 Darrell Jackson	.12	.06	.04
296 Dave Rader	.12	.06	.04		387a Fred Stanley (name in red)	.20	.10	.06
297 Tim Johnson	.12	.06	.04		387b Fred Stanley (name in yellow)	3.00	1.50	.90
298 Ken Holtzman	.20	.10	.06		388 Mike Paxton	.12	.06	.04
299 Steve Henderson	.12	.06	.04		389 Pete LaCock	.12	.06	.04
300 Ron Guidry	.70	.35	.20		390 Fergie Jenkins	.40	.20	.12
301 Mike Edwards	.12	.06	.04		391 Tony Armas	.12	.06	.04
302 Dodgers Team (Tom Lasorda)	.60	.30	.20		392 Milt Wilcox	.12	.06	.04
303 Bill Castro	.12	.06	.04		393 Ozzie Smith	3.50	1.75	1.00
304 Butch Wynegar	.20	.10	.06		394 Reggie Cleveland	.12	.06	.04
305 Randy Jones	.20	.10	.06		395 Ellis Valentine	.12	.06	.04
306 Denny Walling	.12	.06	.04		396 Dan Meyer	.12	.06	.04
307 Rick Honeycutt	.20	.10	.06		397 Roy Thomas	.12	.06	.04
308 Mike Hargrove	.20	.10	.06		398 Barry Foote	.12	.06	.04
309 Larry McWilliams	.12	.06	.04		399 Mike Proly	.12	.06	.04
310 Dave Parker	1.00	.50	.30		400 George Foster	.50	.25	.15
311 Roger Metzger	.12	.06	.04		401 Pete Falcone	.12	.06	.04
312 Mike Barlow	.12	.06	.04		402 Merv Rettenmund	.12	.06	.04
313 Johnny Grubb	.12	.06	.04		403 Pete Redfern	.12	.06	.04
314 *Tim Stoddard*	.20	.10	.06		404 Orioles Team (Earl Weaver)	.60	.30	.20
315 Steve Kemp	.25	.13	.08		405 Dwight Evans	.60	.30	.20
316 Bob Lacey	.12	.06	.04		406 Paul Molitor	1.50	.70	.45
317 Mike Anderson	.12	.06	.04		407 Tony Solaita	.12	.06	.04
318 Jerry Reuss	.20	.10	.06		408 Bill North	.12	.06	.04
319 Chris Speier	.12	.06	.04		409 Paul Splittorff	.20	.10	.06
320 Dennis Eckersley	.40	.20	.12		410 Bobby Bonds	.25	.13	.08
321 Keith Hernandez	1.50	.70	.45		411 Frank LaCorte	.12	.06	.04
322 Claudell Washington	.20	.10	.06		412 Thad Bosley	.12	.06	.04
323 Mick Kelleher	.12	.06	.04		413 Allen Ripley	.12	.06	.04
324 Tom Underwood	.12	.06	.04		414 George Scott	.20	.10	.06
325 Dan Driessen	.20	.10	.06		415 Bill Atkinson	.12	.06	.04
326 Bo McLaughlin	.12	.06	.04		416 *Tom Brookens*	.35	.20	.11
327 Ray Fosse	.12	.06	.04		417 Craig Chamberlain	.12	.06	.04
328 Twins Team (Gene Mauch)	.50	.25	.15		418 Roger Freed	.12	.06	.04
329 Bert Roberge	.12	.06	.04		419 Vic Correll	.12	.06	.04
330 Al Cowens	.12	.06	.04		420 Butch Hobson	.12	.06	.04
331 Rich Hebner	.12	.06	.04		421 Doug Bird	.12	.06	.04
332 Enrique Romo	.12	.06	.04		422 Larry Milbourne	.12	.06	.04
333 Jim Norris	.12	.06	.04		423 Dave Frost	.12	.06	.04
334 Jim Beattie	.20	.10	.06		424 Yankees Team (Dick Howser)	.70	.35	.20
335 Willie McCovey	1.50	.70	.45		425 Mark Belanger	.20	.10	.06
336 George Medich	.12	.06	.04		426 Grant Jackson	.12	.06	.04
337 Carney Lansford	.30	.15	.09		427 Tom Hutton	.12	.06	.04
338 Johnny Wockenfuss	.12	.06	.04		428 Pat Zachry	.12	.06	.04
339 John D'Acquisto	.12	.06	.04		429 Duane Kuiper	.12	.06	.04
340 Ken Singleton	.20	.10	.06		430 Larry Hisle	.12	.06	.04
341 Jim Essian	.12	.06	.04		431 Mike Krukow	.20	.10	.06
342 Odell Jones	.12	.06	.04		432 Willie Norwood	.12	.06	.04
343 Mike Vail	.12	.06	.04		433 Rich Gale	.12	.06	.04
344 Randy Lerch	.12	.06	.04		434 Johnnie LeMaster	.12	.06	.04
345 Larry Parrish	.20	.10	.06		435 Don Gullett	.20	.10	.06
346 Buddy Solomon	.12	.06	.04		436 Billy Almon	.12	.06	.04
347 *Harry Chappas*	.20	.10	.06		437 Joe Niekro	.20	.10	.06
348 Checklist 243-363	.50	.25	.15		438 Dave Revering	.12	.06	.04
349 Jack Brohamer	.12	.06	.04		439 Mike Phillips	.12	.06	.04
350 George Hendrick	.20	.10	.06		440 Don Sutton	.90	.45	.25
351 Bob Davis	.12	.06	.04		441 Eric Soderholm	.12	.06	.04
352 Dan Briggs	.12	.06	.04		442 Jorge Orta	.12	.06	.04
353 Andy Hassler	.12	.06	.04		443 Mike Parrott	.12	.06	.04
354 Rick Auerbach	.12	.06	.04		444 Alvis Woods	.12	.06	.04
355 Gary Matthews	.20	.10	.06		445 Mark Fidrych	.20	.10	.06
356 Padres Team (Jerry Coleman)	.50	.25	.15		446 Duffy Dyer	.12	.06	.04
357 Bob McClure	.12	.06	.04		447 Nino Espinosa	.12	.06	.04
358 Lou Whitaker	1.25	.60	.40		448 Jim Wohlford	.12	.06	.04
359 Randy Moffitt	.12	.06	.04		449 Doug Bair	.12	.06	.04
360 Darrell Porter	.12	.06	.04		450 George Brett	3.50	1.75	1.00
361 Wayne Garland	.12	.06	.04		451 Indians Team (Dave Garcia)	.50	.25	.15
362 Danny Goodwin	.12	.06	.04		452 Steve Dillard	.12	.06	.04
363 Wayne Gross	.12	.06	.04		453 Mike Bacsik	.12	.06	.04
364 Ray Burris	.12	.06	.04		454 Tom Donohue	.12	.06	.04
365 Bobby Murcer	.25	.13	.08		455 Mike Torrez	.20	.10	.06
366 Rob Dressler	.12	.06	.04		456 Frank Taveras	.12	.06	.04
367 Billy Smith	.12	.06	.04		457 Bert Blyleven	.50	.25	.15
368 *Willie Aikens*	.20	.10	.06		458 Billy Sample	.12	.06	.04
369 Jim Kern	.12	.06	.04		459 Mickey Lolich	.12	.06	.04
370 Cesar Cedeno	.25	.13	.08		460 Willie Randolph	.25	.13	.08
371 Jack Morris	1.00	.50	.30		461 Dwayne Murphy	.20	.10	.06
372 Joel Youngblood	.12	.06	.04		462 Mike Sadek	.12	.06	.04
373 *Dan Petry*	.30	.15	.09		463 Jerry Royster	.12	.06	.04
374 Jim Gantner	.20	.10	.06		464 John Denny	.12	.06	.04
375 Ross Grimsley	.12	.06	.04		465 Rick Monday	.20	.10	.06
376 Gary Allenson	.12	.06	.04		466 Mike Squires	.12	.06	.04
377 Junior Kennedy	.12	.06	.04		467 Jesse Jefferson	.12	.06	.04
378 Jerry Mumphrey	.12	.06	.04		468 Aurelio Rodriguez	.20	.10	.06
379 Kevin Bell	.12	.06	.04		469 Randy Niemann	.12	.06	.04
380 Garry Maddox	.20	.10	.06		470 Bob Boone	.20	.10	.06
381 Cubs Team (Preston Gomez)	.50	.25	.15		471 Hosken Powell	.12	.06	.04

		NR MT	EX	VG			NR MT	EX	VG
472	Willie Hernandez	.20	.10	.06	563	Will McEnaney	.12	.06	.04
473	Bump Wills	.12	.06	.04	564	Rick Manning	.12	.06	.04
474	Steve Busby	.12	.06	.04	565	Dennis Leonard	.20	.10	.06
475	Cesar Geronimo	.12	.06	.04	566	Bud Harrelson	.20	.10	.06
476	Bob Shirley	.12	.06	.04	567	Skip Lockwood	.12	.06	.04
477	Buck Martinez	.12	.06	.04	568	*Gary Roenicke*	.25	.13	.08
478	Gil Flores	.12	.06	.04	569	Terry Kennedy	.25	.13	.08
479	Expos Team (Dick Williams)	.50	.25	.15	570	Roy Smalley	.20	.10	.06
480	Bob Watson	.20	.10	.06	571	Joe Sambito	.12	.06	.04
481	Tom Paciorek	.12	.06	.04	572	Jerry Morales	.12	.06	.04
482	*Rickey Henderson*	50.00	30.00	15.00	573	Kent Tekulve	.20	.10	.06
483	Bo Diaz	.20	.10	.06	574	Scot Thompson	.12	.06	.04
484	Checklist 364-484	.50	.25	.15	575	Ken Kravec	.12	.06	.04
485	Mickey Rivers	.20	.10	.06	576	Jim Dwyer	.12	.06	.04
486	Mike Tyson	.12	.06	.04	577	Blue Jays Team (Bobby Mattick)	.50	.25	.15
487	Wayne Nordhagen	.12	.06	.04	578	Scott Sanderson	.20	.10	.06
488	Roy Howell	.12	.06	.04	579	Charlie Moore	.12	.06	.04
489	Preston Hanna	.12	.06	.04	580	Nolan Ryan	3.75	1.75	1.00
490	Lee May	.20	.10	.06	581	Bob Bailor	.12	.06	.04
491	Steve Mura	.12	.06	.04	582	Brian Doyle	.20	.10	.06
492	Todd Cruz	.12	.06	.04	583	Bob Stinson	.12	.06	.04
493	Jerry Martin	.12	.06	.04	584	Kurt Bevacqua	.12	.06	.04
494	Craig Minetto	.12	.06	.04	585	Al Hrabosky	.20	.10	.06
495	Bake McBride	.12	.06	.04	586	Mitchell Page	.12	.06	.04
496	Silvio Martinez	.12	.06	.04	587	Garry Templeton	.20	.10	.06
497	Jim Mason	.12	.06	.04	588	Greg Minton	.12	.06	.04
498	Danny Darwin	.20	.10	.06	589	Chet Lemon	.20	.10	.06
499	Giants Team (Dave Bristol)	.50	.25	.15	590	Jim Palmer	1.25	.60	.40
500	Tom Seaver	2.00	1.00	.60	591	Rick Cerone	.12	.06	.04
501	Rennie Stennett	.12	.06	.04	592	Jon Matlack	.20	.10	.06
502	Rich Wortham	.12	.06	.04	593	Jesus Alou	.12	.06	.04
503	Mike Cubbage	.12	.06	.04	594	Dick Tidrow	.12	.06	.04
504	Gene Garber	.12	.06	.04	595	Don Money	.12	.06	.04
505	Bert Campaneris	.20	.10	.06	596	Rick Matula	.12	.06	.04
506	Tom Buskey	.12	.06	.04	597	Tom Poquette	.12	.06	.04
507	Leon Roberts	.12	.06	.04	598	Fred Kendall	.12	.06	.04
508	U.L. Washington	.12	.06	.04	599	Mike Norris	.12	.06	.04
509	Ed Glynn	.12	.06	.04	600	Reggie Jackson	2.50	1.25	.70
510	Ron Cey	.25	.13	.08	601	Buddy Schultz	.12	.06	.04
511	Eric Wilkins	.12	.06	.04	602	Brian Downing	.20	.10	.06
512	Jose Cardenal	.12	.06	.04	603	Jack Billingham	.12	.06	.04
513	Tom Dixon	.12	.06	.04	604	Glenn Adams	.12	.06	.04
514	Steve Ontiveros	.12	.06	.04	605	Terry Forster	.20	.10	.06
515	Mike Caldwell	.12	.06	.04	606	Reds Team (John McNamara)	.50	.25	.15
516	Hector Cruz	.12	.06	.04	607	Woodie Fryman	.20	.10	.06
517	Don Stanhouse	.12	.06	.04	608	Alan Bannister	.12	.06	.04
518	Nelson Norman	.12	.06	.04	609	Ron Reed	.20	.10	.06
519	Steve Nicosia	.12	.06	.04	610	Willie Stargell	1.50	.70	.45
520	Steve Rogers	.20	.10	.06	611	Jerry Garvin	.12	.06	.04
521	Ken Brett	.12	.06	.04	612	Cliff Johnson	.12	.06	.04
522	Jim Morrison	.12	.06	.04	613	Randy Stein	.12	.06	.04
523	Ken Henderson	.12	.06	.04	614	John Hiller	.20	.10	.06
524	Jim Wright	.12	.06	.04	615	Doug DeCinces	.20	.10	.06
525	Clint Hurdle	.12	.06	.04	616	Gene Richards	.12	.06	.04
526	Phillies Team (Dallas Green)	.70	.35	.20	617	Joaquin Andujar	.20	.10	.06
527	Doug Rau	.12	.06	.04	618	Bob Montgomery	.12	.06	.04
528	Adrian Devine	.12	.06	.04	619	Sergio Ferrer	.12	.06	.04
529	Jim Barr	.12	.06	.04	620	Richie Zisk	.20	.10	.06
530	Jim Sundberg	.12	.06	.04	621	Bob Grich	.20	.10	.06
531	Eric Rasmussen	.12	.06	.04	622	Mario Soto	.20	.10	.06
532	Willie Horton	.20	.10	.06	623	Gorman Thomas	.20	.10	.06
533	Checklist 485-605	.50	.25	.15	624	Lerrin LaGrow	.12	.06	.04
534	Andre Thornton	.25	.13	.08	625	Chris Chambliss	.25	.13	.08
535	Bob Forsch	.20	.10	.06	626	Tigers Team (Sparky Anderson)	.60	.30	.20
536	Lee Lacy	.12	.06	.04	627	Pedro Borbon	.12	.06	.04
537	*Alex Trevino*	.20	.10	.06	628	Doug Capilla	.12	.06	.04
538	Joe Strain	.12	.06	.04	629	Jim Todd	.12	.06	.04
539	Rudy May	.12	.06	.04	630	Larry Bowa	.25	.13	.08
540	Pete Rose	4.00	2.00	1.25	631	Mark Littell	.12	.06	.04
541	Miguel Dilone	.12	.06	.04	632	Barry Bonnell	.12	.06	.04
542	Joe Coleman	.12	.06	.04	633	Bob Apodaca	.12	.06	.04
543	Pat Kelly	.12	.06	.04	634	Glenn Borgmann	.12	.06	.04
544	*Rick Sutcliffe*	3.25	1.75	1.00	635	John Candelaria	.20	.10	.06
545	Jeff Burroughs	.20	.10	.06	636	Toby Harrah	.20	.10	.06
546	Rick Langford	.12	.06	.04	637	Joe Simpson	.12	.06	.04
547	John Wathan	.20	.10	.06	638	*Mark Clear*	.20	.10	.06
548	Dave Rajsich	.12	.06	.04	639	Larry Biittner	.12	.06	.04
549	Larry Wolfe	.12	.06	.04	640	Mike Flanagan	.25	.13	.08
550	Ken Griffey	.25	.13	.08	641	Ed Kranepool	.20	.10	.06
551	Pirates Team (Chuck Tanner)	.50	.25	.15	642	Ken Forsch	.12	.06	.04
552	Bill Nahorodny	.12	.06	.04	643	John Mayberry	.20	.10	.06
553	Dick Davis	.12	.06	.04	644	Charlie Hough	.20	.10	.06
554	Art Howe	.12	.06	.04	645	Rick Burleson	.20	.10	.06
555	Ed Figueroa	.20	.10	.06	646	Checklist 606-726	.50	.25	.15
556	Joe Rudi	.20	.10	.06	647	Milt May	.12	.06	.04
557	Mark Lee	.12	.06	.04	648	Roy White	.20	.10	.06
558	Alfredo Griffin	.25	.13	.08	649	Tom Griffin	.12	.06	.04
559	Dale Murray	.12	.06	.04	650	Joe Morgan	1.50	.70	.45
560	Dave Lopes	.25	.13	.08	651	Rollie Fingers	.50	.25	.15
561	Eddie Whitson	.20	.10	.06	652	Mario Mendoza	.12	.06	.04
562	Joe Wallis	.12	.06	.04	653	Stan Bahnsen	.12	.06	.04

		NR MT	EX	VG
654	Bruce Boisclair	.12	.06	.04
655	Tug McGraw	.25	.13	.08
656	Larvell Blanks	.12	.06	.04
657	Dave Edwards	.12	.06	.04
658	Chris Knapp	.12	.06	.04
659	Brewers Team (George Bamberger)			
		.50	.25	.15
660	Rusty Staub	.30	.15	.09
661	Orioles Future Stars (Mark Corey, Dave Ford, Wayne Krenchicki)	.12	.06	.04
662	Red Sox Future Stars (Joel Finch, Mike O'Berry, Chuck Rainey)	.12	.06	.04
663	Angels Future Stars (Ralph Botting, Bob Clark, *Dickie Thon*)	.30	.15	.09
664	White Sox Future Stars (Mike Colbern, *Guy Hoffman*, Dewey Robinson)	.20	.10	.06
665	Indians Future Stars (Larry Andersen, Bobby Cuellar, Sandy Wihtol)	.12	.06	.04
666	Tigers Future Stars (Mike Chris, Al Greene, Bruce Robbins)	.12	.06	.04
667	Royals Future Stars (Renie Martin, Bill Paschall, *Dan Quisenberry*)	1.00	.50	.30
668	Brewers Future Stars (Danny Boitano, Willie Mueller, Lenn Sakata)	.12	.06	.04
669	Twins Future Stars (Dan Graham, Rick Sofield, *Gary Ward*)	.35	.20	.11
670	Yankees Future Stars (Bobby Brown, Brad Gulden, Darryl Jones)	.20	.10	.06
671	A's Future Stars (Derek Bryant, Brian Kingman, *Mike Morgan*)	.20	.10	.06
672	Mariners Future Stars (Charlie Beamon, Rodney Craig, Rafael Vasquez)	.12	.06	.04
673	Rangers Future Stars (Brian Allard, Jerry Don Gleaton, Greg Mahlberg)	.12	.06	.04
674	Blue Jays Future Stars (Butch Edge, Pat Kelly, Ted Wilborn)	.12	.06	.04
675	Braves Future Stars (Bruce Benedict, Larry Bradford, Eddie Miller)	.12	.06	.04
676	Cubs Future Stars (Dave Geisel, Steve Macko, Karl Pagel)	.12	.06	.04
677	Reds Future Stars (Art DeFreites, *Frank Pastore*, Harry Spilman)	.12	.06	.04
678	Astros Future Stars (Reggie Baldwin, Alan Knicely, *Pete Ladd*)	.12	.06	.04
679	Dodgers Future Stars (Joe Beckwith, *Mickey Hatcher*, Dave Patterson)	.50	.25	.15
680	Expos Future Stars (*Tony Bernazard*, Randy Miller, John Tamargo)	.20	.10	.06
681	Mets Future Stars (Dan Norman, *Jesse Orosco, Mike Scott*)	10.00	5.00	3.00
682	Phillies Future Stars (Ramon Aviles, *Dickie Noles*, Kevin Saucier)	.20	.10	.06
683	Pirates Future Stars (Dorian Boyland, Alberto Lois, Harry Saferight)	.12	.06	.04
684	Cardinals Future Stars (George Frazier, *Tom Herr*, Dan O'Brien)	.50	.40	.20
685	Padres Future Stars (Tim Flannery, Brian Greer, Jim Wilhelm)	.12	.06	.04
686	Giants Future Stars (Greg Johnston, Dennis Littlejohn, Phil Nastu)	.12	.06	.04
687	Mike Heath	.12	.06	.04
688	Steve Stone	.20	.10	.06
689	Red Sox Team (Don Zimmer)	.60	.30	.20
690	Tommy John	.60	.30	.20
691	Ivan DeJesus	.12	.06	.04
692	Rawly Eastwick	.12	.06	.04
693	Craig Kusick	.12	.06	.04
694	Jim Rooker	.12	.06	.04
695	Reggie Smith	.20	.10	.06
696	Julio Gonzalez	.12	.06	.04
697	David Clyde	.12	.06	.04
698	Oscar Gamble	.20	.10	.06
699	Floyd Bannister	.20	.10	.06
700	Rod Carew	1.00	.50	.30
701	*Ken Oberkfell*	.30	.15	.09
702	Ed Farmer	.12	.06	.04
703	Otto Velez	.12	.06	.04
704	Gene Tenace	.20	.10	.06
705	Freddie Patek	.12	.06	.04
706	Tippy Martinez	.12	.06	.04
707	Elliott Maddox	.12	.06	.04
708	Bob Tolan	.12	.06	.04
709	Pat Underwood	.12	.06	.04
710	Graig Nettles	.35	.20	.11
711	Bob Galasso	.12	.06	.04
712	Rodney Scott	.12	.06	.04
713	Terry Whitfield	.12	.06	.04
714	Fred Norman	.12	.06	.04
715	Sal Bando	.20	.10	.06
716	Lynn McGlothen	.12	.06	.04
717	Mickey Klutts	.12	.06	.04

		NR MT	EX	VG
718	Greg Gross	.12	.06	.04
719	Don Robinson	.20	.10	.06
720	Carl Yastrzemski	1.25	.60	.40
721	Paul Hartzell	.12	.06	.04
722	Jose Cruz	.20	.10	.06
723	Shane Rawley	.20	.10	.06
724	Jerry White	.12	.06	.04
725	Rick Wise	.20	.10	.06
726	Steve Yeager	.20	.06	.04

1980 Topps
Superstar 5X7 Photos

In actuality, these cards measure 4-7/8" by 6-7/8". These were another Topps "test" issue that was bought out almost entirely by investors. The 60 cards have a color photo on the front and a blue ink facsimile autograph. Backs have the player's name, team position and card number. The issue was printed on different cardboard stocks, with the first on thick cardboard with a white back and the second on thinner cardboard with a gray back. Prices below are for the more common gray backs; white backs are valued about three times the figures shown. The issue was distributed in selected geographical areas, but they were hoarded quickly. Those who hoarded them still probably have much of their supply as the set has never taken off, despite the presence of many big-name stars.

		NR MT	EX	VG
	Complete Set:	7.00	3.50	2.00
	Common Player:	.10	.05	.03
1	Willie Stargell	.30	.15	.09
2	Mike Schmidt	.30	.15	.09
3	Johnny Bench	.50	.25	.15
4	Jim Palmer	.35	.20	.11
5	Jim Rice	.40	.20	.12
6	Reggie Jackson	.25	.13	.08
7	Ron Guidry	.20	.10	.06
8	Lee Mazzilli	.10	.05	.03
9	Don Baylor	.15	.08	.05
10	Fred Lynn	.20	.10	.06
11	Ken Singleton	.10	.05	.03
12	Rod Carew	.25	.13	.08
13	Steve Garvey	.25	.13	.08
14	George Brett	.30	.15	.09
15	Tom Seaver	.40	.20	.12
16	Dave Kingman	.15	.08	.05
17	Dave Parker	.10	.05	.03
18	Dave Winfield	.40	.20	.12
19	Pete Rose	1.00	.50	.30
20	Nolan Ryan	.40	.20	.12
21	Graig Nettles	.15	.08	.05
22	Carl Yastrzemski	.60	.30	.20
23	Tommy John	.25	.13	.08
24	George Foster	.15	.08	.05
25	James Rodney Richard	.10	.05	.03
26	Keith Hernandez	.30	.15	.09
27	Bob Horner	.15	.08	.05
28	Eddie Murray	.40	.20	.12
29	Steve Kemp	.10	.05	.03
30	Gorman Thomas	.10	.05	.03
31	Sixto Lezcano	.10	.05	.03

		NR MT	EX	VG
32	Bruce Sutter	.15	.08	.05
33	Cecil Cooper	.15	.08	.05
34	Larry Bowa	.10	.05	.03
35	Al Oliver	.15	.08	.05
36	Ted Simmons	.15	.08	.05
37	Garry Templeton	.10	.05	.03
38	Jerry Koosman	.10	.05	.03
39	Darrell Porter	.10	.05	.03
40	Roy Smalley	.10	.05	.03
41	Craig Swan	.10	.05	.03
42	Jason Thompson	.10	.05	.03
43	Andre Thornton	.10	.05	.03
44	Rick Manning	.10	.05	.03
45	Kent Tekulve	.10	.05	.03
46	Phil Niekro	.30	.15	.09
47	Buddy Bell	.15	.08	.05
48	Randy Jones	.10	.05	.03
49	Brian Downing	.10	.05	.03
50	Amos Otis	.10	.05	.03
51	Rick Bosetti	.10	.05	.03
52	Gary Carter	.40	.20	.12
53	Larry Parrish	.15	.08	.05
54	Jack Clark	.20	.10	.06
55	Bruce Bochte	.10	.05	.03
56	Cesar Cedeno	.15	.08	.05
57	Chet Lemon	.10	.05	.03
58	Dave Revering	.10	.05	.03
59	Vida Blue	.15	.08	.05
60	Davey Lopes	.15	.08	.05

1981 Topps

This is another 726-card set of 2-1/2" by 3-1/2" cards from Topps. The cards have the usual color photo with all cards from the same team sharing the same color borders. The player's name appears under the photo with his team and position appearing on a baseball cap at the lower left. The Topps logo returned in a small baseball in the lower right corner. Card backs include the usual stats along with a headline and a cartoon if there was room. Specialty cards include previous season record-breakers, highlights of the playoffs and World Series, along with the final appearance of team cards.

		MT	NR MT	EX
Complete Set:		90.00	65.00	35.00
Common Player:		.08	.06	.03
1	Batting Leaders (George Brett, Bill Buckner)	.70	.50	.30
2	Home Run Leaders (Reggie Jackson, Ben Oglivie, Mike Schmidt)	.40	.30	.15
3	Runs Batted In Leaders (Cecil Cooper, Mike Schmidt)	.30	.25	.12
4	Stolen Base Leaders (Rickey Henderson, Ron LeFlore)	.25	.20	.10
5	Victory Leaders (Steve Carlton, Steve Stone)	.20	.15	.08
6	Strikeout Leaders (Len Barker, Steve Carlton)	.20	.15	.08
7	Earned Run Avg. Leaders (Rudy May, Don Sutton)	.15	.11	.06
8	Leading Firemen (Rollie Fingers, Tom Hume, Dan Quisenberry)	.10	.08	.04
9	Pete LaCock	.08	.06	.03
10	Mike Flanagan	.12	.09	.05

		MT	NR MT	EX
11	Jim Wohlford	.08	.06	.03
12	Mark Clear	.08	.06	.03
13	Joe Charbonneau	.15	.11	.06
14	John Tudor	1.25	.90	.50
15	Larry Parrish	.15	.11	.06
16	Ron Davis	.10	.08	.04
17	Cliff Johnson	.08	.06	.03
18	Glenn Adams	.08	.06	.03
19	Jim Clancy	.12	.09	.05
20	Jeff Burroughs	.10	.08	.04
21	Ron Oester	.08	.06	.03
22	Danny Darwin	.08	.06	.03
23	Alex Trevino	.08	.06	.03
24	Don Stanhouse	.08	.06	.03
25	Sixto Lezcano	.08	.06	.03
26	U.L. Washington	.08	.06	.03
27	Champ Summers	.08	.06	.03
28	Enrique Romo	.08	.06	.03
29	Gene Tenace	.10	.08	.04
30	Jack Clark	.50	.40	.20
31	Checklist 1-121	.08	.06	.03
32	Ken Oberkfell	.08	.06	.03
33	Rick Honeycutt	.08	.06	.03
34	Aurelio Rodriguez	.10	.08	.04
35	Mitchell Page	.08	.06	.03
36	Ed Farmer	.08	.06	.03
37	Gary Roenicke	.08	.06	.03
38	Win Remmerswaal	.08	.06	.03
39	Tom Veryzer	.08	.06	.03
40	Tug McGraw	.20	.15	.08
41	Rangers Future Stars (Bob Babcock, John Butcher, Jerry Don Gleaton)	.10	.08	.04
42	Jerry White	.08	.06	.03
43	Jose Morales	.08	.06	.03
44	Larry McWilliams	.08	.06	.03
45	Enos Cabell	.08	.06	.03
46	Rick Bosetti	.08	.06	.03
47	Ken Brett	.10	.08	.04
48	Dave Skaggs	.08	.06	.03
49	Bob Shirley	.08	.06	.03
50	Dave Lopes	.12	.09	.05
51	Bill Robinson	.08	.06	.03
52	Hector Cruz	.08	.06	.03
53	Kevin Saucier	.08	.06	.03
54	Ivan DeJesus	.08	.06	.03
55	Mike Norris	.08	.06	.03
56	Buck Martinez	.08	.06	.03
57	Dave Roberts	.08	.06	.03
58	Joel Youngblood	.08	.06	.03
59	Dan Petry	.12	.09	.05
60	Willie Randolph	.15	.11	.06
61	Butch Wynegar	.08	.06	.03
62	Joe Pettini	.08	.06	.03
63	Steve Renko	.08	.06	.03
64	Brian Asselstine	.08	.06	.03
65	Scott McGregor	.10	.08	.04
66	Royals Future Stars (Manny Castillo, Tim Ireland, Mike Jones)	.08	.06	.03
67	Ken Kravec	.08	.06	.03
68	Matt Alexander	.08	.06	.03
69	Ed Halicki	.08	.06	.03
70	Al Oliver	.15	.11	.06
71	Hal Dues	.08	.06	.03
72	Barry Evans	.08	.06	.03
73	Doug Bair	.08	.06	.03
74	Mike Hargrove	.08	.06	.03
75	Reggie Smith	.15	.11	.06
76	Mario Mendoza	.08	.06	.03
77	Mike Barlow	.08	.06	.03
78	Steve Dillard	.08	.06	.03
79	Bruce Robbins	.08	.06	.03
80	Rusty Staub	.15	.11	.06
81	Dave Stapleton	.08	.06	.03
82	Astros Future Stars (Danny Heep, Alan Knicely, Bobby Sprowl)	.08	.06	.03
83	Mike Proly	.08	.06	.03
84	Johnnie LeMaster	.08	.06	.03
85	Mike Caldwell	.08	.06	.03
86	Wayne Gross	.08	.06	.03
87	Rick Camp	.08	.06	.03
88	Joe Lefebvre	.08	.06	.03
89	Darrell Jackson	.08	.06	.03
90	Bake McBride	.08	.06	.03
91	Tim Stoddard	.08	.06	.03
92	Mike Easler	.10	.08	.04
93	Ed Glynn	.08	.06	.03
94	Harry Spilman	.08	.06	.03
95	Jim Sundberg	.10	.08	.04
96	A's Future Stars (Dave Beard, Ernie Camacho, Pat Dempsey)	.12	.09	.05
97	Chris Speier	.08	.06	.03

		MT	NR MT	EX
98	Clint Hurdle	.08	.06	.03
99	Eric Wilkins	.08	.06	.03
100	Rod Carew	1.25	.90	.50
101	Benny Ayala	.08	.06	.03
102	Dave Tobik	.08	.06	.03
103	Jerry Martin	.08	.06	.03
104	Terry Forster	.10	.08	.04
105	Jose Cruz	.15	.11	.06
106	Don Money	.08	.06	.03
107	Rich Wortham	.08	.06	.03
108	Bruce Benedict	.08	.06	.03
109	Mike Scott	1.00	.70	.40
110	Carl Yastrzemski	1.50	1.25	.60
111	Greg Minton	.08	.06	.03
112	White Sox Future Stars (Rusty Kuntz, Fran Mullins, Leo Sutherland)	.08	.06	.03
113	Mike Phillips	.08	.06	.03
114	Tom Underwood	.08	.06	.03
115	Roy Smalley	.08	.06	.03
116	Joe Simpson	.08	.06	.03
117	Pete Falcone	.08	.06	.03
118	Kurt Bevacqua	.08	.06	.03
119	Tippy Martinez	.08	.06	.03
120	Larry Bowa	.20	.15	.08
121	Larry Harlow	.08	.06	.03
122	John Denny	.08	.06	.03
123	Al Cowens	.08	.06	.03
124	Jerry Garvin	.08	.06	.03
125	Andre Dawson	.90	.70	.35
126	Charlie Leibrandt	.50	.40	.20
127	Rudy Law	.08	.06	.03
128	Gary Allenson	.08	.06	.03
129	Art Howe	.08	.06	.03
130	Larry Gura	.08	.06	.03
131	Keith Moreland	.45	.35	.20
132	Tommy Boggs	.08	.06	.03
133	Jeff Cox	.08	.06	.03
134	Steve Mura	.08	.06	.03
135	Gorman Thomas	.12	.09	.05
136	Doug Capilla	.08	.06	.03
137	Hosken Powell	.08	.06	.03
138	Rich Dotson	.30	.25	.12
139	Oscar Gamble	.10	.08	.04
140	Bob Forsch	.10	.08	.04
141	Miguel Dilone	.08	.06	.03
142	Jackson Todd	.08	.06	.03
143	Dan Meyer	.08	.06	.03
144	Allen Ripley	.08	.06	.03
145	Mickey Rivers	.10	.08	.04
146	Bobby Castillo	.08	.06	.03
147	Dale Berra	.08	.06	.03
148	Randy Niemann	.08	.06	.03
149	Joe Nolan	.08	.06	.03
150	Mark Fidrych	.12	.09	.05
151	Claudell Washington	.12	.09	.05
152	John Urrea	.08	.06	.03
153	Tom Poquette	.08	.06	.03
154	Rick Langford	.08	.06	.03
155	Chris Chambliss	.12	.09	.05
156	Bob McClure	.08	.06	.03
157	John Wathan	.12	.09	.05
158	Fergie Jenkins	.30	.25	.12
159	Brian Doyle	.08	.06	.03
160	Garry Maddox	.12	.09	.05
161	Dan Graham	.08	.06	.03
162	Doug Corbett	.08	.06	.03
163	Billy Almon	.08	.06	.03
164	Lamarr Hoyt (LaMarr)	.20	.15	.08
165	Tony Scott	.08	.06	.03
166	Floyd Bannister	.12	.09	.05
167	Terry Whitfield	.08	.06	.03
168	Don Robinson	.08	.06	.03
169	John Mayberry	.10	.08	.04
170	Ross Grimsley	.08	.06	.03
171	Gene Richards	.08	.06	.03
172	Gary Woods	.08	.06	.03
173	Bump Wills	.08	.06	.03
174	Doug Rau	.08	.06	.03
175	Dave Collins	.10	.08	.04
176	Mike Krukow	.10	.08	.04
177	Rick Peters	.08	.06	.03
178	Jim Essian	.08	.06	.03
179	Rudy May	.08	.06	.03
180	Pete Rose	3.25	2.50	1.25
181	Elias Sosa	.08	.06	.03
182	Bob Grich	.15	.11	.06
183	Dick Davis	.08	.06	.03
184	Jim Dwyer	.08	.06	.03
185	Dennis Leonard	.10	.08	.04
186	Wayne Nordhagen	.08	.06	.03
187	Mike Parrott	.08	.06	.03
188	Doug DeCinces	.15	.11	.06
189	Craig Swan	.08	.06	.03
190	Cesar Cedeno	.15	.11	.06
191	Rick Sutcliffe	.40	.30	.15
192	Braves Future Stars (Terry Harper, Ed Miller, Rafael Ramirez)	.25	.20	.10
193	Pete Vuckovich	.10	.08	.04
194	Rod Scurry	.10	.08	.04
195	Rich Murray	.08	.06	.03
196	Duffy Dyer	.08	.06	.03
197	Jim Kern	.08	.06	.03
198	Jerry Dybzinski	.08	.06	.03
199	Chuck Rainey	.08	.06	.03
200	George Foster	.25	.20	.10
201	Record Breaker (Johnny Bench)	.40	.30	.15
202	Record Breaker (Steve Carlton)	.40	.30	.15
203	Record Breaker (Bill Gullickson)	.08	.06	.03
204	Record Breaker (Ron LeFlore, Rodney Scott)	.10	.08	.04
205	Record Breaker (Pete Rose)	.80	.60	.30
206	Record Breaker (Mike Schmidt)	.50	.40	.20
207	Record Breaker (Ozzie Smith)	.20	.15	.08
208	Record Breaker (Willie Wilson)	.20	.15	.08
209	Dickie Thon	.10	.08	.04
210	Jim Palmer	.80	.60	.30
211	Derrel Thomas	.08	.06	.03
212	Steve Nicosia	.08	.06	.03
213	Al Holland	.10	.08	.04
214	Angels Future Stars (Ralph Botting, Jim Dorsey, John Harris)	.08	.06	.03
215	Larry Hisle	.10	.08	.04
216	John Henry Johnson	.08	.06	.03
217	Rich Hebner	.08	.06	.03
218	Paul Splittorff	.08	.06	.03
219	Ken Landreaux	.08	.06	.03
220	Tom Seaver	1.25	.90	.50
221	Bob Davis	.08	.06	.03
222	Jorge Orta	.08	.06	.03
223	Roy Lee Jackson	.08	.06	.03
224	Pat Zachry	.08	.06	.03
225	Ruppert Jones	.08	.06	.03
226	Manny Sanguillen	.08	.06	.03
227	Fred Martinez	.08	.06	.03
228	Tom Paciorek	.08	.06	.03
229	Rollie Fingers	.60	.45	.25
230	George Hendrick	.10	.08	.04
231	Joe Beckwith	.08	.06	.03
232	Mickey Klutts	.08	.06	.03
233	Skip Lockwood	.08	.06	.03
234	Lou Whitaker	.60	.45	.25
235	Scott Sanderson	.08	.06	.03
236	Mike Ivie	.08	.06	.03
237	Charlie Moore	.08	.06	.03
238	Willie Hernandez	.12	.09	.05
239	Rick Miller	.08	.06	.03
240	Nolan Ryan	2.25	1.75	.90
241	Checklist 122-242	.08	.06	.03
242	Chet Lemon	.10	.08	.04
243	Sal Butera	.08	.06	.03
244	Cardinals Future Stars (Tito Landrum, Al Olmsted, Andy Rincon)	.15	.11	.06
245	Ed Figueroa	.08	.06	.03
246	Ed Ott	.08	.06	.03
247	Glenn Hubbard	.10	.08	.04
248	Joey McLaughlin	.08	.06	.03
249	Larry Cox	.08	.06	.03
250	Ron Guidry	.50	.40	.20
251	Tom Brookens	.10	.08	.04
252	Victor Cruz	.08	.06	.03
253	Dave Bergman	.08	.06	.03
254	Ozzie Smith	.90	.70	.35
255	Mark Littell	.08	.06	.03
256	Bombo Rivera	.08	.06	.03
257	Rennie Stennett	.08	.06	.03
258	Joe Price	.12	.09	.05
259	Mets Future Stars (Juan Berenguer, Hubie Brooks, Mookie Wilson)	2.50	2.00	1.00
260	Ron Cey	.15	.11	.06
261	Rickey Henderson	6.00	4.50	2.50
262	Sammy Stewart	.08	.06	.03
263	Brian Downing	.12	.09	.05
264	Jim Norris	.08	.06	.03
265	John Candelaria	.12	.09	.05
266	Tom Herr	.15	.11	.06
267	Stan Bahnsen	.08	.06	.03
268	Jerry Royster	.08	.06	.03
269	Ken Forsch	.08	.06	.03
270	Greg Luzinski	.20	.15	.08
271	Bill Castro	.08	.06	.03
272	Bruce Kimm	.08	.06	.03
273	Stan Papi	.08	.06	.03

		MT	NR MT	EX
274	Craig Chamberlain	.08	.06	.03
275	Dwight Evans	.25	.20	.10
276	Dan Spillner	.08	.06	.03
277	Alfredo Griffin	.12	.09	.05
278	Rick Sofield	.08	.06	.03
279	Bob Knepper	.12	.09	.05
280	Ken Griffey	.15	.11	.06
281	Fred Stanley	.08	.06	.03
282	Mariners Future Stars (Rick Anderson, Greg Biercevicz, Rodney Craig)	.08	.06	.03
283	Billy Sample	.08	.06	.03
284	Brian Kingman	.08	.06	.03
285	Jerry Turner	.08	.06	.03
286	Dave Frost	.08	.06	.03
287	Lenn Sakata	.08	.06	.03
288	Bob Clark	.08	.06	.03
289	Mickey Hatcher	.10	.08	.04
290	Bob Boone	.08	.06	.03
291	Aurelio Lopez	.08	.06	.03
292	Mike Squires	.08	.06	.03
293	*Charlie Lea*	.15	.11	.06
294	Mike Tyson	.08	.06	.03
295	Hal McRae	.15	.11	.06
296	Bill Nahorodny	.08	.06	.03
297	Bob Bailor	.08	.06	.03
298	Buddy Solomon	.08	.06	.03
299	Elliott Maddox	.08	.06	.03
300	Paul Molitor	.40	.30	.15
301	Matt Keough	.08	.06	.03
302	Dodgers Future Stars (Jack Perconte, *Mike Scioscia, Fernando Valenzuela*)	5.50	4.25	2.25
303	Johnny Oates	.08	.06	.03
304	John Castino	.08	.06	.03
305	Ken Clay	.08	.06	.03
306	Juan Beniquez	.08	.06	.03
307	Gene Garber	.08	.06	.03
308	Rick Manning	.08	.06	.03
309	*Luis Salazar*	.20	.15	.08
310	Vida Blue	.08	.06	.03
311	Freddie Patek	.08	.06	.03
312	Rick Rhoden	.12	.09	.05
313	Luis Pujols	.08	.06	.03
314	Rich Dauer	.08	.06	.03
315	*Kirk Gibson*	6.00	4.50	2.50
316	Craig Minetto	.08	.06	.03
317	Lonnie Smith	.10	.08	.04
318	Steve Yeager	.08	.06	.03
319	Rowland Office	.08	.06	.03
320	Tom Burgmeier	.08	.06	.03
321	*Leon Durham*	.25	.20	.10
322	Neil Allen	.10	.08	.04
323	Jim Morrison	.08	.06	.03
324	Mike Willis	.08	.06	.03
325	Ray Knight	.12	.09	.05
326	Biff Pocoroba	.08	.06	.03
327	Moose Haas	.08	.06	.03
328	Twins Future Stars (*Dave Engle*, Greg Johnston, Gary Ward)	.12	.09	.05
329	Joaquin Andujar	.12	.09	.05
330	Frank White	.12	.09	.05
331	Dennis Lamp	.08	.06	.03
332	Lee Lacy	.08	.06	.03
333	Sid Monge	.08	.06	.03
334	Dane Iorg	.08	.06	.03
335	Rick Cerone	.08	.06	.03
336	Eddie Whitson	.08	.06	.03
337	Lynn Jones	.08	.06	.03
338	Checklist 243-363	.25	.20	.10
339	John Ellis	.08	.06	.03
340	Bruce Kison	.08	.06	.03
341	Dwayne Murphy	.10	.08	.04
342	Eric Rasmussen	.08	.06	.03
343	Frank Taveras	.08	.06	.03
344	Byron McLaughlin	.08	.06	.03
345	Warren Cromartie	.08	.06	.03
346	Larry Christenson	.08	.06	.03
347	*Harold Baines*	3.75	2.75	1.50
348	Bob Sykes	.08	.06	.03
349	Glenn Hoffman	.08	.06	.03
350	J.R. Richard	.12	.09	.05
351	Otto Velez	.08	.06	.03
352	Dick Tidrow	.08	.06	.03
353	Terry Kennedy	.12	.09	.05
354	Mario Soto	.10	.08	.04
355	Bob Horner	.25	.20	.10
356	Padres Future Stars (George Stablein, Craig Stimac, Tom Tellmann)	.08	.06	.03
357	Jim Slaton	.08	.06	.03
358	Mark Wagner	.08	.06	.03
359	Tom Hausman	.08	.06	.03

		MT	NR MT	EX
360	Willie Wilson	.30	.25	.12
361	Joe Strain	.08	.06	.03
362	Bo Diaz	.10	.08	.04
363	Geoff Zahn	.08	.06	.03
364	*Mike Davis*	.35	.25	.14
365	Graig Nettles	.12	.09	.05
366	Mike Ramsey	.08	.06	.03
367	Denny Martinez	.10	.08	.04
368	Leon Roberts	.08	.06	.03
369	Frank Tanana	.12	.09	.05
370	Dave Winfield	1.00	.70	.40
371	Charlie Hough	.15	.11	.06
372	Jay Johnstone	.10	.08	.04
373	Pat Underwood	.08	.06	.03
374	Tom Hutton	.08	.06	.03
375	Dave Concepcion	.20	.15	.08
376	Ron Reed	.08	.06	.03
377	Jerry Morales	.08	.06	.03
378	Dave Rader	.08	.06	.03
379	Lary Sorensen	.08	.06	.03
380	Willie Stargell	1.00	.70	.40
381	Cubs Future Stars (Carlos Lezcano, Steve Macko, Randy Martz)	.08	.06	.03
382	*Paul Mirabella*(FC)	.12	.09	.05
383	Eric Soderholm	.08	.06	.03
384	Mike Sadek	.08	.06	.03
385	Joe Sambito	.08	.06	.03
386	Dave Edwards	.08	.06	.03
387	Phil Niekro	.70	.50	.30
388	Andre Thornton	.12	.09	.05
389	Marty Pattin	.08	.06	.03
390	Cesar Geronimo	.08	.06	.03
391	Dave Lemanczyk	.08	.06	.03
392	Lance Parrish	.70	.50	.30
393	Broderick Perkins	.08	.06	.03
394	Woodie Fryman	.10	.08	.04
395	Scot Thompson	.08	.06	.03
396	Bill Campbell	.08	.06	.03
397	Julio Cruz	.08	.06	.03
398	Ross Baumgarten	.08	.06	.03
399	Orioles Future Stars (*Mike Boddicker*, Mark Corey, *Floyd Rayford*)	1.25	.90	.50
400	Reggie Jackson	1.50	1.25	.60
401	A.L. Championships (Royals Sweep Yankees)	.50	.40	.20
402	N.L. Championships (Phillies Squeak Past Astros)	.40	.30	.15
403	World Series (Phillies Beat Royals In 6)	.25	.20	.10
404	World Series Summary (Phillies Win First World Series)	.25	.20	.10
405	Nino Espinosa	.08	.06	.03
406	Dickie Noles	.08	.06	.03
407	Ernie Whitt	.10	.08	.04
408	Fernando Arroyo	.08	.06	.03
409	Larry Herndon	.10	.08	.04
410	Bert Campaneris	.12	.09	.05
411	Terry Puhl	.08	.06	.03
412	*Britt Burns*	.12	.09	.05
413	Tony Bernazard	.08	.06	.03
414	John Pacella	.08	.06	.03
415	Ben Oglivie	.10	.08	.04
416	Gary Alexander	.08	.06	.03
417	Dan Schatzeder	.08	.06	.03
418	Bobby Brown	.08	.06	.03
419	Tom Hume	.08	.06	.03
420	Keith Hernandez	.80	.60	.30
421	Bob Stanley	.08	.06	.03
422	Dan Ford	.08	.06	.03
423	Shane Rawley	.15	.11	.06
424	Yankees Future Stars (Tim Lollar, Bruce Robinson, Dennis Werth)	.08	.06	.03
425	Al Bumbry	.10	.08	.04
426	Warren Brusstar	.08	.06	.03
427	John D'Acquisto	.08	.06	.03
428	John Stearns	.08	.06	.03
429	Mick Kelleher	.08	.06	.03
430	Jim Bibby	.08	.06	.03
431	Dave Roberts	.08	.06	.03
432	Len Barker	.10	.08	.04
433	Rance Mulliniks	.08	.06	.03
434	Roger Erickson	.08	.06	.03
435	Jim Spencer	.08	.06	.03
436	Gary Lucas	.08	.06	.03
437	Mike Heath	.08	.06	.03
438	John Montefusco	.10	.08	.04
439	Denny Walling	.08	.06	.03
440	Jerry Reuss	.12	.09	.05
441	Ken Reitz	.08	.06	.03
442	Ron Pruitt	.08	.06	.03
443	Jim Beattie	.08	.06	.03

	MT	NR MT	EX
444 Garth Iorg	.08	.06	.03
445 Ellis Valentine	.08	.06	.03
446 Checklist 364-484	.25	.20	.10
447 Junior Kennedy	.08	.06	.03
448 Tim Corcoran	.08	.06	.03
449 Paul Mitchell	.08	.06	.03
450 Dave Kingman	.10	.08	.04
451 Indians Future Stars (Chris Bando, Tom			
Brennan, Sandy Wihtol)	.12	.09	.05
452 Renie Martin	.08	.06	.03
453 Rob Wilfong	.08	.06	.03
454 Andy Hassler	.08	.06	.03
455 Rick Burleson	.10	.08	.04
456 *Jeff Reardon*	1.00	.70	.40
457 Mike Lum	.08	.06	.03
458 Randy Jones	.10	.08	.04
459 Greg Gross	.08	.06	.03
460 Rich Gossage	.40	.30	.15
461 Dave McKay	.08	.06	.03
462 Jack Brohamer	.08	.06	.03
463 Milt May	.08	.06	.03
464 Adrian Devine	.08	.06	.03
465 Bill Russell	.12	.09	.05
466 Bob Molinaro	.08	.06	.03
467 Dave Stieb	.40	.30	.15
468 Johnny Wockenfuss	.08	.06	.03
469 Jeff Leonard	.20	.15	.08
470 Manny Trillo	.10	.08	.04
471 Mike Vail	.08	.06	.03
472 Dyar Miller	.08	.06	.03
473 Jose Cardenal	.08	.06	.03
474 Mike LaCoss	.08	.06	.03
475 Buddy Bell	.15	.11	.06
476 Jerry Koosman	.15	.11	.06
477 Luis Gomez	.08	.06	.03
478 Juan Eichelberger	.08	.06	.03
479 Expos Future Stars (Bobby Pate, *Tim*			
Raines, Roberto Ramos)	9.00	6.75	3.50
480 Carlton Fisk	.80	.60	.30
481 Bob Lacey	.08	.06	.03
482 Jim Gantner	.10	.08	.04
483 Mike Griffin	.08	.06	.03
484 Max Venable	.08	.06	.03
485 Garry Templeton	.12	.09	.05
486 Marc Hill	.08	.06	.03
487 Dewey Robinson	.08	.06	.03
488 *Damaso Garcia*	.12	.09	.05
489 John Littlefield (photo actually Mark			
Riggins)	.08	.06	.03
490 Eddie Murray	1.50	1.25	.60
491 Gordy Pladson	.08	.06	.03
492 Barry Foote	.08	.06	.03
493 Dan Quisenberry	.20	.15	.08
494 *Bob Walk*	.50	.40	.20
495 Dusty Baker	.12	.09	.05
496 Paul Dade	.08	.06	.03
497 Fred Norman	.08	.06	.03
498 Pat Putnam	.08	.06	.03
499 Frank Pastore	.08	.06	.03
500 Jim Rice	1.00	.70	.40
501 Tim Foli	.08	.06	.03
502 Giants Future Stars (Chris Bourjos, Al			
Hargesheimer, Mike Rowland)	.08	.06	.03
503 Steve McCatty	.08	.06	.03
504 Dale Murphy	2.50	2.00	1.00
505 Jason Thompson	.08	.06	.03
506 Phil Huffman	.08	.06	.03
507 Jamie Quirk	.08	.06	.03
508 Rob Dressler	.08	.06	.03
509 Pete Mackanin	.08	.06	.03
510 Lee Mazzilli	.10	.08	.04
511 Wayne Garland	.08	.06	.03
512 Gary Thomasson	.08	.06	.03
513 Frank LaCorte	.08	.06	.03
514 George Riley	.08	.06	.03
515 Robin Yount	2.00	1.50	.80
516 Doug Bird	.08	.06	.03
517 Richie Zisk	.10	.08	.04
518 Grant Jackson	.08	.06	.03
519 John Tamargo	.08	.06	.03
520 Steve Stone	.12	.09	.05
521 Sam Mejias	.08	.06	.03
522 Mike Colbern	.08	.06	.03
523 John Fulgham	.08	.06	.03
524 Willie Aikens	.08	.06	.03
525 Mike Torrez	.10	.08	.04
526 Phillies Future Stars (Marty Bystrom, Jay			
Loviglio, Jim Wright)	.08	.06	.03
527 Danny Goodwin	.08	.06	.03
528 Gary Matthews	.12	.09	.05
529 Dave LaRoche	.08	.06	.03

	MT	NR MT	EX
530 Steve Garvey	1.25	.90	.50
531 John Curtis	.08	.06	.03
532 Bill Stein	.08	.06	.03
533 Jesus Figueroa	.08	.06	.03
534 *Dave Smith*	.40	.30	.15
535 Omar Moreno	.08	.06	.03
536 Bob Owchinko	.08	.06	.03
537 Ron Hodges	.08	.06	.03
538 Tom Griffin	.08	.06	.03
539 Rodney Scott	.08	.06	.03
540 Mike Schmidt	1.50	1.25	.60
541 Steve Swisher	.08	.06	.03
542 Larry Bradford	.08	.06	.03
543 Terry Crowley	.08	.06	.03
544 Rich Gale	.08	.06	.03
545 Johnny Grubb	.08	.06	.03
546 Paul Moskau	.08	.06	.03
547 Mario Guerrero	.08	.06	.03
548 Dave Goltz	.10	.08	.04
549 Jerry Remy	.08	.06	.03
550 Tommy John	.50	.40	.20
551 Pirates Future Stars (Vance Law, Tony			
Pena, Pascual Perez)	2.00	1.50	.80
552 Steve Trout	.08	.06	.03
553 Tim Blackwell	.08	.06	.03
554 Bert Blyleven	.25	.20	.10
555 Cecil Cooper	.20	.15	.08
556 Jerry Mumphrey	.08	.06	.03
557 Chris Knapp	.08	.06	.03
558 Barry Bonnell	.08	.06	.03
559 Willie Montanez	.08	.06	.03
560 Joe Morgan	.70	.50	.30
561 Dennis Littlejohn	.08	.06	.03
562 Checklist 485-605	.25	.20	.10
563 Jim Kaat	.30	.25	.12
564 Ron Hassey	.08	.06	.03
565 Burt Hooton	.10	.08	.04
566 Del Unser	.08	.06	.03
567 Mark Bomback	.08	.06	.03
568 Dave Revering	.08	.06	.03
569 Al Williams	.08	.06	.03
570 Ken Singleton	.12	.09	.05
571 Todd Cruz	.08	.06	.03
572 Jack Morris	.60	.45	.25
573 Phil Garner	.10	.08	.04
574 Bill Caudill	.08	.06	.03
575 Tony Perez	.35	.25	.14
576 Reggie Cleveland	.08	.06	.03
577 Blue Jays Future Stars (Luis Leal, Brian			
Milner, *Ken Schrom*)	.20	.15	.08
578 *Bill Gullickson*	.20	.15	.08
579 Tim Flannery	.08	.06	.03
580 Don Baylor	.15	.11	.06
581 Roy Howell	.08	.06	.03
582 Gaylord Perry	.70	.50	.30
583 Larry Milbourne	.08	.06	.03
584 Randy Lerch	.08	.06	.03
585 Amos Otis	.10	.08	.04
586 Silvio Martinez	.08	.06	.03
587 Jeff Newman	.08	.06	.03
588 Gary Lavelle	.08	.06	.03
589 Lamar Johnson	.08	.06	.03
590 Bruce Sutter	.25	.20	.10
591 John Lowenstein	.08	.06	.03
592 Steve Comer	.08	.06	.03
593 Steve Kemp	.12	.09	.05
594 Preston Hanna	.08	.06	.03
595 Butch Hobson	.08	.06	.03
596 Jerry Augustine	.08	.06	.03
597 Rafael Landestoy	.08	.06	.03
598 George Vukovich	.08	.06	.03
599 Dennis Kinney	.08	.06	.03
600 Johnny Bench	1.50	1.25	.60
601 Don Aase	.08	.06	.03
602 Bobby Murcer	.15	.11	.06
603 John Verhoeven	.08	.06	.03
604 Rob Picciolo	.08	.06	.03
605 Don Sutton	.70	.50	.30
606 Reds Future Stars (Bruce Berenyi, Geoff			
Combe, Paul Householder)	.08	.06	.03
607 Dave Palmer	.08	.06	.03
608 Greg Pryor	.08	.06	.03
609 Lynn McGlothen	.08	.06	.03
610 Darrell Porter	.10	.08	.04
611 Rick Matula	.08	.06	.03
612 Duane Kuiper	.08	.06	.03
613 Jim Anderson	.08	.06	.03
614 Dave Rozema	.08	.06	.03
615 Rick Dempsey	.12	.09	.05
616 Rick Wise	.10	.08	.04
617 Craig Reynolds	.08	.06	.03

		MT	NR MT	EX
618	John Milner	.08	.06	.03
619	Steve Henderson	.08	.06	.03
620	Dennis Eckersley	.20	.15	.08
621	Tom Donohue	.08	.06	.03
622	Randy Moffitt	.08	.06	.03
623	Sal Bando	.12	.09	.05
624	Bob Welch	.20	.15	.08
625	Bill Buckner	.15	.11	.06
626	Tigers Future Stars (Dave Steffen, Jerry Ujdur, Roger Weaver)	.08	.06	.03
627	Luis Tiant	.20	.15	.08
628	Vic Correll	.08	.06	.03
629	Tony Armas	.12	.09	.05
630	Steve Carlton	1.25	.90	.50
631	Ron Jackson	.08	.06	.03
632	Alan Bannister	.08	.06	.03
633	Bill Lee	.10	.08	.04
634	Doug Flynn	.08	.06	.03
635	Bobby Bonds	.15	.11	.06
636	Al Hrabosky	.10	.08	.04
637	Jerry Narron	.08	.06	.03
638	Checklist 606	.25	.20	.10
639	Carney Lansford	.15	.11	.06
640	Dave Parker	.60	.45	.25
641	Mark Belanger	.10	.08	.04
642	Vern Ruhle	.08	.06	.03
643	Lloyd Moseby	.90	.70	.35
644	Ramon Aviles	.08	.06	.03
645	Rick Reuschel	.15	.11	.06
646	Marvis Foley	.08	.06	.03
647	Dick Drago	.08	.06	.03
648	Darrell Evans	.25	.20	.10
649	Manny Sarmiento	.08	.06	.03
650	Bucky Dent	.12	.09	.05
651	Pedro Guerrero	1.25	.90	.50
652	John Montague	.08	.06	.03
653	Bill Fahey	.08	.06	.03
654	Ray Burris	.08	.06	.03
655	Dan Driessen	.12	.09	.05
656	Jon Matlack	.10	.08	.04
657	Mike Cubbage	.08	.06	.03
658	Milt Wilcox	.08	.06	.03
659	Brewers Future Stars (John Flinn, Ed Romero, Ned Yost)	.08	.06	.03
660	Gary Carter	1.00	.70	.40
661	Orioles Team (Earl Weaver)	.30	.25	.12
662	Red Sox Team (Ralph Houk)	.30	.25	.12
663	Angels Team (Jim Fregosi)	.25	.20	.10
664	White Sox Team (Tony LaRussa)	.25	.20	.10
665	Indians Team (Dave Garcia)	.25	.20	.10
666	Tigers Team (Sparky Anderson)	.30	.25	.12
667	Royals Team (Jim Frey)	.25	.20	.10
668	Brewers Team (Bob Rodgers)	.25	.20	.10
669	Twins Team (John Goryl)	.25	.20	.10
670	Yankees Team (Gene Michael)	.35	.25	.14
671	A's Team (Billy Martin)	.30	.25	.12
672	Mariners Team (Maury Wills)	.25	.20	.10
673	Rangers Team (Don Zimmer)	.25	.20	.10
674	Blue Jays Team (Bobby Mattick)	.25	.20	.10
675	Braves Team (Bobby Cox)	.25	.20	.10
676	Cubs Team (Joe Amalfitano)	.25	.20	.10
677	Reds Team (John McNamara)	.25	.20	.10
678	Astros Team (Bill Virdon)	.25	.20	.10
679	Dodgers Team (Tom Lasorda)	.35	.25	.14
680	Expos Team (Dick Williams)	.25	.20	.10
681	Mets Team (Joe Torre)	.30	.25	.12
682	Phillies Team (Dallas Green)	.25	.20	.10
683	Pirates Team (Chuck Tanner)	.25	.20	.10
684	Cardinals Team (Whitey Herzog)	.30	.25	.12
685	Padres Team (Frank Howard)	.25	.20	.10
686	Giants Team (Dave Bristol)	.25	.20	.10
687	Jeff Jones	.08	.06	.03
688	Kiko Garcia	.08	.06	.03
689	Red Sox Future Stars (Bruce Hurst, Keith MacWhorter, Reid Nichols)	2.00	1.50	.80
690	Bob Watson	.10	.08	.04
691	Dick Ruthven	.08	.06	.03
692	Lenny Randle	.08	.06	.03
693	Steve Howe	.20	.15	.08
694	Bud Harrelson	.08	.06	.03
695	Kent Tekulve	.10	.08	.04
696	Alan Ashby	.08	.06	.03
697	Rick Waits	.08	.06	.03
698	Mike Jorgensen	.08	.06	.03
699	Glenn Abbott	.08	.06	.03
700	George Brett	2.25	1.75	.90
701	Joe Rudi	.12	.09	.05
702	George Medich	.08	.06	.03
703	Alvis Woods	.08	.06	.03
704	Bill Travers	.08	.06	.03
705	Ted Simmons	.25	.20	.10

		MT	NR MT	EX
706	Dave Ford	.08	.06	.03
707	Dave Cash	.08	.06	.03
708	Doyle Alexander	.12	.09	.05
709	Alan Trammell	.30	.25	.12
710	Ron LeFlore	.08	.06	.03
711	Joe Ferguson	.08	.06	.03
712	Bill Bonham	.08	.06	.03
713	Bill North	.08	.06	.03
714	Pete Redfern	.08	.06	.03
715	Bill Madlock	.25	.20	.10
716	Glenn Borgmann	.08	.06	.03
717	Jim Barr	.08	.06	.03
718	Larry Biittner	.08	.06	.03
719	Sparky Lyle	.12	.09	.05
720	Fred Lynn	.35	.25	.14
721	Toby Harrah	.10	.08	.04
722	Joe Niekro	.20	.15	.08
723	Bruce Bochte	.08	.06	.03
724	Lou Piniella	.20	.15	.08
725	Steve Rogers	.10	.08	.04
726	Rick Monday	.15	.11	.06

1981 Topps
Home Team 5 X 7 Photos

MARIO SOTO
Cincinnati Reds
PITCHER

Once again testing the popularity of large cards, Topps issued 4-7/8" by 6-7/8" cards in two different sets. The Home Team cards feature a large color photo, facsimile autograph and white border on the front. Backs have the player name, team, position and a checklist at the bottom. The 102 cards were sold in limited areas corresponding to the teams' geographic home. It was also possible to order the whole set by mail. Eleven teams are involved in the issue, with the number of players from each team ranging from 6 to 12. Although it is an attractive set featuring many stars, ready availability and many collectors' aversion to large cards keep prices relatively low today.

		MT	NR MT	EX
	Complete Set:	40.00	30.00	16.00
	Common Player:	.20	.15	.08
(1)	Dusty Baker	.25	.20	.10
(2)	Don Baylor	.40	.30	.15
(3)	Rick Burleson	.20	.15	.08
(4)	Rod Carew	.90	.70	.35
(5)	Ron Cey	.30	.25	.12
(6)	Steve Garvey	.90	.70	.35
(7)	Bobby Grich	.30	.25	.12
(8)	Butch Hobson	.20	.15	.08
(9)	Burt Hooton	.20	.15	.08
(10)	Steve Howe	.20	.15	.08
(11)	Dave Lopes	.25	.20	.10
(12)	Fred Lynn	.50	.40	.20
(13)	Rick Monday	.25	.20	.10
(14)	Jerry Reuss	.25	.20	.10
(15)	Bill Russell	.25	.20	.10
(16)	Reggie Smith	.30	.25	.12
(17)	Bob Welch	.40	.30	.15
(18)	Steve Yeager	.20	.15	.08
(19)	Buddy Bell	.30	.25	.12
(20)	Cesar Cedeno	.30	.25	.12
(21)	Jose Cruz	.30	.25	.12

		MT	NR MT	EX
(22)	Art Howe	.20	.15	.08
(23)	Jon Matlack	.20	.15	.08
(24)	Al Oliver	.40	.30	.15
(25)	Terry Puhl	.20	.15	.08
(26)	Mickey Rivers	.25	.20	.10
(27)	Nolan Ryan	.70	.50	.30
(28)	Jim Sundberg	.25	.20	.10
(29)	Don Sutton	.60	.45	.25
(30)	Bump Wills	.20	.15	.08
(31)	Tim Blackwell	.20	.15	.08
(32)	Bill Buckner	.40	.30	.15
(33)	Britt Burns	.20	.15	.08
(34)	Ivan DeJesus	.20	.15	.08
(35)	Rich Dotson	.25	.20	.10
(36)	Leon Durham	.25	.20	.10
(37)	Ed Farmer	.20	.15	.08
(38)	Lamar Johnson	.20	.15	.08
(39)	Dave Kingman	.40	.30	.15
(40)	Mike Krukow	.25	.20	.10
(41)	Ron LeFlore	.25	.20	.10
(42)	Chet Lemon	.25	.20	.10
(43)	Bob Molinaro	.20	.15	.08
(44)	Jim Morrison	.20	.15	.08
(45)	Wayne Nordhagen	.20	.15	.08
(46)	Ken Reitz	.20	.15	.08
(47)	Rick Reuschel	.30	.25	.12
(48)	Mike Tyson	.20	.15	.08
(49)	Neil Allen	.20	.15	.08
(50)	Rick Cerone	.20	.15	.08
(51)	Bucky Dent	.25	.20	.10
(52)	Doug Flynn	.20	.15	.08
(53)	Rich Gossage	.60	.45	.25
(54)	Ron Guidry	.60	.45	.25
(55)	Reggie Jackson	.90	.70	.35
(56)	Tommy John	.50	.40	.20
(57)	Ruppert Jones	.20	.15	.08
(58)	Rudy May	.20	.15	.08
(59)	Lee Mazzilli	.25	.20	.10
(60)	Graig Nettles	.40	.30	.15
(61)	Willie Randolph	.30	.25	.12
(62)	Rusty Staub	.40	.30	.15
(63)	Frank Taveras	.20	.15	.08
(64)	Alex Trevino	.20	.15	.08
(65)	Bob Watson	.25	.20	.10
(66)	Dave Winfield	.90	.70	.35
(67)	Bob Boone	.25	.20	.10
(68)	Larry Bowa	.40	.30	.15
(69)	Steve Carlton	.70	.50	.30
(70)	Greg Luzinski	.40	.30	.15
(71)	Garry Maddox	.25	.20	.10
(72)	Bake McBride	.20	.15	.08
(73)	Tug McGraw	.40	.30	.15
(74)	Pete Rose	1.75	1.25	.70
(75)	Dick Ruthven	.20	.15	.08
(76)	Mike Schmidt	.90	.70	.35
(77)	Manny Trillo	.25	.20	.10
(78)	Del Unser	.20	.15	.08
(79)	Tom Burgmeier	.20	.15	.08
(80)	Dennis Eckersley	.40	.30	.15
(81)	Dwight Evans	.50	.40	.20
(82)	Carlton Fisk	.60	.45	.25
(83)	Glenn Hoffman	.20	.15	.08
(84)	Carney Lansford	.30	.25	.12
(85)	Tony Perez	.50	.40	.20
(86)	Jim Rice	.70	.50	.30
(87)	Bob Stanley	.20	.15	.08
(88)	Dave Stapleton	.20	.15	.08
(89)	Frank Tanana	.25	.20	.10
(90)	Carl Yastrzemski	1.25	.90	.50
(91)	Johnny Bench	.90	.70	.35
(92)	Dave Collins	.25	.20	.10
(93)	Dave Concepcion	.40	.30	.15
(94)	Dan Driessen	.25	.20	.10
(95)	George Foster	.50	.40	.20
(96)	Ken Griffey	.30	.25	.12
(97)	Tom Hume	.20	.15	.08
(98)	Ray Knight	.25	.20	.10
(99)	Joe Nolan	.20	.15	.08
(100)	Ron Oester	.20	.15	.08
(101)	Tom Seaver	.70	.50	.30
(102)	Mario Soto	.25	.20	.10

Definitions for grading conditions are located in the Introduction section at the front of this book.

1981 Topps National 5X7 Photos

This set is the other half of Topps' efforts with large cards in 1981. Measuring 4-7/8" by 6-7/8", the National photo issue was limited to 15 cards. They were sold in areas not covered by the Home Team sets and feature ten cards which carry the same photos as found in the Home Team set, but with no checklist on the backs. Five cards are unique to the National set: George Brett, Cecil Cooper, Jim Palmer, Dave Parker and Ted Simmons. With their wide distribution and a limited demand, there are currently plenty of these cards to meet the demand, thus keeping prices fairly low.

		MT	NR MT	EX
	Complete Set:	5.00	3.75	2.00
	Common Player:	.30	.25	.12
(1)	Buddy Bell	.30	.25	.12
(2)	Johnny Bench	.60	.45	.25
(3)	George Brett	.90	.70	.35
(4)	Rod Carew	.60	.45	.25
(5)	Cecil Cooper	.40	.30	.15
(6)	Steve Garvey	.70	.50	.30
(7)	Rich Gossage	.40	.30	.15
(8)	Reggie Jackson	.70	.50	.30
(9)	Jim Palmer	.70	.50	.30
(10)	Dave Parker	.60	.45	.25
(11)	Jim Rice	.50	.40	.20
(12)	Pete Rose	1.25	.90	.50
(13)	Mike Schmidt	.70	.50	.30
(14)	Tom Seaver	.60	.45	.25
(15)	Ted Simmons	.50	.40	.20

1981 Topps Scratchoffs

Sold as a separate issue with bubble gum, this 108-card set was issued in three-card panels that measure 3-1/4" by 5-1/4". Each individual card measures 1-13/16" by 3-1/4" and contains a small player photo alongside a series of black dots designed to be scratched off as part of a baseball game. Cards of National League players have a green backgrounds, while American

League players have a red background. While there are 108 different players in the set, there are 144 possible panel combinations. An intact panel of three cards is valued approximately 20-25" more the sum of the individual cards.

	MT	NR MT	EX
Complete Set:	3.50	2.75	1.50
Common Player:	.02	.02	.01

		MT	NR MT	EX
1	George Brett	.12	.09	.05
2	Cecil Cooper	.04	.03	.02
3	Reggie Jackson	.12	.09	.05
4	Al Oliver	.04	.03	.02
5	Fred Lynn	.06	.05	.02
6	Tony Armas	.02	.02	.01
7	Ben Oglivie	.02	.02	.01
8	Tony Perez	.06	.05	.02
9	Eddie Murray	.10	.08	.04
10	Robin Yount	.08	.06	.03
11	Steve Kemp	.04	.03	.02
12	Joe Charboneau	.04	.03	.02
13	Jim Rice	.10	.08	.04
14	Lance Parrish	.08	.06	.03
15	John Mayberry	.02	.02	.01
16	Richie Zisk	.02	.02	.01
17	Ken Singleton	.04	.03	.02
18	Rod Carew	.10	.08	.04
19	Rick Manning	.02	.02	.01
20	Willie Wilson	.04	.03	.02
21	Buddy Bell	.04	.03	.02
22	Dave Revering	.02	.02	.01
23	Tom Paciorek	.02	.02	.01
24	Champ Summers	.02	.02	.01
25	Carney Lansford	.04	.03	.02
26	Lamar Johnson	.02	.02	.01
27	Willie Aikens	.02	.02	.01
28	Rick Cerone	.02	.02	.01
29	Al Bumbry	.02	.02	.01
30	Bruce Bochte	.02	.02	.01
31	Mickey Rivers	.02	.02	.01
32	Mike Hargrove	.02	.02	.01
33	John Castino	.02	.02	.01
34	Chet Lemon	.04	.03	.02
35	Paul Molitor	.06	.05	.02
36	Willie Randolph	.04	.03	.02
37	Rick Burleson	.02	.02	.01
38	Alan Trammell	.08	.06	.03
39	Rickey Henderson	.10	.08	.04
40	Dan Meyer	.02	.02	.01
41	Ken Landreaux	.02	.02	.01
42	Damaso Garcia	.02	.02	.01
43	Roy Smalley	.02	.02	.01
44	Otto Velez	.02	.02	.01
45	Sixto Lezcano	.02	.02	.01
46	Toby Harrah	.02	.02	.01
47	Frank White	.04	.03	.02
48	Dave Stapleton	.02	.02	.01
49	Steve Stone	.04	.03	.02
50	Jim Palmer	.08	.06	.03
51	Larry Gura	.02	.02	.01
52	Tommy John	.06	.05	.02
53	Mike Norris	.02	.02	.01
54	Ed Farmer	.02	.02	.01
55	Bill Buckner	.04	.03	.02
56	Steve Garvey	.10	.08	.04
57	Reggie Smith	.04	.03	.02
58	Bake McBride	.02	.02	.01
59	Dave Parker	.06	.05	.02
60	Mike Schmidt	.12	.09	.05
61	Bob Horner	.04	.03	.02
62	Pete Rose	.20	.15	.08
63	Ted Simmons	.06	.05	.02
64	Johnny Bench	.12	.09	.05
65	George Foster	.06	.05	.02
66	Gary Carter	.10	.08	.04
67	Keith Hernandez	.08	.06	.03
68	Ozzie Smith	.06	.05	.02
69	Dave Kingman	.06	.05	.02
70	Jack Clark	.06	.05	.02
71	Dusty Baker	.04	.03	.02
72	Dale Murphy	.12	.09	.05
73	Ron Cey	.04	.03	.02
74	Greg Luzinski	.04	.03	.02
75	Lee Mazzilli	.02	.02	.01
76	Gary Matthews	.04	.03	.02
77	Cesar Cedeno	.04	.03	.02
78	Warren Cromartie	.02	.02	.01
79	Steve Henderson	.02	.02	.01
80	Ellis Valentine	.02	.02	.01
81	Mike Easler	.02	.02	.01

		MT	NR MT	EX
82	Garry Templeton	.04	.03	.02
83	Jose Cruz	.04	.03	.02
84	Dave Collins	.02	.02	.01
85	George Hendrick	.02	.02	.01
86	Gene Richards	.02	.02	.01
87	Terry Whitfield	.02	.02	.01
88	Terry Puhl	.02	.02	.01
89	Larry Parrish	.04	.03	.02
90	Andre Dawson	.08	.06	.03
91	Ken Griffey	.04	.03	.02
92	Dave Lopes	.02	.02	.01
93	Doug Flynn	.02	.02	.01
94	Ivan DeJesus	.02	.02	.01
95	Dave Concepcion	.04	.03	.02
96	John Stearns	.02	.02	.01
97	Jerry Mumphrey	.02	.02	.01
98	Jerry Martin	.02	.02	.01
99	Art Howe	.02	.02	.01
100	Omar Moreno	.02	.02	.01
101	Ken Reitz	.02	.02	.01
102	Phil Garner	.02	.02	.01
103	Jerry Reuss	.04	.03	.02
104	Steve Carlton	.10	.08	.04
105	Jim Bibby	.02	.02	.01
106	Steve Rogers	.02	.02	.01
107	Tom Seaver	.10	.08	.04
108	Vida Blue	.04	.03	.02

A player's name in *italic* type indicates a rookie card. An (FC) indicates a player's first card for that particular card company.

NOTE: A card number in parentheses ( ) indicates the card set is unnumbered.

1981 Topps Stickers

The 262 stickers in this full-color set measure 1-15/16" by 2-9/16" and are numbered on both the front and back. They were produced for Topps by the Panini Company of Italy. The set includes a series of "All-Star" stickers printed on silver or gold "foil". An album to house the stickers was also available.

		MT	NR MT	EX
Complete Set:		17.00	12.50	6.75
Common Player:		.03	.02	.01
Sticker Album:		.80	.60	.30
1	Steve Stone	.06	.05	.02
2	Tommy John, Mike Norris	.06	.05	.02
3	Rudy May	.03	.02	.01
4	Mike Norris	.03	.02	.01
5	Len Barker	.03	.02	.01
6	Mike Norris	.03	.02	.01
7	Dan Quisenberry	.06	.05	.02
8	Rich Gossage	.10	.08	.04
9	George Brett	.25	.20	.10
10	Cecil Cooper	.08	.06	.03
11	Reggie Jackson, Ben Oglivie	.06	.05	.02
12	Gorman Thomas	.06	.05	.02
13	Cecil Cooper	.08	.06	.03
14	George Brett, Ben Oglivie	.20	.15	.08
15	Rickey Henderson	.25	.20	.10
16	Willie Wilson	.08	.06	.03
17	Bill Buckner	.06	.05	.02
18	Keith Hernandez	.12	.09	.05
19	Mike Schmidt	.25	.20	.10
20	Bob Horner	.10	.08	.04
21	Mike Schmidt	.25	.20	.10
22	George Hendrick	.06	.05	.02
23	Ron LeFlore	.04	.03	.02
24	Omar Moreno	.03	.02	.01
25	Steve Carlton	.20	.15	.08
26	Joe Niekro	.06	.05	.02

		MT	NR MT	EX				MT	NR MT	EX
27	Don Sutton	.10	.08	.04		116	Tony Armas	.04	.03	.02
28	Steve Carlton	.20	.15	.08		117	Dave Revering	.03	.02	.01
29	Steve Carlton	.20	.15	.08		118	Wayne Gross	.03	.02	.01
30	Nolan Ryan	.20	.15	.08		119	Dwayne Murphy	.04	.03	.02
31	Rollie Fingers, Tom Hume	.08	.06	.03		120	Jeff Newman	.03	.02	.01
32	Bruce Sutter	.08	.06	.03		121	Rick Langford	.03	.02	.01
33	Ken Singleton	.06	.05	.02		122	Mike Norris	.03	.02	.01
34	Eddie Murray	.20	.15	.08		123	Bruce Bochte	.03	.02	.01
35	Al Bumbry	.03	.02	.01		124	Tom Paciorek	.03	.02	.01
36	Rich Dauer	.03	.02	.01		125	Dan Meyer	.03	.02	.01
37	Scott McGregor	.04	.03	.02		126	Julio Cruz	.03	.02	.01
38	Rick Dempsey	.04	.03	.02		127	Richie Zisk	.04	.03	.02
39	Jim Palmer	.15	.11	.06		128	Floyd Bannister	.04	.03	.02
40	Steve Stone	.06	.05	.02		129	Shane Rawley	.04	.03	.02
41	Jim Rice	.20	.15	.08		130	Buddy Bell	.06	.05	.02
42	Fred Lynn	.10	.08	.04		131	Al Oliver	.06	.05	.02
43	Carney Lansford	.06	.05	.02		132	Mickey Rivers	.04	.03	.02
44	Tony Perez	.10	.08	.04		133	Jim Sundberg	.03	.02	.01
45	Carl Yastrzemski	.30	.25	.12		134	Bump Wills	.03	.02	.01
46	Carlton Fisk	.12	.09	.05		135	Jon Matlack	.04	.03	.02
47	Dave Stapleton	.03	.02	.01		136	Danny Darwin	.03	.02	.01
48	Dennis Eckersley	.06	.05	.02		137	Damaso Garcia	.04	.03	.02
49	Rod Carew	.20	.15	.08		138	Otto Velez	.03	.02	.01
50	Brian Downing	.04	.03	.02		139	John Mayberry	.04	.03	.02
51	Don Baylor	.08	.06	.03		140	Alfredo Griffin	.04	.03	.02
52	Rick Burleson	.04	.03	.02		141	Alvis Woods	.03	.02	.01
53	Bobby Grich	.06	.05	.02		142	Dave Stieb	.06	.05	.02
54	Butch Hobson	.03	.02	.01		143	Jim Clancy	.04	.03	.02
55	Andy Hassler	.03	.02	.01		144	Gary Matthews	.06	.05	.02
56	Frank Tanana	.04	.03	.02		145	Bob Horner	.08	.06	.03
57	Chet Lemon	.04	.03	.02		146	Dale Murphy	.25	.20	.10
58	Lamar Johnson	.03	.02	.01		147	Chris Chambliss	.04	.03	.02
59	Wayne Nordhagen	.03	.02	.01		148	Phil Niekro	.12	.09	.05
60	Jim Morrison	.03	.02	.01		149	Glenn Hubbard	.03	.02	.01
61	Bob Molinaro	.03	.02	.01		150	Rick Camp	.03	.02	.01
62	Rich Dotson	.04	.03	.02		151	Dave Kingman	.08	.06	.03
63	Britt Burns	.03	.02	.01		152	Bill Caudill	.03	.02	.01
64	Ed Farmer	.03	.02	.01		153	Bill Buckner	.06	.05	.02
65	Toby Harrah	.04	.03	.02		154	Barry Foote	.03	.02	.01
66	Joe Charboneau	.04	.03	.02		155	Mike Tyson	.03	.02	.01
67	Miguel Dilone	.03	.02	.01		156	Ivan DeJesus	.03	.02	.01
68	Mike Hargrove	.04	.03	.02		157	Rick Reuschel	.06	.05	.02
69	Rick Manning	.03	.02	.01		158	Ken Reitz	.03	.02	.01
70	Andre Thornton	.06	.05	.02		159	George Foster	.08	.06	.03
71	Ron Hassey	.03	.02	.01		160	Johnny Bench	.25	.20	.10
72	Len Barker	.03	.02	.01		161	Dave Concepcion	.06	.05	.02
73	Lance Parrish	.12	.09	.05		162	Dave Collins	.04	.03	.02
74	Steve Kemp	.04	.03	.02		163	Ken Griffey	.06	.05	.02
75	Alan Trammell	.15	.11	.06		164	Dan Driessen	.04	.03	.02
76	Champ Summers	.03	.02	.01		165	Tom Seaver	.20	.15	.08
77	Rick Peters	.03	.02	.01		166	Tom Hume	.03	.02	.01
78	Kirk Gibson	.15	.11	.06		167	Cesar Cedeno	.06	.05	.02
79	Johnny Wockenfuss	.03	.02	.01		168	Rafael Landestoy	.03	.02	.01
80	Jack Morris	.12	.09	.05		169	Jose Cruz	.06	.05	.02
81	Willie Wilson	.08	.06	.03		170	Art Howe	.03	.02	.01
82	George Brett	.25	.20	.10		171	Terry Puhl	.03	.02	.01
83	Frank White	.06	.05	.02		172	Joe Sambito	.03	.02	.01
84	Willie Aikens	.03	.02	.01		173	Nolan Ryan	.20	.15	.08
85	Clint Hurdle	.03	.02	.01		174	Joe Niekro	.06	.05	.02
86	Hal McRae	.06	.05	.02		175	Dave Lopes	.04	.03	.02
87	Dennis Leonard	.04	.03	.02		176	Steve Garvey	.20	.15	.08
88	Larry Gura	.03	.02	.01		177	Ron Cey	.06	.05	.02
89	American League Pennant Winner (Kansas City Royals Team)	.04	.03	.02		178	Reggie Smith	.06	.05	.02
90	American League Pennant Winner (Kansas City Royals Team)	.04	.03	.02		179	Bill Russell	.04	.03	.02
91	Paul Molitor	.10	.08	.04		180	Burt Hooton	.03	.02	.01
92	Ben Oglivie	.04	.03	.02		181	Jerry Reuss	.06	.05	.02
93	Cecil Cooper	.08	.06	.03		182	Dusty Baker	.04	.03	.02
94	Ted Simmons	.08	.06	.03		183	Larry Parrish	.04	.03	.02
95	Robin Yount	.15	.11	.06		184	Gary Carter	.20	.15	.08
96	Gorman Thomas	.06	.05	.02		185	Rodney Scott	.03	.02	.01
97	Mike Caldwell	.03	.02	.01		186	Ellis Valentine	.03	.02	.01
98	Moose Haas	.03	.02	.01		187	Andre Dawson	.12	.09	.05
99	John Castino	.03	.02	.01		188	Warren Cromartie	.03	.02	.01
100	Roy Smalley	.03	.02	.01		189	Chris Speier	.03	.02	.01
101	Ken Landreaux	.03	.02	.01		190	Steve Rogers	.03	.02	.01
102	Butch Wynegar	.04	.03	.02		191	Lee Mazzilli	.04	.03	.02
103	Ron Jackson	.03	.02	.01		192	Doug Flynn	.03	.02	.01
104	Jerry Koosman	.04	.03	.02		193	Steve Henderson	.03	.02	.01
105	Roger Erickson	.03	.02	.01		194	John Stearns	.03	.02	.01
106	Doug Corbett	.03	.02	.01		195	Joel Youngblood	.03	.02	.01
107	Reggie Jackson	.25	.20	.10		196	Frank Taveras	.03	.02	.01
108	Willie Randolph	.04	.03	.02		197	Pat Zachry	.03	.02	.01
109	Rick Cerone	.03	.02	.01		198	Neil Allen	.03	.02	.01
110	Bucky Dent	.04	.03	.02		199	Mike Schmidt	.25	.20	.10
111	Dave Winfield	.20	.15	.08		200	Pete Rose	.40	.30	.15
112	Ron Guidry	.12	.09	.05		201	Larry Bowa	.06	.05	.02
113	Rich Gossage	.10	.08	.04		202	Bake McBride	.03	.02	.01
114	Tommy John	.10	.08	.04		203	Bob Boone	.04	.03	.02
115	Rickey Henderson	.25	.20	.10		204	Garry Maddox	.04	.03	.02
						205	Tug McGraw	.06	.05	.02
						206	Steve Carlton	.20	.15	.08

		MT	NR MT	EX
207	National League Pennant Winner			
	(Philadelphia Phillies Team)	.04	.03	.02
208	National League Pennant Winner			
	(Philadelphia Phillies Team)	.04	.03	.02
209	Phil Garner	.04	.03	.02
210	Dave Parker	.12	.09	.05
211	Omar Moreno	.03	.02	.01
212	Mike Easler	.04	.03	.02
213	Bill Madlock	.06	.05	.02
214	Ed Ott	.03	.02	.01
215	Willie Stargell	.20	.15	.08
216	Jim Bibby	.03	.02	.01
217	Garry Templeton	.06	.05	.02
218	Sixto Lezcano	.03	.02	.01
219	Keith Hernandez	.12	.09	.05
220	George Hendrick	.04	.03	.02
221	Bruce Sutter	.08	.06	.03
222	Ken Oberkfell	.03	.02	.01
223	Tony Scott	.03	.02	.01
224	Darrell Porter	.04	.03	.02
225	Gene Richards	.03	.02	.01
226	Broderick Perkins	.03	.02	.01
227	Jerry Mumphrey	.03	.02	.01
228	Luis Salazar	.03	.02	.01
229	Jerry Turner	.03	.02	.01
230	Ozzie Smith	.10	.08	.04
231	John Curtis	.03	.02	.01
232	Rick Wise	.03	.02	.01
233	Terry Whitfield	.03	.02	.01
234	Jack Clark	.10	.08	.04
235	Darrell Evans	.08	.06	.03
236	Larry Herndon	.03	.02	.01
237	Milt May	.03	.02	.01
238	Greg Minton	.03	.02	.01
239	Vida Blue	.06	.05	.02
240	Eddie Whitson	.03	.02	.01
241	Cecil Cooper	.20	.15	.08
242	Willie Randolph	.20	.15	.08
243	George Brett	.40	.30	.15
244	Robin Yount	.30	.25	.12
245	Reggie Jackson	.40	.30	.15
246	Al Oliver	.20	.15	.08
247	Willie Wilson	.20	.15	.08
248	Rick Cerone	.15	.11	.06
249	Steve Stone	.15	.11	.06
250	Tommy John	.25	.20	.10
251	Rich Gossage	.25	.20	.10
252	Steve Garvey	.30	.25	.12
253	Phil Garner	.15	.11	.06
254	Mike Schmidt	.40	.30	.15
255	Garry Templeton	.20	.15	.08
256	George Hendrick	.15	.11	.06
257	Dave Parker	.25	.20	.10
258	Cesar Cedeno	.20	.15	.08
259	Gary Carter	.30	.25	.12
260	Jim Bibby	.15	.11	.06
261	Steve Carlton	.30	.25	.12
262	Tug McGraw	.20	.15	.08

1981 Topps Traded

The 132 cards in this extension set are numbered from 727 to 858, technically making them a high-numbered series of the regular Topps set. The set was not packaged in gum packs, but rather placed in a specially designed red box and sold through baseball card dealers only. While many complained about the method, the fact remains, even at higher prices, the set has done well for its owners as it

features not only mid-season trades, but also single-player rookie cards of some of the hottest prospects. The cards measure 2-1/2" by 3-1/2".

		MT	NR MT	EX
Complete Set:		25.00	19.00	10.00
Common Player:		.10	.08	.04
727	Danny Ainge(FC)	.50	.40	.20
728	Doyle Alexander	.20	.15	.08
729	Gary Alexander	.10	.08	.04
730	Billy Almon	.10	.08	.04
731	Joaquin Andujar	.15	.11	.06
732	Bob Bailor	.10	.08	.04
733	Juan Beniquez	.10	.08	.04
734	Dave Bergman	.10	.08	.04
735	Tony Bernazard	.10	.08	.04
736	Larry Biittner	.10	.08	.04
737	Doug Bird	.10	.08	.04
738	Bert Blyleven	.50	.40	.20
739	Mark Bomback	.10	.08	.04
740	Bobby Bonds	.20	.15	.08
741	Rick Bosetti	.10	.08	.04
742	Hubie Brooks	1.25	.90	.50
743	Rick Burleson	.15	.11	.06
744	Ray Burris	.10	.08	.04
745	Jeff Burroughs	.15	.11	.06
746	Enos Cabell	.10	.08	.04
747	Ken Clay	.10	.08	.04
748	Mark Clear	.10	.08	.04
749	Larry Cox	.10	.08	.04
750	Hector Cruz	.10	.08	.04
751	Victor Cruz	.10	.08	.04
752	Mike Cubbage	.10	.08	.04
753	Dick Davis	.10	.08	.04
754	Brian Doyle	.10	.08	.04
755	Dick Drago	.10	.08	.04
756	Leon Durham	.25	.20	.10
757	Jim Dwyer	.10	.08	.04
758	Dave Edwards	.10	.08	.04
759	Jim Essian	.10	.08	.04
760	Bill Fahey	.10	.08	.04
761	Rollie Fingers	.90	.70	.35
762	Carlton Fisk	1.25	.90	.50
763	Barry Foote	.10	.08	.04
764	Ken Forsch	.10	.08	.04
765	Kiko Garcia	.10	.08	.04
766	Cesar Geronimo	.10	.08	.04
767	Gary Gray	.10	.08	.04
768	Mickey Hatcher	.15	.11	.06
769	Steve Henderson	.10	.08	.04
770	Marc Hill	.10	.08	.04
771	Butch Hobson	.10	.08	.04
772	Rick Honeycutt	.10	.08	.04
773	Roy Howell	.10	.08	.04
774	Mike Ivie	.10	.08	.04
775	Roy Lee Jackson	.10	.08	.04
776	Cliff Johnson	.10	.08	.04
777	Randy Jones	.15	.11	.06
778	Ruppert Jones	.10	.08	.04
779	Mick Kelleher	.10	.08	.04
780	Terry Kennedy	.20	.15	.08
781	Dave Kingman	.40	.30	.15
782	Bob Knepper	.15	.11	.06
783	Ken Kravec	.10	.08	.04
784	Bob Lacey	.10	.08	.04
785	Dennis Lamp	.10	.08	.04
786	Rafael Landestoy	.10	.08	.04
787	Ken Landreaux	.10	.08	.04
788	Carney Lansford	.20	.15	.08
789	Dave LaRoche	.10	.08	.04
790	Joe Lefebvre	.10	.08	.04
791	Ron LeFlore	.15	.11	.06
792	Randy Lerch	.10	.08	.04
793	Sixto Lezcano	.10	.08	.04
794	John Littlefield	.10	.08	.04
795	Mike Lum	.10	.08	.04
796	Greg Luzinski	.25	.20	.10
797	Fred Lynn	.50	.40	.20
798	Jerry Martin	.10	.08	.04
799	Buck Martinez	.10	.08	.04
800	Gary Matthews	.20	.15	.08
801	Mario Mendoza	.10	.08	.04
802	Larry Milbourne	.10	.08	.04
803	Rick Miller	.10	.08	.04
804	John Montefusco	.10	.08	.04
805	Jerry Morales	.10	.08	.04
806	Jose Morales	.10	.08	.04
807	Joe Morgan	1.00	.70	.40
808	Jerry Mumphrey	.10	.08	.04
809	Gene Nelson(FC)	.30	.25	.12

		MT	NR MT	EX
810	Ed Ott	.10	.08	.04
811	Bob Owchinko	.10	.08	.04
812	Gaylord Perry	1.25	.90	.50
813	Mike Phillips	.10	.08	.04
814	Darrell Porter	.15	.11	.06
815	Mike Proly	.10	.08	.04
816	Tim Raines	7.00	5.25	2.75
817	Lenny Randle	.10	.08	.04
818	Doug Rau	.10	.08	.04
819	Jeff Reardon	.50	.40	.20
820	Ken Reitz	.10	.08	.04
821	Steve Renko	.10	.08	.04
822	Rick Reuschel	.25	.20	.10
823	Dave Revering	.10	.08	.04
824	Dave Roberts	.10	.08	.04
825	Leon Roberts	.10	.08	.04
826	Joe Rudi	.20	.15	.08
827	Kevin Saucier	.10	.08	.04
828	Tony Scott	.10	.08	.04
829	Bob Shirley	.10	.08	.04
830	Ted Simmons	.40	.30	.15
831	Lary Sorensen	.10	.08	.04
832	Jim Spencer	.10	.08	.04
833	Harry Spilman	.10	.08	.04
834	Fred Stanley	.10	.08	.04
835	Rusty Staub	.30	.25	.12
836	Bill Stein	.10	.08	.04
837	Joe Strain	.10	.08	.04
838	Bruce Sutter	.50	.40	.20
839	Don Sutton	1.25	.90	.50
840	Steve Swisher	.10	.08	.04
841	Frank Tanana	.20	.15	.08
842	Gene Tenace	.15	.11	.06
843	Jason Thompson	.10	.08	.04
844	Dickie Thon	.15	.11	.06
845	Bill Travers	.10	.08	.04
846	Tom Underwood	.10	.08	.04
847	John Urrea	.10	.08	.04
848	Mike Vail	.10	.08	.04
849	Ellis Valentine	.10	.08	.04
850	Fernando Valenzuela	4.50	3.50	1.75
851	Pete Vuckovich	.15	.11	.06
852	Mark Wagner	.10	.08	.04
853	Bob Walk	.50	.40	.20
854	Claudell Washington	.15	.11	.06
855	Dave Winfield	1.75	1.25	.70
856	Geoff Zahn	.10	.08	.04
857	Richie Zisk	.15	.11	.06
858	Checklist 727-858	.10	.08	.04

1982 Topps

At 792 cards, this was the largest issue produced up to that time, eliminating the need for double-printed cards. The 2-1/2" by 3-1/2" cards feature a front color photo with a pair of stripes down the left side. Under the player's photo are found his name, team and position. A facsimile autograph runs across the front of the picture. Specialty cards include great performances of the previous season, All-Stars, statistical leaders and "In Action" cards (indicated by "IA" in listings below). Managers and hitting/pitching leaders have cards, while rookies are shown as "Future Stars" on group cards.

	MT	NR MT	EX
Complete Set:	90.00	65.00	35.00

		MT	NR MT	EX
	Common Player:	.08	.06	.03
1	1981 Highlight (Steve Carlton)	.50	.40	.20
2	1981 Highlight (Ron Davis)	.08	.06	.03
3	1981 Highlight (Tim Raines)	.30	.25	.12
4	1981 Highlight (Pete Rose)	.70	.50	.30
5	1981 Highlight (Nolan Ryan)	.30	.25	.12
6	1981 Highlight (Fernando Valenzuela)	.30	.25	.12
7	Scott Sanderson	.08	.06	.03
8	Rich Dauer	.08	.06	.03
9	Ron Guidry	.35	.25	.14
10	Ron Guidry IA	.15	.11	.06
11	Gary Alexander	.08	.06	.03
12	Moose Haas	.08	.06	.03
13	Lamar Johnson	.08	.06	.03
14	Steve Howe	.10	.08	.04
15	Ellis Valentine	.08	.06	.03
16	Steve Comer	.08	.06	.03
17	Darrell Evans	.25	.20	.10
18	Fernando Arroyo	.08	.06	.03
19	Ernie Whitt	.10	.08	.04
20	Garry Maddox	.12	.09	.05
21	Orioles Future Stars (Bob Bonner, *Cal Ripken*, Jeff Schneider)	12.00	9.00	4.75
22	Jim Beattie	.08	.06	.03
23	Willie Hernandez	.10	.08	.03
24	Dave Frost	.08	.06	.03
25	Jerry Remy	.08	.06	.03
26	Jorge Orta	.08	.06	.03
27	Tom Herr	.12	.09	.05
28	John Urrea	.08	.06	.03
29	Dwayne Murphy	.10	.08	.04
30	Tom Seaver	.70	.50	.30
31	Tom Seaver IA	.30	.25	.12
32	Gene Garber	.08	.06	.03
33	Jerry Morales	.08	.06	.03
34	Joe Sambito	.08	.06	.03
35	Willie Aikens	.08	.06	.03
36	Rangers Batting & Pitching Ldrs. (George Medich, Al Oliver)	.12	.09	.05
37	Dan Graham	.08	.06	.03
38	Charlie Lea	.08	.06	.03
39	Lou Whitaker	.40	.30	.15
40	Dave Parker	.35	.25	.14
41	Dave Parker IA	.15	.11	.06
42	Rick Sofield	.08	.06	.03
43	Mike Cubbage	.08	.06	.03
44	Britt Burns	.08	.06	.03
45	Rick Cerone	.08	.06	.03
46	Jerry Augustine	.08	.06	.03
47	Jeff Leonard	.15	.11	.06
48	Bobby Castillo	.08	.06	.03
49	Alvis Woods	.08	.06	.03
50	Buddy Bell	.15	.11	.06
51	Cubs Future Stars (*Jay Howell*, Carlos Lezcano, Ty Waller)	.40	.30	.15
52	Larry Andersen	.08	.06	.03
53	Greg Gross	.08	.06	.03
54	Ron Hassey	.08	.06	.03
55	Rick Burleson	.10	.08	.04
56	Mark Littell	.08	.06	.03
57	Craig Reynolds	.08	.06	.03
58	John D'Acquisto	.08	.06	.03
59	*Rich Gedman*(FC)	.50	.40	.20
60	Tony Armas	.12	.09	.05
61	Tommy Boggs	.08	.06	.03
62	Mike Tyson	.08	.06	.03
63	Mario Soto	.10	.08	.04
64	Lynn Jones	.08	.06	.03
65	Terry Kennedy	.12	.09	.05
66	Astros Batting & Pitching Ldrs. (Art Howe, Nolan Ryan)	.25	.20	.10
67	Rich Gale	.08	.06	.03
68	Roy Howell	.08	.06	.03
69	Al Williams	.08	.06	.03
70	Tim Raines	1.75	1.25	.70
71	Roy Lee Jackson	.08	.06	.03
72	Rick Auerbach	.08	.06	.03
73	Buddy Solomon	.08	.06	.03
74	Bob Clark	.08	.06	.03
75	Tommy John	.30	.25	.12
76	Greg Pryor	.08	.06	.03
77	Miguel Dilone	.08	.06	.03
78	George Medich	.08	.06	.03
79	Bob Bailor	.08	.06	.03
80	Jim Palmer	.60	.45	.25
81	Jim Palmer IA	.30	.25	.12
82	Bob Welch	.20	.15	.08
83	Yankees Future Stars (*Steve Balboni, Andy McGaffigan, Andre Robertson*)(FC)	.50	.40	.20

	MT	NR MT	EX
84 Rennie Stennett	.08	.06	.03
85 Lynn McGlothen	.08	.06	.03
86 Dane Iorg	.08	.06	.03
87 Matt Keough	.08	.06	.03
88 Biff Pocoroba	.08	.06	.03
89 Steve Henderson	.08	.06	.03
90 Nolan Ryan	1.50	1.25	.60
91 Carney Lansford	.12	.09	.05
92 Brad Havens	.08	.06	.03
93 Larry Hisle	.10	.08	.04
94 Andy Hassler	.08	.06	.03
95 Ozzie Smith	.40	.30	.15
96 Royals Batting & Pitching Ldrs. (George Brett, Larry Gura)	.35	.25	.14
97 Paul Moskau	.08	.06	.03
98 Terry Bulling	.08	.06	.03
99 Barry Bonnell	.08	.06	.03
100 Mike Schmidt	1.50	1.25	.60
101 Mike Schmidt IA	.70	.50	.30
102 Dan Briggs	.08	.06	.03
103 Bob Lacey	.08	.06	.03
104 Rance Mulliniks	.08	.06	.03
105 Kirk Gibson	1.25	.90	.50
106 Enrique Romo	.08	.06	.03
107 Wayne Krenchicki	.08	.06	.03
108 Bob Sykes	.08	.06	.03
109 Dave Revering	.08	.06	.03
110 Carlton Fisk	.50	.40	.20
111 Carlton Fisk IA	.15	.11	.06
112 Billy Sample	.08	.06	.03
113 Steve McCatty	.08	.06	.03
114 Ken Landreaux	.08	.06	.03
115 Gaylord Perry	.40	.30	.15
116 Jim Wohlford	.08	.06	.03
117 Rawly Eastwick	.08	.06	.03
118 Expos Future Stars (Terry Francona, Brad Mills, Bryn Smith)(FC)	.25	.20	.10
119 Joe Pittman	.08	.06	.03
120 Gary Lucas	.08	.06	.03
121 Ed Lynch	.08	.06	.03
122 Jamie Easterly	.08	.06	.03
123 Danny Goodwin	.08	.06	.03
124 Reid Nichols	.08	.06	.03
125 Danny Ainge	.20	.15	.08
126 Braves Batting & Pitching Ldrs. (Rick Mahler, Claudell Washington)	.10	.08	.04
127 Lonnie Smith	.10	.08	.04
128 Frank Pastore	.08	.06	.03
129 Checklist 1-132	.12	.09	.05
130 Julio Cruz	.08	.06	.03
131 Stan Bahnsen	.08	.06	.03
132 Lee May	.10	.08	.04
133 Pat Underwood	.08	.06	.03
134 Dan Ford	.08	.06	.03
135 Andy Rincon	.08	.06	.03
136 Lenn Sakata	.08	.06	.03
137 George Cappuzzello	.08	.06	.03
138 Tony Pena	.20	.15	.08
139 Jeff Jones	.08	.06	.03
140 Ron LeFlore	.10	.08	.04
141 Indians Future Stars (Chris Bando, Tom Brennan, Von Hayes)(FC)	1.25	.90	.50
142 Dave LaRoche	.08	.06	.03
143 Mookie Wilson	.12	.09	.05
144 Fred Breining	.08	.06	.03
145 Bob Horner	.20	.15	.08
146 Mike Griffin	.08	.06	.03
147 Denny Walling	.08	.06	.03
148 Mickey Klutts	.08	.06	.03
149 Pat Putnam	.08	.06	.03
150 Ted Simmons	.20	.15	.08
151 Dave Edwards	.08	.06	.03
152 Ramon Aviles	.08	.06	.03
153 Roger Erickson	.08	.06	.03
154 Dennis Werth	.08	.06	.03
155 Otto Velez	.08	.06	.03
156 A's Batting & Pitching Ldrs. (Rickey Henderson, Steve McCatty)	.25	.20	.10
157 Steve Crawford	.08	.06	.03
158 Brian Downing	.12	.09	.05
159 Larry Biittner	.08	.06	.03
160 Luis Tiant	.15	.11	.06
161 Batting Leaders (Carney Lansford, Bill Madlock)	.20	.15	.08
162 Home Run Leaders (Tony Armas, Dwight Evans, Bobby Grich, Eddie Murray, Mike Schmidt)	.35	.25	.14
163 Runs Batted In Leaders (Eddie Murray, Mike Schmidt)	.40	.30	.15
164 Stolen Base Leaders (Rickey Henderson, Tim Raines)	.35	.25	.14

	MT	NR MT	EX
165 Victory Leaders (Denny Martinez, Steve McCatty, Jack Morris, Tom Seaver, Pete Vuckovich)	.20	.15	.08
166 Strikeout Leaders (Len Barker, Fernando Valenzuela)	.20	.15	.08
167 Earned Run Avg. Leaders (Steve McCatty, Nolan Ryan)	.20	.15	.08
168 Leading Relievers (Rollie Fingers, Bruce Sutter)	.20	.15	.08
169 Charlie Leibrandt	.12	.09	.05
170 Jim Bibby	.08	.06	.03
171 Giants Future Stars (Bob Brenly, Chili Davis, Bob Tufts)	.90	.70	.35
172 Bill Gullickson	.10	.08	.04
173 Jamie Quirk	.08	.06	.03
174 Dave Ford	.08	.06	.03
175 Jerry Mumphrey	.08	.06	.03
176 Dewey Robinson	.08	.06	.03
177 John Ellis	.08	.06	.03
178 Dyar Miller	.08	.06	.03
179 Steve Garvey	.80	.60	.30
180 Steve Garvey IA	.40	.30	.15
181 Silvio Martinez	.08	.06	.03
182 Larry Herndon	.10	.08	.04
183 Mike Proly	.08	.06	.03
184 Mick Kelleher	.08	.06	.03
185 Phil Niekro	.50	.40	.20
186 Cardinals Batting & Pitching Ldrs. (Bob Forsch, Keith Hernandez)	.25	.20	.10
187 Jeff Newman	.08	.06	.03
188 Randy Martz	.08	.06	.03
189 Glenn Hoffman	.08	.06	.03
190 J.R. Richard	.12	.09	.05
191 Tim Wallach(FC)	2.00	1.50	.80
192 Broderick Perkins	.08	.06	.03
193 Darrell Jackson	.08	.06	.03
194 Mike Vail	.08	.06	.03
195 Paul Molitor	.35	.25	.14
196 Willie Upshaw	.12	.09	.05
197 Shane Rawley	.15	.11	.06
198 Chris Speier	.08	.06	.03
199 Don Aase	.08	.06	.03
200 George Brett	1.50	1.25	.60
201 George Brett IA	.70	.50	.30
202 Rick Manning	.08	.06	.03
203 Blue Jays Future Stars (Jesse Barfield, Brian Milner, Boomer Wells)	4.00	3.00	1.50
204 Gary Roenicke	.08	.06	.03
205 Neil Allen	.08	.06	.03
206 Tony Bernazard	.08	.06	.03
207 Rod Scurry	.08	.06	.03
208 Bobby Murcer	.15	.11	.06
209 Gary Lavelle	.08	.06	.03
210 Keith Hernandez	.60	.45	.25
211 Dan Petry	.10	.08	.04
212 Mario Mendoza	.08	.06	.03
213 Dave Stewart(FC)	3.00	2.25	1.25
214 Brian Asselstine	.08	.06	.03
215 Mike Krukow	.10	.08	.04
216 White Sox Batting & Pitching Ldrs. (Dennis Lamp, Chet Lemon)	.10	.08	.04
217 Bo McLaughlin	.08	.06	.03
218 Dave Roberts	.08	.06	.03
219 John Curtis	.08	.06	.03
220 Manny Trillo	.10	.08	.04
221 Jim Slaton	.08	.06	.03
222 Butch Wynegar	.08	.06	.03
223 Lloyd Moseby	.20	.15	.08
224 Bruce Bochte	.08	.06	.03
225 Mike Torrez	.10	.08	.04
226 Checklist 133-264	.12	.09	.05
227 Ray Burris	.08	.06	.03
228 Sam Mejias	.08	.06	.03
229 Geoff Zahn	.08	.06	.03
230 Willie Wilson	.20	.15	.08
231 Phillies Future Stars (Mark Davis, Bob Dernier, Ozzie Virgil)(FC)	1.50	1.25	.60
232 Terry Crowley	.08	.06	.03
233 Duane Kuiper	.08	.06	.03
234 Ron Hodges	.08	.06	.03
235 Mike Easler	.10	.08	.04
236 John Martin	.08	.06	.03
237 Rusty Kuntz	.08	.06	.03
238 Kevin Saucier	.08	.06	.03
239 Jon Matlack	.10	.08	.04
240 Bucky Dent	.12	.09	.05
241 Bucky Dent IA	.10	.08	.04
242 Milt May	.08	.06	.03
243 Bob Owchinko	.08	.06	.03
244 Rufino Linares	.08	.06	.03
245 Ken Reitz	.08	.06	.03

		MT	NR MT	EX
246	Mets Batting & Pitching Ldrs. (Hubie Brooks, Mike Scott)	.20	.15	.08
247	Pedro Guerrero	.70	.50	.30
248	Frank LaCorte	.08	.06	.03
249	Tim Flannery	.08	.06	.03
250	Tug McGraw	.15	.11	.06
251	Fred Lynn	.30	.25	.12
252	Fred Lynn IA	.15	.11	.06
253	Chuck Baker	.08	.06	.03
254	*Jorge Bell*(FC)	9.00	6.75	3.50
255	Tony Perez	.30	.25	.12
256	Tony Perez IA	.15	.11	.06
257	Larry Harlow	.08	.06	.03
258	Bo Diaz	.10	.08	.03
259	Rodney Scott	.08	.06	.03
260	Bruce Sutter	.20	.15	.08
261	Tigers Future Stars (Howard Bailey, Marty Castillo, Dave Rucker)	.08	.06	.03
262	Doug Bair	.08	.06	.03
263	Victor Cruz	.08	.06	.03
264	Dan Quisenberry	.20	.15	.08
265	Al Bumbry	.10	.08	.04
266	Rick Leach	.15	.11	.06
267	Kurt Bevacqua	.08	.06	.03
268	Rickey Keeton	.08	.06	.03
269	Jim Essian	.08	.06	.03
270	Rusty Staub	.15	.11	.06
271	Larry Bradford	.08	.06	.03
272	Bump Wills	.08	.06	.03
273	Doug Bird	.08	.06	.03
274	*Bob Ojeda*(FC)	.70	.50	.30
275	Bob Watson	.10	.08	.04
276	Angels Batting & Pitching Ldrs. (Rod Carew, Ken Forsch)	.25	.20	.10
277	Terry Puhl	.08	.06	.03
278	John Littlefield	.08	.06	.03
279	Bill Russell	.10	.08	.04
280	Ben Oglivie	.10	.08	.04
281	John Verhoeven	.08	.06	.03
282	Ken Macha	.08	.06	.03
283	Brian Allard	.08	.06	.03
284	Bob Grich	.15	.11	.06
285	Sparky Lyle	.12	.09	.05
286	Bill Fahey	.08	.06	.03
287	Alan Bannister	.08	.06	.03
288	Garry Templeton	.12	.09	.05
289	Bob Stanley	.08	.06	.03
290	Ken Singleton	.12	.09	.05
291	Pirates Future Stars (Vance Law, Bob Long, *Johnny Ray*)(FC)	1.00	.70	.40
292	Dave Palmer	.08	.06	.03
293	Rob Picciolo	.08	.06	.03
294	Mike LaCoss	.08	.06	.03
295	Jason Thompson	.08	.06	.03
296	Bob Walk	.12	.09	.05
297	Clint Hurdle	.08	.06	.03
298	Danny Darwin	.08	.06	.03
299	Steve Trout	.08	.06	.03
300	Reggie Jackson	1.00	.70	.40
301	Reggie Jackson IA	.50	.40	.20
302	Doug Flynn	.08	.06	.03
303	Bill Caudill	.08	.06	.03
304	Johnnie LeMaster	.08	.06	.03
305	Don Sutton	.50	.40	.20
306	Don Sutton IA	.25	.20	.10
307	Randy Bass	.08	.06	.03
308	Charlie Moore	.08	.06	.03
309	Pete Redfern	.08	.06	.03
310	Mike Hargrove	.08	.06	.03
311	Dodgers Batting & Pitching Leaders (Dusty Baker, Burt Hooton)	.12	.09	.05
312	Lenny Randle	.08	.06	.03
313	John Harris	.08	.06	.03
314	Buck Martinez	.08	.06	.03
315	Burt Hooton	.10	.08	.04
316	Steve Braun	.08	.06	.03
317	Dick Ruthven	.08	.06	.03
318	Mike Heath	.08	.06	.03
319	Dave Rozema	.08	.06	.03
320	Chris Chambliss	.10	.08	.04
321	Chris Chambliss IA	.10	.08	.04
322	Garry Hancock	.08	.06	.03
323	Bill Lee	.10	.08	.04
324	Steve Dillard	.08	.06	.03
325	Jose Cruz	.15	.11	.06
326	Pete Falcone	.08	.06	.03
327	Joe Nolan	.08	.06	.03
328	Ed Farmer	.08	.06	.03
329	U.L. Washington	.08	.06	.03
330	Rick Wise	.10	.08	.04
331	Benny Ayala	.08	.06	.03
332	Don Robinson	.10	.08	.04
333	Brewers Future Stars (*Frank DiPino*, Marshall Edwards, Chuck Porter)	.12	.09	.05
334	Aurelio Rodriguez	.10	.08	.04
335	Jim Sundberg	.10	.08	.04
336	Mariners Batting & Pitching Ldrs. (Glenn Abbott, Tom Paciorek)	.10	.08	.04
337	Pete Rose AS	.80	.60	.30
338	Dave Lopes AS	.12	.09	.05
339	Mike Schmidt AS	.60	.45	.25
340	Dave Concepcion AS	.12	.09	.05
341	Andre Dawson AS	.25	.20	.10
342a	George Foster AS (no autograph)	2.25	1.75	.90
342b	George Foster AS (autograph on front)	.40	.30	.15
343	Dave Parker AS	.20	.15	.08
344	Gary Carter AS	.35	.25	.14
345	Fernando Valenzuela AS	.35	.25	.14
346	Tom Seaver AS	.35	.25	.14
347	Bruce Sutter AS	.12	.09	.05
348	Derrel Thomas	.08	.06	.03
349	George Frazier	.08	.06	.03
350	Thad Bosley	.08	.06	.03
351	Reds Future Stars (Scott Brown, Geoff Combe, Paul Householder)	.08	.06	.03
352	Dick Davis	.08	.06	.03
353	Jack O'Connor	.08	.06	.03
354	Roberto Ramos	.08	.06	.03
355	Dwight Evans	.25	.20	.10
356	Denny Lewallyn	.08	.06	.03
357	Butch Hobson	.08	.06	.03
358	Mike Parrott	.08	.06	.03
359	Jim Dwyer	.08	.06	.03
360	Len Barker	.10	.08	.04
361	Rafael Landestoy	.08	.06	.03
362	Jim Wright	.08	.06	.03
363	Bob Molinaro	.08	.06	.03
364	Doyle Alexander	.12	.09	.05
365	Bill Madlock	.20	.15	.08
366	Padres Batting & Pitching Ldrs. (Juan Eichelberger, Luis Salazar)	.10	.08	.04
367	Jim Kaat	.25	.20	.10
368.	Alex Trevino	.08	.06	.03
369	Champ Summers	.08	.06	.03
370	Mike Norris	.08	.06	.03
371	Jerry Don Gleaton	.08	.06	.03
372	Luis Gomez	.08	.06	.03
373	*Gene Nelson*	.15	.11	.06
374	Tim Blackwell	.08	.06	.03
375	Dusty Baker	.12	.09	.05
376	Chris Welsh	.08	.06	.03
377	Kiko Garcia	.08	.06	.03
378	Mike Caldwell	.08	.06	.03
379	Rob Wilfong	.08	.06	.03
380	Dave Stieb	.25	.20	.10
381	Red Sox Future Stars (Bruce Hurst, Dave Schmidt, Julio Valdez)	.25	.20	.10
382	Joe Simpson	.08	.06	.03
383a	Pascual Perez (no position on front)	35.00	26.00	14.00
383b	Pascual Perez (position on front)	.12	.09	.05
384	Keith Moreland	.12	.09	.05
385	Ken Forsch	.08	.06	.03
386	Jerry White	.08	.06	.03
387	Tom Veryzer	.08	.06	.03
388	Joe Rudi	.12	.09	.05
389	George Vukovich	.08	.06	.03
390	Eddie Murray	1.25	.90	.50
391	Dave Tobik	.08	.06	.03
392	Rick Bosetti	.08	.06	.03
393	Al Hrabosky	.10	.08	.04
394	Checklist 265-396	.12	.09	.05
395	Omar Moreno	.08	.06	.03
396	Twins Batting & Pitching Ldrs. (Fernando Arroyo, John Castino)	.10	.08	.04
397	Ken Brett	.10	.08	.04
398	Mike Squires	.08	.06	.03
399	Pat Zachry	.08	.06	.03
400	Johnny Bench	.90	.70	.35
401	Johnny Bench IA	.40	.30	.15
402	Bill Stein	.08	.06	.03
403	Jim Tracy	.08	.06	.03
404	Dickie Thon	.10	.08	.04
405	Rick Reuschel	.15	.11	.06
406	Al Holland	.08	.06	.03
407	Danny Boone	.08	.06	.03
408	Ed Romero	.08	.06	.03
409	Don Cooper	.08	.06	.03
410	Ron Cey	.15	.11	.06
411	Ron Cey IA	.10	.08	.04
412	Luis Leal	.08	.06	.03

#	Name	MT	NR MT	EX
413	Dan Meyer	.08	.06	.03
414	Elias Sosa	.08	.06	.03
415	Don Baylor	.15	.11	.06
416	Marty Bystrom	.08	.06	.03
417	Pat Kelly	.08	.06	.03
418	Rangers Future Stars (John Butcher, Bobby Johnson, *Dave Schmidt*)(FC)	.20	.15	.08
419	Steve Stone	.12	.09	.05
420	George Hendrick	.10	.08	.04
421	Mark Clear	.08	.06	.03
422	Cliff Johnson	.08	.06	.03
423	Stan Papi	.08	.06	.03
424	Bruce Benedict	.08	.06	.03
425	John Candelaria	.12	.09	.05
426	Orioles Batting & Pitching Ldrs. (Eddie Murray, Sammy Stewart)	.35	.25	.14
427	Ron Oester	.08	.06	.03
428	Lamarr Hoyt (LaMarr)	.08	.06	.03
429	John Wathan	.10	.08	.04
430	Vida Blue	.15	.11	.06
431	Vida Blue IA	.10	.08	.04
432	Mike Scott	.25	.20	.10
433	Alan Ashby	.08	.06	.03
434	Joe Lefebvre	.08	.06	.03
435	Robin Yount	1.00	.70	.40
436	Joe Strain	.08	.06	.03
437	Juan Berenguer	.08	.06	.03
438	Pete Mackanin	.08	.06	.03
439	*Dave Righetti*(FC)	2.50	2.00	1.00
440	Jeff Burroughs	.10	.08	.04
441	Astros Future Stars (Danny Heep, Billy Smith, Bobby Sprowl)	.08	.06	.03
442	Bruce Kison	.08	.06	.03
443	Mark Wagner	.08	.06	.03
444	Terry Forster	.10	.08	.04
445	Larry Parrish	.12	.09	.05
446	Wayne Garland	.08	.06	.03
447	Darrell Porter	.10	.08	.04
448	Darrell Porter IA	.10	.08	.04
449	*Luis Aguayo*(FC)	.12	.09	.05
450	Jack Morris	.50	.40	.20
451	Ed Miller	.08	.06	.03
452	*Lee Smith*(FC)	.90	.70	.35
453	Art Howe	.08	.06	.03
454	Rick Langford	.08	.06	.03
455	Tom Burgmeier	.08	.06	.03
456	Cubs Batting & Pitching Ldrs. (Bill Buckner, Randy Martz)	.15	.11	.06
457	Tim Stoddard	.08	.06	.03
458	Willie Montanez	.08	.06	.03
459	Bruce Berenyi	.08	.06	.03
460	Jack Clark	.30	.25	.12
461	Rich Dotson	.12	.09	.05
462	Dave Chalk	.08	.06	.03
463	Jim Kern	.08	.06	.03
464	Juan Bonilla	.08	.06	.03
465	Lee Mazzilli	.10	.08	.04
466	Randy Lerch	.08	.06	.03
467	Mickey Hatcher	.10	.08	.04
468	Floyd Bannister	.12	.09	.05
469	Ed Ott	.08	.06	.03
470	John Mayberry	.10	.08	.04
471	Royals Future Stars (*Atlee Hammaker*, Mike Jones, Darryl Motley)	.25	.20	.10
472	Oscar Gamble	.10	.08	.04
473	Mike Stanton	.08	.06	.03
474	Ken Oberkfell	.08	.06	.03
475	Alan Trammell	.50	.40	.20
476	Brian Kingman	.08	.06	.03
477	Steve Yeager	.08	.06	.03
478	Ray Searage	.08	.06	.03
479	Rowland Office	.08	.06	.03
480	Steve Carlton	.80	.60	.30
481	Steve Carlton IA	.40	.30	.15
482	Glenn Hubbard	.10	.08	.04
483	Gary Woods	.08	.06	.03
484	Ivan DeJesus	.08	.06	.03
485	Kent Tekulve	.10	.08	.04
486	Yankees Batting & Pitching Ldrs. (Tommy John, Jerry Mumphrey)	.20	.15	.08
487	Bob McClure	.08	.06	.03
488	Ron Jackson	.08	.06	.03
489	Rick Dempsey	.10	.08	.04
490	Dennis Eckersley	.20	.15	.08
491	Checklist 397-528	.12	.09	.05
492	Joe Price	.08	.06	.03
493	Chet Lemon	.10	.08	.04
494	Hubie Brooks	.20	.15	.08
495	Dennis Leonard	.10	.08	.04
496	Johnny Grubb	.08	.06	.03
497	Jim Anderson	.08	.06	.03
498	Dave Bergman	.08	.06	.03
499	Paul Mirabella	.08	.06	.03
500	Rod Carew	.80	.60	.30
501	Rod Carew IA	.40	.30	.15
502	Braves Future Stars (Steve Bedrosian, *Brett Butler*, Larry Owen)	2.00	1.50	.80
503	Julio Gonzalez	.08	.06	.03
504	Rick Peters	.08	.06	.03
505	Graig Nettles	.25	.20	.10
506	Graig Nettles IA	.12	.09	.05
507	Terry Harper	.08	.06	.03
508	*Jody Davis*(FC)	.40	.30	.15
509	Harry Spilman	.08	.06	.03
510	Fernando Valenzuela	1.50	1.25	.60
511	Ruppert Jones	.08	.06	.03
512	Jerry Dybzinski	.08	.06	.03
513	Rick Rhoden	.12	.09	.05
514	Joe Ferguson	.08	.06	.03
515	Larry Bowa	.20	.15	.08
516	Larry Bowa IA	.12	.09	.05
517	Mark Brouhard	.08	.06	.03
518	Garth Iorg	.08	.06	.03
519	Glenn Adams	.08	.06	.03
520	Mike Flanagan	.12	.09	.05
521	Billy Almon	.08	.06	.03
522	Chuck Rainey	.08	.06	.03
523	Gary Gray	.08	.06	.03
524	Tom Hausman	.08	.06	.03
525	Ray Knight	.12	.09	.05
526	Expos Batting & Pitching Ldrs. (Warren Cromartie, Bill Gullickson)	.10	.08	.04
527	John Henry Johnson	.08	.06	.03
528	Matt Alexander	.08	.06	.03
529	Allen Ripley	.08	.06	.03
530	Dickie Noles	.08	.06	.03
531	A's Future Stars (Rich Bordi, Mark Budaska, Kelvin Moore)	.08	.06	.03
532	Toby Harrah	.10	.08	.04
533	Joaquin Andujar	.10	.08	.04
534	Dave McKay	.08	.06	.03
535	Lance Parrish	.50	.40	.20
536	Rafael Ramirez	.10	.08	.04
537	Doug Capilla	.08	.06	.03
538	Lou Piniella	.15	.11	.06
539	Vern Ruhle	.08	.06	.03
540	Andre Dawson	.50	.40	.20
541	Barry Evans	.08	.06	.03
542	Ned Yost	.08	.06	.03
543	Bill Robinson	.08	.06	.03
544	Larry Christenson	.08	.06	.03
545	Reggie Smith	.15	.11	.06
546	Reggie Smith IA	.10	.08	.04
547	Rod Carew AS	.35	.25	.14
548	Willie Randolph AS	.12	.09	.05
549	George Brett AS	.60	.45	.25
550	Bucky Dent AS	.12	.09	.05
551	Reggie Jackson AS	.50	.40	.20
552	Ken Singleton AS	.12	.09	.05
553	Dave Winfield AS	.40	.30	.15
554	Carlton Fisk AS	.20	.15	.08
555	Scott McGregor AS	.12	.09	.05
556	Jack Morris AS	.20	.15	.08
557	Rich Gossage AS	.20	.15	.08
558	John Tudor	.30	.25	.12
559	Indians Batting & Pitching Ldrs. (Bert Blyleven, Mike Hargrove)	.15	.11	.06
560	Doug Corbett	.08	.06	.03
561	Cardinals Future Stars (Glenn Brummer, Luis DeLeon, Gene Roof)	.08	.06	.03
562	Mike O'Berry	.08	.06	.03
563	Ross Baumgarten	.08	.06	.03
564	Doug DeCinces	.15	.11	.06
565	Jackson Todd	.08	.06	.03
566	Mike Jorgensen	.08	.06	.03
567	Bob Babcock	.08	.06	.03
568	Joe Pettini	.08	.06	.03
569	Willie Randolph	.15	.11	.06
570	Willie Randolph IA	.10	.08	.04
571	Glenn Abbott	.08	.06	.03
572	Juan Beniquez	.08	.06	.03
573	Rick Waits	.08	.06	.03
574	Mike Ramsey	.08	.06	.03
575	Al Cowens	.08	.06	.03
576	Giants Batting & Pitching Ldrs. (Vida Blue, Milt May)	.15	.11	.06
577	Rick Monday	.12	.09	.05
578	Shooty Babitt	.08	.06	.03
579	*Rick Mahler*(FC)	.30	.25	.12
580	Bobby Bonds	.15	.11	.06
581	Ron Reed	.08	.06	.03
582	Luis Pujols	.08	.06	.03

#	Player	MT	NR MT	EX
583	Tippy Martinez	.08	.06	.03
584	Hosken Powell	.08	.06	.03
585	Rollie Fingers	.30	.25	.12
586	Rollie Fingers IA	.15	.11	.06
587	Tim Lollar	.08	.06	.03
588	Dale Berra	.08	.06	.03
589	Dave Stapleton	.08	.06	.03
590	Al Oliver	.20	.15	.08
591	Al Oliver IA	.10	.08	.04
592	Craig Swan	.08	.06	.03
593	Billy Smith	.08	.06	.03
594	Renie Martin	.08	.06	.03
595	Dave Collins	.10	.08	.04
596	Damaso Garcia	.08	.06	.03
597	Wayne Nordhagen	.08	.06	.03
598	Bob Galasso	.08	.06	.03
599	White Sox Future Stars (Jay Loviglio, Reggie Patterson, Leo Sutherland)	.08	.06	.03
600	Dave Winfield	.60	.45	.25
601	Sid Monge	.08	.06	.03
602	Freddie Patek	.08	.06	.03
603	Rich Hebner	.08	.06	.03
604	Orlando Sanchez	.08	.06	.03
605	Steve Rogers	.10	.08	.04
606	Blue Jays Batting & Pitching Ldrs. (John Mayberry, Dave Stieb)	.15	.11	.06
607	Leon Durham	.10	.08	.04
608	Jerry Royster	.08	.06	.03
609	Rick Sutcliffe	.25	.20	.10
610	Rickey Henderson	2.75	2.00	1.00
611	Joe Niekro	.20	.15	.08
612	Gary Ward	.10	.08	.04
613	Jim Gantner	.10	.08	.04
614	Juan Eichelberger	.08	.06	.03
615	Bob Boone	.12	.09	.05
616	Bob Boone IA	.10	.08	.04
617	Scott McGregor	.10	.08	.04
618	Tim Foli	.08	.06	.03
619	Bill Campbell	.08	.06	.03
620	Ken Griffey	.15	.11	.06
621	Ken Griffey IA	.10	.08	.04
622	Dennis Lamp	.08	.06	.03
623	Mets Future Stars (Ron Gardenhire, *Terry Leach*, Tim Leary)(FC)	.90	.70	.35
624	Fergie Jenkins	.25	.20	.10
625	Hal McRae	.15	.11	.06
626	Randy Jones	.10	.08	.04
627	Enos Cabell	.08	.06	.03
628	Bill Travers	.08	.06	.03
629	Johnny Wockenfuss	.08	.06	.03
630	Joe Charboneau	.10	.08	.04
631	Gene Tenace	.10	.08	.04
632	Bryan Clark	.08	.06	.03
633	Mitchell Page	.08	.06	.03
634	Checklist 529-660	.12	.09	.05
635	Ron Davis	.10	.08	.04
636	Phillies Batting & Pitching Ldrs. (Steve Carlton, Pete Rose)	.50	.40	.20
637	Rick Camp	.08	.06	.03
638	John Milner	.08	.06	.03
639	Ken Kravec	.08	.06	.03
640	Cesar Cedeno	.15	.11	.06
641	Steve Mura	.08	.06	.03
642	Mike Scioscia	.10	.08	.04
643	Pete Vuckovich	.10	.08	.04
644	John Castino	.08	.06	.03
645	Frank White	.12	.09	.05
646	Frank White IA	.10	.08	.04
647	Warren Brusstar	.08	.06	.03
648	Jose Morales	.08	.06	.03
649	Ken Clay	.08	.06	.03
650	Carl Yastrzemski	1.25	.90	.50
651	Carl Yastrzemski IA	.60	.45	.25
652	Steve Nicosia	.08	.06	.03
653	Angels Future Stars (*Tom Brunansky*, Luis Sanchez, Daryl Sconiers)	2.25	1.75	.90
654	Jim Morrison	.08	.06	.03
655	Joel Youngblood	.08	.06	.03
656	Eddie Whitson	.08	.06	.03
657	Tom Poquette	.08	.06	.03
658	Tito Landrum	.08	.06	.03
659	Fred Martinez	.08	.06	.03
660	Dave Concepcion	.15	.11	.06
661	Dave Concepcion IA	.10	.08	.04
662	Luis Salazar	.08	.06	.03
663	Hector Cruz	.08	.06	.03
664	Dan Spillner	.08	.06	.03
665	Jim Clancy	.12	.09	.05
666	Tigers Batting & Pitching Ldrs. (Steve Kemp, Dan Petry)	.15	.11	.06
667	Jeff Reardon	.25	.20	.10
668	Dale Murphy	2.00	1.50	.80
669	Larry Milbourne	.08	.06	.03
670	Steve Kemp	.12	.09	.05
671	Mike Davis	.10	.08	.04
672	Bob Knepper	.12	.09	.05
673	Keith Drumright	.08	.06	.03
674	Dave Goltz	.10	.08	.04
675	Cecil Cooper	.20	.15	.08
676	Sal Butera	.08	.06	.03
677	Alfredo Griffin	.12	.09	.05
678	Tom Paciorek	.08	.06	.03
679	Sammy Stewart	.08	.06	.03
680	Gary Matthews	.12	.09	.05
681	Dodgers Future Stars (Mike Marshall, Ron Roenicke, *Steve Sax*)(FC)	3.75	2.75	1.50
682	Jesse Jefferson	.08	.06	.03
683	Phil Garner	.10	.08	.04
684	Harold Baines	.70	.50	.30
685	Bert Blyleven	.20	.15	.08
686	Gary Allenson	.08	.06	.03
687	Greg Minton	.08	.06	.03
688	Leon Roberts	.08	.06	.03
689	Lary Sorensen	.08	.06	.03
690	Dave Kingman	.20	.15	.08
691	Dan Schatzeder	.08	.06	.03
692	Wayne Gross	.08	.06	.03
693	Cesar Geronimo	.08	.06	.03
694	Dave Wehrmeister	.08	.06	.03
695	Warren Cromartie	.08	.06	.03
696	Pirates Batting & Pitching Ldrs. (Bill Madlock, Buddy Solomon)	.15	.11	.06
697	John Montefusco	.08	.06	.03
698	Tony Scott	.08	.06	.03
699	Dick Tidrow	.08	.06	.03
700	George Foster	.25	.20	.10
701	George Foster IA	.12	.09	.05
702	Steve Renko	.08	.06	.03
703	Brewers Batting & Pitching Ldrs. (Cecil Cooper, Pete Vuckovich)	.15	.11	.06
704	Mickey Rivers	.10	.08	.04
705	Mickey Rivers IA	.10	.08	.04
706	Barry Foote	.08	.06	.03
707	Mark Bomback	.08	.06	.03
708	Gene Richards	.08	.06	.03
709	Don Money	.08	.06	.03
710	Jerry Reuss	.12	.09	.05
711	Mariners Future Stars (Dave Edler, *Dave Henderson*, Reggie Walton)	.90	.70	.35
712	Denny Martinez	.10	.08	.04
713	Del Unser	.08	.06	.03
714	Jerry Koosman	.12	.09	.05
715	Willie Stargell	.70	.50	.30
716	Willie Stargell IA	.30	.25	.12
717	Rick Miller	.08	.06	.03
718	Charlie Hough	.12	.09	.05
719	Jerry Narron	.08	.06	.03
720	Greg Luzinski	.20	.15	.08
721	Greg Luzinski IA	.12	.09	.05
722	Jerry Martin	.08	.06	.03
723	Junior Kennedy	.08	.06	.03
724	Dave Rosello	.08	.06	.03
725	Amos Otis	.10	.08	.04
726	Amos Otis IA	.10	.08	.04
727	Sixto Lezcano	.08	.06	.03
728	Aurelio Lopez	.08	.06	.03
729	Jim Spencer	.08	.06	.03
730	Gary Carter	.70	.50	.30
731	Padres Future Stars (Mike Armstrong, Doug Gwosdz, Fred Kuhaulua)	.08	.06	.03
732	Mike Lum	.08	.06	.03
733	Larry McWilliams	.08	.06	.03
734	Mike Ivie	.08	.06	.03
735	Rudy May	.08	.06	.03
736	Jerry Turner	.08	.06	.03
737	Reggie Cleveland	.08	.06	.03
738	Dave Engle	.08	.06	.03
739	Joey McLaughlin	.08	.06	.03
740	Dave Lopes	.12	.09	.05
741	Dave Lopes IA	.10	.08	.04
742	Dick Drago	.08	.06	.03
743	John Stearns	.08	.06	.03
744	*Mike Witt*(FC)	1.25	.90	.50
745	Bake McBride	.08	.06	.03
746	Andre Thornton	.12	.09	.05
747	John Lowenstein	.08	.06	.03
748	Marc Hill	.08	.06	.03
749	Bob Shirley	.08	.06	.03
750	Jim Rice	.90	.70	.35
751	Rick Honeycutt	.08	.06	.03
752	Lee Lacy	.08	.06	.03
753	Tom Brookens	.08	.06	.03

		MT	NR MT	EX
754	Joe Morgan	.50	.40	.20
755	Joe Morgan IA	.20	.15	.08
756	Reds Batting & Pitching Ldrs. (Ken Griffey, Tom Seaver)	.30	.25	.12
757	Tom Underwood	.08	.06	.03
758	Claudell Washington	.12	.09	.05
759	Paul Splittorff	.08	.06	.03
760	Bill Buckner	.15	.11	.06
761	Dave Smith	.12	.09	.05
762	Mike Phillips	.08	.06	.03
763	Tom Hume	.08	.06	.03
764	Steve Swisher	.08	.06	.03
765	Gorman Thomas	.12	.09	.05
766	Twins Future Stars (Lenny Faedo, *Kent Hrbek, Tim Laudner*)(FC)	5.00	3.75	2.00
767	Roy Smalley	.08	.06	.03
768	Jerry Garvin	.08	.06	.03
769	Richie Zisk	.10	.08	.04
770	Rich Gossage	.35	.25	.14
771	Rich Gossage IA	.15	.11	.06
772	Bert Campaneris	.12	.09	.05
773	John Denny	.08	.06	.03
774	Jay Johnstone	.10	.08	.04
775	Bob Forsch	.10	.08	.04
776	Mark Belanger	.10	.08	.04
777	Tom Griffin	.08	.06	.03
778	Kevin Hickey	.08	.06	.03
779	Grant Jackson	.08	.06	.03
780	Pete Rose	2.25	1.75	.90
781	Pete Rose IA	1.00	.70	.40
782	Frank Taveras	.08	.06	.03
783	*Greg Harris*(FC)	.15	.11	.06
784	Milt Wilcox	.08	.06	.03
785	Dan Driessen	.10	.08	.04
786	Red Sox Batting & Pitching Ldrs. (Carney Lansford, Mike Torrez)	.12	.09	.05
787	Fred Stanley	.08	.06	.03
788	Woodie Fryman	.10	.08	.04
789	Checklist 661-792	.12	.09	.05
790	Larry Gura	.08	.06	.03
791	Bobby Brown	.08	.06	.03
792	Frank Tanana	.12	.09	.05

		MT	NR MT	EX
45	Bob Knepper	.04	.03	.02
49	Ken Landreaux	.03	.02	.01
53	Burt Hooton	.03	.02	.01
57	Andre Dawson	.12	.09	.05
61	Gary Carter	.20	.15	.08
65	Joel Youngblood	.03	.02	.01
69	Ellis Valentine	.03	.02	.01
73	Garry Maddox	.04	.03	.02
77	Bob Boone	.04	.03	.02
81	Omar Moreno	.03	.02	.01
85	Willie Stargell	.20	.15	.08
89	Ken Oberkfell	.03	.02	.01
93	Darrell Porter	.04	.03	.02
97	Juan Eichelberger	.03	.02	.01
101	Luis Salazar	.03	.02	.01
105	Enos Cabell	.03	.02	.01
109	Larry Herndon	.03	.02	.01
143	Scott McGregor	.04	.03	.02
148	Mike Flanagan	.06	.05	.02
151	Mike Torrez	.04	.03	.02
156	Carney Lansford	.06	.05	.02
161	Fred Lynn	.10	.08	.04
166	Rich Dotson	.04	.03	.02
171	Tony Bernazard	.03	.02	.01
176	Bo Diaz	.04	.03	.02
181	Alan Trammell	.15	.11	.06
186	Milt Wilcox	.03	.02	.01
191	Dennis Leonard	.04	.03	.02
196	Willie Aikens	.03	.02	.01
201	Ted Simmons	.08	.06	.03
206	Hosken Powell	.03	.02	.01
211	Roger Erickson	.03	.02	.01
215	Graig Nettles	.06	.05	.02
216	Reggie Jackson	.25	.20	.10
221	Rickey Henderson	.25	.20	.10
226	Cliff Johnson	.03	.02	.01
231	Jeff Burroughs	.04	.03	.02
236	Tom Paciorek	.03	.02	.01
241	Pat Putnam	.03	.02	.01
246	Lloyd Moseby	.06	.05	.02
251	Barry Bonnell	.03	.02	.01

NOTE: A card number in parentheses ( ) indicates the set is unnumbered.

A player's name in *italic* type indicates a rookie card. An (FC) indicates a player's first card for that particular card company.

1982 Topps Insert Stickers

This 48-player set is actually an abbreviated version of the regular 1982 Topps sticker set with different backs. Used to promote the 1982 sticker set, Topps inserted these stickers in its baseball card wax packs. They are identical to the regular 1982 stickers, except for the backs, which advertise that the Topps sticker album will be "Coming Soon." The 48 stickers retain the same numbers used in the regular sticker set, resulting in the smaller set being skip-numbered.

		MT	NR MT	EX
Complete Set:		2.00	1.50	.80
Common Player:		.03	.02	.01
17	Chris Chambliss	.04	.03	.02
21	Bruce Benedict	.03	.02	.01
25	Leon Durham	.06	.05	.02
29	Bill Buckner	.06	.05	.02
33	Dave Collins	.04	.03	.02
37	Dave Concepcion	.06	.05	.02
41	Nolan Ryan	.15	.11	.06

1982 Topps Stickers

The 1982 Topps sticker set is complete at 260 stickers and includes another series of "foil" All-Stars. The stickers measure 1-15/16" by 2-9/16" and feature full-color photos surrounded by a red border for American League players or a blue border for National League players. They are numbered on both the front and back and were designed to be mounted in a special album.

		MT	NR MT	EX
Complete Set:		15.00	11.00	6.00
Common Player:		.03	.02	.01
Sticker Album:		.80	.60	.30
1	Bill Madlock	.06	.05	.02
2	Carney Lansford	.06	.05	.02
3	Mike Schmidt	.25	.20	.10
4	Tony Armas, Dwight Evans, Bobby Grich, Eddie Murray	.12	.09	.05
5	Mike Schmidt	.25	.20	.10
6	Eddie Murray	.20	.15	.08
7	Tim Raines	.03	.02	.01
8	Rickey Henderson	.25	.20	.10
9	Tom Seaver	.20	.15	.08

#	Name	MT	NR MT	EX
10	Denny Martinez, Steve McCatty, Jack Morris, Pete Vuckovich	.06	.05	.02
11	Fernando Valenzuela	.15	.11	.06
12	Len Barker	.03	.02	.01
13	Nolan Ryan	.20	.15	.08
14	Steve McCatty	.03	.02	.01
15	Bruce Sutter	.08	.06	.03
16	Rollie Fingers	.10	.08	.04
17	Chris Chambliss	.04	.03	.02
18	Bob Horner	.08	.06	.03
19	Dale Murphy	.25	.20	.10
20	Phil Niekro	.12	.09	.05
21	Bruce Benedict	.03	.02	.01
22	Claudell Washington	.04	.03	.02
23	Glenn Hubbard	.03	.02	.01
24	Rick Camp	.03	.02	.01
25	Leon Durham	.06	.05	.02
26	Ken Reitz	.03	.02	.01
27	Dick Tidrow	.03	.02	.01
28	Tim Blackwell	.03	.02	.01
29	Bill Buckner	.06	.05	.02
30	Steve Henderson	.03	.02	.01
31	Mike Krukow	.04	.03	.02
32	Ivan DeJesus	.03	.02	.01
33	Dave Collins	.04	.03	.02
34	Ron Oester	.03	.02	.01
35	Johnny Bench	.25	.20	.10
36	Tom Seaver	.20	.15	.08
37	Dave Concepcion	.06	.05	.02
38	Ken Griffey	.06	.05	.02
39	Ray Knight	.06	.05	.02
40	George Foster	.08	.06	.03
41	Nolan Ryan	.20	.15	.08
42	Terry Puhl	.03	.02	.01
43	Art Howe	.03	.02	.01
44	Jose Cruz	.06	.05	.02
45	Bob Knepper	.06	.05	.02
46	Craig Reynolds	.03	.02	.01
47	Cesar Cedeno	.06	.05	.02
48	Alan Ashby	.03	.02	.01
49	Ken Landreaux	.03	.02	.01
50	Fernando Valenzuela	.15	.11	.06
51	Ron Cey	.06	.05	.02
52	Dusty Baker	.04	.03	.02
53	Burt Hooton	.04	.03	.02
54	Steve Garvey	.20	.15	.08
55	Pedro Guerrero	.12	.09	.05
56	Jerry Reuss	.06	.05	.02
57	Andre Dawson	.12	.09	.05
58	Chris Speier	.03	.02	.01
59	Steve Rogers	.03	.02	.01
60	Warren Cromartie	.03	.02	.01
61	Gary Carter	.20	.15	.08
62	Tim Raines	.20	.15	.08
63	Scott Sanderson	.03	.02	.01
64	Larry Parrish	.06	.05	.02
65	Joel Youngblood	.03	.02	.01
66	Neil Allen	.03	.02	.01
67	Lee Mazzilli	.04	.03	.02
68	Hubie Brooks	.06	.05	.02
69	Ellis Valentine	.03	.02	.01
70	Doug Flynn	.03	.02	.01
71	Pat Zachry	.03	.02	.01
72	Dave Kingman	.08	.06	.03
73	Garry Maddox	.04	.03	.02
74	Mike Schmidt	.25	.20	.10
75	Steve Carlton	.20	.15	.08
76	Manny Trillo	.04	.03	.02
77	Bob Boone	.04	.03	.02
78	Pete Rose	.40	.30	.15
79	Gary Matthews	.04	.03	.02
80	Larry Bowa	.06	.05	.02
81	Omar Moreno	.03	.02	.01
82	Rick Rhoden	.04	.03	.02
83	Bill Madlock	.06	.05	.02
84	Mike Easler	.04	.03	.02
85	Willie Stargell	.20	.15	.08
86	Jim Bibby	.03	.02	.01
87	Dave Parker	.12	.09	.05
88	Tim Foli	.03	.02	.01
89	Ken Oberkfell	.03	.02	.01
90	Bob Forsch	.04	.03	.02
91	George Hendrick	.04	.03	.02
92	Keith Hernandez	.12	.09	.05
93	Darrell Porter	.04	.03	.02
94	Bruce Sutter	.08	.06	.03
95	Sixto Lezcano	.03	.02	.01
96	Garry Templeton	.04	.03	.02
97	Juan Eichelberger	.03	.02	.01
98	Broderick Perkins	.03	.02	.01
99	Ruppert Jones	.03	.02	.01
100	Terry Kennedy	.04	.03	.02
101	Luis Salazar	.03	.02	.01
102	Gary Lucas	.03	.02	.01
103	Gene Richards	.03	.02	.01
104	Ozzie Smith	.10	.08	.04
105	Enos Cabell	.03	.02	.01
106	Jack Clark	.10	.08	.04
107	Greg Minton	.03	.02	.01
108	Johnnie LeMaster	.03	.02	.01
109	Larry Herndon	.03	.02	.01
110	Milt May	.03	.02	.01
111	Vida Blue	.06	.05	.02
112	Darrell Evans	.08	.06	.03
113	Len Barker	.03	.02	.01
114	Julio Cruz	.03	.02	.01
115	Billy Martin	.08	.06	.03
116	Tim Raines	.20	.15	.08
117	Pete Rose	.40	.30	.15
118	Bill Stein	.03	.02	.01
119	Fernando Valenzuela	.15	.11	.06
120	Carl Yastrzemski	.25	.20	.10
121	Pete Rose	.50	.40	.20
122	Manny Trillo	.15	.11	.06
123	Mike Schmidt	.40	.30	.15
124	Dave Concepcion	.20	.15	.08
125	Andre Dawson	.25	.20	.10
126	George Foster	.20	.15	.08
127	Dave Parker	.25	.20	.10
128	Gary Carter	.30	.25	.12
129	Steve Carlton	.30	.25	.12
130	Bruce Sutter	.25	.20	.10
131	Rod Carew	.40	.30	.15
132	Jerry Remy	.15	.11	.06
133	George Brett	.40	.30	.15
134	Rick Burleson	.15	.11	.06
135	Dwight Evans	.25	.20	.10
136	Ken Singleton	.20	.15	.08
137	Dave Winfield	.30	.25	.12
138	Carlton Fisk	.25	.20	.10
139	Jack Morris	.25	.20	.10
140	Rich Gossage	.25	.20	.10
141	Al Bumbry	.04	.03	.02
142	Doug DeCinces	.06	.05	.02
143	Scott McGregor	.04	.03	.02
144	Ken Singleton	.06	.05	.02
145	Eddie Murray	.20	.15	.08
146	Jim Palmer	.15	.11	.06
147	Rich Dauer	.03	.02	.01
148	Mike Flanagan	.04	.03	.02
149	Jerry Remy	.03	.02	.01
150	Jim Rice	.20	.15	.08
151	Mike Torrez	.04	.03	.02
152	Tony Perez	.10	.08	.04
153	Dwight Evans	.10	.08	.04
154	Mark Clear	.03	.02	.01
155	Carl Yastrzemski	.25	.20	.10
156	Carney Lansford	.06	.05	.02
157	Rick Burleson	.04	.03	.02
158	Don Baylor	.08	.06	.03
159	Ken Forsch	.03	.02	.01
160	Rod Carew	.20	.15	.08
161	Fred Lynn	.10	.08	.04
162	Bob Grich	.06	.05	.02
163	Dan Ford	.03	.02	.01
164	Butch Hobson	.03	.02	.01
165	Greg Luzinski	.08	.06	.03
166	Rich Dotson	.04	.03	.02
167	Billy Almon	.03	.02	.01
168	Chet Lemon	.04	.03	.02
169	Steve Trout	.03	.02	.01
170	Carlton Fisk	.12	.09	.05
171	Tony Bernazard	.03	.02	.01
172	Ron LeFlore	.04	.03	.02
173	Bert Blyleven	.08	.06	.03
174	Andre Thornton	.06	.05	.02
175	Jorge Orta	.03	.02	.01
176	Bo Diaz	.04	.03	.02
177	Toby Harrah	.04	.03	.02
178	Len Barker	.03	.02	.01
179	Rick Manning	.03	.02	.01
180	Mike Hargrove	.04	.03	.02
181	Alan Trammell	.15	.11	.06
182	Al Cowens	.03	.02	.01
183	Jack Morris	.12	.09	.05
184	Kirk Gibson	.15	.11	.06
185	Steve Kemp	.04	.03	.02
186	Milt Wilcox	.03	.02	.01
187	Lou Whitaker	.12	.09	.05
188	Lance Parrish	.12	.09	.05
189	Willie Wilson	.08	.06	.03
190	George Brett	.25	.20	.10

		MT	NR MT	EX
191	Dennis Leonard	.04	.03	.02
192	John Wathan	.04	.03	.02
193	Frank White	.06	.05	.02
194	Amos Otis	.04	.03	.02
195	Larry Gura	.03	.02	.01
196	Willie Aikens	.03	.02	.01
197	Ben Oglivie	.06	.05	.02
198	Rollie Fingers	.10	.08	.04
199	Cecil Cooper	.08	.06	.03
200	Paul Molitor	.10	.08	.04
201	Ted Simmons	.08	.06	.03
202	Pete Vuckovich	.04	.03	.02
203	Robin Yount	.15	.11	.06
204	Gorman Thomas	.04	.03	.02
205	Rob Wilfong	.03	.02	.01
206	Hosken Powell	.03	.02	.01
207	Roy Smalley	.03	.02	.01
208	Butch Wynegar	.04	.03	.02
209	John Castino	.03	.02	.01
210	Doug Corbett	.03	.02	.01
211	Roger Erickson	.03	.02	.01
212	Mickey Hatcher	.03	.02	.01
213	Dave Winfield	.20	.15	.08
214	Tommy John	.10	.08	.04
215	Graig Nettles	.06	.05	.02
216	Reggie Jackson	.25	.20	.10
217	Rich Gossage	.10	.08	.04
218	Rick Cerone	.03	.02	.01
219	Willie Randolph	.06	.05	.02
220	Jerry Mumphrey	.03	.02	.01
221	Rickey Henderson	.20	.15	.08
222	Mike Norris	.03	.02	.01
223	Jim Spencer	.03	.02	.01
224	Tony Armas	.04	.03	.02
225	Matt Keough	.03	.02	.01
226	Cliff Johnson	.03	.02	.01
227	Dwayne Murphy	.04	.03	.02
228	Steve McCatty	.03	.02	.01
229	Richie Zisk	.04	.03	.02
230	Lenny Randle	.03	.02	.01
231	Jeff Burroughs	.04	.03	.02
232	Bruce Bochte	.03	.02	.01
233	Gary Gray	.03	.02	.01
234	Floyd Bannister	.04	.03	.02
235	Julio Cruz	.03	.02	.01
236	Tom Paciorek	.03	.02	.01
237	Danny Darwin	.03	.02	.01
238	Buddy Bell	.06	.05	.02
239	Al Oliver	.06	.05	.02
240	Jim Sundberg	.04	.03	.02
241	Pat Putnam	.03	.02	.01
242	Steve Comer	.03	.02	.01
243	Mickey Rivers	.04	.03	.02
244	Bump Wills	.03	.02	.01
245	Damaso Garcia	.04	.03	.02
246	Lloyd Moseby	.06	.05	.02
247	Ernie Whitt	.03	.02	.01
248	John Mayberry	.03	.02	.01
249	Otto Velez	.03	.02	.01
250	Dave Stieb	.06	.05	.02
251	Barry Bonnell	.03	.02	.01
252	Alfredo Griffin	.04	.03	.02
253	1981 N.L. Championship (Gary Carter)	.10	.08	.04
254	1981 A.L. Championship (Mike Heath, Larry Milbourne)	.03	.02	.01
255	1981 World Champions (Los Angeles Dodgers Team)	.04	.03	.02
256	1981 World Champions (Los Angeles Dodgers Team)	.04	.03	.02
257	1981 World Series - Game 3 (Fernando Valenzuela)	.10	.08	.04
258	1981 World Series - Game 4 (Steve Garvey)	.10	.08	.04
259	1981 World Series - Game 5 (Jerry Reuss, Steve Yeager)	.03	.02	.01
260	1981 World Series - Game 6 (Pedro Guerrero)	.08	.06	.03

1982 Topps Traded

Topps released its second straight 132-card Traded set in September of 1982. Again, the 2-1/2" by 3-1/2" cards feature not only players who had been traded during the season, but also promising rookies who were given their first individual cards. The cards follow the basic design of the regular issues, but have

their backs printed in red rather than the regular-issue green. As in 1981, the cards were not available in normal retail outlets and could only be purchased through regular baseball card dealers. Unlike the previous year, the cards are numbered 1-132 with the letter "T" following the number.

		MT	NR MT	EX
Complete Set:		30.00	22.50	12.50
Common Player:		.10	.08	.04
1T	Doyle Alexander	.20	.15	.08
2T	Jesse Barfield	2.25	1.75	.90
3T	Ross Baumgarten	.10	.08	.04
4T	Steve Bedrosian	.80	.60	.30
5T	Mark Belanger	.15	.11	.06
6T	Kurt Bevacqua	.10	.08	.04
7T	Tim Blackwell	.10	.08	.04
8T	Vida Blue	.25	.20	.10
9T	Bob Boone	.20	.15	.08
10T	Larry Bowa	.25	.20	.10
11T	Dan Briggs	.10	.08	.04
12T	Bobby Brown	.10	.08	.04
13T	Tom Brunansky	1.50	1.25	.60
14T	Jeff Burroughs	.15	.11	.06
15T	Enos Cabell	.10	.08	.04
16T	Bill Campbell	.10	.08	.04
17T	Bobby Castillo	.10	.08	.04
18T	Bill Caudill	.10	.08	.04
19T	Cesar Cedeno	.20	.15	.08
20T	Dave Collins	.15	.11	.06
21T	Doug Corbett	.10	.08	.04
22T	Al Cowens	.10	.08	.04
23T	Chili Davis	1.00	.70	.40
24T	Dick Davis	.10	.08	.04
25T	Ron Davis	.10	.08	.04
26T	Doug DeCinces	.20	.15	.08
27T	Ivan DeJesus	.10	.08	.04
28T	Bob Dernier	.20	.15	.08
29T	Bo Diaz	.15	.11	.06
30T	Roger Erickson	.10	.08	.04
31T	Jim Essian	.10	.08	.04
32T	Ed Farmer	.10	.08	.04
33T	Doug Flynn	.10	.08	.04
34T	Tim Foli	.10	.08	.04
35T	Dan Ford	.10	.08	.04
36T	George Foster	.40	.30	.15
37T	Dave Frost	.10	.08	.04
38T	Rich Gale	.10	.08	.04
39T	Ron Gardenhire	.10	.08	.04
40T	Ken Griffey	.25	.20	.10
41T	Greg Harris	.15	.11	.06
42T	Von Hayes	1.25	.90	.50
43T	Larry Herndon	.15	.11	.06
44T	Kent Hrbek	5.00	3.75	2.00
45T	Mike Ivie	.10	.08	.04
46T	Grant Jackson	.10	.08	.04
47T	Reggie Jackson	3.00	2.25	1.25
48T	Ron Jackson	.10	.08	.04
49T	Fergie Jenkins	.40	.30	.15
50T	Lamar Johnson	.10	.08	.04
51T	Randy Johnson	.10	.08	.04
52T	Jay Johnstone	.15	.11	.06
53T	Mick Kelleher	.10	.08	.04
54T	Steve Kemp	.15	.11	.06
55T	Junior Kennedy	.10	.08	.04
56T	Jim Kern	.10	.08	.04
57T	Ray Knight	.20	.15	.08
58T	Wayne Krenchicki	.10	.08	.04
59T	Mike Krukow	.15	.11	.06

		MT	NR MT	EX
60T	Duane Kuiper	.10	.08	.04
61T	Mike LaCoss	.10	.08	.04
62T	Chet Lemon	.15	.11	.06
63T	Sixto Lezcano	.10	.08	.04
64T	Dave Lopes	.15	.11	.06
65T	Jerry Martin	.10	.08	.04
66T	Renie Martin	.10	.08	.04
67T	John Mayberry	.15	.11	.06
68T	Lee Mazzilli	.15	.11	.06
69T	Bake McBride	.10	.08	.04
70T	Dan Meyer	.10	.08	.04
71T	Larry Milbourne	.10	.08	.04
72T	Eddie Milner(FC)	.20	.15	.08
73T	Sid Monge	.10	.08	.04
74T	Jose Morales	.10	.08	.04
75T	Keith Moreland	.20	.15	.08
76T	John Montefusco	.10	.08	.04
77T	Jim Morrison	.10	.08	.04
78T	Rance Mulliniks	.10	.08	.04
79T	Steve Mura	.10	.08	.04
80T	Gene Nelson	.10	.08	.04
81T	Joe Nolan	.10	.08	.04
82T	Dickie Noles	.10	.08	.04
83T	Al Oliver	.30	.25	.12
84T	Jorge Orta	.10	.08	.04
85T	Tom Paciorek	.10	.08	.04
86T	Larry Parrish	.20	.15	.08
87T	Jack Perconte	.10	.08	.04
88T	Gaylord Perry	1.25	.90	.50
89T	Rob Picciolo	.10	.08	.04
90T	Joe Pittman	.10	.08	.04
91T	Hosken Powell	.10	.08	.04
92T	Mike Proly	.10	.08	.04
93T	Greg Pryor	.10	.08	.04
94T	Charlie Puleo(FC)	.15	.11	.06
95T	Shane Rawley	.20	.15	.08
96T	Johnny Ray	.80	.60	.30
97T	Dave Revering	.10	.08	.04
98T	Cal Ripken	10.00	7.50	4.00
99T	Allen Ripley	.10	.08	.04
100T	Bill Robinson	.10	.08	.04
101T	Aurelio Rodriguez	.15	.11	.06
102T	Joe Rudi	.20	.15	.08
103T	Steve Sax	4.00	3.00	1.50
104T	Dan Schatzeder	.10	.08	.04
105T	Bob Shirley	.10	.08	.04
106T	Eric Show(FC)	.70	.50	.30
107T	Roy Smalley	.15	.11	.06
108T	Lonnie Smith	.15	.11	.06
109T	Ozzie Smith	3.50	2.75	1.50
110T	Reggie Smith	.20	.15	.08
111T	Lary Sorensen	.10	.08	.04
112T	Elias Sosa	.10	.08	.04
113T	Mike Stanton	.10	.08	.04
114T	Steve Stroughter	.10	.08	.04
115T	Champ Summers	.10	.08	.04
116T	Rick Sutcliffe	.50	.40	.20
117T	Frank Tanana	.20	.15	.08
118T	Frank Taveras	.10	.08	.04
119T	Garry Templeton	.20	.15	.08
120T	Alex Trevino	.10	.08	.04
121T	Jerry Turner	.10	.08	.04
122T	Ed Vande Berg(FC)	.15	.11	.06
123T	Tom Veryzer	.10	.08	.04
124T	Ron Washington	.10	.08	.04
125T	Bob Watson	.15	.11	.06
126T	Dennis Werth	.10	.08	.04
127T	Eddie Whitson	.15	.11	.06
128T	Rob Wilfong	.10	.08	.04
129T	Bump Wills	.10	.08	.04
130T	Gary Woods	.10	.08	.04
131T	Butch Wynegar	.15	.11	.06
132T	Checklist 1-132	.10	.08	.04

1983 Topps

The 1983 Topps set totals 792 cards. Missing among the regular 2-1/2" by 3-1/2" cards are some form of future stars cards, as Topps was saving them for the now-established late season "Traded" set. The 1983 cards carry a large color photo as well as a smaller color photo on the front, quite similar in design to the 1963 set. Team colors frame the card, which, at the bottom, have the player's name, position and team. At the upper right-hand corner is a Topps Logo. The backs are horizontal and include statistics, personal information and 1982 highlights.

Specialty cards include record-breaking performances, league leaders, All-Stars, numbered checklists "Team Leaders" and "Super Veteran" cards which are horizontal with a current and first-season picture of the honored player.

		MT	NR MT	EX
	Complete Set:	90.00	68.00	36.00
	Common Player:	.08	.06	.03
1	Record Breaker (Tony Armas)	.12	.09	.05
2	Record Breaker (Rickey Henderson)	.35	.25	.14
3	Record Breaker (Greg Minton)	.08	.06	.03
4	Record Breaker (Lance Parrish)	.20	.15	.08
5	Record Breaker (Manny Trillo)	.08	.06	.03
6	Record Breaker (John Wathan)	.08	.06	.03
7	Gene Richards	.08	.06	.03
8	Steve Balboni	.10	.08	.04
9	Joey McLaughlin	.08	.06	.03
10	Gorman Thomas	.12	.09	.05
11	Billy Gardner	.08	.06	.03
12	Paul Mirabella	.08	.06	.03
13	Larry Herndon	.10	.08	.04
14	Frank LaCorte	.08	.06	.03
15	Ron Cey	.15	.11	.06
16	George Vukovich	.08	.06	.03
17	Kent Tekulve	.10	.08	.04
18	Super Veteran (Kent Tekulve)	.10	.08	.04
19	Oscar Gamble	.10	.08	.04
20	Carlton Fisk	.40	.30	.15
21	Orioles Batting & Pitching Ldrs. (Eddie Murray, Jim Palmer)	.35	.25	.14
22	Randy Martz	.08	.06	.03
23	Mike Heath	.08	.06	.03
24	Steve Mura	.08	.06	.03
25	Hal McRae	.15	.11	.06
26	Jerry Royster	.08	.06	.03
27	Doug Corbett	.08	.06	.03
28	Bruce Bochte	.08	.06	.03
29	Randy Jones	.10	.08	.04
30	Jim Rice	.70	.50	.30
31	Bill Gullickson	.08	.06	.03
32	Dave Bergman	.08	.06	.03
33	Jack O'Connor	.08	.06	.03
34	Paul Householder	.08	.06	.03
35	Rollie Fingers	.30	.25	.12
36	Super Veteran (Rollie Fingers)	.15	.11	.06
37	Darrell Johnson	.08	.06	.03
38	Tim Flannery	.08	.06	.03
39	Terry Puhl	.08	.06	.03
40	Fernando Valenzuela	.50	.40	.20
41	Jerry Turner	.08	.06	.03
42	Dale Murray	.08	.06	.03
43	Bob Dernier	.08	.06	.03
44	Don Robinson	.10	.08	.04
45	John Mayberry	.10	.08	.04
46	Richard Dotson	.12	.09	.05
47	Dave McKay	.08	.06	.03
48	Lary Sorensen	.08	.06	.03
49	Willie McGee(FC)	1.25	.90	.50
50	Bob Horner	.20	.15	.08
51	Cubs Batting & Pitching Ldrs. (Leon Durham, Fergie Jenkins)	.15	.11	.06
52	Onix Concepcion(FC)	.08	.06	.03
53	Mike Witt	.30	.25	.12
54	Jim Maler	.08	.06	.03
55	Mookie Wilson	.12	.09	.05
56	Chuck Rainey	.08	.06	.03
57	Tim Blackwell	.08	.06	.03

		MT	NR MT	EX
58	Al Holland	.08	.06	.03
59	Benny Ayala	.08	.06	.03
60	Johnny Bench	.60	.45	.25
61	Super Veteran (Johnny Bench)	.30	.25	.12
62	Bob McClure	.08	.06	.03
63	Rick Monday	.12	.09	.05
64	Bill Stein	.08	.06	.03
65	Jack Morris	.35	.25	.14
66	Bob Lillis	.08	.06	.03
67	Sal Butera	.08	.06	.03
68	*Eric Show*	.30	.25	.12
69	Lee Lacy	.08	.06	.03
70	Steve Carlton	.60	.45	.25
71	Super Veteran (Steve Carlton)	.30	.25	.12
72	Tom Paciorek	.08	.06	.03
73	Allen Ripley	.08	.06	.03
74	Julio Gonzalez	.08	.06	.03
75	Amos Otis	.10	.08	.04
76	Rick Mahler	.12	.09	.05
77	Hosken Powell	.08	.06	.03
78	Bill Caudill	.08	.06	.03
79	Mick Kelleher	.08	.06	.03
80	George Foster	.20	.15	.08
81	Yankees Batting & Pitching Ldrs. (Jerry Mumphrey, Dave Righetti)	.15	.11	.06
82	Bruce Hurst	.15	.11	.06
83	*Ryne Sandberg*(FC)	9.00	6.75	3.50
84	Milt May	.08	.06	.03
85	Ken Singleton	.12	.09	.05
86	Tom Hume	.08	.06	.03
87	Joe Rudi	.12	.09	.05
88	Jim Gantner	.10	.08	.04
89	Leon Roberts	.08	.06	.03
90	Jerry Reuss	.12	.09	.05
91	Larry Milbourne	.08	.06	.03
92	Mike LaCoss	.08	.06	.03
93	John Castino	.08	.06	.03
94	Dave Edwards	.08	.06	.03
95	Alan Trammell	.50	.40	.20
96	Dick Howser	.08	.06	.03
97	Ross Baumgarten	.08	.06	.03
98	Vance Law	.10	.08	.04
99	Dickie Noles	.08	.06	.03
100	Pete Rose	1.75	1.25	.70
101	Super Veteran (Pete Rose)	.80	.60	.30
102	Dave Beard	.08	.06	.03
103	Darrell Porter	.10	.08	.04
104	Bob Walk	.08	.06	.03
105	Don Baylor	.15	.11	.06
106	Gene Nelson	.08	.06	.03
107	Mike Jorgensen	.08	.06	.03
108	Glenn Hoffman	.08	.06	.03
109	Luis Leal	.08	.06	.03
110	Ken Griffey	.15	.11	.06
111	Expos Batting & Pitching Ldrs. (Al Oliver, Steve Rogers)	.15	.11	.06
112	Bob Shirley	.08	.06	.03
113	Ron Roenicke	.08	.06	.03
114	Jim Slaton	.08	.06	.03
115	Chili Davis	.20	.15	.08
116	Dave Schmidt	.10	.08	.04
117	Alan Knicely	.08	.06	.03
118	Chris Welsh	.08	.06	.03
119	Tom Brookens	.08	.06	.03
120	Len Barker	.10	.08	.04
121	Mickey Hatcher	.10	.08	.04
122	Jimmy Smith	.08	.06	.03
123	George Frazier	.08	.06	.03
124	Marc Hill	.08	.06	.03
125	Leon Durham	.10	.08	.04
126	Joe Torre	.10	.08	.04
127	Preston Hanna	.08	.06	.03
128	Mike Ramsey	.08	.06	.03
129	Checklist 1-132	.12	.09	.05
130	Dave Stieb	.20	.15	.08
131	Ed Ott	.08	.06	.03
132	Todd Cruz	.08	.06	.03
133	Jim Barr	.08	.06	.03
134	Hubie Brooks	.15	.11	.06
135	Dwight Evans	.25	.20	.10
136	Willie Aikens	.08	.06	.03
137	Woodie Fryman	.10	.08	.04
138	Rick Dempsey	.10	.08	.04
139	Bruce Berenyi	.08	.06	.03
140	Willie Randolph	.12	.09	.05
141	Indians Batting & Pitching Ldrs. (Toby Harrah, Rick Sutcliffe)	.12	.09	.05
142	Mike Caldwell	.08	.06	.03
143	Joe Pettini	.08	.06	.03
144	Mark Wagner	.08	.06	.03
145	Don Sutton	.40	.30	.15
146	Super Veteran (Don Sutton)	.20	.15	.08
147	Rick Leach	.08	.06	.03
148	Dave Roberts	.08	.06	.03
149	Johnny Ray	.15	.11	.06
150	Bruce Sutter	.20	.15	.08
151	Super Veteran (Bruce Sutter)	.12	.09	.05
152	Jay Johnstone	.10	.08	.04
153	Jerry Koosman	.12	.09	.05
154	Johnnie LeMaster	.08	.06	.03
155	Dan Quisenberry	.20	.15	.08
156	Billy Martin	.12	.09	.05
157	Steve Bedrosian	.25	.20	.10
158	Rob Wilfong	.08	.06	.03
159	Mike Stanton	.08	.06	.03
160	Dave Kingman	.20	.15	.08
161	Super Veteran (Dave Kingman)	.10	.08	.04
162	Mark Clear	.08	.06	.03
163	Cal Ripken	2.25	1.75	.90
164	Dave Palmer	.08	.06	.03
165	Dan Driessen	.10	.08	.04
166	John Pacella	.08	.06	.03
167	Mark Brouhard	.08	.06	.03
168	Juan Eichelberger	.08	.06	.03
169	Doug Flynn	.08	.06	.03
170	Steve Howe	.10	.08	.04
171	Giants Batting & Pitching Ldrs. (Bill Laskey, Joe Morgan)	.15	.11	.06
172	Vern Ruhle	.08	.06	.03
173	Jim Morrison	.08	.06	.03
174	Jerry Ujdur	.08	.06	.03
175	Bo Diaz	.10	.08	.04
176	Dave Righetti	.35	.25	.14
177	Harold Baines	.25	.20	.10
178	Luis Tiant	.15	.11	.06
179	Super Veteran (Luis Tiant)	.10	.08	.04
180	Rickey Henderson	1.00	.70	.40
181	Terry Felton	.08	.06	.03
182	Mike Fischlin	.08	.06	.03
183	*Ed Vande Berg*	.12	.09	.05
184	Bob Clark	.08	.06	.03
185	Tim Lollar	.08	.06	.03
186	Whitey Herzog	.10	.08	.04
187	Terry Leach	.12	.09	.05
188	Rick Miller	.08	.06	.03
189	Dan Schatzeder	.08	.06	.03
190	Cecil Cooper	.20	.15	.08
191	Joe Price	.08	.06	.03
192	Floyd Rayford	.08	.06	.03
193	Harry Spilman	.08	.06	.03
194	Cesar Geronimo	.08	.06	.03
195	Bob Stoddard	.08	.06	.03
196	Bill Fahey	.08	.06	.03
197	*Jim Eisenreich*(FC)	.15	.11	.06
198	Kiko Garcia	.08	.06	.03
199	Marty Bystrom	.08	.06	.03
200	Rod Carew	.70	.50	.30
201	Super Veteran (Rod Carew)	.35	.25	.14
202	Blue Jays Batting & Pitching Ldrs. (Damaso Garcia, Dave Stieb)	.12	.09	.05
203	Mike Morgan	.15	.11	.06
204	Junior Kennedy	.08	.06	.03
205	Dave Parker	.40	.30	.15
206	Ken Oberkfell	.08	.06	.03
207	Rick Camp	.08	.06	.03
208	Dan Meyer	.08	.06	.03
209	*Mike Moore*(FC)	1.25	.90	.50
210	Jack Clark	.30	.25	.12
211	John Denny	.08	.06	.03
212	John Stearns	.08	.06	.03
213	Tom Burgmeier	.08	.06	.03
214	Jerry White	.08	.06	.03
215	Mario Soto	.10	.08	.04
216	Tony LaRussa	.10	.08	.04
217	Tim Stoddard	.08	.06	.03
218	Roy Howell	.08	.06	.03
219	Mike Armstrong	.08	.06	.03
220	Dusty Baker	.12	.09	.05
221	Joe Niekro	.15	.11	.06
222	Damaso Garcia	.08	.06	.03
223	John Montefusco	.08	.06	.03
224	Mickey Rivers	.10	.08	.04
225	Enos Cabell	.08	.06	.03
226	Enrique Romo	.08	.06	.03
227	Chris Bando	.08	.06	.03
228	Joaquin Andujar	.10	.08	.04
229	Phillies Batting & Pitching Ldrs. (Steve Carlton, Bo Diaz)	.20	.15	.08
230	Fergie Jenkins	.25	.20	.10
231	Super Veteran (Fergie Jenkins)	.12	.09	.05
232	Tom Brunansky	.30	.25	.12
233	Wayne Gross	.08	.06	.03

#	Name	MT	NR MT	EX
234	Larry Andersen	.08	.06	.03
235	Claudell Washington	.10	.08	.04
236	Steve Renko	.08	.06	.03
237	Dan Norman	.08	.06	.03
238	*Bud Black*(FC)	.25	.20	.10
239	Dave Stapleton	.08	.06	.03
240	Rich Gossage	.30	.25	.12
241	Super Veteran (Rich Gossage)	.15	.11	.06
242	Joe Nolan	.08	.06	.03
243	Duane Walker	.08	.06	.03
244	Dwight Bernard	.08	.06	.03
245	Steve Sax	.35	.25	.14
246	George Bamberger	.08	.06	.03
247	Dave Smith	.12	.09	.05
248	Bake McBride	.08	.06	.03
249	Checklist 133-264	.12	.09	.05
250	Bill Buckner	.15	.11	.06
251	*Alan Wiggins*(FC)	.08	.06	.03
252	Luis Aguayo	.08	.06	.03
253	Larry McWilliams	.08	.06	.03
254	Rick Cerone	.08	.06	.03
255	Gene Garber	.08	.06	.03
256	Super Veteran (Gene Garber)	.08	.06	.03
257	Jesse Barfield	.50	.40	.20
258	Manny Castillo	.08	.06	.03
259	Jeff Jones	.08	.06	.03
260	Steve Kemp	.12	.09	.05
261	Tigers Batting & Pitching Ldrs. (Larry Herndon, Dan Petry)	.10	.08	.04
262	Ron Jackson	.08	.06	.03
263	Renie Martin	.08	.06	.03
264	Jamie Quirk	.08	.06	.03
265	Joel Youngblood	.08	.06	.03
266	Paul Boris	.08	.06	.03
267	Terry Francona	.08	.06	.03
268	*Storm Davis*(FC)	.70	.50	.30
269	Ron Oester	.08	.06	.03
270	Dennis Eckersley	.20	.15	.08
271	Ed Romero	.08	.06	.03
272	Frank Tanana	.12	.09	.05
273	Mark Belanger	.10	.08	.04
274	Terry Kennedy	.12	.09	.05
275	Ray Knight	.12	.09	.05
276	Gene Mauch	.10	.08	.04
277	Rance Mulliniks	.08	.06	.03
278	Kevin Hickey	.08	.06	.03
279	Greg Gross	.08	.06	.03
280	Bert Blyleven	.20	.15	.08
281	Andre Robertson	.08	.06	.03
282	Reggie Smith	.12	.09	.05
283	Super Veteran (Reggie Smith)	.10	.08	.04
284	Jeff Lahti	.08	.06	.03
285	Lance Parrish	.40	.30	.15
286	Rick Langford	.08	.06	.03
287	Bobby Brown	.08	.06	.03
288	*Joe Cowley*(FC)	.12	.09	.05
289	Jerry Dybzinski	.08	.06	.03
290	Jeff Reardon	.15	.11	.06
291	Pirates Batting & Pitching Ldrs. (John Candelaria, Bill Madlock)	.15	.11	.06
292	Craig Swan	.08	.06	.03
293	Glenn Gulliver	.08	.06	.03
294	Dave Engle	.08	.06	.03
295	Jerry Remy	.08	.06	.03
296	Greg Harris	.08	.06	.03
297	Ned Yost	.08	.06	.03
298	Floyd Chiffer	.08	.06	.03
299	George Wright	.08	.06	.03
300	Mike Schmidt	1.25	.90	.50
301	Super Veteran (Mike Schmidt)	.60	.45	.25
302	Ernie Whitt	.10	.08	.04
303	Miguel Dilone	.08	.06	.03
304	Dave Rucker	.08	.06	.03
305	Larry Bowa	.15	.11	.06
306	Tom Lasorda	.12	.09	.05
307	Lou Piniella	.15	.11	.06
308	Jesus Vega	.08	.06	.03
309	Jeff Leonard	.12	.09	.05
310	Greg Luzinski	.15	.11	.06
311	Glenn Brummer	.08	.06	.03
312	Brian Kingman	.08	.06	.03
313	Gary Gray	.08	.06	.03
314	Ken Dayley(FC)	.15	.11	.06
315	Rick Burleson	.10	.08	.04
316	Paul Splittorff	.08	.06	.03
317	Gary Rajsich	.08	.06	.03
318	John Tudor	.15	.11	.06
319	Lenn Sakata	.08	.06	.03
320	Steve Rogers	.10	.08	.04
321	Brewers Batting & Pitching Ldrs. (Pete Vuckovich, Robin Yount)	.20	.15	.08
322	Dave Van Gorder	.08	.06	.03
323	Luis DeLeon	.08	.06	.03
324	Mike Marshall	.30	.25	.12
325	Von Hayes	.20	.15	.08
326	Garth Iorg	.08	.06	.03
327	Bobby Castillo	.08	.06	.03
328	Craig Reynolds	.08	.06	.03
329	Randy Niemann	.08	.06	.03
330	Buddy Bell	.15	.11	.06
331	Mike Krukow	.10	.08	.04
332	*Glenn Wilson*(FC)	.30	.25	.12
333	Dave LaRoche	.08	.06	.03
334	Super Veteran (Dave LaRoche)	.08	.06	.03
335	Steve Henderson	.08	.06	.03
336	Rene Lachemann	.08	.06	.03
337	Tito Landrum	.08	.06	.03
338	Bob Owchinko	.08	.06	.03
339	Terry Harper	.08	.06	.03
340	Larry Gura	.08	.06	.03
341	Doug DeCinces	.15	.11	.06
342	Atlee Hammaker	.10	.08	.04
343	Bob Bailor	.08	.06	.03
344	Roger LaFrancois	.08	.06	.03
345	Jim Clancy	.10	.08	.04
346	Joe Pittman	.08	.06	.03
347	Sammy Stewart	.08	.06	.03
348	Alan Bannister	.08	.06	.03
349	Checklist 265-396	.12	.09	.05
350	Robin Yount	.70	.50	.30
351	Reds Batting & Pitching Ldrs. (Cesar Cedeno, Mario Soto)	.12	.09	.05
352	Mike Scioscia	.10	.08	.04
353	Steve Comer	.08	.06	.03
354	Randy Johnson	.08	.06	.03
355	Jim Bibby	.08	.06	.03
356	Gary Woods	.08	.06	.03
357	*Len Matuszek*(FC)	.08	.06	.03
358	Jerry Garvin	.08	.06	.03
359	Dave Collins	.10	.08	.04
360	Nolan Ryan	1.50	1.25	.60
361	Super Veteran (Nolan Ryan)	.30	.25	.12
362	Bill Almon	.08	.06	.03
363	*John Stuper*(FC)	.08	.06	.03
364	Brett Butler	.20	.15	.08
365	Dave Lopes	.12	.09	.05
366	Dick Williams	.08	.06	.03
367	Bud Anderson	.08	.06	.03
368	Richie Zisk	.10	.08	.04
369	Jesse Orosco	.15	.11	.06
370	Gary Carter	.50	.40	.20
371	Mike Richardt	.08	.06	.03
372	Terry Crowley	.08	.06	.03
373	Kevin Saucier	.08	.06	.03
374	Wayne Krenchicki	.08	.06	.03
375	Pete Vuckovich	.10	.08	.04
376	Ken Landreaux	.08	.06	.03
377	Lee May	.10	.08	.04
378	Super Veteran (Lee May)	.10	.08	.04
379	Guy Sularz	.08	.06	.03
380	Ron Davis	.08	.06	.03
381	Red Sox Batting & Pitching Ldrs. (Jim Rice, Bob Stanley)	.25	.20	.10
382	Bob Knepper	.12	.09	.05
383	Ozzie Virgil	.10	.08	.04
384	*Dave Dravecky*(FC)	.70	.50	.30
385	Mike Easler	.10	.08	.04
386	Rod Carew AS	.35	.25	.14
387	Bob Grich AS	.10	.08	.04
388	George Brett AS	.50	.40	.20
389	Robin Yount AS	.25	.20	.10
390	Reggie Jackson AS	.50	.40	.20
391	Rickey Henderson AS	.40	.30	.15
392	Fred Lynn AS	.15	.11	.06
393	Carlton Fisk AS	.15	.11	.06
394	Pete Vuckovich AS	.10	.08	.04
395	Larry Gura AS	.08	.06	.03
396	Dan Quisenberry AS	.12	.09	.05
397	Pete Rose AS	.70	.50	.30
398	Manny Trillo AS	.10	.08	.04
399	Mike Schmidt AS	.60	.45	.25
400	Dave Concepcion AS	.12	.09	.05
401	Dale Murphy AS	.70	.50	.30
402	Andre Dawson AS	.20	.15	.08
403	Tim Raines AS	.35	.25	.14
404	Gary Carter AS	.35	.25	.14
405	Steve Rogers AS	.10	.08	.04
406	Steve Carlton AS	.35	.25	.14
407	Bruce Sutter AS	.12	.09	.05
408	Rudy May	.08	.06	.03
409	Marvis Foley	.08	.06	.03
410	Phil Niekro	.40	.30	.15

		MT	NR MT	EX
411	Super Veteran (Phil Niekro)	.20	.15	.08
412	Rangers Batting & Pitching Ldrs. (Buddy Bell, Charlie Hough)	.15	.11	.06
413	Matt Keough	.08	.06	.03
414	Julio Cruz	.08	.06	.03
415	Bob Forsch	.10	.08	.04
416	Joe Ferguson	.08	.06	.03
417	Tom Hausman	.08	.06	.03
418	Greg Pryor	.08	.06	.03
419	Steve Crawford	.08	.06	.03
420	Al Oliver	.20	.15	.08
421	Super Veteran (Al Oliver)	.12	.09	.05
422	George Cappuzzello	.08	.06	.03
423	Tom Lawless(FC)	.10	.08	.04
424	Jerry Augustine	.08	.06	.03
425	Pedro Guerrero	.35	.25	.14
426	Earl Weaver	.10	.08	.04
427	Roy Lee Jackson	.08	.06	.03
428	Champ Summers	.08	.06	.03
429	Eddie Whitson	.08	.06	.03
430	Kirk Gibson	.50	.40	.20
431	Gary Gaetti(FC)	5.00	3.75	2.00
432	Porfirio Altamirano	.08	.06	.03
433	Dale Berra	.08	.06	.03
434	Dennis Lamp	.08	.06	.03
435	Tony Armas	.12	.09	.05
436	Bill Campbell	.08	.06	.03
437	Rick Sweet	.08	.06	.03
438	Dave LaPoint(FC)	.40	.30	.15
439	Rafael Ramirez	.08	.06	.03
440	Ron Guidry	.30	.25	.12
441	Astros Batting & Pitching Ldrs. (Ray Knight, Joe Niekro)	.12	.09	.05
442	Brian Downing	.12	.09	.05
443	Don Hood	.08	.06	.03
444	Wally Backman(FC)	.25	.20	.10
445	Mike Flanagan	.12	.09	.05
446	Reid Nichols	.08	.06	.03
447	Bryn Smith	.10	.08	.04
448	Darrell Evans	.20	.15	.08
449	Eddie Milner	.12	.09	.05
450	Ted Simmons	.20	.15	.08
451	Super Veteran (Ted Simmons)	.12	.09	.05
452	Lloyd Moseby	.15	.11	.06
453	Lamar Johnson	.08	.06	.03
454	Bob Welch	.15	.11	.06
455	Sixto Lezcano	.08	.06	.03
456	Lee Elia	.08	.06	.03
457	Milt Wilcox	.08	.06	.03
458	Ron Washington	.08	.06	.03
459	Ed Farmer	.08	.06	.03
460	Roy Smalley	.08	.06	.03
461	Steve Trout	.08	.06	.03
462	Steve Nicosia	.08	.06	.03
463	Gaylord Perry	.40	.30	.15
464	Super Veteran (Gaylord Perry)	.20	.15	.08
465	Lonnie Smith	.10	.08	.04
466	Tom Underwood	.08	.06	.03
467	Rufino Linares	.08	.06	.03
468	Dave Goltz	.10	.08	.04
469	Ron Gardenhire	.08	.06	.03
470	Greg Minton	.08	.06	.03
471	Royals Batting & Pitching Ldrs. (Vida Blue, Willie Wilson)	.15	.11	.06
472	Gary Allenson	.08	.06	.03
473	John Lowenstein	.08	.06	.03
474	Ray Burris	.08	.06	.03
475	Cesar Cedeno	.12	.09	.05
476	Rob Picciolo	.08	.06	.03
477	Tom Niedenfuer(FC)	.15	.11	.06
478	Phil Garner	.10	.08	.04
479	Charlie Hough	.12	.09	.05
480	Toby Harrah	.10	.08	.04
481	Scot Thompson	.08	.06	.03
482	Tony Gwynn(FC)	20.00	15.00	8.00
483	Lynn Jones	.08	.06	.03
484	Dick Ruthven	.08	.06	.03
485	Omar Moreno	.08	.06	.03
486	Clyde King	.08	.06	.03
487	Jerry Hairston	.08	.06	.03
488	Alfredo Griffin	.10	.08	.04
489	Tom Herr	.12	.09	.05
490	Jim Palmer	.50	.40	.20
491	Super Veteran (Jim Palmer)	.20	.15	.08
492	Paul Serna	.08	.06	.03
493	Steve McCatty	.08	.06	.03
494	Bob Brenly	.10	.08	.04
495	Warren Cromartie	.08	.06	.03
496	Tom Veryzer	.08	.06	.03
497	Rick Sutcliffe	.20	.15	.08
498	Wade Boggs(FC)	35.00	27.50	15.00
499	Jeff Little	.10	.08	.04
500	Reggie Jackson	.70	.50	.30
501	Super Veteran (Reggie Jackson)	.35	.25	.14
502	Braves Batting & Pitching Ldrs. (Dale Murphy, Phil Niekro)	.50	.40	.20
503	Moose Haas	.08	.06	.03
504	Don Werner	.08	.06	.03
505	Garry Templeton	.12	.09	.05
506	Jim Gott(FC)	.25	.20	.10
507	Tony Scott	.08	.06	.03
508	Tom Filer	.15	.11	.06
509	Lou Whitaker	.40	.30	.20
510	Tug McGraw	.15	.11	.06
511	Super Veteran (Tug McGraw)	.10	.08	.04
512	Doyle Alexander	.12	.09	.05
513	Fred Stanley	.08	.06	.03
514	Rudy Law	.08	.06	.03
515	Gene Tenace	.10	.08	.04
516	Bill Virdon	.08	.06	.03
517	Gary Ward	.10	.08	.04
518	Bill Laskey	.08	.06	.03
519	Terry Bulling	.08	.06	.03
520	Fred Lynn	.25	.20	.10
521	Bruce Benedict	.08	.06	.03
522	Pat Zachry	.08	.06	.03
523	Carney Lansford	.12	.09	.05
524	Tom Brennan	.08	.06	.03
525	Frank White	.12	.09	.05
526	Checklist 397-528	.12	.09	.05
527	Larry Biittner	.08	.06	.03
528	Jamie Easterly	.08	.06	.03
529	Tim Laudner	.10	.08	.04
530	Eddie Murray	.80	.60	.30
531	Athletics Batting & Pitching Ldrs. (Rickey Henderson, Rick Langford)	.30	.25	.12
532	Dave Stewart	.20	.15	.08
533	Luis Salazar	.08	.06	.03
534	John Butcher	.08	.06	.03
535	Manny Trillo	.10	.08	.04
536	Johnny Wockenfuss	.08	.06	.03
537	Rod Scurry	.08	.06	.03
538	Danny Heep	.08	.06	.03
539	Roger Erickson	.08	.06	.03
540	Ozzie Smith	.30	.25	.12
541	Britt Burns	.08	.06	.03
542	Jody Davis	.12	.09	.05
543	Alan Fowlkes	.08	.06	.03
544	Larry Whisenton	.08	.06	.03
545	Floyd Bannister	.12	.09	.05
546	Dave Garcia	.08	.06	.03
547	Geoff Zahn	.08	.06	.03
548	Brian Giles	.08	.06	.03
549	Charlie Puleo	.15	.11	.06
550	Carl Yastrzemski	.80	.60	.30
551	Super Veteran (Carl Yastrzemski)	.40	.30	.15
552	Tim Wallach	.30	.25	.12
553	Denny Martinez	.10	.08	.04
554	Mike Vail	.08	.06	.03
555	Steve Yeager	.08	.06	.03
556	Willie Upshaw	.10	.08	.04
557	Rick Honeycutt	.08	.06	.03
558	Dickie Thon	.10	.08	.04
559	Pete Redfern	.08	.06	.03
560	Ron LeFlore	.10	.08	.04
561	Cardinals Batting & Pitching Ldrs. (Joaquin Andujar, Lonnie Smith)	.12	.09	.05
562	Dave Rozema	.08	.06	.03
563	Juan Bonilla	.08	.06	.03
564	Sid Monge	.08	.06	.03
565	Bucky Dent	.12	.09	.05
566	Manny Sarmiento	.08	.06	.03
567	Joe Simpson	.08	.06	.03
568	Willie Hernandez	.12	.09	.05
569	Jack Perconte	.08	.06	.03
570	Vida Blue	.15	.11	.06
571	Mickey Klutts	.08	.06	.03
572	Bob Watson	.10	.08	.04
573	Andy Hassler	.08	.06	.03
574	Glenn Adams	.08	.06	.03
575	Neil Allen	.08	.06	.03
576	Frank Robinson	.12	.09	.05
577	Luis Aponte	.08	.06	.03
578	David Green	.08	.06	.03
579	Rich Dauer	.08	.06	.03
580	Tom Seaver	.70	.50	.30
581	Super Veteran (Tom Seaver)	.30	.25	.12
582	Marshall Edwards	.08	.06	.03
583	Terry Forster	.10	.08	.04
584	Dave Hostetler	.08	.06	.03
585	Jose Cruz	.15	.11	.06
586	Frank Viola(FC)	6.00	4.50	2.50

		MT	NR MT	EX
587	Ivan DeJesus	.08	.06	.03
588	Pat Underwood	.08	.06	.03
589	Alvis Woods	.08	.06	.03
590	Tony Pena	.12	.09	.05
591	White Sox Batting & Pitching Ldrs.			
	(LaMarr Hoyt, Greg Luzinski)	.15	.11	.06
592	Shane Rawley	.12	.09	.05
593	Broderick Perkins	.08	.06	.03
594	Eric Rasmussen	.08	.06	.03
595	Tim Raines	.50	.40	.20
596	Randy Johnson	.08	.06	.03
597	Mike Proly	.08	.06	.03
598	Dwayne Murphy	.10	.08	.04
599	Don Aase	.08	.06	.03
600	George Brett	1.00	.70	.40
601	Ed Lynch	.08	.06	.03
602	Rich Gedman	.12	.09	.05
603	Joe Morgan	.40	.30	.15
604	Super Veteran (Joe Morgan)	.15	.11	.06
605	Gary Roenicke	.08	.06	.03
606	Bobby Cox	.08	.06	.03
607	Charlie Leibrandt	.10	.08	.04
608	Don Money	.08	.06	.03
609	Danny Darwin	.08	.06	.03
610	Steve Garvey	.70	.50	.30
611	Bert Roberge	.08	.06	.03
612	Steve Swisher	.08	.06	.03
613	Mike Ivie	.08	.06	.03
614	Ed Glynn	.08	.06	.03
615	Garry Maddox	.12	.09	.05
616	Bill Nahorodny	.08	.06	.03
617	Butch Wynegar	.08	.06	.03
618	LaMarr Hoyt	.08	.06	.03
619	Keith Moreland	.10	.08	.04
620	Mike Norris	.08	.06	.03
621	Mets Batting & Pitching Ldrs. (Craig			
	Swan, Mookie Wilson)	.12	.09	.05
622	Dave Edler	.08	.06	.03
623	Luis Sanchez	.08	.06	.03
624	Glenn Hubbard	.10	.08	.04
625	Ken Forsch	.08	.06	.03
626	Jerry Martin	.08	.06	.03
627	Doug Bair	.08	.06	.03
628	Julio Valdez	.08	.06	.03
629	Charlie Lea	.08	.06	.03
630	Paul Molitor	.30	.25	.12
631	Tippy Martinez	.08	.06	.03
632	Alex Trevino	.08	.06	.03
633	Vicente Romo	.08	.06	.03
634	Max Venable	.08	.06	.03
635	Graig Nettles	.20	.15	.08
636	Super Veteran (Graig Nettles)	.12	.09	.05
637	Pat Corrales	.08	.06	.03
638	Dan Petry	.10	.08	.04
639	Art Howe	.08	.06	.03
640	Andre Thornton	.12	.09	.05
641	Billy Sample	.08	.06	.03
642	Checklist 529-660	.12	.09	.05
643	Bump Wills	.08	.06	.03
644	Joe Lefebvre	.08	.06	.03
645	Bill Madlock	.15	.11	.06
646	Jim Essian	.08	.06	.03
647	Bobby Mitchell	.08	.06	.03
648	Jeff Burroughs	.10	.08	.04
649	Tommy Boggs	.08	.06	.03
650	George Hendrick	.10	.08	.04
651	Angels Batting & Pitching Ldrs. (Rod			
	Carew, Mike Witt)	.30	.25	.12
652	Butch Hobson	.08	.06	.03
653	Ellis Valentine	.08	.06	.03
654	Bob Ojeda	.15	.11	.06
655	Al Bumbry	.10	.08	.04
656	Dave Frost	.08	.06	.03
657	Mike Gates	.08	.06	.03
658	Frank Pastore	.08	.06	.03
659	Charlie Moore	.08	.06	.03
660	Mike Hargrove	.08	.06	.03
661	Bill Russell	.10	.08	.04
662	Joe Sambito	.08	.06	.03
663	Tom O'Malley	.08	.06	.03
664	Bob Molinaro	.08	.06	.03
665	Jim Sundberg	.10	.08	.04
666	Sparky Anderson	.12	.09	.05
667	Dick Davis	.08	.06	.03
668	Larry Christenson	.08	.06	.03
669	Mike Squires	.08	.06	.03
670	Jerry Mumphrey	.08	.06	.03
671	Lenny Faedo	.08	.06	.03
672	Jim Kaat	.20	.15	.08
673	Super Veteran (Jim Kaat)	.12	.09	.05
674	Kurt Bevacqua	.08	.06	.03

		MT	NR MT	EX
675	Jim Beattie	.08	.06	.03
676	Biff Pocoroba	.08	.06	.03
677	Dave Revering	.08	.06	.03
678	Juan Beniquez	.08	.06	.03
679	Mike Scott	.20	.15	.08
680	Andre Dawson	.40	.30	.15
681	Dodgers Batting & Pitching Ldrs. (Pedro			
	Guerrero, Fernando Valenzuela)	.25	.20	.10
682	Bob Stanley	.08	.06	.03
683	Dan Ford	.08	.06	.03
684	Rafael Landestoy	.08	.06	.03
685	Lee Mazzilli	.10	.08	.04
686	Randy Lerch	.08	.06	.03
687	U.L. Washington	.08	.06	.03
688	Jim Wohlford	.08	.06	.03
689	Ron Hassey	.08	.06	.03
690	Kent Hrbek	.70	.50	.30
691	Dave Tobik	.08	.06	.03
692	Denny Walling	.08	.06	.03
693	Sparky Lyle	.12	.09	.05
694	Super Veteran (Sparky Lyle)	.10	.08	.04
695	Ruppert Jones	.08	.06	.03
696	Chuck Tanner	.08	.06	.03
697	Barry Foote	.08	.06	.03
698	Tony Bernazard	.08	.06	.03
699	Lee Smith	.20	.15	.08
700	Keith Hernandez	.50	.40	.20
701	Batting Leaders (Al Oliver, Willie Wilson)			
		.15	.11	.06
702	Home Run Leaders (Reggie Jackson,			
	Dave Kingman, Gorman Thomas)	.25	.20	.10
703	Runs Batted In Leaders (Hal McRae, Dale			
	Murphy, Al Oliver)	.35	.25	.14
704	Stolen Base Leaders (Rickey Henderson,			
	Tim Raines)	.35	.25	.14
705	Victory Leaders (Steve Carlton, LaMarr			
	Hoyt)	.20	.15	.08
706	Strikeout Leaders (Floyd Bannister, Steve			
	Carlton)	.20	.15	.08
707	Earned Run Average Leaders (Steve			
	Rogers, Rick Sutcliffe)	.12	.09	.05
708	Leading Firemen (Dan Quisenberry, Bruce			
	Sutter)	.15	.11	.06
709	Jimmy Sexton	.08	.06	.03
710	Willie Wilson	.20	.15	.08
711	Mariners Batting & Pitching Ldrs. (Jim			
	Beattie, Bruce Bochte)	.12	.09	.05
712	Bruce Kison	.08	.06	.03
713	Ron Hodges	.08	.06	.03
714	Wayne Nordhagen	.08	.06	.03
715	Tony Perez	.25	.20	.10
716	Super Veteran (Tony Perez)	.12	.09	.05
717	Scott Sanderson	.08	.06	.03
718	Jim Dwyer	.08	.06	.03
719	Rich Gale	.08	.06	.03
720	Dave Concepcion	.15	.11	.06
721	John Martin	.08	.06	.03
722	Jorge Orta	.08	.06	.03
723	Randy Moffitt	.08	.06	.03
724	Johnny Grubb	.08	.06	.03
725	Dan Spillner	.08	.06	.03
726	Harvey Kuenn	.10	.08	.04
727	Chet Lemon	.10	.08	.04
728	Ron Reed	.08	.06	.03
729	Jerry Morales	.08	.06	.03
730	Jason Thompson	.08	.06	.03
731	Al Williams	.08	.06	.03
732	Dave Henderson	.15	.11	.06
733	Buck Martinez	.08	.06	.03
734	Steve Braun	.08	.06	.03
735	Tommy John	.25	.20	.10
736	Super Veteran (Tommy John)	.12	.09	.05
737	Mitchell Page	.08	.06	.03
738	Tim Foli	.08	.06	.03
739	Rick Ownbey	.08	.06	.03
740	Rusty Staub	.15	.11	.06
741	Super Veteran (Rusty Staub)	.10	.08	.04
742	Padres Batting & Pitching Ldrs. (Terry			
	Kennedy, Tim Lollar)	.12	.09	.05
743	Mike Torrez	.10	.08	.04
744	Brad Mills	.08	.06	.03
745	Scott McGregor	.10	.08	.04
746	John Wathan	.10	.08	.04
747	Fred Breining	.08	.06	.03
748	Derrel Thomas	.08	.06	.03
749	Jon Matlack	.10	.08	.04
750	Ben Oglivie	.10	.08	.04
751	Brad Havens	.08	.06	.03
752	Luis Pujols	.08	.06	.03
753	Elias Sosa	.08	.06	.03
754	Bill Robinson	.08	.06	.03

		MT	NR MT	EX
755	John Candelaria	.12	.09	.05
756	Russ Nixon	.08	.06	.03
757	Rick Manning	.08	.06	.03
758	Aurelio Rodriguez	.10	.08	.04
759	Doug Bird	.08	.06	.03
760	Dale Murphy	1.50	1.25	.60
761	Gary Lucas	.08	.06	.03
762	Cliff Johnson	.08	.06	.03
763	Al Cowens	.08	.06	.03
764	Pete Falcone	.08	.06	.03
765	Bob Boone	.12	.09	.05
766	Barry Bonnell	.08	.06	.03
767	Duane Kuiper	.08	.06	.03
768	Chris Speier	.08	.06	.03
769	Checklist 661-792	.12	.09	.05
770	Dave Winfield	.50	.40	.20
771	Twins Batting & Pitching Ldrs. (Bobby Castillo, Kent Hrbek)	.20	.15	.08
772	Jim Kern	.08	.06	.03
773	Larry Hisle	.10	.08	.04
774	Alan Ashby	.08	.06	.03
775	Burt Hooton	.10	.08	.04
776	Larry Parrish	.12	.09	.05
777	John Curtis	.08	.06	.03
778	Rich Hebner	.08	.06	.03
779	Rick Waits	.08	.06	.03
780	Gary Matthews	.12	.09	.05
781	Rick Rhoden	.12	.09	.05
782	Bobby Murcer	.12	.09	.05
783	Super Veteran (Bobby Murcer)	.10	.08	.04
784	Jeff Newman	.08	.06	.03
785	Dennis Leonard	.10	.08	.04
786	Ralph Houk	.10	.08	.04
787	Dick Tidrow	.08	.06	.03
788	Dane Iorg	.08	.06	.03
789	Bryan Clark	.08	.06	.03
790	Bob Grich	.12	.09	.05
791	Gary Lavelle	.08	.06	.03
792	Chris Chambliss	.10	.08	.04

1983 Topps All-Star Glossy Set Of 40

This set was a "consolation prize" in a scratch-off contest in regular packs of 1983 cards. The 2-1/2" by 3-1/2" cards have a large color photo surrounded by a yellow frame on the front. In very small type on a white border is printed the player's name. Backs carry the player's name, team, position and the card number along with a Topps identification. A major feature is that the surface of the front is glossy, which most collectors find very attractive. With many top stars, the set is a popular one, but the price has not moved too far above the issue price.

		MT	NR MT	EX
Complete Set:		12.00	9.00	4.75
Common Player:		.15	.11	.06
1	Carl Yastrzemski	1.00	.70	.40
2	Mookie Wilson	.15	.11	.06
3	Andre Thornton	.15	.11	.06
4	Keith Hernandez	.40	.30	.15
5	Robin Yount	.40	.30	.15
6	Terry Kennedy	.15	.11	.06
7	Dave Winfield	.60	.45	.25

		MT	NR MT	EX
8	Mike Schmidt	1.00	.70	.40
9	Buddy Bell	.20	.15	.08
10	Fernando Valenzuela	.50	.40	.20
11	Rich Gossage	.25	.20	.10
12	Bob Horner	.20	.15	.08
13	Toby Harrah	.15	.11	.06
14	Pete Rose	1.25	.90	.50
15	Cecil Cooper	.20	.15	.08
16	Dale Murphy	1.00	.70	.40
17	Carlton Fisk	.30	.25	.12
18	Ray Knight	.15	.11	.06
19	Jim Palmer	.40	.30	.15
20	Gary Carter	.50	.40	.20
21	Richard Zisk	.15	.11	.06
22	Dusty Baker	.15	.11	.06
23	Willie Wilson	.20	.15	.08
24	Bill Buckner	.15	.11	.06
25	Dave Stieb	.20	.15	.08
26	Bill Madlock	.20	.15	.08
27	Lance Parrish	.30	.25	.12
28	Nolan Ryan	.50	.40	.20
29	Rod Carew	.60	.45	.25
30	Al Oliver	.20	.15	.08
31	George Brett	1.00	.70	.40
32	Jack Clark	.25	.20	.10
33	Rickey Henderson	.70	.50	.30
34	Dave Concepcion	.20	.15	.08
35	Kent Hrbek	.30	.25	.12
36	Steve Carlton	.50	.40	.20
37	Eddie Murray	.60	.45	.25
38	Ruppert Jones	.15	.11	.06
39	Reggie Jackson	.70	.50	.30
40	Bruce Sutter	.20	.15	.08

1983 Topps Foldouts

Another Topps test issue, these 3-1/2" by 5-5/16" cards were printed in booklets like souvenir postcards. Each of the booklets have a theme of currently playing statistical leaders in a specific category such as home runs. The cards feature a color player photo on each side. A black strip at the bottom gives the player's name, position and team along with statistics in the particular category. A facsimile autograph crosses the photograph. Booklets carry nine cards, with eight having players on both sides and one doubling as the back cover, for a total of 17 cards per booklet. There are 85 cards in the set, although some players appear in more than one category. Naturally, most of the players pictured are stars. Even so, the set is a problem as it seems to be most valuable when complete and unseparated, so the cards are difficult to display.

		MT	NR MT	EX
Complete Set:		6.00	4.50	2.50
Common Folder:		1.00	.70	.40
1	Pitching Leaders (Vida Blue, Bert Blyleven, Steve Carlton, Fergie Jenkins, Tommy John, Jim Kaat, Jerry Koosman, Joe Niekro, Phil Niekro, Jim Palmer, Gaylord Perry, Jerry Reuss, Nolan Ryan, Tom Seaver, Paul Splittorff, Don Sutton, Mike Torrez)	1.75	1.25	.70
2	Home Run Leaders (Johnny Bench, Ron Cey, Darrell Evans, George Foster, Reggie Jackson, Dave Kingman, Greg Luzinski, John Mayberry, Rick Monday, Joe Morgan, Bobby Murcer, Graig Nettles, Tony Perez, Jim Rice, Mike Schmidt, Rusty Staub, Carl			

		MT	NR MT	EX
Yastrzemski)		2.50	2.00	1.00
3	Batting Leaders (George Brett, Rod Carew, Cecil Cooper, Steve Garvey, Ken Griffey, Pedro Guerrero, Keith Hernandez, Dane Iorg, Fred Lynn, Bill Madlock, Bake McBride, Al Oliver, Dave Parker, Jim Rice, Pete Rose, Lonnie Smith, Willie Wilson)			
		2.50	2.00	1.00
4	Relief Aces (Tom Burgmeier, Bill Campbell, Ed Farmer, Rollie Fingers, Terry Forster, Gene Garber, Rich Gossage, Jim Kern, Gary Lavelle, Tug McGraw, Greg Minton, Randy Moffitt, Dan Quisenberry, Ron Reed, Elias Sosa, Bruce Sutter, Kent Tekulve)			
		1.00	.70	.40
5	Stolen Base Leaders (Don Baylor, Larry Bowa, Al Bumbry, Rod Carew, Cesar Cedeno, Dave Concepcion, Jose Cruz, Julio Cruz, Rickey Henderson, Ron LeFlore, Davey Lopes, Garry Maddox, Omar Moreno, Joe Morgan, Amos Otis, Mickey Rivers, Willie Wilson)			
		1.00	.70	.40

1983 Topps Stickers

Topps increased the number of stickers in its set to 220 in 1983, but retained the same 1-15/16" by 2-9/16" size. The stickers are again numbered on both the front and back. Similar in style to previous sticker issues, the set includes 28 "foil" stickers, and various special stickers highlighting the 1982 season, playoffs and World Series. An album was also available.

		MT	NR MT	EX
Complete Set:		15.00	11.00	6.00
Common Player:		.03	.02	.01
Sticker Album:		.80	.60	.30
1	Hank Aaron	.40	.30	.15
2	Babe Ruth	.60	.45	.25
3	Willie Mays	.40	.30	.15
4	Frank Robinson	.30	.25	.12
5	Reggie Jackson	.20	.15	.08
6	Carl Yastrzemski	.25	.20	.10
7	Johnny Bench	.20	.15	.08
8	Tony Perez	.10	.08	.04
9	Lee May	.06	.05	.02
10	Mike Schmidt	.25	.20	.10
11	Dave Kingman	.08	.06	.03
12	Reggie Smith	.06	.05	.02
13	Graig Nettles	.06	.05	.02
14	Rusty Staub	.06	.05	.02
15	Willie Wilson	.06	.05	.02
16	LaMarr Hoyt	.03	.02	.01
17	Reggie Jackson, Gorman Thomas	.15	.11	.06
18	Floyd Bannister	.04	.03	.02
19	Hal McRae	.06	.05	.02
20	Rick Sutcliffe	.08	.06	.03
21	Rickey Henderson	.25	.20	.10
22	Dan Quisenberry	.06	.05	.02
23	Jim Palmer	.30	.25	.12
24	John Lowenstein	.03	.02	.01
25	Mike Flanagan	.04	.03	.02
26	Cal Ripken	.20	.15	.08
27	Rich Dauer	.03	.02	.01
28	Ken Singleton	.06	.05	.02
29	Eddie Murray	.20	.15	.08
30	Rick Dempsey	.04	.03	.02

		MT	NR MT	EX
31	Carl Yastrzemski	.40	.30	.15
32	Carney Lansford	.06	.05	.02
33	Jerry Remy	.03	.02	.01
34	Dennis Eckersley	.06	.05	.02
35	Dave Stapleton	.03	.02	.01
36	Mark Clear	.03	.02	.01
37	Jim Rice	.20	.15	.08
38	Dwight Evans	.08	.06	.03
39	Rod Carew	.20	.15	.08
40	Don Baylor	.08	.06	.03
41	Reggie Jackson	.40	.30	.15
42	Geoff Zahn	.03	.02	.01
43	Bobby Grich	.06	.05	.02
44	Fred Lynn	.10	.08	.04
45	Bob Boone	.04	.03	.02
46	Doug DeCinces	.06	.05	.02
47	Tom Paciorek	.03	.02	.01
48	Britt Burns	.03	.02	.01
49	Tony Bernazard	.03	.02	.01
50	Steve Kemp	.04	.03	.02
51	Greg Luzinski	.20	.15	.08
52	Harold Baines	.10	.08	.04
53	LaMarr Hoyt	.03	.02	.01
54	Carlton Fisk	.12	.09	.05
55	Andre Thornton	.15	.11	.06
56	Mike Hargrove	.04	.03	.02
57	Len Barker	.03	.02	.01
58	Toby Harrah	.04	.03	.02
59	Dan Spillner	.03	.02	.01
60	Rick Manning	.03	.02	.01
61	Rick Sutcliffe	.08	.06	.03
62	Ron Hassey	.03	.02	.01
63	Lance Parrish	.30	.25	.12
64	John Wockenfuss	.03	.02	.01
65	Lou Whitaker	.12	.09	.05
66	Alan Trammell	.15	.11	.06
67	Kirk Gibson	.15	.11	.06
68	Larry Herndon	.03	.02	.01
69	Jack Morris	.12	.09	.05
70	Dan Petry	.04	.03	.02
71	Frank White	.06	.05	.02
72	Amos Otis	.04	.03	.02
73	Willie Wilson	.25	.20	.10
74	Dan Quisenberry	.06	.05	.02
75	Hal McRae	.06	.05	.02
76	George Brett	.25	.20	.10
77	Larry Gura	.03	.02	.01
78	John Wathan	.04	.03	.02
79	Rollie Fingers	.10	.08	.04
80	Cecil Cooper	.08	.06	.03
81	Robin Yount	.30	.25	.12
82	Ben Oglivie	.06	.05	.02
83	Paul Molitor	.10	.08	.04
84	Gorman Thomas	.06	.05	.02
85	Ted Simmons	.06	.05	.02
86	Pete Vuckovich	.04	.03	.02
87	Gary Gaetti	.08	.06	.03
88	Kent Hrbek	.30	.25	.12
89	John Castino	.03	.02	.01
90	Tom Brunansky	.06	.05	.02
91	Bobby Mitchell	.03	.02	.01
92	Gary Ward	.04	.03	.02
93	Tim Laudner	.03	.02	.01
94	Ron Davis	.03	.02	.01
95	Willie Randolph	.06	.05	.02
96	Roy Smalley	.03	.02	.01
97	Jerry Mumphrey	.03	.02	.01
98	Ken Griffey	.06	.05	.02
99	Dave Winfield	.30	.25	.12
100	Rich Gossage	.10	.08	.04
101	Butch Wynegar	.04	.03	.02
102	Ron Guidry	.12	.09	.05
103	Rickey Henderson	.40	.30	.15
104	Mike Heath	.03	.02	.01
105	Dave Lopes	.06	.05	.02
106	Rick Langford	.03	.02	.01
107	Dwayne Murphy	.04	.03	.02
108	Tony Armas	.06	.05	.02
109	Matt Keough	.03	.02	.01
110	Dan Meyer	.03	.02	.01
111	Bruce Bochte	.03	.02	.01
112	Julio Cruz	.03	.02	.01
113	Floyd Bannister	.04	.03	.02
114	Gaylord Perry	.30	.25	.12
115	Al Cowens	.03	.02	.01
116	Richie Zisk	.04	.03	.02
117	Jim Essian	.03	.02	.01
118	Bill Caudill	.03	.02	.01
119	Buddy Bell	.20	.15	.08
120	Larry Parrish	.06	.05	.02
121	Danny Darwin	.03	.02	.01

		MT	NR MT	EX				MT	NR MT	EX
122	Bucky Dent	.04	.03	.02	213	Gene Garber	.03	.02	.01
123	Johnny Grubb	.03	.02	.01	214	Bob Horner	.08	.06	.03
124	George Wright	.03	.02	.01	215	Glenn Hubbard	.03	.02	.01
125	Charlie Hough	.06	.05	.02	216	Claudell Washington	.04	.03	.02
126	Jim Sundberg	.04	.03	.02	217	Bruce Benedict	.03	.02	.01
127	Dave Stieb	.20	.15	.08	218	Phil Niekro	.12	.09	.05
128	Willie Upshaw	.06	.05	.02	219	Leon Durham	.20	.15	.08
129	Alfredo Griffin	.04	.03	.02	220	Jay Johnstone	.04	.03	.02
130	Lloyd Moseby	.06	.05	.02	221	Larry Bowa	.06	.05	.02
131	Ernie Whitt	.03	.02	.01	222	Keith Moreland	.06	.05	.02
132	Jim Clancy	.04	.03	.02	223	Bill Buckner	.06	.05	.02
133	Barry Bonnell	.03	.02	.01	224	Fergie Jenkins	.08	.06	.03
134	Damaso Garcia	.04	.03	.02	225	Dick Tidrow	.03	.02	.01
135	Jim Kaat	.08	.06	.03	226	Jody Davis	.06	.05	.02
136	Jim Kaat	.06	.05	.02	227	Dave Concepcion	.06	.05	.02
137	Greg Minton	.03	.02	.01	228	Dan Driessen	.04	.03	.02
138	Greg Minton	.03	.02	.01	229	Johnny Bench	.20	.15	.08
139	Paul Molitor	.10	.08	.04	230	Ron Oester	.03	.02	.01
140	Paul Molitor	.08	.06	.03	231	Cesar Cedeno	.06	.05	.02
141	Manny Trillo	.04	.03	.02	232	Alex Trevino	.03	.02	.01
142	Manny Trillo	.04	.03	.02	233	Tom Seaver	.20	.15	.08
143	Joel Youngblood	.03	.02	.01	234	Mario Soto	.20	.15	.08
144	Joel Youngblood	.03	.02	.01	235	Nolan Ryan	.30	.25	.12
145	Robin Yount	.15	.11	.06	236	Art Howe	.03	.02	.01
146	Robin Yount	.12	.09	.05	237	Phil Garner	.04	.03	.02
147	Willie McGee	.08	.06	.03	238	Ray Knight	.06	.05	.02
148	Darrell Porter	.04	.03	.02	239	Terry Puhl	.03	.02	.01
149	Darrell Porter	.04	.03	.02	240	Joe Niekro	.06	.05	.02
150	Robin Yount	.15	.11	.06	241	Alan Ashby	.03	.02	.01
151	Bruce Benedict	.03	.02	.01	242	Jose Cruz	.06	.05	.02
152	Bruce Benedict	.03	.02	.01	243	Steve Garvey	.20	.15	.08
153	George Hendrick	.04	.03	.02	244	Ron Cey	.06	.05	.02
154	Bruce Benedict	.03	.02	.01	245	Dusty Baker	.04	.03	.02
155	Doug DeCinces	.06	.05	.02	246	Ken Landreaux	.03	.02	.01
156	Paul Molitor	.10	.08	.04	247	Jerry Reuss	.06	.05	.02
157	Charlie Moore	.03	.02	.01	248	Pedro Guerrero	.12	.09	.05
158	Fred Lynn	.10	.08	.04	249	Bill Russell	.04	.03	.02
159	Rickey Henderson	.20	.15	.08	250	Fernando Valenzuela	.30	.25	.12
160	Dale Murphy	.25	.20	.10	251	Al Oliver	.25	.20	.10
161	Willie Wilson	.08	.06	.03	252	Andre Dawson	.15	.11	.06
162	Jack Clark	.10	.08	.04	253	Tim Raines	.20	.15	.08
163	Reggie Jackson	.20	.15	.08	254	Jeff Reardon	.08	.06	.03
164	Andre Dawson	.15	.11	.06	255	Gary Carter	.20	.15	.08
165	Dan Quisenberry	.06	.05	.02	256	Steve Rogers	.03	.02	.01
166	Bruce Sutter	.08	.06	.03	257	Tim Wallach	.08	.06	.03
167	Robin Yount	.15	.11	.06	258	Chris Speier	.03	.02	.01
168	Ozzie Smith	.10	.08	.04	259	Dave Kingman	.08	.06	.03
169	Frank White	.06	.05	.02	260	Bob Bailor	.03	.02	.01
170	Phil Garner	.04	.03	.02	261	Hubie Brooks	.06	.05	.02
171	Doug DeCinces	.06	.05	.02	262	Craig Swan	.03	.02	.01
172	Mike Schmidt	.25	.20	.10	263	George Foster	.08	.06	.03
173	Cecil Cooper	.06	.05	.02	264	John Stearns	.03	.02	.01
174	Al Oliver	.06	.05	.02	265	Neil Allen	.03	.02	.01
175	Jim Palmer	.15	.11	.06	266	Mookie Wilson	.20	.15	.08
176	Steve Carlton	.15	.11	.06	267	Steve Carlton	.30	.25	.12
177	Carlton Fisk	.12	.09	.05	268	Manny Trillo	.04	.03	.02
178	Gary Carter	.20	.15	.08	269	Gary Matthews	.06	.05	.02
179	Joaquin Andujar	.04	.03	.02	270	Mike Schmidt	.25	.20	.10
180	Ozzie Smith	.10	.08	.04	271	Ivan DeJesus	.03	.02	.01
181	Cecil Cooper	.06	.05	.02	272	Pete Rose	.40	.30	.15
182	Darrell Porter	.04	.03	.02	273	Bo Diaz	.04	.03	.02
183	Darrell Porter	.04	.03	.02	274	Sid Monge	.03	.02	.01
184	Mike Caldwell	.03	.02	.01	275	Bill Madlock	.25	.20	.10
185	Mike Caldwell	.03	.02	.01	276	Jason Thompson	.03	.02	.01
186	Ozzie Smith	.10	.08	.04	277	Don Robinson	.03	.02	.01
187	Bruce Sutter	.08	.06	.03	278	Omar Moreno	.03	.02	.01
188	Keith Hernandez	.12	.09	.05	279	Dale Berra	.03	.02	.01
189	Dane Iorg	.03	.02	.01	280	Dave Parker	.10	.08	.04
190	Dane Iorg	.03	.02	.01	281	Tony Pena	.06	.05	.02
191	Tony Armas	.04	.03	.02	282	John Candelaria	.06	.05	.02
192	Tony Armas	.04	.03	.02	283	Lonnie Smith	.04	.03	.02
193	Lance Parrish	.12	.09	.05	284	Bruce Sutter	.25	.20	.10
194	Lance Parrish	.12	.09	.05	285	George Hendrick	.04	.03	.02
195	John Wathan	.04	.03	.02	286	Tom Herr	.06	.05	.02
196	John Wathan	.04	.03	.02	287	Ken Oberkfell	.03	.02	.01
197	Rickey Henderson	.12	.09	.05	288	Ozzie Smith	.10	.08	.04
198	Rickey Henderson	.12	.09	.05	289	Bob Forsch	.04	.03	.02
199	Rickey Henderson	.12	.09	.05	290	Keith Hernandez	.15	.11	.06
200	Rickey Henderson	.12	.09	.05	291	Garry Templeton	.06	.05	.02
201	Rickey Henderson	.12	.09	.05	292	Broderick Perkins	.03	.02	.01
202	Rickey Henderson	.12	.09	.05	293	Terry Kennedy	.20	.15	.08
203	Steve Carlton	.15	.11	.06	294	Gene Richards	.03	.02	.01
204	Steve Carlton	.12	.09	.05	295	Ruppert Jones	.03	.02	.01
205	Al Oliver	.06	.05	.02	296	Tim Lollar	.03	.02	.01
206	Dale Murphy, Al Oliver	.20	.15	.08	297	John Montefusco	.03	.02	.01
207	Dave Kingman	.08	.06	.03	298	Sixto Lezcano	.03	.02	.01
208	Steve Rogers				299	Greg Minton	.03	.02	.01
209	Bruce Sutter	.08	.06	.03	300	Jack Clark	.25	.20	.10
210	Tim Raines	.20	.15	.08	301	Milt May	.03	.02	.01
211	Dale Murphy	.40	.30	.15	302	Reggie Smith	.06	.05	.02
212	Chris Chambliss	.04	.03	.02	303	Joe Morgan	.10	.08	.04

		MT	NR MT	EX
304	John LeMaster	.03	.02	.01
305	Darrell Evans	.08	.06	.03
306	Al Holland	.03	.02	.01
307	Jesse Barfield	.08	.06	.03
308	Wade Boggs	.60	.45	.25
309	Tom Brunansky	.06	.05	.02
310	Storm Davis	.04	.03	.02
311	Von Hayes	.06	.05	.02
312	Dave Hostetler	.03	.02	.01
313	Kent Hrbek	.12	.09	.05
314	Tim Laudner	.03	.02	.01
315	Cal Ripken	.20	.15	.08
316	Andre Robertson	.03	.02	.01
317	Ed Vande Berg	.03	.02	.01
318	Glenn Wilson	.04	.03	.02
319	Chili Davis	.06	.05	.02
320	Bob Dernier	.03	.02	.01
321	Terry Francona	.03	.02	.01
322	Brian Giles	.03	.02	.01
323	David Green	.03	.02	.01
324	Atlee Hammaker	.03	.02	.01
325	Bill Laskey	.03	.02	.01
326	Willie McGee	.12	.09	.05
327	Johnny Ray	.06	.05	.02
328	Ryne Sandberg	.25	.20	.10
329	Steve Sax	.10	.08	.04
330	Eric Show	.04	.03	.02

1983 Topps Stickers Boxes

RICKEY HENDERSON

These eight cards were printed on the back panels of 1983 Topps sticker boxes, on card per box. The blank-backed cards measure the standard 2-1/2" by 3-1/2" and feature a full-color photo with the player's name at the top. The rest of the back panel advertises the sticker album, while the front of the box has an action photo of Reggie Jackson. The boxes are numbered on the front. Prices in the checklist that follows are for complete boxes.

		MT	NR MT	EX
	Complete Set:	6.50	5.00	2.50
	Common Player:	.75	.60	.30
1	Fernando Valenzuela	1.00	.70	.40
2	Gary Carter	1.25	.90	.50
3	Mike Schmidt	1.25	.90	.50
4	Reggie Jackson	1.25	.90	.50
5	Jim Palmer	1.00	.70	.40
6	Rollie Fingers	.75	.60	.30
7	Pete Rose	1.50	1.25	.60
8	Rickey Henderson	1.25	.90	.50

1983 Topps Traded

These 2-1/2" by 3-1/2" cards mark a continuation of the traded set introduced in 1981. The 132 cards retain the basic design of the year's regular issue, with their numbering being 1-132 with the "T" suffix. Cards in the set include traded players, new managers and promising rookies. Sold only through dealers, the set was in heavy demand as it contained the first cards of Darryl Strawberry, Ron Kittle, Julio

Franco and Mel Hall. While some of those cards were very hot in 1983, it seems likely that some of the rookies may not live up to their initial promise.

		MT	NR MT	EX
	Complete Set:	70.00	52.00	27.00
	Common Player:	.10	.08	.04
1T	Neil Allen	.10	.08	.04
2T	Bill Almon	.10	.08	.04
3T	Joe Altobelli	.10	.08	.04
4T	Tony Armas	.20	.15	.08
5T	Doug Bair	.10	.08	.04
6T	Steve Baker	.10	.08	.04
7T	Floyd Bannister	.20	.15	.08
8T	Don Baylor	.30	.25	.12
9T	Tony Bernazard	.10	.08	.04
10T	Larry Biittner	.10	.08	.04
11T	Dann Bilardello	.10	.08	.04
12T	Doug Bird	.10	.08	.04
13T	Steve Boros	.10	.08	.04
14T	Greg Brock(FC)	.30	.25	.12
15T	Mike Brown	.10	.08	.04
16T	Tom Burgmeier	.10	.08	.04
17T	Randy Bush(FC)	.20	.15	.08
18T	Bert Campaneris	.20	.15	.08
19T	Ron Cey	.25	.20	.10
20T	Chris Codiroli(FC)	.15	.11	.06
21T	Dave Collins	.15	.11	.06
22T	Terry Crowley	.10	.08	.04
23T	Julio Cruz	.10	.08	.04
24T	Mike Davis	.15	.11	.06
25T	Frank DiPino	.10	.08	.04
26T	Bill Doran(FC)	.90	.70	.35
27T	Jerry Dybzinski	.10	.08	.04
28T	Jamie Easterly	.10	.08	.04
29T	Juan Eichelberger	.10	.08	.04
30T	Jim Essian	.10	.08	.04
31T	Pete Falcone	.10	.08	.04
32T	Mike Ferraro	.10	.08	.04
33T	Terry Forster	.15	.11	.06
34T	Julio Franco(FC)	3.00	2.25	1.25
35T	Rich Gale	.10	.08	.04
36T	Kiko Garcia	.10	.08	.04
37T	Steve Garvey	1.50	1.25	.60
38T	Johnny Grubb	.10	.08	.04
39T	Mel Hall(FC)	.90	.70	.35
40T	Von Hayes	.50	.40	.20
41T	Danny Heep	.10	.08	.04
42T	Steve Henderson	.10	.08	.04
43T	Keith Hernandez	1.00	.70	.40
44T	Leo Hernandez	.10	.08	.04
45T	Willie Hernandez	.25	.20	.10
46T	Al Holland	.10	.08	.04
47T	Frank Howard	.15	.11	.06
48T	Bobby Johnson	.10	.08	.04
49T	Cliff Johnson	.10	.08	.04
50T	Odell Jones	.10	.08	.04
51T	Mike Jorgensen	.10	.08	.04
52T	Bob Kearney	.10	.08	.04
53T	Steve Kemp	.15	.11	.06
54T	Matt Keough	.10	.08	.04
55T	Ron Kittle(FC)	.60	.45	.25
56T	Mickey Klutts	.10	.08	.04
57T	Alan Knicely	.10	.08	.04
58T	Mike Krukow	.15	.11	.06
59T	Rafael Landestoy	.10	.08	.04
60T	Carney Lansford	.25	.20	.10
61T	Joe Lefebvre	.10	.08	.04
62T	Bryan Little	.10	.08	.04
63T	Aurelio Lopez	.10	.08	.04

		MT	NR MT	EX
64T	Mike Madden	.10	.08	.04
65T	Rick Manning	.10	.08	.04
66T	Billy Martin	.20	.15	.08
67T	Lee Mazzilli	.15	.11	.06
68T	Andy McGaffigan	.10	.08	.04
69T	Craig McMurtry(FC)	.20	.15	.08
70T	John McNamara	.10	.08	.04
71T	Orlando Mercado	.10	.08	.04
72T	Larry Milbourne	.10	.08	.04
73T	Randy Moffitt	.10	.08	.04
74T	Sid Monge	.10	.08	.04
75T	Jose Morales	.10	.08	.04
76T	Omar Moreno	.10	.08	.04
77T	Joe Morgan	1.00	.70	.40
78T	Mike Morgan	.10	.08	.04
79T	Dale Murray	.10	.08	.04
80T	Jeff Newman	.10	.08	.04
81T	Pete O'Brien(FC)	1.25	.90	.50
82T	Jorge Orta	.10	.08	.04
83T	Alejandro Pena(FC)	.60	.45	.25
84T	Pascual Perez	.20	.15	.08
85T	Tony Perez	.60	.45	.25
86T	Broderick Perkins	.10	.08	.04
87T	Tony Phillips(FC)	.20	.15	.08
88T	Charlie Puleo	.10	.08	.04
89T	Pat Putnam	.10	.08	.04
90T	Jamie Quirk	.10	.08	.04
91T	Doug Rader	.10	.08	.04
92T	Chuck Rainey	.10	.08	.04
93T	Bobby Ramos	.10	.08	.04
94T	Gary Redus(FC)	.40	.30	.15
95T	Steve Renko	.10	.08	.04
96T	Leon Roberts	.10	.08	.04
97T	Aurelio Rodriguez	.15	.11	.06
98T	Dick Ruthven	.10	.08	.04
99T	Daryl Sconiers	.10	.08	.04
100T	Mike Scott	.50	.40	.20
101T	Tom Seaver	1.75	1.25	.70
102T	John Shelby(FC)	.40	.30	.15
103T	Bob Shirley	.10	.08	.04
104T	Joe Simpson	.10	.08	.04
105T	Doug Sisk(FC)	.15	.11	.06
106T	Mike Smithson(FC)	.20	.15	.08
107T	Elias Sosa	.10	.08	.04
108T	Darryl Strawberry(FC)	60.00	45.00	24.00
109T	Tom Tellmann	.10	.08	.04
110T	Gene Tenace	.15	.11	.06
111T	Gorman Thomas	.25	.20	.10
112T	Dick Tidrow	.10	.08	.04
113T	Dave Tobik	.10	.08	.04
114T	Wayne Tolleson(FC)	.20	.15	.08
115T	Mike Torrez	.15	.11	.06
116T	Manny Trillo	.15	.11	.06
117T	Steve Trout	.10	.08	.04
118T	Lee Tunnell(FC)	.15	.11	.06
119T	Mike Vail	.10	.08	.04
120T	Ellis Valentine	.10	.08	.04
121T	Tom Veryzer	.10	.08	.04
122T	George Vukovich	.10	.08	.04
123T	Rick Waits	.10	.08	.04
124T	Greg Walker(FC)	.80	.60	.30
125T	Chris Welsh	.10	.08	.04
126T	Len Whitehouse	.10	.08	.04
127T	Eddie Whitson	.15	.11	.06
128T	Jim Wohlford	.10	.08	.04
129T	Matt Young(FC)	.20	.15	.08
130T	Joel Youngblood	.10	.08	.04
131T	Pat Zachry	.10	.08	.04
132T	Checklist 1-132	.10	.08	.04

1984 Topps

Another 792-card regular set from Topps. For the

second straight year, the 2-1/2" by 3-1/2" cards featured a color action photo on the front along with a small portrait photo in the lower left. The team name runs in big letters down the left side, while the player's name and position runs under the large action photo. In the upper right-hand corner is the Topps logo. have a team logo in the upper right corner, along with statistics, personal information and a few highlights. The backs have an unusual and hard-to-read red and purple coloring. Specialty cards include past season highlights, team leaders, major league statistical leaders, All-Stars, active career leaders and numbered checklists. Again, promising rookies were saved for the traded set. Late in 1984, Topps introduced a specially boxed "Tiffany" edition of the 1984 set, with the cards printed on white cardboard with a glossy finish. A total of 10,000 sets were produced. Prices for Tiffany edition superstars can run from six to eight times the value of the "regular" edition, while common cards sell in the 40¢ range.

		MT	NR MT	EX
	Complete Set:	90.00	67.00	35.00
	Common Player:	.08	.06	.03
1	1983 Highlight (Steve Carlton)	.30	.25	.12
2	1983 Highlight (Rickey Henderson)	.30	.25	.12
3	1983 Highlight (Dan Quisenberry)	.10	.08	.04
4	1983 Highlight (Steve Carlton, Gaylord Perry, Nolan Ryan)	.30	.25	.12
5	1983 Highlight (Bob Forsch, Dave Righetti, Mike Warren)	.15	.11	.06
6	1983 Highlight (Johnny Bench, Gaylord Perry, Carl Yastrzemski)	.40	.30	.15
7	Gary Lucas	.08	.06	.03
8	*Don Mattingly*(FC)	30.00	23.00	12.00
9	Jim Gott	.10	.08	.04
10	Robin Yount	.70	.50	.30
11	Twins Batting & Pitching Leaders (Kent Hrbek, Ken Schrom)	.20	.15	.08
12	Billy Sample	.08	.06	.03
13	Scott Holman	.08	.06	.03
14	Tom Brookens	.08	.06	.03
15	Burt Hooton	.10	.08	.04
16	Omar Moreno	.08	.06	.03
17	John Denny	.08	.06	.03
18	Dale Berra	.08	.06	.03
19	*Ray Fontenot*(FC)	.10	.08	.04
20	Greg Luzinski	.12	.09	.05
21	Joe Altobelli	.08	.06	.03
22	Bryan Clark	.08	.06	.03
23	Keith Moreland	.10	.08	.04
24	John Martin	.08	.06	.03
25	Glenn Hubbard	.10	.08	.04
26	Bud Black	.10	.08	.04
27	Daryl Sconiers	.08	.06	.03
28	Frank Viola	.80	.60	.30
29	Danny Heep	.08	.06	.03
30	Wade Boggs	7.00	5.25	2.75
31	Andy McGaffigan	.08	.06	.03
32	Bobby Ramos	.08	.06	.03
33	Tom Burgmeier	.08	.06	.03
34	Eddie Milner	.08	.06	.03
35	Don Sutton	.30	.25	.12
36	Denny Walling	.08	.06	.03
37	Rangers Batting & Pitching Leaders (Buddy Bell, Rick Honeycutt)	.12	.09	.05
38	Luis DeLeon	.08	.06	.03
39	Garth Iorg	.08	.06	.03
40	Dusty Baker	.12	.09	.05
41	Tony Bernazard	.08	.06	.03
42	Johnny Grubb	.08	.06	.03
43	Ron Reed	.10	.08	.04
44	Jim Morrison	.08	.06	.03
45	Jerry Mumphrey	.08	.06	.03
46	Ray Smith	.08	.06	.03
47	Rudy Law	.08	.06	.03
48	Julio Franco(FC)	1.00	.70	.40
49	John Stuper	.08	.06	.03
50	Chris Chambliss	.10	.08	.04
51	Jim Frey	.08	.06	.03
52	Paul Splittorff	.08	.06	.03
53	Juan Beniquez	.08	.06	.03
54	Jesse Orosco	.10	.08	.04
55	Dave Concepcion	.15	.11	.06
56	Gary Allenson	.08	.06	.03
57	Dan Schatzeder	.08	.06	.03

#	Player	MT	NR MT	EX
58	Max Venable	.08	.06	.03
59	Sammy Stewart	.08	.06	.03
60	Paul Molitor	.20	.15	.08
61	*Chris Codiroli*	.10	.08	.04
62	Dave Hostetler	.08	.06	.03
63	Ed Vande Berg	.08	.06	.03
64	Mike Scioscia	.08	.06	.03
65	Kirk Gibson	.40	.30	.15
66	Astros Batting & Pitching Leaders (Jose Cruz, Nolan Ryan)	.25	.20	.10
67	Gary Ward	.10	.08	.04
68	Luis Salazar	.08	.06	.03
69	Rod Scurry	.08	.06	.03
70	Gary Matthews	.12	.09	.05
71	Leo Hernandez	.08	.06	.03
72	Mike Squires	.08	.06	.03
73	Jody Davis	.10	.08	.04
74	Jerry Martin	.08	.06	.03
75	Bob Forsch	.10	.08	.04
76	Alfredo Griffin	.10	.08	.04
77	Brett Butler	.10	.08	.04
78	Mike Torrez	.10	.08	.04
79	Rob Wilfong	.08	.06	.03
80	Steve Rogers	.10	.08	.04
81	Billy Martin	.12	.09	.05
82	Doug Bird	.08	.06	.03
83	Richie Zisk	.10	.08	.04
84	Lenny Faedo	.08	.06	.03
85	Atlee Hammaker	.08	.06	.03
86	*John Shelby*(FC)	.25	.20	.10
87	Frank Pastore	.08	.06	.03
88	Rob Picciolo	.08	.06	.03
89	*Mike Smithson*(FC)	.15	.11	.06
90	Pedro Guerrero	.35	.25	.14
91	Dan Spillner	.08	.06	.03
92	Lloyd Moseby	.12	.09	.05
93	Bob Knepper	.10	.08	.04
94	Mario Ramirez	.08	.06	.03
95	Aurelio Lopez	.08	.06	.03
96	Royals Batting & Pitching Leaders (Larry Gura, Hal McRae)	.10	.08	.04
97	LaMarr Hoyt	.08	.06	.03
98	Steve Nicosia	.08	.06	.03
99	*Craig Lefferts*(FC)	.20	.15	.08
100	Reggie Jackson	.60	.45	.25
101	Porfirio Altamirano	.08	.06	.03
102	Ken Oberkfell	.08	.06	.03
103	Dwayne Murphy	.10	.08	.04
104	Ken Dayley	.08	.06	.03
105	Tony Armas	.12	.09	.05
106	Tim Stoddard	.08	.06	.03
107	Ned Yost	.08	.06	.03
108	Randy Moffitt	.08	.06	.03
109	Brad Wellman	.08	.06	.03
110	Ron Guidry	.30	.25	.12
111	Bill Virdon	.08	.06	.03
112	Tom Niedenfuer	.10	.08	.04
113	Kelly Paris	.08	.06	.03
114	Checklist 1-132	.08	.06	.03
115	Andre Thornton	.12	.09	.05
116	George Bjorkman	.08	.06	.03
117	Tom Veryzer	.08	.06	.03
118	Charlie Hough	.12	.09	.05
119	Johnny Wockenfuss	.08	.06	.03
120	Keith Hernandez	.40	.30	.15
121	*Pat Sheridan*(FC)	.15	.11	.06
122	Cecilio Guante(FC)	.10	.08	.04
123	Butch Wynegar	.08	.06	.03
124	Damaso Garcia	.08	.06	.03
125	Britt Burns	.08	.06	.03
126	Braves Batting & Pitching Leaders (Craig McMurtry, Dale Murphy)	.25	.20	.10
127	Mike Madden	.08	.06	.03
128	Rick Manning	.08	.06	.03
129	Bill Laskey	.08	.06	.03
130	Ozzie Smith	.20	.15	.08
131	Batting Leaders (Wade Boggs, Bill Madlock)	.50	.40	.20
132	Home Run Leaders (Jim Rice, Mike Schmidt)	.50	.40	.20
133	Runs Batted In Leaders (Cecil Cooper, Dale Murphy, Jim Rice)	.40	.30	.15
134	Stolen Base Leaders (Rickey Henderson, Tim Raines)	.30	.25	.12
135	Victory Leaders (John Denny, LaMarr Hoyt)	.10	.08	.04
136	Strikeout Leaders (Steve Carlton, Jack Morris)	.25	.20	.10
137	Earned Run Average Leaders (Atlee Hammaker, Rick Honeycutt)	.10	.08	.04
138	Leading Firemen (Al Holland, Dan Quisenberry)	.12	.09	.05

#	Player	MT	NR MT	EX
139	Bert Campaneris	.12	.09	.05
140	Storm Davis	.12	.09	.05
141	Pat Corrales	.08	.06	.03
142	Rich Gale	.08	.06	.03
143	Jose Morales	.08	.06	.03
144	Brian Harper	.08	.06	.03
145	Gary Lavelle	.08	.06	.03
146	Ed Romero	.08	.06	.03
147	Dan Petry	.10	.08	.04
148	Joe Lefebvre	.08	.06	.03
149	Jon Matlack	.10	.08	.04
150	Dale Murphy	1.00	.70	.40
151	Steve Trout	.08	.06	.03
152	Glenn Brummer	.08	.06	.03
153	Dick Tidrow	.08	.06	.03
154	Dave Henderson	.12	.09	.05
155	Frank White	.12	.09	.05
156	Athletics Batting & Pitching Leaders (Tim Conroy, Rickey Henderson)	.25	.20	.10
157	Gary Gaetti	.70	.50	.30
158	John Curtis	.08	.06	.03
159	Darryl Cias	.08	.06	.03
160	Mario Soto	.10	.08	.04
161	*Junior Ortiz*(FC)	.10	.08	.04
162	Bob Ojeda	.12	.09	.05
163	Lorenzo Gray	.08	.06	.03
164	Scott Sanderson	.08	.06	.03
165	Ken Singleton	.12	.09	.05
166	Jamie Nelson	.08	.06	.03
167	Marshall Edwards	.08	.06	.03
168	Juan Bonilla	.08	.06	.03
169	Larry Parrish	.12	.09	.05
170	Jerry Reuss	.12	.09	.05
171	Frank Robinson	.12	.09	.05
172	Frank DiPino	.08	.06	.03
173	*Marvell Wynne*(FC)	.20	.15	.08
174	Juan Berenguer	.08	.06	.03
175	Graig Nettles	.20	.15	.08
176	Lee Smith	.15	.11	.06
177	Jerry Hairston	.08	.06	.03
178	Bill Krueger	.08	.06	.03
179	Buck Martinez	.08	.06	.03
180	Manny Trillo	.10	.08	.04
181	Roy Thomas	.08	.06	.03
182	*Darryl Strawberry*	15.00	11.00	6.00
183	Al Williams	.08	.06	.03
184	Mike O'Berry	.08	.06	.03
185	Sixto Lezcano	.08	.06	.03
186	Cardinals Batting & Pitching Leaders (Lonnie Smith, John Stuper)	.10	.08	.04
187	Luis Aponte	.08	.06	.03
188	Bryan Little	.08	.06	.03
189	*Tim Conroy*(FC)	.12	.09	.05
190	Ben Oglivie	.10	.08	.04
191	Mike Boddicker	.12	.09	.05
192	*Nick Esasky*(FC)	2.00	1.50	.80
193	Darrell Brown	.08	.06	.03
194	Domingo Ramos	.08	.06	.03
195	Jack Morris	.30	.25	.12
196	Don Slaught(FC)	.12	.09	.05
197	Garry Hancock	.08	.06	.03
198	*Bill Doran*	.60	.45	.25
199	Willie Hernandez	.12	.09	.05
200	Andre Dawson	.35	.25	.14
201	Bruce Kison	.08	.06	.03
202	Bobby Cox	.08	.06	.03
203	Matt Keough	.08	.06	.03
204	*Bobby Meacham*(FC)	.15	.11	.06
205	Greg Minton	.08	.06	.03
206	*Andy Van Slyke*(FC)	2.50	2.00	1.00
207	Donnie Moore	.08	.06	.03
208	*Jose Oquendo*(FC)	.15	.11	.06
209	Manny Sarmiento	.08	.06	.03
210	Joe Morgan	.30	.25	.12
211	Rick Sweet	.08	.06	.03
212	Broderick Perkins	.08	.06	.03
213	Bruce Hurst	.15	.11	.06
214	Paul Householder	.08	.06	.03
215	Tippy Martinez	.08	.06	.03
216	White Sox Batting & Pitching Leaders (Richard Dotson, Carlton Fisk)	.15	.11	.06
217	Alan Ashby	.08	.06	.03
218	Rick Waits	.08	.06	.03
219	Joe Simpson	.08	.06	.03
220	Fernando Valenzuela	.40	.30	.15
221	Cliff Johnson	.08	.06	.03
222	Rick Honeycutt	.08	.06	.03
223	Wayne Krenchicki	.08	.06	.03
224	Sid Monge	.08	.06	.03
225	Lee Mazzilli	.10	.08	.04
226	Juan Eichelberger	.08	.06	.03

		MT	NR MT	EX
227	Steve Braun	.08	.06	.03
228	John Rabb	.08	.06	.03
229	Paul Owens	.08	.06	.03
230	Rickey Henderson	1.00	.70	.40
231	Gary Woods	.08	.06	.03
232	Tim Wallach	.15	.11	.06
233	Checklist 133-264	.08	.06	.03
234	Rafael Ramirez	.08	.06	.03
235	*Matt Young*	.15	.11	.06
236	Ellis Valentine	.08	.06	.03
237	John Castino	.08	.06	.03
238	Reid Nichols	.08	.06	.03
239	Jay Howell	.10	.08	.04
240	Eddie Murray	.60	.45	.25
241	Billy Almon	.08	.06	.03
242	Alex Trevino	.08	.06	.03
243	Pete Ladd	.08	.06	.03
244	Candy Maldonado(FC)	.25	.20	.10
245	Rick Sutcliffe	.15	.11	.06
246	Mets Batting & Pitching Leaders (Tom Seaver, Mookie Wilson)	.25	.20	.10
247	Onix Concepcion	.08	.06	.03
248	*Bill Dawley*(FC)	.10	.08	.04
249	Jay Johnstone	.10	.08	.04
250	Bill Madlock	.12	.09	.05
251	Tony Gwynn	2.00	1.50	.80
252	Larry Christenson	.08	.06	.03
253	Jim Wohlford	.08	.06	.03
254	Shane Rawley	.12	.09	.05
255	Bruce Benedict	.08	.06	.03
256	Dave Geisel	.08	.06	.03
257	Julio Cruz	.08	.06	.03
258	Luis Sanchez	.08	.06	.03
259	Sparky Anderson	.12	.09	.05
260	Scott McGregor	.10	.08	.04
261	Bobby Brown	.08	.06	.03
262	*Tom Candiotti*(FC)	.25	.20	.10
263	Jack Fimple	.08	.06	.03
264	Doug Frobel	.08	.06	.03
265	*Donnie Hill*(FC)	.15	.11	.06
266	Steve Lubratich	.08	.06	.03
267	*Carmelo Martinez*(FC)	.25	.20	.10
268	Jack O'Connor	.08	.06	.03
269	Aurelio Rodriguez	.10	.08	.04
270	*Jeff Russell*(FC)	.20	.15	.08
271	Moose Haas	.08	.06	.03
272	Rick Dempsey	.10	.08	.04
273	Charlie Puleo	.08	.06	.03
274	Rick Monday	.10	.08	.04
275	Len Matuszek	.08	.06	.03
276	Angels Batting & Pitching Leaders (Rod Carew, Geoff Zahn)	.20	.15	.08
277	Eddie Whitson	.08	.06	.03
278	Jorge Bell	1.00	.70	.40
279	Ivan DeJesus	.08	.06	.03
280	Floyd Bannister	.12	.09	.05
281	Larry Milbourne	.08	.06	.03
282	Jim Barr	.08	.06	.03
283	Larry Biittner	.08	.06	.03
284	Howard Bailey	.08	.06	.03
285	Darrell Porter	.10	.08	.04
286	Lary Sorensen	.08	.06	.03
287	Warren Cromartie	.08	.06	.03
288	Jim Beattie	.08	.06	.03
289	Randy Johnson	.08	.06	.03
290	Dave Dravecky	.10	.08	.04
291	Chuck Tanner	.08	.06	.03
292	Tony Scott	.08	.06	.03
293	Ed Lynch	.08	.06	.03
294	U.L. Washington	.08	.06	.03
295	Mike Flanagan	.12	.09	.05
296	Jeff Newman	.08	.06	.03
297	Bruce Berenyi	.08	.06	.03
298	Jim Gantner	.10	.08	.04
299	John Butcher	.08	.06	.03
300	Pete Rose	1.50	1.25	.60
301	Frank LaCorte	.08	.06	.03
302	Barry Bonnell	.08	.06	.03
303	Marty Castillo	.08	.06	.03
304	Warren Brusstar	.08	.06	.03
305	Roy Smalley	.08	.06	.03
306	Dodgers Batting & Pitching Leaders (Pedro Guerrero, Bob Welch)	.15	.11	.06
307	Bobby Mitchell	.08	.06	.03
308	Ron Hassey	.08	.06	.03
309	*Tony Phillips*	.15	.11	.06
310	Willie McGee	.35	.25	.14
311	Jerry Koosman	.12	.09	.05
312	Jorge Orta	.08	.06	.03
313	Mike Jorgensen	.08	.06	.03
314	Orlando Mercado	.08	.06	.03

		MT	NR MT	EX
315	Bob Grich	.12	.09	.05
316	Mark Bradley	.08	.06	.03
317	Greg Pryor	.08	.06	.03
318	Bill Gullickson	.08	.06	.03
319	Al Bumbry	.10	.08	.04
320	Bob Stanley	.08	.06	.03
321	Harvey Kuenn	.10	.08	.04
322	Ken Schrom	.08	.06	.03
323	Alan Knicely	.08	.06	.03
324	*Alejandro Pena*	.30	.25	.12
325	Darrell Evans	.15	.11	.06
326	Bob Kearney	.08	.06	.03
327	Ruppert Jones	.08	.06	.03
328	Vern Ruhle	.08	.06	.03
329	Pat Tabler(FC)	.20	.15	.08
330	John Candelaria	.12	.09	.05
331	Bucky Dent	.12	.09	.05
332	*Kevin Gross*(FC)	.35	.25	.14
333	Larry Herndon	.10	.08	.04
334	Chuck Rainey	.08	.06	.03
335	Don Baylor	.15	.11	.06
336	Mariners Batting & Pitching Leaders (Pat Putnam, Matt Young)	.10	.08	.04
337	Kevin Hagen	.08	.06	.03
338	Mike Warren	.08	.06	.03
339	Roy Lee Jackson	.08	.06	.03
340	Hal McRae	.12	.09	.05
341	Dave Tobik	.08	.06	.03
342	Tim Foli	.08	.06	.03
343	Mark Davis	.08	.06	.03
344	Rick Miller	.08	.06	.03
345	Kent Hrbek	.40	.30	.15
346	Kurt Bevacqua	.08	.06	.03
347	Allan Ramirez	.08	.06	.03
348	Toby Harrah	.10	.08	.04
349	Bob Gibson	.08	.06	.03
350	George Foster	.20	.15	.08
351	Russ Nixon	.08	.06	.03
352	Dave Stewart	.15	.11	.06
353	Jim Anderson	.08	.06	.03
354	Jeff Burroughs	.10	.08	.04
355	Jason Thompson	.08	.06	.03
356	Glenn Abbott	.08	.06	.03
357	Ron Cey	.12	.09	.05
358	Bob Dernier	.08	.06	.03
359	*Jim Acker*(FC)	.12	.09	.05
360	Willie Randolph	.12	.09	.05
361	Dave Smith	.10	.08	.04
362	David Green	.08	.06	.03
363	Tim Laudner	.08	.06	.03
364	Scott Fletcher(FC)	.15	.11	.06
365	Steve Bedrosian	.12	.09	.05
366	Padres Batting & Pitching Leaders (Dave Dravecky, Terry Kennedy)	.12	.09	.05
367	Jamie Easterly	.08	.06	.03
368	Hubie Brooks	.15	.11	.06
369	Steve McCatty	.08	.06	.03
370	Tim Raines	.40	.30	.15
371	Dave Gumpert	.08	.06	.03
372	Gary Roenicke	.08	.06	.03
373	Bill Scherrer	.08	.06	.03
374	Don Money	.08	.06	.03
375	Dennis Leonard	.10	.08	.04
376	*Dave Anderson*(FC)	.15	.11	.06
377	Danny Darwin	.08	.06	.03
378	Bob Brenly	.08	.06	.03
379	Checklist 265-396	.08	.06	.03
380	Steve Garvey	.50	.40	.20
381	Ralph Houk	.10	.08	.04
382	Chris Nyman	.08	.06	.03
383	Terry Puhl	.08	.06	.03
384	*Lee Tunnell*	.10	.08	.04
385	Tony Perez	.20	.15	.08
386	George Hendrick AS	.10	.08	.04
387	Johnny Ray AS	.12	.09	.05
388	Mike Schmidt AS	.35	.25	.14
389	Ozzie Smith AS	.15	.11	.06
390	Tim Raines AS	.25	.20	.10
391	Dale Murphy AS	.40	.30	.15
392	Andre Dawson AS	.20	.15	.08
393	Gary Carter AS	.30	.25	.12
394	Steve Rogers AS	.10	.08	.04
395	Steve Carlton AS	.25	.20	.10
396	Jesse Orosco AS	.10	.08	.04
397	Eddie Murray AS	.35	.25	.14
398	Lou Whitaker AS	.20	.15	.08
399	George Brett AS	.35	.25	.14
400	Cal Ripken AS	.35	.25	.14
401	Jim Rice AS	.30	.25	.12
402	Dave Winfield AS	.30	.25	.14
403	Lloyd Moseby AS	.12	.09	.05

		MT	NR MT	EX
404	Ted Simmons AS	.15	.11	.06
405	LaMarr Hoyt AS	.10	.08	.04
406	Ron Guidry AS	.20	.15	.08
407	Dan Quisenberry AS	.12	.09	.05
408	Lou Piniella	.15	.11	.06
409	*Juan Agosto*(FC)	.15	.11	.06
410	Claudell Washington	.10	.08	.04
411	Houston Jimenez	.08	.06	.03
412	Doug Rader	.08	.06	.03
413	*Spike Owen*(FC)	.20	.15	.08
414	Mitchell Page	.08	.06	.03
415	Tommy John	.25	.20	.10
416	Dane Iorg	.08	.06	.03
417	Mike Armstrong	.08	.06	.03
418	Ron Hodges	.08	.06	.03
419	John Henry Johnson	.08	.06	.03
420	Cecil Cooper	.15	.11	.06
421	Charlie Lea	.08	.06	.03
422	Jose Cruz	.12	.09	.05
423	Mike Morgan	.08	.06	.03
424	Dann Bilardello	.08	.06	.03
425	Steve Howe	.10	.08	.04
426	Orioles Batting & Pitching Leaders (Mike Boddicker, Cal Ripken)	.25	.20	.10
427	Rick Leach	.08	.06	.03
428	Fred Breining	.08	.06	.03
429	*Randy Bush*	.15	.11	.06
430	Rusty Staub	.12	.09	.05
431	Chris Bando	.08	.06	.03
432	*Charlie Hudson*(FC)	.20	.15	.08
433	Rich Hebner	.08	.06	.03
434	Harold Baines	.25	.20	.10
435	Neil Allen	.08	.06	.03
436	Rick Peters	.08	.06	.03
437	Mike Proly	.08	.06	.03
438	Biff Pocoroba	.08	.06	.03
439	Bob Stoddard	.08	.06	.03
440	Steve Kemp	.10	.08	.04
441	Bob Lillis	.08	.06	.03
442	Byron McLaughlin	.08	.06	.03
443	Benny Ayala	.08	.06	.03
444	Steve Renko	.08	.06	.03
445	Jerry Remy	.08	.06	.03
446	Luis Pujols	.08	.06	.03
447	Tom Brunansky	.20	.15	.08
448	Ben Hayes	.08	.06	.03
449	Joe Pettini	.08	.06	.03
450	Gary Carter	.40	.30	.15
451	Bob Jones	.08	.06	.03
452	Chuck Porter	.08	.06	.03
453	Willie Upshaw	.10	.08	.04
454	Joe Beckwith	.08	.06	.03
455	Terry Kennedy	.10	.08	.04
456	Cubs Batting & Pitching Leaders (Fergie Jenkins, Keith Moreland)	.15	.11	.06
457	Dave Rozema	.08	.06	.03
458	Kiko Garcia	.08	.06	.03
459	Kevin Hickey	.08	.06	.03
460	Dave Winfield	.40	.30	.15
461	Jim Maler	.08	.06	.03
462	Lee Lacy	.08	.06	.03
463	Dave Engle	.08	.06	.03
464	Jeff Jones	.08	.06	.03
465	Mookie Wilson	.12	.09	.05
466	Gene Garber	.08	.06	.03
467	Mike Ramsey	.08	.06	.03
468	Geoff Zahn	.08	.06	.03
469	Tom O'Malley	.08	.06	.03
470	Nolan Ryan	1.25	.90	.50
471	Dick Howser	.08	.06	.03
472	Mike Brown	.08	.06	.03
473	Jim Dwyer	.08	.06	.03
474	Greg Bargar	.08	.06	.03
475	*Gary Redus*	.25	.20	.10
476	Tom Tellmann	.08	.06	.03
477	Rafael Landestoy	.08	.06	.03
478	Alan Bannister	.08	.06	.03
479	Frank Tanana	.12	.09	.05
480	Ron Kittle(FC)	.25	.20	.10
481	*Mark Thurmond*(FC)	.10	.08	.04
482	Enos Cabell	.08	.06	.03
483	Fergie Jenkins	.20	.15	.08
484	Ozzie Virgil	.08	.06	.03
485	Rick Rhoden	.12	.09	.05
486	Yankees Batting & Pitching Leaders (Don Baylor, Ron Guidry)	.15	.11	.06
487	Ricky Adams	.08	.06	.03
488	Jesse Barfield	.25	.20	.10
489	Dave Von Ohlen	.08	.06	.03
490	Cal Ripken	.60	.45	.25
491	Bobby Castillo	.08	.06	.03

		MT	NR MT	EX
492	Tucker Ashford	.08	.06	.03
493	Mike Norris	.08	.06	.03
494	Chili Davis	.12	.09	.05
495	Rollie Fingers	.25	.20	.10
496	Terry Francona	.08	.06	.03
497	Bud Anderson	.08	.06	.03
498	Rich Gedman	.10	.08	.04
499	Mike Witt	.15	.11	.06
500	George Brett	.70	.50	.30
501	Steve Henderson	.08	.06	.03
502	Joe Torre	.08	.06	.03
503	Elias Sosa	.08	.06	.03
504	Mickey Rivers	.10	.08	.04
505	Pete Vuckovich	.10	.08	.04
506	Ernie Whitt	.10	.08	.04
507	Mike LaCoss	.08	.06	.03
508	Mel Hall	.20	.15	.08
509	Brad Havens	.08	.06	.03
510	Alan Trammell	.40	.30	.15
511	Marty Bystrom	.08	.06	.03
512	Oscar Gamble	.10	.08	.04
513	Dave Beard	.08	.06	.03
514	Floyd Rayford	.08	.06	.03
515	Gorman Thomas	.10	.08	.04
516	Expos Batting & Pitching Leaders (Charlie Lea, Al Oliver)	.12	.09	.05
517	John Moses	.12	.09	.05
518	*Greg Walker*	.45	.35	.20
519	Ron Davis	.08	.06	.03
520	Bob Boone	.10	.08	.04
521	Pete Falcone	.08	.06	.03
522	Dave Bergman	.08	.06	.03
523	Glenn Hoffman	.08	.06	.03
524	Carlos Diaz	.08	.06	.03
525	Willie Wilson	.15	.11	.06
526	Ron Oester	.08	.06	.03
527	Checklist 397-528	.08	.06	.03
528	Mark Brouhard	.08	.06	.03
529	*Keith Atherton*(FC)	.20	.15	.08
530	Dan Ford	.08	.06	.03
531	Steve Boros	.08	.06	.03
532	Eric Show	.12	.09	.05
533	Ken Landreaux	.08	.06	.03
534	*Pete O'Brien*	1.00	.70	.40
535	Bo Diaz	.10	.08	.04
536	Doug Bair	.08	.06	.03
537	Johnny Ray	.12	.09	.05
538	Kevin Bass	.15	.11	.06
539	George Frazier	.08	.06	.03
540	George Hendrick	.10	.08	.04
541	Dennis Lamp	.08	.06	.03
542	Duane Kuiper	.08	.06	.03
543	*Craig McMurtry*	.12	.09	.05
544	Cesar Geronimo	.08	.06	.03
545	Bill Buckner	.15	.11	.06
546	Indians Batting & Pitching Leaders (Mike Hargrove, Lary Sorensen)	.10	.08	.04
547	Mike Moore	.10	.08	.04
548	Ron Jackson	.08	.06	.03
549	*Walt Terrell*	.50	.40	.20
550	Jim Rice	.40	.30	.15
551	Scott Ullger	.08	.06	.03
552	Ray Burris	.08	.06	.03
553	Joe Nolan	.08	.06	.03
554	Ted Power(FC)	.12	.09	.05
555	Greg Brock	.15	.11	.06
556	Joey McLaughlin	.08	.06	.03
557	Wayne Tolleson	.10	.08	.04
558	Mike Davis	.10	.08	.04
559	Mike Scott	.20	.15	.08
560	Carlton Fisk	.30	.25	.12
561	Whitey Herzog	.10	.08	.04
562	Manny Castillo	.08	.06	.03
563	Glenn Wilson	.10	.08	.04
564	Al Holland	.08	.06	.03
565	Leon Durham	.10	.08	.04
566	Jim Bibby	.08	.06	.03
567	Mike Heath	.08	.06	.03
568	Pete Filson	.08	.06	.03
569	Bake McBride	.08	.06	.03
570	Dan Quisenberry	.12	.09	.05
571	Bruce Bochy	.08	.06	.03
572	Jerry Royster	.08	.06	.03
573	Dave Kingman	.15	.11	.06
574	Brian Downing	.12	.09	.05
575	Jim Clancy	.10	.08	.04
576	Giants Batting & Pitching Leaders (Atlee Hammaker, Jeff Leonard)	.10	.08	.04
577	Mark Clear	.08	.06	.03
578	Lenn Sakata	.08	.06	.03
579	Bob James	.08	.06	.03

#	Player	MT	NR MT	EX
580	Lonnie Smith	.10	.08	.04
581	*Jose DeLeon*(FC)	.60	.45	.25
582	Bob McClure	.08	.06	.03
583	Derrel Thomas	.08	.06	.03
584	Dave Schmidt	.08	.06	.03
585	Dan Driessen	.10	.08	.04
586	Joe Niekro	.15	.11	.06
587	Von Hayes	.15	.11	.06
588	Milt Wilcox	.08	.06	.03
589	Mike Easler	.10	.08	.04
590	Dave Stieb	.15	.11	.06
591	Tony LaRussa	.10	.08	.04
592	Andre Robertson	.08	.06	.03
593	Jeff Lahti	.08	.06	.03
594	Gene Richards	.08	.06	.03
595	Jeff Reardon	.15	.11	.06
596	Ryne Sandberg	1.50	1.25	.60
597	Rick Camp	.08	.06	.03
598	Rusty Kuntz	.08	.06	.03
599	*Doug Sisk*	.10	.08	.04
600	Rod Carew	.50	.40	.20
601	John Tudor	.12	.09	.05
602	John Wathan	.10	.08	.04
603	Renie Martin	.08	.06	.03
604	John Lowenstein	.08	.06	.03
605	Mike Caldwell	.08	.06	.03
606	Blue Jays Batting & Pitching Leaders (Lloyd Moseby, Dave Stieb)	.15	.11	.06
607	Tom Hume	.08	.06	.03
608	Bobby Johnson	.08	.06	.03
609	Dan Meyer	.08	.06	.03
610	Steve Sax	.20	.15	.08
611	Chet Lemon	.10	.08	.04
612	Harry Spilman	.08	.06	.03
613	Greg Gross	.08	.06	.03
614	Len Barker	.10	.08	.04
615	Garry Templeton	.12	.09	.05
616	Don Robinson	.10	.08	.04
617	Rick Cerone	.08	.06	.03
618	Dickie Noles	.08	.06	.03
619	Jerry Dybzinski	.08	.06	.03
620	Al Oliver	.20	.15	.08
621	Frank Howard	.10	.08	.04
622	Al Cowens	.08	.06	.03
623	Ron Washington	.08	.06	.03
624	Terry Harper	.08	.06	.03
625	Larry Gura	.10	.08	.04
626	Bob Clark	.08	.06	.03
627	Dave LaPoint	.10	.08	.04
628	Ed Jurak	.08	.06	.03
629	Rick Langford	.08	.06	.03
630	Ted Simmons	.15	.11	.06
631	Denny Martinez	.10	.08	.04
632	Tom Foley	.08	.06	.03
633	Mike Krukow	.10	.08	.04
634	Mike Marshall	.15	.11	.06
635	Dave Righetti	.25	.20	.10
636	Pat Putnam	.08	.06	.03
637	Phillies Batting & Pitching Leaders (John Denny, Gary Matthews)	.10	.08	.04
638	George Vukovich	.08	.06	.03
639	Rick Lysander	.08	.06	.03
640	Lance Parrish	.35	.25	.14
641	Mike Richardt	.08	.06	.03
642	Tom Underwood	.08	.06	.03
643	Mike Brown	.08	.06	.03
644	Tim Lollar	.08	.06	.03
645	Tony Pena	.12	.09	.05
646	Checklist 529-660	.08	.06	.03
647	Ron Roenicke	.08	.06	.03
648	Len Whitehouse	.08	.06	.03
649	Tom Herr	.12	.09	.05
650	Phil Niekro	.30	.25	.12
651	John McNamara	.08	.06	.03
652	Rudy May	.08	.06	.03
653	Dave Stapleton	.08	.06	.03
654	Bob Bailor	.08	.06	.03
655	Amos Otis	.10	.08	.04
656	Bryn Smith	.08	.06	.03
657	Thad Bosley	.08	.06	.03
658	Jerry Augustine	.08	.06	.03
659	Duane Walker	.08	.06	.03
660	Ray Knight	.12	.09	.05
661	Steve Yeager	.08	.06	.03
662	Tom Brennan	.08	.06	.03
663	Johnnie LeMaster	.08	.06	.03
664	Dave Stegman	.08	.06	.03
665	Buddy Bell	.15	.11	.06
666	Tigers Batting & Pitching Leaders (Jack Morris, Lou Whitaker)	.15	.11	.06
667	Vance Law	.10	.08	.04
668	Larry McWilliams	.08	.06	.03
669	Dave Lopes	.10	.08	.04
670	Rich Gossage	.25	.20	.10
671	Jamie Quirk	.08	.06	.03
672	Ricky Nelson	.08	.06	.03
673	Mike Walters	.08	.06	.03
674	Tim Flannery	.08	.06	.03
675	Pascual Perez	.10	.08	.04
676	Brian Giles	.08	.06	.03
677	Doyle Alexander	.12	.09	.05
678	Chris Speier	.08	.06	.03
679	Art Howe	.08	.06	.03
680	Fred Lynn	.25	.20	.10
681	Tom Lasorda	.12	.09	.05
682	Dan Morogiello	.08	.06	.03
683	*Marty Barrett*(FC)	1.00	.70	.40
684	Bob Shirley	.08	.06	.03
685	Willie Aikens	.08	.06	.03
686	Joe Price	.08	.06	.03
687	Roy Howell	.08	.06	.03
688	George Wright	.08	.06	.03
689	Mike Fischlin	.08	.06	.03
690	Jack Clark	.25	.20	.10
691	*Steve Lake*(FC)	.10	.08	.04
692	Dickie Thon	.10	.08	.04
693	Alan Wiggins	.08	.06	.03
694	Mike Stanton	.08	.06	.03
695	Lou Whitaker	.40	.30	.15
696	Pirates Batting & Pitching Leaders (Bill Madlock, Rick Rhoden)	.15	.11	.06
697	Dale Murray	.08	.06	.03
698	Marc Hill	.08	.06	.03
699	Dave Rucker	.08	.06	.03
700	Mike Schmidt	.80	.60	.30
701	NL Active Career Batting Leaders (Bill Madlock, Dave Parker, Pete Rose)	.35	.25	.14
702	NL Active Career Hit Leaders (Tony Perez, Pete Rose, Rusty Staub)	.35	.25	.14
703	NL Active Career Home Run Leaders (Dave Kingman, Tony Perez, Mike Schmidt)	.30	.25	.12
704	NL Active Career RBI Leaders (Al Oliver, Tony Perez, Rusty Staub)	.15	.11	.06
705	NL Active Career Stolen Bases Leaders (Larry Bowa, Cesar Cedeno, Joe Morgan)	.12	.09	.05
706	NL Active Career Victory Leaders (Steve Carlton, Fergie Jenkins, Tom Seaver)	.30	.25	.12
707	NL Active Career Strikeout Leaders (Steve Carlton, Nolan Ryan, Tom Seaver)	.35	.25	.14
708	NL Active Career ERA Leaders (Steve Carlton, Steve Rogers, Tom Seaver)	.25	.20	.10
709	NL Active Career Save Leaders (Gene Garber, Tug McGraw, Bruce Sutter)	.12	.09	.05
710	AL Active Career Batting Leaders (George Brett, Rod Carew, Cecil Cooper)	.30	.25	.12
711	AL Active Career Hit Leaders (Bert Campaneris, Rod Carew, Reggie Jackson)	.30	.25	.12
712	AL Active Career Home Run Leaders (Reggie Jackson, Greg Luzinski, Graig Nettles)	.20	.15	.08
713	AL Active Career RBI Leaders (Reggie Jackson, Graig Nettles, Ted Simmons)	.20	.15	.08
714	AL Active Career Stolen Bases Leaders (Bert Campaneris, Dave Lopes, Omar Moreno)	.10	.08	.04
715	AL Active Career Victory Leaders (Tommy John, Jim Palmer, Don Sutton)	.25	.20	.10
716	AL Active Strikeout Leaders (Bert Blyleven, Jerry Koosman, Don Sutton)	.15	.11	.06
717	AL Active Career ERA Leaders (Rollie Fingers, Ron Guidry, Jim Palmer)	.15	.11	.06
718	AL Active Career Save Leaders (Rollie Fingers, Rich Gossage, Dan Quisenberry)	.15	.11	.06
719	Andy Hassler	.08	.06	.03
720	Dwight Evans	.20	.15	.08
721	Del Crandall	.08	.06	.03
722	Bob Welch	.15	.11	.06
723	Rich Dauer	.08	.06	.03
724	Eric Rasmussen	.08	.06	.03
725	Cesar Cedeno	.12	.09	.05
726	Brewers Batting & Pitching Leaders (Moose Haas, Ted Simmons)	.12	.09	.05
727	Joel Youngblood	.08	.06	.03
728	Tug McGraw	.12	.09	.05
729	Gene Tenace	.10	.08	.04
730	Bruce Sutter	.20	.15	.08
731	Lynn Jones	.08	.06	.03

		MT	NR MT	EX
732	Terry Crowley	.08	.06	.03
733	Dave Collins	.10	.08	.04
734	Odell Jones	.08	.06	.03
735	Rick Burleson	.10	.08	.04
736	Dick Ruthven	.08	.06	.03
737	Jim Essian	.08	.06	.03
738	*Bill Schroeder*(FC)	.20	.15	.08
739	Bob Watson	.10	.08	.04
740	Tom Seaver	.50	.40	.20
741	Wayne Gross	.08	.06	.03
742	Dick Williams	.08	.06	.03
743	Don Hood	.08	.06	.03
744	Jamie Allen	.08	.06	.03
745	Dennis Eckersley	.15	.11	.06
746	Mickey Hatcher	.10	.08	.04
747	Pat Zachry	.08	.06	.03
748	Jeff Leonard	.12	.09	.05
749	Doug Flynn	.08	.06	.03
750	Jim Palmer	.50	.40	.20
751	Charlie Moore	.08	.06	.03
752	Phil Garner	.10	.08	.04
753	Doug Gwosdz	.08	.06	.03
754	Kent Tekulve	.10	.08	.04
755	Garry Maddox	.10	.08	.04
756	Reds Batting & Pitching Leaders (Ron Oester, Mario Soto)	.10	.08	.04
757	Larry Bowa	.15	.11	.06
758	Bill Stein	.08	.06	.03
759	Richard Dotson	.12	.09	.05
760	Bob Horner	.15	.11	.06
761	John Montefusco	.08	.06	.03
762	Rance Mulliniks	.08	.06	.03
763	Craig Swan	.08	.06	.03
764	Mike Hargrove	.08	.06	.03
765	Ken Forsch	.08	.06	.03
766	Mike Vail	.08	.06	.03
767	Carney Lansford	.12	.09	.05
768	Champ Summers	.08	.06	.03
769	Bill Caudill	.08	.06	.03
770	Ken Griffey	.12	.09	.05
771	Billy Gardner	.08	.06	.03
772	Jim Slaton	.08	.06	.03
773	Todd Cruz	.08	.06	.03
774	Tom Gorman	.08	.06	.03
775	Dave Parker	.30	.25	.12
776	Craig Reynolds	.08	.06	.03
777	Tom Paciorek	.08	.06	.03
778	*Andy Hawkins*(FC)	.40	.30	.15
779	Jim Sundberg	.10	.08	.04
780	Steve Carlton	.50	.40	.20
781	Checklist 661-792	.08	.06	.03
782	Steve Balboni	.10	.08	.04
783	Luis Leal	.08	.06	.03
784	Leon Roberts	.08	.06	.03
785	Joaquin Andujar	.10	.08	.04
786	Red Sox Batting & Pitching Leaders (Wade Boggs, Bob Ojeda)	.40	.30	.15
787	Bill Campbell	.08	.06	.03
788	Milt May	.08	.06	.03
789	Bert Blyleven	.20	.15	.08
790	Doug DeCinces	.12	.09	.05
791	Terry Forster	.10	.08	.04
792	Bill Russell	.10	.08	.04

1984 Topps
All-Star Glossy Set Of 22

These 2-1/2" by 3-1/2" cards were a result of the

success of Topps' efforts the previous year with glossy cards on a mail-in basis. A 22-card set, the cards are divided evenly between the two leagues. Each All-Star Game starter for both leagues, the managers and the honorary team captains have an All-Star Glossy card. The cards feature a large color photo on the front with an All-Star banner across the top and the league emblem in the lower left. The player's anme and position appear below the photo. Backs have a name, team, position and card number along with the phrase "1983 All-Star Game Commemorative Set". The '84 Glossy All-Stars were distributed one card per pack in Topps rack packs that year.

		MT	NR MT	EX
Complete Set:		6.00	4.50	2.50
Common Player:		.20	.15	.08
1	Harvey Kuenn	.20	.15	.08
2	Rod Carew	.50	.40	.20
3	Manny Trillo	.20	.15	.08
4	George Brett	.80	.60	.30
5	Robin Yount	.40	.30	.15
6	Jim Rice	.50	.40	.20
7	Fred Lynn	.25	.20	.10
8	Dave Winfield	.50	.40	.20
9	Ted Simmons	.25	.20	.10
10	Dave Stieb	.25	.20	.10
11	Carl Yastrzemski	.80	.60	.30
12	Whitey Herzog	.20	.15	.08
13	Al Oliver	.25	.20	.10
14	Steve Sax	.30	.25	.12
15	Mike Schmidt	.80	.60	.30
16	Ozzie Smith	.30	.25	.12
17	Tim Raines	.50	.40	.20
18	Andre Dawson	.35	.25	.14
19	Dale Murphy	.80	.60	.30
20	Gary Carter	.50	.40	.20
21	Mario Soto	.20	.15	.08
22	Johnny Bench	.60	.45	.25

1984 Topps
All-Star Glossy Set Of 40

For the second straight year in 1984, Topps produced a 40-card All-Star "Collector's Edition" set as a "consolation prize" for its sweepstakes game. By collecting game cards and sending them in with a bit of cash, the collector could receive one of eight different five-card series. As the previous year, the 2-1/2" by 3-1/2" cards feature a nearly full-frame color photo on its glossy finish front. Backs are printed in red and blue.

		MT	NR MT	EX
Complete Set:		16.00	12.00	6.50
Common Player:		.15	.11	.06
1	Pete Rose	1.25	.90	.50
2	Lance Parrish	.30	.25	.12
3	Steve Rogers	.15	.11	.06
4	Eddie Murray	.60	.45	.25
5	Johnny Ray	.20	.15	.08

		MT	NR MT	EX
6	Rickey Henderson	.70	.50	.30
7	Atlee Hammaker	.15	.11	.06
8	Wade Boggs	3.00	2.25	1.25
9	Gary Carter	.50	.40	.20
10	Jack Morris	.30	.25	.12
11	Darrell Evans	.20	.15	.08
12	George Brett	1.00	.70	.40
13	Bob Horner	.20	.15	.08
14	Ron Guidry	.30	.25	.12
15	Nolan Ryan	.50	.40	.20
16	Dave Winfield	.60	.45	.25
17	Ozzie Smith	.25	.20	.10
18	Ted Simmons	.20	.15	.08
19	Bill Madlock	.20	.15	.08
20	Tony Armas	.15	.11	.06
21	Al Oliver	.20	.15	.08
22	Jim Rice	.50	.40	.20
23	George Hendrick	.15	.11	.06
24	Dave Stieb	.20	.15	.08
25	Pedro Guerrero	.25	.20	.10
26	Rod Carew	.60	.45	.25
27	Steve Carlton	.50	.40	.20
28	Dave Righetti	.30	.25	.12
29	Darryl Strawberry	3.00	2.25	1.25
30	Lou Whitaker	.30	.25	.12
31	Dale Murphy	1.00	.70	.40
32	LaMarr Hoyt	.15	.11	.06
33	Jesse Orosco	.15	.11	.06
34	Cecil Cooper	.20	.15	.08
35	Andre Dawson	.35	.25	.14
36	Robin Yount	.40	.30	.15
37	Tim Raines	.50	.40	.20
38	Dan Quisenberry	.15	.11	.06
39	Mike Schmidt	1.00	.70	.40
40	Carlton Fisk	.30	.25	.12

		MT	NR MT	EX
(1b)	George Brett (bronze)	15.00	11.00	6.00
(1c)	George Brett (silver)	80.00	60.00	32.00
(2a)	Rod Carew (aluminum)	1.25	.90	.50
(2b)	Rod Carew (bronze)	12.50	9.50	5.00
(2c)	Rod Carew (silver)	50.00	37.00	20.00
(3a)	Steve Carlton (aluminum)	1.25	.90	.50
(3b)	Steve Carlton (bronze)	12.50	9.50	5.00
(3c)	Steve Carlton (silver)	50.00	37.00	20.00
(4a)	Rollie Fingers (aluminum)	1.00	.70	.40
(4b)	Rollie Fingers (bronze)	10.00	7.50	4.00
(4c)	Rollie Fingers (silver)	20.00	15.00	8.00
(5a)	Steve Garvey (aluminum)	1.25	.90	.50
(5b)	Steve Garvey (bronze)	12.50	9.50	5.00
(5c)	Steve Garvey (silver)	50.00	37.00	20.00
(6a)	Reggie Jackson (aluminum)	1.50	1.25	.60
(6b)	Reggie Jackson (bronze)	15.00	11.00	6.00
(6c)	Reggie Jackson (silver)	80.00	60.00	32.00
(7a)	Joe Morgan (aluminum)	1.00	.70	.40
(7b)	Joe Morgan (bronze)	10.00	7.50	4.00
(7c)	Joe Morgan (silver)	20.00	15.00	8.00
(8a)	Jim Palmer (aluminum)	1.00	.70	.40
(8b)	Jim Palmer (bronze)	10.00	7.50	4.00
(8c)	Jim Palmer (silver)	20.00	15.00	8.00
(9a)	Pete Rose (aluminum)	2.50	2.00	1.00
(9b)	Pete Rose (bronze)	25.00	18.50	10.00
(9c)	Pete Rose (silver)	110.00	82.00	44.00
(10a)	Nolan Ryan (aluminum)	1.25	.90	.50
(10b)	Nolan Ryan (bronze)	12.50	9.50	5.00
(10c)	Nolan Ryan (silver)	50.00	37.00	20.00
(11a)	Mike Schmidt (aluminum)	1.50	1.25	.60
(11b)	Mike Schmidt (bronze)	15.00	11.00	6.00
(11c)	Mike Schmidt (silver)	80.00	60.00	32.00
(12a)	Tom Seaver (aluminum)	1.25	.90	.50
(12b)	Tom Seaver (bronze)	12.50	9.50	5.00
(12c)	Tom Seaver (silver)	50.00	37.00	20.00

1984 Topps
Gallery of Immortals

The Gallery of Immortals set of aluminum, bronze and silver replicas was the first miniature set of 12 from Topps and the start of an annual tradition (in 1985, the name was changed to Gallery of Champions).Each mini is an exact replica (one-quarter scale) of the featured player's official Topps baseball card card, both front and back, in minute detail. The bronze and silver sets include a dozen three-dimensional raised metal cards packaged in a velvet-lined case that bears the title of the set in gold-embossed letters. A certificate of authenticity is included with each set. A Tom Seaver pewter metal mini-card was given as a premium to dealers who purchsed bronze and silver sets (value $75). A Darryl Strawberry bronze was given as a premium to dealers who purchased cases of the 1984 Topps Traded sets (value #12). Additionally, a Steve Carlton bronze was issued as a premium in 1983 to dealers who purchased 1983 Topps Traded sets (value $50).

	MT	NR MT	EX
Complete Aluminum Set:	30.00	22.00	12.00
Complete Bronze Set:	175.00	131.00	70.00
Complete Silver Set:	600.00	450.00	240.00
(1a) George Brett (aluminum)	1.50	1.25	.60

1984 Topps Rub Downs

This set, produced by Topps in 1984, consists of 32 "Rub Down" sheets featuring 112 different players. Each sheet measures 2-3/8" by 3-15/16" and includes small, color baseball player figures along with bats, balls and gloves. The pictures can be transferred to another surface by rubbing the paper backing. The sheets, which were sold as a spearate issue, are somewhat reminiscent of earlier tattoo sets issued by Topps. The sheets are not numbered.

	MT	NR MT	EX
Complete Set:	9.00	6.75	3.50
Common Player:	.10	.08	.04
(1) Tony Armas, Harold Baines, Lonnie Smith	.10	.08	.04
(2) Don Baylor, George Hendrick, Ron Kittle, Johnnie LeMaster	.10	.08	.04
(3) Buddy Bell, Ray Knight, Lloyd Moseby	.10	.08	.04
(4) Bruce Benedict, Atlee Hammaker, Frank White	.10	.08	.04
(5) Wade Boggs, Rick Dempsey, Keith Hernandez	.60	.45	.25
(6) George Brett, Andre Dawson, Paul Molitor, Alan Wiggins	.30	.25	.12
(7) Tom Brunansky, Pedro Guerrero, Darryl Strawberry	.40	.30	.15
(8) Bill Buckner, Rich Gossage, Dave Stieb, Rick Sutcliffe	.15	.11	.06

		MT	NR MT	EX
(9)	Rod Carew, Carlton Fisk, Johnny Ray, Matt Young	.25	.20	.10
(10)	Steve Carlton, Bob Horner, Dan Quisenberry	.25	.20	.10
(11)	Gary Carter, Phil Garner, Ron Guidry	.25	.20	.10
(12)	Ron Cey, Steve Kemp, Greg Luzinski, Kent Tekulve	.10	.08	.04
(13)	Chris Chambliss, Dwight Evans, Julio Franco	.15	.11	.06
(14)	Jack Clark, Damaso Garcia, Hal McRae, Lance Parrish	.20	.15	.08
(15)	Dave Concepcion, Cecil Cooper, Fred Lynn, Jesse Orosco	.15	.11	.06
(16)	Jose Cruz, Gary Matthews, Jack Morris, Jim Rice	.20	.15	.08
(17)	Ron Davis, Kent Hrbek, Tom Seaver	.25	.20	.10
(18)	John Denny, Carney Lansford, Mario Soto, Lou Whitaker	.10	.08	.04
(19)	Leon Durham, Dave Lopes, Steve Sax	.15	.11	.06
(20)	George Foster, Gary Gaetti, Bobby Grich, Gary Redus	.15	.11	.06
(21)	Steve Garvey, Bill Russell, Jerry REmy, George Wright	.20	.15	.08
(22)	Moose Haas, Bruce Sutter, Dickie Thon, Andre Thornton	.10	.08	.04
(23)	Toby Harrah, Pat Putnam, Tim Raines, Mike Schmidt	.30	.25	.12
(24)	Rickey Henderson, Dave Righetti, Pete Rose	.70	.50	.30
(25)	Steve Henderson, Bill Madlock, Alan Trammell	.20	.15	.08
(26)	LaMarr Hoyt, Larry Parrish, Nolan Ryan	.25	.20	.10
(27)	Reggie Jackson, Eric Show, Jason Thompson	.30	.25	.12
(28)	Tommy John, Terry Kennedy, Eddie Murray, Ozzie Smith	.25	.20	.10
(29)	Jeff Leonard, Dale Murphy, Ken Singleton, Dave Winfield	.30	.25	.12
(30)	Craig McMurtry, Cal Ripken, Steve Rogers, Willie Upshaw	.25	.20	.10
(31)	Ben Oglivie, Jim Palmer, Darrell Porter	.20	.15	.08
(32)	Tony Pena, Fernando Valenzuela, Robin Yount	.20	.15	.08

1984 Topps Stickers

The largest sticker set issued by Topps, the 1984 set consists of 386 stickers, each measuring 1-15/16" by 2-9/16". The full color photos have stars in each of the corners and are numbered on both the front and the back. The back includes information about the sticker album and a promotion to order stickers through the mail.

		MT	NR MT	EX
Complete Set:		15.00	11.00	6.00
Common Player:		.03	.02	.01
Sticker Album:		.80	.60	.30
1	Steve Carlton	.15	.11	.06
2	Steve Carlton	.12	.09	.05
3	Rickey Henderson	.20	.15	.08
4	Rickey Henderson	.15	.11	.06

		MT	NR MT	EX
5	Fred Lynn	.12	.09	.05
6	Fred Lynn	.10	.08	.04
7	Greg Luzinski	.08	.06	.03
8	Greg Luzinski	.06	.05	.02
9	Dan Quisenberry	.08	.06	.03
10	Dan Quisenberry	.06	.05	.02
11	1983 Championship (LaMarr Hoyt)	.03	.02	.01
12	1983 Championship (Mike Flanagan)	.04	.03	.02
13	1983 Championship (Mike Boddicker)	.04	.03	.02
14	1983 Championship (Tito Landrum)	.03	.02	.01
15	1983 Championship (Steve Carlton)	.12	.09	.05
16	1983 Championship (Fernando Valenzuela)	.12	.09	.05
17	1983 Championship (Charlie Hudson)	.03	.02	.01
18	1983 Championship (Gary Matthews)	.04	.03	.02
19	1983 World Series (John Denny)	.03	.02	.01
20	1983 World Series (John Lowenstein)	.03	.02	.01
21	1983 World Series (Jim Palmer)	.10	.08	.04
22	1983 World Series (Benny Ayala)	.03	.02	.01
23	1983 World Series (Rick Dempsey)	.03	.02	.01
24	1983 World Series (Cal Ripken)	.15	.11	.06
25	1983 World Series (Sammy Stewart)	.03	.02	.01
26	1983 World Series (Eddie Murray)	.15	.11	.06
27	Dale Murphy	.25	.20	.10
28	Chris Chambliss	.04	.03	.02
29	Glenn Hubbard	.04	.03	.02
30	Bob Horner	.08	.06	.03
31	Phil Niekro	.12	.09	.05
32	Claudell Washington	.04	.03	.02
33	Rafael Ramirez	.03	.02	.01
34	Bruce Benedict	.04	.03	.02
35	Gene Garber	.03	.02	.01
36	Pascual Perez	.04	.03	.02
37	Jerry Royster	.03	.02	.01
38	Steve Bedrosian	.06	.05	.02
39	Keith Moreland	.06	.05	.02
40	Leon Durham	.06	.05	.02
41	Ron Cey	.06	.05	.02
42	Bill Buckner	.06	.05	.02
43	Jody Davis	.06	.05	.02
44	Lee Smith	.06	.05	.02
45	Ryne Sandberg	.10	.08	.04
46	Larry Bowa	.04	.03	.02
47	Chuck Rainey	.04	.03	.02
48	Fergie Jenkins	.06	.05	.02
49	Dick Ruthven	.03	.02	.01
50	Jay Johnstone	.04	.03	.02
51	Mario Soto	.06	.05	.02
52	Gary Redus	.04	.03	.02
53	Ron Oester	.04	.03	.02
54	Cesar Cedeno	.06	.05	.02
55	Dan Driessen	.04	.03	.02
56	Dave Concepcion	.06	.05	.02
57	Dann Bilardello	.03	.02	.01
58	Joe Price	.03	.02	.01
59	Tom Hume	.03	.02	.01
60	Eddie Milner	.03	.02	.01
61	Paul Householder	.04	.03	.02
62	Bill Scherrer	.04	.03	.02
63	Phil Garner	.04	.03	.02
64	Dickie Thon	.04	.03	.02
65	Jose Cruz	.06	.05	.02
66	Nolan Ryan	.15	.11	.06
67	Terry Puhl	.03	.02	.01
68	Ray Knight	.06	.05	.02
69	Joe Niekro	.06	.05	.02
70	Jerry Mumphrey	.10	.08	.04
71	Bill Dawley	.03	.02	.01
72	Alan Ashby	.04	.03	.02
73	Denny Walling	.04	.03	.02
74	Frank DiPino	.04	.03	.02
75	Pedro Guerrero	.12	.09	.05
76	Ken Landreaux	.03	.02	.01
77	Bill Russell	.04	.03	.02
78	Steve Sax	.10	.08	.04
79	Fernando Valenzuela	.15	.11	.06
80	Dusty Baker	.04	.03	.02
81	Jerry Reuss	.04	.03	.02
82	Alejandro Pena	.04	.03	.02
83	Rick Monday	.06	.05	.02
84	Rick Honeycutt	.03	.02	.01
85	Mike Marshall	.06	.05	.02
86	Steve Yeager	.04	.03	.02

#	Name	MT	NR MT	EX		#	Name	MT	NR MT	EX
87	Al Oliver	.06	.05	.02		177	John Denny	.06	.05	.02
88	Steve Rogers	.03	.02	.01		178	LaMarr Hoyt	.03	.02	.01
89	Jeff Reardon	.08	.06	.03		179	Tim Raines	.30	.25	.12
90	Gary Carter	.20	.15	.08		180	Dale Murphy	.40	.30	.15
91	Tim Raines	.15	.11	.06		181	Andre Dawson	.25	.20	.10
92	Andre Dawson	.12	.09	.05		182	Steve Rogers	.15	.11	.06
93	Manny Trillo	.04	.03	.02		183	Gary Carter	.30	.25	.12
94	Tim Wallach	.06	.05	.02		184	Steve Carlton	.25	.20	.10
95	Chris Speier	.03	.02	.01		185	George Hendrick	.15	.11	.06
96	Bill Gullickson	.04	.03	.02		186	Johnny Ray	.15	.11	.06
97	Doug Flynn	.04	.03	.02		187	Ozzie Smith	.20	.15	.08
98	Charlie Lea	.03	.02	.01		188	Mike Schmidt	.40	.30	.15
99	Bill Madlock	.06	.05	.02		189	Jim Rice	.30	.25	.12
100	Wade Boggs	.25	.20	.10		190	Dave Winfield	.30	.25	.12
101	Mike Schmidt	.15	.11	.06		191	Lloyd Moseby	.15	.11	.06
102a	Jim Rice	.06	.05	.02		192	LaMarr Hoyt	.15	.11	.06
102b	Reggie Jackson	.06	.05	.02		193	Ted Simmons	.15	.11	.06
103	Hubie Brooks	.06	.05	.02		194	Ron Guidry	.20	.15	.08
104	Jesse Orosco	.04	.03	.02		195	Eddie Murray	.40	.30	.15
105	George Foster	.08	.06	.03		196	Lou Whitaker	.25	.20	.10
106	Tom Seaver	.20	.15	.08		197	Cal Ripken	.40	.30	.15
107	Keith Hernandez	.15	.11	.06		198	George Brett	.40	.30	.15
108	Mookie Wilson	.06	.05	.02		199	Dale Murphy	.15	.11	.06
109	Bob Bailor	.03	.02	.01		200a	Cecil Cooper	.03	.02	.01
110	Walt Terrell	.04	.03	.02		200b	Jim Rice	.25	.20	.10
111	Brian Giles	.06	.05	.02		201	Tim Raines	.10	.08	.04
112	Jose Oquendo	.06	.05	.02		202	Rickey Henderson	.15	.11	.06
113	Mike Torrez	.03	.02	.01		203	Eddie Murray	.20	.15	.08
114	Junior Ortiz	.03	.02	.01		204	Cal Ripken	.20	.15	.08
115	Pete Rose	.40	.30	.15		205	Gary Roenicke	.03	.02	.01
116	Joe Morgan	.12	.09	.05		206	Ken Singleton	.06	.05	.02
117	Mike Schmidt	.25	.20	.10		207	Scott McGregor	.04	.03	.02
118	Gary Matthews	.06	.05	.02		208	Tippy Martinez	.03	.02	.01
119	Steve Carlton	.15	.11	.06		209	John Lowenstein	.04	.03	.02
120	Bo Diaz	.04	.03	.02		210	Mike Flanagan	.04	.03	.02
121	Ivan DeJesus	.04	.03	.02		211	Jim Palmer	.10	.08	.04
122	John Denny	.03	.02	.01		212	Dan Ford	.12	.09	.05
123	Garry Maddox	.03	.02	.01		213	Rick Dempsey	.04	.03	.02
124	Von Hayes	.08	.06	.03		214	Rich Dauer	.03	.02	.01
125	Al Holland	.03	.02	.01		215	Jerry Remy	.03	.02	.01
126	Tony Perez	.06	.05	.02		216	Wade Boggs	.50	.40	.20
127	John Candelaria	.06	.05	.02		217	Jim Rice	.20	.15	.08
128	Jason Thompson	.03	.02	.01		218	Tony Armas	.06	.05	.02
129	Tony Pena	.06	.05	.02		219	Dwight Evans	.08	.06	.03
130	Dave Parker	.12	.09	.05		220	Bob Stanley	.04	.03	.02
131	Bill Madlock	.08	.06	.03		221	Dave Stapleton	.06	.05	.02
132	Kent Tekulve	.04	.03	.02		222	Rich Gedman	.04	.03	.02
133	larry McWilliams	.03	.02	.01		223	Glenn Hoffman	.06	.05	.02
134	Johnny Ray	.04	.03	.02		224	Dennis Eckersley	.08	.06	.03
135	Marvell Wynne	.03	.02	.01		225	John Tudor	.06	.05	.02
136	Dale Berra	.03	.02	.01		226	Bruce Hurst	.04	.03	.02
137	Mike Easler	.03	.02	.01		227	Rod Carew	.20	.15	.08
138	Lee Lacy	.03	.02	.01		228	Bobby Grich	.06	.05	.02
139	George Hendrick	.04	.03	.02		229	Doug DeCinces	.06	.05	.02
140	Lonnie Smith	.04	.03	.02		230	Fred Lynn	.10	.08	.04
141	Willie McGee	.08	.06	.03		231	Reggie Jackson	.20	.15	.08
142	Tom Herr	.06	.05	.02		232	Tommy John	.10	.08	.04
143	Darrell Porter	.04	.03	.02		233	Luis Sanchez	.03	.02	.01
144	Ozzie Smith	.10	.08	.04		234	Bob Boone	.04	.03	.02
145	Bruce Sutter	.06	.05	.02		235	Bruce Kison	.04	.03	.02
146	Dave LaPoint	.03	.02	.01		236	Brian Downing	.04	.03	.02
147	Neil Allen	.03	.02	.01		237	Ken Forsch	.03	.02	.01
148	Ken Oberkfell	.04	.03	.02		238	Rick Burleson	.04	.03	.02
149	David Green	.03	.02	.01		239	Dennis Lamp	.03	.02	.01
150	Andy Van Slyke	.04	.03	.02		240	LaMarr Hoyt	.03	.02	.01
151	Garry Templeton	.06	.05	.02		241	Richard Dotson	.04	.03	.02
152	Juan Bonilla	.03	.02	.01		242	Harold Baines	.10	.08	.04
153	Alan Wiggins	.03	.02	.01		243	Carlton Fisk	.12	.09	.05
154	Terry Kennedy	.04	.03	.02		244	Greg Luzinski	.08	.06	.03
155	Dave Dravecky	.04	.03	.02		245	Rudy Law	.06	.05	.02
156	Steve Garvey	.15	.11	.06		246	Tom Paciorek	.03	.02	.01
157	Bobby Brown	.04	.03	.02		247	Floyd Bannister	.04	.03	.02
158	Ruppert Jones	.03	.02	.01		248	Julio Cruz	.04	.03	.02
159	Luis Salazar	.03	.02	.01		249	Vance Law	.03	.02	.01
160	Tony Gwynn	.12	.09	.05		250	Scott Fletcher	.04	.03	.02
161	Gary Lucas	.10	.08	.04		251	Toby Harrah	.04	.03	.02
162	Eric Show	.04	.03	.02		252	Pat Tabler	.04	.03	.02
163	Darrell Evans	.08	.06	.03		253	Gorman Thomas	.06	.05	.02
164	Gary Lavelle	.03	.02	.01		254	Rick Sutcliffe	.08	.06	.03
165	Atlee Hammaker	.03	.02	.01		255	Andre Thornton	.06	.05	.02
166	Jeff Leonard	.06	.05	.02		256	Bake McBride	.03	.02	.01
167	Jack Clark	.10	.08	.04		257	Alan Bannister	.03	.02	.01
168	Johnny LeMaster	.03	.02	.01		258	Jamie Easterly	.03	.02	.01
169	Duane Kuiper	.03	.02	.01		259	Lary Sorenson	.03	.02	.01
170	Tom O'Malley	.06	.05	.02		260	Mike Hargrove	.03	.02	.01
171	Chili Davis	.06	.05	.02		261	Bert Blyleven	.06	.05	.02
172	Bill Laskey	.03	.02	.01		262	Ron Hassey	.04	.03	.02
173	Joel Youngblood	.06	.05	.02		263	Jack Morris	.12	.09	.05
174	Bob Brenly	.06	.05	.02		264	Larry Herndon	.03	.02	.01
175	Atlee Hammaker	.15	.11	.06		265	Lance Parrish	.12	.09	.05
176	Rick Honeycutt	.15	.11	.06		266	Alan Trammell	.15	.11	.06

		MT	NR MT	EX
267	Lou Whitaker	.12	.09	.05
268	Aurelio Lopez	.03	.02	.01
269	Dan Petry	.04	.03	.02
270	Glenn Wilson	.04	.03	.02
271	Chet Lemon	.04	.03	.02
272	Kirk Gibson	.06	.05	.02
273	Enos Cabell	.04	.03	.02
274	Johnny Wockenfuss	.03	.02	.01
275	George Brett	.25	.20	.10
276	Willie Aikens	.03	.02	.01
277	Frank White	.04	.03	.02
278	Hal McRae	.06	.05	.02
279	Dan Quisenberry	.06	.05	.02
280	Willie Wilson	.08	.06	.03
281	Paul Splittorff	.03	.02	.01
282	U.L. Washington	.03	.02	.01
283	Bud Black	.06	.05	.02
284	John Wathan	.04	.03	.02
285	Larry Gura	.03	.02	.01
286	Pat Sheridan	.03	.02	.01
287a	Rusty Staub	.06	.05	.02
287b	Dave Righetti	.25	.20	.10
288a	Bob Forsch	.03	.02	.01
288b	Mike Warren	.06	.05	.02
289	Al Holland	.10	.08	.04
290	Dan Quisenberry	.15	.11	.06
291	Cecil Cooper	.06	.05	.02
292	Moose Haas	.03	.02	.01
293	Ted Simmons	.08	.06	.03
294	Paul Molitor	.10	.08	.04
295	Robin Yount	.15	.11	.06
296	Ben Oglivie	.04	.03	.02
297	Tom Tellmann	.50	.40	.20
298	Jim Gantner	.04	.03	.02
299	Rick Manning	.03	.02	.01
300	Don Sutton	.06	.05	.02
301	Charlie Moore	.04	.03	.02
302	Jim Slaton	.03	.02	.01
303	Gary Ward	.04	.03	.02
304	Tom Brunansky	.08	.06	.03
305	Kent Hrbek	.12	.09	.05
306	Gary Gaetti	.10	.08	.04
307	John Castino	.03	.02	.01
308	Ken Schrom	.03	.02	.01
309	Ron Davis	.03	.02	.01
310	Lenny Faedo	.03	.02	.01
311	Darrell Brown	.06	.05	.02
312	Frank Viola	.06	.05	.02
313	Dave Engle	.03	.02	.01
314	Randy Bush	.03	.02	.01
315	Dave Righetti	.12	.09	.05
316	Rich Gossage	.12	.09	.05
317	Ken Griffey	.06	.05	.02
318	Ron Guidry	.12	.09	.05
319	Dave Winfield	.15	.11	.06
320	Don Baylor	.08	.06	.03
321	Butch Wynegar	.03	.02	.01
322	Omar Moreno	.03	.02	.01
323	Andre Robertson	.03	.02	.01
324	Willie Randolph	.04	.03	.02
325	Don Mattingly	.50	.40	.20
326	Graig Nettles	.06	.05	.02
327	Rickey Henderson	.25	.20	.10
328	Carney Lansford	.08	.06	.03
329	Jeff Burroughs	.04	.03	.02
330	Chris Codiroli	.03	.02	.01
331	Dave Lopes	.06	.05	.02
332	Dwayne Murphy	.04	.03	.02
333	Wayne Gross	.03	.02	.01
334	Bill Almon	.03	.02	.01
335	Tom Underwood	.04	.03	.02
336	Dave Beard	.03	.02	.01
337	Mike Heath	.03	.02	.01
338	Mike Davis	.04	.03	.02
339	Pat Putnam	.03	.02	.01
340	Tony Bernazard	.03	.02	.01
341	Steve Henderson	.03	.02	.01
342	Richie Zisk	.04	.03	.02
343	Dave Henderson	.06	.05	.02
344	Al Cowens	.03	.02	.01
345	Bill Caudill	.03	.02	.01
346	Jim Beattie	.06	.05	.02
347	Ricky Nelson	.04	.03	.02
348	Roy Thomas	.06	.05	.02
349	Spike Owen	.04	.03	.02
350	Jamie Allen	.03	.02	.01
351	Buddy Bell	.06	.05	.02
352	Billy Sample	.03	.02	.01
353	George Wright	.03	.02	.01
354	Larry Parrish	.06	.05	.02
355	Jim Sundberg	.04	.03	.02

		MT	NR MT	EX
356	Charlie Hough	.06	.05	.02
357	Pete O'Brien	.06	.05	.02
358	Wayne Tolleson	.03	.02	.01
359	Danny Darwin	.03	.02	.01
360	Dave Stewart	.04	.03	.02
361	Mickey Rivers	.04	.03	.02
362	Bucky Dent	.04	.03	.02
363	Willie Upshaw	.06	.05	.02
364	Damaso Garcia	.04	.03	.02
365	Lloyd Moseby	.06	.05	.02
366	Cliff Johnson	.03	.02	.01
367	Jim Clancy	.04	.03	.02
368	Dave Stieb	.06	.05	.02
369	Alfredo Griffin	.04	.03	.02
370	Barry Bonnell	.04	.03	.02
371	Luis Leal	.03	.02	.01
372	Jesse Barfield	.06	.05	.02
373	Ernie Whitt	.03	.02	.01
374	Rance Mulliniks	.06	.05	.02
375	Mike Boddicker	.06	.05	.02
376	Greg Brock	.06	.05	.02
377	Bill Doran	.06	.05	.02
378	Nick Esasky	.06	.05	.02
379	Julio Franco	.08	.06	.03
380	Mel Hall	.06	.05	.02
381	Bob Kearney	.03	.02	.01
382	Ron Kittle	.06	.05	.02
383	Carmelo Martinez	.06	.05	.02
384	Craig McMurtry	.03	.02	.01
385	Darryl Strawberry	.30	.25	.12
386	Matt Young	.04	.03	.02

1984 Topps Stickers Boxes

For the second straight year, Topps printed baseball cards on the back of its sticker boxes. The 1984 set, titled "The Super Bats" features 24 hitting leaders. The cards are blank-backed and measure 2-1/2" by 3-1/2". Two cards were printed on each of 12 different boxes. The player's name appears inside a bat above his photo. Prices listed are for complete boxes.

		MT	NR MT	EX
Complete Set:		8.50	6.50	3.50
Common Player:		.75	.60	.30
1	Al Oliver, Lou Whitaker	1.00	.70	.40
2	Ken Oberkfell, Ted Simmons	.75	.60	.30
3	Hal McRae, Alan Wiggins	.75	.60	.30
4	Lloyd Moseby, Tim Raines	1.00	.70	.40
5	Lonnie Smith, Willie Wilson	.75	.60	.30
6	Keith Hernandez, Robin Yount	.75	.60	.30
7	Wade Boggs, Johnny Ray	1.50	1.25	.60
8	Willie McGee, Ken Singleton	.75	.60	.30
9	Ray Knight, Alan Trammell	1.00	.70	.40
11	Rod Carew, George Hendrick	1.25	.90	.50
12	Bill Madlock, Eddie Murray	1.25	.90	.50
13	Jose Cruz, Cal Ripken, Jr.	1.25	.90	.50

1984 Topps Super

The next installment in Topps' continuing production of large-format cards, these 4-7/8" by 6-7/8" cards were sold in cellophane packs with a complete

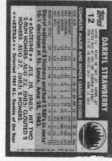

set being 30 cards. Other than their size and the change in n card number on the back, there is nothing to distinguish the Supers from the regular 1984 players are all big name stars, and are likely to remain in demand.

		MT	NR MT	EX
Complete Set:		10.00	7.50	4.00
Common Player:		.20	.15	.08
1	Cal Ripken	.70	.50	.30
2	Dale Murphy	.90	.70	.35
3	LaMarr Hoyt	.20	.15	.08
4	John Denny	.20	.15	.08
5	Jim Rice	.50	.40	.20
6	Mike Schmidt	.90	.70	.35
7	Wade Boggs	1.25	.90	.50
8	Bill Madlock	.20	.15	.08
9	Dan Quisenberry	.20	.15	.08
10	Al Holland	.20	.15	.08
11	Ron Kittle	.20	.15	.08
12	Darryl Strawberry	1.25	.90	.50
13	George Brett	.90	.70	.35
14	Bill Buckner	.25	.20	.10
15	Carlton Fisk	.30	.25	.12
16	Steve Carlton	.50	.40	.20
17	Ron Guidry	.35	.25	.14
18	Gary Carter	.50	.40	.20
19	Rickey Henderson	.70	.50	.30
20	Andre Dawson	.35	.25	.14
21	Reggie Jackson	.60	.45	.25
22	Steve Garvey	.50	.40	.20
23	Fred Lynn	.30	.25	.12
24	Pedro Guerrero	.25	.20	.10
25	Eddie Murray	.60	.45	.25
26	Keith Hernandez	.50	.40	.20
27	Dave Winfield	.50	.40	.20
28	Nolan Ryan	.50	.40	.20
29	Robin Yount	.40	.30	.15
30	Fernando Valenzuela	.40	.30	.15

1984 Topps Traded

The popular Topps Traded set returned for its fourth year in 1984 with another 132-card set. The 2-1/2" by 3-1/2" cards have an identical design to the regular Topps cards except that the back cardboard is white and the card numbers carry a "T"

suffix. As before, the set was sold only through hobby dealers. Also as before, players who changed teams, new managers and promising rookies are included in the set. The presence of several promising young rookies in especially high demand from investors and speculators had made this one of the most expensive Topps issues of recent years. A glossy-finish "Tiffany" version of the set was also issued, valued at four to five times the price of the normal Traded cards.

		MT	NR MT	EX
Complete Set:		90.00	67.50	35.00
Common Player:		.10	.08	.04
1T	Willie Aikens	.10	.08	.04
2T	Luis Aponte	.10	.08	.04
3T	Mike Armstrong	.10	.08	.04
4T	Bob Bailor	.10	.08	.04
5T	Dusty Baker	.20	.15	.08
6T	Steve Balboni	.20	.15	.08
7T	Alan Bannister	.10	.08	.04
8T	Dave Beard	.10	.08	.04
9T	Joe Beckwith	.10	.08	.04
10T	Bruce Berenyi	.10	.08	.04
11T	Dave Bergman	.10	.08	.04
12T	Tony Bernazard	.10	.08	.04
13T	Yogi Berra	.20	.15	.08
14T	Barry Bonnell	.10	.08	.04
15T	Phil Bradley(FC)	1.75	1.25	.70
16T	Fred Breining	.10	.08	.04
17T	Bill Buckner	.25	.20	.10
18T	Ray Burris	.10	.08	.04
19T	John Butcher	.10	.08	.04
20T	Brett Butler	.20	.15	.08
21T	Enos Cabell	.10	.08	.04
22T	Bill Campbell	.10	.08	.04
23T	Bill Caudill	.10	.08	.04
24T	Bob Clark	.10	.08	.04
25T	Bryan Clark	.10	.08	.04
26T	Jaime Cocanower	.10	.08	.04
27T	Ron Darling(FC)	6.00	4.50	2.50
28T	Alvin Davis(FC)	4.00	3.00	1.50
29T	Ken Dayley	.10	.08	.04
30T	Jeff Dedmon(FC)	.15	.11	.06
31T	Bob Dernier	.10	.08	.04
32T	Carlos Diaz	.10	.08	.04
33T	Mike Easler	.15	.11	.06
34T	Dennis Eckersley	.30	.25	.12
35T	Jim Essian	.10	.08	.04
36T	Darrell Evans	.25	.20	.10
37T	Mike Fitzgerald(FC)	.15	.11	.06
38T	Tim Foli	.10	.08	.04
39T	George Frazier	.10	.08	.04
40T	Rich Gale	.10	.08	.04
41T	Barbaro Garbey	.15	.11	.06
42T	Dwight Gooden(FC)	45.00	34.00	18.00
43T	Rich Gossage	.40	.30	.15
44T	Wayne Gross	.10	.08	.04
45T	Mark Gubicza(FC)	5.00	3.75	2.00
46T	Jackie Gutierrez	.10	.08	.04
47T	Mel Hall	.20	.15	.08
48T	Toby Harrah	.15	.11	.06
49T	Ron Hassey	.10	.08	.04
50T	Rich Hebner	.10	.08	.04
51T	Willie Hernandez	.30	.25	.12
52T	Ricky Horton(FC)	.40	.30	.15
53T	Art Howe	.10	.08	.04
54T	Dane Iorg	.10	.08	.04
55T	Brook Jacoby(FC)	1.25	.90	.50
56T	Mike Jeffcoat(FC)	.15	.11	.06
57T	Dave Johnson	.15	.11	.06
58T	Lynn Jones	.10	.08	.04
59T	Ruppert Jones	.10	.08	.04
60T	Mike Jorgensen	.10	.08	.04
61T	Bob Kearney	.10	.08	.04
62T	Jimmy Key(FC)	3.00	2.25	1.25
63T	Dave Kingman	.40	.30	.15
64T	Jerry Koosman	.25	.20	.10
65T	Wayne Krenchicki	.10	.08	.04
66T	Rusty Kuntz	.10	.08	.04
67T	Rene Lachemann	.10	.08	.04
68T	Frank LaCorte	.10	.08	.04
69T	Dennis Lamp	.10	.08	.04
70T	Mark Langston(FC)	9.00	6.75	3.50
71T	Rick Leach	.10	.08	.04
72T	Craig Lefferts	.15	.11	.06
73T	Gary Lucas	.10	.08	.04
74T	Jerry Martin	.10	.08	.04
75T	Carmelo Martinez	.25	.20	.10
76T	Mike Mason(FC)	.15	.11	.06

		MT	NR MT	EX
77T	Gary Matthews	.25	.20	.10
78T	Andy McGaffigan	.10	.08	.04
79T	Larry Milbourne	.10	.08	.04
80T	Sid Monge	.10	.08	.04
81T	Jackie Moore	.10	.08	.04
82T	Joe Morgan	1.00	.70	.40
83T	Graig Nettles	.50	.40	.20
84T	Phil Niekro	1.00	.70	.40
85T	Ken Oberkfell	.10	.08	.04
86T	Mike O'Berry	.10	.08	.04
87T	Al Oliver	.30	.25	.12
88T	Jorge Orta	.10	.08	.04
89T	Amos Otis	.15	.11	.06
90T	Dave Parker	.80	.60	.30
91T	Tony Perez	.60	.45	.25
92T	Gerald Perry(FC)	1.25	.90	.50
93T	Gary Pettis(FC)	.25	.20	.10
94T	Rob Picciolo	.10	.08	.04
95T	Vern Rapp	.10	.08	.04
96T	Floyd Rayford	.10	.08	.04
97T	Randy Ready(FC)	.25	.20	.10
98T	Ron Reed	.15	.11	.06
99T	Gene Richards	.10	.08	.04
100T	Jose Rijo(FC)	1.50	1.25	.60
101T	Jeff Robinson(FC)	.50	.40	.20
102T	Ron Romanick(FC)	.20	.15	.08
103T	Pete Rose	6.00	4.50	2.50
104T	Bret Saberhagen(FC)	15.00	11.00	6.00
105T	Juan Samuel(FC)	2.50	2.00	1.00
106T	Scott Sanderson	.10	.08	.04
107T	Dick Schofield(FC)	.35	.25	.14
108T	Tom Seaver	2.50	2.00	1.00
109T	Jim Slaton	.10	.08	.04
110T	Mike Smithson	.10	.08	.04
111T	Lary Sorensen	.10	.08	.04
112T	Tim Stoddard	.10	.08	.04
113T	Champ Summers	.10	.08	.04
114T	Jim Sundberg	.15	.11	.06
115T	Rick Sutcliffe	.50	.40	.20
116T	Craig Swan	.10	.08	.04
117T	Tim Teufel(FC)	.30	.25	.12
118T	Derrel Thomas	.10	.08	.04
119T	Gorman Thomas	.25	.20	.10
120T	Alex Trevino	.10	.08	.04
121T	Manny Trillo	.15	.11	.06
122T	John Tudor	.25	.20	.10
123T	Tom Underwood	.10	.08	.04
124T	Mike Vail	.10	.08	.04
125T	Tom Waddell	.10	.08	.04
126T	Gary Ward	.10	.08	.04
127T	Curt Wilkerson	.10	.08	.04
128T	Frank Williams(FC)	.25	.20	.10
129T	Glenn Wilson	.20	.15	.08
130T	Johnny Wockenfuss	.10	.08	.04
131T	Ned Yost	.10	.08	.04
132T	Checklist 1-132	.10	.08	.04

1985 Topps

Holding the line at 792 cards, Topps did initiate some major design changes in its 2-1/2" by 3-1/2" cards in 1985. The use of two photos on the front was discontinued in favor of one large color photo. The Topps logo appears in the upper left-hand corner. At the bottom runs a diagonal rectangular box with the team name. It joins a team logo, and below that point runs the player's position and name. The backs feature statistics, biographical information and a

trivia question. Some interesting specialty sets were introduced in 1985, including the revival of the father/son theme from 1976, a subset of the 1984 U.S. Olympic Baseball Team members and a set featuring #1 draft choices since the inception of the baseball draft in 1965. Again in 1985, a glossy-finish "Tiffany" edition of the regular set was produced, though the number was cut back to 5,000 sets. Values range from four times regular value for common cards to five-six times for high-demand stars and rookie cards.

		MT	NR MT	EX
Complete Set:		90.00	67.00	36.00
Common Player:		.06	.05	.02
1	Record Breaker (Carlton Fisk)	.15	.11	.06
2	Record Breaker (Steve Garvey)	.20	.15	.08
3	Record Breaker (Dwight Gooden)	1.00	.70	.40
4	Record Breaker (Cliff Johnson)	.08	.06	.03
5	Record Breaker (Joe Morgan)	.15	.11	.06
6	Record Breaker (Pete Rose)	.60	.45	.25
7	Record Breaker (Nolan Ryan)	.30	.25	.12
8	Record Breaker (Juan Samuel)(FC)	.20	.15	.08
9	Record Breaker (Bruce Sutter)	.12	.09	.05
10	Record Breaker (Don Sutton)	.20	.15	.08
11	Ralph Houk	.08	.06	.03
12	Dave Lopes	.08	.06	.03
13	Tim Lollar	.06	.05	.02
14	Chris Bando	.06	.05	.02
15	Jerry Koosman	.10	.08	.04
16	Bobby Meacham	.06	.05	.02
17	Mike Scott	.15	.11	.06
18	Mickey Hatcher	.06	.05	.02
19	George Frazier	.06	.05	.02
20	Chet Lemon	.08	.06	.03
21	Lee Tunnell	.06	.05	.02
22	Duane Kuiper	.06	.05	.02
23	*Bret Saberhagen*	5.00	3.75	2.00
24	Jesse Barfield	.25	.20	.10
25	Steve Bedrosian	.12	.09	.05
26	Roy Smalley	.06	.05	.02
27	Bruce Berenyi	.06	.05	.02
28	Dann Bilardello	.06	.05	.02
29	Odell Jones	.06	.05	.02
30	Cal Ripken	.50	.40	.20
31	Terry Whitfield	.06	.05	.02
32	Chuck Porter	.06	.05	.02
33	Tito Landrum	.06	.05	.02
34	Ed Nunez(FC)	.08	.06	.03
35	Graig Nettles	.15	.11	.06
36	Fred Breining	.06	.05	.02
37	Reid Nichols	.06	.05	.02
38	Jackie Moore	.06	.05	.02
39	Johnny Wockenfuss	.06	.05	.02
40	Phil Niekro	.25	.20	.10
41	Mike Fischlin	.06	.05	.02
42	Luis Sanchez	.06	.05	.02
43	Andre David	.06	.05	.02
44	Dickie Thon	.08	.06	.03
45	Greg Minton	.06	.05	.02
46	Gary Woods	.06	.05	.02
47	Dave Rozema	.06	.05	.02
48	Tony Fernandez(FC)	1.00	.70	.40
49	Butch Davis	.06	.05	.02
50	John Candelaria	.10	.08	.04
51	Bob Watson	.08	.06	.03
52	Jerry Dybzinski	.06	.05	.02
53	Tom Gorman	.06	.05	.02
54	Cesar Cedeno	.10	.08	.04
55	Frank Tanana	.10	.08	.04
56	Jim Dwyer	.06	.05	.02
57	Pat Zachry	.06	.05	.02
58	Orlando Mercado	.06	.05	.02
59	Rick Waits	.06	.05	.02
60	George Hendrick	.08	.06	.03
61	Curt Kaufman	.06	.05	.02
62	Mike Ramsey	.06	.05	.02
63	Steve McCatty	.06	.05	.02
64	*Mark Bailey*(FC)	.10	.08	.04
65	Bill Buckner	.12	.09	.05
66	Dick Williams	.06	.05	.02
67	*Rafael Santana*(FC)	.20	.15	.08
68	Von Hayes	.10	.08	.04
69	*Jim Winn*(FC)	.10	.08	.04
70	Don Baylor	.12	.09	.05
71	Tim Laudner	.06	.05	.02
72	Rick Sutcliffe	.12	.09	.05
73	Rusty Kuntz	.06	.05	.02

#	Name	MT	NR MT	EX
74	Mike Krukow	.08	.06	.03
75	Willie Upshaw	.08	.06	.03
76	Alan Bannister	.06	.05	.02
77	Joe Beckwith	.06	.05	.02
78	Scott Fletcher	.08	.06	.03
79	Rick Mahler	.06	.05	.02
80	Keith Hernandez	.30	.25	.12
81	Lenn Sakata	.06	.05	.02
82	Joe Price	.06	.05	.02
83	Charlie Moore	.06	.05	.02
84	Spike Owen	.08	.06	.03
85	Mike Marshall	.15	.11	.06
86	Don Aase	.06	.05	.02
87	David Green	.06	.05	.02
88	Bryn Smith	.06	.05	.02
89	Jackie Gutierrez	.06	.05	.02
90	Rich Gossage	.20	.15	.08
91	Jeff Burroughs	.08	.06	.03
92	Paul Owens	.06	.05	.02
93	*Don Schulze*(FC)	.10	.08	.04
94	Toby Harrah	.08	.06	.03
95	Jose Cruz	.10	.08	.04
96	Johnny Ray	.12	.09	.05
97	Pete Filson	.06	.05	.02
98	Steve Lake	.06	.05	.02
99	Milt Wilcox	.06	.05	.02
100	George Brett	.50	.40	.20
101	Jim Acker	.06	.05	.02
102	Tommy Dunbar	.06	.05	.02
103	Randy Lerch	.06	.05	.02
104	Mike Fitzgerald	.08	.06	.03
105	Ron Kittle	.10	.08	.04
106	Pascual Perez	.08	.06	.03
107	Tom Foley	.06	.05	.02
108	Darnell Coles(FC)	.15	.11	.06
109	Gary Roenicke	.06	.05	.02
110	Alejandro Pena	.08	.06	.03
111	Doug DeCinces	.10	.08	.04
112	Tom Tellmann	.06	.05	.02
113	Tom Herr	.10	.08	.04
114	Bob James	.06	.05	.02
115	Rickey Henderson	.40	.30	.15
116	Dennis Boyd(FC)	.15	.11	.06
117	Greg Gross	.06	.05	.02
118	Eric Show	.08	.06	.03
119	Pat Corrales	.06	.05	.02
120	Steve Kemp	.08	.06	.03
121	Checklist 1-132	.06	.05	.02
122	Tom Brunansky	.12	.09	.05
123	Dave Smith	.08	.06	.03
124	Rich Hebner	.06	.05	.02
125	Kent Tekulve	.08	.06	.03
126	Ruppert Jones	.06	.05	.02
127	*Mark Gubicza*	.90	.70	.35
128	Ernie Whitt	.08	.06	.03
129	Gene Garber	.06	.05	.02
130	Al Oliver	.12	.09	.05
131	Father - Son (Buddy Bell, Gus Bell)	.12	.09	.05
132	Father - Son (Dale Berra, Yogi Berra)	.20	.15	.08
133	Father - Son (Bob Boone, Ray Boone)	.12	.09	.05
134	Father - Son (Terry Francona, Tito Francona)	.08	.06	.03
135	Father - Son (Bob Kennedy, Terry Kennedy)	.08	.06	.03
136	Father - Son (Bill Kunkel, Jeff Kunkel)(FC)	.08	.06	.03
137	Father - Son (Vance Law, Vern Law)	.10	.08	.04
138	Father - Son (Dick Schofield, Dick Schofield)	.08	.06	.03
139	Father - Son (Bob Skinner, Joel Skinner)	.08	.06	.03
140	Father - Son (Roy Smalley, Roy Smalley)	.08	.06	.03
141	Father - Son (Dave Stenhouse, Mike Stenhouse)	.08	.06	.03
142	Father - Son (Dizzy Trout, Steve Trout)	.08	.06	.03
143	Father - Son (Ossie Virgil, Ozzie Virgil)	.08	.06	.03
144	Ron Gardenhire	.06	.05	.02
145	*Alvin Davis*	2.00	1.50	.80
146	Gary Redus	.08	.06	.03
147	Bill Swaggerty	.06	.05	.02
148	Steve Yeager	.06	.05	.02
149	Dickie Noles	.06	.05	.02
150	Jim Rice	.35	.25	.14
151	Moose Haas	.06	.05	.02
152	Steve Braun	.06	.05	.02
153	Frank LaCorte	.06	.05	.02
154	Argenis Salazar(FC)	.06	.05	.02
155	Yogi Berra	.12	.09	.05
156	Craig Reynolds	.06	.05	.02
157	Tug McGraw	.10	.08	.04
158	Pat Tabler	.08	.06	.03
159	Carlos Diaz	.06	.05	.02
160	Lance Parrish	.25	.20	.10
161	Ken Schrom	.06	.05	.02
162	*Benny Distefano*(FC)	.10	.08	.04
163	Dennis Eckersley	.12	.09	.05
164	Jorge Orta	.06	.05	.02
165	Dusty Baker	.08	.06	.03
166	Keith Atherton	.06	.05	.02
167	Rufino Linares	.06	.05	.02
168	Garth Iorg	.06	.05	.02
169	Dan Spillner	.06	.05	.02
170	George Foster	.15	.11	.06
171	Bill Stein	.06	.05	.02
172	Jack Perconte	.06	.05	.02
173	Mike Young(FC)	.12	.09	.05
174	Rick Honeycutt	.06	.05	.02
175	Dave Parker	.25	.20	.10
176	Bill Schroeder	.06	.05	.02
177	Dave Von Ohlen	.06	.05	.02
178	Miguel Dilone	.06	.05	.02
179	Tommy John	.20	.15	.08
180	Dave Winfield	.35	.25	.14
181	*Roger Clemens*(FC)	10.00	7.50	4.00
182	Tim Flannery	.06	.05	.02
183	Larry McWilliams	.06	.05	.02
184	Carmen Castillo(FC)	.10	.08	.04
185	Al Holland	.06	.05	.02
186	Bob Lillis	.06	.05	.02
187	Mike Walters	.06	.05	.02
188	Greg Pryor	.06	.05	.02
189	Warren Brusstar	.06	.05	.02
190	Rusty Staub	.12	.09	.05
191	Steve Nicosia	.08	.06	.03
192	Howard Johnson(FC)	4.00	3.00	1.50
193	*Jimmy Key*	1.00	.70	.40
194	Dave Stegman	.06	.05	.02
195	Glenn Hubbard	.06	.05	.02
196	Pete O'Brien	.12	.09	.05
197	Mike Warren	.06	.05	.02
198	Eddie Milner	.06	.05	.02
199	Denny Martinez	.08	.06	.03
200	Reggie Jackson	.40	.30	.15
201	Burt Hooton	.08	.06	.03
202	Gorman Thomas	.10	.08	.04
203	Bob McClure	.06	.05	.02
204	Art Howe	.06	.05	.02
205	Steve Rogers	.08	.06	.03
206	Phil Garner	.08	.06	.03
207	Mark Clear	.06	.05	.02
208	Champ Summers	.06	.05	.02
209	Bill Campbell	.06	.05	.02
210	Gary Matthews	.10	.08	.04
211	Clay Christiansen	.06	.05	.02
212	George Vukovich	.06	.05	.02
213	Billy Gardner	.06	.05	.02
214	John Tudor	.10	.08	.04
215	Bob Brenly	.06	.05	.02
216	Jerry Don Gleaton	.06	.05	.02
217	Leon Roberts	.06	.05	.02
218	Doyle Alexander	.10	.08	.04
219	Gerald Perry	.35	.25	.14
220	Fred Lynn	.20	.15	.08
221	Ron Reed	.06	.05	.02
222	Hubie Brooks	.10	.08	.04
223	Tom Hume	.06	.05	.02
224	Al Cowens	.06	.05	.02
225	Mike Boddicker	.10	.08	.04
226	Juan Beniquez	.06	.05	.02
227	Danny Darwin	.06	.05	.02
228	Dion James(FC)	.20	.15	.08
229	Dave LaPoint	.08	.06	.03
230	Gary Carter	.35	.25	.14
231	Dwayne Murphy	.08	.06	.03
232	Dave Beard	.06	.05	.02
233	Ed Jurak	.06	.05	.02
234	Jerry Narron	.06	.05	.02
235	Garry Maddox	.10	.08	.04
236	Mark Thurmond	.06	.05	.02
237	Julio Franco	.50	.40	.20
238	*Jose Rijo*	.40	.30	.15
239	Tim Teufel	.12	.09	.05
240	Dave Stieb	.12	.09	.05
241	Jim Frey	.06	.05	.02
242	Greg Harris	.06	.05	.02
243	Barbaro Garbey	.10	.08	.04

#	Name	MT	NR MT	EX
244	Mike Jones	.06	.05	.02
245	Chili Davis	.10	.08	.04
246	Mike Norris	.06	.05	.02
247	Wayne Tolleson	.06	.05	.02
248	Terry Forster	.08	.06	.03
249	Harold Baines	.15	.11	.06
250	Jesse Orosco	.08	.06	.03
251	Brad Gulden	.06	.05	.02
252	Dan Ford	.06	.05	.02
253	*Sid Bream*(FC)	.40	.30	.15
254	Pete Vuckovich	.08	.06	.03
255	Lonnie Smith	.08	.06	.03
256	Mike Stanton	.06	.05	.02
257	Brian Little (Bryan)	.06	.05	.02
258	Mike Brown	.06	.05	.02
259	Gary Allenson	.06	.05	.02
260	Dave Righetti	.20	.15	.08
261	Checklist 133-264	.06	.05	.02
262	*Greg Booker*(FC)	.12	.09	.05
263	Mel Hall	.08	.06	.03
264	Joe Sambito	.06	.05	.02
265	Juan Samuel(FC)	.50	.40	.20
266	Frank Viola	.20	.15	.08
267	*Henry Cotto*(FC)	.15	.11	.06
268	Chuck Tanner	.06	.05	.02
269	*Doug Baker*(FC)	.10	.08	.04
270	Dan Quisenberry	.10	.08	.04
271	1968 #1 Draft Pick (Tim Foli)	.08	.06	.03
272	1969 #1 Draft Pick (Jeff Burroughs)	.08	.06	.03
273	1974 #1 Draft Pick (Bill Almon)	.08	.06	.03
274	1976 #1 Draft Pick (Floyd Bannister)	.10	.08	.04
275	1977 #1 Draft Pick (Harold Baines)	.15	.11	.06
276	1978 #1 Draft Pick (Bob Horner)	.15	.11	.06
277	1979 #1 Draft Pick (Al Chambers)	.08	.06	.03
278	1980 #1 Draft Pick (Darryl Strawberry)	1.00	.70	.40
279	1981 #1 Draft Pick (Mike Moore)	.08	.06	.03
280	1982 #1 Draft Pick (*Shawon Dunston*)(FC)	.90	.70	.35
281	1983 #1 Draft Pick (Tim Belcher)(FC)	1.00	.70	.40
282	1984 #1 Draft Pick (*Shawn Abner*)(FC)	.60	.45	.25
283	Fran Mullins	.06	.05	.02
284	Marty Bystrom	.06	.05	.02
285	Dan Driessen	.08	.06	.03
286	Rudy Law	.06	.05	.02
287	Walt Terrell	.08	.06	.03
288	*Jeff Kunkel*(FC)	.10	.08	.04
289	Tom Underwood	.06	.05	.02
290	Cecil Cooper	.12	.09	.05
291	Bob Welch	.12	.09	.05
292	Brad Komminsk(FC)	.08	.06	.03
293	*Curt Young*(FC)	.35	.25	.14
294	*Tom Nieto*(FC)	.10	.08	.04
295	Joe Niekro	.10	.08	.04
296	Ricky Nelson	.06	.05	.02
297	Gary Lucas	.06	.05	.02
298	Marty Barrett	.15	.11	.06
299	Andy Hawkins	.08	.06	.03
300	Rod Carew	.40	.30	.15
301	John Montefusco	.06	.05	.02
302	Tim Corcoran	.06	.05	.02
303	*Mike Jeffcoat*	.08	.06	.03
304	Gary Gaetti	.25	.20	.10
305	Dale Berra	.06	.05	.02
306	Rick Reuschel	.10	.08	.04
307	Sparky Anderson	.08	.06	.03
308	John Wathan	.08	.06	.03
309	Mike Witt	.12	.09	.05
310	Manny Trillo	.08	.06	.03
311	Jim Gott	.06	.05	.02
312	Marc Hill	.06	.05	.02
313	Dave Schmidt	.06	.05	.02
314	Ron Oester	.06	.05	.02
315	Doug Sisk	.06	.05	.02
316	John Lowenstein	.06	.05	.02
317	*Jack Lazorko*(FC)	.10	.08	.04
318	Ted Simmons	.12	.09	.05
319	Jeff Jones	.06	.05	.02
320	Dale Murphy	.60	.45	.25
321	*Ricky Horton*	.30	.25	.12
322	Dave Stapleton	.06	.05	.02
323	Andy McGaffigan	.06	.05	.02
324	Bruce Bochy	.06	.05	.02
325	John Denny	.06	.05	.02
326	Kevin Bass	.10	.08	.04
327	Brook Jacoby	.30	.25	.12
328	Bob Shirley	.06	.05	.02
329	Ron Washington	.06	.05	.02
330	Leon Durham	.08	.06	.03
331	Bill Laskey	.06	.05	.02
332	Brian Harper	.06	.05	.02
333	Willie Hernandez	.08	.06	.03
334	Dick Howser	.06	.05	.02
335	Bruce Benedict	.06	.05	.02
336	Rance Mulliniks	.06	.05	.02
337	Billy Sample	.06	.05	.02
338	Britt Burns	.06	.05	.02
339	Danny Heep	.06	.05	.02
340	Robin Yount	.40	.30	.15
341	Floyd Rayford	.06	.05	.02
342	Ted Power	.06	.05	.02
343	Bill Russell	.08	.06	.03
344	Dave Henderson	.10	.08	.04
345	Charlie Lea	.06	.05	.02
346	*Terry Pendleton*(FC)	.70	.50	.30
347	Rick Langford	.06	.05	.02
348	Bob Boone	.08	.06	.03
349	Domingo Ramos	.06	.05	.02
350	Wade Boggs	3.50	2.75	1.50
351	Juan Agosto	.06	.05	.02
352	Joe Morgan	.30	.25	.12
353	Julio Solano	.06	.05	.02
354	Andre Robertson	.06	.05	.02
355	Bert Blyleven	.12	.09	.05
356	Dave Meier	.06	.05	.02
357	Rich Bordi	.06	.05	.02
358	Tony Pena	.10	.08	.04
359	Pat Sheridan	.06	.05	.02
360	Steve Carlton	.40	.30	.15
361	Alfredo Griffin	.08	.06	.03
362	Craig McMurtry	.06	.05	.02
363	Ron Hodges	.06	.05	.02
364	Richard Dotson	.10	.08	.04
365	Danny Ozark	.06	.05	.02
366	Todd Cruz	.06	.05	.02
367	Keefe Cato	.06	.05	.02
368	Dave Bergman	.06	.05	.02
369	*R.J. Reynolds*(FC)	.25	.20	.10
370	Bruce Sutter	.12	.09	.05
371	Mickey Rivers	.08	.06	.03
372	Roy Howell	.06	.05	.02
373	Mike Moore	.06	.05	.02
374	Brian Downing	.10	.08	.04
375	Jeff Reardon	.12	.09	.05
376	Jeff Newman	.06	.05	.02
377	Checklist 265-396	.06	.05	.02
378	Alan Wiggins	.06	.05	.02
379	Charles Hudson	.08	.06	.03
380	Ken Griffey	.10	.08	.04
381	Roy Smith	.06	.05	.02
382	Denny Walling	.06	.05	.02
383	Rick Lysander	.06	.05	.02
384	Jody Davis	.10	.08	.04
385	Jose DeLeon	.08	.06	.03
386	*Dan Gladden*(FC)	.30	.25	.12
387	*Buddy Biancalana*(FC)	.12	.09	.05
388	Bert Roberge	.06	.05	.02
389	1984 United States Baseball Team (Rod Dedeaux)	.06	.05	.02
390	1984 United States Baseball Team (Sid Akins)(FC)	.10	.08	.04
391	1984 United States Baseball Team (Flavio Alfaro)	.06	.05	.02
392	1984 United States Baseball Team (Don August)(FC)	.40	.30	.15
393	1984 United States Baseball Team (Scott Bankhead)(FC)	.70	.50	.30
394	1984 United States Baseball Team (Bob Caffrey)(FC)	.08	.06	.03
395	1984 United States Baseball Team (Mike Dunne)(FC)	.40	.30	.15
396	1984 United States Baseball Team (Gary Green)(FC)	.08	.06	.03
397	1984 United States Baseball Team (John Hoover)	.06	.05	.02
398	1984 United States Baseball Team (Shane Mack)(FC)	.40	.30	.15
399	1984 United States Baseball Team (John Marzano)(FC)	.20	.15	.08
400	1984 United States Baseball Team (Oddibe McDowell)(FC)	.80	.60	.30
401	1984 United States Baseball Team (Mark McGwire)(FC)	18.00	13.50	7.25
402	1984 United States Baseball Team (Pat Pacillo)(FC)	.20	.15	.08
403	1984 United States Baseball Team (Cory Snyder)(FC)	6.00	4.50	2.50

#	Player	MT	NR MT	EX
404	1984 United States Baseball Team (Billy Swift)(FC)	.30	.25	.12
405	Tom Veryzer	.06	.05	.02
406	Len Whitehouse	.06	.05	.02
407	Bobby Ramos	.06	.05	.02
408	Sid Monge	.06	.05	.02
409	Brad Wellman	.06	.05	.02
410	Bob Horner	.15	.11	.06
411	Bobby Cox	.06	.05	.02
412	Bud Black	.06	.05	.02
413	Vance Law	.08	.06	.03
414	Gary Ward	.08	.06	.03
415	Ron Darling	1.25	.90	.50
416	Wayne Gross	.06	.05	.02
417	*John Franco*(FC)	.90	.70	.35
418	Ken Landreaux	.06	.05	.02
419	Mike Caldwell	.06	.05	.02
420	Andre Dawson	.30	.25	.12
421	Dave Rucker	.06	.05	.02
422	Carney Lansford	.10	.08	.04
423	Barry Bonnell	.06	.05	.02
424	*Al Nipper*(FC)	.15	.11	.06
425	Mike Hargrove	.06	.05	.02
426	Verne Ruhle	.06	.05	.02
427	Mario Ramirez	.06	.05	.02
428	Larry Andersen	.06	.05	.02
429	Rick Cerone	.06	.05	.02
430	Ron Davis	.06	.05	.02
431	U.L. Washington	.06	.05	.02
432	Thad Bosley	.06	.05	.02
433	Jim Morrison	.06	.05	.02
434	Gene Richards	.06	.05	.02
435	Dan Petry	.08	.06	.03
436	Willie Aikens	.06	.05	.02
437	Al Jones	.06	.05	.02
438	Joe Torre	.08	.06	.03
439	Junior Ortiz	.06	.05	.02
440	Fernando Valenzuela	.30	.25	.12
441	Duane Walker	.06	.05	.02
442	Ken Forsch	.06	.05	.02
443	George Wright	.06	.05	.02
444	Tony Phillips	.06	.05	.02
445	Tippy Martinez	.06	.05	.02
446	Jim Sundberg	.08	.06	.03
447	Jeff Lahti	.06	.05	.02
448	Derrel Thomas	.06	.05	.02
449	*Phil Bradley*	.80	.60	.30
450	Steve Garvey	.40	.30	.15
451	Bruce Hurst	.12	.09	.05
452	John Castino	.06	.05	.02
453	Tom Waddell	.06	.05	.02
454	Glenn Wilson	.08	.06	.03
455	Bob Knepper	.08	.06	.03
456	Tim Foli	.06	.05	.02
457	Cecilio Guante	.06	.05	.02
458	Randy Johnson	.06	.05	.02
459	Charlie Leibrandt	.08	.06	.03
460	Ryne Sandberg	.50	.40	.20
461	Marty Castillo	.06	.05	.02
462	Gary Lavelle	.06	.05	.02
463	Dave Collins	.08	.06	.03
464	*Mike Mason*(FC)	.10	.08	.04
465	Bob Grich	.10	.08	.04
466	Tony LaRussa	.08	.06	.03
467	Ed Lynch	.06	.05	.02
468	Wayne Krenchicki	.06	.05	.02
469	Sammy Stewart	.06	.05	.02
470	Steve Sax	.20	.15	.08
471	Pete Ladd	.06	.05	.02
472	Jim Essian	.06	.05	.02
473	Tim Wallach	.12	.09	.05
474	Kurt Kepshire	.06	.05	.02
475	Andre Thornton	.10	.08	.04
476	*Jeff Stone*(FC)	.12	.09	.05
477	Bob Ojeda	.10	.08	.04
478	Kurt Bevacqua	.06	.05	.02
479	Mike Madden	.06	.05	.02
480	Lou Whitaker	.30	.25	.12
481	Dale Murray	.06	.05	.02
482	Harry Spilman	.06	.05	.02
483	Mike Smithson	.06	.05	.02
484	Larry Bowa	.10	.08	.04
485	Matt Young	.06	.05	.02
486	Steve Balboni	.08	.06	.03
487	*Frank Williams*	.15	.11	.06
488	Joel Skinner(FC)	.08	.06	.03
489	Bryan Clark	.06	.05	.02
490	Jason Thompson	.06	.05	.02
491	Rick Camp	.06	.05	.02
492	Dave Johnson	.08	.06	.03
493	*Orel Hershiser*(FC)	6.00	4.50	2.50
494	Rich Dauer	.06	.05	.02
495	Mario Soto	.08	.06	.03
496	Donnie Scott	.06	.05	.02
497	Gary Pettis	.15	.11	.06
498	Ed Romero	.06	.05	.02
499	Danny Cox(FC)	.20	.20	.10
500	Mike Schmidt	.60	.45	.25
501	Dan Schatzeder	.06	.05	.02
502	Rick Miller	.06	.05	.02
503	Tim Conroy	.06	.05	.02
504	Jerry Willard	.06	.05	.02
505	Jim Beattie	.06	.05	.02
506	*Franklin Stubbs*(FC)	.25	.20	.10
507	Ray Fontenot	.06	.05	.02
508	John Shelby	.08	.06	.03
509	Milt May	.06	.05	.02
510	Kent Hrbek	.25	.20	.10
511	Lee Smith	.10	.08	.04
512	Tom Brookens	.06	.05	.02
513	Lynn Jones	.06	.05	.02
514	Jeff Cornell	.06	.05	.02
515	Dave Concepcion	.12	.09	.05
516	Roy Lee Jackson	.06	.05	.02
517	Jerry Martin	.06	.05	.02
518	Chris Chambliss	.08	.06	.03
519	Doug Rader	.06	.05	.02
520	LaMarr Hoyt	.06	.05	.02
521	Rick Dempsey	.08	.06	.03
522	Paul Molitor	.15	.11	.06
523	Candy Maldonado	.10	.08	.04
524	Rob Wilfong	.06	.05	.02
525	Darrell Porter	.08	.06	.03
526	Dave Palmer	.06	.05	.02
527	Checklist 397-528	.06	.05	.02
528	Bill Krueger	.06	.05	.02
529	Rich Gedman	.10	.08	.04
530	Dave Dravecky	.08	.06	.03
531	Joe Lefebvre	.06	.05	.02
532	Frank DiPino	.06	.05	.02
533	Tony Bernazard	.06	.05	.02
534	Brian Dayett(FC)	.06	.05	.02
535	Pat Putnam	.06	.05	.02
536	*Kirby Puckett*(FC)	15.00	11.00	6.00
537	Don Robinson	.08	.06	.03
538	Keith Moreland	.08	.06	.03
539	Aurelio Lopez	.06	.05	.02
540	Claudell Washington	.08	.06	.03
541	Mark Davis	.06	.05	.02
542	Don Slaught	.06	.05	.02
543	Mike Squires	.06	.05	.02
544	Bruce Kison	.06	.05	.02
545	Lloyd Moseby	.10	.08	.04
546	Brent Gaff	.06	.05	.02
547	Pete Rose	.60	.45	.25
548	Larry Parrish	.10	.08	.04
549	Mike Scioscia	.08	.06	.03
550	Scott McGregor	.08	.06	.03
551	Andy Van Slyke	.35	.25	.14
552	Chris Codiroli	.06	.05	.02
553	Bob Clark	.06	.05	.02
554	Doug Flynn	.06	.05	.02
555	Bob Stanley	.06	.05	.02
556	Sixto Lezcano	.06	.05	.02
557	Len Barker	.08	.06	.03
558	Carmelo Martinez	.08	.06	.03
559	Jay Howell	.08	.06	.03
560	Bill Madlock	.12	.09	.05
561	Darryl Motley	.06	.05	.02
562	Houston Jimenez	.06	.05	.02
563	Dick Ruthven	.06	.05	.02
564	Alan Ashby	.06	.05	.02
565	Kirk Gibson	.35	.25	.14
566	Ed Vande Berg	.06	.05	.02
567	Joel Youngblood	.06	.05	.02
568	Cliff Johnson	.06	.05	.02
569	Ken Oberkfell	.06	.05	.02
570	Darryl Strawberry	3.00	2.25	1.25
571	Charlie Hough	.08	.06	.03
572	Tom Paciorek	.06	.05	.02
573	*Jay Tibbs*(FC)	.15	.11	.06
574	Joe Altobelli	.06	.05	.02
575	Pedro Guerrero	.25	.20	.10
576	Jaime Cocanower	.06	.05	.02
577	Chris Speier	.06	.05	.02
578	Terry Francona	.06	.05	.02
579	*Ron Romanick*	.10	.08	.04
580	Dwight Evans	.12	.09	.05
581	Mark Wagner	.06	.05	.02
582	Ken Phelps(FC)	.20	.15	.08
583	Bobby Brown	.06	.05	.02
584	Kevin Gross	.10	.08	.04

#	Player	MT	NR MT	EX
585	Butch Wynegar	.06	.05	.02
586	Bill Scherrer	.06	.05	.02
587	Doug Frobel	.06	.05	.02
588	Bobby Castillo	.06	.05	.02
589	Bob Dernier	.06	.05	.02
590	Ray Knight	.10	.08	.04
591	Larry Herndon	.08	.06	.03
592	*Jeff Robinson*	.30	.25	.12
593	Rick Leach	.06	.05	.02
594	Curt Wilkerson(FC)	.08	.06	.03
595	Larry Gura	.06	.05	.02
596	Jerry Hairston	.06	.05	.02
597	Brad Lesley	.06	.05	.02
598	Jose Oquendo	.06	.05	.02
599	Storm Davis	.10	.08	.04
600	Pete Rose	1.00	.70	.40
601	Tom Lasorda	.10	.08	.04
602	*Jeff Dedmon*	.12	.09	.05
603	Rick Manning	.06	.05	.02
604	Daryl Sconiers	.06	.05	.02
605	Ozzie Smith	.15	.11	.06
606	Rich Gale	.06	.05	.02
607	Bill Almon	.06	.05	.02
608	Craig Lefferts	.08	.06	.03
609	Broderick Perkins	.06	.05	.02
610	Jack Morris	.25	.20	.10
611	Ozzie Virgil	.06	.05	.02
612	Mike Armstrong	.06	.05	.02
613	Terry Puhl	.06	.05	.02
614	Al Williams	.06	.05	.02
615	Marvell Wynne	.06	.05	.02
616	Scott Sanderson	.06	.05	.02
617	Willie Wilson	.12	.09	.05
618	Pete Falcone	.06	.05	.02
619	Jeff Leonard	.10	.08	.04
620	*Dwight Gooden*	9.00	6.75	3.50
621	Marvis Foley	.06	.05	.02
622	Luis Leal	.06	.05	.02
623	Greg Walker	.12	.09	.05
624	Benny Ayala	.06	.05	.02
625	*Mark Langston*	2.00	1.50	.80
626	German Rivera	.06	.05	.02
627	*Eric Davis*(FC)	15.00	11.00	6.00
628	Rene Lachemann	.06	.05	.02
629	Dick Schofield	.12	.09	.05
630	Tim Raines	.35	.25	.14
631	Bob Forsch	.08	.06	.03
632	Bruce Bochte	.06	.05	.02
633	Glenn Hoffman	.06	.05	.02
634	Bill Dawley	.06	.05	.02
635	Terry Kennedy	.08	.06	.03
636	Shane Rawley	.10	.08	.04
637	Brett Butler	.08	.06	.03
638	*Mike Pagliarulo*(FC)	.80	.60	.30
639	Ed Hodge	.06	.05	.02
640	Steve Henderson	.06	.05	.02
641	Rod Scurry	.06	.05	.02
642	Dave Owen	.06	.05	.02
643	Johnny Grubb	.06	.05	.02
644	Mark Huismann(FC)	.06	.05	.02
645	Damaso Garcia	.06	.05	.02
646	Scot Thompson	.06	.05	.02
647	Rafael Ramirez	.06	.05	.02
648	Bob Jones	.06	.05	.02
649	Sid Fernandez(FC)	.90	.70	.35
650	Greg Luzinski	.10	.08	.04
651	Jeff Russell	.08	.06	.03
652	Joe Nolan	.06	.05	.02
653	Mark Brouhard	.06	.05	.02
654	Dave Anderson	.06	.05	.02
655	Joaquin Andujar	.08	.06	.03
656	Chuck Cottier	.06	.05	.02
657	Jim Slaton	.06	.05	.02
658	Mike Stenhouse	.06	.05	.02
659	Checklist 529-660	.06	.05	.02
660	Tony Gwynn	.80	.60	.30
661	Steve Crawford	.06	.05	.02
662	Mike Heath	.06	.05	.02
663	Luis Aguayo	.06	.05	.02
664	*Steve Farr*(FC)	.30	.25	.12
665	Don Mattingly	10.00	7.50	4.00
666	Mike LaCoss	.06	.05	.02
667	Dave Engle	.06	.05	.02
668	Steve Trout	.06	.05	.02
669	Lee Lacy	.06	.05	.02
670	Tom Seaver	.30	.25	.12
671	Dane Iorg	.06	.05	.02
672	Juan Berenguer	.06	.05	.02
673	Buck Martinez	.06	.05	.02
674	Atlee Hammaker	.06	.05	.02
675	Tony Perez	.15	.11	.06
676	*Albert Hall*(FC)	.15	.11	.06
677	Wally Backman	.08	.06	.03
678	Joey McLaughlin	.06	.05	.02
679	Bob Kearney	.06	.05	.02
680	Jerry Reuss	.08	.06	.03
681	Ben Oglivie	.08	.06	.03
682	Doug Corbett	.06	.05	.02
683	Whitey Herzog	.08	.06	.03
684	Bill Doran	.12	.09	.05
685	Bill Caudill	.06	.05	.02
686	Mike Easler	.08	.06	.03
687	Bill Gullickson	.06	.05	.02
688	Len Matuszek	.06	.05	.02
689	Luis DeLeon	.06	.05	.02
690	Alan Trammell	.35	.25	.14
691	Dennis Rasmussen(FC)	.30	.25	.12
692	Randy Bush	.06	.05	.02
693	Tim Stoddard	.06	.05	.02
694	Joe Carter(FC)	2.75	2.00	1.00
695	Rick Rhoden	.10	.08	.04
696	John Rabb	.06	.05	.02
697	Onix Concepcion	.06	.05	.02
698	Jorge Bell	.40	.30	.15
699	Donnie Moore	.06	.05	.02
700	Eddie Murray	.50	.40	.20
701	Eddie Murray AS	.30	.25	.12
702	Damaso Garcia AS	.08	.06	.03
703	George Brett AS	.35	.25	.14
704	Cal Ripken AS	.30	.25	.12
705	Dave Winfield AS	.20	.15	.08
706	Rickey Henderson AS	.30	.25	.12
707	Tony Armas AS	.08	.06	.03
708	Lance Parrish AS	.15	.11	.06
709	Mike Boddicker AS	.08	.06	.03
710	Frank Viola AS	.12	.09	.05
711	Dan Quisenberry AS	.10	.08	.04
712	Keith Hernandez AS	.20	.15	.08
713	Ryne Sandberg AS	.20	.15	.08
714	Mike Schmidt AS	.30	.25	.12
715	Ozzie Smith AS	.12	.09	.05
716	Dale Murphy AS	.35	.25	.14
717	Tony Gwynn AS	.35	.25	.14
718	Jeff Leonard AS	.10	.08	.04
719	Gary Carter AS	.20	.15	.08
720	Rick Sutcliffe AS	.12	.09	.05
721	Bob Knepper AS	.08	.06	.03
722	Bruce Sutter AS	.10	.08	.04
723	Dave Stewart	.12	.09	.05
724	Oscar Gamble	.08	.06	.03
725	Floyd Bannister	.10	.08	.04
726	Al Bumbry	.08	.06	.03
727	Frank Pastore	.06	.05	.02
728	Bob Bailor	.06	.05	.02
729	Don Sutton	.30	.25	.12
730	Dave Kingman	.15	.11	.06
731	Neil Allen	.06	.05	.02
732	John McNamara	.06	.05	.02
733	Tony Scott	.06	.05	.02
734	John Henry Johnson	.06	.05	.02
735	Garry Templeton	.08	.06	.03
736	Jerry Mumphrey	.06	.05	.02
737	Bo Diaz	.08	.06	.03
738	Omar Moreno	.06	.05	.02
739	Ernie Camacho	.06	.05	.02
740	Jack Clark	.20	.15	.08
741	John Butcher	.06	.05	.02
742	Ron Hassey	.06	.05	.02
743	Frank White	.10	.08	.04
744	Doug Bair	.06	.05	.02
745	Buddy Bell	.12	.09	.05
746	Jim Clancy	.08	.06	.03
747	Alex Trevino	.06	.05	.02
748	Lee Mazzilli	.08	.06	.03
749	Julio Cruz	.06	.05	.02
750	Rollie Fingers	.20	.15	.08
751	Kelvin Chapman	.06	.05	.02
752	Bob Owchinko	.06	.05	.02
753	Greg Brock	.08	.06	.03
754	Larry Milbourne	.06	.05	.02
755	Ken Singleton	.08	.06	.03
756	Rob Picciolo	.06	.05	.02
757	Willie McGee	.30	.25	.12
758	Ray Burris	.06	.05	.02
759	Jim Fanning	.06	.05	.02
760	Nolan Ryan	.60	.45	.25
761	Jerry Remy	.06	.05	.02
762	Eddie Whitson	.06	.05	.02
763	Kiko Garcia	.06	.05	.02
764	Jamie Easterly	.06	.05	.02
765	Willie Randolph	.10	.08	.04
766	Paul Mirabella	.06	.05	.02

		MT	NR MT	EX
767	Darrell Brown	.06	.05	.02
768	Ron Cey	.10	.08	.04
769	Joe Cowley	.06	.05	.02
770	Carlton Fisk	.40	.30	.15
771	Geoff Zahn	.06	.05	.02
772	Johnnie LeMaster	.06	.05	.02
773	Hal McRae	.10	.08	.04
774	Dennis Lamp	.06	.05	.02
775	Mookie Wilson	.10	.08	.04
776	Jerry Royster	.06	.05	.02
777	Ned Yost	.06	.05	.02
778	Mike Davis	.08	.06	.03
779	Nick Esasky	.08	.06	.03
780	Mike Flanagan	.10	.08	.04
781	Jim Gantner	.08	.06	.03
782	Tom Niedenfuer	.08	.06	.03
783	Mike Jorgensen	.06	.05	.02
784	Checklist 661-792	.06	.05	.02
785	Tony Armas	.10	.08	.04
786	Enos Cabell	.06	.05	.02
787	Jim Wohlford	.06	.05	.02
788	Steve Comer	.06	.05	.02
789	Luis Salazar	.06	.05	.02
790	Ron Guidry	.25	.20	.10
791	Ivan DeJesus	.06	.05	.02
792	Darrell Evans	.12	.09	.05

1985 Topps
All-Star Glossy Set Of 22

This was the second straight year for this set of 22 cards featuring the starting players, the honorary captains and the managers in the All-Star Game. The set is virtually identical to that of the previous year in design with a color photo, All-Star banner, league emblem, and player's name and position on the front. What makes the cards special is their high gloss finish. The cards were available as inserts in Topps rack packs. With their combination of attractive appearance and big-name stars, these 2-1/2" by 3-1/2" cards will probably continue to enjoy a great deal of popularity.

		MT	NR MT	EX
Complete Set:		6.00	4.50	2.50
Common Player:		.20	.15	.08
1	Paul Owens	.20	.15	.08
2	Steve Garvey	.50	.40	.20
3	Ryne Sandberg	.40	.30	.15
4	Mike Schmidt	.60	.45	.25
5	Ozzie Smith	.30	.25	.12
6	Tony Gwynn	.60	.45	.25
7	Dale Murphy	.80	.60	.30
8	Darryl Strawberry	1.00	.70	.40
9	Gary Carter	.50	.40	.20
10	Charlie Lea	.20	.15	.08
11	Willie McCovey	.40	.30	.15
12	Joe Altobelli	.20	.15	.08
13	Rod Carew	.50	.40	.20
14	Lou Whitaker	.30	.25	.12
15	George Brett	.80	.60	.30
16	Cal Ripken	.60	.45	.25
17	Dave Winfield	.50	.40	.20
18	Chet Lemon	.20	.15	.08
19	Reggie Jackson	.60	.45	.25

		MT	NR MT	EX
20	Lance Parrish	.30	.25	.12
21	Dave Stieb	.25	.20	.10
22	Hank Greenberg	.20	.15	.08

1985 Topps
All-Star Glossy Set Of 40

Similar to previous years' glossy sets, the 1985 All-Star "Collector's Edition" glossy set of 40 could be obtained through the mail in eight five-card subsets. To obtain the 2-1/2" by 3-1/2" cards, collectors had to accumulate sweepstakes insert cards from Topps packs, and pay 75¢ postage and handling. Under the circumstances, the complete set of 40 cards was not inexpensive. They are however, rather attractive and popular cards, and the set size enabled Topps to include some players who didn't make their 22-card set.

		MT	NR MT	EX
Complete Set:		15.00	11.00	6.00
Common Player:		.15	.11	.06
1	Dale Murphy	1.00	.70	.40
2	Jesse Orosco	.15	.11	.06
3	Bob Brenly	.15	.11	.06
4	Mike Boddicker	.15	.11	.06
5	Dave Kingman	.25	.20	.10
6	Jim Rice	.50	.40	.20
7	Frank Viola	.30	.25	.12
8	Alvin Davis	.35	.25	.14
9	Rick Sutcliffe	.20	.15	.08
10	Pete Rose	1.25	.90	.50
11	Leon Durham	.15	.11	.06
12	Joaquin Andujar	.15	.11	.06
13	Keith Hernandez	.40	.30	.15
14	Dave Winfield	.60	.45	.25
15	Reggie Jackson	.70	.50	.30
16	Alan Trammell	.35	.25	.14
17	Bert Blyleven	.20	.15	.08
18	Tony Armas	.15	.11	.06
19	Rich Gossage	.25	.20	.10
20	Jose Cruz	.15	.11	.06
21	Ryne Sandberg	.40	.30	.15
22	Bruce Sutter	.20	.15	.08
23	Mike Schmidt	1.00	.70	.40
24	Cal Ripken	.70	.50	.30
25	Dan Petry	.15	.11	.06
26	Jack Morris	.30	.25	.12
27	Don Mattingly	3.50	2.75	1.50
28	Eddie Murray	.60	.45	.25
29	Tony Gwynn	.60	.45	.25
30	Charlie Lea	.15	.11	.06
31	Juan Samuel	.30	.25	.12
32	Phil Niekro	.35	.25	.14
33	Alejandro Pena	.15	.11	.06
34	Harold Baines	.25	.20	.10
35	Dan Quisenberry	.15	.11	.06
36	Gary Carter	.50	.40	.20
37	Mario Soto	.15	.11	.06
38	Dwight Gooden	2.50	2.00	1.00
39	Tom Brunansky	.20	.15	.08
40	Dave Stieb	.20	.15	.08

1985 Topps
All-Time Record Holders

This 44-card boxed set was produced by Topps for the Woolworth's chain stores. Many hobbyists refer to this as the "Woolworth's" set, but that name does not appear anywhere on the cards. Featuring a combination of black and white and color photos of baseball record holders from all eras, the set is in the standard 2-1/2" by 3-1/2" format. Backs, printed in blue and orange, give career details and personal date. Because it combined old-timers with current players, the set did not achieve a great deal of collector popularity.

		MT	NR MT	EX
Complete Set:		5.00	3.75	2.00
Common Player:		.05	.04	.02
1	Hank Aaron	.25	.20	.10
2	Grover Alexander	.10	.08	.04
3	Ernie Banks	.12	.09	.05
4	Yogi Berra	.15	.11	.06
5	Lou Brock	.12	.09	.05
6	Steve Carlton	.12	.09	.05
7	Jack Chesbro	.07	.05	.03
8	Ty Cobb	.30	.25	.12
9	Sam Crawford	.07	.05	.03
10	Rollie Fingers	.07	.05	.03
11	Whitey Ford	.12	.09	.05
12	Johnny Frederick	.05	.04	.02
13	Frankie Frisch	.07	.05	.03
14	Lou Gehrig	.30	.25	.12
15	Jim Gentile	.05	.04	.02
16	Dwight Gooden	.60	.45	.25
17	Rickey Henderson	.15	.11	.06
18	Rogers Hornsby	.12	.09	.05
19	Frank Howard	.07	.05	.03
20	Cliff Johnson	.05	.04	.02
21	Walter Johnson	.15	.11	.06
22	Hub Leonard	.05	.04	.02
23	Mickey Mantle	1.00	.70	.40
24	Roger Maris	.12	.09	.05
25	Christy Mathewson	.12	.09	.05
26	Willie Mays	.20	.15	.08
27	Stan Musial	.20	.15	.08
28	Dan Quisenberry	.05	.04	.02
29	Frank Robinson	.12	.09	.05
30	Pete Rose	.40	.30	.15
31	Babe Ruth	.60	.45	.25
32	Nolan Ryan	.12	.09	.05
33	George Sisler	.10	.08	.04
34	Tris Speaker	.10	.08	.04
35	Ed Walsh	.07	.05	.03
36	Lloyd Waner	.07	.05	.03
37	Earl Webb	.05	.04	.02
38	Ted Williams	.30	.25	.12
39	Maury Wills	.07	.05	.03
40	Hack Wilson	.07	.05	.03
41	Owen Wilson	.05	.04	.02
42	Willie Wilson	.07	.05	.03
43	Rudy York	.05	.04	.02
44	Cy Young	.12	.09	.05

NOTE: A card number in parentheses ( ) indicates the set is unnumbered.

1985 Topps
Gallery of Champions

This second annual aluminum, bronze, and silver miniature issues honors 12 award winners from the previous season (MVP, Cy Young, Rookie of Year, Fireman, etc.). Each mini is an exact reproduction, at one-quarter scale of the player's official Topps baseball card, both front and back. The bronze and silver sets were issued in a specially-designed velvet-like case. Aluminum sets came cello-wrapped. A Dwight Gooden pewter replica was given as a premium to dealers who bought bronze and silver sets (value $75). A Pete Rose bronze was issued as a premium to dealers purchasing cases of 1985 Topps Traded sets (value $12).

	MT	NR MT	EX
Complete Aluminum Set:	30.00	22.00	12.00
Complete Bronze Set:	175.00	131.00	70.00
Complete Silver Set:	600.00	450.00	240.00
(1a) Tony Armas (aluminum)	.70	.50	.30
(1b) Tony Armas (bronze)	7.50	5.75	3.00
(1c) Tony Armas (silver)	20.00	15.00	8.00
(2a) Alvin Davis (aluminum)	1.00	.70	.40
(2b) Alvin Davis (bronze)	10.00	7.50	4.00
(2c) Alvin Davis (silver)	30.00	22.00	12.00
(3a) Dwight Gooden (aluminum)	3.00	2.25	1.25
(3b) Dwight Gooden (bronze)	25.00	18.50	10.00
(3c) Dwight Gooden (silver)	125.00	94.00	50.00
(4a) Tony Gwynn (aluminum)	1.25	.90	.50
(4b) Tony Gwynn (bronze)	12.00	9.00	4.75
(4c) Tony Gwynn (silver)	50.00	37.00	20.00
(5a) Willie Hernandez (aluminum)	.70	.50	.30
(5b) Willie Hernandez (bronze)	7.50	5.75	3.00
(5c) Willie Hernandez (silver)	20.00	15.00	8.00
(6a) Don Mattingly (aluminum)	8.00	6.00	3.25
(6b) Don Mattingly (bronze)	50.00	37.00	20.00
(6c) Don Mattingly (silver)	200.00	150.00	80.00
(7a) Dale Murphy (aluminum)	1.50	1.25	.60
(7b) Dale Murphy (bronze)	15.00	11.00	6.00
(7c) Dale Murphy (silver)	80.00	60.00	32.00
(8a) Dan Quisenberry (aluminum)	.70	.50	.30
(8b) Dan Quisenberry (bronze)	7.50	5.75	3.00
(8c) Dan Quisenberry (silver)	20.00	15.00	8.00
(9a) Ryne Sandberg (aluminum)	1.25	.90	.50
(9b) Ryne Sandberg (bronze)	12.50	9.50	5.00
(9c) Ryne Sandberg (silver)	50.00	37.00	20.00
(10a) Mike Schmidt (aluminum)	1.50	1.25	.60
(10b) Mike Schmidt (bronze)	15.00	11.00	6.00
(10c) Mike Schmidt (silver)	80.00	60.00	32.00
(11a) Rick Sutcliffe (aluminum)	.70	.50	.30
(11b) Rick Sutcliffe (bronze)	7.50	5.75	3.00
(11c) Rick Sutcliffe (silver)	20.00	15.00	8.00
(12a) Bruce Sutter (aluminum)	.70	.50	.30
(12b) Bruce Sutter (bronze)	7.50	5.75	3.00
(12c) Bruce Sutter (silver)	20.00	15.00	8.00

1985 Topps Rub Downs

Similar in size and design to the Rub Downs of the previous year, the 1985 set again consisted of 32 unnumbered sheets featuring 112 different players.

The set was sold by Topps as a separate issue.

		MT	NR MT	EX
Complete Set:		8.00	6.00	3.25
Common Player:		.10	.08	.04

		MT	NR MT	EX
(1)	Tony Armas, Harold Baines, Lonnie Smith	.10	.08	.04
(2)	Don Baylor, George Hendrick, Ron Kittle, Johnnie LeMaster	.10	.08	.04
(3)	Buddy Bell, Tony Gwynn, Lloyd Moseby	.25	.20	.10
(4)	Bruce Benedict, Atlee Hammaker, Frank White	.10	.08	.04
(5)	Mike Boddicker, Rod Carew, Carlton Fisk, Johnny Ray	.25	.20	.10
(6)	Wade Boggs, Rick Dempsey, Keith Hernandez	.60	.45	.25
(7)	George Brett, Andre Dawson, Paul Molitor, Alan Wiggins	.30	.25	.12
(8)	Tom Brunansky, Pedro Guerrero, Darryl Strawberry	.40	.30	.15
(9)	Bill Buckner, Tim Raines, Ryne Sandberg, Mike Schmidt	.30	.25	.12
(10)	Steve Carlton, Bob Horner, Dan Quisenberry	.25	.20	.10
(11)	Gary Carter, Phil Garner, Ron Guidry	.25	.20	.10
(12)	Jack Clark, Damaso Garcia, Hal McRae, Lance Parrish	.20	.15	.08
(13)	Dave Concepcion, Cecil Cooper, Fred Lynn, Jesse Orosco	.15	.11	.06
(14)	Jose Cruz, Jack Morris, Jim Rice, Rick Sutcliffe	.20	.15	.08
(15)	Alvin Davis, Steve Kemp, Greg Luzinski, Kent Tekulve	.20	.15	.08
(16)	Ron Davis, Kent Hrbek, Juan Samuel	.20	.15	.08
(17)	John Denny, Carney Lansford, Mario Soto, Lou Whitaker	.15	.11	.06
(18)	Leon Durham, Willie Hernandez, Steve Sax	.15	.11	.06
(19)	Dwight Evans, Julio Franco, Dwight Gooden	.40	.30	.15
(20)	George Foster, Gary Gaetti, Bobby Grich, Gary Redus	.15	.11	.06
(21)	Steve Garvey, Jerry Remy, Bill Russell, George Wright	.20	.15	.08
(22)	Kirk Gibson, Rich Gossage, Don Mattingly, Dave Stieb	.90	.70	.35
(23)	Moose Haas, Bruce Sutter, Dickie Thon, Andre Thornton	.10	.08	.04
(24)	Rickey Henderson, Dave Righetti, Pete Rose	.70	.50	.30
(25)	Steve Henderson, Bill Madlock, Alan Trammell	.15	.11	.06
(26)	LaMarr Hoyt, Larry Parrish, Nolan Ryan	.25	.20	.10
(27)	Reggie Jackson, Eric Show, Jason Thompson	.30	.25	.12
(28)	Terry Kennedy, Eddie Murray, Tom Seaver, Ozzie Smith	.25	.20	.10
(29)	Mark Langston, Ben Oglivie, Darrell Porter	.15	.11	.06
(30)	Jeff Leonard, Gary Matthews, Dale Murphy, Dave Winfield	.30	.25	.12
(31)	Craig McMurtry, Cal Ripken, Steve Rogers, Willie Upshaw	.25	.20	.10
(32)	Tony Pena, Fernando Valenzuela, Robin Yount	.20	.15	.08

1985 Topps Stickers

 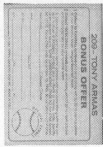

Topps went to a larger size for its stickers in 1985. Each of the 376 stickers measures 2-1/8" by 3" and is numbered on both the front and the back. The backs contain either an offer to obtain an autographed team ball or a poster. An album was also available.

		MT	NR MT	EX
Complete Set:		16.00	12.00	6.50
Common Player:		.03	.02	.01
Sticker Album:		.80	.60	.30

		MT	NR MT	EX
1	Steve Garvey	.25	.20	.10
2	Steve Garvey	.25	.20	.10
3	Dwight Gooden	.25	.20	.10
4	Dwight Gooden	.25	.20	.10
5	Joe Morgan	.10	.08	.04
6	Joe Morgan	.10	.08	.04
7	Don Sutton	.10	.08	.04
8	Don Sutton	.10	.08	.04
9	1984 A.L. Championships (Jack Morris)	.06	.05	.02
10	1984 A.L. Championships (Milt Wilcox)	.03	.02	.01
11	1984 A.L. Championships (Kirk Gibson)	.08	.06	.03
12	1984 N.L. Championships (Gary Matthews)	.04	.03	.02
13	1984 N.L. Championships (Steve Garvey)	.10	.08	.04
14	1984 N.L. Championships (Steve Garvey)	.15	.11	.06
15	1984 World Series (Jack Morris)	.06	.05	.02
16	1984 World Series (Kurt Bevacqua)	.03	.02	.01
17	1984 World Series (Milt Wilcox)	.03	.02	.01
18	1984 World Series (Alan Trammell)	.08	.06	.03
19	1984 World Series (Kirk Gibson)	.08	.06	.03
20	1984 World Series (Alan Trammell)	.12	.09	.05
21	1984 World Series (Chet Lemon)	.03	.02	.01
22	Dale Murphy	.25	.20	.10
23	Steve Bedrosian	.10	.08	.04
24	Bob Horner	.10	.08	.04
25	Claudell Washington	.06	.05	.02
26	Rick Mahler	.06	.05	.02
27	Rafael Ramirez	.04	.03	.02
28	Craig McMurtry	.04	.03	.02
29	Chris Chambliss	.04	.03	.02
30	Alex Trevino	.03	.02	.01
31	Bruce Benedict	.04	.03	.02
32	Ken Oberkfell	.03	.02	.01
33	Glenn Hubbard	.04	.03	.02
34	Ryne Sandberg	.15	.11	.06
35	Rick Sutcliffe	.08	.06	.03
36	Leon Durham	.06	.05	.02
37	Jody Davis	.06	.05	.02
38	Bob Dernier	.04	.03	.02
39	Keith Moreland	.06	.05	.02
40	Scott Sanderson	.04	.03	.02
41	Lee Smith	.06	.05	.02
42	Ron Cey	.06	.05	.02
43	Steve Trout	.06	.05	.02
44	Gary Matthews	.06	.05	.02
45	Larry Bowa	.04	.03	.02
46	Mario Soto	.06	.05	.02
47	Dave Parker	.12	.09	.05
48	Dave Concepcion	.06	.05	.02
49	Gary Redus	.06	.05	.02
50	Ted Power	.06	.05	.02

		MT	NR MT	EX			MT	NR MT	EX
51	Nick Esasky	.04	.03	.02	142	Tom Herr	.04	.03	.02
52	Duane Walker	.06	.05	.02	143	Dave LaPoint	.03	.02	.01
53	Eddie Milner	.03	.02	.01	144	Neil Allen	.04	.03	.02
54	Ron Oester	.03	.02	.01	145	David Green	.03	.02	.01
55	Cesar Cedeno	.04	.03	.02	146	Tony Gwynn	.20	.15	.08
56	Joe Price	.03	.02	.01	147	Rich Gossage	.12	.09	.05
57	Pete Rose	.20	.15	.08	148	Terry Kennedy	.04	.03	.02
58	Nolan Ryan	.15	.11	.06	149	Steve Garvey	.15	.11	.06
59	Jose Cruz	.06	.05	.02	150	Alan Wiggins	.03	.02	.01
60	Jerry Mumphrey	.04	.03	.02	151	Garry Templeton	.08	.06	.03
61	Enos Cabell	.03	.02	.01	152	Ed Whitson	.04	.03	.02
62	Bob Knepper	.04	.03	.02	153	Tim Lollar	.03	.02	.01
63	Dickie Thon	.04	.03	.02	154	Dave Dravecky	.04	.03	.02
64	Phil Garner	.04	.03	.02	155	Graig Nettles	.04	.03	.02
65	Craig Reynolds	.06	.05	.02	156	Eric Show	.03	.02	.01
66	Frank DiPino	.03	.02	.01	157	Carmelo Martinez	.03	.02	.01
67	Terry Puhl	.03	.02	.01	158	Bob Brenly	.03	.02	.01
68	Bill Doran	.06	.05	.02	159	Gary Lavelle	.03	.02	.01
69	Joe Niekro	.04	.03	.02	160	Jack Clark	.10	.08	.04
70	Pedro Guerrero	.12	.09	.05	161	Jeff Leonard	.04	.03	.02
71	Fernando Valenzuela	.15	.11	.06	162	Chili Davis	.06	.05	.02
72	Mike Marshall	.08	.06	.03	163	Mike Krukow	.03	.02	.01
73	Alejandro Pena	.04	.03	.02	164	Johnnie LeMaster	.03	.02	.01
74	Orel Hershiser	.10	.08	.04	165	Atlee Hammaker	.03	.02	.01
75	Ken Landreaux	.06	.05	.02	166	Dan Gladden	.06	.05	.02
76	Bill Russell	.06	.05	.02	167	Greg Minton	.03	.02	.01
77	Steve Sax	.06	.05	.02	168	Joel Youngblood	.03	.02	.01
78	Rick Honeycutt	.03	.02	.01	169	Frank Williams	.04	.03	.02
79	Mike Scioscia	.03	.02	.01	170	Tony Gwynn	.20	.15	.08
80	Tom Niedenfuer	.06	.05	.02	171	Don Mattingly	.30	.25	.12
81	Candy Maldonado	.03	.02	.01	172	Bruce Sutter	.15	.11	.06
82	Tim Raines	.15	.11	.06	173	Dan Quisenberry	.10	.08	.04
83	Gary Carter	.20	.15	.08	174	Tony Gwynn	.40	.30	.15
84	Charlie Lea	.03	.02	.01	175	Ryne Sandberg	.35	.25	.14
85	Jeff Reardon	.08	.06	.03	176	Steve Garvey	.30	.25	.12
86	Andre Dawson	.06	.05	.02	177	Dale Murphy	.40	.30	.15
87	Tim Wallach	.04	.03	.02	178	Mike Schmidt	.40	.30	.15
88	Terry Francona	.04	.03	.02	179	Darryl Strawberry	.50	.40	.20
89	Steve Rogers	.03	.02	.01	180	Gary Carter	.30	.25	.12
90	Bryn Smith	.03	.02	.01	181	Ozzie Smith	.20	.15	.08
91	Bill Gullickson	.04	.03	.02	182	Charlie Lea	.15	.11	.06
92	Dan Driessen	.03	.02	.01	183	Lou Whitaker	.25	.20	.10
93	Doug Flynn	.03	.02	.01	184	Rod Carew	.30	.25	.12
94	Mike Schmidt	.20	.15	.08	185	Cal Ripken	.40	.30	.15
95	Tony Armas	.30	.25	.12	186	Dave Winfield	.30	.25	.12
96	Dale Murphy	.15	.11	.06	187	Reggie Jackson	.40	.30	.15
97	Rick Sutcliffe	.10	.08	.04	188	George Brett	.40	.30	.15
98	Keith Hernandez	.12	.09	.05	189	Lance Parrish	.25	.20	.10
99	George Foster	.08	.06	.03	190	Chet Lemon	.15	.11	.06
100	Darryl Strawberry	.30	.25	.12	191	Dave Stieb	.15	.11	.06
101	Jesse Orosco	.04	.03	.02	192	Gary Carter	.20	.15	.08
102	Mookie Wilson	.04	.03	.02	193	Mike Schmidt	.30	.25	.12
103	Doug Sisk	.03	.02	.01	194	Tony Armas	.15	.11	.06
104	Hubie Brooks	.06	.05	.02	195	Mike Witt	.10	.08	.04
105	Ron Darling	.04	.03	.02	196	Eddie Murray	.20	.15	.08
106	Wally Backman	.04	.03	.02	197	Cal Ripken	.20	.15	.08
107	Dwight Gooden	.15	.11	.06	198	Scott McGregor	.04	.03	.02
108	Mike Fitzgerald	.04	.03	.02	199	Rick Dempsey	.04	.03	.02
109	Walt Terrell	.03	.02	.01	200	Tippy Martinez	.08	.06	.03
110	Ozzie Virgil	.04	.03	.02	201	Ken Singleton	.04	.03	.02
111	Mike Schmidt	.25	.20	.10	202	Mike Boddicker	.06	.05	.02
112	Steve Carlton	.15	.11	.06	203	Rich Dauer	.03	.02	.01
113	Al Holland	.03	.02	.01	204	John Shelby	.04	.03	.02
114	Juan Samuel	.06	.05	.02	205	Al Bumbry	.04	.03	.02
115	Von Hayes	.04	.03	.02	206	John Lowenstein	.04	.03	.02
116	Jeff Stone	.06	.05	.02	207	Mike Flanagan	.04	.03	.02
117	Jerry Koosman	.04	.03	.02	209	Tony Armas	.04	.03	.02
118	Al Oliver	.04	.03	.02	210	Wade Boggs	.60	.45	.25
119	John Denny	.03	.02	.01	211	Bruce Hurst	.06	.05	.02
120	Charles Hudson	.03	.02	.01	212	Dwight Evans	.06	.05	.02
121	Garry Maddox	.06	.05	.02	213	Mike Easler	.04	.03	.02
122	Bill Madlock	.06	.05	.02	214	Bill Buckner	.04	.03	.02
123	John Candelaria	.06	.05	.02	215	Bob Stanley	.04	.03	.02
124	Tony Pena	.06	.05	.02	216	Jackie Gutierrez	.03	.02	.01
125	Jason Thompson	.03	.02	.01	217	Rich Gedman	.04	.03	.02
126	Lee Lacy	.04	.03	.02	218	Jerry Remy	.03	.02	.01
127	Rick Rhoden	.06	.05	.02	219	Marty Barrett	.04	.03	.02
128	Doug Frobel	.06	.05	.02	220	Reggie Jackson	.20	.15	.08
129	Kent Tekulve	.04	.03	.02	221	Geoff Zahn	.03	.02	.01
130	Johnny Ray	.04	.03	.02	222	Doug DeCinces	.06	.05	.02
131	Marvell Wynne	.08	.06	.03	223	Rod Carew	.20	.15	.08
132	Larry McWilliams	.03	.02	.01	224	Brian Downing	.04	.03	.02
133	Dale Berra	.03	.02	.01	225	Fred Lynn	.06	.05	.02
134	George Hendrick	.06	.05	.02	226	Gary Pettis	.04	.03	.02
135	Bruce Sutter	.08	.06	.03	227	Mike Witt	.06	.05	.02
136	Joaquin Andujar	.04	.03	.02	228	Bob Boone	.06	.05	.02
137	Ozzie Smith	.10	.08	.04	229	Tommy John	.06	.05	.02
138	Andy Van Slyke	.04	.03	.02	230	Bobby Grich	.06	.05	.02
139	Lonnie Smith	.06	.05	.02	231	Ron Romanick	.04	.03	.02
140	Darrell Porter	.03	.02	.01	232	Ron Kittle	.06	.05	.02
141	Willie McGee	.06	.05	.02	233	Richard Dotson	.06	.05	.02

		MT	NR MT	EX
234	Harold Baines	.08	.06	.03
235	Tom Seaver	.15	.11	.06
236	Greg Walker	.06	.05	.02
237	Roy Smalley	.04	.03	.02
238	Greg Luzinski	.06	.05	.02
239	Julio Cruz	.03	.02	.01
240	Scott Fletcher	.03	.02	.01
241	Rudy Law	.04	.03	.02
242	Vance Law	.03	.02	.01
243	Carlton Fisk	.20	.15	.08
244	Andre Thornton	.06	.05	.02
245	Julio Franco	.08	.06	.03
246	Brett Butler	.06	.05	.02
247	Bert Blyleven	.08	.06	.03
248	Mike Hargrove	.04	.03	.02
249	George Vukovich	.04	.03	.02
250	Pat Tabler	.04	.03	.02
251	Brook Jacoby	.06	.05	.02
252	Tony Bernazard	.03	.02	.01
253	Ernie Camacho	.03	.02	.01
254	Mel Hall	.06	.05	.02
255	Carmen Castillo	.04	.03	.02
256	Jack Morris	.12	.09	.05
257	Willie Hernandez	.06	.05	.02
258	Alan Trammell	.15	.11	.06
259	Lance Parrish	.12	.09	.05
260	Chet Lemon	.10	.08	.04
261	Lou Whitaker	.06	.05	.02
262	Howard Johnson	.06	.05	.02
263	Barbaro Garbey	.06	.05	.02
264	Dan Petry	.03	.02	.01
265	Aurelio Lopez	.03	.02	.01
266	Larry Herndon	.03	.02	.01
267	Kirk Gibson	.06	.05	.02
268	George Brett	.25	.20	.10
269	Dan Quisenberry	.06	.05	.02
270	Hal McRae	.06	.05	.02
271	Steve Balboni	.06	.05	.02
272	Pat Sheridan	.06	.05	.02
273	Jorge Orta	.04	.03	.02
274	Frank White	.04	.03	.02
275	Bud Black	.03	.02	.01
276	Darryl Motley	.03	.02	.01
277	Willie Wilson	.04	.03	.02
278	Larry Gura	.03	.02	.01
279	Don Slaught	.03	.02	.01
280	Dwight Gooden	.20	.15	.08
281	Mark Langston	.30	.25	.12
282	Tim Raines	.15	.11	.06
283	Rickey Henderson	.10	.08	.04
284	Robin Yount	.15	.11	.06
285	Rollie Fingers	.10	.08	.04
286	Jim Sundberg	.03	.02	.01
287	Cecil Cooper	.06	.05	.02
288	Jaime Cocanower	.04	.03	.02
289	Mike Caldwell	.03	.02	.01
290	Don Sutton	.06	.05	.02
291	Rick Manning	.04	.03	.02
292	Ben Oglivie	.04	.03	.02
293	Moose Haas	.15	.11	.06
294	Ted Simmons	.04	.03	.02
295	Jim Gantner	.03	.02	.01
296	Kent Hrbek	.12	.09	.05
297	Ron Davis	.03	.02	.01
298	Dave Engle	.03	.02	.01
299	Tom Brunansky	.06	.05	.02
300	Frank Viola	.06	.05	.02
301	Mike Smithson	.04	.03	.02
302	Gary Gaetti	.06	.05	.02
303	Tim Teufel	.04	.03	.02
304	Mickey Hatcher	.04	.03	.02
305	John Butcher	.03	.02	.01
306	Darrell Brown	.03	.02	.01
307	Kirby Puckett	.06	.05	.02
308	Dave Winfield	.15	.11	.06
309	Phil Niekro	.12	.09	.05
310	Don Mattingly	.70	.50	.30
311	Don Baylor	.08	.06	.03
312	Willie Randolph	.04	.03	.02
313	Ron Guidry	.06	.05	.02
314	Dave Righetti	.06	.05	.02
315	Bobby Meacham	.04	.03	.02
316	Butch Wynegar	.04	.03	.02
317	Mike Pagliarulo	.08	.06	.03
318	Joe Cowley	.03	.02	.01
319	John Montefusco	.03	.02	.01
320	Dave Kingman	.08	.06	.03
321	Rickey Henderson	.20	.15	.08
322	Bill Caudill	.03	.02	.01
323	Dwayne Murphy	.04	.03	.02
324	Steve McCatty	.04	.03	.02

		MT	NR MT	EX
325	Joe Morgan	.06	.05	.02
326	Mike Heath	.03	.02	.01
327	Chris Codiroli	.06	.05	.02
328	Ray Burris	.04	.03	.02
329	Tony Phillips	.03	.02	.01
330	Carney Lansford	.04	.03	.02
331	Bruce Bochte	.03	.02	.01
332	Alvin Davis	.15	.11	.06
333	Al Cowens	.03	.02	.01
334	Jim Beattie	.03	.02	.01
335	Bob Kearney	.03	.02	.01
336	Ed Vande Berg	.03	.02	.01
337	Mark Langston	.08	.06	.03
338	Dave Henderson	.04	.03	.02
339	Spike Owen	.03	.02	.01
340	Matt Young	.04	.03	.02
341	Jack Perconte	.04	.03	.02
342	Barry Bonnell	.03	.02	.01
343	Mike Stanton	.03	.02	.01
344	Pete O'Brien	.08	.06	.03
345	Charlie Hough	.06	.05	.02
346	Larry Parrish	.06	.05	.02
347	Buddy Bell	.08	.06	.03
348	Frank Tanana	.06	.05	.02
349	Curt Wilkerson	.03	.02	.01
350	Jeff Kunkel	.03	.02	.01
351	Billy Sample	.03	.02	.01
352	Danny Darwin	.03	.02	.01
353	Gary Ward	.03	.02	.01
354	Mike Mason	.03	.02	.01
355	Mickey Rivers	.04	.03	.02
356	Dave Stieb	.08	.06	.03
357	Damaso Garcia	.04	.03	.02
358	Willie Upshaw	.06	.05	.02
359	Lloyd Moseby	.08	.06	.03
360	George Bell	.08	.06	.03
361	Luis Leal	.04	.03	.02
362	Jesse Barfield	.06	.05	.02
363	Dave Collins	.03	.02	.01
364	Roy Lee Jackson	.04	.03	.02
365	Doyle Alexander	.04	.03	.02
366	Alfredo Griffin	.04	.03	.02
367	Cliff Johnson	.04	.03	.02
368	Alvin Davis	.15	.11	.06
369	Juan Samuel	.10	.08	.04
370	Brook Jacoby	.08	.06	.03
371	Dwight Gooden, Mark Langston	.30	.25	.12
372	Mike Fitzgerald	.04	.03	.02
373	Jackie Gutierrez	.03	.02	.01
374	Dan Gladden	.08	.06	.03
375	Carmelo Martinez	.06	.05	.02
376	Kirby Puckett	.20	.15	.08

1985 Topps Super

Still trying to sell collectors on the idea of jumbo-sized cards, Topps returned for a second year with its 4-7/8" by 6-7/8" "Super" set. In fact, the set size was doubled from the previous year, to 60 cards. The Supers are identical to the regular-issue 1985 cards of the same players, only the card numbers on back were changed. The cards were again sold three per pack for 50¢.

	MT	NR MT	EX
Complete Set:	14.00	10.50	5.50
Common Player:	.20	.15	.08

		MT	NR MT	EX
1	Ryne Sandberg	.50	.40	.20
2	Willie Hernandez	.20	.15	.08
3	Rick Sutcliffe	.25	.20	.10
4	Don Mattingly	2.25	1.75	.90
5	Tony Gwynn	.70	.50	.30
6	Alvin Davis	.35	.25	.14
7	Dwight Gooden	2.00	1.50	.80
8	Dan Quisenberry	.20	.15	.08
9	Bruce Sutter	.25	.20	.10
10	Tony Armas	.20	.15	.08
11	Dale Murphy	.90	.70	.35
12	Mike Schmidt	.90	.70	.35
13	Gary Carter	.50	.40	.20
14	Rickey Henderson	.70	.50	.30
15	Tim Raines	.50	.40	.20
16	Mike Boddicker	.20	.15	.08
17	Alejandro Pena	.20	.15	.08
18	Eddie Murray	.60	.45	.25
19	Gary Matthews	.20	.15	.08
20	Mark Langston	.30	.25	.12
21	Mario Soto	.20	.15	.08
22	Dave Stieb	.20	.15	.08
23	Nolan Ryan	.50	.40	.20
24	Steve Carlton	.50	.40	.20
25	Alan Trammell	.40	.30	.15
26	Steve Garvey	.50	.40	.20
27	Kirk Gibson	.35	.25	.14
28	Juan Samuel	.35	.25	.14
29	Reggie Jackson	.60	.45	.25
30	Darryl Strawberry	.90	.70	.35
31	Tom Seaver	.50	.40	.20
32	Pete Rose	1.25	.90	.50
33	Dwight Evans	.30	.25	.12
34	Jose Cruz	.20	.15	.08
35	Bert Blyleven	.25	.20	.10
36	Keith Hernandez	.50	.40	.20
37	Robin Yount	.40	.30	.15
38	Joaquin Andujar	.20	.15	.08
39	Lloyd Moseby	.20	.15	.08
40	Chili Davis	.20	.15	.08
41	Kent Hrbek	.35	.25	.14
42	Dave Parker	.30	.25	.12
43	Jack Morris	.35	.25	.14
44	Pedro Guerrero	.30	.25	.12
45	Mike Witt	.20	.15	.08
46	George Brett	.90	.70	.35
47	Ozzie Smith	.30	.25	.12
48	Cal Ripken	.70	.50	.30
49	Rich Gossage	.25	.20	.10
50	Jim Rice	.50	.40	.20
51	Harold Baines	.25	.20	.10
52	Fernando Valenzuela	.40	.30	.15
53	Buddy Bell	.25	.20	.10
54	Jesse Orosco	.20	.15	.08
55	Lance Parrish	.35	.25	.14
56	Jason Thompson	.20	.15	.08
57	Tom Brunansky	.25	.20	.10
58	Dave Righetti	.30	.25	.12
59	Dave Kingman	.25	.20	.10
60	Dave Winfield	.50	.40	.20

1985 Topps 3-D

These 4-1/4" by 6" cards were something new. Printed on plastic, rather than paper, the player picture on the card is actually raised above the surface much like might be found on a relief map; a true 3-D baseball card. The plastic cards include the player's name, a Topps logo and card number across the top, and a team logo on the side. The backs are blank but have two peel-off adhesive strips so that the card may be attached to a flat surface. There are 30 cards in the set, the bulk of whom are stars.

		MT	NR MT	EX
Complete Set:		14.00	10.50	5.50
Common Player:		.20	.15	.08
1	Mike Schmidt	.90	.70	.35
2	Eddie Murray	.70	.50	.30
3	Dale Murphy	.90	.70	.35
4	George Brett	.90	.70	.35
5	Pete Rose	1.25	.90	.50
6	Jim Rice	.60	.45	.25
7	Ryne Sandberg	.50	.40	.20
8	Don Mattingly	2.50	2.00	1.00
9	Darryl Strawberry	.90	.70	.35
10	Rickey Henderson	.80	.60	.30
11	Keith Hernandez	.50	.40	.20
12	Dave Kingman	.20	.15	.08
13	Tony Gwynn	.80	.60	.30
14	Reggie Jackson	.70	.50	.30
15	Gary Carter	.60	.45	.25
16	Cal Ripken	.80	.60	.30
17	Tim Raines	.50	.40	.20
18	Dave Winfield	.60	.45	.25
19	Dwight Gooden	2.00	1.50	.80
20	Dave Stieb	.20	.15	.08
21	Fernando Valenzuela	.50	.40	.20
22	Mark Langston	.30	.25	.12
23	Bruce Sutter	.25	.20	.10
24	Dan Quisenberry	.20	.15	.08
25	Steve Carlton	.60	.45	.25
26	Mike Boddicker	.20	.15	.08
27	Goose Gossage	.30	.25	.12
28	Jack Morris	.40	.30	.15
29	Rick Sutcliffe	.25	.20	.10
30	Tom Seaver	.60	.45	.25

1985 Topps Traded

By 1985, the Topps Traded set had become a yearly feature, and Topps continued the tradition with another 132-card set. The 2-1/2" by 3-1/2" cards followed the pattern of being virtually identical in design to the regular cards issued by Topps. Sold only through established hobby dealers, the set features traded veterans and promising rookies. A glossy-finish "Tiffany" edition of the set is valued at four times normal Traded card value for commons, up to five or six times normal value for superstars and hot rookies.

		MT	NR MT	EX
Complete Set:		16.00	12.00	6.50
Common Player:		.10	.08	.04
1T	Don Aase	.10	.08	.04
2T	Bill Almon	.10	.08	.04
3T	Benny Ayala	.10	.08	.04
4T	Dusty Baker	.15	.11	.06
5T	George Bamberger	.10	.08	.04
6T	Dale Berra	.10	.08	.04
7T	Rich Bordi	.10	.08	.04
8T	Daryl Boston(FC)	.20	.15	.08
9T	Hubie Brooks	.25	.20	.10

		MT	NR MT	EX
10T	Chris Brown(FC)	.25	.20	.10
11T	Tom Browning(FC)	1.25	.90	.50
12T	Al Bumbry	.10	.08	.04
13T	Ray Burris	.10	.08	.04
14T	Jeff Burroughs	.15	.11	.06
15T	Bill Campbell	.10	.08	.04
16T	Don Carman(FC)	.40	.30	.15
17T	Gary Carter	.70	.50	.30
18T	Bobby Castillo	.10	.08	.04
19T	Bill Caudill	.10	.08	.04
20T	Rick Cerone	.10	.08	.04
21T	Bryan Clark	.10	.08	.04
22T	Jack Clark	.35	.25	.14
23T	Pat Clements(FC)	.20	.15	.08
24T	Vince Coleman(FC)	4.00	3.00	1.50
25T	Dave Collins	.15	.11	.06
26T	Danny Darwin	.15	.11	.06
27T	Jim Davenport	.10	.08	.04
28T	Jerry Davis	.10	.08	.04
29T	Brian Dayett	.10	.08	.04
30T	Ivan DeJesus	.10	.08	.04
31T	Ken Dixon	.10	.08	.04
32T	Mariano Duncan(FC)	.20	.15	.08
33T	John Felske	.10	.08	.04
34T	Mike Fitzgerald	.10	.08	.04
35T	Ray Fontenot	.10	.08	.04
36T	Greg Gagne(FC)	.35	.25	.14
37T	Oscar Gamble	.15	.11	.06
38T	Scott Garrelts(FC)	.50	.40	.20
39T	Bob Gibson	.10	.08	.04
40T	Jim Gott	.10	.08	.04
41T	David Green	.10	.08	.04
42T	Alfredo Griffin	.15	.11	.06
43T	Ozzie Guillen(FC)	.80	.60	.30
44T	Eddie Haas	.10	.08	.04
45T	Terry Harper	.10	.08	.04
46T	Toby Harrah	.15	.11	.06
47T	Greg Harris	.10	.08	.04
48T	Ron Hassey	.10	.08	.04
49T	Rickey Henderson	1.00	.70	.40
50T	Steve Henderson	.10	.08	.04
51T	George Hendrick	.15	.11	.06
52T	Joe Hesketh(FC)	.20	.15	.08
53T	Teddy Higuera(FC)	2.25	1.75	.90
54T	Donnie Hill	.10	.08	.04
55T	Al Holland	.10	.08	.04
56T	Burt Hooton	.15	.11	.06
57T	Jay Howell	.15	.11	.06
58T	Ken Howell(FC)	.15	.11	.06
59T	LaMarr Hoyt	.10	.08	.04
60T	Tim Hulett(FC)	.15	.11	.06
61T	Bob James	.10	.08	.04
62T	Steve Jeltz(FC)	.15	.11	.06
63T	Cliff Johnson	.10	.08	.04
64T	Howard Johnson	1.50	1.25	.60
65T	Ruppert Jones	.10	.08	.04
66T	Steve Kemp	.15	.11	.06
67T	Bruce Kison	.10	.08	.04
68T	Alan Knicely	.10	.08	.04
69T	Mike LaCoss	.10	.08	.04
70T	Lee Lacy	.10	.08	.04
71T	Dave LaPoint	.20	.15	.08
72T	Gary Lavelle	.10	.08	.04
73T	Vance Law	.15	.11	.06
74T	Johnnie LeMaster	.10	.08	.04
75T	Sixto Lezcano	.10	.08	.04
76T	Tim Lollar	.10	.08	.04
77T	Fred Lynn	.30	.25	.12
78T	Billy Martin	.20	.15	.08
79T	Ron Mathis	.10	.08	.04
80T	Len Matuszek	.10	.08	.04
81T	Gene Mauch	.15	.11	.06
82T	Oddibe McDowell	.60	.45	.25
83T	Roger McDowell(FC)	.90	.70	.35
84T	John McNamara	.10	.08	.04
85T	Donnie Moore	.10	.08	.04
86T	Gene Nelson	.10	.08	.04
87T	Steve Nicosia	.10	.08	.04
88T	Al Oliver	.30	.25	.12
89T	Joe Orsulak(FC)	.20	.15	.08
90T	Rob Picciolo	.10	.08	.04
91T	Chris Pittaro	.10	.08	.04
92T	Jim Presley(FC)	.80	.60	.30
93T	Rick Reuschel	.25	.20	.10
94T	Bert Roberge	.10	.08	.04
95T	Bob Rodgers	.10	.08	.04
96T	Jerry Royster	.10	.08	.04
97T	Dave Rozema	.10	.08	.04
98T	Dave Rucker	.10	.08	.04
99T	Vern Ruhle	.10	.08	.04
100T	Paul Runge(FC)	.15	.11	.06

		MT	NR MT	EX
101T	Mark Salas(FC)	.15	.11	.06
102T	Luis Salazar	.10	.08	.04
103T	Joe Sambito	.10	.08	.04
104T	Rick Schu(FC)	.20	.15	.08
105T	Donnie Scott	.10	.08	.04
106T	Larry Sheets(FC)	.50	.40	.20
107T	Don Slaught	.10	.08	.04
108T	Roy Smalley	.15	.11	.06
109T	Lonnie Smith	.15	.11	.06
110T	Nate Snell	.10	.08	.04
111T	Chris Speier	.10	.08	.04
112T	Mike Stenhouse	.10	.08	.04
113T	Tim Stoddard	.10	.08	.04
114T	Jim Sundberg	.15	.11	.06
115T	Bruce Sutter	.25	.20	.10
116T	Don Sutton	.60	.45	.25
117T	Kent Tekulve	.15	.11	.06
118T	Tom Tellmann	.10	.08	.04
119T	Walt Terrell	.15	.11	.06
120T	Mickey Tettleton(FC)	1.00	.70	.40
121T	Derrel Thomas	.10	.08	.04
122T	Rich Thompson	.10	.08	.04
123T	Alex Trevino	.10	.08	.04
124T	John Tudor	.25	.20	.10
125T	Jose Uribe(FC)	.25	.20	.10
126T	Bobby Valentine	.10	.08	.04
127T	Dave Von Ohlen	.10	.08	.04
128T	U.L. Washington	.10	.08	.04
129T	Earl Weaver	.15	.11	.06
130T	Eddie Whitson	.10	.08	.04
131T	Herm Winningham(FC)	.20	.15	.08
132T	Checklist 1-132	.10	.08	.04

1986 Topps

GARY CARTER

The 1986 Topps set consists of 792 cards. Fronts of the 2-1/2" by 3-1/2" cards feature color photos with the Topps logo in the upper right-hand corner while the player's position is in the lower left-hand corner. Above the picture is the team name, while it is the player's name. The borders are a departure from previous practice, as the top 7/8" is black, while the remainder was white. There are no card numbers 51 and 171 in the set; the card that should have been #51, Bobby Wine, shares #57 with Bill Doran, while #171, Bob Rodgers, shares #141 with Chuck Cottier. Once again, a 5,000-set glossy-finish "Tiffany" edition was produced. Values are four to six times higher than the same card in the regular issue.

		MT	NR MT	EX
	Complete Set:	40.00	30.00	15.00
	Common Player:	.05	.04	.02
1	Pete Rose	.90	.70	.35
2	Rose Special 1963-66	.30	.25	.12
3	Rose Special 1967-70	.30	.25	.12
4	Rose Special 1971-74	.30	.25	.12
5	Rose Special 1975-78	.30	.25	.12
6	Rose Special 1979-82	.30	.25	.12
7	Rose Special 1983-85	.30	.25	.12
8	Dwayne Murphy	.07	.05	.03
9	Roy Smith	.05	.04	.02
10	Tony Gwynn	.40	.30	.15
11	Bob Ojeda	.07	.05	.03
12	*Jose Uribe(FC)*	.20	.15	.08

#	Player	MT	NR MT	EX
13	Bob Kearney	.05	.04	.02
14	Julio Cruz	.05	.04	.02
15	Eddie Whitson	.05	.04	.02
16	Rick Schu(FC)	.07	.05	.03
17	Mike Stenhouse	.05	.04	.02
18	Brent Gaff	.05	.04	.02
19	Rich Hebner	.05	.04	.02
20	Lou Whitaker	.25	.20	.10
21	George Bamberger	.05	.04	.02
22	Duane Walker	.05	.04	.02
23	*Manny Lee*(FC)	.15	.11	.06
24	Len Barker	.07	.05	.03
25	Willie Wilson	.12	.09	.05
26	Frank DiPino	.05	.04	.02
27	Ray Knight	.07	.05	.03
28	Eric Davis	2.50	2.00	1.00
29	Tony Phillips	.05	.04	.02
30	Eddie Murray	.40	.30	.15
31	Jamie Easterly	.05	.04	.02
32	Steve Yeager	.05	.04	.02
33	Jeff Lahti	.05	.04	.02
34	Ken Phelps(FC)	.07	.05	.03
35	Jeff Reardon	.12	.09	.05
36	Tigers Leaders (Lance Parrish)	.12	.09	.05
37	Mark Thurmond	.05	.04	.02
38	Glenn Hoffman	.05	.04	.02
39	Dave Rucker	.05	.04	.02
40	Ken Griffey	.10	.08	.04
41	Brad Wellman	.05	.04	.02
42	Geoff Zahn	.05	.04	.02
43	Dave Engle	.05	.04	.02
44	*Lance McCullers*(FC)	.25	.20	.10
45	Damaso Garcia	.05	.04	.02
46	Billy Hatcher(FC)	.20	.15	.08
47	Juan Berenguer	.05	.04	.02
48	Bill Almon	.05	.04	.02
49	Rick Manning	.05	.04	.02
50	Dan Quisenberry	.07	.05	.03
51	Not Issued			
52	Chris Welsh	.05	.04	.02
53	*Len Dykstra*(FC)	.60	.45	.25
54	John Franco	.12	.09	.05
55	Fred Lynn	.15	.11	.06
56	Tom Niedenfuer	.07	.05	.03
57a	Bobby Wine	.05	.04	.02
57b	Bill Doran	.10	.08	.04
58	Bill Krueger	.05	.04	.02
59	Andre Thornton	.07	.05	.03
60	Dwight Evans	.12	.09	.05
61	Karl Best	.05	.04	.02
62	Bob Boone	.07	.05	.03
63	Ron Roenicke	.05	.04	.02
64	Floyd Bannister	.10	.08	.04
65	Dan Driessen	.07	.05	.03
66	Cardinals Leaders (Bob Forsch)	.07	.05	.03
67	Carmelo Martinez	.07	.05	.03
68	Ed Lynch	.05	.04	.02
69	Luis Aguayo	.05	.04	.02
70	Dave Winfield	.30	.25	.12
71	Ken Schrom	.05	.04	.02
72	Shawon Dunston	.20	.15	.08
73	Randy O'Neal(FC)	.07	.05	.03
74	Rance Mulliniks	.05	.04	.02
75	Jose DeLeon	.07	.05	.03
76	Dion James	.07	.05	.03
77	Charlie Leibrandt	.07	.05	.03
78	Bruce Benedict	.05	.04	.02
79	Dave Schmidt	.07	.05	.03
80	Darryl Strawberry	.70	.50	.30
81	Gene Mauch	.07	.05	.03
82	Tippy Martinez	.05	.04	.02
83	Phil Garner	.07	.05	.03
84	Curt Young	.07	.05	.03
85	Tony Perez	.15	.11	.06
86	Tom Waddell	.05	.04	.02
87	Candy Maldonado	.10	.08	.04
88	Tom Nieto	.05	.04	.02
89	Randy St. Claire(FC)	.07	.05	.03
90	Garry Templeton	.07	.05	.03
91	Steve Crawford	.05	.04	.02
92	Al Cowens	.05	.04	.02
93	Scot Thompson	.05	.04	.02
94	Rick Bordi	.05	.04	.02
95	Ozzie Virgil	.05	.04	.02
96	Blue Jay Leaders (Jim Clancy)	.07	.05	.03
97	Gary Gaetti	.20	.15	.08
98	Dick Ruthven	.05	.04	.02
99	Buddy Biancalana	.05	.04	.02
100	Nolan Ryan	.50	.40	.20
101	Dave Bergman	.05	.04	.02
102	*Joe Orsulak*	.15	.11	.06
103	Luis Salazar	.05	.04	.02
104	Sid Fernandez	.12	.09	.05
105	Gary Ward	.07	.05	.03
106	Ray Burris	.05	.04	.02
107	Rafael Ramirez	.05	.04	.02
108	Ted Power	.05	.04	.02
109	Len Matuszek	.05	.04	.02
110	Scott McGregor	.07	.05	.03
111	Roger Craig	.07	.05	.03
112	Bill Campbell	.05	.04	.02
113	U.L. Washington	.05	.04	.02
114	Mike Brown	.05	.04	.02
115	Jay Howell	.07	.05	.03
116	Brook Jacoby	.10	.08	.04
117	Bruce Kison	.05	.04	.02
118	Jerry Royster	.05	.04	.02
119	Barry Bonnell	.05	.04	.02
120	Steve Carlton	.30	.25	.12
121	Nelson Simmons	.05	.04	.02
122	Pete Filson	.05	.04	.02
123	Greg Walker	.10	.08	.04
124	Luis Sanchez	.05	.04	.02
125	Dave Lopes	.07	.05	.03
126	Mets Leaders (Mookie Wilson)	.07	.05	.03
127	*Jack Howell*(FC)	.30	.25	.12
128	John Wathan	.07	.05	.03
129	Jeff Dedmon(FC)	.05	.04	.02
130	Alan Trammell	.30	.25	.12
131	Checklist 1-132	.05	.04	.02
132	Razor Shines	.05	.04	.02
133	Andy McGaffigan	.05	.04	.02
134	Carney Lansford	.10	.08	.04
135	Joe Niekro	.10	.08	.04
136	Mike Hargrove	.05	.04	.02
137	Charlie Moore	.05	.04	.02
138	Mark Davis	.05	.04	.02
139	Daryl Boston	.10	.08	.04
140	John Candelaria	.10	.08	.04
141a	Bob Rodgers	.05	.04	.02
141b	Chuck Cottier	.05	.04	.02
142	Bob Jones	.05	.04	.02
143	Dave Van Gorder	.05	.04	.02
144	Doug Sisk	.05	.04	.02
145	Pedro Guerrero	.20	.15	.08
146	Jack Perconte	.05	.04	.02
147	Larry Sheets	.20	.15	.08
148	Mike Heath	.05	.04	.02
149	Brett Butler	.07	.05	.03
150	Joaquin Andujar	.07	.05	.03
151	Dave Stapleton	.05	.04	.02
152	Mike Morgan	.05	.04	.02
153	Ricky Adams	.05	.04	.02
154	Bert Roberge	.05	.04	.02
155	Bob Grich	.10	.08	.04
156	White Sox Leaders (Richard Dotson)	.07	.05	.03
157	Ron Hassey	.05	.04	.02
158	Derrel Thomas	.05	.04	.02
159	Orel Hershiser	1.00	.70	.40
160	Chet Lemon	.07	.05	.03
161	Lee Tunnell	.05	.04	.02
162	Greg Gagne	.10	.08	.04
163	Pete Ladd	.05	.04	.02
164	Steve Balboni	.07	.05	.03
165	Mike Davis	.07	.05	.03
166	Dickie Thon	.07	.05	.03
167	Zane Smith(FC)	.15	.11	.06
168	Jeff Burroughs	.07	.05	.03
169	George Wright	.05	.04	.02
170	Gary Carter	.25	.20	.10
171	Not Issued			
172	Jerry Reed	.05	.04	.02
173	Wayne Gross	.05	.04	.02
174	Brian Snyder	.05	.04	.02
175	Steve Sax	.15	.11	.06
176	Jay Tibbs	.05	.04	.02
177	Joel Youngblood	.05	.04	.02
178	Ivan DeJesus	.05	.04	.02
179	*Stu Cliburn*(FC)	.10	.08	.04
180	Don Mattingly	3.50	2.75	1.50
181	Al Nipper	.05	.04	.02
182	Bobby Brown	.05	.04	.02
183	Larry Andersen	.05	.04	.02
184	Tim Laudner	.05	.04	.02
185	Rollie Fingers	.20	.15	.08
186	Astros Leaders (Jose Cruz)	.07	.05	.03
187	Scott Fletcher	.07	.05	.03
188	Bob Dernier	.05	.04	.02
189	Mike Mason	.05	.04	.02
190	George Hendrick	.07	.05	.03
191	Wally Backman	.07	.05	.03

#	Player	MT	NR MT	EX
192	Milt Wilcox	.05	.04	.02
193	Daryl Sconiers	.05	.04	.02
194	Craig McMurtry	.05	.04	.02
195	Dave Concepcion	.12	.09	.05
196	Doyle Alexander	.10	.08	.04
197	Enos Cabell	.05	.04	.02
198	Ken Dixon	.05	.04	.02
199	Dick Howser	.05	.04	.02
200	Mike Schmidt	.50	.40	.20
201	Record Breaker (Vince Coleman)(FC)	.30	.25	.12
202	Record Breaker (Dwight Gooden)	.40	.30	.15
203	Record Breaker (Keith Hernandez)	.20	.15	.08
204	Record Breaker (Phil Niekro)	.15	.11	.06
205	Record Breaker (Tony Perez)	.10	.08	.04
206	Record Breaker (Pete Rose)	.50	.40	.20
207	Record Breaker (Fernando Valenzuela)	.20	.15	.08
208	Ramon Romero	.05	.04	.02
209	Randy Ready	.10	.08	.04
210	Calvin Schiraldi(FC)	.10	.08	.04
211	Ed Wojna	.05	.04	.02
212	Chris Speier	.05	.04	.02
213	Bob Shirley	.05	.04	.02
214	Randy Bush	.05	.04	.02
215	Frank White	.10	.08	.04
216	A's Leaders (Dwayne Murphy)	.07	.05	.03
217	Bill Scherrer	.05	.04	.02
218	Randy Hunt	.05	.04	.02
219	Dennis Lamp	.05	.04	.02
220	Bob Horner	.10	.08	.04
221	Dave Henderson	.10	.08	.04
222	Craig Gerber	.05	.04	.02
223	Atlee Hammaker	.05	.04	.02
224	Cesar Cedeno	.10	.08	.04
225	Ron Darling	.15	.11	.06
226	Lee Lacy	.05	.04	.02
227	Al Jones	.05	.04	.02
228	Tom Lawless	.05	.04	.02
229	Bill Gullickson	.05	.04	.02
230	Terry Kennedy	.07	.05	.03
231	Jim Frey	.05	.04	.02
232	Rick Rhoden	.10	.08	.04
233	Steve Lyons(FC)	.07	.05	.03
234	Doug Corbett	.05	.04	.02
235	Butch Wynegar	.05	.04	.02
236	Frank Eufemia	.05	.04	.02
237	Ted Simmons	.12	.09	.05
238	Larry Parrish	.10	.08	.04
239	Joel Skinner	.05	.04	.02
240	Tommy John	.20	.15	.08
241	Tony Fernandez	.20	.15	.08
242	Rich Thompson	.05	.04	.02
243	Johnny Grubb	.05	.04	.02
244	Craig Lefferts	.05	.04	.02
245	Jim Sundberg	.07	.05	.03
246	Phillies Leaders (Steve Carlton)	.15	.11	.06
247	Terry Harper	.05	.04	.02
248	Spike Owen	.05	.04	.02
249	Rob Deer(FC)	.40	.30	.15
250	Dwight Gooden	2.00	1.50	.80
251	Rich Dauer	.05	.04	.02
252	Bobby Castillo	.05	.04	.02
253	Dann Bilardello	.05	.04	.02
254	Ozzie Guillen	.35	.25	.14
255	Tony Armas	.07	.05	.03
256	Kurt Kepshire	.05	.04	.02
257	Doug DeCinces	.10	.08	.04
258	Tim Burke(FC)	.25	.20	.10
259	Dan Pasqua(FC)	.20	.15	.08
260	Tony Pena	.10	.08	.04
261	Bobby Valentine	.05	.04	.02
262	Mario Ramirez	.05	.04	.02
263	Checklist 133-264	.05	.04	.02
264	Darren Daulton(FC)	.12	.09	.05
265	Ron Davis	.05	.04	.02
266	Keith Moreland	.07	.05	.03
267	Paul Molitor	.15	.11	.06
268	Mike Scott	.15	.11	.06
269	Dane Iorg	.05	.04	.02
270	Jack Morris	.20	.15	.08
271	Dave Collins	.07	.05	.03
272	Tim Tolman	.05	.04	.02
273	Jerry Willard	.05	.04	.02
274	Ron Gardenhire	.05	.04	.02
275	Charlie Hough	.08	.06	.03
276	Yankees Leaders (Willie Randolph)	.07	.05	.03
277	Jaime Cocanower	.05	.04	.02
278	Sixto Lezcano	.05	.04	.02
279	Al Pardo	.05	.04	.02
280	Tim Raines	.30	.25	.12
281	Steve Mura	.05	.04	.02
282	Jerry Mumphrey	.05	.04	.02
283	Mike Fischlin	.05	.04	.02
284	Brian Dayett	.05	.04	.02
285	Buddy Bell	.10	.08	.04
286	Luis DeLeon	.05	.04	.02
287	John Christensen(FC)	.10	.08	.04
288	Don Aase	.05	.04	.02
289	Johnnie LeMaster	.05	.04	.02
290	Carlton Fisk	.30	.25	.12
291	Tom Lasorda	.07	.05	.03
292	Chuck Porter	.05	.04	.02
293	Chris Chambliss	.07	.05	.03
294	Danny Cox	.10	.08	.04
295	Kirk Gibson	.30	.25	.12
296	Geno Petralli(FC)	.07	.05	.03
297	Tim Lollar	.05	.04	.02
298	Craig Reynolds	.05	.04	.02
299	Bryn Smith	.05	.04	.02
300	George Brett	.50	.40	.20
301	Dennis Rasmussen	.12	.09	.05
302	Greg Gross	.05	.04	.02
303	Curt Wardle	.05	.04	.02
304	Mike Gallego(FC)	.12	.09	.05
305	Phil Bradley	.15	.11	.06
306	Padres Leaders (Terry Kennedy)	.07	.05	.03
307	Dave Sax	.05	.04	.02
308	Ray Fontenot	.05	.04	.02
309	John Shelby	.05	.04	.02
310	Greg Minton	.05	.04	.02
311	Dick Schofield	.05	.04	.02
312	Tom Filer	.05	.04	.02
313	Joe DeSa	.05	.04	.02
314	Frank Pastore	.05	.04	.02
315	Mookie Wilson	.10	.08	.04
316	Sammy Khalifa	.05	.04	.02
317	Ed Romero	.05	.04	.02
318	Terry Whitfield	.05	.04	.02
319	Rick Camp	.05	.04	.02
320	Jim Rice	.30	.25	.12
321	Earl Weaver	.07	.05	.03
322	Bob Forsch	.07	.05	.03
323	Jerry Davis	.05	.04	.02
324	Dan Schatzeder	.05	.04	.02
325	Juan Beniquez	.05	.04	.02
326	Kent Tekulve	.07	.05	.03
327	Mike Pagliarulo	.20	.15	.08
328	Pete O'Brien	.10	.08	.04
329	Kirby Puckett	1.75	1.25	.70
330	Rick Sutcliffe	.12	.09	.05
331	Alan Ashby	.05	.04	.02
332	Darryl Motley	.05	.04	.02
333	Tom Henke(FC)	.15	.11	.06
334	Ken Oberkfell	.05	.04	.02
335	Don Sutton	.25	.20	.10
336	Indians Leaders (Andre Thornton)	.07	.05	.03
337	Darnell Coles	.07	.05	.03
338	Jorge Bell	.25	.20	.10
339	Bruce Berenyi	.05	.04	.02
340	Cal Ripken	.40	.30	.15
341	Frank Williams	.05	.04	.02
342	Gary Redus	.05	.04	.02
343	Carlos Diaz	.05	.04	.02
344	Jim Wohlford	.05	.04	.02
345	Donnie Moore	.05	.04	.02
346	Bryan Little	.05	.04	.02
347	Teddy Higuera	1.00	.70	.40
348	Cliff Johnson	.05	.04	.02
349	Mark Clear	.05	.04	.02
350	Jack Clark	.20	.15	.08
351	Chuck Tanner	.05	.04	.02
352	Harry Spilman	.05	.04	.02
353	Keith Atherton	.05	.04	.02
354	Tony Bernazard	.05	.04	.02
355	Lee Smith	.10	.08	.04
356	Mickey Hatcher	.05	.04	.02
357	Ed Vande Berg	.05	.04	.02
358	Rick Dempsey	.07	.05	.03
359	Mike LaCoss	.05	.04	.02
360	Lloyd Moseby	.10	.08	.04
361	Shane Rawley	.10	.08	.04
362	Tom Paciorek	.05	.04	.02
363	Terry Forster	.07	.05	.03
364	Reid Nichols	.05	.04	.02
365	Mike Flanagan	.10	.08	.04
366	Reds Leaders (Dave Concepcion)	.07	.05	.03
367	Aurelio Lopez	.05	.04	.02
368	Greg Brock	.07	.05	.03
369	Al Holland	.05	.04	.02
370	Vince Coleman	1.50	1.25	.60
371	Bill Stein	.05	.04	.02

#	Player	MT	NR MT	EX
372	Ben Oglivie	.07	.05	.03
373	*Urbano Lugo*(FC)	.07	.05	.03
374	Terry Francona	.05	.04	.02
375	Rich Gedman	.10	.08	.04
376	Bill Dawley	.05	.04	.02
377	Joe Carter	.30	.25	.12
378	Bruce Bochte	.05	.04	.02
379	Bobby Meacham	.05	.04	.02
380	LaMarr Hoyt	.05	.04	.02
381	Ray Miller	.05	.04	.02
382	*Ivan Calderon*(FC)	.40	.30	.15
383	*Chris Brown*	.30	.25	.12
384	Steve Trout	.05	.04	.02
385	Cecil Cooper	.10	.08	.04
386	*Cecil Fielder*(FC)	.12	.09	.05
387	Steve Kemp	.07	.05	.03
388	Dickie Noles	.05	.04	.02
389	Glenn Davis(FC)	3.50	2.75	1.50
390	Tom Seaver	.40	.30	.15
391	Julio Franco	.10	.08	.04
392	John Russell(FC)	.10	.08	.04
393	Chris Pittaro	.05	.04	.02
394	Checklist 265-396	.05	.04	.02
395	Scott Garrelts	.07	.05	.03
396	Red Sox Leaders (Dwight Evans)	.07	.05	.03
397	*Steve Buechele*(FC)	.20	.15	.08
398	*Earnie Riles*(FC)	.15	.11	.06
399	Bill Swift	.12	.09	.05
400	Rod Carew	.30	.25	.12
401	Turn Back The Clock (Fernando Valenzuela)	.15	.11	.06
402	Turn Back The Clock (Tom Seaver)	.15	.11	.06
403	Turn Back The Clock (Willie Mays)	.20	.15	.08
404	Turn Back The Clock (Frank Robinson)	.15	.11	.06
405	Turn Back The Clock (Roger Maris)	.20	.15	.08
406	Scott Sanderson	.05	.04	.02
407	Sal Butera	.05	.04	.02
408	Dave Smith	.07	.05	.03
409	*Paul Runge*	.07	.05	.03
410	Dave Kingman	.15	.11	.06
411	Sparky Anderson	.07	.05	.03
412	Jim Clancy	.07	.05	.03
413	Tim Flannery	.05	.04	.02
414	Tom Gorman	.05	.04	.02
415	Hal McRae	.10	.08	.04
416	Denny Martinez	.07	.05	.03
417	R.J. Reynolds	.07	.05	.03
418	Alan Knicely	.05	.04	.02
419	Frank Wills	.05	.04	.02
420	Von Hayes	.10	.08	.04
421	Dave Palmer	.05	.04	.02
422	Mike Jorgensen	.05	.04	.02
423	Dan Spillner	.05	.04	.02
424	Rick Miller	.05	.04	.02
425	Larry McWilliams	.05	.04	.02
426	Brewers Leaders (Charlie Moore)	.07	.05	.03
427	Joe Cowley	.05	.04	.02
428	Max Venable	.05	.04	.02
429	Greg Booker	.05	.04	.02
430	Kent Hrbek	.20	.15	.08
431	George Frazier	.05	.04	.02
432	Mark Bailey	.05	.04	.02
433	Chris Codiroli	.05	.04	.02
434	Curt Wilkerson	.05	.04	.02
435	Bill Caudill	.05	.04	.02
436	Doug Flynn	.05	.04	.02
437	Rick Mahler	.05	.04	.02
438	Clint Hurdle	.05	.04	.02
439	Rick Honeycutt	.05	.04	.02
440	Alvin Davis	.30	.25	.12
441	Whitey Herzog	.07	.05	.03
442	Ron Robinson(FC)	.12	.09	.05
443	Bill Buckner	.10	.08	.04
444	Alex Trevino	.05	.04	.02
445	Bert Blyleven	.12	.09	.05
446	Lenn Sakata	.05	.04	.02
447	Jerry Don Gleaton	.05	.04	.02
448	*Herm Winningham*	.15	.11	.06
449	Rod Scurry	.05	.04	.02
450	Graig Nettles	.15	.11	.06
451	Mark Brown	.05	.04	.02
452	Bob Clark	.05	.04	.02
453	Steve Jeltz	.07	.05	.03
454	Burt Hooton	.07	.05	.03
455	Willie Randolph	.10	.08	.04
456	Braves Leaders (Dale Murphy)	.25	.20	.10
457	*Mickey Tettleton*	.60	.45	.25
458	Kevin Bass	.10	.08	.04
459	Luis Leal	.05	.04	.02
460	Leon Durham	.07	.05	.03

#	Player	MT	NR MT	EX
461	Walt Terrell	.07	.05	.03
462	Domingo Ramos	.05	.04	.02
463	Jim Gott	.05	.04	.02
464	Ruppert Jones	.05	.04	.02
465	Jesse Orosco	.07	.05	.03
466	Tom Foley	.05	.04	.02
467	Bob James	.05	.04	.02
468	Mike Scioscia	.07	.05	.03
469	Storm Davis	.10	.08	.04
470	Bill Madlock	.12	.09	.05
471	Bobby Cox	.05	.04	.02
472	Joe Hesketh	.07	.05	.03
473	Mark Brouhard	.05	.04	.02
474	John Tudor	.10	.08	.04
475	Juan Samuel	.12	.09	.05
476	Ron Mathis	.05	.04	.02
477	Mike Easler	.07	.05	.03
478	Andy Hawkins	.05	.04	.02
479	*Bob Melvin*(FC)	.12	.09	.05
480	*Oddibe McDowell*	.30	.25	.12
481	Scott Bradley(FC)	.10	.08	.04
482	Rick Lysander	.05	.04	.02
483	George Vukovich	.05	.04	.02
484	Donnie Hill	.05	.04	.02
485	Gary Matthews	.10	.08	.04
486	Angels Leaders (Bob Grich)	.07	.05	.03
487	Bret Saberhagen	.40	.30	.15
488	Lou Thornton	.05	.04	.02
489	Jim Winn	.05	.04	.02
490	Jeff Leonard	.07	.05	.03
491	Pascual Perez	.07	.05	.03
492	Kelvin Chapman	.05	.04	.02
493	Gene Nelson	.05	.04	.02
494	Gary Roenicke	.05	.04	.02
495	Mark Langston	.20	.15	.08
496	Jay Johnstone	.07	.05	.03
497	John Stuper	.05	.04	.02
498	Tito Landrum	.05	.04	.02
499	Bob Gibson	.05	.04	.02
500	Rickey Henderson	.40	.30	.15
501	Dave Johnson	.07	.05	.03
502	Glen Cook	.05	.04	.02
503	Mike Fitzgerald	.05	.04	.02
504	Denny Walling	.05	.04	.02
505	Jerry Koosman	.10	.08	.04
506	Bill Russell	.07	.05	.03
507	*Steve Ontiveros*(FC)	.12	.09	.05
508	Alan Wiggins	.05	.04	.02
509	Ernie Camacho	.05	.04	.02
510	Wade Boggs	2.25	1.75	.90
511	Ed Nunez	.05	.04	.02
512	Thad Bosley	.05	.04	.02
513	Ron Washington	.05	.04	.02
514	Mike Jones	.05	.04	.02
515	Darrell Evans	.12	.09	.05
516	Giants Leaders (Greg Minton)	.07	.05	.03
517	*Milt Thompson*(FC)	.25	.20	.10
518	Buck Martinez	.05	.04	.02
519	Danny Darwin	.05	.04	.02
520	Keith Hernandez	.30	.25	.12
521	Nate Snell	.05	.04	.02
522	Bob Bailor	.05	.04	.02
523	Joe Price	.05	.04	.02
524	Darrell Miller(FC)	.07	.05	.03
525	Marvell Wynne	.05	.04	.02
526	Charlie Lea	.05	.04	.02
527	Checklist 397-528	.05	.04	.02
528	Terry Pendleton	.15	.11	.06
529	Marc Sullivan	.05	.04	.02
530	Rich Gossage	.20	.15	.08
531	Tony LaRussa	.07	.05	.03
532	*Don Carman*	.25	.20	.10
533	Billy Sample	.05	.04	.02
534	Jeff Calhoun	.05	.04	.02
535	Toby Harrah	.07	.05	.03
536	Jose Rijo	.10	.08	.04
537	Mark Salas	.07	.05	.03
538	Dennis Eckersley	.12	.09	.05
539	Glenn Hubbard	.05	.04	.02
540	Dan Petry	.07	.05	.03
541	Jorge Orta	.05	.04	.02
542	Don Schulze	.05	.04	.02
543	Jerry Narron	.05	.04	.02
544	Eddie Milner	.05	.04	.02
545	Jimmy Key	.15	.11	.06
546	Mariners Leaders (Dave Henderson)	.07	.05	.03
547	*Roger McDowell*	.40	.30	.15
548	Mike Young	.05	.04	.02
549	Bob Welch	.12	.09	.05
550	Tom Herr	.10	.08	.04

	MT	NR MT	EX
551 Dave LaPoint	.07	.05	.03
552 Marc Hill	.05	.04	.02
553 Jim Morrison	.05	.04	.02
554 Paul Householder	.05	.04	.02
555 Hubie Brooks	.10	.08	.04
556 John Denny	.05	.04	.02
557 Gerald Perry	.12	.09	.05
558 Tim Stoddard	.05	.04	.02
559 Tommy Dunbar	.05	.04	.02
560 Dave Righetti	.20	.15	.08
561 Bob Lillis	.05	.04	.02
562 Joe Beckwith	.05	.04	.02
563 Alejandro Sanchez	.05	.04	.02
564 Warren Brusstar	.05	.04	.02
565 Tom Brunansky	.12	.09	.05
566 Alfredo Griffin	.07	.05	.03
567 Jeff Barkley	.05	.04	.02
568 Donnie Scott	.05	.04	.02
569 Jim Acker	.05	.04	.02
570 Rusty Staub	.10	.08	.04
571 Mike Jeffcoat	.05	.04	.02
572 Paul Zuvella	.05	.04	.02
573 Tom Hume	.05	.04	.02
574 Ron Kittle	.10	.08	.04
575 Mike Boddicker	.07	.05	.03
576 Expos Leaders (Andre Dawson)	.12	.09	.05
577 Jerry Reuss	.07	.05	.03
578 Lee Mazzilli	.07	.05	.03
579 Jim Slaton	.05	.04	.02
580 Willie McGee	.15	.11	.06
581 Bruce Hurst	.12	.09	.05
582 Jim Gantner	.07	.05	.03
583 Al Bumbry	.05	.04	.02
584 *Brian Fisher*(FC)	.30	.25	.12
585 Garry Maddox	.07	.05	.03
586 Greg Harris	.05	.04	.02
587 Rafael Santana	.05	.04	.02
588 Steve Lake	.05	.04	.02
589 Sid Bream	.10	.08	.04
590 Bob Knepper	.07	.05	.03
591 Jackie Moore	.05	.04	.02
592 Frank Tanana	.10	.08	.04
593 Jesse Barfield	.20	.15	.08
594 Chris Bando	.05	.04	.02
595 Dave Parker	.20	.15	.08
596 Onix Concepcion	.05	.04	.02
597 Sammy Stewart	.05	.04	.02
598 Jim Presley	.25	.20	.10
599 *Rick Aguilera*(FC)	.20	.15	.08
600 Dale Murphy	.50	.40	.20
601 Gary Lucas	.05	.04	.02
602 *Mariano Duncan*	.15	.11	.06
603 Bill Laskey	.05	.04	.02
604 Gary Pettis	.05	.04	.02
605 Dennis Boyd	.07	.05	.03
606 Royals Leaders (Hal McRae)	.07	.05	.03
607 Ken Dayley	.05	.04	.02
608 Bruce Bochy	.05	.04	.02
609 Barbaro Garbey	.05	.04	.02
610 Ron Guidry	.15	.11	.06
611 Gary Woods	.05	.04	.02
612 Richard Dotson	.10	.08	.04
613 Roy Smalley	.05	.04	.02
614 Rick Waits	.05	.04	.02
615 Johnny Ray	.10	.08	.04
616 Glenn Brummer	.05	.04	.02
617 Lonnie Smith	.07	.05	.03
618 Jim Pankovits	.05	.04	.02
619 Danny Heep	.05	.04	.02
620 Bruce Sutter	.12	.09	.05
621 John Felske	.05	.04	.02
622 Gary Lavelle	.05	.04	.02
623 Floyd Rayford	.05	.04	.02
624 Steve McCatty	.05	.04	.02
625 Bob Brenly	.05	.04	.02
626 Roy Thomas	.05	.04	.02
627 Ron Oester	.05	.04	.02
628 *Kirk McCaskill*(FC)	.35	.25	.14
629 *Mitch Webster*(FC)	.25	.20	.10
630 Fernando Valenzuela	.30	.25	.12
631 Steve Braun	.05	.04	.02
632 Dave Von Ohlen	.05	.04	.02
633 Jackie Gutierrez	.05	.04	.02
634 Roy Lee Jackson	.05	.04	.02
635 Jason Thompson	.05	.04	.02
636 Cubs Leaders (Lee Smith)	.07	.05	.03
637 Rudy Law	.05	.04	.02
638 John Butcher	.05	.04	.02
639 Bo Diaz	.07	.05	.03
640 Jose Cruz	.10	.08	.04
641 Wayne Tolleson	.05	.04	.02

	MT	NR MT	EX
642 Ray Searage	.05	.04	.02
643 Tom Brookens	.05	.04	.02
644 Mark Gubicza	.12	.09	.05
645 Dusty Baker	.07	.05	.03
646 Mike Moore	.05	.04	.02
647 Mel Hall	.07	.05	.03
648 Steve Bedrosian	.10	.08	.04
649 Ronn Reynolds	.05	.04	.02
650 Dave Stieb	.12	.09	.05
651 Billy Martin	.12	.09	.05
652 Tom Browning	.25	.20	.10
653 Jim Dwyer	.05	.04	.02
654 Ken Howell	.07	.05	.03
655 Manny Trillo	.07	.05	.03
656 Brian Harper	.05	.04	.02
657 Juan Agosto	.05	.04	.02
658 Rob Wilfong	.05	.04	.02
659 Checklist 529-660	.05	.04	.02
660 Steve Garvey	.30	.25	.12
661 Roger Clemens	3.00	2.25	1.25
662 Bill Schroeder	.05	.04	.02
663 Neil Allen	.05	.04	.02
664 Tim Corcoran	.05	.04	.02
665 Alejandro Pena	.07	.05	.03
666 Rangers Leaders (Charlie Hough)	.07	.05	.03
667 Tim Teufel	.05	.04	.02
668 Cecilio Guante	.05	.04	.02
669 Ron Cey	.10	.08	.04
670 Willie Hernandez	.07	.05	.03
671 Lynn Jones	.05	.04	.02
672 Rob Picciolo	.05	.04	.02
673 Ernie Whitt	.07	.05	.03
674 Pat Tabler	.07	.05	.03
675 Claudell Washington	.07	.05	.03
676 Matt Young	.05	.04	.02
677 Nick Esasky	.07	.05	.03
678 Dan Gladden	.07	.05	.03
679 Britt Burns	.05	.04	.02
680 George Foster	.15	.11	.06
681 Dick Williams	.05	.04	.02
682 Junior Ortiz	.05	.04	.02
683 Andy Van Slyke	.15	.11	.06
684 Bob McClure	.05	.04	.02
685 Tim Wallach	.12	.09	.05
686 Jeff Stone	.05	.04	.02
687 Mike Trujillo	.05	.04	.02
688 Larry Herndon	.07	.05	.03
689 Dave Stewart	.12	.09	.05
690 Ryne Sandberg	.35	.25	.14
691 Mike Madden	.05	.04	.02
692 Dale Berra	.05	.04	.02
693 Tom Tellmann	.05	.04	.02
694 Garth Iorg	.05	.04	.02
695 Mike Smithson	.05	.04	.02
696 Dodgers Leaders (Bill Russell)	.07	.05	.03
697 Bud Black	.05	.04	.02
698 Brad Komminsk	.05	.04	.02
699 Pat Corrales	.05	.04	.02
700 Reggie Jackson	.35	.25	.14
701 Keith Hernandez AS	.15	.11	.06
702 Tom Herr AS	.07	.05	.03
703 Tim Wallach AS	.07	.05	.03
704 Ozzie Smith AS	.10	.08	.04
705 Dale Murphy AS	.30	.25	.12
706 Pedro Guerrero AS	.12	.09	.05
707 Willie McGee AS	.12	.09	.05
708 Gary Carter AS	.20	.15	.08
709 Dwight Gooden AS	.40	.30	.15
710 John Tudor AS	.07	.05	.03
711 Jeff Reardon AS	.07	.05	.03
712 Don Mattingly AS	.90	.70	.35
713 Damaso Garcia AS	.05	.04	.02
714 George Brett AS	.30	.25	.12
715 Cal Ripken AS	.25	.20	.10
716 Rickey Henderson AS	.25	.20	.10
717 Dave Winfield AS	.20	.15	.08
718 Jorge Bell AS	.20	.15	.08
719 Carlton Fisk AS	.12	.09	.05
720 Bret Saberhagen AS	.15	.11	.06
721 Ron Guidry AS	.10	.08	.04
722 Dan Quisenberry AS	.07	.05	.03
723 Marty Bystrom	.05	.04	.02
724 Tim Hulett	.07	.05	.03
725 Mario Soto	.07	.05	.03
726 Orioles Leaders (Rick Dempsey)	.07	.05	.03
727 David Green	.05	.04	.02
728 Mike Marshall	.12	.09	.05
729 Jim Beattie	.05	.04	.02
730 Ozzie Smith	.15	.11	.06
731 Don Robinson	.07	.05	.03
732 *Floyd Youmans*(FC)	.20	.15	.08

		MT	NR MT	EX
733	Ron Romanick	.05	.04	.02
734	Marty Barrett	.10	.08	.04
735	Dave Dravecky	.07	.05	.03
736	Glenn Wilson	.07	.05	.03
737	Pete Vuckovich	.07	.05	.03
738	Andre Robertson	.05	.04	.02
739	Dave Rozema	.05	.04	.02
740	Lance Parrish	.20	.15	.08
741	Pete Rose	.40	.30	.15
742	Frank Viola	.15	.11	.06
743	Pat Sheridan	.05	.04	.02
744	Lary Sorensen	.05	.04	.02
745	Willie Upshaw	.07	.05	.03
746	Denny Gonzalez	.05	.04	.02
747	Rick Cerone	.05	.04	.02
748	Steve Henderson	.05	.04	.02
749	Ed Jurak	.05	.04	.02
750	Gorman Thomas	.10	.08	.04
751	Howard Johnson	.12	.09	.05
752	Mike Krukow	.07	.05	.03
753	Dan Ford	.05	.04	.02
754	*Pat Clements*	.12	.09	.05
755	Harold Baines	.15	.11	.06
756	Pirates Leaders (Rick Rhoden)	.07	.05	.03
757	Darrell Porter	.07	.05	.03
758	Dave Anderson	.05	.04	.02
759	Moose Haas	.05	.04	.02
760	Andre Dawson	.20	.15	.08
761	Don Slaught	.05	.04	.02
762	Eric Show	.07	.05	.03
763	Terry Puhl	.05	.04	.02
764	Kevin Gross	.07	.05	.03
765	Don Baylor	.12	.09	.05
766	Rick Langford	.05	.04	.02
767	Jody Davis	.10	.08	.04
768	Vern Ruhle	.05	.04	.02
769	*Harold Reynolds*(FC)	.60	.45	.25
770	Vida Blue	.10	.08	.04
771	John McNamara	.05	.04	.02
772	Brian Downing	.07	.05	.03
773	Greg Pryor	.05	.04	.02
774	Terry Leach	.05	.04	.02
775	Al Oliver	.10	.08	.04
776	Gene Garber	.05	.04	.02
777	Wayne Krenchicki	.05	.04	.02
778	Jerry Hairston	.05	.04	.02
779	Rick Reuschel	.10	.08	.04
780	Robin Yount	.40	.30	.15
781	Joe Nolan	.05	.04	.02
782	Ken Landreaux	.05	.04	.02
783	Ricky Horton	.07	.05	.03
784	Alan Bannister	.05	.04	.02
785	Bob Stanley	.05	.04	.02
786	Twins Leaders (Mickey Hatcher)	.07	.05	.03
787	Vance Law	.07	.05	.03
788	Marty Castillo	.05	.04	.02
789	Kurt Bevacqua	.05	.04	.02
790	Phil Niekro	.25	.20	.10
791	Checklist 661-792	.05	.04	.02
792	Charles Hudson	.06	.05	.02

1986 Topps
All-Star Glossy Set Of 22

As in previous years, Topps continued to make the popular glossy-surfaced cards as an insert in rack packs. The All-Star Glossy set of 22 2-1/2" by 3-1/2" cards shows little design change from previous years.

Cards feature a front color photo and All-Star banner at the top. The bottom has the player's name and position. The set includes the All-Star starting teams as well as the managers and honorary captains.

		MT	NR MT	EX
Complete Set:		6.00	4.50	2.50
Common Player:		.20	.15	.08
1	Sparky Anderson	.20	.15	.08
2	Eddie Murray	.50	.40	.20
3	Lou Whitaker	.30	.25	.12
4	George Brett	.80	.60	.30
5	Cal Ripken	.60	.45	.25
6	Jim Rice	.50	.40	.20
7	Rickey Henderson	.60	.45	.25
8	Dave Winfield	.50	.40	.20
9	Carlton Fisk	.30	.25	.12
10	Jack Morris	.30	.25	.12
11	A.L. All-Star Team	.20	.15	.08
12	Dick Williams	.20	.15	.08
13	Steve Garvey	.50	.40	.20
14	Tom Herr	.20	.15	.08
15	Graig Nettles	.20	.15	.08
16	Ozzie Smith	.30	.25	.12
17	Tony Gwynn	.60	.45	.25
18	Dale Murphy	.80	.60	.30
19	Darryl Strawberry	.80	.60	.30
20	Terry Kennedy	.20	.15	.08
21	LaMarr Hoyt	.20	.15	.08
22	N.L. All-Star Team	.20	.15	.08

1986 Topps
All-Star Glossy Set Of 60

The Topps All-Star & Hot Prospects Glossy Set of 60 cards represents an expansion of a good idea. The 2-1/2" by 3-1/2" cards had a good following when they were limited to stars, but Topps realized that the addition of top young players would spice up the set even further, so in 1986 it was expanded from 40 to 60 cards. The cards themselves are basically all color glossy pictures with the player's name in very small print in the lower left-hand corner. To obtain the set, it was necessary to send $1 plus six special offer cards from wax packs to Topps for each series. At 60 cards, that meant the process had to be repeated six times as there were 10 cards in each series, making the set quite expensive from the outset.

		MT	NR MT	EX
Complete Set:		15.00	11.00	6.00
Common Player:		.15	.11	.06
1	Oddibe McDowell	.25	.20	.10
2	Reggie Jackson	.70	.50	.30
3	Fernando Valenzuela	.35	.25	.14
4	Jack Clark	.25	.20	.10
5	Rickey Henderson	.70	.50	.30
6	Steve Balboni	.15	.11	.06
7	Keith Hernandez	.40	.30	.15
8	Lance Parrish	.30	.25	.12
9	Willie McGee	.25	.20	.10
10	Chris Brown	.40	.30	.15
11	Darryl Strawberry	.90	.70	.35

		MT	NR MT	EX
12	Ron Guidry	.30	.25	.12
13	Dave Parker	.25	.20	.10
14	Cal Ripken	.70	.50	.30
15	Tim Raines	.50	.40	.20
16	Rod Carew	.60	.45	.25
17	Mike Schmidt	.90	.70	.35
18	George Brett	.90	.70	.35
19	Joe Hesketh	.15	.11	.06
20	Dan Pasqua	.20	.15	.08
21	Vince Coleman	1.00	.70	.40
22	Tom Seaver	.50	.40	.20
23	Gary Carter	.50	.40	.20
24	Orel Hershiser	.40	.30	.15
25	Pedro Guerrero	.30	.25	.12
26	Wade Boggs	1.25	.90	.50
27	Bret Saberhagen	.30	.25	.12
28	Carlton Fisk	.25	.20	.10
29	Kirk Gibson	.35	.25	.14
30	Brian Fisher	.20	.15	.08
31	Don Mattingly	3.00	2.25	1.25
32	Tom Herr	.15	.11	.06
33	Eddie Murray	.60	.45	.25
34	Ryne Sandberg	.40	.30	.15
35	Dan Quisenberry	.15	.11	.06
36	Jim Rice	.50	.40	.20
37	Dale Murphy	.90	.70	.35
38	Steve Garvey	.50	.40	.20
39	Roger McDowell	.25	.20	.10
40	Earnie Riles	.15	.11	.06
41	Dwight Gooden	1.25	.90	.50
42	Dave Winfield	.50	.40	.20
43	Dave Stieb	.20	.15	.08
44	Bob Horner	.20	.15	.08
45	Nolan Ryan	.50	.40	.20
46	Ozzie Smith	.25	.20	.10
47	Jorge Bell	.50	.40	.20
48	Gorman Thomas	.15	.11	.06
49	Tom Browning	.25	.20	.10
50	Larry Sheets	.20	.15	.08
51	Pete Rose	1.25	.90	.50
52	Brett Butler	.15	.11	.06
53	John Tudor	.20	.15	.08
54	Phil Bradley	.20	.15	.08
55	Jeff Reardon	.20	.15	.08
56	Rich Gossage	.25	.20	.10
57	Tony Gwynn	.60	.45	.25
58	Ozzie Guillen	.25	.20	.10
59	Glenn Davis	.35	.25	.14
60	Darrell Evans	.15	.11	.06

1986 Topps Box Panels

Following the lead of Donruss, which introduced the concept in 1985, Topps produced special cards on the bottom panels of wax boxes. Individual cards measure 2-1/2" by 3-1/2", the same as regular cards. Design of the cards is virtually identical with regular '86 Topps, though the top border is in red, rather than black. The cards are lettered "A" through "P", rather than numbered on the back.

	MT	NR MT	EX
Complete Panel Set:	12.00	9.00	4.75
Complete Singles Set:	4.75	3.50	2.00
Common Panel:	2.00	1.50	.80
Common Single Player:	.15	.11	.06
Panel	3.50	2.75	1.50

		MT	NR MT	EX
A	Jorge Bell	.20	.15	.08
B	Wade Boggs	.60	.45	.25
C	George Brett	.35	.25	.14
D	Vince Coleman	.35	.25	.14
	Panel	2.00	1.50	.80
E	Carlton Fisk	.15	.11	.06
F	Dwight Gooden	.40	.30	.15
G	Pedro Guerrero	.15	.11	.06
H	Ron Guidry	.15	.11	.06
	Panel	3.50	2.75	1.50
I	Reggie Jackson	.30	.25	.12
J	Don Mattingly	.90	.70	.35
K	Oddibe McDowell	.15	.11	.06
L	Willie McGee	.15	.11	.06
	Panel	3.00	2.25	1.25
M	Dale Murphy	.35	.25	.14
N	Pete Rose	.50	.40	.20
O	Bret Saberhagen	.15	.11	.06
P	Fernando Valenzuela	.20	.15	.08

1986 Topps Gallery Of Champions

For the third consecutive year Topps issued 12 "metal mini-cards" as a dealer-ordering incentive. The metal replicas were minted 1/4-size (approximately 1-1/4" by 1-3/4") of the regular cards and come in silver, aluminum and bronze. The bronze and silver sets were issued in leather-like velvet-lined display cases. A bronze 1952 Topps Mickey Mantle was given as a premium for dealers purchasing 1986 Traded sets, while a pewter Don Mattingly was issued as a premium to those ordering the aluminum, bronze and silver sets. The Mantle bronze is valued at $12 and the Mattingly pewter at $100.

		MT	NR MT	EX
Complete Aluminum Set:		30.00	22.00	12.00
Complete Bronze Set:		175.00	131.00	70.00
Complete Silver Set:		650.00	487.00	260.00
(1a)	Wade Boggs (aluminum)	3.00	2.25	1.25
(1b)	Wade Boggs (bronze)	25.00	18.50	10.00
(1c)	Wade Boggs (silver)	125.00	94.00	50.00
(2a)	Vince Coleman (aluminum)	1.25	.90	.50
(2b)	Vince Coleman (bronze)	12.00	9.00	4.75
(2c)	Vince Coleman (silver)	50.00	37.00	20.00
(3a)	Darrell Evans (aluminum)	.70	.50	.30
(3b)	Darrell Evans (bronze)	7.50	5.75	3.00
(3c)	Darrell Evans (silver)	20.00	15.00	8.00
(4a)	Dwight Gooden (aluminum)	2.00	1.50	.80
(4b)	Dwight Gooden (bronze)	20.00	15.00	8.00
(4c)	Dwight Gooden (silver)	100.00	75.00	40.00
(5a)	Ozzie Guillen (aluminum)	.70	.50	.30
(5b)	Ozzie Guillen (bronze)	7.50	5.75	3.00
(5c)	Ozzie Guillen (silver)	20.00	15.00	8.00
(6a)	Don Mattingly (aluminum)	8.00	6.00	3.25
(6b)	Don Mattingly (bronze)	50.00	37.00	20.00
(6c)	Don Mattingly (silver)	200.00	150.00	80.00
(7a)	Willie McGee (aluminum)	1.00	.70	.40
(7b)	Willie McGee (bronze)	10.00	7.50	4.00
(7c)	Willie McGee (silver)	30.00	22.00	12.00
(8a)	Dale Murphy (aluminum)	1.50	1.25	.60
(8b)	Dale Murphy (bronze)	15.00	11.00	6.00
(8c)	Dale Murphy (silver)	80.00	60.00	32.00
(9a)	Dan Quisenberry (aluminum)	.70	.50	.30

		MT	NR MT	EX
(9b)	Dan Quisenberry (bronze)	7.50	5.75	3.00
(9c)	Dan Quisenberry (silver)	20.00	15.00	8.00
(10a)	Jeff Reardon (aluminum)	.70	.50	.30
(10b)	Jeff Reardon (bronze)	7.50	5.75	3.00
(10c)	Jeff Reardon (silver)	20.00	15.00	8.00
(11a)	Pete Rose (aluminum)	2.50	2.00	1.00
(11b)	Pete Rose (bronze)	25.00	18.50	10.00
(11c)	Pete Rose (silver)	110.00	82.00	44.00
(12a)	Bret Saberhagen (aluminum)	1.00	.70	.40
(12b)	Bret Saberhagen (bronze)	10.00	7.50	4.00
(12c)	Bret Saberhagen (silver)	30.00	22.00	12.00

1986 Topps
Mini League Leaders

MIKE SCHMIDT

Topps had long experimented with bigger cards, but in 1986, they also decided to try smaller ones. These 2-1/8" by 2-15/16" cards feature top players in a number of categories. Sold in plastic packs as a regular Topps issue, the 66-card set is attractive as well as innovative. The cards feature color photos and a minimum of added information on the fronts where only the player's name and Topps logo appear. Backs limited information as well, but do feature whatever information was required to justify the player's inclusion in a set of league leaders.

		MT	NR MT	EX
Complete Set:		6.50	5.00	2.50
Common Player:		.09	.07	.04
1	Eddie Murray	.40	.30	.15
2	Cal Ripken	.40	.30	.15
3	Wade Boggs	.80	.60	.30
4	Dennis Boyd	.09	.07	.04
5	Dwight Evans	.15	.11	.06
6	Bruce Hurst	.15	.11	.06
7	Gary Pettis	.09	.07	.04
8	Harold Baines	.15	.11	.06
9	Floyd Bannister	.09	.07	.04
10	Britt Burns	.09	.07	.04
11	Carlton Fisk	.20	.15	.08
12	Brett Butler	.15	.11	.06
13	Darrell Evans	.15	.11	.06
14	Jack Morris	.25	.20	.10
15	Lance Parrish	.25	.20	.10
16	Walt Terrell	.09	.07	.04
17	Steve Balboni	.09	.07	.04
18	George Brett	.50	.40	.20
19	Charlie Leibrandt	.09	.07	.04
20	Bret Saberhagen	.20	.15	.08
21	Lonnie Smith	.09	.07	.04
22	Willie Wilson	.15	.11	.06
23	Bert Blyleven	.15	.11	.06
24	Mike Smithson	.09	.07	.04
25	Frank Viola	.20	.15	.08
26	Ron Guidry	.20	.15	.08
27	Rickey Henderson	.40	.30	.15
28	Don Mattingly	1.25	.90	.50
29	Dave Winfield	.30	.25	.12
30	Mike Moore	.09	.07	.04
31	Gorman Thomas	.09	.07	.04
32	Toby Harrah	.09	.07	.04
33	Charlie Hough	.09	.07	.04
34	Doyle Alexander	.09	.07	.04
35	Jimmy Key	.15	.11	.06

		MT	NR MT	EX
36	Dave Stieb	.15	.11	.06
37	Dale Murphy	.50	.40	.20
38	Keith Moreland	.09	.07	.04
39	Ryne Sandberg	.30	.25	.12
40	Tom Browning	.15	.11	.06
41	Dave Parker	.20	.15	.08
42	Mario Soto	.09	.07	.04
43	Nolan Ryan	.30	.25	.12
44	Pedro Guerrero	.20	.15	.08
45	Orel Hershiser	.30	.25	.12
46	Mike Scioscia	.09	.07	.04
47	Fernando Valenzuela	.25	.20	.10
48	Bob Welch	.15	.11	.06
49	Tim Raines	.30	.25	.12
50	Gary Carter	.30	.25	.12
51	Sid Fernandez	.15	.11	.06
52	Dwight Gooden	.70	.50	.30
53	Keith Hernandez	.25	.20	.10
54	Juan Samuel	.20	.15	.08
55	Mike Schmidt	.50	.40	.20
56	Glenn Wilson	.09	.07	.04
57	Rick Reuschel	.15	.11	.06
58	Joaquin Andujar	.09	.07	.04
59	Jack Clark	.20	.15	.08
60	Vince Coleman	.60	.45	.25
61	Danny Cox	.09	.07	.04
62	Tom Herr	.09	.07	.04
63	Willie McGee	.15	.11	.06
64	John Tudor	.15	.11	.06
65	Tony Gwynn	.40	.30	.15
66	Checklist	.09	.07	.04

1986 Topps Stickers

The 1986 Topps stickers are 2-1/8" by 3". The 200-piece set features 316 different subjects, with some stickers including two or three players. Numbers run only to 315, however. The set includes some specialty stickers such as League Championships and World Series themes. Stickers are numbered both front and back and included a chance to win a trip to spring training as well as an offer to buy a complete 1986 Topps regular set. An album for the stickers was available in stores.

		MT	NR MT	EX
Complete Set:		15.00	11.00	6.00
Common Player:		.03	.02	.01
Sticker Album:		.70	.50	.30
1	Pete Rose	.25	.20	.10
2	Pete Rose	.25	.20	.10
3	George Brett	.12	.09	.05
4	Rod Carew	.10	.08	.04
5	Vince Coleman	.12	.09	.05
6	Dwight Gooden	.15	.11	.06
7	Phil Niekro	.08	.06	.03
8	Tony Perez	.06	.05	.02
9	Nolan Ryan	.10	.08	.04
10	Tom Seaver	.10	.08	.04
11	N.L. Championship Series (Ozzie Smith)			
		.06	.05	.02
12	N.L. Championship Series (Bill Madlock)			
		.04	.03	.02
13	N.L. Championship Series (Cardinals Celebrate)	.03	.02	.01
14	A.L. Championship Series (Al Oliver)			
		.04	.03	.02

		MT	NR MT	EX
15	A.L. Championship Series (Jim Sundberg)			
		.03	.02	.01
16	A.L. Championship Series (George Brett)			
		.10	.08	.04
17	World Series (Bret Saberhagen)	.06	.05	.02
18	World Series (Dane Iorg)	.03	.02	.01
19	World Series (Tito Landrum)	.03	.02	.01
20	World Series (John Tudor)	.04	.03	.02
21	World Series (Buddy Biancalana)	.03	.02	.01
22	World Series (Darryl Motley, Darrell Porter)	.03	.02	.01
23	World Series (George Brett, Frank White)			
		.10	.08	.04
24	Nolan Ryan	.15	.11	.06
25	Bill Doran	.08	.06	.03
26	Jose Cruz	.04	.03	.02
27	Mike Scott	.08	.06	.03
28	Kevin Bass	.04	.03	.02
29	Glenn Davis	.10	.08	.04
30	Mark Bailey	.06	.05	.02
31	Dave Smith	.10	.08	.04
32	Phil Garner	.03	.02	.01
33	Dickie Thon	.06	.05	.02
34	Bob Horner	.12	.09	.05
35	Dale Murphy	.25	.20	.10
36	Glenn Hubbard	.04	.03	.02
37	Bruce Sutter	.08	.06	.03
38	Ken Oberkfell	.04	.03	.02
39	Claudell Washington	.04	.03	.02
40	Steve Bedrosian	.04	.03	.02
41	Terry Harper	.03	.02	.01
42	Rafael Ramirez	.06	.05	.02
43	Rick Mahler	.03	.02	.01
44	Joaquin Andujar	.06	.05	.02
45	Willie McGee	.10	.08	.04
46	Ozzie Smith	.06	.05	.02
47	Vince Coleman	.12	.09	.05
48	Danny Cox	.04	.03	.02
49	Tom Herr	.04	.03	.02
50	Jack Clark	.08	.06	.03
51	Andy Van Slyke	.04	.03	.02
52	John Tudor	.08	.06	.03
53	Terry Pendleton	.03	.02	.01
54	Keith Moreland	.06	.05	.02
55	Ryne Sandberg	.15	.11	.06
56	Lee Smith	.04	.03	.02
57	Steve Trout	.06	.05	.02
58	Jody Davis	.08	.06	.03
59	Gary Matthews	.04	.03	.02
60	Leon Durham	.04	.03	.02
61	Rick Sutcliffe	.06	.05	.02
62	Dennis Eckersley	.04	.03	.02
63	Bob Dernier	.03	.02	.01
64	Fernando Valenzuela	.15	.11	.06
65	Pedro Guerrero	.12	.09	.05
66	Jerry Reuss	.06	.05	.02
67	Greg Brock	.06	.05	.02
68	Mike Scioscia	.03	.02	.01
69	Ken Howell	.04	.03	.02
70	Bill Madlock	.04	.03	.02
71	Mike Marshall	.06	.05	.02
72	Steve Sax	.06	.05	.02
73	Orel Hershiser	.06	.05	.02
74	Andre Dawson	.12	.09	.05
75	Tim Raines	.12	.09	.05
76	Jeff Reardon	.06	.05	.02
77	Hubie Brooks	.04	.03	.02
78	Bill Gullickson	.04	.03	.02
79	Bryn Smith	.04	.03	.02
80	Terry Francona	.04	.03	.02
81	Vance Law	.03	.02	.01
82	Tim Wallach	.04	.03	.02
83	Herm Winningham	.04	.03	.02
84	Jeff Leonard	.06	.05	.02
85	Chris Brown	.20	.15	.08
86	Scott Garrelts	.03	.02	.01
87	Jose Uribe	.04	.03	.02
88	Manny Trillo	.04	.03	.02
89	Dan Driessen	.04	.03	.02
90	Dan Gladden	.06	.05	.02
91	Mark Davis	.04	.03	.02
92	Bob Brenly	.03	.02	.01
93	Mike Krukow	.04	.03	.02
94	Dwight Gooden	.35	.25	.14
95	Darryl Strawberry	.25	.20	.10
96	Gary Carter	.10	.08	.04
97	Wally Backman	.06	.05	.02
98	Ron Darling	.06	.05	.02
99	Keith Hernandez	.12	.09	.05
100	George Foster	.06	.05	.02
101	Howard Johnson	.06	.05	.02
102	Rafael Santana	.04	.03	.02
103	Roger McDowell	.06	.05	.02
104	Steve Garvey	.15	.11	.06
105	Tony Gwynn	.20	.15	.08
106	Graig Nettles	.06	.05	.02
107	Rich Gossage	.10	.08	.04
108	Andy Hawkins	.04	.03	.02
109	Carmelo Martinez	.04	.03	.02
110	Garry Templeton	.04	.03	.02
111	Terry Kennedy	.06	.05	.02
112	Tim Flannery	.08	.06	.03
113	LaMarr Hoyt	.03	.02	.01
114	Mike Schmidt	.25	.20	.10
115	Ozzie Virgil	.06	.05	.02
116	Steve Carlton	.10	.08	.04
117	Garry Maddox	.03	.02	.01
118	Glenn Wilson	.06	.05	.02
119	Kevin Gross	.03	.02	.01
120	Von Hayes	.04	.03	.02
121	Juan Samuel	.06	.05	.02
122	Rick Schu	.08	.06	.03
123	Shane Rawley	.06	.05	.02
124	Johnny Ray	.06	.05	.02
125	Tony Pena	.06	.05	.02
126	Rick Reuschel	.12	.09	.05
127	Sammy Khalifa	.06	.05	.02
128	Marvell Wynne	.04	.03	.02
129	Jason Thompson	.03	.02	.01
130	Rick Rhoden	.04	.03	.02
131	Bill Almon	.03	.02	.01
132	Joe Orsulak	.06	.05	.02
133	Jim Morrison	.06	.05	.02
134	Pete Rose	.40	.30	.15
135	Dave Parker	.12	.09	.05
136	Mario Soto	.03	.02	.01
137	Dave Concepcion	.10	.08	.04
138	Ron Oester	.03	.02	.01
139	Buddy Bell	.06	.05	.02
140	Ted Power	.03	.02	.01
141	Tom Browning	.06	.05	.02
142	John Franco	.08	.06	.03
143	Tony Perez	.06	.05	.02
144	Willie McGee	.08	.06	.03
145	Dale Murphy	.15	.11	.06
146	Tony Gwynn	.40	.30	.15
147	Tom Herr	.15	.11	.06
148	Steve Garvey	.30	.25	.12
149	Dale Murphy	.40	.30	.15
150	Darryl Strawberry	.40	.30	.15
151	Graig Nettles	.15	.11	.06
152	Terry Kennedy	.15	.11	.06
153	Ozzie Smith	.20	.15	.06
154	LaMarr Hoyt	.15	.11	.06
155	Rickey Henderson	.40	.30	.15
156	Lou Whitaker	.25	.20	.10
157	George Brett	.40	.30	.15
158	Eddie Murray	.40	.30	.15
159	Cal Ripken	.40	.30	.15
160	Dave Winfield	.30	.25	.12
161	Jim Rice	.30	.25	.12
162	Carlton Fisk	.25	.20	.10
163	Jack Morris	.25	.20	.10
164	Wade Boggs	.15	.11	.06
165	Darrell Evans	.06	.05	.02
166	Mike Davis	.06	.05	.02
167	Dave Kingman	.08	.06	.03
168	Alfredo Griffin	.04	.03	.02
169	Carney Lansford	.04	.03	.02
170	Bruce Bochte	.10	.08	.04
171	Dwayne Murphy	.08	.06	.03
172	Dave Collins	.04	.03	.02
173	Chris Codiroli	.10	.08	.04
174	Mike Heath	.03	.02	.01
175	Jay Howell	.12	.09	.05
176	Rod Carew	.20	.15	.08
177	Reggie Jackson	.20	.15	.08
178	Doug DeCinces	.10	.08	.04
179	Bob Boone	.12	.09	.05
180	Ron Romanick	.15	.11	.06
181	Bob Grich	.08	.06	.03
182	Donnie Moore	.06	.05	.02
183	Brian Downing	.10	.08	.04
184	Ruppert Jones	.10	.08	.04
185	Juan Beniquez	.04	.03	.02
186	Dave Stieb	.06	.05	.02
187	Jorge Bell	.20	.15	.08
188	Willie Upshaw	.08	.06	.03
189	Tom Henke	.04	.03	.02
190	Damaso Garcia	.10	.08	.04
191	Jimmy Key	.06	.05	.02
192	Jesse Barfield	.10	.08	.04

		MT	NR MT	EX
193	Dennis Lamp	.03	.02	.01
194	Tony Fernandez	.06	.05	.02
195	Lloyd Moseby	.04	.03	.02
196	Cecil Cooper	.08	.06	.03
197	Robin Yount	.15	.11	.06
198	Rollie Fingers	.08	.06	.03
199	Ted Simmons	.04	.03	.02
200	Ben Oglivie	.04	.03	.02
201	Moose Haas	.04	.03	.02
202	Jim Gantner	.03	.02	.01
203	Paul Molitor	.06	.05	.02
204	Charlie Moore	.03	.02	.01
205	Danny Darwin	.06	.05	.02
206	Brett Butler	.06	.05	.02
207	Brook Jacoby	.08	.06	.03
208	Andre Thornton	.12	.09	.05
209	Tom Waddell	.04	.03	.02
210	Tony Bernazard	.04	.03	.02
211	Julio Franco	.08	.06	.03
212	Pat Tabler	.04	.03	.02
213	Joe Carter	.08	.06	.03
214	George Vukovich	.03	.02	.01
215	Rich Thompson	.04	.03	.02
216	Gorman Thomas	.06	.05	.02
217	Phil Bradley	.10	.08	.04
218	Alvin Davis	.06	.05	.02
219	Jim Presley	.08	.06	.03
220	Matt Young	.04	.03	.02
221	Mike Moore	.04	.03	.02
222	Dave Henderson	.06	.05	.02
223	Ed Nunez	.04	.03	.02
224	Spike Owen	.03	.02	.01
225	Mark Langston	.06	.05	.02
226	Cal Ripken	.20	.15	.08
227	Eddie Murray	.20	.15	.08
228	Fred Lynn	.06	.05	.02
229	Lee Lacy	.03	.02	.01
230	Scott McGregor	.04	.03	.02
231	Storm Davis	.04	.03	.02
232	Rick Dempsey	.06	.05	.02
233	Mike Boddicker	.06	.05	.02
234	Mike Young	.06	.05	.02
235	Sammy Stewart	.06	.05	.02
236	Pete O'Brien	.08	.06	.03
237	Oddibe McDowell	.15	.11	.06
238	Toby Harrah	.04	.03	.02
239	Gary Ward	.04	.03	.02
240	Larry Parrish	.04	.03	.02
241	Charlie Hough	.04	.03	.02
242	Burt Hooton	.03	.02	.01
243	Don Slaught	.04	.03	.02
244	Curt Wilkerson	.04	.03	.02
245	Greg Harris	.03	.02	.01
246	Jim Rice	.15	.11	.06
247	Wade Boggs	.60	.45	.25
248	Rich Gedman	.04	.03	.02
249	Dennis Boyd	.04	.03	.02
250	Marty Barrett	.04	.03	.02
251	Dwight Evans	.06	.05	.02
252	Bill Buckner	.04	.03	.02
253	Bob Stanley	.03	.02	.01
254	Tony Armas	.04	.03	.02
255	Mike Easler	.10	.08	.04
256	George Brett	.25	.20	.10
257	Dan Quisenberry	.06	.05	.02
258	Willie Wilson	.06	.05	.02
259	Jim Sundberg	.06	.05	.02
260	Bret Saberhagen	.12	.09	.05
261	Bud Black	.06	.05	.02
262	Charlie Leibrandt	.06	.05	.02
263	Frank White	.04	.03	.02
264	Lonnie Smith	.06	.05	.02
265	Steve Balboni	.06	.05	.02
266	Kirk Gibson	.15	.11	.06
267	Alan Trammell	.15	.11	.06
268	Jack Morris	.10	.08	.04
269	Darrell Evans	.04	.03	.02
270	Dan Petry	.04	.03	.02
271	Larry Herndon	.04	.03	.02
272	Lou Whitaker	.06	.05	.02
273	Lance Parrish	.08	.06	.03
274	Chet Lemon	.03	.02	.01
275	Willie Hernandez	.10	.08	.04
276	Tom Brunansky	.08	.06	.03
277	Kent Hrbek	.12	.09	.05
278	Mark Salas	.03	.02	.01
279	Bert Blyleven	.06	.05	.02
280	Tim Teufel	.03	.02	.01
281	Ron Davis	.04	.03	.02
282	Mike Smithson	.06	.05	.02
283	Gary Gaetti	.08	.06	.03

		MT	NR MT	EX
284	Frank Viola	.06	.05	.02
285	Kirby Puckett	.12	.09	.05
286	Carlton Fisk	.12	.09	.05
287	Tom Seaver	.15	.11	.06
288	Harold Baines	.06	.05	.02
289	Ron Kittle	.04	.03	.02
290	Bob James	.03	.02	.01
291	Rudy Law	.04	.03	.02
292	Britt Burns	.03	.02	.01
293	Greg Walker	.06	.05	.02
294	Ozzie Guillen	.06	.05	.02
295	Tim Hulett	.03	.02	.01
296	Don Mattingly	.70	.50	.30
297	Rickey Henderson	.20	.15	.08
298	Dave Winfield	.10	.08	.04
299	Butch Wynegar	.03	.02	.01
300	Don Baylor	.06	.05	.02
301	Eddie Whitson	.03	.02	.01
302	Ron Guidry	.06	.05	.02
303	Dave Righetti	.08	.06	.03
304	Bobby Meacham	.06	.05	.02
305	Willie Randolph	.08	.06	.03
306	Vince Coleman	.15	.11	.06
307	Oddibe McDowell	.15	.11	.06
308	Larry Sheets	.06	.05	.02
309	Ozzie Guillen	.06	.05	.02
310	Earnie Riles	.04	.03	.02
311	Chris Brown	.10	.08	.04
312	Brian Fisher, Roger McDowell	.08	.06	.03
313	Tom Browning	.04	.03	.02
314	Glenn Davis	.10	.08	.04
315	Mark Salas	.03	.02	.01

1986 Topps Super

REGGIE JACKSON

A third year of oversize, 4-7/8" by 6-7/8", versions of Topps' regular issue cards saw the set once again hit the 60-card mark. Besides being four times the size of a normal card, the Supers differ only in the number on the back of the card.

		MT	NR MT	EX
Complete Set:		9.00	6.75	3.50
Common Player:		.20	.15	.08
1	Don Mattingly	2.25	1.75	.90
2	Willie McGee	.35	.25	.14
3	Bret Saberhagen	.35	.25	.14
4	Dwight Gooden	1.50	1.25	.60
5	Dan Quisenberry	.20	.15	.08
6	Jeff Reardon	.25	.20	.10
7	Ozzie Guillen	.25	.20	.10
8	Vince Coleman	.70	.50	.30
9	Harold Baines	.25	.20	.10
10	Jorge Bell	.50	.40	.20
11	Bert Blyleven	.25	.20	.10
12	Wade Boggs	1.25	.90	.50
13	Phil Bradley	.25	.20	.10
14	George Brett	.80	.60	.30
15	Hubie Brooks	.20	.15	.08
16	Tom Browning	.25	.20	.10
17	Bill Buckner	.20	.15	.08
18	Brett Butler	.20	.15	.08
19	Gary Carter	.50	.40	.20
20	Cecil Cooper	.25	.20	.10
21	Darrell Evans	.25	.20	.10
22	Dwight Evans	.20	.15	.08
23	Carlton Fisk	.30	.25	.12

		MT	NR MT	EX
24	Steve Garvey	.50	.40	.20
25	Kirk Gibson	.35	.25	.14
26	Rich Gossage	.25	.20	.10
27	Pedro Guerrero	.30	.25	.12
28	Ron Guidry	.30	.25	.12
29	Tony Gwynn	.70	.50	.30
30	Rickey Henderson	.70	.50	.30
31	Keith Hernandez	.50	.40	.20
32	Tom Herr	.20	.15	.08
33	Orel Hershiser	.50	.40	.20
34	Jay Howell	.20	.15	.08
35	Reggie Jackson	.60	.45	.25
36	Bob James	.20	.15	.08
37	Charlie Leibrandt	.20	.15	.08
38	Jack Morris	.35	.25	.14
39	Dale Murphy	.80	.60	.30
40	Eddie Murray	.60	.45	.25
41	Dave Parker	.35	.25	.14
42	Tim Raines	.50	.40	.20
43	Jim Rice	.50	.40	.20
44	Dave Righetti	.30	.25	.12
45	Cal Ripken	.70	.50	.30
46	Pete Rose	1.00	.70	.40
47	Nolan Ryan	.50	.40	.20
48	Ryne Sandberg	.50	.40	.20
49	Mike Schmidt	.80	.60	.30
50	Tom Seaver	.50	.40	.20
51	Bryn Smith	.20	.15	.08
52	Lee Smith	.20	.15	.08
53	Ozzie Smith	.30	.25	.12
54	Dave Stieb	.20	.15	.08
55	Darryl Strawberry	.80	.60	.30
56	Gorman Thomas	.20	.15	.08
57	John Tudor	.20	.15	.08
58	Fernando Valenzuela	.40	.30	.15
59	Willie Wilson	.25	.20	.10
60	Dave Winfield	.50	.40	.20

		MT	NR MT	EX
12	Bobby Grich	.09	.07	.04
13	Tony Gwynn	.35	.25	.14
14	Keith Hernandez	.25	.20	.10
15	Reggie Jackson	.30	.25	.12
16	Dave Kingman	.12	.09	.05
17	Carney Lansford	.09	.07	.04
18	Fred Lynn	.12	.09	.05
19	Bill Madlock	.12	.09	.05
20	Don Mattingly	2.00	1.50	.80
21	Willie McGee	.20	.15	.08
22	Hal McRae	.09	.07	.04
23	Dale Murphy	.40	.30	.15
24	Eddie Murray	.35	.25	.14
25	Ben Oglivie	.09	.07	.04
26	Al Oliver	.12	.09	.05
27	Dave Parker	.20	.15	.08
28	Jim Rice	.30	.25	.12
29	Pete Rose	.90	.70	.35
30	Mike Schmidt	.40	.30	.15
31	Gorman Thomas	.09	.07	.04
32	Willie Wilson	.12	.09	.05
33	Dave Winfield	.30	.25	.12

1986 Topps Tattoos

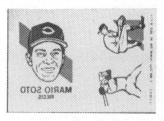

Topps returned to tattoos in 1986, marketing a set of 24 different tattoo sheets. Each sheet of tattoos measures 3-7/16" by 14" and includes both player and smaller action tattoos. As the action tattoos were uniform and not of any particular player, they add little value to the sheet. The player tattoos measure 1-3/16" by 2-3/8". With 24 sheets, eight players per sheet, there are 192 players represented in the set. The sheets are numbered.

		MT	NR MT	EX
Complete Set:		5.00	3.75	2.00
Common Player:		.20	.15	.08
1	Julio Franco, Rich Gossage, Keith Hernandez, Charlie Leibrandt, Jack Perconte, Lee Smith, Dickie Thon, Dave Winfield	.25	.20	.10
2	Jesse Barfield, Shawon Dunston, Dennis Eckersley, Brian Fisher, Moose Haas, Mike Moore, Dale Murphy, Bret Saberhagen	.30	.25	.12
3	George Bell, Bob Brenly, Steve Carlton, Jose DeLeon, Bob Horner, Bob James, Dan Quisenberry, Andre Thornton	.25	.20	.10
4	Mike Davis, Leon Durham, Darrell Evans, Glenn Hubbard, Johnny Ray, Cal Ripken, Ted Simmons	.25	.20	.10
5	John Candelaria, Rick Dempsey, Steve Garvey, Ozzie Guillen, Gary Matthews, Jesse Orosco, Tony Pena	.25	.20	.10
6	Bruce Bochte, George Brett, Cecil Cooper, Sammy Khalifa, Ron Kittle, Scott McGregor, Pete Rose, Mookie Wilson	.45	.35	.20
7	John Franco, Carney Lansford, Don Mattingly, Graig Nettles, Rick Reuschel, Mike Schmidt, Larry Sheets, Don Sutton	.45	.35	.20
8	Cecilio Guante, Willie Hernandez, Mike Krukow, Fred Lynn, Phil Niekro, Ed Nunez, Ryne Sandberg, Pat Tabler	.25	.20	.10
9	Brett Butler, Chris Codiroli, Jim Gantner, Charlie Hough, Dave Parker, Rick Rhoden, Glenn Wilson, Robin Yount	.20	.15	.08
10	Tom Browning, Ron Darling, Von Hayes, Chet Lemon, Tom Seaver, Mike Smithson, Bruce Sutter, Alan Trammell	.25	.20	.10

1986 Topps Super Star

Labeled "Topps' Collector Series" in a red band at the top of the front, this set marked the second year of Topps' production of a special boxed set for the Woolworth chain of stores, through Woolworth's name does not appear anywhere on the card. The cards, which measure 2-1/2" by 3-1/2", feature a color photo with its lower right corner rolled up to reveal the words "Super Star" on a bright yellow border. The player's name appears in the lower left corner. The 66-card set features stars and retains a certain measure of popularity on that basis.

		MT	NR MT	EX
Complete Set:		5.00	3.75	2.00
Common Player:		.09	.07	.04
1	Tony Armas	.09	.07	.04
2	Don Baylor	.12	.09	.05
3	Wade Boggs	1.00	.70	.40
4	George Brett	.40	.30	.15
5	Bill Buckner	.09	.07	.04
6	Rod Carew	.30	.25	.12
7	Gary Carter	.30	.25	.12
8	Cecil Cooper	.12	.09	.05
9	Darrell Evans	.12	.09	.05
10	Dwight Evans	.15	.11	.06
11	George Foster	.12	.09	.05

		MT	NR MT	EX
11	Tony Armas, Jose Cruz, Jay Howell, Rick Mahler, Jack Morris, Rafael Ramirez, Dave Righetti, Mike Young	.20	.15	.08
12	Alvin Davis, Doug DeCinces, Andy Hawkins, Dennis Lamp, Keith Moreland, Jim Presley, Mario Soto, John Tudor	.20	.15	.08
13	Hubie Brooks, Jody Davis, Dwight Evans, Ron Hassey, Charles Hudson, Kirby Puckett, Jose Uribe	:20	.15	.08
14	Tony Bernazard, Phil Bradley, Bill Buckner, Brian Downing, Dan Driessen, Ron Guidry, LaMarr Hoyt, Garry Maddox	.20	.15	.08
15	Buddy Bell, Joe Carter, Tony Fernandez, Tito Landrum, Jeff Leonard, Hal McRae, Willie Randolph, Juan Samuel	.20	.15	.08
16	Dennis Boyd, Vince Coleman, Scott Garrelts, Alfredo Griffin, Donnie Moore, Tony Perez, Ozzie Smith, Frank White	.25	.20	.10
17	Rich Gedman, Kent Hrbek, Reggie Jackson, Mike Marshall, Terry Pendleton, Tim Raines, Mark Salas, Claudell Washington	.25	.20	.10
18	Chris Brown, Tom Brunansky, Glenn Davis, Ron Davis, Burt Hooton, Darryl Strawberry, Frank Viola, Tim Wallach	.30	.25	.12
19	Jack Clark, Bill Doran, Toby Harrah, Bill Madlock, Pete O'Brien, Larry Parrish, Mike Scioscia, Garry Templeton	.20	.15	.08
20	Gary Carter, Andre Dawson, Dwight Gooden, Orel Hershiser, Oddibe McDowell, Roger McDowell, Dwayne Murphy, Jim Rice	.40	.30	.15
21	Steve Balboni, Mike Easler, Charlie Lea, Lloyd Moseby, Steve Sax, Rick Sutcliffe, Gary Ward, Willie Wilson	.20	.15	.08
22	Wade Boggs, Dave Concepcion, Kirk Gibson, Tom Herr, Lance Parrish, Jeff Reardon, Bryn Smith, Gorman Thomas	.30	.25	.12
23	Carlton Fisk, Bob Grich, Pedro Guerrero, Willie McGee, Paul Molitor, Mike Scott, Dave Stieb, Lou Whitaker	.20	.15	.08
24	Bert Blyleven, Damaso Garcia, Phil Garner, Tony Gwynn, Rickey Henderson, Ben Oglivie, Nolan Ryan, Fernando Valenzuela	.30	.25	.12

1986 Topps Traded

JOSE CANSECO

This 132-card set of 2-1/2" by 3-1/2" cards is one of the most popular sets of recent times. As always, the set features traded veterans, including such players as Phil Niekro and Tom Seaver. They are not, however, the reason for the excitement. The demand is there because of a better than usual crop of rookies who also appear in the sets. Among those are Jose Canseco, Wally Joyner, Pete Incaviglia, Todd Worrell and the first card of Bo Jackson. As in the previous two years, a glossy-finish "Tiffany" edition of 5,000 Traded sets was produced. The "Tiffany" cards are worth four to six times the value of the regular Traded cards.

	MT	NR MT	EX
Complete Set:	30.00	22.50	12.50
Common Player:	.08	.06	.03

		MT	NR MT	EX
1T	Andy Allanson(FC)	.20	.15	.08
2T	Neil Allen	.08	.06	.03
3T	Joaquin Andujar	.10	.08	.04
4T	Paul Assenmacher(FC)	.20	.15	.08
5T	Scott Bailes(FC)	.20	.15	.08
6T	Don Baylor	.15	.11	.06
7T	Steve Bedrosian	.15	.11	.06
8T	Juan Beniquez	.08	.06	.03
9T	Juan Berenguer	.08	.06	.03
10T	Mike Bielecki(FC)	.35	.25	.14
11T	Barry Bonds(FC)	1.25	.90	.50
12T	Bobby Bonilla(FC)	.90	.70	.35
13T	Juan Bonilla	.08	.06	.03
14T	Rich Bordi	.08	.06	.03
15T	Steve Boros	.08	.06	.03
16T	Rick Burleson	.10	.08	.04
17T	Bill Campbell	.08	.06	.03
18T	Tom Candiotti	.08	.06	.03
19T	John Cangelosi(FC)	.20	.15	.08
20T	Jose Canseco(FC)	8.00	6.00	3.25
21T	Carmen Castillo	.08	.06	.03
22T	Rick Cerone	.08	.06	.03
23T	John Cerutti(FC)	.20	.15	.08
24T	Will Clark(FC)	12.00	9.00	4.75
25T	Mark Clear	.08	.06	.03
26T	Darnell Coles	.12	.09	.05
27T	Dave Collins	.10	.08	.04
28T	Tim Conroy	.08	.06	.03
29T	Joe Cowley	.08	.06	.03
30T	Joel Davis(FC)	.12	.09	.05
31T	Rob Deer	.15	.11	.06
32T	John Denny	.08	.06	.03
33T	Mike Easler	.10	.08	.04
34T	Mark Eichhorn(FC)	.20	.15	.08
35T	Steve Farr	.08	.06	.03
36T	Scott Fletcher	.15	.11	.06
37T	Terry Forster	.10	.08	.04
38T	Terry Francona	.08	.06	.03
39T	Jim Fregosi	.08	.06	.03
40T	Andres Galarraga(FC)	1.75	1.25	.70
41T	Ken Griffey	.12	.09	.05
42T	Bill Gullickson	.08	.06	.03
43T	Jose Guzman(FC)	.35	.25	.14
44T	Moose Haas	.08	.06	.03
45T	Billy Hatcher	.20	.15	.08
46T	Mike Heath	.08	.06	.03
47T	Tom Hume	.08	.06	.03
48T	Pete Incaviglia(FC)	.50	.40	.20
49T	Dane Iorg	.08	.06	.03
50T	Bo Jackson(FC)	10.00	7.50	4.00
51T	Wally Joyner(FC)	2.50	2.00	1.00
52T	Charlie Kerfeld(FC)	.15	.11	.06
53T	Eric King(FC)	.20	.15	.08
54T	Bob Kipper(FC)	.12	.09	.05
55T	Wayne Krenchicki	.08	.06	.03
56T	John Kruk(FC)	.40	.30	.15
57T	Mike LaCoss	.08	.06	.03
58T	Pete Ladd	.08	.06	.03
59T	Mike Laga	.08	.06	.03
60T	Hal Lanier	.08	.06	.03
61T	Dave LaPoint	.12	.09	.05
62T	Rudy Law	.08	.06	.03
63T	Rick Leach	.08	.06	.03
64T	Tim Leary	.08	.06	.03
65T	Dennis Leonard	.10	.08	.04
66T	Jim Leyland	.08	.06	.03
67T	Steve Lyons	.12	.09	.05
68T	Mickey Mahler	.08	.06	.03
69T	Candy Maldonado	.15	.11	.06
70T	Roger Mason(FC)	.10	.08	.04
71T	Bob McClure	.08	.06	.03
72T	Andy McGaffigan	.08	.06	.03
73T	Gene Michael	.08	.06	.03
74T	Kevin Mitchell(FC)	7.00	5.25	2.75
75T	Omar Moreno	.08	.06	.03
76T	Jerry Mumphrey	.08	.06	.03
77T	Phil Niekro	.40	.30	.15
78T	Randy Niemann	.08	.06	.03
79T	Juan Nieves(FC)	.25	.20	.10
80T	Otis Nixon(FC)	.12	.09	.05
81T	Bob Ojeda	.12	.09	.05
82T	Jose Oquendo	.08	.06	.03
83T	Tom Paciorek	.08	.06	.03
84T	Dave Palmer	.08	.06	.03
85T	Frank Pastore	.08	.06	.03
86T	Lou Piniella	.12	.09	.05
87T	Dan Plesac(FC)	.40	.30	.15
88T	Darrell Porter	.10	.08	.04
89T	Rey Quinones(FC)	.20	.15	.08
90T	Gary Redus	.10	.08	.04
91T	Bip Roberts	.08	.06	.03

		MT	NR MT	EX
92T	Billy Jo Robidoux(FC)	.15	.11	.06
93T	Jeff Robinson	.12	.09	.05
94T	Gary Roenicke	.08	.06	.03
95T	Ed Romero	.08	.06	.03
96T	Argenis Salazar	.08	.06	.03
97T	Joe Sambito	.08	.06	.03
98T	Billy Sample	.08	.06	.03
99T	Dave Schmidt	.08	.06	.03
100T	Ken Schrom	.08	.06	.03
101T	Tom Seaver	.60	.45	.25
102T	Ted Simmons	.20	.15	.08
103T	Sammy Stewart	.08	.06	.03
104T	Kurt Stillwell(FC)	.30	.25	.12
105T	Franklin Stubbs	.12	.09	.05
106T	Dale Sveum(FC)	.25	.20	.10
107T	Chuck Tanner	.08	.06	.03
108T	Danny Tartabull(FC)	1.00	.70	.40
109T	Tim Teufel	.08	.06	.03
110T	Bob Tewksbury(FC)	.15	.11	.06
111T	Andres Thomas(FC)	.30	.25	.12
112T	Milt Thompson	.12	.09	.05
113T	Robby Thompson(FC)	.40	.30	.15
114T	Jay Tibbs	.08	.06	.03
115T	Wayne Tolleson	.08	.06	.03
116T	Alex Trevino	.08	.06	.03
117T	Manny Trillo	.10	.08	.04
118T	Ed Vande Berg	.08	.06	.03
119T	Ozzie Virgil	.08	.06	.03
120T	Bob Walk	.08	.06	.03
121T	Gene Walter(FC)	.12	.09	.05
122T	Claudell Washington	.12	.09	.05
123T	Bill Wegman(FC)	.20	.15	.08
124T	Dick Williams	.08	.06	.03
125T	Mitch Williams(FC)	.60	.45	.25
126T	Bobby Witt(FC)	.40	.30	.15
127T	Todd Worrell(FC)	.60	.45	.25
128T	George Wright	.08	.06	.03
129T	Ricky Wright	.08	.06	.03
130T	Steve Yeager	.08	.06	.03
131T	Paul Zuvella	.08	.06	.03
132T	Checklist	.08	.06	.03

1986 Topps 3-D

This set is a second effort in the production of over-size (4-1/2" by 6") plastic cards on which the player figure is embossed. Cards were sold one per pack for approximately 50¢. The 30 players in the set are among the game's top stars. The embossed color photo is bordered at bottom by a strip of contrasting color on which the player name appears. At the top, a row of white baseballs each contain a letter of the team nickname. Backs have no printing, and contain two self-adhesive strips with which the cards can be attached to a hard surface.

		MT	NR MT	EX
Complete Set:		11.00	8.25	4.50
Common Player:		.20	.15	.08
1	Bert Blyleven	.30	.25	.12
2	Gary Carter	.60	.45	.25
3	Wade Boggs	1.25	.90	.50
4	Dwight Gooden	1.00	.70	.40
5	George Brett	.80	.60	.30
6	Rich Gossage	.30	.25	.12
7	Darrell Evans	.20	.15	.08

		MT	NR MT	EX
8	Pedro Guerrero	.30	.25	.12
9	Ron Guidry	.30	.25	.12
10	Keith Hernandez	.50	.40	.20
11	Rickey Henderson	.70	.50	.30
12	Orel Hershiser	.50	.40	.20
13	Reggie Jackson	.60	.45	.25
14	Willie McGee	.30	.25	.12
15	Don Mattingly	2.25	1.75	.90
16	Dale Murphy	.80	.60	.30
17	Jack Morris	.30	.25	.12
18	Dave Parker	.30	.25	.12
19	Eddie Murray	.60	.45	.25
20	Jeff Reardon	.30	.25	.12
21	Dan Quisenberry	.20	.15	.08
22	Pete Rose	1.00	.70	.40
23	Jim Rice	.50	.40	.20
24	Mike Schmidt	.80	.60	.30
25	Bret Saberhagen	.30	.25	.12
26	Darryl Strawberry	.80	.60	.30
27	Dave Stieb	.20	.15	.08
28	John Tudor	.20	.15	.08
29	Dave Winfield	.50	.40	.20
30	Fernando Valenzuela	.40	.30	.15

1987 Topps

Many collectors feel that Topps' 1987 set of 792 card is a future classic. The 2-1/2" by 3-1/2" design is closely akin to the 1962 set in that the player photo is set against a woodgrain border. Instead of a rolling corner, as in 1962, the player photos in '87 feature a couple of clipped corners at top left and bottom right, where the team logo and player name appear. The player's position is not given on the front of the card. For the first time in several years, the trophy which designates members of Topps All-Star Rookie Team returned to the card design. As in the previous three years, Topps issued a glossy-finish "Tiffany" edition of their 792-card set. However, it was speculated that as many as 50,000 sets were produced as opposed to the 5,000 sets printed in 1985 and 1986. Because of the large print run, the values for the Tiffany cards are only 3-4 times higher than the same card in the regular issue.

		MT	NR MT	EX
Complete Set:		35.00	26.00	14.00
Common Player:		.05	.04	.02
1	Record Breaker (Roger Clemens)	.35	.25	.14
2	Record Breaker (Jim Deshaies)	.07	.05	.03
3	Record Breaker (Dwight Evans)	.07	.05	.03
4	Record Breaker (Dave Lopes)	.07	.05	.03
5	Record Breaker (Dave Righetti)	.07	.05	.03
6	Record Breaker (Ruben Sierra)	.25	.20	.10
7	Record Breaker (Todd Worrell)	.07	.05	.03
8	Terry Pendleton	.07	.05	.03
9	Jay Tibbs	.05	.04	.02
10	Cecil Cooper	.10	.08	.04
11	Indians Leaders (Jack Aker, Chris Bando, Phil Niekro)	.07	.05	.03
12	Jeff Sellers(FC)	.15	.11	.06
13	Nick Esasky	.07	.05	.03
14	Dave Stewart	.12	.09	.05
15	Claudell Washington	.07	.05	.03
16	Pat Clements	.05	.04	.02

#	Player	MT	NR MT	EX
17	Pete O'Brien	.10	.08	.04
18	Dick Howser	.05	.04	.02
19	Matt Young	.05	.04	.02
20	Gary Carter	.20	.15	.08
21	Mark Davis	.05	.04	.02
22	Doug DeCinces	.07	.05	.03
23	Lee Smith	.10	.08	.04
24	Tony Walker	.05	.04	.02
25	Bert Blyleven	.12	.09	.05
26	Greg Brock	.07	.05	.03
27	Joe Cowley	.05	.04	.02
28	Rick Dempsey	.07	.05	.03
29	Jimmy Key	.10	.08	.04
30	Tim Raines	.25	.20	.10
31	Braves Leaders (Glenn Hubbard, Rafael Ramirez)	.07	.05	.03
32	Tim Leary	.07	.05	.03
33	Andy Van Slyke	.12	.09	.05
34	Jose Rijo	.07	.05	.03
35	Sid Bream	.07	.05	.03
36	*Eric King*	.20	.15	.08
37	Marvell Wynne	.05	.04	.02
38	Dennis Leonard	.07	.05	.03
39	Marty Barrett	.07	.05	.03
40	Dave Righetti	.12	.09	.05
41	Bo Diaz	.07	.05	.03
42	Gary Redus	.05	.04	.02
43	Gene Michael	.05	.04	.02
44	Greg Harris	.05	.04	.02
45	Jim Presley	.10	.08	.04
46	Danny Gladden	.05	.04	.02
47	Dennis Powell	.07	.05	.03
48	Wally Backman	.07	.05	.03
49	Terry Harper	.05	.04	.02
50	Dave Smith	.07	.05	.03
51	Mel Hall	.07	.05	.03
52	Keith Atherton	.05	.04	.02
53	Ruppert Jones	.05	.04	.02
54	Bill Dawley	.05	.04	.02
55	Tim Wallach	.10	.08	.04
56	Brewers Leaders (Jamie Cocanower, Paul Molitor, Charlie Moore, Herm Starrette)	.07	.05	.03
57	*Scott Nielsen*(FC)	.10	.08	.04
58	Thad Bosley	.05	.04	.02
59	Ken Dayley	.05	.04	.02
60	Tony Pena	.07	.05	.03
61	*Bobby Thigpen*(FC)	.35	.25	.14
62	Bobby Meacham	.05	.04	.02
63	Fred Toliver(FC)	.07	.05	.03
64	Harry Spilman	.05	.04	.02
65	Tom Browning	.10	.08	.04
66	Marc Sullivan	.05	.04	.02
67	Bill Swift	.05	.04	.02
68	Tony LaRussa	.07	.05	.03
69	Lonnie Smith	.07	.05	.03
70	Charlie Hough	.07	.05	.03
71	*Mike Aldrete*(FC)	.20	.15	.08
72	Walt Terrell	.07	.05	.03
73	Dave Anderson	.05	.04	.02
74	Dan Pasqua	.10	.08	.04
75	Ron Darling	.12	.09	.05
76	Rafael Ramirez	.05	.04	.02
77	Bryan Oelkers	.05	.04	.02
78	Tom Foley	.05	.04	.02
79	Juan Nieves	.10	.08	.04
80	*Wally Joyner*	1.50	1.25	.70
81	Padres Leaders (Andy Hawkins, Terry Kennedy)	.07	.05	.03
82	*Rob Murphy*(FC)	.15	.11	.06
83	Mike Davis	.07	.05	.03
84	Steve Lake	.05	.04	.02
85	Kevin Bass	.07	.05	.03
86	Nate Snell	.05	.04	.02
87	Mark Salas	.05	.04	.02
88	Ed Wojna	.05	.04	.02
89	Ozzie Guillen	.10	.08	.04
90	Dave Stieb	.10	.08	.04
91	Harold Reynolds	.10	.08	.04
92a	Urbano Lugo (no trademark on front)	.30	.25	.12
92b	Urbano Lugo (trademark on front)	.07	.05	.03
93	Jim Leyland	.05	.04	.02
94	Calvin Schiraldi	.05	.04	.02
95	Oddibe McDowell	.07	.05	.03
96	Frank Williams	.05	.04	.02
97	Glenn Wilson	.07	.05	.03
98	Bill Scherrer	.05	.04	.02
99	Darryl Motley	.05	.04	.02
100	Steve Garvey	.20	.15	.08
101	*Carl Willis*(FC)	.10	.08	.04
102	Paul Zuvella	.05	.04	.02
103	Rick Aguilera	.06	.05	.02
104	Billy Sample	.05	.04	.02
105	Floyd Youmans	.07	.05	.03
106	Blue Jays Leaders (George Bell, Willie Upshaw)	.07	.05	.03
107	John Butcher	.05	.04	.02
108	Jim Gantner (photo reversed)	.07	.05	.03
109	R.J. Reynolds	.05	.04	.02
110	John Tudor	.10	.08	.04
111	Alfredo Griffin	.07	.05	.03
112	Alan Ashby	.05	.04	.02
113	Neil Allen	.05	.04	.02
114	Billy Beane	.05	.04	.02
115	Donnie Moore	.05	.04	.02
116	Bill Russell	.07	.05	.03
117	Jim Beattie	.05	.04	.02
118	Bobby Valentine	.05	.04	.02
119	Ron Robinson	.05	.04	.02
120	Eddie Murray	.30	.25	.12
121	*Kevin Romine*(FC)	.12	.09	.05
122	Jim Clancy	.07	.05	.03
123	*John Kruk*	.30	.25	.12
124	Ray Fontenot	.05	.04	.02
125	Bob Brenly	.05	.04	.02
126	*Mike Loynd*(FC)	.15	.11	.06
127	Vance Law	.07	.05	.03
128	Checklist 1-132	.05	.04	.02
129	Rick Cerone	.05	.04	.02
130	Dwight Gooden	.80	.60	.30
131	Pirates Leaders (Sid Bream, Tony Pena)	.07	.05	.03
132	*Paul Assenmacher*	.15	.11	.06
133	Jose Oquendo	.05	.04	.02
134	*Rich Yett*(FC)	.12	.09	.05
135	Mike Easler	.07	.05	.03
136	Ron Romanick	.05	.04	.02
137	Jerry Willard	.05	.04	.02
138	Roy Lee Jackson	.05	.04	.02
139	*Devon White*(FC)	.90	.70	.35
140	Bret Saberhagen	.15	.11	.06
141	Herm Winningham	.05	.04	.02
142	Rick Sutcliffe	.10	.08	.04
143	Steve Boros	.05	.04	.02
144	Mike Scioscia	.07	.05	.03
145	Charlie Kerfeld	.07	.05	.03
146	*Tracy Jones*(FC)	.25	.20	.10
147	Randy Niemann	.05	.04	.02
148	Dave Collins	.07	.05	.03
149	Ray Searage	.05	.04	.02
150	Wade Boggs	1.25	.90	.50
151	Mike LaCoss	.05	.04	.02
152	Toby Harrah	.07	.05	.03
153	*Duane Ward*(FC)	.12	.09	.05
154	Tom O'Malley	.05	.04	.02
155	Eddie Whitson	.05	.04	.02
156	Mariners Leaders (Bob Kearney, Phil Regan, Matt Young)	.07	.05	.03
157	Danny Darwin	.05	.04	.02
158	Tim Teufel	.05	.04	.02
159	Ed Olwine	.05	.04	.02
160	Julio Franco	.10	.08	.04
161	Steve Ontiveros	.05	.04	.02
162	*Mike LaValliere*	.25	.20	.10
163	Kevin Gross	.07	.05	.03
164	Sammy Khalifa	.05	.04	.02
165	Jeff Reardon	.10	.08	.04
166	Bob Boone	.07	.05	.03
167	*Jim Deshaies*	.25	.20	.10
168	Lou Piniella	.07	.05	.03
169	Ron Washington	.05	.04	.02
170	Future Stars *(Bo Jackson)*	3.50	2.75	1.50
171	*Chuck Cary*(FC)	.10	.08	.04
172	Ron Oester	.05	.04	.02
173	Alex Trevino	.05	.04	.02
174	Henry Cotto	.05	.04	.02
175	Bob Stanley	.05	.04	.02
176	Steve Buechele	.07	.05	.03
177	Keith Moreland	.07	.05	.03
178	Cecil Fielder	.05	.04	.02
179	Bill Wegman	.10	.08	.04
180	Chris Brown	.07	.05	.03
181	Cardinals Leaders (Mike LaValliere, Ozzie Smith, Ray Soff)	.07	.05	.03
182	Lee Lacy	.05	.04	.02
183	Andy Hawkins	.05	.04	.02
184	*Bobby Bonilla*	.90	.70	.35
185	Roger McDowell	.10	.08	.04
186	Bruce Benedict	.05	.04	.02
187	Mark Huismann	.05	.04	.02
188	Tony Phillips	.05	.04	.02

		MT	NR MT	EX
189	Joe Hesketh	.05	.04	.02
190	Jim Sundberg	.07	.05	.03
191	Charles Hudson	.05	.04	.02
192	Cory Snyder(FC)	.70	.50	.30
193	Roger Craig	.07	.05	.03
194	Kirk McCaskill	.07	.05	.03
195	Mike Pagliarulo	.10	.08	.04
196	Randy O'Neal	.05	.04	.02
197	Mark Bailey	.05	.04	.02
198	Lee Mazzilli	.07	.05	.03
199	Mariano Duncan	.05	.04	.02
200	Pete Rose	.60	.45	.25
201	*John Cangelosi*	.12	.09	.05
202	Ricky Wright	.05	.04	.02
203	*Mike Kingery*(FC)	.15	.11	.06
204	Sammy Stewart	.05	.04	.02
205	Graig Nettles	.10	.08	.04
206	Twins Leaders (Tim Laudner, Frank Viola)			
		.07	.05	.03
207	George Frazier	.05	.04	.02
208	John Shelby	.05	.04	.02
209	Rick Schu	.05	.04	.02
210	Lloyd Moseby	.07	.05	.03
211	John Morris(FC)	.07	.05	.03
212	Mike Fitzgerald	.05	.04	.02
213	*Randy Myers*(FC)	.50	.40	.20
214	Omar Moreno	.05	.04	.02
215	Mark Langston	.12	.09	.05
216	Future Stars (*B.J. Surhoff*)(FC)	.50	.40	.20
217	Chris Codiroli	.05	.04	.02
218	Sparky Anderson	.07	.05	.03
219	Cecilio Guante	.05	.04	.02
220	Joe Carter	.12	.09	.05
221	Vern Ruhle	.05	.04	.02
222	Denny Walling	.05	.04	.02
223	Charlie Leibrandt	.07	.05	.03
224	Wayne Tolleson	.05	.04	.02
225	Mike Smithson	.05	.04	.02
226	Max Venable	.05	.04	.02
227	*Jamie Moyer*(FC)	.20	.15	.08
228	Curt Wilkerson	.05	.04	.02
229	*Mike Birkbeck*(FC)	.15	.11	.06
230	Don Baylor	.10	.08	.04
231	Giants Leaders (Bob Brenly, Mike Krukow)			
		.07	.05	.03
232	*Reggie Williams*	.10	.08	.04
233	*Russ Morman*(FC)	.10	.08	.04
234	Pat Sheridan	.05	.04	.02
235	Alvin Davis	.10	.08	.04
236	Tommy John	.15	.11	.06
237	Jim Morrison	.05	.04	.02
238	Bill Krueger	.05	.04	.02
239	Juan Espino	.05	.04	.02
240	Steve Balboni	.07	.05	.03
241	Danny Heep	.05	.04	.02
242	Rick Mahler	.05	.04	.02
243	Whitey Herzog	.07	.05	.03
244	Dickie Noles	.05	.04	.02
245	Willie Upshaw	.07	.05	.03
246	Jim Dwyer	.05	.04	.02
247	Jeff Reed(FC)	.07	.05	.03
248	Gene Walter	.07	.05	.03
249	Jim Pankovits	.05	.04	.02
250	Teddy Higuera	.15	.11	.06
251	Rob Wilfong	.05	.04	.02
252	Denny Martinez	.05	.04	.02
253	Eddie Milner	.05	.04	.02
254	*Bob Tewksbury*	.12	.09	.05
255	Juan Samuel	.10	.08	.04
256	Royals Leaders (George Brett, Frank White)			
		.10	.08	.04
257	Bob Forsch	.07	.05	.03
258	Steve Yeager	.05	.04	.02
259	*Mike Greenwell*(FC)	4.00	3.00	1.50
260	Vida Blue	.07	.05	.03
261	*Ruben Sierra*(FC)	3.00	2.25	1.25
262	Jim Winn	.05	.04	.02
263	Stan Javier(FC)	.07	.05	.03
264	Checklist 133-264	.05	.04	.02
265	Darrell Evans	.10	.08	.04
266	*Jeff Hamilton*(FC)	.25	.20	.10
267	Howard Johnson	.10	.08	.04
268	Pat Corrales	.05	.04	.02
269	Cliff Speck	.05	.04	.02
270	Jody Davis	.07	.05	.03
271	Mike Brown	.05	.04	.02
272	Andres Galarraga	1.00	.70	.40
273	Gene Nelson	.05	.04	.02
274	*Jeff Hearron*(FC)	.05	.04	.02
275	LaMarr Hoyt	.05	.04	.02
276	Jackie Gutierrez	.05	.04	.02

		MT	NR MT	EX
277	Juan Agosto	.05	.04	.02
278	Gary Pettis	.05	.04	.02
279	Dan Plesac	.30	.25	.12
280	Jeffrey Leonard	.07	.05	.03
281	Reds Leaders (Bo Diaz, Bill Gullickson, Pete Rose)			
		.10	.08	.04
282	Jeff Calhoun	.05	.04	.02
283	Doug Drabek(FC)	.25	.20	.10
284	John Moses	.05	.04	.02
285	Dennis Boyd	.07	.05	.03
286	Mike Woodard(FC)	.07	.05	.03
287	Dave Von Ohlen	.05	.04	.02
288	Tito Landrum	.05	.04	.02
289	Bob Kipper	.07	.05	.03
290	Leon Durham	.07	.05	.03
291	Mitch Williams(FC)	.60	.45	.25
292	Franklin Stubbs	.07	.05	.03
293	Bob Rodgers	.05	.04	.02
294	Steve Jeltz	.05	.04	.02
295	Len Dykstra	.12	.09	.05
296	*Andres Thomas*	.25	.20	.10
297	Don Schulze	.05	.04	.02
298	Larry Herndon	.05	.04	.02
299	Joel Davis	.07	.05	.03
300	Reggie Jackson	.30	.25	.12
301	Luis Aquino(FC)	.10	.08	.04
302	Bill Schroeder	.05	.04	.02
303	Juan Berenguer	.05	.04	.02
304	Phil Garner	.05	.04	.02
305	John Franco	.10	.08	.04
306	Red Sox Leaders (Rich Gedman, John McNamara, Tom Seaver)			
		.07	.05	.03
307	*Lee Guetterman*(FC)	.15	.11	.06
308	Don Slaught	.05	.04	.02
309	Mike Young	.05	.04	.02
310	Frank Viola	.15	.11	.06
311	Turn Back The Clock (Rickey Henderson)			
		.10	.08	.04
312	Turn Back The Clock (Reggie Jackson)			
		.10	.08	.04
313	Turn Back The Clock (Roberto Clemente)			
		.15	.11	.06
314	Turn Back The Clock (Carl Yastrzemski)			
		.10	.08	.04
315	Turn Back The Clock (Maury Wills)	.07	.05	.03
316	Brian Fisher	.07	.05	.03
317	Clint Hurdle	.05	.04	.02
318	Jim Fregosi	.05	.04	.02
319	*Greg Swindell*(FC)	1.00	.70	.40
320	*Barry Bonds*	.90	.70	.35
321	Mike Laga	.05	.04	.02
322	Chris Bando	.05	.04	.02
323	*Al Newman*	.07	.05	.03
324	Dave Palmer	.05	.04	.02
325	Garry Templeton	.07	.05	.03
326	Mark Gubicza	.10	.08	.04
327	*Dale Sveum*	.20	.15	.08
328	Bob Welch	.10	.08	.04
329	Ron Roenicke	.05	.04	.02
330	Mike Scott	.12	.09	.05
331	Mets Leaders (Gary Carter, Keith Hernandez, Dave Johnson, Darryl Strawberry)			
		.10	.08	.04
332	Joe Price	.05	.04	.02
333	Ken Phelps	.07	.05	.03
334	*Ed Correa*	.15	.11	.06
335	Candy Maldonado	.07	.05	.03
336	*Allan Anderson*(FC)	.25	.20	.10
337	Darrell Miller	.05	.04	.02
338	Tim Conroy	.05	.04	.02
339	Donnie Hill	.05	.04	.02
340	Roger Clemens	.90	.70	.35
341	Mike Brown	.05	.04	.02
342	Bob James	.05	.04	.02
343	Hal Lanier	.05	.04	.02
344a	Joe Niekro (copyright outside yellow on back)			
		.30	.25	.12
344b	Joe Niekro (copyright inside yellow on back)			
		.07	.05	.03
345	Andre Dawson	.20	.15	.08
346	Shawon Dunston	.07	.05	.03
347	Mickey Brantley(FC)	.07	.05	.03
348	Carmelo Martinez	.07	.05	.03
349	Storm Davis	.10	.08	.04
350	Keith Hernandez	.20	.15	.08
351	Gene Garber	.05	.04	.02
352	Mike Felder(FC)	.07	.05	.03
353	Ernie Camacho	.05	.04	.02
354	Jamie Quirk	.05	.04	.02
355	Don Carman	.07	.05	.03
356	White Sox Leaders (Ed Brinkman, Julio Cruz)			
		.07	.05	.03

#	Player	MT	NR MT	EX
357	Steve Fireovid(FC)	.07	.05	.03
358	Sal Butera	.05	.04	.02
359	Doug Corbett	.05	.04	.02
360	Pedro Guerrero	.15	.11	.06
361	Mark Thurmond	.05	.04	.02
362	Luis Quinones(FC)	.12	.09	.05
363	Jose Guzman	.12	.09	.05
364	Randy Bush	.05	.04	.02
365	Rick Rhoden	.07	.05	.03
366	Mark McGwire	3.00	2.25	1.25
367	Jeff Lahti	.05	.04	.02
368	John McNamara	.05	.04	.02
369	Brian Dayett	.05	.04	.02
370	Fred Lynn	.15	.11	.06
371	Mark Eichhorn	.15	.11	.06
372	Jerry Mumphrey	.05	.04	.02
373	Jeff Dedmon	.05	.04	.02
374	Glenn Hoffman	.05	.04	.02
375	Ron Guidry	.12	.09	.05
376	Scott Bradley	.05	.04	.02
377	John Henry Johnson	.05	.04	.02
378	Rafael Santana	.05	.04	.02
379	John Russell	.05	.04	.02
380	Rich Gossage	.15	.11	.06
381	Expos Leaders (Mike Fitzgerald, Bob Rodgers)	.07	.05	.03
382	Rudy Law	.05	.04	.02
383	Ron Davis	.05	.04	.02
384	Johnny Grubb	.05	.04	.02
385	Orel Hershiser	.30	.25	.12
386	Dickie Thon	.07	.05	.03
387	T.R. Bryden(FC)	.10	.08	.04
388	Geno Petralli	.05	.04	.02
389	Jeff Robinson	.07	.05	.03
390	Gary Matthews	.07	.05	.03
391	Jay Howell	.07	.05	.03
392	Checklist 265-396	.05	.04	.02
393	Pete Rose	.40	.30	.15
394	Mike Bielecki	.07	.05	.03
395	Damaso Garcia	.05	.04	.02
396	Tim Lollar	.05	.04	.02
397	Greg Walker	.07	.05	.03
398	Brad Havens	.05	.04	.02
399	Curt Ford(FC)	.07	.05	.03
400	George Brett	.35	.25	.14
401	Billy Jo Robidoux	.07	.05	.03
402	Mike Trujillo	.05	.04	.02
403	Jerry Royster	.05	.04	.02
404	Doug Sisk	.05	.04	.02
405	Brook Jacoby	.10	.08	.04
406	Yankees Leaders (Rickey Henderson, Don Mattingly)	.15	.11	.06
407	Jim Acker	.05	.04	.02
408	John Mizerock	.05	.04	.02
409	Milt Thompson	.07	.05	.03
410	Fernando Valenzuela	.25	.20	.10
411	Darnell Coles	.07	.05	.03
412	Eric Davis	.90	.70	.35
413	Moose Haas	.05	.04	.02
414	Joe Orsulak	.05	.04	.02
415	Bobby Witt	.30	.25	.12
416	Tom Nieto	.05	.04	.02
417	Pat Perry(FC)	.07	.05	.03
418	Dick Williams	.05	.04	.02
419	Mark Portugal(FC)	.10	.08	.04
420	Will Clark	5.00	3.75	2.00
421	Jose DeLeon	.07	.05	.03
422	Jack Howell	.07	.05	.03
423	Jaime Cocanower	.05	.04	.02
424	Chris Speier	.05	.04	.02
425	Tom Seaver	.30	.25	.12
426	Floyd Rayford	.05	.04	.02
427	Ed Nunez	.05	.04	.02
428	Bruce Bochy	.05	.04	.02
429	Future Stars (Tim Pyznarski)(FC)	.10	.08	.04
430	Mike Schmidt	.40	.30	.15
431	Dodgers Leaders (Tom Niedenfuer, Ron Perranoski, Alex Trevino)	.07	.05	.03
432	Jim Slaton	.05	.04	.02
433	Ed Hearn(FC)	.10	.08	.04
434	Mike Fischlin	.05	.04	.02
435	Bruce Sutter	.12	.09	.05
436	Andy Allanson	.15	.11	.06
437	Ted Power	.05	.04	.02
438	Kelly Downs(FC)	.30	.25	.12
439	Karl Best	.05	.04	.02
440	Willie McGee	.10	.08	.04
441	Dave Leiper(FC)	.10	.08	.04
442	Mitch Webster	.07	.05	.03
443	John Felske	.05	.04	.02
444	Jeff Russell	.05	.04	.02
445	Dave Lopes	.07	.05	.03
446	Chuck Finley(FC)	.12	.09	.05
447	Bill Almon	.05	.04	.02
448	Chris Bosio(FC)	.25	.20	.10
449	Future Stars (Pat Dodson)(FC)	.10	.08	.04
450	Kirby Puckett	.30	.25	.12
451	Joe Sambito	.05	.04	.02
452	Dave Henderson	.10	.08	.04
453	Scott Terry(FC)	.12	.09	.05
454	Luis Salazar	.05	.04	.02
455	Mike Boddicker	.07	.05	.03
456	A's Leaders (Carney Lansford, Tony LaRussa, Mickey Tettleton, Dave Von Ohlen)	.07	.05	.03
457	Len Matuszek	.05	.04	.02
458	Kelly Gruber(FC)	.07	.05	.03
459	Dennis Eckersley	.10	.08	.04
460	Darryl Strawberry	.35	.25	.14
461	Craig McMurtry	.05	.04	.02
462	Scott Fletcher	.07	.05	.03
463	Tom Candiotti	.05	.04	.02
464	Butch Wynegar	.05	.04	.02
465	Todd Worrell	.30	.25	.12
466	Kal Daniels(FC)	1.25	.90	.50
467	Randy St. Claire	.05	.04	.02
468	George Bamberger	.05	.04	.02
469	Mike Diaz(FC)	.15	.11	.06
470	Dave Dravecky	.07	.05	.03
471	Ronn Reynolds	.05	.04	.02
472	Bill Doran	.07	.05	.03
473	Steve Farr	.05	.04	.02
474	Jerry Narron	.05	.04	.02
475	Scott Garrelts	.05	.04	.02
476	Danny Tartabull	.90	.70	.35
477	Ken Howell	.05	.04	.02
478	Tim Laudner	.05	.04	.02
479	Bob Sebra(FC)	.10	.08	.04
480	Jim Rice	.25	.20	.10
481	Phillies Leaders (Von Hayes, Juan Samuel, Glenn Wilson)	.07	.05	.03
482	Daryl Boston	.05	.04	.02
483	Dwight Lowry	.05	.04	.02
484	Jim Traber(FC)	.15	.11	.06
485	Tony Fernandez	.10	.08	.04
486	Otis Nixon	.05	.04	.02
487	Dave Gumpert	.05	.04	.02
488	Ray Knight	.07	.05	.03
489	Bill Gullickson	.05	.04	.02
490	Dale Murphy	.40	.30	.15
491	Ron Karkovice(FC)	.10	.08	.04
492	Mike Heath	.05	.04	.02
493	Tom Lasorda	.07	.05	.03
494	Barry Jones(FC)	.12	.09	.05
495	Gorman Thomas	.10	.08	.04
496	Bruce Bochte	.05	.04	.02
497	Dale Mohorcic(FC)	.15	.11	.06
498	Bob Kearney	.05	.04	.02
499	Bruce Ruffin(FC)	.20	.15	.08
500	Don Mattingly	2.25	1.75	.90
501	Craig Lefferts	.05	.04	.02
502	Dick Schofield	.05	.04	.02
503	Larry Andersen	.05	.04	.02
504	Mickey Hatcher	.05	.04	.02
505	Bryn Smith	.05	.04	.02
506	Orioles Leaders (Rich Bordi, Rick Dempsey, Earl Weaver)	.07	.05	.03
507	Dave Stapleton	.05	.04	.02
508	Scott Bankhead	.15	.11	.06
509	Enos Cabell	.05	.04	.02
510	Tom Henke	.07	.05	.03
511	Steve Lyons	.05	.04	.02
512	Dave Magadan(FC)	.35	.25	.14
513	Carmen Castillo	.05	.04	.02
514	Orlando Mercado	.05	.04	.02
515	Willie Hernandez	.07	.05	.03
516	Ted Simmons	.10	.08	.04
517	Mario Soto	.07	.05	.03
518	Gene Mauch	.07	.05	.03
519	Curt Young	.07	.05	.03
520	Jack Clark	.15	.11	.06
521	Rick Reuschel	.10	.08	.04
522	Checklist 397-528	.05	.04	.02
523	Earnie Riles	.05	.04	.02
524	Bob Shirley	.05	.04	.02
525	Phil Bradley	.10	.08	.04
526	Roger Mason	.05	.04	.02
527	Jim Wohlford	.05	.04	.02
528	Ken Dixon	.05	.04	.02
529	Alvaro Espinoza(FC)	.07	.05	.03
530	Tony Gwynn	.35	.25	.14
531	Astros Leaders (Yogi Berra, Hal Lanier, Denis Menke, Gene Tenace)	.07	.05	.03

		MT	NR MT	EX
532	Jeff Stone	.05	.04	.02
533	Argenis Salazar	.05	.04	.02
534	Scott Sanderson	.05	.04	.02
535	Tony Armas	.07	.05	.03
536	*Terry Mulholland*(FC)	.10	.08	.04
537	Rance Mulliniks	.05	.04	.02
538	Tom Niedenfuer	.07	.05	.03
539	Reid Nichols	.05	.04	.02
540	Terry Kennedy	.07	.05	.03
541	*Rafael Belliard*(FC)	.10	.08	.04
542	Ricky Horton	.07	.05	.03
543	Dave Johnson	.07	.05	.03
544	Zane Smith	.07	.05	.03
545	Buddy Bell	.07	.05	.03
546	Mike Morgan	.05	.04	.02
547	Rob Deer	.10	.08	.04
548	*Bill Mooneyham*(FC)	.10	.08	.04
549	Bob Melvin	.05	.04	.02
550	*Pete Incaviglia*	.40	.30	.15
551	Frank Wills	.05	.04	.02
552	Larry Sheets	.07	.05	.03
553	*Mike Maddux*(FC)	.15	.11	.06
554	Buddy Biancalana	.05	.04	.02
555	Dennis Rasmussen	.10	.08	.04
556	Angels Leaders (Bob Boone, Marcel Lachemann, Mike Witt)	.07	.05	.03
557	*John Cerutti*	.15	.11	.06
558	Greg Gagne	.05	.04	.02
559	Lance McCullers	.07	.05	.03
560	Glenn Davis	.25	.20	.10
561	*Rey Quinones*	.15	.11	.06
562	*Bryan Clutterbuck*(FC)	.10	.08	.04
563	John Stefero	.05	.04	.02
564	Larry McWilliams	.05	.04	.02
565	Dusty Baker	.07	.05	.03
566	Tim Hulett	.05	.04	.02
567	*Greg Mathews*(FC)	.20	.15	.08
568	Earl Weaver	.07	.05	.03
569	Wade Rowdon(FC)	.07	.05	.03
570	Sid Fernandez	.10	.08	.04
571	Ozzie Virgil	.05	.04	.02
572	Pete Ladd	.05	.04	.02
573	Hal McRae	.07	.05	.03
574	Manny Lee	.05	.04	.02
575	Pat Tabler	.07	.05	.03
576	Frank Pastore	.05	.04	.02
577	Dann Bilardello	.05	.04	.02
578	Billy Hatcher	.07	.05	.03
579	Rick Burleson	.07	.05	.03
580	Mike Krukow	.07	.05	.03
581	Cubs Leaders (Ron Cey, Steve Trout)	.07	.05	.03
582	Bruce Berenyi	.05	.04	.02
583	Junior Ortiz	.05	.04	.02
584	Ron Kittle	.07	.05	.03
585	*Scott Bailes*	.15	.11	.06
586	Ben Oglivie	.07	.05	.03
587	Eric Plunk(FC)	.10	.08	.04
588	Wallace Johnson	.05	.04	.02
589	Steve Crawford	.05	.04	.02
590	Vince Coleman	.25	.20	.10
591	Spike Owen	.05	.04	.02
592	Chris Welsh	.05	.04	.02
593	Chuck Tanner	.05	.04	.02
594	Rick Anderson	.05	.04	.02
595	Keith Hernandez AS	.12	.09	.05
596	Steve Sax AS	.07	.05	.03
597	Mike Schmidt AS	.20	.15	.08
598	Ozzie Smith AS	.07	.05	.03
599	Tony Gwynn AS	.20	.15	.08
600	Dave Parker AS	.10	.08	.04
601	Darryl Strawberry AS	.20	.15	.08
602	Gary Carter AS	.15	.11	.06
603a	Dwight Gooden AS (no trademark on front)	.80	.60	.30
603b	Dwight Gooden AS (trademark on front)	.30	.25	.12
604	Fernando Valenzuela AS	.12	.09	.05
605	Todd Worrell AS	.10	.08	.04
606a	Don Mattingly AS (no trademark on front)	1.75	1.25	.70
606b	Don Mattingly AS (trademark on front)	.70	.50	.30
607	Tony Bernazard AS	.05	.04	.02
608	Wade Boggs AS	.40	.30	.15
609	Cal Ripken AS	.15	.11	.06
610	Jim Rice AS	.15	.11	.06
611	Kirby Puckett AS	.15	.11	.06
612	George Bell AS	.12	.09	.05
613	Lance Parrish AS	.10	.08	.04
614	Roger Clemens AS	.30	.25	.12
615	Teddy Higuera AS	.10	.08	.04
616	Dave Righetti AS	.10	.08	.04
617	Al Nipper	.05	.04	.02
618	Tom Kelly	.05	.04	.02
619	Jerry Reed	.05	.04	.02
620	Jose Canseco	3.50	2.75	1.50
621	Danny Cox	.07	.05	.03
622	*Glenn Braggs*(FC)	.40	.30	.15
623	*Kurt Stillwell*(FC)	.25	.20	.10
624	Tim Burke	.05	.04	.02
625	Mookie Wilson	.07	.05	.03
626	Joel Skinner	.05	.04	.02
627	Ken Oberkfell	.05	.04	.02
628	Bob Walk	.05	.04	.02
629	Larry Parrish	.07	.05	.03
630	John Candelaria	.07	.05	.03
631	Tigers Leaders (Sparky Anderson, Mike Heath, Willie Hernandez)	.07	.05	.03
632	Rob Woodward(FC)	.07	.05	.03
633	Jose Uribe	.07	.05	.03
634	Future Stars *(Rafael Palmeiro)*(FC)	1.25	.90	.50
635	Ken Schrom	.05	.04	.02
636	Darren Daulton	.05	.04	.02
637	Bip Roberts	.05	.04	.02
638	Rich Bordi	.05	.04	.02
639	Gerald Perry	.10	.08	.04
640	Mark Clear	.05	.04	.02
641	Domingo Ramos	.05	.04	.02
642	Al Pulido	.05	.04	.02
643	Ron Shepherd	.05	.04	.02
644	John Denny	.05	.04	.02
645	Dwight Evans	.12	.09	.05
646	Mike Mason	.05	.04	.02
647	Tom Lawless	.05	.04	.02
648	*Barry Larkin*	2.00	1.50	.80
649	Mickey Tettleton	.05	.04	.02
650	Hubie Brooks	.07	.05	.03
651	Benny Distefano	.05	.04	.02
652	Terry Forster	.07	.05	.03
653	*Kevin Mitchell*	3.75	2.75	1.50
654	Checklist 529-660	.05	.04	.02
655	Jesse Barfield	.15	.11	.06
656	Rangers Leaders (Bobby Valentine, Rickey Wright)	.07	.05	.03
657	Tom Waddell	.05	.04	.02
658	*Robby Thompson*	.30	.25	.12
659	Aurelio Lopez	.05	.04	.02
660	Bob Horner	.10	.08	.04
661	Lou Whitaker	.15	.11	.06
662	Frank DiPino	.05	.04	.02
663	Cliff Johnson	.05	.04	.02
664	Mike Marshall	.10	.08	.04
665	Rod Scurry	.05	.04	.02
666	Von Hayes	.07	.05	.03
667	Ron Hassey	.05	.04	.02
668	Juan Bonilla	.05	.04	.02
669	Bud Black	.05	.04	.02
670	Jose Cruz	.07	.05	.03
671a	Ray Soff (no "D*" before copyright line)	.20	.15	.08
671b	Ray Soff ("D*" before copyright line)	.05	.04	.02
672	Chili Davis	.07	.05	.03
673	Don Sutton	.15	.11	.06
674	Bill Campbell	.05	.04	.02
675	Ed Romero	.05	.04	.02
676	Charlie Moore	.05	.04	.02
677	Bob Grich	.07	.05	.03
678	Carney Lansford	.07	.05	.03
679	Kent Hrbek	.15	.11	.06
680	Ryne Sandberg	.25	.20	.10
681	George Bell	.25	.20	.10
682	Jerry Reuss	.07	.05	.03
683	Gary Roenicke	.05	.04	.02
684	Kent Tekulve	.07	.05	.03
685	Jerry Hairston	.05	.04	.02
686	Doyle Alexander	.07	.05	.03
687	Alan Trammell	.25	.20	.10
688	Juan Beniquez	.05	.04	.02
689	Darrell Porter	.07	.05	.03
690	Dane Iorg	.05	.04	.02
691	Dave Parker	.15	.11	.06
692	Frank White	.07	.05	.03
693	Terry Puhl	.05	.04	.02
694	Phil Niekro	.20	.15	.08
695	Chico Walker	.05	.04	.02
696	Gary Lucas	.05	.04	.02
697	Ed Lynch	.05	.04	.02
698	Ernie Whitt	.07	.05	.03
699	Ken Landreaux	.05	.04	.02

		MT	NR MT	EX
700	Dave Bergman	.05	.04	.02
701	Willie Randolph	.07	.05	.03
702	Greg Gross	.05	.04	.02
703	Dave Schmidt	.05	.04	.02
704	Jesse Orosco	.07	.05	.03
705	Bruce Hurst	.10	.08	.04
706	Rick Manning	.05	.04	.02
707	Bob McClure	.05	.04	.02
708	Scott McGregor	.07	.05	.03
709	Dave Kingman	.10	.08	.04
710	Gary Gaetti	.15	.11	.06
711	Ken Griffey	.07	.05	.03
712	Don Robinson	.07	.05	.03
713	Tom Brookens	.05	.04	.02
714	Dan Quisenberry	.07	.05	.03
715	Bob Dernier	.05	.04	.02
716	Rick Leach	.05	.04	.02
717	Ed Vande Berg	.05	.04	.02
718	Steve Carlton	.25	.20	.10
719	Tom Hume	.05	.04	.02
720	Richard Dotson	.07	.05	.03
721	Tom Herr	.07	.05	.03
722	Bob Knepper	.07	.05	.03
723	Brett Butler	.07	.05	.03
724	Greg Minton	.05	.04	.02
725	George Hendrick	.07	.05	.03
726	Frank Tanana	.07	.05	.03
727	Mike Moore	.05	.04	.02
728	Tippy Martinez	.05	.04	.02
729	Tom Paciorek	.05	.04	.02
730	Eric Show	.07	.05	.03
731	Dave Concepcion	.10	.08	.04
732	Manny Trillo	.07	.05	.03
733	Bill Caudill	.05	.04	.02
734	Bill Madlock	.10	.08	.04
735	Rickey Henderson	.30	.25	.12
736	Steve Bedrosian	.10	.08	.04
737	Floyd Bannister	.07	.05	.03
738	Jorge Orta	.05	.04	.02
739	Chet Lemon	.07	.05	.03
740	Rich Gedman	.07	.05	.03
741	Paul Molitor	.12	.09	.05
742	Andy McGaffigan	.05	.04	.02
743	Dwayne Murphy	.07	.05	.03
744	Roy Smalley	.05	.04	.02
745	Glenn Hubbard	.05	.04	.02
746	Bob Ojeda	.07	.05	.03
747	Johnny Ray	.07	.05	.03
748	Mike Flanagan	.07	.05	.03
749	Ozzie Smith	.15	.11	.06
750	Steve Trout	.07	.05	.03
751	Garth Iorg	.05	.04	.02
752	Dan Petry	.07	.05	.03
753	Rick Honeycutt	.05	.04	.02
754	Dave LaPoint	.07	.05	.03
755	Luis Aguayo	.05	.04	.02
756	Carlton Fisk	.20	.15	.08
757	Nolan Ryan	.30	.25	.12
758	Tony Bernazard	.05	.04	.02
759	Joel Youngblood	.05	.04	.02
760	Mike Witt	.07	.05	.03
761	Greg Pryor	.05	.04	.02
762	Gary Ward	.07	.05	.03
763	Tim Flannery	.05	.04	.02
764	Bill Buckner	.07	.05	.03
765	Kirk Gibson	.20	.15	.08
766	Don Aase	.05	.04	.02
767	Ron Cey	.07	.05	.03
768	Dennis Lamp	.05	.04	.02
769	Steve Sax	.15	.11	.06
770	Dave Winfield	.25	.20	.10
771	Shane Rawley	.07	.05	.03
772	Harold Baines	.12	.09	.05
773	Robin Yount	.25	.20	.10
774	Wayne Krenchicki	.05	.04	.02
775	Joaquin Andujar	.07	.05	.03
776	Tom Brunansky	.10	.08	.04
777	Chris Chambliss	.07	.05	.03
778	Jack Morris	.20	.15	.08
779	Craig Reynolds	.05	.04	.02
780	Andre Thornton	.07	.05	.03
781	Atlee Hammaker	.05	.04	.02
782	Brian Downing	.07	.05	.03
783	Willie Wilson	.10	.08	.04
784	Cal Ripken	.30	.25	.12
785	Terry Francona	.05	.04	.02
786	Jimy Williams	.05	.04	.02
787	Alejandro Pena	.07	.05	.03
788	Tim Stoddard	.05	.04	.02
789	Dan Schatzeder	.05	.04	.02
790	Julio Cruz	.05	.04	.02

		MT	NR MT	EX
791	Lance Parrish	.15	.11	.06
792	Checklist 661-792	.05	.04	.02

1987 Topps
All-Star Glossy Set Of 22

For the fourth consecutive year, Topps produced an All-Star Game commemorative set of 22 cards. The glossy cards, which measure 2-1/2" by 3-1/2", were included in rack packs. Using the same basic card design as in previous efforts with a few minor changes, the 1987 edition features American and National League logos on the card fronts. Card #'s 1-12 feature representatives from the American League, while #'s 13-22 are National Leaguers.

		MT	NR MT	EX
	Complete Set:	5.00	3.75	2.00
	Common Player:	.15	.11	.06
1	Whitey Herzog	.15	.11	.06
2	Keith Hernandez	.40	.30	.15
3	Ryne Sandberg	.40	.30	.15
4	Mike Schmidt	.70	.50	.30
5	Ozzie Smith	.30	.25	.12
6	Tony Gwynn	.50	.40	.20
7	Dale Murphy	.80	.60	.30
8	Darryl Strawberry	.80	.60	.30
9	Gary Carter	.40	.30	.15
10	Dwight Gooden	.60	.45	.25
11	Fernando Valenzuela	.30	.25	.12
12	Dick Howser	.15	.11	.06
13	Wally Joyner	1.25	.90	.50
14	Lou Whitaker	.30	.25	.12
15	Wade Boggs	1.00	.70	.40
16	Cal Ripken	.50	.40	.20
17	Dave Winfield	.40	.30	.15
18	Rickey Henderson	.50	.40	.20
19	Kirby Puckett	.40	.30	.15
20	Lance Parrish	.30	.25	.12
21	Roger Clemens	.60	.45	.25
22	Teddy Higuera	.30	.25	.12

1987 Topps
All-Star Glossy Set Of 60

Using the same design as the previous year, the 1987 Topps All-Star Glossy set includes 48 All-Star performers plus 12 potential superstars branded as "Hot Prospects". The card fronts are uncluttered, save the player's name found in very small print at the bottom. The set was available via a mail-in offer. Six subsets make up the 60-card set, with each subset being available for $1.00 plus six special offer cards that were found in wax packs.

1986 BASEBALL HIGHLIGHTS

6 OF 33 CARDS

Don Sutton earns his 300th victory

At Anaheim Stadium on June 18, 1986 Don became the 19th pitcher in history to win 300 games. He defeated the Rangers, 5-1, in fine Complete Game effort.

		MT	NR MT	EX
Complete Set:		14.00	10.50	5.50
Common Player:		.15	.11	.06
1	Don Mattingly	3.50	2.75	1.50
2	Tony Gwynn	.60	.45	.25
3	Gary Gaetti	.25	.20	.10
4	Glenn Davis	.30	.25	.12
5	Roger Clemens	.70	.50	.30
6	Dale Murphy	.90	.70	.35
7	Lou Whitaker	.30	.25	.12
8	Roger McDowell	.15	.11	.06
9	Cory Snyder	.50	.40	.20
10	Todd Worrell	.20	.15	.08
11	Gary Carter	.50	.40	.20
12	Eddie Murray	.60	.45	.25
13	Bob Knepper	.15	.11	.06
14	Harold Baines	.20	.15	.08
15	Jeff Reardon	.20	.15	.08
16	Joe Carter	.25	.20	.10
17	Dave Parker	.25	.20	.10
18	Wade Boggs	1.25	.90	.50
19	Danny Tartabull	.35	.25	.14
20	Jim Deshaies	.20	.15	.08
21	Rickey Henderson	.70	.50	.30
22	Rob Deer	.15	.11	.06
23	Ozzie Smith	.25	.20	.10
24	Dave Righetti	.25	.20	.10
25	Kent Hrbek	.30	.25	.12
26	Keith Hernandez	.40	.30	.15
27	Don Baylor	.15	.11	.06
28	Mike Schmidt	.90	.70	.35
29	Pete Incaviglia	.50	.40	.20
30	Barry Bonds	.50	.40	.20
31	George Brett	.90	.70	.35
32	Darryl Strawberry	.90	.70	.35
33	Mike Witt	.15	.11	.06
34	Kevin Bass	.15	.11	.06
35	Jesse Barfield	.20	.15	.08
36	Bob Ojeda	.15	.11	.06
37	Cal Ripken	.70	.50	.30
38	Vince Coleman	.25	.20	.10
39	Wally Joyner	1.75	1.25	.70
40	Robby Thompson	.20	.15	.08
41	Pete Rose	1.25	.90	.50
42	Jim Rice	.50	.40	.20
43	Tony Bernazard	.15	.11	.06
44	Eric Davis	1.00	.70	.40
45	George Bell	.50	.40	.20
46	Hubie Brooks	.15	.11	.06
47	Jack Morris	.30	.25	.12
48	Tim Raines	.50	.40	.20
49	Mark Eichhorn	.20	.15	.08
50	Kevin Mitchell	.25	.20	.10
51	Dwight Gooden	.80	.60	.30
52	Doug DeCinces	.15	.11	.06
53	Fernando Valenzuela	.35	.25	.14
54	Reggie Jackson	.70	.50	.30
55	Johnny Ray	.15	.11	.06
56	Mike Pagliarulo	.20	.15	.08
57	Kirby Puckett	.50	.40	.20
58	Lance Parrish	.30	.25	.12
59	Jose Canseco	3.00	2.25	1.25
60	Greg Mathews	.25	.20	.10

1987 Topps Baseball Highlights

The "Baseball Highlights" boxed set of 33 cards was prepared by Topps for distribution at stores in the Woolworth's chain. Each card measures 2-1/2" by 3-1/2" in size and features a memorable baseball event that occurred during the 1986 season. The glossy set sold for $1.99 in Woolworth's stores.

		MT	NR MT	EX
Complete Set:		5.00	3.75	2.00
Common Player:		.09	.07	.04
1	Steve Carlton	.30	.25	.12
2	Cecil Cooper	.12	.09	.05
3	Rickey Henderson	.35	.25	.14
4	Reggie Jackson	.30	.25	.12
5	Jim Rice	.25	.20	.10
6	Don Sutton	.20	.15	.08
7	Roger Clemens	.50	.40	.20
8	Mike Schmidt	.35	.25	.14
9	Jesse Barfield	.15	.11	.06
10	Wade Boggs	.70	.50	.30
11	Tim Raines	.30	.25	.12
12	Jose Canseco	1.00	.70	.40
13	Todd Worrell	.15	.11	.06
14	Dave Righetti	.15	.11	.06
15	Don Mattingly	1.25	.90	.50
16	Tony Gwynn	.35	.25	.14
17	Marty Barrett	.09	.07	.04
18	Mike Scott	.12	.09	.05
19	World Series Game #1 (Bruce Hurst)	.12	.09	.05
20	World Series Game #1 (Calvin Schiraldi)	.09	.07	.04
21	World Series Game #2 (Dwight Evans)	.12	.09	.05
22	World Series Game #2 (Dave Henderson)	.09	.07	.04
23	World Series Game #3 (Len Dykstra)	.12	.09	.05
24	World Series Game #3 (Bob Ojeda)	.09	.07	.04
25	World Series Game #4 (Gary Carter)	.30	.25	.12
26	World Series Game #4 (Ron Darling)	.15	.11	.06
27	Jim Rice	.30	.25	.12
28	Bruce Hurst	.09	.07	.04
29	World Series Game #6 (Darryl Strawberry)	.35	.25	.14
30	World Series Game #6 (Ray Knight)	.09	.07	.04
31	World Series Game #6 (Keith Hernandez)	.25	.20	.10
32	World Series Games #7 (Mets Celebrate)	.12	.09	.05
33	Ray Knight	.09	.07	.04

1987 Topps Box Panels

Offering baseball cards on retail boxes for a second

straight year, Topps reduced the size of the cards to 2-1/8" by 3". Four different wax pack boxes were available, each featuring two cards that were placed on the sides of the boxes. The card fronts are identical in design to the regular issue cards. The backs are printed in blue and yellow and carry a commentary imitating a newspaper format. The cards are numbered A through H.

		MT	NR MT	EX
Complete Panel Set:		5.00	3.75	2.00
Complete Singles Set:		2.00	1.50	.80
Common Panel:		.75	.60	.30
Common Single Player:		.15	.11	.06
	Panel	1.25	.90	.50
A	Don Baylor	.15	.11	.06
B	Steve Carlton	.30	.25	.12
	Panel	.75	.60	.30
C	Ron Cey	.15	.11	.06
D	Cecil Cooper	.15	.11	.06
	Panel	1.75	1.25	.70
E	Rickey Henderson	.40	.30	.15
F	Jim Rice	.25	.20	.10
	Panel	1.25	.90	.50
G	Don Sutton	.20	.15	.08
H	Dave Winfield	.30	.25	.12

1987 Topps Coins

For the first time since 1971, Topps issued a set of baseball "coins". Similar in design to the 1964 edition of Topps coins, the metal discs measure 1-1/2" in diameter. The aluminum coins were sold on a limited basis in retail outlets. Three coins and three sticks of gum were found in a pack. The coin fronts feature a full-color photo along with the player's name, team ans position in a white band at the bottom of the coin. Gold-colored rims are found for American League players; National League players have silver-colored rims. Backs are silver in color and carry the coin number, player's name and personal and statistical information.

		MT	NR MT	EX
Complete Set:		10.00	7.50	4.00
Common Player:		.15	.11	.06
1	Harold Baines	.15	.11	.06
2	Jesse Barfield	.15	.11	.06
3	George Bell	.20	.15	.08
4	Wade Boggs	.70	.50	.30
5	George Brett	.30	.25	.12
6	Jose Canseco	1.00	.70	.40
7	Joe Carter	.15	.11	.06
8	Roger Clemens	.40	.30	.15
9	Alvin Davis	.15	.11	.06
10	Rob Deer	.15	.11	.06
11	Kirk Gibson	.20	.15	.08
12	Rickey Henderson	.25	.20	.10
13	Kent Hrbek	.20	.15	.08
14	Pete Incaviglia	.20	.15	.08
15	Reggie Jackson	.25	.20	.10
16	Wally Joyner	.60	.45	.25
17	Don Mattingly	1.25	.90	.50
18	Jack Morris	.20	.15	.08

19	Eddie Murray	.25	.20	.10
20	Kirby Puckett	.30	.25	.12
21	Jim Rice	.25	.20	.10
22	Dave Righetti	.20	.15	.08
23	Cal Ripken	.25	.20	.10
24	Cory Snyder	.25	.20	.10
25	Danny Tartabull	.20	.15	.08
26	Dave Winfield	.25	.20	.10
27	Hubie Brooks	.15	.11	.06
28	Gary Carter	.25	.20	.10
29	Vince Coleman	.20	.15	.08
30	Eric Davis	.70	.50	.30
31	Glenn Davis	.15	.11	.06
32	Steve Garvey	.25	.20	.10
33	Dwight Gooden	.40	.30	.15
34	Tony Gwynn	.30	.25	.12
35	Von Hayes	.15	.11	.06
36	Keith Hernandez	.20	.15	.08
37	Dale Murphy	.30	.25	.12
38	Dave Parker	.20	.15	.08
39	Tony Pena	.15	.11	.06
40	Nolan Ryan	.25	.20	.10
41	Ryne Sandberg	.20	.15	.08
42	Steve Sax	.15	.11	.06
43	Mike Schmidt	.30	.25	.12
44	Mike Scott	.15	.11	.06
45	Ozzie Smith	.15	.11	.06
46	Darryl Strawberry	.40	.30	.15
47	Fernando Valenzuela	.20	.15	.08
48	Todd Worrell	.15	.11	.06

1987 Topps Gallery Of Champions

Designed as a tribute to the 1986 season's winners of baseball's most prestigious awards, the Gallery of Champions are metal "cards" that are one-quarter size replicas of the regular issue Topps cards. The bronze and silver sets were issued in leather-like velvet-lined display cases; the aluminum sets came cello-wrapped. Hobby dealers who purchased one bronze set or a 16-set case of aluminum "cards" received one free Jose Canseco pewter metal mini-card (value $60). The purchase of a silver set included five Canseco pewters. A 1953 Willie Mays bronze was given to dealers who brought cases of 1987 Topps Traded sets (value $10).

		MT	NR MT	EX
Complete Aluminum Set:		30.00	22.00	12.00
Complete Bronze Set:		175.00	131.00	70.00
Complete Silver Set:		700.00	525.00	280.00
(1a)	Jesse Barfield (aluminum)	.70	.50	.30
(1b)	Jesse Barfield (bronze)	7.50	5.75	3.00
(1c)	Jesse Barfield (silver)	20.00	15.00	8.00
(2a)	Wade Boggs (aluminum)	3.00	2.25	1.25
(2b)	Wade Boggs (bronze)	25.00	18.50	10.00
(2c)	Wade Boggs (silver)	125.00	94.00	50.00
(3a)	Jose Canseco (aluminum)	3.00	2.25	1.25
(3b)	Jose Canseco (bronze)	25.00	18.50	10.00
(3c)	Jose Canseco (silver)	125.00	94.00	50.00
(4a)	Joe Carter (aluminum)	.70	.50	.30
(4b)	Joe Carter (bronze)	7.50	5.75	3.00
(4c)	Joe Carter (silver)	20.00	15.00	8.00
(5a)	Roger Clemens (aluminum)	2.00	1.50	.80

		MT	NR MT	EX
(5b)	Roger Clemens (bronze)	20.00	15.00	8.00
(5c)	Roger Clemens (silver)	90.00	67.00	36.00
(6a)	Tony Gwynn (aluminum)	1.25	.90	.50
(6b)	Tony Gwynn (bronze)	12.00	9.00	4.75
(6c)	Tony Gwynn (silver)	50.00	37.00	20.00
(7a)	Don Mattingly (aluminum)	8.00	6.00	3.25
(7b)	Don Mattingly (bronze)	50.00	37.00	20.00
(7c)	Don Mattingly (silver)	200.00	150.00	80.00
(8a)	Tim Raines (aluminum)	1.00	.70	.40
(8b)	Tim Raines (bronze)	10.00	7.50	4.00
(8c)	Tim Raines (silver)	30.00	22.00	12.00
(9a)	Dave Righetti (aluminum)	1.00	.70	.40
(9b)	Dave Righetti (bronze)	10.00	7.50	4.00
(9c)	Dave Righetti (silver)	30.00	22.00	12.00
(10a)	Mike Schmidt (aluminum)	1.50	1.25	.60
(10b)	Mike Schmidt (bronze)	15.00	11.00	6.00
(10c)	Mike Schmidt (silver)	80.00	60.00	32.00
(11a)	Mike Scott (aluminum)	.70	.50	.30
(11b)	Mike Scott (bronze)	7.50	5.75	3.00
(11c)	Mike Scott (silver)	20.00	15.00	8.00
(12a)	Todd Worrell (aluminum)	.70	.50	.30
(12b)	Todd Worrell (bronze)	10.00	7.50	4.00
(12c)	Todd Worrell (silver)	20.00	15.00	8.00

1987 Topps Glossy Rookies

The 1987 Topps Glossy Rookies set of 22 cards was introduced with Topps' new 100-card "Jumbo Packs". Intended for sale in supermarkets, the jumbo packs contained one glossy card. Measuring the standard 2-1/2" by 3-1/2" size, the special insert cards feature the top rookies from the previous season.

		MT	NR MT	EX
	Complete Set:	10.00	7.50	4.00
	Common Player:	.20	.15	.08
1	Andy Allanson	.20	.15	.08
2	John Cangelosi	.20	.15	.08
3	Jose Canseco	3.00	2.25	1.25
4	Will Clark	1.50	1.25	.60
5	Mark Eichhorn	.40	.30	.15
6	Pete Incaviglia	.70	.50	.30
7	Wally Joyner	2.00	1.50	.80
8	Eric King	.30	.25	.12
9	Dave Magadan	.60	.45	.25
10	John Morris	.20	.15	.08
11	Juan Nieves	.40	.30	.15
12	Rafael Palmeiro	1.00	.70	.40
13	Billy Jo Robidoux	.20	.15	.08
14	Bruce Ruffin	.40	.30	.15
15	Ruben Sierra	1.25	.90	.50
16	Cory Snyder	.80	.60	.30
17	Kurt Stillwell	.60	.45	.25
18	Dale Sveum	.40	.30	.15
19	Danny Tartabull	.80	.60	.30
20	Andres Thomas	.40	.30	.15
21	Robby Thompson	.40	.30	.15
22	Todd Worrell	.40	.30	.15

Definitions for grading conditions are located in the Introduction of this price guide.

1987 Topps Mini League Leaders

Returning for 1987, the Topps "Major League Leaders" set was increased in size from 66 to 76 cards. The 2-1/8" by 3" cards feature wood grain borders that encompass a white-bordered full-color photo. The card backs are printed in yellow, orange and brown and list the player's official ranking based on his 1986 American or National League statistics. The players featured are those who finished the top five in their leagues' various batting and pitching statistics. The cards were sold in plastic-wrapped packs, seven cards plus a game card per pack.

		MT	NR MT	EX
	Complete Set:	6.00	4.50	2.50
	Common Player:	.09	.07	.04
1	Bob Horner	.20	.15	.08
2	Dale Murphy	.50	.40	.20
3	Lee Smith	.09	.07	.04
4	Eric Davis	.60	.45	.25
5	John Franco	.15	.11	.06
6	Dave Parker	.20	.15	.08
7	Kevin Bass	.09	.07	.04
8	Glenn Davis	.20	.15	.08
9	Bill Doran	.15	.11	.06
10	Bob Knepper	.09	.07	.04
11	Mike Scott	.20	.15	.08
12	Dave Smith	.09	.07	.04
13	Mariano Duncan	.09	.07	.04
14	Orel Hershiser	.30	.25	.12
15	Steve Sax	.20	.15	.08
16	Fernando Valenzuela	.25	.20	.10
17	Tim Raines	.30	.25	.12
18	Jeff Reardon	.15	.11	.06
19	Floyd Youmans	.09	.07	.04
20	Gary Carter	.30	.25	.12
21	Ron Darling	.20	.15	.08
22	Sid Fernandez	.15	.11	.06
23	Dwight Gooden	.60	.45	.25
24	Keith Hernandez	.25	.20	.10
25	Bob Ojeda	.09	.07	.04
26	Darryl Strawberry	.50	.40	.20
27	Steve Bedrosian	.15	.11	.06
28	Von Hayes	.15	.11	.06
29	Juan Samuel	.20	.15	.08
30	Mike Schmidt	.50	.40	.20
31	Rick Rhoden	.09	.07	.04
32	Vince Coleman	.20	.15	.08
33	Danny Cox	.09	.07	.04
34	Todd Worrell	.15	.11	.06
35	Tony Gwynn	.40	.30	.15
36	Mike Krukow	.09	.07	.04
37	Candy Maldonado	.09	.07	.04
38	Don Aase	.09	.07	.04
39	Eddie Murray	.40	.30	.15
40	Cal Ripken	.40	.30	.15
41	Wade Boggs	.80	.60	.30
42	Roger Clemens	.60	.45	.25
43	Bruce Hurst	.15	.11	.06
44	Jim Rice	.30	.25	.12
45	Wally Joyner	.80	.60	.30
46	Donnie Moore	.09	.07	.04
47	Gary Pettis	.09	.07	.04
48	Mike Witt	.09	.07	.04
49	John Cangelosi	.09	.07	.04

		MT	NR MT	EX
50	Tom Candiotti	.09	.07	.04
51	Joe Carter	.20	.15	.08
52	Pat Tabler	.09	.07	.04
53	Kirk Gibson	.25	.20	.10
54	Willie Hernandez	.09	.07	.04
55	Jack Morris	.25	.20	.10
56	Alan Trammell	.30	.25	.12
57	George Brett	.50	.40	.20
58	Willie Wilson	.15	.11	.06
59	Rob Deer	.09	.07	.04
60	Teddy Higuera	.15	.11	.06
61	Bert Blyleven	.15	.11	.06
62	Gary Gaetti	.20	.15	.08
63	Kirby Puckett	.35	.25	.14
64	Rickey Henderson	.40	.30	.15
65	Don Mattingly	1.25	.90	.50
66	Dennis Rasmussen	.15	.11	.06
67	Dave Righetti	.20	.15	.08
68	Jose Canseco	1.00	.70	.40
69	Dave Kingman	.15	.11	.06
70	Phil Bradley	.15	.11	.06
71	Mark Langston	.15	.11	.06
72	Pete O'Brien	.09	.07	.04
73	Jesse Barfield	.15	.11	.06
74	George Bell	.25	.20	.10
75	Tony Fernandez	.15	.11	.06
76	Tom Henke	.09	.07	.04
77	Checklist	.09	.07	.04

1987 Topps Stickers

For the seventh consecutive year, Topps issued stickers to be housed in a specially designed yearbook. The stickers, which measure 2-1/8" by 3", offer a full-color front with a peel-off back printed in blue ink on white stock. The sticker fronts feature either one full-size player picture or two half-size individual stickers. The sticker yearbook measures 9" by 10-3/4" and contains 36 glossy, magazine-style pages, all printed in full color. Mike Schmidt, 1986 National League MVP, is featured on the cover. The yearbook sold in retail outlets for 35¢, while stickers were sold five in a pack for 25¢. The number in parentheses in the following checklist is the sticker number the player shares the sticker with.

		MT	NR MT	EX
Complete Set:		18.00	13.50	7.25
Common Player:		.03	.02	.01
Sticker Album:		.70	.50	.30
1	1986 Highlights (Jim Deshaies) (172)	.04	.03	.02
2	1986 Highlights (Roger Clemens) (175)	.15	.11	.06
3	1986 Highlights (Roger Clemens) (176)	.15	.11	.06
4	1986 Highlights (Dwight Evans) (177)	.06	.05	.02
5	1986 Highlights (Dwight Gooden) (178)	.15	.11	.06
6	1986 Highlights (Dwight Gooden) (180)	.15	.11	.06
7	1986 Highlights (Dave Lopes) (181)	.03	.02	.01
8	1986 Highlights (Dave Righetti) (182)	.06	.05	.02

		MT	NR MT	EX
9	1986 Highlights (Dave Righetti) (183)	.10	.08	.04
10	1986 Highlights (Ruben Sierra) (185)	.15	.11	.06
11	1986 Highlights (Todd Worrell) (186)	.06	.05	.02
12	1986 Highlights (Todd Worrell) (187)	.06	.05	.02
13	N.L. Championship Series (Lenny Dykstra)	.06	.05	.02
14	N.L. Championship Series (Gary Carter)	.08	.06	.03
15	N.L. Championship Series (Mike Scott)	.06	.05	.02
16	A.L. Championship Series (Gary Pettis)	.03	.02	.01
17	A.L. Championship Series (Jim Rice)	.08	.06	.03
18	A.L. Championship Series (Bruce Hurst)	.04	.03	.02
19	1986 World Series (Bruce Hurst)	.04	.03	.02
20	1986 World Series (Wade Boggs)	.15	.11	.06
21	1986 World Series (Lenny Dykstra)	.06	.05	.02
22	1986 World Series (Gary Carter)	.08	.06	.03
23	1986 World Series (Dave Henderson)	.04	.03	.02
24	1986 World Series (Howard Johnson)	.04	.03	.02
25	1986 World Series (Mets Celebrate)	.08	.06	.03
26	Glenn Davis	.15	.11	.06
27	Nolan Ryan (188)	.10	.08	.04
28	Charlie Kerfeld (189)	.03	.02	.01
29	Jose Cruz (190)	.04	.03	.02
30	Phil Garner (191)	.06	.05	.02
31	Bill Doran (192)	.06	.05	.02
32	Bob Knepper (195)	.03	.02	.01
33	Denny Walling (196)	.10	.08	.04
34	Kevin Bass (197)	.04	.03	.02
35	Mike Scott	.10	.08	.04
36	Dale Murphy	.25	.20	.10
37	Paul Assenmacher (198)	.06	.05	.02
38	Ken Oberkfell (200)	.06	.05	.02
39	Andres Thomas (201)	.08	.06	.03
40	Gene Garber (202)	.03	.02	.01
41	Bob Horner	.08	.06	.03
42	Rafael Ramirez (203)	.03	.02	.01
43	Rick Mahler (204)	.03	.02	.01
44	Omar Moreno (205)	.03	.02	.01
45	Dave Palmer (206)	.03	.02	.01
46	Ozzie Smith	.12	.09	.05
47	Bob Forsch (207)	.03	.02	.01
48	Willie McGee (209)	.06	.05	.02
49	Tom Herr (210)	.06	.05	.02
50	Vince Coleman (211)	.08	.06	.03
51	Andy Van Slyke (212)	.06	.05	.02
52	Jack Clark (215)	.08	.06	.03
53	John Tudor (216)	.04	.03	.02
54	Terry Pendleton (217)	.03	.02	.01
55	Todd Worrell	.10	.08	.04
56	Lee Smith	.06	.05	.02
57	Leon Durham (218)	.03	.02	.01
58	Jerry Mumphrey (219)	.06	.05	.02
59	Shawon Dunston (220)	.06	.05	.02
60	Scott Sanderson (221)	.06	.05	.02
61	Ryne Sandberg	.15	.11	.06
62	Gary Matthews (222)	.04	.03	.02
63	Dennis Eckersley (225)	.06	.05	.02
64	Jody Davis (226)	.06	.05	.02
65	Keith Moreland (227)	.04	.03	.02
66	Mike Marshall (228)	.06	.05	.02
67	Bill Madlock (229)	.06	.05	.02
68	Greg Brock (230)	.04	.03	.02
69	Pedro Guerrero (231)	.08	.06	.03
70	Steve Sax	.12	.09	.05
71	Rick Honeycutt (232)	.03	.02	.01
72	Franklin Stubbs (235)	.03	.02	.01
73	Mike Scioscia (236)	.10	.08	.04
74	Mariano Duncan (237)	.03	.02	.01
75	Fernando Valenzuela	.15	.11	.06
76	Hubie Brooks	.06	.05	.02
77	Andre Dawson (238)	.08	.06	.03
78	Tim Burke (240)	.04	.03	.02
79	Floyd Youmans (241)	.03	.02	.01
80	Tim Wallach (242)	.04	.03	.02
81	Jeff Reardon (243)	.06	.05	.02
82	Mitch Webster (244)	.15	.11	.06
83	Bryn Smith (245)	.03	.02	.01
84	Andres Galarraga (246)	.12	.09	.05
85	Tim Raines	.15	.11	.06
86	Chris Brown	.08	.06	.03

		MT	NR MT	EX
87	Bob Brenly (247)	.03	.02	.01
88	Will Clark (249)	.25	.20	.10
89	Scott Garrelts (250)	.04	.03	.02
90	Jeffrey Leonard (251)	.06	.05	.02
91	Robby Thompson (252)	.06	.05	.02
92	Mike Krukow (255)	.03	.02	.01
93	Danny Gladden (256)	.03	.02	.01
94	Candy Maldonado (257)	.04	.03	.02
95	Chili Davis	.04	.03	.02
96	Dwight Gooden	.30	.25	.12
97	Sid Fernandez (258)	.04	.03	.02
98	Len Dykstra (259)	.06	.05	.02
99	Bob Ojeda (260)	.04	.03	.02
100	Wally Backman (261)	.04	.03	.02
101	Gary Carter	.15	.11	.06
102	Keith Hernandez (262)	.10	.08	.04
103	Darryl Strawberry (265)	.15	.11	.06
104	Roger McDowell (266)	.08	.06	.03
105	Ron Darling (267)	.08	.06	.03
106	Tony Gwynn	.20	.15	.08
107	Dave Dravecky (268)	.04	.03	.02
108	Terry Kennedy (269)	.08	.06	.03
109	Rich Gossage (270)	.10	.08	.04
110	Garry Templeton (271)	.04	.03	.02
111	Lance McCullers (272)	.04	.03	.02
112	Eric Show (275)	.04	.03	.02
113	John Kruk (276)	.12	.09	.05
114	Tim Flannery (277)	.06	.05	.02
115	Steve Garvey	.15	.11	.06
116	Mike Schmidt	.25	.20	.10
117	Glenn Wilson (278)	.06	.05	.02
118	Kent Tekulve (280)	.06	.05	.02
119	Gary Redus (281)	.08	.06	.03
120	Shane Rawley (282)	.03	.02	.01
121	Von Hayes	.06	.05	.02
122	Don Carman (283)	.04	.03	.02
123	Bruce Ruffin (285)	.04	.03	.02
124	Steve Bedrosian (286)	.06	.05	.02
125	Juan Samuel (287)	.06	.05	.02
126	Sid Bream (288)	.06	.05	.02
127	Cecilio Guante (289)	.03	.02	.01
128	Rick Reuschel (290)	.04	.03	.02
129	Tony Pena (291)	.04	.03	.02
130	Rick Rhoden	.06	.05	.02
131	Barry Bonds (292)	.10	.08	.04
132	Joe Orsulak (295)	.03	.02	.01
133	Jim Morrison (296)	.12	.09	.05
134	R.J. Reynolds (297)	.04	.03	.02
135	Johnny Ray	.06	.05	.02
136	Eric Davis	.30	.25	.12
137	Tom Browning (298)	.10	.08	.04
138	John Franco (300)	.06	.05	.02
139	Pete Rose (301)	.20	.15	.08
140	Bill Gullickson (302)	.04	.03	.02
141	Ron Oester (303)	.04	.03	.02
142	Bo Diaz (304)	.40	.30	.15
143	Buddy Bell (305)	.04	.03	.02
144	Eddie Milner (306)	.08	.06	.03
145	Dave Parker	.10	.08	.04
146	Kirby Puckett	.35	.25	.14
147	Rickey Henderson	.40	.30	.15
148	Wade Boggs	.60	.45	.25
149	Lance Parrish	.25	.20	.10
150	Wally Joyner	.70	.50	.30
151	Cal Ripken	.40	.30	.15
152	Dave Winfield	.30	.25	.12
153	Lou Whitaker	.25	.20	.10
154	Roger Clemens	.50	.40	.20
155	Tony Gwynn	.40	.30	.15
156	Ryne Sandberg	.25	.20	.10
157	Keith Hernandez	.25	.20	.10
158	Gary Carter	.30	.25	.12
159	Darryl Strawberry	.50	.40	.20
160	Mike Schmidt	.40	.30	.15
161	Dale Murphy	.40	.30	.15
162	Ozzie Smith	.20	.15	.08
163	Dwight Gooden	.50	.40	.20
164	Jose Canseco	.80	.60	.30
165	Curt Young (307)	.04	.03	.02
166	Alfredo Griffin (308)	.12	.09	.05
167	Dave Stewart (309)	.06	.05	.02
168	Mike Davis (310)	.06	.05	.02
169	Bruce Bochte (311)	.03	.02	.01
170	Dwayne Murphy (312)	.04	.03	.02
171	Carney Lansford (313)	.20	.15	.08
172	Joaquin Andujar (1)	.04	.03	.02
173	Dave Kingman	.08	.06	.03
174	Wally Joyner	.40	.30	.15
175	Gary Pettis (2)	.15	.11	.06
176	Dick Schofield (3)	.15	.11	.06
177	Donnie Moore (4)	.06	.05	.02

		MT	NR MT	EX
178	Brian Downing (5)	.15	.11	.06
179	Mike Witt	.06	.05	.02
180	Bob Boone (6)	.15	.11	.06
181	Kirk McCaskill (7)	.03	.02	.01
182	Doug DeCinces (8)	.06	.05	.02
183	Don Sutton (9)	.10	.08	.04
184	Jessie Barfield	.10	.08	.04
185	Tom Henke (10)	.15	.11	.06
186	Willie Upshaw (11)	.06	.05	.02
187	Mark Eichhorn (12)	.06	.05	.02
188	Damaso Garcia (27)	.10	.08	.04
189	Jim Clancy (28)	.03	.02	.01
190	Lloyd Moseby (29)	.04	.03	.02
191	Tony Fernandez (30)	.06	.05	.02
192	Jimmy Key (31)	.06	.05	.02
193	George Bell	.20	.15	.08
194	Rob Deer	.06	.05	.02
195	Mark Clear (32)	.03	.02	.01
196	Robin Yount (33)	.10	.08	.04
197	Jim Gantner (34)	.04	.03	.02
198	Cecil Cooper (37)	.06	.05	.02
199	Teddy Higuera (38)	.08	.06	.03
200	Paul Molitor (38)	.08	.06	.03
201	Dan Plesac (39)	.08	.06	.03
202	Billy Jo Robidoux (40)	.03	.02	.01
203	Earnie Riles (42)	.03	.02	.01
204	Ken Schrom (43)	.03	.02	.01
205	Pat Tabler (44)	.03	.02	.01
206	Mel Hall (45)	.03	.02	.01
207	Tony Bernazard (47)	.03	.02	.01
208	Joe Carter	.10	.08	.04
209	Ernie Camacho (48)	.06	.05	.02
210	Julio Franco (49)	.06	.05	.02
211	Tom Candiotti (50)	.08	.06	.03
212	Brook Jacoby (51)	.06	.05	.02
213	Cory Snyder	.30	.25	.12
214	Jim Presley	.08	.06	.03
215	Mike Moore (52)	.08	.06	.03
216	Harold Reynolds (53)	.04	.03	.02
217	Scott Bradley (54)	.03	.02	.01
218	Matt Young (57)	.03	.02	.01
219	Mark Langston (58)	.06	.05	.02
220	Alvin Davis (59)	.06	.05	.02
221	Phil Bradley (60)	.06	.05	.02
222	Ken Phelps (62)	.04	.03	.02
223	Danny Tartabull	.20	.15	.08
224	Eddie Murray	.20	.15	.08
225	Rick Dempsey (63)	.06	.05	.02
226	Fred Lynn (64)	.06	.05	.02
227	Mike Boddicker (65)	.04	.03	.02
228	Don Aase (66)	.06	.05	.02
229	Larry Sheets (67)	.06	.05	.02
230	Storm Davis (68)	.04	.03	.02
231	Lee Lacy (69)	.08	.06	.03
232	Jim Traber (71)	.03	.02	.01
233	Cal Ripken	.20	.15	.08
234	Larry Parrish	.06	.05	.02
235	Gary Ward (72)	.03	.02	.01
236	Pete Incaviglia (73)	.10	.08	.04
237	Scott Fletcher (74)	.03	.02	.01
238	Greg Harris (77)	.08	.06	.03
239	Pete O'Brien	.06	.05	.02
240	Charlie Hough (78)	.04	.03	.02
241	Don Slaught (79)	.03	.02	.01
242	Steve Buechele (80)	.04	.03	.02
243	Oddibe McDowell (81)	.06	.05	.02
244	Roger Clemens (82)	.15	.11	.06
245	Bob Stanley (83)	.03	.02	.01
246	Tom Seaver (84)	.12	.09	.05
247	Rich Gedman (87)	.03	.02	.01
248	Jim Rice	.15	.11	.06
249	Dennis Boyd (88)	.25	.20	.10
250	Bill Buckner (89)	.04	.03	.02
251	Dwight Evans (90)	.06	.05	.02
252	Don Baylor (91)	.06	.05	.02
253	Wade Boggs	.40	.30	.15
254	George Brett	.25	.20	.10
255	Steve Farr (92)	.03	.02	.01
256	Jim Sundberg (93)	.03	.02	.01
257	Dan Quisenberry (94)	.04	.03	.02
258	Charlie Leibrandt (97)	.04	.03	.02
259	Argenis Salazar (98)	.06	.05	.02
260	Frank White (99)	.04	.03	.02
261	Willie Wilson (100)	.04	.03	.02
262	Lonnie Smith (102)	.10	.08	.04
263	Steve Balboni	.04	.03	.02
264	Darrell Evans	.06	.05	.02
265	Johnny Grubb (103)	.15	.11	.06
266	Jack Morris (104)	.08	.06	.03
267	Lou Whitaker (105)	.08	.06	.03
268	Chet Lemon (107)	.04	.03	.02

		MT	NR MT	EX
269	Lance Parrish (108)	.08	.06	.03
270	Alan Trammell (109)	.10	.08	.04
271	Darnell Coles (110)	.04	.03	.02
272	Willie Hernandez (111)	.04	.03	.02
273	Kirk Gibson	.15	.11	.06
274	Kirby Puckett	.20	.15	.08
275	Mike Smithson (112)	.04	.03	.02
276	Mickey Hatcher (113)	.12	.09	.05
277	Frank Viola (114)	.06	.05	.02
278	Bert Blyleven (117)	.06	.05	.02
279	Gary Gaetti	.10	.08	.04
280	Tom Brunansky (118)	.06	.05	.02
281	Kent Hrbek (119)	.08	.06	.03
282	Roy Smalley (120)	.03	.02	.01
283	Greg Gagne (122)	.04	.03	.02
284	Harold Baines	.10	.08	.04
285	Ron Hassey (123)	.04	.03	.02
286	Floyd Bannister (124)	.06	.05	.02
287	Ozzie Guillen (125)	.06	.05	.02
288	Carlton Fisk (126)	.06	.05	.02
289	Tim Hulett (127)	.03	.02	.01
290	Joe Cowley (128)	.04	.03	.02
291	Greg Walker (129)	.04	.03	.02
292	Neil Allen (131)	.10	.08	.04
293	John Cangelosi	.04	.03	.02
294	Don Mattingly	.90	.70	.35
295	Mike Easler (132)	.03	.02	.01
296	Rickey Henderson (133)	.12	.09	.05
297	Dan Pasqua (134)	.04	.03	.02
298	Dave Winfield (137)	.10	.08	.04
299	Dave Righetti	.12	.09	.05
300	Mike Pagliarulo (138)	.06	.05	.02
301	Ron Guidry (139)	.20	.15	.08
302	Willie Randolph (140)	.04	.03	.02
303	Dennis Rasmussen (141)	.04	.03	.02
304	Jose Canseco (142)	.40	.30	.15
305	Andres Thomas (143)	.04	.03	.02
306	Danny Tartabull (144)	.08	.06	.03
307	Robby Thompson (165)	.04	.03	.02
308	Pete Incaviglia, Cory Snyder (166)	.12	.09	.05
309	Dale Sveum (167)	.06	.05	.02
310	Todd Worrell (168)	.06	.05	.02
311	Andy Allanson (169)	.03	.02	.01
312	Bruce Ruffin (170)	.04	.03	.02
313	Wally Joyner (171)	.20	.15	.08

1987 Topps Traded

The Topps Traded set consists of 132 cards as have all Traded sets issued by Topps since 1981. The cards measure the standard 2 1/2" by 3 1/2" and are identical in design to the regular edition set. The purpose of the set is to update player trades and feature rookies not included in the regular issue. As they had done the previous three years, Topps produced a glossy-coated "Tiffany" edition of the Traded set. The Tiffany edition cards are valued at two to three times greater than the regular Traded cards.

		MT	NR MT	EX
Complete Set:		12.00	9.00	4.75
Common Player:		.06	.05	.02
1T	Bill Almon	.06	.05	.02
2T	Scott Bankhead	.08	.06	.03
3T	Eric Bell(FC)	.15	.11	.06

		MT	NR MT	EX
4T	Juan Beniquez	.06	.05	.02
5T	Juan Berenguer	.06	.05	.02
6T	Greg Booker	.06	.05	.02
7T	Thad Bosley	.06	.05	.02
8T	Larry Bowa	.10	.08	.04
9T	Greg Brock	.10	.08	.04
10T	Bob Brower(FC)	.15	.11	.06
11T	Jerry Browne(FC)	.30	.25	.12
12T	Ralph Bryant(FC)	.12	.09	.05
13T	DeWayne Buice(FC)	.15	.11	.06
14T	Ellis Burks(FC)	1.50	1.25	.60
15T	Ivan Calderon	.12	.09	.05
16T	Jeff Calhoun	.06	.05	.02
17T	Casey Candaele(FC)	.10	.08	.04
18T	John Cangelosi	.06	.05	.02
19T	Steve Carlton	.30	.25	.12
20T	Juan Castillo(FC)	.06	.05	.02
21T	Rick Cerone	.06	.05	.02
22T	Ron Cey	.10	.08	.04
23T	John Christensen	.06	.05	.02
24T	Dave Cone(FC)	1.75	1.25	.70
25T	Chuck Crim(FC)	.15	.11	.06
26T	Storm Davis	.06	.05	.02
27T	Andre Dawson	.40	.30	.15
28T	Rick Dempsey	.08	.06	.03
29T	Doug Drabek	.10	.08	.04
30T	Mike Dunne	.40	.30	.15
31T	Dennis Eckersley	.12	.09	.05
32T	Lee Elia	.06	.05	.02
33T	Brian Fisher	.10	.08	.04
34T	Terry Francona	.06	.05	.02
35T	Willie Fraser(FC)	.15	.11	.06
36T	Billy Gardner	.06	.05	.02
37T	Ken Gerhart(FC)	.15	.11	.06
38T	Danny Gladden	.06	.05	.02
39T	Jim Gott	.06	.05	.02
40T	Cecilio Guante	.06	.05	.02
41T	Albert Hall	.06	.05	.02
42T	Terry Harper	.06	.05	.02
43T	Mickey Hatcher	.06	.05	.02
44T	Brad Havens	.06	.05	.02
45T	Neal Heaton	.06	.05	.02
46T	Mike Henneman(FC)	.30	.25	.12
47T	Donnie Hill	.06	.05	.02
48T	Guy Hoffman	.06	.05	.02
49T	Brian Holton(FC)	.15	.11	.06
50T	Charles Hudson	.06	.05	.02
51T	Danny Jackson(FC)	.30	.25	.12
52T	Reggie Jackson	.40	.30	.15
53T	Chris James(FC)	.40	.30	.15
54T	Dion James	.10	.08	.04
55T	Stan Jefferson(FC)	.20	.15	.08
56T	Joe Johnson(FC)	.08	.06	.03
57T	Terry Kennedy	.08	.06	.03
58T	Mike Kingery	.08	.06	.03
59T	Ray Knight	.10	.08	.04
60T	Gene Larkin(FC)	.25	.20	.10
61T	Mike LaValliere	.10	.08	.04
62T	Jack Lazorko	.06	.05	.02
63T	Terry Leach	.06	.05	.02
64T	Tim Leary	.06	.05	.02
65T	Jim Lindeman(FC)	.15	.11	.06
66T	Steve Lombardozzi(FC)	.06	.05	.02
67T	Bill Long(FC)	.20	.15	.08
68T	Barry Lyons(FC)	.15	.11	.06
69T	Shane Mack	.20	.15	.08
70T	Greg Maddux(FC)	.60	.45	.25
71T	Bill Madlock	.15	.11	.06
72T	Joe Magrane(FC)	.90	.70	.35
73T	Dave Martinez(FC)	.25	.20	.10
74T	Fred McGriff(FC)	2.00	1.50	.80
75T	Mark McLemore(FC)	.10	.08	.04
76T	Kevin McReynolds(FC)	.60	.45	.25
77T	Dave Meads(FC)	.15	.11	.06
78T	Eddie Milner	.06	.05	.02
79T	Greg Minton	.06	.05	.02
80T	John Mitchell(FC)	.15	.11	.06
81T	Kevin Mitchell	1.25	.90	.50
82T	Charlie Moore	.06	.05	.02
83T	Jeff Musselman(FC)	.25	.20	.10
84T	Gene Nelson	.06	.05	.02
85T	Graig Nettles	.12	.09	.05
86T	Al Newman	.06	.05	.02
87T	Reid Nichols	.06	.05	.02
88T	Tom Niedenfuer	.08	.06	.03
89T	Joe Niekro	.10	.08	.04
90T	Tom Nieto	.06	.05	.02
91T	Matt Nokes(FC)	.70	.50	.30
92T	Dickie Noles	.06	.05	.02
93T	Pat Pacillo	.15	.11	.06
94T	Lance Parrish	.20	.15	.08

		MT	NR MT	EX
95T	Tony Pena	.10	.08	.04
96T	Luis Polonia(FC)	.30	.25	.12
97T	Randy Ready	.06	.05	.02
98T	Jeff Reardon	.12	.09	.05
99T	Gary Redus	.08	.06	.03
100T	Jeff Reed	.06	.05	.02
101T	Rick Rhoden	.10	.08	.04
102T	Cal Ripken, Sr.	.06	.05	.02
103T	Wally Ritchie(FC)	.15	.11	.06
104T	Jeff Robinson(FC)	.40	.30	.15
105T	Gary Roenicke	.06	.05	.02
106T	Jerry Royster	.06	.05	.02
107T	Mark Salas	.06	.05	.02
108T	Luis Salazar	.06	.05	.02
109T	Benny Santiago(FC)	1.25	.90	.50
110T	Dave Schmidt	.08	.06	.03
111T	Kevin Seitzer(FC)	1.00	.70	.40
112T	John Shelby	.06	.05	.02
113T	Steve Shields(FC)	.08	.06	.03
114T	John Smiley(FC)	.40	.30	.15
115T	Chris Speier	.06	.05	.02
116T	Mike Stanley(FC)	.20	.15	.08
117T	Terry Steinbach(FC)	.70	.50	.30
118T	Les Straker(FC)	.20	.15	.08
119T	Jim Sundberg	.08	.06	.03
120T	Danny Tartabull	.35	.25	.14
121T	Tom Trebelhorn	.08	.06	.03
122T	Dave Valle(FC)	.12	.09	.05
123T	Ed Vande Berg	.06	.05	.02
124T	Andy Van Slyke	.20	.15	.08
125T	Gary Ward	.06	.05	.02
126T	Alan Wiggins	.06	.05	.02
127T	Bill Wilkinson(FC)	.15	.11	.06
128T	Frank Williams	.08	.06	.03
129T	Matt Williams(FC)	2.00	1.50	.80
130T	Jim Winn	.06	.05	.02
131T	Matt Young	.06	.05	.02
132T	Checklist 1T-132T	.06	.05	.02

1988 Topps

The 1988 Topps set features a clean, attractive design that should prove to be very popular with collectors for many years to come. The full-color player photo is surrounded by a thin yellow frame which is encompassed by a white border. The player's name appears in the lower right corner in a colored band which appears to wrap around the player photo. The player's team nickname is located in large letters at the top of the card. The Topps logo is placed in the lower left corner of the card. The card backs feature black print on orange and gray stock and includes the usual player personal and career statistics. Many of the cards contain a new feature entitled "This Way To The Clubhouse", which explains how the player joined his current team, be it by trade, free agency, etc. The 792-card set includes a number of special subsets including "Future Stars", "Turn Back The Clock", All-Star teams, All-Star rookie selections, and Record Breakers. All cards measure 2-1/2" by 3-1/2". For the fifth consecutive year, Topps issued a glossy "Tiffany" edition of its 792-card regular-issue set. The Tiffany cards have a value of 3-4 times greater than the same card in the regular issue. The Tiffany edition could be purchased by collectors directly from Topps for $99. The company

placed ads for the Tiffany set in publications such as USA Today and The Sporting News.

		MT	NR MT	EX
Complete Set:		25.00	20.00	10.00
Common Player:		.04	.03	.02
1	'87 Record Breakers (Vince Coleman)	.08	.06	.03
2	'87 Record Breakers (Don Mattingly)	.60	.45	.25
3a	'87 Record Breakers (Mark McGwire) (white triangle by left foot)	.70	.50	.30
3b	'87 Record Breakers (Mark McGwire) (no triangle by left foot)	.50	.40	.20
4a	'87 Record Breakers (Eddie Murray) (no mention of record on front)	.10	.08	.04
4b	'87 Record Breakers (Eddie Murray) (record stated on card front)	2.00	1.50	.80
5	'87 Record Breakers (Joe Niekro, Phil Niekro)	.10	.08	.04
6	'87 Record Breakers (Nolan Ryan)	.10	.08	.04
7	'87 Record Breakers (Benito Santiago)	.15	.11	.06
8	Kevin Elster(FC)	.25	.20	.10
9	Andy Hawkins	.04	.03	.02
10	Ryne Sandberg	.15	.11	.06
11	Mike Young	.04	.03	.02
12	Bill Schroeder	.04	.03	.02
13	Andres Thomas	.06	.05	.02
14	Sparky Anderson	.06	.05	.02
15	Chili Davis	.06	.05	.02
16	Kirk McCaskill	.06	.05	.02
17	Ron Oester	.04	.03	.02
18a	*Al Leiter* (no "NY" on shirt, photo actually Steve George)(FC)	1.00	.70	.40
18b	*Al Leiter* ("NY" on shirt, correct photo)(FC)	.80	.60	.30
19	*Mark Davidson*(FC)	.12	.09	.05
20	Kevin Gross	.06	.05	.02
21	Red Sox Leaders (Wade Boggs, Spike Owen)	.15	.11	.06
22	Greg Swindell	.15	.11	.06
23	Ken Landreaux	.04	.03	.02
24	Jim Deshaies	.06	.05	.02
25	Andres Galarraga	.12	.09	.05
26	Mitch Williams	.06	.05	.02
27	R.J. Reynolds	.04	.03	.02
28	*Jose Nunez*(FC)	.20	.15	.08
29	Argenis Salazar	.04	.03	.02
30	Sid Fernandez	.08	.06	.03
31	Bruce Bochy	.04	.03	.02
32	Mike Morgan	.04	.03	.02
33	Rob Deer	.06	.05	.02
34	Ricky Horton	.06	.05	.02
35	Harold Baines	.10	.08	.04
36	Jamie Moyer	.06	.05	.02
37	Ed Romero	.04	.03	.02
38	Jeff Calhoun	.04	.03	.02
39	Gerald Perry	.08	.06	.03
40	Orel Hershiser	.20	.15	.08
41	Bob Melvin	.04	.03	.02
42	*Bill Landrum*(FC)	.10	.08	.04
43	Dick Schofield	.04	.03	.02
44	Lou Piniella	.06	.05	.02
45	Kent Hrbek	.12	.09	.05
46	Darnell Coles	.06	.05	.02
47	Joaquin Andujar	.06	.05	.02
48	Alan Ashby	.04	.03	.02
49	Dave Clark(FC)	.10	.08	.04
50	Hubie Brooks	.08	.06	.03
51	Orioles Leaders (Eddie Murray, Cal Ripken)	.12	.09	.05
52	Don Robinson	.06	.05	.02
53	Curt Wilkerson	.04	.03	.02
54	Jim Clancy	.06	.05	.02
55	Phil Bradley	.08	.06	.03
56	Ed Hearn	.04	.03	.02
57	*Tim Crews*(FC)	.15	.11	.06
58	Dave Magadan	.10	.08	.04
59	Danny Cox	.06	.05	.02
60	Rickey Henderson	.25	.20	.10
61	*Mark Knudson*(FC)	.10	.08	.04
62	Jeff Hamilton	.08	.06	.03
63	Jimmy Jones(FC)	.10	.08	.04
64	*Ken Caminiti*(FC)	.25	.20	.10
65	Leon Durham	.06	.05	.02
66	Shane Rawley	.06	.05	.02
67	Ken Oberkfell	.04	.03	.02
68	Dave Dravecky	.06	.05	.02
69	*Mike Hart*(FC)	.10	.08	.04

#	Player	MT	NR MT	EX
70	Roger Clemens	.50	.40	.20
71	Gary Pettis	.04	.03	.02
72	Dennis Eckersley	.10	.08	.04
73	Randy Bush	.04	.03	.02
74	Tom Lasorda	.06	.05	.02
75	Joe Carter	.10	.08	.04
76	Denny Martinez	.04	.03	.02
77	Tom O'Malley	.04	.03	.02
78	Dan Petry	.06	.05	.02
79	Ernie Whitt	.06	.05	.02
80	Mark Langston	.10	.08	.04
81	Reds Leaders (John Franco, Ron Robinson)	.06	.05	.02
82	*Darrel Akerfelds*(FC)	.12	.09	.05
83	Jose Oquendo	.04	.03	.02
84	Cecilio Guante	.04	.03	.02
85	Howard Johnson	.08	.06	.03
86	Ron Karkovice	.04	.03	.02
87	Mike Mason	.04	.03	.02
88	Earnie Riles	.04	.03	.02
89	*Gary Thurman*(FC)	.20	.15	.08
90	Dale Murphy	.30	.25	.12
91	*Joey Cora*(FC)	.12	.09	.05
92	Len Matuszek	.04	.03	.02
93	Bob Sebra	.04	.03	.02
94	*Chuck Jackson*(FC)	.15	.11	.06
95	Lance Parrish	.12	.09	.05
96	*Todd Benzinger*(FC)	.30	.25	.12
97	Scott Garrelts	.04	.03	.02
98	*Rene Gonzales*(FC)	.15	.11	.06
99	Chuck Finley	.06	.05	.02
100	Jack Clark	.12	.09	.05
101	Allan Anderson	.06	.05	.02
102	Barry Larkin	.35	.25	.14
103	Curt Young	.06	.05	.02
104	Dick Williams	.04	.03	.02
105	Jesse Orosco	.06	.05	.02
106	*Jim Walewander*(FC)	.12	.09	.05
107	Scott Bailes	.06	.05	.02
108	Steve Lyons	.04	.03	.02
109	Joel Skinner	.04	.03	.02
110	Teddy Higuera	.08	.06	.03
111	Expos Leaders (Hubie Brooks, Vance Law)	.06	.05	.02
112	*Les Lancaster*(FC)	.15	.11	.06
113	Kelly Gruber	.04	.03	.02
114	Jeff Russell	.04	.03	.02
115	Johnny Ray	.06	.05	.02
116	Jerry Don Gleaton	.04	.03	.02
117	*James Steels*(FC)	.10	.08	.04
118	Bob Welch	.08	.06	.03
119	*Robbie Wine*(FC)	.12	.09	.05
120	Kirby Puckett	.40	.30	.15
121	Checklist 1-132	.04	.03	.02
122	Tony Bernazard	.04	.03	.02
123	Tom Candiotti	.04	.03	.02
124	Ray Knight	.06	.05	.02
125	Bruce Hurst	.08	.06	.03
126	Steve Jeltz	.04	.03	.02
127	Jim Gott	.04	.03	.02
128	Johnny Grubb	.04	.03	.02
129	Greg Minton	.04	.03	.02
130	Buddy Bell	.08	.06	.03
131	Don Schulze	.04	.03	.02
132	Donnie Hill	.04	.03	.02
133	Greg Mathews	.06	.05	.02
134	Chuck Tanner	.04	.03	.02
135	Dennis Rasmussen	.08	.06	.03
136	Brian Dayett	.04	.03	.02
137	Chris Bosio	.06	.05	.02
138	Mitch Webster	.06	.05	.02
139	Jerry Browne	.06	.05	.02
140	Jesse Barfield	.10	.08	.04
141	Royals Leaders (George Brett, Bret Saberhagen)	.12	.09	.05
142	Andy Van Slyke	.10	.08	.04
143	Mickey Tettleton	.04	.03	.02
144	*Don Gordon*(FC)	.08	.06	.03
145	Bill Madlock	.08	.06	.03
146	*Donell Nixon*(FC)	.15	.11	.06
147	Bill Buckner	.08	.06	.03
148	Carmelo Martinez	.06	.05	.02
149	Ken Howell	.04	.03	.02
150	Eric Davis	.60	.45	.25
151	Bob Knepper	.06	.05	.02
152	*Jody Reed*(FC)	.40	.30	.15
153	John Habyan	.04	.03	.02
154	Jeff Stone	.04	.03	.02
155	Bruce Sutter	.10	.08	.04
156	Gary Matthews	.06	.05	.02
157	Atlee Hammaker	.04	.03	.02
158	Tim Hulett	.04	.03	.02
159	*Brad Arnsberg*(FC)	.12	.09	.05
160	Willie McGee	.10	.08	.04
161	Bryn Smith	.06	.05	.02
162	Mark McLemore	.06	.05	.02
163	Dale Mohorcic	.04	.03	.02
164	Dave Johnson	.06	.05	.02
165	Robin Yount	.20	.15	.08
166	*Rick Rodriguez*(FC)	.10	.08	.04
167	Rance Mulliniks	.04	.03	.02
168	Barry Jones	.04	.03	.02
169	*Ross Jones*(FC)	.12	.09	.05
170	Rich Gossage	.12	.09	.05
171	Cubs Leaders (Shawon Dunston, Manny Trillo)	.06	.05	.02
172	*Lloyd McClendon*(FC)	.10	.08	.04
173	Eric Plunk	.04	.03	.02
174	Phil Garner	.04	.03	.02
175	Kevin Bass	.06	.05	.02
176	Jeff Reed	.04	.03	.02
177	Frank Tanana	.06	.05	.02
178	Dwayne Henry(FC)	.06	.05	.02
179	Charlie Puleo	.04	.03	.02
180	Terry Kennedy	.06	.05	.02
181	Dave Cone	.80	.60	.30
182	Ken Phelps	.06	.05	.02
183	Tom Lawless	.04	.03	.02
184	Ivan Calderon	.08	.06	.03
185	Rick Rhoden	.06	.05	.02
186	Rafael Palmeiro	.35	.25	.14
187	Steve Kiefer(FC)	.06	.05	.02
188	John Russell	.04	.03	.02
189	*Wes Gardner*(FC)	.20	.15	.08
190	Candy Maldonado	.06	.05	.02
191	John Cerutti	.06	.05	.02
192	Devon White	.20	.15	.08
193	Brian Fisher	.06	.05	.02
194	Tom Kelly	.04	.03	.02
195	Dan Quisenberry	.06	.05	.02
196	Dave Engle	.04	.03	.02
197	Lance McCullers	.06	.05	.02
198	Franklin Stubbs	.06	.05	.02
199	*Dave Meads*	.12	.09	.05
200	Wade Boggs	.80	.60	.30
201	Rangers Leaders (Steve Buechele, Pete Incaviglia, Pete O'Brien, Bobby Valentine)	.06	.05	.02
202	Glenn Hoffman	.04	.03	.02
203	Fred Toliver	.04	.03	.02
204	Paul O'Neill(FC)	.12	.09	.05
205	*Nelson Liriano*(FC)	.20	.15	.08
206	Domingo Ramos	.04	.03	.02
207	*John Mitchell*(FC)	.15	.11	.06
208	Steve Lake	.04	.03	.02
209	Richard Dotson	.06	.05	.02
210	Willie Randolph	.06	.05	.02
211	Frank DiPino	.04	.03	.02
212	Greg Brock	.06	.05	.02
213	Albert Hall	.04	.03	.02
214	Dave Schmidt	.04	.03	.02
215	Von Hayes	.06	.05	.02
216	Jerry Reuss	.06	.05	.02
217	Harry Spilman	.04	.03	.02
218	Dan Schatzeder	.04	.03	.02
219	Mike Stanley	.08	.06	.03
220	Tom Henke	.06	.05	.02
221	Rafael Belliard	.04	.03	.02
222	Steve Farr	.04	.03	.02
223	Stan Jefferson	.08	.06	.03
224	Tom Trebelhorn	.04	.03	.02
225	Mike Scioscia	.06	.05	.02
226	Dave Lopes	.06	.05	.02
227	Ed Correa	.04	.03	.02
228	Wallace Johnson	.04	.03	.02
229	Jeff Musselman	.08	.06	.03
230	Pat Tabler	.06	.05	.02
231	Pirates Leaders (Barry Bonds, Bobby Bonilla)	.10	.08	.04
232	Bob James	.04	.03	.02
233	Rafael Santana	.04	.03	.02
234	Ken Dayley	.04	.03	.02
235	Gary Ward	.06	.05	.02
236	Ted Power	.04	.03	.02
237	Mike Heath	.04	.03	.02
238	*Luis Polonia*	.20	.15	.08
239	Roy Smalley	.04	.03	.02
240	Lee Smith	.08	.06	.03
241	Damaso Garcia	.04	.03	.02
242	Tom Niedenfuer	.06	.05	.02
243	Mark Ryal(FC)	.04	.03	.02
244	Jeff Robinson	.04	.03	.02

	MT	NR MT	EX
245 Rich Gedman	.06	.05	.02
246 Mike Campbell (FC)	.20	.15	.08
247 Thad Bosley	.04	.03	.02
248 Storm Davis	.08	.06	.03
249 Mike Marshall	.10	.08	.04
250 Nolan Ryan	.40	.30	.15
251 Tom Foley	.04	.03	.02
252 Bob Brower	.06	.05	.02
253 Checklist 133-264	.04	.03	.02
254 Lee Elia	.04	.03	.02
255 Mookie Wilson	.06	.05	.02
256 Ken Schrom	.04	.03	.02
257 Jerry Royster	.04	.03	.02
258 Ed Nunez	.04	.03	.02
259 Ron Kittle	.06	.05	.02
260 Vince Coleman	.15	.11	.06
261 Giants Leaders (Will Clark, Candy Maldonado, Kevin Mitchell, Robby Thompson, Jose Uribe)	.10	.08	.04
262 Drew Hall (FC)	.12	.09	.05
263 Glenn Braggs	.08	.06	.03
264 Les Straker	.15	.11	.06
265 Bo Diaz	.06	.05	.02
266 Paul Assenmacher	.04	.03	.02
267 Billy Bean (FC)	.10	.08	.04
268 Bruce Ruffin	.06	.05	.02
269 Ellis Burks	1.25	.90	.50
270 Mike Witt	.06	.05	.02
271 Ken Gerhart	.06	.05	.02
272 Steve Ontiveros	.04	.03	.02
273 Garth Iorg	.04	.03	.02
274 Junior Ortiz	.04	.03	.02
275 Kevin Seitzer	.60	.45	.25
276 Luis Salazar	.04	.03	.02
277 Alejandro Pena	.06	.05	.02
278 Jose Cruz	.06	.05	.02
279 Randy St. Claire	.04	.03	.02
280 Pete Incaviglia	.12	.09	.05
281 Jerry Hairston	.04	.03	.02
282 Pat Perry	.04	.03	.02
283 Phil Lombardi (FC)	.06	.05	.02
284 Larry Bowa	.06	.05	.02
285 Jim Presley	.08	.06	.03
286 Chuck Crim	.12	.09	.05
287 Manny Trillo	.06	.05	.02
288 Pat Pacillo	.15	.11	.06
289 Dave Bergman	.04	.03	.02
290 Tony Fernandez	.10	.08	.04
291 Astros Leaders (Kevin Bass, Billy Hatcher)	.06	.05	.02
292 Carney Lansford	.08	.06	.03
293 Doug Jones (FC)	.30	.25	.12
294 Al Pedrique (FC)	.12	.09	.05
295 Bert Blyleven	.10	.08	.04
296 Floyd Rayford	.04	.03	.02
297 Zane Smith	.06	.05	.02
298 Milt Thompson	.04	.03	.02
299 Steve Crawford	.04	.03	.02
300 Don Mattingly	1.50	1.25	.60
301 Bud Black	.04	.03	.02
302 Jose Uribe	.04	.03	.02
303 Eric Show	.06	.05	.02
304 George Hendrick	.06	.05	.02
305 Steve Sax	.12	.09	.05
306 Billy Hatcher	.06	.05	.02
307 Mike Trujillo	.04	.03	.02
308 Lee Mazzilli	.06	.05	.02
309 Bill Long	.15	.11	.06
310 Tom Herr	.06	.05	.02
311 Scott Sanderson	.04	.03	.02
312 Joey Meyer (FC)	.30	.25	.12
313 Bob McClure	.04	.03	.02
314 Jimy Williams	.04	.03	.02
315 Dave Parker	.12	.09	.05
316 Jose Rijo	.06	.05	.02
317 Tom Nieto	.04	.03	.02
318 Mel Hall	.06	.05	.02
319 Mike Loynd	.04	.03	.02
320 Alan Trammell	.15	.11	.06
321 White Sox Leaders (Harold Baines, Carlton Fisk)	.08	.06	.03
322 Vicente Palacios (FC)	.15	.11	.06
323 Rick Leach	.04	.03	.02
324 Danny Jackson	.20	.15	.08
325 Glenn Hubbard	.04	.03	.02
326 Al Nipper	.04	.03	.02
327 Larry Sheets	.06	.05	.02
328 Greg Cadaret (FC)	.15	.11	.06
329 Chris Speier	.04	.03	.02
330 Eddie Whitson	.04	.03	.02
331 Brian Downing	.06	.05	.02

	MT	NR MT	EX
332 Jerry Reed	.04	.03	.02
333 Wally Backman	.06	.05	.02
334 Dave LaPoint	.06	.05	.02
335 Claudell Washington	.06	.05	.02
336 Ed Lynch	.04	.03	.02
337 Jim Gantner	.04	.03	.02
338 Brian Holton	.08	.06	.03
339 Kurt Stillwell	.08	.06	.03
340 Jack Morris	.15	.11	.06
341 Carmen Castillo	.04	.03	.02
342 Larry Andersen	.04	.03	.02
343 Greg Gagne	.04	.03	.02
344 Tony LaRussa	.04	.03	.02
345 Scott Fletcher	.06	.05	.02
346 Vance Law	.06	.05	.02
347 Joe Johnson	.04	.03	.02
348 Jim Eisenreich	.04	.03	.02
349 Bob Walk	.04	.03	.02
350 Will Clark	1.00	.70	.40
351 Cardinals Leaders (Tony Pena, Red Schoendienst)	.06	.05	.02
352 Billy Ripken (FC)	.20	.15	.08
353 Ed Olwine	.04	.03	.02
354 Marc Sullivan	.04	.03	.02
355 Roger McDowell	.08	.06	.03
356 Luis Aguayo	.04	.03	.02
357 Floyd Bannister	.06	.05	.02
358 Rey Quinones	.04	.03	.02
359 Tim Stoddard	.04	.03	.02
360 Tony Gwynn	.25	.20	.10
361 Greg Maddux	.35	.25	.14
362 Juan Castillo	.04	.03	.02
363 Willie Fraser	.06	.05	.02
364 Nick Esasky	.06	.05	.02
365 Floyd Youmans	.04	.03	.02
366 Chet Lemon	.06	.05	.02
367 Tim Leary	.06	.05	.02
368 Gerald Young (FC)	.30	.25	.12
369 Greg Harris	.04	.03	.02
370 Jose Canseco	1.25	.90	.50
371 Joe Hesketh	.04	.03	.02
372 Matt Williams	.80	.60	.30
373 Checklist 265-396	.04	.03	.02
374 Doc Edwards	.04	.03	.02
375 Tom Brunansky	.08	.06	.03
376 Bill Wilkinson	.12	.09	.05
377 Sam Horn (FC)	.20	.15	.08
378 Todd Frohwirth (FC)	.15	.11	.06
379 Rafael Ramirez	.04	.03	.02
380 Joe Magrane	.40	.30	.15
381 Angels Leaders (Jack Howell, Wally Joyner)	.12	.09	.05
382 Keith Miller (FC)	.20	.15	.08
383 Eric Bell	.06	.05	.02
384 Neil Allen	.04	.03	.02
385 Carlton Fisk	.20	.15	.08
386 Don Mattingly AS	.60	.45	.25
387 Willie Randolph AS	.06	.05	.02
388 Wade Boggs AS	.35	.25	.14
389 Alan Trammell AS	.08	.06	.03
390 George Bell AS	.10	.08	.04
391 Kirby Puckett AS	.12	.09	.05
392 Dave Winfield AS	.12	.09	.05
393 Matt Nokes AS	.15	.11	.06
394 Roger Clemens AS	.15	.11	.06
395 Jimmy Key AS	.06	.05	.02
396 Tom Henke AS	.06	.05	.02
397 Jack Clark AS	.06	.05	.02
398 Juan Samuel AS	.06	.05	.02
399 Tim Wallach AS	.06	.05	.02
400 Ozzie Smith AS	.08	.06	.03
401 Andre Dawson AS	.10	.08	.04
402 Tony Gwynn AS	.15	.11	.06
403 Tim Raines AS	.12	.09	.05
404 Benny Santiago AS	.10	.08	.04
405 Dwight Gooden AS	.15	.11	.06
406 Shane Rawley AS	.06	.05	.02
407 Steve Bedrosian AS	.08	.06	.03
408 Dion James	.06	.05	.02
409 Joel McKeon (FC)	.04	.03	.02
410 Tony Pena	.06	.05	.02
411 Wayne Tolleson	.04	.03	.02
412 Randy Myers	.10	.08	.04
413 John Christensen	.04	.03	.02
414 John McNamara	.04	.03	.02
415 Don Carman	.06	.05	.02
416 Keith Moreland	.06	.05	.02
417 Mark Ciardi (FC)	.10	.08	.04
418 Joel Youngblood	.04	.03	.02
419 Scott McGregor	.06	.05	.02
420 Wally Joyner	.35	.25	.14

		MT	NR MT	EX
421	Ed Vande Berg	.04	.03	.02
422	Dave Concepcion	.06	.05	.02
423	*John Smiley*	.30	.25	.12
424	Dwayne Murphy	.06	.05	.02
425	Jeff Reardon	.08	.06	.03
426	Randy Ready	.04	.03	.02
427	*Paul Kilgus*(FC)	.20	.15	.08
428	John Shelby	.04	.03	.02
429	Tigers Leaders (Kirk Gibson, Alan Trammell)	.08	.06	.03
430	Glenn Davis	.12	.09	.05
431	Casey Candaele	.04	.03	.02
432	Mike Moore	.04	.03	.02
433	*Bill Pecota*(FC)	.15	.11	.06
434	Rick Aguilera	.04	.03	.02
435	Mike Pagliarulo	.08	.06	.03
436	Mike Bielecki	.04	.03	.02
437	*Fred Manrique*(FC)	.12	.09	.05
438	*Rob Ducey*(FC)	.12	.09	.05
439	Dave Martinez	.08	.06	.03
440	Steve Bedrosian	.10	.08	.04
441	Rick Manning	.04	.03	.02
442	*Tom Bolton*(FC)	.15	.11	.06
443	Ken Griffey	.06	.05	.02
444	Cal Ripken, Sr.	.04	.03	.02
445	Mike Krukow	.06	.05	.02
446	Doug DeCinces	.06	.05	.02
447	*Jeff Montgomery*(FC)	.30	.25	.12
448	Mike Davis	.06	.05	.02
449	*Jeff Robinson*	.35	.25	.14
450	Barry Bonds	.10	.08	.04
451	Keith Atherton	.04	.03	.02
452	Willie Wilson	.08	.06	.03
453	Dennis Powell	.04	.03	.02
454	Marvell Wynne	.04	.03	.02
455	*Shawn Hillegas*(FC)	.15	.11	.06
456	Dave Anderson	.04	.03	.02
457	Terry Leach	.04	.03	.02
458	Ron Hassey	.04	.03	.02
459	Yankees Leaders (Willie Randolph, Dave Winfield)	.08	.06	.03
460	Ozzie Smith	.12	.09	.05
461	Danny Darwin	.04	.03	.02
462	Don Slaught	.04	.03	.02
463	*Fred McGriff*	1.00	.70	.40
464	Jay Tibbs	.04	.03	.02
465	Paul Molitor	.10	.08	.04
466	Jerry Mumphrey	.04	.03	.02
467	Don Aase	.04	.03	.02
468	Darren Daulton	.04	.03	.02
469	Jeff Dedmon	.04	.03	.02
470	Dwight Evans	.10	.08	.04
471	Donnie Moore	.04	.03	.02
472	Robby Thompson	.06	.05	.02
473	Joe Niekro	.06	.05	.02
474	Tom Brookens	.04	.03	.02
475	Pete Rose	.20	.15	.08
476	Dave Stewart	.08	.06	.03
477	Jamie Quirk	.04	.03	.02
478	Sid Bream	.06	.05	.02
479	Brett Butler	.06	.05	.02
480	Dwight Gooden	.40	.30	.15
481	Mariano Duncan	.04	.03	.02
482	Mark Davis	.04	.03	.02
483	*Rod Booker*(FC)	.12	.09	.05
484	Pat Clements	.04	.03	.02
485	Harold Reynolds	.06	.05	.02
486	*Pat Keedy*(FC)	.10	.08	.04
487	Jim Pankovits	.04	.03	.02
488	Andy McGaffigan	.04	.03	.02
489	Dodgers Leaders (Pedro Guerrero, Fernando Valenzuela)	.08	.06	.03
490	Larry Parrish	.06	.05	.02
491	B.J. Surhoff	.10	.08	.04
492	Doyle Alexander	.06	.05	.02
493	Mike Greenwell	1.25	.90	.50
494	*Wally Ritchie*	.12	.09	.05
495	Eddie Murray	.25	.20	.10
496	Guy Hoffman	.04	.03	.02
497	Kevin Mitchell	.30	.25	.12
498	Bob Boone	.06	.05	.02
499	Eric King	.06	.05	.02
500	Andre Dawson	.15	.11	.06
501	Tim Birtsas(FC)	.06	.05	.02
502	Danny Gladden	.04	.03	.02
503	*Junior Noboa*(FC)	.10	.08	.04
504	Bob Rodgers	.04	.03	.02
505	Willie Upshaw	.06	.05	.02
506	John Cangelosi	.04	.03	.02
507	Mark Gubicza	.10	.08	.04
508	Tim Teufel	.04	.03	.02
509	Bill Dawley	.04	.03	.02
510	Dave Winfield	.20	.15	.08
511	Joel Davis	.04	.03	.02
512	Alex Trevino	.04	.03	.02
513	Tim Flannery	.04	.03	.02
514	Pat Sheridan	.04	.03	.02
515	Juan Nieves	.06	.05	.02
516	Jim Sundberg	.06	.05	.02
517	Ron Robinson	.04	.03	.02
518	Greg Gross	.04	.03	.02
519	Mariners Leaders (Phil Bradley, Harold Reynolds)	.06	.05	.02
520	Dave Smith	.06	.05	.02
521	Jim Dwyer	.04	.03	.02
522	*Bob Patterson*(FC)	.12	.09	.05
523	Gary Roenicke	.04	.03	.02
524	Gary Lucas	.04	.03	.02
525	Marty Barrett	.06	.05	.02
526	Juan Berenguer	.04	.03	.02
527	Steve Henderson	.04	.03	.02
528a	Checklist 397-528 (#455 is Steve Carlton)	.40	.30	.15
528b	Checklist 397-528 (#455 is Shawn Hillegas)	.06	.05	.02
529	Tim Burke	.04	.03	.02
530	Gary Carter	.15	.11	.06
531	Rich Yett	.04	.03	.02
532	Mike Kingery	.04	.03	.02
533	*John Farrell*(FC)	.30	.25	.12
534	John Wathan	.06	.05	.02
535	Ron Guidry	.12	.09	.05
536	John Morris	.04	.03	.02
537	Steve Buechele	.04	.03	.02
538	Bill Wegman	.04	.03	.02
539	Mike LaValliere	.06	.05	.02
540	Bret Saberhagen	.25	.20	.10
541	Juan Beniquez	.04	.03	.02
542	*Paul Noce*(FC)	.10	.08	.04
543	Kent Tekulve	.06	.05	.02
544	Jim Traber	.06	.05	.02
545	Don Baylor	.08	.06	.03
546	John Candelaria	.06	.05	.02
547	*Felix Fermin*(FC)	.12	.09	.05
548	*Shane Mack*	.15	.11	.06
549	Braves Leaders (Ken Griffey, Dion James, Dale Murphy, Gerald Perry)	.08	.06	.03
550	Pedro Guerrero	.15	.11	.06
551	Terry Steinbach	.15	.11	.06
552	Mark Thurmond	.04	.03	.02
553	Tracy Jones	.10	.08	.04
554	Mike Smithson	.04	.03	.02
555	Brook Jacoby	.08	.06	.03
556	*Stan Clarke*(FC)	.12	.09	.05
557	Craig Reynolds	.04	.03	.02
558	Bob Ojeda	.06	.05	.02
559	*Ken Williams*(FC)	.20	.15	.08
560	Tim Wallach	.08	.06	.03
561	Rick Cerone	.04	.03	.02
562	Jim Lindeman	.10	.08	.04
563	Jose Guzman	.06	.05	.02
564	Frank Lucchesi	.04	.03	.02
565	Lloyd Moseby	.06	.05	.02
566	*Charlie O'Brien*(FC)	.12	.09	.05
567	Mike Diaz	.06	.05	.02
568	Chris Brown	.06	.05	.02
569	Charlie Leibrandt	.06	.05	.02
570	Jeffrey Leonard	.06	.05	.02
571	*Mark Williamson*(FC)	.12	.09	.05
572	Chris James	.15	.11	.06
573	Bob Stanley	.04	.03	.02
574	Graig Nettles	.08	.06	.03
575	Don Sutton	.12	.09	.05
576	*Tommy Hinzo*(FC)	.12	.09	.05
577	Tom Browning	.08	.06	.03
578	Gary Gaetti	.10	.08	.04
579	Mets Leaders (Gary Carter, Kevin McReynolds)	.08	.06	.03
580	Mark McGwire	1.00	.70	.40
581	Tito Landrum	.04	.03	.02
582	*Mike Henneman*	.20	.15	.08
583	Dave Valle(FC)	.06	.05	.02
584	Steve Trout	.04	.03	.02
585	Ozzie Guillen	.06	.05	.02
586	Bob Forsch	.06	.05	.02
587	Terry Puhl	.04	.03	.02
588	*Jeff Parrett*(FC)	.20	.15	.08
589	Geno Petralli	.04	.03	.02
590	George Bell	.20	.15	.08
591	Doug Drabek	.06	.05	.02
592	Dale Sveum	.06	.05	.02
593	Bob Tewksbury	.04	.03	.02

		MT	NR MT	EX
594	Bobby Valentine	.04	.03	.02
595	Frank White	.06	.05	.02
596	John Kruk	.08	.06	.03
597	Gene Garber	.04	.03	.02
598	Lee Lacy	.04	.03	.02
599	Calvin Schiraldi	.04	.03	.02
600	Mike Schmidt	.40	.30	.15
601	Jack Lazorko	.04	.03	.02
602	Mike Aldrete	.06	.05	.02
603	Rob Murphy	.06	.05	.02
604	Chris Bando	.04	.03	.02
605	Kirk Gibson	.15	.11	.06
606	Moose Haas	.04	.03	.02
607	Mickey Hatcher	.04	.03	.02
608	Charlie Kerfeld	.04	.03	.02
609	Twins Leaders (Gary Gaetti, Kent Hrbek)			
		.08	.06	.03
610	Keith Hernandez	.15	.11	.06
611	Tommy John	.12	.09	.05
612	Curt Ford	.04	.03	.02
613	Bobby Thigpen	.08	.06	.03
614	Herm Winningham	.04	.03	.02
615	Jody Davis	.06	.05	.02
616	*Jay Aldrich*(FC)	.10	.08	.04
617	Oddibe McDowell	.06	.05	.02
618	Cecil Fielder	.04	.03	.02
619	*Mike Dunne*	.20	.15	.08
620	Cory Snyder	.15	.11	.06
621	Gene Nelson	.04	.03	.02
622	Kal Daniels	.15	.11	.06
623	Mike Flanagan	.06	.05	.02
624	Jim Leyland	.04	.03	.02
625	Frank Viola	.12	.09	.05
626	Glenn Wilson	.06	.05	.02
627	*Joe Boever*(FC)	.12	.09	.05
628	Dave Henderson	.08	.06	.03
629	Kelly Downs	.08	.06	.03
630	Darrell Evans	.08	.06	.03
631	Jack Howell	.06	.05	.02
632	*Steve Shields*	.12	.09	.05
633	*Barry Lyons*	.12	.09	.05
634	Jose DeLeon	.06	.05	.02
635	Terry Pendleton	.06	.05	.02
636	Charles Hudson	.04	.03	.02
637	*Jay Bell*(FC)	.15	.11	.06
638	Steve Balboni	.06	.05	.02
639	Brewers Leaders (Glenn Braggs, Tony Muser)			
		.06	.05	.02
640	Garry Templeton	.06	.05	.02
641	Rick Honeycutt	.04	.03	.02
642	Bob Dernier	.04	.03	.02
643	*Rocky Childress*(FC)	.12	.09	.05
644	Terry McGriff(FC)	.06	.05	.02
645	*Matt Nokes*	.50	.40	.20
646	Checklist 529-660	.04	.03	.02
647	Pascual Perez	.06	.05	.02
648	Al Newman	.04	.03	.02
649	*DeWayne Buice*	.15	.11	.06
650	Cal Ripken	.25	.20	.10
651	*Mike Jackson*(FC)	.15	.11	.06
652	Bruce Benedict	.04	.03	.02
653	Jeff Sellers	.06	.05	.02
654	Roger Craig	.06	.05	.02
655	Len Dykstra	.08	.06	.03
656	Lee Guetterman	.04	.03	.02
657	Gary Redus	.04	.03	.02
658	Tim Conroy	.04	.03	.02
659	Bobby Meacham	.04	.03	.02
660	Rick Reuschel	.08	.06	.03
661	Turn Back The Clock (Nolan Ryan)	.08	.06	.03
662	Turn Back The Clock (Jim Rice)	.08	.06	.03
663	Turn Back The Clock (Ron Blomberg)			
		.04	.03	.02
664	Turn Back The Clock (Bob Gibson)	.08	.06	.03
665	Turn Back The Clock (Stan Musial)	.12	.09	.05
666	Mario Soto	.06	.05	.02
667	Luis Quinones	.04	.03	.02
668	Walt Terrell	.06	.05	.02
669	Phillies Leaders (Lance Parrish, Mike Ryan)			
		.06	.05	.02
670	Dan Plesac	.08	.06	.03
671	Tim Laudner	.04	.03	.02
672	*John Davis*(FC)	.15	.11	.06
673	Tony Phillips	.04	.03	.02
674	Mike Fitzgerald	.04	.03	.02
675	Jim Rice	.20	.15	.08
676	Ken Dixon	.04	.03	.02
677	Eddie Milner	.04	.03	.02
678	Jim Acker	.04	.03	.02
679	Darrell Miller	.04	.03	.02
680	Charlie Hough	.06	.05	.02

		MT	NR MT	EX
681	Bobby Bonilla	.12	.09	.05
682	Jimmy Key	.08	.06	.03
683	Julio Franco	.08	.06	.03
684	Hal Lanier	.04	.03	.02
685	Ron Darling	.10	.08	.04
686	Terry Francona	.04	.03	.02
687	Mickey Brantley	.04	.03	.02
688	Jim Winn	.04	.03	.02
689	*Tom Pagnozzi*(FC)	.12	.09	.05
690	Jay Howell	.06	.05	.02
691	Dan Pasqua	.08	.06	.03
692	Mike Birkbeck	.06	.05	.02
693	Benny Santiago	.60	.45	.25
694	*Eric Nolte*(FC)	.12	.09	.05
695	Shawon Dunston	.08	.06	.03
696	Duane Ward	.04	.03	.02
697	Steve Lombardozzi	.08	.06	.03
698	Brad Havens	.04	.03	.02
699	Padres Leaders (Tony Gwynn, Benny Santiago)			
		.12	.09	.05
700	George Brett	.30	.25	.12
701	Sammy Stewart	.04	.03	.02
702	Mike Gallego	.04	.03	.02
703	Bob Brenly	.04	.03	.02
704	Dennis Boyd	.06	.05	.02
705	Juan Samuel	.10	.08	.04
706	Rick Mahler	.04	.03	.02
707	Fred Lynn	.10	.08	.04
708	Gus Polidor(FC)	.06	.05	.02
709	George Frazier	.04	.03	.02
710	Darryl Strawberry	.30	.25	.12
711	Bill Gullickson	.04	.03	.02
712	John Moses	.04	.03	.02
713	Willie Hernandez	.06	.05	.02
714	Jim Fregosi	.04	.03	.02
715	Todd Worrell	.08	.06	.03
716	Lenn Sakata	.04	.03	.02
717	Jay Baller(FC)	.06	.05	.02
718	Mike Felder	.04	.03	.02
719	Denny Walling	.04	.03	.02
720	Tim Raines	.20	.15	.08
721	Pete O'Brien	.06	.05	.02
722	Manny Lee	.04	.03	.02
723	Bob Kipper	.04	.03	.02
724	Danny Tartabull	.15	.11	.06
725	Mike Boddicker	.06	.05	.02
726	Alfredo Griffin	.06	.05	.02
727	Greg Booker	.04	.03	.02
728	Andy Allanson	.06	.05	.02
729	Blue Jays Leaders (George Bell, Fred McGriff)			
		.10	.08	.04
730	John Franco	.08	.06	.03
731	Rick Schu	.04	.03	.02
732	Dave Palmer	.04	.03	.02
733	Spike Owen	.04	.03	.02
734	Craig Lefferts	.04	.03	.02
735	Kevin McReynolds	.20	.15	.08
736	Matt Young	.04	.03	.02
737	Butch Wynegar	.04	.03	.02
738	Scott Bankhead	.04	.03	.02
739	Daryl Boston	.04	.03	.02
740	Rick Sutcliffe	.08	.06	.03
741	Mike Easler	.06	.05	.02
742	Mark Clear	.04	.03	.02
743	Larry Herndon	.04	.03	.02
744	Whitey Herzog	.06	.05	.02
745	Bill Doran	.06	.05	.02
746	Gene Larkin	.15	.11	.06
747	Bobby Witt	.08	.06	.03
748	Reid Nichols	.04	.03	.02
749	Mark Eichhorn	.06	.05	.02
750	Bo Jackson	.50	.40	.20
751	Jim Morrison	.04	.03	.02
752	Mark Grant	.04	.03	.02
753	Danny Heep	.04	.03	.02
754	Mike LaCoss	.04	.03	.02
755	Ozzie Virgil	.04	.03	.02
756	Mike Maddux	.06	.05	.02
757	*John Marzano*	.15	.11	.06
758	*Eddie Williams*(FC)	.20	.15	.08
759	A's Leaders (Jose Canseco, Mark McGwire)			
		.40	.30	.15
760	Mike Scott	.10	.08	.04
761	Tony Armas	.06	.05	.02
762	Scott Bradley	.04	.03	.02
763	Doug Sisk	.04	.03	.02
764	Greg Walker	.06	.05	.02
765	Neal Heaton	.06	.05	.02
766	Henry Cotto	.04	.03	.02
767	*Jose Lind*(FC)	.25	.20	.10
768	Dickie Noles	.04	.03	.02

		MT	NR MT	EX
769	Cecil Cooper	.08	.06	.03
770	Lou Whitaker	.20	.15	.08
771	Ruben Sierra	.50	.40	.20
772	Sal Butera	.04	.03	.02
773	Frank Williams	.04	.03	.02
774	Gene Mauch	.06	.05	.02
775	Dave Stieb	.08	.06	.03
776	Checklist 661-792	.04	.03	.02
777	Lonnie Smith	.06	.05	.02
778a	*Keith Comstock* (white team letters)(FC)			
		7.00	5.25	2.75
778b	*Keith Comstock* (blue team letters)(FC)			
		.25	.20	.10
779	*Tom Glavine*(FC)	.35	.25	.14
780	Fernando Valenzuela	.15	.11	.06
781	*Keith Hughes*(FC)	.15	.11	.06
782	*Jeff Ballard*(FC)	.30	.25	.12
783	Ron Roenicke	.04	.03	.02
784	Joe Sambito	.04	.03	.02
785	Alvin Davis	.10	.08	.04
786	Joe Price	.04	.03	.02
787	Bill Almon	.04	.03	.02
788	Ray Searage	.04	.03	.02
789	Indians Leaders (Joe Carter, Cory Snyder)	.08	.06	.03
790	Dave Righetti	.12	.09	.05
791	Ted Simmons	.08	.06	.03
792	John Tudor	.08	.06	.03

		MT	NR MT	EX
14	Ryne Sandberg	.40	.30	.15
15	Mike Schmidt	.60	.45	.25
16	Ozzie Smith	.25	.20	.10
17	Eric Davis	.60	.45	.25
18	Andre Dawson	.25	.20	.10
19	Darryl Strawberry	.60	.45	.25
20	Gary Carter	.40	.30	.15
21	Mike Scott	.15	.11	.06
22	Billy Williams	.25	.20	.10

1988 Topps
All-Star Glossy Set Of 60

This standard-size collectors set includes 60 full-color glossy cards featuring All-Stars and Prospects in six separate 10-card sets. In 1986, Topps issued a similar set that included only All-Stars. Card fronts have a white border and a thin red line framing the player photo, with the player's name in the lower left corner. Card backs, in red and blue, include very basic player information (name, team and position), along with the card set logo and card number. Topps glossy collector sets were marketed via a special offer printed on a card packaged in all Topps wax packs. For six special offer cards and $1.25, collectors received one of the six 10-card sets; 18 special offer cards and $7.50 earned the entire 60-card collection.

		MT	NR MT	EX
Complete Set:		14.00	10.50	5.50
Common Player:		.15	.11	.06
1	Andre Dawson	.30	.25	.12
2	Jesse Barfield	.20	.15	.08
3	Mike Schmidt	.70	.50	.30
4	Ruben Sierra	.40	.30	.15
5	Mike Scott	.20	.15	.08
6	Cal Ripken	.70	.50	.30
7	Gary Carter	.50	.40	.20
8	Kent Hrbek	.30	.25	.12
9	Kevin Seitzer	.70	.50	.30
10	Mike Henneman	.25	.20	.10
11	Don Mattingly	3.50	2.75	1.50
12	Tim Raines	.40	.30	.15
13	Roger Clemens	.80	.60	.30
14	Ryne Sandberg	.40	.30	.15
15	Tony Fernandez	.20	.15	.08
16	Eric Davis	.80	.60	.30
17	Jack Morris	.30	.25	.12
18	Tim Wallach	.20	.15	.08
19	Mike Dunne	.25	.20	.10
20	Mike Greenwell	1.00	.70	.40
21	Dwight Evans	.20	.15	.08
22	Darryl Strawberry	.80	.60	.30
23	Cory Snyder	.30	.25	.12
24	Pedro Guerrero	.25	.20	.10
25	Rickey Henderson	.60	.45	.25
26	Dale Murphy	.70	.50	.30
27	Kirby Puckett	.50	.40	.20
28	Steve Bedrosian	.20	.15	.08
29	Devon White	.25	.20	.10
30	Benny Santiago	.25	.20	.10
31	George Bell	.40	.30	.15
32	Keith Hernandez	.40	.30	.15

1988 Topps
All-Star Glossy Set Of 22

The fifth edition of Topps' special All-Star inserts (22 cards) were included in the company's 1988 rack packs. The 1987 American and National League All-Star lineup, plus honorary captains Jim Hunter and Billy Williams, are featured on the standard-size All-Star inserts. The glossy full-color card fronts contain player photos centered between a red and yellow "1987 All-Star" logo printed across the card top and the player name (also red and yellow) which is printed across the bottom margin. A National or American League logo appears in the lower left corner. Card backs are printed in red and blue on a white background, with the title and All-Star logo emblem printed above the player name and card number.

		MT	NR MT	EX
Complete Set:		4.00	3.00	1.50
Common Player:		.15	.11	.06
1	John McNamara	.15	.11	.06
2	Don Mattingly	1.50	1.25	.60
3	Willie Randolph	.15	.11	.06
4	Wade Boggs	.80	.60	.30
5	Cal Ripken	.50	.40	.20
6	George Bell	.30	.25	.12
7	Rickey Henderson	.50	.40	.20
8	Dave Winfield	.40	.30	.15
9	Terry Kennedy	.15	.11	.06
10	Bret Saberhagen	.25	.20	.10
11	Jim Hunter	.25	.20	.10
12	Davey Johnson	.15	.11	.06
13	Jack Clark	.25	.20	.10

		MT	NR MT	EX
33	Dave Stewart	.15	.11	.06
34	Dave Parker	.25	.20	.10
35	Tom Henke	.15	.11	.06
36	Willie McGee	.20	.15	.08
37	Alan Trammell	.30	.25	.12
38	Tony Gwynn	.60	.45	.25
39	Mark McGwire	1.25	.90	.50
40	Joe Magrane	.25	.20	.10
41	Jack Clark	.25	.20	.10
42	Willie Randolph	.15	.11	.06
43	Juan Samuel	.25	.20	.10
44	Joe Carter	.25	.20	.10
45	Shane Rawley	.15	.11	.06
46	Dave Winfield	.50	.40	.20
47	Ozzie Smith	.25	.20	.10
48	Wally Joyner	.70	.50	.30
49	B.J. Surhoff	.20	.15	.08
50	Ellis Burks	.80	.60	.30
51	Wade Boggs	1.25	.90	.50
52	Howard Johnson	.20	.15	.08
53	George Brett	.70	.50	.30
54	Dwight Gooden	.80	.60	.30
55	Jose Canseco	2.50	2.00	1.00
56	Lee Smith	.15	.11	.06
57	Paul Molitor	.20	.15	.08
58	Andres Galarraga	.30	.25	.12
59	Matt Nokes	.40	.30	.15
60	Casey Candaele	.15	.11	.06

1988 Topps American Baseball

This 88-card set, unlike Topps' United Kingdom football cards, was made available for distribution by U.S. hobby dealers. The cards were packaged in checklist-backed boxes with an American flag on the top flap. The 2-1/4" by 3" cards feature full-color player photos printed on white stock with a red line framing the photo. The team name, printed in individual team colors, intersects the red frame at the top of the card. A bright yellow name banner appears below the photo. Card backs have bright blue borders and cartoon-style horizontal layouts. The card number appears within a circle of red stars upper left, beside the player's name and team logo. A red banner containing the player career stats runs the length of the card back. The lower half of the flip side features a caricature of the player and a one-line caption. Below the cartoon, a short "Talkin' Baseball" paragraph provides elementary baseball information, obviously designed to acquaint soccer-playing European collectors with American baseball rules and terminology. A glossy edition of the set was issued and is valued at 2-3 times greater than the regular issue.

		MT	NR MT	EX
Complete Set:		7.00	5.25	2.75
Common Player:		.08	.06	.03
1	Harold Baines	.15	.11	.06
2	Steve Bedrosian	.10	.08	.04
3	George Bell	.25	.20	.10
4	Wade Boggs	1.00	.70	.40
5	Barry Bonds	.20	.15	.08
6	Bob Boone	.08	.06	.03

		MT	NR MT	EX
7	George Brett	.40	.30	.15
8	Hubie Brooks	.08	.06	.03
9	Ivan Calderon	.10	.08	.04
10	Jose Canseco	1.25	.90	.50
11	Gary Carter	.30	.25	.12
12	Joe Carter	.15	.11	.06
13	Jack Clark	.20	.15	.08
14	Will Clark	.50	.40	.20
15	Roger Clemens	.60	.45	.25
16	Vince Coleman	.20	.15	.08
17	Alvin Davis	.15	.11	.06
18	Eric Davis	.70	.50	.30
19	Glenn Davis	.20	.15	.08
20	Andre Dawson	.25	.20	.10
21	Mike Dunne	.15	.11	.06
22	Dwight Evans	.10	.08	.04
23	Tony Fernandez	.15	.11	.06
24	John Franco	.10	.08	.04
25	Gary Gaetti	.20	.15	.08
26	Kirk Gibson	.25	.20	.10
27	Dwight Gooden	.60	.45	.25
28	Pedro Guerrero	.20	.15	.08
29	Tony Gwynn	.35	.25	.14
30	Billy Hatcher	.08	.06	.03
31	Rickey Henderson	.35	.25	.14
32	Tom Henke	.08	.06	.03
33	Keith Hernandez	.25	.20	.10
34	Orel Hershiser	.30	.25	.12
35	Teddy Higuera	.10	.08	.04
36	Charlie Hough	.08	.06	.03
37	Kent Hrbek	.25	.20	.10
38	Brook Jacoby	.10	.08	.04
39	Dion James	.08	.06	.03
40	Wally Joyner	.50	.40	.20
41	John Kruk	.15	.11	.06
42	Mark Langston	.15	.11	.06
43	Jeffrey Leonard	.08	.06	.03
44	Candy Maldonaldo	.08	.06	.03
45	Don Mattingly	2.00	1.50	.80
46	Willie McGee	.15	.11	.06
47	Mark McGwire	1.00	.70	.40
48	Kevin Mitchell	.08	.06	.03
49	Paul Molitor	.15	.11	.06
50	Jack Morris	.15	.11	.06
51	Lloyd Moseby	.10	.08	.04
52	Dale Murphy	.40	.30	.15
53	Eddie Murray	.30	.25	.12
54	Matt Nokes	.40	.30	.15
55	Dave Parker	.20	.15	.08
56	Larry Parrish	.08	.06	.03
57	Kirby Puckett	.35	.25	.14
58	Tim Raines	.30	.25	.12
59	Willie Randolph	.08	.06	.03
60	Harold Reynolds	.08	.06	.03
61	Cal Ripken	.35	.25	.14
62	Nolan Ryan	.25	.20	.10
63	Bret Saberhagen	.20	.15	.08
64	Juan Samuel	.15	.11	.06
65	Ryne Sandberg	.25	.20	.10
66	Benny Santiago	.15	.11	.06
67	Mike Schmidt	.40	.30	.15
68	Mike Scott	.10	.08	.04
69	Kevin Seitzer	.40	.30	.15
70	Larry Sheets	.08	.06	.03
71	Ruben Sierra	.15	.11	.06
72	Ozzie Smith	.15	.11	.06
73	Zane Smith	.08	.06	.03
74	Cory Snyder	.15	.11	.06
75	Dave Stewart	.10	.08	.04
76	Darryl Strawberry	.50	.40	.20
77	Rick Sutcliffe	.15	.11	.06
78	Danny Tartabull	.20	.15	.08
79	Alan Trammell	.25	.20	.10
80	Fernando Valenzuela	.20	.15	.08
81	Andy Van Slyke	.15	.11	.06
82	Frank Viola	.15	.11	.06
83	Greg Walker	.10	.08	.04
84	Tim Wallach	.10	.08	.04
85	Dave Winfield	.30	.25	.12
86	Mike Witt	.08	.06	.03
87	Robin Yount	.25	.20	.10
88	Checklist	.08	.06	.03

NOTE: A card number in parentheses ( ) indicates the set is unnumbered.

1988 Topps Big Baseball

1988 Topps Big Baseball cards (2-5/8" by 3-3/4") were issued in three series, 88 cards per series (a total set of 264 cards). Each series features current star players, sold in 7-card packages. The glossy cards are similar in format, both front and back, to the 1956 Topps 340-card set. Each card features a posed head shot and a close-up action photo on the front, framed by a wide white border and a dark blue inner border. A white outlines highlights the player closeup. The player's name appears below his head shot, in reversed type on a splash of color that fades from yellow to orange to red to pink. On the card back, the player's name is printed in large red letters across the top, followed by his team name and position in black. Personal info is printed in a red rectangle beside a Topps baseball logo bearing the card number. A triple cartoon strip, in full-color, illustrates career highlights, performance, personal background, etc. A red, white and blue statistics box (pitching, batting, fielding) is printed across the bottom.

		MT	NR MT	EX
Complete Set:		22.00	16.50	8.75
Common Player:		.05	.04	.02
1	Paul Molitor	.12	.09	.05
2	Milt Thompson	.05	.04	.02
3	Billy Hatcher	.05	.04	.02
4	Mike Witt	.05	.04	.02
5	Vince Coleman	.12	.09	.05
6	Dwight Evans	.10	.08	.04
7	Tim Wallach	.10	.08	.04
8	Alan Trammell	.15	.11	.06
9	Will Clark	.25	.20	.10
10	Jeff Reardon	.08	.06	.03
11	Dwight Gooden	.50	.40	.20
12	Benny Santiago	.12	.09	.05
13	Jose Canseco	1.25	.90	.50
14	Dale Murphy	.30	.25	.12
15	George Bell	.20	.15	.08
16	Ryne Sandberg	.20	.15	.08
17	Brook Jacoby	.08	.06	.03
18	Fernando Valenzuela	.15	.11	.06
19	Scott Fletcher	.05	.04	.02
20	Eric Davis	.60	.45	.25
21	Willie Wilson	.10	.08	.04
22	B.J. Surhoff	.10	.08	.04
23	Steve Bedrosian	.08	.06	.03
24	Dave Winfield	.25	.20	.10
25	Bobby Bonilla	.15	.11	.06
26	Larry Sheets	.08	.06	.03
27	Ozzie Guillen	.08	.06	.03
28	Checklist 1-88	.05	.04	.02
29	Nolan Ryan	.20	.15	.08
30	Bob Boone	.05	.04	.02
31	Tom Herr	.08	.06	.03
32	Wade Boggs	.90	.70	.35

		MT	NR MT	EX
33	Neal Heaton	.05	.04	.02
34	Doyle Alexander	.05	.04	.02
35	Candy Maldonado	.08	.06	.03
36	Kirby Puckett	.25	.20	.10
37	Gary Carter	.20	.15	.08
38	Lance McCullers	.08	.06	.03
39a	Terry Steinbach (black Topps logo on front)	.12	.09	.05
39b	Terry Steinbach (white Topps logo on front)	.12	.09	.05
40	Gerald Perry	.10	.08	.04
41	Tom Henke	.05	.04	.02
42	Leon Durham	.05	.04	.02
43	Cory Snyder	.12	.09	.05
44	Dale Sveum	.05	.04	.02
45	Lance Parrish	.12	.09	.05
46	Steve Sax	.12	.09	.05
47	Charlie Hough	.05	.04	.02
48	Kal Daniels	.15	.11	.06
49	Bo Jackson	.25	.20	.10
50	Ron Guidry	.10	.08	.04
51	Bill Doran	.08	.06	.03
52	Wally Joyner	.40	.30	.15
53	Terry Pendleton	.08	.06	.03
54	Marty Barrett	.08	.06	.03
55	Andres Galarraga	.15	.11	.06
56	Larry Herndon	.05	.04	.02
57	Kevin Mitchell	.08	.06	.03
58	Greg Gagne	.05	.04	.02
59	Keith Hernandez	.15	.11	.06
60	John Kruk	.10	.08	.04
61	Mike LaValliere	.08	.06	.03
62	Cal Ripken	.30	.25	.12
63	Ivan Calderon	.08	.06	.03
64	Alvin Davis	.10	.08	.04
65	Luis Polonia	.08	.06	.03
66	Robin Yount	.20	.15	.08
67	Juan Samuel	.12	.09	.05
68	Andres Thomas	.05	.04	.02
69	Jeff Musselman	.05	.04	.02
70	Jerry Mumphrey	.05	.04	.02
71	Joe Carter	.12	.09	.05
72	Mike Scioscia	.05	.04	.02
73	Pete Incaviglia	.10	.08	.04
74	Barry Larkin	.15	.11	.06
75	Frank White	.08	.06	.03
76	Willie Randolph	.08	.06	.03
77	Kevin Bass	.05	.04	.02
78	Brian Downing	.08	.06	.03
79	Willie McGee	.10	.08	.04
80	Ellis Burks	.40	.30	.15
81	Hubie Brooks	.08	.06	.03
82	Darrell Evans	.08	.06	.03
83	Robby Thompson	.05	.04	.02
84	Kent Hrbek	.15	.11	.06
85	Ron Darling	.12	.09	.05
86	Stan Jefferson	.05	.04	.02
87	Teddy Higuera	.10	.08	.04
88	Mike Schmidt	.30	.25	.12
89	Barry Bonds	.15	.11	.06
90	Jim Presley	.08	.06	.03
91	Orel Hershiser	.25	.20	.10
92	Jesse Barfield	.10	.08	.04
93	Tom Candiotti	.05	.04	.02
94	Bret Saberhagen	.12	.09	.05
95	Jose Uribe	.05	.04	.02
96	Tom Browning	.10	.08	.04
97	Johnny Ray	.08	.06	.03
98	Mike Morgan	.05	.04	.02
100	Jim Sundberg	.05	.04	.02
101	Roger McDowell	.08	.06	.03
102	Randy Ready	.05	.04	.02
103	Mike Gallego	.05	.04	.02
104	Steve Buechele	.05	.04	.02
105	Greg Walker	.08	.06	.03
106	Jose Lind	.12	.09	.05
107	Steve Trout	.05	.04	.02
108	Rick Rhoden	.08	.06	.03
109	Jim Pankovits	.05	.04	.02
110	Ken Griffey	.08	.06	.03
111	Danny Cox	.08	.06	.03
112	Franklin Stubbs	.05	.04	.02
113	Lloyd Moseby	.08	.06	.03
114	Mel Hall	.08	.06	.03
115	Kevin Seitzer	.25	.20	.10
116	Tim Raines	.25	.20	.10
117	Juan Castillo	.05	.04	.02
118	Roger Clemens	.50	.40	.20
119	Mike Aldrete	.08	.06	.03
120	Mario Soto	.05	.04	.02
121	Jack Howell	.05	.04	.02

		MT	NR MT	EX
122	Rick Schu	.05	.04	.02
123	Jeff Robinson	.10	.08	.04
124	Doug Drabek	.08	.06	.03
125	Henry Cotto	.05	.04	.02
126	Checklist 89-176	.05	.04	.02
127	Gary Gaetti	.12	.09	.05
128	Rick Sutcliffe	.10	.08	.04
129	Howard Johnson	.08	.06	.03
130	Chris Brown	.08	.06	.03
131	Dave Henderson	.08	.06	.03
132	Curt Wilkerson	.05	.04	.02
133	Mike Marshall	.10	.08	.04
134	Kelly Gruber	.05	.04	.02
135	Julio Franco	.10	.08	.04
136	Kurt Stillwell	.12	.09	.05
137	Donnie Hill	.05	.04	.02
138	Mike Pagliarulo	.10	.08	.04
139	Von Hayes	.08	.06	.03
140	Mike Scott	.10	.08	.04
141	Bob Kipper	.05	.04	.02
142	Harold Reynolds	.08	.06	.03
143	Bob Brenly	.05	.04	.02
144	Dave Concepcion	.08	.06	.03
145	Devon White	.12	.09	.05
146	Jeff Stone	.05	.04	.02
147	Chet Lemon	.05	.04	.02
148	Ozzie Virgil	.05	.04	.02
149	Todd Worrell	.10	.08	.04
150	Mitch Webster	.05	.04	.02
151	Rob Deer	.08	.06	.03
152	Rich Gedman	.08	.06	.03
153	Andre Dawson	.15	.11	.06
154	Mike Davis	.05	.04	.02
155	Nelson Liriano	.08	.06	.03
156	Greg Swindell	.10	.08	.04
157	George Brett	.30	.25	.12
158	Kevin McReynolds	.15	.11	.06
159	Brian Fisher	.08	.06	.03
160	Mike Kingery	.05	.04	.02
161	Tony Gwynn	.25	.20	.10
162	Don Baylor	.10	.08	.04
163	Jerry Browne	.05	.04	.02
164	Dan Pasqua	.08	.06	.03
165	Rickey Henderson	.25	.20	.10
166	Brett Butler	.08	.06	.03
167	Nick Esasky	.05	.04	.02
168	Kirk McCaskill	.05	.04	.02
169	Fred Lynn	.10	.08	.04
170	Jack Morris	.12	.09	.05
171	Pedro Guerrero	.12	.09	.05
172	Dave Stieb	.10	.08	.04
173	Pat Tabler	.08	.06	.03
174	Floyd Bannister	.05	.04	.02
175	Rafael Belliard	.05	.04	.02
176	Mark Langston	.10	.08	.04
177	Greg Mathews	.08	.06	.03
178	Claudell Washington	.05	.04	.02
179	Mark McGwire	1.00	.70	.40
180	Bert Blyleven	.10	.08	.04
181	Jim Rice	.20	.15	.08
182	Mookie Wilson	.08	.06	.03
183	Willie Fraser	.05	.04	.02
184	Andy Van Slyke	.10	.08	.04
185	Matt Nokes	.10	.08	.04
186	Eddie Whitson	.05	.04	.02
187	Tony Fernandez	.10	.08	.04
188	Rick Reuschel	.08	.06	.03
189	Ken Phelps	.05	.04	.02
190	Juan Nieves	.08	.06	.03
191	Kirk Gibson	.20	.15	.08
192	Glenn Davis	.15	.11	.06
193	Zane Smith	.05	.04	.02
194	Jose DeLeon	.08	.06	.03
195	Gary Ward	.05	.04	.02
196	Pascual Perez	.05	.04	.02
197	Carlton Fisk	.12	.09	.05
198	Oddibe McDowell	.08	.06	.03
199	Mark Gubicza	.10	.08	.04
200	Glenn Hubbard	.05	.04	.02
201	Frank Viola	.15	.11	.06
202	Jody Reed	.12	.09	.05
203	Len Dykstra	.08	.06	.03
204	Dick Schofield	.05	.04	.02
205	Sid Bream	.05	.04	.02
206	Guillermo Hernandez	.05	.04	.02
207	Keith Moreland	.05	.04	.02
208	Mark Eichhorn	.05	.04	.02
209	Rene Gonzales	.08	.06	.03
210	Dave Valle	.05	.04	.02
211	Tom Brunansky	.10	.08	.04
212	Charles Hudson	.05	.04	.02

		MT	NR MT	EX
213	John Farrell	.10	.08	.04
214	Jeff Treadway	.12	.09	.05
215	Eddie Murray	.25	.20	.10
216	Checklist 177-264	.05	.04	.02
217	Greg Brock	.08	.06	.03
218	John Shelby	.05	.04	.02
219	Craig Reynolds	.05	.04	.02
220	Dion James	.05	.04	.02
221	Carney Lansford	.08	.06	.03
222	Juan Berenguer	.05	.04	.02
223	Luis Rivera	.08	.06	.03
224	Harold Baines	.12	.09	.05
225	Shawon Dunston	.08	.06	.03
226	Luis Aguayo	.05	.04	.02
227	Pete O'Brien	.08	.06	.03
228	Ozzie Smith	.12	.09	.05
229	Don Mattingly	1.50	1.25	.60
230	Danny Tartabull	.15	.11	.06
231	Andy Allanson	.05	.04	.02
232	John Franco	.08	.06	.03
233	Mike Greenwell	.80	.60	.30
234	Bob Ojeda	.08	.06	.03
235	Chili Davis	.08	.06	.03
236	Mike Dunne	.12	.09	.05
237	Jim Morrison	.05	.04	.02
238	Carmelo Martinez	.05	.04	.02
239	Ernie Whitt	.05	.04	.02
240	Scott Garrelts	.05	.04	.02
241	Mike Moore	.05	.04	.02
242	Dave Parker	.10	.08	.04
243	Tim Laudner	.05	.04	.02
244	Bill Wegman	.05	.04	.02
245	Bob Horner	.08	.06	.03
246	Rafael Santana	.05	.04	.02
247	Alfredo Griffin	.05	.04	.02
248	Mark Bailey	.05	.04	.02
249	Ron Gant	.12	.09	.05
250	Bryn Smith	.05	.04	.02
251	Lance Johnson	.10	.08	.04
252	Sam Horn	.10	.08	.04
253	Darryl Strawberry	.40	.30	.15
254	Chuck Finley	.05	.04	.02
255	Darnell Coles	.08	.06	.03
256	Mike Henneman	.10	.08	.04
257	Andy Hawkins	.08	.06	.03
258	Jim Clancy	.08	.06	.03
259	Atlee Hammaker	.05	.04	.02
260	Glenn Wilson	.05	.04	.02
261	Larry McWilliams	.05	.04	.02
262	Jack Clark	.12	.09	.05
263	Walt Weiss	.80	.60	.30
264	Gene Larkin	.08	.06	.03

1988 Topps Box Panels

After a one-year hiatus during which they appeared on the sides of Topps wax pack display boxes, Topps retail box cards returned to box bottoms in 1988. Topps first issued box-bottom cards in 1986, following the introduction of the concept by Donruss in 1985. Topps 1988 box-bottom series includes 16 standard-size baseball cards, four cards per each of four different display boxes. Card fronts follow the same design as the 1988 Topps basic issue; full-color player photos, framed in yellow, surrounded by a white border; diagonal player name lower right; team name in large letters at the top of the card front.

Card backs are "numbered" A through P and are printed in black and orange.

		MT	NR MT	EX
Complete Panel Set:		7.00	5.25	2.75
Complete Singles Set:		2.50	2.00	1.00
Common Panel:		1.00	.70	.40
Common Single Player:		.08	.06	.03
	Panel	1.00	.70	.40
A	Don Baylor	.12	.09	.05
B	Steve Bedrosian	.12	.09	.05
C	Juan Beniquez	.08	.06	.03
D	Bob Boone	.08	.06	.03
	Panel	1.75	1.25	.70
E	Darrell Evans	.12	.09	.05
F	Tony Gwynn	.30	.25	.12
G	John Kruk	.15	.11	.06
H	Marvell Wynne	.08	.06	.03
	Panel	2.75	2.00	1.00
I	Joe Carter	.15	.11	.06
J	Eric Davis	.50	.40	.20
K	Howard Johnson	.12	.09	.05
L	Darryl Strawberry	.35	.25	.14
	Panel	2.50	2.00	1.00
M	Rickey Henderson	.20	.15	.08
N	Nolan Ryan	.35	.25	.14
O	Mike Schmidt	.08	.06	.03
P	Kent Tekulve	.08	.06	.03

1988 Topps Coins

This edition of 60 lightweight metal coins is similar in design to Topps' 1964 set. The 1988 coins are 1-1/2" in diameter and feature full-color player closeups under crimped edges in silver, gold and pink. Curved under the photo is a red and white player name banner pinned by two gold stars. Coin backs list the coin number, player name, personal information and career summary in black letters on a silver background.

		MT	NR MT	EX
Complete Set:		8.00	6.00	3.25
Common Player:		.10	.08	.04
1	George Bell	.25	.20	.10
2	Roger Clemens	.40	.30	.15
3	Mark McGwire	.60	.45	.25
4	Wade Boggs	.70	.50	.30
5	Harold Baines	.15	.11	.06
6	Ivan Calderon	.10	.08	.04
7	Jose Canseco	.80	.60	.30
8	Joe Carter	.15	.11	.06
9	Jack Clark	.15	.11	.06
10	Alvin Davis	.15	.11	.06
11	Dwight Evans	.15	.11	.06
12	Tony Fernandez	.15	.11	.06
13	Gary Gaetti	.15	.11	.06
14	Mike Greenwell	.40	.30	.15
15	Charlie Hough	.10	.08	.04
16	Wally Joyner	.30	.25	.12
17	Jimmy Key	.10	.08	.04
18	Mark Langston	.15	.11	.06
19	Don Mattingly	1.00	.70	.40
20	Paul Molitor	.15	.11	.06
21	Jack Morris	.15	.11	.06

		MT	NR MT	EX
22	Eddie Murray	.20	.15	.08
23	Kirby Puckett	.25	.20	.10
24	Cal Ripken	.25	.20	.10
25	Bret Saberhagen	.15	.11	.06
26	Ruben Sierra	.15	.11	.06
27	Cory Snyder	.15	.11	.06
28	Terry Steinbach	.15	.11	.06
29	Danny Tartabull	.15	.11	.06
30	Alan Trammell	.15	.11	.06
31	Devon White	.15	.11	.06
32	Robin Yount	.15	.11	.06
33	Andre Dawson	.15	.11	.06
34	Steve Bedrosian	.15	.11	.06
35	Benny Santiago	.15	.11	.06
36	Tony Gwynn	.25	.20	.10
37	Bobby Bonilla	.15	.11	.06
38	Will Clark	.30	.25	.12
39	Eric Davis	.40	.30	.15
40	Mike Dunne	.15	.11	.06
41	John Franco	.10	.08	.04
42	Dwight Gooden	.40	.30	.15
43	Pedro Guerrero	.15	.11	.06
44	Dion James	.10	.08	.04
45	John Kruk	.15	.11	.06
46	Jeffrey Leonard	.10	.08	.04
47	Carmelo Martinez	.10	.08	.04
48	Dale Murphy	.30	.25	.12
49	Tim Raines	.20	.15	.08
50	Nolan Ryan	.20	.15	.08
51	Juan Samuel	.15	.11	.06
52	Ryne Sandberg	.20	.15	.08
53	Mike Schmidt	.30	.25	.12
54	Mike Scott	.15	.11	.06
55	Ozzie Smith	.15	.11	.06
56	Darryl Strawberry	.40	.30	.15
57	Rick Sutcliffe	.15	.11	.06
58	Fernando Valenzuela	.15	.11	.06
59	Tim Wallach	.15	.11	.06
60	Todd Worrell	.15	.11	.06

1988 Topps Gallery Of Champions

These bronze replicas are exact reproductions at one-quarter scale of Topps official 1988 cards, both front and back. The set includes 12 three-dimensional raised metal cards packaged in a velvet-lined case that bears the title of the set in gold embossed letters. A deluxe limited edition of the set (1,000) was produced in sterling silver and an economy version in aluminum. Topps first issued the metal mini-cards in 1984 (the initial set was called Gallery of Immortals). Since 1985, the metal cards have honored award-winning players from the previous season. A Mark McGwire pewter replica was given as a premium to dealers ordering the aluminum, bronze and silver sets ($50 value). The special pewter card is distinguished from the regular issue by a diagonal name banner in the lower right corner (regular) replicas have a rectangular name banner printer parallel to the lower edge of the card). A 1955 Topps Duke Snider bronze (value $10) was available to dealers purchasing cases of the 1988 Topps Traded sets.

		MT	NR MT	EX
	Complete Aluminum Set:	20.00	15.00	8.00
	Complete Bronze Set:	125.00	94.00	50.00
	Complete Silver Set:	500.00	375.00	200.00
(1a)	Steve Bedrosian (aluminum)	.70	.50	.30
(1b)	Steve Bedrosian (bronze)	7.50	5.75	3.00
(1c)	Steve Bedrosian (silver)	20.00	15.00	8.00
(2a)	George Bell (aluminum)	1.00	.70	.40
(2b)	George Bell (bronze)	10.00	7.50	4.00
(2c)	George Bell (silver)	20.00	15.00	8.00
(3a)	Wade Boggs (aluminum)	3.00	2.25	1.25
(3b)	Wade Boggs (bronze)	25.00	18.50	10.00
(3c)	Wade Boggs (silver)	125.00	94.00	50.00
(4a)	Jack Clark (aluminum)	1.00	.70	.40
(4b)	Jack Clark (bronze)	10.00	7.50	4.00
(4c)	Jack Clark (silver)	20.00	15.00	8.00
(5a)	Roger Clemens (aluminum)	2.00	1.50	.80
(5b)	Roger Clemens (bronze)	20.00	15.00	8.00
(5c)	Roger Clemens (silver)	90.00	67.00	36.00
(6a)	Andre Dawson (aluminum)	1.00	.70	.40
(6b)	Andre Dawson (bronze)	10.00	7.50	4.00
(6c)	Andre Dawson (silver)	20.00	15.00	8.00
(7a)	Tony Gwynn (aluminum)	1.25	.90	.50
(7b)	Tony Gwynn (bronze)	12.00	9.00	4.75
(7c)	Tony Gwynn (silver)	50.00	37.00	20.00
(8a)	Mark Langston (aluminum)	.70	.50	.30
(8b)	Mark Langston (bronze)	7.50	5.75	3.00
(8c)	Mark Langston (silver)	20.00	15.00	8.00
(9a)	Mark McGwire (aluminum)	3.00	2.25	1.25
(9b)	Mark McGwire (bronze)	25.00	18.50	10.00
(9c)	Mark McGwire (silver)	125.00	94.00	50.00
(10a)	Dave Righetti (aluminum)	1.00	.70	.40
(10b)	Dave Righetti (bronze)	10.00	7.50	4.00
(10c)	Dave Righetti (silver)	20.00	15.00	8.00
(11a)	Nolan Ryan (aluminum)	1.00	.70	.40
(11b)	Nolan Ryan (bronze)	10.00	7.50	4.00
(11c)	Nolan Ryan (silver)	20.00	15.00	8.00
(12a)	Benny Santiago (aluminum)	1.00	.70	.40
(12b)	Benny Santiago (bronze)	10.00	7.50	4.00
(12c)	Benny Santiago (silver)	20.00	15.00	8.00

		MT	NR MT	EX
11	Casey Candaele	.20	.15	.08
12	Randy Myers	.60	.45	.25
13	Mark McGwire	2.00	1.50	.80
14	Luis Polonia	.25	.20	.10
15	Terry Steinbach	.40	.30	.15
16	Mike Dunne	.40	.30	.15
17	Al Pedrique	.20	.15	.08
18	Benny Santiago	.70	.50	.30
19	Kelly Downs	.40	.30	.15
20	Joe Magrane	.40	.30	.15
21	Jerry Browne	.20	.15	.08
22	Jeff Musselman	.25	.20	.10

1988 Topps Mini League Leaders

WADE BOGGS

The third consecutive issue of Topps mini-cards (2-1/8" by 3") includes 77 cards spotlighting the top five ranked pitchers and batters. This set is unique in that it was the first time Topps included full-color player photos on both the front and back. Glossy action shots on the card fronts fade into a white border with a Topps logo in an upper corner. The player's name is printed in bold black letters beneath the photo. Horizontal reverses feature circular player photos on a blue and white background with the card number, player name, personal information, 1987 ranking and lifetime/1987 stats printed in red, black and yellow lettering.

		MT	NR MT	EX
	Complete Set:	6.00	4.50	2.50
	Common Player:	.09	.07	.04
1	Wade Boggs	.80	.60	.30
2	Roger Clemens	.60	.45	.25
3	Dwight Evans	.15	.11	.06
4	DeWayne Buice	.09	.07	.04
5	Brian Downing	.09	.07	.04
6	Wally Joyner	.60	.45	.25
7	Ivan Calderon	.15	.11	.06
8	Carlton Fisk	.20	.15	.08
9	Gary Redus	.09	.07	.04
10	Darrell Evans	.15	.11	.06
11	Jack Morris	.25	.20	.10
12	Alan Trammell	.30	.25	.12
13	Lou Whitaker	.20	.15	.08
14	Bret Saberhagen	.20	.15	.08
15	Kevin Seitzer	.50	.40	.20
16	Danny Tartabull	.25	.20	.10
17	Willie Wilson	.15	.11	.06
18	Teddy Higuera	.15	.11	.06
19	Paul Molitor	.20	.15	.08
20	Dan Plesac	.15	.11	.06
21	Robin Yount	.25	.20	.10
22	Kent Hrbek	.25	.20	.10
23	Kirby Puckett	.35	.25	.14
24	Jeff Reardon	.15	.11	.06
25	Frank Viola	.20	.15	.08
26	Rickey Henderson	.40	.30	.15
27	Don Mattingly	1.25	.90	.50
28	Willie Randolph	.15	.11	.06
29	Dave Righetti	.20	.15	.08
30	Jose Canseco	1.00	.70	.40
31	Mark McGwire	.90	.70	.35
32	Dave Stewart	.09	.07	.04

1988 Topps Glossy Rookies

The Topps 1988 Rookies special insert cards follow the same basic design as the All-Star inserts. The set consists of 22 standard-size cards. Large, glossy color player photos are printed on a white background below a red, yellow and blue "1987 Rookies" banner. A red and yellow player name appears beneath the photo. Red, white and blue card backs bear the title of the special insert set, the Rookies logo emblem, player name and card number.

		MT	NR MT	EX
	Complete Set:	10.00	7.50	4.00
	Common Player:	.20	.15	.08
1	Billy Ripken	.30	.25	.12
2	Ellis Burks	1.50	1.25	.60
3	Mike Greenwell	2.00	1.50	.80
4	DeWayne Buice	.20	.15	.08
5	Devon White	.40	.30	.15
6	Fred Manrique	.20	.15	.08
7	Mike Henneman	.40	.30	.15
8	Matt Nokes	.60	.45	.25
9	Kevin Seitzer	1.25	.90	.50
10	B.J. Surhoff	.40	.30	.15

		MT	NR MT	EX
33	Phil Bradley	.15	.11	.06
34	Mark Langston	.15	.11	.06
35	Harold Reynolds	.09	.07	.04
36	Charlie Hough	.09	.07	.04
37	George Bell	.25	.20	.10
38	Tom Henke	.09	.07	.04
39	Jimmy Key	.15	.11	.06
40	Dion James	.09	.07	.04
41	Dale Murphy	.50	.40	.20
42	Zane Smith	.09	.07	.04
43	Andre Dawson	.25	.20	.10
44	Lee Smith	.09	.07	.04
45	Rick Sutcliffe	.15	.11	.06
46	Eric Davis	.60	.45	.25
47	John Franco	.15	.11	.06
48	Dave Parker	.20	.15	.08
49	Billy Hatcher	.09	.07	.04
50	Nolan Ryan	.25	.20	.10
51	Mike Scott	.20	.15	.08
52	Pedro Guerrero	.20	.15	.08
53	Orel Hershiser	.30	.25	.12
54	Fernando Valenzuela	.25	.20	.10
55	Bob Welch	.15	.11	.06
56	Andres Galarraga	.25	.20	.10
57	Tim Raines	.30	.25	.12
58	Tim Wallach	.15	.11	.06
59	Len Dykstra	.15	.11	.06
60	Dwight Gooden	.60	.45	.25
61	Howard Johnson	.15	.11	.06
62	Roger McDowell	.15	.11	.06
63	Darryl Strawberry	.50	.40	.20
64	Steve Bedrosian	.15	.11	.06
65	Shane Rawley	.09	.07	.04
66	Juan Samuel	.20	.15	.08
67	Mike Schmidt	.50	.40	.20
68	Mike Dunne	.15	.11	.06
69	Jack Clark	.25	.20	.10
70	Vince Coleman	.20	.15	.08
71	Willie McGee	.15	.11	.06
72	Ozzie Smith	.20	.15	.08
73	Todd Worrell	.15	.11	.06
74	Tony Gwynn	.40	.30	.15
75	John Kruk	.20	.15	.08
76	Rick Rueschel	.15	.11	.06
77	Checklist	.09	.07	.04

1988 Topps Stickercards

Actually a part of the 1988 Topps Stickers issue, this set consists of 67 cards. The cards are the backs of the peel-off stickers and measure 2-1/8" by 3". To determine total value, combine the prices of the stickers (found in the 1988 Topps Stickers checklist) on the stickercard front with the value assigned to the stickercard in the following checklist.

		MT	NR MT	EX
Complete Set:		2.00	1.50	.80
Common Player:		.02	.02	.01
1	Jack Clark	.03	.02	.01
2	Andres Galarraga	.03	.02	.01
3	Keith Hernandez	.04	.03	.02
4	Tom Herr	.02	.02	.01
5	Juan Samuel	.03	.02	.01
6	Ryne Sandberg	.04	.03	.02
7	Terry Pendleton	.02	.02	.01
8	Mike Schmidt	.06	.05	.02

		MT	NR MT	EX
9	Tim Wallach	.02	.02	.01
10	Hubie Brooks	.02	.02	.01
11	Shawon Dunston	.02	.02	.01
12	Ozzie Smith	.03	.02	.01
13	Andre Dawson	.04	.03	.02
14	Eric Davis	.06	.05	.02
15	Pedro Guerrero	.03	.02	.01
16	Tony Gwynn	.05	.04	.02
17	Jeffrey Leonard	.02	.02	.01
18	Dale Murphy	.06	.05	.02
19	Dave Parker	.03	.02	.01
20	Tim Raines	.04	.03	.02
21	Darryl Strawberry	.06	.05	.02
22	Gary Carter	.04	.03	.02
23	Jody Davis	.02	.02	.01
24	Ozzie Virgil	.02	.02	.01
25	Dwight Gooden	.08	.06	.03
26	Mike Scott	.02	.02	.01
27	Rick Sutcliffe	.02	.02	.01
28	Sid Fernandez	.02	.02	.01
29	Neal Heaton	.02	.02	.01
30	Fernando Valenzuela	.03	.02	.01
31	Steve Bedrosian	.02	.02	.01
32	John Franco	.02	.02	.01
33	Lee Smith	.02	.02	.01
34	Wally Joyner	.06	.05	.02
35	Don Mattingly	.12	.09	.05
36	Mark McGwire	.08	.06	.03
37	Willie Randolph	.02	.02	.01
38	Lou Whitaker	.03	.02	.01
39	Frank White	.02	.02	.01
40	Wade Boggs	.10	.08	.04
41	George Brett	.06	.05	.02
42	Paul Molitor	.02	.02	.01
43	Tony Fernandez	.02	.02	.01
44	Cal Ripken	.06	.05	.02
45	Alan Trammell	.04	.03	.02
46	Jesse Barfield	.03	.02	.01
47	George Bell	.04	.03	.02
48	Jose Canseco	.10	.08	.04
49	Joe Carter	.03	.02	.01
50	Dwight Evans	.02	.02	.01
51	Rickey Henderson	.05	.04	.02
52	Kirby Puckett	.05	.04	.02
53	Cory Snyder	.03	.02	.01
54	Dave Winfield	.04	.03	.02
55	Terry Kennedy	.02	.02	.01
56	Matt Nokes	.03	.02	.01
57	B.J. Surhoff	.02	.02	.01
58	Roger Clemens	.08	.06	.03
59	Jack Morris	.03	.02	.01
60	Bret Saberhagen	.03	.02	.01
61	Ron Guidry	.03	.02	.01
62	Bruce Hurst	.02	.02	.01
63	Mark Langston	.02	.02	.01
64	Tom Henke	.02	.02	.01
65	Dan Plesac	.02	.02	.01
66	Dave Righetti	.03	.02	.01
67	Checklist	.02	.02	.01

1988 Topps Stickers

This set of 313 stickers (on 198 cards) offers a new addition for 1988 - 66 different players are pictured on the reverse of the sticker cards. The stickers come in two sizes (2-1/8" by 3" or 1-1/2" by 2-1/8"). Larger stickers fill an entire card, smaller ones are attached in pairs. A 36-page sticker yearbook produced by Topps has a designated space inside for each sticker, with one page per team and special pages of 1987 Highlights, World Series, All-Stars and Future Stars. No printing appears on the full-color action shot stickers except for a small black number in the lower left corner. Sticker card backs carry a Super Star header, player close-up and stats. Stickers were sold in packages of five (with gum) for 25 cents per pack. Unlike the 1987 Topps Stickers set, different pairings can be found, rather than the same two players/numbers always sharing the same sticker. To determine total value, combine the value of the stickercard (found in the 1988 Topps Stickercard checklist) with the values assigned the stickers in the following checklist.

	MT	NR MT	EX
Complete Set:	15.00	11.00	6.00
Common Player:	.02	.02	.01
Sticker Album:	.60	.45	.25

		MT	NR MT	EX
1	1987 Highlights (Mark McGwire)	.20	.15	.08
2	1987 Highlights (Benny Santiago)	.04	.03	.02
3	1987 Highlights (Don Mattingly)	.25	.20	.10
4	1987 Highlights (Vince Coleman)	.04	.03	.02
5	1987 Highlights (Bob Boone)	.02	.02	.01
6	1987 Highlights (Steve Bedrosian)	.02	.02	.01
7	1987 Highlights (Nolan Ryan)	.08	.06	.03
8	1987 Highlights (Darrell Evans)	.02	.02	.01
9	1987 Highlights (Mike Schmidt)	.10	.08	.04
10	1987 Highlights (Don Baylor)	.04	.03	.02
11	1987 Highlights (Eddie Murray)	.08	.06	.03
12	1987 Highlights (Juan Beniquez)	.02	.02	.01
13	1987 Championship Series (John Tudor)	.04	.03	.02
14	1987 Championship Series (Jeff Reardon)	.04	.03	.02
15	1987 Championship Series (Tom Brunansky)	.06	.05	.02
16	1987 Championship Series (Jeffrey Leonard)	.04	.03	.02
17	1987 Championship Series (Gary Gaetti)	.10	.08	.04
18	1987 Championship Series (Cardinals Celebrate)	.04	.03	.02
19	1987 World Series (Danny Gladden)	.04	.03	.02
20	1987 World Series (Bert Blyleven)	.08	.06	.03
21	1987 World Series (John Tudor)	.06	.05	.02
22	1987 World Series (Tom Lawless)	.04	.03	.02
23	1987 World Series (Curt Ford)	.04	.03	.02
24	1987 World Series (Kent Hrbek)	.12	.09	.05
25	1987 World Series (Frank Viola)	.10	.08	.04
26	Dave Smith	.02	.02	.01
27	Jim Deshaies	.02	.02	.01
28	Billy Hatcher	.02	.02	.01
29	Kevin Bass	.02	.02	.01
30	Mike Scott	.04	.03	.02
31	Danny Walling	.02	.02	.01
32	Alan Ashby	.02	.02	.01
33	Ken Caminiti	.02	.02	.01
34	Bill Doran	.02	.02	.01
35	Glenn Davis	.12	.09	.05
36	Ozzie Virgil	.02	.02	.01
37	Ken Oberkfell	.02	.02	.01
38	Ken Griffey	.02	.02	.01
39	Albert Hall	.02	.02	.01
40	Zane Smith	.02	.02	.01
41	Andres Thomas	.02	.02	.01
42	Dion James	.02	.02	.01
43	Jim Acker	.02	.02	.01
44	Tom Glavine	.04	.03	.02
45	Dale Murphy	.25	.20	.10
46	Jack Clark	.10	.08	.04
47	Vince Coleman	.04	.03	.02
48	Ricky Horton	.02	.02	.01
49	Terry Pendleton	.02	.02	.01
50	Tom Herr	.02	.02	.01
51	Joe Magrane	.04	.03	.02
52	Tony Pena	.02	.02	.01
53	Ozzie Smith	.04	.03	.02
54	Todd Worrell	.04	.03	.02
55	Willie McGee	.10	.08	.04
56	Andre Dawson	.15	.11	.06
57	Ryne Sandberg	.06	.05	.02
58	Keith Moreland	.02	.02	.01
59	Greg Maddux	.04	.03	.02
60	Jody Davis	.02	.02	.01
61	Rick Sutcliffe	.08	.06	.03
62	Jamie Moyer	.02	.02	.01

		MT	NR MT	EX
63	Leon Durham	.02	.02	.01
64	Lee Smith	.02	.02	.01
65	Shawon Dunston	.02	.02	.01
66	Franklin Stubbs	.02	.02	.01
67	Mike Scioscia	.02	.02	.01
68	Orel Hershiser	.06	.05	.02
69	Mike Marshall	.04	.03	.02
70	Fernando Valenzuela	.15	.11	.06
71	Mickey Hatcher	.02	.02	.01
72	Matt Young	.02	.02	.01
73	Bob Welch	.04	.03	.02
74	Steve Sax	.04	.03	.02
75	Pedro Guerrero	.12	.09	.05
76	Tim Raines	.15	.11	.06
77	Casey Candaele	.02	.02	.01
78	Mike Fitzgerald	.02	.02	.01
79	Andres Galarraga	.04	.03	.02
80	Neal Heaton	.02	.02	.01
81	Hubie Brooks	.02	.02	.01
82	Floyd Youmans	.02	.02	.01
83	Herm Winningham	.02	.02	.01
84	Denny Martinez	.02	.02	.01
85	Tim Wallach	.08	.06	.03
86	Jeffrey Leonard	.04	.03	.02
87	Will Clark	.10	.08	.04
88	Kevin Mitchell	.04	.03	.02
89	Mike Aldrete	.02	.02	.01
90	Scott Garrelts	.02	.02	.01
91	Jose Uribe	.02	.02	.01
92	Bob Brenly	.02	.02	.01
93	Robby Thompson	.02	.02	.01
94	Don Robinson	.02	.02	.01
95	Candy Maldonado	.04	.03	.02
96	Darryl Strawberry	.25	.20	.10
97	Keith Hernandez	.06	.05	.02
98	Ron Darling	.04	.03	.02
99	Howard Johnson	.04	.03	.02
100	Roger McDowell	.02	.02	.01
101	Dwight Gooden	.30	.25	.12
102	Kevin McReynolds	.04	.03	.02
103	Sid Fernandez	.02	.02	.01
104	Dave Magadan	.04	.03	.02
105	Gary Carter	.08	.06	.03
106	Carmelo Martinez	.02	.02	.01
107	Eddie Whitson	.02	.02	.01
108	Tim Flannery	.02	.02	.01
109	Stan Jefferson	.02	.02	.01
110	John Kruk	.10	.08	.04
111	Chris Brown	.04	.03	.02
112	Benny Santiago	.04	.03	.02
113	Garry Templeton	.02	.02	.01
114	Lance McCullers	.02	.02	.01
115	Tony Gwynn	.20	.15	.08
116	Steve Bedrosian	.06	.05	.02
117	Von Hayes	.02	.02	.01
118	Kevin Gross	.02	.02	.01
119	Bruce Ruffin	.02	.02	.01
120	Juan Samuel	.04	.03	.02
121	Shane Rawley	.02	.02	.01
122	Chris James	.04	.03	.02
123	Lance Parrish	.04	.03	.02
124	Glenn Wilson	.02	.02	.01
125	Mike Schmidt	.25	.20	.10
126	Andy Van Slyke	.08	.06	.03
127	Jose Lind	.04	.03	.02
128	Al Pedrique	.02	.02	.01
129	Bobby Bonilla	.04	.03	.02
130	Sid Bream	.02	.02	.01
131	Mike LaValliere	.02	.02	.01
132	Mike Dunne	.04	.03	.02
133	Jeff Robinson	.02	.02	.01
134	Doug Drabek	.02	.02	.01
135	Barry Bonds	.10	.08	.04
136	Dave Parker	.08	.06	.03
137	Nick Esasky	.02	.02	.01
138	Buddy Bell	.02	.02	.01
139	Kal Daniels	.04	.03	.02
140	Barry Larkin	.04	.03	.02
141	Eric Davis	.25	.20	.10
142	John Franco	.02	.02	.01
143	Bo Diaz	.02	.02	.01
144	Ron Oester	.02	.02	.01
145	Dennis Rasmussen	.02	.02	.01
146	Eric Davis	.40	.30	.15
147	Ryne Sandberg	.30	.25	.12
148	Andre Dawson	.20	.15	.08
149	Mike Schmidt	.40	.30	.15
150	Jack Clark	.20	.15	.08
151	Darryl Strawberry	.40	.30	.15
152	Gary Carter	.30	.25	.12
153	Ozzie Smith	.20	.15	.08

		MT	NR MT	EX
154	Mike Scott	.20	.15	.08
155	Rickey Henderson	.40	.30	.15
156	Don Mattingly	.90	.70	.35
157	Wade Boggs	.60	.45	.25
158	George Bell	.30	.25	.12
159	Dave Winfield	.30	.25	.12
160	Cal Ripken	.40	.30	.15
161	Terry Kennedy	.15	.11	.06
162	Willie Randolph	.15	.11	.06
163	Bret Saberhagen	.25	.20	.10
164	Mark McGwire	.35	.25	.14
165	Tony Phillips	.02	.02	.01
166	Jay Howell	.02	.02	.01
167	Carney Lansford	.02	.02	.01
168	Dave Stewart	.02	.02	.01
169	Alfredo Griffin	.02	.02	.01
170	Dennis Eckersley	.04	.03	.02
171	Mike Davis	.02	.02	.01
172	Luis Polonia	.02	.02	.01
173	Jose Canseco	.60	.45	.25
174	Mike Witt	.06	.05	.02
175	Jack Howell	.02	.02	.01
176	Greg Minton	.02	.02	.01
177	Dick Schofield	.02	.02	.01
178	Gary Pettis	.02	.02	.01
179	Wally Joyner	.25	.20	.10
180	DeWayne Buice	.02	.02	.01
181	Brian Downing	.02	.02	.01
182	Bob Boone	.02	.02	.01
183	Devon White	.04	.03	.02
184	Jim Clancy	.02	.02	.01
185	Willie Upshaw	.02	.02	.01
186	Tom Henke	.02	.02	.01
187	Ernie Whitt	.02	.02	.01
188	George Bell	.20	.15	.08
189	Lloyd Moseby	.02	.02	.01
190	Jimmy Key	.02	.02	.01
191	Dave Stieb	.02	.02	.01
192	Jesse Barfield	.04	.03	.02
193	Tony Fernandez	.10	.08	.04
194	Paul Molitor	.06	.05	.02
195	Jim Gantner	.02	.02	.01
196	Teddy Higuera	.04	.03	.02
197	Glenn Braggs	.02	.02	.01
198	Rob Deer	.02	.02	.01
199	Dale Sveum	.02	.02	.01
200	Bill Wegman	.02	.02	.01
201	Robin Yount	.06	.05	.02
202	B.J. Surhoff	.04	.03	.02
203	Dan Plesac	.06	.05	.02
204	Pat Tabler	.04	.03	.02
205	Mel Hall	.02	.02	.01
206	Scott Bailes	.02	.02	.01
207	Julio Franco	.04	.03	.02
208	Cory Snyder	.06	.05	.02
209	Chris Bando	.02	.02	.01
210	Greg Swindell	.04	.03	.02
211	Brook Jacoby	.02	.02	.01
212	Brett Butler	.02	.02	.01
213	Joe Carter	.10	.08	.04
214	Mark Langston	.08	.06	.03
215	Rey Quinones	.02	.02	.01
216	Ed Nunez	.02	.02	.01
217	Jim Presley	.02	.02	.01
218	Phil Bradley	.04	.03	.02
219	Alvin Davis	.10	.08	.04
220	Dave Valle	.02	.02	.01
221	Harold Reynolds	.02	.02	.01
222	Scott Bradley	.02	.02	.01
223	Gary Matthews	.02	.02	.01
224	Eric Bell	.02	.02	.01
225	Terry Kennedy	.02	.02	.01
226	Dave Schmidt	.02	.02	.01
227	Billy Ripken	.04	.03	.02
228	Cal Ripken	.20	.15	.08
229	Ray Knight	.02	.02	.01
230	Larry Sheets	.02	.02	.01
231	Mike Boddicker	.02	.02	.01
232	Tom Niedenfuer	.02	.02	.01
233	Eddie Murray	.20	.15	.08
234	Ruben Sierra	.12	.09	.05
235	Steve Buechele	.02	.02	.01
236	Charlie Hough	.02	.02	.01
237	Oddibe McDowell	.02	.02	.01
238	Mike Stanley	.02	.02	.01
239	Pete Incaviglia	.04	.03	.02
240	Pete O'Brien	.02	.02	.01
241	Scott Fletcher	.02	.02	.01
242	Dale Mohorcic	.02	.02	.01
243	Larry Parrish	.04	.03	.02
244	Wade Boggs	.35	.25	.14

		MT	NR MT	EX
245	Dwight Evans	.04	.03	.02
246	Sam Horn	.04	.03	.02
247	Jim Rice	.06	.05	.02
248	Marty Barrett	.02	.02	.01
249	Mike Greenwell	.15	.11	.06
250	Ellis Burks	.10	.08	.04
251	Roger Clemens	.12	.09	.05
252	Rich Gedman	.02	.02	.01
253	Bruce Hurst	.06	.05	.02
254	Bret Saberhagen	.15	.11	.06
255	Frank White	.02	.02	.01
256	Dan Quisenberry	.02	.02	.01
257	Danny Tartabull	.06	.05	.02
258	Bo Jackson	.08	.06	.03
259	George Brett	.25	.20	.10
260	Charlie Leibrandt	.02	.02	.01
261	Kevin Seitzer	.10	.08	.04
262	Mark Gubicza	.04	.03	.02
263	Willie Wilson	.04	.03	.02
264	Frank Tanana	.02	.02	.01
265	Darrell Evans	.02	.02	.01
266	Bill Madlock	.04	.03	.02
267	Kirk Gibson	.06	.05	.02
268	Jack Morris	.12	.09	.05
269	Matt Nokes	.06	.05	.02
270	Lou Whitaker	.04	.03	.02
271	Eric King	.02	.02	.01
272	Jim Morrison	.02	.02	.01
273	Alan Trammell	.20	.15	.08
274	Kent Hrbek	.12	.09	.05
275	Tom Brunansky	.04	.03	.02
276	Bert Blyleven	.04	.03	.02
277	Gary Gaetti	.04	.03	.02
278	Tim Laudner	.04	.03	.02
279	Gene Larkin	.02	.02	.01
280	Jeff Reardon	.02	.02	.01
281	Danny Gladden	.02	.02	.01
282	Frank Viola	.04	.03	.02
283	Kirby Puckett	.20	.15	.08
284	Ozzie Guillen	.06	.05	.02
285	Ivan Calderon	.02	.02	.01
286	Donnie Hill	.02	.02	.01
287	Ken Williams	.04	.03	.02
288	Jim Winn	.02	.02	.01
289	Bob James	.02	.02	.01
290	Carlton Fisk	.04	.03	.02
291	Richard Dotson	.02	.02	.01
292	Greg Walker	.02	.02	.01
293	Harold Baines	.10	.08	.04
294	Willie Randolph	.06	.05	.02
295	Mike Pagliarulo	.04	.03	.02
296	Ron Guidry	.04	.03	.02
297	Rickey Henderson	.10	.08	.04
298	Rick Rhoden	.02	.02	.01
299	Don Mattingly	.70	.50	.30
300	Dave Righetti	.04	.03	.02
301	Claudell Washington	.02	.02	.01
302	Dave Winfield	.08	.06	.03
303	Gary Ward	.02	.02	.01
304	Al Pedrique	.02	.02	.01
305	Casey Candaele	.02	.02	.01
306	Kevin Seitzer	.10	.08	.04
307	Mike Dunne	.04	.03	.02
308	Jeff Musselman	.02	.02	.01
309	Mark McGwire	.20	.15	.08
310	Ellis Burks	.10	.08	.04
311	Matt Nokes	.06	.05	.02
312	Mike Greenwell	.15	.11	.06
313	Devon White	.04	.03	.02

1988 Topps Traded

In addition to new players and traded veterans, 21

members of the U.S.A. Olympic Baseball team are showcased in this 132-card set, numbered 1T-132T. The standard-size (2-1/2" by 3-1/2") set follows the same design as the basic Topps issue - white borders, large full-color photos, team name (or U.S.A.) in large bold letters at the top of the card face, player name on a diagonal stripe across the lower right corner. Topps has issued its traded series each year since 1981 in boxed complete sets available through hobby dealers.

	MT	NR MT	EX
Complete Set:	23.00	18.00	9.00
Common Player:	.06	.05	.02
1T Jim Abbott (U.S.A.)(FC)	9.00	6.75	3.50
2T Juan Agosto	.06	.05	.02
3T Luis Alicea(FC)	.15	.11	.06
4T Roberto Alomar(FC)	.50	.40	.20
5T Brady Anderson(FC)	.40	.30	.15
6T Jack Armstrong(FC)	.15	.11	.06
7T Don August	.15	.11	.06
8T Floyd Bannister	.08	.06	.03
9T Bret Barberie (U.S.A.)(FC)	.40	.30	.15
10T Jose Bautista(FC)	.15	.11	.06
11T Don Baylor	.10	.08	.04
12T Tim Belcher	.20	.15	.08
13T Buddy Bell	.10	.08	.04
14T Andy Benes (U.S.A.)(FC)	3.25	2.50	1.25
15T Damon Berryhill(FC)	.25	.20	.10
16T Bud Black	.06	.05	.02
17T Pat Borders(FC)	.20	.15	.08
18T Phil Bradley	.10	.08	.04
19T Jeff Branson (U.S.A.)(FC)	.40	.30	.15
20T Tom Brunansky	.12	.09	.05
21T Jay Buhner(FC)	.25	.20	.10
22T Brett Butler	.08	.06	.03
23T Jim Campanis (U.S.A.)(FC)	.40	.30	.15
24T Sil Campusano(FC)	.25	.20	.10
25T John Candelaria	.08	.06	.03
26T Jose Cecena(FC)	.15	.11	.06
27T Rick Cerone	.06	.05	.02
28T Jack Clark	.15	.11	.06
29T Kevin Coffman(FC)	.10	.08	.04
30T Pat Combs (U.S.A.)(FC)	1.25	.90	.50
31T Henry Cotto	.06	.05	.02
32T Chili Davis	.08	.06	.03
33T Mike Davis	.08	.06	.03
34T Jose DeLeon	.08	.06	.03
35T Richard Dotson	.10	.08	.04
36T Cecil Espy(FC)	.08	.06	.03
37T Tom Filer	.06	.05	.02
38T Mike Fiore (U.S.A.)(FC)	.60	.45	.25
39T Ron Gant(FC)	.30	.25	.12
40T Kirk Gibson	.15	.11	.06
41T Rich Gossage	.15	.11	.06
42T Mark Grace(FC)	3.50	2.75	1.50
43T Alfredo Griffin	.08	.06	.03
44T Ty Griffin (U.S.A.)(FC)	1.50	1.25	.60
45T Bryan Harvey(FC)	.30	.25	.12
46T Ron Hassey	.06	.05	.02
47T Ray Hayward(FC)	.08	.06	.03
48T Dave Henderson	.10	.08	.04
49T Tom Herr	.10	.08	.04
50T Bob Horner	.10	.08	.04
51T Ricky Horton	.08	.06	.03
52T Jay Howell	.08	.06	.03
53T Glenn Hubbard	.06	.05	.02
54T Jeff Innis(FC)	.15	.11	.06
55T Danny Jackson	.15	.11	.06
56T Darrin Jackson(FC)	.10	.08	.04
57T Roberto Kelly(FC)	.50	.40	.20
58T Ron Kittle	.10	.08	.04
59T Ray Knight	.08	.06	.03
60T Vance Law	.08	.06	.03
61T Jeffrey Leonard	.08	.06	.03
62T Mike Macfarlane(FC)	.20	.15	.08
63T Scotti Madison(FC)	.15	.11	.06
64T Kirt Manwaring(FC)	.20	.15	.08
65T Mark Marquess (U.S.A.)	.06	.05	.02
66T Tino Martinez (U.S.A.)(FC)	1.25	.90	.50
67T Billy Masse(FC)	.40	.30	.15
68T Jack McDowell(FC)	.20	.15	.08
69T Jack McKeon	.06	.05	.02
70T Larry McWilliams	.06	.05	.02
71T Mickey Morandini (U.S.A.)(FC)	.60	.45	.25
72T Keith Moreland	.08	.06	.03
73T Mike Morgan	.06	.05	.02
74T Charles Nagy (U.S.A.)(FC)	.40	.30	.15
75T Al Nipper	.06	.05	.02
76T Russ Nixon	.06	.05	.02
77T Jesse Orosco	.08	.06	.03
78T Joe Orsulak	.06	.05	.02
79T Dave Palmer	.06	.05	.02
80T Mark Parent(FC)	.20	.15	.08
81T Dave Parker	.12	.09	.05
82T Dan Pasqua	.10	.08	.04
83T Melido Perez(FC)	.30	.25	.12
84T Steve Peters(FC)	.15	.11	.06
85T Dan Petry	.08	.06	.03
86T Gary Pettis	.08	.06	.03
87T Jeff Pico(FC)	.20	.15	.08
88T Jim Poole (U.S.A.)(FC)	.40	.30	.15
89T Ted Power	.06	.05	.02
90T Rafael Ramirez	.06	.05	.02
91T Dennis Rasmussen	.10	.08	.04
92T Jose Rijo	.08	.06	.03
93T Earnie Riles	.06	.05	.02
94T Luis Rivera(FC)	.08	.06	.03
95T Doug Robbins (U.S.A.)(FC)	.40	.30	.15
96T Frank Robinson	.10	.08	.04
97T Cookie Rojas	.06	.05	.02
98T Chris Sabo(FC)	.90	.70	.35
99T Mark Salas	.06	.05	.02
100T Luis Salazar	.06	.05	.02
101T Rafael Santana	.06	.05	.02
102T Nelson Santovenia(FC)	.20	.15	.08
103T Mackey Sasser(FC)	.10	.08	.04
104T Calvin Schiraldi	.06	.05	.02
105T Mike Schooler(FC)	.20	.15	.08
106T Scott Servais (U.S.A.)(FC)	.40	.30	.15
107T Dave Silvestri (U.S.A.)(FC)	.40	.30	.15
108T Don Slaught	.06	.05	.02
109T Joe Slusarski (U.S.A.)(FC)	.40	.30	.15
110T Lee Smith	.10	.08	.04
111T Pete Smith(FC)	.10	.08	.04
112T Jim Snyder	.06	.05	.02
113T Ed Sprague (U.S.A.)(FC)	.60	.45	.25
114T Pete Stanicek(FC)	.15	.11	.06
115T Kurt Stillwell	.10	.08	.04
116T Todd Stottlemyre(FC)	.30	.25	.12
117T Bill Swift	.06	.05	.02
118T Pat Tabler	.08	.06	.03
119T Scott Terry(FC)	.10	.08	.04
120T Mickey Tettleton	.06	.05	.02
121T Dickie Thon	.08	.06	.03
122T Jeff Treadway(FC)	.20	.15	.08
123T Willie Upshaw	.08	.06	.03
124T Robin Ventura(FC)	2.50	2.00	1.00
125T Ron Washington	.06	.05	.02
126T Walt Weiss(FC)	.70	.50	.30
127T Bob Welch	.10	.08	.04
128T David Wells(FC)	.08	.06	.03
129T Glenn Wilson	.08	.06	.03
130T Ted Wood (U.S.A.)(FC)	.60	.45	.25
131T Don Zimmer	.06	.05	.02
132T Checklist 1T-132T	.06	.05	.02

1989 Topps

Ten top young players who led the June 1988 draft picks are featured on "#1 Draft Pick" cards in this full-color basic set of 792 standard-size baseball cards. An additional five cards salute 1989 Future Stars, 22 cards highlight All-Stars, seven contain Record Breakers, five are designated Turn Back The Clock, and six contain checklists. This set features the familiar white borders, but two inner photo corners (upper left and lower right) have been rounded off and the rectangular player name was replaced by a curved name banner in bright red or blue that leads to the team name in large script in the lower right corner. The card backs are printed in black on a red background and include personal information and complete minor and major league stats. Another new addition in this set is the special Monthly Scoreboard chart that lists monthly stats (April through September) in two of several categories (hits, run, home runs, stolen bases, RBIs, wins, strikeouts, games or saves).

		MT	NR MT	EX
	Complete Set:	22.00	16.50	8.75
	Common Player:	.03	.02	.01
1	Record Breaker (George Bell)	.08	.06	.03
2	Record Breaker (Wade Boggs)	.35	.25	.14
3	Record Breaker (Gary Carter)	.10	.08	.04
4	Record Breaker (Andre Dawson)	.08	.06	.03
5	Record Breaker (Orel Hershiser)	.10	.08	.04
6	Record Breaker (Doug Jones)	.06	.05	.02
7	Record Breaker (Kevin McReynolds)	.08	.06	.03
8	Dave Eiland(FC)	.20	.15	.08
9	Tim Teufel	.03	.02	.01
10	Andre Dawson	.15	.11	.06
11	Bruce Sutter	.08	.06	.03
12	Dale Sveum	.06	.05	.02
13	Doug Sisk	.03	.02	.01
14	Tom Kelly	.03	.02	.01
15	Robby Thompson	.06	.05	.02
16	Ron Robinson	.03	.02	.01
17	Brian Downing	.06	.05	.02
18	Rick Rhoden	.06	.05	.02
19	Greg Gagne	.03	.02	.01
20	Steve Bedrosian	.08	.06	.03
21	White Sox Leaders (Greg Walker)	.06	.05	.02
22	Tim Crews	.06	.05	.02
23	Mike Fitzgerald	.03	.02	.01
24	Larry Andersen	.03	.02	.01
25	Frank White	.06	.05	.02
26	Dale Mohorcic	.03	.02	.01
27	Orestes Destrade(FC)	.12	.09	.05
28	Mike Moore	.03	.02	.01
29	Kelly Gruber	.03	.02	.01
30	Doc Gooden	.40	.30	.15
31	Terry Francona	.03	.02	.01
32	Dennis Rasmussen	.08	.06	.03
33	B.J. Surhoff	.08	.06	.03
34	Ken Williams	.06	.05	.02
35	John Tudor	.08	.06	.03
36	Mitch Webster	.06	.05	.02
37	Bob Stanley	.03	.02	.01
38	Paul Runge	.03	.02	.01
39	Mike Maddux	.03	.02	.01
40	Steve Sax	.12	.09	.05
41	Terry Mulholland	.03	.02	.01
42	Jim Eppard(FC)	.08	.06	.03
43	Guillermo Hernandez	.06	.05	.02
44	Jim Snyder	.03	.02	.01
45	Kal Daniels	.12	.09	.05
46	Mark Portugal	.03	.02	.01
47	Carney Lansford	.06	.05	.02
48	Tim Burke	.03	.02	.01
49	Craig Biggio(FC)	.70	.50	.30
50	George Bell	.20	.15	.08
51	Angels Leaders (Mark McLemore)	.06	.05	.02
52	Bob Brenly	.03	.02	.01
53	Ruben Sierra	.30	.25	.12
54	Steve Trout	.03	.02	.01
55	Julio Franco	.08	.06	.03
56	Pat Tabler	.06	.05	.02
57	Alejandro Pena	.06	.05	.02
58	Lee Mazzilli	.06	.05	.02
59	Mark Davis	.03	.02	.01
60	Tom Brunansky	.10	.08	.04
61	Neil Allen	.03	.02	.01
62	Alfredo Griffin	.06	.05	.02
63	Mark Clear	.03	.02	.01
64	Alex Trevino	.03	.02	.01
65	Rick Reuschel	.08	.06	.03
66	Manny Trillo	.03	.02	.01
67	Dave Palmer	.03	.02	.01
68	Darrell Miller	.03	.02	.01
69	Jeff Ballard	.06	.05	.02
70	Mark McGwire	.60	.45	.25
71	Mike Boddicker	.06	.05	.02
72	John Moses	.03	.02	.01
73	Pascual Perez	.06	.05	.02

		MT	NR MT	EX
74	Nick Leyva	.03	.02	.01
75	Tom Henke	.06	.05	.02
76	Terry Blocker(FC)	.12	.09	.05
77	Doyle Alexander	.06	.05	.02
78	Jim Sundberg	.06	.05	.02
79	Scott Bankhead	.03	.02	.01
80	Cory Snyder	.15	.11	.06
81	Expos Leaders (Tim Raines)	.08	.06	.03
82	Dave Leiper	.03	.02	.01
83	Jeff Blauser(FC)	.15	.11	.06
84	#1 Draft Pick (Bill Bene)(FC)	.50	.40	.20
85	Kevin McReynolds	.12	.09	.05
86	Al Nipper	.03	.02	.01
87	Larry Owen	.03	.02	.01
88	Darryl Hamilton(FC)	.12	.09	.05
89	Dave LaPoint	.06	.05	.02
90	Vince Coleman	.12	.09	.05
91	Floyd Youmans	.03	.02	.01
92	Jeff Kunkel	.03	.02	.01
93	Ken Howell	.03	.02	.01
94	Chris Speier	.03	.02	.01
95	Gerald Young	.10	.08	.04
96	Rick Cerone	.03	.02	.01
97	Greg Mathews	.06	.05	.02
98	Larry Sheets	.06	.05	.02
99	Sherman Corbett(FC)	.12	.09	.05
100	Mike Schmidt	.35	.25	.14
101	Les Straker	.06	.05	.02
102	Mike Gallego	.03	.02	.01
103	Tim Birtsas	.03	.02	.01
104	Dallas Green	.03	.02	.01
105	Ron Darling	.10	.08	.04
106	Willie Upshaw	.06	.05	.02
107	Jose DeLeon	.06	.05	.02
108	Fred Manrique	.06	.05	.02
109	Hipolito Pena(FC)	.12	.09	.05
110	Paul Molitor	.12	.09	.05
111	Reds Leaders (Eric Davis)	.10	.08	.04
112	Jim Presley	.06	.05	.02
113	Lloyd Moseby	.06	.05	.02
114	Bob Kipper	.03	.02	.01
115	Jody Davis	.06	.05	.02
116	Jeff Montgomery	.06	.05	.02
117	Dave Anderson	.03	.02	.01
118	Checklist 1-132	.03	.02	.01
119	Terry Puhl	.03	.02	.01
120	Frank Viola	.12	.09	.05
121	Garry Templeton	.06	.05	.02
122	Lance Johnson(FC)	.10	.08	.04
123	Spike Owen	.03	.02	.01
124	Jim Traber	.06	.05	.02
125	Mike Krukow	.06	.05	.02
126	Sid Bream	.06	.05	.02
127	Walt Terrell	.06	.05	.02
128	Milt Thompson	.03	.02	.01
129	Terry Clark(FC)	.20	.15	.08
130	Gerald Perry	.08	.06	.03
131	Dave Otto(FC)	.08	.06	.03
132	Curt Ford	.03	.02	.01
133	Bill Long	.06	.05	.02
134	Don Zimmer	.03	.02	.01
135	Jose Rijo	.06	.05	.02
136	Joey Meyer	.08	.06	.03
137	Geno Petralli	.03	.02	.01
138	Wallace Johnson	.03	.02	.01
139	Mike Flanagan	.06	.05	.02
140	Shawon Dunston	.08	.06	.03
141	Indians Leaders (Brook Jacoby)	.06	.05	.02
142	Mike Diaz	.06	.05	.02
143	Mike Campbell	.08	.06	.03
144	Jay Bell	.06	.05	.02
145	Dave Stewart	.08	.06	.03
146	Gary Pettis	.03	.02	.01
147	DeWayne Buice	.03	.02	.01
148	Bill Pecota	.06	.05	.02
149	Doug Dascenzo(FC)	.25	.20	.10
150	Fernando Valenzuela	.15	.11	.06
151	Terry McGriff	.03	.02	.01
152	Mark Thurmond	.03	.02	.01
153	Jim Pankovits	.03	.02	.01
154	Don Carman	.06	.05	.02
155	Marty Barrett	.06	.05	.02
156	Dave Gallagher(FC)	.20	.15	.08
157	Tom Glavine	.08	.06	.03
158	Mike Aldrete	.06	.05	.02
159	Pat Clements	.03	.02	.01
160	Jeffrey Leonard	.06	.05	.02
161	#1 Draft Pick (Gregg Olson)(FC)	1.00	.70	.40
162	John Davis	.03	.02	.01
163	Bob Forsch	.06	.05	.02
164	Hal Lanier	.03	.02	.01

		MT	NR MT	EX
165	Mike Dunne	.08	.06	.03
166	*Doug Jennings*(FC)	.20	.15	.08
167	Future Star *(Steve Searcy)*(FC)	.25	.20	.10
168	Willie Wilson	.08	.06	.03
169	Mike Jackson	.06	.05	.02
170	Tony Fernandez	.10	.08	.04
171	Braves Leaders (Andres Thomas)	.06	.05	.02
172	Frank Williams	.03	.02	.01
173	Mel Hall	.06	.05	.02
174	*Todd Burns*(FC)	.25	.20	.10
175	John Shelby	.03	.02	.01
176	Jeff Parrett	.08	.06	.03
177	#1 Draft Pick *(Monty Fariss)*(FC)	.50	.40	.20
178	Mark Grant	.03	.02	.01
179	Ozzie Virgil	.03	.02	.01
180	Mike Scott	.10	.08	.04
181	*Craig Worthington*(FC)	.40	.30	.15
182	Bob McClure	.03	.02	.01
183	Oddibe McDowell	.06	.05	.02
184	*John Costello*	.20	.15	.08
185	Claudell Washington	.06	.05	.02
186	Pat Perry	.03	.02	.01
187	Darren Daulton	.03	.02	.01
188	Dennis Lamp	.03	.02	.01
189	Kevin Mitchell	.50	.40	.20
190	Mike Witt	.06	.05	.02
191	*Sil Campusano*	.20	.15	.08
192	Paul Mirabella	.03	.02	.01
193	Sparky Anderson	.06	.05	.02
194	*Greg Harris*(FC)	.25	.20	.10
195	Ozzie Guillen	.06	.05	.02
196	Denny Walling	.03	.02	.01
197	Neal Heaton	.03	.02	.01
198	Danny Heep	.03	.02	.01
199	*Mike Schooler*	.30	.25	.12
200	George Brett	.30	.25	.12
201	Blue Jays Leaders (Kelly Gruber)	.06	.05	.02
202	*Brad Moore*(FC)	.12	.09	.05
203	Rob Ducey	.03	.02	.01
204	Brad Havens	.03	.02	.01
205	Dwight Evans	.10	.08	.04
206	Roberto Alomar	.40	.30	.15
207	Terry Leach	.03	.02	.01
208	Tom Pagnozzi	.06	.05	.02
209	*Jeff Bittiger*(FC)	.12	.09	.05
210	Dale Murphy	.30	.25	.12
211	Mike Pagliarulo	.08	.06	.03
212	Scott Sanderson	.03	.02	.01
213	Rene Gonzales	.06	.05	.02
214	Charlie O'Brien	.03	.02	.01
215	Kevin Gross	.06	.05	.02
216	Jack Howell	.06	.05	.02
217	Joe Price	.03	.02	.01
218	Mike LaValliere	.06	.05	.02
219	Jim Clancy	.06	.05	.02
220	Gary Gaetti	.12	.09	.05
221	Cecil Espy	.08	.06	.03
222	#1 Draft Pick *(Mark Lewis)*(FC)	.50	.40	.20
223	Jay Buhner	.10	.08	.04
224	Tony LaRussa	.06	.05	.02
225	*Ramon Martinez*(FC)	.35	.25	.14
226	Bill Doran	.06	.05	.02
227	John Farrell	.08	.06	.03
228	*Nelson Santovenia*	.25	.20	.10
229	Jimmy Key	.08	.06	.03
230	Ozzie Smith	.12	.09	.05
231	Padres Leaders (Roberto Alomar)	.10	.08	.04
232	Ricky Horton	.06	.05	.02
233	Future Star (Gregg Jefferies)(FC)	2.50	2.00	1.00
234	Tom Browning	.08	.06	.03
235	John Kruk	.06	.05	.02
236	Charles Hudson	.03	.02	.01
237	Glenn Hubbard	.03	.02	.01
238	Eric King	.03	.02	.01
239	Tim Laudner	.03	.02	.01
240	Greg Maddux	.10	.08	.04
241	Brett Butler	.06	.05	.02
242	Ed Vande Berg	.03	.02	.01
243	Bob Boone	.06	.05	.02
244	Jim Acker	.03	.02	.01
245	Jim Rice	.20	.15	.08
246	Rey Quinones	.03	.02	.01
247	Shawn Hillegas	.06	.05	.02
248	Tony Phillips	.03	.02	.01
249	Tim Leary	.06	.05	.02
250	Cal Ripken	.30	.25	.12
251	*John Dopson*(FC)	.25	.20	.10
252	Billy Hatcher	.06	.05	.02
253	*Jose Alvarez*(FC)	.12	.09	.05
254	Tom LaSorda	.06	.05	.02
255	Ron Guidry	.12	.09	.05

		MT	NR MT	EX
256	Benny Santiago	.12	.09	.05
257	Rick Aguilera	.03	.02	.01
258	Checklist 133-264	.03	.02	.01
259	Larry McWilliams	.03	.02	.01
260	Dave Winfield	.25	.20	.10
261	Cardinals Leaders (Tom Brunansky)	.06	.05	.02
262	*Jeff Pico*	.20	.15	.08
263	Mike Felder	.03	.02	.01
264	*Rob Dibble*(FC)	.25	.20	.10
265	Kent Hrbek	.15	.11	.06
266	Luis Aquino	.03	.02	.01
267	Jeff Robinson	.06	.05	.02
268	Keith Miller	.06	.05	.02
269	Tom Bolton	.06	.05	.02
270	Wally Joyner	.20	.15	.08
271	Jay Tibbs	.03	.02	.01
272	Ron Hassey	.03	.02	.01
273	Jose Lind	.08	.06	.03
274	Mark Eichhorn	.06	.05	.02
275	Danny Tartabull	.15	.11	.06
276	Paul Kilgus	.08	.06	.03
277	Mike Davis	.06	.05	.02
278	Andy McGaffigan	.03	.02	.01
279	Scott Bradley	.03	.02	.01
280	Bob Knepper	.06	.05	.02
281	Gary Redus	.03	.02	.01
282	*Cris Carpenter*(FC)	.30	.25	.12
283	Andy Allanson	.03	.02	.01
284	Jim Leyland	.03	.02	.01
285	John Candelaria	.06	.05	.02
286	Darrin Jackson	.08	.06	.03
287	Juan Nieves	.06	.05	.02
288	Pat Sheridan	.03	.02	.01
289	Ernie Whitt	.06	.05	.02
290	John Franco	.08	.06	.03
291	Mets Leaders (Darryl Strawberry)	.12	.09	.05
292	*Jim Corsi*(FC)	.15	.11	.06
293	Glenn Wilson	.06	.05	.02
294	Juan Berenguer	.03	.02	.01
295	Scott Fletcher	.06	.05	.02
296	Ron Gant	.10	.08	.04
297	*Oswald Peraza*(FC)	.15	.11	.06
298	Chris James	.08	.06	.03
299	*Steve Ellsworth*(FC)	.12	.09	.05
300	Darryl Strawberry	.35	.25	.14
301	Charlie Leibrandt	.06	.05	.02
302	Gary Ward	.06	.05	.02
303	Felix Fermin	.06	.05	.02
304	Joel Youngblood	.03	.02	.01
305	Dave Smith	.06	.05	.02
306	Tracy Woodson(FC)	.10	.08	.04
307	Lance McCullers	.06	.05	.02
308	Ron Karkovice	.03	.02	.01
309	Mario Diaz(FC)	.10	.08	.04
310	Rafael Palmeiro	.20	.15	.08
311	Chris Bosio	.03	.02	.01
312	Tom Lawless	.03	.02	.01
313	Denny Martinez	.06	.05	.02
314	Bobby Valentine	.03	.02	.01
315	Greg Swindell	.10	.08	.04
316	Walt Weiss	.50	.40	.20
317	*Jack Armstrong*	.15	.11	.06
318	Gene Larkin	.08	.06	.03
319	Greg Booker	.03	.02	.01
320	Lou Whitaker	.15	.11	.06
321	Red Sox Leaders (Jody Reed)	.06	.05	.02
322	John Smiley	.10	.08	.04
323	Gary Thurman	.10	.08	.04
324	*Bob Milacki*(FC)	.25	.20	.10
325	Jesse Barfield	.08	.06	.03
326	Dennis Boyd	.06	.05	.02
327	*Mark Lemke*(FC)	.20	.15	.08
328	Rick Honeycutt	.03	.02	.01
329	Bob Melvin	.03	.02	.01
330	Eric Davis	.35	.25	.14
331	Curt Wilkerson	.03	.02	.01
332	Tony Armas	.06	.05	.02
333	Bob Ojeda	.06	.05	.02
334	Steve Lyons	.03	.02	.01
335	Dave Righetti	.10	.08	.04
336	Steve Balboni	.06	.05	.02
337	Calvin Schiraldi	.03	.02	.01
338	Jim Adduci(FC)	.06	.05	.02
339	Scott Bailes	.03	.02	.01
340	Kirk Gibson	.15	.11	.06
341	Jim Deshaies	.03	.02	.01
342	Tom Brookens	.03	.02	.01
343	Future Star *(Gary Sheffield)*(FC)	1.75	1.25	.70
344	Tom Trebelhorn	.03	.02	.01
345	Charlie Hough	.06	.05	.02

		MT	NR MT	EX
346	Rex Hudler(FC)	.06	.05	.02
347	John Cerutti	.06	.05	.02
348	Ed Hearn	.03	.02	.01
349	*Ron Jones*(FC)	.30	.25	.12
350	Andy Van Slyke	.12	.09	.05
351	Giants Leaders (Bob Melvin)	.06	.05	.02
352	Rick Schu	.03	.02	.01
353	Marvell Wynne	.03	.02	.01
354	Larry Parrish	.06	.05	.02
355	Mark Langston	.08	.06	.03
356	Kevin Elster	.08	.06	.03
357	Jerry Reuss	.06	.05	.02
358	*Ricky Jordan*(FC)	1.25	.90	.50
359	Tommy John	.10	.08	.04
360	Ryne Sandberg	.20	.15	.08
361	Kelly Downs	.08	.06	.03
362	Jack Lazorko	.03	.02	.01
363	Rich Yett	.03	.02	.01
364	Rob Deer	.06	.05	.02
365	Mike Henneman	.08	.06	.03
366	Herm Winningham	.03	.02	.01
367	*Johnny Paredes*(FC)	.20	.15	.08
368	Brian Holton	.06	.05	.02
369	Ken Caminiti	.06	.05	.02
370	Dennis Eckersley	.10	.08	.04
371	Manny Lee	.03	.02	.01
372	Craig Lefferts	.03	.02	.01
373	Tracy Jones	.08	.06	.03
374	John Wathan	.06	.05	.02
375	Terry Pendleton	.08	.06	.03
376	Steve Lombardozzi	.03	.02	.01
377	Mike Smithson	.03	.02	.01
378	Checklist 265-396	.03	.02	.01
379	Tim Flannery	.03	.02	.01
380	Rickey Henderson	.30	.25	.12
381	Orioles Leaders (Larry Sheets)	.06	.05	.02
382	*John Smoltz*(FC)	.40	.30	.15
383	Howard Johnson	.08	.06	.03
384	Mark Salas	.03	.02	.01
385	Von Hayes	.08	.06	.03
386	Andres Galarraga AS	.08	.06	.03
387	Ryne Sandberg AS	.10	.08	.04
388	Bobby Bonilla AS	.08	.06	.03
389	Ozzie Smith AS	.08	.06	.03
390	Darryl Strawberry AS	.15	.11	.06
391	Andre Dawson AS	.10	.08	.04
392	Andy Van Slyke AS	.08	.06	.03
393	Gary Carter AS	.10	.08	.04
394	Orel Hershiser AS	.12	.09	.05
395	Danny Jackson AS	.08	.06	.03
396	Kirk Gibson AS	.08	.06	.03
397	Don Mattingly AS	.60	.45	.25
398	Julio Franco AS	.06	.05	.02
399	Wade Boggs AS	.35	.25	.14
400	Alan Trammell AS	.08	.06	.03
401	Jose Canseco AS	.50	.40	.20
402	Mike Greenwell AS	.20	.15	.08
403	Kirby Puckett AS	.12	.09	.05
404	Bob Boone AS	.06	.05	.02
405	Roger Clemens AS	.15	.11	.06
406	Frank Viola AS	.08	.06	.03
407	Dave Winfield AS	.12	.09	.05
408	Greg Walker	.06	.05	.02
409	Ken Dayley	.03	.02	.01
410	Jack Clark	.12	.09	.05
411	Mitch Williams	.06	.05	.02
412	Barry Lyons	.03	.02	.01
413	Mike Kingery	.03	.02	.01
414	Jim Fregosi	.03	.02	.01
415	Rich Gossage	.10	.08	.04
416	Fred Lynn	.10	.08	.04
417	Mike LaCoss	.03	.02	.01
418	Bob Dernier	.03	.02	.01
419	Tom Filer	.03	.02	.01
420	Joe Carter	.10	.08	.04
421	Kirk McCaskill	.06	.05	.02
422	Bo Diaz	.06	.05	.02
423	Brian Fisher	.06	.05	.02
424	Luis Polonia	.06	.05	.02
425	Jay Howell	.06	.05	.02
426	Danny Gladden	.03	.02	.01
427	Eric Show	.06	.05	.02
428	Craig Reynolds	.03	.02	.01
429	Twins Leaders (Greg Gagne)	.06	.05	.02
430	Mark Gubicza	.08	.06	.03
431	Luis Rivera	.06	.05	.02
432	*Chad Kreuter*(FC)	.20	.15	.08
433	Albert Hall	.03	.02	.01
434	*Ken Patterson*(FC)	.15	.11	.06
435	Len Dykstra	.08	.06	.03
436	Bobby Meacham	.03	.02	.01

		MT	NR MT	EX
437	#1 Draft Pick *(Andy Benes)*	1.00	.70	.40
438	Greg Gross	.03	.02	.01
439	Frank DiPino	.03	.02	.01
440	Bobby Bonilla	.10	.08	.04
441	Jerry Reed	.03	.02	.01
442	Jose Oquendo	.03	.02	.01
443	*Rod Nichols*(FC)	.15	.11	.06
444	Moose Stubing	.03	.02	.01
445	Matt Nokes	.15	.11	.06
446	Rob Murphy	.03	.02	.01
447	Donell Nixon	.03	.02	.01
448	Eric Plunk	.03	.02	.01
449	Carmelo Martinez	.03	.02	.01
450	Roger Clemens	.40	.30	.15
451	Mark Davidson	.06	.05	.02
452	*Israel Sanchez*	.12	.09	.05
453	Tom Prince(FC)	.08	.06	.03
454	Paul Assenmacher	.03	.02	.01
455	Johnny Ray	.06	.05	.02
456	Tim Belcher	.08	.06	.03
457	Mackey Sasser	.06	.05	.02
458	*Donn Pall*(FC)	.20	.15	.08
459	Mariners Leaders (Dave Valle)	.06	.05	.02
460	Dave Stieb	.08	.06	.03
461	Buddy Bell	.06	.05	.02
462	Jose Guzman	.08	.06	.03
463	Steve Lake	.03	.02	.01
464	Bryn Smith	.03	.02	.01
465	Mark Grace	1.50	1.25	.60
466	Chuck Crim	.03	.02	.01
467	Jim Walewander	.03	.02	.01
468	Henry Cotto	.03	.02	.01
469	*Jose Bautista*	.20	.15	.08
470	Lance Parrish	.12	.09	.05
471	*Steve Curry*(FC)	.20	.15	.08
472	Brian Harper	.03	.02	.01
473	Don Robinson	.03	.02	.01
474	Bob Rodgers	.03	.02	.01
475	Dave Parker	.10	.08	.04
476	Jon Perlman(FC)	.06	.05	.02
477	Dick Schofield	.03	.02	.01
478	Doug Drabek	.06	.05	.02
479	*Mike Macfarlane*	.20	.15	.08
480	Keith Hernandez	.20	.15	.08
481	Chris Brown	.06	.05	.02
482	*Steve Peters*	.12	.09	.05
483	Mickey Hatcher	.03	.02	.01
484	Steve Shields	.03	.02	.01
485	Hubie Brooks	.08	.06	.03
486	Jack McDowell	.08	.06	.03
487	Scott Lusader(FC)	.08	.06	.03
488	Kevin Coffman	.06	.05	.02
489	Phillies Leaders (Mike Schmidt)	.12	.09	.05
490	*Chris Sabo*	.40	.30	.15
491	Mike Birkbeck	.03	.02	.01
492	Alan Ashby	.03	.02	.01
493	Todd Benzinger	.10	.08	.04
494	Shane Rawley	.06	.05	.02
495	Candy Maldonado	.06	.05	.02
496	Dwayne Henry	.03	.02	.01
497	Pete Stanicek	.12	.09	.05
498	Dave Valle	.03	.02	.01
499	*Don Heinkel*(FC)	.15	.11	.06
500	Jose Canseco	1.00	.70	.40
501	Vance Law	.06	.05	.02
502	Duane Ward	.03	.02	.01
503	Al Newman	.03	.02	.01
504	Bob Walk	.03	.02	.01
505	Pete Rose	.20	.15	.08
506	Kirt Manwaring	.10	.08	.04
507	Steve Farr	.03	.02	.01
508	Wally Backman	.06	.05	.02
509	Bud Black	.03	.02	.01
510	Bob Horner	.08	.06	.03
511	Richard Dotson	.06	.05	.02
512	Donnie Hill	.03	.02	.01
513	Jesse Orosco	.06	.05	.02
514	Chet Lemon	.06	.05	.02
515	Barry Larkin	.20	.15	.08
516	Eddie Whitson	.03	.02	.01
517	Greg Brock	.06	.05	.02
518	Bruce Ruffin	.03	.02	.01
519	Yankees Leaders (Willie Randolph)	.03	.02	.01
520	Rick Sutcliffe	.08	.06	.03
521	Mickey Tettleton	.03	.02	.01
522	*Randy Kramer*(FC)	.12	.09	.05
523	Andres Thomas	.06	.05	.02
524	Checklist 397-528	.03	.02	.01
525	Chili Davis	.06	.05	.02
526	Wes Gardner	.06	.05	.02
527	Dave Henderson	.08	.06	.03

	MT	NR MT	EX			MT	NR MT	EX
528 *Luis Medina*(FC)	.30	.25	.12	616 *Steve Rosenberg*(FC)		.15	.11	.06
529 Tom Foley	.03	.02	.01	617 *Mark Parent*		.15	.11	.06
530 Nolan Ryan	.35	.25	.14	618 Rance Mulliniks		.03	.02	.01
531 Dave Hengel(FC)	.08	.06	.03	619 Checklist 529-660		.03	.02	.01
532 Jerry Browne	.03	.02	.01	620 Barry Bonds		.10	.08	.04
533 Andy Hawkins	.03	.02	.01	621 Rick Mahler		.03	.02	.01
534 Doc Edwards	.03	.02	.01	622 Stan Javier		.03	.02	.01
535 Todd Worrell	.08	.06	.03	623 Fred Toliver		.03	.02	.01
536 Joel Skinner	.03	.02	.01	624 Jack McKeon		.03	.02	.01
537 Pete Smith	.08	.06	.03	625 Eddie Murray		.25	.20	.10
538 Juan Castillo	.03	.02	.01	626 Jeff Reed		.03	.02	.01
539 Barry Jones	.03	.02	.01	627 Greg Harris		.03	.02	.01
540 Bo Jackson	.50	.40	.20	628 Matt Williams		.10	.08	.04
541 Cecil Fielder	.03	.02	.01	629 Pete O'Brien		.06	.05	.02
542 Todd Frohwirth	.06	.05	.02	630 Mike Greenwell		.60	.45	.25
543 Damon Berryhill	.15	.11	.06	631 Dave Bergman		.03	.02	.01
544 Jeff Sellers	.03	.02	.01	632 *Bryan Harvey*		.20	.15	.08
545 Mookie Wilson	.06	.05	.02	633 Daryl Boston		.03	.02	.01
546 Mark Williamson	.06	.05	.02	634 Marvin Freeman(FC)		.08	.06	.03
547 Mark McLemore	.03	.02	.01	635 Willie Randolph		.06	.05	.02
548 Bobby Witt	.08	.06	.03	636 Bill Wilkinson		.06	.05	.02
549 Cubs Leaders (Jamie Moyer)	.03	.02	.01	637 Carmen Castillo		.03	.02	.01
550 Orel Hershiser	.20	.15	.08	638 Floyd Bannister		.06	.05	.02
551 Randy Ready	.03	.02	.01	639 Athletics Leaders (Walt Weiss)		.15	.11	.06
552 Greg Cadaret	.06	.05	.02	640 Willie McGee		.10	.08	.04
553 Luis Salazar	.03	.02	.01	641 Curt Young		.06	.05	.02
554 Nick Esasky	.06	.05	.02	642 Argenis Salazar		.03	.02	.01
555 Bert Blyleven	.10	.08	.04	643 *Louie Meadows*(FC)		.12	.09	.05
556 Bruce Fields(FC)	.06	.05	.02	644 Lloyd McClendon		.03	.02	.01
557 *Keith Miller*(FC)	.15	.11	.06	645 Jack Morris		.12	.09	.05
558 Dan Pasqua	.08	.06	.03	646 Kevin Bass		.06	.05	.02
559 Juan Agosto	.03	.02	.01	647 *Randy Johnson*(FC)		.25	.20	.10
560 Rock Raines	.25	.20	.10	648 Future Star *(Sandy Alomar)*(FC)		1.25	.90	.50
561 Luis Aguayo	.03	.02	.01	649 Stewart Cliburn		.03	.02	.01
562 Danny Cox	.06	.05	.02	650 Kirby Puckett		.25	.20	.10
563 Bill Schroeder	.03	.02	.01	651 Tom Niedenfuer		.06	.05	.02
564 Russ Nixon	.03	.02	.01	652 Rich Gedman		.06	.05	.02
565 Jeff Russell	.03	.02	.01	653 *Tommy Barrett*(FC)		.12	.09	.05
566 Al Pedrique	.03	.02	.01	654 Whitey Herzog		.06	.05	.02
567 David Wells	.08	.06	.03	655 Dave Magadan		.08	.06	.03
568 Mickey Brantley	.03	.02	.01	656 Ivan Calderon		.06	.05	.02
569 *German Jimenez*(FC)	.08	.06	.03	657 Joe Magrane		.08	.06	.03
570 Tony Gwynn	.30	.25	.12	658 R.J. Reynolds		.03	.02	.01
571 Billy Ripken	.06	.05	.02	659 Al Leiter		.15	.11	.06
572 Atlee Hammaker	.03	.02	.01	660 Will Clark		.50	.40	.20
573 #1 Draft Pick *(Jim Abbott)*	2.00	1.50	.80	661 Turn Back The Clock (Dwight Gooden)				
574 Dave Clark	.06	.05	.02			.20	.15	.08
575 Juan Samuel	.10	.08	.04	662 Turn Back The Clock (Lou Brock)		.08	.06	.03
576 Greg Minton	.03	.02	.01	663 Turn Back The Clock (Hank Aaron)		.15	.11	.06
577 Randy Bush	.03	.02	.01	664 Turn Back The Clock (Gil Hodges)		.06	.05	.02
578 John Morris	.03	.02	.01	665 Turn Back The Clock (Tony Oliva)		.06	.05	.02
579 Astros Leaders (Glenn Davis)	.08	.06	.03	666 Randy St. Claire		.03	.02	.01
580 Harold Reynolds	.06	.05	.02	667 Dwayne Murphy		.06	.05	.02
581 Gene Nelson	.03	.02	.01	668 Mike Bielecki		.03	.02	.01
582 Mike Marshall	.10	.08	.04	669 Dodgers Leaders (Orel Hershiser)		.12	.09	.05
583 *Paul Gibson*(FC)	.15	.11	.06	670 Kevin Seitzer		.25	.20	.10
584 Randy Velarde(FC)	.10	.08	.04	671 Jim Gantner		.03	.02	.01
585 Harold Baines	.10	.08	.04	672 Allan Anderson		.06	.05	.02
586 Joe Boever	.03	.02	.01	673 Don Baylor		.08	.06	.03
587 Mike Stanley	.03	.02	.01	674 Otis Nixon		.03	.02	.01
588 *Luis Alicea*	.15	.11	.06	675 Bruce Hurst		.08	.06	.03
589 Dave Meads	.03	.02	.01	676 Ernie Riles		.03	.02	.01
590 Andres Galarraga	.12	.09	.05	677 Dave Schmidt		.03	.02	.01
591 Jeff Musselman	.06	.05	.02	678 Dion James		.03	.02	.01
592 John Cangelosi	.03	.02	.01	679 Willie Fraser		.03	.02	.01
593 Drew Hall	.10	.08	.04	680 Gary Carter		.15	.11	.06
594 Jimy Williams	.03	.02	.01	681 Jeff Robinson		.10	.08	.04
595 Teddy Higuera	.08	.06	.03	682 Rick Leach		.03	.02	.01
596 Kurt Stillwell	.06	.05	.02	683 *Jose Cecena*		.15	.11	.06
597 *Terry Taylor*(FC)	.12	.09	.05	684 Dave Johnson		.06	.05	.02
598 Ken Gerhart	.06	.05	.02	685 Jeff Treadway		.10	.08	.04
599 Tom Candiotti	.03	.02	.01	686 Scott Terry		.08	.06	.03
600 Wade Boggs	.90	.70	.35	687 Alvin Davis		.10	.08	.04
601 Dave Dravecky	.06	.05	.02	688 Zane Smith		.06	.05	.02
602 Devon White	.10	.08	.04	689 Stan Jefferson		.03	.02	.01
603 Frank Tanana	.06	.05	.02	690 Doug Jones		.10	.08	.04
604 Paul O'Neill	.03	.02	.01	691 Roberto Kelly		.25	.20	.10
605a Bob Welch (missing Complete Major				692 Steve Ontiveros		.03	.02	.01
League Pitching Record line)	2.50	2.00	1.00	693 *Pat Borders*		.20	.15	.08
605b Bob Welch (contains Complete Major				694 Les Lancaster		.06	.05	.02
League Pitching Record line)	.08	.06	.03	695 Carlton Fisk		.20	.15	.08
606 Rick Dempsey	.06	.05	.02	696 Don August		.08	.06	.03
607 #1 Draft Pick *(Willie Ansley)*(FC)	.50	.40	.20	697 Franklin Stubbs		.03	.02	.01
608 Phil Bradley	.08	.06	.03	698 Keith Atherton		.03	.02	.01
609 Tigers Leaders (Frank Tanana)	.06	.05	.02	699 Pirates Leaders (Al Pedrique)		.06	.05	.02
610 Randy Myers	.08	.06	.03	700 Don Mattingly		1.25	.90	.50
611 Don Slaught	.03	.02	.01	701 Storm Davis		.08	.06	.03
612 Dan Quisenberry	.06	.05	.02	702 Jamie Quirk		.03	.02	.01
613 *Gary Varsho*(FC)	.20	.15	.08	703 Scott Garrelts		.03	.02	.01
614 Joe Hesketh	.03	.02	.01	704 *Carlos Quintana*(FC)		.35	.25	.14
615 Robin Yount	.25	.20	.10	705 Terry Kennedy		.06	.05	.02

	MT	NR MT	EX
706 Pete Incaviglia	.08	.06	.03
707 Steve Jeltz	.03	.02	.01
708 Chuck Finley	.03	.02	.01
709 Tom Herr	.06	.05	.02
710 Dave Cone	.30	.25	.12
711 *Candy Sierra*(FC)	.12	.09	.05
712 Bill Swift	.03	.02	.01
713 #1 Draft Pick *(Ty Griffin)*	1.00	.70	.40
714 Joe Morgan	.03	.02	.01
715 Tony Pena	.06	.05	.02
716 Wayne Tolleson	.03	.02	.01
717 Jamie Moyer	.03	.02	.01
718 Glenn Braggs	.06	.05	.02
719 Danny Darwin	.03	.02	.01
720 Tim Wallach	.08	.06	.03
721 *Ron Tingley*(FC)	.12	.09	.05
722 Todd Stottlemyre	.15	.11	.06
723 Rafael Belliard	.03	.02	.01
724 Jerry Don Gleaton	.03	.02	.01
725 Terry Steinbach	.08	.06	.03
726 Dickie Thon	.03	.02	.01
727 Joe Orsulak	.03	.02	.01
728 Charlie Puleo	.03	.02	.01
729 Rangers Leaders (Steve Buechele)	.06	.05	.02
730 Danny Jackson	.12	.09	.05
731 Mike Young	.03	.02	.01
732 Steve Buechele	.03	.02	.01
733 *Randy Bockus*(FC)	.06	.05	.02
734 Jody Reed	.10	.08	.04
735 Roger McDowell	.08	.06	.03
736 Jeff Hamilton	.06	.05	.02
737 *Norm Charlton*(FC)	.25	.20	.10
738 Darnell Coles	.06	.05	.02
739 Brook Jacoby	.08	.06	.03
740 Dan Plesac	.08	.06	.03
741 Ken Phelps	.06	.05	.02
742 Future Star *(Mike Harkey)*(FC)	.30	.25	.12
743 Mike Heath	.03	.02	.01
744 Roger Craig	.06	.05	.02
745 Fred McGriff	.40	.30	.15
746 *German Gonzalez*(FC)	.20	.15	.08
747 Wil Tejada(FC)	.06	.05	.02
748 Jimmy Jones	.03	.02	.01
749 Rafael Ramirez	.03	.02	.01
750 Bret Saberhagen	.12	.09	.05
751 Ken Oberkfell	.03	.02	.01
752 Jim Gott	.03	.02	.01
753 Jose Uribe	.03	.02	.01
754 Bob Brower	.03	.02	.01
755 Mike Scioscia	.06	.05	.02
756 *Scott Medvin*(FC)	.20	.15	.08
757 *Brady Anderson*	.30	.25	.12
758 Gene Walter	.03	.02	.01
759 Brewers Leaders (Rob Deer)	.06	.05	.02
760 Lee Smith	.08	.06	.03
761 *Dante Bichette*(FC)	.20	.15	.08
762 Bobby Thigpen	.08	.06	.03
763 Dave Martinez	.06	.05	.02
764 #1 Draft Pick *(Robin Ventura)*	1.00	.70	.40
765 Glenn Davis	.20	.15	.08
766 Cecilio Guante	.03	.02	.01
767 *Mike Capel*(FC)	.15	.11	.06
768 Bill Wegman	.03	.02	.01
769 Junior Ortiz	.03	.02	.01
770 Alan Trammell	.15	.11	.06
771 Ron Kittle	.06	.05	.02
772 Ron Oester	.03	.02	.01
773 Keith Moreland	.06	.05	.02
774 Frank Robinson	.08	.06	.03
775 Jeff Reardon	.08	.06	.03
776 Nelson Liriano	.06	.05	.02
777 Ted Power	.03	.02	.01
778 Bruce Benedict	.03	.02	.01
779 Craig McMurtry	.03	.02	.01
780 Pedro Guerrero	.12	.09	.05
781 *Greg Briley*(FC)	.70	.50	.30
782 Checklist 661-792	.03	.02	.01
783 *Trevor Wilson*(FC)	.15	.11	.06
784 #1 Draft Pick *(Steve Avery)*(FC)	.60	.45	.25
785 Ellis Burks	.50	.40	.20
786 Melido Perez	.08	.06	.03
787 *Dave West*(FC)	.50	.40	.20
788 Mike Morgan	.03	.02	.01
789 Royals Leaders (Bo Jackson)	.15	.11	.06
790 Sid Fernandez	.08	.06	.03
791 Jim Lindeman	.03	.02	.01
792 Rafael Santana	.03	.02	.01

**NOTE: A card number in parentheses ( )
indicates the set is unnumbered.**

1989 Topps Traded

For the ninth straight year, Topps issued its annual 132-card "Traded" set at the end of the 1989 baseball season. The set, which was packaged in a special box and sold by hobby dealers, includes traded players and rookies who were not in the regular 1989 Topps set.

	MT	NR MT	EX
Complete Set:	15.00	11.00	6.00
Common Player:	.05	.04	.02
1T Don Aase	.05	.04	.02
2T Jim Abbott	1.25	.90	.50
3T Kent Anderson(FC)	.25	.20	.10
4T Keith Atherton	.05	.04	.02
5T Wally Backman	.05	.04	.02
6T Steve Balboni	.05	.04	.02
7T Jesse Barfield	.05	.04	.02
8T Steve Bedrosian	.05	.04	.02
9T Todd Benzinger	.05	.04	.02
10T Geronimo Berroa(FC)	.10	.08	.04
11T Bert Blyleven	.05	.04	.02
12T Bob Boone	.05	.04	.02
13T Phil Bradley	.08	.06	.03
14T Jeff Brantley(FC)	.25	.20	.10
15T Kevin Brown(FC)	.20	.15	.08
16T Jerry Browne	.05	.04	.02
17T Chuck Cary	.20	.15	.08
18T Carmen Castillo	.05	.04	.02
19T Jim Clancy	.05	.04	.02
20T Jack Clark	.10	.08	.04
21T Bryan Clutterbuck	.05	.04	.02
22T Jody Davis	.05	.04	.02
23T Mike Devereaux(FC)	.10	.08	.04
24T Frank DiPino	.05	.04	.02
25T Benny DiStefano	.05	.04	.02
26T John Dopson	.20	.15	.08
27T Len Dykstra	.10	.08	.04
28T Jim Eisenreich	.05	.04	.02
29T Nick Esasky	.08	.06	.03
30T Alvaro Espinosa(FC)	.25	.20	.10
31T Darrell Evans	.08	.06	.03
32T Junior Felix(FC)	.80	.60	.30
33T Felix Fermin	.05	.04	.02
34T Julio Franco	.15	.11	.06
35T Terry Francona	.05	.04	.02
36T Cito Gaston	.05	.04	.02
37T Bob Geren (incorrect photo)(FC)	.50	.40	.20
38T Tom Gordon(FC)	1.25	.90	.50
39T Tommy Gregg(FC)	.25	.20	.10
40T Ken Griffey	.15	.11	.06
41T Ken Griffey Jr.(FC)	3.50	2.75	1.50
42T Kevin Gross	.05	.04	.02
43T Lee Guetterman	.05	.04	.02
44T Mel Hall	.05	.04	.02
45T Erik Hanson(FC)	.30	.25	.12
46T Gene Harris(FC)	.25	.20	.10
47T Andy Hawkins	.05	.04	.02
48T Rickey Henderson	.35	.25	.14
49T Tom Herr	.05	.04	.02
50T Ken Hill(FC)	.20	.15	.08
51T Brian Holman(FC)	.25	.20	.10
52T Brian Holton	.10	.08	.04
53T Art Howe	.05	.04	.03
54T Ken Howell	.05	.04	.02
55T Bruce Hurst	.05	.04	.02
56T Chris James	.05	.04	.02
57T Randy Johnson(FC)	.20	.15	.08

		MT	NR MT	EX
58T	Jimmy Jones	.05	.04	.02
59T	Terry Kennedy	.05	.04	.02
60T	Paul Kilgus	.05	.04	.02
61T	Eric King	.08	.06	.03
62T	Ron Kittle	.08	.06	.03
63T	John Kruk	.08	.06	.03
64T	Randy Kutcher(FC)	.08	.06	.03
65T	Steve Lake	.05	.04	.02
66T	Mark Langston	.25	.20	.10
67T	Dave LaPoint	.05	.04	.02
68T	Rick Leach	.05	.04	.02
69T	Terry Leach	.05	.04	.02
70T	Jim Levebvre	.05	.04	.02
71T	Al Leiter	.05	.04	.02
72T	Jeffrey Leonard	.05	.04	.02
73T	Derek Lilliquist(FC)	.25	.20	.10
74T	Rick Mahler	.05	.04	.02
75T	Tom McCarthy(FC)	.25	.20	.10
76T	Lloyd McClendon	.20	.15	.08
77T	Lance McCullers	.05	.04	.02
78T	Oddibe McDowell	.05	.04	.02
79T	Roger McDowell	.05	.04	.02
80T	Larry McWilliams	.05	.04	.02
81T	Randy Milligan(FC)	.20	.15	.08
82T	Mike Moore	.15	.11	.06
83T	Keith Moreland	.05	.04	.02
84T	Mike Morgan	.05	.04	.02
85T	Jamie Moyer	.05	.04	.02
86T	Rob Murphy	.05	.04	.02
87T	Eddie Murray	.30	.25	.12
88T	Pete O'Brien	.05	.04	.02
89T	Gregg Olson	.60	.45	.25
90T	Steve Ontiveros	.05	.04	.02
91T	Jesse Orosco	.05	.04	.02
92T	Spike Owen	.05	.04	.02
93T	Rafael Palmeiro	.08	.06	.03
94T	Clay Parker(FC)	.20	.15	.08
95T	Jeff Parrett	.05	.04	.02
96T	Lance Parrish	.05	.04	.02
97T	Dennis Powell	.05	.04	.02
98T	Rey Quinones	.05	.04	.02
99T	Doug Rader	.05	.04	.02
100T	Willie Randolph	.08	.06	.03
101T	Shane Rawley	.05	.04	.02
102T	Randy Ready	.05	.04	.02
103T	Bip Roberts	.05	.04	.02
104T	Kenny Rogers(FC)	.25	.20	.10
105T	Ed Romero	.05	.04	.02
106T	Nolan Ryan	1.00	.70	.40
107T	Luis Salazar	.05	.04	.02
108T	Juan Samuel	.08	.06	.03
109T	Alex Sanchez(FC)	.20	.15	.08
110T	Deion Sanders(FC)	.90	.70	.35
111T	Steve Sax	.15	.11	.06
112T	Rick Schu	.05	.04	.02
113T	Dwight Smith(FC)	1.50	1.25	.60
114T	Lonnie Smith	.05	.04	.02
115T	Billy Spiers(FC)	.40	.30	.15
116T	Kent Tekulve	.05	.04	.02
117T	Walt Terrell	.05	.04	.02
118T	Milt Thompson	.05	.04	.02
119T	Dickie Thon	.05	.04	.02
120T	Jeff Torborg	.05	.04	.02
121T	Jeff Treadway	.05	.04	.02
122T	Omar Vizquel(FC)	.30	.25	.12
123T	Jerome Walton(FC)	4.00	3.00	1.50
124T	Gary Ward	.05	.04	.02
125T	Claudell Washington	.05	.04	.02
126T	Curt Wilkerson	.05	.04	.02
127T	Eddie Williams	.05	.04	.02
128T	Frank Williams	.05	.04	.02
129T	Ken Williams	.05	.04	.02
130T	Mitch Williams	.15	.11	.06
131T	Steve Wilson(FC)	.20	.15	.08
132T	Checklist	.05	.04	.02

1989 Topps
All-Star Glossy Set Of 60

For the seventh straight year Topps issued this "send-away" glossy set. Divided into six 10-card sets, it was available only by sending in special offer cards from the 1989 Topps wax packs. The 2-1/2" by 3-1/2" cards feature full-color photos bordered in white with a thin yellow frame. The player's name appears in small print in the lower right corner. Red-and-blue-printed flip sides provide basic

information including player's name, team, and position. Any of the six 10-card sets were available for $1.25 and six special offer cards. The set was also made available in its complete 60-card set form for $7.50 and 18 special offer cards.

		MT	NR MT	EX
Complete Set:		12.00	9.00	4.75
Common Player:		.15	.11	.06
1	Kirby Puckett	.50	.40	.20
2	Eric Davis	.70	.50	.30
3	Joe Carter	.20	.15	.08
4	Andy Van Slyke	.20	.15	.08
5	Wade Boggs	1.00	.70	.40
6	Dave Cone	.25	.20	.10
7	Kent Hrbek	.15	.11	.06
8	Darryl Strawberry	.70	.50	.30
9	Jay Buhner	.15	.11	.06
10	Ron Gant	.15	.11	.06
11	Will Clark	1.00	.70	.40
12	Jose Canseco	1.50	1.25	.60
13	Juan Samuel	.15	.11	.06
14	George Brett	.25	.20	.10
15	Benny Santiago	.20	.15	.08
16	Dennis Eckersley	.15	.11	.06
17	Gary Carter	.15	.11	.06
18	Frank Viola	.20	.15	.08
19	Roberto Alomar	.30	.25	.12
20	Paul Gibson	.15	.11	.06
21	Dave Winfield	.20	.15	.08
22	Howard Johnson	.35	.25	.14
23	Roger Clemens	.40	.30	.15
24	Bobby Bonilla	.25	.20	.10
25	Alan Trammell	.20	.15	.08
26	Kevin McReynolds	.20	.15	.08
27	George Bell	.20	.15	.08
28	Bruce Hurst	.15	.11	.06
29	Mark Grace	1.00	.70	.40
30	Tim Belcher	.20	.15	.08
31	Mike Greenwell	.80	.60	.30
32	Glenn Davis	.15	.11	.06
33	Gary Gaetti	.15	.11	.06
34	Ryne Sandberg	.30	.25	.12
35	Rickey Henderson	.35	.25	.14
36	Dwight Evans	.15	.11	.06
37	Doc Gooden	.50	.40	.20
38	Robin Yount	.25	.20	.10
39	Damon Berryhill	.15	.11	.06
40	Chris Sabo	.20	.15	.10
41	Mark McGwire	1.00	.70	.40
42	Ozzie Smith	.25	.20	.10
43	Paul Molitor	.20	.15	.08
44	Andres Galarraga	.30	.25	.12
45	Dave Stewart	.15	.11	.06
46	Tom Browning	.15	.11	.06
47	Cal Ripken	.50	.40	.20
48	Orel Hershiser	.40	.30	.15
49	Dave Gallagher	.20	.15	.08
50	Walt Weiss	.20	.15	.08
51	Don Mattingly	2.50	2.00	1.00
52	Tony Fernandez	.20	.15	.08
53	Rock Raines	.20	.15	.08
54	Jeff Reardon	.15	.11	.06
55	Kirk Gibson	.20	.15	.08
56	Jack Clark	.20	.15	.08
57	Danny Jackson	.15	.11	.06
58	Tony Gwynn	.60	.45	.25
59	Cecil Espy	.15	.11	.06
60	Jody Reed	.15	.11	.06

1989 Topps Big Baseball

Known by collectors as Topps "Big Baseball," the cards in this 330-card set measure 2-5/8" by 3-3/4" and are patterned after the 1956 Topps cards. The glossy card fronts are horizontally-designed and include two photos of each player, a posed head shot alongside an action photo. The backs include 1988 and career stats, but are dominated by a color cartoon featuring the player. The set was issued in three series of 110 cards each.

		MT	NR MT	EX
Complete Set:		25.00	20.00	10.00
Common Player:		.05	.04	.02
1	Orel Hershiser	.15	.11	.06
2	Harold Reynolds	.08	.06	.03
3	Jody Davis	.05	.04	.02
4	Greg Walker	.05	.04	.02
5	Barry Bonds	.08	.06	.03
6	Bret Saberhagen	.12	.09	.05
7	Johnny Ray	.05	.04	.02
8	Mike Fiore	.20	.15	.08
9	Juan Castillo	.05	.04	.02
10	Todd Burns	.05	.04	.02
11	Carmelo Martinez	.05	.04	.02
12	Geno Petralli	.05	.04	.02
13	Mel Hall	.05	.04	.02
14	Tom Browning	.08	.06	.03
15	Fred McGriff	.15	.11	.06
16	Kevin Elster	.05	.04	.02
17	Tim Leary	.05	.04	.02
18	Jim Rice	.05	.04	.02
19	Bret Barberie	.15	.11	.06
20	Jay Buhner	.05	.04	.02
21	Atlee Hammaker	.05	.04	.02
22	Lou Whitaker	.05	.04	.02
23	Paul Runge	.05	.04	.02
24	Carlton Fisk	.08	.06	.03
25	Jose Lind	.05	.04	.02
26	Mark Gubicza	.08	.06	.03
27	Billy Ripken	.05	.04	.02
28	Mike Pagliarulo	.05	.04	.02
29	Jim Deshaies	.05	.04	.02
30	Mark McLemore	.05	.04	.02
31	Scott Terry	.05	.04	.02
32	Franklin Stubbs	.05	.04	.02
33	Don August	.05	.04	.02
34	Mark McGwire	1.00	.70	.40
35	Eric Show	.05	.04	.02
36	Cecil Espy	.05	.04	.02
37	Ron Tingley	.05	.04	.02
38	Mickey Brantley	.05	.04	.02
39	Paul O'Neill	.05	.04	.02
40	Ed Sprague	.35	.25	.14
41	Len Dykstra	.05	.04	.02
42	Roger Clemens	.25	.20	.10
43	Ron Gant	.05	.04	.02
44	Dan Pasqua	.05	.04	.02
45	Jeff Robinson	.05	.04	.02
46	George Brett	.15	.11	.06
47	Bryn Smith	.05	.04	.02
48	Mike Marshall	.05	.04	.02
49	Doug Robbins	.15	.11	.06
50	Don Mattingly	1.50	1.25	.60
51	Mike Scott	.08	.06	.03
52	Steve Jeltz	.05	.04	.02
53	Dick Schofield	.05	.04	.02
54	Tom Brunansky	.08	.06	.03
55	Gary Sheffield	1.00	.70	.40
56	Dave Valle	.05	.04	.02
57	Carney Lansford	.08	.06	.03
58	Tony Gwynn	.15	.11	.06
59	Checklist	.05	.04	.02
60	Damon Berryhill	.05	.04	.02
61	Jack Morris	.05	.04	.02
62	Brett Butler	.05	.04	.02
63	Mickey Hatcher	.05	.04	.02
64	Bruce Sutter	.05	.04	.02
65	Robin Ventura	.80	.60	.30
66	Junior Oritiz	.05	.04	.02
67	Pat Tabler	.05	.04	.02
68	Greg Swindell	.08	.06	.03
69	Jeff Branson	.20	.15	.08
70	Manny Lee	.05	.04	.02
71	Dave Magadan	.05	.04	.02
72	Rich Gedman	.05	.04	.02
73	Rock Raines	.08	.06	.03
74	Mike Maddux	.05	.04	.02
75	Jim Presley	.05	.04	.02
76	Chuck Finley	.05	.04	.02
77	Jose Oquendo	.05	.04	.02
78	Rob Deer	.05	.04	.02
79	Jay Howell	.05	.04	.02
80	Terry Steinbach	.08	.06	.03
81	Eddie Whitson	.05	.04	.02
82	Ruben Sierra	.20	.15	.08
83	Bruce Benedict	.05	.04	.02
84	Fred Manrique	.05	.04	.02
85	John Smiley	.05	.04	.02
86	Mike Macfarlane	.05	.04	.02
87	Rene Gonzales	.05	.04	.02
88	Charles Hudson	.05	.04	.02
90	Les Straker	.05	.04	.02
91	Carmen Castillo	.05	.04	.02
92	Tracy Woodson	.05	.04	.02
93	Tino Martinez	.70	.50	.30
94	Herm Winningham	.05	.04	.02
95	Kelly Gruber	.05	.04	.02
96	Terry Leach	.05	.04	.02
97	Jody Reed	.05	.04	.02
98	Nelson Santovenia	.05	.04	.02
99	Tony Armas	.05	.04	.02
100	Greg Brock	.05	.04	.02
101	Dave Stewart	.05	.04	.02
102	Roberto Alomar	.08	.06	.03
103	Jim Sundberg	.05	.04	.02
104	Albert Hall	.05	.04	.02
105	Steve Lyons	.05	.04	.02
106	Sid Bream	.05	.04	.02
107	Danny Tartabull	.08	.06	.03
108	Rick Dempsey	.05	.04	.02
109	Rich Renteria	.05	.04	.02
110	Ozzie Smith	.08	.06	.03
111	Steve Sax	.08	.06	.03
112	Kelly Downs	.05	.04	.02
113	Larry Sheets	.05	.04	.02
114	Andy Benes	1.00	.70	.40
115	Pete O'Brien	.05	.04	.02
116	Kevin McReynolds	.08	.06	.03
117	Juan Berenguer	.05	.04	.02
118	Billy Hatcher	.05	.04	.02
119	Rick Cerone	.05	.04	.02
120	Andre Dawson	.08	.06	.03
121	Storm Davis	.05	.04	.02
122	Devon White	.05	.04	.02
123	Alan Trammell	.08	.06	.03
124	Vince Coleman	.08	.06	.03
125	Al Leiter	.05	.04	.02
126	Dale Sveum	.05	.04	.02
127	Pete Incaviglia	.05	.04	.02
128	Dave Stieb	.08	.06	.03
129	Kevin Mitchell	.30	.25	.12
130	Dave Schmidt	.05	.04	.02
131	Gary Redus	.05	.04	.02
132	Ron Robinson	.05	.04	.02
133	Darnell Coles	.05	.04	.02
134	Benny Santiago	.08	.06	.03
135	John Farrell	.05	.04	.02
136	Willie Wilson	.05	.04	.02
137	Steve Bedrosian	.05	.04	.02
138	Don Slaught	.05	.04	.02
139	Darryl Strawberry	.25	.20	.10
140	Frank Viola	.10	.08	.04
141	Dave Silvestri	.20	.15	.08
142	Carlos Quintana	.05	.04	.02
143	Vance Law	.05	.04	.02
144	Dave Parker	.05	.04	.02

		MT	NR MT	EX				MT	NR MT	EX
145	Tim Belcher	.05	.04	.02		236	Jerry Browne	.05	.04	.02
146	Will Clark	.90	.70	.35		237	Rick Rhoden	.05	.04	.02
147	Mark Williamson	.05	.04	.02		238	Bo Jackson	.50	.40	.20
148	Ozzie Guillen	.05	.04	.02		239	Randy Velarde	.05	.04	.02
149	Kirk McCaskill	.05	.04	.02		240	Jack Clark	.05	.04	.02
150	Pat Sheridan	.05	.04	.02		241	Wade Boggs	.80	.60	.30
151	Terry Pendleton	.05	.04	.02		242	Lonnie Smith	.05	.04	.02
152	Roberto Kelly	.05	.04	.02		243	Mike Flanagan	.05	.04	.02
153	Joey Meyer	.05	.04	.02		244	Willie Randolph	.05	.04	.02
154	Mark Grant	.05	.04	.02		245	Oddibe McDowell	.05	.04	.02
155	Joe Carter	.08	.06	.03		246	Ricky Jordan	.35	.25	.14
156	Steve Buechele	.05	.04	.02		247	Greg Briley	.20	.15	.08
157	Tony Fernandez	.08	.06	.03		248	Rex Hudler	.05	.04	.02
158	Jeff Reed	.05	.04	.02		249	Robin Yount	.20	.15	.08
159	Bobby Bonilla	.08	.06	.03		250	Lance Parrish	.05	.04	.02
160	Henry Cotto	.05	.04	.02		251	Chris Sabo	.20	.15	.08
161	Kurt Stillwell	.05	.04	.02		252	Mike Henneman	.05	.04	.02
162	Mickey Morandini	.25	.20	.10		253	Gregg Jefferies	1.00	.70	.40
163	Robby Thompson	.05	.04	.02		254	Curt Young	.05	.04	.02
164	Rick Schu	.05	.04	.02		255	Andy Van Slyke	.08	.06	.03
165	Stan Jefferson	.05	.04	.02		256	Rod Booker	.05	.04	.02
166	Ron Darling	.05	.04	.02		257	Rafael Palmeiro	.05	.04	.02
167	Kirby Puckett	.25	.20	.10		258	Jose Uribe	.05	.04	.02
168	Bill Doran	.05	.04	.02		259	Ellis Burks	.20	.15	.08
169	Dennis Lamp	.05	.04	.02		260	John Smoltz	.10	.08	.04
170	Ty Griffin	.60	.45	.25		261	Tom Foley	.05	.04	.02
171	Ron Hassey	.05	.04	.02		262	Lloyd Moseby	.05	.04	.02
172	Dale Murphy	.08	.06	.03		263	Jim Poole	.15	.11	.06
173	Andres Galarraga	.08	.06	.03		264	Gary Gaetti	.08	.06	.03
174	Tim Flannery	.05	.04	.02		265	Bob Dernier	.05	.04	.02
175	Cory Snyder	.05	.04	.02		266	Harold Baines	.08	.06	.03
176	Checklist	.05	.04	.02		267	Tom Candiotti	.05	.04	.02
177	Tommy Barrett	.05	.04	.02		268	Rafael Ramirez	.05	.04	.02
178	Dan Petry	.05	.04	.02		269	Bob Boone	.05	.04	.02
179	Billy Masse	.20	.15	.08		270	Buddy Bell	.05	.04	.02
180	Terry Kennedy	.05	.04	.02		271	Rickey Henderson	.15	.11	.06
181	Joe Orsulak	.05	.04	.02		272	Willie Fraser	.05	.04	.02
182	Doyle Alexander	.05	.04	.02		273	Eric Davis	.25	.20	.10
183	Willie McGee	.05	.04	.02		274	Jeff Robinson	.05	.04	.02
184	Jim Gantner	.05	.04	.02		275	Damaso Garcia	.05	.04	.02
185	Keith Hernandez	.05	.04	.02		276	Sid Fernandez	.05	.04	.02
186	Greg Gagne	.05	.04	.02		277	Stan Javier	.05	.04	.02
187	Kevin Bass	.05	.04	.02		278	Marty Barrett	.05	.04	.02
188	Mark Eichhorn	.05	.04	.02		279	Gerald Perry	.05	.04	.02
189	Mark Grace	.25	.20	.10		280	Rob Ducey	.05	.04	.02
190	Jose Canseco	1.00	.70	.40		281	Mike Scioscia	.05	.04	.02
191	Bobby Witt	.05	.04	.02		282	Randy Bush	.05	.04	.02
192	Rafael Santana	.05	.04	.02		283	Tom Herr	.05	.04	.02
193	Dwight Evans	.05	.04	.02		284	Glenn Wilson	.05	.04	.02
194	Greg Booker	.05	.04	.02		285	Pedro Guerrero	.10	.08	.04
195	Brook Jacoby	.05	.04	.02		286	Cal Ripken	.10	.08	.04
196	Rafael Belliard	.05	.04	.02		287	Randy Johnson	.15	.11	.06
197	Candy Maldonado	.05	.04	.02		288	Julio Franco	.08	.06	.03
198	Mickey Tettleton	.08	.06	.03		289	Ivan Calderon	.05	.04	.02
199	Barry Larkin	.08	.06	.03		290	Rich Yett	.05	.04	.02
200	Frank White	.05	.04	.02		291	Scott Servais	.20	.15	.08
201	Wally Joyner	.15	.11	.06		292	Bill Pecota	.05	.04	.02
202	Chet Lemon	.05	.04	.02		293	Ken Phelps	.05	.04	.02
203	Joe Magrane	.05	.04	.02		294	Chili Davis	.05	.04	.02
204	Glenn Braggs	.05	.04	.02		295	Manny Trillo	.05	.04	.02
205	Scott Fletcher	.05	.04	.02		296	Mike Boddicker	.05	.04	.02
206	Gary Ward	.05	.04	.02		297	Geronimo Berroa	.05	.04	.02
207	Nelson Liriano	.05	.04	.02		298	Todd Stottlemyre	.05	.04	.02
208	Howard Johnson	.15	.11	.06		299	Kirk Gibson	.05	.04	.02
209	Kent Hrbek	.08	.06	.03		300	Wally Backman	.05	.04	.02
210	Ken Caminiti	.05	.04	.02		301	Hubie Brooks	.05	.04	.02
211	Mike Greenwell	.50	.40	.20		302	Von Hayes	.05	.04	.02
212	Ryne Sandberg	.25	.20	.10		303	Matt Nokes	.05	.04	.02
213	Joe Slusarski	.25	.20	.10		304	Doc Gooden	.20	.15	.08
214	Donnel Nixon	.05	.04	.02		305	Walt Weiss	.10	.08	.04
215	Tim Wallach	.05	.04	.02		306	Mike LaValliere	.05	.04	.02
216	John Kruk	.05	.04	.02		307	Cris Carpenter	.10	.08	.04
217	Charles Nagy	.25	.20	.10		308	Ted Wood	.20	.15	.08
218	Alvin Davis	.08	.06	.03		309	Jeff Russell	.05	.04	.02
219	Oswald Peraza	.05	.04	.02		310	Dave Gallagher	.05	.04	.02
220	Mike Schmidt	.30	.25	.12		311	Andy Allanson	.05	.04	.02
221	Spike Owen	.05	.04	.02		312	Craig Reynolds	.05	.04	.02
222	Mike Smithson	.05	.04	.02		313	Kevin Seitzer	.08	.06	.03
223	Dion James	.05	.04	.02		314	Dave Winfield	.10	.08	.04
224	Ernie Whitt	.05	.04	.02		315	Andy McGaffigan	.05	.04	.02
225	Mike Davis	.05	.04	.02		316	Nick Esasky	.05	.04	.02
226	Gene Larkin	.05	.04	.02		317	Jeff Blauser	.05	.04	.02
227	Pat Combs	.50	.40	.20		318	George Bell	.10	.08	.04
228	Jack Howell	.05	.04	.02		319	Eddie Murray	.10	.08	.04
229	Ron Oester	.05	.04	.02		320	Mark Davidson	.05	.04	.02
230	Paul Gibson	.05	.04	.02		321	Juan Samuel	.05	.04	.02
231	Mookie Wilson	.05	.04	.02		322	Jim Abbott	1.00	.70	.40
232	Glenn Hubbard	.05	.04	.02		323	Kal Daniels	.05	.04	.02
233	Shawon Dunston	.05	.04	.02		324	Mike Brumley	.05	.04	.02
234	Otis Nixon	.05	.04	.02		325	Gary Carter	.05	.04	.02
235	Melido Perez	.05	.04	.02		326	Dave Henderson	.05	.04	.02

		MT	NR MT	EX
327	Checklist	.05	.04	.02
328	Garry Templeton	.05	.04	.02
329	Pat Perry	.05	.04	.02
330	Paul Molitor	.08	.06	.03

1989 Topps Box Panels

Continuing its practice of printing baseball cards on the bottom panels of its wax pack boxes, Topps in 1989 issued a special 16-card set, printing four cards on each of four different box-bottom panels. The cards are identical in design to the regular 1989 Topps cards. They are designated by letter (from A through P) rather than by number.

		MT	NR MT	EX
	Complete Panel Set:	5.00	3.75	2.00
	Complete Singles Set:	2.00	1.50	.80
	Common Panel:	.50	.40	.20
	Common Single Player:	.08	.06	.03
	Panel	.50	.40	.20
A	George Brett	.25	.20	.10
B	Bill Buckner	.08	.06	.03
C	Darrell Evans	.08	.06	.03
D	Rich Gossage	.08	.06	.03
	Panel	1.00	.70	.40
E	Greg Gross	.08	.06	.03
F	Rickey Henderson	.30	.25	.12
G	Keith Hernandez	.15	.11	.06
H	Tom Lasorda	.08	.06	.03
	Panel	2.50	2.00	1.00
I	Jim Rice	.15	.11	.06
J	Cal Ripken	.35	.25	.14
K	Nolan Ryan	.50	.40	.20
L	Mike Schmidt	.25	.20	.10
	Panel	1.00	.70	.40
M	Bruce Sutter	.15	.11	.06
N	Don Sutton	.10	.08	.04
O	Kent Tekulve	.08	.06	.03
P	Dave Winfield	.25	.20	.10

1989 Topps Dream Team

This 33-card, glossy set was produced by Topps

for K-Mart, where it was sold in stores nationwide. The standard-size cards feature mostly action shots on the front, and include the Topps "Dream Team" logo at the top, with the K-Mart logo in the lower right corner. The first 11 cards in the set picture the top rookies of 1988, while next 11 picture the top A.L. rookies of the '80s, and the final 11 cards highlight the top N.L. rookies of the decade.

		MT	NR MT	EX
	Complete Set:	5.00	3.75	2.00
	Common Player:	.10	.08	.04
1	Mark Grace	.70	.50	.30
2	Ron Gant	.15	.11	.06
3	Chris Sabo	.15	.11	.06
4	Walt Weiss	.15	.11	.06
5	Jay Buhner	.15	.11	.06
6	Cecil Espy	.10	.08	.04
7	Dave Gallagher	.15	.11	.06
8	Damon Berryhill	.10	.08	.04
9	Tim Belcher	.20	.15	.08
10	Paul Gibson	.10	.08	.04
11	Gregg Jefferies	.90	.70	.40
12	Don Mattingly	1.50	1.25	.60
13	Harold Reynolds	.15	.11	.06
14	Wade Boggs	.80	.60	.30
15	Cal Ripken	.25	.20	.10
16	Kirby Puckett	.40	.30	.15
17	George Bell	.15	.11	.06
18	Jose Canseco	.50	.40	.20
19	Terry Steinbach	.20	.15	.08
20	Roger Clemens	.40	.30	.15
21	Mark Langston	.20	.15	.08
22	Harold Baines	.15	.11	.06
23	Will Clark	.50	.40	.20
24	Ryne Sanberg	.25	.20	.10
25	Tim Wallach	.10	.08	.04
26	Shawon Dunston	.10	.08	.04
27	Rock Raines	.15	.11	.06
28	Darryl Strawberry	.35	.25	.14
29	Tony Gwynn	.35	.25	.14
30	Tony Pena	.10	.08	.04
31	Doc Gooden	.35	.25	.12
32	Fernando Valenzuela	.15	.11	.06
33	Pedro Guerrero	.15	.11	.06

1989 Topps Highlights

This 33-card set was produced by Topps for the Woolworth store chain and was sold in a special box with a checklist on the back. The glossy-coated cards commemorate the most memorable moments in baseball from the the 1988 season, and include the logo "Woolworth's Baseball Highlights" along the top. The player photos are framed in red, yellow and white and feature the player's name beneath the photo. The backs include a description of the various highlights. Orel Hershiser is pictured on four of the cards, and Jose Canseco appears on two.

	MT	NR MT	EX
Complete Set:	6.00	4.50	2.50
Common Player:	.09	.07	.04

#	Player	MT	NR MT	EX
1	Jose Canseco	1.25	.90	.50
2	Kirk Gibson	.15	.11	.06
3	Frank Viola	.15	.11	.06
4	Orel Hershiser	.15	.11	.06
5	Walt Weiss	.20	.15	.11
6	Chris Sabo	.20	.15	.11
7	George Bell	.15	.11	.06
8	Wade Boggs	1.00	.70	.40
9	Tom Browning	.12	.09	.05
10	Gary Carter	.12	.09	.05
11	Andre Dawson	.15	.11	.06
12	John FRanco	.09	.07	.04
13	Randy Johnson	.15	.11	.06
14	Doug Jones	.09	.07	.04
15	Kevin McReynolds	.20	.15	.11
16	Gene Nelson	.09	.07	.04
17	Jeff Reardon	.09	.07	.04
18	Pat Tabler	.09	.07	.04
19	Tim Belcher	.25	.20	.10
20	Dennis Eckersley	.15	.11	.06
21	Orel Hershiser	.20	.15	.08
22	Gregg Jefferies	1.00	.70	.40
23	Jose Canseco	1.25	.90	.50
24	Kirk Gibson	.20	.15	.08
25	Orel Hershiser	.20	.15	.08
26	Mike Marshall	.09	.07	.04
27	Mark McGwire	1.00	.70	.40
28	Rick Honeycutt	.09	.07	.04
29	Tim Belcher	.20	.15	.08
30	Jay Howell	.12	.09	.05
31	Mickey Hatcher	.09	.07	.04
32	Mike Davis	.09	.07	.04
33	Orel Hershiser	.15	.11	.06

#	Player	MT	NR MT	EX
16	Gerald Young	.09	.07	.04
17	Kirk Gibson	.12	.09	.05
18	Orel Hershiser	.25	.20	.10
19	Steve Sax	.12	.09	.05
20	John Tudor	.09	.07	.04
21	Hubie Brooks	.09	.07	.04
22	Andres Galarraga	.15	.11	.06
23	Otis Nixon	.09	.07	.04
24	Dave Cone	.15	.11	.06
25	Sid Fernandez	.12	.09	.05
26	Doc Gooden	.30	.25	.12
27	Kevin McReynolds	.20	.15	.08
28	Darryl Strawberry	.35	.25	.14
29	Juan Samuel	.09	.07	.04
30	Bobby Bonilla	.12	.09	.05
31	Sid Bream	.09	.07	.04
32	Andy Van Slyke	.12	.09	.05
33	Vince Coleman	.12	.09	.05
34	Jose DeLeon	.09	.07	.04
35	Joe Magrane	.12	.09	.05
36	Ozzie Smith	.12	.09	.05
37	Todd Worrell	.09	.07	.04
38	Tony Gwynn	.30	.25	.12
39	Brett Butler	.12	.09	.05
40	Will Clark	1.00	.70	.40
41	Jim Gott	.09	.07	.04
42	Rick Reuschel	.12	.09	.05
43	Checklist	.09	.07	.04
44	Eddie Murray	.20	.15	.08
45	Wade Boggs	.80	.60	.30
46	Roger Clemens	.30	.25	.12
47	Dwight Evans	.12	.09	.05
48	Mike Greenwell	.70	.50	.30
49	Bruce Hurst	.12	.09	.05
50	Johnny Ray	.09	.07	.04
51	Doug Jones	.09	.07	.04
52	Greg Swindell	.15	.11	.06
53	Gary Pettis	.09	.07	.04
54	George Brett	.15	.11	.06
55	Mark Gubicza	.15	.11	.06
56	Willie Wilson	.09	.07	.04
57	Teddy Higuera	.12	.09	.05
58	Paul Molitor	.15	.11	.06
59	Robin Yount	.25	.20	.10
60	Allan Anderson	.09	.07	.04
61	Gary Gaetti	.12	.09	.04
62	Kirby Puckett	.40	.30	.15
63	Jeff Reardon	.09	.07	.04
64	Frank Viola	.12	.09	.05
65	Jack Clark	.12	.09	.05
66	Rickey Henderson	.25	.20	.10
67	Dave Winfield	.15	.11	.06
68	Jose Canseco	1.00	.70	.40
69	Dennis Eckersley	.12	.09	.05
70	Mark McGwire	.80	.60	.30
71	Dave Stewart	.12	.09	.05
72	Alvin Davis	.12	.09	.05
73	Mark Langston	.12	.09	.05
74	Harold Reynolds	.12	.09	.05
75	George Bell	.15	.11	.06
76	Tony Fernandez	.15	.11	.06
77	Fred McGriff	.25	.20	.10

1989 Topps Mini League Leaders

This 77-card set from Topps features baseball's statistical leaders from the 1988 season, and is referred to as a "mini" set because of the cards' small (2-1/8" by 3") size. The glossy cards feature action photos that have a soft focus on all edges. The player's team and name appear along the bottom of the card. The back features a head-shot of the player along with his 1988 season ranking and stats.

	MT	NR MT	EX
Complete Set:	5.00	3.75	2.00
Common Player:	.09	.07	.04

#	Player	MT	NR MT	EX
1	Dale Murphy	.35	.25	.14
2	Gerald Perry	.09	.07	.04
3	Andre Dawson	.20	.15	.08
4	Greg Maddux	.20	.15	.08
5	Rafael Palmeiro	.15	.11	.06
6	Tom Browning	.12	.09	.05
7	Kal Daniels	.15	.11	.06
8	Eric Davis	.60	.45	.25
9	John Franco	.09	.07	.04
10	Danny Jackson	.09	.07	.04
11	Barry Larkin	.15	.11	.06
12	Jose Rijo	.12	.09	.05
13	Chris Sabo	.20	.15	.08
14	Mike Scott	.09	.07	.04
15	Nolan Ryan	.50	.40	.20

1989 Topps American Baseball

For the second consecutive year Topps released an 88-card set of baseball cards available in both the United States and the United Kingdom. The mini-sized cards (2-1/4" by 3") feature full-color photos on the card fronts. The cards are printed on white stock with a low gloss finish. The player action photo is outlined in red, white, and blue and framed in white. The card backs are printed horizontally and include a characterization cartoon along with biographical information and statistics. The cards are sold in packs of five cards with a stick of bubble gum.

		MT	NR MT	EX
Complete Set:		7.00	5.25	2.75
Common Player:		.08	.06	.03
1	Brady Anderson	.08	.06	.03
2	Harold Baines	.15	.11	.06
3	George Bell	.15	.11	.06
4	Wade Boggs	1.00	.70	.40
5	Barry Bonds	.20	.15	.08
6	Bobby Bonilla	.20	.15	.08
7	George Brett	.15	.11	.06
8	Hubie Brooks	.08	.06	.03
9	Tom Brunansky	.08	.06	.03
10	Jay Buhner	.08	.06	.03
11	Brett Butler	.08	.06	.03
12	Jose Canseco	1.25	.90	.50
13	Joe Carter	.15	.11	.06
14	Jack Clark	.08	.06	.03
15	Will Clark	.80	.60	.30
16	Roger Clemens	.30	.25	.12
17	Dave Cone	.08	.06	.03
18	Alvin Davis	.08	.06	.03
19	Eric Davis	.30	.25	.12
20	Glenn Davis	.08	.06	.03
21	Andre Dawson	.12	.09	.05
22	Bill Doran	.08	.06	.03
23	Dennis Eckersley	.08	.06	.03
24	Dwight Evans	.08	.06	.03
25	Tony Fernandez	.08	.06	.03
26	Carlton Fisk	.08	.06	.03
27	John Franco	.08	.06	.03
28	Andres Galarraga	.15	.11	.06
29	Ron Gant	.08	.06	.03
30	Kirk Gibson	.08	.06	.03
31	Doc Gooden	.25	.20	.10
32	Mike Greenwell	.50	.40	.20
33	Mark Gubicza	.08	.06	.03
34	Pedro Gurrero	.12	.09	.05
35	Ozzie Guillen	.08	.06	.03
36	Tony Gwynn	.15	.11	.06
37	Rickey Henderson	.15	.11	.06
38	Orel Hershiser	.15	.11	.06
39	Teddy Higuera	.08	.06	.03
40	Charlie Hough	.08	.06	.03
41	Kent Hrbek	.12	.09	.05
42	Bruce Hurst	.08	.06	.03
43	Bo Jackson	.50	.40	.20
44	Gregg Jefferies	.60	.45	.25
45	Rickey Jordan	.25	.20	.10
46	Wally Joyner	.15	.11	.06
47	Mark Langston	.12	.09	.05
48	Mike Marshall	.08	.06	.03
49	Don Mattingly	2.00	1.50	.80
50	Fred McGriff	.35	.25	.14
51	Mark McGwire	1.00	.70	.40
52	Kevin McReynolds	.15	.11	.06
53	Paul Molitor	.08	.06	.03
54	Jack Morris	.08	.06	.03
55	Dale Murphy	.15	.11	.06
56	Eddie Murray	.10	.08	.04
57	Pete O'Brien	.08	.06	.03
58	Rafael Palmeiro	.08	.06	.03
59	Gerald Perry	.08	.06	.03
60	Kirby Puckett	.30	.25	.12
61	Rock Raines	.15	.11	.06
62	Johnny Ray	.08	.06	.03
63	Rick Reuschel	.08	.06	.03
64	Cal Ripken	.15	.11	.06
65	Chris Sabo	.15	.11	.06
66	Juan Samuel	.08	.06	.03
67	Ryane Sandberg	.15	.11	.06
68	Benny Santiago	.15	.11	.06
69	Steve Sax	.08	.06	.03
70	Mike Schmidt	.20	.15	.11
71	Ruben Sierra	.20	.15	.11
72	Ozzie Smith	.15	.11	.06
73	Cory Snyder	.08	.06	.03
74	Dave Stewart	.08	.06	.03
75	Darryl Strawberry	.25	.20	.10
76	Greg Swindell	.15	.11	.06
77	Alan Trammell	.15	.11	.06

		MT	NR MT	EX
78	Fernando Valenzuela	.08	.06	.03
79	Andy Van Slyke	.20	.15	.08
80	Frank Viola	.20	.15	.08
81	Claudell Washington	.08	.06	.03
82	Walt Weiss	.08	.06	.03
83	Lou Whitaker	.08	.06	.03
84	Dave Winfield	.20	.15	.08
85	Mike Witt	.08	.06	.03
86	Gerald Young	.08	.06	.03
87	Robin Yount	.20	.15	.08
88	Checklist	.08	.06	.03

1990 Topps

The 1990 Topps set again included 792 cards, and sported a newly-designed front that featured six different color schemes. The set led off with a special four-card salute to Nolan Ryan, and featured various other specials, including All-Stars, Number 1 Draft Picks, Record Breakers, manager cards, rookies, and "Turn Back the Clock" cards. The set also includes a special card commemorating A. Bartlett Giamatti, the late Baseball Commissioner. The backs are printed in black on a chartreuse background with the card number in the upper left corner. The set features 725 different individual player cards, the most ever, including 138 players making their first appearance in a regular Topps set.

		MT	NR MT	EX
Complete Set:		25.00	20.00	10.00
Common Player:		.03	.02	.01
1	Nolan Ryan	.35	.25	.14
2	Nolan Ryan (The Mats Years)	.20	.15	.08
3	Nolan Ryan (The Angels Years)	.20	.15	.08
4	Nolan Ryan (The Astros Years)	.20	.15	.08
5	Nolan Ryan (The Rangers)	.20	.15	.08
6	1989 Record Breaker (Vince Coleman)	.10	.08	.04
7	1989 Record Breaker (Rickey Henderson)	.20	.15	.08
8	1989 Record Breaker (Cal Ripken)	.15	.11	.06
9	Eric Pluank	.03	.02	.01
10	Barry Larkin	.15	.11	.06
11	Paul Gibson	.04	.03	.02
12	Joe Girardi(FC)	.15	.11	.06
13	Mark Williamson	.03	.02	.01
14	Mike Fetters(FC)	.20	.15	.08
15	Teddy Higuera	.06	.05	.02
16	Kent Anderson	.10	.08	.04
17	Kelly Downs	.05	.04	.02
18	Carlos Quintana	.09	.07	.04
19	Al Newman	.03	.02	.01
20	Mark Gubicza	.12	.09	.05
21	Jeff Torborg	.03	.02	.01
22	Bruce Ruffin	.03	.02	.01
23	Randy Velarde	.07	.05	.03
24	Joe Hesketh	.03	.02	.01
25	Willie Randolph	.08	.06	.03
26	Don Slaught	.03	.02	.01
27	Rick Leach	.03	.02	.01
28	Duane Ward	.04	.03	.02
29	John Cangelosi	.03	.02	.01
30	David Cone	.10	.08	.04
31	Henry Cotto	.03	.02	.01

		MT	NR MT	EX
32	John Farrell	.05	.04	.02
33	Greg Walker	.05	.04	.02
34	*Tony Fossas*(FC)	.07	.05	.03
35	Benito Santiago	.12	.09	.05
36	John Costello	.04	.03	.02
37	Domingo Ramos	.03	.02	.01
38	Wes Gardner	.04	.03	.02
39	Curt Ford	.04	.03	.02
40	Jay Howell	.06	.05	.02
41	Matt Williams	.15	.11	.06
42	Jeff Robinson	.05	.04	.02
43	Dante Bichette	.07	.05	.03
44	*Roger Salkeld* (Number 1 Draft Pick)(FC)			
		.30	.25	.12
45	Dave Parker	.09	.07	.04
46	Rob Dibble	.07	.05	.03
47	Brian Harper	.04	.03	.02
48	Zane Smith	.03	.02	.01
49	Tom Lawless	.03	.02	.01
50	Glenn Davis	.08	.06	.03
60	George Brett	.15	.11	.06
61	*Deion Sanders*	.70	.50	.30
62	Ramon Martinez	.10	.08	.04
63	Mike Pagliarulo	.04	.03	.02
64	Danny Darwin	.03	.02	.01
65	Devon White	.07	.05	.03
66	*Greg Litton*(FC)	.25	.20	.10
67	Scott Sanderson	.04	.03	.02
68	Dave Henderson	.06	.05	.02
69	Todd Frohwirth	.03	.02	.01
70	Mike Greenwell	.30	.25	.12
71	Allan Anderson	.05	.04	.02
72	*Jeff Huson*(FC)	.20	.15	.08
73	Bob Milacki	.05	.04	.02
74	*Jeff Jackson* (Number 1 Draft Pick)(FC)			
		.30	.25	.12
75	Doug Jones	.05	.04	.02
76	Dave Valle	.03	.02	.01
77	Dave Bergman	.03	.02	.01
78	Mike Flanagan	.04	.03	.02
79	Ron Kittle	.05	.04	.02
80	Jeff Russell	.05	.04	.02
81	Bob Rodgers	.03	.02	.01
82	Scott Terry	.04	.03	.02
83	*Hensley Meulens*	.30	.25	.12
84	Ray Searage	.03	.02	.01
85	Juan Samuel	.05	.04	.02
86	Paul Kilgus	.03	.02	.01
87	*Rick Lueken*(FC)	.15	.11	.06
88	Glenn Braggs	.05	.04	.02
89	*Clint Zavaras*(FC)	.15	.11	.06
90	Jack Clark	.06	.05	.02
91	*Steve Frey*(FC)	.20	.15	.08
92	Mike Stanley	.03	.02	.01
93	Shawn Hillegas	.03	.02	.01
94	Herm Winningham	.03	.02	.01
95	Todd Worrell	.05	.04	.02
96	Jody Reed	.04	.03	.02
97	Curt Schilling(FC)	.10	.08	.04
98	Jose Gonzalez(FC)	.10	.08	.04
99	*Rich Monteleone*(FC)	.15	.11	.06
100	Will Clark	.70	.50	.30
101	Shane Rawley	.04	.03	.02
102	Stan Javier	.04	.03	.02
103	Marvin Freeman	.09	.07	.04
104	Bob Knepper	.03	.02	.01
105	Randy Myers	.05	.04	.02
106	Charlie O'Brien	.03	.02	.01
107	Fred Lynn	.05	.04	.02
108	Rod Nichols	.04	.03	.02
109	Roberto Kelly	.08	.06	.03
110	Tommy Helms	.03	.02	.01
111	Ed Whited	.20	.15	.08
112	Glenn Wilson	.03	.02	.01
113	Manny Lee	.03	.02	.01
114	Mike Bielecki	.05	.04	.02
115	Tony Pena	.06	.05	.02
116	Floyd Bannister	.04	.03	.02
117	Mike Sharperson(FC)	.09	.07	.04
118	Erik Hanson	.10	.08	.04
119	Billy Hatcher	.04	.03	.02
120	John Franco	.05	.04	.02
121	Robin Ventura	.35	.25	.14
122	Shawn Abner	.03	.02	.01
123	Rich Gedman	.04	.03	.02
124	Dave Dravecky	.04	.03	.02
125	Kent Hrbek	.07	.05	.03
126	Randy Kramer	.03	.02	.01
127	Mike Devereaux	.06	.05	.02
128	Checklist 1-132	.03	.02	.01
129	Ron Jones	.10	.08	.04
130	Bert Blyleven	.05	.04	.02
131	Matt Nokes	.06	.05	.02
132	Lance Blankenship(FC)	.10	.08	.04
133	Ricky Horton	.03	.02	.01
134	*Earl Cunningham* (Number 1 Draft Pick)(FC)			
		.60	.45	.25
135	Dave Magadan	.05	.04	.02
136	Kevin Brown	.06	.05	.02
137	*Marty Pevey*(FC)	.15	.11	.06
138	Al Leiter	.04	.03	.02
139	Greg Brock	.04	.03	.02
140	Andre Dawson	.12	.09	.05
141	*John Hart*(FC)	.15	.11	.06
142	*Jeff Wetherby*(FC)	.20	.15	.08
143	Rafael Belliard	.03	.02	.01
144	Bud Black	.03	.02	.01
145	Terry Steinbach	.07	.05	.03
146	*Rob Richie*(FC)	.20	.15	.08
147	Chuck Finley	.04	.03	.02
148	Edgar Martinez(FC)	.09	.07	.04
149	Steve Farr	.04	.03	.02
150	Kirk Gibson	.09	.07	.04
151	Rick Mahler	.03	.02	.01
152	Lonnie Smith	.05	.04	.02
153	Randy Milligan	.05	.04	.02
154	Mike Maddux	.05	.04	.02
155	Ellis Burks	.25	.20	.10
156	Ken Patterson	.04	.03	.02
157	Craig Biggio	.15	.11	.06
158	Craig Lefferts	.04	.03	.02
159	Mike Felder	.03	.02	.01
160	Dave Righetti	.06	.05	.02
161	Harold Reynolds	.06	.05	.02
162	*Todd Zeile*(FC)	1.25	.90	.50
163	Phil Bradley	.05	.04	.02
164	*Jeff Juden* (Number 1 Draft Pick)(FC)			
		.35	.25	.14
165	Walt Weiss	.08	.06	.03
166	Bobby Witt	.04	.03	.02
167	*Kevin Appier*(FC)	.20	.15	.08
168	Jose Lind	.04	.03	.02
169	Richard Dotson	.03	.02	.01
170	George Bell	.12	.09	.05
171	Russ Nixon	.03	.02	.01
172	Tom Lampkin(FC)	.10	.08	.04
173	Tim Belcher	.12	.09	.05
174	Jeff Kunkel	.03	.02	.01
175	Mike Moore	.07	.05	.02
176	Luis Quinones	.03	.02	.01
177	Mike Henneman	.05	.04	.02
178	Chris James	.06	.05	.02
179	Brian Holton	.04	.03	.02
180	Rock Raines	.10	.08	.04
181	Juan Agosto	.03	.02	.01
182	Mookie Wilson	.05	.04	.02
183	Steve Lake	.03	.02	.01
184	Danny Cox	.04	.03	.02
185	Ruben Sierra	.20	.15	.08
186	Dave LaPoint	.03	.02	.01
187	*Rick Wrona*(FC)	.12	.09	.05
188	Mike Smithson	.03	.02	.01
189	Dick Schofield	.04	.03	.02
190	Rick Reuschel	.06	.05	.02
191	Pat Borders	.08	.06	.03
192	Don August	.04	.03	.02
193	Andy Benes	.35	.25	.14
194	GlenAllen Hill(FC)	.25	.20	.10
195	Tim Burke	.05	.04	.02
196	Gerald Young	.04	.03	.02
197	Doug Drabek	.07	.05	.03
198	Mike Marshall	.06	.05	.02
199	*Sergio Valdez*(FC)	.20	.15	.08
200	Don Mattingly	.90	.70	.35
201	Cito Gaston	.03	.02	.01
202	Mike Macfarlane	.03	.02	.01
203	*Mike Roesler*(FC)	.15	.11	.06
204	Bob Dernier	.03	.02	.01
205	Mark Davis	.09	.07	.04
206	Nick Esasky	.07	.05	.02
207	Bob Ojeda	.04	.03	.02
208	Brook Jacoby	.04	.03	.02
209	Greg Mathews	.04	.03	.02
210	Ryne Sandberg	.15	.11	.06
211	John Cerutti	.04	.03	.02
212	Joe Orsulak	.03	.02	.01
213	Scott Bankhead	.05	.04	.02
214	Terry Francona	.03	.02	.01
215	Kirk McCaskill	.04	.03	.02
216	Rickey Jordan	.30	.25	.12
217	Don Robinson	.04	.03	.02
218	Wally Backman	.04	.03	.02

		MT	NR MT	EX			MT	NR MT	EX
219	Donn Pall	.03	.02	.01	310	Steve Bedrosian	.05	.04	.02
220	Barry Bonds	.10	.08	.04	311	Dwight Smith	.90	.70	.35
221	*Gary Mielke*(FC)	.20	.15	.08	312	Dan Quisenberry	.05	.04	.02
222	Kurt Stillwell	.05	.04	.02	313	Gus Polidor	.03	.02	.01
223	Tommy Gregg	.06	.05	.02	314	*Donald Harris* (Number 1 Draft Pick)(FC)			
224	*Delino DeShields*(FC)	.25	.20	.10			.30	.25	.12
225	Jim Deshaies	.05	.04	.02	315	Bruce Hurst	.06	.05	.02
226	Mickey Hatcher	.03	.02	.01	316	Carney Lansford	.06	.05	.02
227	*Kevin Tapani*(FC)	.15	.11	.06	317	*Mark Guthrie*(FC)	.20	.15	.08
228	Dave Martinez	.03	.02	.01	318	Wallace Johnson	.03	.02	.01
229	David Wells	.03	.02	.01	319	Dion James	.04	.03	.02
230	Keith Hernandez	.07	.05	.03	320	Dave Steib	.07	.05	.03
231	Jack McKeon	.03	.02	.01	321	Joe Morgan	.03	.02	.01
232	Darnell Coles	.04	.03	.02	322	Junior Ortiz	.03	.02	.01
233	Ken Hill	.10	.08	.06	323	Willie Wilson	.04	.03	.02
234	Mariano Duncan	.05	.04	.02	324	Pete Harnisch(FC)	.10	.08	.04
235	Jeff Reardon	.04	.03	.02	325	Robby Thompson	.06	.05	.02
236	Hal Morris(FC)	.10	.08	.06	326	*Tom McCarthy*	.10	.08	.04
237	*Kevin Ritz*(FC)	.20	.15	.08	327	Ken Williams	.03	.02	.01
238	Felix Jose(FC)	.10	.08	.04	328	Curt Young	.03	.02	.01
239	Eric Show	.04	.03	.02	329	Oddibe McDowell	.06	.05	.02
240	Mark Grace	.40	.30	.15	330	Ron Darling	.09	.07	.04
241	Mike Krukow	.04	.03	.02	331	*Juan Gonzalez*(FC)	.40	.30	.15
242	Fred Manrique	.03	.02	.01	332	Paul O'Neill	.07	.05	.03
243	Barry Jones	.03	.02	.01	333	Bill Wegman	.03	.02	.01
244	Bill Schroeder	.03	.02	.01	334	Johnny Ray	.05	.04	.02
245	Roger Clemens	.25	.20	.10	335	Andy Hawkins	.05	.04	.02
246	Jim Eisenreich	.03	.02	.01	336	Ken Griffey Jr.	1.25	.90	.50
247	Jerry Reed	.03	.02	.01	337	Lloyd McClendon	.06	.05	.02
248	Dave Anderson	.03	.02	.01	338	Dennis Lamp	.03	.02	.01
249	*Mike Smith*(FC)	.20	.15	.08	339	Dave Clark	.04	.03	.02
250	Jose Canseco	.70	.50	.30	340	Fernando Valenzuela	.06	.05	.02
251	Jeff Blauser	.05	.04	.02	341	Tom Foley	.03	.02	.01
252	Otis Nixon	.03	.02	.01	342	Alex Trevino	.03	.02	.01
253	Mark Portugal	.03	.02	.01	343	Frank Tanana	.04	.03	.02
254	Francisco Cabrera	.25	.20	.10	344	*George Canale*(FC)	.25	.20	.10
255	Bobby Thigpen	.07	.05	.03	345	Harold Baines	.09	.07	.04
256	Marvell Wynne	.03	.02	.01	346	Jim Presley	.04	.03	.02
257	Jose DeLeon	.07	.05	.03	347	Junior Felix	.50	.40	.20
258	Barry Lyons	.03	.02	.01	348	*Gary Wayne*(FC)	.12	.09	.05
259	Lance McCullers	.05	.04	.02	349	*Steve Finley*(FC)	.20	.15	.08
260	Eric Davis	.30	.25	.12	350	Bret Saberhagen	.10	.08	.04
261	Whitey Herzog	.03	.02	.01	351	Roger Craig	.03	.02	.01
262	Checklist 133-264	.03	.02	.01	352	Bryn Smith	.05	.04	.02
263	*Mel Stottlemyre Jr.*(FC)	.15	.11	.06	353	Sandy Alomar	.25	.20	.10
264	Bryan Clutterbuck	.03	.02	.01	354	*Stan Belinda*(FC)	.20	.15	.08
265	Pete O'Brien	.06	.05	.02	355	Marty Barrett	.05	.04	.02
266	German Gonzalez	.04	.03	.02	356	Randy Ready	.03	.02	.01
267	Mark Davidson	.03	.02	.01	357	Dave West	.20	.15	.08
268	Rob Murphy	.03	.02	.01	358	Andres Thomas	.04	.03	.02
269	Dickie Thon	.03	.02	.01	359	Jimmy Jones	.03	.02	.01
270	Dave Stewart	.08	.06	.03	360	Paul Molitor	.09	.07	.04
271	Chet Lemon	.05	.04	.02	361	*Randy McCament*(FC)	.25	.20	.10
272	Bryan Harvey	.04	.03	.02	362	Damon Berryhill	.06	.05	.02
273	Bobby Bonilla	.15	.11	.06	363	Dan Petry	.03	.02	.01
274	*Goose Gozzo*(FC)	.20	.15	.08	364	Rolando Roomes(FC)	.15	.11	.06
275	Mickey Tettleton	.07	.05	.03	365	Ozzie Guillen	.05	.04	.02
276	Gary Thurman	.03	.02	.01	366	Mike Heath	.03	.02	.01
277	Lenny Harris(FC)	.12	.09	.05	367	Mike Morgan	.03	.02	.01
278	Pascual Perez	.04	.03	.02	368	Bill Doran	.06	.05	.02
279	Steve Buechele	.04	.03	.02	369	Todd Burns	.04	.03	.02
280	Lou Whitaker	.07	.05	.03	370	Tim Wallach	.07	.05	.03
281	Kevin Bass	.05	.04	.02	371	Jimmy Key	.08	.06	.03
282	Derek Lilliquist	.10	.08	.04	372	Terry Kennedy	.03	.02	.01
283	*Joey Belle*(FC)	.80	.60	.30	373	Alvin Davis	.08	.06	.03
284	*Mark Gardner*(FC)	.30	.25	.12	374	*Steve Cummings*(FC)	.20	.15	.08
285	Willie McGee	.06	.05	.02	375	Dwight Evans	.08	.06	.03
286	Lee Guetterman	.03	.02	.01	376	Checklist 265-396	.03	.02	.01
287	Vance Law	.03	.02	.01	377	*Mickey Weston*(FC)	.20	.15	.08
288	Greg Briley	.15	.11	.06	378	Luis Salazar	.03	.02	.01
289	Norm Charlton	.10	.08	.04	379	Steve Rosenberg	.03	.02	.01
290	Robin Yount	.20	.15	.08	380	Dave Winfield	.15	.11	.06
291	Dave Johnson	.03	.02	.01	381	Frank Robinson	.03	.02	.01
292	Jim Gott	.04	.03	.02	382	Jeff Musselman	.03	.02	.01
293	Mike Gallego	.04	.03	.02	383	John Morris	.04	.03	.02
294	Craig McMurtry	.03	.02	.01	384	Pat Combs	.50	.40	.20
295	Fred McGriff	.25	.20	.10	385	Fred McGriff (All-Star)	.20	.15	.08
296	Jeff Ballard	.07	.05	.03	386	Julio Franco (All-Star)	.10	.08	.04
297	Tom Herr	.06	.05	.02	387	Wade Boggs (All-Star)	.20	.15	.08
298	Danny Gladden	.05	.04	.02	388	Cal Ripken (All-Star)	.15	.11	.06
299	Adam Peterson(FC)	.09	.07	.04	389	Robin Yount (All-Star)	.20	.15	.08
300	Bo Jackson	.50	.40	.20	390	Ruben Sierra (All-Star)	.20	.15	.08
301	Don Aase	.03	.02	.01	391	Kirby Puckett (All-Star)	.20	.15	.08
302	*Marcus Lawton*(FC)	.08	.06	.03	392	Carlton Fisk (All-Star)	.08	.06	.03
303	Rick Cerone	.03	.02	.01	393	Bret Saberhagen (All-Star)	.10	.08	.04
304	Marty Clary(FC)	.08	.06	.03	394	Jeff Ballard (All-Star)	.08	.06	.03
305	Eddie Murray	.15	.11	.06	395	Jeff Russell (All-Star)	.08	.06	.03
306	Tom Niedenfuer	.03	.02	.01	396	A. Bartlett Giamatti	.10	.08	.04
307	Bip Roberts	.08	.06	.03	397	Will Clark (All-Star)	.25	.20	.10
308	Jose Guzman	.05	.04	.02	398	Ryne Sandberg (All-Star)	.15	.11	.06
309	*Eric Yelding*(FC)	.20	.15	.08	399	Howard Johnson (All-Star)	.15	.11	.06

#	Player	MT	NR MT	EX
400	Ozzie Smith (All-Star)	.10	.08	.04
401	Kevin Mitchell (All-Star)	.20	.15	.08
402	Eric Davis (All-Star)	.20	.15	.08
403	Tony Gwynn (All-Star)	.15	.11	.06
404	Craig Biggio (All-Star)	.15	.11	.06
405	Mike Scott (All-Star)	.08	.06	.03
406	Joe Magrane (All-Star)	.08	.06	.03
407	Mark Davis (All-Star)	.08	.06	.03
408	Trevor Wilson	.06	.05	.02
409	Tom Brunansky	.09	.07	.04
410	Joe Boever	.06	.05	.02
411	Ken Phelps	.03	.02	.01
412	Jamie Moyer	.04	.03	.02
413	*Brian Dubois*(FC)	.20	.15	.08
414	*Frank Thomas* (Number 1 Draft Pick)(FC)	.60	.45	.25
415	Shawon Dunston	.06	.05	.02
416	*Dave Johnson*(FC)	.12	.09	.05
417	Jim Gantner	.06	.05	.02
418	Tom Browning	.08	.06	.03
419	*Beau Allred*(FC)	.20	.15	.08
420	Carlton Fisk	.08	.06	.03
421	Greg Minton	.03	.02	.01
422	Pat Sheridan	.03	.02	.01
423	Fred Toliver	.03	.02	.01
424	Jerry Reuss	.05	.04	.02
425	Bill Landrum	.05	.04	.02
426	Jeff Hamilton	.05	.04	.02
427	Carmem Castillo	.03	.02	.01
428	*Steve Davis*(FC)	.12	.09	.05
429	Tom Kelly	.03	.02	.01
430	Pete Incaviglia	.06	.05	.02
431	Randy Johnson	.10	.08	.04
432	Damaso Garcia	.03	.02	.01
433	*Steve Olin*(FC)	.12	.08	.04
434	Mark Carreon(FC)	.09	.07	.04
435	Kevin Seitzer	.09	.07	.04
436	Mel Hall	.05	.04	.02
437	Les Lancaster	.05	.04	.02
438	Greg Myers(FC)	.10	.08	.04
439	Jeff Parrett	.06	.05	.02
440	Alan Trammell	.09	.07	.04
441	Bob Kipper	.03	.02	.01
442	Jerry Browne	.07	.05	.02
443	Cris Carpenter	.09	.07	.04
444	*Kyle Abbott* (Number 1 Daft Pick)(FC)	.30	.25	.12
445	Danny Jackson	.05	.04	.02
446	Dan Pasqua	.05	.04	.02
447	Atlee Hammaker	.03	.02	.01
448	Greg Gagne	.04	.03	.02
449	Dennis Rasmussen	.04	.03	.02
450	Rickey Henderson	.20	.15	.08
451	Mark Lemke(FC)	.10	.08	.04
452	Luis de los Santos(FC)	.10	.08	.04
453	Jody Davis	.03	.02	.01
454	Jeff King(FC)	.15	.11	.06
455	Jeffrey Leonard	.06	.05	.02
456	Chris Gwynn(FC)	.09	.07	.03
457	Gregg Jefferies	.50	.40	.20
458	Bob McClure	.03	.02	.01
459	Jim Lefebvre	.03	.02	.01
460	Mike Scott	.09	.07	.03
461	*Carlos Martinez*(FC)	.25	.20	.10
462	Denny Walling	.03	.02	.01
463	Drew Hall	.03	.02	.01
464	*Jerome Walton*	1.50	1.25	.60
465	Kevin Gross	.06	.05	.02
466	Rance Mulliniks	.03	.02	.01
467	Juan Nieves	.04	.03	.02
468	Billy Ripken	.04	.03	.02
469	John Kruk	.07	.05	.02
470	Frank Viola	.09	.07	.04
471	Mike Brumley	.03	.02	.01
472	Jose Uribe	.04	.03	.02
473	Joe Price	.03	.02	.01
474	Rich Thompson	.04	.03	.02
475	Bob Welch	.06	.05	.02
476	Brad Komminsk	.03	.02	.02
477	Willie Fraser	.03	.02	.02
478	Mike LaValliere	.04	.03	.02
479	Frank White	.06	.05	.02
480	Sid Fernandez	.09	.07	.04
481	Garry Templeton	.05	.04	.02
482	*Steve Carter*(FC)	.20	.15	.08
483	Alejandro Pena	.04	.03	.02
484	Mike Fitzgerald	.03	.02	.01
485	John Candelaria	.05	.04	.02
486	Jeff Treadway	.05	.04	.02
487	Steve Searcy	.05	.04	.02
488	Ken Oberkfell	.03	.02	.01

#	Player	MT	NR MT	EX
489	Nick Leyva	.03	.02	.01
490	Dan Plesac	.07	.05	.03
491	*Dave Cochrane*(FC)	.20	.15	.08
492	Ron Oester	.04	.03	.02
493	*Jason Grimsley*(FC)	.25	.20	.10
494	Terry Puhl	.03	.02	.01
495	Lee Smith	.06	.05	.02
496	Cecil Espy	.06	.05	.02
497	Dave Schmidt	.03	.02	.01
498	Rick Schu	.03	.02	.01
499	Bill Long	.04	.03	.02
500	Kevin Mitchell	.35	.25	.14
501	Matt Young	.03	.02	.01
502	Mitch Webster	.04	.03	.02
503	Randy St. Claire	.03	.02	.01
504	Tom O'Malley	.03	.02	.01
505	Kelly Gruber	.08	.06	.03
506	Tom Glavine	.10	.08	.04
507	Gary Redus	.04	.03	.02
508	Terry Leach	.03	.02	.01
509	Tom Pagnozzi	.03	.02	.01
510	Doc Gooden	.25	.20	.10
511	Clay Parker	.07	.05	.03
512	Gary Pettis	.03	.02	.01
513	Mark Eichorn	.03	.02	.01
514	Andy Allanson	.03	.02	.01
515	Len Dykstra	.06	.05	.02
516	Tim Leary	.05	.04	.02
517	Roberto Alomar	.15	.11	.06
518	Bill Krueger	.03	.02	.01
519	Bucky Dent	.03	.02	.01
520	Mitch Williams	.09	.07	.03
521	Craig Worthington	.15	.11	.06
522	Mike Dunne	.04	.03	.02
523	Jay Bell	.03	.02	.01
524	Daryl Boston	.03	.02	.01
525	Wally Joyner	.20	.15	.08
526	Checklist 397-528	.03	.02	.01
527	Ron Hassey	.03	.02	.01
528	*Kevin Wickander*(FC)	.20	.15	.08
529	Greg Harris	.03	.02	.01
530	Mark Langston	.10	.08	.04
531	Ken Caminiti	.06	.05	.02
532	Cecilio Guante	.03	.02	.01
533	Tim Jones(FC)	.07	.05	.03
534	Louie Meadows	.07	.05	.03
535	John Smoltz	.15	.11	.06
536	*Bob Geren*	.15	.11	.06
537	Mark Grant	.03	.02	.01
538	*Billy Spiers*	.20	.15	.08
539	Neal Heaton	.03	.02	.01
540	Danny Tartabull	.09	.07	.03
541	Pat Perry	.03	.02	.01
542	Darren Daulton	.03	.02	.01
543	Nelson Liriano	.03	.02	.01
544	Dennis Boyd	.05	.04	.02
545	Kevin McReynolds	.09	.07	.04
546	Kevin Hickey	.05	.04	.02
547	Jack Howell	.05	.04	.02
548	Pat Clements	.03	.02	.01
549	Don Zimmer	.03	.02	.01
550	Julio Franco	.09	.07	.04
551	Tim Crews	.03	.02	.01
552	*Mike Smith*(FC)	.15	.11	.06
553	*Scott Scudder*(FC)	.20	.15	.11
554	Jay Buhner	.08	.06	.03
555	Jack Morris	.07	.05	.03
556	Gene Larkin	.03	.02	.01
557	*Jeff Innis*	.15	.11	.08
558	Rafael Ramirez	.04	.03	.02
559	Andy McGaffigan	.04	.03	.02
560	Steve Sax	.08	.06	.03
561	Ken Dayley	.03	.02	.01
562	Chad Kreuter	.10	.08	.04
563	Alex Sanchez	.10	.08	.04
564	*Tyler Houston* (Number 1 Draft Pick)(FC)	.50	.40	.20
565	Scott Fletcher	.05	.04	.02
566	Mark Knudson	.06	.05	.02
567	Ron Gant	.08	.06	.03
568	John Smiley	.07	.05	.03
569	Ivan Calderon	.05	.04	.02
570	Cal Ripken	.15	.11	.06
571	Brett Butler	.06	.05	.02
572	Greg Harris	.09	.07	.04
573	Danny Heep	.03	.02	.01
574	Bill Swift	.04	.03	.02
575	Lance Parrish	.07	.05	.03
576	*Mike Dyer*(FC)	.20	.15	.08
577	Charlie Hayes(FC)	.10	.08	.04
578	Joe Magrane	.09	.07	.04

#	Name	MT	NR MT	EX		#	Name	MT	NR MT	EX
579	Art Howe	.03	.02	.01		670	Dennis Eckersley	.09	.07	.04
580	Joe Carter	.15	.11	.06		671	Bob Boone	.09	.07	.04
581	Ken Griffey	.05	.04	.02		672	Roy Smith	.03	.02	.01
582	Rick Honeycutt	.03	.02	.01		673	Joey Meyer	.03	.02	.01
583	Bruce Benedict	.03	.02	.01		674	Spike Owen	.05	.04	.02
584	*Phil Stephenson*(FC)	.09	.07	.04		675	Jim Abbott	.80	.60	.30
585	Kal Daniels	.10	.08	.04		676	Randy Kutcher(FC)	.07	.05	.03
586	Ed Nunez	.03	.02	.01		677	Jay Tibbs	.03	.02	.01
587	Lance Johnson	.08	.06	.03		678	Kirt Manwaring	.10	.08	.04
588	Rick Rhoden	.03	.02	.01		679	Gary Ward	.04	.03	.02
589	Mike Aldrete	.03	.02	.01		680	Howard Johnson	.12	.09	.05
590	Ozzie Smith	.10	.08	.04		681	Mike Schooler	.07	.05	.03
591	Todd Stottlemyre	.08	.06	.03		682	Dann Bilardello	.03	.02	.01
592	R.J. Reynolds	.03	.02	.01		683	*Kenny Rogers*	.10	.08	.04
593	Scott Bradley	.03	.02	.01		684	*Julio Machado*(FC)	.20	.15	.08
594	*Luis Sojo*(FC)	.20	.15	.08		685	Tony Fernandez	.09	.07	.04
595	Greg Swindell	.10	.08	.04		686	Carmelo Martinez	.06	.05	.02
596	Jose DeJesus(FC)	.10	.08	.04		687	Tim Birtsas	.03	.02	.01
597	Chris Bosio	.07	.05	.03		688	Milt Thompson	.06	.05	.02
598	Brady Anderson	.05	.04	.02		689	Rich Yett	.03	.02	.01
599	Frank Williams	.03	.02	.01		690	Mark McGwire	.50	.40	.20
600	Darryl Strawberry	.30	.15	.08		691	Chuck Cary	.03	.02	.01
601	Luis Rivera	.04	.03	.02		692	Sammy Sosa	.50	.40	.20
602	Scott Garrelts	.07	.05	.03		693	Calvin Schiraldi	.03	.02	.01
603	Tony Armas	.03	.02	.01		694	*Mike Stanton*(FC)	.15	.11	.06
604	Ron Robinson	.03	.02	.01		695	Tom Henke	.06	.05	.02
605	Mike Scioscia	.07	.05	.03		696	B.J. Surhoff	.07	.05	.03
606	Storm Davis	.07	.05	.03		697	Mike Davis	.03	.02	.01
607	Steve Jeltz	.03	.02	.01		698	*Omar Vizquel*	.10	.08	.04
608	*Eric Anthony*(FC)	2.00	1.50	.80		699	Jim Leyland	.03	.02	.01
609	Sparky Anderson	.03	.02	.01		700	Kirby Puckett	.25	.20	.10
610	Pedro Guererro	.12	.09	.05		701	*Berenie Williams*(FC)	.25	.20	.10
611	Walt Terrell	.05	.04	.02		702	Tony Phillips	.04	.03	.02
612	Dave Gallagher	.07	.05	.02		703	*Jeff Brantley*	.12	.09	.05
613	Jeff Pico	.04	.03	.02		704	*Chip Hale*(FC)	.20	.15	.08
614	Nelson Santovenia	.09	.07	.04		705	Claudell Washington	.07	.05	.03
615	Rob Deer	.07	.05	.03		706	Geno Petralli	.03	.02	.01
616	Brian Holman	.10	.08	.04		707	Luis Aquino	.03	.02	.01
617	Geronimo Berroa	.08	.06	.03		708	Larry Sheets	.03	.02	.01
618	Eddie Whitson	.05	.04	.02		709	Juan Berneguer	.03	.02	.01
619	Rob Ducey	.08	.06	.03		710	Von Hayes	.09	.07	.04
620	*Tony Castillo*(FC)	.20	.15	.08		711	Rick Aguilera	.05	.04	.02
621	Melido Perez	.07	.05	.03		712	Todd Benzinger	.09	.07	.04
622	Sid Bream	.05	.04	.02		713	*Tim Drummond*(FC)	.15	.11	.06
623	Jim Corsi	.05	.04	.02		714	*Marquis Grissom*(FC)	.70	.50	.30
624	Darrin Jackson	.04	.03	.02		715	Greg Maddux	.15	.11	.06
625	Roger McDowell	.07	.05	.03		716	Steve Balboni	.03	.02	.01
626	Bob Melvin	.03	.02	.01		717	Ron Kakovice	.03	.02	.01
627	Jose Rijo	.07	.05	.03		718	Gary Sheffield	.40	.30	.15
628	Candy Maldonado	.04	.03	.02		719	*Wally Whitehurst*(FC)	.15	.11	.06
629	Eric Hetzel(FC)	.10	.08	.04		720	Andres Galarraga	.15	.11	.06
630	Gary Gaetti	.10	.08	.04		721	Lee Mazzilli	.03	.02	.01
631	*John Wetteland*(FC)	.20	.15	.08		722	Felix Fermin	.03	.02	.01
632	Scott Lusader	.06	.05	.02		723	Jeff Robinson	.05	.04	.02
633	Dennis Cook(FC)	.15	.11	.06		724	Juan Bell(FC)	.10	.08	.04
634	Luis Polonia	.06	.05	.02		725	Terry Pendleton	.07	.05	.03
635	Brian Downing	.06	.05	.02		726	Gene Nelson	.03	.02	.01
636	Jesse Orosco	.03	.02	.01		727	Pat Tabler	.05	.04	.02
637	Craig Reynolds	.03	.02	.01		728	Jim Acker	.03	.02	.01
638	Jeff Montgomery	.07	.05	.03		729	Bobby Valentine	.03	.02	.01
639	Tony LaRussa	.03	.02	.01		730	Tony Gwynn	.20	.15	.08
640	Rick Sitcliffe	.06	.05	.02		731	Don Carman	.05	.04	.02
641	*Doug Strange*(FC)	.15	.11	.06		732	Ernie Riles	.03	.02	.01
642	Jack Armstrong	.04	.03	.02		733	John Dopson	.09	.07	.04
643	Alfredo Griffin	.04	.03	.02		734	Kevin Elster	.06	.05	.02
644	Paul Assenmacher	.04	.03	.02		735	Charlie Hough	.06	.05	.02
645	Jose Oquendo	.06	.05	.02		736	Rick Dempsey	.03	.02	.01
646	Checklist 529-660	.03	.02	.01		737	Chris Sabo	.15	.11	.06
647	Rex Hudler	.03	.02	.01		738	*Gene Harris*	.10	.08	.04
648	Jim Clancy	.03	.02	.01		739	Dale Sveum	.04	.03	.02
649	*Dan Murphy*(FC)	.15	.11	.06		740	Jesse Barfield	.08	.06	.03
650	Mike Witt	.06	.05	.02		741	Steve Wilson	.10	.08	.04
651	Rafael Santana	.06	.05	.02		742	Ernie Whitt	.05	.04	.02
652	Mike Boddicker	.06	.05	.02		743	Tom Candiotti	.05	.04	.02
653	John Moses	.03	.02	.01		744	*Kelly Mann*(FC)	.20	.15	.08
655	*Paul Coleman* (Number 1 Draft Pick)(FC)					745	Hubie Brooks	.06	.05	.02
		.30	.25	.12		746	Dave Smith	.06	.05	.02
656	Mackey Sasser	.05	.04	.02		747	Randy Bush	.03	.02	.01
657	Terry Mulholland	.06	.05	.02		748	Doyle Alexander	.06	.05	.02
658	Donell Nixon	.03	.02	.01		749	Mark Parent	.04	.03	.02
659	Greg Cadaret	.03	.02	.01		750	Dale Murphy	.10	.08	.04
660	Vince Coleman	.10	.08	.04		751	Steve Lyons	.04	.03	.02
661	Turn Back The Clock - 1985	.07	.05	.03		752	Tom Gordon	.50	.40	.20
662	Turn Back The Clock - 1980	.07	.05	.03		753	Chris Speier	.03	.02	.01
663	Turn Back The Clock - 1975	.07	.05	.03		754	Bob Walk	.05	.04	.02
664	Turn Back The Clock - 1970	.07	.05	.03		755	Rafael Palmeiro	.08	.06	.03
665	Turn Back The Clock - 1965	.07	.05	.03		756	Ken Howell	.03	.02	.01
666	Brian Fisher	.05	.04	.02		757	*Larry Walker*(FC)	.25	.20	.10
667	Curt Wilkerson	.03	.02	.01		758	Mark Thurmond	.03	.02	.01
668	*Joe Oliver*(FC)	.25	.20	.10		759	Tom Trebelhorn	.03	.02	.01
669	Tom Lasorda	.03	.02	.01		760	Wade Boggs	.40	.30	.15

		MT	NR MT	EX
761	Mike Jackson	.05	.04	.02
762	Doug Dascenzo	.07	.05	.03
763	Denny Martinez	.07	.05	.03
764	Tim Teufel	.05	.04	.02
765	Chili Davis	.07	.05	.03
766	Brian Meyer(FC)	.10	.08	.04
767	Tracy Jones	.06	.05	.02
768	Chuck Crim	.04	.03	.02
769	Greg Hibbard(FC)	.15	.11	.06
770	Cory Snyder	.09	.07	.04
771	Pete Smith	.06	.05	.02
772	Jeff Reed	.03	.02	.01
773	Dave Leiper	.03	.02	.01
774	Ben McDonald(FC)	1.75	1.25	.70
775	Andy Van Slyke	.09	.07	.04
776	Charlie Leibrandt	.04	.03	.02
777	Tim Laudner	.03	.02	.01
778	Mike Jeffcoat	.03	.02	.01
779	Lloyd Moseby	.06	.05	.02
780	Orel Hershiser	.15	.11	.06
781	Mario Diaz	.03	.02	.01
782	Jose Alvarez	.03	.02	.01
783	Checklist 661-792	.03	.02	.01
784	Scott Bailes	.03	.02	.01
785	Jim Rice	.07	.05	.03
786	Eric King	.04	.03	.02
787	Rene Gonzales	.03	.02	.01
788	Frank DiPino	.03	.02	.01
789	John Wathan	.03	.02	.01
790	Gary Carter	.07	.05	.03
791	Alvaro Espinosa	.15	.11	.06
792	Gerald Perry	.06	.05	.02

		MT	NR MT	EX
17	John Kruk	.40	.30	.15
18	Barry Larkin	.30	.25	.12
19	Mike LaValliere	.15	.11	.06
20	Greg Mathews	.15	.11	.06
21	Kevin Mitchell	.20	.15	.08
22	Dan Plesac	.20	.15	.08
23	Bruce Ruffin	.15	.11	.06
24	Ruben Sierra	.50	.40	.20
25	Cory Snyder	.40	.30	.15
26	Kurt Stillwell	.20	.15	.08
27	Dale Sveum	.12	.09	.05
28	Danny Tartabull	.30	.25	.12
29	Andres Thomas	.15	.11	.06
30	Robby Thompson	.15	.11	.06
31	Jim Traber	.09	.07	.04
32	Mitch Williams	.15	.11	.06
33	Todd Worrell	.30	.25	.12

1988 Toys "R" Us Rookies

This 33-card boxed edition was produced by Topps for exclusive distribution at Toys "R" Us stores. The glossy standard-size cards spotlight rookies in both closeups and action photos on a bright blue background inlaid with yellow. The Toys "R" Us logo frames the top left corner, above a curving white banner that reads "Topps 1988 Collectors' Edition Rookies". A black Topps logo hugs the upper right-hand edge of the photo. The player name, red-lettered on a tube of yellow, frames the bottom. Card backs are horizontal, blue and pink on a bright pink background and include the player name, personal information and career highlights and stats.

		MT	NR MT	EX
Complete Set:		5.00	3.75	2.00
Common Player:		.09	.07	.04
1	Todd Benzinger	.20	.15	.08
2	Bob Brower	.09	.07	.04
3	Jerry Browne	.09	.07	.04
4	DeWayne Buice	.09	.07	.04
5	Ellis Burks	.70	.50	.30
6	Ken Caminiti	.12	.09	.05
7	Casey Candaele	.09	.07	.04
8	Dave Cone	.50	.40	.20
9	Kelly Downs	.20	.15	.08
10	Mike Dunne	.15	.11	.06
11	Ken Gerhart	.12	.09	.05
12	Mike Greenwell	.70	.50	.30
13	Mike Henneman	.12	.09	.05
14	Sam Horn	.20	.15	.08
15	Joe Magrane	.20	.15	.08
16	Fred Manrique	.12	.09	.05
17	John Marzano	.12	.09	.05
18	Fred McGriff	.15	.11	.06
19	Mark McGwire	1.00	.70	.40
20	Jeff Musselman	.12	.09	.05
21	Randy Myers	.20	.15	.08
22	Matt Nokes	.40	.30	.15
23	Al Pedrique	.12	.09	.05
24	Luis Polonia	.15	.11	.06
25	Billy Ripken	.25	.20	.10
26	Benny Santiago	.25	.20	.10
27	Kevin Seitzer	.70	.50	.30
28	John Smiley	.20	.15	.08
29	Mike Stanley	.09	.07	.04

1987 Toys "R" Us

Marked as a collectors' edition set and titled "Baseball Rookies," the 1987 Toys "R" Us issue was produced by Topps for the toy store chain. The set is comprised of 33 glossy-coated cards, each measuring 2-1/2" by 3-1/2". The card fronts are very colorful, employing nine different colors including deep black borders. The backs, printed in blue and orange, contain career highlights and composite minor and major league statistics. The set was distributed in a specially designed box and sold for $1.99 in retail outlets.

		MT	NR MT	EX
Complete Set:		5.00	3.75	2.00
Common Player:		.09	.07	.04
1	Andy Allanson	.12	.09	.05
2	Paul Assenmacher	.12	.09	.05
3	Scott Bailes	.12	.09	.05
4	Barry Bonds	.30	.25	.12
5	Jose Canseco	1.50	1.25	.60
6	John Cerutti	.15	.11	.06
7	Will Clark	.90	.70	.35
8	Kal Daniels	.25	.20	.10
9	Jim Deshaies	.15	.11	.06
10	Mark Eichhorn	.12	.09	.05
11	Ed Hearn	.09	.07	.04
12	Pete Incaviglia	.40	.30	.15
13	Bo Jackson	.60	.45	.25
14	Wally Joyner	1.00	.70	.40
15	Charlie Kerfeld	.09	.07	.04
16	Eric King	.12	.09	.05

		MT	NR MT	EX
30	Terry Steinbach	.20	.15	.08
31	B.J. Surhoff	.25	.20	.10
32	Bobby Thigpen	.12	.09	.05
33	Devon White	.25	.20	.10

1989 Toys "R" Us Rookies

This glossy set of 33 top rookies was produced by Topps for the Toys 'R' Us chain and was sold in a special box. Each player's name and position appear below the full-color photo, while the Toys 'R' Us logo and "Topps 1989 Collector's Edition" appear along the top. Major and minor league stats are on the back. The set is numbered alphabetically.

		MT	NR MT	EX
Complete Set:		5.00	3.75	2.00
Common Player:		.09	.07	.04
1	Roberto Alomar	.20	.15	.08
2	Brady Anderson	.09	.07	.04
3	Tim Belcher	.20	.15	.08
4	Damon Berryhill	.12	.09	.05
5	Jay Buhner	.12	.09	.05
6	Sherman Corbett	.09	.07	.04
7	Kevin Elster	.12	.09	.05
8	Cecil Espy	.12	.09	.05
9	Dave Gallagher	.12	.09	.05
10	Ron Gant	.12	.09	.05
11	Paul Gibson	.09	.07	.04
12	Mark Grace	.90	.70	.35
13	Bryan Harvey	.12	.09	.05
14	Darrin Jackson	.09	.07	.04
15	Gregg Jefferies	1.00	.70	.40
16	Ron Jones	.15	.11	.06
17	Rickey Jordan	.70	.50	.30
18	Roberto Kelly	.25	.20	.10
19	Al Leiter	.09	.07	.04
20	Jack McDowell	.09	.07	.04
21	Melido Perez	.12	.09	.05
22	Jeff Pico	.09	.07	.04
23	Jody Reed	.12	.09	.05
24	Chris Sabo	.25	.20	.10
25	Nelson Santovenia	.15	.11	.06
26	Mackey Sasser	.09	.07	.04
27	Mike Schooler	.12	.09	.05
28	Gary Sheffield	.90	.70	.35
29	Pete Smith	.12	.09	.05
30	Pete Stanicek	.09	.07	.04
31	Jeff Treadway	.09	.07	.04
32	Walt Weiss	.25	.20	.10
33	Dave West	.35	.25	.14

1969 Transogram

Produced by the Transogram toy company, the 2-1/2" by 3-1/2" cards were printed on the bottom of toy baseball player statue boxes. The cards feature a color photo of the player surrounded by a rounded white border. Below the photo is the player's name in red and his team and other personal details all printed in black. The overall background is yellow. The cards were designed to be cut off the box, but

collectors prefer to find the box intact and better still, with the statue inside. Although the 60-card set features a lot of stars, and is fairly scarce, it does not not have a lot of popularity today.

		NR MT	EX	VG
Complete Set:		550.00	275.00	160.00
Common Player:		.80	.40	.25
(1)	Hank Aaron	30.00	15.00	9.00
(2)	Richie Allen	4.00	2.00	1.25
(3)	Felipe Alou	3.00	1.50	.90
(4)	Matty Alou	3.00	1.50	.90
(5)	Luis Aparicio	15.00	7.50	4.50
(6)	Joe Azcue	2.00	1.00	.60
(7)	Ernie Banks	10.00	5.00	3.00
(8)	Lou Brock	20.00	10.00	6.00
(9)	John Callison	3.00	1.50	.90
(10)	Jose Cardenal	2.00	1.00	.60
(11)	Danny Cater	2.00	1.00	.60
(12)	Roberto Clemente	25.00	12.50	7.50
(13)	Willie Davis	1.00	.50	.30
(14)	Mike Epstein	2.00	1.00	.60
(15)	Jim Fregosi	1.00	.50	.30
(16)	Bob Gibson	8.00	4.00	2.50
(17)	Tom Haller	2.00	1.00	.60
(18)	Ken Harrelson	3.00	1.50	.90
(19)	Willie Horton	3.00	1.50	.90
(20)	Frank Howard	1.50	.70	.45
(21)	Tommy John	8.00	4.00	2.50
(22)	Al Kaline	10.00	5.00	3.00
(23)	Harmon Killebrew	10.00	5.00	3.00
(24)	Bobby Knoop	2.00	1.00	.60
(25)	Jerry Koosman	.80	.40	.25
(26)	Jim Lefebvre	2.00	1.00	.60
(27)	Mickey Mantle	125.00	62.00	37.00
(28)	Juan Marichal	8.00	4.00	2.50
(29)	Lee May	3.00	1.50	.90
(30)	Willie Mays	30.00	15.00	9.00
(31)	Bill Mazeroski	4.00	2.00	1.25
(32)	Tim McCarver	4.00	2.00	1.25
(33)	Willie McCovey	10.00	5.00	3.00
(34)	Denny McLain	1.50	.70	.45
(35)	Dave McNally	3.00	1.50	.90
(36)	Rick Monday	3.00	1.50	.90
(37)	Blue Moon Odom	.80	.40	.25
(38)	Tony Oliva	1.50	.70	.45
(39)	Camilo Pascual	3.00	1.50	.90
(40)	Tony Perez	7.00	3.50	2.00
(41)	Rico Petrocelli	1.00	.50	.30
(42)	Rick Reichardt	.80	.40	.25
(43)	Brooks Robinson	25.00	12.50	7.50
(44)	Frank Robinson	8.00	4.00	2.50
(45)	Cookie Rojas	2.00	1.00	.60
(46)	Pete Rose	30.00	15.00	9.00
(47)	Ron Santo	1.50	.70	.45
(48)	Tom Seaver	10.00	5.00	3.00
(49)	Rusty Staub	4.00	2.00	1.25
(50)	Mel Stottlemyre	1.00	.50	.30
(51)	Ron Swoboda	.80	.40	.25
(52)	Luis Tiant	3.00	1.50	.90
(53)	Joe Torre	4.00	2.00	1.25
(54)	Cesar Tovar	2.00	1.00	.60
(55)	Pete Ward	2.00	1.00	.60
(56)	Roy White	3.00	1.50	.90
(57)	Billy Williams	15.00	7.50	4.50
(58)	Don Wilson	2.00	1.00	.60
(59)	Jim Wynn	.80	.40	.25
(60)	Carl Yastrzemski	25.00	12.50	7.50

1970 Transogram

ROBERTO CLEMENTE
OUTFIELD   PITTSBURGH PIRATES

Like the 1969 cards, the 1970 Transogram cards were available on boxes of Transogram baseball statues. The cards are slightly larger at 2-9/16" by 3-1/2". The 30-card set has the same pictures as the 1969 set except for Joe Torre. All players in the '70 set were included in the '69 Transogram issue except for Reggie Jackson, Sam McDowell and Boog Powell. Three cards and three statues were part of each Transogram box in 1970. When available, most collectors prefer to find the cards as uncut panels of three, better yet, as complete boxes.

		NR MT	EX	VG
Complete Set:		275.00	150.00	80.00
Common Player:		.80	.40	.25
(1)	Hank Aaron	30.00	15.00	9.00
(2)	Ernie Banks	8.00	4.00	2.50
(3)	Roberto Clemente	25.00	12.50	6.00
(4)	Willie Davis	1.00	.50	.30
(5)	Jim Fregosi	1.00	.50	.30
(6)	Bob Gibson	8.00	4.00	2.50
(7)	Frank Howard	1.50	.70	.45
(8)	Reggie Jackson	40.00	20.00	12.00
(9)	Cleon Jones	.80	.40	.25
(10)	Al Kaline	10.00	5.00	3.00
(11)	Harmon Killebrew	10.00	5.00	3.00
(12)	Jerry Koosman	.80	.40	.25
(13)	Willie McCovey	10.00	5.00	3.00
(14)	Sam McDowell	3.00	1.50	.90
(15)	Denny McLain	1.50	.70	.45
(16)	Juan Marichal	8.00	4.00	2.50
(17)	Willie Mays	30.00	15.00	9.00
(18)	Blue Moon Odom	.80	.40	.25
(19)	Tony Oliva	1.50	.70	.45
(20)	Rico Petrocelli	1.00	.50	.30
(21)	Boog Powell	4.00	2.00	1.25
(22)	Rick Reichardt	.80	.40	.25
(23)	Frank Robinson	10.00	5.00	3.00
(24)	Pete Rose	30.00	15.00	9.00
(25)	Ron Santo	1.50	.70	.45
(26)	Tom Seaver	10.00	5.00	3.00
(27)	Mel Stottlemyre	1.00	.50	.30
(28)	Joe Torre	4.00	2.00	1.25
(29)	Jim Wynn	.80	.40	.25
(30)	Carl Yastrzemski	25.00	12.50	7.50

1970 Transogram Mets

JERRY KOOSMAN
PITCHER   NEW YORK METS

The Transogram Mets set is a second set that the company produced in 1970. The cards are 2-9/16" by 3-1/2" and feature members of the World Champions Mets team. There are 15 cards in the set which retains the basic color picture with player's names in red and team, position and biographical details in ablack format. As with the other Transogram sets, the cards are most valuable when they are still part of their original box with the statues. Values decrease for them if the cards are removed from the box. While the Mets set does not have the attraction of many Hall of Famers as was the case with the regular set, it does make a very nice item for the Mets team collector.

		NR MT	EX	VG
Complete Set:		110.00	55.00	35.00
Common Player:		.80	.40	.25
(1)	Tommie Agee	3.00	1.50	.90
(2)	Ken Boswell	2.00	1.00	.60
(3)	Donn Clendenon	3.00	1.50	.90
(4)	Gary Gentry	2.00	1.00	.60
(5)	Jerry Grote	3.00	1.50	.90
(6)	Bud Harrelson	3.00	1.50	.90
(7)	Cleon Jones	.80	.40	.25
(8)	Jerry Koosman	.80	.40	.25
(9)	Ed Kranepool	3.00	1.50	.90
(10)	Tug McGraw	7.00	3.50	2.00
(11)	Nolan Ryan	75.00	38.00	23.00
(12)	Art Shamsky	2.00	1.00	.60
(13)	Tom Seaver	15.00	7.50	4.50
(14)	Ron Swoboda	.80	.40	.25
(15)	Al Weis	2.00	1.00	.60

1983 True Value White Sox

HAROLD BAINES
Right Field   3

Issued by the Chicago White Sox and True Value hardware stores, these 2-5/8" by 4-1/8" cards are a rather expensive and scarce regional set. The 23-card set was originally scheduled as part of a promotion in which cards were given out at special Tuesday night games. The idea was sound, but rainouts forced the cancellation of some games so those scheduled cards were never given out. They were, however, smuggled out to hobby channels making it possible, although not easy, to assemble complete sets. The cards feature a large color photo with a wide white border. A red and blue White Sox logo is in the lower left corner, while the player's name, position and team number are in the lower right. Backs feature a True Value ad along with statistics. The three cards which were never given out through the normal channels are considered more scarce than the others. They are Marc Hill, Harold Baines and Salome Barojas.

		MT	NR MT	EX
Complete Set:		30.00	22.00	12.00
Common Player:		.40	.30	.15
1	Scott Fletcher	.60	.45	.25
2	Harold Baines	5.00	3.75	2.00
5	Vance Law	.50	.40	.20
7	Marc Hill	3.25	2.50	1.25

		MT	NR MT	EX
10	Tony LaRussa	.50	.40	.20
11	Rudy Law	.40	.30	.15
14	Tony Bernazard	.40	.30	.15
17	Jerry Hairston	.40	.30	.15
19	Greg Luzinski	1.00	.70	.40
24	Floyd Bannister	.60	.45	.25
25	Mike Squires	.40	.30	.15
30	Salome Barojas	3.25	2.50	1.25
31	LaMarr Hoyt	.50	.40	.20
34	Richard Dotson	.70	.50	.30
36	Jerry Koosman	.70	.50	.30
40	Britt Burns	.50	.40	.20
41	Dick Tidrow	.40	.30	.15
42	Ron Kittle	1.75	1.25	.70
44	Tom Paciorek	.40	.30	.15
45	Kevin Hickey	.40	.30	.15
53	Dennis Lamp	.40	.30	.15
67	Jim Kern	.40	.30	.15
72	Carlton Fisk	2.25	1.75	.90

1984 True Value White Sox

TOM SEAVER
Pitcher 41

True Value hardware stores and the Chicago White Sox gave their Tuesday night baseball card promotion at Comiskey Park another try in 1984. The cards measure 2-5/8" by 4-1/8" with 30 cards comprising the set. In addition to the players, there are cards for manager Tony LaRussa, the coaching staff, and former Sox greats Luis Aparicio and Minnie Minoso. Cards designs are very similar to the 1983 cards. As the cards were given out two at a time, it was very difficult to acquire a complete set. Additionally, as numbers available vary because of attendance, some cards are scarcer than others.

		MT	NR MT	EX
Complete Set:		25.00	18.50	10.00
Common Player:		.40	.30	.15
1	Scott Fletcher	.60	.45	.25
3	Harold Baines	2.25	1.75	.90
5	Vance Law	.50	.40	.20
7	Marc Hill	.40	.30	.15
8	Dave Stegman	.40	.30	.15
10	Tony LaRussa	.50	.40	.20
11	Rudy Law	.40	.30	.15
16	Julio Cruz	.40	.30	.15
17	Jerry Hairston	.40	.30	.15
19	Greg Luzinski	.90	.70	.35
20	Jerry Dybzinski	.40	.30	.15
24	Floyd Bannister	.60	.45	.25
25	Mike Squires	.40	.30	.15
27	Ron Reed	.40	.30	.15
29	Greg Walker	1.50	1.25	.60
30	Salome Barojas	.40	.30	.15
31	LaMarr Hoyt	.50	.40	.20
32	Tim Hulett	1.00	.70	.40
34	Richard Dotson	.70	.50	.30
40	Britt Burns	.40	.30	.15
41	Tom Seaver	3.00	2.25	1.25
42	Ron Kittle	1.00	.70	.40
44	Tom Paciorek	.40	.30	.15
50	Juan Agosto	.40	.30	.15
59	Tom Brennan	1.00	.70	.40
72	Carlton Fisk	2.00	1.50	.80
——	Minnie Minoso	2.00	1.50	.80
——	Luis Aparicio	2.00	1.50	.80

		MT	NR MT	EX
——	Nancy Faust (organist)	1.00	.70	.40
——	The Coaching Staff (Ed Brinkman, Dave Duncan, Art Kusnyer, Tony LaRussa, Jim Leyland, Dave Nelson, Joe Nossek)	.40	.30	.15

1986 True Value

A 30-card set of 2-1/2" by 3-1/2" cards was available in three-card packets at True Value hardware stores with a purchase of $5 or more. Cards feature a photo enclosed by stars and a ball and bat at the bottom. The player's name and team are in the lower left while his position and a Major League Baseball logo are in the lower right. The True Value logo is in the upper left. Above the picture runs the phrase "Collector Series." Backs feature some personal information and brief 1985 statistics. Along with the player cards, the folders contained a sweepstakes card offering trips to post-season games and other prizes.

		MT	NR MT	EX
Complete Panel Set:		9.00	6.75	3.50
Complete Singles Set:		3.00	2.25	1.25
Common Panel:		.40	.30	.15
Common Single Player:		.05	.04	.02
	Panel	1.00	.70	.40
1	Pedro Guerrero	.08	.06	.03
2	Steve Garvey	.15	.11	.06
3	Eddie Murray	.20	.15	.08
	Panel	2.75	2.00	1.00
4	Pete Rose	.30	.25	.12
5	Don Mattingly	.80	.60	.30
6	Fernando Valenzuela	.10	.08	.04
	Panel	.60	.45	.25
7	Jim Rice	.15	.11	.06
8	Kirk Gibson	.10	.08	.04
9	Ozzie Smith	.08	.06	.03
	Panel	1.00	.70	.40
10	Dale Murphy	.20	.15	.08
11	Robin Yount	.10	.08	.04
12	Tom Seaver	.15	.11	.06
	Panel	.80	.60	.30
13	Reggie Jackson	.15	.11	.06
14	Ryne Sandberg	.10	.08	.04
15	Bruce Sutter	.05	.04	.02
	Panel	1.00	.70	.40
16	Gary Carter	.15	.11	.06
17	George Brett	.20	.15	.08
18	Rick Sutcliffe	.05	.04	.02
	Panel	.40	.30	.15
19	Dave Stieb	.05	.04	.02
20	Buddy Bell	.05	.04	.02
21	Alvin Davis	.08	.06	.03
	Panel	.60	.45	.25
22	Cal Ripken, Jr.	.20	.15	.08
23	Bill Madlock	.05	.04	.02
24	Kent Hrbek	.10	.08	.04
	Panel	.50	.40	.20
25	Lou Whitaker	.08	.06	.03
26	Nolan Ryan	.15	.11	.06
27	Dwayne Murphy	.05	.04	.02
	Panel	1.75	1.25	.70
28	Mike Schmidt	.20	.15	.08
29	Andre Dawson	.10	.08	.04

		MT	NR MT	EX
30	Wade Boggs	.50	.40	.20

1932 U.S. Caramel

Produced by the U.S. Caramel Company, Boston, this set is not limited to baseball. Rather, it is a set of 31 "Famous Athletes" of which some 27 are baseball players. The 2-1/2" by 3" cards have a black and white picture on the front with a red background and white border. The player's name appears in white above the picture. The backs feature the player's name, position, team and league as well as a redemption ad and card number. The cards were among the last of the caramel card sets and are very scarce today. The cards could be redeemed for a baseball and baseball glove. Card #16 was recently discovered and is not included in the complete set price.

		NR MT	EX	VG
Complete Set:		15000.00	7500.00	4500.
Common Player:		250.00	125.00	75.00
1	Edward T. (Eddie) Collins	575.00	287.00	172.00
2	Paul (Big Poison) Waner	350.00	175.00	105.00
4	William (Bill) Terry	350.00	175.00	105.00
5	Earl B. Combs (Earle)	350.00	175.00	105.00
6	William (Bill) Dickey	575.00	287.00	172.00
7	Joseph (Joe) Cronin	375.00	187.00	112.00
8	Charles (Chick) Hafey	350.00	175.00	105.00
10	Walter (Rabbit) Maranville	350.00	175.00	105.00
11	Rogers (Rajah) Hornsby	650.00	325.00	195.00
12	Gordon (Mickey) Cochrane	350.00	175.00	105.00
13	Lloyd (Little Poison) Waner	350.00	175.00	105.00
14	Tyrus (Ty) Cobb	1300.00	650.00	390.00
16	Charles (Lindy) Lindstrom	20000.00	10000.00	6000.
17	Al. Simmons	350.00	175.00	105.00
18	Anthony (Tony) Lazzeri	350.00	175.00	105.00
19	Walter (Wally) Berger	250.00	125.00	75.00
20	Charles (Large Charlie) Ruffing	350.00	175.00	105.00
21	Charles (Chuck) Klein	350.00	175.00	105.00
23	James (Jimmy) Foxx	650.00	325.00	195.00
24	Frank J. (Lefty) O'Doul	250.00	125.00	75.00
26	Henry (Lou) Gehrig	1500.00	750.00	450.00
27	Robert (Lefty) Grove	425.00	212.00	127.00
28	Edward Brant (Brandt)	250.00	125.00	75.00
29	George Earnshaw	250.00	125.00	75.00
30	Frank (Frankie) Frisch	375.00	187.00	112.00
31	Vernon (Lefty) Gomez	375.00	187.00	112.00
32	George (Babe) Ruth	2500.00	1250.00	750.00

A player's name in *italic* type indicates a rookie card. An (FC) indicates a player's first card for that particular card company.

1989 Upper Deck

Brady Anderson

This premiere "Collector's Choice' issue from Upper Deck contains 700 cards (2-1/2" by 3-1/2") with full-color photos on both sides. The first 26 cards feature Star Rookies. The set also includes 26 special portrait cards with team checklist backs and seven numberical checklist cards (one for each 100 numbers). Team Checklist cards feature individual player portraits by artist Vernon Wells. Major 1988 award winners (Cy Young, Rookie of Year, MVP) are honored on 10 cards in the set, in addition to their individual player cards. There are also special cards for the Most Valuable Players in both League Championship series and the World Series. The card fronts feature head-and-shoulder poses framed by a white border. A vertical brown and green artist's rendition of the runner's lane that leads from home plate to first base is found along the right margin. The backs carry full-color action poses that fill the card back, except for a compact (yet complete) stats chart. A high-number series, cards 701-800, featuring rookies and traded players, was released in mid-season in foil packs mixed within the complete set, in boxed complete sets and in high number set boxes.

		MT	NR MT	EX
Complete Set: 1-700		55.00	41.00	22.00
Common Player: 1-700		.08	.06	.03
Complete Set: 1-800		100.00	70.00	40.00
Common Player: 701-800		.10	.08	.04
1	Star Rookie (*Ken Griffey, Jr.*)	9.00	6.75	3.50
2	Star Rookie (*Luis Medina*)	.30	.25	.12
3	Star Rookie (*Tony Chance*)	.20	.15	.08
4	Star Rookie (*Dave Otto*)	.08	.06	.03
5	Star Rookie (*Sandy Alomar, Jr.*)	1.25	.90	.50
6	Star Rookie (*Rolando Roomes*)	.40	.30	.15
7	Star Rookie (*David West*)	.40	.30	.15
8	Star Rookie (*Cris Carpenter*)	.30	.25	.12
9	Star Rookie (*Gregg Jefferies*)	2.50	2.00	1.00
10	Star Rookie (*Doug Dascenzo*)	.25	.20	.10
11	Star Rookie (*Ron Jones*)	.35	.25	.14
12	Star Rookie (*Luis de los Santos*)	.25	.20	.10
13a	Star Rookie (*Gary Sheffield*) (SS position on front is upside down)	8.00	6.00	3.25
13b	Star Rookie (*Gary Sheffield*) (SS position on front is correct)	2.25	1.75	.90
14	Star Rookie (*Mike Harkey*)	.40	.30	.15
15	Star Rookie (*Lance Blankenship*)	.25	.20	.10
16	Star Rookie (*William Brennan*)	.20	.15	.08
17	Star Rookie (*John Smoltz*)	.60	.45	.25
18	Star Rookie (*Ramon Martinez*)	.40	.30	.15
19	Star Rookie (*Mark Lemke*)	.20	.15	.08
20	Star Rookie (*Juan Bell*)	.50	.40	.20
21	Star Rookie (*Rey Palacios*)	.20	.15	.08
22	Star Rookie (*Felix Jose*)	.25	.20	.10
23	Star Rookie (*Van Snider*)	.25	.20	.10
24	Star Rookie (*Dante Bichette*)	.25	.20	.10
25	Star Rookie (*Randy Johnson*)	.35	.25	.14
26	Star Rookie (*Carlos Quintana*)	.30	.25	.12
27	Star Rookie Checklist 1-26	.08	.06	.03
28	*Mike Schooler*	.25	.20	.10
29	Randy St. Claire	.08	.06	.03
30	*Jerald Clark*	.25	.20	.10
31	Kevin Gross	.08	.06	.03

	MT	NR MT	EX			MT	NR MT	EX
32	*Dan Firova*	.20	.15	.08	120	Ryne Sandberg	.25	.20	.10
33	Jeff Calhoun	.08	.06	.03	121	Bruce Benedict	.08	.06	.03
34	Tommy Hinzo	.08	.06	.03	122	Hubie Brooks	.10	.08	.04
35	*Ricky Jordan*	1.75	1.25	.70	123	Mike Moore	.08	.06	.03
36	Larry Parrish	.08	.06	.03	124	Wallace Johnson	.08	.06	.03
37	Bret Saberhagen	.15	.11	.06	125	Bob Horner	.10	.08	.04
38	Mike Smithson	.08	.06	.03	126	Chili Davis	.08	.06	.03
39	Dave Dravecky	.08	.06	.03	127	Manny Trillo	.08	.06	.03
40	Ed Romero	.08	.06	.03	128	Chet Lemon	.08	.06	.03
41	Jeff Musselman	.08	.06	.03	129	John Cerutti	.08	.06	.03
42	Ed Hearn	.08	.06	.03	130	Orel Hershiser	.25	.20	.10
43	Rance Mulliniks	.08	.06	.03	131	Terry Pendleton	.10	.08	.04
44	Jim Eisenreich	.08	.06	.03	132	Jeff Blauser	.10	.08	.04
45	*Sil Campusano*	.20	.15	.08	133	Mike Fitzgerald	.08	.06	.03
46	Mike Krukow	.08	.06	.03	134	Henry Cotto	.08	.06	.03
47	*Paul Gibson*	.20	.15	.08	135	Gerald Young	.12	.09	.05
48	Mike LaCoss	.08	.06	.03	136	Luis Salazar	.08	.06	.03
49	Larry Herndon	.08	.06	.03	137	Alejandro Pena	.08	.06	.03
50	Scott Garrelts	.08	.06	.03	138	Jack Howell	.08	.06	.03
51	Dwayne Henry	.08	.06	.03	139	Tony Fernandez	.12	.09	.05
52	Jim Acker	.08	.06	.03	140	Mark Grace	1.75	1.25	.70
53	Steve Sax	.15	.11	.06	141	Ken Caminiti	.08	.06	.03
54	Pete O'Brien	.08	.06	.03	142	Mike Jackson	.08	.06	.03
55	Paul Runge	.08	.06	.03	143	Larry McWilliams	.08	.06	.03
56	Rick Rhoden	.08	.06	.03	144	Andres Thomas	.08	.06	.03
57	*John Dopson*	.25	.20	.10	145	Nolan Ryan	.40	.30	.15
58	Casey Candaele	.08	.06	.03	146	Mike Davis	.08	.06	.03
59	Dave Righetti	.12	.09	.05	147	DeWayne Buice	.08	.06	.03
60	Joe Hesketh	.08	.06	.03	148	Jody Davis	.08	.06	.03
61	Frank DiPino	.08	.06	.03	149	Jesse Barfield	.10	.08	.04
62	Tim Laudner	.08	.06	.03	150	Matt Nokes	.20	.15	.08
63	Jamie Moyer	.08	.06	.03	151	Jerry Reuss	.08	.06	.03
64	Fred Toliver	.08	.06	.03	152	Rick Cerone	.08	.06	.03
65	Mitch Webster	.08	.06	.03	153	Storm Davis	.10	.08	.04
66	John Tudor	.10	.08	.04	154	Marvell Wynne	.08	.06	.03
67	John Cangelosi	.08	.06	.03	155	Will Clark	.80	.60	.30
68	Mike Devereaux	.15	.11	.06	156	Luis Aguayo	.08	.06	.03
69	Brian Fisher	.08	.06	.03	157	Willie Upshaw	.08	.06	.03
70	Mike Marshall	.12	.09	.05	158	Randy Bush	.08	.06	.03
71	Zane Smith	.08	.06	.03	159	Ron Darling	.12	.09	.05
72a	Brian Holton (ball not visible on card front, photo actually Shawn Hillegas)	2.00	1.50	.80	160	Kal Daniels	.15	.11	.06
72b	Brian Holton (ball visible, correct photo)	.15	.11	.06	161	Spike Owen	.08	.06	.03
					162	Luis Polonia	.08	.06	.03
73	Jose Guzman	.10	.08	.04	163	Kevin Mitchell	.50	.40	.20
74	Rick Mahler	.08	.06	.03	164	*Dave Gallagher*	.25	.20	.10
75	John Shelby	.08	.06	.03	165	Benito Santiago	.15	.11	.06
76	Jim Deshaies	.08	.06	.03	166	Greg Gagne	.08	.06	.03
77	Bobby Meacham	.08	.06	.03	167	Ken Phelps	.08	.06	.03
78	Bryn Smith	.08	.06	.03	168	Sid Fernandez	.10	.08	.04
79	Joaquin Andujar	.08	.06	.03	169	Bo Diaz	.08	.06	.03
80	Richard Dotson	.08	.06	.03	170	Cory Snyder	.15	.11	.06
81	Charlie Lea	.08	.06	.03	171	Eric Show	.08	.06	.03
82	Calvin Schiraldi	.08	.06	.03	172	Rob Thompson	.08	.06	.03
83	Les Straker	.08	.06	.03	173	Marty Barrett	.08	.06	.03
84	Les Lancaster	.08	.06	.03	174	Dave Henderson	.10	.08	.04
85	Allan Anderson	.08	.06	.03	175	Ozzie Guillen	.08	.06	.03
86	Junior Ortiz	.08	.06	.03	176	Barry Lyons	.08	.06	.03
87	Jesse Orosco	.08	.06	.03	177	*Kelvin Torve*(FC)	.30	.25	.12
88	Felix Fermin	.08	.06	.03	178	Don Slaught	.08	.06	.03
89	Dave Anderson	.08	.06	.03	179	Steve Lombardozzi	.08	.06	.03
90	Rafael Belliard	.08	.06	.03	180	*Chris Sabo*	.80	.60	.30
91	Franklin Stubbs	.08	.06	.03	181	Jose Uribe	.08	.06	.03
92	Cecil Espy	.08	.06	.03	182	Shane Mack	.08	.06	.03
93	Albert Hall	.08	.06	.03	183	Ron Karkovice	.08	.06	.03
94	Tim Leary	.08	.06	.03	184	Todd Benzinger	.12	.09	.05
95	Mitch Williams	.08	.06	.03	185	Dave Stewart	.10	.08	.04
96	Tracy Jones	.10	.08	.04	186	Julio Franco	.10	.08	.04
97	Danny Darwin	.08	.06	.03	187	Ron Robinson	.08	.06	.03
98	Gary Ward	.08	.06	.03	188	Wally Backman	.08	.06	.03
99	Neal Heaton	.08	.06	.03	189	Randy Velarde	.08	.06	.03
100	Jim Pankovits	.08	.06	.03	190	Joe Carter	.12	.09	.05
101	Bill Doran	.08	.06	.03	191	Bob Welch	.10	.08	.04
102	Tim Wallach	.10	.08	.04	192	Kelly Paris	.08	.06	.03
103	Joe Magrane	.10	.08	.04	193	Chris Brown	.08	.06	.03
104	Ozzie Virgil	.08	.06	.03	194	Rick Reuschel	.10	.08	.04
105	Alvin Davis	.12	.09	.05	195	Roger Clemens	.50	.40	.20
106	Tom Brookens	.08	.06	.03	196	Dave Concepcion	.10	.08	.04
107	Shawon Dunston	.10	.08	.04	197	Al Newman	.08	.06	.03
108	Tracy Woodson	.10	.08	.04	198	Brook Jacoby	.10	.08	.04
109	Nelson Liriano	.08	.06	.03	199	Mookie Wilson	.08	.06	.03
110	Devon White	.12	.09	.05	200	Don Mattingly	1.50	1.25	.60
111	Steve Balboni	.08	.06	.03	201	Dick Schofield	.08	.06	.03
112	Buddy Bell	.08	.06	.03	202	Mark Gubicza	.10	.08	.04
113	*German Jimenez*	.08	.06	.03	203	Gary Gaetti	.15	.11	.06
114	Ken Dayley	.08	.06	.03	204	Dan Pasqua	.10	.08	.04
115	Andres Galarraga	.15	.11	.06	205	Andre Dawson	.20	.15	.08
116	Mike Scioscia	.08	.06	.03	206	Chris Speier	.08	.06	.03
117	Gary Pettis	.08	.06	.03	207	Kent Tekulve	.08	.06	.03
118	Ernie Whitt	.08	.06	.03	208	Rod Scurry	.08	.06	.03
119	Bob Boone	.08	.06	.03	209	Scott Bailes	.08	.06	.03
					210	Rickey Henderson	.35	.25	.14

		MT	NR MT	EX
211	Harold Baines	.12	.09	.05
212	Tony Armas	.08	.06	.03
213	Kent Hrbek	.20	.15	.08
214	Darrin Jackson	.08	.06	.03
215	George Brett	.35	.25	.14
216	Rafael Santana	.08	.06	.03
217	Andy Allanson	.08	.06	.03
218	Brett Butler	.08	.06	.03
219	Steve Jeltz	.08	.06	.03
220	Jay Buhner	.10	.08	.04
221	Bo Jackson	.60	.45	.25
222	Angel Salazar	.08	.06	.03
223	Kirk McCaskill	.08	.06	.03
224	Steve Lyons	.08	.06	.03
225	Bert Blyleven	.10	.08	.04
226	Scott Bradley	.08	.06	.03
227	Bob Melvin	.08	.06	.03
228	Ron Kittle	.08	.06	.03
229	Phil Bradley	.10	.08	.04
230	Tommy John	.12	.09	.05
231	Greg Walker	.08	.06	.03
232	Juan Berenguer	.08	.06	.03
233	Pat Tabler	.08	.06	.03
234	*Terry Clark*	.20	.15	.08
235	Rafael Palmeiro	.25	.20	.10
236	Paul Zuvella	.08	.06	.03
237	Willie Randolph	.08	.06	.03
238	Bruce Fields	.08	.06	.03
239	Mike Aldrete	.08	.06	.03
240	Lance Parrish	.15	.11	.06
241	Greg Maddux	.12	.09	.05
242	John Moses	.08	.06	.03
243	Melido Perez	.10	.08	.04
244	Willie Wilson	.10	.08	.04
245	Mark McLemore	.08	.06	.03
246	Von Hayes	.10	.08	.04
247	Matt Williams	.12	.09	.05
248	John Candelaria	.08	.06	.03
249	Harold Reynolds	.08	.06	.03
250	Greg Swindell	.12	.09	.05
251	Juan Agosto	.08	.06	.03
252	Mike Felder	.08	.06	.03
253	Vince Coleman	.15	.11	.06
254	Larry Sheets	.08	.06	.03
255	George Bell	.25	.20	.10
256	Terry Steinbach	.10	.08	.04
257	*Jack Armstrong*	.20	.15	.08
258	Dickie Thon	.08	.06	.03
259	Ray Knight	.08	.06	.03
260	Darryl Strawberry	.40	.30	.15
261	Doug Sisk	.08	.06	.03
262	Alex Trevino	.08	.06	.03
263	Jeff Leonard	.08	.06	.03
264	Tom Henke	.08	.06	.03
265	Ozzie Smith	.15	.11	.06
266	Dave Bergman	.08	.06	.03
267	Tony Phillips	.08	.06	.03
268	Mark Davis	.08	.06	.03
269	Kevin Elster	.10	.08	.04
270	Barry Larkin	.20	.15	.08
271	Manny Lee	.08	.06	.03
272	Tom Brunansky	.12	.09	.05
273	*Craig Biggio*	.50	.40	.20
274	Jim Gantner	.08	.06	.03
275	Eddie Murray	.25	.20	.10
276	Jeff Reed	.08	.06	.03
277	Tim Teufel	.08	.06	.03
278	Rick Honeycutt	.08	.06	.03
279	Guillermo Hernandez	.08	.06	.03
280	John Kruk	.10	.08	.04
281	*Luis Alicea*	.20	.15	.08
282	Jim Clancy	.08	.06	.03
283	Billy Ripken	.08	.06	.03
284	Craig Reynolds	.08	.06	.03
285	Robin Yount	.30	.25	.12
286	Jimmy Jones	.08	.06	.03
287	Ron Oester	.08	.06	.03
288	Terry Leach	.08	.06	.03
289	Dennis Eckersley	.12	.09	.05
290	Alan Trammell	.20	.15	.08
291	Jimmy Key	.10	.08	.04
292	Chris Bosio	.08	.06	.03
293	Jose DeLeon	.08	.06	.03
294	Jim Traber	.08	.06	.03
295	Mike Scott	.12	.09	.05
296	Roger McDowell	.10	.08	.04
297	Garry Templeton	.08	.06	.03
298	Doyle Alexander	.08	.06	.03
299	Nick Esasky	.08	.06	.03
300	Mark McGwire	.70	.50	.30
301	*Darryl Hamilton*	.20	.15	.08
302	Dave Smith	.08	.06	.03
303	Rick Sutcliffe	.10	.08	.04
304	Dave Stapleton	.08	.06	.03
305	Alan Ashby	.08	.06	.03
306	Pedro Guerrero	.15	.11	.05
307	Ron Guidry	.12	.09	.05
308	Steve Farr	.08	.06	.03
309	Curt Ford	.08	.06	.03
310	Claudell Washington	.08	.06	.03
311	Tom Prince	.08	.06	.03
312	*Chad Kreuter*	.20	.15	.08
313	Ken Oberkfell	.08	.06	.03
314	Jerry Browne	.08	.06	.03
315	R.J. Reynolds	.08	.06	.03
316	Scott Bankhead	.08	.06	.03
317	Milt Thompson	.08	.06	.03
318	Mario Diaz	.10	.08	.04
319	Bruce Ruffin	.08	.06	.03
320	Dave Valle	.08	.06	.03
321a	*Gary Varsho* (batting righty on card back, photo actually Mike Bielecki)	2.00	1.50	.80
321b	*Gary Varsho* (batting lefty on card back, correct photo)	.30	.25	.12
322	Paul Mirabella	.08	.06	.03
323	Chuck Jackson	.08	.06	.03
324	Drew Hall	.10	.08	.04
325	Don August	.10	.08	.04
326	*Israel Sanchez*	.20	.15	.08
327	Denny Walling	.08	.06	.03
328	Joel Skinner	.08	.06	.03
329	Danny Tartabull	.20	.15	.08
330	Tony Pena	.08	.06	.03
331	Jim Sundberg	.08	.06	.03
332	Jeff Robinson	.12	.09	.05
333	Odibbe McDowell	.08	.06	.03
334	Jose Lind	.10	.08	.04
335	Paul Kilgus	.10	.08	.04
336	Juan Samuel	.12	.09	.05
337	Mike Campbell	.10	.08	.04
338	Mike Maddux	.08	.06	.03
339	Darnell Coles	.08	.06	.03
340	Bob Dernier	.08	.06	.03
341	Rafael Ramirez	.08	.06	.03
342	Scott Sanderson	.08	.06	.03
343	B.J. Surhoff	.10	.08	.04
344	Billy Hatcher	.08	.06	.03
345	Pat Perry	.08	.06	.03
346	Jack Clark	.15	.11	.06
347	Gary Thurman	.12	.09	.05
348	*Timmy Jones*	.20	.15	.08
349	Dave Winfield	.30	.25	.12
350	Frank White	.08	.06	.03
351	Dave Collins	.08	.06	.03
352	Jack Morris	.15	.11	.06
353	Eric Plunk	.08	.06	.03
354	Leon Durham	.08	.06	.03
355	Ivan DeJesus	.08	.06	.03
356	*Brian Holman*	.20	.15	.08
357a	Dale Murphy (photo on card front reversed)	150.00	112.00	60.00
357b	Dale Murphy (correct photo)	.35	.25	.14
358	Mark Portugal	.08	.06	.03
359	Andy McGaffigan	.08	.06	.03
360	Tom Glavine	.10	.08	.04
361	Keith Moreland	.08	.06	.03
362	Todd Stottlemyre	.15	.11	.06
363	Dave Leiper	.08	.06	.03
364	Cecil Fielder	.08	.06	.03
365	Carmelo Martinez	.08	.06	.03
366	Dwight Evans	.10	.08	.04
367	Kevin McReynolds	.15	.11	.06
368	Rich Gedman	.08	.06	.03
369	Len Dykstra	.10	.08	.04
370	Jody Reed	.12	.09	.05
371	Jose Canseco	1.25	.90	.50
372	Rob Murphy	.08	.06	.03
373	Mike Henneman	.10	.08	.04
374	Walt Weiss	.40	.30	.15
375	*Rob Dibble*	.25	.20	.10
376	Kirby Puckett	.30	.25	.12
377	Denny Martinez	.08	.06	.03
378	Ron Gant	.12	.09	.05
379	Brian Harper	.08	.06	.03
380	*Nelson Santovenia*	.20	.15	.08
381	Lloyd Moseby	.08	.06	.03
382	Lance McCullers	.08	.06	.03
383	Dave Stieb	.10	.08	.04
384	Tony Gwynn	.30	.25	.12
385	Mike Flanagan	.08	.06	.03
386	Bob Ojeda	.08	.06	.03
387	Bruce Hurst	.10	.08	.04

		MT	NR MT	EX			MT	NR MT	EX
388	Dave Magadan	.10	.08	.04	479	Bob Brenly	.08	.06	.03
389	Wade Boggs	1.00	.70	.40	480	Otis Nixon	.08	.06	.03
390	Gary Carter	.25	.20	.10	481	Johnny Ray	.08	.06	.03
391	Frank Tanana	.08	.06	.03	482	Geno Petralli	.08	.06	.03
392	Curt Young	.08	.06	.03	483	Stu Cliburn	.08	.06	.03
393	Jeff Treadway	.10	.08	.04	484	Pete Incaviglia	.10	.08	.04
394	Darrell Evans	.10	.08	.04	485	Brian Downing	.08	.06	.03
395	Glenn Hubbard	.08	.06	.03	486	Jeff Stone	.08	.06	.03
396	Chuck Cary	.08	.06	.03	487	Carmen Castillo	.08	.06	.03
397	Frank Viola	.15	.11	.06	488	Tom Niedenfuer	.08	.06	.03
398	Jeff Parrett	.10	.08	.04	489	Jay Bell	.08	.06	.03
399	*Terry Blocker*	.15	.11	.06	490	Rick Schu	.08	.06	.03
400	Dan Gladden	.08	.06	.03	491	*Jeff Pico*	.25	.20	.10
401	*Louie Meadows*	.20	.15	.08	492	*Mark Parent*	.20	.15	.08
402	Tim Raines	.25	.20	.10	493	Eric King	.08	.06	.03
403	Joey Meyer	.10	.08	.04	494	Al Nipper	.08	.06	.03
404	Larry Andersen	.08	.06	.03	495	Andy Hawkins	.08	.06	.03
405	Rex Hudler	.08	.06	.03	496	Daryl Boston	.08	.06	.03
406	Mike Schmidt	.70	.50	.30	497	Ernie Riles	.08	.06	.03
407	John Franco	.10	.08	.04	498	Pascual Perez	.08	.06	.03
408	*Brady Anderson*	.30	.25	.12	499	Bill Long	.08	.06	.03
409	Don Carman	.08	.06	.03	500	Kirt Manwaring	.10	.08	.04
410	Eric Davis	.40	.30	.15	501	Chuck Crim	.08	.06	.03
411	Bob Stanley	.08	.06	.03	502	Candy Maldonado	.08	.06	.03
412	Pete Smith	.10	.08	.04	503	Dennis Lamp	.08	.06	.03
413	Jim Rice	.25	.20	.10	504	Glenn Braggs	.08	.06	.03
414	Bruce Sutter	.10	.08	.04	505	Joe Price	.08	.06	.03
415	Oil Can Boyd	.08	.06	.03	506	Ken Williams	.08	.06	.03
416	Ruben Sierra	.40	.30	.15	507	Bill Pecota	.08	.06	.03
417	Mike LaValliere	.08	.06	.03	508	Rey Quinones	.08	.06	.03
418	Steve Buechele	.08	.06	.03	509	*Jeff Bittiger*	.15	.11	.06
419	Gary Redus	.08	.06	.03	510	Kevin Seitzer	.30	.25	.12
420	Scott Fletcher	.08	.06	.03	511	Steve Bedrosian	.10	.08	.04
421	Dale Sveum	.08	.06	.03	512	Todd Worrell	.10	.08	.04
422	Bob Knepper	.08	.06	.03	513	Chris James	.10	.08	.04
423	Luis Rivera	.08	.06	.03	514	Jose Oquendo	.08	.06	.03
424	Ted Higuera	.10	.08	.04	515	David Palmer	.08	.06	.03
425	Kevin Bass	.08	.06	.03	516	John Smiley	.12	.09	.05
426	Ken Gerhart	.08	.06	.03	517	Dave Clark	.08	.06	.03
427	Shane Rawley	.08	.06	.03	518	Mike Dunne	.10	.08	.04
428	Paul O'Neill	.08	.06	.03	519	Ron Washington	.08	.06	.03
429	Joe Orsulak	.08	.06	.03	520	Bob Kipper	.08	.06	.03
430	Jackie Gutierrez	.08	.06	.03	521	Lee Smith	.10	.08	.04
431	Gerald Perry	.10	.08	.04	522	Juan Castillo	.08	.06	.03
432	Mike Greenwell	.60	.45	.25	523	Don Robinson	.08	.06	.03
433	Jerry Royster	.08	.06	.03	524	Kevin Romine	.08	.06	.03
434	Ellis Burks	.60	.45	.25	525	Paul Molitor	.15	.11	.06
435	Ed Olwine	.08	.06	.03	526	Mark Langston	.10	.08	.04
436	Dave Rucker	.08	.06	.03	527	Donnie Hill	.08	.06	.03
437	Charlie Hough	.08	.06	.03	528	Larry Owen	.08	.06	.03
438	Bob Walk	.08	.06	.03	529	Jerry Reed	.08	.06	.03
439	Bob Brower	.08	.06	.03	530	Jack McDowell	.10	.08	.04
440	Barry Bonds	.12	.09	.05	531	Greg Mathews	.08	.06	.03
441	Tom Foley	.08	.06	.03	532	John Russell	.08	.06	.03
442	Rob Deer	.08	.06	.03	533	Don Quisenberry	.08	.06	.03
443	Glenn Davis	.15	.11	.06	534	Greg Gross	.08	.06	.03
444	Dave Martinez	.08	.06	.03	535	Danny Cox	.08	.06	.03
445	Bill Wegman	.08	.06	.03	536	Terry Francona	.08	.06	.03
446	Lloyd McClendon	.08	.06	.03	537	Andy Van Slyke	.15	.11	.06
447	Dave Schmidt	.08	.06	.03	538	Mel Hall	.08	.06	.03
448	Darren Daulton	.08	.06	.03	539	Jim Gott	.08	.06	.03
449	Frank Williams	.08	.06	.03	540	Doug Jones	.10	.08	.04
450	Don Aase	.08	.06	.03	541	Criag Lefferts	.08	.06	.03
451	Lou Whitaker	.15	.11	.06	542	Mike Boddicker	.08	.06	.03
452	Goose Gossage	.12	.09	.05	543	Greg Brock	.08	.06	.03
453	Ed Whitson	.08	.06	.03	544	Atlee Hammaker	.08	.06	.03
454	Jim Walewander	.08	.06	.03	545	Tom Bolton	.08	.06	.03
455	Damon Berryhill	.12	.09	.05	546	*Mike Macfarlane*	.20	.15	.08
456	Tim Burke	.08	.06	.03	547	*Rich Renteria*	.15	.11	.06
457	Barry Jones	.08	.06	.03	548	John Davis	.08	.06	.03
458	Joel Youngblood	.08	.06	.03	549	Floyd Bannister	.08	.06	.03
459	Floyd Youmans	.08	.06	.03	550	Mickey Brantley	.08	.06	.03
460	Mark Salas	.08	.06	.03	551	Duane Ward	.08	.06	.03
461	Jeff Russell	.08	.06	.03	552	Dan Petry	.08	.06	.03
462	Darrell Miller	.08	.06	.03	553	Mickey Tettleton	.08	.06	.03
463	Jeff Kunkel	.08	.06	.03	554	Rick Leach	.08	.06	.03
464	*Sherman Corbett*	.20	.15	.08	555	Mike Witt	.08	.06	.03
465	Curtis Wilkerson	.08	.06	.03	556	Sid Bream	.08	.06	.03
466	Bud Black	.08	.06	.03	557	Bobby Witt	.10	.08	.04
467	Cal Ripken, Jr.	.35	.25	.14	558	Tommy Herr	.08	.06	.03
468	John Farrell	.10	.08	.04	559	Randy Milligan	.08	.06	.03
469	Terry Kennedy	.08	.06	.03	560	*Jose Cecena*	.20	.15	.08
470	Tom Candiotti	.08	.06	.03	561	Mackey Sasser	.08	.06	.03
471	Roberto Alomar	.40	.30	.15	562	Carney Lansford	.08	.06	.03
472	Jeff Robinson	.12	.09	.05	563	Rick Aguilera	.08	.06	.03
473	Vance Law	.08	.06	.03	564	Ron Hassey	.08	.06	.03
474	Randy Ready	.08	.06	.03	565	Dwight Gooden	.50	.40	.20
475	Walt Terrell	.08	.06	.03	566	Paul Assenmacher	.08	.06	.03
476	Kelly Downs	.10	.08	.04	567	Neil Allen	.08	.06	.03
477	*Johnny Paredes*	.20	.15	.08	568	Jim Morrison	.08	.06	.03
478	Shawn Hillegas	.08	.06	.03	569	Mike Pagliarulo	.10	.08	.04

	MT	NR MT	EX
570 Ted Simmons	.10	.08	.04
571 Mark Thurmond	.08	.06	.03
572 Fred McGriff	.40	.30	.15
573 Wally Joyner	.25	.20	.10
574 *Jose Bautista*	.20	.15	.08
575 Kelly Gruber	.08	.06	.03
576 Cecilio Guante	.08	.06	.03
577 Mark Davidson	.08	.06	.03
578 Bobby Bonilla	.12	.09	.05
579 Mike Stanley	.08	.06	.03
580 Gene Larkin	.10	.08	.04
581 Stan Javier	.08	.06	.03
582 Howard Johnson	.10	.08	.04
583a Mike Gallego (photo on card back reversed)	2.00	1.50	.80
583b Mike Gallego (correct photo)	.15	.11	.06
584 David Cone	.35	.25	.14
585 *Doug Jennings*	.20	.15	.08
586 Charlie Hudson	.08	.06	.03
587 Dion James	.08	.06	.03
588 Al Leiter	.15	.11	.06
589 Charlie Puleo	.08	.06	.03
590 Roberto Kelly	.25	.20	.10
591 Thad Bosley	.08	.06	.03
592 Pete Stanicek	.10	.08	.04
593 *Pat Borders*	.25	.20	.10
594 *Bryan Harvey*	.25	.20	.10
595 Jeff Ballard	.10	.08	.04
596 Jeff Reardon	.10	.08	.04
597 Doug Drabek	.08	.06	.03
598 Edwin Correa	.08	.06	.03
599 Keith Atherton	.08	.06	.03
600 Dave LaPoint	.08	.06	.03
601 Don Baylor	.10	.08	.04
602 Tom Pagnozzi	.08	.06	.03
603 Tim Flannery	.08	.06	.03
604 Gene Walter	.08	.06	.03
605 Dave Parker	.12	.09	.05
606 Mike Diaz	.08	.06	.03
607 Chris Gwynn	.10	.08	.04
608 Odell Jones	.08	.06	.03
609 Carlton Fisk	.15	.11	.06
610 Jay Howell	.08	.06	.03
611 Tim Crews	.08	.06	.03
612 Keith Hernandez	.20	.15	.08
613 Willie Fraser	.08	.06	.03
614 Jim Eppard	.08	.06	.03
615 Jeff Hamilton	.08	.06	.03
616 Kurt Stillwell	.08	.06	.03
617 Tom Browning	.10	.08	.04
618 Jeff Montgomery	.08	.06	.03
619 Jose Rijo	.08	.06	.03
620 Jamie Quirk	.08	.06	.03
621 Willie McGee	.12	.09	.05
622 Mark Grant	.08	.06	.03
623 Bill Swift	.08	.06	.03
624 Orlando Mercado	.08	.06	.03
625 *John Costello*	.20	.15	.08
626 Jose Gonzalez	.08	.06	.03
627a Bill Schroeder (putting on shin guards on card back, photo actually Ronn Reynolds)	2.00	1.50	.80
627b Bill Schroeder (arms crossed on card back, correct photo)	.15	.11	.06
628a Fred Manrique (throwing on card back, photo actually Ozzie Guillen)	2.00	1.50	.80
628b Fred Manrique (batting on card back, correct photo)	.15	.11	.06
629 Ricky Horton	.08	.06	.03
630 Dan Plesac	.10	.08	.04
631 Alfredo Griffin	.08	.06	.03
632 Chuck Finley	.08	.06	.03
633 Kirk Gibson	.20	.15	.08
634 Randy Myers	.10	.08	.04
635 Greg Minton	.08	.06	.03
636 Herm Winningham	.08	.06	.03
637 Charlie Leibrandt	.08	.06	.03
638 Tim Birtsas	.08	.06	.03
639 Bill Buckner	.10	.08	.04
640 Danny Jackson	.15	.11	.06
641 Greg Booker	.08	.06	.03
642 Jim Presley	.08	.06	.03
643 Gene Nelson	.08	.06	.03
644 Rod Booker	.08	.06	.03
645 Dennis Rasmussen	.10	.08	.04
646 Juan Nieves	.08	.06	.03
647 Bobby Thigpen	.10	.08	.04
648 Tim Belcher	.10	.08	.04
649 Mike Young	.08	.06	.03
650 Ivan Calderon	.08	.06	.03
651 *Oswaldo Peraza*	.20	.15	.08

	MT	NR MT	EX
652a Pat Sheridan (no position on front)	35.00	27.50	15.00
652b Pat Sheridan (position on front)	.08	.06	.03
653 Mike Morgan	.08	.06	.03
654 Mike Heath	.08	.06	.03
655 Jay Tibbs	.08	.06	.03
656 Fernando Valenzuela	.20	.15	.08
657 Lee Mazzilli	.08	.06	.03
658 Frank Viola	.08	.06	.03
659 Jose Canseco	.08	.06	.03
660 Walt Weiss	.08	.06	.03
661 Orel Hershiser	.08	.06	.03
662 Kirk Gibson	.08	.06	.03
663 Chris Sabo	.08	.06	.03
664 Dennis Eckersley	.08	.06	.03
665 Orel Hershiser	.08	.06	.03
666 Kirk Gibson	.08	.06	.03
667 Orel Hershiser	.08	.06	.03
668 Angels Checklist (Wally Joyner)	.08	.06	.03
669 Astros Checklist (Nolan Ryan)	.08	.06	.03
670 Athletics Checklist (Jose Canseco)	.08	.06	.03
671 Blue Jays Checklist (Fred McGriff)	.08	.06	.03
672 Braves Checklist (Dale Murphy)	.08	.06	.03
673 Brewers Checklist (Paul Molitor)	.08	.06	.03
674 Cardinals Checklist (Ozzie Smith)	.08	.06	.03
675 Cubs Checklist (Ryne Sandberg)	.08	.06	.03
676 Dodgers Checklist (Kirk Gibson)	.08	.06	.03
677 Expos Checklist (Andres Galarraga)	.08	.06	.03
678 Giants Checklist (Will Clark)	.08	.06	.03
679 Indians Checklist (Cory Snyder)	.08	.06	.03
680 Mariners Checklist (Alvin Davis)	.08	.06	.03
681 Mets Checklist (Darryl Strawberry)	.08	.06	.03
682 Orioles Checklist (Cal Ripken, Jr.)	.08	.06	.03
683 Padres Checklist (Tony Gwynn)	.08	.06	.03
684 Phillies Checklist (Mike Schmidt)	.08	.06	.03
685 Pirates Checklist (Andy Van Slyke)	.08	.06	.03
686 Rangers Checklist (Ruben Sierra)	.08	.06	.03
687 Red Sox Checklist (Wade Boggs)	.08	.06	.03
688 Reds Checklist (Eric Davis)	.08	.06	.03
689 Royals Checklist (George Brett)	.08	.06	.03
690 Tigers Checklist (Alan Trammell)	.08	.06	.03
691 Twins Checklist (Frank Viola)	.08	.06	.03
692 White Sox Checklist (Harold Baines)	.08	.06	.03
693 Yankees Checklist (Don Mattingly)	.08	.06	.03
694 Checklist 1-100	.08	.06	.03
695 Checklist 101-200	.08	.06	.03
696 Checklist 201-300	.08	.06	.03
697 Checklist 301-400	.08	.06	.03
698 Checklist 401-500	.08	.06	.03
699 Checklist 501-600	.08	.06	.03
700 Checklist 601-700	.08	.06	.03
701 Checklist 701-800	.20	.15	.08
702 Jessie Barfield	.10	.08	.04
703 Walt Terrell	.10	.08	.04
704 Dickie Thon	.10	.08	.04
705 Al Leiter	.10	.08	.04
706 , Dave LaPoint	.10	.08	.04
707 Charlie Hayes(FC)	.15	.11	.06
708 Andy Hawkins	.10	.08	.04
709 Mickey Hatcher	.10	.08	.04
710 Lance McCullers	.10	.08	.04
711 Ron Kittle	.10	.08	.04
712 Bert Blyleven	.10	.08	.04
713 Rick Dempsey	.10	.08	.04
714 Ken Williams	.10	.08	.04
715 Steve Rosenberg(FC)	.15	.11	.06
716 Joe Skalski(FC)	.20	.15	.08
717 Spike Owen	.10	.08	.04
718 Todd Burns	.10	.08	.04
719 Kevin Gross	.10	.08	.04
720 Tommy Herr	.10	.08	.04
721 Rob Ducey	.10	.08	.04
722 Gary Green(FC)	.15	.11	.06
723 Gregg Olson(FC)	3.25	2.50	1.25
724 Greg W. Harris(FC)	.15	.11	.06
725 Craig Worthington(FC)	.50	.40	.20
726 Tom Howard(FC)	.35	.25	.14
727 Dale Mohorcic	.10	.08	.04
728 Rich Yett	.10	.08	.04
729 Mel Hall	.10	.08	.04
730 Floyd Youmans	.10	.08	.04
731 Lonnie Smith	.15	.11	.06
732 Wally Backman	.10	.08	.04
733 Trevor Wilson	.10	.08	.04
734 Jose Alvarez	.10	.08	.04
735 Bob Milacki(FC)	.15	.11	.06
736 Tom Gordon(FC)	7.00	5.25	2.75
737 Wally Whitehurst(FC)	.25	.20	.10
738 Mike Aldrete	.10	.08	.04

1990 UPPER DECK
Singles

Limited Amount of each card is available!!! Call now avoid sellouts!!

The following cards are being sold in 50 card lots. Minimum order is $50.00. Delivery expected March thru June. All sales are final. Payment in full is required on all orders. If, by chance, a player is not in the set, a full refund will be issued. Prices are subject to change without notice due to market fluctuations.

Abbott 1.75	Hamelin 1.25	Parker, C 10
Alomar, S 30	Henderson, R 15	Ripken, Jr 10
Anthony, E 2.40	Jackson, Bo 50	Ryan 75
Avery 50	Jackson, (special) 50	Ryan 5000K 1.95
Benes, A 75	Jefferies 50	Saberhagen 10
Biggio 25	Johnson, H 10	Sandberg 10
Boggs 1.50	Jordan, R 20	Sanders, D 75
Brett 20	Kelly, R 15	Schmidt (special) 1.25
Briley 25	Lilliquist 10	Sheffield 50
Canale 35	Litton 15	Sierra 20
Canseco 50	Lovullo 10	Smith, Dw 90
Clark, W 75	Maas, K 40	Smoltz 10
Clark, W. (special) ...50	Machado 25	Sosa 95
Clemens 25	Martinez, R 10	Spiers 20
Coolbaugh 40	Martinez, T 50	Stevens 20
Felix, Junior 50	Mercker 75	Strawberry 20
Finley, S 15	Mattingly 60	Swindell 10
Geren 25	McDonald, Ben 2.50	Tapani 25
Girardi 10	Mc Griff 20	Vaughn, G 1.50
Gooden 25	McGwire 40	Ventura 85
T. Gordon 1.25	Meulens 20	Vizquel 10
Gonzalez, J 75	Mitchell 40	Walker 90
Gozzo 25	Murphy, D 10	Walton, F 2.95
Grace 40	Murray, E 10	Wetteland 25
Greenwell 30	Navarro 25	Williams, Matt 25
Greene, T 75	Offerman, J 1.95	Wilson, Steve 10
Griffey Jr 2.75	Olerud, J 3.45	Worthington 10
Grissom 75	Olsen, G 40	Yount 25
Gwynn, T 15	Palmeiro 10	Zeile 2.50
Hayes, C 10		

Any cards not listed above, Call for prices!

If you already have an existing order with Big Bob and you have a question about your order
Call Customer Service: 203-876-2847 Satisfaction Guaranteed

---

1. Thank you for your business.
2. Phone reservations required on all orders.
3. Phone reservations held for 7 days.
4. Full payment on all orders.
5. All cases are double boxes.
6. All sales are final. No refunds.
7. Minimum order $50.00.
8. All postage on cases exact UPS only.
9. Prices are subject to change without notice due to market fluctuations.

For Orders Call "Big Bob" at:
1-800-432-2028
In Connecticut Call (203) 874-0061

"BIG BOB'S"
BASEBALL CARDS, INC.
19 Seemans Lane, Milford, CT 06460

	MT	NR MT	EX
739 Keith Miller	.10	.08	.04
740 Randy Milligan	.10	.08	.04
741 Jeff Parrett	.10	.08	.04
742 Steve Finley(FC)	.35	.25	.14
743 Junior Felix(FC)	2.75	2.00	1.00
744 Pete Harnisch(FC)	.15	.11	.06
745 Bill Spiers(FC)	.50	.40	.20
746 Hensley Meulens(FC)	.70	.50	.30
747 Juan Bell	.20	.15	.08
748 Steve Sax	.15	.11	.06
749 Phil Bradley	.10	.08	.04
750 Rey Quinones	.10	.08	.04
751 Tommy Gregg(FC)	.15	.11	.06
752 Kevin Brown(FC)	.10	.08	.04
753 Derek Lilliquist(FC)	.15	.11	.06
754 Todd Zeile(FC)	6.00	4.50	2.50
755 Jim Abbott(FC)	11.00	8.25	4.50
756 Ozzie Canseco(FC)	1.75	1.25	.70
757 Nick Esasky	.10	.08	.04
758 Mike Moore	.15	.11	.06
759 Rob Murphy	.10	.08	.04
760 Rick Mahler	.10	.08	.04
761 Fred Lynn	.10	.08	.04
762 Kevin Blankenship(FC)	.10	.08	.04
763 Eddie Murray	.15	.11	.06
764 Steve Searcy(FC)	.10	.08	.04
765 Jerome Walton(FC)	12.00	9.00	4.75
766 Erik Hanson(FC)	.25	.20	.10
767 Bob Boone	.15	.11	.06
768 Edgar Martinez(FC)	.15	.11	.06
769 Jose DeJesus(FC)	.10	.08	.04
770 Greg Briley(FC)	1.25	.90	.50
771 Steve Peters(FC)	.10	.08	.04
772 Rafael Palmeiro	.15	.11	.06
773 Jack Clark	.15	.11	.06
774 Nolan Ryan	5.00	3.75	2.00
775 Lance Parrish	.10	.08	.04
776 Joe Girardi(FC)	.35	.25	.14
777 Willie Randolph	.10	.08	.04
778 Mitch Williams	.30	.25	.12
779 Dennis Cook(FC)	.20	.15	.08
780 Dwight Smith(FC)	5.00	3.75	2.00
781 Lenny Harris(FC)	.20	.15	.08
782 Torey Louvullo(FC)	.15	.11	.06
783 Norm Charlton(FC)	.10	.08	.04
784 Chris Brown	.10	.08	.04
785 Todd Benzinger	.10	.08	.04
786 Shane Rawley	.10	.08	.04
787 Omar Vizquel(FC)	.25	.20	.10
788 LaVel Freeman(FC)	.40	.30	.15
789 Jeffrey Leonard	.10	.08	.04
790 Eddie Williams(FC)	.10	.08	.04
791 Jamie Moyer	.10	.08	.04
792 Bruce Hurst	.10	.08	.04
793 Julio Franco	.15	.11	.06
794 Claudell Washington	.10	.08	.04
795 Jody Davis	.10	.08	.04
796 Odibbe McDowell	.10	.08	.04
797 Paul Kilgus	.10	.08	.04
798 Tracy Jones	.10	.08	.04
799 Steve Wilson(FC)	.25	.20	.10
800 Pete O'Brien,			

1990 Upper Deck

Cal Ripken Jr.

Following the success of its first issue, Upper Deck released the first 700 cards of the 1990 set. The cards contain full-color photos on both sides and are 2-1/2" by 3-1/2" in size. The artwork of

Vernon Wells is featured on the front of all team checklist cards. The 1990 set also introduces two new Wells illustrations - a tribute to Mike Schmidt upon his retirement and one commemorating Nolan Ryan's 5,000 career strikeouts. The cards are similar in design to the 1989 issue. The Wade Boggs card depicts the Red Sox star in four stages of his batting swing via a quad-action photograph, much like the Jim Abbott card of 1989. A high- number series (701-800) is expected to become available mid-season.

		MT	NR MT	EX
	Complete Set:	50.00	37.50	20.00
	Common Player:	.06	.05	.02
1	Star Rookie Checklist	.06	.05	.02
2	Randy Nosek(FC)	.15	.11	.06
3	Tom Dress(FC)	.15	.11	.06
4	Curt Young	.06	.05	.02
5	Angels Checklist	.06	.05	.02
6	Luis Salazar	.06	.05	.02
7	Phillies Checklist	.06	.05	.02
8	Jose Bautista	.08	.06	.03
9	Marquis Grissom(FC)	1.00	.70	.40
10	Dodgers Checklist	.06	.05	.02
11	Rick Aguilera	.08	.06	.03
12	Padres Checklist	.06	.05	.02
13	Deion Sanders(FC)	1.00	.70	.40
14	Marvell Wynee	.06	.05	.02
15	David West	.15	.11	.06
16	Pirates Checklist	.06	.05	.02
17	Sammy Sosa(FC)	.80	.60	.30
18	Yankees Checklist	.06	.05	.02
19	Jack Howell	.06	.05	.02
20	Mike Schmidt (Special Card)	1.50	1.25	.60
21	Robin Ventura(FC)	1.00	.70	.40
22	Brian Meyer(FC)	.20	.15	.08
23	Blaine Beatty(FC)	.20	.15	.08
24	Mariners Checklist	.06	.05	.02
25	Greg Vaughn(FC)	2.00	1.50	.80
26	Xavier Hernandez(FC)	.15	.11	.06
27	Jason Grimsley(FC)	.25	.20	.10
28	Eric Anthony(FC)	3.00	2.25	1.25
29	Expos Checklist	.06	.05	.02
30	David Wells	.06	.05	.02
31	Hal Morris(FC)	.15	.11	.06
32	Royals Checklist	.06	.05	.02
33	Kelly Mann(FC)	.15	.11	.06
34	Nolan Ryan (Special Card)	1.75	1.25	.70
35	Scott Service(FC)	.20	.15	.08
36	Athletics Checklist	.06	.05	.02
37	Tino Martinez(FC)	.60	.45	.25
38	Chili Davis	.09	.07	.04
39	Scott Sanderson	.06	.05	.02
40	Giants Checklist	.06	.05	.02
41	Tigers Checklist	.06	.05	.02
42	Scott Coolbaugh(FC)	.40	.30	.15
43	Jose Cano(FC)	.15	.11	.06
44	Jose Vizcaino(FC)	.20	.15	.08
45	Bob Hamelin(FC)	1.25	.90	.50
46	Jose Offerman(FC)	2.25	1.75	.90
47	Kevin Blankenship	.10	.08	.04
48	Twins Checklist	.06	.05	.02
49	Tommy Greene(FC)	.90	.70	.35
50	Will Clark (Special Card)	.50	.40	.20
51	Rob Nelson(FC)	.09	.07	.04
52	Chris Hammond(FC)	.15	.11	.06
53	Indian Checklist	.06	.05	.02
54a	Ben McDonald (Orioles Logo)(FC)	100.00	75.00	40.00
54b	Ben McDonald (Rookies Label)(FC)	2.50	2.00	1.00
55	Andy Benes(FC)	1.00	.70	.40
56	John Olerud(FC)	2.75	2.00	1.00
57	Red Sox Checklist	.06	.05	.02
58	Tony Armas	.06	.05	.02
59	George Canale(FC)	.50	.40	.20
60a	Orioles Checklist (Jamie Weston)	5.00	3.75	2.00
60b	Orioles Checklist (Mickey Weston)	.08	.06	.03
61	Mike Stanton(FC)	.15	.11	.06
62	Mets Checklist	.06	.05	.02
63	Kent Mercker(FC)	.90	.70	.35
64	Francisco Cabrera(FC)	.30	.25	.20
65	Steve Avery(FC)	.70	.50	.30
66	Jose Canseco	.70	.50	.20
67	Matt Merullo(FC)	.15	.11	.06
68	Cardinals Checklist	.06	.05	.02
69	Ron Karkovice	.06	.05	.02
70	Kevin Maas(FC)	.50	.40	.20

		MT	NR MT	EX				MT	NR MT	EX
71	Dennis Cook	.10	.08	.04		161	Paul O'Neill	.09	.07	.04
72	Juan Gonzalez(FC)	1.00	.70	.40		162	Jeff McKnight(FC)	.20	.15	.08
73	Cubs Checklist	.06	.05	.02		163	Alvaro Espinosa(FC)	.15	.11	.06
74	Dean Palmer(FC)	.40	.30	.15		164	Scott Scudder(FC)	.20	.15	.08
75	Bo Jackson (Special Card)	.50	.40	.20		165	Jeff Reed	.06	.05	.02
76	Rob Richie(FC)	.20	.15	.08		166	Gregg Jefferies	.60	.45	.25
77	Bobby Rose(FC)	.40	.30	.15		167	Barry Larkin	.15	.11	.06
78	Brian DuBois(FC)	.15	.11	.06		168	Gary Carter	.10	.08	.04
79	White Sox Checklist	.06	.05	.02		169	Robby Thompson	.09	.07	.04
80	Gene Nelson	.06	.05	.02		170	Rolando Roomes	.15	.11	.06
81	Bob McClure	.06	.05	.02		171	Mark McGwire	.50	.40	.20
82	Rangers Checklist	.06	.05	.02		172	Steve Sax	.10	.08	.04
83	Greg Minton	.06	.05	.02		173	Mark Williamson	.06	.05	.02
84	Braves Checklist	.06	.05	.02		174	Mitch Williams	.15	.11	.06
85	Willie Fraser	.06	.05	.02		175	Brian Holton	.06	.05	.02
86	Neal Heaton	.06	.05	.02		176	Rob Deer	.08	.06	.03
87	Kevin Tapani(FC)	.25	.20	.10		177	Tim Raines	.12	.09	.05
88	Astros Checklist	.06	.05	.02		178	Mike Felder	.06	.05	.02
89a	Jim Gott (Incorrect Photo)	20.00	15.00	8.00		179	Harold Reynolds	.10	.08	.04
89b	Jim Gott (Photo of Gott)	.10	.08	.04		180	Terry Francona	.06	.05	.02
90	Lance Johnson(FC)	.09	.07	.04		181	Chris Sabo	.15	.11	.06
91	Brewers Checklist	.06	.05	.02		182	Darryl Strawberry	.20	.15	.08
92	Jeff Parrett	.08	.06	.03		183	Willie Randolph	.10	.08	.04
93	Julio Machado(FC)	.25	.20	.10		184	Billy Ripken	.06	.05	.02
94	Ron Jones	.10	.08	.04		185	Mackey Sasser	.08	.06	.03
95	Blue Jays Checklist	.06	.05	.02		186	Todd Benzinger	.08	.06	.03
96	Jerry Reuss	.06	.05	.02		187	Kevin Elster	.07	.05	.03
97	Brian Fisher	.06	.05	.02		188	Jose Uribe	.06	.05	.02
98	Kevin Ritz(FC)	.25	.20	.10		189	Tom Browning	.10	.08	.04
99	Reds Checklist	.06	.05	.02		190	Keith Miller	.09	.07	.04
100	Checklist 1-100	.06	.05	.02		191	Don Mattingly	.80	.60	.30
101	Gerald Perry	.06	.05	.02		192	Dave Parker	.12	.09	.05
102	Kevin Appier(FC)	.30	.15	.08		193	Roberto Kelly	.12	.09	.05
103	Julio Franco	.10	.08	.04		194	Phil Bradley	.09	.07	.04
104	Craig Biggio	.30	.25	.12		195	Ron Hassey	.07	.05	.03
105	Bo Jackson	.70	.50	.30		196	Gerald Young	.06	.05	.02
106	Junior Felix	.70	.50	.30		197	Hubie Brooks	.08	.06	.03
107	Mike Harkey(FC)	.25	.20	.10		198	Bill Doran	.09	.07	.04
108	Fred McGriff	.25	.20	.10		199	Al Newman	.06	.05	.02
109	Rick Sitcliffe	.08	.06	.03		200	Checklist 101-200	.06	.05	.02
110	Pete O'Brien	.08	.06	.03		201	Terry Puhl	.06	.05	.02
111	Kelly Gruber	.10	.08	.04		202	Frank DiPino	.06	.05	.02
112	Pat Borders	.10	.08	.04		203	Jim Clancy	.06	.05	.02
113	Dwight Evans	.10	.08	.04		204	Bob Ojeda	.07	.05	.03
114	Dwight Gooden	.20	.15	.08		205	Alex Trevino	.06	.05	.02
115	Kevin Batistel(FC)	.15	.11	.06		206	Dave Henderson	.10	.08	.04
116	Eric Davis	.25	.20	.10		207	Henry Cotto	.06	.05	.02
117	Kevin Mitchell	.40	.30	.15		208	Rafael Belliard	.06	.05	.02
118	Ron Oester	.06	.05	.02		209	Stan Javier	.07	.05	.03
119	Brett Butler	.09	.07	.04		210	Jerry Reed	.06	.05	.02
120	Danny Jackson	.06	.05	.02		211	Doug Dascenzo	.08	.06	.03
121	Tommy Gregg	.06	.05	.02		212	Andres Thomas	.07	.05	.03
122	Ken Caminiti	.08	.06	.03		213	Greg Maddux	.20	.15	.08
123	Kevin Brown	.10	.08	.04		214	Mike Schooler	.09	.07	.04
124	George Brett	.15	.11	.06		215	Lonnie Smith	.09	.07	.04
125	Mike Scott	.10	.08	.04		216	Jose Rijo	.10	.08	.04
126	Cory Snyder	.10	.08	.04		217	Greg Gagne	.08	.06	.03
127	George Bell	.15	.11	.06		218	Jim Gantner	.08	.06	.03
128	Mark Grace	.50	.40	.20		219	Allan Anderson	.09	.07	.04
129	Devon White	.10	.08	.04		220	Rick Mahler	.06	.05	.02
130	Tony Fernandez	.15	.11	.06		221	Jim Deshaies	.09	.07	.04
131	Dan Aase	.06	.05	.02		222	Keith Hernandez	.10	.08	.04
132	Rance Mulliniks	.06	.05	.02		223	Vince Coleman	.12	.09	.05
133	Marty Barrett	.08	.06	.03		224	David Cone	.20	.15	.08
134	Nelson Liriano	.07	.05	.03		225	Ozzie Smith	.20	.15	.08
135	Mark Carreon(FC)	.15	.11	.06		226	Matt Nokes	.10	.08	.04
136	Candy Maldonado	.06	.05	.02		227	Barry Bonds	.10	.08	.04
137	Tim Birtsas	.06	.05	.02		228	Felix Jose	.10	.08	.04
138	Tom Brookens	.06	.05	.02		229	Dennis Powell	.06	.05	.02
139	John Franco	.08	.06	.03		230	Mike Gallego	.06	.05	.02
140	Mike LaCoss	.06	.05	.02		231	Shawon Dunston	.09	.07	.04
141	Jeff Treadway	.07	.05	.03		232	Ron Gant	.10	.08	.04
142	Pat Tabler	.07	.05	.02		233	Omar Vizquel	.10	.08	.04
143	Darrell Evans	.06	.05	.02		234	Derek Lilliquist	.10	.08	.04
144	Rafael Ramirez	.06	.05	.02		235	Erik Hanson	.10	.08	.04
145	Oddibe McDowell	.09	.07	.04		236	Kirby Puckett	.50	.40	.20
146	Brian Downing	.09	.07	.04		237	Bill Spiers	.25	.20	.10
147	Curtis Wilkerson	.06	.05	.02		238	Dan Gladden	.07	.05	.03
148	Ernie Whitt	.07	.05	.02		239	Bryan Clutterbuck(FC)	.07	.05	.03
149	Bill Schroeder	.06	.05	.02		240	John Moses	.06	.05	.02
150	Domingo Ramos	.06	.05	.02		241	Ron Darling	.12	.09	.05
151	Rick Honeycutt	.06	.05	.02		242	Joe Magrane	.12	.09	.05
152	Don Slaught	.06	.05	.02		243	Dave Magadan	.09	.07	.03
153	Mitch Webster	.06	.05	.02		244	Glenn Guerrero	.15	.11	.06
154	Tony Phillips	.07	.05	.02		245	Glenn Davis	.10	.08	.04
155	Paul Kilgus	.06	.05	.02		246	Terry Steinbach	.12	.09	.05
156	Ken Griffey Jr.	2.25	1.75	.90		247	Fred Lynn	.09	.07	.04
157	Gary Sheffield	.50	.40	.20		248	Gary Redus	.06	.05	.02
158	Wally Backman	.06	.05	.02		249	Kenny Williams	.06	.05	.02
159	B.J. Surhoff	.08	.06	.03		250	Sid Bream	.06	.05	.02
160	Louie Meadows	.08	.06	.03		251	Bob Welch	.08	.06	.03

		MT	NR MT	EX			MT	NR MT	EX
252	Bill Buckner	.07	.05	.03	343	Ellis Burks	.25	.20	.10
253	Carney Lansford	.09	.07	.04	344	Tony Gwynn	.20	.15	.08
254	Paul Molitor	.12	.09	.05	345	*Jerome Walton*	2.25	1.75	.90
255	Jose DeJesus	.15	.11	.06	346	Roberto Alomar	.10	.08	.04
256	Orel Hershiser	.25	.20	.10	347	*Carlos Martinez*(FC)	.15	.11	.06
257	Tom Brunansky	.10	.08	.04	348	Chet Lemon	.07	.05	.03
258	Mike Davis	.06	.05	.02	349	Willie Wilson	.07	.05	.03
259	Jeff Ballard	.12	.09	.05	350	Greg Walker	.07	.05	.03
260	Scott Terry	.09	.07	.04	351	Tom Bolton	.06	.05	.02
261	Sid Fernandez	.10	.08	.04	352	German Gonzalez(FC)	.08	.06	.03
262	Mike Marshall	.08	.06	.03	353	Harold Baines	.10	.08	.04
263	Howard Johnson	.20	.15	.08	354	Mike Greenwell	.50	.40	.20
264	Kirk Gibson	.09	.07	.04	355	Ruben Sierra	.20	.15	.08
265	Kevin McReynolds	.15	.11	.06	356	Anres Galarraga	.12	.09	.05
266	Cal Ripken Jr.	.15	.11	.06	357	Andre Dawson	.15	.11	.06
267	Ozzie Guillen	.07	.05	.03	358	*Jeff Brantley*(FC)	.10	.08	.04
268	Jim Traber	.06	.05	.02	359	Mike Bielecki	.08	.06	.03
269	Bobby Thigpen	.09	.07	.04	360	Ken Oberkfell	.06	.05	.02
270	Joe Orsulak	.06	.05	.02	361	Kurt Stillwell	.07	.05	.03
271	Bob Boone	.09	.07	.04	362	Brian Holman	.09	.07	.04
272	Dave Stewart	.09	.07	.04	363	Kevin Seitzer	.12	.09	.05
273	Tim Wallach	.09	.07	.04	364	Alvin Davis	.15	.11	.06
274	Luis Aquino	.06	.05	.02	365	Tom Gordon	.90	.70	.35
275	Mike Moore	.10	.08	.04	366	Bobby Bonilla	.10	.08	.04
276	Tony Pena	.08	.06	.03	367	Carlton Fisk	.10	.08	.04
277	Eddie Murray	.15	.11	.06	368	*Steve Carter*(FC)	.15	.11	.06
278	Milt Thompson	.07	.05	.03	369	Joel Skinner	.06	.05	.02
279	Alejandro Pena	.06	.05	.02	370	John Cangelosi	.06	.05	.02
280	Ken Dayley	.06	.05	.02	371	Cecil Espy	.08	.06	.03
281	Carmen Castillo	.06	.05	.02	372	*Gary Wayne*(FC)	.25	.20	.10
282	Tom Henke	.08	.06	.03	373	Jim Rice	.08	.06	.03
283	Mickey Hatcher	.06	.05	.02	374	*Mike Dyer*(FC)	.15	.11	.06
284	Roy Smith(FC)	.06	.05	.02	375	Joe Carter	.12	.09	.05
285	Manny Lee	.06	.05	.02	376	Dwight Smith	1.00	.70	.40
286	Dan Pasqua	.07	.05	.02	377	*John Wtteland*(FC)	.25	.20	.10
287	Larry Sheets	.06	.05	.02	378	Ernie Riles	.06	.05	.02
288	Garry Templeton	.07	.05	.03	379	Otis Nixon	.06	.05	.02
289	Eddie Williams	.07	.05	.03	380	Vance Law	.06	.05	.02
290	Brady Anderson	.07	.05	.03	381	Dave Bergman	.06	.05	.02
291	Spike Owen	.07	.05	.03	382	Frank White	.07	.05	.03
292	Storm Davis	.09	.07	.04	383	Scott Bradley	.06	.05	.02
293	Chris Bosio	.09	.07	.04	384	Israel Sanchez	.06	.05	.02
294	Jim Eisenreich	.07	.05	.03	385	Gary Pettis	.06	.05	.02
295	Don August	.07	.05	.03	386	Donn Pall(FC)	.06	.05	.02
296	Jeff Hamilton	.07	.05	.03	387	John Smiley	.10	.08	.04
297	Mickey Tettleton	.10	.08	.04	388	Tom Candiotti	.07	.05	.03
298	Mike Scioscia	.09	.07	.04	389	Junior Ortiz	.06	.05	.02
299	Kevin Hickey(FC)	.06	.05	.02	390	Steve Lyons	.06	.05	.02
300	Checklist 201-300	.06	.05	.02	391	Brian Harper	.06	.05	.02
301	Shawn Abner	.06	.05	.02	392	Fred Manrique	.06	.05	.02
302	Kevin Bass	.08	.06	.03	393	Lee Smith	.08	.06	.03
303	Bip Roberts(FC)	.08	.06	.03	394	Jeff Kunkel	.06	.05	.02
304	Joe Girardi	.10	.08	.04	395	Claudell Washington	.08	.06	.03
305	Danny Darwin	.06	.05	.02	396	John Tudor	.07	.05	.02
306	Mike Heath	.06	.05	.02	397	Terry Kennedy	.07	.05	.03
307	Mike Macfarlane	.06	.05	.02	398	Lloyd McClendon	.09	.07	.04
308	Ed Whitson	.08	.06	.03	399	Craig Lefferts	.06	.05	.02
309	Tracy Jones	.07	.05	.02	400	Checklist 301-400	.06	.05	.02
310	Scott Fletcher	.07	.05	.02	401	Keith Moreland	.06	.05	.02
311	Darnell Coles	.07	.05	.02	402	Rich Gedman	.07	.05	.03
312	Mike Brumley	.06	.05	.02	403	Jeff Robinson	.07	.05	.03
313	Bill Swift	.06	.05	.02	404	Randy Ready	.06	.05	.02
314	Charlie Hough	.07	.05	.03	405	Rick Cerone	.06	.05	.02
315	Jim Presley	.08	.06	.03	406	Jeff Blauser	.07	.05	.03
316	Luis Polonia	.07	.05	.03	407	Larry Anderson	.06	.05	.02
317	Mike Morgan	.06	.05	.02	408	Joe Boever	.08	.06	.03
318	Lee Guetterman	.06	.05	.02	409	Felix Fermin	.06	.05	.02
319	Jose Oquendo	.08	.06	.03	410	Glenn Wilson	.06	.05	.02
320	Wayne Tollenson	.06	.05	.02	411	Rex Hudler	.06	.05	.02
321	Jody Reed	.07	.05	.03	412	Mark Grant	.06	.05	.02
322	Damon Berryhill	.09	.07	.04	413	Dennis Martinez	.08	.06	.03
323	Roger Clemens	.40	.30	.15	414	Darrin Jackson	.06	.05	.02
324	Ryne Sandberg	.15	.11	.06	415	Mike Aldrete	.06	.05	.02
325	Benito Santiago	.10	.08	.04	416	Roger McDowell	.09	.07	.04
326	Bret Saberhagen	.15	.11	.06	417	Jeff Reardon	.10	.08	.04
327	Lou Whitaker	.10	.08	.04	418	Darren Daulton	.06	.05	.02
328	Dave Gallagher	.10	.08	.04	419	Tim Laudner	.08	.06	.03
329	Mike Pagliarulo	.07	.05	.03	420	Don Carman	.07	.05	.03
330	Doyle Alexander	.07	.05	.03	421	Lloyd Moseby	.09	.07	.04
331	Jeffrey Leonard	.09	.07	.04	422	Doug Drabek	.09	.07	.04
332	Torey Lovullo	.20	.15	.08	423	Lenny Harris	.09	.07	.04
333	Pete Incaviglia	.09	.07	.04	424	Jose Lind	.07	.05	.03
334	Rickey Henderson	.15	.11	.06	425	*Dave Johnson*(FC)	.30	.25	.12
335	Rafael Palmeiro	.10	.08	.04	426	Jerry Browne	.09	.07	.04
336	Ken Hill	.10	.08	.04	427	*Eric Yelding*(FC)	.12	.09	.05
337	Dave Winfield	.12	.09	.05	428	Brad Komminsk(FC)	.06	.05	.02
338	Alfredo Griffin	.07	.05	.03	429	Jody Davis	.06	.05	.02
339	Andy Hawkins	.07	.05	.03	430	Mariano Duncan(FC)	.09	.07	.04
340	Ted Power	.06	.05	.02	431	Mark Davis	.12	.09	.05
341	Steve Wilson	.10	.08	.04	432	Nelson Santovenia	.10	.08	.04
342	Jack Clark	.10	.08	.04	433	Bruce Hurst	.10	.08	.04

		MT	NR MT	EX
434	*Jeff Huson*(FC)	.15	.11	.06
435	Chris James	.09	.07	.04
436	*Mark Guthrie*(FC)	.15	.11	.06
437	Charlie Hayes(FC)	.10	.08	.04
438	Shane Rawley	.08	.06	.03
439	Dickie Thon	.06	.05	.02
440	Juan Berenguer	.06	.05	.02
441	Kevin Romine	.06	.05	.02
442	Bill Landrum	.09	.07	.04
443	Todd Frohwirth	.07	.05	.03
444	Craig Worthington	.10	.08	.04
445	Fernando Valenzuela	.09	.07	.04
446	*Joey Belle*(FC)	1.00	.70	.40
447	*Ed Whited*(FC)	.15	.11	.06
448	Dave Smith	.09	.07	.04
449	Dave Clark	.07	.05	.03
450	Juan Agosto	.06	.05	.02
451	Dave Valle	.06	.05	.02
452	Kent Hrbek	.15	.11	.06
453	Von Hayes	.10	.08	.04
454	Gary Gaetti	.15	.11	.06
455	Greg Briley	.40	.30	.15
456	Glenn Braggs	.08	.06	.03
457	Kirt Manwaring	.10	.08	.04
458	Mel Hall	.07	.05	.03
459	Brook Jacoby	.08	.06	.03
460	Pat Sheridan	.06	.05	.02
461	Rob Murphy	.06	.05	.02
462	Jimmy Key	.10	.08	.04
463	Nick Esasky	.10	.08	.04
464	Rob Ducey	.09	.07	.04
465	Carlos Quintana	.09	.07	.04
466	*Larry Walker*(FC)	.50	.40	.20
467	Todd Worrell	.10	.08	.04
468	Kevin Gross	.09	.07	.04
469	Terry Pendleton	.09	.07	.04
470	Dave Martinez	.07	.05	.02
471	Gene Larkin	.06	.05	.02
472	Len Dykstra	.09	.07	.04
473	Barry Lyons	.06	.05	.02
474	Terry Mulholland(FC)	.10	.08	.04
475	*Chip Hale*(FC)	.15	.11	.06
476	Jesse Barfield	.08	.06	.03
477	Dan Plesac	.09	.07	.04
478a	Scott Garrelts (Photo actually Bill Bathe)	10.00	7.50	4.00
478b	Scott Garrelts (Correct photo)	.10	.08	.04
479	Dave Righetti	.10	.08	.04
480	Gus Polidor(FC)	.06	.05	.02
481	Mookie Wilson	.09	.07	.04
482	Luis Rivera	.06	.05	.02
483	Mike Flanagan	.07	.05	.03
484	Dennis "Oil Can" Boyd	.07	.05	.03
485	John Cerutti	.07	.05	.03
486	John Costello	.07	.05	.03
487	Pascual Perez	.07	.05	.03
488	Tommy Herr	.09	.07	.04
489	Tom Foley	.06	.05	.02
490	Curt Ford	.06	.05	.02
491	Steve Lake	.06	.05	.02
492	Tim Teufel	.06	.05	.02
493	Randy Bush	.06	.05	.02
494	Mike Jackson	.06	.05	.02
495	Steve Jeltz	.06	.05	.02
496	Paul Gibson	.08	.06	.03
497	Steve Balboni	.06	.05	.02
498	Bud Black	.06	.05	.02
499	Dale Sveum	.06	.05	.02
500	Checklist 401-500	.06	.05	.02
501	Timmy Jones	.06	.05	.02
502	Mark Portugal	.06	.05	.02
503	Ivan Calderon	.07	.05	.03
504	Rick Rhoden	.06	.05	.02
505	Willie McGee	.09	.07	.04
506	Kirk McCaskill	.08	.06	.03
507	Dave LaPoint	.07	.05	.03
508	Jay Howell	.10	.08	.04
509	Johnny Ray	.08	.06	.03
510	Dave Anderson	.06	.05	.02
511	Chuck Crim	.06	.05	.02
512	Joe Hesketh	.06	.05	.02
513	Dennis Eckersley	.10	.08	.04
514	Greg Brock	.08	.06	.03
515	Tim Burke	.08	.06	.03
516	Frank Tanana	.07	.05	.03
517	Jay Bell	.07	.05	.03
518	Guillermo Hernandez	.07	.05	.03
519	Randy Kramer(FC)	.08	.06	.03
520	Charles Hudson	.06	.05	.02
521	Jim Corsi(FC)	.08	.06	.03
522	Steve Rosenberg	.08	.06	.03

		MT	NR MT	EX
523	Cris Carpenter	.10	.08	.04
524	*Matt Winters*(FC)	.12	.09	.05
525	Melido Perez	.08	.06	.03
526	Chris Gwynn	.08	.06	.03
527	Bert Blyleven	.09	.07	.04
528	Chuck Cary	.07	.05	.03
529	Daryl Boston	.06	.05	.02
530	Dale Mohorcic	.06	.05	.02
531	Geronimo Berroa(FC)	.09	.07	.04
532	Edgar Martinez	.09	.07	.04
533	Dale Murphy	.15	.11	.06
534	Jay Buhner	.09	.07	.04
535	John Smoltz	.15	.11	.06
536	Andy Van Slyke	.15	.11	.06
537	Mike Henneman	.09	.07	.04
538	Miguel Garcia(FC)	.07	.05	.03
539	Frank Williams	.06	.05	.02
540	R.J. Reynolds	.06	.05	.02
541	Shawn Hillegas	.06	.05	.02
542	Walt Weiss	.10	.08	.04
543	*Greg Hibbard*(FC)	.15	.11	.06
544	Nolan Ryan	1.00	.70	.40
545	*Todd Zeile*(FC)	2.25	1.75	.90
546	Hensley Meulens	.20	.15	.08
547	Tim Belcher	.10	.08	.04
548	Mike Witt	.08	.06	.03
549	Greg Cadaret	.06	.05	.02
550	Franklin Stubbs	.06	.05	.02
551	*Tony Castillo*(FC)	.12	.09	.05
552	Jeff Robinson	.08	.06	.03
553	*Steve Olin*(FC)	.12	.09	.05
554	Alan Trammell	.10	.08	.04
555	Wade Boggs	.70	.50	.30
556	Will Clark	1.00	.70	.40
557	Jeff King(FC)	.10	.08	.04
558	Mike Fitzgerald	.06	.05	.02
559	Ken Howell	.06	.05	.02
560	Bob Kipper	.06	.05	.02
561	Scott Bankhead	.09	.07	.04
562	*Jeff Innis*(FC)	.10	.08	.04
563	Randy Johnson	.10	.08	.04
564	*Wally Whithurst*	.10	.08	.04
565	*Gene Harris*(FC)	.10	.08	.04
566	Norm Charlton	.09	.07	.04
567	Robin Yount	.25	.20	.10
568	*Joe Oliver*(FC)	.25	.20	.10
569	Mark Parent	.07	.05	.03
570	John Farrell	.07	.05	.03
571	Tom Glavine	.10	.08	.04
572	Rod Nichols(FC)	.06	.05	.02
573	Jack Morris	.09	.07	.04
574	Greg Swindell	.12	.09	.05
575	Steve Searcy(FC)	.09	.07	.04
576	Ricky Jordan	.50	.40	.20
577	Matt Williams	.35	.25	.14
578	Mike LaValliere	.07	.05	.03
579	Bryn Smith	.08	.06	.03
580	Bruce Ruffin	.06	.05	.02
581	Randy Myers	.08	.06	.03
582	*Rick Wrona*(FC)	.15	.11	.06
583	Juan Samuel	.09	.07	.04
584	Les Lancaster	.07	.05	.03
585	Jeff Musselman	.07	.05	.03
586	Rob Dibble	.09	.07	.04
587	Eric Show	.07	.05	.03
588	Jesse Orosco	.06	.05	.02
589	Herm Winningham	.06	.05	.02
590	Andy Allanson	.06	.05	.02
591	Dion James	.06	.05	.02
592	Carmelo Martinez	.06	.05	.02
593	Luis Quinones(FC)	.08	.06	.03
594	Dennis Rasmussen	.08	.06	.03
595	Rich Yett	.06	.05	.02
596	Bob Walk	.08	.06	.03
597	Andy McGaffigan	.07	.05	.03
598	Billy Hatcher	.07	.05	.03
599	Bob Knepper	.06	.05	.02
600	Checklist 501-600	.06	.05	.02
601	Joey Cora(FC)	.10	.08	.04
602	*Steve Finley*	.15	.11	.06
603	Kal Daniels	.10	.08	.04
604	Gregg Olson	.50	.40	.20
605	Dave Steib	.09	.07	.04
606	*Kenny Rogers*(FC)	.15	.11	.06
607	Zane Smith	.06	.05	.02
608	*Bob Geren*(FC)	.25	.20	.10
609	Chad Kreuter	.10	.08	.04
610	Mike Smithson	.06	.05	.02
611	*Jeff Wetherby*(FC)	.15	.11	.06
612	*Gary Mielke*(FC)	.15	.11	.06
613	Pete Smith	.08	.06	.03

		MT	NR MT	EX
614	*Jack Daugherty*(FC)	.15	.11	.06
615	Lance McCullers	.08	.06	.03
616	Don Robinson	.06	.05	.02
617	Jose Guzman	.06	.05	.02
618	Steve Bedrosian	.08	.06	.03
619	Jamie Moyer	.06	.05	.02
620	Atlee Hammaker	.06	.05	.02
621	*Rick Lueken*(FC)	.15	.11	.06
622	Greg W. Harris	.09	.07	.04
623	Pete Harnisch	.10	.08	.04
624	Jerald Clark	.10	.08	.04
625	Jack McDowell	.07	.05	.03
626	Frank Viola	.12	.09	.05
627	Ted Higuera	.09	.07	.04
628	*Marty Pevey*(FC)	.15	.11	.06
629	Bill Wegman	.06	.05	.02
630	Eric Plunk	.06	.05	.02
631	Drew Hall	.06	.05	.02
632	Doug Jones	.08	.06	.03
633	Geno Petralli	.06	.05	.02
634	Jose Alvarez	.06	.05	.02
635	Bob Milacki(FC)	.10	.08	.04
636	Bobby Witt	.07	.05	.03
637	Trevor Wilson	.08	.06	.03
638	Jeff Russell	.08	.06	.03
639	Mike Krukow	.07	.05	.03
640	Rick Leach	.06	.05	.02
641	Dave Schmidt	.06	.05	.02
642	Terry Leach	.06	.05	.02
643	Calvin Schiraldi	.06	.05	.02
644	Bob Melvin	.06	.05	.02
645	Jim Abbott	1.25	.90	.50
646	*Jaime Navarro*(FC)	.20	.15	.08
647	Mark Langston	.10	.08	.04
648	Juan Nieves	.08	.06	.03
649	Damaso Garcia	.06	.05	.02
650	Charlie O'Brien	.06	.05	.02
651	Eric King	.06	.05	.02
652	Mike Boddicker	.08	.06	.03
653	Duan Ward	.07	.05	.03
654	Bob Stanley	.06	.05	.02
655	Sandy Alomar Jr.	.50	.40	.20
656	Danny Tartabull	.10	.08	.04
657	Randy McCarment	.15	.11	.06
658	Charlie Leibrandt	.07	.05	.03
659	Dan Quisenberry	.07	.05	.03
660	Paul Assenmacher	.06	.05	.02
661	Walt Terrell	.07	.05	.03
662	Tim Leary	.07	.05	.03
663	Randy Milligan	.08	.06	.03
664	Bo Diaz	.06	.05	.02
665	Mark Lemke	.07	.05	.03
666	Jose Gonzalez	.08	.06	.03
667	Chuck Finley	.07	.05	.03
668	John Kruk	.08	.06	.03
669	Dick Schofield	.07	.05	.03
670	Tim Crews	.06	.05	.02
671	John Dopson	.09	.07	.04
672	*John Orton*(FC)	.15	.11	.06
673	*Eric Hetzel*(FC)	.10	.08	.04
674	Lance Parrish	.08	.06	.03
675	Ramon Martinez	.10	.08	.04
676	Mark Gubicza	.10	.08	.04
677	Greg Litton	.20	.15	.08
678	Greg Mathews	.07	.05	.03
679	Dave Dravecky	.07	.05	.03
680	Steve Farr	.07	.05	.03
681	Mike Devereaux	.09	.07	.04
682	Ken Griffey Sr.	.08	.06	.03
683a	*Mickey Weston* (Incorrectly says Jamie)(FC)	15.00	11.00	6.00
683b	*Mickey Weston* (corrected)(FC)	.30	.25	.12
684	Jack Armstrong	.07	.05	.03
685	Steve Buechele	.07	.05	.03
686	Bryan Harvey	.07	.05	.03
687	Lance Blankenship	.09	.07	.04
688	Dante Bichette	.09	.07	.04
689	Todd Burns	.09	.07	.04
690	Dan Petry	.06	.05	.02
691	*Kent Anderson*(FC)	.15	.11	.06
692	Todd Stottlemyre	.08	.06	.03
693	Wally Joyner	.15	.11	.06
694	*Mike Rochford*(FC)	.10	.08	.04
695	Floyd Bannister	.07	.05	.03
696	Rick Reuschel	.09	.07	.04
697	Jose DeLeon	.09	.07	.04
698	Jeff Montgomery	.08	.06	.03
699	Jeff Montgomery	.08	.06	.03
700a	Checklist 601-700 (Jamie Weston)	5.00	3.75	2.00

		MT	NR MT	EX
700b	Checklist 601-700	.10	.08	.04

1989 Very Fine Pirates

This 30-card set Pittsburgh Pirates team set was sponsored by Veryfine fruit juices, and was issued in the form of two uncut, perforated panels, each containing 15 standard-size cards. A third panel featured color action photographs. The panels were distributed in a stadium promotion to fans attending the April 23 Pirates game at Three Rivers Stadium. The cards display the Pirates traditional black and gold color scheme, and include the player's names and uniform number along the bottom. The "Veryfine" logo appears in the lower right corner. The backs include player data and complete stats.

		MT	NR MT	EX
Complete 3-Panel Set:		20.00	15.00	8.00
Complete Singles Card Set:		12.00	9.00	4.75
Common Player:		.20	.15	.08
	Junior Ortiz	.20	.15	.08
2	Gary Redus	.30	.25	.12
3	Jay Bell	.30	.25	.12
5	Sid Bream	.30	.25	.12
6	Rafael Belliard	.25	.20	.10
10	Jim Leyland	.30	.25	.12
11	Glenn Wilson	.30	.25	.12
12	Mike La Valliere	.30	.25	.12
13	Jose Lind	.40	.30	.15
14	Ken Oberkfell	.25	.20	.10
15	Doug Drabek	.50	.40	.20
16	Bob Kipper	.20	.15	.08
17	Bob Walk	.25	.20	.10
18	Andy Van Slyke	1.00	.70	.40
23	R.J. Reynolds	.30	.25	.12
24	Barry Bonds	1.25	.90	.50
25	Bobby Bonilla	1.25	.90	.50
26	Neal Heaton	.30	.25	.12
30	Benny Distefano	.30	.25	.12
35	Jim Gott	.35	.25	.14
41	Mike Dunne	.30	.25	.12
43	Bill Landrum	.40	.30	.15
44	John Cangelosi	.25	.20	.10
49	Jeff Robinson	.35	.25	.12
52	Dorn Taylor	.60	.45	.25
54	Brian Fisher	.25	.20	.10
57	John Smiley	.50	.40	.20
3137	Ray Miller, Tommy Sandt	.20	.15	.08
3236	Bruce Kimm, Gene Lamont	.20	.15	.08
3945	Milt May, Rich Donnelly	.20	.15	.08

NOTE: A card number in parentheses ( ) indicates the set is unnumbered.

1950 W576
Callahan Hall Of Fame

KENESAW MOUNTAIN LANDIS
Elected to the Hall of Fame 1944. First High Commissioner of Baseball; born at Millville, Ohio, November 20, 1866; died November 24, 1944, age 78.

Lean, dynamic, white-haired Judge Landis brought to baseball one of the greatest and fairest legal minds in America, plus a fanatical love for the game and uncompromising insistence on all-exclusive cleanness and honesty. The Judge knew baseball and knew human nature just as thoroughly. For many years, prior to his appointment as Commissioner he served distinctively and fearlessly on the Federal Bench.

As baseball's High Commissioner, Landis ruled the game impartially and understandingly—but with an iron hand —from 1920 until his death. To him must go the credit for rebuilding a strong and enduring foundation for baseball and restoring public confidence in its integrity after the disruption "Black Sox" scandal following the 1919 Chicago-Cincinnati World Series. His verdict in that case barred 8 White Sox players—including several of the game's brightest stars—from organized ball for life.

Scores of his decisions were tough to take, but all were made for the everlasting good of the game. The Judge's constructive work raised high the standard of baseball, set basic ideals which will endure as long as the game endures.

KENESAW M. LANDIS

These cards, which feature drawings of Hall of Famers, were produced from 1950 through 1956 and sold by the Baseball Hall of Fame in Cooperstown. The cards measure 1-3/4" by 2-1/2" and include a detailed player biography on the back. When introduced in 1950 the set included all members of the Hall of Fame up to that time, and then new cards were added each year as more players were elected. Therefore, cards of players appearing in all previous editions are lesser in value than those players who appeared in just one or two years. When the set was discontinued in 1956 it consisted of 82 cards, which is now considered a complete set. The cards are not numbered and are listed here alphabetically.

		NR MT	EX	VG
	Complete Set:	450.00	230.00	135.00
	Common Player:	3.00	1.50	.90
(1)	Grover Alexander	5.00	2.50	1.50
(2)	"Cap" Anson	5.00	2.50	1.50
(3)	J. Franklin "Home Run" Baker	6.00	3.00	1.75
(4)	Edward G. Barrow	6.00	3.00	1.75
(5a)	Charles "Chief" Bender (different biography)	6.00	3.00	1.75
(5b)	Charles "Chief" Bender (different biography)	6.00	3.00	1.75
(6)	Roger Bresnahan	3.00	1.50	.90
(7)	Dan Brouthers	3.00	1.50	.90
(8)	Mordecai Brown	3.00	1.50	.90
(9)	Morgan G. Bulkeley	3.00	1.50	.90
(10)	Jesse Burkett	3.00	1.50	.90
(11)	Alexander Cartwright	3.00	1.50	.90
(12)	Henry Chadwick	3.00	1.50	.90
(13)	Frank Chance	3.00	1.50	.90
(14)	Albert B. Chandler	20.00	10.00	6.00
(15)	Jack Chesbro	3.00	1.50	.90
(16)	Fred Clarke	3.00	1.50	.90
(17)	Ty Cobb	30.00	15.00	9.00
(18a)	Mickey Cochran (name incorrect)	30.00	15.00	9.00
(18b)	Mickey Cochrane (name correct)	5.00	2.50	1.50
(19a)	Eddie Collins (different biography)	5.00	2.50	1.50
(19b)	Eddie Collins (different biography)	5.00	2.50	1.50
(20)	Jimmie Collins	3.00	1.50	.90
(21)	Charles A. Comiskey	3.00	1.50	.90
(22)	Tom Connolly	6.00	3.00	1.75
(23)	"Candy" Cummings	3.00	1.50	.90
(24)	Dizzy Dean	20.00	10.00	6.00
(25)	Ed Delahanty	3.00	1.50	.90
(26a)	Bill Dickey (different biography)	20.00	10.00	6.00
(26b)	Bill Dickey (different biography)	20.00	10.00	6.00
(27)	Joe DiMaggio	70.00	35.00	21.00
(28)	Hugh Duffy	3.00	1.50	.90
(29)	Johnny Evers	3.00	1.50	.90
(30)	Buck Ewing	3.00	1.50	.90
(31)	Jimmie Foxx	6.00	3.00	1.75
(32)	Frank Frisch	3.00	1.50	.90
(33)	Lou Gehrig	30.00	15.00	9.00

		NR MT	EX	VG
(34)	Charles Gehringer	3.00	1.50	.90
(35)	Clark Griffith	3.00	1.50	.90
(36)	Lefty Grove	5.00	2.50	1.50
(37)	Leo "Gabby" Hartnett	6.00	3.00	1.75
(38)	Harry Heilmann	3.00	1.50	.90
(39)	Rogers Hornsby	6.00	3.00	1.75
(40)	Carl Hubbell	5.00	2.50	1.50
(41)	Hughey Jennings	3.00	1.50	.90
(42)	Ban Johnson	3.00	1.50	.90
(43)	Walter Johnson	6.00	3.00	1.75
(44)	Willie Keeler	3.00	1.50	.90
(45)	Mike Kelly	3.00	1.50	.90
(46)	Bill Klem	6.00	3.00	1.75
(47)	Napoleon Lajoie	3.00	1.50	.90
(48)	Kenesaw M. Landis	3.00	1.50	.90
(49)	Ted Lyons	6.00	3.00	1.75
(50)	Connie Mack	6.00	3.00	1.75
(51)	Walter Maranville	6.00	3.00	1.75
(52)	Christy Mathewson	6.00	3.00	1.75
(53)	Tommy McCarthy	3.00	1.50	.90
(54)	Joe McGinnity	3.00	1.50	.90
(55)	John McGraw	5.00	2.50	1.50
(56)	Charles Nichols	3.00	1.50	.90
(57)	Jim O'Rourke	3.00	1.50	.90
(58)	Mel Ott	5.00	2.50	1.50
(59)	Herb Pennock	3.00	1.50	.90
(60)	Eddie Plank	3.00	1.50	.90
(61)	Charles Radbourne	3.00	1.50	.90
(62)	Wilbert Robinson	3.00	1.50	.90
(63)	Babe Ruth	70.00	35.00	21.00
(64)	Ray "Cracker" Schalk	6.00	3.00	1.75
(65)	Al Simmons	6.00	3.00	1.75
(66a)	George Sisler (different biography)	3.00	1.50	.90
(66b)	George Sisler (different biography)	3.00	1.50	.90
(67)	A. G. Spalding	3.00	1.50	.90
(68)	Tris Speaker	3.00	1.50	.90
(69)	Bill Terry	6.00	3.00	1.75
(70)	Joe Tinker	3.00	1.50	.90
(71)	"Pie" Traynor	3.00	1.50	.90
(72)	Clarence A. "Dizzy" Vance	6.00	3.00	1.75
(73)	Rube Waddell	3.00	1.50	.90
(74)	Hans Wagner	20.00	10.00	6.00
(75)	Bobby Wallace	6.00	3.00	1.75
(76)	Ed Walsh	3.00	1.50	.90
(77)	Paul Waner	5.00	2.50	1.50
(78)	George Wright	3.00	1.50	.90
(79)	Harry Wright	6.00	3.00	1.75
(80)	Cy Young	6.00	3.00	1.75
---a)	Museum Exterior View (different biography)	6.00	3.00	1.75
---b)	Museum Exterior View (different biography)	6.00	3.00	1.75
---a)	Museum Interior View (different biography)	6.00	3.00	1.75
---b)	Museum Interior View (different biography)	6.00	3.00	1.75

1985 Wendy's Tigers

This 22-card set of cards measuring 2-1/2" by 3-1/2", which carry both Wendy's Hamburgers and Coca-Cola logos was produced by Topps. The cards feature a color photo with the player's team, name and position underneath the picture and the Wendy's logo in the lower left and Coke logo in the upper right. Backs are identical to 1985 Topps cards except they have different card numbers and are done in a red and black color scheme. Cards were distributed three to a pack along with a "Header" checklist in a cellophane package at selected Wendy's outlets in Michigan only.

		MT	NR MT	EX
	Complete Set:	8.00	6.00	3.25
	Common Player:	.15	.11	.06
1	Sparky Anderson	.30	.25	.12
2	Doug Bair	.15	.11	.06
3	Juan Berenguer	.15	.11	.06
4	Dave Bergman	.15	.11	.06
5	Tom Brookens	.15	.11	.06
6	Marty Castillo	.15	.11	.06
7	Darrell Evans	.40	.30	.15
8	Barbaro Garbey	.15	.11	.06
9	Kirk Gibson	1.00	.70	.40
10	Johnny Grubb	.15	.11	.06
11	Willie Hernandez	.25	.20	.10
12	Larry Herndon	.15	.11	.06
13	Rusty Kuntz	.15	.11	.06
14	Chet Lemon	.25	.20	.10
15	Aurelio Lopez	.15	.11	.06
16	Jack Morris	.80	.60	.30
17	Lance Parrish	.80	.60	.30
18	Dan Petry	.25	.20	.10
19	Bill Scherrer	.15	.11	.06
20	Alan Trammell	1.00	.70	.40
21	Lou Whitaker	.80	.60	.30
22	Milt Wilcox	.15	.11	.06

1954 Wilson Franks

The 2-5/8" by 3-3/4" cards are among the most popular and difficult to find baseball card sets issued with hot dogs during the 1950s. The cards feature color-added photos on the front where the player's name, team and position appear at the top. The front also has a facsimile autograph and a color picture of a package of Wilson's frankfurters. The card backs feature personal information, a short career summary and 1953 and career statistics. The 20-card set includes players from a number of teams and was distributed nationally in the frankfurter packages. The problem with such distribution is that the cards are very tough to find without grease stains from the hot dogs.

		NR MT	EX	VG
	Complete Set:	4000.00	2000.00	1200.
	Common Player:	125.00	62.00	37.00
(1)	Roy Campanella	475.00	237.00	142.00
(2)	Del Ennis	125.00	62.00	37.00
(3)	Carl Erskine	140.00	70.00	42.00
(4)	Ferris Fain	125.00	62.00	37.00
(5)	Bob Feller	400.00	200.00	120.00
(6)	Nelson Fox	200.00	100.00	60.00
(7)	Johnny Groth	125.00	62.00	37.00
(8)	Stan Hack	125.00	62.00	37.00
(9)	Gil Hodges	300.00	150.00	90.00
(10)	Ray Jablonski	125.00	62.00	37.00
(11)	Harvey Kuenn	150.00	75.00	45.00
(12)	Roy McMillan	125.00	62.00	37.00
(13)	Andy Pafko	125.00	62.00	37.00
(14)	Paul Richards	125.00	62.00	37.00
(15)	Hank Sauer	125.00	62.00	37.00
(16)	Red Schoendienst	140.00	70.00	42.00

		NR MT	EX	VG
(17)	Enos Slaughter	300.00	150.00	90.00
(18)	Vern Stephens	125.00	62.00	37.00
(19)	Sammy White	125.00	62.00	37.00
(20)	Ted Williams	1800.00	900.00	540.00

1988 Woolworth

This 33-card boxed set was produced by Topps for exclusive distribution at Woolworth stores. The set includes 18 individual player cards and 15 World Series game action photo cards. World Series cards include two for each game of the Series, plus a card of 1987 Series MVP Frank Viola. Card front carry a Woolworth's Baseball Highlights heading on a red and yellow banner above the blue-bordered super glossy player photo. A white-lettered caption beneath the photo consists of either the player's name or a World Series game notation. Card backs are red, white and blue and contain the Topps logo, card number and "Collector's Series" label above a "1987 Baseball Highlights" logo and a brief description of the photo on the front.

		MT	NR MT	EX
	Complete Set:	5.00	3.75	2.00
	Common Player:	.09	.07	.04
1	Don Baylor	.12	.09	.05
2	Vince Coleman	.15	.11	.06
3	Darrell Evans	.12	.09	.05
4	Don Mattingly	1.50	1.25	.60
5	Eddie Murray	.30	.25	.12
6	Nolan Ryan	.30	.25	.12
7	Mike Schmidt	.35	.25	.14
8	Andre Dawson	.20	.15	.08
9	George Bell	.25	.20	.10
10	Steve Bedrosian	.12	.09	.05
11	Roger Clemens	.50	.40	.20
12	Tony Gwynn	.35	.25	.14
13	Wade Boggs	1.00	.70	.40
14	Benny Santiago	.35	.25	.14
15	Mark McGwire	.80	.60	.30
16	Dave Righetti	.15	.11	.06
17	Jeffrey Leonard	.09	.07	.04
18	Gary Gaetti	.12	.09	.05
19	World Series Game #1 (Frank Viola)	.12	.09	.05
20	World Series Game #1 (Dan Gladden)	.09	.07	.04
21	World Series Game #2 (Bert Blyleven)	.12	.09	.05
22	World Series Game #2 (Gary Gaetti)	.12	.09	.05
23	World Series Game #3 (John Tudor)	.12	.09	.05
24	World Series Game #3 (Todd Worrell)	.12	.09	.05
25	World Series Game #4 (Tom Lawless)	.09	.07	.04
26	World Series Game #4 (Willie McGee)	.12	.09	.05
27	World Series Game #5 (Danny Cox)	.09	.07	.04
28	World Series Game #5 (Curt Ford)	.09	.07	.04
29	World Series Game #6 (Don Baylor)	.12	.09	.05
30	World Series Game #6 (Kent Hrbek)	.15	.11	.06

		MT	NR MT	EX
31	World Series Game #7 (Kirby Puckett)	.25	.20	.10
32	World Series Game #7 (Greg Gagne)	.09	.07	.04
33	World Series MVP (Frank Viola)	.12	.09	.05

Z

1982 Zellers Expos

Tim Raines
Sliding
Glissade

Produced and distributed by the Zellers department stores in Canada, this 60-card set was produced in the form of 20 three-card panels. The cards feature a photo of the player surrounded by rings and a yellow background. A red "Zellers" is above the photo and on either side of it are the words "Baseball Pro Tips" in English on the left and in French on the right. The player's name and the title of the playing tip are under the photo. Backs have the playing tip in both languages. Single cards measure 2-1/2" by 3-1/2" while the whole panel is 7-1/2" by 3-1/2". Although a number of stars are depicted, this set is not terribly popular as collectors do not generally like the playing tips idea. Total panels are worth more than separated cards.

		MT	NR MT	EX
	Complete Set:	12.00	9.00	4.75
	Common Player:	.40	.30	.15
1	Gary Carter (Catching Position)	1.00	.70	.40
2	Steve Rogers (Pitching Stance)	.50	.40	.20
3	Tim Raines (Sliding)	1.00	.70	.40
4	Andre Dawson (Batting Stance)	.80	.60	.30
5	Terry Francona (Contact Hitting)	.40	.30	.15
6	Gary Carter (Fielding Pop Fouls)	1.00	.70	.40
7	Warren Cromartie (Fielding at First Base)	.40	.30	.15
8	Chris Speier (Fielding at Shortstop)	.40	.30	.15
9	Billy DeMars (Signals)	.40	.30	.15
10	Andre Dawson (Batting Stroke)	.80	.60	.30
11	Terry Francona (Outfield Throws)	.40	.30	.15
12	Woodie Fryman (Holding the Runner-Left Handed)	.40	.30	.15
13	Gary Carter (Fielding Low Balls)	1.00	.70	.40
14	Andre Dawson (Playing Centerfield)	.80	.60	.30
15	Bill Gullickson (The Slurve)	.50	.40	.20
16	Gary Carter (Catching Stance)	1.00	.70	.40
17	Scott Sanderson (Fielding as a Pitcher)	.40	.30	.15
18	Warren Cromartie (Handling Bad Throws)	.40	.30	.15
19	Gary Carter (Hitting Stride)	1.00	.70	.40
20	Ray Burris (Holding the Runner-Right Handed)	.40	.30	.15

1978 Zest Soap

MANNY MOTA

Produced by Topps for a Zest Soap promotion, the five cards in this set are almost identical to the regular 1978 Topps issue, except the backs are printed in both Spanish and English and the card numbers are different. The cards measure 2-1/2" by 3-1/2". Because of the player selection and the bilingual backs, it seems obvious that this set was aimed at the Hispanic community.

		NR MT	EX	VG
	Complete Set:	5.00	2.50	1.50
	Common Player:	.75	.40	.25
1	Joaquin Andujar	1.00	.50	.30
2	Bert Campaneris	1.25	.60	.40
3	Ed Figueroa	.75	.40	.25
4	Willie Montanez	.75	.40	.25
5	Manny Mota	1.25	.60	.40

Exclusive Special Section—

Minor League Team Set Price Guide: 1940–1989

With the tremendous demand for "rookie cards" dominating the baseball card hobby the past few years, it is only logical that the next step up the same hobby ladder would be an increasing interest in minor league cards — sometimes referred to as "pre-rookie" cards. The description is an accurate one, because that's precisely what a player's minor league card is — a card issued prior to his Major League "rookie card."

Minor league baseball cards are nothing new. In fact, they've been around for over 100 years and are almost as old as the game itself. Many minor league players were pictured in the old 19th Century tobacco cards that today's advanced collectors refer to as "N-Cards," after their designation in the old American Card Catalog (ACC). Minor leaguers also made up a significant portion of many of the early 20th Century baseball card sets, including the famous T-206 set and several other frequently-collected card issues.

Minor league cards also appeared in various other sets throughout the long long history of the hobby, but for the vast majority of collectors — those who focus their attention on more recent issues — the history of "modern" minor league cards probably dates back to the decade of the 1940s, which saw the release of a very limited number of minor league team sets that more closely resemble those of today. The price guide listings in this special section, therefor, begin with the 1940 minor league issues.

There were relatively few minor league card sets issued during the Fifties and Sixties, but the face of minor league collecting changed dramatically in the 1970s, when Mike Aronstein, owner of a card company in Amawalk, N.Y., entered the field by producing a team set for the Gastonia Rangers to sell at their souvenir stand. The idea spread to other minor league clubs, and each year TCMA increased the number of sets it produced. Within five years, TCMA was producing nearly 40 sets, more than half of them in color.

Aronstein was still virtually alone in the field as the Eighties began, but in 1982 another player — veteran hobby dealer Larry Fritsch of Wisconsin — joined the minor league field, issuing card sets for teams in the Midwest League. By 1983 TCMA was issuing over 50 team sets a season, while Fritsch was contributing nearly a dozen more. A year later Richard Cramer joined in with a series of Pacific Coast League sets, and more and more teams began issuing sets on their own, recruiting local businesses to sponsor them.

The minor league card industry enjoyed another surge in the mid-'80s, when the Pennsylvania-based Pro Cards — headed by Jeff Rogovin and Jeff Metzger — challenged other card producers by aggressively signing as many minor league teams to contracts as they could. Pro Cards produced more than 80 team sets in 1986 and more than 100 by 1988. Meanwhile, Mike Aronstein, the man who started it all back in the mid-'70s, decided to leave the minor league card business and sold his entire stock of TCMA cards — nearly five million pieces — to Hampton, Va., hobby dealer Don Harrison of The Tenth Inning.

Still more players, though, continued to enter the the already-crowded field, and by the late Eighties the names of Bill Pucko, Grand Slam, Best Cards, the Star Co. and others were added to the roster of minor league card producers. Some companies had negotiated exclusive contracts with various clubs, but fans of many teams had two — or even more — sets to choose from.

Collecting minor league cards is in many ways similar to collecting Major League cards — and, for the most part, their values are determined by the same factors: condition, scarcity and popularity. The prices again depend on supply and demand, and just as with Major League cards, the stars and superstars are more valuable. Actually, in minor league sets the star cards are comparatively much more valuable. It is not uncommon, for instance, for a minor league team set's entire value to be based on a single player. After all, most minor league clubs — especially those in the lower classes — are lucky to have even one player on their roster who will become a superstar on the Major League level. The vast majority of players pictured on minor league cards never make it to the majors, and their cards, therefore, have little or no collector interest or value.

It is important to note that even though a single player is often the key to an entire set's value, minor league cards are rarely bought, sold or traded as individual cards. Minor league cards are almost exclusively collected and traded as complete sets, partly to deter potential counterfeiters, who may be tempted to reproduce a single valuable card but would probably not be inclined to copy an entire set of cards that have little or no value.

The prices in this special section were compiled by Mary Huston, a leading authority in the field and the editor/publisher of the *Minor League Monthly Price Guide*, a highly-respected publication among minor league specialists. The listings appear chronologically by year, and then alphabetically by team within each year. The number of cards in each set appears in parentheses immediately after the team name. The third column lists the major players in the set, while the fourth column indicates the issuer of the set, and the final column lists the set's current value in Near Mint to Mint condition. Subscription information regarding the *Minor League Monthly Price Guide* is available by writing to Mary Huston at 11903 Woodworth Road, Box 125, North Lima, OH 44452.

Exclusive Special Section—
Minor League Team Set Price Guide: 1940–1989

Compiled for SCD By Mary Huston

Team	Stars in Set	Issuer	Mint
1940 Issues			
Sacramento Solons (20)	Tony Freitas	Hughes	2400.
1943 Issues			
Milwaukee Brewers (21)	Charlie Grimm	Grand Studio	750.
Seattle Rainers (25)	Christopher	Centennial	1350.
1944 Issues			
Seattle Rainers (25)	Roy Johnson	Centennial	1250.
1945 Issues			
Seattle Rainers (27)	S. Johnson	Centennial	1000.
1946 Issues			
Oakland Oaks (23)	Raimondi	Remar	875.
w/team card			1450.
Sacramento Solons (21)	Gerry Staley	Sunbeam	675.
1947 Issues			
Hollywood Stars (19)	G. Stewart	Signal Oil	475.
w/Williams			700.
L.A. Angels (18)	Red Adams	Signal Oil	375.
Oakland Oaks (19)	Casey Stengel	Signal Oil	700.
Oakland Oaks (25)	Casey Stengel	Remar	450.
Oakland Oaks (24)	Casey Stengel	Smith's	525.
w/Marshall			775.
Sacramento Solons (15)	Tony Freitas	Signal Oil	1350.
w/Ripple			1650.
Sacramento Solons (26)	Tony Freitas	Sunbeam	525.
Seattle Rainers (32)	Rollie Hemsley	Centennial	625.
Seattle Rainers (16)	JoJo White	Signal Oil	1350.
Tacoma Tigers (24)	Priced as individual cards	Morley	27.00
1948 Issues			
Hollywood Stars (5)	Gus Zernial	Signal Oil	625.
L.A. Angels (5)	Eddie Malone	Signal Oil	650.
Oakland Oaks (1)	Team picture	Remar	1200.
Oakland Oaks (24)	Stengel/Martin	Signal Oil	485.
Oakland Oaks (25)	Stengel/Martin	Smith's	500.
1949 Issues			
Bowman PCL (36)	JoJo White	Bowman	6900.
Hollywood Stars (9)	Priced as individual cards	Hage's Ice Cream	27.00
L.A. Angels (13)	Priced as individual cards	Hage's Ice Cream	27.00
Oakland Oaks (5)	Priced as individual cards	Hage's Ice Cream	27.00
Oakland Oaks (32)	Billy Martin	Remar	400.
Omaha Cardinals (20)	Joe Presko	Team	475.
Portland Beavers (9)	Priced as individual cards	Hage's Ice Cream	27.00
Sacramento Solons (9)	Priced as individual cards	Hage's Ice Cream	27.00
San Diego Padres (37)	Priced as individual cards	Hage's Ice Cream	27.00
San Francisco Seals (12)	Priced as individual cards	Hage's Ice Cream	27.00
San Francisco Seals (30)	—	Sommer & Kaufman	800.
Seattle Raniers (11)	Jo Jo White Priced as individual cards	Hage's Ice Cream	35.00
Stockton Ports (12)	Bongiovanni	Sunbeam	600.
1950 Issues			
Hollywood Stars (2)	Priced as individual cards	Hage's Ice Cream	26.00

Team	Stars in Set	Issuer	Mint
L.A. Angels (9)	Priced as individual cards	Hage's Ice Cream	26.00
Oakland Oaks (5)	Priced as individual cards	Hage's Ice Cream	26.00
Oakland Oaks (27)	Bamberger	Remar	340.
Portland Beavers (4)	Priced as individual cards	Hage's Ice Cream	26.00
Sacramento Solons (15)	Priced as individual cards	Hage's Ice Cream	26.00
San Diego Padres (75)	Priced as individual cards	Hage's Ice Cream	27.00
S.F. Seals (5)	Priced as individual cards	Hage's Ice Cream	26.00
S.F. Seals (13)	Cliff Melton	Popcorn	820.00
Seattle Rainiers (10)	Priced as individual cards	Hage's Ice Cream	26.00
Stockton Ports	—	Sunbeam	700.00
1951 Issues			
Hollywood Stars (6)	Priced as individual cards	Hage's Ice Cream	26.00
San Diego Padres (40)	Priced as individual cards	Hage's Ice Cream	26.00
Vancouver Capilanos (24)	Bud Beasley	Sears & Roebuck	775.00
1952 Issues			
Columbus Cardinals	Priced as individual cards	Team	42.00
Canadian Prov. (120) League	—	LaVal Dairies	1400.
PCL Players (64)	Chuck Connors	Mother's Cookies	950.
Stockton Ports (11)	Tony Freitas	Knowles	675.
Vancouver Capilanos (23)	Van Fletcher	Sears & Roebuck	375.
1953 Issues			
Fargo Mooreheads (16)	Roger Maris	—	600.
PCL Players (63)	O'Doul Bamberger	Mother's Cookies	650.
Vancouver Capilanos (18)	Van Fletcher	Sears & Roebuck	525.
1954 Issues			
Sacramento Solons (6)	Al Cicotte	MD Super Service	375.
Seattle Rainiers (26)	Priced as individual cards	Team	32.00
Vancouver Capilanos (14)	Danny Holden	Sears & Roebuck	480.
1955 Issues			
Des Moines Bruins (21)	Pepper Martin	Homestead Franks	1100.
Seattle Rainiers (22)	Priced as individual cards	Team	22.00
1956 Issues			
Seattle Rainiers (27)	Priced as individual cards	Team	21.00
1957 Issues			
Omaha Cardinals (20)	Johnny Keane	Team	375.
Seattle Rainiers (12)	Priced as individual cards	Hygrade Meats	160.
Seattle Rainiers (24)	Priced as individual cards	Team	25.00

1958 Issues

Team	Stars in Set	Issuer	Mint
Buffalo Bisons (9)	Luke Easter	Bond Bread	450.
Sacramento Solons (10)	Sibby Sisty	Union Oil	200.
Seattle Rainiers (19)	Vada Pinson	Popcorn	575.

1959 Issues

Team	Stars in Set	Issuer	Mint
Seattle Rainiers (38)	Priced as individual cards	Team	35.00
Spokane Indians (22)	Norm Sherry	Darigold Farms	700.

1960 Issues

Team	Stars in Set	Issuer	Mint
Denver Bears (10)	Ossie Virgil	Armour	460.
Richmond Virginians (6)	Bob Martyn	Team	220.
Seattle Rainiers (18)	Dave Stenhouse	Henry House	2000.
Seattle Rainiers (18)	Priced as individual cards	Team	17.00
Seattle Rainiers (9)	R. Ripplemeyer	Union Oil	150.
Spokane Indians	—	Darigold Farms	385.
Tacoma Giants (21)	Marichal/Alou	National Bank Wash	425.
Tacoma Giants (12)	Juan Marichal	Tacoma Ath. Com.	300.
Toronto Maple Leafs (23)	Frank Funk	Shopsy's Franks	375.

1961 Issues

Team	Stars in Set	Issuer	Mint
Columbus Jets (2)	Larry Elliot	Jeff Morey	60.00
Hawaii Islanders (10)	Diego Segui	Union Oil	250.
Portland Beavers (13)	"Duke" Carmel	Union Oil	170.
San Diego Padres (12)	Herb Score	Union Oil	150.
Seattle Rainiers (29)	Priced as individual cards	Team	17.00
Seattle Rainiers (11)	Bob Tillman	Union Oil	125.
Spokane Indians (11)	Doug Camilli	Union Oil	250.
Syracuse Chiefs (2)	Ron Stillwell	Jeff Morey	60.00
Tacoma Giants (10)	Gaylord Perry	Union Oil	125.
Toronto Maple Leafs (24)	Chuck Tanner	Beehive Starch	360.

1962 Issues

Team	Stars in Set	Issuer	Mint
Atlanta Crackers (24)	McCarvery	Kahn's	550.
Omaha Dodgers (22)	Ken McMullen	Mel Bailey	325.
Richmond Virginians	—	Team	175.
Seattle Rainiers (20)	Priced as individual cards	Team	12.00
Tulsa Oilers (24)	Dal Maxvil	Pepsi	160.

1963 Issues

Team	Stars in Set	Issuer	Mint
Rochester Red Wings (9)	Ossie Virgil	Scheible Press	200.
Seattle Rainiers (11)	Bill Spanswick	Milwaukee Sausage	3000.
Seattle Rainiers (15)	Priced as individual cards	Team	12.00
Tulsa Oilers (24)	Jim Beauchamp	Pepsi	160.

1964 Issues

Team	Stars in Set	Issuer	Mint
Buffalo Bisons (3)	Cleon Jones	Team	260.
Seattle Rainiers (18)	—	Team	13.00

1965 Issues

Team	Stars in Set	Issuer	Mint
Seattle Rainiers (23)	Priced as individual cards	Team	13.00

1966 Issues

Team	Stars in Set	Issuer	Mint
Columbus Yankees (20)	Ronnie Boyer	RC Cola	350.
Seattle Rainiers (29)	Priced as individual cards	Team	17.00
St. Petersburg (20) Cardinals	S. Anderson	Foremost	75.00
Toledo Mud Hens (25)	Bobby Murcer	Team	375.
Tulsa Oilers (24)	Alex Johnsn	Pepsi	150.

1967 Issues

Team	Stars in Set	Issuer	Mint
Seattle Rainiers (19)	Priced as individual cards	Team	12.00

1968 Issues

Team	Stars in Set	Issuer	Mint
Seattle Rainiers (18)	Ethan Blackaby	Team	225.

1970 Issues

Team	Stars in Set	Issuer	Mint
Wichita Aeros (18)	Dick Tidrow	Mac's	475.

1971 Issues

Team	Stars in Set	Issuer	Mint
Richmond Braves (18)	Dusty Baker	Team	95.00
Syracuse Chiefs (8)	Danny Walton	Jeff Morey	105.

1972 Issues

Team	Stars in Set	Issuer	Mint
Cedar Rapids (29) Cardinals	Gary Geiger w/team photo	TCMA	150. 225.
Puerto Rico (231)	Mike Schmidt	Eva Ediciones	850.
Puerto Rico Album (1)	—		50.00
Seattle Rainiers	Priced as individual cards	Team	27.00
Tacoma Twins (16)	Tom Kelly	Team	30.00

1973 Issues

Team	Stars in Set	Issuer	Mint
Cedar Rapids Astros (28)	Luis Pujols	TCMA	85.00
Seattle Rainiers Scorecard Insert	Priced as individual cards	Team	20.00
Sherbrooke Pirates (18)	Tony Armas	Team	195.
Syracuse Chiefs (29) w/Pazik card (30)	Mickey Mantle	Team	150. 250.
Tacoma Twins (21)	Bill Campbell	Caruso	12.00
Wichita Aeros (19) w/Variations (21)	Tony La Russa	Kansas State Bank	75.00 100.

1974 Issues

Team	Stars in Set	Issuer	Mint
Albuquerque Dukes (16)	Jerry Royster	Caruso	12.00
Albuquerque Dukes (23)	Rich Rhoden	Team	450.
Cedar Rapids Astros (28)	Luis Puhols	TCMA	87.00
Gastonia Rangers (24)	Len Barker	TCMA	110.
Hawaii Islanders (8)	Bill Almon	Caruso	12.00
Omaha Royals (10)	Dennis Leonard	Falstaff Beer	170.
Phoenix Giants (11)	Rocky Bridges	Caruso	12.00
Sacramento Solons (18)	Gorman Thomas	Caruso	12.00
Salt Lake City (10)	—	Caruso	10.00
Seattle Rainiers (20)	Lynn Jones	Team	170.
Spokane Indians (18)	—	Caruso	12.00
Syracuse Chiefs (29) w/Frazier card (30)	Mickey Mantle	Team	125. 225.
Tacoma Twins (27)	Frazier	Caruso	12.00
Wichita Aeros (28) w/Variation (29)	Pete LaCock	One Day Film	90.00 130.

1975 Issues

Team	Stars in Set	Issuer	Mint
Albuquerque Dukes (21)	Jerry Royster	Caruso	10.00
Anderson Rangers (25)	Tom Brookens	TCMA	62.00
Appleton Foxes (29)	Kevin Bell	TCMA	62.00
Burlington Bees (29)	Moose Haas	TCMA	67.00
Cal League All Stars (30)	Lee Mazilli	Broder	75.00
Cedar Rapids Giants (32)	Jim Ray	TCMA	75.00
Clinton Pilots (30)	Jim Leyland	TCMA	67.00
Dubuque Packers (33)	Terry Puhl	TCMA	70:00
Ft. Lauderdale Yankees (29) w/Figueroa (30)	Mike Heath	Sussman	75.00 150.
Hawaii Islanders (21)	Bill Almon	Caruso	20.00
Int'l League All Stars (31)	Gay Carter	TCMA	32.00
Iowa Oaks (21)	Joe Niekro	TCMA	90.00
Lafayette Drillers (32)	Jack Clark	TCMA	125.
Lynchburg Rangers (26)	Pat Putnam	TCMA	57.00
OK City 89ers (24)	Rick Waits	Team	10.00
Omaha Royals (18)	U.L. Washington		125.
PCL All Stars (36)	Jerry Royster	Broder	75.00
Phoenix Giants (26)	Larry Herndon	Circle K	6.00
Phoenix Giants (21)	Bob Knepper	Caruso	12.00
Quad City Angels (34)	Rance Mulliniks	TCMA	67.00
Sacramento Solons (22)	Gorman Thomas	Caruso	10.00
Salt Lake City (20)	Dave Collins	Caruso	10.00
San Antonio Brewers (22)	Wil Aaron	TCMA	59.00
Shreveport Captains (23)	Rick Langford	TCMA	67.00
Spokane Indians (21)	Roy Smalley	Caruso	10.00
Syracuse Chiefs (24) w/Bladt card (25)	Whitey Ford	Team	100. 200.
Tacoma Twins (21)	Randy Bass	KMMO	6.00
Tidewater Tides (24)	Craig Swan	Stewart Sandwich	155.
Tucson Toros (21)	Roger Nelson	Caruso	10.00
Tucson Toros (21)	Chet Lemon	Team	25.00
Tulsa Oilers (24)	Larry Herndon	7-11	65.00
West Palm Beach (29)	Tony Bernazard	Sussman	25.00
Waterbury Dodgers (22)	R. Landestoy	TCMA	62.00
Waterloo Royals (34) w/Variation card (35)	Willie Wilson	TCMA	80.00 130.

1976 Issues

Team	Stars in Set	Issuer	Mint
Appleton Foxes (29)	Mitch Lukevics	TCMA	50.00
Arkansas Travelers (12)	Ken Oberkfell	TCMA	125.
Asheville Tourists (25)	Pat Putnam	TCMA	70.00
Batavia Trojans (29)	Tim Glass	Team	150.
Baton Rouge Cougars (21)	Terry Leach	TCMA	75.00

Team	Stars in Set	Issuer	Mint
Burlington Bees (33)	George Frazier	TCMA	59.00
Cedar Rapids Giants (37)	Grimes	TCMA	40.00
w/Variations (39)			90.00
Clinton Pilots (35)	Mcguel Garcia	TCMA	75.00
w/Late Issue cards (37)			125.
Dubuque Packers (40)	Alan Knicely	TCMA	50.00
Ft. Lauderdale (30) Yankees	Willie Upshaw	Sussman	80.00
Hawaii Islanders (21)	Joe Pepitone	Caruso	25.00
Indianapolis Indians (26)	Ray Knight	Team	35.00
OK City 89ers (24)	Willie Hernandez	Team	65.00
Omaha Royals (27)	John Wathan	Top Trophies	100.
Phoenix Giants (24)	Jack Clark	Cramer	35.00
Phoenix Giants (24)	Jack Clark	Coke	10.00
Phoenix Giants (20)	Jack Clark	Caruso	20.00
Phoenix Giants (24)	Jack Clark	VNB	15.00
Quad City Angels (39)	Carney Lansford	TCMA	125.
w/Mercedes card (40)			140.
Sacramento Solons (23)	Len Barker	Caruso	25.00
Salt Lake City (22)	—	Caruso	10.00
San Antonio Brewers (26)	Jim Clancy	Knowltons	60.00
Seattle Rainiers (20)		Cramer	10.00
Shreveport Captains (23)	Rod Scurry	TCMA	60.00
w/Weinberg card (24)			110.
w/Team card (25)			200.
Spokane Indians (21)	Moose Haas	Caruso	25.00
Tacoma Twins (24)	Dave McKay	Dairy Queen	30.00
Tucson Toros (24)	Jeff Newman	Team	10.00
Tucson Toros (20)	Jeff Newman	Caruso	10.00
Tulsa Oilers (26)	Ken Boyer	Goof's Pants	90.00
Waterloo Royals (33)	Dan Quisenberry	TCMA	80.00
Wausau Mets (25)	Mario Ramirez	TCMA	70.00
Williamsport Tomahawks (23)	Wil Arron	TCMA	65.00

1977 Issues

Team	Stars in Set	Issuer	Mint
Appleton Foxes (29)	Steve Trout	TCMA	60.00
w/Correct Minoso (30)			90.00
Arkansas Travelers (12)	Tito Landrum	TCMA	75.00
w/All Variations (21)			200.
Asheville Tourists (29)	Brian Allard	TCMA	39.00
Bristol Red Sox (20)	John Tudor	TCMA	185.
Burlington Bees (25)	Rey Quinones	TCMA	65.00
w/Halls & Mercado (27)			115.
Cedar Rapids Giants (24)	Bob Brenly	TCMA	65.00
w/Laubhan card (25)			140.
Charleston Patriots (25)	Pascual Perez	TCMA	35.00
Clinton Dodgers (29)	Dave Stewart	TCMA	135.
Cocoa Astros (25)	Dave Smith	TCMA	37.00
Columbus Clippers (22)	Ed Whitson	TCMA	250.
w/Variations (24)			350.
Daytona Bch. Islanders (27)	Ken Phelps	TCMA	35.00
Evansville Triplets (25)	Parrish/Morris	TCMA	375.
Ft. Lauderdale (31) Yankees	Pat Tabler	Sussman	90.00
Hawaii Islanders (24)	Steve Mura	Caruso	20.00
Holyoke Millers (26)	George Frazier	TCMA	27.00
Indianapolis Indians (27)	Mario Soto	Team	13.00
Jacksonville Suns (22)	Dan Quisenberry	TCMA	80.00
Lodi Dodgers (25)	Rudy Law	TCMA	70.00
Lynchburg Mets (30)	Neil Allen	TCMA	100.
w/Reardon Card (31)			200.
w/Both Variations (33)			300.
w/Greenstein Var. (34)			400.
Modesto A's (23)	R. Henderson	Chong	325.
Newark Co-Pilots (29)	Brian Fisher	TCMA	37.00
OK City 89ers	—	Team	110.
Omaha Royals (19)	—	Top Trophies	75.00
Orlando Twins (22)	John Castino	TCMA	65.00
w/Terry Felton (23)			90.00
Phoenix Giants (24)	Bob Knepper	Coke Prem.	25.00
Phoenix Giants (24)	Bob Knepper	Cramer	5.00
Phoenix Giants (24)	Bob Knepper	VNB	25.00
Quad City Angels (29)	Mark Clear	TCMA	50.00
Reading Phillies (23)	Tod Cruz	TCMA	360.
Rochester Red Wings (24)	Ken Boyer	McCurdy's	125.
Salem Pirates (24)	Tony Pena	TCMA	75.00
w/Var. & Late iss. (35)			225.
Salt Lake City (24)	Rance Mullniks	Cramer	6.00
San Jose Missions (25)	Odom	Mr. Chef's	8.00
Shreveport Captains (23)	Don Robinson	TCMA	100.
Spartanburg Phillies (24)	Ozzie Virgil	TCMA	130.
Spokane Indians (24)	Jim Gantner	Cramer	7.00
St. Petersburg (25) Cardinals	—	TCMA	85.00
w/Mike Nagle Card (26)			135.

Team	Stars in Set	Issuer	Mint
Tacoma Twins (27)	Rob Wilfong	Dairy	27.00
w/Unissued cards (30)		Queen	33.00
Tucson Toros (24)	Len Barker	Cramer	6.00
Visalia Oaks (17)	Ray Smith	TCMA	32.00
Waterloo Indians (29)	Tom Brennan	TCMA	60.00
w/Late Issue cards (31)			110.
w/Brennan Variation (32)			170.
Wausau Mets (24)	Kelvin Chapman	TCMA	50.00
West Haven Yanks (25)	Mike Heath	TCMA	190.

1978 Issues

Team	Stars in Set	Issuer	Mint
Albuquerque Dukes (20)	Pedro Guerrero	Cramer	20.00
Appleton Foxes (25)	Lamar Hoyt	TCMA	45.00
Arkansas Travelers (23)	Tommy Herr	TCMA	195.
Asheville Tourists (29)	Ed Lynch	TCMA	40.00
Burlington Bees (28)	Kevin Bass	TCMA	45.00
Cedar Rapids Giants (24)	Chili Davis	TCMA	90.00
Charleston Charlies (20)	Vern Ruhle	TCMA	18.00
Charleston Pirates (24)	Junior Ortiz	TCMA	35.00
Clinton Dodgers (33)	Mitch Webster	TCMA	55.00
w/Late Issue card (34)			90.00
Columbus Clippers (27)	Mike Easler	TCMA	18.00
Daytona Bch. Astros (26)	Ricky Adams	TCMA	25.00
Denver Bears (25)	Schatzeder Bernazard	Tiefel & Assoc.	8.00
Dunedin Blue Jays (27)	Jesse Barfield	TCMA	110.
Geneva Cubs (24)	Danny Rohn	Team	200.
Greenwood Braves (24)	Cletis Boyer	TCMA	25.00
Holyoke Millers (24)	Mike Dempsey	TCMA	20.00
Indianapolis Indians (27)	Mario Soto	Team	22.00
Knoxville Knox Sox (25)	Harold Baines	TCMA	260.
w/Wolf Error (26)			330.
Lodi Dodgers (25)	Ron Roenicke	TCMA	35.00
w/Variation card (26)			55.00
Memphis Chicks (10)	Felipe Alou	Brittling Cafeterias	12.00
Modesto A's (26)	Mike Davis	Chong	65.00
Newark Co-Pilots (45)	Doug Jones	TCMA	45.00
OK City 89ers (26)	Keith Moreland	Team	70.00
Orlando Twins (23)	Doc Estes	TCMA	25.00
Phoenix Giants (25)	Greg Minton	Cramer	4.00
Quad City Angels (30)	Brad Havens	TCMA	100.
Richmond Braves (20)	Rick Mahler	TCMA	20.00
Rochester Red Wings (17)	Frank Robinson	TCMA	23.00
Salem Pirates (18)	Luis Salazar	TCMA	27.00
Salt Lake City (24)	Dickie Thon	Cramer	7.00
San Jose Missions (24)	Bill Plummer	Mr. Chef's	30.00
Spokane Indians (24)	Ned Yost	Cramer	6.00
Springfield Redbirds (24)	Ken Oberkfell	R. West	75.00
St. Petersburg Cards (29)	Tito Landrum	TCMA	45.00
Syracuse Chiefs (22)	Danny Ainge	TCMA	25.00
Tacoma Yankees (25)	Hoyt Wilhelm	Cramer	6.00
Tidewater Tides (27)	Mike Scott	TCMA	25.00
Tucson Toros (25)	Len Barker	Cramer	6.00
Waterloo Indians (26)	Ramon Romero	TCMA	25.00
Wausau Mets (25)	Brent Gaff	TCMA	40.00
Wisconsin Rapids (18)	M. Funderburk	TCMA	25.00

1979 Issues

Team	Stars in Set	Issuer	Mint
Albuquerque Dukes (23)	Mike Scioscia	TCMA	35.00
Albuquerque Dukes (23)	Pedro Guerrero	University Volkswagen	200.
Appleton Foxes (25)	Kevin Hickey	TCMA	50.00
Arkansas Travelers (23)	Joe DeSa	TCMA	17.00
Asheville Tourists (28)	Gene Nelson	TCMA	115.
Buffalo Bisons (21)	Pena/Dravecky	TCMA	100.
Burlington Bees (25)	Doug Jones	TCMA	25.00
Cedar Rapids Giants (32)	Rob Deer	TCMA	110.
Charleston Charlies (19)	Dave Bergman	TCMA	15.00
w/Corrected cards (21)			35.00
Clinton Dodgers (28)	Steve Sax	TCMA	125.
Columbus Clippers (29)	Gene Michael	TCMA	17.00
Elmira Pioneer (28) Red Sox	Gutierrez	TCMA	95.00
Hawaii Islanders (24)	Eichelberger	Cramer	6.00
Hawaii Islanders (24)	Eichelberger	TCMA	10.00
Holyoke Millers (30)	Kevin Bass	TCMA	10.00
Indianapolis Indians (32)	Ron Oester	Team	27.00
Iowa Oaks (14)	Harold Baines	Police	170.
Jackson Mets (25)	Wally Backman	TCMA	13.00
Knoxville Knox Sox (26)	Richard Dotson	TCMA	100.
Lodi Dodgers (21)	Mike Marshall	TCMA	90.00
Memphis Chicks (24)	Tim Raines	TCMA	200.
Modesto A's (23)	Mike Davis	Chong	50.00
Nashville Sounds (25)	Bill Dawley	Team	30.00
Newark Co-Pilots (24)	Kevin Rose	TCMA	28.00
Ogden A's (26)	R. Henderson	TCMA	55.00
OK City 89ers (24)	Luis Aguayo	Team	60.00
Phoenix Giants (24)	Mike Rowland	Cramer	6.00
Portland Beavers (24)	Vance Law	TCMA	12.00

Team	Stars in Set	Issuer	Mint
Quad City 89ers (27)	Joe Hicks	TCMA	50.00
Richmond Braves (25)	Jamie Easterly	TCMA	10.00
Rochester Red Wings (20)	Joe Kerrigan	TCMA	10.00
Salt Lake City (23)	Rance Mulliniks	TCMA	12.00
Savannah Braves (26)	Steve Bedrosian	TCMA	20.00
Spokane Indians (25)	Bill Plummer	TCMA	10.00
Syracuse Chiefs (20)	Ernie Whitt	TCMA	19.00
Syracuse Chiefs (24)	Willie Upshaw	Team	47.00
Tacoma Tugs (26)	Ron Hassay	TCMA	19.00
Tidewater Tides (25)	Jeff Reardon	TCMA	25.00
Toledo Mud Hens (22)	Gary Ward	TCMA	10.00
Tucson Toros (24)	Ed Lynch	TCMA	11.00
Tulsa Drillers (24)	Roy Clark	TCMA	15.00
Vancouver Canadians (25)	Ed Romero	TCMA	10.00
Waterbury A's (25)	Mike Davis	TCMA	95.00
Waterloo Indians (36)	Carmen Castillo	TCMA	115.
West Haven Yankees (30)	Willie McGee	TCMA	59.00
Wisconsin Rapids (23)	Rich Stelmazek	TCMA	52.00

1980 Issues

Team	Stars in Set	Issuer	Mint
Albuquerque Dukes (27)	Dave Stewart	TCMA	37.00
Anderson Braves (29)	Brook Jacoby	TCMA	20.00
Appleton Foxes (30)	Greg Walker	TCMA	115.
Arkansas Travelers (25)	Luis DeLeon	TCMA	15.00
Asheville Tourists (28)	Pete O'Brien	TCMA	25.00
Batavia Trojans (30)	Kelly Gruber	TCMA	85.00
Buffalo Bisons (16)	Dave Dravecky	TCMA	13.00
Burlington Bees (29)	Juan Castillo	TCMA	45.00
Cedar Rapids Reds (26)	Les Straker	TCMA	10.00
Charleston Charlies (17)	John Butcher	TCMA	10.00
Charlotte O's (28)	Cal Ripken, Jr.	W3TV	250.
Charlotte O's (24)	Cal Ripken, Jr.	Police	900.
Clinton Giants (27)	Rob Deer	TCMA	100.
Columbus Astros (22)	Johnny Ray	TCMA	60.00
Columbus Clippers (25)	Dave Righetti	Police	10.00
Columbus Clippers (28)	Dave Righetti	TCMA	30.00
El Paso Diablos (24)	Tom Brunansky	TCMA	12.00
Elmira Pioneer (44) Red Sox	Oil Can Boyd	TCMA	90.00
Evansville Triplets (24)	Rick Leach	TCMA	10.00
Glens Falls (b/w) (29)	Orlando Cepeda	TCMA	175.
Glens Falls (color) (30)	Orlando Cepeda	TCMA	25.00
Hawaii Islanders (25)	Tim Flannery	TCMA	10.00
Holyoke Millers (25)	Frank DiPino	TCMA	10.00
Indianapolis Indians (32)	Bill Dawley	Team	35.00
Iowa Oaks (14)	Lamar Hoyt	Police	180.
w/Variations (16)			380.
Knoxville Blue Jays (28)	Jesse Barfield	TCMA	175.
Lynn Sailors (24)	Karl Best	TCMA	10.00
Memphis Chicks (30)	Charlie Lea	TCMA	35.00
Modesto A's (29)	Keith Lieppman	Chong	40.00
Nashville Sounds (24)	Willie McGee	Team	20.00
w/Filer card (25)			30.00
Ogden A's (23)	Dave Bears	TCMA	10.00
OK City 89ers (24)	Luis Aguayo	Team	60.00
Omaha Royals (24)	Ken Phelps	Police	60.00
Orlando Twins (22)	Tim Laudner	TCMA	120.00
Peninsula Pilots (27)	Franco (b/w)	TCMA	50.00
Peninsula Pilots (27)	Franco (color)	TCMA	25.00
Phoenix Giants (26)	Max Venable	VNB	5.00
Portland Beavers (27)	Rhoden/Pena	TCMA	13.00
Quad City Cubs (32)	C. Martinez	TCMA	125.
Reading Phillies (24)	Sandberg Dernier/Bell	TCMA	400.
San Jose Missions (23)	Rick Mahler	TCMA	10.00
Rochester Red Wings (21)	Boddicker	TCMA	5.00
Salt Lake City (26)	Ken Schrom	TCMA	10.00
San Jose Missions (21)	Bud Black	Jack in the Box	30.00
Spokane Indians (24)	Dave Henderson	TCMA	12.00
Syracuse Chiefs (23)	Danny Ainge	TCMA	25.00
Syracuse Chiefs (24)	Lloyd Moseby	Team	40.00
Tacoma Tigers (28)	Tom Brennan	TCMA	10.00
Tidewater Tides (24)	Mookie Wilson	TCMA	27.00
Toledo Mud Hens (20)	Ron Washington	TCMA	12.00
Tucson Toros (24)	Danny Heep	TCMA	10.00
Tulsa Drillers (26)	Nick Capra	TCMA	10.00
Utica Blue Jays (33)	Juan Castillo	TCMA	45.00
Vancouver Canadians (22)	Dave LaPoint	TCMA	9.00
Waterbury Reds (22)	Nick Esasky	TCMA	110.
Waterloo Indians (35)	Von Hayes	TCMA	110.
Wausau Timbers (25)	Jim Presley	TCMA	80.00
West Haven White Caps (31)	Keith Comstock	TCMA	10.00
Wichita Aeros (22)	Lee Smith	TCMA	15.00
Wisconsin Rapids (27)	Hrbek/Gaetti	TCMA	225.

1981 Issues

Team	Stars in Set	Issuer	Mint
Albuquerque Dukes (26)	Mike Marshall	TCMA	75.00
Appleton Foxes (29)	Cecil Espy	TCMA	12.00
Arkansas Travelers (23)	Jim Gott	TCMA	25.00
Batavia Trojans (30)	R. Washington	TCMA	20.00
Birmingham Barons (25)	Howard Johnson	TCMA	140.
Bristol Red Sox (22)	Ed Jurak	TCMA	15.00
Buffalo Bisons (25)	Jose DeLeon	TCMA	10.00
Burlington Bees (29)	Randy Ready	TCMA	35.00
Cedar Rapids Reds (26)	Ron Robinson	TCMA	25.00
Charleston Charlies (24)	Hayes/Bando	TCMA	20.00
Charleston Royals (26)	Mark Hulsmann	TCMA	20.00
Charlotte O's (25)	John Shelby	Team	70.00
Chattanooga Lookouts (25)	Carmen Castillo	TCMA	25.00
Clinton Giants (29)	Matt Young	TCMA	25.00
Columbus Clippers (25)	Dave Righetti	Police	12.00
Columbus Clippers (28)	Righetti/Tabler	TCMA	45.00
Durham Bulls (24)	Jeff Dedmon	TCMA	25.00
Edmonton Trappers (24)	Fran Mullins	Red Rooster	5.00
El Paso Diablos (24)	Jones/Candiotti	TCMA	11.00
Evansville Triplets (22)	Marty Castillo	TCMA	10.00
Glens Falls (24)	Greg Walker	TCMA	35.00
Hawaii Islanders (23)	Eric Show	TCMA	9.00
Holyoke Millers (26)	Rasmussen Petitis	TCMA	15.00
Holyoke Millers (25)	Rasmussen Petitis	Team	60.00
Indianapolis Indians (32)	—	Team	23.00
Lynn Sailors (29)	Bud Black	TCMA	20.00
Miami Orioles (21)	Al Padro	TCMA	10.00
w/Late Issue cards (23)			125.
Modesto A's (30)	—	Chong	27.00
Nashville Sounds (25)	Mattingly	Team	30.00
OK City 89ers (26)	Ryne Sandberg	TCMA	28.00
Omaha Royals (24)	Atlee Hammaker	TCMA	15.00
Pawtucket Red Sox (24)	Boggs/Hurst	TCMA	74.00
Phoenix Giants (27)	Bob Brenly	VNB	12.00
Portland Beavers (27)	Luis Tiant	TCMA	10.00
Quad City Cubs (33)	Henry Cotto	TCMA	12.00
Reading Phillies (24)	Julio Franco	TCMA	135.
Redwood Pioneers (30)	Warren Spahn	TCMA	12.00
Richmond Braves (25)	Bedrosian/Butler	TCMA	16.00
Rochester Red Wings (23)	Cal Ripken, Jr.	TCMA	28.00
Rochester Red Wings (25)	Cal Ripken, Jr.	WTF	57.00
Salt Lake City (26)	Brunansky	TCMA	12.00
Shreveport Captains (23)	Dan Gladden	TCMA	12.00
Spokane Indians (32)	Ed Vandeburg	TCMA	9.00
Syracuse Chiefs (24)	Ken Schrom	TCMA	9.00
Syracuse Chiefs (24)	Ken Schrom	Team	35.00
Tacoma Tigers (32)	Mike Davis	TCMA	10.00
Tidewater Tides (29)	Terry Leach	TCMA	15.00
Toledo Mud Hens (22)	Ron Washington	TCMA	9.00
Tucson Toros (26)	Johnny Ray	TCMA	30.00
Tulsa Drillers (30)	Darling/O'Brien	TCMA	20.00
Vancouver Canadians (25)	Kevin Bass	TCMA	9.00
Vero Bch. Dodgers (27)	R.J. Reynolds	TCMA	30.00
Waterbury Reds (23)	Gary Redus	TCMA	32.00
Waterloo Indians (34)	Bob Feller	TCMA	30.00
Wausau Timbers (29)	Presley/Calderon	TCMA	60.00
West Haven A's (23)	Keith Atherton	TCMA	9.00
Wisconsin Rapids (23)	Jim Eisenreich	TCMA	39.00

1982 Issues

Team	Stars in Set	Issuer	Mint
Albuquerque Dukes (27)	Orel Hershiser	TCMA	65.00
Alexandria Dukes (27)	Joe Orsulak	TCMA	29.00
Amarillo Gold Sox (25)	Mark Parent	TCMA	30.00
Appleton Foxes (31)	Darryl Boston	Fritsch	6.00
Arkansas Travelers (24)	Andy Van Slyke	TCMA	95.00
Auburn Astros (19)	Carlos Alfonso	TCMA	17.00
Beloit Brewers (27)	Bill Wegman	Fritsch	6.00
Birmingham Barons (24)	Paul Gibson	TCMA	12.00
Buffalo Bisons (18)	Mike Bielecki	TCMA	14.00
Burlington Rangers (30)	Dwayne Henry	Fritsch	5.00
Burlington Rangers (26)	Wilkerson	TCMA	20.00
w/Avery card (27)			70.00
Cedar Rapids Reds (27)	Eric Davis	TCMA	50.00
Charleston Charlies (24)	Neal Heaton	TCMA	10.00
Charleston Royals (24)	Jackson/Cone	TCMA	42.00
Charlotte O's (31)	John Stefero	Team	55.00
Chattanooga Lookouts (25)	Kelly Gruber	TCMA	25.00
Clinton Giants (32)	Matt Nokes	Fritsch	15.00
Columbus Clippers (25)	Mattingly	Police	40.00
Columbus Clippers (26)	Mattingly	TCMA	275.
Danville Suns (28)	Devon White	Fritsch	10.00
Daytona Bch. Astros (25)	Glenn Davis	TCMA	39.00
Durham Bulls (25)	Brian Fisher	TCMA	95.00
Edmonton Trappers (25)	Ron Kittle	TCMA	17.00
El Paso Diablos (24)	James/Ready	TCMA	20.00
Evansville Triplets (25)	Berenguer	TCMA	12.00
Ft. Myers Royals (23)	Huisman	TCMA	17.00
Glens Falls (23)	Joel Skinner	TCMA	175.
Hawaii Islanders (25)	Tony Gwynn	TCMA	49.00
Holyoke Millers (26)	Mooneyham	TCMA	12.00

Representative Minor League Cards

1981 TCMA

1982 TCMA

1983 TCMA

1984 Police Set

1985 Nashville Sounds

1987 Best Cards

1988 CMC Tides

1989 Best Cards

1989 Star Co.

Team	Stars in Set	Issuer	Mint		Team	Stars in Set	Issuer	Mint
Holyoke Millers (29)	Mooneyham	Team	50.00		Iowa Cubs (30)	Joe Carter	TCMA	35.00
Idaho Falls A's (33)	Dave Leiper	TCMA	17.00		w/Variation card (31)			75.00
Indianapolis Indians (32)	Nick Esasky	Team	17.00		Kinston Blue Jays (28)	Joe Schroeder	Tony Kelly	95.00
Iowa Cubs (32)	Hall/Tabler	TCMA	19.00		Knoxville Blue Jays (22)	John Cerruti	TCMA	20.00
Jackson Mets (25)	Strawberry	TCMA	150.		Las Vegas Stars (22)	McReynolds	BHN	18.00
Knoxville Blue Jays (23)	Dennis Howard	TCMA	12.00		Louisville Red Birds (30)	Van Slyke	Riley's	15.00
Louisville Red Birds (30)	Willie McGee	Ehrlers	20.00			Worrell		
		Dairy			Lynchburg Mets (23)	Deight Gooden	TCMA	65.00
Lynchburg Mets (23)	Mitchell/Milligan	TCMA	95.00		Lynn Pirates (27)	Rafael Belliard	TCMA	60.00
Lynn Sailors (18)	Reynolds	TCMA	25.00		Madison Muskies (32)	Joe Canseco	Fritsch	35.00
	Presley				Memphis Chicks (24)	Santovenia		29.00
Madison Muskies (34)	Steve Keifer	Fritsch	5.00		Miami Marlins (28)	Santiago	TCMA	130.
Miami Marlins (22)	Lee Granger	TCMA	12.00		Midland Cubs (26)	Billy Hatcher	TCMA	20.00
Modesto A's (27)	Tettleton	Chong	29.00		Modesto A's (30)	Tettleton	Chong	24.00
Nashville Sounds (28)	Mark Salas	Team	7.00		Nashua Angels (27)	Mooneyham	TCMA	12.00
OK City 89ers (25)	Julio Franco	TCMA	20.00		Nashville Sounds (25)	Pagliarulo	Team	12.00
Omaha Royals (27)	Pat Sheridan	TCMA	15.00		OK City 89ers (24)	Tom Henke		13.00
w/Variations (29)			70.00		Omaha Royals (26)	Danny Jackson	TCMA	27.00
Oneonta Yankees (17)	John Elway	TCMA	130.		Orlando Twins (22)	Rich Yett	TCMA	10.00
Orlando Twins (24)	Gagne/Teufel	TCMA	29.00		w/Late Issue card (23)			60.00
Orlando Twins (24)	Frank Viola	TCMA	70.00		Pawtucket Red Sox (26)	Marty Barrett	TCMA	59.00
('81 Southern League Champs Set)					Peoria Suns (30)	Devon White	Fritsch	10.00
Phoenix Giants (27)		VNB	6.00		Phoenix Giants (28)	Randy Kutcher	BHN	20.00
Portland Beavers (25)	Pascual Perez	TCMA	17.00		Portland Beavers (22)	Juan Samuel	TCMA	95.00
Quad City Cubs (28)	Darrin Jackson	TCMA	17.00		w/Late Issue cards (25)			150.
Reading Phillies (22)	Steve Jeltz	TCMA	35.00		Quad City Cubs (27)	S. Dunston	TCMA	55.00
Redwood Pioneers (27)	Craig Gerber	TCMA	17.00		Reading Phillies (24)	Lavalliere	TCMA	150.
Richmond Braves (31)	Gerald Perry	TCMA	30.00			Samuel		
w/Variation card (32)			80.00		Redwood Pioneers (32)	Kirk McKaskill	TCMA	15.00
Rochester Red Wings (22)	Shelby	TCMA	12.00		Richmond Braves (25)	Brook Jacoby	TCMA	20.00
	Boddicker				Rochester Red Wings (25)	Mike Young	TCMA	20.00
Salt Lake City (25)	Dave Valle	TCMA	9.00		Salt Lake City (26)	Phil Bradley	TCMA	15.00
Spokane Indians (26)	Brunansky	TCMA	9.00		San Jose Bees (26)	Bruce Fields	Barry Colla	10.00
Springfield Cardinals (24)	Danny Cox	Fritsch	9.00		Springfield Cardinals (26)	Bob Green	Fritsch	11.00
Syracuse Chiefs (26)	George Bell	TCMA	25.00		St. Petersburg (30)	Danny Cox	TCMA	27.00
w/Late Issue cards (29)			80.00		Syracuse Chiefs (26)	Fernandez/Bell	TCMA	47.00
Syracuse Chiefs (24)	Fernandez	Team	60.00		Tacoma Tigers (31)	Donnie Hill	TCMA	10.00
Tacoma Tigers (37)	Mike Gallego	TCMA	10.00		w/Late Issue cards (36)			110.
w/Late Issue cards (39)			75.00		Tampa Tarpons (29)	Browning/O'Neil	TCMA	39.00
Tidewater Tides (26)	Ron Darling	TCMA	37.00		Tidewater Tides (29)	Strawberry	TCMA	75.00
Toledo Mud Hens (24)	Frank Viola	TCMA	30.00			& Everybody		
w/Late Issue cards (27)			100.			Greg Gagne	TCMA	12.00
Tucson Toros (28)	Bill Doran	TCMA	19.00		Toledo Mud Hens (25)			
Tulsa Drillers (24)	Tom Henke	TCMA	10.00		w/Late Issue cards (29)			112.
w/Late Issue cards (28)			65.00		Tri-Cities Triplets (28)	Bob Sebra	TCMA	20.00
Vancouver Canadians (24)	Doug Jones	TCMA	10.00		Tucson Toros (25)	Pankovits	TCMA	12.00
Vero Beach Dodgers (29)	Fernandez	TCMA	125.		w/Late Issue card (26)			62.00
	Bream				Tulsa Drillers (25)	Bob Brower	TCMA	15.00
Waterbury Reds (23)	Tartabull	TCMA	32.00		Vero Bch. Dodgers (29)	Mariano Duncan	TCMA	25.00
Waterloo Indians (28)	Jose Roman	Fritsch	5.00		Visalia Oaks (25)	Kirby Puckett	Fritsch	60.00
Waterloo Indians (25)	Mike Jeffcoat	TCMA	12.00		Waterbury Reds (19)	Eric Davis	TCMA	90.00
w/Late Issue cards (28)			87.00		Waterloo Indians (29)	Jose Roman	Fritsch	5.00
Wausau Timbers (31)	Ivan Calderon	Fritsch	8.00		Wausau Timbers (31)	—	Fritsch	5.00
West Haven A's (29)	Donnie Hill	TCMA	17.00		Wichita Aeros (24)	Angel Salazar	Dog "N"	12.00
Wichita Aeros (20)	Ken Phelps	Team	12.00				Shake	
Wisconsin Rapids (27)	Mark Portugal	Fritsch	6.00		Wisconsin Rapids (28)	Allan Anderson	Fritsch	12.00

1983 Issues

1984 Issues

Team	Stars in Set	Issuer	Mint		Team	Stars in Set	Issuer	Mint
Albany-Colonie A's (20)	Ontiveros	TCMA	175.		Albany-Colonie A's (26)	Tettleton	TCMA	14.00
Albuquerque Dukes (25)	Orel Hershiser	TCMA	55.00		Albuquerque Dukes (26)	Reynolds	Cramer	7.00
Alexandria Dukes (31)	Bobby Bonilla	TCMA	50.00			Bream		
Anderson Braves (33)	Andres Thomas	TCMA	20.00		Arkansas Travelers (26)	Todd Worrell	TCMA	14.00
Appleton Foxes (30)	John Cangelosi	Fritsch	8.00		Beaumont Golden Gators (25)	Walter/Jones	TCMA	11.00
Arkansas Travelers (25)	Pendleton	TCMA	95.00		Buffalo Bisons (25)	Allanson	TCMA	11.00
Beaumont Golden (23)	John Kruk	TCMA	70.00		Butte Copper Kings (27)	Manny Estrada	TCMA	14.00
Gators					Cedar Rapids Reds (28)	Stillwell	TCMA	20.00
Beloit Brewers (30)	Chris Bosio	Fritsch	12.00		Charlotte O's (27)	Ken Gerhart	TCMA	12.00
Birmingham Barons (25)	Dwight Lowry	TCMA	12.00		Chattanooga Lookouts (29)	Brantley/Nixon	TCMA	12.00
Buffalo Bisons (25)	Dave Gallagher	TCMA	15.00		Columbus Clippers (25)	Pagliarulo	Police	7.00
Burlington Rangers (25)	Randy Kramer	Fritsch	6.00		Columbus Clippers (25)	Pagliarulo	TCMA	18.00
Burlington Rangers (28)	Randy Kramer	TCMA	15.00		Daytona Bch. Astros (25)	Robbie Wine	Team	55.00
Butte Copper Kings (33)	Kevin Seitzer	TCMA	55.00		Durham Bulls (30)	Andres Thomas	TCMA	16.00
Cedar Rapids Reds (26)	Kal Daniels	Fritsch	15.00		Edmonton Trappers (26)	—	Cramer	5.00
Cedar Rapids Reds (28)	Daniels/Murphy	TCMA	32.00		El Paso Diablos (25)	Higuera, Sveum	TCMA	19.00
Charleston Charlies (22)	Jerry Reed	TCMA	11.00		Evansville Triplets (22)	Bob Melvin	TCMA	11.00
Charleston Royals (25)	Van Snider	TCMA	25.00		Everett Giants (35)	—	Cramer	5.00
Chattanooga Lookouts (28)	Tartabull	TCMA	160.		Greensboro Hornets (26)	Roberto Kelly	TCMA	25.00
	Langston				Greenville Hornets (26)	Duane Ward	Team	40.00
Clinton Giants (30)	Alonzo Powell	Fritsch	10.00		Hawaii Islanders (25)	Bob Walk	Cramer	6.00
Columbus Astros (24)	Glenn Davis	TCMA	49.00		Idaho Falls A's (30)	Felix Jose	Team	75.00
Columbus Clippers (27)	Rasmussen	TCMA	45.00		Indianapolis Indians (32)	Joe Hesketh	Team	10.00
Daytona Bch. Astros (27)	Mak Knudsn	TCMA	15.00		Iowa Cubs (31)	Joe Carter	TCMA	29.00
Durham Bulls (29)	Duane Ward	TCMA	12.00		Jackson Mets (15)	Strawberry	Mike Feder	70.00
El Paso Diablos (25)	Crews/Riles	TCMA	12.00		Jackson Mets (25)	Dykstra	TCMA	35.00
Erie Cardinals (25)	Tom Pagnozzi	TCMA	18.00			Carreon		
Evansville Triplets (25)	Marty Castillo	TCMA	12.00		Las Vegas Stars (25)	John Kruk	Cramer	12.00
Glens Falls (24)	Tom Brennan	TCMA	75.00		Little Falls Mets (26)	West/Gozzo	TCMA	29.00
Greensboro Hornets (30)	Ozzie Canseco	TCMA	36.00		Louisville Red Birds (20)	Coleman	Riley's	15.00
Idaho Falls A's (34)	Camilo Pascual	TCMA	20.00			Pendleton		
Indianapolis Indians (32)	Bill Dawley	Team	12.00		Madison Muskies (25)	Steinbach	Police	15.00
					Maine Guides (23)	Dave Gallagher	TCMA	12.00

Team	Stars in Set	Issuer	Mint
Memphis Chicks (25)	David Cone	TCMA	29.00
Midland Cubs (24)	Varsho/Dunston	TCMA	29.00
Modesto A's (28)	Jose Canseco	Chong	150.00
Nashville Sounds (25)	Dan Pasqua	Team	7.00
Newark Orioles (25)	Eric Bell	TCMA	11.00
OK City 89ers (25)	Henke/Buechele	TCMA	11.00
Omaha Royals (30)	Charlie Liebrandt	TCMA	11.00
Pawtucket Red Sox (25)	Roger Clemens	TCMA	55.00
w/Variations (29)			75.00
Phoenix Giants (25)	Deer/Gladden	Cramer	9.00
Portland Beavers (22)	Don Carman	Cramer	7.00
Prince William (34)	Felix Fermin	TCMA	13.00
Richmond Braves (27)	Milt Thompson	TCMA	12.00
Rochester Red Wings (19)	Larry Sheets	TCMA	12.00
Salt Lake City (24)	Tartabull/Presley	Cramer	15.00
Savannah Cardinals (26)	Lloyd Merritt	TCMA	12.00
Shreveport Captains (24)	Matt Nokes	First Base	15.00
Syracuse Chiefs (32)	Tony Fernandez	TCMA	20.00
Tacoma Tigers (25)	Steve Keifer	Cramer	5.00
Tidewater Tides (28)	Kevin Mitchell	TCMA	30.00
Tidewater (1)	Strawberry card		35.00
Toledo Mud Hens (24)	Havens/Yett	TCMA	10.00
Tucson Toros (25)	Glenn Davis	Cramer	11.00
Tulsa Drillers (22)	Jose Guzman	Team	12.00
Vancouver Canadians (25)	Tom Candiotti	Cramer	5.00
Visalia Oaks (25)	Allan Anderson	TCMA	15.00
Wichita Aeros (23)	Eric Davis	Rock's Dugout	60.00

1985 Issues

Team	Stars in Set	Issuer	Mint
Albany-Colonie Yanks (30)	Doug Drabek	TCMA	32.00
w/Late Issue cards (35)			42.00
Albuquerque Dukes (25)	Franklin Stubbs	Cramer	5.00
Beaumont Golden Gators (25)	B. Santiago	TCMA	27.00
Beloit Brewers (26)	Dean Freeland	TCMA	17.00
Bend Phillies (24)	Ron Jones	Cramer	10.00
Birmingham Barons (25)	Mike Henneman	Team	30.00
Buffalo Bisons (26)	Joel Skinner	TCMA	10.00
Burlington Rangers (28)	Sid Akins	TCMA	10.00
Calgary Cannons (25)	Tartabull	Cramer	20.00
Cedar Rapids Reds (32)	—	TCMA	18.00
Charlotte O's (29)	Rob Dibble	TCMA	10.00
w/Late Issue cards (31)			15.00
Chattanooga Lookouts (26)	—	Team	60.00
Columbus Clippers (25)	Dan Pasqua	Police	5.00
Columbus Clippers (26)	Fisher/Barrett	TCMA	18.00
w/Late Issue cards (28)			22.00
Daytona Bch. Islanders (30)	Billy Ripken	Team	27.00
Durham Bulls (32)	Blankenship	TCMA	15.00
Edmonton Trappers (25)	Wally Joyner	Cramer	15.00
Elmira Pioneers (25)	Quintana Anderson	TCMA	22.00
Everett Giants I (24)	Rick Nelson	Cramer	4.00
Everett Giants II (24)	Ty Dabney	Cramer	4.00
Ft. Myers Royals (30)	Seitzer de los Santos	TCMA	36.00
Fresno Giants (32)		Police	40.00
Greensboro Hornets (28)	Jim Corsi	TCMA	10.00
Greenville Braves (26)	Andres Thomas	Pizza Hut	25.00
Greenville Braves (26)	Andres Thomas	Team	25.00
Hawaii Islanders (25)	Rick Reuschel	Cramer	7.00
Huntsville Stars (25)	Jose Canseco	D. Jennings	10.00
Indianapolis Indians (36)	Gallaraga	Team	25.00
Int'l League All Stars (42)	Kevin Mitchell	TCMA	40.00
w/Greenwell & withdrawn cards (45)			60.00
Iowa Cubs (34)	Noce/Hatcher	TCMA	15.00
Kinston Blue Jays (26)	Borders/Liriano	TCMA	20.00
Las Vegas Stars (25)	John Kruk	Cramer	10.00
Little Falls Mets (27)	Todd Welborn	TCMA	15.00
Louisville Red Birds (30)	Coleman Worrell	Riley's	15.00
Lynchburg Mets (27)	Abner/Elster	TCMA	30.00
Madison Muskies (25)	Felix Jose	Police	8.00
Madison Muskies (25)	Jose/Burns	TCMA	13.00
Maine Guides (30)	Gallagher	TCMA	12.00
Mexico City Tigers (29)	Renteria	TCMA	9.00
Midland Angels (25)	Devon White	TCMA	21.00
Modesto A's (25)	Mark McGwire	Chong	70.00
w/McGwire Error (29)			120.
Nashua Pirates (29)	Felix Fermin	TCMA	13.00
Nashville Sounds (25)	Mike Laga	Team	6.00
Newark Orioles (25)	Sherwin Cijntje	TCMA	10.00
OK City 89ers (30)	Oddibe McDowell	TCMA	20.00
Omaha Royals (31)	David Cone	TCMA	25.00
Orlando Twins (26)	Mark Davidson	TCMA	10.00
Osceola Astros (30)	Young/Caminiti	Team	65.00
Patucket Red Sox (20)	Mike Greenwell	TCMA	75.00
Phoenix Giants (25)	Jeff Robinson	Cramer	8.00
Portland Beavers (25)	Chris James	Cramer	20.00

Team	Stars in Set	Issuer	Mint
Prince William (31)	Lind/Smiley	TCMA	14.00
Reading Phillies (25)	Marvin Freeman	Procards	7.00
Richmond Braves (26)	Milt Thompson	TCMA	11.00
Rochester Red Wings (29)	John Shelby	TCMA	11.00
w/Late Issue cards (31)			16.00
Spokane Indians (24)	Steve Garvey	Cramer	6.00
Spokane Indians (24)	Jerald Clark	Cramer	6.00
Springfield Cards (25)	John Costello	TCMA	10.00
Syracuse Chiefs (31)	Fred McGriff	TCMA	35.00
Tacoma Tigers (25)	Ontiveros/Rijo	Cramer	8.00
Tidewater Tides (27)	Fernandez	TCMA	37.00
w/Late Issue card (28)	Mitchell/Dykstra		39.00
Toledo Mud Hens (25)	Allan Anderson	TCMA	13.00
w/Late Issue card (26)			17.00
Tucson Toros (25)	Davis/Kerfield	Cramer	11.00
Tulsa Drillers (28)	Ruben Sierra	Team	75.00
Utica Blue Sox (26)	Ross Jones	TCMA	9.00
Vancouver Canadians (25)	Sveum/Leary	Cramer	9.00
Vero Bch. Dodgers (27)	Woodson Brennan	TCMA	11.00
Visalia Oaks (25)	Bell/Larkin	TCMA	10.00
Waterbury Indians (25)	Snyder/Jones	TCMA	27.00

1986 Issues

Team	Stars in Set	Issuer	Mint
Albany-Colonie Yanks (32)	Kelly/Reed	TCMA	10.00
Albuquerque Dukes (28)	Jeff Hamilton	Procards	6.00
Appleton Foxes (28)	Randy Velarde	Procards	6.00
Arkansas Travelers (26)	Joe Magrane	Procards	132.00
Asheville Tourists (29)	Cameron Drew	Procards	10.00
Auburn Astros (27)	Ed Whited	Procards	9.00
Bakersfield Dodgers	Ramon Martinez	Procards	22.00
Beaumont Golden Gators (25)	Alomar/Mack	Procards	18.00
Bellingham Mariners (29)	Greg Briley	Cramer	7.00
Beloit Brewers (26)	Carl Moraw	Procards	5.00
Bend Phillies (25)	Charles Malone	Cramer	5.00
Birmingham Barons (28)	Bobby Thigpen	Team	25.00
Buffalo Bisons (26)	Joe DeSa	Procards	5.00
Burlington Expos (28)	Jeff Huson	Procards	8.00
Calgary Cannons (26)	Harold Reynolds	Procards	6.00
Cedar Rapids Reds (28)	Marty Brown	TCMA	9.00
Charleston Rainbows (29)	Knabenshue	Procards	7.00
Charlotte O's (30)	Billy Ripken	Team	20.00
Chattanooga Lookouts (25)	Campbell (error)	Procards	6.00
Clearwater Phillies (26)	Ron Jones	Procards	10.00
Clinton Giants (29)	Dean Freeland	Procards	6.00
Columbia Mets (28)	Gregg Jefferies	Procards	95.00
Columbia Astros (25)	Gerald Young	Procards	7.00
Columbus Clippers (25)	Dan Pasqua	Police	6.00
Columbus Clippers (26)	Drabek/Pasqua	Procards	9.00
Daytona Bch. Islanders (28)	Jones Threadgill	Procards	5.00
Durham Bulls (27)	Gant/Blauser	Procards	12.00
Edmonton Trappers (27)	Devon White	Procards	8.00
El Paso Diablos (23)	Freeman Stanicek	Procards	7.00
Elmira Pioneers (30)	Cooper	Procards	12.00
Erie Cardinals (30)	Todd Zeile	Procards	25.00
w/Late Issue card (31)			35.00
Eugene Emeralds (25)	Sean Berry	Cramer	5.00
Everett Giants (36)		Popcorn Cards	4.00
Everett Giants (32)	Matt Williams	Cramer	10.00
Florida State (50) League All Stars	Jones/Anderson	Procards	42.00
Ft. Myers Royals (29)	Jose DeJesus	Procards	6.00
Fresno Giants (32)	Dennis Cook	Police	35.00
Ft. Lauderdale Yanks (23)	Jason Maas	Procards	9.00
Geneva Cubs (27)	Ced Landrum	Procards	5.00
Glens Falls Tigers (24)	Steve Searcy	Procards	7.00
Grensboro Hornets (27)	Pratt/Quintana	Procards	9.00
Greenville Braves (23)	Tom Glavine	Team	10.00
Hagerstown Suns (29)	Ballard/Milacki	Procards	10.00
Hawaii Islanders (23)	Fermin/Espy	Procards	7.00
Huntsville Stars (25)	McGwire Steinbach	D. Jennings	12.00
Indianapolis Indians (36)	John Dopson	Team	10.00
Iowa Cubs (26)	Martinez/Noce	Procards	7.00
Jackson Mets (27)	Elster/Abner Milligan	TCMA	17.00
Jacksonville Expos (26)	Santovenia	TCMA	9.00
Jamestown Expos (30)	Blowers	Procards	6.00
Kenosha Twins (27)	Steve Gasser	Procards	6.00
Kinston Eagles (25)	Scott Melvin	Procards	5.00
Knoxville Blue Jays (27)	Liriano/Borders Campusanao	Procards	8.00
Lakeland Tigers (25)	John Smoltz	Procards	15.00
Las Vegas Stars (26)	Santiago	Procards	11.00
w/Bowa card (27)			17.00
Little Falls Mets (29)	Roseboro	Procards	6.00
Louisville Red Birds (30)	Dunne Lindeman	Team	12.00

Team	Stars in Set	Issuer	Mint
Lynchburg Mets (28)	West/Gozzo	Procards	15.00
Macon Pirates (27)	Tony Chance	Procards	6.00
Madison Muskies (27)	Walt Weiss	Police	10.00
Madison Muskies (28)	Walt Weiss	Procards	12.00
Maine Guides (26)	Snyder/Jones	Procards	16.00
Medford A's (25)	Blankenship	Cramer	6.00
Memphis Chicks (26) (Gold Border)	Jackson/Snider	Time Out Sports	30.00
Memphis Chicks (26) (Silver Border)	Jackson/Snider	Time Out Sports	40.00
Miami Marlins (29)	Von Ohlen	Procards	5.00
Midland Angels (26)	McLemore	Procards	5.00
Modesto A's (27)	Jose/Walton	Chong	12.00
Modesto A's (27)	Jose/Walton	Procards	8.00
Nashua Pirates (28)	Gregg/Lind	Procards	7.00
Nashville Sounds (24)	Matt Nokes	Team	11.00
New Britain Red Sox (25)	Burks/Reed	Procards	37.00
OK City 89ers (26)	Brower/Sierra (error)	Procards	8.00
Omaha Royals (20)	Cone/Seitzer	Procards	16.00
Omaha Royals (25)	Cone/Seitzer	TCMA	22.00
Orlando Twins (24)	Gene Larkin	Procards	5.00
Osceola Astros (29)	John Fishel	Procards	6.00
Palm Springs Angels (28)	Doug Jennings Smokey Bear	Police	17.00
Palm Springs Angels (29)	Jennings Bichette	Procards	7.00
Pawtucket Red Sox (28)	Greenwell Benziger	Procards	49.00
Peninsula White Sox (28)	Peterson	Procards	6.00
Peoria Chiefs (27)	Mark Grace	Procards	65.00
Phoenix Firebirds (26)	Mike Aldrette	Procards	6.00
Pittsfield Cubs (25)	Maddux Palmeiro	Procards	25.00
Portland Beavers (22)	Chris James	Procards	6.00
Prince William (27)	Smiley/Chance	Procards	6.00
Quad City Angels (33)	Jeff Manto	Procards	9.00
Reading Phillies (26)	Ricky Jordan	Procards	27.00
Richmond Braves (27)	Gerald Perry	Procards	7.00
Rochester Red Wings (26)	Jim Traber	Procards	7.00
Salem Angels (25)	Colin Charland	Cramer	6.00
Salem Red Birds (29)	Chad Kreuter	Procards	7.00
San Jose Bees (28)	Steve Howe	Procards	5.00
Shreveport Captains (28)	Mackey Sasser	Procards	7.00
Southern League (25) All Stars	Canseco Jackson/McGwire D. Jennings	Procards	10.00
Spokane Indians (25)	George Brett	Cramer	6.00
Spokane Indians (24)	Ricky Bones	Univ. City	40.00
St. Petersburg Cards (29)	John Costello	Procards	5.00
Stars of the Future (40)	Fred McGriff	TCMA	13.00
Stockton Ports (26)	Rob DeWolf	Procards	5.00
Sumter Braves (30)	Mark Lemke	Procards	9.00
Syracuse Chiefs (27)	Fred McGriff	Procards	18.00
Tacoma Tigers (25)	Polonia/Nelson	Procards	7.00
Tampa Tarpons (27)	Rob Lopez	Procards	5.00
Tidewater Tides (28)	Myers/Magadan	Procards	11.00
Toledo Mud Hens (24)	Allan Anderson	Procards	6.00
Tri-Cities Triplets (14)	Thomas Ealy	Cramer	5.00
Tucson Toros (26)	Robbie Wine	Procards	6.00
Tulsa Drillers (27)	Jerry Browne	Team	11.00
Vancouver Canadians (27)	Braggs/Surhoff	Procards	14.00
Ventura Gulls (28)	Stoltemeyre Ducey	Procards	10.00
Vermont Reds (24)	Treadway Dibble	Procards	12.00
Vero Bch. Dodgers (27)	Jeff Hartman	Procards	5.00
Visalia Oaks (24)	Tim Senne	Procards	5.00
Waterbury Indians (26)	Bell/Farrell	Procards	6.00
Waterloo Indians (32)	Luis Medina	Procards	9.00
Watertown Pirates (27)	Bill Copp	Procards	6.00
Wausau Timbers (29)	Mike Schooler	Procards	6.00
West Palm Bch. (28)	Randy Johnson	Procards	8.00
Winston-Salem Spirits (29)	Dascenzo/Pico	Procards	7.00
Winter Haven Red Sox (27)	Brady Anderson	Procards	12.00

1987 Issues

Team	Stars in Set	Issuer	Mint
Albany-Colonie Yanks (23)	Velarde/Geren	Procards	7.00
Albuquerque Dukes (30)	Chris Gwynn	Team	11.00
Appleton Foxes (30)	Kenny Jackson	Procards	5.00
Arkansas Travelers (25)	Alicea/Hill	Procards	7.00
Asheville Tourists (28)	Whited/Simms	Procards	7.00
Auburn Astros (25)	Andres Mota	Procards	6.00
Bakersfield Dodgers (29)	Juan Bell	Procards	9.00
Bellingham Mariners (34)	Ken Griffey, Jr.	Team	24.00
Beloit Brewers (26)	Vaughn/Jaha	Procards	13.00
Birmingham Barons (28)	Adam Peterson	Best	7.00
Buffalo Bisons (29)	Allanson/Bell	Pucko	9.00
Burlington Expos (29)	Tony Welborn	Procards	6.00
Calgary Cannons (24)	Campbell/Nixon	Procards	6.00

Team	Stars in Set	Issuer	Mint
Cedar Rapids Reds (28)	Jefferson Scudder	Procards	8.00
Charleston Rainbows (23)	Matt Maysey	Procards	5.00
Charleston Wheelers (28)	Carl Grovum	Procards	5.00
Charlotte O's (30)	Bob Milacki	Team	11.00
Chattanooga Lookouts (26)	Schooler/Briley	Best	8.00
Chattanooga Lookouts (26) w/Coke Emblem	Mike Schooler	Best/Coke	14.00
Clearwater Phillies (27)	Chuck Malone	Procards	6.00
Clinton Giants (29)	Mark Leonard	Procards	6.00
Columbia Mets (29)	Jamie Roseboro	Procards	6.00
Columbus Astros (25)	Drew/Caminiti	Procards	8.00
Columbus Clippers (25)	Roberto Kelly	Police	6.00
Columbus Clippers (27)	Roberto Kelly	Procards	8.00
Columbus Clippers (25)	Roberto Kelly	TCMA	9.00
Daytona Bch. Admirals (26)	Dress/Merullo	Procards	5.00
Denver Zephyrs (27)	Joey Meyer	Procards	6.00
Dunedin Blue Jays (29)	D. Martinez	Procards	5.00
Durham Bulls (28)	Lemke/Mercker	Procards	7.00
Edmonton Trappers (23)	Bill Merrifield	Procards	5.00
El Paso Diablos (27)	Lavell Freeman	Procards	6.00
Elmira Pioneers (34)	Black Border	Cain	7.00
Elmira Pioneers (36)	Red Border	Cain	11.00
Erie Cardinals (29)	Darren Nelson	Procards	5.00
Eugene Emeralds (30)	T. Gordon	Procards	28.00
Everett Giants (34)	Mike Remlinger	Cramer	6.00
Fayetteville Generals (27)	Ken Williams	Procards	6.00
Ft. Myers Royals (34)	T. Gordon	Procards	14.00
Ft. Lauderdale Yanks (30)	Maas/Williams	Procards	9.00
Gastonia Rangers (29)	Sammy Sosa	Procards	9.00
Geneva Cubs (26)	Steve Owens	Procards	5.00
Glens Falls Tigers (25)	John Smoltz	Procards	8.00
Greensboro Hornets (26)	Scott Cooper	Procards	8.00
Greenville Braves (28)	Ron Gants	Best	10.00
Hagerstown Suns (29)	Ron Dillard	Procards	5.00
Harrisburg Senators (26)	Fermin/Gregg	Procards	8.00
Hawaii Islanders (27)	Ken Williams	Procards	5.00
Huntsville Stars (29)	Weiss/Jose	Team	8.00
Idaho Falls Braves (27)	Jeff Dodig	Procards	5.00
Indianapolis Indians (36)	Dennis Martinez	Team	8.00
I.L. League All Stars (45)	Leiter/Glavine Elster	TCMA	9.00
Iowa Cubs (25)	Palmeiro Berryhill	Team	14.00
Jackson Mets (25)	Jefferies/West	Team	15.00
Jacksonville Expos (29)	Randy Johnson	Procards	8.00
Jamestown Expos (30)	John Vanderwal	Procards	5.00
Kenosha Twins (29)	Derek Parks	Procards	7.00
Kinston Indians (24)	Hinzo/Webster	Procards	6.00
Knoxville Blue Jays (27)	Pat Borders	Procards	8.00
Lakeland Tigers (26)	Donnie Rowland	Procards	5.00
Las Vegas Stars (27)	Shawn Abner	Procards	11.00
Little Falls Mets (29)	Todd Hundley	Procards	9.00
Louisville Red Birds (30)	Magrane/Jones	Team	10.00
Lynchburg Mets (28)	Alan Hayden	Procards	6.00
Macon Pirates (25)	Rick Reed	Procards	8.00
Madison Muskies (23)	Ozzie Canseco	Police	9.00
Madison Muskies (25)	Ozzie Canseco	Procards	8.00
Maine Guides (23)	Ron Jones	Procards	5.00
Maine Guides (25) w/Error cards (27)	Mike Maddux	TCMA	8.00 / 13.00
Memphis Chicks (27)	Goose Gozzo	Best	8.00
Memphis Chicks (27)	Goose Gozzo	Procards	7.00
Miami Marlins (25)	Rick Richardi	Procards	5.00
Midland Angels (30)	Doug Jennings	Procards	7.00
Modesto A's (27)	Tony LaRussa	Chong	9.00
Modesto A's (25)	Blankenship	Procards	6.00
Myrtle Bch. Blue Jays (30)	Junior Felix	Procards	13.00
Nashville Sounds (25) w/Orsino Hill card (26)	Sabo/Treadway	Team	10.00 / 15.00
New Britain Red Sox (25)	Carlos Quintana	Procards	10.00
Newark Orioles (29)	Steve Finley	Procards	10.00
OK City 89ers (27)	Mike Stanley	Procards	8.00
Omaha Royals (26)	De Los Santos	Procards	9.00
Oneonta Yankees (33)	Imes/Williams	Procards	10.00
Orlando Twins (26)	Steve Gasser	Procards	6.00
Osceola Astros (29)	Bran Meyer	Procards	6.00
Palm Springs Angels (32)	Jeff Manto	Procards	7.00
Pan Am Set (33)	Abbott	Independent	90.00
w/extra Carpenter (34)	Carpenter		100.00
Pawtucket Red Sox (27)	Burks/Benzinger	Procards	5.00
Pawtucket Red Sox (25)	Burks/Benzinger	TCMA	13.00
Peninsula White Sox (29)	Mark Davis	Procards	6.00
Peoria Chiefs (6)	Jerome Walton	Pizza World	55.00
Peoria Chiefs (29)	Jerome Walton	Procards	40.00
Phoenix Firebirds (28)	Matt Williams	Procards	9.00
Pittsfield Cubs (26)	Mark Grace	Procards	45.00
Pocatello Giants (32)	Diego Segui	The Bon	35.00
Port Charlotte (27)	Chad Kreuter	Procards	6.00
Portland Beavers (25)	Allan Anderson	Procard	6.00

Team	Stars in Set	Issuer	Mint
Prince Williams Yanks (29)	Meulens/Maas	Procards	15.00
Quad City Angels (31)	Mike Knapp	Procards	6.00
Reading Phillies (26)	Ricky Jordan	Procards	15.00
Richmond Braves	Jeff Blauser	Bob's Photo	25.00
Richmond Braves (30)	Blauser/Glavine	Crown Oil	12.00
Richmond Braves (29)	Blauser/Glavine	TCMA	9.00
Rochester Red Wings (27)	Ballard/Ripken	Procards	7.00
Rochester Red Wings (29)	Ballard/Ripken	TCMA	9.00
Salem Angels (34)	Mike Erb	Procards	5.00
Salem Buccaneers (30)	King/Chance	Procards	6.00
Salinas Spurs (32)	Smokey Bear	Police	75.00
Salt Lake City Trappers (29)	—	Taco Time	10.00
San Antonio Dodgers (25)	Mike Devereaux	Team	7.00
San Bernadino Spirits (23)	Larry Smith	Procards	5.00
San Jose Bees (30)	Steve McCatty	Procards	5.00
Savannah Cardinals (26)	Geronimo Pena	Procards	6.00
Shreveport Captains (28)	Dennis Cook	Procards	8.00
Southern Lg. All Stars (25)	Gant/Berroa	D. Jennings	6.00
Spartanburg Phillies (28)	Vince Holyfield	Procards	5.00
Spokane Indians (25)	Paul Faries	Procards	6.00
Springfield Cards (28)	Todd Zeile	Best	17.00
St. Petersburg Cards (27)	Brett Harrison	Procards	5.00
Stockton Ports (26)	Gary Sheffield	Procards	15.00
Sumter Braves (30)	Bell/Deak	Procards	7.00
Syracuse Chiefs (23)	Stottlemyre Ducey	Procards	8.00
Syracuse Chiefs (33)	Stottlemyre Ducey	TCMA	8.00
Tacoma Tigers (23)	Tim Belcher	Procards	6.00
Tampa Tarpons (30)	Chris Hammond	Procards	7.00
Texas Lg. All Stars (36)	Jefferies/Alomar		16.00
Tidewater Tides (33)	Elster/Gooden	Procards	8.00
Tidewater Tides (30)	Elster/Gooden	TCMA	12.00
Toledo Mud Hens (30)	Searcy/Gibson	Procards	7.00
Toledo Mud Hens (25)	Steve Searcy	TCMA	7.00
Tucson Toros (25)	Gerald Young	Procards	7.00
Tucson Toros (24)	Gerald Young	Jones Photo	39.00
Tulsa Drillers (28)	Jose Cecena	Team	6.00
Utica Blue Sox (33)	Rambo Thatcher	Procards	8.00
Vancouver Canadians (25)	Dunne/Lind	Procards	6.00
Vermont Reds (26)	Marty Brown	Procards	6.00
Vero Bch. Dodgers (31)	Ramon Martinez	Procards	14.00
Visalia Oaks (27)	Chris Calvert	Procards	5.00
West Palm Bch. (28)	Jeff Huson	Procards	7.00
Waterloo Indians (29)	Mike Walker	Procards	5.00
Watertown Pirates (31)	Steve Carter	Procards	6.00
Wausau Timbers (28)	Jose Tartabull	Procards	6.00
Wicita Pilots (25)	R. Alomar S.Alomar	Team	15.00
Williamsport Bills (27)	Luis Medina	Procards	7.00
Winston-Salem Spirits (27)	Curtis/Girardi	Procards	6.00
Winter Haven Red Sox (30)	Tod Pratt	Procards	8.00
Wytheville Cubs (31)	Greg Jackson	Procards	5.00

1988 Issues

Team	Stars in Set	Issuer	Mint
Albany Yankees (27)	Hensley Meulens	Procards	7.00
Albuquerque Dukes (25)	Devereaux Gwynn	CMC	5.00
Albuquerque Dukes (29)	Devereaux Gwynn	Procards	5.00
Appleton Foxes (30)	T. Gordon	Procards	13.00
Arkansas Travelers (25)	Todd Zeile	Grand Slam	9.00
Asheville Tourists (31)	Joe Ortiz	Procards	5.00
Auburn Astros (29)	Andy Mota	Procards	5.00
Augusta Pirates (33)	Steve Carter	Procards	5.00
Bakersfield Dodgers (34)	Adam Brown	Cal League	5.00
Baseball America (30) AA Prospects Set	Walton Martinez	Best Procards	18.00
Baseball City Royals (25)	Kevin Appier	Star Co.	6.00
w/Late Issue cards (27)			10.00
Batavia Clippers (31)	Tony Trevino	Procards	5.00
Bellingham Mariners (30)	Tim Stargell	Legoe	6.00
Beloit Brewers (25)	Mark Chapman	Grand Slam	5.00
Bend Bucks (35)	G. Disarcina	Lego	7.00
Billings Mustangs (31)	Benny Colvard	Procards	5.00
Birmingham Barons (29)	Carlos Martinez	Best	6.00
Boise Hawks (29)	Mark Krumback	Procards	5.00
Bristol Tigers (32)	Rico Brogna	Procards	7.00
Buffalo Bisons (25)	Prince/Gregg	CMC	6.00
Buffalo Bisons (31)	Prince/Gregg	Procards	6.00
Buffalo Bisons (8)	Rocky Bridges	Team	7.00
Burlington Braves (31)	Mike Stanton	Procards	6.00
Burlington Indians (31)	Mark Lewis	Procards	23.00
Butte Copper Kings (29)	Monty Fariss	Sport Pro	11.00
Cal. Lg. All Stars (50)	Ken Griffey, Jr.	Cal. Lg.	12.00
Calgary Cannons (25)	Greg Briley	CMC	6.00
Calgary Cannons (28)	Greg Briley	Procards	6.00

Team	Stars in Set	Issuer	Mint
Carolina Lg. All Stars (40)	Cooper Pina/Bell	Star Co.	8.00
Cedar Rapids Reds (31)	Scott Scudder	Procards	6.00
Charleston Rainbows (30)	Mike Myers	Procards	5.00
Charleston Wheelers (28)	—	Best	6.00
Charlotte Knights (25)	Pete Harnisch	Team	9.00
Charlotte Rangers (23)	Sammy Sosa	Star Co.	7.00
w/Late Issue card (24)			9.00
Chattanooga Lookouts (32)	Killebrew	Team	8.00
Chattanooga Lookouts (26)	Chris Hammond	Best	6.00
Clearwater Phillies (26)	Royal Thomas	Star Co.	6.00
Clinton Giants (29)	Beck/Owens	Procards	5.00
Colorado Spgs. Sky Sox (25)	Luis Medina	CMC	6.00
Colorado Spgs. Sky Sox (29)	Luis Medina	Procards	6.00
Columbia Mets (27)	Jamie Roseboro	Grand Slam	6.00
Columbus Astros (28)	Charlie Kerfeld	Best	6.00
Columbus Clippers (26)	Velarde/Buhner	CMC	7.00
Columbus Clippers (28)	Velarde/Buhner	Police	6.00
Columbus Clippers (29)	Velarde/Buhner	Procards	6.00
Denver Zephyrs (25)	Lavell Freeman	CMC	5.00
Denver Zephyrs (30)	Lavell Freeman	Procards	5.00
Dunedin Blue Jays (24)	Pedro Munoz	Star Co.	6.00
Durham Bulls (blue) (24)	Michael Bell	Star Co.	8.00
w/Blue Costner card (25)			11.00
Durham Bulls (orange) (26)	Kevin Costner	Star Co.	8.00
Eastern Lg. All Star (52) Game Set	Walton/Hrkey	Procards	13.00
Edmonton Trappers (25)	Dante Bichette	CMC	6.00
Edmonton Trappers (31)	Dante Bichette	Procards	6.00
El Paso Diablos (30)	Sheffield Vaughn	Best	15.00
El Paso Diablos (30) Platinum Set	Sheffield Vaughn	Best	20.00
Elmira Pioneers (30)	Tim Naehring	Cain	6.00
Eugene Emeralds (30)	Bob Hamelin	Best	7.00
Fayetteville Generals (28)	Mike Wilkins	Procards	5.00
Florida State Lg. (52) All Stars	Geronimo Pena	Star Co.	6.00
Fresno Suns (27)	Ernie Young	Cal. League	5.00
Fresno Suns (29)	Ernie Young	Procards	5.00
Ft. Lauderdale Yanks (24)	Tony Morrison	Star Co.	6.00
Gastonia Rangers (30)	Brant Alyea	Procards	5.00
Geneva Cubs (30)	Mike Sodders	Procards	5.00
Glens Falls Tigers (27)	Rob Richie	Procards	5.00
Great Falls Dodgers (27)	Bene/Offerman	Team	19.00
Greensboro Hornets (26)	Steve Hester	Procards	6.00
Greenville Braves (24)	Mark Lemke	Best	6.00
Hagerstown Suns (25)	Steve Finley	Star Co.	6.00
w/Late Issue cards (27)			10.00
Hamilton Redbirds (30)	Tim Redman	Procards	5.00
Harrisburg Senators (30)	King/Chance	Procards	5.00
Huntsville Stars (25)	Scott Hemond	Team	5.00
Idaho Falls Braves (31)	D. Campbell	Procards	5.00
Indianapolis Indians (25)	Randy Johnson	CMC	6.00
Indianapolis Indians (31)	Randy Johnson	Procards	6.00
Iowa Cubs (25)	Grace/Smith	CMC	14.00
Iowa Cubs (30)	Grace/Smith	Procards	13.00
Jackson Mets (25)	Angelo Cuevas	Grand Slam	6.00
Jacksonville Expos (29)	Jeff Huson	Best	7.00
Jacksonville Expos (32)	Jeff Huson	Procards	6.00
Jamestown Expos (31)	Marquis Grissom	Procards	15.00
Kenosha Twins (29)	Willie Banks	Procards	7.00
Kinston Indians (24)	Joey Belle	Star Co.	14.00
Knoxville Blue Jays (26)	Alex Sanchez	Best	7.00
Lakeland Tigers (25)	Phil Clark	Star Co.	6.00
Las Vegas Stars (25)	S. Alomar R. Alomar	CMC	8.00
Las Vegas Stars (28)	S. Alomar R. Alomar	Procards	6.00
Legends of Minor (11) League Baseball	Luke Easter	Little Sun	5.00
Little Falls Mets (29)	Lee May	Pucko	5.00
Louisville Red Birds (25)	Cris Carpenter	CMC	6.00
Louisville Red Birds (26)	Cris Carpenter	Procards	6.00
Louisville Red Birds	Cris Carpenter	Team	13.00
Lynchburg Red Sox (27)	Mickey Pina	Star Co.	9.00
w/Logo card (28)			10.00
Madison Muskies (25)	Ozzie Canseco	Police	6.00
Maine Phillies (25)	Ricky Jordan	CMC	6.00
Maine Phillies (27)	Ricky Jordan	Procards	5.00
Managers Set (21)	Kevin Costner	Star Co.	7.00
Martinsville (32)	John Marshall	Star Co.	5.00
Memphis Chick (27)	Goose Gozzo	Best	5.00
Miami Marlins (24)	Brian Morrison	Star Co.	5.00
Midland Angels (25)	Jeff Manto	Grand Slam	6.00
Midwest Lg. All Stars (59)	Gordon Canseco	Grand Slam	9.00
Modesto A's (28)	Ron Coomer	Cal. League	5.00
Modesto A's (36)	Walt Weiss	Team	6.00
Myrtle Bch. Blue Jays (28)	Derek Bell	Procards	10.00

Team	Stars in Set	Issuer	Mint
Nashville Sounds 925)	Snider/Dibble	CMC	6.00
Nashville Sounds (26)	Snider/Dibble	Procards	6.00
Nashville Sounds (25)	Keith Brown	Team	6.00
New Britan Red Sox (25)	Todd Pratt	Procards	6.00
OK City 89ers (25)	Tom O'Malley	CMC	5.00
OK City 89ers (27)	Tom O'Malley	Procards	5.00
Omaha Royals (25)	De Los Santos	CMC	5.00
Omaha Royals (29)	De Los Santos	Procards	5.00
Oneonta Yankees (34)	Pat Kelly	Procards	6.00
Orlando Twins (29)	Derek Parks	Best	6.00
Osceola Astros (25)	Mike Simms	Star Co.	6.00
Palm Springs Angels (31)	Colin Charland	Cal. League	5.00
Palm Springs Angels (32)	Colin Charland	Procards	5.00
Pawtucket Red Sox (25)	Carlos Quintana	CMC	6.00
Pawtucket Red Sox (26)	Carlos Quintana	Procards	6.00
Peoria Chiefs (35)	Grace/Walton	Team	12.00
Phoenix Firebirds (25)	Matt Williams	CMC	9.00
Phoenix Firebirds (29)	Matt Williams	Procards	9.00
Pittsfield Cubs (25)	Jerome Walton	Procards	20.00
Pocatello Giants (31)	David Slavin	Procards	5.00
Portland Beavers (25)	Allan Anderson	CMC	6.00
Portland Beavers (27)	Allan Anderson	Procards	6.00
Prince William Yanks (25)	Williams/Maas	Star Co.	7.00
Pulaski Braves (25)	Glen Gardner	Procards	5.00
Quad City Angels (30)	David Holdridge	Grand Slam	6.00
Reading Phillies (27)	Chuck Malone	Procards	5.00
Reno Silver Fox (24)	Robbie Rogers	Cal. League	5.00
Richmond Braves (24)	Jeff Blauser	Bob's Photo	50.00
Richmond Braves (25)	Gant/Blauser	CMC	6.00
Richmond Braves (27)	Gant/Blauser	Procards	6.00
Riverside Red Wave (28)	Ricky Bones	Cal. League	5.00
Riverside Red Wave (28)	Ricky Bones	Procards	5.00
Rochester Red Wings (25)	Jeff Ballard	CMC	6.00
Rochester Red Wings (30)	Jeff Ballard	Procards	6.00
Rochester Red Wings (30)	Jeff Ballard	Team	6.00
Rochester Red Wings (36)	Harnisch/Finley	Pucko	12.00
Governor's Cup Set			
Rockford Expos (34)	Deshields	Team	11.00
Salem Buccaneers (25)	Rick Reed	Star Co.	6.00
Salt Lake Trappers (30)	Bill Murray	Team	6.00
San Antonio Missions (28)	R. Martinez	Best	9.00
San Antonio Missions (28)	R. Martinez	Best	15.00
Platinum Set			
San Bernadino Spirit (28)	Ken Griffey, Jr.	Best	19.00
San Bernadino Spirit (28)	Ken Griffey, Jr.	Best	25.00
Platinum Set			
San Bernadino Spirit (28)	Ken Griffey, Jr.	Cal. Lg.	10.00
San Jose Giants (29)	Mark Leonard	Cal. Lg.	5.00
San Jose Giants (30)	Mark Leonard	Procards	5.00
Savannah Cardinals (29)	John Sellick	Procards	5.00
Shreveport Captains (25)	Joe Olker	Procards	5.00
South Atlantic Lg. (28)	Bell/Vella	Grand Slam	7.00
All Stars			
South Bend White Sox (28)	Mike Maksudian	Grand Slam	5.00
Southern Lg. All Stars (40)	Mark Lemke	D. Jennings	5.00
Southern Oregon A's (28)	Stan Royer	Procards	9.00
Spartanburg Phillies (24)	Rambo/Vatcher	Star Co.	6.00
Spartanburg Phillies (26)	James Vatcher	Procards	6.00
Spokane Indians (26)	Humphreys Houston	Procards	5.00
Springfield Cardinals (28)	Ray Lankford	Best	7.00
St. Catharines (35) Blue Jays	Wood Williams	Procards	6.00
St. Lucie Mets (25)	Juan Villanueva	Star Co.	6.00
St. Petersburg Cards (25) w/Late Issues (27)	Geronimo Pena	Star Co.	6.00 / 10.00
Stockton Ports (31)	Spiers/Jaha	Cal. League	6.00
Stockton Ports (33)	Spiers/Jaha	Procards	6.00
Sumter Braves (32)	D. Burlingame	Procards	6.00
Syracuse Chiefs (25)	Berroa/Ducey	CMC	5.00
Syracuse Chiefs (30)	Berroa/Ducey	Procards	5.00
Tacoma Tigers (25)	Blankenship Jose	CMC	6.00
Tacoma Tigers (28)	Blankenship Jose	Procards	6.00
Tampa Tarpons (25)	Jerry Kutzler	Star Co.	5.00
Texas Lg. All Stars (39)	Sheffield/Zeile	Grand Slam	8.00
Tidewater Tides (25)	Gregg Jefferies	Candl Coin	20.00
Tidewater Tides (26)	Gregg Jefferies	CMC	16.00
Tidewater Tides (26)	Error Set (Jefferies)	CMC	30.00
Tidewater Tides (29)	Gregg Jefferies	CMC	14.00
Toledo Mud Hens (25)	Steve Searcy	CMC	5.00
Toledo Mud Hens (28)	Steve Searcy	Procards	5.00
Triple A All Stars (45)	Jefferies Sheffield/Alomar	CMC	14.00
Triple A All Star (55) Game Set	Jefferies Alomar	Procards	12.00
Tucson Toros (25)	Craig Biggio	CMC	7.00
Tucson Toros (28)	Craig Biggio	Procards	7.00
Tucson Toros (24)	Craig Biggio	Jones Photo	37.00
Tulsa Drillers (28)	Monty Fariss	Team	10.00
Utica Blue Sox (29)	Derek Lee	Pucko	5.00
Vancouver Canadians (25)	Adam Peterson	CMC	5.00
Vancouver Canadians (27)	Adam Peterson	Procards	5.00
Vermont Mariners (26)	Greg Brinkman	Procards	5.00
Vero Bch. Dodgers (26)	Dave Hansen	Star Co.	5.00
Virginia Generals (23) w/Late Issues (26)	Tom Johnson	Star Co.	5.00 / 9.00
Visalia Oaks (30)	John Eccles	Cal. Lg.	5.00
Visalia Oaks (28)	John Eccles	Procards	5.00
Waterloo Indians (29)	Tom Kramer	Procards	5.00
Watertown Pirates (35)	K. Richardson	Pucko	6.00
Wausau Timbers (28)	Chuck Carr	Grand Slam	5.00
West Palm Bch. Expos (26)	Kingwood	Star Co.	5.00
Wichita Pilots (27)	Knabenshue	Rock's Dugout	7.00
Williamsport Bills (27)	Casey Webster	Procards	5.00
Winston-Salem Spirits (22)	Derrick May	Star Co.	5.00
Winter Haven Red Sox (27)	Phil Plantier	Star Co.	6.00
Whytheville Cubs (31)	Weinheimer	Procards	5.00

1989 Issues

Team	Stars in Set	Issuer	Mint
Albany Yankees (30)	Sanders Meulens	Best	8.00
Albany Yankees (29)	Sanders Meulens	Procards	7.00
Albany Yankees	H. Meulens	Star Co.	8.00
Albuquerque Dukes (25)	R. Martinez	CMC	5.00
Albuquerque Dukes (30)	R. Martinez	Procards	5.00
Albuquerque Dukes (29)	R. Martinez	Albuq. Tribune	10.00
Appleton Foxes (31)	Bill Drohan	Procards	5.00
Arkansas Travelers (25)	Ray Lankford	Grand Slam	5.00
Asheville Tourists (30)	Willie Ansley	Procards	9.00
Auburn Astros (31)	Howard Prager	Procards	6.00
Augusta Pirates (32)	Estep/Merchant	Procards	5.00
Bakersfield Dodgers (29)	Bene/Offerman	Cal. Lg.	6.00
Baseball City Royals (27)	Jim Hudson	Star Co.	5.00
Batavia Clippers (31)	Michael Owens	Procards	5.00
Beloit Brewers (26)	Oreste Marrero	Star Co.	5.00
Billings Mustangs (31)	—	Procards	5.00
Birmingham Barons (30)	Robin Ventura	Best	8.00
Birmingham Barons (31)	Robin Ventura	Procards	7.00
Bluefield Orioles (31)	—	Star Co.	5.00
Boise Hawks (31)	Stan Cook	Procards	5.00
Bristol Tigers (31)	—	Star Co.	5.00
Buffalo Bisons (25)	Jay Bell	CMC	5.00
Buffalo Bisons (27)	Bell/King Carter	Procards	5.00
Burlington Braves (32)	Don Campbell	Procards	6.00
Burlington Braves (30)	Don Campbell	Star Co.	5.00
Burlington Indians (29)	—	Star Co.	5.00
Butte Copper Kings	—	Sport-Pro	9.00
Butte Copper Kings All Star Set	Seitzer	Sport-Pro	11.00
Cal. Lg. All Stars	Harris/Bene Offerman	Cal. Lg.	7.00
Calgary Cannons (25)	Jay Buhner	CMC	5.00
Calgary Cannons (24)	Jay Buhner	Procards	5.00
Canton-Akron Indians (28)	Allred/Neel	Best	6.00
Canton-Akron Indians (28)	Allred	Procards	6.00
Canton-Akron Indians (25)	Allred/Belle	Star Co.	9.00
Cedar Rapids Reds (30)	Benny Colvard	Best	5.00
Cedar Rapids Reds (29)	Benny Colvard	Procards	5.00
Cedar Rapids Reds	Benny Colvard	Star Co.	5.00
Charleston Rainbows (28)	Matt Witkowski	Procards	5.00
Charleston Wheelers (27)	Matt Franco	Best	5.00
Charleston Wheelers (28)	Matt Franco	Procards	5.00
Charlotte Knights (25)	Ty Griffin	Team	10.00
Charlotte Rangers	—	Star Co.	5.00
Chattanooga Lookouts (26)	R. Jefferson	Best	5.00
Chattanooga Lookouts (25)	R. Jefferson	Grand Slam	5.00
Clearwater Phillies (27)	David Holdridge	Star Co.	6.00
Clinton Giants (31)	Dave Slavin	Procards	5.00
Colorado Spgs. Sky Sox (25)	Tommy Hinzo	CMC	5.00
Colorado Spgs. Sky Sox (28)	Tommy Hinzo	Procards	5.00
Columbia Mets (30)	Todd Hundley	Best	5.00
Columbia Mets (29)	Todd Hundley	Grand Slam	5.00
Columbus Clippers (30)	Maas/Cary	CMC	5.00
Columbus Clippers (25)	Maas/Cary	Police	5.00
Columbus Clippers (28)	Maas/Cary	Procards	5.00
Columbus Mudcats (28)	Eric Anthony	Best	10.00
Columbus Mudcats (31)	Eric Anthony	Procards	8.00
Columbus Mudcats (24)	Eric Anthony	Star	8.00
Denver Zephyrs (25)	Greg Vaughn	CMC	6.00
Denver Zephyrs (28)	Greg Vaughn	Procards	6.00
Dunedin Blue Jays (26)	Ed Sprague	Star Co.	5.00

Team	Stars in Set	Issuer	Mint	Team	Stars in Set	Issuer	Mint
Durham Bulls (29)	Steve Avery	Star Co.	7.00	Pawtucket Red Sox (28)	Quintana	Procards	5.00
Durham Bulls (28)	Steve Avery	Team	15.00	Peninsula Pilots (26)	Knoblauh	Star Co.	5.00
Eastern Lg. Diamond		Procards	10.00	Peoria Chiefs	Ty Griffin	Team	7.00
Diplomacy Set				Phoenix Firebirds (25)	Dennis Cook	CMC	6.00
Edmonton Trappers (25)	K. Anderson	CMC	5.00	Phoenix Firebirds (29)	Dennis Cook	Procards	5.00
Edmonton Trappers (25)	K. Anderson	Procards	5.00	Pittsfield Mets (28)	Langbehn	Star Co.	5.00
Elizabethton Twins (31)	—	Star Co.	5.00	Portland Beavers (25)	Chip Hale	CMC	5.00
Elmira Pioneers (32)	Kevin Morton	Pucko	7.00	Portland Beavers (26)	Chip Hale	Procards	5.00
El Paso Diablos (30)	Sandy Guerrero	Grand Slam	6.00	Prince William Cannons (29)	Bill Masse	Star Co.	5.00
Erie Orioles (29)	Pete Rose Jr.	Star Co.	8.00	Pulaski Braves (28)	Hutchinson	Procards	6.00
Eugene Emeralds (25)	—	Best	5.00	Quad City Angels (31)	Mike Erb	Best	5.00
Everett Giants	—	Star Co.	5.00	Quad City Angels (30)	Mike Erb	Grand Slam	5.00
Fayetteville Generals (29)	Rusty Meacham	Procards	5.00	Reading Phillies (27)	Chuck Malone	Best	6.00
Frederick Keys (27)	Pete Rose, Jr.	Star Co.	9.00	Reading Phillies (27)	Chuck Malone	Procards	6.00
Ft. Lauderdale Yanks (29)	Skip Nelloms	Star Co.	5.00	Reading Phillies (27)	Chuck Malone	Star Co.	6.00
Gastonia Rangers	Trey McCoy	Best	5.00	Reno Silver Sox (26)	Wesbrook	Cal. Lg.	5.00
Gastonia Rangers (30)	Trey McCoy	Procards	6.00	Richmond Braves (25)	Mercker/Lemke	CMC	5.00
Gastonia Rangers (25)	Trey McCoy	Star Co.	5.00	Richmond Braves	Mercker/Lemke	Team	5.00
Geneva Cubs	—	Procards	6.00	Riverside Red Wave (30)	M. Humphreys	Best	5.00
Great Falls Dodgers	Jones/Goodwin	Sport-Pro	13.00	Riverside Red Wave (31)	M. Humphreys	Cal. Lg.	5.00
Great Falls All Star Set	Jose Offerman	Sport-Pro	11.00	Riverside Red Wave (31)	Mike Humphreys	Procards	5.00
Greensboro Hornets (29)	Mike Mulvaney	Procards	5.00	Rochester Red Wings (25)	Juan Bell	CMC	5.00
Greenville Braves (29)	Bell/Avery	Best	8.00	Rochester Red Wings	Juan Bell	Procards	5.00
Greenville Braves (30)	Mike Bell	Procards	5.00	Salem Buccaneers (27)	K. Richardson	Star Co.	5.00
Greenville Braves (25)	Mike Bell	Star Co.	5.00	Salinas Spurs (27)	—	Cal. Lg.	5.00
Hagerstown Suns (29)	D. Bettendorf	Best	5.00	Salinas Spurs (25)	Kerry Shaw	Procards	5.00
Hagerstown Suns (26)	Don Burford, Jr.	Procards	5.00	San Antonio Dodgers (28)	Offerman	Best	6.00
Hagerstown Suns (22)	Don Burford, Jr.	Star Co.	5.00		Hershiser		
Hamilton Redbirds (29)	Tim Redman	Star Co.	5.00	San Bernadino Spirit (29)	Harmon	Best	6.00
Harrisburg Senators (26)	Kevin Burdick	Procards	5.00	San Jose Giants (31)	Jamie Cooper	Best	6.00
Harrisburg Senators (23)	Kevin Burdick	Star Co.	5.00	San Jose Giants (30)	Jamie Cooper	Cal. Lg.	6.00
Helena Brewers	Bo Dodson	Sport-Pro	8.00	San Jose Giants (30)	Jamie Cooper	Procards	5.00
Helena All Star Set	—	Sport-Pro	11.00	San Jose Giants (28)	Jamie Cooper	Star Co.	6.00
High School (23)	T. Houston	Little Sun	14.00	Sarasota White Sox (25)	—	Star Co.	5.00
Prospects - Set				Savannah Cardinals (30)	—	Procards	5.00
Huntsville Stars (29)	Ozzie Canseco	Best	6.00	Scranton Red Barons (25)	Steve Stanicek	CMC	5.00
Idaho Falls Braves	Tyler Houston	Procards	7.00	Scranton Red Barons (28)	Steve Stanicek	Procards	5.00
Indianapolis Indians (25)	Jeff Huson	CMC	5.00	Shreveport Captains (27)	Dean Freeland	Procards	5.00
Indianapolis Indians (32)	Jeff Huson	Procards	5.00	South Atlantic League	—	Grand Slam	5.00
Iowa Cubs (25)	Smith/Harkey	CMC	7.00	All Stars			
Iowa Cubs (28)	Smith/Harkey	Procards	5.00	Spartanburg Phillies (30)	Morandini	Procards	6.00
Jackson Mets (30)	Todd Welborn	Grand Slam	5.00	Spartanburg Phillies (26)	Morandini	Star Co.	6.00
Jacksonville Expos (29)	Deshields	Best	7.00	Spokane Padres	—	Sport-Pro	7.00
Jacksonville Expos (29)	Deshields	Procards	6.00	Springfield Cards (30)	Mike Fiore	Best	5.00
Jamestown Expos (30)	—	Procards	5.00	St. Catharine's	—	Procards	5.00
Johnson City Cards	—	Star Co.	5.00	Blue Jays			
Kenosha Twins (29)	Steve Dunn	Procards	6.00	St. Lucie Mets (27)	Roseboro	Star Co.	5.00
Kenosha Twins (29)	Steve Dunn	Star Co.	5.00	St. Petersburg Cards (29)	Cormier	Star Co.	5.00
Kingsport Mets	—	Star Co.	5.00	Stockton Ports (32)	John Jaha	Best	5.00
Kinston Indians (27)	Mark Lewis	Star Co.	6.00	Stockton Ports (28)	John Jaha	Cal. Lg.	5.00
Knoxville Blue Jays (31)	Bell/Gozzo	Best	6.00	Stockton Ports (31)	John Jaha	Procards	5.00
Knoxville Blue Jays (31)	Derek Bell	Procards	6.00	Stockton Ports (28)	John Jaha	Star Co.	5.00
Knoxville Blue Jays (25)	Bell/Gozzo	Star Co.	5.00	Sumter Braves (33)	Gardner	Procards	5.00
Lakeland Tigers	Rico Brogna	Star Co.	5.00	Syracuse Chiefs (25)	Sanchez/Felix	CMC	6.00
Las Vegas Stars (25)	S. Alomar, Jr.	CMC	6.00	Syracuse Chiefs (27)	Sanchez/Felix	Procards	6.00
Las Vegas Stars (29)	S. Alomar, Jr.	Procards	6.00	Tacoma Tigers (25)	Blankenship	CMC	5.00
London Tigers (32)	Phil Clark	Procards	5.00	Tacoma Tigers (32)	Blankenship	Procards	5.00
Louisville Red Birds (25)	Todd Zeile	CMC	6.00	Texas Lg. All Stars	—	Grand Slam	5.00
Louisville Red Birds (28)	Todd Zeile	Procards	6.00	Tidewater Tides (29)	Dave West	CMC	6.00
Louisville Red Birds	Todd Zeile	Team	12.00	Tidewater Tides	Dave West	Procards	6.00
Lynchburg Red Sox	Phil Plantier	Star Co.	5.00	Toledo Mud Hens 925)	Cuyler/Ritz	CMC	5.00
Madison Muskies (22)	Tony Ariola	Star Co.	5.00	Toledo Mud Hens (30)	Milt Cuyler	Procards	5.00
Martinsville Phillies	—	Star Co.	5.00	Triple A All Star (55)	Zeile/Alomar	Procards	10.00
Medford A's (31)	Michael Conte	Best	5.00	Game Set			
Memphis Chicks (28)	Bob Hamelin	Best	5.00	Tucson Toros (25)	Kerfeld	CMC	5.00
Memphis Chicks (28)	Bob Hamelin	Procards	5.00	Tucson Toros (26)	Eric Anthony	Jones	30.00
Memphis Chicks (24)	Bob Hamelin	Star Co.	5.00			Photo	
Miami Marlins (25)	—	Star Co.	5.00	Tucson Toros (28)	Kerfeld	Procards	5.00
Midland Angels (30)	Bobby Rose	Grand Slam	5.00	Tulsa Drillers (26)	Monty Fariss	Grand Slam	6.00
Modesto A's (23)	Stan Royer	Cal. Lg.	6.00	Utica Blue Sox (34)	John Smith	Pucko	6.00
Modesto A's (35)	Canseco	Chong	8.00	Vancouver Canadians (25)	Lance Johnson	CMC	5.00
	McGwire			Vancouver Canadians (27)	Lance Johnson	Procards	5.00
Myrtle Bch. Blue Jays (30)	Ray Giannelli	Procards	5.00	Vero Bch. Dodgers (29)	Opperman	Star Co.	6.00
Nashville Sounds (25)	Roomes	CMC	5.00	Visalia Oaks (29)	Willie Banks	Cal. Lg.	6.00
Nashville Sounds (28)	Roomes	Procards	5.00	Visalia Oaks (31)	Willie Banks	Procards	5.00
Nashville Sounds	Roomes	Team	5.00	Waterloo Diamonds	S. Meadows	Procards	5.00
New Britain Red Sox (27)	Cooper/Zupcic	Procards	7.00	Waterloo Diamonds	—	Star Co.	5.00
New Britain Red Sox (25)	Cooper/Zupcic	Star Co.	8.00	Watertown Indians (29)	Tepper	Star Co.	5.00
Niagara Falls Rapids (30)	John Desilva	Pucko	6.00	Wausau Timbers (28)	Chris Howard	Grand Slam	5.00
OK City 89ers (25)	Coolbaugh	CMC	5.00	Welland Pirates (35)	David Bird	Pucko	6.00
OK City 89ers (29)	Coolbaugh	Procards	5.00	West Palm Bch. Expos (29)	Barberie	Star Co.	5.00
Omaha Royals (25)	Kevin Appier	CMC	5.00	Wichita Wrangers	Andy Benes	Rock's	9.00
Omaha Royals (27)	Kevin Appier	Procards	5.00			Dugout	
Oneonta Yankees	—	Procards	6.00	Wichita Wrangers	Andy Benes	Rock's	9.00
Orlando Twins (31)	Sorrento	Best	5.00	Stadium Set		Dugout	
Orlando Twins (30)	Derek Parks	Procards	5.00	Williamsport Bills (25)	Martinez	Procards	6.00
Osceola Astros (27)	Scott Servais	Star Co.	5.00	Williamsport Bills (25)	Martinez	Star Co.	6.00
Palm Springs Angels (32)	Wiley Lee	Cal. Lg.	5.00	Winston-Salem Spirit (22)	John Jensen	Star Co.	5.00
Palm Springs Angels (28)	Wiley Lee	Procards	5.00	Winter Haven Red Sox (29)	Erik Laseke	Star Co.	5.00
Pawtucket Red Sox (25)	Quintana	CMC	5.00	Wytheville Cubs (30)	E. Cunningham	Star Co.	9.00

1990 ALPHABETICAL

ROOKIE CARD CHECKLIST

A

Kyle Abbott .... 1990 Fleer #444
Kyle Abbott .... 1990 Score #673
Beau Allred .... 1990 Donruss #691
Beau Allred ....1990 Topps #419
Moises Alou .... 1990 Fleer #650
Moises Alou .... 1990 Score #592
Kent Anderson .... 1990 Donruss #490
Kent Anderson .... 1990 Score #412
Kent Anderson ....1990 Topps #16
Kent Anderson ....1990 Upper Deck #691
Eric Anthony .... 1990 Donruss #34
Eric Anthony .... 1990 Fleer #222
Eric Anthony .... 1990 Score #584
Eric Anthony ....1990 Topps #608
Eric Anthony ....1990 Upper Deck #28
Kevin Appier .... 1990 Fleer #100
Kevin Appier .... 1990 Score #625
Kevin Appier ....1990 Topps #167
Kevin Appier ....1990 Upper Deck #102
Luis Aquino .... 1990 Donruss #179
Luis Aquino .... 1990 Fleer #101
Luis Aquino .... 1990 Score #432
Luis Aquino ....1990 Topps #707
Luis Aquino ....1990 Upper Deck #274
Pat Austin .... 1990 Score #626

B

Billy Bates ....1990 Score #608
Kevin Batiste ....1990 Upper Deck #115
Blaine Beatty ....1990 Score #632
Blaine Beatty ....1990 Upper Deck #23
Stan Belinda ....1990 Score #634
Stan Belinda ....1990 Topps #354
Joey Belle .... 1990 Donruss #390
Joey Belle .... 1990 Fleer #485
Joey Belle .... 1990 Score #508
Joey Belle ....1990 Topps #283
Joey Belle ....1990 Upper Deck #546
Mike Benjamin .... 1990 Fleer #51
Greg Blosser .... 1990 Score #681
Mike Blowers .... 1990 Donruss #656
Mike Blowers .... 1990 Fleer #438
Mike Blowers .... 1990 Score #624
Jeff Brantley .... 1990 Donruss #466
Jeff Brantley .... 1990 Fleer #52
Jeff Brantley .... 1990 Score #371
Jeff Brantley ....1990 Topps #703
Jeff Brantley ....1990 Upper Deck #358
Terry Bross .... 1990 Donruss #502
Scott Bryant .... 1990 Score #667

C

Francisco Cabrera .... 1990 Donruss #646
Francisco Cabrera ....1990 Topps #254
Francisco Cabrera ....1990 Upper Deck #64
George Canale .... 1990 Donruss #699
George Canale .... 1990 Fleer #641
George Canale .... 1990 Score #656
George Canale ....1990 Topps #344
George Canale ....1990 Upper Deck #59
Jose Cano ....1990 Upper Deck #43
Steve Carter ....1990 Topps #482
Steve Carter ....1990 Upper Deck #368
Tony Castillo .... 1990 Donruss #592
Tony Castillo ....1990 Topps #620
Tony Castillo ....1990 Upper Deck #551
Colin Charland .... 1990 Fleer #640
Dave Cochrane ....1990 Topps #491
Paul Coleman .... 1990 Score #662
Paul Coleman ....1990 Topps #654
Pat Combs .... 1990 Donruss #44
Pat Combs .... 1990 Fleer #553
Pat Combs .... 1990 Score #623
Pat Combs ....1990 Topps #384
Scott Coolbaugh .... 1990 Donruss #43
Scott Coolbaugh .... 1990 Fleer #293
Scott Coolbaugh .... 1990 Score #612
Scott Coolbaugh ....1990 Upper Deck #214
Steve Cummings .... 1990 Donruss #698
Steve Cummings ....1990 Topps #374
Earl Cunningham .... 1990 Score #670
Earl Cunningham ....1990 Topps #134
Milt Cuyler .... 1990 Score #583

D

Jack Daugherty .... 1990 Donruss #461
Jack Daugherty .... 1990 Fleer #294
Jack Daugherty ....1990 Score #564
Jack Daugherty ....1990 Topps #52
Jack Daugherty ....1990 Upper Deck #614
Steve Davis .... 1990 Score #187
Steve Davis ....1990 Topps #428
Delino Deshields .... 1990 Donruss #42
Delino Deshields .... 1990 Fleer #652
Delino Deshields .... 1990 Score #645
Delino Deshields ....1990 Topps #224
Tom Drees .... 1990 Fleer #644
Tom Drees ....1990 Upper Deck #3
Tim Drummond .... 1990 Donruss #510
Tim Drummond ....1990 Topps #713
Brian Dubois .... 1990 Donruss #38
Brian Dubois .... 1990 Fleer #601
Brian Dubois .... 1990 Score #657
Brian Dubois ....1990 Topps #413
Brian Dubois ....1990 Upper Deck #78
Mike Dyer .... 1990 Donruss #642
Mike Dyer .... 1990 Fleer #372

Mike Dyer ....1990 Score #571
Mike Dyer ....1990 Topps #576
Mike Dyer ....1990 Upper Deck #374

E

Gary Eave .... 1990 Donruss #713
Gary Eave .... 1990 Score #621
Wayne Edwards .... 1990 Fleer #652
Cal Eldred .... 1990 Score #669
Alvaro Espinoza .... 1990 Donruss #245
Alvaro Espinoza .... 1990 Fleer #441
Alvaro Espinoza .... 1990 Score #101
Alvaro Espinoza ....1990 Topps #791
Alvaro Espinoza ....1990 Upper Deck #163

F

Mike Fetters .... 1990 Donruss #35
Mike Fetters .... 1990 Fleer #131
Mike Fetters ....1990 Topps #14
Steve Finley .... 1990 Donruss #215
Steve Finley .... 1990 Fleer #176
Steve Finley .... 1990 Score #339
Steve Finley ....1990 Topps #349
Steve Finley ....1990 Upper Deck #602
Jeff Fischer ....1990 Score #654
Darrin Fletcher ....1990 Score #622
Tony Fossas .... 1990 Donruss #457
Tony Fossas .... 1990 Fleer #323
Tony Fossas .... 1990 Score #567
Tony Fossas ....1990 Topps #34
Steve Frey .... 1990 Fleer #649
Steve Frey ....1990 Topps #91

G

Mark Gardner .... 1990 Donruss #40
Mark Gardner .... 1990 Fleer #646
Mark Gardner ....1990 Score #639
Mark Gardner ....1990 Topps #284
Bob Geren .... 1990 Donruss #395
Bob Geren .... 1990 Fleer #442
Bob Geren .... 1990 Score #464
Bob Geren ....1990 Topps #536
Bob Geren ....1990 Upper Deck #608
Greg Gohr ....1990 Score #679
Juan Gonzalez .... 1990 Donruss #33
Juan Gonzalez .... 1990 Fleer #297
Juan Gonzalez .... 1990 Score #637
Juan Gonzalez ....1990 Topps #331
Juan Gonzalez ....1990 Upper Deck #72
Tom Goodwin ....1990 Score #668
Mauro Gozzo .... 1990 Donruss #655
Mauro Gozzo .... 1990 Fleer #82
Mauro Gozzo .... 1990 Score #610
Mauro Gozzo ....1990 Topps #274
Willie Green ....1990 Score #682
Tommy Greene .... 1990 Donruss #576
Tommy Greene .... 1990 Fleer #584
Tommy Greene .... 1990 Score #640
Tommy Greene ....1990 Upper Deck #49
Jason Grimsley .... 1990 Fleer #653
Jason Grimsley .... 1990 Score #649
Jason Grimsley ....1990 Topps #493
Jason Grimsley ....1990 Upper Deck #27
Marquis Grissom .... 1990 Donruss #36
Marquis Grissom ....1990 Score #591

Marquis Grissom ....1990 Topps #714
Marquis Grissom ....1990 Upper Deck #9
Mark Guthrie .... 1990 Donruss #622
Mark Guthrie ....1990 Topps #317
Mark Guthrie ....1990 Upper Deck #436

H

Chip Hale .... 1990 Donruss #690
Chip Hale ....1990 Score #588
Chip Hale ....1990 Topps #704
Chip Hale .... 1990 Score #588
Chip Hale ....1990 Upper Deck #475
Bob Hamelin ....1990 Upper Deck #45
Dave Hansen .... 1990 Fleer #642
Donald Harris ....1990 Score #661
Donald Harris ....1990 Topps #314
John Hart ....1990 Topps #141
Mike Hartley .... 1990 Fleer #651
Mike Hartley ....1990 Score #641
Scott Hemond .... 1990 Fleer #646
Scott Hemond ....1990 Score #598
Xavier Hernandez .... 1990 Donruss #682
Xavier Hernandez ....1990 Upper Deck #26
Greg Hibbard .... 1990 Donruss #384
Greg Hibbard .... 1990 Fleer #534
Greg Hibbard .... 1990 Score #369
Greg Hibbard ....1990 Topps #769
Greg Hibbard ....1990 Upper Deck #543
Shawn Holman .... 1990 Fleer #606
Shawn Holman ....1990 Score #620
Steve Hosey ....1990 Score #666
Tyler Houston ....1990 Score #677
Tyler Houston ....1990 Topps #564
Dann Howitt .... 1990 Fleer #644
Mike Huff .... 1990 Fleer #649
Mike Huff ....1990 Score #597
Jeff Huson .... 1990 Donruss #693
Jeff Huson .... 1990 Fleer #350
Jeff Huson .... 1990 Score #615
Jeff Huson ....1990 Topps #72
Jeff Huson ....1990 Upper Deck #434

I

Jeff Innis .... 1990 Donruss #408
Jeff Innis .... 1990 Fleer #206
Jeff Innis ....1990 Topps #557
Jeff Innis ....1990 Upper Deck #562

J

Jeff Jackson ....1990 Score #678
Jeff Jackson ....1990 Topps #74
Keith Jones ....1990 Score #676
Terry Jorgenson ....1990 Score #655
Jeff Juden ....1990 Topps #164
Dave Justice .... 1990 Donruss #704
Dave Justice .... 1990 Fleer #586
Dave Justice ....1990 Score #650

K

Jeff King .... 1990 Donruss #480
Jeff King .... 1990 Fleer #469
Jeff King .... 1990 Score #549
Jeff King ....1990 Topps #454
Jeff King ....1990 Upper Deck #557
Matt Kinzer .... 1990 Fleer #652

Deion Sanders .... 1990 Fleer #454
Deion Sanders .... 1990 Score #586
Deion Sanders ....1990 Topps #61
Deion Sanders ....1990 Upper Deck #13
Scott Scudder .... 1990 Donruss #435
Scott Scudder .... 1990 Fleer #434
Scott Scudder .... 1990 Score #518
Scott Scudder ....1990 Topps #553
Scott Scudder ....1990 Upper Deck #164
Rudy Seanez .... 1990 Fleer #640
Joe Skalski .... 1990 Fleer #618
Mike Smith (Pirates) ....1990 Score #635
Mike Smith (Pirates) ....1990 Topps #552
Mike Smith (Orioles) .... 1990 Topps #249
Luis Sojo ....1990 Topps #594
Paul Sorrento .... 1990 Donruss #626
Paul Sorrento .... 1990 Score #647
Sammy Sosa .... 1990 Donruss #489
Sammy Sosa .... 1990 Fleer #548
Sammy Sosa .... 1990 Score #558
Sammy Sosa ....1990 Topps #692
Sammy Sosa ....1990 Upper Deck #17
Mike Stanton .... 1990 Donruss #508
Mike Stanton .... 1990 Fleer #596
Mike Stanton ....1990 Score #609
Mike Stanton ....1990 Topps #694
Mike Stanton ....1990 Upper Deck #61
Phil Stephenson ....1990 Score #642
Phil Stephenson ....1990 Topps #584
Lee Stevens .... 1990 Fleer #145
Mel Stottlemyre Jr. ....1990 Topps #263
Doug Strange .... 1990 Donruss #535
Doug Strange ....1990 Topps #641

T
Kevin Tapani .... 1990 Donruss #473
Kevin Tapani ....1990 Topps #227
Kevin Tapani ....1990 Upper Deck #87
Stu Tate .... 1990 Fleer #643
Frank Thomas ....1990 Score #663
Frank Thomas ....1990 Topps #414

V
Sergio Valdez .... 1990 Donruss #405
Sergio Valdez ....1990 Topps #199
Greg Vaughn .... 1990 Donruss #37
Greg Vaughn .... 1990 Fleer #339
Greg Vaughn ....1990 Score #585
Greg Vaughn ....1990 Topps #57
Greg Vaughn ....1990 Upper Deck #25
Maurice Vaughn ....1990 Score #675
Jose Vizcaino .... 1990 Fleer #410
Jose Vizcaino .... 1990 Score #613
Jose Vizcaino ....1990 Upper Deck #44
Omar Vizquel .... 1990 Donruss #483
Omar Vizquel .... 1990 Fleer #528
Omar Vizquel .... 1990 Score #264
Omar Vizquel ....1990 Topps #698
Omar Vizquel ....1990 Upper Deck #233

W
Larry Walker .... 1990 Donruss #578
Larry Walker .... 1990 Fleer #363
Larry Walker ....1990 Score #631
Larry Walker ....1990 Topps #757

Larry Walker ....1990 Upper Deck #466
Jerome Walton .... 1990 Donruss #285
Jerome Walton .... 1990 Fleer #44
Jerome Walton ....1990 Score #229
Jerome Walton ....1990 Topps #464
Jerome Walton ....1990 Upper Deck #345
Gary Wayne .... 1990 Donruss #318
Gary Wayne .... 1990 Fleer #387
Gary Wayne ....1990 Score #527
Gary Wayne ....1990 Topps #348
Gary Wayne ....1990 Upper Deck #372
Lenny Webster ....1990 Score #638
Mickey Weston ....1990 Score #616
Mickey Weston ....1990 Topps #377
Mickey Weston ....1990 Upper Deck #683
Jeff Wetherby ....1990 Score #540
Jeff Wetherby ....1990 Topps #142
Jeff Wetherby ....1990 Upper Deck #611
John Wetteland .... 1990 Donruss #671
John Wetteland .... 1990 Fleer #411
John Wetteland .... 1990 Score #388
John Wetteland ....1990 Topps #631
John Wetteland ....1990 Upper Deck #377
Ed Whited ....1990 Score #644
Ed Whited ....1990 Topps #111
Ed Whited ....1990 Upper Deck #447
Wally Whitehurst ....1990 Score #599
Wally Whitehurst ....1990 Topps #719
Wally Whitehurst ....1990 Upper Deck #564
Kevin Wickander ....1990 Topps #528
Dean Wilkins .... 1990 Fleer #47
Dean Wilkins ....1990 Score #630
Bernie Williams .... 1990 Donruss #689
Bernie Williams ....1990 Score #619
Bernie Williams ....1990 Topps #701
Dana Williams .... 1990 Fleer #648
Matt Winters .... 1990 Fleer #124
Matt Winters ....1990 Upper Deck #524
Rick Wrona .... 1990 Donruss #512
Rick Wrona .... 1990 Score #557
Rick Wrona ....1990 Topps #187
Rick Wrona ....1990 Upper Deck #582

Y
Eric Yelding .... 1990 Donruss #123
Eric Yelding .... 1990 Score #411
Eric Yelding ....1990 Topps #309
Eric Yelding ....1990 Upper Deck #427

Z
Clint Zavaras .... 1990 Donruss #662
Clint Zavaras ....1990 Topps #89
Todd Zeile .... 1990 Donruss #29
Todd Zeile .... 1990 Fleer #265
Todd Zeile .... 1990 Score #600
Todd Zeile ....1990 Topps #162
Todd Zeile ....1990 Upper Deck #545
Alan Zinter ....1990 Score #671
Eddie Zosky ....1990 Score #665

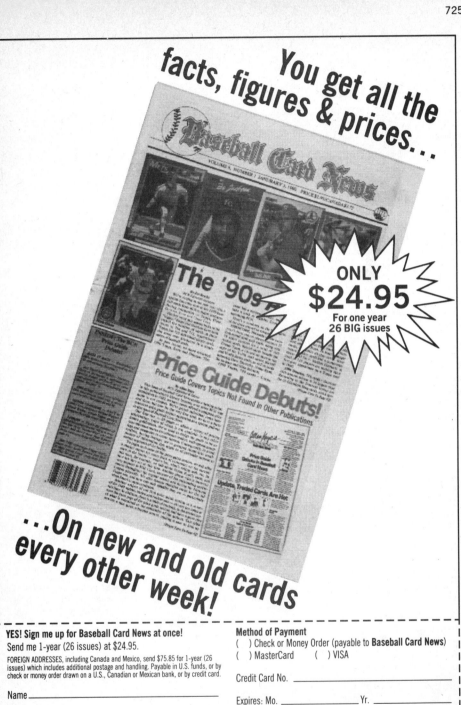

Representative Minor League Cards

1979 Cramer Phoenix

1983 TCMA

1984 Columbus Clippers

1985 TCMA

1986 ProCards

1985 Everett Giants

1988 Salt Lake City

1988 Eastern League

1989 Lookout Legends II

Representative Minor League Cards

1984 Cramer PCL

1984 Sequoia

1985 TCMA

1985 Burger King

1987 Salt Lake City

1986 Sun Belt Press

1988 Bill Pucko Buffalo

1988 CMC

1988 Donn Jennings

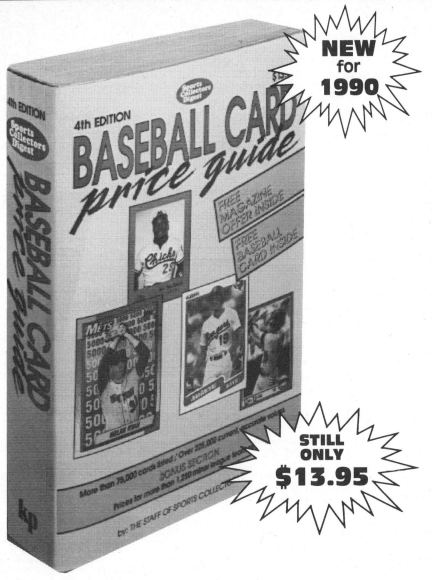

NEW for 1990

STILL ONLY $13.95

Notes

Notes